BRADFORD'S CROSSWORD SOLVER'S DICTIONARY

Collins

HarperCollins Publishers
Westerhill Road
Bishopbriggs
Glasgow
G64 2QT
Great Britain

Seventh Edition (paperback) 2008

© **Anne R. Bradford 1986, 1993,
1997, 2000, 2003, 2005**
This edition:
© **Anne R. Bradford 2008**

First edition published by
Longman; second, third and fourth
editions published by Peter Collin
Publishing Ltd

ISBN 978-0-00-727464-2

Collins® is a registered trademark of
HarperCollins Publishers Limited

www.collinslanguage.com

A catalogue record for this book is
available from the British Library

Technical support and typesetting
by Thomas Callan

Printed in Italy by
LEGO Spa, Lavis (Trento), Italy

Contents

Author's Preface	v
Solving Crossword Clues	vi
How to use the Dictionary	ix
About the Author	xi
The Crossword Club	xiii
Crossword Solver's Dictionary	**1–845**

Author's Preface

It is hard to believe that 50 years have flown by since I started reversing the standard dictionary in order to have easier access to crossword solutions. This has truly been my life's work yet the fascination is as strong as ever. What a delight when reading a dictionary definition to come across a totally unexpected meaning tucked in there – the equivalent, I feel sure, to the thrill a treasure seeker must get when the metal detector changes tone.

This 7th edition includes further sections listed by word-length, and hopefully will encourage confidence in users to attempt ever more complicated puzzles. You have my word for it!

My thanks, as ever, to my supporters at Collins, and beyond.

Anne R. Bradford 2007

Solving Crossword Clues

Crossword puzzles tend to be basically 'quick' or 'cryptic'. A 'quick' crossword usually relies on a one- or two-word clue which is a simple definition of the answer required. Many words have different meanings, so that the clue 'ball' could equally well lead to the answer 'sphere', 'orb', or 'dance'. The way to solve 'quick' crosswords is to press on until probable answers begin to interlink, which is a good sign that you are on the right track.

'Cryptic' crosswords are another matter. Here the clue usually consists of a basic definition, given at either the beginning or end of the clue, together with one or more definitions of parts of the answer. Here are some examples taken from all-time favourites recorded over the years:

1. *'Tradesman who bursts into tears'* (**Stationer**)

   Tradesman is a definition of stationer. *Bursts* is cleverly used as an indication of an anagram, which *into tears* is of stationer.

2. *'Sunday school tune'* (**Strain**)

   Here *Sunday* is used to define its abbreviation S, *school* is a synonym for train, and put together they give strain, which is a synonym of *tune*.

3. *'Result for everyone when head gets at bottom'* (**Ache**)
   (used as a 'down' clue)

   This is what is known as an '& lit' clue, meaning that the setter has hit on a happy composition which could literally be true. *Everyone* here is a synonym for each, move the *head* (first letter) of the word to the *bottom*, and the answer is revealed, the whole clue being the definition of the answer in this case.

4. *'Tin out East'* (**Sen**)

   In this example, *tin*, implying 'money', requires its chemical symbol Sn to go *out*(side) *East*, or its abbreviation, E, the whole clue being a definition of a currency (sen) used in the East.

5. *'Information given to communist in return for sex'* (**Gender**)

   Information can be defined as gen; *communist* is almost always red, *in return* indicates 'reversed', leading to gen-der, a synonym for *sex*.

6. *'Row about no enclosure of this with sardines'* (**Tin-opener**)

   Row is a synonym for tier, *about* indicates 'surrounding', *no enclosure* can be no pen, leading to ti-no pen-er, and another '& lit' clue.

7. *'Cake-sandwiches-meat, at Uncle Sam's party'* (**Clambake**)

   Meat here is lamb, *sandwiches* is used as a verb, so we have C-lamb-ake, which is a kind of party in America. *Uncle Sam* or US is often used to indicate America.

8. *'Initially passionate meeting of boy and girl could result in it'* (**Pregnancy**)

   Initially is usually a sign of a first letter, in this case 'p' for *passionate* + Reg (a *boy*) and Nancy (a *girl*), and another clever '& lit'.

With 'cryptic' clues the solver needs to try to analyse the parts to see what he or she is looking for – which word or words can be the straight definition, and which refer to the parts or hint at anagrams or other subterfuges. Whilst it would be unrealistic to claim total infallibility, practice has shown that in most crosswords some 90% of the answers are to be found in this work.

Anne R. Bradford

How to use the Dictionary

This dictionary is the result of over fifty years' analysis of some 300,000 crossword clues, ranging from plain 'quick' crosswords requiring only synonyms to the different level of cryptic puzzles. Therefore the words listed at each entry may be connected to the keyword in various ways, such as:

- – a straightforward synonym

- – a commonly-associated adjective

- – an associated or proper noun

- – a pun or other devious play on words

Keywords are listed alphabetically; in cases where the heading consists of more than one word, the first of these words is taken to be the keyword, and in cases where the end of a word is bracketed, the material up to the opening bracket is taken to be the keyword. Keywords marked with the symbol ▸ refer the user to other entries where additional information may be found. Keywords marked with the symbol ▹ give leads to anagrams and other ploys used by crossword setters. If the keywords found in the clue do not lead directly to the required answer, the solver should look under words given as cross-references to other entries. These are indicated by the symbol →, with the cross-referenced word shown in capitals.

Some additional entries have been divided into two parts – a general entry similar to the standard entries which appear elsewhere, and a panel entry which contains a list of more specific or encyclopedic material. So, for example, the entry 'Artist(ic)' includes not only a list of general words connected with 'Artist' or 'Artistic' in some way, such as 'Bohemian', 'Cubist', 'Fine' and 'Virtuoso', but also a panel with the heading 'Artists' containing a list of the names of specific artists, such as 'Bellini', 'Constable', and 'Rembrandt'. For added help, the words in these panels are arranged by length, with all three-letter words grouped together in alphabetical order, then all four-letter words, then all five-letter words, and so on.

About the Author

Anne Bradford's love of words began to make itself evident even in her schooldays, when, as Head Girl of her school, she instituted a novel punishment – instead of making rulebreakers write lines, she had them write out pages from a dictionary, on the grounds that this was a more useful exercise. Little did she know this was soon to be her own daily routine!

In time, crosswords became a magnificent obsession for Anne. All lovers of crosswords can understand the irresistible lure of solving them, but Anne's interest went much deeper than most people's, and when she stopped work in 1957 to have her first child, she found herself starting to note down answers to particularly tricky clues as an aid to memory, in case she should come across them again in another puzzle. It was from this simple beginning that this crossword dictionary evolved.

Over the space of 25 years, Anne continued to build on her collection of solutions, analysing every crossword clue as she solved it and adding it to her steadily growing bank of entries. This unique body of material eventually reached such proportions that she had the idea of offering it to her fellow crossword-solvers as a reference book, and since then, the book has gone from strength to strength, providing valuable help to countless cruciverbalists over a number of editions.

Anne Bradford continues to devote time each day to solving crosswords, averaging some 20 a week – both quick and cryptic – and still avidly collects new solutions for her *Crossword Solver's Dictionary* at a rate of around 150 a week, compiling each solution by hand (without the use of a computer!). This latest edition therefore includes much new material, gleaned by a true crossword lover who not only solves crosswords but, as an active member of the Crossword Club, can offer the user an insight into the mind of a cunning crossword compiler.

The Crossword Club

If you are interested in crosswords, you might like to consider joining the Crossword Club. Membership is open to all who enjoy tackling challenging crosswords and who appreciate the finer points of clue-writing and grid-construction. The Club's magazine, Crossword, contains two prize puzzles each month. A sample issue and full details are available on request.

The Crossword Club
Coombe Farm
Awbridge
Romsey, Hants.
SO51 0HN
UK

email: bh@thecrosswordclub.co.uk
website address: www.thecrosswordclub.co.uk

Aa

A, An Ack, Adult, Ae, Alpha, Angstrom, Are, Argon, D, Ein, Her, If, L, One, Per, They
A1 Tiptop
AA Milne
Aardvark Ant-bear, Ant-eater, Earth-hog, Ground-hog
Aaron's Rod Hagtaper
Aba, Abba Patriarch
Abacus Counter, Soroban
Abaft Astern, Sternson
Abalone Ormer, Paua, Perlemoen
Abandon(ed), Abandonment Abdicate, Abnegate, Abort, Adrift, Amoral,
  Apostasy, Back down, Cade, Cancel, Castaway, Corrupt, Decommission, Defect,
  Derelict, → DESERT, Desuetude, Discard, Disown, Dissolute, Ditch, Drop, Dump,
  Elan, Evacuate, Expose, Flagrant, Forhoo(ie), Forhow, Forlend, Forsake, Gomorra,
  Immoral, Jack(-in), Jettison, Jilt, Leave, Loose, Louche, Maroon, Old, Orgiastic,
  Profligate, Quit, Rakish, Rat, Relinquish, Renounce, Reprobate, Scrap, Shed, Sink,
  Strand, Vacate, Waive, Wanton, Yield
Abase Degrade, Demean, Disgrace, Grovel, → HUMBLE, Kowtow, Lessen
Abash Daunt, Discountenance, Mortify
Abate(ment) Allay, Appal, Decrescent, Defervescence, Diminish, Let up, Lyse, Lysis,
  Moderate, Reduce, Remit, → SUBSIDE
▷ **Abate** *may indicate* a contention
Abattoir Knackery, Slaughterhouse
Abbey Abbacy, Bath, Buckfast, Cloister, Downside, Fonthill, Fountains, Glastonbury,
  Györ, Je(r)vaulx, Medmenham, Melrose, Minster, Nightmare, Northanger, Priory,
  Rievaulx, Tintern, Westminster, Whitby, Woburn
Abbot Aelfric, Archimandrite, Brother, Friar
Abbreviate, Abbreviation Abridge, Ampersand, Compendium, Condense, Curtail,
  → SHORTEN, Sigla
ABC Absey
Abdicate, Abdication Cede, Demission, Disclaim, Disown, Resign
Abdomen Belly, C(o)eliac, Epigastrium, Gaster, Hypochondrium, Opisthosoma,
  Paunch, Pleon, → STOMACH, Tummy, Venter
Abduct(ed), Abduction Enlèvement, Kidnap, Rapt, Ravish, Shanghai, Steal
Aberdeen Granite City
Aberrant, Aberration Abnormal, Aye-aye, Deviant, Idolon, Perverse
Abet(tor) Aid, Back, Candle-holder, Second
Abeyance, Abeyant Dormant, Shelved, Sleeping, Store
Abhor(rent) → DETEST, Execrable, → HATE, Loathe, Odious, Shun
Abide Adhere, Dwell, Inhere, → LAST, Lie, Live, Observe, Remain, Stand, Tarry
Abigail Maid, Masham
Ability Aptitude, Calibre, Capacity, Cocum, → COMPETENCE, Efficacy, ESP, Facility,

Faculty, Ingine, Initiative, Instinct, Lights, Potential, Power, Prowess, Savey, Savoir-faire, Savv(e)y, Skill, Talent

Abject Base, Craven, Grovel, Humble, Servile, Slave

Abjure Eschew, Forswear, Recant, Renege, Reny

Ablaze Afire, Ardent

Able Ablins, Accomplished, → ADEPT, Aiblins, Apt, Capable, → COMPETENT, Fere, Literate, Proficient, Seaman, Yibbles

Abnormal(ity) Anomalous, Atypical, → DEVIANT, Dysfunction, Ectopic, Erratic, Etypical, Freakish, Malocclusion, Odd, Peloria, Preternatural, → QUEER, Sport, Teras, Trisome, Unnatural, Varus

Aboard On

Abode Domicile, Dwelling, Habitat, → HOME, Lain, Libken, Limbo, Midgard, Remain, Seat

Abolish, Abolition(ist) Annihilate, Annul, Axe, → BAN, D, Delete, Destroy, Eradicate, Erase, Extirpate, John Brown, Nullify, Repeal, Rescind, Wilberforce

Abomasum Read

Abominable, Abominate, Abomination Bane, Cursed, → HATE, Nefandous, Nefast, Revolting, Snowman, Vile, Yeti

Aboriginal, Aborigine Adivasi, Ainu, Aranda, Autochthon, Binghi, Boong, Buck, Bushmen, Carib, Evolué, Fringe-dweller, Gin, Gurindji, Indigenous, Jacky(-Jacky), Kamilaroi, Kipper, Koori, Lubra, Maori, Mary, Motu, Myall, Pintubi, Pitjant(jat)jara, Pre-Dravidian, Sakai, San, Sican, Siwash, Truganini, Vedda(h), Warlpiri, Yupik

Abort(ion), Abortive Apiol, Cancel, Ecbolic, Miscarry, Moon-calf, Slip, Sooterkin, Teras, Termination

Abound(ing) Bristle, Copious, Enorm, Overflow, Rife, Swarm, Teem

About A, Almost, Anent, Around, C, Ca, Circa, Circiter, Concerning, Encompass, Environs, Going, Near, Of, On, Over, Re, Regarding, Soon at

▷ **About** *may indicate* one word around another

Above Abune, Aforementioned, Aloft, Over, Overhead, Overtop, Owre, Sopra, Superior, Supra-, Suspicion, Upon

Abracadabra Cantrip, Heypass

Abrade, Abrasive Carbanado, Carborundum®, Chafe, Emery, Erode, File, Garnet paper, → GRATE, Rub, Sand, Scrape, Scrat, Scuff

Abraham Lincoln, Patriarch, Urite

Abreast Alongside, Au courant, Au fait, Beside, Level, Up

Abridge(ment) Audley, Compress, Condense, Cut, Digest, Dock, Epitome, Pot, Shorten, Trim

Abroad Afield, Away, Distant, Forth, Offshore, Out, Overseas

▷ **Abroad** *may indicate* an anagram

Abrogate Abolish, Repeal, Replace

▷ **Abrupt** *may indicate* a shortened word

Abrupt(ly) Bold, Brusque, Curt, Gruff, Offhand, Premorse, Prerupt, Short, Staccato, Terse

Abscess Gumboil, Impost(h)ume, Ulcer, Warble

Abscond Absquatulate, Decamp, Desert, Elope, Flee, Leg-bail, Levant, Skase, Welch

Abseil(ing) Dulfer, Rappel, Roping-down

Absence, Absent(ee), Absent-minded(ness) Abs, Abstracted, Away, Distant, Distracted, Distrait, Exeat, Exile, Hookey, Malingerer, Missing, Mitch, Sabbatical, Scatty, Skip, Truant, Vacuity, Void, Wanting, Wool-gathering

Absinthe Wormwood

Absolute(ly) Bang, Complete, Dead, Deep-dyed, Downright, Fairly, Implicit,

Ipso facto, Just, Meer, Mere, Mondo, Nominative, Plenary, Plumb, Quite, Real, Sheer, Total, Truly, Unconditional, Unmitigated, Unqualified, Utter, Veritable, Very
Absolve, Absolution Acquit, Assoil, Assoilzie, Clear, Exculpate, Excuse, Pardon, Shrive
Absorb(ed), Absorbent, Absorbing, Absorption Assimilate, Autism, Blot, Consume, Desiccant, Devour, Digest, Dope, Drink, → ENGROSS, Enrapt, Imbibe, Ingest, Intent, Merge(r), Occlude, Occupy, Osmosis, Porous, Preoccupation, Preoccupied, Rapt, Sorbefacient, Spongy, Unputdownable
Absquatulate Skedaddle
Abstain(er), Abstemious, Abstinence, Abstinent Band of Hope, Celibacy, Chastity, Continent, Desist, Eschew, Forbear, Forgo, Maigre, Nazarite, Nephalism, Pioneer, Rechab(ite), Refrain, Resist, Sober, Temperate, TT
Abstract(ed), Abstraction Abrege, Abridge, Academic, Appropriate, Brief, Deduct, Digest, Discrete, Distrait, Epitome, Essence, Metaphysical, Musing, Notional, Précis, Preoccupied, Prepossessed, Prescind, Remove, Resumé, Reverie, Stable, Steal, Summary, Syllabus, Tachism
Abstruse Arcane, Deep, Esoteric, Obscure, Recondite
Absurd(ity) Alician, Apagoge, Fantastic, Farcical, Folly, Inept, Irrational, Laputan, Ludicrous, Madness, Nonsense, Paradox, Preposterous, Ridiculous, Silly, Solecism, Stupid, Toshy, Whim-wham
Abundance, Abundant A-gogo, Ample, Aplenty, Bounty, Copious, Excess, Flood, Flush, Fouth, Fowth, Fruitful, Galore, Lashings, Lavish, Mickle, Mine, Mint, Muckle, Oodles, Oodlins, Opulent, Over, Plenitude, Plenteous, → PLENTIFUL, Plenty, Pleroma, Plethora, Plurisie, Profusion, Prolific, Relative, Replete, Rich, Rife, Routh, Rowth, Sonce, Sonse, Store, Stouth and routh, Surfeit, Tallents, Teeming, Tons, Uberous
Abuse, Abusive Assail, Becall, Billingsgate, Blackguard, Chemical, Cruelty, Flak, Fustilarian, Fustil(l)irian, Hail, Ill-treat, Insult, Invective, Jobbery, Limehouse, Malpractice, Maltreat, Miscall, → MISTREAT, Misuse, Mofo, Obloquy, Opprobrium, Philippic, Rail, Rampallian, Rate, Rayle, Revile, Ritual, Satanic, Satire, Scarab(ee), Scurrilous, Serve, Sexual, Slang, Slate, Sledging, Snash, Solvent, Strap, Substance, Thersitical, Tirade, Vilify, Violate, Vituperation
Abut Adjoin, Border, Touch
Abysm(al), Abyss Avernus, Barathrum, Barranca, Chasm, Deep, Gulf, Swallet, Tartarean, Tartarus
AC Current, Erk
Acacia Bablah, Boree, Brigalow, Eumong, Eumung, Gidgee, Gidjee, Koa, Mimosa, Mulga, Myall, Sallee, Shittim, Wattle
Academic(ian) A, Acca, Acker, Della-Cruscan, Don, Erudite, Fellow, Hypothetic(al), Immortals, Literati, Master, Pedantic, PRA, Prof(essor), RA, Reader, Rector
Academy, Academic Athenaeum, Dollar, Donnish, French, Loretto, Lyceum, Military, Naval, Royal, St Cyr, Sandhurst, School, Seminary, The Shop, West Point
Acanthus Blankursine, Ruellia
Accelerate, Acceleration, Accelerator Antedate, Betatron, Bevatron, Collider, Cosmotron, Cyclotron, Festinate, G, Gal, Grav, Gun, Hasten, Increase, Linac, Linear, Rev, Signatron, Speed, Stringendo, Synchrotron
Accent(ed), Accentuate Acute, Beat, Breve, Brogue, Bur(r), Circumflex, Cut-glass, Doric, Drawl, Enclitic, Enhance, Gammat, Grave, Hacek, Intonation, Kelvinside, Long, Macron, Marcato, Martelé, Mockney, Morningside, Mummerset, Nasal, Orthotone, Oxford, Oxytone, Paroxytone, Perispomenon, Pitch, Primary, Proparoxytone, Rhythm, Secondary, Stress, Tittle, Tone, Tonic, Twang

Accentor Dunnock
Accept(able), Acceptance, Accepted A, Accede, Admit, Adopt, Agree, Allow, Approbate, Bar, Believe, Buy, Can-do, Common, Consent, Cool, Cosher, Decent, Done, Embrace, Grant, Idee recue, Kosher, Meet, Obey, On, Pocket, Putative, Resipiscence, Settle, Stand, Suppose, Swallow, Take, Tolerate, U, Valid, Wear, Widespread
Access(ible) Avenue, Blue-jacking, Card, Come-at-able, Conditional, Credit, Direct, Door, Entrée, → **ENTRY**, Fit, Get-at-able, Hack, Ingo, Key, Log in, Log on, Passe-partout, Password, Phreaking, Random, Recourse, Remote, Sequential, Spasm, Wayleave
Accessory, Accessories Abettor, Addition, Aide, Ally, Ancillary, Appendage, Appurtenance, Attribute, Bandanna, Bells and whistles, Cribellum, Cuff-links, Findings, Fitment, Staffage, Trappings, Trimming
Accident(al) Adventitious, Bechance, Blowdown, Blunder, Calamity, → **CHANCE**, Circumstance, Contingency, Contretemps, Crash, Dent, Disaster, Fall, Fluke, Fortuitous, Hap, Hit and run, Mischance, Mishap, Promiscuous, Rear-ender, Shunt, Smash, Smash-up, Spill, Stramash, Unmeant, Wreck
Accidie Acedia, Sloth, Torpor
Acclaim Accolade, Applaud, Brava, Bravo, Cheer, Eclat, Fame, Fanfare, Hail, Kudos, Ovation, Praise, Salute
Accolade Award, Brace, Honour, Palm, Token, Tribute
Accommodate, Accommodation Adapt, Almshouse, B and B, Bedsit, Berth, Billet, Board, Botel, Bunkhouse, Camp, Chalet, Compromise, Crashpad, Digs, Flotel, Gaff, Gite, Grace and favour, Homestay, Hostel, Hotel, House, Lend, Loan, Lodge, Lodgement, Minshuku, Motel, → **OBLIGE**, Parador, Pension, Quarters, Rapprochement, Recurve, Room, Sheltered, Single-end, Sorehon, Stabling, Stateroom, Steerage, Storage, Wharepuni, Xenodochium
▷ **Accommodating** *may indicate* one word inside another
Accompany(ing), Accompanied (by), Accompaniment, Accompanist Accessory, Alberti, And, Attend, Backing, Chaperone, Chum, Concomitant, Consort, Continuo, Descant, → **ESCORT**, Fixings, Harmonise, Herewith, Obbligato, Obligate, Obligato, Repetiteur, Soundtrack, Trimmings, Vamp
Accomplice Abettor, Aide, → **ALLY**, Collaborator, Confederate, Federarie, Partner, Shill, Stale, Swagsman
Accomplish(ed), Accomplishment Able, → **ACHIEVE**, Arch, Attain, Clever, Complete, Consummate, Done, Effect, Master, Over, Perform, Polished, Prowess, Realise, Ripe, Savant, Success, Tour de force
Accord(ingly), According to After, Agree, Ala, Allow, As per, Attune, Chime, Consensus, Give, Grant, Harmony, Jibe, Meech Lake, Meet, Sort, Thus
According to nature SN
Accordion Button, Concertina, Flutina, Piano, Squeeze-box
Accost Abord, Approach, Greet, Hail, Importune, Molest, Solicit, Tackle
Account(s) AC, Anecdote, Appropriation, Audit, Battels, Behalf, Bill, Budget, Cause, Charge, Checking, Chequing, Chronicle, Control, Current, Deposit, Discretionary, Drawing, Enarration, Expense, Explain, Exposition, ISA, Joint, Lawin, Ledger, Log, Long, Memoir, Narration, Nominal, Nostro, Numbered, Procès-verbal, Real, Reason, Recital, Regest, Register, → **REPORT**, Repute, Resumé, Sake, Short, Suspense, Swindlesheet, Tab, Tale, Thesis, Trust, Version, Vostro
Accountable Responsible
Accountant Auditor, Bean counter, CA, Cost, Forensic, Hyde, Liquidator, Reckoner, Vestry-clerk

Accredit Attribute
Accumulate, Accumulation Accrue, Adsorb, Aggregate, → **AMASS**, Augment, Backlog, Build, Collect, Gather, Hoard, Lodg(e)ment, Pile, Rack up, Run up, Stockpile, Uplay
Accuracy, Accurate(ly) Bang-on, Cocker, → **CORRECT**, Dead-on, Fair, Fidelity, Minute, Precise, Right, Spot-on, True, Veracious, Word-perfect
Accursed Argued, Blest, Blist, Sacred
Accusation, Accuse(d) Allege, Arraign, Attaint, Bill, Blame, Censure, Challenge, Charge, Criminate, Denounce, Dite, Gravamen, Impeach, Incriminate, Panel, Plaint, Suspect, Tax, Threap, Threep, Traduce, Wight, Wite, Wyte
Accustom(ed) Acquaint, Attune, Enure, General, Habituate, Harden, Inure, Teach, Wont, Woon
Ace(s) Basto, Blackjack, Crabs, Dinger, → **EXPERT**, Jot, Master, Mournival, One, Quatorze, Spadille, Spadill(i)o, Spot, Tib, Virtuoso, Wonderful
Acerbate Intensify
Ache, Aching Aitch, Die, Long, Mulligrubs, Nag, Otalgia, Pain, Stitch, Work, Yearn, Yen
Achieve(ment) Accomplish, Acquisition, Attain, Come, Compass, Cum laude, → **EFFECT**, Exploit, Feat, Fulfil, Gain, Hatchment, Masterpiece, Realise, Res gestae, Satisfice, Satisfy, Stroke, Succeed, Threepeat, Triumph, Trock, Troke, Truck
Acid(ity) Acrimony, Corrosive, Drop, EPA, Etchant, Hydroxy, Reaction, Ribosomal, Ribozyme, Solvent, Sour, Tart, Vinegar, Vitriol

---

ACIDS

2 letters:	Iodic	Marine	Chloric
pH	L-dopa	Niacin	Chromic
	Lewis	Nitric	Creatin
3 letters:	Malic	Oxalic	Cystine
DNA	Mucic	Oxygen	Ellagic
HCL	Oleic	Pectic	Eugenic
LSD	Orcin	Phenol	Ferulic
Oxo	Osmic	Picric	Folacin
RNA	Trona	Quinic	Fumaric
		Serine	Fusidic
4 letters:	*6 letters:*	Sialic	Glycine
Acyl	Adipic	Sorbic	Guanine
Dopa	Bromic	Tannic	Leucine
Pyro	Capric	Tiglic	Malonic
Uric	Cholic	Toluic	Meconic
Wood	Citric	Valine	Melanic
	Cyanic		Muramic
5 letters:	Erucic	*7 letters:*	Nitrous
Algin	Formic	Abietic	Nucleic
Amide	Gallic	Acrylic	Orcinol
Amino	Lactic	Alanine	Peracid
Auric	Lauric	Alginic	Proline
Boric	Leucin	Benzoic	Prussic
Caro's	Lipoic	Butyric	Pteroic
Fatty	Lysine	Caproic	Pyruvic
Folic	Maleic	Cerotic	Racemic

Sebacic
Selenic
Silicic
Stannic
Stearic
Suberic
Terebic
Titanic
Valeric
Vanadic
Xanthic
Xylonic

8 letters:
Abscisic
Adenylic
Arginine
Ascorbic
Aspartic
Butanoic
Caprylic
Carbamic
Carbolic
Carbonic
Chlorous
Cinnamic
Creatine
Cresylic
Crotonic
Cyclamic
Cysteine
Decanoic
Ethanoic
Fulminic
Glutamic
Glyceric
Glycolic
Guanylic
Hippuric
Iopanoic
Itaconic
Linoleic
Lysergic
Manganic

Margaric
Muriatic
Myristic
Nonanoic
Palmitic
Periodic
Phthalic
Retinoic
Rhodanic
Succinic
Sulfonic
Tantalic
Tartaric
Telluric
Tungstic
Tyrosine
Uridylic
Valproic

9 letters:
Aqua-regia
Cevitamic
Citydylic
Dichromic
Histidine
Hydrazoic
Hydriodic
Isocyanic
Linolenic
Methanoic
Nalidixic
Nicotinic
Ornithine
Panthenic
Pentanoic
Polybasic
Propanoic
Propenoic
Saccharic
Salicylic
Sassolite
Selenious
Sulphonic
Sulphuric

Tellurous
Threonine

10 letters:
Aquafortis
Asparagine
Barbituric
Carboxylic
Citrulline
Dithionous
Dodecanoic
Glucoronic
Glutamatic
Glutaminic
Hyaluronic
Isoleucine
Margaritic
Methionine
Neuraminic
Orthoboric
Pelargonic
Perchloric
Phosphonic
Phosphoric
Proprionic
Pyrogallic
Ricinoleic
Thiocyanic
Thymidylic
Trans-fatty
Tryptophan

11 letters:
Arachidonic
Butanedioic
Decanedioic
Ethanedioic
Ferricyanic
Ferrocyanic
Gibberellic
Hydnocarpic
Hydrobromic
Hydrocyanic
Hyponitrous

Methacrylic
Octanedioic
Pantothenic
Permanganic
Phosphorous
Ribonucleic
Sarcolactic
Taurocholic

12 letters:
Dicraboxylic
Hydrochloric
Hydrofluoric
Hypochlorous
Indoleacetic
Orthosilicic
Persulphuric
Phenylalanin
Polyadenalic
Propanedioic
Prostacyclin
Pyroligneous
Terephthalic

13 letters:
Galactosamine
Heptadecanoic
Indolebutyric
Phenylalanine
Prostaglandin
Pyrosulphuric
Thiosulphuric

14 letters:
Metaphosphoric
Pyrophosphoric

15 letters:
Orthophosphoric
Pteroylglutamic

16 letters:
Deoxyribonucleic

Acknowledge(ment) Accept, Admit, Allow, Answer, Avow, Confess, Credit, Grant,
Mea culpa, Nod, Own, Receipt, Recognise, Resipiscence, Respect, Righto, Roger,
Salute, Ta, Touché, Wilco, Yo
Acme Apex, Apogee, Climax, Comble, Crest, Peak, Summit, Top, Zenith
Acolyte Nethinim, Novice, Server, Thurifer
Acorn(s), Acorn-shell Balanus, Glans, Mast, Rac(c)ahout, Valonia

Acoustic(s) Harmonics, Phonics, Sonics
Acquaint(ance), Acquainted Advise, Cognisant, Enlighten, Familiar, → INFORM,
Knowledge, Nodding, Notify, Tell, Versed
Acquiesce(nce), Acquiescent Accept, Bow, Conform, Resigned, Righto, Roger,
Wilco, Yield
Acquire, Acquisition Acquest, Cop, Earn, Ern, Gain, → GET, Glom, Irredentist,
Land, Obtain, Procure, Purchase, Steal, Take-over, Target, Usucap(t)ion
Acquit(tal) Assoil, Cleanse, Clear, Exonerate, Free, Loose, Loste, Pardon
Acre(s) A, Area, Bigha, Hide, Rival, Rood
Acrid, Acrimony Bitter(ness), Empyreuma, Pungent, Rough, Sour, Surly
Acrobat(s), Acrobatics Equilibrist, Gymnast, Hot dog, Jerry-come-tumble,
Ropedancer, Speeler, Splits, Trampoline, Tumbler, Wing-walker
Acropolis Citadel, Parthenon
Across A, Ac, Athwart, Opposite, Over, Through
Act(ing), Action, Acts A, Actus reus, Affirmative, Antic, Assist, Assumpsit,
Auto, Barnstorm, Barrier, Behave, Bit, Business, Camp, Campaign, Case, Caster,
Cause, Charade, Class, Come, Conduct, Consolation, Coup, Daff, Deal, → DEED,
Delaying, Deputise, Detinue, Direct, Do, DORA, Double, Enabling, Enclosure,
Epitasis, Excitement, Exert, Exploit, Factory, Feat, Feign, Forth-putting, Function,
Furthcoming, Habeas corpus, Histrionic, Homestead, Identic, Impersonate,
Improbation, Incident, Industrial, Juristic, Lance-jack, Litigate, Locutionary,
Measure, Method, Movement, Mum, Mutiny, Navigation, Overt, Partypiece, Pas,
Perform(ance), Perlocutionary, Personate, Play, Positive, Pp, Practice, Pretence,
Private, Procedure, Process, Public, Qua, Qui tam, Reflex, Replevin, Represent,
Riot, Rising, Roleplay, Routine, Sasine, Scenery, Secondary, Septennial, Serve,
Showdown, Shtick, Sick-out, Simulate, Speech, Stamp, Stanislavski, Statute, Steps,
Suit, Synergy, Terminer, Test, Theatricise, Thellusson, Thing, Transitory, Treat,
Trover, Truck, Turn, Twig, Uniformity, Union, Vicegerent, War, Windlass
Actinium Ac
Actinon An
Activate Arm, Engage, Goad, Spark, Spur, Stur, Styre, Trigger
Active, Activist, Activity A, Agile, Alert, At, Athletic, Brisk, Busy, Cadre, Deedy,
DIY, Do(ing), Dynamited, Dynamo, Ecowarrior, Effectual, Energetic, Energic,
Erupting, Exercise, Extra-curricular, Floruit, Fluster, Game, Go-go, Goings-on,
Hum, Hyper, Leish, Licht, Live, Mobile, Motile, Nimble, Ongo, On the go, Op,
Operant, Optical, Play, Rambunctious, Residual, Sideline, Sprightly, Springe, Spry,
Sthenic, Stir, Surge, Third house, Vacuum, Voice, Wick, Wimble, Ya(u)ld
Actor(s), Actor-like Agent, Alleyn, Artist, Ashe, Barnstormer, Benson, Betterton,
Bit player, Burbage, Cast, Character, Company, Diseur, Donat, Equity, Gable,
Garrick, Gielgud, Guiser, Ham, Hamfatter, Heavy, Histrio(n), Jay, Juve(nile),
Kean, Luvvie, MacReady, Mime, Mummer, Olivier, Performer, Player, Playfair,
Protagonist, Roscian, Roscius, Savoyard, Sim, Stager, Strolling, Super, Thespian,
Tragedian, Tree, Tritagonist, Trouper, Understudy, Utility man, Wolfit
Actress Bankhead, Duse, Ingenue, Loren, Pierrette, Siddons, Soubrette, Terry, West
Actual(ity), Actually De facto, Entelechy, Literal, Live, Material, Real, Real-life,
Tangible, True, Very
Acumen Insight, Sense
Acupressure Jin shin do, Shiatsu
Acupuncture Stylostixis
Acute Astute, Dire, Fitché, Incisive, → INTENSE, Keen, Quick-witted, Sharp
Adage Aphorism, Gnome, Maxim, Motto, Paroemia, Proverb, Saw, Saying, Truism

Adam Bede, Delved
Adamant Firm, Inexorable, Insistent, Obdurate, Rigid, Unbending
Adapt(er), Adaptable, Adaptations, Adaptor Bushing, Ecad, Flexible, Persona,
  Pliant, Reorient, Resilient, Tailor, Timeserver, Transform, Versatile
Add(ed), Addendum, Adder Accrue, Adscititious, → **APPENDIX**, Attach, Cast,
  Coopt, Dub, Ech(e), Eik, Eke, Elaborate, Embroider, Enhance, Fortify, Insert, Lace,
  Puff, Reckon, Score, Spike, Sum, Summate, Tack on, Tot(e), Total, Viper
Addict(ion), Addicted Abuser, Acidhead, Base head, Blunthead, Buff, Couch
  potato, Dependency, Devotee, Dope-fiend, Etheromaniac, Fan, Fiend, Freak,
  Hophead, Hype, Jones, Joypopper, Junkie, Lover, Mainliner, Mania, Need, Pillhead,
  Pillpopper, Pothead, Shithead, Slave, Space-cadet, Speedfreak, User, Vinolent,
  Wino
Addison Spectator
Addition(al) Accession, Addend, Additive, Adscititious, Adulterant, Advene,
  Also, And, Annexure, (As an) in, Bolt-on, Braata, Codicil, Corollary, Eik, Eke,
  Encore, Epithesis, Etc, Extender, Extension, → **EXTRA**, Extramural, Footnote,
  → **IN ADDITION**, Increment, Makeweight, Monkey, New, Odd, On, On top, Other,
  Padding, Paragog(u)e, Parergon, Plus, PS, Rider, Ripieno, Spare, Suffect, Suffix,
  Supplementary, Surcharge, Thereto, Top-up, Verandah
Address, Address system Accommodation, Accost, Adroit, Allocution,
  Apostrophe, Apostrophise, Appellation, Art, → **ATLAS**, Ave, Bub, Buster, Call,
  Compellation, Dedication, Delivery, Den, Diatribe, Direction, Discourse, Election,
  Epilogue, Epirrhema, Esquire, Gettysburg, Gospodin, Hail, Home, Homily, IP, Lala,
  Lecture, Mester, Mister, Mush, Mynheer, Nkosi, Ode, Orate, Parabasis, Pastoral,
  Poste-restante, Prelection, Rig, Salute, Sermon, Sir(ree), Speech, Stance, Tact,
  Tannoy®, → **TITLE**, Towkay, Tuan, Valedictory, Wambenger, Web, Wus, Y'all
Adduce Cite
Adelphic Adam
Adept Able, Adroit, Buff, Dab, Deacon, Don, → **EXPERT**, Fit, Handy, Mahatma
Adequate Condign, Does, Due, Egal, Equal, Ere-now, Passable, Proper,
  → **SUFFICIENT**, Tolerable, Valid
Adhere(nt), Adherence, Adhesive Allegiance, Ally, Araldite®, Bond, Burr, Child,
  Cling, Conform, Cow Gum®, Dextrin, Disciple, Emplastic, Epoxy, Fidelity, Follower,
  Glue, Goldsize, Guebre, Gum, Hot-melt, Impact, Jain(a), Loyalist, Mucilage,
  Nomism, Partisan, Resin, Sectator, Servitor, Stand pat, Sticker, Supporter,
  Synechia, Votary, Waterglass
Adjacent, Adjoining Bordering, Conterminous, Contiguous, Handy, Nigh
Adjective Adnoun, Epithet, Gerundive
Adjourn(ment) Abeyance, Defer, Delay, → **POSTPONE**, Prorogate, Recess, Rise,
  Suspend
Adjudicate, Adjudicator Arbiter, Judge, Jury, Referee, Try, Umpire
Adjunct Addition, Aid, Ancillary, Rider
Adjust(able), Adjustment, Adjuster Accommodate, Adapt, Attune, Coapt,
  Dress, Ease, Fine-tune, Fit, Focus, Gang, Gauge, Gerrymander, J'adoube, Modify,
  Modulate, Orientate, Prepare, Reduce, Regulate, Reorientate, Reset, Scantle,
  Scotopia, Sliding, Suit, Temper, Toe-in, Tram, Trim, True, Tune, Tweak, Vernier
▷ **Adjust** *may indicate* an anagram
Adjutant Aide, Argala, Officer, Stork
Adler Irene
Ad-lib Wing it
Administer, Administration, Administrator Adhibit, Anele, Apply,

Arrondissement, Bairiki, Bureaucrat, Control, Corridors of power, → **DIRECT**, Dispence, Dispense, Executive, Intendant, Intinction, → **MANAGE**, Raj, Regime, Registrar, Run, Secretariat, Soke, Steward

Admirable, Admiration, Admire(d), Admirer Clinker, Clipper, Conquest, Crichton, Esteem, Estimable, → **EXCELLENT**, Flame, Fureur, Gaze, Ho, Iconise, Idolater, Laudable, Partisan, Regard, Ripping, Splendid, Toast, Tribute, Venerate, Wonder, Wow

Admiral Adm, AF, Anson, Beatty, Beaufort, Benbow, Blake, Bligh, Boscawen, Butterfly, Byng, Byrd, Capitan, Drake, Effingham, Fisher, Hood, Hornblower, Howard, Jellicoe, Keyes, Marrowfat, Navarch, Nelson, Raeder, Red, Rodney, Spee, Sturdee, Togo, Vanessa, Van Nieman, Van Tromp, White

Admission, Admit(ting), Admittance Accept, Access, Agree, Allow, Avow, Concede, → **CONFESS**, Enter, Entrée, Entry, Estoppel, Grant, Induct, Ingress, Initiate, Intromit, Ordain, Ordination, Owe, Own, Recognise, Shrift, Take, Tho(ugh), Yield

Admonish, Admonition Caution, Chide, Lecture, Moralise, Pi-jaw, Rebuke, Reprimand, → **SCOLD**, Tip, Warn

Ado Bother, Bustle, Fuss

Adolescent Developer, Grower, Halflin, Immature, Juvenile, Neanic, Teenager, Veal, Youth

Adonais Keats

Adonis Pheasant's Eye

Adopt(ed) Accept, Affect, Affiliate, Assume, Dalt, Embrace, Espouse, Father, Foster, Mother

Adoration, Adore Doat, Dote, Homage, Idolise, Latria, Love, Pooja(h), Puja, Revere, Venerate, Worship

Adorn(ed), Adornment Aplustre, Attrap, Banderol, Bedeck, Bedight, Bejewel, Caparison, Clinquant, Deck, Dight, Drape, Embellish, Emblaze, Emblazon, Embroider, Enchase, Equip, Festoon, Flourish, Furnish, Garnish, Grace, Graste, Ornament, Riband, Tattoo, Tatu, Tinsel, Trappings

Adrenaline Epinephrin(e)

Adroit Adept, Clever, Dextrous, Expert, Skilful

Adulate, Adulation Flatter(y), Praise, → **WORSHIP**

Adullam Cave

Adult Amadoda, Consenting, Grown-up, Man, Mature, Upgrown, X

Adulterant, Adulterate Cut, Debase, Impurify, Lime, Mix, Multum, → **POLLUTE**, Sophisticate, Weaken

Adulterer, Adultery Avoutery, Cuckold, Fornication, Francesca, Lenocinium

Advance(d) A, Abord, Accelerate, Anabasis, Ante, Approach, Ascend, Assert, Better(ment), Charge, Develop, Extreme, Far, Fore, Forge, Forward, Further, Gain, Get on, Grubstake, Haut(e), Hi-tec(h), Impress, Imprest, Incede, Late, Lend, → **LOAN**, March, Mortgage, On(ward), Overture, Pass, Piaffe, Posit, Postulate, Precocious, Prefer, Prest, Process, Progress, → **PROMOTE**, Propose, Propound, Retainer, Ripe, Rise, Scoop, Sub, Submit, Tiptoe, Upfront, Voorskot

Advantage(ous) Accrual, Aid, → **ASSET**, Avail, Batten, Benefit, Bisque, Boot, Edge, Emolument, Expedient, Exploit, Favour, Fruit, Gain, Grouter, Handicap, Handle, Head-start, Help, Interess, Interest, Lever(age), Nonmonetary, Odds, One-up, Oyster, Pecuniary, Percentage, Plus, Privilege, Prize, Pro, Purchase, Salutary, Stead, Strength, Toe-hold, Upper-hand, Upside, Use, Van, Whiphand, Whipsaw

Advent(ist) Coming, Shaker

Adventure(r), Adventuress, Adventurous Argonaut, Assay, Aunter, Buccaneer,

Casanova, Conquistador, Dareful, Daring, Emprise, Enterprise, Escapade,
→ **EXPLOIT**, Filibuster, Gest, Lark, Mata Hari, Mercenary, Merchant, Picaresque,
Picaro, Picaroon, Risk, Routier, Rutter, Swashbuckler, Vamp, Voyage

Adversary Antagonist, Cope(s)mate, Enemy, Foe

Adverse, Adversity Calamity, Cross, Down, Harrow, Misery, Reversal, Setback,
Untoward, Woe

Advert(ise), Advertisement, Advertising Ad, Air, Allude, Attack, Bark, Bill,
Blipvert, Circular, Classified, Coign(e), Coin, Commercial, Copy, Display, Dodger,
Flier, Flyer, Flyposting, Flysheet, Hard sell, Hype, Infomercial, Jingle, Madison
Avenue, Mailshot, Niche, Noise, → **NOTICE**, Out, Packshot, Parade, Personnel,
Placard, Plug, → **POSTER**, Promo, Promote, Promulgate, Prospectus, Puff,
Quoin, Refer, Semisolus, Sky-write, Splash, Spot, Stunt, Subliminal, Teaser, Tele-,
Throwaway, Tout, Trailer, Trawl, Want(s) (ad)

Advice Conseil, Counsel, → **GUIDANCE**, Guideline, Information, Invoice, Opinion,
Read, Recommendation, Reed, Re(e)de

Advise(d), Adviser, Advisable Acquaint, Avise(ment), CAB, Cabal, Camarilla,
Counsel, Egeria, Enlighten, Expedient, Genro, Induna, Inform, Instruct, Mentor,
Oracle, Peritus, Politic, Prudent, Ralph, → **RECOMMEND**, Tutor, Urge, Wise

Advocate(d) Agent, Argue, Attorney, Back, Counsel, Devil's, Endorse, Exponent,
Gospel, Intercede, Lawyer, Move, Paraclete, Peat, Peddle, Pleader, Pragmatist,
Preach, Proponent, Silk, Syndic, Urge

Aerial Aeolian, Aery, Antenna, Beam, Clover, Clover leaf, Communal, Dipole, Dish,
Ethereal, Ferrite-rod, Folded dipole, Frame, Ground-plane, Long-wire, Loop,
Minidish, Parabolic, Rhombic, Satellite dish, Slot, Yagi

Aerobatics Stunt

Aerobics Pilates, Step

Aerodrome → **AIRPORT**, Rotor-station

Aerofoil Spoiler

▸ **Aeroplane** see **AIRCRAFT**

Aerosol Atomiser, Mace®

Aesir Loki

Aesthetic Arty, Tasteful

Affable Amiable, Avuncular, Benign, Gracious, Suave, Urbane

Affair(s) Amour, Business, Concern, Current, Effeir, Effere, Event, External, Fight,
Fling, Foreign, Go, Indaba, Internal, Intrigue, Matter, Pash, Pi(d)geon, Pidgin, Ploy,
Relationship, Res, Romance, Shebang, Subject, Thing

Affect(ed), Affectation, Affection(ate) Air, Airtsy-mairtsy, Alter, Arty, Breast,
Camp, Chi-chi, Concern, Crachach, Crazy, Endearment, Euphuism, Foppery, Grip,
Hit, Impress, Ladida, Lovey-dovey, Mimmick, Minauderie, Mincing, Minnick,
Minnock, Mouth-made, Phoney, → **POSE**, Poseur, Precieuse, Preciosity, Pretence,
Prick-me-dainty, Smitten, Spoilt, Stag(e)y, Storge, Susceptible, Sway, Sympathetic,
Tender, Topophilia, Touched, Touchy-feely, Twee, Unction, Unnatural, Upend

Affiliate, Affiliation Adopt, Associate, Merge, Unite

Affinity Bro, Kin(ship), Penchant, Rapport, Tie

Affirm(ative), Affirmation Assert, Attest, Maintain, Predicate, Profess,
Protestation, Uh-huh, → **VERIFY**, Yebo

Affix(ed) Append, Ascribe, → **ATTACH**, Connect, Fasten, On

Afflict(ed), Affliction Aggrieve, Ail, Asthma, Cross, Cup, Curse, Disease,
Furnace, Harass, Hurt, Lumbago, Molest, Nosology, Palsy, Persecute, Pester,
Plague, Scourge, Smit, Sore, → **SORROW**, Stricken, Teen, Tene, Tic, Tribulation,
→ **TROUBLE**, Try, Unweal, Visitation, Woe

Affluence, Affluent Abundance, Dinky, Fortune, Grey panther, Opulence, Wealth
Afford Allow, Bear, Give, Manage, Offer, Provide, Spare, Yield
Affray Brawl, Fight, Mêlée, Scuffle, Skirmish
Affront Assault, Defy, Facer, → INSULT, → OFFEND, Outrage, Scandal, Slight, Slur
Afghan(istan) Bactria, Dard, Hound, Kaf(f)ir, Pakhto, Pakhtu, Pashto, Pashtu, Pathan, Pushto(o), Pushtu
Afloat Aboard, Abroach, Adrift, Natant
Afoot Astir, Up
Aforesaid Above, Same
Afraid Adrad, Alarmed, Chicken, Fearful, Funk, Rad, Regretful, Scared, Timorous, Windy, Yellow
Africa(n) Abyssinian, Adamawa, Akan, Algerian, Amakwerekwere, Angolan, Ashanti, Baganda, Bambara, Bantu, Barbary, Barotse, Basotho, Basuto, Bechuana, Beento, Bemba, Beninese, Berber, Biafran, Bintu, Black, Boer, Botswana, Bushman, Caffre, Cairene, Carthaginian, Chewa, Chichewa, Ciskei, Congo(l)ese, Cushitic, Damara, Dinka, Duala, Dyula, Efik, Eritrean, Ethiopian, Eve, Fang, Fanti, Fingo, Flytaal, Fula(h), Gabonese, Galla, Gambian, Ganda, Gazankulu, Grikwa, Griqua, Guinean, Gullah, Hamite, Hausa, Herero, Hottentot, Hutu, Ibibi, Ibo, Igbo, Impi, Kabyle, Kaffer, Kaf(f)ir, Kenyan, Khoikhoi, Kikuyu, Kongo, Lango, Lesotho, Liberian, Libyan, Lowveld, Lozi, Luba, Luo, Maghreb, Maghrib, Malawi, Malian, Malinke, Mande, Mandingo, Masai, Mashona, Matabele, Mende, Moor, Moroccan, Mossi, Mozambican, Mswahili, Munt(u), Mzee, Nama, Nama(qua), Namibian, Negrillo, → NEGRO, Ngoni, Nguni, Nilot(e), Nubian, Nuer, Numidian, Nyanja, Oromo, Ovambo, Pedi, Pied noir, Pondo, Rastafarian, Rhodesian, Rwandan, San, Senegalese, Shilluk, Shluh, Shona, Somali, Songhai, Sotho, Soweto, Sudanese, Susu, Swahili, Swazi, Temne, Tiv, Togolese, Tonga, Transkei, Transvaal, Tshi, Tsonga, Tswana, Tuareg, Tutsi, Twi, Ugandan, Venda, Voltaic, Waswahili, Watu(t)si, Wolof, X(h)osa, Yoruban, Zairean, Zulu
Afrikaan(s), Afrikaner Cape Dutch, Crunchie, Hairyback, Mynheer, Taal, Volk, Voortrekker
After(wards) About, A la, At, Behind, Beyond, Eft, Epi-, → LATER, On, Once, Past, Rear, Since, Sine, Subsequent, Syne
Afterbirth Secundines, Sooterkin
Afterimage Photogene
▷ **After injury** *may indicate* an anagram
Aftermath Consequence, Fall out, Legacy, Mow(ing), Rawing, Rawn, Rowan, Rowen, Rowing, Sequel(a)
Afternoon A, Arvo, PM, Postmeridian, Undern
Afterpiece, Afterthought Addendum, Codicil, Epimetheus, Exode, Footnote, Note, PS, Supplement
Again Afresh, Agen, Anew, Back, Bis, De novo, Ditto, Do, Eft, Eftsoons, Encore, Iterum, More, Moreover, O(v)er, Re-, Recurrence, Reprise, Than, Then
Against A, Anti, Beside, Con, Counter, Gainsayer, Into, Nigh, On, Opposing, To, V, Versus
Agape Feast, Hiant, Ringent, Yawning
Agate Chalcedonyx, Moss, Murr(h)a, Onyx, Ruin
Agave Century plant, Henequen, Lily, Maenad, Maguey
Age(d), Ages, Aging Absolute, Achievement, Ae, Aeon, Aet, Alcheringa, Anno domini, Antique, Archaise, Atomic, Augustan, Azilian, Bronze, Calpa, Century, Chellean, Coon's, Copper, Cycle, Dark, Date, Day, Doddery, Eld, Elizabethan, Eon, Epact, Epoch(a), Era, Eternity, Generation, Gerontic, Golden, Grey, Heroic,

Hoar, Hore, Ice, Information, Iron, Jazz, Jurassic, Kaliyuga, Kalpa, La Tene, Lias, Magdalenian, Maglemosian, Mature, Mental, Mesolithic, Middle, Millennium, Neolithic, New, New Stone, Of, Old, Oligocene, Paleolithic, Passé, Periclean, Period, Phanerozoic, Progeria, Reindeer, S(a)eculum, Saros, Senescence, Silver, Solera, Space, Stone, Third, Villanovan, Yellow, Yonks, Yug(a)

Agency, Agent Agitator, Alkylating, Ambassador, Antistatic, Art, Autolysin, Bailiff, Bargaining, Barm, Bond, Broker, BSI, Bureau, Catalyst, Cat's paw, Cause, Chelating, Child support, Commis, Complexone, Comprador(e), Confidential, Consul, Consular, Countryside, Crown, Customs, Dating, Del credere, Developing, Disclosing, Distributor, Doer, Double, Emissary, Environment, Envoy, Enzyme, Escort, Estate, Exciseman, Executant, Executor, Factor, Fed, Finger, Flack, Forwarding, Free, Galactagogue, G-man, Go-between, Hand, Hirudin, House, Implement, Indian, Influence, Institorial, Instrument, Intermediary, Kinase, Law, Legate, Literary, Magic bullet, Man, Means, Medium, Mercantile, Mitogen, Mole, Moral, Mutagen, Narc, Narco, Nerve, Ninja, Nucleating, OO, -or, Order paper, Oxidizing, Parliamentaire, Parliamentary, Patent, Pathogen, Peace corps, Penetration, Pinkerton, Press, Procurator, Proxy, Realtor, Reducing, Rep(resentative), Resident, Reuters, Riot, Road, Runner, Salesman, Secret (service), Setter, Shipping, SIS, Sleeper, Solvent, Soman, Spook, Spy, Stock, Surfactant, Syndic, Tass, Teratogen, Third party, Ticket, Training, Travel, UNESCO, Vakeel, Vakil, Virino, Voice, Welfare, Wetting, Wire service

Agenda Business, Hidden, Programme, Remit, Schedule

Aggie Agnes, Ines, Nessa, Nesta

Aggravate Annoy, Exasperate, Inflame, Irk, Needle, Nettle, Provoke, Try, Vex

Aggregate, Aggregation Ballast, Congeries, Detritus, Etaerio, Granulite, Gravel, Omnium, Ore, Sum, Total

Aggression, Aggressive, Aggressor Arsey, Attack, Bare-knuckle, Bellicose, Belligerent, Biffo, Bullish, Butch, Defiant, Enemy, Feisty, Foe, Gungho, Hard-hitting, Hawk, Invader, In-your-face, Militant, On-setter, Pushing, Rambo, Rampant, Road rage, Shirty, Truculent, Wild

Agile Acrobatic, Deft, Lissom(e), Nifty, Nimble, Quick, Spry, Supple, Swank, Twinkletoes

Agitate(d), Agitation, Agitator Activist, Ado, Agitprop, Betoss, Boil, Bolshie, Bother, Chartist, Churn, Commotion, Commove, Convulse, Demagogue, Discompose, Distraught, → **DISTURB**, Doodah, Ebullient, Emotion, Excite, Extremist, Fan, Fantad, Fanteeg, Fantigue, Fantod, Ferment, Firebrand, Flurry, Fluster, Flutter, Fraught, Frenzy, Fuss, Goad, Heat, Hectic, Jabble, Lather, Militant, Overwrought, Panicky, Pedetic, Perturb, Poss, Pother, Rattle, Restless, Rouse, Ruffle, Seethed, Shake, Sod, Stir(-up), Swivet, Tailspin, Taking, Tempest, Tew, Thermal, Tizzy, Toss, Tremor, Trepidation, Trouble, Turmoil, Tweak, Twitchy, Unrest, Upset, Welter, Whisk, Wrought up, Ytost

▷ **Agitate** *may indicate* an anagram

Agley Awry, Unevenly

Aglow Alight, Tipsy

▶ **Agnes** *see* **AGGIE**

Agnostic Laodicean

Ago Lang syne, → **SINCE**

Agog Astir, Athirst, Eager, Keen, Pop-eyed

Agonise, Agony Ache, Anguish, Brood, Dread, Ecstasy, Heartache, → **PAIN**, Throe(s), Torment, Torture

Agree(ing), Agreed, Agreement Accede, Accept, Accord, Acquiescence, Agt,

Allow, Amen, Analog(ue), Analogy, Apply, As one, Assent, Assort, Atone,
Ausgleich, Aye, Bilateral, Bipartite, Bond, Camp David, Cartel, Champerty,
Charterparty, Chime, Closing, Coincide, Collective, Comart, Community, Compact,
Comply, Comport, Concert, Concord(at), Concur, Conform, Congree, Congruent,
Consension, Consensus, → **CONSENT**, Consonant, Contract, Contrahent,
Convention, Correspond, Cotton, Covenant, Cushty, Dayton Accords, Deal, Deffo,
Deign, Done, Entente, Equate, Escrow, Fadge, Gatt, Gentleman's, Handfast,
Harmony, Homologous, Indenture, Jibe, Knock-for-knock, League, Like-minded,
Mercosur, Munich, National, Net Book, Nod, Nudum pactum, Okay, Pact, Pair,
Placet, Plant, Plea bargaining, Prenuptial, Procedural, Productivity, Rabat(te),
Repo, Repurchase, Right(o), Right on, Roger, Sanction, Schengen, Service,
Settlement, Side, Sort(ance), Specialty, Sponsion, Square, Standstill, Substantive,
Suit, Sweetheart, Sympathy, Synchronise, Synesis, Syntony, Tally, Technology,
Threshold, Trade, Treaty, Uh-huh, Union, Unison, Unspoken, Wilco, Wukkas, Yea,
Yea-say, Yes
Agreeable Amene, Harmonious, Pleasant, Sapid, Sweet, Well-disposed, Willing,
Winsome
Agriculture, Agricultural(ist) Arval, Geoponic, Georgic, Inari, Permaculture, Slash
and burn, Smallholding, Tull
Aground Ashore, Beached, Sew, Stranded
Ague Dumb
▷ **Ague(ish)** *may indicate* an anagram
Ah Ach, Ay
Ahead Anterior, Before, Foreship, Forward, Frontwards, In store, Onward,
Precocious, Up
Aiblins Perhap, Perhaps, Yibbles
Aid(s), Aide Accessory, Adjutant, Artificial, Assist, Decca, → **DEPUTY**, First,
Foreign, Galloper, Gift, Grant, Hearing, Help, Key, Legal, Lend-lease, Monitor,
Optophone, Orthosis, PA, Realia, Relief, Serve, Sex, Subsidy, Subvention, Succour,
Support, Teaching, Visual, Yeoman('s) service, Zimmer®
AIDS Slim
Ail(ment) Affect, Afflict(ion), Complaint, Croup, Disease, Malady, Narks,
Occupational, Pink-eye, Pip, Sickness
Aim Approach, Aspire, Bead, Bend, End, Ettle, Eye, Goal, Hub, Intent, Level, Mark,
Mint, Mission, Object, Peg, Plan, Plank, Point, Point blank, Purpose, Reason, Sake,
Seek, Sight(s), Target, Tee, Telos, Train, View, Visie, Vizy, Vizzie, Zero-in
Aimless Adrift, Drifting, Erratic, Haphazard, Random, Unmotivated
Air(s), Airer, Airy Aerate, Aerial, Aero, Affectation, Allure, Ambiance, Ambience,
Aquarius, Arietta, Atmosphere, Attitude, Aura, Bearing, Breath, Calypso, Canzona,
Canzone, Cavatina, Compressed, Dead, Demaine, Descant, Ditty, Draught, Dry,
Emphysema, Ether(eal), Expose, Fan, Filmy, Front, Gemini, Heat-island, Heaven,
Horse, Inflate, Libra, Lift, Light, Liquid, Look, Lullaby, Madrigal, Manner, Melody,
Microburst, Mien, Night, Nitre, Oat, Open, Ozone, Parade, Periptery, Pneumatic,
Radio, Screen, Scuba, Serenade, Serenata, Serene, Shanty, Side, Sky, Slipstream,
Solo, Song, Strain, Swank, Thin, Trigon, → **TUNE**, Vent, Ventilate, Vital, Wake,
Wind
Airborne Ab
Air-conditioning Plenum system
Aircraft, Airship Aerodyne, Aerostat, Angels, AST, Auster, Autoflare, Autogiro,
Autogyro, Aviette, Avion, Biplane, Blimp, Brabazon, Bronco, Camel, Canard,
Canberra, Chaser, Chopper, Coleopter, Comet, Concorde, Convertiplane, Corsair,

Crate, Cropduster, Cyclogiro, Delta-wing, Dirigible, Doodlebug, Drone, Eagle, F, Ferret, Fixed-wing, Flivver, Flying wing, Fokker, Freedom-fighter, Freighter, Galaxy, Glider, Gotha, Gyrodyne, Gyroplane, Hang-glider, Harrier, Hawkeeze, Heinkel, Helicopter, Hercules, Hunter, Hurricane, Interceptor, Intruder, Jet star, Jumbo, Jump-jet, Kite, Lancaster, Liberator, Lifting-body, Messerschmitt, Microjet, Microlight, Microlite, MIG, Mirage, Monoplane, Mosquito, Moth, Multiplane, Nightfighter, Nightfinder, Oerlikon, Orion, Ornithopter, Orthopter, Parasol, Penguin, Phantom, → **PLANE**, Provider, Prowler, Pusher, Ramjet, Rigid, Rotaplane, Runabout, Scramjet, Semi-rigid, Skiplane, Skyhawk, Sopwith, Sopwith Camel, Spitfire, SST, Starfighter, Starlifter, Stealth bomber, STOL, Stratocruiser, Stratotanker, Stuka, Super Sabre, Sweptwing, Swing-wing, Tankbuster, Taube, Taxiplane, Thunderbolt, Thunderchief, Tomcat, Tornado, Tracker, Trident, Tri-jet, Triplane, Tube, Turbofan, Turbo-jet, Turbo-prop, Turboramjet, Vigilante, Viking, Viscount, Vomit comet, Voodoo, VTOL, Wild weasel, Zeppelin
Aircraftsman, Airman AC, Aeronaut, Erk, Fokker, Kiwi, LAC, RAF
Aircraftswoman Penguin, Pinguin
▶ **Airfield** see **AIRPORT**
Air force Luftwaffe
Airlift Thermal
Airline, Airway Aeroflot, Anthem, BAC, BEA, Duct, Larynx, Lot, Lyric, Purple, Qantas, SAS, S(ch)norkel, TWA, Weasand(-pipe), Windpipe
▶ **Airman** see **AIRCRAFTSMAN, FLIER**
Airport Drome, Entebbe, Faro, Gander, Gatwick, Heliport, Idlewild, Kennedy, La Guardia, Landing strip, Lod, Luton, Lydda, Lympne, Orly, Prestwick, Runway, Shannon, Stansted, Stolport, Terminal, Vertiport, Wick
Air-raid Blitz, Mission
Air-tight Hermetic, Indisputable, Sealed
Aisle Gangway
Aitch Ache, Aspirate, H
Ajax Loo
Aka Alias
Akin Alike, Cognate, Congener, Kindred
Alabaster Oriental
Alarm Alert, Arouse, Bell, Bleep, Caution, Concern, Dismay, Eek, False, Fire, Fricht, Fright, Ghast, Hairy, Larum, Panic, Perturb, Rock, Rouse, Siren, Smoke, Startle, Tirrit, Tocsin, Warn, Yike(s)
Alas Ah, Alack, Ay, Eheu, Ha, Haro, Harrow, Io, Lackadaisy, Lackaday, O, Oh, Ohone, O me, Ou, Sadly, Waesucks, Waly, Well-a-day, Wellanear, Wel(l)away, Woe
Alaskan AK, Sourdough, Yupik
Alban Berg
Albanian Arna(o)ut
Albatross Alcatras, Golf, Gooney(-bird), Millstone, Omen, Onus, Wandering
Albeit Tho(ugh)
Albert Chain, Chevalier, Consort, Hall, Herring, Slang
Album Autograph, Looseleaf, Photo, Record, Stamp
Albumen, Albumin Chalaza, Glair, Leucosin, Mucin, Myogen, Protein, Ricin, Serum, White
Alchemic, Alchemist, Alchemy Adept, Brimstone, Faust(us), Hermetic(s), Multiplier, Orpiment, Paracelsus, Quicksilver, Sal ammoniac, Sorcery, Spagyric, Spagyrist, Witchcraft
Alcides Hercules

Alcohol(ic) Absolute, Acrolein, Aldehyde, Amyl, Bibulous, Booze, Borneol, Catechol, Cetyl, Chaptalise, Cholesterol, Choline, Citronellol, Cresol, Denatured, Diol, Dipsomaniac, Drinker, Ethal, Ethanol, Ethyl, Farnesol, Feni, Fenny, Firewater, Fusel-oil, Geraniol, Glycerin(e), Grain, Grog, Gut-rot, Hard, Hard stuff, Inebriate, Inositol, Isopropyl, Jakey, Jungle juice, Lauryl, Linalool, Lush, Mahua, Mahwa, Mannite, Mannitol, Mercaptan, Mescal, Methanol, Meths, Methyl, Mow(r)a, Nerol, Phytol, Plonko, Propyl, Rotgut, Rubbing, Rubby, Scrumpy, Secondary, Snake juice, Sorbitol, Sphingosine, Spirits, Spirits of wine, Spirituous, Sterol, Taplash, Terpineol, Tincture, Tocopherol, Triol, Wash, Wino, Wood, Xylitol

Alcove Apse, Bay, Bole, Carrel(l), Dinette, Inglenook, Lunette, Niche, Nook, Recess, Tokonoma

Alcyonarian Sea-feather

Aldehyde Acrolein, Aldol, Vanillin

Alder Fothergilla

Alderman Bail(l)ie, CA

Alderney CI, Cow

Ale, Alehouse Audit, Barleybree, Barley-broo, Barley-broth, Barley wine, Beer, Brown, CAMRA, Church, Four, Heather, Humming, Humpty-dumpty, Lamb's wool, Light, Mild, Morocco, Nappy, Nog, Nogg, October, Pale, Plain, Porter, Purl, Real, Small, Stout, Swats, Tiddleywink, Tipper, White, Whitsun, Wort, Yard, Yill, Yorkshire stingo

Alert Amber, Arrect, Astir, Attentive, Aware, Conscious, Gleg, Gogo, Intelligent, Open-eyed, Qui vive, Red, Scramble, Sharp, Sprack, Sprag, Stand-to, Tentie, Up and coming, Vigilant, Volable, Wary, Watchful, Wide-awake

Alewife Barkeeper, Gaspereau

Alexander, Alexandrine Alex, Arius, Macedonian, Pope, Sandy, Sasha, Sawn(e)y, Selkirk, Senarius

Alfalfa Lucern(e), Luzern

Alfred Dreyfus, Garnet, Jingle

Alfresco Barbecue, Plein-air

Alga(e) Anabaena, Blanketweed, Chlorella, Conferva, Desmid, Diatom, Dulse, Heterocontae, Isokont, Jelly, Nostoc, Periphyton, Phycology, Pleuston, Pond scum, Prokaryon, Protococcus, Red, Seaweed, Spirogyra, Star-jelly, Stonewort, Ulothrix, Ulotrichales, Valonia, Volvox, Witches' butter, Zooxanthella

Algebra Boolean, Linear, Quadratics

Algerian Kabyle, Nimidian

Algonquin Innu

Alias Aka, Byname, Epithet, Moni(c)ker, Nick(name), Pen-name, Pseudonym

Alibi Excuse, Watertight

Alien(ate), Alienation A-effect, Amortise, Disaffect, Ecstasy, Erotic, Estrange, ET, Exotic, External, Foreign, Forinsecal, Fremd, Hostile, Martian, Metic, Outlandish, Outsider, Philistine, Repugnant, Strange(r)

Alight Alowe, Availe, Detrain, Disembark, Dismount, In, Lambent, Land, Lit, Perch, Pitch, Rest, Settle

Align Arrange, Associate, Collimate, Dress, Juxtapose, Marshal, Orient, Straighten

▶ **Alike** see LIKE

Alimentary Oesophagus, Pharynx

Aliquot Submultiple

Alive Alert, Animated, Breathing, Extant, Quick

Alkali(ne), Alkaloid Antacid, Apomorphine, Atropine, Base, Bebeerine, Berberine, Betane, Borax, Brucine, Caffein(e), Capsaicin, Chaconine, Choline, Cinchon(id)ine,

Codeine, Colchicine, Corydaline, Curarine, Emetin(e), Ephedrine, Ergotamine, Gelsemin(in)e, Guanidine, Harmalin(e), Harmin(e), Hydrastine, Hyoscine, Hyoscyamine, Ibogaine, Lixivium, Lobeline, Lye, Mescalin, Narceen, Narceine, Nicotine, Papaverine, Physostigmine, Pilocarpin(e), Piperine, Potash, Potass, Quinine, Reserpine, Rhoeadine, Scopaline, Scopolamine, Soda, Solanine, Sparteine, Thebaine, Theine, Theobromine, Theophylline, Totaquine, Tropine, Veratridine, Veratrin(e), Vinblastine, Vinca, Vincristine, Volatile, Yohimbine

Alkane Hexane

All A, → ENTIRE, Entity, Finis, Omni, Pan, Quite, Sum, → TOTAL, Toto, Tutti, Whole

Allah Bismillah, God

All at once Holus-bolus, Suddenly

Allay Alleviate, Calm, Disarm, Lessen, Quieten, Soothe

Allegation, Allege Accuse, Assert, Aver, Claim, Obtend, Plead, Purport, Represent, Smear

Allegiance Faith, Foy, Loyalty

Allegory, Allegorical Apologue, Fable, Mystic, Myth, Parable

Allergy Atopy, Aversion, Bagassosis, Hay fever, Hives

Alleviate Allay, Alleg(g)e, Calm, Mitigate, Mollify, Palliate, → RELIEVE, Temper

Alley Aisle, Blind, Bonce, Bowling, Corridor, Ennog, Ginnel, Lane, Laura, Marble, Passage, Rope-walk, Silicon, Tin Pan, Twitten, Vennel, Walk, Wynd

Alliance Agnation, Axis, Bloc, Cartel, Coalition, Combine, Compact, Confederation, Dreibund, Dual, Federacy, → LEAGUE, Marriage, NATO, Quadruple, Syndicate, Triple, Union

Alligator Al(l)igarta, Avocado, Caiman, Cayman

Alliteration Cynghanedd, Head-rhyme

Allocate, Allocation Allot, Apportion(ment), Assign, Designate, Distribute, Earmark, Placement, Priorate, Ration, Share, Zone

Allot(ment), Allow(ance), Allowed, Allowing Admit, Affect, Alimony, Allocation, Although, Aret(t), Assign, Attendance, Award, Batta, Beteem(e), Brook, Budget, Charter, Cloff, Confess, Cor(r)ody, Diet, Discount, Dole, Draft, Enable, Entitle, Excuse, Expenses, Feod, Give, Grant, House-bote, Husbandage, Indulge, Jobseekers', Latitude, Legit(imate), Let, Licit, Luit(en), Machining, Mag, Mobility, Okay, Palimony, Parcel, Pension, Percentage, → PERMIT, Personal, Pittance, Plot, Portion, Quarterage, Quota, Ratio, Ration, Rebate, Rood, Salt-money, Sanction, Separation, Sequel, Share(-out), Shrinkage, Sizings, Stint, Stipend, Subsistence, Suffer, Tare, Tax, Teene, Though, Tolerance, Tolerate, Tret, Viaticum, Weighting, Yield

Allotment-holder Cleruch

▶ **Allow** see ALLOT

Alloy Albata, Alnico®, Amalgam, Babbitt, Bell-metal, Billon, Brass, Britannia metal, Bronze, Cermet, Chrome(l), Compound, Constantan, Cupronickel, Duralumin®, Electron, Electrum, Eutectoid, Ferrochrome, Gunmetal, Invar®, Iridosmine, Kamacite, Latten, Magnalium, Magnox, Manganin®, Marmem, Mischmetal, Mix, Monel®, Nichrome®, Nickel-silver, Nicrosilal, Nimonic, Nitinol, Occamy, Oreide, Orichalc, Ormolu, Oroide, Osmiridium, Paktong, Pewter, Pinchbeck, Platinoid, Porous, Potin, Pot metal, Prince's metal, Shakudo, Shibuichi, Similor, Solder, Speculum, Spelter, Steel, Stellite®, Tambac, Terne, Tombac, Tombak, Tutenag, Zircal(l)oy, Zircoloy

▷ **Alloy** *may indicate* an anagram

Allright A1, Assuredly, Fit, Hale, Hunky(-dory), Jake, OK, Safe, Tickety-boo, Well

All-round Overhead, Versatile

All-seeing Panoptic
Allspice Jamaica pepper, Pimiento
All the same Nath(e)less, Nevertheless
Allude, Allusion Hint, Imply, Innuendo, Mention, Refer, Reference, Suggest
Allure, Alluring Agaçant(e), Charm, Circe, Decoy, Entice, Femme fatale, Glam,
  Glamour, Inviting, It, Magnet(ic), SA, Seduce, Seductive, Tempt, Trap, Trepan,
  Vamp
Alluvium Carse
Ally, Allied Accomplice, Agnate, Aide, Alley, Alliance, Backer, Belamy, Cognate,
  Colleague, Dual, Foederatus, German(e), Holy, Marble, Marmoreal, Partner,
  Plonker, Related, Taw, Unholy
Almanac Calendar, Clog, Ephemeris, Nautical, Nostradamus, Whitaker's, Wisden,
  Zadkiel
Almighty Creator, Dollar, God, Jehovah, Omnipotent
Almond Amygdal, Emulsion, Jordan, Marchpane, Marzipan, Orgeat, Praline,
  Ratafia, Sugared, Valencia
Almost Anear, Anigh, Close on, Most, Near, Nigh(ly), Practically, Ripe, Une(a)th,
  Virtually, Well-nigh, Welly
Alms Awmous, Charity, Dole, Handout, Zakat
Aloe Agave, Pita
Alone Hat, Jack, Lee-lane, Onely, Pat, Secco, Separate, Single, Singly, Sola, Solo,
  Solus, Tod, Unaccompanied, Unaided, Unattended, Unholpen
Along, Alongside Abeam, Aboard, Abreast, Apposed, Beside, By, Parallel
Aloof Abeigh, Apart, Asocial, Cool, Detached, Distant, Hou inch, Indrawn,
  Mugwump, Offish, Remote, Reserved, Reticent, Skeigh, Snooty, Stand-offish,
  Toffee-nosed, Unapproachable
Alpaca Paco
Alphabet ABC, Absey, Augmented Roman, Black-out, Brahmi, Braille, Chalcidian,
  Christcross, Cyrillic, Deaf, Devanagari, Estrang(h)elo, Futhark, Futhorc, Futhork,
  Glagol, Glagolitic, Glossic, Grantha, Hangul, Horn-book, International, IPA, ITA,
  Kana, Kanji, Katakana, Kufic, Latin, Manual, Nagari, Og(h)am, Pangram, Phonetic,
  Pinyin, Romaji, Roman, Runic, Signary, Syllabary
Alpine, Alps Australian, Bernese, Cottian, Dinaric, Gentian, Graian, Julian,
  Laburnum, Lepontine, Maritime, Matterhorn, Ortles, Pennine, Rhaetian, Savoy,
  Southern, Transylvanian, Tyrol, Western
Also Add, And, Eke, Item, Likewise, Moreover, Plus, Too, Und
Altar, Altar-cloth, Altarpiece Butsudan, Diptych, Dossal, Dossel, High, Polyptych,
  Retable, Shrine, Tabula, Triptych
Alter, Alteration Adapt, Adjust, Bushel, Change, Changeover, Cook, Correct,
  Customise, Distort, Evolve, Falsify, Lib, Modify, Modulate, Mutate, Recast, Revise,
  Transpose, Up-end, → VARY
▷ **Alter(native)** *may indicate* an anagram
Altercation Barney, Brawl, Fracas, Row, Words, Wrangle
Alternate, Alternating, Alternation, Alternative Boustrophedon, Bypass,
  Exchange, Instead, Metagenesis, → OPTION, Ossia, Other, Rotate, Second string,
  Solidus, Staggered, Systaltic, Tertian, Variant, Vicissitude
▷ **Alternately** *may indicate* every other letter
Althaea Mallow, Malva
Although Admitting, Albe(e), All-be, But, Even, Howsoever, Howsomever,
  Whereas, While
Altitude Elevation, Height, Meridian, Rated

Alto Countertenor
Altogether Algate(s), All-to-one, Completely, Entirely, Holus-bolus, Idea, In all, Nude, Nudity, Purely, Slick, Tout, Uncut, Wholly
▷ **Altogether** *may indicate* words to be joined
Altruistic Heroic, Humane, Philanthropic, Selfless, Unselfish
Alum Potash
Aluminium, Alumino-silicate Al, Bauxite, Gibbsite, Sillimanite, Stilbite, Tinfoil
Alumnus Graduate, OB
Always Algate(s), Ay(e), Constant, E'er, Eternal, Ever(more), Forever, I, Immer, Semper, Sempre, Still
Amalgamate Coalesce, Consolidate, Fuse, Merge, Unite
Amalthea Cornucopia
Amarylli(d)s Leocojum, Lily, Polianthes
Amass Accumulate, Assemble, Collect, Gather, Heap, Hoard, Pile, Upheap
Amateur(s) A, AA, Armchair, Beginner, Corinthian, Dilettante, DIY, Enthusiast, Ham, Inexpert, L, Laic, Lay, Neophyte, Novice, Prosumer, Sunday painter, Tiro, Tyro
Amatory Eros, Erotic, Fervent
Amaze(d), Amazement, Amazing Astonish, Astound, Awe, Awhape, Bewilder, Cor, Criv(v)ens, Dumbfound, Far out, Flabbergast, Gee-whiz, Gobsmack, Goodnow, Grace, Incredible, Jesus wept, Magical, Monumental, O, Open-eyed, Open-mouthed, Perplex, Poleaxe, Pop-eyed, Prodigious, Stagger, Stupefaction, Stupendous, Thunderstruck, Unreal
Amazon(ian) Ant, ATS, Brimstone, Britannia, Dragon, Hippolyta, Hoyden, Jivaro, Orellana, Penthesilea, Shield-maid, Shield-may, Thalestris, Tupi, Virago
Ambassador At-large, Diplomat, Elchee, Elchi, Eltchi, Envoy, Extraordinary, HE, Internuncio, Leaguer, Ledger, Legate, Leiger, Minister, Nuncio, Plenipo, Plenipotentiary
Amber Colophony, Lammer, Ligure, Resin, Retinite, Succinum
Ambience Aura, Milieu, Setting
Ambiguous, Ambiguity Amphibology, Cryptic, Delphic, Double, Double entendre, Enigmatic, Epicene, Equivocal, Loophole, Oracular, Weasel words
Ambit Scope
Ambition, Ambitious Aim, Arrivisme, Aspiring, Careerism, Drive, Emulate, Go-ahead, Goal, Go-getter, High-flier, Keen, Office-hunter, Purpose, Pushy, Rome-runner, Thrusting
Amble Meander, Mosey, Pace, Poddle, Saunter, Single-foot, Stroll
Ambrose Emrys
Ambrosia(l) Amreeta, Amrita, Beebread, Fragrant, Odorant, Ragweed, Savoury
Ambulance, Ambulanceman Badger, Blood-wagon, Field, Meat wagon, Pannier, Paramedic, Van, Yellow-flag, Zambu(c)k
Ambulatory Stoa
Ambush(ed) Ambuscade, Belay, Bushwhack, Embusque, Latitant, Lurch, Perdu(e), Trap, Watch, Waylay
Amelia Bloomer
Ameliorate Amend, Ease, Improve, Remedy
Amen Ammon, Approval, Inshallah, Verify
Amenable Putty
Amend(ment) Alter, Change, Correct, Expiate, Expurgate, Fifth, Protocol, Redress, Reform, Repair, Restore, → REVISE, Satisfy
▷ **Amend** *may indicate* an anagram

Ament Catkin, Idiot
America(n) A, Algonki(a)n, Algonqu(i)an, Am, Angeleno, Basket Maker, Caddo, Cajun, Carib, Chicano, Chickasaw, Chinook, Copperskin, Digger, Doughface, Down-easter, Federalist, Flathead, Fox, Gringo, Huron, Interior, Joe, Jonathan, Latino, Miskito, Mistec, Mixtec, Native, New World, Norteno, Olmec, Paisano, Salish, Stateside, Statesman, Statist, Tar-heel, Tico, Tupi, Uncle Sam, US(A), WASP, Yankee, Yanqui
Americium Am
Amethyst Oriental
Amiable Friendly, Genial, Gentle, Inquiline, Mungo, Sweet, Warm
Amid(st) Among, Atween, Between, Inter, Twixt
Amide Asparagine
Amine Putrescine, Spermine
Amino-acid Dopa, Tyrosine, Valine
Amiss Awry, Ill, Up, Wrong
Ammonia(c) Amide, Amine, Choline, Ethylamine, Hartshorn, Oshac
Ammonite Serpent-stone
Ammunition Ammo, Bandoleer, Bandolier, Buckshot, Bullets, Chain-shot, Dum-dum, Grape(shot), Grenade, Round, Shot, Slug, Tracer
Amnesia Anterograde, Fugal, Fugue, Lethe, Retrograde
Amnesty Oblivion, Pardon
Amoeba Melboean
Amok Rampaging
Among Amid(st), In, Inter al, Within
Amorous(ly) Casanova, Erotic, Fervent, Lustful, Smickly, Spoony, Warm
Amorphous Formless, Shapeless, Vague
Amount Come, Dose, Element, Figure, Handful, Lashings, Levy, Lot, Number, Ocean, Pot(s), Premium, Price, Quantity, Quantum, Span, Stint, Sum, Throughput, Volume, Whale, Wheel
Amour Affair(e), Intrigue, Love
Ampersand Tironian sign
Amphetamine Benny, Benzedrine, Speed
Amphibian, Amphibious Amb(l)ystoma, Amtrack, Anura, Axolotl, Batrachian, Caecilia, Caecilian, Desman, Eft, Frog, Guana, Hassar, Labyrinthodont, Mermaid, Mudpuppy, Newt, Olm, Proteus, Rana, Salamander, Salientia, Seal, Tadpole, Toad, Urodela(n), Urodele, Weasel
Amphipod Sand-screw, Shrimp
Amphitheatre Bowl, Circus Maximus, Coliseum, Colosseum, Ring, Stage
Ample, Amplitude Bellyful, Copious, Enough, Generous, Good, Large, Opulent, Profuse, Rich, Roomy, Round, Sawtooth, Uberous, Voluminous
Amplifier, Amplify Booster, Double, Eke, Enlarge, Hailer, Laser, Loud hailer, Maser, Megaphone, Push-pull, Solion, Tannoy®, Transistor, Treble
Amulet Abraxas, Charm, Churinga, Fetish, Greegree, Grigri, Grisgris, Haemon, Pentacle, Periapt, Phylactery, Sea-bean, Talisman, Tiki, Toadstone, Token
Amuse(ment), Amusing(ly) Caution, Cottabus, Disport, Diversion, Divert, Divertimento, Divertissement, Drole, Droll, Game, Gas, Giocoso, Glee, Hoot, Killing, Levity, Light, Occupy, Pleasure, Popjoy, Priceless, Regale, Rich, Scream, Slay, Solace, → SPORT, Tickle, Titillate, Wacky
Amy Johnson, Robsart
▶ **An** see **A**
Ana(s) Story, Teal

Anabaptist Abecedarian, Dipper, Dopper, Hutterite, Knipperdolling
Anableps Four-eyes
Anachronism Archaism, Solecism
Anaconda Water boa
Anacreon Te(i)an
Anaemia Aplastic, Cooley's, Fanconi's, Favism, Haemolytic, Megaloblastic, Pernicious, Sickle-cell, Thalassaemia
Anaesthetic, Anaesthetise, Anaesthetist Analgesic, Avertin®, Benzocaine, Bupivacaine, Caudal, Chloralose, Chloroform, Cocaine, Endotracheal, Epidural, Ether, Eucain(e), Freeze, Gas, General, Halothane, Infiltrate, Intravenous, Jabber, Ketamine, Lidocaine, Lignocaine, Local, Metopryl, Morphia, Novocaine, Number, Opium, Orthocaine, Pentothal, Phenacaine, Procaine, Rhigolene, Special K, Spinal, Stovaine, Topical, Trike, Urethan(e)
Anagram Jumble
Anal, Anus Poepol, Proctal, Tewel
Analgesic Aspirin, Bute, Codeine, Diclofenac, Disprin, Fentanyl, Ketamine, Menthol, Methadone, Morphia, Moxa, Opium, Painkiller, Paracetamol, Pethidine, Phencyclidine, Quina, Salicin(e), Sedative
Analogous, Analogy Akin, Corresponding, Like, Parallel, Similar
Analyse(r), Analysis Alligate, Anagoge, Anatomy, Assess, Blot, Breakdown, Combinatorial, Conformational, Construe, Diagnosis, Emic, Eudiometer, Examine, Explication, Factor, Force-field, Fourier, Gravimetric, Harmonic, Input-output, Job, Kicksorter, Lexical, Linguistic, Logical, Miscue, Numerical, Parse, Pollen, Process, Psych out, Qualitative, Quantitive, Quantitative, Risk, Rundown, Sabermetrics, Scan(sion), Semantics, Sift, Spectral, Spectroscopic, Spectrum, Systems, Test, Transactional, Volumetric
▷ **Analysis** *may indicate* an anagram
Analyst Alienist, Investment, Jung, Lay, Psychiatrist, Shrink, Trick cyclist
Anarchist, Anarchy Black Bloc(k), Black Hand, Bolshevist, Chaos, Kropotkin, Nihilism, Provo, Rebel, Revolutionary, Trotskyite
Anathema Ban, Curse, Execration, Oath, Warling
Anatole, Anatolian France, Hittite, Turk
Anatomy, Anatomist Bones, Framework, Herophilus, Histology, Malpighi, Morbid, Prosector, Schneider, Spiegel, Worm
Ancestor, Ancestral, Ancestry Adam, Avital, Descent, Extraction, For(e)bear, Forefather, Gastraea, Humanoid, Lin(e)age, Parent, Predecessor, Proband, Profectitious, Progenitor, Propositus, Roots, Sire, Tipuna, Tree, Tupina
Anchor(age) Atrip, Berth, Bower, Cell, Deadman, Drag, Drift, Drogue, Eremite, Grapnel, Hawse, Hermit, Kedge, Kedger, Killick, Killock, Laura, Moor, Mud-hook, Mushroom, Nail, Ride, Roads(tead), Rode, Root, Scapa Flow, Sea, Sheet, Spithead, Stock, Stream, Toehold, Waist, Weather
Anchorite Recluse
Anchovy Fish, Pear
Ancient Antediluvian, Archaic, Auld-warld, Bygone, Early, Gonfanoner, Historic, Hoary, Iago, Immemorial, Lights, Neolithic, Ogygian, → **OLD(ER)**, Old-world, Primeval, Primitive, Pristine, Ur, Veteran
Ancient city Carthage, Ur
Ancillary Adjunct, Secondary, Subservient
And Als(o), Ampassy, Ampersand, Amperzand, Ampussyand, Besides, Et, Furthermore, Item, 'n', Plus, Tironian sign, Und
Andalusite Macle

Andiron Chenet, Dog, Firedog
Andrew(es) Aguecheek, Lancelot, Merry
Androgynous Epicene
Android Automaton, Golem, Robot
Anecdote(s) Ana, Exemplum, Story, Tale, Yarn
Anemometer Wind-sleeve, Windsock
Anemone Actinia, Pasque-flower, Windflower
Anew De integro, De novo
Angel(s) Abdiel, Adramelech, Apollyon, Archangel, Ariel, Arioch, Asmadai, Azrael,
   Backer, Banker, Beelzebub, Belial, Benefactor, Cake, Cherub, Clare, Destroying,
   Deva, Dominion, Dust, Eblis, Falls, Fuzzy-wuzzy, Gabriel, Guardian, Heavenly
   host, Hierarchy, Host, Iblis, Investor, Israfel, Ithuriel, Lucifer, Michael, Nurse,
   Power, Principality, Raphael, Recording, Rimmon, St, Seraph, Spirit, Throne, Uriel,
   Uzziel, Virtue, Watcher, Zadkiel, Zephiel
Angela Brazil
Angelica Archangel
Angel's wings Begonia
Anger, Angry → ANNOY, Bate, Bile, Black, Bristle, Choler(ic), Conniption, Cross,
   Dander, Displeased, Dudgeon, Enrage, Exasperation, Face, Fury, Gram, Heat, Het
   up, Horn-mad, Huff, Incense, Inflame, Infuriate, Iracund, Irascible, Ire, Kippage,
   Livid, Mad, Monkey, Moody, Nettle, Pique, Provoke, Radge, Rage, Rampant, Ratty,
   Renfierst, Rile, Roil, Rouse, Sore, Spleen, Steam, Stroppy, Tamping, Tantrum,
   Tarnation, Teen(e), Temper, Tene, Tooshie, Vex, Vies, Warm, Waspish, Waxy,
   Wound up, Wrath, Wroth, Yond
Angina Sternalgia, Vincent's
Angle(d), Angler, Angular, Angles, Angling Acute, Argument, Aspect, Attitude,
   Axil, Azimuthal, Canthus, Cast, Catch, Chiliagon, Coign, Complementary,
   Conjugate, Contrapposto, Corner, Cos, Critical, Diedral, Diedre, Dihedral, Elbow,
   Elevation, Ell, Exterior, Facial, Fish, Fish-hook, Fork, Geometry, Gonion, Hade, Hip,
   Hour, Hyzer, In, Incidence, Interior, L, Laggen, Laggin, Loft, Mitre, Mung, Negative,
   Oblique, Obtuse, Parallax, Pediculate, Perigon, Peterman, Piend, Piscator,
   Pitch, Pitch-cone, Plane, Polyhedral, Position, Positive, Quoin, Radian, Rake,
   Re-entrant, Reflex, Right, Rodster, Round, Sally, Saltchucker, Sine, Sinical, Slip,
   Solid, Spherical, Stalling, Steeve, Steradian, Straight, Supplementary, Sweepback,
   The gentle craft, Trotline, Vertical, Viewpoint, Visual, Walton, Washin, Weather,
   Wide-gab
Anglesey Mona
Anglican(s) CE-men, Conformist, Episcopal
Anglo-Catholic High-church
Anglo-Indian Qui-hi, Qui-hye, Topi-wallah
Angora Goat, Mohair, Rabbit
Angst Dread
Anguish(ed) Agony, Distress, Gip, Grief, Gyp, Hag-ridden, Heartache, Misery,
   → PAIN, Pang, Sorrow, Throes, → TORMENT, Torture, Woe
Angus Aberdeen
Animal(s) Acrita, Anoa, Armadillo, Atoc, Bag, Bandog, Barbastel, Beast, Bestial,
   Brute, Cariacou, Carnal, Chalicothere, Cleanskin, Coati, Creature, Criollo, Critter,
   Ethology, Fauna, Felis, Gerbil, Herd, Ichneumon, Jacchus, Jerboa, Kinkajou, Klipdas,
   Mammal, Marmoset, Marmot, Menagerie, Moose, Noctule, Oribi, Pack, Parazoon,
   Pet, Political, Protozoa, Pudu, Quagga, Rac(c)oon, Rhesus, Sensual, Sloth, Stud,
   Symphile, Tarsier, Teledu, Urson, Waler, Xenurus, Yale, Yapock, Zerda, Zoo

Animal-catcher Utricularia
Animate(d), Animation Activate, Actuate, Arouse, Biophor, Ensoul, Excite, Fire, Hortatory, Hot, Inspire, Live, Morph, Mosso, Perky, Pixil(l)ation, Rouse, Spiritoso, Spritely, Suspended, Verve, Vivacity, Vivify
Animosity Enmity, Friction, Hostility, Ill-will, Malice, Pique, Rancour
Ankle Coot, Cuit, Cute, Hock, Hucklebone, Knee, Malleolus, Talus
Ankle(t), Ankle covering Cootikin, Cuitikin, Cutikin, Gaiter, Jess
Anna, Anne, Annie Boleyn, Hathaway, Laurie, Oakley, Page, Pavlova, Pice, Sewell, Sister
Annal(s) Acta, Archives, Chronicles, Register
Annatto Roucou
Annex(e) Acquire, Add, Affiliate, Attach, Codicil, Extension, Subjoin
Annihilate Destroy, Erase, Exterminate, Obliterate, Slay
Anniversary Birthday, Feast, Jubilee, Obit, Triennial, Wedding, Yahrzeit
Annotate, Annotator Comment, Interpret, Note, Postil, Scholiast
Announce(r), Announcement Banns, Bellman, Biil(ing), Blazon, Bulletin, Communiqué, Declare, Decree, Divulgate, Gazette, Herald, Hermes, Inform, Intimate, Meld, Newsflash, Noise, Post, Preconise, Proclaim, Profess, Promulgate, Pronunciamente, Publish, Release, → REPORT, Rescript, Speaker(ine), State, Toastmaster, Town crier, Trumpet
Annoy(ance), Annoyed, Annoying Aggravate, Aggrieve, Anger, Antagonise, Badger, Blight, Bother, Bug, Bugbear, Chagrin, Choleric, Cross, Deuce(d), Disturb, Doggone, Doh, Drat, Fash, Fleabite, Frab, Fumed, Gall, Gatvol, Hack off, Hang, Harass, Hatter, Hector, Hip, Huff, Hump, Humph, Incense, Irk, → IRRITATE, Mickey-taking, Miff, Mischief, Molest, Moryah, Nag, Nark, Nettle, Noisome, Noy(ance), Peeve, Pesky, Pester, Pipsqueak, Pique, Plague, Provoke, Rankle, Rats, Ratty, Resentful, Ride, Rile, Roil, Rub, Shirty, Tiresome, Tracasserie, Try, Vex, Wazzock
Annual, Annuity Book, Contingent, Deferred, Etesian, → FLOWER, Half-hardy, Hardy, Immediate, Life, Pension, Perpetuity, Rente, Tontine, Yearbook, Yearly
Annul(ment) Abolish, Abrogate, Cashier, Cassation, Dissolution, Invalidate, Irritate, Negate, Recision, Repeal, Rescind, Reversal, Revoke, Vacatur, → VOID
Annular Toric
Anodyne Balm, Narcotic, Paregoric, Sedative
Anoint(ing) Anele, Cerate, Chris(o)m, Embrocate, Grease, Hallow, Nard, Smear
Anomaly Eccentric, Gravity, Magnetic, Mean, True
▷ **Anomaly** *may indicate* an anagram
Anon Again, Anew, Later, Soon
Anonymous Adespota, Anon, A.N.Other, Faceless, Grey, Impersonal, Somebody, Unnamed
Anorak Nerd, Wonk
Another Extra
Answer(ing), Answer(s) Account, Acknowledge, Amoebaean, Ans, Antiphon, Because, Comeback, Crib (sheet), Defence, Dusty, Echo, Key, Lemon, Light, No, Oracle, Rebuttal, Rebutter, Rein, Rejoin(der), Repartee, Reply, Rescript, Respond, Response, Responsum, Retort, Return, Riposte, Serve, Sol, Solution, Solve, Verdict, Yes
Ant(s), Anthill Amazon, Army, Bull(dog), Carpenter, Colony, Driver, Dulosis, Emmet, Ergataner, Ergates, Ergatomorph, Fire, Formic, Formicary, Leafcutter, Legionary, Myrmecoid, Myrmidon, Nasute, Neuter, Pharaoh, Pismire, Sauba, Slave, Soldier, Termite, Thief, Umbrella, Velvet, White, Wood

Antacid Magnesia, Peptic
Antagonist(ic), Antagonise Adverse, Estrange, Hostile, Oppugnant, Peare, Peer
Antarctica Adelie Land, Byrd Land, Graham Land, Wilkes Land
Ant-bear Tamanoir
Ante Bet, Punt, Stake
Ant-eater Aardvark, Banded, Echidna, Edental, Giant, Manis, Numbat, Pangolin, Scaly, S(e)ladang, Spiny, Tamandu, Tamandua, Tapir
Antelope Addax, Antilope, Blackbuck, Blaubok, Blesbok, Bloubok, Bluebuck, Bongo, Bontebok, Bubal(is), Bushbuck, Cabric, Chamois, Chikara, Chiru, Dikdik, Duiker, Duyker, Dzeren, Eland, Elk, Gazelle, Gemsbok, Gerenuk, Gnu, Goa, Goral, Grysbok, Harnessed, Hartbees, Hartebeest, Impala, Inyala, Kaama, Kid, Klipspringer, Kob, Kongoni, Koodoo, Kudu, Lechwe, Madoqua, Marshbuck, Mhorr, Mohr, Nagor, Nilgai, Nilgau, Nyala, Nylghau, Oribi, Oryx, Ourebi, Ox, Pale-buck, Pallah, Prongbuck, Pronghorn, Pronk, Puku, Pygarg, Reebok, Reedbuck, Rhebok, Sable, Saiga, Sasin, Sassaby, Serow, Sitatunga, Situtunga, Springbok, Steenbok, Steinbock, Stemback, Stembok, Suni, Takin, Thar, Topi, Tragelaph, Tsessebe, Waterbuck, Wildebeest
Antenna Aerial, Dipole, Dish, Feeler, Horn, Sensillum, TVRO
Anterior Anticous, Earlier, Front, Prior
Anthelmintic Worm
Anthem Chant, Die Stem, Hymn, Introit, Isodica, Marseillaise, Motet(t), National, Psalm, Red Flag, Responsory, Song, Star Spangled Banner, Stem, Theme, Tract, Troparion
Anthology Album, Ana, Chrestomathy, Digest, Divan, Florilegium, Garland, Pick, Spicilege
Anthony Absolute, Adverse, Trollope
Anthracite Blind-coal
Anthrax Sang
Anthropo(i)d Peripatus, Sivapithecus
Anthropologist Heyerdahl, Mead
Anti Against, Agin, Con, Hostile
Anti-aircraft AA
Anti-bacterial, Antibiotic Actinomycin, Amoxicillin, Ampicillin, Aureomycin®, Avoparcin, Bacitracin, Bacteriostat, Cecropin, Cephalosporin, Cipro®, Ciprofloxacin, Cloxacillin, Colistin, Cortisone, Co-trimoxazole, Doxorubicin, Doxycycline, Drug, Erythromycin, Gentamicin, Gramicidin, Griseofulvin, Interferon, Interleukin, Kanamycin, Lincomycin, Lineomycin, Magainin, Methicillin, Mitomycin, Neomycin, Nystatin, Opsonin, Oxacillin, Oxytetracycline, Penicillin, Polymixin, Quinolone, Rifampicin, Rifamycin, Spectinomycin, Streptomycin, Streptothricin, Terramycin®, Tetracycline, Tyrocidine, Tyrothricin, Vancomycin, Virginiamycin, Wide-spectrum
Antibody Agglutinin, Amboceptor, Antitoxin, Blocker, H(a)emolysin, Hybroid, Isoagglutinin, Lysin, Monoclonal, Opsonin, Precipitin, Reagin
Antic(s) Caper, Dido, Frolic, Gambado, Hay, Prank, Shenanigan, Stunt
Anti-carlist Queenite
Anticipate, Anticipation Antedate, Augur, Await, Drool, → EXPECT, Forecast, Foresee, Foresight, Forestall, Foretaste, Forethought, Hope, Intuition, Preparation, Prevenancy, Prolepsis, Prospect, Second-guess, Type
Anticlimax Bathos, Damp squib, Deflation, Letdown
Anticline Upwrap
Anticlockwise Dextrorse, Laevorotatory, Widdershins, Withershins

Anticoagulant C(o)umarin, Heparin, Hirudin, Prostacyclin, Warfarin
Anticommunist McCarthyism
Anticyclone High
Antidote Adder's wort, Alexipharmic, Angelica, Antivenin, Arrowroot, Bezoar,
Contrayerva, Cure, Dimercaprol, Emetic, Guaco, Interleukin, Mithridate, Nostrum,
Orvietan, Remedy, Ribavirin, Senega, Theriac(a), (Venice-)Treacle
Anti-freeze Glycerol, Lagging
Antigen Agglutinogen, Hapten(e)
Antihistamine Dimenhydrinate
Anti-imperialist Guelf, Guelph
Antimacassar Tidy
Antimonopoly Trust buster
Antimony Kohl, Sb, Stibium, Tartar emetic
Antioxidant Lycopene
Anti-parliamentarian Poujadist
Antipasto Caponata
Antipathy Allergy, Aversion, Detest, → DISLIKE, Enmity, Intolerance,
Repugnance
Anti-perfectionist Cobden
Antiphon The Reproaches
Antipodean Abo, Antarctic, Antichthon, Enzed, Underworld
Antipope Novatian(us)
Anti-protectionist Cobden
Antiquated, Antique, Antiquarian Ancient, Archaic, A(u)stringer, Bibelot, Curio,
Dryasdust, FAS, Fog(e)y, Fogram(ite), Fossil, Old-fangled, Ostreger, Relic
Anti-reformer Obscurant
Anti-revolutionary White
Anti-Roman Ghibel(l)ine
Anti-royalist Whig
Anti-Semitic Pamyat
Antiseptic Acriflavine, Carbolic, Cassareep, Creosote, Disinfectant, Eupad, Eusol,
Formaldehyde, Formalin, Formol, Germicide, Guaiacol, Iodine, Lister, Lysol®,
Phenol, Sterile, Tar, Thymol, Tutty
Anti-slavery Free-soil, Wilberforce
Anti-smoker ASH, Misocapnic
Antisocial Hostile, Ishmaelitish, Misanthropic, Oik
Antithesis Contrary, Converse, Opposite
Anti-three Noetian
Antitoxin Antibody, Antivenin, Guaco, Serum, Vaccine
Anti-union Secesher
Antivitamin Pyrithiamine
Antler(s) Bosset, Crown, Horn, Palm, Rights, Staghorn, Surroyal, Tine
Ant-proof Bilian
▶ **Anus** see ANAL
Anvil Bick-iron, Block, Incus, Stiddie, Stithy
Anxiety, Anxious Angst, Brood, Care(ful), Cark, Concern, Disquiet, Dysthymia,
Fanteeg, Fantigue, Fantod, Fraught, Grave, Heebie-jeebies, Hypochondria,
Inquietude, Itching, Jimjams, Jumpy, Keen, Nerviness, Reck, Restless, Scruple,
Separation, Solicitous, Stress, Suspense, Sweat, Tension, Toey, Trepidation,
Twitchy, Unease, Unquiet, Upset, Uptight, White-knuckle, Worriment
Any Arrow, Ary, Some

Anybody, Anyone Everyman, One, Whoso, You
Anyhow, Anyway Anyroad(s), However, Leastways, Regardless
Anything Aught, Diddly-squat, Oucht, Owt, Whatnot
▷ **Anyway** *may indicate* an anagram
Apache Arizona, AZ
Apart Aloof, Aside, Asunder, Atwain, Beside, Separate
Apartheid Racism, Verkrampte
Apartment Atrium, Ben, Condominium, Digs, Duplex, Efficiency, Flat, Insula,
   Mansion, Pad, Paradise, Penthouse, Pied-a-terre, Quarters, Room, Simplex,
   Solitude, Suite, Tenement, Unit, Walk-up
Apathetic, Apathy Accidie, Acedia, Incurious, Indifferent, Languid, Lethargic,
   Listless, Lobotomized, Pococurante, Stoical, Torpid
Ape(-like), Apeman Anthropoid, Barbary, Big-foot, Bonobo, Catarrhine, Copy,
   Dryopithecine, Gelada, Gibbon, Gorilla, → IMITATE, Magot, Mimic, → MONKEY,
   Orang, Paranthropus, Parrot, Pithecoid, Pongo, → PRIMATE, Proconsul, Sacred,
   Simian, Simulate, Yowie
Aperient Cascara, Laxative, Senna
Aperitif → DRINK, Pernod®
Aperture Balistraria, Chink, Fenestella, Hole, Keyhole, Opening, Orifice, Osculum,
   Peephole, Pinhole, Porta, Relative, Spiracle, Swallow, Window
Apex Acme, Culmen, Gonion, Keystone, Knoll, Knowe, Solar, Summit, Vortex
Aphid Ant-cow, Phylloxera
Aphorism Adage, Epigram, Gnome, Pensée, Proverb, Sutra
Aphrodisiac, Aphrodite Cytherean, Erotic, Idalian, Paphian, Philter, Philtre,
   Spanish fly, Urania, Yohimbine
Aplomb Assurance, Cool, Equanimity, Poise, Sangfroid, Serenity
Apocryphal Spurious, Tobit
Apograph Roneo®
Apollo Belvedere, Pythian, Sun
Apology Excuse, Justifier, Mockery, Oops, Pardon, Scuse, Sir-reverence
Apostate Citer, → HERETIC, Pervert, Rat, Recreant, Renegade, Runagate, Turncoat
Apostle, Apostolic Cuthbert, → DISCIPLE, Evangelist, Johannine, Jude, Matthew,
   Pauline, Spoon, Thad(d)eus, Twelve
Apostrophe, Apostrophise Elision, O(h), Soliloquy, Tuism
Apothegm Dictum, Maxim, Motto
Appal(ling) Abysmal, Affear(e), Aghast, Dire, Dismay, Egregious, Frighten, Horrify,
   Piacular, Shock, Tragic
▷ **Appallingly** *may indicate* an anagram
Apparatus Alembic, Alkalimeter, Appliance, Aspirator, Autoclave, Caisson,
   Calorimeter, Chemostat, Churn, Clinostat, Coherer, Colorimeter, Commutator,
   Condenser, Cosmotron, Critical, Cryostat, Davis, Defibrillator, → DEVICE, Digester,
   Ebullioscope, Effusiometer, Electrograph, Electrophorus, Electroscope, Eprouvette,
   Equipment, Eudiometer, Exciter, Fixings, Gadget, Gasogene, Gazogene, Golgi,
   Graith, Gyroscope, Heliograph, Helioscope, Hemocytometer, Hodoscope,
   Holophote, Hydrophone, Hygrostat, Incubator, Injector, Inspirator, Installation,
   Instrument, Jacquard, Kipp's, Kymograph, Lease-rod, Life-preserver, Loom,
   Masora(h), Microreader, Mimeograph, Multi-gym, Nephoscope, Nitrometer,
   Oscillograph, Oxygenator, Pasteuriser, Percolator, Phonometer, Photophone,
   Photostat®, Phytotron, Plate-warmer, Plethysmograph, Plumber's snake,
   Potometer, Projector, Proto®, Pulmotor®, Radiosonde, Replenisher, Resistor,
   Respirator, Respirometer, Resuscitator, Retort, Rotisserie, Rounce, Scintiscanner,

Scrubber, Scuba, Semaphore, Set, Skimmer, Slide rest, Snorkel, Soundboard, Sphygmograph, Spirophore, Stellarator, Steriliser, Still, Substage, Switchgear, Tackle, Tackling, Talk-you-down, Telecine, Teleprinter, Teleseme, Tellurian, Thermopile, Tokamak, Transformer, Transmitter, Tromp(e), Tuner, Ventouse, Wheatstone's bridge, Whip-and-derry, ZETA

Apparel Attire, Besee, → **COSTUME**, Garb, Raiment, Wardrobe, Wardrop

Apparent(ly) Ap, Clear, Detectable, Manifest, Ostensible, Outward, Overt, Plain, Prima facie, Seeming, Semblance, Visible

▷ **Apparent** *may indicate* a hidden word

Apparition Dream, Eidolon, Fetch, Ghost, → **ILLUSION**, Phantom, Shade, Spectre, Visitant, Wraith

Appeal(ing) Ad, Beg, Cachet, Catchpenny, Charisma, Charm, Cri de coeur, Cry, Entreat, Entreaty, Epirrhema, Fetching, Invocation, It, Miserere, O, Oomph, Plead, SA, Screeve, Sex(iness), Solicit, SOS, Suit

Appear(ance) Advent, Air, Apport, Arrival, Aspect, Broo, Brow, Burst, Cast, Compear, Debut, Emerge, Enter, Exterior, Eye, Facade, Facies, Far(r)and, Farrant, Fa(s)cia, Feature, Format, Garb, Guise, Habitus, Hue, Image, Kithe, Kythe, Looks, Loom, → **MANNER**, Mien, Occur, Ostensibly, Ostent, Outward, Person, Phase, Phenomenon, Physiognomy, Presence, Prosopon, Represent, Rig, Rise, Seem, Semblance, Show, Spring, Superficies, Theophany, View, Visitation, Wraith

Appease(ment) Allay, Alleviate, Calm, Conciliation, Danegeld, Mitigate, → **MOLLIFY**, Munichism, Pacify, Placate, Propitiate, Satisfy, Soothe, Sop

Append(age) Adjunct, Affix, Aglet, Allantois, Annex, Antennule, Aril, Arista, Cercus, Chelicera, Codpiece, Ctene, Fang, Flagellum, Hanger-on, Lobe, Lug, Palp(us), Paraglossa, Parapodium, Pedipalp, Postfix, Stipel, Stipule, Suffix, Swimmeret, Tail, Tailpiece, Tentacle, Ugly, Uropod, Uvula

Appendix Addendum, Apocrypha, Codicil, Grumbling, Label, Pendant, Pendent, Rider, Schedule, Vermiform

Appetite, Appetitive, Appetise(r) Amuse-bouche, Antepast, Antipasto, Aperitif, Appestat, Bhagee, Bhajee, Bulimia, Bulimy, Canapé, Concupiscence, Concupy, Crudités, Desire, Dim-sum, Entremes(se), Entremets, Flesh, Hunger, Limosis, Malacia, Meze, Mezze, Nacho, Orectic, Orexis, Passion, Pica, Polyphagia, Relish, Tapa(s), Titillate, Twist, Ventripotent, Yerd-hunger, Yird-hunger

Applaud, Applause Acclaim, Bravo, → **CHEER**, Clap, Claque, Eclat, Encore, Extol, Hum, Kentish fire, Olé, Ovation, Praise, Root, Ruff, Tribute

Apple Adam's, Alligator, Bad, Baldwin, Balsam, Biffin, Blenheim orange, Braeburn, Bramley, Cashew, Charlotte, Codlin(g), Cooker, Costard, Crab, Custard, Dead Sea, Discord, Eater, Granny Smith, Greening, Jenneting, John, Jonathan, Leather-coat, Love, Mammee, May, McIntosh (red), Medlar, Nonpareil, Oak, Pacific Rose, Pearmain, Pippin, Pomace, Pome(roy), Pom(e)water, Pomroy, Potato, Punic, Pupil, Pyrus, Quarantine, Quarenden, Quar(r)ender, Quarrington, Quodlin, Redstreak, Reinette, Rennet, Ribston(e), Ripstone, Rotten, Ruddock, Russet, Seek-no-further, Snow, Sops-in-wine, Sorb, Sturmer, Sturmer (Pippin), Sugar, Sweeting, Thorn, Toffee, Windfall, Winesap

Apple juice Malic

Apple-picker Atalanta

Applicant Ordinand, Postulant

Application, Apply, Appliance(s) Address, Adhibit, Appeal, Appose, Assiduity, Barrage, Blender, Devote, Diligence, Dressing, Exercise, Foment, Give, Implement, Inlay, Juicer, Lay, Liquidiser, Lotion, Mixer, Ointment, Opodeldoc, Petition, Plaster,

Poultice, Put, Request, Resort, Respirator, Rub, Sinapism, Stupe, Toggle, Truss,
→ USE, Vice, White goods

Appliqué Hawaiian

Appoint(ee), Appointment Advowson, Assign, Berth, Date, Delegate,
Depute, Designate, Dew, Due, Executor, Induction, Installation, Make, Name,
→ NOMINATE, Nominee, Office, Ordain, Position, Post, Posting, Rendezvous,
Room, Set, Tryst

▷ **Appointed** *may indicate* an anagram

Apportion(ment) Allocate, Allot, Mete, Parcel, Ration, Share, Weigh

Apposite Apt, Cogent, Germane, Pat, Pertinent, Relevant, Suitable

Appraise, Appraisal Analyse, → EVALUATE, Gauge, Guesstimate, Judge,
Once-over, Tape, → VALUE, Vet

Appreciate, Appreciation Acknowledgement, Cherish, Clap, Dig, Endear, Esteem,
Gratefulness, Increase, Phwoar, Prize, Realise, Recognise, Regard, Relish, Rise,
Sense, Stock, Taste, Thank you, Treasure, → VALUE

Apprehend, Apprehension Afears, Alarm, Arrest, → CATCH, Collar, Fear, Grasp,
Insight, Intuit, Perceive, Quailing, See, Suspense, Take, Toey, Trepidation, Uh-oh,
Unease, Uptake

Apprehensive Jumpy, Nervous, Uneasy

Apprentice(ship) Article, Commis, Cub, Devil, Garzone, Improver, Indent(ure),
Jockey, L, Learner, Lehrjahre, Novice, Noviciate, Novitiate, Printer's devil,
Pupillage, Snob, Tiro, Trainee, Turnover, Tyro(ne)

Approach(ing), Approachable Abord, Access, Accost, Advance, Affable, Anear,
Appropinquate, Appulse, Avenue, Close, Come, Converge, Cost(e), Draw nigh,
Drive, Driveway, Fairway, Feeler, Gate, Imminent, Line, Near, Nie, Overture, Pitch,
Procedure, Road, Run-up, Towards, Verge

Appropriate Abduct, Abstract, Annex, Apposite, Apt, Asport, Assign, Bag,
Borrow, Collar, Commandeer, Commensurate, Confiscate, Convenient, Due,
Embezzle, Expedient, Fit, Germane, Good, Happy, Hijack, Hog, Impound, Jump,
Just, Meet, Nick, Pertinent, Pilfer, Plagiarise, Pocket, Pre-empt, Proper, Purloin,
Right, Seise, Seize, Sequester, Sink, Snaffle, Steal, Suit, Swipe, Take, Timely,
Trouser, Usurp

Approval, Approve(d), Approbation Adopt, Allow, Amen, Applaud, Attaboy,
Aye, Blessing, Bravo, Brownie points, Change, → COUNTENANCE, Credit, Cushty,
Dig, Endorse, Favour, Hear hear, Homologate, Hubba-hubba, Imprimatur,
Initial, Kitemark, Know, Laud, Nod, Okay, Olé, Orthodox, Plaudit, Rah, Ratify,
Rubber-stamp, Sanction, Stotter, Thumbs-up, Tick, Tribute, Yay, Yes, Zindabad

Approximate(ly), Approximation Almost, Circa, Close, Coarse, Estimate, Guess,
Imprecise, Near, Roughly

Apricot Mebos

April, April fool Apr, Huntiegowk, Hunt-the-gowk

Apron Barm-cloth, Bib, Blacktop, Brat, Bunt, Canvas, Dick(e)y, Ephod, Fig-leaf,
Gremial, Ice, Napron, Pinafore, Pinner, Pinny, Placket, Stage, Tablier, Tier, Waist

Apse Concha, Exedra, Niche, Recess, Tribune

Apt(ly) Apposite, Appropriate, Apropos, Ben trovato, Capable, Evincive, Fit, Gleg,
Happy, Liable, Pat, Prone, Suitable, Tends

Aptitude Ability, Bent, Faculty, Flair, Gift, Knack, Skill, Talent, Tendency

Aqua(tic) Euglena, Flustra, Lentic, Lotic, Regia, Zizania

Aqualung Rebreather, Scuba

Aquamarine Madagascar

Aqueduct Canal, Channel, Conduit, Hadrome, Xylem

Arab(ian), Arabia, Arabic Abdul, Adeni, Algorism, Ali, Baathist, Bahraini, Bahrein,
Bedouin, Druse, Druz(e), Effendi, Fedayee(n), Gamin, Geber, Hashemite, Himyarite,
Horse, Iraqi, Jawi, Lawrence, Moor, Mudlark, Nabat(a)ean, Nas(s)eem, Nes(h)ki,
Omani, Omar, PLO, Qatari, Rag(head), Saba, Sab(a)ean, Saracen, Saudi, Semitic,
Sheikh, Street, Syrian, UAR, Urchin, Yemen
Arabis Cress
Arachnid Podogona, Ricinulei, → **SPIDER**
Arbiter, Arbitrator ACAS, Censor, Daysman, Judge, Negotiator, Ombudsman,
Prud'homme, Ref(eree), Umpire
Arbitrary Despotic, Haphazard, Peculiar, Random, Wanton
Arboreal, Arbour Bower, Dendroid, Pergola, Trellis
Arc Azimuth, Bow, Carbon, → **CURVE**, Flashover, Fogbow, Halo, Island, Limb,
Mercury, Octant, Quadrant, Rainbow, Reflex, Seadog, Trajectory, White rainbow
Arcade Amusement, Burlington, Cloister, Gallery, Loggia, Mall, Penny, Triforium
Arcadia(n) Idyllic, Nemoral, Sylvan
Arcane Esoteric, Obscure, Occult, Orphism, Recherché, Rune, Secret
Arch(ed), Arching Acute, Admiralty, Arblaster, Arcade, Arcature, Archivolt,
Arcuate, Camber, Chief, Coom, Counterfort, Crafty, Cross-rib, Crown-green,
Ctesiphon, → **CUNNING**, Curve, Elfin, Embow, Espiegle, Fallen, Flying buttress,
Fog-bow, Fornicate, Fornix, Gill, Gothic, Hance, Haunch, Hog, Horseshoe, Instep,
Intrados, Keel, Keystone, Lancet, Leery, Lierne, Limb-girdle, Marble, Neural,
Norman, Ogee, Ogive, Opisthotonos, Order, Parthian, Pectoral, Pelvic, Pointed,
Portal, Proscenium, Recessed, Relieving, Roach, Roguish, Roman, Safety, Saucy,
Segmental, Shouldered, Skew, Soffit, Span, Squinch, Stilted, Trajan, Triumphal,
Vault, Zygoma
Archaeological, Archaeologist Carter, Dater, Dig, Evans, Industrial, Layard,
Leakey, Mycenae, Petrie, Pothunter, Sutton Hoo, Wheeler, Woolley
Archangel Azrael, Gabriel, Israfeel, Israfel, Israfil, Jerahmeel, Michael, Raguel,
Raphael, Sariel, Satan, Uriel, Yellow
Arch-binder Voussoir
Archbishop Anselm, Augustine, Cosmo, Cranmer, Davidson, Dunstan, Ebor,
Elector, Hatto, Lanfranc, Lang, Langton, Laud, Metropolitan, Primate, Temple,
Trench, Tutu, Whitgift
Archdeacon Ven
Archduke Trio
Archer Acestes, Bow-boy, → **BOWMAN**, Cupid, Eros, Hood, Philoctetes, Sagittary,
Tell, Toxophilite
Archetype Avatar, Form, Model, Pattern
Archibald, Archie, Archy Ack-ack, Cockroach, Oerlikon, Rice, Roach
Archilochian Epode
Archipelago Alexander, Antarctic, Azores, Bismarck, Camaguey, East Indian, Fiji,
Franz Josef Land, Gulag, Japan, Kerguelen, Malay, Maldives, Marquesas, Mergui,
Novaya Zemlya, Palmer, Paumotu, St Pierre and Miquelon, Severnaya Zemlya,
Spitsbergen, Sulu, Svalbard, Tierra del Fuego, Tonga, Tuamoto, West Indies
Architect(ure), Architectural Arcology, Baroque, Bauhaus, Bricolage, Brutalism,
Byzantine, Churrigueresque, Composite, Computer, Corinthian, Creator,
Data-flow, Decorated, Designer, Domestic, Doric, Early English, Elizabethan,
Entablature, Federation, Flamboyant, Georgian, Gothic, Greek Revival, Ionic,
Italian, Jacobean, Landscape, Lombard, Mission, Moderne, Moorish, Moresque,
Mudejar, Naval, Neoclassical, Neo-gothic, Norman, Palladian, Pelasgian,
Perpendicular, Planner, Plateresque, Prostyle, Queen Anne, Romanesque,

Saracenic, Saxon, Spandrel, Spandril, Tectonic, Tudor, Tudorbethan, Tuscan, Vitruvian

ARCHITECTS

4 letters:	Utzon	Lutyens	10 letters:
Adam	Wyatt	Venturi	Inigo Jones
Kent		Vignola	Mackintosh
Loos	6 letters:		Trophonius
Nash	Casson	8 letters:	Van der Rohe
Shaw	Foster	Bramante	
Webb	Nissen	Palladio	11 letters:
Wood	Repton	Piranesi	Abercrombie
Wren	Spence	Saarinen	Butterfield
	Street	Vanbrugh	Le Corbusier
5 letters:	Wright		
Gaudi		9 letters:	12 letters:
Inigo	7 letters:	Hawksmoor	Brunelleschi
Nervi	Behrens	Macquarie	
Pugin	Bernini	Vitruvius	14 letters:
Scott	Columbo		Vitruvius Pollo
Soane	Gropius		

Architrave Epistyle, Platband
Archive(s) Backfile, Muniment, PRO, Records, Register
Archon Draco
Arch-villain Ringleader
Arctic Estotiland, Frigid, Hyperborean, In(n)uit, Inupiat, Polar, Tundra
Ardent, Ardour Aflame, Aglow, Boil, Broiling, Burning, Fervent, Fervid, Fiery, Fire, Flagrant, Heat, Het, → HOT, Hot-brained, In, Mettled, Mettlesome, Passion(ate), Perfervid, Rage, Spiritous, Vehement, Warm-blooded, Zealous, Zeloso
Arduous Laborious, Uphill
Are A, Exist, 're
Area Acre, Aleolar, Apron, Arctogaea, Are, Bailiwick, Belt, Bovate, Broca's, Built-up, Carucate, Catchment, Centare, Centiare, Centre, Conurbation, Craton, Curtilage, Dec(i)are, Dedans, Depressed, Dessiatine, Development, Disaster, District, Domain, Endemic, Eruv, Extent, Farthingland, Gau, Goal, Grey, Growth, Heartland, Hectare, Henge, Hide, Husbandland, Imperium, Input, Karst, Landmass, Lathe, Latitude, Lek, Locality, Lodg(e)ment, Manor, Metroplex, Milieu, Morgen, Mush, Neogaea, No-go, Notogaea, Orb, Oxgang, Oxgate, Oxland, Parish, Patch, Penalty, Place, Pleasance, Plot, Precinct, Province, Purlieu, Quad, Quadrat, Quarter, Range, Redevelopment, Refugium, → REGION, Renosterveld, Rest, Restricted, Retrochoir, Rood, Sector, Service, Shire, Site, Slurb, Special, Staging, Sterling, Subtopia, Support, Target, Technical, Terrain, Territory, Theatre, Tie, Tract, Tundra, Tye, Urban, Ure, White, Work station, Yard, Zone
Arena Circus, Cockpit, Dohyo, Field, Lists, Maidan, Olympia, → RING, Rink, Stadium, Tiltyard, Velodrome, Venue
Argal Ergo
Argent Ag, Silver
Argentina RA
Argon Ar

Argonaut Acastus, Jason, Lynceus, Meleager, Nautilus
Argot Flash, Idiom, Jargon, Lingo, Scamto, Shelta
Argue, Argument(ative) Altercation, Antistrophon, Argie-bargie, Argle-bargle,
    Argy-bargy, Bandy, Beef, Blue, Brush, Case, Casuism, Choplogic, Conflict, Contend,
    Contest, Cosmological, Debate, Deprecate, Diallage, Difference, Dilemma, Dispute,
    Dissent, Elenchus, Elenctic, Enthymeme, Eristic, Exchange, Expostulate, Forensic,
    Free-for-all, Generalisation, Hysteron proteron, Logic, Logomachy, Moot, Ob
    and soller, Object, Ontological, Paralogism, Patter, Pettifog, Plead, Polemic,
    Polylemma, Premiss, Propound, Quarrel, Quibble, Quodlibet, Rammy, Ratiocinate,
    → **REASON**, Remonstrate, Row, Run-in, Sophism, Sophistry, Sorites, Spar, Stickle,
    Straw man, Stroppy, Summation, Syllogism, Teleological, Theme, Thetic, Third
    man, Tiff, Transcendental, Trilemma, Wrangle, Yike
Argyle Argathelian
Aria Ballad, Cabaletta, Melody, Song
Arid Dry, Parched
Ariel Pen
Arise Appear, Be, Develop, Emanate, Emerge, Upgo, Wax
Aristocracy, Aristocrat(ic) Blood, Boyar, Buckeen, Classy, Debrett, Duc, Elite,
    Eupatrid, Gentle, Gentry, Grandee, High-hat, Junker, Nob, Noble, Optimate,
    Passage, Patrician, Thane, Tony, U-men, Upper-crust, Well-born
Aristotle Peripatetic, Stagirite, Stagyrite
Arithmetic(ian) Algorism, Algorith, Arsmetrick, Cocker, Euclid, Logistic, Modular,
    Sums
Ark(wright) Chest, Noah
Arly Thicket
Arm(ed), Arms Akimbo, Arsenal, Bearing, Brachial, Branch, Bundooks, Canting,
    Cove, Crest, Cross bow, Embattle, Equip, Escutcheon, Fin, Firth, Frith, Gnomon,
    Halbert, Hatchment, Heel, Heraldic, Inlet, Jib, Krupp, Limb, Loch, Long, Member,
    Olecranon, Pick-up, Quillon, Radius, Ramous, Rocker, Rotor, SAA, Secular,
    Shield, Shotgun, Side, Small, Smooth-bore, Spiral, Tappet, Tentacle, Timer, Tone,
    Tooled-up, Transept, Tremolo, Ulnar, → **WEAPON**, Whip
▷ **Arm** *may indicate* an army regiment, etc.
Armada Spanish
Armadillo Dasypod, Dasypus, Fairy, Giant, Pangolin, Peba, Pichiciago, Tatou(ay),
    Xenurus
Armature Keeper, Shuttle
Armenian Haikh, Yezedi
Armistice Truce
Armour(ed) Ailette, Armature, Armet, Barbette, Beaver, Besagew, Bevor, Brasset,
    Breastplate, Brigandine, Buckler, Byrnie, Camail, Cannon, Casspir, Cataphract,
    Chaffron, Chain, Chamfrain, Chamfron, Character, Chausses, Corium, Cors(e)let,
    Couter, Cuirass, Cuish, Cuisse, Culet, Curat, Curiet, Cush, Defence, Fauld,
    Garniture, Gear, Genouillère, Gere, Gorget, Greave, Habergeon, Hauberk,
    Hoplology, Jack, Jambeau, Jazerant, Jesserant, Lamboys, Loricate, Mail, Male,
    Mentonnière, Nasal, Nosepiece, Palette, Panoply, Panzer, Pauldron, Petta, Placcat,
    Placket, Plastron, Plate, Poitrel, Poleyn, Pouldron, Rerebrace, Sabaton, Scale,
    Secret, → **SHIELD**, Solleret, Spaudler, Splint, Stand, Tace, Tank, Taslet, Tasse(t),
    Thorax, Tonlet, Tuille, Vambrace, Vantbrass, Ventail, Visor, Voider, Weed
Armpit Axilla, Oxter
Armstrong Louis, Satchmo
Army Arrière-ban, BEF, Blue Ribbon, Church, Colours, Confederate, Crowd, Federal,

Field, Fyrd, Golden (Horde), Horde, Host, IRA, Junior Service, Land, Landwehr,
Lashkar, Legion, Line, Military, Militia, Mobile Command, Multitude, New Model,
Para-military, Red, SA, Sabaoth, Salvation, SAS, Sena, Service, Soldiers, Standing,
Swarm, TA, Territorial, Thin red line, Volunteer, War, Wehrmacht
▷ **Army** *may indicate* having arms
Aroma(tic) Allspice, Aniseed, Aryl, Balmy, Coriander, Fenugreek, Fragrant,
Odorous, Pomander, Spicy, Stilbene, Vanillin, Wintergreen
Around About, Ambient, Circa, Near, Peri-, Skirt, Tour
▷ **Around** *may indicate* one word around another
Arouse, Arousal Alarm, → EXCITE, Fan, Fire, Incite, Inflame, Must(h), Needle,
Provoke, Stimulate, Stole, Suscitate, Touch up, Urolagnia, Waken
Arrange(r), Arrangement Adjust, Array, Attune, Bandobast, Bank, Bundobust,
Concert, Concinnity, Configuration, Design, Display, Dispose, Do, Edit, Engineer,
Finger, Fix, Foreordain, Format, Formation, Formwork, Grade, Ikebana, Layout,
Marshal, Modus vivendi, Orchestrate, Orchestration, Ordain, → ORDER, Ordnance,
Organise, Pack, Pattern, Perm, Permutation, Plan, Position, Prepare, Prepense,
Quincunx, Redactor, Regulate, Run, Schedule, Schema, Scheme, Score, Set, Settle,
Sort, Spacing, Stack, Stage-manage, Stereoisomerism, Stow, Straighten, Style,
System, Tabulate, Tactic, Taxis, Tidy, Transcribe, Vertical
▷ **Arrange** *may indicate* an anagram
Arras Tapestry
Array(ed) Attire, Bedight, Deck, Herse, Logic, Marshal, Muster, Panoply, Phased,
Seismic
Arrear(s) Aft, Ahint, Backlog, Behind, Debt, Owing
Arrest(ed), Arresting Abort, Alguacil, Alguazil, Ament, Apprehend, Attach, Attract,
Blin, Book, Bust, Caption, Capture, Cardiac, Catch, Check, Citizen's, Collar, Detain,
False, Furthcoming, Hold, House, Knock, Lift, Lightning, Nab, Nail, Nick, Nip,
Nobble, Pinch, Pull, Restrain, Retard, Riveting, Round-up, Run-in, Salient, Sease,
Seize, Snaffle, Stasis, Stop, Sus(s)
Arris Groin
Arrival, Arrive, Arriving Accede, Advent, Attain, Come, Get, Happen, Hit,
Inbound, Influx, Johnny-come-lately, Land, Latecomer, Natal, Nativity, Pitch up,
Reach, Show, Strike
Arrogance, Arrogant Assumption, Bold, Bravado, Cavalier, Cocksure,
Contemptuous, Disdain, Dogmatic, Effrontery, Haughty, Haut(eur), High,
High-hat, Hogen-mogen, Hoity-toity, Hubris, Imperious, Jumped up, Lordly,
Morgue, Overweening, Presumption, Proud, Side, Snobbish, Stuck-up, Surquedry,
Toploftical, Turkeycock, Uppish, Uppity, Upstart
Arrogate Appropriate, Assume, Claim, Impute, Usurp
Arrow, Arrow-head Acestes, Any, Ary, Blunt, Bolt, Broad(head), Cloth-yard shaft,
Dart, Dogbolt, Filter, Flechette, Flight, Missile, Pheon, Pointer, Quarrel, Reed,
Sagittate, Shaft, Sheaf, Straight
Arrowroot Kuzu, Maranta, Pia
Arsenal Ammo, Armo(u)ry, Depot, Magazine, Side, Toulon
Arsenate, Arsenic(al), Arsenide As, Erythrite, Realgar, Resalgar, Rosaker,
Salvarsan, Scorodite, Skutterudite, Smaltite, Speiss, Zarnich
Arson(ist) Firebug, Pyromania
Art(s), Arty, Art school, Art style Abstract, Alla prima, Applied, Ars, Arte
Povera, Bauhaus, Bloomsbury, Bonsai, Britart, Brut, Chiaroscuro, Clair-obscure,
Clare-obscure, Clip, Cobra, Commercial, Conceptual, Constructivism, Contrapposto,
Craft, Cubism, Culture vulture, Cunning, Curious, Dada, Daedal(e), Deco, Decorative,

Dedal, De Stijl, Die Brucke, Diptych, Divisionism, Earth, Ekphrasis, Environmental, Es, Expressionism, Fauvism, Feat, Fine, Finesse, Flemish, Folk, Fugue, Futurism, Genre, Graphic, Guile, Impressionist, Jugendstil, Kakemono, Kano, Ka pai, Kinetic, Kirigami, Kitsch, Knack, Liberal, Mandorla, Mannerism, Martial, Mehndi, Minimal, Modern(e), Montage, Motivated, Music, Mystery, Nabis, Nazarene, Neoclassical, Neo-impressionism, New Wave, Noli-me-tangere, Norwich, Nouveau, Optical, Origami, Orphic Cubism, Orphism, Outsider, Pastiche, Performance, Performing, Perigordian, Plastic, Pointillism, Pop, Postimpressionism, Postmodern, Practical, Pre-Raphaelite, Primitive, Psychedelic, Public, Quadratura, Quadrivium, Relievo, Sienese, → SKILL, Still-life, Suprematism, Surrealism, Synchronism, Tachism(e), Tatum, Tenebrism, Toreutics, Trecento, Triptych, Trivium, Trompe l'oeil, Trouvé, Tsutsumu, Useful, Verism, Virtu, Visual, Vorticism

▷ **Art** *may indicate* an -est ending

Artefact(s) Neolith, Tartanalia, Tartanry, Xoanon

▷ **Artefact** *may indicate* an anagram

Artemis Selene

Artemus Ward

Artery Aorta, Carotid, Coronary, Duct, Femoral, Frontal, Iliac, Innominate, M1, Maxillary, Phrenic, Pulmonary, Radial, Route, Spermatic, Temporal

Artful Cute, Dodger, Foxy, Ingenious, Quirky, Shifty, Sly, Subtle, Tactician

Arthropod Limulus, Peripatus, Prototracheata, Tardigrade, Trilobite, Water-bear

Artichoke Cardoon, Jerusalem

Article(s) A, An, Apprentice, Column, Commodity, Cutting, Definite, Feature, Five, Indefinite, Indenture, Item, Leader, Leading, Paper, Piece, Pot-boiler, Shipping, Sidebar, Specify, The, Thing, Thinkpiece, Thirty-nine, Treatise, Ware

Articulation, Articulate(d) Clear, Coherent, Coudé, Diarthrosis, Distinct, Eloquent, Enounce, Express, Fluent, Fortis, Gimmal, Gomphosis, Hinged, Intonate, Jointed, Jymold, Lenis, Limbed, Lisp, Pretty-spoken, Pronounce, Schindylesis, Trapezial, Utter, Vertebrae, Voice

Artifice(r), Artificial Bogus, Chouse, Contrived, Dodge, Ersatz, Factitious, Finesse, Guile, Hoax, In vitro, Logodaedaly, Man-made, Mannered, Opificer, Postiche, Pretence, Prosthetic, Pseudo, Reach, Ruse, Sell, Set, Sham, Spurious, Stratagem, → STRATEGY, Synthetic, Theatric, → TRICK, Unnatural, Wile, Wright

Artificial respiration Kiss of life, Schafer's method

Artillery Battery, Cannon, Field, Fougade, Fougasse, Guns, Mortar, Ordnance, Pyroballogy, RA, Rafale, Ramose, Ramus, Train

Artiodactyl Camel, Chevrotain, Deerlet

Artisan Craftsman, Decorator, Joiner, Journeyman, Mechanic, Peon, Pioner, Pyoner, Shipwright, Workman

Artist(ic) Barbizan, Blaue Reiter, Bohemian, Cartoonist, Colourist, Cubist, Dadaist, Daedal(e), Deccie, Decorator, Die Brucke, Etcher, Fauve, Fine, Foley, Gentle, Gilder, ICA, Impressionist, Left Bank, Limner, Linear, Maestro, Master, Mime, Miniaturist, → MUSICIAN, Nabis, Nazarene, Oeuvre, Orphism, → PAINTER, Pavement, Paysagist, Piss, Plein-airist, Pre-Raphaelite, Primitive, Quick-change, RA, Romantic, Screever, → SCULPTOR, Sien(n)ese, Tachisme, Trapeze, Trecentist, Virtuose, Virtuoso

---

ARTISTS

3 letters:		4 letters:	
Arp	Cox	Cuyp	Dali
	Rap	Dadd	Doré
			Dufy

Etty
Goya
Hals
John
Klee
Lely
Miró
Opie
Phiz

5 letters:
Aiken
Appel
Bacon
Bakst
Bosch
Corot
Crome
Degas
Dulac
Dürer
Ensor
Ernst
Hoare
Hooch
Klimt
Leech
Léger
Lippi
Lotto
Lowry
Makar
Manet
Monet
Munch
Orpen
Redon
Riley
Rodin
Seago
Steen
Steer
Tatum
Watts

6 letters:
Boudin
Braque
Brucke

Calder
Callot
Derain
D'Orsay
Escher
Fuseli
Giotto
Greuze
Guardi
Haydon
Ingres
Knight
Le Nain
Millet
Moreau
Renoir
Ribera
Rivera
Romney
Rothko
Rubens
Seurat
Signac
Sisley
Stubbs
Tissot
Titian
Turner
Warhol
Zeuxis

7 letters:
Apelles
Audubon
Bellini
Bernini
Bonnard
Cézanne
Chagall
Chardin
Cimabue
Collier
Courbet
Cranach
Da Vinci
Duchamp
El Greco
Epstein
Gauguin

Hobbema
Hockney
Hogarth
Hokusai
Holbein
Hoppner
Kneller
Matisse
Millais
Morisot
Morland
Murillo
Nattier
Picasso
Pissaro
Poussin
Prudhon
Raeburn
Raphael
Rouault
Sargent
Sickert
Spencer
Tiepolo
Uccello
Utamaro
Utrillo
Van Dyke
Van Eyck
Van Gogh
Vermeer
Watteau
Zeuxian
Zoffany

8 letters:
Daubigny
Eastlake
Kirchner
Landseer
Leonardo
Magritte
Mantegna
Masaccio
Mondrian
Nevinson
Perugino
Piranesi
Reynolds

Rousseau
Topolski
Veronese
Whistler

9 letters:
Beardsley
Bonington
Canaletto
Carpaccio
Constable
Correggio
Delacroix
Donatello
Fragonard
Gericault
Giorgione
Grunewald
Hiroshige
Kandinsky
Rembrandt
Velasquez

10 letters:
Alma-Tadema
Botticelli
Burne-Jones
Guillaumin
Madox Brown
Modigliani
Rowlandson
Signorelli
Sutherland
Tintoretto
Van der Goes

12 letters:
Gainsborough
Lichtenstein
Michelangelo
Winterhalter

14 letters:
Jackson Pollock

15 letters:
Hieronymus Bosch
Toulouse-Lautrec

Artless Candid, Ingenuous, Innocent, Naive, Open, Seely, Simple

Art nouveau Jugendstil

Arturo Toscanini

Arum Acorus, Green-dragon, Lily, Taro

As Aesir, Als, Arsenic, Coin, Eg, Forasmuch, Kame, Qua, Ridge, 's, Since, So, Thus, Ut, While

As above US, Ut supra

Asafoetida Hing

As before Anew, Ditto, Do, Stet

Asbestos Amiant(h)us, Amosite, Chrysolite, Crocidolite, Earthflax, Fireproof, Rockwood

Ascend(ant), Ascent, Ascension Anabasis, Climb, Dominant, Escalate, Gradient, Lift, Pull, Ramp, Right, Rise, Sclim, Sklim, Slope, Up, Upgang, Uphill, Uprise, Zoom

Ascertain Determine, Discover, → **ESTABLISH**, Prove

Ascetic Agapetae, Anchor(et), Anchorite, Ancress, Ashramite, Austere, Dervish, Diogenes, Encratite, Eremital, Essene, Fakir, Faquir, Gymnosophist, Hermit, Jain(ite), Monk, Nazarite, Nazirite, Nun's flesh, Sad(d)hu, Simeon Stylites, Stylite, Sufic, Therapeutae, Yogi(n)

Ascidian Chordate, Urochordate

Asclepiad Stapelia

Ascribe Assign, → **ATTRIBUTE**, Blame, Imply, Impute

Asdic Sonar

As far as Quoad

As good as Equal, Tantamount

Ash(es), Ashy Aesc, Aizle, Bone, Breeze, Cinders, Cinereal, Clinker(s), Easle, Embers, Fly, Kali, Lahar, Pallor, Pearl, Pozz(u)olana, Prickly, Rowan, Ruins, Soda, Sorb, Spodo-, Tephra, Urn, Varec, Wednesday, Weeping, White, Witchen, Yg(g)drasil(l)

Ashamed Abashed, Embarrassed, Hangdog, Mortified, Repentant, Shent

Ashore Aland, Beached, Grounded, Stranded

Ash-pan Backet

Asia(n), Asiatic Altaic, Azari, Balinese, Bangladeshi, Bengali, Cambodian, Cantonese, E, Evenki, Ewenki, Gook, Hun, Hyksos, Indian, Karen(ni), Kashmir, Kirghiz, Korean, Kurd, Kyrgyz, Lao, Malay, Mongol, Naga, Negrito, Nepalese, Phrygian, Pushtu, Samo(y)ed, Shan, Siamese, Sogdian, Tamil, Tartar, Tibetan, Tocharian, Tokharian, Turanian, Turk(o)man

Asia Minor Anatolia, Ionic

Aside Apart, By, Despite, Private, Separate, Shelved, Sotto voce

Asinine Crass, Dull, Idiotic, Puerile, Stupid

Ask Bed, Beg, Beseech, Bid, Cadge, Demand, Desire, Enquire, Entreat, Evet, Implore, Intreat, Invite, Newt, Petition, Prithee, Pump, Quiz, Request, Require, Rogation, Seek, Solicit, Speer, Speir, Touch

Askance Asconce, Askew, Oblique, Sideways

Askew Agee, Aglee, Agley, Ajee, Aslant, Awry, Crooked, Skivie

Asleep Dormant, Inactive, Napping

Asparagus Asperge, Sparrow-grass, Spear, Sprew, Sprue

Aspect Angle, Bearing, Brow, Face, Facet, Facies, Feature, Look, Mien, Nature, Outlook, Perfective, Perspective, Side, → **VIEW**, Visage, Vista

Aspersion Calumny, Innuendo, Libel, Slander, Slur, Smear

Asphalt Bitumen, Blacktop, Gilsonite®, Jew's pitch, Pitch, Pitch Lake, Uinta(h)ite

Aspirant, Aspirate, Aspiration, Aspire Ambition, Breath, Buckeen, Challenger,

Desire, Dream, Endeavour, Ettle, Goal, H, Hope(ful), Pretend, Pursue, Rough, Spiritus, Wannabe(e), Would be, Yearn

Ass Buridan's, Burnell, Burro, Cardophagus, Chigetai, Clot, Couscous, Cuddie, Dick(e)y, Donkey, Dziggetai, Funnel, Golden, Hemione, Hemionus, Hinny, Jack, Jenny, Jerusalem pony, Kiang, K(o)ulan, Kourbash, Kourmiss, Kouskous, Kumiss, Kurbash, Kyang, Liripipe, Liripoop, Moke, Neddy, Nitwit, Onager, Quagga, Sesterce, Simp, → STUPID PERSON

Assail(ant) Assault, Attack, Batter, Bego, Belabour, Bepelt, Beset, Bombard, Harry, Impugn, Onsetter, Oppugn, Pillory, Ply, Revile

Assassin(ate), Assassination Booth, Brave, Bravo, Brutus, Casca, Character, Frag, Gunman, Highbinder, Hitman, Killer, Ninja, Sword, Sworder, Thuggee, Tyrannicide

Assault ABH, Assail, Assay, Attack, Battery, Bombard, GBH, Hamesucken, Head-butt, Indecent, Invasion, Maul, Mug, → RAID, Scalade, Stoor, Storm, Stour, Stowre

Assay Cupel, Examine, Proof, Test, Wet

Assemble, Assembly Agora, Audience, Ball, Bottom-hole, Bundestag, Chapter, Chatuaqua, Cho(u)ltry, Church, Co, Collation, → COLLECTION, Comitia, Company, Conclave, Concourse, Congeries, Congress, Consistory, Constituent, Convene, Conventicle, Convention, Convocation, Convoke, Corroboree, Cortes, Council, Court, Curia, Dail Eireann, Dewain, Diet, Divan, Donnybrook, Ecclesia, Eisteddfod, Erect, Feis(anna), Folkmoot, Folkmote, Force, Forgather, Gather(ing), Gemot(e), General, Gorsedd, Group, Headstock, Hoi polloi, Jirga, Kgotla, Knesset, Landtag, Legislative, Lekgotla, Levee, Loya jirga, Majlis, Make, Mass, → MEETING, Mejlis, Moot, Muster, National, Panegyry, Panoply, Parishad, Parliament, Patron, Pattern, Plenum, Pnyx, Powwow, Prefabrication, Presence, Primary, Quorum, Rally, Rechate, Recheate, Reichstag, Repair, Resort, Riksdag, Roll up, Sanghat, Sanhedrin, Sanhedron, Sejm, Senate, Skupshtina, Sobranje, Soc, Society, Stort(h)ing, Synagogue, Synedrion, Synod, T(h)ing, Tribunal, Troop, Unlawful, Vidhan Sabha, Volksraad, Wapens(c)haw, Wapins(c)haw, Wappens(c)haw, Wardmote, Weapon-s(c)haw, Witan, Witenagemot, Zemstvo

Assent Accede, Acquiesce, Agree, Amen, Aye, Comply, Concur, Jokol, Nod, Placet, Royal, Sanction, Viceregal, Yea, Yield

Assert(ing), Assertion Affirm, Allege, Bumptious, Constate, Contend, → DECLARE, Ipse-dixit, → MAINTAIN, Pose, Predicate, Proclaim, Pronounce, Protest, Rumour, Swear (blind), Thetical

Assess(ment) Affeer, Appraise, Audition, Cense, Estimate, Evaluate, Gauge, Guesstimate, → JUDGE, Levy, Means test, Measure, Perspective, Rating, Referee, Risk, Scot and lot, Size up, Special, Stent, Summative, Tax, Value, Weigh

Asset(s) Advantage, Capital, Chargeable, Chattel, Current, Fixed, Floating, Goodwill, Intangible, Inventory, Liquid, Net, Plant, Property, Resource, Talent, Virtue, Wasting

Assiduous Attentive, Busy, Constant, Diligent, Studious, Thorough

Assign(ation), Assignment Allocate, → ALLOT, Apply, Appoint, Aret, Ascribe, Attribute, Award, Date, Dedicate, Duty, Entrust, Errand, Fix, Give, Grant, Impute, Point, Quota, Refer, Transfer, Tryst

Assimilate(d) Absorb, Blend, Digest, Esculent, Fuse, Imbibe, Incorporate, Merge

Assist(ance), Assistant Acolyte, Adjunct, Aid(e), Aide-de-camp, Ally, Alms, Attaché, Au pair, Best boy, Busboy, Cad, Chainman, Collaborate, Counterhand, Counter-jumper, Dresser, Ex parte, Facilitate, Factotum, Famulus, Feldschar, Felds(c)her, Gofer, → HAND, Handlanger, Help, Henchman, Legal aid, Matross, Mentor, National, Offsider, Omnibus, Proproctor, Public, Reinforce, Relief, Second,

Server, Servitor, Shill, Sidesman, Smallboy, Social, Stead, Subsidiary, Subsidy, Suffragan, Supernumerary, → **SUPPORT**, Usher

Assize Botley, Circuit, Court, Maiden, Oyer

Associate, Association Accomplice, Affiliate, Alliance, Amphictyony, Ass, Attach, Bedfellow, Brotherhood, Cartel, Chapel, Chum, Clang, Club, Cohort, Combine, Comecon, Community, Compeer, Complice, Comrade, Concomitant, Confrère, → **CONNECT**, Consort(ium), Co-partner, Correlate, Crony, Enclisis, Fellow, Fraternise, Free, Gesellschaft, Guild, Hobnob, Housing, Inquiline, Intime, Join, Kabele, Kebele, League, Liaison, Lloyds, Mell, Member, Mess, Mix, Moshav, Oddfellows, Pal, Parent teacher, Partner, Phoresy, Press, Probus, Professional, Relate, Residents', Ring, Round Table, Samit(h)i, Sangh(at), Sidekick, Sodality, Stablemate, Staff, Symbiosis, Syndicate, Tenant's, Toc H, Toenadering, Trade, UN(A), Union, Verein, Whiteboy, Word, Yoke-mate

Assort(ed), Assortment Paraphernalia, Pick-'n'-mix, Various

▷ **Assorted** *may indicate* an anagram

Assuage Allay, Appease, Beet, Calm, Ease, Mease, Mitigate, Mollify, Slake, Soften, Soothe

As such Qua

Assume, Assuming, Assumption Adopt, Affect, Arrogate, Attire, Axiom, Believe, Don, Donné(e), Feign, Hypothesis, Lemma, Occam's Razor, Posit, Postulate, Preconception, Premise, Premiss, Presuppose, Pretentious, Principle, Putative, Saltus, Suppose, Surmise, Take

▷ **Assumption** *may indicate* 'attire'

Assure(d), Assurance Aplomb, Aver, Avouch, Belief, Calm, → **CERTAIN**, Comfort, Confidence, Confirm, Earnest, Gall, Guarantee, Life, Pledge, Poise, Warranty

Assuredly Indeed, Perdie, Verily, Yea

Astatine At

Astern Abaft, Apoop, Rear

Asteroid Ceres, Eros, Eros 433, Hermes, Hygiea, Juno, Pallas, Phaethon, Pholus, Star, Starfish, Trojan, Vesta

Astir Afoot, Agate, Agog

Astonish(ed), Astonishing, Astonishment, Astound Abash, Admiraunce, Amaze, Banjax, Bewilder, Confound, Corker, Crikey, Daze, Donnert, Dum(b)found, Dumbstruck, Eye-popping, Flabbergast, Gobsmack, Heavens, Mind-boggling, Open-eyed, Open-mouthed, Phew, Pop-eyed, Prodigious, Rouse, Singular, Stagger, Startle, Stun, Stupefaction, Stupefy, Stupendous, Surprise, Thunderstruck, Wow

Astray Abord, Amiss, Errant, Lost, Will, Wull

Astride Athwart, Spanning, Straddle-back

Astringent Acerbic, Alum, Catechu, Dhak, Gambi(e)r, Harsh, Kino, Krameria, Myrobalan, Rhatany, Sept-foil, Severe, Sour, Styptic, Tormentil, Witch-hazel

Astrologer, Astrology, Astrological Archgenethliac, Chaldean, Culpeper, Faust, Figure-caster, Genethliac, Judicial, Lilly, Midheaven, Moore, Nostradamus, Soothsayer, Starmonger, Zadkiel

Astronaut Cosmonaut, Gagarin, Glenn, Lunarnaut, Spaceman, Spacer, Taikonaut

Astronomer, Astronomy, Astronomical Almagest, Aristarchus, Barnard, Bessel, Bradley, Brahe, Callipic, Cassini, Celsius, Copernicus, Eddington, Encke, Eratosthenes, Eudoxus, Flamsteed, Galileo, Gamma-ray, Hale, Halley, Herschel, Hertzsprung, Hewish, Hipparchus, Hoyle, Hubble, Huggins, Infra red, Jeans, Kepler, Lagrange, Laplace, Leverrier, Lockyer, Lovell, Meton, Neutrino, Omar Khayyam, Oort, Physical, Planetology, Ptolemy, Radar, Radio, Reber, Roche, Roemer, Russell, Ryle, Schwarzschild, Selenography, Selenology, Sosigenes,

Stargazer, Star read, Telescopy, Tycho Brahe, Ultraviolet, Urania, Uranic, Uranography, X-ray, Zwicky

Astrophel Penthia

Astrophysicist Seifert

Astute Acute, Canny, Crafty, Cunning, Downy, Perspicacious, Shrewd, Subtle, Wide, Wily

As usual Solito

As well Additionally, Also, Both, Even, Forby, Too

Asylum Bedlam, Bin, Bughouse, Frithsoken, Funny-farm, Girth, Grith, Haven, Institution, Loony bin, Lunatic, Madhouse, Magdalene, Nuthouse, Political, Rathouse, Refuge, Retreat, Sanctuary, Shelter, Snake-pit

Asymmetric(al) Contrapposto, Lopsided, Skew

At Astatine, In, Kip, To, Up-bye

Atahualpa Inca

At all Ava, Ever, Oughtlings

At all events Algate

Atavistic Reversion, Throw-back

Atheist Doubter, Godless, Infidel, Sceptic

Athenian, Athene Attic, Cleruch, Pallas, Pericles, Solon, Timon

Athlete, Athletic(s) Agile, Agonist, Blue, Coe, Discobolus, Field, Gymnast, Hurdler, Jock, Leish, Miler, Milo, Nurmi, Olympian, Pacemaker, Quarter-miler, Runner, Sexual, Sportsman, Sprinter, Track

Athodyd Ram-jet

Athwart Across, Awry, Oblique, Traverse

Atlantic Millpond, Pond

Atlas Dialect, Linguistic, Maps, Range, Silk

▷ **At last** *may indicate* a cobbler

Atmosphere Aeropause, Afterdamp, Air, Ambience, Aura, Chemosphere, Elements, Epedaphic, Ether, F-layer, Geocorona, Ionosphere, Lid, Magnetosphere, Mesosphere, Meteorology, Miasma, Ozone, Standard, Thermosphere, Tropopause, Troposphere, Upper, Vibe(s), Vibrations

At most Al piu

Atoll Bikini, Eniwetok, Kwajalein, Male, Motu, Tarawa

Atom(ic), Atoms, Atomism Boson, Electron, Excimer, Free, Gram, Ion, Iota, Isobare, Isotone, Isotope, Labelled, Ligand, Logical, Molecule, Monad, Monovalent, Muonic, Nematic, Nuclide, Odoriphore, Particle, Pile, Primeval, Radionuclide, Recoil, Sellafield, Side-chain, Steric, Stripped, Substituent, Tagged, Windscale, Xylyl

Atomiser Airbrush

At once Ek dum, Holus-bolus, Immediate, Instanter, Presto, Statim, Straight away, Swith, Tight, Tit(e), Titely, Tout de suite, Tyte

Atone(ment) Aby(e), Acceptilation, Appease, Assoil, Expiate, Penance, Redeem, Redemption, Yom Kippur

Atop Upon

▷ **At random** *may indicate* an anagram

Atrocious, Atrocity Abominable, Brutal, Diabolical, Flagitious, Heinous, Horrible, Monstrous, Outrage, Vile

Atrophy Degeneration, Marasmus, Sudeck's, Sweeny, Wasting

▷ **At sea** *may indicate* an anagram

Attach(ed), Attachment Accessory, Accrete, Adhesion, Adhibition, Adnate, Adnation, Adscript, Affix, Allonge, Annexe, Bolt, Bro, Byssus, Cleat, Covermount,

Devotement, Devotion, Distrain, Dobby, Feller, Garnish, Glom, Glue, → JOIN, Netsuke, Obconic, Pin, Reticle, Snell, Stick, Tie, Weld

Attack(ing), Attacker Access, Affect, Airstrike, Alert, Anti, Apoplexy, Asperse, Assail, Assault, At, Banzai, Batten, Bego, Belabour, Beset, Bestorm, Blitz(krieg), Bodrag(ing), Bombard, Bordraging, Bout, Broadside, Bushwhack, Camisade, Camisado, Campaign, Cannonade, Charge, Clobber, Club, Counteroffensive, Coup de main, Denounce, Descent, Diatribe, Feint, Fit, Flèche, Foray, Gas, Get, Handbag, Heart, Iconoclast, Ictus, Impingement, Impugn, Incursion, Inroad, Invade, Inveigh, Lampoon, Lese-majesty, Let fly, Maraud, Molest, Mug, Offensive, Onding, Onfall, Onrush, Onset, Onslaught, Oppugn, Panic, Pillage, Polemic, Predacious, Pre-emptive, Push, Quart(e), Raid, Rough, Sail, Sandbag, Savage, Seizure, Sic(k), Siege, Skitch, Snipe, Sortie, Storm, Strafe, Strike, Swoop, Thrust, Tilt, Vilify, Vituperate, Wage, Warison, Wolf-pack, Zap

Attain(ment) Accomplish, Arrive, Earn, Fruition, Get, Land, Reach

Attempt Bash, Bid, Burl, Crack, Debut, Effort, Egma, Endeavour, Essay, Go, Mint, Nisus, Seek, Shot, Show, Shy, Stab, Strive, → TRY, Venture, Whack, Whirl

Attend(ance), Attendant Accompany, Aide, Apple-squire, Await, Batman, Bearer, Be at, Behold, Bulldog, Caddy, Cavass, Chaperone, Chasseur, Checker, Corybant, Courtier, Cuadrilla, Cupbearer, Custrel, Doula, Entourage, Equerry, Escort, Esquire, Famulus, Footman, Gate, Gillie, Hand-maiden, Harken, Hear, → HEED, Hello, Holla, Iras, Kavass, Led captain, → LISTEN, Loblolly-boy, Maenad, Marshal, Mute, Note, Orderly, Outrider, Outrunner, Page, Panisc, Panisk, Paranymph, People, Pew-opener, Presence, Pursuivant, Respect, Roll-up, S(a)ice, Satellite, Second, Server, Sowar, Steward, Syce, Trainbearer, Trolleydolly, Turn-out, Up at, Valet, Varlet, Visit, Wait, Watch, Whiffler, Zambuck

Attention, Attentive Achtung, Alert, Assiduity, Court, Coverage, Dutiful, Ear, Gallant, Gaum, Gorm, Heed, Interest, Mind, Notice, Present, Psst, Punctilious, Qui vive, → REGARD, Selective, Solicitous, Spellbound, Tenty, Thought

Attenuate, Attenuation Lessen, Neper, Rarefy, Thin, Weaken

Attest Affirm, Certify, Depose, Guarantee, Notarise, Swear, → WITNESS

Attic Bee-bird, Cockloft, Garret, Greek, Koine, Loft, Mansard, Muse, Salt, Sky parlour, Solar, Soler, Sollar, Soller, Tallat, Tallet, Tallot

Attila Etzel, Hun

Attire Accoutre, Adorn, Apparel, Clobber, → DRESS, Garb, Habit

Attitude Air, Aspect, Behaviour, Demeanour, Light, → MANNER, Mindset, Nimby, Outlook, Pose, Posture, Propositional, Sense, Song, Stance, Tone, Uppity, Viewpoint

Attorney Advocate, Counsellor, DA, District, Lawyer, Private, Proctor, Prosecutor, Public

Attract(ion), Attractive, Attractor Attrahent, Bait, Barrie, Becoming, Bewitch, Bonny, Bootylicious, Catchy, Charisma, → CHARM, Cheesecake, Clou, Comely, Crowd puller, Cute, Cynosure, Dinky, Dipolar, Dish(y), Draught, → DRAW, Dreamboat, Duende, Engaging, Entice, Epigamic, Eye candy, Eye-catching, Eyeful, Fanciable, Fascinate, Feature, Fetching, Fox(y), Goodly, Gravity, Great, Groovy, Heartthrob, Himbo, Hot stuff, Hunky, Inducement, Inviting, It, Loadstone, Lodestone, Looker, Lovable, Lovely, Lure, Luscious, Magnes, Magnet(ism), Mecca, Mediagenic, Meretricious, Nubile, Personable, Photogenic, Picturesque, Pull, Sematic, Sexpot, Shagtastic, Sideshow, Sightly, Slick, Snazzy, Soote, Speciosity, Spunk, Stotter, Striking, Studmuffin, Stunner, Taking, Taky, Tasteful, Tempt, Theme-park, Weber, Winning, Winsome, Zaftig, Zoftig

Attribute, Attribution Accredit, Allot, Ap(p)anage, Ascribe, Asset, By, Credit, Gift,

Impute, Lay, Metonym, Owe, Proprium, Quality, Refer, Shtick, Strength

Attune Accord, Adapt, Temper

Atypical Aberrant

Aubergine Brinjal, Brown jolly, Egg-plant, Mad-apple

Aubrey Beardsley

Auburn Abram, Chestnut, Copper, Titian, Vill(age)

Auction(eer) Barter, Bridge, Cant, Dutch, Hammer, Knock out, Outcry, Outro(o)per, Roup, Sale, Subhastation, Tattersall, Vendue

Audacious, Audacity Bald-headed, Bold, Brash, Cheek, Chutspah, Cool, Der-doing, Devil-may-care, Effrontery, Face, Hardihood, Indiscreet, Insolence, Intrepid, Neck, Nerve, Rash, Sauce

Audience, Auditorium Assembly, Court, Durbar, Gate, Hearing, House, Interview, Pit, Sphendone, Theatre, Tribunal

Audiovisual AV

Audit(or) Accountant, Check, Ear, Environmental, Examine, Green, Inspect, Listener, Medical, Position

Audition Cattle-call, Screen-test

Auditory Acoustic, Oral

Audrey Hoyden

Auger Miser

Augment(ed) Boost, Eche, Eke, Ich, Increase, Supplement, Swell, Tritone

Augury Ornithoscopy

August Awe-inspiring, Grand, Imperial, Imposing, Lammas, Majestic, Noble, Royal, Solemn, Stately, Stern

Augustine, Augustus Austin, Hippo, John

Auk Guillemot, Ice-bird, Puffin, Roch, Rotch(e)

Aunt(ie) Agony, Augusta, Beeb, Giddy, Maiden, Naunt, Sainted, Tia

Aura Aroma, Emanation, Halo, Mystique, Nimbus, Odour, Vibe(s), Vibrations

Aureole Coronary, Halo, Nimbus

Auricle Ear, Otic

Aurora Eos, Leigh, Matutinal, Merry dancers, Northern lights

Auspice(s) Aegis, Patronage

Auster S-wind

Austere, Austerity Ascetic, Astringent, Bleak, Dantean, Hard, → **HARSH**, Moral, Plain, Rigour, Severe, Spartan, Stern, Stoic, Stoor, Strict, Vaudois, Waldensian

Austin Friar

Australia(n) Alf, Antichthone, Antipodean, Aussie, Balt, Banana-bender, Bananalander, Billjim, Canecutter, Cobber, Coon, Currency, Current, Darwinian, Digger, Gin, Godzone, Gumsucker, Gurindji, Jackie, Jacky, Koori, Larrikin, Lucky Country, Murree, Murri, Myall, Norm, Ocker, Ossie, Oz, Pintupi, Roy, Sandgroper, Strine, Wallaby, Yarra-yabbies

Austrian Cisleithan, Tyrolean

Authentic(ate) Certify, Des(h)i, Echt, Genuine, Honest, Notarise, Official, Real, Sign, Simon-pure, Test, True, Validate

Author(ess) Anarch, Auctorial, Inventor, Me, Parent, Volumist, Wordsmith, → **WRITER**

▷ **Author** *may refer to* author of puzzle

Authorise(d), Authorisation Accredit, Clearance, Countersign, Delegate, Empower, Enable, Exequatur, Imprimatur, Legal, Legit, → **LICENCE**, Official, OK, Passport, → **PERMIT**, Plenipotentiary, Retainer, Sanction, Sign, Stamp, Warrant

Authority, Authoritarian, Authoritative Canon, Charter, Circar, Cocker,

Commission, Commune, Crisp, Definitive, Domineering, Dominion, Establishment, Ex cathedra, Expert, Fascist, Free hand, Gravitas, Hegemony, Inquirendo, Jackboot, Leadership, Licence, Local, Magisterial, Mandate, Mantle, Mastery, Name, Oracle, Permit, Potency, → **POWER**, Prefect, Prestige, Pundit, Remit, Right, Rod, Say-so, Sceptre, Sircar, Sirkar, Source, Supremacy, Unitary, Warrant

Autobiography Memoir

Autocrat(ic) Absolute, Caesar, Cham, Despot, Khan, Neronian, Tsar, Tyrant

Autograph Signature

Autolycus Scrapman

Automatic, Automaton Android, Aut, Browning, Deskill, Instinctive, Machine, Mechanical, Pistol, Quarter-boy, Quarter-jack, Reflex, Robot, RUR, Zombi

Auto-pilot George

Autopsy Necropsy

Auto-suggestion Coueism

Autumn(al) Fall, Filemot, Leaf-fall, Libra, Philamot

Auxiliary Adjunct, Adjuvant, Adminicle, Aide, Be, Feldsher, Foederatus, Have, Helper, Ido, Subsidiary

Avail(able) Benefit, Dow, Eligible, Going, Handy, Off-the-shelf, On call, On tap, Open, Out, Pickings, → **READY**, Serve, Use, Utilise

Avalanche Bergfall, Deluge, Landfall, Landslide, Landslip, Lauwine, Slide, Slip, Snowdrop

Avant-garde Modernistic, Spearhead

Avarice, Avaricious Cupidity, Golddigger, Greed, Money-grubbing, Pleonexia, Sordid

Avatar Epiphany, Incarnation, Rama

Avaunt Away, Go

Avenge(r) Eriny(e)s, Eumenides, Goel, Kurdaitcha, Nightrider, Punish, Redress, Requite, → **REVENGE**, Steed, Wreak

Avenue Alley, Arcade, Boulevard, Channel, Corso, Cradle-walk, Hall, Madison, Mall, Midway, Passage, Vista, Way, Xyst(us)

Aver Affirm, Assert, Asseverate, Depose, Swear, Vouch

Average Adjustment, Av, Batting, Dow Jones, Mean, Mediocre, Middle-brow, Middling, Moderate, Moving, Norm, Par, Particular, Run, Run-of-the-mill, Soso, Standard, Weighted

Averse, Aversion, Avert Against, Antipathy, Apositia, Disgust, Dislike, Distaste, Hatred, Horror, Opposed, Pet, Phobic, Risk, Scunner, Stave off

Avert Avoid, → **DEFLECT**, Forfend, Parry, Ward

Aviary Volary, Volery

Aviator Airman, Alcock, Bleriot, Brown, Byrd, Earhart, Flier, Hinkler, Icarus, Johnson, Lindbergh, Pilot, Red Baron, Richthofen

Avid Agog, → **EAGER**, Greedy, Keen

Avifauna Ornis

Avignon Pont

Avocado Aguacate, Guac(h)amole, Pear

Avocet Scooper

Avoid(er), Avoidance Abstain, Ba(u)lk, Boycott, Bypass, Cop-out, Cut, Dodge, Duck, Elude, Escape, Eschew, Evade, Evitate, Evite, Fly, Forbear, Gallio, Hedge, Miss, Obviate, Parry, Prevaricate, Scutage, Secede, Shelve, Shun, Sidestep, Skirt, Spare, Spurn, Waive

Avoirdupois Size, Weight

Avow(ed) Acknowledged, Affirm, Declare, Own, Swear

Await Abide, Bide, Expect, Tarry

Awake(ning) Aware, Conscious, Conversion, Fly, Rouse, Vigilant

Award Academy, Accolade, Acquisitive, Addeem, Addoom, Allot, Alpha, Arbitrament, Aret(t), Bafta, Bar, Bestow, Bursary, Cap, Clasp, Clio, Crown, Emmy, Exhibition, Genie, Golden Raspberry, Golden Starfish, Grammy, Grant, Honours, Juno, Logie, Lourie, Medal, Meed, Mete, MOBO, Oscar, Padma Shri, Palatinate, Palme d'Or, Premium, Present(ation), Prix Goncourt, → **PRIZE**, Queen's, Razzie, Scholarship, Tony, Trophy, Vir Chakra, Yuko

Aware(ness) Alert, C(o)enesthesis, Cognisant, Conscious, Conversant, ESP, Est, Hep, Hip, Informed, Knowing, Liminal, Mindshare, Onto, Panaesthesia, Prajna, Presentiment, Samadhi, Scienter, Sensible, Sensile, Sensitive, Sentience, Streetwise, Switched on, Vigilant, Weet, Wit, Wot

Away Abaxial, Absent, Afield, Apage, Avaunt, By, For-, Fro(m), Go, Hence, Off, Out, Past

▷ **Away** *may indicate* a word to be omitted

Awe(d) D(o)ulia, Dread, Fear, Intimidate, Loch, Overcome, Popeyed, Regard, Respect, Reverent, Scare, Solemn, Wonderment

Awe-inspiring Numinous

Awful(ly) Alas, Deare, Dere, Dire, Fearful, Horrendous, O so, Piacular, Rotten, Terrible

▷ **Awfully** *may indicate* an anagram

Awkward Angular, Bolshy, Bumpkin, Clumsy, Complicated, Corner, Crabby, Cubbish, Cumbersome, Cussed, Dub, Embarrassing, Farouche, Fiddly, Fix, Gangly, Gauche, Gawky, Handless, Howdy-do, Inconvenient, Inept, Kittle-cattle, Lanky, Loutish, Lurdan(e), Lurden, Maladdress, Mauther, Mawr, Naff, Nasty, Nonconformist, Ornery, Perverse, Refractory, Slummock, So-and-so, Spot, Sticky, Stiff, Stroppy, Stumblebum, Swainish, Uneasy, Ungainly, Unwieldy, Wry

Awl(-shaped) Brog, Els(h)in, Nail, Stob, Subulate

Awn(ing) Barb, Beard, Canopy, Ear, Shade, Velarium

Awry Agley, Amiss, Askent, Askew, Cam, Haywire, Kam(me), Pear-shaped, Wonky

Axe Abolish, Adz(e), Bardiche, Bill, Celt, Chop(per), Cleaver, Curtal, Eatche, Gisarme, Gurlet, Halberd, Halbert, Hatchet, Holing, Ice, Jeddart staff, Jethart-staff, Labrys, Lochaber, Mattock, Palstaff, Palstave, Partisan, Piolet, Retrench, Sax, Slate, Sparth(e), Sperthe, Spontoon, Stone, Thunderbolt, Tomahawk, Twibill

Axeman Bassist, Guitarist

Axe-shaped Securiform

Axiom Adage, Motto, Peano's, Proverb, Saw, Saying

Axis Alliance, Anorthic, Anticous, Axle, Caulome, Chital, Cob, Columella, Epaxial, Henge, Hinge, Major, Minor, Modiolus, Myelon, Neutral, Optic, Pivot, Polar, Principal, Rachis, Radical, Spindle, Sympodium, Visual, X, Y, Z

Axle, Axle-shoulder Arbor, Axis, Driving, Fulcrum, Hurter, Journal, Live, Mandrel, Mandril, Pivot, Spindle, Stub

Ay I, Indeed

Aye Always, Eer, Ever, Yea, Yes

Ayesha She

Azo-dye Para-red

Aztec Nahuatl

Bb

B Bachelor, Black, Book, Born, Boron, Bowled, Bravo, Flipside

Babble(r) Blather, Brook, Chatter, Gibber, Haver, Lallation, Lurry, Prate, Prattle, Runnel, Tonguester, Twattle, Waffle

Babel Charivari, Confusion, Din, Dovercourt, Medley

Baboon Ape, Bobbejaan, Chacma, Cynocephalus, Dog-ape, Drill, Gelada, Hamadryas, Mandrill, Sphinx

Baby Bairn, Band-Aid®, Blue, Bub, Bunting, Changeling, Coddle, Designer, Duck, Grand, Infant, Jelly, Neonate, Nursling, Pamper, Papoose, Plunket, Preverbal, Rhesus, Sis, Small, Sook, Suckling, Tar, Test tube, Thalidomide, Tot, War, Wean

Babylonian Mandaean, Semiramis, Sumerian

Bacchanalian, Bacchus Ivied, Upsee, Ups(e)y

Bacchantes Maenads

Bachelor BA, Bach, Benedict, Budge, Celibate, En garçon, Knight, Pantagamy, Parti, Seal, Single, Stag, Wifeless

Bacillus Comma, Germ, Klebs-Loffler, Micrococcus, Tubercle, Virus

Back(ing), Back up, Backward Abet, Accompany, Addorse, Again, Ago, Anticlockwise, Antimacassar, Arear, Arrear, Arrière, Assist, Baccare, Backare, Bankroll, Buckram, Champion, Chorus, Consent, Defender, Dorsal, Dorse, Dorsum, Dos, Ebb, Empatron, Encourage, Endorse, Finance, Frae, Fro, Full, Fund, Gaff, Half, Help, Hind, Historic, Incremental, La-la, Late, Notaeum, Notal, Notum, On, Patronise, Pendu, Poop, Pronotum, Punt, Rear(most), Retral, Retro(grade), Retrogress, Retrorse, Retrospective, Return, Rev, Reverse, Ridge, Root, Running, Shy, Spinal, Sponsor, Stern, Sternboard, → **SUPPORT**, Sweeper, Tail, Telson, Tergum, Third, Thrae, Three-quarter, Tonneau, Ulu, Uphold, Verso, Vie, Vo, Wager, Watteau

▷ **Back(ing)** *may indicate* a word spelt backwards

Back and forth Boustrophedon

Backbiter, Backbiting Catty, Defame, Detract, Libel, Molar, Slander

Backbone Chine, Grit, Guts, Mettle, Spina, Spine

Backchat Lip, Mouth, Sass

Backer Angel, Benefactor, Patron, Punter, Seconder, Sponsor

Backfire Boomerang

Backgammon Acey-deucy, Blot, Lurch, Tick-tack, Trick-track, Tric-trac, Verquere

Background Antecedence, Chromakey, Cyclorama, Field, Fond, History, Horizon, Microwave, Muzak, Setting, Ulterior

Backhander Bribe, Payola, Reverso, Sweetener

Backroom Boffin, Boy, Moor

Backslide(r), Backsliding Apostate, Lapse, Regress, Relapse, Revert

Backwash Rift

Backwater Bogan, Ebb, Logan, Retreat, Slough, Wake

Backwoods Boondocks, Boonies, Hinterland

Backyard Court, Patio

Bacon Bard, Canadian, Collar, Danish, Essayist, Flitch, Francis, Gammon, Lardo(o)n, Pancetta, Pig, Pork, Rasher, Roger, Spec(k), Streaky, Verulam

Bacteria, Bacterium Acidophilus, Actinomycete, Aerobe, Amphitricha, Bacilli, Bacteriological, Botulinum, → **BUG**, Campylobacter, Chlamydia, Clostridia, Cocci, Coliform, Culture, Detritivore, Diplococcus, Escherichia, → **GERM**, Gonococcus, Gram-negative, Gram-positive, Intestinal flora, Klebsiella, Legionella, Listeria, Lysogen, Meningococcus, Microbe, Micrococcus, Microphyte, Mother, MRSA, Mycoplasma, Nitrous, Nostoc, Packet, Pasteurella, Pathogen, Pneumococcus, Probiotic, Prokaryote, Proteus, Pseudomonas, Pus, Ray-fungus, Rhizobium, Rickettsia, Salmonella, Schizomycete, Septic, Serotype, Serum, Shigella, Spirilla, Spirochaete, Spore, Staph, Staphylococcus, Strep(tococcus), Streptobacillus, Streptomyces, Sulphur, Superbug, Thermophil(e), Treponemata, Vibrio, Vinegar-plant, Yersinia, Zoogloea

Bad, Badness Addled, Chronic, Crook, Defective, Diabolic, Dud, Duff, Dystopia, Egregious, Execrable, Faulty, God-awful, Half-pie, Heinous, Ill, Immoral, Inferior, Injurious, Lither, Mal, Naughty, Nefandrous, Nefarious, Nice, Off, Ominous, Oncus, Onkus, Piacular, Poor, Rancid, Rank, Ropy, Scampish, Scoundrel, Sinful, Spoiled, Turpitude, Undesirable, Unspeakable, Useless, Wack, Wick, → **WICKED**

▷ **Bad(ly)** *may indicate* an anagram

Badge Brassard, Brooch, Button, Chevron, Cockade, Cockleshell, Comm, Cordon, Crest, Emblem, Ensign, Epaulet, Episemon, Fáinne, Film, Flash, Garter, Gorget, ID, Insigne, Insignia, Kikumon, Mark, Mon, Numerals, Pilgrim's sign, Rosette, Scallop, Shield, Shouldermark, → **SIGN**, Symbol, Tiger, Token, Vernicle, Vine branch, Vine-rod, Wings

Badger → **ANNOY**, Bait, Bedevil, Beset, Brock, Browbeat, Bug, Bullyrag, Cete, Dassi(e), Ferret, Gray, Grey, → **HARASS**, Hassle, Heckle, Hog, Honey, Hound, Nag, Pester, Plague, Provoke, Ratel, Ride, Roil, Sand, Sow, Stinking, Teledu, Wisconsin

Bad habit Cacoethes, Vice

Badinage Banter, Chaff, Raillery

Bad luck Ambs-ace, Ames-ace, Deuce-ace, Hard cheese, Hard lines, Hoodoo, Jinx, Jonah, Shame, Voodoo

Bad-tempered Carnaptious, Curmudgeon, Curnaptious, Curst, Grouchy, Grum(py), Irritable, Moody, Nowty, Patch, Shirty, Splenetic, Stroppy

Bad woman Harridan, Loose, Mort

Baffle(d), Baffling Anan, Balk, Bemuse, Bewilder, Confound, Confuse, Elude, Evade, Floor, Flummox, Foil, Fox, Get, Hush-kit, Mate, Muse, Mystify, Nark, Nonplus, Perplex, Pose, Puzzle, Stump, Throw, Thwart

Bag(gage), Bags Acquire, Air, Alforja, Allantois, Amaut, Amowt, Ascus, Ballonet, Besom, Bladder, Blue, Body, Bounty, Bulse, Bum, Buoyancy, Caba(s), Caecum, Callet, Capture, Carpet, Carrier, Carryall, Case, Cecum, Clutch, Cly, Cod, Colostomy, Cool, Corduroy, Crone, Crumenal, Cyst, Daypack, Dilli, Dilly, Dime, Diplomatic, Ditty, Doggy, Dorothy, Douche, Duffel, Dunnage, → **EFFECTS**, Emery, Excess, Flannels, Flotation, Follicle, Galligaskins, Game, → **GEAR**, Gladstone, Grab, Grip, Gripsack, Grow, Holdall, Ice, Impedimenta, Jelly, Jiffy®, Kill, Knapsack, Ladies' companion, Lavender, Lithocyst, Marsupium, Materiel, Meal-poke, Minx, Mixed, Money, Monkey, Moon, Mummy, Musette, Musk, Muzzle, Mystery, Nap, Net, Nunny, Organiser, Overnight, Oxford, Packsack, Pantaloons, Plastic, Plus fours, Pochette, Pock(et), Pocketbook, Pockmanky, Pockmantie, Poke, Politzer's, Poly(thene), Port(manteau), Portmantle, Portmantua, Post, Pot, Pouch, Pounce, Pudding, Punch, Purse, Rake, Red, Reticule, Ridicule, Rucksack, Sabretache,

Sac(cule), Sachet, Sack, Saddle, Sag, Satchel, Scent, School, Scrip, Scrotum, Sea, Shopper, Sick, Slattern, Sleeping, Sponge, Sporran, Stacks, Strossers, Sugar, Survival, Tea, Tote, → TRAP, Trews, Trollop, Trouse(r), Tucker (box), Udder, Unmentionables, Utricle, Valise, Vanity, Viaticals, Waist, Wallet, Water, Weekend, Win, Woolpack, Work, Wrap, Ziplock

Bagatelle Bauble, Fico, Trifle, Trinket

Bagpipe Biniou, Chorus, Cornemuse, Drone, Gaita, Musette, Pibroch, Piffero, Skirl, Sourdeline, Uillean, Zampogna

Bahama(s), Bahamian BS, Conch

Bail(er), Bailment Bond, Ladle, Mainpernor, Mainprise, Mutuum, Replevin, Replevy, Scoop

Bailey Bridge, Castle wall, Ward

Bailiff Adam, Bandog, Beagle, Bum, Factor, Foud, Grieve, Huissier, Hundreder, Hundredor, Land-agent, Nuthook, Philistine, Reeve, Shoulder-clapper, Shoulder-knot, Steward, Tipstaff, Water

Bairn Baby, → CHILD, Infant, Wean

Bait Badger, Berley, Brandling, Burley, Capelin, Chum, Dap, Decoy, Entice, Gentle, Gudgeon, Harass, Hellgram(m)ite, Incentive, Lobworm, Lug(worm), Lure, Mawk, → RAG, Ragworm, Sledge, Teagle, Tease, Tempt

Bake(r), Baked, Baking Alaska, Batch, Baxter, → COOK, Fire, Kiln-dry, Pieman, Roast, Scorch, Shirr

Baker's daughter Own

Baker Street Irregular

Balance(d) Account, Beam, Compensation, Counterpoise, Counterweight, Equate, Equilibrium, Equipoise, Equiponderate, Even, Fixed, Funambulate, Gyroscope, Gyrostat, Hydrostatic, Invisible, Isostasy, Launce, Libra, Librate, Meet, Otolith, Peise, Perch, Peyse, Poise, → REMAINDER, Remnant, Residual, Rest, Running, Scale, Sea-legs, Spring, Stand, Steelyard, Symmetry, Torsion, → TOTAL, Trial, Trim, Tron(e), Visible

Balcony Circle, Gallery, Loggia, Mirador, Moucharaby, Porch, Quarter-gallery, Sundeck, Tarras, Terrace, Veranda(h)

Bald, Baldness Alopecia, Apterium, Awnless, Barren, Calvities, Coot, Crude, Egghead, Fox-evil, Glabrous, Hairless, Madarosis, Open, Peelgarlic, Pilgarlic(k), Pollard, Psilosis, Slaphead, Smoothpate, Stark, Tonsured

Balderdash Drivel, Flapdoodle, Nonsense, Rot

Baldmoney Emeu, Meu, Spignel

Bale Bl, Bundle, Evil, Lave, Pack, Sero(o)n, Truss

Baleful Evil, Malefic, Malignant

▶ **Balk** *see* BAULK

Balkan Albanian, Bosnian, Bulgarian, Macedon, Rumanian, Serb, Vlach

Ball(s) Aelopile, Aelopyle, Aeolipile, Aeolipyle, Agglomerate, Alley, Ally, Ammo, Aniseed, Apple, Beach, Bead, Beamer, Birthing, Bobble, Boll, Bolus, Bosey, Bouncer, Break, Buckshot, Buzzer, Caltrap, Caltrop, Camphor, Cap, Cherry, Chin, Chinaman, Chopper, Clew, Clue, Condyle, Cotill(i)on, Cramp, Creeper, Croquette, Crystal, Cue, Curve, Daisy-cutter, → DANCE, Delivery, Dink, Dodge, Dollydrop, Dot, Dribbler, Eight, Ensphere, Eolipile, Eolipyle, Eolopile, Eolopyle, Falafel, Felafel, Fungo, Gazunder, → GLOBE, Glomerate, Gobstopper, Googly, Gool(e)ys, Goolies, Grub, Gutta, Gutter, Hank, Hop, Hummer, Inswinger, Ivory, Jinglet, Jump, Knob, Knur(r), Leather, Leg-break, Leg-cutter, Lob, Long-hop, Marble, Masked, Masque(rade), Matzo, Medicine, Minié, Mirror, Moth, Nur(r), O, Object, Off-break, Off-cutter, Off-spin, Orb, Outswinger, Over, Overarm, Pakora, Pea, Pellet, Pill, Poi, Pomander,

Pompom, Pompon, Prom, Puck, Punch, Quenelle, Rabbit, Rissole, Root, Round, Rover, Rundle, Seamer, Shooter, Shot, Sliotar, Sneak, Sphere, Spinner, Stress, Strike, Swinger, Taw, Testes, Thenar, Three, Tice, Time, Track(er), Witches, Wood, Yorker, Zorb®

Ballad Bab, Bothy, Broadside, Bush, Calypso, Carol, Fanzone, Folk-song, Lay, Lillibullero, Lilliburlero, Mento, Singsong, → **SONG**, Torch-song

Ballast Kentledge, Makeweight, Stabiliser, Trim, Weight

Ball-boy Dry-bob

Ballerina Coryphee, Dancer, Pavlova, Prima

Ballet, Ballet movement, Ballet-system Battement, Bharat Natyam, Bolshoi, Cambré, Chainé, Changement, Checkmate, Daphnis and Chloe, Développé, Don Pasquale, Écarté, Echappé, Enchainement, Entrechat, Firebird, Fouette, Giselle, Jeté, Kirov, Laban, Labanotation, Leg business, Pas de basque, Pas de bourrée, Pas de chat, Petit battement, Pirouette, Plie, Pointe, Pointer, Port de bras, Relevé, Saut, Swan Lake

Ballet-interlude Divertimento

Ballistic Wildfire

Balloon(ist) Aeronaut, Aerostat, Airship, Bag, Barrage, Billow, Blimp, Bloat, Dirigible, Dumont, Fumetto, Hot air, Lead, Montgolfier, Pilot, Rawinsonde, Sonde, Trial, Weather, Zeppelin

Ballot Butterfly, Election, → **POLL**, Referendum, Second, Suffrage, Ticket, Vote

Ballot-box Urn

Ballpoint Bic®, Biro®

Balm(y) Anetic, Arnica, Balsam, Calamint, Fragrant, Garjan, Gilead, Gurjun, Lemon, Lenitive, Lotion, → **MILD**, Mirbane, Myrbane, Nard, Oil, Opobalsam, Ottar, Redolent, Remedy, Soothe, Spikenard, Tiger, Tolu, Unguent

Balmoral Bonnet

Baloney Bunk, Hooey, Nonsense

Balsam Canada, Copaiba, Copaiva, Friar's, Nard, Noli-me-tangere, Peruvian, Resin, Spikenard, Tamanu, Tolu(ic), Touch-me-not, Tous-les-mois, Turpentine

Balt Esth, Lett

Baltic Estonian, Lettic

Bamboo Kendo, Split cane, Tabasheer, Whangee

Bamboozle(d) Cheat, Dupe, Flummox, Hoodwink, Mystify, Nose-led, Perplex, Trick

Ban Abolish, Accurse, Anathema, Black(ing), Censor, Debar, D-notice, Embargo, Estop, Excommunicate, Forbid, For(e)say, For(e)speak, Gate, Green, Moratorium, No, Outlaw, Prohibit, Proscribe, Suppress, Taboo, Tabu, Test, Veto

Banal Corny, Dreary, Flat, Hackneyed, Jejune, Mundane, Platitudinous, → **TRITE**, Trivial

Banana(s) Abaca, Hand, → **MAD**, Matoke, Musa, Plantain, Scitamineae, Split, Strelitzia, Top

Band(s) Absorption, Alice, Ambulacrum, Anadem, Anklet, Armlet, Barrulet, Belt, Border, Braid, Brake, Brass, Brassard, Brassart, Caravan, CB, Channel, Chinstrap, Chromosome, Cingulum, Circlet, Citizens', Clarain, Cohort, Collar, Collet, Combo, Company, Conduction, Corslet, Coterie, Crape, Crew, Deely boppers, Elastic, Endorse, Energy, Enomoty, Facia, Falling, Fascia, Fasciole, Ferret, Ferrule, Fess, Filament, Fillet, Frequency, Frieze, Frog, Frontlet, Galloon, Gamelan, → **GANG**, Garage, Garland, Garter, Gasket, Gaskin, Geneva, German, Gird, Girth, Guard, → **HOOP**, Hope, Iron, Jazz, Jug, Kitchen, Label, Laticlave, Lytta, Maniple, Mariachi, Massed, Military, Mourning, Myrmidon, Noise, One-man, Orchestra, Orchestrina, Pack, Parral, Parrel, Parsal, Parsel, Pass, Patte, Pipe, Plinth, Property, Purfle,

Puttee, Retinaculum, Rib, Ribbon, Rigwiddie, Rigwoodie, Rim, Ring, Robbers, Rubber, Rymme, Sash, Scarf, Screed, Scrunchie, Scrunchy, Sect, Shadow, Shallal, Shash, Sheet, Shoe, Snood, Steel, Strake, Strap, Stratum, String, Stripe, Swath(e), Sweat, Tambu-bambu, Tape, Tendon, Thoroughbrace, Throat-latch, Tie, Tippet, Torques, Tourniquet, Train, Tribute, Troop, Troupe, Tumpline, Turm, Tyre, Unite, Valence, Vinculum, Virl, Vitrain, Vitta, Wanty, Wedding, Weed, Weeper, Welt, With(e), Wristlet, Zona, Zone, Zonule

Bandage Bind, Blindfold, Capeline, Dressing, Fillet, Ligature, Lint, Living, Pledget, Roller, Scapular, Sling, Spica, Suspensor, Swaddle, Swathe, T, Tape, Truss, Tubigrip®, Wadding

Bandicoot Bilby, Pig-rat

Bandit Apache, Bravo, Brigand, Desperado, Fruit-machine, Gunslinger, Klepht, Moss-trooper, Outlaw, Pirate, Rapparee, → **ROBBER**, Squeegee, Turpin

Bandsman, Band-leader Alexander, Bugler, Conductor, Maestro, Miller, Wait

Bandy Bow, Exchange, Revie, Toss, Vie

Bane Curse, Evil, Harm, Poison

Bang(er) Amorce, Big, Cap, Chipolata, Clap, Cracker, Crock, Explode, Flivver, Fringe, Haircut, Heap, Implode, Jalopy, Maroon, Rattletrap, Report, → **SAUSAGE**, Sizzler, Slam, Sonic, Thrill, Wurst

Bangle Anklet, Armlet, Bracelet, Kara

Banish(ment) Ban, Deport, Depose, Exile, Expatriate, Expel, Extradition, Forsay, Maroon, Ostracise, → **OUTLAW**, Relegate, Rusticate

Banjo Ukulele

Bank(ing) An(n)icut, Asar, Backs, Bar, Bay, Bk, Blood, Bluff, Bottle, Brae, Brim, Bund, Camber, Cay, Central, Chesil, Clearing, Cloud, Commercial, Cooperative, Data, Depend, Deposit, Dogger, Down, Dune, Dyke, Earthwork, Escarp, Fog, Gene, Giro, Glacis, Gradient, Gradin(e), Hele, Hill, Home, Incline, Jodrell, Land, Left, Lender, Levee, Link, Lombard Street, Memory, Merchant, Mound, Nap, National, Needle, Nore, Overslaugh, Oyster, Parapet, Penny, Piggy, Pot, Private, Rake, Ramp, Rampart, Reef, → **RELY**, Reserve, Retail, Rivage, Riverside, Rodham, Row, Sandbar, Savings, Seed, Shallow, Shelf, Side, Slope, Soil, Sperm, Staithe, State, Sunk, Telephone, Terrace, Terreplein, Tier, Vault, West, World

Banker Agent, Financial, Fugger, Gnome, Lombard, Medici, → **RIVER**, Rothschild, Shroff, Teller

▷ **Banker** *may indicate* a river

Banknote(s) Flimsy, Greenback, Snuff-paper

Bankrupt(cy) Break, Broke, Bung, Bust, Cadaver, Carey Street, Crash, Debtor, Deplete, Duck, Dyvour, Fail, Fold, Insolvent, Lame duck, Notour, Penniless, Receivership, Ruin, Rump, Scat, Sequestration, Skatt, Smash

▷ **Bankrupt** *may indicate* 'red' around another word

Bank system Giro

Bann(s) Out-ask

Banner Banderol(e), Bandrol, Bannerol, → **FLAG**, Gumphion, Labarum, Oriflamme, Sign, Streamer

Banquet Beanfeast, Dine, Feast, Junket, Spread

Banquette Firestep

Bant Diet, Reduce

Banter Backchat, Badinage, Borak, Chaff, Dicacity, Dieter, Jest, → **JOKE**, Persiflage, Picong, Rag, → **RAILLERY**, Rally, Ribaldry, Roast, Tease

Bantu Bosotho, Gazankulu, Herero, Lebowa, Qwaqwa, Shangaan, Sotho, Transkei, Tutsi, X(h)osa

Bap Bread, Roll, Tommy

Baptise(d), Baptism, Baptist Affusion, Amrit, Christen, Dip, Dipper, Dopper, Dunker, Illuminati, Immersion, John, Mersion, Sabbatarian, Sprinkle, Tinker

Bar(s) Address, Angle-iron, Anti-roll, Astragal, Asymmetric, Axletree, Bail, Ban, Barrelhouse, Baulk, Beam, Bierkeller, Bilboes, Billet, Bistro, Blackball, Blacklist, Block(ade), Bloom, Bolt, Boom, Bottega, Brasserie, Buffet, Bull, Bumper, But, Buvette, Café(-chantant), Café-concert, → **CAGE**, Came, Cantina, Capo, Capstan, Channel, Cocktail, Coffee, Colour, Counter, Cramp(on), Cross(head), Crow, Crush, Currency, Dive, Double-tree, Draw, Drift, Dumbbell, Efficiency, Espresso, Estop(pel), Except, Exclude, Fen, Fid, Flinders, Fonda, Forbid, Foreclose, Forestall, Fret, Gad, Gemel, Glazing, Grate, Grid, Grog-shop, Hame, Handspike, Heck, → **HINDRANCE**, Horizontal, Hound, Hyphen, Impediment, Ingoes, Ingot, Ingowes, Inn, Inner, Judder, Juice, Karaoke, Keeper, Kickstand, Knuckleduster, Latch, Let, Lever, Limbo, Line, Local, Lounge, Macron, Mandrel, Mandril, Measure, Menu, Milk, Mousing, Muesli, Mullion, Nail, Nanaimo, Navigation, No-go, Norman, Obstacle, Onely, Orgue, Outer, Overslaugh, Oxygen, Parallel, Perch, Pile, Pinch, Pole, Posada, Prescription, Private, Prohibit, Pub, Public, Putlog, Rabble, Rack, Rail, Ramrod, Rance, Randle-balk, Randle-perch, Randle-tree, Raw, Reach, Restrict, Rib, Risp, Rod, Roll, Roo, Rung, Saddle, Salad, Saloon, Sans, Save, Saving, Scroll, Semantron, Shaft, Shanty, Shet, Shut, Singles, Skewer, Slice, Slot, Snack, Snug, Spacer, Spar, Speakeasy, Sperre, Spina, Spit, Splinter, Sprag, Stancher, Stanchion, Status, Stave, Sternson, Stick, Stirre, Stretcher, Stripe, Strut, Sway, Swee, T, Tael, Tap(-room), Tapas, Taphouse, Tavern(a), Temple, Toll, Tombolo, Tommy, Tool, Torsion, Tow, Trace, Trangle, Transom, Trapeze, Triblet, Trundle, Type, Vinculum, Wall, Ward, Wet, Whisker, Window, Wine, Wire, Wrecking, Z, Zed, Zygon

Barabbas Robber

Barb(ed) Bur(r), Fluke, Harl, Herl, → **HOOK**, Jag(g), Jibe, Pheon, Prickle, Ramus, Tang, Thorn, Vexillum

Barbados, Barbadian Bajan, Bim(m)

Barbara Allen, Major

Barbarian, Barbaric Boor, Crude, Fifteen, Foreigner, Goth, Heathen, Hottentot, Hun, Inhuman, Lowbrow, Outlandish, Philistine, Rude, Savage, Tartar, Tatar(ic)

Barbary Ape, Roan

Barbecue Braai(vleis), Cook-out, Flame-grill, Grill, Hangi, Hibachi, Roast, Spit

Barbel Beard

Barber Epilate, Figaro, Scrape(r), Shaver, Strap, Todd, Tonsor, Trimmer

Barbiturate Goofball

Bard(ic) Ariosto, Gorsedd, Griot, Heine, Meat, Minstrel, Muse, Ossian, Scald, Scop, Skald, Taliesin

Bare, Bare-headed Adamic, Aphyllous, Bald, Barren, Blank, Bodkin, Cere, Décolleté, Denude, Hush, Lewd, Marginal, Moon, → **NAKED**, Open, Plain, Scablands, Scant, Sear, Stark, Topless, Uncase, Uncover, Unveil

Barefoot Discalced, Unshod

Barely At a pinch, At a stretch, Hand-to-mouth, Hardly, Just, Merely, Scarcely, Scrimp

Bargain(ing) Bargoon, Barter, Braata, Chaffer, Champerty, → **CHEAP**, Collective, Contract, Coup, Deal, Dicker, Distributive, Effort, Find, Go, Haggle, Higgle, Horse-trade, Huckster, Integrative, Option, → **PACT**, Plea, Productivity, Scoop, Snip, Steal, Supersaver, Time, Trade, Trock, Troke, Truck, Wanworth, Wheeler-dealing

Barge Birlinn, Bucentaur, Budgero(w), Butty, Gabbard, Gabbart, Galley-foist, Hopper, Intrude, Jostle, Keel, Lighter, Nudge, Obtrude, Pra(a)m, Ram, Scow, → **SHIP**, Trow, Wherry

▷ **Barge** *may indicate* an anagram

Bargee, Bargeman Keeler, Keelman, Legger, Lighterman, Ram, Trow

Barium Ba, Witherite

Bark Angostura, Ayelp, Azedarach, Bass, Bast, Bay, Bowwow, Calisaya, Cambium, Canella, Caribbee, Cascara, Cascara sagrada, Cascarilla, Cassia, China, Cinchona, Cinnamon, Cork, Cortex, Cusparia, Honduras, Jamaica, Jesuit's, Kina, Kinakina, Latration, Liber, Mezereum, Myrica, Parchment, Peel, Pereira, Peruvian, Phloem, Quebracho, Quest, Quill, Quillai, Quina, Quinquina, Red, Rind, Sagrada, Salian, Sassafras, Scrape, Scurf, Shag, → **SHIP**, Skin, Slippery elm, Tan, Tap(p)a, Totaquine, Waff, Waugh, Winter's, Woof, Wow, Yaff, → **YAP**, Yellow, Yelp, Yip

Bar-keep(er), Barmaid, Barman Advocate, Ale-wife, Bencher, Curate, Hebe, Luckie, Lucky, Tapster, Underskinker

Barley (water) Awn, Bear, Bere, Bigg, Hordeum, Malt, Orgeat, Pearl, Pot, Scotch, Truce, Tsamba

Barm(y) Yeast

Barmecide, Barmecidal Imaginary

Barn Bank, Byre, Cowshed, Dutch, Farm, Grange, Mow, Perchery, Skipper, Tithe

Barnaby Rudge

Barnacle Acorn, Cypris, Goose(neck), Limpet

Barometer Aneroid, Glass, Orometer, Statoscope, Sympiesometer, Torricellian tube, Weatherglass

Baron B, Corvo, Drug, Munchausen, Noble, Thyssen, Tycoon

Baronet Bart

Baronne Dudevant Sand

Baroque Fancy, Gothic, Ornate, Rococo

▷ **Baroque** *may indicate* an anagram

Barrack(s), Barracking Asteism, Boo, Cantonment, Casern(e), Cat-call, Garrison, Heckle, Irony, Jeer, Quarters

Barrage Balloon, Fusillade, Heat, Salvo

Barred Banned, Edh, Trabeculated

Barrel Bl, Butt, Cade, Capstan, Cascabel, Cask, Clavie, Cylinder, Drum, Hogshead, Keg, Kibble, Morris-tube, Oildrum, Organ, Pièce, Pork, Run(d)let, Tan-vat, Thrall, Tierce, Tun, Vat, Water, Wood

Barrel-organ Apollonicum, Hurdy-gurdy, Street piano

Barren Addle, Arid, Badlands, Blind, Blunt, Clear, Dry, Eild, → **EMPTY**, Farrow, Hardscrabble, Hirstie, Jejune, Sterile, Unbearing, Waste, Wasteland, Wilderness, Yeld, Yell

Barrier Bail, Barrage, Bayle, Block, Breakwater, Cauld, Checkrail, Cheval de frise, Chicane, Cordon (sanitaire), Crash, Crush, → **DAM**, Defence, Drawgate, Dyke, Fence, Fraise, Gate, Heat, Hedge, Hurdle, Mach, Obstruct, Pain, Potential, Rail(-fence), Rampart, Restraint, Revetment, Roadblock, Rope, Screen, Skreen, Sonic, Sound, Spina, Stockade, Thermal, Tollgate, Trade, Transsonic, Turnpike, Turnstile, → **WALL**

Barrister Advocate, Attorney, Counsel, Devil, Lawyer, Revising, Rumpole, Sergeant (at law), Serjeant(-at-law), Silk, Templar, Utter

Barrow Dolly, Handcart, Henge, How, Hurley, Kurgan, Molehill, Mound, Pushcart, Tram, Trolley, Truck, Tumulus

Barrow-boy Coster, Trader

Bar-tail Scamel, Staniel, Stannel

Barter Chaffer, Chop, Coup, Dicker, → EXCHANGE, Haggle, Hawk, Niffer, Sco(u)rse, Swap, → TRADE, Traffic, Truck

Basalt Diabase, Melaphyre, Tachylite, Tephrite, Toadstone, Trap(pean), Traprock, Wacke

Base Adenine, Air, Alkali, Bed, Beggarly, Billon, Bottom, Caitiff, Camp, Choline, Codon, Cytosine, Degenerate, Degraded, Dog, Down, E, Erinite, → ESTABLISH, First, Floor, Foot, Foothold, Footstall, Found, Foundation, Fundus, Guanine, Harlot, Histamine, Hydroxide, Ignoble, Indamine, Infamous, Install, Knowledge, Leuco, Lewis, → LOW, → MEAN, Nefarious, Nook, Oasis®, Parasaniline, Partite, Patten, Platform, Plinth, Podium, Premise, Ptomaine, Purin(e), Pyrimidine, Pyrrolidine, Raca, Radix, Rascally, Ratty, Rests, Ribald, Root, Rosaniline, Schiff, Servile, Shameful, Shand, Sheeny, Socle, Soda, Spaceport, Staddle, → STAND, Station, Substrate, Ten, Thymine, Torus, Triacid, Turpitude, Unworthy, Uracil, Vile

Baseball Apple, Nine

Baseless Idle, Unfounded, Ungrounded

Base-line Datum

Basement Bargain, Below stairs

Bash Belt, Bonk, Clout, Go, Hit, Rave, Shot, Slog, Strike, Swat, Swipe

Bashful Awed, Blate, Coy, Modest, Retiring, Shamefast, Sheep-faced, Sheepish, → SHY

Basic(s), Basically, Basis ABC, Abcee, Alkaline, Aquamanale, Aquamanile, Crude, Elemental, → ESSENTIAL, Fiducial, Fond, Fundamental, Ground(work), Gut, In essence, Integral, Intrinsic, Logic, Meat and potatoes, Nitty-gritty, No-frills, No-nonsense, Pou sto, Presumption, Primordial, Principle, Radical, Rudimentary, Spit-and-sawdust, Staple, Substance, Underlying, Uracil

Basilica St Peter's

Basilisk Cannon, Lizard

Basin Aquamanale, Aquamanile, Artesian, Aspergillum, Aspersorium, Benitier, Bidet, Bowl, Canning, Catch, Catchment, Cirque, Corrie, Cwm, Dish, Dock, Doline, Donets, Drainage, Foxe, Geosyncline, Great, Impluvium, Kuzbass, Kuznetsk, Lavabo, Laver, Minas, Monteith, Ocean, Okavango, Pan, Park, Piscina, Playa, Porringer, Pudding, Reservoir, River, Scapa Flow, Sink, Slop, Stoop, Stoup, Sugar, Tank, Tarim, Tidal, Washhand

Bask Apricate, Revel, Sun, Sunbathe, → WALLOW

Basket, Basket-work Baalam, Bass, Bassinet, Bread, Buck, Cabas, Calathus, Canephorus, Car, Cesta, Chip, Cob, Coop, Corbeil(le), Corbicula, Corf, Creel, Cresset, Dosser, Fan, Flasket, Flax kit, Frail, Gabian, Hamper, Hask, Junket, Kago, Kajawah, Kipe, Kit, Kite, Leap, Litter, Maund, Mocock, Mocuck, Moses, Murlain, Murlan, Murlin, Osiery, Pannier, Ped, Petara, Pitara(h), Plate, Pollen, Pottle, Punnet, Rip, Round file, Scull, Scuttle, Seed-lip, Skep, Skull, Trolley, Trout, Trug, Van, Wagger-pagger(-bagger), Waste(-paper), Wattlework, Whisket, Wicker(-work), Will(e), Wisket, Work

Basketball Tip-off

Basket-bearer Canephor(a), Canephore, Canephorus

Basket-maker Alfa, Cane, Halfa, Wicker

Basque Euskarian

Bass Alberti, Ale, Alfie, B, Black, Continuo, Deep, Double, El-a-mi, Figured, Fish, Ground, Largemouth, Low, Ostinato, Serran, Smallmouth, String, Thorough, Walking

Bast Liber

Bastard, Bastard-wing Alula, Base, By-blow, Filius nullius, Git, Haram(za)da, Illegitimate, Mamzer, Momzer, Mongrel, Sassaby, Side-slip, Slink, Spuriae, Spurious, Whoreson
▷ **Bastard** *may indicate* an anagram
Baste Enlard, Sew, Stitch, Tack
Bastion Citadel, Lunette, Moineau
Bat(sman), Bat's wing, Batter, Batting, Batty Aliped, Ames, Assail, Barbastelle, Baton, Belfry, Blink, Chiroptera, Close, Club, Cosh, Crackers, Cudgel, Dad, Die Fledermaus, Eyelid, False vampire, Flittermouse, Flying fox, Fruit, Grace, Hammerhead, Hatter, Haywire, Hit, Hobbs, Hook, Horseshoe, In, Ink mouse, Insectivorous, Kalong, Language, Leisler, Man, Mastiff, Maul, May, Mormops, Mouse-eared, Myopic, Nictate, Nictitate, Night, Nightwatchman, Noctilio, Nora, Nurdle, Opener, Patagium, Pinch-hit, Pipistrel(le), Poke, Pummel, Racket, Racquet, Ram, Rearmouse, Reremice, Reremouse, Roussette, Ruin, Sauch, Saugh, Scotch hand, Serotine, Sledge, Spectre, Stick, Stonewall, Straight, Striker, Swat, Switch hitter, Trap-stick, Vampire, Vespertilionid, Viv, Whacky, Willow, Wood
Batch Bake, Bunch, Clutch
Bath(room) Aerotone, Aeson's, Bagnio, Bain-marie, Balneotherapy, Bed, Blanket, Blood, Bubble, Caldarium, Cor, Dip, En suite, Epha, Foam, Hammam, Hip, Hummaum, Hummum, Jacuzzi®, Laver, Mik vah, Mud, Mustard, Oil, Piscina, Plunge, Salt, Sauna, Shower, Sitz, Slipper, Soak, Spa, Sponge, Steam, Stew, Stop, Tepidarium, Therm, Tub, Turkish, Tye, Vapour, Whirlpool, Wife
Bathe, Bathing Balneal, Balneation, Balneology, Balneotherapy, Bay(e), Beath, Bogey, Bogie, Dip, Dook, Douk, Embay, Foment, Immerse, Lave, Lip, Skinny-dip, Souse, Splash, Stupe, → SWIM, Tub, → WASH
Batman Valet
Baton Mace, Rod, Sceptre, Staff, Truncheon
Batrachian Frog, Toad
▷ **Bats, Batting** *may indicate* an anagram
Battalion Bn, Corps, Troop
Batten Dropper, Fasten, Tie
Batter(ed) Bombard, Bruise, Buffet, Decrepit, Pound
Battery Accumulator, Artillery, Drycell, Field, Galvanic, Heliac, Henhouse, Li(thium)-ion, Nicad, Penlight, Pra(a)m, Primary, Solar, Storage, Troop, Voltaic, Waffle, Water
Battle(s), Battleground Action, Affair, Ben, Clash, Cockpit, Combat, → CONFLICT, Encounter, Engagement, Field, → FIGHT, Fray, Front, Hosting, Joust, Naumachy, Pitched, Royal, Running, Sarah, Sciamachy, Skiamachy, Spurs, Stoor, Stour, Stowre, Theatre, Wage, → WAR

BATTLES

3 letters:	Laon	Allia	Marne
Kut	Loos	Arcot	Parma
Ulm	Mons	Arras	Pydna
	Nile	Boyne	Sedan
4 letters:	Zama	Bulge	Somme
Alma		Crecy	Tours
Chad	*5 letters:*	Ipsus	Valmy
Ivry	Accra	Issus	Ypres
Jena	Alamo	Lewes	

6 letters:
Actium
Arbela
Argyle
Arnhem
Barnet
Camlan
Cannae
Cressy
Crimea
Lutzen
Maldon
Midway
Naseby
Sadowa
Senlac
Shiloh
Tobruk
Varese
Verdun
Vigrid
Wagram
Wipers

7 letters:
Aboukir
Alamein
Argonne
Bautzen
Beaches
Britain
Bull Run
Cambrai
Chalons
Colenso
Coronel
Corunna
Dunkirk

Evesham
Flodden
Flowers
Glencoe
Jericho
Jutland
Lepanto
Magenta
Marengo
Nations
Newbury
Orleans
Picardy
Plassey
Poltava
Pultowa
Salamis
Vitoria
Warburg

8 letters:
Antietam
Ardennes
Ayacucho
Blenheim
Borodino
Bosworth
Clontarf
Culloden
Edgehill
Erzurium
Flanders
Fontenay
Hastings
Inkerman
Jemappes
Le Cateau
Manassas

Marathon
Metaurus
Navarino
Omdurman
Palo Alto
Philippi
Poitiers
Ragnarok
Saratoga
Syracuse
Talavera
Waterloo

9 letters:
Agincourt
Balaclava
Caporetto
El Alamein
Gallipoli
Ladysmith
Otterburn
Oudenarde
Pharsalus
Princeton
Ramillies
Sedgemoor
Solferino
St Vincent
Theomachy
Trafalgar
Worcester

10 letters:
Armageddon
Austerlitz
Bennington
Bunker Hill
Camperdown

Gettysburg
Lundy's Lane
Petersburg
Quatre Bras
Shipka Pass
Stalingrad
Steenkerke

11 letters:
Armentières
Bannockburn
Belleau Wood
Chattanooga
Hohenlinden
Marston Moor
Prestonpans
Thermopylae
Wounded Knee

12 letters:
Flodden Field
Monte Cassino
Roncesvalles

13 letters:
Bosworth Field
Little Bighorn
Passchendaele
Spanish Armada

14 letters:
Castlebar Races
Stamford Bridge

15 letters:
Missionary Ridge
Plains of Abraham
Teutoberger Wald

Battle-axe Amazon, Bill, Gorgon, Halberd, Ogress, Sparth(e), Termagant,
 Termagent, Turmagant, Turmagent
Battlement Barmkin, Crenellate, Merlon, Rampart
Battle-order Phalanx
Battleship Carrier, Destroyer, Dreadnought, Gunboat, Man-o'-war, Pocket,
 Potemkin
Bauble Bagatelle, Gaud, Gewgaw, Trifle
Bauhaus Gropius
Baulk Demur, Gib, Hen, Impede, Jib, Reest, Reist, Shy, Thwart
Bavardage Fadaise
Bawd(y) Hare, Raunchy, Sculdudd(e)ry, Skulduddery
Bawl Bellow, Gollar, Howl, Weep

Bay Ab(o)ukir, Aere, Arm, Baffin, Bantry, Bark, Bell, Bengal, Bight, Biscay, Bonny, Botany, Broken, Byron, Cape Cod, Cardigan, Chesapeake, Cienfuegos, Cleveland, Colwyn, Corpus Christi, Cove, Covelet, Creek, Daphne, Delagoa, Delaware, Discovery, Dublin, Dundalk, Dvina, False, Famagusta, Fleet, Frobisher, Fundy, Galway, Gdansk, Georgian, Gibraltar, Glace, Golden, Great Australian Bight, Green, Guanabara, Guantanamo, Gulf, Hangzhou, Harbour, Hawke's, Herne, Horse, → HOWL, Hudson, Inhambane, Inlet, Ise, James, Jervis, Jiazhou, Kavalla, Kuskokwim, Laura, Laurel, Layby, Loading, Lobito, Loblolly, Lutzow-Holm, MA, Magdalena, Manila, Massachusetts, Montego, Morton, Narragansett, New York, Niche, Oleander, Omaha, Oriel, Passamaquoddy, Pegasus, Pigs, Plenty, Plymouth, Port Phillip, Poverty, Recess, Red, Roan, St Austell, St Michel, San Pedro, Scene, San Francisco, Santiago, Setubal, Shark, Sick, Sligo, Suvla, Swansea, Table, Tampa, Tasman, Thunder, Tor, Toyama, Tralee, Trincomalee, Ungava, Vae, Vigo, Vlore, Voe, Vyborg, Waff, Walfish, Walvis, Wash, Whitley, Wick, Yowl
Bayonet Jab, Skewer, Stab, Sword
Bazaar Alcaiceria, Emporium, Fair, Fete, Market, Pantechnicon, Sale, Sook, Souk
BBC Auntie
Be Exist, Live, Occur
Beach Bondi, Chesil, Coast, Daytona, Ground, Hard, Lido, Littoral, Machair, Miami, Omaha, Palm, Plage, Raised, Sand, Seaside, Shingle, Shore, Storm, Strand, Waikiki
Beachcomber Arenaria
Beacon Belisha, Fanal, Landing, Lightship, Need-fire, Pharos, Racon, Radar, Radio, Robot, Signal
Bead(s), Beaded Adderstone, Aggri, Aggry, Astragal, Baily's, Ballotini, Bauble, Blob, Bugle, Cabling, Chaplet, Crab-stones, Dewdrop, Drop, Droplet, Gadroon, Gaud, Job's tears, Kumbaloi, Mala, Moniliform, Ojime, Passament, Passement, Paternoster, Poppet, Poppit, Prayer, Rosary, St Cuthbert's, Se(a)wan, Subha, Sweat, Tear, Wampum(peag), Worry
Beadle Apparitor, Bederal, Bedral, Bumble, Herald, Paritor, Shammes, Verger
Beagle Spy
Beak AMA, Bailie, Bill, Cad, Cere, Coronoid, Egg-tooth, Gar, JP, Kip(p), Magistrate, Master, Metagnathous, Mittimus, Nasute, Neb, Nose, Pecker, Prow, Ram, Rostellum, Rostrum, Shovel
Beaker Bell, Cup, Goblet
Beakless Erostrate
Beak-shaped Coracoid
Beam(ing) Arbor, Balance, Bar, Ba(u)lk, Binder, Boom, Bowstring, Box, Breastsummer, Bressummer, Broadcast, Bum(p)kin, Cantilever, Carline, Carling, Cathead, Collar, Crossbar, Crosshead, Crosspiece, Deck, Electron, Girder, Grin, Hammer, Hatch, Herisson, Holophote, I, Irradiate, Joist, Ke(e)lson, Landing, Laser, Lentel, Lintel, Manteltree, Molecular, Needle, Outrigger, Particle, Pencil, Principal, Purlin, Putlock, Putlog, Radio, → RAFTER, → RAY, Rayon, Refulgent, Rident, Ridgepole, Rood, Roof-tree, Sandwich, Scale, Scantling, Searchlight, Shaft, Shine, Shore, Sleeper, Smile, Soffit, Solive, Stanchion, Stemson, Sternpost, Straining, Streamer, Stringer, Stringpiece, Summer, Support, Tailing, Tie, Timber, Trabeate, Trabecula, Transom, Trave, Trimmer, Truss, Universal, Viga, Walking, Weigh-bauk, Yard, Yardarm
Beamish Galumphing, Nephew
Bean Abrus, Adsuki, Aduki, Adzuki, Arabica, Asparagus pea, Baked, Berry, Black, Black-eye, Borlotti, Broad, Bush, Butter, Cacao, Calabar, Castor, Cluster, Cocoa,

Coffee, Cow-pea, Dwarf, Fabaceous, Fava, Flageolet, French, Frijol(e), Garbanzo, Goa, Gram, Green, Haricot, Harmala, Head, Horse, Jack, Jelly, Jumping, Kachang putch, Kidney, Lablab, Lentil, Lima, Locust, Molucca, Moong, Moth, Mung, Nelumbo, Nib, Noddle, Ordeal, Pichurim, Pinto, Runner, St Ignatius's, Scarlet, Scarlet runner, Shell, Snap, Soy(a), String, Sugar, Sword, Tonga, Tonka, Tonquin, Urd, Wax, Winged, Yard-long

Beanfeast → PARTY, Spree, Wayzgoose

Bear(er), Bear lover Abide, Abrooke, Andean, Arctic, Arctophile, Baloo, Balu, Beer, Bigg, Breed, Brook, Brown, Bruin, Brunt, → CARRY, Cave, Churl, Cinnamon, Coati-mondi, Coati-mundi, Cub, Demean, Dree, Ean, → ENDURE, Engender, Exert, Fur-seal, Gonfalonier, Great, Grizzly, Hack, Ham(m)al, Harbinger, Have, Hold, Honey, Humf, Hump(h), Jampani, Keb, Kinkajou, Koala, Kodiak, Koolah, Lioncel(le), Lionel, Lug, Mother, Nandi, Nanook, Owe, Paddington, Panda, Polar, Pooh, Rac(c)oon, Roller, Rupert, Russia, Sackerson, Seller, Shoulder, Sit, Sloth, Spectacled, Stand, Stay, Stomach, → SUFFER, Sunbear, Sustain, Targeteer, Teddy, Teem, Thole, Throw, Tolerate, Tote, Transport, Undergo, Upstay, Ursine, Water, Whelp, White, Wield, Woolly, Yield

Bearberry Manzanita, Uva-ursi

Beard(ed) Aaron, Alfalfa, Anchor, Arista, Assyrian, Aureole, Awn, Balaclava, Barb, Barbiche, Beaver, Belgrave, Cadiz, Cathedral, Charley, Charlie, Confront, Defy, Ducktail, Face, Five o'clock shadow, Forked, Fungus, Goatee, Hair(ie), Hairy, Hear(ie), Imperial, Jewish, Kesh, Lincolnesque, Mephistopheles, Old Dutch, Olympian, Outface, Peak, Pencil, Raleigh, Rivet, Roman T, Screw, Shenandoah, Spade, Stibble, Stiletto, Stubble, Swallowtail, Tile, Trojan, Tuft, Uncle Sam, Vandyke, Whiskerando, Whiskery, Ziff

Beardless Callow, Clean, Tahr, Tehr

▷ **Bearhug** *may indicate* Teddy or similar around a word

Bearing(s) Air, Allure, Amenaunce, Armorial, Aspect, Azimuth, Babbitt, Ball, Behaviour, Bush, Carriage, Deportment, Direction, E, Endurance, Gait, Hatchment, Haviour, Heading, → HERALDIC, Hugger-mugger, Lioncel(le), Lionel, Manner, Martlet, Mascle, Middy, Mien, N, Needle, Nor, Pheon, Port, Presence, Reference, Relevant, Roller, S, Subordinary, Teeming, Tenue, Thrust, W, Yielding

▷ **Bearing** *may indicate* compass points

Beast → ANIMAL, Arna, Behemoth, Brute, Caliban, Caribou, Chimera, → CREATURE, Dieb, Dragon, Dzeren, Gargoyle, Gayal, Genet, Grampus, Hippogriff, Hodog, Hog, Hy(a)ena, Hydra, Jumart, Kinkajou, Lion, Mammoth, Marmot, Mastodon, Mhorr, Monoceros, Oliphant, Opinicus, Oryx, Panda, Potto, Quagga, Rac(c)oon, Rhytina, Rother, Rumptifusel, Sassaby, Steer, Sumpter, Tarand, Teg, Theroid, Triceratops, Triton, Wart-hog, Whangam, Yahoo, Yak, Yale, Zizel

Beat(ing), Beaten, Beater Anoint, Arsis, Athrob, Bandy, Bang, Baste, Bastinado, Batter, Battue, Belabour, Belt, Bepat, Best, Blatter, Bless, Bo Diddley, Bubble, Cadence, Cane, Cat, Chastise, Clobber, Club, Clump, Cob, Conquer, Cream, Cudgel, Cuff, Curry, Debel, → DEFEAT, Ding, Donder, Dress, Drub, Duff up, Excel, Fatigue, Faze, Feague, Feeze, Fibbed, Firk, Flagellate, Flail, Flam, Float, Flog, Floor, Flush, Fly, Fustigate, Hipster, Hollow, Horsewhip, Ictus, Inteneration, Jole, Joll, Joule, Jowl, Knock, Knubble, Lace, Laidie, Laidy, Lambast(e), Larrup, Lash, Lather, Laveer, Lay, Lick, Lilt, Lounder, Mall, Malleate, Mersey, Nubble, Outclass, Outdo, Outflank, Outstrip, Paik, Palpitate, Pandy, Paradiddle, Pash, Paste, Ploat, Pommel, Pound, Prat, Pug, Pulsate, Pulsatile, Pulse, Pulsedge, Pummel, Pun, Quop, Raddle, Ram, Ratten, Resolve, Retreat, Rhythm, Ribroast, Rope's end, Round, Rowstow, Ruff(le),

Scourge, Scutch, Slat, Smight, Smite, Soak, Sock, Strap, Strap-oil, Strike, Swinge, Swingle, Systole, Taber, Tabor, Tabrere, Tachycardia, Tact, Tala, Tattoo, Thesis, Thrash, Thresh, Throb, Thud, Thump, Thwack, Tick, Tired, Top, Torture, Tricrotic, Trounce, Tuck, Tund, Verberate, Vibrate, Wallop, Wappend, Weary, Welt, Wham, Whip, Whisk, Whitewash, Wraught, Ybet, Yerk, Yirk

▷ **Beaten-up** *may indicate* an anagram

Beat it Skedaddle, Vamo(o)se

Beatitude Macarism

Beau Admirer, Blade, Brummel, Cat, Damoiseau, Dandy, Flame, Geste, Lair, Lover, Masher, Nash, Spark, Tibbs

Beaufort Scale, Windscale

Beaut(y) Advantage, Bathing, Belle, Bellibone, Bombshell, Camberwell, Charmer, Colleen, Comeliness, Corker, Dish, Doll, Glory, Houri, Hyperion, Lana, Monism, Picture, Pride, Pulchritude, Purler, Sheen, Smasher, Stunner

Beautiful, Beautify Astrid, Bonny, Bright, Embellish, Enhance, Exquisite, Fair, Fine, Gorgeous, Junoesque, Ornament, Pink, Radiant, Smicker, Specious, To kalon

Beauty spot Patch, Tempe, Tika

Beaver Beard, Castor, Eager, Grind, Mountain, Oregon, Rodent, Sewellel

Because (of) As, Forasmuch, Forwhy, Hence, In, Inasmuch, Sens, Since

Beckon Gesture, Nod, Summons, Waft, Wave

Become, Becoming Apt, Besort, Decent, Decorous, Enter, Fall, Fit, Flatter, Get, Go, Grow, Happen, Occur, Seemly, Suit, Wax, Worth

Bed(s), Bedding, Bedstead Air, Allotment, Amenity, Apple-pie, Arroyo, Bacteria, Base, Bassinet, → BEDCOVER, Berth, Bottom, Bottomset, Box, Bundle, Bunk, Caliche, Camp, Carrycot, Channel, Charpoy, Cill, Cot(t), Couch(ette), Counterpane, Couvade, Coverlet, Cradle, Crib, Cross, Cul(t)ch, Day, Divan, Doona, Doss, Duvet, Erf, False, Feather, Filter, Fluidized, Flying, Four-poster, Futon, Gault, Greensand, Hammock, Inlay, Kago, Kang, Kip, Knot, Knot garden, Layer, Lazy, Lilo®, Litter, Marriage, Mat, Matrix, Mattress, Murphy, Nap, Nest, Nookie, Oyster, Pad, Paillasse, Pallet, Palliasse, Pan, Parterre, Passage, Patch, Pavement, Pay, Pig, Plank, Plant, Plot, Procrustean, Puff, Quilt, Retire, River, Rollaway, Roost, Rota, Sack, Scalp, Settle, Shakedown, Sill, Sitter, Sleep, Sofa, Standing, Stratum, Stretcher, Sun, Tanning, T(h)alweg, Test, Thill, Trough, Truckle, Trundle, Twin, Wadi, Wady, Ware, Water, Wealden, Wedding

Bedaub Cake, Deck, Smear

Bed-bug B, B flat, Chinch, Flea, Louse, Vermin

Bedchamber, Bedroom Boudoir, Bower, Chamber, Cubicle, Dorm(itory), Dormer, Dorter, Ruelle, Ward

Bedcover Palampore, Palempore

Bedeck Adonise, Adorn, Array, Festoon

▷ **Bedevilled** *may indicate* an anagram

Bedjacket Nightingale

Bedlam Chaos, Furore, Madness, Nuthouse, Tumult, Uproar

Bed-rest Dutch-wife

Bedwetting Enuresis

Bee Athenia, Bumble, Carpenter, Cuckoo, Deborah, Debra, Deseret, Dog, Drone, Drumbledor, Dumbledore, Group, Hiver, Honey, Humble, Killer, King, Lapidary, Leaf-cutter, Mason, Melissa, Mining, Nurse, Queen, Quilting, Raising, Solitary, Spell, Spell-down, Spelling, Swarm, Worker, Working

Beech Antarctic, Copper, Fagus, Hornbeam, Mast, Taw(h)ai, Tree

Bee-eater Merops, Rainbow-bird

Beef(y) Baron, Bleat, Brawny, Bresaola, Bull(y), Bullock, Carpaccio, Charqui, Chateaubriand, Chuck, Clod, Complain, Corned, Filet mignon, Groan, Grouse, Hough, Jerk, Kobe, Liebig, Mart, Mice, Moan, Mousepiece, Muscle, Neat, Ox, Pastrami, Peeve, Plate, Porterhouse, Rother, Salt-junk, Sauerbraten, Sey, Silverside, Sirloin, Stolid, Stroganoff, Topside, Tournedos, Tranche, Undercut, Vaccine, Wellington

Beefeater Billman, Exon, Gin, Oxpecker, Warder, Yeoman

Bee-glue Propolis

Beehive Alveary, Apiary, Ball, Gum, Skep

Beelzebub Devil

Beer Ale, Alegar, Amber fluid, Amber liquid, Bantu, Barley sandwich, Bitter, Black, Bock, Chaser, Draught, Drink, Dry, Entire, Export, Gill, Ginger, Granny, Grog, Guest, Heavy, Herb, Home-brew, Kaffir, Keg, Kvass, Lager, Lambic, Lite, Lush, Malt, March, Middy, Mild, Mum, Near, Nog, October, Pils(e)ner, Pint, Pony, Porter, Real, Real ale, Rice, Root, Saki, Scoobs, Sherbet, Skeechan, Small, Spruce, Stingo, Stout, Swankey, Swats, Swipes, Switchel, Table, Taplash, Tinnie, Tipper, Tshwala, Tube, Wallop, Wheat, Zythum

Beer garden Brasserie

Bee's nest Bink

Beet Blite, Chard, Fat-hen, Goosefoot, Mangel(wurzel), Seakale, Silver, Spinach, Sugar

Beetle Ambrosia, Anobiid, Argos tortoise, Asiatic, Bacon, Bark, Batler, Bee, Blister, Bloody-nosed, Boll weevil, Bombardier, Bruchid, Bug, Bum-clock, Buprestidae, Buprestus, Burying, Bustle, Buzzard-clock, Cabinet, Cadelle, Cane, Cantharis, Carabid, Cardinal, Carpet, Carrion, Chafer, Christmas, Churchyard, Cicindela, Click, Clock, Cockchafer, Cockroach, Coleoptera, Coleopterous, Colorado, Coprophagan, Curculio, Darkling, Deathwatch, Dermestid, Devil's coach-horse, Diamond, Diving, Dor(r), Dor-fly, Dumbledore, Dung, Dyticus, Dytiscus, Elater, Elytron, Elytrum, Firefly, Flea, Furniture, Glow-worm, Gold(smith), Goliath, Gregor, Ground, Hammer, Hangover, Hercules, Hop-flea, Hornbug, Huhu, Humbuzz, Impend, Japanese, Jewel, June, Khapra, Ladybird, Ladybug, Lamellicorn, Larder, Leaf, Leather, Longhorn, Longicorn, Mall(et), Maul, May-bug, Meloid, Minotaur, Museum, Musk, Oakpruner, Oil, Overhang, Pill, Pinchbuck, Pine, Pine-chafer, Potato, Project, Protrude, Race(-bug), Rhinoceros, Rhynchophora, Roach, Rosechafer, Rove, Sacred, Saw palmetto, Scamper, Scarab(ee), Scavenger, Scolytus, Scurry, Sexton, Shard, Skelter, Sledge(-hammer), Snapping, Snout, Soldier, Spanish fly, Spider, Spring, Stag, Tenebrio, Tiger, Toktokkie, Tortoise, Tumble-bug, Tumble-dung, Turnip-flea, Typographer, Vedalia, VW, Water, Weevil, Whirligig, Wireworm, Woodborer, Wood-engraver

Beetle-crushers Cops

Befall Happen, Occur

Before(hand) A, Advance, Ante, Avant, By, Coram, Earlier, Early, Ere, Erst(while), → FORMER, Or, Pre, Previously, Prior, Pro, Sooner, Till, To, Until, Van, Zeroth

Before food Ac

Befriend Assist, Cotton, Fraternise, Support

Befuddle(ment) Bemuse, Dwaal, Inebriate, Stupefy

Beg(gar), Beggarly, Begging Abr(ah)am-man, Ask, Badgeman, Beseech, Besognio, Bey, Bezonian, Blighter, Blue-gown, Cadge, Calendar, Clapper-dudgeon, Crave, → ENTREAT, Exoration, Flagitate, Fleech, Gaberlunzie, Gangrel, Hallan-shaker, Implore, Impoverish, Irus, Jarkman, Lackall, Lazar(us), Lazzarone, Lumpenproletariat, Maund, Mendicant, Mooch, Mouch, Mump, Niggardly, Obtest,

Palliard, Panhandle, Pauper, Penelophon, Penniless, → **PLEAD**, Pled, Pray, Prig, Prog, Ptochocracy, Rag, Randie, Randy, Ruffler, Ruin(ate), Sadhu, Schnorr(er), Screeve, Scrounge, Shool(e), Skelder, Skell, Solicit, Sue, Supplicate, Thig(ger), Toe-rag, Touch, Undo, Uprightman, Whipjack

Beget Gender, Kind

Beggar rule Ptochocracy

Begging bowl Clackdish, Clapdish

Begin(ner), Beginning Ab ovo, Alpha, Author, B, Babyhood, Black, Cause, Clapdash, Commence, Daw, Dawn, Deb, Debut, Embryo, Enter, Exordium, Fall-to, Fledgling, Genesis, Germ, Go, Greenhorn, Inaugural, Inception, Inchoate, Incipient, Incipit, Initial, Initiate, Intro, Johnny-raw, L, Lead, Learn, Learner, Logos, Nascent, Neophyte, → **NOVICE**, Oncome, Onset, Ope(n), Ord, → **ORIGIN**, Outbreak, Pose, Prelim(inary), Presidium, Primer, Rookie, Seed, Set, → **START**, Startup, Takeoff, Tenderfoot, Tiro, To-fall, Tyro(ne), Yearn

Begone Aroint, Aroynt, Avaunt, Scram, Shoo, Vamo(o)se

Begonia Elephant's-ear(s)

Begorrah Bedad, Musha

Begrudge Envy, Resent

Beguile(r) Bewitch, Charm, Coax, Distract, Divert, Enchant, Ensnare, Entice, Flatter, Gull, Intrigue, Jack-a-lantern, Tice, Wile

Behalf Ex parte, For, Part, Sake

Behave, Behaviour, Behaving Acquired, Act, Conduct, Consummatory, Convenance, Decorum, Demean, Deportment, Do, Epimeletic, Etepimeletic, Ethics, Form, Goings-on, Guise, Horme, → **MANNER**, Meme, Nature, Netiquette, Noblesse oblige, Obey, Orientation, Praxeology, Quit, React, Response, Satisficing, Strong meat, Tribalism, Unreasonable

Behead Decapitate, Decollate, Guillotine

Behind(hand) Abaft, Aft(er), Ahind, Ahint, Apoop, Arear, Arere, Arrear, Arse, Astern, Beneath, Bottom, Bum, Buttocks, Croup, Derrière, Fud, Late, Overdue, Post, Prat, → **REAR**, Slow, Tushie

Behold(en) Affine, Ecce, Eye, Here's, Indebted, La, Lo, Look, Observe, See, View, Voilà

Beige Greige, Tan

Being Cratur, Creature, Ens, Entia, Entity, Esse, Essence, Existence, Human, Man, Metaphysics, Mode, Nature, Omneity, Ontology, → **PERSON**, Saul, Soul, Subsistent, Substance, Supreme, Ubiety, Wight

Bejabers Arrah

Belch Boak, Boke, Brash, Burp, Emit, Eruct, Erupt, Rift, Spew, Yex

Belcher Foulard, Handkerchief, Hanky, Toby

Beldam(e) Crone, Hag, Harridan, Scold

Belfry Campanile, Tower

Belgian Flemish, Walloon

Belief, Believe, Believed, Believer, Believing Accredit, Anata, Ativism, Bigot, Buy, Christian, Conviction, Creationism, Credence, Credit, Creed, Cult, Culture, Deem, Deist, Doctrine, Doxastic, Doxy, Dukkha, Faith, Formulism, Gnostic, Heresy, Heterodoxy, Hold, Holist, Idea, Ideology, Islam, Ism, Ludism, Manichaeism, Meme, Messianist, Methink, Mysticism, Notion, → **OPINION**, Orthopraxy, Ovist, Pacifism, Pantheism, Persuasion, Physicism, Pluralism, Presumption, Religion, Reputed, Seeing, S(h)aivism, Shema, Solfidian, Superstition, Suspect, Swallow, Tenet, Thanatism, Theist, Theosophy, Think, Threap, Threep, Traducianism, Transcendentalism, Trinitarian, Triphysite, Trow, Trust, Ubiquitarianism,

Umma(h), Unitarian, Universalism, Wear, Ween, Wis(t)

Belittle Cheapen, Cry down, Decry, Depreciate, Derogate, Detract, Diminish, Discredit, Disparage, Downgrade, Humble, Pooh-pooh, Slight

Bell(s) Acton, Angelus, Ben, Big Ben, Bob, Bow, Bronte, Cachecope, Canterbury, Carillon, Chime, Chinese pavilion, Crotal, Curfew, Currer, Daisy, Diving, Division, Ellis, Gong, Grandsire, Jar, Low, Lutine, Market, Mass, Minute, Mort, Muffin, Pancake, Passing, Pavilion, Peal, Peter, Pinger, Pudding, Ring, Roar, Sacring, Sanctus, Shark, Sleigh, Tailor, Tantony, Tenor, Tent, Tintinnabulum, Tocsin, Toll, Tom, Triple, Tubular, Vair, Vaire, Verry, Vesper

Bell-bird Arapunga, Campanero

Belle Beauty, Starr, Toast, Venus

Bell-founder Belleter

Bellicose, Belligerent Chippy, Combatant, Gung-ho, Hostile, Jingoist, Martial, Militant, Truculent, Warmonger

Bellow(s) Buller, Holla, Holler, Moo, Rant, Rave, Roar, Rout, Saul, Thunder, Troat, Tromp(e), Trumpet, Windbag

Bell-ringer, Bell-ringing Bob, Campanology, Changes, Clapper, Course, Grandsire, Handstroke, Hunting, Maximus, Quasimodo, Rope, Sally, Tocsin, Toller

Belly Abdomen, Alvine, Bag, Beer, Beer-gut, Boep, Bunt, Calipee, Celiac, Coeliac, Gut, Kite, Kyte, Pod, → **STOMACH**, Swell, Tum(my), Venter, Wame, Weamb, Wem(b), Womb

Belong, Belonging(s) Apply, Appurtenant, Chattels, Effects, Incident, Inhere, Intrinsic, Paraphernalia, Pertain, → **PROPERTY**, Relate, Traps

Beloved Acushla, Alder-lief, Amy, Boyfriend, David, Dear, Doy, Esme, Inamorata, Joy, Lief, Morna, Pet, Popular, Precious

Below Beneath, Inf(erior), Infra, Nether, Sub, Subjacent, Under, Unneath

Belt(ed) Baldric(k), Band, Bandoleer, Bandolier, Baudric(k), Bible, Black, Cartridge, Chastity, Cholera, Clitellum, Clobber, Clock, Commuter, Conveyor, Copper, Cotton, Crios, Demolition, Equator, Fan, Flog, Fold and thrust, Galvanic, Garter, Gird(le), Girt, Great, Green, Hip, Hydraulic, Inertial, Judoka, Kuiper, Lap, Larrup, Life, Lonsdale, Mitre, Money, Muesli, Orion's, Orogenic, Polt, Pound, Radiation, Roller, Rust, Safety, Sam Browne, Sanitary, Sash, Seat, Speed, Stockbroker, Storm, Strap, Stratosphere, Sun, Surcingle, Suspender, Swipe, Sword, Taiga, Tear, Thump, Tore, Tract, Van Allen, Wampum, Wanty, Webbing, Wing, Zodiac, Zone, Zoster

Belt up Sh

Belvedere Gazebo, Mirador

Bemoan → **LAMENT**, Mourn, Sigh, Wail

Bemuse Infatuate, Stonn(e), Stun, Stupefy, Throw

Ben Battle, Hur, Jonson, Mountain, Nevis, Spence

Bench Banc, Banker, Bink, Bleachers, Counter, Court, Cross, Exedra, Form, Front, King's, Knifeboard, Magistrates, Optical, Pew, Queen's, Rout seat, Rusbank, → **SEAT**, Settle, Siege, Stillage, Thoft, Thwart, Treasury, Trestle, Widow's

Benchmark Criteria, Yardstick

Bend(er), Bending, Bends Angle, Arc, Arch, Articular, Becket, Bight, Binge, Bow, Buck(le), Bust, Camber, Carrick, Chicane, Circumflect, Corner, Crank(le), Cringe, → **CROOK**, Curl, Curve, Diffraction, Dog-leg, Double up, Elbow, Engouled, Epinasty, Es(s), Expansion, Falcate, Fawn, Flex(ural), Flexion, Flexure, Fold, Geller, Geniculate, Genu, Genuflect, Grecian, Hairpin, Hinge, Hook, Horseshoe, Hunch, Incline, Inflect, Kink, Knee(cap), Kneel, Knot, Kowtow, Meander, Mould, Nutant, Ox-bow, Pitch, Plash, Plié, Ply, Recline, Reflex, Retorsion, Retortion, Retroflex, Riband, S, Scarp, Sheet, Souse, Spree, Spring, Stave, Stoop, Swan-neck, Trend,

Twist, U, Ups(e)y, Uri, Wale, Warp, → YIELD, Z

▷ **Bendy** *may indicate* an anagram

Beneath Below, Sub, Under, Unworthy

Benedict(ine) Black Monk, Cluniac, Cluny, Dom, Eggs, Maurist, Olivetan, OSB, Tironensian, Tyronensian

Benediction Blessing, God-speed

Benefactor Angel, Backer, Barmecide, Carnegie, Donor, Maecenas, → PATRON, Philanthropist, Promoter

Beneficial, Beneficiary, Benefit, Benefice Advantage, → AID, Alms, Ameliorate, Asset, Avail, Behalf, Behoof, Behove, Bonus, Boon, Boot, Charity, Collature, Commendam, Commensal, Devisee, Disablement, Dole, Donee, Endorsee, Enure, FIS, Fringe, Housing, Incapacity, Incumbent, Inheritor, Injury, Inure, Invalidity, Legal aid, Living, Manna, Maternity, Ménage, Neckverse, Pay, Perk, Perquisite, Plus, Portioner, Postulate, Prebend, Profit, Sake, Salutary, Sanative, Sickness, Sinecure, Spin-off, Stipend, Supplementary, Symbiotic, Unemployment, Use, Usufruct

Benevolence, Benevolent Charitable, Clement, Dobbie, Dobby, Humanitarian, Kind, Liberal, Pecksniffian, Philanthropy, Sprite

Benighted Ignorant

Benign Affable, Altruistic, Gracious, Kindly, Trinal

Benin DY

Benito Duce, Mussolini

Benjamin Franklin

Bennett Alan, Phil

Bent Akimbo, Bowed, Brae, Coudé, Courb, Crooked, Curb, Determined, Dorsiflex, Falcate, Fiorin, Flair, Geniculate, Habit, Heath, Inclination, Ingenium, Intent, Inverted, Leant, Peccant, Penchant, Ply, Predisposition, Reclinate, Redtop, Round-shouldered, Scoliotic, Stooped, Talent, Taste, Twisted

▷ **Bent** *may indicate* an anagram

Bent grass Fiorin, Redtop

Bentham Utilitarian

Benzine Kinone, Phene, Toluene, Toluol

Bequeath, Bequest Bestow, Chantr(e)y, Demise, Endow, Heirloom, → LEAVE, Legacy, Mortification, Pass down, Pittance, Transmit, Will

Berate(d) Censure, Chide, Jaw, Reproach, Scold, Shent, Slate, Vilify

Berber Almoravide, Kabyle, Moor, Rif(i), Riff, Shluh, Tuareg

Bereave(d), Bereavement Deprive, Loss, Mourning, Orb, Sorrow, Strip, Widow

Beret Green

Berg Alban, Floe

Bermuda Shorts

Bernard Levin, Shaw

Bernini Baroque

Berry Acai, Allspice, Bacca, Blackcurrant, Cubeb, Fruit, Goosegog, Haw, Konini, Miracle, Pepo, Peppercorn, Persian, Pigeon, Pimento, Poke, Pottage, Rhein, Rhine, Sal(l)al, Slae, Sloe, Sop, Tomatillo

Berserk Amok, Ape-shit, Baresark, Frenzy, Gungho, Rage

Berth Anchorage, Bunk, Cabin, Couchette, Dock, Moor, Seat, Space

Beryl Aquamarine, Emerald, Heliodor, Morganite, Silica

Beryllium Be

Beseech Beg, Crave, Entreat, Implore, Invoke, Obsecrate

Beset Amidst, Assail, Assiege, Badger, Bego, Environ, Harry, Perplex, Scabrid, Siege

Beside(s) Adjacent, Alone, And, At, Au reste, Else, Forby(e), Further(more),

Moreover, Next, On, Withal, Yet

Besiege(d) Beset, Best(ed), Blockade, Gherao, Girt, Invest, Obsess, Plague, Surround

▷ **Besiege** *may indicate* one word around another

Besmirch(ed) Bloody, Bludie, Smear, Soil, Sully

Besom Cow, Kow

Besot(ted) Dotard, Infatuate, Intoxicate, Lovesick, Stupefy

Bespangle Adorn, Gem

Bespeak, Bespoken Address, Bee, Beta, Engage, Hint

Best A1, Ace, Aristocrat, Beat, Choice, Conquer, Cream, Creme, Damnedest, Deluxe, Elite, Eximious, Finest, Flagship, Flower, Foremost, Greatest, Ideal, Optima, Outdo, Outwit, Overcome, Peak, Peerless, Pick, Pièce de résistance, Pink, Plum, Purler, Quintessence, Ream, Sunday, Super, The, The tops, Tiptop, Top, Topper, Transcend, Vanquish, Wale

Bestiality Zoophalia

Bestiary Physiologus

Best man Paranymph

Bestow(al) Accord, Bequeath, Donate, Endow, → GIVE, Impart, Investiture, Present

Bestride Cross

Bet(ting), Betting System A cheval, Ante, Antepost, Back, Banco, Chance, Daily double, Double, Each way, Flutter, Gaff, Gamble, Go, Hedge, Impone, Lay, Long shot, Martingale, Mise, Note, Pari-mutuel, Parlay, Perfecta, Pip, Pot, Punt, Quadrella, Quinella, Ring, Risk, Roll up, Saver, Set, Spec, Sport, Spread, Stake, Superfecta, Tattersalls, Tatts, Totalisator, Totalise, Tote, Treble, Treble chance, Triella, Trifecta, → WAGER, Yankee

Betel Catechu, Paan, Pan, Pawn, Siri(h)

Betimes Anon, Early, Soon

Betise Solecism

Betray(al), Betrayer Abandon, Abuse, Belewe, Bewray, Cornuto, Desert, Divulge, Dob, Dobbin, Double-cross, Gethsemane, Giveaway, Grass, Judas, Renegade, Renege, Rumble, Sell, Sellout, Shop, Sing, Sinon, Stab, Traditor, Traitor, Treachery, Treason, Turncoat

Betroth(ed), Betrothal Assure, Engage, Ensure, Espouse, Fiancé(e), Handfasting, Pledge, Promise, Subarr(h)ation

Better Abler, Amend, Apter, Bigger, Buck, Cap, Convalescent, Fairer, Finer, Gambler, Gamester, Imponent, Improve, Meliorate, Mend, Outdo, Outpoint, Outshine, Outsmart, Outstrip, Outwit, Preponderate, Punter, Race-goer, Reform, Superior, Surpass, Throw, Top, Turfite, Worst

Between Amid, Bet, Betwixt, Inter, Interjacent, Linking, Mesne, Twixt

Bevel Angle, Cant, Oblique, Slope, Splay

Beverage Ale, Cocoa, Coffee, Cordial, Cup, → DRINK, Hydromel, Nectar, Tea

Bevy Flock, Group, Herd, Host

Beware Cave, Fore, Heed, Mind, Mistrust, Pas op

Bewilder(ed), Bewildering, Bewilderment Amaze, At sea, Baffle, Buffalo, Confuse, Consternation, Daze, Flummox, Mate, Maze, Mind-boggling, Mystify, Perplex, Stun, Taivert, Wander, Will, Wull

Bewitch(ed), Bewitching Charm, Delight, Elf-shot, Enchant, Ensorcell, Glam(orous), Hex, Hoodoo, Jinx, Obeah, Obiah, Strike

Beyond Above, Ayont, Besides, Farther, Outwith, Over, Past, Thule, Trans, Ulterior

Bias(ed) Angle, Aslant, Bent, Chauvinism, Discriminatory, Grid, Imbalance, Loaded, One-sided, Partial, Parti pris, Partisan, Penchant, Preconception, Predilection, → PREJUDICE, Prepossess, Set, Sexism, Skew, Slope, Tendency, Unjust, Warp

Bib, Bibulous Apron, Beery, Feeder, Pout, Tope, Tucker

Bibelot Objet d'art

Bible Adulterous, Alcoran, Alkoran, Antilegomena, Apocrypha, ASV, Authority, AV, Avesta, Bamberg, Book, Breeches, Bug, Coverdale, Cranmer, Cromwell, Douai, Douay, Family, Ferrara, Fool, Forgotten sins, Gemara, Geneva, Gideon, Good book, Goose, Gospel, Gutenberg, Hagiographa, Heptateuch, Hexapla, Hexateuch, Holy, Idle, Isagogic, Itala, Italic, King James (version), Leda, Matthew Parker, Mazarin(e), Midrash, Missal, Murderer, New English, NT, Omasum, Ostrog, OT, Pentateuch, Peshito, Peshitta, Peshitto, Polyglot, Psalter, Revised Version, RSV, RV, Scriptures, Septuagint, Stomach, Talmud, Tanach, Tantra, Targum, Taverner, Taverners, Thirty-six-line, Treacle, Tyndale, Unrighteous, Vinegar, Vulgate, Whig, Wicked, Wife-hater, Wyclif(fe), Zurich

Biblical scholar Rechabite, USPG, Wycliffe

Bibliophagist, Bibliophile Bookworm

Bicarb Saleratus

Bicker Argue, Bowl, Brawl, Coggie, Dispute, Tiff, Wrangle

Bicycle, Bike(r) Bambi, Bone-shaker, Chopper, Coaster, Crog(gy), Dandy-horse, Dirt, Draisene, Draisine, Exercise, Fixed-wheel, Hobby, Hobbyhorse, Mixte, Moped, Mount, Mountain, Multicycle, Ordinary, Pedal, Penny-farthing, Quad, Raleigh®, Recumbent, Roadster, Safety, Scooter, Spin, Stationary, Tandem, Trail, Tree, Velocipede

Bid(der), Bidding (system) Acol, Apply, Blackwood, Call, Canape, Command, Contract, Cue, Declare, Double, Forcing, Gone, Hostile, Invite, Jump, Misère, Nod, NT, → OFFER, Order, Pass, Pre-empt, Proposal, Psychic, Puffer, Redouble, Shut-out, Summon, Take-over, Tell, Tender, Vied, White bonnet

Biddy Gammer, Hen

Biennial Trieteric

Bier Hearse, Litter

Big Beamy, Bulky, Bumper, Burly, Cob, Enormous, Fat, Ginormous, Gross, → LARGE, Loud, Mansize, Massive, Mighty, Obese, Skookum, Slockdoliger, Slockdologer, Soc(k)dologer, Sogdolager, Sogdoliger, Stonker, Strapping, Swopper, Thumping, Tidy, Vast, Whacker, Whopper

Bigamy, Bigamist, Bigamous Bluebeard, Diandrous

Bighead Ego

Bight Canterbury, Great Australian, Heligoland

Bigot(ed) Chauvinist, Dogmatist, Fanatic, Hide-bound, Intolerant, Narrow-minded, Racialist, Racist, Sexist, Wowser, Zealot

Bigshot, Bigwig Cheese, Law lord, Nib, Nob, Oner, Oneyer, Oneyre, Swell, → VIP

Bijou Doll-like

▶ **Bike** *see* BICYCLE

Bikini Atoll, Tanga

Bile, Bilious(ness) Cholaemia, Choler, Gall, Icteric, Melancholy, Scholaemia, Venom, Yellow

Bilge Leak, Pump, Rhubarb, Rot, Waste

Bilingual Diglot

Bilk Default

Bill(ed), Billy Ac(c), Accommodation, Accompt, Account, Act, Ad, Addition, Appropriation, Barnacle, Beak, Becke, Budd, Buffalo, Can, Caress, Carte, Chit(ty), Cody, Coo, Coronoid, Demand, Dixy, Docket, Double, Due, Exactment, Fin, Finance, Foreign, Gates, Goat, Hybrid, Inland, Invoice, Kaiser, → LAW, Lawin(g), Legislation, Liam, Liar, List, Measure, Menu, Neb, Ness, Nib, → NOTE, Notice,

Platypus, Pork barrel, Portland, Poster, Private, Programme, Pruning, Public, Puffing, Reckoning, Reform, Remanet, Rhamphotheca, Rostral, Rostrum, Score, Short, Shot, Show, Sickle, Silly, Sparth(e), Sperthe, Spoon, Sticker, Tab, Tomium, Trade, Treasury, True, Twin, Victualling, Willy

Billet Berth, Casern, Cess, Chit, Coupon, Note, Quarter

Billet doux Capon, Valentine

Billiards, Billiards player, Billiards stroke Bar, Cannon-game, Cueist, Jenny, Lagging, Long jenny, Massé, Pocket, Pool, Potter, Pyramids, Short jenny, Snooker, String, Whitechapel

Billion Gillion, Milliard, Tera

Bill of sale Bs

Billow Roil, Roller, Rule, Surge, Swell, Wave

▶ **Billy** *see* **BILL**

Bin Bing, Box, Chilly, Container, Crib, Dump, Hell, Litter, Loony, Receptacle, Sin, Snake-pit, Stall, Wagger-pagger, Wheelie, Wheely

Binary ASCII, Semidetached

Bind(er), Binding Adherent, Adhesive, Akedah, Alligate, Apprentice, Astrict, Astringent, Bale, Bandage, Bandeau, Bandster, Bias, Bibliopegist, Brail, Burst, Calf, Cerlox®, Chain, Cinch, Circuit, Clamp, Colligate, Complain, Cord, Cummerbund, Deligation, Drag, Edge, Embale, Enchain, Engage, Enslave, Enwind, → **FASTEN**, Fetter, Galloon, Gird, Girdle, Grolier, Half-leather, Hay-wire, Hold, Incumbent, Indenture, Iron, Keckle, Lash(er), Law-calf, Leash, Ligament, Ligature, Mail, Marl, Morocco, Muslin, Obi, Obligate, Oblige, Oop, Organdie, Oup, Parpen, Perfect, Pinion, Raffia, Restrict, Ring, → **ROPE**, Roxburghe, Seize, Sheaf, Spiral, Strap, Stringent, Stygian, Swathe, Syndesis, Tape, Tether, Thirl, Thong, Three-quarter, Tie, Tree-calf, Truss, Twine, Valid, Whip, Withe, Yapp, Yerk, Yoke

Bindweed Bearbine, Convolvulus, With(y)wind

Bing Crosby, Go, Heap

Binge Bat, Beano, Bend(er), Blind, Carouse, → **DRINK**, Drinking-bout, Party, Riot, Soak, Souse, Splore, Spree, Toot, Tout

Bingo Beano, Housey-housey, Keno, Lotto, Tombola

Binocular(s) Glasses, Jumelle, OO, Stereoscope

Biochemical, Biochemist(ry) Ames, DNA, Proteomics

Biographer, Biography Boswell, CV, Hagiography, History, Life, Memoir, Plutarch, Potted, Prosopography, Suetonius, Vita

Biology, Biologist Algology, Cladistics, Genetics, Mendel, Morphology, Phenetics, Photodynamics, Somatology, Stoechiology, Stoich(e)iology, Taxonomy, Teratology, Transgenics

Bioscope Kinema

Birch Birk, Cane, Cow, Flog, Hazel, Kow, Larch, Reis, Rice, Rod, Silver, Swish, Twig, Weeping, Whip, White, Withe

Bird(s) Al(l)erion, Altricial, Aves, Avian, Bertram, Brood, Damsel, Doll, Early, Flier, Fowl, Gal, → **GIRL**, Grip, Hen, Jail, Left, Limicoline, Ornis, Ornithology, Pecker, Pen, Perching, Poultry, Praecoces, Prison, Quod, Raptor, Roaster, Sentence, Sis, Skirt, Time

BIRDS

2 letters:	3 letters:	Boo	Fum
Ka	Ani	Cob	Jay
Oi	Auk	Emu	Kae

Kea
Maw
Mew
Moa
Nun
Owl
Pea
Pie
Ree
Roc
Ruc
Tit
Tui

4 letters:
Barb
Chat
Cirl
Cobb
Coly
Coot
Crax
Crow
Dodo
Dove
→ DUCK
Emeu
Erne
Eyas
Fung
Gled
Gnow
Guan
Guga
Gull
Hawk
Hern
Huia
Huma
Ibis
Iynx
Jynx
Kagu
Kaka
Kite
Kiwi
Knot
Koel
Kora
Lark
Loom

Loon
Lory
Mina
Monk
Myna
Nene
Otis
Pavo
Pawn
Pern
Piet
Pink
Pown
Pyot
Rail
Rhea
Roch
Rook
Ruff
Ruru
Rype
Shag
Smee
Sora
Swan
Taha
Tara
Teal
Tern
Tick
Tody
Tuli
Weka
Wren
Xema
Yale
Yite

5 letters:
Agami
Ardea
Ariel
Bennu
Booby
Bosun
Capon
Colin
Colly
Crake
Crane
Diver

Egret
Finch
Fleet
Galah
Glede
Goose
Goura
Grebe
Heron
Hobby
Homer
Isaac
Junco
Kawau
Kight
Liver
Lowan
Macaw
Madge
Manch
Mavis
Merle
Mimus
Mohua
Monal
Murre
Mynah
Nandu
Nelly
Noddy
Ousel
Ox-eye
Peggy
Pekan
Pewit
Picus
Pilot
Piper
Pipit
Pitta
Poaka
Poker
Potoo
Prion
Quail
Quest
Quist
Raven
Reeve
Robin
Rotch

Ryper
Saker
Scape
Scart
Scaup
Scops
Scray
Scrub
Serin
Shama
Sitta
Skart
Snipe
Solan
Soree
Spink
Sprug
Squab
Stare
Stilt
Stint
Stork
Swift
Sylph
Terek
Tewit
Topaz
Twite
Umber
Umbre
Urubu
Veery
Vireo
Wader
Whaup
Widow
Wonga
Yaffa

6 letters:
Aquila
Avocet
Avoset
Bantam
Barbet
Bishop
Bittor
Bittur
Bonxie
Boubou
Brolga

Bulbul
Canary
Chough
Chukar
Condor
Corbie
Coucal
Cuckoo
Curlew
Cushat
Darter
Dikkop
Dipper
Drongo
Duiker
Dunlin
Duyker
Elanet
Evejar
Falcon
Fulmar
Gambet
Gander
Gannet
Garuda
Gentle
Gentoo
Go-away
Godwit
Gooney
Goslet
Grakle
Grouse
Hagden
Hagdon
Haglet
Hermit
Hoopoe
Houdan
Jabiru
Jacana
Jaeger
Kakapo
Kotare
Kotuku
Lanner
Leipoa
Linnet
Lintie
Loerie
Loriot

Lourie
Lungie
Magpie
Martin
Matata
Menura
Merlin
Merops
Missel
Mistle
Monaul
Mopoke
Mossie
Motmot
Musket
Mutton
Nandoo
Oriole
Oscine
Osprey
Oxbird
Parrot
Parson
Pavone
Peahen
Peeper
Peewee
Peewit
Pernis
Petrel
Phoebe
Pigeon
Piopio
Plover
Pouter
Progne
Puffin
Pukeko
Pullet
Queest
Quelea
Quoist
Redcap
Reeler
Roller
Scamel
Scarth
Scaury
Scraye
Sea-cob
Sea-mew

Seapie
Shrike
Simara
Simorg
Simurg
Siskin
Skarth
Smeath
Soland
Sorage
Strich
Sultan
Sylvia
Tailor
Takahe
Tarcel
Tassel
Tewhit
Thrush
Tom-tit
Toucan
Towhee
Trogon
Turaco
Turbit
Turkey
Tyrant
Tystie
Verdin
Walker
Waxeye
Whidah
Whydah
Willet
Woosel
Yaffle
Ynambu
Yucker
Zoozoo

7 letters:
Amokura
Anhinga
Antbird
Apteryx
Axebird
Babbler
Bécasse
Bee-kite
Bittern
Bittour

Bluecap
Blue-eye
Blue jay
Bluetit
Boobook
Bullbat
Bunting
Buphaga
Bush-tit
Bustard
Buzzard
Cacique
Cariama
Cheeper
Chewink
Chicken
Coal-tit
Cole-tit
Colibri
Corella
Cotinga
Courlan
Courser
Cow-bird
Creeper
Crombec
Cropper
Diamond
Dinorus
Dottrel
Dovekie
Dunnock
Emu-wren
Fantail
Fern-owl
Figbird
Finfoot
Flicker
Frigate
Gleerie
Gobbler
Goburra
Gorcrow
Goshawk
Grackle
Grallae
Hacklet
Hadedah
Hagbolt
Hagdown
Halcyon

Harrier
Hemipod
Hoatzin
Humming
Ice-bird
Jacamar
Jackdaw
Kahawai
Kamichi
Kestrel
Killdee
Kinglet
Koekoea
Lapwing
Leghorn
Limpkin
Manakin
Maribou
Martlet
Mesites
Minivet
Mudlark
Oilbird
Ortolan
Oscines
Ostrich
Pandion
Peacock
Peafowl
Pelican
Penguin
Phoenix
Pickmaw
Piculet
Pinnock
Pintado
Pintail
Pochard
Pockard
Poe-bird
Poy-bird
Quetzal
Rainbow
Rasores
Ratitae
Redpoll
Redwing
Regulus
Rooster
Rosella
Rotchie

Ruddock
Sakeret
Sawbill
Scooper
Scourie
Sea-mell
Simurgh
Sirgang
Sitella
Skimmer
Skylark
Snow-cap
Spadger
Sparrow
Squacco
Staniel
Stinker
Sturnus
Sunbird
Swallow
Tanager
Tanagra
Tarrock
Tattler
Teacher
Teuchat
Tiercel
Tinamou
Titanis
Titlark
Titling
Tokahea
Totanus
Touraco
Tumbler
Tweeter
Vulture
Vulturn
Wagtail
Warbler
Waxbill
Waxwing
Whooper
Widgeon
Wimbrel
Witwall
Woosell
Wren-tit
Wrybill
Wryneck
Yang-win

8 letters:
Aasvogel
Accentor
Adjutant
Aigrette
Alcatras
Altrices
Amadavat
Aquiline
Arapunga
Arenaria
Avadavat
Barnacle
Bellbird
Blackcap
Bluebird
Blue-wing
Boatbill
Boattail
Bobolink
Bob-white
Buln-buln
Caracara
Cardinal
Cargoose
Cheewink
Chirn-owl
Cockatoo
Cockerel
Coquette
Curassow
Dabchick
Didapper
Dip-chick
Dobchick
Dotterel
Estridge
Fauvette
Fernbird
Fish-hawk
Flamingo
Gambetta
Gang-gang
Garefowl
Garganey
Greenlet
Grosbeak
Guacharo
Hackbolt
Hangbird
Hangnest

Hawfinch
Hazelhen
Hemipode
Hernshaw
Hickymal
Hoactzin
Hornbill
Killdeer
Kingbird
Kiskadee
Landrail
Lanneret
Laverock
Longspur
Lorikeet
Lyrebird
Magotpie
Megapode
Mire-drum
Miromiro
Morepork
Murrelet
Nightjar
Notornis
Nuthatch
Ovenbird
Oxpecker
Paradise
Parakeet
Peetweet
Percolin
Petchary
Pheasant
Philomel
Pihoihoi
Podargus
Poorwill
Prunella
Puffbird
Quarrian
Quarrion
Rainbird
Rallidae
Redshank
Redstart
Reedling
Reed-wren
Rice-bird
Ringtail
Riroriro
Sandpeep

Scolopar	Baldicoot	Jack-snipe	Thornbill
Screamer	Baltimore	Kittiwake	Trochilus
Sea-eagle	Beccaccia	Lintwhite	Trumpeter
Shake-bag	Beccafico	Mallemuck	Turnstone
Shoebill	Beefeater	Merganser	Volucrine
Silktail	Bergander	Mistletoe	Water cock
Sittella	Blackbird	Mollymawk	Water-rail
Skua-gull	Blackhead	Mousebird	Wind-hover
Snowbird	Blackpoll	Night-hawk	Woodspite
Stanniel	Blood bird	Nutjobber	Xanthoura
Struthio	Bower-bird	Nutpecker	
Surfbird	Brambling	Olive-back	**10 letters:**
Swiftlet	Broadbill	Ossifraga	Aberdevine
Tantalus	Bullfinch	Ossifrage	Bearded tit
Tapacolo	Campanero	Pardalote	Bluebreast
Tapaculo	Cassowary	Partridge	Bluethroat
Teru-tero	Chaffinch	Peaseweep	Brain-fever
Thrasher	Chatterer	Peregrine	Bubbly-jock
Thresher	Chickadee	Phalarope	Budgerigar
Throstle	Coachwhip	Pictarnie	Butter-bump
Ticklace	Cockatiel	Pine finch	Chiff-chaff
Titmouse	Cormorant	Porphyrio	Crested tit
Tom-noddy	Corncrake	Ptarmigan	Demoiselle
Toucanet	Crocodile	Razorbill	Dickcissel
Tragopan	Cross-bill	Riflebird	Didunculus
Trembler	Currawong	Rosy-finch	Dive-dapper
Troopial	Dove prion	Sabrewing	Dollarbird
Troupial	Dowitcher	Salangane	Ember-goose
Tubenose	Estreldid	Sandpiper	Eyas-musket
Umbrella	Fieldfare	Sapsucker	Fallow-chat
Umbrette	Fig-pecker	Satinbird	Fly-catcher
Water-hen	Fire-crest	Scansores	Four o'clock
Wheatear	Fledgling	Sea-turtle	Fringillid
Whimbrel	Francolin	Secretary	Goatsucker
Whinchat	Friarbird	Seedeater	Gobemouche
Whipbird	Frogmouth	Sheldrake	Grassfinch
Whitecap	Gallinule	Shoveller	Greenfinch
White-eye	Gerfalcon	Silver eye	Greenshank
Wildfowl	Gier-eagle	Skunk-bird	Hen-harrier
Wirebird	Goldcrest	Solitaire	Honey-eater
Woodchat	Goldfinch	Spoonbill	Honey guide
Woodcock	Goosander	Standgale	Kingfisher
Woodlark	Grassquit	Stonechat	Kookaburra
Woodwale	Grenadier	Stormbird	Locust-bird
Yoldring	Guillemot	Storm-cock	Mallee fowl
	Happy Jack	Sugarbird	Marsh-robin
9 letters:	Helldiver	Swart-back	Meadowlark
Accipiter	Heronshaw	Sword-bill	Night-churr
Aepyornis	Hornywink	Talegalla	Noisy miner
Albatross	Icteridae	Thickhead	Nutcracker
Aylesbury	Impundulu	Thick-knee	Peckerwood

Pettichaps
Pettychaps
Pick-cheese
Pine-marten
Pratincole
Quaker-bird
Racket-tail
Rafter-bird
Rain-plover
Ramphastos
Regent-bird
Rhinoceros
Roadrunner
Ruby-throat
Saddleback
Saddlebill
Sanderling
Sandgrouse
Sea swallow
Shearwater
Sheathbill
Sicklebill
Silverbill
Snowy egret
Spatchcock
Stone-snipe
Tanagridae
Tropicbird
Wattlebird
Weaver bird
Whisky-jack
Whisky-john
Wonga-wonga
Woodpecker

Woodpigeon
Yaffingale
Yellowbird
Yellowhead
Yellowlegs
Yellowyite

11 letters:
Apostlebird
Bokmakierie
Bristlebird
Butcherbird
Cape sparrow
Fallow-finch
Fringilline
Gnatcatcher
Grallatores
Happy-family
Honey-sucker
House martin
Humming-bird
Ichthyornis
Java sparrow
Leatherhead
Mockingbird
Moss-bluiter
Moss-cheeper
Nightingale
Pied wagtail
Plantcutter
Pyrrhuloxia
Reed-warbler
Scissortail
Snowbunting

Sparrow-hawk
Stilt-plover
Stone-curlew
Storm petrel
Stymphalian
Thunderbird
Tree-creeper
Wall creeper
Whitethroat
Woodcreeper
Woodswallow
Woodwarbler
Yellow-ammer

12 letters:
Bronze-pigeon
Drongo-cuckoo
Drongo-shrike
Flowerpecker
Hedge-warbler
Honey creeper
Peppershrike
Ring-dotterel
Sage-thrasher
Sedge-warbler
Serpent-eater
Standard-wing
Stonechatter
Stormy petrel
Throstle-cock
Whippoorwill
Willy wagtail
Yellow-hammer
Yellow-yowley

13 letters:
Archaeopteryx
Cetti's warbler
Cock-of-the-rock
Mocking thrush
Oyster-catcher
Pipiwharauroa
Plantain-eater
Willow-wagtail
Willow warbler
Wilson's petrel

14 letters:
Manx shearwater
Tawny frogmouth
Woodchat shrike

15 letters:
Montagu's harrier

16 letters:
Tyrant flycatcher
White-fronted tern

17 letters:
Pectoral sandpiper
Spotted flycatcher

18 letters:
Paradise flycatcher

▷ **Bird** *may indicate* a prison sentence
Bird-catcher Avicularia, Fowler, Papageno
Bird-like Hirundine, Sturnine
Bird's nest(ing) Caliology, Monotropa, Soup
Bird-watcher Augur, Twitcher
Birkenhead F.E.Smith
Birmingham Brum(magem)
Birth Burden, Congenital, Delivery, Drop, Extraction, Genesis, Happy event, Jataka, Lineage, Multiple, Nativity, Natural, Origin, Parage, Parity, Parturition, Virgin
Birthday Anniversary, Genethliac
Birthmark Blemish, Mole, Mother-spot, Naevus, Port wine stain, Stigmata, Strawberry
Birthright Heritage, Mess, Patrimony
Birthwort Aristolochia
Biscuit Abernethy, Bath-oliver, Biscotto, Bourbon, Brandysnap, Brown George, Butterbake, Captain's, Charcoal, Cookie, Cracker, Cracknel, Crispbread,

Dandyfunk, Digestive, Dog, Dunderfunk, Fairing, Flapjack, Florentine, Fortune
cookie, Four-by-two, Garibaldi, Ginger nut, Gingersnap, Hardtack, Kiss, Langue
de chat, Lebkuchen, Macaroon, Marie, Mattress, Matza(h), Matzo(h), Nut,
Oatcake, Oliver, Osborne, Parkin, Perkin, Petit four, Petticoat tail, Pig's ear,
Pilot, Poppadom, Poppadum, Pretzel, Ratafia, Rice, Rusk, Rye-roll, Sea, Ship's,
Shortbread, Snap, Soda, Sweetmeal, Tack, Tararua, Tea, Wafer, Water, Wine,
Zwieback

Bisexual AC/DC, Freemartin, Switch-hitter

Bishop(ric) Aaronic, Abba, Aidan, Ambrose, Bench, Berkeley, Bp, Cambrensis,
Cantuar, Chad, Coadjutor, Coverdale, Diocesan, Dunelm, Ebor, Ely, Eparch,
Episcopate, Eusebian, Exarch, Exon, Golias, Hatto, Henson, Latimer, Lord,
Magpie, Metropolitan, Norvic, Odo, Ordainer, Patriarch, Peter, Petriburg, Piece,
Polycarp, Pontiff, Prelate, Priest, Primate, Primus, Proudie, Roffen, RR, Sarum,
Sleeve, Suffragan, The purple, Titular, Tulchan, Weaver, Weed, Winton,
Wrexham

Bismarck Otto

Bismuth Bi

Bison Bonas(s)us, Buffalo, Ox, Wisent

Bit Baud, Cantle(t), Centre, Chad, Cheesecake, Chip, Coin, Crumb, Curb, Curn,
Drib, Excerpt, Flibbert, Fraction, Gag, Haet, Hate, Ion, Jaw, Jot, Mite, Modicum,
Morsel, Mote, Mu, Nit, Ort, Ounce, Pelham, Peni, Penny, → PIECE, Port, Rap, Rare,
Ratherish, Scintilla, Scrap, Section, Shaving, Shiver, Shred, Smidgen, Smidgeon,
Smidgin, Snaffle, Snatch, Snippet, Some, Soupcon, Spale, Speck, Splinter, Spot,
Spudding, Suspicion, Tad, Tait, Tate, Threepenny, Trace, Unce, Vestige, What,
Whit

Bite(r), Biting, Bitten Canapé, Caustic, Chelicera, Chew, Eat, Engouled, Erose,
Etch, Gnash, Gnat, Hickey, Hickie, Incisor, Knap, Masticate, Midge, Molar,
Mordacious, Mordant, Morsel, Morsure, Nibble, Nip(py), Occlude, Peck, Pium,
Premorse, Rabid, Sarcastic, Sharp, Shrewd, Snap, Sound, Spammie, Tart

Bitter(ness) Absinth, Acerb, Acid, Acrid, Acrimonious, Ale, Aloe, Angostura, Bile,
Cassareep, Caustic, Eager, Edge, Ers, Fell, Gall, Keen, Marah, Maror, Myrrh, Pique,
Rancorous, Rankle, Resentful, Sarcastic, Sardonic, Snell, Sore, Spleen, Tart(aric),
Venom, Verjuice, Virulent, Vitriolic, Wersh, Wormwood, Wry

Bittern Boomer, Bull-of-the-bog, Butterbump, Heron, Sedge, Siege

Bittersweet Dulcamara, Staff-tree

Bitumen Albertite, Asphalt, Blacktop, Elaterite, Gilsonite®, Maltha, Mineral tar,
Pissasphalt, Pitch, Tar, Tarseal, Uintaite

Bivalve Clam, Cockle, Lamellibranch, Mollusc, Muscle, Mussel, Oyster, Pelecypod,
Piddock, Razorshell, Scallop, Tuatua, Whelk

Bivouac Camp

Bizarre Antic, Curious, Eccentric, Exotic, Fantastic, Far-out, Freaky, Gonzo,
Grotesque, Odd, Off-the-wall, Outlandish, Outré, Pythonesque, Queer, Strange,
Surreal, Weird

▷ **Bizarre** *may indicate* an anagram

Blab Babble, Gossip, Prate, Squeal

Black(en), Blackness, Black-out Amadoda, Atramental, B, BB, Bess, Blae, Boong,
Cape Coloured, Carbon, Char, Charcoal, Cilla, Coloured, Coon, Cypress, Darkie,
Darky, Death, Denigrate, Dinge, Dwale, Ebon(y), Eclipse, Ethiop, Fuzzy-wuzzy,
Geechee, Gladwellise, Graphite, Grime, Heben, Hole, Ink(y), Ivory, Japan, Jeat, Jet,
Jim Crow, Kohl, Lepidomelane, Malign, Market, Melanic, Melano, Moke, Moor,
Muntu, Myall, Negritude, Negro, Niello, Niger, Nigrescent, Nigritude, Obliterate,

Obscure, Outage, Oxford, Piceous, Pitch, Platinum, Pongo, Prince, Pudding, Puke, Quashee, Quashie, Raven, Sable, Sambo, Scab, School, Sericon, Sheep, Slae, Sloe, Snowball, Sodium, Solvent, Sombre, Soot, Sooterkin, Spade, Spook, Stygian, Swart(y), Swarth(y), Tar, Uncle Tom, Weeds
Black art Necromancy, Nigromancy
Blackball Ban, Exclude, Pill, Pip, Reject
Blackberry Acini, Bramble, Mooch, Mouch
Blackbird Collybird, Crow, Jackdaw, Ousel, Raven, Woosel
Blackcurrant Quinsy-berry
Black eye(d) Half-mourning, Mouse, Shiner, Susan
Blackguard Leg, Nithing, Raff, Revile, Rotter, Scoundrel, Sweep
Blackhead Comedo
Black hole Collapsar
Blackjack Billie, Billy, Cosh, Flag, Sphalerite, Tankard, Truncheon, Vingt(-et)-un
Blackleg Fink, Rat, Scab, Snob
Black-letter Gothic
Black magic Goety
Blackmail(er) Bleed, Chantage, Chout, Exact, Extort, Ransom, Shakedown, Strike, Vampire
Blackout ARP, Eclipse, Faint, Swoon
Black Sea Pontic, Pontus Euxinus
Black sheep Neer-do-well, Reprobate
Blacksmith Brontes, Burn-the-wind, Farrier, Forger, Harmonious, Plater, Shoer, Vulcan
Blackthorn Sloe
Bladder(wort) Air, Balloon, Blister, Cholecyst, Cyst, Gall, Hydatid, Isinglass, Popweed, Sac, Sound, Swim, Urinary, Utricle, Varec(h), Vesica, Vesicle
Blade(s) Acrospire, Bilbo, Brand, Brown Bill, Cleaver, Co(u)lter, Cutlass, Dandy, Espada, Faible, Foible, Forte, Gleave, Gouge, Guillotine, Hydrofoil, Knife, Lance, Lawnmower, Leaf, Man, Mouldboard, Oar, Omoplate, Palmetto, Peel, Propeller, Rachilla, Rapier, Razor, Rip, Rotor, Scimitar, Scull, Scythe, Skate, Spade-, Spatula, Spatule, Spear, Spoon, Stiletto, Stock, Strigil, Sweep, → **SWORD**, Symitar, Toledo, Turbine, Vane, Vorpal, Web
Blair Eric, Lionel, Tony
Blame(worthy) Accuse, Censure, Condemn, Confound, Decry, Dirdam, Dirdum, Dispraise, Fault, Guilt, Inculpate, Odium, Rap, Reprehensible, Reproach, Reprove, Stick, Thank, Twit, Wight, Wite, Wyte
Blameless Innocent, Irreproachable, Lily-white, Unimpeachable
Blanch Bleach, Etiolate, Scaud, Whiten
Blancmange Carrageen, Flummery, Mould, Shape, Timbale
Bland Anodyne, Glop, Mild, Pigling, Sleek, Smooth, Spammy, Suave, Tame, Unctuous
Blandish(ment) Agremens, Agrement, Cajole, → **COAX**, Flatter, Treacle, Wheedle
Blank Burr, Cartridge, Empty, Erase, Flan, Ignore, Lacuna, Mistigris, Planchet, Shot, Space, Tabula rasa, → **VACANT**
Blanket Afghan, Bluey, Chilkat, Counterpane, Cover, Electric, Fire, General, Hudson's Bay, Kaross, Mackinaw, Manta, Obscure, Overall, Poncho, Quilt, Rug, Saddle, Sarape, Security, Serape, Shabrack, Smog, Space, Stroud, Wagga, Wet, Whittle
Blare Horn, Trumpet
Blarney Cajolery, Flattery, Nonsense, Sawder, Taffy

Blasé Worldly

Blaspheme, Blasphemous Abuse, → CURSE, Defame, Profanity, Revile

Blast(ed) Blight, Blore, Blow, Bombard, Dang, Darn, Dee, Drat, Dynamite, Explode, Fanfare, Flaming, Flurry, Fo(e)hn, Gale, Gust, Noser, Oath, Parp, Pryse, Rats, Scarth, Scath(e), Sere, Shot, Sideration, Skarth, Stormer, Tantara, Toot, Tromp(e), Trump(et), Volley

Blatant Flagrant, Hard-core, Noticeable, Open, Strident, Vulgar

Blather Baloney, Gabble

Blaze(r) Beacon, Bonfire, Burn, Cannel, Conflagration, Firestorm, → FLAME, Flare, Glare, Jacket, Low(e), Lunt, Palatinate, Race, Ratch, Sati, Star, Sun, Tead(e)

Bleach Agene, Blanch, Chemic, Chloride, Decolorate, Etiolate, Janola®, Keir, Kier, Peroxide, Whiten, Whitster

Bleak Ablet, Bare, Blay, Bley, Cheerless, Dour, Dreary, Dreich, Gaunt, Raw, Wintry

Bleary Blurred, Smudged

Bleat Baa, Blat, Bluster, Maa

Bleed(er), Bleeding Cup, Ecchymosis, Epistaxis, Extravasate, Fleam, Haemorrhage, Leech, Menorrhagia, Menorrh(o)ea, Metrorrhagia, Milk, Purpura, Root-pressure

Bleep Earcon, Pager

Blefuscudian Big-endian, Little-endian

Blemish Birthmark, Blot, Blotch, Blur, Botch, Defect, Flaw, Mackle, Mark, Milium, Mote, Naevus, Scar, Smirch, Spot, Stain, Sully, Taint, Tash, Vice, Wart, Wen

Blench Flinch, Recoil, Wince

Blend(ing) Amalgam, Coalesce, Commix, Contemper, Contrapuntal, Counterpoint, Electrum, Fuse, Go, Harmonize, Hydrate, Interfuse, Interlace, Liquidise, Meld, Melt, → MERGE, Mingle, Mix, Osmose, Portmanteau, Scumble, Sfumato, Synalepha

▷ **Blend** *may indicate* an anagram

Blenny Eel-pout, Gunnel, Shanny

Bless(ing), Blessed(ness) Amen, Approval, Asset, Beatitude, Benedicite, Benediction, Benison, Benitier, Bensh, Bismillah, Boon, Brachah, Brocho, Charmed, Consecrate, Cup, Damosel, Darshan, Elysium, Ethereal, Felicity, Gesundheit, Godsend, Grace, Gwyneth, Holy (dam), Kiddush, Luck, Macarise, Mercy, Mixed, Sain, Saint, Sanctify, Sanctity, Sheva Brachoth, Sheva Brochos, Toronto, Urbi et orbi, Xenium

Bless me Lawk(s)

Blight Afflict, Ague, American, Apple, Bespot, Blast, Destroy, Eyesore, Fire, Planning, Potato, Rot, → RUIN, Rust, Sandy, Shadow, Viticide, Waldersterben, Wither

Blighter Cuss, Perisher, Varment, Varmint

Blimey Coo, Cor, Crimini, O'Riley, Strewth

Blimp Airship, Colonel

Blind(ness), Blind spot Amaurosis, Amblyopia, Artifice, Austrian, Beesome, Bisson, Blend, Blotto, Carousal, Cecity, Chi(c)k, Cog, Concealed, Dazzle, Drop serene, Eyeless, Feint, Festoon, Gravel, Hemeralopia, Homer, Hood, Jalousie, Legless, Meropia, Mole, Night, Nyctalopia, Onchocerciasis, Persian, Persiennes, Pew, Prestriction, Rash, Roller, Roman, Scotoma, Seel, Shade, Shutter, Snow, Stimie, Stimy, Stymie, Sun, Teichopsia, Typhlology, Venetian, Window, Word, Yblent

Blindfish Amblyopsis

Blindfold Bandage, Hoodwink, Muffle, Seal, Wimple

Blindworm Anguis

Blink, Blinker(s), Blinkered, Blinking Bat, Blepharism, Blinders, Bluff, Broken, Eye-flap, Flash, Haw, Idiot, Insular, Nictate, Owl-eyed, Owly, Twink, Wapper, Wink

Bliss(ful) Beatitude, Bouyan, Composer, Delight, → ECSTASY, Eden, Elysium, Happy, Idyll, Ignorance, Married, Millenium, Nirvana, Paradise, Rapture, Sion, Tir-na-nog, Valhalla, Walhalla, Wedded

Blister(ed), Blistering Blab, Blain, Bleb, Bubble, Bullate, Cold sore, Epispastic, Fever, Herpes, Overgall, Pemphigus, Phlyct(a)ena, Scorching, Tetter, Vesicant, Vesicle, Visicate, Water

Blitz Attack, Bombard, Onslaught, Raid

Blizzard Buran, Gale, Snowstorm, Whiteout

Bloat(er) Buckling, Puff, Strout, Swell, Tumefy, Two-eyed steak

Blob Bead, Bioblast, Drop, Globule, O, Pick, Spot, Tear

Bloc Alliance, Cabal, Cartel, Party

Block(er), Blockage, Blocked, Blocking Altar, Anvil, Ashlar, Atresia, → BAR, Barricade, Barrier, Battle-axe, Brake, Breeze, Brick, Briquet(te), Building, Bung, Bunt, Catasta, Cavity, Chinese, Choke, Chunk, Cinder, Cleat, Clint, Clog, Clot, Cloy, Compass, Congest, Constipated, Cut-off, Cyclopean, Cylinder, Dado, → DAM, Dead-eye, Debar, Dentel, Dentil, Die, Dit, Domino, Electrotint, Embolism, Emphractic, Encompass, Euphroe, Fipple, Hack-log, Heart, High-rise, Hunk, Ice, Ileus, Impasse, Impede, Impost, Ingot, Insula, Interclude, Interrupt, Investment, Jam, Licence, Lifestyle, Line, Lingot, Lodgment, Log-jam, Lump, Mental, Ministroke, Mitre, Monkey, Mounting, Mutule, Nerve, Nifedipine, Nog, Notepad, Oasis®, Obstacle, → OBSTRUCT, Occlude, Office, Opossum, Oppilate, Pad, Page, Parry, Perched, Pile-cap, Pile-up, Pillow, Plinth, Plummer, Power, Pre-empt, Prevent, Process, Psychological, Quad, Ram, Saddle, Scotch, Sett, Siege, Snatch, Stalemate, Stap, Starting, Stenosis, Stimie, Stimy, Stone, Stonewall, Stop, Stumbling, Stymie, Sun, Swage, Tamp, Thwart, Tint, Tower, Tranche, Trig, Triglyph, Truck, Uphroe, Upping-stock, Vibropac®, Wig, Wood(cut), Wrest, Writer's, Zinco, Zugzwang

Blockbuster Epic

Blockhead Jolterhead, Mome, Nitwit, Noodle, Pig sconce, Stupid

Bloke Beggar, Chap, Cove, Fellow, Gent, Man, Oik

Blond(e) Ash, Cendré, Fair, Flaxen, Goldilocks, Peroxide, Platinised, Platinum, Strawberry, Tallent, Tow-haired, Towhead

Blood(y), Blood letting A, Ancestry, B, Bad, Bally, Blue, Blut, Claret, Clot, Cold, Cruor, Cup, Ecchymosis, Ensanguine, Epigons, Factor, First, Full, → GORE, Haemal, Haemorrhage, Ichor, Internecine, Introduce, Kin, Kinship, Knut, Menses, Microcyte, New, Nut, O, Opsonin, Parentage, Persue, Pigeon's, Plasma, Platelet, Plurry, Properdin, Pup, Race, Rare, Red, Rh negative, Rh positive, Ruby, Sang, Schistosoma, Serum, Show, Stroma, Toff, Venisection, Welter, Whole, Young

Blood disease, Blood disorder, Blood-poisoning Hypinosis, Isch(a)emia, Leukemia, Lipaemia, Oligaemia, Purpura, Pyaemia, Sapraemia, Septicemia, Spanaemia, Thalassemia, Thrombocytopenia, Toxaemia, Uraemia

Bloodhound Lime, Lyam, Rach(e), Ratch, Sleuth, Spartan

Bloodless Anaemic, Isch(a)emic, Wan, White

Blood-letter Leech, Phlebotomist, Sangrado

Blood money Eric

▸ **Blood-poisoning** *see* BLOOD DISEASE

Blood-pressure Hypertension, Hypotension

Bloodshot Red-eyed

Blood-sport Hunting, Shooting, Venery

Blood-sucker Asp, Dracula, Flea, Gnat, Ked, Leech, Louse, Mosquito, Parasite, Reduviid, Sponger, Tick, Vampire(-bat)

Bloom(er), Blooming Anthesis, Bally, Blossom, Blow, Blush, Boner, Cobalt, Dew, Effloresce, Error, Film, Florence, Florescent, Flowery, Flush, Gaffe, Glaucous, Heyday, Knickers, Loaf, Miscalculation, Nickel, Out, Pruina, Rationals, Reh, Remontant, Rosy, Ruddy, Thrive, Underwear

▷ **Bloomer** *may indicate* a flower

Blossom Blow, Burgeon, Catkin, Festoon, Flourish, Flower, May, Orange, Pip

Blot Atomy, Blob, Cartel, Delete, Disgrace, Dry, Eyesore, Obscure, Smear, Smudge, Southern, Splodge, Splotch

Blotch(y) Blemish, Giraffe, Monk, Mottle(d), Spot, Stain

Blotto Legless

Blouse Choli, Garibaldi, Gimp, Guimpe, Kerbaya, Middy, Pneumonia, Sailor, Shirtwaist, Smock, Tunic, Waist(er), Windjammer

Blow(er) Appel, Bang, Bash, Bat, Bellows, Biff, Billow, Blip, Bloom, Brag, Breeze, Buckhorse, Buffet, Bump, Burst, Calamity, Clap, Clat, Claut, Clip, Clout, Clump, Conk, Coup, Cuff, Dad, Daud, Dawd, Dev(v)el, Dinnyhayser, Dint, Dod, Douse, Dowse, Estramacon, Etesian, Facer, Fan, Fillip, Gale, Grampus, Gust, Hammer, Haymaker, Hit, Hook, Ictus, Impact, Insufflate, Karate, Kibosh, Knuckle sandwich, KO, Lame, Lander, Left-hander, Lick, Lounder, Muff, Neck-herring, Northerly, Noser, Oner, One-two, Paddywhack, Paik, Pash, Phone, Piledriver, Plague, Plug, Plump(er), Polt, Pow, Puff, Punch, Purler, Rats, Rattler, Rib-roaster, Roundhouse, Sas(s)arara, Scat, Settler, Short, Sideswipe, Side-winder, Sis(s)erary, Skiff, Skite, Skyte, Slat, Slog, Slug, Snell, Snot, Sock, Sockdolager, Sockdologer, Southwester, Spanking, Spat, Spout, Squall, Squander, Stripe, Stroke, Strooke, Stunning, Sufflate, Supercharger, Swash, Swat, Swinger, Telephone, Thump, Thwack, Tingler, Tootle, Trump(et), Tuck, Undercut, Upper-cut, Waft, Wallop, Wap, Waste, Welt, Whammy, Whample, Whang, Whap, Wheeze, Wherret, Whiffle, Whirret, Whistle, → **WIND**, Winder, Wipe, Wuther

Blown-up Elated, Enlarged, Exploded

Blow-out Binge, Bloat, Exhale, Feast, Feed, Flat, Fulminate, Lava, Nosh-up, Snuff, Spiracle, → **SPREAD**

Blowpipe Hod, Peashooter, Sarbacane, Sumpit(an)

Blub(ber) Cry, Fat, Snotter, Sob, Speck, → **WEEP**, Whimper

Bludge Sinecure

Bludgeon Bully, Club, Cosh, Cudgel, Sap

Blue(s) Abattu, Accablé, Adult, Anil, Aquamarine, Azure, Azurn, Beard, Berlin, Bice, Bleuâtre, Blow, Bottle, Butterfly, C, Caesious, Cafard, Cambridge, Cantab, Celeste, Cerulean, City, Clair de lune, Classic, Cobalt, Coomassie, Copenhagen, Cornflower, Country, Coventry, Cyan, Danish, Danube, Dejected, Dirty, Disconsolate, Doldrums, → **DOWN**, Duck-egg, Eatanswill, Eggshell, Electric, Facetiae, Firmament, Fritter, Gentian, Germander, Glaucous, Glum, Hauyne, Heliotrope, Hump, Indecent, Indigo, Indol(e), Iron, Isatin(e), Lapis lazuli, Lavender, Lewd, Lionel, Low, Mazarine, Methylene, Midnight, Monastral®, Mope, Morose, Murder, Nattier, Naughty, Navy, Nile, Obscene, Ocean, Off-colour, Oxford, Peacock, Periwinkle, Perse, Petrol, Phycocyan, Porn, Powder, Prussian, Rabbi, Ribald, Riband, Right, Ripe, Robin's egg, Royal, Sad, Sapphire, Saxe, Saxon(y), Scurrilous, → **SEA**, Shocking, Sky, Slate, Smalt(o), Smutty, Sordid, Spirit, Splurge, Squander, Stafford, Steel, Stocking, Teal, Thenard's, Tony, Tory, Trist, True, Trypan, Turnbull's, Turquoise, Ultramarine, Unhappy, Urban, Verditer, Washing,

Watchet, Wedgwood®, Welkin, Woad, Zaffer, Zaffre

▷ **Blue** *may indicate* an anagram

Bluebell Blawort, Blewart, Campanula, Harebell

Bluebottle Blawort, Blewart, Blowfly, Blowie, Brommer, Brummer, Cop, Cornflower, Fly, Policeman

▶ **Blue-legged** *see* BLUESTOCKING

Blueprint Cyanotype, Draft, Drawing, Plan, Recipe

Bluestocking, Blue-legged Basbleu, Carter, Erudite, Femme savante, Hamburg(h), Mrs Montagu, Précieuse, Sheba

Bluff(ing) Blunt, Cle(e)ve, Cliff, Clift, Crag, Fake, Flannel, Four-flush, Frank, Hal, Headland, Height, Hoodwink, Kidology, Pose, Precipice, Steep, Trick

Blunder(er), Blundering Barry (Crocker), Betise, Bévue, Bish, Bloomer, Blooper, Boob, Break, Bull, Bumble, Clanger, Clinker, Cock-up, Err, Faux pas, Floater, Flub, Fluff, Gaff(e), Goof, Howler, Inexactitude, Irish, Josser, Malapropism, → MISTAKE, Muddle, Mumpsimus, Slip, Solecism, Stumble, Trip

Blunt(ed), Bluntly Abrupt, Alleviate, Bald, Bate, Bayt, Brash, Brusque, Candid, Deaden, Disedge, Downright, Forthright, Frank, Hebetate, Mole, Morned, Obtund, Obtuse, Outspoken, Pointblank, Rebate, Retund, Retuse, Roundly, Snub, Straight-out, Stubby

Blur(red), Blurring Cloud, Confuse, Fog, Fuzz, Halation, Mackle, Macule, Muzzy, Pixilation, → SMUDGE, Stump, Tortillon

Blurb Ad, Puff

Blush(ing) Colour, Cramoisy, Crimson, Erubescent, Erythema, Incarnadine, Mantle, → REDDEN, Rouge, Rubescent, Ruby, Rufescent, Rutilant

Bluster(ing), Blusterer, Blustery Arrogance, Bellow, Blore, Brag, Hector, Rage, Rant, Rodomontade, Roister, Sabre-rattler, Squash, Swagger, Vapour, Windbag, Wuthering

Boar Barrow, Calydonian, Erymanthian, Hog, Pentheus, Sanglier, Sounder, Tusker, Wild

Board(s), Boarding Abat-voix, Admiralty, Aquaplane, Baffle, Banker, Barge, Beaver, Billet, Bristol, Bulletin, Catchment, Centre, Cheese, Chevron, Circuit, Collegium, Committee, Contignation, Counter, Cribbage, Dagger, Dart, Daughter, Deal, Directors, Diving, Draft, Draining, Drawing, Embark, Embus, Emery, Enter, Entrain, Fare, Fascia, Featheredge, Fibro, Fibrolite®, Flannelgraph, Full, Gib(raltar), Gutter, Hack, Half, Half-royal, Hawk, Hoarding, Idiot, Instrument, Insulating, Ironing, Kip, Lag, Leader, Ledger, Lodge, Magnetic, Malibu, Masonite®, Match, Message, Mill, Monkey, Mortar, Moulding, Notice, Otter, Ouija, Palette, Pallet, Panel, Parochial, Particle, Patch, Pedal, Peg(board), Pension, Planch(ette), Plank, Plug, Ply(wood), Punch, Quango, Ribbon-strip, Roof, Running, Sandwich, Sarking, Scale, Scaleboard, School, Score, Screen, Sheathing, Shelf, Shifting, Shingle, Shooting, Side-table, Sign, Skim, Skirting, Sleeve, Snow, Sounding, Splasher, Spring, Stage, Strickle, Stringboard, Supervisory, Surf, Switch, → TABLE, Telegraph, Thatch, Theatre, Trencher, Verge, Wainscot, Wobble, Wokka, Wood chip

▷ **Board** *may refer to* chess or draughts

Boarder Interne, Pensioner, PG, Roomer

Boarding house Digs, Kip, Lodgings, Pension

Boast(er), Boastful, Boasting Big-note, Blew, Blow, Blowhard, Bluster, Bobadil, Bounce, Brag, Braggadocio, Breeze, Bull, Cock-a-hoop, Crake, Crow, Fanfaronade, Gas, Gascon(nade), Glory, Hot air, Jact(it)ation, Line, Ostent(atious), Prate, Rodomontade, Scaramouch, Skite, Swagger, Swank, Tall, Thrasonic, Vainglory, Vapour, Vaunt, Yelp

Boat Ark, Barge, Bark, Bawley, Billyboy, Black skipjack, Canal, Cat, Clinker-built, Coaster, Cock, Codder, Corvette, Cott, Cruiser, Curragh, Cutter, Double scull, Dragon, Eight, Flagship, Flatboat, Fly(ing), Fore-and-after, Four, Foyboat, Goldie, Gravy, Gulet, Hatch, Hooker, Hydroplane, Isis, Jolly, Keel, Kit, Lapstrake, Lap streak, Launch, Liberty, Long, Lymphad, Mackinaw, Monkey, Monohull, Mosquito, Motor, Narrow, Outrigger, Pair-oar, Pedalo, Pont, Privateer, PT, Pucan, Puffer, Pulwar, Q, Revenue cutter, Sailer, Sauce, Scooter, Sculler, Sea Dog®, Shallop, She, → SHIP, Sidewheeler, Skiff, Slogger, Smack, Stake, Sternwheeler, Swing, Tangle-netter, Tanker, Tender, Tilt, Torpid, Trek-ox, Vaporetto, Vedette, → VESSEL, Vidette, Wager, Weekender, Whiff

Boater → HAT, Punter, Straw

Boatman Bargee, Charon, Cockswain, Coxswain, George, Gondolier, Harris, Hoveller, Phaon, Voyageur, Waterman, Wet-bob

Boat population Tank(i)a

Boat-shaped Carina, Scaphoid

Boatswain Bosun, Serang, Smee

Bob Acres, Beck, Curtsey, Deaner, Dip, Dock, Dop, Duck, Float, Hod, Hog, Jerk, Major, Maximus, Minor, Page-boy, Peal, Plain, Plumb, Plummet, Popple, Rob, Royal, S, Shingle, Skip, Sled(ge), Sleigh

Bobbin Quill, Reel, Shuttle, Spindle, Spool

Bobble Pompom

Bobby Bluebottle, Busy, Copper, Flatfoot, Patrolman, Peeler, Pig, → POLICEMAN

Bobby-dazzler Dinger, Stunner

Bock Stein

Bode Augur

Bodice Basque, Bolero, Bustier, Chemise, Chemisette, Choli, Corsage, Gilet, Halter, Jirkinet, Liberty, Plastron, Polonie, Polony, Spencer, Tucker, Watteau

Bodkin Eyeleteer, Needle, Poniard, Stilet(to)

Body, Bodies, Bodily Administration, Amount, Anatomic, Astral, Barr, Board, Bouk, Buik, Buke, Bulk, Cadaver, Cadre, Carcase, Carcass, Carnal, Caucas, Centrosome, Chapel, Chapter, Chassis, Chondriosome, Ciliary, Clay, Coachwork, Coccolite, Cohort, Column, Comet, Committee, Contingent, Cormus, Corpor(e)al, Corps, Corpse, Corpus, Corse, Cytode, Detail, Earth, Elaiosome, Flesh, Food, Frame, Fuselage, Gazo(o)n, Golgi, Goner, Grey, → GROUP, Heavenly, Hull, Immune, Incarnate, Inclusion, Kenning, Ketone, Lewy, Lich, Lifting, Like, Lithites, Malpighian, → MASS, Militia, Mitochondrion, Moit, Mote, Mummy, Nacelle, Nucleole, Nucleolus, Olivary, Ore, Pack, Personal, Phalanx, Pineal, Plant, Platelet, Platoon, Polar, Politic, Posse, Purview, Quango, Relic(t), Remains, Review, Ruck, Satellite, Senate, Solid, Soma, Soredium, Sound-box, Soyle, Spinar, Spore, Squadron, Square, Staff, Statoblast, Stiff, Syndicate, Tagma, Testis, Thallus, Torse, Torso, Trunk, Turm, Ulema, Vitreous, Wolffian, X

▷ **Body** *may indicate an anagram*

Body builder Steroid

Bodyguard Amulet, → ESCORT, Gentleman-at-arms, House-carl, Minder, Praetorian, Protector, Retinue, Schutzstaffel, → SHIELD, SS, Triggerman, Varangian, Yeomen

Body segment Arthromere, Genome, Metamere

Boer Afrikaner, Kruger, Van der Merwe

Boffin Brain

Bog(gy) Allen, Blanket, Can, Carr, Clabber, Fen, Gents, Glaur, Hag, Lair, Latrine, Letch, Loo, Machair, Marish, Marsh, Merse, Mire, Moory, Morass, Moss(-flow),

Mud, Muskeg, Peat, Petary, Quag, Raised, Serbonian, Slack, Slade, Slough, Spew, Spouty, Stodge, Sump, Vlei, Washroom, WC, Yarfa, Yarpha

Bog(e)y Boggart, Bug(aboo), Bugbear, Chimera, Colonel, Eagle, Mumbo jumbo, Nis(se), Par, Poker, Rawhead, Scarer, Spectre, Troll

Boggle Astonish, Bungle, Demur, Hesitate, Perplex, Shy

Bog-trotter Tory

Bogus Assumed, Counterfeit, Fake, False, Histrionic, Phoney, → **SHAM**, Snide, Snobbish, Spoof, Spurious

Bohemian Arty, Beatnik, Demi-monde, Gypsy, Hippy, Hussite, Mimi, Offbeat, Taborite, Trustafarian

Boil(er), Boiled, Boiling (point) Angry, Anthrax, Blain, Botch, Brew, Bubble, C, Carbuncle, Coction, Cook, Cree, Dartre, Decoct, Ebullient, Foam, Furuncle, Gathering, Hen, Herpes, Kettle, Leep, Ligroin, Pimple, Pinswell, Poach, Poule, Rage, Reflux, Samovar, Seethe, Simmer, Sod, Sore, Steam, Stew, Stye, Tea-kettle, Water tube

Boisterous Gilp(e)y, Goustrous, Gusty, Hoo, Knockabout, Noisy, Rambunctious, Randy, Riotous, Rorty, Rough, Stormy, Strepitoso, Termagant, Turbulent, Wild

Bold(ly), Boldness Assumptive, Brash, Brass, Bravado, Bravery, Bravura, Brazen, Brussen, Caleb, Crust, Daredevil, Defiant, Derring-do, Diastaltic, Familiar, Free, Gallus, Hardihood, Heroics, High-spirited, Impudent, Intrepid, Malapert, Mature, Outspoken, Parrhesia, Pert, Plucky, Presumptive, Rash, Risoluto, Sassy, Temerity, Unshrinking

Bole Stem, Trunk

Bolivar Liberator

Bollard Cone, Kevel

Bolshevik, Bolshie Communist, Maximalist, Rebel, Soviet

Bolster Cushion, Dutch wife, Pillow, → **PROP**

Bolt Arrow, Captive, Carriage, Coach, Cuphead, Dash, Dead, Eat, Elope, Expansion, Explosive, Fish, Flee, Gobble, Gollop, Gorge, Gulp, Latch, Levant, Levin, Lightning, Lock, Machine, Missile, Panic, Pig, Pintle, Ragbolt, Rivet, Roll, Scoff, Slot, Snib, Sperre, Stud, Tap, Through, Thunder, Toggle, U, Wing, Wolf, Wring

Bolus Ball

Bomb(ed), Bomber, Bombing Atom, Attack, B, Blitz, Blockbuster, Borer, Buzz, Candle, Car, Carpet, Cluster, Cobalt, Daisycutter, Depth charge, Deterrent, Dirty, Doodlebug, Drogue, Egg, Fission, Flop, Flying, Fragmentation, Fusion, Glide, Greek fire, Grenade, H, Harris, Homicide, Hydrogen, Lancaster, Land-mine, Letter, Liberator, Loft, Logic, Mail, Megaton, Millennium, Mills, Minnie, Mint, Molotov cocktail, Mortar, Nail, Napalm, Necklace, Neutron, Nuclear, Nuke, Packet, Parcel, Petar, Petard, Petrol, Pineapple, Pipe, Plaster, Plastic, Prang, Precision, Radium, Ransom, Robot, Sex, Shell, Skip, Smart, Smoke, Sneak-raid, Stealth, Stick, Stink, Stratofortress, Stuka, Suicide, Tactical, Terrorist, Thermonuclear, Time, Torpedo, Turkey, V1, Volcanic, Walleye

Bombard(ment) Attack, Battery, Blitz, Cannonade, Drum-fire, Mortar, Pelt, Shell, Stone, Stonk, Strafe, Straff

Bombardon Tuba

Bombast(ic) Euphuism, Fustian, Grandiose, Hot air, Magniloquence, Orotund, Pomp, Rant, Timid, Tumid, Turgent

Bombay Nasik

Bombay duck Bum(m)alo

▶ **Bomber** see **BOMB**

Bona fide Echt, Genuine

Bonanza Luck, Windfall
Bonaparte Boney, → NAPOLEON, Plon-plon
Bond(s), Bondage, Bondsman Adhesive, Affinity, Agent, Assignat, Baby, Bail, Bearer, Cedula, Cement, Chain, Chemical, Compact, Connect, Consols, Coordinate, Copula, Corporate, Covalent, Covenant, Daimyo, Dative, Debenture, Deep-discount, Double, Duty, Electrovalent, English, Ernie, Escrow, Esne, Fetter, Fleming, Flemish, Geasa, Gilt, Grammy, Granny, Heart, Herringbone, Hydrogen, Hyphen, Income, Investment, Ionic, James, Junk, Knot, Liaise, Ligament, Link(age), Long, Manacle, Managed, Metallic, Mortar, Municipal, Nexus, Noose, Pair, Peptide, Performance, → PLEDGE, Post-obit, Premium, Property, Rapport, Recognisance, Relationship, Revenue, Running, Samurai, Security, Semipolar, Serf, Servitude, Shackle, Shogun, Single, Singlet, Slave, Solder, Stacked, Starr, Superglue, Surety, Thete, Thral(l)dom, Three-per-cent, → TIE, Treasury, Triple, Valence, Valency, Vassal, Vinculum, Yearling, Yoke, Zebra
Bone(s), Bony Acromion, Anableps, Angular, Apatite, Astragalus, Atlas, Axis, Baculum, Calcaneus, Caluarium, Cannon, Capitate, Capitellum, Carina, Carpel, Carpus, Cartilage, Catacomb, Centrum, Chine, Clavicle, Cly, Coccyx, Coffin, Columella, Concha, Condyle, Coracoid, Coral, Costa, Coxa, Crane, Cranium, Cuboid, Cuneiform, Cuttlefish, Dentary, Diaphysis, Dib, Dice, Diploe, Dolos, Endosteal, Ethmoid, Femur, Fetter, Fibula, Fillet, Frontal, Funny, Ganoid, Gaunt, Hamate, Haunch, Hause-bane, Horn, Humerus, Hyoid, Ilium, Incus, Innominate, Interclavicle, Involucrum, Ischium, Ivory, Jugal, Kneecap, Knuckle, Lacrimal, Lamella, Luez, Lunate, Luz, Malar, Malleolus, Malleus, Mandible, Manubrium, Marrow, Mastoid, Maxilla, Medulla, Membrane, Metacarpal, Metatarsal, Napier's, Nasal, Navicular, Occipital, Olecranon, Omoplate, Orthopaedics, Os, Ossicle, Palatine, Parasphenoid, Parietal, Patella, Pecten, Pectoral, Pedal, Pelvis, Pen, Percoid, Perone, Petrous, Phalanx, Pisiform, Ploughshare, Premaxilla, Pubis, Pygostyle, Quadrate, Rachial, Rack, Radialia, Radius, Relic, Rib, Rump-post, Sacrum, Scaphoid, Scapula, Sclere, Sepium, Sequestrum, Sesamoid, Share, Skeleton, Skull, Sphenoid, Splint, Splinter, Spur, Squamosal, Stapes, → STEAL, Sternebra, Sternum, Stifle, Stirrup, Suboperculum, T, Talus, Tarsus, Temporal, Tibia, Tibiotarsus, Tot, Trapezium, Triquetral, Trochanter, Trochlea, True-rib, Tympanic, Ulna, Vertebrae, Vomer, Whirl, Wish, Wormian, Zygomatic
Bone-head Capitellum, Capitulum
Bonehouse Ossuary
Boneshaker Dandy-horse, Draisene, Draisine
Bonfire Bale-fire, Beltane, Blaze, Chumping, Clavie, Feu de joie, Pyre
Boniface Inn-keeper, Landlord, Taverner
Bonne-bouche Cate
Bonnet Balmoral, Bongrace, Cap, Cornette, Cowl, Easter, Glengarry, Hood, Hummel, Hummle, Kiss-me, Mobcap, Mutch, Poke, Scotch, Sun, Toorie, War
Bonny Blithe, Gay, Merry, Sonsy, Weelfar'd
Bonsai Saikei
Bonus Bisque, Bounty, Braata, Bye, Christmas box, Danger money, Dividend, Escalator, Extra, Hand-out, Lagniappe, No-claim, → PREMIUM, Reversionary, Reward, Scrip, Spin-off, Windfall
Boob Gaffe, Nork, Simpleton, Stumer
Booby Dunce, Hick, Patch, Patchcocke, Patchoke, → STUPID
Boojum Snark
Book(s), Bookish, Bookwork Academic, Album, Antilegomena, Antiphonary, Appointment, Audio, B, Backlist, Bedside, Bestiary, Bestseller, Black, Block, Blotter,

Blue, Cash, Chrestomathy, Classic, Closed, Coffee-table, Diary, Digest, Directory, Diurnal, Ench(e)iridion, Engage, Enter, Erudite, Exercise, Facetiae, Folio, Good, Gradual, Gradus, Guide, Hardback, Hymnal, Imprint, Issue, Lectionary, Ledger, Lib, Liber, Literary, Manual, Memorandum, Missal, Monograph, Muster, Octavo, Octodecimo, Office, Open, Order, Page-turner, Paperback, Pass, Pedantic, Phrase, Pica, Plug, Polyglot, Potboiler, Pseudepigrapha, Publication, Quair, Quarto, Quire, → **RESERVE**, Road, Script, Sext, Sexto, Sextodecimo, Sixmo, Sixteenmo, Sketch, Softback, Spelling, Spine-chiller, Statute, Studious, Study, Style, Swatch, Symbolical, Table, Tablet, Talking, Text(ual), Thriller, Title, Titule, Tome, Trade, Transfer, Twelvemo, Unputdownable, Visiting, Visitor's, Vol(ume), Waste, White, Work, Year

---

BOOKS

2 letters:
NT
OT

3 letters:
Dan
Eph
Gal
Hab
Hag
Jud
Lam
Log
Rag
Red
Rom
Sir
Sus

4 letters:
Acts
Amos
Edda
Ezek
Ezra
Joel
John
Jude
Luke
Macc
Mark
Mook
Obad
Veda

5 letters:
Atlas

Bible
Chron
Hosea
Kells
Kings
Manga
Micah
Nahum
Pop-up
Snobs
Sutra
To-bit

6 letters:
Aeneid
Baruch
Caxton
Course
Daniel
Eccles
Esdras
Esther
Exeter
Exodus
Haggai
Herbal
I Ching
Isaiah
Jashar
Jasher
Joshua
Judges
Prayer
Primer
Prompt
Psalms
Ration

Reader
Romans
Scroll
Tanach

7 letters:
Chumash
Cookery
Ezekiel
Genesis
Grolier
Malachi
Martyrs
Matthew
Numbers
Obadiah
Octapla
Omnibus
Orarium
Ordinal
Psalter
Susanna
Timothy

8 letters:
Breviary
Clarissa
Domesday
Doomsday
Georgics
Grimoire
Habakkuk
Haggadah
Haggadoh
Hermetic
Libretto
Megillah

Ordinary
Philemon
Porteous
Portesse
Prophets
Proverbs
Triodion
Vercelli
Vesperal

9 letters:
Apocrypha
Ephesians
Formulary
Galatians
Gazetteer
Kama Sutra
Leviticus
Maccabees
Portolano
Reference
Remainder
Satyricon
Sibylline
Sybilline
Telephone
Tripitaka
Vade-mecum
Zephadiah

10 letters:
Apocalypse
Chronicles
Compendium
Cyclopedia
Dictionary
Heptameron

Heptateuch
Hitopadesa
Incunabula
Passionary
Persuasion
Teratology

11 letters:
Commonplace

Concordance
Corinthians
Deuteronomy
Evangeliary
Hagiographa
Nomenclator
Philippians
Revelations

12 letters:
Bodice-ripper
Ecclesiastes
Encyclopedia
Lamentations
Panchatantra
Paralipomena
Processional
Responsorial

Twelve Tables

13 letters:
Penny dreadful
Pharmacopoeia
Thessalonians

Bookbinder, Bookbinding Fanfare, Grolier, Mutton-thumper, Organdie
Book-case Credenza, Press, Satchel
Bookie(s), Bookmaker Binder, John, Layer, Librettist, Luke, Mark, Matthew, Printer, Ringman, To-bit
Booking Reservation
Bookkeeper, Bookkeeping Clerk, Double entry, Librarian, Posting, Recorder, Satchel, Single-entry
Booklet B, Brochure, Folder
Book-like Solander
Book-lover Incunabulist
Bookmark Flag, Tassel
Book-scorpion Chelifer
Bookseller Bibliopole, Colporteur, Conger, Sibyl, Stallman
Bookworm Sap, Scholar
Boom(ing) Baby, Beam, Boost, Bowsprit, Bump, Fishpole, Increase, Jib, Orotund, Prosper, Resound, Roar, Sonic, Spar, Supersonic, Swinging, Thrive, Torpedo, Wishbone
Boomer Bittern, Bull-of-the-bog, Butter-bump, Kangaroo, Mire-drum
Boomerang Backfire, Kiley, Kyley, Kylie, Recoil, Ricochet, Throwstick, Woomera
Boon Bene, Benefit, Blessing, Bounty, Cumshaw, Gift, Godsend, Mills, Mitzvah, Prayer, Windfall
Boor(ish) Borel, Bosthoon, Chuffy, Churl, Clodhopper, Crass, Goth, Grobian, Hog, Ill-bred, Jack, Keelie, Kern(e), Kernish, Kill-courtesy, Lob, Lout, Lumpen, Ocker, Peasant, Philistine, Trog, Uncouth, Yahoo, Yob, Yokel
Boost(er) Adrenalin, Afterburner, Bolster, Ego, Encourage, Fillip, Help, Hoist, Impetus, Increase, Injection, Lift, Promote, Raise, Rap, Reheat, Reinforce, Reinvigorate, Spike, Step up, Supercharge, Tonic, Wrap
Boot(s) Addition, Adelaide, Ankle-jack, Avail, Balmoral, Beetle-crushers, Benefit, Blucher, Bottine, Bovver, Brogan, Brogue, Buskin, Cerne, Chukka, Cockers, Cold, Combat, Concern, Cothurn(us), Cowboy, Cracowe, Crowboot, Denver, Derby, Desert, Dismiss, Field, Finn(e)sko, Finsko, Fire, Football, Galage, Galosh, Gambado, Go-go, Granny, Gum, Heave-ho, Hessian, High shoe, Hip, Jack, Jemima, Jodhpur, Kamik, Kletterschuh, Lace-up, Larrigan, Last, Mitten, Moon, Muchie, Muc(k)luc(k), Mukluk, Pac, Para, Profit, Riding, Rock, Russian, Sabot, → SACK, Seven league, → SHOE, Surgical, Thigh, Toe, Tonneau, Tops, Trunk, Ugh, Vibram®, Vibs, Wader, Warm, Weller, Wellie, Wellington, Welly
Booth Assassin, Crame, Kiosk, Polling, Stall, Stand, Telephone, Voting
Bootlegger Cooper, Coper, Runner
Bootless Futile, Idle, Unprofitable, Vain
Booty Creach, Creagh, Haul, Loot, Prey, Prize, Spoil(s), Spolia optima, Swag
Booze(r) → DRINK, Liquor, Pub, Spree, Tipple

Borage Bugloss, Comfrey, Gromwell, Myosote
Borax Tincal
Border(s), Borderland, Borderline Abut, Adjoin, Apron, Bed, Bind, Bound, Boundary, Braid, Checkpoint, Coast, Cot(t)ise, Dado, Dentelle, → **EDGE**, Engrail, Fimbria, Frieze, Fringe, Frontier, Furbelow, Guilloche, Head-rig, Hedgerow, Hem, Herbaceous, Impale, Kerb, Lambrequin, Limb, Limbate, Limbo, Limen, Limes, Limit, Limitrophe, Lip, List, March, Marchland, → **MARGIN**, Mat, Mattoid, Meith, Mete, Mount, Neighbour, Orle, Pand, Pelmet, Penumbra, Perimeter, Purfle, Purlieu, Rand, Rim, Roadside, Roon, Royne, Rubicon, Rund, Rymme, Scottish, Selvage, Selvedge, Side, Skirt, Skirting, Strand, Strip, Surround, Swage, The Marches, Trench, Tressure, Valance, Valence, → **VERGE**
▷ **Borders** *may indicate* first and last letters
Bore(d), Boredom, Borer, Boring Aiguille, Airshaft, Anobium, Anorak, Apathy, Aspergillum, Aspergillus, Aspersoir, Auger, Awl, Beetle, Bind, Bit, Broach, Brog, Bromide, Calibre, Chokebore, Deadly, Drag, → **DRILL**, Dry, Dusty, Dweeb, Eagre, Eat, Eger, Elshin, Elsin, Endured, Ennui, Ennuye, Foozle, Gim(b)let, Gouge, Gribble, Grind, Had, Heigh-ho, Ho-hum, Irk, Jumper, Land, Listless, Longicorn, Longueur, Miser, Mole, Nerd, Noyance, Nudni(c)k, Nuisance, Nyaff, Operose, Pain, Pall, Penetrate, Perforate, Pest, Pholas, Pierce, Pill, Platitude, Probe, Prosaic, Prosy, Punch, Ream(ingbit), Rime, Saddo, Sat, Schmoe, Scolytus, Screw, Severn, Shothole, Snooze, Snore, Sondage, Spleen, Spod, Spudding-un, Sting, Stob, Stupid, Tediosity, Tedious, Tedisome, Tedium, Tedy, Terebra, Teredo, Termes, Termite, Thirl, Tire, Trepan, Trocar, Tunnel, Turn-off, → **WEARY**, Well, Wimble, Windbag, Wonk, Woodworm, Workaday, Worldweary, Xylophaga, Yawn
Borgia Cesare, Lucretia
Boric Sassolin, Sassolite
Born B, Free, Great, Nascent, Nat(us), Né(e)
Borneo Kalimantan
Boron B
Borough Borgo, Close, Pocket, Port, Quarter, Rotten, Township, Wick
Borrow(ed), Borrowing Adopt, Appropriate, Cadge, Copy, Derivative, Eclectic, George, Hum, Leverage, Scunge, Straunge, → **TAKE**, Touch
Bosh Humbug, Nonsense, Rot
Bosom Abraham's, Breast, Bristols, Close, Gremial, Inarm, Intimate, Poitrine
Boson Gauge, Squark
Boss(ed), Bossy Big White Chief, Blooper, Burr, Cacique, Director, Dominate, Domineer, Gadroon, Governor, Headman, Honcho, Hump, Inian, Inion, Jewel, Knob, Knop, Knot, Leader, Maestro, → **MANAGER**, Massa, → **MISTAKE**, Mistress, Netsuke, Noop, Nose-led, Omphalos, Oubaas, Overlord, Overseer, Owner, Pannikin, Pellet, Protuberance, Ruler, Run, Sherang, Straw, Stud, Superintendent, Supremo, Taskmaster, Umbo(nate)
Boston Hub
Bot Oestrus
Botany, Botanist Banks, Bryology, Candolle, Carpology, Cockayne, Dendrologist, Frees, Garden, Godet, Graminology, Herbist, Linnaeus, Mendel, Phytogenesis, Phytology, Pteridology, Tradescant, Weigel
Botch(ed) Bungle, Clamper, Cock-up, Flub, Fudge, Mismanage, Pig's ear, Spoil, Tink
Both Together, Two
Bother(some) Ado, Aggro, Brush, Care, Deave, Deeve, Disturb, Drat, Fash, Fluster, Fuss, Get, Hassle, Hector, Incommode, Irk, Irritate, Moither, Nark, Nuisance,

Perturb, Pesky, Pest(er), Pickle, Reke, Todo, → **TROUBLE**

Bottle(s) Ampul(la), Bacbuc, Balthasar, Balthazar, Belshazzar, Borachio, Bundle, Carafe, Carboy, Chapine, Cock, Cork, Costrel, Courage, Cruet, Cruse, Cucurbital, Cutter, Dead-man, Decanter, Demijohn, Fearlessness, Feeding, Fiasco, Filette, Flacket, Flacon, Flagon, Flask, Glass can, Goatskin, Gourd, Guts, Half-jack, Hen, Imperial, Jeroboam, Junk, Klein, Lachrymal, Lagena, Magnetic, Magnum, Marie-Jeanne, Matrass, Medicine, Melchior, Methuselah, Mettle, Mickey, Middy, Nansen, Nebuchadnezzar, → **NERVE**, Nursing, Phial, Pig, Pilgrim, Pitcher, Pooter, Pycnometer, Rehoboam, Resource, Retort, Salmanaser, Salmanazar, Scent, Screwtop, Siphon, Smelling, Split, Squeeze, Squeezy, Sucking, Tear, Tube, Twenty-sixer, Vial, Vinaigret(te), Wad, Water, Water bouget, Weighing, Winchester, Wine, Woulfe

▷ **Bottle(d)** *may indicate* an anagram or a hidden word

Bottom Anus, Aris, Arse, Ass, Base, Batty, Beauty, Bed, Benthos, Bilge, Booty, Breech, Bum, Butt, Buttocks, Croup(e), Croupon, Demersal, Derrière, Doup, Dowp, End, Fanny, Floor, Foot, Foundation, Fud, Fundus, Haunches, Hunkers, Hurdies, Keel(son), Kick, Lumbar, Nadir, Nates, Planning, Podex, Posterior, Pottle-deep, Prat, Pyramus, Rear, Rock, Root, Rump, Seat, Ship, Sill, Sole, Staddle, Tail, Tush, Weaver

Bottom drawer Glory box

Bottomless Subjacent

Botulism Limberneck

Boudoir Bower, Room

Bouffant Pouf

Bough Branch, Limb

Bought Coft

Boulder Erratic, Gibber, Niggerhead, Rock, → **STONE**

Boule Senate

Bounce(r), Bouncing, Bouncy Bang, Blague, Bound, Caper, Dandle, Dap, Dead-cat, Doorman, Dop, Dud, Eject, Evict, Fib, Jounce, Keepy-uppy, Kite, Lie, Lilt, Resilient, Ricochet, Spiccato, Spring, Stot, Tale, Tamp, Valve, Verve, Vitality, Yorker, Yump

▷ **Bouncing** *may indicate* an anagram

Bound(er), Boundary Adipose, Apprenticed, Articled, Bad, Barrier, Beholden, Border, Bourn(e), Bubalis, Cad, Cavort, Certain, Circumference, Curvet, Decreed, Demarcation, Demarkation, Dool, Dule, Duty, End, Engirt, Entrechat, Erub, Eruv, Event horizon, Exciton, Fence, Four, Frape, Frontier, Galumph, Gambado, Gambol, Girt, Harestane, Hedge, Heel, Held, Hoarstone, Hops, Hourstone, Ibex, Interface, Izard, Jump, Kangaroo, K/T, → **LEAP**, Limes, Limit, Linch, Lollop, Lope, March-stone, Meare, Meer, Meith, Mere, Merestone, Mete, Moho, Muscle, Obliged, Ourebi, Outward, Pale, Parameter, Perimeter, Periphery, Plate, Prance, Precinct, Prometheus, Purlieu, Redound, Ring-fence, Roller, Roo, Roped, Rubicon, Scoup, Scowp, Serf, Side, Sideline, Six(er), Skelp, Skip, Spang, Spring, Sten(d), Stoit, Stylolite, Terminator, T(h)alweg, Tied, Touchline, Upstart, Vault, Verge, Wallaby

▷ **Bounds** *may indicate* outside letters

Bounty, Bountiful Aid, Bligh, Boon, Christian, Generosity, → **GIFT**, Goodness, Grant, Head money, Honorarium, Largess(e), Lavish, Queen Anne's, Queen's

Bouquet Aroma, Attar, Aura, Compliment, Corsage, Fragrancy, Garni, Nose, Nosegay, Perfume, Plaudit, Posy, Scent, Spiritual, Spray

Bourbon Alfonso

Bourgeois(ie) Biedermeier, Common, Middle class, Pleb(eian), Pooter(ish)

Bout Bender, Bust, Contest, Dose, Go, Jag, Match, Spell, Spree, Turn, Venery, Venewe, Venue

Boutique Shop

Bovine Stolid

Bow(ing), Bower, Bowman Alcove, Arbour, Arc, Arch, → **ARCHER**, Arco, Arson, Bandy, Beck, Bend, Boudoir, Butterfly, Clara, Congé(e), Crescent, Crook, Cupid, → **CURVE**, Defer, Dicky, Drail, Droop, Duck, Echelles, Eros, Eugh, Eyes, Fiddle(r), Fiddlestick, Foredeck, Halse, Hawse, Honour, Jook, Jouk, Kneel, Kotow, Laval(l)ière, Lean, Long, Loof, Lout, Lowt, Luff, Martellato, Moulinet, Namaste, Nameste, Nod, Nutate, Obeisance, Obtemper, Paganini, Pergola, Prore, Quarrel, Reverence, Salaam, Seamer, Shelter, Slope, Sound, Spiccato, Stick, → **SUBMIT**, Tie, Torrent, Yew, Yield

Bowdler(ize) Edit(or), Water

Bowels Entrails, Guts, Innards, Viscera

▷ **Bower** *may indicate* using a bow

Bowl(ing), Bowler, Bowl over, Bowls B, Basin, Begging, Bicker, Bocce, Bocci(a), Boccie, Bodyline, Bool, Bosey, Bouncer, Cage-cup, Calabash, Candlepins, Cap, Carpet, Caup, Chalice, Cheese, Chinaman, Christie, Christy, Cog(g)ie, Concave, Coolamon, Crater, Cup, Deliver, Derby, → **DISH**, Dismiss, Dome, Drake, Dumbfound, Dust, Ecuelle, End, Finger, Fivepin, Goldfish, Googly, Grub, Hog, Hoop, Jack, Jeroboam, Jorum, Kegler, Krater, Lavabo, Laver, Leg-spin, Lightweight, Lob, Locke, Mazer, Monteith, Night, Offbreak, Old, Over-arm, Overpitch, Pace, Pan, Pétanque, Piggin, Pitch, Porringer, Pot-hat, Pottinger, Punch, Raku, Rice, Rink, Roll, Roundarm, Seam(er), Skip, Skittle(s), Spare, Speed, Spinner, Spofforth, Stadium, Stagger, Stummel, Sucrier, Super, Ten-pin, Tom, Underarm, Underhand, Underwood, Voce, Wassail, Wood, York(er)

Box(ing) Baignoire, Ballot, Bandbox, Bareknuckle, Bento, Bijou, Bimble, Binnacle, Black, Blue, Bonk, Booth, Buist, Bunk, Bush, Caddy, Call, Camera, Canister, Case, Cash, Casket, Cassolette, Chest, Chinese, Christmas, Ciborium, Clog, Coach, Coffer, Coffin, Coffret, Coin, Confessional, Cool, Crate, Cuff, Dabba, Deed, Dialog(ue), Dispatch, Ditty, Dog, Drawer, Encase, Enclose, → **FIGHT**, File, Fist, Fund, Fuse, Fuzz, Glory, Glove, Go-kart, Grass, Hat, Hay, Hedge, Honesty, Horse, Humidor, Hutch, Ice, Idiot, Inherce, Inro, Inter, Jewel, Journal, Junction, Jury, Keister, Kick, Kiosk, Kite, Knevell, Ladle, Letter, Light, Live, Locker, Lodge, Loge, Loose, Lunch, Match, Message, Mill, Mitre, Mocock, Mocuck, Money, Musical, Nest(ing), Omnibus, Orgone, Package, Packing, Paint, Pandora's, Papeterie, Patch, Pattress, Peepshow, Peg, Penalty, Petara, Pew, Phylactery, Pill, Pillar, Pitara, Pix, Poor, Post, Pounce(t), Powder, Press, Prompt, Protector, Puff, Pugilism, Pyxis, Register, Resonance, Ring, Rope-a-dope, Royal, Saggar(d), Sagger, Sand, Savate, Scent, Scrap, Seggar, Sentry, Set-top, Shadow, Shoe, Shooting, Side, Signal, Skinner, Skip(pet), Slipcase, Smudge, Sneeze, Soap, Solander, Sound, Sound body, → **SPAR**, Spice, Spit, Spring, Squawk, Squeeze, Strong, Stuffing, Swell, Tabernacle, Tee, Tefillin, Telephone, Telly, Thai, Tick, Tin, Tinder, Tool, Touch, Trunk, Tube, Tuck, TV, Urn, Vanity, Vasculum, Vinaigrette, Voice, Weather, Window, Wine, Witness, Yakhdan

Boxer Ali, Amycus, Babyweight, Bantamweight, Bruiser, Bruno, Canine, Carnera, Carpentier, Carthorse, Chinaman, Cooper, Crater, Cruiserweight, Dog, Eryx, Farr, Featherweight, Flyweight, Ham, Heavyweight, Lightweight, McCoy, Middleweight, Mosquito-weight, Pandora, Pollux, Pug, Pugil(ist), Rebellion, Rocky, Shadow, Southpaw, Strawweight, Welterweight, Wilde

Boxing-glove Hurlbat, Muffle, Whirlbat, Whorlbat

Boy(s) Amoretto, Apprentice, Ball, Bevin, Blue-eyed, Breeches, Bub(by), Cabin, Callant, Catamite, Champagne, Chiel(d), → **CHILD**, Chokra, Chummy, Cub, Cupid, Dandiprat, Errant, Galopin, Garçon, Gorsoon, Gossoon, Green Mountain, Groom, Grummet, Ha, Hansel, Jack, Kid, Klonkie, Knave, Knave-bairn, Kwedien, Lackbeard, → **LAD**, Loblolly, Loon(ie), Minstrel, Nibs, Nipper, Office, Page, Poster, Pot, Prentice, Principal, Putto, Rent, Roaring, Rude, Shaver, Ship's, Son, Spalpeen, Sprig, Stripling, Tad, Tar, Ted(dy), Tiger, Toy, Urchin, Whipping, Wide, → **YOUTH**

▷ **Boy** *may indicate* an abbreviated name

Boycott Avoid, Ban, Bat, Black, Blacklist, Exclude, Hartal, Isolate, Ostracise, Shun, Swadeshi

Boyfriend Beau, Date, Fella, Fellow, Steady

Boyle Juno

Bp Bishop, DD, RR

Brace(s), Bracing Accolade, Couple, Crosstree, Fortify, Gallace, Gallows, Gallus(es), Gird, Hound, Invigorate, Ozone, Pair, Pr, Rear-arch, Rere-arch, Sea air, Skeg, Spider, Splint, Steady, Stiffener, Strut, → **SUPPORT**, Suspenders, Tauten, Thorough, Tone, Tonic, Two

Bracelet Armil(la), Armlet, Bangle, Cuff, Darbies, Handcuff, Identity, Manacle, Manilla

Brachiopod Ecardines, Lamp-shell, Spirifer

Bracken Brake, Fern, Pteridium, Tara

Bracket Ancon, Angle-iron, Bibb, Brace, Cantilever, Console, Corbel, Couple, Cripple, Lance rest, Misericord(e), Modillion, Mutule, Parenthesis, Potence, Pylon, Rigger, Sconce, Square, Straddle, Strata, → **STRUT**, Trivet, Truss

Bract Glume(lla), Involucel, Involucre, Leaf, Lemma, Palea, Palet, Phyllary, Spathe

Brad Nail, Pin, Rivet, Sprig

Brag(gart), Bragging Basilisco, Birkie, Bluster, Boast, Bobadil, Boister, Braggadocio, Bull, Cockalorum, Crow, Falstaff, Fanfaronade, Gab, Gascon, Hot-air, Loudmouth, Parolles, Puckfist, Puff, Rodomontader, Skite, Slam, Swagger, Thrason, Thrasonic, Tongue-doubtie, Tongue-doughty, Vainglorious, Vapour, Vaunt

Brahma(n) San(n)yasi(n)

Braid A(i)glet, Aiguillette, Fishbone, French, Frog, Galloon, Lacet, Plait, Plat, Rickrack, Ricrac, Scrambled eggs, Seaming-lace, Sennet, Sennit, Sinnet, Soutache, Tress, Trim, Twist, Weave

Braille (system) Moon

Brain(box), Brains, Brainstorm, Brainy, Brain disease, Brain-power Amygdala, Appestat, Bean, Boffin, Bright, Cerebellum, Cerebrum, Cortex, Diencephalon, Dura mater, Encephalon, Epencephalon, Fornix, Genius, Gyrus, Harn(s), Head, Hippocampus, Hydrocephalus, Hypothalamus, Inspiration, Insula, Intelligence, IQ, Kuru, Left, Limbic, Loaf, Lobe, Mastermind, Mater, Medulla, Medulla oblongata, Metencephalon, Mind, Noddle, Noesis, Nous, Peduncle, Pericranium, Pia mater, Pons, Pontile, Prosencephalon, Rhinencephalon, Rhombencephalon, Sconce, Sense, Sensorium, Striatum, Subcortex, Tapagnosia, Tectum, Telencephalon, Thalamencephalon, Thalamus, Upper stor(e)y, Vermis, Wetware

▷ **Brain(s)** *may indicate* an anagram

Brainless Anencephaly, Bimbo, Stupid, Thick

Brainwash(ing) Indoctrinate, Menticide, Propaganda

Brake, Braking ABS, Adiantum, Aerodynamic, Air, Anchors, Antilock, Bracken, Centrifugal, Curb, Disc, Dive, Drag, Drum, Estate car, Fern, Fly, Foot, Grove, Hand,

Hydraulic, Nemoral, Overrun, Ratchet, Rein, Shoe, Shooting, → **SLOW**, Spinney, Sprag, Tara, Thicket, Vacuum, Westinghouse

Bramble, Brambly Batology, Blackberry, Boysenberry, Brier, Cloudberry, Rubus, Thorn, Wait-a-bit, Youngberry

Bran Cereal, Chesil, Chisel, Oats, Pollard

Branch(ed), Branches, Branching, Branch office Affiliate, Antler, Arm, BO, Bough, Cladode, Cow, Dendron, Dept, Diversify, Diverticulum, Divide, Filiate, Fork, Grain, Jump, Kow, Lateral, Leaf-trace, Limb, Lobe, Loop, Lye, Lylum, Offshoot, Olive, Patulous, Raguly, Ramate, Ramulus, Reis, Rice, Shroud, Special, Spray(ey), Sprig, Spur, Tributary, Turning, Turn-off, Twig, Wattle, Yard

Branch-rib Lierne

Brand Broadsword, Buist, Burn, Cauterise, Chop, Class, Dealer, Denounce, Earmark, Ember, Excalibur, Falchion, Faulchin, Faulchion, Flambeau, Home, Idiograph, Inust, Iron, Label, Line, → **MARK**, Marque, Name, Own, Power, Sear, Sere, Stigma, Sweard, Sword, Torch, Wipe

Brandish Bless, Flaunt, Flourish, Hurtle, Waffle, Wampish, Wave

Brandy Aguardiente, Applejack, Apricot, Aqua vitae, Armagnac, Bingo, Calvados, Cape smoke, Cold without, Dop, Eau de vie, Fine, Framboise, Grappa, Mampoer, Marc, Mobbie, Mobby, Nantes, Nantz, Napoleon, Palinka, Peach, Quetsch, Slivovic(a), Slivovitz, Smoke

Bras Arms

Brash Cocky, Flashy, Impudent, Jack-the-lad, Jumped-up, Pushy, Rain, Rash

Brass(y), Brassware Alpha-beta, Benares, Brazen, Cheek, Club, Corinthian, Cornet, Dinanderie, Face, Front, Harsh, High, Horn, Horse, Latten, Lip, Loot, Lota(h), Loud, Matrix, → **MONEY**, Moola(h), Oof, Oricalche, Orichalc, Pyrites, Sass, Snash, Sopranino, Talus, Top, Trombone, Wood

Brassard Armlet

Brass hat Brig

Brassica Brussels (sprout), → **CABBAGE**, Colza, Turnip

Brassière Gay deceiver

Brat Bairn, Bra(t)chet, Enfant terrible, Gait(t), Gamin, Geit, Get, Git, Gyte, Imp, Lad, Terror, Urchin

Brave(ry) Amerind, Apache, Bold, Conan, Corragio, Courage, Creek, Dare, → **DEFY**, Doughty, Dress, Face, Fearless, Gallant, Game, Gamy, Gutsy, Hardy, Heroism, Indian, Injun, Intrepid, Lion, Lion-hearted, Manful, Manly, → **MEXICAN**, Nannup, → **NORTH AMERICAN**, Plucky, Prow(ess), Sannup, Skookum, → **SOUTH AMERICAN**, Spunk, Stout, Uncas, Valiant, Valour, Wight

Bravo Acclaim, B, Bandit, Bully, Desperado, Euge, Murderer, Olé, Shabash, Spadassin, Villain

Brawl(er) Affray, Bagarre, Bicker, Brabble, Donnybrook, Dust, Fight, Flite, Flyte, Fracas, Fratch, Fray, Melee, Prawl, Rammy, Roarer, Roughhouse, Row, Scuffle, Set-to, Shindig, Stoush, Tar, Wrangle

Brawn Beef, Burliness, Headcheese, He-man, Might, Muscle, Power, Rillettes, Sinew

Bray Cry, Heehaw, Stamp, Vicar, Whinny

Brazen Bold, Brassy, Flagrant, Impudent, Shameless, Unabashed

Brazier Brasero, Fire, Hibachi, Mangal, Scaldino

Brazil(ian) Caboclo, Carioca, Para, Yanomami, Yanomamo

Breach Assault, Break, Chasm, Cleft, Gap(e), Great schism, Infraction, Redan, Rupture, Saltus, Schism, Solecism, Solution, Trespass, Violate

Bread, Bread crumbs Afrikomen, Azym(e), Bagel, Baguette, Bannock, Bap,

Barmbrack, Barm cake, Batch, Baton, Brewis, Brioche, Brownie, Bun, Cash, Chal(l)ah, Chametz, Chapati, Cheat, Ciabatta, Cob, Coburg, Corn, Corsned, Croissant, Crostini, Croute, Crouton, Crumpet, Crust, Currency, Damper, Dibs, Dika, Doorstep, Elephant's-foot, Eulogia, Fancy, Flatbread, Focaccia, French, Garlic, Gluten, Graham, Granary, Grissini, Guarana, Hallah, Hametz, Hometz, Horse, Host, Indian, Injera, Jannock, Johnny-cake, Kaffir, Laver, Lavish, Leavened, Loaf, Long tin, Manchet, Maori, Milk-sop, → **MONEY**, Monkey, Na(a)n, Pain, Panada, Panary, Pane, Paneity, Paratha, Pikelet, Pit(t)a, Pone, Poori, Poppadom, Poultice, Prozymite, Pumpernickel, Puree, Puri, Raspings, Ravel, Roll, Rooty, Roti, Round, Rusk, Rye, Sally Lunn, Schnecken, Shewbread, Shive, Simnel, Sippet, Smor(re)brod, Soda, Soft-tommy, Sop, Sourdough, Staff of life, Standard, Stollen, Stottie, Sugar, Sweet, Tartine, Tea, Tommy, Tortoise-plant, Twist, Wastel, Wrap, Zakuski, Zwieback

Breadfruit Ja(c)k

Breadwinner Earner, Pa

Break, Break-down, Break-in, Break-up, Broken Adjourn, Apn(o)ea, Aposiopesis, Bait, Breach, Breather, Caesura, Caesure, Cantle, Cark, Cesure, Chinaman, Chip, Cleave, Coffee, Comb, Comma, Commercial, Comminute, Compost, Conk, Crack, Crock, Crumble, Deave, Debacle, Deeve, Demob, Destroy, Diffract, Disband, Disintegrate, Disperse, Disrupt, Erupt, Exeat, Fast, Fault, Four, → **FRACTURE**, Fragment, Fritter, Frush, Gaffe, Give, Greenstick, Half-term, Half-time, Hernia, Hiatus, Holiday, Infringe, Interim, Interlude, Intermission, Interrupt, → **INTERVAL**, Irrupt, Kark, Knap, Knickpoint, Lacuna, Lapse, Leave, Lysis, Moratorium, Nickpoint, Nooner, Outage, Part, Pause, Phreak, Playtime, Poach, Polarise, Price, Reave, Recess, Recrudescent, Relief, Rend, Resorption, Respite, Rest, Rift, Ruin, Rupture, Saltus, Schism(a), Secede, Service, Shatter, Shiver, Smash, Smokeho, Smoko, Snap, Split, Stave, Stop, Stop-over, Stove, Sunder, Take five, Take ten, Tame, Tea-ho, Tear, Time-out, Torn, Transgress, Truce, Twist, Vacation, Violate

Breakable Brittle, Delicate, Fissile, Frail, Friable

Breakdown Analyse, Autolysis, Cataclasm, Collapse, Conk, Crack-up, Glitch, Glycolosis, Glycolysis, Histolysis, Hydrolysis, Lyse, Lysis, Nervous, Ruin

Breaker Billow, Circuit, Comber, Ice, Roller, Smasher, Surf

Breakfast B, Brunch, Chota-hazri, Continental, Deskfast, Disjune, English, Kipper, Petit déjeuner, Power, Wedding

Breakneck Headlong

Breakwater Groyne, Jetty, Mole, Pier, Tetrapod

Bream Fish, Porgy, Sar(gus), Sea, Silver, Tai, White

Breast(s), Breastbone, Breastwork Bazuma, Blob, Bosom, Brave, Brisket, Bristols, Bust, Chimney, Counter, Diddy, Duddy, Dug, Falsies, Garbonza, Gazunga, Heart-spoon, Jubbies, Jugs, Knockers, Norg, Nork, Pigeon, Rampart, Redan, Sangar, Stem, Sternum, Sungar, Supreme, Tit, Xiphisternum

Breastplate Armour, Byrnie, Curat, Curiet, Pectoral, Plastron, Rational, Rest, Shield, Thorax, Xiphiplastron

Breath(e), Breathing, Breather Aerobe, Apneusis, Aqualung, Aspirate, Bated, Branchia, Caesural, Cheyne-Stokes, Circular, Cypress-knee, Eupnoea, Exhalation, Expiration, Flatus, Gasp, Gill, H, Halitosis, Hauriant, Haurient, Hobday, Hypernoea, Hyperventilation, Hypopnoea, Inhale, Inspiration, Knee, Lung, Nares, Nostril, Orthopnoea, Oxygenator, Pant, Plosion, Pneuma, Prana, Pulmo, Rale, Respire, Respite, Rest, Rhonchus, Rough, Scuba, Smooth, Snore, Snorkel, Snortmast, Snotter, Snuffle, Spiracle, Spirit, Spiritus, Stertor, Stridor, Tachypnoea,

Vent, Wheeze, Whiff, Whift, Whisper, Whist, Wind, Windpipe

Breathless(ness) Anhelation, Apnoea, Asthma, Dyspnoea, Emphysema, Orthopnoea, Puffed-out, Tachypnoea, Wheezing

Breathtaking Amazing, Asphyxia

Breech(es) Bible, Buckskin, Chaps, Flog, Galligaskins, Hose, Jodhpurs, Kneecords, Knickerbockers, Petticoat, Plushes, Riding, Smallclothes, Smalls, Trews, Trouse(rs), Trunk hose, Trusses

Breed(er), Breeding(-place) Bear, Beget, Cleck, Endogamous, Engender, Engend(r)ure, Eugenics, Fast, Generation, Gentilesse, Gentrice, Hetero, Hotbed, In-and-in, Lineage, → MANNERS, Origin, Panmixia, Procreate, Propagate, Pullulate, Race, Raise, Rear, Seminary, Sire, Species, Stock, Strain, Stud, Telegony, Thremmatology, Tribe, Voltinism

Breeze, Breezy Air, Breath, Brisk, Cakewalk, Catspaw, Chipper, Doctor, Draught, Fresh, Gentle, Gust, Land, Light, Mackerel, Moderate, Sea, Slant, Sniffler, Strong, Tiff, Zephyr

Brethren Bohemian, Darbyite, Elder, Exclusive, Herrnhuter, Kin, Open, Plymouth, Trinity

Breton Armoric, Brezonek

Breve Minim, Note, O

Breviary Portesse, Portous

▸ **Brevity** see **BRIEF**

Brew(ery), Brewer, Brewing Ale, Billycan, Brose, Browst, Bummock, → CONCOCT, Contrive, Dictionary, Distillery, Ferment, Infusion, Liquor, Malt, Percolate, Perk, Potion, Steep, Witches', Yeast, Yill, Zymurgy

Briar Bramble, Canker, Lawyer

Bribe(ry) Backhander, Barratry, Barretry, Bonus, Boodle, Bung, Carrot, Dash, Embracery, Get at, Graft, Grease, Hamper, Hush-money, Insult, Kickback, Oil, Palm, Palm-grease, Palm-oil, Payola, Schmear, Slush, Soap, Sop, Square, Straightener, Suborn, Sweeten(er), Tamper, Tempt, Tenderloin, Vail, Vales

Bric-a-brac Bibelot, Curio, Rattle-trap, Smytrie, Tatt, Virtu

Brick(s), Brickwork Adobe, Air, Bat, Bath, Bonder, Bondstone, Boob, Breeze, Bullnose, Bur(r), Clanger, Clinker, Closer, Course, Dutch clinker, Fletton, Gaffe, Gault, Gold, Hard stocks, Header, Ingot, Klinker, Lateritious, Lego®, Malm, Nogging, Red, Rubber, Soldier, Sport, Stalwart, Stretcher, Terra-cotta, Testaceous, Tile, Trojan, Trump

Brickbat Missile

Bricklayer Churchill

Bride(s) Bartered, Danaides, Ellen, Hen, Spouse, War, Wife, Ximena

Bridesmaid Paranymph

Bridge(head), Bridge player Acol, Air, Al Sirat, Aqueduct, Auction, Avignon, Bailey, Balance, Barre, Bascule, Bestride, Bifrost, Biritch, Board, Bridle-chord, Brig, Brooklyn, Cable-stayed, Cantilever, Capo, Capodastro, Capotasto, Catwalk, Chevalet, Chicago, Chicane, Clapper, Clifton, Contract, Counterpoise, Cross, Cut-throat, Deck, Declarer, Drawbridge, Duplicate, Flying, Flyover, Foot, Four-deal, Gangplank, Gangway, Gantry, Girder, Golden Gate, Hog's back, Humber, Humpback, Humpbacked, Ice, Irish, Jigger, Land, Lattice, Leaf, Lifting, Ligger, Link, London, Menai, Millau, Millennium, Nasion, Overpass, Pivot, Plafond, Ponceau, Ponticello, Pontifice, Pont levis, Pontoon, Raft, Rainbow, Rialto, Rubber, Sighs, Sinvat, Skew, Snow, → SPAN, Spanner, Stamford, Straddle, Suspension, Swing, Tay, Temper, Tête-de-pont, Through, Transporter, Traversing, Trestle, Truss, Turn, Vertical lift, Viaduct, Vint, Waterloo, Weigh, Wheatstone, Wire

Bridge pair EW, NS, SN, WE

Bridge protector Ice-apron

Bridge system Acol

Bridle Bit, Branks, Bridoon, Bristle, Browband, Crownpiece, Curb, Double, Hackamore, Halter, Headstall, Musrol, Noseband, Rein, Scold's

Bridle path Orbit, Track

Brief(s), Briefing, Briefly, Brevity Acquaint, Awhile, Barristerial, Bluette, Brachyology, Breviate, Cape, Compact, → **CONCISE**, Conspectus, Crisp, Curt, Dossier, Fill in, Fleeting, Instruct, Laconic, Nearly, Pants, Pennorth, Pithy, Prime, Scant, → **SHORT(EN)**, Short-term, Short-winded, Sitrep, Sparse, Succinct, Summing, Tanga, Terse, Transient, Undies, Update, Watching

Brig Br, Hermaphrodite, Jail, Nancy Bell, → **SHIP**, Snow

Brigade Boys', Corps, Fire, Fur, Girls', Green-ink, International, Naval, Red, Troop

Brigand Bandit, Bandolero, Cateran, Haidu(c)k, Heiduc, Heyduck, Klepht, Pillager, Pirate, → **ROBBER**, Rob Roy, Trailbaston

Bright, Brightness Afterglow, Alert, Ashine, Bertha, Brainy, Breezy, Brilliant, Brisk, Cheery, Chiarezza, Cla(i)re, Clara, Clear, Clever, Cuthbert, Effulgent, Elaine, Facula, Fair, Floodlit, Florid, Garish, Gay, Glad, Glow, Helen, Hono(u)r, Hubert, Light, Lit, Loud, Lucid, Luculent, Lustre, Net(t), Nit, Nitid, Radiant, Ro(a)ry, Rorie, Rosy, Scintillating, Sematic, Sharp, Sheeny, Sheer, Shere, Skyre, Smart, Spark(y), Stilb, Sunlit, Sunny, Vive, Vivid, White

Bright spot Facula

Brilliant, Brilliance Ace, Aine, Blaze, Brainy, Bravura, Def, Effulgent, Eurian, Flashy, Galaxy, Gay, Gemmy, Gifted, Glossy, High flyer, Inspired, Lambent, Leam, Lucent, Lustre, Mega-, Meteoric, Nitid, Pear, → **RADIANT**, Refulgent, Resplendent, Shiny, Spangle, Splendour, Star, Virtuoso, → **VIVID**, Water

Brim Edge, Lip, Rim, Ugly

Brimstone Hellfire, S, Sulphur

Brindisi Skolion, Toast

Brindled Piebald, Tabby, Tawny

Brine Muriatic, Ozone, Pickle, Saline, Salt

Bring Afferent, Bear, Carry, Cause, Conduct, Convey, Earn, Evoke, Fet, Fetch, Foist, Hatch, Induce, Land, Precipitate, Produce, Wreak

Bring up Breed, Educate, Exhume, Foster, Nurture, Raise, → **REAR**

Brink → **EDGE**, Lip, Rim, Shore, → **VERGE**

Brio Elan

Brisk(ly), Briskness Active, Alacrity, Alert, Allegro, Breezy, Busy, Chipper, Con moto, Crank, Crisp, Crouse, Fresh, Gaillard, Galliard, Jaunty, Kedge, Kedgy, Kidge, Lively, Nippy, Peart, Perk, Pert, Rattling, Roaring, Scherzo, Sharp, Smart, Snappy, Spanking, Spirited, Sprightly, Vivace, Yare, Zippy

Bristle, Bristling, Bristly Aciculum, Arista, Awn, Barb, Bewhiskered, Birse, Bridle, Campodeiform, Chaeta, Flurry, Fraught, Frenulum, Glochidium, Gooseflesh, Hackles, Hair, Hérissé, Hispid, Horrent, Horripilation, Nereid, Polychaete, Seta, Setose, Striga, Strigose, Stubble, Styloid, Vibraculum, Villus, Whisker

Bristle-tail Campodea

Brit Silt

Brit(ish), Briton(s) All-red, Anglo, Herring, Iceni, Insular, Isles, Kipper, Limey, Pict, Pom, Rooinek, Saxon, Silurian, UK

Britain Alban(y), Albion, GB, Old Dart

Britannia, Britannia metal Tutania

Brittany Armorica

Brittle Bruckle, Crackly, Crimp, Crisp, Delicate, → **FRAGILE**, Frush, Hot-short, Redsear, Red-share, Red-shire, Redshort, Shivery, Spall, Spalt

▷ **Brittle** *may indicate* an anagram

Broach Approach, Open, Raise, Spit, Suggest, Tap, Widen

Broad(ly) Crumpet, Dame, Doll, Doxy, Drab, General, Generic, Hippy, Largo, Latitudinous, Loose, Outspoken, Ovate, Pro, Roomy, Spatulate, Tart, Thick, Tolerant, Wide, Woman

Broad-beaked Latirostrate

Broadcast(er), Broadcasting Ad(vertise), Air, Announce, Beam, Breaker, CB, Disperse, Disseminate, Downlink, Emission, Ham, IBA, Monophonic, Multicast, Network, Newscast, OB, On, Outside, Pirate, Programme, Promulgate, Put out, Radiate, Radio, Relay, RTE, Run, Satellite, → **SCATTER**, Scattershot, Screen(ed), SECAM, Seed, Simulcast, Sky, Sow, Sperse, Spread, Sprinkle, Stereophonic, Transmission, Ventilate, Wavelength

Broad-nosed Platyrrhine

Broadside Barrage, Criticism, Salvo, Tire

Broadway Boulevard, Esplanade, Great White Way, Motorway

Brocade Arrasene, Baldachin, Baldaquin, Baudekin, Bawdkin, Kincob, Zari

Brochure Leaflet, Pamphlet, Programme, Tract

Brogue Accent, → **SHOE**

Broke(n) Bankrupt, Bust(ed), Duff, Evans, Fritz, Impoverished, Insolvent, Kaput, On the rocks, Puckeroo, Shattered, Skint, Stony, Stove, Strapped

▷ **Broken** *may indicate* an anagram

Broken off Prerupt

Broker Agent, Banian, Banyan, Go-between, Jobber, Mediator, → **MERCHANT**, Power, Shadchan, Uncle

Bromide Halide, Haloid, Truism

Bromine Br

Bronchitis, Bronchitic Chesty, Husk

Bronte(s) Bell, Cyclops

Brontosaurus Apatosaurus

Bronze, Bronze age Bell, Bras(s), Brown, Eugubine, Gunmetal, Hallstatt(ian), Helladic, Kamakura, Manganese, Minoan, Mycenean, Ormolu, Phosphor, Schillerspar, Sextans, Talos, Tan, Third

Brooch Breastpin, Cameo, Clasp, Fibula, Luckenbooth, Ouch, Owche, Pin, Preen, Prop, Spang, Sunburst

Brood(y) Clock, Clucky, Clutch, Cogitate, Cour, Cover, Covey, Eye, Eyrie, Hatch, Hover, Incubate, Introspect, Kindle, Litter, Meditate, Mill, Mull, Nest, Nid, Perch, Pet, → **PONDER**, Repine, Roost, Sit, Sulk, Team

Brook Abide, Babbling, Becher's, Beck, Branch, Burn, Countenance, Creek, Endure, Ghyll, Gill, Kerith, Kill, Pirl, Purl, Rill(et), River, Rivulet, Runlet, Runnel, Springlet, Stand, Stomach, Stream, Suffer, Tolerate

Broom Besom, Brush, Butcher's, Cow, Cytisus, Genista, Gorse, Greenweed, Knee-holly, Kow, New, Orobranche, Retama, Spart, Sweeper, Whisk

Brose Atholl, Pease

Broth Bouillon, Bree, Brew(is), Cullis, Dashi, Kail, Kale, Muslin-kale, Pot liquor, Pottage, Scotch, Skilly, → **SOUP**, Stock

Brothel Bagnio, Bordel(lo), Cathouse, Corinth, Crib, Den, Flash-house, Honkytonk, Hothouse, Kip, Knocking shop, Red-light, Seraglio, Sporting house, Stew, Vaulting-house

Brother(hood) Ally, Bhai, Billie, Billy, Blood, Boet, Brethren, Bro, Bud, Comrade,

Félibre, Fellow, Fra, Freemason, Lay, → MONK, Moose, Plymouth, Pre-Raphaelite, Sib(ling), Theatine, Trappist, Worker

Brow Crest, Forehead, Glabella, Ridge, Sinciput, Superciliary, Tump-line

Browbeat Badger, Bully, Butt, Cow, Hector, Nut

Brown(ed) Abram, Adust, Amber, Apricate, Auburn, Au gratin, Bay, Biscuit, Bisque, Bister, Bistre, Bole, Br, Braise, Brindle, Bronzed, Brunette, Bruno, Burnet, Burnt umber, Camel, Capability, Caramel, Caromel, Chamois, Cinnamon, Cook, Coromandel, Drab, Dun, Duncan, Fallow, Filemot, Fulvous, Fusc(ous), Grill, Hazel, Infuscate, Ivor, John, Khaki, Liver, March, Meadow, Mocha, Mousy, Mulatto, Mushroom, Nut, Ochre, Olive, Oxblood, Philamot, Rufous, Rugbeian, Russet, Rust, Scorch, Seal, Sepia, Sienna, Snuff, Soare, Sore, Sorrel, Spadiceous, Tan, Tawny, Tenné, Testaceous, Toast, Tom, Umber, Vandyke, Wallflower, Wholemeal, Windsor

Browne Sam

Brownie Dobbie, Dobby, Dobie, Goblin, Hob, Kobold, Leprechaun, Nis(se), Rosebud, Sprite

Browse(r) Graze, Netscape®, Pasture, Read, Scan, Stall-read, Surf

Bruce Robert

Bruise Contund, Contuse, Crush, Damage, Ding, Ecchymosis, Frush, Golp(e), Hurt, Intuse, Livedo, Lividity, Mark, Mouse, Pound, Purpure, Rainbow, Shiner, Ston(n), Stun, Surbate, Vibex

Brummagem Tatty

Brunette Dark, Latin

Brush (off), Brushwood Bavin, Bottle, Brake, Broom, Carbon, Chaparral, Clash, Clothes, Dandy, Dismiss, Dust, Encounter, Fan, Filbert, Filecard, Firth, Fitch, Frith, Grainer, Hag, Hagg, Hair-pencil, Hog, Kiss, Liner, Loofah, Mop, Paint, Pallet, Pig, Pope's head, Putois, Rebuff, Rice, Rigger, Sable, Scrap, Scrub, Scuff, Shaving, Skim, Striper, Thicket, Touch, Whisk, Wire

Brusque Abrupt, Blunt, Brief, Curt, Downright, Pithy, Short

Brussels Carpet, Lace

Brutal, Brute Animal, Barbaric, Beast, Bête, Caesar, Caliban, Cruel, Hun, Iguanodon, Inhuman, Nazi, Nero, Ostrogoth, Pitiless, Quagga, Rambo, Roughshod, Ruffian, Thresher-whale, Yahoo

Brutus Wig

Bryophyte Moss, Tree-moss

Bubble(s), Bubbly Air-bell, Air-lock, Barmy, Bead(ed), Bell, Bleb, Blister, Boil, Buller, Cavitate, Champagne, Cissing, Ebullition, Effervesce, Embolus, Enthuse, Espumoso, Foam, → FROTH, Gassy, Globule, Gurgle, Head, Magnetic, Mantle, Mississippi, Popple, Rale, Reputation, Roundel, Rowndell, Seed, Seethe, Simmer, Soap, South Sea, Vesicle, Widow

Bubble and squeak Colcannon

Buccaneer Corsair, Dampier, Drake, Freebooter, Morgan, Picaroon, Pirate

Buck (up) Bongo, Brace, Cheer, Dandy, Deer, Dollar, Elate, Encheer, Hart, Jerk, Leash, Male, Ourebi, Pitch, Pricket, Ram, Rusa, Sore, Sorel(l), Sorrel, Spade, Spay(a)d, → STAG, Staggard, Stud, Water, Wheel

Buckaroo Cowboy, Cowpoke

Bucket(s) Bail, Bale, Clamshell, Ice, Jacob's ladder, Kibble, Ladle, Noria, Pail, Piggin, Rust, Scuttle, Situla, Slop, Stoop(e), Stope, Stoup, Tub

Buckeye Ohio

Buckle Artois, Clasp, Contort, Crumple, Deform, Dent, Fasten, Warp

▷ **Buckle** *may indicate* an anagram

Buckle-beggar Patrico

Buckler Ancile, Rondache, → SHIELD, Targe

▷ **Bucks** *may indicate* an anagram

Buckshee Free

Buckthorn Cascara, Wahoo

Buckwheat Brank, Sarrasin, Sarrazin

Bucolic Aeglogue, Eglogue, Idyllic, Pastoral, Rural, Rustic

Bud(ding), Buddy Botoné, Bottony, Bulbil, Burgeon, Cacotopia, Clove, Cobber, Deb, Eye, Gem(ma), Germinate, Hibernaculum, Holly, Knop, Knosp, Knot, Nascent, Pal, Scion, Serial, Shoot, Sprout, Statoblast, Taste, Turion

Buddha, Buddhism, Buddhist Abhidhamma, Ahimsa, Amitabha, Anata, Anatta, Anicca, Arhat, Asoka, Bodhisattva, Dalai Lama, Dukkha, Esoteric, Foism, Gautama, Hinayana, Jain, Jataka, Jodo, Kagyu, Mahatma, Mahayana, Maitreya, Maya, Nichiren, Pali, Pitaka, Pure Land, Rinzai, Ryobu, Sakya-muni, Sangha, Shinto, Siddhartha Gautama, Sila, Soka Gakkai, Soto, Sutra, Tantric, Theravada, Tripitaka, Triratna, Vajrayana, Zen(o)

Budge Jee, Move, Stir, Submit

Budget Allocation, Estimate, Operating, Plan, Programme, Save, Shoestring

Buff Beige, Birthday suit, Eatanswill, Fan, Fawn, Nankeen, Natural, Nude, Nut, Polish, → RUB, Streak

Buffalo African, Anoa, Arna, Asiatic, Bison, Bonasus, Bugle, Cap, Cape, Carabao, Ox, Perplex, Takin, Tamarao, Tamarau, Timarau, Water, Zamouse

Buffer Bootblack, Cofferdam, Cutwater, Fender, Sleek-stone

Buffet Bang, Blow, Box, Carvery, Counter, Cuff, Finger-food, Fork luncheon, Fork-supper, Hit, Lam, Maltreat, Perpendicular, Shove, Sideboard, Smorgasborg, Strike, Strook(e)

Buffoon(ery) Antic, Clown, Droll, Goliard, Harlequin, Horseplay, Iniquity, Jester, Mime(r), Mome, Mountebank, Mummer, Nutter, Pantagruel, Pantaloon(ery), Pickle-herring, Pierrot, Punchinello, Scaramouch, Scogan, Scoggin, Scurrile, Slouch, Tomfool, Vice, Wag, Zany

Bug(s) Anoplura, Antagonise, Arthropod, Assassin, Bacteria, Bedevil, Beetle, Berry, Bishop's mitre, Cabbage, Capsid, Chinch, Cimex, Coccidae, Cockchafer, Corixid, Creepy-crawly, Croton, Damsel, Debris, Dictograph®, Eavesdrop, E-coli, Error, Germ, Ground, Harlequin, Hassle, Hemiptera, → INSECT, Jitter, June, Kissing, Lace, Lightning, Listeria, Maori, May, Mealy, Micrococcus, Mike, Millennium, Mite, Nettle, Pill, Reduviid, Rhododendron, Rile, Shield, Skeeter, Sow, Squash, Tap, Vex, Water-measurer, Wheel, Wiretap

Bugbear Anathema, Bête noire, Bogey, Bogle, Bogy, Eten, Ettin, Poker, Rawhead

Buggy Beach, Car, Cart, Pushchair, Shay, Tipcart, Trap

Bughouse Fleapit, Loco

Bugle, Bugle call Boots and saddles, Chamade, Clarion, Cornet, Flugelhorn, Hallali, Last post, Ox, Reveille, Taps, → TRUMPET, Urus

Build, Building(s), Building site Accrue, Anabolism, Ar(a)eostyle, Assemble, Bhavan, Big, Bricks and mortar, Capitol, Chapterhouse, Colosseum, Commons, Construction, Containment, Corncrib, Cot, → CREATE, Cruck, Curia, Develop, Dipteros, Drystone, Duplex, Edifice, Edify, Erect, Fabric, Heapstead, High-rise, Hut, Infill, Insula, Kaaba, Ken, Linhay, Listed, Low-rise, Lyceum, Minaret, Monopteron, Mould, Observatory, Odeon, Odeum, Outhouse, Palazzo, Pataka, Phalanstery, Phalanx, Pile, Portakabin®, Premises, Prytaneum, Quonset®, Raise, Ribbon, Rotunda, Skyscraper, Stance, Statehouse, Structure, Suspension, Synthesis, System, Tectonic, Telecottage, Temple, Tenement, Tholos, Tower,

Town hall, Triplex®, Whata

Builder Brick, Constructor, Engineer, Mason, Millwright, Stonemason, Waller

▷ **Building** *may indicate* an anagram

Bulb Camas(h), Camass, Chive, Cive, Corm, Flash, Globe, Lamp, Light, Olfactory, Pearl, Rupert's drop, Scallion, Set, Shallot, Squill

Bulge, Bulging Astrut, Bag, Bias, Biconvex, Bug, Bulbous, Bunchy, Cockle, Entasis, Expand, Exsert, Inion, Prolate, Protrude, Protuberant, Relievo, Rotund, Strout, Strut, → SWELL, Tumid

Bulk(y) Aggregate, Ample, Big, Body, Corpulent, Density, Extent, Gross, Hull, Immensity, Massive, Preponderance, Roughage, Scalar, → SIZE, Stout, Vol(ume), Weight

Bull(s), Bullock, Bully Anoa, Apis, Bakha, Beef, Blarney, Bludgeon, Bluster, Bouncer, Bovine, Brag, Brave, Browbeat, Buchis, Bucko, Centre, Cuttle, Despot, Dragoon, Drawcansir, Encierro, Englishman, Eretrian, Fancyman, Farnese, Flashman, Flatter, Gold, Gosh, Hapi, Harass, Hawcubite, Haze(r), Hector, Hoodlum, Huff, Intimidate, Investor, Iricism, Irish(ism), John, Killcow, Lambast, Maltreat, Merwer, Mick(e)(y), Mistake, Mithraism, Mohock, Nandi, Neat, Pamplona, Papal, Piker, Pistol, Placet, Poler, Rhodian, Roarer, Rot, Ruffian, Sitting, Souteneur, Stag, Stale, Strong-arm, Swash-buckler, Taurine, Taurus, Toitoi, Tommy-rot, Tosh, Trash, Tripe, Twaddle, Tyran(ne), Tyrannise, Tyrant, Unigenitus, Victimise, Winged, Zo(bo)

Bulldog Marshal, Tenacious

Bulldoze(r) Angledozer, Coerce, Earthmover, Leveller, Overturn

Bullet Ammo, Balata, Ball, Baton round, Biscayan, Blank, Dumdum, Fusillade, Lead towel, Magic, Minié, Minié ball, Missile, Pellet, Percussio, Plastic, Round, Rubber, Shot, Slug, Soft-nosed, Tracer

Bulletin All points, Memo, Message, Newscast, Newsletter, Report, Summary

Bull-fight(er) Banderillero, Banderillo, Corrida, Cuadrilla, Escamillo, Matador, Picador, Rejoneador, Tauromachy, Toreador, Torero

Bull-head Cottoid, Father-lasher, Pogge, Sea-poacher

Bull-rider Europa

Bull-roarer Rhombos, Tu(r)ndun

Bull's eye Carton, God, Humbug, Target

▶ **Bully** *see* BULL

Bulrush Pandanaceous, Raupo, Reed, Reed-mace, Tule

Bulwark Bastion, Defence, Rampart, Resistor

Bum Ass, Beg, Deadbeat, Prat, Sponge, Thumb, Tramp, Vagabond

Bumble Beadle, Bedel(l)

▷ **Bumble** *may indicate* an anagram

Bumboat woman Buttercup

Bumf Spam

Bump(er), Bumps Big, Blow, Bradyseism, Bucket, Clour, Collide, Dunch, Encephalocele, Fender, Hillock, Immense, Inian, Inion, Joll, Jo(u)le, Jowl, Keltie, Kelty, Knar, Knock, Mamilla, Mogul, Organ, Overrider®, Phrenology, Reveille, Rouse, Speed, Thump

Bumph Loo-roll

Bumpkin Bucolic, Bushwhacker, Clodhopper, Hawbuck, Hayseed, Hick, Jock, Lout, Oaf, Put(t), Rube, Rustic, Yokel, Zany

Bumptious Arrogant, Brash, Randie, Randy, Uppity

Bun Barmbrack, Bath, Black, Chelsea, Chignon, Chou, Currant, Devonshire split, Hot-cross, Huffkin, Mosbolletjie, Roll, Teacake, Toorie, Wad

Bunch Acinus, Anthology, Bob, Botryoid, Bouquet, Byndle, Cluster, Fascicle, Finial, Flock, → **GROUP**, Hand, Handful, Lot, Lump, Nosegay, Panicle, Raceme, Spray, Staphyline, Tassel, Tee, Truss, Tuft

Bundle Axoneme, Bale, Bavin, Bluey, Bottle, Byssus, Desmoid, Dorlach, Drum, Fag(g)ot, Fascicle, Fascine, Fibre, Fibrovascular, Kemple, Knitch, Lemniscus, Matilda, → **PACK(AGE)**, Parcel, Sack, Sheaf, Shiralee, Shock, Shook, Stook, Swag, Tie, Top, Trousseau, Truss, Vascular, Wad, Wadge, Wap

Bung Cork, Dook, Obturate, Plug, Stopgap, Stopper

Bungalow Dak

Bungle(r) Blunder, Blunk, Bodge, Boob, Botch, Bumble, Bummle, Dub, Duff, Fluff, Foozle, Foul, Foul up, Goof, Gum up, Mash, Mess, Mis(h)guggle, Muddle, Muff, Mull, Prat, Screw, Spoil

Bunk(er), Bunkum Abscond, Absquatulate, Balderdash, Baloney, Berth, Blah, Bolt, Casemate, Claptrap, Clio, Entrap, Guy, Hazard, History, Hokum, Humbug, Malarky, Nonsense, Rot, Sandtrap, Scuttle, Stokehold, Tosh, Trap, Tripe

Bunter Billy, Owl

Bunthorne Aesthete, Poet

Bunting Bird, Cirl, Flag, Fringilline, Ortolan, Snow, Streamer, Yellow-hammer, Yowley

Buoy (up) Bell, Breeches, Can, Dan, Daymark, Dolphin, Float, Life, Marker, Nun, Raft, Reassure, Ring, Seamark, Sonar, Sonobuoy, Spar, Sustain, Wreck

Buoyant Afloat, Blithe, Floaty, Resilient

Burble Blat, Gibber

Burden Albatross, Beare, Bob, Cargo, Cark, Chant, Chorus, Cross, Cumber, Deadweight, Drone, Droore, Encumber, Encumbrance, Fa-la, Fardel, Folderol, Fraught, Freight, Gist, Handicap, Hum, Lade, → **LOAD**, Lumber, Millstone, Monkey, Oercome, Onus, Oppress, Put-upon, Refrain, Rumbelow, Saddle, Servitude, Shanty, Substance, Tax, Tenor, Torch, Trouble, Weight, White man's, Woe, Yoke

Burdensome Irksome, Onerous, Oppressive, Weighty

Burdock Clote(-bar), Clothur, Cockle-bar, Hardoke, Weed

Bureau Agency, Agitprop, Breakfront, Cominform, Davenport, Desk, Interpol, Kominform, Marriage, → **OFFICE**, Volunteer

Bureaucracy, Bureaucrat(ic) CS, Impersonal, Jack-in-office, Mandarin, Red tape, Tapist, Wallah

Burgeon(ing) Asprout, Blossom, Bud, Grow, Sprout

Burgess, Burgher Citizen, Freeman

Burgh Parliamentary, Police, Royal

Burglar, Burgle Area-sneak, Cat, Crack(sman), House-breaker, Intruder, Peterman, Picklock, Raffles, Robber, Screw, Thief, Yegg

Burgundy Macon, Vin

Burial(place) Catacomb, Charnel, Committal, Crypt, Cubiculum, Darga, Funeral, God's acre, Golgotha, Grave, Interment, Kurgan, Lair, Last rites, Sepulchre, Sepulture, Tomb, Tumulus, Vault, Zoothapsis

Burin Graver

Burlesque Caricatura, Caricature, Comedy, Farce, Heroicomical, Hudibrastic(s), Hurlo-thrumbo, Lampoon, Macaronic, Parody, Satire, Skimmington, Skit, Spoof, Travesty

Burlington RA

Burly Bluff, Stout, Strapping

Burmese Karen(ni), Mon(-Khmer), Naga, Shan

Burn(er), Burning, Burnt Adust, Afire, Alow(e), Ardent, Argand, Arson, Ash,

Auto-da-fé, Bats-wing, Beck, Bishop, Blaze, Blister, Blowtorch, Brand, Bren(ne), Brent, Brook, Bunsen, Causalgia, Caustic, Cauterise, Char, Chark, Chinese, Cinder, Coal, Coke, Combust, Conflagration, Cremate, Crozzled, Crucial, Deflagrate, Destruct, Eilding, Ember, Emboil, Empyreuma, Fervid, Fircone, → **FIRE**, Fishtail, Flagrant, Flare, Flash, Fresh(et), Gleed, Gut, Holocaust, Ignite, In, Incendiary, Incense, Incinerate, Inure, Inust(ion), Itch, Kill, Live, Lunt, Offering, On, Oxidise, Oxyacetylene, Pilot, Plo(a)t, Powder, Pyric, Pyromania, Rill, Sati, Scald, Scorch, Scouther, Scowder, Scowther, Sear, Sienna, Sike, Singe, Sizzle, Smart, Smoulder, Suttee, Swale, Third-degree, Thurible, Torch, Umber, Urent, Ustion, Ustulation, Weeke, Welsbach, Wick

Burp Belch

Burr(ing) Brei, Brey, Clote, Croup, Dialect, Knob, Rhotacism

Burrow(er), Burrowing Dig, Earth, Fossorial, Gopher, Groundhog, Hole, How, Howk, Mole, Nuzzle, Root, Sett, Terricole, Tunnel, Viscacha, Warren, Wombat, Worm

Bursar(y) Camerlengo, Camerlingo, Coffers, Grant, Purser, Scholarship, Tertiary, Treasurer

Bursitis Beat

Burst(ing) Blowout, Brast, Break, Dehisce, Disrupt, Dissilient, Ebullient, Erumpent, Erupt, → **EXPLODE**, Flare-up, Fly, Implode, Pop, Sforzato, Shatter, Spasm, Spirt, Split, Sprint, Spurt, Stave, Tetterous

Bury Cover, Eard, Earth, Embowel, Engrave, Enhearse, Graff, Graft, Imbed, Inearth, Inhearse, Inherce, Inhume, Inter, Inurn, Landfill, Repress, Sepulture, Sink, Ye(a)rd, Yird

Bus Aero, Bandwagon, Car, Charabanc, Coach, Crew, Double-decker, Greyhound, Hondey, Hopper, ISA, Jitney, Mammy-wagon, Purdah, Rattletrap, Single-decker, Tramcar, Trolley, Walking

Bus conductor Cad, Clippy

Bush(y), Bush-man Bitou, Bramble, Brier, Bullace, Busket, Calico, Clump, Cotton, Dumose, Firethorn, Hawthorn, Hibiscus, Ivy-tod, Kapok, Kiekie, Mallee, Matagouri, Mulberry, Outback, Poinsettia, Poly-poly, President, Prostanthera, Sallee, San, Shepherd, Shrub, Sloe, Sugar, Thicket, Tire, Tod(de), Tumatakuru

Bush-baby Durukuli, Galago, Nagapie, Night-ape

Bushel Ardeb, Bu, Co(o)mb, Cor, Ephah, Fou, Homer, Peck, Weight, Wey

Bushwalker Hoon

Business Affair, Agency, Biz, Bricks and clicks, Brokerage, Bus, Cartel, Cerne, Chaebol(s), Co, Commerce, Company, Concern, Conglomerate, Craft, Duty, Enterprise, Ergon, Establishment, Exchange, Fasti, Firm, Funny, Game, Gear, Hong, Industry, Lifestyle, Line, Métier, Monkey, Office, Palaver, Pi(d)geon, Pidgin, Practice, Professional, Racket, Shebang, Shop, Show, To-do, Trade, Traffic, Transaction, Tread, Turnover, Unincorporated, Vocation, Zaibatsu, Zaikai

Businessman Babbitt, Capitalist, City, Entrepreneur, Financier, Realtor, Taipan, Trader, Tycoon

Busk(er) Bodice, Corset, Entertainer, German-band

Buskin(s) Brod(e)kin, Cothurn(us), Shoe

Buss Kiss, Osculate, Smack

Bussu Troelie, Troely, Troolie

Bust Beano, Boob, Brast, Break, Chest, Falsies, Figurehead, Herm(a), Insolvent, Mamma, Rupture, Sculp, Shatter(ed), Spree, Statue, Term(inus), To-tear, To-torne, Ups(e)y

▷ **Bust** *may indicate* an anagram

Bustard Bird, Otis, Turkey

Buster Keaton

Bustle Ado, Beetle, Do, Dress-improver, Flap, Pad, Scurry, → STIR, Swarm, Tournure, Whew

Busy Active, At (it), Deedy, → DETECTIVE, Dick, Eident, Employ, Engaged, Ergate, Eye, Goer, Hectic, Hive, Humming, Occupied, Ornate, Prodnose, Stir, Stirabout, Tec, Throng, Worksome

Busybody Bustler, Meddler, Noser, Pragmatic, Snooper, Trout, Yenta

But Aber, Algates, Bar, Except, However, Keg, Merely, Nay, Only, Save, Sed, Simply, Tun, Without

Butch He-man, Macho

Butcher(y) Cumberland, Decko, Dekko, Flesher, Ice, Kill, Killcow, Look, Massacre, Ovicide, Sever, Shambles, Shochet, Shufti, Slaughter, Slay, Slink

Butler Bedivere, Bread-chipper, Jeeves, Khansama(h), Major-domo, RAB, Rhett, Samuel, Servant, Sewer, Sommelier, Steward

Butt (in) Aris, Barrel, Bumper, Bunt, Clara, Dimp, Dunch, Enter, Geck, Glasgow kiss, Goat, Header, Horn, Jesting-stock, Laughing-stock, Mark, Nut, Outspeckle, Pantaloon, Pipe, Push, Ram, Roach, Scapegoat, Snipe, Stompie, → STOOGE, Straight man, Stump, Target, Tun, Ups

Butter Adulation, Apple, Billy, Brandy, Butyric, Cacao, Cocoa, Coconut, Drawn, Flatter, Galam, Garcinia, Ghee, Ghi, Goa, Goat, Illipi, Illupi, Kokum, Mahua, Mahwa, Maitre d'hotel, Mow(r)a, Nut, Nutter, Palm, Pat, Peanut, Print, Ram, Rum, Scrape, Shea, Spread, Vegetable

▷ **Butter** *may indicate* a goat or such

Buttercup Bumboat woman, Crow-foot, Crow-toe, Goldilocks, Ranunculus, Reate, Thalictrum

Butterfingers Muff

Butterfish Nine-eyes

Butterfly Apollo, Argus, Birdwing, Blue, Brimstone, Brown, Cabbage white, Camberwell beauty, Cardinal, Chequered skipper, Cleopatra, Clouded yellow, Comma, Common blue, Copper, Dilettante, Eclosion, Emperor, Fritillary, Gate-keeper, Grayling, Hair-streak, Heath, Hesperid, Imaginal, Kallima, Large copper, Large white, Leaf, Lycaena, Marbled-white, Meadow brown, Milk-weed, Monarch, Morpho, Mourning-cloak, Nerves, Nymphalid, Nymphean, Orange-tip, Owl, Painted lady, Papilionidae, Peacock, Pieris, Psyche, Purple emperor, Red admiral, Rhopalocera, Ringlet, Satyr(idae), Satyrinae, Scotch argus, Silverspot, Skipper, Small white, Speckled wood, Stamper, Sulphur, Swallow-tail, Thecla, Thistle, Tiger swallowtail, Tortoiseshell, Two-tailed pasha, Vanessa, Wall brown, White admiral

Buttermilk Bland, Lassi

Butternut Souari

Butter-tree Mahua, Mahwa, Mow(r)a

Buttocks Aristotle, Arse, Ass, Bahookie, Booty, Bottom, Can, Coit, Derrière, Doup, Duff, Fanny, Fundament, Gluteus maximus, Heinie, Hinder-end, Hinderlan(d)s, Hurdies, Jacksie, Jacksy, Keester, Keister, Mooning, Nache, Nates, Posterior, Prat, Quoit, Seat, Tush

Button(s) Barrel, Bellboy, Fastener, Frog, Hot, Knob, Mute, Netsuke, Olivet, Page(boy), Panic, Pearl, Press, Push, Snooze, Stud, Switch, Toggle, Toolbar

Buttonhole Accost, Boutonniere, Detain, Doorstep, Eye, Flower

Buttress Brace, Counterfort, Flying, Hanging, Pier, Prop, Stay, Support, Tambour

Butty Chum, Oppo

Buxom Bonnie, Busty, Plump, Sonsy, Well-endowed

Buy(ing), Buyer Believe, Bribe, Coemption, Coff, Corner, Customer, Emption, Engross, Impulse, Monopsonist, Oligopsony, Panic, Purchase, Redeem, Regrate, Shop, Shout, Spend, Take, Trade, Vendee

▷ **Buyer** *may indicate* money

Buzz(er) Bee, Birr, Bombilate, Bombinate, Button, Fly, Hum, Rumour, Scram, Whirr, Whisper, Zed, Zing, Zoom

Buzzard Bee-kite, Bird, Buteo, Hawk, Honey, Pern, Puttock, Turkey, Vulture

By Alongside, At, Gin, Gone, In, Near, Neighbouring, Nigh, Of, On, Past, Per, Through, With, X

Bye Extra

Bye-bye Adieu, Farewell, Tata

Bygone B.C., Dead, Departed, Past, Yore

By Jove Egad

Bypass Avoid, Circuit, Coronary, → **DETOUR**, Evade, Ignore, Omit, Shunt, Skirt

By-product Epiphenomenon, Spill-over, Spin-off

Byre Cowshed, Manger, Stable, Trough

By so much The

Byte Nybble

By the way Apropos, Incidentally, Obiter

Byway Alley, Lane, Path

Byword Ayword, Nayword, Phrase, Proverb, Slogan

Byzantine Catapan, Comnenus, Complicated, Exarch, Intricate, Intrince, Theme

Cc

C Around, Caught, Celsius, Cent, Centigrade, Charlie, Conservative, San

Cab Boneshaker, Crawler, Drosky, Fiacre, Four-wheeler, Growler, Gurney, Hackney, Hansom, Mini, Noddy, Taxi, Vettura

Cabal(ler) Arlington, Ashley, Buckingham, Clifford, Clique, Conspiracy, Coterie, Faction, Junto, Lauderdale, Party, Plot

Cab(b)alistic Abraxis, Mystic, Notarikon, Occult

Cabaret Burlesque, Floorshow

Cabbage(-head), Cabbage soup Bok choy, Borecole, Brassica, Castock, Cauliflower, Cavalo nero, Chinese, Choucroute, Cole, Collard, Crout, Custock, Drumhead, Gobi, Kerguelen, Kohlrabi, Kraut, Loaf, Loave, Pak-choi, Pamphrey, Pe-tsai, Sauerkraut, Savoy, Shchi, Shtchi, Skunk, Thieve, Turnip, Wild, Wort

Caber Fir, Janker, Log, Sting

Cabin Berth, Bibby, Bothy, Box, Cabana, Caboose, Camboose, Coach, Cottage, Crannog, Crib, Cuddy, Den, Gondola, Hovel, Hut, Izba, Lodge, Loghouse, Long-house, Pod, Pressure, Room, Roundhouse, Saloon, Shanty, Stateroom, Trunk

Cabin-boy Grummet

Cabinet Armoire, Bahut, Cabale, Case, Cellaret, Chiffonier, Closet, Commode, Console, Cupboard, Filing, Kitchen, Ministry, Secretaire, Shadow, Shrinal, Unit, Vitrine

Cabinet maker Chippendale, Ebeniste, Hepplewhite, Joiner, PM

Cable(way), Cable-car Chain, Coax(ial), Extension, Flex, Halser, Hawser, Jumper, Jump leads, Junk, Landline, Lead, Lead-in, Lifeline, Null-modern, Oil-filled, Outhaul, Outhauler, Rope, Shroud, Slatch, Snake, Téléférique, → **TELEGRAM**, Telegraph, Telepherique, Telpher(age), Topping lift, Trunking, Wire, Yoke

Cache Deposit, Hidlin(g)s, → **HOARD**, Inter, Stash, Store, Treasure

Cachet Prestige

Cackle Cluck, Gaggle, Gas, Haw, Snicker, Titter

Cacography Scrawl

Cacophony Babel, Caterwaul, Charivari, Discord, Jangle

Cactus, Cactus-like Alhagi, Barel, Cereus, Cholla, Christmas, Dildo, Easter, Echino-, Hedgehog, Jointed, Jojoba, Maguey, Mescal, Mistletoe, Nopal, Ocotillo, Opuntia, Organ-pipe, Peyote, Pitahaya, Prickly pear, Retama, Saguaro, Stapelia, Star, Strawberry, Torch-thistle, Tuna, Xerophytic

Cad Base, Boor, Bounder, Churl, Cocoa, Heel, Oik, Rascal, Rotter, Skunk, Varlet

Cadaver(ous) Body, Corpse, Deathly, Ghastly, Goner, Haggard, Stiff

Caddy Porter, Tea, Teapoy

Cadence Beat, Close, Euouae, Evovae, Fa-do, Flow, Lilt, Meter, Perfect, Plagal, Rhythm

Cadenza Fireworks

Cadet(s) Junior, OTC, Plebe, Recruit, Rookie, Scion, Snooker, Space, Syen, Trainee, Younger

Cadge(r) Bludge, Bot, Bum, Impose, Mutch, → SCROUNGE, Sponge
Cadmium Cd
Caesar Nero
Caesium Cs
Café(teria) Automat, Bistro, Brasserie, Buvette, Canteen, Commissary, Cybercafe, Diner, Dinette, Donko, Eatery, Estaminet, Filtré, Greasy spoon, Hashhouse, Internet, Juke joint, Netcafé, Pizzeria, Pull-in, Snackbar, Tearoom, Transport, Truckstop
Cage Bar, Battery, Box, Cavie, Confine, Coop, Corf, Dray, Drey, Enmew, Faraday, Fold, Frame, Grate, Hutch, Keavie, Mew, Mortsafe, Pen, → PRISON, Safety, Squirrel, Trave
Cahoots Hugger-mugger
Cairn Barp, Clearance, Dog, Horned, Man, Mound, Raise
Caisson Bends
Caitiff Meanie
Cajole(ry) Beflum, Beguile, Blandish, Blarney, Carn(e)y, → COAX, Cuittle, Humbug, Inveigle, Jolly, Persuade, Wheedle, Whilly, Wiles
Cake Agnus dei, Angel, Baba, Babka, Baklava, Banbury, Bannock, Bara brith, Barmbrack, Battenberg, Birthday, Brioche, Brownie, Buckwheat, Bun, Carcake, Cattle, Chapat(t)i, Chillada, Chupati, Chupattie, Chupatty, Clapbread, Clot, Coburg, Cookie, Corn dodger, Cotton, Croquante, Croquette, Cruller, Crumpet, Currant, Dainty, Devil's food, Drizzle, Dundee, Eccles, Eclair, Fancy, Farl(e), Filter, Fish, Flapjack, Frangipane, Frangipani, Fritter, Galette, Genoa, Gingerbread, Girdle, → HARDEN, Hockey, Hoe, Idli, Jannock, Johnny, Jumbal, Jumbles, Koeksister, Kruller, Kuchen, Kueh, Lamington, Lardy, Latke, Layer, Linseed, Macaroon, Madeira, Madeleine, Maid of honour, Marble, Meringue, Millefeuille, Mud, Muffin, Napoleon, Nut, Oatmeal, Oil, Pan, Panettone, Paratha, Parkin, Parliament, Pastry, Pat, Patty, Pavlova, Pepper, Petit four, Pikelet, → PLASTER, Pomfret, Pone, Pontefract, Poori, Popover, Pound, Profiterole, Puff, Puftaloon(a), Puri, Queencake, Ratafia, Ready-mix, Religieuse, Rice, Rock, Rosti, Roti, Rout, Rum baba, Rusk, Sachertorte, Saffron, Sally Lunn, Salt, Sandwich, Savarin, Scone, Seed, Set, Simnel, Singing-hinny, Slab, Slapjack, Soul, Spawn, Spice, Sponge, Stollen, Stottie, Sushi, Swiss roll, Tablet, Tansy, Tea(bread), Tipsy, Torte, Tortilla, Twelfth, Upside down, Vetkoek, Wad, Wafer, Waffle, Wedding, Wonder, Yeast, Yule log
▷ **Cake** *may indicate* an anagram
Cake-shaped Placentiform
Cakestand Curate
Cakewalk Doddle
Calaboose Jail, Loghouse
Calamitous, Calamity Blow, Catastrophe, Dire, → DISASTER, Distress, Fatal, Ill, Jane, Ruth, Storm, Tragic, Unlucky, Visitation, Woe
Calcareous Ganoin, Lithite
Calcium Ca, Colemanite, Dogger, Dripstone, Otolith, Quicklime, Scawtite, Whewellite
Calculate(d), Calculation, Calculator Abacus, Actuary, Comptometer, Compute(r), Cost, Design, Estimate, Extrapolate, Log, Napier's bones, Number-crunch, Prorate, Quip(p)u, Rate, → RECKON, Slide-rule, Sofar, Soroban, Tactical, Tell
Calculus Cholelith, Differential, Functional, Infinitesimal, Integral, Lambda, Lith, Lithiasis, Predicate, Propositional, Science, Sentential, Sialolith, Stone, Tartar, Urolith
Caledonian Kanak

Calendar Advent, Agenda, Almanac, Chinese, Diary, Fasti, Gregorian, Hebrew, Intercalary, Jewish, Journal, Julian, Luach, Lunisolar, Menology, Newgate, New Style, Ordo, Perpetual, Revolutionary, Roman, Sothic
Calender(ing) Dervish, Mangle, Swissing
Calf Ass, Bobby, Box, Cf, Deacon, Divinity, Dogie, Dogy, Freemartin, Golden, Law, Leg, Maverick, Mottled, Poddy, Sleeper, Slink, Smooth, Stirk, Sural, Tollie, Tolly, Tree, Veal, Vitular
Caliban Moon-calf
Calibrate, Calibre Bore, Capacity, Graduate, Mark, → **QUALITY**, Text
Californium Cf
Caliph Abbasid(e), Omar, Vathek
Call(ed), Calling, Call on, Call up Adhan, Appeal, Arraign, Art, Awaken, Azan, Banco, Bawl, Beck, Behote, Bevy, Bid, Boots and saddles, Business, Buzz, Career, Chamade, Cite, Claim, Clang, Clarion, Cleep, Clepe, Close, Cold, Conference, Conscript, Convene, Convoke, Cooee, Cry, Curtain, Dial, Drift, Dub, Evoke, Gam, Go, Hail, Hallali, Haro, Heads, Heave-ho, Hech, Hete, Hey, Hight, Ho, Hot(e), Howzat, Huddup, Hurra(h), Invocation, Job, Junk, Last (post), Line, Local, Margin, Métier, Misère, Mobilise, Mot, Name, Nap, Need, Nemn, Nempt, Nominate, No trumps, Olé, Page, Peter, Phone, Photo, Post, Proo, Pruh, Pursuit, Rechate, Recheat, Retreat, Reveille, Ring, Roll, Rort, Rouse, Route, Sa-sa, See, Sennet, → **SHOUT**, Shut-out, Slam, Slander, Slogan, Soho, Sola, SOS, STD, Style, Subpoena, Summon(s), Tails, Tantivy, Taps, Telephone, Term, Toho, Toll, Trumpet, Trunk, Visit, Vocation, Waken, Wake-up, Whoa-ho-ho, Wo ha ho, Yell, Yo, Yodel, Yodle, Yo-ho(-ho), Yoicks, Yoo-hoo
Calla(s) Aroid, Lily, Maria
Caller Fresh, Guest, Herring, Inspector, Muezzin, Rep, Traveller, → **VISITOR**
Calligraphy Kakemono
Callipers Odd legs
Callisthenics T'ai chi (ch'uan)
Callosity, Call(o)us Bunion, Cold, Corn, Hard, Horny, Obtuse, Ringbone, Seg, Thylose, Tough, Tylosis, Unfeeling
Callow Crude, Green, Immature, Jejune
Calm Abate, Alegge, Aleye, Allay, Allege, Appease, Ataraxy, Composed, Cool, Doldrums, Easy, Easy-osy, Eevn, Equable, Equanimity, Even, Eye, Flat, Glassy, Halcyon, Loun(d), Lown(d), Lull, Mellow, Mild, Milden, Millpond, Nonchalant, Pacify, Peaceable, Peaceful, Philosophical, Phlegmatic, Placate, Placid, Quell, Quiet, Relax(ed), Repose, Restrained, Seraphic, Serena, Serene, Settle, Simmer down, Sleek, → **SOOTHE**, Sopite, Steady, Still, Stilly, Subside, Tranquil(lise), Unturbid, Windless
Calorie Gram, Kilogram
Calumniate, Calumny Aspersion, Backbite, Defame, Libel, Malign, Sclaunder, Slander, Slur
Calvary Golgotha
Calvin(ist) Accusative, Coolidge, Genevan, Hopkins, Huguenot, Infralapsarian, Predestination, Sublapsarian, Supralapsarian
Calydonian Boar
Calypso Ogygia, Siren, Soca, Sokah, → **SONG**
Cam Cog, River, Snail, Tappet
Camaraderie Fellowship, Rapport, Team spirit
Camber Hog, Slope
Cambium Phellogen

Cambodian Khmer (Rouge), Montagnard
Cambria(n) Menevian, Wales
Cambridge Cantab, Squat, Uni
Came Arrived
Camel, Camel train Aeroplane, Arabian, Artiodactyla, Bactrian, Caisson, Colt, Dromedary, Kafila, Llama, Oont, Sopwith, Tulu
Cameo Anaglyph, Camaieu, Carving
Camera, Camera man All-round, Box, Brownie®, Camcorder, Candid, Chambers, Cine, Compact, Digital, Disc, Electron, Flash, Gamma, Gatso®, Grip(s), Iconoscope, Instant, Kodak®, Lucida, Miniature, Minicam, Movie, Nannycam, Obscura, Orthicon, Palmcorder, Panoramic, Pantoscope, Periphery, Phone-cam, Pinhole, Polaroid®, Process, Programmed, Reflex, Retina, Schmidt, SLR, Somascope, Speed, Spycam, Steadicam®, Stop-frame, Subminiature, Video, Vidicon, Viewfinder, Webcam
Camouflage Conceal, → DISGUISE, Mark, Maskirovka, War-dress
▷ **Camouflaged** *may indicate* an anagram
Camp(er) Affectation, Aldershot, Auschwitz, Banal, Base, Belsen, Bivouac, Boma, Boot, Buchenwald, Caerleon, Cantonment, Castral, Colditz, Concentration, Dachau, David, Death, Depot, D(o)uar, Dumdum, Epicene, Faction, Fat, Flaunt, Gulag, Happy, Health, High, Holiday, L(a)ager, Labour, Lashkar, Leaguer, Low, Manyat(t)a, Motor, Oflag, Outlie, Peace, Prison, Side, Siwash, Stagey, Stalag, Stative, Swagman, Tent, Theatrical, Transit, Treblinka, Valley Forge, Work, Zare(e)ba, Zariba, Zereba, Zeriba
Campaign(er) Barnstorm, Battle, Blitz, Blitzkrieg, Canvass, Crusade, Doorknock, Drive, Field, Jihad, Lobby, Mission, Offensive, Pankhurst, Promotion, Roadshow, Run, Satyagraha, Smear, Stint, Strategist, The stump, Tree-hugger, Venture, Veteran, War, Warray, Warrey, Whispering, Whistle-stop, Witchhunt
Campanula Rampion
Campeador Chief, Cid
Camp-follower Lascar, Leaguer-lady, Leaguer-lass, Sutler
Camphor Menthol
Campion Knap-bottle, Lychnis, Ragged robin, Silene
▷ **Camptown** *may indicate* de-
Can(s) Able, Billy, Bog, Capable, Churn, Cooler, Dow, Gaol, Garbage, Gents, Headphones, Is able, Jerry, Jug, Karsy, Loo, May, Nick, Pail, Pot, Preserve, → PRISON, Privy, Six-pack, Stir, Tank, Tin, Trash, Watering
Canada, Canadian Abenaki, Acadian, Bella Bella, Bella Coola, Beothuk, Bois-brûlé, Canuck, Comox, Dene, Dogrib, Hare, Heiltsuk, Herring choker, Inuit, Johnny Canuck, Joual, Maliseet, Metis, Montagnais, Naskapi, Nuxalk, Péquiste, Quebeccer, Quebecker, Québecois, Salishan, Salteaux, Saulteaux, Slavey, Stoney, Tsimshian, Ungava, Yukon
Canal Alimentary, Ampul, Anal, Birth, Caledonian, Channel, Conduit, Corinth, Cruiseway, Da Yunhe, Duct, Duodenum, Ea, Enteron, Erie, Foss(e), Gota, Grand (Trunk), Grande Terre, Grand Union, Groove, Gut, Haversian, Houston Ship, Kiel, Klong, Labyrinth, Lode, Manchester Ship, Meatus, Midi, Mittelland, Moscow, Navigation, New York State Barge, Oesophagus, Panama, Pharynx, Pipe, Pound, Regent's, Resin, Rhine-Herne, Ring, Root, Sault Sainte Marie, Scala, Schlemm's, Semi-circular, Ship, Shipway, Soo, Spinal, Stone, Suez, Suo, Urethra, Vagina, Waterway, Welland, Zanja
Canal-boat Barge, Fly-boat, Gondola, Vaporetto
Canapé Cate, Snack, Titbit

Canary Bird, Grass, Roller, Serin, Singer, Yellow
Cancel(led) Abrogate, Adeem, Annul, Counteract, Countermand, Cross, Delete, Destroy, Erase, Kill, Negate, Nullify, Obliterate, Override, Rained off, Red line, Remit, Repeal, Rescind, Retrait, Revoke, Scrub, Undo, Unmake, Void, Wipe, Write off
Cancer(ian), Cancerous Big C, Carcinoma, Crab, Curse, Kaposi's sarcoma, Leukaemia, Lymphoma, Moon child, Oat-cell, Oncogenic, Tropic, Tumour, Wolf
Candela Cd
▶ **Candelabra** *see* CANDLE(STICK)
Candid, Candour Albedo, Blunt, Camera, Franchise, Frank, Honesty, Open, Outspoken, Plain(-spoken), Round, Upfront
Candida Fungus
Candidate(s) Agrege, Applicant, Aspirant, Contestant, Entrant, Field, Nomenklatura, Nominee, Office-seeker, Ordinand, Postulant, Running mate, Stalking horse, Testee
Candied, Candy Angelica, Caramel, Cotton, Eryngo, Eye, Glace, Maple, Rock, Snow, Succade, Sugar, → SWEET
Candle(stick), Candelabra Amandine, Bougie, Chanukiah, C(i)erge, Dip, Fetch, Girandole, Hanukiah, International, Jesse, Lampadary, Light, Long-sixes, Menorah, Mould, New, Padella, Paschal, Pricket, Roman, Rushlight, Sconce, Serge, Shammash, Shammes, Shortsix, Slut, Sperm, Standard, Tace, Tallow, Tallow-dip, Taper, Tea-light, Torchère, Tricerion, Vigil light, Wax, Waxlight
Candlefish Eulachon, Oolakon, Oulachon, Oulakon, Ulic(h)an, Ulic(h)on, Ulikon
▶ **Candy** *see* CANDIED
Cane Arrow, Baculine, Bamboo, Baste, Beat, Birk, Crabstick, Dari, Dhurra, Doura, Dur(r)a, Ferula, Ferule, Goor, Gur, Jambee, Malacca, Narthex, Penang-lawyer, Pointer, Raspberry, Rat(t)an, Rod, Split, Stick, Sugar, Swagger-stick, Swish, Switch, Swordstick, Tan, Tickler, Vare, Wand, Whangee, Wicker(-work)
Canine Biter, C, Dhole, Dog, Eye-tooth
Canker Corrosion, Curse, Lesion, Ulcer
Cannabis Benj, Bhang, Bifter, Blow, Boneset, Durban poison, Ganja, Ganny, Grass, Hash, Hemp, Henry, Louie, Number, Pot, Skunk, Zol
Cannibal Anthropophagus, Heathen, Long pig, Man-eater, Ogre, Thyestean, Wendigo
Cannon Amusette, Barrage, Basilisk, Bombard, Breechloader, Carom, Carronade, Chaser, Collide, Criterion, Culverin, Drake, Drop, Falcon, Gun, Howitzer, Kiss, Long-tom, Loose, Monkey, Mons Meg, Nursery, Oerlikon, Saker, Stern-chaser, Water, Zamboorak, Zomboruk, Zumbooru(c)k
Cannot Canna, Cant, Downa(e), Downay
Canny Careful, Frugal, Prudent, Scot, Shrewd, Slee, Sly, Thrifty, Wice, Wily, Wise
Canoe(ist) Bidarka, Bidarkee, Canader, Canadian, Dugout, Faltboat, Kayak, Log, Mokoro, Monoxylon, Montaria, Oomiack, Paddler, Peterborough, Piragua, Pirogue, Rob Roy, Surf, Waka, Woodskin
Canon(ise) Austin, Besaint, Brocard, Camera, Cancrizens, Chapter, Chasuble, Code, Crab, Infinite, Isidorian, → LAW, Line, Mathurin(e), Minor, Nocturn, Norbertine, Nursery, Pitaka, Polyphony, Prebendary, Precept, Premonstrant, Premonstratensian, Retrograde, Rota, Round, Rule, Square, Squier, Squire, Standard, Tenet, Unity, White
Canopy Awning, Baldachin, Baldaquin, Chuppah, Ciborium, Clamshell, Dais, He(a)rse, Huppah, Majesty, Marquee, Marquise, Pavilion, Shamiana(h), State, Tabernacle, Tent, Tester, Veranda(h)

Cant Argot, Bevel, Heel, Incline, Jargon, Mummery, Patois, Patter, Rogue's Latin, Shelta, Slang, Slope, Snivel, Snuffle, Tip

Cantankerous Cussed, Fire-eater, Ornery, Querulous, Testy, Tetchy

Cantata Kinderspiel, Motet, Tobacco

Canteen Chuck-wagon, Mess, Munga, Naafi

Canter Amble, Hypocrite, Jog, Lope, Run, Tit(t)up, Tripple

Canto Air, Fit(te), Fitt, Fytte, Melody, Verse

Canton Aargau, Appenzell, Basle, District, Eyalet, Fribourg, Glarus, Graubunden, Jura, Lucerne, Neuchatel, Quarter, St Gall, Schaffhausen, Schwyz, Solothurn, Thurgau, Ticino, Unterwalden, Uri, Valais, Vaud, Zug, Zurich

Cantor Haz(z)an

Cantred Commot(e)

Canvas Awning, Binca®, Burlap, Dra(b)bler, Fly-sheet, Lug-sail, Mainsail, Marquee, Oil-cloth, Paint, Raven's-duck, Reef, → **SAIL**, Staysail, Stuns(ai)l, Tent, Trysail, Wigan, Woolpack

Canvass(er), Canvassing Agent, Doorstep, Drum, Mainstreeting, Poll, Solicit

▷ **Canvasser** *may indicate* a painter or a camper

Canyon Box, Canada, Defile, Grand, Grand Coulee, Nal(l)a, Nallah, Submarine

Cap(ped) Abacot, Amorce, Balaclava, Balmoral, Barret, Baseball, Bathing, Bellhop, Bendigo, Ber(r)et, Biggin, Biretta, Black, Blakey, Blue, Blue-bonnet, Bonnet-rouge, Bycoket, Call, Calotte, Calpac(k), Calyptrate, Capeline, Caul, Chaco, Chape, Chapeau, Chaperon, Chapka, Chechia, Cheese-cutter, Cloth, Cockernony, Coif, College, Coonskin, Cope, Cornet, Cowl, Cradle, Crest, → **CROWN**, Czapka, Davy Crockett, Deerstalker, Dunce's, Dutch, Fatigue, Ferrule, Filler, Flat, Fool's, Forage, Gandhi, Garrison, Gimme, Glengarry, Grannie, Granny, → **HAT**, Havelock, Hummel bonnet, Iceberg, International, Jockey, Juliet, Kalpak, Kepi, Kilmarnock, Kippa, Kippoth, Kipput, Kiss-me(-quick), Knee, Legal, Liberty, Lid, Mob, Monmouth, Monteer, Montero, Mor(r)ion, Mortar-board, Muffin, Mutch, Newsboy, Night, Outdo, Pagri, Patellar, Percussion, Perplex, Phrygian, Pile, Pileus, Pinner, Polar, Puggaree, Quoif, Root, Schapska, Shako, Skullcap, Square, Squirrel-tail, Statute, Stocking, Summit, → **SURPASS**, Taj, Tam(-o'-shanter), Thimble, Thinking, Thrum, Toe, Toorie, Top, Toque, Toy, Trenchard, Trencher, Truck, Tuque, Turk's, Watch, Wishing, Yarmulka, Yarmulke, Zuchetto

Capable, Capability Able, Brown, Capacity, Competent, Deft, Effectual, Efficient, Firepower, Qualified, Skilled, Susceptible, Up to

Capacitance, Capacity Ability, Aptitude, C, Cab, Carrying, Competence, Content, Cor, Cubic, Endowment, Function, Gift, Legal, Limit, Log, Potency, Potential, Power, Qua, Rated, Receipt, Scope, Size, Skinful, Tankage, Thermal, Tonnage, Valence, Vital, Volume

Caparison Robe, Trap(pings)

Cape Agulhas, Almuce, Blanc(o), Bon, Burnouse, Byron, Calimere Point, Canaveral, Canso, Cardinal, Chelyuskin, Cloak, Cod, Comorin, Delgado, Dezhnev, Domino, Dungeness, East(ern), Fairweather, Faldetta, Fanion, Fanon, Farewell, Fear, Fichu, Finisterre, Flattery, Gallinas Point, Good Hope, Guardafui, Harp, Hatteras, Head(land), Helles, Hoe, Hogh, Hook of Holland, Horn, Inverness, Kennedy, Leeuwin, Lindesnes, Lizard, Manteel, Mant(e)let, Mantilla, Mantle, Matapan, May, Miseno, Mo(z)zetta, Muleta, Naze, Ness, Nordkyn, North, Northern, Ortegal, Palatine, Parry, Pelerine, Peninsula, Point, Poncho, Promontory, Race, Ras, Ray, Reinga, Roca, Ruana, Runaway, Sable, St Vincent, Sandy, Scaw, Skagen, Skaw, Sontag, Southwest, Talma, Tippet, Trafalgar, Ushant, Verde, Waterproof, Western, Wrath, York

Caper(ing) Antic, Bean, Boer, Capparis, Capriole, Cavort, Dance, Dido, Flisk, Frisk, Frolic, Gambado, Gambol, Harmala, Harmalin(e), Harmel, Harmin(e), Prance, Prank, Saltant, Scoup, Scowp, Skip, Tit(t)up
Capet Marie Antoinette
Cape Town SA
Capital(s) A1, Assets, Block, Boodle, Bravo, Bully, Cap, Chapiter, Chaptrel, Doric, Equity, Euge, Excellent, Fixed, Flight, Float, Floating, Fonds, Great, Helix, Human, Initial, Ionic, Lethal, Lulu, Metropolis, Principal, Refugee, Risk, Rustic, Seat, Seed, Share, Social, Splendid, Sport, Stellar, Stock, Super, Topping, UC, Upper case, Working

CAPITALS

3 letters:	Kiel	Batum	Korov
Fes	Kiev	Belém	Kyoto
Fez	Kobe	Berne	Lagos
Gap	Laon	Bisho	Lassa
Jos	Laos	Boise	Laval
Ray	Leon	Bourg	Le Puy
Rio	Lima	Braga	Lhasa
Ude	Lomé	Cairo	Liege
Ufa	Male	Cuzco	Lille
Zug	Metz	Cuzev	Lyons
	Nara	Dacca	Macao
4 letters:	Nuuk	Dakar	Melun
Acra	Oslo	Delhi	Meroe
Aden	Pegu	Dhaka	Minsk
Albi	Pune	Dijon	Monza
Apia	Riga	Dilli	Namur
Auch	Rome	Dover	Nancy
Baki	San'a	Dutse	Natal
Baku	Sian	Emisa	Nimes
Bari	Sion	Enugu	Nukus
Bern	Susa	Goias	Oskub
Bida	Suva	Gotha	Palma
Boac	Vila	Guaco	Paris
Bonn	Xian	Hanoi	Parma
Brno		Harar	Patna
Caen	*5 letters:*	Hefei	Pella
Cali	Aarau	Hofei	Perth
Chur	Abiya	Hsian	Petra
Cluj	Abuja	Ikeja	Pinsk
Cork	Accra	Jammu	Poona
Dili	Adana	Jinan	Praha
Doha	Agana	Kabul	Praia
Faro	Aijal	Kandy	Quito
Graz	Akure	Karor	Rabat
Homs	Amman	Kazan	Rouen
Hums	Aosta	Kizyl	Salem
Ipoh	Arlon	Konia	Sanaa
Jolo	Assen	Konya	Scone

Seoul
Simla
Sofia
Stans
Sucré
Tepic
Tokyo
Trier
Tunis
Turin
Uxmal
Vadso
Vaduz
Yanan
Yenan
Zomba

6 letters:
Abakan
Albany
Almaty
Andros
Ankara
Annecy
Anyang
Asmara
Astana
Athens
Austin
Bagdad
Baguio
Bamako
Bangui
Banjui
Bassau
Bastia
Batumi
Bauchi
Beirut
Berlin
Bhopal
Bogota
Bruges
Brunei
Cahors
Canton
Colima
Colmar
Cracow
Darwin
Denver

Dessau
Dispur
Dodoma
Dublin
Edessa
Erfurt
Fuchou
Geneva
Giyani
Gondar
Habana
Harare
Havana
Helena
Hobart
Hohhot
Ibadan
Ilorin
Imphal
Jaipur
Jalapa
Johore
Kaduna
Kaunas
Kigali
Kohima
Kuwait
Lahore
Lisbon
Loanda
Lokoja
London
Luanda
Lusaka
Macapá
Maceió
Madrid
Maikop
Majuro
Malabo
Manama
Manaus
Manila
Maputo
Marsan
Maseru
Mekele
Merano
Merida
Moroni
Moscow

Munich
Murcia
Muscat
Nagpur
Nassau
Nevers
Niamey
Nouméa
Ottawa
Oviedo
Owerri
Palmas
Panaji
Panjim
Peking
Pierre
Prague
Puebla
Punaka
Quebec
Ranchi
Recife
Regina
Rennes
Riyadh
Roseau
Ryazan
Saigon
Sardes
Sardis
Sarnen
Sendai
Skopje
Sokoto
Sparta
St Gall
St Paul
Taipei
Tallin
Tarawa
Tarbes
Tarsus
Tehran
Tetuan
Thebes
Thimbu
Tirana
Tobruk
Toledo
Toluca
Topeka

Ulundi
Umtata
Vesoul
Vienna
Warsaw
Xining
Yangon
Yaunde
Zagreb
Zurich
Zwolle

7 letters:
Abidjan
Ajaccio
Alençon
Algiers
Altdorf
Antioch
Atlanta
Auxerre
Baghdad
Bangkok
Barnaul
Begawan
Beijing
Belfast
Belfort
Bien Hoa
Bijapur
Bikaner
Bishkek
Bobigny
Bologna
Calabar
Caracas
Cardiff
Cayenne
Cetinje
Coblenz
Coimbra
Colombo
Conakry
Concord
Cordoba
Cuttack
Douglas
Durango
Foochow
Funchal
Gangtok

Goiania
Guiyang
Haarlem
Halifax
Hanover
Hassett
Herisau
Honiara
Huhehot
Iqaluit
Isfahan
Izhevsk
Jackson
Jakarta
Kaesong
Kaifeng
Kampala
Karachi
Kashmir
Kharkov
Khartum
Koblenz
Konakri
Kuching
Kunming
Lanchow
Lansing
Lanzhou
Lashkar
Liestal
Limoges
Lincoln
Louvain
Lucerne
Lucknow
Madison
Malacca
Managua
Masbate
Mathura
Mbabane
Memphis
Messene
Morelia
Munster
Nairobi
Nalchik
Nanjing
Nanking
Nicosia
Nineveh

Novi Sad
Olomouc
Oshogbo
Pachuca
Palermo
Palikit
Papeete
Phoenix
Pishpek
Plovdiv
Potenza
Potsdam
Punakha
Quimper
Raleigh
Rangoon
San José
San Juan
Santa Re
Sao Tomé
Sapporo
Saransk
Stanley
St John's
Taiyuan
Tallinn
Tangier
Tbilisi
Teheran
Tel Aviv
Thimphu
Tiemcen
Toronto
Trenton
Trieste
Tripoli
Umuahia
Urumshi
Valetta
Venture
Vilnius
Vilnyus
Xanthus
Yaounde
Yerevan

8 letters:
Abeokuta
Abu Dhabi
Adelaide
Agartala

Ashgabet
Asuncion
Auckland
Bar-le-Duc
Belgrade
Belmopan
Beyrouth
Boa Vista
Brasilia
Brisbane
Brussels
Budapest
Cagliari
Calcutta
Campeche
Canberra
Cape Town
Castries
Chambéry
Chaumont
Cheyenne
Chisinau
Coahuila
Columbia
Columbus
Culiacan
Curitiba
Damascus
Dehra Dun
Djibouti
Dushanbe
Ecbatana
Edmonton
Eraklion
Florence
Freetown
Fribourg
Funafuti
Gaborone
Godthaab
Golconda
Hannover
Hargeisa
Hartford
Helsinki
Honolulu
Istanbul
Jayapura
Kandahar
Katmandu
Khartoum

Kilkenny
Kingston
Kinshasa
Kinossat
Kirkwall
Kishinev
Lausanne
Liaoyand
Lilongwe
Luneburg
Mandalay
Mechelen
Mexicali
Monrovia
Monterey
Nanchang
Nanching
Nanterre
Narbonne
Ndjamena
Pamplona
Pergamum
Peshawar
Pnom-Penh
Port Said
Port-Vila
Pretoria
Pristina
Roskilde
Saltillo
Salvador
Salzburg
Santiago
Sao Paulo
Sarajevo
Seremban
Shah Alam
Shanghai
Shenyang
Shillong
Silvassa
Srinigar
St Helier
Tashkent
The Hague
Thonburi
Torshavn
Toulouse
Usumbura
Valletta
Victoria
Vladimir

Warangai
Windhoek
Winnipeg
Yinchuan

9 letters:
Amsterdam
Annapolis
Ashkhabad
Ayutthaya
Banda Aceh
Bandar Ser
Bangalore
Benin City
Birobijan
Bucharest
Bujumbura
Cartagena
Changchun
Changshar
Chengchow
Cherkessk
Chihuahua
Darmstadt
Des Moines
Edinburgh
Fongafale
Fortaleza
Frankfort
Grand Turk
Heraklion
Hyderabad
Innsbruck
Islamabad
Jalalabad
Jerusalem
Karlsruhe
Kathmandu
Kingstown
Knoxville
Kuch Bihar
Leningrad
Ljubljana
Magdeburg
Maiduguri
Marrakesh
Melbourne
Mogadishu
Montauban
Monterrey
Nashville

Nelspriut
Nuku'alofa
Perigueux
Perpignan
Phnom Penh
Podgorica
Polokwane
Port Blair
Port Louis
Porto Novo
Port Royal
Putrajaya
Pyongyang
Reykjavik
Rio Branco
Samarkand
San Merino
Singapore
Solothurn
St George's
Stockholm
Stuttgart
Thorshavn
Trebizond
Ulan Bator
Vientiane
Zhengzhou

10 letters:
Addis Ababa
Basse-terre
Baton Rouge
Bellinzona
Birobidzan
Bratislava
Bridgetown
Campobosso
Carson City
Chandigarh
Charleston
Cooch Behar
Copenhagen
Eisenstadt
Frauenfeld
Georgetown
Harrisburg
Heidelberg
Hermosillo
Joao Pessoa
Klagenfurt
Kragujevac

Launceston
Leeuwarden
Libreville
Little Rock
Maastricht
Mexico City
Middelburg
Mogadiscio
Montevideo
Montgomery
Montpelier
Nouakchott
Panama City
Paramaribo
Persepolis
Podgoritsa
Porto Velho
Providence
Rawalpindi
Sacramento
Trivandrum
Tskhinvali
Valladolid
Washington
Wellington
Whitehorse
Willemstad
Winchester
Yashkar-Ola

11 letters:
Bhubaneswar
Brazzaville
Buenos Aires
Campo Grande
Charlestown
Dares Salaam
Fredericton
Gandhinagar
Guadalajara
Hermoupolis
Johore Bahru
Kuala Lumpur
Montbeliard
Nakhichevan
Ouagadougou
Pandemonium
Pondicherry
Port Moresby
Porto Alegre
Port of Spain

Rio Gallegas
Saarbrucken
San Salvador
Springfield
St Peter Port
Tallahassee
Tegucigalpa
Thohoyandou
Ulaanbaatar
Vatican City
Vladikavkaz
Yellowknife

12 letters:
Antananarivo
Anuradhapura
Bloemfontein
Chilpancingo
Fort-de-France
Indianapolis
Johannesburg
Kota Kinabalu
Mont-de-Marsan
Muzzafarabad
Pandaemonium
Petrozavodsk
Port-au-Prince
Port Harcourt
Rio de Janeiro
Salt Lake City
Santo Domingo
Schaffhausen
Schoemansdal
Seringapatam
Tenochtitian
Villahermosa
Williamsburg
Yamoussoukro

13 letters:
Belo Horizonte
Charlottetown
Florianopolis
Funafuti Atoll
Guatemala City
Hertogenbosch
Jefferson City
Yaren District

14 letters:
Andorra la Vella

Constantinople	Puerto Princesa	*15 letters:*	*16 letters:*
Kuala Trengganu	's Hertogenbosch	Chalons-sur-Marne	Pietermaritzburg
Oaxaca de Juarez		Charlotte Amalie	Trixtia Gutiérrez
		Clermont-Ferrand	

Capitalise Carpe diem
Capitalist Financier, Moneyer, Sloane
▷ **Capitalist** *may indicate* a citizen of a capital
Capitulate Acquiesce, Comply, → **SURRENDER**
Capless Bare
▷ **Capless** *may indicate* first letter missing
Capone Al, Scarface
▷ **Capriccioso** *may indicate* an anagram
Caprice, Capricious Arbitrary, Boutade, Capernoitie, Cap(p)ernoity, Conceit, Desultory, Erratic, Fancy, Fickle, Fitful, Freak, Humoresk, Humoresque, Irony, Megrim, Mood, Perverse, Quirk, Vagary, Wayward, Whim(sy)
Capsize Crank, Overbalance, Purl, Tip, Turn turtle, Upset, Whemmle, Whomble
▷ **Capsized** *may indicate* a word upside down
Capstan Sprocket, Windlass
Capsule Amp(o)ule, Bowman's, Cachet, Habitat, Internal, Ootheca, Orbiter, Ovisac, Pill, Space, Spacecraft, Spansule, Spermatophore, Suppository, Time, Urn
Captain Ahab, Bligh, Bobadil, Bones, Brassbound, Capt, Channel, Chief, Cid, Commander, Condottiere, Cook, Copper, Cuttle, Flint, Group, Hornblower, Kettle, Kidd, Leader, Macheath, Master, Nemo, Old man, Owner, Patron, Patroon, Post, Privateer, Protospatharius, Skip(per), Standish, Subah(dar), Subedar, Swing, Trierarch
Caption Cutline, Heading, Headline, Inscription, Masthead, Roller, Sub-title, Title
Captious Critical, Peevish
Captivate(d), Captivating Beguile, Bewitch, Charm, Enamour, Enthrall, Epris(e), Take, Winsome
Captive, Captivity Bonds, Duress, POW, Prisoner, Slave
Capture Abduct, Annex, Bag, Catch, Collar, Cop, Electron, Enchain, Enthral(l), Grab, Land, Motion, Net, Prize, Rush, Seize, Snabble, Snaffle, Snare, → **TAKE**
Capuchin Cebus, Monkey, Sajou
Car Alvis, Astra, Audi, Austin, Auto, Banger, Beetle, Berlin, Biza, BL, Bluebird, Bomb, Boneshaker, Brake, Bubble, Buffet, Bugatti, Buick, Bumper, Bus, Cab(riolet), Cadillac, Catafalco, Catafalque, Chariot, Chorrie, Classic, Clunker, Coach, Company, Concept, Convertible, Cortina, Coupé, Courtesy, Crate, Daimler, Diner, Dodgem®, Drag(ster), Drophead, Dunger, Elf, Estate, E-type, Fastback, Fiat, Flivver, Ford, Formula, Freight, Friday, Gas guzzler, Ghost, Gondola, Griddle, GT, Hardtop, Hatchback, Heap, Hearse, Hillman, Hot hatch, Hot-rod, Irish, Jaguar, Jalop(p)y, Jamjar, Jammy, Jam sandwich, Jaunting, Jim Crow, Kart, Kit, Knockabout, Lada, Lagonda, Lancia, Landaulet, Landrover, Lift-back, Limo, Limousine, Merc(edes), MG, Mini, Model T, Morgan, Morris, Nacelle, Notchback, Observation, Opel, Pace, Palace, Panda, Parlo(u)r, Patrol, Popemobile, Production, Prowl, Pullman, Racer, Ragtop, Railroad, Rattletrap, Restaurant, Roadster, Roller, Rolls (Royce), Rover, RR, Runabout, Runaround, Rust bucket, Saloon, Scout, Sedan, Service, Shooting-brake, Skoda, Sleeper, Sleeping, Soft-top, Speedster, Sports, Squad, Station wagon, Steam, Stock, Stretch-limo, Subcompact, Sunbeam, Supermini, SUV, Tank, Telepherique, Telpher, Three-wheeler, Tin Lizzie, Tonneau, Tourer, Tram, Triumph, Trolley, Tumble, Turbo, Two-seater, Vehicle, Veteran,

Vintage, Voiture, VW, Wheeler, Wheels

Caramel Brûlé

Carat Point

Caravan Caf(f)ila, Convoy, Fleet, Kafila, Motor home, Safari, Trailer

Caravanserai Choltry, Choutry, Inn, Khan

Caraway Aj(o)wan, Carvy, Seed

Car-back Boot, Dick(e)y, Tonneau

Carbamide Urea

Carbide Silicon

Carbine Gun, Musket

Carbohydrate Agar, Agarose, Callose, Carrageenan, Cellulose, Chitin, Dextran, Disaccharide, Glycogen, Heptose, Hexose, Inulin, Ketose, Laminarin, Mannan, Mucilage, Pectin, Pectose, Pentosan(e), Pentose, Saccharide, Sorbitol, Starch, Sucrose, Sugar

Carbolic Orcin

Carbon(ate) Activated, Ankerite, Austenite, Buckminsterfullerene, Buckyball, C, Charcoal, Coke, Dialogite, Diamond, Drice, Dry ice, Flame, Flimsy, Fullerene, Gas black, Graphite, Lampblack, Martensite, Natron, Petroleum coke, Scawtite, Soot, Spode, Spodium, Urao, Witherite, Zaratite

Carbon deficiency Acapnia

Carboy Demijohn

Carbuncle Anthrax, Ruby

Carcase, Carcass Body, Cadaver, Carrion, Corpse, Cutter, Krang, Kreng, Morkin, Mor(t)ling

Card(s), Cardboard Ace, Affinity, Amex®, Arcana, Baccarat, Basto, Bill, Birthday, Bower, Business, Calling, Canasta, Cartes, Cash, Caution, Charge, Cheque, Chicane, Cigarette, Club, Comb, Communion, Community, Compass, Court(esy), Credit, Cue, Curse of Scotland, Dance, Debit, Deck, Deuce, Devil's (picture) books, Diamond, Donor, Drawing, Ecarté, Eccentric, Euchre, Expansion, Face, False, Flash, Flaught, Flush, → **GAME**, Gold, Green, Hand, Hard, Health, Heart, Hole, Honour, ID, Identification, Identity, Intelligent, Jack, Jambone, Jamboree, Joker, Kanban, Key, King, Laser, Leading, Letter, Loo, Loyalty, Magnetic, Manille, Master, Matador, Maximum, Meishi, Meld, Memory, Mise, Mistigris, Mogul, Mournival, Notelet, Oddity, Ombre, Pack, Past, Pasteboard, Payment, PC, Phone, Picture, Placard, Place, Plastic, Playing, Postal, Proximity, Punch(ed), Quatorze, Quatre, Queen, Queer, Quiz, Race, Rail, Ration, Red, Rippler, Rove, Royal marriage, Score, Scraperboard, Scratch, Screwball, Scribble, Shade, Show, SIM, Singleton, Smart, Soda, Solo, Sound, Spade, Spadille, Squeezer, Stiffener, Store, Strawboard, Swab, Swipe, Swish, Switch, Swob, Swot, Talon, Tarok, Tarot, Tease(r), Tenace, Test, Thaumatrope, Ticket, Tiddy, Time, Top-up, Tose, Toze, Trading, Trey, Trump, Two-spot, Union, Valentine, Visa, Visiting, Wag, Warrant, Weirdie, Whitechapel, Wild, Yellow, Zener

Cardigan Ballet-wrap, Jacket, Wam(m)us, Wampus, Woolly

Cardinal Camerlingo, Chief, College, Eight, Eminence, Eminent, Grosbeak, Hat, HE, Hume, Legate, Manning, Mazarin, Medici, Newman, Number, Pivotal, Polar, Prefect, Prelate, Radical, Red, Red-hat, Richelieu, Sacred college, Seven, Sin, Spellman, Ten, Virtue, Vital, Wolsey, Ximenes

Card-player Dealer, Pone

Care(r), Caring Attention, Burden, Cark, Caution, Cerne, Cherish, Community, → **CONCERN**, Cosset, Grief, Heed, Intensive, Kaugh, Keep, Kiaugh, Maternal, Mind, Pains, Palliative, Parabolanus, Primary, Providence, Reck(e), Reke, Residential,

Respite, Retch, Shared, Solicitude, → **TEND**, Tenty, Worry

Careen(ing) Parliament-heel

Career Course, Hurtle, Life, Line, Run, Rush, Speed, Start, Tear, Vocation

▷ **Career** *may indicate* an anagram

Carefree → **CARELESS(LY)**, Dozy, Happy-go-lucky, Irresponsible, → **NEGLIGENT**, Oops, Perfunctory, Rollicking, Thoughtless

Careful(ly) Canny, Chary, Discreet, Gentle, Hooly, Leery, Meticulous, Mindful, Painstaking, Penny-pinching, Penny-wise, Pernickety, Provident, Prudent, Scrimp, Studious, Tentie, Tenty, Thorough, Vigilant, Ware, Wary

Careless(ly) Casual, Cheery, Debonair, Easy, Free-minded, Gallio, Improvident, Imprudent, Inadvertent, Insouciance, Irresponsible, Lax, Lighthearted, Négligé, → **NEGLIGENT**, Nonchalant, Oops, Oversight, Perfunctory, Raffish, Rash, Remiss, Resigned, Riley, Rollicking, Slam-bang, Slapdash, Slaphappy, Slipshod, Sloven(ly), Slubber, Taupie, Tawpie, Thoughtless, Unguarded, Unmindful, Untenty, Unwary

▷ **Carelessly** *may indicate* an anagram

Caress Bill, Coy, Embrace, Fondle, Kiss, Lallygag, Lollygag, Noursle, Nursle, Pet, Straik, Stroke, Touch

Caretaker Concierge, Curator, Custodian, Dvornik, Granthi, Guardian, Interim, Janitor, Nightwatchman, Sexton, Shammash, Shammes, Superintendent, Verger, Warden

Careworn Haggard, Lined, Tired, Weary

Cargo Boatload, Bulk, Burden, Fraught, Freight, Lading, Last, → **LOAD**, Payload, Shipload, Shipment

Caribbean Belonger, Puerto Rican, Soca, Sokah, Taino, WI

Caribou Tuktoo, Tuktu

Caricature, Caricaturist Ape, Beerbohm, Burlesque, Caran d'Ache, Cartoon, Cruikshank, Doyle, Farce, Gillray, Rowlandson, Skit, Spy, Tenniel, Toon, Travesty

Carlin Pug

Carmelite Barefoot, White (Friar)

Carmen AA, BL, Chai, RAC

Carnage Bloodshed, Butchery, Massacre, Slaughter

Carnal Bestial, Lewd, Sensual, Sexual, Worldly

Carnation Clove pink, Dianthus, Gillyflower, Malmaison, Picotee, Pink

Carnival Fair, Fasching, Festival, Fete, Mas, Moomba, Revelry

Carnivore Cacomistle, Cacomixl, Coati, Creodont, Fo(u)ssa, Genet, Glutton, Grison, Meerkat, Ratel, Stoat, Suricate, Viverridae, Wolverine

Carob Algarroba, Locust, St John's bread

Carol(ler) Noel, Sing, Song, Wait, Wassail, Yodel

Carousal, Carouse Bend, Birl(e), Bouse, Bride-ale, Compotation, Drink, Mallemaroking, Mollie, Orge, Orgy, → **REVEL**, Roist, Screed, Spree, Upsee, Upsey, Upsy, Wassail

Carp(er) Beef, Cavil, Censure, Complain, Crab, Critic, Crucian, Crusian, Gibel, Goldfish, Id(e), Koi, Kvetch, Mirror, Mome, Nag, Nibble, Nitpick, Roach, Roundfish, Scold, Twitch, Whine, Yerk, Yirk

Carpenter Beveller, Bush, Cabinet-maker, Carfindo, Chips, Fitter, Joiner, Joseph, Menuisier, Quince, Tenoner, Woodworker, Wright

▷ **Carpenter** *may indicate* an anagram

Carpet Aubusson, Axminster, Beetle, Berate, Bessarabian, Broadloom, Brussels, Castigate, Chide, Dhurrie, Drugget, Durrie, Dutch, Kali, Kelim, Khilim, Kidderminster, Kilim, Kirman, Lecture, Lino, Magic, Mat, Moquette, Persian, Rate, Red, Reprimand, Reproach, Rug, Runner, Shagpile, Shark, Shiraz, Stair, Turkey,

Wall-to-wall, Wig, Wilton

Carrageen Sea-moss

Carriage Air, Ar(a)ba, Aroba, Bandy, Barouche, Bearing, Berlin(e), Bier, Brake, Brit(sch)ka, Britska, Britzka, Brougham, Buckboard, Buggy, Cab, Calash, Calèche, Car, Cariole, Caroche, Carriole, Carryall, Cartage, Chaise, Charabanc, Charet, Chariot, Chassis, Chay, Clarence, Coach, Coch, Composite, Conveyance, Coupé, Curricle, Demeanour, Dennet, Deportment, Désobligeante, Diner, Dormeuse, Dos-a-dos, Do-si-do, Drag, Dros(h)ky, Ekka, Equipage, Fiacre, Fly, Four-in-hand, Gait, Gig, Gladstone, Go-cart, Growler, Gun, Haulage, Herdic, Horseless, Hurly-hacket, Landau(let), Landing, Limber, Mien, Non-smoker, Norimon, Observation-car, Phaeton, Pick-a-back, Pochaise, Pochay, Poise, Port(age), Portance, Postchaise, Posture, Poyse, Pram, Pullman, Purdah, Railcar, Railway, Randem, Rath(a), Remise, Rickshaw, Rockaway, Shay, Sled, Sleeper, Smoker, Sociable, Spider, Spider phaeton, Stanhope, Sulky, Surrey, Tarantas(s), Taxi, T-cart, Tender, Tenue, Tilbury, Tim-whiskey, Tonga, Trail, Trap, Vetture, Victoria, Voiture, Wagonette, Waterage, Whirligig, Whisk(e)y

Carrier Aircraft, Airline, Arm, Baldric, Barkis, Barrow, Bomb-ketch, Bulk, Caddy, Cadge, Camel, Coaster, Common, Conveyor, Escort, Fomes, Fomites, Frog, Grid, Hamper, Haversack, Hod, Janker, Jill, Majority, Minority, Nosebag, Noyade, Obo, Packhorse, Personnel, Pigeon, Porter, Rucksack, Satchel, Schistosoma, Semantide, Sling, Straddle, Stretcher, → **TRAY**, Vector, Wave

Carrion Cadaver, Carcase, Carcass, Flesh, Ket, Stapelia

Carrots Seseli, Titian

Carry(ing) Asport, Bear, Chair, Convey, Enlevé, Escort, Ferry, Frogmarch, Hawk, Hent, Humf, Hump, Humph, Kurvey, Land, Pack, Pickaback, Port, Stock, Sustain, Tide over, Tote, → **TRANSPORT**, Trant, Wage, With, Yank

Carry on Continue, Create, Wage

Carry out Execute, Mastermind, Pursue

Cart Bandy, Barrow, Bogey, Buck, Cape, Car(r)iole, Chapel, Democrat, Democrat wagon, Dog, Dolly, Dray, Furphy, Gambo, Gill, Golf, Governess, Gurney, Hackery, Jag, Jill, Lead, Mail, Pie, Rickshaw, Scot, Scotch, Shandry, T, Tax(ed), Telega, Trolley, Tumbrel, Tumbril, Village, Wag(g)on, Wain, Whitechapel

Cartel Duopoly, Ring, Syndicate

Carthaginian Punic

Carthorse Aver, Shire

Carthusian Bruno

Cartilage Antitragus, Arytenoid, Chondral, Chondrin, Chondrus, Cricoid, Darwin's tubercle, Disc, Epiglottis, Gristle, Hyaline, Lytta, Meniscus, Semilunar, Tendron, Thyroid, Tragus, Worm, Xiphoid

Cartload Seam

Cartographer Cabot, Chartist, Kremer, Mercator, OS, Speed

Carton Box, Case, Crate, Sydney, Tub

Cartoon(ist) Animated, Bairnsfather, Caricature, Comic, Disney, Drawn, Emmet, Fougasse, Fumetto, Garland, Leech, Low, Manga, Mel, Partridge, Popeye, Robinson, Rube Goldberg, Short, Spy, Strip, Tenniel, Thurber, Tidy, Tintin, Trog

Cartridge Ball, Blank, Bullet, Cartouche, Cassette, Crystal, Doppie, Live, Magazine, Magnetic, QIC, Rim-free, Shell, Spent

Cart-track Rut

Cartwheel Handspring

Caruncle Aril, Carnosity

Carve(d), **Carver**, **Carving** Abated, Alcimedon, Armchair, Bas relief, Camaieu,

Cameo, Chisel, Cilery, Crocket, Cut, Dismember, Doone, Enchase, Engrave, Entail, Entayle, Fiddlehead, Gibbons, Glyptic, Hew, Incise, Inscribe, Insculp, Intaglio, Knotwork, Netsuke, Nick, Petroglyph, Scrimshaw, Sculp(t), Slice, Tondo, Trophy, Truncheon, Tympanum, Whakairo, Whittle

Caryatid Column, Telamon

Casanova Heartbreaker, Leman

Cascade Cataract, Fall, Lin(n), Stream, Waterfall

Cascara Buckthorn, Honduras bark, Rhamnus, Wahoo

Case(s), Casing Abessive, Ablative, Accusative, Action, Adessive, Allative, Altered, Appeal, Aril, Ascus, Assumpsit, Attaché, Basket, Beer, Bere, Bittacle, Blimp, Box, Brief, Bundwall, Burse, C, Ca, Cabinet, Calyx, Canister, Canterbury, Capsule, Cartouch(e), Cartridge, Cause celebre, Cellaret, Chase, Chitin, Chrysalis, Cocoon, Compact, Crate, Croustade, Crust, Dative, Declension, Detinue, Dispatch, Dossier, Dressing, Elative, Elytron, Enallage, Ensheath, Essive, Etui, Etwee, Example, Flan, Flapjack, Frame, Genitive, Grip, Hanaper, Hard, Hatbox, Hold-all, Housewife, Hull, Humidor, Husk, Imperial, → **IN CASE**, Index, Indusium, Inessive, Instance, Kalamdan, Keister, Locative, Locket, Lorica, Manche, Matter, Mezuzah, Music, Nacelle, Nominative, Non-suit, Nutshell, Objective, Oblique, Ochrea, Ocrea, Outpatient, Packing, Pair, Papeterie, Patient, Pencil, Penner, Phylactery, Plight, Plummer-block, Pod, Port, Possessive, Prima facie, Puparium, Quiver, Recce, Reconnoitre, Sabretache, Sad, Scabbard, Sheath(e), Shell, Situation, Six-pack, Sporran, Stead, Sted, Subjective, Suit, Tantalus, Tea-chest, Telium, Test, Theca, Tichborne, Trial, Trunk, Valise, Vasculum, Vocative, Volva, Walise, Walking, Wallet, Wardian, Wing, Worst, Writing

Case-harden Nitrode

Casein Curd

Casement Frame, Roger, Sash, Window

Cash Blunt, Bonus, Bounty, Change, Coin, Dosh, Dot, Float, Hard, Idle money, Imprest, Lolly, → **MONEY**, Needful, Ochre, Oscar, Pence, Petty, Ready, Realise, Redeem, Rhino, Spondulicks, Spot, Stumpy, Tender, Tin, Wampum, Wherewithal

Cashier Annul, Break, Depose, Disbar, Dismiss, Oust, Teller, Treasurer

Cashmere Circassienne

Casino Monte Carlo

Cask(et) Armet, Barrel, Barrico, Bas(i)net, Box, Breaker, Butt, Cade, Casque, Cassette, Drum, Firkin, Galeate, Harness, Heaume, Hogshead, Keg, Leaguer, Octave, Pin, Pipe, Puncheon, Pyxis, Run(d)let, Salade, Sallet, Sarcophagus, Scuttlebutt, Shrine, Solera, Tierce, Tun, Wine

Cask-stand Stillion

Cassava Manioc, Tapioca, Yucca

Casserole Diable, Osso bucco, Pot, Salmi, Terrine, Tzimmes

Cassette Cartridge, Tape, Video

Cassia Cleanser, Senna

Cassio Lieutenant

Cassiterite Needle-tin, Tinstone

Cassock Gown, Soutane, Subucula

Cast (down, off, out), Casting Abattu, Actors, Add, Angle, Appearance, Bung, Cire perdue, Die, Discard, Ecdysis, Ectype, Eject, Endocranial, Exorcise, Exuviae, Exuvial, Fling, Found, Fusil, Grape, Heave, Hob, Hue, Hurl, Impression, Ingo(w)es, Keb, Look, Lose, Mew, Molt, Moulage, Mould, Pick, Plaster(stone), Players, Put, Reject, Shed, Shoot, Sling, Slive, Slough, Spoil, Stookie, Tailstock, → **THROW**, Toss, Tot, Warp, Wax, Ytost

▷ **Cast** *may indicate* an anagram or a piece of a word missing
Castanet Crotal(um), Knackers
Castaway Adrift, Crusoe, Gunn, Left, Outcast, Selkirk, Stranded, Weft
▷ **Cast by** *may indicate* surrounded by
Caste Brahmin, Burakumin, Class, Dalit, Group, Harijan, Hova, Kshatriya, Rajpoot, Rajpout, Rank, Scheduled, Sect, Sudra, Untouchable, Vaisya, Varna
Caster Truckle
Castigate Berate, Chastise, Criticise, Denounce, Keelhaul, Lash, Punish, Rate
Cast-iron Spiegeleisen
Castle(d) Bouncy, Broch, C, Chateau, Citadel, Fastness, Fort, Kasba(h), Maiden, Man, Mot(t)e, Move, Rook, Stronghold, Villa

CASTLES

4 letters:	Belvoir	Doubting	Trausnitz
Sand	Braemar	Egremont	
Trim	Calzean	Elephant	10 letters:
	Canossa	Elsinore	Caerphilly
5 letters:	Chillon	Inverary	Kenilworth
Blois	Colditz	Kronberg	Pontefract
Conwy	Culzean	Malperdy	
Corfe	Despair	Pembroke	11 letters:
Hever	Harlech	Perilous	Carisbrooke
Leeds	Lincoln	Rackrent	Chateauroux
Spain	Otranto	Richmond	Eilean Donan
	Schloss	Stirling	Gormenghast
6 letters:	Skipton	Stokesay	
Casbah	Warwick	Stormont	12 letters:
Forfar	Windsor	Tintagel	Fotheringhay
Glamis		Urquhart	Herstmonceux
Howard	8 letters:	Wartburg	Sissinghurst
Ludlow	Balmoral		
Raglan	Bamburgh	9 letters:	13 letters:
	Bastille	Dangerous	Carrickfergus
7 letters:	Berkeley	Dunsinane	
Adamant	Carbonek	Edinburgh	14 letters:
Amboise	Chepstow	Lancaster	Motte and bailey
Arundel	Crotchet	Sherborne	

Castor-oil Ricinus
Castrate(d), Castrato Alter, Cut, Doctor, Emasculate, Eunuch, Evirate, Farinelli, Geld, Glib, Lib, Manzuoli, Moreschi, Mutilate, Neuter, Senesino, Spado, Spay, Swig
Castro Fidel
Casual Accidental, Adventitious, Airy, Blasé, Chance, Chav(ette), Flippant, Grass, Haphazard, Idle, Incidental, Informal, Jaunty, Lackadaisical, Nonchalant, Odd(ment), Offhand, Off-the-cuff, Orra, Passing, Promiscuous, Random, Scratch, Sporadic, Stray, Temp, Throwaway
Casualty Caduac, Chance-medley, → VICTIM
Casuist Jesuit
Cat Catamount, Dandy, Domestic, Fat, Felid, Feline, Flog, Gossip, Hipster, Jazzer, Lair, Lash, Mewer, Mog, Native, Neuter, Nib, Oriental, Painter, Palm, Pardal, Practical,

Puss, Sacred, Scourge, Serval, Sick, Singed, Spew, Spue, Swinger, Top, Vomit

CATS

3 letters:
Gib
Gus
Kit
Rex
Tom

4 letters:
Eyra
Lion
Lynx
Manx
Musk
Pard
Puma

5 letters:
Alley
Civet
Felix
Fossa
Genet
Hodge
Korat
Manul
Ounce
Quoll
Rasse
Rumpy
Tabby
Tiger
Tigon
Zibet

6 letters:
Angora
Birman
Bobcat

Cougar
Foussa
Jaguar
La Perm
Malkin
Margay
Mouser
Musang
Ocelot
Ocicat
Somali
Sphynx
Tibert
Tybalt
Weasel
Zibeth

7 letters:
Burmese
Caracal
Cheetah
Clowder
Dasyure
Foumart
Genette
Leopard
Linsang
Maltese
Nandine
Pallas's
Panther
Persian
Pharaoh
Polecat
Ragdoll
Siamese
Tiffany
Tigress

Viverra

8 letters:
Balinese
Baudrons
Cacomixl
Cheshire
Devon Rex
Kilkenny
Long-hair
Mountain
Munchkin
Ringtail
Snowshoe
Tiffanie

9 letters:
Asparagus
Binturong
Bluepoint
Chantilly
Chartreux
Delundung
Grimalkin
Himalayan
Maine Coon
Marmalade
Mehitabel
Niebelung
Sealpoint
Shorthair
Tobermory
Tonkinese

10 letters:
Abyssinian
Cacomistle
Cornish Rex

Jaguarondi
Jaguarundi
Selkirk Rex
Turkish Van

11 letters:
Colourpoint
Egyptian Mau
Havana Brown
Russian Blue
Tongkingese

12 letters:
American Curl
Scottish Fold

13 letters:
Tortoise-shell
Turkish Angora

14 letters:
Asian Shorthair
Australian Mist
Siberian Forest

15 letters:
Norwegian Forest

16 letters:
American Wirehair

19 letters:
Californian
Spangled

Catacomb Cemetery, Crypt, Hypogeum, Vault
Catalepsy Catatony, Trance
Catalogue Cattle dog, Dewey, Dictionary, Index, Inventory, List, Litany, Magalog, Messier, Ragman, Ragment, Raisonné, Record, Register, Specialogue, Star, Subject, Table, Tabulate, Thematic, Union
Catalyst Accelerator, Agent, Influence, Kryptonite, Stereospecific, Unicase, Ziegler
Catamite Gunsel, Ingle, Pathic
Catapult Ballista, Ging, Launch, Mangon(el), Perrier, Petrary, Propel, Scorpion,

Shanghai, Sling, Slingshot, Stone-bow, Tormentum, Trebuchet, Wye, Y

Cataract Cascade, Film, Pearl, Pearl-eye, Torrent, Waterfall, Web and pin

Catarrh Coryza, Rheum

Catastrophe Apocalypse, Calamity, → **DISASTER**, Doom, Epitasis, Fiasco, Meltdown

Catatonia Stupor

Cat-call Boo, Jeer, Mew, Miaow, Miaul, Razz, Wawl, Whistle, Wrawl

Catch(y), Caught Air, Apprehend, Attract, Bag, Benet, Bone, C, Capture, Chape, Clasp, Cog, Collar, Contract, Cop, Corner, Cotton on, Ct, Deprehend, Detent, Dolly, Engage, Enmesh, Ensnare, Entoil, Entrap, Fang, Field, Fumble, Gaper, Get, Glee(some), Grasp, Had, Hank, Haud, Haul, Hear, Hitch, Hold, Hook, Inmesh, Keddah, Keight, Kep(pit), Kheda, Kill, Land, Lapse, Lasso, Latch, Lime, Lock, Morse, Nab, Nail, Net, Nick, Nim, Nobble, Noose, Overhear, Overhent, Overtake, Parti, Pawl, Rap, Release, Rope, Round, Rub, Safety, Sean, Sear, See(n), Seize, → **SNAG**, Snap, Snare, Snib, Snig, → **SONG**, Surprise, Swindle, Tack, Take, Tickle, Trammel, Trap, Trawl, Trick, Tripwire, Troll, Twenty two, Twig, Understand, Wrestle

Catchword Motto, Shibboleth, Slogan, Tag

Catechism Carritch, Shorter, Test

Categorise, Category → **CLASS**, Etic, Genre, Genus, Label, Order, Pigeonhole, Range, Stereotype, Taxon, Triage

Cater(er) Acatour, Cellarer, Feed, Manciple, → **PROVIDE**, Purveyor, Serve, Steward, Supply, Victualler, Vivandière

Caterpillar Army worm, Aweto, Boll worm, Cabbageworm, Cotton-worm, Cutworm, Eruciform, Geometer, Gooseberry, Hop-dog, Hornworm, Inchworm, Larva, Looper, Osmeterium, Palmer, Tent, Webworm, Woolly-bear

Catfish Hassar, Woof

Cathartic Turbeth

Cathedral Amiens, Basilica, Birmingham, Burgos, Chartres, Chester, → **CHURCH**, Cologne, Cortona, Dome, Duomo, Durham, Ely, Evreux, Gloucester, Guildford, Hereford, Hertford, Huesca, Kirkwall, Lateran, Lichfield, Lincoln, Lugo, Minster, Mullingar, Notre Dame, Rheims, Ripon, St Albans, St Davids, St Paul's, Salisbury, Santiago de Compostela, Sens, Teruel, Up(p)sala, Viseu, Wakefield, Wells, Westminster, Winchester, Worcester, York

Catherine Braganza, Parr

Catherine-wheel Girandole

Cathode Electrode, Filament, Ray

Catholic Assumptionist, Broad, Defenders, Doolan, Eclectic, Ecumenical, Fenian, General, Irvingism, Jebusite, Latin, Lazarist, Left-footer, Liberal, Marian, Opus Dei, Ostiary, Papalist, Papaprelatist, Papist, Passionist, Recusant, Redemptionist, Roman, Salesian, Spike, Taig, Te(a)gue, Teigue, Theatine, Thomist, Tike, Tory, Tridentine, Tyke, Universal, Ursuline, Waldenses, Wide

Catkin Amentum, Chat, Lamb's tail, Pussy-willow, Salicaceous

Cat-lover Ailurophile

Catmint Nep, Nepeta

Cato Porcian, Uticensis

Cats-eye Chatoyant, Cymophane

Catsmeat Lights

Catspaw Pawn, Tool

Cat's tail Reed-mace, Typha

Cat's whiskers Vibrissa

Cattle(pen) Aberdeen Angus, Africander, Ankole, Aver, Ayrshire, Beefalo, Belgian
Blue, Bestial, Black, Brahman, British White, Buffalo, Carabao, Charbray, Charolais,
Chillingham, Dexter, Drove, Durham, Fee, Friesland, Galloway, Gaur, Gayal,
Guernsey, Gyal, Heard, Herd, Hereford, Highland, Holstein (Friesian), Illawarra,
Jersey, Kerry, Kine, Kouprey, Kraal, Ky(e), Kyloe, Lairage, Limousin, Lincoln,
Longhorn, Luing, Neat, Nout, Nowt, Owsen, Oxen, Piemontese, Rabble, Redpoll,
Rother, Santa Gertrudis, Shorthorn, Simment(h)al, Soum, South Devon, Sowm,
Steer, Stock, Store, Stot, Sussex, Tamarao, Tamarau, Teeswater, Welsh Black
Cattle disease Actinobacillosis, Actinomycosis, Anthrax, Black water, Dry-bible,
Footrot, Gallsickness, Heart-water, Hoove, Johne's, Listeriosis, Lumpy jaw, Mange,
Mastitis, Milk lameness, Moorill, New Forest, Quarter-ill, Red-water, Rinderpest,
Scours, Scrapie, Texas fever, Wire-heel, Woody-tongue
Cattle food Fodder
Cattleman Cowboy, Herder, Maverick, Rancher, Ringer, Stock-rider
Catty Kin, Spiteful
Caucasian Aryan, Azabaijani, Azeri, Cherkess, European, Georgian, Iberian,
Kabardian, Melanochroi, Paleface, Semite, Shemite, White, Yezdi, Yezidee, Zezidee
Caucus Assembly, Cell, Gathering, Race
▶ **Caught** see CATCH
Caul Baby-hood, Kell, Membrane, Sillyhow
Cauldron Kettle, Pot
Cauliflower Curd, Ear, Floret
Caulk Fill, Pay, Pitch, Snooze
Causation, Cause(d), Causes Aetiology, Agent, Beget, Breed, Bring, Compel,
Create, Crusade, Determinant, Due, Effect, Efficient, Encheason, Engender, Factor,
Final, First, Flag-day, Formal, Gar(re), Generate, Ideal, Induce, Lead, Lost, Make,
Material, Motive, Movement, Natural, → OCCASION, Parent, Probable, Provoke,
Proximate, Reason, Root, Sake, Secondary, Source, Teleology, Topic, Ultimate,
Wreak
Causeway Giant's, Tombolo
Caustic Acid, Acrimonious, Alkaline, Burning, Common, Erodent, Escharotic, Lime,
Lunar, Moxa, Pungent, Sarcastic, Scathing, Seare, Soda, Tart, Vitriol, Waspish,
Withering
Cauterise, Cauterisation Brand, Burn, Disinfect, Inustion, Moxibustion, Sear
Caution, Cautious (person) Achitophel, Admonish, Ahithophel, Alert, Amber,
Awarn, Beware, Cagey, Card, Care, Cave, Caveat, Chary, Circumspect, Credence,
Cure, Defensive, Deliberate, Discretion, Fabian, Gingerly, Guard(ed), Heedful,
Leery, Prudent, Rum, Scream, Skite, Tentative, Timorous, Vigilant, Ware,
→ WARN, Wary, Yellow card
Cavalcade Pageant, Parade, Procession, Sowarree, Sowarry
Cavalier Brusque, Cicisbeo, Devil-may-care, Gallant, Lively, Malignant, Offhand,
Peart, Rider, Royalist
Cavalry(man) Blues, Car(a)bineer, Car(a)binier, Cornet, Cossack, Dragoon, Equites,
Heavies, Horse, Horse Guards, Household, Hussar, Ironsides, Knights, Lancers,
Life Guards, Light-horse, Plunger, Ressaldar, Risaldar, Rough-rider, Rutter, Sabres,
Silladar, Spahi, Uhlan, Yeomanry
Cave(rn), Caves, Cave-dwelling Acherusia, Aladdin's, Alert, Altamira, Antar,
Antre, Beware, Cellar, Collapse, Corycian, Den, Domdaniel, Erebus, Fingal's, Fore,
Grot(to), Hollow, Jenolan, Lascaux, Look-out, Lupercal, Mammoth, Nix, Pot-hole,
Proteus, Sepulchre, Snow, Spel(a)ean, Speleology, Spelunker, Speos, Tassili,
Trophonian, Vault, Waitomo, Ware, Weem, Wookey Hole

Cave-dweller Troglodyte
Caveman Adullam, Aladdin, Fingal, Neanderthal, Primitive, Troglodyte, Troll
Caviare Beluga, Osietra, Roe, Sevruga, Sturgeon
Cavil Carp, Haggle, Quibble
Cavity Acetabulum, Amygdale, Amygdule, Androclinium, Archenteron, Atrial, Body, Camera, Camouflet, Celom, Chamber, Clinandrium, Coelenteron, Coelom(e), Concepticle, Concha, Countermark, Crater, Crypt, Dent, Domatium, Druse, Enteron, Follicle, Foss, Gap, Geode, Glenoid, Hold, Hole, Lacuna, Locule, Mediastinum, Miarolitic, Orbita, Orifice, Pocket, Pulp, Resonant, Segmentation, Sinus, Stomod(a)eum, Tear, Thunderegg, Tympanum, Vacuole, Vein, Ventricle, Vesicle, Vitta, Vomica, Vug, Vugg, Vugh, Well
Cavort(ing) Jag
Cavy Agouti, Capybara, Hograt, Paca
Cease(fire) Abate, Blin, Cut, Desist, Die, Disappear, Halt, Intermit, Lin, Lose, Pass, Refrain, Remit, Sessa, → **STOP**, Truce
Ceaseless Eternal, Incessant
Cecil Rhodes
Cedar(wood) Arolla, Atlas, Deodar, Incense, Jamaica, Japanese, Toon
Cede Grant, Yield
Ceiling Absolute, Barrel, Coffered, Cove, Cupola, Dome, Glass, Lacunar, Laquearia, Limit, Plafond, Roof, Service, Soffit, Stained glass
Celebrate(d), Celebration, Celebrity Ale, Beanfeast, Besung, Bigwig, Binge, Carnival, Cel, Chant, Commemorate, Distinguished, Do, Emblazon, Encaenia, Epithalamion, Epithalamium, Fame, Feast, Fest, Festivity, Fete, Fiesta, Gala, Gaudeamus, Gaudy, Glorify, Grog-up, Harvest home, Hold, Holiday, Honour, Jamboree, Jol, Jollifications, Jollities, Jubilee, Keep, Large it, Laud, Legend, Lion, Loosing, Lowsening, Maffick, Mardi Gras, Mass, Mawlid al-Nabi, Megastar, Monstre sacre, Name, Noted, Nuptials, Observe, Occasion, Orgy, Panathenaea, Pinata, Praise, Randan, Rejoice, Renown, Repute, Revel, Rite, Roister, Saturnalia, Sing, Spree, Star, Storied, Sung, Superstar, Treat, Triumph, Wassail, Wet
Celerity Dispatch, Haste, Speed, Velocity
Celery Alexanders, Smallage, Stick
Celestial Chinese, Divine, Ethereal, Heavenly, Supernal, Uranic
Celibate, Celibacy Bachelor, Chaste, Paterin(e), Rappist, Rappite, Shakers, Single, Spinster
Cell(s), Cellular Battery, Bullpen, Cadre, Chamber, Chapel, Condemned, Crypt, Cubicle, Death, Dungeon, Group, Laura, Padded, Peter, → **PRISON**, Safety, Strip, Tank, Unit

---

CELLS

1 letter:	*4 letters:*	Oxum	Flame
T	Axon	Soma	Giant
	Comb	Stem	Gland
3 letters:	Cone	Zeta	Guard
Dry	Cyte		Islet
Pec	Fuel	*5 letters:*	Linin
Sex	Germ	Ascus	Lymph
Wet	Hair	Basal	Nerve
	HeLa	Canal	Nicad
	Mast	Clark	Solar

Sperm
Spore
Stone
Swarm
Water
White
X-body

6 letters:
Button
Censor
Collar
Cybrid
Cytoid
Diaxon
Gamete
Goblet
Hadley
Killer
Morula
Mother
Neuron
Oocyte
Plasma
Sensor
Sickle
Somite
Target
Thread
Zygote

7 letters:
Bimorph
Cadmium
Cambium
Cathode
Daniell
Energid
Gemmule
Gravity
Helper T
Initial
Lithite
Myotome
Myotube
Neurite
Neurone
Neutron
Plastid
Primary
Schwann

Sertoli
Somatic
Spireme
Sporule
Storage
Tapetum
Vesicle
Voltaic

8 letters:
Akaryote
Auxocyte
Basidium
Basophil
Blasteme
Blastula
Congenic
Cytology
Daughter
Defensin
Ectomere
Endoderm
Endosarc
Ependyma
Epiblast
Eukaryon
Galvanic
Gonidium
Gonocyte
Hapteron
Hemocyte
Meiocyte
Meristem
Monocyte
Myoblast
Neoblast
Palisade
Parietal
Platelet
Purkinje
Receptor
Retinula
Schizont
Selenium
Seredium
Squamous
Standard
Sweatbox
Symplast
Synergid
Tracheid

Unipolar
Zoosperm
Zoospore

9 letters:
Adipocyte
Antipodal
Astrocyte
Athrocyte
Auxospore
Basophile
Coenocyte
Companion
Corpuscle
Desmosome
Ectoplasm
Embryo-sac
Fibrocyte
Haemocyte
Hybridoma
Idioblast
Internode
Iridocyte
Karyology
Laticifer
Leclanché
Leucocyte
Leukocyte
Merozoite
Microcyte
Micromere
Myelocyte
Myofibril
Organelle
Periplasm
Periplast
Phagocyte
Phellogen
Proembryo
Secondary
Spermatid
Sporocyte
Suspensor
Syncytium
Synkaryon
Thymocyte
Trabecula
Tracheide

10 letters:
Ameloblast

Archespore
Blastoderm
Blastomere
Centrosome
Choanocyte
Chromaffin
Chromosome
Cnidoblast
Eosinophil
Epithelium
Fibroblast
Gametocyte
Histiocyte
Leucoblast
Leukoblast
Lymphocyte
Macrophage
Melanocyte
Mesenchyme
Myeloblast
Neuroblast
Neutrophil
Normoblast
Osteoblast
Osteoclast
Perikaryon
Phelloderm
Protoplast
Spermatium
Spherocyte
Suppressor
Totipotent
White-blood

11 letters:
Aplanospore
Arthrospore
Endothelium
Erythrocyte
Granulocyte
Interneuron
Kinetoplast
Lymphoblast
Megaloblast
Melanoblast
Microgamete
Microvillus
Motor neuron
Odontoblast
Poikilocyte
Propoceptor

Schistocyte
Spheroplast
Suppressor T
Trophoblast

12 letters:
Aplanogamete
Chondroblast

Electrolytic
Gametrangium
Haematoblast
Interstitial
Paraphysisis
Photovoltaic
Reticulocyte
Spermatocyte

Spermatozoid
Spermatozoon
Spongioblast

13 letters:
Chromatophore
Mitochondroin
Photoelectric

Photoreceptor

14 letters:
Spermatogonium
Weston standard

Cellar Basement, Bodega, Coalhole, Dunny, Hypogeum, Ratskeller, Storm, Vault, Vaut, Wine
Cell division Amitosis
Cellist, Cello Casals, Du Pré, Hermit, Prisoner, Tortelier
Celluloid, Cellulose Acetate, Cel, Viscose, Xylonite
Celt(ic) Belgic, Breton, Brython, Cornish, Druid, Gadhel, Gael, Goidel, Helvetii, Kelt, La Tène, P, Q, Taffy, Welsh
Cement Araldite®, Blast-furnace, Compo, Concrete, Fix, Flaunch, Glue, Grout, Gunite, High-alumina, Hydraulic, Lute, Maltha, Mastic, Mortar, Paste, Pointing, Porcelain, Portland, Putty, Rice-glue, Roman, Rubber, Slurry, → STICK, Trass, Water
Cemetery Aceldama, Arenarium, Arlington, Boneyard, Boot Hill, Campo santo, Catacomb, Churchyard, God's Acre, Golgotha, Graveyard, Musall, Necropolis, Père Lachaise, Potter's field, Saqqara, Urnfield
Censer Cassolette, Navicula, Thurible
Censor(ious), Censure Accuse, Admonition, Animadvert, Appeach, Ban, Banner, Berate, Blame, Blue-pencil, Bowdler, Braid, Cato, Comstockery, → CONDEMN, Critical, Criticise, Damn, Dang, Decry, Dispraise, Edit, Excommunicate, Excoriate, Expurgate, Gag, Obloquy, Opprobrium, Rap, Repress, Reprimand, Reproach, Reprobate, Reprove, Satirise, Scold, Scrub, Slam, Slate, Stricture, Suppress, Tax, Tirade, Traduce, Wig
Census, Census taker Count, Numerator, Poll
Cent Bean, Coin, Ct, Penny, Red
Centaur Ch(e)iron, Horseman, Nessus, Sagittary, Therianthropic
Centenary, Centennial Anniversary, Colorado
Centipede Chilopoda, Earwig, Polypod, Scolopendra, Scutiger
Central, Centre Active, Amid, Assessment, Attendance, Axis, Broca's, Bunt, Call, Cardinal, Chakra, Civic, Community, Contact, Core, Cost, Day, Daycare, Dead, Detention, Detoxification, Deuteron, Deuton, Downtown, Drop-in, Epergne, Eye, Field, Focus, Frontal, Garden, Health, Heart, Heritage, Hotbed, Hothouse, Hub, Incident, Inmost, Internal, Interpretive, Kernel, Kingpin, Law, Leisure, Lincoln, Live, Main, Mecca, Median, Medulla, Mid(st), Mission, Music, Nave, Nerve, Nucleus, Omphalos, Pompidou, Profit, Property, Reception, Rehabilitation, Remand, Respiratory, Shopping, Social Education, Storm, Teachers', Trauma, Visitor, Waist, Weather
Central heating Cen, CH
▷ **Centre** *may indicate* middle letters
Centrepiece Epergne
Century Age, C, Era, Magdeburg, Period, Siècle, Ton
Cephalopod Ammonite, Calamary, Cuttle, Loligo, Nautilus, Octopus, Sepia, Squid
Ceramic(s) Agateware, Arcanist, China, Earthen, Ferrite, Porcelain, Pottery, Sialon, Tiles

Cereal Amelcorn, Barley, Blé, Bran, Buckwheat, Bulgar, Bulg(h)ur, Cassava, Corn, Cornflakes, Couscous, Emmer, Farina, Gnocchi, Grain, Granola, Groats, Hominy, Maize, Mandioc(a), Mandiocca, Mani(h)oc, Manihot, Mealie, Millet, Muesli, Oats, Paddy, Popcorn, Rye(corn), Sago, Samp, Sarassin, Seed, Semolina, Sorghum, Spelt, Tapioca, Tef(f), Triticale, Triticum, Wheat, Zea

Cerebrate, Cerebration Pore, Thought

Ceremonial, Ceremony Aarti, Amrit, Baptism, Barmitzvah, Chado, Chanoyu, Common Riding, Coronation, Doseh, Durbar, Encaenia, Enthronement, Etiquette, Eucharist, Flypast, Form(al), Formality, Gongyo, Habdalah, Havdalah, Havdoloh, Heraldry, Investiture, Matsuri, Maundy, Mummery, Observance, Occasion, Ordination, Pageantry, Parade, Pomp, Powwow, Protocol, Rite, Ritual, Sacrament, Sado, Seder, Service, State, Tea, Topping-out, Trooping (the Colour), Unveiling, Usage

Cerium Ce

Cert(ain), Certainty Absolute, Actual, Assured, Banker, Bound, Cast-iron, Cinch, Cocksure, Confident, Convinced, Decided, Exact, Fact, Fate, Indubitable, Inevitable, Infallible, Keen, Monte, Moral, Nap, Needly, One, Positive, Poz, Precise, Racing, Shoo-in, Siccar, Sicker, Snip, Some, → **SURE**, Sure-fire, Truth, Yes

Certainly Agreed, Ay, Certes, Fegs, Forsooth, Indeed, Iwis, Jokol, OK, Oke, Pardi(e), Pardy, Perdie, Siccar, Sicker, → **SURE**, Truly, Verily, Yea, Yes, Yokul, Ywis

Certificate, Certified, Certify Affirm, Assure, Attest, Bene decessit, Birth, Bond, Chit, Cocket, Confirm, Credential, Death, Debenture, Depose, Diploma, Docket, Document, Enseal, Gold, Guarantee, Landscrip, Licence, Lines, Medical, MOT, Notarise, Paper, Patent, Proven, Savings, School, Scrip, Scripophily, Security, Share, Stamp note, Stock, Sworn, Talon, Testamur, Testimonial, Treasury, U, Unruly, Voucher, Warrant

Cesspit Bog, Dungmere, Sinkhole, Slurry

Cetacean Dolphin, Porpoise, Whale

Ceylon(ese) Serendip, Vedda(h)

Chafe(r), Chafing Chunter, Fray, Fret, Harass, Intertrigo, Irritate, Pan, → **RUB**, Seethe, Worry

Chaff(y) Badinage, Banter, Bran, Chip, Cornhusk, Dross, Hay, Husk, Rag, Raillery, Rally, Ramentum, Refuse, Roast, Rot, Tease, Twit

Chaffer(ing) Bandy, Bargain, Haggle, Higgle, Hucksterage, Traffic

Chaffinch Whitewing

Chagrin Envy, Mortify, Spite, Vexation

Chain(s), Chained Acre's-breadth, Albert, Anklet, Band, Bicycle, Bind, Bond, Bracelet, Branched, Bucket, Cable, Catena, Chatelaine, Choke, Cistron, Closed, Cordillera, Cyclic, Daisy, Decca, Dixie, Drive, Duplex, Dynasty, Engineer's, Esses, Fanfarona, Fetter, Fob, Food, Furlong, Gleipnir, Golden, Grand, Gunter's, Gyve, Heavy, Human, Learner's, Lockaway, Markov, Mayor, Micella(r), Micelle, → **MOUNTAIN**, Noria, Open, Pennine, Pitch, Range, Rockies, Rode, Roller, Safety, Seal, → **SERIES**, Shackle, Side, Slang, Snigging, Snow, Sprocket, Straight, String, Strobila, Supply, Surveyor's, Suspensor, Team, Tug, Voluntary, Watch

Chain-gang Coffle

Chair Basket, Bath, Bench, Bentwood, Berbice, Bergère, Birthing, Bosun's, Butterfly, Camp, Cane, Captain's, Carver, Club, Curule, Deck, Dining, Director's, Easy, Electric, Emeritus, Estate, Fauteuil, Fiddle-back, Folding, Frithstool, Garden, Gestatorial, Guérite, High, Jampan, Jampanee, Jampani, Ladder-back, Lounger, Love-seat, Lug, Merlin, Morris, Musical, Nursing, Personal, Pew, Preside, Recliner, Rocker, Rush-bottomed, → **SEAT**, Sedan, Steamer, Stool, Straight, Sugan, Swivel,

Throne, Wainscot, Wheel, Windsor, Wing

Chair-back Ladder, Splat

Chairman Convener, Emeritus, Landammann, Mao, MC, Pr(a)eses, Prof, Prolocutor, Sheraton, Speaker

Chalaza Albumen, Treadle, Treddle

Chaldean Babylonian, Ur

Chalet Cabana, Cot, Skio

Chalice Poisoned

Chalk(y) Calcareous, Cauk, Cawk, Crayon, Credit, Cretaceous, Dentin, French, Senonian, Soapstone, Spanish, Steatite, Tailor's, White(n), Whit(en)ing

Challenge(r), Challenging Acock, Assay, Call, Cartel, Champion, Charge, Confront, Contest, Dare, Defy, Gage, Gauntlet, Glove, Hazard, Hen(ner), Iconoclasm, Impugn, Insubordinate, Oppugn, Provoke, Query, Question, Recuse, Sconce, Shuttle, Tackle, Taker, Tall order, Tank, Threat, Vie, Wero, Whynot

Chamber(s) Airlock, Atrium, Auricle, Bladder, Bubble, Camarilla, Camera, Casemate, Cavern, Cavitation, Cavity, Cell(a), Chanty, Close-stool, Cloud, Cofferdam, Combustion, Cubicle, Decompression, Dene-hole, Dolmen, Echo, Float, Fumatorium, Fume, Gas, Gazunder, Gilded, Hall, Horrors, Hypogea, Inspection, Ionization, Jerry, Jordan, Kiva, Lethal, Locule, Lok Sabha, Lower, Magma, Manhole, Mattamore, Mesoscaphe, Plenum, Po(t), Presence, Priest('s)-hole, Privy, Reaction, Resonance-box, Roum, Second, Serdab, Silo, Spark, Star, Steam-chest, Swell-box, Synod, Thalamus, Undercroft, Upper, Utricle, Vault, Ventricle, Wilson cloud, Zeta

Chamberlain Camerlengo, Camerlingo, Censor

Chameleon American, Anole, Ethiopian, Lizard, Tarand

Chamfer Bevel, Groove

Chamois Ibex, Izard, Shammy

Champ Bite, Chafe, Chew, Chomp, Eat, Gnash, Gnaw, Hero, Mash, Morsure, Munch

Champagne Boy, Bubbly, Charlie, Fizz, Gigglewater, Pop, Sillery, Simkin, Simpkin, Stillery, Troyes, Widow

Champion(s) Ace, Adopt, Ali, Apostle, Belt, Campeador, Cid, Cock, Crusader, Cupholder, Defend, Don Quixote, Doucepere, Douzeper, Dymoke, Enoch, Espouse, Gladiator, Gun, Harry, → HERO, Horse, Kemp, Kemper(yman), King, Knight, Maintain, Matchless, Messiah, Messias, Neil, Paladin, Palmerin, Peerless, Perseus, Promachos, Proponent, Protagonist, Roland, St Anthony, St David, St Denis, St George, St James, St Patrick, Seven, Spiffing, Spokesman, Star, Support, Tribune, Upholder, Victor, Wardog, → WINNER, Yokozuna

Championship Five Nations, Open, Seven, Six Nations, Super Bowl, Title, Tri-nations

Chance (upon), Chancy Accident, Aleatory, Aunter, Bet, Break, Buckley's, Cast, Casual, Cavel, Coincidence, Contingent, Dice, Earthly, Even, Fat, → FATE, Fighting, First refusal, Fluke, Fortuitous, Fortuity, Fortune, → GAMBLE, Game, Hap, Happenstance, Hobnob, Iffy, Kevel, Light, Loaves and fishes, Look-in, Lot, → LOTTERY, Luck, Main, Meet, Mercy, Occur, Odds, Odds-on, Opening, Opportunity, Outside, Peradventure, Posse, Potluck, Probability, Prospect, Random, Rise, Risk, Run into, Russian roulette, Serendipity, Slant, Spec, Sporting, Stake, Stochastic, Sweep, Toss-up, Treble, Turn, Tychism, Ventre, Venture, Wager

Chancel Adytum, Bema, Nave

Chancellor Adolf, Bismarck, Dollfuss, Kohl, Logothete, Minister, More, Wolsey

Chancery Court, Hanaper

Chandelier Candlestick, Corona, Drop, Electrolier, Gasolier, Girandole, Lustre, Pendant

Chandler Acater, Acatour, Raymond
Chaney Lon
Change(able), Changes, Changing Adapt, Adjust, Agio, Aleatoric, → ALTER, Amendment, Attorn, Backtrack, Barter, Become, Bob-major, Capricious, Cash, Catalysis, Chameleon, Channel-hop, Chop, Cline, Commute, Convert, Coppers, Cut, Denature, Departure, Development, Dichrony, Edit, Enallage, Esterify, Eustatic, Evolve, Exchange, Fickle, Find, Flighty, Float, Fluctuate, Flux, Guard, Gybe, Inflect, Innovate, Kembla, Killcrop, Labile, Loose, Make-over, Menopause, Metabolic, Metabolise, Metamorphose, Metamorphosis, Mew, Mobile, Modify, Morph, Mutable, Mutalis mutandis, Mutanda, Mutation, Ontogeny, Parallax, Peal, Pejoration, Peripet(e)ia, Permute, Port, Prisere, Prophase, Protean, Quantum leap, Realise, Recant, Rectify, Reform, Refraction, Regime, Rejig, Reshuffle, Resipiscence, Rest, Reverse, Revise, Revolutionise, Rework, Sandhi, Scourse, Sd, Sea, Seesaw, Sere, Sex, Shake-out, Shake-up, Shift, Silver, Small, Sublimation, Substitute, Swap, Swing, Switch, Tempolabile, Tolsel, Tolsey, Tolzey, Transfer, Transfiguration, Transform, Transition, Transmogrify, Transmute, Transpose, Transubstantial, Turn, Uncertain, Upheaval, U-turn, Vagary, Variant, Variation, Vary, Veer, Versatile, Vicissitude, Volatile, Volte-face, Wankle, Washers, Waver, Weathercock, Wheel, Wow
▷ **Change(d)** *may indicate* an anagram
Changeling Auf, Killcrop, Oaf, Turncoat
Channel Access, Aflaj, Aqueduct, Artery, Beagle, Bed, Billabong, Bristol, Canal, Canaliculus, Chimb, Chime, Chine, Chute, Conduit, Culvert, Cut, Cutting, Distribution, Ditch, Drain, Duct, Dyke, Ea, English, Estuary, Euripus, Fairway, Falaj, Feeder, Floodway, Flume, Foss, Funnel, Furrow, Gat, Gate, Geo, Gio, Glyph, Grough, Gully, Gut, Gutter, Head-race, Ingate, Katabothron, Katavothron, Khor, Kill, Kos, Lane, Latch, Leat, Leet, Limber, Major, Meatus, Medium, Minch, Moat, Mozambique, Multiplex, Narrows, North, Penstock, Pentland Firth, Pescadores, Pipeline, Qanat, Race, Raceway, Rebate, Rigol(l), Rigolets, Rivulet, Run, St George's, Sea-gate, Seaway, Sewer, Shunt, Sinus, Sky, Sloot, Sluice, Sluit, Sny(e), Solent, Solway Firth, Sound, Sow, Spillway, Sprue, Strait, Suez, Sure, Swash, Tailrace, Tideway, Tracheole, Trough, Ureter, Vallecula, Vein, Wasteweir, Watercourse, Waterspout, Wireway, Yucatan
Chant Anthem, Antiphon, Canticle, Cantillate, Cantus, Chaunt, Daimoku, Decantate, Euouae, Evovae, Gregorian, Haka, Harambee, Hymn, Intone, Introit, Mantra(m), Motet, Pennillion-singing, Plainsong, Proper, Psalm, Sing, Slogan, Te Deum, The Reproaches, Yell
Chantilly Cream, Lace
Chaos, Chaotic Abyss, Anarchy, Confusion, Disorder, Fitna, Fractal, Hun-tun, Jumble, Mess, Mixter-maxter, Muss, Shambles, Shambolic, Snafu, Tohu bohu
▷ **Chaotic** *may indicate* an anagram
Chap(s) Beezer, Bloke, Bo, Bod, Bor, Cat, Chafe, Cheek, Chilblain, Chop, Cleft, Cod, Codger, Cove, Crack, Customer, Dog, Fella, Fellow, Flews, Genal, Gent, Gink, Guy, Hack, Joll, Jowl, Kibe, Lad, → MAN, Mouth, Mum, Ocker, Rent, Rime, Spray, Spreathe, Spreaze, Spreethe, Spreeze, Wang
Chapel Bethel, Bethesda, Beulah, Cha(u)ntry, Chevet, Ebenezer, Feretory, Galilee, Lady, Oratory, Parabema, Prothesis, Sacellum, Sistine
Chaperon(e) Beard, Cap, Duenna, Escort, Gooseberry, Griffin, Griffon, Gryphon, Muffin
Chaplain CF, Ordinary, Padre, Priest, Skypilot, Slope
Chaplet Anadem, Coronet, Fillet, Garland, Wreath

▷ **Chaps** *may indicate* an anagram

Chapter Accidents, C, Canon, Cap, Capitular, Ch, Chap, Cr, Division, Episode, Lodge, Phase, Section, Social, Sura(h), Verse

Char(woman) Adust, Burn, Cleaner, Coal, Daily, Duster, Mop(p), Mrs Mop(p), Scorch, Sear, Singe, Smoulder, Toast, Togue, Torgoch

Charabanc Bus, Chara, Coach

Character(s) Aesc, Alphabet, Ampersand, Ampussyand, Atmosphere, Aura, Backslash, Brand, Calibre, Case, Cipher, Clef, Cliff, Climate, Coloration, Complexion, Contour, Credit, Delimiter, Devanagari, Digamma, Digit, Dramatis personae, Emoticon, Ess, Essence, Eta, Ethos, → **FEATURE**, Fish, Fist, Form, Grain, Graphics, Grass, Grit, Hieroglyphic, Homophone, Ideogram, Ideograph, Italic, Kanji, Kern, Kind, La(m)bda, Letter, Logogram, Make-up, Mark, Mu, Nagari, → **NATURE**, Non-person, Nu, Ogam, Ogham, Pahlavi, Pantaloon, Part, Pehlevi, Person(a), Personage, → **PERSONALITY**, Phonogram, Physiognomy, Pi, Polyphone, Protagonist, Psi, Raisonneur, Reference, Reference-mark, Repute, Rho, Role, Rune, Runic, Sampi, San, Self, Sirvente, Slash, Sonancy, Space, Sphenogram, Stamp, Subscript, Superscript(ion), Swung dash, Syllabary, Symbol, Tab, Testimonial, Ton(e), Trait, Uncial, Unit, Vav, Vee, Waw, Wen, Wild card, Wyn(n), Yogh, Zeta

Characterise(d), Characterism, Characteristic(s) Acquired, Attribute, Aura, Cast, Colour, Distinctive, Earmark, Ethos, Facies, Feature, Hair, Hallmark, Has, Headmark, Idiomatic, Idiosyncrasy, Jizz, Lineament, Mien, Nature, Notate, Peculiar, Persona, Phenotype, Point, Property, Quality, Signature, Stigma, Strangeness, Streak, Style, → **TRAIT**, Transfer, Typical, Vein, Way

Characterless Anon, Inane, Wet

Charade Enigma, Pretence, Riddle

Charcoal Activated, Carbon, Coke, Fusain, Sugar

Charge(s), Charged, Charger Access, Accusal, Accuse, Aerate, Agist, Allege, Annulet, Arraign, Ascribe, Assault, Baton, Bear, Behest, Blame, Brassage, Brush, Buckshot, Bum rap, Care, Carrying, Cathexis, Commission, Community, Complaint, Congestion, Cost, Count, Cover, Criminate, Damage, Debit, Delate, Delf, Delph, Demurrage, Depth, Depute, Directive, Dittay, Dockage, Due, Duty, Electric, Electron, Entrust, Entry, Exit, Expense, Fare, Fee, Fill, Fixed, Flag fall, Fleur-de-lis, Floating, Flock, Freight, Fullage, Fuse, Fusil, Fuze, Gazump, Giron, Gravamen, Gyron, → **HERALDIC**, Hot, Hypothec, Impeach, Impute, Indict, Inescutcheon, Inform, Instinct, Ion, Isoelectric, Last, Lien, Lioncel(le), Lionel, Live, Load, Mandate, Mine, Mount, Nuclear, Objure, Obtest, Onrush, Onslaught, Onus, Ordinary, Orle, Overhead, Pastoral, Pervade, Pew-rent, Plaint, Positive, Premium, Prime, Prix fixe, Q, Quayage, Rack-rent, Rap, Rate, Red-dog, Rent, Report, Reprise, Reverse, Roundel, Run, → **RUSH**, Saddle, Service, Specific, Stampede, Steed, Tariff, Tax, Tear, Terms, Tilt, Toll, → **TRAY**, Tressure, Trickle, Trust, Tutorage, Upfill, Vaire, Vairy, Verdoy, Vigorish, Ward, Warhead, Wharfage

Chariot(eer) Auriga, Automedon, Biga, Cart, Charet, Curricle, Hur, Phaethon, Quadriga, Vimana, Wagon, Wain

Charisma Oomph, Personality

Charitable, Charity Alms, Alms-deed, Awmous, Benign, Breadline, Caritas, Cause, Chugger, Dole, Dorcas, Eleemosynary, Kiwanis, Largesse, Leniency, Liberal, Lion, Love, Mercy, Oddfellow, Openhanded, Oxfam, Pelican, Zakat

Charivari Rough music, Uproar

Charlatan Cheat, Crocus, Empiric, Escroc, Faker, Imposter, Katerfelto,

Mountebank, Poseur, Quack(salver), Saltimbanco

Charlemagne Carlovingian

Charles, Charley, Charlie Beard, Car, Champagne, Chan, Chaplin, Checkpoint, Elia, Lamb, (Old) Rowley, Pretender, Rug-gown, Sap, Tail-end, Watchman

Charles de Gaulle Airport

Charlock Runch

Charlotte Bronte, Russe, Yonge

Charm(er), Charming Abracadabra, Abrasax, Abraxas, Allure, Amulet, Appeal, Aroma, Attraction, Beguile, Bewitch, Captivate, Charisma, Circe, Comether, Cute, Cutie, Delectable, Emerods, Enamour, Enchant, Engaging, → ENTRANCE, Fascinate, Fay, Fetish, Grace, Greegree, Gri(s)gris, Hand of glory, Houri, Juju, Magnetic, Mascot, Mojo, Obeah, Obi(a), Periapt, Phylactery, Porte-bonheur, Pretty, Prince, Quaint, Quark, Ravish, Siren, Smoothie, Spellbind, Suave, Sweetness, Taking, Talisman, Tefillah, Telesm, Tephillah, Tiki, Trinket, Unction, Voodoo, Winning, Winsome

▷ **Charming** *may indicate* an anagram

Chart(ed), Charting Abac, Bar, Breakeven, Card, Control, Diagram, Eye, Flip, Flow, Gantt, Graph, Histogram, Horoscope, Hydrography, Isogram, Isopleth, List, Magna Carta, → MAP, Mappemond, Movement, Nomogram, Organisation, Pie, Plane, Plot, Portolano, Ringelmann, Run, Social, Sociogram, Table, Test, Timetable, Waggoner, Weather, Z

Charta, Charter Atlantic, Book, Citizen's, Covenant, Hire, Lease, Let, Novodamus, Rent, Social (Chapter), Tenants', Time, Voyage

Chary Cagey, Careful, Cautious, Frugal, Shy, Wary

Charybdis Maelstrom, Whirlpool

Chase(r), Chasing Cannock, Chace, Chevy, Chivy, Ciseleur, Ciselure, Course, Cranbome, Decorate, Drink, Game, Harass, Hound, → HUNT, Jumper, Oxo, Pursuit, Race, Scorse, Sic(k), Steeple, Sue, Suit, Wild-goose

Chasm Abyss, Crevasse, Fissure, Gap, Gorge, Gulf, Schism, Yawn

Chaste, Chastity Agnes, Attic, Celibate, Classic, Clean, Continent, Fatima, Florimell, Ines, Innocent, Modesty, Nessa, → PURE, Vestal, Virginal, Virtue

Chasten, Chastise(d), Chastisement Beat, Correct, Discipline, Disple, Lash, Rib-roast, Rollicking, Scold, Scourge, Shame-faced, Spank, Strap, Whip

Chat, Chatter(box) Babble, Bavardage, Blab(ber), Blether, Campanero, Causerie, Chelp, Chinwag, Clack, Clishmaclaver, Confab(ulate), Converse, Cosher, Coze, Crack, Dialogue, Froth, Gab(ble), Gas, Gossip, Gup, Hobnob, Jabber, Jargon, Jaw, Kilfud, Madge, Mag(pie), Natter, Patter, Pie, Pourparler, Prate, Prattle, Rabbit, Rabble, Rap, Rattle, Scuttlebutt, Shmoose, Shoot the breeze, Stone, Talk, Talkee-talkee, Tattle, Tongue-work, Twattle, Waffle, Whin, Windbag, Witter, Wongi, Yacketyyak, Yad(d)a-yad(d)a-yad(d)a, Yak, Yap, Yarn, Yatter, Yellow-breasted, Yoking

Chateau Castle, Cru, Malmaison, Schloss

Chateaubriand René

Chattel Asset, Chose, Deodand

Chaucer(ian) Dan, OE

Chauffeur Cabby, Coachy, Driver, Sice, Syce

Chauvinist Alf, Bigot, Jingo, MCP, Partisan, Patriot, Sexist

Cheap A bon marché, Bargain, Base, Catchpenny, Cheesy, Chintzy, Cut-price, Downmarket, Giveaway, Ignoble, Knockdown, Low, Off-peak, Poor, Sacrifice, Shoddy, Stingy, Tatty, Tawdry, Ticky-tacky, Tinhorn, Tinpot, Tinselly, Trivial, Tuppenny, Two-bit, Twopenny, Undear, Vile

▷ **Cheap** *may indicate* a d- or p- start to a word

Cheapside Bow

Cheat(ers), Cheating Bam, Bamboozle, Beguile, Bilk, Bite(r), Bob, Bonnet, Bucket, Bullock, Burn, Cardsharp(er), Charlatan, Chiaus, Chicane(ry), Chisel, Chouse, Clip, Cod, Cog(ger), Colt, Con, Cozen, Crib, Cross, Cross-bite(r), Cuckold, Cully, Defraud, Delude, Diddle, Dingo, Dish, Do, Doublecross, Duckshove, Dupe, Escroc, Faitor, Fiddle, Finagle, Flam, Fleece, Fob, Foister, Fox, Fraud, Gaff, Gip, Glasses, Gull-catcher, Gum, Gyp, Hoax, Hocus, Hoodwink, Hornswoggle, Horse, Intake, Jockey, Leg, Magsman, Mulct, Mump, Nick, Pasteboard, Picaro(on), Poop, Queer, Rib, Rig, Rogue, Rook, Rush, Scam, Screw, Screw over, Shaft, Sharper, Short-change, Slur, Smouch, Snap, Stack, Stiff, Sting, Swindle, Thimble-rigging, Trepan, Trim, Two-time, Welch, Welsh, Wheedle

Check Arrest, Audit, Bauk, Ba(u)lk, Bill, Bridle, Collate, Compesce, Control, Count, Cramp, Cross-index, Curb, Dam, Damp, Detain, Detent, Discovered, Dogs-tooth, Examine, Foil, Frustrate, Halt, Hamper, Hobble, Houndstooth, Inhibit, Inspect, Jerk, Jerque, Let, Limit, Mate, Monitor, Observe, Overhaul, Parity, Perpetual, Prevent, Rain, Reality, Rebuff, Rebuke, Rein, Repress, Reprime, Repulse, Reread, → **RESTRAIN**, Revoke, Saccade, Screen, Service, Setback, Shepherd's, Shorten, Sit-upon, Sneap, Sneb, Snib, Snub, Sound, Spot, → **STEM**, Stent, Stint, Stop, Stunt, Tab, Tally, Tartan, Tattersall, Test, Thwart, Tick, Trash, Verify, Vet

Checkers Chinese, Piece

Check-out Till

Cheddar Cheese, Gorge

Cheek(y) Alforja, Audacity, Brass-neck, Buccal, Chap, Chollers, Chutzpah, Cool, Crust, Flippant, Fresh, Gena(l), Gum, Hard-faced, Hussy, Impertinent, Impudent, Joll, Jowl, Lip, Malapert, Malar, Masseter, Neck, Nerve, Noma, Pert, Presumption, Quean, Sass, Sauce, Sideburns, Wang, Yankie, Zygoma

Cheep Chirp, Chirrup, Peep

Cheer(s), Cheerful(ness), Cheering Acclaim, Agrin, Applaud, Banzai, Barrack, Blithe, Bonnie, Bravo, Bright, Bronx, Bubbly, Buck, Buoy, Cadgy, Canty, Carefree, Cherry, Chin-chin, Chipper, Chirpy, → **COMFORT**, Crouse, Debonair, Drink, Ease, Elate, Elevate, Enliven, Exhilarate, Festive, Genial, Gladden, Happy-go-lucky, Hearten, Hilarity, Holiday, Hooch, Hoorah, Hurra(h), Huzzah, Insouciance, Jocund, Jovial, Kia-ora, L'allegro, Light-hearted, Lightsome, Lively, Meal, Olé, Ovate, Peart, Perky, Please, Praise, Prosit, Rah, Riant, Rivo, Root, Rumbustious, Shout, Sko(a)l, Slainte, Sonsie, Sunny, Ta, Tata, Thanks, Three, Tiger, Tiggerish, Toodle-oo, Upbeat, Warm, Winsome, Yell

Cheerless Dismal, Drab, Drear, Gloomy, Glum, Wint(e)ry

Cheese, Cheesy American, Amsterdam, Appenzell, Asiago, Bel Paese, Blue, Blue vein, Boc(c)oncini, Boursin, Brie, Caboc, Caerphilly, Cambazola, Camembert, Cantal, Casein, Caseous, Cheddar, Cheshire, Chessel, Chèvre, Colby, Cottage, Coulommiers, Cream, Crowdie, Curd, Damson, Danish blue, Derby, Dolcelatte, Double Gloucester, Dunlop, Edam, Emmental(er), Emmenthal(er), Ermite, Esrom, Ewe, Fet(a), Fontina, Fromage frais, Fynbo, Gloucester, Goat, Gorgonzola, Gouda, Grana Padano, Grand Panjandrum, Green, Gruyère, Halloumi, Hard, Havarti, Huntsman, Ilchester, Islay, Jarlsberg®, Junket, Kebbock, Kebbuck, Kenno, Killarney, Lancashire, Leicester, Limburg(er), Lymeswold®, Macaroni, Mascarpone, Mousetrap, Mozzarella, Mu(e)nster, Mycella, Neufchatel, Oka, Orkney, Paneer, Parmesan, Pecorino, Pont l'Eveque, Port Salut, Pot, Provolone, Quark, Raclette, Rarebit, Reblochon, Red Leicester, Rennet, Ricotta, Romano, Roquefort, Sage Derby, Samso, Sapsago, Skyr, Stilton®, Stone, Stracchino, Swiss,

Taleggio, Tilsit, Tofu, Truckle, Vacherin, VIP, Wensleydale

Cheesecake Pin-up, Talmouse

Cheese-scoop Pale

Chef Commis, Escoffier

Chekhov Anton

Chemical Acanthin, Acid, Acrolein, Adrenalin®, Agent Orange, Alar, Aldehyde, Alkali, Allomone, Alum, Amide, Anabolic, Barilla, Bradykinin, Bute, Camphene, Camphor, Carbide, Carnallite, Caseose, Catalyst, Cephalin, Cerebroside, Depside, Developer, Dopamine, Encephalin, Enkephalin(e), Enol, Ethanal, Fixer, Fluoride, Formyl, Freon, Fungicide, Gamone, Glutamine, Glycol, Halon, Harmin, Heavy, Hecogenin, Heptane, Hexylene, Hexylresorcinol, Histamine, Hypo, ICI, Imine, Imipramine, Indican, Interleukin, Larvicide, Lewisite, Morphactin, Naioxone, Natron, Neurotransmitter, Nitre, Nonylphenol, Oestrogen, Olefin, Olein, Oxide, Oxysalt, Pentane, Pentene, Pentyl, Peptide, Periclase, Phenol, Phenyl, Pheromone, Potash, Potassa, Psoralen, Ptomaine, Reagent, Resorcin, Resorcinol, Restrainer, Serotonin, Soman, Soup, Stearate, Strontia, Styrene, Sulphide, Terpene, Thio-salt, Toluol, Toner, Trimer, Weedicide, Weedkiller

Chemise Cymar, Sark, Serk, Shift, Shirt, Simar(re), Smock, Symar

Chemist(ry) Adams, Alchemy, Alchymy, Analyst, Apothecary, Bunsen, Butenandt, Cavendish, Charles, Cleve, Dalton, Davy, Debye, Dewar, Dispenser, Druggist, Drugstore, FCS, Gahn, Hevesy, Inorganic, Lavoisier, Liebig, LSA, Macadam, MPS, Nernst, Newlands, Nobel, Nuclear, Organic, Paracelsus, Pasteur, Pharmacist, Physical, Pothecary, Pottingar, Proust, Prout, Redwood, RIC, Sabatier, Sanger, Schiff, Spageric, Spagiric, Spagyric, Spicer, Stinks, Stoechiometry, Stoich(e)iometry, Technical, Urey, Von Babo, Welsbach, Zymurgy

Cheops Khufu

Cheque Blank, Bouncer, Giro, Gregory, Open, Rubber, Stumer, Tab, Traveller's

Chequer Dice

Cherish(ed) Dear, Dote, Enshrine, Entertain, Esteem, Foment, Foster, Harbour, Inshrine, Nestle, Nurse, Pamper, Pet, Precious, Treasure

Cheroot Cigar, Manil(l)a

Cherry (tree) Amarelle, Amazon, Ball, Barbados, Bigaroon, Bigarreau, Bird, Blackheart, Cerise, Choke, Cornelian, Gean, Ground, Heart, Jerusalem, Kearton, Kermes, Kermesite, Malpighia, Marasca, Maraschino, May-duke, Maz(z)ard, Merry, Morel(lo), Prunus, Red, Sweet, Whiteheart

Cherry-pie Heliotrope

Cherub Angel, Putto, Seraph

Chervil Cow-parsley

Chess (move), Chess player, Chess term Black, Blindfold, Endgame, Euwe, Fianchetto, FIDE, J'adoube, Karpov, Kasparov, Lightning, Miranda, Patzer, Plank, Rapid transit, Shogi, Speed, White, Zugzwang, Zwischenzug

Chessman Bishop, Black, Castle, Horse, King, Knight, Pawn, Pin, Queen, Rook, White

Chest(y) Ark, Bahut, Bosom, Box, Breast, Buist, Bunker, Bureau, Bust, Caisson, Cap-case, Case, Cassone, Chapel, Charter, Chiffonier, Coffer, Coffin, Coffret, Commode, Community, Cub, Dresser, Girnel, Hope, Inro, Kist, Larnax, Locker, Lowboy, Meal-ark, Medicine, Ottoman, Pectoral, Pereion, Pigeon, Pleural, Safe, Scrine, Scryne, Sea, Shrine, Slop, Steam, Sternum, Tallboy, Tea, Thorax, Toolbox, Treasure, Trunk, Wangan, Wangun, Wanigan, War, Wind

Chester Deva

Chestnut Auburn, Badious, Ch, Chincapin, Chinese, Chinkapin, Chinquapin, Cliché,

Conker, Dwarf, Favel(l), Hoary, Horse, Marron, Marron glacé, Moreton Bay, Roan, Russet, Saligot, Soare, Sorrel, Spanish, Sweet, Water

Chest protector → ARMOUR, Bib

Chevalier Bayard, Knight, Pretender

Chevron Dancette, Stripe

Chew(ing) Bite, Champ, Chaw, Cud, Eat, Fletcherism, Gnaw, Gum, Manducate, Masticate, Maul, Meditate, Moop, Mou(p), Munch, Ruminate, Siri(h), Spearmint

Chewink Ground-robin

Chiastolite Macle

Chic Dapper, Debonair, Elegant, Heroin, In, Kick, Modish, Posh, Radical, Smart, Soigné, Stylish, Swish, Tonish, Trim

Chicago Windy City

Chicane(ry) Artifice, Deception, Fraud, Wile

Chichester Yachtsman

Chichi Precious

Chick(en) Australorp, Battery, Biddy, Boiler, Broiler, Capon, Cheeper, Chittagong, Chuckie, Clutch, Cochin, Coronation, Coward, Cowherd, Eirack, Gutless, Hen, Howtowdie, Kiev, Layer, Marengo, Minorca, Mother Carey's, Niderling, Pavid, Poltroon, Poot, Pope's nose, Poult, Pout, Prairie, Precocial, Pullus, Quitter, Roaster, Spatchcock, Spring, Squab, Supreme, Timorous, Unheroic, Windy, Wyandotte, Yellow

Chickenfeed Maize, Peanuts

Chickenpox Varicella

Chickpea Chana, Garbanzo

Chickweed Snow-in-summer

Chicory Endive, Radiccio, Succory, Witloof

Chide Admonish, Berate, Dress, Objurgate, Rate, Rebuke, Reprove, Row, Scold, Tick off, Twit, Upbraid

Chief(tain) Arch, Ardrigh, Ariki, Boss, Caboceer, Cacique, Calif, Caliph, Capital, Capitan, Capitayn, Capo, Caradoc, Cazique, Ch, Chagan, Dat(t)o, DG, Dominant, Emir, Finn (MacCool), First, Foremost, Geronimo, Grand, Haggis, → HEAD, Hereward, Jarl, Kaid, King, Leader, → MAIN, Mass, Mugwump, Nawab, Nizam, Nkosi, Oba, Overlord, Paramount, Pendragon, Premier, Primal, Prime, Principal, Quanah, Raja(h), Rajpramukh, Rangatira, Rangatiratanga, Ratoo, Ratu, Sachem, Sagamore, Sarpanch, Sudder, Supreme, Tanist, Tank, Top

Chiffonier Cabinet, Commode

Chilblain Kibe

Child(ish), Childhood, Children Aerie, Alannah, Ankle biter, Babe, Baby, Bach(ch)a, Badger, Bairn, Bambino, Bantling, Boy, Brat, Brood, Butter-print, Ch, Changeling, Cherub, Chick, Chickabiddy, Chit, Collop, Cub, Dream, Elfin, Eyas, Feral, Foster, Foundling, Gait, Gangrel, Ge(i)t, Girl, Gyte, Heir, Hellion, Hurcheon, Imp, Infancy, Infant, Inner, Issue, It, Jailbait, Jejune, Juvenile, Kid, Kiddie(wink), Kiddy, Kinder, Lad, Latchkey, Limb, Litter, Littlie, Littling, Love, Mamzer, Mardy, Minion, Minor, Mite, Munchkin, Naive, Nipper, Nursling, Offspring, Pantywaist, Papoose, Piccaninny, Pickin, Problem, Progeny, Puerile, Puss, Putto, Ragamuffin, Rip, Romper, Rug rat, Scion, Second, Seed, Small fry, Smout, Smowt, Sprog, Street arab, Subteen, Tacker, Ted, Teeny-bopper, Tike, Toddle(r), Tot(tie), Totty, Trot, Tweenager, Tweenie, Tyke, Urchin, Waif, Wean, Weanel, Weanling, Weeny-bopper, Whelp, Younker, Youth

Childbearing, Childbirth Couvade, Dystocia, Intrapartum, Lamaze, Obstetrics, Parity, Puerperal, Tocology, Tokology

Child-killer Herod
Childless Atocous, Atokous, Barren, Nullipara, Sp
Chill(er), Chilly Bleak, Cauldrife, → COLD, Frappé, Freeze, Freon®, Frigid, Frosty, Gelid, Ice, Iciness, Mimi, Oorie, Ourie, Owrie, Parky, Raw, Refrigerate, Rigor, Scare
Chilli Bird's eye, → PEPPER, Pimentón
Chime(s) Bell, Cymar, Jingle, Peal, Semantron, Tink, → TOLL, Wind
Chimera Graft
Chimney (pot), Chimney corner Can, Cow(l), Femerall, Flare stack, Flue, Funnel, Lamp, Lug, Lum, Smokestack, Stack, Stalk, Steeplejack, Tallboy, Tunnel
Chimp(anzee) Ape, Bonobo, Jocko, Pygmy
Chin, Chinwag Chitchat, Double, Genial, Jaw, Jowl, Mentum
China(man), Chinese Ami, Amoy, Boxer, Cameoware, Cantonese, Cathay, Celestial, Ch, Chelsea, Chink(y), Chow, Coalport, Cochin, Cock, Communist, Confucius, Crackle, Crockery, Delft, Derby, Dresden, Eggshell, Etrurian, Flowery land, Friend, Fukien, Google, Googly, Goss, Hakka, Han, Hizen, Hmong, Imari, Ironstone, Kanji, Kaolin, Kuo-yu, Limoges, Manchu, Manchurian, Mandarin, Mangi, Maoist, Mate, Meissen, Min, Ming, Minton, National, Oppo, Pal, Pareoean, Pekingese, Pe-tsai, Pinyin, Porcelain, → POTTERY, Putonghua, Queensware, Red, Rockingham, Royal Worcester, Semiporcelain, Seric, Sèvres, Shanghai, Sinaean, Sinic, Sino-, Spode®, Sun Yat-sen, Tai-ping, Taoist, Teng, Tocharian, Tungus, Uigur, Wal(l)y, Ware, Wedgwood®, Whiteware, Willowware, Worcester, Wu, Yellow peril
Chine Chink, Chynd, Ridge
Chink Chinaman, Chop, Cleft, Clink, Cloff, Crack, Cranny, Crevice, Gap, Rent, Rift, Rima, Sinic, Window
Chintz Kalamkari
Chip(s) Blue, Bo(a)st, Carpenter, Counter, Cut, Deep-fried, EPROM, EROM, Fish, Flake, Fragment, Game, Hack, Knap, Log, Nacho(s), Neural, Nick, Pin, Potato, Shaving, Silicon, Spale, Spall, Span, Teraflop, Tortilla, Transputer, Virus
▷ **Chip** *may indicate* an anagram
Chipmunk Gopher, Hackee, Suslik, Zizel
Chipper Jaunty, Spry, Wedge
Chiron Centaur
Chiropody Podiatry
Chiropractic McTimoney
Chirp(y), Chirrup Cheep, Cherup, Chirm, Chirr, Cicada, Peep, Pip, Pipe, Pitter, Stridulate, Trill, Tweet, Twitter
Chisel(ler), Chisel-like Bam, Boaster, Bolster, Bur, Burin, Carve, Cheat, Clip, Drove, Firmer, Gad, → GOUGE, Half-round, Mason, Paring, Scalpriform, Scauper, Scorper, Sculpt, Slick, Socket, Sting
Chit Docket, Girl, Note, Voucher
Chivalry, Chivalrous Brave, Bushido, Courtly, Gallant, Grandisonian, Quixotic
Chivvy Badger, Harass, Pursue
Chloride, Chlorine Calomel
Chlorophyll Leaf-green
Chock Trig
Chocolate Aero, Brown, Cacao, Carob, Cocoa, Dragee, Ganache, Milk, Neapolitan, Noisette, Pinole, Plain, Theobroma, Truffle, Vegelate, Vermicelli
Choice, Choose, Choosy, Chosen Adopt, Anthology, Appoint, Aryan, Cherry-pick, Cull, Dainty, Decide, Druthers, Eclectic, Elect, Elite, Esnecy, Fine, Fork, Free will, Hercules, Hobson's, Leet, Leve, Lief, List, Multiple, Opt, Option, Or, Ossian, Peach, Peculiar, → PICK, Picking, Plum(p), Precious, Predilect, Prefer, Proairesis, Rare,

Recherché, → SELECT, Superb, Try(e), Via media, Volition, Wale

Choiceless Beggar

Choir, Choral, Chorister, Chorus Antiphony, Antistrophe, Anvil, Apse, Burden, Choragus, Choregus, Chorister, Dawn, Decani, Faburden, Fauxbourdon, Group, Hallelujah, Harmony, Hymeneal, Motet, Ninth, Parabasis, Precentor, Quirister, → REFRAIN, Ritual, Singing, Stop, Strophe, Treble, Triad, → UNISON

Choir-master Choragus, Choregus, Precentor

Choke(r) Block, Clog, Gag, Garotte, Glut, Silence, Smoor, Smore, Smother, Stap, Stifle, Stop, Strangle(hold), Strangulate, → THROTTLE

Choky Can, Prison

Choler Yellow bile

Cholera Hog

Cholesterol Spinacene, Squalene

Choliamb Scazon

▶ **Choose** see CHOICE

Chop, Chops, Chopper(s), Choppy Adze, Ax(e), Celt, Charge, Cheek, Chump, Cleave, Côtelette, Cuff, Cutlet, Dice, Fell(er), Flew, Hack, Helicopter, Hew, Ivory, Karate, Lop, Mince, Mouth, Rotaplane, Rough, Standing, Suey, Teeth, To-rend, Underhand, Wang

Chopin Pantoufle, Shoe

Chopstick(s) Waribashi

Chord(s) Altered, Arpeggio, Barré, Broken, Common, Diameter, Eleventh, Harmony, Intonator, Latus rectum, Neapolitan sixth, Nerve, Ninth, Picardy third, Riff, Seventh, Sixth, Submediant, Thirteenth, Triad, Vocal

Chore Darg, Duty, Fag, Task

Chorea Sydenham's

Choreographer Arranger, Ashton, Balanchine, Cecchetti, Cranko, Fokine, Laban, Massine

Chorus Antistrophe, Dawn, Ninth, Stop, Strophe

Chosen Korea

Chough Chewet

Chowder Bouillabaisse, Skink, Soup

Christ Ecce homo, Messiah, Pantocrator, Paschal Lamb, Prince of Peace, Saviour, The Good Shepherd, The Redeemer, X, Xt

Christen(ing) Baptise, Launch, Name-day

Christian(ity) Abcee, Abecedarian, Absey, Adventist, Albigenses, Anabaptist, Beghard, Believer, Cathar(ist), Charismatic, Colossian, Coptic, Dior, Donatist, D(o)ukhobor, Ebionite, Galilean, Giaour, Gilbertine, Gnostic, Godsquad, Goy, Heteroousian, Holy roller, Homo(i)ousian, Hutterite, Jehovah's Witness, Lutheran, Maronite, Marrano, Melchite, Melkite, Methodist, Monarchian, Monophysite, Moral, Mozarab, Muscular, Mutineer, Nazarene, Nestorian, Phalange, Pilgrim, Presbyterian, Protestant, Quaker, Quartodeciman, RC, Sabotier, Scientist, SCM, Shambe, Solifidian, Traditor, Uniat(e), Unitarian, Valdenses, Waldensian, Wesleyan, Xian, Zwinglian

Christian Scientist Eddy

Christmas(time) C(h)rimbo, Chrissie, Dec, Island, Nativity, Noel, Nowel(l), Yuletide

Christopher Kit, Robin, Sly, Wren

Chromatin Karyotin

Chromium Cr

Chromosome Aneuploid, Autosome, Centromere, Cistron, Euchromatin, Genome, Haploid, Homologous, Id(ant), Karyotype, Lampbrush, Operon, Philadelphia,

Ploid(y), Polytene, Prophage, Telomere, Trisomy, X, Y

Chronicle(r) Anglo-Saxon, Annal, Brut, Calendar, Diary, Froissart, Hall, History, Holinshed, Logographer, Moblog, Paralipomena, Parian, Paris, → **RECORD**, Register, Stow

Chrysalis Nymph, Pupa

Chrysanthemum Corn-marigold, Feverfew, Korean

Chrysolite Olivine, Peridot

Chub Cheven, Chevin, Fish

Chubby Butterball, Plump

Chuck (out) Berry, Buzz, Chook(ie), Discard, Eject, Food, Four-jaw, Grub, Independent-jaw, Pat, Pitch, Scroll, Shy, Sling, Three-jaw, Toss, Turf

Chuckle Chortle, Giggle, Gurgle

Chukka Polo

Chum(my) Ally, Boet, Buddy, Cobber, Cock, Companion, Comrade, Crony, Mate, Pal, Sociable, Sodality

Chump Fool, Mug(gins), Noddle, Sap, → **STUPID PERSON**

Chunk(y) Boxy, Chubby, Gob, Piece, Slab, Squat, Wad

Church Abbey, Armenian, Autocephalous, Basilica, Bethel, Bethesda, Broad, Brood, Byzantine, → **CATHEDRAL**, CE, Ch, Chapel, Chevet, Clergy, Collegiate, Congregational, Coptic, Delubrum, Easter (Orthodox), Eastern, EC, Ecumenical, Episcopal, Episcopalian, Established, Faith, Fold, Free, Greek, High, House, Institutional, Kirk, Lateran, Latin, Low, Lutheran, Maronite, Melchite, Methodist, Minster, Moonie, Moravian, Mormon, Mother, National, New, New Jerusalem, Old Light, Oratory, Orthodox, Parish, Peculiar, Pentecostal, Preaching-house, Prebendal, Presbyterian, Ratana, RC, Reformed, Relief, Rome, Russian Orthodox, Shrine, Smyrna, Station, Stave, Steeple, Steeplehouse, Temple, Triumphant, Unification, Unitarian, United Free, United Reformed, Visible, Wee Free, Western, Wool

Churchgoer, Churchman, Churchwarden Antiburgher, Azymite, Baptist, Believer, Cameronian, Classis, Clay, Cleric, Clerk, Congregation, Deacon, Dom, Dopper, Elder, Evangelist, Hatto, Ignorantine, Incumbent, Invisible, Knox, Lector, Lutheran, Methodist, Militant, Moderator, Moonie, Mormon, MU, Newman, Oncer, Parson, PE, Pew-opener, Pipe, Pontiff, Prebendary, Precentor, Predicant, Predikant, Prelate, Presbyterian, Priest, Protestant, Puritan, Racovian, Rector, Romanist, Ruridecanal, Sacristan, Sidesman, Sim, Simeonite, Socinian, Subdeacon, Succentor, Swedenborgian, Tantivy, Triumphant, Ubiquitarian, Unitarian, Verger, Visible, Wesleyan, Worshipper, Wren

Church house Deanery, Manse, Parsonage, Presbytery, Rectory, Vicarage

Churchill Tank, Winston

Churchyard God's acre

Churl(ish) Attercop, Boor, Crabby, Curmudgeonly, Cynical, Ethercap, Ettercap, Gruff, Ill-natured, Nabal, Peasant, Rustic, Serf, Surly

Churn Bubble, Kirn, Seethe

Chute Flume, Runway

CIC Shogun, Sirdar

Cicada Greengrocer, Locust, Periodical, Tettix

Cicatrix Scar

Cicely Myrrh, Sweet

Cicero Cic, Orator, Tully

Cid Campeador, Chief, Hero

Cider Drink, Hard, Perry, Scrumpy, Sweet

Ci-devant Ex

Cigar(ette), Cigarette cards Beedi(e), Bidi, Bifter, Bumper, Burn, Camberwell carrot, Cancer stick, Caporal, Cartophily, Cheroot, Cigarillo, Claro, Coffin nail, Conch, Concha, Corona, Dog-end, Doob, Durry, Fag, Filter-tip, Gasper, Giggle(-stick), Havana, Joint, Locofoco, Long-nine, Loosies, Maduro, Manilla, Number, Panatella, Paper-cigar, Perfecto, Puritano, Reefer, Regalia, Roach, Roll-up, Segar, Smoke, Snout, Splif(f), Stogie, Stog(e)y, Stompie, Twist, Weed, Whiff, Woodbine, Zol

Cinch Belt, Certainty, Duck soup, Easy, Girth, Stroll

Cinchona Kina, Quina

Cinder(s) Ash, Breeze, Clinker, Dander, Embers, Slag

Cinderella Drudge, Stepdaughter

Cinema(s) Art house, Big screen, Biograph, Bioscope, Circuit, Drive-in, Films, Fleapit, Flicks, Grindhouse, Megaplex, Movies, Multiplex, Multiscreen, Mutoscope, New Wave, Nickelodeon, Nouvelle Vague, Odeon, Pictures, Plaza, Theatre, Tivoli

Cinnabar Vermilion

Cinnamon, Cinnamon stone Canella, Cassia(bark), Essonite, Hessonite, Saigon, Spice

Cipher Chi-rho, Code, Cryptogram, Nihil, Nobody, → **NOTHING**, Number, O, Steganogram, Zero

Circle Almacantar, Almucantar, Annulet, Antarctic, Arctic, Circassian, Co, Colure, Company, Compass, Corn, Corolla, Coterie, Cromlech, Crop, Cycloid, Cyclolith, Dip, Disc, Dress, Druidical, Eccentric, Ecliptic, Embail, Enclose, Engird, Epicyclic, Equant, Equator, Equinoctial, Euler's, Family, Fraternity, Full, Galactic, Girdle, Gloriole, Great, Gyre, Halo, Henge, Hoop, Horizon, Hour, Hut, Inner, Inorb, Lap, Longitude, Loop, Magic, Malebolge, Mandala, Meridian, Mohr's, Mural, Nimbus, O, Orb, Orbit, Parhelic, Parquet, Parterre, Penannular, Peristalith, Pitch, Polar, Quality, Rigol, → **RING**, Rondure, Rotate, Roundlet, Seahenge, Sentencing, Set, Setting, Small, Sphere, Stemme, Stone, Stonehenge, Striking, Surround, Tinchel, Traffic, Transit, Tropic, Turning, Umbel, Upper, Vertical, Vicious, Vienna, Virtuous, Volt, Wheel

Circuit(ous) Ambit, AND, Autodyne, Bridge, Bypass, Chipset, Closed, Comparator, Daughterboard, Diocese, Discriminator, Dolby®, Equivalent, Eyre, Gate, Gyrator, IC, Integrated, Interface, Lap, Limiter, Live, Logic, Loop, Microprocessor, Motherboard, NAND, NOR, NOT, Open, OR, Perimeter, Phantom, Phase, Printed, Quadripole, Reactance, Ring, Round, Scaling, Series, Short, Smoothing, Squelch, Stage, Three-phase, Tour, Windlass

Circuit-breaker Fuse

Circular Annular, Court, Flysheet, Folder, Leaflet, Mailshot, Orby, Round, Spiral, Unending, Wheely

Circulate, Circulation Astir, Bloodstream, Cyclosis, Disseminate, Flow, Gyre, Issue, Mingle, Mix, Orbit, Pass, Publish, Report, Revolve, Rotate, Scope, Send round, Spread, Stir, Troll, Utter

▷ **Circulating** *may indicate* an anagram

Circumcise(r), Circumcision Bris, Brith, Brit milah, Infibulate, Milah, Mohel, Pharaonic, Sandek

Circumference Boundary, Girth, Perimeter, Size

Circumflex Perispomenon

Circumlocution Bafflegab, Periphrasis, Tautology

Circumnavigation Periplus

Circumscribe(d) Define, Demarcate, Enclose, Eruv, Restrain

Circumspect Chary, Guarded, Prudential, Wary
Circumstance(s), Circumstantial Case, Detail, Event, Fact, Formal, → INCIDENT, Mitigating, Precise, Shebang, Situation, Stede
Circumvent Bypass, Dish, Evade, Outflank, Outwit, Usurp
Circus, Circus boy Arena, Big top, Eros, Flea, Flying, Harrier, Hippodrome, Marquee, Maximus, Media, Monty Python, Ring, Sanger, Slang, Three-ring
Cissy Nelly
Cistercian Trappist
Cistern Feed-head, Flush-box, Sump, Tank, Tub, Vat
Citadel Acropolis, Alhambra, Castle, Fort(ress), Keep, Kremlin, Sea-girt
Citation, Cite Adduce, Allegation, Instance, Mention, Name, Quote, Recall, Reference, Repeat, Sist, Summon
Citizen(s), Citizenship Burgess, Burgher, Civism, Cleruch, Denizen, Dicast, Ephebe, Franchise, Freeman, Jus sanguinis, Jus soli, Kane, National, Oppidan, Patrial, People, Propr(a)etor, Quirites, Resident, Roman, Second-class, Senior, Snob, Subject, Trainband, Trierarch, Venireman, Vigilante, Voter
Citroen DS
Citron, Citrous Bergamot
Citrus Acid, Calamondin, Cedrate, Lemon, Lime, Mandarin, Min(n)eola, Orange, Pomelo, Tangerine, Ugli
City Agra, Athens, Atlantis, Babylon, Burgh, Cardboard, Carthage, Cosmopolis, Ctesiphon, Dodge, EC, Empire, Eternal, Forbidden, Free, Garden, Gath, Heavenly, Hilversum, Holy, Imperial, Inner, LA, Leonine, Medina, Megalopolis, Metropolis, Micropolis, Municipal, Mycenae, Ninevah, NY, Persepolis, Petra, Pompeii, Rhodes, Salem, Smoke, Sparta, Tech, Teheran, Town, Ur, Vatican, Weltstadt, Wen
Civet Binturong, Cat, Fo(u)ssa, Genet(te), Herpestes, Linsang, Musang, Nandine, Palm, Paradoxine, Paradoxure, Rasse, Suricate, Toddy-cat, Viverra, Zibet
Civil(ian), Civilisation, Civilised, Civility Amenity, Christian, Cit, Citizen, Civ(vy), Comity, Courtesy, Culture, Fertile crescent, Humane, Indus Valley, Kultur, Maya, Municipal, Nok, Non-combatant, Polite, Politesse, Push-button, Secular, Temporal, Urbane
Civil Service CS
Clad(ding) Sarking, Weatherboard
Clag(gy) Stickjaw
Claim(s) Appeal, Arrogate, Assert, Asseverate, Bag, Challenge, Charge, Darraign(e), Darrain(e), Darrayn, Demand, Deraign, Droit, Encumbrance, Haro, Harrow, Lien, List, Maintain, Nochel, Plea, Pose, Posit, Postulate, Pretence, Pretend, Profess, Pulture, Purport, Puture, Revendicate, Right, Set-off, Small, Sue, Title
Claimant Irredentist, Petitioner, Pot-waller, Pretender, Prospector, Tichborne, Usurper
Clairvoyance, Clairvoyancy ESP, Fey, Insight, Lucidity, Psiphenomena, Taisch, Taish, Tel(a)esthesia, Telegnosis
Clam Bivalve, Chowder, Cohog, Geoduck, Giant, Gweduc, Hardshell, Littleneck, Mollusc, Mya, Quahang, Quahog, Round, Soft-shell, Steamer, Tridacna, Venus
Clamant Vociferous
Clamber Climb, Crawl, Scramble, Spra(i)ckle, Sprauchle
Clammy Algid, Damp, Dank, Moist, Sticky, Sweaty
Clamour(ing), Clamorous Blatant, Brouhaha, Din, Hubbub, Hue, Outcry, Racket, Raird, Reird, Rout, Shout, Strepitant, Uproar, Utis, Vociferate
Clamp Beartrap, Clinch, Coupler, Denver boot, Fasten, Grip, Holdfast, Jumar, Pinchcock, Potato-pit, Serrefine, Stirrup, Tread, Vice, Wheel

Clan(sman) Cameron, Clique, Gens, Gentile, Group, Horde, Kiltie, Kindred, Name, Ngati, Phratry, Phyle, Sect, Sept, Society, Stewart, Stuart, Tribe

Clandestine Covert, Furtive, Secret, Underhand

Clang(er), Clanging, Clank Bell, Belleter, Boob, Boo-boo, Clash, Gong, Jangle, Plangent, Ring

Clap(per), Clapping Applaud, Blow, Castanet, Chop, Crotal, Dose, Jinglet, Peal, Plaudite, Thunder, Tonant

Claptrap Bilge, Blab, Bombast, Bunkum, Eyewash, Hokum, Rot, Tripe

Claque(ur) Fans, Hat, Laudator, Sycophant

Clara Bow, Butt

Claret Blood, Loll-shraub, Loll-shrob, Vin

Clarify, Clarifier Clear, Despumate, Dilucidate, Explain, Explicate, Fine, Finings, Purge, Refine, Render, Simplify

Clarinet Reed

Clarion Brassy, Clear, Trumpet

Clary Orval, Sage

Clash(ing) Bang, Clangour, Clank, Claver, Coincide, Collide, Conflict, Friction, Gossip, → IMPACT, Incident, Irreconcilable, Jar, Loud, Missuit, Riot, Shock, Showdown, Strike, Swash

Clasp(ing) Adpress, Agraffe, Amplexus, Barrette, Brooch, Button, Catch, Chape, Clip, Embrace, Fibula, Grasp, Hasp, Hesp, Hook, Hug, Inarm, Interdigitate, Link, Morse, Ochreate, Ouch, Slide, Tach(e), Tie, Unite

Class(ification), Classify, Classified, Classy Acorn, Arrange, Assort, Bourgeois(ie), Bracket, Brand, Breed, Business, Cabin, Canaille, Caste, → CATEGORY, Chattering, Cheder, Cl, Clan, Clerisy, Clinic, Club, Composite, Course, Criminal, Dalit, Dewey, Digest, Division, Economy, Estate, Evening, Faction, First, Form, Genera, Gentry, Genus, → GRADE, Group, Harvard, Haryan, Heder, Hubble, Ilk, Keep-fit, Kohanga Reo, League, Life, Linn(a)ean, List, Lower, Mammal, Master, Meritocracy, Middle, Night, Number, Nursery, Order, Phenetics, Phylum, Pigeon-hole, Pleb(eian), Proper, Race, Range, Rank, Rate, Rating, Raypoot, Raypout, Reception, Remove, Salariat, Second, Secret, Seminar, Shell, Siege, Social, Sort(ation), Spectral, Steerage, Stratum, Stream, Syntax, Taxonomy, Teach-in, Third, Tony, Tourist, Tribe, Tutorial, → TYPE, U, Universal, Upper, Varna, Water, Working, World, Year

Classic(al), Classics, Classicist Ageless, Ancient, Basic, Derby, Elzevir, Grecian, Greek, Humane, Leger, Literature, Pliny, Purist, Roman, Standard, Traditional, Vintage

Clatch Blunk, Smear, Spoil

Clatter Bicker, Charivari, Clack, Din, Noise, Rattle

Clause Adjunct, Apodosis, Article, Basket, Complement, Condition, Conscience, Coordinate, Dependent, Disability, Endorsement, Escalator, Escape, Exclusion, Exemption, Filioque, Four, Golden parachute, Grandfather, Independent, Main, Member, Noun, Object, Omnibus, Option, Poison-pill, Predicator, Principal, Protasis, Proviso, Reddendum, Reported, Reservation, Rider, Salvo, Saving, Sentence, Subject, Subordinate, Sunset, Tenendum, Testatum, Testing, Warrandice

Claw Chela, Claut, Crab, Dewclaw, Edate, Falcula, Grapple, Griff(e), Hook, Nail, Nipper, Pounce, Scrab, Scramb, Sere, Talent, → TALON, Tear, Telson, Tokay, Unguis

Clay Allophane, Argil, Argillite, Barbotine, B(e)auxite, Bentonite, Blaes, Blaise, Blaize, Bole, Boulder, Calm, Cam, Caum, Ceramic, Charoset(h), China, Cimolite, Cloam, Clunch, Cob, Cornish, Earth, Engobe, Fango, Figuline, Fire, Fuller's earth,

Gault, Glei, Gley, Gumbotil, Hardpan, Haroset(h), Illite, Kaolin, Kokowai, Laterite, Lithomarge, Loam, London, Lute, Malm, Marl, Meerschaum, Mire, Mortal, Mud, Oxford, Papa, Pipeclay, Pipestone, Pise, Plastic, Plastilina, Porcelain, Potter's, Pottery, Puddle, Pug, Saggar(d), Sagger, Scroddle(d), Seggar, Sepiolite, Slip, Slurry, Smectite, Terra sigillata, Thill, Till(ite), Tumphy, Varve, Warrant, Warren, Wax

Clean(er), Cleaning Absterge, Bathbrick, Besom, Bleach, Bream, Broom, Careen, Catharise, Catharsis, Char(e), Chaste, Clear, Daily, Debride, Decontaminate, Dentifrice, Depurate, Deterge(nt), Dhobi, Dialysis, Dicht, Do, Douche, Dredge, Dust(er), Eluant, Emunge, Enema, Erase, Ethnic, Evacuant, Evacuate, Expurgate, Fay, Fettle, Fey, Floss, Flush, Full, Grave, Groom, Gut, Heels, Hoover®, Hygienic, Immaculate, Innocent, Launder, Lave, Lustrum, Lye, Mouthwash, Mrs Mop(p), Mundify, Net, Overhaul, Porge, Pull-through, Pumice, Pure, Purgative, Purge, Ramrod, Rebite, Rub, Rump, Sandblast, Scaffie, Scavenge, Scour, Scrub, Shampoo, Shot-blast, Snow-white, Soap, Soogee, Soogie, Soojey, Sponge, Spotless, Squeaky, Squeegee, Sterile, Sujee, Swab, Sweep, Tidy, Toothpick, Ultrasonic, Vac(uum), Valet, → WASH, Whistle, Wipe

Clear(ance), Clearly Absolve, Acquit, Aloof, Apparent, Bell, Berth, Bold, Bore, Brighten, Bus, Categorical, Clarify, Crystal, Decode, Definite, Delouse, Diaphanous, Dispel, Distinct, Downright, Earn, Eidetic, Evacuate, Evident, Exculpate, Exonerate, Explicit, Fair, Five-by-five, Gain, Headroom, Hyaline, Intelligible, Iron, Laund, Leap, Legible, Limpid, Lucid, Luculent, Manifest, Mop, Neat, Negotiate, Net(t), → NOT CLEAR, Observable, Obvious, Ope(n), Overleap, Palpable, Patent, Pellucid, Perspicuous, Plain, Play, Pratique, Predy, Pure, Quit, Rack, Realise, Remble, Rid, Ripple, Serene, Sheer, Shere, Slum, Stark, Sweep, Thro(ugh), Thwaite, Transire, Translucent, Transparent, Unblock, Unclog, Uncork(ed), Unequivocal, Vault, Vivid, Void, Well, Windage, Wipe

Clearing Assart, Glade, Opening, Shire, Slash

Cleat Bitt, Wedge

Cleave, Cleavage, Cleft Adhere, Bisulcate, Chimney, Chine, Chink, Cling, Cloff, Cohere, Cut, Divide, Division, Divorce(ment), Fissure, Gap, Ghaut, Goose-grass, Grike, Gryke, Harelip, Pharynx, Rift, Riva, Scissure, Severance, Slack, Space, Spathose, Split, Sulcus

Clef Soprano, Treble

Clematis Montana, Old man's beard, Traveller's joy, Virgin's-bower

Clemenceau Tiger

Clemency, Clement Ahimsa, Grace, Lenience, Lenity, Mercy, Mildness, Quarter, Temperate

Cleopatra Needle

Clergy(man), Cleric(al) Abbé, Canon, Cantor, Cardinal, Chancellor, Chaplain, Cleric, Clerk, Cloth, Curate, Curé, Deacon, Dean, Ecclesiast(ic), Goliard, Incumbent, Josser, Levite, Ministerial, Ministry, Minor canon, Non-juror, Non-usager, Notarial, Paperwork, Parson, Pastor, Pontifex, Pontiff, Preacher, Prebendary, Precentor, Prelate, Presbyter, Presenter, Priest, Primate, Prior, Proctor, Rabbi, Rector, Red-hat, Reverend, Rome-runner, Scribal, Secretarial, Shaveling, Shepherd, Sky pilot, Slope, Spin-text, Spirituality, Squarson, Subdeacon, Theologian, Vartabed, Vicar

Clergy-hater Misoclere

Clerk(s) Actuary, Baboo, Babu, Basoche, Circar, Cleric, Cratchit, Cursitor, Enumerator, Filing, Heep, Lay, Limb, Notary, Paper-pusher, Parish, Pen-driver, Penman, Penpusher, Petty Bag, Poster, Prot(h)onotary, Protocolist, Recorder, Salaryman, Scribe, Secretariat, Shipping, Sircar, Sirkar, Tally, Vicar, Writer

Clever(ness) Able, Adroit, Astute, Brainy, Bright, Canny, Cool, Cute, Daedal(e), Deep-browed, Deft, Genius, Gleg, Ingenious, Intellectual, Jackeen, Know-all, Natty, Nimblewit, Sage(ness), Shrewd, Skilful, Smart(y), Smarty-pants, Souple, Subtle

Clevis Becket

Cliché Banality, Boilerplate, Commonplace, Corn, Journalese, Platitude, Saying, Tag

Click(er), Clicking Castanet, Catch, Forge, Pawl, Rale, Ratch(et), Snick, Succeed, Tchick, Ticktack

Client Customer, Fat, Gonk, John, Patron, Thin, Trick

Cliff(s) Beachy Head, Bluff, Cleve, Corniche, Crag, Craig, Escarp, Palisade(s), Precipice, Sca(u)r

Cliffhanger Samphire, Serial, Thriller

Climate Ambience, Atmosphere, Attitude, Continental, Mood, Sun, Temperament, Temperature, Weather

Climax Apex, Apogee, Catastasis, Come, Crescendo, Crest, Crisis, Culminate, Edaphic, End, Head, Height, Heyday, Orgasm, Payoff, Top, Zenith

Climb(er), Climbing Aid, Alpinist, Aralia, Aristolochia, Artificial, Ascend, Bignonian, Breast, Briony, Bryony, Clamber, Clematis, Clusia, Cowage, Cowhage, Cowitch, Crampon, Creeper, Cucumber, Dodder, Heart-pea, Hedera, Ivy, Jamming, Kie-kie, Kudzu, Lawyer, Layback, Liana, Liane, → **MOUNT**, Munro-bagger, Pareira, Parvenu, Pea, Peg, Prusik, Rat(t)an, Rise, Root, Scale, Scan, Scandent, Scansores, Sclim, Scramble, Shin, Shinny, Sklim, Smilax, Social, Speel, Steeplejack, Sty(e), Swarm, Timbo, Tuft-hunter, Udo, Up(hill), Uprun, Vine, Wistaria, With(y)wind, Woodbine, Zoom

Clinch Attach, Carriwitchet, Determine, Ensure, Fix, Quibble, Rivet, Secure, Settle

Cling(er), Clinging Adhere, Bur(r), Cherish, Cleave, Embrace, Hold, Hug, Ring, Tendril

Clinic Antenatal, Dental, Dispensary, Hospital, Hospitium, Mayo, Well-woman

Clink Gingle, Jail, Jingle, Lock up, Prison, Stir, Ting, Tinkle

Clinker Ash, Slag

Clint Limestone

Clip(ped), Clipper, Clipping Alberta, Banana, Barrette, Bicycle, Brash, Bulldog, Butterfly, Cartridge, Chelsea, Clasp, Crocodile, Crop-ear, Crutch, Curt, Curtail, Cut, Cutty Sark, Dag, Dock, Dod, Excerpt, Fleece, Jubilee, Jumar, Krab, Lop, Money, Outtake, Pace, Paper, Pare, Peg, Prerupt, Prune, Roach, Scissel, Secateur, Shear, Ship, Shore, Shorn, Snip, Spring, Staccato, Tie, Tie-tack, Tinsnips, Topiarist, Trim

Clippy Cad, Conductor

Clique Cabal, Clan, Club, Coterie, Faction, Four Hundred, Gang, Junta, Ring, Set

Clive Arcot

Cloak(room), Cloaks Aba, Abaya, Abba, Abolla, Amice, Bathroom, Buffalo-robe, Burnous, Capa, Cape, Capote, Caracalla, Cardinal, Cassock, Chasuble, Chimer(e), Chlamydes, Chlamys, Chuddah, Chuddar, Conceal, Cope, Cover, Disguise, Dissemble, Djellaba(h), Domino, Gabardine, Gaberdine, Gal(l)abea(h), Gal(l)abi(y)a(h), Gal(l)abi(y)eh, Gentlemen, Gents, Grego, Hall-robe, Heal, Hele, Himation, Hood, Inverness, Jelab, Jellaba, Joseph, Kaross, Korowai, Manta, Manteau, Manteel, Mant(e)let, Mantle, → **MASK**, Mourning, Mousquetaire, Mozetta, Opera, Paenula, Paletot, Pallium, Paludamentum, Pelisse, Pilch, Poncho, Powder-room, Rail, Revestry, Rocklay, Rokelay, Roquelaure, Sagum, Sarafan, Scapular, → **SCREEN**, Shroud, Swathe, Talma, Toga, Vestiary, Vestry, Visite

Clobber Anoint, Apparel, Dress, Garb, Habiliments, Lam, Tack

Clock Alarm, Ammonia, Analogue, Astronomical, Atomic, Beetle, Big Ben, Biological, Blowball, Body, Bracket, Bundy, Caesium, Carriage, Cartel, Clepsydra,

Cuckoo, Dandelion, Digital, Doomsday, Dutch, Floral, Grandfather, Grandmother, Hit, Knock, Long case, Meter, Paenula, Parliament, Quartz, Repeater, Sandglass, Solarium, Speaking, Speedo, Strike, Sundial, Taximeter, Tell-tale, Time(r), Turret, Wag at the wa', Water

Clockmaker Fromanteel, Graham, Harrison, Knibb, Mudge, Tompion

Clockwise Deasil, Deasiul, Deasoil, Deiseal, Deisheal

Clockwork Precision, Regular

Clod Clumsy, Divot, Glebe, Lump, Mool, Mould, Put(t), Scraw, Sod, Stupid, Turf

Clog Accloy, Ball, Block, Clam, Crowd, Dance, Fur, Galosh, Golosh, Hamper, Jam, Lump, Mire, Obstruct, Overshoe, Patten, Sabot

Cloisonné Shippo

Cloister Arcade, Confine, Cortile, Immure, Monastery, Mure, Refuge, Seclude

Clone, Cloning Ramet, Replicant, Reproduce, Therapeutic

Cloots Worricow

Close(d), Closing, Closure Airless, Alongside, Atresia, Block, Boon, By, Cadence, Clammy, Clap, Clench, Complete, Cone off, Court, Dear, Debar, Dense, → END, Epilogue, Ewest, Finale, Forby, Gare, Grapple, Handy, Hard, Hard by, Humid, Imminent, Inbye, Infibulate, Intent, Intimate, Lock, Lucken, Marginal, Mean, Miserly, Muggy, Mure, Narre, Narrow, Near, Nearhand, Neist, Nie, Niggardly, Nigh, Nip and tuck, Obturate, Occlude, Occlusion, Oppressive, Parochial, Penny-pinching, Placket, Precinct, Reserved, Reticent, Seal, Secret, Serre, Serried, Serry, Shet, Shut(ter), Shutdown, Silly, Slam, Snug, Stap, Sticky, Stuffy, Sultry, Tailgate, Temenos, Tight, Uproll, Wafer, Warm, Yard

Close-cropped Crewcut, Not-pated

Close-fitting Skintight, Slinky, Tight

Closet Cabinet, Confine, Cubicle, Cupboard, Dooket, Earth, Locker, Safe, Wardrobe, WC, Zeta

Close-up Detail, Fill, Shut, Stop, Zoom

Closing-time Eleven, End

Clot(ting) Agglutinate, Ass, Clag, Clump, Coagulate, Congeal, Crassamentum, Cruor, Curdle, Dag, Embolism, Embolus, Gel, Globule, Gob, Gout, Grume, Incrassate, Incrust, Jell, Lapper, Lopper, → LUMP, Mass, Prothrombin, Splatch, Stupid, Thicken, Thrombosis, Thrombus

Cloth Aba, Abaya, Abba, Antependium, Bribe, Carmelite, Clergy, Cloot, Clout, Communion, Dishrag, Duster, → FABRIC, → FELT, Frocking, Frontal, Gremial, G-string, Jharan, Loin, Lungi, Manta, → MATERIAL, Nap, Napery, Napje, Nappie, Neckerchief, Needlework, Netting, Pack, Painted, Pall, Pane, Pilch, Priesthood, Print(er), Pull-through, Purificator, Puttee, Putty, Rag, Raiment, Roll, Roon, Runner, Sashing, Serviette, Sheet, Sheeting, Shoddy, Stripe, Stuff, Stupe, Sudarium, Supper, Sweatband, T, Tapestry, Tea, → TEXTILE, Throw, Tissue, Toilet, Vernicle, Veronica, Washrag, Whole

---

CLOTH

1 letter:	Web	Ciré	Haik
J®		Doek	Harn
	4 letters:	Drab	Hyke
3 letters:	Aida	Duck	Ikat
Abb	Amis	Fent	Kelt
Rep	Baft	Flax	Knit
Say	Bark	Gair	Lamé

Lawn
Leno
Line
Mull
Nude
Pina
Puke
Repp
Rund
Shag
Slop
Sulu
Wire
Wool

5 letters:
Atlas
Baize
Beige
Binca
Budge
Chino
Crape
Crash
Crepe
Denim
Dobby
Drill
Duroy
Fanon
Foulé
Frisé
Gauze
Gazar
Grass
Gunny
Haick
Honan
Jaspe
Kanga
Kente
Khadi
Khaki
Kikoi
Linen
Llama
Loden
Lurex®
Lycra®
Moiré
Mongo

Monk's
Mummy
Mungo
Ninon
Nylon
Orlon®
Panel
Panne
Perse
Pilot
Piqué
Plaid
Plush
Poult
Rayon
Satin
Scrim
Serge
Slops
Surah
Surat
Surge
Tabby
Tamin
Tammy
Terry
Tibet
Toile
Towel
Tulle
Tweed
Tweel
Twill
Union
Voile
Wigan

6 letters:
Aertex®
Alpaca
Angora
Armure
Barège
Beaver
Bouclé
Broche
Burlap
Burnet
Burrel
Byssus
Caddis

Calico
Camlet
Camlot
Canvas
Chintz
Cilice
Cloqué
Coburg
Coutil
Covert
Crepon
Cubica
Cyprus
Damask
Devoré
Dimity
Domett
Dossal
Dossel
Dowlas
Dralon®
Duffel
Duffle
Dupion
Durrie
Etamin
Faille
Fannel
Frieze
Gloria
Greige
Gurrah
Haique
Harden
Herden
Hodden
Hoddin
Humhum
Hurden
Jersey
Kersey
Khanga
Kincob
Lampas
Madras
Medley
Melton
Merino
Mohair
Mongoe
Moreen

Muleta
Muslin
Mutton
Nankin
Oxford
Pongee
Rateen
Ratine
Russel
Samite
Satara
Sateen
Saxony
Sendal
Shalli
Sherpa
Sindon
Soneri
Stroud
Tactel®
Tamine
Tartan
Tencel®
Thibet
Tricot
Velour
Velure
Velvet
Vicuna
Wadmal
Wincey
Winsey

7 letters:
Abattre
Alamode
Alepine
Baracan
Batiste
Brocade
Cabbage
Cambric
Camelot
Challie
Challis
Cheviot
Chiffon
Crombie
Cypress
Delaine
Dhurrie

Doeskin
Dorneck
Dornick
Drabbet
Drapery
Droguet
Drugget
Duvetyn
Etamine
Faconné
Fannell
Fishnet
Flannel
Foulard
Fustian
Galatea
Genappe
Gingham
Gore-tex®
Grogram
Hessian
Holland
Hopsack
Jaconet
Jamdani
Khaddar
Kitenge
Lockram
Mockado
Nankeen
Oilskin
Organza
Orleans
Ottoman
Paisley
Percale
Rabanna
Raploch
Raschel
Ratteen
Rattine
Ripstop
Sacking
Sagathy
Scarlet
Schappe
Silesia
Sinamay
Spandex®
Stammel
Supplex®

Tabaret
Tabinet
Taffeta
Tiffany
Tussore
Viyella®
Wadmaal
Webbing
Woolsey
Worsted
Zanella

8 letters:
Aircraft
Algerine
American
Armozeen
Armozine
Arresine
Bagheera
Barathea
Barracan
Bayadere
Bearskin
Bobbinet
Brocatel
Cameline
Cashmere
Casimere
Celanese
Chambray
Chamelot
Chenille
Ciclaton
Corduroy
Corporal
Coteline
Coutille
Cretonne
Drabette
Duchesse
Dungaree
Duvetine
Duvetyne
Eolienne
Gambroon
Gossamer
Homespun
Jacquard
Jeanette
Lava-lava

Lustring
Mackinaw
Mantling
Marcella
Marocain
Mazarine
Moleskin
Moquette
Nainsook
Organdie
Osnaburg
Pashmina
Pleather
Prunella
Rodevore
Sarcenet
Sarsenet
Sealskin
Shabrack
Shalloon
Shantung
Sicilian
Swanskin
Tabbinet
Tarlatan
Toilinet
Whipcord
Wild silk
Zibeline

9 letters:
Aeroplane
Alcantara
Balzarine
Bengaline
Bombasine
Calamanco
Cassimere
Cerecloth
Charmeuse®
Ciclatoun
Corporale
Cottonade
Courtelle®
Crepoline
Crimplene®
Crinoline
Evenweave
Fabrikoid®
Farandine
Filoselle

Folk-weave
Gaberdine
Georgette
Grenadine
Grosgrain
Haircloth
Horsehair
Indiennes
Levantine
Longcloth
Mandilion
Mandylion
Marseille
Matelassé
Messaline
Moygashel
Open-weave
Overcheck
Paramatta
Penistone
Percaline
Persienne
Pinstripe
Polyester
Ravenduck
Sailcloth
Sharkskin
Silkalene
Silkaline
Stockinet
Swansdown
Tarpaulin
Tricotine
Velveteen
Wire gauze
Worcester
Zibelline

10 letters:
Balbriggan
Baldachino
Broadcloth
Brocatelle
Candlewick
Farrandine
Fearnought
Ferrandine
Florentine
Geotextile
Kerseymere
Lutestring

			12 letters:
Mousseline	Toilinette	Drap-de-berry	Brilliantine
Needlecord	Tuftaffeta	Dreadnought	Cavalry twill
Parramatta	Winceyette	Hammercloth	Crepe de chine
Polycotton		Interfacing	Leather-cloth
Ravensduck	11 letters:	Kendal green	
Russel-cord	Abercrombie	Marquisette	13 letters:
Seersucker	Bedford cord	Nun's veiling	Gros de Londres
Shabracque	Canton crepe	Sempiternum	Linsey-woolsey
Shiveshive	Cheesecloth	Stockinette	
Sicilienne	Cloth of gold	Stretch knit	
Tattersall	Dotted Swiss	Swiss muslin	

Cloth-designing Batik

Clothe(s), Clothing, Clothed Accoutrements, Apparel, Array, Attire, Baggies, Besee, Bib and tucker, Cape, Casuals, Chasuble, Choli, Cits, Clad, Clericals, Clobber, Coat, Combinations, Coordinates, Costume, Cour, Cover, Croptop, Dicht, Dight, Don, Drag, → **DRESS**, Duds, Emboss, Endue, Finery, Frippery, Garb, Garments, Gear, Gere, Get-up, Glad rags, Grave, Gymslip, Habit, Haute couture, Hejab, Innerwear, Judogi, Jumps, Kimono, Layette, Lederhosen, Long-togs, Mitumba, Mocker, Muff, Outfit, Pannicle, Plain, Playsuit, Raggery, Rag trade, Raiment, Rami, Rigout, Robes, Samfoo, Samfu, Schmutter, Scungies, Shirtwaister, Shmatte, Shroud, Slops, Sunday best, Swaddling, Swathe, Swothling, Tackle, Togs, Tracksuit, Trappings, Trews, Trousseau, Tweeds, Two-piece, Vernicle, Vestiary, Vestiture, Vestment, Wardrobe, Watteau, Weeds, Widow's weeds, Workwear, Yclad, Ycled

Clothes basket, Clothes horse Airer, Petara, Winterhedge

Cloud(ing), Clouded, Cloudiness, Cloudy Altocumulus, Altostratus, Banner, Benight, C, Cataract, Cirrocumulus, Cirrostratus, Cirrus, Coalsack, Coma, Contrail, Crab Nebula, Cumulonimbus, Cumulus, Dim, Dull, Emission nebula, Fog, Fractocumulus, Fractostratus, Funnel, Goat's hair, Haze, Horsehead Nebula, Infuscate, Magellanic, Mare's tail, Milky, Mist, Molecular, Mushroom, Nacreous, Nephele, Nephelometer, Nepho-, Nimbostratus, Nimbus, Nubecula, Nubilous, Nuée ardente, Obnubilation, Obscure, Octa, Okta, Oort, Overcast, Pall, Pother, Protostar, Rack, Roily, Stain, Storm, Stratocumulus, Strat(o)us, Thunder(head), Turbid, Virga, War, Water-dog, Woolpack, Zero-zero

Cloudberry Mountain bramble

Cloudless Serene

Clough Dale, Gorge, Ravine

Clout Belt, Cloth, Hit, Influence, Lap(pie), Lapje, Pull, Raddle

Clove Chive, Eugenia, Rose-apple, Split

Clover Alfalfa, Alsike, Berseem, Calvary, Cinque, Cow-grass, Four-leaf, Hare's foot, Hop, Japan, Ladino, Lespedeza, Medic(k), Melilot, Owl's, Pin, Rabbit-foot, Red, Serradella, Serradilla, Shamrock, Souple, Sucklers, Sweet, Trefoil, Trilobe, White

Clown(ish) Airhead, Antic, Antick, August(e), Boor, Bor(r)el, Buffoon, Carl, Chough, Chuff, Clout-shoe, Coco, → **COMEDIAN**, Comic, Costard, Daff, Feste, Froth, Girner, Gobbo, Goon, Gracioso, Grimaldi, Harlequin, Hob, Idiot, Jack-pudding, Jester, Joey, Joker, Joskin, Leno, Merry Andrew, Mountebank, Nedda, Nervo, Peasant, Pickle-herring, Pierrot, Put, Rustic, Slouch, Thalian, Touchstone, Trinculo, Wag, Zany

Cloy(ing) Choke, Clog, Glut, Pall, Satiate, Surfeit, Sweet

Club(s), Club-like Adelphi, Airn, Almack's, Alpeen, Apex, Army and Navy, Arsenal, Artel, Association, Athen(a)eum, Baffy, Band(y), Basto, Bat, Bath, Beefsteak, Blackjack, Blaster, Bludgeon, Boodles, Bourdon, Brassie, Breakfast, Brook's, Bulger, C, Card, Carlton, Caterpillar, Cavalry, Chartered, Chigiriki, Clavate, Cleek, Clip-joint, Combine, Compassion, Conservative, Constitutional, Cordeliers, Cosh, Cotton, Country, Crockford's, Cudgel, Devonshire, Disco(theque), Driver, Driving iron, Drones, Fan, Fascio, Feuillant, Fustigate, Garrick, Glee, Golf, Guards, Guild, Hampden, Hell-fire, Hercules', Honky-tonk, Indian, Investment, Iron, Jacobin, Jigger, Jockey, Junior Carlton, Kennel, Kierie, Kiri, Kitcat, Kiwanis, Knobkerrie, Landsdowne, Lathi, Laughter, League, Leander, Lions, Lofter, Luncheon, Mace, Mallet, Mashie, Maul, Mell, Mere, Meri, Mess, Midiron, Monday, National Liberal, Niblick, Night(stick), Nightspot, Nitery, Nulla(-nulla), Oddfellows, Paris, Patu, Pitching wedge, Polt, Pregnant, Priest, Provident, Pudding, Putter, Quarterstaff, RAC, R & A, Reform, Ring, Rota, Rotarian, Rotary, Round Table, Sand wedge, Savage, Savile, Shillelagh, Slate, Society, Soroptimist, Sorosis, Spoon, Spot, Spurs, Strike, Strip, Supper, Texas wedge, Thatched House, Tong, Travellers, Trefoil, Truncheon, Trunnion, Union, United Services, Variety, Waddy, Wedge, White's, Wood, Yacht, Youth

Club-foot Kyllosis, Po(u)lt-foot, Talipes, Varus

Clubman Member

Club-rush Deer-hair, Scirpus, Sedge

Cluck Chirrup, Dent

Clue Across, Anagram, Ball, Charade, Clavis, Dabs, Down, → **HINT**, Inkling, Key, Lead, Light, Rebus, Scent, Scooby(doo), Signpost, Thread, Tip

Clueless Ignorant

Clump Cluster, Finial, Knot, Mass, Mot(te), Patch, Plump, Tread, Tuft, Tump, Tussock

▷ **Clumsily** *may indicate* an anagram

Clumsy Artless, Awkward, Bauchle, Bungling, Butterfingers, Cack-handed, Calf, Chuckle, Clatch, Clodhopper, Cumbersome, Dub, Dutch, Galoot, Gauche, Gimp, Ham(-fisted), Heavy-handed, Horse-godmother, Inapt, Inelegant, Inept, Inexpert, Klutz, Lob, Loutish, Lubbard, Lubber, Lummox, Lumpish, Maladdress, Maladroit, Mauther, Mawr, Mawther, Messy, Mor, Nerd, Nurd, Oafish, Off-ox, Palooka, Plonking, Rough, S(c)hlemiel, Schlemihl, Spastic, Spaz(zy), Squab, Stot, Swab, Swob, Taupie, Tawpie, Two-fisted, Unco, Ungain, Unskilful, Unsubtle, Unwieldy

Cluster Acervate, Assemble, Asterism, Bunch, Clump, Collection, Concentre, Constellate, Conurbation, Corymb, Cyme, Gather, Gear, Globular, Glomeration, Knot, Oakleaf, Packet, Plump, Raceme, Sheaf, Sorus, Strap, Thyrse, Tone, Truss, Tuffe, Tuft, Umbel, Verticillaster

Clutch Battery, Brood, Chickens, Clasp, Cling, Eggs, Friction, Glaum, Grab, → **GRASP**, Gripe, Nest, Seize, Sitting, Squeeze

Clutter Confusion, Litter, Mess, Rummage

Coach Battlebus, Berlin, Bogie, Bus, Car, Carriage, Chara, Clerestory, Crammer, Diligence, Dilly, Double-decker, Drag, Edifier, Fly, Four-in-hand, Gig, Hackney, Handler, Landau(let), Life, Microbus, Mourning, Phaeton, Post chaise, Pullman, Railcar, Rattler, Repetiteur, Saloon, Shay, Sleeper, Slip, Sobriety, Stage, Surrey, Tally(-ho), Teach(er), Thoroughbrace, Train(er), Tutor, Voiture

Coach-horse Rove-beetle

Coachman Automedon, Bunene, Coachy, Dragsman, Jarvey, Jehu, John

Coagulant, Coagulate, Coagulation Cautery, Clot, Congeal, Curds, Jell, Rennet, Run, Runnet, Set, Solidify, Thicken

Coal Anthracite, Bituminous, Black diamonds, Block, Brown, Burgee, Cannel, Cherry, Clinker, Coking, Coom, Crow, Culm, Dice, Edge, Eldin, Ember, Fusain, Gas, Gathering, Hard, Jud, Knob, Lignite, Maceral, Mineral, Nut, Open-cast, Paper, Parrot, Purse, Sapropelite, Score, Sea, Slack, Soft, Splint, Steam, Stone, Vitrain, Wallsend, White, Wood
Coalesce(nce) Amalgamate, Concrete, Fuse, Merge, Sintery, Synaloepha, Unite
Coalfish Saith
Coalition Alliance, Bloc, Janata, Merger, Rainbow, Tie
Coal-tar Cresol, Indene
Coal-tub Corf, Dan, Scuttle
Coarse(ness) Base, Bawdy, Blowzy, Bran, Broad, Common, Crude, Dowlas, Earthy, Fisherman, Foul, Gneissose, Grained, Grobian, Gross, Grossièreté, Haggery, Ham, Illbred, Indelicate, Low-bred, Plebeian, Rabelaisian, Rank, Rappee, Raunchy, Ribald, Rough, Rudas, Rude, Sackcloth, Schlub, Semple, Slob, Sotadic, Unrefined, Vulgar
Coast(al) Barbary, Beach, Bight, Caird, Causeway, Coromandel, Costa, Drift, Freewheel, Glide, Gold, Hard, Ivory, Littoral, Longshore, Malabar, Maritime, Murman(sk), Orarian, Riviera, Seaboard, Seafront, Seaside, → **SHORE**, Slave, Sledge, Strand, Toboggan, Trucial
Coaster Beermat, Drog(h)er, Mat, Roller, Ship
Coastguard CG, Gobby
Coastline Watermark
Coast-road Corniche
Coat(ed), Coating Abaya, Ab(b)a, Achkan, Acton, Admiral, Afghan, Anarak, Anodise, Anorak, Balmacaan, Barathea, Basan, Bathrobe, Belton, Benjamin, Blazer, Bloomed, Box, British warm, Buff, Buff-jerkin, Calcimine, Car, Chesterfield, Cladding, Claw-hammer, Clearcole, Cloak, Clutch, Cocoon, Coolie, Cover, Covert, Creosote, Crust(a), Cutaway, Dip, Doggett's, Drape, Dress, Duffel, Duster, Electroplate, Enamel, Encrust, Envelope, Ermelin, Ermine, Exine, Extine, Fearnought, Film, Fleece, Frock, Fur, Gabardine, Galvanise, Gambeson, Ganoin, Glaze, Grego, Ground, Ha(c)queton, Hair, Happi, Impasto, Integument, Inverness, Iridise, Jack(et), Jemmy, Jerkin, Jodhpuri, Joseph, Jump, Jupon, Lacquer, Lammie, Lammy, Lanugo, Layer, Laying, Loden, Lounge, Mac, Mackinaw, Matinee, Metallise, Morning, Newmarket, → **OVERCOAT**, Paint, Paletot, Palla, Parka, Parkee, Passivate, Patinate, Pebbledash, Pelage, Pelisse, Perfuse, Peridium, Petersham, Plate, Polo, Pos(h)teen, Primer, Primine, Prince Albert, Raglan, Redingote, Resin, Resist, Riding, Roquelaure, Sack, Saque, Sclera, Scratch, Seal, Sheepskin, Shellac, Sherardise, Sherwani, Silver, Skinwork, Spencer, Sports, Stadium, Surtout, Swagger, Swallowtail(ed), Tabard, Taglioni, Tail, Tar, Teflon, Tent, Top, Trench, Truss, Trusty, Tunic, Tuxedo, Ulster(ette), Underseal, Veneer, Verdigris, Warm, Wash, Windjammer, Wool, Wrap-rascal, Zamarra, Zamarro, Zinc
Coat of arms Crest, Hatchment
Coat-tail Flap
Coax Blandish, Blarney, Cajole, Carn(e)y, Cuittle, Entice, Flatter, Lure, Persuade, Wheedle, Whillywha(w)
Cob Hazel(nut), Horse
Cobalt Co, Zaffer, Zaffre
Cobble(s), Cobbled, Cobbler(s) Bunkum, Claptrap, Cosier, Cozier, Mend, Patch, Pie, Rot, Snob, Soutar, Souter, Sowter, Stone, Sutor, Twaddle, Vamp
Cobra King

Cobweb(by) Arachnoid, Araneous, Gossamer, Snare, Trap
Cocaine Basuco, C, Charlie, Coke, Crystal, Freebase, Moonrock, Nose candy, Number, Ready-wash, Snow
Coccid Wax-insect
Cochlear Scala
Cock(y) Alectryon, Ball, Capon, Chanticleer, Chaparral, Erect, Escape, Fighting, Flip, Fowl, France, Fugie, Half, Hay, Heath, Jack-the-lad, Jaunty, Midden, Penis, Roadrunner, Robin, Rooster, Shake-bag, Snook, Strut, Swaggering, Tap, Tilt, Turkey, Vain, Valve, Vane
Cock-a-hoop Crowing, Elated
Cockatoo Bird, Corella, Galah, Leadbeater's, Major Mitchell, Parrot
Cockboat Cog
Cockchafer Humbuzz, Maybug
Cock crow Skreigh of the day
Cocker Blenheim, Cuiter, Spaniel
Cockeyed Agee, Askew, Skewwhiff
Cockfight Main
Cockle Bulge, Crease, Wrinkle
▷ **Cockle(s)** *may indicate* an anagram
Cockney 'Arriet, 'Arry, Bow, Eastender, Londoner, Londonese
▷ **Cockney** *may indicate* a missing h
Cockpit Greenhouse, Well
Cockroach Archy, Beetle, Black beetle, Croton bug, German, Oriental, Orthoptera
▶ **Cockscomb** *see* **COXCOMB**
Cocktail Alexander, Aperitif, Atomic, Bellini, Between the sheets, Black Russian, Bloody Mary, Brandy Alexander, Buck's fizz, Bumbo, Caipirinha, Cobbler, Cold duck, Crusta, Daiquiri, → **DRINK**, Egg-flip, Fruit, Fustian, Gibson, Gimlet, Grasshopper, Harvey Wallbanger, Highball, → **HORSE**, Horse's neck, Julep, Mai-Tai, Manhattan, Margarita, Martini®, Melange, Mix, Molotov, Moscow mule, Old-fashioned, Piña colada, Pink lady, Planter's punch, Prawn, Punch, Rickey, Rusty nail, Sangaree, Sangria, Sazerac®, Screwdriver, Sherry cobbler, Side-car, Singapore sling, Slammer, Snakebite, Snowball, Spritzer, Stengah, Stinger, Swizzle, Tom Collins, Twist, White-lady
Cocoa Criollo, Nib(s)
Coconut Coco-de-mer, Coir, Copra, Head, Madafu, Poonac, Toddy-palm
Cocoon Dupion, Mother, Pod, Swathe, Trehala
Cod Bag, Cape, Coalfish, Fish, Gade, Gadus, Haberdine, Keeling, Kid, Lob, Man, Morrhua, Murray, Red, Saith, Saltfish, Stockfish, Torsk, Tusk, Whiting
Coda End(ing), Epilogue, Rondo, Tail
Coddle Cosset, Molly, Nancy, Pamper, Pet, Poach
Code, Coding, Codification Access, Alphanumeric, Amalfitan, Area, Bar, Barred, Binary, Bushido, Canon, Character, Cipher, City, Civil, Clarendon, Codex, Colour, Computing, Condition, Country, Cryptogram, Cryptograph, Dialling, Disciplinary, Dogma, Dress, DX, EBCDIC, Enigma, Error, Escape, Ethics, Fuero, Genetic, Gray, Green Cross, Hammurabic, Highway, Hollerith, Iddy-umpty, Justinian, MAC, Machine, Morse, Napoleon(ic), National, Object, Omerta, Opcode, Penal, PGP, Pindaric, Postal, Price, Rulebook, Scytale, Sharia, Shulchan Aruch, Signal, Sort, Source, STD, Talmud, Time, Twelve Tables, Zip
Code-breaker, Code-breaking Bletchley Park, Malpractitioner
Codger Buffer, Fellow
Codicil Addition, Label, PS, Rider

Codon Initiator
Coefficient Absorption, Correlation, Differential, Diffusion, Distribution, Modulus, Partition, Pearson's correlation, Permeability, Saturation, Spearman's rank-order, Transmission, Young modulus
Coelacanth Latimeria
Coerce, Coercion Big stick, Bully, Compel, Dragoon, Gherao, Pressure, Railroad, Restrain, Threaten
Coffee, Coffee beans, Coffee pot Americano, Arabica, Brazil, Cafetiere, Cappuccino, Decaff, Demi-tasse, Espresso, Expresso, Filter, Gaelic, Gloria, Granules, Instant, Irish, Java, Latte, Macchiato, Mocha, Peaberry, Percolator, Robusta, Rye, Skinny latte, Tan, Triage, Turkish
Coffee-house Lloyd's
Coffer Ark, Box, Casket, Cassone, Chest, Lacunar, Locker
Coffin Bier, Box, Casket, Hearse, Kist, Larnax, Sarcophagus, Shell, Wooden kimono, Wooden overcoat
Cog(ged) Contrate, Mitre-wheel, Nog, Pinion, Tooth
Cogent Compelling, Forceful, Good, Sound, Telling
Cogitate Deliberate, Mull, Muse, Ponder
Cognate Paronym
Cohabit Bed, Indwell, Share
Co-heir Parcener
Cohere(nt) Agglutinate, Clear, Cleave, Cling, Logical, Stick
Cohort Colleague, Crony, Soldier
Coif Calotte, Cap, Hood
Coiffure Hairdo, Pompadour, Tête
Coil(s), Coiled Armature, Bight, Bought, Choke, Circinate, Clew, Clue, Convolute(d), Convolve, Curl, Current, Fake, Fank, Furl, Hank, Helix, Ignition, Induction, Loading, Mortal, Moving, Primary, Resistance, Rouleau, Scorpioid, Solenoid, Spark, Spiral, Spiraster, Spire, Tesla, Tickler, Toroid, Twine, Twirl, → **WIND**, Wound, Wreath, Writhe, Yoke
Coin Base, Bean, Bit, Broad(piece), Cash, Change, Coign(e), Contorniate, Copper, Create, Doctor, Dosh, Double-header, Dump(s), Fiver, Han(d)sel, Imperial, Invent, Make, Mill, Mint, → **MONEY**, Neoterise, Numismatic, Nummary, Piece, Plate, Pocket-piece, Proof, Razoo, Rock, Shiner, Slip, Smelt, Specie, Stamp, Sterling, Strike, Subsidiary, Sum, Tenner, Thin'un, Token, Touchpiece, Unity

---

COINS

1 letter:	Bar	Lei	Sol
D	Bob	Lek	Som
	Cob	Leu	Sou
2 letters:	Dam	Lev	Won
As	Ecu	Lew	Yen
DM	Fen	Mil	Zuz
Kr	Fil	Mna	
Rd	Fin	Moy	4 letters:
Xu	Flu	Ore	Anna
	Hao	Pul	Baht
3 letters:	Jun	Pya	Bani
Avo	Kip	Red	Birr
Ban	Lat	Sen	Buck

Cedi	Tael	Liard	Zimbi
Cent	Taka	Litai	Zloty
Chon	Tala	Litas	
Dibs	Tein	Livre	**6 letters:**
Dime	Toea	Louis	Agorol
Doit	Tray	Lyart	Aureus
Dong	Trey	Maile	Balboa
Dram	Vatu	Manat	Bawbee
Duro	Yuan	Maneh	Bender
Euro	Zack	Mohur	Bezant
Fiat		Mongo	Boddle
Fils	**5 letters:**	Mopus	Byzant
Inti	Agora	Naira	Canary
Jack	Angel	Nakfa	Centas
Jane	Asper	Ngwee	Colone
Jiao	Aurar	Noble	Copeck
Kina	Baiza	Obang	Couter
Kobo	Bekah	Oscar	Dalasi
Kuna	Belga	Paisa	Danace
Kyat	Bodle	Paolo	Deaner
Lari	Brown	Pence	Décime
Lion	Butat	Pengo	Denier
Lipa	Butut	Penie	Derham
Lira	Chiao	Penni	Dirham
Loti	Colon	Penny	Dirhem
Luma	Conto	Plack	Dodkin
Maik	Crore	Pound	Dollar
Mark	Crown	Rider	Double
Merk	Daric	Royal	Drachm
Mina	Dibbs	Ruble	Ekuele
Mite	Dinar	Rupee	Escudo
Mule	Diram	Sceat	Filler
Obol	Dobra	Scudo	Florin
Para	Ducat	Scute	Forint
Paul	Eagle	Semis	Gilder
Peag	Eyrir	Sente	Gourde
Peni	Franc	Shand	Guinea
Peso	Fugio	Soldo	Gulden
Pice	Gazet	Souon	Halala
Pula	Gerah	Sucre	Heller
Puli	Gopik	Sycee	Hryvna
Punt	Groat	Tenge	Jitney
Rand	Grosz	Thebe	Kobang
Real	Haler	Tical	Koruna
Reis	Krona	Ticky	Kroner
Rial	Krone	Tiyin	Kroona
Riel	Kroon	Tolar	Kruger
Ryal	Kurus	Toman	Kwacha
Sene	Laari	Tyyin	Kwanza
Sent	Laree	Unite	Lepton
Slog	Leone	Zaire	Likuta

Loonie	Cardecu	**8 letters:**	Fourpence
Makuta	Carolus	Brockage	Half-eagle
Mancus	Centavo	Cardecue	Half-tiger
Markka	Chetrum	Cruzeiro	Luckpenny
Mawpus	Cordoba	Denarius	Maple leaf
Mongoe	Crusado	Doubloon	Ninepence
Pa'anga	Drachma	Ducatoon	Pistareen
Paduan	Ekpwele	Emalengi	Rennminbi
Pagoda	Guarani	Farthing	Rix-dollar
Pataca	Guilder	Groschen	Rose noble
Pennia	Hryvnya	Johannes	Schilling
Peseta	Jacobus	Kreutzer	Sou marque
Pesewa	Joannes	Llangeni	Sovereign
Qintar	Kopiyka	Louis d'or	Spur-royal
Rappen	Kreuzer	Maravedi	Yellowboy
Rouble	Lemoira	Millieme	Zwanziger
Rupiah	Lisente	Napoleon	
Santum	Metical	Ngultrum	**10 letters:**
Satang	Millime	Picayune	Chervonets
Sceatt	Milreis	Pistolet	Krugerrand
Seniti	Moidore	Planchet	Portcullis
Sequin	Ostmark	Portague	Reichsmark
Shekel	Ouguiya	Portigue	Siege-piece
Sickle	Patrick	Quadrans	
Siglos	Piastre	Rigmarie	**11 letters:**
Somoni	Piefort	Semuncia	Bonnet-piece
Stater	Pistole	Sesterce	Deutschmark
Stiver	Pollard	Shilling	Double eagle
Stotin	Quarter	Skilling	Sword-dollar
Talent	Quetzal	Solidare	Tetradrachm
Tanner	Ringgit	Spur-rial	
Tester	Ruddock	Spur-ryal	**12 letters:**
Teston	Rufiyaa	Stotinka	Antoninianus
Thaler	Sextans	Twopence	
Tickey	Solidus	Xeraphin	**13 letters:**
Toonie	Spanker	Zecchino	Half-sovereign
Tugrik	Tambala		Rennminbi yuan
Turner	Testoon	**9 letters:**	
Vellon	Testril	Boliviano	**14 letters:**
Wakiki	Thick'un	Britannia	Three-farthings
	Thrimsa	Centesimo	
7 letters:	Thrymsa	Dandiprat	**18 letters:**
Afghani	Tughrik	Dandyprat	Maria Theresa
Austral	Unicorn	Didrachma	dollar
Bolivar	Xerafin	Dupondius	

Coinage Currency, Invention, Nonce-word
Coincide(nt), Coincidence Accident, Chance, Consilience, Conterminous, Fit, Fluke, Homotaxis, Overlap, Rabat(to), Simultaneous, Synastry, Synchronise, Tally
Coke Chark, Coal, Cocaine, Kola
Col Pass, Poort, Saddle

Cold(-blooded) Ague, Algid, Aloof, Arctic, Austere, Biting, Bitter, Bleak, C, Catarrh, Cauld(rife), Charity, Chill(y), Colubrine, Common, Coryza, Ectotherm, Emotionless, Frappé, Frem(d), Fremit, Frigid, Frost(y), Gelid, Glacial, Hiemal, Icy, Impersonal, Jeel, Nippy, Nirlit, Parky, Passionless, Perishing, Piercing, Poikilotherm(ic), Polar, Psychro-, Remote, Rheumy, Rigor, Rume, Snap, Snell, Sniffles, Sour, Standoffish, Starving, Streamer, Subzero, Taters, Weed, Wintry

Cold sore Herpes, Shiver

Coldstream Borderer, Guard

Cole Colza, King, Nat, Porter

Colic Batts, Bots, Botts, Gripe, Lead, Painter's, Sand, Upset, Zinc

Collaborate, Collaborator, Collaboration Assist, Combine, → **COOPERATE**, Keiretsu, Quisling, Synergy, Vichy, Vichyite

Collage Paste up

Collapse Apoplexy, Breakdown, Buckle, Cave, Conk, Crash, Crumble, Crumple, Debacle, Downfall, Fail(ure), Fall, Flake out, Fold, Founder, Give, Implode, Inburst, Landslide, Meltdown, Phut, Purler, Rack, Rot, Ruin, Scat(ter), Sink, Slump, Stroke, Subside, Sunstroke, Swoon, Telescope, Tumble, Wilt, Wrack, Zonk

▷ **Collapsing** *may indicate* an anagram

Collar(ed) Arrest, Astrakhan, Bermuda, Bertha, Berthe, Bib, Bishop, Blue, Brecham, Buster, Butterfly, Button-down, Buttonhole, Capture, Carcanet, Chevesaile, Choke(r), Clerical, Collet, Dog, Esses, Eton, Falling-band, Flea, Gorget, Grandad, Hame, Head(stall), Holderbat, Horse, Jabot, Jampot, Karenni, Mandarin, Moran, Mousquetaire, Nab, Nail, Neckband, Necklet, Ox-bow, Peter Pan, Piccadell, Piccadillo, Piccadilly, Pikadell, Pink, Polo, Puritan, Rabatine, Rabato, Rebater, Rebato, Revers, Rollneck, Roman, Ruff, Sailor, Seize, Shawl, Steel, Storm, Tackle, Tappet, Tie-neck, Torque, Turndown, Turtleneck, Vandyke, Whisk, White, Wing, Yoke

Collation Comparison, Meal, Repast

Colleague(s) Ally, Associate, Bedfellow, Confrère, Mate, Oppo, Partner, Team

Collect(ion), Collective(ly), Collector Accrue, Agglomerate, Aggregate, Album, Alms, Amass, Amildar, Ana, Anthology, Arcana, Assemble, Aumil, Bank, Bow, Budget, Bunch, Bundle, Burrell, Caboodle, Calm, Cap, Cete, Clowder, Compendium, Compile, Congeries, Conglomerate, Covey, Cull, Dossier, Dustman, Earn, Egger, Exaltation, Exordial, Fest, (Fest)schrift, Fetch, Florilegium, Gaggle, Garbo, Garner, Gather, Get, Gilbert, Glean, Glossary, Grice, Heap, Herd, Hive, Idant, In all, Jingbang, Job lot, Kit, Kitty, Levy, Loan, Magpie, Meal, Meet, Meinie, Mein(e)y, Menagerie, Menyie, Miscellany, Mish-mash, Montem, Murmuration, Museum, Muster, Nide, Offertory, Omnibus, Omnium-gatherum, Paddling, Pile, Plate, Pod, Post, Prayer, Quest, Raft, Raise, Rammle, Recheat, Rhapsody, Scramble, Sedge, Serene, Set, Shoe, Siege, Skein, Smytrie, Sord, Sottisier, Sounder, Spring, Stand, Tahsildar, Team, Troop, Unkindness, Uplift, Watch, Wernher, Whipround, Wisp

▷ **Collection** *may indicate* an anagram

Collection-box Brod, Ladle, Rammle

Collectorate Taluk

College(s) Academy, All Souls, Alma mater, Ampleforth, Balliol, Brasenose, Business, C, Caius, Campus, CAT, Cheltenham, Clare, Classical, Coed, Commercial, Community, Corpus, Cow, Cranwell, Downing, Dulwich, Electoral, Emmanuel, Eton, Exeter, Foundation, Freshwater, Girton, Hall, Heralds', Jail, Junior, Keble, King's, Lancing, Linacre, Lincoln, LSE, Lycée, Lyceum, Madras(s)a(h), Madressah, Magdalen(e), Marlborough, Medrese, Medresseh, Merton, Newnham, Nuffield,

Open, Oriel, Pembroke, Poly, Polytechnic, Pontifical, Protonotariat, Queen's, Ruskin, Sacred, St Johns, Saliens, Sandhurst, Selwyn, Seminary, Sixth-form, Somerville, Sorbonne, Staff, Tech(nical), Technikon, Tertiary, Theologate, Training, Trinity, Tug, UMIST, Up, Village, Wadham, Winchester, Yeshwa(h)

Collide, Collision Afoul, Barge, Bird-strike, Bump, Cannon, Carom(bole), Clash, Dash, Elastic, Fender-bender, Foul, Head-on, Hurtle, Impact, Inelastic, Into, Kiss, Meet, Pile-up, Prang, Rencounter, Smash-up, Strike, Thwack

Collie Bearded, Border, Dog, Kelpie, Kelpy, Rough, Sheepdog

Collier Geordie, Hoastman, Miner, Necklace, Patience, Ship

Colloid Aerogel, Gel, Lyophil(e), Sol

Collude, Collusive Abet, Cahoots, Conspire, Deceive

Colon Aspinwall, Sigmoid, Spastic, Transverse

Colonel Blimp, Bogey, Chinstrap, Col, Everard, Goldstick, Newcome, Nissen, Pride

Colonial(ist), Colonist Ant, Antenatal, Boer, Creole, Emigré, Oecist, Oikist, Overseas, Phoenician, Pioneer, Planter, Polyp(e), Settler, Sicel(iot), Sikel(ian), Sikeliot, Stuyvesant, Swarm, Territorial, Voter

Colonnade Eustyle, File, Gallery, Peristyle, Porch, Portico, Stoa

Colony Aden, Cape, Charter, Cleruchy, Crown, Dependency, Halicarnassian, Hive, Hongkong, Kaffraria, Nudist, Penal, Plymouth, Presidio, Proprietary, Rookery, Settlement, Swarm, Termitarium, Warren, Zambia, Zimbabwe

Colophony Rosin

Colossal → **ENORMOUS**, Epochal, Gigantic, Huge, Vast

Colosseum Amphitheatre

Colour(ed), Colouring, Colours Achromatic, Bedye, Blee, Blush, C, Cap, Chromatic, Chrome, Complementary, Complexion, Crayon, Criant, Cross, Distort, Dye, False, Film, Flag, Florid, Flying, Gouache, Haem, → **HUE**, Ink, Irised, Kalamkari, Leer, Local, Lutein, Metif, Nankeen, Orpiment, Palette, Pantone®, Pastel, Pied, Pigment, Pochoir, Polychrome, Primary, Prism, Prismatic, Process, Puke, Queen's, Raddle, Reddle, Regimental, Rinse, Riot, Ruddle, Secondary, Sematic, Shade, Solid, Spectrum, Startle, Tertiary, Tie-dye, Tinctorial, Tinc(ture), Tinge, Tint, Tone, Uvea, Wash

---

COLOURS

2 letters:	Gold	Camel	Rouge
Or	Grey	Chica	Sepia
	Jade	Coral	Taupe
3 letters:	Lake	Cream	Tenné
Bay	Lime	Eosin	Tenny
Jet	Navy	Green	Umber
Red	Pink	Gules	
Tan	Plum	Ivory	**6 letters:**
	Puce	Khaki	Anatta
4 letters:	Rose	Lemon	Anatto
Anil	Ruby	Lilac	Auburn
Bice	Sand	Lovat	Bisque
Blue	Teal	Mauve	Bister
Buff	Vert	Ochre	Bistre
Cyan		Olive	Cerise
Ecru	**5 letters:**	Peach	Day-Glo®
Fawn	Beige	Pearl	Isabel

Maroon	Filemot	Cinnamon	**10 letters:**
Orange	Gamboge	Lavender	Aquamarine
Reseda	Magenta	Off-white	French navy
Roucou	Oatmeal	Pea-green	Tartrazine
Sienna	Old gold	Philamot	Vermillion
Titian	Old rose	Philomot	
	Saffron		**11 letters:**
7 letters:	Scarlet	**9 letters:**	Ultramarine
Annatta	Umbrage	Alizarine	
Annatto		Anthocyan	**12 letters:**
Apricot	**8 letters:**	Chocolate	Cappagh-brown
Arnotto	Alizarin	Royal blue	
Caramel	Burgundy	Solferino	
Crimson	Cardinal	Turquoise	
Emerald	Chestnut	Vermilion	

Colour blindness Daltonism, Deuteranopia, Dichrom(at)ism, Monochromatic, Protanomaly, Protanopia, Protanopic, Tritanopia

▷ **Coloured** *may indicate* an anagram

Colourful Abloom, Brave, Flamboyant, Flowery, Iridescent, Kaleidoscope, Opalescent, Splashy, Vivid

Colourless Albino, Bleak, Drab, Dull, Hyalite, Pallid, Pallor, Wan, White

Colt Cade, Foal, Gun, Hogget, Sta(i)g, Teenager, Two-year-old

Columbine Aquilegia

Column(s), Column foot Agony, Anta, Atlantes, Clustered, Commentary, Control, Corinthian, Correspondence, Cylinder, Decastyle, Diastyle, Doric, Editorial, Eustyle, Fifth, File, Fractionating, Geological, Gossip, Hypostyle, Impost, Lat, Lonelyhearts, Monolith, Nelson's, Newel, Obelisk, Pericycle, Peripteral, Peristyle, Persian, Personal, Pilaster, → **PILLAR**, Pilotis, Prostyle, Pycnostyle, Rouleau, Row, Short, Spina, Spinal, Spine, Stalactite, Stalagmite, Steering, Stylobate, Systyle, Tabulate, Telamone, Third, Tige, Tore, Torus, Trajan's, Vertebral

Columnist Advertiser, Caryatid, Newsman, Stylite, Telamon, Writer

Coma(tose) Apoplexy, Crown, Sedated, Sleep, Torpor, Trance

Comb(er), Combed, Combing Afro, Alveolate, Beehive, Breaker, Card, Copple, Crest, Curry, Dredge, Fine-tooth, Hackle, Heckle, Hot, Kaim, Kame, Kangha, Kemb, Noils, Pecten, Rake, Red(d), Ripple(r), Rose, Scribble, Search, Side, Small tooth, Smooth, Tease(l), Toaze, Tooth, Tose, Toze, Trawl, Tuft, Wave

Combat(ant), Combative Argument, → **BATTLE**, Competitor, Conflict, Contest, Dispute, Duel, → **FIGHT**, Gladiator, Joust, Judicial, Jujitsu, Just, Karate, Kendo, List, Mêlée, Militant, Oppose, Paintball, Protagonist, Spear-running, Unarmed, War

Combination, Combine(d), Combining Accrete, Alligate, Ally, Amalgam, Associate, Axis, Bloc, Cartel, Cleave, Clique, Coalesce, Coalition, Composite, Concoction, Conflated, Conglomerate, Consortium, Coordinate, Crasis, Fuse, Group, Harvester, Incorporate, Integration, Interfile, Join, Junta, Kartell, League, Meld, Merge(r), Mingle, Mixture, Perm(utation), Piece, Pool, Quill, Ring, Solvate, Splice, Syncretize, Synthesis, Terrace, Trivalent, Trona, Unite, Valency, Wed, Zaibatsu

Comb-like Ctenoid, Pecten

Combustible, Combustion Ardent, Fiery, Inflammable, Phlogistic, Phlogiston, Spontaneous, Wildfire

▷ **Combustible** *may indicate* an anagram

Come, Coming (back), Coming out Advent, Anear, Anon, Appear, Approach, Ar(r), Arise, Arrive, Attend, Debouch, Derive, Emerge, Future, Happen, Iceman, Issue, Millenarian, Orgasm, Parousia, Pass, Pop, Respond, Second, Via

Come again Eh

Comeback Boomerang, Bounce, Echo, Homer, Quip, Rally, Rearise, Rebound, Recovery, Repartee, Reply, Retort, Retour, Return, Reversion, Riposte

Comedian Benny, Buffoon, Chaplin, → **CLOWN**, Comic, Durante, Emery, Goon, Groucho, Hope, Joker, Karno, Keaton, Leno, Quipster, Robey, Scream, Screwball, Stand-up, Tate, Tati, Tummler, Wag, Wise, Yell

Comedo Blackhead

Comedown Avale, Bathetic, Bathos, Disappointment, Drop, Letdown, Shower

Comedy Alternative, Black, Com, Drama, Ealing, Errors, Farce, High, Humour, Keystone, Knockabout, Lazzo, Low, Millamant, Musical, Romcom, Situation, Slapstick, Stand-up, Thalia, Travesty

Comely Beseen, Bonny, Fair, Goodly, Graceful, Jolly, Likely, Pleasing, Pretty, Proper

Comestible(s) Cate, Eats, Fare

Comet Chiron, Geminid, Halley's, Kohoutek, Meteor, Oort cloud, Reindeer, Shoemaker-Levy 9, Vomet, Xiphias

Come through Weather

Comfort(able), Comforter, Comforting, Comfy Amenity, Analeptic, Armchair, Balm, Bein, Bildad, Calm, Canny, Cheer, Cherish, Clover, Cold, Consolation, Console, Convenience, Cose, Cosh, Cosy, Couthie, Couthy, Creature, Crumb, Cushy, Dummy, Dutch, Ease, Easy, Eliphaz, Featherbed, Gemutlich, Heeled, Homely, Job's, Mumsy, Noah, Plum, Plushy, Reassure, Relaxed, Relief, Relieve, Rug, Scarf, Sinecure, Snug, Solace, Soothe, Succour, There, Tosh, Trig, Warm, Wealthy, Well, Well-to-do, Zophar

Comic(al) Beano, Buff, Buffo(on), Bumpkin, Buster, Chaplin, Clown, → **COMEDIAN**, Dandy, Droll, Eagle, Facetious, Fields, → **FUNNY**, Gagster, Hardy, Horror, Jester, Knock-about, Laurel, Leno, Mag, Manga, Quizzical, Rich, Robey, Strip, Tati, Trial, Zany

Comma Inverted, Oxford

Command(eer), Commanding, Commandment(s) Behest, Bid, Categorical imperative, Charge, Coerce, Control, Decalogue, Direct, Direction, Dominate, Domineer, Easy, Edict, Fiat, Fiaunt, Fighter, Firman, Haw, Hest, High, Imperious, Impress, Injunction, Instruction, Jussive, Mandate, Maritime, Mastery, Mitzvah, Mobile, → **ORDER**, Precept, Press, Query language, Requisition, Rule, Seize, Ukase, Warn, Warrant, Will, Wish, Writ

Commander Admiral, Ag(h)a, Ameer, Barleycorn, Bey, Bloke, Blucher, Boss, Brennus, Brig, Caliph, Centurion, Cid, Decurion, Dreyfus, Emir, Emperor, Field cornet, Generalissimo, Hetman, Hipparch, Imperator, Killadar, Leader, Manager, Marshal, Master, Meer, Mir, Moore, Officer, Overlord, Pendragon, Polemarch, Pr(a)efect, Raglan, Seraskier, Shogun, Sirdar, Taxiarch, Trierarch, Turcopolier, Vaivode, Voivode, Waivode, Warlord, Wing

Commando Chindit(s), Fedayee(n), Green Beret, Raider, Ranger, SAS

Commemorate, Commemoration Encaenia, Epitaph, Eulogy, Keep, Memorial, Monument, Plaque, Remember

Commence Begin, Initiate, Open, Start

Commend(ation) Belaud, Bestow, Encomium, Entrust, Laud, Panegyric, → **PRAISE**, Roose, Tribute

Commensal Epizoon, Messmate

Commensurate Adequate, Enough, Equivalent, Relevant

Comment(ary), Commentator Analyst, Animadvert, Annotate, Apercu, Comm, Coryphaeus, Coverage, Critic, Critique, Descant, Discuss, Editorial, Essay, Exegete, Explain, Exposition, Expound, Footnote, Gemara, Gloss(ographer), Glosser, Hakam, Kibitz, Margin, Marginalia, Midrashim, Note, Obiter dictum, Observation, Par, Platitude, Play-by-play, Postil, Remark, Running, Scholiast, Scholion, Scholium, Voice-over, Zohar

Commerce, Commercial Ad, Barter, Cabotage, Jingle, Marketable, Mercantile, Mercenary, Merchant, Shoppy, Simony, Trade, Traffic

Commercial traveller Drummer, Rep

Commiserate, Commiseration Compassion, Pity, Sympathise

Commissar People's, Political

Commission(er), Commissioned Authorise, Boundary, Brevet, Brokage, Brokerage, Charge, Charity, Countryside, Delegation, Depute, ECE, Employ, Engage, Envoy, Errand, European, Factor, Gosplan, High, Husbandage, Job, Kickback, Law, Magistrate, Mandate, Office(r), Official, Ombudsman, Order, Percentage, Perpetration, Place, Poundage, Price, Rake-off, Resident, Roskill, Roving, Royal, Task, Task force, Trust, Wreck

Commit(tal), Commitment Aret(t), Consign, Contract, Decision, Dedication, Delegate, Devotion, Do, Engage, Entrust, Enure, Impeachment, Perpetrate, Pledge, Rubicon

Committee ACRE, Board, Body, Commission, Commune, Council, Delegacy, Group, Hanging, Joint, Junta, Politburo, Presidium, Propaganda, Review body, Riding, Samiti, School, Select, Standing, Steering, Syndicate, Table, Vigilance, Watch, Works

Commode, Commodious Ample, Closestool, Roomy, Spacious

Commodities, Commodity Article, Futures, Gapeseed, Item, Physicals, Soft, Staple, Ware

Common(ly), Commoner, Commons As per usual, Average, Cad, Conventional, Diet, Dirt, Doctor's, Ealing, Eatables, Enclosure, Endemic, Epicene, Everyday, Familiar, Fare, Folk, General, Green, Greenham, House, Law, Lay, Low, Lower House, Mark, Mere, MP, Mutual, Naff, Non-U, Normal, People, Pleb, Prevalent, Prole, Public, Related, Rife, Roturier, Ryfe, Scran, Sense, Shared, Stray, Tie, Tiers d'état, Trite, Tritical, Tuft, Tye, Use, → USUAL, Vile, Vul(gar), Vulgo, Vulgus, Widespread, Wimbledon

Commonplace Banal, Copybook, Hackneyed, Homely, Humdrum, Idée reçue, Mot, Ordinary, Philistine, Plain, Platitude, Prosaic, Quotidian, Trite, Workaday

Commonsense Gumption, Nous, Savoir-faire, Smeddum, Wit

Commonwealth Protectorate, Puerto Rico, Res publica

Commotion Bluster, Bustle, Carfuffle, Clangour, Clatter, Curfuffle, Dirdam, Dirdum, Do, Dust, Ferment, Flap, Flurry, Fraise, Fuss, Hell, Hoo-ha(h), Hurly-burly, Hurry, Pother, Pudder, Racket, Romage, Rort, Ruckus, Ruction, Rumpus, Shemozzle, Shindig, Shindy, Shivaree, Steery, Stir, Stirabout, Storm, Stushie, Tirrivee, Tirrivie, To-do, Toss, Tumult, Turmoil, Upheaval, Uproar, Whirl, Wroth

Communal, Commune Agapemone, Collective, Com, Meditate, Mir, Paris, Phalanstery, Public, Talk, Township

Communicate, Communication Ampex, Announce, Baud, Bluetooth, Boyau, Cable, Channelling, Conversation, Convey, Cybernetic, E-mail, Expansive, Impart, Infobahn, Inform, Intelpost, Intelsat, Internet, Message, Nonverbal, Note, Oracy, Prestel®, Proxemics, Put across, Reach, Road, Semiotics, Signal, Tannoy®, Telepathy, Teletex, Telex, Telstar, Tieline, Transmit, Utraquist, Viewdata

Communion Creed, Fellowship, Host, Housel, Intinction, Lord's Supper, Species, Viaticum

Communiqué Announcement, Statement

Communism, Communist Apparat(chik), Aspheterism, Bolshevist, Brook Farm, Com, Comecon, Cominform, Comintern, Commo, Comsomol, Deviationist, Engels, Essene, Fourier, Khmer Rouge, Komsomol, Leninite, Maoist, Marxist, Nomenklatura, Perfectionist, Pinko, Politburo, Populist, Red, Revisionism, Soviet, Spartacist, Stalinism, Tanky, Titoist, Trot, Vietcong, Vietminh

Communities, Community Agapemone, Alterne, Ashram, Biome, Body, Brook Farm, Brotherhood, Clachan, Climax, Closed, Coenobitism, Coenobium, Colonia, Colony, Consocies, District, EC, Ecosystem, EEC, Enclave, European, Faith, Frat(e)ry, Global, Kahal, Kibbutz, Mesarch, Neighbourhood, Pantosocracy, People, Phalanx, Phyle, Preceptory, Public, Pueblo, Republic, Seral, Sere, Settlement, Shtetl, Sisterhood, Society, Speech, Street, Toon, Town, Tribe, Ujamaa, Village, Virtual, Volost, Zupa

Commute(r) Change, Convert, Reduce, Straphanger, Travel

Como Lake, Perry

Compact Agreement, Cement, Concise, Conglobe, Covenant, Covin, Coyne, Dense, Entente, Fast, Firm, Flapjack, Hard, Knit, League, Match, Neat, Pledge, Powder, Solid, Tamp, Terse, Tight, Treaty, Well-knit

Companion(able) Achates, Arm candy, Associate, Attender, Barnacle, Bedfellow, Bonhomie, Bud(dy), Butty, CH, China, Comate, Compeer, Comrade, Consort, Contubernal, Crony, Cupman, Duenna, Ephesian, Escort, Feare, Felibre, → **FELLOW**, Fere, Franion, Furked, Handbook, Helpmate, Mate, Native, Pal, Pard, Pheer(e), Playmate, Pot, Sidekick, Skaines mate, Stable, Thane, Thegn, Trojan, Vade-mecum

Company, Companies Actors, Artel, Ass, Assembly, Band, Bank, Battalion, Bevy, → **BUSINESS**, Bv, Cahoot, Cartel, Cast, Cavalcade, Chartered, CIA, Circle, City, Close, Club, Co, Conger, Consort, Cordwainers, Core, Corporation, Corps, Coy, Crew, Crowd, Decury, Dotcom, East India, Enterprise, Entourage, Faction, Finance, Fire, → **FIRM**, Flock, Free, Gang, Garrison, Ging, Guild, Haberdashers, Heap, Holding, Hudson's Bay, ICI, Inc, Indie, In-house, Intercourse, Investment, Jingbang, Joint-stock, Limited, Listed, Livery, Management, Maniple, Muster, Order, Organisation, Parent, Plc, Pride, Private, Public, Public limited, Quoted, Rep(ertory), Room, SA, Sedge, Set, Set out, Shell, Siege, Sort, SpA, Stationers', Stock, Subsidiary, Syndicate, Table, Team, Thiasus, Touring, Troop, Troupe, Trust, Twa, Two(some), Visitor, White

Compare(d), Comparison Analogy, Balance, Beside, Bracket, Collate, Confront, Contrast, Correspond, Cp, Equate, Liken, Match, Odious, Parallel, Relation, Simile, Weigh

Compartment Ballonet, Bay, Booth, Box, Carriage, Casemate, Cell, Chamber, Cofferdam, Cubbyhole, Cubicle, Dog box, Locellate, Locker, Loculament, Loculus, Panel, Partition, Pigeonhole, Pocket, Pod, Room, Room(ette), Severy, Smoker, Stall, Till, Trunk, Watertight

Compass Ambit, Area, Beam, Binnacle, Bounds, Bow, Dividers, Extent, Gamut, Goniometer, Gyro, Gyromagnetic, Gyroscope, Infold, Magnetic, Mariner's, Needle, Orbit, Pelorus, Pencil, Perimeter, Prismatic, Radio, → **RANGE**, Reach, Rhumb, Room, Scale, Sweep, Tessitura, Trammel, Width

Compassion(ate) Aroha, Bleed(ing), Clemency, Commiseration, Empathy, Heart, Humane, Kuan Yin, Kwan Yin, Mercy, Pity, Samaritan, Sympathy, Ubuntu

Compatible Consistent, Fit, Harmonious

Compatriot National

Compel(ling), Compelled, Compulsion, Compulsive, Compulsory Addiction,

Coact, Coerce, Cogent, Command, Constrain, Dragoon, Duress, Enforce, Extort, Fain, → **FORCE**, Force majeure, Gar, Make, Mandatory, Oblige, Pathological, Steamroller, Strongarm, Tyrannise

Compendium Breviate

Compensate, Compensation Amend(s), Balance, Boot, Comp, Counterbalance, Counterpoise, Damages, Demurrage, Guerdon, Indemnity, Offset, Payment, Recoup, Redress, Reparation, Reprisal, Requital, Restitution, Restore, Retaliation, Salvage, Satisfaction, Solatium, Wergild, X-factor

Compère Emcee, Host, MC, Presenter

Compete Contend, Emulate, Enter, Match, Outvie, Play, Rival, Vie

Competence, Competent Ability, Able, Adequate, Can, Capacity, Dab, Dow, Efficient, Fit, Responsible, Sui juris, Worthy

Competition, Competitive, Competitor Agonist, Backmarker, Battle, Bee, Biathlon, Buckjumping, Candidate, Comper, Concours, Contention, Contest, Cup, Drive, Entrant, Event, Field, Finals, Freestyle, Gamesman, Gymkhana, Head-to-head, Heptathlon, Imperfect, Judoka, Jump off, Karateka, Knockout, Match, Match-play, Monopolistic, Open, Opponent, Outsider, Pairs, Panellist, Pentathlon, Perfect, Player, Premiership, Pro-am, Puissance, Race, Rally, Regatta, Repechage, Rival(ise), Rodeo, Runner-up, Show-jumping, Stableford, Super G, Tenson, Test, Tiger, Tournament, Tourney, Trial, Triallist, Wap(p)enshaw, Wild card

Compile(r), Compilation Anthology, Arrange, Collect, Edit, Prepare, Segue, Synthesis, Zadkiel

Complacent Babbitt, Fatuous, Joco, Pleasant, Self-satisfied, Smug

Complain(t), Complainer Adenoids, Affection, Affliction, Alas, Alastrim, Alopecia, Anaemia, Angashore, Angina, Asthma, Barrack, Beef, Bellyache, Bitch, Bleat, BSE, Carp, Cavil, Charge, Chorea, Colic, Crab, Cramp, Criticise, Diatribe, Disorder, Dropsy, Epidemic, Ergot, Exanthema, Girn, Gout, Gravamen, Groan, Grouch, Grouse, Growl, Grudge, Grumble, Grutch, Harangue, Hives, Hone, Hypochondria, Ileitis, → **ILLNESS**, Jeremiad, Kvetch, Lupus, Malady, Mange, Mean(e), Mein, Mene, Moan, Morphew, Mumps, Murmur, Nag, Natter, Neuralgia, Ologoan, Pertussis, Plica, Poor-mouth, Protest, Pule, Pyelitis, Querimony, Rail, Remonstrate, Repine, Report, Rickets, Sapego, Sciatica, Scold, Sigh, Silicosis, Squawk, Staggers, Thrush, Tic, Tinea, Upset, Wheenge, Whimper, Whine, Whinge, Yammer, Yawp

Complaisant Agreeable, Flexible, Suave, Supple

Complement Alexin, Amount, Balance, Finish, Gang, Lot, Reciprocate

▷ **Complement** *may indicate* a hidden word

Complete(ly), Completion Absolute, Accomplish, Achieve, All, Arrant, Attain, Clean, Congenital, Consummate, Crown, Do, End, Entire, Finalise, Finish, Flat, Follow through, Fruition, Fulfil, Full, Full-blown, Hollow, Incept, Integral, In toto, One, Ouroboros, Out, Out and out, Perfect, Plenary, Quite, Ready, Root and branch, Rounded, Self-contained, Sew-up, Sheer, Spang, Sum, Teetotal, Thorough, Total, Unanimous, Unbroken, Uncut, Unequivocal, Unmitigated, Utter, Whole (hog), Wrap

Complex(ity) Abstruse, Advanced, Arcane, Castration, Compound, Difficult, Electra, Golgi, Hard, Heath Robinson, Immune, Inferiority, Intricate, Intrince, Involute, Knot, Manifold, MHC, Military-industrial, Mixed, Multinucleate, Nest, Network, Obsession, Oedipus, Paranoid, Persecution, Phaedra, Plexiform, Superiority, Syndrome, Tangle, Web

Complexion Aspect, Blee, Hue, Leer, Temper, Tint, View

Compliance, Compliant, Comply Agree, Amenable, Assent, Conform, Deference, Docile, Follow, Hand-in-glove, Obey, Observe, Obtemper, Sequacious, Surrender, Wilco, Yield

Complicate(d), Complication Bewilder, Complex, Deep, Elaborate, Embroil, Implex, Intricate, Involution, Involve, Inweave, Node, Nodus, Perplex, Ramification, Rigmarole, Sequela, Snarl, Tangle, Tirlie-wirlie

▷ **Complicated** *may indicate* an anagram

Compliment(s) Baisemain, Bouquet, Congratulate, Devoirs, Douceur, Encomium, Flatter, Flummery, Greetings, Praise, Soap, Trade-last, Tribute

Component(s) Base, Coherer, Constituent, Contact, CRT, Daisy-wheel, Element, Factor, Formant, Guidance, Impedor, Inductor, Ingredient, Longeron, → **PART**, Pre-amp, Profile, Reactance, Resistor, Subunit, Tensor

Compose(d), Composure Aplomb, Arrange, Calm, Choreograph, Consist, Cool, → **CREATE**, Equanimity, Even, Face, Improvise, Indite, Lull, Notate, Orchestrate, Placid, Poise, Produce, Reconcile, Sangfroid, Sedate, Serenity, Settle, Soothe, Tranquil, Unruffled, Write

Composer Contrapunt(al)ist, Hymnist, Inditer, Inventor, Maker, Melodist, Musician, → **POET**, Serialist, Six, Songsmith, Songwriter, Symphonist, Triadist, Tunesmith, Writer

---

COMPOSERS

3 letters:
Bax

4 letters:
Adam
Arne
Bach
Berg
Blow
Brel
Bull
Byrd
Cage
Dima
Graf
Ives
Kern
Lalo
Monk
Nono
Orff
Peri
Raff
Wolf

5 letters:
Auber
Auric
Balfe

Berio
Bizet
Bliss
Bloch
Boito
Boyce
Brian
Bruch
Crumb
D'Indy
Dukas
Elgar
Falla
Fauré
Field
Finzi
Glass
Gluck
Grieg
Harty
Haydn
Henze
Holst
Ibert
Lasso
Lehar
Liszt
Loewe
Lully

Parry
Prout
Ravel
Reger
Rossi
Satie
Sousa
Spohr
Suppe
Tosti
Verdi
Watts
Weber
Weill
Zappa

6 letters:
Alfven
Arnold
Azione
Barber
Bartók
Bennet
Berlin
Boulez
Brahms
Bridge
Burney
Busoni

Chopin
Coates
Delius
Duparc
Dvorák
Flotow
Franck
German
Glière
Glinka
Gounod
Handel
Hummel
Joplin
Kodaly
Lassus
Ligeti
Mahler
Mingus
Morley
Mozart
Ogolon
Pierne
Rameau
Rubbra
Schutz
Tallis
Varese
Wagner

Walton	Rodgers	Schubert	Monteverdi
Webern	Rodrigo	Schumann	Mussorgsky
	Romberg	Scriabin	Palestrina
7 letters:	Rossini	Sessions	Ponchielli
Albeniz	Roussel	Sibelius	Rawsthorne
Alberti	Salieri	Sondheim	Saint-Saëns
Allegri	Smetana	Sullivan	Schoenberg
Amadeus	Stainer	Taverner	Stravinsky
Bantock	Strauss	Telemann	Villa-Lobos
Bellini	Tartini	Vangelis	Williamson
Berlioz	Tippett		
Berners	Vivaldi	**9 letters:**	**11 letters:**
Borodin	Warlock	Bacharach	Charpentier
Britten	Xenakis	Balakirev	Frescobaldi
Brubeck	Youmans	Beethoven	Humperdinck
Copland		Bernstein	Leoncavallo
Corelli	**8 letters:**	Boulanger	Mendelssohn
Debussy	Alaleona	Broughton	Stockhausen
De Falla	Albinoni	Buxtehude	Tchaikovsky
Delibes	Boughton	Chaminade	Wolf Ferrari
Dohnany	Bruckner	Cherubini	
Dowland	Chabrier	Donizetti	**12 letters:**
Gibbons	Chausson	Dunstable	Khachaturian
Ireland	Couperin	Hindemith	Rachmaninoff
Janácek	Gershwin	Meyerbeer	Shostakovich
Lambert	Gesualdo	Offenbach	
Mancini	Glazunov	Pachelbel	**13 letters:**
Martinu	Grainger	Pergolesi	Havergal Brian
Menotti	Granados	Prokofiev	Maxwell Davies
Milhaud	Honegger	Scarlatti	
Nielsen	Kreutzer	Schnittke	**14 letters:**
Novello	Marcello	Zemlinsky	Rimsky-Korsakov
Ormandy	Mascagni		
Poulenc	Massenet	**10 letters:**	**15 letters:**
Puccini	Messager	Birtwistle	Vaughan Williams
Purcell	Messiaen	Boccherini	
Purnell	Paganini	Carmichael	
Quilter	Respighi	Cole Porter	

▷ **Composing** *may indicate* an anagram

Composite Aster, Costmary, Foalfoot, Gerbera, Groundsel, Hawkweed, Hybrid, Integral, Motley, Opinicus, Rag(weed), Sphinx, Synthesized, Thistle

Composition, Compositor Albumblatt, Aleatory, Azione, Bagatelle, Beaumontage, Beaumontague, Canon, Capriccio, Caprice, Cob, Concerto, Concertstuck, Creation, Dite, Essay, Etude, Exaration, Fantasia, Inditement, Ingredient, Line, Loam, Met, Montage, Morceau, Nonet(te), Nonetto, Opus, Oratorio, Part-writing, Pastiche, Piece, Pieta, Poem, Polyphony, Polyrhythm, Printer, Quartette, Raga, Rhapsody, Round, Setting, Ship, Sing, Smoot, Sonata, Sonatina, Structure, Suite, Symphony, Synthesis, Terracotta, Texture, Toccata, Treatise, Trio, Typesetter, Verismo, Voluntary, Work

Compost Dressing, Fertilizer, Humus, Vraic, Zoo doo

Compound, Compound stop Addition, Admixture, Amalgam, Anti-inflammatory, Anti-knock, Bahuvrihi, Blend, → CAMP, Composite, Constitute, Coordination, Cpd, Cutting, Derivative, Ethiops, Mix, Mixture, Multiply, Racemate, Rooting, Tatpurusha, Type

COMPOUNDS

3 letters:
Azo

4 letters:
Alum
Clay
EDTA
Enol
Haem
Heme
TEPP
Urea

5 letters:
Algin
Allyl
Aloin
Amide
Amino
Azide
Azine
Azole
Diazo
Diene
Dimer
Diode
Erbia
Ester
Furan
Halon
Imide
Imine
Lipid
Nitro
Olein
Oxide
Oxime
Potin
Pyran
Salol
Sarin
Soman
Tabun
Thiol

Trona
Vinyl

6 letters:
Acetal
Alkane
Alkene
Ammine
Arsine
Baryta
Borane
Calque
Cetane
Chrome
Cresol
Epimer
Fluate
Glycol
Halide
Haloid
Hexene
Isatin
Isomer
Ketone
Kinone
Lithia
Niello
Octane
Phenol
Pinene
Potash
Purine
Pyrone
Retene
Silane
Speiss
Tannin
Tartar
Tetryl
Thymol
Triene
Trimer
Uranyl

7 letters:
Acetone
Acridin
Aglycon
Ammonia
Argyrol®
Aspirin
Barilla
Benzene
Betaine
Borazon
Bromide
Caliche
Calomel
Camphor
Carbide
Chelate
Choline
Cinerin
Creatin
Cumarin
Cyanide
Diamine
Diazine
Diazole
Dioxide
Dvandva
Epoxide
Erinite
Ethanol
Eugenol
Fenuron
Ferrite
Flavone
Hormone
Hydrate
Hydride
Indican
Indoxyl
Lactate
Lactone
Menthol
Metamer
Monomer

Niobite
Nitride
Nitrile
Nitrite
Oxazine
Oxonium
Pentane
Peptide
Peptone
Polyene
Polymer
Prodrug
Protein
Quassia
Quinoid
Quinone
Realgar
Skatole
Steroid
Sulfide
Syncarp
Taurine
Terpene
Toluene
Tritide
Uridine
Wolfram
Zymogen

8 letters:
Acridine
Aglycone
Aldehyde
Alizarin
Arginine
Asbestos
Astatide
Butyrate
Caffeine
Carbaryl
Catenane
Cephalin
Ceramide
Chloride

Chromene
Coenzyme
Coumarin
Creatine
Cyanogen
Datolite
Dieldrin
Dopamine
Ethoxide
Farnesol
Fluoride
Furfuran
Glycogen
Hydroxyl
Indoform
Isologue
Ketoxime
Lecithin
Luteolin
Massicot
Melamine
Monoxide
Oligomer
Pentosan
Peroxide
Phthalin
Piperine
Ptomaine
Purpurin
Pyrazole
Rock-alum
Rotenone
Selenate
Silicide
Siloxane
Sodamide
Stilbene
Sulphide
Sulphone
Tautomer
Tetroxid
Thiazide
Thiazine
Thiazole
Thiophen
Thiotepa
Thiourea
Titanate
Tolidine
Triazine
Triazole

Trilling
Trioxide
Tyramine
Urethane
Xanthate
Xanthine
Zirconia

9 letters:
Aflatoxin
Alicyclic
Aliphatic
Anhydride
Biguanide
Carbazole
Carnitine
Celloidin
Cellulose
Cementite
Cetrimide
Chromogen
Copolymer
Cortisone
Deuteride
Dibromide
Dipeptide
Disulfram
Endorshin
Ferrocene
Flavanone
Fool's gold
Fulleride
Glycoside
Greek fire
Guanosine
Haematein
Histamine
Hydantoin
Hydrazide
Hydroxide
Imidazole
Impsonite
Ionophore
Jasmonate
Limestone
Menadione
Mepacrine
Merbromin
Methoxide
Monoamine
Organotin

Pentoxide
Phenazine
Phenoxide
Pheromone
Phosphide
Piperonal
Polyamine
Porphyrin
Qinghaosu
Quercetus
Quinoline
Saltpetre
Sapogenin
Serotonin
Telluride
Tetroxide
Thiophene
Veratrine

10 letters:
Adrenaline
Amphoteric
Argyrodite
Azobenzene
Bradykinin
Cellosolve®
Cytochroma
Dichloride
Dimethoate
Disulphide
Enkephalin
Ethambutol
Indophenon
Isocyanate
Lumisterol
Mercaptide
Nitrazepam
Nucleoside
Nucleotide
Phenformin
Phenocaine
Picrotoxin
Piperazine
Piperidine
Propionate
Putrescine
Pyrethroid
Pyrimidine
Sildenafil
Sulphonium
Thimerosal

Tocopherol

11 letters:
Acetanilide
Amphetamine
Coprosterol
Dimercaprol
Electrolyte
Fluorescein
Galantamina
Ghitathione
Haliocarbon
Hydrocarbon
Neostigmine
Nitrosamine
Resveratrol
Sesquioxide
Sphingosine
Tributyltin

12 letters:
Carbohydrate
Formaldehyde
Haematoxylin
Hydroquinone
Permanganate
Phenanthrine
Polyurethane
Sulphonamide
Testosterone
Thiosinamine
Triglyceride
Trimethadine

13 letters:
Catecholamine
Cycloheximide
Isoproterenol
Mercurochrome
Metronidazole
Nitroglycerin
Nortriptyline
Phenothiazine
Physostigmine
Sulphonylurea
Trinucleotide

14 letters:
Cyanocobalamin
Oxyhaemoglobin
Phenolphthalin

Polycarboxylic	Sulphonmethane	*15 letters:*	*17 letters:*
Polyunsaturate	Trohalomethane	Perfluorocarbon	Pentachlorophenol
		Succinylcholine	

▷ **Compound(ed)** *may indicate* an anagram

Comprehend, Comprehensive All-in, Catch-all, Catholic, Compass, Compendious, Contain, Exhaustive, Fathom, Follow, Full-scale, General, Global, Grasp, Include, Indepth, Ken, Large, Omnibus, Panoramic, Perceive, School, Sweeping, Thoroughgoing, Tumble, → **UNDERSTAND**, Wide

Compress(ed), Compression, Compressor Astrict, Astringe, Axial-flow, Bale, Coarctate, Contract, Pack, Pump, Solidify, Squeeze, Stupe, Thlipsis, Turbocharger

Comprise Contain, Embody, Embrace, Include

Compromise, Compromising Avoision, Brule, Commit, Concession, Endanger, Give and take, Happy medium, Honeytrap, Involve, Middleground, Modus vivendi, Settlement, Time-server, Trade off, Via media

▶ **Compulsion** *see* **COMPEL**

Compunction Hesitation, Regret, Remorse, Scruple, Sorrow

Computer(s) Analog(ue), Apple (Mac)®, Desknote, Desktop, Digital, Eniac, Front-end, Host, Laptop, Mainframe, Micro, Notebook, Number-cruncher, Palmtop, PC, Personal, Proxy server, TALISMAN, Turing machine

Computer hardware, Computer memory Busbar, Chip, Dataglove®, DRAM, EAROM, EPROM, Floptical, IDE, Modem, Neurochip, Pentium®, Plug'n'play, Processor, PROM, RAM, ROM, Router, Tower, Track(er)ball

Computer language ADA, ALGOL, ASCII, AWK, Basic, C, COBOL, COL, CORAL, Fortran, ICL, Java®, LISP, LOGO, OCCAM, PASCAL, Perl, PROLOG, Scratchpad, Small-talk, SNOBOL, SQL, Weblish

Computer network, Computer systems Arpa, ARPANET, BIOS, Cambridge ring, ERNIE, Ethernet, Evernet, Executive, Extranet, Fileserver, Freenet, HOLMES, Hypermedia, Internet, Intranet, JANET, LAN, Linux, MARC, MIDI, Neural, Peer-to-peer, Stand-alone, Tally, TAURUS, Telnet, Token ring, Unix, Usenet, WAN, Web, Wide-area, WIMP

Computer programs, Computer software Abandonware, Acrobat, ActiveX, Agent, Antivirus, Applet, Application, Assembler, Autotune, Bloatware, Bootstrap, Bot, CADMAT, Cancelbot, Careware, Chatbot, Checksum, Client, Columbus, Crippleware, CU See Me, Debugger, Diagnostic, Dictionary, Emacs, Est, E-wallet, Extreme, Facemail, Firewall, Firmware, Flash, Freeware, Groupware, HAL, Hypermedia, iTunes®, Linker, Loader, Macro, Malware, Middleware, Mmorpg, Object, OCR, Parser, Payware, Plug-in, Relocator, RISC, Servlet, Shareware, Shovelware, Spellchecker, Spyware, Stiffware, Systems, Translator, Trialware, Utility, Vaporware, Warez, Web browser, Webcast, Web crawler, Windows®, Word processor, Worm

Computer terms Address bus, Algorism, Authoring, Autosave, Backslash, Bitmap, Bookmark, Boot, Bot army, Breakpoint, Calculate, Calculus, Chatroom, Clickstream, Clipboard, Coder, Counter, Cybercafe, Cyber(netics), Domain name, Earcon, Estimate, FAT, Figure, GIGO, Gopher, High-end, Hybrid, Hypertext, Inbox, Inputter, Integrator, Interface, IT, Kludge, Linear, Logic, Mail merge, Measure, Morphing, Mouseover, Mung, Network, Neural, Numlock, Nybble, Object, On-line, Outbox, Package, Packet sniffer, Pageview, Patch, Pel, Phishing, Pixel, Platform, Public-key, Pushdown, README file, Read-out, Realtime, Reboot, Reckoner, Rogue dialler, Rootserver, Screensaver, Search engine, Server, Shell, Smart, Smurfing, Soft return, Source, Spim, Spreadsheet, Sprite, String, Subroutine,

Superserver, Systems, Tape streamer, Thick client, Thin client, Time slice, Toggle, Unicode, Username, Vaccine, Voice response, Voxel, Webbie, WebBoard, Webfarm, Wiki, WORM, Wysiwyg, Yottabyte, Zettabyte

Computer user(s) Alpha geek, Anorak, Brain, Browser, Cast(er), Chiphead, Cyberpunk, Cybersurfer, Digerati, Hacker, Liveware, Luser, Mouse potato, Nerd, Nethead, Netizen, Nettie, Otaku, Pumpking, Troll, White hat

Comrade Achates, Ally, Buddy, Bully-rook, Butty, China, Fellow, Friend, Kamerad, Mate, Oliver, Pal, Pard, Roland, Tovarich, Tovaris(c)h

Con(man) Against, Anti, Bunco, Diddle, Dupe, Fleece, Hornswoggle, Jacob, Lag, Learn, Peruse, Read, Scam, Scan, Steer, Sucker, Swindle, Tweedler

Concave Dished, Invexed

Conceal(ed), Concealment Blanket, Blind, Closet, Clothe, Cover, Curtain, Disguise, Dissemble, Doggo, Drown, Feal, Heal, Heel, Hele, → **HIDE**, Latent, Misprision, Occult, Palm, Perdu(e), Recondite, Screen, Scriene, Secrete, Shroud, Sleeve, Smother, Snow job, Stash, Subreption, Ulterior, Whitewash, Wrap

Concede, Concession Acknowledge, Admit, Allow, Budge, Carta, Charter, Compromise, Confess, Favour, Forfeit, Franchise, Grant, Munich, Ou, Ow, Owe, Own, Privilege, Ship, Sop, Synchoresis

Conceit(ed) Bumptious, Caprice, Carriwitchet, Cat-witted, Concetto, Crank, Crotchet, Device, Dicty, Egoist, Egomania, Fancy, Fastuous, Figjam, Flory, Fop, Fume, Hauteur, Idea, Mugwump, Notion, Podsnappery, Prig, Princock, Princox, Puppyism, Quiblin, Self-assumption, Side, Snotty, Stuck-up, Swellhead, Toffee-nose, Vain(glory), Wind

Conceive, Conceivable Beget, Create, Credible, Imagine, Possible, Surmise

Concentrate(d), Concentration Aim, Application, Attend, Bunch, Cathexis, Centre, Collect, Condense, Dephlegmate, Distil, Elliptical, Essence, Extract, Focalise, Focus, Intense, Kurtosis, Listen, Major, Mantra, Mass, Molality, Molarity, Navel-gazing, Potted, Reduce, Rivet, Samadhi, Titrate, Titre, Undivided

Concept(ion) Alethic, Brain, Hent, Ideal, Ideation, Image, Immaculate, Myth, Notion, Sortal, Stereotype

Concern(ed), Concerning About, After, Ail, Altruism, Anent, As to, Bother, Business, Care, Cerne, Company, Disturb, Firm, Going, Heed, In re, Intéressé, Interest, Into, Lookout, → **MATTER**, Mell, Misease, Over, Part, Pidgin, Pigeon, Re, Reck, Regard, Reke, Respect, Retch, Solicitude, Touch, Trouble, Versant, Worry

▷ **Concerned** *may indicate* an anagram

Concert (place) Agreement, Benefit, Chamber, Charivari, Cooperation, Device, Dutch, Gig, Hootanannie, Hootananny, Hootenanny, Hootnannie, Hootnanny, Odeon, Odeum, Pop, Prom(enade), Recital, Singsong, Smoker, Subscription, Symphony, Together, Unison, Unity, Wit

Concertina Bandoneon, Pleat, Squeezebox, Squiffer

Concerto Brandenburg, Emperor, Grosso

▶ **Concession** *see* CONCEDE

Conch Shell, Strombus

Conchie CO

Conciliate, Conciliator Allay, Calm, Disarm, Dove, Ease, Mollify, Placate, Reconcile

Concise Compact, Curt, Encapsulated, Laconic, Short, Succinct, Terse, Tight

Conclave Assembly, Caucus, Confab, Meeting

Conclude(d), Conclusion, Conclusive Achieve, A fortiori, Afterword, Amen, Binding, Button-up, Cease, Clinch, Close, Complete, Dead, Decide, Deduce, → **END**, Envoi, Explicit, Finding, Fine, Finis, → **FINISH**, Foregone, Gather, Illation, Infer, Lastly, Limit, Non sequitur, Omega, Over, Peroration, Point, Postlude, Punchline,

Reason, Resolve, Settle, Showdown, Summary, Terminate, Upshot, Uptie

Conclusive Cogent, Convincing, Estoppel, Final

Concoct(ion) Brew, Compound, Creation, Plan, Trump (up)

Concord Concent, Consonance, Harmony, Peace, Plane, Sympathy, Treaty, Unity

Concorde SST

Concourse Assembly, Confluence, Esplanade, Throng

Concrete, Concretion Actual, Aggregate, Beton, Bezoar, Breeze, Cake, Calculus, Caprolite, Clot, Dogger, Gunite, Hard, Lean, Mass, Minkstone, No-fines, Pile-cap, Positive, Prestressed, Reify, Reinforced, Siporex, Solid, Tangible, Tremie

Concubine Apple-squire, Campaspe, Harem, Hetaria, Madam, Mistress, Odalisk, Sultana

Concur Accord, Agree, Coincide, Comply, → **CONSENT**, Gree

Concurrent(ly) Meantime

Concuss(ion) Clash, Shock, Stun

Condemn(ation) Accuse, Blame, Blast, Cast, Censor, Censure, Convict, Damn, Decry, Denounce, Deprecate, Doom, Judge, Kest, Obelise, Proscribe, Revile, Sentence, Theta, Upbraid

Condense(d), Condenser Abbe, Abbreviate, Abridge, Brief, Capacitator, Compress, Contract, Distil, Encapsulate, Epitomise, Jet, Liebig, Précis, Rectifier, Reduce, Shorten, Shrink, Summarise, Surface, Vernier, Vinificator

Condescend Deign, Patronise, Stoop, Vouchsafe

Condiment Caraway, Catsup, Cayenne, Chutney, Cum(m)in, Flavour, Horse radish, Kava, Ketchup, Mustard, Pepper, Relish, Salt, Sambal, Sambol, Sauce, Spice, Tracklement, Turmeric, Vinegar, Zedoary

Condition(al), Conditioning Autism, Circ(s), Circumstance, Classical, Congenital, Connote, Contingent, Dropsy, Experimental, Fettle, Going, Hammertoe, Hood, If, → **IN GOOD CONDITION**, Kelter, Kernicterus, Kilter, Latah, Necessary, Nick, Order, Pass, Pavlovian, Plight, Pliskie, Ply, Point, Position, Predicament, Prepare, Prerequisite, Presupposition, Protasis, Proviso, Provisory, Repair, Reservation, Reserve, Rider, Ropes, Sine qua non, Sis, Spina bifida, Standing, State, Sted, Stipulation, String, Sufficient, Term, Tid, Tox(a)emia, Trim, Trisomy, Unless, Vir(a)emia, White finger

Condom(s) Blob, Cap, Franger, French letter, Gumboot, Johnny, Letter, Prophylactic, Rubber, Rubber goods, Safe, Scumbag, Sheath

Condone Absolve, Excuse, Forgive, Overlook

Conduct(or), Conductress Accompany, Administer, Anode, Arm, Arrester, Barbirolli, Bearing, Beecham, Behaviour, Bulow, Bus-bar, Cad, Chobdar, Clippie, Coil, Comport, Demean(our), Deportment, Direct, Disorderly, Drive, Editor, Electrode, Escort, Feedthrough, Fetch, Goings-on, Haitink, Hallé, Ignitron, Karajan, Kempe, Klemperer, Lark, Lead, Liber, Lightning, Maestro, Mantovani, Mho, Microchip, Nerve, N-type, Officiate, Ormandy, Outer, Parts, Photodiode, → **PILOT**, Previn, Probe, Prosecute, Protocol, Psychagogue, Psychopomp, P-type, Rattle, Safe, Sargent, Scudaller, Scudler, Shunt, Skudler, Solicit, Solti, Stokowski, Tao, Thermal, Thermistor, Toscanini, Transact, → **USHER**, Varactor, Varistor, Wave guide, Wire, Wood, Zener diode

▷ **Conducting** *may indicate* an '-ic' ending

Conduit Aqueduct, Canal, Carrier, Duct, Main, Penstock, Pipe, Tube, Utilidor

Cone(s), Conical, Cone-shaped Alluvial, Cappie, Circular, Conoidal, Egmont, Ellipse, Female, Fir, Fusion, Moxa, Nose, Pastille, Peeoy, Pineal, Pingo, Pioy(e), Pottle, Puy, Pyramid, Retinal, Segar, Spire, Storm, Strobilus, Taper, Tee, Traffic, Volcanic, Wind, Windsock

Coney Daman, Doe, Hyrax

Confection(er) Candy, Candyfloss, Caramel, Chocolate, Concoction, Conserve, Countline, Ice, Kiss, Marzipan, Noisette, Nougat, Quiddery, Rock, Sweet, Sweetmeat, Tablet

Confederal, Confederacy, Confederate, Confederation Accessory, Alliance, Ally, Association, Body, Bund, Bunkosteerer, Cover, F(o)edarie, Gueux, Illinois, League, Partner, Senegambia, Union

Confer(ence) Bestow, Bretton Woods, Cf, Collogue, Colloqium, Colloquy, Congress, Council, Diet, Do, Dub, Fest, Forum, Grant, Huddle, Hui, Imparlance, Imperial, Indaba, Intercommune, Lambeth, Meeting, Munich, Negotiate, News, Palaver, Parley, Pawaw, Pear, Potsdam, Pourparler, Powwow, Press, Pugwash, Quadrant, Seminar, Settle, Summit, Symposium, Synod, → **TALK**, Teach-in, Video, Vouchsafe, Yalta

Confess(ion), Confessor Acknowledge, Admit, Agnise, Avowal, Concede, Declare, Disclose, Edward, Own, Peccavi, Recant, Shrift, Shriver, Sing, Tetrapolitan, Whittle

Confide(nce), Confident(ial), Confidant Aplomb, Aside, Assertive, Assured, Bedpost, Belief, Bottle, Can do, Certitude, Cocksure, Cocky, Cred, Crouse, Entre nous, Entrust, Extravert, Extrovert, Faith, Feisty, Gatepost, Hardy, Hope, Hush-hush, Intimate, Morale, Nerve, Pack, Private, Privy, Sanguine, Secret, Secure, Self-assured, Self-possessed, Sub rosa, Sure, Tell, Trust, Unbosom, Under the rose, Vaulting

Confine(d), Confines, Confinement Ambit, Bail, Bale, Cage, CB, Chain, Constrain, Contain, Coop, Cramp, Crib, Detain, Emmew, Encase, Enclose, Endemic, Enmew, Ensheath, Gaol, Gate, Gender-moon, House arrest, Immanacle, Immew, Immure, Impound, → **IMPRISON**, Incage, Incarcerate, Incommunicado, Inertial, Inhoop, Intern, Local, Mail, March, Mew, Mure, Narrow, Pen, Pent, Pinion, Poky, Restrict, Rule 43, Rules, Section, Solitary, Tether, Thirl, Trammel

Confirm(ed), Confirmation Addict, Ascertain, Assure, Attest, Bear, Certify, Chris(o)m, Christen, Chronic, Clinch, Corroborate, Dyed-in-the-wool, Endorse, Homologate, Obsign, OK, Ratify, Sacrament, Sanction, Seal, Strengthen, Ten-four, Tie, Validate, Vouch

Confiscate, Confiscation Attainder, Deprive, Dispossess, Distrain, Escheat, Garnishee, Impound, Infangenethef, Raupatu, Seize, Sequestrate

Conflagration Blaze, Holocaust, Inferno, Wildfire

Conflict(ing) Agon, Armageddon, At odds, Battle, Boilover, Camp, Casus belli, Clash, Close, Contend, Contravene, Controversy, Disharmony, Diverge, Encounter, Feud, Fray, Inconsistent, Jar, Lists, Mêlée, Muss, Off-key, Oppose, Psychomachia, Rift, Scrape, Strife, → **STRUGGLE**, Tergiversate, War

Conform(ist), Conformity Accord, Adjust, Comply, Conservative, Consistence, Correspond, Normalise, Obey, Observe, Propriety, Standardize, Stereotype(d), Suit, Trimmer, Yield

Confound(ed) Abash, Amaze, Astound, Awhape, Baffle, Bewilder, Blamed, Blasted, Blest, Blinking, Bumbaze, Contradict, Darn, Dismay, Drat, Dumbfound, Elude, Floor, Jigger, Mate, Murrain, Nonplus, Perishing, Perplex, Rabbit, Spif(f)licate, Stump, Throw

▷ **Confound** *may indicate* an anagram

Confrère Ally

Confront(ation) Appose, Beard, Breast, Eyeball, Face, Face down, Head-to-head, Incident, Loggerheads, Mau-Mau, Meet, Militance, Nose, Oppose, Outface, Showdown, Tackle, Toe-to-toe

Confuse(d), Confusedly, Confusion Addle, Anarchy, Astonishment, At sea,

Babel, Baffle, Bazodee, Bedevil, Befog, Befuddle, Bemuse, Bewilder, Blur, Bobby-die, Burble, Bustle, Chaos, Cloud, Clutter, Complicate, Debacle, Didder, Discombobulate, Disconcert, Disorient, Distract, Dither, Dizzy, Dudder, Dust, Dwaal, Egarement, Embrangle, Embroglio, Embroil, Farrago, Flap, Flat spin, Flummox, Flurry, Fluster, Fog, Fox, Fuddle, Gaggle, Galley-west, Hash, Havoc, Hazy, Helter-skelter, Hubble-bubble, Huddle, Hugger-mugger, Hurly-burly, Hurry-scurry, Hurry-skurry, Imbrangle, Imbroglio, → **IN CONFUSION**, Indistinct, Litter, Lost, Lurry, Maelstrom, Maffled, Mayhem, Maze, Melange, Melee, Mess, Mingle, Mish-mash, Mither, Mixter-maxter, Mixtie-maxtie, Mix-up, Mizzle, Mizzy maze, Moider, Moither, Moonstruck, Morass, → **MUDDLE**, Mudge, Muss(e), Muzzy, Obfuscate, Overset, Pellmell, Perplex, Pi(e), Pose, Ravel, Razzle-dazzle, Razzmatazz, Rout, Rummage, S(c)hemozzle, Scramble, Skimble-skamble, Snafu, Spin, Stump, Stupefy, Swivet, Synchysis, Tangle, Throw, Tizzy, Topsy-turvy, Turbulence, Tzimmes, Welter, Whemmle, Whomble, Whummle, Woolly, Woozy

▷ **Confuse(d)** *may indicate* an anagram

Confute Confound, Contradict, Deny, Disprove, Infringe, Redargue, Refel

Congeal Coagulate, Freeze, Gel, Gunge, Set, Solidify

Congenial Agreeable, Amiable, Compatible, Connate, Couthie, Couthy, Happy, Kindred, Simpatico, Sympathique

Congenital Connate, Inborn, Innate, Inveterate

Congest(ed), Congestion Coryza, Cram, Crowd, Engorge, Impact, Jam, Logjam, Turgid

Conglomerate, Conglomeration Aggregate, Banket, Empire, Gather, Heap, Mass

Congo(u) Shaba, Tea

Congratulate, Congratulation Applaud, Felicitate, Laud, Mazeltov, Preen, Salute

Congregate, Congregation(alist) Assembly, Barnabite, Body, Brownist, Class, Community, Conclave, Ecclesia, Flock, Fold, Gathering, Host, Laity, Oratory, Propaganda, Synagogue

Congress(man) ANC, Assembly, Conclave, Continental, Council, Eisteddfod, Intercourse, Legislature, Pan-Africanist, Rally, Senator, Solon, Synod, Vienna

Conifer(ous) Araucaria, Cedar, Cypress, Cyrus, Evergreen, Larch, Macrocarpo, Picea, Pine, Spruce, Taiga, Taxus, Thuja, Yew

Conject(ure) Fancy, Goldbach's, Guess, Guesswork, Speculate, Surmise, Theory, View

Conjoin Alligate, Ally, Connect, Knit

Conjugate, Conjugation Couple, Hermitian, Join, Nuptial, Synopsis, Typto, Zygosis

Conjunction Alligation, Ampersand, And, Combination, Consort, Coordinating, Nor, Polysyndeton, Subordinating, Superior, Synod, Syzygy, Together, Union, Unition, Unless

Conjure(r), Conjuror Angekkok, Charm, Contrive, Heypass, Heypresto, Hocus-pocus, Illusionist, Imagine, Invoke, Mage, Magic, Mystery-man, Palmer, Prestidigitator, Prestigiator, Thaumaturgus

Conk Nose

Connect(ed), Connection, Connector About, Accolade, Adaptor, Affinity, Agnate, Anastomosis, And, Associate, Attach, Band, Bind, Bridge, Bridle, Cable, Clientele, Coherent, Colligate, Conjugate, Couple, Cross-link, Delta, Dovetail, Downlink, Drawbar, Fishplate, Fistula, Hook-up, → **IN CONNECTION WITH**, Interlink, Interlock, Join, Jumper, Kinship, Liaison, Lifeline, Link, Linkup, Marry, Merge, Mesh, Nexus, On, Online, Patch, Pons, Raphe, Rapport, Relate, Relative, Respect, Sentence, Shuttle, Splice, S-R, Synapse, Syntenosis, Syssarcosis, Tendon, Through,

Tie, Tie-in, Union, Y, Yoke, Zygon

Connecticut Ct

Connive, Connivance Abet, Cahoots, Collude, Condone, Conspire, Plot

Connoisseur Aesthete, Cognoscente, Epicure, Expert, Fancier, Gourmet, Judge, Maven, Mavin, Oenophil

Connotate, Connotation Imply, Infer, Intent, Meaning

Conquer(or), Conquering, Conquest Alexander, Beat, Conquistador, Cortes, Crush, Debel, Genghis Khan, Hereward, → MASTER, Moor, Norman, Ostrogoth, Overcome, Overpower, Overrun, Pizarro, Saladin, Subjugate, Tame, Tamerlane, Vanquish, Victor, Vincent

Conquistador Cortes, Cortez

Conscience, Conscientious Casuistic, Duteous, Heart, Inwit, Morals, Painstaking, Pang, Remorse, Scruple(s), Sense, Superego, Syneidesis, Synteresis, Thorough, Twinge

Conscious(ness) Awake, Aware, Chit, Limen, Mindful, On to, Persona, Sensible, Sentient, Witting

Conscript(ion) Blood-tax, Choco, Commandeer, Draft(ee), Impress, Inductee, Landsturm, Levy, Nasho, → RECRUIT, Register

Consecrate(d), Consecration Bless, Enoch, Hallow, Noint, Oint, Sacring, Sanctify, Venerate

Consecutive Sequential, Successive

Consensus Agreement, Harmony, Unanimity

Consent Accord, Acquiesce, Affo(o)rd, Agree, Approbate, Comply, Concur, Grant, Informed, Permit, Ratify, Volens, Yes-but, Yield

Consequence, Consequent(ial), Consequently Aftermath, Consectaneous, Corollary, Effect, End, Importance, Issue, Karma, Knock-on, Logical, Moment, Outcome, Ramification, Repercussion, → RESULT, Sequel, Thence, Threat, Thus, Upshot

Conservative Blimpish, Blue, C, Cautious, Diehard, Disraeli, Fabian, Hard-hat, Hidebound, Hunker, Neanderthal, Old guard, Old-line, Preppy, Progressive, Rearguard, Redneck, Right(-wing), Safe, Square, Thrifty, Tory, True blue, Unionist, Verkramp, Young Fogey

Conservatory Hothouse, Orangery, Solarium

Conserve, Conservation(ist) Can, Comfiture, Husband(ry), Jam, Jelly, Maintain, Maintenance, Noah, NT, Protect, Save

Consider(able), Considerate, Consideration Animadvert, Attention, Avizandum, By-end, Case, Cerebrate, Chew over, Cogitate, Contemplate, Count, Courtesy, Debate, Deem, Deliberate, Entertain, Envisage, Factor, Fair, Feel, Forethought, Gay, Gey, Heed, Importance, Inasmuch, Judge, Many, Materially, Meditate, Muse, Pay, Perpend, Poise, Ponder, Premeditate, Pretty, Rate, Reck, Reckon, Reflect, Regard, Respect, Scruple, See, Sensitive, Several, Shortlist, Solicitous, Song, Speculate, Steem, Study, Substantial, Think, Tidy, Vast, View, Ween, Weigh

Consign(ment) Allot, Award, Batch, Bequeath, Delegate, Deliver, Drop shipment, Entrust, Lading, Ship, Transfer

Consist(ent), Consistency Agree, Coherent, Comprise, Enduring, Even, Liaison, Rely, Sound, Steady, Texture

Consolation, Console Ancon, Appease, Balm, Comfort, Games, Relief, Solace, Sop

Consolidate Coalesce, Combine, Compact, Gel, Merge, Pun, Unify

Consommé Julienne, Soup

Consonant(s) Affricate, Agma, Agreeing, Cacuminal, Cerebral, Explosive, Fortis, Fricative, Harmonious, Implosive, Labial, Lateral, Lenis, Media, Mouillé, Plosive,

Sonorant, Spirant, Surd, Tenuis, Velar

Consort Ally, Associate, Maik, Mate, Moop, Moup, Partner, Spouse

Consortium Coalition, Combine, Ring

Conspicuous Arresting, Blatant, Clear, Eminent, Glaring, Kenspeck(le), Landmark, Light, Manifest, Patent, Salient, Shining, Showy, Signal, Striking

Conspiracy, Conspirator, Conspire, Conspiring Brutus, Cabal, Casca, Cassius, Catiline, Cato St, Champerty, Cinna, Collaborate, Colleague, Collogue, Collude, Complot, Connive, Covin, Covyne, Guy, Highbinder, In cahoots, Intrigue, Oates, Omerta, → **PLOT**, Ring, Scheme

Constable Beck, Catchpole, Cop, Dogberry, Dull, Elbow, Harman(-beck), Headborough, High, John, Officer, Painter, Petty, Pointsman, → **POLICEMAN**, Posse, Special, Thirdborough, Tipstaff, Verges

Constancy, Constant Abiding, Boltzmann, C, Changeless, Chronic, Coefficient, Cosmological, Devotion, Dielectric, Diffusion, Dilys, Dirac, Eccentricity, Eternal, Faith, Firm, Fixed, Fundamental, G, Gas, Gravitational, H, Honesty, Hubble's, K, Lambert, Leal(ty), Logical, Loyal, Magnetic, Often, Parameter, → **PERPETUAL**, Planck's, Pole star, Resolute, Sad, Solar, Staunch, Steadfast, Steady, Time, True, Unfailing, Uniform, Usual

Constellation Andromeda, Antlia, Apus, Aquarius, Aquila, Ara, Argo, Aries, Auriga, Bootes, Caelum, Camelopardalis, Camelopardus, Canes Venatici, Canis Major, Canis Minor, Carina, Cassiopeia, Centaurus, Cepheus, Cetus, Cham(a)eleon, Circinus, Columba, Coma Berenices, Coma Cluster, Corvus, Crater, Cygnus, Cynosure, Delphinus, Delta, Dolphin, Dorado, Draco, Equuleus, Eridanus, Fornax, Galaxy, Gemini, Great Bear, Gru(i)s, Hercules, Horologium, Hydra, Hydrus, Indus, Lacerta, Leo, Leo Minor, Lepus, Libra, Little Bear, Little Dipper, Lupus, Lynx, Lyra, Mensa, Monoceros, Musca, Norma, Octans, Ophiuchus, Orion, Pavo, Pegasus, Perseus, Phoenix, Pictor, Piscis Austrinus, → **PLANET**, Puppis, Pyxis, Reticulum, Sagitta, Sagittarius, Scorpius, Sculptor, Scutum, Serpens, Sextans, Southern Cross, Spica, → **STAR**, Telescopium, The Rule, Triangulum (Australe), Tucana, Twins, Unicorn, Vela, Virgin, Virgo, Volans, Vulpecula, Wag(g)oner, Whale, Zodiacal

Consternation Alarm, Dismay, Doodah, Fear, Horror

Constipate(d), Constipation Astrict, Bind, Block, Costive, Stegnotic, Stenosis

Constituency, Constituent Borough, Component, Element, Immediate, Part, Principle, Seat, Ultimate, Voter

▷ **Constituents** *may indicate* an anagram

Constitute, Constitution(al) Appoint, Charter, Clarendon, Compose, Comprise, Congenital, Creature, Establishment, Form, Fuero, Health, Physique, Policy, Polity, Seat, State, Synthesis, Upmake, Walk

Constrain(ed), Constraint Bind, Bondage, Boundary, Coerce, Confine, Coop, Curb, Duress(e), Force, Hard, Oblige, Pressure, Repress, Stenosis, Taboo, Trammel

Constrict(ed), Constriction Bottleneck, Choke, Coarctate, Contract, Cramp, Hour-glass, Impede, Limit, Narrow, Phimosis, Squeeze, Stegnosis, Stenosis, Strangle, Strangulate, Thlipsis, Tighten, Venturi

Construct(ion), Constructor, Constructive Build, Compile, Engineer, Erect, Fabricate, Facture, Fashion, Form, Frame, Idolum, Make, Manufacture, Partners, Seabee, Stressed-skin, Tectonic, Weave

Construe Deduce, Explain, Expound, Infer

Consul Ambassador, Attaché, Horse, Lucullus, Praetor

Consult(ant), Consultation Avisement, Confer, Deliberate, Discuss, Emparl, Imparl, Joint, Peritus, See, Sexpert, Shark watcher, Surgery, Vide

Consume(r), Consumption, Consumptive Bolt, Burn, Caterpillar®, Conspicuous,

Decay, Devour, Diner, Eat, Engross, Exhaust, Expend, Feed, Glutton, Hectic, Mainline, Scoff, Spend, Swallow, TB, Use, Waste, Wear

Consummate, Consummation Achieve, Crown, Keystone, Seal

Contact Abut, Adpress, Contingence, Fax, Hook-up, Lens, Liaise, Liaison, Meet, Radio, Reach, Shoe, Taction, → **TOUCH**, Touchy-feely, Wiper

Contagious, Contagion Infection, Noxious, Poison, Taint, Variola, Viral

Contain(er) Amphora, Ampulla, Aquafer, Aquifer, Barrel, Bass, Bidon, Bin, Boat, Bottle, Box, Buddle, Cachepot, Can, Canakin, Canikin, Canister, Cannikin, Cantharus, Capsule, Carafe, Carboy, Carry, Carton, Case, Cask, Cassette, Chase, Chest, Churn, Coffer, Comprise, Coolamon, Crate, Crater, Crucible, Cup, Cupel, Decanter, Dracone, Dredger, Enclose, Encompass, Enseam, Esky®, Feretory, Flagon, Flask, Flat, Gabion, Gourd, Growler, → **HOLD**, House, Igloo, Include, Incubator, Intray, Jar, Jeroboam, Jerrican, Jerrycan, Jug, Keg, Kirbeh, Leaguer, Lekythos, Monkey, Monstrance, Mould, Olpe, Out-tray, Pail, Pinata, Piscina, Pitcher, Pithos, Pod, Pottle, Punnet, Reliquary, Repository, Restrain, Sac(k), Saggar, Scyphus, Shaker, Situla, Skin, Skip, Snaptin, Spittoon, Stamnos, Stillage, Tank, Tantalus, Terrarium, Tinaja, Trough, Tub, Tun, Tupperware®, Urn, Vase, Vessel, Vinaigrette, Wardian case, Wineskin, Woolpack, Workbag

Contaminate(d) Adulterate, Corrupt, Defile, Denature, Flyblown, Impure, Infect, Pollute, Soil, Stain, Tarnish

Contemplate, Contemplation Consider, Ecce, Envisage, Hesychasm, Meditate, Muse, Ponder, Reflect, Retrospection, Rue, Samadhi, Spell, Study, Think, Watch

Contemporary AD, Coetaneous, Current, Equal, Fellow, Modern, Modish, Present, Verism

Contempt(ible), Contemptuous Abject, Ageism, Aha, Arsehole, Bah, BEF, Cheap, Contumely, Crud, Crumb, Crummy, Cullion, Cynical, Derision, Despisal, Dis(s), Disparaging, Disrespect, Dog-bolt, Fig, Hangdog, Ignominious, Insect, Low, Mean, Measly, Misprision, Och, Odious, Paltry, Phooey, Pish, Poof, Poxy, Pshaw, Ratfink, Rats, Razoo, Scabby, Scarab, Schlub, Scofflaw, → **SCORN**, Scumbag, Scurvy, Sexism, Shabby, Shithead, Slimeball, Sneeze, Sniffy, Snooty, Snot, Snotty, Soldier, Sorry, Squirt, Squit, Supercilious, Toad, Toerag, Tossy, Vilipend, Weed, Whipster, Wretched

Contend(er) Argue, Candidate, Claim, Clash, Compete, Cope, Debate, Dispute, Fight, Grapple, Oppose, Rival, Stickle, → **STRIVE**, Struggle, Submit, → **VIE**, Wrestle

Content Apaid, Apay, Appay, Blissful, Happy, Inside, Please, Satisfy, Volume

▷ **Content** *may indicate* a hidden word

Contention, Contentious Argument, Bellicose, Cantankerous, Case, Combat, Competitive, Logomachy, Perverse, Polemical, Rivalry, Strife, Struggle, Sturt

Contest(ant) Agon, Battle, Beauty, Biathlon, Bout, Catchweight, Challenge, Championship, Combat, Competition, Concours, Darraign, Decathlon, Defend, Deraign, Dogfight, Duathlon, Duel(lo), Entrant, Eurovision, Event, Examinee, Finalist, Free-for-all, Fronde, Handicap, Heptathlon, Kemp, Kriegspiel, Lampadephoria, Match, Matchplay, Olympiad, Pancratium, Paralympics, Pentathlon, Pingle, Play-off, Prizer, Race, Rival, Roadeo, Rodeo, Scrap, Set-to, Skirmish, Slam, Slugfest, Strife, Struggle, Tenson, Tetrathlon, Tournament, Triathlon, Tug-of-war, Vie, War, With

Context Intentional, Opaque, Transparent

Continent(al) Abstinent, Asia, Atlantis, Austere, Chaste, Dark, Epeirogeny, Euro, European, Gallic, Gondwanaland, Laurasia, Lemuria, Mainland, Moderate, Pang(a)ea, Shelf, Teetotal, Temperate, Walloon

Contingency, Contingent Accident, Arm, Casual, Chance, Conditional, Dependent,

Event, Fluke, Group, Prospect

Continual(ly), Continuous Adjoining, Away, Chronic, Connected, Eer, Endlong, Eternal, Ever, Frequent, Incessant, Non-stop, On(going), Unbroken, Unceasing

Continue, Continuation, Continuing, Continuity Abye, Duration, Dure, During, Enduring, Enjamb(e)ment, Follow-on, Go on, Hold, Keep, Last, Link, Ongoing, Onward, Persevere, Persist, Proceed, Prolong, Remain, Resume, Sequence, Stand, Subsist, Survive, Sustain, Synaphe(i)a, Tenor

▷ **Continuously** *may indicate* previous words to be linked

Contort(ion) Deform, Gnarl, Jib, Twist, Warp, Wreathe, Wry

Contour Curve, Graph, Isallobar, Isobase, Isocheim, Isochime, Isogeothermal, Line, Profile, Silhouette, Streamline, Tournure

Contraband Hot, Illicit, Prohibited, Smuggled

Contraception, Contraceptive Billings method, Cap, Coil, Condom, Diaphragm, Dutch cap, Etonogestrol, IU(C)D, Lippes loop, Loop, Minipill, Oral, Pessary, Pill, Precautions, Prophylactic, Rubber(s), Sheath, Vimule®

Contract(ion), Contractor Abbreviate, Abridge, Affreightment, Agreement, Appalto, Astringency, Bargain, Biceps, Bottomry, Braxton-Hicks, Bridge, Builder, Catch, Champerty, Charter, Clonus, Condense, Consensual, Constringe, Contrahent, Convulsion, Covenant, Cramp, Crasis, Curtail, Debt, Diastalsis, Dupuytren's, Dwindle, Engage, Entrepreneur, Escrow, Fitzgerald-Lorentz, Flex, Gainsay, Gooseflesh, Guarantee, Hand-promise, Hire, Incur, Indenture, Jerk, Ketubah, Knit, Lease, Levator, Lorentz-Fitzgerald, Make, Miosis, Myosis, Narrow, Obligee, Outsource, Party, Peristalsis, Privilege, Promise, Pucker, Purse, Restriction, Risus (sardonicus), Service, Shrink, Shrivel, Sign, Slam, Social, Spasm, Specialty, Squinch, Steelbow, Stenosis, Stipulation, Straddle, Supplier, Sweetheart, Synaloepha, Syngraph, Systole, Telescope, Tetanise, Tetanus, Tic, Tighten, Time bargain, Tonicity, Tontine, Treaty, Triceps, Trismus cynicus, Wrinkle, Yellow-dog, Z

Contradict(ion), Contradictory Ambivalent, Antilogy, Antinomy, Belie, Bull, Contrary, Counter, Dementi, Deny, Disaffirm, Disprove, Dissent, → **GAINSAY**, Negate, Oxymoron, Paradox, Sot, Stultify, Sublate, Threap, Threep, Traverse

Contraption Contrivance

Contrarily, Contrary Adverse, A rebours, Arsy-versy, But, Captious, Converse, Counter, Counterfleury, Crosscurrent, Cross-grained, Cross-purpose, Froward, Hostile, Inverse, Mary, Opposite, Oppugnant, Ornery, Perverse, Rebuttal, Retrograde, Wayward, Withershins

Contrast Chiaroscuro, Clash, Colour, Compare, Differ, Foil, Relief

Contravene Infringe, Oppose, Thwart, Violate

Contribute, Contribution Abet, Add, Assist, Chip in, Conduce, Donate, Dub, Furnish, Go, Help, Input, Kick in, Mite, Offering, Share, Sub, Subscribe, Whack, Widow's mite

▷ **Contributing to** *may indicate* a hidden word

Contrite, Contrition Penance, Penitent, Remorse, Repentant, Rue, → **SORRY**

Contrivance, Contrive(r) Art, Chicaner, Contraption, Cook, Deckle, Deus ex machina, Device, Devise, Dodge, Engine, Engineer, Finesse, Frame, Gadget, Gimmick, Gin, Hatch, Hokey, Intrigue, Invention, Machinate, Manage, Manoeuvre, Page, Plan, Plot, Procure, Rest, Rowlock, Scheme, Secure, Stage, Trump, Wangle, Weave

Control(ler), Controllable Ada, Appestat, Autopilot, Big Brother, Birth, Boss, Bridle, Cabotage, Chair, Check, Chokehold, Christmas tree, Corner, Corset, Curb, Cybernetics, Descendeur, Dirigible, Dirigism(e), Dominate, Dominion, Dynamic,

Elevon, Etatiste, Fast-forward, Fet(ch), Finger, Flood, Fly-by-wire, Gain, Gar, George, Gerent, Govern, Ground, Gubernation, Harness, Have, Heck, Helm, Influence, Influx, Joystick, Keypad, Knee-swell, Lead, Lever, → **MANAGE**, Martinet, Mastery, Moderate, Mouse, Nipple, Noise, Numerical, Operate, Override, Pilot, Placebo, Police, Population, Possess, Power, Preside, Price, Process, Puppeteer, Quality, Radio, Regulate, Regulo®, Rein, Remote, Rent, Repress, Restrain, Rheostat, Ride, Ripple, Rule, Run, School, Servo, Snail, Solion, Steady, Steer, Stop, Stranglehold, Stringent, Subdue, Subject, Subjugate, Supervise, Suzerain, Svengali, Sway, Takeover, Tame, Thermostat, Throttle, Tiller, Tone, Traction, Valve, Weld, Wield, Zapper

Controversial, Controversy Argument, Contention, Debate, Dispute, Eristic(al), Furore, Hot potato, Polemic(al), Tendentious

Conundrum Acrostic, Egma, Enigma, Puzzle, Riddle, Teaser

Convalesce(nt), Convalescence Anastatic, Mend, Rally, Recover, Recuperate, Rest-cure

▶ **Convene** *see* **CONVOKE**

Convenience, Convenient Behoof, Commode, Eft, Expedient, Facility, Gain, Gents, Handsome, → **HANDY**, Hend, Lav, Leisure, Near, Opportune, Pat, Privy, Public, Suitable, Toilet, Use, Well

Convent Abbatial, Cloister, Fratry, Friary, House, → **MONASTERY**, Motherhouse, Nunnery, Port-royal, Priory, Retreat

Convention(al) Academic, Accepted, Babbitt, Blackwood, Bourgeois, Caucus, Conclave, Conformity, → **CUSTOMARY**, Diet, Done, Formal, Geneva, Habitude, Iconic, Lame, Lingua franca, Mainstream, Meeting, Middlebrow, Middle-of-the-road, More, National, Nomic, Orthodox, Pompier, Proper, Readymade, Schengen, Staid, Starchy, Stereotyped, Stock, Straight, Synod, Uptight, Usage, Warsaw

Converge(nce) Approach, Focus, Meet, Toe-in

Conversation(alist), Converse, Conversant Abreast, Antithesis, Board, Buck, Cackle, Causerie, Chat, Chitchat, Colloquy, Commune, Confab, Crosstalk, Deipnosophist, Dialogue, Discourse, Eutrapelia, Eutrapely, Hobnob, Interlocution, Jaw-jaw, Natter, Opposite, Palaver, Parley, Persiflage, Rap, Rhubarb, Shop, Shoptalk, Socialise, → **TALK**, Transpose, Trialogue, Wongi, Word

Conversion, Converter, Convert(ible) Adapt, Alter, Assimilate, Azotobacter, Bessemer, Cash, Catalytic, Catechumen, Change, Commute, Cyanise, Diagenesis, Disciple, Encash, Etherify, Evangelize, Exchange, Expropriate, Fixation, Gummosis, Hodja, Kho(d)ja, Landau, L-D, Liquid, Marrano, Metanoia, Neophyte, Noviciate, Novitiate, Persuade, Prill, Proselyte, Put, Ragtop, Realise, Rebirth, Reclamation, Recycle, Revamp, Sheik(h), Souper, Tablet, Taw, Torque, Transduce, Transform, Transmute, Try

▷ **Conversion, Converted** *may indicate* an anagram

Convex(ity) Arched, Bowed, Camber, Curved, Entasis, Extrados, Gibbous, Lenticle, Nowy

Convey(ance) Assign, BS, Carousel, Carriage, Carry, Charter, Coach, Conduct, Cycle, Deed, Deliver, Eloi(g)n, Enfeoffment, Giggit, Grant, Guide, Lease, Litter, Lorry, Mailcar(t), Pirogue, Pneumatic, Re-lease, Sac, Screw, Soc, Tip, Title deed, Tote, Tram, Transfer, Transit, Transmit, Transport, Vehicle

Convict(ion) Attaint, Belief, Bushranger, Certitude, Cockatoo, Cogence, Crawler, Credo, Creed, Criminal, Demon, Dogma, Faith, Felon, Forçat, Government man, Lag, Magwitch, Old chum, → **PERSUASION**, Plerophory, Ring, Trusty, Vehemence, Yardbird

Convince(d), Convincing Assure, Cogent, Doubtless, Luculent, Persuade, Plausible, Satisfy, Sold, Sure

Convivial(ity) Boon, Bowl, Festive, Gay, Genial, Jovial, Social

Convoke Assemble, Call, Convene, Summon

Convolute(d), Convolution Coiled, Gyrus, Helical, Intricate, Spiral, Tortuous, Twisty, Whorl, Writhen

Convolvulus Bindweed, Dodder

Convoy Caravan, Column, Conduct, Escort, Fur brigade, Pilot, Train, Wagon-train

Convulse, Convulsion(s), Convulsive Agitate, Clonic, Clonus, Commotion, Disturb, DT, Eclampsia, → FIT, Galvanic, Paroxysm, Spasm, Throe, Tic

Cook(s), Cooker(y), Cooking Aga®, Babbler, Babbling brook, Bake, Balti, Beeton, Benghazi, Bhindi, Bouche, Braise, Broil, Cacciatore, Calabash, Captain, Charbroil, Chargrill, Chef, Coddle, Concoct, Cordon bleu, Cuisine, Deep-fry, Delia, Devil, Do, Doctor, Dumple, Easy over, Edit, Escoffier, Fake, Falsify, Fiddle, Fireless, Flambé, Forge, Fricassee, Fry, Fudge, Gastronomy, Greasy, Grill, Haute cuisine, Haybox, Hibachi, Lyonnaise, Marengo, Marinière, Meunière, Microwave, Nouvelle cuisine, Poach, Prepare, Pressure, Provencale, Ribroast, Rig, Ring, Roast, Roger, Sauté, Sous-chef, Spit, Steam, Stew, Stir-fry, Stove, Tandoori, Tikka, Tire

▷ **Cook** *may indicate* an anagram

Cool(er), Cooling, Coolness Aloof, Aplomb, Calm, Can, Chill, Collected, Composed, Cryogen, Cryostat, Defervescence, Desert, Dispassionate, Distant, Esky®, Fan, Frappé, Fridge, Frigid, Frosty, Gaol, Goglet, Hip, Ice(box), Jail, Jug, Keel, La Nina, Maraging, Phlegm, Prison, Quad, Quod, Reefer, Refresh, Regenerative, Reserved, Sangfroid, Serene, Skeigh, Splat, Stir, Sweat, Temperate, Thou(sand), Trendy, Unruffled, Wint(e)ry

Coop Cage, Cavie, Confine, Gaol, Hutch, Mew, Pen, Rip

Cooper Gary, Henry, Tubman

Cooperate, Cooperation, Cooperative Collaborate, Combine, Conspire, Contribute, Coop, Give and take, Liaise, Play, Synergy, Teamwork, Together, Worker's

Coordinate(s), Coordinated, Coordination Abscissa, Abscisse, Agile, Arrange, Cartesian, Ensemble, Harmony, Nabla, Orchestrate, Ordonnance, Peer, Polar, Right ascension, Spherical, Synergy, Teamwork, Twistor, Waypoint, X, Y, Z

Coot Stupid, Sultan

Cop(s) Bag, Bull, Catch, Dick, Keystone, Peeler, Peon, → POLICEMAN, Silent

Copal Dammar, Resin

Cope Chlamys, Deal, Face, Handle, Make do, → MANAGE, Mantle, Meet, Negotiate, Pallium, Poncho

Coping (stone) Balustrade, Capstone, Skew

Copious Abundant, Affluent, Ample, Fecund, Fluent, Fruitful, Fulsome, Plentiful, Profuse

Copper As, Atacamite, Blister, Bluebottle, Bobby, Bornite, Busy, Cash, Cent, Chessylite, → COIN, Cu, D, Dam, Double, Erinite, Flatfoot, Lawman, Lota(h), Malachite, Mountain-blue, Ormolu, Peacock, Pence, Penny, Pfennig, Pie, Pig, Plack, → POLICEMAN, Red, Rosser, Rozzer, S, Sen(s), Slop, Special, Traybit, Venus, Verdet, Washer, Washtub, Wire bar

Copse Thicket

Copulate Boff, Intercourse, Line, Mate, Roger, Tup

Copy(ing), Copier, Copyist, Copywriter Adman, Aemule, Ape, Apograph, Autotype, Calk, Calque, Camera-ready, Carbon, Clerk, Clone, Counterpart, Crib, Cyclostyle, Diazo, Ditto, Download, Dyeline, Echo, Echopraxia, Ectype, Edition,

Eidograph, Electro, Emulate, Engross, Estreat, Example, Facsimile, Fair, Fax, Flimsy, Forge, Hard, Hectograph, → IMITATE, Issue, Jellygraph, Knocking, Manifold, Manuscript, Match, Me-tooer, Microdot, Milline, Mimeograph®, Mimic, Mirror, MS, Offprint, Parrot, Photostat®, Plagiarism, Polygraph, Read-out, Repeat, Replica, Repro, Reproduce, Review, Rip, Roneo®, Scribe, Script, Scrivener, Sedulous, Show, Simulate, Skim, Soft, Spit, Stencil, Stuff, Tall, Telautograph®, Telefax, Tenor, Tenure, Trace, Transcribe, Transume, Vidimus, Xerox®

Copyright C, Landgrab

Coquette Agacerie, Flirt, Rosina, Tease, Vamp

Cor Bath, Crumbs, Ephah, Homer

Coracle Currach, Curragh

Coral (reef) Alcyonaria, Aldabra, Atoll, Brain, Cup, Deadmen's fingers, Gorgonia(n), Laccadives, Madrepore, Millepore, Pink, Precious, Red, Reef, Sea fan, Sea ginger, Sea-pen, Sea whip, Seed, Staghorn, Stony, Zoothome

Cord, Cord-like Aiguillette, Band, Bedford, Bind, Boondoggle, Cat-gut, Chenille, Communication, Creance, Drawstring, Elephant, Flex, Fourragère, Funicle, Gasket, Heddle, Lace, Laniard, Lanyard, Ligature, Line, Moreen, Myelon, Nerve, Net, Ocnus, Picture, Piping, Quipo, Quipu, Rep(s), Restiform, Rip, Rope, Sash, Sennit, Service, Shroudline, Sinnet, Spermatic, Spinal, → STRING, Tendon, Tie, Tieback, Torsade, Twine, Twitch, Umbilical, Vocal, Wick

Cordial Anise(ed), Anisette, Benedictine, Cassis, Drink, Elderflower, Gracious, Grenadine, Hearty, Hippocras, Kind, Neighbourly, Oporice, Orangeade, Persico(t), Pleasant, Ratafia, Rosa-solis, Roso(g)lio, Shrub, Tar-water, Warm

Cordon Band, Beltcourse, Picket, Ring, Sanitaire, Surround

Corduroy Rep(p)

Cordyline Ti-tree

Core Barysphere, Calandria, Campana, Centre, Chog, Essence, Filament, Hard, Heart, Hub, Kernel, Nife, Nitty-gritty, Plerome, Quintessence, Slug

Co-religionist Brother

Coriander Cilantro

Corinthian(s) Casuals, Caulis, Epistolaters

Cork(ed), Corker Balsa, Bouché, Bung, Float(er), Humdinger, Mountain, Oner, Phellem, Phellogen, Plug, Seal, Shive, Stopper, Suber(ate)

Corkscrew Bore, Opening, Spiral

Cormorant Duiker, Duyker, Scart(h), Skart(h)

Corn(y) Bajr(a), Banal, Blé, Cereal, Cob, Dolly, Durra, Emmer, Epha, Flint, Gait, Graddan, Grain, Green, Grist, Guinea, Icker, Indian, Kaffir, Kanga pirau, Mabela, Maize, Mealie, Muid, Negro, Nubbin, Pickle, Pinole, Posho, Rabi, Rye, Seed, Shock, Stitch, Straw, Sugar, Sweet, Thrave, Trite, Zea

Corncrake Landrail

Cornel Dogberry, Tree

Corner Amen, Angle, Bend, Canthus, Cantle, Canton, Cranny, Dangerous, Diêdre, Elbow, Entrap, Hog, Hole, Hospital, Long, Lug, Monopoly, NE, Niche, Nook, NW, Penalty, Predicament, Quoin, SE, Short, Speakers', Spot, SW, Tack, Tight, Trap, Tree, Vertex

Cornerstone Coi(g)n, Encoignure, Skew-corbel, Skew-put, Skew-table

Cornet Cone, Cornopean, Field, Horn

Cornice Surbase

Cornish(man) Cousin Jack

Cornstalks Strammel, Straw, Strummel, Stubble

Cornucopia Amalthea, Horn

Cornwall SW
Corollary Conclusion, Dogma, Porism, Rider, Theory, Truism
Corona Aureole, Cigar, Larmier, Nimbus, Wreath
Coronation Enthronement
Coroner Procurator fiscal
Corporal Bardolph, Bodily, Bombardier, Brig(adier), Lance-pesade, Lance-prisade, Lance-prisado, Lance-speisade, Master, Naik, NCO, Nym, Pall, Physical, Trim
Corporation Belly, Body, Closed, Commune, Company, Conglomerate, Guild, Kite, Kyte, Paunch, Public, Public service, Stomach, Swag-belly, Tum, Wame, Wem
Corps Body, C, Crew, Diplomatic, Peace, RAC, REME, Unit
Corpse Blob, Body, Cadaver, Carcass, Carrion, Dust, Goner, Like, Mort, Relic, Remains, Stiff, Zombi(e)
Corpulence, Corpulent Adipose, Fat, Fleshy, Gross, Obese, Poddy, Stout, Thickset, Tubby
Corpuscle Cell, Erythrocyte, Malpighian, Meissner's, Microcyte, Neutrophil, Pacinian, Phagocyte, Poikilocyte
Correct(ive), Correcting, Correctly, Correctness, Correction, Corrector Accurate, Alexander, Align, Amend, Aright, Blue-pencil, Bodkin, Castigate, Chasten, Chastise, Check, Decorous, Diorthortic, Emend, Ethical, Exact, Fair, Fix, Grammatical, Legit, Mend, Politically, Preterition, Probity, Proofread, Proper, Propriety, Punctilious, Punish, Purism, Rebuke, Rectify, Rectitude, Redress, Remedial, Reprove, Revise, Right(en), Scold, Spot-on, Sumpsimus, Tickety-boo, Trew, True, Twink, U
▷ **Corrected** *may indicate* an anagram
Correspond(ence), Correspondent, Corresponding Accord, Agree, Analogy, Assonance, Coincident, Communicate, Congruence, Counterpart, Epistolist, Equate, Equivalence, Eye-rhyme, Fit, Foreign, Hate mail, Homolog(ue), Identical, Lobby, Match, On all fours, One to one, Par, Parallel, Parity, Relate, Snail mail, Symmetry, Tally, Veridical, War, Write
Corridor Air, Aisle, Berlin, Entry, Gallery, Greenway, Lobby, Passage, Polish, Re-entry
Corroborate Confirm, Support, Verify
Corrode(d), Corrosion, Corrosive Acid, Acid rain, Brinelling, Burn, Canker, Decay, Eat, Erode, Etch, Fret, Gnaw, Hydrazine, Mordant, → ROT, Rubiginous, Rust, Waste
Corrugate Gimp
Corrupt(er), Corrupting, Corruption Abuse, Adulterate, Bastardise, Bent, Bobol, Bribable, Canker, Cesspit, Debase, Debauch, Debosh, Decadent, Defile, Degenerate, Depravity, Dissolute, Dry rot, Emancipate, Embrace(o)r, Embrasor, Empoison, Etch, Evil, Fester, Gangrene, Graft(er), Immoral, Impaired, Impure, Infect, Inquinate, Jobbery, Leprosy, Malversation, Nefarious, Obelus, Payola, Perverse, Poison, Pollute, Power, Putrid, Rakery, Ret(t), Rigged, Rot, Scrofulous, Seduce, Sepsis, Septic, Sleaze, Sodom, Sophisticate, Spoil, Suborn, Tammany, Twist, Venal, Vice, Vitiate
Corsage Buttonhole, Pompadour, Posy, Spray
Corsair Barbary, Picaroon, Pirate, Privateer, Robber, Rover
Corset, Corslet Belt, Bodice, Busk, Girdle, Lorica, Roll-on, Stays, Thorax, Waspie
Corsican Napoleon
Cortege Parade, Retinue, Train
Cortex Cerebral, Renal
Cortisone Hecogenin
Corundum Emery, Sapphire

Corvo Rolfe
Corybant Roisterer
Cosh Sap
Cosmetic Beautifier, Blusher, Bronzer, Chapstick, Conditioner, Eye-black, Eyeliner, Eye-shadow, Face-pack, Foundation, Fucus, Highlighter, Kohl, Liner, Lip gloss, Lip liner, Lipstick, Lotion, Maquillage, Mascara, Mousse, Mudpack, Paint, Pearl-powder, Powder, Reface, Rouge, Talcum, Toner
▶ **Cosmic** *see* COSMOS
Cosmonaut Gagarin, Spaceman, Tereshkova
Cosmopolitan International, Urban
Cosmos, Cosmic Globe, Heaven, Infinite, Mundane, Nature, Universe, World
Cossack Ataman, Hetman, Mazeppa, Russian, Tartar, Zaporogian
Cosset Caress, Coddle, Fondle, Pamper
Cost(s), Costly Bomb, Carriage, Charge, Current, Damage, Direct, Earth, Escuage, Estimate, Exes, → EXPENSE, Factor, Fixed, Hire, Historic(al), Indirect, Loss, Marginal, Opportunity, Outlay, Overhead, Precious, Price, Prime, Quotation, Rate, Running, Sacrifice, Sumptuous, Toll, Unit, Upkeep, Usurious, Variable
Costa Rica(n) Tico
Costermonger Barrow-boy, Kerb-merchant, Pearly
Costume(s) Apparel, Attire, Camagnole, Cossie, Dress, Ensemble, Get-up, Gi(e), Guise, Judogi, Livery, Maillot, Motley, Nebris, Polonaise, Rig, Ruana, Surcoat, Tanga, Togs, Uniform, Wardrobe, Wear
Cosy Cosh, Gemutlich, Intime, Snug
Cot Moses basket
Coterie Cell, Cenacle, Circle, Clan, Clique, Club, Ring, Set, Society
Cottage(r) Bach, Batch, Bordar, Bothie, Bothy, Bower, Box, Bungalow, Cabin, Cape Cod, Chalet, Cot, Crib, Dacha, Home-croft, Hut, Lodge, Mailer
Cotton Absorbent, Agree, AL, Alabama, Balbriggan, Batiste, Batting, Bengal, Calico, Candlewick, Ceiba, Chambray, Chino, Chintz, Collodion, Coutil(le), Cretonne, Denim, Dho(o)ti, Dimity, Ducks, Fustian, Galatea, Gossypine, Gossypium, Humhum, Ihram, Jaconet, Lavender, Lawn, Lea, Lille, Lint, Lisle, Longcloth, Manchester, Marcella, Muslin, Nainsook, Nankeen, Nankin, Osnaburg, Pongee, Sea-island, Seersucker, Silesia, Stranded, Surat, T-cloth, Thread, Twig, Upland, Velveteen
Cotton soil Regar, Regur
Cotyledon Seed-leaf
Couch Bed, Casting, Davenport, Daybed, → DIVAN, Express, Grass, Lurk, Palanquin, Palkee, Palki, Quick, Recamier, Sedan, Settee, Sofa, Studio, Triclinium, Vis-à-vis, Winnipeg, Word
Coué Auto-suggestion
Cougar Cat, Painter, Puma
Cough(ing) Bark, Chin, Croup, Expectorate, Hack, Harrumph, Hawk, Hem, Hoast, Hooping, Kink, Pertussis, Phthisis, Rale, Tisick, Tussis, Ugh, Whooping
Could Couth
Council (meeting), Councillor, Counsel(lor) Achitophel, Admonish, Admonitor, Advice, Advocate, Ahithophel, Alfred, Amphictryon, Anziani, Aread, A(r)re(e)de, Assembly, Attorney, Aulic, Aunt, Ayuntamiento, Board, Body, Boule, Bundesrat, Burgess, Cabinet, Casemate, Committee, Consistory, Corporation, County, Cr, Decurion, Dergue, Devil, Dietine, Divan, Douma, Duma, Ecumenical, Egeria, Europe, European, Executive, Exhort, General, Great, Greenbag, Hebdomadal, Indaba, Induna, Industrial, Info, Islands, Jirga, Junta, Kabele, Kebele, King's, Kite,

Landst(h)ing, Lateran, Leader, Legislative, Loan, Majlis, Mentor, Nestor, Nicaean, Nicene, Panchayat, Paraclete, Parish, Powwow, Press, Privy, Provincial, Queen's, Rede, Regional, Reichsrat, Robber, Runanga, Samaritan, Sanhedrim, Sanhedrin, Security, Senate, Shoora, Shura, Sobranje, Sobranye, Soviet, States, Syndicate, Synedrion, Synod, Thing, Town, Tradeboard, Trades, Trent, Tridentine, Trullan, Vatican, Volost, Wages, Whitley, Witan, Witenagemot, Works, Zemstvo, Zila, Zila parishad, Zillah

Count(ed), Counter(balance), Counting Abacus, Add, Algoriam, Anti, Balance, Bar, Basie, Blood, Buck, Buffet, Calculate, Cavour, Census, Chip, Compute, Coost, Crystal, Desk, Dracula, Dump, Earl, Enumerate, Fish, Geiger, Geiger-Muller, Graf(in), Grave, Itemise, Jet(t)on, Landgrave, Margrave, Marker, Matter, Merel(l), Meril, Milton work, Nobleman, Number, Numerate, Obviate, Olivia, Oppose, Palatine, Palsgrave, Paris, Pollen, Presume, Proportional, Rebut, → **RECKON**, Refute, Rejoinder, Rely, Retaliate, Retort, Rhinegrave, Scaler, Scintillation, Score, Sperm, Squail, Statistician, Stop, Sum, Table, Tally, Tell, Tiddleywink, Ugolino, Weigh, Zeppelin

Countenance Approve, Brow, Endorse, Face, Favour, Mug, Sanction, Support, Visage

Counteract(ing) Ant-, Antidote, Cancel, Correct, Frustrate, Offset, Talion

Counterbalance Bascule, Offset, Undo, Weigh

Counter-charge Recrimination

Counterclockwise L(a)evorotatory

Counterfeit(er) Bastard, Belie, Bogus, Boodle, Brum, Coiner, Duffer, Dummy, Fantasm, Flash, Forge, Imitant, Paperhanger, Phantasm, Phoney, Pinchbeck, Postiche, Pseudo, Queer, Rap, Schlenter, Sham, Shan(d), Simulate, Slang, Slip, Smasher, Snide, Spurious, Stumer

Counterfoil Stub

Counterglow Gegenschein

Counter-irritant Seton

Countermand Abrogate, Annul, Cancel, Override, Rescind, Retract, Revoke

Counterpart Copy, Double, Obverse, Oppo, Parallel, Shadow, Similar, Spit(ting), Tally, Twin

Counterpoint Contrapuntal, Descant

Countersign Endorse, Password

Counterthrust Riposte

Counties, County Co, Comital, District, Metropolitan, Palatine, Parish, Seat, Shire, Six

COUNTIES

2 letters:	Cork	Clwyd	Meath
NI	Down	Derry	Moray
Sy	Fife	Dyfed	Notts
	Kent	Essex	Omagh
3 letters:	Mayo	Flint	Perth
Ely	Ross	Gwent	Powys
Som		Herts	Sligo
	5 letters:	Hunts	Wilts
4 letters:	Angus	Kerry	Worcs
Avon	Cavan	Laois	
Beds	Clare	Louth	

6 letters:
Antrim
Armagh
Barset
Carlow
Dorset
Dublin
Durham
Galway
Offaly
Surrey
Sussex
Tyrone

7 letters:
Cumbria
Donegal
Gwynedd
Kildare
Leitrim
Norfolk
Rutland
Suffolk
Torfaen
Wexford
Wicklow

8 letters:
Cheshire
Cornwall
Finnmark
Kesteven
Kilkenny
Limerick

Longford
Lothians
Monaghan
Somerset

9 letters:
Berkshire
Buteshire
Caithness
Champagne
Cleveland
Fermanagh
Hampshire
Loamshire
Roscommon
The Mearns
Tipperary
Waterford
Westmeath
Yorkshire

10 letters:
Banffshire
Ceredigion
Derbyshire
Devonshire
Humberside
Lancashire
Merseyside
Midlothian
Nairnshire
Perthshire
Shropshire
Sutherland

West Sussex

11 letters:
Breconshire
East Lothian
Lanarkshire
Londonderry
Oxfordshire
Radnorshire
Tyne and Wear
West Lothian

12 letters:
Berwickshire
Denbighshire
Kinrossshire
Lincolnshire
Mid-Glamorgan
Peeblesshire
Renfrewshire
Selkirkshire
Warwickshire
West Midlands
Westmoreland
Wigtownshire

13 letters:
Dumfriesshire
Herefordshire
Monmouthshire
Pembrokeshire
Roxburghshire
Staffordshire
Stirlingshire

West Glamorgan
West Yorkshire

14 letters:
Brecknockshire
Dumbartonshire
Glamorganshire
Invernessshire
Leicestershire
Merionithshire
Northumberland
North Yorkshire
South Glamorgan
South Yorkshire

15 letters:
Caernarvonshire
Carmarthenshire
Gloucestershire
Kincardineshire
Montgomeryshire
Neath Port Talbot
Ross and Cromarty
Vale of Glamorgan

16 letters:
Clackmannanshire
Northamptonshire

17 letters:
Kircudbrightshire

Countless Infinite, Innumerable, Myriad, Umpteen, Untold
Country(side), Countrified Annam, Bangladesh, Bolivia, Boondocks, Bucolic, Champaign, Clime, Colchis, Edom, Enchorial, Farmland, Fatherland, Greenwood, High, Karoo, Karroo, → LAND, Lea, Lee, Low, Mongolia, Motherland, Nation, Parish, Paysage, People, Province, Realm, Region, Republic, Rural, Satellite, Scenery, Soil, State, Sultanate, The sticks, Thrace, Tundra, Tweedy, Venezuela, Weald, Wold, Yemen
Country girl Amaryllis
Country house Hall, Manor, Quinta
Countryman Arcadian, Bacon, Boor, Culchie, Hick, Hillbilly, Hodge, National, Native, Peasant, Ruralist, Un, Yokel
Coup Blow, Deal, KO, Move, Putsch, Scoop, Stroke, Treason
Coupé Cabriolet, Landaulet
Couple(r), Coupling Acoustic, Ally, Band, Brace, Bracket, Connect, Direct, Duet, Duo, Dyad, Fishplate, Flange, Galvanic, Gemini, Geminy, Hitch, Interlock, Item, → JOIN, Marrow, Marry, Mate, Meng(e), Ment, Ming, Octave, Pair, Pr, Relate,

Shackle, Tenace, Tie, Tirasse, Turnbuckle, Tway, Union, Universal, Voltaic, Wed, Yoke

Couple of ducks Spectacles

Couplet Distich, Heroic

Coupon(s) Ration, Ticket, Voucher

Courage(ous) Balls, Ballsy, Bottle, Bravado, Bravery, Bulldog, Cojones, Dutch, Fortitude, Gallantry, Game, Gimp, Grit, Gumption, Guts, Hardihood, Heart, Heroism, Lion-heart, Macho, Manful, Mettle, Moral, Moxie, Nerve, Pluck, Prowess, Rum, Spirit, Spunk, Stalwart, Steel, Stomach, Valiant, Valour, Wight

Courgette Zucchini

Courier Estafette, Guide, Harbinger, Herald, → MESSENGER, Postillion, Postman

Course(s) Access, Afters, Aim, Aintree, Antipasto, Appetiser, Arroyo, Ascot, Assault, Atlantic, Back straight, Barge, Bearing, Beat, Belt, Canal, Career, Chantilly, Chase, Circuit, Civics, Collision, Consommé, Conversion, Correspondence, Crash, Current, Curriculum, Cursus, Daltonism, Damp(-proof), Dessert, Diadrom, Dish, Dromic, Easting, Entrée, Epsom, Fish, Food, Foundation, Going, Golf, Goodwood, Greats, Heat, Induction, Isodomon, Lane, Lap, Layer, Leat, Leet, Line, Lingfield, Links, Longchamp, Magnetic, Main, Meal, Meat, Mess, Newbury, Newmarket, Nine-hole, Northing, Nulla, → OF COURSE, Orbit, Orthodromic, Period, Policy, PPE, Practicum, Procedure, Process, Programme, Progress, Pursue, Quadrivium, Race, Raik, Refresher, Regimen, Rhumb, Ride, Ring, Rink, Road, Rota, Route, Routine, Run, Rut, Sandown, Sandwich, Semester, Seminar, Series, Slalom, Sorbet, Soup, Southing, Stadium, Starter, Stearage, Steerage, Step(s), Stratum, Streak, Stretch, Stretching, String, Syllabus, Tack, Tanride, Tenor, Track, Trade, Trend, Troon, Vector, Via media, Water table, Way, Wearing, Wentworth, Westing

Court(ship), Courtier Address, Admiralty, Appellate, Arbitration, Arches, Areopagus, Atrium, Attention, Audience, Audiencia, Aula, Banc, Bar, Basecourt, Bench, Beth Din, Bishop's, Boondock, Caerleon, Camelot, Canoodle, Caravanserai, Cassation, Centre, Chancery, Chase, Clay, Commercial, Commissary, Commission, Conscience, Conservancy, Consistory, County, Criminal, Crown, CS, Ct, Curia, Curia Regis, Curtilage, Cutcher(r)y, Date, Dedans, Deuce, Dicastery, Diplock, District, Doctor's Commons, Domestic, Duchy, Durbar, Dusty Feet, En tout cas, Evora, Eyre, Federal, Fehm(gericht), Fehmgerichte, Fiars, Forensic, Forest, Forum, Fronton, Galleria, Garth, Go steady, Grass, Guildenstern, Halimot(e), Hampton, Hard, High, Hof, Holy See, Hustings, Hypaethron, Inferior, Intermediate, Invite, Jack, Justice, Juvenile, Kachahri, Kacheri, Kangaroo, Keys, King, King's Bench, Kirk Session, Knave, Law, Leet, Lobby, Lyon, Magistrate's, Majlis, Marshalsea, Mash, Moot, Old Bailey, Open, Parvis, Patio, Peristyle, Petty Sessions, Philander, Piepowder, Police, Porte, Praetorium, Prerogative, Presbytery, Prize, Probate, Provincial, Provost, Quad, Quarter Sessions, Queen, Queen's Bench, Racket, Request, Retinue, Romance, Rosenkrantz, Royal, St James's, Sanhedrim, Sanhedrin, See, Service, Session, Sheriff, Shire-moot, Spoon, Stannary, Star Chamber, Sudder, Sue, Superior, Supreme, Swanimote, Sweetheart, Thane, Thegn, Traffic, Trial, Tribunal, Vehm, Vehmgericht(e), Vestibulum, Walk out, Ward, Wench, Woo, World, Wow, Yard, Youth

Courteous, Courtesy Affable, Agrement, Bow, Chivalry, Civil, Comity, Devoir, Etiquette, Fair, Genteel, Gracious, Hend, Polite, Politesse, Refined, Urbanity, Well-mannered

Courtesan Aspasia, Bianca, Bona-roba, Delilah, Demi-monde, Demi-rep, Geisha, Hetaera, Lais, Lampadion, Lorette, Madam, Phryne, Plover, Pornocracy, Prostitute, Stallion, Thais

Courtly Chivalrous, Cringing, Dignified, Flattering, Refined
Court-martial Drumhead
Courtyard Area, Close, Cortile, Enceinte, Garth, Marae, Patio, Quad
Cousin(s) Bette, Cater, Country, Coz, Cross, German, Kin, Kissing, Parallel, Robin, Second, Skater
Couturier Dior, Dressmaker
Cove Abraham's, Arm, Bay, Bight, Buffer, Creek, Cure, Gink, Grot, Guy, Hithe, Hythe, Inlet, Lulworth, Nook
Covenant(er) Abrahamic, Alliance, Appurtenant, Bond, Contract, Hillmen, Pledge, Restrictive, Warranty, Whiggamore
Coventry Isolation
Cover(ed), Covering Adventitia, Air, A l'abri, Amnion, Antependium, Antimacassar, Apron, Aril, Attire, Awning, Barb, Bard(s), Bark, Bedspread, Bestrew, Bind, Blanket, Bodice, Brood, Bubblewrap, Bury, Camouflage, Canopy, Cap, Caparison, Cape, Capsule, Casing, Casque, Catch-all, Caul, Ceil, Ciborium, Cladding, Clapboard, Cleithral, Clithral, Coat, Cocoon, Coleorhiza, Conceal, Cope, Copyright, Cosy, Counterpane, Cour, Covert, Cowl, Crust, Curtain, Deadlight, Debruised, Deck, Deputise, Dividend, Dome, Drape(t), Dripstone, Duchesse, Dust-sheet, Duvet, Eiderdown, Encase, Endue, Enguard, Enlace, Enshroud, Envelop(e), Enwrap, Exoderm(is), Exoskeleton, Extra, Face, Falx, Fanfare, Felting, Fielder, Figleaf, Fingerstall, First-day, Flashing, Fother, Front, Gaiter, Gambado, Gobo, Grolier, Ground, Groundsheet, Hap, Harl, Hat, Hatch, Havelock, Heal, Heel, Hejab, Hele, Hell, Helmet, Hijab, Hood, Housing, Hubcap, Immerse, Incase, Indument, Indusium, Inmask, Insulate, Insurance, Insure, Jacket, Lag, Lambrequin, Lay, Leap, Leep, Legging, Legwarmer, Lid, Liner, Loose, Manche, Mantle, Mask, Metal, Mount, Muffle, Mulch, Notum, Numnah, Obscure, OC, Occlude, On, Operculum, Orillion, Orlop, Overlap, Overlay, Palampore, Palempore, Pall, Pand, Parcel, Pasties, Patch, Pebbledash, Pelmet, Periderm, Perigone, Pillow sham, Plaster, Plate, Pleura, Point, Pseudonym, Pullover, Quilt, Radome, Regolith, Robe, Roof, Roughcast, Rug, Sally, Screen, Serviette, Setting, Sheath, Sheet, Shell, Shelter, Shield, Shower, Shrink-wrap, Shroud, Shuck, Skin, Smokescreen, Solleret, Span, Spat, Splashback, Stand-by, Stifle, Superimpose, Swathe, Tampian, Tampion, Tapadera, Tapis, Tarpaulin, Teacosy, Tectorial, Tegmen, Tegument, Tent, Test(a), Tester, Thatch, Thimble, Thumbstall, Tick(ing), Tidy, Tile, Tilt, Tonneau, Top, Trapper, Trench, Trip, Turtleback, Twill, Twilt, Umbrella, Upholster, Valance, Veil, Vele, Veneer, Ventail, Vesperal, Vest, Visor, Volva, Wainscot, Warrant, Waterdeck, Whelm, Whitewash, Wrap, Wrappage, Wrapper, Yapp, Yashmak
Covert(ly) Clandestine, Copse, Privy, → SECRET, Shy, Sidelong, Sub rosa, Surreptitious, Tectrix, Ulterior
Covet(ed), Covetous Avaricious, Crave, Desiderata, Desire, Eager, Envy, Greedy, Hanker, Yearn
Cow Adaw, Alderney, Amate, Appal, Awe, Ayrshire, Boss(y), Bovine, Brahmin, Browbeat, Cash, Charolais, Colly, Crummy, Danton, Daunt, Dexter, Dsomo, Dun, Galloway, Gally, Goujal, Guernsey, Hawkey, Hawkie, Heifer, Hereford, Intimidate, Jersey, Kouprey, Kyloe, Lea(h), Mart, Milch, Mog(gie), Moggy, Mooly, Muley, Mulley, Neat, Overawe, Redpoll, Red Sindhi, Rother(-beast), Sacred, Santa Gertrudis, Scare, Simmental, Slattern, Springing, Stirk, Subact, Teeswater, Threaten, Unnerve, Vaccine, Zebu, Z(h)o
Coward(ice), Cowardly Bessus, Cat, Chicken, Cocoa, Craven, Cuthbert, Dastard, Dingo, Dunghill, Fraidy-cat, Fugie, Funk, Gutless, Hen, Hilding, Jessie, Lily-livered, Meacock, Milk-livered, Niddering, Nidderling, Nidering, Niderling, Niding,

Nithing, Noel, Panty-waist, Poltroon, Pusillanimous, Recreant, Scaramouch, Scaredy cat, Sganarelle, Slag, Sook, Squib, Viliaco, Viliago, Villagio, Villiago, White feather, Yellow, Yellow-belly

Cowboy, Cowgirl Broncobuster, Buckaroo, Cowpoke, Cowpuncher, Gaucho, Inexpert, Io, Jerrybuilder, Leger, Llanero, Puncher, Ranchero, Ritter, Roper, Vaquero, Waddie, Waddy, Wrangler

Cow-catcher Fender, Reata

Cower Croodle, Crouch, Fawn, Quail, Ruck, Skulk, Wince

Cowl Bonnet, Capuchin, Granny, Hood, Kilmarnock

Cowpat Dung, Tath

Cowpox Vaccinia

Cowshed, Cowstall Byre, Crib, Shippen, Shippon, Stable, Stall, Staw

Cowslip Culver-key, Pa(i)gle

Cox Steerer

Coxcomb Aril, Caruncle, Copple, Crest, Dandy, Dude, Fop, Jackanapes, Popinjay, Yellow-rattle

Coy Arch, Coquettish, Demure, Laithfu', Mim, Nice, Shamefast, → **SHY**, Skeigh, Skittish

Coyote SD

CPRS Think tank

Crab(by), Crablike Apple, Attercop, Blue swimmer, Boston, Calling, Cancer, Cancroid, Cantankerous, Capernoity, Cock, Coconut, Daddy, Decapoda, Diogenes, Ethercap, Ettercap, Fiddler, Ghost, Grouch, Hard-shell, Hermit, Horseman, Horseshoe, King, Land, Limulus, Mantis, Mitten, Mud, Nebula, Ochidore, Oyster, Pagurian, Partan, Pea, Perverse, Podite, Roast, Robber, Rock, Sand, Saucepan-fish, Scrawl, Sentinel, Sidle, Soft-shell, Soldier, Spectre, Spider, Velvet, Velvet-fiddler, Woolly-hand, Xiphosura, Zoea

▷ **Crab** *may indicate* an anagram

Crab-apple Scrog-bush, Scrog-buss

Crab-eater Urva

Crabs-eye Abrus

Crack(ed), Cracker(s), Cracking Ad-lib, Admirable, Bananas, Biscuit, Bonbon, Break, Cat, Catalytic, Chap, Chasm, Chat, Chink, Chip, Chop, Clap, Cleave, Cleft, Cloff, Confab, Cranny, Craquelure, Craqueture, Craze, Cream, Crepitate, Crevasse, Crevice, Crispbread, Dawn, Decipher, Decode, Doom, Dunt, Elite, Expert, Fatiscent, Fent, Firework, First-rate, Fisgig, Fissure, Fizgig, Flaw, Flip-flop, Fracture, Go, Graham, Grike, Gryke, Gully, Hairline, Hit, Jibe, Joint, Knacker, Leak, Liar, Little-endian, Matzo, Moulin, Oner, Peterman, Pleasantry, Pore, Praise, Prawn, Quarter, Quip, Rap, Report, Rhagades, Rictus, Rift, Rille, Rima, Rime, Rimous, Rive, Rock, Saltine, Sand, Seam, Shaky, Snap, Soda, Solve, Split, Squib, Sulcus, Toe, Top, Try, Waterloo, Wind shake, Yegg

Crackerjack Ace, Nailer, Trump

Crackle, Crackling Craze, Crepitation, Crepitus, Crinkle, Decrepitate, Fizz, Glaze, Rale, Skin, Static

Crackpot Nutter

Cracksman Burglar, Peterman, Raffles

Cradle Bassinet, Berceau, Book rest, Cat's, Cot, Crib, Cunabula, Hammock, Knife, Nestle, Newton's, Rocker

Craft(y) Arch, Art, Aviette, Barbola, Boat, Canal boat, Cautel, Cunning, Disingenuous, Finesse, Fly, Guile, Hydroplane, Ice-breaker, Insidious, Kontiki, Landing, Machiavellian, Mister, Mystery, Oomiack, Reynard, Saic, Shallop, Ship,

Shuttle, → **SKILL**, Slee, Sleeveen, Slim, Slippy, Sly, Slyboots, State, Subdolous, Subtil(e), Subtle, Suttle, Trade, Triphibian, Umiak, Underhand, Versute, → **VESSEL**, Wile, Workmanship

▷ **Craft** *may indicate* an anagram

Craftsman AB, Artificer, Artisan, Artist, Chippy, Cutler, Ebonist, Fabergé, Finisher, Gondolier, Guild, Hand, Joiner, Journeyman, Mason, Mechanic, Morris, Opificer, Wainwright, Wright

Crag(gy) Coralline, Eyrie, Height, Heuch, Heugh, Krantz, Noup, Rock

Cram(mer) Bag, Candle-waster, Cluster, Craig, Fill, Gag, Gavage, Neck, Pang, Prime, Revise, Rugged, Scar(p), Shoehorn, Spur, Stap, Stodge, Stow, Swat, Tuck

Cramp(ed) Agraffe, Charleyhorse, Confine, Constrict, Crick, Hamper, Hamstring, Incommodious, Musician's, Myalgia, Pinch, Poky, Potbound, Restrict, Rigor, Squeeze, Stunt, Tetany, Writer's

Crane, Crane-driver Brolga, Cherry picker, Container, Davit, Deck, Demoiselle, Derrick, Dogman, Dragline, Gantry, Gooseneck, Grabbing, Herd, Heron, Hooper, Ichabod, Jenny, Jib, Jigger, Kenworthy, Luffing-jib, Numidian, Rail, Sarus, Sedge, Shears, Sheer, Siege, Stork, Stretch, Tower, Tulip, Whooper, Whooping, Winch

Crane-fly Leatherjacket, Tipulidae

Cranium Harnpan

Crank(y) Bell, Eccentric, Grouch, Handle, Lever, Mot, Perverse, Whim, Wince, Winch, Wind

Crash Bingle, Collapse, Disk, Ditch, Dush, Fail, Fall, Fragor, Intrude, Linen, Nosedive, Pile up, Prang, Rack, Ram, Rote, Shunt, Slam, Smash, South Sea Bubble, Thunderclap, Topple

▷ **Crashes** *may indicate* an anagram

Crass Coarse, Crude, Rough, Rude

Crate Biplane, Box, Case, Ceroon, Crib, Hamper, Sero(o)n, Soapbox, Tube

Crater Alphonsus, Aniakchak, Aristarchus, Aristotle, Askja, Autolycus, Bail(l)y, Blowhole, Caldera, Cavity, Cissing, Clavius, Copernicus, Fra Mauro, Grimaldi, Hipparchus, Hole, Hollow, Kepler, Kilauea, Maar, Meteor, Newton, Pit, Plato, Ptolemaeus, Pythagoras, Schickard, Sinus iridium, Theophilus, Tycho

Cravat Ascot, Neckatee, Neck-cloth, Oerlay, Overlay, Scarf, Soubise, Steenkirk, Tie

Crave, Craving Appetite, Aspire, Beg, Beseech, Covet, Desire, Entreat, Gasp, Greed, Hanker, Hunger, Itch, Libido, Long, Lust, Malacia, Methomania, Munchies, Opsomania, Orexis, Pica, Polyphagia, Sitomania, The munchies, Thirst, Yearn, Yen

Craven Abject, Coward, Dastard, Hen, Recreant

Crawl(er) All fours, Australian, Back, Clamber, Creep, Cringe, Drag, Front, Grovel, Lag, Lickspittle, Pub, Reptile, Scramble, Scrome, Side, Skulk, Snail, Swim, Sycophant, Tantony, Trail, Trudgen, Yes-man

Crayfish Astacology, Gilgie, Jilgie, Marron, Yabbie, Yabby

Crayon Chalk, Colour, Conté®, Pastel, Pencil, Sauce

Craze(d), Crazy Absurd, Ape, Apeshit, Barmy, Bats, Batty, Berserk, Bonkers, Break, Cornflake, Crack(ers), Crackpot, Cult, Daffy, Dement, Derange, Dingbats, Dippy, Distraught, Doiled, Doilt, Doolally, Doolally tap, Dottle, Dotty, Fad, Flake, Flaw, Folie, Frantic, Furious, Furore, Furshlugginer, Gaga, Geld, Gonzo, Gyte, Haywire, Headbanger, Insane, Loco, Loony, Loopy, Lunatic, Madden, Maenad(ic), Mania, Manic, Mattoid, Melomania, Meshug(g)a, Moonstruck, Nuts, Porangi, Potty, Psycho(path), Rage, Rave, Scatty, Screwball, Skivie, Slatey, Stunt, Typomania, Unhinge, Wacko, Wacky, Wet, W(h)acky, Whim, Wowf, Zany

▷ **Crazy** *may indicate* an anagram

Creak(y) Cry, Grate, Grind, Rheumatic, Scraich, Scraigh, Scroop, Seam, Squeak

Cream(y) Barrier, Bavarian, Best, Chantilly, Cherry-pick, Clotted, Cold, Cornish, Crème fraîche, Devonshire, Double, Elite, Foundation, Frangipane, Glacier, Heavy, Ivory, Jollop, Lanolin, Liniment, Lotion, Mousse, Off-white, Ointment, Opal, Paragon, Pastry, Pick, Ream, Rich, Salad, Salve, Sillabub, Single, Skim, Smitane, Sour, Sun(screen), Syllabub, Vanishing, Whipped, Whipping

Crease Bowling, Crumple, → **FOLD**, Goal, Lirk, Pitch, Pleat, Popping, Return, Ridge, Ruck(le), Ruga, Rugose, Wrinkle

Create, Creation, Creative Arty, Brainstorm, Build, Coin, Compose, Continuous, Devise, Dreamtime, Engender, Establish, Fabricate, Forgetive, Form, Found, Generate, Genesis, Godhead, Hexa(h)emeron, Ideate, Imaginative, → **INVENT**, Omnific, Oratorio, Originate, Produce, Shape, Synthesis, Universe

Creator Ahura Mazda, Author, Demiurge, God, Inventor, Maker, Ormazd, Ormuzd

Creature Animal, Ankole, Basilisk, Beast, Being, Bigfoot, Chevrotain, Cratur, Critter, Crittur, Man, Nekton, Saprobe, Sasquatch, Sphinx, Whiskey, Wight

Credence, Credential(s) Certificate, Document, Papers, Qualifications, Shelf, Testimonial

Credibility Street

Credible, Credit(s), Creditor Ascribe, Attribute, Belief, Billboard, Byline, Carbon, Crawl, Esteem, Extended, Family, Honour, HP, Kite, Kudos, LC, Lender, Mense, Post-war, Probable, Reliable, Renown, Revolving, Shylock, Social, Strap, Street, Tally, Tax, Tick, Title, Trust, Weight, Youth

Credulous Charlie, Gullible, Naive, Simple, Trusting

Creed Apostle's, Athanasian, Belief, Doctrine, Faith, Ism, Nicene, Ophism, Outworn, Sect, Tenet

Creek Antietam, Bay, Breaches, Cooper, Cove, Crick, Dawson, Estuary, Fleet, Geo, Gio, Goe, Indian, Inlet, Kill, Pow, Slough, Vae, Voe, Wick

Creel Basket, Hask, Scull, Skull

Creep(er), Creeping, Creeps Ai, Ampelopsis, Arbutus, Aseismic, Boston ivy, Cleavers, Crawl, Function, Grew, Grovel, Grue, Heebie-jeebies, Heeby-jeebies, Herpetic, Honey, Inch, Insect, Ivy, Mission, Nerd, Nuthatch, Pussyfoot, Repent, Reptant, Sarmentous, Sidle, Sittine, Skulk, Slink, Snake, Sneak(sby), Sobole(s), Soil, Steal, Toad, Tropaeolum, Truckle, Vinca, Vine, Virginia, Wickthing, Willies

Creeping Jenny Moneywort

Cremate, Cremation, Crematorium Burn, Char, Cinerarium, Ghat, Ghaut, Incinerate, Pyre, Sati, Suttee, Ustrinium

Creole Gullah, Haitian, Kriol, Papiamento, Tok Pisin

Crepe Blini, Blintz(e), Canton, Pancake

Crescent Barchan(e), Bark(h)an, Fertile, Growing, Lune(tte), Lunulate, Lunule, Meniscus, Moon, Red, Sickle, Waxing

Cress Cardamine, Garden, Hoary, Isatis, Pepperwort, Swine's, Thale, Wart, Water, Yellow

Crest(ed) Acme, Chine, Cimier, Cockscomb, Comb, Copple, Crista, Height, Kirimon, Knap, Mon, Peak, Pileate, Pinnacle, Plume, Ridge, Summit, Tappit, Tee, → **TOP**, Tufty

Cretaceous Chalky, Senonian

Cretan Candiot(e), Minoan, Teucer

Crevasse Bergschrund, Chasm, Gorge, Rimaye

Crevice Chine, Cranny, Fissure, Interstice, Ravine, Vallecula

Crew Boasted, Company, Complement, Core, Deckhand, Eight, Equipage, Four, Lot, Manners, Men, Oars, Prize, Sailors, Salts, Seamen, Ship men, Team, Teme, Torpid

Crew-cut Not(t)

Crib Cheat, Cot, Cowhouse, Cratch, Filch, Horse, → **KEY**, Manger, Pony, Purloin, Putz, Shack, Stall, Steal, Trot

Crick Cramp, Kink, Spasm

Cricket(er) Balm, Bat, Botham, Bowler, Bradman, CC, Cicada, Dry-bob, French, Grade, Grasshopper, Grig, Hopper, Jerusalem, Katydid, Keeper, Knott, Leg, Long-leg, Long-off, Long-on, Longstop, March, May, Mid-on, Mole, Muggleton, Nightwatchman, Opener, Packer, Point, Pyjama, Shield, Single-wicket, Slip, Sobers, Stool, Stridulate, Tate, Test, Tettix, Tip and run, Vigoro, Warner, Wart-biter, Windball, Windies, Wisden, XI(gent)

Crier Bellman, Herald, Muezzin, Niobe, Outrooper

Crime Attentat, Barratry, Caper, Chantage, Chaud-mellé, Computer, Corpus delicti, Ecocide, Fact, Felony, Fraud, Graft, Hate, Heist, Iniquity, Inside job, Malefaction, Mayhem, Misdeed, Misdemeanour, → **OFFENCE**, Organised, Ovicide, Peccadillo, Perjury, Pilferage, Ram raid, Rap, Rape, Rebellion, → **SIN**, Tort, Transgression, Treason, Victimless, Villa(i)ny, War, White-collar, Wrong

Crimea Balaclava

Criminal Bandit, Bent, Bushranger, Chummy, Con, Cosa Nostra, Counterfeiter, Crack-rope, → **CROOK**, Culpable, Culprit, Delinquent, Escroc, Fagin, Felon, Flagitious, Forensic, Gangster, Heavy, Heinous, Highbinder, Hitman, Hood(lum), Jailbird, Ladrone, Lag, Larcener, Lifer, Looter, Lowlife, Maf(f)ia, Malefactor, Maleficent, Malfeasant, Mens rea, Mob(ster), Molester, Ndrangheta, Nefarious, Nefast, Offender, Outlaw, Perp(etrator), Peterman, Racketeer, Receiver, Recidivist, Reprehensible, Rustler, Sinner, Snakehead, Thug, Triad, Triggerman, Underworld, Villain, Wicked, Wire, Yakuza, Yardie, Yegg

▷ **Criminal** *may indicate* an anagram

Criminologist Lombroso

Crimp Pleat

Crimson Carmine, Incarnadine, Modena, Red, Scarlet

Cringe, Cringing Cower, Creep, Crouch, Fawn, Grovel, Shrink, Sneaksby, Truckle

Crinkle, Crinkly Rugate, Rugose

Crinoline Farthingale, Hoop

Cripple(d) Damage, Debilitate, Disable, Game, Hamstring, Handicap, Injure, → **LAME**, Lameter, Lamiter, Maim, Paralyse, Polio, Scotch, Spoil

Crisis Acme, Crunch, Drama, Emergency, Exigency, Fastigium, Fit, Flap, Head, Identity, Make or break, Midlife, Panic, Pass, Quarterlife, Shake-out, Solution, Test

Crisp Brisk, Clear, Crimp, Crunchy, Fresh, Potato, Sharp, Short, Succinct, Terse

Crispin Sutor(ial)

Criss-cross Alternate, Fret, Interchange, Vein

Criteria, Criterion Benchmark, Gauge, Koch's postulates, Measure, Precedent, Proof, Rayleigh, Rule, Shibboleth, → **STANDARD**, Test, Touchstone

Critic(al), Criticise, Criticism Acute, Agate, Animadversion, Archer, Aristarch, Armchair, Arnold, Attack, Badmouth, Bagehot, Barrack, Bellettrist, Berate, Bird, Blame, Boileau, Boo, Bucket, Captious, Carp, Castigate, Cavil, Censor(ious), → **CENSURE**, Climacteric, Clobber, Comment, Condemn, Connoisseur, Crab, Criticaster, → **CRUCIAL**, Crunch, Dangle, Decisive, Denigrate, Denounce, Deprecate, Desperate, Diatribe, Do down, Dutch uncle, Earful, Etain, Exacting, Excoriate, Fastidious, Fateful, Feuilleton, Flak, Flay, Fulminous, Gosse, Harrumph, Higher, Important, Impugn, Inge, Inveigh, Judge, Judgemental, Knife-edge, Knock(er), Lash, Leavis, Life and death, Literary, Masora(h), Mas(s)orete, Mordacious, Nag, Nasute, Nibble, Nice, Niggle, Overseer, Pan, Pater, Puff, Pundit, Quibble, Rap, Rebuke, Reprehend, Review(er), Rip, Roast, Ruskin,

Scalp, Scarify, Scathe, Scorn, Second guess, Serious, Severe, Shaw, Sideswipe,
Slag, Slam, Slashing, Slate, Sneer, Snipe, Stick, Stricture, Strop, Tense, Textual,
Thersitic, Threap, Touch and go, Ultracrepidate, Urgent, Vet, Vitriol, Vituperation,
Watershed, Zoilism

Croak Creak, Crow, Die, Grumble, Gutturalise

Croatian Cravates, Glagolitic, Serb

Crochet Lace, Weave

Crock Chorrie, Crate, Jar, Mug, Pig, Pitcher, Pot, Potshard, Potshare, Potsherd,
Stean(e)

Crockery Ceramics, China, Dishes, Earthenware, Oddment, Sunbeam, Ware

▷ **Crocks** *may indicate* an anagram

Crocodile Cayman, File, Flat dog, Garial, Gavial, Gharial, Gotcha lizard, Line, Mud
gecko, Mugger, River-dragon, Saltie, Saltwater, Sebek, Teleosaur(ian)

Crocus Autumn, Naked lady, Prairie, Saffron

Croesus Lydia

Croft Pightle

Cromwell Ironside, Lord Protector, Noll, Oliver, Protector, Richard, Roundhead

Crone(s) Beldam(e), Ewe, Graeae, Hag, Mawkin, Ribibe, Rudas, Sibyl, Sybil, Trot,
Trout, → **WITCH**

Crony Anile, Chum, Intimate, Mate, Pal, Sidekick

Crook(ed) Adunc, Ajee, Aslant, Asymmetric, Awry, Bad, Bend, Bow, Cam,
Camsheugh, Camsho(ch), Criminal, Cromb, Crome, Crosier, Crummack,
Crummock, Crump, Curve, Dishonest, Elbow, Fraud, Heister, Hook, Indirect,
Kam(me), Kebbie, Lituus, Malpractitioner, Operator, Shank, Shyster, Sick,
Skew(whiff), Slick(er), Squint, Staff, Swindler, Thraward, Thrawart, Thrawn,
Twister, Wonky, Yeggman

▷ **Crooked** *may indicate* an anagram

Croon(er), Crooning Bing, Como, Lament, Lull, Monody, Murmur, Sing

Crop(s), Cropped, Cropping Basset, Browse, Cash, Catch, Clip, Cover, Craw,
Cut, Distress, Dock, Emblements, Energy, Epilate, Eton, Foison, Forage, Harvest,
Hog, Ingluvies, Kharif, Ladino, Milo, Not(t), Plant, Poll, Produce, Rabi, Riding,
Rod, Root, Shingle, Silage, Standing, Stow, Strip, Subsistence, Succession, Top,
Truncate, White

Cropper Downfall, Header, Purler

Croquet (term) Peel, Rover, Wire

Croquette Kromesky, Quenelle, Rissole

Cross(ing), Crossbred Angry, Ankh, Ansate, Archiepiscopal, Banbury, Basta(a)rd,
Beefalo, Bestride, Bois-brule, Boton(n)e, Buddhist, Burden, Calvary, Cantankerous,
Canterbury, Capital, Cattalo, Celtic, Channel, Chi, Chiasm(a), Choleric, Cleche,
Clover-leaf, Compital, Constantine, Crosslet, Crosswalk, Crotchety, Crucifix, Crux,
Decussate, Demi-wolf, Dihybrid, Double, Dso(mo), Dzobo, Eleanor, Encolpion,
Faun, Fiery, Fitché, Fleury, Foil, Footbridge, Ford, Frabbit, Fractious, Frampold,
Franzy, Funnel, Fylfot, Geneva, George, Grade, Greek, Holy rood, Humette, Hybrid,
Ill, Imp, Indignant, Interbreed, Intersect, Intervein, Iona, Iracund, Irate, Irked, Iron,
Jerusalem, Jomo, Jumart, Kiss, Krest, Ladino, Latin, Level, Liger, Lorraine, Lurcher,
Maltese, Mameluco, Market, Mermaid, Military, Misfortune, Mix, Moline, Mongrel,
Mule, Narky, Nattery, Node, Norman, Northern, Nuisance, Oblique, Obverse,
Ordinary, Orthodox, Overpass, Overthwart, Papal, Patonce, Patriarchal, Pattée,
Pectoral, Pedestrian, Pelican, Plumcot, Plus, Pommé, Potence, Potent, Preaching,
Puffin, Quadrate, Railway, Ratty, Reciprocal, Red, Roman, Rood, Rose, Rosy,
Rouen, Rouge, Rubicon, Ruthwell, Sain, St Andrew's, St Anthony's, St George's, St

Patrick's, St Peter's, Saltier, Saltire, Sambo, Satyr, Shirty, Sign, Snappy, Southern, Splenetic, Strid, Svastika, Swastika, T, Tangelo, Tau, Tayberry, Ten, Testy, Thraw, Thwart, Tiglon, Tigon, Times, Toucan, Transit, Transom, Transverse, Traverse, Tree, Unknown, Urdé, Vexed, Vext, Victoria, → **VOTE**, Weeping, Whippet, Wry, X, Yakow, Zambo, Zebra(ss), Zebrinny, Zebroid, Zebrula, Zebrule, Zedonk, Z(h)o, Zobu

▷ **Cross** *may indicate* an anagram
▶ **Cross-bar** *see* **CROSSPIECE**
▶ **Crossbeam** *see* **CROSSPIECE**
Cross-bearer Crucifer
Cross-bill Metagnathous
Cross-bones Marrowbones
Cross-bow Arbalest, Bal(l)ista
Cross-country Langlauf, Overland
Cross-dressing Eonism
Cross-examine Grill, Interrogate, Question, Targe
Cross-eyed Skelly(-eyed), Squint
Crossfertilisation Allogamy, Heterosis, Hybrid vigour, Xenogamy
Cross-grained Ill-haired, Mashlam, Mashlim, Mas(h)lin, Mashlock, Mashlum, Stubborn
Crosspiece, Cross-bar, Cross-beam, Cross-timber Bar, Cancelli, Footrail, Inter-tie, Lierne, Phillipsite, Putlock, Putlog, Quillon, Serif, Seriph, Stempel, Stemple, Stretcher, Stull, Swingle-tree, Toggle, Transom, Trave, Whiffle-tree, Whipple-tree, Yoke
Crossroads Carfax, Carfox, Carrefour, Compital, Soap
Crossword Cryptic, Grid, Puzzle, Quickie
Crotchet(y) Eccentric, Fad, Fancy, Grouch, Kink, Quarter-note, Toy
Crouch Bend, Cringe, Falcade, Fancy, Lordosis, Ruck, Set, Squat, Squinch
Croup Angina, Cough, Kink, Rump
Crow Boast, Brag, Carrion, Chewet, Chough, Corbie, Corvus, Crake, Currawong, Daw, Flute-bird, Gorcrow, Hooded, Hoodie, Huia, Jackdaw, Jim(my), Murder, Piping, Raven, Rook, Saddleback, Scald, Skite, Squawk, Swagger, Vaunt
Crowbar Gavelock, James, Jemmy, Lever
Crowd(ed) Abound, Army, Bike, Boodle, Bumper, Bunch, Byke, Caboodle, Clutter, Concourse, Congest(ed), Cram, Crush, Crwth, Dedans, Doughnut, Drove, Fill, Flock, Galere, Gang, Gate, Gathering, Herd, Horde, → **HOST**, Huddle, Hustle, Jam, Lot, Meinie, Mein(e)y, Menyie, Mob, Mong, Multitude, Ochlo-, Pack, Pang, Populace, Press, Rabble, Raft, Ram, Ratpack, Ring, Ruck, Scrooge, Scrouge, Scrowdge, Scrum, Serr(é), Shoal, Shove, Slew, Slue, Squash, Squeeze, Stuff, Swarm, Swell, Three, Throng, Trinity, Varletry
Crowfoot Gilcup, Reate
Crown Acme, Bays, Bull, Camp, Cantle, Cap, Capernoity, Cidaris, Civic, Coma, Corona, Cr, Diadem, Ecu, Engarland, Enthrone, Fillet, Garland, Gloria, Haku, Head, Headdress, Instal, Iron, Ivy, Krantz, Laurel, Monarch, Mural, Naval, Nole, Noll, Noul(e), Nowl, Olive, Optical, Ore, Ovation, Pate, Peak, Pschent, Sconce, Stephen's, Taj, Thick'un, Tiara, → **TOP**, Triple, Triumphal, Trophy, Vallary, Vertex
Crucial Acute, Critical, Essential, Key, Pivotal, Quintessential, Vital, Watershed
Crucible Cruset, Melting-pot, Vessel
Crucifix(ion), Crucify Calvary, Cross, Golgotha, Mortify, Rood, Torment, Torture
Crude(ness) Bald, Brash, Brute, Coarse, Earthy, Halfbaked, Immature, Incondite, Primitive, Raunch, Raw, Rough, Rough and ready, Rough-hewn, Rough-wrought, Tutty, Uncouth, Vulgar, Yahoo

Cruel(ty) Barbarous, Bloody, Brutal, Dastardly, De Sade, Draconian, Fell, Fiendish, Flinty, Hard, Heartless, Immane, Inhuman, Machiavellian, Mental, Neronic, Pitiless, Raw, Remorseless, Sadistic, Stern, Tiger, Tormentor, Vicious

▷ **Cruel** *may indicate* an anagram

Cruet Ampulla, Condiments, Decanter

Cruise(r) Booze, Busk, Cabin, Nuke, Prowl, Rove, Sail, Ship, Tom, Travel, Trip, Voyager

Crumb(le), Crumbly, Crumbs Coo, Decay, Disintegrate, Ee, Fragment, Friable, Law, Leavings, Moulder, Mull, Murl, Nesh, Nirl, Ort, Panko, Particle, Ped, Raspings, Rot, Rotter

Crumpet Dish, Girl, Muffin, Nooky, Pash, Pikelet

Crumple Collapse, Crunkle, Crush, Raffle, Scrunch, Wrinkle

Crunch(y) Abdominal, Chew, Craunch, Crisp, Gnash, Graunch, Grind, Munch, Occlude, Scranch

Crusade(r) Baldwin, Campaign, Cause, Pilgrim, Tancred, Templar

Crush(ed), Crusher Acis, Anaconda, Annihilate, Bow, Champ, Comminute, Conquer, Contuse, Cranch, Crunch, Defeat, Destroy, Graunch, Grind, Hug, Jam, Knapper, Levigate, Mangle, Mash, Mill, Molar, Mortify, Oppress, Overcome, Overwhelm, Pash, Policeman, Pound, Press, Pulp, Pulverise, Quash, Quell, Ruin, Schwarmerei, Scotch, Scrum, Scrumple, Smash, Squabash, Squash, Squeeze, Squelch, Squish, Stamp, Stave, Steam-roll, Stove, Suppress, Telescope, Trample, Tread

Crust(y) Argol, Beeswing, Cake, Coating, Coffin, Continental, Cover, Crabby, Craton, Fur, Gratin, Heel, Horst, Kissing, Kraton, Lithosphere, Oceanic, Orogen, Osteocolla, Pie, Reh, Rind, Rine, Sal, Salband, Scab, Shell, Sial, Sima, Sinter, Sordes, Surly, Tartar, Teachie, Terrane, Tetchy, Upper, Wine-stone

Crustacea(n) Amphipod, Barnacle, Brachyuran, Branchiopoda, Camaron, Cirriped, Cirripede, Cirripid, Cladoceran, Copepod, Crab, Crayfish, Cumacean, Cyclops, Cyprid, Cypris, Daphnia, Decapod(a), Entomostraca, Euphausia, Fishlouse, Foot-jaw, Gribble, Isopod, Krill, Langoustine, Lobster, Macrura, Malacostracan, Marine borer, Maron, Nauplius, Ostracoda, Pagurian, Phyllopod, Prawn, Rhizocephalan, Sand-hopper, Sand-skipper, Scampi, Scampo, Schizopod, Sea slater, Shellfish, Shrimp, Slater, Squilla, Stomatopod, Woodlouse, Yabbie, Yabby

Crutch Morton's, Potent

Crux Essence, Nub

Cry(ing) Aha, Alalagmus, Alew, Banzai, Bark, Battle, Bawl, Bell, Bill, Blat, Bleat, Bleb, Blub(ber), Boo, Boohoo, Boom, Bray, Bump, Caramba, Caw, Cheer, Chevy, Chirm, Chivy, Clang, Crake, Croak, Crow, Dire, Euoi, Eureka, Evoe, Exclaim, Fall, Field-holler, Gardyloo, Gathering, Geronimo, Gowl, Greet, Halloo, Harambee, Haro, Harrow, Havoc, Heigh, Hemitrope, Herald, Hinny, Hoicks, Holler, Honk, Hoo, Hoop, Hosanna, Hout(s)-tout(s), Howl, Humph, Io, Kaw, Low, Mewl, Miaou, Miau(l), Miserere, Mourn, Night-shriek, O(c)hone, Oi, Olé, Ow, Pugh, Rabbito(h), Rallying, Rivo, Sab, Scape, Scream, Screech, Sell, Sese(y), Sessa, → **SHOUT**, Shriek, Slogan, Snivel, Snotter, Sob, Soho, Sola, Squall, Squawk, Street, Sursum corda, Tally-ho, Tantivy, Umph, Vagitus, View-halloo, Vivat, Vociferate, Wail, War, Watchword, Waterworks, Waul, Wawl, Weep, Westward ho, Whee(ple), Whimper, Whine, Whinny, Whoa, Whoop, Winge, Wolf, Yammer, Yelp, Yicker, Yikker, Yip, Yippee, Yodel, Yo-heave-ho, Yo-ho-ho, Yoick, Yoop, Yowl

Crypt(ic) Catacomb, Cavern, Chamber, Crowde, Encoded, Favissa, Grotto, Hidden, Obscure, Occult, Secret, Sepulchre, Short, Steganographic, Tomb, Unclear, Undercroft, Vault

Cryptaesthesia ESP
Cryptogam Acotyledon, Acrogen, Fern(-ally), Moss, Pteridophyte
Cryptographer Decoder, Ventris
Crystal(s), Crystal-gazer, Crystalline, Crystallise Allotriomorphic, Axinite, Baccara(t), Beryl, Candy, Citrine, Clathrate, Clear, Cleveite, Copperas, Coumarin, Cumarin, Dendrite, Druse, Effloresce, Elaterin, Enantiomorph, Epitaxy, Erionite, Fuchsin(e), Geode, Glass, Hemihedron, Hemimorphic, Hemitrope, Ice-stone, Ideal, Imazadole, Jarosite, Lead, Liquid, Lithium, Love-arrow, Macle, Macro-axis, Melamine, Mixed, Nicol, Orthogonal, Orthorhombic, Pellucid, Penninite, Pericline, Phenocryst, Piezo, Piezoelectric, Pinacoid, Pinakoid, Prism, Pseudomorph, Purin(e), Quartz, R(h)aphide, R(h)aphis, Rhinestone, Rock, Rotenone, Rubicelle, Scryer, Shoot, Skatole, Skryer, Smectic, Snowflake, Sorbitol, Spar, Spherulite, Spicule, Table, Tolan(e), Trichite, Trilling, Twin(ned), Wafer, Watch-glass, Xanthene, Xenocryst, Yag
Cub Baby, Kit, Novice, Pup, Whelp, Wolf
Cube, Cubic, Cubist Bath, Braque, Cu, Die, Magic, Necker, Nosean, Quadrate, Rubik's®, Serac, Smalto, Snub, Solid, Stere, Stock, Tesseract
Cubicle Alcove, Booth, Carrel(l), Stall
Cuckold Actaeon, Cornute, Graft, Homer, Lenocinium, Vulcan's badge, Wittol
Cuckoo Ament, Ani, April fool, Bird, Brain-fever bird, Gouk, Gowk, Inquiline, Insane, Koekoea, Koel, → **MAD**, Mental, Piet-my-vrou, Stupid
▷ **Cuckoo** *may indicate* an anagram
Cuckoopint Arum
Cucumber Bitter-apple, Choko, Colocynth, Coloquintida, Dill, Elaterium, Gherkin, Pickle, Sea-slug, Squirting, Trepang, Wolly
Cuddle Canoodle, Caress, Clinch, Embrace, Fondle, Hug, Nooky, Smooch, Smuggle, Snog, Snuggle
Cudgel Alpeen, Ballow, Bludgeon, Brain, Club, Cosh, Drub, Fustigate, Oaken towel, Plant, Rack, Rung, Shillelagh, Souple, Stick, Swipple, Tan, Towel, Truncheon
Cue Cannonade, Catchword, Feed, Feed-line, Half-butt, Hint, Mace, → **PROMPT**, Reminder, Rod, Sign, Signal, Wink
Cuff Box, Buffet, Clout, French, Iron, Muffettee, Rotator, Strike, Swat
Cuirass Armour, Corselet, Lorica
Cuisine Bourgeoise, Cookery, Food, Lean, Menu, Minceur, Nouvelle
Cul-de-sac Blind, Dead-end, Impasse, Loke
Cull Gather, Pick, Select, Thin, Weed
Culminate, Culmination Apogean, Apogee, Climax, Conclusion, Crest, End, Head
Culpable Blameworthy, Guilty
Cult Aum Shinrikyo, Cabiri, Candomble, Cargo, Creed, Fertility, Macumba, New Age, Personality, Rastafarian, Sect, Shango, Shinto, Snake, Voodoo, Wicca, Worship
Cultivate(d), Cultivation Agronomy, Arty, Civilise, Dig, Dress, Ear, Ere, Farm, Genteel, Grow, Hoe, Hydroponics, Improve, Labour, Pursue, Raise, Reclaim, Refine, Sative, Sophisticated, Tame, Tasteful, Till, Tilth
Culture(d), Cultural Acheulean, Acheulian, Agar, Art(y), Aurignacian, Azilian, Bel esprit, Brahmin, Canteen, Capsian, Civil(isation), Clactonian, Club, Compensation, Corporate, Enterprise, Ethnic, Experiment, Explant, Gel, Gravettian, Grecian, Halafian, Hallstatt, Hip-hop, Humanism, Kultur(kreis), La Tène, Learning, Levallois, Magdalenian, Maglemosean, Maglemosian, Meristem, Minoan, Mousterian, Organisational, Perigordian, Polish, Pure, Refinement, Solutrean, Sophisticated, Starter, Strepyan, Suspension, Tardenoisian, Tissue, Villanovan, Water

Cumbersome Clumsy, Heavy, Lumbering, → UNWIELDY
Cunctator Dilatory
Cuneiform Wedge(d)
Cunning Arch, Art, Artifice, Astute, Cautel, Craft(y), Deceit, Deep, Devious, Down, Finesse, Foxy, Insidious, Leery, Machiavellian, Quaint, Skill, Slee(kit), Sleight, Slim, Sly(boots), Smart, Sneaky, Subtle, Vulpine, Wile
Cup(s), Cupped Aecidium, America's, Beaker, Bledisloe, Calcutta, Calix, Calyculus, Cantharus, Chalice, Claret, Communion, Cotyle, Cruse, Cupule, Cyathus, Cylix, Davis, Demitasse, Deoch-an-doruis, Deuch-an-doris, Dish, Doch-an-dorach, Dop, Egg, European, FA, Fairs, Final, Fingan, Finjan, Fruit, Gemma, Glenoid, Goblet, Grace, Grease, Hanap, Horn, Kylix, Loving, Melbourne, Merry, Monstrance, Moustache, Mug, Noggin, Nut, Pannikin, Parting, Planchet, Plate, Poley, Posset, Pot, Procoelous, Quaff, Quaich, Quaigh, Rhyton, Rider, Ryder, Sangrado, Scyphus, Sippy, Stem, Stirrup, Tantalus, Tass(ie), Tastevin, Tazza, Tea-dish, Tig, Tot, → TROPHY, Tyg, UEFA, Volva, Waterloo, World
Cup-bearer Ganymede, Hebe
Cupboard Airing, Almery, Almirah, A(u)mbry, Beauf(f)et, Cabinet, Chiffonier, Chiff(o)robe, Closet, Coolgardie safe, Court, Credenza, Dresser, Fume, Livery, Locker, Meat-safe, Press, Walk-in
Cup-holder Hanaper, Hebe, Plinth, Saucer, Zarf, Zurf
Cupid Amoretto, Amorino, Archer, Blind, Cherub, Dan, Eros, Love, Putto
Cupola Belfry, Dome, Tholos
Cup-shaped Poculiform
Cur Dog, Messan, Mongrel, Mutt, Pi-dog, Scab, Scoundrel, Whelp, Wretch, Yap
Curare, Curari Ourali, Poison, Wourali
Curassow Crax
Curate Barman, Minister, Nathaniel, Padré, Perpetual, Priest
Curator Aquarist
Curb Bit, Brake, Bridle, Check, Clamp, Coaming, Dam, Edge, Puteal, Rein, Restrain, Rim, Snub, Well
Curd(s) Bean, Cheese, Junket, Lapper(ed)-milk, Lemon, Skyr, Tofu
Curdle Clot, Congeal, Earn, Erne, Lopper, Posset, Ren, Rennet, Run, Set, Sour, → TURN, Whig, Yearn
Cure(d), Curative Ameliorate, Amend, Antidote, Antirachitic, Bloater, Cold turkey, Dry-salt, Dun, Euphrasy, Fix, Ginseng, Heal, Hobday, Hydropathy, Jadeite, Jerk, Kipper, Laetrile, Medicinal, Nature, Nostrum, Panacea, Park-leaves, Prairie oyster, → PRESERVE, Reast, Recover, Recower, Reest, Re(i)st, Relief, Remede, Remedy, Restore, Salt, Salve, Serum, Smoke, Smoke-dry, Tan, → TREATMENT, Tutsan, Water
▷ **Cure** *may indicate* an anagram
Curfew Bell, Gate, Prohibit, Proscribe
Curie Ci
Curio, Curiosity, Curious Agog, Bibelot, Freak, Inquisitive, Into, Meddlesome, Nos(e)y, Objet d'art, Objet de vertu, Odd, Peculiar, Prurience, Rarity, Rum, → STRANGE, Wondering
▷ **Curious(ly)** *may indicate* an anagram
Curium Cm
Curl(s), Curler, Curling, Curly Bev, Bonspiel, Cirrus, Coil, Crimp, Crimple, Crinkle, Crisp, Crocket, Dildo, Earlock, Frisette, Friz(z), Frizzle, Heart-breaker, Hog, Inwick, Kiss, Leaf, Loop, Love-lock, Outwick, Perm, Pin, Quiff, Repenter, Ringlet, Roll, Roulette, Scroll, Shaving, Spiral, Spit, Tong, Trunk, Twiddle, → TWIST,

Ulotrichous, Undée, Wave, Wind
Curlew Bird, Whaup, Whimbrel
Curmudgeon Boor, Churl, Grouch, Route, Runt
Currant Berry, Flowering, Raisin, Rizard, Rizzar(t), Rizzer
Currency Cash, Circulation, → COIN, Coinage, Decimal, Euro, Finance, Fractional, Jiao, Kip, Koruna, Monetary, → MONEY, Prevalence, Reserve, Soft
▷ **Currency** *may indicate* a river
Current Abroad, AC, Actual, Alternating, Amp(ere), Amperage, California, Canary, Contemporaneous, Cromwell, Dark, DC, Direct, Draught, Drift, Dynamo, Ebbtide, Eddy, Electric, El Nino, Emission, Equatorial, Euripus, Existent, Flow, Foucault, Galvanic(al), Going, Gyre, Headstream, Humboldt, Hummock, I, Immediate, Inst, Intermittent, Japan, Kuroshio, Labrador, Maelstrom, Millrace, Modern, Newsy, North Atlantic, Now, Ongoing, Output, Peru, Present, Prevalent, Pulsating, Race, Rapid, Rife, Rip, Roost, Running, Stream, Thames, Thermal, Thermionic, Tide, Tideway, Topical, Torrent, Turbidity, Underset, Undertow, Updraught
Curriculum Core, Cursal, National, Programme
Curry Bhuna, Brush, Comb, Cuittle, Dhansak, Fawn, Groom, Ingratiate, Korma, Madras, Spice, Tan, Tandoori, Turmeric, Vindaloo
Curse Abuse, Anathema, Badmouth, Ban, Bane, Beshrew, → BLASPHEME, Blast, Chide, Dam(me), Damn, Dee, Drat, Ecod, Egad, Excommunicate, Execrate, Heck, Hex, Hoodoo, Imprecate, Jinx, Malgre, Malison, Maranatha, Mau(l)gré, Mockers, Moz(z), Mozzle, Nine (of diamonds), Oath, Paterson's, Pize, Plague, Rant, Rats, Scourge, 'Snails, Spell, Swear, Upbraid, Weary, Winze, Wo(e)
Cursive Estrang(h)elo, Run
Cursor Mouse, Turtle
Cursorily, Cursory Casual, Hasty, Lax, Obiter, Passing, Perfunctory, Sketchy, Speedy, Superficial
Curt Abrupt, Blunt, Crusty, Laconic, Offhand, Short, Snappy
Curtail(ment) Abate, Apocope, Crop, Cut, Reduce, Shorten
Curtain(s), Curtain raiser, Curtain-rod Air, Arras, Backdrop, Bamboo, Canopy, Casement, Caudle, Cloth, Cyclorama, Death, Demise, Drape, Drop, Dropcloth, Dropscene, Fatal, Hanging, Iron, Lever de rideau, Louvre, Net, Pall, Portière, Purdah, Safety, Scene, Screen, Scrim, Shower, Tab, Tableau, Tormentor, Tringle, Upholstery, Vail, Valance, Veil, Vitrage, Window
Curtsey Bob, Bow, Dip, Dop, Honour
Curve(d), Curvaceous, Curvature, Curving, Curvy Adiabatic, Aduncate, Anticlastic, Apophyge, Arc, Arch, Archivolt, Assurgent, Axoid, Bend, Bezier, Bight, Bow, Brachistochrone, Camber, Cardioid, Catacaustic, Catenary, Caustic, Characteristic, Chordee, Cissoid, Conchoid, Contrapposto, Crescent, Cycloid, Demand, Diacaustic, Dogleg, Entasis, Epicycloid, Epinastic, Epitrochoid, Ess, Evolute, Exponential, Extrados, Felloe, Felly, Folium, French, Gaussian, Geodesic, Gooseneck, Growth, Hance, Harmonogram, Helix, Hodograph, Hollow-back, Hook, Hyperbola, Hypocycloid, Inswing, Intrados, Isochor, J, Jordan, Kyphosis, Laffer, Learning, Lemniscate, Limacon, Liquidus, Lituus, Lordosis, Loxodrome, Normal, Nowy, Ogee, Parabola, Phillips, Pothook, Pott's disease, Pulvinate, Reclinate, Record, Rhumb, RIAA, Roach, Rondure, Rotundate, Scoliosis, Sheer, Sigmoid flexure, Sinuate, Sinusoid, Slice, Spiral, Spiric, Strophoid, Supply, Survival, Swayback, Synclastic, Tautochrone, Tie, Tractrix, Trajectory, Trochoid, Tumble-home, Twist, Undulose, U-turn, Volute, Witch (of Agnesi)
Cushion(s) Air, Allege, Bolster, Buffer, Bustle, Frog, Ham, Hassock, Kneeler, → PAD, Pillow, Pin, Pouf(fe), Pulvillus, Scatter, Soften, Squab, Upholster, Whoopee

Cusp Horn, Spinode, Tine

Custard (apple) Crème caramel, Flam(m), Flan, Flaune, Flawn, Flummery, Pastry, Pa(w)paw, Zabaglione

Custodian, Custody Care, Claviger, Guard, Hold, Janitor, Keeping, Protective, Sacrist, Steward, Trust, Ward

Custom(ised), Customs (officer), Customary Agriology, Coast-waiters, Consuetude, Conventional, Couvade, Dedicated, De règle, Dhamma, Dharma, Douane, Exciseman, Familiar, Fashion, Folklore, → **HABIT**, Land-waiter, Lore, Manner, Montem, Mores, Nomic, Octroi, Ordinary, Practice, Praxis, Relic, Rite, Routine, Rule, Sororate, Spanish, Sunna, Tax, Thew, Tidesman, Tide-waiter, Tikanga, Time-honoured, Tradition, Unwritten, Usance, Used, Usual, Won, Wont, Woon, Zollverein

Customer Client, Cove, Patron, Prospect, Purchaser, Shillaber, Shopper, Smooth, Stiff, Trade, Trick, Ugly

Cut(ter), Cutting Abate, Abjoint, Ablate, Abridge, Abscission, Abscond, Acute, Adeem, Adze, Aftermath, Ali Baba, Amputate, Apocope, Axe, Bang, Bisect, Bit, Bite, Bowdlerise, Boycott, Brilliant, Broach, Caesarean, Caique, Canal, Cantle, Caper, Carver, Castrate, Caustic, Censor, Chap, Cheese, Chisel, Chopper, Chynd, Circumscribe, Cleaver, Clinker-built, Clip, Colter, Commission, Concise, Coppice, Coulter, Coupé, Crew, Crop, Cruel, Cube, Culebra, Curtail, Deadhead, Decrease, Dedekind, Dicer, Die, Director's, Discide, Disengage, Dismember, Dissect, Division, Divorce, Dock, Dod, Edge, Edit, Emarginate, Embankment, Engraver, Entail, Entayle, Epistolary, Epitomise, Eschew, Estrepe, Excalibur, Excide, Excise, Exscind, Exsect, Exude, Fashion, Fell, Filet mignon, Fillet, Flench, Flense, Flinch, Form, Froe, Frow, Gaillard, Garb, Gash, Go-down, Grater, Graven, Gride, Gryde, Hack, Handsaw, Hew(er), Ignore, Incision, Incisor, Indent, Intersect, Jigsaw, Joint, Junk, Kerf, Kern, Kirn, Lacerate, Lance, Leat, Lesion, Lin, Lop, Math, Medaillon, Microtome, Milling, Minimise, Mohel, Mortice, Mortise, Mower, Nache, Nick, Not, Notch, Nott, Occlude, Omit, Open, Operate, Osteotome, Oxyacetylene, Padsaw, Pare, Pink, Plant, Pliers, Ploughshare, Poll, Pollard, Pone, Power, Precisive, Press, Proin, Quota, Race, Rake off, Rase, Razor, Reap, Rebate, Reduction, Re-enter, Resect, Retrench, Revenue, Ring, Ripsaw, Roach, Rose, Rout, Saddle, Sarcastic, Sarky, Saw(n), Scarf, Scathing, Scion, Scission, Scissor, Score, Scrap, Sculpt, Scye, Scythe, Secant, Secateurs, Sect, Section, Sever, Sey, Share(out), Shaver, Shears, Shingle, Ship, Shive, Shorn, Short, Shred, Shun, Sickle, Side, Sirloin, Skin, Skip, Slane, Slash, Slicer, Slip, Slit, Sloop, Sned, Snee, Snib, Snick, Snip, Snub, Spade, Speedy, Spin, Spud, Steak, Stencil, Stereotomy, Stir, Stramac, Stramazon, Strimmer®, Style, Surgeon, Swath(e), Tailor(ess), Tap, Tart, Tenderloin, Tenotomy, Tomial, Tomium, Tonsure, Tooth, Topside, Transect, Trash, Trench, Trenchant, Trepan, Trim, Truant, Truncate, Urchin, Whang, Whittle, Winey

▷ **Cut** *may indicate* an anagram

▷ **Cutback** *may indicate* a reversed word

Cute Ankle, Pert, Pretty, Taking

Cuticle Epidermis, Eponychium, Periplast, Pleuron, Skin

Cut in Interpose, Interrupt

Cutlass Machete, Sword

Cutlery Canteen, Flatware, Fork, Knife, Setting, Silver, Spoon, Sunbeam, Tableware, Trifid

Cutlet Schnitzel

Cut off Elide, Enisle, Estrange, Inisle, Insulate, Intercept, → **ISOLATE**, Lop, Prune

Cut-throat Razor, Ruinous

Cuttlebone, Cuttlefish Octopus, Pen, Polyp(e)s, Polypus, Sea-sleeve, Sepia, Sepiost(aire), Sepium, Squid
CV Biodata
Cyanide Acrylonitrile, Nitrile, Potassium, Prussiate
Cycad Coontie, Coonty
Cyclamen Sow-bread
Cycle, Cyclist, Cycling Anicca, Arthurian, Bike, Biorhythm, Business, Cal(l)ippic, Calvin, Carbon, Carnot, Cell, Circadian, Citric acid, Closed, Daisy, Diesel, Eon, Era, Fairy, Four-stroke, Freewheel, Frequency, Geological, Gigahertz, Heterogony, Hydrologic, Indiction, Keirin, Ko, Krebs, Life, Light-year, Lunar, Madison, Metonic, Moped, Nitrogen, Oestrus, Orb, Otto, Pedal, Peloton, Period, Product life, Rankine, Repulp, Revolution, Ride, Roadster, Rock, Rota, Round, Samsara, Saros, Scorch, Series, Sheng, Solar, Song, Sonnet, Sothic, Spin, Sunspot, TCA, Trade, Trick, Trike, Turn, UCI, Urea, Vicious, Water, Wheeler, Wheelman, Wu
Cyclone Cockeye(d) bob, Storm, Tornado, Typhoon, Willy-willy
Cyclops Arges, Arimasp(i), Brontes, Polyphemus, Steropes
Cylinder, Cylindrical Air, Clave, Column, Drum, Licker-in, Magic, Master, Pipe, Pitch, Roll, Rotor, Slave, Spool, Steal, Stele, Swift, Terete, Torose, Treadmill, Tube, Vascular
Cymbal(s) High-hat, Hi-hat, Zel
Cynic(al) Crab, Diogenes, Doubter, Hard-bitten, Hard-boiled, Menippus, Pessimist, Sardonic, Sceptic, Thersites, Timon
Cynosure Centre, Focus
Cynthia Artemis, Moon
Cypress Bald, Lawson's, Leyland(ii), Monterey, Retinospora, Swamp, Tree
Cypriot Enosis, Eoka
Cyst Atheroma, Bag, Blister, Chalazion, Dermoid, Hydatid, Impost(h)ume, Meibomian, Ranula, Sac, Sebaceous, Vesicle, Wen
Czechoslovakia(n) CZ, Moravian, Sudetenland

Dd

D Daughter, Delta, Died, Edh, Eth, Penny

Dab(s) Bit, Daub, Fish, Flounder, Pat, Print, Ringer, Smear, Spot, Stupe, Whorl

Dabble(r) Amateur, Clatch, Dally, Dilettante, Plouter, Plowter, Potter, Smatter, Splash, Stipple, Trifle

Dachshund Teckel

Dactyl Anapaest

Dad(dy) Blow, Dev(v)el, Father, Generator, Hit, Male, Pa(pa), Pater, Polt, Pop, Slam, Sugar, Thump

Daddy-longlegs Crane-fly, Jennyspinner, Leather-jacket, Spinning-jenny, Tipula

Daffodil Asphodel, Jonquil, Lent-lily, Narcissus

Daft Absurd, Crazy, Potty, Ridiculous, Silly, Simple, Stupid

Dag Jag, Pierce, Pistol, Prick, Stab, Tag, Wool

Dagger(s) An(e)lace, Ataghan, Baselard, Bayonet, Bodkin, Crease, Creese, Da(h), Diesis, Dirk, Double, Dudgeon, Han(d)jar, Hanger, Jambiya(h), Katar, Khanjar, Kindjahl, Kirpan, Kreese, Kris, Lath, Misericord(e), Obelisk, Obelus, Poi(g)nado, Poniard, Pugio, Puncheon, Pusser's, Quillon, Rondel, Sgian-dubh, Skean, Skene(-occle), Spanish, Stiletto, Swordbreaker, Whiniard, Whinyard, W(h)inger, Yatag(h)an

Dahlia Cosmea

Daily Adays, Char, Circadian, Cleaner, Diurnal, Domestic, Guardian, Help, Journal, Mail, Mirror, Mrs Mopp, Paper, Per diem, Quotidian, Rag, Regular, Scotsman, Sun, Tabloid

Dainty Cate(s), Cute, Delicacy, Elegant, Elfin, Entremesse, Entremets, Exquisite, Genty, Junket, Lickerish, Liquorish, Mignon(ne), Minikin, → **MORSEL**, Neat, Nice, Particular, Petite, Pussy, Sunket, Twee

Dairy Creamery, Loan, Parlour

Dairymaid Dey, Patience

Dais Estate, Machan, Platform, Podium, Pulpit, Stage, Tribune

Daisy African, Barberton, Bell, Felicia, Gerbera, Gowan, Hen and chickens, Livingstone, Marguerite, Marigold, Michaelmas, Moon, Ox-eye, Ragweed, Shasta, Transvaal, Vegetable sheep

Dale(s) Dell, Dene, Dingle, Glen, Nidder, Ribbles, Swale, Vale, Valley, Wensley, Wharfe, Yorkshire

Dally Coquet(te), Dawdle, Finger, Flirt, Play, Spoon, Sport, Toy, Trifle, Wait

Dam An(n)icut, Arch, Aswan, Aswan High, Bar, Barrage, Barrier, Block, Boulder, Bund, Cabora Bassa, Cauld, Check, Gravity, Hoover, Kariba, Kielder, Ma, Mangla, Mater, Obstacle, Obstruct, Pen, Sennar, Stank, → **STEM**, Sudd, Tank, Three Gorges, Turkey nest, Volta River, Weir, Yangtze

Damage(d), Damages, Damaging Appair, Bane, Banjax, Bruise, Buckle, Charge, Chip, Collateral, Contuse, Cost, Cripple, Dent, Desecrate, Detriment, Devastate, Devastavit, Distress, Estrepe, Exemplary, Fault, Flea-bite, Foobar, Fubar,

Fuck up, Harm, Havoc, Hedonic, Hit, Hole, Hurt, Impair, Injury, Insidious, Loss, Mar, Mayhem, Moth-eaten, Mutilate, Nobble, Opgefok, Pair(e), Prang, Price, Punitive, Ratten, Ravage, Retree, Sabotage, Scaith, Scath(e), Scotch, Scratch, Skaith, Smirch, Solatium, → **SPOIL**, Tangle, Tear, Tigger, Toll, Value, Vandalise, Violate, Wear and tear, Wing, Wound, Wreak, Wreck, Write off

▷ **Damage(d)** *may indicate* an anagram

Dambuster Ondatra

Dame Crone, Dowager, Edna, Gammer, Lady, Matron, Nature, Naunt, Partlet, Peacherino, Sis, Title(d), Trot, Woman

Damn(ation), Damned Accurst, Attack, Blame, Condemn, Curse, Cuss, D, Darn, Dee, Execrate, Faust, Hell, Hoot, Jigger, Malgre, Perdition, Predoom, Sink, Swear, Tarnal, Tarnation, Tinker's, Very

Damp(en), Damping Aslake, Black, Blight, Check, Clam(my), Dank, Dewy, Fousty, Fusty, Humid, Moist, Muggy, Raw, Rheumy, Rising, Roric, Soggy, Sordo, Sultry, Unaired, Viscous, → **WET**, White

Damper Barrier, Check, Dashpot, Killjoy, Mute, Sordino, Sourdine

Damsel Girl, Lass, Maiden, Wench

Damson Plumdamas

Dan Box, Cupid, Leno, Olivetan, Scuttle, Tribe

Dance(r), Dancing Astaire, Baladin(e), Ballabile, Ballant, Ballerina, Ballroom, Bayadère, Bob, Body-popping, Caper, Chorus-girl, Cinderella, Comprimario, Contredanse, Corybant, Coryphee, Dervish, Diaghilev, Dinner, Dolin, Exotic, Figurant, Foot, Gandy, Gigolo, Hetaera, Hetaira, Hoofer, Kick-up, Knees-up, Leap, Maenad, Modern, Nautch-girl, Night, Nijinsky, Nod, Nureyev, Oberek, Old-time, Partner, Pavlova, Petipa, Pierette, Prom(enade), Raver, Ring, St Vitus, Salome, Saltatorious, Skipper, Spot, Spring, Step, Strut, Table, Tea, Terpsichore, Thé dansant, Tread, Trip(pant), Vogue(ing), Whirl

---

DANCES

3 letters:	Clog	Polo	Conga
Bop	Dump	Rain	Disco
Fan	Fado	Reel	Fling
Gig	Folk	Rope	Furry
Hay	Frug	Sand	Galop
Hey	Giga	Shag	Ghost
Hop	Go-go	Slam	Gigue
Ice	Haka	Spin	Glide
Jig	Hora	Stag	Gopak
Lap	Hula	Taxi	Horah
Pas	Jive	Wire	Limbo
Poi	Jota		Loure
Sun	Juba	5 letters:	Mambo
Tap	Juke	Bamba	Mooch
Toe	Kolo	B and S	Natch
War	Line	Belly	Paspy
	Lion	Bogle	Pavan
4 letters:	Loup	Brawl	Paven
Alma	Mosh	Break	Pavin
Ball	Nach	Carol	Polka
Barn	Pogo	Ceroc®	Ragga

Robot
Round
Rueda
Rumba
Salsa
Samba
Shake
Skank
Skirt
Snake
Stomp
Sword
Tango
Torch
Truck
Twist
Valse
Volta
Waltz

6 letters:
Almain
Apache
Ballet
Bolero
Boogie
Boston
Branle
Bubble
Canary
Can-can
Cha-cha
Fading
Floral
German
Hustle
Jump-up
Kathak
Lavolt
Maxixe
Minuet
Morris
Pavane
Redowa
Shimmy
Smooch
Square
Trophe
Valeta
Veleta
Waggle

7 letters:
Bambuca
Beguine
Bourrée
Bransle
Brantle
Cantico
Capuera
Carioca
Coranto
Cossack
Country
Courant
Csardas
Farruca
Forlana
Foxtrot
Furlana
Gavotte
Halling
Hoe-down
Lambada
Lancers
Landler
Lavolta
Macabre
Mazurka
Measure
Moresco
Morisco
Morrice
Moshing
One-step
Pericon
Planxty
Polacca
Pyrrhic
Ridotto
Ringlet
Romaika
Roundel
Roundle
Routine
Sardana
Sashaya
Shuffle
Tanagra
Tordion
Toyi-toy
Trenise
Two-step

Ziganka

8 letters:
Alegrias
Boogaloo
Bunnyhop
Bunnyhug
Cachucha
Cakewalk
Canticoy
Capoeira
Chaconne
Cotillon
Courante
Egg-dance
Excuse-me
Fandango
Flamenco
Flip-flop
Galliard
Habanera
Hay-de-guy
Haymaker
Headbang
Hey-de-guy
Heythrop
Hoolican
Hornpipe
Hula-hula
Irish jig
Joncanoe
Junkanoo
Kantikoy
Kapa haka
Kazachok
Kazatzka
Lindy hop
Macarena
Marinera
Matachin
Medicine
Merengue
Murciana
Orchesis
Reindeer
Rigadoon
Robotics
Ronggeng
Saraband
Snowball
Soft-shoe

Taglioni
Trucking

9 letters:
Allemande
Bergamask
Bergomask
Bossanova
Caballero
Cha-cha-cha
Chipaneca
Cotillion
Ecossaise
Eightsome
Farandole
Formation
Gallopade
Hoolachan
Jitterbug
Kathakali
Malaguena
Pas de deux
Paso doble
Passepied
Paul Jones
Polonaise
Poussette
Quadrille
Quickstep
Ring-shout
Roundelay
Siciliana
Siciliano
Sink-a-pace
Tambourin
Tripudium
Variation
Zapateado

10 letters:
Antimasque
Breakdance
Carmagnole
Charleston
Cinderella
Cinque-pace
Corroboree
Gay Gordon's
Hay-de-guise
Hay-de-guyes
Hey-de-guise

Hey-de-guyes
Hokey-cokey
Passamezzo
Petronella
Rug-cutting
Saltarello
Seguidilla
Sicilienne
Sinke-a-pace
Strathspey
Tarantella
Tripudiate
Turkey trot
Tyrolienne

Walk-around

11 letters:
Antistrophe
Black bottom
Buck and wing
Cracovienne
Eurhythmics
Lambeth walk
Palais glide
Passacaglia
Pastourelle
Progressive
Schottische

Shimmy-shake
Varsovienne

12 letters:
Bharat Natyam
Labanotation
Passemeasure
Passy-measure
Virginia reel

13 letters:
Highland fling
Virginian reel

14 letters:
Divertissement
Jack-in-the-green

15 letters:
Soft shoe shuffle

16 letters:
Circassian circle

18 letters:
Sir Roger de
  Coverley

Dance hall Disco, Palais
Dance movement Arabesque, Balancé, Battement, Batterie, Brisé, Chassé,
  Dos-à-dos, Dosido, Entrechat, Fishtail, Fouetté, Glissade, Jeté, Lassu, Pantalon,
  Pas de basque, Pas de chat, Pas seul, Pigeonwing, Pirouette, Plié, Poule, Poussette,
  Routine, Sauté, Step
Dance tune Toy
▷ **Dancing** *may indicate* an anagram
Dancing party Ball, Ridotto
Dandelion Kok-saghyz, Piss-a-bed, Scorzonera, Taraxacum
Dander Anger, Gee, Passion, Saunter, Temper
Dandle Dance, Doodle, Fondle, Pet
Dandruff Furfur, Scurf
Dandy Adonis, Beau, Blood, Boulevardier, Buck(een), Cat, Coxcomb, Dapper,
  → **DUDE**, Exquisite, Fantastico, Fop, Gem, Jay, Jessamy, Johnny, Kiddy, Knut,
  Lair, Macaroni, Masher, Modist, Monarcho, Muscadin, Nash, Nut, Posh, Puss
  -gentleman, Roy, Smart, Spark, Spiff, Swell, Ted, Toff, U, Yankee-doodle
Dandy-horse Draisene, Draisine
Dane(s) Clemence, Dansker, Ogier, Ostmen
Danger(ous) Apperil, Breakneck, Chancy, Crisis, Dic(e)y, Dire, Dodgy, Emprise,
  Fear, Hairy, Hazard, Hearie, High-risk, Hot, Insecure, Jeopardy, Lethal, Menace,
  Mine, Nettle, Nocuous, Objective, Parlous, Periculous, → **PERIL**, Pitfall, Plight,
  Precarious, Quicksand, Risk, Serious, Severe, Snag, Snare, Tight, Tight spot, Trap,
  Wonchancy
Dangle A(i)glet, Aiguillette, Critic, Flourish, Hang, Loll, Swing
Daniel Dan, Defoe, Deronda, Lion-tamer, Portia, Quilp
Dank Clammy, Damp, Humid, Moist, Wet, Wormy
Daphne Agalloch, Agila, Eaglewood, Lace-bark, Laura, Laurel, Mezereon
Dapper Dressy, Natty, Neat, Smart, Spiff, Spruce, Sprush, Spry, → **TRIM**
Darbies Cuffs, Irons, Snaps
Dare, Dare-devil, Daring Adventure, Audacious, Bold, Brave, Challenge, Courage,
  Dan, Da(u)nton, Defy, Durst, Emprise, Face, Gallant, Gallus, Hardihood, Hazard,
  Hen, Intrepid, Moxie, Neck, Prowess, Racy, Stuntman, Swashbuckler, Taunt,
  Venture
Dark(en), Darkie, Darkness Aphelia, Aphotic, Apophis, Black, Blind, Byronic,
  Cimmerian, Cloud, Colly, Depth, Dim, Dingy, Dirk(e), Dusky, Eclipse, Erebus, Evil,
  Gloom, Glum, Inky, Inumbrate, Jet, Kieran, Mare, Maria, Melanous, Mulatto,

Murk(y), Negro, Night, Obfuscate, Obscure, Ominous, Ousel, Ouzel, Pall, Phaeic, Pitch-black, Pit-mirk, Rooky, Sable, Sad, Secret, Shades, Shady, Shuttered, Sinister, Solein, Sombre, Sooty, Sphacelate, Stygian, Sullen, Swarthy, Tar, Tenebr(i)ous, Tenebrose, Unfair, Unlit, Wog, Woosel, Yellowboy, Yellowgirl

Darling Acushla, Alannah, Asthore, Beloved, Charlie, Cher, Chéri(e), Chick-a-biddy, Chick-a-diddle, Chuck-a-diddle, Dear, Dilling, Do(a)ting-piece, Duck(s), Favourite, Grace, Honey, Idol, Jarta, Jo(e), Lal, Love, Luv, Mavourneen, Mavournin, Minikin, Minion, Oarswoman, Own, Peat, Pet, Poppet, Precious, Sugar, Sweetheart, Yarta, Yarto

Darn Begorra, Blow, Doggone, Hang, Mend, Repair, Sew

Dart(s), Darter Abaris, Arrow, Banderilla, Dace, Dash, Deadener, Dodge, Fleat, Fléchette, Flirt, Flit, Harpoon, Javelin, Launch, Leap, Scoot, Shanghai, Skrim, Speck, Spiculum, Sprint, Strike, Thrust, Wheech

Dash(ing), Dashed Backhander, Bally, Blade, Blight, Blow, Buck, Charge, Collide, Cut, Dad, Dah, Damn, Dapper, Dart(le), Daud, Dawd, Debonair, Ding, Dod, Elan, En, Fa(s)cia, Flair, Fly, Go-ahead, Hang, Hurl, → **HURRY**, Hustle, Hyphen, Impetuous, Jabble, Jaw, Jigger, Lace, Line, Minus, Modicum, Morse, Natty, Nip, Panache, Pebble, Race, Rakish, Ramp, Rash, Rule, Run, Rush, Sally, Scamp(er), Scapa, Scarper, Scart, Scoot, Scrattle, Scurry, Scuttle, Shatter, Showy, Soupçon, Souse, Spang, Speed, Splash, Splatter, Sprint, Strack, Streak, Stroke, → **STYLE**, Swung, Throw, Touch, Viretot

Dashboard Fascia

Dashwood Hell-fire club

Dastard(ly) Base, Coward, Craven, Nid(d)erling, Poltroon

Data(base), Datum Archie, Cyberspace, Donne(e), Evidence, Facts, Fiche, File, Floating-point, Gen, HOLMES, Info, Input, Material, Matrix, Newlyn, News, Ordnance, Read-out, Soft copy, Triple

Date(d), Dates, Dating AD, Age, AH, Almanac, Appointment, Blind, Boyfriend, Calendar, Carbon, Carbon-14, Computer, Court, Deadline, Engagement, Epoch, Equinox, Era, Escort, Exergue, Expiry, Fission-track, Fixture, Girlfriend, Ides, Julian, Meet, Outmoded, → **OUT OF DATE**, Passé, Past, Radioactive, Radio-carbon, Radiometric, Rubidium-strontium, See, System, → **TRYST**, Ult(imo), Value

Daub Begrime, Blob, Dab, Gaum, Mess, Moil, Noint, Plaister, Plaster, → **SMEAR**, Smudge, Splodge, Teer, Wattle

Daughter (in law) Child, D, Elect, Girl, Jephthah's, Niece, Offspring, Skevington's

Daunt Adaw, Amate, Awe, Deter, Dishearten, Intimidate, Overawe, Quail, Stun, Stupefy, Subdue

Dauphin Delphin

David Dai, Psalmist

Davit Crane, Derrick, Hoist

Davy Crockett, Jones

Daw Bird, Magpie, Margery

Dawdle(r) Dally, Draggle, Drawl, Idle, Lag(gard), → **LOITER**, Potter, Shirk, Slowcoach, Tarry, Troke, Truck

Dawn(ing) Aurora, Cockcrow, Daw, Daybreak, Daylight, Day-peep, Dayspring, Enlightenment, Eoan, Eos, False, Light, Morrow, Occur, Prime, Roxane, Sparrowfart, Start, Sunrise, Ushas

Day(s) Account, Ahemeral, All Fools', All Hallows', All Saints', All Souls', Anniversary, Annunciation, Anzac, April Fool's, Armistice, Ascension, Australia, Bad hair, Baker, Banian, Barnaby, Bastille, Borrowing, Boxing, Broad, Calendar, Calends, Calpa, Canada, Canicular, Civil, Columbus, Commonwealth, Contango,

Continental, D, Daft, Date, Decoration, Degree, Distaff, Dog, Dominion, Double, Duvet, Early, Ember, Empire, Epact, Fast, Fasti, Father's, Feast, Ferial, Field, Flag, Fri, Gang, Gaudy, Groundhog, Guy Fawkes', Halcyon, High, Hogmanay, Holy, Holy Innocents', Holy-rood, Hundred, Ides, Inauguration, Independence, Intercalary, Judgment, Juridical, Kalends, Kalpa, Labo(u)r, Lady, Laetare, Lammas, Last, Law(ful), Lay, Leap, Mardi, Market, May, Memorial, Michaelmas, Midsummer, Mon, Morrow, Mother's, Muck-up, Mufti, Mumping, Name, Ne'erday, New Year's, Nones, Nychthemeron, Oak-apple, Octave, Open, Orangeman's, Pancake, Paper, Pay, Poppy, Post, Pound, Present, Press(ed), Primrose, Pulvering, Quarter, Rag, Rainy, Red-letter, Remembrance, Rent, Rest, Robin, Rock, Rogation, Rood(-mas), Rosh Chodesh, Sabbath, Saint's, St Swithin's, St Thomas's, St Valentine's, Salad, Sat, Scambling, Settling, Shick-shack, Show, Sidereal, Snow, Solar, Solstice, Speech, Sports, Station, Sun, Supply, Tag, Term, Thanksgiving, Thurs, Ticket, Time, Transfer, Trial, Triduum, Tues, Twelfth, Utas, Valentine's, Varnishing, VE, Veterans', Victoria, Visiting, VJ, Waitangi, Wed, Wedding, Working

Daybreak Cockcrow, Cockleert

Daydream(er), Daydreaming Brown study, Castle(s) in the air, Dwam, Dwaum, Fancy, Imagine, Muse, Reverie, Rêveur, Walter Mitty, Woolgathering

Daylight Artificial, Dawn, Space, Sun

Daze(d) Amaze, Bemuse, Confuse, Dwaal, Gally, Muddle, Muzzy, Petrify, Punch drunk, Reeling, Spaced out, → STUN, Stupefy, Stupor, Trance

Dazzle(d), Dazzling Bewilder, Blend, Blind, Eclipse, Foudroyant, Glare, Meteoric, Outshine, Radiance, Resplendent, Splendour, Yblent

Deacon Cleric, Doctor, Minister

Deactivate Unarm

Dead(en) Abrupt, Accurate, Alamort, Asgard, Asleep, Blunt, Brown bread, Bung, Cert, Cold, Complete, D, Deceased, Defunct, Doggo, Expired, Extinct, Gone(r), Inert, Infarct, Late, Lifeless, Morkin, Muffle, Mute, Napoo, Niflheim, Numb, Obsolete, Obtund, Ringer, She'ol, Slain, Smother, Stillborn, True, Utter, Waned

Dead end, Deadlock Blind alley, Cut-off, Dilemma, Impasse, Logjam, Stalemate, Stoppage

Dead-leaf colour Filemot, Philamot, Philomot

Deadline Date, Epitaph, Limit

Deadlock Stand-off, Sticking-point

Deadly Baleful, Dull, Fell, Funest, Internecine, → LETHAL, Malign, Mortal, Mortific, Pestilent, Thanatoid, Unerring, Venomous

Deadly nightshade Belladonna, Dwale

Deadpan Expressionless

Dead reckoning Dr

Dead tree Rampick, Rampike

Deaf(en), Deafness Adder, Asonia, Deave, Deeve, Dunny, Heedless, Paracusis, Presbyc(o)usis, Surd(ity)

Deal(er), Dealing(s), Deal with Address, Agent, Agreement, Allot(ment), Arb, Arbitrageur, Bargain, Breadhead, Brinjarry, Broker, Business, Cambist, Chandler, Chapman, Commerce, Cope, Coup, Cover, Croupier, Dispense, Distributor, Do, Dole, Eggler, Exchange, Fripper, Goulash, Hand(le), Help, Inflict, Insider, Interbroker, Jiggery-pokery, Jobber, Lashing, Lay on, Lay out, Lot, Manage, Mercer, Merchant, Mickle, Middleman, Monger, Mort, Negotiate, New, Operator, Package, Pine, Plain, Productivity, Pusher, Raft, Raw, Red, Sale, Serve, Side, Sort, Spicer, Square, Stockist, Stockjobber, Takeover, Tape, Timber, Totter, Tout(er), → TRADE, Traffic, Transaction, Treat, Truck, Wheeler, White, Wholesaler,

Wield, Woolstapler, Yardie

Dean Acheson, Arabin, Colet, Decani, Doyen, Forest, Head, Inge, Nellie, Provost, RD, Rural, Rusk, Slade, Spooner, Swift, Vale, Vicar-forane, V rev

Dear(er), Dearest, Dear me Ay, Bach, Beloved, Cara, Caro, Cher(e), Cherie, Chou, Chuckie, Darling, Duck(s), Expensive, High, Honey(bun), Lamb, Leve, Lief, Lieve, Loor, Love, Machree, Mouse, My, Pet, Pigsney, Pigsnie, Pigsny, Steep, Sweet, Sweetie, Toots(ie), Up

Dearth Famine, Lack, Paucity, Scantity, Scarcity, → SHORTAGE

Deaspiration Psilosis

Death(ly) Auto-da-fe, Bane, Bargaist, Barg(h)est, Biolysis, Black, Cataplexis, Charnel, Clinical, Cot, Curtains, Cypress, Demise, Departure, Dormition, End, Eschatology, Euthanasia, Exit, Extinction, Fatality, Funeral, Fusillation, Gangrene, Grim Reaper, Hallal, Heat, Infarction, Jordan, Karoshi, Lead colic, Lethee, Leveller, Living, Loss, Mors, Napoo, Necrosis, Nemesis, Night, Obit, Quietus, Reaper, Sati, Sergeant, SIDS, Small-back, Strae, Sudden, Suttee, Terminal, Thanatism, Thanatology, Thanatopsis, Thanatos

Death-flood Styx

Deathless(ness) Athanasy, Eternal, Eterne, Immortal, Struldberg, Timeless, Undying

Debacle Cataclysm, Collapse, Disaster, Fiasco

Debag Dack

Debar Deny, Exclude, Forbid, → PREVENT, Prohibit

Debase(d) Adulterate, Allay, Bemean, Cheapen, Corrupt, Demean, Depreciate, Dialectician, Dirty, Grotesque, Hedge, Lower, Pervert, Traduce, Vitiate

Debate Argue, Combat, Contention, Contest, Deliberate, Dialectic, Discept, Discourse, Discuss(ion), → DISPUTE, Flyte, Forensics, Full-dress, Moot, Paving, Polemics, Powwow, Reason, Teach-in, Warsle, Wrangle, Wrestle

Debauch(ed), Debauchee, Debauchery Corrupt, Decadent, Defile, Degenerate, Dissipate, Dissolute, Heliogabalus, Libertine, Licence, Orgy, Profligate, Raddled, Rake-hell, Riot, Roist, Royst, Seduce, Spree, Stuprate, Wet, Whore

Debenture Bond, Security

Debilitate(d), Debility Asthenia, Atonic, Cachexia, Feeble, Languid, Weak

Debit Charge, Debt, Direct

Debonair Cavalier, Gay, Gracious, Jaunty

Debris Bahada, Bajada, Detritus, Eluvium, Moraine, Moslings, Refuse, → RUBBLE, Ruins, Shrapnel, Tel, Tephra, Waste, Wreckage

▷ **Debris** *may indicate* an anagram

Debt(or) Abbey-laird, Alsatia, Arrears, Arrestee, Bonded, Dr, Due, Floating, Funded, Insolvent, IOU, Liability, Moratoria, National, Obligation, Oxygen, Poultice, Public, Queer Street, Score, Subordinated, Tie, Unfunded

Debt-collector Bailiff, Forfaiter, Remembrancer

Debut Launch, Opening, Outset, Presentation

Debutante Bud, Deb

Decade Rosary, Ten

Decadence, Decadent Babylonian, Decaying, Degeneration, Dissolute, Effete, Fin-de-siècle, Libertine

Decamp Abscond, Absquatulate, Bolt, Bunk, Depart, Flee, Guy, Levant, Mizzle, Slide, Slope, Vamoose

Decant Pour, Unload

Decapitate, Decapitation Aphesis, → BEHEAD, Guillotine

▷ **Decapitated** *may indicate* first letter removed

Decay(ed), Decaying Alpha, Appair, Beta, Biodegrade, Blet, Canker, Caries, Caseation, Consenescence, Crumble, Decadent, Declension, Decline, Decompose, Decrepit, Dieback, Disintegrate, Dissolution, Doat, Doddard, Doddered, Dote, Dricksie, Druxy, Dry rot, Fail, F(o)etid, Forfair, Gangrene, Heart-rot, Impair, Moulder, Pair(e), Perish, Plaque, Putrefy, Radioactive, Ret, Rot, Saprogenic, Sap-rot, Seedy, Sepsis, Spoil, Tabes, Thoron, Wet-rot

Decease(d) Death, Decedent, Demise, Die, Stiff

Deceit(ful), Deceive(r) Abuse, Artifice, Bamboozle, Barrat, Befool, Bitten, Blind, Bluff, Braide, → **CHEAT**, Chicane, Chouse, Con, Cozen, Cuckold, Defraud, Deke (out), Delude, Diddle, Dissemble, Do brown, Double-cross, Double-tongued, Dupe, Duplicity, False(r), Fastie, Fast-talk, Fiddle, Flam, Fool, Four-flusher, Fox, Fraud, Gag, Gerrymander, Gloze, Guile, Gull, Hoax, Hoodwink, Hornswoggle, Humbug, Hype, Illusion, Imposition, Inveigle, Invention, Jiggery-pokery, Kid, Liar, Malengine, Mamaguy, Mata Hari, Mendacious, Mislead, Mislippen, Phenakism, Poop, Poupe, Pretence, Prevaricate, Punic, Rig, Ruse, Sell, Sham, Sinon, Sleekit, Snow job, Spruce, Stratagem, Subreption, Swindle, Swizzle, Tregetour, Trick, Trump, Two-faced, Two-time, Weasel, Wile

Decency, Decent Chaste, Decorum, Fitting, Healsome, Honest, Kind, Modest, Moral, Passable, Seemly, Sporting, Wholesome

Decentralise Disperse

Deception, Deceptive Artifice, Bluff, Catchpenny, Catchy, Cheat, Chicanery, Codology, → **DECEIT**, Disguise, Dupe, Duplicity, Eyewash, Fallacious, False, Flam, Fraud, Gag, Gammon, Guile, Gullery, Have-on, Hocus-pocus, Hokey-pokey, Hum, Hunt-the-gowks, Hype, Ignes-fatui, Ignis-fatuus, Illusion, Insidious, Kidology, Lie, Moodies, Phantasmal, Runaround, Ruse, Sell, Sleight, Smoke and mirrors, Specious, Sting, The moodies, → **TRICK**, Trompe l'oeil, Two-timing, Underhand

Decide(r), Decided, Decision, Decisive Addeem, Adjudge, Agree, A(r)re(e)de, Ballot, Barrage, Bottom-line, Cast, Clinch, Conclude, Conclusive, → **DECISION**, Deem, Definite, Determine, Distinct, Engrenage, Firm, Fix, Jump-off, Mediate, Opt, Parti, Predestination, Pronounced, Rescript, → **RESOLVE**, Result, Rule, Run-off, See, Settle, Split, Sudden death, Tiebreaker, Try

Decimal Mantissa, Recurring, Repeating, Terminating

Decimate Destroy, Lessen, Weaken

Decipher(ing) Cryptanalysis, Decode, Decrypt, Descramble, Discover, Interpret

▷ **Decipher(ed)** *may indicate* an 'o' removed

Decision Arbitrium, Arrêt, Crossroads, Crunch, Decree, Engrenage, Fatwa, Fetwa, Firman, Judg(e)ment, Placit(um), Referendum, Resolution, Resolve, Responsa, Ruling, Sentence, Sudden death, Verdict

Decisive Climactic, Clincher, Critical, Crux, Definite, Final, Pivotal

Deck Adorn, Array, Attrap, Bejewel, Boat, Cards, Clad, Daiker, Daub, Decorate, Dizen, Embellish, Equip, Flight, Focsle, Forecastle, Garland, Hang, Helideck, Hurricane, Lower, Main, Mess, Monkey poop, Orlop, Ornament, Pack, Pedestrian, Platform, Poop, Prim, Promenade, Quarter, Saloon, Spar, Sun, Tape, Upper, Void, Well

Declare, Declaration, Declaim, Decree Absolute, Affidavit, Affirm, Air, Allege, Announce, Annunciate, Aread, A(r)re(e)de, Assert, Asseverate, Aver, Avow, Balfour, Bann(s), Bayyan, Breda, Dictum, Diktat, Doom, Edict, Elocute, Enact, Fatwa(h), Fiat, Firman, Go, Grace, Harangue, Hatti-sherif, Independence, Indulgence, Insist, Interlocutory, Irade, Law, Mandate, Manifesto, Mecklenburg, Meld, Motu proprio, Mou(th), Nisi, Noncupate, Novel(la), Nullity, Nuncupate, Orate, Ordain, Order, Ordinance, Parlando, Pontificate, Predicate, Proclaim, Profess, Promulgate,

Pronounce, Protest, Psephism, Publish, Rant, Recite, Rescript, Resolve, Rights, Rule, Ruling, SC, Sed, Senatus consultum, Senecan, Shahada, Signify, Speak, Spout, State, Statutory, Testify, Testimony, UDI, Ultimatum, Unilateral, Vie, Voice, Vouch, Word

▷ **Declaring** *may indicate* a word beginning 'Im'

Decline, Declining Age, Ail, Atrophy, Catabasis, Comedown, Decadent, Degeneration, Degringoler, Deny, Descend, Deteriorate, Devall, Die, Diminish, Dip, Dissent, Downhill, Downtrend, Downturn, Droop, Dwindle, Ebb, Fade, Fall, Flag, Forbear, Paracme, Peter, Quail, Recede, Recession, Refuse, Retrogression, Rot, Rust, Sag, Senile, Set, Sink, Slide, Slump, Stoop, Twilight, Wane, Welke, → **WILT**, Withdraw, Wither

Decoct(ion) Apozem, Cook, Devise, Ptisan, Tisane

Decode(d) En clair

Decolleté Low, Neckline

Decompose, Decomposition Biodegradable, Crumble, Decay, Disintegrate, Hydrolysis, Mor, Pyrolysis, Rot, Wither

Decompression Bends

Decor Background, Scenery

Decorate(d), Decoration, Decorative Adorn, Angelica, Aogai, Arpillera, Attrap, Award, Bargeboard, Baroque, Beaux-arts, Bedizen, Biedermeier, Bordure, Braid, Brattishing, Braze, Brooch, Cartouche, Centrepiece, Chambranle, Champlevé, Chinoiserie, Christingle, Cinquefoil, Cloissoné, Coffer, Cresting, Crocket, Cul-de-lampe, Daiker, Decoupage, Dentelle, Diamante, Doodad, Dragée, Dragging, Emblazon, Emboss, Embrave, Engrail, Enrich, Epergne, Etch, Fancy, Festoon, Filigree, Finery, Finial, Fleuret(te), Fleuron, Floriated, Flushwork, Fluting, Fourragère, Frieze, Frill, Frog, Frost, Furbish, Gammadion, Garniture, Gaud, Gild, Glitter, Goffer, Gradino, Grecque key, Grotesque, Guilloche, Historiated, Ice, Illuminate, Impearl, Inlay, Intarsia, Intarsio, Interior, Knotwork, Leglet, Linen-fold, Linen-scroll, Marquetry, MC, Medal(lion), Mola, Motif, Moulding, Oath, OBE, Order, → **ORNAMENT**, Ornate, Orphrey, Overglaze, Ovolo, Paint, Paper, Parament, Pâté-sur-pâté, Photomural, Pinata, Pipe, Pokerwork, Polychromy, Pompom, Prettify, Prink, Purfle, Purple heart, Quilling, Rag-rolling, Rangoli, Repoussé, Rich, Rosemaling, Ruche, Scallop, Schwarzlot, Scrimshander, Scrimshaw, Serif, Set-off, Sgraffito, Skeuomorph, Soutache, Spangle, Staffage, Stomacher, Storiated, Strapwork, Studwork, Tailpiece, Tattoo, TD, Titivate, Tool, Topiary, Trim, Veneer, Vergeboard, Wallpaper, Well-dressing, Wirework

Decorous, Decorum Becoming, Demure, Etiquette, Fitness, Parliamentary, Prim, → **PROPER**, Propriety, Sedate, Seemlihe(a)d, → **SEEMLY**, Staid

Decoy Allure, Bait, Bonnet, Button, Call-bird, Coach, Crimp, Entice, Lure, Piper, Roper, Ruse, Shill, Stale, Stalking-horse, Stool-pigeon, Tice, Tole, Toll, Trap, Trepan

Decrease Decrew, Diminish, Dwindle, Iron, Lessen, Press, Ramp down, Reduce, Rollback, Slim, Step-down, Subside, Wane, Wanze

Decree → **DECLAIM**, Saw

Decrepit Dilapidated, Doddery, Failing, Feeble, Frail, Moth-eaten, Time-worn, Tumbledown, Warby, Weak

Decry Condemn, Crab, Denounce, Derogate, Detract, Downgrade

Dedicate(d), Dedication Corban, Devote, Dinah, Endoss, Hallow, Inscribe, Oblate, Pious, Sacred, Single-minded, Votive

Deduce, Deduction, Deductive A priori, Assume, Conclude, Consectary, Corollary, Derive, Discount, Dockage, Gather, Illation, Infer(ence), Natural, Obvert,

Off-reckoning, Reason, Rebate, Recoup, Reprise, Stoppage, Surmise, Syllogism

Deed(s) Achievement, Act(ion), Atweel, Backbond, Back letter, Charta, Charter, Derring-do, Disposition, Escrol(l), Escrow, Exploit, Fact(um), Feat, Indeed, Indenture, Manoeuvre, Mitzvah, Muniments, Premises, Settlement, Specialty, Starr, → TITLE, Trust

Deem Consider, Judge, Opine, Ordain, Proclaim, Repute, Think

Deep(en), Deeply Abstruse, Bass(o), Brine, Briny, Enhance, Excavate, Grum, Gulf, Hadal, Intense, Low, Mindanao, Mysterious, → OCEAN, Profound, Re-enter, Rich, Sea, Sonorous, Throaty, Upsee, Ups(e)y

Deep-rooted Inveterate

Deer(-like) Axis, Bambi, Barasing(h)a, Barking, Blacktail, Brocket, Buck, Cariacou, Caribou, Carjacou, Cervine, Chevrotain, Chital, Doe, Elaphine, Elk, Fallow, Gazelle, Hart, Hog, Jumping, Moose, Mouse, Mule, Muntjac, Muntjak, Musk, Père David's, Pricket, Pudu, Pygarg, Red, Rein, Roe, Rusa, Sambar, Sambur, Selenodont, Sika, Sorel(l), Spade, Spay(d), Spayad, Spitter, Spottie, Stag(gard), Tragule, Ungulate, Virginia, Wapiti, Water, White-tailed

Deer-hunter Tinchel

Deface Disfigure, Spoil

▷ **Defaced** *may indicate* first letter missing

Defame, Defamatory, Defamation Abase, Bad mouth, Blacken, Calumny, Cloud, Denigrate, Detract, Dishonour, Impugn, Libel, Malign, Mud, Mudslinging, Obloquy, Sclaunder, Scurrilous, Slander, Smear, Stigmatise, Traduce, Vilify

Default(er) Absentee, Bilk, Dando, Delinquent, Flit, Levant, Neglect, Omission, Waddle, Welsh

Defeat(ed), Defeatist Beat, Best, Caning, Capot, Codille, Conquer, Counteract, Debel, Defeasance, Demolish, Discomfit, Dish, Ditch, Donkey-lick, Fatalist, Floor, Foil, Foyle, Hammer, Hiding, Kippered, Laipse, Lick, Loss, Lurch, Marmelize, Master, Mate, Moral, Negative, Out, Outclass, Outdo, Outplay, Outvote, Outwit, → OVERCOME, Overpower, Overreach, Overthrow, Overwhelm, Pip, Plaster, Quitter, Reverse, Rout, Rubicon, Scupper, Set, Shellacking, Sisera, Skunk, Squabash, Stump, Tank, Thrash, Thwart, Tonk, Trounce, Vanquish, War, Waterloo, Whap, Whip, Whitewash, Whop, Whup, Wipe-out, Worst

Defecate, Defecation Horse, Mute, Poop, Scumber, Shit, Skummer, Tenesmus

Defect(ion), Defective, Defector Abandon, Amateur, Apostasy, Bug, Coma, Crack, Crawling, Deficient, Failing, Faulty, Flaw, → FORSAKE, Frenkel, Halt, Hamartia, Kink, Low, Manky, Mass, Mote, Natural, Paralexia, Point, Psellism, Rachischisis, Renegade, Renegate, Ridgel, Ridgil, Rig, Rogue, Runagate, Schottky, Shortcoming, Spina bifida, Terrace, Treason, Trick, Want, Weakness, Wreath

Defence, Defend(er), Defensible, Defensive Abat(t)is, Alexander, Alibi, Antibody, Antidote, Antihistamine, Apologia, Back, Back four, Bailey, Barbican, Barmkin, Barricade, Bastion, Battery, Battlement, Berm, Bestride, Bridgehead, Bulwark, Calt(h)rop, Catenaccio, CD, Champion, Chapparal, Civil, Curtain, Demibastion, Ditch, Embrasure, Goalie, Hedgehog, Herisson, Hold, J(i)u-jitsu, Justify, Kaim, Keeper, Laager, Laer, Last-ditch, Libero, Linebacker, Maginot-minded, Maintain, Martello tower, MIDAS, Moat, Motte and bailey, Muniment, Outwork, Palisade, Parapet, Pentagon, Perceptual, Propugnation, Protect, Rampart, Redan, Redoubt, Resist, Ringwall, → SHELTER, Shield, Stonewall, Strategic, Support, Sweeper, Tenable, Tenail(le), Testudo, Tower, Trench, Trou-de-loup, Uphold, Vallation, Vallum, Vindicate, Wall, Warran(t), Zonal

Defenceless Helpless, Inerm, Naked, Sitting duck, Vulnerable

Defendant Accused, Apologist, Respondent, Richard Roe

Defer(ence), Deferential, Deferring Bow, Complaisance, Delay, Dutiful, Homage, Moratory, Morigerous, Obeisant, Pace, Polite, Postpone, Procrastinate, Protocol, Respect, Shelve, Submit, Suspend, Waive, Yield

Defiance, Defiant, Defy Acock, Bold, Brave, Contumacy, Dare, Daring, Disregard, Do or die, Outbrave, Outdare, Rebellion, Recusant, Resist, Stubborn, Titanism, Truculent, Unruly

Deficiency, Deficient Absence, Acapnia, Anaemia, Beriberi, Defect, Inadequate, Incomplete, Kwashiorkor, Lack, Osteomalacia, Scant, Scarcity, SCID, Shortage, Shortfall, Spanaemia, Want

▷ **Deficient** *may indicate* an anagram

Deficit Anaplerotic, Arrears, Defective, Ischemia, Loss, Poor, Shortfall

Defile(ment) Abuse, Array, Barranca, Barranco, Besmear, Col, Conspurcation, Desecrate, Dishonour, Donga, Enseam, → **FOUL**, Gate, Gorge, Gully, Inquinate, Inseem, Kloof, Moil, Pass, Pollute, Poort, Ravine, Ray, Roncesvalles, Smear, Spoil, → **SULLY**

Define(d), Definition, Definitive Decide, Demarcate, Determine, Diorism, Distinct, Explain, Fix, Limit, Parameter, Set, Tangible, Term

Definite(ly) Classic, Clear, Deffo, Emphatic, Firm, Hard, Indeed, Pos, Positive, Precise, Specific, Sure, Yes

Deflate Burst, Collapse, Flatten, Lower, Prick, Puncture

Deflect(or), Deflection Avert, Bend, Detour, Diverge, Divert, Glance, Holophote, Otter, Paravane, Refract, Snick, Swerve, Throw, Trochotron, Veer, Windage

Deform(ed), Deformity Anamorphosis, Blemish, Crooked, Disfigure, Distort, Gammy, Hammer-toe, Harelip, Misborn, Mishapt, Mooncalf, Mutilate, Phocomelia, Phocomely, Polt-foot, Saddle-nose, Stenosed, Talipes, Valgus, Varus, Warp

▷ **Deformed** *may indicate* an anagram

Defraud Bilk, Cheat, Cozen, Gull, Gyp, Mulct, Shoulder, Sting, Swindle, Trick

Defray Bear, Cover, Meet

Defrost Thaw

Deft Adept, Agile, Dab, Dexterous, Elegant, Handy, Nimble

Defunct Deceased, Extinct, Obsolete

▶ **Defy** *see* **DEFIANCE**

Degenerate, Degeneration, Degenerative Acorn-shell, Ascidian, Atrophy, Balanus, Base, Cirrhipedea, Cirrhipedia, Cirrhopod(a), Cirripedea, Cirripedia, Decadent, Deprave, Descend, Deteriorate, Eburnation, Effete, Fatty, Kaliyuga, Necrobiosis, Pejorate, Pervert, Rakehell, Relapse, Retrogress, Salp, Tunicate

Degrade, Degradation Abase, Cheapen, Culvertage, Debase, Demission, Demote, Depose, Diminish, Disennoble, Embase, Humble, Imbase, Imbrute, Lessen, Lower, → **SHAME**, Waterloo

Degree(s) Aegrotat, As, Attila (the Hun), Azimuthal, BA, Baccalaureate, BCom, BD, B es S, C, Class, D, Desmond (Tutu), Doctoral, Double first, Douglas (Hurd), Engler, Extent, External, F, First, Geoff (Hurst), German, Gradation, Grade, Grece, Gree(s), Greece, Gre(e)se, Grice, Griece, Grize, → **IN A HIGH DEGREE**, Incidence, K, Lambeth, Latitude, Letters, Level, Levitical, Licentiate, Longitude, MA, Measure, Mediant, Nth, Nuance, Order, Ordinary, Pass, Peg, PhD, Pin, Poll, Rate, Remove, Second, Stage, Status, Step, Submediant, Subtonic, Supertonic, Third, Trevor (Nunn), Water

Dehiscence Suture

Dehydrate(d) Exsiccate, Thirsty

Deification, Deify Apotheosis

Deign Condescend, Stoop
Deity Avatar, Cabiri, Demogorgon, Divine, Faun, → **GOD**, → **GODDESS**, Idolise,
Immortalise, Krishna, Numen, Pan, Satyr, Zombi(e)
Deject(ed), Dejection Abase, Abattu, Alamort, Amort, Blue, Chap-fallen, Crab,
Crestfallen, Despondent, Dismay, Dispirited, Down, Downcast, Gloomy, Hangdog,
Humble, Melancholy
Delay(ed) Adjourn(ment), Ambage, Avizandum, Behindhand, Check, Cunctator,
Defer, Demurrage, Detention, Fabian, Filibuster, For(e)slow, Forsloe, Frist,
Hesitate, Hinder, Hitch, Hold up, Hysteresis, Impede, Laches, Lag, Late, Laten, Let,
Linger, Loiter, Mora(torium), Obstruct, Pause, Procrastinate, Prolong, Prorogue,
Remanet, Reprieve, Respite, Retard, Setback, Slippage, Sloth, Slow, → **STALL**,
Stand-over, Stay, Stonewall, Suspend, Temporise, Wait
Delectable Delicious, Luscious, Tasty
Delegate, Delegation Agent, Amphictyon, Apostolic, Appoint, Assign,
Decentralise, Depute, Devolution, Mission, Nuncio, Offload, Representative,
Secondary, Transfer, Vicarial, Walking
Delete Cancel, Cut, Erase, Excise, Expunge, Purge, Rase, Scratch, Scrub, Strike,
Twink out
Deliberate(ly) Adagio, Consider, Debate, Intentional, Meditate, Moderate, Muse,
Overt, Ponder, Prepensely, Ruminate, Studied, Voulu, Weigh, Witting
Delicacy, Delicate Airy-fairy, Beccafico, Blini, Canape, Cate, Caviare, Dainty,
Difficult, Discreet, Ectomorph, Eggshell, Elfin, Ethereal, Fastidious, Filigree, Fine,
Finespun, Finesse, Flimsy, Fragile, → **FRAIL**, Friand, Gossamer, Guga, Hothouse,
Inconie, Incony, Kickshaw, Kidglove, Ladylike, Light, Lobster, Morbidezza, Nesh,
Nicety, Niminy-piminy, Ortolan, Oyster, Pastel, Reedy, Roe, Sensitive, Soft,
Subtle(ty), Sunket, Sweetmeat, Taste, Tender, Tenuous, Ticklish, Tidbit, Titbit,
Truffle
Delicious Ambrosia, Delectable, Exquisite, Fragrant, Goloptious, Goluptious,
Gorgeous, Lekker, Lip-smacking, Mor(e)ish, Mouthwatering, Scrummy,
Scrumptious, Tasty, Toothsome, Yummo, Yummy, Yum-yum
▷ **Delight** *may indicate* 'darken'
Delight(ed), Delightful Bewitch, Bliss, Charm, Chuff, Delice, Dreamy, Edna,
Elated, Elysian, Enamour, Enjoyable, Enrapture, Exuberant, Felicity, Fetching,
Frabjous, Gas, Glad, Glee, Gratify, Honey, Joy, Nice, Overjoy, Over the moon, Please,
Pleasure, Precious, → **RAPTURE**, Regale, Revel, Scrummy, Super, Taking, Tickle,
Turkish, Whacko, Whee, Whoopee, Wizard, Yippee, Yum-yum
Delineate Draft, Sketch, Trace
Delinquent Bodgie, Criminal, Halbstarker, Juvenile, Negligent, Offender, Ted
Delirious, Delirium Deranged, DT, Fever, Frenetic, Frenzy, Insanity, Mania,
Phrenetic, Phrenitis, Spaced out, Spazz, Wild
Deliver(ance), Deliverer, Delivery(man) Accouchement, Ball, Birth, Bowl, Breech,
Caesarean, Consign, Convey, Courier, Deal, Doosra, Drop, Elocution, Escape,
Express, Extradition, Give, Jail, Lead, Liberate, Lob, Orate, Over, Pronounce,
Receipt, Recorded, Redeem, Release, Relieve, Render, Rendition, → **RESCUE**, Rid,
Round(sman), Salvation, Save, Say, Seamer, Sell, Shipment, Speak, Special, Tice,
Transfer, Underarm, Underhand, Utter, Wide, Yorker
Dell Dale, Dargle, Dene, Dimble, Dingle, Dingl(e)y, Glen, Valley
Delphic Pythian
Delphinium Larkspur
Delta Camargue, D, Del, Flood-plain, Kronecker, Nabla, Nile, Oil Rivers, Triangle
Delude, Delusion Bilk, Cheat, Deceive, Fallacy, Fool, Hoax, Megalomania,

→ **MISLEAD**, Paranoia, Schizothymia, Trick, Zoanthropy

Deluge Avalanche, Flood, Ogygian, Saturate, Submerge, → **SWAMP**

De luxe Extra, Plush, Special

Delve Burrow, Dig, Excavate, Exhume, Explore, Probe, Search

Demagogue Agitator, Fanariot, Leader, Mobsman, Phanariot, Speaker, Tribune

Demand(ing) Appetite, Call, Claim, Cry, Dun, Exact, Excess, Exigent, Fastidious, Final, Hest, → **INSIST**, Mandate, Market, Need, Order, Postulate, Pressure, Request, Requisition, Rush, Sale, Stern, Stipulate, Stringent, Summon, Ultimatum, Want

Demean(ing) Belittle, Comport, Debase, Degrade, Humble, Infra dig, Lower, Maltreat

Demeanour Air, Bearing, Conduct, Expression, Front, Gravitas, Mien, Port, Presence

Dement(ed) Crazy, Hysterical, Insane, Mad, Wacko

Demi-god Aitu, Daemon, Garuda, Hero

Demi-mondaine Cocotte, → **LOOSE WOMAN**, Prostitute

Demise Death, Decease, Finish

Demo March, Parade, Protest, Rally, Sit-in

Democracy, Democrat, Democratic D, Hunker, Industrial, Liberal, Locofoco, Menshevik, Montagnard, People's, Popular, Republic, Sansculotte, Social, Tammany

Demoiselle Crane, Damselfish

Demolish, Demolition Bulldoze, Devastate, Devour, Dismantle, Floor, KO, Level, Rack, → **RAZE**, Smash, Tear down, Wreck

▶ **Demon** *see* **DEVIL**

Demoness Lilith

Demonstrate, Demonstration, Demonstrator Agitate, Barrack, Display, Endeictic, Evénement, Evince, Explain, Hunger march, Maffick, Manifest, March, Morcha, Ostensive, Peterloo, Portray, Protest, Prove, Provo, Send-off, → **SHOW**, Sit-in, Touchy-feely, Vigil

Demoralize Bewilder, Corrupt, Destroy, Shatter, Unman, Weaken

Demote, Demotion Comedown, Degrade, Disbench, Disrate, Embace, Embase, Reduce, Relegate, Stellenbosch

Demur Hesitate, Jib, Object

Demure Coy, Mim, Modest, Prenzie, Primsie, Sedate, Shy

Den Dive, Domdaniel, Earth, Hell, Hide-away, Holt, Home, Lair, Lie, Lodge, Opium, Room, Shebeen, Study, Sty, Wurley

Denial, Deny, Denier Abnegate, Antinomian, Aspheterism, Bar, Contradict, Controvert, Démenti, Disavow, Disenfranchise, Disown, Forswear, → **GAINSAY**, Nay, Negate, Nick, Nihilism, Protest, Refuse, Refute, Renague, Renay, Reneg(e), Renegue, Reney, Renig, Renounce, Reny, Repudiate, Sublate, Traverse, Withhold

Denigrate Besmirch, Blacken, Defame, Tar

Denim Jeans

Denizen Diehard, Inhabitant, Resident

Denomination Category, Cult, Sect, Variety

Denote Import, Indicate, Mean, Signify

Denouement Anagnorisis, Catastrophe, Climax, Coda, Exposure, Outcome, Showdown

Denounce, Denunciation Ban, Commination, Condemn, Criticise, Decry, Delate, Diatribe, Fulminate, Hatchet job, Hereticate, Proclaim, Proscribe, Shop, Stigmatise, Thunder, Upbraid

Denry Card

Dense, Density Charge, Compact, Critical, Current, D, Double, Firm, Flux, Intense, Neutral, Opaque, Optical, Packing, Reflection, Relative, Single, Solid, Spissitude, Tesla, Thick, Transmission, Vapour, Woofy

Dent(ed) Batter, Concave, Dancette, Depress, Dimple, Dinge, Dint, Nock, V

Dental, Dentist(ry) DDS, Entodontics, Extractor, Kindhart, LDS, Odontic, Periodontic, Toothy

Dentures Biteplate, Bridge, Bridgework, False teeth, Plate, Prosthodontia, Store teeth, Wallies

▶ **Deny** *see* DENIAL

Deodorant Anti-perspirant, Roll-on

Deoxidise Outgas, Reduce

Depart(ed), Departing, Departure Abscond, Absquatulate, Bunk, D, Dead, Decession, Defunct, Die, Digress, Divergence, Exit, Exodus, Flight, → GO, Leave, Lucky, Outbound, Rack off, Remue, Send-off, Vacate, Vade, Vamoose, Walkout

Department Achaea, Ain, Aisne, Allier, Alpes de Provence, Alpes-Maritimes, Angers, Arcadia, Ardeche, Ardennes, Argo, Argolis, Ariege, Arrondissement, Arta, Attica, Aube, Aude, Aveyron, Bas-Rhin, Belfort, Beziers, Bouches-du-Rhône, Branch, Bureau, Calvados, Cantal, Charente, Charente-Maritime, Cher, Commissariat, Corrèze, Cote d'Or, Cotes d'Armor, Cotes du Nord, Creuse, DEFRA, Deme, Deux-Sevres, Division, Dordogne, Doubs, Drôme, El(e)ia, Essonne, Eure, Eure-et-Loir, Faculty, Finistere, Fire, FO, Gard, Gers, Gironde, Greencloth, Guadeloupe, Gulag, Hanaper, Haute-Garonne, Haute-Loire, Haute-Marne, Haute-Normandie, Hautes-Alpes, Haute-Saône, Haute Savoie, Hautes-Pyrenees, Haute-Vienne, Haut-Rhin, Hauts-de-Seine, Herault, Home, Ille-et-Vilaine, Indre, Indre-et-Loire, Isere, Jura, Landes, Loire, Loiret, Loir-et-Cher, Lot, Lot-et-Garonne, Lozere, Maine-et-Loire, Manche, Marne, Mayenne, Meurthe-et-Moselle, Meuse, Ministry, Morbihan, Moselle, Nièvre, Nome, Nomos, Nord, Office, Oise, Orne, Pas-de-Calais, Province, Puy de Dôme, Pyrénées(-Atlantique), Pyrénées-Orientales, Region, Rehabilitation, Rhône, Sanjak, Saône-et-Loire, Sarthe, Savoie, Secretariat(e), Section, Seine-et-Marne, Seine Maritime, Seine St Denis, Somme, Sphere, State, Tarn(-et-Garonne), Treasury, Tuscany, Val de Marne, Val d'Oise, Var, Vaucluse, Vendée, Vienne, Voiotia, War, Wardrobe, Yonne, Yvelines

Depend(ant), Dependence, Dependency, Dependent Addicted, Child, Client, Colony, Conditional, Contingent, Count, Dangle, E, Fief, Habit, Hang, Hinge, Icicle, Lean, Minion, Pensioner, Relier, Rely, Retainer, Ross, Sponge, Statistical, Subject, Subordinate, Trust, Turn on, Vassal

Dependable Reliable, Reliant, Secure, Sheet-anchor, Solid, Sound, Staunch, Sure, → TRUSTWORTHY

Depict Delineate, Display, Draw, Limn, Paint, Portray, Present, Represent

Depilate, Depilatory Grain, Rusma, Slate

Deplete Diminish, Drain, Exhaust, Reduce

Deplorable, Deplore Base, Bemoan, Chronic, Complain, Deprecate, Dolorous, Grieve, Lament, Mourn, Piteous, Regret, Rue

Deploy(ment) Extend, Herse, Unfold, Use

▷ **Deploy(ment)** *may indicate* an anagram

Depopulate Deracinate

Deport(ation), Deportment Address, Air, Banish, → BEARING, Carriage, Demeanour, Mien, Renvoi, Renvoy, Repatriation

Depose, Deposition Affirm, Banish, Dethrone, Displace, Dispossess, Overthrow, Pieta, Testify

Deposit(s), Depository Aeolian, Alluvial, Alluvium, Aquifer, Arcus, Argol, Arles, Atheroma, Bank, Bathybius, Bergmehl, Calc-sinter, Calc-tuff, Caliche, Cave-earth, Coral, Crag, Delta, Depone, Diatomite, Diluvium, Drift, Evaporite, Fan, File, Firn, Fort Knox, Fur, Gyttja, Illuvium, Kieselguhr, Land, Laterite, Lay, Lay-by, Limescale, Lodge(ment), Loess, Löss, Measure, Moraine, Natron, Outwatch, Park, Pay dirt, Placer, Plank, Plaque, Precipitate, Put, Repose, Residuum, Saburra, Salamander, Saprolite, → **SEDIMENT**, Silt, Sinter, Sludge, Stockwork, Stratum, Surety, Tartar, Terramara, Terramare, Till, Time, Tophus, Tripoli, Turbidite

Depot Barracoon, Base, Camp, Depository, Station, Terminus, Treasure-city, Warehouse

Deprav(ed), Depravity Bestial, Cachexia, Cachexy, Caligulism, → **CORRUPT**, Dissolute, Evil, Immoral, Low, Reprobate, Rotten, Sodom, Total, Turpitude, Ugly, Vice, Vicious, Vile

Deprecate Censure, Deplore, Expostulate, Reproach

Depreciate Abase, Belittle, Derogate, Detract, Discount

Depredate, Depredation Pillage, Plunder, Rob

Depress(ed), Depressing, Depression Accablé, Agitated, Alamort, Alveolus, Amort, Astrobleme, Attrist, Black dog, Blight, Blue devils, Blues, Cafard, Caldron, Canada, Canyon, Chill, Col, Combe, Couch, Crab, Crush, Cyclone, Dampen, Deject, Dell, Demission, Dene, Dent, Despair, → **DIMPLE**, Dip, Dismal, Dispirit, Dolina, Doline, Doomy, Downlifting, Drear, Drere, Dumpish, Endogenous, Exanimate, Flatten, Fonticulus, Foss(ula), Fossa, Fovea, Frog, Geosyncline, Ghilgai, Gilgai, Gilgie, Glen, Gloom, Graben, Grinch, Ha-ha, Hammer, Heart-spoon, Hilar, Hilum, Hilus, Hollow, Howe, Hyp, Hypothymia, Joes, Kettle, Kick(-up), Lacuna, Leaden, Low(ness), Low-spirited, Megrims, Moping, Morose, Neck, Ocean basin, Pan, Pit, Polje, Postnatal, Prostrate, Qattara, Recession, Re-entrant, Retuse, Sad, Saddle, Sag, Salt-cellar, Salt-pan, Scrobicule, Sink, Sinkhole, Sinus, Sitzmark, Slot, → **SLUMP**, Slumpflation, Soakaway, Spiritless, Stomodaeum, Sump, Swag, Swale, Swallowhole, Trench, Trough, Umbilication, Vale, Vallecula, Valley, Wallow, Weigh down, Wet blanket

Deprivation, Deprive(d) Amerce, Bereft, Deny, Disenfranchise, Disfrock, Disseise, Disseize, Expropriate, Famine, Foreclose, Geld, Have-not, Hunger, Reduce, Remove, Rob, Sensory, Withhold

Depth Draught, Draw, F, Fathom, Gravity, Intensity, Isobath, Pit, Profundity

Deputise, Deputy Act, Agent, Aide, Assistant, Commis(sary), Delegate, Legate, Lieutenant, Locum, Loot, Mate, Number two, Prior, Proxy, Represent, Secondary, Sidekick, Standby, Sub, Subchanter, Substitute, Succentor, Surrogate, Vicar, Vice, Viceregent, Vidame

Derange(d) Craze, Détraqué, Disturb, Insane, Manic, Troppo, Unhinge, Unsettle

Derby Boot, Demolition, Donkey, Eponym, Hat, Kentucky, Kiplingcotes, Race, Roller

Derek Bo

Derelict Abandoned, → **DECREPIT**, Deserted, Negligent, Outcast, Ramshackle

Deride, Derision, Derisive Contempt, Gup, Guy, Hiss, Hoot, Jeer, Mock, Nominal, Pigs, Raspberry, → **RIDICULE**, Sardonic, Scoff, Scorn, Snifty, Snort, Yah, Ya(h)boo

Derive, Derivation, Derivative Amine, Ancestry, Creosote, Deduce, Descend, Extract, Get, Kinone, Of, Offshoot, Origin, Pedigree, Picoline, Secondary, Tyramine

▶ **Dermatitis** *see* **SKIN DISEASE**

Derogate, Derogatory Belittle, Decry, Defamatory, Demeaning, Detract, Discredit, Pejorative, Personal, Slighting, Snide

Deronda Daniel

Derrick Crane, Davit, Hoist, Jib, Spar, Steeve

Dervish Calender, Doseh, Mawlawi, Mevlevi, Revolver, Santon, Whirling

Descant Comment, Discourse, Faburden, Melody, Song

Descartes René

Descend(ant), Descent Ancestry, Avail, Avale, Bathos, Blood, Cadency, Catabasis, Chute, Cion, Decline, Degenerate, Derive, Dismount, Dive, Drop, Epigon, Extraction, Heir, Heraclid, → LINEAGE, Offspring, Pedigree, Posterity, Progeny, Prone, Rappel, Said, Say(y)id, Scarp, Scion, Seed, Shelve, Sien(t), Sink, Stock, Syen, Vest, Volplane

Describe, Description, Descriptive Blurb, Define, Delineate, Depict, Designate, Draw, Epithet, Exposition, Expound, Graphic, Job, Narrate, Outline, Paint, Portray, Rapportage, Recount, Relate, Report, Sea-letter, Signalment, Sketch, Specification, Synopsis, Term, Trace, Vignette, Write-up

▷ **Describing** *may indicate* 'around'

Descry Behold, Discern, Get, Notice, Perceive

Desecrate, Desecration Abuse, Defile, Dishallow, Profane, Sacrilege, Unhallow

▷ **Desecrated** *may indicate* an anagram

Desert(er), Deserted, Deserts Abandon, Absquatulate, Apostasy, Arabian, Arid, Ar Rimal, Arunta, Atacama, AWOL, Badland, Barren, Bledowska, Bug, Bunk, Colorado, Come-uppance, D, Dahna, Defect, Desolate, Dissident, Due, Empty, Eremic, Etosha Pan, Factious, Fail, Fezzan, Foresay, Forhoo, Forhow, Forlorn, Forsake, Forsay, Frondeur, Garagum, Gibson, Gila, Gobi, Great Basin, Great Indian, Great Sandy, Great Victoria, Heterodox, Indian, Jump ship, Kalahari, Kara Kum, Kavir, Kyzyl Kum, Libyan, Lurch, Meeds, Merit, Mohave, Mojave, Nafud, Namib, Negev, Nubian, Ogaden, Painted, Pategonian, Pindan, Rat, Refus(e)nik, Reg, → RENEGADE, Reward, Rub'al-Khali, Run, Runaway, Sahara, Sahel, Sands, Secede, Shamo, Simpson, Sinai, Sonoran, Sturt, Syrian, Tacna-Arica, Tergiversate, Thar, Turncoat, Ust(y)urt, Victoria, Void, Wadi, Waste, Western Sahara, Wilderness, Worthiness

Deserve(d) Condign, Earn, → MERIT, Rate, Well-earned, Worthy

Desiccate(d) Dry, Sere

Design(er) Adam, Aim, Arabesque, Architect, Armani, Ashley, Batik, Between-subjects, Broider, Calligram(me), Cardin, Cartoon, Castrametation, Chop, Cloisonné, Create, Cul de lampe, Damascene, Decal(comania), Decor, Deep, Depict, Devise, Dévoré, Dior, Draft, Embroidery, End, Engender, Engine(r), Engineer, Erté, Etch, Fashion, Feng-shui, Former, Hepplewhite, Hitech, Iconic, Impresa, Imprese, Industrial, Intend(ment), Intent(ion), Interior, Issigonis, Layout, Limit-state, Linocut, Logo, Marquetry, Mascle, Matched pairs, Mean, Meander, Mehndi, Millefleurs, Modiste, Monogram, Morris, Mosaic, Motif, Multifoil, Paisley, Pattern, → PLAN, Plot, Propose, Pyrography, Quant, Retro, Ruse, Schema, Scheme, Seal, Sheraton, Sketch, Specification, Stencil, Stubble, Stylist, Sunburst, Tatow, Tattoo, Tattow, Tatu, Think, Tooling, Trigram, Versace, Vignette, Watermark, Weiner, Werkstalte, Whittle, Within-subjects

Designate Earmark, Note, Style, Title

Desirable, Desire, Desirous Ambition, Appetite, Aspire, Avid, Best, Cama, Conation, Concupiscence, Covet, Crave, Cupidity, Dreamboat, Earn, Eligible, Epithymetic, Fancy, Gasp, Hanker, Hope, Hots, Hunger, Itch, Kama(deva), Le(t)ch, Libido, List, Long, Luscious, Lust, Mania, Nymphomania, Orectic, Owlcar, Pica, Plum, Reck, Request, Residence, Salt, Slaver, Streetcar, Thirst, Velleity, Vote, Wanderlust, Want, Whim, Will, Wish, Yearn, Yen

Desist Abandon, Cease, Curb, Pretermit, Quit, Stop

Desk Almemar, Ambo, Bonheur-du-jour, Bureau, Carrel(l), Cash, Check-in,

Cheveret, City, Copy, Davenport, Desse, Devonport, Enquiry, E(s)critoire, Faldstool, Lectern, Lettern, Litany, Pay, Pedestal, Prie-dieu, Pulpit, Reading, Roll-top, Scrutoire, Secretaire, Vargueno, Writing

Desman Pyrenean

Desolate, Desolation Bare, Barren, Desert, Devastate, Disconsolate, Forlorn, Gaunt, Godforsaken, Gousty, Moonscape, Waste, Woebegone

Despair, Desperate, Desperation Acharne, Anomy, De profundis, Despond, Dire, Dismay, Extreme, Frantic, Gagging, Giant, Gloom, Hairless, Headlong, Last-ditch, Last-gasp, Life and death, Reckless, Unhopeful, Urgent, Wanhope

▸ **Despatch** *see* DISPATCH

Desperado Bandit, Bravo, Ruffian, Terrorist

Despicable Abject, Base, Bleeder, Caitiff, Cheap, Churl, Contemptible, Heinous, Ignoble, Ignominious, Low-down, Mean, Moer, Poep(ol), Puke, Ratbag, Ratfink, Scumbag, Shabby, Toerag, Wretched

Despise Condemn, Contemn, Forhow, Hate, Ignore, Scorn, Spurn, Vilify, Vilipend

Despite For, Malgré, Notwithstanding, Pace, Though, Venom

Despoil Mar, Ravage, Vandalise

Despondent Dejected, Downcast, Forlorn, Gloomy, Sad

Despot(ism) Autarchy, Autocrat, Bonaparte, Caesar, Darius, Dictator, Napoleon, Nero, Satrap, Stratocrat, Tsar, Tyrant, Tzar

Dessert Afters, Baked Alaska, Baklava, Bavarian cream, Bavarois, Bombe, Charlotte, Charlotte russe, Clafoutis, Cobbler, Compote, Coupe, Crème brulée, Crème caramel, Dulce de leche, Entremets, Flummery, Fool, Granita, Junket, Kissel, Knickerbocker glory, Kulfi, Marquise, Mousse, Mud pie, Nesselrode, Pannacotta, Parfait, Pashka, Pavlova, Peach Melba, → PUDDING, Rasmalai, Sabayon, Sawine, Semifreddo, Shoofly pie, Split, Strudel, Sundae, Syllabub, Tartufo, Tiramisu, Tortoni, Trifle, Vacherin, Whip, Zabaglione

Destine(d), Destination Design, End, Fate, Foredoom, Goal, Home, Intend, Joss, Meant, Port, Purpose, Vector, Weird

Destiny Doom, → FATE, Karma, Kismet, Lot, Manifest, Moira, Yang, Yin

Destitute Bankrupt, Bare, Broke, Devoid, Dirt-poor, Helpless, Impoverished, Indigent, Needy, Penniless, Poor, Sterile, Void

Destroy(er) Annihilate, Antineutrino, Antineutron, Antiparticle, Apollyon, Atomise, Blight, Can, D, Decimate, Deep-six, Deface, Delete, Demolish, Denature, Destruct, Dish, Dismember, Dissolve, Eat, Efface, End, Eradicate, Erase, Estrepe, Exterminate, Extirpate, Flivver, Fordo, Graunch, Harry, Iconoclast, Incinerate, → KILL, KO, Murder, Obliterate, Overkill, Perish, Predator, Ravage, Raze, Ruin, Saboteur, Sack, Scuttle, Slash, Smash, Spif(f)licate, Spoil, Sterilize, Stew-can, Stonker, Stultify, Subvert, Trash, Undo, Uproot, Vandal, Vitiate, Waste, Whelm, Wreck, Zap

Destruction, Destructive Adverse, Autolysis, Bane, Can, Collapse, Deathblow, Deleterious, Devastation, Doom, Downfall, Ecocide, End, Götterdämmerung, Grave, Havoc, Holocaust, Insidious, Internecine, Kali, Lethal, Loss, Maleficent, Pernicious, Pogrom, Quelea, Rack, Ragnarok, Ravage, Sabotage, Speciocide, Stroy, Wrack

Desultory Aimless, Cursory, Fitful, Idle

Detach(ed), Detachment Abstract, Alienate, Aloof, Body, Calve, Clinical, Cut, Detail, Discrete, Insular, Isle, Isolate, Loose, Outlying, Outpost, Patrol, Picket, Picquet, Separate, Sever, Staccato, Stoic, Unfasten, Unhinge

Detached work Ravelin

Detail(s), Detailed Annotate, Dock, Elaborate, Embroider, Expatiate, Explicit,

Expound, Instance, → **ITEM**, Itemise, Minutiae, Nicety, Particular(ise), Pedantry, Point, Recite, Relate, Respect, Send, Spec, Special, Specification, Technicality

▷ **Detailed** *may indicate* last letter missing

Detain(ee), Detention Arrest, Buttonhole, Collar, Custody, Delay, Detinue, Gate, Glasshouse, Hinder, Intern, Keep, POW, Preventive, Retard, Stay, → **WITHHOLD**

Detect(or), Detective Agent, Arsène, Asdic, Bloodhound, Brown, Bucket, Busy, Catch, Chan, CID, Cuff, Dick, Discover, Divine, Doodlebug, Dupin, Espy, Eye, Fed, Find, Flambeau, Flic, Fortune, French, Geigercounter, Geophone, Gumshoe, Hanaud, Hercule, Holmes, Interpol, Investigator, Jack, Lecoq, Lupin, Maigret, Metal, Microwave, Mine, Minitrack®, Nail, Nose, Peeper, PI, Pinkerton, Plant, Poirot, Private, Private eye, Prodnose, Radar, Reagent, Rumble, Scent, Scerne, Sense, Sensor, Shadow, Shamus, Sherlock, → **SLEUTH**, Sleuth-hound, Sofar, Sonar, Sonobuoy, Spot, Tabaret, Take, Tec, Thorndyke, Toff, Trace, Trent, Vance, Wimsey, Yard

Detent Pawl, Trigger

Deter(rent) Block, Check, Daunt, Dehort, Delay, Dissuade, Prevent, Restrain, Turn-off

Detergent Cationic, Cleaner, Non-ionizing, Solvent, Surfactant, Syndet, Tepol, Whitener

Deteriorate, Deterioration Decadence, Degenerate, Derogate, Entropy, Pejoration, Rust, Worsen

▷ **Deterioration** *may indicate* an anagram

▷ **Determination** *may indicate* 'last letter'

Determine(d), Determination Arbitrament, Ardent, Ascertain, Assign, Assoil, Bent, Condition, Dead-set, → **DECIDE**, Define, Doctrinaire, Dogged, Do-or-die, Dour, Drive, Earnest, Fix, Govern, Grit(ty), Headstrong, Hell-bent, Indomitable, Influence, Intent, Judgement, Law, Liquidate, Out, Point, Pre-ordain, Purpose, Quantify, → **RESOLUTE**, Resolve, Rigwiddie, Rigwoodie, Self-will, Set, Settle, Shape, Stalwart, Steely, Type, Weigh

Detest(able) Abhor, Despise, Execrable, Execrate, Hate, Loathsome, Pestful, Vile

Detonate, Detonator Blast, Explode, Fire, Fuse, Fuze, Ignite, Kindle, Plunger, Primer, Saucisse, Saucisson, Tetryl, Trip-wire

Detour Bypass, Deviate, Divert

Detract Belittle, Decry, Diminish, Discount, Disparage

Detriment(al) Adverse, Damage, Harm, Injury, Loss, Mischief

Deuce Dickens, Old Harry, Twoer

Deuteron Diplon

Devalue Debase, Impair, Reduce, Undermine

Devastate Demolish, Destroy, Gut, Lay waste, Overwhelm, Ravage, Ruin, Sack, Traumatise, Waste, Wreck

Develop(er), Developed, Developing, Development Advance, Amidol®, Aplasia, Breakthrough, Breed, Bud, Build, Burgeon, Catechol, Creep, Educe, Elaborate, Enlarge, Epigenetic, Escalate, Evolve, Expand, Expatriate, Foetus, Full-fledged, Fulminant, Genesis, Germinate, Gestate, Grow, Hatch, Hothouse, Hydroquinone, Hypo, Imago, Improve, Incipient, Incubate, Lamarckism, Larva, Mature, Metamorphose, Metol, Morphogenesis, Morphosis, Mushroom, Nurture, Oidium, Ontogenesis, Pathogeny, Pullulate, Pupa, Pyro, Pyrogallol, Quinol, Ribbon, Ripe(n), Sarvodaya, Sensorimeter, Separate, Shape, Soup, Speciation, Sprawl, Subtopia, Technography, Teens, Tone, Unfold, Upgrow

▷ **Develop** *may indicate* an anagram

Deviant, Deviate, Deviation Aberrance, Abnormal, Anomaly, Average, Brisure,

Deflect, Depart, Derogate, Digress, Diverge, Divert, Error, Kinky, Kurtosis, List, Mean, Pervert, Quartile, Sheer, Solecism, Sport, Standard, Stray, Swerve, Transvestite, → TURN, Valgus, Varus, Veer, Wander, Wend

Device Allegory, → APPARATUS, Appliance, Artifice, Contraption, Contrivance, Deus ex machina, Dodge, Emblem, Expedient, Gadget, Gimmick, Gubbins, Instrument, Logo, Mnemonic, Motto, Pattern, Plan, Safeguard, → STRATAGEM, Subterfuge, Tactic, Tag, Thing, Trademark, Trick

DEVICES

3 letters:
Bug
FET
LED
Mux
Pad
POP
Zip

4 letters:
Capo
Drag
Fret
Fuse
Gobo
Grab
Orle
Plug
Rest
Shoe
Spur
Stop
Tram
Trap

5 letters:
Audio
Balun
Chaff
Choke
Chuck
Clamp
Cleat
Cramp
Crank
Diode
E-nose
Frame
Gizmo
Gland
Input

Maser
Meter
Mixer
Modem
Mouse
Optic®
Otter
Pager
Petar
Prism
Probe
Quipu
Relay
Rotor
Saser
Scale
Scart
Servo
Shear
Sieve
Siren
Snare
Sonde
Spool
Sprag
SQUID
Stent
Timer
Tromp
Truss
Valve
V-chip
Waldo

6 letters:
Analog
Atlatl
Beeper
Biodot
Blower
Bungee

Buzzer
Charge
Chouri
Choury
Cotter
Cut-out
Dasher
Deckle
De-icer
Detent
Dimmer
Dongle
Elevon
Engine
Etalon
Faller
Feeder
Filter
Friend®
Imager
Jigger
Joypad
Keeper
Kludge
Nanite
Petard
Pick-up
Pinger®
Possum
Preset
Quippu
Rabble
Reverb
Rocker
Roller
Router
Selsyn
Sensor
Shaker
Stoner
Switch

Swivel
Temple
Tipple
Tracer
Tremie
Triode
Trompe
Turtle
Tympan
Viewer
Wafter
Walker
Widget
Zapper

7 letters:
Bearing
Bendlet
Bleeper
Chopper
Cleaver
Clicker
Compass
Counter
Coupler
Dashpot
Digibox®
Divider
Doubler
Fuzzbox
Gas mask
Genlock
Gimbals
Grapnel
Hushkit
Imprese
Inhaler
Isotron
Jetpack
Krytron
Lighter

Machine
Minicom
Monitor
Pelorus
Pessary
Pickoff
Plunger
Ratchet
Reactor
Roll-bar
Rotator
Rowlock
Scanner
Shut-off
Shutter
Shuttle
Sniffer
Snorkel
Snuffer
Sounder
Spoiler
Starter
Stinger
Storage
Sundial
Swatter
Synchro
Toaster
Tokamak
Tonepad
Vernier
Vocoder

8 letters:
Airscoop
Alcolock
Analogue
Anti-icer
Atomiser
Autodial
Ballcock
Barostat
Betatron
Bootjack
Calutron
Commutor
Conveyor
Coupling
Demister
Detector
Diagraph

Diestock
Ecraseur
Eggtimer
Enlarger
Episcope
Episemon
Expander
Geophone
Heat pump
Hotplate
Ignitron
Launcher
Monogram
Nailhead
Occluder
Odograph
Odometer
Orthosis
Paravane
Playback
Pulsator
Push-pull
Pyrostat
Radiator
Resister
Shoehorn
Shredder
Silencer
Slip ring
Snow-eyes
Snowshoe
Solenoid
Spray gun
Spreader
Squeegee
Sweatbox
Swellbox
Terminal
Thin-film
Trembler
Varactor
Varistor
Vibrator

9 letters:
Aspirator
Autometer
Capacitor
Compasses
Convector
Converter

Corkscrew
Decoherer
Defroster
Delayline
Detonator
Dispenser
Dynamotor
Eccentric
Excelsior
Exerciser
Generator
Gyroscope
Headstock
Hendiadys
Hodoscope
Hydrofoil
Hydrostat
Hygrostat
Insulator
Keylogger
Konimeter
Kymograph
Megaphone
Mekometer
Metronome
Milometer
Nebuliser
Octophone
Optophone
Overdrive
Pacemaker
Parachute
Pedometer
Periscope
Photocell
Pitchbend
Polariser
Polygraph
Powerpack
Propeller
Rectifier
Regulator
Remontoir
Resonator
Responsor
Rheotrope
Rotachute
Rotameter®
Satellite
Scrambler
Separator

Sequencer
Simulator
Smokejack
Sonograph
Spaceband
Spindryer
Sprinkler
Stairlift
Steadicam
Stretcher
Tabulator
Tape drive
Tasimeter
Telegraph
Telemeter
Telepoint
Thermette
Thyristor
Tonometer
Trackball
Tremulant
Well sweep

10 letters:
Acetometer
Anemoscope
Applicator
Attenuator
Autowinder
Blackberry®
Calculator
Ceilometer
Centrifuge
Chronotron
Clapometer
Commutator
Comparator
Compressor
Copyholder
Cyclometer
Cyclostyle
Daisy-wheel
Databogger
Derailleur
Descendeur
Eprouvette
Groundprox
Humidistat
Hygroscope
Jawbreaker
Jaws of Life

Jellygraph	Transducer	Smokerlyzer	Telautograph
Kicksorter	Transistor	Snickometer	Teleprompter
Metrostyle	Turnbuckle	Solarimeter	Thermocouple
Microphone	Ventilator	Space heater	Turbidimeter
Microprobe	Vertoscope®	Spectograph	Viscosimeter
Microscope	Videophone	Speedometer	
Mileometer	Viewfinder	Swingometer	**13 letters:**
Noisemaker	Viscometer	Telestrator	Baton-sinister
Otter-board	Zener diode	Thermoscope	Dead man's pedal
Peripheral		Trackerball	Metal detector
Phonoscope	**11 letters:**	Transceiver	Phonendoscope
Phonospore	Afterburner	Transformer	Rack and pinion
Remontoire	Annunciator	Transmitter	Shock-absorber
Respirator	Autochanger	Transponder	Smoke detector
Self-feeder	Baffle-plate		
Siderostat	Carburettor	**12 letters:**	**14 letters:**
Snowplough	Distributor	Breathalyser	Anamorphoscope
Spirograph	Epidiascope	Concentrator	Dead man's handle
Stabiliser	Floor turtle	Desert cooler	Interferometer
Stimpmeter	Fluoroscope	Ebulliometer	Intervalometer
Suppressor	Insufflator	Intrauterine	Peltier element
Switchgear	Intoximeter	Lithotripter	Plethysmograph
Tachograph	Lie detector	Object finder	Scintillometer
Tachometer	Microfitter	Oscillograph	Spinthariscope
Telewriter	Microreader	Picturephone	
Thermistor	Microwriter	Sensitometer	**15 letters:**
Thermopile	Multiplexer	Snooperscope	Radiogoniometer
Thermostat	Recuperator	Spectroscope	
Tourniquet	Self-starter	Supercharger	

Devil(ish), Demon Abaddon, Afree, Afrit, Ahriman, Amaimon, Apollyon, Asmodeus, Atua, Auld Hornie, Azazel, Barbason, Beelzebub, Belial, Buckra, Cartesian, Clootie, Cloots, Dasyure, Davy Jones, Deev, Deil, Demogorgon, Demon, Deuce, Devling, Diable, Diabolic, Dickens, Div, Drudge, Dust, Eblis, Falin, Familiar, Fend, Fiend, Fient, Ghoul, Goodman, Goodyear, Grill, Hangie, Hornie, Iblis, Imp, Incubus, Infernal, Lamia, Legion, Lilith, Lord of the Flies, Lori, Lucifer, Mahoun(d), Man of Sin, Manta, Mara, Maxwell's, Mazikeen, Mephisto(pheles), Mischief, Nick, Nickie-ben, Old Bendy, Old Nick, Old One, Old Pandemonium, Old Poker, Old Roger, Old Split-foot, Old Toast, Printer's, Ragamuffin, Rahu, Ralph, Satan, Sathanas, Satyr, Scour, Scratch, Screwtape, Season, Setebos, Shaitan, Shedeem, Snow, Sorra, Succubine, Succubus, Tailard, Tasmanian, Tempter, Titivil, Tutivillus, Wendigo, Wicked, Wicked One, Wirricow, Worricow, Worrycow, Zernebock
Devious Braide, Cunning, Deep, Eel(y), Erroneous, Evasive, Implex, Indirect, Scheming, Shifty, Stealthy, Subtle, Tortuous, Tricky
Devise(d) Arrange, Concoct, Contrive, Decoct, Hatch, Hit-on, Imagine, Invenit, Invent, Plot, Thermette
Devitrified Ambitty
Devoid Barren, Destitute, Empty, Vacant, Wanting
Devolve Occur, Result, Transmit
Devote(e), Devotion(al), Devoted Addiction, Aficionado, Angelus, Attached, Bhakti, Buff, Bunny, Consecrate, Corban, Dedicate, Employ, Fan, Fervid, Fetishism,

Fiend, Holy, Hound, Loyalty, Novena, Ophism, Passion, Pious, Puja, Religioso, Saivite, Sea-green incorruptible, S(h)akta, Sivaite, Solemn, True, Zealous

Devour(ing) Consume, Eat, Engorge, Engulf, Manducate, Moth-eat, Scarf, Scoff, Snarf, → **SWALLOW**, Vorant

▷ **Devour** *may indicate* one word inside another

Devout Holy, Pia, Pious, Reverent, Sant, Sincere, Solemn

Dew(y) Bloom, Moist, Mountain, Rime, Roral, Roric, Rorid, Roscid, Serein, Serene, Tranter

Dexterity, Dexterous Adept, Adroit, Aptitude, Cleverness, Craft, Deft, Feat(e)ous, Featuous, → **HANDY**, Knack, Shrewd, Sleight, Slick

Diabolic Cruel, → **DEVILISH**, Infernal

Diacritic (mark) Acute, Angstrom, Cedilla, Circumflex, Diaresis, Eth, Grave, Háček, Thorn, Tilde, Umlaut

Diadem Coronet, Fillet, Garland, Tiara

Diagnose, Diagnosis, Diagnostic Amniocentesis, Fetal, Findings, Identify, Iridology, Pulse, Scan, Scintigraphy

Diagonal(ly) Bend(wise), Bias, Cater(-corner), Catty-cornered, Counter, Oblique, Slant, Solidus, Twill

Diagram Argand, Block, Butterfly, Chart, Chromaticity, Compass rose, Decision tree, Dendogram, Drawing, Fault-tree, Feynman, Figure, Flow, Graph, Graphics, Grid, Hertzsprung-Russell, Indicator, Logic, Map, Plan, Plat, Run-chart, Scintigram, Scatter, Schema, Stem-and-leaf, Stemma, Stereogram, Tephigram, Topo, Venn, Wind rose

Dial(ling) Card, Face, Mug, Phiz, Phone, Pulse, Ring, STD, Visage

Dialect Accent, Aeolic, Alemannic, Arcadic, Attic, Basuto, Burr, Castilian, Doric, Eldin, Eolic, Erse, Eye, Franconian, Friulian, Gallo-Romance, Gascon, Geechee, Geordie, Greenlander, Hegelian, Idiom, Ionic, Isogloss, Jargon, Jockney, Joual, Khalka, Koine, Konkani, Ladin, Lallans, Landsmaal, Langobardic, Langue d'oc, Langue d'oil, Langue d'oui, Lingo, Low German, Mackem, Min, Norman, Norn, Old Icelandic, Old North French, Parsee, Patois, Pedi, Prakrit, Rhotic, Riffian, Romans(c)h, Salish, Savoyard, Scouse, Sesotho, Syriac, Taal, Talkee-talkee, Talky-talky, Tongue, Tshi, Tuscan, Twi, Vernacular, Wu, Yealdon, Yenglish, Yinglish

Dialogue Colloquy, Conversation, Critias, Discussion, Exchange, Interlocution, Lazzo, Pastourelle, Speech, Stichomythia, Talk, Upspeak

Dialysis Kidney, Peritoneal

Diameter Breadth, Calibre, Gauge, Systyle, Tactical, Width

Diamond(s), Diamond-shaped Adamant, Black, Boart, Brilliant, Bristol, Carbonado, Cullinan, D, DE, Delaware, Eustace, False, Florentine, Hope, Ice, Industrial, Isomer, Jim, Koh-i-Noor, Lasque, Lattice, Lozenge, Paragon, Pick, Pitch, Pitt, Quarry, Rhinestone, Rhomb, Rock, Rose-cut, Rosser, Rough, Rustre, Sancy, Solitaire, Spark, Sparklers, Squarial, Suit

Diana Artemis, Di

Diapason Normal, Open, Ottava, Stopped

Diaphanous Clear, Sheer, Translucent

Diaphoretic Sweater

Diaphragm Cap, Iris, Mid-riff, Phrenic, Stop

Diaresis Trema

▶ **Diarist** *see* **DIARY**

Diarrhoea Collywobbles, Delhi belly, Gippy tummy, Lientery, Montezuma's revenge, Runs, Scours, Squitters, The shits, Trots, Verbal, Weaning-brash, Wood-evil

Diary, Diarist Chronicle, Dale, Day-book, Evelyn, Hickey, Journal, Kilvert, Log, Nobody, Pepys, Pooter, Record, Video

Diaspora Exodus, Galuth

Diatribe Harangue, Invective, Philippic, Tirade

Dice(r), Dicey Aleatory, Astragals, Bale, Bones, Chop, Craps, Cube, Doctor, Dodgy, Fulham, Fullams, Fullans, Gourd(s), Highman, Jeff, Mandoline, Novum, Poker, Shoot, Snake-eyes, Tallmen

Dichotomy Split

Dick(y), Dickey Clever, Deadeye, Front, Ill, Moby, OED, Policeman, Rumble, Shaky, Shirt, Spotted, Tec, Tonneau, Tucker, Tumbledown, Unstable, Wankle, Weak, Whittington

▷ **Dick** *may indicate* a dictionary

Dickens Boz, Deuce, Devil, Mephistopheles

Dicker Bargain, Barter, Haggle, Trade

▷ **Dicky** *may indicate* an anagram

Dictate, Dictator(ial) Amin, Authoritarian, Autocrat, Big Brother, Caesar, Castro, Cham, Command, Czar, Decree, Demagogue, Despot, Duce, Franco, Fu(e)hrer, Gauleiter, Hitler, Impose, Lenin, Ordain, Overbearing, Peremptory, Peron, Salazar, Shogun, Stalin, Tell, Tito, Totalitarian, Tsar, Tyrant, Tzar

Diction Language, Lexis, Palavinity, Speech, Style

Dictionary Alveary, Calepin, Chambers, Data, Etymologicon, Fowler, Gazetteer, Glossary, Gradus, Hobson-Jobson, Idioticon, Johnson's, Larousse, Lexicon, Lexis, OED, Onomasticon, Thesaurus, Vocabulary, Webster, Wordbook

Dictum Obiter, Say-so

Did Began, Couth, Fec(it), Gan

Didactic Sermonical

Diddle Cheat, Con, Hoax

Dido Antic, Caper, Carthaginian, Elissa

Die(d), Dying Ache, Cark, Choke, Crater, Croak, Cube, D, Decadent, Desire, End, Evanish, Exit, Expire, Fade, Fail, Flatline, Forfair, Fulham, Fulhan, Fullam, Go, Go west, Hallmark, Highman, Hop, Kark, Long, Morendo, Moribund, Ob(iit), Orb, Pass, Peg out, Perdendosi, Perish, Peter, Slip the cable, Snuff, Snuff it, Solidum, Sphacelation, Stamp, Sterve, Succumb, Suffer, Swage, Swelt, Terminal, Tine, Touch, Wane

Diehard Blimp, Fanatic, Intransigent, Reactionary, Standpatter, Zealot

Diesel Red

Diet(er) Assembly, Augsburg, Bant(ing), Cacatrophy, Council, Dail, Eat, Fare, Hay, Intake, Kashrut(h), Ketogenic, Landtag, Lent, Macrobiotic, Parliament, Pleading, Reduce, Regimen, Reichstag, Slim, Solid, Sprat, Staple, Strict, Tynwald, Vegan, Vegetarian, Weightwatcher, Worms

Dietetics Sit(i)ology

Differ(ence), Differing, Different(ly) Allo, Barney, Change, Cline, Contrast, Contretemps, Deviant, Diesis, Disagree, Discord, Discrepant, Disparate, Dispute, Dissent, Dissimilitude, Distinct, Diverge, Diverse, Else, Elsewise, Epact, Nuance, Omnifarious, Other, Othergates, Otherguess, Otherness, Otherwise, Potential, Separate, Several, Symmetric, Tiff, Unlike, Variform, Various, Vary

Differential, Differentiate, Differentiation Calculus, Del, Distinguish, Nabla, Product, Secern, Taxeme, Wage

Difficult(y) Abstruseness, Ado, Aporia, Arduous, Augean, Badass, Balky, Ballbuster, Bitter, Block, Bolshie, Bother, Catch, Choosy, Complication, Corner, Crotchety, Deep, Depth, Dysphagia, Extreme, Fiddly, Formidable, Gordian, → **HARD**, Hassle,

Hazard, Hiccough, Hiccup, Hobble, Hole, Hoor, Ill, Impasse, Indocile, Intractable, Intransigent, Jam, Kink, Knot, Lob's pound, Lurch, Mulish, Net, Nodus, Obstacle, Parlous, Pig, Pitfall, Plight, Predicament, Quandary, Queer St, Recalcitrant, Rough, Rub, Scabrous, Scrape, Scrub, Setaceous, Shlep, Snag, Soup, Steep, Stey, Stick, Sticky, Stiff, Strait, Stubborn, Stymie, Thorny, Ticklish, Tight spot, Trial, Tricky, Troublous, Une(a)th, Uphill, Via dolorosa

Diffident Bashful, Meek, Modest, Reserved, Shy

Diffuse, Diffusion Barophoresis, Disperse, Disseminate, Endosmosis, Exude, Osmosis, Pervade, Radiate, Spread, Thermal

Dig(s), Digger, Digging, Dig up Antipodean, Australian, Backhoe, Beadle, Bed(e)ral, Bedsit, Billet, Bot, Burrow, Costean, Delve, Enjoy, Excavate, Flea-bag, Fossorial, Gaulter, Gibe, Gird, Graip, Grub, Howk, Jab, Kip, Lair, Like, Lodgings, Mine, Navvy, Nervy, Nudge, Pad, Pioneer, Probe, Prod, Raddleman, Resurrect, Root, Ruddleman, Sap, See, Spade, Spit, Spud, Star-nose, Taunt, Till, Tonnell, Trench, Tunnel, Undermine, Unearth

Digest(ible), Digestion, Digestive Abridgement, Absorb, Abstract, Aperçu, Archenteron, Assimilate, Codify, Concoct, Endue, Epitome, Eupepsia, Eupepsy, Fletcherism, Gastric, Indew, Indue, Light, Pandect, Pem(m)ican, Pepsin(e), Peptic, Précis, Salt-cat, Steatolysis, → SUMMARY

Digit(s) Binary, Bit, Byte, Check, Dactyl, Figure, Finger, Hallux, Mantissa, Number, Pollex, Prehallux, Thumb, Toe

Dignified, Dignify August, Elevate, Exalt, Handsome, Honour, Lordly, Majestic, Manly, Proud, Solemn, Stately

Dignitary Bigwig, Dean, Name, Personage, Provost, → VIP

Dignity Aplomb, Bearing, Cathedra, Decorum, Face, Glory, Grandeur, High horse, Maestoso, Majesty, Nobility, Poise, Pontificate, Presence, Scarf, Tiara

Digraph Ash, Eng, Ng

Digress(ion) Apostrophe, Deviate, Diverge, Ecbole, Episode, Excurse, Excursus, Maunder, Veer, Wander

Dike Bank, Channel, Cludgie, Dam, Ditch, → DYKE, Embank(ment), Estacade, Lav(atory), Levee, Wall

Dilapidated, Dilapidation Clapped out, Clunker, Decrepit, Desolate, Disrepair, Eroded, Rickle, Ruined, Rust bucket, Tumbledown

Dilate, Dilation, Dilatation Amplify, Develop, Diastole, Ecstasis, Enlarge, Expand, Increase, Mydriasis, Sinus, Swell, Telangiectasia, Tent, Varix

Dilatory Protracting, Slow, Sluggish, Tardy

Dilemma Casuistry, Choice, Cleft, Dulcarnon, Fix, Horn, Predicament, Quandary, Why-not

Dilettante Aesthete, Amateur, Butterfly, Dabbler, Playboy

Diligence, Diligent Active, Application, Assiduous, Coach, Conscience, Eident, Industry, Intent, Painstaking, Sedulous, Studious

Dill Anise, Pickle

Dilute, Dilution Adulterate, Deglaze, Delay, Diluent, Lavage, Qualify, Simpson, Thin, Water, Weaken

Dim(ness), Dimming, Dimwit Becloud, Blear, Blur, Brownout, Caligo, Clueless, Crepuscular, Dense, Dusk, Eclipse, Fade, Faint, Feint, Gormless, Ill-lit, Indistinct, Mist, Nebulous, Ninny, Obscure, Overcast, Owl, Pale, Shadow, Unsmart

Dimension(s) Area, Breadth, Extent, Fourth, Height, Length, Measure, New, Scantling, Size, Third, Volume, Width

Diminish(ed), Diminishing, Diminuendo, Diminution, Diminutive Abatement, Assuage, Baby, Bate, Calando, Contract, Cot(t)ise, Deactivate, Decline,

Decrease, Détente, Detract, Disparage, Dissipate, Dwarf, Dwindle, Erode, Fourth, Hypocorism(a), Lessen, Lilliputian, Minify, Minus, Mitigate, Petite, Pigmy, Ritardando, Scarp, Small, Stultify, Subside, Toy, Trangle, Wane, Whittle

Dimple(d) Dent, Depression, Hollow, Orange-peel

Din Babel, Charivary, Chirm, Commotion, Deen, Discord, Gunga, Hubbub, → **NOISE**, Racket, Raird, Randan, Reel, Reird, Uproar, Utis

Dine(r), Dining Aristology, Café, Eat, Feast, Mess, Refect, Sup, Trat(toria)

Dingbat Doodad, Weirdo

Dinghy Pram, Shallop, Ship, Skiff

Dingo Warrigal

Dingy Crummy, Dark, Dirty, Drear, Dun, Fusc(ous), Grimy, Isabel(la), Isabelline, Lurid, Oorie, Ourie, Owrie, Shabby, Smoky

Dining-room Cafeteria, Cenacle, Commons, Frater, Hall, Langar, Mess hall, Refectory, Restaurant, Triclinium

Dinner Banquet, Collation, Feast, Hall, Kail, Kale, Meal, Prandial, Progressive, Repast, Spread

Dinosaur Allosaurus, Ankylosaur, Apatosaurus, Atlantosaurus, Baryonyx, Brachiosaurus, Brontosaurus, Ceratopsian, Ceratosaurus, Ceteosaurus, Chalicothere, Coelurosaur, Compsognathus, Cotylosaur, Cynodont, Dinothere, Diplodocus, Dolichosaurus, Duck-billed, Elasmosaur, Galeopithecus, Glyptodon, Hadrosaur, Ichthyosaur(us), Iguanodon, Megalosaur, Mosasaur, Ornithischian, Ornithopod, Ornithosaur, Oviraptor, Pelycosaur, Perissodactyl, Placoderm, Plesiosaur, Prehistoric, Prosauropod, Pteranodon, Pterodactyl, Pterosaur, Rhynchocephalian, Saurischian, Sauropod, Smilodon, Stegadon(t), Stegosaur, Teleosaurus, Theropod, Titanosaurus, Titanothere, Triceratops, Tyrannosaurus, Uintothere, Velociraptor

Dint Brunt, Dent, Depression, Force, Means, Power

Diocese Bishopric, District, Eparchate, See

Diode Esaki, Tunnel, Zener

Diogenes Cynic

Dioxide Cassiterite, Needle-tin

Dip(per) Bagna cauda, Baptise, Basin, Bathe, Bob, Brantub, Dabble, Dap, Dean, Dib, Diver, Dop, Double, Duck, Dunk, Foveola, Geosyncline, Guacomole, H(o)ummus, Houmous, Hum(m)us, Immerge, Immerse, Intinction, Ladle, Lucky, Magnetic, Ouzel, Paddle, Rinse, Rollercoaster, Sag, Salute, Sheep-wash, Star, Submerge, Tapenade, Taramasalata, Tzatziki, Ursa

Diphthong Synaeresis, Synizesis

Diploma Bac, Charter, Parchment, Qualification, Scroll, Sheepskin

Diplomacy, Diplomat(ic) Alternat, Ambassador, Attaché, CD, Chargé d'affaires, Chateaubriand, Cheque-book, Consul, DA, Dean, Dollar, Doyen, El(t)chi, Envoy, Fanariot, Fetial, Finesse, Gunboat, Legation, Lei(d)ger, Megaphone, Phanariot, Plenipotentiary, Shuttle, Suave, → **TACT**

▷ **Dippy** *may indicate* a bather

Dipsomania Oenomania

Dire Dreadful, Fatal, Fell, Hateful, Ominous, Urgent

Direct(or), Directly Administer, Advert, Aim, Airt, Auteur, Aventre, Board, Boss, Cann, Cast, Chairperson, Channel, Charge, Command, Compere, Con(n), Conduct, Control, Cox, Dead, Due, Dunstable road, Eisenstein, Enjoin, Executive, Explicit, Fast-track, Fellini, First-hand, Forthright, Frontal, Guide, Helm, Hitchcock, Huston, Immediate, Impresario, Instruct, Intendant, Kapellmeister, Lead, Lean, Manager, Mastermind, Navigate, Nonexecutive, Orson (Welles), Outright, Pagnol, Pilot, Play,

Point-blank, Ready, Reed, Refer, Régisseur, Rudder, Send, Set, Signpost, Stear, → **STEER**, Straight, Tati, Teach, Tell, Truffaut, Unvarnished, Vector, Welles

Direction Aim, Airt, Arrow, Astern, Bearings, Course, Cross-reference, E, End-on, Guidance, Guide, Heading, Keblah, L, Line, N, Orders, Passim, R, Route, Rubric, S, Sanction, Send, Sense, Side, Slap, Tack, Tenor, Thataway, Tre corde, Trend, W, Way, Wedelns

Direction-finder Asdic, Compass, Decca, Quadrant, Radar, Sextant, Sonar

Directory Crockford, Data, Debrett, Encyclop(a)edia, French, Kelly, List, Red book, Register, Root, Web, Yellow Pages®

Dirge Ballant, Coronach, Dirige, Epicedium, Knell, Monody, Requiem, Song, Threnody

Dirigible Airship, Balloon, Blimp, Zeppelin

Dirk Anelace, Dagger, Skean, Whinger, Whiniard, Whinyard

Dirt(y) Augean, Bed(r)aggled, Begrime, Bemoil, Cacky, Chatty, Clag, Clarty, Colly, Contaminate, Coom, Crock, Crud, Draggle, Dung, Dust, Earth, Festy, Filth, Foul, Gore, Grime, Grufted, Grungy, Impure, Manky, Moit, Mote, Muck, Obscene, Ordure, Pay, Pollute, Ray, Scody, Sculdudd(e)ry, Scum, Scungy, Scuzzy, Skanky, Skulduddery, Smirch, Smut(ch), Soil, Sooty, Sordes, Sordor, Squalid, Stain, Trash, Unclean, Unsatisfactory, Unwashed, Warb, Yucky, Yukky

Dis Hades, Hell

Disability, Disable(d) Cripple, Gimp, Handicapped, Incapacitate, Kayo, Lame, Maim, Paralyse, Scissor-leg, Scotch, Wreck

Disadvantage Detriment, Downside, Drawback, Handicap, Mischief, Out, Penalise, Penalty, Supercherie, Upstage, Wrongfoot, Zugswang

Disagree(ing), Disagreeable, Disagreement Argue, Argy-bargy, Bad, Clash, Conflict, Contest, Debate, Differ, Discrepant, Dispute, Dissent, Dissonant, Evil, Fiddlesticks, Friction, Heterodoxy, Pace, Plagu(e)y, Rift, Troll, Unpleasing

Disallow Forbid, Overrule

Disappear(ing) Cook, Dispel, Evanesce, Evanish, Evaporate, Fade, Kook, Latescent, Melt, Occult, Pass, Skedaddle, Slope, → **VANISH**

Disappoint(ment), Disappointed Anticlimax, Balk, Baulk, Bombshell, Bummer, Chagrin, Comedown, Crestfallen, Delude, Disgruntle, Frustrate, Gutted, Heartsick, Lemon, Letdown, Regret, Sell, Setback, Shucks, Sick, Suck-in, Sucks, Swiz(zle), Thwart, Underwhelm

Disapproval, Disapprove Ach, Animadvert, Boo, Catcall, Censure, Deplore, Deprecate, Discountenance, Expostulate, Fie, Frown, Harrumph, Hiss, Napoo, Object, Pejorative, Po-faced, Raspberry, Razz, Reject, Reproach, Reprobate, Squint, Tush, Tut, Tut-tut, Umph, Veto, Whiss

Disarm(ament), Disarming Bluff, Defuse, Demobilise, Nuclear, Winsome

Disarrange Disturb, Muddle, Ruffle, Tousle, Unsettle

Disarray Disorder, Mess, Rifle, Tash, Undress

Disaster, Disastrous Adversity, Apocalypse, Bale, Calamity, Cataclysm(ic), Catastrophe, Debacle, Dire, Doom, Evil, Fatal, Fiasco, Flop, Impostor, Meltdown, Mishap, Pitfall, Rout, Ruin, Screw-up, Seism, Shipwreck, Titanic, Tragedy, Wipeout

Disavow Abjure, Deny, Disclaim, Recant, Retract

Disbelief, Disbelieve(r) Acosmism, Anythingarian, Atheism, Doubt, Gawp, Incredulity, Mistrust, Nothingarianism, Occamist, Phew, Phooey, Puh-lease, Puh-leeze, Question, Sceptic, Shoot, Voetsak

Disburse Distribute, Expend, Outlay, Spend

Disc, Disk Bursting, Button, CD, Cheese, Compact, Coulter, Counter, Diaphragm, Dogtag, EP, Epiphragm, Flexible, Floppy, Frisbee®, Gold, Gong, Hard, Hard card,

Harrow, Impeller, Intervertebral, Laser, LP, Magnetic, Mono, O, Optic(al), Parking, Paten, Patin, Planchet, Plate, Platinum, Puck, RAM, Rayleigh, Record, Reflector, Rosette, Roundel, Roundlet, Rowel, Rundle, Sealed unit, Silver, Slipped, Slug, Stereo, Stylopodium, Sun, Swash plate, System, Tax, Token, Video, Wafer, Wharve, Whorl, Winchester, Wink, WORM, Zip®

Discard(ed) Abandon, Burn, Crib, Defy, Dele, Jettison, Kill, Leave, Obsolete, Off, Offload, Oust, → **REJECT**, Scrap, Shed, Shuck, Slough, Sluff, Supersede, Throw over, Trash

Discern(ing), Discernment Acumen, Acute, Clear-eyed, Descry, Detect, Discrimination, Eagle-eyed, Flair, Insight, Perceive, Percipient, Perspicacity, Realise, Sapient, Scry, See, Skry, → **TASTE**, Tell, Wate

Discharge Absolve, Acquit, Arc, Assoil, Blennorrhoea, Blow off, Brush, Cashier, Catamenia, Catarrh, Conditional, Corona, Dejecta, Deliver, Demob, Disembogue, Disgorge, Dismiss, Disruptive, Dump, Efflux, Effusion, Egest, Ejaculate, Eject, Embogue, Emission, Emit, Encopresis, Enfilade, Evacuate, Excrete, Execute, Exemption, Expulsion, Exude, Fire, Flashover, Flower, Flux, Frass, Free, Gleet, Glow, Lava, Lay off, Leak, Let off, Leucorrhoea, Lochia, Loose, Maturate, Menses, Mitimus, Mute, Offload, Otorrhoea, Oust, Ozaena, Pay, Perform, Period, Planuria, Purulence, Pus, Pyorrhoea, Quietus, Rheum, Rhinorrhoeal, Sack, Salvo, Sanies, Secretion, Show, Shrive, Snarler, Spark, Suppurate, Teem, Unload, Vent, Void, Water, Whites

Disciple(s) Adherent, Apostle, Babi, Baruch, Catechumen, Chela, Follower, John, Judas, Luke, Mark, Matthew, Peter, Simon, Son, Student, The Seventy, Thomist, Votary

Disciplinarian, Discipline Apollonian, Ascesis, Chasten, Chastise, Correct, Despot, Drill, Exercise, Feng shui, Inure, Martinet, Mathesis, Punish, Regimentation, Regulate, Sadhana, School, Science, Spartan, Stickler, Subject, Taskmaster, Train, Tutor

▶ **Disc jockey** see **DJ**

Disclaim(er) Deny, Disown, No(t)chel, Recant, Renounce, → **REPUDIATE**, Voetstoots

Disclose, Disclosure Apocalypse, Confess, Divulge, Expose, Impart, Leak, Manifest, Propale, → **PUBLISH**, Report, Reveal, Spill, Tell, Unheal, Unhele, Unrip, Unveil

Discoloration, Discolour(ed) Bloodstain, Bruise, Cyanosis, Dyschroa, Ecchymosis, Fox, Livedo, Livid, Livor, Stain, Streak, Tarnish, Tinge, Weather

Discomfit(ure) Abash, Confuse, Disconcert, Disturb, Frustrate, Lurch, Shend

Discomfort(ed) Ache, All-overish, Angst, Dysphoria, Gyp, Heartburn, Pain, Unease

Disconcert(ing) Abash, Astound, Confuse, Disturb, Embarrass, Faze, Feeze, Flurry, Fluster, Nonplus, Off-putting, Phase, Pheese, Pheeze, Phese, → **RATTLE**, Shatter, Tease, Throw, Upset, Wrong-foot

▷ **Disconcert(ed)** *may indicate* an anagram

Disconnect(ed) Asynartete, Detach, Disjointed, Off-line, Sever, Staccato, Uncouple, Undo, Unplug

Disconsolate Desolate, Doleful, Downcast, → **GLOOMY**

Discontent(ed) Disquiet, Dissatisfied, Humph, Repined, Sour, Umph

Discontinue, Discontinuance, Discontinuity Abandon, Cease, Desist, Desuetude, Drop, Moho, Prorogue, Stop, Terminate

Discord(ant) Absonant, Ajar, Charivari, Conflict, Din, Dispute, Eris, Faction, Hoarse, Jangle, Jar, Raucous, Ruction, Strife

▷ **Discord(ant)** *may indicate* an anagram

Discount Agio, Cashback, Deduct, Disregard, Forfaiting, Invalidate, Quantity,
→ **REBATE**, Trade
Discountenance Disfavour, Efface, Embarrass
Discourage(ment) Caution, Chill, Dampen, Dash, Daunt, Deject, Demoralise,
Deter, Dishearten, Disincentive, Dismay, Dissuade, Enervate, Frustrate, Intimidate,
Opposition, Stifle, Unman
Discourse Address, Argument, Conversation, Descant, Diatribe, Dissertate, Eulogy,
Expound, Homily, Lecture, Lucubrate, Orate, Philippic, Preach, Relate, Rigmarole,
Sermon, Wash
Discourteous, Discourtesy Impolite, Insult, Rude, Slight, Uncivil, Unmannerly
Discover(y), Discoverer Amundsen, Anagnorisis, Ascertain, Betray, Breakthrough,
Columbus, Cook, Descry, Detect, Discern, Discure, Eureka, → **FIND**, Heureka,
Heuristic, Learn, Locate, Manifest, Moresby, Protegé, Rumble, Serendip,
Serendipity, Spy, Tasman, Trace, Treasure trove, Unearth, Unhale, Unmask, Unveil
▷ **Discovered in** *may indicate* an anagram or a hidden word
Discredit(able) Debunk, Decry, Disgrace, Explode, Infamy, Scandal, Smear,
Unworthy
Discreet, Discretion Cautious, Circumspect, Freedom, Judicious, Option, Polite,
Politic, Prudence, Prudent, Trait, Wise
Discrepancy Difference, Gap, Lack, Shortfall, Variance
Discrete Distinct, Separate, Unrelated
Discriminate, Discriminating, Discrimination Ag(e)ism, Colour bar, Diacritic,
Differentiate, Discern, Distinguish, Elitism, Handism, Invidious, Lookism,
Nasute, Racism, Rankism, Reverse, Secern, Segregate, Select, Sexism, Siz(e)ism,
Speciesism, Subtle, Taste
Discursive Roving
Discuss(ed), Discussion Agitate, Air, Canvass, Commune, Conf(erence), Consult,
Debate, Dialectic, Dialogue, Dicker, Disquisition, En l'air, Examine, Excursus,
Expatiate, Handle, Hob and nob, Interlocution, Korero, Moot, Negotiation, Over,
Palaver, Parley, Pourparler, Prolegomenon, Quodlibet, Rap, Re, Symposium, Talk,
Tapis, Treatment, Ventilate, Vex
Disdain(ful) Belittle, Contempt, Coy, Deride, Despise, Geck, Poof, Pooh-pooh, Puh,
Rats, Sassy, → **SCORN**, Scout, Sdei(g)n, Sniffy, Spurn, Supercilious, Ugh
Disease(d) Affection, Ailment, Communicable, Complaint, Deficiency, Epidemic,
Fever, Functional, Industrial, Infection, Malady, Noso-, Nosocomial, Notifiable,
Occupational, Organic, Pest(ilence), Rot, Scourge, Sickness

DISEASES

2 *letters:*	Haw	Clap	5 *letters:*
CD	Pip	Conk	Bang's
MD	Pox	Gout	Black
ME	Sod	Keel	Borna
MS	→ **STD**	Kuru	Brand
TB	TSE	Loco	Dread
VD	Wog	Lues	Dutch
		Lyme	Ebola
3 *letters:*	4 *letters:*	Roup	Edema
ALS	Aids	Wind	Ergot
BSE	Boba	Yaws	Favus
Flu	Bunt		Fifth

Gapes
Hoove
Kwok's
Lupus
Lurgi
Lurgy
Mesel
Mumps
Ngana
Palsy
Pinta
Polio
Pott's
Rabid
Scall
Sprue
Surra
Tinea
Virus
Weil's
Worms

6 letters:
Anbury
Aphtha
Blight
Blotch
Border
Cancer
Canker
Chagas'
Chorea
Cowpox
Crohn's
Cruels
Dartre
Dengue
Eczema
Farcin
Graves'
Herpes
Income
Johne's
Mad cow
Marck's
Meazel
Mildew
Morbus
Mosaic
Nagana

Oedema
Paget's
Parrot
Rabies
Sapego
Scurvy
Social
Still's
Thrush
Tunnel
Typhus
Ulitis
Urosis
Yuppie
Zoster

7 letters:
Ascites
Batten's
Bright's
British
Caisson
Cholera
Coeliac
Crewels
Dieback
Dourine
Endemic
English
Frounce
Hansen's
Hardpad
Hydatid
Icterus
Kissing
Leprosy
Lockjaw
Maidism
Malaria
Marburg
Miller's
Mimesis
Mooneye
Moor-ill
Murrain
Mycosis
Myiasis
Pébrine
Podagra
Porrigo

Purples
Redfoot
Rickets
Ring rot
Rosette
Scabies
Scrapie
Sequela
Serpigo
Tetanus
Tetters
Typhoid
Variola
Wilson's
Zymosis

8 letters:
Addison's
Alastrim
Aujesky's
Beri-beri
Blackleg
Bornholm
Club root
Crown rot
Cushing's
Cynanche
Diabetes
Dutch elm
Economo's
Fishskin
Fowl pest
Gaucher's
Glanders
Glaucoma
Gummosis
Hodgkin's
Hookworm
Impetigo
Jaundice
Kala-azar
Leaf-roll
Leaf-spot
Liver-rot
Loose-cut
Menière's
Minamata
Mycetoma
Myopathy
Myxedema

Nosology
Pandemic
Pathogen
Pellagra
Phthisis
Phytosis
Porrigro
Progeria
Pullorum
Rachitis
Raynaud's
Rose-rash
Scaly leg
Scrofula
Shingles
Smallpox
Soft sore
Suppeago
Swayback
Swinepox
Syphilis
Tay-Sachs
The bends
Trembles
Venereal
Vincent's
Zoonosis

9 letters:
Bilharzia
Blackhead
Black knot
Brown lung
Chancroid
Chlorosis
Christmas
Cirrhosis
Contagion
Diathesis
Distemper
Dysentery
Enteritis
Exanthema
Filanders
Gonorrhea
Idiopathy
Ixodiasis
Kawasaki's
Lathyrism
Leucaemia

Leukaemia
Loose smut
Myxoedema
Navicular
Nephritis
Nephrosis
Newcastle
New Forest
Pellagrin
Pemphigus
Phossy-jaw
Porphyria
Seborrhea
Siderosis
Silicosis
Toxicosis
Trichosis
Tularemia
Yuppie flu

10 letters:
Acromegaly
Alzheimer's
Amoebiasis
Asbestosis
Autoimmune
Babesiosis
Bagassosis
Bluetongue
Byssinosis
Chickenpox
Dandy-fever
Diphtheria
Erysipelas
Filariasis

Framboesia
Gonorrhoea
Heartwater
Hemophilia
Iatrogenic
Ichthyosis
Impaludism
Leuchaemia
Limber-neck
Lou Gehrig's
Louping ill
Moniliasis
Muscardine
Neuropathy
Nosography
Ornithosis
Parkinson's
Scarlatina
Seborrhoea
Topagnosia
Tularaemia

11 letters:
Anthracosis
Brittle-bone
Cardiopathy
Consumption
Green monkey
Haemophilia
Hebephrenia
Huntington's
Isle of Wight
Kwashiorkor
Listeriosis
Myxomatosis

Parasitosis
Paratyphoid
Psittacosis
Rickettsial
Scleroderma
Septicaemia
Thalassemia
Trench mouth
Trichinosis
Woolsorter's
Yellow-fever

12 letters:
Avitaminosis
Enterobiasis
Fascioliasis
Finger and toe
Foot and mouth
Furunculosis
Hoof and mouth
Legionnaires'
Molybdenosis
Motor neurone
Osteomalacia
Osteoporosis
Scheuermann's
Shaking palsy
Slapped cheek
Thalassaemia
Tuberculosis
Uncinariasis

13 letters:
Elephantiasis
Leichmaniasis

Leptospirosis
Osteomyelitis
Poliomyelitis
Sclerodermata
Syringomyelia
Toxoplasmosis
Tsutsugamushi

14 letters:
Cystic fibrosis
Histoplasmosis
Leucodystrophy
Onchocerciasis
Pasteurellosis
Pneumoconiosis
Psillid yellows
River blindness
Sporotrichosis
Trichomoniasis
Trichophytosis
Vincent's angina

15 letters:
Schistosomiasis
Trypanosomiasis

16 letters:
Pneumonoconiosis
Sleeping sickness
Sweating sickness

17 letters:
Friedreich's ataxia
Multiple sclerosis

▷ **Diseased** *may indicate* an anagram

Disembark Alight, Detrain, Land

Disembarrass Extricate, Rid, Unthread

Disembowel Eviscerate, Exenterate, Gralloch, Gut, Viscerate

Disenchant Disabuse, Dismay, Embitter

Disencumber Free, Rid, Unburden

Disengage(d), Disengagement Clear, Detach, Divorce, Liberate, Loosen, Release, Untie

Disentangle Debarrass, Extricate, Red(d), Solve, Unravel, Unsnarl

Disestablishmentarian Cosmist

Disfavour Doghouse, Maugre

Disfigure(ment), Disfigured Agrise, Agryze, Camsho, Deface, Deform, Goitre, Mutilate, Scar, Spoil, Tash, Ugly

▷ **Disfigured** *may indicate* an anagram

Disgorge Discharge, Spew, Spill, Vent, Void

Disgrace Atimy, Attaint, Baffle, Blot, Contempt, Contumely, Degrade, Discredit, Dishonour, Dog-house, Ignominy, Indignity, Infamy, Obloquy, Opprobrium, Scandal, Shame, Shend, Slur, Soil, Stain, Stigma, Yshend

Disgraceful Diabolical, Fie, Ignoble, Ignominious, Indign, Infamous, Mean, Notorious, Shameful, Turpitude

Disgruntled Brassed off, Malcontent, Resentful, Sore

▷ **Disgruntled** *may indicate* an anagram

Disguise(d) Alias, Blessing, Camouflage, Cloak, Colour, Conceal, Cover, Covert, Dissemble, Hide, Hood, Incog(nito), Mantle, Mask, Masquerade, Obscure, Peruke, Pretence, Pseudonym, Ring, Shades, Travesty, Veil, Vele, Veneer, Visagiste, Visor, Vizard

▷ **Disguised** *may indicate* an anagram

Disgust(ing) Ach-y-fi, Ad nauseam, Aversion, Aw, Bah, Cloy, Discomfort, Execrable, Faugh, Fie, Foh, Fulsome, Grisly, Grody, Irk, Loathsome, Manky, Mawkish, Minging, Nauseous, Noisome, Obscene, Odium, Oughly, Ouglie, Pah, Pho(h), Pish, Pshaw, Pugh, Repel, Repugnant, Repulse, → **REVOLT**, Revulsion, Scomfish, Scumfish, Scunner, Scuzz, → **SICKEN**, Si(e)s, Sir-reverence, Slimeball, Squalid, Tush, Ugh, Ugsome, Vile, Yech, Yu(c)k, Yucko, Yukky

Dish(y) Adonis, Allot, Apollo, Ashet, Basin, Belle, Bowl, Chafing, Charger, Cocotte, Cook-up, Cutie, Dent, Diable, Dole, Dreamboat, Epergne, Flasket, Grail, Kitchen, Laggen, Laggin, Lanx, Luggie, Mazarine, Muffineer, Ovenware, Pan, Pannikin, Paten, Patera, Patin(e), Petri, Plate, Platter, Porringer, Ramekin, Ramequin, Receptacle, Rechauffé, Remove, Sangraal, Sangrail, Sangreal, Satellite, Saucer, Scallop, Scorifier, Scupper, Serve, Service, Side, Smasher, Special, Toll, Watchglass

---

DISHES

3 letters:	Dolma	Bharta	Roesti
Poi	Gomer	Bhoona	Salmis
	Kasha	Bridie	Sowans
4 letters:	Kibbe	Chilli	Sowens
Fool	Kofta	Cou-cou	Subgum
Kiev	Korma	Cuscus	Surimi
Mess	Laksa	Entrée	Tamale
Olla	Maror	Fondue	Tsamba
Puri	Perog	Haggis	
Sate	Pilau	Hotpot	**7 letters:**
Soss	Pilow	Kimchi	Biriani
Taco	Poori	Kishke	Bobotie
Tian	Raita	Masale	Burrito
	Ramen	Mornay	Calzone
5 letters:	Rosti	Mousse	Cassava
Adobo	Salmi	Muesli	Ceviche
Balti	Satay	Nachos	Comport
Bhaji	Sushi	Paella	Compote
Bhuna	Tamal	Pakora	Crowdie
Bitok	Tikka	Panada	Crubeen
Boxty	Tripe	Pirogi	Crumble
Brose		Quiche	Custard
Champ	**6 letters:**	Ragout	Cuvette
Curry	Bhagee	Regale	Dariole

Dhansak
Dopiaza
Egg roll
Fajitas
Fal-a-fel
Fel-a-fel
Foo yung
Friture
Grav lax
Marengo
Mousaka
Padella
Pierogi
Poutine
Rarebit
Ravioli
Sasatie
Sashimi
Seviche
Soufflé
Stir-fry
Stovies
Tempura
Terrine
Timbale
Tostada

8 letters:
Brandade
Caponata
Chop suey
Chow mein
Coolamon
Coq au vin
Coquille
Couscous
Crostini
Dog's-body
Entremes
Feijoada
Flummery
Frittata

Gado-gado
Halloumi
Handroll
Jalfrezi
Kedgeree
Keftedes
Kickshaw
Kouskous
Kreplach
Linguini
Matelote
McCallum
Meunière
Moussaka
Pandowdy
Pastrami
Porridge
Pot-au-feu
Pot-roast
Raclette
Shashlik
Sillabub
Souvlaki
Squarial
Sukiyaki
Syllabub
Teriyaki
Tzatziki
Vindaloo
White-pot
Yakimono
Yakitori

9 letters:
Carbonara
Carpaccio
Cevapcici
Compotier
Egg-fo-yang
Enchilada
Entremets
Fricassee

Galantine
Gravad lax
Guacamole
Howtowdie
Jambalaya
Manicotti
Marinière
Matelotte
Pastitsio
Pepper-pot
Reistafel
Rijstafel
Rogan josh
Shashlick
Souvlakia
Succotash
Surf n'turf

10 letters:
Blanquette
Bombay duck
Cacciatore
Coulibiaca
Couscousou
Doner kebab
Egg-foo-yung
Jugged hare
Koulibiaca
Mousseline
Nasi goreng
Parmigiana
Plat du jour
Provençale
Quesadilla
Rijsttafel
Salmagundi
Sauerkraut
Scallopine
Shish kebab
Spitchcock
Spring roll
Stroganoff

Teppan-yaki

11 letters:
Buck-rarebit
Fritto misto
Saltimbocca
Sauerbraten
Smorgasbord
Spanakopita
Surf and turf
Welsh rabbit

12 letters:
Eggs Benedict
Shepherd's pie
Solomon Gundy
Steak tartare
Sweet and sour
Taramasalata
Welsh rarebit

13 letters:
Fish and brewis
Rumbledethump
Skirl in the pan
Toad-in-the-hole

14 letters:
Beef stroganoff
Chilli con carne
Rumbledethumps
Scotch woodcock

15 letters:
Bubble and squeak
Eggs in moonshine

16 letters:
Potatoes and point

17 letters:
Cauliflower cheese

Dishabille Disarray, Négligé, Undress
Dishearten Appal, Core(r), Cow, Daunt, Depress, Discourage, Dispirit
Dishevel(led) Blowsy, Blowzy, Daggy, Mess, Rumpled, Touse, Tousle, Touzle, Tumble, Uncombed, Unkempt, Windswept
Dishonest(y) Bent, Crooked, Cross, Dodgy, False, Fraud, Graft, Hooky, Hot, Improbity, Jiggery-pokery, Knavery, Malpractice, Malversation, Shonky, Snide, Stink, Twister, Underhand, Venal, Wrong'un
Dishonour Abatement, Defile, Disgrace, Disparage, Ignominy, Seduce, → SHAME,

Violate, Wrong

Disillusion Disenchant, Sour

Disincline(d), Disinclination Apathy, Averse, Loth, Off, Reluctant

Disinfect(ant) Acriflavin(e), Carbolic, Cineol(e), Cleanse, Dip, Eucalyptole, Formalin, Formol, Fuchsine, Fumigate, Lysol®, Phenol, Purify, Sheep-dip, Sheep-wash, TCP, Terebene

Disingenuous Insincere, Mask, Oblique, Two-faced

Disinherit Deprive, Dispossess

Disintegrate, Disintegration Break, Collapse, Crumble, Decay, Erode, Fragment, Lyse, Lysis, Osteoclasis, Rd, Rutherford

Disinter Exhume, Unearth

Disinterested Apathetic, Impartial, Incurious, Mugwump, Unbiased

Disjoint(ed) Bitty, Dismember, Incoherent, Rambling, Scrappy

▶ **Disk** *see* **DISC**

Dislike Abhor, Allergy, Animosity, Animus, Antipathy, Aversion, Derry, Disesteem, Displeasure, Distaste, Gross out, Hate, Lump, Mind, Needle, Scunner, Warling

Dislocate, Dislocation Break, Diastasis, Displace, Fault, Luxate, Slip, Subluxate

Dislodge Budge, Displace, Expel, Luxate, Oust, Rear, Tuft, Unship, Uproot

Disloyal(ty) False, Treason, Unfaithful, Untrue

Dismal Black, Bleak, Cheerless, Dark, Dowie, Dowly, Drack, Dreary, Funereal, → **GLOOMY**, Grey, Long-faced, Morne, Obital, Sepulchral, Sombre, Sullen, Trist(e), Wae, Woebegone, Wormy

Dismantle(d), Dismantling Decommission, Derig, Divest, Get-out, Sheer-hulk, Strike, Strip, Unrig

Dismast Unstep

Dismay Amate, Appal, Confound, Consternation, Coo, Daunt, Fie, Ha, Horrify, Lordy, Lumme, Qualms, Strewth

Dismiss(al), Dismissive Airy, Annul, Ax, Boot, Bounce, Bowl(er), Bum's rush, Cancel, Cashier, Catch, Chuck, Congé, Constructive, Daff, Discard, Discharge, Dooced, Expulsion, Fire, Heave-ho, Kiss-off, Lay off, Marching orders, Mitten, Och, Prorogue, Push, Recall, Reform, Reject, Remove, R.O., Road, Sack, Scout, Send, Shoo, Shrug off, Skittle out, Spit, Spurn, Stump, Suka wena, Via, Voetsak, Voetsek, Walking papers, York

Dismount Alight, Hecht

Disobedience, Disobedient, Disobey Contumacy, Defy, Flout, Insubordination, Rebel, Sit-in, Wayward

Disorder(ly), Disordered Affective, Ague, Ailment, Anarchy, Ariot, Asthma, Ataxia, Catatonia, Chaos, Chlorosis, Clutter, Confuse, Consumption, Contracture, Conversion, Defuse, Derange, Deray, Diabetes, Dishevel, Dissociative, Dysthymic, Dystrophy, Echolalia, Entropy, Epilepsy, Farrago, Greensickness, Grippe, Haemophilia, Hallucinosis, Heartburn, Huntingdon's chorea, Hypallage, Inordinate, Irregular, Mange, Mare's nest, ME, Mental, Mess, Misrule, Mistemper, → **MUDDLE**, Muss(y), Neurosis, Oncus, Onkus, Pandemonium, Panic, Para-, Pell-mell, Personality, Phenylketonuria, Porphyria, Psychomatic, Psychopathic, Psychosis, Ragmatical, Rile, Roughhouse, Rowdy, SAD, St Vitus' Dance, Schizophrenia, Seborrh(o)ea, Shell-shock, Slovenly, Sydenham's chorea, Tarantism, Thalass(a)emia, Thought, Tousle, Turbulence, Unhinge, Unruly, Upheaval, Upset, Virilism

▷ **Disorder(ed)** *may indicate* an anagram

Disorganised At sea, Deranged, Haywire, Scatterbrain, Shambolic, Structureless

Disown Deny, Disclaim, Disinherit, Renounce, Repudiate, Unget
Disparage, Disparaging Abuse, Belittle, Decry, Defame, Denigrate, Depreciate, Detract, Discredit, Lessen, Pejorative, Poor mouth, Racist, → **SLANDER**, Slur, Snide, Traduce, Vilify
Dispassionate Calm, Clinical, Composed, Cool, Impartial, Objective, Serene
Dispatch Bowl, Celerity, Consign, Destroy, Dismiss, Expede, Expedite, Express, Gazette, Kibosh, Kill, Missive, Post, Pronto, Remit, Report, → **SEND**, Ship, Slaughter, Slay, Special
Dispel Disperse, Scatter
Dispensation, Dispense(r), Dispense with Absolve, Administer, Aerosol, Apothecary, Automat, Ax(e), Cashpoint, Chemist, Container, Distribute, Dose, Dropper, Exempt, Handout, Indult, Scrap, Spinneret, Vendor, Visitation
Dispersable, Disperse, Dispersion Deflocculate, Diaspora, Diffract, Diffuse, Disband, Dissolve, Lyophil(e), Scail, Scale, → **SCATTER**, Skail, Sow, Strew
Dispirit(ed), Dispiriting Chapfallen, Crestfallen, Dampen, Dash, Daunt, Discourage, Dishearten, Exorcism, Gloomy, Listless, Sackless
Displace(ment), Displaced Antevert, Blueshift, Depose, Disturb, Ectopia, Ectopy, Fault, Heterotopia, Lateroversion, Load, Luxate, Move, Oust, Proptosis, Ptosis, Reffo, Shift, Stir, Subluxation, Unseat, Unsettle, Uproot, Valgus, Varus, Volumetric
Display, Display ground Air, Array, Blaze, Blazon, Brandish, Bravura, Depict, Eclat, Epideictic, Etalage, Evidence, Evince, Exhibition, Exposition, Express, Extend, Extravaganza, Exude, Fireworks, Flash, Flaunt, Float, Gondola, Hang, Head-down, Head-up, Heroics, Lay out, LCD, LED, Lek, Liquid crystal, Manifest, Mount, Muster, Ostentation, Outlay, Overdress, Pageant, Parade, Paraf(f)le, Peepshow, Pixel, Pomp, Propale, Pyrotechnics, Rode, Rodeo, Roll-out, Scene, Shaw, → **SHOW**, Sight, Spectacle, Splash, Splurge, Sport, Spree, State, Stunt, Tableau, Tattoo, Tournament, Up, Vaunt, Wear
Displease(d), Displeasure Anger, Dischuffed, Humph, Irritate, Provoke, Umbrage
Disport Amuse, Divert, Play
Dispose(d), Disposal, Disposition Apt, Arrange, Bestow, Cast, Despatch, Dump, Eighty-six, Kibosh, Lay(-out), Ordonnance, Prone, Sale, Sell, Service, Settle, Stagger
▷ **Disposed, Disposition** *may indicate* an anagram
Disposition Affectation, Attitude, Bent, Bias, Humour, Inclination, Kidney, Lie, Nature, Penchant, Propensity, Talent, Temper(ament), Trim
Dispossess(ed) Abate, Attaint, Bereft, Depose, Deprive, Evict, Oust
Disproportion(ate) Asymmetric, Extreme, Imbalance, Unequal
Disprove, Disproof, Disproval Debunk, Discredit, Negate, Rebut, Rebuttal, Redargue, Reductio ad absurdum, Refel, Refute
Dispute(d), Disputant Argue, Barney, Brangle, Cangle, Case, Chaffer, Challenge, Chorizont(ist), Contend, Contest, Contravene, Contretemps, Controversy, Debate, Demarcation, Deny, Differ, Discept, Discuss, Eristic, Fracas, Fray, Haggle, Kilfud-yoking, Lock-out, Militate, Ob and soller, Odds, Oppugn, Plea, Polemic, Pro-and-con, Quarrel, → **QUESTION**, Quibble, Rag, Resist, Spar, Stickle, Threap(it), Threep(it), Tiff, Tissue, Tug-of-love, Variance, Wrangle
Disqualify Debar, Incapacitate, Recuse, Reject, Unfit
Disquiet(ed) Agitate, Concern, Discomboberate, Discombobulate, → **DISTURB**, Pain, Perturb(ation), Solicit, Turmoil, Uneasy, Unnerve, Unrest, Vex
Disraeli Dizzy, Tancred
Disregard(ed) Anomie, Anomy, Contempt, Defy, Disfavour, Flout, Forget, Ignore, Oblivion, Omit, Overlook, Oversee, Pass, Pretermit, Slight, Spare, Violate, Waive
Disrepair Dilapidation, Fritz, Ruin

Disreputable, Disrepute Base, Disgrace, Grubby, Louche, Low, Lowlife, Notorious, Raffish, Ragamuffin, Reprobate, Rip, Scuzz(ball), Seamy, Seamy side, Shady, Shameful, Shy, Sleazy

Disrespect(ful) Contempt, Derogatory, Discourtesy, Flip(pant), Impiety, Impolite, Irreverent, Profane, Slight, Uncivil

Disrupt(ion) Breach, Cataclasm, Dislocate, Disorder, Distract, Hamper, Interrupt, Jetlag, Mayhem, Perturb, Quonk, Screw, Upheaval

▷ **Disruption** *may indicate* an anagram

Dissatisfaction Displeasure, Distaste, Humph, Umph

Dissect(ion) Analyse, Dismember, Examine, Necrotomy, Zootomy

Dissemble(r) Conceal, Feign, Fox, Hypocrite, Impostor

Dissent(er), Dissension, Dissenting Contend, Differ, Disagree, Discord, Dissident, Faction, Flak, Heretic, Jain, Leveller, Lollard, Noes, Non-CE, Non-con(formist), Occasional conformist, Old Believer, Pantile, Protest, Raskolnik, Recusant, Sectary, Separat(ion)ist, Splinter group, → **STRIFE**, Vary

Dissertation Essay, Excursus, Lecture, Thesis, Treatise

▸ **Dissident** *see* **DESERTER**

Dissimilar Different, Diverse, Heterogeneous, Unlike

Dissipate(d) Debauch, Diffuse, Disperse, Dissolute, Gay, Revel, Scatter, Shatter, Squander, Waste

▷ **Dissipated** *may indicate* an anagram

Dissociate Separate, Sever, Withdraw

Dissolute Degenerate, Demirep, Falstaffian, Hell, Lax, Libertine, Licentious, Loose, Rake-helly, Rakish, Rip, Roué, Wanton

▷ **Dissolute** *may indicate* an anagram

Dissolution Dismissal, Divorce, End, Repeal, Separation

Dissolve Deliquesce, Digest, Disband, Disunite, Lap, Liquesce, Melt, Repeal, Terminate, Thaw

Dissonance Wolf

Dissuade Dehort, Deter, Discourage

Distaff Clotho, Female, Lady, Rock, Stick

Distance Absciss(a), Afield, Apothem, Breadth, Coss, Declination, Eloi(g)n, Farness, Focal, Foot, Headreach, Height, Hyperfocal, Intercalumniation, Interval, Klick, Kos(s), Latitude, League, Length, Mean, Mean free path, Middle, Mileage, Northing, Outland, Parasang, Parsec, Range, Reserve, Rod, Skip, Span, Spitting, Stade, Striking, Way, Yojan, Zenith

Distant Aloof, Cold, Far, Frosty, Hyperfocal, Icy, Long, Northing, Offish, Outland, Polar, Remote, Tele-, Timbuctoo, Yonder

Distaste(ful) Gross-out, Repugnant, Ropy, Scunner, Unpalatable, Unpleasant, Unsavoury

Distemper Ailment, Colourwash, Equine, Hard-pad, Paint, Panleucopenia, Tempera

Distend(ed), Distension Bloat, Dilate, Ectasia, Emphysema, Expand, Hoove, Inflate, Meteorism, → **STRETCH**, Swell, Turgid, Tympanites, Varicocele, Varicose

Distil(late), Distillation, Distiller, Distilling Alcohol, Alembic, Anthracine, Azeotrope, Brew, Condense, Destructive, Drip, Fractional, Naphtha, Pelican, Pyrene, Pyroligneous, Rosin, Turps, Vacuum, Vapour

▷ **Distillation** *may indicate* an anagram

Distinct(ive) Apparent, Characteristic, Clear, Determinate, Different, Discrete, Evident, Grand, Individual, Peculiar, Plain, Separate, Several, Signal, → **SPECIAL**, Stylistic, Trenchant, Vivid

Distinction Beaut(y), Blue, Cachet, Credit, Diacritic, Difference, Dignity, Diorism,
 Disparity, Division, Eclat, Eminence, Honour, Lustre, Mark, Mystique, Nicety,
 Note, Nuance, OM, Prominence, Quiddity, Rank, Renown, Speciality, Style, Title
Distinguish(ed), Distinguishing Classify, Contrast, Demarcate, Denote, Diacritic,
 Different(iate), Discern, Discriminate, Divide, Elevate, Eximious, Mark, Notable,
 Perceive, Prestigious, Prominent, Secern, Signal, Stamp, Tell
Distort(ion), Distorted Anamorphosis, Bend, Colour, Contort, Deface, Deform,
 Dent, Fudge, Garble, Helium speech, Jaundiced, Mangle, Misshapen, Pervert,
 Rubato, Thraw, Time-warp, Travesty, Twist, → **WARP**, Wow, Wrest, Wring, Wry
▷ **Distort(ed)** *may indicate* an anagram
Distract(ed), Distraction Absent, Agitate, Amuse, Avocation, Bewilder, Divert,
 Embroil, Éperdu, Forhaile, Frenetic, Lost, Madden, Mental, Nepenthe, Perplex,
 Scatty, Sidetrack, Sledge, Upstage
▷ **Distract(ed)** *may indicate* an anagram
Distrain(t) Na(a)m, Poind, Sequestrate, Stress
Distraught Deranged, Elfish, Elvan, Frantic, Mad, Troubled
Distress(ed), Distressing Afflict, Ail, Alack, Anger, Anguish, Antique, Distraint,
 Dolour, Exigence, Extremity, Grieve, Harass, Harrow, Heartbreak, Hurt, Ill, → **IN
 DISTRESS**, Irk, Misease, Misfortune, Need, Oppress, Pain, Poignant, Prey, Sad,
 Shorn, Sore, SOS, Straits, Traumatic, Tribulation, → **TROUBLE**, Une(a)th, Unstrung
Distribute(d), Distribution, Distributor Allocate, Allot, Binomial, Busbar,
 Carve, Chi-square, Colportage, Deal, Deliver(y), Deploy, Dish, Dispense, Dispose,
 Exponential, F, Frequency, Gamma, Gaussian, Geometric, Issue, Lie, Lot, Mete,
 Normal, Out, Pattern, Poisson, Prorate, Renter, Repartition, Serve, Share
▷ **Distributed** *may indicate* an anagram
District Alsatia, Amhara, Arcadia, Ards, Area, Arrondissement, Bail(l)iwick,
 Banat, Banate, Bannat, Barrio, Belt, Canton, Cantred, Circar, Classis, Community,
 Congressional, Diocese, End, Exurb, Federal, Fitzrovia, Gau, Ghetto, Hundred,
 Lathe, Liberty, Locality, Loin, Manor, Metropolitan, → **NEIGHBOURHOOD**, Oblast,
 Pachalic, Pale, Pargana, Parish(en), Paroch, Pashalik, Patch, Peak, Pergunnah,
 Phocis, Precinct, Province, Quarter, Quartier, Rape, → **REGION**, Ride, Riding, Ruhr,
 Rural, Sanjak, Section, Sheading, Sircar, Sirkar, Soc, Soke(n), Stake, Stannary,
 Suburb, Sucken, Talooka, Taluk, Tenderloin, Township, Urban, Venue, Vicinage,
 Walk, Wapentake, Way, Wealden, Zila, Zillah, Zone
Distrust(ful) Caution, Doubt, Misanthropic, Suspect, Wariness
Disturb(ance), Disturbed Ado, Aerate, Affray, Agitate, Atmospherics, Autism,
 Betoss, Brabble, Brainstorm, Brash, Brawl, Broil, Carfuffle, Collieshangie, Concuss,
 Delirium, Dementia, Derange, Desecrate, Disquiet, Dust, Dysfunction, Feeze,
 Firestorm, Fracas, Fray, Fret, Harass, Hoopla, Incident, Incommode, Infest,
 Interrupt, Jee, Kerfuffle, Kick-up, Kurfuffle, Muss, Outbreak, Perturb(ation),
 Prabble, Rammy, Ramp, Riot, Ripple, Romage, Rookery, Roughhouse, Rouse,
 Ruckus, Ruction, Ruffle, Rumpus, Shake, Shellshock, Shindy, Shook-up, Stashie,
 Static, Steer, Stir, Sturt, Tremor, Trouble, Turbulent, Unquiet, Unrest, Unsettle,
 Upheaval, Uproot, → **UPSET**, Vex
▷ **Disturb(ed)** *may indicate* an anagram
Disunite Alienate, Dissever, Divide, Divorce, Split
Disuse Abandon, Abeyance, Desuetude, Discard, Lapse
Ditch Barathron, Barathrum, Channel, Crash-land, Cunette, Delf, Delph, Dike,
 Discard, Donga, Drainage, Drop, Dyke, Euripus, Foss(e), Graft, Grip, Gully,
 Ha(w)-ha(w), Jettison, Khor, Level, Lode, Moat, Na(l)la(h), Nulla(h), Rean, Reen,
 Rhine, Rid, Sea, Sheuch, Sheugh, Sike, Sloot, Sluit, Spruit, Stank, Syke, Trench

Dither(ing) Agitato, Bother, Dicker, Faff, Hesitate, Indecisive, Pussyfoot, Twitter
Dittany Gas-plant
Ditty, Ditties Air, Arietta, Canzonet, Departmental, Jingle, Lay, Song
Diuretic Frusemide, Furosemide, Spironolactone
Diva Callas, Patti, Singer
Divan Compilement, Congress, Couch, Council, Settee, Sofa
Dive(r), Diving Armstand, Backflip, Belly-flop, Crash, Dart, Den, Duck, File,
  Full-gainer, Half-gainer, Header, Honkytonk, Jackknife, Joint, Ken, Nitery, Nose,
  Pass, Pickpocket, Pike, Plummet, Plunge, Plutocrat, Power, Saturation, Scoter,
  Skin, Sound, Stage, Stoop, Submerge, Swallow, Swan, Swoop, Tailspin, Urinant
Diver(s) Didapper, Duck, Embergoose, Flop, Frogman, Gainer, Grebe, Guillemot,
  Loom, Loon, Lungie, Many, Merganser, Pearl, Pike, Plong(e), Pochard, Poker,
  Puffin, Sawbill, Scuba, Snake-bird, Speakeasy, Sundry, Urinator, Various, Zoom
Diverge(nce) Branch, Deviate, Divaricate, Spread, Swerve, Variant, Veer
Divers Miscellaneous, Some
Diverse, Diversify Alter, Chequer, Dapple, Different, Eclectic, Interlard,
  Intersperse, Manifold, Motley, Multifarious, Separate, Variegate, Various, Vary
Diversion, Divert(ing) Amuse, Avocation, Beguile, Deflect, Detour, Disport,
  Dissuade, Distract, Entertain, Game, Hare, Hobby, Interlude, Pastime, Pleasure,
  Prolepsis, Ramp, Red-herring, Refract, Reroute, Ruse, Shunt, Sideshow, Sidetrack,
  Siphon, Smokescreen, Sport, Stalking-horse, Steer, Stratagem, Sublimation, Sway,
  Switch, Tickle, Upstage, Yaw
▷ **Diverting** *may indicate* an anagram
Divest Denude, Rid, Strip, Undeck, Undress
Divide(d), Division Abkhazia, Adzharia, Apportion, Balk, Band, Bipartite,
  Bisect, Branch, Cantle, Chancery, Cleft, Comminute, Commot(e), Continental,
  Counter-pale, Cut, Deal, Demerge, Digital, Dimidiate, Dissever, Estrange, Fork,
  Great, Indent, Parcel, Part, Partitive, Party wall, Pentomic, Plebs, Polarise, Ramify,
  Rend, Rift, Separate, Sever, Share, → **SPLIT**, Stanza, Sunder, Tribalism, Trisect,
  Utgard, Watershed, Zone
Dividend Bonus, Div, Interim, Into, Peace, Share
Divination, Diviner Anthroposcopy, Arithmancy, Augury, Auspices, Axinomancy,
  Belomancy, Bibliomancy, Botanomancy, Capnomancy, Cartomancy, Ceromancy,
  Chiromancy, Cleromancy, Coscinomancy, Crithomancy, Crystal-gazing,
  Crystallomancy, Doodlebug, Dowser, Empyromancy, Geloscopy, Geomancy,
  Gyromancy, Hariolation, Haruspex, Hepatoscopy, Hieromancy, Hieroscopy,
  Hydromancy, I Ching, Intuition, Lampadomancy, Leconomancy, Lithomancy,
  Magic, Mantic, Myomancy, Omphalomancy, Oneiromancy, Onychomancy,
  Ornithomancy, Ornithoscopy, Osteomancy, Palmistry, Pegomancy, Pessomancy,
  Pyromancy, Radiesthesia, Rhabdomancy, Scapulimancy, Sciomancy, Seer, Sibyl,
  Sideromancy, Sortes, Sortilege, Spae(man), Spodomancy, Taghairm, Tais(c)h,
  Theomancy, Tripudiary, Vaticanator, Xylomancy, Zoomancy
Divine, Divine presence, Divinity Acoemeti, Ambrose, Atman, Avatar,
  Beatific, Celestial, Clergyman, Conjecture, Curate, DD, Deduce, Deity, Douse,
  Dowse, Ecclesiastic, Forecast, Foretell, Fuller, → **GOD**, → **GODDESS**, Godhead,
  Guess, Hariolate, Heavenly, Holy, Hulse, Immortal, Inge, Isiac, Kami, Mantic,
  Numen, Numinous, Olympian, Pontiff, Predestinate, Predict, Presage, Priest,
  Prophesy, RE, Rector, RI, Rimmon, Scry, Sense, Seraphic, Shechinah, Shekinah,
  Spae, Superhuman, Supernal, Theandric, Theanthropic, Theologise, Theology,
  Triune
Division, Divisible Amitosis, Angiosperm, Arcana, Arm, Arrondissement,

Bajocian, Banat(e), Bannet, Bar, Bizone, Branch, Brome, Caesura, Canton, Cantred, Cantref, Cassini's, Caste, Category, Cell, Champart, Chapter, Classification, Cleft, Cloison, Clove, Comitatus, Commot(e), Commune, Compartment, Coralline Crag, Corps, County, Crevasse, Curia, Department, Dichotomy, Disagreement, Disunity, Duan, Eyalet, Family, Farren, Fissile, Fork, Grisons, Guberniya, Gulf, Gulph, Hedge, Hide, Hundred, Inning, Isogloss, Keuper, Kim(m)eridgian, Lathe, Leet, Legion, Lindsey, List, Lobe, Long, M(e)iosis, Mitosis, Mofussil, Nome, Pachytene, Pargana, Part, Partition, Passus, Pergunnah, Period, Phratry, Phyle, Phylum, Pipe, Pitaka, Platoon, Polarisation, Presidency, Queen's Bench, Quotition, Rape, Red Crag, Reduction, Region, Replum, Reservation, Riding, Sanjak, Schism, Section, Sector, Segment, Semeion, Sept(ate), Sever, Share, Sheading, Shed, Shire, Short, Stage, Subheading, Tahsil, Tanach, Taxis, Telophase, Tepal, Thanet, Trichotomy, Trio, Trivium, Troop, Tuath, Unit, Vilayet, Volost, Wapentake, Ward, Watershed

Divisor Aliquant, Aliquot

Divorce(d) Alienate, Diffarreation, Disaffiliate, Dissolve, Disunion, Div, Estrange, Get(t), Part, Separate, Sequester, → **SUNDER**, Talak, Talaq

Divot Clod, Sod, Turf

Divulge Confess, Disclose, Expose, Publish, Reveal, Split, Tell, Unveil, Utter

DIY Flatpack

Dizziness, Dizzy Beaconsfield, Ben, Capricious, Dinic, Disraeli, Giddy, Giglot, Lightheaded, Mazey, Mirligoes, Scotodinia, Swimming, Vertiginous, → **VERTIGO**, Woozy

DJ Deejay, Mixmaster, Monkey-suit, Presenter, Selecta, Shockjock, Tuxedo, Veejay

DNA Antisense, Centromere, Chromatin, Cistron, Codon, Complementary, Cytosine, Exon, Gene, Heteroduplex, Homopolymer, Intron, Junk, Microsatellite, Mitochondrial, Muton, Nucleosome, Operator, Papovavirus, Plasmid, Poxvirus, Procaryote, Profiling, Prokaryote, Purine, Recombinant, Replication fork, Replicon, RNA, Satellite, Selfish, Southern blot, Synthetic, Telomere, Thymidine, Transposon, Vector, Watson-Crick model

Do(es), Doing Accomplish, Achieve, Act, Anent, Banquet, Beano, Begin, Blow-out, Char, Cheat, Chisel, Cod, Con, Cozen, Deed, Dich, Dish, Div, Doth, Dupe, Effectuate, Enact, Execute, Fare, Function, Gull, Handiwork, Hoax, Mill, Perform, Provide, Same, Serve, Settle, Shindig, Spif(f)licate, Suffice, Thrash, Thrive, Ut

▷ **Do** *may indicate* an anagram

Do away Abolish, Banish, Demolish, Kill

Docile Agreeable, Amenable, Biddable, Dutiful, Facile, Meek, Submissive, Tame, Tractable, Yielding

Dock(er), Docked, Docks Abridge, Barber, Basin, Bistort, Bob, Camber, Canaigre, Clip, Crop, Curta(i)l, Cut, Deduct, De-tail, Dry, Floating, Grapetree, Graving, Knotweed, Longshoreman, Lop, Marina, Moor, Off-end, Pare, Patience, Pen, Pier, Quay, Rhubarb, Rumex, Rump, Scene, Seagull, Shorten, Snakeweed, Sorrel, Sourock, Stevedore, Tilbury, Watersider, Wet, Wharf, Wharfie, Yard

Docket Invoice, Label, Tag

Dockyard Arsenal, Rosyth

Doctor(s) Allopath, Alter, Arnold, Asclepiad, Barefoot, Barnardo, Bleeder, BMA, Bones, Breeze, Bright, Brighton, Brown, Caius, Castrate, Chapitalize, Clinician, Cook, Cup(per), Cure(r), Dale, Diagnose, Dr, Dryasdust, Erasmus, Extern(e), Fake, Falsify, Family, Faustus, Feldsher, Fell, Fiddle, Finlay, Flying, Foster, Fundholder, Galen, Geriatrician, Geropiga, GP, Hakeem, Hakim, Healer, Homeopath, Houseman, Hyde, Imhotep, Intern, Internist, Jekyll, Jenner, Johnson, Kildare, Lace, Leach, Leech, Linacre, Load, Locum, Luke, Manette, Massage, MB, MD, Medicate,

Medico, Middleton, Mindererus, Minister, Misrepresent, MO, MOH, Molla(h), Moreau, Mulla(h), Neuter, No, Ollamh, Ollav, Paean, Panel, Pangloss, Paracelsus, Paramedic, Pedro, PhD, Physician, Pill(s), Practitioner, Quack, Quacksalver, Rabbi, RAMC, Registrar, Resident, Rig, Rorschach, Salk, Sangrado, Saw, Sawbones, School, Script, Seraphic, Seuss, Shaman, Slammer, Slop, Spin, Stum, Surgeon, Syn, Syntax, Thorne, Treat, Vaidya, Vet, Water, Watson, Who, Witch

▷ **Doctor(ed)** *may indicate* an anagram

Doctrine Adoptianism, Adoptionism, Antinomian, Apollinarian, Archology, Arianism, Averr(h)oism, Bonism, Brezhnev, Cab(b)ala, Calvanism, Catastrophism, Chiliasm, Consubstantiation, Credo, Creed, Determinism, Ditheletism, Docetism, Dogma, Doxie, Doxy, Dualism, Esotery, Federalism, Fideism, Finalism, Functionalism, Gnosticism, Gospel, Henotheism, Holism, Idealism, Immaterialism, Immersionism, Indeterminism, Infralapsarianism, Islam, Ism, Jansenism, Krypsis, Laches, Lore, Malthusian, Manich(a)eism, Materialism, Metempsychosis, Molinism, Monadism, Monergism, Monism, Monothel(et)ism, Monroe, Neomonianism, Nestorianism, Neutral monism, Nihilism, Panentheism, Pantheism, Pelagianism, Physiocracy, Pluralism, Pragmatism, Predestination, Premillennialism, Preterition, Probabilism, Psilanthropism, Pythagorean(ism), Real presence, Reformism, Satyagrahi, Scotism, Secularism, Sharia, Sheria, Shibboleth, Solidism, Strong meat, Subjectivism, Sublapsarianism, Subpanation, Substantialism, Swedenborgianism, Syndicalism, Synergism, System, Teleology, → **TENET**, Terminism, Theory, Theravada, Thomism, Transubstantiation, Trialism, Tridentine, Tutiorism, Universalism, Utilitarianism, Voluntarism, Wasm, Weismannism, Whiteboyism, Zoism, Zwinglian

Document(s), Documentary Brevet, Bumf, Bumph, Carta, Certificate, Charge sheet, Charter, Contract, Conveyance, Covenant, Daftar, Deed, Diploma, Docket, Doco, Dompass, Dossier, Fiat, Form, Grand Remonstrance, Holograph, Latitat, Logbook, Mandamus, Offer, Papers, Policy, Precept, Production, Pro forma, Public, Ragman, Ragment, Record, Resort, Roll, Roul(e), Screed, Source, Stamp note, Voucher, Warrant, Waybill, Writ, Write up

Dod Pet, Poll

Dodder(y) Old, Shake, Stagger, Strangleweed, Totter, Tremble

Doddle Easy

Dodge, Dodgy Artful, Avoid, Bell-ringing, Column, Elude, Evade, Evasion, Iffy, Jink, Jook, Jouk, Racket, Ruse, Shirk, Sidestep, Skip, Slalom, Slinter, Tip, Trick, Twist, Urchin, Weave, Welsh, Wheeze, Wire, Wrinkle

Doe(s) Deer, Faun, Hind

Doff Avail(e), Avale, Remove, Rouse, Shed, Tip

Dog(s) Assistance, Bowwow, Canes, Canidae, Canine, Feet, Fire, Fog, Heading, Hot, Hunter, Kennel, Leading, Native, Nodding, Pursue, Ratter, Sea, Search, Seeing-eye, Shadow, Sleeve, Sleuthhound, Spotted, Stalk, Starter, Strong-eye, Sun, Tag, Tail, Top, Tracker, Trail, Truffle, Tumbler, Wammul, Water, Water dog, Working, Yellow

DOGS

3 letters:	Pug	Bird	Dane
Cur	Rab	Brak	Fido
Eye	Yap	Bran	Heel
Gun		Bush	Iron
Pig	4 letters:	Cant	Kuri
Pom	Barb	Chow	Kuta

Kuti
Leam
Lyam
Mutt
Oath
Peke
Puli
Rach
Sled
Stag
Tike
Toby
Tosa
Tray
Tyke
Wolf

5 letters:
Akita
Alans
Apsos
Argos
Boots
Boxer
Brach
Cairn
Coach
Dhole
Dingo
Guard
Guide
Haunt
Hound
Husky
Hyena
Kurre
Laika
Lorel
Luath
Merle
Moera
Pidog
Pluto
Pooch
Rache
Ratch
Rover
Shock
Spitz
Spoor
Whelp

Zorro

6 letters:
Afghan
Bandog
Barbet
Barker
Basset
Beagle
Bitser
Blanch
Borzoi
Bounce
Bowler
Briard
Caesar
Canaan
Chenet
Cocker
Collie
Dangle
Eskimo
Gelert
Goorie
Heeler
Jackal
Katmir
Kelpie
Kennet
Ketmir
Kratim
Lassie
Mauthe
Messan
Moppet
Pariah
Piedog
Police
Poodle
Pye-dog
Ranger
Saluki
Setter
Shaggy
Shough
Sirius
Sothic
Talbot
Teckel
Touser
Towser

Vizsla
Westie
Yapper
Yorkie

7 letters:
Andiron
Basenji
Bobbery
Boerbul
Bouvier
Brachet
Bulldog
Courser
Griffon
Harrier
Hearing
Iceland
Lowchen
Lurcher
Maltese
Maremma
Mastiff
Mongrel
Orthrus
Pointer
Prairie
Raccoon
Reynard
Samoyed
Sapling
Sausage
Shar-Pei
Sheltie
Shih tzu
Showghe
Sloughi
Sniffer
Spaniel
→ **TERRIER**
Volpino
Whiffet
Whippet
Yapster

8 letters:
Aardwolf
Aberdeen
Airedale
Alsatian
Blenheim

Bouvrier
Bratchet
Brittany
Carriage
Cerberus
Chow-chow
Doberman
Elkhound
Hovawart
Huntaway
Kangaroo
Keeshond
Komondor
Labrador
Landseer
Malamute
Malemute
Papillon
Pekinese
Pembroke
Pinscher
Samoyede
Sealyham
Sheepdog
Springer
Turnspit
Warragal
Warrigal

9 letters:
Buckhound
Chihuahua
Coonhound
Dachshund
Dalmatian
Deerhound
Dobermann
Draghound
Gazehound
Great Dane
Greyhound
Harlequin
Kerry blue
Lhasa apso
Molossian
Pekingese
Retriever
Schnauzer
Staghound
Wolfhound

10 *letters:*	Trindle-tail	Tibetan mastiff	17 *letters:*
Bedlington	Trundle-tail	Tibetan spaniel	Anatolian Shepherd
Bloodhound	Wishtonwish	Tibetan terrier	Dobermann-
Blueheeler			pinscher
Fox terrier	12 *letters:*	15 *letters:*	
Otterhound	Border collie	Bernese mountain	18 *letters:*
Pomeranian	Gazelle hound	Estreia mountain	Large
Rottweiler	Japanese chin	Hamilton stovare	Munsterlander
Schipperke	Newfoundland	Mexican hairless	Old English
Shin-barker	Saint Bernard	Norwegian buhund	sheepdog
Tripehound	Welsh terrier	Portuguese water	Rhodesian
Weimaraner	West Highland	Swedish vallhund	ridgeback
11 *letters:*	13 *letters:*	16 *letters:*	20 *letters:*
Bichon frise	Affenpinscher	Australian cattle	Landseer
Irish setter	Dandie Dinmont	Doberman-pinscher	Newfoundland
Jack Russell	Scotch terrier	Lancashire heeler	21 *letters:*
Labradoodle	Sussex spaniel	Pyrenean mountain	Polish Lowland
Montmorency		Russian wolfhound	sheepdog
Skye terrier	14 *letters:*	Shetland sheepdog	
Tibetan apso	Italian spinone		
Trendle-tail	Norwich terrier		

Dog-bane Apocynum
Doge Dandolo
Dogfish Huss, Rigg
Dogged Determined, Die-hard, Dour, Indefatigable, Pertinacious, Stubborn, Sullen
Doggerel Crambo, Jingle, Laisse, Rat-rhyme
Dog letter R
Dogma(tic) Assertive, Belief, Conviction, Creed, Doctrinal, En têté, Ideology, Ipse
   dixit, Opinionative, Pedagogic, Peremptory, Pontifical, Positive, → TENET
Do-gooder Piarist, Reformer, Salvationist, Samaritan, Scout
Dogsbody Bottle-washer, Gofer, Skivvy
Dog star Canicula, Lassie, Sirius, Sothic
Do it Dich
Dolce Stop, Sweet
Dole Alms, Batta, B(u)roo, Give, Grief, Maundy, Payment, Pittance, Pog(e)y, Ration,
   → SHARE, Tichborne, Vail, Vales
Doll(y) Barbie®, Bimbo, Common, Corn, Creeper, Crumpet, Dress, Dutch, Golliwog,
   Kachina, Kewpie®, Maiden, Marionette, Matryoshka, Maumet, Mommet,
   Mummet, Ookpik®, Ornament, Paris, Parton, Peggy, Poppet, Puppet, Ragdoll,
   Russian, Sis(ter), Sitter, Tearsheet, Toy, Trolley, Varden, Washboard, Wax
Dollar(s) Balboa, Boliviano, Buck, Cob, Cob money, Euro, Fin, Greenback, Iron man,
   Peso, Petrol, Piastre, Pink, S, Sand, Sawbuck, Sawhorse, Scrip, Smacker, Spin,
   Sword, Top, Wheel
Dollop Glob, Helping, Share
▷ **Dolly** *may indicate* an anagram
Dolly-bird Dish
Dolour Grief, Pain, Sorrow
Dolphin Amazon, Arion, Beluga, Bottlenose, Cetacean, Coryphene, Delphinus,
   Grampus, Lampuka, Lampuki, Mahi-mahi, Meer-swine, Porpess(e), Risso's,

River, Sea-pig

Dolt Ass, Blockhead, Clodhopper, Noodle, Oaf, Ouph(e), Owl, → **STUPID**

Domain Archaea, Bacteria, Bourn(e), Demain, Demesne, Eminent, Emirate, Empire, Estate, Eukarya, Manor, Predicant, Public, Rain, Realm, Region, Reign

Dome(-shaped) Al-Aqsa, Cap, Cupola, Cupula, Dagoba, Geodesic, Head, Imperial, Louvre, Millennium, Onion, Periclinal, Rotunda, Salt, Stupa, Tee, Tholos, Tholus, Tope, Vault, Xanadu

Domestic(ate) Char, Cleaner, Dom, Esne, Familiar, Home-keeping, Homely, House, Housetrain, Humanise, Interior, Internal, Intestine, Maid, Menial, → **SERVANT**, Swadeshi, Tame, Woman

Domicile Abode, Dwelling, Hearth, Home, Ménage

Dominate, Dominance, Dominant, Domination Ascendancy, Baasskap, Ballbreaker, Bethrall, Clou, Coerce, Control, Enslave, Hegemony, Henpeck, Maisterdome, Mesmerise, Momism, Monopolise, O(v)ergang, Override, Overshadow, Power, Preponderant, Preside, Rule, Soh, → **SUBDUE**, Subjugate, Tower

Domineer(ing) Authoritarian, Boss, Henpeck, Lord, Ride, Swagger, Tyrannize

Dominica(n) Jacobite, Monk, OP, Preaching friar, Predicant, Savonarola, WD

Dominie Maister, Master, Pastor, Sampson, Schoolmaster

Dominion Dom, Empire, Khanate, NZ, Realm, Reame, Reign, → **RULE**, Supremacy, Sway, Territory

Domino(es) Card, Fats, Mask, Matador

Don Academic, Address, Assume, Caballero, Camorrist, Endue, Fellow, Garb, Giovanni, Indew, Juan, Lecturer, Mafia, Prof, Quixote, Reader, Señor, Spaniard, Tutor, Wear

Dona(h) Duckie, Love

Donate, Donation Aid, Bestow, Contribution, Gift, Give, Peter's pence, Present, Wakf, Waqf

Done Achieved, Complete, Crisp, Ended, Executed, Had, Over, Spitcher, Tired, Weary

Donjon Dungeon, Keep

Donkey Ass, Burro, Cardophagus, Cuddie, Cuddy, Dapple, Dick(e)y, Dunce, Eeyore, Fussock, Genet(te), Jackass, Jennet, Jenny, Jerusalem pony, Kulan, Modestine, Moke, Mule, Neddy, Nodding, Onager, Stupid, Years

Donor Benefactor, Bestower, Settlor, Universal

Doo Dove

Doodle(r) Scribble, Yankee

Doodlebug Antlion, Larva, V1

Doofer Thingumabob

Doom(ed) Condemned, Damnation, Date, Destine, Destiny, → **FATE**, Fay, Fey, Fie, Goner, Ill-starred, Lot, Predestine, Preordain, Ragnarok, Ruined, Sentence, Spitcher, Star-crossed, Weird

Doone Carver, Lorna

Door(s), Doorstep, Doorway Aperture, Communicating, Damnation, Drecksill, Dutch, Elephant, Entry, Exit, Fire, Folding, Front, Gull-wing, Haik, Hake, Hatch, Heck, Ingress, Jib, Lintel, Louver, Louvre, Muntin, Oak, Open, Overhead, Patio, Portal, Postern, Revolving, Rory, Screen, Sliding, Stable, Stage, Storm, Street, Swing, Tailgate, Trap, Up and over, Vomitory, Wicket, Yett

Doorkeeper, Doorman Bouncer, Commissionaire, Guardian, Janitor, Ostiary, Porter, Tiler, Tyler, Usher

Doormat Subservient, Weakling

Doorpost Architrave, Dern, Durn, Jamb, Yate, Yett

Dope Acid, Amulet, Bang, Coke, Crack, → DRUG, Gen, Goose, Info, Lowdown, Narcotic, Nobble, Rutin, Sedate, Soup, → STUPID PERSON, Tea

Doppelganger Double, Ringer

Dorcas Gazelle, Needle, Shepherdess

Dorian, Doric Metope, Mutule

Doris Day, Lessing, Mollusc

Dormant Abed, Comatose, Hibernating, Inactive, Inert, Joist, Latent, Quiescent, Resting, → SLEEPING, Torpescent

Dormer Luthern

Dormitory Barrack, Bunkhouse, Dorter, Dortour, Hall, Hostel, Quarters

Dormouse Loir

Dorothy Bag, Dot, Sayers

Dorsal Back, Neural, Notal

Dory Fish, John

Dosage, Dose Absorbed, Acute, Administer, Aperient, Booster, Cascara, Cumulative, Drachm, Draught, Drench, Drug, Hit, Kilogray, Lethal, → MEASURE, Permissible, Physic, Posology, Potion, Powder, Rem, Threshold, Tolerance

Doss (house) Dharmsala, Dharmshala, Kip, Padding-ken, Spike

Dossier File, Record

Dot(s), Dotted, Dotty Absurd, Bind(h)i, Bullet, Centred, Criblé, Dieresis, Dit, Dower, Dowry, Ellipsis, Engrailed, Leader, Lentiginose, Limp, Micro, Morse, Occult, Or, Particle, Pinpoint, Pixel, → POINT, Polka, Precise, Punctuate, Punctulate, Punctum, Schwa, Semé(e), Set, Speck, Spot, Sprinkle, Stigme, Stipple, Stud, Tap, Tittle, Trema, Umlaut

Dote, Dotage, Doting, Dotard Adore, Anile, Anility, Cocker, Dobbie, Idolise, Imbecile, Pet, Prize, Senile, Spoon(e)y, Tendre, Twichild

Double(s) Amphibious, Ancipital, Bi-, Bifold, Binate, Clone, Counterpart, Crease, Dimeric, Doppel-ganger, Doppio, Dual, Duo, Duple(x), Duplicate, Equivocal, Fetch, Fold, Foursome, Geminate, Gimp, Image, Ingeminate, Ka, Look-alike, Loop, Martingale, Pair, Parlay, Polyseme, Reflex, Replica, Ringer, Run, Similitude, Spit, Trot, Turnback, Twae, → TWIN, Two(fold)

Double-barrelled Tautonym

Double-cross, Double dealing Ambidext(e)rous, Two-time

Double-entendre Polyseme, Polysemy

Doublet Peascod, Pourpoint, TT

Doubt(s), Doubter, Doubtful Agnostic, Ambiguous, Aporia, Askance, But, Debatable, Discredit, Distrust, Dubiety, Dubitate, Hesitate, Hum, Iffy, Incertitude, Misgiving, Mistrust, → NO DOUBT, Precarious, Qualm, Query, → QUESTION, Rack, Scepsis, Sceptic, Scruple, Second thoughts, Shady, Shy, Sic, Skepsis, Sus, Suspect, Suspicious, Suss, Thomas, Thos, Umph, Uncertain, Unsure, Waver

Doubtless Certain, Iwis, Probably, Sure, Truly, Ywis

Douceur Bonus, Sop, Sweetener

Douche Bath, Gush, Rinse, Shower, Wash

Dough(y) Boodle, Cake, Calzone, Cash, Duff, Gnocchi, Hush-puppy, Knish, Loot, Magma, Masa, Money, Paste, Pop(p)adum, Ready, Sad, Sour, Spondulicks, Strudel

Doughboy Dumpling, Soldier

Doughnut Beavertail®, Cruller, Knish, Koeksister, Olycook, Olykoek, Sinker, Torus

Doughty Brave, Intrepid, Resolute, Stalwart, Valiant

Dour Glum, Hard, Mirthless, Morose, Reest, Reist, Sinister, Sullen, Taciturn

Douse Dip, Drench, Extinguish, Snuff, Splash

Dove Collared, Columbine, Culver, Cushat, Diamond, Doo, Ground, Ice-bird, Mourning, Pacifist, → PIGEON, Queest, Quoist, Ring, Rock, Stock, Turtle

Dove-cot(e) Columbarium, Columbary, Louver, Louvre, Lover

Dovetail Fit, Lewis(son), Mortise, Tally, Tenon

Dowager Elder, Widow

Dowdy Frumpish, Mopsy, Mums(e)y, Shabby, Sloppy, Slovenly

Dowel Peg, Pin

Down(s), Downbeat, Downsize, Downward, Downy A bas, Abase, Abattu, Alow, Amort, Bank, Below, Berkshire, Blue, Cast, Catabasis, Chapfallen, Comous, Cottony, Crouch, Darling, Dejected, Dowl(e), Drink, Epsom, Feather, Fledge, Floccus, Flue, Fluff, Fly, Fuzz, Goonhilly, Ground, Hair, Hill, Humble, Humiliate, Jeff, Kennet, Lanugo, Losing, Low, Lower, Nap, Neck, Oose, Ooze, Owing, Pappus, Pennae, Pile, Plumage, Powder, Quash, Repress, Sebum, Slim, Thesis, Thistle, Tomentum, Under, Unserviceable, Urinant, Vail, Wold, Wretched

Downcast Abject, Chapfallen, Despondent, Disconsolate, Dumpish, Hangdog, Hopeless, Melancholy, Woebegone

Downfall, Downpour Cataract, Collapse, Deluge, Fate, Flood, Hail, Onding, Overthrow, Rain, Ruin, Shower, Thunder-plump, Torrent, Undoing, Waterspout

Downgrade(d) Déclassé, Disrate

Downright Absolute, Arrant, Bluff, Candid, Clear, Complete, Flat, Plumb, Plump, Pure, Rank, Sheer, Stark, Utter

Downstairs Below

Downturn Slump

Downwind Leeward

Dowry Dot, Dower, Lobola, Lobolo, Merchet, Portion, Settlement, Tocher

Dowse(r), Dowsing Divine, Enew, Fireman, Radionics, Rhabdomancy, Water-witch

Doxology Gloria, Glory

Doxy Harlot, Loose woman, Wench

Doyen Dean, Senior

Doze Catnap, Ca(u)lk, Dove(r), Nap, Nod, Semi-coma, Sleep, Slip, Slumber

Dozen(s) Baker's, Long, Round, Thr(e)ave, Twal, Twelve

Dr Debtor, Doctor, Dram

Drab Ash-grey, Cloth, Dell, Dingy, Dull, Dun, Ecru, Isabel(line), Lifeless, Livor, Mumsy, Olive, Prosaic, Pussel, Quaker-colour, Rig, Road, Scarlet woman, Slattern, Sloven, Subfusc, Tart, Trull, Wanton, Whore

Drabble Bemoil, Draggle

Dracula Bat, Count, Vampire

Draft Cheque, Draw, Ebauche, Essay, Landsturm, Minute, MS, Outline, Plan, Press, Project, Rough, Scheme, Scroll, Scrowle, → SKETCH

Drag Car, Drail, Dredge, Drogue, Elicit, Eonism, Epicene, Extort, Fiscal, Form, Hale, Harl, → HAUL, Induced, Keelhaul, La Rue, Lug, Nuisance, Parasite, Pressure, Profile, Puff, Pull, Rash, Sag, Schlep, Shockstall, Shoe, Skidpan, Sled, Snig, Sweep, Toke, Tote, Tow, Trail, Trailing vortex, Train, Travail, Travois, Trawl, Treck, Trek, Tug, Tump, Vortex

Draggle Drail, Lag, Straggle

Dragon Aroid, Basilisk, Bel, Bellemère, Chaperon(e), Chindit, Draco, Drake, Fafnir, Fire-drake, Gargouille, Komodo, Kung-kung, Ladon, Lindworm, Opinicus, Peist, Puk, Python, Rouge, Safat, Shrew, Typhoeus, Wantley, Wivern, Worm, Wyvern

Dragonfly Aeschna, Demoiselle, Devil's darning needle, Nymph, Odonata

Dragon's teeth Cadmus, Spartae, Sparti

Dragoon Coerce, Force, Press, Trooper

Drain(ed), Drainage, Draining, Drainpipe Bleed, Brain, Buzz, Catchment, Catchwater, Channel, Cloaca, Condie, Cundy, Delf, Delph, Dewater, Ditch, Dry, Ea(u), → EMPTY, Emulge(nt), Exhaust, Field, Fleet, Grating, Grip, Gully, Gutter, Ketavothron, Kotabothron, Lade, Leach, Leech, Limber, Lose, Lymphatic, Milk, Mole, Nala, Nalla(h), Nulla(h), Penrose, Pump, Rack, Rone, Sap, Scupper, Seton, Sew(er), Sheuch, Sheugh, Shore, Silver, Sink, Siver, Sluice, Sluse, Soakaway, Sough, Spend, Stank, Storm, Sump, Sure, Syver, Tile, Trench, Trocar, Unwater, Ureter, U-trap, Weary, Well

Dram Drink, Drop, Nipperkin, Nobbler, Portion, Snifter, Tickler, Tiff, Tot, Wet

Drama(tic), Drama school Auto, Azione, Catastasis, Charade, Closet, Comedy, Costume, Drastic, Epic, ER, Farce, Heroic, Histrionic, Kabuki, Kathakali, Kitchen sink, Legit, Legitimate, Mask, Masque, Mime, Moralities, No, Nogaku, Noh, Piece, Play, RADA, Scenic, Sensational, Singspiel, Stagy, Striking, Tetralogy, Theatric, Thespian, Tragedy, Unities, Wagnerian, Wild

Dramatist Adamov, Aeschylus, Albee, Aristophanes, Beaumarchais, Beaumont, Brecht, Bridie, Calderon, Congreve, Corneille, Coward, Drinkwater, Eumenides, Euripides, Fletcher, Frisch, Fry, Gay, Genet, Gogol, Goldoni, Havel, Ibsen, Ionesco, Jarry, Kyd, Lyly, Massinger, Menander, Middleton, Molière, Odets, O'Neill, Osborne, Otway, Pinero, Pirandello, Plautus, → PLAYWRIGHT, Racine, Rostand, Rowe, Rowley, Schiller, Seneca, Shadwell, Shaffer, Sherriff, Sophocles, Stoppard, Strindberg, Synge, Terence, Udall, Vanbrugh, Voltaire, Webster, Wedekind, Wesker, Wilde, Wilder, Will, → WRITER, Yeats

Dram-shop Bar, Boozingken, Bousingken

Drape(ry) Adorn, Coverlet, Coverlid, Curtain, Festoon, Fold, Hang, Mantling, Swathe, Valance, Veil, Vest

Draper Clothier, Gilpin, Haberdasher, Hosier, Mercer, Outfitter, Ruth, Scotch cuddy, Tailor

Drastic Dire, Dramatic, Extreme, Harsh, Purge, Senna, → SEVERE, Violent

Drat Bother, Dang, Darn

Draught(s), Draughtsman(ship) Aloetic, Aver, Breeze, Dam, Design, Drench, Drink, Fish, Gulp, Gust, Haal, Hippocrene, King, Line, Men, Nightcap, Outline, Plan, Potation, Potion, Pull, Quaff, Sketch, Sleeping, Slug, Swig, Tracer, Up-current, Veronal, Waucht, Waught, Williewaught

▷ **Draught** *may refer to* fishing

Draught-board Dam-board, Dambrod

Dravidian Tamil

Draw (off), Drawer(s), Drawing, Drawn Adduct, Allure, Attract, Bleed, Blueprint, Bottom, Cartoon, Charcoal, Cock, Crayon, Dead-heat, Delineate, Dentistry, Derivation, Describe, Detail, Diagram, Dis(em)bowel, Doodle, Dr, Draft, Drag, Dress, Educe, Elevation, Elongate, Entice, Equalise, Evaginate, Extract, Fet(ch), Freehand, Fusain, Gather, Gaunt, Glorybox, Graphics, Gut, Haggard, Hale, Halve, Haul, Indraft, Induce, Indue, Inhale, Isometric, Lead, Lengthen, Limn, Line, Longbow, Lottery, Mechanical, Monotint, No-score, Orthograph, Pantalet(te)s, Panty, Pastel, Perpetual check, Petroglyph, Profile, Protract, Pull, Rack, Raffle, Remark, Scenography, Scent, Score, Seductive, Sepia, Sesquipedalian, Shottle, Shuttle, Silverpoint, Siphon, Sketch, Slub, Snig, Spin, Stalemate, Stretch, Study, Stumps, Sweepstake, Syphon, Tap, Taut, Technical, Tempt, Tenniel, Tie, Till, Toke, Tole, Tombola, Top, Tose, Tow(age), Toze, Traction, Trice, Troll, Tug, Unsheathe, Uplift, Wash, Working

▷ **Draw** *may indicate* something to smoke

Drawback Catch, Downside, Ebb, Handicap, Impediment, → OBSTACLE, Rebate,

Retraction, Shrink, Snag

Drawbridge Bascule, Pontlevis

Drawl Dra(u)nt, Haw, Slur, Twang

▷ **Drawn** *may indicate* an anagram

Drawn up Atrip, Drafted

Dray Cart, Lorry, Wagon

Dread(ed) Angst, Anxiety, Awe, Fear, → **HORROR**, Rasta, Redoubt, Thing

Dreadful Awful, Chronic, Dearn, Dern, Dire, Formidable, Funk, Ghastly, Horrendous, Penny, Sorry, Terrible, Willies

Dream(er), Dream home, Dream state, Dreamy Alchera, Alcheringa, Aspire, Castle, Desire, Drowsy, Dwalm, Dwa(u)m, Fantast, Fantasy, Faraway, Gerontius, Idealise, Illusion, Imagine, Languor, Long, Mare, Mirth, Moon, Morpheus, Muse, Nightmare, On(e)iric, Pensive, Phantasmagoria, Phantom, Pipe, → **REVERIE**, Rêveur, Romantic, Somniate, Spac(e)y, Stargazer, Surreal, Sweven, Trance, Trauma, Vague, Vision, Walter Mitty, Wet

Dreary Bleak, Desolate, Dismal, Doleful, Dreich, Dull, Gloom, Gousty, Gray, Grey, Oorie, Ourie, Owrie, Sad

Dredge(r) Caster, Scoop

Dreg(s) Bottom, Draff, Dunder, F(a)eces, Fecula, Gr(e)aves, Grounds, Lag(s), Lees, Legge, Mother, Mud, Riffraff, Scaff, Sediment, Settlings, Silt, Snuff, Ullage

Dreikanter Ventifact

Drench Dowse, Sluice, Sluse, Soak, Souse, Steep, Submerge

Dress(ing), Dressed Academic, Accoutre, Adjust, Adorn, Aguise, Align, Ao dai, Array, Attire, Attrap, Bandage, Bandoline, Bedizen, Black-tie, Bloomer, Blouson, Boast, Bodice, Boun, Bowne, Brilliantine, Busk, Caftan, Cataplasm, Charpie, Cheongsam, Chimer, Cimar, Clad, Clericals, → **CLOTHING**, Coat, Cocktail, Comb, Compost, Compress, Corsage, Corset, Costume, Court, Curry, Cymar, Dandify, Dashiki, Deck, Deshabille, Dight, Dink, Dirndl, Dizen, Doll, Dolly Varden, Dolman, Don, Drag, Dub, Dubbin, Elastoplast®, Empire, Endue, Enrobe, Evening, Fancy, Far(r)andine, Farthingale, Fatigues, Ferrandine, Fertiliser, Fig, Finery, Flamenco, French, Frock, Full, Gamgee tissue, Garb, Garnish, Gauze, Girt, Gown, Graith, Granny, Guise, Gymslip, → **HABIT**, Highland, Ihram, Italian, Jaconet, Kabuki, Ketchup, K(h)anga, Kimono, Kirtle, Kitenge, Line, Lint, Lounger, Marie Rose, Maxi, Mayo(nnaise), Merveilleuse, Midi, Mineral, Mob, Morning, Mother Hubbard, Mufti, Mulch, Muu-muu, National, Oil, Ore, Patch, Peplos, Pinafore, Plaster, Pledget, Plumage, Polonaise, Pomade, Potash, Poultice, Power, Prank, Preen, Prepare, Princess (line), Rag, Raiment, Rainbow, Ranch, Rational, Ray, Rehearsal, Rémoulade, Rig, Robe, Russet, Russian, Rybat, Sack, Sacque, Salad, Salad cream, Samfoo, Samfu, Sari, Sarong, Sartorial, Sauce, Scutch, Seloso, Separates, Sheath, Shift, Shirt, Shirtwaist(er), Simar(re), Smock, Sterile, Stole, Stupe, Subfusc, Subfusk, Suit, Sundress, Symar, Tartan, Tasar, Taw, Tent, Tenue, Tew, Thousand Island, Tiff, Tire, Tog, Toga, Toilet, Tonic, Top, Treat, Trick, Trim, Trollopee, Tunic, Tusser, Tussore, Tuxedo, Uniform, Vest, Vinaigrette, Wear, Wedding, Well, White-tie, Wig, Window, Yclad, Ycled

Dressage Demivolt(e), Manège, Passade, Passage, Pesade, Piaffe

▷ **Dressed up, Dressing** *may indicate* an anagram

Dresser Adze, Almery, Bureau, Chest, Couturier, Deuddarn, Dior, Lair, Lowboy, Sideboard, Transvestite, Tridarn, Welsh

Dressing-gown Bathrobe, Negligée, Peignoir

Dressing-room Apodyterium, Vestiary, Vestry

Dressmaker Costumier, Dorcas, Modiste, Seamstress, Tailor

Drew Steeld, Stelled

Dribble Drip, Drivel, Drop, Seep, Slaver, Slobber, Slop, Trickle

Dried fish Bum(m)alo, Bummaloti, Haberdine, Speld(r)in(g), Stockfish

▸ **Dried fruit** see **DRY FRUIT**

Drift(ing), Drifter Becalmed, Continental, Cruise, Current, Digress, Diluvium, Drumlin, Float, Genetic, Heap, Impulse, Longshore, Maunder, Natant, North Atlantic, Plankton, Purport, Rorke, Slide, Tendence, Tendency, → **TENOR**, Waft, Wander, Zooplankton

Drill(ing) Appraisal, Archimedean, Auger, Bore, Burr, Close order, Directional, Educate, Exercise, Fire, Form, Hammer, Jackhammer, Jerks, Kerb, Monkey, Pack, PE, Pierce, Pneumatic, Power, PT, Radial, Reamer, Ridge, Rimer, Rock, Seeder, Sow, Square-bashing, Teach, Train, Twill, Twist, Usage, Wildcat

Drink(er), Drunk(enness) AA, Absorb, Adrian Quist, Alkie, Alky, Babalas, Bacchian, Barfly, Bender, Beverage, Bev(v)y, Bezzle, Bib(ite), Bibber, Binge, Birl(e), Bladdered, Bland, Blatted, Blind, Blitzed, Bloat, Blootered, Blotto, Bombed, Boose, Booze, Borachio, Bosky, Bottled, Bouse, Bowl, Bowsey, Bowsie, Bracer, Brandy, Bumper, Burst, Capernoitie, Cap(p)ernoity, Carafe, Carousal, Cat-lap, Chaser, Chota peg, Compotation, Cooler, → **CORDIAL**, Corked, Cot case, Crapulent, Crapulous, Cratur, Crocked, Cuppa, Cut, Demitasse, Digestif, Dipsomaniac, Double, Down, Drain, Draught, Drop, Ebriate, Ebriose, Elixir, Energy, Entire, Eye-opener, Finger, Fleein', Flush, Flying, Fou, Fuddle-cap, Fuddled, Full, Glug, Half-seas-over, Heart-starter, Heavy wet, High, Hobnob, Hogshead, Honkers, Hooker, Hophead, Imbibe, Indulge, Inhaust, Intemperate, Irrigate, Ivresse, Jag, Jakey, Jar, Juice, Juicehead, Kaylied, Knock back, Lager lout, Langered, Lap, Legless, Lethean, Libation, → **LIQUOR**, Lit, Loaded, Lord, Lower, Lush(y), Maggoty, Maltworm, Maudlin, Merry, Methomania, Methysis, Mixer, Moony, Mortal, Mug, Mullered, Neck, Nog(gin), Obfuscated, Oenomania, Oiled, One, Oppignorate, Overshot, Paid, Paint, Partake, Particular, Peg, Pickled, Pick-me-up, Pie-eyed, Pint(a), Piss-artist, Pissed, Pisshead, Pisspot, Piss-up, Pixil(l)ated, Pledge, Plonk(o), Plottie, Potation, Poteen, Potion, Primed, Quaff, Rat-arsed, Ratted, Roaring, Rolling, Rotten, Round, Rouse, Rumfustian, Rummer, St Martin's evil, Screamer, Screwed, Sea, Shebeen, Skink, Shicker, Shotover, Silenus, Sip(ple), Skinned, Slake, Slewed, Sloshed, Slued, Slug, Slurp, Smashed, Smile, Smoothie, Snort, Soak, Soused, Sozzled, Sponge, Spongy, Spunge, Squiffy, Steaming, Stewed, Stimulant, Stinko, Stocious, Stoned, Stonkered, Stotious, Stukkend, Stuporous, Suiplap, Sup, Swacked, Swallow, Swig, Swill, Tank, Tanked up, Temulence, Tiddl(e)y, Tiff, Tift, Tight, Tincture, Tipper, Tipple, Tipsy, Tope, Toss, Tossicated, Tost, Two-pot, Two-pot screamer, Usual, Wash, Wat, Wauch, Waught, Well-oiled, Wet, Whiffled, Williewaught, Winebag, Wine bibber, Wino, Wrecked, Zonked

---

DRINKS

2 letters:	Dop	Rye	Bock
It	Fap	Tea	Bull
	G&T	Tot	Coke®
3 letters:	Hom	Vin	Flip
Ale	Kir		Grog
Ava	L&P	*4 letters:*	Homa
Bub	Mum	Arak	Kava
Cha	Pop	Asti	Kola
Cup	Rum	Beer	Malt

Marc
Mead
Nipa
Ouzo
Port
Purl
Raki
Sack
Sake
Saki
Soda
Soft
Soma
Sour
Sura
Tape
Tass
Tent
Yill

5 letters:
Assai
Bingo
Bombo
Bumbo
Cider
Cocoa
Copus
Crush
Doris
Float
Glogg
Haoma
Hogan
Hooch
Joram
Jorum
Julep
Kefir
Kelty
Kvass
Lassi
Mâcon
Malwa
Mauby
Meath
Medoc
Meths
Mobby
Morat
Mulse

Nappy
Negus
Nipa
Pekoe
Pepsi®
Perry
Pimms
Polly
Pombe
Punch
Rakee
Rumbo
Rummy
Sarsa
Sarza
Shake
Short
Shrub
Sling
Stout
Toddy
Tonic
Totty
Vodka
Xeres

6 letters:
Amrita
Apozem
Arrack
Bishop
Burton
Busera
Cassis
Caudle
Cauker
Chasse
Claret
Coffee
Cognac
Cooper
Doctor
Eggnog
Enzian
Geneva
Gimlet
Grappa
Graves
Gutrot
Hootch
Kalied
Keltie

Kephir
Kirsch
Kumiss
Kümmel
Maotai
Meathe
Mescal
Mickey
Mobbie
Nectar
Obarni
Old Tom
Oolong
Orgeat
Oulong
Oxymel
Pastis
Pernod®
Plotty
Porter
Posset
Pulque
Rickey
Rotgut
Saloop
Samshu
Shandy
Sherry
Smiler
Squash
Stingo
Strega
Strunt
Taffia
Tisane
Waragi
Whisky
Yaqona
Zythum

7 letters:
Absinth
Akvavit
Alcopop
Amoroso
Aquavit
Bacardi®
Bitters
Campari®
Caribou
Chablis

Chianti
Cobbler
Curaçao
Curaçoa
Daquiri
Eggflip
Fairish
Fustian
Guarana
Italian
Koumiss
Limeade
Madeira
Malmsey
Mineral
Nobbler
Oenomel
Oloroso
Persico
Philter
Philtre
Pilsner
Pink gin
Quickie
Ratafia
Reviver
Rosiner
Rosolio
Sangria
Sazerac
Screech
Scrumpy
Sherbet
Sherris
Sloe gin
Snifter
Soda pop
Stengah
Swizzle
Tequila
Tio Pepe®
Wassail
Whiskey

8 letters:
Absinthe
Aleberry
Ambrosia
Anisette
Aperitif
Armagnac

Babbelas	Riesling	Milk punch	Athole Brose
Bordeaux	Root beer	Milkshake	Benedictine
Brown cow	Rosoglio	Mint julep	Black and tan
Burgundy	Sangaree	Moonshine	Black velvet
Calvados	Schnapps	Moose milk	Boiler-maker
Champers	Skokiaan	Nipperkin	Doch-an-doris
Charneco	Snowball	Orangeade	Half-and-half
Ciderkin	Spritzer	Refresher	Niersteiner
Coca-cola®	Switchel	Sauternes	Screwdriver
Cocktail	Tequilla	Slivovica	Soapolallie
Cold duck	Vermouth	Slivovitz	Tom and Jerry
Daiquiri	Witblits	Snakebite	Whiskey sour
Dog's nose		Soda water	
Dubonnet®	**9 letters:**	Stiffener	**12 letters:**
Eau de vie	Applejack	Sundowner	Bloody Caesar
Geropiga	Aqua vitae	The cratur	Deoch-an-doris
Gin sling	Ayahuasco	Whisky mac	Doch-an-dorach
Gluhwein	Badminton		Doch-an-doruis
Highball	Buck's fizz	**10 letters:**	Humpty-dumpty
Hollands	Burnt sack	Blackstone	Jimmy Woodser
Homebrew	Calabogus	Bloody Mary	Marcobrunner
Hydromel	Champagne	Buttermilk	Old-fashioned
Lemonade	Chocolate	Chartreuse®	Sarsaparilla
Light ale	Claret cup	Hippomanes	
Mahogany	Cream soda	Lolly water	**13 letters:**
Nepenthe	Cuba libre	Maraschino	Cobbler's punch
Nightcap	Eccoccino	Mickey Finn	Deoch-an-doruis
Persicot	Febrifuge	Piña colada	Mild and bitter
Pilsener	Firewater	Pousse-café	Mops and brooms
Ragmaker	Gingerade	Shandygaff	Prairie oyster
Red biddy	Grenadine	Tom Collins	
Regmaker	Hippocras		**14 letters:**
Resinata	Lambswool	**11 letters:**	John Barleycorn
Resinate	Manhattan	Aguardiente	
Rice beer	Metheglin	Amontillado	

Drink store Cellar
Drip Bore, Dew-drop, Dribble, Drop, Gutter, IV, Leak, Post-nasal, Saline, Seep, Splatter, Stillicide, Trickle, Wimp
Dripstone Label, Larmier
Drive(r), Driving, Drive out AA, Acquired, Actuate, Amber gambler, Ambition, Automatic, Backseat, Banish, Beetle, Belt, Bullocky, Ca', Cabby, Campaign, Carman, Chain, Charioteer, Chauffeur, Coachee, Coact, Crankshaft, Crew, Crowd, Designated, Disk, Dislodge, Dr, Drover, Drum, Economy, Eject, Emboss, Energy, Enew, Enforce, Engine, Expatriate, Faze, Feeze, Ferret, Fire, Firk, Flexible, Fluid, Force, Four-stroke, Four-wheel, Front-wheel, Fuel, Gadsman, Goad, Hack, Hammer, Haste, Heard, Helmsman, Herd, Hie, Hoon, Hoosh, Hot-rod, Hoy, Hunt, Hurl, Impact, Impel, Impetus, Impinge, Impulse, Jarvey, Jehu, Jockey, Juggernaut, Key(ring), Lash, Libido, Locoman, Lunge, Mahout, Make, Mall, Miz(z)en, Motor, Motorman, Offensive, Overland, Peg, Penetrate, Phase, Piston, Pocket, Power, Powertrain, Propel, Puncher, Put, Quill, RAC, Rack, Ram, Rear-wheel, Rebut,

Reinsman, Ride, Road, Roadhog, Run, Sales, Scorch, Screw, Scud, Senna, Sex, Shepherd, Shoo, Spank, Spin, Spur, Start, Steer, Stroke, Sumpter-horse, Sunday, Sweep, Swift, Tape, Task-master, Teamster, Tee, Test, Thrust, Thumb, Toad, Tool, Tootle, Torrential, Trot, Truckie, Tup, Twoccer, Two-stroke, Urge, Urgence, USB, Vetturino, Wagoner, Warp, Whist, Wood, Wreak

Drivel Balderdash, Blether(skate), Drip, Drool, Humbug, Maunder, Nonsense, Pabulum, Pap, Rot, Salivate, Slabber, Slaver

Driving club AA, Iron, RAC

Drizzle Drow, Haze, Mist, Mizzle, Roke, Scotch mist, Scouther, Scowther, Serein, Skiffle, Smir(r), Smur, Spit

Droll Bizarre, Comic, Funny, Jocular, Queer, Waggish

Drone Bee, Buzz, Dog-bee, Doodle, Dor(r), Drant, Draunt, Drawl, Grind, Hanger-on, Hum, Idler, Parasite, Tamboura, Thrum, Windbag

Drool Drivel, Gibber, Salivate, Slaver

Droop(y), Drooping Cernuous, Decline, Flaccid, Flag, Languish, Lill, Limp, Lob, Loll, Lop, Nutate, Oorie, Ourie, Owrie, Peak, Pendulous, Ptosis, → **SAG**, Slink, Slouch, Slump, Weeping, Welk(e), Wilt, Wither

Drop(s), Dropping Acid, Airlift, Apraxia, Bag, Bead, Beres, Blob, Cadence, Calve, Cascade, Cast, Chocolate, Cowpat, Dap, Delayed, Descent, Deselect, Dink, Dip, Downturn, Drappie, Drib(let), Ease, Ebb, Escarp(ment), Fall, Floor, Flop, Fruit, Fumet, Gallows, Glob(ule), Gout(te), Guano, Gutta, Guttate, Instil, Knockout, Land, Minim, Modicum, Muff, Mute, Omit, Pilot, Plonk, Plummet, Plump, Plunge, Plunk, Precepit, Precipice, (Prince) Rupert's, Rain, Scat, Scrap, Shed, Sip, Skat, Spraint, Stilliform, Tass, Taste, Tear, Turd, Virga, Wrist

Drop-out Beatnik, Hippie, Hippy

Drop-shot Dink

Dropsy Anasarca, Ascites, Edema, Oedema

Dross Chaff, Dregs, Recrement, Scoria, Scorious, Scum, Sinter, Slack, Slag, Waste

Drought Dearth, Drouth, Lack, Thirst

Drove(r) Band, Crowd, Flock, Herd, Host, Masses, Mob, Overlander, Puncher

Drown(ed), Drowning Drench, Drent, Drook, Drouk, Engulf, Inundate, Noyade, Overcome, Sorrows, Submerge

Drowse, Drowsiness, Drowsy Blet, Comatose, Doze, Hypnagogic, Hypnopompic, Lethargic, Nap, Narcolepsy, Narcosis, Nod, Snooze

Drub Anoint, Thrash

Drudge(ry) Devil, Dogsbody, Donkey-work, Fag, Grind, Hack, Jackal, Johnson, Plod, Scrub, Slave(y), Snake, Sweat, Swink, Thraldom, Toil, Trauchle, Treadmill

Drug(ged) Acaricide, ACE inhibitor, Antabuse®, Anti-depressant, Antimetabolite, Antipyrine, Bag, Barbiturate, Base, Blow, Bolus, Bomber, Boo, Botanical, Chalybeate, Cholagogue, Clofibrate, Clot buster, Dadah, Deck, Depot, Depressant, Designer, DET, Diuretic, Dope, Downer, E, Ecbolic, Ecphractic, Elixir, Emmenagogue, Errhine, Euphoriant, Fantasy, Fertility, Fig, Galenical, Gateway, Gear, Hallucinogen, Hard, High, Homeopathy, Immunosuppressant, Knockout drops, Largactic, Lifestyle, Line, Load, Mainline, Medicine, Mind-expanding, Miracle, Modified release, Monged, Nervine, Nobble, Obstruent, OD, Opiate, Orlistat, Painkiller, Paregoric, Parenteral, Peace, Pharmaceutics, Pharmacology, Pharmacopoeia, Poison, Popper, Prophylactic, Psychedelic, Psychoactive, Psychodelic, Recreational, Roborant, Scag, Sedate, Shit, Sialogogue, Smart, Snort, Soft, Soporific, Sorbefacient, Speedball, Spermicide, Spike, Stimulant, Stone(d), Stupefacient, Stupefy, Styptic, Substance, Sudorific, Synthetic, Tout, Tranquiliser,

Truth, Upper, Vasoconstrictor, Vermicide, Weed, White stuff, Wonder, Wrap, Zeolitic

DRUGS

1 letter:
Q

3 letters:
AZT
Eve
Hop
Ice
INH
LSD
PCP®
STP
Tab
Tea

4 letters:
Acid
Adam
Bang
Bute
Dopa
Hemp
Junk
Sida
Soma
SSRI
Toot

5 letters:
Aloes
Benny
Bhang
Candy
Crank
Dagga
Ganja
Grass
Hocus
Intal®
L-dopa
Mummy
Opium
Quina
Rutin
Salep
Salop

Senna
Speed
Sugar
Sulfa
Taxol
Zyban®

6 letters:
Amulet
Amytal®
Ativan®
Charas
Curare
Dragée
Heroin
Inulin
Joypop
Lariam®
Mescla
Mummia
Nubain®
Peyote
Pituri
Prozac®
Saloop
Statin
Sulpha
Valium®
Viagra®
Zantac®

7 letters:
Aricept®
Atabrin
Atebrin®
Botanic
Cascara
Charlie
Churrus
Codeine
Damiana
Dapsone
Diconal®
Ecstasy
Eserine
Eucaine

Guarana
Hashish
Henbane
Hypnone
Insulin
Jellies
Librium®
Metopon
Miltown®
Mogadon®
Morphia
Nurofen®
Patulin
Quinine
Relenza®
Ritalin®
Seconal®
Septrin®
Seroxat®
Steroid
Suramin
Tacrine
Trional
Turpeth
Veronal®
Xenical®

8 letters:
Adjuvant
Ataraxic
Banthine
Benadryl®
Curarine
Diazepam
Fentanyl
Goofball
Hyoscine
Ketamine
Laetrile
Laudanum
Mersalyl
Mescalin
Methadon
Miticide
Moonrock
Morphine

Naloxone
Narcotic
Nembutal
Nepenthe
Nystatin
Oxytocic
Psilocin
Quaalude®
Retrovir®
Rifampin
Rohypnol®
Scopolia
Serevent®
Snowball
Special K
Tetronal
Thiazide
Varidase®
Veratrin
Viricide
Zerumbet

9 letters:
Acyclovir
Analeptic
Angel-dust
Anovulant
Antrycide
Augmentin
Barbitone
Biguanide
Busulphan
Captopril
Carbachol
Cisplatin
Clozapine
Compound Q
Corticoid
Cyclizine
Digitalis
Dramamine®
Electuary
Ephedrine
Foscarnet
Frusemide
Ibuprofen

Indinavir
Iprindole
Isoniazid
Jaborandi
Lidocaine
Lorazepam
Meloxicam
Mepacrine
Methadone
Minoxidil
Mydriasis
Naltrexol
Novocaine
Nux vomica
Oxycontin®
Paludrine®
Pethidine
Phenytoin
Practolol
Quinidine
Quinquina
Reserpine
Ritonavir
Synergist
Tamoxifen
Temazepam
Teniacide
Totaquine
Trinitrum
Verapamil
Veratrine
Vermifuge
Wobbly egg
Zanamivir

10 letters:
Amantadine
Ampicillin
Antagonist
Anxiolytic
Atracurium
Belladonna
Benzedrine
Bufotenine
Cimetidine
Clomiphene
Clonazepam
Colestipol
Disulfiram
Ergotamine
Ethambutol

Fluoxetine
Formestane
Gabapentim
Imipramine
Indapamide
Isoamirine
Isoniazide
Ivermectin
Mefloquine
Methyldopa
Mickey Finn
Nalbuphine
Nifedipine
Nitrazepam
Papaverine
Paroxetine
Penicillin
Pentaquine
Phenacetin
Prednisone
Primaquine
Probenecid
Psilocybin
Quinacrine
Raloxifine
Rifampicin
Salbutamol
Saquinavir
Selegiline
Stramonium
Sucralfate
Tacrolimus
Taeniacide
Taeniafuge
Ziduvudine

11 letters:
Alendronate
Allopurinol
Aminobutene
Amoxycillin
Amphetamine
Anastrozole
Beta-blocker
Carbimazole
Carminative
Chloroquine
Ciclosporin
Cinnarizine
Clenbuterol
Clindamycin

Cyclosporin
Deserpidine
Distalgesic
Finasteride
Fluconazole
Fluvoxamine
Galantamine
Gemfibrozil
Haloperidol
Idoxuridine
Ipratropium
Isoxsuprine
Magic bullet
Meprobamate
Neostigmine
Nikethamide
Ondansetron
Paracetamol
Pentamidine
Pentazocine
Phentermine
Pravastatin
Propranolol
Purple heart
Risperidone
Succedaneum
Sulfadoxine
Terfenadine
Thalidomide
Theobromine
Tolbutamide
Tous-les-mois
Tropomyosin
Varicomycin
Vinblastine
Vincristine

12 letters:
Alpha-blocker
Anthelmintic
Antiperiodic
Arsphenamine
Azathioprine
Chlorambucil
Eflornithine
Fenfluramine
Fluphenazine
Glanciclover
Gonadotropin
Guanethidine
Indomethacin

Isoprenaline
Isotretinoin
Mecamylamine
Methaqualone
Methotrexate
Mifepristone
Perphenazine
Physotigmine
Promethazine
Salicylamide
Streptomycin
Sulfadiazine
Trimethoprim

13 letters:
Amitriptyline
Anthelminthic
Antihistamine
Carbamazepine
Depressometer
Flunitrazepam
Materia medica
Nitroglycerin
Penicillamine
Phencyclidine
Pyrimethamine
Spectinomycin
Sulfadimidine
Sulfathiazole
Sulphadiazine
Thiabendazole
Triamcinolone

14 letters:
Bendrofluozide
Bisphosphonate
Butyrhophenone
Combretastatin
Cyclobarbitone
Discodermolide
Flucloxacillin
Norethisterone
Pentobarbitone
Phenacyclidine
Phenobarbitone
Phenylbutazone
Spironolactone
Sulphanilamide

Druid Gorsedd

Drum(mer), Drumming, Drumbeat Arête, Atabal, Barrel, Beatbox, Bodhran, Bongo, Brake, Carousel, Chamade, Conga, Cymograph, Daiko, Dash-wheel, Devil's tattoo, Dhol, Djembe, Dr, Drub, Ear, Flam, Gran cassa, Kettle, Kymograph, Lambeg, Mridamgam, Mridang(a), Mridangam, Myringa, Naker, Ngoma, Oil, Pan, Paradiddle, Percussion, Rappel, Rataplan, Reel, Rep, Ridge, Rigger, Roll, Ruff, Ruffle, Salesman, Side, Skin, Snare, Steel, Tabla, Tabour, Tabret, Taiko, Tambourine, Tam-tam, Tap, Tattoo, Thrum, Timbal, Timp(ano), Tom-tom, Touk, Traps, Traveller, Tuck, Tymbal, Tympanist, Tympano, Whim, Winding, Work

Drum-belly Hoven

Drumstick Attorney, Leg, Rute

▶ **Drunk(ard)** *see* DRINK

▷ **Drunken** *may indicate* an anagram

Drupe(l) Etaerio, Tryma

Druse Crystal

Dry(ing), Drier, Dryness Air, Anhydrous, Arefaction, Arefy, Arid, Blot, Bone, Brut, Corpse, Crine, Dehydrate, Desiccate, Detox, Drain, Dull, Ensear, Evaporate, Exsiccator, Firlot, Fork, Harmattan, Hasky, Hi(r)stie, Humidor, Hydrate, Jejune, Jerk, Khor, Kiln, Mummify, Oast, → PARCH, Prosaic, Reast, Reist, Rizzar, Rizzer, Rizzor, Scarious, Sciroc, Scorch, Sear, Season, Sec(co), Seco, Sere, Shrivel, Siccative, Siroc(co), Sober, Sponge, Steme, Stove, Ted, Thirsty, Thristy, Toasted, Torrefy, Torrid, Towel, Tribble, Trocken, TT, Unwatery, Watertight, Welt, Wilt, Win(n), Windrow, Wipe, Wither, Wizened, Wry, Xeransis, Xerasia, Xero(sis), Xeroderma, Xerophthalmia, Xerostomia

Dryad Eurydice, Nymph

Dry fruit, Dried fruit Achene, Akene, Currant, Mebos, Prune, Raisin, Samara, Silicula, Siliqua, Silique, Sultana

Dry mouth Xerostoma

DT's Dingbats, Hallucinations, Zooscopic

Dual Double, Twin, Twofold

Dub Array, → CALL, Entitle, Hete, Knight, Name

Dubious Doubtful, Equivocal, Fishy, Fly-by-night, Hesitant, Iffy, Improbable, Questionable, Scepsis, Sceptical, Sesey, Sessa, → SHADY, Shonky, Suspect, Touch and go, Unlikely

▷ **Dubious** *may indicate* an anagram

Dubliner Jackeen

Duce Leader, Musso(lini)

Duchess Anastasia, Malfi, Peeress, Titled

Duchy Anhalt, Brabant, Brunswick, Cornwall, Dukedom, Franconia, Grand, Holstein, Limburg, Luxembourg, Nassu, Omnium, Realm, Savoy, Swabia, Valois, Westphalian

Duck(ling), Ducked Amphibian, Avoid, Aylesbury, Bald-pate, Bargander, Bergander, Blob, Blue, Bluebill, Bob, Bombay, Broadbill, Bufflehead, Bum(m)alo, Butterball, Canard, Canvasback, → COUPLE OF DUCKS, Dead, Dearie, Decoy, Dip, Diving, Dodge, Dodo, Douse, Drook, Drouk, Dunk(er), Eider, Enew, Escape, Evade, Ferruginous, Flapper, Gadwall, Garganey, Garrot, Golden-eye, Goosander, Greenhead, Hareld, Harlequin, Heads, Herald, Immerse, Indian runner, Jook, Jouk, Lame, Long-tailed, Mallard, Mandarin, Muscovy, Musk, Nil, Nodding, Nun, O, Oldsquaw, Old Tom, Orpington, Paddling, Pair of spectacles, Palmated, Paradise, Pekin(g), Pintail, Plunge, Pochard, Poker, Putangitangi, Redhead, Ruddy, Runner, Rush, St Cuthbert's, Scaup, Scoter, Sheld(d)uck, Shieldrake, Shovel(l)er, Shun,

Sitting, Smeath, Smee(th), Smew, Sord, Souse, Sowse, Spatula, Spirit, Sprigtail, Steamer, Surf(scoter), Teal, Team, Tufted, Tunker, Ugly, Velvet scoter, Whio, Whistling, Widgeon, Wigeon, Wood, Zero

Duckbill Ornithorhynchus, Platypus

Duckwalk Waddle

Duckweed Lemna

Ducky Sweet, Twee

Duct Bile, Canal(iculus), Channel, Conduit, Diffuser, Diffusor, Emunctory, Epididymus, Fistula, Gland, Lachrymal, Lacrimal, Laticifer, Lumen, Parotid, Pipe, Tear, Thoracic, Tube, Ureter, Vas deferens, Wolffian

Dud Bouncer, Failure, Flop, Shan(d), Stumer

Dude Cat, Coxcomb, Dandy, Fop, Lair, Macaroni, Popinjay, Roy

Dudgeon Anger, Hilt, Huff, Pique

Due(s) Adequate, Arrearage, Claim, Debt, Deserts, Forinsec, Geld, Heriot, Just, Lot, Mature, Needful, Owing, Reddendo, Rent, Right, → SUITABLE, Thereanent, Toll, Tribute, Worthy

Duel(list) Mensur, Monomachy, Principal, Tilt

Duenna Chaperone, Dragon

Duff Bungle, Dough, Nelly, NG, Plum, Pudding, Rustle

Duffer Bungler, Rabbit, Useless

Dug Ploughed, Teat, Titty, Udder

Dugong Halicore, Sea-cow, Sea-pig, Sirenian

Dug-out Abri, Canoe, Piragua, Pirogue, Shelter, Trench, Trough

Duke(dom) Alva, Clarence, D, Ellington, Fist, Iron, Milan, Orsino, Peer, Prospero, Rohan, Wellington

Dulcimer Cembalo, Citole, Cymbalo, Santir, Sant(o)ur

Dull(ard), Dullness Anodyne, Anorak, Bald, Banal, Barren, Besot, Bland, Blear, Blunt, Boeotian, Boring, Cloudy, Commonplace, Dead (and alive), Deadhead, Dense, Dim, Dinge, Dingy, Ditchwater, Doldrums, Dowf, Dowie, Drab, Drear, Dreich, Dry, Dunce, Faded, Flat, Fozy, Grey, Heavy, Hebetate, Ho-hum, Humdrum, Illustrious, Insipid, Jejune, Lacklustre, Lifeless, Log(y), Lowlight, Mat(t), Matte, Monotonous, Mopish, Mull, Obtund, Obtuse, Opacity, Opiate, Ordinary, Overcast, Owlish, Pall, Pedestrian, Perstringe, Podunk, Prosaic, Prose, Prosy, Rebate, Rust, Slow, Solein, Sopite, Staid, Stick, Stodger, Stodgy, Stolid, Stuffy, Stultify, → STUPID, Sunless, Tame, Tarnish, Tedious, Ticky-tacky, Toneless, Torpor, Treadmill, Tubby, Unimaginative, Vapid, Wonk, Wooden, Zoid

Dumb(ness) Alalia, Aphonic, Crambo, Hobbididance, Inarticulate, Mute, Silent, Stupid

Dumbfound(ed) Amaze, Astound, Flabbergast, Stun, Stupefy, Stupent

Dumb ox Aquinas

Dummy Comforter, Copy, Effigy, Fathead, Flathead, Mannequin, Mannikin, Mock-up, Model, Pacifier, Quintain, Soother, Table, Teat, Waxwork

Dump(ing), Dumps Abandon, Blue, Core, Dejection, Dispirited, Doldrums, Empty, Eyesore, Fly-tipping, Hole, Jettison, Jilt, Junk, Mine, Scrap, Screen, Shoot, Store(house), Tip, Toom, Unlade, Unload

Dumpling Dim sum, Dough(boy), Gnocchi, Gyoza, Knaidel, Knaidloch, Kneidlach, Knish, Kreplach, Matzoball, Norfolk, Quenelle, Ribaude, Suet, Won ton

Dumpy Pudgy, Squat

Dun Annoy, Cow, Importune, Pester, → SUE, Tan

Duncan Isadora

Dunce Analphabet, Booby, Dolt, Donkey, Dullard, Fathead, Schmo, Schmuck, Schnook, Stupid

Dune Areg, Bar, Barchan(e), Bark(h)an, Erg, Sandbank, Seif, Star, Whaleback

Dung(hill) Argol, Buttons, Chip, Cock, Coprolite, Cowpat, Droppings, Fewmet, Fumet, Fumiculous, Guano, Hing, Manure, Midden, Mixen, Mute, Night soil, Ordure, Puer, Pure, Scat, Scumber, Shairn, Shard, Sharn, Siege, Skat, Skummer, Sombrerite, Sombrero, Spawn brick, Spraint, Stercoraceous, Tath

Dungarees Overalls

Dung-eating Merdiverous

Dungeon Bastille, Cell, Confine, Donjon, Durance, Oubliette, Souterrain

Dunk Immerse, Sop, Steep

Dunnock Accentor

Duo Couple, Pair, Twosome

Dupe Catspaw, Chiaus, Chouse, Cony, Cull(y), Delude, Geck, Gull, Hoax, Hoodwink, Mug, Pawn, Pigeon, Plover, Sitter, Soft mark, Sucker, Swindle, → **TRICK**, Victim

Duplex Twofold

Duplicate, Duplicator Clone, Copy, Counterpart, Cyclostyle, Double, Facsimile, Match, Ozalid®, Replica, Reproduce, Roneo®, Spare

Durable Enduring, Eternal, Eterne, Hardy, Lasting, Permanent, Stout, Tough

Duralumin® Y-alloy

Duration Extent, Period, Span

Duress Coercion, Pressure, Restraint

Durham Palatine

During Amid, Dia-, For, In, Over, Throughout, While, Whilst

Dusk(y) Dark, Dewfall, Dun, Eve, Gloaming, Gloom, Owl-light, Phaeic, Twilight, Umbrose

Dust(y) Arid, Ash, Bo(a)rt, Calima, Clean, Coom, Cosmic, Culm, Derris, Devil, Duff, Earth, Fuss, Gold, Khak(i), Lemel, Limail, Lo(e)ss, Miller, Nebula, Pellum, Pollen, Pother, Pouder, Poudre, Powder, Pozz(u)olana, Pudder, Rouge, Seed, Shaitan, Slack, Stour, Talc, Volcanic, Wipe

▷ **Dusted** *may indicate* an anagram

Duster Cloth, Feather, Red, Talcum, Torchon

Dustman Doolittle, Garbo(logist), Scaffie

Dust measure Konimeter, Koniscope

Dutch(man), Dutchwoman Batavian, Boor, Butterbox, Cape, Courage, D(u), Double, Elm, Erasmus, Flying, Frow, Kitchen, Knickerbocker, Middle, Missis, Missus, Mynheer, Parnell shout, Patron, Pennsylvania, Sooterkin, Taal, Wife

Dutiful, Duty Active, Ahimsa, Allegiance, Average, Blench, Bond, Charge, Corvee, Countervailing, Customs, Death, Debt, Deontology, Detail, Devoir, Docile, Drow, Due, Duplicand, End, Estate, Excise, Fatigue, Feu, Function, Heriot, Homage, Imposition, Impost, Incumbent, Lastage, Likin, Mission, Mistery, Mystery, Obedient, Obligation, Octroi, Office, Onus, Pia, Picket, Pious, Point, Preferential, Prisage, Probate, Rota, Sentry-go, Shift, Stamp, Stillicide, Stint, Succession, Tariff, → **TASK**, Tax, Toll, Transit, Trow, Watch, Zabeta

Duvet Doona, Quilt

Dwarf(ism) Achondroplasia, Agate, Alberich, Andvari, Ateleiosis, Bashful, Belittle, Bes, Black, Bonsai, Brown, Doc, Dopey, Droich, Drow, Durgan, Elf, Gnome, Grumpy, Happy, Hobbit, Homuncule, Hop o' my thumb, Knurl, Laurin, Little man, Man(n)ikin, → **MIDGET**, Mime, Minikin, Minim, Nanism, Nectabanus, Ni(e)belung, Nurl, Overshadow, Pacolet, Pigmy, Pygmy, Red, Regin, Ront, Rumpelstiltskin, Runt, Skrimp, Sleepy, Sneezy, → **STUNT**, Tiddler, Titch, Tokoloshe, Tom Thumb,

Toy, Troll, Trow, White

Dwell(er), Dwelling Abide, Be, Bungalow, Cabin, Cell, Cot(tage), Descant,
Discourse, Domicile, Habitation, Harp, Heteroscian, Hogan, House, Hut, Laura,
Lavra, Live, Lodge, Longhouse, Maison(n)ette, Mansion, Messuage, Midgard,
Midgarth, Mithgarthr, Palafitte, Pied-à-terre, Pueblo, Reside, Roof, Sty, Tenement,
Tepee, Terramara, Tipi, Weem, Wigwam, Won(ing), Wonning, Woon

Dwindle Decline, Diminish, Fade, Lessen, Peter, Shrink, Wane

Dye(ing), Dyestuff, Dye-seller Acid, Alkanet, Amaranth, Anil, Anthracene,
Anthraquinone, Archil, Azo(benzine), Azurine, Bat(t)ik, Benzidine, Brazil(e)in,
Burnt umber, Camwood, Canthaxanthin, Carthamine, Catechin, Chay(a), Chica,
Chicha, Chico, Choy, Cinnabar, Cobalt, Cochineal, Colour, Congo, Coomassie blue,
Corkir, Crocein, Crotal, Crottle, Cudbear, Dinitrobenzene, Direct, Embrue, Engrain,
Envermeil, Eosin, Flavin(e), Fluoxene, Fuchsin(e), Fustic, Fustoc, Gambi(e)r,
Gentian violet, Grain, Haematoxylin, Henna, Hue, Ikat, Imbrue, Imbue, Incardine,
Indamine, Indican, Indigo, Indigocarmine, Indigotin, Indirubin, Indoxyl, Indulin(e),
Ingrain, Kalamkari, Kamala, Kermes, Kohl, Korkir, Madder, Magenta, Mauvein(e),
Mauvin(e), Methyl violet, Murex, Myrobalan, Nigrosin(e), Orcein, Orchel(la),
Orchil, Para-red, Phenolphthalein, Phthalein, → **PIGMENT**, Ponceau, Primuline,
Puccoon, Purple, Purpurin, Pyronine, Quercitron, Quinoline, Raddle, Resorcinol,
Rhodamine, Rosanilin(e), Safranin(e), Salter, Shaya, → **STAIN**, Stone-rag,
Stone-raw, Sumac(h), Sunfast, Tannin, Tartrazine, Tie-dye, Tinct, Tint, Tropaeolin,
Turmeric, Turnsole, Valonia, Vat, Wald, Weld, Woad, Woald, Wold, Xanthium,
Xylidine

▶ **Dying** *see* **DIE**

Dyke Aboideau, Aboiteau, Bund, Devil's, → **DIKE**, Gall, Offa's, Ring

Dynamic(s) Ballistics, Energetic, Forceful, Gogo, High-powered, Kinetics, Potent

Dynamite Blast, Explode, Gelignite, Giant powder, TNT, Trotyl

Dynamo Alternator, Armature

Dynasty Angevin, Bourbon, Capetian, Carolingian, Chin(g), Ch'ing, Chou, Era,
Frankish, Gupta, Habsburg, Han, Hapsburg, Holkar, Honan, House(hold), Hyksos,
Khan, Manchu, Maurya, Merovingian, Ming, Omayyad, Osman, Pahlavi, Ptolemy,
Qajar, Q'ing, Rameses, Romanov, Rule, Safavid, Saga, Sassanid, Seleucid, Seljuk,
Shang, Song, Sui, Sung, Tai-ping, Tang, Tudor, Umayyad, Wei, Yi, Yuan, Zhou

Dysentery Amoebic, Bloody flux, Slugellosis

Dyslexia Strephosymbolia

Dyspeptic Cacogastric

Dysprosium Dy

Dystrophy Duchenne's, Muscular

Ee

E Boat, East, Echo, Energy, English, Spain

Each All, Apiece, Ea, → **EVERY**, Ilka, Per, Severally

Eager(ly) Agog, Antsy, Ardent, Avid, Beaver, Bore, Bright-eyed, Dying, Earnest, Enthusiastic, Fain, Fervent, Fervid, Frack, Game, Gung-ho, Hot, Intent, → **KEEN**, Perfervid, Prone, Race, Raring, Rath(e), Ready, Roost, Sharp-set, Sore, Spoiling, Thirsty, Toey, Wishing, Yare

Eagle Al(l)erion, Altair, American, Aquila, Bald, Bateleur, Berghaan, Bird, Double, Erne, Ethon, Fish, Gier, Golden, Harpy, Hawk, Legal, Lettern, Nisus, Ossifrage, Sea, Spread, Tawny, Wedge-tailed

Ear(drum), Ear trouble Ant(i)helix, Attention, Audience, Auricle, Barotitis, Cauliflower, Cochlea, Concha, Conchitis, Deafness, Dionysius, Dolichotus, External, Glue, Hearing, Helix, Icker, Incus, Inner, Internal, Jenkins, Kieselguhr, Labyrinth, Labyrinthitis, Listen, Locusta, Lop, Lug, Malleus, Middle, Modiolus, Myringa, Myringitis, Nubbin, Otalgia, Otalgy, Otic, Paracusis, Paramastoid, Parotic, Pavilion, Periotic, Petrosal, Phonic, Pinna, Presby(a)c(o)usis, Prootic, Spike, Stapes, Thick, Tin, Tragus, Tympanitis, Utricle

Earl(dom) Belted, Mar, Peer, Sandwich

Earlier, Early Above, Ago, Ahead, Alsoon, AM, Antelucan, Auld, Betimes, Cockcrow, Daybreak, Ere-now, Ex, Germinal, Incipient, Or, Precocious, Precursor, Prehistoric, Premature, Prevernal, Previous, Primeur, Primeval, Primordial, Prior, Rath(e), Rath(e)ripe, Rear, Rudimentary, Soon, Timely, Tim(e)ous

▷ **Early** *may indicate* belonging to an earl

Early man Eoanthropus, Flat-earther

▷ **Early stages of** *may indicate* first one or two letters of the word(s) following

Earmark Allocate, Bag, Book, Characteristic, Flag, → **RESERVE**, Tag, Target, Ticket

Earn(er), Earning(s) Achieve, Addle, Breadwinner, Curdle, Deserve, Digerati, Ern, Gain, Income, Invisible, Make, Merit, O.T.E., Rennet, Runnet, Win, Yearn

Earnest(ly) Ardent, Arle(s)(-penny), Deposit, Fervent, Imprest, Intent, Promise, Serious, Token, Wistly, Zealous

Earring Drop, Hoop, Keeper, Pendant, Sleeper, Snap, Stud

Earshot Hail, Hearing

Earth(y) Alkaline, Antichthon, Art, Asthenosphere, Barbados, Brown, Capricorn, Clay, Cloam, Clod, Cologne, Craton, Diatomite, Dirt, Drey, Dust, E, Eard, Edaphic, Epigene, Foxhole, Friable, Fuller's, Gaea, Gaia, Gault, Ge, Globe, Green, Ground, Heavy, Horst, Infusiorial, Kadi, Lair, Leaf-mould, Lemnian, Lithosphere, Loam, Malm, Mankind, Mantle, Mools, Mould, Mouls, Papa, Pise, Planet, Rabelaisian, Racy, Rare, Red, Samian, Seat, Sett, Sod, → **SOIL**, Subsoil, Taurus, Telluric, Tellus, Terra, Terrain, Terramara, Terrene, Topsoil, Tripoli, Virgo, Wad, Ye(a)rd, Yellow, Yird

Earth-bound Chthonian

Earthenware Arretine, Biscuit, Ceramic, Creamware, Crock(ery), Delf(t),

Della-robbia, Delph, Faience, Figuline, Maiolica, Majolica, Pig, Pot, Queen's ware, Raku, Samian, Sanitary, Terracotta

Earthquake Aftershock, Aseismic, Bradyseism, Foreshock, Mercalli, Richter, Seism, Shake, Shock, Temblor, Trembler, Tremor

Earth's surface Sal, Sial

Earthwork Agger, Bank, Cursus, Gazon, Parados, Rampart, Remblai, Vallum

Earthworm Angledug, Angletwitch, Angleworm, Annelid, Bait, Night-crawler

Earwig Clipshear(s), Eavesdrop, Forkit-tail, Forky-tail

Ease, Easing, Easygoing Alleviate, Carefree, Clear, Clover, Comfort, Content, Defuse, Deregulate, Détente, Easy-osy, Facility, Genial, Hands down, Informal, Lax, Mellow, Mid(dy), Mitigate, Otiosity, Palliate, Peace, Pococurante, Quiet, Relieve, Reposal, Repose, Soothe

East(erly), Eastward Anglia, Asia, Chevet, E, Eassel, Eassil, Eothen, Eurus, Far, Levant, Middle, Near, Orient, Ost, Sunrise

Easter Festival, Island, Pace, Pasch, Pasque

Eastern(er), Eastern language Asian, Kolarian, Oriental, Virginian

East European Lettic, Slovene

Easy, Easily ABC, Breeze, Cakewalk, Carefree, Child's play, Cinch, Cushy, Degage, Doddle, Duck soup, Eath(e), Ethe, Facile, Free, Gift, Glib, Hands down, Independent, Jammy, Kid's stuff, Lax, Light, Midshipman, Natural, Nimps, No-brainer, Oldster, Picnic, Pie, Pushover, Romp, Simple, Sitter, Snotty, Soft, Tolerant, Turkey shoot, User-friendly, Walk-over, Well, Yare

▷ **Easy** *may indicate* an anagram

Eat(able), Eater, Eating Bite, Bolt, Champ, Chop, Commensal, Consume, Corrode, Edible, Edite, Endew, Endue, Erode, Esculent, Etch, Fare, Feast, → **FEED**, Fret, Gastronome, Gnaw, Go, Gobble, Graze, Grub, Have, Hoe into, Hog, Hyperorexia, Hyperphagia, Ingest, Manducate, Muckamuck, Munch, Nosh, Nutritive, Omnivore, Partake, Phagomania, Phagophobia, Predate, Refect, Scoff, Stuff, Sup, Swallow, Syssitia, Take, Taste, Trencherman, Trophesy, Tuck away, Tuck into, Whale

Eavesdrop(per) Cowan, Earwig, Icicle, Listen, Overhear, Pry, Snoop, Stillicide, Tab-hang, Tap, Wiretap

Ebb(ing) Abate, Decline, Recede, Refluent, Sink, → **WANE**

Ebony Black, Cocus-wood, Coromandel, Hebenon, Jamaican

Ebullient Brash, Effervescent, Exuberant, Fervid

Eccentric Abnormal, Antic, Cam, Card, Character, Crank, Curious, Daffy, Dag, Deviant, Dingbat, Ditsy, Ditzy, E, Farouche, Fay, Fey, Fie, Freak, Fruitcake, Geek, Gonzo, Iffish, Irregular, Kinky, Kook(y), Mattoid, Nutcase, Nutter, Odd(ball), Offbeat, Off-centre, Off the wall, Original, Outré, → **PECULIAR**, Phantasime, Pixil(l)ated, Queer, Quirky, Quiz, Rake, Raky, Recondite, Rum, Scatty, Screwball, Screwy, Squirrelly, Wack(y), Way-out, Weird(o), W(h)acko

▷ **Eccentric** *may indicate* an anagram

Ecclesiastic(es), Ecclesiasticus Abbé, Clergyman, Clerical, Lector, Secular, Sir(ach), Theologian, The Preacher

Echelon Formation

Echinoderm Asteroidea, Basket-star, Brittle-star, Comatulid, Crinoid, Heart-urchin, Sea-egg, Sea-lily, Sea-urchin, Starfish

Echo, Echo-sounder Angel, Answer, Ditto, E, Fathometer®, Imitate, Iterate, Rebound, Repeat, Repercussion, Reply, Resonant, → **RESOUND**, Respeak, Reverb(erate), Revoice, Ring, Rote, Tape

Eclat Flourish, Glory, Prestige, Renown

Eclectic Babist, Broad, Complex, Diverse, Liberal

Eclipse Annular, Block, Cloud, Deliquium, Excel, Hide, Lunar, Obscure, Occultation, Outmatch, Outweigh, Overshadow, Partial, Penumbra, Rahu, Solar, Total, Transcend, Upstage

Eclogue Bucolic, Idyll, Pastoral

Eco-community Seral

Ecology Bionomics

Economic(s), Economise Budget, Conserve, Dismal science, Eke, Entrench, Finance, Home, Husband, Intrench, Pinch, Retrench, Scrimp, Skimp, Spare, Sparing, Stagflation, → **STINT**, Supply-side, Welfare

Economist Angell, Bentham, Chrematist, Cole, Friedman, Keynes, Malthus, Marginalist, Meade, Mill, Pareto, Physiocrat, Ricardo, Tinbergen, Tobin, Toynbee, Veblen, Webb

Economy, Economic(al), Economics Agronomy, Black, Careful, Cliometrics, Command, Conversation, Frugal, Hidden, Knowledge, Market, Mitumba, Mixed, Neat, New, Parsimony, Planned, Political, Pusser's logic, Retrenchment, Shoestring, Siege, Stakeholder, Stumpflation, Thrift, Tiger, Token

Ecstasy, Ecstatic Bliss, Delight, Delirious, Dove, E, Exultant, Joy, Liquid, Lyrical, Nympholepsy, Pythic, Rapture, Rhapsodic, Sent, Trance, Transport

Ecumenical Catholic, Lateran

Eczema Pompholyx, Tetter

Edda Elder, Prose, Younger

Eddy Backset, Curl, Duane, Gurge, Maelstrom, Nelson, Pirl, Purl, Rotor, Sousehole, Swelchie, Swirl, Vortex, Weel, Well, Whirlpool, Wiel

Eden Bliss, Fall, Heaven, Paradise, PM, Utopia

Edentate Ant-eater, Armadillo, Sloth, Tatou, Xenarthra

Edge, Edging, Edgy Advantage, Arris, Bleeding, Border, Bordure, Brim, Brink, Brittle, Brown, Burr, Chamfer, Chimb, Chime, Chine, Coaming, Costa, Cutting, Dag, Deckle, End, Flange, Flounce, Frill, Fringe, Frontier, Furbelow, Gunnel, Gunwale, Hem, Hone, Inch, Inside, Kerb, Knife, Leading, Leech, Limb(ate), Limbus, Limit, Lip, List, Lute, Marge(nt), Margin, Nosing, Orle, Outside, Parapet, Periphery, Picot, Pikadell, Piping, Rand, Rim, Rund, Rymme, Selvage, Selvedge, Sidle, Skirt, Strand, Trailing, Trim, Tyre, Verge, Wear, Whet

▶ **Edible** *see* **EAT(ABLE)**

Edict(s) Ban, Bull, Clementines, Decree, Decretal, Extravagantes, Fatwa, Firman, Interim, Irade, Nantes, Notice, Pragmatic, Proclamation, Pronunciamento, Rescript, Sext, Ukase

Edifice Booth, Building, Structure, Stupa, Superstructure

Edify Instruct, Teach

Edinburgh Auld Reekie

Edit(or), Editorial Abridge, Article, City, Copy (read), Cut, Dele, Dramaturg(e), Ed, Emend, Expurgate, Footsteps, Garble, Leader, Nantes, Prepare, Recense, Redact, Revise, Seaman

▷ **Edited** *may indicate* an anagram

Edith Sitwell

Edition Aldine, Bulldog, Bullpup, Ed, Extra, Ghost, Hexapla(r), Impression, Issue, Library, Limited, Number, Omnibus, Trade, Variorum, Version

Edmond, Edmund Burke, Gosse, Ironside(s), Rostand, Spenser

Educate(d) Baboo, Babu, Enlighten, Evolué, Informed, Instruct, Learned, Noursle, Nousell, Nousle, Nurture, Nuzzle, Polymath, Preppy, Scholarly, School, → **TEACH**, Train, Yuppie

Education(alist) Adult, Basic, B.Ed, Classical, Conductive, Didactics, Further,

Heurism, Learning, Literate, Mainstream, Montessori, Paedotrophy, Pedagogue, Pestalozzi, Physical, Piarist, Primary, Schooling, Special, Steiner, Teacher, Tertiary, Upbringing

Educe Elicit, Evoke, Extract, Infer

Edward Confessor, Ed, Elder, Lear, Martyr, Ned, Ted

Eel Conger, Congo, Electric, Elver, Glass, Grig, Gulper, Gunnel, Hagfish, Kingklip, Lamper, Lamprey, Lant, Launce, Leptocephalus, Moray, Murray, Murr(e)y, Olm, Paste, Salt, Sand(ling), Silver belly, Snake, Snig, Spitchcock, Tuna, Vinegar, Wheat, Wolf

Eerie Spooky, Uncanny, Unked, Weird

Efface Cancel, Delete, Dislimn, → ERASE, Expunge, Obliterate

Effect(s), Effective(ness), Effectual Able, Achieve, Acting, Auger, Babinski, Bags, Barkhausen, Belongings, Bit, Bohr, Border, Bricolage, Butterfly, Causal, C(h)erenkov, Chromakey, Coanda, Coastline, Competent, Compton, Consequence, Coriolis, Do, Domino, Doppler, Dr(y)ice, Eclat, Edge, Efficacious, Enact, End, Estate, Execute, Experimenter, Fet, Foley, Fringe, Functional, Fungibles, Gear, Goods, Greenhouse, Ground, Gunn, Hall, Halo, Hawthorne, Home, Horns and halo, Impact, Implement(al), Impression, Introgenic, Josephson, Joule(-Thomson), Kerr, Keystone, Knock-on, Magnus, Meissner, Militate, Moire, Mossbauer, Mutual, Neat, Nisi, Notch, Operant, Optical, Outcome, Ovshinsky, Oxygen, Parallax, Peltier, Perficient, Personal, Phi, Photoelectric, Photovoltaic, Piezoelectric, Piezomagnetic, Pinch, Placebo, Pogo, Position, Potent, Practical, Primary, Promulgate, Raman, Ratchet, Recency, Redound, Repercussion, → RESULT, Ripple, Schottky, Seebeck, Shadow, Shore, Side, Skin, Slash-dot, Sound, Sovereign, Special, Spectrum, Spin-off, Stage, Stark, Striking, Stroop, Submarine, Tableau, Teeth, Telling, Thermoelectric, Thomson, Toxic, Tunnel, Tyndall, Upshot, Valid, Viable, Virtual, Win, Withdrawal, Work, Zeeman

Effeminate Airtsy-mairtsy, Camp, Carpet-knight, Carpet-monger, Cissy, Cookie-pusher, Dildo, Epicene, Female, Gussie, Jessie, Milksop, (Miss) Nancy, Molly(coddle), Nellie, Nelly, Panty-waist, Poovy, Pretty, Prissy, Punce, Sissy, Swish, Tender, Tenderling, Tonk, Unman, Wuss(y)

Effervescence, Effervescent Bubbling, Ebullient, Fizz, Frizzante, Pétillant, Soda

▷ **Effervescent** *may indicate* an anagram

Effete Camp, Epigon(e)

Efficacious, Efficacy Effective, Operative, Potent, Sovereign, Value

Efficiency, Efficient Able, Businesslike, Capable, Competent, Current, Despatch, Electrode, Ergonomics, Luminous, Productivity, Quantum, Smart, Spectral luminous, Streamlined, Strong, Thermal, Volumetric

Effigy Figure, Guy, Idol, Image, Statua, Statue

Efflorescence Bloom, Blossom, Reh

Effluence, Effluent, Effluvia Air, Aura, Billabong, Discharge, Fume, Gas, Halitus, Miasma, Odour, Outflow, Outrush

Effort Achievement, Attempt, Best, Conatus, Concerted, Drive, Endeavour, Essay, Exertion, Fit, Frame, Hardscrabble, Herculean, Labour, Molimen, Nisus, Pains, Rally, Spurt, Stab, Strain, Struggle, Team, → TRY, Work, Yo

Effortless Lenis

Effrontery Audacity, Brass, Cheek, Face, Gall, Neck, Nerve, Temerity

Effulgent Bright, Radiant, Shining

Effuse, Effusion, Effusive Emanate, Exuberant, Exude, Gush, Lyric, Ode, Outburst, Prattle, Rhapsody, Sanies, Screed, Spill

Eft After

Eg As, Example

Egest Eliminate, Evacuate, Excrete, Void

Egg(s) Abet, Benedict, Berry, Blow, Bomb, Caviar(e), Cavier, Chalaza, Cheer, Cleidoic, Clutch, Cockney, Collop, Coral, Curate's, Darning, Easter, Edge, Fabergé, Fetus, Flyblow, Foetus, Free-range, Glair(e), Goad, Goog, Graine, Hoy, Incite, Instigate, Layings, Mine, Nest, Nidamentum, Nit, Oocyte, Oophoron, Ostrich, Ova, Ovum, Pace, Pasch, Plover's, Prairie oyster, Press, Raun, Roe, Rumble-tumble, Scotch, Scrambled, Seed, Setting, Spat, Spawn, Spur(ne), Tar(re), Thunder, Tooth, Tread(le), Urge, Whore's, Wind, Yelk, Yolk, Zygote

Egghead Don, Highbrow, Intellectual, Mensa, Pedant

Egg-plant Aubergine, Brinjal

Egg-producer Gametophyte, Hen, Ovipositor

Egg-shaped Obovate, Oval, Ovate

Egg-white Albumen, Glair

Ego(ism), Egoist Che, Conceit, I, Narcissism, Not-I, Pride, Self, Solipsism, Ubu, Vanity

Egocentric Solipsistic

Egregious Eminent, Flagrant, Glaring, Shocking

Egypt(ian), Egyptologist Arab, Cairene, Carter, Cheops, Chephren, Cleopatra, Copt(ic), ET, Gippo, Goshen, Gyppo, Imhotep, Nasser, Nefertiti, Nilote, Nitrian, Osiris, Ptolemy, Rameses, Syene, UAR, Wafd, Wog

Eiderdown Bedspread, Duvet, Quilt

Eight(h), Eighth day Acht, Byte, Crew, Cube, Middle, Nundine, Octa, Octad, Octal, Octastrophic, Octave, Octet, Ogdoad, Okta, Ottava, Ure, Utas

Eighteen Majority

Eighty Fourscore, R

Einsteinium Es

Either Also, Both, O(u)ther, Such

Ejaculate Blurt, Discharge, Emit, Exclaim

Eject Bounce, Disgorge, Dismiss, Emit, Erupt, Expel, Oust, Propel, Spew, Spit, Spue, Vent

Eke Augment, Eche, Enlarge, Husband, Supplement

Elaborate Detail, Develop, Dressy, Enlarge, Evolve, Florid, Imago, Improve, Intricate, Ornate, Rich, Stretch

Elan Dash, Drive, Esprit, → **FLAIR**, Gusto, Lotus, Panache, Spirit, Vigour

Elapse Glide, Intervene, Pass

Elastic(ity) Adaptable, Bungee, Buoyant, Dopplerite, Elater, Flexible, Give, Resilient, Rubber, Spandex®, Springy, Stretchy, Tone, Tonus

Elastomer Adiprene®

Elate(d), Elation Cheer, Euphoric, Exalt, Exhilarate, Gladden, Hault, High, Ruff(e), Uplift

Elbow, Elbow tip Akimbo, Ancon, Angle, Bender, Cubital, Hustle, Joint, Jostle, Justle, Kimbo, Noop, Nudge, Olecranon, Tennis

Elder(ly), Eldest Ainé(e), Ancestor, Ancient, Bourtree, Chief, Classis, Eigne, Geriatric, Guru, Kaumatua, Kuia, OAP, Presbyter, → **SENIOR**, Sire, Susanna, Wallwort

Eldorado Ophir

Eleanor(a) Bron, Duse, Nora(h)

Elect(ed), Election(eer), Electoral Choice, Choose, Chosen, Co-opt, Eatanswill, Elite, General, Gerrymander, Hustings, In, Israelite, Khaki, Off-year, Opt, Pick, PR, Primary, Psephology, Rectorial, Return, Select, Stump

Electrical discharge Corposant, Ion, Zwitterion
Electrical instrument Battery, Charger, Galvaniser, Mains, Resistor, Rheostat, Shoe
Electrical unit Amp(ere), Coulomb, Farad, Kilowatt, Ohm, Volt, Watt
Electric eye Pec
Electrician Gaffer, Lineman, Ohm, Siemens, Sparks, Tesla
Electricity Galvanism, HT, Juice, Mains, Negative, Positive, Power, Static, Utility, Vitreous
Electrify Astonish, Galvanise, Startle, Stir, Thrill
Electrode Anode, Cathode, Dynode, Element, Photocathode
Electrolyte Ampholyte
Electromagnet(ic) Abampere, Armature, Oersted, Solenoid, Weber
Electron(ic), Electronics, Electronic device Cooper pairs, Exciton, FET, Fly-by-wire, Linac, Lone pair, Martenot, Polaron, Possum®, Quantum, Thermionics, Valence, Valency
Elegance, Elegant Artistic, Bijou, Chic, Classy, Dainty, Daynt, Debonair, Fancy, Feat, Finesse, Gainly, Galant, Grace, Jimp, Luxurious, Polished, Recherché, Refined, Ritzy, → SMART, Soigné(e), Suave, Swish, Tall, Urbane
Elegy Dirge, Lament, Poem
Element(s), Elementary Abcee, Abecedarian, Absey, Barebones, → COMPONENT, Detail, → ESSENCE, Essential, Factor, Feature, Fuel, Heating, Ideal, Identity, Insertion, Milieu, Peltier, Pixel, Primary, Principle, Rare earth, Rudimental, Simple, Strand, Trace, Tramp, Transition, Weather

ELEMENTS

3 letters:
Air
Tin (Sn)

4 letters:
Atom
Fire
Gold (Au)
Iron (Fe)
Lead (Pb)
Neon (Ne)
Ylem
Zinc (Zn)

5 letters:
Alloy
Argon (Ar)
Boron (B)
Earth
Morph(eme)
Niton
Radon (Rn)
Terra
Water
Xenon (Xe)

6 letters:
Barium (Ba)
Carbon (C)
Cerium (Ce)
Cesium (Cs)
Cobalt (Co)
Copper (Cu)
Curium (Cm)
Erbium (Er)
Helium (He)
Indium (In)
Iodine (I)
Nickel (Ni)
Osmium (Os)
Oxygen (O)
Radium (Ra)
Silver (Ag)
Sodium (Na)

7 letters:
Arsenic (As)
Bismuth (Bi)
Bromine (Br)
Cadmium (Cd)
Caesium (Cs)
Calcium (Ca)

Dubnium (Db)
Fermium (Fm)
Gallium (Ga)
Hafnium (Hf)
Hahnium (Hn)
Halogen
Hassium (Hs)
Holmium (Ho)
Iridium (Ir)
Isotope
Krypton (Kr)
Lithium (Li)
Mercury (Hg)
Niobium (Nb)
Rhenium (Re)
Rhodium (Rh)
Silicon (Si)
Sulphur (S)
Terbium (Tb)
Thorium (Th)
Thulium (Tm)
Uranide
Uranium (U)
Wolfram
Yttrium (Y)

8 letters:
Actinide
Actinium (Ac)
Antimony (Sb)
Astatine (At)
Chlorine (Cl)
Chromium (Cr)
Didymium
Europium (Eu)
Fluorine (F)
Francium (Fr)
Hydrogen (H)
Illinium
Inchoate
Lutetium (Lu)
Masurium
Nebulium
Nitrogen (N)
Nobelium (No)
Platinum (Pt)
Polonium (Po)
Rubidium (Rb)
Samarium (Sm)
Scandium (Sc)
Selenium (Se)
Tantalum (Ta)

Thallium (Tl)
Titanium (Ti)
Tungsten (W)
Vanadium (V)

9 letters:
Alabamine
Aluminium (Al)
Americium (Am)
Berkelium (Bk)
Beryllium (Be)
Brimstone
Columbium
Germanium (Ge)
Joliotium
Lanthanum (La)
Magnesium (Mg)

Manganese (Mn)
Metalloid
Neodymium (Nd)
Neptunium (Np)
Palladium (Pd)
Plutonium (Pu)
Potassium (K)
Ruthenium (Ru)
Strontium (Sr)
Tellurium (Te)
Virginium
Ytterbium (Yb)
Zirconium (Zr)

10 letters:
Dysprosium (D)
Gadolinium (Gd)

Lanthanide
Lawrencium (Lr)
Meitnerium (Mt)
Molybdenum (Mo)
Phlogiston
Phosphorus (P)
Promethium (Pm)
Seaborgium (Sg)
Technetium (Tc)

11 letters:
Californium (Cf)
Einsteinium (Es)
Mendelevium (Md)
Transuranic
Unnilennium (Une)
Unnilhexium (Unh)

Unniloctium (Uno)
Ununquadium
 (Uuq)

12 letters:
Kurchatovium
Nielsbohrium
Praseodymium (Pr)
Protactinium (Pa)
Unnilpentium (Unp)
Unnilseptium (Uns)

13 letters:
Rutherfordium
Transactinide
Unniliquadium
 (Unq)

Elephant(ine) African, Babar, Hathi, Indian, Jumbo, Kheda, Mammoth, Mastodon, Oliphant, Pachyderm, Pad, Pink, Proboscidean, Rogue, Subungulata, Trumpeter, Tusker, White
Elephant-headed Ganesa
Elephant's ears Begonia
Elevate(d), Elevation, Elevator Agger, Attitude, Cheer, Colliculus, El, Eminence, Ennoble, Foothill, Glabella, Grain, Heighten, Hoist, Jack, Lift, Machan, Montic(u)le, Monticulus, Promote, → **RAISE**, Random, Relievo, Ridge, Rise, Steeve, Sublimate, Up(lift), Uplying, Upraise, Wallclimber
Eleven Elf, Hendeca-, Legs, Side, Tail-ender, Team, XI
Elf, Elves Alfar, Chiricaune, Fairy, Goblin, Imp, Kobold, Ouph, Pigwiggen, Pixie, Ribhus, Sprite
Elicit Evoke, Extract, Toase, Toaze, Tose, Toze
Eligible Available, Catch, Fit, Nubile, Parti, Qualified, Worthy
Eliminate, Elimination Cull, Delete, Discard, Exclude, Execute, Extirpate, Heat, Liquidate, Omit, Preclude, Purge, Red-line, Rid, Separate, Slay, Void, Zap
Elision Synal(o)epha, Syncope
Elite Best, Choice, Crack, → **CREAM**, Elect, Flower, Liberal, Meritocracy, Ton, Top drawer, Twelve pitch, U, Zaibatsu
Elixir Amrita, Arcanum, Bufo, Cordial, Daffy, Essence, Medicine, Panacea, Quintessence, Tinct
Elizabeth Bess(ie), Gloriana, Oriano
Elk Deer, Gang, Irish, Moose
Elkoshite Nahum
Ellipse, Elliptic Conic, Oblong, Oval
Elm Dutch, Slippery, Wahoo, Weeping, Wich, Winged, Wych
Elmer Gantry
Elongate Extend, Lengthen, Protract, Stretch
Elope Abscond, Decamp
Eloquence, Eloquent Articulate, Demosthenic, Facundity, Fluent, Honey-tongued, Oracy, Rhetoric, Speaking, Vocal
Else(where) Absent, Alibi, Aliunde, Other
Elucidate Explain, Expose, Interpret

Elude, Elusive Avoid, Dodge, Escape, → EVADE, Evasive, Foil, Intangible, Jink, Slippy, Subt(i)le, Will o' the wisp
▸ **Elves** *see* ELF
Elysium Tir-nan-Og
Em Mut(ton), Pica
Emaciated, Emaciation Atrophy, Erasmus, Gaunt, Haggard, Lean, Skinny, Sweeny, Tabid, Thin, Wanthriven, Wasted
Email Flame, Spam
Emanate, Emanation Arise, Aura, Discharge, Exude, Issue, Miasma, Radiate, Spring
Emancipate, Emancipation Deliver, Forisfamiliate, Free, → LIBERATE, Manumission, Uhuru
Emasculate Bobbitt, Castrate, Debilitate, Evirate, Geld, Unsex
Embalm Anoint, Mummify, Preserve
Embankment Berm, Bund, Causeway, Dam, Dyke, Earthwork, Levee, Mattress, Mound, Rampart, Remblai, Sconce, Staith(e), Stopbank, Terreplein
Embargo → BAN, Blockade, Edict, Restraint
Embark Begin, Board, Enter, Inship, Launch, Sail
Embarrass(ed), Embarrassing, Embarrassment Abash, Ablush, Awkward, Barro, Besti, Buttock-clenching, Chagrin, Cheap, Disconcert, Gêne, Haw, Mess, Mortify, Pose, Predicament, Scundered, Scunnered, Shame, Sheepish, Squirming, Straitened, Toe-curling, Tongue-tied, Upset, Whoopsie, Writhing
▷ **Embarrassed** *may indicate* an anagram
Embassy Consulate, Embassade, Legation, Mission
Embed(ded) Fix, Immerse, Inlaid, Set
Embellish(ed), Embellishment Adorn, Beautify, Bedeck, Deck, Decorate, Dress, Embroider, Enrich, Frill, Garnish, Garniture, Mordent, → ORNAMENT, Ornate, Prettify, Rel(l)ish, Roulade, Turn
Ember(s) Ash, Cinder, Clinker, Gleed
Embezzle(ment) Defalcate, Malversation, Peculate, Purloin, Shoulder, → STEAL
Embitter(ed) Acerbate, Aggravate, Enfested, Rankle, Sour
Emblem(atic) Badge, Bear, Colophon, Daffodil, Device, Figure, Ichthys, Impresa, Insignia, Kikumon, Leek, Lis, Maple leaf, Oak, Pip, Rose, Roundel, Shamrock, Sign, Spear-thistle, → SYMBOL, Tau-cross, Thistle, Token, Totem(ic), Triskelion, Wheel
Embody, Embodied, Embodiment Epitome, Fuse, Impanation, Incarnation, Incorporate, Personify, Quintessence
Embolism Clot, Infarct
Emboss(ed) Adorn, Chase, Cloqué, Engrave, Matelassé, Pounce, Raise, Repoussé, Toreutic
Embrace(d) Abrazo, Accolade, Arm, Canoodle, Clasp, Clinch, Clip, Coll, Complect, Comprise, Cuddle, Embosom, Encircle, Enclasp, Enclose, Enfold, Enlacement, Envelop, Espouse, Fold, Grab, Halse, Haulst, Hause, Hesp, Hug, Imbrast, Inarm, Inclasp, Inclip, Include, Inlace, Kiss, Lasso, Neck, Press, Stemme, Twine, Welcome, Wrap
▷ **Embraces, Embracing** *may indicate* a hidden word
Embrocate, Embrocation Anoint, Arnica, Liniment
Embroider(y) Appliqué, Arrasene, Assisi, Battalia-pie, Braid, Brede, Couching, Crewellery, Crewel-work, Cross-stitch, Cutwork, Drawn threadwork, Embellish, Exaggerate, Eyelet, Fag(g)oting, Fancywork, Featherstitch, Filet, Framework, Gros point, Handiwork, Knotting, Lace(t), Laid work, Mola, Needlepoint, Needlework, Open-work, Opus anglicanum, Orfray, Ornament, Orphrey, Orris, Petit point,

Pinwork, Pulled threadwork, Purl, Sampler, Sew, Smocking, Stitch, Stitchery, Stumpwork, Tambour, Tent, Wrap

Embroideress Mimi

Embroil Confuse, Entangle, Involve, Trouble

Embryo(nic) Blastocyst, Blastospore, Blastula, Conceptus, Epicotyl, Fo(e)tus, Gastrula, Germ, Mesoblast, Morula, Nepionic, Neurula, Origin, Rudiment, Undeveloped

Emend Adjust, Alter, Edit, Reform

Emerald Beryl, Gem, Green, Oriental, Smaragd, Uralian

Emerge(ncy), Emerging Anadyomene, Arise, Craunch, Crise, Crisis, Crunch, Debouch, Eclose, Emanate, Enation, Erupt, Exigency, Hard-shoulder, Issue, Lash-up, Last-ditch, Loom, Need, Outcrop, Pinch, SOS, Spring, Stand-by, Stand-in, Strait, Surface

▷ **Emerge from** *may indicate* an anagram or a hidden word

Emerson Waldo

Emetic Apomorphine, Cacoon, Epicac, Evacuant, Ipecacuanha, Puker, Sanguinaria, Stavesacre, Tartar, Vomitory

Emigrant, Emigration Chozrim, Colonist, Italiot, Jordim, Redemptioner, Settler, When-we, Yordim

Emile Zola

Emily Ellis

Eminence, Eminent Alp, Altitude, Cardinal, Distinguished, Eximious, Grand, Height, Hill, Hywel, Inselberg, Knoll, Light, Lion, Lofty, Luminary, Noble, → NOTABLE, Note, Palatine, Prominence, Renown, Repute, Stature, Tor, Trochanter, → VIP, Wallah

Emirate Dubai

Emissary Agent, Envoy, Legate, Marco Polo

Emission, Emit Discharge, Emanate, Field, Give, Issue, Spallation, Thermionic, Utter, Vent

Emmer Amelcorn, Wheat

Emollient Paregoric

Emolument Income, Perk, Remuneration, Salary, Stipend, Tip, Wages

Emotion(s), Emotional Affection, Anger, Anoesis, Atmosphere, Breast, Chord, Ecstasy, Empathy, Excitable, Feeling, Flare up, Freak-out, Gusty, Hate, Heartstrings, Hoo, Hysteria, Intense, Joy, Limbic, Nympholepsy, Passion, Reins, Roar, Sensibility, Sensitive, Sentiment, Spirit, Theopathy, Torrid, Transport, Weepy

Emotionless Deadpan, Glassy

Empathy Identifying, Rapport, Rapprochement, Sympathy

Emperor Agramant(e), Akbar, Akihito, Antoninus, Augustus, Babur, Barbarossa, Bonaparte, Caesar, Caligula, Caracalla, Charlemagne, Claudius, Commodus, Concerto, Constantine, Diocletian, Domitian, Ferdinand, Gaius, Genghis Khan, Gratian, Great Mogul, Hadrian, Haile Selassie, Heraclius, Hirohito, Imp, Imperator, Inca, Jimmu, Justinian, Kaiser, Keasar, Kesar, King, Maximilian, Menelik, Mikado, Ming, Mogul, Montezuma, Mpret, Napoleon, Negus, Nero, Nerva, Otho, Otto, Penguin, Peter the Great, Purple, Pu-yi, Rex, Rosco, Ruler, Severus, Shah Jahan, Shang, Sovereign, Sultan, Tenno, Theodore, Theodosius, Tiberius, Titus, Trajan, Tsar, Valens, Valentinian, Valerian, Vespasian, Vitellius, Wenceslaus

Emphasis, Emphasize, Emphatic Accent, Birr, Bold, Dramatise, Ek se, Forcible, Foreground, Forzando, Hendiadys, Italic, Marcato, Positive, Resounding, Sforzando, → STRESS, Underline, Underscore, Vehement

Empire Assyria, British, Byzantine, Celestial, Chain, Chinese, Domain, Empery,

First, French, Georgia, Holy Roman, Indian, Kingdom, Latin, NY, Ottoman, Parthia, Persian, Principate, Realm, Reich, Roman, Russian, Second, Turkish, Western

Empiricism Positivism

Emplacement Battery, Platform

Employ(ment) Business, Calling, Designated, Engage, Exercitation, Hire, Occupy, Pay, Place, Portfolio, Practice, Pursuit, Service, Shiftwork, Trade, Use, Using, Utilise, Vocation

Employee(s) Barista, Clock-watcher, Factotum, Hand, Help, Hireling, Intrapreneur, Minion, Munchkin, Networker, Payroll, Pennyboy, Personnel, Rainmaker, Servant, Staff, Staffer, Valet, Walla(h), Worker, Workforce, Workpeople

Employer Baas, Boss, Malik, Master, Melik, Padrone, User

▷ **Employs** *may indicate* an anagram

Emporium Bazaar, Shop, Store

Empower Authorise, Enable, Entitle, Permit

Empress Eugenie, Josephine, Messalina, Queen, Sultana, Tsarina, VIR

Empty Addle, Bare, Barren, Blank, Boss, Buzz, Claptrap, Clear, Deplete, Deserted, Devoid, Disembowel, Drain, Exhaust, Expel, Forsaken, Futile, Gousty, Gut, Hent, Hollow, Inane, Jejune, Lade, Lave, Null, Phrasy, Pump, Shallow, Teem, Toom, Tume, Unfurnished, Unoccupied, Unpeople, Vacant, Vacate, Vacuous, Vain, Viduous, → **VOID**

▷ **Empty** *may indicate* an 'o' in the word or an anagram

Emulate Ape, Copy, Envy, Equal, Imitate, Match

Emulsion Pseudosolution, Tempera

Enable Authorise, Empower, Potentiate, Qualify, Sanction

Enact Adopt, Effect, Ordain, Personate, Portray

Enamel(led), Enamel work Aumail, Champlevé, Cloisonné, Della-robbia, Dentine, Fabergé, Ganion, Lacquer, Nail, Polish, Porcelain, Schwarzlot, Shippo, Smalto, Stoved, Vitreous

Encampment Bivouac, Douar, Dowar, Duar, Laager, Laer, Settlement

Encase(d), Encasement Box, Crate, Emboîtement, Encapsulate, Enclose, Obtect

Enchant(ing), Enchanted, Enchantment Bewitch, Captivate, Charm, Delight, Gramary(e), Incantation, Magic, Necromancy, Orphean, Rapt, Sorcery, Spellbind, Thrill

Enchanter, Enchantress Archimage, Archimago, Armida, Circe, Comus, Fairy, Lorelei, Magician, Medea, Mermaid, Prospero, Reim-kennar, Sorcerer, Vivien, Witch

Encircle(d) Belt, Enclose, Encompass, Enlace, Entrold, Gird, Hoop, Inorb, Introld, Orbit, Pale, Ring, Stemme, → **SURROUND**, Wreathe

Enclave Cabinda, Ceuta, → **ENCLOSURE**, Melilla, Pocket, San Marino

Enclose(d), Enclosing, Enclosure Bawn, Beset, Boma, Box, Cage, Carol, Carrel, Case, Circumscribe, Common, Compound, Corral, Court, Embale, Embowel, Embower, Enceinte, Enchase, Encircle, Enclave, Enhearse, Enlock, Enshrine, Fence, Fold, Forecourt, Garth, Haggard, Haw, Hem, Henge, Hope, Impound, In, Incapsulate, Inchase, Infibulate, Inlock, Insert, Interclude, Lairage, Pale, Peel, Pele, Pen(t), Petavius, Pightle, Pin, Pinfold, Pit, Playpen, Plenum, Rail, Rath, Recluse, Ree(d), Ring, Run, Saddling, Saleyard, Seal, Sekos, Sept, Seraglio, Serail, Several, Sin bin, Steeld, Stell, Stive, Stockade, Sty, → **SURROUND**, Tine, Unsaddling, Vibarium, Ward, Winner's, Wrap, Yard

Encode Cipher, Scramble

Encomium Eulogy, Praise, Sanction, Tribute

Encompass Bathe, Begird, Beset, Environ, Include, Surround

Encore Again, Agen, Ancora, Bis, Ditto, Do, Iterum, Leitmotiv, Recall, Repeat, Reprise

Encounter Battle, Brush, Combat, Contend, Cope, Dogfight, Face, Hit, Incur, Intersect, Interview, → **MEET**, One-one, Rencontre, Ruffle, Skirmish, Tilt

Encourage(ment), Encouraging Abet, Acco(u)rage, Alley-oop, Animate, Attaboy, Bolster, Boost, Brighten, Buck, Cheer, Cohortative, Comfort, Commend, Dangle, Egg, Elate, Embolden, Empatron, Exhort, Fillip, Fire, Fortify, Foster, Fuel, Gee, Hearten, Heigh, Help, Hope, Hortatory, Incite, Inspirit, Nourish, Nurture, Pat, Patronise, Proceleusmatic, Prod, Protreptic, Push, Reassure, Root, Stimulate, Support, Tally-ho, Train, Upcheer, Uplift, Urge, Wean, Yay, Yo

Encroach(ment) Impinge, Infringe, Inroad, Intrude, Invade, Overlap, Overstep, Poach, Purpresture, Trespass, Usurp

Encrypt(ion) Coding, Public key

Encumber, Encumbrance Burden, Charge, Clog, Dead weight, Deadwood, Dependent, → **HANDICAP**, Impede, Load, Obstruct, Saddle

Encyclopaedic Comprehensive, Diderot, Extensive, Universal, Vast

End(ing) Abolish, Abut, Aim, Ambition, Amen, Anus, Arse, Big, Bitter, Bourn(e), Butt, Cease, Climax, Close, Closure, Cloture, Coda, Conclude, Crust, Culminate, Curtain, Curtains, Cut off, Dead, Death, Decease, Denouement, Desinence, Desistance, Destroy, Determine, Dissolve, Domino, Effect, Envoi, Envoy, Epilogue, Exigent, Expire, Explicit, Extremity, Fatal, Fattrels, Feminine, Final(e), Fine, Finis, → **FINISH**, Finite, Gable, Grave, Heel, Ish, Izzard, Izzet, Kill, Kybosh, Last, Let up, Little, Loose, Masculine, Mill, Nirvana, No side, Ort, Outro, Period, Peter, Pine, Point, Purpose, Quench, Receiving, Remnant, Rescind, Result, Roach, Round off, Runback, Scotch, Scrag, Shank, Slaughter, Sopite, Split, Sticky, Stub, Supernaculum, Surcease, Swansong, Tag, Tail, Tailpiece, Telesis, Telic, Telos, Term, Terminal, Terminate, Terminus, Thrum, Tip, Toe, Top, Ultimate, Up, Upshot, West, Z

Endanger Hazard, Imperil, Periclitate, Risk, Threaten

Endear(ing), Endearment Adorable, Affection, Asthore, Caress, Cariad, Ducks, Ducky, Enamour, Hinny, Honey(-bunch), Honey-chile, Ingratiate, Jarta, Luv, Machree, Mavourneen, Peat, Pet, Sweet nothings

Endeavour Aim, Effort, Enterprise, Essay, Morse, Strain, Strive, Struggle, Try, Venture

Endemic Local, Prevalent

Endive Escarole

Endless Continuous, Ecaudate, Eternal, Eterne, Infinite, Interminable, Perpetual, Undated

▷ **Endlessly** *may indicate* a last letter missing

End of the world Ragnarok

Endorse(ment) Adopt, Affirm, Allonge, Approve, Assurance, Back, Certify, Confirmation, Docket, Initial, Okay, Oke, Ratify, Rubber stamp, Sanction, Second, Sign, Subscript, → **SUPPORT**, Underwrite, Visa

Endow(ment) Assign, Bequeath, Bestow, Bless, Cha(u)ntry, Dot, Dotation, Enrich, Foundation, Gift, Leave, Patrimony, State, Vest, Wakf, Waqf

Endurance, Endure(d), Enduring Abought, Aby(e), Bear, Bide, Brook, Dree, Dure, Face, Fortitude, Have, Hold, → **LAST**, Livelong, Lump, Patience, Perseverance, Pluck, Ride, Stamina, Stand, Stay, Stomach, Stout, Support, Sustain, Swallow, Tether, Thole, Timeless, Tolerance, Undergo, Wear, Weather

Endymion Bluebell

Enema Barium, Catharsis, Clyster, Purge

Enemy Adversary, Antagonist, Boer, Devil, Fifth column, Foe(n), Fone, Opponent, Public, Time

Energetic, Energise, Energy Active, Alternative, Amp, Animation, Arduous, Atomic, Bond, Cathexis, Chakra, Chi, Dash, Doer, Drive, Dynamic, Dynamo, E, Enthalpy, Entropy, EV, Fermi, Fireball, Firebrand, Firecracker, Force, Fossil, Free, Fructan, Fusion, Geothermal, Gism, Go, Graviton, Hartree, H.D.R., Horme, Input, Instress, Internal, → **JET**, Jism, Jissom, Joie de vivre, Joule, Karma, Kinetic, Kundalini, Lattice, Libido, Lossy, Luminous, Magnon, Moxie, Nuclear, Orgone, Pep, Phonon, Potency, Potential, → **POWER**, Powerhouse, Prana, QI, Quantum, Quasar, Rad, Radiant, Radiatory, Renewable, Roton, Rydberg, Sappy, Second-wind, Solar, Stamina, Steam, Sthenic, Stingo, Tidal, Trans-uranic, Vehement, Verve, Vibrational, Vigour, Vim, Vital, Wave, Whammo, Wind(-farm), Zappy, Zing, Zip

Enervate Exhaust

Enfold Clasp, Embrace, Envelop, Hug, Stemme, Swathe, Wrap

Enforce(ment) Administer, Coerce, Control, Exact, Implement, Impose

Eng Agma

Engage(d), Engagement, Engaging Absorb, Accept, Appointment, At, Attach, Bespoken, Betrothal, Bind, Book, Busy, Contract, Date, Embark, Employ, Engross, Enlist, Enmesh, Enter, Fascinate, Gear, Gig, Hire, Hold, Interest, Interlock, Lock, Mesh, Met, Occupy, Pledge, Promise, Prosecute, Reserve, Residency, Skirmish, Sponsal, Sponsion, Spousal, Sprocket, Trip, Wage, Winsome

▷ **Engagement** *may indicate* a battle

Engender Beget, Breed, Cause, Occasion, Produce

Engine, Engine part Air, Analytical, Athodyd, Beam, Booster, Bricole, Bypass, Carburettor, Catapult, Compound, Diesel, Donkey, Dynamo, Fan-jet, Fire, Four-cycle, Four-stroke, Gas, Gin, Heat, Humdinger, Internal combustion, Ion, Iron horse, Jet, Lean-burn, Light, Little-end, Locomotive, Machine, Mangonel, → **MOTOR**, Nacelle, Oil, Onager, Orbital, Otto, Outboard, Overhead valve, Petard, Petrary, Petrol, Petter, Pilot, Plasma, Podded, Pony, Pug, Pulp, Pulsejet, Push-pull, Put-put, Radial, Ramjet, Reaction, Reciprocating, Retrorocket, Rocket, Rose, Rotary, Scorpion, Scramjet, Search, Side-valve, Sleeve valve, Stationary, Steam, Stirling, Sustainer, Tank, Terebra, Testudo, Thermometer, Top-end, Traction, Trompe, Turbine, Turbofan, Turbojet, Turboprop, Two-handed, Two-stroke, V, Vernier, V-type, Wankel, Warwolf, Water, Wildcat, Winch, Winding

Engineer(ing), Engineers Aeronautical, AEU, Armstrong, Arrange, Baird, Barnes Wallis, Bazalgette, BE, Bessemer, Brindley, Brinell, Brunel, CE, Chartered, Concurrent, Contrive, De Lessops, Diesel, Fokker, Genetic, Greaser, Ground, Heinkel, Interactive, Junkers, Kennelly, Knowledge, Liability, Manhattan District, Manoeuvre, Marconi, Marine, Mastermind, McAdam, Mechanical, Mechatronics, Military, Mime, Operator, Organise, Otto, Planner, Porsche, Process, RE, Repairman, Reverse, Rig, Rogallo, Sales, Sanitary, Sapper, Savery, Scheme, Siemens, Smeaton, Social, Software, Sound, Stage, Stephenson, Strauss, Systems, Telford, Tesla, Traffic, Trevithick, Wangle, Wankel, Watt, Whittle, Whitworth

England Albany, Albion, Blighty, Demi-paradise, Eden, John Bull, Merrie, Merry, Middle, The Old Dart

English(man) Anglican, Anglice, Baboo, Babu, Basic, Brit, Bro talk, Canajan, Choom, E, Ebonics, Eng, Estuary, Gringo, Hawaiian, Hong Kong, Indian, Irish, Jackeroo, John Bull, King's, Kipper, Limey, Middle, Mister, Modern, Newspeak, Norman, Officialese, Old, Oxford, Philippine, Pidgin, Plain, Pom(my), Pommie, Pongo, Pork-pudding, Queen's, Qui-hi, Qui-hye, Rock, Rooinek, Rosbif, Sassenach,

Saxon, Scotic, Seaspeak, Shopkeeper, Side, Singapore, Singlish, South African, South Asian, Southron, Spanglish, Standard, Strine, Wardour Street, Woodbine, Yanqui, Yinglish

Engorge Devour, Glut, Swallow

Engraft Inset

Engrave(r), Engraving Aquatint, Blake, Carve, Cerography, Cerotype, Chalcography, Character, Chase, Cut, Die-sinker, Dry-point, Durer, Enchase, Eng, Etch, Glyptic, Glyptograph, Hogarth, Impress, Inchase, Inciser, Inscribe, Insculp, Intagliate, Inter, Lapidary, Line, Mezzotint, Niello, Photoglyphic, Photogravure, Plate, Scalp, Scrimshander, Scrimshandy, Scrimshaw, Steel, Stillet, Stipple, Stylet, Stylography, Turn, Wood, Xylographer

Engross(ed) Absorb, Engage, Enwrap, Immerse, Monopolise, → OCCUPY, Preoccupy, Prepossess, Rapt, Sink, Writ large

Engulf Overwhelm, Swamp, Whelm

Enhance Add, Augment, Better, Elevate, Embellish, Exalt, Heighten, Intensify

Enigma(tic) Charade, Conundrum, Dilemma, Gioconda, Gnomic, Mystery, Oracle, Poser, Problem, → PUZZLE, Quandary, Question, Rebus, Riddle, Secret, Sphinxlike, Teaser

Enjoin Command, Direct, Impose, Prohibit, Require

Enjoy(able), Enjoyment Apolaustic, Appreciate, Ball, Brook, Delectation, Fruition, Glee, Groove, Gusto, Have, High jinks, Lekker, Like, Own, Possess, Relish, Ripping, Savour, Taste, Wallow

Enlarge(ment), Enlarger Accrue, Acromegaly, Add, Aneurism, Aneurysm, Augment, Blow-up, Diagraph, Dilate, Exostosis, Expand, Expatiate, Explain, Increase, → MAGNIFY, Piece, Ream, Rebore, Sensationalize, Swell, Telescope, Tumefy, Upbuild, Varicosity

Enlighten(ed), Enlightenment Awareness, Bodhisattva, Dewali, Divali, Edify, Educate, Explain, Haskalah, Illumine, Instruct, Liberal, Nirvana, Revelation, Satori, Verlig(te)

Enlist Attest, Conscript, Draft, Engage, Enrol, Induct, Join, Levy, Muster, Prest, Recruit, Rope in, Roster, Volunteer

Enliven(ed) Animate, Arouse, Brighten, Cheer, Comfort, Exhilarate, Ginger, Invigorate, Merry, Pep, Refresh, Warm

Enmity Animosity, Aversion, Bad blood, Hatred, Malice, Nee(d)le, Rancour, Spite

Ennoble(ment) Dub, Elevate, Ermine, Exalt, Honour, Raise

Ennui Boredom, Tedium

Enormous Colossal, Exorbitant, Googol, Huge, Humongous, Humungous, → IMMENSE, Jumbo, Mammoth, Mega, Plonking, Vast, Walloper, Walloping

Enough Adequate, → AMPLE, Anow, Basta, Belay, Enow, Fill, Geyan, Nuff, Pax, Plenty, Qs, Sate, Satis, Suffice, Sufficient, Via, When

Enounce Affirm, Declare, State

Enquire, Enquiring, Enquiry Ask, Case, Check, Curious, Eh, Examine, Inquest, Inquire, Organon, Public, Request, Research, Scan, See, Stewards', Trial

Enrage(d) Bemad, Emboss, Enfelon, Imboss, → INCENSE, Inflame, Infuriate, Livid, Madden, Wild

Enrapture(d) Enchant, Ravish, Sent, Transport

Enrich Adorn, Endow, Enhance, Fortify, Fructify, Oxygenate

Enrol(ment) Attest, Empanel, Enlist, Enter, Incept, → JOIN, List, Matriculate, Muster, Register

Ensconce(d) Establish, Settle, Shelter, Snug

Ensemble Band, Octet(te), Orchestra, Outfit, Ripieno, Set, Tout, Whole

Enshrine Cherish, Sanctify

Ensign Ancient, Badge, Banner, Duster, → **FLAG**, Gonfalon, Officer, Pennon, Red, White

Enslave(ment) Addiction, Bondage, Captivate, Chain, Enthral, Thrall, Yoke

Ensue Follow, Result, Succeed, Supervene, Transpire

Entail Involve, Necessitate, Require

Entangle(ment) Ball, Cot, Elf, Embrangle, Embroil, Encumber, Ensnarl, Entrail, Fankle, Implicate, → **KNOT**, Mat, Ravel, Retiarius, Taigle, Trammel

Enter, Entry Admit, Board, Broach, Come, Enrol, Field, Infiltrate, Ingo, Inscribe, Insert, Intromit, Invade, Lodge, Log, Penetrate, Pierce, Record, Run, Submit, Table, Wild card

Enterprise, Enterprising Adventure, Ambition, Aunter, Cash cow, Dash, Emprise, Free, Go ahead, Goey, Go-getter, Gumption, Industry, Minefield, Plan, Private, Public, Push, Spirit, Starship, Stunt, Up and coming, Venture

Entertain(er), Entertaining, Entertainment Accourt, Acrobat, Afterpiece, All-dayer, All-nighter, Amphitryon, Amuse, Balladeer, Ballet, Beguile, Burlesque, Busk, Cabaret, Carnival, Cater, Charade, Cheer, Chout, Circus, Comedian, Comic, Concert, Conjure, Consider, Cottabus, Crack, Craic, Cuddy, Diseur, Diseuse, Distract, Divert, Divertissement, ENSA, Extravaganza, Fete, Fleshpots, Floorshow, Foy, Fun, Gaff, Gala, Gas, Gaudy, Gig, Harbour, Harlequin, Have, Hospitality, Host(ess), Impressionist, Infotainment, Interest, Interlude, Intermezzo, Jester, Juggler, Karaoke, Kidult, Kursaal, Lauder, Levee, Light, Masque, Melodrama, Minstrel, Movieoke, Musical, Music hall, Olio, Opera, Palladium, Panto, Pap, Party, Peepshow, Performer, Piece, Pierrot, Play, Raree-show, Reception, Regale, Review, Revue, Ridotto, Roadshow, Rodeo, Serenade, Showbiz, Sideshow, Singer, Snake-charmer, Soirée, Son et lumière, Striptease, Table, Tamasha, Tattoo, Treat, Variety, Vaudeville, Ventriloquist, Wattle

Enthral(l) Charm, Enchant, Enslave, Spellbind

Enthuse, Enthusiasm, Enthusiast(ic) Acclamatory, Amateur, Ardent, Ardour, Buff, Bug, Buzz, Cat, Cheerleader, Crazy, Crusader, Delirium, Demon, Devotee, Ebullience, Ecstatic, Estro, Fandom, Fiend, Fire, Flame, Freak, Furor(e), Geek, Get-up-and-go, Gung-ho, Gusto, Hacker, Hearty, Hype, Into, Keen, Lyrical, Mad, Mane, Mania, Muso, Nethead, Nympholept, Oomph, Outpour, Overboard, Passion, Perfervid, Preoccupation, Rah-rah, Raring, Rave, Relish, Rhapsodise, Schwärmerei, Sold, Spirit, Teeny-bopper, Verve, Warmth, Whole-hearted, Wonk, Zealot, Zest

Entice(ment), Enticing Allure, Angle, Cajole, Carrot, Decoy, Lure, Persuade, Seductive, → **TEMPT**, Tole, Toll, Trepan

Entire(ly), Entirety Absolute, All, Bag and baggage, Clean, Complete, Full Monty, Genuine, Inly, Intact, Integral, In toto, Livelong, Lot, Purely, Root and branch, Systemic, Thorough, Total, Tout, → **WHOLE**

Entitle(ment) Empower, Enable, Legitim, Name, Right

Entity Being, Body, Existence, Holon, Monad, Tao, Tensor, Thing, Virino

Entomologist Fabré

Entourage Cortège

Entrail(s) Bowels, Chawdron, Giblets, Gralloch, Guts, Ha(r)slet, Humbles, Lights, Numbles, Offal, Quarry, Tripe, Umbles, Viscera

Entrance(d), Entrant, Entry Access, Adit, Admission, Anteroom, Arch, Atrium, Attract, Avernus, Bewitch, Charm, Closehead, Contestant, Door, Doorstop, Double, Dromos, Eye, Fascinate, Foyer, Gate, Ghat, Hypnotise, In-door, Infare, Inflow, Ingate, Ingress, Inlet, Introitus, Jawhole, Jaws, Jib-door, Mesmerise, Mouth, Narthex, Pend, Porch, Portal, Porte-cochère, Postern, Propylaeum, Propylon,

Ravish, Reception, Record, Regest, Registration, Single, Spellbound, Starter, Stem, Stoa, Stoma, Stulm, Torii

Entreat(y) Appeal, Ask, Beg, Beseech, Flagitate, Impetrate, → **IMPLORE**, Orison, Petition, Plead, Pray, Precatory, Prevail, Prig, Rogation, Solicit, Sue, Supplicate

Entrée Access, Dish, Entry, Ingate

Entrench(ment) Coupure, Encroach, Fortify, Trespass

Entrepreneur Businessman, E-tailer, Executor, Impresario, Wheeler-dealer

Entrust Aret(t), Confide, Consign, Delegate, Give

▶ **Entry** *see* **ENTRANCE**

Entwine Complect, Impleach, Intervolve, Lace, Twist, Weave

Enumerate, Enumeration Catalogue, Count, Detail, Fansi, List, Tell

Enunciate, Enunciation Articulate, Declare, Deliver, Diction, Elocution, Proclaim

Envelop(e) Arachnoid, Bangtail, Chorion, Corolla, Corona, Cover(ing), Cuma, Enclose, Entire, First day cover, Floral, Invest, Involucre, Jiffy(bag)®, Muffle, Mulready, Perianth, Sachet, Sae, Serosa, Shroud, Smother, Surround, Swathe, Window

Environment(s), Environmental(ist) ACRE, Ambience, Ecofreak, Econut, Eco-warrior, Element, Entourage, Ergonomics, Green, Greenpeace, Habitat, Milieu, Realo, SEPA, Setting, Sphere, Surroundings, Umwelt, Vicinity

Envisage Contemplate, Imagine, Suppose

Envoi Farewell, RIP

Envoy Agent, Diplomat, Elchee, El(t)chi, Hermes, Legate, Plenipotentiary

Envy, Enviable, Envious Begrudge, Covet, Jaundiced, Jealousy, Penis, Plum

Enzyme ACE, Aldolase, Allosteric, Allozyme, Amylase, Amylopsin, Apyrase, Arginase, Asparaginase, Autolysin, Bromel(a)in, Carbohydrase, Carbonic anhydrase, Carboxylase, Casease, Catalase, Cathepsin, Cellulase, Cholinesterase, Chymopapain, Chymotrypsin, Coagulase, Collagenase, Constitutive, Cyclase, Cytase, Deaminase, Decarboxylase, Dehydrogenase, Diastase, Dipeptidase, Elastase, ELISA, Enolase, Enterokinase, Erepsin, Esterase, Fibrinolysin, Flavoprotein, Guanase, Histaminase, Hyaluronidase, Hydrase, Hydrolase, Inducible, Inulase, Invertase, Isomerase, Kallikrein, Kinase, Lactase, Lecithinase, Ligase, Lipase, Luciferase, Lyase, Lysin, Lysozyme, Maltase, Mutase, Neuraminidase, Nuclease, Oxdoreductase, Oxidase, Oxygenase, Papain, Pectase, Pectinesterase, Penicillinase, Pepsin(e), Peptidase, Permease, Peroxidase, Phosphatase, Phosphorylase, Plasmin, Polymerase, Protease, Proteinase, PSA, Ptyalin, Reductase, Ren(n)in, Restriction, Ribonuclease, Saccharase, Steapsin, Streptodornase, Streptokinase, Subtilisin, Sulfatase, Sulphatase, Telomerase, Thrombin, Thrombokinase, Thromboplastin, Transaminase, Transcriptase, Transferase, Trehalase, Trypsin, Tyrosinase, Urease, Urokinase, Zymase

Eon Arch(a)ean, Epoch

Epaminondas Theban

Ephemera(l) Brief, Day, Drake, Fungous, Mayfly, Momentary, Passing, Transient, Transitory, Trappings

Epic Aeneid, Ben Hur, Beowulf, Calliope, Colossal, Dunciad, Edda, Epopee, Epyllion, Gilgamesh, Heroic, Homeric, Iliad, Kalevala, Lusiad(s), Mahabharata, Nibelungenlied, Odyssey, Ramayana, Rhapsody, Saga

Epicene Hermaphrodite

Epicure(an) Apicius, Apolaustic, Connoisseur, Friand, Gastronome, Gastrosopher, Glutton, → **GOURMAND**, Gourmet, Hedonist, Sybarite

Epidemic Pandemic, Pestilence, Plague, Prevalent, Rampant, Rash

Epigram Adage, Apophthegm, Gnomic, Mot, Proverb

Epigraph Citation, Inscription, RIP

Epilepsy, Epileptic Clonic, Eclampsia, Falling evil, Falling sickness, Fit, Grand mal, Petit mal, Turn

Epilogue Appendix, Coda, Postscript

Epiphany Twelfthtide

Epiphenomenon ESP

Epiphyte Air-plant

Episcopalian PE, Prelatic

Episode, Episodic Chapter, Incident, Page, Picaresque, Scene

Epistle(s) Catholic, General, Lesson, Letter, Missive, Pastoral, Titus

Epitaph Ci-git, Hic jacet, Inscription, RIP

Epithet Adj(ective), Antonomasia, Apathaton, Byword, Curse, Expletive, Panomphaean, → TERM, Title

Epitome, Epitomise Abridge, Abstract, Digest, Image, Model, Summary, Typify

Epoch Age, Eocene, Era, Holocene, Magnetic, Miocene, Neogene, Oligocene, Palaeocene, Palaeolithic, Perigordian, Period, Pl(e)iocene, Pleistocene

Epsom salts Kieserite

Equable, Equably Calm, Just, Pari passu, Placid, Smooth, Tranquil

Equal(ly), Equality, Equal quantities Alike, All square, A(n)a, As, Balanced, Commensurate, Compeer, Egal(ity), Emulate, Equinox, Equiparate, Equity, Even, Even-steven, Ex aequo, Fe(a)re, Feer, Fiere, Fifty-fifty, For, Identical, Identity, Is, Iso-, Isocracy, Isonomy, Level, Level-pegging, Maik, Make, Match, Mate, Owelty, Par, Parametric, Pari passu, → PEER, Peregal, Pheer(e), Rise, Rival, → SO, Square, Upsides, Wyoming, Ylike

Equanimity Aplomb, Balance, Poise, Serenity

Equate, Equation(s) Balance, Chemical, Cubic, Defective, Differential, Diophantine, Dirac, Exponential, Gas, Identity, Linear, Logistic, Maxwell's, Parametric, Personal, Polar, Quadratic, Reduce, Relate, Rhizic, Schrödinger, Simultaneous, Van der Waals', Wave

Equator(ial) Celestial, Galactic, Line, Magnetic, Thermal, Tropical

Equerry Courtier, Officer, Page

Equilibrium Balance, Composure, Homeostasis, Isostasy, Poise, Punctuated, Stable, Stasis, Steady state, Tautomerism, Thermodynamic

Equinox Autumnal, Vernal

Equip(ment), Equipage Accoutrement, Adorn, Aguise, Aguize, Apparatus, Apparel, Appliance, Armament, Array, Attire, Carriage, Clobber, Codec, Deadstock, Deck, Dight, Expertise, → FURNISH, Gear, Gere, Get-up, Graith, Habilitate, Hand-me-up, Kit, Material, Matériel, Mechanise, Muniments, Outfit, Paraphernalia, Plant, Receiver, Retinue, Rig, Sonar, Spikes, Stereo, Stock, Stuff, Tack(le), Tool, Trampet(te), Trampoline, Turn-out

Equity Actors, Equality, Justice, Law, Negative, Owner's, Union

Equivalence, Equivalent Akin, Amounting to, Correspondent, Dose, Equal, Equipollent, Ewe, Formal, In-kind, Same, Tantamount

Equivocal Ambiguous, Dubious, Evasive, Fishy, Oracular, Vague

Equivocate Flannel, Lie, Palter, Prevaricate, Quibble, Tergiversate, Waffle, Weasel

Er Um

Era Age, Archaean, C(a)enozoic, Christian, Common, Cretaceous, Cryptozoic, Decade, Dynasty, Ediocaron, Eozoic, Epoch, Hadean, Hegira, Hej(i)ra, Hijra, Jurassic, Lias, Mesozoic, Palaeozoic, Period, Precambrian, Proterozoic, Republican, Vulgar

Eradicate, Erase Abolish, Delete, Demolish, Destroy, Dislimn, Efface, Expunge,

Extirp, Obliterate, Purge, Root, Scrat, Scratch, Stamp-out, Strike off, Uproot, Uptear

Erasmus Humanist

Eratosthenes Sieve

Erbium Er

Erect(ion), Erector Attolent, Boner, Build, Construct(ion), Elevate, Hard-on, Henge, Horn, Perpendicular, Priapism, Prick, Rear, Rigger, Stiffy, Straight-pight, Tentigo, Upright, Vertical

Ergo Argal, Hence, Therefore

Erica Heather, Ling

Ermine Fur, Minever, Miniver, Stoat

Ernie Bondsman

Erode, Erosion Abrade, Corrasion, Denude, Destroy, Deteriorate, Detrition, Etch, Fret, Hush, Planation, Spark, Wash, Wear, Yardang

Eros, Erotic(a) Amatory, Amorino, Amorous, Aphrodisiac, Carnal, Cupid, Curiosa, Lascivious, Philtre, Prurient, Salacious, Steamy

Err(or) Aliasing, Anachronism, Bish, Blip, Blooper, Blunder, Boner, Bug, Clanger, Comedy, Corrigendum, EE, Execution, Fat-finger, Fault, Fluff, Glaring, Heresy, Human, Inaccuracy, Inherited, Jeofail, K'thibh, Lapse, Lapsus, Literal, Mackle, Mesprise, Mesprize, Misgo, Misprint, Misprise, Misprize, Misstep, → MISTAKE, Mumpsimus, Out, Parachronism, Probable, Rounding, Rove, Runtime, Sampling, Semantic, Sin, Slip, Slip-up, Solecism, Standard, Stray, Trip, Truncation, Typo, Typographical, Unforced, Wander

Errand Chore, Commission, Fool's, Message, Mission, Sleeveless, Task

Errand-boy Cad, Galopin, Page

Erratic Haywire, Temperamental, Unstable, Vagary, Vagrant, Wayward

Erroneous False, Inaccurate, Mistaken, Non-sequitur

Ersatz Artificial, Synthetic

Erudite, Erudition Academic, Didactic, Learned, Savant, Scholar, Well-read, Wisdom

Erupt(ion), Erupture Belch, Brash, Burst, Ecthyma, Eject, Emit, Emphlysis, Exanthem(a), Exanthemata, → EXPLODE, Fissure, Flare, Fumarole, Hives, Hornito, Lichen, Mal(l)ander, Mallender, Morphew, Outbreak, Outburst, Papilla, Paroxysm, Plinian, Pompholyx, Pustule, Rash, Rose-drop, Scissure

Escalate, Escalator Accrescence, Expand, Granary, Grow, Lift, Travolator

Escape(e), Escapade, Escapist Abscond, Atride, Avoid, Bale out, Bolt, Bolthole, Breakout, Caper, Close call, Eject, Elope, Elude, Elusion, Esc, Eschewal, Evade, Exit, Fire, Flee, Flight, Frolic, Fugacity, Gaolbreak, Hole, Hoot, Houdini, Houdini act, Hout, Lam, Leakage, Leg-it, Let-off, Levant, Loop(-hole), Meuse, Mews, Muse, Narrow, Near thing, Outlet, Prank, Refuge, Rollick, Runaway, Sauve qui peut, Scapa, Scarper, Seep(age), Shave, Slip, Vent, Walter Mitty, Wilding, Wriggle

Escapement Anchor, Foliot, Recoil

Eschew Abandon, Avoid, For(e)go, Ignore, → SHUN

Escort Accompany, Attend, Bodyguard, Chaperone, Comitatus, Conduct, Convoy, Cortège, Corvette, Date, Destroyer, Entourage, Frigate, Gallant, Gigolo, Guide, Lead, Outrider, Protector, Retinue, See, Send, Set, Squire, Take, Tend, Usher, Walker

Escutcheon Achievement, Crest, Shield

Esker OS

Eskimo Aleut, Caribou, Husky, In(n)uit, Inuk, Inukitut, Thule, Yupik

Esoteric Abstruse, Acroamatic, Arcane, Inner, Mystic, Occult, Orphic, Private,

Rarefied, Recondite, Secret

ESP Psi

Especial(ly) Chiefly, Esp, Espec, Outstanding, Particular

Esperanto Ido, Zamenhof

Espionage Industrial, Spying, Surveillance

Esplanade Promenade, Walk

Esprit Insight, Spirit, Understanding, Wit

Esquire Armiger(o), Esq, Gent

Essay(s) Article, Attempt, Causerie, Critique, Dabble, Disquisition, Dissertation, Endeavour, Festschrift, Go, Paper, Prolusion, Stab, Theme, Thesis, Tractate, Treatise, Try

Essayist Addison, Bacon, Carlyle, Columnist, Elia, Ellis, Emerson, Hazlitt, Holmes, Hunt, Huxley, Lamb, Locke, Montaigne, Pater, Prolusion, Ruskin, Scribe, Steele, → **WRITER**

Essence Alma, Atman, Attar, Aura, Being, Core, Element, Entia, Esse, Extract, Fizzen, Flavouring, Foison, Gist, Heart, Hom(e)ousian, Inbeing, Inscape, Kernel, Marrow, Mauri, Mirbane, Myrbane, Nub, Nutshell, Oil, Ottar, Otto, Perfume, Per-se, Pith, Quiddity, Ratafia, Soul, Ylang-ylang

Essential(ly) Basic, Central, Crucial, Entia, Formal, Fundamental, Imperative, In, Indispensable, Inherent, Integral, Intrinsic, Kernel, Key, Lifeblood, Linch-pin, Marrow, Material, Must, Necessary, Need, Nitty-gritty, Nuts and bolts, Part-parcel, Per-se, Prana, Prerequisite, Quintessence, Radical, Requisite, Sine qua non, Soul, Vital, Whatness

Establish(ed) Abide, Anchor, Ascertain, Base, Build, Chronic, Create, Deploy, Embed, Enact, Endemic, Engrain, Ensconce, Entrench, Erect, Evince, Fix, → **FOUND**, Haft, Imbed, Ingrain, Instal(l), Instate, Instil, Institute, Inveterate, Ordain, Pitch, Pre-set, Prove, Raise, Root(ed), Set, Stable, Standing, Stell, Substantiate, Trad, Trite, Valorise, Verify

Establishment Building, Business, CE, Church, Co, Concern, Creation, Hacienda, Household, Institution, Lodge, Proving ground, Salon, School, Seat, Succursal, System, Traditional

Estate, Estate-holder Allod(ium), Alod, Assets, Commons, Demesne, Domain, Dominant, Dowry, Fazenda, Fee-simple, Fee-tail, Fen, First, Fourth, General, Hacienda, Hagh, Haugh, Having, Hay, Housing, Industrial, Land-living, Latifundium, Legitim, Life, Manor, Messuage, Odal, Personal(ty), Plantation, Press, → **PROPERTY**, Real, Runrig, Second, Situation, Spiritual, Standing, Talooka, Taluk(a), Temporal, Termer, Termor, Thanage, Third, Trading, Trust, Udal, Zamindari, Zemindari

Estate agent Realtor

Esteem(ed), Estimable Account, Admiration, Appreciation, Count, Have, Honour, Izzat, Los, Precious, Prestige, Price, Pride, Prize, Rate, → **REGARD**, Reputation, Respect, Store, Value, Venerate, Wonder, Worthy

Ester Benzocaine, C(o)umarin, Depside, Glyceride, Olein, Palmitin, Phthalate, Psilocybin, Triglyceride, Urethan(e)

▶ **Estimable** *see* **ESTEEM**

Estimate, Estimation Appraise, Assess, Calculate, Carat, Conceit, Cost, Esteem, Extrapolation, Forecast, Gauge, Guess(timate), Inexact, Interval, Opinion, Point, Projection, Quotation, Rate, Rating, Reckon, Regard, Sight, Value, Weigh

Estrange Alienate, Disunite, Wean

Estuary Bay, Clyde, Creek, Dee, Delta, Firth, Gironde, Humber, Inlet, Mouth, Orwell, Ostial, Para, Rio de la Plata

Esurient Arid, Insatiable

Etc(etera) Et al(ia), So on

Etch(ing) Aquafortis, Aquatint(a), Bite, → ENGRAVE, Incise, Inscribe

Eternal, Eternity Aeonian, Ageless, Endless, Everlasting, Eviternal, Ewigkeit, Forever, Immortal, Infinity, Never-ending, Perdurable, Perpetual, Sempiternal, Tarnal, Timeless

Ether Atmosphere, Ch'i, Crown, Gas, Petroleum, Sky, Yang, Yin

Ethereal Airy, Delicate, Fragile, Heavenly, Nymph

Ethic(al), Ethics Deontics, Ideals, Marcionite, Moral, Principles, Work

Ethiopia(n) African, Amharic, Asmara, Cushitic, Falasha, Galla, Geez, Kabele, Kebele, Ogaden

Ethnic Racial, Roots

Ethyl ET

Etiquette Code, Conduct, Kawa, → MANNERS, Politesse, Propriety, Protocol, Ps and Qs, Punctilio

Etna Empedocles, Vessel, Volcano

Etonian Oppidan, Victim

Etruscan Tyrrhenian

Etymologist, Etymology Hobson-Jobson, Isodore

Eucalyptus Blackbutt, Bloodwood, Cadaga, Cadagi, Coolabah, Gum-tree, Ironbark, Jarrah, Mallee, Marri, Morrell, Sallee, Sally, Stringybark, Sugar gum, Tallow wood, Tewart, Tooart, Tuart, Wandoo, Woolly butt, Yate

Eucharist Communion, Housel, Mass, Supper, Viaticum

Eugene Aram, Onegin

Eugenia Jambal, Jambolan(a), Jambu(l)

Eulogy Encomium, Laudatory, Panegyric, Praise, Tribute

Euphausia Krill, Shrimp

Euphemism Fib, Gosh, Gracious, Heck, Hypocorism

Euphoria, Euphoric Cock-a-hoop, Ecstasy, Elation, High, Jubilation, Mindfuck, Nirvana, Rapture, Rush

Euphrasia Eyebright

Eurasian Chee-chee, Chi-chi

Europe(an) Balt, Bohunk, Catalan, Community, Continent, Croat, E, Esth, Faringee, Faringhi, Feringhee, Fleming, Hungarian, Hunky, Japhetic, Lapp, Lithuanian, Palagi, Polack, Ruthene, Ruthenian, Serb, Slavonian, Slovene, Topi-wallah, Transleithan, Tyrolean, Vlach, Yugoslav

Europium Eu

Eustace Diamonds

Euthanasia Exit

Evacuate, Evacuation Excrete, Expel, Getter, Medevac, Planuria, Planury, Scramble, Stercorate, Stool, Vent, Void, Withdraw

Evade, Evasion, Evasive Ambages, Avoid, Circumvent, Cop-out, Coy, Dodge, Duck, Elude, Equivocate, Escape, Fence, Fudge, Hedge, Loophole, Mealymouthed, Parry, Prevaricate, Quibble, Quillet, Salvo, Scrimshank, Shack, Shifty, Shirk, Shuffling, Sidestep, Skive, Skrimshank, Slippy, Stall, Subterfuge, Tergiversate, Waive, Weasel, Weasel out, Whiffler

Evaluate, Evaluation Appraise, Assess, Estimate, Gauge, Job, Ponder, Rate, Review, Waid(e), Weigh

Evanescent Cursory, Fleeting, Fugacious

Evangelical, Evangelist(ical) Buchman, Clappy-doo, Converter, Crusader, Fisher, Godsquad, Gospeller, Happy-clappy, Jansen, Jesus freak, John, Luke, Marist,

Mark, Matthew, Missioner, Moody, Morisonian, Peculiar, Preacher, Revivalist, Salvationist, Sankey, Sim(eonite), Stundist, Wild

Evaporate, Evaporation Condense, Dehydrate, Desorb, Dry, Exhale, Steam, Steme, Ullage, Vaporise

Eve(ning) All Hallow's, Nightfall, St Agnes's, Soirée, Subfusk, Sunset, Tib(b)s, Twilight, Vesperal, Vespertinal, Vigil, Yester

Evelyn Diarist, Hope

Even(ly), Evenness Aid, Albe(e), Albeit, All, Average, Balanced, Clean, Drawn, Dusk, Een, Ene, Equable, Equal, Erev, Fair, Fair play, Flush, Forenight, Iron, J'ouvert, Level, Level-pegging, Meet, Pair, Par, Plain, Plane, Plateau, Quits, Rib, Smooth, Square, Standardise, Toss-up, Yet

Evening flight Ro(a)ding

Evensong Vespers

Event Bash, Case, Circumstance, Contingency, Discus, Encaenia, Episode, Fest, Field, Gymkhana, Happening, Happy, Heat, Incident, Iron man, Landmark, Leg, Liquidity, Media, Milestone, Occasion, Occurrence, Ongoing, Outcome, Pass, Regatta, Result, Stick-on, Three-day, Three-ring circus, Track, Triple

Even-toed Artiodactyl

Eventual(ity), Eventually Case, Contingent, Finally, Future, In time, Nd, Sooner or later

Ever Always, Ay(e), Constantly, Eternal, Eviternity

Everglade Vlei

Evergreen Abies, Ageless, Arbutus, Cembra, Cypress, Gaultheria, Golden lie, Ivy, Myrtle, Olearia, Periwinkle, Pinaster, Privet, Thuja, Thuya, Washington, Winterberry, Yacca

Everlasting Cat's ear, Changeless, Enduring, Eternal, Immortal, Immortelle, Perdurable, Recurrent, Tarnal

Every(one), Everything All, Complete, Each, Et al, Existence, Full Monty, Ilk(a), In toto, Monty, Sub chiz, Sum, The works, To a man, Tout, Tout le monde, Universal, Varsal

Everyday Banal, Informal, Mundane, Natural, Ordinary, Plain, Routine

Everywhere Omnipresent, Passim, Rife, Throughout, Ubique, Ubiquity

Evict(or) Disnest, Disseisor, Eject, Expel, Oust

Evidence, Evident Adminicle, Apparent, Argument, Axiomatic, Circumstantial, Clear, Confessed, Credentials, Direct, Distinct, Document, Empirical, Exemplar, Flagrant, Hearsay, Indicate, Internal, King's, Manifest, Marked, Naked, Obvious, Overt, → **PATENT**, Plain, Premise, Prima facie, Probable, Proof, Queen's, Record, Sign, Smoking gun, State's, Surrebuttal, Testimony, Understandable

Evil Ahriman, Alastor, Amiss, Bad, Badmash, Bale, Beelzebub, Budmash, Corrupt, Depraved, Eale, Falling, Guilty, Harm, Heinous, Hydra, Ill, Immoral, Iniquity, King's, Malefic, Malign, Mare, Mischief, Monstrous, Necessary, Night, Perfidious, Rakshas(a), Shrewd, Sin, → **SINISTER**, Theodicy, Turpitude, Vice, Wicked

Evil eye Jettatura

Evince Disclose, Exhibit, Indicate, → **MANIFEST**, Show

Eviscerate(d) Debilitate, Disembowel, Drawn, Gralloch

Evoke Arouse, Awaken, Elicit, Move, Stir

Evolution(ary) Convergent, Countermarch, Development, Emergent, Growth, Holism, Lamarck, Lysenkoism, Moner(on), Neo-Lamarckism, Orthogenesis, Phylogeny, Social, Spencerman, Stellar, Transformism, Turning

▷ **Evolution** *may indicate* an anagram

Evolve Speciate

Ewe Crone, Gimmer, Keb, Rachel, Sheep, Teg, Theave

Ewer Aquamanale, Aquamanile, → JUG

Ex Former, Late, Quondam, Ten

Exacerbate Aggravate, Embitter, Exasperate, Irritate, Needle

Exact(ing), Exactitude, Exactly Accurate, Authentic, Careful, Dead, Definite, Due, Elicit, Estreat, Even, Exigent, Extort, Fine, Formal, It, Jump, Literal, Literatim, Mathematical, Meticulous, Nice(ty), Pat, Point-device, → PRECISE, Require, Slap-bang, Spang, Specific, Spot-on, Strict, Stringent, T, To a 't', Verbatim

Exaction Blackmail, Extortion, Impost, Montem, Sorelion, Tax

Exaggerate(d), Exaggeration Agonistic, Amplify, Ballyhoo, Boast, Brag, Camp, Colour, Distend, Dramatise, → EMBROIDER, Goliathise, Hoke, Hyperbole, Inflate, Lie, Line-shoot, Magnify, Munch(h)ausen, Mythomania, Overdo, Overdraw, Overegg, Overpaint, Overplay, Overrate, Overstate, Overstretch, Over-the-top, Romance, Shoot a line, Steep, Stretch, Tall, Theatrical

Exalt(ed), Exaltation Attitudes, Deify, Dignify, Elation, Enhance, Ennoble, Erect, Extol, Glorify, High, Jubilance, Larks, Lofty, Magnific, → PRAISE, Raise, Rapture, Ruff(e), Sama, Sublime, Supernal, Throne

Exam(ination), Examine, Examinee, Examiner Agrégé, A-level, Analyse, Analyst, Appose, Assess, Audit, Auscultation, Autopsy, Baccalauréat, Biopsy, Case, Check-out, Check-up, Cognosce, Collate, Comb, Common Entrance, Consideration, Cross-question, CSE, Deposal, Depose, Disquisition, Dissect, Docimasy, Eleven plus, Endoscopy, Entrance, Expiscate, Explore, Eyeball, Finals, GCE, GCSE, Going-over, Grade(s), Great-go, Greats, Gulf, Haruspex, Hearing, Inspect, Inter, Interrogate, Interview, Introspection, Jerque, Jury, Little-go, Local, Mark, Matriculation, Medical, Mocks, Moderator, Mods, Mug, O-level, Once-over, Oral, Ordalian, Ordeal, Overhaul, Palp(ate), Paper, Peruse, Physical, Post-mortem, Prelims, Probe, Pry, Psychoanalyse, Pump, → QUESTION, Quiz, Ransack, Recce, Reconnaissance, Resit, Responsions, Review, Sayer, Scan, Schools, Scrutator, Scrutineer, Scrutinise, Search, Seek, Shroff, Sift, Sit, Smalls, Survey, Sus(s), Test, Trial, Tripos, Try, Unseen, Vet, Viva, Voir dire

Example Apotheosis, Assay-piece, Byword, Epitome, Erotema, Foretaste, → FOR EXAMPLE, Illustration, Instance, Lead, Lesson, Model, Paradigm, Paragon, → PATTERN, Praxis, Precedent, Prototype, Role model, Say, Shining, Showpiece, Specimen, Standard, Stormer, Such as, Touchstone, Type, Typify

Exasperate, Exasperating, Exasperation Anger, Embitter, Galling, Irk, Irritate, Nettle, Provoke

Excavate, Excavation, Excavator Armadillo, Burrow, Catacomb, Crater, Cutting, Delf, Delph, → DIG, Dike, Disinter, Ditch, Dragline, Dredge, Drive, Earthwork, Gaulter, Graft, Heuch, Heush, Hollow, JCB, Mine, Pichiciago, Pioneer, Pioner, Pyoner, Quarry, Shaft, Sink, Sondage, Steam-shovel, Stope, Well

Exceed, Exceeding(ly) Amain, Not half, Outdo, Overstep, Surpass, Transcend, Very

Excel(lence), Excellency, Excellent A1, Ace, Admirable, A-per-se, Assay-piece, Awesome, Bangin(g), Bang on, Beat, Beaut, Better, Bitchin', Blinder, Bodacious, Boffo, Bonzer, Booshit, Boss, Bottler, Bravo, Brill, Bully, Capital, Castor, Champion, Cheese, Choice, Class(y), Classical, Copacetic, Copesettic, Copybook, Corking, Crack, Crackerjack, Crucial, Daisy, Def, Dic(k)ty, Dilly, Dominate, Doozy, Elegant, Excelsior, Exemplary, Eximious, Exo, Extraordinaire, Fab, Fantastic, First rate, Five-star, Goodness, Great, Grit, Grouse, HE, High, Humdinger, Hunky(-dory), Inimitable, Jake, Jammy, Jim-dandy, Kiff, Knockout, Lalapalooza, Laudable, Lollapalooza, Lummy, Matchless, Mean, Mega-, Merit, Neat, Noble, Out and outer, Outbrag, Outdo, Outstanding, Outtop, Overdo, Overtop, Paragon, Peachy, Peerless,

Phat, Prime, Pure, Quality, Rad, Rare, Rattling, Ring, Rinsin', Ripping, Ripsnorter,
Say-piece, Shagtastic, → **SHINE**, Shit-hot, Sick-dog, Sik, Socko, Spanking, Spiffing,
Stellar, Stonking, Stupendous, Sublime, Superb, Super-duper, Superior, Supreme,
Swell, Terrific, Tip-top, Top flight, Top-hole, Topnotch, Topping, Transcend,
Transcendent, Triff, Virtue, Wal(l)y, War, Way-out, Wicked, Worth
Except(ion) Bar, But, Else, Exc, Nobbut, Omit, Save, Than, Then, Unless
Exceptional Abnormal, Anomaly, Cracker, Egregious, Especial, Extraordinary, Gas,
Rare, Ripsnorter, Select, Singular, Special, Uncommon, Zinger
Excerpt(s) Digest, Extract, Passage, Scrap
Excess(ive), Excessively All-fired, Basinful, Exaggeration, Exorbitant, Extortionate,
Extravagant, Flood, Fulsome, Glut, Hard, Inordinate, → **LAVISH**, Mountain,
Needless, Nimiety, OD, Old, OTT, Outrage, Over, Overage, Overblown, Overcome,
Overdose, Overkill, Overmuch, Overspill, Over-the-top, Owercome, Plethora,
Preponderance, Profuse, Salt, Satiety, Spate, Spilth, Steep, Superabundant,
Superfluity, Surfeit, Surplus, Terrific, Thundering, Too, Troppo, Ultra, Undue,
Unequal, Woundily
Exchange Baltic, Bandy, Barter, Bourse, Cambist, Catallactic, Change, Chop,
Commute, Contango, Convert, Cope, Corn, Ding-dong, Employment, Enallage,
Excambion, Foreign, Inosculate, Interplay, Ion, Labour, Logroll, → **MARKET**,
Mart, Needle, Niffer, Paraphrase, PBX, Post, Quid pro quo, Rally, Rate, Recourse,
Redeem, Rialto, Royal, Scorse, Scourse, Sister-chromated, Stock, Swap, Switch,
Swop, Telephone, Tolsel, Tolsey, Tolzey, → **TRADE**, Traffic, Transfusion,
Trophallaxis, Truck
Exchequer Remembrancer
Excise(man), Excise district Ablate, Bobbitt, Crop, Expunge, Gauger, Resect, Ride,
Tax
Excite(ment), Excited, Exciting, Excitability Ablaze, Aboil, Abuzz, Aerate,
Agitate, Agog, Amove, Animate, Aphrodisiac, Arouse, Athrill, Atwitter, Awaken,
Brouhaha, Buck-fever, Climatic, Combustible, Commotion, Delirium, Electrify,
Emove, Enthuse, Erethism, Eventful, Feisty, Fever, Fire, Flap, Flat spin, Frantic,
Frenzy, Frisson, Furore, Fuss, Galvanise, Gas, Grip, Headiness, Heat, Hectic,
Het, Hey-go-mad, Hilarity, Hobson-Jobson, Hoopla, Hothead, Hyped, Hyper,
Hypomania, Hysterical, Impel, Incite, Inebriate, Inflame, Intoxicate, Jimjams,
Kick, Kindle, Liven, Metastable, Must, Neurotic, Oestrus, Orgasm, Overheat,
Overwrought, Panic, Passion, Pride, Prime, Provoke, Racy, Radge, Red-hot, Rile,
Roil, → **ROUSE**, Rousement, Ruff(e), Rut, Send, Sexy, Spin, Splash, Spur, Startle,
Stimulate, Stir(e), Suscitate, Temperamental, Tetanoid, Tetany, Tew, Thrill,
Titillate, Trickle, Turn-on, Twitter, Upraise, Va-va-voom, Waken, Whee, Whet,
Whoopee, Work up, Yahoo, Yerk, Yippee, Yoicks
▷ **Excite(d)** *may indicate* an anagram
Exclaim, Exclamation (mark) Ahem, Aue, Begorra, Bliksem, Blurt, Bo, Ceas(e),
Crikey, Criv(v)ens, Dammit, Ecphonesis, Eina, Eish, Ejaculate, Epiphonema,
Eureka, Expletive, Fen(s), Good-now, Hadaway, Haith, Halleluiah, Hallelujah,
Heigh-ho, Hem, Hip, Hookey Walker, Hosanna, Inshallah, Interjection, Moryah,
Omigod, Oops, Phew, Pling, Pow, Protest, Pshaw, Sasa, Screamer, Sese(y), Sessa,
Unberufen, Vociferate, Walker, Whau, Whoops, Wirra, Wow, Yay, Yippee,
Yo-ho-ho, Yummy, Zounds
Exclave Cabinda
Exclude, Excluding, Exclusion Ban, Bar, Block, Competitive, Debar, Deforcement,
Disbar, Drop, Eliminate, Ex, Except, Excommunicate, Freeze out, Omit, Ostracise,
Outbar, Outwith, Pauli, Shut out, Social

Exclusive Cliquish, Closed-shop, Complete, Debarment, Elect, Monopoly, Particular, Pure, Rare, Scoop, Select, Single, Sole

Excommunicate Curse

Excoriate Flay, Slam

Excrement, Excretion, Excretory Dirt, Doo-doo, Dung, Emunctory, Faeces, Flyspeck, Frass, Jobbie, Keech, Meconium, Oliguria, Ordure, Poo(p), Poo-poo, Puer, Pure, Refuse, Scatology, Shit(e), Sir-reverence, Stercoraceous, Strangury, Turd, Urea, Waste, Whoopsie

Excrescence Aril, Carnosity, Caruncle, Enate, Gall, Growth, Knob, Knurl, Lump, Nurl, Pimple, Pin, Spavin(e), Strophiole, Talpa, Twitter(-bone), Wart

Excruciate, Excruciating Agonising, Rack, Torment, Torture

Exculpate Acquit, Clear, Forgive

Excursion Airing, Cruise, Dart, Digression, Jaunt, Junket, Outing, Road, Sally, Sashay, Sortie, Tour, Trip

Excuse, Excusable Absolve, Alibi, Amnesty, Bunbury, Condone, Essoin, Essoyne, Evasion, Exempt, Exonerate, Faik, Forgive, Let off, Mitigate, Occasion, Off come, Out, Overlook, Palliate, → **PARDON**, Pretext, Release, Salvo, Venial, Viable, Whitewash

Execrate Abhor, Ban, Boo, Curse

Execute(d), Executioner, Executive, Executor Abhorson, Accomplish, Account, Administrate, Behead, Carnifex, Deathsman, Despatch, Discharge, Dispatch, Exor, Finish, Fry, Gan, Gar(r)otte, Gin, Guardian, Hang, Headsman, Implement, Ketch, Kill, Koko, Literary, Lynch, Management, Martyr, Noyade, Official, Perform, Perpetrate, Pierrepoint, Politburo, Scamp, Top, Trustee, Tyburn

Exemplar(y) Byword, Impeccable, Laudable, Model, Paragon, Perfect, St, Warning

Exemplify Cite, Epitomise, Illustrate, Instantiate, Satisfy

Exempt(ion) Dispensation, Exclude, Exeem, Fainites, Fains, Free, Immune, Impunity, Indemnity, Overslaugh, Quarter, Spare, Tyburn ticket, Vains

Exercise(s) Aerobics, Air, Antic, Apply, Bench press, Burpee, Cal(l)isthenics, Callanetics®, Chi kung, Cloze, Constitutional, Drill, Employ, Enure, Eurhythmics, Exert, Falun dafa, Falun gong, Floor, Gradus, Inure, Isometrics, Kata, Keepy-uppy, Kegel, Krav Maga, Lesson, Limber, Manual, Medau, Op, Operation, PE, Physical jerks, Pilates, Ply, Plyometrics, Popmobility, Practice, Practise, Preacher curl, Press-up, Prolusion, PT, Pull-up, Pump iron, Push-up, Qigong, Sadhana, Shintaido, Sit-up, Solfeggi(o), Step (aerobics), Stretch, Tai chi (ch'uan), Thema, Theme, Thesis, Train, Trampoline, Trunk curl, Use, Vocalise, Warm-down, Warm-up, Wield, Work, Work-out, Xyst(us), Yomp

▷ **Exercise(d)** *may indicate* an anagram

Exert(ion) Conatus, → **EFFORT**, Exercise, Labour, Operate, Strain, Strive, Struggle, Trouble, Wield

Ex-European Japhetic

Exhalation, Exhale Breath, Fume, Miasma, Reek, Sigh, Steam, Transpire, Vapour

Exhaust(ed), Exhausting, Exhaustion, Exhaustive All-in, Backbreaking, Beaten, Beggar, Bugger(ed), Burn, Burn-out, Bushed, Clapped out, Consume, Deadbeat, Debility, Deplete, Detailed, Dissipate, Do, Done, Drain, Eduction, Effete, Emission, Empty, End, Enervate, Fatigue, Fordo, Forfeuchen, Forfochen, Forfoughen, Forfoughten, Forjaskit, Forjeskit, Forspent, Forswink, Frazzle, Gruelling, Heat, Heatstroke, Inanition, Jet-lagged, Jet-stream, Jiggered, Knacker, Mate, Milk, Out, Outwear, Play out, Poop, Powfagged, Puckerood, Puggled, Rag, Ramfeezle, Rundown, Sap, Shatter, Shot, Shotten, Spend, Spent, Stonkered, Tailpipe, Tire, Trauchled, Use, Used up, Wabbit, Wappend, Warby, Washed-up, Wasted,

Waygone, → **WEARY**, Wind, Worn, Zonked

Exhibit(ion), Exhibitioner, Exhibitionist Aquashow, Bench, Circus, Concours, Demo, Demonstrate, Demy, Diorama, Discover, Display, Evince, Expo, Expose, Fair, Hang, Indicate, → **MANIFEST**, Olympia, Pageant, Panopticon, Parade, Present, Retrospective, Salon, Scene, Set forth, Show(piece), Showcase, Show-off, Showplace, Viewing

Exhilarate(d) Bubble, Cheer, Elate, Enliven

Exhort(ation) Admonish, Allocution, Caution, Counsel, Incite, Lecture, Par(a)enesis, Persuade, Protreptic, Urge

Exhume Delve, Disinter, Resurrect, Unearth

Exigency, Exigent Demanding, Emergency, Pressing, Taxing, Urgent, Vital

Exile Adam, Babylon, Banish, Deport, Emigré, Eve, Expatriate, Exul, Galut(h), Ostracise, Outlaw, Relegate, Tax, Wretch

Exist(ence), Existing Be(ing), Corporeity, Dwell, Enhypostasia, Entelechy, Esse, Extant, Identity, Inbeing, In esse, Inherent, Life, Live, Ontology, Perseity, Solipsism, Status quo, Substantial, Ubiety

Existentialist Camus, Sartre

Exit Débouché, Door, Egress, Gate, Leave, Log off, Log out, Outlet

Exodus Book, Departure, Flight, Hegira, Hejira

Ex-official Outler

Exogamous Outbred

Exonerate(d) Absolve, Acquit, Clear, Excuse, Exempt, Shriven

Exorbitant Excessive, Expensive, Slug, Steep, Tall, Undue

Exorcise, Exorcist Benet, Lay

Exordium Opening, Preface, Prelude

Exotic Alien, Chinoiserie, Ethnic, Fancy, Foreign, Free, Outlandish, Strange

Expand, Expanse, Expansion Amplify, Boom, Branch out, Bulking, Develop, Diastole, Dilate, Distend, Ectasis, Elaborate, → **ENLARGE**, Escalate, Flesh out, Grow, Increase, Magnify, Ocean, Outspread, Snowball, Spread, Stretch, Swell, Vastitude, Wax, Wire-draw

Expatiate Amplify, Descant, Dwell, Enlarge, Perorate

Expatriate Banish, Colonial, Emigrate, Émigré, Exile, Outcast

Expect(ant), Expectation, Expected, Expecting Agog, Anticipate, Ask, Await, Due, Foresee, Gravid, Hope, Lippen, Look, Natural, Par, Pip, Predict, Pregnant, Presume, Prim, Prospect, Require, → **SUPPOSE**, Tendance, Think, Thought, Usual, Ween

Expectorant, Expectorate Expel, Guaiacol, Hawk, Spit

Expedient Advisable, Artifice, Contrivance, Fend, Make-do, Makeshift, Measure, Politic, Resort, Resource, Shift, Stopgap, Suitable, Wise

Expedite, Expedition, Expeditious Advance, Alacrity, Anabasis, Celerity, Crusade, Dispatch, Excursion, Fastness, Field trip, Hasten, Hurry, Kon-Tiki, Pilgrimage, Post-haste, Quest, Safari, Short cut, Speed, Trek, Trip, Voyage

Expel Amove, Dispossess, Drum out, Egest, Evacuate, Evict, Exile, Exorcize, Hoof, Oust, Out(cast), Read out, Void

Expend(iture) Budget, Consume, Cost, Dues, Gavel, Goings-out, Mise, Occupy, Oncost, Outgo(ing), Outlay, Poll, Squander, Tithe, Toll, Use, Waste

Expendable Cannon-fodder

Expense(s), Expensive Charge(ful), Cost(ly), Current, Dear, Executive, Exes, Fee, High, Law, Oncost, Outgoing, Outlay, Overhead, Price, Salt, Steep, Sumptuary, Upmarket, Valuable

Experience(d) Accomplished, A posteriori, Assay, Blasé, Come up, Discovery,

Empiric, Encounter, Expert, → FEEL, Felt, Find, Foretaste, Freak-out, Gust, Hands-on, Have, Incur, Know, Learn, Live, Mature, Meet, Mneme, Near-death, Old hand, Old-stager, Ordeal, Out-of-body, Pass, Plumb, Seasoned, See, Senior, Sense, Sensory, Spin, Stager, Stand, Street-smart, Streetwise, Taste, Transference, Trial, Trip, Trocinium, Try, Undergo, Versed, Veteran, Work, Worldly wise

Experiment(al) Attempt, Avant-garde, Ballon d'assai, Control, Empirical, Essay, Michelson-Morley, Peirastic, Pilot, Sample, Shy, Single-blind, Taste, Tentative, → TRIAL, Trial balloon, Try, Venture, Vivisection

Expert(ise) Accomplished, Ace, Adept, Adroit, Arch, Authority, Boffin, Buff, Cambist, Cocker, Cognoscente, Competent, Connoisseur, Crack, Craft, Dab(ster), Dan, Deft, Demon, Don, Egghead, Finesse, Fundi, Gourmet, Gun, Hotshot, Karateka, Know-all, Know-how, Luminary, Maestro, Masterly, Mastery, Maven, Mavin, Meister, Nark, Old hand, Oner, Oneyer, Oneyre, Peritus, Practised, Pro, Proficient, Pundit, Ringer, Savvy, Science, Shroff, Skill(y), Sly, Specialist, Technique, Technocrat, Troubleshooter, Ulema, Used, W(h)iz

Expiate, Expiation, Expiatory Amends, Atone, Penance, Piacular

Expire(d), Expiry Blow, Collapse, Croak, → DIE, End, Exhale, Invalid, Ish, Lapse, Neese, Pant, Sneeze, Terminate

Explain(able), Explanation Account, Annotate, Appendix, Aread, Arede, Arreede, Clarify, Conster, Construe, Decline, Define, Describe, Eclaircissement, Elucidate, Explicate, Exponible, Expose, Expound, Extenuate, Gloss, Glossary, Gloze, Justify, Parabolize, Salve, Solve, Upknit

Explanation, Explanatory Apology, Commentary, Exegesis, Exegetic, Exposition, Farse, Gloss, Gloze, Hypothesis, Key, Note, Preface, Reading, Rigmarole, Solution, Theory

Expletive Arrah, Darn, Exclamation, Oath, Ruddy, Sapperment

Explicit Clean-cut, Clear, Definite, Express, Frank, Full-on, Outspoken, → PRECISE, Specific

Explode, Explosion, Explosive Agene, Airburst, Amatol, Ammonal, ANFO, Antimatter, Aquafortis, Backfire, Bang, Bangalore torpedo, Big bang, Blast, Booby-trap, Burst, C4, Cap, Cheddite, Chug, Controlled, Cordite, Cramp, Crump, Cyclonite, Debunk, Demolitions, Detonate, Dualin, Dunnite, Dust, Egg, Erupt, Euchloric, Euchlorine, Fireball, Firecracker, Firedamp, Firework, Fulminant, Fulminate, Gasohol, Gelatine, Gelignite, Grenade, Guncotton, Gunpaper, Gunpowder, HE, High, Iracund, Jelly, Landmine, Low, Lyddite, Megaton, Melinite, Mine, Nail-bomb, Napalm, Nitre, Nitro(glycerine), Outburst, Ozonide, Paravane, Payload, Petar(d), Petre, Phut, Plastic, Plastique, Pluff, Pop, Population, Pow, Priming, Propellant, Ptarmic, Pustular, Report, Roburite, SAM, Semtex®, Sheet, Shrapnel, Snake, Sneeze, Soup, Squib, Supernova, Tetryl, Thunderflash, Tinderbox, TNT, Tonite, Trinitrobenzene, Trotyl, Volatile, Volcanic, Warhead, Xyloidin(e)

Exploit(s), Exploiter, Exploitation Act, Adventure, Coup, Coyote, Deed, Develop, Escapade, Feat, Gest, Harness, Ill-use, Impose, Kulak, Manoeuvre, Milk, Mission, Parlay, Play on, Rachmanism, Ramp, Res gestae, Stunt, Sweat, Tap, Use, Utilise

Explore(r), Exploration Amerigo, Amundsen, Baffin, Balboa, Bandeirante, Banks, Barents, Bellingshausen, Bering, Boone, Burton, Cabot, Cartier, Chart, Columbus, Cook, Cordoba, Cortes, Da Gama, Dampier, Darwin, De Soto, Dias, Diaz, Discover, Dredge, Eric, Eriksson, Examine, Feel, Field trip, Flinders, Frobisher, Fuchs, Humboldt, Investigate, Livingstone, Magellan, Map, Marco Polo, Mungo Park, Nansen, Navigator, Park, Pathfinder, Peary, Pioneer, Potholer, Probe, Przewalski, Rale(i)gh, Research, Rhodes, Ross, Scott, Scout, Search, Shackleton, Spaceship, Speke, Stanley, Sturt, Tasman, Vancouver, Vasco da Gama, Vespucci, Voyageur

▷ **Explosive** *may indicate* an anagram
Exponent Advocate, Example, Index, Interpreter, Logarithm
Export(s) Despatch, Invisible, Klondike, Klondyke, Ship, Visible
Expose(d), Exposure Air, Anagogic, Bare, Bleak, Blot, Blow, Burn, Crucify, Debag, Debunk, Denude, Desert, Disclose, Double, Endanger, En prisé, Exhibit, Flashing, Glareal, Indecent, Insolate, Moon, Nude, Object, Open, Out, Over, Paramo, Propale, Reveal, Showdown, Snapshot, Streak, Strip, Subject, Sun, Time, Uncover, Unmask, Windswept
Exposition Aperçu
Expostulate, Expostulation Argue, Arrah, Protest, Remonstrate
Expound(er) Discourse, Discuss, Exegete, Explain, Open, Prelict, Red, Scribe, Ulema
Express(ed), Expression, Expressive Air, APT, Aspect, Breathe, Cacophemism, Circumbendimus, Cliché, Colloquialism, Conceive, Concetto, Couch, Countenance, Declare, Denote, Eloquent, Embodiment, Epithet, Estafette, Explicit, Face, Fargo, Formulate, Godspeed, Good-luck, Gup, Hang-dog, Hell's bells, Idiom, Isit, Limited, Locution, Lyrical, Manifest, Metonym, Mien, Mot (juste), Neologism, Non-stop, Orient, Paraphrase, Phrase, Pleonasm, Pony, Precise, Pronouncement, Pronto, Put, Quep, Register, Say(ne), Show, Soulful, → **SPEAK**, State, Strain, Succus, Term, Token, Tone, Topos, Trope, Utterance, Vent, → **VOICE**
Expressionless Aphasia, Blank, Boot-faced, Deadpan, Impassive, Inscrutable, Po(ker)-faced, Vacant, Wooden
Expressman Fargo
Expropriate Dispossess, Pirate, Seize, Usurp
Expulsion Discharge, Eccrisis, Ejection, Eviction, Exile, Pride's Purge, Sacking, Synaeresis
Expunge Cancel, Delete, Erase, Obliterate
Expurgate Bowdlerize, Castrate, Censor, Purge
Exquisite Beautiful, Choice, Ethereal, Fine, Intense, Lair, Macaroni, Pink, Princox, Refined, Soigné(e), Too-too
Ex-serviceman Vet
Extemporise Ad lib, Improvise, Pong
Extend(ed), Extension Add, Aspread, Augment, Conservative, Cremaster, Draw, Eke, Elapse, Ell, Elongate, Enlarge, Escalate, Expand, Exsert, Extrapolation, Fermata, Grow, Increase, Jumboise, Length, Long, Long-range, Long-stay, Long-term, Offer, Outgrowth, Overbite, Overlap, Pong, Porrect, Proffer, Prolong, Propagate, Protract, Reach, Retrochoir, Span, Spread, Steso, → **STRETCH**, Substantial, Widen
Extensive, Extent Ambit, Area, Capacious, Catch-all, Compass, Comprehensive, Degree, Distance, Duration, Large, Latitude, Length, Limit, → **MAGNITUDE**, Panoramic, Range, Reach, Scale, Size, Spacious, Span, Spread-eagle, Sweeping, Wholesale, Wide, Widespread
Extenuate Diminish, Lessen, Mitigate, Palliate
Exterior Aspect, Crust, Derm, Exoteric, Facade, Outer, → **OUTSIDE**, Shell, Surface, Veneer
Exterminate, Extermination Abolish, Annihilate, Destroy, Holocaust, Uproot
External Exoteric, Exterior, Extraneous, Foreign, Outer
Extinct(ion) Archaeopteryx, Bygone, Chalicothere, Creodont, Dead, Death, Defunct, D(e)inothere, Dodo, Obsolete, Quagga, Quietus, Rasure, Saururae, Theodont
Extinguish Douse, Dout, Dowse, Dowt, Extirpate, Obscure, Quash, Quell, Quench, Slake, Slo(c)ken, Smother, Snuff, Stamp out, Stifle, Suppress

Extirpate End, Erase, Excise, Obliterate, Root, Uproot

Extol Commend, Enhance, Eulogise, Exalt, Laud, Puff

Extort(ion), Extortionate, Extortioner Barathrum, Blackmail, Bleed, Bloodsucker, Chantage, Chout, Churn, Compel, Exact, Force, Gombeen, Montem, Outwrest, Rachman, Rack, Racketeer, Ransom, Rapacious, Screw, Shank, Squeeze, Sweat, Urge, Vampire, Wrest, Wring

Extra Accessory, Additament, Addition(al), Additive, Adjunct, And, Annexe, Attachment, Bisque, Bonus, By(e), Debauchery, Encore, Etcetera, Frill, Further, Gash, Lagniappe, Left-over, Leg bye, Make-weight, More, Nimiety, No ball, Odd, Optional, Out, Over, Overtime, Perk, Plus, Plusage, Reserve, Ripieno, → SPARE, Spilth, Staffage, Sundry, Super, Supernumerary, Supplementary, Suppletive, Surplus, Trop, Undue, Walking-gentleman, Walking-lady, Wide, Woundy

Extract(ion), Extractor Apozem, Bleed, Breeding, Catechu, Clip, Corkscrew, Decoction, Descent, Distil, Draw, Educe, Elicit, Emulsin, Enucleate, Essence, Estreat, Excerpt, Exodontics, Extort, Gist, Gobbet, Insulin, Kino, Liver, Malta, Milk, Mine, Oust, Parentage, Passage, Pericope, Pick, Piece, Pituitary, Pry, Pyrene, Pyrethrin, Quintessence, Render, Retour, Smelt, Snippet, Soundbite, Squeeze, Stope, Suck, Summary, Tap, Tincture, Trie, Try, Vanilla, Vegemite®, Ventouse, Winkle, Worm, Wring, Yohimbine

Extradition Renvoi

Extraneous Extrinsic, Foreign, Irrelevant, Outlying, Spurious

Extraordinary Amazing, By-ordinar, Case, Curious, Humdinger, Important, Phenomenal, Preternatural, Rare, Singular, Startling, Strange, Unusual

Extravagance, Extravagant, Extravaganza Bombastic, Excessive, Fancy, Feerie, Flamboyant, Glitzy, Heroic, High-flown, High roller, Hyperbole, Lavish, Luxury, Outré, Prodigal, Profligate, Profuse, Rampant, Reckless, Riotise, Romantic, Splash, Splurge, Squander, Sumptuous, Superfluous, Waste

Extreme(ly), Extremist Acute, All-fired, Almighty, Butt, Deep-dyed, Desperate, Die-hard, Drastic, Edge, Exceptional, Farthermost, Gross, In spades, → INTENSE, Jacobin, Mega-, Militant, Mondo, National Front, Nazi, Opposite, OTT, Parlous, Pretty, Radical, Root and branch, Steep, Tendency, Terminal, Thule, Too, Tremendous, Ultimate, Ultima thule, Ultra, Unco, Utmost, Utter, → VERY, Vitally, Wing

▷ **Extreme** *may indicate* a first or last letter

Extremity Bourn(e), Crisis, Digit, Ending, Finger(-tip), Limb, Limit, Outrance, Pole, Tip, Toe, Utterance

Extricate Liberate, Loose, Outwind, Rescue, Untangle

Extrinsic Aliunde, External, Irrelevant, Outward

Extrovert Lad, Outgoing

Extrude Debar, Eject, Project

Exuberance, Exuberant Brio, Copious, Ebullient, Effusive, Gusto, Hearty, Lavish, Mad, Overflowing, Profuse, Rambunctious, Rumbustious, Skippy, Streamered

Exudation, Exude Bleed, Ectoplasm, Emit, Extravasate, Guttate, Ooze, Secrete, Still, Sweat, Swelter, Ulmin, Weep

Exult(ant) Crow, Elated, → GLOAT, Glorify, Jubilant, Paeonic, Rejoice, Tripudiate, Triumphant, Whoop

Eye(s), Eye-ball, Eyeful, Eye movement, Eyepiece Aperture, Beady, Canthus, Compound, Cringle, Eagle, Ee, Eine, Electric, Emmetropia, Evil, Glad, Glass, Glim, Glom, Goggles, Hurricane, Huygen's, Iris, Jack, Keek, Klieg, Lamp, Lazy, Lens, London, Magic, Mincepie, Mind's, Mongoloid, Naked, → OBSERVE, Ocellar, Ocular, Ogle, Ommateum, Ommatidium, Optic, Orb, Pedicel, Peeper, PI, Pigsnie,

Pigsn(e)y, Pineal, Private, Pupil, Regard, Retina, Rhabdom, Roving, Saccade, Sclera, Screw, Seeing, Sheep's, Shufti, Shufty, Sight, Spy, Stemma, Storm-centre, Tec, Third, Uvea, Watch, Water-pump, Weather, Whally, Windows, Winker

Eyebright Euphrasy

Eyebrow Bree, Brent-hill, Glib, Penthouse, Superciliary

Eyeglass Loupe

Eyelash Cilium, Winker

Eyelet Cringle, Grommet, Hole

Eyelid Canthus, Ectropion, Haw, Palpebral, Winker

Eye-rod Rhabdom

Eye-shadow Kohl

Eyesore Blot, Disfigurement, Sty(e)

Eye-stalk Ommatophore, Stipes

Eye trouble Amblyopia, Ametropia, Aniseikonia, Anisomatropia, Aphakia, Asthenopia, Astigmatism, Caligo, Cataract, Ceratitis, Coloboma, Cycloplegia, Diplopia, Entropion, Erythropsia, Exophthalmus, Glaucoma, Gravel-blind, Hemeralopia, Hemi(an)op(s)ia, Hypermetropia, Hyperopia, Iritis, Keratitis, Leucoma, Lippitude, Micropsia, Miosis, Monoblepsis, Muscae volitantes, Myosis, Nebula, Nyctalopia, Nystagmus, Ommateum, Palinop(s)ia, Photophobia, Photopsia, Pin and web, Pink-eye, Presbyopia, Retinitis, Retinoblastoma, Sandy blight, Scotoma(ta), Shiner, Stigmatism, Strabismus, Strephosymbolia, Strong, Stye, Synechia, Teichopsia, Thylose, Thylosis, Trachoma, Trichiasis, Tritanopia, Tylosis, Wall-eye, Xeroma, Xerophthalmia

Eye-wash Collyrium

Eyrie Nest

Ezra Pound

Ff

F Fahrenheit, Fellow, Feminine, Fluorine, Following, Force, Foxtrot

Fab Super

Fabian, Fabius Dilatory, Washington

Fable(s) Aesop, Allegory, Apologue, Exemplum, Fiction, Hitopadesa, La Fontaine, Legend, Marchen, Milesian, Myth, Panchatantra, Parable, Romance, Tale, Tarand

Fabric Acetate, → CLOTH, Contexture, Framework, Interfacing, Interlining, Orlon®, Plissé

Fabricate, Fabrication Artefact, Concoct, Construct, Contrive, Cook, Fake, Fangle, Figment, Forge, → INVENT, Lie, Porky, Trump, Weave, Web

Fabulous (beast), Fabulous place Apocryphal, Apologue, Chichevache, Chimera, Cockatrice, Eldorado, Fictitious, Fung, Gear, Griffin, Hippogriff, Hippogryph, Huma, Incredible, Jabberwock(y), Kylin, Legendary, Magic, Manticora, Manticore, Merman, Monoceros, Mythical, Opinicus, Orc, Phoenix, Roc, Romantic, Simorg, Simurg(h), Snark, Sphinx, Tarand, Tragelaph, Unicorn, Unreal, Utopia, Wivern, Wyvern, Yale

Facade Front(age), Frontal, Mask, Pretence

Face, Facing Abide, Affront, Ashlar, Ashler, Aspect, Audacity, Bold, Brave, Brazen, Caboched, Caboshed, Cheek, Chiv(v)y, Coal, Confront, Countenance, Culet, Dalle, Dare, Dartle, Deadpan, Dial, Eek, Elevation, Encounter, Facade, Fat, Favour, Features, Fineer, Fortune, → FRONT, Gardant, Girn, Gonium, Grid, Groof, Groue, Grouf, Gurn, Hatchet, Head-on, Jib, Kisser, Light, Lining, Look, Lore, Mascaron, Meet, Metope, Moe, Mug, Mush, Obverse, Opposite, Outstare, Outward, Pan, Paper tiger, Pavilion, Phisnomy, Phiz(og), Physiognomy, Poker, Puss, Revet, Revetment, Roughcast, Rud, Rybat, Side, Snoot, Socle, Straight, Stucco, Three-quarter, Type, Veneer, Vis(age), Visnomy, Withstand, Zocco(lo)

Face-ache Noli-me-tangere

Face-lift Rhytidectomy

Face-saving Redeeming, Salvo

Facet(ed) Angle, Aspect, Bezel, Culet, Face, Pavilion, Polyhedron

Facetious Frivolous, Jocular, Waggish, Witty

Facile Able, Adept, Complaisant, Ductile, Easy, Fluent, Glib

Facilitate, Facility Amenity, Assist, Benefit, Capability, Committed, → EASE, Expedite, Fluency, Gift, ISO, Knack, Skill

Facsimile Copy, Photostat®, Replica, Repro

Fact(s), Factual Actual, Brass tacks, Case, Corpus delicti, Correct, Data, Datum, Detail, French, Gospel, Griff, Info, Literal, Mainor, Material, Nay, Poop, Really, Statistics, Truism, Truth, Veridical, Yes

Faction Bloc, Cabal, Camp, Caucus, Clique, Contingent, Ghibelline, Guelph, Junto, Red Army, Schism, Sect, Tendency, Wing

Factor Agent, Aliquot, Broker, Cause, Chill, Clotting, Coagulation, Co-efficient, Common, → COMPONENT, Divisor, Edaphic, Element, F, Feel-good, Growth,

House, Intrinsic, Load, Modulus, Multiple, Power, Q, Quality, Reflection, Representative, Rh, Rhesus, Risk, Safety, Steward, Unit, Utilization, Wind chill, X

Factory Cannery, Etruria, Gasworks, Glassworks, Hacienda, Maquiladora, Mill, Plant, Refinery, Sawmill, Steelworks, Sweatshop, Tinworks, Wireworks, Works, Workshop

Factotum Circar, Handyman, Servant, Sircar, Sirkar

Faculty Aptitude, Arts, Capacity, Department, Ear, Ease, Indult, Knack, Moral, Power, School, Sense, Speech, → **TALENT**, Teachers, Wits

Fad(dish) Crank, Craze, Cult, Fashion, Foible, Ismy, Thing, Vogue, Whim

Fade(d), Fading Blanch, Die, Diminuendo, Dinge, Elapsion, Etiolate, Evanescent, Fall, Filemot, Lessen, Mancando, Pale, Passé, Perdendo(si), Peter, Smorzando, Smorzato, Stonewashed, Vade, Vanish, Wallow, Wilt, Wither

Faeces Cesspit, Dingleberry, Dung, Kak, Meconium, Motion, Mute, Number two, Scybalum, Skatole, Stercoraceous, Stools

Fag-end Ash, Butt, Dout, Lag, Snipe, Stub

Fag(ging) Chore, Cigarette, Drag, Drudge, Fatigue, Gasper, Homosexual, Menial, Pennalism, Quean, Reefer, Snout, Tire, Toil, Weary

Fag(g)ot(s) Bavin, Bundle, Fascine, Firewood, Homosexual, Kid, Knitch, Twigs

Fail(ing), Failure Achalasia, Ademption, Anile, Anuria, Awry, Backfire, Blemish, Blow, Bomb, Bummer, Cark, Chicken, → **COLLAPSE**, Conk, Crack up, Crash, Cropper, Debacle, Decline, Defalcation, Default, Defect, Demerit, Demise, Die, Dog, Dry, Dud, Fault, Feal, Fiasco, Fink out, Flame out, Flivver, Flop, Flow, Flunk, Fold, Founder, Frost, Glitch, Gutser, Infraction, Lapse, Lemon, Lose, Malfunction, Manqué, Mis-, Miscarry, Misfire, Misprision, Miss, Muff, Nerd, No-hoper, No-no, Omit, Outage, Oversight, Pip, Plough, Plow, Pluck, Pratfall, Reciprocity, Refer, Refusal, Respiratory, Shambles, Short(coming), Short circuit, Shortfall, Slippage, Smash, Spin, Stumer, Tank, Turkey, Vice, Wash-out, Weakness, White elephant, Wipeout

Fain Lief

Faineant Gallio

Faint(ness) Black-out, Conk, Darkle, Dim, Dizzy, Dwalm, Fade, Lassitude, Pale, Stanck, Swarf, Swarve, Swelt, Swerf, Swerve, Swoon, Swound, Syncope, Unclear, Wan, Whitish

Faint-heart Boneless, Coward, Craven, Eery, Timid, Wet

Fair Adequate, Aefauld, Aefwld, A(e)fald, Barnet, Bartholomew, Bazaar, Beauteous, Beautiful, Belle, Blond, Bon(n)ie, Bonny, Brigg, Decent, Dishy, Donnybrook, Equal, Equitable, Evenhanded, Exhibition, Expo(sition), Feeing-market, → **FESTIVAL**, Fête, Fine, Fiona, Funfair, Gaff, Gala, Gey, Goose, Gwyn, Hiring, Honest, Hopping, Isle, → **JUST**, Kermess, Kermis, Kirmess, Market, Mart, Mediocre, Mela, Mop, Nundinal, Objective, OK, Paddington, Passable, Play, Pro rata, Rosamond, Sabrina, Sporting, Square, Statute, Steeple, Straight, Tavistock, Tidy, Tolerable, Tow-headed, Trade, Tryst, Unbias(s)ed, Vanity, Wake, Widdicombe, Xanthe

Fair-buttocked Callipygean

Fairing Ornament, Spat

Fairly Clearly, Enough, Evenly, Midway, Moderately, Pari passu, Pretty, Properly, Quite, Ratherish

Fairway Dog-leg, Pretty

Fairy, Fairies Banshee, Befana, Cobweb, Dobbie, Dobby, Elf(in), Fay, Gloriana, Good people, Hob, Hop o' my thumb, Leprechaun, Lilian, Little people, Mab, Morgane(tta), Morgan le Fay, Moth, Nis, Peri, Pigwidgin, Pigwiggen, Pisky, Pixie, Pouf, Puck, Punce, Queen Mab, Sandman, Seelie, Sidhe, Spirit, Sprite, Sugar-plum,

Tink(erbell), Titania, Tooth, Unseelie, Urchin-shows

Faith(ful) Accurate, Achates, Belief, Constant, Creed, Devoted, Doctrine, Faix, Fay, Feal, Fegs, Fideism, Fiducial, Haith, Implicit, Islam, Lay, Loyal, Plerophory, Punic, Puritanism, Quaker, Religion, Shahada, Shema, Solifidian, Staunch, Strict, Troth, → **TRUE**, True-blue, Trust, Truth, Umma(h)

Faithless Atheist, Disloyal, False, Giaour, Hollow, Infidel, Nullifidian, Perfidious, Punic

Fake(r), Faking Bodgie, Bogus, Copy, Counterfeit, Duff(er), Ersatz, False, Fold, Forgery, Fraud, Fudge, Imitation, Imposter, Impostor, Paste, Phoney, Pirate(d), Postiche, Pretend, Pseudo, Sham, Spurious, Toy, Trucage, Truquage, Truqueur, Unreal

Falcon Cast, Gentle, Hawk, Hobby, Iceland, Kestrel, Lanner(et), Merlin, Nyas, Peregrine, Prairie, Saker, Sakeret, Spar-hawk, Sparrow-hawk, Stallion, Staniel, Stannel, Stanyel, Stone, Tassel-gentle, Tassell-gent, Tercel-gentle, Tercel-jerkin

Falklander Kelper

Fall(s), Fallen, Falling Abate, Accrue, Angel, Arches, Astart, Autumn, Boyoma, Cadence, Cascade, Cataract, Churchill, Chute, Collapse, Crash, Cropper, Cross press, Declension, Decrease, Degenerate, Descent, Dip, Domino effect, Douse, Downswing, Dowse, → **DROP**, Ebb, Firn, Flag, Flop, Flump, Folding press, Free, Grabble, Grand, Gutser, Gutzer, Horseshoe, Idaho, Iguaçu, Incidence, Kabalega, Kaieteur, Lag, Landslide, Lapse, Lin(n), Niagara, Oct(ober), Onding, Owen, Perish, Plonk, Plummet, Plump, Plunge, Prolapse, Ptosis, Purl(er), Rain, Reaction, Relapse, Ruin, Sheet, Sin, Sleet, Snow, Soss, Spill, Stanley, Sutherland, Tailor, Takakkau, Topple, Toss, Trip, Tugela, Tumble, Victoria, Voluntary, Wipeout, Yellowstone, Yosemite

Fallacious, Fallacy Elench(us), Error, Gamblers', Idolon, Idolum, Ignoratio elenchi, Illogical, Illusion, Material, Naturalistic, Pathetic, Sophism, Specious, Unsound

Fallible Human, Imperfect

▷ **Falling** *may indicate* an anagram or a word backwards

Fallow Barren, Lea, Tan, Uncared, Uncultivated, Untilled

False, Falsify, Falsification, Falsehood Adulterate, Assumed, Bastard, Bodgie, Bogus, Braide, Bricking, Calumny, Canard, Cavil, Charlatan, Cook, Deceitful, Disloyal, Dissemble, Doctor, Fake, Feigned, Fiddle, Forge, Illusory, Knave, Lying, Meretricious, Mock, Obreption, Perjury, Pinchbeck, Postiche, Pretence, Pseudo, Rap, Refute, Roorback, Sham, Specious, Spoof, Spurious, Treacherous, Trumped-up, Two-faced, Untrue, Veneer

False notions Idola

Falter Hesitate, Limp, Stoiter, Totter, Waver

Fame, Famous Bruit, Cause célèbre, Celebrity, Distinguished, Eminent, Glitterati, Gloire, Glory, Greatness, History, Humour, Illustrious, Kudos, Legendary, Luminous, Megastar, Mononym, Name, Noted, Notorious, Prestige, Reclamé, Renown, Repute, Robert, Rumour, Splendent, Spur, Stardom, Word

Familiar(ise), Familiarity Accustom, Acquaint, Assuefaction, Au fait, Auld, Chummy, Comrade, Conversant, Couth, Crony, Dear, Demon, Easy, Free, Friend, Habitual, Homely, Homey, Incubus, Intimate, Known, Liberty, Maty, Old, Old-hat, Privy, Python, Used, Versed, Warhorse

Family Ainga, Ancestry, Bairn-team, Blood, Breed, Brood, Clan, Class, Close-knit, Cognate, Consanguine, County, Descent, Dynasty, Extended, Eye, House(hold), Issue, Kin, Kind, Kindred, Line, Mafia, Medici, Name, Nuclear, One-parent, Orange, People, Phratry, Progeny, Quiverful, Race, Sept, Sib(b), Sibship, Stem, Stirps, Strain, Taffy, Talbot, Tribe, Whanau

Family tree Pedigree, Stemma
Famine Dearth, Lack, Scarcity
Famish(ed) Esurient, Hungry, Ravenous, Starving
▷ **Famished** *may indicate* an 'o' in the middle of a word
Fan(s), Fan-like Adherent, Admirer, Aficionado, Alligator, Alluvial, Arouse, Bajada, Barmy-army, B-boy, Blow, Cat, Clapper, Claque, Colmar, Cone, Cool, Cuscus, Devotee, Diadrom, Dryer, Enthusiast, Extractor, Fiend, Flabellum, Following, Goth, Grebo, Groupie, Headbanger, Hepcat, Khuskhus, Muso, Nut, Outspread, Partisan, Popette, Punka(h), Rhipidate, Ringsider, Sail, Spectator, Spread, Supporter, Tail, Tifosi, Ventilate, Votary, Voteen, Washingtonia, Wind machine, Wing, Winnow, Zealot, Zelant
▷ **Fan** *may indicate* an anagram
Fanatic(al) Bigot, Devotee, Energumen, Enthusiastic, Extremist, Fiend, Frenetic, Glutton, Mad, Maniac, Nut, Partisan, Phrenetic, Picard, Rabid, Santon, Ultra, Wowser, Zealot
Fancy, Fanciful Caprice, Chim(a)era, Conceit, Concetto, Crotchet, Daydream, Dream, Dudish, Elaborate, Fangle, Fantasy, Fit, Flam, Florid, Frothy, Guess, Hallo, Idea(te), Idolon, → IMAGINE, Inclination, Lacy, Liking, Maya, Mind, My, Nap, Notion, Opine, Ornamental, Ornate, Picture, Pipe dream, Predilection, Reverie, Rococo, Suppose, Thought, Unreal, Urge, Vagary, Visionary, Ween, Whigmaleerie, Whigmaleery, Whim(sy), Woolgather
▷ **Fancy** *may indicate* an anagram
Fane Banner, Pronaos
Fanfare Flourish, Sennet, Show, Tantara, Trump, Tucket
Fang Tooth, Tusk
Fanny Adams, Bottom, Gas-lit, Price
Fantasist, Fantasy, Fantastic Absurd, Antic, Bizarre, Caprice, Chimera, Cloud-cuckoo land, Cockaigne, Cockayne, Escapism, Fab, Fanciful, Grotesque, Hallucination, Idol, Illusion, Kickshaw(s), Lucio, Mega, Myth, Outré, Phantasmagoria, Pipe-dream, Queer, Reverie, Romance, Schizoid, Unreal, Untrue, Walter Mitty, Wannabe(e), → WHIM, Whimsical, Wild, Wishful thinking
Far Apogean, Away, Distal, Distant, Eloi(g)n, Extreme, Outlying, Remote, Thether, Thither
Farce(ur) Burletta, Charade, Comedy, Exode, Feydeau, Lazzo, Mime, Mockery, Pantomime, Rex, Screaming, Sham, Travesty
Fare Apex, Charge, Cheer, Commons, Do, Eat, Excess, Excursion, → FOOD, Go, Passage, Passage money, Passenger, Rate, Table, Traveller
Farewell Adieu, Adios, Aloha, Apopemptic, Bye, Cheerio, Departure, Godspeed, → GOODBYE, Leave, Prosper, Sayonara, Send off, So long, Toodle-oo, Toodle-pip, Totsiens, Vale, Valediction
Far-fetched Fanciful, Improbable, Recherché
Farm(ing), Farmhouse Agronomy, Arable, Bocage, Bowery, City, Cold Comfort, Collective, Cooperative, Croft, Cultivate, Dairy, Deep-litter, Dry, Emmerdale, Estancia, Extensive, Factory, Fat, Fish(ery), Funny, Geoponical, Grange, Hacienda, Health, Home, Homestead, Husbandry, Intensive, Kibbutz, Kolkhoz, Land, Ley, Loaf, Location, Mailing, Mains, Mas, Mixed, No-tillage, Onstead, Orley, Oyster, Pen, Plaas, Plough, Poultry, Ranch, Rent, Set-aside, Sewage, Shamba, Sheep station, Smallholding, Sovkhoz, Station, Stead(ing), Sted(d), Stedde, Steed, Stock, Store, Stump, Subsistence, Tank, Till, Toon, Toun, Town, Trash, Tree, Trout, Truck, Wick, Wind
Farmer Blockie, Boer, Campesino, Carl, Cockatoo, Cocklaird, Cocky, Collins Street,

Colon, Cow cocky, Crofter, Estanciero, Gebur, Gentleman, George, Giles, Hick, Hobby, Macdonald, Metayer, Nester, NFU, Peasant, Pitt Street, Queen St, Ryot, Share-cropper, Smallholder, Sodbuster, Squatter, Stubble-jumper, Tax, Tenant, Tiller, Whiteboy, Yeoman, Zeminda(r)

Farmhand Cadet, Churl, Cottar, Cotter, Cottier, Cowman, Ditcher, Hand, He(a)rdsman, Hind, Ploughman, Redneck, Rouseabout, Roustabout, Shearer, Stockman

▸ **Farmhouse** see **FARM**

Farmyard Barton, Homestall, Villatic

Farouche Awkward, Shy, Sullen

Farrago Hotch-potch, Jumble, Medley, Mélange

Farrier Marshal, Smith

Farrow Litter, Mia, Sow

Far-sighted Presbyte

Fart Poep, Trump

Farthing Brass, F, Fadge, Har(r)ington, Mite, Q, Quadragesimal, Rag

Fascia Band, Fillet, Platband

Fascinate, Fascinating Allure, Attract, Bewitch, → **CHARM**, Dare, Enchant, Engross, Enthral(l), Fetching, Inthral, Intrigue, Kill, Mesmeric, Rivet, Siren, Witch

Fascist Blackshirt, Blue shirt, Brownshirt, Dictator, Falange, Falangist, Iron Guard, Lictor, Nazi, Neo-Nazi, NF, Phalangist, Rexist, Sinarchist, Sinarquist

Fashion(able), Fashioned Aguise, À la (mode), Bristol, Build, Chic, Construct, Convention, Cool, Corinthian, Craze, Create, Cult, Custom, Cut, Dernier cri, Design, Directoire, Du jour, Elegant, Entail, Fad, Feat, Feign, Forge, Form, Genteel, Go, Hew, High, Hip, Hot, In, Invent, Kitsch, Look, → **MAKE**, Man-about-town, Manière, Manners, Mode, Mondain(e), Mould, Newgate, Pink, Preppy, Rage, Rag trade, Rate, Roy, Sc, Shape, Smart, Smith, Snappy, Snazzy, Stile, Stylar, Style, Swish, Tailor, Ton, Ton(e)y, Tonish, → **TREND(Y)**, Turn, Twig, Vogue, Way, Wear, With-it, Work, Wrought

Fast(ing), Faster Abstain, Apace, Ashura, Breakneck, Citigrade, Clem, Clinging, Cracking, Daring, Dharna, Dhurna, Double-quick, Elaphine, Express, Fizzer, Fleet, Immobile, Lent, Lightning, Loyal, Maigre, Meteoric, Moharram, Muharram, Muharrem, Pac(e)y, Posthaste, Presto, Pronto, Quadragesimal, Quick, Raffish, Raking, Ramadan, Ramadhan, Rash, Rathe, Relay, Siyam, Spanking, Speedy, Stretta, Stretto, Stuck, Supersonic, Sure, Swift, Tachyon, Thick, Tight, Tisha b'Av, TishaBov, Tishah-Baav, Tishah-b(e)Ab, Tishah-b(e)Av, Whistle-stop, Yarer, Yom Kippur

Fast and loose Fickle, Prick-the-garter, Strap-game

Fasten(er), Fastening Anchor, Attach, Bar, Belay, Bind, Bolt, Buckle, Button, Chain, Clamp, Clasp, Click, Clinch, Clip, Cramp, Cufflink, Dead-eye, Diamond-hitch, Dome, Espagnolette, Eye-bolt, Frog, Gammon, Hasp, Hesp, Hook, Lace, Latch, Lock, Moor, Morse, Nail, Netsuke, Nip, Nut, Padlock, Parral, Patent, Pectoral, Pin, Preen, Press stud, Reeve, Rivet, Rope, Rove, Seal, → **SECURE**, Sew up, Shut, Spar, Sprig, Staple, Stitch, Suspender, Swift(er), Tach(e), Tag, Tape, Tassel, Tether, Thong, Tintack, Toggle, U-bolt, Velcro®, Wedge, Zip

Fastidious Chary, Critical, Dainty, Fusspot, Fussy, Neat, Nice, Particular, Precieuse, Precious, Purism, Queasy, Squeamish

Fat(s), Fatten, Fatty Adipic, Adipocere, Adipose, Aldermanly, Aliphatic, Arcus, Atheroma, Bard, Batten, Battle, Blubber, Brown, Butter, Calipash, Calipee, Cellulite, Cholesterol, Chubbed, Chubby, Corpulent, Creesh, Degras, Dika-oil, Dosh, Dripping, Embonpoint, Enarm, Endomorph, Ester, Flab, Flesh, Flick, Fozy, Fubsy,

Galam-butter, Grease, Gross, Keech, Kitchen-fee, Lanolin, Lard, Leaf, Lipaemia, Lipid, Lipoma, Love handles, Margarine, Marge, Marrow, Moti, Motu, Obese, Oil, Oleomargarine, OS, Palmitin, Pinguid, Plump, Poddy, Podgy, Polyunsaturated, Portly, Puppy, Pursy, Rich, Rolypoly, Rotund, Saddlebags, Saginate, Saim, Saturated, Schmal(t)z, Seam(e), Sebacic, Sebum, Shortening, Soil, Spare tyre, Spe(c)k, Squab, Stearic, Steatopygia, Steatorrhea, Suberin, Suet, Tallow, Tin, Tomalley, Triglyceride, Tub, Unsaturated, Vanaspati, Waller, Well-padded, Wool

Fatal(ism), Fate(s), Fated, Fateful Apnoea, Atropos, Cavel, Chance, Clotho, Deadly, Death, Decuma, Destiny, Doom, End, Fay, Fell, Joss, Karma, Kismet, Lachesis, Lethal, Lot, Meant, Moera, Moira, Mortal, Mortiferous, Nemesis, Norn(a), Parca, Pernicious, Portion, Predestination, Skuld, Urd, Verdande, Waterloo, Weird, Weird sisters

Father(ly) Abba, Abbot, Abuna, Adopt, Apostolic, Bapu, Begetter, Breadwinner, Brown, City, Conscript, Curé, Dad, Engender, Foster, Founding, Fr, Generator, Genitor, Getter, Gov, Governor, Guv, Male, NASCAR dad, Pa, Padre, Papa, Pappy, Parent, Pater(nal), Paterfamilias, Patriarch, Père, Pilgrim, Pop(pa), Popper, Priest, Rev, Seraphic, Sire, Stud, Thames, Tiber, William

Father-lasher Sea-scorpion

Fathom Delve, Depth, Dig, F, Plumb, Plummet, Understand

Fatigue Battle, Combat, Compassion, Exhaust, Fag, Jade, Jet lag, ME, Metal, Neurasthenia, Overdo, Overwatch, Tire, Weariness, Weary

Fatuous Gaga, Idiotic, Silly, Stupid

Faucet Cock, Spigot, Tap

Fault(y) Arraign, Bad, Beam, Blame(worthy), Blunder, Bug, Cacology, Carp, Compound, Culpa, Culpable, Defect, Demerit, Dip, Dip-slip, Drop-out, Duff, → **ERROR**, Failing, Flaw, Frailty, Gall, Glitch, Gravity, Henpeck, Hitch, Imperfect, Literal, Massif, → **MISTAKE**, Nag, Nibble, Niggle, Nit-pick, Oblique, Oblique-slip, Out, Outcrop, Overthrust, Para, Peccadillo, Pre-echo, Rate, Reprehend, Rift, Rupes Recta, San Andreas, Sclaff, Set-off, Short, Slip, Snag, Step, Strike, Strike-slip, Technical, Thrust, Trap, Trough, Underthrust, Upbraid, Vice

Faultless Immaculate, Impeccable, Lily-white, Perfect

Fauna Mesobenthos, Wild life

Fauvist Matisse

Faux pas Blunder, Boner, Gaffe, Leglen-girth, Solecism

Favour(able), Favoured, Favourite Advance, Advantage(ous), Aggrace, Agraste, Alder-liefest, Approval, Auspicious, Back, Befriend, Behalf, Benign, Bless, Boon, Bribe, Cert, Chosen, Cockade, Curry, Darling, Ex gratia, Fancy, Favonian, Form horse, Good turn, Grace, Graste, Gratify, Gree, Hackle, Hot, In, Indulge, Kickback, Minion, Nod, Odour, Particular, Peat, Persona grata, Pet, Pettle, Popular, → **PREFER**, Promising, Propitious, Resemble, Rib(b)and, Roseate, Rose-knot, Rosette, Side, Smile, Toast, Token, Win-win

Fawn(er), Fawning Adulate, Bambi, Beige, Blandish, Brown-nose, Camel, Crawl, Creep, Cringe, Deer, Ecru, Flatter, Fleech, Grovel, Ko(w)tow, Lickspittle, Obsequious, Servile, Slavish, Smarm, Smoo(d)ge, Subservient, Sycophant, Tasar, Toady, Truckle, Tussah, Tusseh, Tusser, Tussore

Fay Fairy, Korrigan, Peri

FBI G-men

Fear Aichmophobia, Angst, Apprehension, Astra(po)phobia, Awe, Bathophobia, Bête noire, Bugbear, Claustrophobia, Cold sweat, Crap, Creeps, Cyberphobia, Dismay, Doubt, Drad, Dread, Dromophobia, Foreboding, → **FOR FEAR**, Fright, Funk, Hang-up, Horror, Kenophobia, Mysophobia, Nyctophobia, Ochlophobia, Panic,

→ **PHOBIA**, Photophobia, Redoubt, Revere, Taphephobia, Taphophobia, Terror, Thalassophobia, Trepidation, Willies

Fearful Afraid, Cowardly, Dire, Horrific, Nervous, Pavid, Rad, Redoubtable, Timorous, Tremulous, Windy

Fearless Bold, Brave, Courageous, Daring, Gallant, Impavid, Intrepid

Fearsome Dire, Formidable

Feasible Goer, Likely, On, Possible, Practical, Probable, Viable

Feast Adonia, Agape, Assumption, Banquet, Barmecide, Beano, Belshazzar's, Blow-out, Candlemas, Carousal, Celebration, Dine, Do, Double, Eat, Encaenia, Epiphany, Epulation, Festival, Fleshpots, Fool's, Gaudeamus, Gaudy, Hakari, Halloween, Hallowmas, Hockey, Hogmanay, Holy Innocents, Id-al-Adha, Id-al-Fitr, Immaculate Conception, Isodia, Junket, Kai-kai, Lady Day, Lamb-ale, Lammas, Love, Luau, Lucullus, Martinmas, Michaelmas, Midnight, Movable, Noel, Passover, Pentecost, Pig, Potlatch, Purim, Regale, Revel, Roodmas, Seder, Shindig, Spread, Succoth, Sukkot(h), Tabernacles, Tuck-in, Wake, Wayzgoose, Weeks, Yule, Zagmuk

Feast-day Mass

Feat Achievement, Deed, Effort, Exploit, Gambado, Handspring, Stunt, Trick

Feather(ed), Feathers Aigrette, Alula, Barbicel, Boa, Braccate, Cock, Contour, Covert, Crissum, Down, Duster, Filoplume, Flags, Fledged, Fletch, Flight, Gemmule, Hackle, Harl, Hatchel, Herl, Lei, Lure, Macaroni, Manual, Oar, Ostrich, Pen(na), Pin, Pinna, Pith, Plumage, Plume, Plumule, Prince's, Pteryla, Ptilosis, → **QUILL**, Rectrix, Remex, Remiges, Rocket-tail, Saddle(-hackle), Scapular, Scapus, Secondary, Semiplume, Shaft, Shag, Sickle, Standard, Stipa, Swansdown, Tectrix, Tertial, Vibrissa, White, Wing covert

Feather-worker Plumassier

Feature(s) Acoustic, Amenity, Appurtenance, Article, Aspect, Attribute, Brow, Character, Chin, Depict, Double, Eye, Eyebrow, Face, Facet, Figure, Hallmark, Highlight, Item, Jizz, Landmark, Lineament, Neotery, Nose, Nucleus, Overfold, Phiz(og), Physiognomy, Signature, Snoot, Spandrel, Star, Temple, Trait, Underlip

Featureless Flat

Febrifuge Atabrin, Atebrin®, Mepacrine, Quina

February Fill-dyke

Fecund(ity) Fertile, Fruitful, Prolific, Uberty

Fed Agent, G-man

Federal, Federation Alliance, Axis, Bund, Commonwealth, Interstate, League, Russian, Statal, Union

Fee Base, Capitation, Charge, Chummage, Commitment, Common, Conditional, Contingency, Corkage, Drop-dead, Dues, Duty, Faldage, Fine, Great, Groundage, Hire, Honorarium, Interchange, Mortuary, Mouter, Multure, Obvention, Pay, Pierage, Premium, Refresher, Retainer, Sub, Subscription, Transfer, Tribute

Feeble Banal, Characterless, Daidling, Debile, Decrepit, Droob, Effete, Feckless, Fizzenless, Flaccid, Foisonless, Footling, Fragile, Fus(h)ionless, Geld, Ineffective, Infirm, Jessie, Limp, Mimsy, Namby-pamby, Pale, Puny, Sassy, Sickly, Slender, Slight, Soppy, Tailor, Tame, Thin, Tootle, Wallydrag, Wallydraigle, Washy, Wastrel, Weak, Weak-kneed, Weak-minded, Weed, Weedy, Wersh, Wet, Wimpish, Worn

Feed(er), Feeding Battle, Bib, Break, Browse, Cake, Cater, Cibation, Clover, Cowfeteria, Cram, Cue, Demand, Dine, Dressing, Drip, → **EAT**, Fatten, Filter, Fire, Fishmeal, Flushing, Fodder, Food, Force, Gavage, Graze, Hay, Line, Lunch, Meal, Nourish, Nurse, Paid, Pecten, Provender, Refect, Repast, Sate, Soil, Stoke, Stooge, Stover, Suckle, Sustain, Tire, Tractor, Wean, Wet nurse

Feedback Negative, Positive

Feel, Feeling(s) Aesthesia, Affetuoso, Animus, Artificial, Atmosphere, Ballottement, Compassion, Darshan, Déja vu, → **EMOTION**, Empathy, Empfindung, Euphoria, → **EXPERIENCE**, Fellow, Finger, Flaw, Frisk, Grope, Groundswell, Handle, Hard, Heart, Heartstrings, Hunch, Intuit, Knock, Know, Palp, Passible, Passion, Phatic, Pity, Premonition, Presentiment, Probe, Realise, Sensate, Sensation, → **SENSE**, Sensitive, Sentiment, Somesthesis, Spirit, Sprachgefühl, Tactual, Touch, Turn, Undercurrent, Vehemence, Vibes, Vibrations, Zeal

Feeler Antenna, Barbel, Exploratory, Overture, Palp, Sensillum, Tentacle

▶ **Feet** *see* FOOT

Feign Act, Affect, Colour, Fake, Malinger, Mime, Mock, → **PRETEND**, Sham, Simulate

Feint Deke, Disguise, Dodge, Faint, Fake, Spoof, Trick

Fel(d)spar Adularia, Albite, Anorthite, Gneiss, Hyalophane, Moonstone, Orthoclase, Petuntse, Petuntze, Plagioclase, Sanidine, Saussurite, Sun-stone

Felicity Bliss, Happiness, Joy, Relevance

▶ **Feline** *see* CAT

Fell Axe, Chop, Cruel, Deadly, Dire, Dread, Fierce, Heath, Hew, Hide, Hill, Inhuman, Knock-down, KO, Lit, Log, Malign, Moor, Pelt, Poleaxe, Ruthless, Sca, Shap, Skittle

Fellow(s), Fellowship Academic, Associate, Bawcock, Birkie, Bloke, Bo, Bro, Bucko, Buffer, Callan(t), Carlot, Cat, Chal, Chap, Chi, China, Chum, Co, Cock, Cod(ger), Collaborator, Co-mate, Communion, Companion, Comrade, Confrère, Cove, Cully, Cuss, Dandy, Dean, Dog, Don, Dude, Equal, F, Fogey, Fop, Gadgie, Gadje, Gaudgie, Gauje, Gink, Guy, Joe, Joker, Josser, Kerel, Lad, Like, M, Mall, Man, Mate, Member, Mister, Mun, Partner, Peer, Professor, Rival, Seniority, Sister, Skate, Sociate, Society, Sodality, Swab, Teaching, Twin, Waghalter, Wallah

Felon(y) Bandit, Convict, Crime, Gangster, Offence, Villain

Felt Bat(t), Drugget, Knew, Met, Numdah, Numnah, Pannose, Roofing, Sensed, Tactile, Underlay, Velour

Female (bodies), Feminine, Feminist Anima, Bint, Bit, Dame, Distaff, Doe, F, Fair sex, Filly, Girl, Harem, Hen, Her, Kermes, Lady, Libber, Maiden, Muliebrity, Pen, Petticoated, Riot girl, Sakti, Shakti, She, Sheila, Shidder, Soft, Spindle, Thelytoky, -trix, → **WOMAN**, Yin

▷ **Female, Feminine** *may indicate* an -ess ending

Fen Bog, Carr, Ea, Jiao, Marsh, Morass, Silicon, Wash

Fence(r), Fencing (position) Appel, Balestra, Bar, Barrier, Botte, Carte, Croisé, Cyclone®, Derobement, Dogleg, Electric, Enclose, Épée, Feint, Flanconade, Flèche, Foils, Fraise, Froissement, Haha, Hay, Hedge, Hot, Hurdle, Iaido, Imbrocate, Inquartata, Kendo, Line, Link, Mensur, Molinello, Montant, Netting, Obstacle, Ox, Oxer, Pale, Paling, Palisade, Palisado, Parry, Passado, Pen, Picket, Post and rail, Quart(e), Quinte, Rabbit-fence, Rabbit-proof, Raddle, Rail, Rasper, Receiver, Reset, Ring, Scrimure, Seconde, Sepiment, Sept(um), Septime, Singlestick, Sixte, Snake, Snow, Stacket, Stockade, Stramac, Stramazon, Sunk, Swordplay, Tac-au-tac, Tierce, Touché, Trellis, Virginia, Wattle, Wear, Weir, Weldmesh®, Wire, Worm

Fend(er) Buffer, Bumper, Cowcatcher, Curb, Mudguard, Parry, Provide, Resist, Skid, Ward, Wing

Fennel Finnochio, Finoc(c)hio, Florence, Herb, Love-in-a-mist, Narthex, Ragged lady

Fent Offcut, Remnant, Slit

Feral Brutal, Fierce, Savage, Wild

Ferdinand Archduke, Bull

Ferment(ation) Barm, Enzym(e), Leaven, Mowburn, Protease, Ptyalin, Seethe, Solera, Storm, Stum, Trypsin, Turn, Vinify, Working, Ye(a)st, Zyme, Zymo-, Zymology, Zymosis, Zymotic, Zymurgy

Fermium Fm

Fern Acrogenous, Adder's-tongue, Adiantum, Archegonial, Asparagus, Aspidium, Asplenium, Azolla, Barometz, Beech, Bird's nest, Bladder, Bracken, Brake, Bristle, Buckler, Bungwall, Ceterach, Cinnamon, Coral, Cryptogam, Cyathea, Cycad, Dicksonia, Door, Elkhorn, Fairy moss, Filicales, Filices, Filmy, Fishbone, Grape, Hard, Hart's-tongue, Ice, Isoetes, Lady, Maidenhair, Male, Man, Mangemange, Marattia, Marsh, Marsilea, Marsilia, Meadow, Miha, Moonwort, Mosquito, Mulewort, Nardoo, Nephrolepis, Northern, Oak, Ophioglossum, Osmunda, Para, Parsley, Peppergrass, Pepperwort, Pig, Pillwort, Polypody, Polystichum, Ponga, Pteridology, Pteris, Punga, Rachilla, Rhizocarp, Rockbrake, Royal, Rusty-back, Salvinia, Scale, Schizaea, Scolopendrium, Seed, Shield, Silver, Snowbrake, Soft tree, Spleenwort, Staghorn, Sweet, Sword, Tara, Tree, Venus's hair, Walking, Wall rue, Water, Woodsia

Ferocious Brutal, Cruel, Fell, Predatory, Rambunctious, Tiger, Wild

Ferret Albin, Black-footed, Business, Fesnyng, Gill, Hob, Jill, Nose, Polecat, Ribbon, Rootle, Snoop, Trace, Unearth

Ferry(man) Charon, Convey, Harper's, Hovercraft, Passage, Plier, Pont, Roll-on, RORO, Sealink, Shuttle, Soyuz, Train, Traject, Tranect

Fertile, Fertility (symbol), Fertilisation Arable, Ashtoreth, Battle, Cleistogamy, Fat, Fecund, Fruitful, Green, Linga, Priapus, Productive, Prolific, Rhiannon, Rich, Uberous

Fertilise(r), Fertilisation Ammonia, Auxin, Bee, Bone-ash, Bone-earth, Bone-meal, Caliche, Caprify, Compost, Cross, Fishmeal, Guano, Heterosis, Humogen, Humus, In-vitro, IVF, Kainite, Manure, Marl, Nitrate, Nitre, Nitro-chalk, Pearl-ash, Phosphate, Pollen, Pollinator, Potash, Potassa, Self, Sham, Stamen, Superphosphate, Top dressing

Fervent, Fervid, Fervour Ardent, Burning, Earnest, Heartfelt, Heat, Hwyl, Intense, Keen, Passionate, White-hot, Zeal, Zeloso

Fester Beal, Putrefy, Rankle, Rot, Suppurate

Festival, Festive, Festivity Adonia, Agon, Aldeburgh, Ale, Al Hijra(h), All Saints' Day, Ambarvalia, Anniversary, Anthesteria, Ashura, Bairam, Baisak(h)i, Bayreuth, Beano, Beltane, Biennale, Bon, Candlemas, Carnival, Celebration, Cerealia, Chanuk(k)ah, Childermas, Church-ale, Circumcision, Commemoration, Convivial, Corpus Christi, Corroboree, Crouchmas, Dassehra, Dewali, Dionysia, Divali, Diwali, Doseh, Druid, Easter, Eisteddfod, Encaenia, En fête, Epiphany, → **FAIR**, Feast, Feis, Fête, Fête-champêtre, Fête-Dieu, Fête-galante, Fiesta, Fleadh, Fringe, Gaff, → **GALA**, Gaudy, Glastonbury, Glyndebourne, Gregory, Hallowmas, Hanukkah, Harvest, Harvest home, High day, Hock-tide, Hogmanay, Holi, → **HOLIDAY**, Holy-ale, Hosay, Hosein, Id-al-fitr, Imbolc, Imbolg, J'ouvert, Kermess, Kermiss, Kirmess, Kumbh Mela, Kwanzaa, Lady-Day, Lailat-ul-Qadr, Lammas, Laylat-al-Miraj, Lemural, Lemuria, Lesser Bairam, Let-off, Lughnasadh, Lupercalia, Matsuri, Mayday, Mela, Merry-night, Michaelmas, Miraj, Mod, Moomba, Navaratra, Navaratri, Noel, Obon, Palilia, Panathenaean, Panegyry, Pardon, Pasch, Passover, Pentecost, Pesa(c)h, Play, Pongal, Pooja(h), Pop, Potlach, Puja, Purim, Quirinalia, Revel, Rosh Hashanah, Rush-bearing, Samhain, Saturnalia, Seder, Semi-double, Shabuath, Shavuath, Shemini Atseres, Shrove(tide), Simchas Torah, Simchat(h) Torah, Simchat Torah, Slugfest, Terminalia, Tet, Thargelia, Thesmophoria, Tide, Transfiguration, Up-Helly-Aa, Utas, Vesak, Vinalia, Visitation, Vulcanalia, Wake,

Wesak, Woodstock, Yom Tob, Yomtov, Yuan Tan, Yule(tide)

Festoon Deck, Decorate, Encarpus, Garland, Swag, Wreathe

Fetch(ing) Arrive, Attract, Bring, Charming, Fet(t), Get, Gofer, Realise

Fête Bazaar, Champêtre, Entertain, → **FESTIVITY**, Gala, Honour, Tattoo

Fetish(ist) Charm, Compulsion, Gimp, Idol, Ju-ju, Obeah, Obi(a), Talisman, Totem, Voodoo

Fetter Basil, Bilboes, Chain, Gyve, Hamshackle, Hopple, Iron, Leg-iron, Manacle, Shackle

Fettle Arrange, Condition, Frig, Potter, Repair

Feu Tenure

Feud Affray, Blood, Clash, Feoff, Fief, Quarrel, Strife, → **VENDETTA**

Feudal (service), Feudalism Arriage, Auld-farrant, Fief, Forinsec, Old, Vassalage

Fever(ish) African coast, Ague, Beaver, Blackwater, Brain, Breakbone, Buck, Cabin, Calenture, Camp, Cat-scratch, Cerebrospinal, Childbed, Dengue, East coast, Enteric, Ferment, Fog, Frenetic, Gastric, Gate, Glandular, Haemorrhagic, Hay, Heatstroke, Hectic, Hyperpyretic, Insolation, Intense, Intermittent, Jail, Japanese river, Jungle, Kala-azar, Lassa, Malaria, Malta, Marsh, Mediterranean, Miliary, Milk, Mono, Mud, Paratyphoid, Parrot, Parturient, Passion, Puerperal, Putrid, Pyretic, Pyrexia, Pyrogenic, Q, Quartan, Quintan, Quotidian, Rabbit, Ratbite, Recurrent, Relapsing, Remittent, Rheumatic, Rift Valley, Rock, Rocky Mountain spotted, Roseola, Sandfly, Scarlatina, Scarlet, Sextan, Ship, Splenic, Spotted, Spring, Stage, Sunstroke, Swamp, Swine, Tap, Temperature, Tertian, Texas, Tick, Trench, Typhoid, Typhus, Undulant, Valley, Verruga, Vomito, West Nile, Whot, Worm, Yellow(jack)

Few(er) Handful, Infrequent, → **LESS**, Limited, Scarce, Some, Wheen

Fey Clairvoyant, Eccentric, Elfin, Weird

Fez Tarboosh, Tarboush, Tarbush

Fiancé(e) Betrothed, Intended, Promised

Fiasco Bomb, Debacle, Disaster, Failure, Flask, Flop, Lash-up, Wash-out

Fiat Command, Decree, Edict, Order, Ukase

Fib Gag, → **LIE**, Prevaricate, Story, Taradiddle, Untruth

Fibre, Fibrous Abaca, Acrilan®, Acrylic, Aramid, Arghan, Backbone, Bass, Bast, Beta, Buaze, Bwazi, Cantala, Carbon, Coir, Constitution, Cotton, Courtelle®, Cuscus, Dietary, Dralon®, Elastane, Elastin, Filament, Filasse, Flax, Funicle, Gore-Tex®, Graded-index, Hair, Hemp, Henequen, Henequin, Herl, Hypha, Ispaghula, Istle, Ixtle, Jipyapa, Jute, Kapok, Kenaf, Kevlar®, Kittul, Lemniscus, Manilla, Monkey-grass, Monofil, Monomode, Moorva, Moral, Multimode, Mungo, Murva, Muscle, Myotube, Nap, Natural, Nerve, Noil(s), Nylon, Oakum, Olefin(e), Optic(al), Orlon®, Peduncle, Piassaba, Piassava, Pina, Pita, Polyarch, Pons, Pontine, Pulu, Raffia, Ramee, Rami, Ramie, Rayon, Rhea, Rock-cork, Roughage, Rove, Shoddy, Sida, Silk, Sisal, Slagwool, Sleave, Slub(b), Spandex, Splenium, Staple, Stepped-index, Sterculia, Strand, Strick, Sunn-hemp, Tampico, Tencel®, Toquilla, Tow, Uralite, Viver, Vulcanized, Wallboard, Watap, Whisker, Wood pulp

Fibula Bone, Brooch, Perone

Fickle(ness) Capricious, Change, False, Inconstant, Light, Mutable, Protean, Shifty, Varying, Volage, Volatile

Fiction(al), Fictitious Bogus, Chick-lit, Cyberpunk, Fable, Fabrication, Legal, Myth, Pap, Phoney, Picaresque, Romance, Science, Slash, Speculative, Splatterpunk, → **STORY**

Fiddle(r), Fiddling Amati, Bow, Calling-crab, Cello, Cheat, Crab, Cremona, Croud, Crouth, Crowd, Crwth, Do, Fidget, Fix, Gju, Ground, Gu(e), Jerrymander, Kit,

Launder, Nero, Peculate, Petty, Potter, Racket, Rebec(k), Rig, Rote, Sarangi, Saw, Sawah, Scam, Scotch, Scrape, Scrapegut, Second, Spiel, Strad, Sultana, → **TAMPER**, Tinker, Toy, Trifle, Tweedle(-dee), Twiddle, Viola, → **VIOLIN**, Wangle

Fidelity Accuracy, Faith, Fealty, Loyalty, Troth

Fidget(y) Fantad, Fanteeg, Fantigue, Fantod, Fike, Fuss, Fyke, Hirsle, Hotch, Jimjams, Jittery, Niggle, Restive, Trifle, Twiddle, Twitch, Uneasy

Fiduciary Trustee

Fief Benefice, Fee

Field(er), Fielding, Fields(man) Aalu, Aaru, Abroad, Aceldama, Aerodrome, Area, Arena, Arish, Arpent, Arrish, Campestral, Campestrian, Catch, Champ(s), Close, Coulomb, Cover, Domain, Electric, Electromagnetic, Electrostatic, Elysian, Entry, Fid, Fine leg, Flodden, Flying, Forte, Fylde, Glebe, Gracie, Gravitational, Grid(iron), Gull(e)y, Hop-yard, Ice, Keep wicket, Killing, Land, Landing, Lare, Lay, Lea(-rig), Leg slip, Ley, Line, Long leg, Long-off, Long-on, Longstop, Lords, Magnetic, Mead(ow), Mid-off, Mid-on, Mid-wicket, Mine, Oil, Padang, Paddock, Paddy, Parrock, Pasture, Peloton, Pitch, Playing, Point, Potter's, Province, Realm, Runners, Salting, Sawah, Scarecrow, Scope, Scout, Shamba, Short leg, Short stop, Silly, Slip, Sphere, Square leg, Stage, Stray, Stubble, Territory, Third man, Tract, Unified, Vector, Visual, W.C., World

▷ **Field** *may indicate* cricket

Field marshal Allenby, Bulow, French, Haig, Ironside, Kesselring, Kitchener, Montgomery, Roberts, Robertson, Rommel, Slim, Wavell

Fieldwork Lunette, Ravelin, Redan, Redoubt, Tenaillon

Fiend Barbason, Demon, → **DEVIL**, Enthusiast, Flibbertigibbet, Frateretto, Hellhound, Hobbididance, Mahn, Modo, Obidicut, Smulkin, Succubus

Fierce(ly) Amain, Billyo, Breem, Breme, Cruel, Draconic, Dragon, Grim, Hard-fought, Intense, Ogreish, Rampant, Renfierst, → **SAVAGE**, Severe, Tigerish, Tigrish, Violent, Wild, Wood, Wud

Fiery Ardent, Argand, Aries, Con fuoco, Dry, Fervent, Hot, Hotspur, Idris, Igneous, Impassioned, Leo, Mettlesome, Phlogiston, Sagittarius, Salamander, Zealous

Fiesta Festival, Fête, Gala, Holiday

Fife Piffero

Fifth Column, Diapente, Hemiol(i)a, Nones, Perfect, Quint, Sesquialtera, Sextans

Fifty Bull, Demi-c, Jubilee, L

Fig Bania, Benjamin-tree, Caprifig, Fico, Figo, Footra, Fouter, Foutra, Foutre, Hottentot, Indian, Moreton Bay, Mouldy, Sycamore, Syconium, Sycomore, Trifle

Fight(er), Fighting Action, Affray, Agonistics, Aikido, Alpino, Altercate, Arms, Bandy, Bare-knuckle, Barney, → **BATTLE**, Bicker, Biffo, Blue, Bout, Box, Brave, Brawl, Bruiser, Bundeswehr, Bush-whack, Campaign, Chaud-mellé, Chindit, Combat, Compete, Conflict, Contest, Crusader, Cuirassier, Defender, Dog, Donnybrook, Duel, Encounter, Engagement, Extremes, Faction, Fecht, Fence, Fisticuffs, Flyting, Fray, Freedom, Free-for-all, Fund, Ghazi, Gladiator, Grap(p)le, Grudge, Gunslinger, Gurkha, Hurricane, Kite, Kumite, Lapith, Marine, Med(d)le, Medley, Mêlée, Mercenary, MIG, Militate, Mill, Mujahed(d)in, Mujahidin, Naumachy, Night, Partisan, Pellmell, Pillow, PLO, Prawle, Press, Pugilist, Pugnacity, Punch up, Rammy, Rapparee, Repugn, Resist, Ring, Ruck, Ruction, Rumble, Running, Savate, Sciamachy, Scold, Scrap, Scrimmage, Scuffle, Shadow, Shine, Skiamachy, Skirmish, Slam, Soldier, Spar, Spat, Spitfire, Squabble, Stealth, Stoush, Straight, Strife, Struggle, Sumo, Swordsman, Tar, Tatar, Thersites, Toreador, Tuilyie, Tuilzie, Tussle, Umbrella, War(-dog), War-horse, War-man, Warrior, Wraxle, Wrestle, Yike, Zero

Figment Delusion, Fiction, Invention
Figure(s), Figurine, Figurative Action, Arabic, Aumail, Bas-relief, Body, Build, Caganer, Canephorus, Caryatid, Cast, Chladni, Cinque, Cipher, Cone, Cube, Cypher, Decahedron, Digit, Ecorché, Effigy, Eight, Ellipse, Enneagon, Enneahedron, Epanadiplosis, Escher, → **FORM**, Fret, Fusil, Gammadion, Girth, Gnomon, Graph, Heptagon, Hexagon, Hour-glass, Icon, Icosahedron, Idol, Ikon, Image, Impossible, Insect, Intaglio, Integer, Interference, Lay, Lissajous, Magot, Manaia, Mandala, Matchstick, Moai, Monogram, Motif, Nonagon, Number, Numeral, Numeric, Octagon, Octahedron, Orant, Outline, Parallelepiped, Parallelogram, Pentacle, Pentalpha, Plane, Polygon, Polyhedron, Poussette, Prism, Puppet, Pyramid, Reckon, Repetend, Repoussoir, Rhomboid, See, → **SHAPE**, Sheela-na-gig, Significant, Simplex, Solid, Sonorous, Statistics, Statue(tte), String, Tanagra, Telamon, Tetragon, Tetrahedron, Torus, Triangle, Trigon, Trihedron, Triskele, Triskelion, Trisoctahedron, Tropology, Ushabti, Waxwork
Figure of speech Allegory, Alliteration, Analogy, Antimask, Antimasque, Antimetabole, Antithesis, Asyndeton, Catachresis, Chiasmus, Deixis, Diallage, Ellipsis, Euphemism, Hendiadys, Hypallage, Hyperbaton, Hyperbole, Hysteron proteron, Irony, Litotes, Meiosis, Metalepsis, Metaphor, Metonymy, Onomatopoeia, Oxymoron, Paral(e)ipsis, Prosopopoeia, Siddhuism, Simile, Solecism, Syllepsis, Synecdoche, Taxeme, Tmesis, Trope, Tropology, Zeugma
Figure study Arithmetic, Mathematics, Numeration
Figure-weaver Draw-boy
Filament Barbule, Byssus, Cirrus, Fibre, Fimbria, Floss, Gossamer, Hair, Hypha, Mycor(r)hiza, Myofibril, Paraphysis, Protonema, → **THREAD**, Whisker, Wreath
Filch Appropriate, Drib, Pilfer, Pinch, Prig, Purloin, Smouch, → **STEAL**
File, Filing(s) Abrade, Archive, Back up, Bastard, Batch, Binary, Box, Burr, Circular, Clyfaker, Coffle, Croc(odile), Crosscut, Database, Data set, Dead-smooth, Disc, Disk, Dossier, Enter, Floatcut, Folder, Generation, Half-round, Index, Indian, Lever-arch, Limation, Line, Lodge, Nail, Pickpocket, Pigeon-hole, Podcast, Pollute, Quannet, Rank, Rasp, Rat-tail, README, Riffler, Risp, Rolodex®, Row, Scalprum, Scratch, Single, Single-cut, String, Swap, Swarf, Text, Tickler, TIF(F)
Filial generation F1
Filibuster Freebooter, Hinder, Obstruct, Pirate, Run on, Stonewall
Filigree Delicate, Fretwork, Sheer
Filipino Igorot, Moro, → **PHILIPPINE(S)**
Fill(ing), Filler Anaplerosis, Balaam, Banoffee, Banoffi, Beaumontag(u)e, Beaumontique, Billow, Bishop, Bloat, Brick-nog, Brim, Bump, Centre, Charge, Cram, Fat-lute, Ganache, Gather, Gorge, Heart, Imbue, Implete, Impregn(ate), Inlay, Instill, Jampack, Line, Mastic, Occupy, Pabulous, Packing, Permeate, Plug, Replenish, Repletive, Salpicon, Sate, Satisfy, Sealant, Shim, Slush, Stack, Stock, Stocking, Stopping, → **STUFF**, Tales, Tank-up, Teem, Top up, Ullage
Fillet(s) Anadem, Annulet, Band, Bandeau, Bandelet, Bone, Cloisonné, Flaunching, Fret, Goujons, Grenadine, Headband, Infula, Label, Lemniscus, List(el), Mitre, Moulding, Reglet, Regula, Ribbon, Rollmop, Slice, Snood, Sphendone, Stria, Striga, Taeniate, Tape, Teniate, Tilting, Tournedos, Vitta
Fillip Boost, Kick, Snap, Stimulus
Filly Colt, Foal, She
Film(s), Filmmaker, Filmy, Filming Acetate, Actioner, Amnion, Animatronics, Anime, Biopic, Blaxploitation, Blockbuster, Bollywood, Buddy, Carry On, Cartoon, Casablanca, Caul, Cel, Chick-flick, Chiller, Chopsocky, Cine, Cinema vérité, Cinerama®, Circlorama®, Cliffhanger, Cling, Clip, Coat, Compilation,

Creature feature, Deepie, Dew, Diorama, Docudrama, Documentary, Dogme, Dust, Epic, ET, Exposure, Fantasia, Feature, Fiche, Flick, Floaty, Footage, Gigi, Gossamer, Hammer, Haze, Hollywood, Horror, Horse opera, Infomercial, Kell, Kidult, Lacquer, Layer, Loid, Mask, Membrane, Microfiche, Mist, Molecular, Monochrome, Montage, Movie, Neo-noir, Newsreel, Noddy, Noir, Non-flam, Oater, Omnimax®, Outtake, Panchromatic, Patina, Pellicle, Photo, Pilot, Plaque, Prequel, Psycho, Quickie, Quota-quickie, Reel, Release, Reversal, Roll, Romcom, Rush, Safety, Scale, Scent-scale, Screen, Scum, Sepmag, Sheet, Shoot-'em-up, Short, Shot, Silent, Skin, Skin flick, Slasher-movie, Slashfest, Slick, Slo-mo, Snuff, Spaghetti western, Splatter, Star Wars, Studio, Super 8, Suspensor, Talkie, Tear-jerker, Technicolor, Titanic, Toon, Trailer, Travelogue, Trippy, Two-shot, Ultrafiche, Varnish, Vicenzi, Video, Video-nasty, Vitaphone®, Web, Weepie, Weepy, Weft, Western, Wuxia
Film star Extra, Vedette
Filter(ing) Band-pass, Clarify, Colour, Dialysis, Dichroic, High-pass, Leach, Low-pass, Percolate, Perk, Polarizing, Seep, Sieve, → SIFT, Sile, Skylight, Strain
Filth(y) Addle, Augean, Bilge, Bogging, Colluvies, Crock, Crud, Defile, Dirt, Dung, Feculent, Foul, Grime, Lucre, Mire, Muck, Obscene, Pythogenic, Refuse, Slime, Smut(ch), Soil, Squalor, Stercoral, Sullage, Yuck
Fin Adipose, Anal, Caudal, Ctene, Dollars, Dorsal, Fiver, Fluke, Pectoral, Pelvic, Pinna, Pinnule, Rib, Skeg, Skegg, Stabiliser, Ventral
Final(e), Finalise Absolute, Closing, Coda, Conclusive, Cup, Decider, End, End-all, Eventual, Exam, Extreme, Grand, Last, Net(t), Peremptory, Sew up, Swansong, Terminal, Ultimate, Utter
Finance, Financial, Financier Ad crumenam, Angel, Back, Banian, Banker, Bankroll, Banyan, Bottomry, Cambism, Chrematistic, Equity, Exchequer, Fiscal, Gnome, Grubstake, Mezzanine, Monetary, Revenue, Sponsor, Subsidise, Treasurer, Underwrite
Finch Bird, Brambling, Bunting, Canary, Charm, Chewink, Crossbill, Darwin's, Fringillid, Gouldian, Grosbeak, Linnet, Marsh-robin, Peter, Redpoll, Rosy, Serin, Siskin, Spink, Twite, Zebra
Find(er), Finding Ascertain, Come across, Detect, Direction, Discover(y), Get, Hit, Inquest, → LOCATE, Meet, Provide, Rumble, Trace, Track down, Trouvaille, Unearth, Verdict
Fine, Fine words Amende, Amerce, Amerciament, Arts, Assess, Beau(t), Bender, Blood-wit(e), Bonny, Boshta, Boshter, Boss, Brandy, Brave, Braw, Bully, Buttock-mail, Champion, Dainty, Dandy, Dick, End, Eriach, Eric(k), Estreat, F, Fair, Famous, Forfeit, Gate, Godly, Good(ly), Gossamer, Gradely, Graithly, Grand, Grassum, Hair, Hairline, Handsome, Heriot, Hunkydory, Immense, Impalpable, Inconie, Incony, Infangthief, Issue, Keen, Leirwite, Log, Maritage, Merchet, Mooi, Mulct, Nifty, Niminy-piminy, Noble, OK, Oke, Okey-doke(y), Outfangthief, → PENALTY, Phat, Precise, Pretty, Pure, Relief, Righto, Safe, Sconce, Sheer, Sicker, Slender, Smart, Spanking, Subtle, Summery, Super, Tax, Thin, Ticket(t)y-boo, Tiptop, Topping, Transmission, Unlaw, Wally, Waly, Well, Wer(e)gild
Fine-collector Cheater
Finery Braws, Fallal, Frills, Frippery, Gaudery, Ornament, Trinket, Wally, Warpaint
Finesse Artifice, Artistry, Delicacy, Skill, Strategy
Fine-weather All-hallond, All-hallow(e)n, All-hollown
Finger(s), Fingernail Annular, Dactyl, Digit, Fork, Green, Handle, Index, Lunula, Medius, Name, Nip, Piggy, Pinky, Pointer, Potato, Prepollex, Pusher, Ring(man), Shop, Sponge, Talaunt, Talon, Tot, Trigger, White
Finger-hole Lill, Ring

Fingerprint(ing) Arch, Dabs, Dactylogram, DNA, Genetic, Loop, Whorl
Fingerstall Hutkin
Finial Bunch, Knob, Ornament, Tee
Finical, Finicky Faddy, Fastidious, Fussy, Particular, Pernickety, Precise
Finish, Finished, Finishing touch Arch, Blanket, Calendar, Close, Coating, Coda, Complete, → CONCLUDE, Crown, Die, Dish, Do, Dope, Dress, → END, Epilog(ue), Epiphenomena, Exact, Full, Gloss, Grandstand, Kibosh, Lacquer, Log off, Mat(t), Mirror, Neat, Outgo, Outwork, Pebbledash, Peg out, Perfect, Photo, Polish off, Refine, Ripe, Round, Satin, Settle, Shot, Spitcher, Surface, Terminate, Through, Top out, Up (tie), Veneer, Wau(l)k, Wind-up
Finite Bounded, Limited
Finn(ish) Esth, Huck(leberry), Karelian, Lapp, Mickey, Mordvin, Suomic, Udmurt, Votyak
Fiord Bay, Hardanger, Inlet, Oslo, Randers, Trondheim
Fir Abies, Balsam, Douglas, Larch, Oregon, Scotch, Scots, Silver, Spruce, Umbrella
Fire(side) Accend, Agni, Aidan, Aiden, Animate, Ardour, Arouse, Arson, Atar, Axe, Bake, Bale, Barbecue, Barrage, Beacon, Behram, Blaze, Boot, Brand, Brazier, Brush, Burn, Bush, Central, Chassé, Conflagration, Corposant, Covering, Delope, Discharge, Dismiss, Élan, Electric, Element, Embolden, Ena, Energy, Enfilade, Enkindle, Enthuse, Flak, Flame, Friendly, Furnace, Greek, Gun, Hearth, Hob, Ignite, Inferno, Ingle, Inspire, Kentish, Kiln, Kindle, Launch, Let off, Light, Liquid, Lowe, Pop, Prime, Prometheus, Pull, Pyre, Quick, Radiator, Rake, Rapid, Red, Red cock, Sack, St Anthony's, St Elmo's, Scorch, Shell, Shoot, Smudge, Spark, Spirit, Spunk, Stoke, Stove, Strafe, Tracer, Trial, Wake, Watch, Wisp, Zeal, Zip
▶ **Firearm** *see* GUN
Fireback Reredos
Fireball Bolide
Firebird Phoenix
Fire-break Epaulement, Greenstrip
Firedamp Blower
Fire-dog Andiron
Fire engine Green Goddess
Fire-extinguisher Halon, Hell-bender, Salamander
Firefly Glow-worm, Lightning-bug, Luciferin, Pyrophorus
Fire-guard Fender
Fireman Abednego, Brigade, Deputy, Prometheus, Stoker, Visiting
Fire-opal Girasol
Fireplace Camboose, Chimney, Grate, Hearth, Hob, Ingle, Loop-hole, Range
Fireplug H, Hydrant
Fireproof Abednego, Asbestos, Incombustible, Inflammable, Meshach, Salamander, Shadrach, Uralite
Firewalker Salamander
Firewood Billet, Faggot, Knitch, Tinder
Firework(s) Banger, Bengal-light, Bunger, Catherine wheel, Cherry bomb, Cracker, Devil, Feu d'artifice, Fisgig, Fizgig, Flip-flop, Fountain, Gerbe, Girandole, Golden rain, Iron sand, Jumping jack, Maroon, Pastille, Peeoy, Petard, Pharaoh's serpent, Pinwheel, Pioy(e), Pyrotechnics, Realgar, Rocket, Roman candle, Serpent, Skyrocket, Slap-bang, Sparkler, Squib, Tantrum, Throwdown, Tourbill(i)on, Volcano, Waterloo cracker, Wheel, Whizzbang
Fire-worshipper Parsee
Firing Baking, Fusillade, Mitten, Salvo, Touchpaper

Firm, Firmness Adamant, Agency, Binding, Business, Collected, Compact, Company, Concern, Concrete, Conglomerate, Consistency, Constant, Crisp, Decided, Determined, Duro, Faithful, Fast, Fixed, Hard, Inc, Insistent, Marginal, Oaky, Obdurate, Obstinate, → RESOLUTE, Sclerotal, Secure, Set, Siccar, Sicker, → SOLID, Sound, Stable, Stalwart, Staunch, Steady, Ste(a)dfast, Steely, Steeve, Stern, Stieve, Stiff, Strict, Sturdy, Sure, Tight, Tough, Unshakeable, Well-knit

Firmament Canopy, Empyrean, Heaven, Sky

First Ab initio, Alpha, Arch, Archetype, Best, Calends, Champion, Chief, Earliest, E(a)rst, Eldest, Foremost, Former, Front, Head, I, Ideal, Imprimis, Initial, 1st, Kalends, Led, Maiden, No 1, One, Opener, Or, Original, Pioneer, Pole, Pole position, Premier, Première, Prima, Primal, Prime, Primo, Principal, Prototype, Rudimentary, Senior, Starters, Top, Uppermost, Victor, Yama

First-aid(ers) Zambu(c)k

First born Ariki, Eigne, Eldest, Heir, Major, Senior

First class, First rate A1, Crack, Prime, Pukka, Supreme, Tiptop, Top(notch)

First day Calends

First fruits Annat, Arles, Primitiae, Windfalls

First man Adam, Ask, Gayomart, Premier, President, Yama, Ymer, Ymir

First offender Eve, Probationer

▶ **First rate** *see* FIRST CLASS

First woman Embla, Eve, Pandora, Premier

Firth Estuary, Forth, Inlet, Moray, Pentland, Solway, Tay

Fish(ing) Angle, Bob, Bottom, Cast, Catch, Chowder, Coarse, Cran, Creel, Deep-sea, Dib, Dredge, Dry, Dry-fly, Episcate, Fly, Flying, Frozen, Fry, Game, Gefilte, Gefulte, Goujons, Guddle, Halieutics, Haul, Hen, Inshore, Ledger, Mess, Net, Otterboard, Overnet, Piscine, Queer, Roe, Rough, Runner, Sacred, Sashimi, Shoal, Skitter, Sleeper, Small mouth, Snigger, Sniggle, Spin, Spot, Surimi, Trawl, Troll, Tub, Walking, Wet, White

---

FISH

2 letters:	Koi	Chad	Huso
Ai	Lax	Char	Huss
Id	Lob	Chub	Ikan
	Par	Chum	Jack
3 letters:	Pod	Coho	Kelt
Aua	Ray	Cray	Keta
Ayu	Rig	Cusk	Lant
Bar	Sar	Dace	Leaf
Bib	Tai	Dare	Ling
But	Top	Dart	Luce
Cat		Dory	Lump
Cod	*4 letters:*	Drum	Maid
Cow	Barb	Fugu	Maze
Dab	Bass	Gade	Moki
Dog	Blay	Goby	Mola
Eel	Bley	Gump	Mort
Gar	Brit	Hake	Opah
Ged	Butt	Harl	Orfe
Hag	Carp	Hoka	Parr
Ide	Cero	Hoki	Peal

Peel
Pike
Pope
Pout
Raun
Rawn
Rigg
Rudd
Ruff
Scad
Scar
Scat
Scup
Seer
Seir
Shad
Sild
Slip
Snig
Sole
Star
Tope
Trot
Tuna
Tusk
Woof

5 letters:
Ablet
Ahuru
Allis
Angel
Apode
Aspro-
Basse
Belta
Blain
Bleak
Bream
Brill
Bully
Capon
Charr
Cisco
Clown
Cobia
Cohoe
Coley
Cuddy
Danio
Dorad

Doras
Doree
Dorse
Elops
Elver
Fluke
Gadus
Gibel
Grunt
Jewie
Jurel
Koura
Laker
Lance
Loach
Lythe
Maise
Maize
Manta
Masus
Mease
Molly
Murre
Murry
Nerka
Padle
Perai
Perca
Perch
Pilot
Piper
Pirai
Platy
Pogge
Powan
Prawn
Roach
Roker
Royal
Ruffe
Saith
Sargo
Saury
Scrod
Sewen
Sewin
Shark
Sheat
Skate
Slope
Smelt

Snoek
Snook
Solen
Speck
Sprat
Sprod
Tench
Tetra
Togue
Torsk
Trout
Tunny
Umber
Wahoo
Whiff
Wirra
Witch
Yabby
Zebra

6 letters:
Alevin
Allice
Anabas
Angler
Archer
Ballan
Barbel
Belone
Beluga
Bichir
Big-eye
Blenny
Bonito
Bounce
Bowfin
Braise
Braize
Bumalo
Burbot
Callop
Caplin
Caranx
Caribe
Cheven
Clupea
Cockle
Comber
Conger
Conner
Cottus

Cudden
Cuddie
Cuddin
Cunner
Cuttle
Darter
Dentex
Diodon
Dipnoi
Discus
Doctor
Dorado
Dun-cow
Ellops
Espada
Finnac
Finnan
Fogash
Fumado
Gadoid
Garvie
Gilgie
Goboid
Goramy
Grilse
Groper
Gulper
Gunnel
Gurami
Gurnet
Haddie
Hapuka
Hassar
Inanga
Jerker
Jilgie
Kipper
Kokiri
Labrus
Lancet
Launce
Lizard
Louvar
Lunker
Mad Tom
Mahsir
Maigre
Marari
Marlin
Meagre
Medaka

Medusa
Megrim
Milter
Minnow
Morgay
Mudcat
Mullet
Murena
Nerite
Oyster
Paddle
Paidle
Pakoko
Parore
Parrot
Patiki
Pholas
Piraya
Plaice
Podley
Pollan
Porgie
Puffer
Redfin
Remora
Rewaru
Robalo
Roughy
Saithe
Salmon
Samlet
Sander
Sardel
Sargus
Sauger
Saurel
Scampi
Sea-bat
Sea-owl
Seeder
Serran
Shanny
Sheath
Shiner
Skelly
Sparid
Splake
Sucker
Tailor
Tarpon
Tautog

Tinker
Toitoi
Tomcod
Trygon
Turbot
Twaite
Ulicon
Ulikon
Vendis
Weever
Wirrah
Wrasse
Yabbie
Zander
Zingel

7 letters:
Ale-wife
Anchovy
Anemone
Asterid
Azurine
Batfish
Bellows
Bergylt
Birchir
Bloater
Bluecap
Boxfish
Brassie
Buffalo
Bumallo
Bummalo
Cabezon
Capelin
Cavalla
Cavally
Ceviche
Cichlid
Codfish
Copepod
Corvina
Cottoid
Crappie
Croaker
Crucian
Crusian
Cutlass
Dogfish
Eelfare
Eel-pout

Escolar
Fantail
Findram
Finnack
Finnock
Flattie
Garfish
Garoupa
Garpike
Garvock
Geelbek
Gemfish
Goldeye
Gourami
Grouper
Growler
Grunion
Gudgeon
Gurnard
Gwiniad
Gwyniad
Haddock
Hagdown
Hagfish
Halibut
Herling
Herring
Hirling
Hogfish
Homelyn
Houting
Ichthys
Inconnu
Jewfish
Kahawai
Keeling
Koi carp
Kokanee
Lampern
Lamprey
Lampuki
Lantern
Lingcod
Lobster
Lubfish
Lyomeri
Mahseer
Matelot
Medacca
Merling
Mojarra

Moon-eye
Morwong
Muraena
Oarfish
Old-wife
Oolakan
Opaleye
Osseter
Oulakan
Oulican
Panchax
Pandora
Peacock
Pegasus
Pigfish
Pinfish
Piranha
Pollack
Pomfret
Pompano
Pupfish
Ragfish
Rasbora
Ratfish
Rat-tail
Redfish
Rorqual
Roughie
Sand dab
Sand-eel
Sardine
Scalare
Scallop
Sculpin
Sea-bass
Sea-cock
Sea-dace
Sea-moth
Sea-pike
Sea-star
Sea-wife
Sevruga
Sillock
Silurid
Skegger
Skipper
Snapper
Sock-eye
Sparoid
Speldin
Sterlet

Sunfish
Sunstar
Surgeon
Teleost
Tiddler
Tilapia
Titling
Torgoch
Torpedo
Tubfish
Ulichon
Vendace
Vendiss
Wall-eye
Whipray
Whistle
Whiting
Wide-gab

8 letters:
Albacore
Albicore
Anableps
Arapaima
Asteroid
Atherine
Billfish
Blennius
Bloodfin
Blowfish
Blueback
Bluefish
Bluegill
Boarfish
Brisling
Bullhead
Bullhorn
Bummallo
Cabezone
Cabrilla
Carangid
Cardinal
Cavefish
Characid
Characin
Chimaera
Coalfish
Corkwing
Cow-pilot
Cucumber
Cyprinid

Dealfish
Dragonet
Drumfish
Eagle-ray
Elephant
Escallop
Eulachon
Fallfish
Fighting
Filefish
Flathead
Flounder
Four-eyes
Frogfish
Gambusia
Ganoidei
Gillaroo
Gilthead
Goatfish
Gobiidae
Graining
Grayling
Hackbolt
Hair-tail
Half-beak
Hard-head
Holostei
Hornbeak
Hornpout
Kabeljou
Killfish
Kingfish
Kingklip
Kukukuma
Lionfish
Luderick
Lumpfish
Lungfish
Mackerel
Mahi-mahi
Mata Hari
Menhaden
Milkfish
Monkfish
Moonfish
Moray eel
Mosquito
Mulloway
Nannygai
Nennigai
Nine-eyes

Oulachon
Paradise
Patutuki
Pickerel
Pilchard
Pipefish
Piraricu
Redbelly
Red roman
Reperepe
Rock-cook
Rockfish
Rockling
Roncador
Rosefish
Saibling
Sailfish
Saltfish
Sardelle
Scabbard
Scaridae
Sciaenid
Scorpion
Scuppaug
Sea-bream
Sea-devil
Seahorse
Sea-lemon
Sea-raven
Sea-robin
Sergeant
Serranus
Skipjack
Smear-dab
Snake-eel
Sparidae
Sparling
Spelding
Speldrin
Stenlock
Sting-ray
Stonecat
Sturgeon
Tarakihi
Tarwhine
Teraglin
Terakihi
Tile-fish
Toadfish
Trevally
Tropical

Tubenose
Tullibee
Weakfish
Whitling
Wolffish

9 letters:
Ahuruhuru
Amberjack
Anabantid
Anchoveta
Barracuda
Blackfish
Butterfly
Carangoid
Cascadura
Ceratodus
Chaetodon
Chavender
Clingfish
Clupeidae
Coregonus
Coryphene
Cyprinoid
Devilfish
Gaspereau
Glassfish
Globefish
Goldfinny
Goldsinny
Golomynka
Goosefish
Greenbone
Greenling
Grenadier
Haberdine
Hornyhead
Hottentot
Houndfish
Ichthyoid
Jacksmelt
Jewelfish
Kabeljouw
Killifish
Labyrinth
Latimeria
Matelotte
Menominee
Mudhopper
Neon tetra
Pikeperch

Porbeagle	Whitebait	Nurse-hound	Plectognath
Porcupine	White-bass	Paddlefish	Pumpkinseed
Queenfish	Wreckfish	Pakirikiri	Scolopendra
Quillback	Yellowfin	Rabbitfish	Seventy-four
Roussette		Red emperor	Snail darter
Scaldfish	*10 letters:*	Red-snapper	Soldierfish
Scalefish	Amblyopsis	Ribbonfish	Stickleback
Schnapper	Barracoota	Rudderfish	Stoneroller
Scorpaena	Barracouta	Scopelidae	Surgeonfish
Selachian	Barramundi	Sea-poacher	Triggerfish
Shubunkin	Bitterling	Sea-surgeon	Trumpetfish
Siluridae	Bombay duck	Serrasalmo	Water souchy
Slickhead	Bottlehead	Sheepshead	Yellowbelly
Snailfish	Butterfish	Ship-holder	
Snakehead	Candlefish	Shovelnose	*12 letters:*
Snipefish	Cockabully	Silverside	Ballan-wrasse
Solenette	Cofferfish	Springfish	Elasmobranch
Spadefish	Cornetfish	Squeteague	Father-lasher
Spearfish	Cyclostome	Teleostome	Heterosomata
Speldring	Damselfish	Titarakura	Histiophorus
Stargazer	Demoiselle	Tripletail	Mangrove Jack
Steenbras	Dollarfish	Yellowtail	Miller's thumb
Stingaree	Etheostoma		Mouthbreeder
Stockfish	Fingerling	*11 letters:*	Mouthbrooder
Stonefish	Flutemouth	Chondrostei	Orange roughy
Surfperch	Groundling	Cyprinodont	Plectognathi
Surmullet	Horned pout	Dolly Varden	Rainbow-trout
Swellfish	Lake-lawyer	Istiophorus	Squirrelfish
Swordfish	Largemouth	Lapidosteus	
Sword-tail	Lumpsucker	Lepidosiren	*13 letters:*
Thornback	Maskalonge	Lophobranch	Leatherjacket
Threadfin	Maskanonge	Maskallonge	Musselcracker
Tittlebat	Maskinonge	Moorish idol	Sailor's choice
Topminnow	Midshipman	Muskellunge	Sergeant Baker
Trachinus	Mossbunker	Ostracoderm	
Troutfish	Mudskipper	Oxyrhynchus	*15 letters:*
Trunkfish	Needlefish	Plagiostome	Crossopterygian

Fish and chips Greasies
Fish-basket Creel, Hask, Kipe
Fish disease Argulus
Fisher(man) Ahab, Andrew, Angler, Black cat, Caper, Codder, Dragman, High-liner, Liner, Pedro, Peter, Piscator, Rodster, Sharesman, Walton
▸ **Fisherwoman** *see* **FISHSELLER**
Fish-hawk Osprey
Fishing-ground Haaf
Fishing-line G(u)imp, Gymp, Paternoster
Fishpond Ocean, Stew, Vivarium
Fishseller, Fisherwoman Fishwife, Molly Malone, Ripp(i)er, Shawley, Shawlie
Fishy Botargo, Suspicious, Vacant
Fission Multiple, Nuclear

Fissure Chasm, Cleft, Crack, Crevasse, Crevice, Gap, Grike, Gryke, Lode, Rent, Rift, Rolando, Sand-crack, Scam, Sylvian, Sylvius, Vallecula, Vein, Zygon

Fist Clench, Dukes, Hand, Iron, Join-hand, Mailed, Neaf(f)e, Neif, Neive, Nief, Nieve, Pud, Punch, Thump, Writing

Fit(s), Fitful, Fitting(s), Fitness Able, Access, Adapt, Ague, Align, Aline, Apoplexy, Appointment, Appropriate, Apropos, Apt, Babbitt, Bayonet, Beseemly, Bout, Canto, Capable, Cataleptic, Cataplexy, Click, Concinnous, Condign, Congruous, Conniption, Convulsion, Culver-tail, Darwinian, Decent, Decorous, Desultory, Dod, Dove-tail, Due, Eclampsia, Egal, Eligible, Ensconce, Epilepsy, Equip, Exies, Expedient, Fairing, Fay, Fiddle, Form, Furniment, Furnishing, Fytte, Gee, Germane, Gusty, Habile, Hale, Hang, Health, Hinge, Huff, Hysterics, Ictus, Inclusive, In-form, Interference, Intermittent, In trim, Just, Kashrut(h), Like, Lune, Marry, Mate, Meet, Mood, Nest, Opportune, Paroxysm, Passus, Pertinent, Prepared, Press, → **PROPER**, Queme, Ready, Rig, Rind, Ripe, Rynd, Seemly, Seizure, Set, Shrink, Sit, Sliding, Snotter, Sort, Sound, Spasm, Spell, Start, Suit(able), Syncope, Tailor, Tantrum, Throe, To prepon, Turn, Up to, Well, Wobbler, Wobbly, Worthy, Wrath

▷ **Fit(ting)** *may indicate* a 't'

Fitment Adaptor, Unit

Fitzgerald Edward, Ella, Scott

Five(s), Fiver Cinque, Flim, Mashie, Pallone, Pedro, Pentad, Quinary, Quintet, Sextan, Towns, V

Five years Lustre, Lustrum

Fix(ed), Fixer, Fixative Affeer, Anchor, Appoint, Appraise, → **ARRANGE**, Assess, Assign, Attach, Bind, Brand, Cement, Clamp, Clew, Clue, Constant, Corking-pin, Cure, Decide, Destinate, Destine, Determine, Do, Embed, Empight, Encastré, Engrain, Establish, Fast, Fasten, Firm, Fit, Freeze, Gammon, Hold, Hypo(sulphite), Immutable, Impaction, Imprint, Inculcate, Ingrain, Jag, Jam, Locate, Lodge, Mend, Nail, Name, Narcotic, Nobble, Orientate, Peg, Persistent, Pin, Place, Point, Quantify, Repair, Resolute, Rig, Rigid, Rivet, Rove, Rut, Scrape, Screw, Seat, Seize, Set, Settle, Ship, Shoo, Skatole, Skewer, Splice, Stage, Staple, Static, Stell, Step, Stew, Stuck, Tie, Toe, Valorize, Weld

Fixture Attachment, Event, Match, Permanence, Rawlplug®, Unit

Fizz(ed), Fizzy Buck's, Effervesce, Gas, Hiss, Pop, Sherbet, Sod, Soda

Fizzle Failure, Flop, Hiss, Washout

▶ **Fjord** *see* **FIORD**

Flabbergast(ed) Amaze, Astound, Floor, Thunderstruck

Flabby Flaccid, Lank, Lax, Limp, Pendulous, Saggy

Flaccid Flabby, Lank, Limp, Soft

Flag(gy), Flags Acorus, Ancient, Ashlar, Banderol, Banner, Black, Blackjack, Blue (Ensign), Blue Peter, Bunting, Burgee, Calamus, Chequered, Colour(s), Dan(n)ebrog, Decline, Droop, Duster, Ensign, Fail, Faint, Falter, Fane, Fanion, Field colours, Gladdon, Gonfalon, Green, Guidon, Hail, Hoist, Irideal, Iris, Jack, Jade, Jolly Roger, Kerbstone, Languish, Lis, Old Glory, Orris, Pave(ment), Pavilion, Pencel, Pennant, Pennon, Penoncel(le), Pensel, Pensil, Peter, Pilot, Pin, Prayer, Quarantine, Rag, Rainbow, Red, Red Duster, Red Ensign, Repeater, Sag, Sedge, Semaphore, Sick, Sink, Slab(stone), Slack, Stand, Standard, Stars and Bars, Stars and Stripes, Streamer, Substitute, Sweet, Tire, Tricolour, Union (Jack), Vane, Vexillology, Waft, Whift, White (Ensign), Wilt, Wither, Yellow (Jack)

Flagday Tagday

Flagellate Beat, Mastigophora, Scourge, Trypanosome, Whip

Flagon Bottle, Carafe, Ewer, Jug, Pitcher, Stoop, Stoup, Vessel

Flagpole Pin, Staff
Flagrant Egregious, Glaring, Heinous, Patent, Wanton
Flagship Admiral, Barge, Victory
Flail Beat, Drub, Swingle, Swip(p)le, Threshel
Flair Art, Bent, Élan, Gift, Knack, Nose, Panache, Style, → **TALENT**
Flak AA, Attack, Criticism
Flake Chip, Flame, Flaught, Flaw, Floccule, Flocculus, Fragment, Peel, Scale, Smut, Snow
Flam Impose
Flamboyant Baroque, Brilliant, Florid, Garish, Grandiose, Ornate, Ostentatious, Paz(z)azz, Piz(z)azz, Swash-buckler
Flame, Flaming Ardent, Blaze, Fire, Flake, Flambé, Flammule, Glow, Kindle, Leman, Lover, Lowe, Musical, Olympic, Oxyacetylene, Reducing, Sensitive, Sweetheart
Flan Pastry, Quiche, Tart
Flanders Mare, Moll
Flange Border, Collar, Collet, Lip, Rim
Flank(s) Accompany, Anta, Flange, Flitch, Ilia, Lisk, Loin, Side, Spur
Flannel Blather, Canton, Cloth, Cotton, Face, Flatter, Outing, Soft-soap, Waffle, Washrag, Zephyr
Flap(ped), Flapper, Flapping Ado, Agnail, Aileron, Alar, Alarm(ist), Aventail(e), Bate, Beat, Bird, Bobbysoxer, Bustle, Chit, Dither, Elevon, Epiglottis, Fipple, Flacker, Flaff, Flag, Flaught, Flutter, Fly, Fuss, Giglet, Giglot, Hover, → **IN A FLAP**, Labium, Labrum, Lapel, Loma, Louvre, Luff, Lug, Operculum, Panic, Spin, Spoiler, Tab, Tag, Tailboard, Tailgate, Tiswas, To-do, Tongue, TRAM, Volucrine, Wave, Whisk
Flare(d), Flares, Flare up Bell, Bell-bottoms, Fishtail, Flame, Flanch, Flaunch, Godet, Magnesium, Scene, Signal, Skymarker, Solar, Spread, Spunk, Ver(e)y, Widen
Flash(y), Flasher, Flashpoint Brash, Coruscate, Cursor, Electronic, Emicant, Essex Man, Fire-flag, Flare, Flaught, Fulgid, Fulgural, Garish, Gaudy, Glaik, Gleam, Glint, Glisten, Glitzy, Green, Green ray, Helium, Indicate, Instant, Jay, Lairy, Levin, Lightning, Loud, Magnesium, Meretricious, Mo, Ostentatious, Photopsy, Raffish, Ribbon, Ring, Roary, Scintillation, Second, Sequin, Showy, Sluice, Snazzy, Spark, Sparkle, Sport, Streak, Strobe, Swank(e)y, Tick, Tigrish, Trice, Twinkle, Vivid, Wire
▷ **Flashing** *may indicate* an anagram
Flask(-shaped) Ampulla, Aryballos, Bottle, Canteen, Carafe, Cask, Coffin, Conceptacle, Costrel, Cucurbit, Dewar, Erlenmeyer, Fiasco, Flacket, Flacon, Florence, Goatskin, Hip, Lekythos, Matrass, Mick(e)(y), Moon, Pocket-pistol, Powder, Reform, Retort, Thermos®, Vacuum, Vial
Flat(s), Flatten(ed), Flattener Adobe, Alkali, Amaze, Ancipital, Apartment, Bachelor, Bald, Banal, Beat, Bed-sit, Blow-out, Bulldoze, Callow, Cape, Complanate, Compress, Condominium, Corymb(ose), Cottage, Coulisse, Dead, Demolish, Dorsiventral, Double, Dress, Dull, Even, Feeble, Flew, Floor, Flue, Fool, Gaff, Garden, Granny, Guyot, Haugh, High-rise, Homaloid, Home-unit, Horizontal, Insipid, Ironed, Jacent, Key, KO, Law, Lay, Level, Lifeless, Llano, Maderised, Marsh, Monotonous, Mud, Nitwit, Norfolk, Oblate, Ownership, Pad, Pancake, Pedestrian, Peneplain, Peneplane, Penthouse, Pentice, Pied-à-terre, Plain, Planar, Plane, Planish, Plat, Plateau, Press, Prone, Prostrate, Recumbent, Rooms, Salt, Scenery, Service, Smooth, Splayfoot, Spread-edged, Squash, Studio, Tableland, Tabular, Tame, Tasteless, Tenement, True, Unsensational, Vapid, Walk-up
Flat-chested Cithara
Flat-faced Socle

Flat-foot(ed) Policeman, Splay

Flat-nosed Camus

Flatter(ing), Flatterer, Flattery Adulate, Becoming, Beslaver, Blandish, Blarney, Bootlick, Butter, Cajole, Candied, Carn(e)y, Claw(back), Complimentary, Comprabatio, Earwiggy, En beau, Eyewash, Fawn, Fillibrush, Flannel, Flannen, Fleech, Flummery, Fulsome, Gloze, Gnathonic(al), Honey, Imitation, Lip-salve, Moody, Palp, Phrase, Poodle-faker, Proneur, Puffery, Sawder, Smarm, Snow job, Soap, Soft soap, Soother, Souk, Spaniel, Stroke, Sugar, Sweet talk, Sycophant, Taffy, Toady, Treacle, Unction, Wheedle, Word

Flatulence Belch, Borborygmus, Burp, Carminative, Colic, Gas, Wind

Flaunt Brandish, Flourish, Gibe, Parade, Skyre, Sport, Strout, Strut, Wave

Flavour(ed), Flavouring Absinth(e), Alecost, Anethole, Angostura, Anise, Aniseed, Aroma, Benne, Bergamot, Bold, Borage, Bouquet garni, Clove, Coriander, Cumin, Dill, Essence, Eucalyptol, Fenugreek, Flor, Garlic, Garni, Gingili, Marinate, Mint, Orgeat, Piperonal, Quark, Race, Ratafia, Relish, Rocambole, Sair, Sassafras, Sesame, Tack, Tang, Tarragon, → **TASTE**, Til, Tincture, Twang, Vanilla

Flaw Blemish, Brack, Bug, Chip, Crack, Defect, Fallacy, → **FAULT**, Gall, Hamartia, Imperfection, Infirmity, Kink, Knothole, Lophole, Red-eye, Rima, Spot, Taint, Tear, Thief, Tragic, Windshake

Flawless Impeccable, Intact

Flax(en) Aleseed, Blonde, Codilla, Harakeke, Harden, Hards, Herden, Herl, Hurden, Line, Linseed, Lint, Lint-white, Linum, Mill-mountain, Poi, Tow

Flay Excoriate, Fleece, Flense, Scourge, Skin, Strip, Uncase, Whip

Flea Aphaniptera, Chigger, Chigoe, Chigre, Daphnid, Hopper, Itch-mite, Lop, Pulex, Sand, Turnip, Water

Flea-bane Erigeron

Fleabite Denier

Fleck Dash, Freak, Spot, Streak

Fledgling Aerie, Eyas, Sorage

Flee(ing) Abscond, Bolt, Decamp, Escape, Eschew, Fly, Fugacity, Lam, Loup, Run, Scapa, Scarper, Scram

Fleece, Fleecy Bleed, Coat, Despoil, Flocculent, Golden, Jib, Lambskin, Lanose, Pash(i)m, Pashmina, Plot, Pluck, Rifte, Ring, Rob, Rook, Shave, Shear, Sheepskin, Skin, Skirtings, → **SWINDLE**, Toison

Fleer Ogle

Fleet(ing) Armada, Brief, Camilla, Convoy, Ephemeral, Evanescent, Fast, First, Flit, Flota, Flotilla, Fugacious, Fugitive, Hasty, Hollow, Lightfoot, Navy, Pacy, Passing, Prison, Spry, Street, Transient, Velocipede

Flesh(y) Beefy, Body, Carneous, Carrion, Corporeal, Corpulent, Creatic, Dead-meat, Digastric, Finish, Goose, Gum, Hypersarcoma, Joint, Jowl, Ket, Longpig, Lush, Meat, Mole, Mons, Mummy, Muscle, Mutton, Proud, Pulp, Quick, Sarcous, Spare tyre, Tissue

Flesh-eating Cannibalism, Carnassial, Creophagus, Omophagic

Fleshless Dry, Maigre, Pem(m)ican

Flex(ible), Flexibility Adaptable, Bend(y), Compliant, Double-jointed, Elastic, Genu, Limber, Lissom(e), Lithe, Pliant, → **RESILIENT**, Rubato, Rubbery, Squeezy, Supple, Tensile, Tonus, Wieldy, Willing, Wiry

▷ **Flexible, Flexuous** *may indicate* an anagram

Flick(er), Flicks Bioscope, Cinema, Fillip, Film, Flip, Flirt, Flutter, Glimmer, Gutter, Movie, Movy, Snap, Snow, Spang-cockle, Switch, Talkie, Twinkle, Waver, Wink, Zap

Flickertail ND

Flier Aerostat, Airman, Alcock, Amy, Aviator, → **BIRD**, Bleriot, Blimp, Brown, Crow, Daedalus, Erk, Fur, George, Gotha, Handout, Icarus, Leaflet, Lindbergh, Montgolfier, Pilot, RAF, Scotsman, Spec, Speedy

Flight(y) Backfisch, Birdbrain, Bolt, Bubble-headed, Capricious, Charter, Contact, Dart, Departure, Escalier, Escape, Exaltation, Exodus, Fast, Fickle, Flaught, Flibbertigibbet, Flip, Flock, Flyby, Fly-past, Free, Fugue, Giddy, Grece, Grese, Gris(e), Guy, Hegira, Hejira, Hejra, Hellicat, Hijra, Lam, Loup-the-dyke, Mercy, Milk-run, Mission, Open-jaw, Pair, R(a)iser, Redeye, Ro(a)ding, Rode, Rout, Skein, Sortie, Stairs, → **STAMPEDE**, Stayre, Steps, Swarm, Test, Top, Tower, Trap, Vol(age), Volatile, Volley, Whisky-frisky, Wing

Flightless Kakapo, Nandoo, Ostrich, Rhea, Struthious

▷ **Flighty** *may indicate* an anagram

Flimsy Finespun, Gimcrack, Gossamer, Jimcrack, Lacy, Sleazy, Sleezy, Tenuous, Thin, Weak, Wispy

Flinch Blench, Cringe, Funk, Quail, Recoil, Shrink, Shudder, Start, Wince

Fling Dance, Flounce, Highland, Hurl, Lance, Pitch, Shy, Slat, Slug, Slump, Spanghew, Spree, Throw, → **TOSS**

Flint Chert, Firestone, Granite, Hag-stone, Hornstone, Microlith, Mischmetal, Optical, Pirate, Rock, Silex, Silica, Stone, Touchstone

Flip(pant), Flipping Airy, Bally, Brash, Cocky, Flick, Frivolous, Impudent, Jerk, Nog, Pert, Purl, Sassy, Saucy, Toss, Turn

Flipper(s) Fin-toed, Paddle, Pinniped(e)

Flirt(ation), Flirting, Flirtatious Bill, Buaya, Carve, Chippy, Cockteaser, Come-hither, Come-on, Coquet(te), Dalliance, Demivierge, Footsie, Gallivant, Heart-breaker, Lumber, Mash, Minx, Neck, Philander(er), Prick-teaser, Rig, Toy, Trifle, Vamp, Wow

Flit Dart, Decamp, Flicker, Flutter, Moonlight, Scoot

Float(er), Floating, Flotation Balsa, Bob, Bubble, Buoy, Caisson, Camel, Carley, Clanger, Drift, Fleet, Flotsam, Flutterboard, Froth, Fucus, Jetsam, Jetson, Levitate, Lifebuoy, Milk, Natant, Neuston, Oropesa, Outrigger, Paddle, Planula, Pontoon, Pram, Quill, Raft, Ride, Sail, Skim, Sponson, Stick, Trimmer, Vacillate, Waft, Waggler, Waterwings

Floating garden Chinampa

Flock(s) Assemble, Bevy, Charm, Chirm, Company, Congregation, Dopping, Drove, Flight, Fold, Forgather, Gaggle, Gather, Gregatim, Herd, Mob, Rally, Sedge, Sord, Spring, Trip, Troop, Tuft, Vulgar, Wing, Wisp, Wool

Flog(ger), Flogging Beat, Birch, Breech, Cane, Cat, Exert, Flay, Hawk, Hide, Knout, Lace, Lambast, Larrup, Lash, Lather, Lick, Orbilius, Rope's end, Scourge, Sell, Strap, Tat, → **THRASH**, Thwack, Tout, Vapulate, Welt, Whip

Flood(ed) Awash, Bore, Cataclysm, Deluge, Deucalion's, Diffuse, Diluvium, Drown, Dump, Eger, Flash, Freshet, Gush, Inundate, Irrigate, Noachic, Overflow, Overswell, Overwhelm, Pour, Rage, Smurf, Spate, Speat, Suffuse, Swamp, Tide, → **TORRENT**, Undam, Washland

Floodgate St(a)unch

Floodlight Ashcan, Blond(e), One-key

Floor(ing) Area, Astound, Baffle, Barbecue, Beat, Benthos, Chess, Deck, Dev(v)el, Down, Entresol, Étage, Fell, Flags(tone), Flatten, Flight, Gravel, Ground, Kayo, KO, Mezzanine, Mould loft, Paralimnion, Parquet, Pelvic, Piano nobile, Pit, Planch, Platform, Puncheon, Screed, Shop, Stage, Story, Stump, Terrazzo, Tessella, Tessera, Thill, Trading, Woodblock

Flop Belly-landing, Bomb, Collapse, Dud, Failure, Fizzer, Fosbury, Lollop, Mare's-nest, Misgo, Phut, Plump, Purler, Washout, Whap, Whitewash

Flora Benthos, Biota, Cybele, Flowers, Intestinal

Florence, Florentine Tuscan

Florid Coloratura, Cultism, Flamboyant, Fresh, Gongorism, High, Red, Rococo, Rubicund, Ruddy, Taffeta

Florida Fa

Floss(y) Dental, Flashy, Florence, Ornate, Silk

▶ **Flotation** *see* FLOAT

Flotilla Armada, Escadrille

Flotsam Detritus, Driftwood, Flotage, Waift, Waveson, Weft

Flounce Falbala, Frill, Furbelow, Huff, Prance, Ruffle, Sashay, Toss

Flounder Blunder, Fluke, Reel, Slosh, Struggle, Stumble, Tolter, Toss, Wallow

Flour Cassava, Couscous(ou), Cribble, Crible, Farina, Graham, Gram, Kouskous, Meal, Middlings, Pinole, Plain, Powder, Red-dog, Rice, Rock, Rye, Self-raising, Soy(a), Strong, Wheatmeal, White, Wholegrain, Wholemeal, Wholewheat, Wood

Flourish(ed), Flourishing Blague, Bless, Bloom, Blossom, Boast, Brandish, Bravura, Burgeon, Cadenza, Epiphonema, Fanfare, Fiorita, Fl, Flare, Floreat, Florescent, Grow, Kicking, Lick, Melisma, Mort, Omar, Palmy, Paraph, Prosper, Rubric, Scroll, Swash, Tantara, Thrive, Tucket, Veronica, Vigorous, Wampish, Wave, Welfare

Flout Disdain, Disobey, Insult, Malign, Mock, Profane, Scorn, Scout

Flow(ing) Abound, Afflux, Cantabile, Cash, Current, Cursive, Cusec, Data, Distil, Ebb, Emanate, Estrang(h)elo, Fleet, Fluent, Fluid, Flush, Flux, Freeform, Gene, Gush, Knickpoint, Lahar, Laminar, Liquid, Loose-bodied, Nappe, Nickpoint, Obsequent, Onrush, Ooze, Popple, Pour, Purl, Rail(e), Rayle, Rill, Rin, Run, Scapa, Seamless, Seep, Seton, Setter, Slip, Slur, Spate, Spurt, Stream, Streamline, Teem, Tidal, Torrent, Trickle, Turbulent, Viscous

Flower (part), Flowering, Flowers, Flower bed Best, Bloom, Bloosme, Blossom, Cream, Develop, Efflorescence, Elite, Fiori, Inflorescence, Parterre, Passion, Plant, Pre-vernal, Prime, Quatrefeuille, Quatrefoil, Remontant, → RIVER, Rogation, Serotine, Spray, Square, Stalked, Stream, Trumpet, Verdoy, Vernal, Wreath

---

FLOWERS

4 letters:
Arum
Cyme
Disa
Flag
Gold
Gool
Gule
Irid
Iris
Knot
Lily
Pink
Rose
Wald
Weld

5 letters:
Agave
Aster
Brook
Bugle
Camas
Daisy
Enemy
Hosta
Oxlip
Padma
Pansy
Phlox
Poppy
Spink
Tansy

Toran
Tulip
Umbel
Yulan

6 letters:
Adonis
Arabis
Camash
Camass
Corymb
Cosmos
Crants
Dahlia
Gollan
Henbit

Madder
Maguey
Mimosa
Nuphar
Onagra
Orchid
Oxslip
Paeony
Pompom
Pompon
Protea
Scilla
Sesame
Silene
Smilax
Spadix

Tassel	Rampion	Scabious	Granadilla
Torana	Sulphur	Stapelia	Heliotrope
Wasabi	Verbena	Trollius	Immortelle
Yarrow		Tuberose	Nasturtium
	8 letters:	Turnsole	Pentstemon
7 letters:	Abutilon	Valerian	Poached egg
Aconite	Amaranth		Poinsettia
Alyssum	Argemone	**9 letters:**	Polyanthus
Amarant	Asphodel	Bald-money	Pulsatilla
Anemone	Bindi-eye	Belamoure	Snapdragon
Astilbe	Bluebell	Buttercup	Stavesacre
Bugloss	Carolina	Cineraria	Tibouchine
Campion	Clematis	Columbine	Touch-me-not
Cowslip	Cyclamen	Edelweiss	
Freesia	Daffodil	Eglantine	**11 letters:**
Fumaria	Floscule	Galingale	Boutonniere
Gentian	Foxglove	Gessamine	Bur-marigold
Gilt-cup	Gardenia	Hellebore	Gillyflower
Glacier	Geranium	Hydrangea	Loose-strife
Gladdon	Gillyvor	Jessamine	Meadow-sweet
Godetia	Gladioli	Melampode	Saintpaulia
Golland	Glory-pea	Pimpernel	
Gowland	Hepatica	Pyrethrum	**12 letters:**
Ipomoea	Hesperis	Rudbeckia	Hortus siccus
Kikumon	Hibiscus	Santonica	None-so-pretty
Lobelia	Kok-sagyz	Saxifrage	Pheasant's eye
Melilot	Larkspur	Speedwell	Tradescantia
Mimulus	Leucojum	Strobilus	
Nosegay	Magnolia		**13 letters:**
Petunia	Marigold	**10 letters:**	Flannelflower
Picotee	Myosotis	Bellamoure	
Primula	Oleander	Buttonhole	
Quamash	Primrose	Coronation	

▷ **Flower** may indicate a river
Flower arrangement, Flower work Barbola, Ikebana, Lei
Flowery Anthea, Anthemia, Damassin, Orchideous, → ORNATE, Pseudocarp, Verbose
▶ **Flu** see INFLUENZA
Fluctuate(r), Fluctuation Ambivalence, Balance, Seiche, Trimmer, Unsteady, Vacillate, Vary, Waver
Flue Chimney, Duct, Funnel, Pipe, Recuperator, Tewel, Uptake, Vent
Fluent(ly) Eloquent, Facile, Flowing, Glib, Liquid, Oracy, Verbose, Voluble
Fluff(y) Bungle, Dowl(e), Down, Dust, Dust bunny, Feathery, Flocculent, Floss, Flue, Fug, Fuzz, Girl, Lint, Mess-up, Muff, Noil, Oose, Ooze, Thistledown
Fluid Aldehyde, Amniotic, Anasarca, Ascites, Broo, Chyle, Cisterna, Colostrum, Condy's, Coolant, Dewdrop, Edema, Enema, Erf, Fixative, Fl, Humour, Joint-oil, Juice, Latex, → LIQUID, Lymph, Movable, Mucus, Oedema, Perfect, Perilymph, Plasma, Sap, Seminal, Serous, Serum, Shifting, Spermatic, Spittle, Succus, Synovia, Vitreum, Vril, Water
▷ **Fluid** may indicate an anagram

Fluke Accident, Anchor, Chance, Fan, Flounder, Ga(u)nch, Grapnel, Killock, Liver, Lobe, Redia, Schistosoma, Scratch, Upcast
Flummery BS, Pudding
Flummox Baffle, Bamboozle, Floor, Nonplus
Flunk Fail
Flunkey Chasseur, Clawback, Haiduck, Heyduck, Jeames, Lackey, Servant, Toady
Fluorescence, Fluorescent Bloom, Day-glo, Epipolism, Glow, Phosphorescence
Fluorine F
Flurry Bustle, Fluster, Haste, Hoo-ha, Shower
Flush(ed) Affluent, Beat, Busted, Even, Ferret, Florid, Flow, Gild, Hectic, Heyday, Hot, Level, Red, Rolling, Rose, Royal, Rud, Scour, Sluice, Spaniel, Start, Straight, Sypher, Thrill, Tierce, Vigour, Wash
Fluster(ed) Befuddle, Confuse, Disconcert, Faze, Flap, Jittery, Pother, Pudder, Rattle, Shake
Flute (player) Bellows-maker, Bohm, Channel, Claribel(la), Crimp, English, Fife, Fipple, Flageolet, German, Glass, Glyph, Groove, Marsyas, Nose, Ocarina, Piccolo, Pipe, Poogye(e), Quena, Shakuhachi, Sulcus, Thisbe, Tibia, Toot, Transverse, Whistle
Flutter Bat, Bet, Fan, Fibrillate, Flacker, Flaffer, Flaught, Flichter, Flicker, Flitter, Fly, → **GAMBLE**, Hover, Palpitate, Play, Pulse, Sensation, Twitter, Waft, Winnow
Flux D, Electric, Flow, Fusion, Luminous, Magnetic, Maxwell, Melt, Neutron, Panta rhei, Radiant, Tesla, Weber
Fly(ing), Flies Abscond, Agaric, Airborne, Alder, Alert, Antlion, Assassin, Astute, Aviation, Awake, Aware, A-wing, Baker, Bedstead, Bee, Black, Blister, Blowfly, Blue-arsed, Bluebottle, Bolt, Bot, Breese, Breeze, Brize, Brommer, Bulb, Bush, Cab, Caddis, Canny, Carriage, Carrot, Cecidomyia, Chalcid, Cheesehopper, Cheese skipper, Cleg, Cluster, Cock-a-bondy, Crane, Cuckoo, → **CUNNING**, Decamp, Deer, Diptera, Dobson, Doctor, Dolphin, Doodlebug, Dragon, Drake, Drone, Drosophila, Dry, Dung, Dutchman, Escape, Face, Fiacre, Flee, Flesh, Flit, Fox, Frit, Fruit, Glide, Glossina, Gnat, Grannom, Greenbottle, Greenhead, Hackle, Hairy Mary, Harl, Harvest, Hedge-hop, Herl, Hessian, Homoptera, Hop, Horn, Horse, Hover, Hurtle, Ichneumon, Instrument, Jenny-spinner, Jock Scott, Lace-wing, Lamp, Lantern, Laputan, March brown, Mosquito, Mossie, Moth, Motuca, Murragh, Musca, Mutuca, Namu, Needle, New Forest, Nymph, Onion, Opening, Ox-warble, Palmer, Para, Pilot, Pium, Plecopteran, Pomace, Rapid, Robber, Saucer, Sciaridae, Scorpion, Scotsman, Screwworm, Scud, Sedge, Silverhorn, Simulium, Smart, Smother, Snake, Snipe, Soar, Spanish, Speed, Spinner, Stable, Stream, Syrphidae, Tabanid, Tachina, Tail, Tear, Thrips, Tipula, Trichopteran, Tsetse, Tube, Turkey brown, Vamoose, Vinegar, Volatic, Volitate, Warble, Watchet, Water, Welshman's button, Wet, Wheat, Wide-awake, Willow, Wily, Wing, Yellow Sally, Yogic, Zebub, Zimb, Zipper
Fly-catcher Attercop, Clamatorial, Cobweb, Darlingtonia, Dionaea, King-bird, Phoebe, Spider, Tanrec, Tyrant
Flying-fox Fruit-bat, Kalong
Flying saucer UFO
Fly-killer Chowri, Chowry, DDT, Swat
Flyover Overpass
Foam(ing) Aerogel, Barm, Bubble, Froth, Lather, Mousse, Oasis®, Polystyrene, Ream, Scum, Seethe, Spindrift, Spooming, Spume, Sud(s), Surf, Wake, Wild water, Yeast, Yest
Fob Chain, Defer, Fub, Pocket, Slang

Focal, Focus Centre, Centrepiece, Converge, Fix, Hinge, Hub, Narrow, Nub, Pinpoint, Point, Prime, Principal, Spotlight, Train

Fodder Alfalfa, Browsing, Buckwheat, Cannon, Clover, Eatage, Emmer, Ensilage, Foon, Forage, Gama-grass, Grama, Guar, Hay, Lucerne, Oats, Oilcake, Pasture, Provender, Rye-grass, Sainfoin, Silage, Soilage, Stover, Straw

Foe Arch, Contender, → ENEMY, Opponent, Rival

Foetus Embryo

Fog Aerosol, Brume, Cloud, Damp, Fret, Haar, (London) Particular, Miasm(a), Mist, Murk, Obscure, Pea-soup(er), Roke, Sea-fret, Sea-haar, Smog, Smoke, Soup, Thick, Vapour, Yorkshire

Fogey Die-hard

Fogg Phileas, Solicitor

Foible Failing, Flaw, Idiosyncrasy, Quirk, Weakness

Foil(ed) Ba(u)lk, Chaff, Cross, Dupe, Epée, Fleurette, Frustrate, Gold, Gold leaf, Lametta, Leaf, Offset, Paillon, Pip, Scotch, Scupper, Silver, Stooge, Stump, Tain, Thwart, Touché

Foist Fob, Insert, Insinuate, Suborn, Wish

Fold(er), Folding, Folded, Folds Anticline, Bend, Binder, Close, Collapse, Concertina, Convolution, Corrugate, Cote, Crash, Crease, Crimp, Crinkle, Crunkle, Diapir, Diptych, Dog-ear, Double, Duo-tang®, Epicanthus, Epiploon, Fake, Fan, File, Fourchette, Fr(a)enum, Frill, Furl, Gather, Groin, Gyrus, Intussuscept, Jack-knife, Lap, Lapel, Lap(p)et, Lirk, Mesentery, Mitre, Monocline, Nappe, Nympha, Obvolute, Octuple, Omentum, Origami, Pastigium, Pen, Pericline, Pintuck, Pleach, → PLEAT, Plica, Plunging, Ply, Prancke, Pran(c)k, Ptyxis, Recumbent, Ruck(le), Ruga, Sheep-pen, Syncline, Triptych, Tuck, Vocal, Wrap

Foliage Coma, Finial, Frond, Frondescence, Greenery, Leafage, Leaves

Folio(s) Crown, Elephant, F(f), File, Foolscap, Imperial, Percy, Royal

Folk(sy) Beaker, Homespun, Kin, People, Public

Follicle Graafian

Follow(er), Following Acolyte, Acolyth, Adhere, Admirer, After, Agree, Amoret, And, Anthony, Attend(ant), Believer, Clientele, Consequence, Copy, Dangle, Disciple, Dog, Echo, Ensew, Ensue, Entourage, Epigon(e), Equipage, F, Fan, Groupie, Heel(er), Henchman, Hereon, Hunt, Jacob, Man, Merry men, Minion, Muggletonian, Myrmidon, Neist, Next, Obey, Pan, Post, Pursue, Rake, Road, Run, Satellite, School, Secundum, Seewing, Segue, Sequel, Seriation, Servitor, Shadow, Sheep, S(h)ivaite, Sidekick, Stag, Stalk, Stear, Steer, Subsequent, Succeed, Sue, Suivez, Supervene, Tag, Tail, Tantony, Trace, Track, Trail, Train, Use, Vocation, Votary

▷ **Follower** 'a follower' *may indicate* B

Folly Antic, Bêtise, Idiocy, Idiotcy, Imprudence, Lunacy, Mistake, Moria, Unwisdom, Vanity

Foment(ation) Arouse, Brew, Embrocation, Excite, Poultice, Stupe

Fond(ness) Amatory, Ardour, Dote, Keen, Loving, Partial, Penchant, Tender, Tendre

Fondant Ice, Sweet

Fondle Canoodle, Caress, Dandle, Grope, Hug, Nurse, Pet, Snuggle

Font Aspersorium, Bénitier, Bitmap, Delubrum, Ennage, Outline, Proportional, Source, True-type, Vector

Food Aliment, Ambrosia, Bakemeat, Balti, Batten, Battill, Battle, Bellytimber, Board, Bolus, Bord, Broth, Browse, Bully, Burger, Cate, Cereal, Chametz, Cheer, Cheese, Chop, Chow, Chuck, Chyme, Cocoyam, Collation, Comestible, Comfort, Commons, Convenience, Course, Curd, Deutoplasm, Dietetics, → DISH, Dodger, Dog's body,

Dunderfunk, Eats, Esculents, Eutrophy, Falafel, Fare, Fast, Fast casual, Felafel, Fodder, Forage, Frankenstein, Freedom, Fuel, Functional, Giffengood, Grub, Hangi, Hometz, Incaparina, Ingesta, Jootha, Jorts, Junk, Kai, Keep, Langar, Leben, Lerp, Long-pig, Maigre, Maki, Manna, Mato(o)ke, Matzoon, Meal, Meat, Muckamuck, Nacho, Nardoo, Nosebag, Nosh, Nourishment, Nourriture, Opsonium, Ort, Oven-ready, Pabulum, Pannage, Pap, Parev(e), Parve, Pasta, Pasture, Peck, Pemmican, Pizza, Prog, Provand, Provender, Provision, Pu(l)ture, Ration(s), Real, Rysttafel, Sambal, Samosa, Sap, Sashimi, Scaff, Scoff, Scran, Sitology, Sizings, Skin, Skran, Slow, Snack, Soil, Soul, Staple, Stodge, Sushi, Table, Tack, Takeaway, Tamale, Taro, Tempeh, Tempura, Teriyake, Tofu, Trimmings, Trophallaxis, Tuck(er), Vegeburger, Veggie-burger, Viand, Victuals, Vivers, Waffle, Yantia, Yittles, Yog(h)urt

Food-plant Laser, Silphium

Foodstore Delicatessen, Grocery, Larder, Pantry, Silo

Fool(hardy), Foolish(ness) Air-head, Anserine, April, Asinico, Assot, Berk, BF, Bob, Booby, Brainless, Brash, Buffoon, Cake, Capocchia, Chump, Clot, Clown, Cockeyed, Coof, Coxcomb, Cuif, Cully, Daft, Dagonet, Daw, Delude, Dessert, Divvy, Doat, Dote, Dummy, Dunce, Empty, Etourdi, Fatuous, Feste, Flannel(led), Folly, Fon, Fond, Fox, Gaby, Gaga, Galah, Git, Glaikit, Goat, Gobbo, Goon, Goose, Gooseberry, Groserts, Gubbins, Gull, Gullible, Halfwit, Hanky-panky, Hare-brained, Haverel, Highland, Huntiegowk, Hunt-the-gowk, Idiotic, Imbecile, Inane, Ineptitude, Injudicious, Jest, Joke, Kid, Kissel, Lark, Loon, Madcap, Mamba, Misguide, Mislead, Mome, Moron, Muggins, Niaiserie, Nignog, Ni(n)compoop, Ninny, Nong, Noodle, Nose-led, Oanshagh, Omadhaun, Patch, Pea-brained, Poop, Poupe, Punk, Rash, Sawney, Scogan, Scoggin, Senseless, Shallow, Shmo, Simp(leton), Snipe, Soft, Sot, Spoony, Stultify, → **STUPID**, Sucker, Tom (noddy), Trifle, Unwitty, Vice, Wantwit, Yorick, Yoyo, Zany

Foolproof Fail-safe

Foot(ing), Footwork, Feet Amphibrach, Amphimacer, Anap(a)est, Antibacchius, Antispast, Athlete's, Bacchius, Ball, Base, Board, Choliamb, Choree, Choriamb, Club, Cold, Cretic, Dactyl, Dance, Dipody, Dochmii, Dochmius, Epitrite, F, Hephthemimer, Hoof, Hoppus, Iamb(us), Immersion, Infantry, Ionic, Molossus, Ockodols, Pad, Paeon, Palama, Pastern, Paw, Pay, Pedate, Pedicure, Penthemimer, Pes, Plates, Podiatry, Podium, Proceleusmatic, Pyrrhic, Roothold, Scazon, Semeia, Serif, Shanks's mare, Shanks's pony, Spade, Splay, Spondee, Standing, Syzygy, Tarsus, Terms, Tootsie, Tootsy, Tootsy-wootsy, Tread, Trench, Tribrach, Trilbies, Triseme, Trochee, Trotter, Tube, Ungula, Verse, Wrong

Football(er) Aerial pingpong, American, Association, Australian Rules, Back, Banyana-banyana, Barbarian, Ba'spiel, Camp, Canadian, Centre, Fantasy, FIFA, Five-a-side, Flanker(back), Fly-half, Futsal, Gaelic, Goalie, Gridder, Half, Hooker, Keeper, Kicker, League, Libero, Lineman, Lock, Midfield, Pack, Pele, Pigskin, RU, Rugby, Rugger, Rules, Safety, Seven-a-side, Sevens, Soccer(oos), Sport, Stand-off, Striker, Subbuteo®, Sweeper, Table, Tight-end, Togger, Total, Touch(back), Wallgame, Wing, Wingman

Footboard Stretcher

Foot-fault Bunion, Corn, Hammer-toe, Verruca

Foothold Lodgement, Purchase, Stirrup

Footlights Floats

Footling Trivial

Footloose Peripatetic

Footman Attendant, Flunkey, Lackey, Pedestrian, Pompey, Yellowplush

Footnote Addendum, PS

Footpad Land-rat, Mugger, Robber

Footpath, Footway Banquette, Catwalk, Clapper, Track

Footplate Horseshoe

Footprint Ecological, Electronic, Ichnite, Ichnolite, Pad, Prick, Pug, Seal, Slot, Trace, Track, Tread, Vestige

Footrest, Footstool Coaster, Cricket, Hassock, Pouffe, Stirrup, Stool, Tramp

Footrot, Footsore Blister, Bunion, Corn, Halt, Surbate, Surbet, Weary, Wire-heel

Footslogger Infantryman

Footwashing Maundy, Nipter

Footwear Gumboot, Jackboot, → SHOE, Slipper, Sock, Spats, Stocking

Fop(pish) Apery, Barbermonger, Beau, Buck, Cat, Coxcomb, Dandy, Dude, Exquisite, Fallal, Fangled, Fantastico, Finical, La-di-da, Macaroni, Monarcho, Muscadin, Popinjay, Skipjack, Toff

For Ayes, Because, Concerning, Cos, Pro, Since, To

Forage Alfalfa, Fodder, Graze, Greenfeed, Ladino, Lucern(e), Pickeer, Prog, Raid, Rummage, Sainfoin, Search

Foray Attack, Creach, Creagh, Raid, Sortie, Spreagh

Forbear(ance), Forbearing Abstain, Clement, Endure, Indulgent, Lenience, Lineage, Longanimity, Mercy, Overgo, Pardon, Parent, Patient, Quarter, → REFRAIN, Suffer, Tolerant, Withhold

Forbid(den), Forbidding Ban, Bar, City, Denied, Don't, Dour, Enjoin, For(e)speak, Gaunt, Grim, Haram, Hostile, Loury, NL, Prohibit, Stern, Taboo, Tabu, Tapu, Tref(a), Verboten, Veto

Force(d), Forceful, Forces, Forcible Activist, Agency, Air-arm, Army, Back emf, Bathmism, Bind, Birr, Bludgeon, Body, Bounce, Brigade, Bring, Brunt, Bulldoze, Cadre, Capillary, Cascade, Centrifugal, Centripetal, Chi, Coerce, Coercive, Cogency, Commando, Compel, Constrain, Coriolis, Cram, Delta, Detachment, Dint, Domineer, Downflow, Dragoon, Drive, Duress(e), Dynamic, Dyne, E, Edge, Electromotive, Emphatic, Energetic, Equilibrant, Erdgeist, Erg, Exchange, Expeditionary, Extort, Extrude, F, Farci, Fifth, Fire brigade, Frogmarch, G, Gar, Gendarmerie, Gilbert, Gism, Gouge, Gravitational, Hale, Host, Hurricane, Impetus, Impose, Impress, Inertial, Instress, Intense, Irgun, Irrupt, Jism, Juggernaut, Kinetic, Kundalini, Labour, Land, Lashkar, Legion, Leverage, Life, Lift, Linn, Lorentz, Magnetomotive, Magnus, Make, Mana, Manpower, Market, Militia, Moment, Momentum, Muscle, Nature-god, Navy, Newton, Numen, Oblige, Od, Odyl(e), OGPU, Old Contemptibles, Orgone, Orotund, Personnel, Phrenism, Physical, Pigs, Pion, Pithy, Plastic, Police, Posse, Potent, Pound, Poundal, Prana, Press(gang), Pressure, Prise, Procrustean, Psyche, Psychic, Pull, Pushy, Put, Qi, Railroad, Rape, Ravish, Reave, Red Army, Regular, Require, Restem, Route, Rush, SAS, Sforzando, Shear, Snorting, Spent, Spetsnaz, Squad, Squirt, Steam(roller), Stick, Stiction, Strained, → STRESS, Strong-arm, Subject, Sword, TA, Task, Telergy, Telling, Territorial, The Bill, Thrust, Torque, Tractive, Troops, Van der Waals', Vehement, Vigorous, Vim, Violence, Vires, Vis, Vis visa, Vital, Vively, Vociferous, Vril, Weak, Wedge, Wrench, Wrest, Wring, Zap

▷ **Force(d)** *may indicate* an anagram

Forced labour Begar

Force-feeding Gavage

Forceps Bulldog, Capsule, Crow(s)bill, Hemostatic, Mosquito, Obstetrical, Pedicellaria, Pincers, Rongeur, Tenaculum, Thumb, Vulsella

Ford Anglia, Capri, Car, Crossing, Drift, Escort, Irish bridge, Sierra, Strid, Tin Lizzy, Wade

Forearm Cubital, Radius, Ulna

▶ **Forebear** *see* **FORBEAR**

Foreboding Anxiety, Augury, Cloudage, Croak, Feeling, Freet, Hoodoo, → **OMEN**, Ominous, Premonition, Presage, Presentiment, Sinister, Zoomantic

Forecast(er), Forecasting Augury, Auspice, Divine, Extrapolation, Horoscope, Long-range, Metcast, Metman, Numerical, Perm, Portend, Precurse, Predict, Presage, Prescience, Prevision, Prognosis, Prognosticate, Prophesy, Quant, Rainbird, Scry, Shipping, Skry, Soothsay, Spae, Tip, Weather

Foreclose Bar, Block, Obstruct, Preclude

Forefather(s) Ancestor, Elder, Forebear, Parent, Rude

Forefront Van, Vaward

Forehead Brow, Front(let), Frontal, Glabella(r), Sincipitum, Temple

Foreign(er) Alien, Amakwerekwere, Arab, Auslander, Barbarian, Easterling, Ecdemic, Eleanor, Ethnic, Étranger, Exclave, Exotic, External, Extraneous, Extrinsic, Forane, Forinsecal, Forren, Fraim, Fremit, Gaijin, German, Gringo, Gweilo, Malihini, Metic, Moit, Mote, Outlander, Outside, Oversea, Peregrine, Remote, → **STRANGE**, Stranger, Taipan, Tramontane, Uitlander, Unfamiliar, Wog

Foreknowledge Prescience

Foreman Baas, Boss, Bosun, Chancellor, Clicker, Gaffer, Ganger, Manager, Overseer, Steward, Superintendent, Tool pusher, Topsman, Walla(h)

Foremost First, Front, Leading, Primary, Prime, Supreme, Upfront, Van

▷ **Foremost** *may indicate* first letters of words following

Forenoon Undern

Forepart Cutwater, Front

Forerunner Augury, Harbinger, Herald, Messenger, Omen, Pioneer, Precursor, Prequel, Trailer, Vaunt-courier

Foresee Anticipate, Divine, Preview, Prophesy, Scry

Foreshadow Adumbrate, Augur, Bode, Forebode, Hint, Portend, Pre-echo, Prefigure, Presage, Type

Foreshow Betoken, Bode, Signify

Foresight Ganesa, Prescience, Prophecy, Prospect, Providence, Prudence, Taish, Vision

Foreskin Prepuce

Forest(ry) Arden, Ashdown, Black, Bohemian, Bracknell, Bush, Caatinga, Charnwood, Chase, Cloud, Dean, Elfin, Epping, Fontainebleau, Gallery, Gapo, Glade, Greenwood, Igapo, Jungle, Managed, Monte, Nandi, Nemoral, New, Petrified, Rain, Savernake, Selva, Sherwood, Silviculture, Taiga, Thuringian, Urman, Virgin, Waltham, → **WOOD**, Woodcraft

Forestall Anticipate, Head-off, Obviate, Pip, Pre-empt, Prevent, Queer, Scoop

Forester Foster, Lumberjack, Verderer, Walker, Woodman, Woodward

Foretaste Antepast, Antipasto, Appetiser, Pregustation, Prelibation, Preview, Sample, Trailer

Foretell(ing), Forewarn Augur, Bode, Caution, Divine, Fatidic, Forecast, Portend, Predict, Premonish, Presage, Previse, Prognosticate, Prophecy, Soothsay, Spae

Forethought Anticipation, Caution, Prometheus, Provision, Prudence

Forever Always, Amber, Ay(e), Eternal, Evermore, Keeps

▶ **Forewarn** *see* **FORETELL**

Foreword Introduction, Preamble, Preface, Proem, Prologue

For example Eg, Say, Vg, ZB

For fear Lest

Forfeit Deodand, Fine, Forgo, → **PENALTY**, Relinquish, Rue-bargain, Sconce

Forge(d), Forger(y) Blacksmith, Copy, Counterfeit, Drop, Dud, Fabricate, Fashion, Foundry, Hammer, Heater, Horseshoe, Ireland, Ironsmith, Lauder, Mint, Paper-hanger, Pigott, Progress, Rivet head, Rivet-hearth, Smith(y), Smithery, Spurious, Stiddie, Stiff, Stithy, Stumer, Tilt, Trucage, Truquage, Utter, Valley, Vermeer, Vulcan, Weld

Forget(ful), Forget-me-not Amnesia, Dry, Fluff, Lethe, Myosotis, Neglect, Oblivious, Omit, Overlook, Wipe

Forgive(ness), Forgiving Absolution, Amnesty, Clement, Condone, Divine, Lenity, Merciful, Overlook, Pardon, Placable, Remission, Remittal, Tolerant

Forgo(ne) Abstain, Expected, Refrain, Renounce, Waive

Forgotten Bygone, Lost, Missed, Sad

Forjeskit Overscutched

Fork(ed), Fork out Bifurcate, Biramous, Branch, Caudine, Cleft, Crotch, Crutch, Divaricate, Forficate, Fourchette, Grain, Graip, Morton's, Osmeterium, Pay, Prong, Replication, Runcible, Slave, Sucket, Tine, Toaster, Toasting, Tormenter, Tormentor, Trident, Trifid, Tuner, Tuning, Y

Forlorn(ness) Abject, Aidless, Desolate, Destitute, Drearisome, Miserable, Nightingale, Sad, Woebegone

▷ **Form** *may indicate* a hare's bed

Form(s) Alumni, Bench, Bumf, Cast, Ceremonial, Charterparty, Class, Clipped, Constitute, Coupon, Create, Document, Dress, Experience, Fashion, Feature, Fig, → **FIGURE**, Formula, Free, Game, Gestalt, Hare, Idea, Image, Inscape, Keto, Lexicalise, Life, Logical, Mode, Mood, Morph(ic), Morphology, Mould, Order, Originate, → **OUT OF FORM**, P45, Penitent, Physique, Protocol, Questionnaire, Redia, Remove, Rite, Ritual, Schedule, Shape, Shell, Sonata, Song, Stage, Stamp, State, Stem, Stereotype, Structure, Style, Symmetry, Talon, Ternary, Version

Formal Ceremonious, Conventional, Dry, Exact, Fit, Literal, Methodic, Official, Pedantic, Perfunctory, Precise, Prim, Routine, Set, Solemn, Starched, Stiff, Stodgy, Tails

Formality Amylum, Ceremony, Ice, Pedantry, Protocol, Punctilio, Starch

Formation Battalion, Brown, Configuration, Diapyesis, Echelon, Eocene, Fours, Growth, Line, Manufacture, Origin, Pattern, Phalanx, Prophase, Reaction, Riss, Serried, Wedge

▷ **Former** *may indicate* something that forms

Former(ly) Ance, Auld, Before, Ci-devant, Earlier, Ere-now, Erst(while), Ex, Late, Maker, Matrix, Old, Once, One-time, Past, Previous, Prior, Pristine, Quondam, Sometime, Then, Umquhile, Whilom, Yesterday

Formidable Alarming, Armipotent, Battleaxe, Fearful, Forbidding, Gorgon, Powerful, Redoubtable, Shrewd, Stoor, Stour, Stowre, Sture, Tiger

Formless Amorphous, Invertebrate, Nebulous, Shapeless

▷ **Form of, Forming** *may indicate* an anagram

Formosan Tai

Formula(te) Define, Devise, Doctrine, Empirical, Equation, Frame, Graphic, Incantation, Invent, Kekule, Lurry, Molecular, Paternoster, Prescription, Protocol, Prunes and prisms, → **RECIPE**, Reduction, Rite, Ritual, Stirling's, Structural

Forsake Abandon, Desert, Quit, Renounce

Forsooth Certes, Certy, Even, Marry, Quotha

For sure Pukka

Forswear Abandon, Abjure, Disavow, Renounce, Reny

Forsyte Fleur, Saga, Soames

Fort(ification), Fortress Acropolis, Alamo, Alhambra, Balclutha, Bastille, Bastion,

Battlement, Bawn, Blockhouse, Bonnet, Breastwork, Bridgehead, Burg, Casbah, Castellated, Castellum, Castle, Citadel, Contravallation, Counterscarp, Crémaillère, Demilune, Deva, Dun, Earthwork, Edinburgh, Enceinte, Epaule, Escarpment, Fastness, Fieldwork, Flanker, Flèche, Fortalice, Fortilage, Fortlet, Fraise, Ft, Gabion(ade), Garrison, Gatehouse, Golconda, Haven, Hedgehog, Hill, Hornwork, Kaim, Kame, Kasba(h), Keep, Knox, La(a)ger, Lauderdale, Louisbourg, Maiden, Malakoff, Martello tower, Masada, Merlon, Mile-castle, Moineau, Motte and bailey, Orillion, Pa(h), Peel, Pele, Pentagon, Place, Przernysl, Rampart, Rath, Ravelin, Redoubt, Reduit, Ring, Salient, Sallyport, Sangar, Sconce, Stavropol, Stronghold, Sumter, Talus, Tenaille, Terreplein, Tête-du-pont, Ticonderoga, Tower, Tower of London, Trench, Vallation, Vitrified, William, Worth
Forte F, Métier, Specialty, Strength
Forth Away, From, Hence, Out
Forthright(ness) Blunt, Candid, Direct, Four-square, Frank, Glasnost, Prompt
Forthwith Anon, Directly, Eft(soons), Immediately
Fortify Arm, Augment, Brace, Casemate, Embattle, Lace, Munify, Soup up, Steel, → **STRENGTHEN**
Fortitude Endurance, Grit, Mettle, Patience, Pluck, → **STAMINA**
Fortune, Fortunate, Fortuitous Auspicious, Blessed, Blest, Coincident, Godsend, Happy, → **LUCKY**, Madoc, Opportune, Providential, Well
Fortune teller, Fortune-telling Auspicious, Bonanza, Bumby, Cartomancy, Chaldee, Cha(u)nce, Destiny, Dukkeripen, Fame, Fate, Felicity, Genethliac, Geomancy, Hap, Hydromancy, I Ching, Lot, Luck, Mint, Motser, Motza, Oracle, Packet, Palmist, Peripety, Pile, Prescience, Pyromancy, Sibyl, Soothsayer, Sortilege, Spaewife, Success, Taroc, Tarok, Tarot, Tyche, Wealth, Windfall
Forty, Forties Capot, F, Hungry, Kemple, Roaring
Forty-ninth Parallel
Forum Arena, Assembly, Debate, Platform, Tribunal
Forward(s) Accede, Advanced, Ahead, Along, Anterior, Arch, Assertive, Assuming, Bright, Early, Flanker, Forrad, Forrit, Forth, Fresh, Future, Hasten, Hooker, Immodest, Impudent, Insolent, Lock, Malapert, On(wards), Pack, Pert, Petulant, Porrect, Precocious, → **PROGRESS**, Promote, Prop, Readdress, Redirect, Scrum, Send, Stem, To(ward), Van, Wing
Fossil(ised), Fossils Amber, Ammonite, Baculite, Belemnite, Blastoid(ea), Calamite, Ceratodus, Chondrite, Conodont, Corallian, Cordaites, Creodont, Crinite, Derived, Encrinite, Eohippus, Eozoon, Eurypterus, Exuviae, Fairy stone, Florula, Florule, Fogy, Goniatite, Graptolite, Hipparion, Hominid, Ichnite, Ichnolite, Ichnology, Ichthyodurolite, Ichthyolite, Index, Jew's stone, Kenyapithecus, Lepidostrobus, Lingulella, Living, Mosasauros, Nummulite, Odontolite, Olenus, Oligocene, Orthoceras, Osteolepis, Ostracoderm, Oxfordian, Pal(a)eo-, Pentacrinus, Petrifaction, Phytolite, Plesiosaur, Pliohippus, Pliosaur, Psilophyton, Pteridosperm, Pterodactyl(e), Pterygotus, Pythonomorph, Relics, Reliquiae, Remanié, Reworked, Sigillaria, Sinanthropus, Sivatherium, Snakestone, Stigmaria, Stromatolite, Taphonomy, Teleosaurus, Tentaculite, Titanotherium, Trace, Trilobite, Uintatherium, Wood-opal, Zinganthropus, Zone, Zoolite
Foster (child, mother), Fostering Adopt, Cherish, Da(u)lt, Develop, Farm out, Feed, Fornent, Further, Harbour, Incubation, Metapelet, Metaplot, Nourish, Nourse(l), Noursle, Nousell, Nurse, Nurture, Nuzzle, → **REAR**
Foul, Foul-smelling Base, Beray, Besmirch, Besmutch, Bewray, Bungle, → **DEFILE**, Dreggy, Drevill, Enseam, Evil, Feculent, Funky, Gross, Hassle, Hing, Mephitic, Mud, Noisome, Olid, Osmeterium, Paw(paw), Professional, Putid, Putrid, → **RANK**,

Reekie, Rotten, Sewage, Soiled, Squalid, Stagnant, Stain, Stapelia, Technical, Unclean, Unfair, Vile, Violation, Virose

▷ **Foul** *may indicate an anagram*

Found (in) Among, Base, Bed, Bottom, Build, Cast, Caught, Emong, Endow, → **ESTABLISH**, Eureka, Institute, Introduce, Met, Occur, Plant, Recovered, Rest, Start, Table

Foundation(s) Base, Bedrock, Corset, Cribwork, Establishment, Footing, Girdle, Grillage, Ground, Groundwork, Hard-core, Hypostasis, Infrastructure, Institution, Matrix, Panty girdle, Pile, Pitching, Roadbed, Rockefeller, Root, Scholarship, Stays, Stereobate, Subjacent, Substrata, Substructure, Trackbed, Underlie, Underlinen

▷ **Foundations** *may indicate* last letters

Founder Author, Bell, Collapse, Crumple, Fail, Inventor, Iron-master, Miscarry, Oecist, Oekist, Patriarch, Perish, Settle, Sink, Steelman, Stumble

Fount Aonian, Digital, Source, Springlet, Wrong

Fountain Acadine, Aganippe, Arethusa, Bubbler, Castalian, Cause, Conduit, Drinking, Fauwara, Forts, Gerbe, Head, Hippocrene, Jet, Pant, Pirene, Salmacis, Scuttlebutt, Soda, Spring, Trevi, Well-spring, Youth

Fountain basin Laver

Four(times), Foursome, Four-yearly Cater, Georges, Horsemen, IV, Mess, Penteteric, Qid, Quartet, Quaternary, Quaternion, Reel, Tessara, Tessera, Tetrad, Tetralogy, Tiddy, Warp

Fourpence Groat

Fourteenth Bastille, Trecento, Valentine

Fourth Deltaic, Estate, Fardel, Farl(e), Firlot, Forpet, Forpit, July, Martlet, Perfect, Quarter, Quartet, Quaternary, Quintan, Sesquitertia, Tritone

Fowl Barnyard, Biddy, Boiler, Brahma, Brissle-cock, Burrow-duck, Capon, Chicken, Chittagong, Cob, Cock, Coot, Domestic, Dorking, Duck, Ember, Gallinaceous, Gallinule, Game, Gleenie, Guinea, Hamburg(h), Heather-bleat(er), → **HEN**, Houdan, Jungle, Kora, Leghorn, Mallee, Moorhen, Orpington, Papageno, Partridge, Pheasant, Pintado, Plymouth Rock, Poultry, Quail, Rooster, Rumkin, Rumpy, Scrub, Solan, Spanish, Spatchcock, Spitchcock, Sultan, Sussex, Teal, Turkey, Wyandotte

Fox(y) Alopecoid, Arctic, Baffle, Blue, Charley, Charlie, Corsac, Cunning, Desert, Fennec, Floor, Flying, Fool, Friend, Fur, Grey, Kit, Lowrie(-tod), Outwit, Pug, Puzzle, Quaker, Red, Reynard, Rommel, Russel, Silver, Skulk, → **SLY**, Swift, Tod, Uffa, Uneatable, Vixen, White, Zerda, Zoril(le), Zorro

Foxglove Cowflop, Deadmen's bells, Digitalis, Witches'-thimble

Foxhole Earth

Foyer Hall, Lobby

Fracas Brawl, Dispute, Mêlée, Prawle, Riot, Rumpus, Scrum, Shindig, Uproar

Fraction Common, Complex, Compound, Continued, Decimal, Improper, Ligroin, Mantissa, Mixed, Packing, Part, Partial, Piece, Proper, Scrap, Simple, Some, Vulgar

Fracture Break, Colles, Comminuted, Complicated, Compound, Crack, Fatigue, Fault, Fissure, Greenstick, Hairline, Impacted, Pathological, Platy, Pott's, Rupture, Shear, Simple, Split, Stress

Fragile Brittle, Crisp, Delicate, Frail, Frangible, Nesh, Slender, Tender, Vulnerable, Weak

Fragment(s) Atom, Bit, Bla(u)d, Brash, Breccia, Brockram, Cantlet, Clastic, Crumb, End, Flinder, Fritter, Frust, Graile, Lapilli, Mammock, Mite, Morceau, Morsel, Ort, → **PARTICLE**, Piece, Piecemeal, Potshard, Potsherd, Relic, Restriction, Rubble, Scrap, Segment, Shard, Shatter, Sheave, Shiver, Shrapnel, Shred, Skerrick, Sliver,

Smithereens, Smithers, Snatch, Splinter

▷ **Fragment of** *may indicate* a hidden word

Fragrance, Fragrant Aromatic, Attar, Bouquet, Conima, Nosy, Odour, Olent, → **PERFUME**, Pot-pourri, Redolent, → **SCENT**, Sent, Spicy, Suaveolent

Frail Brittle, Creaky, Delicate, Feeble, Flimsy, → **FRAGILE**, Puny, Slight, Slimsy, Tottery, Weak

Framboesia Morula, Yaws

Frame(work) Adjust, Airer, Angle, Armature, Bail, Bayle, Body, Bow, Brickbat, Build, Cadge, Cadre, Cage, Case, Casement, Casing, Cent(e)ring, Centreing, Chase, Chassis, Clamper, Climbing, Coaming, Cold, Compages, Companion, Cowcatcher, Cradle, Cratch, Cribwork, Deckel, Deckle, Draw, Dutchwife, Entablature, Everest pack, Fabric, Fender, Fiddley, Fit-up, Flake, Form, Frisket, Gallows, Gambrel, Gantry, Garden, Gate, Gauntry, Grid-iron, Haik, Hake, Heck, Horse, Hull, Jungle gym, Lattice, Limit, Louvre, Mantel, Mixter, Mood, Mount, Mullion, Muntin(g), Newsreel, Ossature, Outrigger, Oxford, Pack, Pannier, Pantograph, Parameter, Partners, Passe-partout, Pergola, Physique, Pillory, Plant, Plot, Plummer-block, Poppet head, Portal, Puncheon, Quilting, Rack, Rave, Redact, Retable, Rib(bing), Rim, Sampling, Sash, Scaffold, Scuncheon, Sect(ion), Set, Setting, Skeleton, Spring-box, Stanchion, Stand, Stern, Still(age), Stitch up, Stocking, Stocks, Straddle, Stretcher, Stretching, Stroma, → **STRUCTURE**, Studwork, Surround, Swift, Tabernacle, Taboret, Tambour, Tent(er), Tepee, Time, Timeline, Trave, Trellis, Tress, Tressel, Trestle, Tribble, Trussing, Vacuum, Victimize, Walking, Wattle, Ways, Window, Yoke, Zarf, Zimmer®

Framley Parsonage

Franc Fr, Leu, Lev, Lew

France Anatole, Marianne, RF, Thibault

Franchise Charter, Contract, Liberty, Pot-wall(op)er, Privilege, Right, Suffrage, Vote, Warrant

Franciscan Custos, Minorite, Observant, Salesian, Scotist, Tertiaries

Francium Fr

Franck Cesar

Frank(ish) Artless, Austrasia, Blunt, → **CANDID**, Direct, Easy, Free, Free-spoken, Honest, Ingenuous, Man-to-man, Merovingian, Natural, Open, Outspoken, Overt, Postage, Postmark, Raw, Ripuarian, Salian, Sincere, Squareshooter, Stamp, Straight, Straightforward, Sty, Upfront

Frankincense Laser, Olibanum, Thus

Frans, Franz Hals, Lehar

Frantic Demoniac, Deranged, Distraught, Frenzied, Hectic, Mad, Overwrought, Phrenetic, Rabid, Violent, Whirl(ing)

▷ **Frantic** *may indicate* an anagram

Frappé Iced

Fraternise, Fraternity Affiliate, Brotherhood, Burschenschaft, Consort, Elk, Fellowship, Lodge, Mingle, Moose, Order, Shrine, Sodality

Fratricide Cain

Fraud(ulent) Barratry, Bobol, Bubble, Charlatan, Cheat, Chisel, Collusion, Covin, Cronk, Deceit, Diddle, Do, Fineer, Gyp, Humbug, Hypocrite, → **IMPOSTOR**, Imposture, Jiggery-pokery, Jobbery, Knavery, Liar, Peculator, Piltdown, Pious, Pseud(o), Put-up, Ringer, Rip-off, Roguery, Rort, Salami technique, Scam, Shoulder surfing, South Sea Bubble, Stellionate, Supercherie, Swindle, Swiz(z), Swizzle, Tartuffe, Trick

Fraught Perilous

Fray(ed) Bagarre, Brawl, Contest, Feaze, Frazzle, Fret, Fridge, Ravel, Riot, Scrimmage, Wigs on the green

Freak Cantrip, Caprice, Chimera, Control, Deviant, Geek, Jesus, Lusus naturae, Mooncalf, Sport, Teras, Whim, Whimsy

Freckle Ephelis, Fern(i)tickle, Fern(i)ticle, Heatspot, Lentigines, Lentigo, Spot, Sunspot

Frederick Barbarossa, Carno, Great

Free(d), Freely Acquit, Assoil, At large, Buckshee, Candid, Canny, Church, Clear, Complimentary, Cuffo, Dead-head, Deliver, Deregulate, Devoid, Disburden, Disburthen, Disengage, Disentangle, Eleutherian, Emancipate, Enfranchise, Enlarge, Excuse, Exeem, Exeme, Exempt, Exonerate, Extricate, Familiar, Footloose, Frank, French, Gratis, House, Idle, Immune, Indemnify, Independent, Kick, Large, Lavish, Lax, Leisure, Let, Liberate, Loose, Manumit, Open, Parole, Pro bono, Quit(e), Range, Ransom, Redeem, → **RELEASE**, Relieve, Rescue, Reskew, Rick, Rid, Sciolto, Scot, Solute, Spare, Spring, Stald, Stall, Trade, Unbowed, Unlock, Unloosen, Unmew, Unmuzzle, Unshackle, Unsnarl, Untangle, Untie, Untwist, Vacant, Verse, Voluntary

▷ **Free** *may indicate* an anagram

Freebooter Cateran, Corsair, Franklin, Marauder, Moss-trooper, Pad, Pindaree, Pindari, Pirate, Rapparee, Snapha(u)nce, Snaphaunch, Thief, Viking

Freedom Abandon, Autonomy, Breadth, Carte blanche, Eleutherian, Exemption, Fear, Fling, Four, Immunity, Impunity, Independence, Laisser aller, Laisser faire, Laissez aller, Laissez faire, Latitude, Liberty, Licence, Moksha, Play, Range, Releasement, Speech, Uhuru, UNITA, Want, Worship

Free gift Bonus, Charism, Perk

Freehold(er) Enfeoff, Franklin, Frank tenement, Odal(l)er, Seisin, Udal(ler), Yeoman

Freelance Eclectic, Independent, Mercenary, Stringer

Freeloader Sponge

▷ **Freely** *may indicate* an anagram

Freeman Burgess, Ceorl, Churl, Franklin, Liveryman, Thegn, Thete, Villein

Freemason(ry), Freemason's son Craft, Lewis, Lodge, Moose, Templar

Free-range Eggs, Outler

Free State Orange

Freethinker Agnostic, Bradlaugh, Cynic, Libertine, Sceptic

Free-trade(r) Cobdenism, Wright

Free-wheel Coast

Freeze(s), Freezer, Freezing Alcarrazo, Arctic, Benumb, Congeal, Cool, Cryogenic, Cryonics, Eutectic, Freon®, Frost, Geal, Harden, Ice, Lyophilize, Moratoria, Nip, Numb, Paralyse, Regelate, Riss, Stiffen, Wage

Freight Cargo, Carriage, Fraught, Goods, Load

French(man), Frenchwoman Alsatian, Anton, Aristo, Basque, Breton, Cajun, Crapaud, Creole, Dawn, Dreyfus, Emil(e), Frog, Gallic(e), Gaston, Gaul, Gombo, Grisette, Gumbo, Huguenot, Joual, Jules, M, Mamselle, Marianne, Midi, Monsieur, Mounseer, Neo-Latin, Norman, Parleyvoo, Pierre, René, Rhemish, Savoyard, Yves

Frenetic Deranged, Frantic, Overwrought

Frenzied, Frenzy Amok, Berserk, Corybantic, Deliration, Delirium, Demoniac, Enrage, Enrapt, Euhoe, Euoi, Evoe, Feeding, Fit, Fury, Hectic, Hysteric, Lune, Maenad, Mania, Must, Nympholepsy, Oestrus, Phrenetic, Rage

Frequency, Frequent(er), Frequently Angular, Attend, Audio, Bandwidth, Channel, Common, Constant, Expected, Familiar, Forcing, Formant, FR, Fresnel, Gene, Habitué, Hang-out, Haunt, Hertz, High, Incidence, Intermediate, Low,

Medium, Megahertz, Natural, Often, Penetrance, Pulsatance, Radio, Recurrent, Regular, Relative, Resort, Spatial, Spectrum, Superhigh, Thick, Ultrahigh, Video
Fresco Intonaco, Sinopia, Tempera
Fresh(en), Freshness Airy, Anew, Aurorean, Brash, Caller, Chilly, Clean, Crisp, Dewy, Entire, Forward, Green, Hot, Insolent, Lively, Maiden, Nas(s)eem, New, Novel, Quick, Rebite, Recent, Roral, Roric, Rorid, Smart, Span-new, Spick, Sweet, Tangy, Uncured, Verdure, Vernal, Virent, Virescent
Freshman Bajan, Bejan(t), Fresher, Frosh, Pennal, Plebe, Recruit, Student
Fret(ful) Chafe, Filigree, Fray, Grate, Grecque, Haze, Impatient, Irritate, Ornament, Peevish, Repine, Rile, Ripple, Roil, Rub, Stop, Tetchy, Tracery, Whittle, Worry
Friable Crisp, Crumbling, Powdery
Friar(s) Augustinian, Austin, Bacon, Barefoot, Black, Brother, Bungay, Capuchin, Carmelite, Conventual, Cordelier, Crutched, Curtal, Dervish, Dominican, Fra(ter), Franciscan, Frate, Grey, Jacobin, Laurence, Limiter, Lymiter, Minim, Minor, Minorite, → **MONK**, Observant, Observantine, Preaching, Predicant, Recollet, Redemptionist, Rush, Tuck, White
Friction Attrition, Conflict, Dissent, Drag, Rift, Rub, Skin, Sliding, Stiction, Stridulation, Tribology, Tripsis, Wear, Xerotripsis
Friday Black, Casual, Girl, Golden, Good, Holy, Man, Person, Savage
Fridge Esky®, Freezer, Icebox, Rub
Fried cake Croquette, Cruller
Friend(ly), Friends Achates, Affable, Ally, Alter ego, Ami(cable), Amigo, Approachable, Associate, Avuncular, Belamy, Benign, Boet(ie), Bosom, Bra, Bro, Bru, Bud(dy), Buster, Butty, Cackermander, Cater-cousin, China, Choma, Chommie, Chum, Circle, Cobber, Cock, Cohort, Compadre, Companion, Companionable, Comrade, Confidant, Cordial, Couthie, Couthy, Crony, Cully, Damon, Downhome, Edwin, Ehoa, En ami, Fairweather, False, Familiar, Feare, Feathered, Feer, Fere, Fiere, Folksy, Gemütlich, Gossib, Gossip, Gregarious, Hail-fellow-well-met, Homeboy, Ingle, Intimate, Inward, Jong, Kith, Litigation, Marrow, Mate, McKenzie, Mentor, Mucker, Near, Next, Oppo, Outgoing, Paisano, Pal, Paranymph, Pen, Penn, Pheere, Privado, Prochain ami, Prochein ami, Pythias, Quaker, Sidekick, Sociable, Societal, Sport, Steady, Tillicum, Tonga, Tosh, Wack(er), Warm, Well-wisher, Wus(s), Yaar
Friendliness, Friendship Amity, Bonhomie, Camaraderie, Contesseration, Entente, Platonic, Rapprochement, Sodality
Frieze Dado, Metope, Penistone, Zoophorus
Fright(en), Frightened, Frightful Afear, Affear(e), Agrise, Agrize, Agryze, Alarm, Aroint, Aroynt, Ashake, Chilling, Cow, Dare, Da(u)nt, Deter, Eek, Eerie, Faceache, Fear(some), Flay, Fleg, Fleme, Fley, Flush, Gallow, Gally, Ghast, Gliff, Glift, Grim, Grisly, Hairy, Horrid, Horrific, Intimidate, Ordeal, Panic, Scar, → **SCARE**, Scarre, Scaur, Schrecklich, Shocking, Sight, Skear, Skeer, Skrik, Spine-chilling, Spook, Stage, Startle, Terrible, Terrify, Terror, Tirrit, Unco, White-knuckle, Windy, Yitten
Frigid Bleak, Cold, Dry, Frory, Frosty, Ice, Indifferent, Serac, Stiff
Frill Armil, Armilla, Bavolet, Falbala, Furbelow, Jabot, Newgate, Oriental, Ornament, Papillote, Ruche, Ruff(le), Tucker, Valance
▷ **Frilly** *may indicate* an anagram
Fringe(s), Fringed Bang, Border, Bullion, Celtic, Ciliated, Ciliolate, Edge, Fall, Fimbria, Frisette, Interference, Laciniate, Loma, Lunatic, Macramé, Macrami, Newgate, Pelmet, Peripheral, Robin, Ruff, Run, Thrum, Toupee, Toupit, Tsitsith,

Tzitzit(h), Valance, Verge, Zizith

Frisian Holstein

Frisk(y) Caper, Cavort, Curvet, Fisk, Flimp, Frolic, Gambol, Search, Skip, Wanton

Fritillary Snake's-head

Fritter Batter, Beignet, Dribble, Dwindle, Fragment, Fribble, Pakora, Piddle, Potter, Puf(f)taloon, Squander, Waste, Wonder

Frivolous, Frivolity Butterfly, Empty(-headed), Etourdi(e), Facetious, Featherbrain, Flighty, Flippant, Frothy, Futile, Giddy, Idle, Inane, Levity, Light, Light-minded, Lightweight, Playboy, Skittish, Trifling, Trivial

Frizz(le), Frizzly Afro, Crape, Crimp, Crinkle, Curly, Fry, Fuzz, Hiss

Frock Dress, Gown, Ordain, Robe, Smock

Frog Anoura, Anura, Batrachia(n), Braid, Bullfrog, Cape nightingale, Crapaud, Depression, Flying, Fourchette, Frenchman, Frush, Goliath, Hairy, Hyla, Marsupial, Mounseer, Nic, Nototrema, Paddock, Paradoxical, Peeper, Pelobatid, Platanna, Puddock, Puttock, Rana, Ranidae, Tree, Wood, Xenopus

Frogman Diver

Frogmouth Mo(re)poke, Podargus

Frog spawn Redd, Tadpole

Frolic(some) Bender, Bust(er), Cabriole, Caper, Cavort, Curvet, Disport, Escapade, → **FRISK(Y)**, Fun, Galravage, Galravitch, Gambol, Gammock, Gil(l)ravage, How's your father, Jink, Kittenish, Lark, Play, Pollick, Prank, Rag, Rand, Rig, Romp, Scamper, Skylark, Splore, Sport, Spree, Stooshie, Tittup, Wanton

From A, Against, Ex, For, Frae, Off, Thrae

Frond Fern, Leaf, Tendril

Front(al), Frontman Antependium, Anterior, Bow, Brass, Brow, Cold, Cover, Dead, Dickey, Dicky, Esplanade, Facade, Face, Fore(head), Forecourt, Foreground, Groof, Grouf, Grufe, Head, Home, Metope, National, Newscaster, Occluded, Paravant, People's, Plastron, Polar, Popular, Pose, Preface, Presenter, Pro, Prom, Prow, Rhodesian, Sector, Sinciput, Stationary, Tabula, Temerity, Van, Vaward, Ventral, Warm, Western

Frontier(sman) Afghan, Barrier, Border, Boundary, Checkpoint, Limit, Limitrophe, List, March, North-west, Outpost, Pathan, Wild West

Front page P1

Front-ranker Pawn

Frost(ing), Frosty, Frostbite Air, Alcorza, Black, Chill, Cranreuch, Cryo-, Freon®, Frigid, Frore(n), Frorne, Glacé, Ground, Hoar, Hore, Ice, Icing, Jack, Mat, Nip, Rime, Silver, Trench foot, White

Froth(y) Barm, Bubble, Cuckoospit, Cuckoospit(tle), Despumate, Foam, Frogspit, Gas, Head, Lather, Mantle, Nappy, Off-scum, Ream, Saponin, Scum, Seethe, Shallow, Spoom, Spoon, Spume, Sud, Yeasty, Yest, Zephir

Frown Glower, Knit, Lour, Lower, Scowl

Frozen Froren, Frorn(e), Frory, Gelid, Glacé, Graupel, Ice-bound, Spellbound, Static, Tundra

Fructification, Fructify, Fructose Aeci(di)um, Basidium, Fertilise, Flower, Fruit, Inulin

Frugal Meagre, Parsimonious, Provident, Prudent, Scant, Skimpy, Spare, Spartan, Thrifty

Fruit(ing), Fruit tree, Fruity Accessory, Achene, Acinus, Akene, Allocarpy, Apothecium, Autocarp, Bacciform, Cedrate, Coccus, Compot(e), Confect, Conserve, Cremocarp, Crop, Dessert, Drupe, Eater, Encarpus, Etaerio, First, Follicle, Forbidden, Fritter, Harvest, Issue, Multiple, Orchard, Poof, Primeur, Primitiae,

Product(ion), Pseudocarp, Regma(ta), Replum, Result, Return, Rich, Ripe,
Schizocarp, Seed, Silicle, Silicula, Siliqua, Silique, Soft, Sorosis, Stoneless, Succade,
Sweetie, Sweety, Syconium, Syncarp, Utricle, Valve, Wall, Xylocarp, Yield

FRUIT

3 letters:
Fig
Haw
Hep
Hip
Hop
Jak
Key
Nut

4 letters:
Akee
Bael
Bito
Date
Gage
Gean
Jack
Kaki
Kiwi
Lime
Pear
Pepo
Plum
Pome
Sloe
Sorb
Star
Tuna
Ugli®
Yuzu

5 letters:
Ackee
Anana
Anona
Apple
Assai
Berry
Bread
Choko
Genip
Gourd
Grape
Guava

Jaffa
Lemon
Lotus
Mango
Melon
Nancy
Naras
Nashi
Nelis
Olive
Papaw
Prune
Rowan
Whort

6 letters:
Almond
Ananas
Babaco
Banana
Banian
Banyan
Carica
Cherry
Chocho
Citron
Citrus
Comice
Damson
Durian
Durion
Emblic
Feijoa
Lichee
Litchi
Longan
Lychee
Mammee
Medlar
Narras
Nelies
Oilnut
Orange
Papaya
Pawpaw

Pepino
Pomace
Pomelo
Pruine
Quince
Raisin
Rennet
Russet
Samara
Sapota
Sharon
Squash
Tomato
Wampee

7 letters:
Apricot
Avocado
Bullace
Chayote
Crab-nut
Cypsela
Geebung
Genipap
Gherkin
Kumquat
Leechee
Litchee
Manjack
Morello
Passion
Pimento
Pinguin
Poperin
Pumpkin
Pupunha
Ruddock
Satsuma
Soursop
Tangelo
Winesap

8 letters:
Abricock
Apricock

Bergamot
Bilberry
Blimbing
Calabash
Dewberry
Fraughan
Goosegog
Hagberry
Hastings
Hedgehog
Kalumpit
Minneola
Mulberry
Physalis
Plantain
Prunello
Rambutan
Rathripe
Sebesten
Shaddock
Sunberry
Tamarind
Tayberry
Teaberry
Waxberry

9 letters:
Algarroba
Apple-john
Aubergine
Bakeapple
Blueberry
Butternut
Canteloup
Carambola
Caryopsis
Cherimoya
Cranberry
Freestone
Haanepoot
Hackberry
Mirabelle
Myrobalan
Naseberry
Nectarine

Neesberry
Ortanique
Persimmon
Plumdamas
Poppering
Ratheripe
Sapodilla
Saskatoon
Shadberry
Sorb-apple
Star-apple
Tangerine
Tomatillo
Victorine
Whimberry
Whinberry

10 letters:
Blackberry
Canteloupe
Cherimoyer
Clementine
Clingstone
Elderberry
Granadilla
Grenadilla
Jargonelle
Mangosteen
Paddymelon
Pick-cheese
Punicaceae
Scaldberry
Watermelon

Youngberry

11 letters:
Boysenberry
Hesperidium
Huckleberry
Lingonberry
Marionberry
Pampelmoose
Pampelmouse
Pomegranate
Pompelmoose
Pompelmouse
Salmonberry

12 letters:
Blackcurrant
Checkerberry
Custard-apple
Service-berry
Whortleberry

13 letters:
Bullock's heart
Sapodilla plum

14 letters:
Worcesterberry

Fruitful(ness) Calathus, Ephraim, Fat, Fecund, Feracious, Fertile, Productive, Prolific, Uberty, Worthwhile

Fruitless Bare, Futile, Sisyphean, Sterile, Useless, Vain

Frump(ish) Dowdy, Judy, Shabby, Unkempt

Frustrate(d) Baffle, Ba(u)lk, Beat, Blight, Bugger, Check, Cheesed off, Confound, Countermine, Dash, Disappoint, Discomfit, Dish, Foil, Hogtie, Outwit, Scotch, Stymie, Tantalise, Thwart

Fry, Fried Blot, Brit, Christopher, Elizabeth, Fricassee, Fritter, Frizzle, Parr, Sauté, Sizzle, Small, Spawn, Whippersnapper, Whitebait

Fuddle(d) Drunk, Fluster, Fuzzle, Maudlin, Ta(i)vert, Tosticated, Woozy

▷ **Fuddle(d)** *may indicate* an anagram

Fudge Cook, Doctor, Dodge, Drivel, Evade, Fiddlesticks, Nonsense, Rot, Stop-press

Fuel Anthracite, Argol, Astatki, Atomic, Avgas, Biodiesel, Biogas, Borane, Briquet(te), Bunker, Butane, Candle-coal, Cannel, Carbonette, Charcoal, Coal, Coalite®, Coke, Derv, Diesel, Eilding, Eldin(g), Ethane, Faggot, Fire(wood), Fossil, Gasohol, Gasoline, Go-juice, Haxamine, Hydrazine, Hydyne, Jud, Kerosene, Kerosine, Kindling, Knitch, Lignite, Mox, Napalm, Naphtha, Nuclear, Orimulsion, Outage, Paraffin, Peat, Propane, Propellant, Smokeless, Solid, Sterno®, Stoke, Tan balls, Triptane, Unleaded, Yealdon

Fug Frowst

Fugitive Absconder, Ephemeral, Escapee, Fleeting, Hideaway, Lot, Outlaw, Refugee, Runagate, Runaway, Runner, Transient, Vagabond

Fugue Ricercar(e), Ricercata

Fulcrum Key-pin, Pivot

Fulfil(ment) Accomplish, Complete, Consummate, Fruition, Honour, Implementation, Meet, Pass, Realise, → SATISFY, Steed, Subrogation

Fulgent Bright, Shining

Full(ness), Fully Abrim, Ample, Arrant, Bouffant, Capacity, Chock-a-block, Chocker, Complete, Copious, Embonpoint, Engorged, Entire, Fat, Fed, Flush, Fou, Frontal, German, High, Hoatching, Hotch, Mill, Plein, Plenary, Plenitude, Pleroma, Plethora, Replete, Rich, Sated, Satiated, Thorough, Torose, Torous, Toss, Turgid, Turgor, Ullage, Up, Wau(l)k, Wholly

Full-faced Caboched, Caboshed

Full-throated Goitred

Fulminate, Fulmination Detonate, Explode, Levin, Lightning, Rail, Renounce, Thunder

Fumarole Hornito, Mofette

Fumble Blunder, Faff, Grope, Misfield, Muff

Fume(s) Bluster, Gas, Halitus, Nidor, Rage, Reech, Reek, Settle, Smoke, Stum, Vapours

Fumigate, Fumigator Disinfect, Pastil(le), Smoke, Smudge

Fun(ny), Funny bone Amusing, Antic, Boat, Buffo, Caper, Clownery, Comedy, Comic(al), Crack, Craic, Delight, Droll, Frolic, Gammock, Gas, Gig, Giocoso, Glaik, Guy, Hilarity, Humerus, Humorous, Hysterical, Ill, Jest, Jouisance, Jouysaunce, Killing, Kinky, Lark, Music, Play, Pleasure, Priceless, Rag, Rib-tickling, Rich, Rummy, Scream, Sidesplitting, Skylark, Sport, Uproarious, Weird(o), Wit, Yell

Funambulist Blondin, Equilibrist, Tight-rope

Function(al) Act, Algebraic, Antilog, Apparatchik, Arccos, Arcsine, Arctan, Assignment, Bodily, Bunfight, Ceremony, Characteristic, Circular, Cosec, Cosh, Cot(h), Cotangent, Dance, Density, Discriminant, Distribution, Dynamic, Exponential, Gamma, Gibbs, Hamilton(ian), Helmholtz, Hyperbolic, Integral, Integrand, Inverse, Jacobian, Job, Logarithm, Map(ping), → OPERATE, Periodic, Polymorphic, Probability, Propositional, Quadric, Quantical, Reception, Recursive, Role, Run, Secant, Sech, Sentential, Service, Sine, Sinh, State, Ste(a)d, Step, Surjection, Tan(h), Tangent, Tick, Transcendental, Trigonometric, Truth, Use, Utensil, Utility, Versin, Vital, Wave, → WORK

Functionless Otiose

Fund(s), Funding, Fundraising Bank, Bankroll, Barrel, Capital, Chest, Consolidated, Emendals, Endow, Evergreen, Finance, Fisc, Fisk, Gild, Green, Hedge, Imprest, Index, Jackpot, Kitty, Managed, Mutual, Nest-egg, Pension, Pool, Pork-barrel, Prebend, Private, Public, Purse, Revolving, Roll-up, Sinking, Slush, Social, Sou-sou, Stabilisation, Stock, Store, Subsidise, Sustentation, Susu, Telethon, Tracker, Treasury, Trust, Vulture, Wage(s), War chest, Wherewithal

Fundamental(ist) Basic(s), Bedrock, Cardinal, Essence, Grass-roots, Hamas, Integral, Missing, Nitty-gritty, Organic, Prime, Principle, Radical, Rudimentary, Taleban, Taliba(a)n, Ultimate

Fund-holder Rentier

Funeral, Funereal Charnel, Cortege, Dismal, Exequy, Feral, Hearse, Obit, Obsequy, Sad-coloured, Solemn, Tangi

Fungicide Benomyl, Biphenyl, Bordeaux mixture, Burgundy mixture, Captan, Diphenyl, Ferbam, Menadione, PCP, Resveratrol, Thiram, Zineb

Fungoid, Fungus Agaric, Amadou, Amanita, Ambrosia, Anthersmut, Anthracnose, Apothecium, Armillaria, Asci(us), Ascomycete, Aspergillus, Barm, Basidium, Beefsteak, Bird's nest, Black, Blackknot, Blewits, Blue-mould, Blue-rot, Boletus, Bootlace, Botrytis, Bracket, Brand, Bread-mould, Bunt, Candida, Ceps, Chantarelle, Chanterelle, Claudosporium, Clubroot, Conk, Coral spot, Corn smut, Cramp-ball, Craterellus, Cryptococcus, Cup, Death-cap, Death-cup, Dermatophytosis, Destroying angel, Discomycetes, Dutch elm, Earth-star, Elf-cup, Empusa, Endophyte, Ergot, Eumycetes, Fairy butter, Favus, Flowers of tan, Funnel-cap, Fuss-ball, Fuzz-ball, Gall, Gibberella, Gill, Honey, Horsehair, Hypersarcoma, Hypha, Imperfect, Ink-cap, Ithyphallus, Jelly, Jew's ear, Jupiter's beard, Lawyer's wig, Liberty cap, Lichen, Magic mushroom, Merulius, Mildew, Milk cap, Monilia, Morel, Mould, Mucor(ales), Mushroom, Mycelium, Mycetes, Mycology, Noble rot, Oak-leather, Oak-wilt, Oidium, Oomycete, Orange-peel, Penicillium, Pest, Peziza, Phallus, Phycomycete, Pileum, Plica Polonica, Polyporus, Porcino,

Pore, Prototroph, Puccinia, Puckfist, Puffball, Pythium, Rhizomorph, Rhizopus, Rhytisma, Russula, Rust, Saccharomyces, Saprolegnia, Saprophyte, Sariodes, Scab, Shaggy cap, Shaggy mane, Shoestring, Slime, Smut, Sooty mould, Spunk, Stinkhorn, Stipe, Stromata, Sulphur tuft, Tarspot, Thalline, Thallophyte, Toadstool, Torula, Tremella, Trichophyton, Truffle, Tuckahoe, Uredine, Ustilago, Velvet shank, Wax cap, Wheat rust, Witches' meat, Wood hedgehog, Wood woollyfoot, Yeast, Yellow brain, Yellow rust, Yellows, Zygomycete, Zygospore

Fungus-eater Mycophagist

Funicular Cable-car

Funk(y) Blue, Dodge, Dread, Fear, Scared, Stylish

Funnel Buchner, Chimney, Choana, Drogue, Flue, Hopper, Infundibulum, Separating, Smokestack, Stack, Stovepipe, Tun-dish, Tunnel, Wine

Fur Astrakhan, Astrex, Beaver(skin), Boa, Broadtail, Budge, Calabre, Caracul, Castor, Chinchilla, Coonskin, Crimmer, Ermelin, Ermine, Fitchew, Flix, Flue, Fun, Galyac, Galyak, Genet, Kolinsky, Krimmer, Lettice, Marten, Minever, Miniver, Mink, Mouton, Musquash, Ocelot, Otter, Palatine, Pane, Pashm, Pean, Pekan, Rac(c)oon, Roskyn, Sable, Sealskin, Sea-otter, Stole, Tincture, Tippet, Vair(e), Victorine, Wolverine, Zibeline, Zorino

Furbish Polish, Renovate, Spruce, Vamp

Furl Clew up, Fold, Roll, Stow, Wrap

Furlough Congé, Leave

Furnace Arc, Athanor, Blast, Bloomery, Bosh, Breeze, Calcar, Cockle, Cremator, Cupola, Destructor, Devil, Electric, Finery, Firebox, Forge, Glory-hole, Incinerator, Kiln, Lear, Lehr, Lime-kiln, Oast, Oon, Open-hearth, Oven, Pot, Producer, Reverberatory, Scaldino, Solar, Stokehold, Stokehole, Tank, Wind

Furnish(ing) Appoint, Array, Deck, Decorate, Endow, Endue, Equip, Feed, Fledge, Gird, Lend, Produce, Provision, Soft, Stock, Supply, Tabaret, Upholster

Furniture, Furniture designer Biedermeier, Chattels, Chippendale, Duncan Phyfe, Encoignure, Escritoire, Etagère, Flatpack, Fyfe, Hepplewhite, Insight, Lumber, Moveable, Queen Anne, Sheraton, Sideboard, Sticks, Stoutherie, Street, Tire, Unit, Washstand, Whatnot

Furore Brouhaha, Commotion, Outburst, Stink, Storm, Uproar

Furrier Trapper

Furrow(ed) Crease, Feer, Feerin(g), Furr, Groove, Gutter, Plough, Pucker, Rill(e), Rugose, Rut, Stria, Sulcus, Vallecula, Wrinkle

Fur-seal Seecatch(ie)

Further(more), Furthest Additional, Advance, Again, Aid, Also, Besides, Deeper, Else, Expedite, Extend, Extra, Extreme, Fresh, Infra, Longer, Mo(e), Mow, Other, Promote, Serve, Speed, Subserve, Then

Furtive(ly) Clandestine, Cunning, Hole and corner, Secret, Shifty, Sly, Sneaky, Stealthy, Stowlins, Stownlins

Fury, Furies, Furious Acharné, Agitato, Alecto, → **ANGER**, Apoplexy, Atropos, Avenger, Eriny(e)s, Eumenides, Exasperation, Frantic, Frenzied, Furor, Hectic, Incensed, → **IRE**, Livid, Maenad, Megaera, Paddy, Rabid, Rage, Red, Savage, Seething, Tisiphone, Virago, Wood, Wrath, Yond

Furze Gorse, Whin

Fuse(d), Fusion Anchylosis, Ankylosis, Blend, Coalesce, Cohere, Colliquate, Conflate, Encaustic, Endosmosis, Flow, Flux, Igniter, Knit, Match, Merge, Merit, Nuclear, Percussion, Portfire, Proximity, Rigelation, Run, Sacralization, Safety, Saucisse, Saucisson, Short, Slow-match, Symphytic, Syncretism, Syngamy, Time, Tokamak, Unite

Fuselage Body, Monocoque, Structure

Fuss(y) Ado, Agitation, Anile, Ballyho, Bobsie-die, Bother, Br(o)uhaha, Bustle, Carfuffle, Carry on, Chichi, Coil, Commotion, Complain, Cosset, Create, Cu(r)fuffle, Dust, Faff, Fantad, Fantod, Fiddle-faddle, Finical, Finikin, Hairsplitter, Hoohah, Hoopla, Mither, Mother, Niggle, Nit-pick, Noise, Old-womanish, Overexact, Overnice, Overwrought, Palaver, Particular, Perjink, Pernickety, Picky, Pother, Precise, Prejink, Primp, Prissy, Pudder, Racket, Razzmatazz, Rout, Song, Song and dance, Spoffish, Spoffy, Spruce, Stashie, Stickler, Stink, → **STIR**, Stishie, Stooshie, Stushie, Tamasha, To-do, Tracasserie

Fustian Bombast, Gas, Pompous, Rant

Futile Empty, Feckless, Idle, Inept, No-go, Nugatory, Null, Otiose, Pointless, Sleeveless, Stultified, Trivial, Useless, → **VAIN**

Future(s), Futurist Again, Be-all, Coming, Demain, Financial, Hence, Horoscope, Index, Interest-rate, Later, Long-range, Offing, Ovist, Paragogic, Posterity, Prospect, To-be, Tomorrow

Fuzz(y) Blur, Crepe, Down, Fluff, Foggy, Lint, Pig, Policeman

Gg

G George, Golf, Gravity

Gab(ble), Gabbler Chatter, Dovercourt, Jabber, Pie, Prattle, Talkative, Yabber

Gable Clark, Corbie, Jerkinhead, Pediment, Pine end

Gabriel Angel, Walter

Gad(about), Gadzooks Gallivant, Lud, Rover, Sbuddikins, Sdeath, Traipse, Trape(s), Viretot

Gadfly Breese, Breeze, Brize

Gadget Adaptor, Appliance, Artifice, Device, Dingbat, Dingus, Doodad, Doodah, Doofer, Doohickey, Gismo, Gizmo, Gubbins, Hickey, Jiggumbob, Jimjam, Notion, Possum, Tool, Utility, Waldo, Widget

Gadolinium Gd

Gadzooks Odsbobs

Gaekwar Baroda

Gael(ic) Celt, Erse, Goidel, Scottish, Teague

Gaff(e), Gaffer Bêtise, Blague, Bloomer, Error, Floater, Foreman, Gamble, Game, Solecism, Spar, Throat, Trysail, Yokel

Gag Brank, Choke, Estoppel, Joke, Pong, Prank, Retch, Silence(r), Smother, Wheeze

Gage Challenge, Pawn, Pledge, Plum

▶ **Gaiety** *see* GAY

Gain(s), Gained Acquire, Appreciate, Attain, Avail, Boodle, Boot, Bunce, Capital, Carry, Catch, Chevisance, Clean-up, Derive, Earn, Edge, Fruit, → GET, Good, Gravy, Land, Lucre, Obtain, Plus, Profit, Purchase, Rake-off, Reap, Thrift, Use, Velvet, Wan, Win, Windfall, Winnings

Gainsay Contradict, Deny

Gait Bearing, Canter, Pace, Piaffer, Rack, Trot

Gaiter(s) Cootikin, Cu(i)tikin, Gambado, Hogger, Legging(s), Puttee, Spat(s), Spattee, Spatterdash, Vamp

Gala Banquet, Festival

Galaxy, Galaxies Active, Andromeda, Blazar, Great Attractor, Heaven, Irregular, Magellanic cloud, Milky Way, Radio, Regular, Seyfert, Spiral, Stars

Galbanum Ferula

Gale(s) Backfielder, Equinoctial, Fresh, Moderate, Near, Peal, Ripsnorter, Sea turn, Snorter, Squall, Storm, Strong, Tempest, Whole, Winder

Gall, Gall bladder Aleppo, Bedeguar, Bile, Bitterness, Canker, Cholecyst, Ellagic, Enrage, Fell, Irritate, Mad-apple, Maugre, Maulgre, Oak(nut), Oak apple, Saddle, Sage-apple, Sandiver, → SAUCE, Tacahout, Vine

Gallant(ry) Admirer, Amorist, Beau, Blade, Buck, Cavalier, Chevalier, Cicisbeo, Courtliness, Lover, Prow, Romeo, Sigisbeo, Spark, Valiance

Galleon Galloon, Ghostly, Ship

Gallery Accademia, Alure, Amphitheatre, Arcade, Assommoir, Belvedere, Brattice, Bretasche, Bretesse, Brettice, Brow, Burrell (Collection), Catacomb,

Celestials, Cupola, Dedans, Fly, Gods, Hayward, Hermitage, Jube, Ladies', Loft, Loggia, Louvre, Machicolation, Mine, Minstrel, National, Organ, Pawn, Picture, Pinacotheca, Pinakothek, Pitti, Prado, Press, Public, Rogues', Scaffoldage, Serpentine, Shooting, Strangers', Tate, Terrace, Traverse, Tribune, Triforium, Uffizi, Veranda(h), Whispering, Whitechapel, Winning

Galley Bireme, Bucentaur, Caboose, Drake, Galliot, Kitchen, Lymphad, Penteconter, Proof

Gallimaufry Macedoine, Mishmash, Stew

Gallium Ga

Gallon(s) Bushel, Cong(ius), Cran, Hin, Imperial, Pottle, Tierce

Galloon Lace, Osiris

Gallop(er) Aide, Canter, Canterbury, Career, Lope, Trot, Wallop

Gallows Bough, Cheat, Drop, Dule-tree, Forks, Gibbet, Nub, Nubbing-cheat, Patibulary, Three-legged mare, Tree, Tyburn, Tyburn-tree, Widow, Woodie

Gallows-bird Crack-halter, Crack-hemp, Crack-rope

Gall-stone Cholelith

Galore Abundance, À gogo, Plenty, Whisky

Galosh Overshoe, Rubber

Galvanise Activate, Buck up, Ginger, Rouse, Zinc

Galvanometer Tangent

Gam Pod

Gambit Manoeuvre, Ploy, Stratagem

Gamble(r), Gambling (place) Adventure, Amber, Ante, Back, Bet, Casino, Chance, Dice(-play), Flutter, Gaff, Hold, Jeff, Martingale, Mise, Pari-mutuel, Parlay, Partingale, Piker, Plunge, Policy, Punt(er), Raffle, Reno, Risk, Roulette, School, Spec, Speculate, Speculator, Sweep(stake), Throw(ster), Tinhorn, Tombola, Tontine, Treble chance, Two-up, → WAGER

Gambol Frisk, Frolic

Game(s) Away, Closed, Commonwealth, Computer, Console, Decider, Electronic, Fair, Frame, Gallant, Gammy, Ground, Gutsy, High-jinks, Highland, Home, Intrepid, Isthmian, Jeu, → LAME, Match, Middle, Mind, MUD, Nemean, Numbers, Olympic, On, Open, Panel, Paralympic, Parlour, Perfect, Platform, Play, Plaything, Pythian, Raffle, Ready, Road, Role-playing, Round, Rubber, Saving, Scholar's, Secular, Spoof, Sport, Square, String, Table, Tie-break, Vie, Waiting, Willing, Zero-sum

GAMES

2 letters:	Pam	Crap	Main
Eo	Pit	Dibs	Mora
Go	Put	Fa-fi	Palm
PE	Sim	Faro	Polo
RU	Swy	Goff	Pool
	Tag	Golf	Putt
3 letters:	Tig	Grab	Ruff
Cat	War	I-spy	Scat
Hob		Keno	Skat
Loo	4 letters:	Kino	Slam
Maw	Base	Laik	Snap
Nap	Brag	Loto	Solo
Nim	Bull	Ludo	Taws

Vint
Wall
Word

5 letters:
Bingo
Bocce
Bowls
Cards
Catch
Chess
Cinch
Craps
Darts
Fives
Gleek
Goose
Halma
House
Jacks
Keeno
Lotto
Lurch
Merel
Meril
Monte
Morra
Noddy
Novum
Omber
Ombre
Poker
Quino
Roque
Rummy
Shogi
Stops
Tarok
Tarot
Trugo
Trump
Two-up
Ulama
Video
Whisk
Whist

6 letters:
Basset
Beetle
Bo-peep

Boston
Boules
Bounce
Casino
Chemmy
Clumps
Crambo
Ecarté
Euchre
Fantan
Footer
Gammon
Gobang
Gomoku
Hockey
Hoopla
Hurley
Kitcat
Merell
Peepbo
Pelota
Piquet
Quinze
Quoits
Shinny
Shinty
Soccer
Socker
Squash
Tenpin
Tipcat
Uckers
Vigoro

7 letters:
Ba'spiel
Bezique
Braemar
Camogie
Canasta
Cassino
Charade
Chicken
Codille
Conkers
Coon-can
Croquet
Curling
Diabolo
Doubles
Hangman

Hurling
In-and-in
Jai alai
Jukskei
Kabaddi
Kalooki
Lottery
Mahjong
Mancala
Marbles
Matador
Muggins
Murphy's
Netball
Old maid
Pachisi
Pallone
Passage
Patball
Peekabo
Peevers
Pharaoh
Pinball
Plafond
Pontoon
Primero
Push-pin
Rackets
Reversi
Ring-taw
Seven-up
Singles
Snooker
Squails
Tag ends
Tenpins
Vingt-un
Zero sum

8 letters:
All-fives
All-fours
Baccarat
Baseball
Bob-apple
Bumpball
Buzkashi
Canfield
Charades
Chequers
Chouette

Conquian
Cottabus
Cribbage
Dominoes
Draughts
Fivepins
Football
Forfeits
Four-ball
Foursome
Gin rummy
Goalball
Handball
Handicap
Hardball
Kalookie
Kickball
Klondike
Klondyke
Korfball
Lacrosse
Leapfrog
Mahjongg
Michigan
Monopoly®
Napoleon
Ninepins
Nintendo®
Octopush
Pachinko
Pall-mall
Pastance
Patience
Peekaboo
Pegboard
Penneech
Penneeck
Penuchle
Petanque
Ping-pong
Pinochle
Pintable
Pope Joan
Push-ball
Pyramids
Reversis
Rolypoly
Roulette
Rounders
Sardines
Scrabble®

Skittles
Slapjack
Softball
Sphairee
Subbuteo®
Teetotum
Trap-ball
Tray-trip
Tredille
Tric-trac
Verquere
Verquire

9 letters:
Acey-deucy
Aunt Sally
Badminton
Bagatelle
Billiards
Black-cock
Black-jack
Bob-cherry
Broomball
Crokinole
Cutthroat
Dodgeball
Duplicate
Fillipeen
Hacky Sack®
Hopscotch
Jingo-ring
Lanterloo
Level-coil
Matrimony
Mistigris
Mournival
Mumchance
Newmarket
Paintball
Parcheesi®
Pelmanism
Punchball
Quadrille
Quidditch®
Shell game
Shoot'em-up

Solitaire
Solo whist
Spoilfive
Stoolball
Strap-game
Tip-and-run
Tredrille
Twenty-one
Vingt-et-un
Water polo

10 letters:
Angel-beast
Backgammon
Basketball
Battledore
Bouillotte
Candlepins
Cat's cradle
Deck tennis
Dumb crambo
Five-stones
Flapdragon
Geocaching
Handy-dandy
Horseshoes
Hot cockles
Jackstones
Jackstraws
Knurr-spell
Lansquenet
Paddleball
Paper chase
Phillipina
Phillipine
Philopoena
Pooh sticks
Preference
Punto-banco
Put and take
Shuffle-cap
Snapdragon
Spillikins
Strip poker
Tablanette
Tchoukball

Thimblerig
Trick-track
Troll-madam
Trou-madame
Volley-ball

11 letters:
Barley-brake
Barley-break
Bumble-puppy
Catch-the-ten
Chemin de fer
Fox and geese
General post
Gerrymander
Hide and seek
Mumbletypeg
Post and pair
Puncto-banco
Racquetball
Rouge et noir
Sancho-pedro
Shovelboard
Speculation
Tick-tack-toe
Tiddlywinks
Troll-my-dame

12 letters:
Bar billiards
Consequences
Fast and loose
Hoodman-blind
Knucklebones
Minister's cat
One-and-thirty
Pitch and putt
Pitch and toss
Shuffleboard
Span-farthing
Troll-my-dames

13 letters:
Blind man's buff
Chicken-hazard
Double or quits

French cricket
Jingling match
Musical chairs
Postman's knock
Prisoner's base
Scavenger hunt
Space Invaders®
Spin-the-bottle
Tenpin bowling
Tickly-benders

14 letters:
British bulldog
Crown and anchor
Ducks and drakes
Fives and threes
Follow-my-leader
Hunt-the-slipper
Pig-in-the-middle
Prick-the-garter
Shove-halfpenny
Snip-snap-snorum
Tenpins bowling
Three-card monte

15 letters:
Chinese whispers
Puss-in-the-corner

16 letters:
Piggy-in-the-
  middle
Snakes and ladders
Trente-et-quarante

17 letters:
Noughts and
  crosses

20 letters:
Kiss-me-quick-in-
  the-ring

Game, Game birds Bag, Fowl, Grouse, Guan, Hare, Meat, Partridge, Pheasant,
  Prairie chicken, Ptarmigan, Quail, → QUARRY, Rype(r), Snipe, Spatchcock,
  Woodcock
Gamekeeper Mellors, Velveteen, Venerer, Warrener

Gamete Ootid
Gaming place Bucket-shop, Casino, Saloon, Table
Gammerstang Taupie, Tawpie
Gammon Baloney, Bilge, Tosh
Gamut Compass, Range
Gander Airport, Look-see
Gandhi Mahatma
Gang Baader-Meinhof, Band(itti), Bikers, Bing, Bunch, Canaille, Chain, Coffle, Core, Crew, Crue, Droog, Elk, Go, Group, Hell's Angels, Horde, Mob, Mods, Nest, Outfit, Pack, Posse, Press, Push, Ratpack, Ring, Rockers, Shearing, Triad, Tribulation, Troop, Yardie
Ganglia Basal
Gangrene Canker, Gas, Noma, Phaged(a)ena, Sphacelate, Thanatosis
Gangster Al, Bandit, Capone, Crook, Dacoit, Dakoit, Hatchet-man, Highbinder, Hood, Mafioso, Mobster, Ochlocrat, Scarface, Skollie, Skolly, Tsotsi, Yakuza, Yardie
Gangway Brow, Catwalk, Road
Gannet Alcatras, Booby, Guga, Solan(d)
Gantry Elmer
Ganymede Cupper
▶ **Gaol(er)** *see* JAIL(ER)
Gap Aperture, Belfort, Breach, Chasm, Chink, Credibility, Day, Deflationary, Diastema, Dollar, Embrasure, Energy, F-hole, Financing, Flaw, Fontanel(le), Gender, Generation, Gulf, Gulph, Hair-space, Hiatus, Hole, Inflationary, Interlude, Interstice, Kirkwood, Lacunae, Leaf, Lin(n), Loophole, M(e)use, Mews, Muset, Musit, Node of Ranvier, Opening, Ostiole, Pass, Rest, Rift, Rima, Shard, Sherd, Skills, Slap, → SPACE, Spark, Street, Synapse, Trade, Truth-value, Vacancy, Vent, Water, Wind, Window
Gape(r), Gaping Comber, Dehisce, Fatiscent, Gant, Ga(u)p, Gerne, Hiant, Mya, Outstare, Rictal, Rictus, Ringent, Rubberneck, Stare, Yawn, Yawp
Garage Barn, Carport, Chopshop, Hangar, Lock-up, Muffler shop
Garb Apparel, Costume, Gear, Gere, Guise, Ihram, Invest, Leotard, Raiment, Toilet
Garbage Bunkum, Junk, Refuse, Rubbish, Trash
Garble Edit, Jumble, Muddle
▷ **Garble** *may indicate* an anagram
Garden(ing), Gardens Arbour, Area, Babylon(ian), Bagh, Bear, Beer, Botanic, Chinampa, Colegarth, Container, Cottage, Covent, Cremorne, Dig, Eden, Erf, Floriculture, Garth, Gethsemane, Hanging, Hesperides, Hoe, Horticulture, Italian, Japanese, Kailyard, Kew, Kitchen, Knot, Landscape, Lyceum, Market, Monastery, NJ, Olitory, Paradise, Parterre, Physic, Plantie-cruive, Pleasance, Plot, Potager, Ranelagh, Rockery, Roji, Roof, Rosarium, Rosary, Rosery, Tea, Tilth, Topiary, Tuileries, Vauxhall, Walled, Welwyn, Window, Winter, Yard, Zoological
Gardener Adam, Capability Brown, Fuchs, Hoy, Jekyll, Landscape, Mali, Mallee, Mary, Nurseryman, Topiarist, Tradescant, Trucker
Gargantuan Enormous, Huge, Pantagruel, Vast
Gargle Gargarism, Mouthwash
Gargoyle Waterspout
Garish Criant, Flashy, Gaudy, Glitzy, Jazzy, Painty, Roary, Rorie, Rory, Technicolour
Garland Anadem, Anthology, Chaplet, Coronal, Crants, Festoon, Lei, Stemma, Toran(a), Vallar(y), Wreath
Garlic Clove, Elephant, Hedge, Rams(on), Rocambole
Garment Aba(ya), Abba, Alb, Ao dai, Barrow, Blouse, Blouson, Bodice, Body

warmer, Bolero, B(o)ub(o)u, B(o)urk(h)a, Brassière, Breeks, Burnous, Burqa,
Busuuti, Caftan, Catsuit, Cerements, Chador, Chasuble, Chausses, Chimer,
Cilice, Cimar, Clout, Cote-hardie, Cotta, Cover-slut, Crop top, Dalmatic, Dashiki,
Dirndl, Dishdash(a), Djibbah, Doublet, Dreadnought, → DRESS, Ephod, Exomion,
Exomis, Fanon, Foundation, Gambeson, Gilet, Gipon, Gown, G-suit, Habiliment,
Habit, Hand-me-down, Himation, Hug-me-tight, Ihram, Izar, Jeistiecor, Jibbah,
Jubbah, Jumpsuit, Jupon, Kaftan, K(h)anga, Kanzu, Kaross, Kilt, Kittel, Leotard,
Levis, Lingerie, Mandilion, Mandylion, Mantle, Mantua, Negligée, One-piece,
Pallium, Pannicle, Pantihose, Pantyhose, Partlet, Pelerine, Pelisse, Penitential,
Peplos, Pilch, Polonaise, Polonie, Polony, Poncho, Popover, Rail, Ramée, Rami(e),
Reach-me-down, Rochet, Rompers, Ruana, Sackcloth, Salopettes, Sanbenito,
Sari, Sarong, Scapular, Shroud, Singlet, Skirt, Skivvy, Slop, Soutane, Step-in, Stola,
Stole, Sulu, Surcoat, Surplice, Swimsuit, Tabard, Tankini, Tank-top, Thong, Toga,
Togs, Trunks, Tunic(le), Two-piece, Unitard, Vestment, Vesture, Waistcoat, Weed,
Woolly, Wrapper, Yukata, Zephyr

Garnet Alabandine, Almandine, Andradite, Carbuncle, Demantoid, Essonite,
Grossular(ite), Hessonite, Melanite, Pyrenite, Pyrope, Rhodolite, Spessartite,
Topazine, Topazolite, Uvarovite

Garnish Adorn, Attach, Crouton, Decorate, Gremolata, Lard, Parsley, Sippet,
Staffage

Garret Attic, Loft, Sol(l)ar, Sol(l)er

Garrison Fort, Man, Presidial

Garrulity, Garrulous Babbling, Gas, Gushy, Sweetiewife, Windbag

Garter Bowyang, Crewel, Flash, G(r)amash, Gramosh, Nicky-tam

Gary Glitter, Player

Gas(sy) Acetylene, Afterdamp, Air, Ammonia, Argon, Argonon, Arsine, Azote,
Blah(-blah), Blather, Blether, Bloat, Blue water, Bottle(d), Butadiene, Butane,
Butene, BZ, Calor®, Carbonic acid, Carburetted, Carrier, Chat, Chlorine,
Chokedamp, Chrom(at)osphere, CN, Coal(-oil), Crypton, CS, Cyanogen, Damp,
Diphosgene, Dispersant, Electrolytic, Emanation, Ethane, Ethene, Ether(ion),
Ethine, Ethylene, Euchlorine, Firedamp, Fizz, Flatulence, Flatus, Flocculus, Flue,
Fluorin(e), Formaldehyde, Fugacity, Gabnash, Greenhouse, H, Halitus, He, Helium,
Hot-air, Hydrogen, Ideal, Inert, Jaw, Ketene, Kr(ypton), Laughing, Lewisite, Lurgi,
Mace®, Marsh, Methane, Methylamine, Mofette, Mustard, Napalm, Natural,
Ne, Neon, Nerve, Nitrogen, Noble, North Sea, Nox, O, Oil, Olefin(e), Orotund,
Oxyacetylene, Oxygen, Ozone, Perfect, Petrol, Phosgene, Phosphine, Plasma, Poep,
Poison, Prate, Producer, Propane, Propellant, Propene, Propylene, Protogalaxy,
Protostar, Radon, Rare, RN, Sarin, Semiwater, Sewage, Sewer, Silane, Solfatara,
Soman, Sour, Stibine, Sulphur dioxide, Swamp, Sweet, Synthesis, Tabun, → TALK,
Taraniki wind, Tear, Tetrafluoroethene, Tetrafluoroethylene, Therm, Thoron,
Town, Utility, V-agent, Vapour, VX, Waffle, War, Water, Whitedamp, → WIND,
Xenon, Yackety-yak

Gasbag Blimp, Envelope, Prattler

Gascon(ade) Boast, Braggart, Skite

Gash Incise, Rift, Score, Scotch, → SLASH

Gas-mask Inhaler

Gasp(ing) Anhelation, Apn(o)ea, Chink, Exhale, Kink, Oh, Pant, Puff, Singult, Sob

Gast(e)ropod Ataata, Conch, Cowrie, Cowry, Dog-whelk, Dorididae, Euthyneura,
Fusus, Glaucus, Haliotis, Harp-shell, Limpet, Mitre, Mollusc, Money cowry, Murex,
Nerita, Nerite, Nudibranch, Opisthobranch, Ormer, Pelican's foot, Pennywinkle,
Periwinkle, Pteropod, Purpura, Sea-ear, Sea-hare, Slug, Snail, Spindle-shell,

Streptoneura, Stromb, Top, Triton, Turbo, Turritella, Unicorn, Wentletrap, Whelk, Winkle

Gate(s), Gateway Alley, Attendance, Bill, Brandenburg, Caisson, Cilician, Crowd, Decuman, Entry, Erpingham, Golden, Head, Iron, Ivory, Kissing, Lock, Lych, Mallee, Menin, Moon, Moravian, Nor, Pearly, Portal, Portcullis, Postern, Praetorian, Propylaeum, Propylon, Pylon, Sallyport, Starting, Tail, Taranaki, Toran(a), Torii, Traitor's, Turnout, Turnstile, Waste, Water, Wicket, Yate, Yet(t)

Gatecrash(er) Interloper, Intrude, Ligger, Sorn, Unasked

Gatepost Sconcheon, Scontion, Scuncheon

▷ **Gateshead** *may indicate* 'g'

Gather(ed), Gathering Accrue, Amass, Assemble, Bee, Braemar, Cluster, Collate, → **COLLECT**, Colloquium, Concourse, Conglomerate, Congregate, Conventicle, Conversazione, Corral, Corroboree, Crop, Crowd, Cull, Derive, Eve, Fest, Frill, Function, Gabfest, Galaxy, Get together, Glean, Glomerate, Hangi, Harvest, Hear, Hootenanny, Hotchpot, Hui, Husking, In, Infer, Jamboree, Kommers, Learn, Lek, Lirk, Love-in, Meinie, Menyie, Multitude, Pleat, Plica, Plissé, Pucker, Purse, Raft, Raising-bee, Rake, Rally, Rave, Reef, Reunion, Round-up, Rout, Ruche, Ruff(le), Salon, Shindig, Shir(r), Shoal, Shovel, Singsong, Social, Spree, Swapmeet, Take, Tuck, Vindemiate, Vintage, Wappensc(h)aw, Witches' sabbath

Gauche Awkward, Clumsy, Farouche, Graceless

Gaudy Classy, Criant, Fantoosh, Flash, Garish, Glitz(y), Meretricious, Tacky, Tinsel

Gauge Absolute, Alidad(e), Anemometer, → **ASSESS**, Block, Bourdon, Broad, Calibre, Denier, Depth, Dial, Estimate, Etalon, Evaluate, Feeler, Judge, Lee, Limit, Loading, Manometer, Marigraph, Measure, Meter, Narrow, Nilometer, Oil, Ombrometer, Oncometer, Perforation, Plug, Pressure, Rain, Rate, Ring, Scantle, Size, Slip, Standard, Steam, Strain, Tape, Template, Tonometer, Tram, Tread, Tyre, Udometer, Vacuum, Water, Weather, Wind, Wire

Gauguin Paul

Gaul Asterix, Cisalpine, Transalpine, Vercingetorix

Gaunt Haggard, Lancaster, Lean, Randletree, Ranneltree, Rannletree, Rantletree, Rawbone, → **THIN**, Wasted

Gauntlet C(a)estus, Gantlope

Gauss G

Gautama Buddha

Gauze, Gauzy Gas mantle, Gossamer, Muslin, Sheer, Tiffany, Wire

Gawky Clumsy, Cow, Gammerstang, Sloucher

Gawp Rubberneck

Gay, Gaiety Blithe, Bonny, Boon, Buxom, Camp, Canty, Daffing, Debonair, Festal, Frolic, Gallant, Gladsome, Glee, Gordon, Grisette, Inverted, Jolly, Lightsome, May, Merry, Nitid, Out, Rackety, Riant, Rorty, Tit(t)upy, Volatile

Gaze Moon, Pore, Regard, Stare

Gazelle Ariel, Gerenuk, Goa, Mhorr, Mohr, Tabitha, Thomson's

Gazette London, Paper

Gear(ing), Gearbox Alighting, Angel, Arrester, Attire, Bags, Bevel, Capital, Clobber, Dérailleur, Differential, Draw, Duds, Engrenage, Epicyclic, Fab, Finery, Granny, Harness, Helical, Herringbone, High, Hypoid, Idle wheel, Involute, Kit, Landing, Lay-shaft, Low, Mesh, Mess, Mitre, Neutral, Notchy, Overdrive, Planetary, Ratio, Reverse, Rig, Riot, Rudder, Running, Spur, Steering, Straight, Sun and planet, Switch, Synchromesh, → **TACKLE**, Timing, Tiptronic®, Top, Trim, Tumbler, Valve, Variable, Worm(-wheel)

Gecko Tokay

Gee Horse, Hump, My, Reist, Sulk, Tout, Towt, Urge

Geiger-counter Scintillator

Geisha Maiko

Gel Hair, Pectin, Pectise, Silica

Gelatine, Gelatinous Blasting, Calipash, Collagen, Glutinous, Isinglass, Size, Tunicin

Geld(ing) Castrate, Lib, Neuter, Sort, Spado

Gelignite Jelly

Geller Uri

Gem Abraxas, Agate, Alexandrite, Almandine, Amazonite, Andradite, Asteria, Baguette, Birthstone, Bloodstone, Boule, Brilliant, Briolette, Cabochon, Cacholong, Cairngorm, Callais, Carbuncle, Carnelian, Cat's eye, Chrysoberyl, Chrysolite, Chrysoprase, Cornelian, Cymophane, Demantoid, Diamante, Diamond, Dumortierite, Emerald, Girasol(e), Girosol, Grossular(ite), Hawk's eye, Heliodor, Heliotrope, Hessonite, Hiddenite, Hyacinth, ID, Idaho, Indicolite, Iolite, Jacinth, Jargo(o)n, Jasper, Jaspis, → JEWEL, Kunzite, Lapis lazuli, Ligure, Marcasite, Marquise, Melanite, Menilite, Mocha stone, Moonstone, Morganite, Onyx, Opal, Pearl, Peridot(e), Plasma, Prase, Pyrope, Rhinestone, Rhodolite, Rose-cut, Rubellite, Ruby, Sapphire, Sard, Sardius, Sardonyx, Scarab, Scaraboid, Smaragd, Solitaire, Sparkler, Spessartite, Starstone, Stone, Sunstone, Tiger's eye, Topazolite, Tourmaline, Turquoise, Uvarovite, Verd antique, Zircon

Gemination, Gemini Diplogenesis, Twins

Gemma Bud, Knosp

Gen Info

Gendarme Flic

Gender Form, Natural, Sex

Gene(tics) Allel(e), Allelomorph, Anticodon, Codon, Complementary, Creation, Designer, Disomic, Dysbindin, Episome, Exon, Factor, Gay, Genome, Hereditary, Heterogamy, Holandric, Hologynic, Intron, Jumping, Lysenkoism, Mendel, Michurinism, Molecular, Muton, Oncogene, Operon, Regulatory, Reporter, Reverse, Selfish, Structural, Synteny, Telegony, Terminator, Transposon, Weismannism

Genealogist, Genealogy Armory, Family, Heraldry, Line, Pedigree, Seannachie, Seannachy, Sennachie, Whakapapa

General Agamemnon, Agricola, Agrippa, Alcibiades, Allenby, Antigonus, Antipater, Antony, Ataman, At large, Banquo, Barca, Blucher, Booth, Botha, Boulanger, Broad, C in C, Clive, Common, Communal, Conde, Cornwallis, Crassus, Current, Custer, De Gaulle, De Wet, Diadochi, Eclectic, Ecumenical, Election, Fairfax, Franco, Gamelin, Gen, GOC, Gordon, Grant, Hadrian, Hannibal, Holofernes, Ike, Inspector, Joshua, Kitchener, Lafayette, Lee, Leslie, Macarthur, Main, Marius, Marshall, Massena, Montcalm, Napier, Napoleon, Omnify, Overall, Overhead, Patton, Pershing, Pompey, Prevailing, Raglan, Regulus, Rife, Rommel, Scipio, Sherman, Shrapnel, Smuts, Stilwell, Strategist, Structural, Sulla, Tom Thumb, Turenne, → UNIVERSAL, Usual, Vague, Wide, Wolfe

Generate, Generation, Generator Abiogenetic, Age, Beat, Beget, Boomerang, Breeder, Charger, Cottonwool, Create, Dynamo, Electrostatic, Epigon, Father, Fuel-cell, House, Kipp, Loin, Lost, Magneto, Motor, Noise, Olds, Powerhouse, Signal, Sire, Spawn, Spontaneous, Stallion, Van de Graaff, Windmill, X, Yield

Generosity, Generous Bounty, Charitable, Free-handed, Free-hearted, Handsome, Kind, Largess(e), → LAVISH, Liberal, Magnanimous, Munificent, Noble(-minded), Open, Open-handed, Open-hearted, Philanthropic, Plump, Profuse, Selfless, Sporting, Unstinting

▶ **Genetic** *see* GENE

Geneva(n) Calvinist, Gin, Hollands

Genial(ity) Affable, Amiable, Benign, Bluff, Bonhomie, Chin, Convivial, Cordial, Human, Kindly, Mellow

Genie Djinn, Mazikeen, Shedeem

Genipap Lana

Genital(s) Ballocks, Bol(l)ix, Bollocks, Box, Cooze, Crack, Crotch, Cunt, Fanny, Front bottom, Labia, Lunchbox, Minge, Muff, Naff, Nympha, Private parts, Privates, Pubes, Pudendum, Pun(a)ani, Pun(a)any, Pussy, Quim, Secrets, Tackle, Tail, Twat, Vagina, Vulva, Wedding tackle, Yoni

Genitive Ethical

Genius Agathodaimon, Brain, Daemon, Einstein, Engine, Flash, Ingine, Inspiration, Ka, Mastermind, Michaelangelo, Numen, Prodigy

Genome Prophage

Genre Splatterpunk, Tragedy

Gent(leman), Gentlemen, Gentlemanly Amateur, Baboo, Babu, Beau, Caballero, Cavalier, Dandy, Duni(e)wassal, Dunniewassal, Esq(uire), Gemman, Gemmen, Ja(u)nty, Knight, Messrs, Milord, Mister, Mr, Nob, Proteus, Ritter, Runner, Rye, Sahib, Senor, Signor, Sir, Sirra(h), Smuggler, Squire, Sri, Stalko, Stir(rah), Swell, Tea, Toff, Tuan, Von, Yeoman

Genteel Conish, Polite, Proper, Refined

Gentian European, Felwort, Violet, Yellow

Gentile(s) Aryan, Ethnic, Goy, Nations, Shi(c)ksa, Uncircumcised

Gentle Amenable, Amenage, Bland, Clement, Delicate, Gradual, Grub, Light, Maggot, Mansuete, Mild, Tame, Tender

Gentry County, Landed, Quality, Squir(e)age

Gents Bog, John, Lav, Loo, WC

Genuflexion Bend, Curts(e)y, Kowtow, Salaam

Genuine Authentic, Bona-fide, Dinkum, Dinky-di, Echt, Frank, Heartfelt, Honest, Intrinsic, Jannock, Jonnock, Kosher, Legit(imate), McCoy, Nain, Proper, Pucka, Pukka, Pure, Pusser, → **REAL**, Real McCoy, Right, Simon-pure, Sincere, Square, Sterling, True, Unsophisticated, Veritable

Genus Class, Form, -ia, Mustela

Geode Druse

Geographer, Geography Chorography, Dialect, Economic, Hakluyt, Linguistic, Mercator, Pausanias, Physical, Political, Strabo

Geology, Geologist Economic, Geodynamics, Historical, Hutton, Isotope, Mineralogy, Phanerozoic, Seismology, Self-rock, Tectonics, Werner

Geometry, Geometrician, Geometer Affine, Analytical, Conics, Coordinate, Descriptive, Differential, Elliptic, Euclid(ean), Hyperbolic, Moth, Non-Euclidean, Parabolic, Plane, Porism, Projective, Riemannian, Solid, Spherics, Topologist

Geordie Guinea, Tynesider

George(s) Autopilot, Best, Borrow, Eliot, Farmer, Lloyd, Orwell, Pilot, Sand

Georgia(n) Abkhaz, Ga, Hanover, Iberian, Mingrel(ian)

Geraint Knight

Geranium Dove's foot, Rose, Stork's bill, Yellow

Gerbil Jird

Germ(s) Bacteria, Bug, Culture, Klebsiella, Seed, Spirilla, Strep, Virus, Wheat, Zyme

German(y) Al(e)main(e), Alemannic, Angle, Anglo-Saxon, Bavarian, Berliner, Blood-brother, Boche, Cimbri, Composer, Cousin, Denglish, Franconian, Frank, Fritz, G, Goth, Habsburg, Hans, Hapsburg, Herr, Hessian, High, Hun, Jerry, Jute, Kaiser, Kraut, Landgrave, Low, Lusatian, Neanderthal, Ossi, Ostrogoth, Otto,

Palsgrave, Pennsylvania, Plattdeutsch, Pruce, Prussian, Salic, Saxon, Squarehead, Tedesco, Teuton(ic), Vandal, Visigoth, Wessi, Wolfgang

Germane Apt, → **PERTINENT**, Relevant

Germanium Ge

Germ-free Aseptic

Germinate Grow, Pullulate, Sprout

Gesticulate, Gesticulation, Gesture(s) Ameslan, Beck(on), Ch(e)ironomy, Fico, Gest(e), Harvey Smith, Mannerism, Mime, Motion, Mudra, Salute, → **SIGN**, Signal, Snook, Token

Get(ting), Get(ting) by, Get(ting) on Acquire, Advance, Aggravate, Annoy, Attain, Bag, Become, Becoming, Brat, Bring, Capture, Cop, Cope, Derive, Fet(ch), Fette, Gain, Gee, Land, Learn, Make, Manage, Milk, Net, Noy, → **OBTAIN**, Pass, Peeve, Procure, Progress, Reach, Realise, Rile, Roil, Secure, See, Sire, Twig, Understand, Win

Getaway Disappearance, Escape, Vamoose

▷ **Getting** *may indicate* an anagram

Getting better Convalescing, Improving, Lysis

Get-up Tog(s)

Geum Avens

Gewgaw Bagatelle, Bauble, Doit, Tat, Trifle

Geyser Soffioni, Therm

Ghanaian Ashanti, Fantee, Fanti, Tshi, Twi

Ghastly Charnel, Gash, Grim, Hideous, Lurid, Macabre, Pallid, Spectral, Ugsome, Welladay, White

Gherkin Cornichon

Ghetto Barrio, Slum

Ghost(ly) Acheri, Apparition, Apport, Banquo, Caddy, Chthonic, Duende, Duppy, Eerie, Eery, Fantasm, Fetch, Gytrash, Haunt, Hint, Holy, Jumbie, Jumby, Larva(e), Lemur, Malmag, No'canny, Paraclete, Pepper's, Phantasm(agoria), Phantom, Revenant, Sampford, Shade, Shadow, Spectre, Spectrology, → **SPIRIT**, Spook, Trace, Truepenny, Umbra, Vision, Visitant, Waff, Wraith

Ghoul Fiend

GI Joe, Yankee

Giant(ess) Alcyoneus, Alifanfaron, Anak, Antaeus, Archiloro, Argus, Ascapart, Atlas, Balan, Balor, Bellerus, Blunderbore, Bran, Briareus, Brobdingnagian, Cacus, Colbrand, Colbronde, Colossus, Coltys, Cormoran, Cottus, Cyclop(e)s, Despair, Enceladus, Ephialtes, Eten, Ettin, Ferragus, Gabbara, Galligantus, Gargantua, Géant, Gefion, Geirred, Gigantic, Gog, Goliath, Grim, Harapha, Hrungnir, Hymir, Idris, Irus, Jotun(n), Jumbo, Krasir, Lestrigon, Leviathan, Magog, Mammoth, Mimir, Monster, Oak, Og, Ogre, Orion, Otus, Pallas, Pantagruel, Patagonian, Polyphemus, Pope, Red, Rounceval, Skrymir, Slaygood, Talos, Talus, Thrym, Titan, Tityus, Tregeagle, Triton, Troll, Tryphoeus, Typhon, Urizen, Utgard, Ymir, Yowie

Gibberish Claptrap, Double Dutch, Greek, Jargon

Gibbet Gallows, Patibulary, Potence, Ravenstone, Tree

Gibbon(s) Hoolock, Hylobate, Orlando, Siamang, Stanley, Wou-wou, Wow-wow

Gibe Barb, Brocard, Chaff, Fleer, Glike, Jeer, Jibe, Quip, Shy, Slant, Wisecrack

Gibraltar Calpe

Giddy (girl), Giddiness Capernoitie, Cap(p)ernoity, Dizzy, Fisgig, Fishgig, Fizgig, Giglot, Glaikit, Glaky, Haverel, Hellicat, Hoity-toity, Jillet, Light, Light-headed, Skipping, Staggers, Sturdy, Turn, Vertigo, Volage(ous), Wheel, Woozy

Gift(s), Gifted Ability, Alms, Aptitude, Bef(f)ana, Bequest, Blessing, Blest, Bonbon,

Bonsel(l)a, Boon, Bounty, Charism(a), Congiary, Corban, Covermount, Cumshaw, Dash, Deodate, → **DONATION**, Etrenne, Fairing, Fidecommissum, Flair, Foy, Free, Freebie, Gab, Garnish, Godsend, Grant, Greek, Handout, Han(d)sel, Hogmanay, Indian, Knack, Koha, Kula, Lagniappe, Largesse, Legacy, Manna, Ne'erday, Nuzzer, Offering, Parting, Peace-offering, PET, Potlatch, → **PRESENT**, Presentation, Prezzie, Propine, Reward, Sop, Talent, Tongues, Treat, Tribute, Wakf, Waqf, Windfall, Xenium

Gig Cart, Dennet, Moze, Whisk(e)y

Gigantic Atlantean, Briarean, Colossal, Goliath, → **HUGE**, Immense, Mammoth, Monster, Patagonian, Rounceval, Titan, Vast

Giggle, Giggling Cackle, Fou rire, Ha, Keckle, Simper, Snicker, Snigger, Tehee, Titter

Gigolo Gallant, Ladykiller, Pimp

Gilbert Bab, Gb, White, WS

Gild(ed), Gilding Checklaton, Embellish, Enhance, Inaurate, Ormolu, S(c)hecklaton, Vermeil

Gill(s) Beard, Branchia, Cart, Ctenidium, Jill, Noggin, Spiracle, Trematic

Gillman's Aqualung

Gilpin Draper, John, Renowned

Gilt Elt, Parcel, Sow

Gimcrack Gewgaw, Tawdry, Trangam

Gimmick Doodad, Doodah, Hype, Ploy, Ruse, Stunt

Gin Bathtub, Geneva, Genever, Hollands, Juniper, Lubra, Max, Mother's ruin, Noose, Old Tom, Pink, Ruin, Schiedam, Schnapp(s), Sloe, Snare, Springe, Toil, Trap, Trepan, Twankay

Ginger Activist, Amomum, Asarum, Cassumunar, Costus, Curcuma, Galanga(l), Galengale, Galingale, Gari, Malaguetta, Nut, Pachak, Pep, Pop, Putchock, Putchuk, Race, Rase, Red(head), Root, Spice, Stem, Turmeric, Zedoary, Zingiber

Gingerbread D(o)um-palm, Lebkuchen, Parkin, Parliament(-cake), Pepper-cake

Gingivitis Ulitis

▶ **Gipsy** *see* **GYPSY**

Giraffe Camelopard, Okapi

Gird Accinge, Belt, Equip, Gibe, Jibe, Quip

Girder Beam, Binder, H-beam, I-beam, Lattice, Loincloth, Spar

Girdle Baldric, Center, Cestus, Chastity, Cincture, Cingulum, Corset, Enzone, Equator, Hippolyte, Hoop, Mitre, Panty, Pectoral, Pelvic, Sash, Shoulder, Surcingle, Surround, Zona, Zone, Zonulet

Girl(s) Backfisch, Ball, Bimbo, Bint, Bird, Bit, Bobby-dazzler, Bobby-soxer, Bohemian, Broad, Burd, Call, Charlie, Chit, Chorus, Coed, Colleen, Cover, Crumpet, Cummer, Cutey, Cutie, Cutty, Dam(o)sel, Deb, Dell, Demoiselle, Dish, Doll, Dollybird, Essex, Filly, Fisgig, Fizgig, Flapper, Flower, Fluff, Fraulein, Frippet, Gaiety, Gal, Gammerstang, Geisha, Gibson, Gill(et), Gilp(e)y, Gouge, Gretel, Grisette, Hen, Hoiden, Hoyden, Hussy, It, Italian, Judy, Kimmer, Kinchinmort, Ladette, Land, Lass(ock), Lorette, Maid(en), Mauther, Mawr, Mawther, May, Miss(y), Moppet, Mor, Mot, Mousmé, Mousmee, Mystery, Nautch, Number, Nymph(et), Oanshagh, Peach, Peacherino, Petticoat, Piece, Pigeon, Popsy, Poster, Principal, Puss, Quean, Queyn, Quin(i)e, Randy, Señorita, Sheila, Shi(c)ksa, Sis(s), Smock, Sweater, Tabby, Taupie, Tawpie, Teddy, Tiller, Tit, Tootsie, Trull, Weeny-bopper, Wench, Widgie, Wimp

▷ **Girl** *may indicate* a female name

Girl friend Baby, Chérie, Confidante, Date, Flame, Hinny, Leman, Moll, Peat

Girth Cinch, Compass, Exploitable, Size, Surcingle

Gist Drift, Essence, Kernel, → **NUB**, Pith, Substance

Give(r), Give up, Giving Abandon, Abstain, Accord, Administer, Afford, Award, Bend, Bestow, Buckle, Cede, Confiscate, Consign, Contribute, Dative, Dispense, Dole, → **DONATE**, Duck, Elasticity, Enable, Endow, Enfeoff, Forswear, Gie, Grant, Hand, Impart, Indian, Jack, Largition, Present, Provide, Render, Resign, Sacrifice, Sag, Spring, Stop, Tip, Vacate, Vouchsafe, Yeve, Yield

Give-away Freebie, Gift-horse

Given If

Give out Bestow, Dispense, Emit, Exude, Peter

Give over Cease, Lin

Glacial, Glaciation Gunz, Mindel, Riss, Wurm

Glacier Aletsch, Crevasse, Drumline, Fox, Franz-Josef, Hanging, Iceberg, Ice-cap, Icefall, Moraine, Moulin, Muir, Rhône, Riss, Serac, Stadial, Stoss, Tasman

Glad(ly), Gladden, Gladness Cheer, Fain, → **HAPPY**, Lettice, Lief, Willing

Glade La(u)nd

Gladiator Retiarius, Spartacus

Glamour(ise), Glamorous Charm, Glitter(ati), Glitz, Halo, It, Prestige, SA, Sexy, Spell

Glamour girl Cheesecake, Odalisk, Odalisque, Pin-up

Glance Allusion, Amoret, Argentite, Blink, Browse, Carom(bole), Copper-head, Coup d'oeil, Dekko, Draw, Eld, Eliad, Eye-beam, Galena, Glad eye, Glimpse, Illiad, Inwick, Lustre, Oeillade, Once-over, Peek, → **PEEP**, Ray, Redruthite, Ricochet, Scan, Sheep's eyes, Shufti, Shufty, Side, Silver, Skellie, Skelly, Slant, Snick, Squint, Squiz, Twire, Vision, Waff

Gland Acinus, Adenoid, Adenoma, Adrenal, Apocrine, Bartholin's, Bulbourethral, Colleterial, Conarium, Cowper's, Crypt, Digestive, Ductless, Duodenal, Eccrine, Endocrine, Epiphysis, Exocrine, Goitre, Green, Holocrine, Hypophysis, Hypothalamus, Ink-sac, Lachrymal, Lacrimal, Liver, Lymph, Mammary, Meibomian, Musk-sac, Nectary, Oil, Osmeterium, Ovary, Pancreas, Paranephros, Parathyroid, Parotid, Parotis, Parotoid, Perineal, Pineal, Pituitary, Pope's eye, Preen, Prostate, Prothoracic, Salivary, Scent, Sebaceous, Sericterium, Shell, Silk, Sublingual, Submaxillary, Suprarenal, Sweat, Sweetbread, Tarsel, Tear, Testicle, Testis, Third eye, Thymus, Thyroid, Tonsil, Uropygial, Vesicle, Vulvovaginal, Zeiss

Glanders Farcy

Glandular (trouble) Adenitis

Glare, Glaring Astare, Blare, Dazzle, Flagrant, Garish, Gleam, Glower, Holophotal, Iceblink, Lour, Low(e), Naked, Shine, Vivid, Whally

Glass(es), Glassware, Glassy Amen, Ampul(la), Aneroid, Avanturine, Aventurine, Baccara(t), Barometer, Bell, Bifocals, Bins, Borosilicate, Bottle, Brimmer, Bumper, Burmese, Burning, Calcedonio, Case, Cheval, Cloche, Cocktail, Cooler, Copita, Cordial, Coupe, Cover, Crookes, Crown, Crystal, Cullet, Cupping, Cut, Dark, Delmonico, Diminishing, Eden, Euphon, Favrile, Fibre, Field, Flint, Float, Flute, Foam, Frigger, Frit, Fulgurite, Gauge, Glare, Goblet, Goggles, Granny, Green, Ground, Hand, Highball, Horn-rims, Humpen, Hyaline, Iceland agate, Jar, Jena, Jigger, Keltie, Kelty, Lace, Lalique, Laminated, Lanthanum, Latticinio, Lead, Lens, Liqueur, Liquid, Log, Lorgnette, Loupe, Lozen(ge), Lunette, Magma, Magnifying, Metal, Mica, Middy, Milk, Millefiori, Minimizing, Mirror, Moldavite, Monocle, Mousseline, Multiplying, Murr(h)ine, Muscovy, Musical, Nitreous, Object, Obsidian, One-way, Opal, Opal(ine), Opera, Optical, Pane, Parison, Paste, Pearlite, Pebble, Peeper, Pele, Pele's hair, Perlite, Perspective, Pier, Pince-nez,

Pinhole, Pitchstone, Plate, Pocket, Pon(e)y, Pressed, Prospective, Prunt, Psyche, Pyrex®, Quarrel-pane, Quarry, Quartz, Reducing, Roemer, Ruby, Rummer, Safety, Schmelz, Schooner, Seam, Seidel, Sheet, Silex, Silica, Sleever, Slide, Smalt(o), Snifter, Soluble, Specs, → **SPECTACLES**, Spun, Stained, Stein, Stem, Stemware, Stone, Storm, Strass, Straw, Sun, Supernaculum, Tachilite, Tachylite, Tachylyte, Tektite, Telescope, Tiffany, Tiring, Toilet, Trifocals, Triplex®, Tumbler, Uranium, Varifocals, Venetian, Venice, Vernal, Vita, Vitrail, Vitreous, Vitrescent, Vitro-di-trina, Volcanic, Watch, Water, Waterford, Weather, Window (pane), Wine, Wire

Glass-gall Sandiver

Glass-house Conservatory, Orangery

Glassite Sandemania

Glass-maker Annealer, Blower, Glazier, Lalique, Pontie, Pontil, Ponty, Puntee, Punty

Glaze(d), Glazing Aspic, Ciré, Coat, Double, Eggwash, Film, Flambé, Frit, Glost, Ice, Majolica, Peach-blow, Salt, Sancai, Slip, Tammy, Temmoku, Velatura

Gleam(ing) Blink, Flash, Glint, Glisten, Glitter, Gloss, Leme, Light, Lustre, Ray, Relucent, Sheen, Shimmer, → **SHINE**

Glean(er) Gather, Harvest, Lease, Stibbler

Glee Exuberance, Joy, Mirth, Song

Glen Affric, Ghyll, Gill, Rushy, Silicon, Vale

Glib Flip, Pat, Slick, Smooth

Glide(r), Glideaway, Gliding Aquaplane, Aviette, Chassé, Coast, Elapse, Float, Illapse, Lapse, Luge, Microlight, Off, On, Portamento, Rogallo, Sail, Sailplane, Sashay, Scorrendo, Scrieve, Skate, Ski, Skim, Sleek, Slide, Slip, Slur, Swim, Volplane

Glimmer(ing) Gleam, Glent, Glint, Glow, Inkling, Light, Stime, Styme, Twinkle, Wink

Glimpse Aperçu, Flash, Glance, Gledge, Glisk, Stime, Styme, Waff, Whiff

Glint Flash, Shimmer, → **SPARKLE**, Trace, Twinkle

Glisten(ing) Ganoid, Glint, Sheen, Shimmer, → **SHINE**, Sparkle

Glitter(ing) Clinquant, Garish, Gemmeous, Glee, Paillon, Sequin, Spang(le), Sparkle, Tinsel

Gloat(ing) Crow, Drool, Enjoy, Exult, Schadenfreude

Globe, Globule Artichoke, Ball, Bead, Celestial, Drop, Earth, Orb, Pearl, Shot, Sphear, Sphere

Globulin Legumin, Protein

Gloom(y) Atrabilious, Benight, Blues, Cheerless, Cimmerian, Cloud, Crepuscular, Damp, Dark, → **DESPAIR**, Dingy, Disconsolate, Dismal, Dool(e), Downbeat, Drab, Drear, Drumly, Dump(s), Dyspeptic, Feral, Funereal, Glum, Grey, Grim, Louring, Mirk, Misery, Mopish, Morne, Morose, Mumps, Murk, Obscurity, Overcast, Sable, Sad, Saturnine, Sepulchral, Solein, Solemn, → **SOMBRE**, Sourpuss, Stygian, Sullen, Tenebrious, Tenebrose, Tenebrous, Unlit, Wan

Glorification, Glorify Aggrandise, Apotheosis, Avatar, Bless, → **EXALT**, Extol, Halo, Laud, Lionise, Praise, Radiance, Splendour

Glorious, Gloria, Glory Chorale, Grand, Halo, Hosanna, Ichabod, Knickerbocker, Kudos, Lustre, Magnificent, Nimbus, Strut, Sublime, Twelfth

Glory-pea Kaka-beak, Kaka-bill, Kowhai

Gloss(y) Ciré, Enamel, Gild, Glacé, Interpret, Japan, Lip, Lustre, Patina, → **POLISH**, Postillate, Sheen, Sleek, Slick, Slide, Slur, Supercalendered, Veneer, Wetlook, Whitewash

Glossary Catalogue, Clavis, Index, K'thibh

Gloucester Cheese

Glove Boxing, Cestus, Dannock, Gage, Gauntlet, Kid, Mermaid's, Mitten, Mousquetaire, Muffle, Oven, Velvet

Glow(er), Glowing, Glowworm Aflame, Ashine, Aura, Bloom, Burn, Calescence, Candent, Candescence, Firefly, Flush, Foxfire, Gegenschein, Gleam, Halation, Iceblink, Incandescence, Lambent, Lamp-fly, Leam, Leme, Luculent, Luminesce, Lustre, Perspire, Phosphorescence, Radiant, Reflet, Rushlight, Shine, Snowblink, Translucent, → WARMTH

Glucin(i)um Gl

Glucose, Glucoside Aesculin, Amygdalin, Dextrose, Digitalin, Indican, Maltose, Salicin(e), Saponin, Solanine

Glue(y) Alkyd, Araldite®, Bee, Cement, Colloidal, Gelatin(e), Gunk, Hot-melt, Ichthyocolla, Isinglass, Marine, Paste, Propolis, Rice, Size, Spetch

Glum Dour, Livery, Lugubrious, Moody, Morose, Ron, Sombre

Glut Choke, Gorge, Sate, Satiate, Saturate, Surfeit

Gluten, Glutinous Goo, Ropy, Seiten, Sticky, Tar, Viscid, Zymome

Glutton(ous), Gluttony Bellygod, Carcajou, Cormorant, Edacity, Feaster, Free-liver, Gannet, Gorb, Gourmand, Greedyguts, Gulosity, Gutser, Gutsy, Gutzer, Hog, Lurcher, Pig, Ratel, Scoffer, Sin, Trencherman, Trimalchio, Wolverine

Glyceride, Glycerine Ester, Olein, Palmitin

Glycoside Hesperidin

Gnarl(ed) Knot, Knuckly, Knur, Nob

Gnash(ing) Bruxism, Champ, Grate

Gnat Culex, Culicidae, Midge, Mosquito

Gnaw(ing) Corrode, Erode, Fret, Lagomorph, Rodent

Gnome Adage, Bank-man, Chad, Cobalt, Financier, Kobold, Maxim, Motto, Proverb, Saw, Sprite

Gnostic(ism) (A)eon, Archontic, Cainite, Mand(a)ean, Marcionism, Ophite, Sabian, Tsabian, Zabian

Gnu Brindled, Horned horse, White-tailed, Wildebeest

Go, Going (after, for, off, on, up, etc) Advance, Afoot, Anabasis, Animation, Assail, Attempt, Bash, Betake, Bing, Brio, Choof, Clamber, Continuance, Crack, Depart, Die, Do, Energy, Fare, Gae, Gang, Gee, Gonna, Green, Hamba, Hark, Heavy, Hence, Hie, Imshi, Imshy, Ish, → LEAVE, March, Match, Off, Path, Pep, Perpetual, Ply, Quit, Raik, Repair, Resort, Resume, Run, Scat, Scram, Segue, Shoo, Shot, Skedaddle, Snick-up, Sour, Spank, Square, Stab, Success, Transitory, Trine, Try, Turn, Vam(o)ose, Verve, Via, Viable, Wend, Work, Yead, Yede, Yeed, Zap, Zing, Zip

Goad Ankus, Brod, Gad, Impel, Incite, → NEEDLE, Prod, Rowel, Spur, Stimulate, Stimulus, Taunt

Goal(posts) Ambition, Basket, Bourn(e), Cage, Destination, Dool, Dream, Drop, Dule, End, Ettle, Field, Golden, Grail, Hail, Home, Horme, Hunk, Limit, Mission, Moksha, Own, Score, Silver, Tap-in, Target, Touch-in, Ultima Thule, Uprights

Goat(-like) Alpine, Amalthea, Angora, Antelope, Antilope, Billy, Bok, Bucardo, Buck, Caprine, Cashmere, Cilician, Gait, Gate, Giddy, Goral, Hircine, Ibex, Izard, Kashmir, Kid, Libido, Markhor, Mountain, Nan(ny), Nubian, Rocky Mountain, Saanen, Sassaby, Serow, Serpent-eater, Steenbok, Steinbock, Tahr, Takin, Tehr, Thar, Toggenburg

Goatsucker Fern-owl, Nightjar

Gob(bet) Clot, Dollop, Mouth, Yap

Gobble Bolt, Devour, Gorge, Gulp, Slubber, Wolf
Gobelin Tapestry
Go-between Broker, Factor, Intermediate, Link, Mediate, Middleman, Pandarus, Pander, Shuttle
Goblet Chalice, Hanap
Goblin Banshee, Bargaist, Barg(h)est, Bodach, Bogey, Bogle, Bogy, Brownie, Bucca, Croquemitaine, Empusa, Erl-king, Esprit follet, Genie, Gnome, Gremlin, Knocker, Kobold, Lob-lie-by-the-fire, Lubberfiend, Lutin, Nis(se), Phooka, Phynnodderree, Pooka, Pouke, Puca, Pug, Red-cap, Red-cowl, Shellycoat, → **SPRITE**, Troll, Trow
Goby Dragonet
God(s) All-seer, Amen, Ancient of Days, → **DEITY**, Deus, Di, Divine, Gallery, Gracious, Holy One, Household, Immortals, Inner Light, Light, Maker, Od(d), Olympian, Prime Mover, Principle, Promachos, Providence, Serpent, The Creator, Tin, Trinity, Truth, Unknown, Vanir, War, Water

GODS

1 letter:	Apis	*5 letters:*	Surya
D	Ares	Aegir	Thoth
	Asur	Aesir	Titan
2 letters:	Aten	Allah	Woden
An	Atum	Ammon	Wotan
As	Baal	Bragi	Yahve
Ra	Brag	Comus	Yahwe
Re	Bran	Cupid	
	Cama	Dagan	*6 letters:*
3 letters:	Deva	Dagon	Adonai
Anu	Dieu	Donar	Aeolus
Bel	Eros	Freyr	Amen-ra
Bes	Faun	Haoma	Amon-ra
Dis	Frey	Horus	Anubis
Gad	Joss	Hymen	Apollo
Geb	Kama	Indra	Ashtar
Jah	Kami	Janus	Asshur
Lar	Llyr	Khnum	Avatar
Lir	Loki	Liber	Balder
Lug	Lugh	Lludd	Boreas
Mot	Mars	Mimir	Brahma
Pan	Mors	Momus	Cabiri
Set	Nebo	Njord	Chemos
Sol	Odin	Numen	Cronus
Tiu	Ptah	Orcus	Delian
Tiw	Rama	Orixa	Elohim
Tum	Seth	Pales	Faunus
Tyr	Siva	Picus	Ganesa
	Soma	Pluto	Garuda
4 letters:	Thor	Rudra	HaShem
Abba	Tyrr	Satyr	Helios
Agni	Yama	Sebek	Hermes
Aitu	Zeus	Shiva	Hughie
Amun		Sinis	Hypnos

Kronos
Mammon
Marduk
Mexitl
Mextli
Mithra
Molech
Moloch
Nereus
Njorth
Oannes
Orisha
Ormazd
Ormuzd
Osiris
Panisc
Panisk
Plutus
Rimmon
Saturn
Somnus
Tammuz
Teraph
Teshup
Thamiz
Thunor
Triton
Uranus
Varuna
Vishnu
Vulcan
Yahweh

Zombie

7 letters:
Alastor
Alpheus
Angus Og
Anteros
Bacchus
Bhagwan
Chemosh
Daikoku
Ganesha
Hanuman
Heimdal
Jehovah
Jupiter
Krishna
Kuan Yin
Kwan Yin
Mercury
Mithras
Neptune
Nisroch
Oceanus
Penates
Phoebus
Priapus
Proteus
Rameses
Sarapis
Sat Guru
Serapis

Setebos
Shamash
Silenus
Thammuz
Zagreus

8 letters:
Achelous
Dionysus
Heimdall
Hyperion
Kamadeva
Mahadeva
Morpheus
Mulciber
Nataraja
Pantheon
Poseidon
Quirinus
Silvanus
Sylvanus
Terminus
Trimurti
Wahiguru
Zephyrus

9 letters:
All-father
Asclepius
Fabulinus
Heimdallr
Jagganath

Tetragram
Thunderer
Vertumnus
Zernebock

10 letters:
Ahura Mazda
Demogorgon
Elegabalus
Hephaestus
Hephaistos
Juggernaut
Karttikaya
Mumbo-jumbo
Prometheus
Trophonius

11 letters:
Adrammelech
Aesculapius
Bodhisattva

12 letters:
Quetzalcoati
Supreme Being
Trismegistus

14 letters:
Tetragrammaton

God-bearing Deiparous
Goddess(es) Divine, Green, Muse

GODDESSES

2 letters:
Ge

3 letters:
Ate
Eos
Hel
Mut
Nox
Nut
Nyx
Ops
Pax

4 letters:
Dian
Eris
Gaea
Gaia
Hera
Idun
Iris
Isis
Juno
Kali
Leda
Leto

Luna
Maat
Maut
Nike
Norn
Pele
Rhea
Sita
Thea

5 letters:
Aruru
Ceres

Diana
Dione
Durga
Erato
Flora
Freya
Grace
Horae
Houri
Hulda
Iduna
Irene
Kotys

Moera	Graiae	**7 letters:**	Cytherea
Moira	Hathor	Artemis	Libitina
Pales	Hecate	Astarte	Rhiannon
Tanit	Hertha	Astraea	Valkyrie
Terra	Hestia	Bellona	Victoria
Tyche	Huldar	Cotytto	Walkyrie
Ushas	Hyaeia	Cynthia	
Venus	Idalia	Demeter	**9 letters:**
Vesta	Ishtar	Fortuna	Aphrodite
	Ithunn	Kotytto	Ashtaroth
6 letters:	Lucina	Lakshmi	Ashtoreth
Aglaia	Pallas	Megaera	Eumenides
Ashnan	Parcae	Minerva	Mnemosyne
Athene	Phoebe	Nemesis	Sarasvati
Aurora	Pomona	Nepthys	
Bastet	Satyra	Parvati	**10 letters:**
Cybele	Selene	Sabrina	Amphitrite
Cyrene	Semele	Strenia	Proserpina
Eastre	Tellus	Victory	Proserpine
Freyja	Tethys		
Frigga	Themis	**8 letters:**	
Graeae	Thetis	Cloacina	

Godfather, Godmother Capo, Cummer, Fairy, Gossip, Kimmer, Rama, Sponsor, Woden

Godless Agnostic, Atheistic, Atheous, Impious, Profane

Godly Deist, Devout, Holy, Pious

Godown Hong

God-willing Deo volente, DV, Inshallah, Mashallah

Go-getter Arriviste, Hustler

Goggle(s) Snow-eyes, Stare

Going wrong Aglee, Agley, Misfiring

▷ **Going wrong** *may indicate* an anagram

Goitre Derbyshire neck, Exophthalmic, Graves' disease, Struma

Gold(en) Age, Amber, Apple, Ass, Au, Aureate, Auriferous, Bendigo, Bough, Bull, Bullion, California, Chryselephantine, Doubloon, Dutch, Eagle, Electron, Electrum, Emerods, Filigree, Filled, Fleece, Fool's, Free, Fulminating, Gate, Gule, Handshake, Hind, Horde, Horn, Ingot, Kolar, Leaf, Lingot, Moidore, Mosaic, Muck, Nugget, Oaker, Obang, Ochre, Ophir, Or, Oreide, Ormolu, Oroide, Pistole, Placer, Pyrites, Red, Reef, Rolled, Silence, Silver-gilt, Sol, Standard, Stream, Stubborn, Talmi, Thrimsa, Tolosa, Treasury, Venice, Virgin, White, Witwatersrand, Yellow

Gold-digger Forty-niner, Prospector

Golden fleece Phrixus

Goldfield Rand

Goldfinch Charm, Chirm, Redcap

Gold leaf Ormolu

Gold rush Kalgoorlie, Klondike

Goldsmith Cellini, Fabergé, Oliver

Golf (ball) Better-ball, Clock, Crazy, Foursome, Gutta, Matchplay, Medal play, Repaint, Round, Stableford

Golfer Alliss, Braid, Cotton, Els, Faldo, Hogan, Lyle, Pivoter, Rees, Roundsman,

Seve, Snead, Teer, Texas scramble, Tiger Woods, Trevino, Wolstenholme, Yipper

Golly Crumbs, Gosh

Gondolier Balloonist, Bargee

Gone Ago, Dead, Defunct, Napoo, Out, Past, Ygo(e), Yod

▷ **Gone off** *may indicate* an anagram

Gone west Had it

Gong Bell, DSO, → MEDAL, Tam-tam, VC

Gonorrhoea Clap

Goo Gleet, Gloop, Gunge, Poise, Ulmin

Goober Monkey nut

Good(ness), Goody-goody Agatha, Agathodaimon, Altruism, Angelic, Bad, Bein, Benefit, Blesses, Bon, Bonzer, Bosker, Bounty, Brod, Budgeree, Canny, Castor, Civil, Clinker, Common, Coo, Cool, Crack(ing), Credit, Dab, Dandy, Def, Dow, Enid, Estimable, Fantabulous, Finger lickin', First-class, G, Gear, Giffen, Glenda, Gosh, Guid, Humdinger, Lois, Lor, Ma foi, Neat, Nobility, → NO GOOD, Pi, Plum, Prime, Proper, Purler, Rattling, Rectitude, Riddance, Right, Rum, Sake, Salutary, Samaritan, Sanctity, Slap-up, Smashing, Spiffing, St, Suitable, Super, Taut, Tollol, Topping, Valid, Virtue, Virtuous, Weal, Welfare, Whacko, Wholesome, Worthy

Goodbye Addio, Adieu, Adios, Aloha, Apopemptic, Arrivederci, Cheerio, Ciao, Congé, Farewell, Haere ra, Hamba kahle, Hooray, Hooroo, Sayonara, See-you, Tata, Toodle-oo, Toodle-pip, Vale

Good evening Den

Goodfellow Brick, Puck, Robin, Samaritan, Worthy

Good-for-nothing Bum, Donnat, Donnot, Dud, Idler, Layabout, Lorel, Lorrell, Losel, Napoo, Sca(l)lawag, Scallywag, Scant o'grace, Sculpin, Shot-clog, Useless, Vaurien, Waff, Waster, Wastrel

Good Friday Parasceve, Pasch of the Cross

Good-humour(ed), Good-natured Amiable, Bonhomie, Gruntled, Kind

Good-looking Bon(n)ie, Bonny, Bonwie, Comely, Fair, Handsome, Personable, Pretty, Wally

Good news Evangel

Good number Thr(e)ave

Good order Eutaxy, Shipshape

Goods Bona, Brown, Cargo, Consumer, Disposable, Durable, Durables, Fancy, Flotsam, Freight, Futures, Gear, Hardware, Insight, Ironware, Lagan, Lay-away, Line, Piece, Products, Property, Schlock, Soft, Sparterie, Truck, Wares, White

Goodwill Amity, Bonhom(m)ie, Favour, Gree

Goody Wrong'un

Goon Bentine, Milligan, Secombe, Sellers

Goose, Geese Anserine, Barnacle, Bernicle, Blue, Brent, Canada, Cape Barren, Colonial, Daftie, Ember, Gaggle, Gander, Gannet, Golden, Greylag, Grope, Harvest, Hawaiian, Idiot, Juggins, MacFarlane's, Magpie, Michaelmas, Mother, Nana, Nene, Pink-footed, Quink, Roger, Saddleback, Silly, Simpleton, Skein, Snow, Solan, Strasbourg, Stubble, → STUPID PERSON, Swan, Team, Wav(e)y, Wawa, Whitehead

Gooseberry Cape, Chaperon(e), Chinese, Coromandel, Detrop, Fool, Gog, Groser(t), Groset, Grossart, Grozer, Honey blob, Kiwi, Physalis, Tomato

Gooseflesh Horripilation

Goosefoot Allgood, Amarantaceae, Beet, Blite, Fat-hen, Mercury, Orache, Saltbush

Gooseherd Quill-driver

Gopher Camass-rat, Minnesota, Pocket

Gordian Knot
Gordon Chinese, Flash, Rioter
Gore Blood, Cloy, Gair, Horn, Inset, Toss
Gorge(s) Abyss, Arroyo, Barranca, Barranco, Canyon, Chasm, Cheddar, Cleft, Couloir, Cram, Defile, Donga, Flume, Gap, Ghyll, Glut, Grand Canyon, Grand Coulee, Gulch, Iron Gate, Khor, Kloof, Lin(n), Nala, Nalla(h), Nulla(h), Olduvai, Overeat, Overfeed, Pass, Ravine, Snarf, Staw, → **STUFF**, Throat, Tire, Tums, Valley, Yosemite
Gorgeous Delectable, Dreamboat, Grand, Splendid, Superb
Gorgon Euryale, Medusa, Ogress, Stheno
▶ **Gorilla** *see* **MONKEY**
Gorse Broom, Furze, Gosse, Ulex, Whin
Gosh Begad, Begorra, Blimey, Coo, Cor, Gadzooks, Gee, Gracious, Gum, Heavens, Lor, My, Och, Odsbobs, Odso
Gospel(s), Gospeller Apocryphal, Creed, Diatessaron, Evangel, Fact, John, Kerygma, Luke, Mark, Matthew, Nicodemus, Prosperity, Protevangelium, Synoptic, Truth, Waldensian
Gossamer(y) Araneous, Byssoid, Cobwebby, Gauzy
Gossip Ana(s), Aunt, Backbite, Blether, Cackle, Cat, Causerie, Chat, Chin, Chitchat, Clash, Claver, Cleck, Clish-clash, Clishmaclaver, Confab, Coze, Crack, Cummer, Dirt, Flibbertigibbet, Gab(nash), Gabfest, Gas, Gash, Goster, Gup, Hearsay, Hen, Jaw, Loose-tongued, Maundrel, Nashgab, Natter, Noise, On dit, Pal, Personalist, Prattle, Prose, Quidnunc, Reportage, Rumour, Scandal(monger), Schmooze, Scuttlebutt, Shmoose, Shmooze, Sweetie-wife, Tabby(cat), Talk(er), Tattle, Tattletale, Tibby, Tittle(-tattle), Twattle, Yatter, Yenta
Got Gat, Obtained
Goth(ic) Alaric, Lurid, Moesia
Gothamite Abderian, New Yorker
Gouge Chisel, Groove, Scoop
Gourd Bottle, Calabash, Courgette, Dishcloth, Guiro, Hercules' club, Loofa, Melon, Monkeybread, Pumpkin, Squash, Zucchini
Gourmand, Gourmet Apicius, → **EPICURE**, Gastronome, Gastrosopher, Lickerish, Table, Trencherman, Ventripotent
Gout Chiragra, Hamarthritis, Podagra, Taste, Tophus
Govern(or), Government Adelantado, Administer, Ag(h)a, Agricola, Alderman, Amban, Amman, Amtman, ANC, Andocracy, Archology, Aristocracy, Autarchy, Autocrat, Autonomy, Bahram, Ban, Bashaw, Beehive, Beg, Beglerbeg, Bencher, Bey, Bridler, Bureaucracy, Burgrave, Cabinet, Caciquism, Caretaker, Castellan, Catapan, Cham, Circar, Classis, Coalition, Command, Commonwealth, Condominium, Congress, Constable, Constitution, Consulate, Cybernetic, Darogha, Democracy, Dergue, Despotism, Dey, Diarchy, Dictatorship, Dinarchy, Directoire, Directory, Dominate, Downing St, Duarchy, Dulocracy, Duumvirate, Dyarchy, Dynast, Earl, Ecclesiarchy, Empery, Eparch, Ergatocracy, Escapement, Ethnarch, Exarch, Fascism, Federal, G, Gauleiter, Gerontocracy, Gov, Grieve, Gubernator, Guv, Gynarchy, Hagiarchy, Hagiocracy, Hague, Hajjaz, Hakim, Haptarchy, Harmost, HE, Helm, Hexarchy, Hierocracy, Honcho, Hospodar, Imperialism, Ins, Inspector, Isocracy, Junta, Kaimakam, Kakistocracy, Kawanatanga, Kebele, Kemalism, Khalifate, Khan, Kremlin, Legate, Local, Majlis, Majorism, Monarchy, Monocracy, Mudir, Nabob, Naik, Nomarch, Nomocracy, Ochlocracy, Oireachtas, Oligarchy, Optic®, Pa, Pacha, Padishah, Pasha, Pater, Pentarch, Père, Petticoat, Physiocracy, Pilate, Placemen, Plutocracy, Podesta, Polity, Polyarchy, Porte, Power, Priest-king, Proconsul, Propraetor, Proveditor, Provedor(e), Providor,

Ptochocracy, Quadrumvirate, Quirinal, Raj, Realpolitik, Rection, Rector, Rectrix, Regency, Regié, Regime(n), Reign, Rein, Ride, → **RULE**, Satrap, Senate, Serkali, Shogun, Signoria, Sircar, Sirkar, Stad(t)holder, Stakhanovism, Statecraft, Steer, Stratocracy, Subadar, Sway, Technocracy, Tetrarchy, Thalassocracy, Thalattocracy, Thatcherism, Thearchy, Theocracy, Theonomy, Timocracy, Totalitarianism, Triarchy, Triumvirate, Tuchun, Tyranny, Vali, Viceregal, Viceroy, Vichy, Wali, Warden, Wealsman, Whitehall, White House, Witan

Governess Duenna, Eyre, Fraulein, Griffin, Mademoiselle, Prism, Vicereine

Government revenue Jaghir(e), Jagir

Gown Banian, Banyan, Dressing, Empire, Geneva, Green, Johnny, Kirtle, Manteau, Manto, Mantua, Manty, Morning, Mother Hubbard, Peignoir, Polonaise, Robe, Sack, Silk, Slammakin, Slammerkin, Slop, Stola, Stuff, Tea, Wrap(per)

Grab Annexe, Bag, Clutch, Cly, Collar, Glaum, Grapnel, Hold, Holt, Rap, Seise, Seize, → **SNATCH**, Steal, Swipe

Gracchi Jewels

Grace(s), Graceful Aglaia, Airy, Amnesty, Anna, Bad, Beauty, Become, Benediction, Bethankit, Blessing, Charis(ma), Charites, Charity, Cooperating, Darling, Dr, Elegance, Euphrosyne, Fluent, Gainly, Genteel, Genty, Godliness, Grazioso, Handsome, Light, Mense, Mercy, Molinism, Mordent, Omnium, Ornament, Polish, Pralltriller, Prayer, Sacrament, Saving, Spirituelle, Streamlined, Style, Thalia, Thanks, Thanksgiving, WG, Willowy

Gracious Benign, By George, Charismatic, Generous, Good, Handsome, Hend, Merciful, Polite

Gradation Ablaut, Cline, Degree, Nuance, Stage

Grade, Gradient Alpha, Analyse, Angle, Assort, Beta, Bubs, Class(ify), Conservation, Dan, Degree, Delta, Echelon, Gamma, Geothermal, Gon, Gride, Hierarchy, Inclination, Kyu, Lapse, Measure, Order, Ordinary, Pressure, Rank, Reserve, Score, Seed, Slope, Stage, Standard, Status, Temperature, Thermocline

Gradual Gentle, Grail, Imperceptible, Inchmeal, Piecemeal, Slow

Graduate, Graduation Alumnus, BA, Bachelor, Calibrate, Capping, Classman, Incept, Laureateship, Licentiate, LlB, MA, Master, Nuance, Optime, Ovate

Graffiti Bomb, Doodle, Tag, Tagger

Graft Anaplasty, Autoplasty, Boodle, Bribery, Bud, Bypass, Cion, Cluster, Crown, Dishonesty, Dub, Enarch, Enrace, Flap, Hard, Heteroplasty, Imp, Implant, Inarch, Inoculate, Payola, Pomato, Racket, Scion, Shoot, Sien(t), Skin, Slip, Syen, Transplant, Whip, Ympe

Grail Chalice, Cup, Sangraal, Sangrail, Sangreal

Grain(y) Bajra, Bajree, Bajri, Bear, Bere, Boll, Bran, Cereal, Corn, Couscous, Crop, Curn, Curn(e)y, Cuscus, Distillers', D(o)urra, Extine, Frumentation, Gr, Graddan, Granule, Groats, Grumose, Intine, Kaoliang, Knaveship, Malt, Mashlam, Mashlin, Mashloch, Mashlum, Maslin, Mealie, Millet, Milo, Minim, Mongcorn, Oats, Panic(k), Pannick, Pickle, Pinole, Pollen, Polynology, Popcorn, Proso, Psyllium, Puckle, Quarter, Quinoa, Rabi, Rag(g)ee, Raggy, Ragi, Rhy, Rye, Sand, Scruple, Seed, Semsem, Sorghum, Thirlage, Tola, Touch, Wheat, Wholemeal

Gram Black, Chich, Chick-pea, Green, Teen, Tene, Urd

Grammar(ian), Grammatical Ablative absolute, Accidence, Amphibology, Anacoluthia, Anacoluthon, Anaphora, Anastrophe, Case, Cataphora, Categorical, Donat, Donet, Generative, Gr, Linguistics, Montague, Paradigm, Paucal, Pivot, Primer, Priscianist, Priscianus, Protasis, Scholiast, Stratificational, Syndetic, Syndeton, Synectics, Synesis, Syntax, Systemics, Tagmeme, Transformational, Trivium, Typto, Universal, Valency

Gramophone Record player, Victrolla®
Grampus Orc, Thresher-whale, Whale
Granary Barn, Girnel, Silo
Grand(eur), Grandiose Big, Canyon, Epical, Flugel, G, Gorgeous, Guignol, High-faluting, Hotel, Imposing, La(h)-di-da(h), Long, Lordly, Magnificent, Majestic, Megalomania, Palatial, Piano(forte), Pompous, Regal, Splendid, Stately, Stoor, Stour, Stowre, Sture, Sublime, Swell, Tour
Grandchild Mokopuna, Niece, Oe, Oy(e)
Grandee Adelantado, Don, Magnifico
Grandfather Ancient, Avital, Clock, Goodsire, Gramps, Gudesire, Gutcher, Luckie-dad, Oldster, Old-timer, Oupa
Grandmother Babushka, Beldam, Gran(nie), Granny, Moses, Nan(a), Ouma
Grandparent(al) Aval, Avital
Grand Prix Race(-cup)
Grandsire Peal
Grange Moated
Granite Aberdeen, Chinastone, Graphic, Greisen, Luxul(l)ianite, Luxulyanite, NH, Pegmatite, Protogine
Grannie Forebear, Knot, Nan(a)
Grant(ed) Accord, Aid, Award, Bestow, Beteem(e), Block, Bounty, Bursary, Carta, Cary, Cede, Charta, Charter, Concession, → **CONFER**, Cy, Datum, Endow, Exhibition, Feoff, Give, Hugh, Land, Lend, Let, Munich, Obreption, Patent, President, Regium donum, Send, Sop, Subsidy, Subvention, Supply, Teene, Ulysses, Vouchsafe, Yeven, Yield
Granule, Granulate(d) Kern, Otolith, Pearl, Plastid, Pound, Prill
Grape(s) Aligoté, Botros, Botryoid, Bullace, Cabernet, Cabernet Sauvignon, Catawba, Chardonnay, Chenin blanc, Colombard, Concord, Delaware, Diamond, Fox, Gamay, Gewurztraminer, Grenache, Haanepoot, Hamburg(h), Hanepoot, Honeypot, Hyacinth, Lambrusco, Malbec, Malmsey, Malvasia, Malvesie, Malvoisie, Marsanne, Merlot, Muscadel, Muscadine, Muscat(el), Noble rot, Oregon, Petite Syrah, Pinot, Pinot blanc, Pinot Chardonnay, Primitivo, Ptisan, Racemose, Raisin, Rape, Riesling, Sauvignon, Scuppernong, Sémillon, Sercial, Shiraz, Sour, Staphyline, Steen, Sultana, Sweet-water, Sylvaner, Syrah, Tokay, Uva, Verdelho, Véronique, Vino, Wineberry, Zinfandel
Grapefruit Pampelmoose, Pomelo, Pompelmouse, Pompelo, Pumple-nose, Shaddock, Ugli®
Grapeshot Mitraille
Grape-sugar Glucose
Grapevine Hearsay, Mocassin telegraph, Moccasin telegraph
Graph, Graphic(s) Bar, Chart, Computer, Contour, Diagram, Histogram, Learning curve, Nomograph, Ogive, Picturesque, Pie (chart), Profile, Sonogram, Table, Turtle, Vivid, Waveform, Waveshape
Graphite Kish, Plumbago
Grapple Clinch, Close, Hook, Lock, Struggle, Wrestle
Grasp(ing) Apprehend, Catch, Clat, Claut, Clinch, → **CLUTCH**, Compass, Comprehend, Fathom, Get, Grab, Grapple, Greedy, Grip(e), Hent, Hug, Prehend, Prehensile, Raptorial, Realise, Rumble, Sense, Snap, Snatch, Twig, Uptak(e)
Grass(land), Grass roots, Grassy Agrostology, Alang, Alfa(lfa), Arrow, Avena, Bahia, Bamboo, Bang, Barbed wire, Barley, Barnyard, Beard, Bennet, Bent, Bermuda, Bhang, Blade, Blady, Blue(-eyed), Blue moor, Bristle, Brome-grass, Bromus, Buffalo, Buffel, Bunch, Bush, Canary, Cane, Canna, Cannach, Carpet,

Cat's tail, Chess, China, Citronella, Cleavers, Clivers, Clover, Cochlearia, Cocksfoot, Cockspur, Cogon, Cord, Cortaderia, Cotton, Couch, Cow, Crab, Culm, Cuscus, Cutty, Dactylis, Danthonia, Dari, Darnel, Deergrass, Dhur(r)a, Diss, Divot, Dogstail, Dog's tooth, Dogwheat, Doob, Doura, Dura, Durra, Eddish, Eel, Eelwrack, Elephant, Emmer, Esparto, Feather, Fescue, Finger, Fiorin, Flinders, Floating, Flote, Fog, Foggage, Foxtail, Gage, Gama-grass, Ganja, Gardener's garters, Glume, Glumella, Goose, Grama, Green(sward), Hair, Halfa, Harestail, Hassock, Haulm, Hay, Haycock, Heath(er), Hemp, Herbage, High veld, Holy, → **INFORM**, Jawar(i), Job's tears, Johnson, Jowar(i), Kangaroo, Kans, Kentucky blue, Khuskhus, Kikuyu, Knoll, Knot, Lalang, Laund, Lawn, Lay, Lea, Lee, Lemon, Locusta, Lolium, Lop, Lucern(e), Lyme, Mabela, Machair, Manna, Marram, Marrum, Mary Jane, Mat, Materass, Matweed, Mead, Meadow(-fescue), Meadow foxtail, Melic, Melick, Millet, Milo, Miscanthus, Monkey, Moor, Nark, Nassella tussock, Nature strip, Nose, Nut, Oat, Orange, Orchard, Oryza, Painted, Palet, Pamir, Pampas, Panic, Paspalum, Pasturage, Peach, Pennisetum, Pepper, Persicaria, Phleum, Plume, Poa, Porcupine, Pot, Purple moor, Puszta, Quack, Quaking, Quick, Quitch, Ramee, Rami(e), Rat, Rat on, Redtop, Reed, Rescue, Rhodes, Rib, Ribbon, Rice, Rips, Roosa, Rough, Rumble(r), Rusa, Rush, Rye(-brome), Sacaton, Sago, Salt, Sand, Savanna(h), Saw, Scorpion, Scraw, Scurvy, Scutch, Sea-reed, Sedge, Seg, Sesame, Shave, Sheep's fescue, Shop, Sing, Sinsemilla, Sisal, Sneak(er), Snitch, Snout, Snow, Sorghum, Sour-gourd, Sourveld, Spanish, Spear, Spelt, Spike, Spinifex, Splay, Split, Squeal, Squirrel-tail, Squitch, Stag, Star(r), Stipa, Stool-pigeon, Storm, Sudan, Sugar, Sward, Swath(e), Sword, Tape, Taramea, Tath, Tea, Tef(f), Tell, Teosinte, Timothy, Toad, Toetoe, Toitoi, Triticale, Triticum, True-love, Tuffet, Turf, Tussac, Tussock, Twitch, Veld(t), Vernal, Vetiver, Viper's, Whangee, Wheat, Wheatgrass, Whitlow, Windlestraw, Wire, Witch, Wood melick, Worm, Yard, Yellow-eyed, Yorkshire fog, Zizania, Zostera, Zoysia

Grasshopper Cicada, Cricket, Grig, Katydid, Locust, Long-horned, Meadow, Tettix, Wart-biter, Weta

Grate(r), Grating Abrade, Burr, Cancelli, Chain, Chirk, Crepitus, Diffraction, → **FRET**, Graticule, Gravelly, Grid, Grill, Guichet, Guttural, Hack, Haik, Hake, Hearth, Heck, Hoarse, Ingle, Jar, Mort-safe, Portcullis, Rasp, Risp, Rub, Ruling, Scrannel, → **SCRAPE**, Scrat, Shred, Siver, Strident, Syver

Grateful Beholden, Cinders, Indebted, Obliged

Gratification, Gratify(ing) Aggrate, Indulge, Kick, Masochism, Narcissism, Oblige, Pleasure, Regale, Reward, Sadism

Gratitude God 'a mercy, Ta, Thanks

Gratuitous, Gratuity Baksheesh, Beer-money, Bonsella, Bonus, Bounty, Cumshaw, Free, Glove-money, Gratis, Mag(g)s, Tip

Grave(yard) Accent, Arlington, Bass, Bier, Burial, Charnel, Chase, Critical, Darga, Demure, Dust, God's acre, Heavy, Heinous, Important, Ingroove, Kistvaen, Kurgan, Long home, Mool, Mould, Mound, Passage, Pit, Sad, Saturnine, Serious, Sober, Sombre, Speos, Staid, Stern, Tomb, Watery

Grave-digger Bederal, Fossor, Sexton

Gravel(ly) Calculus, Channel, Chesil, Chisel, Eskar, Esker, Glareous, Grail(e), Grit, Hoggin(g), Murram, Nonplus, Pay, Pea, Pingo, Shingle

Gravity Barycentric, G, Geotaxis, Geotropism, Great Attraction, Magnitude, Mascon, Quantum, Specific, Weight, Zero

Gravy Baster, Bisto®, Browning, Coin, Jus, Sauce

Gravy-boat Argyle, Argyll

▶ **Gray** see **GREY**

Grayling Umber

Graze, Grazing, Grazier Abrade, Agist, Bark, Brush, Crease, Crop, Feed, Gride, Gryde, Heft, Herdwick, Leasow(e), Machair, Moorburn, Muirburn, Pascual, Pastoralist, Pasture, Rake, Rangeland, Scrape, Scrawn, Shave, Sheepwalk, Shieling, Zero

Grease, Greasy Bribe, Creesh, Dope, Dubbing, Elaeolite, Elbow, Enseam, Glit, Lanolin, Lard, Lubricate, Ointment, Pinguid, Seam(e), Shearer, Sheep-shearer, Smarm, Smear, Suint, Unctuous

Great(ly), Greater, Greatest, Greats Alfred, Ali, Astronomical, Bully, Capital, Colossus, Extreme, Gargantuan, Gatsby, Gay, Gey, Gran(d), Grit, Gt, Guns, Hellova, Helluva, Immortal, Important, Lion, Macro, Magnus, Main, Major, Massive, Mega, Mickle, Mochell, Modern, Much, Muchel(l), Muckle, No end, OS, Profound, Rousing, Stoor, Stour, Stupendous, Sture, Sublime, Super, Superb, Swingeing, Synergy, Tall, Titan(ic), Top notch, Tremendous, Unco, Untold, Utmost, Vast, Voluminous, Zenith

Great deal Mort

Grebe Cargoose

Grecian Bend, Nose

Greed(y) Avarice, Avid, Bulimia, Bulimy, Cupidity, Edacious, Esurient, Gannet, Gare, Grabby, Grip(ple), Gulosity, Harpy, Insatiable, Killcrop, Lickerish, Liquorish, Mercenary, Money-grubbing, Piggery, Pleonexia, Rapacity, Selfish, Shark's manners, Solan, Voracity, Wolfish

Greek(s) Achaean, Achaian, Achilles, Aeolic, Agamemnon, Ajax, Ancient, Aonian, Arcadia, Archimedes, Argive, Aristides, Athenian, Attic, Boeotian, Byzantine, Cadmean, Cleruch, Corinthian, Cretan, Cumae, Cyzicus, Delphian, Demotic, Ding, Diomedes, Dorian, Doric, Elea, Eoka, Eolic, Epaminondas, Ephebe, Epirus, Euclid, Evzone, Fanariot, Gr, Helladic, Hellene, Hellenic, Homer, Hoplite, Ionian, Isocrates, Italiot(e), Javan, Katharev(o)usa, Klepht, Koine, Laconian, Lapith, Late, Leonidas, Linear B, Locrian, Lucian, Lysander, Macedonia, Medieval, Middle, Modern, Molossian, Momus, Nestor, Nike, Nostos, Orestes, Paestum, Patroclus, Pelasgic, Pelopid, Perseus, Phanariot, Pythagoras, Romaic, Samiot, Seminole, Spartacus, Spartan, Stagirite, Strabo, Sybarite, Tean, Teian, Theban, Thersites, Theseus, Thessal(on)ian, Thracian, Timon, Typto, Uniat, Xenophon, Zorba

Green(ery) Almond, Apple, Avocado, Baggy, Bice, Biliverdin, Bleaching, Bottle, Bowling, Caesious, Callow, Celadon, Cerulein, Chard, Chartreuse, Chlorophyll, Chrome, Citron, Cole, Collard, Common, Copper, Corbeau, Crown, Cyan, Dioptase, Eau de nil, Eco-, Ecofriendly, Emerald, Emerande, Envious, Erin, Fingers, Foliage, Forest, Fundie, Fundy, Gaudy, Glaucous, Go, Goddess, Grass, Gretna, Gull, Immature, Inexpert, Jade, Jungle, Kendal, Kensal, Khaki, Lawn, Leafage, Lime, Lincoln, Loden, Lovat, Mead, Monastral®, Moss, Moulding, Naive, New, Nile, Oasis, Olive, Paris, Pea, Peridot, Pistachio, Porraceous, Putting, Raw, Realo, Reseda, Rifle, Rink, Sage, Sap, Scheele's, Sea, Sludge, Smaragdine, Sward, Teal, Tender, Terre-vert, Turacoverdin, Tyro, Unfledged, Uninitiated, Unripe, Untrained, Uranite, Verdant, Verd antique, Verdigris, Verdure, Vert, Virent, Virid, Vir(id)escent, Young

Greenheart Bebeeru

Greenhorn Baby, Dupe, Put(t), Rookie, Sucker

Greenhouse Conservatory, Orangery, Phytotron, Polytunnel

Greens Broccoli, Cabbage, Calabrese, Cash, Money, Sprout, Vegetable(s)

Greet, Greeting(s) Abrazo, Accost, All hail, Arvo, Banzai, Benedicite, Bid, Blubber, Bonsoir, Chimo, Ciao, Gorillagram, Hail, Hallo, Halse, Handclasp, Handshake,

Haway, Heil, Heita, Hello, Herald, Hi, High-five, Hiya, Hongi, How, How d'ye do,
Howsit, Jai Hind, Jambo, Kia ora, Kiss, Kissagram, Mihi, Namaskar, Namaste,
Respects, Salaam, Salam alaikum, Salute, Salve, Sd, Shalom, Shalom aleichem,
Sorry, Strippagram, Strippergram, Tena koe, Tena korua, Tena koutou, Wave,
→ WELCOME, Wotcher, Yo

Gregarious Social

Gregorian Chant, NS, Plagal

▶ **Gremlin** *see* GOBLIN

Grenade, Grenadier Bomb, Egg, Hand, Pineapple, Rat-tail, Rifle, Stun

Greta Garbo

Grey(ing), Gray Age, Agnes, Argent, Ashen, Ashy, Battleship, Beige, Bloncket,
C(a)esius, Charcoal, Cinereous, Dapple, Dorian, Dove, Drab, Ecru, Feldgrau, Field,
Glaucous, Gloomy, Gr, Gridelin, Griesie, Gries(l)y, Grise, Grisy, Grizzled, Gunmetal,
Gy, Hoary, Hodden, Hore, Inn, Iron, Leaden, Liard, Livid, Lloyd, Lucia, Lyart,
Mouse-coloured, Neutral, Olive drab, Oyster, Pearl, Perse, Pewter, Poliosis, Putty,
Sclate, Slaty, Steel, Taupe, Zane

Greyfriars Bunter, Magnet

Greyhound Grew, Italian, Lapdog, Longtail, Ocean, Persian, Saluki, Sapling,
Whippet

Grey matter Cinerea

Grid(dle), Gridiron Bar, Barbecue, Brandreth, Cattle, Control, Dot matrix, Grate,
Graticule, Grating, National, Network, Reseau, Reticle, Roo-bar, Screen, Starting,
Suppressor, Tava(h), Tawa, Windscale

Gride Creak, Grate

Grief, Grievance, Grieve, Grievous Axe, Bemoan, Bitter, Complaint, Condole, Cry,
Dear(e), Deere, Distress, Dole, Dolour, Gram(e), Gravamen, Grudge, Heartbreak,
Hone, Illy, Io, → MISERY, Monody, Noyous, O(c)hone, Overset, Pain, Pathetic,
Plaint, Rue, Score, Sore, Sorrow, Teen, Tene, Tragic, Wayment, Weeping, Woe,
Wrong

Griffin Gripe, Grype, Novice, Pony

Grill(er), Grilling Braai, Brander, Broil, Carbonado, Crisp, Devil, Gridiron,
Inquisition, Interrogate, Kebab, Mixed, Pump, Question, Rack, Radiator, Reja,
Yakimona

Grim Dire, Dour, Forbidding, Gaunt, Glum, Gurly, Hard, Macabre, Stern

▷ **Grim** *may indicate* an anagram

Grimace Face, Girn, Moe, Mop, Moue, Mouth, Mow, Murgeon, Pout, Wince

Grime(s), Grimy Colly, Dirt, Peter, Rechie, Reechie, Reechy, Soil, Sweep

Grin Fleer, Girn, Risus, Simper, Smirk, Sneer

Grind(ing), Grinder Bray, Bruxism, Chew, Crunch, → CRUSH, Droil, Drudgery,
Gnash, Grate, Graunch, Grit, Home, Kern, Kibble, Labour, Levigate, Mano, Metate,
Mill, Mince, Molar, Muller, Offhand, Pug, Pulverise, Slog, Stamp, Triturate

Grip(ping), Gripper Ascendeur, Bite, Chuck, Clam, Clamp, Clip, Clutch, Craple,
Embrace, Engrasp, Enthral, Get, Grapple, → GRASP, Haft, Hair, Hairpin,
Hand(fast), Handhold, Hend, Hold, Hug, Key, Kirby®, Lewis, Obsess, Pincer,
Pinion, Pistol, Prehensile, Purchase, Raven, Rhine, Sally, Setscrew, Sipe, Strain,
Streigne, Traction, Twist, Valise, Vice, Walise, Wrestle

Gripe(s) Colic, Complain, Ditch, Grasp, Griffin, Ileus, Pain, Tormina

Grisly Gory, Macabre

Grist Burden

Gristle, Gristly Cartilage, Chondroid, Lytta, Raven's bone

Grit(s), Gritty Blinding, Clench, Gnash, Granular, Grate, Guts, Hominy, Mattress,

Millstone, Nerve, Pluck, Resolution, Sabulose, Sand, Shingle, Swarf, Valour, Yorkshire

Grizzle(d) Grey

Groan(er) Bewail, Bing, Moan, Titus

Grocer Grasshopper, Jorrocks, Pepperer, Symbol

Groggy Dazed, Shaky

Groin Gnarr, Inguinal, Lisk

Groom(ed) Brush, Coistrel, Coistril, Comb, Curry, Dress, Fettler, Kempt, Ostler, Palfrenier, Paranymph, Preen, Primp, Prink, S(a)ice, Smarten, Spouse, Strapper, Syce, Tiger, Tracer, Train, Wrangler

▷ **Groom** *may indicate* an anagram

Groove(s), Grooved, Groovy Bezel, Canal, Cannelure, Chamfer, Channel, Chase, Clevis, Coulisse, Croze, Dièdre, Exarate, Fissure, Flute, Fuller, Furr, Furrow, Glyph, Gouge, Hill and dale, Kerf, Key-seat, Keyway, Lead-in, Lead-out, Oche, Pod, Rabbet, Race(way), Raggle, Raphe, Rare, Rebate, Rif(f)le, Rifling, Rigol(l), Rout, → **RUT**, Scrobe, Sipe, Slot, Sulcus, Throat, Track, Trough, Vallecula

Grope(r) Feel, Fumble, Grabble, Hapuka, Ripe, Scrabble

Gross All-up, Coarse, Complete, Crass, Dense, Earn, Earthy, Flagrant, Frankish, Fustilugs, Giant, Gr, Loathsome, Material, Obese, Outsize, Overweight, Pre-tax, Rank, Ribald, Rough, Stupid, Sum, Whole

▷ **Gross** *may indicate* an anagram

Grotesque Antic, Bizarre, Fantastic, Fright, Gargoyle, Magot, Outlandish, Rabelaisian, Rococo, Teras

Grotto Cave, Lupercal

Ground(s) Abthane, Arena, Astroturf, Basis, Bottom, Breeding, Campus, Cause, Common, Criterion, Crushed, Deck, Dregs, Eard, Earth, Edgbaston, Epig(a)eal, Epig(a)ean, Epig(a)eous, Floor, Footing, Gathering, Grated, Grist, Grouts, Happy hunting, Headingley, High, Hunting, Justification, Lees, Leeway, Lek, Lords, Lot, Marl, Meadow, Mealed, Middle, Occasion, Oval, Parade, Piste, Pitch, Plat, Pleasure, Plot, Policy, Proving, Quad, → **REASON**, Rec(reation), Réseau, Ring, Sandlot, Sediment, Slade, Soil, Solum, Sports, Stadium, Stamping, Strand, Terra, Terrain, Tom Tiddler's, Touch, Tract, Turf, Udal, Vantage, Venue, Waste(land), Yard, Yird

▷ **Ground** *may indicate* an anagram

Groundbait Chum

Ground-crew Erk

Ground-rent Crevasse

Groundsheet Hutchie

Groundsman Greenkeeper

Group Abelian, Acyl, Affinity, 'A'list, Band, Batch, Battle, Beatles, Bee, Bevy, Bloc(k), Blood, Bloomsbury, Body, Bracket, Bratpack, Break-out, Bruges, Caboodle, Cadre, Camarilla, Camp, Cartel, Category, Caucus, Cave, Cell, Chain, Chordata, Circle, Clade, Clan, Class(is), Clique, Cluster, Clutch, Cohort, Colony, Combo, Commune, Community, Concertina, Confraternity, Congregation, Consort(ium), Contact, Contingent, Control, Convoy, Coterie, Covey, Crew, Deme, Demi-monde, Denomination, Department, Detail, Enclave, Encounter, Ensemble, Faction, Family, Fascio, Focus, Fold, Fraternity, Front, Galère, Gang, Gemeinschaft, Gender, Generation, Genotype, Genus, Gesellschaft, Ginger, Globe, Guild, Hapu, Heading, Hexad, Hirsel, House, Income, In-crowd, Ketone, Kit, Knot, League, Lichfield, Local, Lumpenproletariat, Marathon, Marshal, Minority, Minyan, Nexus, Order, Outfit, Oxford, Pack(et), Panel, Parti, Party, Passel, Peer, Phalange, Phratry, Phylum, Platoon, Pleiad, Plump, Pocket, Pod, Point, Pool, Pop, Pressure,

Prosthetic, Push, Quincunx, Raceme, Racemose, Rap, Reading, Ring, Rush, School, Sector, Seminar, Series, Set, Several, Sex, Shower, Society, Sort, Sorus, Splinter, Strain, Stream, String, Study, Subfamily, Sub-general, Sub-order, Support, Symbol, Syndicate, T, Tales, Taxon, Tetrad, Tithing, Topological, Trainband, T-Rex, Tribe, Tribune, Trilogy, Trio, Troop, Troupe, TU, Umbrella, Unit, User, Vigilante, Workshop, Zaibatsu, Zupa

Grouse Black, Blackcock, Bleat, Blue, Caper(caillie), Capercailzie, Covey, Gorcock, Greyhen, Gripe, Growl, Grumble, Hazel-hen, Heath-cock, Heathfowl, Heath-hen, Jeremiad, Moan, Moorcock, Moorfowl, Moor-pout, Muir-poot, Muir-pout, Mutter, Natter, Peeve, Pintail, Prairie-hen, Ptarmigan, Red, Red game, Resent, Ruffed, Rype(r), Sage, Sharp-tailed, Snarl, Spruce, Twelfth, Wheenge, W(h)inge, Willow

Grove Academy, Arboretum, Bosk, Bosquet, Copse, Glade, Hurst, Lyceum, Motte, Nemoral, Orchard, Orchat, Silva, Tope

Grovel Cheese, Crawl, Creep, Fawn, Ko(w)tow, Worm

Grow(ing), Grow out, Growth Accrete, Accrue, Acromegaly, Adenoma, Aggrandisement, Angioma, Apophysis, Arborescence, Auxesis, Bedeguar, Boom, Braird, Breer, Burgeon, Car(b)uncle, Chancre, Cholelith, Chondroma, Compensatory, Condyloma, Corn, Crescendo, Crop, Culture, Cyst, Down, Ectopia, Edema, Ellagic, Enate, Enchondroma, Enlarge, Epinasty, Epitaxy, Excrescence, Exostosis, Expansion, Fibroid, Flor, Flourish, Flush, Gain, Gall, Germinate, Get, Goitre, Hepatocele, Hummie, Hyperostosis, Hyponasty, Increase, Keratosis, Knur(r), Lichen, Lipoma, Mole, Monopodial, Mushroom, Myoma, Nur(r), Oedema, Oncology, Osselet, Osteoma, Osteophyte, Pharming, Polyp, Proleg, Proliferate, Rampant, Rank, Scirrhus, Septal, Snowball, Spavin, → **SPROUT**, Stalagmite, Stand, Stipule, Sympodial, Tariff, Thigmotropism, Thrive, Trichome, → **TUMOUR**, Tylosis, Vegetable, Wart, Wax, Weed, Wox

▷ **Grow(n)** *may indicate* an anagram

Growl(ing) Fremescent, Gnar, Groin, Grr, Gurl, Roar(e), Roin, Royne, Snar(l)

Grown up Adult, Mature, Risen

Grub(by) Assart, Aweto, Bardie, Bardy, Bookworm, Caddis, Caterpillar, Cheer, Chow, Chrysalis, Deracinate, Dig, Eats, Fare, Fodder, → **FOOD**, Gentle, Groo-groo, Gru-gru, Larva, Leatherjacket, Mawk, Mess, Nosh, Palmerworm, Peck, Pupa, Root(le), Rout, Rowt, Sap, Slave, Stub, Tired, Wireworm, Witchetty, Wog, Worm

Grudge, Grudging Chip, Derry, Envy, Grievance, Grutch, Resent, Score, Sparse, Spite, Spleen

Gruel Brochan, Bross, Loblolly, Skilligalee, Skilligolee, Skilly

Gruesome Ghastly, Grisly, Grooly, Horror, Livid, Macaberesque, Macabre, → **MORBID**, Sick

Gruff Guttural, Hoarse, Surly

Grumble Beef, Bellyache, Bitch, Bleat, Chunter, Crab, Croak, Girn, Gripe, Grizzle, Groin, Growl, Moan, Murmur, Mutter, Nark, Natter, Repine, Rumble, Whinge, Yammer

Grump(y) Attercop, Bearish, Cross, Ettercap, Grouchy, Moody, Sore-headed, Surly

Grunt Groin, Grumph, Humph, Oink, Pigfish, Spanish, Ugh, Wheugh

Guano Dung, Sombrerite

Guanoco Llama

Guarantee Accredit, Assure, Avouch, Certify, Ensure, Gage, Hallmark, Insure, Mainprise, Money-back, Pignerate, Pignorate, → **PLEDGE**, Plight, Seal, Secure, Sponsion, Surety, Underwrite, → **VOUCHSAFE**, Warn, Warrandice, Warrant(y)

Guard(ed), Guards Acolouthos, Advance, Apron, Beefeaters, Blues, Bostangi, Bouncer, Bracer, Cabiri, Cage, Cag(e)y, Cerberus, Chaperon(e), Chary,

Cheesemongers, Cherry-pickers, Coast, Coldstream, Colour, Cordon, Crinoline, Curator, Custodian, Custos, Diehards, Dragoons, Duenna, Equerry, Escort, Eunuch, Excubant, Exon, Fence, Fender, Gaoler, Gauntlet, Grenadiers, Greys, Hedge, Home, Horse, INS, Iron, Jaga, Jailer, Keep, Lancers, Life, Lilywhites, Look out, Mask, Mort-safe, National, Nightwatch(man), Nutcrackers, Out-rider, Out-sentry, Pad, Palace, Patrol, Picket, Point, Praetorian, → **PROTECT**, Provost, Quillon, Rail, Red, Ride, Roof, Screw, Secure, Security, Sentinel, Sentry, Shadow, Shield, Shin, Shopping, Shotgun, SS, Strelitz, Streltzi, Swiss, Switzer, Tapadera, Tapadero, Tile, Toecap, Tsuba, Turnkey, Vambrace, Vamplate, Varangian, Vigilante, Visor, Wage, Wait(e), Ward, Wary, Watch (and ward), Watchdog, Watchman, Wear, Weir, Wire, Yeoman

Guardian Altair, Argus, Curator, Custodian, Custos, Dragon, Gemini, Granthi, Hafiz, Janus, Julius, Miminger, Templar, Trustee, Tutelar(y), Tutor, Warder, Watchdog, Xerxes

Gudgeon Fish, Pin, Trunnion

Guenon Grivet, Vervet

Gue(r)rilla Bushwhacker, Chetnik, Contra, ETA, Fedayee, Gook, Haiduk, Heyduck, Irregular, Khmer Rouge, Komitaji, Maquis, Mujahadeen, Mujahed(d)in, Mujahedeen, Mujahideen, Partisan, Phalanx, Red Brigade, Tamil Tiger, Terrorist, Tupamaro, Urban, Viet Cong, Zapata, Zapatista

Guess Aim, Aread, Arede, Arreede, Conjecture, Divine, Estimate, Harp, Hazard, Hunch, Imagine, Infer, Level, Mor(r)a, Mull, Psych out, Shot, Speculate, Suppose, Surmise, Theorise, Venture

Guessing game Handy-dandy, Mor(r)a, Quiz

Guest(s) Caller, Company, House-party, Inquiline, Invitee, Parasite, Paying, PG, Symbion(t), Symphile, Synoecete, Umbra, Visitant, → **VISITOR**, Xenial

Guesthouse B & B, Minshuku, Taverna, Xenodochium

Guff Bosh, Gas

Guianian S(a)ouari

Guidance, Guide, Guideline, Guiding Advice, Antibarbus, Auspice, Baedeker, Bradshaw, Cicerone, Clue, Command, Concordance, Conduct, Counsel, Courier, Curb, Cursor, Director(y), Docent, Dragoman, Drive, → **ESCORT**, Field, Gillie, Graticule, Helm, Heuristic, Homing, Index, Inertial, Inspire, Itinerary, Jig, Key, Lad, Landmark, Lead, Lodestar, Map, Mark, Marriage, Mentor, Michelin, Missile, Model, Navaid, Navigate, Nose, Pelorus, Pilot, Pointer, Postil(l)ion, Principle, Queen's, Rainbow, Range, Ranger, Reference, Rein, Relate, Rudder, Sabot, Shepherd, Sherpa, Shikaree, Shikari, Sight, Sign, Sixer, Stear, Steer, Stire, Template, Templet, Terminal, Terrestrial, Tiller, Train, Travelogue, Tutelage, Vocational, Voyageur, Waymark, Weise, Weize, Wise

Guild Artel, Basoche, Company, Freemason, Gyeld, Hanse, Hoastman, League, Mistery, Mystery, Society, Tong, Union

Guile Art, Cunning, Deceit, Dole, Malengine

Guillotine Closure, Louisiette, Maiden, Marianne

Guilt(y) Affluenza, Angst, Blame, Cognovit, Flagitious, Mea culpa, Nocent, Peccavi, Remorse, Wicked

Guinea(s) Canary, Geordie, Gns, Job, Ls, Meg, Spade

Guinea-fowl Pintado

Guinea-pig Abyssinian, Agoute, Agouti, Cavie, Cavy, Paca

Guinea-worm Dracunculus

Guise Form, Manner, Shape

Guitar(ist) Acoustic, Axe(man), Bass, Bottleneck, Cithern, Cittern, Dobro®, Electric,

Fender®, Gittarone, Gittern, Hawaiian, Humbucker, Lute, Lyre, Pedal steel, Plankspanker, Samisen, Sancho, Sanko, Shamisen, Sitar, Slide, Spanish, Steel, Uke, Ukulele

Gulf Aden, Anadyr, Aqaba, Bay, Bothnia, California, Cambay, Campeche, Carpentaria, Chasm, Chihli, Corinth, Cutch, Darien, Dvina, Exmouth, Fonseca, Genoa, Gonaives, Hauraki, Honduras, Iskenderun, Isthmus, Izmit, Joseph Bonaparte, Kutch, Lepanto, Leyte, Lingayen, Lions, Mannar, Martaban, Maw, Mexico, Ob, Patras, Persian, Pozzuoli, Queen Maud, Rapallo, Riga, St Lawrence, St Vincent, Salerno, Salonika, Saronic, Saros, Siam, Sidra, Spencer, Taganrog, Taranto, Tongking, Tonkin, Trieste, Tunis, Van Diemen, Venice, Vorago

Gull(s) Black-backed, Bonxie, Cheat, Cob(b), Cod, Cony, Cozen, Dupe, Fool, Geck, Glaucous, Have, Hoodwink, Ivory, Kittiwake, Laridae, Larus, Maw, Mew, Mollyhawk, Pickmaw, Pigeon, Queer, Rook, Sabine's, Saddleback, Scaury, Scourie, Scowrie, Sea-cob, Sea-mew, Sell, Simp, Skua, Sucker, Swart-back, Tern, Tystie, Xema

Gullet Crop, Enterate, Maw, Oesophagus, Throat, Weasand-pipe

Gullible Green, Mug punter, Naive, Sucker

Gulliver Lemuel

Gully Couloir, Donga, Fielder, Geo, Gio, Goe, Grough, Gulch, Infielder, Pit, Rake, Ravine, Sloot, Sluit, Wadi

Gulp Bolt, Draught, Gollop, Quaff, Slug, Sob, → SWALLOW, Swig, Swipe, Wolf

Gum (tree) Acacia, Acajou, Acaroid, Agar, Algin, Angico, Arabic, Arabin, Arar, Arctic, Asafoetida, Bablah, Balata, Balm, Bandoline, Bdellium, Benjamin, Benzoin, Bloodwood, Blue, Boot, Bubble, Cerasin, Chicle, Chuddy, Chutty, Coolabah, Courbaril, Cow®, Dextrin(e), Dragon's-blood, Ee-by, Eucalyptus, Euphorbium, Flooded, Frankincense, Galbanum, Gamboge, Ghost, Gingival, → GLUE, Goat's-thorn, Gosh, Grey, Guar, Ironbark, Karri, Kauri, La(b)danum, Lac, Lentisk, Mastic(h), Mucilage, Myrrh, Nicotine, Olibanum, Opopanax, Oshac, Red, River red, Sagapenum, Sarcocolla, Scribbly, Size, Sleep, Snow, Spearmint, Spirit, Starch, Sterculia, Stringybark, Sugar, Sweet, Tacamahac, Tragacanth, Tupelo, Ulmin, Water, White, Xanthan

Gumbo Okra

Gumboil Parulis

Gumption Nous, Spirit

Gun(fire), Guns, Gunfight Amusette, Archibald, Archie, Arquebus, Automatic, Barker, Baton, Bazooka, Beanbag, Beretta, Big Bertha, Biscayan, Blunderbuss, Bofors, Bombard, Breech(-loader), Bren, Broadside, Brown Bess, Browning, Bulldog, Bullpup, Bundook, Burp, Caliver, Cannonade, Carbine, Carronade, Cement, Chokebore, Coehorn, Colt®, Dag, Derringer, Electron, Elephant, Escopette, Falcon(et), Field, Fieldpiece, Firearm, Fire lock, Flame, Flash, Flintlock, Four-pounder, Fowler, Fowlingpiece, Garand, Gas, Gat(ling), Gingal(l), Grease, HA, Hackbut, Half-cock, Harquebus, Heater, Hired, Howitzer, Jezail, Jingal, Kalashnikov, Lewis, Long Tom, Luger®, Machine, Magazine, Magnum, Maroon, Martini-Henry®, Matchlock, Mauser®, Maxim, Metal, Minnie, Minute, Mitrailleuse, Morris Meg, Mortar, Musket(oon), Muzzle-loader, Nail, Needle, Neutron, Noonday, Oerlikon, Ordnance, Over and under, Owen, Paderero, Paterero, Ped(e)rero, Pelican, Perrier, Petronel, Piece, Pistol(et), Pompom, Pump (action), Punt, Purdey®, Quaker, Radar, Ray, Repeater, Rev, Revolver, Riot, Rod, Roscoe, Saker, Sarbacane, Scatter, Self-cocker, Shooter, Shooting iron, Shoot-out, Sidearm, Siege, Smoothbore, Snapha(u)nce, Spear, Speed, Spray, Squirt, Staple, Starting, Sten, Sterculia, Sterling, Stern-cannon, Stern-chaser, Stun, Swivel, Taser®, Tea,

Thirty eight, Thompson, Tier, Time, Tommy, Tool, Tupelo, Turret, Uzi, Walther, Wesson, Young, Zip

Gunge Gowl, Paste

Gunman Ace, Assassin, Bandit, Earp, Greaser, Pistoleer, Sniper, Starter

Gunner, Gunner's assistant Arquebusier, Arsenal, Artillerist, Cannoneer, Cannonier, Culverineer, Gr, Matross, RA

Gunpowder Charcoal, Pebble-powder, Saucisse, Saucisson

Gunwale Gunnel, Portland, Portlast, Portoise

Guppy Million

Gurgle Burble, Clunk, Glug, Gobble, Gollar, Goller, Guggle, Ruckle, Squelch

Gurnard Tubfish

Guru Lifestyle, Sadhu, Teacher

Gush(ing) Blether, Effusive, → **FLOOD**, Flow, Jet, Outpour, Rail, Raile, Regurgitate, Rhapsodize, Scaturient, Spirt, Spout, Spurt, Too-too

Gusset Godet, Gore, Insert, Inset, Mitre

Gust Blast, Blore, Flaught, Flaw, Flurry, Puff, Sar, Waff

Gusto Élan, Relish, Verve, Zest

Gut(s), Gutty Archenteron, Balls, Beer, Bowel(s), Chitterlings, Cloaca, Disembowel, Draw, Duodenum, Enteral, Enteron, Entrails, Fore, Gill, Hind, Ileum, Insides, Kyle, Mesenteron, Mid, Minikin, Omental, Omentum, Purtenance, Remake, Sack, Sand, Snell, Stamina, Staying-power, Strip, Thairm, Tripe, Ventriculus, Viscera

Gutta-percha Jelutong, Pontianac, Pontianak

Gutter(ing) Arris, Channel, Conduit, Coulisse, Cullis, Grip, Gully, Kennel, Rhone, Rigol(l), Roan, Rone, Sough, Spout, Strand, Swale, Swayl, Sweal, Sweel

Guttersnipe Arab, Gamin, Thief

Guttural Faucal, Throaty

Guy Backstay, Bo, Burgess, Cat, Chaff, Clewline, Decamp, Deride, Effigy, Fall, Fawkes, Fellow, Gink, Josh, Mannering, Parody, Rib, Rope, Scarecrow, Stay, Tease, Vang, Wise

Guzzle(d) Gannet, Gorge, Go(u)rmandize, Overeat, Snarf

Gwyn Nell

Gym(nasium), Gymnast(ic) Acrobat, Akhara, Arena, Contortionist, Dojo, Jungle, Lyceum, Palaestra, PE, PT, Rhythmic, Sokol, Tumbler, Turner

Gymnosophist Yogi

Gypsum Alabaster, Gesso, Plaster, Satin-stone, Selenite, Terra alba

Gypsy, Gipsy Bohemian, Cagot, Caird, Caqueux, Chai, Chal, Chi, Collibert, Egyptian, Esmeralda, Faw, Gipsen, Gitano, Hayraddin, Lavengro, Meg, Pikey, Rom(any), Rye, Scholar, Tinker, Traveller, Tsigane, Tzigane, Tzigany, Vagabond, Vlach, Walach, Wanderer, Zigan, Zigeuner, Zincala, Zincalo, Zingaro

Gyrate Revolve, Rotate, → **SPIN**, Twirl

Hh

H Ache, Aitch, Aspirate, Height, Hospital, Hotel, Hydrant, Hydrogen

Haberdasher(y) Clothier, Ferret, Hosier, Notions

Habit(s), Habitual, Habituate, Habitué Accustom, Addiction, Apparel, Assuefaction, Assuetude, Bent, Cacoethes, Chronic, Clothes, Coat, Consuetude, Crystal, Custom, Diathesis, Dress, Ephod, Frequenter, Garb, Inure, Inveterate, Motley, Mufti, Nature, Outfit, Pathological, Practice, Raiment, Regular, Riding, Robe, Rochet, Routine, Scapular, Schema, Season, Second nature, Set, Soutane, Suit, Surplice, Toge, Trait, Trick, Tway, Usual, Way, Won, Wont, Xerotes

Habitat Element, Environment, Haunt, Home, Locality, Station

Hacienda Ranch

Hack(er) Blackhat, Chip, Chop, Cough, Cut, Drudge, Garble, Gash, Ghost, Grub-Street, Hag, Hash, Hedge-writer, Heel, Hew, Horse, Journo, Mangle, Mutilate, Nag, Notch, Pad, Paper-strainer, Penny-a-liner, Phreak, Pick, Pot-boiler, Rosinante, Script kiddie, Spurn, Steed, Tadpole, Taper, Tussis, Unseam, White hat

Hackle(s) Comb, Rough

Hackney(ed) Banal, Cab, Cliché, Corny, Percoct, Stale, Threadbare, Tired, Trite, Worn

Haddock Arbroath smokie, Findram, Finnan, Fish, Norway, Rizzered, Smoky, Speldin(g), Speldrin(g), Whitefish

Hades Dis, Hell, Orcus, Pit, Tartarus

Had (to) Moten, Must, Obliged, Threw

Haematite Oligist

Haemoglobin Chelate

Haemorrhoids Farmer Giles, Piles

Hafnium Hf

Hag(-like) Anile, Beldame, Besom, Carlin(e), Crone, Harpy, Harridan, Hell-cat, Hex, Moss, Nickneven, Occasion, Rudas, Runnion, Trot, Underwood, Witch

Haggard Drawn, → GAUNT, Pale, Rider

Haggis Kishke

Haggle Argue, Badger, → BARGAIN, Barter, Chaffer, Dicker, Horse-trade, Niffer, Palter, Prig

Ha-ha Dike, So there, Sunk-fence

Hahnium Hn

Hail(er) Acclaim, Ahoy, Ave, Bull-horn, Cheer, Fusillade, Graupel, Greet, Hi, Ho, Megaphone, Salue, Salute, Shower, Signal, Skoal, Skol, Sola, Stentor, Storm, Trumpet, Whoa-ho-ho

Hair(y), Haircut, Hairlike, Hair problem/condition, Hair style Afro, Ailes de pigeon, Ainu, Alopecia, Backcomb, Baldy, Bang, Barnet, Beard, Beehive, Bezoar, Bingle, Bob, Bouffant, Braid, Brede, Bristle, Brutus, Bumfluff, Bun, Bunches, Butch, Cadogan, Camel, Capillary, Catogan, Chignon, Cilia, Cleopatra, Coat, Cockernony, Coif, Coiffure, Comal, Comate, Comb-over, Cornrow, Corymbus, Cowlick, Crepe,

Crew-cut, Crinal, Cronet, Crop, Cue, Curlicue, DA, Dangerous, Dreadlocks, Dubbing, Duck's arse, Ducktail, Earmuffs, Elf locks, En brosse, Esau, Excrement, Eyelash, Feather, Feather-cut, Fetlock, Filament, Flat-top, Floccus, Forelock, French pleat, French roll, Frenulum, Fringe, Fur, Garconne, Glib(s), Glochidium, Guard, Hackles, Heard, Heer(i)e, Hispid, Hog, Indumentum, Kemp, Kesh, Lanugo, Lash, List, Lock, Lovelock, Lowlights, Madarosis, Mane, Marcel, Mohican, Mop, Mullet, Muttonchops, Not(t), Number two, Pageboy, Pappus, Pashm, Pele(s), Pelt, Perm(anent), Pigtail, Pika, Pile, Pilus, Pincurl, Plait, Plica, Plica Polonica, Pompadour, Ponytail, Poodle cut, Porcupine, Pouf(fe), Pow, Psilosis, Puberulent, Pubescent, Pudding basin, Punk, Queue, Quiff, Radicle, Rat-tail, Red mullet, Rhizoid, Roach, Root, Scaldhead, Scalp lock, Scopate, Scopula, Sericeous, Set, Shag, Shingle, Shock, Sideburns, Sidelock, Snell, Spikes, Stinging, Strammel, Strand, Strigose, Strummel, Switch, Sycosis, Tête, Thatch, Tomentose, Tonsure, Toorie, Topknot, Tour(ie), Tragus, Tress, Trichoid, Trichology, Trichome, Trichosis, Trim, Velutinous, Vibrissi, Villi, Villosity, Villus, Wedge, Widow's peak, Wig, Wisp, → **WOOL**, Xerasia

Hair-cream, Hair-oil Conditioner, Pomade

Hairdresser Barber, Coiffeur, Comb, Crimper, Friseur, Marcel, Salon, Stylist, Trichologist

Hairless Bald, Callow, Glabrate, Glabrescent, Glabrous, Irate

Hairline Brow, Nape

Hairnet Kell, Snood

Hairpiece Frisette, Merkin, Postiche, Strand, Toupee, → **WIG**

Hairpin Barrette, Bodkin, Slide, U, U-turn

Hair-shirt Ab(b)a, Cilice

Haiti RH

Hal Prince

Halberd Spontoon

Halcyon Calm, Kingfisher, Mild

Hale(r) Drag, Healthy, Koruna, Raucle, Robust, Well

Half, Halved Bifid, Demi, Dimidiate, Dirempt, Divide, Hemi, Moiety, Semi, Share, Split, Stand-off, Term

Half-a-dozen Six, VI

Half-asleep, Half-conscious Dove, Dozy

Half-baked Foolish, Mediocre, Samel, Slack-bake

Half-breed, Half-caste Bastard, Baster, Creole, Eurasian, Mameluco, Mestee, Mestiza, Mestizo, Metif, Métis(se), Miscegen, Mongrel, Mulatto, Mustee, Octaroon, Quadroon, Quarteroon, Quintero, Quintroon, Sambo, Yellow-boy, Yellow-girl, Zambo

Half-guinea Smelt

Half-hearted Reluctant, Tepid

Half-hour Bell

Half-pence, Half-penny Mag, Maik, Mail(e), Make, Obolus, Patrick, Portcullis, Posh, Rap, Wood's

Half-turn Caracol(e), Demivolt

Half-wit Changeling, Mome, Simpleton, → **STUPID**

Hall Anteroom, Apadana, Atrium, Auditorium, Aula, Basilica, Carnegie, Casino, Chamber, Citadel, City, Concert, Concourse, Corridor, Dance, Divinity, Dojo, Domdaniel, Dome, Dotheboys, Ex(h)edra, Festival, Foyer, Gallen, Hardwick, Holkham, Judgement, Kedleston, Liberty, Lobby, Locksley, Megaron, Mess, Moot, Music, Narthex, Newby, Odeon, Palais, Palais de danse, Passage, Prytaneum, Rathaus, Rideau, Salle, Saloon, Stationer's, Tammany, Tara, Tolsel, Town, Trullen,

Valhalla, Vestibule, Walhall(a), Wildfell
Hallmark(ed) Brand, Contrôlé, Logo, Seal, Stamp
▶ **Hallo** *see* **HELLO**
Hallow Revere, Worship
Hallucinate, Hallucination, Hallucinogen Autoscopy, DT's, Fantasy,
   Formication, Freak, Freak out, Illusion, Image, Mirage, Negative, Photism, Psilocin,
   Psilocybin, Psychedelic, Trip
Halo Antheolion, Areola, Aura, Aureola, Corona, Galactic, Gloria, Gloriole,
   Mandorla, Nimbus, Rim, Vesica, Vesica piscis
Halogen Iodine
Halt(er) Abort, Arrest, Block, Brake, Bridle, Cavesson, Cease, Check, Full stop,
   Game, Hackamore, Heave-to, Hilch, Lame(d), Limp, Noose, Prorogue, Rope, Stall,
   Standstill, Staw, → **STOP**, Stopover, Toho, Tyburn-tippet, Whoa
Ham(s) Amateur, Barnstormer, Flitch, Gammon, Haunch, Hock, Hoke, Hough,
   Hunker, Jambon, Jay, Mutton, Nates, Overact, Overplay, Parma, Pigmeat, Prat,
   Prosciutto, Radio, Serrano, Tiro, Westphalian, York
Hamfisted Maladroit, Unheppen
Hamite Berber, Nilot(e)
Hamlet Aldea, Auburn, Cigar, Clachan, Dane, Dorp, Hero, Kraal, Stead, Thorp(e),
   Vill(age), Wick
Hammer(ed), Hammerhead About-sledge, Ballpeen, Ballpein, Beetle, Bully,
   Bush, Celt, Claw, Drop, Excudit, Flatten, Fore, Fuller, Gavel, Hack, Incuse, Jack,
   Kevel, Knap, Knapping, Kusarigama, Lump, Madge, Mall(et), Malleate, Martel,
   Maul, Mjol(l)nir, Monkey, Nevel, Oliver, Pane, Pean, Peen, Pein, Pene, Percussion,
   Piledriver, Planish, Plessor, Plexor, Pneumatic, Rawhide, Repoussé, Rip,
   Sheep's-foot, Shingle, Sledge, Steam, Stone, Strike, Tack, Tenderizer, Tendon, Tilt,
   Trip, Umbre, Water, Wippen
▷ **Hammered** *may indicate* an anagram
Hammerthrower Thor
Hammock Cott
▷ **Hammy** *may indicate* an anagram
Hamper Basket, Cabin, Ceroon, Cramp, Cumber, Delay, Encumber, Entrammel,
   Hamstring, Handicap, Hobble, Hog-tie, Obstruct, Pad, Pannier, Ped, Pinch,
   Restrict, Rub, Sero(o)n, Shackle, Tangle, Trammel, Tuck
Hamster Cricetus, Idea
Hamstring Cramp, Hock, Hox, Lame, Popliteal, Thwart
Hand(s), Hand over, Hand down, Hand-like, Handwriting Assist(ance),
   Bananas, Bequeath, Cacography, Calligraphy, Charge, Chicane, Chirography,
   Clap(ping), Claque, Club, Clutch, Copperplate, Court, Crew, Cursive, Dab, Daddle,
   Danny, Dawk, Dead, Deal, Deck, Deliver, Devolve, Donny, Dukes, Dummy, Famble,
   Fin, Fist, Flipper, Flush, Free, Glad, Graphology, Help, Helping, Hidden, Hond,
   Hour, Impart, Iron, Israel, Italian, Jambone, Jamboree, Jemmy, Kana, L, Lone, Man,
   Manual, Manus, Maulers, Medieval, Minute, Mitt(en), Nes(h)ki, Niggle, Operative,
   Orthography, Pad, Palaeography, Palm(atifid), Part, Pass, Paw, Podium, Post, Pud,
   R, Referral, Rein (arm), Round, Running, Script, Second, Secretary, Signature, Span,
   Spencerian, Stage, Station, Straight, Sweep, Text, Tiger, Uncial, Upper, Whip,
   Widow, Worker, Yarborough
Handbag Caba(s), Grip, Indispensable, Pochette, Purse, Reticule, Valise
Handbook Baedeker, Companion, Enchiridion, Guide, Manual, Vade-mecum
Handcuff(s) Bracelet, Darbies, Golden, Irons, Manacle, Mittens, Nippers, Snaps,
   Wristlet

Handful Few, Gowpen, Grip, Problem, Pugil, Rip(p), V

Handicap Bisque, Burden, Cambridgeshire, Ebor, Encumber, Hamper, Impede, Impost, Lame, Liability, Lincolnshire, Mental, → **OBSTACLE**, Off, Physical, Restrict, Weigh(t), Welter-race

Handicraft Marquetry

Handkerchief, Hanky Bandan(n)a, Belcher, Billy, Buffon, Clout, Fogle, Foulard, Kleenex®, Madam, Madras, Monteith, Mouchoir, Muckender, Napkin, Nose-rag, Orarium, Romal, Rumal, Sudary, Tissue, Wipe(r)

Handle(d) Ansate, Bail, Bale, Behave, Bitstock, Brake, Broomstick, Cope, Crank, Dead man's, Deal, Doorknob, Dudgeon, Ear, Feel, Finger, Forename, Gaum, Gorm, Grab, Grip, Gunstock, Haft, Helve, Hilt, Hold, Knob, Knub, Lug, → **MANAGE**, Manipulate, Manubrium, Maul, Moniker, Name, Nib, Palp, Paw, Pistol-grip, Pommel, Process, Rounce, Shaft, Snath, Snead, Sneath, Sned, Staff, Staghorn, Stale, Starting, Steal(e), Steel, Steil, Stele, Stilt, Stock, Tiller, Title, To-name, Touch, Transact, Treat, Use, Whipstock, Wield, Withe

Handmaid(en) Iras, Manicurist, Valkyrie

Hand-out Alms, Charity, Dole, Gift, Release, Sample

Handshake Golden

Hand-signal Beck(on), Point, Wave

Handsome Adonis, Apollo, Attractive, Bonny, Brave, Comely, Dashing, Dishy, Featuous, Fine, Gracious, Kenneth, Liberal

Handspring, Handstand Cartwheel, Diamodov

Hand-warmer Muff, Pome

Hand-washer Pilate

▶ **Handwriting** *see* **HAND**

Handy(man) Accessible, Close, Convenient, Deft, Dext(e)rous, Digit, Factotum, Get-at-able, Jack(-of-all-trades), Near, Nigh, Palmate, Palmist, Ready, Skilful, Spartan, Useful

Hang, Hanger, Hanging(s) Append, Arras, Aweigh, Chick, Chik, Coat, Dangle, Darn, Depend, Dewitt, Dossal, Dossel, Dosser, Drape, Droop, Execute, Frontal, Gobelin, Hinge, Hoove, Hove(r), Kakemono, Kilt, Lime, Lobed, Loll, Lop, Lynch, Mooch, Noose, Nub, Pend(ant), Sag, Scenery, Scrag, Set, Sit, Sling, Suspend, Suspercollate, Swing, Tapestry, Tapet, Tapis, The rope, Toran(a)

Hanger-on Bur, Lackey, Leech, Limpet, Liripoop, Parasite, Satellite, Sycophant, Tassel, Toady

Hangman, Hangmen Bull, Calcraft, Dennis, Derrick, Gregory, Ketch, Marwood, Nubbing-cove, Pierrepoint, Topsman

Hangnail Agnail

Hangover Canopy, Cornice, Crapulence, Drape, DT's, Head, Hot coppers, Katzenjammer, Mistletoe, Remnant, Tester

Hank Bobbin, Coil, Fake, Lock, Skein

Hanker(ing) Desire, Envy, Hunger, Itch, Long, Yearn, Yen

Hannibal Punic

Hansard Minutes

Haphazard Casual, Chance, Helter-skelter, Higgledy-piggledy, Hit and miss, Hitty-missy, Promiscuous, → **RANDOM**, Rough and tumble, Scattershot, Slapdash, Willy-nilly

Happen(ing), Happen to Afoot, Be, Befall, Befortune, Betide, Come, Crop up, Event(uate), Fall-out, Materialise, → **OCCUR**, Pan, Pass, Prove, Subvene, Thing, Tide, Transpire, Worth

Happiness, Happy Apposite, Ave, Beatific, Beatitude, Blessed, Bliss, Bluebird,

Bonny, Carefree, Cheery, Chuffed, Cock-a-hoop, Dwarf, Ecstatic, Elated, Eud(a)emony, Exhilarated, Felicity, Felix, Fool's paradise, Fortunate, Glad(some), Gleeful, Golden, Goshen, Gruntled, Halcyon, Half-cut, Hedonism, High-feather, Jovial, Joy, Kvell, Larry, Light-hearted, Merry, Opportune, Radiant, Rapture, Sandboy, Seal, Seel, Sele, Serene, Sunny, Tipsy, Trigger, Warrior

Hara-kiri Eventration, Seppuku, Suicide

Harangue Declaim, Diatribe, Earwigging, Lecture, Oration, Perorate, Philippic, Sermon, Speech, Spruik, Tirade

Harass(ed) Afflict, Annoy, Badger, Bait, Beleaguer, Beset, Bother, Chivvy, Distract, Dun, Gall, Grill, Grind, Grounden, Hassle, Haze, Heckle, Hector, Henpeck, Hound, Irritate, Needle, Persecute, Pester, Plague, Press, Tailgate, Thwart, Trash, Vex

Harbinger Herald, Omen, Precursor, Usher

Harbour(ed) Alee, Anchorage, Basin, Brest, Cherish, Dock, Entertain, Foster, Herd, Hide, Hythe, Incubate, Lodge, Manukau, Marina, Mulberry, Pearl, PLA, Poole, Port, Quay, Reset, Scapa Flow, → **SHELTER**, Watemata, Wellington

Hard(en), Hardness Abstruse, Adamant(ine), Adularia, Augean, Austere, Bony, Brindell, Brinell, Brittle, Bronze, Cake, Calcify, Callous, Caramel, Cast-iron, Chitin, Concrete, Cornute, Crusty, Dentin(e), Difficult, Dour, Draconian, Ebonite, Endure, Enure, Exacting, Firm, Flint(y), Geal, Granite, Gruelling, H, Hawkish, Hellish, Herculean, HH, Horny, Indurate, Inure, Iron(y), Jasper, Knotty, Liparite, Lithoid, Metallic, Metally, Moh, Moh's scale, Murder, Nails, Obdurate, Obdure, Osseous, Ossify, Permafrost, Permanent, Petrify, Picrite, Raw, Rugged, Ruthless, Scirrhus, Schist, Scleral, Set, Severe, Solid, Sore, Steel(y), Steep, Stereo, Stern, Sticky, Stiff, Stoic, Stony, Teak, Temper, Temporary, Tough, Wooden

Hardback Case-bound

Hard-core Riprap, Scalpins

Hard-headed Stegochepalian

Harding Warden

Hardliner Hawk

Hardly Borderline, Ill, Just, Scarcely, Uneath(es), Unnethes

Hard-pressed Strait, Taxed

Hardship Affliction, Grief, Mill, Mishap, Penance, Privation, Rigour, Trial, Trouble

Hardware → **COMPUTER HARDWARE**, Gear, Ironmongery

Hardy Brave, Dour, Durable, Gritty, Manful, Oliver, Ollie, Rugged, Spartan, Sturdy, Thomas

Hare Arctic, Baud(rons), Bawd, Belgian, Doe, Dolicholis, Down, Electric, Husk, Jack-rabbit, Jugged, Jumping, Lam, Leporine, Malkin, Mara, March, Mawkin, Mountain, Mouse, Ochotona, Pika, Piping, Puss, Scut, Snowshoe, Spring, Wat

Hare-brained Giddy, Madcap, Scatty

Harem Gynaeceum, Gynoecium, Seraglio, Serai(l), Zenana

Hark(en) Ear, Hear, List(en)

Harlequin Chequered, Columbine, Pantaloon

Harlot Blue gown, Drab, Hussy, Loon, Loose, Paramour, Plover, Pusle, Pussel, Quail, Rahab, Scrubber, Slut, Strumpet, Whore

Harm(ed), Harmful Aggrieve, Bane, Blight, Damage, Deleterious, Detriment, Endamage, Evil, Hurt, Inimical, Injury, Insidious, Maleficent, Malignant, Maltreat, Mischief, Nocuous, Noxious, Pernicious, Sinister, Spoil, Wroken, Wrong

Harmless Benign, Canny, Drudge, Informidable, Innocent, Innocuous, Innoxious, Inoffensive

Harmonica Harp, Orpheus

Harmonious, Harmonise, Harmonist, Harmony Agree(ment), Alan, Allan, Allen, Alternation, Assort, Atone, Attune, Balanced, Barbershop, Blend, Chord, Close, Concent, Concentus, Concert, Concinnity, Concord, Congruous, Consonant, Consort, Coordinate, Correspondence, Counterpoint, Descant, Diapason, Diatessaron, Doo-wop, Euphony, Eur(h)ythmy, Faburden, Feng-shui, Go, Jibe, Keeping, Match, Melody, Mesh, Musical, Overblow, Overtone, Rappite, Solidarity, Symmetry, Sympathy, Symphonious, Sync, Thorough-bass, Tone, Tune, Unanimity, Unison, Unity

Harmotome Cross-stone

Harness(maker) Breeching, Bridle, Cinch, D-ring, Equipage, Frenum, Gear, Girth, Hitch, Inspan, Lorimer, Loriner, Pad-tree, Partnership, Swingletree, Tack(le), Throat-stop, Tie, Trace, Trappings, Whippletree, Yoke

Harp(sichord) Aeolian, Cembalo, Clairschach, Clarsach, Clavier, Drone, Dwell, Irish, Jew's, Lyre, Nebel, Trigon, Triple, Virginal, Welsh, Wind, Zither

Harpagon L'avare, Miser

Harpoon(er) Bart, Fis(h)gig, Fizgig, Grain, Iron, Lily iron, Peg, Spear, Specktioneer, Toggler, Tow-iron, Trident

Harpy Aello, Celeno, Eagle, Ocypete

Harridan Hag, Harpy, Shrew, Termagant, Xantippe, Zantippe, Zentippe

Harrier Hen, Montagu's

Harriet Hetty, Martineau

Harris Boatman, Isle, Rolf

Harrow(ing) Alas, Appal, Brake, Disc, Drag, Frighten, Herse, Lacerant, Pitch-pole, Plough, Rake, Rend, Shock

Harry Aggravate, Badger, Bother, Champion, Chase, Chivvy, Coppernose, Dragoon, Flash, Fret, Hal, Harass, Hassle, Hector, Herry, Houdini, Hound, Lauder, Lime, Maraud, Molest, Nag, Pester, Plague, Rag, Reave, Reive, Rieve, Rile, Tate, Tchick, Torment

▷ **Harry** *may indicate* an anagram

Harsh(ness) Abrasive, Acerbic, Austere, Barbaric, Brassy, Cacophonous, Cruel, Desolate, Discordant, Draconian, Extreme, Glary, Grating, Gravelly, Grim, Gruff, Guttural, Hard, Inclement, Oppressive, Raucle, Raucous, Raw, Rigour, Rude, Ruthless, Scabrid, Scrannel, Screechy, → SEVERE, Sharp, Spartan, Stark, Stern, Stoor, Stour, Stowre, Strict, Strident, Unkind

Hart Deer, Spade, Spay, Spay(a)d, Venison

Harte Bret

Hartebeest Bubal, Kaama, Kongoni

Harum-scarum Bayard, Chaotic, Madcap, Rantipole

Harvest(er), Harvest home Combine, Crop, Cull, Fruit, → GATHER, Hairst, Hawkey, Hay(sel), Hockey, Horkey, In(ning), Ingather, Kirn, Lease, Nutting, Pick, Produce, Rabi, Random, Reap, Shock, Spatlese, Spider, Tattie-howking, Thresh, Vendage, Vendange

Has Habet, Hath, Owns, 's

Has-been Effete, Ex, Outmoded

Hash(ish) Bungle, Charas, Discuss, Garble, Garboil, Hachis, Lobscouse, Mince, Pi(e), Ragout

▷ **Hashed** *may indicate* an anagram

Hasn't Hant, Nas

Hassle Aggro, Bother, Moider, M(o)ither

Hassock Kneeler, Pouf(fe), Stool, Tuffet

Haste(n), Hastening, Hastily, Hasty Cursory, Despatch, Expedite, Express,

Festinately, Fly, Hare, Headlong, Hie, Hotfoot, → **HURRY**, Hurry-scurry, Impetuous, Precipitant, Race, Ramstam, Rash, Rush, Scuttle, Speed, Spur, Stringendo, Subitaneous, Sudden, Tear, Tilt, Urge

Hastings Banda, Bustles, Senlac, Warren

Hat Akubra®, Ascot, Astrakhan, Balibuntal, Balmoral, Basher, Beanie, Beany, Bearskin, Beaver, Beret, Bicorn, Billycock, Biretta, Bluebonnet, Boater, Bobble, Bollinger, Bonnet, Bowler, Boxer, Brass, Breton, Broad-brim, Bronx, Busby, Cabbage tree, Cap, Capotain, Cartwheel, Castor, Chaco, Chapeau, Cheese-cutter, Chimneypot, Christie, Christy, Claque, Cloche, Cocked, Cockle-hat, Coolie, Cossack, Cowboy, Crusher, Curch, Deerstalker, Derby, Dolly Varden, Dunstable, Envoy, Fedora, Fez, Flat-cap, Fore-and-after, Gaucho, Gibus, Gimme, Glengarry, Hard, Hattock, Headdress, Head-rig, Hennin, Homburg, Kamelaukion, Kepi, Lamington, Leghorn, Lid, Lum, Matador, Mitre, Mob-cap, Mountie's, Mushroom, Nab, Opera, Pagri, Panama, Petasus, Picture, Pilion, Pill-box, Pilleus, Pilos, Pith, Pixie, Planter's, Plateau, Plug, Poke(-bonnet), Pork-pie, Pot, Profile, Puggaree, Puritan, Ramil(l)ies, Red, Runcible, Safari, Sailor, Scarlet, Shako, Shovel, Silk, Skimmer, Skull-cap, Slouch, Snap-brim, Snood, Sola(-helmet), Solah, Sola-topi, Sombrero, Songkok, Souwester, Steeple-crown, Stetson®, Stovepipe, Straw, Sugarloaf, Sunbonnet, Sundown, Sunhat, Tam (o' Shanter), Tarboosh, Tarb(o)ush, Tarpaulin, Ten-gallon, Terai, Thrummed, Tile, Tin, Tit(fer), Toorie, Top(per), Topee, Topi, Toque, Tricorn(e), Trilby, Turban, Tyrolean, Ugly, Wide-awake, Witch's

Hat-band Weeper

Hatch(ment), Hatching Achievement, Altricial, Booby, Breed, Brew, Brood, Cleck, Clutch, Companion, Concoct, Cover, Devise, Eclosion, Emerge, Escape, Incubate, Service, Set, Trap-door

Hatchet(-shaped) Axe, Bill, Chopper, Claw, Cleaver, Dolabriform, Tomahawk

▷ **Hatching** *may indicate* an anagram

Hatchway (surround) Companionway, Fiddley, Guichet, Porthole, Scuttle, Service

Hate(ful), Hatred Abhor, Abominable, Abominate, Anims, Aversion, Bugbear, Detest, Enmity, Haterent, Loathe, Misogyny, Odium, Pet, Phobia, Racism, Resent, Spite, Ug(h), Vitriol

Hatless Bareheaded, Unbeavered

Hat-plant S(h)ola

Hatter Mad

Hatty Etta

Haughty, Haughtiness Aloof, Aristocratic, Arrogant, Bashaw, Cavalier, Disdainful, Dorty, Fastuous, High, Hogen-mogen, Hoity-toity, Hye, Imperious, Lofty, Morgue, Orgillous, Orgulous, Paughty, → **PROUD**, Scornful, Sdeignful, Sniffy, Stiff-necked, Toplofty, Upstage

Haul(age), Haulier Bag, Bouse, Bowse, Brail, Carry, Cart, Catch, Drag, Heave, Hove, Kedge, Long, Loot, Plunder, Pull, Rug, Sally, Scoop, Snake, Snig, TIR, Touse, Touze, Tow(se), Towze, Transporter, Trice, Winch, Yank

Haunch Hance, Hip, Huckle, Hunkers, Quarter

Haunt(s) Catchy, Den, Dive, Frequent, Ghost, Hang-out, Honky-tonk, Houf(f), Howf(f), Infest, Obsess, Purlieu, Resort, Spot, Spright

Hauteur Bashawism, Height, Morgue, Vanity

Havana Cigar

Have, Having Bear, Ha(e), Han, Hoax, Hold, Of, → **OWN**, Possess, Sell

Haven Asylum, Harbour, Hithe, Hythe, Oasis, Port, Refuge, Refugium, Retreat, Safe, Shelter, Tax

Haver(s) Blether, Clanjamfray, Dither, Gibber, Nigel

▶ **Haversack** *see* RUCKSACK
Havoc Desolation, Devastation, Hell, Ravage, Waste
▷ **Havoc** *may indicate* an anagram
Haw Drawl, Hip, Sloe
Hawaiian Kanaka
Hawk(er), Hawkish Accipitrine, Auceps, Badger, Bastard, Buzzard, Cadger,
  Camelot, Caracara, Cast, Cheapjack, Cooper's, Cry, Duck, Eagle, Elanet, Eyas,
  Falcon, Fish, Gerfalcon, Goshawk, Haggard, Hardliner, Harrier, Harrumph,
  Hobby, Honey-buzzard, Keelie, Kestrel, Kite, Lammergeier, Lanner(et), Marsh,
  Merlin, Molla(h), Monger, Moolah, Mosquito, Mullah, Musket, Night, Nyas,
  Osprey, Ossifrage, Passager, Pearlie, Pearly, Peddle, Pedlar, Peregrine, Pigeon,
  Privet, Ringtail, Sacre(t), Sell, Slab, Slanger, Soar(e), Sorage, Sore(-eagle), Sparrow,
  Spiv, Staniel, Stone, Sutler, Tallyman, Tarsal, Tarsel(l), Tassel, Tercel(et), Tiersel,
  Trant(er), Trucker, Warlike
Hawkeye IA, Iowa
Hawk-keeper Austringer, Ostreger
Hawser Line, Rope
Hawthorn Albespine, Albespyne, May(flower), Quickset
Hay(cock), Hey Antic, Cock, Contra-dance, Fodder, Goaf, Hi, Kemple, Math, Mow,
  Pleach, Pook, Salt, Stack, Straw, Truss, Windrow
Hayfever Pollenosis, Pollinosis
Haymaker Blow, Slog
Hayseed Chaw-bacon, Hodge, Joskin, Rustic
Hazard(ous) Bet, Breakneck, Bunker, Chance, Danger, Dare, Die, Dye, Game,
  Gremlin, Guess, Imperil, In-off, Jeopardy, Losing, Main, Minefield, Moral, Nice,
  Niffer, Occupational, Perdu(e), Peril, Pitfall, Play, Pothole, Queasy, → RISK, Stake,
  Trap, Venture, Vigia, Wage, Winning
Haze, Hazy Blear, Cloud, Filmy, Fog, → MIST, Mock, Muzzy, Nebulous, Smaze,
  Smog, Tease
▷ **Haze** *may indicate* an anagram
Hazel(wort) Amenta, Asarabacca, Catkin, Cob, Corylus, Filbert
HC Encomia, Encomium
He, HE A, Helium, Tag, Tig, → TNT, Tom
Head(s), Heading, Headman, Head shaped, Heady Aim, Apex, Ard-ri(gh),
  Beachy, Bean, Behead, Bill, Block, Bonce, Boss, Bound, Brain, Brainpan, Bregma,
  Brow, But(t), Caboceer, Cape, Capitani, Capitate, Capitulum, Capo, Captain,
  Caption, Caput, Caudillo, Cephalic, Chaton, Chief, Chump, Coarb, Coconut,
  Coma, Commander, Conk, Cop, Coppin, Costard, Cranium, Crest, Crisis, Crown,
  Crumpet, Cylinder, Dateline, Director, Dome, Dummy, Each, Ear, Exarch,
  Figure, Flamborough, Foam, Foreland, Froth, General, Glomerate, Grand Mufti,
  Hegumen(os), Herm(a), Hoe, Hogh, Huff-cap, Inion, Jowl, Karmapa, Keyword,
  Knob, Knowledge-box, Lead(er), Lid, Lizard, Loaf, Loave, Loo, Lore, Malik,
  Manager, Mayor, Maz(z)ard, Melik, Mocuddum, Mogul, Mokaddam, Mr Big, Mull,
  Muqaddam, Nab, Nana, Napper, Nappy, Ness, Nob, Noddle, Noggin, Noll, Noup,
  Nowl, Nut, Obverse, Occiput, Onion, Panicle, Panorama, Parietal, Pash, Pate,
  Pater(familias), Patriarch, Pick-up, Point, Poll, Pow, Prefect, President, Pressure,
  Principal, Promontory, Provost, Ras, Read-write, Ream, Rector, Rubric, Sarpanch,
  Scalp, Scaup, Scaw, Scholarch, Scolex, Sconce, Short, Sinciput, Skaw, Skull, Sound,
  Source, Spume, Squeers, Starosta, Strapline, Subject, Superior, Taipan, Talking,
  Tanadar, Tete, Thanadar, Throne, Tight, Tintagel, Title, Toilet, Top, Topic, Tsantsa,
  Twopenny, Upperworks, Vaivode, Velocity, Voivode, Yorick, Zupan

▷ **Head** *may indicate* the first letter of a word

Headache Cephalalgia, Encephalalgia, Hangover, Megrim, Migraine, Neuralgia, Red out, Scotodinia, Splitter

Headband Fillet, Garland, Infula, Sphendone, T(a)enia

Headdress, Headcover Ampyx, Balaclava, Bandeau, Bas(i)net, Bonnet, Burnous(e), Busby, Calotte, Caul, Chaplet, Circlet, Comb, Commode, Cor(o)net, Cowl, Coxcomb, Crownet, Curch, Doek, Dopatta, Dupatta, Fascinator, Fontange, Fool's cap, Frontlet, Hat(tock), Helm(et), Joncanoe, Juliet cap, Kaffiyeh, Kell, Kerchief, Kuffiyeh, Kufiah, Kufiya(h), Mantilla, Mitre, Mobcap, Modius, Mortarboard, Nubia, Periwig, Pill-box, Plug-hat, Porrenger, Porringer, Romal, Sakkos, Ship-tire, Silly-how, Skullcap, Sphendome, Stephane, Taj, Tarbush, Tiara, Tire-vallant, Tower, Tulban, Turban, War bonnet, Wig, Wimple

Header Bonder, Dive, Fall, Rowlock

Headhunter Naga

Headland Beachy Head, Bill, Cape, Cape Horn, Dungeness, Finisterre, Foreland, Head-rig, Hoe, Hogh, Land's End, Morro, Naze, Ness, Noup, → **PROMONTORY**, Ras, Ross, St Vincent, Scaw, Skaw

Headless Acephalous

Headlight(s) Beam, Brights, Dip, Halo

Headline Banner, Caption, Drophead, Frown, Kicker, Ribbon, Scare-head, Screamer, Streamer, Title

Headlock Chancery

Headlong Breakneck, Pell-mell, Precipitate, Ramstam, Reckless, Steep, Sudden, Tantivy, Tearaway

▶ **Headman** *see* **HEAD**

Headmaster Principal, Squeers

Headphone(s) Cans, Earpiece, Walkman®

Headquarters Base, Command, Depot, Guardhouse, Guildhall, Pentagon, SHAEF, SHAPE, Station

▷ **Heads** *may indicate* a lavatory

Headstrong Obstinate, Rash, Stubborn, Unruly, Wayward, Wilful

Head-to-tail Tête-bêche

Headway Advancement, Headroom, Progress

Head-word Lemma

Heal(ing) Aesculapian, Ayurveda, Balsam, Chiropractic, Cicatrise, Cleanse, Curative, Cure, Esculapian, G(u)arish, Hele, Hippocratise, Intention, Knit, Mend, Mental, New Thought, Olosis, Osteopathy, Restore, Sain, Salve, Sanitory, Spiritual, Therapeutic, Vulnerary

Healer Althea, Asa, Doctor, Homeopath, Naturopath, Osteopath, Sangoma, Shaman, Time

Health(y) Bouncing, Bracing, Chin-chin, Constitution, Doer, Fit, Flourishing, Gesundheit, Hail, Hale, Hartie-hale, Heart, Holism, Kia-ora, L'chaim, Lustique, Lusty, Medicaid, Medicare, Pink, Prosit, Public, Robust, Rosy, Salubrious, Sane, Slainte, Sound, Toast, Tope, Valentine, Valetudinarian, Vigour, Well, WHO, Wholesome

Heap(ed) Acervate, Agglomerate, Amass, Bing, Boneshaker, Bulk, Car, Clamp, Coacervate, Cock, Congeries, Cumulus, Drift, Hog, Jalopy, Lot, Pile, Raff, Raft, Rick(le), Ruck, Scrap, Shell, Slag, Stash, Tass, Toorie, Up-piled

Hear(ing) Acoustic, Attend, Audience, Audile, Avizandum, Captain's mast, Catch, Clairaudience, Dirdum, Ear, Harken, Learn, List(en), Oyer, Oyez, Panel, Paracusis, Pick up, Session, Subpoena, Try

▷ **Hear(say)** *may indicate* a word sounding like one given

Hearsay Account, Gossip, Report, Rumour, Surmise

Hearse Bier, Catafalco, Catafalque, Meat wagon, Shillibeer

Heart(en), Heartily, Hearty, Heart-shaped AB, Agood, Auricle, Backslapping, Beater, Bleeding, Bluff, Bosom, Bradycardia, Cant, Cardiac, Centre, Cheer, Cockles, Columella, Cordate, Cordial, Core, Courage, Crossed, Daddock, Embolden, Encourage, Essence, Floating, Gist, H, Hale, Herz, Inmost, Jarta, Kernel, Lepid, Lonely, Memoriter, Mesial, Mid(st), Middle, Nub, Nucleus, Obcordate, Purple, Robust, Root, Sacred, Sailor, Seafarer, Seaman, Sinoatrial, Staunch, Tachycardia, Tar, Ticker, Yarta, Yarto

Heart-break Crève-coeur, Grief, Sorrow

Heartburn Brash, Cardialgia, Pyrosis

Heartfelt Deep, Genuine, Real, Sincere, Soulful

Hearth Cupel, Finery, Fireside, Home, Ingle, Killogie

Heartless Callous, Cored, Cruel, Three-suited

Heart's ease Pansy

Heart trouble Bradycardia, Fallot's tetralogy, Fibrillation, Murmur, Tachycardia

Heat(ed), Heater, Heating Anneal, Ardour, Arousal, Atomic, Barrage, Beath, Blood, Brazier, Calcine, Califont, Caloric, Calorifier, Central, Chafe, Convector, Dead, Decay, Dielectric, Dudgeon, Eccaleobion, Element, Eliminator, Endothermic, Enthalpy, Estrus, Etna, Excite, Exothermic, Fan, Ferment, Fever, Fire, Fluster, Fug, Furnace, Het, Hibachi, Hyperthermia, Hypocaust, Immersion, Incalescence, Induction, J, Kindle, Latent, Liquate, Lust, Moxibustion, Normalise, Oestrus, Panel, Prelim, Prickly, Q, Radiant, Radiator, Rankine, Recalescence, Red, Render, Repechage, Rut, Salt, Scald, Sinter, Sizzle, Solar, Space, Specific, Spice, Stew, Storage, Stove, Swelter, Teend, Temperature, Tind, Tine, Torrefy, Total, Tynd(e), Underfloor, Warming-pan, Warmth, White, Zip®

Heath(land) Bearberry, Bent, Briar, Brier, Egdon, Epacrid, Erica, Geest, Lande, Manoao, Manzanita, Moor, Muir, Stead, Ted

Heathen(s) Ethnic, Gentile, Infidel, Litholatrous, Nations, Pagan, Pa(i)nim, Paynim, Philistine, Primitive, Profane, Proselyte of the gate

Heather Bell, Broom, Calluna, Epacrid, Erica, Foxberry, Ling, Rhodora, Sprig

▷ **Heating** *may indicate* an anagram

Heave(d) Cast, Fling, Frost, Heeze, Hoise, Hoist, Hump, Hurl, Popple, Retch, Shy, Sigh, Vomit

▷ **Heave** *may indicate* 'discard'

Heaven(s), Heavenly Air, Aloft, Ama, Ambrosial, Arcady, Asgard, Bliss, Celestial, Celia, Divine, Ecstasy, Elysian, Elysium, Empyrean, Ethereal, Fiddler's Green, Firmament, Hereafter, Himmel, Holy, Hookey Walker, Land o' the Leaf, Leal, Lift, Mackerel, New Jerusalem, Olympus, Paradise, Pole, Rapture, Seventh, Shangri-la, Sion, Sky, Supernal, Svarga, Swarga, Swerga, Tir na n'Og, Uranian, Welkin, Zion

Heavy(weight), Heavily, Heaviness Ali, Clumpy, Dutch, Elephantine, Embonpoint, Endomorph, Grave, Hefty, Last, Leaden, Lumpish, Onerous, Osmium, Pesante, Ponderous, Sad, Scelerate, Stodgy, Stout, Top, Upsee, Ups(e)y, Weighty, Wicked

Hebe Barmaid

Hebrew Aramaic, Eli, Heb, Jesse, Karaism, Levi, Mishnayoth, Modern, Rabbinical, Yid

Hebridean Harris

Heckle Badger, Gibe, Harass, Hatchel, Jeer, Needle, Spruik

Hectic Ding-dong, Feverish, Frenetic

Hector Badger, Bluster, Browbeat, Bully, → **HARASS**, Nag

Hedge, Hedging Box, Bullfinch, Enclosure, Equivocate, Evade, Haw, Hay, Lay off, Meuse, Mews, Muse, Pleach, Privet, Quickset, Raddle, Sepiment, Shield, Stonewall, Texas, Thicket, Waffle

Hedgehog Gymnure, Hérisson, Tenrec, Tiggywinkle, Urchin

Hedge-parson Bucklebeggar, Patercove

Hedge-sparrow Accentor

Hedonist Cyreniac, Epicurean, Playboy, Sybarite

Heed(ed), Heedful Attend, Listen, → **MIND**, Notice, Obey, Observe, Rear, Reck, Regard(ant), Reke, Respect, Rought, Tent, Tinker's cuss

Heedless Careless, Inattentive, Incautious, Rash, Scapegrace, Scatterbrain

Heel Achilles, Cad, Calcaneum, Cant, Careen, Cuban, Dogbolt, Foot, French, Kitten, List, Louse, Rogue, Seel, Spike, Stacked, Stiletto, Tilt, Wedge

Heel-tap Snuff

Hefty Brawny, Heavy, Solid, Weighty

Heifer Io, Quey, Stirk

Height(en), Heights Abraham, Altitude, Cairngorm, Ceiling, Dimension, Elevation, Embroider, Eminence, Enhance, Golan, H, Hill, Hypsometry, Level, Might, Peak, Procerity, Spot, Stature, Stud, Sum, → **SUMMIT**, Tor, X

Heinous Abominable, Atrocious, Flagrant

Heir Alienee, Claimant, Coparcener, Dauphin, Devisee, Distributee, Eigne, H(a)eres, Institute, Intitule, Legatee, Parcener, Scion, Sprig, Tanist

Heirless Escheat, Intestate

Held Captive, Hostage, Sostenuto, Ten(uto)

▷ **Held by** *may indicate* a hidden word

Helen Elaine, Nell(y)

Helicopter, Heliport Airstop, Chopper, Egg-beater, Gunship, Hover, Iroquois, Medevac, Rotodyne, Sea Cobra, Sea King, Sea Knight, Sea Sprite, Sea Stallion, Sikorsky, Sky-hook, Whirlybird

Helios Hyperion

Heliotrope Cherry-pie

Helium He

Helix Alpha, Double, Parastichy

Hell(ish) Abaddon, Abyss, Ades, Agony, Amenthes, Annw(yf)n, Avernus, Below, Blazes, Chthonic, Dis, Erebus, Furnace, Gehenna, Hades, Heck, Inferno, Jahannam, Lower regions, Malebolge, Naraka, Netherworld, Orcus, Pandemonium, Perditious, Pit, Ruin, Sheol, Stygian, Tartar(ean), Tartarus, Tophet, Torment

Hellbender Menopome, Mud-puppy

Hellebore Itchweed, Setterwort

Hellenic Dorian

Hellespont Dardanelles

Hello, Hallo, Hullo Aloha, Chin-chin, Ciao, Dumela, Golden, Hi, Ho(a), Hoh, Howdy, Howzit, Yoo-hoo

Helm(sman) Cox, Navigator, Pilot, Steer, Tiller, Timon(eer)

Helmet Armet, Balaclava, Basinet, Beaver, Burganet, Burgonet, Cask, Casque, Comb, Crash, Galea, Heaume, Knapscal, Knapscull, Knapskull, Montero, Mor(r)ion, Nasal, Pickelhaube, Pith, Plumed, Pot, Pressure, Salade, Sal(l)et, Shako, Skid-lid, Smoke, Topee, Topi

Helot Esne, Slave

Help(er), Helping, Helpful Abet, Accomplice, Adjuvant, Advantage, Aid(ance), Aidant, Aide, Alexis, Alleviate, Ally, Asset, → **ASSIST**, Avail, Back, Beet-master,

Beet-mister, Befriend, Benefit, Bestead, Boon, Brownie, Char(woman), Coadjutor, Complice, Conducive, Daily, Dollop, Dose, Ezra, Forward, Further(some), Go, Hand, Henchman, Hint, Home, Hyphen, Instrumental, Leg-up, Life-saver, Maid, Mayday, Monitor, Obliging, Ophelia, Order, Patronage, Ration, Recourse, Relieve, Servant, Serve, Slice, SOS, Stead, Sted, Subserve, Subvention, Succour, Taste, Therapeutic, Use

Helpless(ness) Adynamia, Anomie, Downa-do, Feeble, Impotent, Paralytic, Useless

Helpmate Consort

Hem Border, Fringe, Hoop, List

He-man Adonis, Hunk, Jock, Macho

Hemisphere, Hemispherical Dominant, Magdeburg, Rose-cut, Western

Hemlock Conia, Cowbane, Insane root, Tsuga

Hemp Abaca, Bhang, Boneset, Bowstring, Carl(ot), Choke-weed, Codilla, Dagga, Fimble, Ganja, Hards, Henequen, Hiniquin, Indian, K(a)if, Kef, Love-drug, Manil(l)a, Mauritius, Moorva, Murva, Neckweed, Pita, Sida, Sunn, Tat, Tow

Hen(s) Ancona, Andalusian, Australorp, Biddy, Buff Orpington, Chock, Cochin, Dorking, Eirack, Fowl, Grig, Houdan, Langshan, Layer, Leghorn, Maori, Marsh, Mother, Mud, Orpington, Partlet, Pertelote, Plymouth Rock, Poulard, Poultry, Pullet, Ree(ve), Rhode Island red, Sitter, Spanish fowl, Sultan, Tappit, Welsummer, Wyandotte

Hence Apage, Avaunt, Ergo, Go, Hinc, So, Therefore, Thus

Henchman Attendant, Follower, Myrmidon, Satellite

Hen-house Battery, Eggery

Henna Camphire

Hennery Run

Hen-pecked Pussy-whipped, Spineless, Woman-tired

Henry Eighth, H, Hal, Hank, Hooray, Hy, James, Navigator, O

Hep Bacca, Berry, Hip

Hepatic Scale-moss

Hepatitis Favism, Jaundice

Herald(ic), Heraldry Abatement, Al(l)erion, Argent, Armory, Azure, Bagwyn, Bars, Baton sinister, Bearing, Bend, Bendwise, Blazonry, Bloody Hand, Blue Mantle, Bordure, Caboched, Cabré, Calygreyhound, Checky, Chevron, Chief, Cicerone, Cinquefoil, Clarenc(i)eux, Cleché, Compone, Company, Couchant, Coue, Counter-passant, Coupee, Coward, Crest, Crier, Debruised, Degraded, Difference, Displayed, Dormant, Endorse, Enfiled, Erased, Fecial, Fess(e), Fetial, File, Flory, Forerunner, Gardant, Garter, Gironny, Golp(e), Gules, Gyronny, Hauriant, Hermes, Honour-point, Issuant, King-of-arms, Lionel, Lis, Lodged, Lyon, Lyon King of Arms, Manchet, Martlet, Messenger, Minocaine, Morné, Mullet, Naiant, Naissant, Nascent, Nombril, Norroy, Nowed, Nowy, Opinicus, Or, Ordinary, Pale, Pallet, Paly, Passant, Pile, Portcullis, Portend, Potent, Precursor, Proclaim, Purpure, Pursuivant, Quartering, Rampant, Red Hand, Regardant, Rouge Croix, Rouge Dragon, Roundel, Roundle, Sable, Salient, Scarp, Sea lion, Segreant, Sejant, Statant, Stentor, Subordinary, Tenné, Trangle, Tressure, Trick, Trippant, Trundle, Umbrated, Undifferenced, Urinant, Usher, Vaunt-courier, Verdoy, Vert, Vol(ant), Vorant, Wivern, Woodhouse, Woodwose, Wyvern, Yale

Herb(s) Aconite, Agrimony, Ajowan, Alecost, Allspice, Angelica, Anise, Aristolochia, Arugula, Avens, Basil, Bay, Bennet, Bergamot, Borage, Capers, Caraway, Cardamom, Centaury, Chamomile, Chervil, C(h)ive, Cilanto, Cohosh, Comfrey, Coriander, Costmary, Cum(m)in, Dill, Dittany, Echinacea, Eruca, Estragon,

Exacum, Eyebright, Felicia, Fennel, Fenugreek, Ferula, Feverfew, Fireweed, Fitch, Fluellin, Forb, Garlic, Garnish, Gentian, Germander, Good-King-Henry, Gunnera, Haworthia, Hyssop, Inula, Kalanchoe, Knapweed, Lamb's ears, Laserpicium, Laserwort, Lewisia, Lovage, Madder, Madwort, Mandrake, Marjoram, Maror, Medic, Mint, Moly, Mustard, Oca, Oleraceous, Oregano, Origan(e), Origanum, Ornithogalum, Orval, Paprika, Parakeelya, Parakelia, Parsley, Paterson's curse, Phlomis, Pia, Pipsissewa, Plantain, Purpie, Purslane, Pussytoes, Reed-mace, Rest-harrow, Rhizocarp, Rodgersia, Rosemary, Rue, Rupturewort, Saffron, Sage, Salad, Saloop, Salsify, Savory, Senna, Sesame, Soapwort, Sorrel, Southernwood, Spearmint, Staragen, Sweet cicely, Tacca, Tansy, Tarragon, Thyme, Tormentil, Turmeric, Typha, Valerian, Veronica, Vervain, Vetch, Weed, Willow, Wormwood, Wort, Yarrow, Yerba

Herbert Alan, AP(H), Lom, Spencer

Herbicide Agent Orange, Atrazine, Defoliant, Diquat, Picloram, Simazine

Herbivore Iguanodon, Sauropod

Hercules Alcides, Huge, Rustam, Rustem

Herd(er), Herdsman Band, Corral, Drive, Drover, Flock, Gang, Marshal, Meinie, Mein(e)y, Menyie, Mob, Pod, Raggle-taggle, Round-up, Shepherd, Tinchel, Vaquero

Here Adsum, Hi, Hic, Hither, Local, Now, Present

Hereditary, Heredity Ancestry, Blood, Breeding, Codon, Dynastic, Eugenics, Exon, Genetics, Id(ant), Idioplasm, Mendelism, Panagenesis

▷ **Herein** *may indicate* a hidden word

Here is laid HS

Heresiarch Nestor

Heresy, Heretic(al) Agnoitae, Albi, Albigensian, Apollinaris, Apostasy, Arian, Bab, Bogomil, Bugger, Cathar, Cerinthus, Docete, Donatist, Dulcinist, Encratite, Eudoxian, Giaour, Gnosticism, Heresearch, Heterodoxy, Lollard, Manichaean, Montanism, Nestorian, Nonconformist, Origen, Patarin(e), Pelagius, Phrygian, Racovian, Rebel, Unitarian, Zendik

Heritage Birthright, Due, NT, Ottilie, Patrimony

Hermaphrodite Androgynous, Gynandromorph, Monochinous, Monoecious, Prot(er)andry

Hermes (rod) Caduceus, Mercury

Hermetic Alchemist, Sealed

Hermit(age), Hermit-like Anchoret, Anchorite, Ascetic, Ashram(a), Augustinian, Austin, Cell, Cloister, Crab, Eremite, Grandmontine, Loner, Marabout, Monk, Museum, Nitrian, Pagurid, Peter, Recluse, Retreat, Robber-crab, Sannyasi, Soldier-crab, Solitary, Troglodyte

Hernia Bubonocele, Cystocoele, Diverticulum, Enterocele, Hiatus, Inguinal, Rectocele, Rupture

Hero(ic) Achilles, Aeneas, Agamemnon, Aitu, Ajax, Alcides, Amadis, Asterix, Bader, Balarama, Bellerophon, Beowulf, Brave, Bunyan, Champ(ion), Cid, Couplet, Crockett, Cuchulain, Cuchullain, Cyrano, Dambuster, Dan Dare, Demigod, Drake, Epic, Eponym, Eric, Everyman, Faust, Fingal, Finn, Finn MacCool, Folk, Garibaldi, Glooscap, Gluscap, Gluskap, God, Goody, Great, Hector, Heracles, Hercules, Hiawatha, Howleglass, Hudibrastic, Icon, Ideal, Idol, Ivanhoe, Jason, Kaleva, Kami, Leonidas, Lion, Lochinvar, Lothair, Marmion, Meleager, Nestor, Noble, Odysseus, Oliver, Onegin, Orion, Owl(e)glass, Ow(l)spiegle, Paladin, Parashurama, Parsifal, Pericles, Perseus, Philoctetes, Priestess, Principal, Ramachandra, Rambo, Raven, Resolute, Revere, Rinaldo, Roderego, Roderick, Roland, Rustem, Rustum, Saladin, Sheik, Siegfried, Sigurd, Superman, Tam o' Shanter, Tancred, Tarzan, Tell,

Theseus, Tragic, Triptolemus, Tristan, Trist(r)am, Ulysses, Valiant, Vercingetorix, Virago, Volsung, White knight, Zorro

Herod Agrippa, Antipas

Heroin Dogfood, Doojie, Dynamite, Gumball, H, Harry, Henry, Horse, Jack, Junk, Scag, Shit, Skag, Smack, Snow, Snowball, Speedball, Sugar

Heroine Andromeda, Ariadne, Candida, Darling, Demigoddess, Hedda, Imogen, Isolde, Judith, Juliet, Leda, Leonora, Manon, Mimi, Nana, Norma, Pamela, Star, Tess, Una

Heron(s) Ardea, Bird, Bittern, Boat-billed, Butter-bump, Egret, Green, Handsaw, Kotuko, Screamer, Sedge, Siege, Squacco, Winnard

Herpes Cold sore, Dartre, Shingles, Shiver

Herring Bismarck, Bloater, Brisling, Brit, Buckling, Caller, Cisco, Clupea, Digby chick(en), Gaspereau, Glasgow magistrate, Kipper, Lake, Ma(a)tjes, Maise, Maize, Mattie, Maze, Mease, Menhaden, Norfolk capon, Ox eye, Rabbitfish, Red, Rollmop, Sea-stick, Shotten, Sild, Silt, Sparling, Teleost, Whitebait

Herringbone Sloping

Hesitant, Hesitate, Hesitation Balance, Boggle, Cunctation, Delay, Demur, Dicker, Dither, Doubtful, Dubitate, Er, Falter, Halting, Haver, Haw, Irresolute, Mammer, Mealy-mouthed, → PAUSE, Qualm, Scruple, Shillyshally, Shrink, Stagger, Stammer, Swither, Tarrow, Teeter, Tentative, Think twice, Um, Ur, Vacillate, Wait, Waver

Hesperus Vesper

Hessian Burlap, Hireling

Heterodoxy Heresy

Heterogeneous Diverse, Motley, Piebald

Heterosexual Hasbian, Straight

Hew(er) Ax, Chop, Cut, Gideon, Hack, Sever

Hex Bewitch, Jinx, Voodoo

Hexameter Dolichurus

▶ **Hey** *see* HAY

Heyday Prime, Summer

Hi Cooee, Hello, Howdie

Hiatus Caesura, Entr'acte, Gap, Hernia, Interact, Interregnum, Interval, Lacuna, Lull

Hibernal, Hibernate, Hibernating Estivate, Hiemal, Hole up, Latitant, Sleep, Winter

Hibernian Irish

Hibiscus Okra, Roselle, Rozelle

Hiccup Glitch, Singultus, Snag, Spasm, Yex

Hick Jake, Oaf, Podunk, Rube, Yokel

Hickory Black, Jackson, Mockernut, Pecan, Scaly-bark, Shagbark

Hidden Buried, Cabalistic, Covert, De(a)rn, Doggo, Hooded, Latent, Obscure, Occult, Pentimento, Recondite, Screened, Secret, Shuttered, Sly, Ulterior, Unseen, Veiled, Wrapped

▷ **Hidden** *may indicate* a concealed word

Hide, Hiding (place) Abscond, Basan, Befog, Bield(y), Blind, Box-calf, Burrow, Bury, Butt, Cache, Camouflage, Ceroon, Coat, → CONCEAL, Cootch, Cordwain, Couch, Cour, Crop, Curtain, Cwtch, Deerskin, Doggo, Earth, Eclipse, Encave, Ensconce, Enshroud, Envelop, Epidermis, Fell, Flaught, Flay, Gloss over, Harbour, Heal, Heel, Hele, Hell, Hole-up, Hoodwink, Incave, Inter, Kip, Kipskin, Lair, Leather, Mai-mai, Mask, Mobble, Nebris, → OBSCURE, Parfleche, Pell, Pelt, Plank, Plant, Priest's hole, Repress, Robe, Saffian, Screen, Secrete, Shadow, Shellac(k), Shroud, Skin,

Spetch, Stash, Strap-oil, Tappice, Thong, Thrashing, Trove, Veil, Wallop, Whang, Wrap

Hideous(ness) Deform(ed), Enormity, Gash, Grotesque, Horrible, Monstrous, Odious, Ugly, Ugsome

Hierarchic, Hierarchy Byzantine, Elite, Theocracy

Hieroglyph Cipher, Pictogram

Higgledy-piggledy Mixtie-maxtie

High(er), Highly, Highness Alt(a), Altesse, Altissimo, Apogee, Atop, Brent, Climax, Doped, Drugged, E-la, Elation, Elevated, Eminent, Exalted, Excelsior, Frequency, Gamy, Haut(e), Intoxicated, Lofty, Maggotty, Mind-blowing, Orthian, Prime, Rancid, Ripe, School, Senior, Sent, Shrill, So, Steep, Stenchy, Stoned, String-out, Strong, Superior, Swollen, Tall, Tension, Tipsy, Top-lofty, Topmost, Treble, Ultrasonic, Up(per), Very, Wired, Zonked

▷ **High** *may indicate* an anagram

High and mighty Haughty, Hogen-mogen

Highball Drink, Lob, Loft

Highbrow Brain, Egghead, Intelligentsia, Long-hair

High-class Best, Superior, U

High-crowned Copataine

Highest Best, Climax, Mostwhat, Ne plus ultra, Progressive, Supreme

Highest note E-la

High-flown Bombastic, Euphuism

Highland(er), Highlands Blue-bonnet, Blue-cap, Cameron, Cat(h)eran, Down, Duniwassal, Dun(n)iewassal, Gael, Irish Scot, Karoo, Kiltie, Masai, Nainsel(l), Plaid(man), Redshank, Riff, Scot, Seaforth, Shire, Teuchter

Highlight Feature, Focus, Heighten, Stress

▶ **High-pitched** *see* HIGH

High-spirited Extravert, Extrovert

High tension HT

Highway Alaska, Alcan, Autobahn, Autopista, Autostrada, Camino Real, Divided, Flyover, Freeway, Information, Interstate, King's, Motorway, Overpass, Pass, Queen's, Road, Rode, Tarseal, Thoroughfare, Tightrope

Highwayman, Highway robber(y) Bandit, Bandolero, Duval, Footpad, Fraternity, Gilderoy, Jack Sheppard, Land-pirate, Land-rat, Latrocinium, MacHeath, Motorist, Rank-rider, Road-agent, Scamp, Skyjacker, Toby, Tobyman, Turpin, Twitcher, Wheel

Hijack(er) Abduct, Pirate

Hike(r) Backpack, Bushbash, Bushwalk, Raise, Rambler, Ramp, Rise, Traipse, Tramp, Trape(s), Upraise

Hilarious, Hilarity Hysterical, Jollity, Mirth, Riot

Hilary Term

Hill(s), Hillock, Hillside Ant, Antidine, Arafar, Areopagus, Aventine, Barrow, Beacon, Ben, Bent, Berg, Beverly, Black, Bluff, Bombay, Brae, Breed's, Brew, Broken, Bunker, Butte, Caelian, Calvan, Capitol(ine), Cheviots, Chiltern, Chin, Cleve, Cone, Coteau, Crag-and-tail, Crest, Damon, Djebel, Drumlin, Dun(e), Dunsinane, Eminence, Esquiline, Fell, Flodden, Gebel, Golan Heights, Golgotha, Gradient, Grampians, Hammock, Height, Helvellyn, Highgate, Holt, Horst, How, Howe, Hummock, Incline, Inselberg, Janiculum, Jebel, Kip(p), Knap, Knoll, Knot, Kop(je), Koppie, Lammermuir, Lavender, Law, Loma, Low, Ludgate, Malvern, Mamelon, Man, Matopo, Mendip, Merrick, Mesa, Monadnock, Monte Cassino, Monticule, Morro, Mound, Mount Lofty Ranges, Nab, Naga, Nanatak, Nilgiri(s), North Downs,

Otway Ranges, Palatine, Pap, Pennines, Pike, Pingo, Pnyx, Quantocks, Quirinal, Rand, Range, Saddleback, Savoy, Scaur, Seven, Silbury, Sion, Stoss, Tara, Tel(l), Toft, Toot, Tor, Tump, Tweedsmuir, Valdai, Viminal, Wolds, Wrekin, Zion

Hillbilly Yap

Hill-dweller Ant

Hillman Areopagite, Nepalese

Hilltop Crest, Knoll, Nab

Hilt Basket, Coquille, Haft, Handle, Hasp, Shaft

Him(self) He, Ipse, Un

Himalaya(n) Nepali, Panda, Sherpa, Tibetan

Hind(most) Back, Deer, Lag, Rear, Starn, Stern

Hinder, Hindrance Back, Bar, Block, Check, Counteract, Cramp, Crimp, Cumber, Debar, → DELAY, Deter, Encumber, Estop, Hamper, Handicap, Harass, Holdback, Impeach, Impede, Inconvenience, Obstacle, Overslaugh, Porlock, Posterior, Pull-back, Rear, Rein, Remora, Rump, Set back, Shackle, Slow, Stop, Stunt, Taigle, Thwart, Trammel

Hindi, Hindu(ism) Arya Samaj, Babu, Bania(n), Banyan, Brahman, Brahmin, Dalit, Gentoo, Gurkha, Harijan, Jaina, Kshatriya, Maharishi, Nagari, Pundit, Rajpoot, Rajput, Rama, Sad(d)hu, Saiva, S(h)akta, Saktas, Sanatana Dharma, Sankhya, Shaiva, Sheik(h), Shudra, Smriti, Sudra, Swami, Swinger, Trimurti, Untouchable, Urdu, Vaishnava, Vais(h)ya, Varna, Vedanta

Hindquarters Backside, Crupper, Haunches

Hinge(d) Butt, Cardinal, Cross-garnet, Drop-leaf, Garnet, Gemel, Gimmer, Ginglymus, Joint, Knee, Mount, Parliament, Pivot, Stamp, Strap

▷ **Hinge(s)** *may indicate* a word reversal

Hingeless Ecardinate

Hinny Ass, Donkey, Joe

Hint Allude, Clew, Clue, Cue, Element, Gleam, Hunch, Idea, Imply, Inkle, Inkling, Innuendo, Insinuate, Intimate, Key, Mint, Nuance, Office, Overtone, Pointer, Preview, Scintilla, Shadow, Soupçon, → SUGGEST, Tang, Tip, Touch, Trace, Trick, Wind, Wink, Wisp, Word, Wrinkle

▷ **Hint** *may indicate* a first letter

Hip(pie), Hippy, Hips Cafard, Cheer, Coxa(l), Drop-out, Huck(le), Hucklebone, Hunkers, Ilium, Informed, Ischium, Pubis, Sciatic, Tonish

Hippopotamus Behemoth, River-horse, Sea-cow, Sea horse

Hire(d), Hiring Affreightment, Charter, Employ, Engage, Fee, Freightage, Job, Lease, Merc(enary), Never-never, Pensionary, Rent, Shape-up, Ticca, Wage

Hirsute Hairy, Pilose, Shaggy

▷ **His** *may indicate* greetings

Hispanic Latino

Hiss(ing) Boo, Fizzle, Goose, Hish, Sibilant, Siffle, Sizzle, Static, Swish

Historian Acton, Adams, Antiquary, Archivist, Arrian, Asellio, Bede, Biographer, Bryant, Buckle, Camden, Carlyle, Centuriator, Chronicler, Etain, Froude, Gibbon, Gildas, Green, Griot, Herodotus, Knickerbocker, Livy, Macaulay, Oman, Paris, Pliny, Plutarch, Ponsonby, Renan, Roper, Sallust, Spengler, Starkey, Strachey, Suetonius, Tacitus, Taylor, Thiers, Thucydides, Toynbee, Trevelyan, Wells, Xenophon

History, Historic(al) Account, Anamnesis, Ancient, Annal, Bunk, Case, Chronicle, Clio, Diachronic, Epoch(a), Ere-now, Ever, Heritage, Legend, Life, Living, Mesolithic, Modern, Natural, Ontogency, Oral, Past, Record, Renaissance

Histrionic Operatic, Theatrical

Hit Bang, Bash, Baste, Bat, Bean, Belt, Bepat, Blip, Blockbuster, Bloop, Blow,

Bludgeon, Boast, Bolo, Bonk, Bunt, Catch, Clobber, Clock, Clout, Club, Collide, Cuff, Dot, Flail, Flick, Flip, Foul, Fourpenny-one, Fungo, Fustigate, Get, Hay, Head-butt, Home(-thrust), Impact, Knock, Lam, Lob, Magpie, Mug, Pandy, Paste, Pepper, Pistol-whip, Polt, Prang, Punto dritto, Ram, Roundhouse, Sacrifice, Score, Sensation, Six, Skier, Sky, Slam, Slap, Slosh, Smash(eroo), Smit(e), Sock, Spank, Spike, Stoush, Straik, Stricken, Strike, Strook, Struck, → **SUCCESS**, Swat, Switch, Thwack, Tip, Tonk, Touché, Undercut, Venewe, Venue, Volley, Wallop, Wham, Wing, Ythundered, Zap, Zonk

Hitch(ed) Catch, Contretemps, Edge, Espouse, Harness, Hike, Hirsle, Hoi(c)k, Hotch, Jerk, Lorry-hop, Rub, Setback, Sheepshank, Sheet bend, Shrug, Snag, Technical, Thumb, Wed

Hitherto Before, Yet

Hittite Uriah

Hive(s) Nettlerash, Skep, Spread, Swarm, Wheal

Hoar(y) Ashen(-grey), Canescent, Froren, Frost, Gaudy-day, Grizzled, Rime

Hoard(ing) Accumulate, Amass, Bill, Billboard, Cache, Coffer, Eke, Heap, Hoord, Husband, Hutch, Mucker, Plant, Pose, Salt away, Save, Sciurine, Snudge, Squirrel, Stash, Stock, Store, Stow, Treasure

Hoarse(ness) Croupy, Frog, Grating, Gruff, Husky, Raucous, Roar(er), Roopit, Roopy, Roup, Throaty

Hoax April-fish, Bam, Canard, Cod, Do, Doff, Fub, Fun, Gag, Gammon, Gowk, Gull, Hum, Huntie-gowk, Kid, Leg-pull, Piltdown, Put-on, Quiz, Sell, Sham, Skit, Spoof, String, Stuff, Supercherie, → **TRICK**

Hob Ceramic, Cooktop, Ferret, Goblin, Lout

Hobble, Hobbling Game, Hamshackle, Hilch, Hitch, Lame, Limp, Pastern, Picket, Spancel, Stagger, Tether

Hobby Avocation, Fad, Falcon, Interest, Pastance, → **PASTIME**, Predator, Pursuit, Recreation, Scrimshaw

Hobby-horse Dada, Obsession, Play-mare

Hobgoblin Bog(e)y, Puck

Hobnail Clinker, Tacket

Hobnob Chat, Mingle

Hobo Bum, → **TRAMP**, Vagrant

Hock Cambrel, Dip, Gambrel, Gambril, Gammon, Ham, Heel, Hough, Hypothecate, Pawn, Pledge, Rhenish, Wine

Hockey Field, Grass, Hurling, Ice, Pond, Shinny, Shinty, Street

Hod Carrier, Tray

Hodge Peasant, Rustic, Yokel

Hoe Claut, Dutch, Grub, Grubbing, Jembe, Nab, Pecker, Prong, Rake, Scuffle, Thrust, Weed

Hog Babiroussa, Babirussa, Boar, Glutton, Guttle, Peccary, Pig, Porker, Puck, Road, Shoat, Shott, Whole

Hogmanay Ne'erday

Hog-rat Hutia

Hogshead Butt, Cask, Muid

Hogwash Bull, Nonsense, Swill, Twaddle

Hoi-polloi Prole(tariat), Rabble

Hoist Boom, Bouse, Crane, Davit, Derrick, Garnet, Gin, Heft, Hills, Jack, Lewis, Lift, Raise, Shearlegs, Shears, Sheerlegs, Sheers, Sway, Teagle, Trice, Whip-and-derry, Wince, Winch, Windas, Windlass

Hold(er), Holding, Hold back, out, up, etc Absorb, Anchor, Backbreaker, Belay,

Believe, Boston crab, Canister, Cease, Cement, Cinch, Clamp, Clasp, Cling, Clutch, Contain, Cotland, Defer, Delay, Detain, Display, Dog, Embrace, Engross, Er, Facebar, Farm, Fast, Fief, Fistful, Frog, Full nelson, Garter, → GRASP, Grip, Grovet, Half-nelson, Hammerlock, Handle, Haud, Have, Headlock, Heft, Heist, Hiccup, Hinder, Hitch, Ho(a), Hoh, Hoy, Hug, Impedance, Impede, Impediment, Impound, Incumbent, Intern, Intray, Japanese stranglehold, Keep, Keepnet, Lease, Maintain, Manure, Nelson, Nurse, Occupant, Own, Port, Proffer, Rack, Reach, Reluct, Reserve, Restrain, Rivet, Rob, Rundale, Runrig, Save, Scissors, Shelve, Shore, Sleeve, Sostenuto, Stand, Suplex, Suspend, Tenancy, Tenement, Tenure, Toehold, Toft, Tray, Tripod, Wristlock, Zarf, Zurf

Hole(s), Holed, Holey Ace, Agloo, Aglu, Albatross, Antrum, Aubrey, Beam, Birdie, Black, Bogey, Bolt, Cat, Cave, Cavity, Cenote, Cissing, Coal, Coalsack, Collapsar, Crater, Cubby, Cup, Dell, Den, Dene, Dog-leg, Dolina, Doline, Dormie, Dormy, Dreamhole, Dry, Dugout, Eagle, Earth, Ethmoid, Eye(let), Faveolate, Finger, Foramen, Funk, Gap, Geat, Glory, Gnamma, Gutta, Hag(g), Hideout, Kettle, Knot, Lenticel, Lill, Limber, Loop, Loup, Lubber's, Lumina, Maar, Mortise, Moulin, Namma, Nineteenth, Oillet, → OPENING, Orifex, Orifice, Ozone, Perforate, Pierce, Pigeon, Pinprick, Pit, Pocket, Pore, Port, Pot, Potato, Priest's, Punctuate, Punctum, Puncture, Rabbet, Rivet, Rowport, Sallyport, Scupper, Scuttle, Scye, Situation, Slot, Snag, Snow, Soakaway, Socket, Sound, Spandrel, Spider, Spiraculum, Starting, Steal, Stew, Stop, Stove, Swallow, Tear, Thirl, Thumb, Touch, Trema, Vent, Ventage, Ventige, Voided, Vug, Watering, Well, White, Wookey

Holiday(s) Bank, Benjo, Break, Busman's, Childermas, Days of Awe, Ferial, Festa, → FESTIVAL, Fête, Fiesta, Furlough, Gala, Half(term), High, Honeymoon, Kwanzaa, Lag b'Omer, Laik, Leasure, Leave, Legal, Leisure, Long, Minibreak, Off-day, Off-time, Outing, Packaged, Pink-eye, Play-day, Playtime, Public, Purim, Recess, Repose, Rest, Roman, Schoolie, Seaside, Shabuoth, Shavuot, Sojourn, Statutory, Stay, Sunday, Tax, Trip, → VACATION, Villegiatura, Wake(s), Whitsun

Holinshed Chronicler

Holland(s) Batavia, Genevese, Gin, Hogen-mogen, Netherlands, NL

Hollow Acetabulum, Alveary, Antar, Antre, Antrum, Armpit, Axilla, Blastula, Boss, Bowl, Cave(rn), Cavity, Chasm, Chott, Cirque, Cleché, Comb(e), Concave, Coomb, Corrie, Crater, Cup(mark), Cwm, Deaf, Dean, Dell, Delve, Den(e), Dent, Dimple, Dingle, Dip, Dish(ing), Dolina, Doline, Empty, Fossette, Frost, Gilgai, Glenoid, Gnamma-hole, Gowpen, Grot(to), Hole, How, Howe, Igloo, Incavo, Insincere, Keck(sy), Kettle(hole), Kex, Khud, Lip-deep, Mortise, Namma-hole, Niche, Omphaloid, Orbita, Pan, Philtrum, Pit, Punt, Redd, Rout, Rut, Scoop, Shott, Sinus, Slade, Sleepy, Slot, Slough, Socket, Swire, Thank-you-ma'am, Trematic, Trough, Vlei, Vola, Wame, Wem

Holly Aquifoliaceae, Eryngo, Ilex, Mate, Yaupon

Hollyhock Althaea, Malva, Rose mallow

Hollywood Bowl, Tinseltown

Holm Isle

Holmes Sherlock, Wendell

Holmium Ho

Holocaust Churban, Shoah

Hologram, Holograph Laser, MS

Holothurian Trepang

Holster Sheath

Holy(man), Holiness Adytum, Alliance, Ariadne, Blessed, → DIVINE, Godly, Grail, Halidom, Helga, Hery, Khalif, Loch, Mountain, Olga, Orders, Pan(h)agia, Pious,

Sacred, Sacrosanct, Sad(d)hu, Saintly, Sanctitude, Sannayasi(n), Santon, Sekos, Sepulchre, Shrine, Starets, Staretz, SV, Tirthankara, War

Holy books, Holy writing Adigranth, Atharvaveda, Bible, Gemara, Granth, Hadith, Koran, Mishnah, NT, OT, Pia, Purana, Rigveda, Sama-Veda, → **SCRIPTURE**, Shaster, Shastra, Smriti, Sura(h), Tanach, Writ, Yajur-Veda

Holy building, Holy city, Holy place Chapel, Church, Kaaba, Mashhad, Mecca, Medina, Meshed, Najaf, Penetralia, Sanctum, Synagogue, Temenos, Temple

Holy Ghost Paraclete

Holy water Amrit

Homage Bow, Cense, Honour, Kneel, Manred, Obeisance, Tribute, Vail

Home(land), Homeward Abode, Apartment, Base, Blighty, Burrow, Cheshire, Chez, Clinic, Community, Convalescent, Domal, Domicile, Earth, Eventide, Family, Fireside, Flat, Funeral, Gaff, Goal, Habitat, Harvest, Heame, Hearth, Heme, Hospice, House, In, Lair, Libken, Lockwood, Lodge, Maisonette, Mental, Mobile, Montacute, Nest, Nursing, Old sod, Pad, Penny-gaff, Plas Newydd, Remand, Res(idence), Rest, Starter, Stately, Tepee, Turangawaewae, Up-along, Villa

Homecoming Nostos

Home counties SE

Homeless Outler, Rootless, Skell

Homer(ic) Comatose, Cor, Epic(ist), Nod, Pigeon, Somnolent

Home-rule Parnellism, Swaraj

Homesick(ness) Heimweh, Mal du pays

Homespun Cracker-barrel, Plain, Raploch, Russet, Simple

Homestead Ranch, Toft

Homework → **DIY**, Prep, Preparation

Homicidal, Homicide Chance-medley, Justifiable, Killing, Manslaughter

Homily Lecture, Midrash, Pi, Postil, Prone, Sermon, Tract

▷ **Homing** *may indicate* coming back

Hominid Oreopitheous

Homogeneous Indiscrete

Homogram, Homograph Abac, Heteronym

Homosexual(ity) Auntie man, Bardash, Batty boy, Bender, Bent, Buftie, Bufty, Camp, Cat, Catamite, Closet queen, Cocksucker, Cottaging, Dike, Dyke, Fag(got), Fairy, Friend of Dorothy, Fruit, Gay, Gaydar, Ginger, Homophile, Invert, Lesbian, Moffie, Muscle Mary, Pederast, Ponce, Poof(tah), Poofter, Poove, Pouf(fe), Poufter, Puff, Punk, Quean, Queer, Quiff, Rough trade, Shirt-lifter, Swish(y), Tonk, Tribade, Uranism, Urning, Woofter

Hone Grind, → **SHARPEN**, Whet

Honest(y), Honestly Aboveboard, Afauld, Afawld, Amin, Candour, Clean, Fair dinkum, Genuine, Incorruptible, Injun, Jake, Jannock, Jonnock, Legitimate, Lunaria, Lunary, Mensch, Open-faced, Penny, Probity, Rectitude, Reputable, Righteous, Round, Sincere, Square, Squareshooter, Straight, Straight-arrow, Straight-out, Trojan, → **TRUE**, Upfront, Upright, Upstanding

Honey Comb, Flattery, Hybdean, Hybla, Hymettus, Mel, Melliferous, Nectar, Oenomel, Oxymel, Palm, Peach, Popsy-wopsy, Sis, Sugar, Sweetheart, Sweetie, Virgin, Wild, Wood

Honeycomb(ed) Cellular, Faveolate, Favose, Waxwork

Honey-eater Bear, Blue-eye, Pooh

Honeypot Haanepoot

Honeysuckle Abelia, Anthemion, Caprifoil, Caprifole, Lonicera, Rewarewa, Suckling, Woodbind, Woodbine

Honour(s), Honourable, Honoured, Honorary, Honorific A, Accolade, Ace, Adore, Birthday, Blue, Bow, CBE, Commemorate, Credit, Curtsey, Dan, Elate, Emeritus, Ennoble, → **ESTEEM**, Ethic, Face-card, Fame, Fête, Gloire, Glory, Grace, Greats, Homage, Insignia, Invest, Izzat, J, Jack, K, King, Knave, Knight, Kudos, Laudation, Laureate, Laurels, MBE, Mention, Military, OBE, Optime, Pundonor, Q, Queen, Remember, Repute, Respect, Revere, Reward, Ten, Tenace, Titular, Tripos, Venerate, Worship, Wranglers

Honourable companion CH

Honourless Yarborough

Hooch Hogan, Hogen, Moonshine

Hood(ed) Almuce, Amaut, Amice, Amowt, Apache, Balaclava, Bashlik, Biggin, Blindfold, Calash, Calèche, Calyptra, Capeline, Capuccio, Capuche, Chaperon(e), Coif, Cope, Cowl, Cucullate(d), Fume, Gangster, Jacobin, Kennel, Lens, Liripipe, Liripoop, Mantle, Mazarine, Nithsdale, Pixie, Robin, Rowdy, Snood, Trot-cosey, Trot-cozy, Visor

Hoodlum Gangster, Roughneck, Thug, Wanksta

Hoodoo Moz(z)

Hoodwink(ed) Blear, Bluff, Cheat, → **DECEIVE**, Gull, Nose-led, Seel

Hoof(ed) Artiodactyla, Cloot, Coffin, Frog, Trotter, Ungula

Hoohah Humdudgeon

Hook(er), Hooked, Hooks Addict, Adunc, Aduncous, Arrester, Barb(icel), Becket, Butcher's, Cant(dog), Catch, Chape, Claw, Cleek, Clip, Cocotte, Corvus, Crampon, Cromb, Crome, Crook, Crotchet, Cup, Drail, Fifi, Fish, Floozy, Fluke, Fly, Gab, Gaff, Gig, Grapnel, Grappling, Hamate, Hamose, Hamulus, Heel, Hitch, Inveigle, Kype, Meat, Pot, Prostitute, Pruning, Retinaculum, Sister, Snell, Sniggle, Swivel, Tala(u)nt, Tart, Tenaculum, Tenter, Tie, Trip, Uncus, Wanton, Welsh

Hookah Bong, Chillum, Hubble-bubble, Kalian, Narg(h)ile, Narghil(l)y, Nargileh, Nargil(l)y, Pipe

Hooligan Apache, Bogan, Casual, Desperado, Droog, Hobbledehoy, Hoon, Keelie, Larrikin, Lout, Ned, Rough(neck), Ruffian, Skollie, Skolly, Tearaway, Ted, Tityre-tu, Tough, Tsotsi, Yahoo, Yob(bo)

Hoop Bail, Band, Circle, Farthingale, Garth, Gird, Girr, Hula®, O, → **RING**, Tire, Trochus, Trundle

Hooray Whoopee, Yippee

Hoot(er) Conk, Deride, Honk, Madge, Nose, Owl, Riot, Screech-owl, Siren, Ululate

Hoover Dam

Hop(per) An(o)ura, Ball, Bin, Cuscus, Dance, Flight, Jeté, Jump, Kangaroo, Leap, Lilt, Long, Opium, Pogo, Roo, Saltate, Scotch, Skip, Spring, Tremié, Vine

Hope(ful) Anticipate, Aspirant, Comer, Contender, Daydream, Desire, Dream, Esperance, Evelyn, Expectancy, Forlorn, Gleam, Good, Pipe-dream, Promising, Roseate, Rosy, Sanguine, Trust, Valley, White, Wish

Hopeless(ness), Hopeless quest Abattu, Anomie, Anomy, Black, Buckley's chance, Despair, Despondent, Forlorn, Goner, Non-starter, Perdu, Pessimist

Hopscotch Peevers

Horace Flaccus, Ode, Satirist

Horatio Nelson

Horatius Cocles

Horde Crowd, Golden, Many, Mass, Mob, Swarm

Horizon A, Apparent, Artificial, B, C, Celestial, Event, Gyro, Rational, Scope, Sea-line, Sensible, Skyline, Visible

Horizontal Advection, Flat, Level, Prone, Supine, Tabular

Hormone ACTH, Adrenalin®, Adrenaline, Aldosterone, Androgen, Androsterone, Angiotensin, Antidiuretic, Autacoid, Auxin, Biosynthesis, Bursicon, Calcitonin, Catecholamine, Cholecystokinin, Corticoid, Corticosteroid, Corticosterone, Cortisone, Cytokinin, Ecdysone, Endocrine, Erythropoietin, Estrogen, Florigen, Folliculin, Gastrin, Gibberellin, Glucagon, Gonadotrophic, Gonadotrop(h)in, Growth, Hydrocortisone, IAA, Inhibin, Insulin, Intermedin, Juvenile, Kinin, Leuteotropic, Lipotropin, Luteinizing, Melanotropine, Melatonin, Mineralo corticord, Noradrenalin(e), Norepinephrine, Oestradiol, Oestriol, Oestrogen, Oestrone, Oxytocin, Pancreozymin, Parathyroid, Progesterone, Progestin, Progestogen, Prolactin, Prostaglandin, Relaxin, Secretagogue, Secretin, Secretion, Serotonin, Sex, Somatomedin, Somatostatin, Somatotrop(h)in, Steroid, Stilboestrol, Testosterone, Thymosin, Thyroid, Thyrotrop(h)in, Thyroxine, Triiodothyronine, TSH, Vasopressin

Horn(y) Acoustic, Advancer, Amalthea, Antenna(e), Antler, Baleen, Basset, Bez, Brass, Buck, Bugle, Cape, Ceratoid, Cor, Cornet, Cornett, Cornopean, Cornu(a), Cornucopia, Cromorna, Cromorne, Cusp, Dilemma, English, Exponential, Flugel-horn, French, Frog, Golden, Gore, Hooter, → **HORNBLOWER**, Hunting, Ivory, Keratin, Klaxon, Lur, Morsing, Mot, Oliphant, Periostracum, Plenty, Post, Powder, Pryse, Ram's, Scur, Shofar, Shophor, Spongin, Tenderling, Trey, Trez, Trumpet, Tusk, Waldhorn

Hornblende Syntagmatite

Hornblower Brain, Horatio, Peel, Triton, Trumpeter

Hornbook Battledoor, Battledore

Horned (sheep) Cabrié, Cabrit, Cornute, Hamate, Lunate, Mouflon, Muflon

Hornless Doddy, Humbel, Humlie, Hummel, Mooly, Mul(l)ey, Poley, Polled

Hornpipe Matelote

Horoscope Figure, Future, Prophecy, Star-map

Horrible, Horror Aw(e)some, Brat, Dire, Dread(ful), Execrable, Ghastly, Grisly, Gruesome, Grysie, Hideous, Loathsome, Minging, Odious, Shock, Terror, Ugh, Vile

Horrid, Horrific, Horrify(ing) Dire, Dismay, Dreadful, Frightful, Ghastly, Gothic, Grim, Grisly, H, Loathy, Odious, Spine chilling, Spiteful, Ugly

Hors d'oeuvres Antipasto, Canapé, Carpaccio, Ceviche, Hoummos, Houmus, Hummus, Mez(z)e, Pâté, Smorgasbord, Smor(re)brod, Smør(re)brød, Zak(o)uski

Horse Airer, Bidet, Bloodstock, Carriage, Cut, Cutting, Dark, Doer, Dray, Drier, Drug, Equine, Form, H, → **HEROIN**, High, Hobby, Iron, Knight, Kt, Light, Malt, Outsider, Pack, Pantomime, Plug, Ride, Rocking, Sawbuck, Screen, Selling-plate, Sense, Stalking, Standard-bred, Stayer, Steeplechaser, Stiff, Stock, Teaser, Trestle, Vaulting, Willing, Wooden

HORSES

2 letters:	Nag	Barb	Jade
GG	Pad	Buck	Mare
	Pot	Cert	Pole
3 letters:	Rip	Colt	Pony
Ass	Tit	Crib	Post
Bay		Dale	Prad
Cob	*4 letters:*	Fell	Roan
Dun	Arab	Foal	Scag
Gee	Aver	Hack	Snow

Span	Entire	Draught	Palomino
Stud	Exmoor	Eclipse	Schimmel
Taki	Favell	Eventer	Shetland
Trot	Ganger	Gelding	Skewbald
Yale	Garran	Hackney	Sleipnir
Yaud	Garron	Hobbler	Springer
	Gennet	Liberty	Stallion
5 letters:	Hogget	Marengo	Stibbler
Arion	Hunter	Marocco	Warragal
Arkle	Jennet	Morocco	Warragle
Bevis	Kanuck	Mustang	Warragul
Borer	Keffel	Palfrey	Warrigal
Caple	Lampos	Pegasus	Welsh cob
Capul	Livery	Piebald	Whistler
Favel	Morgan	Pointer	Yarraman
Filly	Mudder	Quarter	Yearling
Genet	Novice	Remount	
Morel	Pad-nag	Saddler	**9 letters:**
Mount	Plater	Sheltie	Appaloosa
Neddy	Pommel	Spanker	Black Bess
Pacer	Poster	Starter	Caballine
Pinto	Quagga	Sumpter	Clavileno
Poler	Randem	Swallow	Coldblood
Punch	Remuda	Swinger	Connemara
Rogue	Roarer	Trigger	Gringolet
Screw	Rouncy	Trotter	Houyhnhnm
Seian	Runner	Walking	Icelandic
Shire	Sabino	Wheeler	Incitatus
Stage	Saddle	Xanthos	Knabstrup
Steed	Shoo-in	Xanthus	Percheron
Tacky	Sorrel		Rosinante
Takhi	String	**8 letters:**	Rozinante
Troop	Stumer	Aquiline	Warmblood
Waler	Summer	Bangtail	
Wheel	Tandem	Bathorse	**10 letters:**
White	Tarpan	Boerperd	Andalusian
	Tracer	Buckskin	Bucephalus
6 letters:	Trojan	Camargue	Buckjumper
Ambler	Vanner	Chestnut	Buttermilk
Bayard		Clay-bank	Clydesdale
Bronco	**7 letters:**	Cocktail	Copenhagen
Brumby	Bobtail	Dartmoor	Lipizzaner
Calico	Breaker	Destrier	Lippizaner
Canuck	Cavalry	Eohippus	Pliohippus
Cayuse	Centaur	Friesian	Przewalski
Chaser	Charger	Galloway	Showjumper
Cooser	Clipper	Highland	Stagecoach
Crollo	Coacher	Holstein	Svadilfari
Curtal	Courser	Hyperion	
Cusser	Cuisser	Kochlani	**11 letters:**
Dobbin	Dappled	Lusitano	Daisy-cutter

High-stepper	*12 letters:*	Thoroughbred	*16 letters:*
Przewalski's	Cleveland Bay		Tennessee Walking
	Hambletonian	*13 letters:*	
	Suffolk Punch	Perissodactyl	

Horseback Croup
Horse-box Stable, Stall
Horse-chestnut Aesculus, Conker
Horse collar Brecham, Hame
Horse complaint, Horse disease, Horse problem, Horse trouble Blind
  staggers, Blood spavin, Bogspavin, Bot(t)s, Broken wind, Capel(l)et, Cracked heels,
  Curb, Dourine, Equinia, Eweneck, Farcy, Fives, Founder, Frush, Glanders, Gourdy,
  Head staggers, Heaves, Hippiatric, Knee spavin, Laminitis, Lampas, Lampers,
  Malander, Mallander, Mallender, Megrims, Miller's disease, Mooneye, Mud
  fever, N(a)gana, Poll-evil, Quartercrack, Quitter, Quittor, Ringbone, Sallenders,
  Sand crack, Scratches, Seedy-toe, Spavie, Spavin, Springhalt, Staggers, Strangles,
  Stringhalt, Summer sores, Surra, Sway-back, Sween(e)y, Thorough-pin, Thrush,
  Toe-crack, Tread, Vives, Weed, Weid, Whistling, Windgall, Wind-sucking,
  Wire-heel, Yellows
Horse-dealer Buster, Coper
Horse-lover Philip
Horseman Ataman, Caballero, Cavalry, Centaur, Conquest, Cossack, Cowboy,
  Death, Dragman, Famine, Farrier, Hobbler, Hussar, Knight, Lancer, Nessus, Ostler,
  Parthian, Picador, Pricker, Quadrille, Revere, → **RIDER**, Slaughter, Spahi, Stradiot,
  Tracer
Horsemanship Manège
Horseplay Caper, Chukka, Knockabout, Polo, Rag, Rant, Romp
Horsepower Hp, Indicated, Ps
Horseradish Ben, Moringa
Horseshoe(-shaped) Henge, Hippocrepian, King-crab, Lunette, Manilla, Oxbow,
  Plate
Horsetail Equisetum
Horse thief Blanco, Rustler
Horticultural, Horticulture, Horticulturist Grower, Pomology, RHS
Hose Chausses, Fishnet, Galligaskins, Gaskins, Lisle, Netherstock(ing), Nylons,
  Panty, Sock, Stockings, Tabi, Tights, Trunk, Tube
Hospitable, Hospitality Cadgy, Convivial, Entertainment, Euxine, Kidgie,
  Lucullan, Open house, Philoxenia, Social, Xenial
Hospital Ambulance, Asylum, Barts, Base, Bedlam, Clinic, Cottage, Day, Dressing
  station, ENT, Field, General, Guys, H, Home, Hospice, Imaret, Isolation, Karitane,
  Lambarene, Lazaretto, Leprosarium, Leprosery, Lock, Loony bin, Lying-in, MASH,
  Mental, Nosocomial, Ozzie, Pest-house, Polyclinic, Rathouse, San, Scutari, Sick
  bay, Snake-pit, Special, Spital, Spittle, Teaching, Trust, UCH
Host(s), Hostess Amphitryon, Army, Barmecide, Bunny girl, Chatelaine, Compere,
  Crowd, Definitive, Emcee, Entertainer, Eucharist, Heavenly, Hirsel, Hotelier,
  Innkeeper, Intermediate, Inviter, Laban, Landlady, Landlord, Legend, Legion,
  Lion-hunter, Lot, Mass, Mavin, MC, Publican, Quickly, Sabaoth, Swarm, Taverner,
  Throng, Trimalchio
Hostage Gherao, Pawn, Pledge, POW
Hostel Asylum, Dharms(h)ala, Dorm, Entry, Halfway house, Inn, YHA, Youth
Hostile, Hostility Adverse, Aggressive, Alien, Animus, Aversion, Bellicose, Bitter,

Chilly, Currish, Diatribe, Feud, Forbidding, Hating, Icy, Ill, Ill-will, Inimical, Inveterate, Oppugnant, Unfriendly, Vitriolic, War

Hot (tempered) Ardent, Big, Blistering, Breem, Breme, Cajun, Calid, Candent, Dog days, Enthusiastic, Facula, Fervid, Feverish, Fiery, Fuggy, Gospeller, Het, In, Incandescent, Irascible, Lewd, Live, Mafted, Mirchi, Mustard, Pepper, Piping, Potato, Quick, Randy, Red, Roaster, Scorcher, Sexpot, Sizzling, Spicy, Stewy, Stifling, Stolen, Sultry, Sweaty, Sweltering, Sweltry, Tabasco®, Thermidor, Torrid, Toustie, Tropical, Zealful

Hotchpotch Bricolage, Farrago, Mish-mash, Powsowdy, Welter

Hotel, Hotelkeeper Bo(a)tel, Boutique, Commercial, Fleabag, Flophouse, Gasthaus, Gasthof, H, Hilton, Host, Hydro, Inn, Motel, Parador, Patron(ne), Posada, Private, Ritz, Roadhouse, Savoy, Tavern, Temperance, Trust, Watergate

Hothead(ed) Impetuous, Rash, Spitfire, Volcano

Hot-house Conservatory, Nursery, Orangery, Vinery

Hot plate Salamander

Hot rod Dragster

Hotspur Harry, Hothead, Rantipole

Hottentot Griqua, Khoikhoi, Strandloper

Hot water Soup, Therm

Hound(s) Afghan, Basset, Beagle, Bellman, Brach, Cad, Canine, Cry, → DOG, Entry, Gabriel's, Hamiltonstovare, Harass, Harrier, Hen-harrier, Ibizan, Javel, Kennet, Lyam, Lym(e), Mute, Otter, Pack, Pharaoh, Pursue, Rache, Ranter, Reporter, Saluki, Talbot, True, Tufter

Hound's bane Palay

Hour(s) Canonical, Complin(e), Elders', Eleventh, Golden, H, Happy, Holy, Hr, Literacy, Little, Lunch, None(s), Office, Orthros, Peak, Prime, Rush, Sext, Sidereal, Small, Staggered, Terce, Tide, Time, Undern, Unsocial, Vespers, Visiting, Witching, Working, Zero

House(s), Housing, Household(er) Abode, Accepting, Adobe, Astrology, Audience, Auditorium, B, Bach, Bastide, Beehive, Beth, Bhavan, Bhawan, Biggin, Bingo, Black, Block, Boarding, Bondage, Brick veneer, Broadcasting, Broiler, Brownstone, Bundestag, Casa, Chalet, Chamber, Chapter, Charnel, Château, Chattel, Chez, Clapboard, Clearing, Coffee, Commercial, Concern, Convent, Cote, Cottage (orné), Council, Counting, Country, Crankcase, Crib, Custom(s), Dacha, Dail, Demain, Demesne, Derry, Des res, Discount, Disorderly, Domal, Domestic, Domicile, Donga, Door, Dower, Drostdy, Drum, Duplex, Dwelling, Dynasty, Edifice, Entertain, Establishment, Este, Eyrie, Familial, Fashion, Fibro(cement), Finance, Firm, Forcing, Frame, Fraternity, Free, Frontager, Full, Gaff, Gambling, Garage, Gite, Government, Grace and favour, Habitat, Habitation, Hacienda, Halfway, Hall, Harbour, Hearth, HK, Ho, Home, Homestead, Ice, Igloo, Inn, Insula, Issuing, Joss, Ken, Lodge, Lofted, Loose, Lot(t)o, Maison(ette), Malting, Manor, Manse, Mansion, Mas, Meeting, Meiney, Meinie, Meiny, Ménage, Menyie, Messuage, Mobility, Monastery, Montagne, Nacelle, Node, Open(-plan), Opera, Pad, Parliament, Pent, Picture, Pilot, Pleasure, Pole, Pondokkie, Post, Prefab, Printing, Public, Quinta, Radome, Ranch, Ratepayer, Register, Residence, Rooming, Rough, Sacrament, Safe, Satis, Schloss, School, Seat, Semi, Shanty, Sheltered, Show, Sign, Social, Software, Spec-built, Sporting, Stable, Station, Steeple, Storey, Succession, Tavern, Tea, Tenement, Terrace, Theatre, Third, Tied, Toft, Tombola, Tower, Town, Tract, Treasure, Tree, Trust, Vaulting, Vicarage, Villa, Villa(-home), Wash, Watch, Weather, Weatherboard, Weigh, Wendy, Whare, Wheel, White, Work, Zero, Zodiac

HOUSES

3 letters:
Leo

4 letters:
Bush
Keys
Syon
York

5 letters:
Lords
Scala
Tudor
Upper
Usher

6 letters:
Orange
Queen's

Seanad
Stuart
Wilton

7 letters:
Althing
Althorp
Bourbon
Commons
Hanover
Kenwood
Knesset
Lodging
Osborne
Stewart
Trinity
Windsor

8 letters:
Burghley
Chequers
Harewood
Hatfield
Holyrood
Lagthing
Longleat
Petworth
Somerset

9 letters:
Admiralty
Chartwell
Knebworth
Lancaster
Odelsting

10 letters:
Chatsworth
Heartbreak
Kirribilli
Odelsthing

11 letters:
Plantagenet
Russborough
Sandringham

12 letters:
Lockwood Home

13 letters:
Seanad Eireann

15 letters:
Representatives

House-boat Wangun, Wan(i)gan
House-builder Jack
House-keeper Chatelaine, Matron, Publican
House-leek Sengreen
Housemaid's knee Bursa
Houseman Betty, Doctor, Intern, Peer
House-warming Infare
Housewife Etui, Needlecase, WI
Housework Chore, DIY
Housing Case, Crankcase, Shabrack, Shelter, Slum, Tenement
Hova Malagash
Hove Plim, Swell
Hovel Cru(i)ve, Den, Pigsty, Shack, Shanty
Hover Hang, Levitate, Lurk, Poise
How Hill, Hollow
How'dyedo, How d'ye do Hallo, Pass, Salve
However As, But, Even-so, Leastwise, Sed, Still, Though, Yet
Howitzer Gun
Howl(er) Banshee, Bawl, Bay, Bloop, Clanger, Hue, Mycetes, Slip up, Squawk, Ululate, War whoop, Wow, Yawl, Yowl
How much The
Hoy Bilander, Ship
HP Never-never
HQ Centre, Headquarters, SHAPE
Hub Boss, Centre, Focus, Hob, Nave, Pivot, Tee
Hubbub Charivari, Chirm, Coil, Din, Level-coil, Palaver, Racket, Row, Stir
Hubris Pride
Huckster Hawker, Kidd(i)er, Pedlar
Huddle Cringe, Gather, Hunch, Ruck, Shrink

Hudson River, Rock

Hue Colour, Dye, Outcry, Proscription, Steven, Tincture, Tinge, Utis

Huff Dudgeon, Hector, Pant, Pet, Pique, Snuff, Strunt, Umbrage, Vex

Hug Bear, Coll, Cuddle, → **EMBRACE**, Squeeze

Huge (number) Astronomical, Brobdingnag, Colossal, Enorm(ous), Gargantuan, Giant, → **GIGANTIC**, Gillion, Ginormous, Humongous, Humungous, Immane, Immense, Leviathan, Lulu, Mega-, Milliard, Monolithic, Monster, Octillion, Prodigious, Socking, Tall, Titanian, Tremendous, Vast, Whacking

Hugo Victor

Huguenot Camisard

Hulk Lout, Ruin, Shale, Shell, Ship

Hull Bottom, Framework, Husk, Inboard, Monocoque, Pod, Sheal, Sheel, Shell, Shiel, Shill, Shiplap

Hullabaloo Outcry, Razzamatazz, Raz(z)mataz(z)

▶ **Hullo** *see* **HELLO**

Hum(ming) Bombilate, Bombinate, Bum, Chirm, Chirr, Drone, Lilt, Moan, Murmur, Nos(e)y, Pong, Ponk, Rank, Reek, Sowf(f), Sowth, Stench, Stink, Stir, Whir(r), Zing

Human(e), Humanist, Humanity Anthropoid, Bang, Colet, Earthling, Erasmus, Incarnate, Kindness, Mandom, Merciful, Mortal, Philanthropic, Species, Sympathy, Ubuntu, Virtual, Wight

Humble Abase, Abash, Afflict, Baseborn, Chasten, Cow, Degrade, Demean, Demiss(ly), Lower, Lowly, Mean, → **MEEK**, Modest, Morigerate, Obscure, Poor, Rude, Small, Truckle

Humbug Berley, Blague, Blarney, Buncombe, Bunk(um), Burley, Cant, Claptrap, Con, Delude, Flam, Flummery, Fraud, Fudge, Gaff, Gammon, Gas, Guff, Gum, Hoax, Hoodwink, Hookey-walker, Kibosh, Liar, Maw-worm, Nonsense, Prig, Shenanigan, Wind

Humdinger Cracker, Lulu

Humdrum Banal, Boredom, Bourgeois, Monotonous, Mundane, Ordinary, Prosaic, Tedious

Humid(ity) Clammy, Damp, Dank, Machie, Machy, Muggy, Saturation, Steam, Sticky, Sultry

Humiliate(d), Humiliation, Humility Abase, Abash, Baseness, Degrade, Disbench, Eating crow, Fast, Indignity, Laughing stock, Lose face, Mortify, Put-down, → **SHAME**, Skeleton, Take-down, Wither

Humming-bird Colibri, Hermit, Rainbow, Sabre-wing, Sapphire-wing, Sappho, Sylph, Thornbill, Topaz, Trochilus

Hummock Tump

Humorist Cartoonist, Comedian, Jester, Leacock, Lear, Punster, Twain, Wodehouse

Humour, Humorous Aqueous, Bile, Blood, Caprice, Cardinal, Chaff, Choler, Coax, Cocker, Coddle, Cosher, Cuiter, Cuittle, Daut, Dawt, Dry, Facetious, Fun, Gallows, Ichor, Indulge, Irony, Jocose, Jocular, Juice, Kidney, Levity, Light, Melancholy, → **MOOD**, Observe, One-liner, Pamper, Phlegm, Pun, Pythonesque, Ribaldry, Salt, Serum, Temper, Trim, Vein, Vitreous, Vitreum, Wetness, Whim, Whimsy, Wit

Humourless Dry, Po(-faced)

Hump(ed) Boy, Bulge, Dorts, Dowager's, Gibbose, Gibbous, Hog, Huff, Hummock, Hunch, Middelmannetjie, Pip, Ramp, Road, Speed bump, Tussock

▶ **Humpback** *see* **HUNCHBACK**

Humphrey Bogart

Humus Compost, Leafmould, Moder, Mor, Mull

Hun Alaric, Atli, Attila, Fritz, German

Hunch, Hunchback Camel, Chum, Crookback, Gobbo, Intuition, Kyphosis, Premonition, Quasimodo, Roundback, Sense, Urchin

Hundred(s), Hundredth Burnham, C, Cantred, Cantref, Cent, Centesimal, Centum, Century, Chiltern, Commot, Days, Desborough, Great, Host, → **IN A HUNDRED**, Long, Northstead, Old, Shire, Stoke, Ton, Wapentake

Hundred and fifty CL, Y

Hundred and sixty T

Hundredweight Centner, Long, Metric, Quintal, Short

Hung Displayed, Executed, Framed, High

Hungarian, Hungary Bohunk, Cheremis(s), Csardas, Magyar, Nagy, Szekely, Tzigane, Ugric, Vogul

Hunger, Hungry Appestat, Appetite, Bulimia, Bulimy, Clem, → **CRAVE**, Desire, Edacity, Empty, Esurient, Famine, Famish, Fast, Hanker, Hunter, Pant, Peckish, Rapacious, Raven, Ravin, Sharp-set, Unfed, Unfuelled, Yaup, Yearn

▷ **Hungry** *may indicate* an 'o' in another word

Hunk(s) Beefcake, Chunk, Dry-fist, Miser(ly), Slab, Wedge

Hunker Squat

Hunt(er), Hunting, Huntress, Huntsman Actaeon, Alew, Archer, Artemis, Atalanta, Battue, Beagle, Bellman, Bounty, Calydon, Chace, Chase(r), Chasseur, Chevy, Cool, Coursing, Crockett, Cynegetic, Dog, Drag(net), Esau, Ferret, Fox, Free-shot, Gun, Halloo, Herne, Hound, Jager, Lamping, Leigh, Letterbox, Lurcher, Montero, National, Nimrod, Orion, Peel, Pig-sticking, Poacher, Poot, Pout, Predator, Pursue, Quest, Quorn, Rabbit, Rach(e), Rake, Ran, Rancel, Ranzel, Ride, Rummage, Run, Scavenge(r), Scorse, Scout, → **SEARCH**, Seek, Shikar(ee), Shikari, Skirter, Slipper, Stag, Stalk, Sticker, Still, Swiler, Terrier, Thimble, Ticker, Tinchel, Tower, Trail, Trap, Treasure, Venatic, Venator, Venerer, Venery, → **WATCH**, Whip, Whipper-in, Witch, Wolfer, Woodman, Woodsman, Yager

Hunting-call Rechate, Recheat, Tally-ho, View-halloo

Hunting-ground Forestation, Walk

Hurdle(r) Barrier, Doll, Fence, Flake, Gate, Hemery, Obstacle, Raddle, Sticks, Wattle

Hurdy (gurdy) Barrel-organ, Hainch, Haunch, Vielle

Hurl(ing) Camogie, Cast, Dash, → **FLING**, Heave, Put(t), Throw, → **TOSS**

Hurly-burly Furore, Noise

Hurrah Cheers, Huzza, Io, Whee

Hurricane Baguio, Tornade, Tornado, Typhoon, → **WIND**

Hurry Belt, Bustle, Chivvy, Chop-chop, Dart, Dash, Drive, Festinate, Fisk, Frisk, Gad, Gallop, Giddap, Giddup, Giddy-up, Hadaway, Hare, Haste, Hie, Hightail, Induce, Mosey, Post-haste, Press, Push, Race, Railroad, → **RUSH**, Scamper, Scoot, Scramble, Scur(ry), Scutter, Scuttle, Skelter, Skurry, Spank, Speed, Streak, Tear, Whirr

Hurt(ful) Abuse, Ache, Aggrieve, Ake, Bruise, Cutting, Damage, De(a)re, Disservice, Harm, Harrow, Hit, → **INJURE**, Lesion, Maim, Nocent, Nocuous, Noisome, Noxious, Noyous, Pain, Pang, Prick(le), Scaith, Wound, Wring

Hurtle Rush, Spin, Streak, Streek

Husband(ry), Husbands Add, Baron, Breadwinner, Consort, Darby, Ear, Eche, Economy, Eke, Ere, Farm, Gander-mooner, Georgic, Goodman, Groom, H, Hoddy-doddy, Hodmandod, Hubby, Ideal, Man, Manage, Mate, Partner, Polyandry, Retrench, Save, Scrape, Scrimp, Spouse, Squirrel, → **STORE**, Tillage

Hush(-hush) Bestill, Gag, Sh, Silent, Smug, St, Tace, Wheesh(t), Whisht

Husk(s), Husky Acerose, Bran, Draff, Eskimo, Hoarse, Hull, Malemute, Seed, Sheal, Shuck

Hussar Cherry-picker, Cherubim
Hussite Calixtin(e), Taborite
Hussy Besom, Hen, Limmer, Loose, Minx, Vamp
Hustle(r) Fast talk, Frogmarch, Jostle, Pro, Push, Railroad, Shoulder, Shove, Skelp
Hut(s) Banda, Booth, Bothie, Bothy, Bustee, Cabin, Caboose, Chalet, Choltry, Gunyah, Hogan, Humpy, Igloo, Mia-mia, Nissen, Pondok(kie), Quonset®, Rancheria, Rancho, Rondavel, Shack, Shanty, Sheal(ing), Shebang, Shed, Shiel(ing), Skeo, Skio, Succah, Sukkah, Tilt, Tolsel, Tolsey, Tolzey, Tramping, Wan(n)igan, Whare, Wi(c)kiup, Wigwam, Wil(t)ja, Wurley, Wurlie
Hutch Buddle, Crate, Pen, Rabbit
Hyacinth Cape, Grape, Starch, Wild
Hybrid Bigener, Bois-brûlé, Cama, Catalo, Centaur, Chamois, Chichi, Chimera, Citrange, Cockatrice, Cross, Dso, Funnel, Geep, Graft, Hippogriff, Hircocervus, Interbred, Jersian, Jomo, Jumart, Lurcher, Mameluco, Mermaid, Merman, Metif, Métis, Mongrel, Mule, Mutation, Noisette, Opinicus, Ortanique, Ox(s)lip, Percolin, Plumcot, Pomato, Ringed, Tangelo, Tiglon, Tigon, Topaz, Ugli, Zho(mo)
▷ **Hybrid** *may indicate* an anagram
Hydra Polyp
Hydrant Fireplug, H
Hydrocarbon Acetylene, Aldrin, Alkane, Alkene, Alkyl, Alkyne, Amylene, Arene, Asphaltite, Benzene, Butadiene, Butane, Butene, Camphane, Camphene, Carotene, Cetane, Cubane, Cycloalkane, Cyclohexane, Cyclopropane, Cymogene, Decane, Diene, Dioxin, Diphenyl, Ethane, Gutta, Halon, Hatchettite, Heavy oil, Hemiterpene, Heptane, Hexane, Hexene, Hexyl(ene), Indene, Isobutane, Isoprene, Ligroin, Limonene, Mesitylene, Naphtha, Naphthalene, Naphthalin(e), Nonane, Octane, Olefin(e), Paraffin, Pentane, Pentene, Pentylene, Phenanthrene, Phene, Pinene, Polyene, Propane, Pyrene, Pyridine, Retene, Squalene, Stilbene, Styrene, Terpene, Toluene, Triptane, Wax, Xylene, Xylol
Hydrogen Deut(er)on, Diplon, Ethene, H, Muonium, Protium, Replaceable, Tritium
Hydrometer Salinometer
Hydrophobic Rabid
Hydroplane Skid
Hydroponic Soil
Hydrozoa(n) Campanularia, Millepore, Portuguese man-of-war, Siphonophore
Hyena Aard-wolf, Earthwolf, Laughing, Nandi bear, Spotted, Strand-wolf, Tiger-wolf
Hygiene, Hygienic Aseptic, Dental, Oral, Sanitary, Sepsis, Sleep
Hymen Maidenhead
Hymn(s) Anthem, Benedictine, Bhajan, Canticle, Carol, Cathisma, Choral(e), Coronach, Dies Irae, Dithyramb, Doxology, Gloria, Hallel, Introit(us), Ithyphallic, Lay, Magnificat, Mantra, Marseillaise, Nunc Dimittis, Ode, P(a)ean, Psalm, Recessional, Rigveda, Sanctus, Secular, Sequence, Stabat Mater, Sticheron, Tantum Ergo, Te Deum, Trisagion, Troparion, Veda
Hymnographer, Hymnologist David, Faber, Heber, Moody, Neale, Parry, Sankey, Watts
Hype(d) Aflutter
Hyperbole, Hyperbolic Auxesis, Exaggeration, Sech
Hypercritical Captious
Hyperion Titan
Hypersensitive Allergic, Idiosyncratic
Hypha(e) Conidiophore, Stroma

Hyphen(ated) Dash, Parasyntheton, Soft
Hypnosis, Hypnotise, Hypnotic, Hypnotism, Hypnotist Braidism, Chloral,
Codeine, Enthral, Entrance, Hypotonia, Magnetic, Meprobamate, Mesmerism,
Psychognosis, Svengali
Hypochondria(c) Atrabilious, Hyp, Nosophobia, Phrenesiac, Valetudinarian
Hypocrisy, Hypocrite, Hypocritical Archimago, Bigot, Byends, Cant, Carper,
Chadband, Creeping Jesus, Deceit, Dissembler, False-faced, Heep, Holy Willie,
Humbug, Insincere, Janus-faced, Mucker, Nitouche, Pecksniff, Pharisaic, Pharisee,
Piety, Prig, Sanctimony, Self-pious, Sepulchre, Tartuf(f)e, Two-faced, Whited
sepulchre
Hypothesis, Hypothetical Avogadro, Biophor, Conditional, Continuum, Gluon,
Graviton, Nebular, Notional, Null, Planetesimal, Sapir-Whorf, Suppositious,
Virtual, Working
Hyrax Cony, Daman, Dassie, Klipdas, Rock rabbit
Hysteria, Hysteric(al) Achiria, Astasia, Conniption, Delirium, Frenzy, Meemie,
Mother

Ii

I A, Ch, Cham, Che, Dotted, Ego, Ich, Indeed, India, Iodine, Italy, J, Je, Me, Muggins, One, Self, Yours truly

Ian Scot

Iberian Celtiberean

Ibex Izard

Ibis Hadedah, Sacred, Waldrapp

Ice(d), Ice-cream, Icing, Icy Alcorza, Anchor, Arctic, Ballicatter, Banana split, Berg, Black, Brash, Camphor, Cassata, Coconut, Cone, Cool, Cornet, Coupe, Cream, Crystal, Diamonds, Drift, Dry, Floe, Frappé, Frazil, Freeze, Frigid, Frore, Frosting, Frosty, Gelato, Gelid, Gems, Glacé, Glacial, Glacier, Glare, Glaze, Glib, Granita, Graupel, Ground, Growler, Hailstone, Hok(e)y-pok(e)y, Hommock, Hummock, Kitty-benders, Knickerbocker glory, Kulfi, Lolly, Macallum, Marzipan, Neapolitan, Oaky, Pack, Pancake, Pingo, Polar, Popsicle®, Rime, Rink, Ross, Royal, Sconce, Serac, Shelf, Sherbet, Slay, Slider, Slob, Sludge, Sorbet, Spumone, Spumoni, Stream, Sugar, Tickly-benders, Topping, Tortoni, Tutti-frutti, Verglas, Virga, Wafer, Water, Wintry

Ice-axe Piolet

Iceberg Calf, Floe, Growler

Ice-box Cooler, Freezer, Fridge, Frig, Yakhdan

▶ **Ice-cream** *see* ICE

Iceland IS

Ice-skating Choctaw, Figure, Glide

Icicle Tangle

Icon Fashion, Idol, Image, Madonna, Sprite

Icterus Jaundice

ID PIN

Id(e) Ego, Fish, Orfe

Idea(s) Archetype, Brainchild, Brainwave, Clou, Clue, Conceit, Concept, Fancy, Figment, Fixed, Germ, Hunch, Idée fixe, Idolum, Image, Inkling, Inspiration, Interpretation, Keynote, Light, → NOTION, Obsession, Plan, Plank, Rationale, Recept, Theory, Thought, Whimsy, Zeitgeist

Ideal(ise) A1, Abstract, Apotheosis, Bee's knees, Cat's whiskers, Dream, Eden, Ego, Goal, Halo, Hero, Model, Monist, Nirvana, Notional, Paragon, Pattern, → PERFECT, Romantic, Siddhi, Sidha, Sublimate, Transcendental, Utopian, Vision

Idealism, Idealist(ic) Dreamer, More, Perfectionist, Quixotic, Romantic, Transcendental, Visionary

Identical Alike, Clone, Congruent, Equal, Menechmian, One, Same, Selfsame, Verbatim, Very

Identification, Identify Bertillonage, Codeword, Credentials, Designate, Diagnosis, Differentiate, Discern, Document, Dog-tag, Earmark, Empathy, Espy, Finger(print), ID, Identikit®, Label, Mark, Monomark, Name, Name-tape, Password, Photofit®,

Pin, Pinpoint, Place, Point up, Recognise, Reg(g)o, Secern, Spot, Swan-hopping, Swan-upping, Verify

Identikit® E-fit

Identity Alias, Appearance, Corporate, Credentials, Equalness, Likeness, Mistaken, Numerical, Oneness, Personal, Qualitative, Seity, Self, Selfhood

Ideology, Ideologue Credo, Hard-liner, Ism

Idiom Americanism, Argot, Britishism, Cant, Expression, Idioticon, Jargon, Language, Pahlavi, Parlance, Pehlevi, Persism, Scotticism, Syri(a)cism, Syrism

Idiosyncrasy, Idiosyncratic Foible, Mannerism, Nature, Quirk, Way, Zany

Idiot(ic), Idiocy Congenital, Dingbat, Dolt, Eejit, Fatuity, Fool, Goose, Half-wit, Imbecile, Inane, Maniac, Moron, Natural, Nerk, Nidget, Noncom, Numpty, Oaf, Ouph(e), → **STUPID**, Tony, Twit, Village, Whacko, Zany

Idle(ness), Idler Beachcomber, Bludger, Boondoggle, Bum, Bumble, Bummle, Cockaigne, Dally, Deadbeat, Diddle, Dilly-dally, Dole-bludger, Donnat, Donnot, Do-nothingism, Drone, Fainéant, Fallow, Farnarkel, Fester, Flaneur, Flim-flam, Footle, Frivolous, Gold brick, Groundless, Hawm, Inaction, Indolent, Inert, Lackadaisical, Laesie, Lallygag, Layabout, Laze, Lazy, Lead-swinger, Lie, Lig, Light, Limer, Loaf, Lollop, Lollygag, Lotophagus, Lounge, Lusk, Micawber, Mike, Mollusc, Mooch, Mouch, Otiose, Otium, Patagonian, Piddle, Ride, Scapegrace, Shiftless, Skive, Sloth, Sluggard, Spiv, Stalko, Stock-still, Stooge, Stroam, Tarry, Transcendental, Trock, Troke, Truant, Truck, Twiddle, Unbusy, Unoccupied, Vain, Vegetate, Veg out, Waste

Idol(ise) Adore, Adulate, Baal(im), Baphomet, Bel, Crush, E(i)luned, Fetich(e), Fetish, God, Heartthrob, Hero, Icon, Image, Joss, Juggernaut, Lion, Mammet, Manito, Manitou, Matinee, Maumet, Mawmet, Molech, Moloch, Mommet, Moorish, Mumbo-jumbo, Stotter, Swami, Teraph(im), Termagant, Vision, Wood, Worship

Idyll(ic) Arcady, Eclogue, Eden, Pastoral, Peneian

Ie Sc

If, If it All-be, An('t), Condition, Gif, Gin, In case, Pot, Provided, Sobeit, Whether

Igloo Snowden

Igneous Pyrogenic

Ignis-fatuus Elf-fire, Fire-dragon, Fire-drake, Friar's lanthorn, Wildfire

Ignite, Ignition Coil, Electronic, Flare, Kindle, Lightning, Spark, Starter

Ignoble Base, Inferior, Mean, Vile

Ignominious, Ignominy Base, Dishonour, Fiasco, Infamous, Scandal, → **SHAME**

Ignorance, Ignorant Agnoiology, Analphabet, Anan, Artless, Benighted, Blind, Clueless, Darkness, Green, Hick, Illiterate, Inerudite, Ingram, Ingrum, Inscient, Know-nothing, Lewd, Lumpen, Misken, Nescience, Night, Oblivious, Oik, Philistine, Purblind, Red-neck, Unaware, Uneducated, Unlettered, Unread, Unschooled, Untold, Unversed, Unwist

Ignore Alienate, Ba(u)lk, Blink, Bypass, Connive, Cut, Discount, Disregard, Forget, Neglect, Omit, Overlook, Override, Overslaugh, Pass, Pass-up, Rump, Scrub round, Slight, Snub

Igor Prince

Iguana Chuckwalla

I know Iwis, Ywis

Iliad Homeric

Ill Adverse, All-overish, Bad, Bilious, Cronk, Crook, Evil, Inauspicious, Income, Off-colour, Poorly, Queer, Sea-sick, → **SICK**, Unweal, Unwell, Valetudinarian, Wog, Wrong

▷ **Ill** *may indicate* an anagram

Ill-adjusted Sad sack
Ill-balanced Lop-sided
Ill-bred Churlish, Plebeian, Uncouth, Unmannerly
▷ **Ill-composed** *may indicate* an anagram
Ill-defined Diagnosis, Hazy, Unclear, Vague
Ill-dressed Frumpish
Illegal, Illicit Adulterine, Black, Bootleg, Breach, Furtive, Ill-gotten, Malfeasance, Misbegotten, Pirated, Shonky, Unlawful
Illegitimate Baseborn, Bastard, By-blow, Come-o'-will, Fitz, Irregular, Love-child, Lucky-piece, Mamzer, Misbegotten, Misborn, Misfortunate, Momzer, Natural, Scarp, Slink, Spurious, Unlineal
Ill-favoured Lean, Offensive, Thin, Ugly
Ill-feeling, Ill-humour Bad blood, Bile, Curt, Dudgeon, Glum, Hate, Miff, Peevish, Pique, Rheumatic
Illiberal Insular, Skinflint, Strict
▶ **Illicit** *see* ILLEGAL
Illiterate Ignoramus, Unlettered, Unread
Ill-looking Peaky, Poorly
Ill-luck Ambs-ace, Ames-ace, Bad trot, Deuce-ace, Misfortune
Ill-mannered, Ill-natured Attercop, Bitchy, Coarse, Crabby, Ethercap, Ettercap, Goop, Gurrier, Guttersnipe, Huffy, Stingy, Sullen, Ugly, Uncouth, Unkind
Illness Aids, Ailment, Attack, Autism, Brucellosis, Complaint, Croup, Death-bed, Diabetes, Disease, DS, Dwalm, Dwaum, Dyscrasia, Eale, Eclampsia, Grippe, Hangover, Hypochondria, Lockjaw, Malady, ME, SAD, Scarlatina, Sickness, Terminal, Toxaemia, Urosis, Weed, Weid, Wog
Ill-nourished Emaciated
Illogical Inconsequent, Non-sequitur
Ill-sighted Owl, Purblind
Ill-smelling F(o)etid, High, Hing, Miasmic, Stinking
▶ **Ill-tempered** *see* ILL-MANNERED
Ill-timed Inopportune, Unseasonable
Illuminate(d), Illumination, Illuminating Aperçu, Brighten, Clarify, Cul-de-lampe, Decorate, Enlighten, Floodlit, Lamplight, Langley, Light, Limn, Miniate, Nernst, Pixel, Radiate, Rushlight
Illusion, Illusory, Illusive Air, Apparition, Barmecide, Deception, Déjà vu, Fallacy, Fancy, Fantasy, Hallucination, Ignis-fatuus, Mare's-nest, Maya, Mirage, Muller-Lyer, Optical, Phantom, Phi-phenomenon, Size-weight, Specious, Transcendental, Trompe l'oeil, Unreality, Will o'the wisp
Illustrate(d), Illustration, Illustrator Artwork, Case, Centrefold, Collotype, Demonstrate, Drawing, Eg, Elucidate, Epitomise, Exemplify, Explain, Figure, Frontispiece, Grangerize, Graphic, Half-tone, Illume, Illumin(at)e, Instance, Instantiate, Keyline, Limner, Lithograph, Pictorial, Plate, Show, Sidelight, Spotlight, Tenniel, Vignette, Visual
Illustrious Bright, Celebrated, Famous, Legendary, Renowned
Ill-will Animosity, Enmity, Grudge, Hostility, Malice, Maltalent, Mau(l)gre, Spite
I'm I'se
Image(s) Atman, Blip, Brand, Corporate, Discus, Effigy, Eidetic, Eidolon, Eikon, Eiluned, Emotion, Enantiomorph, Fine-grain, Graphic, Graven, Hologram, Hypnagogic, Icon, Iconograph, Ident, Idol, Invultuation, Joss, Latent, Likeness, Matte, Mirror, Morph, Murti, Paranthelion, Paraselene, Pentimento, Phantasmagoria, Photogram, Photograph, Pic(ture), Pixel(l)ated, Pixil(l)ated,

Poetic, Profile, Public, Real, Recept, Reflectogram, Reflectograph, Representation,
Scintigram, Search, Shadowgraph, Simulacrum, Spectrum, Spitting, Split,
Stereotype, Symbol, Teraph(im), Thumbnail, Tiki, Tomogram, Totem, Venogram,
Video, Virtual, Xoanon
Imagine(d), Imaginary (land), Imagination, Imaginative Assume,
Bandywallop, Believe, Boojum, Bullamakanka, Cloud-cuckoo-land, Cockaigne,
Cockayne, Conceive, Conjure, Cyborg, Dystopia, Envisage, Esemplasy, Faery,
Faine, Fancy, Feign, Fictional, Fictitious, Fictor, Figment, Figure, Hallucinate,
Hobbit, Ideate, Invent, Mind's eye, Moral, Oz, Picture, Poetical, Prefigure, Pretend,
Recapture, Replicant, Scotch mist, Snark, Straw, → **SUPPOSE**, Surmise, Think,
Tulpa, Vicarious, Visualise, Whangam
Imbecile Anile, Fool, Idiot, → **STUPID**
▷ **Imbecile** *may indicate* an anagram
Imbibe Absorb, Drink, Lap, Quaff, Suck, Swallow
Imbricate Overlie
Imbroglio Complication, Maze
Imbrue, Imbue Colour, Impregnate, Indoctrinate, Infuse, Inoculate, Permeate,
Soak, Steep
Imitate, Imitation, Imitator Act, Ape, Burlesque, Copy(cat), Counterfeit, Dud,
Echo, Echopraxia, Emulate, Epigon(e), Ersatz, Fake, False, Faux, Follow, Marinist,
Me-too, Mime, Mimetic, Mimic(ry), Mini-me, Mockery, Monkey, Onomatopoeia,
Parody, Parrot, Paste, Pastiche, Pinchbeck, Potichomania, Rip-off, Sham, Simulate,
Stumer, Take-off, Travesty
Immaculate Conception, Flawless, Lily-white, Perfect, Pristine, Spotless, Virgin
Immanentist Pantheist
Immaterial Insignificant, Spiritual, Trifling
Immature(ly), Immaturity Callow, Crude, Embryo, Ergate(s), Green, Inchoate,
Larval, Neotenic, Non-age, Puberal, Puberulent, Pupa, Raw, Sophomoric, Tender,
Unbaked, Underage, Unformed, Unripe, Young
▷ **Immature** *may indicate* a word incompleted
Immediate(ly) Alsoon, At once, B(e)live, Direct, Eftsoons, Ekdum, First-time,
Forthwith, Imminent, Incontinent, Instantaneous, Instanter, Lickety-split, Near,
Next, → **NOW**, Now-now, On the knocker, Outright, Present, Pronto, Right-off,
Short-term, Slapbang, Spontaneous, Stat, Statim, Straight, Straight off, Sudden,
Then, Tout de suite
Immense Astronomical, Brobdingnag, Cosmic, Enormous, → **GIGANTIC**, Huge,
Vast, Wide
Immerse Baptise, Demerge, Demerse, Drench, Embathe, Emplonge, Enew, Engage,
Imbathe, Plunge, Soak, Steep
Immigrant, Immigration, Immigrate Aliya(h), Aussiedler, Brain gain,
Carpet-bagger, Cayun, Chalutz, Freshie, Greener, Greenhorn, Halutz, Illegal,
Incomer, Issei, Merino, Metic, New chum, Nisei, Non-quota, Olim, Outsider,
Overstayer, Pilgrim, Pommy, Quota, Redemption(er), Reffo, Sanei, Sansei, Settler,
Wetback, Whenwe
Imminent Approaching, Close, Immediate, Pending
Immobility, Immobile, Immobilise(r) Akinesia, Cataplexy, Catatonia, Hog-tie,
Inertia, Pinion, Rigidity, Taser, Tether
Immoderate Excessive, Extreme, Inordinate, Intemperate, Lavish, Undue,
Unreasonable
Immodest(y) Brash, Brazen, Forward, Impudicity, Indelicate, Unchaste
Immolation Sacrifice, Sati, Suttee

Immoral(ity) Corrupt, Degenerate, Dissolute, Evil, Lax, Libertine, Licentious, Loose, Nefarious, Peccable, Reprobate, Scarlet, Turpitude, Unholy, Unsavoury, Vice, Vicious, Wanton

Immortal(ity) Agelong, Amarant(h), Amarantin, Amritattva, Athanasy, Deathless, → **DIVINE**, Enoch, Eternal, Ever-living, Famous, Godlike, Memory, Sin, Struldbrug, Timeless, Undying

Immovable Fast, Firm, Obdurate, Rigid, Stable, Stubborn

Immune, Immunisation, Immunise(r), Immunity Acquired, Active, Amboceptor, Anamnestic, Anergy, Bar, Cree, Diplomatic, Free, Humoral, Inoculate, Klendusic, Natural, Non-specific, Passive, Pasteurism, Pax, Premunition, Properdin, Serum, Tachyphylaxis, Vaccine

Immure Confine, Encloister, Imprison

Imp(ish) Devilet, Elf, Flibbertigibbet, Gamin(e), Hobgoblin, Limb, Lincoln, Litherly, Nickum, Nis(se), Puck, Ralph, Rascal, Spright, Sprite

Impact Bearing, Bump, Clash, Collision, Feeze, High, Impinge, Jar, Jolt, Pack, Percuss, Pow, Slam, Souse, Strike home, Wham

Impair(ed), Impairment Appair, Cripple, Damage, Disease, Enfeeble, → **HARM**, Injure, Lame, Mar, Mental, Odd, Pair(e), Paralogia, Stale, Vitiate

Impala Pallah

Impale Elance, Ga(u)nch, Skewer, Spike, Transfix

Impart Bestow, Convey, Divulge, Impute, Infect, Shed, Tell

Impartial Candid, Detached, Equitable, Even-handed, Fair, Just, Neutral, Unbiased

Impasse, Impassable Deadlock, Dilemma, Invious, Jam, Mexican standoff, Snooker, Stalemate, Zugzwang

Impassioned Emotional, Fervid, Fiery, Heated, Zealous

Impassive Apathetic, Deadpan, Stoical, Stolid

Impatience, Impatient Chafing, Chut, Dysphoria, Fiddle-de-dee, Fiddlesticks, Fidgety, Fretful, Hasty, Hoot(s), Irritable, Och, Peevish, Peremptory, Petulant, Pish, Restless, Tilly-fally, Till(e)y-vall(e)y, Tut

Impeach Accuse, Challenge, Charge, Delate, Indict

Impeccable Faultless, Novice

Impecunious Penniless, Poor, Short

Impedance, Impede, Impediment Burr, Clog, Dam, Diriment, Encumber, Halt, Hamstring, Handicap, → **HINDER**, Hog-tie, Let, Log, Obstacle, Obstruct, Reactance, Rub, Shackle, Snag, Stammer, Stymie, Tongue-tie, Trammel, Veto, Z

Impel(led) Actuate, Coerce, Drave, Drive, Drove, Goad, Inspire, → **URGE**

Impend(ing) Imminent, Looming, Toward

Impenetrable Adamantine, Air-tight, Dense, Hard, Impervious, Proof, Watertight

Imperative Categorical, Dire, Hypothetical, Jussive, Mood, Need-be, Pressing, Vital

Imperceptible, Imperceptive Blind Freddie, Intangible, Invisible, Latent, Minimal, Subtle

Imperfect(ion) Aplasia, Aplastic, Blotch, Defect, Deficient, Faulty, Feathering, Flawed, Half-pie, Kink, Kinkle, Lame, Poor, Rough, Second, Unideal

Imperial(ist), Imperious Beard, C(a)esarian, Commanding, Haughty, Majestic, Masterful, Mint, Peremptory, Regal, Rhodes, Royal, Tuft

Imperil Endanger, Risk

Imperishable Eternal, Immortal, Indestructible

Impermeable Airtight, Athermanous, Proof, Resistant

Impersonal Abstract, Cold, Detached, Inhuman, Institutional

Impersonate, Impersonation, Impersonator Amphitryon, Ape, As, Double, Imitate, Impression, Mimic, Pose, Spoof

Impertinence, Impertinent Crust, Flip(pant), Fresh, Impudent, Irrelevant, Rude, Sass, Sauce

Imperturbable Cool, Placid, Stoic, Tranquil

Impervious(ness) Athermancy, Callous, Hardened, Obdurate, Proof, Tight

Impetigo Scrumpox

Impetuous, Impetuosity Birr, Brash, Bullheaded, Élan, → **HASTY**, Headstrong, Heady, Hothead, Impulsive, Rash, Rhys, Tearaway, Vehement, Violent, Young Turk

Impetus Birr, Drift, Incentive, MacGuffin, Momentum, Propulsion, Slancio, Steam, Swing

Impious Blasphemous, Godless, Irreverent, Unholy

Implant(ation) AID, Cochlear, Embed, Engraft, Enroot, Graft, Inset, Instil, Nidation, Silicone, Sow

Implausible Lame, Off-the-wall

Implement Agent, Backscratcher, Biffer, Celt, Cultivator, Disgorger, Eolith, Execute, Flail, Follow out, Fork, Fulfil, Hacksaw, Harrow, Hayfork, Mop, Muller, Pin, Pitchfork, Plectrum, Plough, Pusher, Rest, Ripple, Scarifier, Scythe, Seed drill, Shoehorn, Sickle, Snuffer, Spatula, Splayd®, Squeegee, Strickle, Tongs, → **TOOL**, Toothpick, Tribrach, Utensil

Implicate, Implication Accuse, Concern, Connotation, Embroil, Incriminate, Innuendo, → **INVOLVE**, Material, Overtone

Implore Beg, Beseech, Crave, → **ENTREAT**, Obsecrate, Petition, Plead, Pray

Imply, Implied Hint, Insinuate, Involve, Predicate, Signify, → **SUGGEST**, Tacit

Impolite Ill-bred, Rude, Uncivil

Import(s) Convey, Denote, Drift, Invisible, Mean, Parallel, Sense, Signify, Spell, Visible

Importance, Important (person) Big, Big cheese, Big wheel, Billing, Calibre, Cardinal, Central, Cheese, Cob, Coming, Consequence, Considerable, Core, Cornerstone, Count, Critical, Crucial, Crux, Earth-shaking, Earth-shattering, Eminent, Epochal, Grave, Gravitas, Gravity, Greatness, Heavy, High, High-muck-a-muck, His nibs, Historic, Honcho, Hotshot, Huzoor, Key, Keystone, Macher, Magnitude, Main, Major, Material, Matters, Megastar, Mighty, Milestone, Moment(ous), Nabob, Nawab, Nib, Note, Numero uno, Obbligato, Overriding, Personage, Pivotal, Pot, Preponderate, Prime, Principal, Red-carpet, Salient, Seminal, Serious, Significant, Something, Special, Stature, Status, Stress, Substantive, Tuft, Urgent, VIP, Weight, Weighty, Worth

Importune, Importunate Beg, Coax, Flagitate, Press(ing), Prig, Solicit, Urgent

Impose(r), Imposing, Imposition Allocate, Assess, August, Burden, Charge, Cheat, Diktat, Dread, Enforce, Enjoin, Epic, Fine, Flam, Foist, Fraud, Grand(iose), Hidage, Homeric, Hum, Impot, Inflict, Kid, Lay, Levy, Lumber, Majestic, Obtrude, Pensum, Pole, Scot, Sponge, Stately, Statuesque, Stonehand, Sublime, Whillywhaw

Impossible Hopeless, Incorrigible, Insoluble, Insurmountable, No-go, No-no, Unacceptable

Impost Excise, Levy, Tax, Toll

Imposter, Impostor Bunyip, Charlatan, Disaster, Faitor, Faitour, → **FAKE**, Fraud, Idol, Pretender, Sham, Triumph, Warbeck

Impotent Barren, Helpless, Spado, Sterile, Weak

Impound(er) Appropriate, Bond, Confiscate, Intern, Pen, Pinder, Poind

Impoverish(ed) Bankrupt, Bare, Beggar, Exhaust, Indigent, Straiten

Impractical Absurd, Academic, Blue-sky, Chim(a)era, Idealist, Inoperable, Laputan, Not on, Other-worldly, Quixotic, Useless

Imprecation Oath, Pize, 'Slife

Imprecise Approximate, Inaccurate, Indeterminate, Intangible, Loose, Nebulous, Rough, Sloppy, Vague

Impregnate Conceive, Enwomb, Imbue, Inseminate, Milt, Permeate, Resinate

Impresario Maestro, Manager, Producer, Showman

Impress(ive), Impression(able) Air, Astonish, Awe, Blur, Blurb, Bowl over, Brand, Cliché, Commanding, Conscript, Crimp, Deboss, Dent, Dramatic, Edition, Effect, Engram(ma), Engrave, Enstamp, Epic, Feel(ing), Fingerprint, Fossil, Frank, Gas, Glorious, Grab, Grandiose, Heroic, Homeric, Idea, Idée, Imitation, Impinge, Imprint, Incuse, Intaglio, Kick ass, Knock, Let, Majestic, Name-drop, Niello, Noble, Note, Palimpsest, Plastic, Plate, Pliable, Powerful, Prent, Presence, Press(gang), Print, Proof, Recruit, Register, Repute, Resplendent, Responsive, Ripsnorter, Rotund, Seal, Seize, Sense, Shanghai, Slay, Smite, Soft, Spectacular, Stamp, Stereotype, Strike, Stunning, Susceptible, Sway, Tableau, Touch, Type, Vibrant, Watermark, Weal, Weighty, Woodcut, Wow

Impressionist Caxton, Cézanne, Impersonator, Liebermann, Lumin(ar)ist, Manet, Matisse, Monet, Morisot, Renoir

Imprint Edition, Engrave, Etch, Stamp

Imprison(ment) Cape, Committal, Confine, Constrain, Custody, Durance, False, Immure, Incarcerate, Intern, Jail, Penal servitude, Quad, Quod, Time

Improbable Buckley's chance, Buckley's hope, Dubious, Far-fetched, Unlikely

Impromptu Ad lib(itum), Extempore, Improvised, Offhand, Spontaneous, Sudden, Unrehearsed

Improper, Impropriety Abnormal, Blue, Demirep, False, Illegitimate, Indecent, Indecorum, Naughty, Outré, Prurient, Solecism, Undue, Unmeet, Unseemly, Untoward

▷ **Improperly** *may indicate* an anagram

Improve(ment), Improver, Improving Advance, Ameliorate, Beat, Benefit, Bete, Break, Buck, Cap, Chasten, Conditioner, Convalesce, Cultivate, Détente, Didactic, Ease, Edify, Edutainment, Embellish, Emend, Enhance, Enrich, Eugenic, Euthenics, File, Gentrify, Kaizen, Meliorate, Mend, Potentiate, Promote, Rally, Refine, Reform, Resipiscence, Retouch, Revamp, Sarvodaya, Slim, Streamline, Surpass, Tart, Tatt, Titivate, Top, Touch-up, Turn round, Tweak, Uptrend, Upturn

Improvident Feckless, Micawber

Improvise(d), Improvisation Adlib, Break, Devise, Drumhead, Extemporise, Invent, Knock-up, Lash-up, Noodle, Ride, Scratch, Sudden, Vamp, Wing

Imprudent Foolhardy, Foolish, Impetuous, Impolitic, Indiscreet, Injudicious, Rash, Reckless, Unwary, Unwise

Impudence, Impudent Audacious, Backchat, Bardy, Bold, Brash, Brassy, Brazen, Cheeky, Cool, Crust, Effrontery, Forward, Gall, Gallus, Hussy, Impertinent, Insolent, Jackanapes, Lip, Malapert, Neck, → **NERVE**, Pert, Sass(y), Sauce, Saucebox, Saucy, Slack-jaw, Temerity, Whippersnapper, Yankie

Impugn Censure, Challenge, Defame, Impeach, Malign

Impulse, Impulsive Beat, Compelling, Conatus, Dictate, Drive, Efferent, Headlong, Horme, Ideopraxist, Impetus, Instigation, → **INSTINCT**, Libido, Madcap, Nerve, Nisus, Premature, Premotion, Send, Signal, Snap, Specific, Spontaneous, Tendency, Thrust, Tic, Urge, Whim

Impure, Impurity Adulterated, Contaminated, Donor, Faints, Feints, Indecent, Lees, Lewd, Regulus, Scum, Unclean

Imputation, Impute Ascribe, Attribute, Charge, Scandal, Slander, Slur

In A, Amid, At, Batting, Chic, Current, Home, Hostel, I', Inn, Intil, Occupying, On, Pop(ular), Pub, Trendy, Within

Inability Anosmia, Aphagia, Aphasia, Apraxia
Inaccessible Abaton, Impervious, Remote, Unattainable, Uncom(e)atable
Inaccurate Distorted, Erroneous, Faulty, Imprecise, Inexact, Out, Rough, Slipshod, Unfaithful
Inactive, Inaction, Inactivity Acedia, Cabbage, Comatose, Dead, Dormant, Extinct, Fallow, Hibernate, Idle, Inert, Languor, Moratorium, Passive, Quiescent, Racemic, Rusty, Sedentary, Sluggish, Stagnation, Torpid, Veg(etate)
In addition Eke, Else, Further, Moreover, Plus, To boot, Too
Inadequate Derisory, Feeble, Inapt, Inferior, Pathetic, Poor, Ropy, Scanty, Slight, Thin, Unequal
Inadvertent(ly) Accidental, Careless, Chance, Unwitting
▷ **In a flap** *may indicate* an anagram
In a high degree So
In a hundred Percent
Inane Empty, Fatuous, Foolish, Imbecile, Silly, Vacant
Inanimate Abiotic, Lifeless
Inappropriate Amiss, Incongrous, Infelicitous, Malapropos, Off-key, Pretentious, Unapt, Unbecoming, Undue, Unmeet, Unsuitable, Untoward
Inapt Maladroit, Unsuitable
Inarticulate(ness) Indistinct, Mumbling, Psellism
Inartistic Artless, Crude
Inattentive, Inattention Absent, Asleep, Deaf, Distrait, Dwaal, Dwa(l)m, Dwaum, Heedless, Loose, Slack, Unheeding, Unobservant
Inaudible Silent, Superhet
Inaugurate Han(d)sel, Initiate, Install, Introduce
Inauspicious Adverse, Ominous, Sinister
▷ **In a whirl** *may indicate* an anagram
▷ **In a word** *may indicate* two clue words linked to form one
Inborn, Inbred Homogamy, Inherent, Innate, Native, Selfed, Sib
Inca Quechua, Quichua
Incalculable Endless, Unpredictable, Untold
Incandescent Alight, Bright, Brilliant, Excited, Radiant
Incantation Charm, Magic, Mantra, Spell
Incapable Can't, Downa-do, Powerless, Unable, Useless
Incarnation Advent, Avatar, Embodiment, Fleshing, Krishna, Rama, Ramachandra
In case Lest, So
Incautious Foolhardy, Rash, Reckless, Unwary
Incendiary Arsonist, Combustible, Firebug, Fire-lighter, Fireship, Napalm, Thermite
Incense(d), Incenser Anger, Aroma, Elemi, Enfelon, Enrage, Homage, Hot, → INFLAME, Joss-stick, Navicula, Onycha, Outrage, Pastil(le), Provoke, Thurible, Thus, Vex, Wrathful
Incentive Carrot, Carrot and stick, Feather-bed, Fillip, Impetus, Motive, Premium, Spur, Stakhanovism, Stimulus, Wage
Incessant Constant, Endless, Unremitting
Incest Backcross, Spiritual
Inch(es) Ait, Column, Edge, Isle, Mil, Miner's, Sidle, Tenpenny, Uncial
Inchoate Formless, Immature, Incipient
Incident(al) Affair, Baur, Bawr, Carry-on, Chance, Circumstance, Episode, Event, Facultative, Handbags, Negligible, Occasion, Occurrent, Page, Peripheral, Scene, Throwaway

Incinerate, Incinerator Burn, Combust, Cremate, Destructor
Incipient Beginning, Germinal, Inchoate
Incise, Incision, Incisive(ness) Bite, Cut, Engrave, Incavo, Lobotomy, McBurney's, Mordant, Notch, Phlebotomy, Punchy, Rhizotamy, Scarf, Scribe, Slit, Surgical, Thoracotomy, Tracheotomy, Trenchant
Incisor Foretooth
Incite(ment) Abet, Drive, Egg, Fillip, Good, Hortative, Hoy, Impassion, Inflame, Instigate, Kindle, Motivate, Prod, Prompt, Provoke, Put, Rouse, Sa sa, Sedition, Set, Sic(k), Sool, → SPUR, Sting, Suborn, Suggest, Tar, Urge
Incline(d), Inclination Acclivity, Angle, Aslant, Aslope, Atilt, Bank, Batter, Bent, Bias, Bow, Camber, Clinamen, Cock, Crossfall, Declivity, Dip, Disposed, Drift, Enclitic, Glacis, → GRADIENT, Grain, Habitus, Hade, Heel, Hill, Italic, Kant, Kip, Lean, Liking, List, Maw, Minded, Nod, On, Partial, Peck, Penchant, Proclivity, Prone, Propensity, Rake, Ramp, Ready, Rollway, Set, Shelve, Slant, → SLOPE, Steep, Steeve, Stomach, Supine, Tend, Tilt, Tip, Trend, Upgrade, Velleity, Verge, Weathering, Will
Include(d), Inclusion, Inclusive Add, All-told, Bracket, Compass, Comprise, Connotate, Contain, Cover, Embody, Embrace, Enclose, Involve, Short-list, Social, Subsume, Therein
Incognito Anonymous, Disguised, Faceless, Secret, Unnamed
Incoherent Confused, Disconnected, Disjointed, Gabbling, Inarticulate, Rambling, Spluttering
Incombustible Clinker
Income Annuity, Benefice, Disposable, Dividend, Earned, Entry, Fixed, Franked, Livelihood, Living, Meal-ticket, Milch cow, National, OTE, Penny-rent, Prebend, Primitiae, Private, Proceeds, Rent, Rente, Rent-roll, Returns, Revenue, Salary, Stipend, Unearned, Unfranked, Wages
Incommunicado Isolated, Silent
Incomparable Supreme, Unequalled, Unique, Unmatched
Incompatible, Incompatibility Contradictory, Dyspathy, Incongruous, Inconsistent, Mismatched, Unsuited
Incompetent Bungler, Deadhead, Helpless, Hopeless, Ill, Inefficient, Inept, Palooka, Slouch, Unable, Unfit
Incomplete Broadbrush, Cagmag, Catalectic, Deficient, Inchoate, Lacking, Partial, Pendent, Rough, Unfinished
Incomprehensible, Incomprehension Acatamathesia, Double Dutch, Hard, Unbelievable
Inconceivable Impossible, Incredible
▷ **In confusion** *may indicate* an anagram
Incongruous, Incongruity Absurd, Discordant, Heterogenous, Irish, Ironic, Sharawadgi, Sharawaggi
In connection with Re
Inconsiderable Light, Slight
Inconsiderate High-handed, Hog, Petty, Presumptuous, Roughshod, Thoughtless, Unkind
Inconsistency, Inconsistent Alien, Anacoluthon, Anomaly, Contradictory, Discrepant, Oxymoronic, Paradoxical, Unequal, Unsteady, Variance
Inconsolable Heartbroken, Niobe
Inconspicuous Unobtrusive
Inconstant Chameleon, Desultory, Fickle, Light, Mutable, → VARIABLE
Inconvenience, Inconvenient Awkward, Bother, Discommode, Fleabite,

Incommodious, → **TROUBLE**, Unseemly, Untoward

Incorporate(d), Incorporation Absorb, Embody, Inc, Integrate, Introgression, Introject, Join, Merge, Subsume

Incorporeal Aery, Airy, Spiritual

Incorrect Catachresis, False, Improper, Invalid, Naughty, Wrong

Incorrigible Hopeless, Obstinate

Incorruptible Copper-bottomed, Honest, Immortal, Pure, Robespierre, Sea-green

Increase(s), Increasing Accelerando, Accelerate, Accession, Accrue, Add, Additur, Aggrandise, Amplify, Amp up, Appreciate, Approve, Augment, Auxetic, Bolster, Boost, Bulge, Crank up, Crescendo, Crescent, Crescive, Deepen, Dilate, Double, Ech(e), Eech, Eik, Eke, Enhance, Enlarge, Escalate, → **EXPAND**, Explosion, Greaten, → **GROW**, Heighten, Ich, Increment, Interbreed, Jack, Jack up, Joseph, Lift, Magnify, Mark up, Mount, Multiply, Plus, Proliferate, Propagate, Ramp up, Redshift, Reflation, Regrate, Rise, Snowball, Swell, Thrive, Up, Upsize, Upswell, Upswing, Wax

Incredible Amazing, Cockamamie, Extraordinary, Fantastic, Steep, Stey, Tall, Unreal

Incredulity, Incredulous Distrust, Infidel, Suspicion, Thunderstruck, Unbelief

Increment Accrual, Augment, Growth, Increase

Incriminate Accuse, Implicate, Inculpate

Incubate, Incubator Brooder, Develop, Eccaleobion, Hatch

Incubus Demon, Load, Nightmare

Inculcate Implant, Infuse

Incumbent Lying, Obligatory, Occupier, Official

Incur Assume, Earn, Involve

Incursion Foray, Inroad, Invasion, Raid, Razzia

Indecent Bare, Blue, Fescennine, Free, Immodest, Immoral, Improper, Lewd, Obscene, Rabelaisian, Racy, Scurril(e), Sotadic, Spicy, Sultry, Unnatural, Unproper, Unseem(ly), X-rated

Indecision, Indecisive Demur, Dithery, Doubt, Hamlet, Havering, Hesitation, Hung jury, Inconclusive, Shilly-shally, Suspense, Swither, Weakkneed

Indeclinable Aptote

Indecorous Graceless, Immodest, Outré, Unbecoming

Indeed Atweel, Ay, Aye, Da, Een, Even, Faith, Haith, I, Insooth, Ja wohl, La, Marry, Quotha, Truly, Verily, Yah, Yea

Indefensible Implausible, Inexcusable, Vincible

Indefinite(ly) A, An, Any, Evermore, Hazy, Nth, Some, Undecided, Vague

Indelible Fast, Permanent

Indelicate Broad, Coarse, Improper, Vulgar, Warm

Indemnify, Indemnification, Indemnity Assythement, Compensation, Double, Insurance

Indent(ed), Indentation Apprentice, Contract, Crenellate, Dancetty, Dimple, Impress, Niche, Notch, Order, Philtrum, Subentire

Independence, Independent Apart, Autocephalous, Autogenous, Autonomy, Crossbencher, Detached, Extraneous, Free(dom), Free-lance, Free spirit, Freethinker, I, Liberty, Mana motuhake, Maverick, Mugwump, Perseity, Self-sufficient, Separate, Separatist, Sui juris, Swaraj, Udal, UDI, Uhuru

Indescribable Incredible, Ineffable

Indestructible Enduring, Impenetrable, Inextirpable

Indeterminate Borderline, Formless, Incalculable, Open-ended, Unknown

Index Alidad(e), All-Ordinaries, Catalogue, Cephalic, Colour, Cranial, Dial,

Dow Jones, Exponent, Facial, Finger, Fist, Fog, Footsie, Forefinger, Gazetteer, Glycaemic, Hang Seng, Kwic, Librorum Prohibitorum, Margin, Misery, Nasal, Nikkei, Opsonic, Power, Price, Refractive, → REGISTER, Rotary, Share, Stroke, Table, Thumb, TPI, UV, Verborum

India(n) Adivisi, Asian, Assamese, Ayah, Baboo, Babu, Bharat(i), Bihari, Canarese, Carib, Chin, Dard, Dravidian, East, File, Goanese, Gond(wanaland), Gujarati, Harijan, Harsha, Hindu, Indic, Ink, Jain, Jat, Jemadar, Kafir, Kanarese, Kannada, Khalsa, Kisan, Kolarian, Kshatriyas, Lepcha, Ma(h)ratta, Maratha, Mazhbi, → MEXICAN, Mission, Mofussil, Mogul, Mulki, Munda, Munshi, Naga, Nagari, Nair, Nasik, Nation, Nayar, → NORTH AMERICAN, Nuri, Ocean, Oriya, Pali, Panjabi, Pargana, Parsee, Parsi, Peshwa, Plains, Prakrit, Punja(u)bee, Punjabi, Red, Sanskrit, Sepoy, Shri, Sikh, Sind(h), → SOUTH AMERICAN, Sowar, Summer, Swadeshi, Taino, Tamil, Telegu, Vakeel, Vakil, West

Indiaman Clive

Indiana, Indianian Hoosier

Indicate, Indication, Indicative, Indicator Adumbrate, Allude, Argue, Bespeak, Blinker, Cite, Clue, Cursor, → DENOTE, Design, Desine, Dial, Dial gauge, Endeixis, Evidence, Evince, Fluorescein, Gesture, Gnomon, Litmus, Manifest, Mean, Mood, Nod, Notation, Performance, Pinpoint, Plan-position, Point, Portend, Proof, Ray, Register, Remarque, Representative, Reveal, Show, → SIGN, Signify, Specify, Symptom, Tip, Token, Trace, Trafficator, Trait, Winker

Indictment Accusation, Arraign, Caption, Charge, Dittay, Reproach, Trounce

Indifference, Indifferent Adiaphoron, Aloof, Apathetic, Apathy, Blasé, Blithe, Callous, Cavalier, Cold, Cool(th), Dead, Detached, Disdain, Easy-osy, Empty, Incurious, Insouciant, Jack easy, Mediocre, Neutral, Nonchalant, Perfunctory, Phlegm, Pococurante, Sangfroid, So-so, Stoical, Supercilious, Supine, Tepid, Unconcerned

Indigence, Indigent Need, Pauper, Penury, Poverty, Want

Indigenous Aboriginal, Endemic, Native

▷ **Indi-gent** *may indicate* Baboo or Babu

Indigestion Apepsia, Apepsy, Dyspepsia, Heartburn

Indignant, Indignation Anger, Annoyed, Incensed, Irate, Outrage, Pique, Resentful, Steamed up, Wrathful

Indignity Affront, Outrage

Indigo Anil, Blue, Bunting, Carmine, Indole, Isatin(e), Wild

Indirect Back-handed, By(e), Devious, Implicit, Mediate, Oblique, Remote, Roundabout, Sidelong, Zig-zag

Indiscreet, Indiscretion Blabbermouth, Folly, Gaffe, Imprudence, Indelicate, Injudicious, Loose cannon, Rash, Unguarded, Wild oats

Indiscriminate Haphazard, Random, Scattershot, Sweeping

Indispensable Basic, Essential, King-pin, Necessary, Sine qua non, Vital

Indispose(d), Indisposition Adverse, Disincline, Ill, Incapacitate, Sick, Unwell

Indisputable Evident

Indistinct Ambiguous, Bleary, Blur, Bumble, Bummle, Faint, Fuzzy, Hazy, Misty, Nebulous, Neutral, Nondescript, Pale, S(c)hwa, Sfumato, → VAGUE

▷ **In distress** *may indicate* an anagram

Indite Compose, Pen, Write

Indium In

Individual(ist), Individuality Apiece, Being, Discrete, Exclusive, Free spirit, Gemma, Haecceity, Identity, Ka, Libertarian, Loner, Man, Man-jack, Morph, One-to-one, Own, Particular, Person, Poll, Respective, Separate, Single, Singular,

Solo, Soul, Special, Unit, Zoon

Indoctrinate Brainwash, Discipline, Instruct

Indo-European Aryan, Jat(s)

Indolence, Indolent Bone idle, Fainéance, Inactive, Languid, Lazy, Otiose, Sloth, Sluggish, Supine

Indomitable Brave, Dauntless, Invincible

Indonesia(n) Batavian, Nesiot, RI

Indoor(s) Within

Indubitably Certainly, Certes, Manifestly, Surely

Induce(ment) Bribe, Carrot, Cause, Coax, Draw, Encourage, Get, Inveigle, Lead, Motivate, → PERSUADE, Prevail, Suasion, Suborn, Tempt

Induct(ion), Inductance Epagoge, Henry, Inaugurate, Initiate, Install, L, Logic, Mutual, Prelude, Remanence

Indulge(nce), Indulgent Absolution, Binge, Coddle, Drink, Favour, Gratify, Humour, Law, Luxuriate, Oblige, Orgy, Pamper, Pander, Pardon, Permissive, Pet, Pettle, Please, → SATISFY, Splurge, Spoil, Spoonfeed, Surfeit, Tolerant, Venery, Voluptuous, Wallow

Industrial, Industrious, Industry Appliance, Application, Basic, Business, Busy, Cottage, Deedy, Diligence, Eident, Energetic, Growth, Labour, Millicent, Ocnus, Operose, Ruhr, Service, Smokestack, Sunrise, Technical, Technics, Tourism, Zaibatsu

▸ **Inebriate** see INTOXICATE

Inedible Inesculent, Noisome, Rotten

Ineffective, Ineffectual Clumsy, Deadhead, Drippy, Droob, Dud, Empty, Fainéant, Fruitless, Futile, Idle, Ill, Impotent, Mickey Mouse, Neutralised, Null, Powerless, Resty, Sterile, Toothless, → USELESS, Void, Weak, Wet

Inefficient Clumsy, Incompetent, Lame, Shiftless, Slack

Inelegant Awkward, Inconcinnity, Stiff, Turgid, Unneat

Ineligible Unqualified

Inept Absurd, Anorak, Cack-handed, Farouche, Nerd, Otaku, Plonker, Sad sack, Schlimazel, Schmo, Unskilled, Wet

Inequality Anomaly, Chebyshev's, Disparity, Injustice, Odds, Tchebyshev's

Inert(ia) Catatonia, Comatose, Dead, Dull, Excipient, Inactive, Languid, Leaden, Mollusc, Neon, Oblomovism, Potato, Rigor, Sluggish, Stagnant, Stagnation, Thowless, Torpid

Inestimable Incalculable, Invaluable, Priceless

Inevitable, Inevitably Automatic, Certain, Fateful, Inescapable, Inexorable, Needs, Perforce, TINA, Unavoidable

Inexact(itude) Cretism, Incorrect, Terminological, Wrong

Inexorable Relentless

Inexpedient Impolitic, Imprudent, Unwise

Inexpensive Bargain, Cheap, Dirt-cheap, Economic

Inexperience(d), Inexpert Amateur, Callow, Colt, Crude, Fresh, → GREEN, Greenhorn, Ham, Ingénue, Jejune, Put(t), Raw, Rookie, Rude, Tender, Unconversant, Unseasoned, Unseen, Unversed, Yardbird, Youthful

Inexplicable Magical, Mysterious, Paranormal, Unaccountable

Infallible Foolproof, Right, Sure-fire, Unerring

Infamous, Infamy Base, Ignominious, Notorious, Opprobrium, Shameful, Villainy

Infant Babe, Baby, Innocent, Lamb, Minor, Oral, Rug rat

Infantry(man) Buff, Foot, Grunt, Jaeger, Phalanx, Pultan, Pulto(o)n, Pultun, → SOLDIER, Tercio, Turco, Voetganger, Zouave

▷ **Infantry** *may refer to* babies

Infatuate(d), Infatuating, Infatuation Assot, Besot, Circean, Crush, Enamoured, Engou(e)ment, Entêté, Fanatic, Foolish, Lovesick, Mash, → **OBSESSION**, Pash, Rave, Turn

Infect(ed), Infecting, Infection, Infectious Angina, Anthrax, Babesiasis, Babesiosis, Candidiasis, Carrier, Catching, Catchy, Cholera, Communicable, Contagious, Contaminate, Corrupt, Cowpox, Cryptococcosis, Diseased, Fascioliasis, Fester, Focal, Fomes, Giardiasis, Gonorrhoea, Herpes, Impetigo, Leishmaniasis, Listeria, Lockjaw, Mycetoma, NSU, Opportunistic, Orf, Overrun, Poison, Polio(myelitis), → **POLLUTE**, Py(a)emia, Quittor, Ringworm, Roup, Salmonella, Sarcoid, Scabies, Septic, Shingles, Smit(tle), Strongylosis, Taint, Tetanus, Thrush, Tinea, Toxocariasis, Trichuriasis, Typhoid, Typhus, Virion, Virulent, Whitlow, Wog, Yersiniosis, Zoonosis, Zymosis

Infeftment Sasine, Seisin

Infer(ence), Inferred Conclude, Conjecture, Deduce, Divine, Educe, Extrapolate, Generalise, Guess, Illation, Imply, Judge, Obversion, Putative, Surmise, Syllogism

▷ **Infer** *may indicate* 'fer' around another word

Inferior Base, Bodgier, Cheap-jack, Cheesy, Coarse, Crummy, Degenerate, Dog, Ersatz, Gimcrack, Grody, Grub-Street, Indifferent, Infra, Jerkwater, Less, Lo-fi, Lower, Low-grade, Minor, Naff, Nether, One-horse, Ornery, Paravail, Petty, Poor, Rop(e)y, Schlock, Second, Second-best, Shlock, Shoddy, Sprew, Sprue, Subjacent, Subordinate, Substandard, Surat, Tatty, Tinpot, Trashy, Under(man), Underneath, Understrapper, Untermensch, Waste, Worse

Infernal Cotton-picking, Demogorgon, Diabolic, Hellish, Phitonian, Tartarean, Unholy

Infertile Barren, Farrow, Sterile

Infest(ed), Infestation Acariasis, Acrawl, Beset, Blight, Dog, Hoatching, Overrun, Pediculosis, Phthiriasis, → **PLAGUE**, Stylopised, Swamp, Swarm, Torment, Trombiculiasis, Trombidiasis, Uncinariasis

Infidel Atheist, Caffre, Giaour, Heathen, Heretic, Kafir, Pagan, Paynim, Saracen

Infield Intown

Infiltrate Encroach, Enter, Instil, Intrude, Pervade

Infinite, Infinity Cosmic, Endless, Eternal, N

Infinitive Split

Infirm Decrepit, Doddery, Feeble, Lame, Shaky, Sick

▷ **Infirm** *may indicate* 'co' around another word

Infirmary Hospital, Sick bay

Inflame(d), Inflammable, Inflammation Afire, Anger, → **AROUSE**, Bloodshot, Enamoured, Enchafe, Enfire, Enkindle, Fever, Fire, Founder, Gleet, Ignite, Impassion, Incense, Infection, Ire, Methane, Napalm, Naphtha, → **RED**, Stimulate, Swelling, Touchwood

---

INFLAMMATIONS

3 letters:	Stye	*6 letters:*	Iritis
Sty		Ancome	Otitis
	5 letters:	Angina	Quinsy
4 letters:	Croup	Bunion	Thrush
Acne	Felon	Coryza	Ulitis
Gout		Eczema	
Noma		Garget	

7 letters:
Bubonic
Catarrh
Colitis
Ecthyma
Ignatis
Ileitis
Onychia
Pinkeye
Prurigo
Rosacea
Sunburn
Sycosis
Tylosis
Uveitis
Whitlow

8 letters:
Adenitis
Aortisis
Bursitis
Carditis
Colpitis
Cystisis
Fibrosis
Hyalitis
Mastitis
Metritis
Mycetoma
Myelitis
Myositis
Neuritis
Orchitis
Osteitis
Ovaritis
Phlegmon
Pleurisy
Pyelitis
Rachitis
Rhinitis
Uvulitis
Vulvitis
Windburn

9 letters:
Arteritis
Arthritis
Balanitis

Barotitis
Cheilitis
Chilblain
Cloacitis
Enteritis
Fasciitis
Frostbite
Gastritis
Glossitis
Keratitis
Laminitis
Nephritis
Onychitis
Parotitis
Phlebitis
Phrenitis
Pneumonia
Proctitis
Pyorrhoea
Retinitis
Scleritis
Sinusitis
Splenitis
Strumitis
Synovitis
Typhlitis
Vaginitis
Vent gleet

10 letters:
Asbestosis
Bronchitis
Cellulitis
Cephalitis
Cerebritis
Cervicitis
Dermatitis
Duodenitis
Erysipelas
Fibrositis
Gingivitis
Hepatitis A
Hepatitis B
Intertrigo
Laryngitis
Meningitis
Oophoritis
Ophthalmia

Papillitis
Paronychia
Phlegmasia
Phlogistic
Stomatitis
Tendinitis
Thrombosis
Tracheitis
Tympanitis
Urethritis
Valvulitis
Vasculitis

11 letters:
Blepharitis
Farmer's lung
Mad staggers
Mastoiditis
Myocarditis
Parotiditis
Peritonitis
Pharyngitis
Pneumonitis
Prostatitis
Salpingitis
Sandy blight
Sclerotitis
Shin splints
Spondylitis
Tennis elbow
Thoroughpin
Thyroiditis
Tonsillitis
Utriculitis
Woody-tongue

12 letters:
Appendicitis
Encephalitis
Endocarditis
Endometritis
Folliculitis
Golfer's elbow
Lymphangitis
Lympodenitis
Mesenteritis
Osteoporosis
Panarthritis

Pancreatitis
Pericarditis
Polymyositis
Polyneuritis
Sacroillitis
Swimmer's itch
Vestibulitis

13 letters:
Cholecystitis
Enterocolitis
Jogger's nipple
Labyrinthitis
Lymphadenitis
Osteomyelitis
Perihepatitis
Perinephritis
Periodontisis
Perityphlitis
Tenosynovitis
Tenovaginitis
Thrombophilia

14 letters:
Conjunctivitis
Diverticulitis
Osteoarthritis
Pyelonephritis
Sleepy staggers
Trichomoniasis
Vincent's angina

15 letters:
Gastroenteritis
Pachymeningitis

16 letters:
Bronchopneumonia

17 letters:
Encephalomyelitis
Meningocephalitis

Inflate(d), Inflation Aerate, Aggrandise, Bloat, Bombastic, Cost-push, Dilate, Distend, Distent, Exaggerate, Grade, Increase, Pneumatic, Pump, Remonetise, RPI,

Spiral, Stagflation, Stagnation, Swell

Inflect(ion) Accidence, Conjugation, Tone

Inflexible, Inflexibility Adamant(ine), Byzantine, Doctrinaire, Hard-ass, Hard-liner, Iron, Obstinate, Ossified, Relentless, Resolute, Rigid, Rigour, Set, Staid, Stubborn, Unbending

Inflict(ion) Deal, Force, Give, Impose, Subject, Trouble, Visit, Wreak

Inflorescence Bostryx, Catkin, Ci(n)cinnus, Drepanium, Glomerule, Panicle, Pleiochasium, Polychasium, Raceme, Umbel, Verticillaster

Inflow Affluence, Influx

Influence(d), Influential Act, Affect, After, Backstairs, Charm, Clamour, Clout, Credit, Determine, Drag, Earwig, Eclectic, Embracery, Éminence grise, Factor, Force, Get at, Govern, Hold, Hypnotise, Impact, Impinge, Impress, Incubus, Inspire, Interfere, Lead, Leverage, Lobby, Macher, Mastery, Militate, Mogul, Octopus, Operation, Outreach, Power, Preponderant, Pressure, Prestige, → PULL, Push, Reach, Rust, Say, Seminal, Significant, Star, Star-blasting, Stimulus, Suggest, Svengali, Sway, Swing, Telegony, Undue, Weigh with, Will, Work, Wull

Influenza Asian, Equine, Flu, Gastric, Grippe, Lurgi, Wog, Yuppie

Influx Inbreak

Inform(ation), Informant, Informed, Informer Acquaint, Advise, Agitprop, Apprise, Au fait, Aware, Beagle, Bit, Burst, Canary, Ceefax®, Clype, Contact, Cookie, Datum, Deep throat, Delate, Dob(ber), Dobber-in, Dope, Education, Exposition, Facts, Fact sheet, Feedback, Fink, Fisgig, Fiz(z)gig, Gen, Genome, Good oil, Grapevine, Grass, Griff, Gunsel, Hep, Immersive, Input, Inside, Instruct, Izvesti(y)a, Light, Lowdown, Media, Moiser, Nark, Nepit, Nit, Nose, Notify, Occasion, Oracle®, Peach, Pem(m)ican, Pentito, Pimp, Poop, Prestel®, Prime, Printout, Propaganda, Prospectus, Rat, Read-out, Revelation, Rheme, Rumble, Shelf, Shop, Sidelight, Sing, Sneak, Snitch, Squeak, Squeal, Stag, Stoolie, Stool-pigeon, Supergrass, Sycophant, Teletext®, Tell, Tidings, Tip-off, Up, Videotext®, Viewdata®, Whistle(-blower), Wire

Informal Casual, Intimate, Irregular, Outgoing, Rough and ready, Unofficial

Infra Under

Infra dig Ignominious

Infrequent Casual, Occasional, Rare, Scant, Seldom, Sparse

Infringe Contravene, Violate

Infuriate Anger, Bemad, Bepester, Enrage, Exasperate, Incense, Madden, Pester, Provoke

Infuse(r), Infusion Brew, Distill, Gallise, Instil, Mash, Ooze, Saloop, Saturate, Steep, Tea, Tea-ball, Tea-egg, Tisane, Toddy, Uva-ursi

Ingenious, Ingenuity Adept, Adroit, Art, Artificial, Clever, Cunning, Cute, Inventive, Natty, Neat, Resourceful, Smart, Subtle, Trick(s)y, Wit

Ingenuous Artless, Candid, Green, Innocent, Naive, Open, Transparent

Ingest Eat, Endue, Incept, Indue, Swallow

In good condition Fit, Shipshape, Taut, Trim

Ingot Bar, Billet, Bullion, Lingot, Sycee, Wedge

Ingrain Fix, Impregnate, Train

Ingrate Thankless, Viper

Ingratiate, Ingratiating Bootlick, Butter, Court, Flatter, Greasy, Silken, Smarm(y)

Ingredient(s) Additive, Admixture, Basis, Content, Element, Factor, Formula, Makings, Staple

Ingrowing, Ingrowth Onychocryptosis, T(h)ylosis

Inhabit(ants) Affect, Children, Denizen, Dweller, Inholder, Inmate, Live, Native, Occupant, People, Resident

Inhale(r), Inhalation Aspirate, Breath(e), Draw, Gas, Inspire, Intal, Sniff, Snort, Snuff, Take, Toot, Tout

Inharmonious Out, Patchy

Inherent Characteristic, Essential, Immanent, Inbred, Innate, Native

Inherit(ance), Inherited, Inheritor Accede, Birthright, Borough-English, Congenital, Feoffee, Gene, Genom, Heirloom, Inborn, Legacy, Legitim, Meek, Mendelism, Particulate, Patrimony, Portion, Reversion, Succeed, Tichborne, Ultimogenitive

Inhibit(ing), Inhibition, Inhibitor ACE, Captopril, Chalone, Chalonic, Deter, Enalapril, Forbid, Hang-up, Protease, Restrain, Retard, Retroactive, Stunt, Suppress, Tightass

Inhuman Barbarous, Brutal, Merciless

Inimical Adverse, Harmful, Hostile

Iniquity, Iniquitous Diabolical, Evil, Offence, Sin, Vice

Initial Acronym, First, Letter, Monogram, Paraph, Prelim(inary), Primary, Rubric

▷ **Initially** *may indicate* first letters

Initiate(d), Initiating, Initiation, Initiative Baptism, Begin, Bejesuit, Blood, Bora, Bring, Ceremony, Debut, Démarche, Enter, Enterprise, Epopt, Esoteric, Gumption, Induct, Instigate, Instruct, → LAUNCH, Nous, Onset, Proactive, Spark, → START

Inject(or), Injection Antiserum, Bang, Blast, Booster, Collagen, Enema, Epidural, Fuel, Hypo, Implant, Innerve, Inoculation, Instil, Introduce, Jab, Jack up, Jag, Mainline, Pop, Reheat, Serum, Shoot, Shoot up, Skin-pop, Solid, Syringe, Transfuse, Venipuncture

Injunction Command, Embargo, Freezing, Mandate, Mareva, Quia timet, Swear, Writ

Injure(d), Injury, Injurious, Injustice ABH, Abuse, Aggrieve, Bale, Bled, Bruise, Concuss, Contrecoup, Contuse, Damage, De(a)re, Disserve, Forslack, Frostbite, Gash, GBH, Harm, → HURT, Ill-turn, Impair, Industrial, Iniquity, Lesion, Malign, Mar, Mayhem, Mistreat, Mutilate, NAI, Needlestick, Nobble, Nocuous, Non-accidental, Noxal, Nuisance, Occupational, Oppression, Outrage, Packet, Paire, Prejudice, Rifle, RSI, Scaith, Scald, Scath(e), Scotch, Sore, Sprain, Teen(e), Tene, Tort, Trauma, Umbrage, Whiplash, Wound, Wrong

▶ **Injury** *see* AFTER INJURY

Ink(y) Atramental, Black, Bray, China, Chinese, Copying, Cyan, Gall, Gold, Indian, Invisible, Magnetic, Marking, Monk, Printer's, Printing, Sepia, Stained, Sympathetic, Tusche

Inkling Clue, Glimpse, Hint, Idea

Inkpot Standish

Inlaid, Inlay(er) Boulle, Buhl, Damascene, Emblemata, Empaestic, Enamel, Enchase, Incrust, Intarsia, Intarsio, Koftgar(i), Marquetrie, Marquetry, Pietra-dura, Piqué, Set, Tarsia, Veneer

Inland Hinterland, Interior, Up

Inlet Arm, Bay, Bohai, Cook, Cove, Creek, Entry, Estuary, Fiord, Firth, Fjord, Fleet, Flow, Geo, Gio, Golden Horn, Gusset, Hope, Infall, Ingate, Jervis Bay, McMurdo Sound, Moray Firth, Pamlico Sound, Pearl Harbor, Plymouth Sound, Pohai, Port Jackson, Puget Sound, Solway Firth, Strait, Sullom Voe, Table Bay, The Wash, Tor Bay, Zuyder Zee

▷ **Inlet** *may indicate* 'let' around another word

Inmate Intern(e), Lodger, Patient, Prisoner, Resident
Inn(s), Innkeeper Albergo, Alehouse, Auberge, Barnard's, Boniface, Caravanserai, Chancery, Change-house, Coaching, Court, Gray's, Halfway-house, Host, Hostelry, Hotel, House, Imaret, In, Inner Temple, Jamaica, Khan, Ladin(ity), Law, Licensee, Lincoln's, Lodging, Luckie, Lucky, Middle Temple, Motel, Padrone, Parador, Patron, Porterhouse, Posada, Posthouse, Pothouse, Publican, Roadhouse, Ryokan, Serai, Tabard, Taphouse, Tavern(er), Victualler
▷ **Inn** *may refer to* the law
Innards Entrails, Giblets, Gizzard, Guts, Harigals, Harslet, Haslet, Omasa, Rein, Viscera
Innate Congenital, Essential, Inborn, Inbred, Inbuilt, Ingenerate, Instinctive, Natural
Inner(most) Bencher, Esoteric, Internal, Intima, Intimate, Lining, Man, Marrow, Medulla, Private, Red, Woman
Innings Chance, Knock, Turn
▸ **Innkeeper** *see* INN
Innocent Absolved, Angelic, Arcadian, Babe, Blameless, Canny, Chaste, Cherub, Childlike, Clean, Dewy-eyed, Doddypoll, Dodipoll, Dove, Encyclical, Green, Guileless, Idyllic, Ingenue, Lamb, Lily-white, Maiden, Naive, Opsimath, Pope, → PURE, Sackless, Seely, Simple, St, Unwitting, White
Innocuous Harmless, Innocent
Innovate, Innovative, Innovation, Innovator Alteration, Cutting edge, Departure, Ground-breaking, Newell, Novelty, Pioneer, Promethean, Radical
Inn-sign Bush
Innu Naskapi
Innumerable Countless, Infinite, Myriad, N
Inoculate, Inoculation Engraft, Immunise, Jab, Protect, Vaccine, Variolate
Inoffensive Mild, Pleasant
Inoperative Futile, Nugatory, Silent, Void
Inopportune Disadvantageous, Inconvenient, Intempestive, Untimely
Inordinate Excessive, Irregular, Undue
▷ **Inordinately** *may indicate* an anagram
In place of For, Qua, Vice, With
Input Direct, OCR
Inquest Debriefing, Hearing, Inquiry, Investigation
Inquire, Inquiring, Inquiry Ask, Demand, Investigation, Maieutic, Nose, Organon, Probe, Query, Question, See, Speer, Speir
Inquisition, Inquisitive, Inquisitor Curious, Interrogation, Meddlesome, Nosy, Prying, Rubberneck, Snooper, Spanish, Stickybeak, Torquemada
▷ **In revolt, In revolution** *may indicate* an anagram
Inroad(s) Breach, Encroachment, Honeycomb, Infall, Invasion
Insane, Insanity Absurd, Batty, Crack-brained, Crazy, Deranged, Headcase, Hebephrenia, Loco, Lune, Mad, Manic, Mattoid, Nutso, Paranoia, Pellagra, Psycho, Schizo, Troppo, Yarra
Insatiable Greedy, Ravenous, Voracious
Insatiate child Killcrop
Inscribe(d), Inscription Chisel, Chronogram, Colophon, Dedicate, Emblazon, Endoss, Engrave, Enter, Epigraph, Epitaph, Exergue, Graffiti, Hic jacet, Hierograph, Lapidary, Legend, Lettering, Neum(e), Posy, Writ
Inscrutable Deadpan, Esoteric, Mysterious, Sphinx
Insect(s) Entomic, Nonentity, Non-person

INSECTS

3 letters:
Ant
Bee
Bot
Bug
Fly
Ked
Lac
Nit
Wax
Wog

4 letters:
Flea
Gnat
Grig
Lice
Mite
Moth
Pium
Pupa
Tick
Wasp
Weta
Zimb

5 letters:
Aphis
Borer
Brise
Cimex
Emmet
Gogga
Louse
Midge
Nymph
Ox-bot
Scale
Stick
Zebub

6 letters:
Acarid
Breese
Breeze
Capsid
Chigoe
Cicada
Cicala

Coccid
Day-fly
Earwig
Elater
Gadfly
Hopper
Hornet
Instar
Locust
Maggot
Mantid
Mantis
Mayfly
Noctua
Psocid
Psylla
Punkie
Redbug
Sawfly
Scarab
Slater
Spider
Tettix
Thrips
Vespid
Walker
Weevil

7 letters:
Antlion
Bristle
Buzzard
Carabid
Chalcid
Chigger
Corixid
Cornfly
Cricket
Culicid
Cutworm
Daphnid
Ergates
Firefly
Gallfly
Girdler
Gordius
Goutfly
Grayfly
Hexapod

Hive-bee
Humbuzz
Katydid
Ladybug
Odonata
Oestrus
Oniscus
Phasmid
Pill-bug
Pyralis
Sandfly
Spectre
Spittle
Stylops
Tabanus
Termite

8 letters:
Alderfly
Bookworm
Circutio
Coccidae
Crane-fly
Dipteras
Firebrat
Fruit fly
Gall-wasp
Glossina
Goatmoth
Greenfly
Horntail
Horsefly
Itchmite
Lacewing
Ladybird
Lygus bug
Mealybug
Metabola
Milliped
Mosquito
Myriapod
Pauropod
Pillworm
Puss-moth
Reduviid
Ruby-tail
Scarabee
Silkworm
Snowflea

Stinkbug
Stonefly
Symphile
Waterbug
Wheelbug
Whitefly
Wireworm
Woodworm

9 letters:
Ametabola
Booklouse
Butterfly
Caddis-fly
Campodeid
Centipede
Cochineal
Cockroach
Damselfly
Dobsonfly
Dor-beetle
Dragonfly
Ephemerid
Hemiptera
Homoptera
Leaf-miner
Mecoptera
Millepede
Millipede
Rearhorse
Robber-fly
Songololo
Synoekete
Tabanidae
Tiger-moth
Woodlouse
Xylophage

10 letters:
Apterygota
Bark mantis
Bluebottle
Casebearer
Chironomid
Cockchafer
Coleoptera
Collembola
Fan-cricket
Fen-cricket

Froghopper	Treehopper	Trichoptera	**13 letters:**
Greendrake	Waterstick		Cotton stainer
Harvestman	Web spinner	**12 letters:**	Daddy-long-legs
Leaf-cutter		Bishop's mitre	Jenny-longlegs
Leafhopper	**11 letters:**	Creepy-crawly	Leatherjacket
Mallophaga	Bristletail	Dictyopteran	Praying mantis
Orthoptera	Collembolan	Heteropteran	Staphylinidae
Phylloxera	Dermapteran	Neuropterous	Water scorpion
Plant-louse	Grasshopper	Orthopterous	
Pond-skater	Greenbottle	Rhipidoptera	**14 letters:**
Psocoptera	Hymenoptera	San Jose scale	Strepsipterous
Rhipiptera	Mole-cricket	Strepsiptera	
Silverfish	Neuropteran	Thousand-legs	
Springtail	Rhopalocera	Thysanoptera	
Thysanuran	Tiger-beetle	Water boatman	

Insecticide Allethrin, Aphicide, Carbaryl, Chromene, Cube, DDT, Deet, Derris, Dieldrin, Endosulfan, Endrin, Flycatcher, Gammexane®, Ivermectin, Lindane®, Malathion®, Menazon, Methoxychlor, Miticide, Naphthalene, Parathion, Paris green, Piperazine, Pyrethrin, Pyrethrum, Rotenone, Spray, Timbo, Toxaphene, Zineb

Insectivore Agoura, Desman, Donaea, Drosera, Hedgehog, Jacamar, Nepenthaceae, Otter-shrew, Sarracenia, Tanrec, Tenrec(idae), Venus flytrap, Zalambdodont

Insecure Infirm, → LOOSE, Precarious, Shaky, Unsafe, Unstable, Unsteady, Vulnerable

Insensitive, Insensitivity Analgesia, Blunt, Callous, Dead, Log, Numb, Obtuse, Pachyderm, Stolid, Tactless, Thick-skinned

Inseparable Indiscrete, One, United

Insert(ed), Insertion, Inset Anaptyxis, Cue, Empiecement, Enchase, Enter, Entry, Foist, Fudge, Godet, Gore, Graft, Gusset, Immit, Imp, Implant, Inchase, Inject, Inlay, Input, Intercalar, Interject, Interpolate, Interpose, Intersperse, Introduce, Intromit, Lexical, Mitre, Pin, Punctuate, Sandwich

Inside(r) Content, Core, Entrails, Gaol, Heart, Indoors, Interior, Internal, Interne, Inward, Inwith, Mole, Tum, → WITHIN

Insidious Artful, Crafty, Sly

Insight Acumen, Anagoge, Aperçu, Enlightenment, Hunch, Inkling, Intuition, → PERCEPTION, Tais(c)h

Insignia Armour, Arms, Badger, Charge, Chevron, Mark, Regalia, Ribbon, Roundel, Tab

Insignificant (person) Dandiprat, Fico, Fiddling, Flea-bite, Fractional, Gnat, Inconsiderable, Insect, Jerkwater, Mickey Mouse, Minimus, Miniscule, Minnow, Nebbich, Nobody, Nominal, Nondescript, Nonentity, One-eyed, Petit, Petty, Pipsqueak, Pissant, Quat, Scoot, Scout, Scrub, Shrimp, Slight, Small potatoes, Small-time, Squirt, Squit, Tenuous, Trifling, Trivial, Two-bit, Unimportant, Venial, Warb, Whiffet, Whippersnapper

Insincere Affected, Artificial, Barmecide, Cant, Double, Double-faced, Empty, Factitious, Faithless, False, Glib, Greenwash, Hollow, Janus-faced, Lip service, Mealy-mouthed, Meretricious, Mouth-made, Pseudo, Shallow, Synthetic, Two-faced

Insinuate, Insinuating, Insinuation Allude, Foist, Hint, Imply, Innuendo, Intimate, Sleek, Slur, Sneck-draw

Insipid Banal, Blab, Bland, Drippy, Fade, Flat, Insulse, Jejune, Lash, Mawkish, Milk

and water, Shilpit, Tame, Tasteless, Vapid, Weak, Wearish, Wersh
Insist(ent) Adamant, Assert, Demand, Dogmatic, Exact, Stickler, → STIPULATE, Stress, Swear, Threap, Threep, Urge
Insolence, Insolent Audacity, Bardy, Brassy, Cheek, Contumely, Cub, Effrontery, Gum, Hubris, Hybris, Impudence, Lip, Rude, Snash, Stroppy, Wanton
Insoluble Cerasin, Hard, Irresolvable, Mysterious
Insolvent Bankrupt, Broke, Destitute, Penniless
Insomnia Agrypnotic, Sleeplessness, Wakefulness, White night
Insouciant Carefree, Careless, Cavalier
Inspect(ion), Inspector Alnage(r), Auditor, Case, Comb, Conner, Darogha, Examine, Go-over, Government, Investigator, Jerque, Keeker, Lestrade, Look-see, Morse, Muster, Once-over, Peep, Perlustrate, Proveditor, Rag-fair, Recce, Review, Sanitary, School, Scrutinise, Spot check, Survey, Test, Vet, Vidimus, Visitation
Inspire(d), Inspiration, Inspiring Actuate, Aerate, Afflatus, Aganippe, Animate, Brainstorm, Brainwave, Breath(e), Castalian, Draw, Duende, Elate, Exalt, Fire, Flash, Geist, Hearten, Hunch, Hwyl, Idea, Illuminate, Impress, Impulse, Induce, Inflatus, Infuse, Kindle, Motivate, Move, Muse, Pegasus, Prompt, Prophetic, Satori, Sniff(le), Stimulus, Taghairm, Theopnautic, Theopneust(y), Uplift, Vatic, Verbal
In spite of Augre
Instability Anomie, Anomy
Install(ation) Elect, Enchase, Enthrone, Inaugurate, Induction, Infrastructure, Insert, Invest, Put (in)
Instalment Episode, Fascicle, Fascicule, Heft, Insert, Livraison, Never-never, Part, Serial, Tranche
Instance, Instant As, Case, Chronon, Example, Flash, Jiffy, Moment, Present, Say, Shake, Spur, Tick, Trice, Twinkling, Urgent
Instead (of) Deputy, For, Lieu, Locum, Vice
Instigate Arouse, Foment, Impel, Incite, Prompt, Spur
Instil(l) Implant, Inculcate, Infuse, Inspire, Teach, Transfuse
Instinct(ive) Automatic, Flair, Gut, Herd, Id, Impulse, Inbred, Innate, Intuition, Life, Nature, Nose, Pleasure principle, Prim(a)eval, Talent, Tendency, Visceral
Institute, Institution Academy, Activate, Asylum, Bank, Begin, Bring, Broadmoor, Charity, College, Collegiate, Erect, Found(ation), I, Inaugurate, Mechanical, MORI, Orphanage, Poorhouse, Protectory, Raise, Redbrick, Retraict, Retrait(e), Retreat, Royal, Smithsonian, Start, Technical, University, Women's, Workhouse
Instruct(ed), Instruction, Instructor ADI, Advice, Algorithm, Apprenticeship, Brief, CAI, Catechism, Chautauquan, Clinic, Coach, Course, Didactic, Direct(ive), Document, Edify, Educate, Enjoin, Ground(ing), Guide, How-to, Inform, Lesson, Loop, Macro, Manual, Mystagogue, Mystagogus, Notify, Order, Precept, Prescription, Program, Recipe, Rubric, Script, Swami, → TEACH, Train, Tutelage, Tutorial, Up
Instrument(al) Ablative, Act, Agent, Dash(board), Helpful, Kit, Mean(s), Mechanical, → MUSICAL INSTRUMENT, Negotiable, → RESPONSIBLE, → TOOL, Transit, Transposing, → UTENSIL, Weapon

INSTRUMENTS

3 letters:	4 letters:		5 letters:
Fan	Celt	Mike	Brake
Gad	Clam	Prog	Curet
	Dupe	Rasp	Fleam
	Fork	Rote	Float
		Tram	

Gadge	Swingle	Dermatome	Somascope
Groma	Swozzle	Dip-circle	Sonograph
Meter	Syringe	Dosemeter	Tasimeter
Miser	Trammel	Dosimeter	Telemeter
Organ	Vocoder	Dropsonde	Telescope
Probe		Endoscope	Tellurian
Sonde	**8 letters:**	Ergograph	Tellurion
Wecht	Barnacle	Eriometer	Tenaculum
	Burdizzo	Extractor	Tonometer
6 letters:	Diagraph	Fadometer	Toothpick
Bougie	Dividers	Fetoscope	Tripmeter
Broach	Ecraseur	Flowmeter	Voltmeter
Etalon	Enlarger	Fluxmeter	Volumeter
Megger®	Iriscope	Focimeter	Wavemeter
Opener	Luxmeter	Graduator	Xylometer
Pallet	Myograph	Haemostat	Zymometer
Pestle	Odometer	Heliostat	
Scythe	Ohmmeter	Hodometer	**10 letters:**
Sector	Otoscope	Hourglass	Acidimeter
Speedo	Oximeter	Konimeter	Almacantar
Strobe	Quadrant	Kymograph	Almucantar
Trocar	Repeater	Lysimeter	Altazimuth
Wimble	Scalprum	Machmeter	Anemometer
	Scissors	Manometer	Araeometer
7 letters:	Snuffler	Marigraph	Buttonhook
Alidade	Speculum	Megaphone	Ceilometer
Cadrans	Strickle	Megascope	Clinometer
Caliper	Trephine	Metronome	Colposcope
Caltrop	Tweezers	Microtome	Comparator
Cautery	Vuvuzela	Milometer	Cryophorus
Compass	Waywiser	Monochord	Cyclograph
Curette		Nocturnal	Cystoscope
Dilator	**9 letters:**	Nut-wrench	Densimeter
Diopter	Algometer	Oedometer	Drosometer
Flesher	Alphonsin	Oncometer	Fibrescope
Forceps	Arcograph	Ondograph	Gaussmeter
Grapple	Areometer	Optometer	Geodimeter®
Monitor	Astrolabe	Optophone	Goniometer
Organic	Atmometer	Osmometer	Gonioscope
Pelican	Auriscope	Osteotome	Gravimeter
Plotter	Auxometer	Pedometer	Heliograph
Pointel	Barometer	Periscope	Hydrometer
Pricker	Baryscope	Pintadera	Hydroscope
Probang	Bolometer	Polygraph	Hygrograph
Scriber	Cauterant	Potometer	Hygrometer
Sextant	Coelostat	Pyrometer	Hypsometer
Shuttle	Crows-bill	Pyroscope	Iconometer
Spatula	Cryoprobe	Raspatory	Integrator
Stapler	Cryoscope	Retractor	Lactoscope
Strigil	Cymograph	Rheometer	Micrograph
Swazzle	Depressor	Skiascope	Micrometer

Microphone
Microscope
Mileometer
Multimeter
Nephograph
Nephoscope
Nitrometer
Opisometer
Orthoscope
Oscillator
Osteoclast
Pantograph
Photometer
Piezometer
Pilliwinks
Planimeter
Protractor
Pulsimeter
Pulsometer
Pycnometer
Radiometer
Radiophone
Radioscope
Radiosonde
Rhinoscope
Scotometer
Siderostat
Spirograph®
Spirometer
Tachograph
Tachometer
Telewriter
Tensimeter
Theodolite
Thermopile
Thorascope
Tribometer
Tromometer
Urinometer
Variometer
Voltameter

11 letters:
Actinometer
Auxanometer
Cardiograph
Chronograph

Chronometer
Chronoscope
Coercimeter
Colonoscope
Coronagraph
Craniometer
Crescograph
Dilatometer
Fluorometer
Fugitometer
Gastroscope
Gradiometer
Helicograph
Intoximeter
Jacob's staff
Laparoscope
Nephroscope
Odontograph
Opeidoscope
Pinnywinkle
Pitchometer
Planetarium
Plastometer
Polarimeter
Polariscope
Proctoscope
Psychograph
Pyranometer
Pyrgeometer
Quantometer
Rangefinder
Rocketsonde
Sclerometer
Screwdriver
Seismograph
Seismoscope
Solarimeter
Spherometer
Stactometer
Stadiometer
Stauroscope
Stereometer
Stereoscope
Stethoscope
Stroboscope
Synthesizer
Tacheometer

Thermometer
Thermoscope
Vaporimeter
Vectorscope
Velocimeter
Voltammeter

12 letters:
Aethrioscope
Bronchoscope
Camera lucide
Cephalometer
Densitometer
Electrometer
Galactometer
Galvanometer
Galvanoscope
Harmonograph
Harmonometer
Inclinometer
Isoteniscope
Kaleidoscope
Katharometer
Keraunograph
Laryngoscope
Meteorograph
Myringoscope
Nephelometer
Oscilloscope
Penetrometer
Pinniewinkle
Psychrometer
Respirometer
Scarificator
Sensitometer
Snooperscope
Spectrometer
Spectroscope
Sphygmograph
Sphygmophone
Synchroscope
Tellurometer
Turbidimeter
Urethroscope
Zenith-sector

13 letters:
Accelerometer
Alcoholometer
Dipleidoscope
Opthalmometer
Pharyngoscope
Phonendoscope
Pneumatograph
Pneumatometer
Potentiometer
Pyrheliometer
Reflectometer
Refractometer
Saccharometer
Sigmoidoscope
Stalagmometer
Tachistoscope
Weatherometer

14 letters:
Diffractometer
Interferometer
Oesophagoscope
Ophthalmometer
Ophthalmoscope
Phosphoroscope
Pyrophotometer
Scintillascope
Scintilloscope
Spinthariscope
Synchronoscope

15 letters:
Phenakestoscope
Radiogoniometer
Telestereoscope

16 letters:
Sphygmoma-
  nometer
Telespectroscope

17 letters:
Spectrophotometer

Insubordinate Contumacious, Faction, Mutinous, Rebel, Refractory
Insubstantial Airy, Brief, Flimsy, Frothy, Illusory, Jackstraw, Slight, Syllabub, Thin,
  Wispy, Ye(a)sty

Insufferable Egregious
Insufficient Exiguous, Inadequate, Poor, Scant, Shortfall
Insular Isolated, Moated, Narrow, Xenophobe
Insulate, Insulation, Insulator Biotite, Corkboard, Dielectric, Electret, Enwind, Grommet, Haybox, Inwind, Lagging, Mica, Non-conductor, Padding, Pugging, Sleeving, Tog
Insult(ing) Abuse, Affront, Aspersion, Barb, Becall, Charientism, Contumely, Cut, Dyslogistic, Embarrass, Facer, Fig, Injurious, Lese-majesty, Mud, Mud-pie, Offend, Opprobrious, Rip on, Skit, Slagging, Sledge, Slight, Slur, Snub, Trauma, Uncomplimentary, Verbal, Yenta, Yente
Insure(r), Insurance Abandonee, Accident, Cover, Endowment, Fidelity, Fire, Group, Guarantee, Hedge, Indemnity, Knock-for-knock, Life, Lloyds, Marine, Medibank, Medicare, Mutual, National, Participating, Pluvius, Policy, Public liability, Reversion, Security, Social, Term, Underwrite, Whole-life
Insurgent, Insurrection Cade, Jacquerie, Mutiny, Outbreak, Pandy, Rebel, Revolt, Sedition, Uprising, Whisky
▷ **Insurgent** *may indicate* 'reversed'
Intact Complete, Entire, Inviolate, Unused, Whole
Intaglio, Intagliate Diaglyph, Incavo
Intake Absorption, Entry, Fuel
Integer, Integral Component, Definite, Entire, Improper, Inbuilt, Indefinite, Needful, Number, Organic, Unitary
Integrate(d), Integration Amalgamate, Assimilate, Combine, Coordinate, Fuse, Harmonious, Holistic, Large-scale, Mainstream, Merge, Postural, Tightknit
Integrity Honesty, Principle, Probity, Rectitude, Strength, Uprightness, Whole
Integument Coat, Primine, Secundine, Sheath, Skin, Velum
Intellect, Intellectual(s) Academic, Aptitude, Belligerati, Brain, Cerebral, Cultural, Dianoetic, Egghead, Eggmass, Far-out, Genius, Grey matter, Highbrow, Intelligent, Intelligentsia, -ist, Learned, Literati, Luminary, Mastermind, Mental(ity), Mind, Noesis, Noetic, Noology, Nous, Profound, Reason, Sublime, Titan
Intelligence, Intelligent Advice, Artificial, Boss, Brainiac, Brains, Bright, CIA, Discerning, Dope, Eggmass, Emotional, Esprit, G, Grey matter, GRU, Humint, Info, Ingenious, IQ, Knowledgeable, Machiavellian, Machine, MI, Mossad, Mother wit, News, Pate, Pointy-headed, Rational, Sconce, Sense, Sharp, Shrewd, Smart, Spetsnaz, Spetznaz, Tidings, Wit
Intelligible Exoteric
Intemperance Acrasia, Crapulent, Excess, Gluttony, Immoderation
Intend(ed), Intending Allot, Betrothed, Contemplate, Design, Destine, Ettle, Fiancé(e), Going, → MEAN, Meditate, Planned, Propose, Purpose
Intense, Intensify, Intensity Acute, Aggravate, Ardent, Compound, Crash, Crescendo, Deep, Depth, Earnest, Earthquake, Emotional, Enhance, Escalate, Estro, Excess, Extreme, Fervent, Keen, Luminous, Might, Profound, Radiant, Redouble, Sharpen, Vehement, Vivid
Intent, Intention(al) À dessein, Animus, Deliberate, Dole, Earnest, Ettle, Hellbent, Manifesto, Mens rea, Mind, Paradoxical, Prepense, Purpose, Rapt, Resolute, Set, Studious, Systematic, Thought, Tire, Witting, Yrapt
Inter Bury, Entomb
Interaction Chemistry, Enantiodromia, Solvation
Interbreed(ing) Miscegenation
Intercalation Embolism
Intercede, Intercession Mediate, Negotiate, Plead, Prayer

Intercept Absciss(a), Abscisse, Check, Hack, Meet, Waylay
Interchange(d) Altercation, Alternate, Clover-leaf, Crossing, Equivalent, Junction, Mutual, Permute, Reciprocate, Substitute, Transpose
Intercom Entryphone®
Intercourse Arse, Ball, Bang, Bed, Blow job, Boff, Bone, Bonk, Buggery, Bukkake, Bump, Coition, Coitus, Commerce, Commixture, Congress, Connection, Consummation, Converse, Copulation, Cottaging, Coupling, Cover, Cunnilingus, Deflowering, Enjoy, Fluff, Fornication, Gam, Gamahuche, Gamaruche, Gangbang, Greens, Hochmagandy, Houghmagandie, Jass, Jazz, Jig(-a)-jig, Jiggy, Jiggy-jiggy, Jump, Knee-trembler, Knock, Know(ledge), Koap, Laying, Leg-over, Lie with, Make, Marriage bed, Nail, Naughty, Necrophilia, Nookie, Nooky, Poke, Poontang, Pussy, Quickie, Ride, Rim, Roger, Root, Rump, Rumpy(-pumpy), Satyriasis, Screw, Sexual, Shaft, Shag, Shtup, Sixty-nine, Sociality, Sodomy, Soixante-neuf, Stuff, Swive, Tail, Teledildonics, The other, Tie, Trade, Tribadism, Trock, Troilism, Truck, Whoredom
Interdict Ban, Forbid, Prohibit, Taboo
Interest(ed), Interesting Amusive, APR, Attention, Behalf, Benefit, Clou, Compound, Concern, Contango, Controlling, Coupon, Dividend, Ear-grabbing, Engage, Engross, Enthusiasm, Fad, Fascinate, Fee-simple, Fee-tail, Grab, Hot, Human, Import, Income, Insurable, Int(o), Intrigue, Landed, Life, Line, Negative, Part, Partisan, Percentage, Readable, Rente, Respect, Revenue, Reversion, Riba, Scene, Sepid, Share, Side, Sideline, Simple, Spice, Stake, Tickle, Topical, Usage, Usance, Use, Usure, Usury, Vested, Vig(orish), Warm
Interfere(r), Interference Busybody, Clutter, Disrupt, Hamper, Hinder, Intrude, Mar, → MEDDLE, Molest, Nose, Officious, Pry, Radio, Shash, Shot noise, Static, Tamper, Teratogen
Interferometer Etalon
Intergrowth Perthite
Interim Break, Meantime, Meanwhile, Temporary
Interior Backblocks, Cyclorama, Domestic, Innards, Innate, Inner, Inside, Outback, Plain, Up-country, Vitals
Interject(ion) Ahem, Begorra(h), Chime-in, Gertcha, Haith, Hoo-oo, Interpolate, Lackaday, Lumme, Nation, Sese(y), Sessa, 'Sheart, 'Slid, Tarnation, Tush
Interlace Mingle, Pleach, Weave, Wreathe
Interlock Dovetail, Engage, Knit, Tangle
Interlocutor Elihu, MC, Questioner
Interloper Gate-crasher, Intruder, Trespasser
Interlude Antimask, Antimasque, Divertimento, Entr'acte, Interruption, Kyogen, Lunch-hour, Meantime, Pause, Verset
Intermediary, Intermediate Agent, Bardo, Comprador(e), Contact man, Go-between, In-between, Instar, Mean, Medial, Mesne, Mezzanine, Middleman, Middle-of-the-road, Thirdsman, Transitional
Interminable Endless, Infinite, Unending
Intermission Apyrexia, Break, Interval, Pause, Recess
Intermittent Broken, Fitful, Off-on, Periodic, Random, Spasmic, Spasmodic, Sporadic
Intern(e) Confine, Doctor, Impound, Restrict, Trainee
Internal Domestic, Inner, Internecine, Inward, Within
International Cap, Cosmopolitan, Fourth, Lion, Second, Test, Trotskyist, UN, Universal
Internet Dotcom, Infobahn, URL, Web, WWW
Interpolate(r), Interpolation Diaskeuast, Insert, Intercalate, Interrupt,

Spatchcock, Tmesis

Interpose Butt in, Horn in, Interject, Interlay, Interprone, Intervene, Spatchcock, Stickle

Interpret(er) Aread, Ar(r)e(e)de, Conster, Construe, Decipher, Decode, Dobhash, Dragoman, Exegete, Explain, Exponent, Expositor, Expound, Glossator, Hermeneutist, Hierophant, Jehovist, Latiner, Lingster, Linguistic, Linkster, Medium, Moonshee, Moonshi, Moralise, Munshi, Oneirocritic, Oneiroscopist, Origenist, Prophet, Read, Rede, Reed(e), Render, Represent, Spokesman, Textualist, → **TRANSLATE**, Truchman, Ulema

Interpretation Anagoge, Anagogy, Construction, Copenhagen, Eisegesis, Euhemerism, Exegesis, Exegete, Gematria, Gloss(ary), Gospel, Halacha(h), Halakah, Hermeneutics, Midrash, Oneirocriticism, Portray, Reading, Rede, Rendition, Spin, Targum, Translation, Tropology

Interrogate, Interrogation Catechism, Debrief(ing), Enquire, Examine, Grill, Maieutic, Pump, → **QUESTION**, Quiz

Interrupt(ion), Interrupter Ahem, Aposiopesis, Blip, Break, Butt, Chequer, Chip in, Disturb, Entr'acte, Heckle, Hiatus, Intercept, Interfere, Interpellate, Interpolate, Interpose, Interregnum, Intrusion, Overtalk, Pause, Portage, Rheotome, Stop, Suspend, Time-out

Intersect(ion) Carfax, Carfox, Carrefour, Chiasm(a), Cross, Crunode, Cut, Decussate, Divide, Groin, Metacentre, Orthocentre, Trace

Intersperse Dot, Interlard, Interpose, Scatter, Sprinkle

Interstice Areole, Interlude, Pore, Space

Intertwine Braid, Impleach, Knit, Lace, Plait, Splice, Twist, Writhe

Interval Between, Break, Breather, Class, Closed, Comma, Confidence, Contour, Diapente, Diastaltic, Diatesseron, Diesis, Distance, Ditone, Duodecimo, Entr'acte, Fifth, Gap, Half-time, Harmonic, Hiatus, Hourly, Interim, Interlude, Interregnum, Interruption, Interspace, Interstice, Limma, Lunitidal, Meantime, Meantone, Meanwhile, Melodic, Microtone, Minor third, Ninth, Octave, Open, Ottava, Perfect, Pycnon, Respite, Rest, Schisma, Semitone, Seventh, Sixth, Space, Span, Spell, Tritone, Twelfth, Unison, Wait

Intervene, Intervention Agency, Arbitrate, Expromission, Interfere, Interjacent, Interrupt, Mediate, Mesne, Theurgy, Up

Interview Audience, Audition, Beeper, Conference, Doorstep, Examine, Hearing, Oral, Press conference, See, Vox pop

Interweave, Interwoven, Interwove Entwine, Interlace, Monogram, Pirnit, Plait, Plash, Pleach, Raddle, Wreathed

Intestate Heirless, Unwilling

Intestinal, Intestine(s) Bowel, Chit(ter)lings, Derma, Duodenum, Enteric, Entrails, Guts, Harigals, Innards, Jejunum, Kishke, Large, Mesenteron, Omenta, Rectum, Small, Splanchnic, Thairm, Tripes, Viscera

Intimacy, Intimate(ly) Achates, À deux, Boon, Bosom, Close, Communion, Connote, Familiar, Friend, Heart-to-heart, Inmost, Innuendo, Intrigue, Nearness, Opine, Pack, Private, Signal, Special, Thick, Throng, Warm, Well

Intimation Clue, Hint, Implication, Inkling, Innuendo, Si quis

Intimidate, Intimidating Awe, Browbeat, Bulldoze, Bully, Cow, Daunt, Dragon, Hector, Niramiai, Psych, Threaten, Tyrannise, Unnerve

Into At, Intil, Within

Intolerant, Intolerable Allergic, Bigotry, Egregious, Excessive, Illiberal, Impatient, Impossible, Ombrophobe, Self-righteous

Intone, Intonation Cadence, Just, Twang

In touch Au fait
Intoxicate(d), Intoxicant, Intoxicating, Intoxication Alcoholic, Areca-nut, Benj, Bhang, Coca, Corn, Cup, Disguise, Fuddle, Ganja, Half-cut, Heady, → **HIGH**, Hocus, Hou high, Inebriate, Jag, Merry, Mescal, Peyote, Pixil(l)ated, Rumbullion, Shroom, Slewed, Soma, Sozzle, Spirituous, Swacked, Temulent, Whiskeyfied, Whiskified, Zonked
Intractable Disobedient, Kittle, Mulish, Obdurate, Perverse, Surly, Unruly, Wilful
Intransigent Adamant, Inflexible, Rigid, Uncompromising
Intransitive Neuter, Objectless
Intrepid Aweless, Bold, Brave, Dauntless, Doughty, Firm, Gallant, → **RESOLUTE**, Valiant
Intricate Complex, Daedal(ian), Daedale, Dedal, Gordian, Intrince, Involute, Knotty, Pernickety, Sinuous, Tirlie-wirlie, Tricky, Vitruvian
Intrigue(r), Intriguing Affaire, Artifice, Brigue, Cabal, Camarilla, Cloak and dagger, Collogue, Conspiracy, Fascinate, Hotbed, Ignatian, Interest, Jesuit, Jobbery, Liaison, Machinate, Plot, Politic, Rat, → **SCHEME**, Stairwork, Strategy, Traffic, Trinketer
Intrinsic(ally) Basically, Genuine, Inherent, Innate, Inner, Per se
▷ **Intrinsically** may indicate something within a word
Introduce(r), Introduction, Introductory Acquaint, Anacrusis, Curtain-raiser, Debut, Emcee, Enseam, Exordial, Foreword, Immit, Import, Induct, Initiate, Inject, Insert, Instil(l), Institutes, Intercalate, Interpolate, Intrada, Introit, Isagogic, Lead-in, Opening, Phase in, Plant, Preamble, Preface, Preliminary, Prelude, Prelusory, Preparatory, Present, Presentment, Proem, Prolegomena, Prolegomenon, Prologue, Proponent, Referral, Standfirst, Start, Usher
▷ **Introduction** may indicate a first letter
Intromission Vicious
Introspective Musing, Reflex, Ruminant
▷ **In trouble** may indicate an anagram
Introvert(ed) Cerebrotonic, Ingrow, In-toed, Invaginate, Reserved, Shy
Intrude(r), Intrusion, Intrusive Abate, Aggress, Annoy, Bother, Burglar, Derby dog, Disturb, → **ENCROACH**, Gatecrash, Hacker, Interloper, Invade, Meddle, Nosey, Personal, Porlocking, Presume, Raid, Sorn, Trespass
Intuition, Intuitive Belief, ESP, Hunch, Insight, Instinct, Inwit, Noumenon, Premonition, Presentiment, Seat-of-the-pants, Telepathy, Theosophy, Visceral
▷ **In two words** may indicate a word to be split
Inuit Caribou, Eskimo, Inuk, Yupik
Inundate, Inundation Flood, Overflow, Overwhelm, Submerge, Swamp
Inure Acclimatise, Accustom, Harden, Season, Steel
Invade(r), Invasion Angle, Attack, Attila, Dane, Descent, Encroach, Goth, Hacker, Hengist, Horsa, Hun, Infest, Inroad, Intruder, Irrupt, Jute, Lombard, Martian, Norman, Norsemen, Ostrogoth, Overlord, Overrun, Permeate, Raid, Trespass, Vandal, Viking, Visigoth
Invalid(ate), Invalidation Bad, Bogus, Bunbury, Cancel, Chronic, Clinic, Defunct, Diriment, Erroneous, Expired, False, Inauthentic, Inform, Inoperative, Irritate, Lapsed, Nugatory, Null, Nullify, Overturn, Quash, Refute, Shut-in, Terminate, Valetudinarian, Vitiate, Void
Invaluable Essential, Excellent, Precious, Useful
Invariable, Invariably Always, Constant, Eternal, Habitual, Perpetual, Steady, Uniform
Invective Abuse, Billingsgate, Diatribe, Philippic, Reproach, Ribaldry, Tirade

Inveigh Declaim, Denounce, Protest, Rail
Invent(ion), Inventive Adroit, Babe, Baby, Brainchild, Chimera, Coin, Contrive, Cook up, → **CREATE**, Daedal, Design, Device, Excogitate, Fabricate, Fain, Fantasia, Feign, Figment, Imaginary, Improvise, Ingenuity, Mint, Myth, Originate, Patent, Plateau, Pretence, Resourceful, Synectics, Whittle, Wit
Inventor Archimedes, Arkwright, Artificer, Author, Babbage, Baird, Bell, Biro, Boys, Bramah, Brix, Cartwright, Celsius, Coiner, Creator, Crompton, Daedalus, Edison, Engineer, Galileo, Geiger, Hansom, Jubal, Marconi, Maxim, Mercator, Mills, Minié, Mint-master, Morse, Nernst, Newcomen, Nobel, Patentee, Savery, Schmidt, Siemens, Solvay, Tesla, Torricelli, Tull, Watt, Wheatstone, Whitney
Inventory Account, Index, Itemise, List, Perpetual, Personality, Register, Steelbow, Stock, Terrier
Inverse, Inversion, Invert(ed) Anastrophe, Antimetabole, Antimetathesis, Capsize, Chiasmus, Entropion, Entropium, First, Homosexuality, Opposite, Overset, Reciprocal, Resupinate, Reverse, Second, Tête-bêche, Turn, Upset
Invertebrate Acanthocephalan, Annelida, Anthozoan, Arrowworm, Arthropod, Brachiopod, Cnidarian, Coelenterate, Crinoid, Ctenophore, Decapod, Echinoderm, Echinoid, Euripterid, Feather star, Gast(e)ropod, Globigerina, Hydrozoan, Mollusc, Onychophoran, Parazoan, Pauropod, Peritrich, Platyhelminth, Polyp, Poriferan, Protostome, Rotifer, Roundworm, Scyphozoan, Sea-cucumber, Sea-lily, → **SHELLFISH**, Slug, Spineless, Spoonworm, Starfish, Tardigrade, Trepang, Trochelminth, Unio, Water bear, Worm, Zoophyte
Invest(or), Investment Agamemnon, Ambient, Angel, Bate, Beleaguer, Besiege, Bet, Blockade, Blue-chip, Capitalist, Collins Street farmer, Contrarian, Dignify, Dub, Embark, Empanoply, Enclothe, Endow, Enrobe, Ethical, Financier, Flutter, Gilt, Girt, Holding, Infeft, Install, Inward, On, Pannicle, Panniculus, Parlay, Place, Portfolio, Put, Ring, Robe, Saver, Share, Siege, Sink, Spec, Speculation, Stag, Stake, Stock, Surround, Tessa, Tie up, Trust, Trustee, Venture, Zaitech
▷ **Invest** *may indicate* one word surrounding another
Investigate, Investigator, Investigation Canvass, Case, Chart, CID, Delve, Examine, Explore, Fed, Ferret, Fieldwork, Go into, Gumshoe, Hunt, Inquest, Inquirendo, Inquiry, Inquisition, McCarthyism, Nose, Organon, Organum, Probe, Pry, Quester, Rapporteur, Research, Scan, Scout, Screen, Scrutinise, Search, Sleuth, Snoop, Study, Suss, Tec, Test, T-man, Track, Try, Zetetic
Investiture Award, Inauguration
Inveterate Chronic, Double-dyed, Dyed-in-the-wool, Engrained, Habitual, Hardened
Invidious Harmful, Hostile, Malign
Invigilator Proctor
Invigorate, Invigorating, Invigoration Analeptic, Brace, Brisk, Cheer, Elixir, Energise, Enliven, Fortify, Insinew, Pep, Refresh, Renew, Stimulate, Tonic, Vital
Invincible Almighty, Brave, Stalwart, Valiant
Inviolatable, Inviolate, Inviolable Intemerate, Sacred, Sacrosanct
Invisible Blind, Hidden, Imageless, Infra-red, Secret, Tusche, Unseen
Invite, Invitation, Inviting Ask, Attract, Bid, Call, Card, Overture, → **REQUEST**, Solicit, Stiffie, Summons, Tempt, Toothsome, Woo
Invocation, Invoke Appeal, Call, Conjure, Curse, Entreat, Epiclesis, Solicit, White rabbits
Invoice Account, Bill, Docket, Itemise, Manifest, Pro forma
Involuntary Automatic, Instinctive, Unwitting
Involve(d), Involvement Active, Commitment, Complicate, Complicit, Concern,

Embroil, Engage, Entail, Envelop, Imbroglio, Immerse, → **IMPLICATE**, Include, Intricate, Meet, Necessitate, Participate, Tangle

▷ **Involved** *may indicate* an anagram

Inward(s) Afferent, Centripuntal, Homefelt, Introrse, Mental, Private, Varus, Within

Iodine I, Kelp, Thyroxin(e)

Iolanthe Peri

Ion Ammonium, Anion, Carbanion, Carborium, Hydrogen, Hydronium, Hydroxyl, Isomer, Onium, Zwitterion

Ionian Iastic, Te(i)an

Iota Atom, Jot, Subscript, Whit

IOU Cedula, Market, PN, Shinplaster, Vowels

IOW Vectis

IRA Provisional, Provo

Iran(ian) Babist, Kurd, Mede, Osset, Pahlavi, Parsee, Pehlevi, Ta(d)jik, Tadzhik

Irascible Choleric, Crusty, Fiery, Peevish, Snappy, Tetchy, Toustie

Irate Angry, Cross, Infuriated, Wrathful

Ire Anger, Bait, Cholera, Fury, Rage, Wrath

Ireland Composer, Deirdre, Gaeltacht, Hibernia, Innisfail, Irena, IRL, Iverna, Twenty-six counties

Irenic Peaceful

Iridescence, Iridescent Chatoyant, Flambé, Opaline, Reflet, Shimmering, Shot, Water-gall

Iridium Ir

Iris Areola, Eye, Flag, Fleur-de-lis, Gladdon, Ixia, Lily, Lis, Orris, Rainbow, Roast-beef plant, Sedge, Seg, Stinking, Sunbow

Irish(man) Bark, Bog-trotter, Boy, Celt(ic), Clan-na-gael, Defender, Dermot, Dubliner, Eamon(n), Eirann, Erse, Fenian, Gael, Gaeltacht, Goidel, Greek, Keltic, Kern(e), Mick(e)(y), Middle, Milesian, Mulligan, Ogamic, Orange(man), Ostmen, Paddy(-whack), Partholon, Pat(rick), Rapparee, Redshank, Reilly, Riley, Rory, Ryan, Sean, Shoneen, Teague, Temper, Ultonian, Whiteboy, Wildgeese

Irk(some) Annoy, Bother, Irritate, Needle, Tedious

Iron(s), Ironwork(s) Airn, Alpha, Angle, Beta, Carron, Cast, Cautery, Chains, Chalybeate, Chancellor, Channel, Climbing, Coquimbite, Corrugated, Cramp(on), Crimp, Cross, Curling, Curtain, Delta, Derringer, Dogs, Eagle-stone, Fayalite, Fe, Ferredoxin, Ferrite, Fetter, Fiddley, Flip-dog, Galvanised, Gamma, Gem, Golfclub, Goose, Grappling, Grim, Grozing, → **GUN**, Gyve, Horse, Ingot, Italian, Kamacite, Laterite, Lily, Lofty, Long, Maiden, Malleable, Marcasite, Mars, Martensite, Mashie, Mashy, Merchant, Meteoric, Mitis (metal), Pea, Pig, Pinking, → **PRESS**, Pro-metal, Rabble, Rations, Rod, Sad, Scrap, Shooting, Short, Smoother, Soft, Soldering, Specular, Spiegeleisen, Steam, Stirrup, Stretching, Strong, Taconite, Taggers, Terne, Tin terne, Toggle, Tow, Wafer, Waffle, Wear, Wedge, White, Wrought

Iron age Latene, Villanovan

Ironic, Irony Antiphrasis, Asteism, Dramatic, Meiosis, Metal, Ridicule, Sarcasm, Satire, Socratic, Tongue-in-cheek, Tragic, Trope, Wry

Ironside Edmund

Ironwood Pyengadu

▶ **Ironwork(s)** *see* **IRON**

Irrational Absurd, Brute, Delirious, Foolish, Illogical, Number, Superstitious, Surd, Wild

Irreconcilable Poles apart

Irrefutable Evident, Positive, Undeniable
Irregular(ity) Abnormal, Alloiostrophus, Anomaly, Aperiodic, A salti, Asymmetric,
  Atypical, Bashi-bazouk, Blotchy, Crazy, Episodic, Erratic, Evection, Fitful, Flawed,
  Formless, Free-form, Guerilla, Heteroclitic, Incondite, Inordinate, Jitter, Kink,
  Occasional, Orthotone, Para-military, Partisan, Patchy, Rambling, Random, Rough,
  Scalene, Scrawl, Sebundy, Sharawadgi, Sharawaggi, Snatchy, Solecism, Sporadic,
  TA, Uneven, Unsteady, Unwonted, Variable, Wayward, Zigzag
▷ **Irregular** *may indicate* an anagram
Irrelevant Academic, Digression, Extraneous, Gratuitous, Immaterial, Inept,
  Non sequitur, Ungermane, Unrelated
Irreligious Heathen, Impious, Pagan, Profane
Irremedial Hopeless, Incurable, Laches
Irrepressible Resilient
Irreproachable Blameless, Spotless, Stainless
Irresistible Almighty, Endearing, Inevitable, Mesmeric, Overwhelming
Irresolute, Irresolution Aboulia, Doubtful, Hesitant, Timid, Unsure, Wavery,
  Weak-willed
Irresponsible Capricious, Feckless, Flighty, Fly-by-night, Slap-happy, Strawen,
  Trigger-happy, Wanton, Wildcat
Irreverent Blasphemous, Disrespectful, Godless, Impious, Profane
Irrigate, Irrigation Canalise, Colonic, Douche, Enema, Flood, Get, Water
Irritable, Irritability, Irritant, Irritate(d), Irritation Acerbate, Anger, Annoy,
  Bête noire, Blister, Bother, Bug, Chafe, Chauff, Chippy, Chocker, Crabbit, Crabby,
  Cross-grained, Crosspatch, Crotchety, Crusty, Dod, Dyspeptic, Eat, Eczema, Edgy,
  Emboil, Enchafe, Erethism, Ewk, Exasperate, Fantod, Feverish, Fiery, Fleabite,
  Frabbit, Fractious, Fraught, Fretful, Gall, Get, Goad, Grate, Gravel, Hasty, Heck,
  Humpy, Intertrigo, Irk, Itch, Jangle, Livery, Mardy, Narky, Needle, Nettle, Niggly,
  Ornery, Peckish, Peevish, Peppery, Pesky, Pestilent(ial), Pet, Petulance, Pinprick,
  Pique, Prickly, Provoke, Rag'd, Ragde, Rankle, Rasp, Rattle, Ratty, Rile, Roil, Rub,
  Ruffle, Savin(e), Scratchy, Shirty, Snappy, Snit, Snitchy, Splenetic, Sting, Tease,
  Techy, Testy, Tetchy, Thorn, Tickle, Tiresome, Toey, Touchy, Uptight, → **VEX**, Waxy,
  Windburn, Yuke
▷ **Irritated** *may indicate* an anagram
Irving Actor, Berlin
Is Est, Ist
Isaiah Is
Isinglass Carlock, Fish-glue, Mica, Sturgeon
Islam(ic) Al Queda, Crescent, Druse, Druz(e), Hamas, Kurd(ish), Senus(si), Sheriat,
  Shia(h), Shiite, Sunni(te), Taleban, Taliban, Wah(h)abi
Island, Isle(t) Ait, Archipelago, Atoll, Cay, Char, Desert, Eyot, Floating, Holm, I,
  Inch, Is, Key, Lagoon, Mainland, Motu, Refuge, Traffic

ISLANDS

2 letters:	Fyn	Sea	Attu
TT	Hoy	Yap	Bali
	Kos		Biak
3 letters:	Man	*4 letters:*	Bute
Aru	May	Amoy	Calf
Cos	Rat	Aran	Cebu
Diu	Rum	Arru	Coll

Cook	Belle	Pelew	Cyprus
Cuba	Bioko	Pemba	Devil's
Dogs	Bohol	Pines	Diomed
Eigg	Bonin	Qeshm	Djerba
Elba	Canna	Qishm	Easter
Erin	Capri	Reil's	Eelpie
Fair	Ceram	Rhode	Ellice
Fiji	Cheju	Samar	Euboea
Guam	Chios	Samoa	Flores
Heat	Clare	Samos	Fraser
Herm	Cocos	Saria	Hainan
Holy	Coney	Seram	Harris
Hova	Coral	South	Hawaii
Idse	Corfu	Spice	Hobart
Iona	Crete	Sumba	Honshu
Java	Delos	Sunda	Hormuz
Jolo	Disko	Thera	Icaria
Jura	Ellis	Thule	Imbros
Keos	Faial	Timor	Indies
King	Farne	Tiree	Insula
Line	Faroe	Tonga	Ionian
Long	Fayal	Upolu	Ischia
Mahe	Funen	Whale	Ithaca
Maui	Haiti	White	Jersey
Mazu	Hondo	Wight	Kodiak
Mona	Ibiza	Youth	Kurile
Muck	Islay	Zante	Kvaley
Mull	Isola		Kyushu
Niue	Iviza	**6 letters:**	Labuan
Oahu	Jerba	Achill	Laputa
Rona	Kiska	Aegean	Lemnos
Ross	Kuril	Aegina	Lesbos
Saba	Lanai	Amager	Leucas
Sark	Lewis	Andros	Leukas
Skye	Leyte	Aurora	Levkas
Spud	Lundy	Avalon	Lipari
Truk	Luzon	Azores	Lizard
Uist	Maewo	Baffin	Lombok
Unst	Malta	Banaba	Madura
Wake	Matsu	Bangka	Majuro
Yell	Melos	Barrow	Marajo
	Nauru	Bedloe	Mercer
5 letters:	Naxos	Bikini	Midway
Aland	Nevis	Borneo	Negros
Apple	North	Bounty	Ogygia
Arran	Oland	Butung	Paphos
Aruba	Ormuz	Caicos	Patmos
Banka	Palau	Canvey	Penang
Banks	Panay	Cayman	Pharos
Barra	Papua	Ceylon	Philae
Batan	Paros	Chiloe	Phuket

Pladdy	Celebes	Palmyra	Barbados
Quemoy	Channel	Paracel	Bathurst
Ramsey	Chatham	Phoenix	Billiton
Rhodes	Cipango	Purbeck	Blefuscu
Rialto	Corsica	Rathlin	Bora-Bora
Robben	Crannog	Reunion	Bornholm
Royale	Curacao	Roanoke	Canaries
Ryukyu	Cythera	Rockall	Caroline
Safety	Diomede	Salamis	Catalina
Saipan	Elvissa	San Juan	Choiseul
Savage	Emerald	Sheppey	Colonsay
Savaii	Eriskay	Shikoku	Cyclades
Scilly	Falster	Society	Dominica
Sicily	Frisian	Socotra	Falkland
Skerry	Fur Seal	Sokotra	Farquhar
Skyros	Gambier	Solomon	Flinders
Snares	Gilbert	Spratly	Foulness
Soemba	Gotland	St Croix	Friendly
Soenda	Grenada	Stewart	Gothland
Staffa	Hawaiki	St Kilda	Gottland
Staten	Howland	St Kitts	Guernsey
Tahiti	Ireland	St Lucia	Hamilton
Taiwan	Iwo Jima	Sumatra	Hatteras
Thanet	Jamaica	Sumbawa	Hebrides
Thasos	Keeling	Suqutra	Hokkaido
Tobago	Laaland	Surtsey	Hong Kong
Tresco	Ladrone	Tenedos	Jan Mayen
Tubuai	La Palma	Tokelau	Kangaroo
Tuvalu	Leeward	Tortola	Kermadec
Unimak	Liberty	Tortuga	Kiribati
Ushant	Lofoten	Tutuila	Ladrones
Veneti	Lolland	Visayan	Lilliput
Virgin	Madeira	Volcano	Lord Howe
	Majorca	Waihake	Luggnagg
7 letters:	Mariana	Watling	Mackinac
Aeolian	Masbate	Western	Maldives
Aldabra	Mayotte	Wrangel	Mallorca
Amboina	Mindoro	Zealand	Malvinas
Andaman	Minicoy	Zetland	Marianas
Antigua	Minorca		Marquesa
Austral	Molokai	**8 letters:**	Marshall
Bahamas	Moreton	Alcatraz	Mauna Loa
Baranof	Mykonos	Alderney	Melville
Barbuda	Nicobar	Aleutian	Mindanao
Basilan	Norfolk	Amindiva	Miquelon
Batavia	Oceania	Anglesey	Moluccas
Battery	Okinawa	Anguilla	Mustique
Bedloe's	Orcades	Antilles	Njazidja
Bermuda	Orkneys	Atlantis	Northern
Bonaire	Pacific	Auckland	Pelagian
Cartier	Palawan	Balearic	Pitcairn

Pleasant
Portland
Pribilof
Principe
Sakhalin
Sandwich
Sardinia
Schouten
Shetland
Soembawa
Somerset
South Sea
Sporades
Sri Lanka
St Helena
St Helier
St Martin
St Thomas
Sulawesi
Svalbard
Sverdrup
Tasmania
Tenerife
Terceira
Thousand
Thursday
Trinidad
Tsushima
Unalaska
Venetian
Victoria
Viti Levu
Windward
Zanzibar

9 letters:
Admiralty
Alexander
Andreanof
Anticosti
Antipodes
Ascension
Barataria
Belle Isle
Benbecula
Chichagof
Christmas
Elephanta
Ellesmere
Falklands

Fortunate
Galapagos
Governors
Greenland
Hainan Tao
Halmahera
Innisfree
Jamestown
Kerguelen
Laccadive
Lampedusa
Lanzarote
Macquarie
Manhattan
Margarita
Marquesas
Mascarene
Mauritius
Melanesia
Nantucket
New Guinea
Polynesia
Rangitoto
Rarotonga
Runnymede
Saghalien
Santorini
Sao Miguel
Shetlands
Sjaelland
Stromboli
St Vincent
Teneriffe
Trobriand
Vancouver
Vanua Levu
Walcheren

10 letters:
Basse-Terre
Bermoothes
Campobello
Cape Barren
Cape Breton
Cephalonia
Corregidor
Dodecanese
Formentera
Grand Manan
Grenadines

Guadeloupe
Heligoland
Hispaniola
Isle Royale
Kiritimati
Langerhans
Madagascar
Manitoulin
Marinduque
Martinique
Micronesia
Montserrat
New Britain
New Georgia
New Ireland
Pescadores
Poor Knight
Puerto Rico
Sahghalien
Samothrace
Sandalwood
Seychelles
Three Kings
Vesteralen
West Indies
Whitsunday

11 letters:
Austronesia
Dry Tortugas
Glubdubdrib
Grand Bahama
Grand Canary
Grande-Terre
Guadalcanal
Lakshadweep
Lesser Sunda
Lindisfarne
Mount Desert
New Siberian
Pantelleria
Philippines
San Salvador
Southampton
South Orkney
Spitsbergen

12 letters:
Bougainville
Cassiterides

Glubbdubdrib
Greater Sunda
Marie Galante
New Caledonia
Newfoundland
Nusa Tenggara
Prince Edward
San Cristobal
Santa Barbara
Seringapatam
South Georgia
Torres Strait

13 letters:
Espiritu Santo
Forneaux Group
Fuerteventura
Juan Fernandez
New Providence
Prince of Wales
Santa Catalina
South Shetland

14 letters:
Amboina oceanic
D'Entrecasteaux
Lesser Antilles
Papua New
 Guinea
Queen Charlotte
Queen Elizabeth
Tristan da Cunha
Turks and Caicos
Vestmannaeyjar

15 letters:
Greater Antilles
Mont-Saint-Michel
Wallis and Futuna

16 letters:
Heard and
 McDonald

17 letters:
Fernando de
 Noronha

Islander Chian, Cretan, D(a)yak, Filipino, Kanaka, Kelper, Laputan, Madeiran, Maltese, Mauritian, Native, Nesiot, Newfie, Orcadian, Parian, Rhodian, Samiot, Sican, Singalese, Taiwanese
Isle of Wight Vectis
Isn't Aint, Nis, Nys
Isolate(d) Ancress, Apart, Backwater, Cleidoic, Cut off, Desolate, Enclave, Enisle, Incommunicado, Inisle, In vacuo, Island, Lone, Maroon, Pocket, Quarantine, Sea-girt, Seclude, Secret, Segregate, Separate, Sequester, Six-finger country, Solitary, Sporadic, Stray
Isomer Carotene, Carotin, Carvacrol, Geranial, Neral, Pinene, Theophylline
Isopod Gribble
Isosceles Triangle
Isotope Actinon, Cobalt-60, Deuterium, Iodine-131, Muonium, Protium, Strontium-90, Thoron, Tritium
Israel(i) Beulah, IL, Meir, Sabra
Issue(s) Bonus, Capitalization, Children, Come, Crux, Debouch, Denouement, Derive, Disclose, Dispense, Edition, Effluence, Egress, → **EMANATE**, Emerge, Emit, Escape, Exit, Exodus, Family, Feigned, Fiduciary, Flotation, Fungible, General, Government, Gush, Immaterial, Ish, Litter, Material, Matter, Mise, Number, Offspring, Outflow, Part, Privatization, Proof, Publish, Result, Rights, Sally, Seed, Side, Son, Spawn, Special, Spring, Stream, Subject, Topic, Turn, Utter
Istanbul Byzantium, Constantinople
Isthmus Darien, Karelian, Kra, Neck, Panama, San Blas, Suez, Tehuantepec
It A, Chic, Hep, Id, Italian, Oomph, SA, 't, Vermouth
Italian, Italy Alpini, Ausonia, Bolognese, Calabrian, Chian, Dago, Ding, Este, Etnean, Etrurian, Etruscan, Eyeti(e), Eytie, Faliscan, Florentine, Genoese, Ghibelline, Guelf, Guelph, Hesperia, Irredentist, It, Latian, Latin, Lombard, Medici, Mezzogiorno, Moro, Oscan, Paduan, Patarin(e), Rocco, Roman, Sabine, Samnite, Sicel, Sienese, Signor(i), Sikel, Spag, Tuscan, Umbrian, Venetian, Vermouth, Volscian, Wop
Italic Swash
Itch(ing), Itchiness Acariasis, Annoy, Cacoethes, Dhobi, Euk, Ewk, Hanker, Heat rash, Jock, Miliaria, Photopsy, Prickle, Prickly heat, Prurience, Prurigo, Pruritis, Psora, Scabies, Scrapie, Seven-year, Tickle, → **URGE**, Urtication, Yeuk, Youk, Yuck, Yuke
Item(ise) Also, Article, Bulletin, Detail, Entry, Flash, Line, List, Number, Piece, Point, Spot, Too, Topic
Iterate Repeat
Itinerant, Itinerary Ambulant, Didakai, Didakei, Did(d)icoy, Dusty Feet, Gipsy, Gypsy, Hobo, Journey, Log, Pedlar, Peripatetic, Pie-powder, Roadman, Roamer, Romany, Rootless, Route, Stroller, Traveller, Vagrom
Itself Per se
Ivan Russian, Terrible
Ivory (tower) Black, Bone, Chryselephantine, Dentine, Distant, Eburnean, Impractical, Incisor, Key, Solitude, Teeth, Tower, Tusk, Vegetable, Whale's bone
Ivy Ale-hoof, Angelica-tree, Aralia, Boston, Bush, Cat's-foot, Climber, Creeper, Evergreen, Gill, Grape, Ground, Hedera, Helix, Japanese, Panax, Poison, Shield, Sweetheart, Udo, Weeping
Izzard Z

Jj

J Curve, Juliet, Pen

Jab(ber) Chatter, Foin, Gabble, Immunologist, Inject, Jaw, Jook, Nudge, One-two, Peck, Poke, Prattle, Prod, Proke, Punch, Puncture, Sook, Sputter, Stab, Stick, Venepuncture, Yak

Jack(s) AB, Apple, Artocarpus, Ass, Ball, Boot, Bower, Bowl(s), Boy, Card, Cheap, Coatcard, Crevalle, Deckhand, Dibs(tones), Five stones, Flag, Frost, Hoist, Honour, Hopper, Horner, Hydraulic, Idle, J, Jock, Jumping, Ketch, Kitty, Knave, Knucklebones, Lazy, London, Loord, Lout, Lumber, Mark, Matlow, Mistress, Nob, Noddy, Pilot, Point, Pot, Pur, Rabbit, Raise, Rating, Ripper, Roasting, Robinson, Russell, Sailor, Salt, Screw, Seafarer, Shaun, Sprat, Spring-heeled, Springtail, Steeple, Sticker, Straw, Tar, Tee, Tradesman, Turnspit, Union, Uplift, Wood, Yellow

Jackal Anubis, Dieb, Hack, Stooge

Jackass Aliboron, Goburra, Kookaburra, Stupid

Jackdaw Bird, Chawk, Chough, Daw, Kae, Raven, Rheims, Thief

Jacket Acton, Afghanistan, Air, Amauti(k), Anorak, Atigi, Bainin, Baju, Bania(n), Banyan, Barbour®, Basque, Battle, Bawneen, Bed, Bellhop, Biker, Blazer, Blouse, Blouson, Body-warmer, Bolero, Bomber, Brigandine, Bumfreezer, Bush, Cagoul(e), Camisole, Can, Caraco, Cardigan, Carmagnole, Casing, → **COAT**, Dinner, Dolman, Donkey, Drape, Dressing, Dressing-sack, Duffel coat, Duffle coat, Dust-cover, Dustwrapper, Duvet, Fearnought, Flak, Fleece, Gambeson, Gendarme, Grego, Habergeon, Hacking, Ha(c)queton, Half-kirtle, Hug-me-tight, Jerkin, Jupon, Kagool, Kaross, Life, Life preserver, Lumber, Mackinaw, Mae West, Mandarin, Mandilion, Mao, Matinée, Mess, Monkey, Nehru, Newmarket, Norfolk, Parka, Pea, Petenlair, Pierrot, Pilot, Polka, Potato, Pyjama, Railly, Reefer, Safari, Sayon, Shearling, Shell, Shooting, Shortgown, Simar(re), Sleeve, Slip-cover, Smoking, Spencer, Sports, Steam, Strait, Tabard, Tailcoat, Toreador, Tunic, Tux(edo), Tweed, Vareuse, Waistcoat, Wam(m)us, Wampus, Water, Windbreaker®, Windcheater, Windjammer, Wrapper, Zouave

Jackknife Dive, Fold, Jockteleg, Pike

Jackpot Cornucopia, Kitty, Pool

Jackson Stonewall

Jackstraw Spellican, Spil(l)ikin

Jacobite(s) Non-compounder, Non juror, Wild Geese

Jacquard Matelasse

Ja(c)ques Melancholy, Tati

Jade(d) Axe-stone, Bidet, Cloy, Crock, Disjaskit, Exhaust, Fatigue, Greenstone, Hack, Hag, Horse, Hussy, Limmer, Minx, Nag, Nephrite, Pounamu, Rip, Rosinante, Sate, Screw, Slut, Spleenstone, Stale, Tired, Trite, Weary, Yaud, Yu(-stone)

Jaeger Skua

Jag(ged) Barbed, Cart, Drinking, Erose, Gimp, Injection, Laciniate, Ragde, Ragged, Serrate, Snag, Spree, Spur, Tooth

Jagger Mick, Pedlar
Jaguar American tiger, Car, Caracal, Cat, E-type, Ounce, Tiger
Jail(er) Adam, Alcaide, Alcatraz, Bedford, Bin, Bridewell, Can, Clink, Commit, Cooler, Gaol, Hoosegow, Imprison, Incarcerate, Jug, Keeper, Kitty, Limbo, Lockup, Marshalsea, Newgate, Nick, Pen, Pokey, → PRISON, Screw, Shop, Slammer, Spandau, Strangeways, Tronk, Turnkey, Warder
Jailbird Con, Lag, Lifer, Trusty
Jain(ism) Mahavira
Jakarta Batavia
Jake Honest, Hunkydory, OK, Rube
Jalopy Banger, Boneshaker, Buggy, Car, Crate, Heap, Shandry(dan), Stock-car
Jam(my) Apple butter, Block, Choke, Clog, Confiture, Crush, Cushy, Dilemma, Gridlock, Hold-up, How d'ye do, Jeelie, Jeely, Lock, Log, Plight, → PREDICAMENT, Preserve, Press, Quince, Seize, Snarl-up, Spot, Squeeze, Stall, Stick, Tailback, Tangle, Traffic, Vice, Vise, Wedge
Jamaica(n) Rasta(farian), Rastaman, Yardie
Jamb Doorpost, Durn, Sconcheon, Scontion, Scuncheon, Upright
James Agee, Bond, Bothwell, Henry, Jacobite, Jemmy, Jesse, Jim, Joyce, Screw, Seamus, Seumas, Sid, Watt
Jane Austen, Calamity, Eyre, Seymour, Shore, Sian
Jangle Clank, Clapperclaw, Clash, Rattle, Wrangle
Janitor Doorman, Porter, Servitor, Sweeper, Tiler
Jankers KP
Jansky Jy
Janus Two-faced
Japan(ese), Japanese drama Ainu, Burakumin, Daimio, Eta, Geisha, Genro, Gloss, Haiku, Heian, Hondo, Honshu, Issei, Kabuki, Kami, Kana, Kirimon, Lacquer, Mandarin, Meiji, Mikado, Mousmé, Mousmee, Nihon, Nip, Nippon, Nisei, No(h), Resin, Sansei, Satsuma, Shinto, Shogun, Taisho, Togo, Tycoon, Yamato, Yellow peril
Jape Jeer, Joke, Prank, Trick
Jar(ring) Albarello, Amphora, Bell, Canopus, Churr, Clash, Crock, Cruet, Din, Dissonant, Distune, Dolium, Enrough, Gallipot, Gas, Grate, Greybeard, Gride, Grind, Gryde, Humidor, Hydria, → JOLT, Kalpis, Kang, Kilner®, Leyden, Mason, Monkey, Off-key, Olla, Pint, Pithos, Pot(iche), Quarrel, Rasp, Rock, Screwtop, Shelta, Shock, Stamnos, Start, Stave, Stean, Steen, Stein, Tankard, Tinaja, Turn, Vessel, Water-monkey
Jargon Argot, Baragouin, Beach-la-mar, Buzzword, Cant, Chinese, Chinook, Eurobabble, Eurospeak, Geekspeak, Gobbledegook, Gobbledygook, Jive, Kennick, Legalese, Lingo, Lingoa geral, Lingua franca, Mumbo-jumbo, Netspeak, Newspeak, Officialese, Parlance, Patois, Patter, Patter-flash, Psychobabble, Shelta, Shoptalk, → SLANG, Technobabble, Technospeak, Vernacular
Jasmine Cape, Frangipani, Gelsemine, Gelsemium, Gessamine, Jessamy, Madagascar, Olea
Jasper Basanite, Bloodstone, Egyptian, Porcelain, Touchstone
Jaundice(d) Cynical, Icterus, Prejudiced, Sallow, Yellow
Jaunt Journey, Outing, Sally, Stroll, Swan, Trip
Jaunty Airy, Akimbo, Chipper, Debonair, Perky, Rakish
▷ **Jaunty** *may indicate* an anagram
Java man Pithecanthropus
Javelin Dart, Gavelock, Harpoon, Jereed, Jerid, Pile, Pilum, Spear

Jaw(s), Jawbone Blab, Chaft, Chap, Chat, Chaw, Cheek, Chide, Chin, Entry, Glass, Gnathic, Gnathite, Gonion, Hypognathous, Jabber, Jobe, Kype, Lantern, Lumpy, Mandible, Masseter, Maxilla, Mesial, Muzzle, Mylohyoid, Natter, Opisthognathous, Overbite, Overshot, Phossy, Pi, Premaxillary, Prognathous, Ramus, Rubber, Shark, Stylet, Underhung, Undershot, Wapper-jaw, Ya(c)kety-Ya(c)k
Jay Bird, J, Sirgang, Whisky-jack, Whisky-john
Jazz(er), Jazzman Acid, Afro-Cuban, Barber, Barrelhouse, Basie, Bebop, Blues, Boogie, Boogie-woogie, Bop, Cat, Cool, Dixieland, Enliven, Gig, Gutbucket, Hardbop, Hipster, Jive, Latin, Lick, Mainstream, Modern, New Orleans, Progressive, Ragtime, Riff, Scat, Skiffle, Slap base, Stomp, Swinger, Tailgate, Trad, Traditional, West Coast
Jealous(y) Envious, Green(-eyed), Green-eyed monster, Grudging, Zelotypia
Jean(s) Chinos, Denims, Levis®, Pants, Trousers, Wranglers®
Jeer(ing) Ballyrag, Barrack, Belittle, Birl, Boo, Burl, Digs, Fleer, Flout, Gird, Heckle, Hoot, Jape, Jibe, → **MOCK**, Rail, Razz, Ridicule, Scoff, Sling off, Sneer, Taunt, Twit, Yah
Jeeves Valet
Jehovah God, Lord, Yahve(h), Yahwe(h)
Jehovah's Witness Russellite
Jehu Charioteer, Driver
Jejune Arid, Barren, Dry, Insipid, Juvenile
Jelly Acaleph(a), Acalephe, Agar(-agar), Aspic, Brawn, Calf's foot, Chaudfroid, Comb, Cow-heel, → **EXPLOSIVE**, Flummery, Gel, Isinglass, Jam, Kanten, K-Y®, Liquid paraffin, Macedoine, Meat, Medusa, Mineral, Mould, Napalm, Neat's foot, Petroleum, Quiddany, Royal, Shape, Tunicin, Vaseline®, Vitreous humour
▷ **Jelly** *may indicate* an anagram
Jellyfish Acaleph(a), Acalephe, Aurelia, Blubber, Box, Cnidaria, Discomedusae, Discophora, Hydromedusa, Hydrozoa, Irukandji, Medusa, Mesogloea, Physalia, Planoblast, Portuguese man-of-war, Quarl, Scyphistoma, Scyphozoan, Sea-blubber, Sea-nettle, Sea-wasp, Strobila
Jemmy Betty, Crowbar, Lever
Jenkins Ear, Roy, Up
Jenny Ass, Lind, Long, Mule, Short, Spinner, Spinning, Spinster, Wren
Jeopardise, Jeopardy Danger, Double, Expose, Hazard, Peril, Risk
Jerboa Desert rat
Jeremiad Lament, Tragedy, Woe
Jeremy Fisher, Jerry
Jerk(y), Jerkily, Jerking, Jerks Aerobics, A salti, Bob, Braid, Cant, Diddle, Ebrillade, Flirt, Flounce, Gym(nastics), Hike, Hitch, Hoi(c)k, Idiot, Jut, Kant, Knee, PE, Peck, Physical, Saccade, Shove, Spasm, Start, Strobe, Surge, Switch, Sydenham's chorea, Tic, Toss(en), Tweak, → **TWITCH**, Wrench, Yank
Jerkin Body warmer, Jacket, Tabard
Jerome Kern, Vulgate
Jerry, Jerry-built Boche, Flimsy, Fritz, Hun, Kraut, Lego, Mouse, Po(t)
Jersey(s) Bailiwick, CI, Cow, Frock, Gansey, Guernsey, Kine, Lily, Maillot, Polo, Roll-neck, Singlet, → **SWEATER**, Sweatshirt, Yellow, Zephyr
Jerusalem Ariel, Hierosolymitan, Sion, Zion
Jess(e) James, Strap
Jest(er), Jesting Badinage, Barm, Baur, Bawr, Bourd(er), Buffoon, Clown, Cod, Comic, Droll, Gleek, Goliard, Inficete, Jape, Jig, Joker, Josh, Merryman, Miller, Motley, Patch, Quip, Raillery, Ribaldry, Rigoletto, Scogan, Scoggin, Sport, Toy,

Trinculo, Wag, Wit, Yorick

Jesuit Bollandist, Ignatius, Loyola, SJ

Jesus → CHRIST, Emmanuel, IHS, Immanuel, INRI, Isa, Jabers, Lord

Jet, Jet lag Airbus®, Aircraft, Beadblast, Black, Burner, Chirt, Douche, Fountain, Geat, Harrier, Ink, Jumbo, Plane, Pump, Soffione, Spirt, Spout, Spray, Spurt, Squirt, Stream, Time-zone disease, Time-zone fatigue, Turbine, Turbo, Vapour, Water

Jettison Discard, Dump, Flotsam, Jetsam, Lagan, Ligan

Jetty Groin, Mole, Pier, Wharf

Jew(ish), Jews Ashkenazi, Chas(s)id, Diaspora, Essene, Falasha, Grecian, Greek, Has(s)id, Hebrew, Hellenist, Kahal, Karaite, Kike, Landsman, Levite, Lubavitch, Maccabee, Marrano, Misnaged, Mitnag(g)ed, Nazarite, Neturei Karta, Nicodemus, Peculiar People, Pharisee, Refusenik, Sabra, Sadducee, Semite, Sephardim, Sheeny, Shemite, Shtetl, Smouch, Smouse, Tobit, Wandering, Yid(dish), Zealot

Jewel(s), Jeweller(y) Agate, Aigrette, Almandine, Artwear, Beryl, Bijouterie, Bling(-bling), Brilliant, Chrysoprase, Cloisonné, Cornelian, Costume, Crown, Diamond, Earbob, Ear-drop, Emerald, Ewe-lamb, Fabergé, Fashion, Ferron(n)ière, Finery, Garnet, → GEM, Girandole, Gracchi, Jade, Junk, Lherzolite, Marcasite, Navette, Olivine, Opal, Parure, Paste, Pavé, Pearl, Pendant, Peridot, Rivière, Rock, Rubin(e), Ruby, Sapphire, Sard, Scarab, Smaragd, Solitaire, Stone, Sunburst, Tom, Tomfoolery, Topaz, Torc, Treasure, Trinket

Jezebel Harlot, Loose, Whore

Jib Ba(u)lk, Boggle, Boom, → DEMUR, Face, Flying, Foresail, Genoa, Milk, Reest, Reist, Stay-sail, Storm

Jibe Barb, Bob, Correspond, Crack, Dig, Fling, Gleek, → JEER, Mock, Quip, Sarcasm, Slant, Taunt

Jiffy Mo, Pronto, Twinkling, Whiff

Jig(gle) Bob, Bounce, Dance, Fling, Frisk, Hornpipe, Jog, Juggle, Morris

Jigger(ed) Beat, Chigoe, Jolley, Ruin

Jill Ferret

Jilt Discard, Reject, Shed, Throw-over

Jim(my) Diamond, Dismal, Jas, Lucky, Pee, Piddle, Riddle

Jingle(r) Clerihew, Clink, Ditty, Doggerel, Rhyme, Tambourine, Tinkle

Jingo(ism) Odzooks, Patriot, War-rant

Jink Elude

Jinn(i) Afreet, Eblis, Genie, Marid, Spirit

Jinx Curse, Hex, Jonah, Kibosh, Moz(z), Spoil, Voodoo, Whammy

Jitter(s), Jittery Coggly, DT, Fidgets, Funk, Jumpy, Nervous, Willies

▷ **Jitter(s)** *may indicate* an anagram

Jo → LOVER, Sweetheart

Job(bing) Agiotage, Appointment, Berth, Career, Chore, Comforter, Crib, Darg, Errand, Gig, Hatchet, Homer, Inside, Métier, Mission, Nixer, Oratorio, Paint, Patient, Pensum, Place(ment), Plum, Position, Post, Problem, Pursuit, Put-up, Sinecure, Snow, Spot, Steady, → TASK, Ticket, Trotter, Truck, Undertaking, Work

▷ **Job** *may indicate* the biblical character

Jock Deejay, DJ, Mac, Sawn(e)y, Scot

Jockey Carr, Cheat, Diddle, Disc, Jostle, Jump, Lester, Manoeuvre, Mouse, Rider, Steve, Suicide, Swindle, Trick, Video, Winter

▷ **Jockey** *may indicate* an anagram

Jocose, Jocular, Jocund Cheerful, Debonair, Facete, Facetious, Jesting, Lepid, Scurril(e), Waggish

Joe(y), Joseph Addison, Dogsbody, GI, Kangaroo, Pal, Roo, Sloppy, Stalin, Surface, Trey

Jog(ger), Joggle, Jog-trot Arouse, Canter, Dog-trot, Dunch, Dunsh, Heich-how, Heigh-ho, Hod, Jiggle, Jolt, Jostle, Memo, Mosey, Nudge, Piaffe, Prompt, Ranke, Remind, Run, Shake, Shog, Tickle, Trot, Whig

Johannesburg Jozi

John(ny) Ajax, Augustus, Barleycorn, Bog, Bright, Brown, Bull, Bunyan, Cloaca, Collins, Doree, Dory, Elton, Evan, Gaunt, Gents, Gilpin, Groats, Halifax, Ia(i)n, Ivan, Lackland, Latecomer, Lav, Little, Loo, Peel, Prester, Stage-door, Throne, Toot, Tout, WC

Johnny-come-lately Upstart

Johnson Cham, Doctor, Idler

Join(er), Joined, Joining Abut, Accede, Accompany, Add, Affix, Alligate, Ally, Amalgamate, And, Annex, Associate, Attach, Braze, Butt-end, Cement, Cleave, Combine, Conflate, Conglutinate, Conjugate, Conjunct, Connect, Cope, → COUPLE, Dovetail, Engraft, Enlist, Enrol, Enter, Federate, Fuse, Glue, Graft, Hasp, Hitch, Hyphen, Include, Inosculate, Interconnect, Jugate, Knit, Link, Marry, Meet, Member, Menuisier, Merge, Mix, Mortar, Mortise, Oop, Oup, Overlaunch, Piece, Piecen, Rebate, Regelation, Rivet, Scarf, Seam, Se-tenant, Sew, Siamize, Snug, Solder, Splice, Spot-weld, Squirrel, Staple, Stylolite, Tenon, Unite, Wed, Weld, Yoke

Joint(ed) Ancon, Ankle, Arthrosis, Articular, Ball and socket, Bar, Baron, Butt, Capillary, Cardan, Carpus, Chine, Clip, Co, Cogging, Collar, Colonial goose, Commissure, Compression, Conjunction, Cuit, Cup and ball, Cut, Dive, Dovetail, Drumstick, Elbow, Enarthrosis, Entrecôte, Expansion, False, Fish, Gambrel, Genu, Gimmal, Gimmer, Ginglymus, Hainch, Haunch, Heel, Hinge, Hip, Hough, Huck, Hunker, J, Joggle, Jolly, Junction, Knee, Knuckle, Lap(ped), Lith, Loin, Marijuana, Meat, Mitre, Mortise, Mouse (buttock), Mouse-piece, Mutton, Mutual, Phalange, Phalanx, Pin, Popliteal, Psoas, Push-fit, Rabbet, Rack, Raphe, Reducer, Reefer, Rhaphe, Ribroast, Roast, Saddle, Scarf, Schindylesis, Seam, Shoulder, Silverside, Sirloin, Splice, Spliff, Stifle, Straight, Strip, Symphysis, Syndesmosis, T, Tarsus, T-bone, Tenon, Together, Toggle, Tongue and groove, Topside, Trochanter, Trochite, Undercut, Universal, Vertebra, Water, Wedging, Weld, Wrist

Joist Accouplement, Bar, Beam, Dormant, Ground plate, Groundsill, H-beam, I-beam, Rib, Rolled-steel, Sleeper, Solive, String, Trimmer

Joke(r), Joke-book, Joking Banter, Bar, Baur, Bawr, Booby-trap, Bourdon, Card, Chaff, Chestnut, → CLOWN, Cod, Comedian, Comic, Crack, Cut-up, Farceur, Farceuse, Fool, Fun, Funster, Gab, Gag, Glike, Guy, Have-on, Hazer, Hoax, Hum, Humorist, In fun, Jape, Jest, Jig, Jocular, Josh, Lark, Legpull, Merry-andrew, Merryman, Mistigris, One, One-liner, Pleasantry, Practical, Prank(ster), Pun, Punchline, Pundigrion, Quip, Rag, Rib-tickler, Rot, Sally, Scherzo, Scogan, Scoggin, Sick, Skylark, Sottisier, Squib, Standing, Wag, Wheeze, Wild, Wisecrack, Wit

Jollity, Jolly 'Arryish, Bally, Cheerful, Convivial, Cordial, Do, Festive, Galoot, Gaucie, Gaucy, Gawcy, Gawsy, Gay, Hilarious, Jocose, Jovial, Marine, Mirth, Rag, RM, Roger, Sandboy, Tar, Very

Jolt Bump, Jar, Jig-a jig, Jog(gle), Jostle, Jounce, Shake, Shog, Start

Jonah Hoodoo, Jinx, Moz(z)

Jones Davy, Emperor, Inigo

Jordan Pot, Urinal

Joris Horseman

▶ **Joseph** *see* JOE

Josh Chaff, Kid, Rib, Tease

Josiah Stamp, Wedgewood

Joss Incense, Luck, Stick

Jostle Barge, Bump, Compete, Elbow, Hog-shouther, Hustle, Push, Shoulder,
→ **SHOVE**, Throng
Jot(ter), Jotting(s) Ace, Fig, Iota, Memo, Mite, Note, Pad, Stime, Styme, Tittle, Whit
Journal Band(e), Blog, Chronicle, Daily, Daybook, Diary, Ephemeris, Gazette,
Hansard, Lancet, Log, Noctuary, Organ, Paper, Periodical, Pictorial, Punch, Rag,
Record, TES, TLS, Trade, Weblog
Journalism, Journalist Cheque-book, Columnist, Commentariat, Contributor,
Diarist, Diurnalist, Ed, Fleet St, Freelance, (GA) Sala, Gonzo, Hack, Hackery,
Hackette, Hatchetman, Inkslinger, Interviewer, Investigative, Keyhole, Lobby,
Muckraker, Newshound, Northcliffe, NUJ, Penny-a-liner, Pepys, Press(man),
Reporter, Reviewer, Scribe, Sob sister, Stead, Stringer, Wireman, → **WRITER**,
Yellow
Journey Circuit, Cruise, Errand, Expedition, Eyre, Foray, Grand Tour, Hadj, Hop,
Jaunce, Jaunse, Jaunt, Long haul, Mush, Odyssey, Passage, Periegesis, Ply, Raik,
Rake, Red-eye, Ride, Run, Sabbath-day's, Sentimental, Soup run, Tour, Travel,
Trek, Viatical, Walkabout
Journeyman Artisan, Commuter, Craftsman, Sterne, Yeoman
Joust Giust, Tilt, Tournament, Tourney
Jove Egad, Gad, Igad, Jupiter, Thunderer
Jovial Bacchic, Boon, Convivial, Cordial, Festive, Genial, Jolly
Jowl(s) Cheek, Chollers, Chops, Jaw
Joy(ful), Joyous Ah, Bliss, Blithe, Charmian, → **DELIGHT**, Dream, Ecstasy, Elation,
Exulting, Fain, Felicity, Festal, Frabjous, Glad, Glee, Gloat, Groove, Hah, Hey,
Jubilant, Nirvana, Rapture, Schadenfreude, Sele, Tra-la, Transport, Treat, Yippee
Joyce Haw Haw, Traitor
JP Beak, Queer cuffin, Quorum
Jubilant, Jubilation, Jubilee Celebration, Cock-a-hoop, Diamond, Ecstatic, Elated,
Exultant, Holiday, Joy, Triumphant
Judaism Semitism
Judas Double-crosser, Iscariot, Traitor, Tree
Judder Put-put, Shake, Vibrate
Jude Obscure
Judge(ment), Judges Absolute, Addoom, Adjudicator, Agonothetes, Alacus,
Alcalde, Arbiter, Areopagite, Aret(t), Arrêt, Assess, Assize, Auto-da-fé, Avizandum,
Banc, Brehon, Cadi, Calculate, Censure, Centumvirus, Circuit(eer), Common
Serjeant, Comparative, Connoisseur, Consider, Coroner, Court, Critic(ise), Daniel,
Dayan, Daysman, Deborah, Decern(e), Decide, Decision, Decreet, Deem(ster),
Dempster, Dicast, Dies non, Differential, Dikast, Discern(ment), District, Ephor,
Ermined, Estimate, Evaluate, Faisal, Faysal, Gauge, Gesse, Gideon, Good-sense,
Guess, Hakeem, Hakim, Hearing, Hold, Honour, Inky-smudge, Interlocutor,
J, Jeffreys, Jephthah, Justice, Justicier, Last, Line, Lud, Lynch, Minos, Mufti,
Non prosequitur, Nonsuit, Official Referee, Old Fury, Opine, Opinion, Ordinary,
Outfangthief, Panel, Paris, Podesta, Providence, Provisional, Puisne, Puny,
Reckon(ing), Recorder, Ref(eree), Regard, Rhadamanthus, Ruler, Samson, Samuel,
Sapience, Scan, Second guess, See, Sentence, Sentiment, Shallow, Sheriff, Sober,
Solomon, Sound, Suppose, Surrogate, Syndic, Tact, Think, Touch, Trior, Try,
Umpire, Value, Verdict, Ween, Weigh up, Wig, Wik, Wisdom, Worship
Judicious Critical, Discreet, Politic, Rational, Sage, Sensible, Shrewd, Sound
Judo, Judo costume Dojo, Gi(e), Kyu, Shiai
Jug(s) Amphora, Aquamanale, Aquamanile, Bellarmine, Bird, Blackjack, Bombard,
Breasts, Can, Cooler, Cream(er), Crock, Enghalskrug, Ewer, Flagon, Gaol, Gotch,

Greybeard, Growler, John Roberts, Malling, Measuring, Olpe, Pitcher, Pound, Pourer, Pourie, → **PRISON**, Quad, Quod, Shop, Stir, Tits, Toby, Urceolus
Juggle(r) Conjuror, Cook, Escamotage, Fake, Fire-eater
Juice, Juicy Aloe vera, Bacca, Cassareep, Cassaripe, Cremor, Current, Fluid, Fruity, Gastric, Hypocist, Ichor, Jungle, La(b)danum, Laser, Latex, Lush, Moist, Must, Oil, Pancreatic, Perry, Petrol, Ptisan, Rare, Sap, Snake, Soma, Spanish, Succ(o)us, Succulent, Tarantula, Thridace, Vril, Walnut, Zest
Juju Charm, Fetish
Jujube Christ's thorn, Lotus, Nabk, Padma, Sweet
Jukebox Nickelodeon
Julian Apostate
July Dogdays
Jumble Cast offs, Chaos, Conglomeration, Farrago, Garble, Huddle, Jabble, Lumber, Mass, Medley, Mingle-mangle, Mish-mash, Mixter-maxter, Mixtie-maxtie, Mixture, Mix(t)y-max(t)y, Pastiche, Praiseach, Printer's pie, Raffle, Ragbag, Scramble, Shuffle, Wuzzle
▷ **Jumbled** *may indicate* an anagram
Jumbo Aircraft, Elephant, Jet, Large-scale, Mammoth, OS, Plane
Jump(er), Jumping, Jumpy Aran, Assemble, Axel, Bate, Batterie, Boomer, Bound, Bungee, Bungy, Bunny-hop, Caper, Capriole, Cicada, Cicata, Crew-neck, Cricket, Croupade, Daffy, Desultory, Entrechat, Euro, Eventer, Flea, Fosbury flop, Gansey, Gazump, Gelande(sprung), Guernsey, Halma, Helicopter, High, Hurdle, Impala, Itchy, Jersey, Joey, Jolly, Kangaroo, Katydid, Knight, Lammie, Lammy, Leap(frog), Lep, Long, Lope, Lutz, Nervous, Nervy, Ollie, Parachute, Pig, Pogo, Polo-neck, Pounce, Prance, Prank, Pronking, Puissance, Quantum, Quersprung, Rap, Salchow, Saltatory, Saltigrade, Saltus, Scissors, Scoup, Scowp, Shy, Skip, Skipjack, Skydiver, → **SPRING**, Star, Start, Straddle, Sweater, Toe(-loop), Trampoline, Triple, Turtle-neck, Vau(l)t, V-neck, Water, Western roll
Jumping jack Pantine
Junction Abutment, Alloyed, Angle, Box, Bregma, Carfax, Close, Clover-leaf, Connection, Crewe, Crossroads, Diffused, Gap, Intersection, Joint, Josephson, Knitting, Meeting, Node, P-n, Point, Raphe, Spaghetti, Stage, Suture, T, Tight, Union
Juneberry Saskatoon, Shadbush
Jungle Asphalt, Blackboard, Boondocks, Bush, Concrete, Forest, Shola, Tangle
Junior Cadet, Chota, Cion, Dogsbody, Fils, Minor, Name-son, Office, Petty, Puisne, Scion, Sub(ordinate), Underling, Understrapper, Younger
Juniper Cade, Pencil-cedar, Red-cedar, Savin(e)
Junk(shop), Junkie Bric-à-brac, Chuck in, Jettison, Litter, Lorcha, Lumber, Refuse, Ship, Tagareen, Tatt, Trash, User
▷ **Junk** *may indicate* an anagram
Junker Prussian
Junket(ing) Beano, Creel, Custard, Feast, Picnic, Rennet, Spree
Juno Lucina
Junta Cabal, Council
Jupiter Jove, Newspaper
Jurassic Bajocian, Lias, R(h)aetic
Jurisdiction Authority, Bailiwick, Domain, Province, Soke(n)
Juror(s), Jury Array, Assize, Blue-ribbon, Dicast, Grand, Hung, Inquest, Judges, Mickleton, Old Fury, Pais, Panel, Party, Petit, Petty, Sail, Special, Strike, Tales, Tribunal, Venire, Venireman, Venue

Just(ice) Adeel, Adil, Alcalde, All, Aristides, Astraea, Balanced, Barely, Condign, Cupar, Deserved, Equal, Equity, E(v)en, Fair, Fair-minded, Forensic, Honest, Impartial, J, Jasper, Jeddart, Jethart, Jurat, Kangaroo, Mere, Moral, Natural, Nemesis, Newly, Nice, Only, Palm-tree, Piso, Poetic, Provost, Puisne, Pure and simple, Quorum, Recent, Restorative, Right(ful), Righteous, Rightness, Rough, Shallow, Silence, Simply, Solely, Sommer, Street, Themis, Tilt, Upright

Justifiable, Justification, Justify Apology, Autotelic, Avenge, Aver, Avowry, Clear, Darraign(e), Darrain(e), Darrayn, Defend, Deraign, Excusable, Explain, Grounds, Rationale, Reason, Vindicate, Warrant

Just so Exactly, Sic, Stories

Jut Beetle, Bulge, Overhang, Project, Protrude, Sail

Jute Burlap, Corchorus, Gunny, Hengist, Hessian, Horsa, Jew's mallow, Urena, Wool bale

Juvenile Childish, Teenage(r), Yonkers, Young, Younkers, Youth

Juxtaposition Parataxis

Kk

K Kelvin, Kilo, King, Kirkpatrick
K2 Dapsang, Godwin Austen
Kaffir Shares, Xosa
Kail, Kale Borecole, Cabbage, Cole, Curly-greens, Ninepins
Kaiser Doorn
Kaleidoscope Dappled, Motley, Myrioscope, Various
Kangaroo Bettong, Boodie-rat, Boomer, Boongary, Bounder, Brush, Cus-cus, Diprotodont, Euro, Forester, Joey, Macropodidae, Notothenium, Old man, Potoroo, Rat, Red, Steamer, Tree, Troop, Wallaby, Wallaroo
Kansas Sunflower
Kaolin Lithomarge
Karate Kung Fu, Shotokan, Wushu
Karma Destiny, Fate, Predestination
Kate Greenaway, Shrew
Kayak Bidarka
Kebab Cevapcici, Doner, Gyro, Satay, Sate, Shashli(c)k, Sosatie, Souvlakia
Keel Bilge, Bottom, Carina, Centreboard, Even, Faint, False, Fin, List, Overturn, Skeg(g), Sliding
Keen(ness), Keener Acid, Acute, Agog, Ardent, Argute, Aspiring, Astute, Athirst, Avid, Aygre, Bemoan, Bewail, Breem, Breme, Cheap, Coronach, Dash, Devotee, Dirge, Eager, Elegy, Enthusiastic, Fanatical, Fell, Greet, Grieve, Hone, Hot, Howl, Into, Lament, Mourn, Mustard, Mute, Narrow, Ochone, Ohone, Overfond, Partial, Peachy, Perceant, Persant, Pie, Raring, Razor, Ready, Red-hot, Rhapsodic, Sharp, Shrewd, Shrill, Snell, Thirsting, Threnodic, Thrillant, Trenchant, Ululate, Wail, Whet, Zeal(ous)
Keep(er), Keeping Ames, Armature, Austringer, Castellan, Castle, Celebrate, Chatelain(e), Citadel, Conceal, Conserve, Curator, Custodian, Custody, Depositary, Depository, Detain, Donjon, Escot, Fastness, Finder, Fort, Gaoler, Goalie, Guardian, Have, Hoard, → **HOLD**, Maintain, Nab, Net, Observe, Ostreger, Own, Park, Pickle, Preserve, Retain, Safe, Safeguard, Save, Stay, Stet, Stock, Store, Stow, Stumper, Support, Sustain, Tower, Warden, Withhold
Keep back Detain, Recoup, Reserve, Retard, Stave
Keepsake Memento, Souvenir, Token
Keep under Cow, Subdue, Submerge
Keg Barrel, Cask, Powder, Tub, Tun, Vat
Kelly('s) Eye, Gene, Ned
Kelvin Absolute, K
Ken Eyeshot, Know(ledge), Purview, Range
Kennel(s) Guard, Home, House, Shelter
Kent Lathe, SE, Superman
Kentuckian, Kentucky Chicken, Corn-cracker, Derby, KY

Kenya(n) Luo, Masai, Mau Mau
Kerala Nair, Nayar
Kerb Edge, Gutter, Roadside
Kerchief Babushka, Bandan(n)a, Headcloth, Romal, Scarf
Kernel Copra, Core, Corn, Grain, Nucleus, Pine, Praline, Prawlin
Kestrel Bird, Hawk, Keelie, Stallion, Staniel, Stannel, Stanyel, Windhover
Ket Carrion, Wool
Ketch Jack
Ketchup Relish, Sauce, Tomato
Kettle Boiler, Cauldron, Dixie, Dixy, Drum, Fanny, Pot, Tea, Turpin, War, Whistling
Key(s), Keyhole A, Ait, Allen, Alt, Ash, B, Backspace, Basic, C, Cay, Central,
    Chip, Church, Cipher, Claver, Clavis, Clew, Clink, Clue, Control, Crib, D, Del(ete),
    Dichotomous, Digital, Dital, Dominant, E, Enter, Esc(ape), Essential, F, Flat,
    Florida, Fruit, Function, G, Greek, High, Holm, Hot, Ignition, Important, Inch,
    Index, INS, Instrumental, Islet, Ivory, Kaie, King-pin, Latch, Legend, Linchpin,
    Locker, Low, Main, Major, Master, Minor, Note, Nut, Octachord, Opener,
    Oustiti, Outsiders, Pass(word), Passe-partout, Piano, Pipe, Pivot, Pony, Prong,
    Reef, Return, Semibreve, Shift, Signature, Skeleton, Spanner, Spline, Stimulate,
    Subdominant, Supertonic, Tab, Table, Tipsy, Tonal, Turning, USB, Vital, Watch,
    Water, Wedge, Woodruff, Yale®
Keyboard, Keypad Azerty, Console, Digitorium, Dvorak, Electronic, Manual,
    Martenot, Numeric(al), Piano, Pianola®, Qwerty, Spinet
Keyholder Occupant, Resident, Tenant, Warder
Key man Islander, Kingpin
Keynote Line, Mese, Theme, Tonic
Keystone Cops, Crux, PA, Pennsylvania, Quoin, Sagitta, Voussoir
Keyword Kwic, Sesame
Khan Aga, Chagan, Cham, Serai, Shere
Kick(ing) Back-heel, Bicycle, Boot, Buzz, Corner, Dribble, Drop, Fling, Flutter, Fly,
    Free, Frog, Garryowen, Goal, Grub, Hack, Heel, High, Hitch, Hoof, Lash, Nutmeg,
    Pause, Penalty, Pile, Place, Punce, Punt, Recalcitrate, Recoil, Recoyle, Savate,
    Scissors, Sixpence, Speculator, Spot, Spur, Spurn, Squib, Stab, Tanner, Tap, Thrill,
    Toe, Up and under, Vigour, Volley, Wince, Yerk, Zip
Kid(s) Arab, Befool, Billy, Brood, Cheverel, Chevrette, Child, Chit, Cisco, Con,
    Delude, Giles, Goat, Hircosity, Hoax, Hocus, Hoodwink, Hum, Joke, Leather, Mag,
    Minor, Misguide, Nipper, Offspring, Outwit, Pretend, Rag, Rib, Spoof, Suede,
    Sundance, → TEASE, Tot, Trick, Whiz(z), Wiz
Kidnap Abduct, Hijack, Plagium, Shanghai, Snatch, Spirit, Steal
Kidney(-shaped) Character, Mettle, Nature, Reins, Renal, Reniform, Sort, Type
Kildare Dr
Kill(ed), Killer, Killing Assassin, Attrit, Axeman, Battue, Behead, Biocidal,
    Boojum, Booth, Bump off, Butcher, Carnage, Carnifex, Category, Chance-medley,
    Choke, Comical, Croak, Crucify, Cull, Deep six, Despatch, Destroy, Electrocute,
    Euthanasia, Execute, Exhibition, Exterminate, Extirpate, For(e)do, Frag, Garotte,
    Germicide, Gun, Handsel, Hatchet man, Hilarious, Homicide, Honour, Humane,
    Ice, Immolate, Infanticide, Jugulate, K, Knacker, Knock off, Liquidate, Lynch,
    Mactation, Matador(e), Mercy, Misadventure, Mortify, Murder, Napoo, Necklace,
    Ninja, NK, Off, Orc(a), Penalty, Pesticide, -phage, Pick off, Pip, Predator, Prolicide,
    Quell, Quietus, Regrate, Sacrifice, Serial, Settle, Shochet, Shoot up, Slaughter,
    Slay(er), Slew, Smite, Snuff, Spike, Stifle, Stonker, Strangle, Swat, Tailor, Thagi,
    Thug(gee), Top, Toreador, Total, Vaticide, Veto, Waste, Zap

Killjoy Crab, Puritan, Sourpuss, Spoilsport, Trouble-mirth, Wowser
Kiln Lime, Oast, Oven
Kilometre Km, Verst
Kilt Drape, Filabeg, Fil(l)ibeg, Fustanella, Phil(l)abeg, Phil(l)ibeg, Plaid, Tartan
Kimono Yukata
Kin(sman) Ally, Family, Kith, Like, Nearest, Relation, Sib(b), Sybbe
Kind(ly) Akin, Amiable, Avuncular, Benefic, Benevolent, Benign, Boon, Breed,
   Brood, Brotherly, Category, Class, Clement, Considerate, Favourable, Gender,
   Generic, Generous, Genre, Gentle, Genus, Good, Gracious, Humane, Ilk, Kidney,
   Kin, Lenient, Manner, Modal, Nature, Nice, Sisterly, → **SORT**, Species, Strain,
   Strene, Thoughtful, Trine, Type, Understanding, Variety, Well-disposed, Ylke
Kindle, Kindling Accend, Fire, Ignite, Incense, Incite, Inflame, → **LIGHT**, Litter,
   Lunt, Stimulate, Teend, Tind, Tine, Touchwood, Tynd(e)
Kindness Aloha, Benevolence, Clemency, Favour, Humanity, Mitzvah, Ubuntu
Kindred Allied, Blood, Like, Related
King(s), Kingly Ard-ri(gh), Butcher, Coatcard, Cobra, Csar, Elvis, English, ER, Evil,
   Highness, Kong, Ksar, Majesty, Monarch, Negus, Pearly, Peishwa(h), Penguin,
   Peshwa, Pharaoh, Philosopher, Potentate, R, Ransom, Reigner, Rex, Rial, Roi,
   Royalet, Ruler, Ryal, Sailor, Seven, Shah, Shepherd, Shilling, Sovereign, Stork, Tsar,
   Tzar

KINGS

2 letters:	Lear	Lludd	Darius
GR	Loki	Louis	Duncan
Og	Nudd	Midas	Edmund
Re	Numa	Minos	Egbert
	Offa	Mpret	Farouk
3 letters:	Olaf	Ninus	Fergus
Asa	Otto	Osric	Harold
Erl	Saul	Penda	Hellen
Ine	Zeus	Priam	Hyksos
Lir		Rufus	Josiah
Log	5 letters:	Uther	Lucomo
Lud	Apple		Ludwig
Zog	Balak	6 letters:	Lycaon
	Basil	Acetes	Memnon
4 letters:	Brute	Aegeus	Miledh
Agag	Creon	Alaric	Nestor
Agis	Cyrus	Alfred	Oberon
Ahab	David	Alonso	Ogyges
Atli	Edgar	Amasis	Paphos
Brut	Edwin	Arthur	Peleus
Ceyx	Etzel	Atreus	Philip
Cnut	Gyges	Attila	Ramses
Cole	Herod	Baliol	Rhesus
Edwy	Hiram	Brutus	Utgard
Fahd	Idris	Canute	Xerxes
Inca	Ixion	Cheops	
Jehu	James	Clovis	7 letters:
Knut	Laius	Daneus	Acestes

Admetus	Stephen	Thutmose	Tyndareus
Athamas	Tarquin	Thyestes	Vortigern
Baldwin	Umberto	Tigranes	Wenceslas
Balliol		Zedekiah	
Beowulf	**8 letters:**		**10 letters:**
Busiris	Adrastus	**9 letters:**	Belshazzar
Caradoc	Aegyptus	Agamemnon	Cadwaladar
Cecrops	Alberich	Ahasuerus	Caractacus
Cepheus	Alcinous	Alexander	Erechtheus
Croesus	Cambyses	Athelstan	Ozymandias
Danaiis	Cophetua	Bretwalda	Wenceslaus
Diomede	Diomedes	Brian Boru	
Elidure	Endymion	Conchobar	**11 letters:**
Evander	Ethelred	Cunobelin	Charlemagne
Gentius	Hezekiah	Cymbeline	Hardicanute
Gordius	Jereboam	Ethelbert	Jehoshaphat
Gunther	Jonathan	Florestan	Melchizedek
Jupiter	Leonidas	Frederick	Prester John
Kenneth	Menander	Gambrinus	Sennacherib
Macbeth	Menelaus	Gargantua	Tutenkhamen
Malcolm	Milesius	Gilgamesh	
Oedipus	Nehemiah	Idomeneus	**12 letters:**
Porsena	Odysseus	Lionheart	Wayland Smith
Ptolemy	Pentheus	Lobengula	
Pyrrhus	Porsenna	Nabonidus	**14 letters:**
Rameses	Rehoboam	Pygmalion	Harold Harefoot
Regulus	Sarpedon	Ras Tafari	Nebuchadnezzar
Servius	Siegmund	Rodomonte	Sweyn Forkbeard
Sigmund	Sisyphus	Sigismund	Uther Pendragon
Solomon	Tantalus	Tarquinus	

Kingdom, Kingship Animal, An(n)am, Aragon, Arles, Armenia, Ashanti, Assyria, Austrasia, Babylonia, Barataria, Belgium, Bhutan, Bohemia, Brandenburg, Brunel, Burgundy, Castile, Cilicia, Connacht, Connaught, Dahomey, Dalriada, Darfur, Denmark, Dominion, Edom, Elam, Fes, Fez, Fife, Granada, He(d)jaz, Heptarchy, Hijaz, Jordan, Latin, Leon, Lesotho, Lydia, Macedon(ia), Mercia, Meroe, Middle, Mineral, Moab, Morocco, Murcia, Naples, Navarre, Nepal, Netherlands, Neustria, Noricum, Northumbria, Norway, Parthia, Plant, Pontic, Realm, Reame, Reign, Royalty, Ruritania, Saba, Samaria, Sardinia, Saudi Arabia, Sennar, Sheba, Siam, Spain, Sphere, Swaziland, Sweden, Thailand, Throne, Tonga, Two Sicilies, Ulster, Vegetable, Wessex, Westphalia, World
Kingfisher Alcyone, Halcyon
Kingmaker Neville, Warwick
King-of-arms Clarenc(i)eux, Garter, Lyon, Norroy (and Ulster)
King's evil Crewels, Cruels, Scrofula
Kingsley Amis, Charles
King's son Dauphin, Delphin, P, Prince
Kink(y) Bent, Buckle, Crapy, Curl, Enmeshed, Flaw, Gasp, Knurl, Null, Nurl, Odd, Perm, Perverted, Quirk, Twist, Wavy
▷ **Kink(y)** *may indicate* an anagram
Kinkajou Honey-bear, Potto

Kip(per) Cure, Dosser, Doze, Limey, Nap, → SLEEPER, Smoke
Kipling Beetle
Kirkpatrick K
Kismet Destiny, Fate, Karma, Predestination
Kiss(er), Kissing Air, Baisemain, Buss, Butterfly, Caress, Contrecoup, Cross, Deep,
　French, Lip, Mouth, Neck, Osculate, Pax(-board), Pax-brede, Peck, Pet, Plonker, Pree,
　Salue, Salute, Smack(er), Smooch, Smouch, Snog, Spoon, Suck face, Thimble, X, Yap
Kit Accoutrement, Christopher, Clobber, Clothes, Dress, Housewife, Jack, Layette,
　Marlowe, Mess, → OUTFIT, Rig, Set, Slops, Sportswear, Strip, Tackle, Uniform
Kitchen Caboose, Cookhouse, Cuisine, Galley, Scullery, Soup, Thieves
Kite Belly, Bird, Box, Chil, Crate, Dragon, Elanet, Forktail, Gled(e), Hawk, Milvus,
　Paunch, Puttock, Rokkaku
Kitten(ish) Cute, Kindle, Sexy
Kittiwake Bird, Gull, Hacklet, Haglet
Kitty Ante, Cat, Fisher, Float, Fund, Jackpot, Pool, Pot, Tronc
Kiwi Apteryx, Chinese gooseberry, NZ, Ratitae
Klu-Klux-Klan Nightrider
Knack Art, Faculty, Flair, Forte, Gift, Hang, Instinct, → TALENT, Technique, Trick
Knacker Castanet, Exhaust
Knapsack Musette
Knapweed Matfelon
Knave(ry) Bezonian, Bower, Boy, Cad, Card, Coatcard, Coistril, Coystril, Custrel,
　Dog, Drôle, Fripon, Jack(-a-napes), Jock, Loon, Makar, Maker, Nob, Noddy, Pam,
　Pur, Rapscallion, → RASCAL, Recreant, Ropery, Scoundrel, Skelm, Taroc, Tarot,
　Tom, Treachery, Varlet, Villain
Knead Conche, Malax(ate), Massage, Mould, Pug, Pummel, Work
Knee(s), Knee-cap, Knee-pan Genicular, Genu, Hock, Housemaid's, Lap,
　Marrowbones, Patella, Poleyn, Popliteal, Punch, Rotula, Whirl bone
Kneel(er) Defer, Genuflect, Hassock, Kowtow, Prie-dieu, Truckle
Knell Bell, Curfew, Dirge, Peal, Ring, Toll
Knicker(bocker), Knickers Bloomers, Culottes, Directoire, Irving, Panties,
　Plus-fours, Shorts, Trousers
Knick-knack Bagatelle, Bibelot, Bric-à-brac, Gewgaw, Pretty(-pretty), Quip, Smytrie,
　Toy, Trangam, Trifle, Victoriana
Knife Anelace, Athame, Barlow, Barong, Bistoury, Blade, Boline, Bolo, Bolster,
　Bowie, Bush, Butterfly, Carver, Carving, Case, Catling, Chakra, Chiv, Clasp, Cleaver,
　Couteau, Cradle, Cuttle, Cutto(e), Da(h), Dagger, Dirk, Fleam, Flick, Fruit, Gamma,
　Gully, Hay, Hunting, Jockteleg, Kard, Keratome, Kukri, Lance(t), Machete, Matchet,
　Moon, Oyster, Palette, Pallet, Panga, Paper, Parang, Peeler, Pen, Pigsticker, Pocket,
　Putty, Scalpel, Scalping, Sgian-dhu, Sgian-dubh, Sheath, Shiv, Simi, Skean-dhu,
　Slash, Snee, Snickersnee, Spade, Stab, Stanley, Steak, Sticker, Stiletto, Switchblade,
　Table, Toothpick, Tranchét, Trench
Knight(hood) Accolon, Aguecheek, Alphagus, Amfortas, Artegal, Balan, Banneret,
　Bayard, Bedivere, Black, Bliant, Bors, Britomart, Caballero, Calidore, Cambel,
　Caradoc, Carpet, Cavalier, Chevalier, Companion, Crusader, Douceper, Douzeper,
　Dub, Equites, Errant, Galahad, Gallant, Gareth, Garter, Gawain, Geraint, Giltspurs,
　Grey, Guyon, Hospitaller, Kay, KB, KBE, Kemper, KG, Lamorack, La(u)ncelot,
　Launfal, Lionel, Lochinvar, Lohengrin, Maecenas, Malta, Mark, Medjidie, Melius,
　Modred, Mordred, N, Noble, Orlando, Paladin, Palmerin, Palomides, Papal,
　Paper, Parsifal, Perceforest, Perceval, Percival, Pharamond, Pinel, Precaptory,
　Preux chevalier, Red Cross, Ritter, Round Table, St Columba, Samurai, Sir,

Tannhauser, Templar, Teutonic, Tor, Trencher, Tristan, Tristram, Valvassor, Vavasour, White

Knit(ting), Knitwear Aran, Contract, Crochet, Double, Entwine, Fair Isle, Hosiery, Intarsia, Interlock, Intertwine, K, Mesh, Porosis, Purl, Seam, Set, Stockinet, Weave, Wrinkle

Knob(by) Berry, Boll, Boss, Botoné, Bottony, Bouton, Bur(r), Cam, Caput, Cascabel, Croche, Gear, Handle, Hill, Inion, Knub, Knur(r), Node, Noop, Pellet, Pommel, Protuberance, Pulvinar, Push-button, Snib, Snub, Snuff, Stud, Torose, Tuber, Tuner

Knobless Enodal

Knock(er), Knock down, off, out, Knockout Bang, Beaut, Biff, Blow, Bonk, Bump, Ca(a), Chap, Clash, Clour, Collide, Con, Criticise, Dad, Daud, Dawd, Degrade, Denigrate, Deride, Dev(v)el, Ding, Dinnyhauser, Dod, Etherise, Eyeful, Floor, Grace-stroke, → **HIT**, Innings, King-hit, KO, Lowse, Lowsit, Mickey Finn, Opportunity, Pan, Pink, Quietus, Rap, Rat-tat, Six, Skittle, Spat, Steal, Stop, Strike, Stun(ner), Tap, Technical, Thump, Tonk, Wow

Knock-kneed Valgus

Knot(ted), Knotty Apollo, Baff, Bend, Bind, Blackwall hitch, Bow, Bowline, Bur(r), Burl, Carrick-bend, Cat's paw, Clinch, Clove hitch, Cluster, Crochet, Diamond hitch, Englishman's, Entangle, Figure of eight, Fisherman's (bend), Flat, French, Gnar, → **GNARL**, Gordian, Granny, Half-hitch, Harness hitch, Hawser-bend, Herculean, Hitch, Interlace, Knag, Knap, Knar, Knur(r), Loop, Love(r's), Macramé, Macrami, Magnus hitch, Marriage-favour, Matthew Walker, Mouse, Nirl, Node, Nowed, Nub, Nur(r), Overhand, Peppercorn, Picot, Porter's, Problem, Prusik, Quipu, Reef, Rolling hitch, Root, Rosette, Running, Seizing, Sheepshank, Sheetbend, Shoulder, Shroud, Sleave, Slip, Slub, Spurr(e)y, Square, Stevedore's, Surgeon's, Sword, Tangle, Tat, Thumb, Tie, Timberhitch, Torose, Truelove, Tubercle, Turk's head, Virgin, Wale, Wall, Weaver's (hitch), Windsor, Witch

Know(how), Knowing(ly), Knowledge(able), Known Acquaintance, Autodidactic, Aware, Carnal, Cognition, Common, Compleat, Comprehend, Cred, Epistemics, Erudite, Expertise, Famous, Fly, Gnosis, Gnostic, Have, Hep, Hip, Info, Information, Insight, Intentional, Intuition, Jnana, Ken, Kith, Kydst, Lare, Light, Lore, Mindful, Omniscience, On, On to, Pansophy, Paragnosis, Party, Polymath, Positivism, Privity, Realise, Recherché, → **RECOGNISE**, Sapient, Savvy, Science, Scienter, Scilicet, Sciolism, Sciosophy, Shrewd, Smattering, Suss, Technology, Telegnosis, Understand(ing), Up, Versed, Wat(e), Weet(e), Well-informed, Well-read, Wis, Wise, Wist, Wit, Wonk, Wot

Know-all Arrogant, Besserwisser, Bumptious, Cognoscenti, Pansophist, Polymath, Poseur, Smart alec(k), Smart-arse, Smart-ass, Wiseacre

Knuckle (bone) Apply, Dolos, Fist, Joint, Ossein, Submit

Koko List

Kookaburra Laughing jackass, Settler's clock

Kop Spion

Koran Scripture, Sura(h)

Korea(n) Chosen, ROK

Kosher Approved, Genuine, Legitimate, Real

Kremlin Fortress

Kri Masora

Krypton Kr

Kudos Credit, Glory, Praise

Kurd Yezidi

Kyanite Disthene

Ll

L Latitude, League, Learner, Left, Length, Liberal, Lima, Litre, Long, Luxembourg, Pound
La Indeed, My
Label Badge, Band, Book-plate, Brand, Crowner, Designer, Docket, File, Identifier, Indie, Mark, Own, Seal, Sticker, Style, Tab, Tag, Tally, Ticket, Trace
Labiate Catmint, Hoarhound, Horehound
Laboratory Lab, Language, Skylab, Space-lab, Studio, Workshop
Labour(er), Laboured, Laborious Aesthetic, Agonise, Arduous, Begar, Birth, Carl, Casual, Chore, Churl, Coolie, Corvée, Cottager, Cottar, Culchie, Dataller, Day, Direct, Docker, Dwell, Emotional, Forced, Gandy-dancer, Ganger, Gibeonite, Grecian, Grind, Grunt, Hard, Hercules, Hod carrier, Hodge, Hodman, Ida, Indirect, Job, Journeyman, Kanaka, Katorga, Leaden, Manpower, Militant tendency, Moil, Navvy, New, Okie, Operose, Opposition, Pain, Peon, Pioneer, Prole, Redneck, Roll, Rouseabout, Roustabout, Rouster, Sisyphean, Slave, Spalpeen, Statute, Stertorous, Stint, Strive, Sudra, Swagman, Sweated, Task, Tedious, The grip, The lump, → TOIL(S), Toss, Travail, Uphill, Vineyard, Wetback, → WORK(ER), Workmen, Yakka
Labrador Innu, Retriever, Tea
Labyrinth Daedalus, Maze, Mizmaze, Warren, Web
▷ **Labyrinthine** *may indicate* an anagram
Lac Lacquer, Lakh, Resin, Shellac, Tomans
Lace, Lacy Alençon, Babiche, Beat, Blonde, Bobbin, Bone, Bourdon, Brussels, Chantilly, Cluny, Colbertine, Dash, Dentelle, Duchesse, Filet, Galloon, Guipure, Honiton, Inweave, Irish, Jabot, Lash, Macramé, Malines, Mechlin, Mignonette, Mode, Net, Orris, Pearlin, Picot, Pillow, Point, Queen Anne's, Reseau, Reticella, Ricrac, Rosaline, Seaming, Shoestring, Shoe-tie, Spiderwork, Spike, Stay, Tat(ting), Tawdry, Thrash, Thread, Torchon, Trim, Trol(le)y, Truss, Tucker, Valenciennes, Venise, Weave, Welt, Window-bar
Lacerate(d) Ganch, Gash, Gaunch, Maul, Rent, Rip, Slash, Tear
Lachrymose Maudlin, Niobe, Tearful, Water-standing, → WEEPY
Lack(ing), Lacks Absence, Aplasia, Bereft, Dearth, Famine, Ha'n't, Insufficiency, Manqué, Minus, → NEED, Poverty, Privation, Remiss, Sans, Shortfall, Shy, Void, Want
Lackadaisical Languid, Listless, Torpid
Lackaday Haro
Lackey Boots, Flunkey, Moth, Page, Poodle, Satellite, Skip-kennel
Lacklustre Dull, Insipid, Matt
Lack of confidence Doubt, Scepsis
Laconic Blunt, Close-mouthed, Curt, Spartan, Succinct, Terse
Lacquer Coromandel, Enamel, Hair(spray), Japan, Shellac, → VARNISH
Lad Boy(o), Bucko, Callan(t), Chiel(d), Child, Geit, Gyte, Knight, Loonie, Master,

Nipper, Shaver, Stableman, Stripling, Tad, Whipper-snapper
Ladder(y) Accommodation, Aerial, Bucket, Companion, Companionway, Etrier, Extension, Fish, Jack, Jacob's, Pompier, Potence, Rope, Run, Salmon, Scalado, Scalar, Scaling, Sea, Squash, Step, Stie, Sty, Stye, Trap, Turntable

▸ **Lade** *see* **LOAD**

Ladle Bail, Dipper, Punch, Scoop, Shank, Toddy

Lady, Ladies Baroness, Bevy, Bountiful, Burd, Dame, Dark, Dinner, Don(n)a, Duenna, Female, First, Frau, Frow, Gemma, Godiva, Hen, Khanum, Leading, Luck, Maam, Madam(e), Martha, Memsahib, Muck, Nicotine, Peeress, Señora, Shopping bag, Signora, Tea, WC, White, Windermere

▷ **Lady** *may indicate* an '-ess' ending

Ladybird Cushcow, Hen, Vedalia

▷ **Ladybird** *may indicate* a female of a bird family

Ladykiller Bluebeard, Lothario, Masher, Wolf

Lady of the Lake Vivian

Lady's fingers Gumbo, Okra

Lady's maid Abigail

Lag(gard) Culture, Dawdle, Delay, Drag, Flag, Hysteresis, Inmate, Jailbird, Jet, Leng, → **LINGER**, Loiter, Prisoner, Retard, Slowcoach, Slowpoke, Time, Tortoise, Trail

Lager Pils(e)ner

Lagoon Aveiro, Barachois, Haff, Pontchartrain, Pool, Salina, Saline, Vistula

▸ **Laic, Laid** *see* **LAY**

Lair Couch, Den, Earth, Haunt, Hideaway, Kennel, Lodge, Warren

Lake(s) Alkali, Basin, Bayou, Carmine, Cirque, Cowal, Crater, Crimson, Cut off, Finger, L, Lacustrine, Lagoon, Lagune, → **LOCH**, Lochan, Lough, Madder, Mead, Mere, Nyanza, Ox-bow, Poets, Pool, Red, Reservoir, Salina, Salt, Shott, Soda, Tank, Tarn, Turlough, Vlei, Wine

---

LAKES

2 letters:	Taal	Myall	Barlee
No	Tana	Nam Co	Bienne
	Thun	Neagh	Bitter
3 letters:		Nyasa	Broads
Ewe	**5 letters:**	Onega	Cayuga
Van	Atlin	Pitch	Corrib
	Chott	Playa	Edward
4 letters:	Cowan	Poopo	Geneva
Amin	Frome	Pskov	Kariba
Bala	Garda	Sevan	Kittle
Biel	Gatun	Tahoe	Ladoga
Bled	Great	Taupo	Lugano
Chad	Huron	Tsana	Malawi
Como	Ilmen	Urmia	Miveru
Erie	Leman	Volta	Mobutu
Erne	Leven		Monona
Eyre	Lower	**6 letters:**	Nakuru
Kivu	Malar	Albert	Nam Tso
Mead	Morar	Argyle	Nyassa
Nyos	Mungo	Averno	Oneida
Pink	Mweru	Baikal	Peipus

Poyang	Vattern	**9 letters:**	Hawes Water
Rudolf		Athabasca	Ijsselmeer
Saimaa	**8 letters:**	Bangweulu	Miraflores
St John	Balkhash	Champlain	Mistassini
Te Anau	Bodensee	Constance	Of the Woods
Tekapo	Carnegie	Ennerdale	Okeechobee
Vanern	Dongting	Everglade	Okefenokee
Varese	Gairdner	Genfersee	Serpentine
Zurich	Grasmere	Great Bear	Tanganyika
	Issyk-kul	Great Salt	Washington
7 letters:	Kinneret	Innisfree	Windermere
Amadeus	Maggiore	Killarney	
Aral Sea	Manitoba	Macquarie	**11 letters:**
Avernus	Masurian	Manapouri	Lesser Slave
Axolotl	Menindee	Maracaibo	Paralimnion
Balaton	Michigan	Naumachia	Stanley Pool
Bizerte	Naumachy	Neuchatel	
Dead Sea	Okanagan	Nicaragua	**12 letters:**
Iliamna	Onondaga	Nipissing	Derwentwater
Katrine	Regillus	Serbonian	Memphremagog
Koko Nor	Reindeer	Thirlmere	Waikaremoana
Lucerne	Schwerin	Trasimene	Winnipegosis
Managua	Superior	Trasimono	
Mendota	Tiberias	Ullswater	**13 letters:**
Nipigon	Titicaca	Wairarapa	Bassenthwaite
Ontario	Tonle Sap	Wast Water	Coniston Water
Red Deer	Tungting	Winnebago	Crummock Water
Rotorua	Veronica	Ysselmeer	Pontchartrain
Sempach	Victoria		
Shkoder	Wakatipu	**10 letters:**	**14 letters:**
St Clair	Wanawaka	Buttermere	Chiputneticook
Toronto	Winnipeg	Chautawqua	Disappointment
Torrens		Clearwater	Ennerdale Water
Turkana		Great Slave	

Lake-dwelling Crannog
Lakeland Cumbria
Lam Flee, Scram
Lama Dalai, Karmapa, Panchen, Tashi
Lamb(skin) Baa, Barometz, Beaver, Budge, Bummer, Cade, Canterbury, Caracul, Cosset, Ean(ling), Elia, Fat, Fell, Grit, Innocent, Keb, Larry, Noisette, Paschal, Persian, Poddy, Rack, Shearling, Target, Yean(ling)
Lambent Flickering, Glowing, Licking
Lambert Constant
Lame(ness) Accloy, Claude, Cripple, Crock, Game, Gammy, Gimp(y), Halt, Hamstring, Hirple, Hors de combat, Maim, Main, Spavined, Springhalt, Stringhalt, Weak
Lament(able), Lamentation, Lamenter Bemoan, Bewail, Beweep, Complain, Croon, Cry, Dirge, Dumka, Dump, Elegy, Funest, Jeremiad, Jeremiah, Keen, Meane, Mein, Mene, Moon, Mourn, Ochone, Paltry, Piteous, Plain, Repine, Sigh, Sorry, Threne, Threnody, Ululate, → **WAIL**, Welladay, Wel(l)away, Yammer

Lamia Deadnettle
Lamina(te) Film, Flake, Folium, Formica®, Lamella, Layer, Plate, Scale, Table, Veneer
Lamp(s) Aladdin's, Aldis, Anglepoise, Arc, Argand, Bowat, Bowet, Buat, Cru(i)sie, Cru(i)zie, Crusy, Davy, Daylight, Eye, Eyne, Flame, Fluorescent, Fog, Geordie, Glow, Head, Hurricane, Incandescent, Induction, Kudlik, Lampion, Lantern, Lava, Lucigen, Mercury vapour, Miner's, Moderator, Neon, Nernst, Nightlight, Padella, Photoflood, Pilot, Platinum, Quartz, Reading, Riding, Safety, Sanctuary, Scamper, Searchlight, Signal, Sodium, Sodium-vapour, Spirit, Standard, Street, Stride, Stroboscope, Sun, Tail, Tantalum, Tiffany, Tilley, Torchier(e), Tungsten, Uplight(er), Veilleuse, Xenon
Lamplighter Leerie, Spill
Lampoon Caricature, Parody, Pasquil, Pasquin(ade), Satire, Skit, Squib
Lamprey Hag, Lampern, Sandpride
Lancaster Burt, Osbert
Lance Dart, Harpoon, Morne, Pesade, Pike, Prisade, Prisado, Rejôn, Spear, Speisade, Thermic, White arm
Lancelet Amphioxus
Lancer Bengal, Picador, Uhlan
Lancet Fleam
Land(s), Landed Acreage, Aina, Alight, Alluvion, Arpent, Bag, Beach, Bigha, Bovate, Byrd, Carse, Carucate, Cavel, Conacre, Corridor, Country, Croft, Crown, Curtilage, Debatable, Demain, Demesne, Disbark, Disembark, Ditch, Doab, Dock, Earth, Edom, Enderby, Estate, Fallow, Farren, Farthingland, Fee, Feod, Feoff, Feud, Fief, Freeboard, Gair, Glebe, Gondwanaland, Gore, Graham, Ground, Hide, Holding, Holm, Holy, Horst, Ind, Innings, Isthmus, Kingdom, La-la, Laurasia, Lea, Leal, Ley, Light, Link, Machair, Maidan, Manor, Marginal, Marie Byrd, Mesnalty, Métairie, Moose pasture, Morgen, Mortmain, Nation, Never-never, Nod, No man's, Odal, Onshore, Oxgang, Oxgate, Pakahi, Palmer, Pangaea, Panhandle, Parcel, Pasture, Peneplain, Peneplane, Peninsula, Piste, Plot, Ploughgate, Point, Polder, Pr(a)edial, Premises, Private, Promised, Property, Public, Purlieu, Queen Maud, Real estate, Realm, Realty, Reservation, Roman candle, Rundale, Runrig, Rupert's, Savanna(h), Set-aside, Settle, Spit, Swidden, Tack, Taluk, Terra(e), Terra-firma, Terrain, Territory, Thwaite, Tie, Tir na n'Og, Touchdown, Turbary, Tye, Udal, Unship, Ure, Van Diemen's, Veld(t), Victoria, Wainage, Waste, Whenua, Wilkes, Yird
▶ **Landfall** see **LANDSLIDE**
Landing (craft, stair, system) Autoflare, Crash, Forced, Gallipoli, Gha(u)t, Half, Halfpace, Hard, Instrument, LEM, Module, Pancake, Pier, Quay, Quayside, Soft, Solar, Sollar, Sol(l)er, Splashdown, Three-point, Three-pricker, Touchdown, Undercarriage
Landlock Embay
Landlord, Land owner Absentee, Balt, Boniface, Bonnet laird, Copyholder, Eupatrid, Fiar, Franklin, Herself, Host, Innkeeper, Junker, Laird, Lessor, Letter, Licensee, Patron, Patroon, Proprietor, Publican, Rachman, Rentier, Squattocracy, Squire, Squirearchy, Squireen, Thane, Zamindar(i), Zemindar
Landmark Meith, Watershed
Landmass Laurasia
Land right Emphyteusis
Landscape Karst, Paysage, Picture, Saikei, Scene, Vista
Landslide, Landfall Avalanche, Earthfall, Éboulement, Lahar, Scree, Slip

Landsman Lubber
Land tenure Frankalmoign, Raiyatwari, Rundale, Runrig, Ryotwari
Lane Boreen, Bus, Corridor, Crawler, Drangway, Drury, Express, Fast, Fetter, Gut,
Inside, Loan, Lois, Loke, Memory, Middle, Mincing, Nearside, Offside, Outside,
Overtaking, Passage, Petticoat, Pudding, Ruelle, Sea-road, Slow, Twitten, Twitting,
Vennel, Wynd
Langerhans Insulin, Islets
Language(s) Argot, Artificial, Assembly, Auxiliary, Basic, Body, Cant, Centum,
Command, Community, Computer, → COMPUTER LANGUAGE, Dead, Dialect,
Formal, Georgian, High-level, Hobson-Jobson, Humanities, Idioglossia, Idiolect,
Idiom, Inclusive, Jargon, Langue, Ledden, Lingo, Lingua franca, Macaroni,
Machine code, Mellowspeak, Meta-, Mixed, Modern, Mother tongue, Native,
Natural, Netspeak, Newspeak, Novelese, Object, Officialese, Page description,
Parlance, Philology, Pidgin, Plain, Polysynthetic, Pragmatics, Private, Procedural,
Programming, Prose, Query, Register, Relay, Rhetoric, Sea-speak, Second, Sign,
Sociolect, → SPEECH, Strong, Style, Symbolic, Synthetic, Target, Technobabble,
Telegraphese, Tone, → TONGUE, Tropology, Tushery, Union, Vedic, Verbiage,
Vernacular, Vocabulary, Wawa, Words, World

LANGUAGES

3 letters:
Ada, Bat, Edo, Fur, Giz, Gur, Ibo, Ido, Kwa, Luo, Mam, Mon, Neo, San, Tai, Tiv, Twi

Krio, Lozi, Manx, Mari, Maya, Motu, Naga, Nuba, Nupe, Pali, Pedi, Pict, Shan, Susu, Taal, Thai, Tshi, Tupi, Urdu

Cajun, Carib, Chewa, Cobol, Dogon, Doric, Fanti, Farsi, Galla, Ganda, Gondi, Hausa, Hindi, Hokan, Indic, Joual, Kafri, Koine, Kriol, Kuo-yu, Ladin, Lamba, Lamut, Latin, Lubon, Lunda, Lyele, Malay, Mande, Maori

Mayan, Munda, Nguni, Norse, Oriya, Oscan, Papua, P-Celt, Sakai, Sango, Satem, Saxon, Shona, Shono, Shuar, Sinha, Sioux, Sotho, Suomi, Swazi, Taino, Tajik, Tamil, Temne, Te reo, Tigre, Tonga, Turki, Ugric, Venda

4 letters:
Ainu, Avar, Cham, Dani, Erse, Geez, Igbo, Inca, Innu, Komi, Xosa, Zulu, Zuni

5 letters:
Aleut, Aryan, Azeri, Balti, Bantu, Batak

Vogul
Welsh
Wolof
Xhosa
Yakut
Yuman
Yupik

6 letters:
Adyahe
Adygei
Adyghe
Altaic
Arabic
Aranda
Aymara
Basque
Basutu
Berber
Bihari
Bokmal
Brahui
Breton
Celtic
Chadic
Coptic
Creole
Cymric
Dardic
Divehi
Eskimo
Evenki
Fantee
Fijian
Finnic
Fulani
Gaelic
Gagauz
German
Gullah
Hebrew
Herero
Italic
Ladino
Lahnda
Lakota
Lepcha
Lu-wian
Lycian
Lydian
Manchu

Micmac
Mishmi
Na-Dene
Nepali
Novial
Nubian
Ostyak
Pahari
Paiute
Pakhti
Papuan
Pashto
Pashtu
Polish
Pushto
Pushtu
Romany
Rwanda
Salish
Shelta
Sindhi
Siouan
Slovak
Somali
Strine
Tanoan
Tartar
Telegu
Telugu
Tigray
Tongan
Tsonga
Tswana
Tuareg
Tungus
Turkic
Udmurt
Ugrian
Uralic
Yoruba
Zyrian

7 letters:
Adamawa
Amerind
Amharic
Aramaic
Ashanti
Austric
Bengali
Bislama

Cabiric
Caddoan
Catalan
Chaldee
Chinook
Chuvash
Cushite
Dzongka
Elamite
Flemish
Frisian
Gagauzi
Gaulish
Hamitic
Hin Motu
Hittite
Janlish
Japlish
Kannada
Khoisan
Kirundi
Kurdish
Kushite
Lallans
Laotian
Lingala
Luganda
Malinke
Marathi
Miao-Yao
Mingrel
Miskito
Mordvin
Nahuatl
Nauruan
Ndebele
Nilotic
Nyungar
Oceanic
Ossetic
Ottoman
Pahlavi
Pehlevi
Pictish
Prakrit
Punjabi
Pushtoo
Quechua
Romance
Romanes
Romansh

Saharan
Samnite
Samoyed
Semitic
Serbian
Servian
Sesotho
Sinhala
Sinitic
Slovene
Sogdian
Sorbian
Spanish
Sudanic
Swahili
Swedish
Tagalog
Tahitan
Tibetan
Tlingit
Turkish
Turkmen
Umbrian
Uralian
Venetic
Volapuk
Voltaic
Walloon
Wendish
Yerkish
Yiddish

8 letters:
Akkadian
Albanian
Arawakan
Assamese
Bulgaric
Cheremis
Cherkess
Chibchan
Chichewa
Croatian
Cushitic
Dzongkha
Ethiopic
Etrurian
Etruscan
Faliscan
Fanagalo
Filipino

Frankish	Tigrinya	Muskogean	Serbo-Croat
Friesian	Tshiluba	Nostratic	Singhalese
Goidelic	Tungusic	Onondagan	Synchronic
Gujarati	Turanian	Provençal	Ural-Altaic
Gujerati	Turkoman	Putonghua	Uto-Aztecan
Gurkhali	Tuvaluan	Roumanian	Vietnamese
Hiri-Motu	Ugaritic	Roumansch	
Illyrian	Volscian	Sabellian	**11 letters:**
Japhetic	Wakashan	Semi-Bantu	Belarussian
Javanese	Warlpiri	Sinhalese	Celtiberean
Judezono	Yugoslav	Sinhalese	Dagestanian
Jugoslav		Tocharian	Interglossa
Kashmiri	**9 letters:**	Tokharian	Interlingua
Kingwana	Abkhazian	Tokharish	Kordofanian
Kolarian	Afrikaans	Tungurian	Langobardic
Kwakiutl	Algonkian	Ukrainian	Micronesian
Landsmal	Algonquin	Ursprache	Nilo-Saharan
Lusatian	Anatolian	Winnebago	Old Paissian
Malagasy	Brythonic		Osco-Umbrian
Mandarin	Cantonese	**10 letters:**	Pama-Nyungan
Mongolic	Chari-Nile	Algonquian	Sino-Tibetan
Mon-Khmer	Cheremiss	Araucanian	Sranantongo
Nez Perce	Cingalese	Athabascan	Tessaraglot
Ossetian	Diglossia	Azerbayani	Tupi-Guarani
Penutian	Dravidian	Beach-la-Mar	
Pilipino	Esperanto	Bêche-la-Mar	**12 letters:**
Polabian	Esthonian	Caprolalia	Billingsgate
Rhaetian	Euskarian	Circassian	Gallo-Romance
Romanian	Franglais	Diachronic	Idiom neutral
Romansch	Goidhelic	Eteocretan	Indo-European
Rumansch	Gujarathi	Finno-Ugric	Platt-deutsch
Rumonsch	Gujerathi	Gallo-Roman	Tibeto-Burman
Salishan	Hottentot	Himyaritic	Volga-Baltaic
Sanscrit	Inuktitut	Hindustani	
Sanskrit	Iroquoian	Langue d'oil	**13 letters:**
Scythian	Kamilaroi	Macedonian	Neo-Melanesian
Setswana	Kiswahili	Malayalaam	Semito-Hamitic
Shemitic	Landsmaal	Melanesian	Serbo-Croatian
Shoshone	Langue d'oc	Mingrelian	
Slavonic	Leizghian	Muskhogean	**14 letters:**
Sumerian	Malayalam	Niger-Congo	Thraco-Phrygian
Tahitian	Marquesan	Papiamento	
Teutonic	Messapian	Police Motu	**16 letters:**
Thracian	Mongolian	Proto-Norse	Malayo-Polynesian
		Rajasthani	

Languid, Languish Die, Divine, Droop, Feeble, Flagging, Listless, Lukewarm, Lydia, Melancholy, Quail, Torpid, Wilt

Languor Lassitude

Lanky Beanpole, Gangly, Gawky, Spindleshanks, Windlestraw

Lanolin Woolfat, Yolk

Lantern Aristotle's, Bowat, Bowet, Buat, Bull's eye, Chinese, Dark(e)y, Epidiascope,

Episcope, Friar's, Glim, Japanese, Jaw, Lanthorn, Magic, Sconce, Stereopticon, Storm, Turnip
Lanthanum La
Laodicean Lukewarm
Lap Circuit, Drink, Gremial, Leg, Lick, Lip, Luxury, Override, Pace, Sypher
Lapdog Messan, Shough, Showghe
▷ **Lapdog** *may indicate* 'greyhound'
Lapel Revers
Laplander, Lapp Saam(e), Sabme, Sabmi, Sami
Lappet Infula
Lapse Backslide, Drop, Error, Expire, Fa', Fall, Nod, Sliding, Trip
Lapwing Hornywink, Teru-tero
Larceny Compound, Grand, Petty, Simple
Larch Hackmatack, Tamarack
Lard Enarm, Leaf, Saim, Seam(e)
Larder Buttery, Pantry, Spence, Springhouse
Large(ness), Largest Ample, Astronomical, Big, Boomer, Bulky, Buster, Colossus, Commodious, Decuman, Enormous, Epical, Extensive, Gargantuan, → **GIGANTIC**, Ginormous, Great, Grit, Gross, Hefty, Helluva, Huge, Hulking, Humdinger, Humongous, Humungous, Kingsize, L, Lunker, Macrocephaly, Massive, Maximin, Maximum, Outsize, Plethora, Prodigious, Rounceval, Rouncival, Skookum, Slew, Slue, Sollicker, Spacious, Spanking, Stonker, Stout, Swingeing, Tidy, Titanic, Vast, Voluminous, Whopping
Large number Centillion, Fermi, Giga, Gillion, Googol, Googolplex, Grillion, Infinitude, Jillion, Lac, Lakh, Legion, Mille, Nation, Nonillion, Quadrillion, Quintillion, Raft, Regiment, Ruck, Scads, Sea, Septillion, Sextillion, Shitload, Slather, Slew, Slue, Squillion, Toman, Trillion, Zillion
Largess Alms, Charity, Frumentation, Generosity
Lariat Lasso, Reata, Riata
Lark Adventure, Aunter, Caper, Dido, Dunstable, Exaltation, Fool, Giggle, Guy, Laverock, Magpie, Mud, Pipit, Prank
Larkspur Stavesacre
Larva Ammacoete, Amphibiotic, Amphiblastule, Aphid lion, Army-worm, Augerworm, Axolotl, Bagworm, Bipinnaria, Bloodworm, Bookworm, Bot(t), Budworm, Cabbage worm, Caddice, Caddis(-worm), Cankerworm, Caterpillar, Cercaria, Chigger, Chigoe, Coenurus, Corn borer, Corn earworm, Cysticercoid, Doodlebug, Grub, Hellgram(m)ite, Hydatid, Indusium, Instar, Jigger, Jointworm, Leather-jacket, Leptocephalus, Maggot, Mealworm, Measle, Microfilaria, Miracidium, Muckworm, Mudeye, Naiad, Nauplius, Neoteny, Nigger, Nymph, Ox-bot, Planula, Pluteus, Porina, Redia, Screwworm, Shade, Silkworm, Strawworm, Tadpole, Trochophore, Trochosphere, Veliger, Water penny, Wireworm, Witchetty, Witchetty grub, Woodworm, Zoea
Laryngitis Croup, Hives
Lascar Seacunny, Tindal
Lascivious(ness) Crude, Goaty, Horny, Lewd, Lubric, Paphian, Satyric, Sotadic, Tentigo, Wanton
Lash(ed), Lashing(s) Cat, Cilium, Firk, Flagellum, Frap, Gammon, Knout, Mastigophora, Mousing, Oodles, Oup, Quirt, Riem, Rope's end, Scourge, Secure, Sjambok, Stripe, Swinge, Tether, Thong, Trice, Whang, → **WHIP**, Wire
Lass(ie) Damsel, Maid, Quean, Queyn, Quin(i)e
Lassitude Accidie, Acedie, Languor, Lethargy

Lasso Lariat, Reata, Rope

Last(ing) Abide, Abye, Aftermost, → **AT LAST**, Boot-tree, Bottom, Cargo, Chronic, Coda, Dernier, Dure, Endmost, Endurance, Endure, Extend, Extreme, → **FINAL**, Hinder, Hindmost, Latest, Latter, Linger, Live, Load, Long-life, Model, Nightcap, Outstay, Perdure, Permanent, Perpetuate, Persist, Rearmost, Spin, Stable, Stand, Stay, Supper, Survive, Swan-song, Thiller, Thule, Tree, Trump, Ult(imate), Ultimo, Utmost, Wear, Weight, Whipper-in, Yester, Z

Last drop Supernaculum

Last resort Pis aller

Last syllable Ultima

Last word(s) Amen, Envoi, Farewell, Ultimatum, Zythum

Latch Bar, Clicket, Clink, Espagnolette, Lock, Night, Sneck, Thumb, Tirling-pin

Late(r), Latest After(wards), Afterthought, Behindhand, Chit-chat, Dead, Deid, Ex, Former, Gen, Infra, Lag, Lamented, New(s), Overdue, Overrunning, Past, Recent, Serotine, Sine, Slow, State-of-the-art, Stop-press, Syne, Tardive, Tardy, Top shelf, Trendy, Umquhile

Late-learner Opsimath

Latent Concealed, Delitescent, Dormant, Maieutic, Potential

Lateral Askant, Edgeways, Sideways

Latex Antiar, Gutta-percha, Jelutong, Ule

Lath Lag, Splat

Lathe Capstan, Mandrel, Mandril, Turret

Lather Flap, Foam, Froth, Sapples, Suds, Tan

Latin(ist) Biblical, Classical, Criollo, Dago, Dog, Erasmus, Eyeti, Greaseball, High, Humanity, Italiot, L, Late, Law, Low, Medieval, Middle, Modern, Neapolitan, New, Pig, Quarter, Rogues', Romanic, Romish, Scattermouch, Silver, Spic, Thieves', Vulgar, Wop

Latin-American Criollo, Tico

Latitude Breadth, Celestial, Ecliptic, Free hand, Horse, L, Leeway, Liberty, Licence, Meridian, Parallel, Play, Roaring forties, Scope, Tropic, Width

Latrine Ablutions, Bog, Cloaca, Furphy, Garderobe, Loo, Privy, Rear

Latter Last, Previous

Latter-day Recent, Saints, Young

Lattice Bravais, Clathrate, Espalier, Grille, Space, Treillage, Trellis

Lattice-leaf Ouvirandra

Latvian Lett

Laud(able), Lauder Commend, Eulogist, Extol, Harry, Praise, Worthily

Lauderdale Caballer

Laugh(ing), Laughable, Laughter Belly, Cachinnate, Cackle, Chortle, Chuckle, Cod, Corpse, Democritus, Deride, Derision, Fit, Fou rire, Gelastic, Giggle, Goster, Guffaw, Ha, He-he, Ho-ho, Homeric, Hoot, Horse, Hout, Howl, Irrision, Isaac, Last, Lauch, Leuch, Levity, Ludicrous, → **MIRTH**, Mock, Nicker, Peal, Present, Riancy, Riant, Rich, Rident, Ridicule, Risus, Scream, Snigger, Snirt(le), Snort, Tehee, Titter, Yo(c)k

Laughing-stock Outspeckle, Sport

Launcelot Gobbo

Launch(ing), Launch pad Begin, Blast-off, Catapult, Chuck, Cosmodrome, ELV, Fire, Float, Hurl, Initiate, Lift-off, Moonshot, Motoscalp, Opening, Pioneer, Presentation, Release, Rolling, Roll out, Send, Shipway, Slipway, Start, Steam, Unstock, Upsend, VTO

Launder, Laund(e)rette, Laundry Bagwash, Clean, Coin-op, Lav, Steamie, Tramp,

Transfer, Wash, Washhouse, Whites

Laurel(s) Aucuba, Bay, Camphor, Cherry, Daphne, Japan, Kalmia, Kudos, Mountain, Pichurim, Rose (bay), Sassafras, Spicebush, Spotted, Spurge, Stan, Sweet-bay, True

Laurence Sterne

Lava Aa, Block, Bomb, Coulée, Cysticercus, Dacite, Flood basalt, Lahar, Lapilli, Magma, Mud, Nuée ardente, Pahoehoe, Palagonite, Pillow, Pitchstone, Plug, Pumice, Pyroclast, Scoria, Tephra, Toadstone

Lavatory Ajax, Bogger, Brasco, Can, Carsey, Carzey, Cludgie, Comfort station, Convenience, Cottage, Dike, Dunnakin, Dunny, Dyke, Earth closet, Elsan®, Facilities, Forica, Furphey, Gents, Heads, Jakes, Jane, John, Kars(e)y, Karzy, K(h)azi, Kleinhuisie, Kybo, Ladies, Lat(rine), Loo, Necessary, Netty, Office, Outhouse, Portaloo®, Privy, Rear(s), Reredorter, Shithouse, Shouse, Siege, Smallest room, Superloo, Throne, Thunderbox, Toilet, Toot, Tout, Urinal, Washroom, WC

Lave Lip, Wash

Lavender Aspic, Sea, Spike

Lavengro Borrow

Laver Moabite, Nori, Ore-weed

Lavish Barmecidal, Copious, Excessive, Exuberant, Flush, Free, Fulsome, Generous, Liberal, Lucullan, Lush, Prodigal, Shower, Slap-up, Sumptuous, Wanton, Waste

Law(s) Abingdon, Act, Agrarian, Anti-trust, Ass, Association, Avogadro's, Babo's, Bar, Barratry, Bernoulli's, → **BILL**, Biogenetic, Blue-sky, Bode's, Bonar, Boyle's, Bragg's, Brehon, Brewster's, Brocard, Buys Ballot's, Byelaw, Cain, Canon, Capitulary, Case, Chancery, Charles's, Civil, Code, Common, Constitution, Corn, Coulomb's, Criminal, Cupar, Curie's, Curie-Weiss, Cy pres, Dalton's, Dead-letter, Decree, Decretals, Decretum, De Morgan's, Deodand, Dharma, Dictate, Digest, Din, Distributive, Dry, Edict, Einstein's, Enact, Excise, Forensic, Forest, Fuero, Fundamental, Fuzz, Game, Gas, Gay-Lussac's, Graham's, Gresham's, Grimm's, Grotian, Haeckel's, Halifax, Hardy-Weinberg, Henry's, Homestead, Hooke's, Hubble's, Hudud, Hume's, International, Irade, Iure, Joule's, Jura, Jure, Jus, Kain, Kashrut(h), Kepler's, Kirchhoff's, Labour, Land, Lay, Leibniz's, Lemon, Lenz's, Lien, Liquor, Lor(d), Losh, Lydford, Lynch, Magdeburg, Mariotte's, Martial, May, Mendel's, Mercantile, Military, Mishna(h), Mishnic, Moral, Mosaic, Murphy's, Natural, Newton's, Noahide, Nomistic, Nomothetic, Octave, Ohm's, Oral, Ordinance, Pandect, Parity, Parkinson's, Pass, Penal, Periodic, Planck's, Plebiscite, Poor, Principle, Private, Public, Regulation, Roman, Rubric, Rule, Salic, Salique, Scout, Sharia(h), Sheria(t), Shield, Shulchan Aruch, Snell's, Sod's, → **STATUTE**, Stefan's, Stokes, Sumptuary, Sunna, Sus(s), Sword, Table, Talmud, Tenet, Thorah, Thorndike's, Torah, Tort, Tradition, Twelve Tables, Ulema, Unwritten, Use, Verner's, Vigilante, Written

Lawless(ness) Anarchy, Anomie, Anomy, Antinomian, Bushranger, Piratical, Rowdy

Lawmaker, Lawman, Lawyer Alfaqui, Ambulance chaser, Attorney, AV, Avocat, Barrack room, Barrister, Bencher, BL, Bluebottle, Bramble, Bush, Canon, Coke, Counsel, DA, Decemvir, Deemster, Defence, Dempster, Doge, Draco, Earp, Enactor, Fiscal, Greenbag, Grotius, Hammurabi, Jurisconsult, Jurist, Legal eagle, Legist, Mooktar, Moses, MP, Mufti, Mukhtar, Nomothete, Notary, Penang, Pettifoggers, Philadelphia, Proctor, Procurator fiscal, Prosecutor, Rabbi, Shirra, Shyster, Silk, Solicitor, Spenlow, Stratopause, Talmudist, Templar, Thesmothete, Vakil, WS

Lawn Cloth, Grass, Green, Linen, Sward, Turf

Lawrence DH, Ross, Shaw, TE

Lawrencium Lr

Lawsuit Case, Cause, Plea, Trover

▶ **Lawyer(s), Lawman** *see* **LAWMAKER**

▷ **Lax** *may indicate* an anagram

Lax(ity) Freedom, Inexact, Laissez-aller, Latitude, Lenience, Loose, Remiss, → **SLACK**, Wide, Wide-open

Laxative Aloin, Aperitive, Cascara, Cassia, Cathartic, Eccoprotic, Elaterin, Elaterium, Glauber's salt, Gregory (powder), Loosener, Physic, Purgative, → **PURGE**, Saline, Senna-pod, Taraxacum

Lay(ing), Layman, Laic, Laid, Laity Air, Amateur, Antepost, Aria, Ballad, Bed, Bet, Blow, Chant, Civil, Ditty, Drop, Earthly, Egg, Embed, Fit, Impose, Lied, Lodge, Man, Minstrel, Oat, Oblate, Ode, Ordinary, Outsider, Oviparous, Oviposit, Parabolanus, Pose, Secular, Set, Sirvente, → **SONG**, Sypher, Temporalty, Tertiary, Tribal, Wager, Warp

Layabout Idler, Loafer, Lotophagus, Ne'er-do-well, Slob

Lay-by Rest stop

Layer(s) Abscission, Aeuron(e), Ancona, Appleton, Battery, Boundary, Cake, Caliche, Cladding, Coating, Crust, D, Depletion, E, Ectoplasm, Ectosarc, Ekman, Epiblast, Epilimnion, Epitaxial, Epitheca, Epithelium, Erathem, E-region, Exine, Exocarp, Film, Flake, Friction, Ganoin, Germ, Gossan, Gozzan, Granum, Ground, Heaviside, → **HEN**, Herb, Hypotheca, Intima, Inversion, Kennelly(-Heaviside), Kerf, Lamella, Lamina, Lap, Leghorn, Lenticle, Lie, Malpighian, Media, Miocene, Ozone, Pan, Patina, Paviour, Photosphere, Ply, Retina, Reversing, Rind, Scale, Sclerite, Screed, Shrub, Skim, Skin, Skiver, Sliver, Spathic, Stratify, Stratopause, Stratum, Substratum, Tabular, Tapetum, Tier, Tremie, Trophoblast, Trophoderm, Uvea, Varve, Vein, Velamen, Veneer

Lay-off Dismiss, Hedge, Redundance

Lay-out Ante, Design, Fell, Format, Map, Mise, Pattern, Spend, Straucht, Straught, Streak, Streek, Stretch

Laze, Laziness, Lazy (person) Bed-presser, Bummer, Cabbage, Couch potato, Faineant, Hallian, Hallion, Hallyon, Indolent, Inert, Lackadaisical, Laesie, Languid, Layabout, Lie-abed, Lig(ger), Lime, Lither, Loaf, Lotus-eater, Lusk, Mollusc, Ne'er-do-well, Oblomovism, Resty, Sloth, Slouch, Slug(-a-bed), Sluggard, Susan, Sweer, Sweir, Veg, Workshy

▷ **Lazily** *may indicate* an anagram

Lea Grass, Meadow

Leach(ing) Cheluviation, Lixivial, Ooze

Lead(er), Leading, Leadership Ag(h)a, Ahead, Akela, Amakosi, Anglesite, Article, Atabeg, Atabek, Ayatollah, Bab, Bellwether, Black, Bluey, Brand, Cable, Cade, Calif, Caliph, Came, Capitano, Capo, Captain, Castro, Caudillo, Causal, Centre, Ceruse, Cheer, Chieftain, Chiliarch, Chin, China white, Choragus, Choregus, CO, Codder, Condottiere, Conducive, Conduct, Coryphaeus, Coryphee, Demagogue, Dictator, Duce, Dux, Editorial, Escort, Ethnarch, Extension, Figurehead, Floor, Foreman, Foremost, Frontrunner, Fu(e)hrer, Fugleman, Gaffer, Gandhi, Garibaldi, Gerent, Go, Graphite, Guide(r), Halter, Hand, Headman, Headmost, Headnote, Hegemony, Heresiarch, Hero, Hetman, Honcho, Idi, Imam, Imaum, Ink(h)osi, Inveigle, Jason, Jefe, Jump, Juve(nile), Kabir, Kame, King, Ksar, Leam, Litharge, Livid, Loss, Lost, Lyam, Lyme, Mahatma, Mahdi, Main, Market, Marshal, Massicot, Masticot, Mayor, Meer, Mehdi, Minium, Mir, Nanak, No 1, Nomarch, Nose, Numero uno, Omrah, Open, Pacemaker, Pacesetter, Padishah, Panchen Lama, Pb, Pilot, Pioneer, Pit, Plumb(um), Plummet, PM, Precentor, Premier(e), President, Price, Rangitara, Ratoo, Rebbe, Rebecca, Red, Role, Ruler, Sachem, Sagamore, Saturn,

Saturn's tree, Scotlandite, Scout, Scuddaler, Scudler, Sharif, Sheik(h), Sixer, Skipper, Skudler, Soaker, Soul, Sounding, Spearhead, Staple, Star, Sultan, Supremo, Taoiseach, Tecumseh, Tetraethyl, Top banana, Top dog, Trail(blazer), Tribune, Tsaddik, Tsaddiq, Tzaddik, Up, Usher, Vaivode, Van(guard), Vanadinite, Va(u)nt, Vaunt-courier, Voivode, Vozhd, Waivode, Wali, Warlord, White, Whitechapel, Wulfenite, Youth, Zaddik, Zia

▷ **Lead(s), Leaders** *may indicate* first letters of words

Leaden Flat, Plumbeous, Saturnine

Lead-glance Galena

Leading to Pre

Leaf(y), Leaves Acanthus, Acrospire, Amphigastrium, Amplexicaul, Ascidia, At(t)ap, Baccy, Betel, Blade, Bract, Carpel, Cataphyll, Cladode, Coca, Compound, Consent, Corolla, Costate, Cotyledon, Dolma, Drop, Duff, Fig, Finial, Foil, Foliage, Foliar, Folio(se), Folium, Frond, Glume, Gold, Green, Holiday, Induviae, Jugum, K(h)at, Maple, Megaphyll, Microphyll, Needle, Nervate, Out, P, Pad, Page, Pan, Phyllid, Phyllome, Qat, Repair, Riffle, Rosula, Salad, Scale, Sclerophyll, Secede, Sepal, Sheet, Siri(h), Skip, Spathe, Sporophyll, Stipule, Tea, Title, Tobacco, TTL, Valve, Vert, Vine, Withdraw

Leafhopper Thrip

Leafless Ebracteate, Scape

Leaflet At(t)ap, Bill, Bracteole, Circular, Dodger, Fly-sheet, Foliolose, Handbill, Pinna, Pinnula, Prophyll, Stipel, → TRACT

League Achaean, Alliance, Arab, Band, Bund, Compact, Decapolis, Delian, Entente, Federation, Gueux, Guild, Hanse(atic), Holy, Ivy, Land, Major, Minor, Nations, Parasang, Primrose, Redheaded, Rugby, Solemn, Super, Union, Ypres, Zollverein, Zupa

Leak(y) Bilge, Drip, Escape, Extravasate, Gizzen, Holed, Holey, Ooze, Pee, Porous, Seepage, Sype, Trickle, Wee, Weep, Wee-wee

Leak-proof Airtight

Leamington Spa

Lean(ing) Abut, Barren, Batter, Bend, Careen, Carneous, Carnose, Griskin, Heel, Hike out, → INCLINE, Lie, Lig(ge), Minceur, Prop, Propend, Rake, Rely, Rest, Scraggy, Scrawny, Skinny, Spare, Stoop, Taste, Tend, Tilt, Tip, Walty, Wiry

Leander Abydos

Lean-to Skillion

Leap(ing), Leapt Assemblé, Bound, Brisé, Cabriole, Caper, Capriole, Cavort, Clear, Croupade, Curvet, Echappé, Entrechat, Falcade, Fishdive, Frisk, Galumph, Gambade, Gambado, Gambol, Jeté, Jump, Loup, Luppen, Ollie, Over, Pigeon-wing, Pounce, Pronk, Quantum, Sally, Salto, Somersa(u)lt, Somerset, → SPRING, Stag, Transilient, Vault, Volte

Leap year Bissextile, Penteteric

Lear Edward, King, Nonsense

Learn(ed), Learner Beginner, Blue, Bluestocking, Chela, Classical, Con, Discover, Distance, Doctor, Don, Erudite, Gather, Get, Glean, Hear, Kond, L, Lear(e), Leir, Lere, Literate, Literati, Literato, Lucubrate, Master, Memorise, Mirza, Mug up, → NOVICE, Opsimath, Pandit, Polymath, Programmed, Pundit, Pupil, Rookie, Savant, Scan, Scholar, Scient, See, Starter, Student, → STUDY, Tiro, Trainee, Tutee, Tyro, Wise

Learning Blended, Culture, Discipline, Discrimination, Distance, Erudition, Index, Insight, Instrumental, Latent, Lifelong, Lore, Machine, New, Open, Opsimathy, Rep, Sleep, Wit

Lease(-holder) Charter, Farm, Feu, Gavel, Hire, Let, Long, Novated, → **RENT**, Set(t), Tack, Tacksman
Leash Lead, Lune, Lyam, Lym(e), Slip, Three, Trash, Triplet
Least Minimum, Rap
Leather(s), Leathery Artificial, Bouilli, Bouilly, Box-calf, Buckskin, Buff, Cabretta, Calf, Capeskin, Chammy, Chamois, Chaps, Checklaton, Cheverel, Chevrette, Cordovan, Cordwain, Corium, Counter, Cowhide, Crispin, Cuir(-bouilli), Deacon, Deerskin, Diphthera, Doeskin, Dogskin, Durant, Fair, Foxing, Goatskin, Grain, Hide, Hog-skin, Horsehide, Japanned, Kid, Kip(-skin), Lacquered, Lamp, Levant, Marocain, Maroquin, Mocha, Morocco, Mountain, Nap(p)a, Neat, Nubuck®, Oak, Ooze, Oxhide, Paste-grain, Patent, Pigskin, Plate, Rand, Rawhide, Rexine®, Riem(pie), Roan, Rock, Rough-out, Russia, Saffian, Shagreen, Shammy, Sharkskin, Shecklaton, Sheepskin, Shoe, Skiver, Slinkskin, Snakeskin, Spetch, Split, Spur, Stirrup, Strand, Strap, Suede, Tan, Taw, Thong, Upper, Wallop, Wash, Waxed, White, Whitleather, Yuft
Leatherneck Marine, RM
Leave(r), Leavings, Leave off Abandon, Abiturient, Abscond, Absit, Absquatulate, Acquittal, Adieu, Avoid, Bequeath, Blessing, Bug, Compassionate, Congé, Congee, Decamp, Depart, Desert, Desist, Devisal, Devise, Ditch, Evacuate, Exeat, Exit, Exodus, Extrude, Forego, Forgo, Forsake, French, Furlough, Gardening, Garlandage, → **GO**, Inspan, Ish, Legate, Liberty, Licence, Maroon, Mass, Maternity, Mizzle, Omit, Orts, Pace, Parental, Park, Part, Paternity, → **PERMISSION**, Permit, → **QUIT**, Residue, Resign, Sabbatical, Scapa, Scat, Scram, Shore, Sick, Skedaddle, Skidoo®, Stick, Strand, Vacate, Vade, Vamo(o)se, Will, Withdraw
Leaven Barm, Ferment, Yeast
Lebanese, Lebanon Druse, RL
Lecher(ous), Lechery Gate, Goaty, Lascivious, Libertine, Lickerish, Lustful, Profligate, Rake, Roué, Salaciousness, Satirisk, Satyr, Silen, Whoremonger, Wolf
Lectern Ambo, Desk, Eagle, Oratory
Lecture(r), Lectures, Lecturing Address, Aristotelian, Chalktalk, Creed, Curtain, Docent, Dissert(ator), Don, Earful, Erasmus, Expound, Homily, Hulsean, Jaw, Jawbation, Jobe, L, Lector, Pi-jaw, Prelect, Privatdocent, Prone, Rate, Read(er), Rede, Reith, Rubber chicken circuit, Scold, Sententious, → **SERMON**, Spout, Talk, Teacher, Teach-in, Wigging, Yaff
Ledge Altar, Berm, Buttery-bar, Channel, Fillet, Gradin(e), Linch, Misericord(e), Nut, Rake, Scarcement, Settle, → **SHELF**, Window (sill)
Ledger Book, Purchase, Register
Lee(s) Dregs, Dunder, Heeltaps, Sediment, Shelter, Ullage
Leech Bleeder, Gnathobdellida, Horse, Medicinal, Parasite, Rhynchobdellida
Leek Allium, Fouat, Fouet, Porraceous, Rocambole, Sengreen
Leer Eliad, Fleer, Oeillade, Ogle, Perv
Leeway Drift
Left (hand), Left-handed, Left-hander, Left-winger Abandoned, Adrift, Balance, Bolshy, Corrie-fisted, Dolly-push, Gallock, Hie, High, Inherited, L, Laeotropic, Laevorotation, Larboard, Links, Loony, Lorn, Near, New, Other, Over, Pink, Port, Portsider, Quit, Rad, Red, Relic, Residuum, Resigned, Secondo, Sinister, Soc(ialist), Southpaw, Thin, Titoism, Trot, Verso, Vo, Went, West, Wind, Yet
Left-over Astatki, Dregs, End, Gone, Lave, Oddment, Offcut, Orra, Remains, Remanet, → **REMNANT**, Residue, Waste
Leg(s), Leggings, Leggy, Leg-wear Antigropelo(e)s, Bandy, Barbados, Barley-sugar, Bow, Breeches, Cabriole, Cannon, Chaparajos, Chaparejos, Chaps,

Crural, Crus, Dib, Drumstick, Fine, Fly-sail, Gaiter, Galligaskins, Gam(b), Gamash, Gambado, Garter, Gaskin, Giambeux, Gigot, Gramash, Gramosh, Ham, Haunch, Hest, Hock, Jamb, Jambeau, Jambeaux, Knock-knee(d), Limb, Long, Member, Milk, Myriapod, Oleo, On(side), Peg, Peraeopod, Periopod, Peroneal, Pestle, Pin, Podite, Proleg, Puttees, Pylon, Relay, Section, Shanks, Shanks's pony, Shaps, Shin, Short, Spats, Spatterdash, Spider, Spindleshanks, Square, Stage, Stump, Thigh, Tights, White

Legacy Bequest, Cumulative, Demonstrative, Dowry, Entail, General, Heirloom, Residuary, Specific, Substitutional

Legal(ism), Legally, Legitimate Bencher, Decriminalised, Forensic, Halacha, Halaka(h), Halakha, Lawful, Licit, Nomism, Scienter, Statutory

Legal book Halacha, Halaka(h), Halakha, Talmud

Leg-armour, Leg-covering Cootikin, Cu(i)tikin, Gambado, Jamb(e), Pad

Legate, Legator Ambassador, Consul, Devisor, Emissary, Envoy, Nuncio

▷ **Legend** *may indicate* leg-end (e.g. foot, talus)

Legend(ary) Arthurian, Caption, Edda, Fable, Folklore, Hadith, Motto, Myth, Saga, Story, Urban, Yowie

Leger Swindler

Leghorn Livorno

Legible Clear, Lucid, Plain

Legion(ary), Legionnaire Alauda, American, Army, British, Cohort, Countless, Deserter, Foreign, Geste, Honour, → **HOST**, Maniple, Many, Throng, Thundering, Zillions

Legislate, Legislator, Legislature Assemblyman, Congress, Decemvir, Decree, MP, Nomothete, Oireachtas, → **PARLIAMENT**, Persian, Senator, Solon, Zemstvo

Legitimate Kosher, Loyal

Legless Amelia, Blotto, Boozy, Caecilia, Drunk, Mermaid, Psyche

Leg-pull Chaff, Joke, Rise, Rot

Legume, Leguminous Bean, Guar, Lentil, Lomentum, Pea, Pipi, Pod, Pulse

Leibniz Monadism

Leigh Amyas

Leisure(ly) Adagio, Ease, Lento, Liberty, Moderato, Otium, Respite, Rest, Vacation

Lemming Morkin

Lemon Answer, Cedrate, Citron, Citrus, Smear-dab, Sole, Yellow

Lemur Angwantibo, Aye-aye, Babacoote, Bush-baby, Colugo, Galago, Half-ape, Indri(s), Loris, Macaco, Malmag, Mongoose, → **MONKEY**, Nagapie, Potto, Ringtail, Sifaka, Spectre, Tana, Tarsier

Lend Advance, Loan, Prest, Sub, Vaunce

Length(y), Lengthen(ing), Lengthwise Archine, Arsheen, Arshin(e), Aune, Barleycorn, Braccio, Cable, Chain, Cubit, Distance, Eke, Ell, → **ELONGATE**, Endways, Ennage, Epenthetic, Expand, Extensive, Focal, Foot, Furlong, Inch, Ley, Mile, Nail, Passus, Perch, Piece, Plethron, Pole, Prolate, Prolix, Prolong, Protract, Reach, Remen, Rod, Rope, Slow, Span, Stadium, Toise, Vara, Verbose, Yard

Lenient Clement, Exurable, Lax, Mild, Permissive, Soft, Tolerant

Lens Achromatic, Acoustic, Anamorphic, Anastigmat, Aplanatic, Apochromat(ic), Bifocal, Bull's eye, Compound, Contact, Corneal, Crookes, Crown, Crystalline, Dielectric, Diopter, Dioptre, Diverging, Electron, Electrostatic, Eye, Eyeglass, Eye-piece, Facet, Fish-eye, Fresnel, Gas-permeable, Gravitational, Hard, Immersion, Lentil, Macro, Magnetic, Metallic, Mirror, Object-glass, Optic, Pantoscope, Phacoid, Piano-concave, Piano-convex, Soft, Soft-focus, Stanhope, Sunglass, Telephoto, Toric, Trifocal, Varifocal, Water, Wide-angle, Zoom

Lent Carême, Fast, Laetare, Out, Quadragesimal, Term
Lentil(s) D(h)al, Dholl, Ervalenta, Lens, Phacoid, Pulse, Puy, Revalenta
Leonora Overture
Leopard Clouded, Hunting, Leap, Libbard, Ounce, Panther, Pard, Snow, Spots
Leopold Bloom
Leotard Maillot
Leper, Leprosy, Leprous Gehazi, Hansen's disease, Lazar, Leontiasis, Lionism, Meazel, Mesel, Outcast, Pariah
Lepidopterist Aurelian, Moth-er, Pendleton, Treacler
Leprechaun Elf, Gremlin, Imp
Lepton Muon
Lesbian Boi, Bull dyke, Crunchie, Diesel, Dike, Dyke, Homophile, Lipstick, Sapphist, Tribade
Lese-majesty Treason
Lesion Cut, Gash, Pannus, Scar, Serpiginous, Sore, Wheal, Whelk
Less(en), Lesser, Lessening Abate, Alaiment, Bate, Contract, Deaden, Decline, Deplete, Derogate, Dilute, → **DWINDLE**, Extenuate, Fewer, Junior, Littler, Meno, Minus, Play down, Reduce, Relax, Remission, Subordinate, Subsidiary, Tail, Under
Lesson Example, Lear(e), Lection, Leir, Lere, Life, Masterclass, Moral, Object, Parashah, Period, Sermon, Shiur, Tutorial
Let (go, off, out), Letting Allow, Cap, Charter, Conacre, Displode, Divulge, Enable, Entitle, Explode, Hire, Impediment, Indulge, Lease, Litten, Loot(en), Luit(en), Lutten, Net, Obstacle, Obstruct, → **PERMIT**, Rent, Reprieve, Sett, Tenancy, Unhand, Warrant
Let down Abseil, Betray, Lower, Sell, Vail
Let-down Disappointment, Non-event
Lethal Deadly, Fatal, Fell, Mortal
Lethargic, Lethargy Accidie, Apathy, Coma, Drowsy, Ennui, Hebetude, Inertia, Lassitude, Listless, Passive, Sleepy, Sluggish, Stupor, Supine, Torpid, Turgid
Letter(s) Ache, Aerogam, Aesc, Airgraph, Aleph, Alif, Alpha, Ascender, A(y)in, Bayer, Begging, Beta, Beth, Block, Breve, Cadmean, Canine, Caph, Capital, Capon, Casket, Chain, Cheth, Chi, Chitty, Circular, Col, Collins, Consonant, Covering, Cue, Cuneiform, Daled, Daleth, Dead, Dear John, Delta, Digamma, Digraph, Dominical, Edh, Ef(f), Emma, Encyclical, Ep(isemon), Epistle, Epsilon, Eta, Eth, Fan, Favour, Form, Fraktur, French, Gamma, Gimel, Grapheme, He, Heth, Initial, Iota, Izzard, Jerusalem, Kaph, Kappa, Koppa, Kufic, Labda, Lambda, Lamed(h), Landlady, Landlord, Lessee, Lessor, Literal, Love, Mail, Mail-shot, Majuscule, Mem, Memo, Miniscule, Minuscule, Missive, Monogram, Mu, Nasal, Night, Note, Notelet, Nu, Nun, Og(h)am, Omega, Omicron, Open, Pahlavi, Paston, Pastoral, Patent, Pe, Pehlevi, Phi, Pi, Plosive, Poison-pen, Polyphone, Postbag, Psi, Pythagorean, Qoph, Resh, Rho, Rhyme, Rom, Runestave, Sad(h)e, Samekh, Samian, Sampi, San, Scarlet, Screed, Screeve, Screwtape, Script, See, Shin, Ship, Siglum, Sigma, Sign, Signal, Sin, Sort, Stiff, Swash, Tau, Tav, Taw, Teth, Theta, Thorn, Toc, Tsade, Typo, Uncial, Upsilon, Vau, Vav, Versal, Vowel, Waw, Wen, Wyn, Wynn, Xi, Yod(h), Yogh, Ypsilon, Zayin, Zed, Zeta
Lettering Cufic, Kufic
Lettuce Batavia, Butterhead, Cabbage, Chicon, Corn-salad, Cos, Frog's, Iceberg, Lactuca, Lamb's, Lollo rosso, Mizuna, Romaine, Salad, Sea, Thridace
Leucoma Albugo
Levant(ine) Coptic, Go, Israelite, Jew, Ottamite, Ottomite
Levee Bank, Dyke, Embankment, Party

Level(ler) A, Abney, Abreast, Aclinic, Ad eundum, Aim, Awash, Bargaining, Base, Break even, Bulldoze, Champaign, Confidence, Countersink, Degree, Dumpy, Echelon, Energy, Equal, → **EVEN**, Extent, Flat, Flight, Flush, Fog, Grade, Logic, O, Occupational, Ordinary, Par, Plane, Plat(eau), Point, Price, Race, Rank, Rase, Raze, Reduced, Savanna, Sea, Spirit, Split, Springing, → **SQUARE**, Status, Stratum, Street, Strew, Strickle, Subsistence, Support, Surveyor's, Tier, Top, Trophic, True, Water, Y
Lever(age) Backfall, Bell-crank, Brake, Cock, Crampon, Crowbar, Dues, Gear, Handspike, Jaw, Jemmy, Joystick, Key, Knee-stop, Landsturm, Pawl, Peav(e)y, Pedal, Prise, Prize, Pry, Purchase, Stick, Sweep, Swipe, Tappet, Throttle, Tiller, Treadle, Treddle, Tremolo arm, Trigger, Tumbler, Typebar
Leviathan Whale
Levitate Float, Hover, Rise
Levity Flippancy, Glee, Humour, Jollity
Levy Capital, Estreat, Impose, Imposition, Leave, Militia, Octroi, Raise, Scutage, Stent, Talliate, Tax, Tithe, Toll
Lewd(ness) Bawdy, Blue, Debauchee, Impure, Libidinous, Lubricity, Obscene, Priapism, Prurient, Silen(us), Unclean
Lewis Carroll, Tenon
Lexicographer, Lexicon Compiler, Craigie, Drudge, Etymologist, Florio, Fowler, Glossarist, Grove, Johnson(ian), Larousse, Liddell, Mental, Murray, OED, Thesaurus, Vocabulist, Webster, Words-man
Liability, Liable Anme, Apt, Current, Debt, Employer's, Incur, Limited, Open, Product, Prone, Subject, Susceptible, White elephant
Liaison Affair, Amour, Contact, Link
Liana Guarana
Libel(lous) Defamatory, Malign, Sclaunder, Slander, Smear, Sully, Vilify
Liberal(ity) Abundant, Adullamites, Ample, Besant, Bounteous, Bountiful, Breadth, Bright, Broad, Catholic, Enlightened, Free(hander), Free-hearted, → **GENEROUS**, Giver, Grey, Grimond, Grit, Handsome, Indulgent, L, Largesse, Lavish, Limousine, Octobrist, Open, → **PROFUSE**, Rad(ical), Samuelite, Simonite, Steel, Tolerant, Trivium, Unstinted, Verlig, Verligte, Whig
Liberate(d), Liberation, Liberator Bolivar, Deliver, Emancipate, Fatah, → **FREE**, Gay, Inkatha, Intolerant, Messiah, PLO, Release, Save, Sucre, Unfetter, UNITA, Women's
Liberian Kroo, Kru
Libertarian, Libertine Chartered, Corinthian, Debauchee, Don Juan, Laxist, Lecher, Lothario, Lovelace, Playboy, Rake, Rip, Roué, Wencher, Wolf
Liberty Bail, Civil, Discretion, Franchise, Freedom, Hall, Mill, Sauce
Library, Librarian Bibliothecary, BL, Bodleian, Bookmobile, British, Chartered, Circulating, Copyright, Cottonian, Film, Gene, Genomic, Harleian, Laurentian, Lending, Mazarin, Mobile, Morgue, PL, Public, Radcliffe, Reference, Rental, Subscription, Tauchnitz
Librettist Boito, Gilbert, Hammerstein, Lyricist
▶ **Lice** see **LOUSE**
Licence, License Abandon, Allow, Authorisation, Carnet, Charter, Dispensation, Driving, Enable, Exequatur, Fling, Franchise, Free(dom), Gale, Imprimatur, Indult, → **LATITUDE**, Let, Marriage, Occasional, Passport, → **PERMIT**, Poetic, Pratique, Provisional, Road-fund, Rope, Slang, Special, Table
Licentious Artistic, Corinthian, Debauchee, Hot, Immoral, Large, Lax, Liberal, Loose, Prurient, Ribald, Sensual, Wanton
Lichen Apothecia, Archil, Corkir, Crotal, Crottle, Cup, Epiphyte, Epiphytic, Graphis,

Korkir, Lecanora, Litmus, Orchel, Orchil(la), Orcine, Orseille, Parella, Parelle, Roccella, Rock tripe, Sea-ivory, Stone-rag, Stone-raw, Tree-moss, Usnea, Wartwort
Lick(ing) Bat, Beat, Deer, Lambent, Lap, Leather, Rate, Salt, Slake, Speed, Tongue, Whip
▸ **Licorice** *see* **LIQUORICE**
Lid Cover, Hat, Kid, Maximum, Opercula, Screwtop, Twist-off
Liddell Alice
Lido Beach, Pool
Lie(s), Liar, Lying Abed, Accubation, Accumbent, Ananias, Bam, Bare-faced, Bask, Billy, Bounce(r), Braide, Cau(l)ker, Cellier, Clipe, Clype, Concoction, Contour, Couchant, Cracker, Cram(mer), Cretism, Cumbent, Deception, Decubitous, Decumbent, Direct, Doggo, Fable, False(r), Falsehood, Falsify, Falsity, Fib, Fiction, Figment, Flam, Gag, Gonk, Hori, Incumbent, Invention, Inveracity, Kip, Lair, Leasing, Lee(ar), Lig(ge), Lurk, Mythomania, Obreption, Oner, Perjury, Plumper, Porky (pie), Procumbent, Prone, Prostrate, Pseudologia, Recline, Recumbent, Repent, Repose, Reptant, Ride, Romance(r), Sham, Sleep, Strapper, Stretcher, Supine, Swinger, Tale, Tappice, Tar(r)adiddle, Thumper, Tissue, Try, Untruth, Whacker, Whid, White, Whopper, Yanker
Lied Art-song, Song
Lie-detector Polygraph
Lien Mortgage, Title
Lieu Locus, Place
Lieutenant Cassio, Flag, Loot, Lt, No 1, Sub(altern)
Life Age, Animation, Being, Bio, Biog(raphy), Brian, Brio, C'est la vie, Chaim, Clerihew, CV, Esse, Eva, Eve, Existence, Good, Heart, High, Mean, Memoir, Nelly, Night, Pep, Plasma, Private, Real, Shelf, Span, Spirit, Still, Subsistence, Time, True, Useful, Vita, Zoe
Life-blood Essence, Lethee
Lifeboat Ark
Life-cell Energid
Life-cycle Redia
Life-force, Life-style Chi, Mana, Port, Qi
Lifeguard Cheesemonger
Lifeless(ness) Abiosis, Algidity, Amort, Arid, Azoic, Barren, Catatonic, Cauldrife, → **DEAD**, Dull, Flat, Inanimate, Inert, Log, Mineral, Possum, Sterile, Stonen, Wooden
Lifelike Breathing, Speaking
Lifeline Umbilicus
Life-rent Usufruct
Life-saver Lineman, Preserver, Raft, Reelman
Lift(ed), Lifter, Lifting Arayse, Arsis, Attollent, Bone, Cable-car, Camel, Chair, Cly, Copy, Crane, Davit, Dead, Dumb waiter, Elate, Elevator, Enhance, Extol, Filch, Fillip, Fireman's, Heave, Heeze, Heezie, Heft, Heist, Hitch, Hoise, Hoist, Hove, Jack, Jigger, Kleptomania, Leaven, Lefte, Lever, Lewis, Nab, Nap, Otis®, Paternoster, Pilfer, Press, Pulley, → **RAISE**, Ride, Scoop, Ski, Sky, Snatch, Spout, Stair, Steal, T-bar, Teagle, Theft, Thumb, Topping, Up, Winch, Windlass
Ligament Annular, Cruciate, Fr(a)enum, Paxwax, Peacock-stone, Spring, Suspensory, Tendon, Urachus
Ligation, Ligature Aesc, Bandage, Bind, Tubal
Light(en), Lighting, Lighter, Lights Aerate, Afterglow, Airy, Albedo, Ale, Alow, Alpenglow, Amber, Ancient, Ans(wer), Arc, Aurora, Back-up, Barge, Batement,

Batswing, Beacon, Beam, Bengal, Beshine, Bezel, Birlinn, Bleach, Brake, Breezy, Bude, Bulb, Calcium, Candle, Cannel, Casco, Casement, Chiaroscuro, Cierge, Clue, Courtesy, Day, Dewali, Diffused, Direct, Diwali, Dream-hole, Drop, Drummond, Earth-shine, Eddystone, Electrolier, Ethereal, Fairy, Fall, Fan, Fantastic, Fastnet, Fetch-candle, Fidibus, Fill, Fire, First, Fixed, Flambeau, Flame, Flare, Flax(y), Flicker, Flippant, Flit(t), Floating, Flood, Fluorescent, Fog (lamp), Frothy, Fuffy, Gas-poker, Gegenschein, Gleam, Glim(mer), Glow, Gossamer, Green, Guiding, Gurney, Haggis, Hazard, Head, House, Idiot, Ignite, Illum(in)e, Incandescence, Indirect, Induction, Inner, Irradiate, Junior, Keel, Key, Kindle, Kiran, Klieg, Lamp, Land, Lantern, Lanthorn, Laser, Leading, LED, Leerie, Leggiero, Levigate, Lime, Link, Linstock, Loadstar, Lobuli, Lodestar, Lozen, Lucarne, Lucigen, Luminaire, Lumine, Luminescence, Luminous, Lunt, Lustre, Lux, Mandorla, Match, Mercurial, Merry-dancers, Mithra(s), Moon, Naphtha, Navigate, Navigation, Neon, New, Nit, Northern, Obstruction, Od(yl), Offal, Optics, Pale, Pane, Parhelion, Pavement, Pennyweight, Phosphene, Phosphorescence, Phot, Photon, Pilot, Pipe, Polar, Pontoon, Portable, Pra(a)m, Producer-gas, Range, Rear, Red, Reflex, Relume, Rembrandt, Reversing, Riding, Rocket, Running, Rush, Safe(ty), Satori, Scoop, Sea-dog, Search, Shine, Shy, Southern, Southern-vigil, Spill, Spot, Spry, Steaming, Strip, Strobe, Stroboscope, Subtle, Sun, Sunshine, Suttle, Svelte, Tail, Tally, Taper, Taps, Tead, Threshold, Tind, Tine, Torch, Torchère, Touchpaper, Traffic, Trivial, Ultraviolet, Unchaste, Unoppressive, UV, Ver(e)y, Vesica, Vesta, Vigil, Watch, Wax, Welsbach burner, White, Windock, Window, Winnock, Zippo, Zodiacal
▷ **Light** *may indicate* an anagram
Lighthouse Beacon, Caisson, Eddystone, Fanal, Fastnet, Phare, Pharos, Sea-mark, Signal
Lightless Aphotic, Dark, Obscure, Unlit
Lightness Buoyancy, Galant, Levity, Pallor
Lightning Ball, Catequil, Chain, Dry, Éclair, Enfouldered, Fireball, Fire flag, Forked, Fulmination, Heat, Levin, Sheet, Thunderbolt, Wildfire, Zigzag
Lightship Nore
Lightweight Nobody, Oz, Trivial
Lignite Jet, Surtarbrand, Surturbrand
Like(ness), Liking À la, As, Broo, Care, Corpse, Dig, Duplicate, Effigy, Eg, Egal, Enjoy, Equal, Fancy, Fellow, Guise, Lich, Palate, Parallel, Peas, Penchant, Please, Predilection, Semblant, Shine, Similar, Simile, Smaak, Sort, Speaking, Taste, Tiki, Uniformity
Likely, Likelihood Apt, Fair, Maximum, Odds-on, Offchance, On, Plausible, Possible, Probable, Probit, Prone, Prospective
Likewise Also, Ditto, Do, Eke, Item, So, Too, Tu quoque
Lilac French, Laylock, Mauve, Pipe-tree, Syringa
Lilliputian Minute
Lilt Swing
Lily African, Agapanthus, Aloe, Amaryllis, Annunciation, Arum, Asphodel, Aspidistra, Belladonna, Blackberry, Calla, Camas(h), Camass, Canada, Candock, Chincherinchee, Colchicum, Colocasia, Convallaria, Corn, Crinum, Dale, Day, Easter, Elaine, Fawn, Fleur de lys, Fritillary, Galtonia, Guernsey, Haemanthus, Hemerocallis, Herb-Paris, Jacobean, Jacob's, Jersey, Kniphofia, Laguna, Lent, Leopard, Lote, Lotos, Lotus, Madonna, Mariposa, Martagon, Meadow, Moorva, Mount Cook, Nelumbo, Nenuphar, Nerine, Nuphar, Orange, Padma, Phormium, Pig, Plantain, Pond, Quamash, Regal, Richardia, Sabadilla, Sansevieria, Sarsa, Scilla, Sego, Skunk cabbage, Smilax, Solomon's seal, Spider, Star of Bethlehem,

Stone, Sword, Tiger, Trillium, Tritoma, Tuberose, Turk's cap, Vellozia, Victoria, Water, Water maize, Yucca, Zephyr

Lily-maid Elaine

Lima Sugar bean

Limb Arm, Bough, Branch, Crural, Exapod, Flipper, Hindleg, Imp, Leg, Leg-end, Member, Phantom, Proleg, Pterygium, Ramus, Scion, Shin, Spald, Spall, Spaul(d), Wing

Limbless Amelia

Limbo Bardo, Isolation

Lime Bass(wood), Beton, Calc, Calcicolous, Caustic, Lind(en), Malm, Mortar, Slaked, Soda, Teil, Tilia, Trap, Unslaked, Viscum, Whitewash

Limerick Doggerel, Twiner, Verse

Limestone Burren, Calc-sinter, Calm, Calp, Ca(u)m, Clint, Coquina, Coral Rag, Cornbrash, Cornstone, Forest Marble, Grike, Karst, Kentish rag, Kunkar, Kunkur, Magnesian, Muschelkalk, Oolite, Pisolite, Rottenstone, Scaglia, Stinkstone, Travertin(e)

Limey Rooinek

Limit(ation), Limited, Limiting Ambit, Bind, Border, Borné, Bound, Bourn(e), Brink, Cap, Cash, Ceiling, Chandrasekhar, Circumscribe, Climax, Compass, Confine, Curb, Deadline, Define, Demark, Determine, Earshot, Eddington, Edge, End, Entail, Esoteric, → **EXTENT**, Extreme, Finite, Frontier, Gate, Goal, Gole, Impound, Induciae, Insular, Limes, Lite, Lynchet, March, Maximum, Meare, Mete, Minimum, Nth, Outedge, Pale, Parameter, Perimeter, Periphery, Predetermine, Qualify, Range, Rate-cap, Ration, Reservation, Restrict, Rim, Roche, Roof, Scant, Shoestring, Sky, Speed, Stint, String, Sumptuary, Tail(lie), Tailye, Tailzie, Term(inus), Tether, Three-mile, Threshold, Thule, Tie, Time, Tropic, Twelve-mile, Utmost, Utter, Verge

▷ **Limit** *may indicate* 'surrounding'

Limner RA

Limousine Daimler, Rolls, Stretch, Zil

Limp Claudication, Dot, Droopy, Flabby, Flaccid, Flaggy, Flimsy, Floppy, Hilch, Hirple, Hitch, Hobble, Hop, Lank, Lifeless, Spancel, Tangle

Limpet Keyhole, Patella, Slipper, Streptoneura

Limpid Clear, Lucid, Pure

Linch Terrace

Lincoln(shire) Abe, Poacher, Yellow-belly

Linden Baucis, Lime, Tilia

Line(d), Lines, Lining Abreast, Aclinic, Agate, Agonic, Allan, Anacreontic, → **ANCESTRY**, Anent, Angle, Apothem, Arew, Asclepiadean, Assembly, Asymptote, Axis, Babbitt, Bakerloo, Bar, Barcode, Baton, Battle, Baulk, Becket, Bikini, Bluebell, Bob, Body, Bombast, Bottom, Boundary, BR, Brail, Branch, Bread, Building, Bush, By, Canal, Carolingian, Carriage, Casing, Cathetus, Cell, Ceriph, Chord, Ciel, Clew, Club, Coach, Coffle, Colour, Column, Contour, Cord(on), Coseismal, Course, Crease, Credit, Crib, Crocodile, Crowfoot, Crow's feet, Curve, Cushion, Dancette, Date, Datum, Dead-ball, Delay, Descent, DEW, Diagonal, Diameter, Diffusion, Directrix, Distaff, Dochmiachal, Dotted, Doublure, Downhaul, Downrigger, Dress, Dynasty, Earing, El, E-la-mi, Encase, Equator, Equinoctial, Equinox, Faint, Fall(s), Fault, Feint, Fess(e), Fettle, File, Finishing, Firing, Firn, Flex, Flight, Frame, Fraunhofer, Front, Frontier, Frost, Furr(ow), Geodesic, Geotherm, Germ, Gimp, Giron, Goal, Graph, Grass, Green, Gridiron, Gymp, Gyron, Hachure, Halyard, Hard, Hatching, Hawser, Header, Hemistich, Heptameter, Hexameter, Hexapody,

High-watermark, Hindenburg, Hockey, Hogscore, Hot, House, Impot, Inbounds, Inbred, Incase, Insole, Interfluve, Intima, Isallobar, Isentrope, Isobar, Isobath, Isobront, Isocheim, Isochime, Isochron(e), Isoclude, Isocryme, Isogloss, Isogonal, Isogram, Isohel, Isohyet, Isolex, Isomagnetic, Isonome, Isopach(yte), Isophone, Isophote, Isopiestic, Isopleth, Isopyenal, Isotach, Isothere, Isotherm, Kill, Knittle, L, Land, Lane, Lansker, Lap, Lariat, Lateral, Latitude, Lead, Leash, Le(d)ger, Ley, Lie, Ling, LMS, Load, Log, Longitude, Lossy, Loxodrome, Lubber, Lugger, Lye, Macron, Maginot, Main, Mainsheet, Mark, Marriage, Mason-Dixon, Median, Meridian, Mesal, Miurus, Monorail, Multiplet, Naman, Nazca, Nidation, Noose, Norsel, Northern, Number, Oche, Octastichon, Ode, Oder-Neisse, Og(h)am, Omentum, Onedin, Ordinate, Orphan, Orthostichy, Painter, Panty, Parallel, Parameter, Parastichy, Party, Paternoster, Path, Penalty, Pencil, Phalanx, Picket, Pinstripe, Plimsoll, Plumb, Poetastery, Police, Policy, Popping-crease, Poverty, Power, Product(ion), Profession, Punch, Pure, Queue, Race, Radial, Radius, Rail, Rank, Raster, Ratlin(e), Ratling, Rattlin, Ray, Receiving, Red, Reticle, Retinue, Rew, Rhumb, Ripcord, Rope, Route, Row, Rugose, Rugous, Rule, Ry, Sarking, Scazon, Score, Script, Secant, Seperatrix, Serif, Seriph, Service, Set, Shielded, Shore, Shout, Shroud, Siding, Siegfried, Sield, Sight, Silver, Six-yard, Slur, Snood, Snow, Soft, Solidus, Sounding, Spectral, Spider, Spilling, Spring, Spunyarn, Squall, SR, Staff, Stance, Stanza, Starting, Static, Stave, Stean, Steen, Stein, Stem, Stich(os), Stock, Story, Strap, Streak, Striate, String, Stripe, Stuff, Subtense, Swap, Swifter, Symphysis, Syzygy, Tag, Tailback, Talweg, Tangent, Teagle, Tea lead, Terminator, Tetrameter, Thalweg, Thin blue, Thin red, Thread, Throwaway, Tidemark, Tie, Timber, Touch, Trade, Transmission, Transoceanic, Transversal, Tree, Trimeter, Tropic, Trot, Trunk, Try, Tudor, Upstroke, Variety, Verse, Vinculum, Virgule, Wad, Wallace's, Washing, Water(shed), White, Widow, Wire, World, Wrinkle, Yellow, Zag, Zip, Zollner's
Lineage Ancestry, Descent, Extraction, Filiation, Parage, Pedigree
Linen Amice, Amis, Barb, Bed, Byssus, Cambric, Crash, Damask, Dornick, Dowlas, Ecru, Flax, Harn, Huckaback, Inkle, Lawn, Lint, Lockram, Moygashel, Napery, Percale, Seersucker, Sendal, Silesia, Table, Toile, Undies
Liner Artist, Bin-bag, Eye, Ocean greyhound, RMS, Ship, Sleeve, Steamer, Steen, Titanic
Linesman Parodist, → POET, Touch-judge
Linger(ing) Chronic, Dawdle, Dwell, Hang, Hove(r), Lag, → LOITER, Straggle, Tarry, Tie
Lingerie Bra, Drawers, Undies
Lingo Argot, Bat, Cant, Jargon, Polglish, Speech
Linguist(ic), Linguistics Glottic, Historical, Philological, Phonemics, Polyglot, Semantics, Structural, Stylistics, Syntax, Tagmemics, Taxeme
Liniment Balm, Carron-oil, Embrocation, Ointment, Opodeldoc, Salve
Link(ed), Linking, Links Associate, Between, Bond, Bridge, Chain, Cleek, Colligate, Concatenation, Connect, Copula, Couple, Cross-reference, Cuff, Desmid, Drag, Ess, Flambeau, Golf, Hookup, Hot, Hotline, Incatenation, Index, Interconnect, Interface, Internet, Intertwine, Karabiner, Krab, Liaise, Machair, Missing, Nexus, On-line, Pons, Preposition, Relate, Tead(e), → TIE, Tie-in, Tie-line, Torch, Unite, Weakest, Yoke
Linkman Lamplighter, Mediator
Linnet Finch, Lintie, Lintwhite, Twite
Linoleum Waxcloth
Lint Charpie, Dossil
Lintel Summer, Transom

Lion(ess) Androcles, Aphid, Chindit, Elsa, Glitterati, Hero, Leo, Maned, Mountain, Nemean, Opinicus, Personage, Pride, Simba

Lionel Trilling

Lion-tamer Dan(iel)

Lip(py), Lips Beestung, Cheek, Fat, Fipple, Flews, Hare, Helmet, Jib, Labellum, Labiate, Labret, Labrum, Ligula, Muffle, Philtrum, → RIM, Rubies, Sass, Sauce, Slack-jaw, Submentum

Lipase Steapsin

Lipstick Chapstick

Liquefy Dissolve, Fuse, Melt

Liqueur, Liquor Abisante, Absinthe, Advokaat, Ale, Almondrado, Amaretto, Anise, Anisette, Apry, Benedictine, Bree, Brew, Broo, Broth, Calvados, Cassis, Cerise, Chartreuse, Chasse, Cherry Marnier®, Cher-suisse, Chicha, Choclair, Chococo, Cocoribe, Cointreau®, Creature, Crème, Crème de cacao, Crème de menthe, Curaçao, Drambuie®, Eau des creoles, Elixir, Enzian, Feni, Fenny, Fraises, Framboise, Fumet, Fustian, Galliano, Geropiga, Grand Marnier®, Hogan, Hogan-mogen, Hogen, Hooch, John Barleycorn, Jungle juice, Kahlua®, Kaoliang, Kir, Kirschwasser, Kirsh(wasser), Kummel, Lager, Lap, Malt, Maraschino, Mastic, Metheglin, Mickey Finn, Midori®, Mirabelle, Mobbie, Mobby, Noyau, Oedema, Ooze, Ouzo, Parfait d'amour, Pasha, Pastis, Pernod®, Persico, Pot, Potation, Pousse-café, Prunelle, Rakee, Raki, Ratafia, Roiano, Roncoco, Rose, Rotgut, Rum, Rum shrub, Sabra, Sambuca, Samshoo, Schnapps, Sciarada, Shypoo, Skink, Stingo, Stock, Stout, Strega®, Strunt, Stuff, Supernaculum, Tape, Taplash, Tequila, Tia Maria®, Tickle-brain, Tiff, Triple sec, Van der Hum®, White lightning, Wine, Witblits, Wort

Liquid(ate), Liquidity, Liquids, Liquefaction Acetal, Amortise, Annihilate, Apprize, Aqua-regia, Azeotrope, Bittern, Bouillon, Bromine, Butanal, Butanol, Butyraldehide, Butyrin, Cacodyl, Cadaverine, Cash, Cash flow, Chloramine, Cinerin, Clyster, Court-bouillon, Creosol, Creosote, Decoction, Dispersant, Dope, Eluate, Erase, Ethanol, Ether, Eucalyptol, Eugenol, Flow, Fluid, Fural, Furfural, Furol, Halothene, Isoprene, Jaw, Kakodyl, Lewisite, Limonene, Linalool, Lye, Massacre, Mess, Minim, Mouillé, Nebula, Picamar, Pipe, Potion, Protoplasm, Ptisan, Pyrrole, Pyrrolidine, Quinoline, Raffinate, Rhigolene, Safrole, Serum, Solution, Solvent, Syrup, Terebene, Thixotropy, Titer, Titre, Tuberculin, Tusche, Ullage, Verjuice, Whey, Wind up, Wort

Liquorice Indian, Jequirity, Nail, Nail-rod, Pomfret, Pontefract-cake, Spanish juice, Sugarallie, Sugarally

Lis Iris, Lily

Lisa Mona

Lisp(er) Ephraimite, Sibilance

Lissom(e) Agile, Lithe, Nimble, Svelte

▷ **List** *may indicate* 'listen'

List(s), Listing A, Active, Agenda, Antibarbarus, Appendix, Army, Atilt, B, Barocco, Barrace, Bead-roll, Bibliography, British, Canon, Cant, Catalog(ue), Categorise, Catelog, Cause, Check, Choice, Civil, Class, Compile, Credits, Danger, Debrett, Docket, Entry, Enumerate, Front, Glossary, Hark, Hearken, Heel, Hit, Hit-parade, Honours, Index, Indian, Interdiction, Inventory, Itemise, Laundry, Lean, Leet, Line-up, Linked, Lloyds, Mailing, Manifest, Menu, Navy, Notitia, Official, Panel, Paradigm, Party, Price, Prize, Register, Repertoire, Reserved, Retired, Roin, Roll, Roon, Roster, Rota, Rund, Schedule, Short, Sick, Slate, Slope, Strip, Syllabus (of Errors), Table, Tariff, Tick, Ticket, Tilt, Timetable, Tip, Transfer, Union, Waiting,

Waybill, White, Wine, Wish
Listen(er) Attend, Auditor, Auscultate, Ear, Eavesdropper, Gobemouche, Hark,
→ **HEED**, Lithe, Lug, Monitor, Oyez, Simon, Sithee, Wire-tap, Yo-ho(-ho)
▷ **Listen to** *may indicate* a word sounding like another
Listless(ness) Abulia, Accidie, Acedia, Apathetic, Atony, Dawney, Draggy, Inanition,
Indolent, Lackadaisical, Languor, Mooning, Mope, Mopus, Sloth, Thowless,
Torpor, Upsitting, Waff
Lit Alight, Landed
▷ **Lit** *may indicate* an anagram
Litany Eirenicon
Literacy Emotional
Literal(ly), Literal sense Etymon, Misprint, Simply, Typo, Verbatim
Literary Academic, Bas bleu, Booksie, Erudite, Lettered
Literary girls Althea, Jenny, Maud, Pippa
Literature Belles lettres, Corpus, Fiction, Gongorism, Hagiology, Midrash, Musar,
Page, Picaresque, Polite, Prose, Responsa, Samizdat, Splatterpunk, Wisdom
Lithe Flexible, Limber, Pliant, Souple, → **SUPPLE**, Svelte, Willowy
Lithium Li
Litigant Barrator, John-a-Nokes, John-a-Stiles, John Doe, Party, Richard Roe, Suer,
Suitor
Litmus Indicator, Lacmus, Lichen, Turnsole
Litre L
Litter Bed, Brancard, Brood, Cacolet, Cat, Cubs, Debris, Deep, Doolie, Duff,
Emu-bob, Farrow, Jampan, Kago, Kajawah, Kindle, Mahmal, Mor, Nest, Norimon,
Palankeen, Palanquin, Palkee, Palki, Pup, → **REFUSE**, Scrap, Sedan, Stretcher,
Sweepings, Team
Little Bagatelle, Billee, Brief, Chota, Curn, Dorrit, Drib, Drop, Fewtrils, Ickle, Insect,
Iota, John, Jot, Leet, Lilliputian, Limited, Lite, Lyte, Mini, Miniscule, Minnow,
Minuscule, → **MINUTE**, Modicum, Morceau, Nell, Paltry, Paucity, Paul, Petite,
Pink, Pittance, Ronte, Runt, Scant, Scut, Shade, Shoestring, Shred, Shrimp, Slight,
Sma', → **SMALL**, Smattering, Smidge(o)n, Smidgin, Some, Soupçon, Spot, Tad,
Teensy, Tich, Tiddly, Tine, Titch, Touch, Tyne, Vestige, Wee, Weedy, Whit, Women
Littoral Coast(al)
Liturgical, Liturgy Divine, Doxology, Hallel, Rite, Versicle
Live(d), Livelihood, Living, Liveliness, Lively, Lives Active, Alert, Allegretto,
Allegro, Am, Animated, Animation, Animato, Are, AV, Awake, Be, Birkie, Bouncy,
Breezy, Brio, Brisk, Cant(y), Capriccio(so), Cheery, Chipper, Chirpy, Cohabit, Con
moto, Con spirito, Crouse, Durante vita, → **DWELL**, Dynamic, Ebullient, Entrain,
Exist, Exuberant, Feisty, Frisky, Galliard, Gamy, Gay, Giocoso, Gracious, Grig,
Hang-out, Hard, High jinks, Hijinks, Hot, Is, Jazz, Kedge, Lad, Lead, Mercurial,
Merry, Outgo, Pacey, Peart, Pep, Piert, Quicksilver, Rackety, Racy, Reside, Rousing,
Salt, Saut, Scherzo, Skittish, Smacking, Spiritoso, Spirituel(le), Sprack, Spry,
Spunky, Sustenance, Swinging, Vibrant, Vigoroso, Vital, Vitality, Vivace, Vive, Vivo,
→ **VOLATILE**, Vyvyan, Wick, Zappy, Zingy, Zippy, Zoe
▶ **Livelihood** *see* **LIVE(D)**
Liver(ish) Foie gras, Hepar, Hepatic(al), Porta, Puce, Resident, Tomalley
Liverpool, Liverpudlian Scouse
Liverwort Gemma-cup, Hepatica, Riccia
Livery(man) Ermine, Flunkeydom, Goldsmith, Skinner, Tiger, Uniform
Livid Blae, Bruised, Cross, → **FURIOUS**, Pale
Living Advowson, Benefice, Biont, Bread, Canonry, Crust, Glebe, Inquiline, Lodging,

Quick, Resident, Simony, Subsistence, Symbiotic, Vicarage, Vital
Livingstone Doctor, Ken
Liza, Lizzie Bess, Betty, Flivver, Hexam, Tin
Lizard Abas, Agama, American chameleon, Amphisbaena, Anguis, Anole, Basilisk,
Bearded, Bearded-dragon, Blindworm, Blue-tongued, Brontosaurus, Chameleon,
Chuckwalla, Dinosaur, Draco, Dragon, Eft, Evet, Fence, Flying, Frilled, Frill-necked,
Galliwasp, Gecko(ne), Gila, Gila monster, Glass snake, Goanna, Gotcha, Guana,
Hatteria, Hellbender, Horned, Iguana, Jew, Kabaragoya, Komodo (dragon),
Lacerta, Legua(a)n, Lounge, Malayan monitor, Mastigure, Menopome, Mokomoko,
Moloch, Monitor, Mosasaur(us), Mountain devil, Newt, Ngarara, Perentie, Perenty,
Reptile, Rock, Sand, Sauria, Scincoid, Seps, Skink, Slow-worm, Snake, Sphenodon,
Stellio(n), Sungazer, Swift, Tegu(exin), Thorny devil, Tokay, Tuatara, Tuatera,
Varan, Wall, Whiptail, Worm, Worral, Worrel, Zandoli, Zonure
Llama Alpaca, Alpaco, Guanaco, Huanaco, Paco, Vicuña
Load(ed), Loader, Loading, Loads Accommodation, Affluent, Back-end, Ballast,
Base, Boot-strap, Boozy, Burden, Cargo, Charge, Cobblers, Dead weight, Disc,
Dope, Drunk, Dummy, Fardel, Fother, Freight, Front-end, Fulham, Full, Gestant,
Glyc(a)emic, Heap, Input, Jag, Lade, Lard, Last, Live, Onus, Pack, Packet, Pay,
Peak, Power, Prime, Rich, Seam, Shipment, Shoal, Some, Span, Super, Surcharge,
→ **TIGHT**, Tod, Traction, Ultimate, Useful, Wealthy, Weight, Wharfinger, Wing
Loaf(er), Loaves Baguette, Barmbrack, Batch, Baton, Beachbum, Beachcomber,
Bloomer, Bludge, Bonce, Boule, Brick, Bum, Bu(r)ster, Cad, Cob, Coburg, Cottage,
Currant, Danish, Farmhouse, French stick, Hawm, Hoe-cake, Idle, → **LAZE**, Long
tin, Lusk, Manchet, Miche, Milk, Mouch, Pan, Pan(h)agia, Plait, Quartern, Roll,
Roti, Shewbread, Showbread, Slosh, Split tin, Square tin, Sugar, Tin, Vantage,
Vienna, Yob
Loam Clay, Loess, Loss, Malm
Loan(s) Advance, Balloon, Benevolence, Bottomry, Bridging, Call, Consolidation,
Debenture, Demand, Droplock, Imprest, Lane, Mutuum, Omnium, Out, Prest,
Respondentia, Roll-over, Soft, Start-up, Sub, Time, Top-up, War
Loathe, Loathing, Loathsome Abhor(rent), Abominate, Carrion, Detest, Hate,
Nauseate, Odious, Scunner, Ug(h)
Lob Loft, Sky, Underarm
Lobby Demo, Division, Entry, Foyer, Gun, Hall, Press, Urge
Lobe(d) Anisocercal, Fluke, Frontal, Insula, Jugum, Lacinia, Lap, Occipital, Optic,
Palmate, Parietal, Pinnule, Prostomium, Runcinate, Segment, Temporal, Uvula,
Vermis
Lobster Cock, Crawfish, Crayfish, Crustacean, Decapoda, Langouste, Newburg,
Norway, Pot, Rock, Scampo, Spiny, Squat, Thermidor, Tomalley
Local(ity) Area, Bro, Des(h)i, Endemic, Home, Inn, Insider, Landlord, Native, Near,
Nearby, Neighbourhood, Number, Parochial, Pub, Regional, Resident, Swadishi,
Tavern, Topical, Vernacular, Vicinal
▷ **Local** *may indicate* a dialect word
Locale Scene, Site
Locate, Location Address, Connect, Find, Fix, Lay, Milieu, Node, Pinpoint, Place,
Plant, Recess, Site, Situate, Situation, Sofar, Spot, Trace, Ubiety, Website, Where, Zone
Loch, Lough Allen, Ashie, Awe, Derg, Earn, Eil, Erne, Etive, Fine, Gare, Garten,
Holy, Hourn, Katrine, → **LAKE**, Larne, Leven, Linnhe, Lomond, Long, Moidart,
Morar, More, Nakeel, Neagh, Ness, Rannoch, Ryan, Shiel, Strangford, Tay,
Torridon
Lock(ing), Locker, Locks, Lock up Bar, Barnet, Bolt, Canal, Central, Chubb®,

Clinch, Combination, Cowlick, Curlicue, Davy Jones, Deadbolt, Detent, Drop, Fastener, Fermentation, Foretop, Gate, Haffet, Haffit, Handcuff, Hasp, Hold, Intern, Key, Latch, Lazaretto, Man, Mortise, Percussion, Prison, Quiff, Ragbolt, Rim, Ringlet, Safety, Sasse, Scalp, Scissors, → SECURE, Sluice, Snap, Spring, Sta(u)nch, Stock, Strand, Tag, Talon, Time, Trap, Tress, Tuft, Tumbler, Vapour, Villus, Ward, Wheel, Wrestle, Yale®

Locket Lucy

Lockjaw Tetanus, Trismus

Locksmith Garret-master, Hairdresser

Locomotive Banker, Bogie, Bul(l)gine, Engine, Iron horse, Mobile, Rocket, Steam, Steamer, Train

Locum Deputy, Relief, Stand-in, Stopgap

Locus Centrode, Horopter, Lemniscate, Place, Spot

Locust, Locust tree Anime, Carob, Cicada, Hopper, Nymph, Robinia, Seventeen-year, Voetganger

Lode Comstock, Lodge, Mother, Reef, Vein

Lodestone Magnes, Magnet

Lodge(r) Billet, Board(er), Box, Cosher, Deposit, Dig, Doss, Encamp, Entertain, Freemason, Grange, Grove, Guest, Harbour, Host, Inmate, Layer, Lie, Masonic, Nest, Orange, Parasite, PG, Porter's, Put up, Quarter, Rancho, Resident, Room(er), Roomie, Stay, Storehouse, Stow, Sweat, Tenant, Tepee, Wigwam

Lodging(s) Abode, B and B, Chummage, Dharms(h)ala, Diggings, Digs, Dosshouse, Ferm, Grange, Grove, Hostel, Inquiline, Kip, Minshuku, Pad, Padding-ken, Pension, Pied-à-terre, Quarters, Resiant, Rooms, Singleen, Sponging-house, Spunging-house, YHA

Loft(iness), Lofty Aerial, Airy, Arrogant, Attic, Celsitude, Chip, Choir, Exalted, Garret, Grand, Haymow, High, Jube, Lordly, Magniloquent, Noble, Olympian, Pulpitum, Rarefied, Rigging, Rood, Roost, Sky, Sublime, Tallat, Tallet, Tallot

Log Billet, Black box, Cabin, Chip, Chock, Deadhead, Diarise, Diary, Hack, Ln, Mantissa, Nap(i)erian, Neper, Patent, → RECORD, Stock, Yule

Logarithm Common, Lod, Mantissa, Nap(i)erian, Natural

Logic(al) Alethic, Analytical, Aristotelian, Boolean, Chop, Deontic, Dialectic(s), Distributed, Doxastic, Epistemics, Formal, Fuzzy, Heuristics, Iff, Mathematical, Modal, Organon, Philosophical, Premise, Pusser's, Ramism, Rational(e), Reason, Sane, Sequacious, Shared, Sorites, Syllogism, Symbolic, Tense, Trivium

Logo Colophon

Loin(s) Flank, Inguinal, Lungie, Lunyie, Reins

Loincloth Dhoti, Lungi, Pareu, Waist-cloth

Loiter(ing) Dally, Dare, Dawdle, Dilatory, Dilly-dally, Idle, Lag, Lallygag, Leng, Lime, → LINGER, Lollygag, Mike, Mooch, Mouch, Potter, Saunter, Scamp, Suss, Tarry

Lola Dolores

Loll Hawm, Lounge, Sprawl

Lollipop, Lolly Ice pole, Lulibub

Lolly Money, Popsicle®, Sweetmeat

London(er) 'Arry, Big Smoke, Cockaigne, Cockney, Co(c)kayne, East-ender, Flat-cap, Jack, Roseland, Smoke, Town, Troynovant, Wen

London pride None-so-pretty

Lone(r), Lonely Remote, Rogue, Saddo, Secluded, Sole, Solitary, Unked, Unket, Unkid

Long(er), Longing, Longs Ache, Aitch, Ake, Appetent, Aspire, Brame, Covet, Desire, Die, Earn, Erne, Far, Greed, Green, Grein, → HANKER, Huey, Hunger,

Inveterate, Island, Itch, L, Lanky, Large, Lengthy, Longa, Lust, Macron, Miss, More, → **NO LONGER**, Nostalgia, Option, Pant, Parsec, → **PINE**, Prolix, Sesquipedalian, Side, Sigh, Tall, Thirst, Trews, Weary, Wish, Wist, Yearn, Yen

Long-eared Spicate

Longitude Celestial, Ecliptic, Meridian

Long-lashed Mastigophora(n)

Long live(d) Banzai, Macrobian, Viva, Vive, Zindabad

Longshoreman Hobbler, Hoveller, Wharfinger

Long-suffering Job, Patient, Stoical

Long-tailed Macrural

Long-winded Prolix, Verbose, Wordy

Loo Ajax, Bog, Can, Chapel, Dike, Game, Gents, Jakes, John, Privy, Toilet

Loofah Towel gourd

Look(s), Look at After-eye, Air, Aspect, Behold, Belgard, Bonne-mine, Busk, Butcher's, Butcher's hook, Clock, Close-up, Crane, Daggers, Decko, Deek, Dekko, Ecce, Ecco, Expression, Eye, Eye-glance, Face, Facies, Gander, Gawp, Gaze, Geek, Glance, Glare, Gleam, Gledge, Glimpse, Glom, Glower, Goggle, Good, Grin, Hallo, Hangdog, Hey, Iliad, Inspect, Keek, La, Leer, Lo, Mien, New, Ogle, Old-fashioned, Peek, Peep, Prospect, Ray, Recce, Refer, → **REGARD**, Scan, Scrutinise, Search, See, Seek, Shade, Sheep's eyes, Shufti, Shufty, Spy, Squint, Squiz, Stare, Survey, Toot, V, Vista, Wet

Look-out (man) Cockatoo, Crow's nest, Dixie, Huer, Mirador, Nit, Sangar, Sentinel, Sentry, Sungar, Tentie, Toot(er), Watch, Watchtower

▷ **Look silly** *may indicate* an anagram

Loom Beamer, Dobby, Emerge, Impend, Jacquard, Lathe, Menace, Picker, Temple, Threaten, Tower

Loon Diver

Loop(ed), Loophole, Loopy Articulatory, Becket, Bight, Billabong, Bouclé, Carriage, Chink, Closed, Coil, Eyelet, Eyesplice, Fake, Frog, Frontlet, Grom(m)et, Ground, Grummet, Hank, Henie's, Hysteresis, Infinite, Kink, Knop, Lasket, Lippes, Local, Lug, Noose, Oillet, Parral, Parrel, Pearl(-edge), Picot, Prusik, Purl, Scrunchie, Staple, Stirrup, Tab, Terry, Toe, Twist

Loos Anita

Loose(n), Loose woman Absolve, Abstrict, Afloat, Anonyma, Baggage, Bail, Besom, Bike, Bunter, Chippie, Chippy, Cocotte, Cutty, Demi-mondaine, Demirep, Demivierge, Desultory, Dissolute, Dissolve, Doxy, Draggletail, Dratchell, Drazel, Ease, Emit, Flipperty-flopperty, Flirt-gill, Floosie, Floozie, Floozy, Floppy, Franion, Free, Gangling, Gay, Hussy, Insecure, Jade, Jezebel, Lax, Light-heeled, Loast, Mob, Mort, Naughty pack, Painted, Pinnace, Profligate, Promiscuous, Quail, Ramp, → **RELAX**, Sandy, Scrubber, Skanky-ho, Slag, Slapper, Slut, Streel, Tart, Tramp, Trull, Ungyve, Unhasp, Unhitch, Unknit, Unknot, Unlace, Unpin, Unreined, Unscrew, Unthread, Untie, Vague, Waistcoateer, Wappend, Whore

Loot Boodle, Booty, Cragh, Creach, Foray, Haul, Mainour, Peel, Pluck, → **PLUNDER**, Ransack, Rape, Reave, Rieve, Rob, Sack, Smug, Spoils, Spoliate, Swag, Treasure, Waif

Lop Behead, Clop, Curtail, Detruncate, Droop, Shroud, Sned, Trash

Lope Stride

Loquacious Chatty, Gabby, Garrulous, Rambling

Lord(s), Lordship, Lordly Adonai, Ahura Mazda, Anaxandron, Arrogant, Boss, Byron, Cyril, Dieu, Domineer, Dominical, Duc, Earl, Elgin, Gad, Gilded Chamber, God, Haw-haw, Herr, Idris, Imperious, Jim, Justice, Kami, Kitchener, Landgrave,

Law, Ld, Liege, Lonsdale, Losh, Lud, Mesne, Misrule, Mynheer, Naik, Oda Nobunaga, Omrah, Ordinary, Ormazd, Ormuzd, Peer, Sea, Seigneur, Seignior, Shaftesbury, Sire, Spiritual, Taverner, Temporal, Tuan, Ullin

Lords and ladies Wake-robin

Lore Cab(b)ala, Edda, Lair, Lare, Riem, Upanis(h)ad

Lorelei Siren

Lorgnette Starers

Lorna Doone

Lorry Artic(ulated), Camion, Crummy, Drag, Flatbed, Juggernaut, Low-loader, Rig, Tipper, Tonner, → **TRUCK**, Wagon

Lose(r) Also-ran, Decrease, Drop, Elude, Forfeit, Hesitater, Leese, Misère, Mislay, Misplace, Nowhere, Spread, Tank, Throw, Tine(r), Tyne, Underdog, Unsuccessful, Waste, Weeper

Loss, Lost Anosmia, Aphesis, Aphonia, Apocope, Apraxia, Astray, Attainder, Boohai, Chord, Cost, Dead, Decrease, Depreciation, Detriment, Disadvantage, Elision, Extinction, Foredamned, Forfeited, Forgotten, Forlorn, Gone, Lore, Lorn, Lurch, Missing, Omission, Outage, Pentimento, Perdition, Perdu, Perished, Preoccupied, Privation, Psilosis, Reliance, Tine, Tinsel, Tint, Toll, Traik, Tribes, Tyne(d), Ullage, Unredeemed, Wastage, Wasted, Will, Write-off, Wull

Loss of memory Amnesia, Black-out, Fugue, Infonesia, Paramnesia

▷ **Lost** *may indicate* an anagram or an obsolete word

Lot(s) Abundant, Amount, Aret(t), Badly, Batch, Boatload, Caboodle, Cavel, Chance, Deal, Dole, Doom, Drove, Due, → **FATE**, Fortune, Group, Hantle, Hap, Heaps, Horde, Host, Item, Job, Kevel, Kismet, Lank, Lashings, Legion, Loads, Luck, Manifold, Many, Mass, Moh, Moira, Mony, Mort, Myriad, Oceans, Omnibus, Oodles, Oodlins, Pack, Parcel, Parking, Plenitude, Plenty, Portion, Power, Purim, Raft, Rich, Scads, Set, Sight, Slather, Slew, Slue, Sortilege, Sortition, Stack, Sum, Tall order, The works, Tons, Vole, Wagonload, Weird

Loth Averse, Circumspect, Sweer(t), Sweir(t), Unwilling

Lothario Lady-killer, Libertine, Poodle-faker, Rake, Womaniser

Lotion After-shave, Blackwash, Calamine, Collyrium, Cream, Eye-wash, Humectant, Setting, Suntan, Unguent, Wash, Yellow wash

Lottery, Lotto Art union, Ballot, Bingo, Cavel, Draw, Gamble, National, Pakapoo, Pools, Postcode, Punchboard, Raffle, Rollover, Scratchcard, Sweepstake, Tattersall's, Tombola

Lotus (eater), Lotus land Asana, Djerba, Lotophagus, Padmasana, White

Loud(ness), Loudly Bel, Big, Blaring, Booming, Brassy, Decibel, F, FF, Flashy, Forte, Fracas, Full-mouthed, Garish, Gaudy, Glaring, Hammerklavier, High, Lumpkin, Noisy, Orotund, Plangent, Raucous, Roarie, Siren, Sone, Stentor(ian), Strident, Tarty, Vocal, Vociferous, Vulgar

Loudspeaker Action, Boanerges, Bullhorn, Hailer, Megaphone, Stentor, Subwoofer, Tannoy®, Tweeter, Woofer

▶ **Lough** *see* **LOCH**

Louis Baker, Roi

Louisianian Cajun

Lounge(r) Cocktail, Da(c)ker, Daiker, Departure, Hawm, Idle, Laze, Lizard, Loll, Lollop, Parlour, Paul's man, Sitkamer, Slouch, Sun, Transit

Louse (up), Lousy, Lice Acrawl, Argulus, Bolix, Bollocks, Chat, Chicken, Cootie, Crab, Crummy, Fish, Head, Isopod(a), Kutu, Nit, Oniscus, Pedicular, Phthiriasis, Plant, Psocoptera, Psylla, Slater, Snot, Sowbug, Sucking, Vermin, Whale

Lout Clod(hopper), Coof, Cuif, Hallian, Hallion, Hallyon, Hick, Hob, Hobbledehoy,

Hooligan, Hoon, Jack, Jake, Keelie, Lager, Larrikin, Litter, Lob(lolly), Loord, Lubber, Lumpkin, Lycra, Oaf, Oik, Rube, Swad, Tout, Tripper, Yahoo, Yob(bo)
Louvre Shutter
Love(d), Lovable, Lover Abelard, Admire, Adore, Adulator, Affection, Agape, Alma, Amabel, Amanda, Amant, Amateur, Ami(e), Amoret, Amoroso, Amour, Angharad, Antony, Ardour, Ariadne, Aroha, Aucassin, Beau, Bidie-in, Blob, Calf, Care, Casanova, Chamberer, Cicisbeo, Concubine, Coquet, Court, Courtly, Cupboard, Cupid, Dona(h), Dotard, Dote, Doxy, Duck(s), Ducky, Dulcinea, Eloise, Eloper, Emotion, Enamorado, Eros, Esme, Fan, Fancy man, Flame, Frauendienst, Free, Goose-egg, Greek, Idolise, Inamorata, Inamorato, Iseult, Isolde, Item, Jo, Kama, Lad, Leander, Leman, Like, Lochinvar, Loe, Loo, Lurve, Man, Nihility, Nil, Nothing, Nought, O, Pairs, Paramour, Pash, Passion, Philander, -phile, Platonic, Precious, Protestant, Psychodelic, Puppy, Revere, Rhanja, Romance, Romeo, Sapphism, Spooner, Stale, Storge, Suitor, Swain, Thisbe, Touch, Toyboy, Troilus, True, Turtle(-dove), Valentine, Venus, Virtu, Woman, Worship, Zeal, Zero
Love-apple Tomato, Wolf's-peach
Love-bite Hickey
Love-child By-blow, Come-by-chance
Love-in-a-mist Nigella
Love letter Capon
Lovely Adorable, Belle, Dishy, Dreamy, Exquisite, Nasty
Love-making → INTERCOURSE, Kama Sutra, Sex, Snog
Love-sick Smit(ten), Strephon
Loving(ly) Amoroso, Amorous, Fond, Tender
Low(est), Low-cut, Lower(ing) Abase, Abate, Abysmal, Amort, Area, Avail(e), Avale, B, Basal, Base(-born), Bass(o), Beneath, Blue, Caddish, Cartoonist, Cheap, Church, Condescend, Contralto, Cow, Croon, Crude, Darken, Debase, Décolleté, Deepmost, Degrade, Demean, Demit, Demote, Depress, Devalue, Dim, Dip, Dispirited, Doldrums, Drawdown, Drop, Early, Embase, Flat, Foot, Frown, Gazunder, Glare, Guernsey, Gurly, Hedge, Humble, Ignoble, Imbase, Inferior, Jersey, Laigh, Lallan, Law, Light, Lite, Mass, Mean, Menial, Moo, Mopus, Morose, Nadir, Net, Nether, Nett, Non-U, Ostinato, Paravail, Plebeianise, Profound, Prole, Relegate, Ribald, Rock-bottom, Sad, Scoundrel, Scowl, Secondo, Settle, Shabby, Short, Soft, Stoop, Subordinate, Sudra, Undermost, Unnoble, Vail, Vulgar, Weak, Wretched
Lowbrow Philistine
Lowdown Gen, Info
▷ **Lower** *may refer to* cattle
Lowland(er) Carse, Gallovidian, Glen, Laigh, Lallans, Merse, Mudflat, Plain, Polder, Sassenach, Vlei
Low-lying Callow, Epigeous, Fens, Inferior, Sump
Low person Boor, Bunter, Cad, Caitiff, Cocktail, Demirep, Ratfink, Snot
Loyal(ty) Adherence, Allegiant, Brick, Dependable, Esprit de corps, Faithful, Fast, Fidelity, Gungho, Leal, Patriotic, Pia, Stalwart, Staunch, → TRUE, True blue, Trusty
Loyalist Hard core, Paisley, Patriot, Tory
Lozenge Cachou, Catechu, Fusil, Jujube, Mascle, Pastille, Pill, Rhomb, Rustre, Tablet, Troche, Voided
LSD Acid, Money
Lubber(ly), Lubbers Booby, Clod, Clumsy, Gawky, Hulk, Lob, Looby, Oaf, Slowback, Swab, Swads
Lubricant, Lubricate, Lubrication Carap-oil, Coolant, Derv, Fluid, Force-feed,

Grease, Oil, Petrolatum, Sebum, Unguent, Vaseline®, Wool-oil

Luce Ged

Lucerne Alfalfa, Medick, Nonsuch

Lucia Mimi

Lucid Bright, Clear, Perspicuous, Sane

Lucifer Devil, Match, Proud

Luck(y) Amulet, Auspicious, Beginner's, Bonanza, Break, Caduac, Canny, Cess, Chance, Charmed, Chaunce, Daikoku, Dip, Fate, Fluke, → **FORTUNE**, Godsend, Hap, Heather, Hit, Jam(my), Joss, Lady, Lot, Mascot, Mozzle, Pot, Prosit, Providential, Pudding-bag, Purple patch, Seal, Seel, Sele, Serendipity, Sess, Sonsie, Sonsy, Star(s), Streak, Success, Talisman, Tinny, Tough, Turn-up, Windfall, Worse

Luckless Hapless, Wight

Lucre Money, Pelf, Tin

Lucy Locket

Lud Gad

Luddite Saboteur, Wrecker

Ludicrous Absurd, Bathetic, Bathos, Farcical, Fiasco, Inane, Irish, Jest, Laughable, Risible

Ludo Uckers

Luff Derrick

Lug Ear, Earflap, Sea-worm, Sowle, Tote, Tow

Luggage Bags, Carryon, Cases, Dunnage, Excess, Grip, Hand, Kit, Petara, Suiter, Traps, Trunk

Luggage-carrier Grid

Lugubrious Dismal, Drear

Luke-warm Laodicean, Lew, Tepid

Lull, Lullaby Berceuse, Calm, Cradlesong, Hushaby, Respite, Rock, Sitzkreig, Soothe, Sopite

Lulu Stunner

Lumber(ing) Clump, Galumph, Jumble, Pawn, Ponderous, Raffle, Saddle, Scamble, Timber

Lumberjack Bushwhacker, Feller, Logger, Logman

Luminance, Luminous, Luminosity, Luminescence Aglow, Arc, Foxfire, Glow, Ignis-fatuus, L, Light, Nit, Phosphorescent, Scintillon, Sea-dog, Wildfire, Will o' the wisp

Lumme Coo, Lor

Lump(y) Aggregate, Bubo, Bud, Bulge, Bur(r), Caruncle, Chuck, Chunk, Clat, Claut, Clod, Clot, Cob, Combine, Dallop, Da(u)d, Dollop, Enhydros, Epulis, Flocculate, Ganglion, Geode, Gnarl, Gob(bet), Goiter, Goitre, Grape, Grip, Hunch, Hunk, Inium, Knarl, Knob, Knub, Knur(r), Knurl, Lob, Lunch, Malleolus, Mass, Mote, Mott, Myxoma, Neuroma, Nibble, Nirl, Node, Nodule, Nodulus, Nub, Nubble, Nugget, Nur(r), Nurl, Osteophyte, Plook, Plouk, Quinsy, Raguly, Sarcoma, Scybalum, Sitfast, Slub, Strophiole, Tragus, Tuber(cle), Wart, Wodge

Lumpsucker Sea-owl

Lunacy, Lunatic Bedlam, Dementia, Demonomania, Folly, Insanity, Mad(ness), Psychosis

Lunar Evection, Mascon

▷ **Lunatic** *may indicate* an anagram

Lunch(time) Bait, Crib, Dejeune, Déjeuner, L, Nacket, Nocket, Nuncheon, Packed, Piece, Ploughman, Pm, Power, Tiff(in), Working

Lung(s) Alveoli, Bellows, Coalminer's, Farmer's, Green, Iron, Lights, Pulmo, Pulmonary, Soul

Lung disease Anthracosis, Byssinosis, Emphysema, Farmer's lung, Pneumoconiosis, Siderosis, Silicosis, Tuberculosis

Lunge Breenge, Breinge, Dive, Stab, Thrust, Venue

Lungfish Dipnoi(an)

Lupin Arsene

Lurch Reel, Stoit, Stumble, Swee

Lure Bait, Bribe, Carrot, Decoy, Devon minnow, Entice, Horn, Inveigle, Jig, Judas, Plug, Roper, Spinner, Spoon, Spoonbait, Spoonhook, Squid, Stale, Temptation, Tice, Tole, Toll, Train, Trepan, Wormfly

Lurgi Illness

Lurid Gruesome, Purple

Lurk(ing) Dare, Latitant, Skulk, Slink, Snoke, Snook, Snowk

Lusatia(n) Wend(ic), Wendish

Luscious Succulent

Lush Alcoholic, Alkie, Alky, Dipso(maniac), Drunk, Fertile, Green, Juicy, Lydian, Sot, Tosspot, Verdant

Lust(ful), Lusty Cama, Concupiscence, Corflambo, Desire, Eros, Frack, Greed, Kama, Lech(ery), Lewd, Megalomania, Obidicut, Randy, Rank, Raunchy, Salacious, Venereous

Lustre, Lustrous Brilliance, Census, Chatoyant, Galena, Gaum, Gilt, Gloss, Gorm, Inaurate, Lead-glance, Pentad, Reflet, Satiny, Schiller, → SHEEN, Water

Lute, Lutist Amphion, Chitarrone, Cither, Dichord, Orpharion, Pandora, Pandore, Theorbo, Vielle

Lutetium Lu

Lutheran Adiaphorist, Calixtin(e), Pietist, Ubiquitarian

Lux Lx

Luxemburg L

Luxuriant, Luxuriate, Luxurious, Luxury (lover) Bask, Clover, Cockaigne, Cockayne, Copious, Deluxe, Dolce vita, Extravagant, Fleshpots, Lavish, Lucullan, Lush, Mollitious, Ornate, Pie, Plush, Posh, Rank, → RICH, Ritzy, Sumptuous, Sybarite, Wallow

Lycanthropist Werewolf

Lydia Languish

Lye Buck

▶ **Lying** see LIE

Lymph Chyle

Lymphoma Burkett's

Lynch(ing), Lyncher Dewitt, Hang, Necktie party, Nightrider

Lynx Bay, Bobcat, Caracal, Desert, Rooikat

Lyre Cithern, Harp, Psaltery, Testudo, Trigon

Lyric(s), Lyrical, Lyricist, Lyrist Cavalier, Dit(t), Epode, Gilbert, Hammerstein, Melic, Ode, Orphean, Paean, Pean, Poem, Rhapsodic, Song, Words

Mm

M Married, Member, Metre, Mike, Mile, Thousand
Mac Mino, Scot, Waterproof
Macabre Gothic, Grotesque, Sick
Macaroni Beau, Blood, Cat, Dandy, Elbow, Exquisite, Fop, Jack-a-dandy, Olio, Pasta, Petitmaitre
Macaroon Biscuit, Signal
Macaulay Layman
Mace Club, Nutmeg, Sceptre, Spice
Mace-bearer Beadle, Bedel, Poker
Macedonian Philip, Stagirite, Stagyrite
Machine(ry) Air-engine, Answering, Apparat(us), Appliance, Automaton, Bathing, Bulldozer, Calender, Centrifuge, Clobbering, Cycle, → DEVICE, Dialyser, Dredge(r), Drum, Dynamotor, Engine, Enginery, Facsimile, Fax, Fourdrinier, Fruit, Gin, Hawk-Eye®, Heck, Hopper, Hot-press, Infernal, Instrument, Jawbreaker, Jukebox, Lathe, Life-support, Linotype®, Linter, Lithotripter, Loom, Ludlow, Milling, Moulinet, Moviola®, Mule, Nintendo®, Party, Pile-driver, Planer, Plant, Pokie, Press, Processor, Propaganda, Pulsator, Robot, Rotavator®, Rototiller, Rowing, Sausage, Sewing, Sigmatron, Slicer, Slot, Spin, Spinning jenny, Stenotype®, Tape, Teaching, Tedder, Throstle, Time, Transfer, Treadmill, Tumbler, Turbine, Turing, Twin tub, Typewriter, Vending, Virtual, War, Washing, Weighing, Willow, Wimshurst, Wind(mill), Wringer
Macho Jock, Laddish
Mackerel Albacore, Brack, Dory, Fish, Horse, Pacific, Pimp, Scad, Scomber, Sky, Spanish, Spotted, Trevally
Mackintosh Burberry®, Mac, Mino, Oilskin, Slicker, Waterproof
Macropus Euro, Wallaroo
Mad(den), Madman, Madness Angry, Balmy, Bananas, Barking, Barmy, Bedlam, Besotted, Bonkers, Crackbrained, Crackpot, Crazy, Cuckoo, Cupcake, Daffy, Delirious, Dement, Distract, Dotty, Enrage, Fay, Fey, Folie, Folly, Frantic, Frenetic(al), Fruitcake, Furioso, Fury, Gelt, Gyte, Harpic, Hatter, Idiotic, Incense, Insane, Insanie, Insanity, Into, Ireful, Irritate, Kook, Loco, Lunatic, Lycanthropy, Madbrained, Maenad, Mango, Mania, Mattoid, Mental, Meshug(g)a, Metric, Midsummer, Moonstruck, Motorway, Mullah, Nuts, Porangi, Psycho, Rabid, Rasputin, Raving, Redwood, Redwud, Scatty, Screwy, Short-witted, Starkers, Tonto, Touched, Troppo, Unhinged, Wacko, Wood, Wowf, Wrath, Wud, Xenomania, Yond, Zany
▷ **Mad(den)** *may indicate* an anagram
Madagascan, Madagascar Aye-aye, Hova, Indri, Lemur, Malagasy, RM
Madam(e) Baggage, Lady, M, Proprietress
Madcap Impulsive, Tearaway
Madder Alizari, Alyari, Chay(a), Gardenia, Genipap, Rose, Rubia, Shaya

Made (it) Built, Did, Fec(it), Ff, Gart, Invented
Madge Pie
▷ **Madly** *may indicate* an anagram
Madonna Lady, Lily, Mary, Pietà, Sistine, Virgin
Madras Chennai
Madrigal Ballet, Fala, Song
Maelstrom Voraginous, Vortex, Whirlpool
Maenad Devotee, Fan
Maestro Artist, Toscanini, Virtuoso
Mafia Camorra, Capo, Cosa nostra, Godfather, Goombah, Mob, Ndrangheta, Omerta, The Mob
Mag Mail
Magazine Arsenal, Clip, Colliers, Contact, Cornhill, Cosmopolitan, Digizine, Economist, E-zine, Field, Girlie, Glossy, Granta, Jazz mag, Lady, Lancet, Life, Listener, Little, Magnet, Organ, Part work, Periodical, Pictorial, Playboy, Powder, Private Eye, Pulp, Punch, She, Skin, Slick, Spectator, Store, Strand, Tatler, Time, Vogue, Warehouse, Weekly, Yoof, Zine
Magdalene St Mary
Maggie Rita
Maggot Bot, Flyblow, Gentiles, Gentle, Grub, Larva, Mawk, Myiasis, Whim, Worm
Magi Balthazar, Gaspar, Melchior
Magic(al), Magician, Magic square Archimage, Art, Baetyl, Black, Black art, Charm, Circle, Conjury, Diablerie, Diablery, Enchanting, Faust, Faustus, Fetish, Genie, Goetic, Goety, Gramary(e), Grimoire, Hermetic, Houdini, Illusionist, Incantation, Makuto, Math, Medea, Merlin, Mojo, Moly, Morgan le Fay, Myal, Nasik, Natural, Necromancer, Obeah, Pawaw, Powwow, Prospero, Reim-kenner, Rhombus, Shamanism, Sorcery, Sortilege, Spell, Speller, Supernatural, Sympathetic, Talisman, Thaumaturgics, Theurgy, Voodoo, Warlock, White, Wizard, Zendik
Magistracy, Magistrate Aedile, Amman, Amtman, Archon, Avoyer, Bailie, Bailiff, Bailli(e), Bench, Burgess, Burgomaster, Cadi, Censor, Consul, Corregidor, Demiurge, Doge(ate), Draco, Edile, Effendi, Ephor, Field cornet, Finer, Foud, Gonfalonier, JP, Judiciary, Jurat, Kotwal, Landamman(n), Landdrost, Lord Provost, Maire, Mayor, Mittimus, Novus homo, Podesta, Portreeve, Pr(a)efect, Pr(a)etor, Prior, Proconsul, Propraetor, Provost, Qadi, Quaestor, Recorder, Reeve, Shereef, Sherif, Stad(t)holder, Stipendiary, Syndic, Tribune, Worship
Magnanimity, Magnanimous Big, Charitable, → GENEROUS, Largeness, Lofty, Noble
Magnate Baron, Bigwig, Industrialist, Mogul, Onassis, Randlord, Tycoon, Vanderbilt, VIP
Magnesia, Magnesium Humite, Kainite, Mg, Periclase
Magnet(ic), Magnetism Animal, Artificial, Attraction, Bar, Charisma, Field, Gauss, Horseshoe, It, Loadstone, Lodestone, Maxwell, Od, Oersted, Permanent, Personal, Polar, Pole, Pole piece, Poloidal, Pull, Remanence, Retentivity, Slug, Solenoid, Terrella, Terrestrial, Tesla, Tole
Magnificence, Magnificent Fine, Gorgeous, Grandeur, Imperial, Laurentian, Lordly, Noble, Pride, Regal, Royal, Splendid, Splendo(u)r, State, Sumptuous, Superb
Magnifier, Magnify(ing) Aggrandise, Augment, Binocle, → ENLARGE, Exaggerate, Increase, Loupe, Megaphone, Microscope, Teinoscope, Telescope
Magniloquent Bombastic, Orotund

Magnitude Absolute, Abundance, Amplitude, Apparent, Earthquake, Extent, Muchness, Photoelectric, Scalar, Size, Visual

Magnolia An(n)ona, Beaver-tree, Champac, Champak, Mississippi, Sweet bay, Umbrella-tree, Yulan

Magpie Bell, Bird, Bishop, Chatterer, Madge, Mag, Margaret, Outer, Pica, Piet, Pyat, Pyet, Pyot

Magus Artist

Magyar Hungarian, Szekely, Szekler, Ugrian, Ugric

Mahogany Acajou, African, Carapa, Cedrela, Philippine, Wood

Mahommedan Dervish, Shiah

Maid(en) Abigail, Aia, Amah, Biddy, Bonibell, Bonne, Bonnibell, Burd, Chamber, Chloe, Clothes-horse, Damosel, Dell, Dey, Dresser, Femme de chambre, First, Girl, Guillotine, Ignis-fatuus, Imago, Inaugural, Io, Iras, Iron, Lorelei, M, Marian, May, Miss, Nymph, Opening, Over, Parlour, Pucelle, Rhian, Rhine, Skivvy, Soubrette, Suivante, Table, Thestylis, Tirewoman, Tweeny, Valkyrie, Virgin, Walkyrie, Wench, Wicket

Maidenhair Fern, Ginkgo

Mail Air, → ARMOUR, Byrnie, Cataphract, Chain, Da(w)k, Direct, E(lectronic), Express, Fan, Habergeon, Hate, Hauberk, Helm, Junk, Letter, Media, Metered, Panoply, Pony express, Post, Ring, Send, Snail, Spam, Surface, Tuille(tte), Voice

Mailbag Pouch

Mailboat Packet

Maim Cripple, Impair, Lame, Main, Mayhem, Mutilate, Vuln

Main(s) Atlantic, Brine, Briny, → CENTRAL, Chief, Cockfight, Conduit, Essential, Foremost, Gas, Generally, Grid, Gross, Head, → KEY, Lead(ing), Major, Pacific, Palmary, Predominant, Prime, Principal, Ring, → SEA, Sheer, Spanish, Staple, Water

Mainland Continent, Pomona

Mainstay Backbone, Bastion, Pillar, Support

Maintain(er), Maintenance Alimony, Allege, Ap(p)anage, Argue, Assert, Aver, Avouch, Avoure, Avow, Claim, Contend, Continue, Defend, Escot, Insist, Keep (up), Lengthman, Preserve, Run, Sustain, Upbear, Uphold, Upkeep

Maize Corn, Hominy, Indian, Indian corn, Mealie, Popcorn, Samp, Silk, Stamp, Zea

Majestic, Majesty August, Britannic, Dignity, Eagle, Grandeur, Imperial, Maestoso, Olympian, Regal, SM, Sovereign, Stately, Sublime, Tuanku

Major (domo) Barbara, Drum, → IMPORTANT, Pipe, PM, Seneschal, Senior, Sergeant, Star, Trumpet, Wig

Majority Absolute, Age, Body, Eighteen, Landslide, Latchkey, Maturity, Moral, Most, Preponderance, Relative, Silent, Working

Make(r), Make do, Making Amass, Brand, Build, Clear, Coerce, Coin, Compel, Compulse, Concoct, Creant, Create, Devise, Earn, Execute, Fabricate, Factive, Fashion, Faute de mieux, Fet(t), Forge, Form, Gar(re), God, Halfpenny, Mail(e), Manage, Marque, Prepare, Production, Reach, Render, Shape, Sort, Temporise, Wright

▷ **Make** *may indicate* an anagram

Make believe Fantasy, Fictitious, Pretend, Pseudo

Make good Abet, Compensate, Remedy, Succeed, Ulling

Make hay Ted

Make off Bolt, Leg it, Mosey, Run, Scarper

Makeshift Bandaid, Crude, Cutcha, Expedient, Jury-rigged, Kacha, Kachcha, Kludge, Kutcha, Lash-up, Mackle, Pis-aller, Rude, Stopgap, Timenoguy

Make up Ad lib, Compensate, Compose, Concealer, Constitution, Cosmetics, Fucus, Gaud, Gawd, Gene, Greasepaint, Identikit®, Kohl, Liner, Lipstick, Maquillage, Mascara, Metabolism, Paint, Pancake, Panstick, Powder, Reconcile, Rouge, Slap, Tidivate, Titivate, Toiletry, Visagiste, War paint, White-face
Maladroit Awkward, Clumsy, Graceless, Inelegant, Unperfect
Malady Disease, Illness
Malagas(e)y Hova, RM
Malaise Affluenza
Malapropism Catachresis, Slipslop
Malaria Ague, Falciparum, Marsh-fever, Paludism, Tap, Vivax
Malawi Nyasa
Malay(an), Malaysian Austronesian, Bahasa, Bajou, Datin, Datuk, D(a)yak, Jawi, Madurese, Moro, Sakai, Tokay, Tuan
Male Alpha, Arrhenotoky, Buck, Bull, Butch, Dog, Ephebe, Ephebus, Gent, Hob, John Doe, Macho, Mansize, Masculine, Ram, Rogue, Spear(side), Stag, Stamened, Telamon, Tom
Malediction Curse, Cuss, Oath, Slander
Malefactor Criminal, Felon, Villain
Malevolent, Malevolence Evil, Fell, Malign, Pernicious, Venomous
Malformation Teratogenesis
Malfunction Glitch, Hiccup
Mali RMM
Malice, Malicious Bitchy, Catty, Cruel, Despiteous, Envy, Hatchet job, Malevolent, Malign, Narquois, Prepense, Schadenfreude, Serpent, Snide, Spite, Spleen, Venom, Virulent, Vitriol
Malign(ant), Malignity Asperse, Backbite, Baleful, Defame, Denigrate, Evil, Gall, Harm, Hate-rent, Hatred, Libel, Poor-mouth, Sinister, Slander, Spiteful, Swart(h)y, Toxin, Vicious, Vilify, Vilipend, Viperous, Virulent
Malinger(er) Dodge, Leadswinger, Scrimshank, Shirk, Skrimshank, Truant
Mall Parade
Mallard Duck, Sord
Malleable Clay, Ductile, Fictile, Pliable
▷ **Malleable** *may indicate* an anagram
Mallet Beetle, Club, Hammer, Mace, Maul, Serving, Stick
Mallow Abutilon, Dwarf, Musk, Sida, Urena
Malodorous Mephitic, Stenchy
Malpractice(s) Sculduggery, Skulduggery
Malt Brewer's grain, Diastase, Grains, Grist, Single, Straik, Wort
Maltese (cross) Falcon, GC
Maltreat Abuse, Harm, Maul, Mishandle, Misuse
Mammal Animal, Anta, Armadillo, Artiodactyl, Binturong, Bobcat, Cacomistle, Cacomixle, Caracal, Cervid, Cetacean, Chalicothere, Charronia, Chevrotain, Chiropteran, Ciscus, Colugo, Creodont, Dhole, Dinothere, Dolphin, Dugong, Eutheria, Fisher, Glires, Glutton, Glyptodon, Grison, Guanaco, Hydrax, Hyrax, Indri, Jaguarondi, Jaguarundi, Kinkajou, Lagomorph, Leporid, Linsang, Loris, Lynx, Manatee, Margay, Marten, Meerkat, Metatherian, Mongoose, Monodelphia, Monotreme, Musteline, Notoungulate, Numbat, Olungo, Otter, Pachyderm, Pangolin, Peccary, Pekan, Perissodactyl, Pika, Pine marten, Pinniped, Platypus, Polecat, Porpoise, Primate, Pronghorn, Prototherian, Pudu, Raccoon, Rasse, Ratel, Rhytina, Sable, Serval, Shrew, Sirenian, Skunk, Sloth, Solenodon, Springhaas, Stegodon(t), Taguan, Tahr, Takin, Tamandu(a), Tanrec, Tapir, Tayra, Teledu,

Tenrec, Theria(n), Titanothere, Tylopod, Uintathere, Vicuña, Viverrid, Weasel, Whale, Wolverine, Zorilla

Mammon Money, Riches, Wealth

Mammoth Epic, Gigantic, Huge, Jumbo, Mastodon, Whopping, Woolly

Man(kind), Manly Adam, Advance, Andrew, Ask(r), Belt, Best, Betty, Bimana(l), Biped, Bloke, Bo, Boxgrove, Boy, Boyo, Bozo, Cad, Cairn, Calf, Castle, Cat, Chal, Chap, Checker, Chequer, Chiel, Cockey, Cod, Contact, Continuity, Crew, Cro-Magnon, Cuffin, Cully, Dog, Don, Draught, Dude, Emmanuel, Essex, Everyman, Family, Fancy, Fella, Feller, Fellow, Folsom, Friday, Front, G, Gayomart, Geezer, Gent, Grimaldi, Guy, He, Heidelberg, Himbo, Hombre, Hominid, Homme, Homo, Homo sapiens, Inner, IOM, Iron, Isle, It, Jack, Java, Joe (Bloggs), Joe Blow, Joe Sixpack, Joe Soap, John(nie), John Doe, Josser, Limit, Link, Lollipop, M, Male, Medicine, Microcosm, Mister, Mon, Mondeo, Mr, Muffin, Mun, Neanderthal, Numbers, Nutcracker, Oreopithecus, Organisation, Ou, Paleolithic, Party, Pawn, Peking, Person, Piece, Piltdown, Pin, Pithecanthropus, Property, Raff, Ray, Remittance, Renaissance, Resurrection, Rhodesian, Right-hand, Rook, Sandwich, Servant, Servitor, Ship, Sinanthropus, Sodor, Soldier, Solo, Spear, Staff, Stag, Standover, Straw, Third, Thursday, Trinil, Twelfth, Tyke, Type, Utility, Valet, Vir, White van, Wight

Man-about-town Boulevardier

Manacle Fetter, Handcuff, Iron, Shackle

Manage(r), Manageable, Management, Managing Adhocracy, Administer, Agent, Amildar, Attain, Aumil, Behave, Boss, Chief, Come by, Conduct, Contrive, Control, Cope, Darogha, Direct, Docile, Exec(utive), Fare, Fend, Find, Floor, Fund, Gerent, Get by, Govern, Grieve, Handle, Head bummer, Honcho, IC, Impresario, Intendant, Line, Logistical, MacReady, Maître d('hotel), Manipulate, Manoeuvre, Middle, Nomenklatura, Organise, Proctor, Procurator, Régisseur, Rig, Roadie, → RUN, Scrape, Shift, Steward, Strategy, Subsist, Succeed, Suit, Superintend, Supervisor, Swing, Tawie, Top, Tractable, Transact, Treatment, Trustee, Wangle, Wield(y), Yare

Manatee Lamantum, Mermaid, Sea-ape

Manchu Fu

Mandarin Bureaucrat, Chinaman, Kuo-Yu, Nodding, Satsuma, Yamen

Mandate Authority, Decree, Fiat, Order

Mandela Madiba, Nelson

Mandrake Springwort

Mandrel Triblet

Mane(d), Manes Crest, Encolure, Jubate, Larva(e), Shades

Manège Horseplay, Train

Manganese Diagolite, Mn, Synadelphite, Wadd

Manger Cratch, Crib, Hack, Stall

Mangle Agrise, Butcher, Distort, Garble, Hack, Hackle, Haggle, Wring(er)

▷ **Mangle** *may indicate* an anagram

Mango Dika

Manhandle Frogmarch, Maul, Rough

Manhater Misanthrope

Manhattan Bowery

Mania Cacoethes, Craze, Frenzy, Paranoia, Passion, Rage

Manichaean Albi

Manifest(ation), Manifestly Apparent, Attest, Avatar, Epiphany, Evident, Evince, Exhibit, Extravert, Extrovert, Feat, List, Marked, Mode, Notably, Obvious,

Open, Show, Undisguised
Manifesto Communist, Plank, Platform, Policy, Pronunciamento
Manifold(ness) Many, Multeity, Multiple
Manila Abaca, Cheroot
Manioc Cassava
Maniple Fannel, Fanon
Manipulate, Manipulative, Manipulator, Manipulation Bend, Chiropractor,
Cog, Control, Cook, Demagogic, Diddle, Fashion, Finagle, Finesse, Gerrymander,
Handle, Jerrymander, Juggle, Legerdemain, Logodaedalus, Masseuse, Milk,
Osteopath, Play off, Ply, Rig, Tweeze, Use, Wangle, → **WIELD**
▷ **Manipulate** *may indicate* an anagram
Manna Alhagi, Food, Trehala, Turkish
Manner(ism), Mannerly, Manners Accent, Airs, À la, Appearance, Attitude,
Bedside, Behaved, Behaviour, Bon ton, Breeding, Carriage, Conduct, Couth,
Crew, Custom, Deportment, Ethos, Etiquette, Farand, Farrand, Farrant, Guise,
Habit, How, Mien, Mister, Mode, Morality, Mores, Of, Ostent, Panache, Politesse,
Presentation, P's & Q's, Quirk, Rate, Sort, Style, Table, Thew(s), Thewe(s), Trick,
Upsee, Upsey, Upsy, Urbanity, Way, Wise
Manoeuvre(s) Alley-oop, Campaign, Castle, Christie, Christy, Démarche, Engineer,
Exercise, Faena, Fianchetto, Fork, Gambit, Half-board, Heimlich, Hot-dog, Jink(s),
Jockey, Manipulate, Op(eration), Pendule, Pesade, Ploy, Pull out, Renversement,
Ruse, Skewer, Stickhandle, Tactic, Takeover, Use, U-turn, Valsalva, Wear, Wheelie,
Whipstall, Wile, Wingover, Zigzag
▷ **Manoeuvre** *may indicate* an anagram
Man-of-war Armada, Bluebottle, Destroyer, Ironclad, Portuguese
Manor (house) Area, Demain, Demesne, Estate, Hall, Kelmscott, Schloss, Vill(a),
Waddesdon
Mansion Broadlands, Burghley House, Casa, Castle Howard, Chatworth House,
Cliveden, Knole, Luton Hoo, Mentmore, Penshurst Place, Queen's House, Seat,
Stourhead, Stowe, Waddesdon Manor, Woburn Abbey
Mantle Asthenosphere, Authority, Burnous(e), Capote, Caracalla, Chlamydate,
Dolman, Elijah, Gas, Pall, Pallium, Paludament, Pelisse, Rochet, Sima, Toga,
Tunic, Vakas, Veil
Mantuan Maro, Virgil
Manual Blue collar, Bradshaw, Cambist, Console, Enchiridion, Great (organ), Guide,
Hand, Handbook, How-to, Portolan(o), Positif, Sign
Manufacture, Manufacturing Fabricate, Industrial, Kanban, Make, Produce
Manure Compost, Dressing, Dung, → **FERTILISER**, Green, Guano, Hen-pen, Lime,
Muck, Sha(i)rn, Tath
Manuscript(s) Book of Kells, Codex, Codicology, Folio, Hand, Holograph,
Longhand, Miniscule, MS, Opisthograph, Palimpsest, Papyrus, Parchment, Script,
Scroll, Scrowl(e), Uncial, Vellum
Manx(man) Cat, IOM, Kelly, Kelt
▷ **Manx** *may indicate* a last letter missing
Many C, CD, Countless, D, Hantle, Herd, Horde, Host, L, Lot, M, Manifold, Mony,
Multi(tude), Myriad, Scad, Sight, Stacks, Tons, Umpteen, Untold
▷ **Many** *may indicate* the use of a Roman numeral letter
Maoist Naxalite, Red Guard
Maori (house) Hauhau, Hori, Jikanga, Mallowpuff, Moa hunter, Tangata whenua,
Te reo, Wahine, Whare
Map(s), Mapping Atlas, A-Z, Card, Cartogram, Chart, Chorography, Choropleth,

Chromosome, Cognitive, Contour, Digital, Face, Genetic, Inset, Key, Loxodromic, Mappemond, Mental, Mosaic, Moving, Mud, OS, Perceptual, Plan, Plot, Portolano, Relief, Road, Sea-card, Sea-chart, Site, Star, Strip, Topography, Weather

Maple Acer, Flowering, Japanese, Manitoba, Mazer, Norway, Plane, Silver, Sugar, Sycamore, Syrup

Map-maker Cartographer, OS, Speed

Maquis Queach, Underground

Mar Blight, Denature, Dere, Impair, Soil, Spoil, Taint

Marabout Sofi, Sufi

Marathon Comrades, Huge, London, Race, Two Oceans

Maraud(er) Amalekite, Attacker, Bandit, Pillager, Pirate, Predator, Prowler, Raid

Marble(s), Marbling Aeginetan, Agate, All(e)y, Arch, Arundelian, Bonce, Bonduc, Bool, Boondoggle, Bowl, Carrara, Chequer, Cipollino, Commoney, Devil's, Dump, Elgin, Humite, Hymettus, Knicker, Languedoc, Lucullite, Marl, Marmarosis, Marmoreal, Marver, Mottle, Nero-antico, Nickar, Nicker, Onychite, Onyx, Paragon, Parian, Pavonazzo, Pentelic(an), Petworth, Phigalian, Plonker, Plunker, Purbeck, Rance, Ringer, Ring-taw, Ruin, Sanity, Scagliola, Spangcockle, Taw, Variegate, Xanthian

Marcel Proust

March(ing) Abut, Adjoin, Advance, Anabasis, Border(er), Borderland, Dead, Defile, Demo, Étape, File, Footslog, Forced, Freedom, Fringe, Galumph, Go, Goosestep, Hikoi, Hunger, Ides, Jarrow, Lide, Limes, Lockstep, Long, Meare, Music, → PARADE, Paso doble, Procession, Progress, Protest, Quick, Rogue's, Route, Slow time, Step, Strunt, Strut, Trio, Tromp, Troop, Wedding, Yomp

▷ **March** *may indicate* 'Little Women' character, Amy, Beth, Jo, Meg

Marco Il Milione, Polo

Mare Dam, Flanders, Horse, M, MacCurdle's, Shanks's, Spanish, Yaud

Margaret Anjou, Meg, Peg, Rita

Margarine Oleo

Marge, Margin(al) Annotate, Bank, Border, Brim, Brink, Curb, Edge, Fimbria, Hair's breadth, Kerb, Lean, Leeway, Limit, Lip, Littoral, Neck, Nose, Peristome, Profit, Rand, Repand, → RIM, Selvedge, Sideline, Spread, Tail, Term

Marginal note Apostil(le), K'ri

Margosa Melia, Nim

Maria(nne) France, Tia

Marie Dressler, Tempest

Marigold Calendula, Kingcup, Tagetes

Marijuana Alfalfa, Camberwell carrot, Dagga, Gage, Ganja, Grass, Greens, Gungeon, Ha-ha, Hay, Herb, J, Jive, Joint, Kaif, Kef, Kif, Leaf, Lid, Locoweed, Mary-Jane, Pot, Roach, Rope, Shit, Sinsemilla, Splay, Spliff, Tea, Toke, Weed

Marina Wharf

Marinade Chermoula, Escabeche

Marine (animal) Aquatic, Bootie, Bootneck, Cephalopod, Chaetognath, Cnidarian, Coelenterate, Comatulid, Ctenophora, Cunjevoi, Enteropneusta, Flustra, Foram(inifer), Galoot, Graptolite, Harumfrodite, Hemichorda, Holothurian, Horse, Hydrocoral, Hydroid, Hydromedusa, Jarhead, Jolly, Lancelet, Leatherneck, Lobster, Mercantile, Mere-swine, Mistress Roper, Oceanic, Physalia, Pollywag, Pollywog, Salpa, Sea-soldier, Seston, Thalassian, Ultra

Mariner AB, Ancient, MN, Noah, RM, Sailor, Salt, Seafarer, Spacecraft, Tar

Marionette(s) Fantoccini, Puppet

Marjoram Amaracus, Origan, Pot, Sweet, Wild, Winter-sweet

Mark(ing), Marked, Marks Accent, Antony, Apostrophe, Asterisk, Astrobleme, Badge, Banker, Bethumb, Birth, Blaze, Blot, Blotch, Brand, Bruise, Bull, But(t), Cachet, Caract, Caret, Caste, CE, Cedilla, Chatter, Chequer, Cicatrix, Class, Clout, Colon, Comma, Coronis, Crease, Criss-cross, Cross, Cup (and ring), Dash, Denote, Dent, Diacritic, Diaeresis, Dieresis, Distinction, DM, Duckfoot quote, Dupe, Emblem, Ensign, Enstamp, Exclamation, Expression, Feer, Fleck, Freckle, Genetic, Glyph, Gospel, Grade, Guillemet, Gybe, Haček, Haemangioma, Hair-line, Hash, Hatch, Heed, High water, Hyphen, Impress(ion), Indicium, Ink, Inscribe, Insignia, Interrogation, Keel, Kite, Kumkum, Lentigo, Line, Ling, Livedo, Logo, Lovebite, Low water, M, Macron, Matchmark, MB, Medical, Merk, Mint, Minute, Mottle, NB, Nota bene, Notal, Note, Notice, Obelisk, Observe, Oche, Paginate, Paraph, Period, Pilcrow, Pit, Plage, Pling, Pock, Point, Popinjay, Port wine, Post, Presa, Printer's, Proof, Punctuation, Question, Quotation, Record, Reference, Register, Regulo, Remarque, Ripple, Roundel, Sanction, Scar, Score, Scratch, Section, See, Service, Shadow, Shilling, Shoal, Sigil, Sign, Smit, Smut, Smutch, Soft touch, Speck, Splodge, Splotch, Stain, Stencil, Stigma(ta), Strawberry, Stress, Stretch, Stroke, Sucker, Swan-upping, Symbol, Tag, Target, Tarnish, Tatow, Tattoo, Tee, Theta, Thread, Tick, Tide, Tika, Tikka, Tilak, Tilde, Tittle, Token, Touchmark, Trace, Track, Trout, Tug(h)ra, Twain, Umlaut, Ure, Victim, Wand, Warchalking, Watch, Weal, Welt

Marker Biological, Bollard, Buck, Cairn, Cross(let), Fanion, Flag, Gnomon, Infinitive, Ink, Inukshuk, Label, Medical, Scorer, Tie

Market(ing), Market day, Market place Advergaming, Agora, Alcaiceria, Available, Baltic, Bazaar, Bear, Billingsgate, Black, Black stump, Borgo, Bull, Buyers', Capital, Captive, Cattle, Change, Chowk, Cinema, Circular, Cluster, Common, Demo, Denet, Direct, Discount, Dragon, EC, Emerging, Emporium, Errand, Exchange, Exhibition, Fair, Farmers', Feeing, Flea, Forum, Forward, Free, Grey, Growth, Insert, Internal, Kerb, Lloyds, Main, Mandi, Mart, Meat, Mercat, Money, Niche, Nundine, Obigosony, Oligopoly, Open, Order-driven, Outlet, Overt, Pamphlet, Perfect, Piazza, Poster, Press, Radio, Reach, Relationship, Sale, Sellers', Servqual, Share, Shop, Single, Social, Societal, Sook, Souk, Spot, Stance, Staple, Stock, Stock Exchange, Tattersall's, Terminal, Test, Third, Tiger, Trade, Tron, Tryst, USP, Vent, Viral, Wall Street

Market garden Truck-farm

Marksman Sharpshooter, Shootist, Shot, Sniper, Tell

Marlborough Blenheim

Marlene Lilli

Marmalade Cat, Mammee-sapota, Preserve, Squish

Marmoset Jacchus, Mico, Midas, Monkey, Wistiti

Marmot Bobac, Bobak, Dassie, Groundhog, Hoary, Hyrax, Rodent, Whistler, Woodchuck

Maroon Brown, Castaway, Enisle, Firework, Inisle, Isolate, Strand

Marquee Pavilion, Tent, Top

Marquess, Marquis Granby, Lorne, Sade

Marquetry Boul(l)e, Buhl, Inlay

Marriage → ALLIANCE, Bed, Beenah, Bigamy, Bridal, Buckle-beggar, Civil, Coemption, Common law, Commuter, Confarreation, Conjugal, Connubial, Coverture, Digamy, Endogamy, Espousal, Exogamy, Gandharva, Genial, Group, Hedge, Hetaerism, Hetairism, Hymen(eal), Jugal, Ketubah, Knot, Lavender, Levirate, Match, Mating, Matrilocal, Matrimony, Mésalliance, Mixed, Monandry, Monogamy, Morganatic, Noose, Nuptial, Open, Pantagamy, Patrilocal, Polygamy,

Punalua, Putative, Sacrament, Shidduch, Shotgun, Tie, Trial, → UNION, Wedding, Wedlock

Marriageable Marrow, Nubile, Parti

Marriage-broker Shadchan

Marrow Courgette, Friend, Gist, Kamokamo, Medulla, Myeloid, Pith, Pumpkin, Squash, Vegetable

Marry, Married Ally, Amate, Buckle, Cleek(it), Confarreate, Couple, Coverture, Espouse, Feme covert, Forsooth, Fuse, Goody, Hitch, Join, Knit, M, Mate, Matron, Memsahib, Missis, Missus, Pair, Pardie, Quotha, Sannup, Splice, Tie, Tie the knot, Troggs, Troth, Umfazi, Unite, W, Wed, Wive

Mars Areography, Ares, Red (planet)

Marsh(y) Bayou, Bog, Chott, Corcass, Emys, Everglades, Fen, Hackney, Maremma, Merse, Mire, Morass, Ngaio, Paludal, Plashy, Pontine, Pripet, Quagmire, Romney, Salina, Salt, Shott, Slade, Slough, Sog, Spew, Spue, Swale, Swamp, Taiga, Terai, Vlei, Wetlands

Marshal Arrange, Array, Commander, Earp, Foch, French, Hickok, MacMahon, Muster, Neil, Ney, Order, Pétain, Provost, Shepherd, Steward, Tedder, Usher, Yardman

Marshmallow Althaea, Mallowpuff

Marsupial Bandicoot, Bilby, Cuscus, Dasyure, Dibbler, Didelphia, Diprotodon(t), Dunnart, Honey mouse, Honey possum, Kangaroo, Koala, Macropod, Metatheria, Notoryctes, Nototherium, Numbat, Opossum, Pademelon, Pad(d)ymelon, Petaurist, Phalanger, Polyprodont, Possum, Potoroo, Pouched mouse, Pygmy glider, Quokka, Quoll, Roo, Tammar, Tasmanian devil, Theria, Thylacine, Tuan, Wallaby, Wambenger, Wombat, Yapo(c)k

Marten Fisher, Mustela, Pekan, Pine, Sable, Woodshock

Martha Vineyard

Martial (arts) Bellicose, Budo, Capoeira, Capuera, Chopsocky, Dojo, Iai-do, Judo, Ju-jitsu, Karate, Kendo, Kick boxing, Kumite, Kung fu, Militant, Muay thai, Ninjitsu, Ninjutsu, Shintaido, Tae Bo®, Tae kwon do, T'ai chi (chuan), Warlike, Wushu

Martin Bird, Luther, Swallow

Martinet Captious, Ramrod, Stickler, Tyrant

Martini® Cocktail, Henry

Martyr(dom), Martyrs Alban, Alphege, Colosseum, Donatist, Justin, Latimer, Metric, MM, Passional, Persecute, Sebastian, Stephen, Suffer, Tolpuddle, Wishart

Marvel(lous) Bodacious, Bully, Épatant, Fab, Fantabulous, Lulu, Magic, Marl, Miracle, Mirific, Phenomenon, Prodigious, Selcouth, Superb, Super-duper, Swell, Terrific, Wonder

Marx(ism), Marxist Aspheterism, Chico, Comintern, Commie, Groucho, Gummo, Harpo, Karl, Lenin, Mao, Menshevik, Revisionism, Tanky, Tipamaro, Zeppo

Mary Bloody, Celeste, Madonna, Moll, Morison, Our Lady, Tum(my), Typhoid, Virgin

Marylebone Station

Marzipan Marchpane

Mascara Eye-black

Mascot Charm, → TALISMAN, Telesm, Token

Masculine, Masculinity He, He-man, Linga(m), M, Machismo, Macho, Male, Manly, Virile

Maser Laser

Mash(er) Beat, Beau, Beetle, Brew, Lady-killer, Pap, Pestle, Pound, Sour, Squash

Mask(ed) Bird cage, Camouflage, Cloak, Cokuloris, Death, Disguise, Dissemble,

Domino, Face pack, False face, Front, Gas, Hide, Larvated, Life, Loo, Loup,
Mascaron, Matte, Oxygen, Persona, Respirator, Screen, Semblance, Shadow,
Stalking-horse, Stocking, Stop out, Template, Visor, Vizard
Mason(ry) Ashlar, Ashler, Brother, Builder, Cowan, Emplecton, Isodoma,
Isodomon, Isodomum, Lodge, Moellon, Nogging, Opus, Perry, Random, Squinch,
Stylobate
Masque(rade), Masquerader Comus, Domino, Guisard, Mum(m), Pose, Pretend
Mass(es) Aggregate, Agnus Dei, Anniversary, Atomic, Banket, Bezoar, Bike,
Body, Bulk, Cake, Chaos, Clot, Congeries, Conglomeration, Consecration, Core,
Crith, Critical, Crowd, Demos, Density, Flake, Flysch, Folk, Geepound, Gramme,
Gravitational, Great, Herd, High, Horde, Hulk, Inertial, Jud, Kermesse, Kermis,
Kilo(gram), Kirmess, Low, Lump, M, Majority, Missa, Mob, Month's mind, Mop,
Nest, Phalanx, Pile, Plebs, Plumb, Pontifical, Populace, Proper, Raft, Requiem,
Rest, Ruck, Salamon, Salmon, Scrum, Sea, Serac, Service, Shock, Sicilian, Size,
Slub, Slug, Solar, Solemn, Solid, Stack, Stroma, Sursum Corda, Te Igitur, Tektite,
Trental, Vesper, Vigil, Volume, Wad, Weight, Welter
Massacre Amritsar, Beziers, Blood-bath, Butcher, Carnage, Glencoe, Havock,
Kanpur, Manchester, Peterloo, Pogrom, Purge, St Bartholomew's Day, Scullabogue,
Scupper, September, Sicilian vespers, Slaughter, Slay, Wounded Knee
Massage, Masseur An mo, Chafer, Chavutti thirumal, Do-in, Effleurage,
Hellerwork, → KNEAD, Malax, Palp, Petrissage, Physio, Rolf(ing), Rubber,
Shampoo, Shiatsu, Stone, Stroke, Swedish, Tapotement, Thai, Tripsis, Tui na
Massif Makalu
Massive Big, Bull, Colossal, Gargantuan, Heavy, Herculean, Huge, Monumental,
Strong, Titan
Mast(ed), Masthead Acorn, Banner, Captain's, Crosstree, Flag, Foretop, High
top, Hounds, Jigger, Jury, M, Mizzen, Mooring, Pannage, Pole, Racahout, Royal,
Ship-rigged, Spar, Top-gallant, Truck, Venetian
Master(ly) Artful, Baalebos, Baas, Beak, Beat, Boss, Buddha, Bwana, Careers,
Checkmate, Conquer, Control, Dan, Dominate, Dominie, Employer, Enslave,
Exarch, Expert, Gov, Grand, Harbour, Herr, Himself, International, Learn, Lord,
MA, Maestro, Mas(s), Massa, Mes(s), Nkosi, Old, Ollamh, Ollav, Oner, Oppress,
Original, Overcome, Overlord, Overpower, Overseer, Passed, Past, Pedant,
Question, Rabboni, Schoolman, Seigneur, Seignior, Signorino, Sir(e), Skipper,
→ SUBDUE, Subjugate, Superate, Surmount, Swami, Tame, Task, Thakin, Towkay,
Tuan, Usher, Vanquish, Virtuoso
Mastermind Brain, Conceive, Direct
Masterpiece Chef d'oeuvre, Creation
Mastersinger Sachs
Master-stroke Coup, Triumph
Masturbate, Masturbation Abuse, Blow, Frig, Gratify, Jerk off, Jock, Onanism,
Toss off, Wank, Whack off
Mat(ted), Matting Bast, Capillary, Coaster, Doily, Dojo, Doyley, Dutch mattress,
Felt, Inlace, Pad, Paunch, Place, Plat, Prayer, Rug, Surf, Table, Taggy, → TANGLE,
Tat(ami), Tatty, Taut, Tautit, Tawt, Tomentose, Welcome, Zarf
Matador Card, Espada, Ordonez, Theseus, Torero
Match(ed) Agree, Alliance, Amate, Balance, Besort, Bonspiel, Bout, Carousel,
Compare, Compeer, Congreve, Contest, Cope, Correlate, Correspond, Counterpane,
Doubles, Emulate, Engagement, Equal(ise), Equate, Even, Exhibition, Fellow, Fit,
Fixture, Four-ball, Friction, Friendly, Fusee, Fuzee, Game, Go, Greensome, Grudge,
International, Joust, Light, Locofoco, Love, Lucifer, Main, Marrow, Marry, Meet,

Mouse, Needle, Pair(s), Paragon, Parti, Pit, Prizefight, Promethean, Reproduce, Return, Rival, Roland, Rubber, Safety, Semifinal, Sevens, Shield, Shoo-in, Shooting, Shouting, Singles, Slanging, Slow, Spunk, Striker, Suit, Sync, → **TALLY**, Team, Test, Tie, Twin, Union, Venue, Vesta, Vesuvian, Wedding

Matchbox label (collecting) Phillumeny

Match girl Bride

Match-holder Lin(t)stock

Matchless Non(e)such, Orinda

Matchmaker Blackfoot, Broker, Pairer, Promoter, Shadchan

Mate, Mating Achates, Adam, Amigo, Amplexus, Bedfellow, Bo, Breed, Buddy, Buffer, Butty, Check, Chess, China, Chum, Cobber, Cock, Comrade, Consort, Crony, Cully, Digger, Eve, Feare, Feer, Fellow, Fere, Fiere, First, Fool's, Helper, Husband, Ilex, Maik, Make, Marrow, Marry, Match, Mister, Mucker, Nick, Oldster, Oppo, → **PAIR**, Pal, Panmixia, Panmixis, Paragon, Partner, Pheer(e), Pirrauru, Running, Scholar's, Second, Serve, Sex, Skaines, Smothered, Soul, → **SPOUSE**, Tea, Tup, Wack, Wacker, Wife, Wus(s)

Material(ism) Agalmatolite, Aggregate, Agitprop, Apt, Armure, Ballast, Blastema, Bole, Borsic, Byssus, Celluloid, Cellulose, Ceramic, Cermet, → **CLOTH**, Cob, Compo, Concrete, Copy, Corfam®, Corporeal, Data, Documentation, Earthy, Fablon®, → **FABRIC**, Factual, Fallout, Fertile, Fettling, Fibrefill, Fibreglass, Fines, Flong, Fomes, Frit(t), Fuel, Gang(ue), Germane, Gypsum, Historical, Hylic, Illusion, Illuvium, Interfacing, Lambskin, Leading, Macintosh, Matter, Metal, Moxa, Oasis®, Oilcloth, Oilskin, Papier-maché, Pertinent, Phantom, Physical, Pina-cloth, Plasterboard, Polystyrene, Polythene, Positive, Protoplasm, Protore, Pug(ging), Raw, Regolith, Relevant, Sackcloth, Sagathy, Samsonite®, Silicone, Skirting, Staff, Stuff, Substance, Swish, Tangible, Tape, Textile, Thermolite®, Thingy, Towelling, Tusser, Wattle and daub, Worldly

Materialise Appear, Apport, Click, Reify

Materialist(ic) Banausian, Hylist, Hyloist, Philistine, Somatist

Mathematician Agnesi, Apollonius, Archimedes, Archytas, Bernoulli, Bessel, Boole, Bourbaki, Briggs, Cantor, Cocker, De Morgan, Descartes, Diophantos, Dunstable, Eratosthenes, Euclid, Euler, Fermat, Fibonacci, Fourier, Friedmann, Gauss, Godel, Goldbach, Gunter, Hawking, Lagrange, Laplace, Leibniz, Lie, Mandelbrot, Mercator, Minkowski, Napier, Newton, Optime, Pascal, Penrose, Playfair, Poisson, Ptolemy, Pythagoras, Pytheas, Riemann, Statistician, Torricelli, Turing, Von Leibnitz, Walker, Wrangler, Zeno

Mathematics, Mathematical, Maths Algebra, Applied, Arithmetic, Arsmetrick, Calculus, Geometry, Higher, Logarithms, Mechanics, New, Numbers, Porism, Pure, Topology, Trig, Trigonometry

Matilda Liar, Swag, Untruthful, Waltzing

Matinee Coat, Idol, Show

Mating Pangamy

Matins Nocturn

Matricide Orestes

Matrimony Bed, Conjugal, Marriage, Sacrament, Spousal, Wedlock

Matrix Active, Array, Boston, Hermitian, Jacobian, Mould, Orthogonal, Pattern, Scattering, Square, Uterus

Matron Dame, Hausfrau, Lucretia, Nurse, Warden

Matt(e) Dense, Dingy, Dull

Matter Alluvium, Bioblast, Biogen, Body, Concern, Condensed, Consequence, Dark, Degenerate, Empyema, Epithelium, Gear, Gluon, Go, Grey, Hyle, Impost(h)ume,

Issue, Mass, Material, Molecule, Multiverse, Phlegm, Pith, Point, Positron, Protoplasm, Pulp, Pus, Quark, Reading, Reck, Reke, Scum, Shebang, Signify, Solid, Stuff, Subject, → SUBSTANCE, Thing, Topic, Tousle, Touzle, White, Ylem
Matthew Arnold
Mattress Bed(ding), Biscuit, Dutch, Featherbed, Foam, Futon, Lilo®, Pa(i)lliasse, Pallet, Spring, Tick
Mature, Maturity Adult, Age, Blossom, Bold, Concoct, Develop, Mellow, Metaplasis, Old, Puberty, Ripe(n), Rounded, Seasoned, Upgrow(n)
Maudlin Fuddled, Mawkish, Sentimental, Slip-slop, Sloppy, Too-too
Maul Hammer, Manhandle, Paw, Rough, Savage
Maundy Money, Nipter, Thursday
Mauretanian, Mauritania(n) Moor, RIM
Mausoleum Helicarnassus, Mole, Sepulchre, Taj Mahal, Tomb
Mauve Lilac, Mallow, Perkin's
Maverick Misfit, Nonconformist, Rogue
Mavis Throstle
Maw Crop, Gorge, Gull(et), Mouth, Oesophagus
Mawkish Sentimental, Sickly
Maxim Adage, Aphorism, Apo(ph)thegm, Axiom, Byword, Gnome, Gorki, Gun, Hiram, Moral, Motto, Proverb, Restaurateur, → RULE, Saw, Saying, Sentence, Sentiment, Watchword
Maximum All-out, Full, Highest, Most, Peak, Utmost
May Blossom, Can, Hawthorn, Merry, Might, Month, Mote, Quickthorn, Shall, Whitethorn
Maybe Happen, Mebbe, Peradventure, Percase, Perchance, Perhaps, Possibly
▷ **May become** *may indicate* an anagram
May day Beltane, SOS
Mayfair WI
Mayfly Ephemera, Ephemeroptera, Green-drake, Sedge
Mayhem Chaos, Crime, Damage, Havoc, Pandemonium
Mayonnaise Aioli, Rémoulade
Mayor Alcaide, Burgomaster, Casterbridge, Charter, Councilman, Portreeve, Provost, Whittington
Maze Honeycomb, Labyrinth, Meander, Theseus, Warren, Wilderness
MC Compere, Host, Ringmaster
MD Doctor, Healer
ME Yuppie flu
Me I, Mi
Mead(ow) Flood, Grass, Haugh, Hydromel, Inch, Ing, Lea(se), Ley, Meath(e), Metheglin, → PASTURE, Runnymede, Saeter, Salting, Water
Meadowsweet Dropwort
Meagre Bare, Exiguous, Measly, Paltry, Pittance, Scant, Scrannel, Scranny, Scrawny, Skimpy, Skinny, Spare, Sparse, Stingy, Thin
Meal(s), Mealie, Mealy Banquet, Barbecue, Barium, Beanfeast, Blow-out, Board, Breakfast, Brunch, Buffet, Cassava, Cereal, Cholent, Chota-hazri, Collation, Corn, Cornflour, Cottoncake, Cottonseed, Cou-cou, Cribble, Dejeune(r), Deskfast, Dinner, Drammock, Ear, Ervalenta, Fare, Farina, Feast, Flour, Food, Grits, Grout, Hangi, High tea, Iftar, Indian, Italian, Kai, Lock, Lunch, Mandioc, Mandioc(c)a, Mani(h)oc, Matzo, Melder, Meltith, Mensal, Mess, Mush, No-cake, Nosh, Nuncheon, Obento, Ordinary, Picnic, Piece, Plate, Poi, Polenta, Porridge, Prandial, Prix fixe, Rac(c)ahout, Refection, Repast, Revalenta, Rijst(t)afel, Salep, Scambling, Scoff,

Seder, Smorgasbord, Snack, Spread, Square, Supper, Table d'hôte, Takeaway, Tea, Thali, Tiffin, Tightener, Twalhours, Undern

Meal-ticket LV

Mean(ing), Meant Aim, Arithmetic(al), Average, Base, Betoken, Bowsie, Caitiff, Connotation, Curmudgeon, Definition, Denotate, Denote, Design, Dirty, Drift, Essence, Ettle, Feck, Footy, Foul, Geometric(al), Gist, Golden, Hang, Harmonic, Humble, Hunks, Ignoble, Illiberal, Imply, Import, Inferior, Insect, Intend, Intermediate, Kunjoos, Lexical, Low, Mang(e)y, Marrow, Medium, Mesquin, Method, Mid, Miserly, Narrow, Near, Norm, Nothing, One-horse, Ornery, Paltry, Par, Penny-pinching, Petty, Piker, Pinch-penny, Pith, Point, Purport, → **PURPOSE**, Quadratic, Ratfink, Revenue, Roinish, Roynish, Scall, Scrub, Scurvy, Semanteme, Semantic(s), Sememe, Sense, Shabby, Signify, Slight, Small, Sneaky, Snoep, Snot, Sordid, Sparing, Spell, Stingy, Stink(ard), Stinty, Substance, Symbol, Thin, Threepenny, Tightwad, Two-bit, Value, Vile, Whoreson

Meander Fret, Ring, Sinuate, Stray, Wander, Weave, Wind

Meaningless Ducdame, Empty, Hollow, Hot air, Insignificant, Nonny, Rumbelow

Means Agency, Dint, Income, Instrumental, Media, Method, Mode, Opulence, Organ, Private, Resources, Staple, Substance, Tactics, Visible, Ways, Wherewithal

Meantime, Meanwhile Among, Emong, Greenwich, Interim

Measles Morbilli, Roseola, Rose-rash, Rubella, Rubeola, Sheep

Measure(d), Measuring, Measurement By(e)law, Calibre, Circular, Crackdown, → **DANCE**, Démarche, → **DIMENSION**, Distance, Dose, Dry, Gavotte, Gross, Imperial, Limit, Linear, Moratorium, Of, Offset, Plumb, Precaution, Prophylactic, Quickstep, Ration, Share, Short, → **SIZE**, Standard, Statute, Step, Strike, Struck, Survey, Token, Wine

---

MEASURING INSTRUMENTS

2 letters:	Wey	Line	Thou
As		Link	Unit
Em	**4 letters:**	Maze	Vara
En	Acre	Mete	Volt
Mu	Aune	Mile	Warp
	Bath	Mole	Yard
3 letters:	Boll	Mott	
Are	Bolt	Muid	**5 letters:**
Bel	Comb	Nail	Anker
Cab	Cord	Omer	Ardeb
Cor	Coss	Pace	Barye
Ell	Cran	Peck	Bekah
Erg	Culm	Pint	Bigha
Fat	Dram	Pipe	Caneh
Hin	Epha	Pole	Carat
Lay	Foot	Pood	Chain
Lea	Gage	Ream	Clove
Ley	Gill	Reau	Combe
Log	Hank	Rood	Coomb
Lug	Hide	Rope	Crore
Mil	Inch	Shot	Cubit
Rod	Koss	Span	Cumec
Tot	Last	Tape	Cusec

Depth
Ephah
Fermi
Float
Gauge
Grain
Groma
Hanap
Homer
Joule
Kaneh
Lento
Liang
Ligne
Lippy
Loure
Mease
Meter
Metre
Middy
Optic®
Perch
Quart
Romer
Ruler
Scale
Skein
Sound
Stade
Stere
Tesla
Therm
Toise
Verst
Wecht
Yojan

6 letters:
Albedo
Alnage
Arpent
Arshin
Barrel
Barren
Beegah
Bovate
Bushel
Chenix
Chopin
Cicero
Cubage

Denier
Double
Etalon
Exergy
Fathom
Firkin
Firlot
Gallon
Height
Hemina
Jigger
Kelvin
Kilerg
League
Lippie
Liquid
Metage
Modius
Morgen
Mutton
Noggin
Oxgang
Parsec
Pascal
Pottle
Radius
Runlet
Sazhen
Stadia
Thread
Tierce
Yojana

7 letters:
Aneroid
Arshine
Breadth
Burette
Caliper
Candela
Chalder
Choenix
Conguis
Coulomb
Cyathus
Decibel
Drastic
Entropy
Furlong
Geodesy
Lambert

Leaguer
Pelorus
Quarter
Refract
Rundlet
Sleever
Spindle
Spondee
Venturi
Virgate

8 letters:
Angstrom
Calliper
Carucate
Chaldron
Crannock
Desyatin
Diameter
Exitance
Fistmele
Foot rule
Hogshead
Kilogray
Luxmeter
Mutchkin
Odometer
Oximeter
Parasang
Poulter's
Puncheon
Tape-line
Teraflop
Viameter
Waywiser

9 letters:
Astrolabe
Atmometer
Bolometer
Cryometer
Decalitre
Decastere
Dosimeter
Ergometer
Eriometer
Kilometre
Konimeter
Lysimeter
Manometer
Mekometer

Nipperkin
Octameter
Oenometer
Pentapody
Potometer
Steradian
Tappet-hen
Telemeter
Titration
Tonometer
Yardstick

10 letters:
Acidometer
Amphimacer
Anemometer
Barleycorn
Bathometer
Centimetre
Coulometer
Cyclometer
Densimeter
Dessiatine
Dessyatine
Drosometer
Eudiometer
Goniometer
Gravimeter
Humidistat
Hydrometer
Hygrometer
Lactometer
Micrometer
Millimetre
Opisometer
Photometer
Piezometer
Resistance
Touchstone
Tromometer
Winchester

11 letters:
Actinometer
Auxanometer
Calorimeter
Dioptometer
Dynamometer
Intoximeter
Jacob's staff
Stereometer

Tacheometry	Coulombmeter	Galactometer	*13 letters:*
Venturi tube	Densitometer	Nephelometer	Saccharometer
Weighbridge	Electrometer	Permittivity	
	Electronvolt	Tellurometer	
12 letters:	Extensimeter	Viscosimeter	
Cathetometer	Extensometer		

Meat(s) Aitchbone, Bacon, Bard, Beef, Biltong, Brawn, Brisket, Brown, Burger, Cabob, Carbonado, Carrion, Charcuterie, Chop, Collop, Confit, Croquette, Cut, Dark, Devon, Dog-roll, Easy, Edgebone, Entrecôte, Escalope, Essence, Fanny Adams, Fleishig, Fleishik, Flesh, Flitch, Force, Galantine, Gigot, Gobbet, Gosht, Griskin, Ham, Haslet, Jerky, Joint, Junk, Kabab, Kabob, Kebab, Kebob, Lamb, Loin, Luncheon, Mart, Mince, Mutton, Noisette, Offal, Olive, Oyster, Pastrami, Paupiette, Pem(m)ican, Piccata, Pith, Pope's eye, Pork, Processed, Prosciutto, Rack, Red, Rillettes, Roast, Saddle, Sasatie, Satay, Scaloppino, Schnitzel, Scran, Scrapple, Sey, Shashlik, Shishkebab, Side, Sirloin, Sosatie, Spam®, Spare rib, Spatchcock, Spaul(d), Steak, Strong, Tenderloin, Tiring, Tongue, Variety, Veal, Venison, Vifda, Virgate, Vivda, Weiner schnitzel, White, Wurst

Meatball(s) Cecils, Croquette, Faggot, Falafel, Felafel, Fricadel, Frikkadell, Goujon, Knish, Kofta, Kromesky, Quenelle, Rissole

Meat extract Brawn, Gravy, Juice, Stock

Meatless Banian, Lent, Maigre, Vegetarian

Mecca Centre, Kaaba, Keblah, Kibla(h), Qibla

Mechanic(s) Apron-man, Artificer, Artisan, Banausic, Bottom, Celestial, Classical, Dynamics, Engineer, Fitter, Fluid, Fundi, Grease monkey, Greaser, Hand, Journeyman, Kinematics, Kinesiology, Kinetics, Newtonian, Operative, Quantum, Rock, Soil, Statics, Statistical, Technician, Wave

▷ **Mechanic(al)** *may indicate* characters from 'A Midsummer Night's Dream'

Mechanical, Mechanism Action, Apparatus, Auto, Banausic, Clockwork, Defence, Dérailleur, Escape, Escapement, Gimmal, Instrument, Machinery, Movement, Organical, Pulley, Pushback, Regulator, Robotic, Servo, Synchroflash, Synchromesh, Trippet, Works

Medal(lion)(s) Award, Bar, Bronze, Congressional, Croix de guerre, Decoration, Dickin, DSM, GC, George, Gold, Gong, Gorget, Military, MM, Numismatic, Pan(h)agia, Purple Heart, Putty, Roundel, Silver, Tony, Touchpiece, VC, Vernicle

Meddle(r), Meddlesome Busybody, Dabble, Finger, Hen-hussy, → INTERFERE, Interloper, Marplot, Mell, Monkey, Officious, Potter, Pragmatic, Pry, Snooper, Spoilsport, Tamper, Tinker, Trifle

Media Mass, Mixed, New, PR

Mediate, Mediator ACAS, Arbitrate, Intercede, Interpose, Intervene, Liaison, Muti, Referee, Thirdsman, Trouble-shooter

Medical, Medicine (chest), Medicament, Medication Aesculapian, Algology, Allopathy, Aloetic, Alternative, Andrology, Anodyne, Antacid, Antibiotic, Antidote, Antisepsis, Antiseptic, Arnica, Asafetida, Aviation, Ayurveda, Bi, Bismuth, Blister, Brunonian, Buchu, Bucku, Calumba, Carminative, Charm, Chinese, Chiropody, Chlorodyne, Chrysarobin, Clinician, Complementary, Cordial, Corpsman, Cubeb, Curative, Defensive, Diapente, Diascordium, Diatessaron, Dose, Draught, Drops, → DRUG, Dutch drops, Electuary, Elixir, Emmenagogue, Empirics, Enema, Epulotic, Excipient, Expectorant, Fall-trank, Febrifuge, Feldsher, Folk, Forensic, Fringe, Galen, Galenism, Gelcap, Genitourinary, Gripe water®, Gutta, Haematinic, Herb, Herbal, Hesperidin, Holistic, Hom(o)eopathy, Horse-drench,

Iatric(al), Imhotep, Industrial, Inhalant, Inro, Internal, Iodine, Ipecac(uanha), Iron, Ko cycle, Lariam®, Laxative, Leechcraft, Legal, Loblolly, Lotion, Magnesia, Menthol, Microbubbles, Mishmi, Mixture, Moxar, Muti, Nephritic, Nervine, Nosology, Nostrum, Nuclear, Nux vomica, Ob-gyn, Officinal, Oncology, Oporice, Orthopoedics, Osteopath, Palliative, Panacea, Paregoric, Patent, Pathology, Pharmacy, Physic, Physical, Pill, Placebo, Polychrest, Polypill, Posology, Potion, Poultice, Preparation, Preventive, Proctology, Psionic, Psychiatry, Quinacrine, Quinine, Quin(quin)a, Radiology, Red Crescent, Red Cross, Relaxative, → REMEDY, Salve, Sanative, Sanguinaria, Senna, Serology, Simple, Space, Specific, Sports, Steel, Stomachic, Stomatology, Stramonium, Stupe, Suppository, Synergast, Syrup, Tabasheer, Tabashir, Tablet, Tar-water, Tetracycline, Therapeutics, TIM, Tisane, Tocology, Tonic, Totaquine, Trade, Traditional Chinese, Traumatology, Treatment, Trichology, Troche, Valerian, Veronal, Veterinary, Virology
Medicine man, Medico Bone-setter, Koradji
Medic(k) Lucern(e), Snail
Medieval Archaic, Feudal, Gothic, Med, Old, Trecento
Mediocre Fair, Indifferent, Middle-of-the-road, Middling, Ordinary, Pap, Respectable, Run-of-the-mill, So-So, Undistinguished
Meditate, Meditation, Meditator, Meditative Brood, Chew, Cogitate, Gymnosophy, Hesychast, Muse, Mystic, Pensive, Ponder, Reflect, Reverie, Revery, Ruminate, Thanatopsis, Transcendental, Vipassana, Weigh, Yoga, Zazen
Mediterranean Levant, Midi, Scattermouch
Medium (A)ether, Agency, Average, Channel, Clairvoyant, Contrast, Culture, Dispersive, Element, Ether, Even, Happy, Home, Intermediary, Interstellar, M, Magilp, Mean, Megilp, Midsize, Midway, Milieu, Oils, Organ, Ouija, Planchette, Press, Radio, Regular, Shaman, Spiritist, Spiritualist, Television, Telly, TV, Vehicle
Medley Charivari, Collection, Gallimaufry, Jumble, Macedoine, Melange, Mishmash, Mix, Pastiche, Patchwork, Pi(e), Pot-pourri, Quodlibet, Ragbag, Salad, Salmagundi, Series, Tat
▷ **Medley** *may indicate* an anagram
Medusa Planoblast
Meek Docile, Griselda, Humble, Milquetoast, Patient, Tame
Meerkat Suricate
Meerschaum Sepiolite
Meet(ing), Meeting place Abide, Abutment, AGM, Appointment, Apropos, Assemble, Assembly, Assignation, Audience, Baraza, Bosberaad, Briefing, Camporee, Caucus, Chapterhouse, Chautauqua, Clash, Conclave, Concourse, Concur, Confluence, Confrontation, Congress, Connivance, Consistory, Consulta, Contact, Conterminous, Convene, Convent(icle), Convention, Converge, Conversazione, Convocation, Correspond, Cybercafé, Defray, Demo, EGM, Encounter, Ends, Experience, Face, Find, Fit, For(e)gather, Forum, Fulfil, Gemot, Giron, Gorsedd, Guild, Gyeld, Gymkhana, Gyron, Howf(f), Hunt, Hustings, Imbizo, Indaba, Infall, Interface, Interview, Join, Junction, Kgotla, Korero, Lekgotla, Liaise, Marae, Moot, Mother's, Obviate, Occlusion, Occur, Oppose, Overflow, Pay, Plenary, Plenum, Pnyx, Pow-wow, Prayer, Prosper, Quadrivial, Quaker, Quorate, Quorum, Race, Races, Rally, Rencontre, Rencounter, Rendezvous, Reunion, Sabbat(h), Satisfy, Séance, See, Seminar, Session, Sit, Social, Sports, Suitable, Summit, Symposium, Synastry, Synaxis, Synod, Tackle, Talkfest, Think-in, Town, Track, Tryst, Venue, Vestry, Wapinshaw, Wardmote, Wharenui, Wharepuni, Workshop
Megalith(ic) Sarsen, Skara Brae, Stonehenge
Megalomaniac Monarcho

Megaphone Bull-horn, Loudhailer
Megapode Mound-bird, Talegalla
Meiosis Understatement
Melancholy, Melancholic Adust, Allicholy, Allycholly, Anatomy, Atrabilious, Cafard, Despond(ency), Dreary, Dump(s), Gloom, Heart-sore, Hipped, Hump, Hyp, Hypochondria, Jaques, Lienal, Panophobia, Pensieroso, Pensive, Saturnine, Sombre, Spleen, Splenetic, Triste, Tristesse, Weltschmerz
Melanesian Kanak
Mêlée Brawl, Commotion, Fracas, Rally, Salmagundi, Scrum
Melia Margosa, Neem, Nim
Mellifluent, Mellifluous Cantabile, Melodic
Mellow Fruity, Genial, Mature, Ripe, Smooth
Melodrama(tic) Bathos, Histrionic, Sensation, Transpontine
Melody, Melodious Air, Arioso, Cabaletta, Canorous, Cantabile, Cantilena, Canto (fermo), Cantus, Chopsticks, Conductus, Counterpoint, Descant, Dulcet, Euphonic, Fading, Musical, Orphean, Plainsong, Ranz-des-vaches, Refrain, Songful, Strain, Theme, Tunable, → TUNE(S)
Melon(like) Cantaloup(e), Cas(s)aba, Charentais, Galia, Gourd, Honeydew, Mango, Musk, Nar(r)as, Ogen, Pepo, Persian, Rock, Spanspek, Winter
Melt(ed), Melting Ablate, Colliquate, → DISSOLVE, Eutectic, Eutexia, Flux, Found, Fuse, Fusil(e), Liquescent, Liquid, Run, Smectic, Syntexis, Thaw, Touch
Member Adherent, Arm, Branch, Bro(ther), Charter, Chin, Confrère, Cornice, Coulisse, Crossbeam, Crypto, Direction, Felibre, Fellow, Forearm, Forelimb, Founder, Gremial, Harpin(g)s, Insider, Keel, Leg, Limb, Lintel, Longeron, M, MBE, Montant, MP, Organ, Part, Partisan, Peer, Politicaster, Politician, Private, Rood-beam, Soroptomist, Stile, Stringer, Strut, Syndic, Toe
Membrane, Membranous Amnion, Arachnoid, Axilemma, Caul, Cell, Chorioallantois, Chorion, Choroid (plexus), Chromoplast, Conjunctiva, Cornea, Cyst, Decidua, Dissepiment, Dura (mater), Endocardium, Endometrium, Endosteum, Ependyma, Exine, Extine, Film, Frenulum, Fr(a)enum, Haw, Head, Hyaloid, Hymen, Indusium, Intima, Intine, Involucre, Mater, Mediastinum, Meninx, Mesentery, Mucosa, Mucous, Neurolemma, Nictitating, Patagium, Pellicle, Pericardium, Pericarp, Perichondrium, Pericranium, Periost(eum), Periton(a)eum, Pia mater, Plasma, Pleura, Putamen, Retina, Rim, Sarcolemma, Scarious, Schneiderian, Sclera, Serosa, Serous, Skin, Synovial, Tectorial, Tela, Third eyelid, Tissue, Tonoplast, Trophoblast, Tympan(ic), Vacuolar, Velamen, Velum, Vitelline, Web, Yolk-sac
Memento, Memoir Keepsake, Locket, Relic, Remembrancer, Souvenir, Token, Trophy
Memo(randum) Bordereau, Cahier, Chit, IOU, Jot, Jurat, Minute, Note, Notepad, → REMINDER
Memoirist Casanova
Memorable, Memorise, Memory Associative, ATLAS, Bubble, Cache, Catchy, Collective, → COMPUTER MEMORY, Con, Core, DRAM, Echoic, Engram(ma), Extended, Flash (bulb), Folk, Get, Highlight, Historic, Hypermnesia, Iconic, Immortal, Immunological, Learn, Living, Long-term, Main, Mainstore, Memoriter, Mind, Mneme, Mnemonic, Mnemosyne, Non-volatile, Noosphere, Notable, Pelmanism, Photographic, Race, Read-write, Recall, Recovered, → REMEMBER, Retention, Retrospection, Ro(a)te, Samskara, Screen, Semantic, Short-term, Souvenir, Sovenance, Static, Video, Virtual, Volatile, Word, Working
Memorial Altar tomb, Cenotaph, Cromlech, Ebenezer, Gravestone, Hatchment,

Headstone, Marker, Monument, Mount Rushmore, Obelisk, Plaque, Relic, Statue, Tomb, Trophy, War

▶ **Memory loss** *see* **LOSS OF MEMORY**

Men(folk) Amadoda, Chaps, Chess, Cuffins, Male, Messrs, Mortals, OR, People, Race, Troops

Menace, Menacing Danger, Dennis, Endanger, Foreboding, Minatory, Peril, Pest, Threat(en)

Menagerie Ark, Circus, Zoo

Mend Beet, Bete, Bushel, Cobble, Correct, Darn, Fix, Heal, Improved, Mackle, Patch, Piece, Recover, Remedy, → **REPAIR**, Set, Sew, Solder, Trouble-shoot

Mendelevium Md

Mendicant Beggar, Calender, Fakir, Franciscan, Servite

Menial Bottlewasher, Drudge, Drug, Eta, Fag, Flunkey, Lowly, Scullion, Servile, Toady, Underling, Wood-and-water joey

Meninx (D)jerba

Menopause Andropause, Climacteric

Menstruation Menarche, Menses

Mental (condition), Mental disorder Alienism, Doolally, Eject, Hallucinosis, Insane, Noetic, Paranoia, Psychic

▷ **Mental** *may indicate* the chin

Mention(ed) Allusion, Bename, Benempt, Broach, Bynempt, Citation, Hint, Honourable, Name, Notice, Quote, Refer, Speech, State, Suggest, Touch

Mentor Guru, Rebbe, Tutor

Menu Agenda, Card, Carte, Carte du jour, Cascading, Drop-down, Fare, List, Table d'hôte, Tariff

Mercantile Commercial, Trade

Mercator Cartographer

Mercenary Arnaout, Condottiere, Freelance, Greedy, Hack, Hessian, Hired gun, Hireling, Landsknecht, Legionnaire, Pindaree, Pindari, Rutter, Sordid, Spoilsman, Swiss Guard, Venal, Wildgeese

Merchandise Cargo, Goods, Line, Produce, Ware(s)

Merchant(man) Abudah, Antonio, Broker, Bun(n)ia, Burgher, Chandler, Chap, Crare, Crayer, Dealer, Factor, Flota, Gossip, Hoastman, Importer, Jobber, Law, Magnate, Marcantant, Mercer, Monger, Négociant, Pedlar, Polo, Provision, Retailer, Seller, Shipper, Speed, Squeegee, Stapler, Sutler, Trader, Vintner, Wholesaler

Mercia Offa

Merciful, Mercy Amnesty, Charity, Clement, Compassionate, Corporal, Grace, Humane, Kind, Kyrie, Lenient, Lenity, Miserere, Misericord(e), Pacable, Pity, Quarter, Ruth, Sparing, Spiritual

Merciless Cruel, Hard, Hard-hearted, Inclement, Pitiless

Mercurial, Mercuric sulphide, Mercury Azoth, Cyllenius, Dog's, Fulminating, Herald, Hermes, Hg, Horn, Hydrargyrum, Messenger, Quicksilver, Red, Red-man, Spurge, Tiemannite, Volatile

Mere(ly) Allenarly, Bare, Common, Lake, Pond, Pool, Pure, Sheer, Tarn, Very

Merge(r), Merging Amalgamate, Blend, Coalesce, Composite, Conflate, Consolidate, Die, Elide, Fusion, Incorporate, Interflow, Interpenetrate, Liquesce, Meld, Melt, Mingle, Syncretism, Synergy, Unify, Unite

Meridian Magnetic, Noonday, Prime

Meringue Pavlova

Merit(ed) CL, Condign, Deserve, Due, Earn, Found, Rate, Virtue, Worth(iness)

Mermaid Dugong, Halicore, Merrow, Siren, Tavern, Undine
Merriment, Merry Andrew, Blithe(some), Bonny, Boon, Cant, Cherry, Chirpy, Crank, Elated, Full, Gaudy, Gay, Gean, Gleesome, Greek, Jocose, Jocular, Jocund, Jolly, Joyous, L'allegro, Lively, Nitid, On, Page, Riant, Sportive, Sunny, Vogie, Waggery, Wassail
Merry-andrew Clown, Jack-pudding, Pickle-herring
Merry-go-round Carousel, Galloper, Whirligig
Merry-making Cakes and ale, Carnival, Festivity, Gaiety, Gaud, Gawd, Revel
Merrythought Clavicle, Collarbone, Wishbone
Mesh Cancellate, Chain, Entangle, Mantle, Net, Reseau, Screen
Mess(y) Balls-up, Bedraggled, Boss, Botch, Canteen, Caudle, Chaos, Clamper, Clutter, Cock-up, Failure, Farrago, Fiasco, Flub, Garboil, G(l)oop, Glop, Gory, Guddle, Gunge, Gunk, Gun-room, Hash, Horlicks, Hotch-potch, Hugger-mugger, Imbroglio, Lash-up, Louse, Mash, Meal, Mismanage, Mix, Mixter-maxter, Modge, Muck, Muff, Mullock, Muss, Mux, Pi(e), Piss-up, Plight, Pollute, Pottage, Screw-up, Scungy, Shambles, Shambolic, Shemozzle, Sight, Slaister, Smudge, Snafu, Soss, Sty, Sully, Untidy, Wardroom, Whoopsie, Yuck(y)
Message(s) Aerogram, Bull, Bulletin, Cable, Contraplex, Dépêche, Despatch, Dispatch, Email, Errand, Error, Flame, Kissagram, Kissogram, Missive, News, Note, Pager, Ping, Posting, Postscript, Radiogram, Rumour, Signal, Slogan, SOS, Stripagram, Strippergram, Subtext, Telegram, Telephone, Teletype®, Telex, Text, Tidings, Toothing, Wire, → **WORD**
Messenger Angel, Angela, Apostle, Azrael, Beadle, Caddie, Caddy, Chaprassi, Chuprassy, Courier, Culver, Despatch-rider, Emissary, Envoy, Forerunner, Gaga, Gillie-wetfoot, Gillie whitefoot, Hatta, Herald, Hermes, Internuncio, Iris, Ladas, Mercury, Nuncio, Page, Peon, Post, Pursuivant, Runner, Send, Shellycoat, Valkyrie
Messiah Christ, Emmanuel, Immanuel, Mahdi, Mashiach, Saviour, Son of man
Met Old Bill, Weather, Weatherman
Metabolism Basal
Metal(s), Metallic, Metalware, Metalwork Ag, Aglet, Aiglet, Aiguillette, Al, Alkali, Aluminium, Antifriction, Antimony, Babbitt, Base, Bell, Billon, Brassy, Britannia, Cadmium, Chrome, Chromium, Cobalt, Copper, Death, Dutch, Dysprosium, Er(bium), Europium, Expanded, Filler, Foil, Fusible, Gallium, Germanium, Gib, Gold, Heavy, Hot, Ingot, Invar®, Iridium, Iron, Jangling, Leaf, Magnolia, Manganese, Mineral, Misch, Mitis, Monel(l), Muntz, Natrium, Nickel, Noble, Nonferrous, Ore, Ormolu, Osmium, Parent, Perfect, Planchet, Platinum, Precious, Prince's, Protore, Regulus, Rhenium, Road, Ruthenium, Samarium, Scrap, Sheet(-iron), Silver, Slug, Sm, Sn, Sodium, Speculum, Speiss, Sprue, Steel, Strontium, Taggers, Tantalum, Terbic, Terbium, Terne, Thallium, Thorium, Thrash, Tin, Tole, Toreutics, Tramp, Transition, Tutania, Tutenag, Type, White, Wolfram, Yellow, Zinc
Metal-worker Founder, Lorimer, Smith, Spurrier, Tubal Cain
Metamorphose Transmogrify
▷ **Metamorphosing** *may indicate* an anagram
Metaphor Conceit, Figure, Image, Kenning, Malonym, Mixed, Symbol, Trope, Tropical
Metaphysics Ontology, Scotism
Mete Inflict
Meteor(ic), Meteorite Achondrite, Aerolite, Aerosiderite, Bolide, Chondrite, Comet, Drake, Falling star, Fireball, Geminid, Iron, Leonid, Perseid, Quadrantid, Siderite, Siderolite, Star(dust), Stony, Tektite

Meter Alidad(e), Electric, Exposure, Flow, Gas, Light, Orifice, Parking, Postage, Postal, Torque, Torsion, Water, White
Methamphetamine Ice
Methane Alkane
Methedrine® Speed
Method(ology), Methodical Art, Billings, Buteyko, Direct, Feldenkrais, Formula, Gram's, Historical, Hi-tec(h), Kenny, Kumon, Line, Manner, Mode, Modus, Modus operandi, Monte Carlo, Montessori, Neat, Orderly, Ovulation, Painstaking, Plan, Ploy, Procedure, Process, Q, Rhythm, Schafer's, Scientific, Socratic, Stanislavski, → SYSTEM, Tactics, Technique, Way, Withdrawal
Methodism, Methodist Huntingdonian, Jumper, Methody, Primitive, Ranter, Scientism, Southcottian, Swaddler, Wesley
Methuselah Bottle, Macrobiote
Meticulous Careful, → EXACT, Finicky, Minute, Precise, Punctilious, Quiddler, Scrupulous, Thorough
Métier Line, Trade, Vocation
Metre Alexandrine, Amphibrach, Amphimacer, Anapaest, Antispast, Arsis, Ballad, Cadence, Choliamb, Choree, Choriamb, Common, Dipody, Galliambic, Iambic, Ithyphallic, Long, M, Prosody, Pyrrhic, Rhythm, Sapphic, Scansion, Scazon, Service, Short, Spondee, Strophe, Tripody, Trochee
Metric (system) MKS
Metroland Subtopia
Metropolitan Eparch
Mettle Ardour, Bravery, Courage, Ginger, Guts, Pith, → PLUCK, Pride, Smeddum, Spirit, Spunk, Steel
Mew Caterwaul, Miaou, Miaow, Pen, Purr, Seagull, Waul, Wrawl
Mews Meuse, Muse(t), Musit, Stables
Mexican (Indian) Atlalt, Aztec, Carib, Chicano, Chichibec, Diaz, Greaser, Gringo, Hairless, Hispanic, Maya, Mixe-Zoque, Mixtec, Montezuma, Nahuatl, Norténo, Olmec, Otomi, Pachuco, Spic, Spik, Taino, Toltec, Wetback, Zapotec, Zuni
Mezzanine Entresol
Mezzo-soprano Tessa
Mica Biotite, Daze, Fuchsite, Glimmer, Isinglass, Lepidolite, Lepidomelane, Muscovite, Paragonite, Phlogopite, Rubellan, Sericite, Talc, Verdite, Vermiculite
Micawber Wilkins
Mick(ey) Greek, Mouse
Micro Mu
Microbe, Microorganism Extremophile, Germ, Lactobacillus, Nanobe, Organism
Microphone Bug, Carbon, Crystal, Lavaliere, Lip, Mike, Phonic Ear®, Radio, Ribbon, Throat
Microscope Compound, Confocal, Darkfield, Dissecting, Electron, Engyscope, Lens, Optical, Phase-contrast, Proton, Reflecting, SEM, Simple, Solar, TEM, Ultraviolet
Microwave Nuke
Mid(st) Amongst, Mongst
Midas Goldinger, Tamarin
Midday Meridian, N, Noon, Noon-tide, Noon-time
Middle, Middling Active, Basion, Centre, Core, Crown, Enteron, Excluded, Eye, Girth, Heart, Innermost, Loins, Median, Mediocre, Meridian, Meseraic, Mesial, Mesne, Meso, Midriff, Moderate, Noon, Passive, Turn, Twixt, Via media, Wa(i)st
Middle age Menopause
Middle-Cambrian Menevian

Middle class Bourgeois, Hova, Mondeo Man
Middle Eastern Arab, Iraqi, Omani
Middleman Broker, Comprador(e), Diaphragm, Interlocutor, Intermediary, Jobber, Median, Navel, Regrater, Regrator
Middlesex Hermaphrodite
Midge Gall, Gnat
Midget Dwarf, Homunculus, Lilliputian, Pygmy, Shrimp
Midianite Prowler
Midlander Brummie
Midlands Mercia
Midnight G, O Am
▸ **Midnight** see PAST MIDNIGHT
Midriff Phrenic, Skirt, Waist
Midshipman Brass-bounder, Easy, Middy, Oldster, Reefer, Snottie, Snotty
▸ **Midst** see MID
Midwife Accoucheur, Doula, Gran(nie), Granny, Howdie, Howdy, Lucina, Mab, Obstetric
Mien Air, Bearing, Demean, Manner
Might(iness), Mighty Force, Main, Mote, Nibs, Potence, → POWER, Prowess, Puissant, Should, Strength
Mignon(ette) Dyer's rocket, Fillet, Reseda, Weld
Migraine Megrim, Scotodinia, Teichopsia
Migrant Economic, Externe, Gastarbeiter, Lemming, Traveller
Migrate, Migration, Migratory Colonise, Diapedesis, Diaspora, Drift, Eelfare, Exodus, Fleet, Great Trek, Run, Tre(c)k, Volkwanderung
Mikado Emperor, Kami
Mike Bug, Stentorphone
Milanese Patarine
Mild(ly) Balmy, Benign, Bland, Clement, Euphemism, Genial, Gentle, Lenient, Litotes, Mansuete, Meek, → MODERATE, Pacific, Patient, Sarcenet, Sars(e)net, Temperate
Mildew Downy, Foxing, Fungus, Mould, Oidium, Powdery, Vine
Mile(s) Admiralty, Coss, Coverdale, Food, Geographical, Irish, Knot, Kos, Li, Milliary, Nautical, Passenger, Roman, Royal, Scots, Sea, Soldier, Square, Standish, Statute, Swedish, Train
Milesian Teague
Milestone Milliary, MS
Milfoil Yarrow
Militant, Military Activist, Aggressive, Battailous, Black Panther, Black Power, Commando, Fortinbras, Hawkish, Hezbollah, Hizbollah, Hizbullah, Hostile, Ireton, Janjaweed, Janjawid, Kshatriya, Landsturm, Landwehr, Lumper, Mameluke, Martial, Presidio, Provisional, Provo, Soldatesque, Stratocracy, West Point
Militia(-man) Fyrd, Guard, Haganah, Minuteman, Reserve, Tanzim, Trainband, Yeomanry
Milk(er), Milky Acidophilus, Beestings, Bland, Bleed, Bonny-clabber, Bristol, Casein, Certified, Colostrum, Condensed, Creamer, Crud, Curd, Dairy, Emulge, Evaporated, Exploit, Galactic, Glacier, Goat's, Homogenised, Jib, Kefir, Kephir, K(o)umiss, Lactation, Lacteal, Latex, Maas, Madafu, Madzoon, Magnesia, Malted, Mamma, Matzoon, Mess, Moo-juice, Opaline, Pasteurised, Pigeon's, Pinta, Posset, Raw, Rice, Sap, Semi-skimmed, Shedder, Skim(med), Soya, Squeeze, Strippings, Stroke, Suckle, Town, UHT, Whig, Whole, Yaourt, Yogh(o)urt

Milking-machine, Milking parlour Loan, Tapper
Milking-pail Leglan, Leglen, Leglin
Milkless Agalactic, Dry, Eild
Milkmaid, Milkman Chalker, Dey, Emulge, Kefir, Kephir, Radha, Rounder, Roundsman, Skimmed
Milksop Coward, Meacock, Namby-pamby, Nance, Pance, Weakling
Milk-vetch Loco
Milkweed Asclepias
Milkwort Senega
Milky Way Via Lactea
Mill(ing), Mills Aswarm, Ball, Barker's, Boxing, Coffee, Crazing, Economist, Gang, Gastric, Grind(er), Hayley, Kibble, Knurl, Malt, Mano, Melder, Molar, Nurl, Oil, Paper, Pepper, Post, Powder, Press, Pug, Quartz, Quern, Reave, Rob, Rolling, Rumour, Satanic, Scutcher, Smock, Spinning, Stamp, Stamping, Strip, Sugar, Surge, Thou, Tide, Tower, Tuck, Water, Wool(len), Works
Miller Dusty, Glen, Grinder, Jester, Joe, Molendinar, Multurer
Millet Bajra, Bajree, Bajrii, Couscous, Dari, Dhurra, Doura, Dur(r)a, Grain, Miliary, Negro-corn, Pearl, Proso, Ragee, Raggee, Ragi, Whisk
Millionaire Astor, Carnegie, Rockefeller, Rothschild, Vanderbilt
Millions, Millionth Crore, Femto-, Milliard, Muckle, Pico-
Millipede Songololo
Millstone Ligger, Rind, Rynd
Mim Perjink
Mime, Mimic(ry) Ape, Batesian, Copycat, Farce, Imitate, Impersonate, Lipsync, Mina, Mullerian, Mummer, Parody, Sturnine
Mimosa Cacoon, Saman
Mince Cecils, Chop, Dice, Grate, Grind, Keema, Prance, Rice
Mind(er) Aide, Beware, Brain, Genius, Handler, Head, → **HEED**, Herd, Id, Intellect, Noology, Noosphere, Nous, One-track, Open, Phrenic, Psyche, Psychogenic, Resent, Sensorium, Tabula rasa, Tend, Thinker, View, Wit, Woundwort
Mine, Mining Acoustic, Antenna, Bomb, Bonanza, Bottom, Bouquet, Burrow, Camouflet, Chemical, Claymore, Colliery, Contact, Creeping, Dane-hole, Data, Dig(gings), Drifting, Egg, Eldorado, Excavate, Explosive, Floating, Flooder, Fougade, Fougasse, Gallery, Gob, Golconda, Gold, Gopher, Grass, Homing, Land, Limpet, Magnetic, Naked-light, Nostromo, Open-cast, Open-cut, Ophir, Pit, Placer, Pressure, Prospect, Rising, Sap, Set(t), Show, Sonic, Stannary, Stope, Strike, Strip, Undercut, Wheal, Win, Workings
Mine-deflector Otter, Paravane
Mine-owner Operator
Miner, Mine-worker, Mine-working Bevin boy, Butty-gang, Collier, Continuous, Corporal, Cutter, Digger, Forty-niner, Geordie, Leaf, Molly Maguire, Noisy, NUM, Oncost(man), Pitman, Shot-firer, Stall, Tippler, Tributer, UDM
Mineral(s) Accessory, Essential, Index

MINERALS

3 letters:	4 letters:	Mica	Trap
YAG	Clay	Sard	Urao
	Foid	Spar	
	Gang	Talc	

5 letters:
Balas
Borax
Chert
Emery
Flint
Fluor
Macle
Mafic
Nitre
Prase
Topaz
Trona
Umber

6 letters:
Acmite
Albite
Augite
Blende
Galena
Gangue
Garnet
Glance
Gypsum
Hauyne
Illite
Jargon
Lithia
Natron
Nosean
Pinite
Pyrite
Quartz
Rutile
Schorl
Silica
Sphene
Spinel
Tincal
Zircon

7 letters:
Alunite
Anatase
Apatite
Axinite
Azurite
Barytes
Biotite
Bornite

Brucite
Calcite
Calomel
Catseye
Cuprite
Cyanite
Diamond
Dysodil
Epidote
Euclase
Eucrite
Fahlore
Felspar
Gahnite
Göthite
Gummite
Hessite
Ice spar
Jadeite
Jargoon
Kainite
Kernite
Kyanite
Leucite
Mellite
Mullite
Nacrite
Olivine
Pennine
Peridot
Pyrites
Realgar
Rosaker
Sylvine
Sylvite
Thorite
Thulite
Tripoli
Turgite
Ulexite
Uralite
Uranite
Uranium
Zeolite
Zeuxite
Zincite
Zoisite
Zorgite

8 letters:
Adularia

Allanite
Analcime
Analcite
Andesine
Ankerite
Antimony
Aphanite
Asbestos
Autunite
Blue john
Boehmite
Boracite
Braunite
Bronzite
Brookite
Calamine
Cerusite
Chlorite
Chromite
Cinnabar
Cleveite
Corundum
Crocoite
Cryolite
Datolite
Dendrite
Diallage
Diaspore
Disthene
Dolomite
Dysodile
Dysodyle
Epsomite
Erionite
Euxenite
Fayalite
Feldspar
Flinkite
Fluorite
Galinite
Gibbsite
Goethite
Gyrolite
Hematite
Idocrase
Ilmenite
Iodyrite
Jarosite
Lazulite
Lazurite
Lewisite

Limonite
Massicot
Meionite
Melilite
Mimetite
Monazite
Nephrite
Noselite
Orpiment
Petuntse
Picotite
Prehnite
Pyroxene
Resalgar
Rock-salt
Sanidine
Saponite
Siderite
Smectite
Sodalite
Stannite
Stibnite
Stilbite
Taconite
Tenorite
Titanite
Troilite
Vesuvian
Xenotime
Zaratite

9 letters:
Alabaster
Allophane
Amazonite
Amphibole
Anglesite
Anhydrite
Anorthite
Aragonite
Argentite
Atacamite
Blackjack
Blacklead
Carnelian
Carnotite
Celestine
Celestite
Cerussite
Chabazite
Chalybite

Cheralite
Chondrule
Cobaltine
Cobaltite
Coccolite
Columbate
Columbite
Covellite
Cystolith
Dolomitic
Elaeolite
Endomorph
Enhydrite
Enstatite
Erythrite
Fibrolite®
Fluorspar
Gehlenite
Germanite
Geyserite
Gmelinite
Goslarite
Haematite
Harmotome
Hercynite
Hiddenite
Hornstone
Kaolinite
Kermesite
Kieserite
Magnesite
Magnetite
Malachite
Manganite
Marcasite
Margarite
Marialite
Microlite
Microlith
Millerite
Mispickel
Mizzonite
Moonstone
Muscovite
Natrolite
Nepheline
Nephelite
Niccolite
Nitratine
Olivenite
Ottrelite

Paramorph
Pargasite
Pectolite
Periclase
Pericline
Perimorph
Phenacite
Pleonaste
Polianite
Pollucite
Powellite
Proustite
Rhodonite
Rubellite
Scapolite
Scheelite
Scolecite
Septarium
Spodumene
Sylvanite
Tantalite
Tremolite
Troostite
Tungstite
Uraninite
Uvarovite
Variscite
Vulpinite
Wavellite
Wernerite
Willemite
Witherite
Wulfenite
Zinkenite

10 letters:
Actinolite
Alabandine
Alabandite
Andalusite
Bastnasite
Calaverite
Carnallite
Chalcocite
Chessylite
Chrysolite
Colemanite
Cordierite
Crocoisite
Dyscrasite
Forsterite

Gadolinite
Garnierite
Glauconite
Halloysite
Heulandite
Honey-stone
Hornblende
Indicolite
Indigolite
Jamesonite
Laurdalite
Meerschaum
Microcline
Oligoclase
Orthoclase
Paragonite
Perovskite
Phosgenite
Piemontite
Polybasite
Polyhalite
Pyrolusite
Pyrrhotine
Pyrrhotite
Redruthite
Riebeckite
Ripidolite
Samarskite
Saphir d'eau
Sapphirine
Saussurite
Serpentine
Smaragdite
Sperrylite
Sphalerite
Staurolite
Tennantite
Thaumasite
Thenardite
Thorianite
Tiemannite
Torbernite
Tourmaline
Triphylite
Vanadinite
Wolframite

11 letters:
Alexandrite
Amblygonite
Annabergite

Apophyllite
Baddeleyite
Bastnaesite
Cassiterite
Chiastolite
Chrysoberyl
Clinochlore
Crocidolite
Dendrachate
Franklinite
Greenockite
Hypersthene
Idiomorphic
Josephinite
Labradorite
Molybdenite
Pentlandite
Phosphorite
Piedmontite
Pitchblende
Plagioclase
Pseudomorph
Psilomelane
Pyrargyrite
Pyrrhotiner
Sal ammoniac
Sillimanite
Smithsonite
Tabular spar
Tetradymite
Vermiculite
Vesuvianite
Ythro-cerite

12 letters:
Adularescent
Arfvedsonite
Arsenopyrite
Babingtonite
Chalcanthite
Chalcopyrite
Cristobalite
Dumortierite
Feldspathoid
Fluorapatite
Hemimorphite
Pyromorphite
Pyrophyllite
Senarmontite
Skutterudite
Strontianite

Synadelphite	*13 letters:*	*15 letters:*
Tetrahedrite	Cummingtonite	Gooseberry-stone
Wollastonite	Rhodochrosite	Montmorillonite

Mineral water Apollinaris, Tonic
Minesweeper Oropesa, Unity
Mingle, Mingling Blend, Circulate, Consort, Interfuse, Mell, Merge, → MIX, Participate, Socialise, Theocrasy, Unite
Mini Cab, Car, Skirt, Teen(s)y
Miniature, Miniaturist Cosway, Microcosm, Midget, Model, Toy, Young
Minimise, Minimum (range) Bare, Downplay, Fewest, Least, Neap, Shoestring, Stime, Styme, Threshold, Undervalue
▷ **Minimum of** *may indicate* the first letter
Minion Flunkey, Lackey, Pet, Subordinate, Tool, Vassal
Minister Ambassador, Attend, Buckle-beggar, Cabinet, Chancellor, Chaplain, Cleric, Coarb, Commissar, Deacon, Dewan, Diplomat, Divine, D(i)wan, Dominee, Dominie, Envoy, First, Foreign, Holy Joe, Mas(s)john, Mes(s)john, Moderator, Nurse, Officiant, Padre, Parson, Pastor, Peshwa, Preacher, Predikant, Presbyter, Prime, Rector, Secretary, Seraskier, → SERVE, Stick, Stickit, Subdeacon, Tend, Visier, Vizier, Wazir, Wizier
Ministry Defence, Department, Dept, DoE, MOD, MOT, Orders, Service
▷ **Ministry** *may indicate* some government department
Mink Kolinsky, Mutation, Vison
Minnow Devon, Penk, Pink, Tiddler
Minoan Knossus
Minor(ity) Child, Comprimario, Ethnic, Faction, Few, Infant, Junior, Less, Minutia, Nonage, One-horse, Peripheral, Petty, Pupillage, Signed, Slight, Small-time, Trivial, Ward
Minotaur Bull-headed
Minstrel Allan-a-Dale, Bard, Blondel, Bones, Busker, Cantabank, Christy, Cornerman, Gleeman, Hamfatter, Joculator, Jongleur, Minnesinger, Nigger, Pierrot, Scop, Singer, Taillefer
Mint Aim, Bugle-weed, Catnip, Coin, Ettle, Fortune, Herb, Horse, Humbug, Labiate, Monarda, Monetise, Nep, New, Penny-royal, Pepper, Pile, Polo®, Poly, Royal, Selfheal, Spear, Stamp, Stone, Strike, Unused, Utter, Water
Minute(s), Minutiae Acta, Alto, Degree, Detailed, Diatom, Entry, Infinitesimal, Little, Micron, Mo, Mu, Nano-, New York, Pinpoint, Resume, Small, Teen(t)sy, Teeny, Tine, Tiny, Trivia, Tyne, Wee
Minx Hellion
Miracle(s), Miraculous Cana, Marvel, Merel(l), Meril, Morris, Mystery, Phenomenon, Supernatural, Thaumatology, Thaumaturgic, Theurgy, Wirtschaftswunder, Wonder, Wonderwork
Mirage Fata morgana, Illusion, Loom, Northern lights
Mire Bog, Glaur, Lair(y), Latch, Lerna, Lerne, Loblolly, Marsh, Mud, Quag, Sludge, Soil
Mirky Dark, Dirk(e)
Mirror(s), Mirrored Alasnam, Antidazzle, Busybody, Cambuscan, Catoptric, Cheval, Claude Lorraine glass, Coelostat, Conde, Conjugate, Dare, Enantiomorph, Glass, Image, Imitate, Keeking-glass, Lao, Magnetic, Merlin, One-way, Pierglass, Primary, Psyche, Rearview, → REFLECT, Reynard, Shisha, Siderostat, Sign, Specular, Speculum, Stone, Tiring-glass, Two-way, Vulcan, Wing

Mirror-image Perversion
Mirth(ful) Cheer, Dream, Festive, Hilarity, Joy, Laughter, Spleen
▷ **Misalliance** *may indicate* an anagram
Misanthrope Cynic, Timon
Misapplication Catachresis, Misuse
Misappropriate, Misappropriation Asport, Detinue, Purloin, Steal
Miscarry Abort, Backfire, Fail, Slink, Warp
Miscegenation Allocarpy
Miscellaneous, Miscellany Assortment, Chow, Collectanea, Diverse, Etceteras,
    Misc, Odds and ends, Odds and sods, Olio, Omnium-gatherum, Potpourri, Raft,
    Ragbag, Sundry, Varia, Variety, Various
Mischance Misfare
Mischief(-maker), Mischievous Ate, Bale, Bane, Cantrip, Cloots, Devilment,
    Diablerie, Dido, Disservice, Gallus, Gremlin, Harm, Hellery, Hellion, Hob,
    Imp, Injury, Jinks, Larrikin, Limb, Litherly, Make-bate, Malicho, Mallecho,
    Monkey-tricks, Nickum, Owl-spiegle, Pestilent, Pickle, Prank, Puckish, Rascal,
    Scally(wag), Scamp, Scapegrace, Shenanigans, Spriteful, Tricksy, Wag, Wicked,
    Widgie
Misconception Delusion, Idol(on), Idolum, Misunderstanding
Misconduct Impropriety, Malfeasance, Malversation
Miscreant Reprobate, Sinner
Misdeed Offence, Peccadillo, Trespass, Wrong
▷ **Misdelivered** *may indicate* an anagram
Misdemeanour Delict, Offence, Peccadillo, Tort, Wrongdoing
Miser(ly) Carl, Cheapskate, Cheese-parer, Close, Curmudgeon, Gare, Grasping,
    Harpagon, Hunks, Marner, Meanie, Mingy, Niggard, Nipcheese, Nipcurn,
    Nipfarthing, Pennyfather, Pinch-commons, Puckfist, Runt, Scrape-good,
    Scrape-penny, Screw, Scrimping, Scrooge, Skinflint, Snudge, Storer, Tightwad,
    Timon
Miserable, Misery, Miserably Abject, Angashore, Bale, Cat-lap, Crummy, Distress,
    Dole, Forlorn, Gloom, Grief, Heartache, Hell, Joyless, Lousy, Perdition, Punk, Sad,
    Scungy, Sorry, Sourpuss, Tragic, Triste, → **UNHAPPY**, Woe(begone), Wretched
Misfire Dud
Misfit Drop-out, Geek, Loner, Maverick, Sad sack
Misfortune Accident, Affliction, Bale, Calamity, Curse, Disaster, Distress, Dole,
    Hex, Ill, Reverse, Rewth, Ruth, Wroath
Misgiving(s) Anxiety, Doubt, Dubiety, Qualms, Scruples
Misguide(d) Impolitic, Off-beam
▷ **Misguided** *may indicate* an anagram
Mishandle Abuse
Mishap Accident, Contretemps, Misaunter, Misfortune, Pile-up, Wroath
Misheard Mondegreen
Mishit, Misstroke Crab, Draw, Edge, Fluff, Muff, Sclaff, Shank, Slice, Thin, Toe,
    Top
Misinterpret(ation) Mondegreen, Wrest
Mislay Leese, Lose
Mislead(ing) Blind, Bum steer, Cover-up, Deceive, Delude, Dupe, Equivocate,
    Fallacious, False, Gag, Red herring, Runaround, Smoke and mirrors
▷ **Misled** *may indicate* an anagram
Mismanage Blunder, Bungle, Muddle
Mismatch Kludge

Misplace(ment) Anachorism, Ectopia
Misplay Fluff, Whitechapel
Misprint Error, Literal, Literal error, Slip, Typo
Mispronunciation Cacoepy, Lallation, Lambdacism
Misrepresent(ation) Abuse, Belie, Calumny, Caricature, Colour, Distort, Falsify, Garble, Lie, Slander, Subreption, Traduce, Travesty
Miss(ing) Abord, Air, Avoid, AWOL, Colleen, Desiderate, Dodge, Drib, Err(or), Fail, Forego, Gal, → GIRL, Kumari, Lack, Lass, Link, Lose, Mademoiselle, Maid, Maiden, Mile, Muff(et), Near, Neglect, Negligence, Omit, Otis, Overlook, Señorita, Shy, Skip, Spinster, Stoke, Unmeet, Wanting, Whiff
▷ **Miss** *may refer to* Missouri
Missal Breviary, Te igitur, Triodion
Misshapen Crooked, Deformed, Dysmelia, Gnarled
Missile Air-to-air, ALCM, Ammo, Anti-ballistic, Arrow, Artillery, Atlas, Ball, Ballistic, Beam Rider, Blue streak, Bolas, Bolt, Bomb, Boomerang, Brickbat, Bullet, Condor, Cruise, Dart, Dingbat, Doodlebug, Dum-dum, Exocet®, Falcon, Fléchette, Genie, Grenade, Guided, HARM, Harpoon, Hawk, Hellfire, Hound Dog, ICBM, Interceptor, Jired, Kiley, Kyley, Kylie, Lance, Mace, MARV, Maverick, Minuteman, MIRV, Missive, Mx, Onion, Patriot, Pellet, Pershing, Phoenix, Polaris, Poseidon, Qual, Quarrel, Rocket, SAM, Scud, Sea Skimmer, Sergeant, Shell, Shillelagh, Shot, Shrike, Side-winder, Smart bomb, Snowball, Sparrow, Spartan, Spear, Sprint, SSM, Standard Arm, Standoff, Styx, Subroc, Surface to air, Surface to surface, Talos, Tartar, Terrier, Thor, Titan, Tomahawk, Torpedo, Tracer, Trident, UAM, Warhead
Mission(ary) Aidan, Alamo, Antioch, Apostle, Assignment, Augustine, Barnabas, Bethel, Caravan, Charge, Delegation, Embassage, Embassy, Errand, Evangelist, Foreign, Iona, Legation, Livingstone, LMS, Message, NASA, Neurolab, Ninian, Op, Paul, Pr(a)efect, Quest, Reclaimer, Redemptorist, Schweitzer, Task, Vocation, Xavier
Missis, Missus, Mrs Devi, Maam, Mrs, Wife
Missive Letter, Message, Note
Missouri Mo
▶ **Misstroke** *see* MISHIT
Mist(y) Australian, Blur, Brume, Cloud, Dew, Drow, Dry-ice, Film, Fog, Haar, Haze, Hoar, Miasma, Moch, Nebular, Niflheim, Rack, Red, Roke, Scotch, Sea-fret, Sfumato, Smir(r), Smog, Smur, Spotted, Vapour
Mistake(n) Barry (Crocker), Bish, Bloomer, Blooper, Blunder, Boner, Boob, Booboo, Boss, Botch, Category, Clanger, Clinker, Confound, Deluded, Domino, Erratum, Error, Fault, Floater, Flub, Fluff, Folly, Gaffe, Goof, Horlicks, Howler, Identity, Incorrect, Lapse, Malapropism, Miss, Muff, Mutual, Nod, Off-beam, Oversight, Plonker, Pratfall, Ricket, Screw-up, → SLIP, Slip-up, Solecism, Stumer, Trip, Typo
▷ **Mistake(n)** *may indicate* an anagram
Mister Babu, Effendi, Mr, Sahib, Señor, Shri, Sir, Sri
Mistletoe Album, Missel, Parasite, Viscum
Mistreat Abuse, Attrite, Manhandle, Violate
Mistress Amie, Aspasia, Canary-bird, Chatelaine, Concubine, Courtesan, Demimondaine, Devi, Doxy, Goodwife, Herself, Hussif, Inamorata, Instructress, Kept woman, Lady, Leman, Maintenon, Martha, Montespan, Mrs, Natural, Paramour, Stepney, Teacher, Wardrobe, Wife
Mistrust(ful) Askant, Doubt, Gaingiving, Suspect, Suspicion
Misunderstand(ing) Disagreement, Discord, Mistake
Misuse Abuse, Catachresis, Defalcate, Malappropriate, Malapropism, Maltreat,

Perversion, Torment

Mite Acaridian, Acarus, Berry bug, Bit, Bulb, Cheese, Child, Dust, Flour, Forage,
Fowl, Gall, Harvest, Itch, Lepton, Little, (Red) spider, Rust, Sarcoptes, Speck, Sugar,
Trombiculid, Tyroglyphid, Varroa, Widow's

Mitigate, Mitigating Abate, Allay, Allieve, Ameliorate, Assuage, Extenuating,
Lenitive, Lessen, Mease, Palliate, Quell, Relief, Relieve

Mitosis Anaphase

Mitre Hat, Tiar(a)

Mitt(en), Mittens Fist, Glove, Hand, Paw, Pockies

Mix(ed), Mixer, Mixture, Mix-up Alloy, Amalgam, Associate, Assortment,
Attemper, Balderdash, Bigener, Bland, Blend, Blunge, Bordeaux, Brew, Carburet,
Card, Caudle, Chichi, Chow, Cocktail, Co-meddle, Compo, Compound,
Conglomerate, Consort, Cross, Cut, Disperse, Diversity, Dolly, Drammock, Embroil,
Emulsion, Eutectic, Farrago, Fold-in, Freezing, Garble, Grill, Griqua, Half-breed,
Heather, Hobnob, Hotchpotch, Hybrid, Imbroglio, Interlace, Intermingle,
Isomorphous, Jumble, Lace, Lard, Lignin, Linctus, Load, Macedoine, Marketing,
Matissé, Meddle, Medley, Melange, Mell, Meng(e), Ment, Mess, Mestizo, Métis,
Ming(le), Miscellaneous, Miscellany, Mishmash, Mong, Motley, Muddle, Muss(e),
Neapolitan, Octaroon, Octoroon, Olio, Olla, Pi(e), Potin, Pousowdie, Powsowdy,
Praiseach, Promiscuous, Raggle-taggle, Ragtag, Salad, Scramble, Shuffle, Soda,
Spatula, Stew, Stir, Temper, Through-other, Trail, Vision, Yblent

▷ **Mixed** *may indicate* an anagram

Mizzle Decamp, Scapa, Scarper

Mnemonic(s) Fleming's rules, Memoria technica, Quipo, Quipu, Reminder

Moab(ite) Balak, Ruth, Wash-pot

Moan(ing) Beef, Bewail, Bleat, Complain, Groan, Hone, Keen, → **LAMENT**, Meane,
Plangent, Sigh, Snivel, Sough, Wail, W(h)inge

Moat Dike, Ditch, Foss(e)

Mob(ster) Army, Assail, Canaille, Crew, Crowd, Doggery, Faex populi, Flash, Gaggle,
Gang, Herd, Hoi-polloi, Hoodlum, Horde, Lynch, Many-headed beast, Ochlocrat,
Press, Rabble, Rabble rout, Raft, Ragtag, Ribble-rabble, Riff-raff, Rout, Scar-face

Mobile, Mobilise, Mobility Donna, Downward, Fluid, Horizontal,
Intergenerational, Movable, Plastic, Rally, Thin, Upward(ly), Vagile, Vertical

Mob-rule Ochlocracy

Mocassin Larrigan, Shoe, Snake

Mock(ery), Mocking Ape, Banter, Chaff, Chyack, Cod, Cynical, Deride, Derisory,
Dor, Ersatz, False, Farce, Fleer, Flout, Gab, Geck, Gibe, Gird, Guy, Imitation, Irony,
Irrisory, Jape, → **JEER**, Jibe, Lampoon, Laugh, Mimic, Narquois, Parody, Paste,
Pillorise, Rail(lery), Rally, Ridicule, Sacrilege, Sardonic, Satirise, Scorn, Scout,
Sham, Simulate, Slag, Sneer, Travesty, Wry

Mocking-bird Mimus, Sage-thrasher

Mode Aeolian, Church, Convention, Dorian, Ecclesiastical, Fashion, Form, Formal,
Greek, Gregorian, Hyperdorian, Hypo(dorian), Hypolydian, Iastic, Ionian, Locrian,
Lydian, Major, Manner, Material, Medieval, Minor, Mixolydian, Phrygian, Plagal,
Rate, Real-time, Sleep, Step, Style, Ton

Model(ler), Modelling Archetype, Bozzeto, Cast, Copy, Demonstration, Diorama,
Doll, Dummy, Ecorché, Effigy, Epitome, Example, Exemplar, Exemplary, Fictor,
Figure, Figurine, Icon, Ideal, Image, Instar, Jig, Last, Lay-figure, Layman, Madame
Tussaud, Manakin, Manikin, Mannequin, Maquette, Mark, Mirror, Mock-up,
→ **MOULD**, Norm, Original, Orrery, Papier-mâché, Parade, Paragon, Pattern,
Phelloplastic, Pilot, Plasticine, Play-Doh®, Pose(r), Posture-maker, Prototype,

Replica, Role, Scale, Sedulous, Sitter, Specimen, Standard, Superwaif, T, Template, Templet, Terrella, Toy, Trilby, Twiggy, Type, Typify, Waif, Waxwork, Working
▷ **Model(s)** *may indicate* an anagram
Modem Subset
Moderate(ly), Moderation Abate, Allay, Alleviate, Assuage, Attemper, Average, Ca'canny, Centre, Chasten, Continent, Diminish, Discretion, Ease, Gentle, Girondist, Ho, Lessen, Lukewarm, Measure, Mediocre, Medium, Menshevik, Mezzo, Middling, Mild, Mitigate, OK, Politique, Reason(able), Restraint, RR, Slake, So-so, Sumptuary, Temper(ate), Temperance, Tolerant, Tone, Via media, Wet
Modern(ise) AD, Aggiornamento, Contemporary, Fresh, Latter(-day), Milly, Neonomian, Neoterical, → **new**, Present-day, Progressive, Recent, Retrofit, Swinger, Trendy, Update, Up-to-date
Modest(y) Aidos, Blaise, Chaste, Coy, Decent, Demure, Discreet, Fair, Humble, Humility, Ladylike, Low-key, Maidenly, Mim, Mussorgsky, Propriety, Prudish, Pudency, Pure, Reserved, Shame, Shy, Unassuming, Unpretending, Unpretentious, Verecund
Modicum Dash
Modifiable, Modification, Modifier, Modify Adapt, Adverb, Alter, Backpedal, Change, Enhance, Extenuate, H, Leaven, Misplaced, Plastic, Qualify, Retrofit, Sandhi, Scumble, Soup, Streamline, Temper, Top, Trim, Vary
Modulation, Module, Modulus Accent, Amplitude, Bulk, Cadence, Command, Distance, Excursion, Frequency, Habitat, Inflexion, Lem, Lunar, Mitigate, Phase, Pulse, Service, Tune, Unit, Vary, Velocity, Young's
Mogul Bigwig, Magnate, Nawab, Padishah, Plutocrat, Potentate, Taipan, VIP
Mohair Moire
Mohammed, Mohammedan (era) Hadith, Hegira, Hejira, Hejra, Hijra, Islamite, Mahdi, Mahoun(d), Moslem, Muezzin, Mussulman, Prophet, Said, Shiite, Sunna(h)
Moist(en), Moisture Baste, Bedew, Damp, Dank, De(a)w, Humect, Latch, Love-in-a-mist, Madefy, Mesarch, Moil, Nigella, Oozy, Slake, Slocken, Soggy, Sponge, Wet
▷ **Moither** *may indicate* an anagram
Molar Grinder, Mill-tooth, Secodont, Tooth, Wang
Molasses Blackstrap, Sorghum, Treacle
Mole(hill) Breakwater, Fen-cricket, Golden, Hydatidiform, Jetty, Marsupial, Miner, Mo(u)diewart, Moudi(e)wart, Mouldiwarp, Naeve, Notoryctes, Orology, Pier, Sea-wall, Shrew, Sleeper, Spot, Spy, Star-nose(d), Talpa, Want(hill), Want knap, Warp
Molecule, Molecular Acceptor, Atom, Buckyball, Carbene, Cavitand, Chiral, Chromophore, Closed chain, Cobalamin, Codon, Coenzyme, Cofactor, Dimer, DNA, Electrogen, Enantiomorph, Footballene, Fullerene, Gram, Hapten, Iota, Isomer, Kinin, Kisspeptin, Ligand, Long-chain, Metabolite, Metameric, Monomer, Nanotube, Peptide, Polymer, Polysaccharide, Quark, Replicon, Ribozyme, Semantide, Stereoisomer, Trimer, Uridine, Vector
Molendinar Mill
Molest(er) Annoy, Bother, Disturb, Harass, Nonce, Scour
Moll(y), Mollie Bloom, Bonnie, Carousal, Cutpurse, Flanders, Girl, Maguire, Malone, May, Sissy
Mollify Appease, Fob, Mease, Mitigate, Pacify, Placate, Relax, Soften, Temper
Mollusc(s) Ammonite, Amphineura, Arca, Argonaut, Ark-shell, Belemnite, Bivalve, Bulla, Capiz, Cephalopod, Chiton, Clam, Cockle, Conch, Cone-shell, Cowrie, Cowry, Cuttle(fish), Dentalium, Doris, Gaper, Gast(e)ropod, Goniatite,

Heart-cockler, Heart-shell, Helix, Horse mussel, Idler, Lamellibranch, Limpet,
Malacology, Marine boxer, Money cowry, Monoplacophora, Murex, Mussel, Mya,
Nautiloid, Nautilus, Neopilina, Octopod, Octopus, Olive, Opisthobranch, Oyster,
Pandora, Paper nautilus, Paper-sailor, Pearly nautilus, Pecten, Pelican's-foot,
Pholas, Piddock, Pinna, Polyp, Poulpe, Protostome, Pteropod, Quahaug, Quahog,
Razor-clam, Razor-fish, Razorshell, Saxicava, Scallop, Scaphopoda, Sea-hare,
Sea-lemon, Sea-slug, Sepia, → **SHELLFISH**, Shipworm, Slipper limpet, Slug,
Snail, Solen, Spat, Spirula, Spoot, Squid, Strombus, Tectibranch, Tellen, Tellin,
Teredo, Toheroa, Top-shell, Triton, Trochophore, Trochus, Trough-shell, Turbo,
Tusk-shell, Unio, Univalve, Veliger, Venus, Venus shell, Vitrina, Wentletrap,
Whelk, Wing-shell, Winkle
Mollycoddle Indulge, Nanny, Pamper
Moloch Thorn-devil
Molten Dissolved, Fusil, Melted
Molybdenum Mo
Moment(s), Momentous Aha, Bending, Bit, Dipole, Electromagnetic, Eureka,
Flash, Hogging, Import, Instant, Jiffy, Magnetic, → **MINUTE**, Mo, Nonce, Point,
Psychological, Pun(c)to, Sagging, Sands, Sec, Senior, Shake, Stound, Stownd, Tick,
Time, Trice, Twinkling, Weighty, Wink
Momentum Angular, Impetus, L, Speed, Thrust
Mona(s) I, IOM
Monaco Grimaldi
Mona Lisa La Gioconda
Monarch(y) Absolute, Autocrat, Butterfly, Caesar, Constitutional, Crown, Dual,
Emperor, HM, K, Karling, King, Limited, Merry, Potentate, Q, Queen, R, Raine,
Reign, Ruler, Tonga, Tsar
Monarchist Cavalier
Monastery Abbey, Abthane, Charterhouse, Chartreuse, Cloister, Community,
Gompa, Hospice, Lamaserai, Lamasery, La Trappe, Laura, Priory, Vihara, Wat
Monastic Abthane, Celibate, Holy, Monkish, Oblate, Secluded
Monday Black, Collop, Handsel, J'ouvert, Meal, Oatmeal, Plough, Whit
Mondrian Piet
Money, Monetary Ackers, Akkas, Allowance, Annat, Ante, Appearance, Archer,
Assignat, Banco, Batta, Blood, Blue, Blunt, Boodle, Bottle, Brass, Bread, Bread
and honey, Broad, Bull's eye, Cabbage, Capital, Cash, Caution, Century, Change,
Chink, Cob, Cock, → **COIN**, Collateral, Confetti, Conscience, Crackle, Cranborne,
Crinkly, Currency, Danger, Dib(s), Dingbat, Dollar, Dosh, Dust, Earnest, Easy, Even,
Fat, Fee, Fiat, Float, Folding, Fonds, Found, Fund, Funny, Gate, Gelt, Gilt, Godiva,
Gold, Grand, Grant, Gravy, Greens, Hard, Head, Hello, Hoot, Hot, Housekeeping,
Hush, Husk, Idle, Ingots, Investment, Jack, Kale, Kembla, Key, Knife, L, Legal
tender, Lolly, Loot, Lucre, M, Mammon, Maundy, Mazuma, Means, Mint, Monkey,
Monopoly, Moola(h), Narrow, Near, Necessary, Needful, Nest-egg, Note, Nugger,
Numismatic, Nummary, Oaker, Ochre, Offertory, Oof, Option, Outlay, P, Packet,
Paper, Passage, Pavarotti, Payroll, Peanuts, Pecuniary, Pelf, Pin, Pine-tree,
Pittance, Plastic, Plum, Pocket, Pony, Posh, Press, Prize, Proceeds, Profit,
Protection, Purse, Push, Quid, Ration, Ready, Rebate, Resources, Revenue, Rhino,
Ring, Risk, Rogue, Rowdy, Salt(s), Score, Scratch, Scrip, Seed, Shell, Shin-plaster,
Ship, Short, Siller, Silly, Silver, Slush, Smart, Soap, Soft, Spondulicks, Stake,
Sterling, Stipend, Stuff, Subsistence, Sugar, Sum, Table, Takings, Tender, Tin,
Toea, Token, Tranche, Treaty, Tribute, Turnover, Viaticum, Wad, Wealth, Wonga
Money-box Penny-pig, Piggy bank

Moneylender Gombeen, Shroff, Shylock, Usurer
Moneymaking Earner, Profitable, Quaestuary
Mongol(ian) Bashkir, Buriat, Buryat, Calmuck, Chuvash, Evenski, Golden Horde, Kalmuck, Kara-Kalpak, Kazak(h), Khalkha, Kubla(i) Khan, Kyrgyz, Lapp, Lepcha, Manchoo, Manchu, Mishmi, Mogul, Pareoean, Samoyed, Shan, Sherpa, Tamerlane, Tatar, Tungus(ic), Uig(h)ur, Ural-altaic, Uzbek
Mongoose Herpestes, Ichneumon, Mangouste, Meerkat, Suricate, Urva
Mongrel Bitser, Cross(bred), → DOG, Goorie, Goory, Hybrid, Kuri, Lurcher, Mutt, Quadroon, Tyke, Underbred, Zo
Monitor(ing) Dataveillance, Detect, Goanna, Iguana, Lizard, Observe, Offer, Ofgas, Ofgem, Oflot, Ofsted, Oftel, Ofwat, Prefect, Preview, Record, Screen, Ship, Track, Warship, Watchdog, Whole-body, Worral, Worrel
Monk(s) Abbey-lubber, Abbot, Acoemeti, Angelico, Archimandrite, Arhat, Asser, Augustinian, Austin, Basilian, Bede, Beghard, Benedictine, Bernardine, Bethlehemite, Bhikhu, Black, Bonaventura, Bonze, Bro, Brother, Bruno, Caedmon, Caloyer, Carthusian, Celestine, Cellarist, Cenobite, Cistercian, Cluniac, Coenobite, Cowl, Crutched Friar, Culdee, Dan, Dervish, Dom, Dominican, Félibre, Feuillant, Fraticelli, Friar, General, Gyrovague, Hegumen, Hermit, Hesychast, Hildebrand, Ignorantine, Jacobin, Jacobite, Jerome, Lama, Maurist, Mechitharist, Mekhitarist, Mendel, Norbertine, Obedientiary, Oblate, Olivetan, Order, Pelagian, Prior, Rakehell, Rasputin, Recluse, Recollect, Religieux, Roshi, Salesian, Sangha, Savonarola, Simeon Stylites, Sub-prior, Talapoin, Theatine, Thelemite, Thelonious, Thomas à Kempis, Tironensian, Trappist, Votary
Monkey Anger, Ape, Aye-aye, Baboon, Bandar, Bobbejaan, Bonnet, Bushbaby, Capuchin, Catar(r)hine, Cebidae, Cebus, Chacma, Coaita, Colobus, Cynomolgus, Diana, Douc, Douroucouli, Drill, Durukuli, Entellus, Galago, Gelada, Gibbon, Gorilla, Grease, Green, Grison, Grivet, Guenon, Guereza, Hanuman, Hoolock, Howler, Hylobates, Indri, Jacchus, Jackey, Jocko, Kippage, Langur, Leaf, Lemur, Loris, Macaco, Macaque, Magot, Malmag, Mandrill, Mangabey, Marmoset, Meddle, Meerkat, Mico, Midas, Mona, Mycetes, Nala, Nasalis, New World, Old World, Orang-utang, Ouakari, Ouistiti, Phalanger, Platyrrhine, Powder, → PRIMATE, Proboscis, Pug, Puzzle, Rage, Ram, Rapscallion, Rascal, Rhesus, Sago(u)in, Saguin, Sai(miri), Sajou, Saki, Sapajou, Satan, Semnopithecus, Siamang, Sifaka, Silen(us), Silverback, Simian, Simpai, Slender loris, Spider, Squirrel, Talapoin, Tamarin, Tamper, Tana, Tarsier, Tee-tee, Titi, Toque, Trip-hammer, Troop, Tup, Uakari, Vervet, Wanderoo, White-eyelid, Wistiti, Wou-wou, Wow-wow, Wrath, Zati
Monkey-nut Earth-pea
Monkey-puzzle Araucaria, Bunya-bunya
Monkshood Aconite
Monocle Eye-glass, Gig-lamp, Lorgnon, Quiz(zing-glass)
Monocot(yledon) Araceae, Endogen, Tradescantia
Monodon Narwhal
Monogram, Monograph Chi-rho, Cipher, Study, Treatise, Tug(h)ra
Monolith Ayers Rock, Cenotaph, Chambers Pillar, Uluru
Monologue Interior, Patter, Rap, Recitation, Soliloquy, Speech
Monopolise, Monopoly Appalto, Bloc, Bogart, Cartel, Corner, Engross, Octroi, Régie, Trust
Monorail Aerobus
Monosyllable Proclitic
Monotonous, Monotony Boring, Dull, → FLAT, Grey, Humdrum, Same(y), Sing-song, Tedious

Monsoon Dry, Hurricane, Typhoon, Wet, → WIND
▷ **Monsoon** *may indicate* weekend (Mon soon)
Monster, Monstrous Alecto, Apollyon, Asmodeus, Bandersnatch, Behemoth,
Bunyip, Caliban, Cerberus, Cete, Charybdis, Chichevache, Chim(a)era, Cockatrice,
Colossal, Cyclops, Dabbat, Deform, Dinoceras, Dismayd, Div, Dragon, Echidna,
Enormous, Erebus, Erinys, Erl-king, Eten, Ettin, Evil-one, Fiend, Fire-drake,
Frankenstein, Freak, Geryon, Ghost, Giant, Gila, Golem, Gorgon, Green-eyed,
Grendel, Harpy, Hippocampus, Hippogriff, Hippogryph, Huge, Hydra, Jabberwock,
Kraken, Lamia, Leviathan, Lilith, Lusus naturae, Mastodon, Medusa, Minotaur,
Misbegotten, Moloch, Mooncalf, Mylodont, Nessie, Nicker, Nightmare, Ogopogo,
Ogre, Ogr(e)ish, Opinicus, Orc, Outrageous, Pongo, Sasquatch, Satyral, Scylla,
Serra, Shadow, Simorg, Simurg(h), Siren, Skull, Snark, Spectre, Sphinx, Spook,
Stegodon, Stegosaur, Succubus, Taniwha, Teras, Teratism, Teratoid, Triceratops,
Troll, Typhoeus, Typhon, Unnatural, Vampire, Vast, Wasserman, Wendego,
Wendigo, Wer(e)wolf, Wyvern, Xiphopagus, Yowie, Ziffius
Monstrance Ostensory
Month(ly) Ab, Abib, Adar, Anomalistic, April, Asadha, Asvina, August, Bhadrapada,
Brumaire, Bul, Calendar, Cheshvan, Chislev, December, Dhu-al-Hijjah,
Dhu-al-Qadah, Draconic, Elul, February, Floréal, Frimaire, Fructidor, Germinal,
Hes(h)van, Iy(y)ar, January, July, Jumada, June, Jysaitha, Kartuka, Kisleu, Kislev,
Lide, Lunar, Lunation, Magha, March, Margasirsa, May, Messidor, Mo, Moharram,
Moon, Muharram, Muharrem, Nisan, Nivôse, Nodical, November, October,
Periodical, Phalguna, Pluviôse, Prairial, Rabia, Rajab, Ramadan, Ramazon,
Rhamadhan, Safar, Saphar, September, Sha(a)ban, Shawwal, S(h)ebat, Sidereal,
Sivan, Solar, Stellar, Synodic, Tammuz, Tebeth, Thermidor, Tishri, Tisri, Tropical,
Vaisakha, Veadar, Vendémiaire, Ventôse
Monument Ancient, Arch, Archive, Cenotaph, Charminar, Column, Cromlech,
Dolmen, Henge, Megalith, Memorial, Menhir, Monolith, National, Pantheon,
Pyramid, Sacellum, Stele(ne), Stone, Stonehenge, Stupa, Talayot, Tombstone,
Trilith, Trilithon, Urn
Mood(y) Active, Anger, Atmosphere, Attitude, Capricious, Conjunctive, Dudgeon,
Emoticon, Enallage, Fettle, Fit, Foulie, Glum, Grammar, Humour, Hump,
Imperative, Indicative, Infinitive, Mercurial, Morale, Optative, Passive, Peat, Pet,
Revivalist, Sankey, Spleen, Subjunctive, Temper, Tid, Tone, Tune, Vein, Vinegar,
Whim
Moon(light), Moony Aah, Alignak, Aningan, Apogee, Artemis, Astarte, Blue,
Callisto, Calypso, Chandra, Cheese, Cynthia, Diana, Epact, Eye, Flit, Full, Gander,
Ganymede, Gibbous, Glimmer, Grimaldi, Harvest, Hecate, Hunter's, Hyperion,
Inconstant, Juliet, Leda, Lucina, Luna(r), Mani, Mascon, McFarlane's Buat,
Midsummer, Mock, Month, Mope, New, Nimbus, Nocturne, Octant, Oliver,
Paddy's lantern, Paraselene, Paschal, Pasiphaë, Phoebe, Plenilune, Proteus, Raker,
Satellite, Selene, Set, Shepherd, Shot, Sickle, Sideline, Silvery, Sonata, Stargaze,
Stone, Syzygy, Thebe, Thoth, Titan, Triton, Umbriel, Wander
Moonraker Astrogeologist, Gothamite
Moonshine(r) Hootch, Poteen, Rot, Shebeener
Moor(ing), Moorish, Moorland Berth, Bodmin, Culloden, Dock, Fen, Flow
country, Grouse, Heath, Iago, Ilkley, Makefast, Marina, Marston, Moresque,
Moroccan, Mudéjar, Othello, Palustrine, Roadstead, Ryepeck, Saracen, Sternfast,
Tether, → TIE, Wharf, Wold
Mop(ping) Dwile, Flibbertigibbet, Girn, Glib, Shag, Squeegee, Squilgee, Swab,
Swob, Thatch, → WIPE

Mope Boody, Brood, Peak, Sulk

Mor Humus

Moral(ity), Morals Apologue, Austere, Deontic, Ethic(al), Ethos, Everyman, Fable, High-minded, Integrity, Precept, Principled, Puritanic, Righteous, Sittlichkeit, Tag, Upright, Virtuous, Well-thewed

Morale Ego, Mood, Spirit, Zeal

Moralise, Moralising Preach, Sententious

Moralist Prig, Prude, Puritan, Whitecap

Morass Bog, Fen, Flow, Marsh, Moss, Quagmire, Slough

Morbid(ity) Anasarca, Ascites, Cachaemia, Dropsy, Ectopia, Ghoul(ish), Gruesome, Pathological, Plethora, Prurient, Religiose, Sick, Sombre, Unhealthy

Mordant Biting, Caustic, Critic(al), Sarcastic, Tooth

Mordent Inverted, Pralltriller, Upper

More Added, Additional, Else, Extra, Increase, Less, Mae, Merrier, Mo(e), → **NO MORE**, Over, Piu, Plus, Stump, Utopia

Moreover Also, Besides, Eft, Either, Eke, Further, Too, Yet

Morgan Buccaneer, Pirate

Moribund Dying, Stagnant, Withered

Mormon Danite, Latter-day Saint, Salt Lake City, Utah, Young

Morning Ack-emma, Am, Antemeridian, Dawn, Daybreak, Early, Forenoon, Levée, Matin(al), Morrow, Sparrowfart

Morning-glory Bindweed, Ipomoea, Turbith, Turpeth

Morning-star Morgenstern, Phosphor(us), Threshel, Venus

Moroccan, Morocco Agadir, French, Leather, Levant, MA, Mo(o)r, Persian, Riff, Tangerine, Venus

Moron Fool, Idiot, Schmuck, → **STUPID**

Morose Acid, Boody, Churlish, Crabby, Cynical, Disgruntled, Gloomy, Glum, Grum, Moody, Sour-eyed, Sullen, Surly

Morph Phase

Morris Car, Dance, Fivepenny, Merel(l), Meril, Nine Men's, Ninepenny

Morrow Future

Morse Code, Endeavour, Iddy-umpty, Walrus

Morsel Bit, Bite, Bouche, Canape, Crumb, Dainty, Morceau, Ort, Scrap, Sippet, Sop, Tidbit, Titbit

Mortal(ity) Averr(h)oism, Being, Deathly, → **FATAL**, Grave, Human, Lethal, Yama

Mortar, Mortar-board Bowl, Cannon, Cement, Co(e)horn, Compo, Grout, Gunite, Hawk, Life, Metate, Mine-thrower, Minnie, Moaning (Minnie), Parget, Plaster, Pot gun, Screed, Square, Squid, Toc emma, Trench(er)

Mortgage(e) Balloon, Bond, Cedula, Chattel, Debt, Dip, Encumbrance, Endowment, First, Hypothecator, Loan, Pension, Pledge, Wadset(t)

Mortification, Mortified, Mortify Abash, Ashame, Chagrin, Crucify, Crush, Gangrene, Humble, Humiliate, Infarct, Necrose, Penance, Sick, Sphacelus, Wormwood

Mosaic Buhl, Cosmati, Inlay, Intarsia, Musive, Opus musivum, Pietra dura, Screen, Tarsia, Terrazzo, Tessella(te), Tessera, Tobacco, Venetian

Moscow Dynamo

Moses Grandma

▶ **Moslem** see **MUSLIM**

Mosque Dome of the Rock, El Aqsa, Jami, Masjid, Medina, Musjid

Mosquito Aedes, Anopheles, Culex, Culicine, Gnat, Parasite, Stegomyia

Moss(y) Acrogen, Agate, Bryology, Bur(r), Carrag(h)een, Ceylon, Club, Fog, Fontinalis,

Hag(g), Hypnum, Iceland, Irish, Lecanoram, → **LICHEN**, Litmus, Liverwort, Long, Lycopod, Marsh, Musci, Muscoid, Parella, Peat, Polytrichum, Reindeer, Rose, Scale, Selaginella, Spanish, Sphagnum, Staghorn, Tree, Usnea, Wall, Wolf's claw
Most Largest, Major, Maxi(mum), Optimum
Mot Quip, Saying
Mote Atom, Particle, Speck
Moth(s) Abraxas, Antler, Arch, Arctiidae, Atlas, Bag, Bee, Bell, Bobowler, Bogong, Bombycid, Brown-tail, Buff-tip, Bugong, Burnet, Cabbage, Cactoblastis, Carpenter, Carpet, Cecropia, Cinnabar, Clearwing, Clifden nonpareil, Clothes, Codlin(g), Corn (-borer), Dagger, Dart-moth, Death's head, Diamondback, Drepanid, Drinker, Eggar, Egger, Emerald, Emperor, Ermine, Flour, Fox, Geometer, Geometrid, Ghost, Giant peacock, Gipsy, Goat, Goldtail, Gooseberry, Grass, Gypsy, Hawk, Herald, Honeycomb, Hook-tip, House, Hummingbird, Imago, Io, Kentish glory, Kitten, Lackey, Lappet, Large emerald, Lasiocampidae, Leafroller, Leopard, Lepidoptera, Lichen, Lobster, Luna, Lymantriidae, Macrolepidoptera, Magpie, Meal, Microlepidoptera, Mother of pearl, Mother Shipton, Muslin, Noctua, Noctuid, Notodonta, Nun, Oak-egger, Owl, Owlet, Peppercorn, Peppered, Pine-beauty, Pine-carpet, Plane, Plume, Polyphemus, Privet hawk, Processionary, Prominent, Psyche, Pug-moth, Purple emperor, Puss, Pyralidae, Red underwing, Sallow-kitten, Saturnia, Saturniid, Scavenger, Silkworm, Silver-Y, Snout, Sphingid, Sphinx, Swift, Tapestry, Thorn, Tiger, Tinea, Tineidae, Tortrix, Turnip, Tussock, Umber, Underwing, Unicorn, Vapourer, Veneer, Wainscot, Wave, Wax, Wheat, Winter, Woodborer, Yellow underwing, Y-moth, Zygaena
Mothball(s) Abeyance, Camphor, Naphtha, Preserver
Mother Bearer, Church, Cognate, Cosset, Courage, Dam(e), Dregs, Ean, Earth, Eve, Foster, Generatrix, Genetrix, Genitrix, Goose, Hubbard, Lees, Ma, Machree, Madre, Mam(a), Mamma, Mater, Maya, Minnie, Mom, Multipara, Mum, Native, Nature, Nourish, Nursing, Parity, Pourer, Primipara, Reverend, Shipton, Superior, Surrogate, Theotokos, Wit
▷ **Mother** *may indicate* a lepidopterist (moth-er)
Motherless Adam, Orphan
Motif Anthemion, Design, Gist, Idée, Theme
Motion Angular, Contrary, Diurnal, Early day, Fast, Gesture, Harmonic, Impulse, Kepler, Kinematics, Kinetic, Link, Move, Oblique, Offer, Parallactic, Parallel, Peculiar, Perpetual, PL, Proper, Proposal, Rack and pinion, Rider, Similar, Slow, Spasm, Wave
Motionless Doggo, Frozen, Immobile, Quiescent, Stagnant, Stasis, Still, Stock-still
Motive, Motivate, Motivation Actuate, Cause, Ideal, Impel, Incentive, Intention, Mainspring, Mobile, Object, → **PURPOSE**, Spur, Ulterior
Motley Jaspé, Medley, Piebald, Pied
Motor(boat) Auto, Car, Dynamo, Electric, Engine, Hot rod, Inboard, Induction, Jato, Linear, Outboard, Rocket, Scooter, Series-wound, Stator, Synchronous, Thruster, Turbine, Universal, Water
Motorcycle, Motorcyclist Bambi, Bikie, Chookchaser, Chopper, Farm-bike, Harley Davidson, Hell's Angel, Minimoto, Moped, Pipsqueak, Scooter, Scramble, Trail bike, Yamaha®
Motorist(s) AA, Driver, Petrolhead, RAC, Tripper
Motorman Austin, Benz, Ford, Morris
Motor race Rally, Scramble, TT
Motorway Autobahn, Autopista, Autoput, Autoroute, Autostrada, Expressway, M(1), Orbital, Superhighway, Throughway, Thruway

Mottle(d) Brindled, Chiné, Jaspé, Marbled, Marly, Mirly, Pinto, Poikilitic, Tabby
Motto Device, Epigraph, Excelsior, Gnome, Impresa, Imprese, Impress(e), Legend, Maxim, Mot, Poesy, Posy, Saw
Mou(e) Grimace, Mim
Mould(ed), Moulder, Mouldable, Moulding, Mouldy Accolade, Architrave, Archivolt, Astragal, Baguette, Balection, Bandelet, Beading, Bend, Black, Blow, Blue, Bolection, Bread, Briquet(te), Cabling, Casement, Cast(ing), Cavetto, Chessel, Chill, Cold, Cornice, Coving, Cyma, Cymatium, Dancette, Dariole, Die, Die-cast, Dogtooth, Doucine, Dripstone, Ductile, Echinus, Egg and dart, Emboss, Flong, → **FORM**, Foughty, Fousty, Fungose, Fungus, Fusarol(e), Fust, Gadroon, Godroon, Gorgerin, Green, Hood-mould, Hore, Humus, Injection, Iron, Jelly, Leaf, Machine, Matrix, Mildew, Model, Mool, Moulage, Mucid, Mucor, Must, Mycetozoan, Myxomycete, Nebule, Necking, Noble rot, Ogee, Ovolo, Palmette, Papier-mâché, Penicillin, Phycomycete, Picture, Pig, Plasm(a), Plastic, Plastisol, Plat, Platband, Plate, Prototype, Prunt, Quarter-round, Reeding, Reglet, Rhizopus, Rot, Rust, Sandbox, Scotia, Shape, Slime, Smut, Soil, Soot(y), Spindle, Storiated, Stringcourse, Stucco, Surbase, Tailor, Talon, Template, Templet, Timbale, Tondino, Torus, Trochilus, Vinew, Water table
Moult(ing) Cast, Metecdysis, Mew, Shed
Mound Agger, Bank, Barp, Barrow, Berm, Cahokia, Cone, Dike, Dun, Embankment, Heap, Hog, Kurgan, Mogul, Molehill, Monticule, Mote, Motte, Orb, Pile, Pingo, Pome, Rampart, Rampire, Remblai, Tel(l), Teocalli, Teopan, Tuffet, Tumulus, Tussock
Mound-bird Megapode
Mount(ed), Mounting, Mountain (peak), Mountains Air, → **ALPINE**, Ascend, Aspiring, Back, Barp, Ben, Berg, Board, Breast, Butter, Chain, Charger, → **CLIMB**, Colt, Cordillera, Cradle, Dew, Display, Djebel, Dolly, Escalade, Frame, Hinge, Horse, Inselberg, Jebel, Massif, Monture, Mt, Nunatak, Orography, Orology, Passe-partout, Pike, Pile, Pin, Pownie, Quad, Ride, Saddlehorse, Saddle up, Scalado, Scale, Sclim, Set, Soar, Stage, → **STEED**, Stie, Strideways, Tel, Tier, Topo, Tor, Turret, Upgo, Volcano

MOUNTAINS

2 letters:	Hoss	Andes	Idris
K2	Jaya	Aneto	Kamet
	Jura	Athos	Kenya
3 letters:	Meru	Atlas	Logan
Apo	Nebo	Badon	Munro
Ida	Oeta	Black	Ozark
Kaf	Ossa	Blanc	Pelée
Ore	Rigi	Coast	Rocky
	Ubac	Djaja	Rydal
4 letters:	Zeil	Eiger	Sayan
Alai		Ellis	Serra
Blue	*5 letters:*	Er Rif	Sinai
Bona	Abora	Ghats	Siple
Cook	Adams	Green	Smoky
Etna	Aldan	Guyot	Snowy
Fuji	Altai	Hekla	Table
Harz	Amara	Horeb	Tabor

Tatra	Taurus	Whitney	Dolomites
Tirol	Umbria	Wicklow	El Capitan
Tyree	Vernon		Grampians
Tyrol	Vosges	**8 letters:**	Guadalupe
Uinta	Zagros	Anapurna	Helvellyn
Urals		Ben Nevis	Highlands
Welsh	**7 letters:**	Cambrian	High Tatra
White	Aetolia	Carstenz	Himalayas
	Ala Dagh	Catskill	Hindu Kush
6 letters:	Aorangi	Caucasus	Jebel Musa
Ala Dag	Aragats	Cevennes	Karakoram
Alaska	Arcadia	Cumbrian	Lenin Peak
Amhara	Bernina	Demavend	Longs Peak
Anadyr	Brocken	Grampian	Marmolada
Arafat	Buffalo	Guerrero	Mont Blanc
Ararat	Calvary	Hymettus	Monte Rosa
Averno	Cariboo	Illimani	Nanda Devi
Balkan	Cascade	Jungfrau	Parnassus
Bogong	Chianti	Kinabalu	Pikes Peak
Carmel	Corbett	King Peak	Ruwenzori
Cho Oyu	Dapsang	Leibnitz	Shivering
Dragon	Estreia	McKinley	Sugar Loaf
Egmont	Everest	Mulhacen	Tirich Mir
Elbert	Helicon	Ngaliema	Trans Alai
Elberz	Kennedy	Ouachita	Tupungato
Elbrus	Khingan	Pennines	Vancouver
Erebus	Kuenlun	Pyrenees	Venusberg
Gilead	Lebanon	Rushmore	Voralberg
Hermon	Lucania	Seamount	Weisshorn
Hoggar	Manaslu	St Helen's	Woodroffe
Hoosac	Markham	Taraniki	Yablonovy
Katmai	Nan Shan	Tian Shan	Zugspitze
Kazbek	Olympic	Tien Shan	
Kunlun	Olympus	Vesuvius	**10 letters:**
Lhotse	Palomar	Victoria	Altazimuth
Makalu	Perdido	Wrangell	Arakan Yoma
Mourne	Pilatus		Armageddon
Olives	Rainier	**9 letters:**	Black Hills
Ortles	Rhodope	Aconcagua	Cantabrian
Pamirs	San Juan	Allegheny	Carpathian
Pelion	Scafell	Annapurna	Delectable
Pindus	Selkirk	Apennines	Dhaulagiri
Pisgah	Skiddaw	Ben Lomond	Equatorial
Pocono	Snowdon	Blackburn	Erymanthus
Robson	Sperrin	Blue Ridge	Erzgebirge
Scopus	Stanley	Cairngorm	Great Gable
Sintra	St Elias	Carstensz	Great Smoky
Sorata	Sudeten	Catskills	Harney Peak
Steele	Tibesti	Caucasian	Horselberg
Tasman	Travers	Connemara	Kongur Shan
Taunus	Troglav	Demavrand	Koscuiszko

		13 letters:	**15 letters:**
Laurentian	Gerlachovka	Carrantuohill	New England Range
Masharbrum	Kilimanjaro	Croagh Patrick	Teutoburger Wald
Masherbrum	Kirkpatrick	Flinders Range	
Matterhorn	Kolyma Range	Great Dividing	**16 letters:**
Monte Corno	Nanga Parbat	Grossglockner	Emperor
Montserrat	Picode Anito	Humphrey's Peak	Seamounts
Pentelicus	Salmon River	Kangchenjunga	Macdonnell Ranges
Pentelikon	Scafell Pike	Massif Central	Owen Stanley
Puncak Jaya	Sierra Madre	Mount Klinovec	Range
Puy de Sancy		Petermann Peak	Thabana-Ntlenyana
Qomolangma	**12 letters:**	San Bernardino	
Sagarmatha	Albert Edward	Stanovoi Range	**17 letters:**
St Michael's	Cascade Range	Tibesti Massif	Continental Divide
Tengri Khan	Eastern Ghats		Transylvanian Alps
Teton Range	Godwin Austen	**14 letters:**	
Vorarlberg	Gran Paradiso	Admiralty Range	**18 letters:**
Washington	Ingleborough	Bohemian Forest	Great Dividing
Waziristan	Kanchenjunga	Carnarvon Range	Range
Wellington	Monte Perdido	Finsteraarhorn	
Wetterhorn	Ruahine Range	Hamersley Range	**19 letters:**
	Sierra Morena	Kaikoura Ranges	Macgillicuddy's
11 letters:	Sierra Nevada	Kommunizma Peak	Reeks
Adirondacks	Slieve Donard	Liverpool Range	
Alaska Range	Southern Alps	Musgrove Ranges	**20 letters:**
Anti-Lebanon	Tararua Range	Queen Maud Range	Salmon River
Appalachian	Victoria Peak	Ruwenzori Range	Mountains
Bartle Frere	Vindhya Range	Sangre de Cristo	
Bimberi Peak	Vinson Massif	Stirling Ranges	
Brooks Range	Wasatch Range	Thadentsonyane	
Drakensberg	Western Ghats	Wind River Range	
Fairweather			

Mountain-building Orogenesis

Mountaineer(ing) Aaron, Abseil, Alpinist, Arnaut, Climber, Hunt, Sherpa, Smythe, Upleader

Mountebank Antic(ke), Baladin(e), Charlatan, Jongleur, Quack, Saltimbanco

Mourn(er), Mournful, Mourning Adonia, Black, Dirge, Dole, Elegiac, Grieve, Grone, Half-mast, Hatchment, Jamie Duff, Keen, Lament, Mute, Niobe, Omer, Ovel, Plangent, Saulie, Shibah, Shivah, Shloshim, Sorrow, Tangi, Threnetic, Threnodial, Weeds, Weep, Willow

Mouse(like), Mousy Black eye, Church, Deer, Dun(nart), Fat, Field, Flitter, Harvest, Honey, House, Icon, Jumping, Kangaroo, Marsupial, Meadow, Muridae, Murine, Optical, Pocket, Pouched, Rodent, Shiner, Shrew, Vermin, Waltzer, White-footed

Mousetrap Samson's post

Mousse Styling

Moustache(d) Algernon, Boxcar, Burnside, Charley, Charlie, Chevron, Excrement, Fu Manchu, Handlebar, Hindenburg, Horseshoe, Kaiser, Mistletoe, Pencil, Pyramid, Regent, Roman T, Ronnie, Soupstrainer, Toothbrush, Walrus, Waxed, Wings, Zapata

Mouth(piece) Aboral, Bazoo, Bocca, Brag, Buccal, Cakehole, Chapper, Check, Crater, Debouchure, Delta, Embouchure, Estuary, Fauces, Fipple, Gab, Gam,

Geggie, Gills, Gob, Gum, Hard, Kisser, Labret, Laughing gear, Lawyer, Lip, Manubrium, Maw, Neb, Orifex, Orifice, Os, Oscule, Ostium, Outfall, Outlet, Port, Potato trap, Rattle-trap, Speaker, Spokesman, Spout, Stoma, Swazzle, Swozzle, Teat, Trap, Trench, Uvula

Mouthful Bite, Gob, Gobbet, Morceau, Morsel, Sip, Sup, Taste

Mouthless Astomatous

Mouth-organ Harmonica, Harp, Palp, Sang

Move(d), Mover, Movable, Moving Act, Actuate, Affect, Andante, Astir, Budge, Carry, Catapult, Chattel, Claw off, Coast, Counter-measure, Coup, Decant, Démarche, Displace, Disturb, Ease, Eddy, Edge, Evoke, Extrapose, False, Flit, Flounce, Fluctuate, Forge, Fork, Frogmarch, Gambit, Gee, Go, Gravitate, Haulier, Hustle, Inch, Inspire, Instigate, Jee, Jink, Kedge, Kinetic, Knight's progress, Link, Mill, Mobile, Mosey, Motivate, Nip, Opening, Overcome, Pan, People, Poignant, Prime, Proceed, Progress, Prompt, Propel, Quicken, Qui(t)ch, Rearrange, Redeploy, Relocate, Remuage, Retrocede, Roll, Rollaway, Rouse, Roust, Sashay, Scoot, Scramble, Scroll, Scuttle, Sealed, Sell, Shift, Shog, Shoo, Shunt, Sidle, Skelp, Slide, Soulful, Spank, Steal, Steer, Step, Stir, Styre, Surf, Sway, Swish, Tack, Tactic, Taxi, Transfer, Translate, Translocate, Transplant, Transport, Travel, Troll, Trundle, Turn, Unstep, Up, Upsticks, Vacillate, Vagile, Veronica, Vire, Volt(e), Waft, Wag, Wapper, Whirry, Whish, Whisk, Whiz, Wuther, Yank, Zoom, Zwischenzug

Movement(s) Action, Advection, Aerotaxis, Akathisia, Al Fatah, Allegro, Allemande, Almain, Andantino, Antic, Antistrophe, Arts and crafts, Azapo, Badinerie, Bandwagon, Brownian, Cadence, Capoeira, Cell, Charismatic, Chartism, Chemonasty, Constructivism, Course, Crusade, Dadaism, Diaspora, Diastole, Ecumenical, Enlightenment, Eoka, Eurhythmics, Expressionism, Faction, Feint, Fianchetto, Fris(ka), Gait, Gallicanism, Geneva, Gesture, Groundswell, Hip-hop, Honde, Imagism, Indraught, Inkatha, Intermezzo, Jhala, Jor, Kata, Keplarian, Kinesis, Kin(a)esthetic, Kinetic, Larghetto, Largo, Lassu, Ligne, Logistics, Manoeuvre, Motion, Mudra, Nastic, Naturalism, Naziism, New Urbanism, New Wave, Nihilism, Official, Operation, Orchesis, Oxford, Pantalon, Parallax, Pase, Passade, Pedesis, Photokinesis, Photonasty, Piaffer, Pincer, Plastique, Play, Populist, Poule, Poulette, Procession, Progress, Provisional, Punk, Puseyism, Reformation, Regression, REM, Renaissance, Resistance, Revivalism, Ribbonism, Risorgimento, Romantic, Rondo, Saccade, Scherzo, Seiche, Sinn Fein, Solifluction, Solifluxion, Spuddle, Stir(e), Sturm und Drang, Swadeshi, Swing, Symbolist, Tachism, Tamil Tigers, Tantrism, Taxis, Tectonic, Telekinesis, Thigmotaxis, Tic, Tide, Tractarianism, Transhumance, Trend, Trenise, Ultramontanism, UNITA, Verismo, Veronica, Wave, Wheel, Women's, Zionism

Movie Bioscope, Buddy, Cine(ma), Disaster, Film, Flick, Nudie, Popcorn, Road, Slasher, Snuff, Splatter, Talkie

Mow(er), Mowing Aftermath, Cut, Grimace, Lattermath, Lawn, Math, Rawing, Rawn, Rowan, Rowen, Rowing, Scytheman, Shear, Sickle, Strimmer®, Tass, Trim

MP Backbencher, Commoner, Gendarme, Knight of the Shire, Member, Politico, Provost, Redcap, Retread, Snowdrop, Stannator, Statist, TD

▶ **Mr** *see* **MISTER**

▶ **Mrs** *see* **MISSIS**

Mrs Copperfield Agnes, Dora

Mrs Siddons Tragic muse

Much Abundant, Far, Glut, Great, Lots, Mickle, Scad, Sore, Viel

Mucilage Gum, → **MUCUS**, Putty, Resin

Muck (up), Mucky Bungle, Dirt, Dung, Island, Leep, Manure, Midden, Mire, Rot,

Sludge, Soil, Sordid, Spoil, Stercoral

Mucker Fall, Pal, Purler

Mucus Blennorrhoea, Catarrh, Phlegm, Pituita, Pituite, Snivel, Snot, Snotter, Sputum

Mud(dy) Adobe, Clabber, Clart, Clay, Cutcha, Dirt, Drilling, Dubs, Fango, Glaur, Glob, Gutter, Kacha, Lahar, Lairy, Limous, → MIRE, Moya, Ooze, Peloid, Pise, Red, Riley, Roily, Salse, Slab, Slake, Sleech, Slime, Slob, Slough, Sludge, Slur(ry), Slush, Slutch, Tocky, Trouble, Turbid, Volcanic

Muddle(d) Befog, Bemuse, Botch, Cock up, Confuse, Disorder, Embrangle, Fluster, Gump, Higgledy-piggledy, Mash, Mêlée, Mess, Mix, Mull, Pickle, Puddle, Shemozzle, Snarl-up, Stupefy, Ta(i)vert, Tangle

▷ **Muddled** *may indicate* an anagram

Mudfish Lepidosiren

Mudguard Splashboard, Wing

Mudlark Ragamuffin, Urchin

Muesli Granola

Muff Boob, Botch, Bungle, Drop, Snoskyn

Muffin Bun, Mule, Popover

Muffle(d), Muffler Baffle, Damp, Envelop, Hollow, Mob(b)le, Mute, Scarf, Silencer, Sourdine, Stifle

Mug(ger), Muggy Assault, Attack, Bash, Beaker, Bock, Can, Club, Con, Croc(odile), Cup, Dial, Dupe, Enghalskrug, Face, Fool, Footpad, Gob, Humid, Idiot, Latron, Learn, Mou, Noggin, Pan, Pot, Puss, Rob, Roll, Sandbag, Sap, Sconce, Simpleton, Steamer, Stein, Sucker, Swot, Tankard, Tax, Thief, Thug(gee), Tinnie, Tinny, Toby, Trap, Ugly, Visage, Yap

Mulatto Griff(e)

Mulberry Artocarpus, Breadfruit, Cecropia, Contrayerva, Cow-tree, Indian, Jack, Morat, Morus, Murrey, Overlord, Sycamine

Mulch Compost

Mulct Fine

Mule Ass, Bab(o)uche, Barren, Donkey, Funnel, Hemionus, Hybrid, Mocassin, Moccasin, Moyl(e), Muffin, Muil, Pack, Rake, Shoe, Slipper, Spinning, Sumpter

Muleteer Arriero

Mull Brood, Chew, Kintyre, Ponder, Promontory, Study

Mullein Aaron's rod

Mullet Goatfish

Mullion Monial

Multi-coloured Scroddled

Multiform Allotropic, Diverse, Manifold

Multiple, Multiplication, Multiplied, Multiplier, Multiply Augment, Breed, Common, Double, → INCREASE, Manifold, Modulus, Populate, Product, Proliferate, Propagate, Scalar, Severalfold

Multi-purpose Polychrest

Multitude Army, Crowd, Hirsel, Horde, Host, Legion, Populace, Shoal, Sight, Throng, Zillion

Mum(my) Boutonné, Carton(n)age, Corpse, Egyptian, Embalm, Mamma, Mine, Mute, Quiet, Sh, Silent, Tacit, Whisht, Wordless

Mumble Grumble, Moop, Moup, Mouth, Mump, Mushmouth, Mutter, Royne, Slur

Mumbo jumbo Hocus pocus, Mammet, Maumet, Mawmet, Mommet

Mummer Actor, Mime, Scuddaler, Scudler, Skudler

Mumps Parotitis

Munch Champ, Chew, Chomp, Expressionist, Moop, Moup, Scranch
Mundane Banal, Common, Earthly, Nondescript, Ordinary, Prosaic, Quotidian, Secular, Subcelestial, Trite, Workaday, Worldly
Municipal Civic
Munificent Bounteous, Generous, Liberal, Profuse
Munition(s) Arms, Artillery, Matériel, Ordnance
Munro Saki
Mural(s) Fresco, Graffiti
Murder(er), Murderess, Murderous Aram, Assassin, Blue, Bluebeard, Bravo, Burke, Butcher, Butler, Cain, Cathedral, Crackhalter, Crippen, Crows, Cutthroat, Do in, Eliminate, Filicide, First degree, Fratricide, Genocide, Hare, Hatchet man, Hit, Hitman, Homicide, Internecine, Judicial, → KILL, Liquidate, Locusta, Made man, Massacre, Matricide, Modo, Parricide, Patricide, Petty treason, Poison, Red, Regicide, Ripper, Ritual, Ritz, Rub out, Second degree, Sikes, Slaughter, Slay, Strangle(r), Take out, Thagi, Throttle, Thug(gee), Ugly man, Vaticide, Whodun(n)it
Murk(y) Black, Dirk(e), Gloom, Obscure, Rookish, Stygian
Murmur(ing) Brool, Bruit, Bur(r), Burble, Coo, Croodle, Croon, Grudge, Heart, Hum, → MUTTER, Purr, Repine, Rhubarb, Rumble, Rumour, Souffle, Sowf(f), Sowth, Sturnoid, Undertone, Whisper
Murphy Chat, Potato, Pratie, Spud, Tater
Muscle, Muscular Abductor, Abs, Accelerator, Accessorius, Adductor, Agonist, Anconeus, Aristotle's lantern, Aryepiglottic, Arytaenoid, Athletic, Attollens, Beef(y), Beefcake, Biceps, Bowr, Brachialus, Brawn, Buccinator, Cardiac, Ciliary, Clout, Complexus, Corrugator, Creature, Cremaster, Delt(oid), Depressor, Diaphragm, Digastric, Dilat(at)or, Duvaricator, Écorché, Effector, Elevator, Erecter, Erector, Evertor, Extensor, Eye-string, Flexor, Force, Gastrocnemius, Gemellus, Glut(a)eus, Gluteus maximus, Gracilis, Hamstring, Hiacus, Iliacus, Intrinsic, Involuntary, Kreatine, Lat, Latissimus dorsi, Laxator, Levator, Lumbricalis, Masseter, Mesomorph, Might, Motor, Mouse, Myalgia, Mylohyoid, Myology, Myotome, Nasalis, Oblique, Occlusor, Omohyoid, Orbicularis, Pathos, Pec(s), Pectoral, Perforans, Perforatus, Peroneus, Plantaris, Platysma, Popliteus, → POWER, Pronator, Protractor, Psoas, Pylorus, Quad(riceps), Quadratus, Rambo, Rectus, Retractor, Rhomboid, Rhomboideus, Ripped, Risorius, Rotator, Sarcolemma, Sarcous, Sartorius, Scalene, Scalenus, Serratus, Sinew, Six-pack, Smooth, Soleus, Sphincter, Spinalis, Splenial, Sthenic, Striated, Striped, Supinator, Suspensory, Temporal, Tenaculum, Tendon, Tensor, Teres, Thenar, Thew, Tibialis, Tonus, Trapezius, Triceps, Vastus, Voluntary, Zygomatic
Muscovite Mica, Talc
Muse(s), Muse's home, Musing Aglaia, Aonia(n), Attic, Calliope, Clio, Cogitate, Consider, Erato, Euphrosyne, Euterpe, Goddess, Helicon, Inspiration, IX, Melpomene, Mull, Nine, Nonet, Pensée, Pierides, Poly(hy)mnia, Ponder, → REFLECT, Ruminate, Study, Teian, Terpsichore, Thalia, Tragic, Urania, Wonder
Museum Alte-Pinakothek, Ashmolean, BM, British, Fitzwilliam, Gallery, Getty, Guggenheim, Heritage centre, Hermitage, Hunterian, Louvre, Metropolitan, Parnassus, Prado, Repository, Rijksmuseum, Science, Smithsonian, Tate, Uffizi, VA, V and A, Waxworks
Mush Cree, Glop, Goo, Mess, Porridge, Puree, Schmaltz, Slop
Mushroom Agaric, Blewits, Boletus, Burgeon, Button, Cep, Champignon, Chanterelle, Darning, Enoki, Escalate, Expand, Fly agaric, → FUNGUS, Girolle, Grisette, Gyromitra, Honey fungus, Horse, Hypha(l), Ink-cap, Liberty cap, Magic, Matsutake, Meadow, Morel, Oyster, Parasol, Penny-bun, Pixy-stool, Porcino,

Russula, Sacred, St George's, Scotch bonnet, Shaggymane, Shiitake, Sickener,
Spread, Start-up, Straw, Truffle, Upstart, Velvet shank, Waxcap
Music Absolute, Light, Lounge, Medieval, Minstrelsy, Mood, → MUSICAL
INSTRUMENTS, Passage work, Phrase, Piece, Pop(ular), Programme, Score,
Sound, Table

MUSIC

2 letters:	Trio	Thema	Rootsy
Oi	Tune	Tonal	Sextet
	Zouk	Trash	Sonata
3 letters:		Truth	Strain
Air	5 letters:	Vocal	Techno
AOR	Alaap	World	Tenuto
Art	Alapa		Thrash
Dub	Bebop	6 letters:	Trance
Emo	Benga	Arioso	Verset
Gat	Canon	Aubade	Zydeco
Jor	Chant	Bebung	
Mas	Cliff	Bouree	7 letters:
Pop	Cu-bop	Decani	Allegro
Rag	Disco	Doo-wop	Andante
Rai	Dream	Enigma	Ars nova
Rap	Early	Equali	Ballade
Rug	Fugue	Façade	Baroque
Ska	Funky	Fugato	Bhangra
Son	Gabba	Fusion	Bluette
	House	Gagaku	Bourree
4 letters:	Indie	Galant	Britpop
Alap	Jhala	Garage	Cadenza
Chin	Kwela	Gospel	Calypso
Duet	Largo	Gothic	Cantata
Folk	March	Grunge	Ceilidh
Funk	Motet	Hip-hop	Chamber
Go-go	Muzak®	Jungle	Chorale
Jazz	Neume	Khayal	Country
Loco	Nonet	Kirtan	Dad rock
Meno	Outro	Kwaito	Euterpe
Note	Piped	Lydian	Fanfare
Opus	Ragga	Mantra	Gangsta
Prom	Rondo	Marabi	Hardbag
Raga	Roots	Mashup	Introit
Rave	Rough	Melody	Klezmer
Riff	Salon	Motown®	Landler
Rock	Salsa	New Age	Marcato
Romo	Salve	Popera	Melisma
Soca	Sheet	Pycnon	Messiah
Soul	Sokah	Ragini	Morceau
Surf	Staff	Redowa	New Wave
Tala	Suite	Reggae	Numbers
Trad	Swing	Rhythm	Nu-metal

Organum
Orphean
Partita
Passion
Pecking
Pibroch
Prelude
Qawwali
Quartet
Quintet
Ragtime
Rastrum
Requiem
Reverse
Romanza
Rondeau
Rondino
Rosalia
Roulade
Sanctus
Scherzo
Secondo
Setting
Skiffle
Soukous
Toccata
Trip hop
Ziganka

8 letters:
Acid rock
Aleatory
Berceuse
Blue beat
Chaconne
Cock rock
Concerto
Concrete
Continuo
Coranach
Coronach
Entracte
Fantasia
Flamenco
Folk rock

Glam rock
Hard core
Hard rock
High life
In nomine
Janizary
Karnatak
Lollipop
Madrigal
Maggiore
Mariachi
Mbaqanga
Modality
Nocturne
Notation
Old-skool
Oratorio
Parlando
Partitur
Pastiche
Postlude
Post-rock
Preludio
Psalmody
Punk rock
Rhapsody
Ricercar
Saraband
Serenade
Serenata
Symphony
Synth-pop
Waltzian

9 letters:
Acid-house
Allemande
Antiphony
Arabesque
Bagatelle
Bluegrass
Breakbeat
Cantilena
Capriccio
Dixieland

Drum'n'bass
Fioritura
Grandioso
Hillbilly
Honky-tonk
Interlude
Klezmorim
Obbligato
Partitura
Pastorale
Plainsong
Polyphony
Prick-song
Quodlibet
Reggaeton
Ricercare
Rock'n'roll
Septimole
Spiritual
Swingbeat
Tambourin
Technopop
Toccatina
Voluntary
Warehouse

10 letters:
Albumblatt
Anacrustic
Chopsticks
Coloratura
Death metal
Desert rock
Electronic
Gangsta rap
Gothic rock
Heavy metal
Hindustani
Humoresque
Incidental
Intermezzo
Jam session
Martellato
Mersey beat
New Country

Percussion
Polyhymnia
Ragamuffin
Rare groove
Ritornello
Rockabilly
Rocksteady
Seguidilla
Toccatella
Twelve-tone
Urban blues

11 letters:
Motor rhythm
Passacaglia
Psychobilly
Raggamuffin
Renaissance
Sinfonietta
Solmisation
Stadium rock
Third stream
Thrash metal

12 letters:
Blue-eyed soul
Boogie-woogie
Concertstück
Contrapuntal
Divertimento
Electroclash
Nunc Dimittis
Pralltriller

13 letters:
Detroit techno
Progressional

14 letters:
Rhythm and blues

15 letters:
Musique concrete
Progressive rock

Musical Arcadian, Azione, Brigadoon, Cats, Chess, Euphonic, Evergreen, Evita, Gigi, Grease, Hair, Harmonious, Kabuki, Kismet, Lyric, Mame, Melodic, Oliver, Opera, Operetta, Orphean, Revue, Showboat
Musical box Juke-box, Polyphon(e)
Musical chairs Level-coil

MUSICAL INSTRUMENTS

2 letters:
Ax
Gu

3 letters:
Axe
Gue
Kit
Oud
Saz
Uke
Zel

4 letters:
Buva
Chyn
Crwd
Drum
Erhu
Fife
Gong
Harp
Horn
Kora
Koto
Lure
Lute
Lyre
Moog®
Oboe
Pipa
Rate
Reed
Rote
Sang
Tuba
Vina
Viol
Zeze

5 letters:
Aulos
Banjo
Bugle
Cello
Clave
Cobza
Corno
Crowd

Crwth
Esraj
Flute
Gazog
Guiro
Gusla
Gusle
Gusli
Kazoo
Mbira
Naker
Nebel
Organ
Piano
Quena
Rebec
Regal
Sanko
Sansa
Sarod
Shalm
Shawm
Sitar
Stick
Tabla
Tabor
Tenor
Tibia
Veena
Viola
Zanze
Zinke

6 letters:
Antara
Biniou
Bisser
Bongos
Citole
Cornet
Cymbal
Euphon
Flugel
Guitar
Kanoon
Maraca
Poogye
Racket
Rebeck

Ribibe
Sancho
Santir
Santur
Shalme
Shofar
Sittar
Spinet
Syrinx
Tom-tom
Trigon
Vielle
Violin
Yidaki
Zither
Zufolo

7 letters:
Alphorn
Anklong
Bagpipe
Bandore
Bandura
Baryton
Bassoon
Bazooka
Celesta
Celeste
Cembalo
Chikara
Cithara
Cittern
Clarino
Clarion
Clavier
Clogbox
Console
Cornett
Dichord
Dulcian
Fagotto
Flutina
Gamelan
Gazogka
Gittern
Hautboy
Helicon
High-hat
Kalimba

Kantela
Kantele
Kithara
Klavier
Lyricon
Mandola
Marimba
Musette
Ocarina
Pandora
Pandore
Pandura
Pianola®
Piccolo
Poogyee
Posaune
Rackett
Ribible
Sackbut
Sambuca
Samisen
Santour
Sarangi
Saxhorn
Saxtuba
Serpent
Tambour
Tambura
Theorbo
Timbrel
Timpano
Trumpet
Tympany
Ukelele
Ukulele
Vihuela
Violone
Whistle
Zuffolo

8 letters:
Angklung
Archlute
Autoharp®
Barytone
Berimbau
Bombarde
Bouzouki
Calliope

Canorous	Tenoroon	Saxophone	Contrabasso
Carillon	Theremin	Seraphine	Harmoniphon
Charango	Triangle	Slughorne	Harpsichord
Cimbalom	Trichord	Snare-drum	Heckelphone
Clarinet	Trombone	Sonometer	Nickelodeon
Clarsach	Virginal	Sopranino	Octave flute
Clavecin	Vocalion	Stockhorn	Orchestrina
Cornetto	Zambomba	Trompette	Orchestrion
Cornpipe	Zampogna	Vibraharp	Phonofiddle
Cromorna		Washboard	Straduarius
Cromorne	**9 letters:**	Xylophone	Synthesizer
Crumhorn	Accordion	Xylorimba	Trump-marine
Dulcimer	Aerophone		Violoncello
Gemshorn	Alpenhorn	**10 letters:**	Wobble-board
Guarneri	Balalaika	Bullroarer	
Guimbard	Bandoneon	Chitarrone	**12 letters:**
Handbell	Bandurria	Clavichord	Chapman stick®
Hautbois	Banjulele	Colascione	Chinese block
Humstrum	Bombardon	Concertina	Clavicembalo
Jew's harp	Chalumeau	Cor anglais	Glockenspiel
Key-bugle	Clarionet	Didgeridoo	Harmoniphone
Langspel	Cornemuse	Flugelhorn	Metallophone
Lyra-viol	Decachord	French horn	Penny-whistle
Mandolin	Dulcitone®	Gramophone	Sarrusophone
Manzello	Euphonium	Hurdy-gurdy	Stock and horn
Martenot	Flageolet	Kettledrum	Stradivarius
Melodeon	Flexatone	Lagerphone	Tromba-marina
Melodica	Flute-à-bec	Light organ	Tubular bells
Melodion	Gittarone	Mellophone	
Mirliton	Gutbucket	Nun's fiddle	**13 letters:**
Oliphant	Harmonica	Ophicleide	Contrabassoon
Ottavino	Harmonium	Orpheoreon	Ondes Martenot
Pan pipes	Idiophone	Pentachord	Panharmonicon
Phorminx	Kent-bugle	Shakuhachi	Physharmonica
Polyphon	Krummhorn	Squeeze-box	
Psaltery	Langspiel	Stylophone®	**14 letters:**
Recorder	Mandoline	Symphonium	Glass harmonica
Reco-reco	Mellotron®	Tambourine	Jingling Johnny
Slughorn	Monochord	Thumb piano	Ondes musicales
Spinette	Mouth-harp	Vibraphone	Piano accordion
Sticcado	Nose flute	Wokka board	
Sticcato	Orpharion		**18 letters:**
Surbahar	Pantaleon	**11 letters:**	Chinese temple
Tamboura	Pastorale	Chordophone	block
Tamburin	Polyphone	Clairschach	

Music-hall Alhambra, Disco, Empire, Odeon
Musician(s), Musicologist Accompanist, Arion, Arist, Beiderbecke, Brain, Buononcini, Casals, Chanter, Clapton, Combo, → **COMPOSER**, Conductor, Crowder, Duet, Ensemble, Executant, Flautist, Gate, Grove, Guido d'Arezzo, Guslar, Handel, Jazzer, Jazzman, Joplin, Mahler, Mariachi, Menuhin, Minstrel, Muso, Noisenik,

Nonet, Octet, Orphean, Pianist, Quartet, Quintet, Rapper, Reed(s)man, Répétiteur, Rubinstein, Septet, Session, Sextet, Sideman, Spohr, String, Techno, Tortelier, Troubador, Trouvère, Violinist, Waits

Musk Civet, Mimulus, Must

Musket Brown Bess, Caliver, Carabine, Eyas, Flintlock, Fusil, Hawk, Jezail, Nyas, Queen's-arm, Weapon

Musketeer Aramis, Athos, D'Artagnan, Fusilier, Ja(e)ger, Porthos, Rifleman, Sam

Muslim (ritual), Moslem Alaouite, Alawite, Ali, Almohad(e), Balochi, Baluchi, Berber, Black, Caliph, Dato, Dervish, Druse, Fatimid, Ghazi, Hadji, Hafiz, Hajji, He'zbolah, Iranian, Islamic, Ismaili, Karmathian, Khotbah, Khotbeh, Khutbah, Mahometan, Mawlawi, Meivievi, Mogul, Mohammedan, Moor, Morisco, Moro, Mufti, Mus(s)ulman, Mutazilite, Nawab, Panislam, Paynim, Pomak, Said, Saracen, Say(y)id, Senus(s)i, Shafiite, Shia(h), Shiite, Sofi, Sonnite, Sufi, Sulu, Sunna, Sunni(te), Tajik, Turk, Ummah, Wahabee, Wahabi(te), Wahhabi

Muslin Butter, Cloth, Coteline, Gurrah, Jamdani, Leno, Mousseline, Mull, Nainsook, Organdie, Tarlatan, Tiffany

Musquash Ondatra

Mussel(s) Bearded, Bivalve, Clabby-doo, Clam, Clappy-doo, Deerhorn, Edible, Horse, Moules marinières, Mytilus, Naiad, Niggerhead, Pearl, Swan, Unio, Zebra

Mussorgsky Modest

Must(y) Amok, Essential, Foughty, Froughy, Frowsty, Frowy, Funky, Fust, Gotta, Man, Maun(na), Mote, Mould, Mucid, Mun, Need(s)-be, Shall, Should, Stum, Wine

▷ **Must** *may indicate* an anagram

Mustard Black, Brown, Charlock, Cress, English, Erysimum, French, Garlic, Gas, Nitrogen, Praiseach, Quinacrine, Runch, Sarepta, Sauce-alone, Senvy, Treacle, Wall, White, Wild, Wintercress

Mustard plaster Sinapism

Musteline Skunk

Muster Array, Assemble, Bangtail, Call up, Mass, Raise, Rally, Really, Recruit, Round-up, Wappenshaw

Mutability Wheel

Mutate, Mutant, Mutation Auxotroph(ic), Change, Saltation, Somatic, Sport, Suppressor, Terata, Transform, Vowel

▷ **Mutation** *may indicate* an anagram

Mute(d) Deaden, Dumb, Harpo, Noiseless, Silent, Sordino, Sordo, Sourdine, Stifle

Mutilate(d), Mutilation Castrate, Concise, Deface, Dismember, Distort, Garble, Hamble, Injure, Maim, Mangle, Mayhem, Obtruncate, Riglin, Tear

▷ **Mutilate(d)** *may indicate* an anagram

Mutineer, Mutiny Bounty, Caine, Christian, Curragh, Indian, Insurrection, Jhansi, Meerut, Nore, Pandy, → **REVOLT**, Rising, Sepoy

Mutter(ing) Chunter, Fremescent, Grumble, Maunder, Mumble, Mump, Murmur, Mussitate, Rhubarb, Roin, Royne, Rumble, Whittie-whattie, Witter

Mutton Braxy, Colonial goose, Em, Ewes, Fanny Adams, Gigot, Macon, Rack, Saddle, Sheep, Theave, Traik

Mutual (aid) Common, Log-roll, Reciprocal, Symbiosis

Muzzle Decorticate, Gag, Jaw, Mouth, Restrain, Snout

My Christ, Coo, Gemini, Golly, Gosh, Ha, Lor, Lumme, M, Musha, Odso, Oh, Our, Tush

Mynah Stare, Starling

Mynheer Stadholder

Myopia, Myopic Hidebound, Mouse-sight, Narrow, Short-sighted, Thick-eyed

Myriad Host, Zillion
Myristic Nutmeg
Myrrh Stacte
Myrtle Bog, Callistemon, Crape, Creeping, Crepe, Eucalyptus, Gale, Jambolana, Tasmanian, Tooart, Trailing, Tuart
Mysterious, Mystery Abdabs, Abdals, Acroamatic, Arcane, Arcanum, Cabbala, Closed book, Craft, Creepy, Cryptic, Dark, Deep, Delphic, Eleusinian, Enigma, Esoteric, Grocer, G(u)ild, Incarnation, Inscrutable, Miracle, Mystagogue, Numinous, Occult, Original sin, Orphic, Penetralia, Riddle, → SECRET, Telestic, Trinity, UFO, Uncanny, Whodunit
▷ **Mysterious(ly)** *may indicate* an anagram
Mystic (word), Mystical Abraxas, Agnostic, Cab(e)iri, Eckhart, Epopt, Fakir, Familist, Gnostic, Hesychast, Mahatma, Occultist, Quietism, Rasputin, Secret, Seer, Sofi, Sufi, Swami, Tantrist, Theosophy, Transcendental, Zohar
Mystify Baffle, Bamboozle, Bewilder, Metagrabolise, Metagrobolise, Perplex, Puzzle
Myth(ology), Mythical (beast) Allegory, Behemoth, Bunyip, Centaur, Cockatrice, Dragon, Euhemerism, Fable, Fantasy, Fictitious, Folklore, Garuda, Geryon, Griffin, Hippocampus, Impundulu, Kelpie, Kylin, Legend, Leviathan, Lore, Lyonnesse, Otnit, Pantheon, Pegasus, Phoenix, Sea horse, Selkie, Solar, Speewah, Sphinx, Sun, Thunderbird, Tokoloshe, Tragelaph, Unicorn, Urban, Wivern, Wyvern, Yale, Yeti

Nn

N Name, Nitrogen, Noon, North, November
Nab Arrest, Capture, Collar, Confiscate, Grab, Seize
Nabob Deputy, Nawab, Wealthy
Nadir Bottom, Depths, Dregs, Minimum
Nag(ging) Badger, Bidet, Brimstone, Callet, Cap, Captious, Complain, Fret,
    Fuss, Harangue, Harp, Henpeck, Horse, Jade, Jaw, Keffel, Peck, Pester, Plague,
    Rosinante, Rouncy, → **SCOLD**, Tit, Xant(h)ippe, Yaff
Nail(ed) Brad, Brod, Catch, Clinker, Clout, Coffin, Fasten, Hob, Keratin, Onyx, Pin,
    Rivet, Screw, Secure, Shoe, Sisera, Sixpenny, Sparable, Sparrow-bill, Spick, Spike,
    Sprig, Staple, Stub, Stud, Tack(et), Talon, Tenpenny, Tenterhook, Thumb, Tingle,
    Toe, Unguis, Wire
Naive(té) Artless, Green, Guileless, Gullible, Ingenuous, Innocence, Open,
    Pollyanna, Simpliste, Simplistic, Unsophisticated, Wide-eyed
Naked Adamical, Artless, Bare, Blunt, Buff, Clear, Cuerpo, Defenceless, Encuerpo,
    Exposed, Gymno-, Kaal gat, Nuddy, Nude, Querpo, Raw, Scud, Simple, Skyclad,
    Stark(ers), Uncovered
Namby-pamby Milksop, Nance, Sissy, Weak, Weakling, White-shoe
Name(d), Names Agnomen, Alias, Allonym, Anonym, Appellation, Appoint,
    Attribute, Baptise, Behight, Byline, Call, Celeb(rity), Christen, Cite, Cleep, Clepe,
    Cognomen, Day, Designate, Dinges, Dingus, Dit, Domain, Dub, Entitle, Epithet,
    Eponym, Exonym, Family, First, Generic, Given, Handle, Hete, Hight, Hypocorism,
    Identify, Identity, Label, Maiden, Marque, Masthead, Mention, Metronymic,
    Middle, Moni(c)ker, Mud, N, Nap, Nemn, Nempt, Nom, Nomen(clature), Noun,
    Onomastics, Onymous, Patronymic, Pennant, Personage, Pet, Place, Praenomen,
    Proper, Proprietary, Pseudonym, Quote, Red(d), Repute, Scilicet, Sign, Signature,
    Sir, Specify, Stage, Street, Substantive, Tag, Teknonymy, Term, → **TITLE**, Titular,
    Titule, Toponymy, Trade, Trivial
Name-dropper Eponym
Nameless Anon, Unchrisom
Namely Ie, Sc, Scilicet, To-wit, Videlicet, Viz
Namesake Homonym
Name unknown Anon, A N Other, NU
Nancy Coddle, Effeminate, Milksop
Nanny Ayah, Foster, Goat, Nurse
Naos Cell(a)
Nap(py) Ale, Bonaparte, Diaper, Doze, Drowse, Fluff, Frieze(d), Fuzz, Happen,
    Hippin(g), Kip, Moze, Oose, Ooze, Oozy, Power, Put(t), Shag, Siesta, → **SLEEP**,
    Slumber, Snooze, Tease, Teasel, Teaze, Tipsy, Tuft
Nape Niddick, Noddle, Nucha, Scrag, Scruff, Scuff, Scuft
Napier Logarithm
Napkin Cloth, Diaper, Doily, Doyley, Linen, Muckender, Paper, Sanitary,

Serviette, Table
Napless Threadbare
Napoleon Badinguet, Bonaparte, Boustrapa, Cognac, Coin, Consul, Corporal Violet,
Corsican, December, Little Corporal, Nantz, Nap, Pig, Rantipole
▷ **Napoleon** *may indicate* a pig
Napper Bonce, Shearman
Narcissus Echo, Egocentric, Jonquil
Narcotic Ava, Benj, B(h)ang, Charas, Churrus, Coca, Codeine, Datura, Dope,
→ **DRUG**, Heroin, Hop, Kava, Laudanum, Mandrake, Marijuana, Meconium,
Methadone, Morphia, Narceen, Narceine, Opiate, Pituri, Sedative, Tea, Trional
Nark Grass, Inform, Irritate, Nose, Pique, Roil, Squealer, Stag
Narrate, Narration, Narrative, Narrator Allegory, Anecdote, Cantata, Describe,
Diegesis, Fable, History, Oblique, Periplus, Plot, Raconteur, Récit, Recite, Recount,
Saga, Scheherazade, Splatterpunk, Story, Tell, Voice-over
Narrow(ing), Narrow-minded Alf, Bigoted, Borné, Bottleneck, Constringe, Cramp,
Ensiform, Grundy(ism), Hidebound, Illiberal, Insular, Kyle, Limited, Meagre, Nary,
One-idead, Parochial, Phimosis, Pinch, Pinch-point, Provincial, Prudish, Puritan,
Scant, Sectarian, Shrink, Slender, Slit, Specialise, Squeak, Stenosed, Strait, Straiten,
Strait-laced, Strict, Suburban, Verkramp, Wafer-thin, Waist
Narwhal Monodon
Nasal Adenoidal, Sonorant, Twang
Nash Beau
Nashville Bath
Nastiness, Nasty Disagreeable, Drevill, Filth, Fink, Ghastly, Lemon, Lo(a)th,
Malign(ant), Noisome, Noxious, Obscene, Odious, Offensive, Ribby, Scummy, Sif,
Sordid, Vile
Nat(haniel) Hawthorne, Winkle
Natal Inborn, Native, Patrial
Natant Afloat, Swimming
Nation(s), National(ist), Nationalism Anthem, Baathist, Broederbond, Casement,
Chetnik, Country, Cuban, Debt, Eta, Federal, Five, Folk, Grand, Hindutva, Indian,
IRA, Israeli, Jingoist, Kuomintang, Land, Mexican, Oman, Pamyat, Parnell,
Patriot, → **PEOPLE**, Plaid Cymru, Polonia, Race, Rainbow, Risorgimento, Scottish,
Shivsena, Six, SNP, Subject, Swadeshi, United, Verkrampte, Vietminh, Wafd,
Yemini, Young Ireland, Zionist
Native(s) Abo(rigin), Aborigine, African, Amerind, Annamese, Arab, Ascian,
Australian, Autochthon, Aztec, Basuto, Belonging, Bengali, Boy, Bushman,
Cairene, Carib, Carioca, Chaldean, Citizen, Colchester, Conch, Creole, Criollo,
Domestic, Dyak, Edo, Enchorial, Eskimo, Fleming, Fuzzy-wuzzy, Genuine,
Habitual, Home-bred, Inborn, Inca, Indigene, Indigenous, Inhabitant, Intuitive,
John Chinaman, Kaffir, Libyan, Local, Malay, Maori, Mary, Micronesian, Moroccan,
Norwegian, Oyster, Polack, Portuguese, Scythian, Son, Spaniard, Te(i)an, Thai,
Tibetan, Uzbeg, Uzbek, Whitstable, Yugoslav
Nativity Birth, Jataka, Putz
Natron Urao
Natter Chat, Gossip, Jack, Prate
Natty Bumppo, Chic, Dapper, Leatherstocking, Smart, Spruce
Natural(ly), Naturalised, Naturalism Artless, Ass, Denizen, Easy, Genuine,
Homely, Idiot, Illegitimate, Inborn, Inbred, Indigenous, Ingenerate, Inherent,
Innate, Moron, Native, Nidget, Nitwit, Nude, Ordinary, Organic, Prat, Real,
Simpleton, Simpliciter, Sincere, True, Undyed, Untaught, Verism

Naturalist Bates, Buffon, Darwin, Wallace, White
Nature Adam, Akin, Character, Disposition, Esse(nce), Ethos, Haecceity, Human, Hypostasis, Inscape, Manhood, Mould, Quiddity, Quintessence, Second, SN, Temperament
Naught Cypher, Failure, Nil, Nothing, Zero
Naughty Bad, Disobedient, Girly, Improper, Indecorous, Light, Marietta, Nonny, Rascal, Remiss, Spright, Sprite, Wayward
Nausea, Nauseous Disgust, Fulsome, Malaise, Queasy, Sickness, Squeamish, Wamble, Wambly
Nave Aisle, Apse, Centre, Hub, Modiolus, Nef
Navel Belly-button, Jaffa, Naff, Nave, Omphalos, Orange, Tummy button, Umbilicus
Navigate, Navigator Albuquerque, Bougainville, Cabot, Cartier, Columbus, Control, Da Gama, Dias, Direct, Franklin, Frobisher, Gilbert, Hartog, Haul, Henry, Hudson, Keel, Magellan, Navvy, Orienteer, Pilot, Raleigh, Sail, Star-read, → **STEER**, Tasman, Traverse, Vancouver, Vespucci
Navigation (aid, system) Asdic, Cabotage, Celestial, Decca, Dectra, Echosounder, Fido, Gee, Inertial, Inland, Loran, Loxodromics, Navarho, Omnirange, Portolan(o), Portulan, Radar, Satnav, Seamark, Shoran, Tacan, Teleran®, Vor
Navvy Workhorse
Navy, Naval AB, Armada, Blue, Fleet, French, Maritime, Merchant, N, Red, RN, Senior Service, Wavy, Wren
Nawab Huzoor, Nabob, Viceroy
Nazi Brownshirt, Gauleiter, Hess, Hitler, Jackboot, SS, Stormtrooper, Wer(e)wolf
NB Niobium, Nota bene
NCO Bombardier, Corp(oral), Havildar, Noncom, Orderly, Sergeant, SM
Neanderthal Mousterian
Neap Low, Tide
Neapolitan Ice
Near(er), Nearest, Nearby, Nearly, Nearness About, Adjacent, All-but, Almost, Anigh, Approach, Approximate, Beside, By, Close, Cy pres, Degree, Even, Ewest, Feckly, Forby, Gain, Handy, Hither, Imminent, Inby(e), Mean, Miserly, Narre, Neist, Next, Nie, Niggardly, Nigh, Oncoming, Outby, Propinquity, Proximity, Short-range, Stingy, Thereabout(s), To, Upon, Warm, Well-nigh
Neat(ly) Bandbox, Cattle, Clean-cut, Clever, Dainty, Dapper, Deft, Dink(y), Doddy, Donsie, Elegant, Feat(e)ous, Featly, Featuous, Gayal, Genty, Gyal, Intact, Jemmy, Jimpy, Lower, Nett, Ninepence, Orderly, Ox(en), Preppy, Pretty, Rother, Shipshape, Short, Smug, Snod, Spruce, Straight, → **TIDY**, Trig, Trim, Unwatered, Well-groomed
Neb Beak, Bill, Nose, Snout
Nebula, Nebulous Aeriform, Celestial, Cloudy, Dark, Emission, Gum, Hazy, Horsehead, Obscure, Planetary, Reflection, Shadowy, Vague
Necessary, Necessarily Bog, Cash, De rigueur, → **ESSENTIAL**, Estovers, Important, Indispensable, Intrinsic, Money, Needful, Ought, Perforce, Prerequisite, Requisite, Vital, Wherewithal
Necessitate, Necessity Ananke, Compel, Constrain, Cost, Emergency, Entail, Exigent, Fate, Indigence, Logical, Mathematical, Moral, Must, Natural, Need, Need-be, Oblige, Perforce, Require, Requisite
Neck(ed) Bottle, Brass, Canoodle, Cervical, Cervix, Channel, Col, Crag, Craig, Crop, Cuff, Embrace, Ewe, Gall, Gorgerin, Halse, Hawse, Inarm, Inclip, Isthmus, Kiss, Mash, Nape, Pet, Polo, Rack, Rubber, Scoop, Scrag, Scruff, Smooch, Snog, Stiff, Strait, Surgical, Swan, Swire, Theorbo, Torticollis, Trachelate, Vee

▷ **Necking** *may indicate* one word around another

Necklace Afro-chain, Anodyne, Brisingamen, Chain, Choker, Collar, Corals, Lava(l)lière, Lunula, Mangalsutra, Negligee, Pearls, Rope, Sautoir, String, Torc, Torque

Neckline Boat, Collar, Cowl, Crew, Décolletage, Lanyard, Palter, Plunging, Sweetheart, Turtle, Vee

Neckwear Ascot, Barcelona, Boa, Bow, Collar, Cravat, Fur, Rail, Steenkirk, Stock, Tie

Necromancer Goetic, Magician, Ormandine, Osmand, Witch, Wizard

Necrosis Infarct, Sphacelus

Nectar Ambrosia, Amrita, Honey, Mead

Ned(dy) Donkey, Kelly, Ludd

Need(ed), Needy Beggarly, Call, Demand, Desiderata, Egence, Egency, Exigency, Gap, Gerundive, Impecunious, Indigent, → **LACK**, Mister, Pressing, PRN, Require, Strait, Strapped, Want

Needle(s) Acerose, Acicular, Aciform, Between, Bodkin, Cleopatra's, Darning, Dip, Dry-point, Electric, Etching, Goad, Gramophone, Hagedorn, Hype, Hypodermic, Ice, Icicle, Inoculate, Knitting, Leucotome, Magnetic, Miff, Monolith, Neeld, Neele, Netting, Obelisk, Packing, Pine, Pinnacle, Pique, Pointer, Prick, R(h)aphis, Sew, Sharp, Spanish, Spicule, Spike, Spine, Stylus, Tattoo, Tease, Thorn, Wire

Needlewoman Cleopatra, Seamstress

Needlework Baste, Crewel, Drawn(-thread), Embroidery, Fag(g)oting, Fancy work, Gros point, Mola, Patchwork, Petit point, Piqué, Plainwork, Rivière, Sampler, Smocking, Spanish, Tapestry, Tattoo, White-seam, Woolwork, Worsted-work

Ne'er-do-well Badmash, Budmash, Bum, Good-for-nothing, Scullion, Shiftless, Skellum, Wastrel

Negation, Negative Ambrotype, Anion, Apophatic, Cathode, Denial, Double, Enantiosis, False, Ne, No, Non, Nope, Nullify, Pejorative, Photograph, Refusal, Resinous, Unresponsive, Veto, Yin

Neglect(ed), Neglectful, Negligence, Negligent Careless, Casual, Cinderella, Contributory, Cuff, Default, Dereliction, Disregard, Disuse, Failure, Forget, Forlorn, Heedless, Inadvertence, Inattention, Incivism, Laches, Malpractice, Misprision, Omission, Oversight, Pass, Pass-up, Rack and ruin, → **REMISS**, Scamp, Shirk, Slight, Slipshod, Undone, Unilateral, Waif, Wanton

▷ **Neglected** *may indicate* an anagram

Negligee Déshabillé, Manteau, Mob, Nightgown, Peignoir, Robe

Negligible Fig, Minimal

Negotiate, Negotiator Arbitrate, Arrange, Bargain, Clear, Confer, Deal, Diplomat, Haggle, Intercede, Interdeal, Intermediary, Liaise, Manoeuvre, Mediator, Parley, Trade, Transact, Treat(y), Weather

Negro(id) → **AFRICAN**, Baganda, Bambara, Barotse, Bemba, Bergdama, Bini, Black, Blackamoor, Buck, Chewa, Creole, Cuffee, Cuffy, Damara, Dinge, Duala, Dyula, Ebon(y), Edo, Efik, Ethiop, Ewe, Fang, Ga, Ganda, Gullah, Hausa, Hottentot, Hutu, Ibibio, Ibo, Igbo, Igorot, Jim Crow, Kikuyu, Kongo, Luba, Luganda, Malinke, Maninke, Mestee, Moke, Moor, Mossi, Mustee, Ndebele, Nilote, Nupe, Nyanja, Nyoro, Ovambo, Pondo, Quashee, Quashie, Sambo, Snowball, Sotho, Spade, Susu, Temne, Thick-lips, Tiv, Tonga, Tsonga, Tswana, Twi, Uncle Tom, Venda, Watu(t)si, Wolof, Xhosa, Yoruba, Zambo, Zulu

Negus Emperor, Rumfruction, Selassie

Nehru Pandit

Neigh Bray, Hinny, Nicker, Whicker, Whinny

Neighbour(ly), Neighbouring, Neighbours Abut(ter), Adjoin, Alongside,

Amicable, Bor, Border, But, Friendly, Joneses, Nearby, Next-door, Vicinal
Neighbourhood(s) Acorn®, Area, Community, District, Environs, Locality,
Precinct, Vicinage, Vicinity
Neither Nor
Nell(ie), Nelly Bly, Dean, Trent
Nelson Columnist, Eddy, Horatio
Nemesis Alastor, Avenger, Deserts, Downfall, Fate, Retribution, Revenge
Neodymium Nd
Neolithic Avebury, Halafian, Skara Brae, Stonehenge
Neon Ne
Nepalese Gurkha
Neper N
Nephrite Yu
Nepotism Kin, Partisan, Patronage
Neptune God, Planet, Poseidon
Neptunium Np
Nerd Anorak, Otaku
Nereid Cymodoce, Nymph, Panope
Nerve(s), Nervous(ness), Nervure, Nerve centre, Nervy Abdabs, Abducens,
Accessory, Acoustic, Afferent, Aflutter, Afraid, Alveolar, Appestat, Auditory, Axon,
Baroreceptor, Bottle, Bouton, Brass neck, Buccal, Chord, Chutzpah, Collywobbles,
Column, Commissure, Cones, Courage, Cranial, Cyton, Depressor, Edgy,
Effector, Efferent, Electrotonus, Epicritic, Excitor, Facial, Fearful, Gall, Ganglion,
Glossopharyngeal, Grit, Guts, Habdabs, Heart-string, High, Highly-strung,
Hyp, Hypoglossal, Impudence, Jitters, Jittery, Jumpy, Median, Mid-rib, Motor,
Moxie, Myelon, Nappy, Neck, Neurological, Nidus, Oculomotor, Olfactory, On
edge, Optic, Pavid, Perikaryon, Proprioceptor, Rad, Radial, Receptor, Restiform,
Restless, Sacral, Sangfroid, Sauce, Sciatic, Screaming abdabs, Screaming meemies,
Sensory, Shaky, Shpilkes, Solar plexus, Splanchnic, Spunk, Squirrel(l)y, Steel,
Strung-up, Synapse, Tense, Tizzy, Toey, Tongue-tied, Trembler, Tremulous,
Trigeminal, Trochlear, Twitchy, Ulnar, Uptight, Vagus, Vapours, Vestibulocochlear,
Wandering, Willies, Windy, Wired, Yips
Nervous disease, Nervous disorder Chorea, Epilepsy, Neuritis, Tetany
▷ **Nervously** *may indicate* an anagram
Ness Cape, Headland, Ras
Nessus Centaur
Nest Aerie, Aery, Aiery, Ayrie, Bike, Bink, Brood, Byke, Cabinet, Cage, Caliology,
Clutch, Dray, Drey, Eyrie, Eyry, Lodge, Love, Nid, Nide, Nidify, Nidus, Norwegian,
Sett, Termitarium, Turkey, Wurley
Nestle Burrow, Coorie, Cose, Courie, Cuddle, Nuzzle, Snug(gle)
Nestor Counsellor, Kea, King, Parrot, Sage
Net(ting), Nets, Network(ing) Anastomosis, Bamboo, BR, Bunt, Butterfly,
Cast, Casting, Catch, Caul, Clap, Clathrate, Clear, Cobweb, → **COMPUTER
NETWORK**, Crinoline, Criss-cross, Crossover, Drift, Earn, Eel-set, Enmesh,
Equaliser, Fetch, File server, Filet, Final, Fish, Flew, Flue, Fyke, Gill, → **GRID**,
Hammock, Heliscoop, Honeycomb, Insect, Kiddle, Lace, Land, Landing, Lattice,
Leap, Line, Linin, Mains, Malines, Mattress, Maze, → **MESH**, Mist, Mosquito,
Neuropil, Old boys', PCN, Plexus, Portal system, Pound, Pout, Purse-seine,
Quadripole, Reseau, Rete, Retiary, Reticle, Reticulate, Reticulum, Ring, Safety,
Sagene, Scoop, Screen, Sean, Seine, Senior, Set(t), Shark, Snood, Speed, Stake,
Sweep-seine, Symplast, System, Tangle, Tela, Telex, Toil, Torpedo, Trammel,

Trap, Trawl, Trepan, Tulle, Tunnel, Wire

Netball Let

Nether Below, Inferior, Infernal, Lower, Under

Nettle(rash) Anger, Annoy, Day, Dead, Hemp, Hives, Horse, Irritate, Labiate, Nark, Ongaonga, Pellitory, Pique, Ramee, Rami, Ramie, Rhea, Rile, Roman, Ruffle, Sting, Urtica(ceae), Urticaria

Neuralgia, Neuritis Migraine, Sciatica, Tic

Neurosis Combat, Compulsion, Obsessive-compulsive, Shellshock

Neuter Castrate, Gib, Impartial, Neutral, Sexless, Spay

Neutral(ise) Alkalify, Angel gear, Buffer zone, Counteract, Degauss, Grey, Impartial, Inactive, Schwa, Sheva, Shiva, Unbiased

Neutron(s) Delayed, Fast, Nucleon, Prompt, Slow, Thermal, Virgin

Never(more) Nary, Nathemo(re), No more, Nowise, St Tib(b)'s Eve

Never-ending Age-long

Nevertheless Algate, Anyhow, But, Even, However, Quand même, Still, Tout de même, Yet

▷ **New** *may indicate* an anagram

New(s), Newborn, News agency Bulletin, Copy, Coranto, Dope, Euphobia, Evangel, Flash, Forest, Fresh, Fudge, Gen, Green, Griff, Info, Innovation, Intelligence, Itar Tass, Item, Kerygma, Latest, Mint, Modern, N, Novel, Oil(s), Original, PA, Paragraph, Pastures, Pristine, Propaganda, Raw, Recent, Report, Reuter, Scoop, Span, Split, Stranger, Tass, Teletext®, Tidings, Ultramodern, Unco, Usenet, Wire service, Word

New boy Gyte

Newcomer Dog, Freshman, Griffin, Immigrant, Jackaroo, Jackeroo, Jillaroo, Johnny-come-lately, Newbie, Novice, Parvenu, Pilgrim, Settler, Tenderfoot, Upstart

Newfoundland Dog, Nana, Vinland

Newgate Calendar

Newly wed Benedick, Benedict, Bride, Groom, Honeymooner, Neogamist

Newman Cardinal, Noggs

New moon Rosh Chodesh

Newsman, News-reader Announcer, Editor, Journalist, Legman, Press, Reporter, Sub, Sysop

Newsmonger, News-vendor Butcher, Gossip, Quidnunc

Newspaper Blat(t), Broadsheet, Courier, Daily, Express, Fanzine, Feuilleton, Freesheet, Gazette, Guardian, Heavy, Herald, Journal, Jupiter, Le Monde, Mercury, National, Organ, Patent inside, Patent outside, Post, Pravda, Press, Print, Rag, Red-top, Scandal sheet, Sheet, Spoiler, Squeak, Sun, Tabloid, Today

Newsreel Actualities

Newt(s) Ask(er), Eft, Evet, Swift, Triton, Urodela

Newton N

New World USA

New Year Hogmanay, Ne'er-day, Rosh Hashana(h), Tet

New York(er) Big Apple, Gotham, Knickerbocker

New Zealand(er) Aotearoa, Enzed, Jafa, Kiwi, Maori, Mooloo, Moriori, Pakeha, Pig Island, Ronz(er), Shagroon, Zelanian

Next Adjacent, Adjoining, After, Alongside, Beside, Following, Immediate, Later, Nearest, Neist, Proximate, Proximo, Sine, Subsequent, Syne

Nib(s) Cocoa, J, Pen, Point, Tip

Nibble Bite, Brouse, Browse, Byte, Crop, Eat, Gnaw, Knap(ple), Moop, Moup, Munch, Nag, Nepit, Nosh, Peck, Pick, Snack

Nice(ty) Accurate, Amene, Appealing, Cool, Dainty, Fastidious, Fine, Finical, Genteel, Lepid, Mooi, Ninepence, Pat, Pleasant, Precise, Quaint, Rare, Refined, Subtil(e), Subtle, Sweet, T

Niche Alcove, Almehrahb, Almery, Ambry, Apse, Aumbry, Awmrie, Awmry, Columbarium, Cranny, Exedra, Fenestella, Mihrab, Recess, Slot

Nicholas Santa

Nick(ed) Appropriate, Arrest, Bin, Blag, Can, Chip, Cly, Colin, Copshop, Cut, Denay, Dent, Deny, → **DEVIL**, Erose, Groove, Hoosegow, Kitty, Knock, Nab, Nap, Nim, Nock, Notch, Pinch, Pook, Pouk, Prison, Scratch, Sneak, → **STEAL**, Steek, Swan-upping, Swipe, Thieve, Whip, Wirricow, Worricow, Worrycow

Nickel (silver) Coin, Garnierite, Jitney, Millerite, Ni, Packfong, Paktong, Zaratite

Nicker Bonduc, Neigh, Whinny

Nickname Alias, Byname, Byword, Cognomen, So(u)briquet, To-name

Nicotine Tobacco, Weed

Nifty Smart, Stylish

Nigeria(n) Biafran, Cross River, Efik, Hausa, Ibibio, Ibo, Igbo, Nupe, WAN, Yoruba

Niggard(ly) Dry-fist, Illiberal, Mean, Miser, Near-(be)gaun, Nippy, Nirlit, Parsimonious, Pinchcommons, Pinchgut, Pinchpenny, Scrunt, Skinflint, Tightwad

Niggle Carp, Gripe, Nag, Potter, Trifle

Night(s), Nightfall Acronical, Acronychal, Arabian, Burns, Darkling, Darkmans, First, Gaudy, Guest, Guy Fawkes, Hen, Leila, Nacht, Nicka-nan, Nutcrack, Nyx, School, Stag, Twelfth, Twilight, Walpurgis, Watch, White

Night-blindness Day-sight, Nyctalopia

Night-cap Biggin, Cocoa, Kilmarnock cowl, Nip, Pirnie, Sundowner

Nightclub Clip joint, Dive, Honkytonk

Night-dew Serein, Serene

Nightdress Wylie-coat

Nightingale Bulbul, Florence, Jugger, Lind, Philomel, Scutari, Swedish, Watch

Nightjar Chuck-will's-widow, Churn-owl, Evejar, Fern-owl, Goatsucker, Poorwill, Potoo

Night-light Moonbeam

Nightmare, Nightmarish Cacod(a)emon, Ephialtes, Incubus, Kafkaesque, Oneirodynia, Phantasmagoria

Night-rider Revere

Nightshade Atropin(e), Belladonna, Bittersweet, Black, Circaea, Deadly, Dwale, Enchanter's, Henbane, Morel, Solanum, Woody

Nightwatchman Charley, Charlie, Rug-gown

Nightwork Lucubrate

Nihilist Anarchist, Red, Sceptic

Nil Nothing, Nought, Zero

Nile Albert, Blue, Luvironza, Victoria, White

Nimble(ness), Nimbly Active, → **AGILE**, Alert, Deft, Deliver, Fleet, Legerity, Light, Light-footed, Lissom(e), Lithe, Quiver, Sciolto, Springe, Spry, Supple, Swack, Wan(d)le, Wannel, Wight, Ya(u)ld

Nimbus Aura, Aureole, Cloud, Gloriole, Halo

Nimrod Hunter

Nincompoop Ass, Imbecile, Ninny, Stupid

Nine, Ninth Choral, Ennead, Muses, Nonary, Nonet, Novenary, Pins, Sancho, Skittles, Tailors, Worthies

Nine hundred Sampi

Nine of diamonds Curse of Scotland

Nineteen(th) Bar, Decennoval
Ninetieth, Ninety N, Nonagesimal
Ninevite Assyrian
Ninny (hammer) Fool, Goose, Idiot, Stupid, Tony
Ninon Nan
Niobium Nb
Nip(per) Bite, Check, Chela, Chill, Claw, Cutpurse, Dip, Dram, Fang, Gook, Jap, Lad,
   Lop, Nep, Nirl, Peck, Pickpocket, Pincers, Pinch, Pook, Pop, Scotch, Sneap, Susan,
   Tad, Taste, Tot, Tweak, Urchin, Vice, Vise
Nipa At(t)ap, Palm
Nipple Dug, Grease, Jogger's, Mastoid, Pap, Teat
Nis Brownie, Goblin, Kobold, Sprite
Nit Egg, Insect, Louse
Nitre Saltpetre
Nitric, Nitrogen Azote, Azotic, Gas, N, Quinoline
Nitroglycerine Glonoin
Nitwit Ass, Flat, Fool, Simpleton, → STUPID
No Aikona, Denial, Na(e), Nah, Naw, Negative, Nix, Nope, Nyet, O, Refusal
Noah Arkite, Beery, Utnapishtim
Nob(by) Grandee, Parage, Prince, Swell, Toff
Nobble Dope, Hilch, Injure, Interfere
▷ **Nobbled** *may indicate* an anagram
Nobelium No
Noble(man), Noblewoman, Nobility Adela, Adele, Adeline, Aneurin, Aristocrat,
   Atheling, Baron(et), Baronne, Bart, Blue blood, Boyar, Brave, Bt, Burgrave, Childe,
   Contessa, Count, County, Daimio, Dom, Don, Doucepere, Douzeper(s), Duc, Duke,
   Duniwassal, Earl, Empress, Eorl, Ethel, Eupatrid, Fine, Galahad, Gent, Glorious,
   Graf, Grandee, Grandeur, Great, Heroic, Hidalgo, Highborn, Infant, Jarl, Junker,
   King, Landgrave, Lord, Magnate, Magnifico, Manly, Margrave, Marquis, Mona,
   Nair, Nayar, Palatine, Patrician, Patrick, Peer, Rank, Rose, Seigneur, Seignior,
   Sheik(h), Stately, Sublime, Thane, Thegn, Titled, Toiseach, Toisech, Vavasour,
   Vicomte, Vidame, Viscount
Noble gas(es) Argon, Helium, Krypton, Neon, Radon, Xenon
Nobody Diarist, Gnatling, Jack-straw, Nebbish, Nemo, None, Nonentity, Nyaff,
   Pipsqueak, Pooter, Quat, Schlepp, Scoot, Shlep, Zero
Nocturnal (creature) Bat, Galago, Moth, Night, Owl
Nod(ding) Agree, Assent, Beck(on), Bob, Browse, Catnap, Cernuous, Dip, Doze,
   Drowsy, Headbang, Mandarin, Nutant, Somnolent
Node, Nodular, Nodule Ascending, Boss, Descending, Enhydros, Geode, Knot,
   Lump, Lymph, Milium, Pea-iron, Ranvier, Root, Septarium, Swelling, Thorn,
   Tophus, Tubercle
No doubt Iwis, Ywis
Noel Christmas, Coward, Yule
Nog(gin) Ale, Cup, → DRINK, Peg
No good Dud, NG, Ropy
No-hoper Gone goose, Goner
Noise, Noisy Ambient, Babel, Bedlam, Big, Blare, Bleep, Blip, Blue murder, Bobbery,
   Boing, Boink, Bruit, Cangle, Charm, Chellup, Clamant, Clamour, Clangour, Clash,
   Clatter, Clitter, Clutter, Coil, Crackle, Creak, Deen, Din, Dirdum, Euphonia,
   Euphony, F, Flicker, Fuss, Hewgh, Howlround, Hubbub, Hue, Hullabaloo, Hum,
   Hurly-burly, Knocking, Loud, Mush, Obstreperous, Ping, Pink, Plangent, Quonk,

Racket, Report, Roar, Robustious, Rorie, Rort, Rory, Row(dow-dow), Rowdedow, Rowdy(dow)(dy), Rucous, Schottky, Schottky-Utis, Scream, Screech, Shindig, Shindy, Shot, Shreek, Shreik, Shriech, Shriek, Solar, Sone, Sonorous, Sound, Strepent, Strepitation, Strepitoso, Stridor, Surface, Thermal, Thunder, Tinnitus, Top, Tumult, → UPROAR, VIP, Vociferous, White, Zoom
Noisome Fetid, Invidious, Noxious, Offensive, Rank
No longer Ex, Past
Nomad(ic) Amalekite, Ammonites, Bedawin, Bed(o)uin, Bedu, Berber, Chal, Edom(ite), Fula(h), Gypsy, Hottentot, Hun, Hunter-gatherer, Hyksos, Itinerant, Kurd, Kyrgyz, Lapp, Rom, Rootless, Rover, Saracen, Sarmatian, Strayer, Tsigane, Tsigany, Tuareg, Turk(o)man, Unsettled, Vagabond, Vagrant, Zigan
Noman Ta(r)tar
No man's land Tom Tiddler's ground
Nome Province
Nomenclature Term
Nominal Formal, Onomastic, Titular, Trifling
Nominate, Nomination Appoint, Baptism, Designate, Elect, Postulate, Present, → PROPOSE, Slate, Specify, Term
Nomogram Abac
No more Gone, Napoo
Nomothete Enactor, Legislator
Non-Aboriginal Wudjula
Non-attender Absentee, Recusant
Non-believer Atheist, Cynic, Infidel, Sceptic
Non-catalyst Zymogen
Nonchalance, Nonchalant Blasé, Casual, Cool, Debonair, Insouciant, Jaunty, Poco
Non-Christian Saracen
Noncommittal Trimmer
Non-communist West
Non-conformist, Non-conformity Beatnik, Bohemian, Chapel, Deviant, Dissent(er), Dissident, Drop-out, Ebenezer, Heresiarch, Heretic, Maverick, Odd-ball, Outlaw, Pantile, Patarine, Rebel, Recusant, Renegade, Renegate, Sectarian, Wesleyan
Nondescript Dull, Grey, Insipid, Neutral, Nyaff
Non-drip Thixotropic
None Nada, Nary, Nil, Nought, Zero
Nonentity Cipher, Nebbich, Nebbish(er), Nebish, Nobody, Pipsqueak, Quat
Non-essential Adiaphoron, Extrinsic, Incidental
Nonesuch Model, Nonpareil, Paradigm, Paragon, Rarity
Nonetheless Mind you
▷ **Nonetheless** *may indicate* an 'o' to be omitted
Non-existent Unbeing, Virtual
Non-finite Verbid
Non-Gypsy Gajo, Gorgio
Non-interference Laissez faire
Non-Jewish Goy, Shi(c)ksa, Shkitzim, Sho(y)getz
Non-juror Usager
Non-Maori Tangata tiriti, Tauiwi
Non-Muslim Raia, Rayah
No-nonsense Hardball
Nonpareil Nonesuch, Pearl, Peerless, Type, Unequal, Unique

Nonplus(sed) Baffle, Bewilder, Blank, Perplex, Stump
Non-professional Amateur, Laic
Non-radiative Auger
Non-resident Extern, Outlier
Non-runner Scratched, Solid
Nonsense Absurdity, Amphigon, Amphigory, Balderdash, Baloney, Bilge,
   Bizzo, Blague, Blah, Blarney, Blat(her), Blatherskite, Blether, Bollocks, Boloney,
   Bora(c)k, Borax, Bosh, Bull, Bulldust, Bullshit, Bull's wool, Buncombe, Bunkum,
   Clamjamfr(a)y, Clamjamphrie, Claptrap, Cobblers, Cock, Cockamamie, Cod,
   Codswallop, Crap, Crapola, Drivel, Dust, Eyewash, Faddle, Falderal, Fandangle,
   Fiddlededee, Fiddle-faddle, Fiddlesticks, Flannel, Flapdoodle, Flim-flam,
   Folderol, Footling, Fudge, Gaff, Galimatias, Gammon, Gas and gaiters, Get away,
   Gibberish, Guff, Gum, Hanky-panky, Haver, Hogwash, Hokum, Hooey, Hoop-la,
   Horsefeathers, Humbug, Jabberwocky, Jive, Kibosh, Kidstakes, Malark(e)y,
   Moonshine, Mouthwash, My eye, Niaiserie, Phooey, Piffle, Pishogue, Pshaw,
   Pulp, Ratbaggery, Rats, Rawmaish, Rhubarb, Rigmarole, Rot, Rubbish, Scat,
   Shenanigans, Shit(e), Squit, Stuff, Tom(foolery), Tommy-rot, Tosh, Trash, Tripe,
   Tush, Twaddle, Unreason, Waffle
Non-sequitur Anacoluthia, Irrelevant
Non-stick PTFE, Teflon®, Tusche
Non-stop Through
Non-U Naff
Non-violence Ahimsa, Pacificism, Satyagraha
Non-white Coloured, Yolk
Noodle(s) Capellini, Crispy, Daw, Fool, Head, Laksa, Lokshen, Manicotti, Mee,
   Moony, Ninny, Pasta, Sammy, Simpleton, Soba, Udon
Nook Alcove, Angle, Corner, Cranny, Niche, Recess, Rookery
Noon Am end, M, Midday, N, Narrowdale
No one Nemo, None
Noose Fank, Halter, Lanyard, Loop, Necktie, Rope, Rope's end, Snare, Twitch
▶ **Nor** *see* NOT
Nordic, Norse(man) Icelander, Norn, Scandinavian, Viking
▶ **Nordic** *see* NORWAY, NORWEGIAN
Norm Canon, Criterion, Rule, Standard
Normal Average, Conventional, Customary, Everyday, General, Natural, Norm,
   Ordinary, Orthodox, Par, Perpendicular, Regular, Standard, Unexceptional, Usu(al)
Normal eyes Emmetropia
Norman French, Rufus
▶ **Norse** *see* NORWAY, NORWEGIAN
North(ern), Northerner Arctic, Boreal, Cispontine, Copperhead, Dalesman,
   Doughface, Eskimo, Geographic, Hyperborean, Magnetic, N, Norland, Runic,
   Septentrion, True, Up
North American (Indian) Ab(e)naki, Algonki(a)n, Algonqui(a)n, Apache, Arapaho,
   Assiniboine, Basket Maker, Blackfoot, Brave, Caddoan, Cajun, Cayuga, Cherokee,
   Cheyenne, Chibcha, Chickasaw, Chinook, Chipewyan, Choctaw, Comanche,
   Copperskin, Creek, Crow, Delaware, Dene, Erie, Five Nations, Fox, Galibi,
   Geronimo, Gwich'in, Haida, Hiawatha, Hopi, Huron, Injun, Innu, Iroquois, Kiowa
   Apache, Kloo(t)ch, Kootenai, Kootenay, Kutenai, Kwakiutl, Lakota, Mahican,
   Malecite, Mandan, Manhattan, Massachuset(ts), Melungeon, Menominee,
   Menomini, Mescalero, Micmac, Mikasuki, Miniconjou, Minneconjou, Mission,
   Mogollon, Mohave, Mohawk, Mohegan, Mohican, Montagnais, Montagnard,

Mound Builder, Mugwump, Musk(h)ogean, Muskogee, Narranganset, Natchez, Navaho, Nez Percé, Nootka, Northern P(a)iute, Oglala, Ojibwa(y), Okanagon, Okinagan, Omaha, Oneida, Onondaga, Osage, P(a)iute, Palouse, Papago, Papoose, Pawnee, Pequot, Pima, Plains, Pocahontas, Pomo, Ponca, Pontiac, Potawatom, Pueblo, Quapaw, Red(skin), Sachem, Sagamore, Sahaptan, Sahapti(a)n, Salish, Sannup, Sauk, Scalper, Seminole, Senecan, Serrano, Shahaptin, Shawnee, Shoshone, Sioux, Sitting Bull, Siwash, Six Nations, Southern P(a)iute, Status, Suquamash, Susquehannock, Tahitan, Taino, Tarahumara, Teton, Tewa, Tiwa, Tlingit, Totemist, Tribe, Tsimshian, Tuscarora, Ute, Uto-Aztecan, Wampanoag, Wichita, Winnebago, Wyandot(te), Yalkama, Yanqui, Yuman, Zuni

Northern Ireland NI, Six Counties

Northwestern Aeolis

Norway, Norwegian Bokmal, Fortinbras, Landsma(a)l, N, Nordic, Norweyan, Nynorsk, Rollo, Scandinavian

Nose, Nosy A(d)jutage, Aquiline, Beak, Bergerac, Boko, Bouquet, Breather, Catarrhine, Conk, Cromwell, Curious, Desman, Droop, Fink, Flair, Gnomon, Grass, Grecian, Greek, Grog-blossom, Honker, Hooter, Index, Informer, Leptorrhine, Meddle, Muffle, Muzzle, Nark, Neb, Nozzle, Nuzzle, Parker, Platyrrhine, Proboscis, Prying, Pug, Rhinal, Roman, Schnozzle, Shove, Smelly, Sneb, Sniff, Snoot, Snout, Snub, Squeal, Stag, Stickybeak, Toffee

Noseband Barnacle, Cavesson, Musrol

Nose-bleed Epistaxis

Nosh Eat, Food, Nibble, Snack

Nostalgia Longing, Retrophilia, Yearning

Nostril(s) Blowhole, Cere, Choana, Nare

Nostrum Elixir, Medicine, Remede, Remedy

Not, Nor Dis-, Na(e), Narrow A, Ne, Neither, Never, No, Pas, Polled, Taint

Notable, Notability Conspicuous, Distinguished, Eminent, Especial, Landmark, Large, Lion, Memorable, Personage, Signal, Striking, Unco, VIP, Worthy

Not allowed NL

▷ **Not allowed** *may indicate* a word to be omitted

Notary Apostolical, Ecclesiastical, Escribano, Scrivener

Notation(al) Benesh, Cantillation, Descriptive, Entry, Formalism, Hexadecimal, Memo, Octal, Polish, Positional, Postfix, Romic, Staff, Tablature

Notch(ed) Crena(l), Crenel, Cut, Dent, Erode, Erose, Gain, Gap, Gimp, Indent, Insection, Jag, Kerf, Mush, Nick, Nock, Raffle, Score, Serrate, Serrulation, Sinus, Snick, Tally, Vandyke

Not clear Blocked, NL, Obscure, Opaque, Pearl

Note(s), Notebook A, Acciaccatura, Accidental, Advance, Adversaria, Advice, Agogic, Apostil(le), Apparatus, Appoggiatura, Arpeggio, Auxiliary, B, Bill(et), Bradbury, Breve, C, Cedula, Chit(ty), Chord, Cob, Comment, Conceit, Continental, Cover, Credit, Crotchet, Currency, D, Debit, Delivery, Demand, Dig, Do(h), Dominant, Double-dotted, E, E-la, F, Fa(h), False, Fame, Fiver, Flat, Flim, G, Gamut, Gloss(ary), Gold, Grace, Greenback, Heed, Hemiole, Identic, Index rerum, IOU, Item(ise), Jot(tings), Jug(-jug), Key, Kudos, La, Large, Leading, Lichanos, Line, Liner, Log, Long, Longa, Lower mordent, Marginalia, Masora(h), Me, Melisma, Melody, Memo(randum), Mese, Mi, Minim, Minute, → **MONEY**, Mordent, Nachschlag, Natural, NB, Nete, Neum(e), Oblong, Observe, Octave, Oncer, Open, Ostmark, Outline, Parhypate, Passing, Postal, Post-it®, Pound, Promissory, Prompt, Prosiambanomenos, Protocol, PS, Quarter, Quaver, Rag-money, Re, Record, Remark, Renown, Request, Right, Root, Scholion, Scholium, Semibreve,

Semiquaver, Semitone, Sensible, Sextolet, Sharp, Shinplaster, Shoulder, Si, Sick, Sixteenth, Sixty-fourth, Sleeve, Smacker, So(h), Sol, Stem, Strike, Subdominant, Submediant, Subtonic, Supertonic, Te, Ten(ner), Third, Thirty-second, Tierce, Tonic, Treasury, Treble, Undecimole, Ut, Variorum, Verbal, Wad, Warison, Whole, Wolf, Wood

Note-case Pochette, Purse, Wallet

▷ **Notes** *may indicate* the use of letters A-G

Noteworthy Eminent, Extraordinary, Memorable, Particular, Signal, Special

Nothing, Nought Cipher, Devoid, Diddlysquat, Emptiness, FA, Gratis, Jack, Love, Nada, Napoo, Naught, Nihil, Niks-nie, Nil, Nix(-nie), Noumenon, Nowt, Nuffin, Nullity, O, Rap, Rien, Sweet FA, Void, Zero, Zilch, Zip(po)

Notice(able) Ad(vertisement), Advance, Advice, Affiche, Apprise, Attention, Avis(o), Banns, Bill, Blurb, Bold, Caveat, Circular, Clock, Cognisance, Crit, D, Descry, Detect, Discern, Dismissal, Enforcement, Gaum, Get, Gorm, Handbill, → **HEED**, Intimation, Marked, Mensh, Mention, NB, No(t)chel, Obit, Observe, Oyez, Perceptible, Placard, Plaque, Playbill, Poster, Press, Proclamation, Prominent, Pronounced, → **REMARK**, Review, See, Short, Si quis, Spot, Spy, Sticker, Tent, Whip

Notify Acquaint, Advise, Apprise, Awarn, Inform, → **TELL**, Warn

Notion(al) Academic, Conceit, → **CONCEPT**, Crotchet, Fancy, Hunch, Idea, Idée, Idolum, Inkling, Opinion, Reverie, Vapour, Whim

Notoriety, Notorious Arrant, Byword, Crying, Egregious, Esclandre, Fame, Flagrant, Infamous, Infamy, Notour, Proverbial, Réclame, → **RENOWN**, Repute

No trump Laical, Lay, NT

Notwithstanding Although, Despite, Even, For, Howbeit, However, Mau(l)gre, Nath(e)less, Natheless(e), Naythles, Nevertheless, Spite

Nougat Montelimar, Sundae

▶ **Nought** *see* **NOTHING**

Noughts and crosses Tic(k)-tac(k)-to(e)

Noumenon Thing-in-itself

Noun Abstract, Agent, Agentive, Aptote, Collective, Common, Concrete, Count, Gerund, Mass, N, Proper, Substantive, Tetraptote, Verbal, Vocative

Nourish(ing), Nourishment Aliment, Battill, Cherish, Cultivate, Feed, Ingesta, Meat, Nurse, Nurture, Nutrient, Promote, Replenish, Sustenance, Trophic

Nous Intellect, Intelligence, Reason

Nova Scotia(n) Acadia, Blue-nose

Novel(ty) Aga-saga, Bildungsroman, Bonkbuster, Book, Campus, Change, Clarissa, Different, Dime, Dissimilar, Emma, Epistolary, Fad, Fiction, Fresh, Gimmick, Gothic, Graphic, Historical, Horror, Idiot, Innovation, Ivanhoe, Kenilworth, Kidnapped, Kim, Middlemarch, → **NEW**, Newfangled, Original, Outside, Page-turner, Pamela, Paperback, Pendennis, Penny dreadful, Persuasion, Picaresque, Pot-boiler, Primeur, Pulp, Rebecca, River, Roman-à-clef, Romance, Roman fleuve, Scoop, Sex and shopping, Shilling-dreadful, Shilling-shocker, Terror, Thesis, Ulysses, Unusual, Whodun(n)it, Yellowback

▷ **Novel** *may indicate* an anagram

▶ **Novelist** *see* **WRITER**

Novice Acolyte, Apprentice, Beginner, Cadet, Chela, Colt, Cub, Greenhorn, Griffin, Jackaroo, Jillaroo, Johnny-raw, Kyu, L, Learner, Neophyte, New chum, Patzer, Postulant, Prentice, Rabbit, Rookie, Tenderfoot, Tyro(ne), Unweaned

Now(adays) AD, Alate, Anymore, Current, Here, Immediate, Instanter, Interim, Nonce, Nunc, Present, Pro tem, This

Nowhere Limbo
Nowt Cattle, Cows, Ky(e), Neat, Nothing
Noxious Harmful, Offensive, Poisonous, Toxic, Toxin, Venomous
Nozzle A(d)jutage, Aerospike, Fishtail, Nose, Nose-piece, Rose, Spout, Stroup,
   Syringe, Tewel, Tuyere, Tweer, Twier, Twire, Twyer(e)
Nuance Gradation, Nicety, Overtone, Shade
Nub Crux, Gist, Knob, Lump, Point
Nubile Beddable, Marriageable, Parti
Nuclear, Nucl(e)ide, Nucleus Cadre, Calandria, Centre, Core, Crux, Daughter,
   Deuteron, Eukaryon, Euratom, Even-even, Even-odd, Heartlet, Hub, Isomer,
   Isotone, Karyon, Kernel, Linin, Mushroom, Nuke, Pith, Prokaryon, Recoil,
   Synkaryon, Triton
▷ **Nucleus** *may indicate* the heart of a word
Nude, Nudism, Nudist, Nudity Adamite, Altogether, Aphylly, Bare, Buff, Eve,
   Exposed, Full-frontal, Gymnosophy, → **NAKED**, Nuddy, Scud, Stark, Stripped,
   Undress
Nudge Dunch, Dunsh, Elbow, Jostle, Poke, Prod
Nudibranch Sea-slug
Nugget Chunk, Cob, Gold, Lump
Nuisance Bore, Bot, Bugbear, Chiz(z), Drag, Impediment, Inconvenience, Mischief,
   Pest, Plague, Public, Terror, Trial
Null(ification), Nullify Abate, Cancel, Counteract, Defeasance, Destroy, Diriment,
   Disarm, Invalid(ate), Negate, Neutralise, Overturn, Recant, Terminate, Undo, Veto,
   Void
Numb(ness) Asleep, Blunt, Dead(en), Stun, Stupor, Torpefy, Torpescent, Torpid,
   Unfeeling
Number(s) Abscissa, Abundant, Accession, Air, Aleph-null, Aleph-zero, Algebraic,
   Algorithm, Aliquant, Aliquot, Amicable, Anaesthetic, Analgesic, Antilog,
   Apocalyptic, Apostrophus, Army, Atomic, Augend, Avogadro, Babylonian, Binary,
   Box, Brinell, Calculate, Cardinal, Cetane, Chromosome, Class, Cocaine, Coefficient,
   Cofactor, Complex, Composite, Concrete, Constant, Coordination, Count, Cyclic,
   Decillion, Deficient, Deficit, Diapason, Digit, Drove, E, Edition, Epidural, Ether,
   Eucaine, Ex-directory, F, Feck, Fraction, Friendly, Frost(bite), Froude, Gas, Gobar,
   Golden, Googol, Handful, Hantle, Hash(mark), Hemlock, Host, Hyperreal,
   Imaginary, Include, Incomposite, Index, Infimum, Integer, Irrational, Isospin,
   Isotopic, Item, Lac, Lakh, Legion(s), Lepton, Livraison, Local, Mach, Magazine,
   Magic, Mass, Melodic, Milliard, Minuend, Minyan, Mixed, Mort, Muckle, Multiple,
   Multiplex, Multiplicity, Multitude, Myriadth, Nasik, Natural, Neutron, No(s),
   Nonillion, Nth, Nuclear, Nucleon, Num, Numerator, Numerical, Octane, Octillion,
   Opiate, Opium, Opposite, Opus, Ordinal, OT, Paginate, Par, Paucal, Peck, Perfect,
   Pile, PIN, Plural, Polygonal, Prime, Production, Proton, Quantum, Quarternion,
   Quorum, Quotient, Radix, Raft, Random, Rational, Real, Reckon, Registration,
   Regulo®, Repunit, Reynolds, Sampi, Scads, Serial, Sight, Slew, Slue, Some,
   Square, Strangeness, Strength, Subtrahend, Summand, Surd, T, Tale, Telephone,
   Tell, Thr(e)ave, Totient, Totitive, Transcendental, Transfinite, Troop, Turn-out,
   Umpteen, Umpty, Urethan(e), Verse, Wave, Whole, Wrong, Zeroth
▷ **Number** *may indicate* a drug
Numeral(s) Arabic, Chapter, Figure, Ghubar, Gobar, Integer, Number, Roman,
   Sheep-scoring
Numerous(ness) Divers, Galore, Legion, Lots, Many, Multeity, Myriad, Teeming
Numskull Blockhead, Booby, Dunce, Stupid

Nun Beguine, Bhikkhuni, Clare, Cluniac, Conceptionist, Dame, Minim, Minoress, Mother Superior, Outsister, Pigeon, Poor Clare, Prioress, Religeuse, Sister, Sister of Mercy, Top, Ursuline, Vestal, Vowess, Zelator, Zelatrice, Zelatrix
▷ **Nun** *may indicate* a biblical character, father of Joshua
Nuptial (chamber) Bridal, Marital, Marriage, Thalamus
Nurse(ry) Aia, Alice, Amah, Ayah, Bonne, Caledonia, Care(r), Cavell, Charge, Cherish, Consultant, Crèche, Day, Deborah, District, Dry, EN, Flo(rence), Foster, Gamp, Glumdalclitch, Harbour, Health visitor, Karitane, Mammy, Midwife, Minister, Mother, Mrs Gamp, Nan(n)a, Nanny, Night, Nightingale, Nourice, Nourish, Parabolanus, Phytotron, Playroom, Playschool, Plunket, Probationer, RN, School, Seminary, SEN, Sister, Staff, Suckle, Tend, VAD, Visiting, Wet
Nursery(man) Conservatory, Crèche, Garden, Hothouse, Rhyme, Seedsman, Slope
▷ **Nursing** *may indicate* one word within another
Nurture Cultivate, Educate, Feed, Foster, Suckle, Tend
Nut(s), Nutcase, Nutshell, Nut tree, Nutty Acajou, Acorn, Almond, Amygdalus, Anacardium, Aphorism, Arachis, Areca, Arnut, Babassu, Barcelona, Barking, Barmy, Bats, Beech-mast, Bertholletia, Betel, Brazil, Briefly, Buffalo, Butterfly, Butternut, Cashew, Castle, Chock, Cob, Coffee, Cola, Conker, Coquilla, Coquina, Core, Cranium, Cream, Cuckoo, Dukka(h), En, Filberd, Filbert, Frog, Gelt, Gilbert, Gland, Glans, Goober, Gum, Hard, Hazel, Head, Hickory, Illipe, Ivory, Kachang puteh, Kernel, Kola, Lichee, Li(t)chi, Litchi, Loaf, Lug, Lunatic, Lychee, Macadamia, Macahuba, Macaw-palm, Macoya, Manic, Marking, Mast, Mockernut, Monkey, Noisette, Noodle, Nucule, Oak, Oil, Pakan, Palmyra, Para, Pate, Pecan, Pekan, Philippina, Philippine, Philopoena, Physic, Pili, Pine, Pistachio, Poison, Praline, Prawlin, Quandang, Quantong, Queensland, Rhus, Sapucaia, Sassafras, Shell, Skull, Slack, Sleeve, Stuffing, Supari, Thumb, Tiger, Tough, Walnut, Weirdo, Wing, Zany, Zealot
▷ **Nut** *may refer to* Egyptian god, father of Osiris
▶ **Nutcase, Nutshell** *see* **NUT**
Nutcracker Cosh
Nutmeg Calabash, Connecticut, CT, Mace, Myristica
Nutrient, Nutriment, Nutrition Eutrophy, Food, Ingesta, Protein, Sustenance, Trace element, Trophic
▷ **Nuts** *may indicate* an anagram
Nuzzle Snoozle
Nyasaland Malawi
Nymph(et) Aegina, Aegle, Amalthea, Arethusa, Callisto, Calypso, Camenae, Carme, Clytie, Constant, Cymodoce, Daphne, Doris, Dryad, Echo, Egeria, Eurydice, Galatea, Hamadryad, Hesperides, Houri, Hyades, Ida, Insect, Larva, Liberty, Lolita, Maelid, Maia, Maiden, Mermaid, Naiad, Nereid, Oceanid, Oenone, Oread, Pupa, Rusalka, Sabrina, Scylla, Siren, Sylph, Syrinx, Tessa, Tethys, Thetis, Water, Wood

Oo

O Blob, Duck, Nought, Omega, Omicron, Oscar, Oxygen, Spangle, Tan, Zero

Oaf Auf, Changeling, Dolt, Fool, Mou, Ocker, Ouph(e), Stupid, Twit, Yahoo

Oak(s) Bog, Bur, Cerris, Classic, Cork, Desert, Dumbarton, Durmast, Flittern, Fumed, Gabriel, Herne, Holly, Holm, Honour, Ilex, Jerusalem, Kermes, Live, Major, Native, Parliament, Pedunculate, Philemon, Poison, Quercus, Red, Roble, Royal, Sessile, Silky, Swamp, Swilcar, → **TREE**, Turkey, Valonia, Watch, White

Oakley Annie

Oar(s), Oarsmen Blade, Ctene, Eight, Leander, Organ, Paddle, Palm, Propel, Rower, Scull, Spoon, Stroke, Sweep

Oasis Biskra, Buraimi, Haven, Hotan, Hotien, Refuge, Spring, Tafilalet, Tafilelt

Oat(meal), Oats Ait, Athole brose, Avena, Brome-grass, Fodder, Grain, Grits, Groats, Gruel, Haver, Loblolly, Parritch, Pilcorn, Pipe, Porridge, Quaker®, Rolled, Wild

Oatcake Bannock, Clapbread, Farle, Flapjack, Jannock

Oath Affidavit, Begorrah, Blast, Burgess, Curse, Dang, Demme, Doggone, Drat, Ecod, Egad, Expletive, God-so, Gospel, Halidom, Hippocratic, Igad, Imprecation, Jabers, Lumme, Lummy, Nouns, Oons, Promise, Sacrament, Sal(a)mon, Sapperment, Saucer, Sdeath, Sfoot, Sheart, Slid, Strewth, Stygian, Swear, Tarnation, Tennis-court, Voir dire, Vow, Zbud, Zounds

Obdurate Adamant, Cruel, Flinty, Hard, Intransigent, Stony, Stubborn, Tenacious

Obedient, Obedience, Obey Bent, Bridlewise, Canonical, Comply, Dutiful, Follow, Hear, Mindful, Obsequious, Observe, Obtemper, Passive, Perform, Pliant, Servant, Yielding

Obeisance → **BOW**, Salaam

Obelisk, Obelus Aguilla, Column, Dagger, Monument, Needle, Pillar

Oberon King, Merle

Obese, Obesity Bariatrics, Corpulent, Fat, Stout

Object(s), Objection(able), Objective(ness), Objector Ah, Aim, Ambition, Argue, Article, Bar, Beef, Case, Cavil, Challenge, Clinical, Cognate, Complain(t), Conchy, Conscientious, Cow, Demur, Detached, Direct, End, Exception, Fuss, → **GOAL**, Her, Him, Impersonal, Improper, Indifferent, Indirect, Intensional, Intention, It, Item, Jib, Loathe, Mind, Moral, Niggle, Non-ego, Noumenon, Ob, Obnoxious, Offensive, Oppose, Outness, Perspective, Plan, Plot, Point, Protest, Proximate, Question, Quibble, Quasi-stellar, Quiddity, Rank, Rebarbative, Recuse, Refuse, Relation, Resist, Retained, Sake, Scruple, Sex, Subject, Sublime, Target, Thing, Transitive, Tut, Ultimate, Unbiased, Virtu, Wart

▷ **Object** *may indicate* a grammatical variant

Objectless Intransitive

Oblate, Oblation Gift, Monk, Offering, Offertory, Prothesis, Sacrifice

Oblige, Obliging, Obligation, Obligatory Accommodate, Affable, Behold, Binding, Burden, Charge, Compel, Complaisant, Compliant, Contract, Corvée,

Debt, De rigueur, Duty, Easy, Encumbent, Force, Giri, Gratify, Impel, Incumbent,
IOU, Mandatory, Must, Necessitate, Novation, Obruk, Obstriction, Peremptory,
Promise, Recognisance, Sonties, Synallagmatic, Tie, Wattle
Oblique(ly) Askance, Askew, Asklent, Asquint, Athwart, Awry, Cross, Diagonal,
Indirect, Perverse, Plagio-, Separatrix, Sidelong, Skew, Skewwhiff, Slanting,
Solidus, Squint, Virgule
▷ **Oblique** *may indicate* an anagram
Obliterate(d) Annul, Black out, Blot, Dele(te), Efface, Expunge, Exterminate, Rase,
Rast, Raze, Wash away, Wipe
Oblivion, Oblivious Forgetful, Lethe, Limbo, Nirvana, Obscurity
Oblong Rectangular
Obloquy Opprobrium
Obnoxious Eyesore, Foul, Horrid, Offensive, Pestilent, Repugnant, Septic, Sod
Obscene(ly), Obscenity Bawdy, Blue, Fescennine, Gross, Hard-core, Indecent,
Lewd, Lubricious, Paw(paw), Porn(o), Salacious, Smut, Vulgar
Obscure, Obscurity Abstruse, Anheires, Becloud, Befog, Blend, Blot out, Cloud,
Cobweb, Conceal, Cover, Cryptic, Darken, Deep, Dim, Disguise, Eclipse, Encrypt,
Envelop, Esoteric, Filmy, Fog, Hermetic, Hide, Indistinct, Jude, Mantle, Mist, Murk,
Nebular, Night, Nubecula, Obfuscate, Obnubilate, Opaque, Oracular, Overcloud,
Overshade, Overshadow, Recherché, Recondite, Shadowy, Tenebrific, Twilit,
Unclear, → VAGUE, Veil, Vele, Wrap
▷ **Obscure(d)** *may indicate* an anagram
Obsequious(ness) Bootlicker, Brown nose, Creeping Jesus, Fawn, Fulsome,
Grovelling, Kowtowing, Menial, Parasitic, Pig, Servile, Slavish, Sleeveen, Slimy,
Subservient, Suck-hole, Sycophantic, Tantony, Toady
Observance, Observant, Observation Adherence, Alert, Attention, Comment,
Custom, Empirical, Espial, Eyeful, Holy, Honour, Lectisternium, Mass, → NOTICE,
Obiter dicta, Perceptive, Percipient, Recce, Remark, Right, Rite, Ritual, Vising
Observatory Arecibo, Atalaya, Greenwich, Herstmonceux, Hurstmonceux, Jodrell
Bank, Lookout, Mount Palomar, Tower
Observe(d), Observer Behold, Bystander, Celebrate, Commentator, Detect, Espy,
Eye, Fly-on-the-wall, Heed, Keep, Mark, NB, Note, Notice, Obey, Onlooker, Optic,
Regard(er), Remark, Rite, Scry, See, Seer, Sight, Spectator, Spial, Spot, Spy, Study,
Take, Twig, View, Voyeur, Watch, Witness
Obsess(ed), Obsession, Obsessive Anal, Besot, Bug, Bugbear, Craze, Dominate,
Fetish, Fixation, Hang-up, Haunt, Hobbyhorse, Hooked, Idée fixe, Infatuation,
Mania, Monomania, Necrophilia, Neurotic, One-track, Preoccupy, Thing, Wonk
Obsidian Pe(a)rlite
Obsolete, Obsolescence, Obsolescent Abandoned, Antique, Archaic, Dated,
Dead, Defunct, Disused, Extinct, Latescent, Obs, Outdated, Outworn, Passé,
Planned
Obstacle Barrage, Barrier, Boyg, Cheval de frise, Chicane, Dam, Drag, Dragon's
teeth, Drawback, Gate, Handicap, Hindrance, Hitch, Hurdle, Node, Oxer, Remora,
Rock, Sandbank, Snag, Stimie, Stumbling-block, Stymie, Tank-trap
Obstetrics Gynaecology, Midwifery, Tocology, Tokology
Obstinacy, Obstinate Asinine, Bigoted, Buckie, Bullish, Contrarian, Contumacious,
Cussed, Die-hard, Dour, Entêté, Froward, Headstrong, Inflexible, Intractable,
Intransigent, Mule, Persistent, Perverse, Pervicacious, Piggish, Pig-headed,
Recalcitrant, Refractory, Restive, Rusty, Self-will, Stiff(-necked), Stubborn,
Thraward, Thrawart, Wilful
Obstreperous Noisy, Stroppy, Truculent, Unruly

Obstruct(ion) Bar, Block, Bottleneck, Chicane, Clog, Crab, Cross, Cumber, Dam, Embolus, Fil(l)ibuster, Gridlock, Hamper, Hand-off, Hedge, Hinder, Hurdle, Ileus, Impede, Let, Obstacle, Occlude, Sab(otage), Sandbag, Snarl-up, Snooker, Stall, Stap, Stonewall, Stop, Stymie, Sudd, Thwart, Trammel, Trump
Obtain Achieve, Acquire, Cop, Exist, Gain, Get, Land, Pan, Prevail, Procure, Realise, Secure, Succeed, Wangle, Win
Obtrude, Obtrusive Expel, Impose, Loud, Prominent, Push, Sorn, Thrust
Obtuse Blunt, Dense, Dull, Purblind, Stupid, Thick
Obverse Complement, Cross, Face, Front, Head
Obviate Forestall, Preclude, Prevent
Obvious Apparent, Axiom, Blatant, Brobdingnag, Clear, Distinct, Evident, Flagrant, Frank, Inescapable, Kenspeck(le), Manifest, Marked, Open(ness), Open and shut, Overt, Palpable, Patent, Pikestaff, Plain, Pronounced, Salient, Self-evident, Stark, Transparent, Truism, Visible
Occasion Call, Cause, Ceremony, Encheason, Event, Fête, Field day, Nonce, → **OPPORTUNITY**, Reason, Rise, Sometime, Tide, Time
Occasional(ly) Casual, Chance, Daimen, Intermittent, Irregular, Motive, Orra, Periodic, Sometimes, Sporadic, While
Occident(al) West, Western(er)
Occlude, Occlusion Absorb, Clog, Coronary, Embolism, Obstruct
Occult(ist) Angekkok, Arcane, Art, Esoteric, I-Ching, Magic, Mysterious
Occupant, Occupation, Occupy(ing) Absorb, Activity, Avocation, Beset, Business, Busy, Denizen, Embusy, Employ, Engage, Engross, Fill, Hold, In, Incumbent, Indwell, Inhabitant, Inmate, Involve, Line, Métier, People, Profession, Pursuit, Reserved, Resident, Runrig, Sideline, Squat, Stay, Tenancy, Tenant, Tenure, Thrift, Trade, Upon, Use, Vocation, Walk of life
Occur(rence) Arise, Be, Betide, Betime, Case, Contingency, Crop up, Event, Fall, Happen, Incident, Instance, Outbreak, Outcrop, Pass, Phenomenon
Ocean(ic), Oceania Abundance, Abyssal, Antarctic, Arctic, Atlantic, Blue, Deep, German, Hadal, Herring-pond, Indian, Melanesia, Micronesia, Pacific, Panthalassa, Pelagic, Polynesia, Sea(way), Southern, Thalassic, Waves, Western
Och aye Troggs
Ochre Burnt, Keel, Lemnian ruddle, Rubric, Ruddle, Sienna
Octave Diapason, Diminished, Eight, Great, Ottava, Perfect, Small, Utas
Octopus Blue-ringed, Cephalopod, Cuero, Devilfish, Paper nautilus, Polyp, Poulp(e), Scuttle, Squid
Octoroon Mestee, Mestizo, Mustee
Od Energy, Force
Odd (person), Oddity Abnormal, Anomaly, Bizarre, Card, Cure, Curio, Droll, Eccentric, Eery, Erratic, Gink, Impair, Imparity, Jimjam, Offbeat, Original, Orra, Outré, Paradox, Parity, Peculiar, Queer, Quiz, Random, Rare, Remote, Rum, Screwball, Singular, → **STRANGE**, Unequal, Uneven, Unmatched, Unusual, Weird, Whims(e)y
▷ **Odd(s)** *may indicate* an anagram or the odd letters in words
Oddfellow OF
Odd job man Joey, Loppy, Orraman, Rouster, Smoot, Thronner
Odds, Oddments Bits, Carpet, Chance, Gubbins, Handicap, Line, Long, Price, Short, SP, Tails, Variance
Ode Awdl, Dit, Epicede, Epicedium, Epinicion, Epinikion, Genethliacon, Horatian, Hymn, Lay, Lyric, Monody, Paeon, Pindaric, Poem, Sapphic, Song, Stasimon, Strophe, Threnody, Verse

Odin One-eyed, Woden
Odium, Odious Comparison, Disestimation, Disgrace, Foul, Hatred, Heinous, Invidious, Ponce, Repugnant, Stigma
Odorous, Odour Air, Bad, BO, Flavour, Funk, Good, Hum, Opopanax, Perfume, Quality, Redolence, Sanctity, Scent, Smell, Whiff
Odourless Silent
Odyssey Epic, Journey, Wandering
Oedipus Complex, Parricide
Oeillade Glance, Leer, Ogle, Wink
Oesophagus Crop
Oestrogen, Oestrus Frenzy, Heat, Isoflavone, Mestranol, Must, Rut, Stilb(o)estrol
Of (me) About, Among, Aus, By, De, From, In, My, Re
▷ **Of** *may indicate* an anagram
Of course Certainly, Natch, Yes
Off Absent, Agee, Ajee, Away, Discount, Distance, Far, From, High, Inexact, Licence, Odd, Reasty, Reesty, Relâche, Start
▷ **Off** *may indicate* an anagram
Offal Cagmag, Carrion, Chidlings, Chitterling, Entrails, Fry, Giblets, Gralloch, Gurry, Haggis, Ha(r)slet, Heart, Innards, Kidney, Lamb's fry, Lights, Liver, Numbles, Pig's fry, Pluck, Sweetbread, Tripe, Variety meat
Off-beat Zoppo
Off-colour Pale, Seedy, Wan
▷ **Off-colour** *may indicate* an anagram
Offence Attack, Crime, Delict, Delinquency, Distaste, Fault, Huff, Hurt, Lapse, Lese majesty, Miff, Misdemeanour, Misprision, Outrage, Peccadillo, Pip, Pique, Piracy, Regrate, Sedition, → **SIN**, Summary, Trespass, Umbrage, Violation
Offend(ed), Offender Affront, Anger, Annoy, Boobhead, Bridles, Culprit, Default, Disoblige, Displease, Distaste, Hip, Huff, Hurt, Hyp, Infringe, Inveigh, Miffy, Miscreant, Nettle, Nonce, Nuisance, Peeve, Perp, Provoke, Sin(ner), Stray, Transgress, Twoccer, Violate, Wrongdoer
Offensive Affront, Aggressive, Alien, Attack, Bombardment, Campaign, Cruel, Derisatory, Embracery, Euphemism, Execrable, Eyesore, Foul, Gobby, Hedgehog, Hedgepig, Indelicate, Invidious, Miasmic, Nasty, Noisome, Obnoxious, Obscene, Peccant, Personal, Push, Putrid, Rank, Repugnant, → **RUDE**, Scandalous, Scurrilous, Sortie, Storm, Ugly, Unbecoming, Unsavoury, War
Offer(ing) Alms, Altarage, Anaphora, Bargain, Bid, Bode, Bouchée, Cadeau, Corban, Deodate, Dolly, Epanophora, Extend, Ex voto, Gift, Godfather, Hold, Inferiae, Introduce, Invitation, Oblation, Overture, Peace, Peddle, Plead, Pose, Potla(t)ch, Present, Propine, → **PROPOSE**, Propound, Sacrifice, Shewbread, Shore, S(h)raddha, Special, Stamp, Stand, Submit, Suggestion, Tender, Utter, Volunteer, Votive, Wave, Xenium
Offhand Airy, Banana, Brusque, Casual, Cavalier, Curt, Extempore, Impromptu, Indifferent, Snappy
Office(s) Agency, Bedelship, Booking, Box, Branch, Broo, Bucket shop, Bureau, Buroo, Caliphate, Chair, Chancery, Clerical, Colonial, Complin(e), Consulate, Crown, Cube farm, Cutcher(r)y, Daftar, Dataria, Dead-letter, Deanery, Den, Divine, Dogate, Employment, Evensong, Foreign, Function, Holy, Home, Job, Land, Last, Left luggage, Lieutenancy, Little, Little hours, Loan, Lost property, Mayoralty, Met(eorological), Ministry, Missa, Mistery, Mudiria, Mutessarifat, Mystery, Nocturn, Nones, Obit, Oval, Palatinate, Papacy, Patent, Penitentiary, Personnel, Petty Bag, Pipe, Place, Plum, Portfolio, Position, Post, Prefecture, Prelacy, Press,

Prime, Printing, Provosty, Record, Regency, Register, Registry, Rite, Scottish, Secretarial, See, Seraskierate, Shogunate, Sinecure, Situation, Sorting, Stationery, Tariff, Tenebrae, Terce, Ticket, Tierce, Tol(l)booth, Tribunate, Vespers, War, Yamen

Officer(s) Acater, Adjutant, Admiral, Ag(h)a, Agistor, Aide, Apparitor, Bailiff, Beatty, Bimbashi, Black Rod, Blimp, Blue Rod, Bombardier, Bos(u)n, Branch, Brass-hat, Brigadier, Bumbailiff, Capt(ain), Catchpole, Catchpoll, Cater, Cellarist, Centurion, Chamberlain, Chancellor, CIGS, Colonel, Commander, Commissioned, Commissioner, Commodore, Compliance, Constable, Cop(per), Co-pilot, Cornet, Coroner, Counter-round, Cursitor, Customs, Darogha, Datary, Deacon, Decurion, Duty, Earl Marshal, Engineer, Ensign, Equerry, Exciseman, Executive, Exon, Field Marshal, Filacer, Filazer, First, First mate, Flag, Flying, Gallant, Ga(u)ger, Gazetted, Gen(eral), GOC, Grand Vizier, Group, Group captain, Gunner, Havildar, Hayward, Hetman, Ima(u)m, Incumbent, Infirmarian, Intendant, Jamadar, Janty, Jauntie, Jaunty, Jemadar, Jemidar, Jonty, Jurat, Justiciar, Lance-sergeant, Liaison, Lictor, Lord High Steward, Lt, Major, Marshal, Mate, Moderator, NCO, Non-commissioned, Number one, Nursing, Official Solicitor, Orderly, Oxon, Pantler, Peace, Petty, Pilot, Pipe major, PO, Police, Posse, Prefect, President, Prison, Probation, Proctor, Procurator fiscal, Provost, Provost-marshal, Purser, Pursuivant, Quartermaster, Quartermaster-sergeant, Radio, Relieving, Remembrancer, Returning, Rodent, Rupert, Safety, Samurai, Sbirro, Scene-of-crime, Schout, Sea Lord, Second mate, Securocrat, Select-man, Serang, Sergeant-major, Sewer, Sexton, Sheriff, Silver-stick, Skipper, SL, SM, Speaker, Staff, Striper, Sub(altern), Suba(h)dar, Subchanter, Sublieutenant, Supercargo, Superintendent, Tahsildar, Tidewaiter, Tindal, Tipstaff, Treasurer, Tribune, Usher, Varlet, Waldgrave, Warden, Wardroom, Warrant, Watch, Woodward, Yeoman

Official(s), Officiate, Officious Aga, Agent, Aleconner, Amban, Amtman, Atabeg, Atabek, Attaché, Authorised, Beadle, Bossy, Bureaucrat, Catchpole, Censor, Chamberlain, Chancellor, Chinovnik, Claviger, Commissar, Commissioner, Consul, Count, Count palatine, Dean, Diplomat, Dockmaster, Dogberry, Ealdorman, Ephor, Equerry, Escheater, Eurocrat, Executive, Fonctionnaire, → **FORMAL**, Functionary, Gauleiter, Gymnasiarch, Handicapper, Hayward, Incumbent, Inspector, Intendant, Jack-in-office, Jobsworth, Keeper, Landdrost, Lictor, Linesman, Mandarin, Marplot, Marshal, Mayor, MC, Meddlesome, Mirza, Mueddin, Mukhtar, Nazir, Notary, Notary public, Ombudsman, Omlah, Overbusy, Palatine, Paymaster, Placeman, Pleaseman, Plenipotentiary, Polemarch, Pontificate, Poohbah, Postmaster, Praefect, Pragmatic, Prefect, Proctor, Procurator, Prog, Proveditor, Provedor(e), Providor, Reeve, Régisseur, Registrar, Remembrancer, Shammash, Shammes, Sherpa, Silentiary, Souldan, Staff, Steward, Suffete, Suit, Syndic, Timekeeper, Tipstaff, Tribune, Trier, Trior, Triumvir, Turncock, Valid, Valuer General, Veep, Verderer, Verger, Vizier, Walla(h), Whiffler, Whip, Woodward, Yamen, Yeoman

Offprint Separate

Off-putting Dehortative, Discouraging, Mañana, Negative, Procrastination, Rebarbative, Repellent, Yips

Offset Balance, Cancel, Compensate, Counter(act), Counterbalance

Offshoot Bough, Branch, Cion, Limb, Lye, Member, Outgrowth, Plant, Scion, Sien, Sient, Swarm, Syen

Offspring Boy, Burd, Chick, Children, Daughter, Descendant, Family, Fry, Get, Girl, Heir, Procreation, Product, Progeny, Seed, Sient, Son, Spawn

Offstage Wings

Often Frequent, Habitual, Repeated

▷ **Often** *may indicate* 'of ten'

Ogee Cyma, Moulding, Talon
Ogle Drake, Eliad, Eye, Glance, Leer, Oeillade, Wodewose
Ogre(ss) Baba Yaga, Boyg, Brute, Eten, Etten, Fiend, Giant, Monster, Orc
Ohio Buckeye
Oil(s), Oily, Oil producer Anele, Anoint, Balm, Black gold, Bribe, Crude,
    Derv, Diesel, Drying, Essence, Essential, Ethereal, Fatty, Fish, Fixed, Frying,
    Fuel, Good, Grease, Heavy, Lamp, Lipid, Long, Lubricant, Midnight, Mineral,
    Monounsaturated, Multigrade, Oint, Oleaginous, Pellitory, Polyunsaturated,
    Pomade, Seed, Short, Sleek, Slick, Smalmy, Smarmy, Smeary, Sweet, Topped crude,
    Unction

OILS

2 letters:	Benne	Cineol	Myrrhol
BP®	Benni	Cohune	Naphtha
	Clove	Croton	Picamar
3 letters:	Colza	Elaeis	Pyrrole
Ben	Copra	Jojoba	Retinol
Emu	Fusel	Magilp	Ricinus
Gas	Grass	Megilp	Saffron
Nim	Niger	Monola®	Safrole
Nut	Olive	Neroli	Spindle
	Ottar	Peanut	Verbena
4 letters:	Poppy	Ramtil	Vitriol
Baby	Pulza	Savine	Wallaba
Bath	Rosin	Semsem	
Bone	Savin	Sesame	8 letters:
Coal	Sebum	Shamoy	Bergamot
Corn	Shale	Tallow	Camphire
Musk	Shark	Virgin	Cod-liver
Neem	Snake	Walnut	Creasote
Nimb	Sperm		Creosote
Oleo	Spike	7 letters:	Gingelli
Otto	Stand	Apiezon®	Gingelly
Palm	Thyme	Bittern	Hazelnut
Poon	Train	Cajeput	Kerosene
Rape	Ulyie	Cajuput	Kerosine
Rock	Ulzie	Camphor	Lavender
Rose	Whale	Cineole	Linalool
Rusa		Coconut	Macassar
Slum	6 letters:	Dittany	North Sea
Tall	Ajowan	Eugenol	Oiticica
Tolu	Almond	Gingili	Pachouli
Tung	Balsam	Linalol	Paraffin
Wool	Banana	Linseed	Photogen
Yolk	Butter	Lumbang	Pristane
	Canola	Menthol	Rapeseed
5 letters:	Carapa	Mirbane	Rosewood
Ajwan	Carron	Moringa	Volatile
Argan	Castor	Mustard	
Attar	Chrism	Myrbane	

9 *letters:*	Photogene	Elaeoptene	Wintergreen
Aleuritis	Safflower	Eucalyptus	
Beech-mast	Sassafras	Guttiferae	*12 letters:*
Candlenut	Spearmint	Petit grain	Benzaldehyde
Carvacrol	Spikenard	Sandalwood	Brilliantine
Eleoptene	Star-anise	Turpentine	
Golomynka	Sunflower	Ylang-ylang	*14 letters:*
Grapeseed	Vanaspati		Glutaraldehyde
Groundnut	Vegetable	*11 letters:*	Parnassus grass
Neat's-foot		Camphorated	
Parathion	*10 letters:*	Chaulmoogra	*15 letters:*
Patchouli	Chaulmugra	Chinese wood	Evening primrose
Patchouly	Citronella	Extra virgin	
Petroleum	Cotton-seed	Stearoptene	

Oilcake Poonac
Oilcan Pourie
Oilcloth American, Lino
Oilman Driller, Prospector, Rigger, Texan
Oil painting Master, Titian
Ointment Balm, Basilicon, Boracic, Boric, Cerate, Collyrium, Cream, Liniment, Lipsalve, Nard, Pomade, Pomatum, Salve, Spikenard, Theriac, Unguent, Vaseline®, Zinc
OK Agree(d), Approve, Authorise, Clearance, Copacetic, Copesettic, Go-head, Green light, Hunky-dory, Initial, Kosher, Mooi, Right(o), Sanction, Sound, U, Vet
Okra Bhindi, Gumbo, Lady's fingers
Old(er), Oldie Ae(t), Aged, Aine(e), Ancient, Antique, Auld, Bean, Decrepit, Dutch, Fogram, Former, Gaffer, Geriatric, Glory, Golden, Gray, Grey, Hills, Hoary, Immemorial, Major, Mature, Methusaleh, Moore, Nestor, Nick, O, OAP, Obsolete, Off, Ogygian, One-time, Outworn, Palae-, Passé, Primeval, Ripe, Rugose, Sen(escent), Senile, Senior, Shot, Signeur, Stale, Trite, Venerable, Veteran, Victorian(a), Worn
Old boy, Old girl Alumnae, Alumnus, Fossil, OB
Old days Once, Past, Yore
Old English OE
Old-fashioned Aging, Ancient, Antediluvian, Antwackie, Arch(aic), Arriéré, Bygone, Corn(y), Dated, Dowdy, Fogey, Fuddy-duddy, Medieval, Museum piece, Neanderthal, No tech, Obsolete, Ogygian, Oldfangled, Outdated, Outmoded, Passé, Podunk, Primeval, Quaint, Relic, Retro, Rinky-dink, Schmaltzy, Shot, Square, Square-toes, Steam, Stick-in-the-mud, Traditional, Uncool, Vieux jeu, Worm-eaten
Old hat Clichéd
Old maid Biddy, Spinster
Old man, Old woman Anile, Aunty, Bodach, Buda, Budi, Burd, Cailleach, Carlin(e), Codger, Crow, Crumbly, Faggot, Fantad, Fantod, Fogey, Fogramite, Fogy, Fussy, Gammer, Geezer, Grandam, Grannam, Greybeard, Greyhen, Husband, Kangaroo, Koro, Kuia, Luckie, Lucky, Matriarch, Methuselah, Mort, Mzee, OAP, Oom, Pantaloon, Patriarch, Presbyte, Rudas, Trot, Trout, Wife, Wight, Woopie, Wrinkly
Old-timer Hourglass, Sundial, Veteran
Oleander Nerium
Olid Fetid, Foul, High, Rancid, Rank

Olio Hash, Medley, Mess, Potpourri, Stew
Olive (grove), Olivine Calamata, Cerulein, Drupe, Dunite, Gethsemane, Kalamata, Lilac, Olea(ster), Peridot, Queen
Oliver Bath, Cromwell, Goldsmith, Hardy, Noll, Protector, Twist
Olympian, Olympus Asgard, Athlete, Celestial, Elis, Pantheon, Quadrennium, Zeus
Omelette Crêpe, Foo yong, Foo yung, Frittata, Fu yung, Pancake, Spanish, Tortilla
Omen Abodement, Absit, Augury, Auspice, Foreboding, Forewarning, Freet, Freit, Portent, Presage, Prodrome, Sign, Token, Warning
Omentum Caul, Epiploon
Ominous Alarming, Baleful, Bodeful, Dire, Dour, Forbidding, Grim, Inauspicious, Oracular, Sinister, Threatening
Omission, Omit Aph(a)eresis, Apocope, Apospory, Apostrophe, Asyndeton, Caret, Disregard, Drop, Elide, Elision, Ellipse, Ellipsis, Failure, Haplography, Haplology, Lipography, Loophole, Miss, Neglect, Nonfeasance, Oversight, Paral(e)ipomenon, Pass, Senza, Skip
Omnibus Anthology, Coach, Collection
Omniscient Encyclopedia
Omnivorous Pantophagous
On (it) Aboard, About, Agreed, An, An't, At, Atop, By, Game, Half-cut, In, Leg, O', Of, Oiled, Over, Pon, Re, Tipsy, Up(on)
▷ **On** *may indicate* an anagram
On account of Over
▷ **On board** *may indicate* chess, draughts, or 'SS' around another word
Once(r) Ance, As was, → **AT ONCE**, Bradbury, Earst, Erst(while), Ever, Ex, Fore, Former, Jadis, Oner, Onst, Secular, Sole, Sometime, Whilom
One(self) A, Ace, Ae, Alike, An(e), Any, Body, Chosen, Eeny, Ego, Ein, Formula, I, Individual, Integer, Me, Monad, Per se, Single(ton), Singular, Solo, Tane, Un, Unify, Unit(y), Unitary, United, Us, We, Yin, You
One-act-er Playlet
One-eared Monaural
One-eyed Arimasp(ian), Cyclops
One-man band Moke
One o'clock 1 am, NNE
One-off Ad hoc
One-rayed Monact
Onerous Arduous, Exacting, Taxing, Tedious, Weighty
Onion(s) Allium, Bengi, Bonce, Bulb, Chibol, Chive, Cibol, Cive, Eschalot, Green, Head, Ingan, Jibbons, Leek, Lyonnaise, Moly, Pearl, Ramp, Ramson, Rocambole, Ropes, Scallion, Scilla, Shal(l)ot, Soubise, Spanish, Spring, Squill, Sybo(e), Sybow, Tree, Welsh
Onlooker Bystander, Kibitzer, Rubberneck, Spectator, Witness
Only Allenarly, Anerly, But, Except, Just, Meer, Merely, Nobbut, Seul, Singly, Sole
Onset Affret, Attack, Beginning, Charge, Dash, Ending, Rush, → **START**, Thrust
Onslaught Attack, Dead-set, Onset, Raid, Spreagh, Storm, Swoop
On time Pat, Prompt, Punctual
Onus Burden, Charge, → **DUTY**, Responsibility
Onward Advance, Ahead, Away, Forth, Forward, Progress
Oodles Heaps, Lashings, Lots, Slather
Oolite Pisolite, Roestone
Oomph Energy, It, SA, Verve
Ooze Drip, Exhale, Exude, Gleet, Mud, Percolate, Pteropod(a), Seep, Sew, Sipe,

Slime, Slob, Spew, Spue, Sweat, Sype, Transude

Opal(escent) Black, Cymophanous, Fire, Gem, Girasol, Girosol, Hyalite, Hydrophane, Liver, Menilite, Noble, Potch, Wood

Opaque, Opacity Dense, Dull, Intense, Leucoma, Obscure, Obtuse, Onycha, Roil, Thick, Turbid

Open(er), Opening, Openness Adit, Aedicule, Ajar, Antithesis, Anus, Apert(ure), Apparent, Apse, Autopsy, Bald, Bare, Bat, Bay, Bole, Breach, Break, Broach, Buttonhole, Candid, Cardia, Cavity, Champaign, Chance, Chasm, Chink, Circumscissile, Clear, Crevasse, Dehisce, Deploy, Dispark, Door, Dup, Embrasure, Exordium, Expansive, Eyelet, Fair, Fenestra, Fissure, Fistula, Flue, Fontanel(le), Foramen, Frank, Free, Gambit, Gap, Gaping, Gat, Gate, Give, Glasnost, Glottis, Guichet, Gullwing, Hagioscope, Hatch, Hatchback, Hatchway, Hiatus, Hilus, → HOLE, Inaugural, Intake, Interstice, Intro, Key, Lacy, Lance, Lead, Loid, Loophole, Loose, Machicolation, Manhole, Meatus, Micropyle, Mofette, Moongate, Mouth, Nare, Oillet, Orifice, Oscule, Osculum, Ostiole, Ostium, Overture, Patent, Peephole, Pert, Pervious, Pick(lock), Placket, Plughole, Pore, Port(age), Porta, Porthole, Preliminary, Premiere, Prise, Pro-am, Public, Pylorus, Receptive, Rent, Riva, Room, Scuttle, Scye, Sesame, Sicilian, Sincere, Slit, Spare, Spirant, Squint, Start, Stenopaic, Stoma, Syrinx, Thereout, Thirl, Touchhole, Transparent, Trapdoor, Trema, Trou, Truthful, Unbar, Unbolt, Unbutton, Uncork, Undo, Unfurl, Unhasp, Unlatch, Unscrew, Unstop, Unsubtle, Untie, Unzip, Upfront, Vent, Vulnerable, Wide, Window

Open air Alfresco, Sub divo, Sub Jove

Opera, Opera house Aida, Ariadne, Ballad, Bouffe, Buffo, Burletta, Carmen, Comic, Comique, Dramma giocoso, Electra, ENO, Ernani, Falstaff, Faust, Fedora, Fidelio, Glyndebourne, Grand, Hansel and Gretel, Horse, Idomeneo, Iolanthe, I Puritani, La Bohème, La Scala, Light, Lohengrin, Lulu, Macbeth, Met, Musical, Nabucco, Norma, Oater, Oberon, Onegin, Open Wingrave, Orfeo, Otello, Parsifal, Pastorale, Patience, Peter Grimes, Pinafore, Rienzi, Rigoletto, Ruddigore, Savoy, Seria, Singspiel, Soap, Space, Tell, The Met, Threepenny, Tosca, Turandot, Verismo, Werther, Work, Zarzuela

Opera-glasses Jumelle

Opera-lover Wagnerite

Opera-singer Baritone, Bass, Contralto, Diva, Savoyard, Soprano

Operate, Operation(s), Operative Act(ion), Activate, Actuate, Agent, Artisan, Attuition, Barbarossa, Bypass, Caesarean, Campaign, Conduct, Couching, Current, Desert Storm, Detective, Exercise, Function, Game, Hobday, Holding, Keystroke, Laparotomy, Leucotomy, Liposuction, Lithotomy, Lobotomy, Logical, Manipulate, Mechanic, Mules, Nose job, Oner, Overlord, Plastic, Practice, Run, Sealion, Shirodkar's, Sortie, Strabotomy, Titration, Ure, Valid, Wertheim, Work

Operator Agent, Conductor, Dealer, Laplace, Manipulator, Nabla, Sawbones, Sparks, Surgeon

Opiate, Opium Buprenorphine, Dope, Drug, Hop, Laudanum, Meconin, Meconium, Morphine, Narcotic, Religion, Soporific, Thebaine

Opinion, Opinionative Attitude, Belief, Bet, Consensus, Cri, Dictum, Dogma, Doxy, Entêté, Esteem, Feeling, Groundswell, Guess, Judgement, Mind, Mumpsimus, Parti pris, Pious, Prejudice, Private, Public, Pulse, Say, Second, Sense, Sentence, Sentiment, SO, Stand, Take, Tenet, Utterance, View, Viewpoint, Voice, Vox pop, Vox populi

Opossum Lie, Marmose, Phalanger, Tarsipes, Vulpine, Water, Yapo(c)k

Oppidan Cit, Townsman, Urban

Opponent(s) Adversary, Antagonist, Anti, E-N, Enemy, E-S, Foe, Gainsayer, Mitnaged, N-E, N-W, S-E, Straw-man, S-W, W-N, W-S

Opportune, Opportunist, Opportunity Appropriate, Apropos, Break, Carpetbagger, → CHANCE, Day, Equal, Facility, Favourable, Ganef, Ganev, Ganof, Godsend, Go-go, Golden, Gonif, Gonof, Heaven-sent, Occasion, Opening, Pat, Photo, Room, Seal, Seel, Sele, Snatcher, Tabula rasa, Tide, Timely, Timous, Well-timed, Window

Oppose(d), Opposer, Opposing, Opposite, Opposition Against, Agin, Anti, Antipathy, Antipodes, Antiscian, Antithesis, Antithetic, Antitype, Antonym, Argue, At, Au contraire, Averse, Battle, Black, Breast, Colluctation, Combat, Confront, Contradict, Contrary, Converse, Counter, Diametric, Dis(en)courage, Disfavour, Dissent, Distance, E contrario, Face, Foreanent, Fornen(s)t, Hinder, Hostile, Impugn, Inimical, Inverse, Militate, Mugwump, Noes, Object, Obscurant, Overthwart, Polar, Reactance, Reaction, Reluct, Repugn, Resist, Retroact, Reverse, Rival, Shadow, Subtend, Syzygy, Teeth, Terr, Thereagainst, Thwart, Toto caelo, Traverse, V, Versus, Vis-à-vis, Withstand

Oppress(ion), Oppressive Airless, Bind, Burden, Close, Crush, Despotic, Incubus, Jackboot, Onerous, Overpower, Persecute, Ride, Snool, Stifling, Sultry, Tyrannise

Opprobrium Disgrace, Envy, Odium, Scandal

Oppugn Attack, Criticise

Opt, Option(al) Alternative, → CHOICE, Choose, Crown-jewel, Decide, Default, Double zero, Elect, Facultative, Fine, Leipzig, Local, Menu, Omissible, Pick, Plump, Select, Share, Soft, Swap, Trade(d), Traditional, Voluntary, Votive, Wale, Zero(-zero)

Optic(al), Optics Active, Adaptive, Electron, Fibre, Fire, Lens, Prism, Reticle, Visual

Optimism, Optimist(ic) Bull, Chiliast, Elated, Expectant, Feelgood, Hopeful, Micawber, Morale, Pangloss, Pollyanna, Rosy, Sanguine, Starry-eyed, Upbeat, Utopiast, Yea-sayer

Opulent Abundant, Affluent, Moneyed, Rich, Wealthy

Opus Piece, Study, Work

Or Au, Either, Ere, Gold, Ossia, Otherwise, Sol

Oracle(s), Oracular Delphi, Dodonian, Mirror, Prophet, Pythian, Pythoness, Sage, Seer, Sibyl(line), Thummim, Urim, Vatic

Oral Acroamatic, Sonant, Spoken, Verbal, Viva, Viva voce, Vocal

Orange An(n)atta, An(n)atto, Arnotto, Aurora, Bergamot, Bigarade, Bilirubin, Bitter, Blood, Blossom, Calamondin, Chica, Claybank, Clockwork, Croceate, Flame, Flamingo, Fulvous, Genip(ap), Jaffa, Kamala, Kamela, Kamila, Karaka, Kumquat, Mandarin, Mock, Naartje, Nacarat, Nartjie, Navel, Ochre, Osage, Pig, Roucou, Ruta, Satsuma, Seville, Shaddock, Sour, Sweet, Tangerine, Tenné, Ugli®, Ulsterman

Orang-utan Ape, Monkey, Satyr

Orate, Oration Address, Declaim, Eloge, Elogium, Elogy, Eulogy, Harangue, Panegyric, Philippics, Speech

Oratorio, Orator(y) Boanerges, Brompton, Brougham, Cantata, Cicero, Creation, Demosthenes, Diction, Elijah, Hwyl, Isocrates, Lectern, Morin, Nestor, Prevaricator, Proseucha, Proseuche, Rhetor, Samson, Spellbinder, Stump, Tub-thumper, Windbag, Yarra-banker

Orb Ball, Eyeball, Firmament, Globe, Mound, Ocellus, Pome, Sphere

Orbit Apse, Apsis, Circuit, Dump, Eccentric, Ellipse, Eye, Graveyard, Osculating, Parking, Path, Periastron, Perigee, Perihelion, Perilune, Periselenium, Polar, Revolution, Stationary, Synchronous

Orcadian Hoy

Orchard Arbour, Grove, Holt

Orchestra(te), Orchestration Chamber, Charanga, Concertgebouw, Concerto, ECO, Ensemble, Gamelan, Hallé, Instrumentation, LPO, LSO, Palm-Court, Pit, Ripieno, Score, SNO, String, Symphony

Orchid Adam and Eve, Adder's mouth, Arethusa, Babe-in-a-cradle, Bee, Bee-orchis, Bird's nest, Bog, Burnt-tip, Butterfly, Calanthe, Calypso, Cattleya, Cooktown, Coralroot, Cymbidium, Cypripedium, Disa, Epidendrum, Fly, Fly orchis, Fragrant, Fringed orchis, Frog, Helleborine, Lady, Lady's slipper, Lady's tresses, Lizard, Man, Marsh, Military, Moccasin-flower, Monkey, Musk, Naked lady, Odontoglossum, Oncidium, Pogonia, Purple-fringed, Puttyroot, Pyramidal, Rattlesnake plantain, Salep, Scented, Slipper, Snakemouth, Soldier, Spider, Spotted, Swamp pink, Swan, Twayblade, Vanda, Vanilla

Ord Beginning, Point

Ordain Arrange, Command, Decree, Destine, Enact, Induct, Japan, Priest

Ordeal Corsned, Disaster, Preeve, Test, → TRIAL, Via Dolorosa

Order(ed), Orderly, Orders Acoemeti, Adjust, Administration, Affiliation, Alphabetical, Anton Piller, Apollonian, Apple-pie, Arrange, Array, Attendant, Attention, Attic, Avast, Bade, Banker's, Bankruptcy, Bath, Batman, Battalia, Bed, Behest, Benedictine, Bespoke, Bid, Book, Call, Camaldolite, Canon, Category, Caveat, CB, Chaprassi, Charter, Cheque, Chit, Chuprassy, Class, Coherent, Command(ment), Committal, Compensation, Composite, Corinthian, Cosmo, Cosmos, Court, Decorum, Decree, Demand, Dictate, Diktat, Direct(ion), Directive, Dispone, Distringas, Dominican, Doric, DSO, Edict, Embargo, Enclosed, Enjoin, En règle, Established, Establishment, Eutaxy, Eviction, Exclusion, Feldsher, Fiat, Fiaunt, Firing, Firman, Form(ation), Franciscan, Fraternity, Freemason, Gagging, Garnishee, Garter, Gilbertine, Ginkgo, Good, Grade, Habeas corpus, Heast(e), Hecht, Hest, Holy, Indent, Injunction, Instruct, Interdict, Ionic, Irade, Khalsa, Kilter, Knights Hospitallers, Kosmos, Language, Large, Lexical, Loblolly boy, Loblolly man, Loose, Mail, Major, Mandamus, Mandate, Marching, Marist, Market, Marshal, Masonic, Medjidie, Merit, Methodical, Minor, Mittimus, Monastic, Money, Monitor, Natural, Neatness, Nunnery, OBE, Oddfellows, Official, OM, Open, Orange, Ord, Ordain, Organic, Pecking, Possession, Postal, Precedence, Precept, Premonstrant, Prescribe, Preservation, Provisional, Pyragyrite, Rank, Receiving, Reception, Règle, Regular, Religious, Restraining, Return, Right, Rule, Ruly, Sailing, Sealed, Search, Seraphic, Series, Settle, Shipshape, Short, Side, Standing, Starter's, State, Statutory, Stop(-loss), Straight, Subpoena, Summons, Supersedere, Supervision, System, Tabulate, Tall, Taxis, Tell, Templar, Teutonic, Third, Thistle, Tidy, Trim, Tuscan, Ukase, Uniformity, Warison, Warrant, Word, Writ

▷ **Ordering** *may indicate an anagram*

Ordinal Book, Number, Second, Sequence

Ordinance Byelaw, Capitulary, Decree, Edict, Law, Prescript, Rescript, Rite, Statute

Ordinary Average, Banal, Bog standard, Canton, Chevron, Comely, Common (or garden), Commonplace, Cot(t)ise, Everyday, Fess(e), Flanch, Flange, Folksy, Grassroots, Hackneyed, Mass, Mediocre, Middling, Mundane, → NORMAL, O, OR, Pedestrian, Plain, Prosy, Pub, Rank and file, Run-of-the-mill, Saltier, Saltire, Simple, Tressure, Trivial, Unexceptional, Uninspired, Usual, Workaday, Your

Ordnance Artillery, Cannon, Guns, Pelican, Supply

Ordure Cess, Dung, Fertiliser, Manure

Ore Alga, Babingtonite, Bauxite, Bornite, Breunnerite, Calamine, Calaverite, Cerusite, Chalcocite, Chalcopyrite, Chloanthite, Coffinite, Coin, Coltan, Copper, Crocoite, Element, Galenite, Glance, Haematite, Hedyphane, Horseflesh, Ilmenite,

Iridosmine, Ironstone, Kidney, Limonite, Mat, Melaconite, Middlings, Millhead, Milling grade, Mineral, Minestone, Morass, Niobite, Oligist, Peacock, Pencil, Phacolite, Pipe, Pitchblende, Proustite, Psilomelane, Pyrargyrite, Pyromorphite, Realgar, Red-lead, Ruby silver, Schlich, Seaweed, Siderite, Sinoptite, Slime, Slug, Smaltite, Speiss, Sphalerite, Stephanite, Stilpnosiderite, Stockwork, Stream-tin, Taconite, Tailing, Tenorite, Tetrahedrite, Tin, Wad(d), White-lead, Yellow cake
Organ(s), Organic Adnexa, American, Anlage, Antimere, Apollonicon, Appendix, Archegonium, Barrel, Biogenic, Calliope, Carpel, Carpogonium, Cercus, Chamber, Chemoreceptor, Choir, Chord, Claspers, Clave, Colour, Conch(a), Console, Corti's, Cribellum, Ctene, Ear, Echo, Electric, Electronic, Electroreceptor, End, Essential, Exteroceptor, Feeler, Fin, Flabellum, Fundus, Gametangium, Gill, Glairin, Gonad, Hammond®, Hand, Hapteron, Harmonica, Harmonium, Haustorium, House, Hydathode, Hydraulos, Imine, Isomere, Kerogen, Kidney, Lien, Light, Liver, Lung-book, Lyriform, Means, Mechanoreceptor, Media, Medulla, Melodion, Ministry, Nasal, Natural, Nectary, Nematocyst, Nephridium, Newspaper, Oogonia, Ovary, Ovipositor, Ovotestis, Palp, Pancreas, Parapodium, Part, Pedal, Photogen, Photophore, Photoreceptor, Physharmonics, Pipe, Pipeless, Placenta, Plastid, Portative, Positive, Procarp, Prothallus, Pulmones, Purtenance, Pyrophone, Radula, Receptor, Recit, Reed, Regal, Relict, Sang, Saprobe, Scent, Sense, Sensillum, Serinette, Serra, Siphon, Spinneret, Spleen, Sporangium, Sporophore, Stamen, Statocyst, Steam, Swell, Syrinx, Tentacle, Textual, Theatre, Theca, Thymus, Tongue, Tonsil, Tool, Tympanum, Uterus, Vegetative, Velum, Verset, Viscera, Viscus, Vitals, Voice, Voluntary, Womb, Wurlitzer®
Organelle Peroxisome
Organise(d), Organisation, Organiser Activate, Aggregator, Anatomy, → **ARRANGE**, Association, Brigade, Caucus, Class(ify), Collect, Comecon, Company, Constitution, Coordinate, Design, Embody, Entrepreneur, Fascio, Firm, Impresario, Infrastructure, Jaycee, Ku Klux Klan, Logistics, Machine, Mafia, Marshal, Mobilise, Octopus, Opus Dei, Orchestrate, Outfit, Personal, PLO, Promotor, Quango, Rally, Regiment, Resistance, Rosicrucian, Run, Setup, Sharpbender, Social, Soroptimist, Sort, Stage, Stahlheim, Steward, System, Tidy, Together, UN, Viet Minh
▷ **Organise(d)** *may indicate* an anagram
Organism Aerobe, Agamic, Auxotroph, Being, Biont, Biotic, Cell, Chimeric, Chlamydia, Ciliate, Clade, Coral, Diplont, Ecad, Endogenous, Entity, Epibenthos, Epizoite, Epizoon, Eucaryote, Euglena, Eukaryote, Eurytherm, Germ, Halobiont, Halophile, Haplont, Hemiparasite, Holophyte, Holoplankton, Homeotherm, Incross, Infauna, Infusoria(n), Lichen, Macrobiote, Medusa, Meroplankton, Metamale, Microbe, Moneron, Morphology, Nekton, Neuston, Paramecium, Pathogen, Periphyton, Phenetics, Plankter, Plankton, Pleuston, Protist, Protista, Protozoan, Radiolarian, Saprobe, Saprotroph, Schizomycete, Streptococcus, Symbion(t), Teratogen, Thermophile, Torula, Virino, Volvox, Vorticella
Organ-part, Organ-stop Bourdon, Clarabella, Diapason, Gamba, Montre, Nasard, Principal, Pyramidon, Quint, Salicet, Stop
Organ-tuner Reed-knife
Orgy Bacchanalia(n), Binge, Blinder, Bust, Carousal, Dionysian, Feast, Revel, Saturnalia, Spree, Wassail
Orient(al) Adjust, Annamite, Chinoiserie, Dawn, Dayak, E, East(ern), Fu Manchu, Hindu, Levant, Leyton, Malay, Mongol, Mongolian, Pareoean, Shan, Sunrise, Tatar, Thai, Tibetan, Turk(o)man
Orifice Aperture, Blastosphere, Gap, Hole, Micropyle, Nare, Opening, Pore, Spiracle, Trema, Vent

Origen's work Tetrapla
Origin(al), Originate, Originating Abo, Adam, Arise, Beginning, Birth, Come, Cradle, Creation, Derive, Editio princeps, Elemental, Emanate, Epicentre, Etymon, Extraction, First, Firsthand, Focus, Found, Generic, Genesis, Genetical, Germ, Grow, Hatch, Incunabula, Initial, Innovate, Invent, Master, Mother, Nascence, Natality, New, Novel, Ord, Primal, Primary, Primigenial, Primordial, Pristine, Prototype, Provenance, Provenience, Rise, Root, Seminal, Source, Spring, Start, Ur, Ylem, Zoism
Oriole Firebird, Hangbird
Orison Blessing, Prayer
Ormer Abalone, Haliotis
Ornament(al), Ornamentation Acroter(ia), Additament, Adorn, Aglet, Aiguillette, Anaglyph, Antefix, Anthemion, Aplustre, Arabesque, Bahuti, Ball-flower, Barbola, Baroque, Barrette, Bead, Bedeck, Bez(z)ant, Billet, Blister, Boss, Bracelet, Breloque, Broider, Brooch, Bugle, Bulla, Cartouche, Chase, Clock, Cockade, Conceit, Corbeil(le), Cornice, Crocket, Cross-quarters, Curin, Curlicue, Decorate, Decoration, Diamanté, Die-work, Diglyph, Dog's-tooth, Doodad, Dreamcatcher, Embellish, Emblem(a), Enrich, Epaulet(te), Epergne, Fallal, Fandangle, Fiddlehead, Figuration, Figurine, Filagree, Filigrain, Filigree, Fillagree, Fleuret, Fleurette, Fleuron, Florid, Fret, Fretwork, Frill, Frounce, Furbelow, Furnish, Gadroon, Gaud, Gingerbread, Gorget, Griff(e), Guilloche, Gutta, Headwork, Heitiki, Helix, Honeysuckle, Illustrate, Inlay, Knotwork, Labret, Lambrequin, Leglet, Lotus, Macramé, Mantling, Mense, Millefleurs, Mordent, Moresque, Motif, Nail-head, Necklet, Netsuke, Nicknackery, Niello, O, Okimono, Ouch, Ovolo, Palmette, Parure, Paternoster, Paua, Pawa, Pectoral, Pendant, Picot, Pipe, Pompom, Pompo(o)n, Poppyhead, Pounce, Pralltriller, Prettify, Prunt, Purfle, Quatrefoil, Rel(l)ish, Rocaille, Rococo, Scalework, Scrollwork, Spangle, Spar, Tassel, Tettix, Tiki, Tool, Torque, Torsade, Tracery, Trappings, Trill, Trimming, Trinket, Triquetra, Turn, Versal, Wally, Water-leaf, Whigmaleerie, Whigmaleery
Ornate Baroque, Churrigueresque, Dressy, Elaborate, Fancy, Florid, Flowery
▷ **Ornate** *may indicate* an anagram
Ornithologist Audubon, Birdman
Orotund Bombastic, Grandiose, Pompous, Rhetorical, Sonant
Orphan Annie, Foundling, Topsy, Ward
Orpiment Arsenic, Zarnich
Orpington Buff, Hen
Ort Bit, Crumb, Morsel, Remnant
Orthodox Bien-pensant, Cocker, Conventional, Hardshell, Proper, Sound, Standard
Orthorhombic Enstatite
Ortolan Bird, Bunting, Rail
Oscar Award, O, Wilde
Oscillate, Oscillation, Oscillator Dynatron, Excitor, Fluctuate, Librate, Local, Parasitic, Relaxation, Ripple, Rock, Seesaw, Seiche, Squeg, Surge, Swing, Vibrate, Waver
Osier Red, Reed, Sallow, Willow
Osmium Os
Osmosis Reverse
Osprey Fish-hawk, Lammergeier, Ossifrage, Pandion
Osseous Bony, Hard, Skeletal, Spiny
Ostensibly Apparent, External, Seeming
Ostentation, Ostentatious Camp, Display, Dog, Éclat, Epideictical, Extravagant,

Fantoosh, Flamboyant, Flash(y), Flaunt, Florid, Flourish, Garish, Gaudy, Highfalutin(g), Parade, Pomp, Ponc(e)y, Pretence, Puff, → **SHOW(ING)**, Side, Splash, Swank, Tacky, Tulip

Ostler Stabler

Ostracise, Ostracism Banish, Blackball, Boycott, Cut, Exclude, Exile, Petalism, Potsherd, Snub, Taboo, Tabu

Ostrich Em(e)u, Estrich, Estridge, Nandoo, Nandu, Ratite, Rhea, Struthio(nes), Titanis

Othello Moor, Morisco

Other(s), Otherwise Additional, Aka, Alia, Alias, Allo-, Alternative, Besides, Different, Distinct, Else, Et al, Et alli, Etc, Excluding, Former, Further, Rest, Significant

Other things Alia

▷ **Otherwise** *may indicate* an anagram

Otiose Idle, Indolent, Ineffective, Lazy, Needless, Superfluous

Otis Bustard

Otter Edal, Paravane, Sea, Tarka

Otto Attar, Chypre, Mahratta

Ottoman Osmanli, Porte, Rumelia, Turk

Oubliette Dungeon, Pit, Prison

Ouch Brooch, Ornament, Ow

Ought All, Should

Ouida Ramée

Ounce Cat, Fluid, Liang, Oz, Panther, Tael, Uncial

Our(selves) Us, We

▶ **Ousel** *see* **OUZEL**

Oust Depose, Dislodge, Eject, Evict, Expel, Fire, Supplant, Unnest, Unseat

Out Absent, Aglee, Agley, Asleep, Aus, Away, Begone, Bowl, Dated, En ville, Exposed, External, Forth, Furth, Haro, Harrow, Hence, Hors, Oust, Skittle, Striking, Stump, Taboo, Uit, Unfashionable, Up, York

▷ **Out** *may indicate* an anagram

Out and out Absolute, Arrant, Rank, Sheer, Stark, Teetotal, Thorough, Totally, Utter

Outback Backblocks, Bundu, The mulga

Outbreak Epidemic, Eruption, Explosion, Flare-up, Plague, Putsch, Rash, Recrudescence

Outburst Access, Blurt, Bluster, Boutade, Evoe, Explosion, Fit, Flaw, Furore, Fusillade, Gush, Gust, Paroxysm, Passion, Philippic, Salvo, Storm, Tantrum, Tumult, Volley

Outcast Cagot, Discard, Eta, Exile, Exul, Ishmael, Leper, Mesel, Pariah, Rogue

Outcome Aftermath, Consequence, Dénouement, Effect, Emergence, End, Event, Issue, → **RESULT**, Sequel, Upshot, Wash-up

Outcrop Basset, Blossom, Crag, Creston, Inlier, Mesa, Rognon, Spur, Tarpit

Outcry Alew, Bray, → **CLAMOUR**, Halloo, Howl, Hue, Humdudgeon, Protest, Racket, Shright, Steven, Uproar, Utas

Outdated, Out of date Archaic, Dinosaur, Effete, Feudal, Fossil, Horse and buggy, Obsolete, Old hat, Outmoded, Passé, Square

Outdo Beat, Best, Cap, Picnic, Surpass, Top, Trump, Worst

Outdoor(s) Alfresco, External, Garden, Open air, Plein-air

Outer External, Extrogenous, Magpie, Superficial, Top

Outfit(ter) Accoutrement, Catsuit, Ensemble, Equipage, Fitout, Furnish, Get-up, Haberdasher, Habit, Kit, Rig, Samfoo, Samfu, Strip, Suit, Team, Trousseau,

Weed(s), Whites

Outflank Overlap

Outflow Anticyclone, Discharge, Effluence, Eruption, Gorge, Issue, Surge

Outgoing Egression, Exiting, Extrovert, Open, Retiring

Outgrowth Ala(te), Aril, Bud, Caruncle, Enation, Epiphenomenon, Exostosis, Flagellum, Ligule, Offshoot, Osteophyte, Propagulum, Root-hair, Sequel, Strophiole, Trichome

Outhouse Lean to, Privy, Shed, Skilling, Skillion, Skipper, Stable

Outing Excursion, Jaunt, Junket, Picnic, Sortie, Spin, Spree, Treat, Trip, Wayzgoose

Outlandish Barbarous, Bizarre, Exotic, Foreign, Peregrine, Rum

Outlaw Allan-a-Dale, Attaint, Badman, Ban, Bandit(ti), Banish, Exile, Fugitive, Hereward, Horn, Jesse James, Proscribe, Put to the horn, Robin Hood, Rob Roy, Ronin, Tory, Waive

Outlay Cost, Expense, Mise

Outlet Débouché, Egress, Escape, Estuary, Exit, Femerall, Market, Opening, Orifice, Outfall, Overflow, Sluice, Socket, Spout, Tuyere, Tweer, Twier, Twire, Twyer(e), Vent

Outline Adumbration, Aperçu, Circumscribe, Configuration, Contorno, Contour, Delineate, Digest, → **DRAFT**, Esquisse, Footprint, Layout, Note, Perimeter, Plan, Profile, Prospectus, Relief, Scenario, Schematic, Shape, Silhouette, Skeletal, Skeleton, Sketch, Summary, Syllabus, Synopsis, T(h)alweg, Trace

Outlook Casement, Perspective, Prospect, View, Vista, Weltanschauung

Outmoded Wasm

▷ **Out of** *may indicate* an anagram

Out of date Corny, Obs, Passé, Scrap, Square, Worn

Out of form Amorphous, Awry

Out of order Fritz

Out of sorts Cachectic, Nohow, Peevish, Poorly

▷ **Out of sorts** *may indicate* an anagram

Out of tune Discordant, Flat, Scordato, Scordatura

Outpost Colony, Picquet

Outpour(ing) Effuse, Flood, Flow, Gush, Libation, Stream, Torrent

Output Data, Emanation, Get, Produce, Production, Turnout, Yield

▷ **Output** *may indicate* an anagram

Outrage(ous) Affront, Appal, Atrocity, Desecrate, Disgust, Egregious, Enorm(ity), Flagitious, Flagrant, Insult, OTT, Rich, Sacrilege, Scandal, Shocking, Ungodly, Unholy, Violate

▷ **Outrageously** *may indicate* an anagram

Outright Clean, Complete, Entire, Point-blank, Utter

Outset Beginning, Start

Outshine Eclipse, Excel, Overshadow, Surpass, Upstage

Outside Ab extra, Crust, Exterior, External, Extramural, Front, Furth, Hors, Periphery, Plein-air, Rim, Rind, Rine, Surface

Outsider Alien, Bolter, Bounder, Cad, Extern, Extremist, Foreigner, Incomer, Oustiti, Palagi, Pariah, Ring-in, Roughie, Stranger, Stumer, Unseeded, Upstart

Outsize Capacious, Giant, Gigantic, Huge, OS

Outskirts Edge, Fringe, Periphery, Purlieu

Outspoken Bluff, Blunt, Broad, Candid, Explicit, Forthright, Frank, Plain, Rabelaisian, Round, Vocal

Outstand(ing) Ace, Beaut(y), Belter, Billowing, Bulge, Chief, Egregious, Eminent, Especial, Exceptional, Extant, First, Fugleman, Highlight, Humdinger, Impasto, Jut,

Lulu, Marked, Matchless, Oner, Overdue, Owing, Paragon, Phenom(enal), Pièce de résistance, Prince, Prize, Prominent, Promontory, Prosilient, Protrude, Proud, Purler, Relief, Relievo, Salient, Signal, Special, Squarrose, Star, Stellar, Strout, Superb, Tour de force, Unpaid, Unsettled

Outstrip Best, Cap, Cote, Distance, Exceed, Overtake

Outward Efferent, Extern(e), External, Extrinsic, Extrorse, Extrovert, Posticous, Postliminary, Superficial

Outweigh Preponderate

Outwit Baffle, Best, Circumvent, Crossbite, Dish, Euchre, Fox, Outthink, Over-reach, → THWART, Trick

Outwork Demilune, Jetty, Moon, Tenail(le), Tenaillon

Outworn Decrepit, Obsolete, Used

Ouzel Ring, Water

Oval(s) Cartouche, Cassini, Ellipse, Henge, Navette, Obovate, Ooidal

Ovary Oophoron

Ovation Applause, Cheer, Standing

Oven(-like) Aga®, Calcar, Camp, Combination, Convection, Cul-de-four, Dutch, Electric, Furnace, Gas, Hangi, Haybox, Horn(it)o, Kiln, Lear, Leer, Lehr, Lime kiln, Maori, Microwave, Muffle, Norwegian, Oast, Oon, Stove, Umu

Over Above, Across, Again, Atop, C, Clear, Done, Finished, Hexad, Left, Maiden, Of, On, Ore, Ort, Owre, Sopra, Spare, Superior, Surplus, Through, Uber, Wicket maiden, Yon

Overact Burlesque, Emote, Ham, Hell, Hoke

Overactive Hyper

Overall(s) Boiler suit, Chaps, Denims, Dungarees, Dust-coat, Fatigues, Jumper, Smicket, Smock, Tablier, Workwear

Overbearing Arrogant, Dogmatic, Domineering, High-muck-a-muck, Imperious, Insolent, Lordly

Overbid Gazump

Overcast Cloudy, Lowering, Sew, Sombre

Overcharge Clip, Extort, Fleece, Gyp, OC, Rack-rent, Rook, Rush, Soak, Sting

Overcoat Balmacaan, Benjamin, Benny, British warm, Chesterfield, → COAT, Crombie, Dolman, Grego, Inverness, Joseph, Paletot, Petersham, Pos(h)teen, Prince Albert, Raglan, Redingote, Spencer, Surtout, Tabard, Taglioni, Ulster, Warm, Wooden, Wrap-rascal

Overcome Beat, Bested, Conquer, Convince, Defeat, Hit for six, Kill, Master, Mither, Moider, Moither, Prevail, Quell, Speechless, Stun, Subdue, Subjugate, Superate, Surmount, Vanquish, Win

Overcrowd Congest, Jam, Pack

Overdo(ne) Exceed, Ham, Hokey, Hokum, OTT, Percoct, Tire

Overdose OD

Overdraft Red

▷ **Overdrawn** *may indicate* 'red' outside another word

Overdress(ing) Dudism, Flossy, Overall

Overdue Behindhand, Belated, Excessive, Late

Overeat(ing) Binge, Gorge, Hypertrophy, Pig out, Satiate

Overemphasize Rub in, Stress

Overfeed Gorge, Sate, Stuff

Overflow(ing) Abrim, Lip, Nappe, Ooze, Ream, Redound, Spillage, Surfeit, Teem

Overfull Brimming, Hept

Overgrow(n) Ivy'd, Jungle, Ramp(ant), Rank, Rhinophyma

Overhang(ing) Beetle, Bulge, Cornice, → JUT, Project, Shelvy
Overhaul Bump, Catch, Overtake, Recondition, Revision, Service, Strip
Overhead(s) Above, Aloft, Ceiling, Cost, Exes, Hair(s), Headgear, Oncost, Rafter, Upkeep, Zenith
Overhear Catch, Eavesdrop, Tap
Overheat Enrage
Overindulge(nt) Crapulent, Crass, Dissipated, Dissolute, Pig
Overjoy Elate, Thrill
Overland Portage
Overlap(ping) Correspond, Equitant, Imbricate, Incubous, Kern(e), Limbous, Obvolute, Stretto, Tace, Tasse
Overlay Ceil, Smother, Stucco, Superimpose, Veneer
Overlearned Pedantic
Overload Burden, Plaster, Strain, Surcharge, Tax
Overlook Condone, Disregard, Excuse, Forget, Miss, Pretermit, Superintend, Waive
Overlord Edwin, Excess, Invasion
Overlying Incumbent, Jessant, Pressing
Overmuch Excessive, Surplus, Too, Undue
Overplay Ham, Hoke
Overpower(ing) Crush, Evince, Mighty, Onerous, Oppress, Overwhelm, Subdue, Surmount, Swelter, Whelm
Overpraise Adulate
Over-refined Dainty, Nice, Pernickety, Precious
Override, Overrule Abrogate, Disallow, Outweigh, Reverse, Talk down, Veto
Overrun Exceed, Extra, Infest, Inundate, Invade, Swarm, Teem
Overseas Abroad, Colonial, Outremer, Transmarine, Ultramarine
Oversee(r) Baas, Boss, Captain, Care, Deputy, Direct, Eyebrow, Foreman, Forewoman, Grieve, Handle, Induna, Moderator, Periscope, Steward, Supercargo, Survey(or)
Oversentimental Byronic, Slushy
Overshadow(ed) Cloud, Dominate, Eclipse, Obscure, Outclass, Umbraculate
Overshoe Arctic, Galosh, Sandal, Snowboot
Oversight Blunder, Care, Error, Gaffe, Lapse, Neglect, Parablepsis
Overstate(ment) Embroider, Exaggerate, Hyperbole
Overstrained Epitonic
Overt Manifest, Patent, Plain, Public
Overtake Catch, For(e)hent, Lap, Leapfrog, Overget, Overhaul, → PASS, Supersede, Usurp
Overthrow Dash, Defeat, Demolish, Depose, Down, Labefact(at)ion, Ruin, Smite, Stonker, Subvert, Supplant, Topple, Unhorse, Usurp, Vanquish, Whemmle, Whommle, Whummle, Worst
Overture Advance, Carnival, Concert, Egmont, French, Hebrides, Intro, Italian, Leonora, Offer, → OPENING, Prelude, Propose, Sinfonia, Toccata, Toccatella, Toccatina
Overturn(ing) Catastrophe, Coup, Cowp, Engulf, Quash, Reverse, Tip, Topple, Up(set), Upend, Whemmle
Overvalue Exaggerate, Salt
Overweening Bashaw, Cocky, Excessive, Imperious, Presumptuous
Overweight Sunk
Overwhelm(ed), Overwhelming Accablé, Assail, → CRUSH, Defeat, Deluge, Engulf, Flabbergast, Foudroyant, Inundate, KO, Mind-boggling, Oppress,

Overcome, Scupper, Smother, Submerge, Swamp, Whup

Overwork(ed) Fag, Hackneyed, Ornament, Slog, Stale, Supererogation, Tax, Tire, Toil

Overwrought Frantic, Hysterical, Ore-rested, Ornate, Rococo

Ovid Naso

Ovum Egg, Oosphere, Seed

Owe(d), Owing Attribute, Due, OD

Owen Glendower

Owl(s) African, Barn, Barred, Blinker, Boobook, Brown, Bubo, Bunter, Chinese, Eagle, Elegant, English, Fish, Glimmergowk, Hawk, Hoo(ter), Horned, Howlet, Jenny, Little, Long-eared, Longhorn, Madge, Moper, Mopoke, Mopus, Night, Ogle, Parliament, Ruru, Saw-whet, Scops, Screech, Sea, Snowy, Strich, Striges, Strigiformes, Tawny, Wood

Own(er), Owning, Ownership Admit, Agnise, Confess, Domain, Dominium, Fess, Have, Hold, Mortmain, Nain, Of, Personal, Possess, Proper, Proprietor, Recognise, Reputed, Title, Use

Ox(en) Anoa, Aquinas, Aurochs, Banteng, Banting, Bison, Bonas(s)us, Buffalo, Bugle, Bullock, Cat(t)alo, Fee, Gaur, Gayal, Gyal, Kouprey, Mart, Musk, Musk-sheep, Neat, Ovibos, Rother, Saola, Sapi-utan, S(e)ladang, Steare, Steer, Stirk, Taurus, Ure, Urus, Water, Water buffalo, Yak, Yoke, Zebu, Z(h)o

Oxford (group) Buchmanism, OU, Puseyism, Shoe

Oxhead Aleph

Oxidation, Oxide Alumina, Anatase, Ceria, Erbium, Eremacausis, Gothite, Gummite, Holmia, Kernite, Lithia, Magnesia, Nitrous, Psilomelane, Quicklime, Red lead, Rutile, Samarskite, Strontia, Thoria, Zaffer, Zaffre

▷ **Oxtail** *may indicate* 'x'

Oxygen (and lack of) Anoxia, Epoxy, Liquid, Lox, Loxygen, O, Vital air

Oyer Hearing, Trial

Oyster (bed), Oyster disease, Oyster-eater Avicula, Bivalve, Bonamia, Bush, Cul(t)ch, Kentish, Lay, Mollusc, Native, Ostrea, Ostreophage, Pandore, Pearl, Plant, Prairie, Salsify, Scalp, Scaup, Seed(ling), Spat, Spondyl, Stew, Vegetable

Oyster-catcher Sea-pie

Oyster-plant Gromwell, Salsify

Oz Amos, Australia

Ozone Air, Atmosphere, Oxygen

Pp

P Papa, Parking, Penny, Piano, Prince

PA Aide, Tannoy

Pabulum Aliment, Cheer, Food, Fuel, Nourishment

Pace, Pacemaker Canter, Clip, Cracking, Dog-trot, Easter, Gait, Geometric, Heel and toe, Jog-trot, Lope, Measure, Military, Pari passu, Pioneer, → **RATE**, Roman, Scout's, Snail's, Spank, Speed, Step, Stride, Stroll, Tempo, Tramp, Tread, Trot

Pachyderm Armadillo, Elephant, Hippo, Mastodon, Rhino

Pacific, Pacify Appease, Bromide, Conciliate, Dove, Ease, Irenic, Lull, Mild, Moderate, Ocean, Placate, Placid, Quiet, Serene, Soothe, Subdue, Sweeten, Tranquil

Pacifist CO, Conciliator, D(o)ukhobor, Dove, Peacenik

Pack(age), Packed, Packing Back, Bale, Blister, Bobbery, Box, Bubble, Bundle, Cards, Cold, Compress, Congest, Cram, Crate, Crowd, Cry, Deck, Dense, Dunnage, Embox, Entity, Everest, Excelsior, Face, Fardel, Floe, Gasket, Gaskin, Glut, Hamper, Hunt, Ice, Jam, Kennel, Knapsack, Load, Matilda, Naughty, Pair, → **PARCEL**, Pikau, Power, Pun, Rout, Rucksack, Set, Shiralee, Shrink-wrap, Steeve, Stow, Suits, Sumpter, Tamp, Tread, Troop, Truss, Wad, Wet, Wolf, Wrap

Packet Boat, Bundle, Deck, Liner, Mailboat, Mint, Parcel, Pay, Red, Roll, Sachet, Steam, Steamboat, Wage

Pack-horse Sumpter

Packman Chapman, Hawker, Hiker, Pedlar, Tinker

Pact Agreement, Alliance, Bargain, Bilateral, Cartel, Contract, Covenant, Locarno, Munich, Stability, Suicide, → **TREATY**, Warsaw

Pad(ding) Batting, Bombast, Brake, Bustle, Compress, Condo, Crash, Cushion, Dabber, Damper, Dossil, Enswathe, Expand, Falsies, Filler, Flat, Frog, Gumshield, Hard, Hassock, Horse, Ink, Launch, Leg-guard, Lily, Nag, Note, Numnah, Patch, Paw, Ped, Pillow, Pincushion, Plastron, Pledget, Plumper, Pouf(fe), Protract, Pudding, Puff, Pulvillus, Pulvinar, Scratch, Shoulder, Stamp, Stuff, Sunk, Swab, Tablet, Thief, Touch, Tournure, Tylopod, Tympan, Velour(s), Velure, Wad, Wase, Writing

Paddington Bear, Station

Paddle, Paddle boat, Paddle-foot Canoe, Dabble, Doggy, Oar, Pinniped, Row, Seal, Side-wheel, Spank, Splash, Stern-wheeler, Wade

Paddock Field, Frog, Holding, Meadow, Park, Sacrifice

Paddy, Paddy field Fury, Ire, Irishman, Mick, Pat(rick), Pet, Rag, Rage, Sawah, Tantrum, Temper, Wax

Padre Chaplain, Cleric, Father, Monk, Priest

Paean Hymn, Ode, Praise, Psalm

Paedophile Nonce

Pagan Animist, Atheist, Gentile, Gentoo, Godless, Heathen, Idolater, Infidel, Odinist, Paynim, Saracen

Page(s), Pageboy Back, Bellboy, Bellhop, Bleep, Boy, Buttons, Callboy, Centrefold,
Flyleaf, Folio, Foolscap, Front, Gate-fold, Groom, Haircut, Hairdo, Home,
Hornbook, Leaf, Master, Messenger, Moth, Octavo, Op-ed, P, Pane, PP, Problem,
Quarto, Ream, Recto, Ro, Servant, Sheet, Side, Splash, Squire, Tear sheet, Tiger,
Title, Varlet, Verso, Web, Yellow
Pageant Antique, Cavalcade, Pomp, Spectacle, Tattoo, Triumph
Pagoda Anking, Anqing, Temple, To
Pah Pish, Tush, Umph
▶ **Paid** *see* **PAY**
Pail Bucket, Kettle, Leglan, Leglen, Leglin, Piggin, Slop
Pain(ful), Pains Ache, Aggrieve, Agony, Ake, Algesis, Angina, Anguish, Arthralgia,
Bad, Bale, Bedsore, Bitter, Bore, Bot(t), Bother, Burn, Causalgia, Colic, Cramp, Crick,
Distress, Dole, Doleur, Dolour, Dool(e), Dysmenorhoea, Dysury, Eina, Excruciating,
Fibrositis, Gastralgia, Gip, Grief, Gripe, Growing, Gyp, Harrow, Heartburn,
Hemialgia, → **HURT**, Ill, Kink, Laborious, Lumbago, Mal, Mastalgia, Mastodynia,
Metralgia, Migraine, Misery, Mulligrubs, Myalgia, Neuralgia, Nociceptive, Pang,
Persuant, Pest, Phantom, Pleurodynia, Prick, Pungent, Rack, Raw, Referred, Sair,
Sciatica, Smart, Sore, Sorrow, Splitting, Sten(d), Sting, Stitch, Strangury, Stung,
Teen(e), Tene, Throe, Topalgia, Torment, Tormina, Torture, Travail, Twinge, Wo(e),
Wrench, Wring
▷ **Pain** *may indicate* bread (French)
Painkiller Aminobutene, Analgesic, Bute, Cocaine, Distalgesic, Endorphin,
Enkephalin, Jadeite, Meperidine, Metopon, Morphine, Number, Pethidine
Painless(ness) Analgesia, Easy
Painstaking Assiduous, Careful, Diligent, Elaborate, Exacting, Meticulous,
Sedulous, Studious, Thorough
Paint(ed), Painting Abstract, Abstract expressionism, Acrylic, Action, Airbrush,
Alla prima, Aquarelle, Arcimboldo, Art autre, Art deco, Artificial, Art nouveau, Ash
Can School, Barbizon, Battlepiece, Bice, Blottesque, Camaieu, Canvas, Cellulose,
Chiaroscuro, Clair-obscure, Clobber, Coat, Colour, Cubism, Dadaism, Daub,
Dayglo, Decorate, Depict, Describe, Diptych, Distemper, Duco, Eggshell, Emulsion,
Enamel, Encaustic, Fard, Fauvism, Finery, Finger, Flatting, Flemish, Fore-edge,
Fresco, Fucus, Genre, Gild, Gloss, Gouache, Gravure, Grease, Grisaille, Hard-edge,
Historical, Icon, Impasto, Impressionism, Intimism(e), Intonaco, Intumescent,
Lead, Limn, Luminous, Magilp, Matt, Megilp, Mehndi, Miniate, Miniature,
Modello, Mona Lisa, Monotint, Mural, Naive, Neo-Impressionism, Neo-Plasticism,
Nightpiece, Nihonga, Nocturne, Non-drip, Oaker, Ochre, Oil, Old Master,
Oleo(graph), Op art, Orphism, Paysage, Pentimento, Pict, Picture, Pigment, Pinxit,
Plein air, Pointillism(e), Portray, Poster, Post-Impressionism, Predella', Primitive,
Quadratura, Raddle, Rag-rolling, Rosemaling, Roughstuff, Sand, Scenography,
Scumble, Secco, Sfumato, Sien(n)ese, Skyscape, Spray, Stencil, Stereochrome, Still
life, Stipple, Suprematism, Tablature, Tachism(e), Tag, Tall-oil, Tanka, Tempera,
Tenebrism, Thangka, Tondo, Ukiyo-e, Umber, Umbrian, Undercoat, Underglaze,
Vanitas, Veduta, Vorticism, War, Wax
Painted woman Courtesan, Harlot, Pict, Tart
Painter(s) Animalier, → **ARTIST**, Ash Can School, Colourist, Cubist, Decorator,
Gilder, Illusionist, Impressionist, Limner, Little Master, Miniaturist, Old Master,
Paysagist, Plein-airist, Primitive, Sien(n)ese, Soutine, Sunday
Pair(ing) Brace, Cooper, Couple(t), Duad, Duo, Dyad(ic), Exciton, Fellows,
Geminate, Item, Jugate, Jumelle, Link, Lone, Match, Mate, Minimal, Ocrea,
Pigeon, Pr, Span, Spouses, Synapsis, Syndyasmian, Syzygy, Tandem, Thummim,

Twa(e), Tway, Two, Urim, Yoke
Paisley Ian, Orange, Shawl
Pakistan(i) Pathan
Pal Ally, Amigo, Bud(dy), China, Chum, Comrade, Crony, Cully, Friend, Mate, Wus(s)
Palace Alcazar, Alhambra, Basilica, Blenheim, Buckingham, Court, Crystal, Edo, Élysée, Escorial, Escurial, Fontainebleau, Forbidden City, Fulham, Gin, Goslar, Holyrood, Holyroodhouse, Hotel, Istana, Lambeth, Lateran, Linlithgow, Louvre, Mansion, Nonsuch, Palatine, Picture, Pitti, Pushkin, Quirinal, St James's, Sans Souci, Schloss, Seraglio, Serail, Shushan, Topkapi, Trianon, Tuileries, Valhalla, Vatican, Versailles
Paladin Champion, Charlemagne, Defender, Douzeper, Fièrabras, Ganelon, → KNIGHT, Ogier, Oliver, Orlando, Rinaldo, Roland
Palanquin Doolie, Kago, Litter, Palkee, Palki, Sedan
Palatable, Palatalized, Palate Cleft, Dainty, Hard, Mouille, Relish, Roof, Sapid, Savoury, Soft, Taste, Toothsome, Uranic, Uraniscus, Uvula, Velum
Palatial Ornate, Splendid
Palatinate, Palatine Officer, Pfalz
Palaver Chatter, Debate, Parley, Powwow, → TALK
Pale, Paling Ashen, Blanch, Bleach, Cere, Dim, English, Etiolate(d), Fade, → FAINT, Fence, Ghostly, Haggard, Insipid, Jewish, Lily (white), Livid, Mealy, Ox-fence, Pallescent, Pastel, Peaky, Peelie-wally, Picket, Sallow, Shilpit, Stang, Verge, Wan, Whey-faced, White, Wishy-washy
Paleography Diplomatics
Pal(a)eolithic Acheulean, Acheulian, Azilian, Chellean, Gravettian, Levallois(ian), Lower, Madelenian, Magdalenian, Middle, Neanderthal, Perigordian, Solutrean, Strepyan, Upper
Paleozoic Permian, Silurian
Palestine, Palestinian Amorite, Fatah, Gadarene, Intifada, Israel, Pal, Per(a)ea, PLO, Samaria
Palette Board, Cokuloris
Palindrome, Palindromic Cancrine, Sotadic
Palisade Barrier, Fence, Fraise, Stacket, Stockade
Pall Bore, Cloy, Curtain, Damper, Glut, Mantle, Mortcloth, Satiate, Shroud
Palladium Defence, Pd, Safeguard
Pallas Athene
Pallet Bed, Cot, Couch, Mattress, Tick
Palliate, Palliative Alleviate, Anetic, Ease, Extenuate, Lessen, Mitigate, Reduce, Relieve, Sedative
Pallid Anaemic, Ashen, Insipid, Pale, Wan, Waxy
Palm Accolade, Areca, Assai, Atap, Babassu, Bangalow, Betel, Buriti, Burrawang, Bussu, Cabbage, Calamus, Carna(h)uba, Chamaerops, Chiqui-chiqui, Coco, Cohune, Conceal, Coquito, Corozo, Corypha, Cycad, Date (tree), Doom, Doum, Elaeis, Euterpe, Fan, Feather, Fob, Foist, Gomuti, Gomuto, Groo-groo, Gru-gru, Hand, Ita, Itching, Ivory, Jip(p)i-Jap(p)a, Jipyapa, Jupati, Kentia, Kittul, Laurels, Loof, Looves, Macahuba, Macaw, Macoya, Moriche, Nikau, Nipa, Oil, Palmyra, Paxiuba, Peach, Pupunha, Raffia, Raphia, Rat(t)an, Royal, Sabal, Sago, Saw palmetto, Sugar, Talipat, Talipot, Thatch, Thenar, Toddy, Triumph, Troelie, Troolie, Trooly, Trophy, Vola, Washingtonia, Wax, Wine, Zamia
Palmer Lilli, Pilgrim
Palmerston Pam
Palmistry Ch(e)irognomy

Palm-leaf Frond
Palpable Evident, Gross, Manifest, Patent, Plain, Tangible
Palpitate, Palpitation Flutter, Pitpat, Pulsate, Throb, Twitter, Vibrate
Palsy Bell's, Cerebral, Paralysis, Shakes
Paltry Bald, Cheap, Exiguous, Mean, Measly, Peanuts, Pelting, Petty, Poor, Puny,
    Scald, Scalled, Shoestring, Sorry, Tin(-pot), Tinny, Trashy, Trifling, Two-bit, Vile,
    Waff, Whiffet
Pamper(ed) Cocker, Coddle, Cosher, Cosset, Cuiter, Feather-bed, Gratify, High-fed,
    → INDULGE, Mollycoddle, Overfeed, Pet, Pompey, Spoon-fed
Pamphlet Brochure, Catalogue, Chapbook, Leaflet, Notice, Sheet, Tract
Pan Agree, Auld Hornie, Bainmarie, Balit, Basin, Betel(-pepper), Braincase, Chafer,
    Dent, Dial, Drip, Dripping, Goat-god, Goblet, God, Hard, Ice-floe, Iron, Karahi,
    Ladle, Lavatory, Muffin, Nature-god, Oil, Pancheon, Panchion, Patella, Patina,
    Peter, Poacher, Preserving, Prospect, Roast, Salt, Search, Skid, Skillet, Slag, Slate,
    Spider, Vessel, Warming, Wo(c)k, Work
Panacea All-heal, Azoth, Catholicon, Cure(-all), Elixir, Ginseng, Parkleaves,
    Remedy, Tutsan
Panache Bravura, Crest, Dash, Flair, Paz(z)azz, Piz(z)azz, Plume, Pzazz, Show,
    Talent
Pancake Blin(i), Blintz(e), Burrito, Crêpe (suzette), Crumpet, Drop(ped)-scone,
    Flam(m), Flapjack, Flaune, Flawn, Fraise, Fritter, Froise, Latke, Pikelet, Poppadum,
    Potato, Quesadilla, Scotch, Slapjack, Spring roll, Suzette, Taco, Tortilla, Tostada,
    Waffle
Pancreas Isles of Langerhans, Sweetbread
Panda Bear-cat, Chi-chi, Chitwah, Common, Giant, Lesser, Red
Pandarus Go-between
Pandemonium Inferno, Uproar
Pander Broker, Indulge, Pimp, Procurer, Toady
Pane Glass, Light, Panel, Quarrel, Quarry, Sheet
Panegyric Encomium, Eulogy, Laudation, Praise, Tribute
Panel(ling) Adoption, Array, Board, Cartouche, Children's, Control, Dashboard,
    Fa(s)cia, Gore, Hatchment, Inset, Instrument, Jury, Lacunar, Mandorla, Mimic,
    Mola, Orb, Patch(board), People's, Reredorse, Reredos(se), Rocker, Screen, Skreen,
    Solar, Stile, Stomacher, Table, Tablet, Valance, Volet, Wainscot
Pang Achage, Ache, Crick, Qualm, Spasm, Stab, Stound, Twinge, Wrench
Pangloss Optimist
Pangolin Ant-eater, Manis
Panhandle(r) Beggar, W. Virginia
Panic Alar(u)m, Amaze, Consternation, Fear, Flap, Flat-spin, Flip, Fright, Funk,
    Guinea-grass, Lather, Millet, Raggee, Raggy, Ragi, Sauve qui peut, → SCARE,
    Scarre, Stampede, Stampedo, State, Stew, Tailspin, → TERROR
Panicle Thyrse
Panjandrum Bashaw
Pannier Basket, Cacolet, Corbeil, Dosser, Saddlebag, Skip, Whisket
Panoply Armour, Array, Pomp
Panorama, Panoramic Cyclorama, Range, Scenery, Veduta, View, Vista
Pansy Gay, Heart's-ease, Herb-trinity, Kiss-me-quick, Nance, Powder-puff, Queer,
    Viola
Pant(s) Bags, Breeches, Capri, Cargo, Chaps, Chinos, Culottes, Deck, Dhoti,
    Drawers, Fatigues, Flaff, Gasp, Gaucho, Harem, Hot, Long johns, Longs, Parachute,
    Pech, Pedal-pushers, Pegh, Puff, Ski, Slacks, Smalls, Stovepipe, Sweat, Throb,

Toreador, Training, Trews, Trousers, Wheeze, Yearn
Pantaloon Columbine, Dupe, Pants
Pantheism Idolatry, Immanency
Panther Bagheera, Black, Cat, Cougar, Grey, Jaguar, Leopard, Pink
Panties Briefs, Knickers, Scanties, Step-ins, Undies
Pantomime, Pantomime character Aladdin, Charade, Cheironomy, Dumb-show,
  Farce, Galanty, Harlequinade, Pierrot, Play
Pantry Buttery, Closet, Larder, Spence, Stillroom
Pap Dug, Mealie, Mush, Nipple, Teat, Udder
Papal, Papist Catholic, Clementine, Concordat, Guelf, Guelph, Legation, Pontifical,
  RC, Roman, Vatican
Paper(s), Paperwork, Papery Allonge, Antiquarian, Art, Atlas, Ballot, Baryta,
  Bible, Blotting, Bond, Brief, Broadsheet, Broadside, Bromide, Brown, Building,
  Bumf, Bumph, Butter, Cap, Carbon, Cartridge, Cellophane®, Chad, Chinese,
  Chiyogami, Cigarette, Colombier, Command, Commercial, Confetti, Corrugated,
  Cream-laid, Cream-wove, Credentials, Crêpe, Crown, Cutch, Daily, Decorate,
  Demy, Document, Dossier, Eggshell, Elephant, Emery, Emperor, Essay, Exam, File,
  Filter, Final, Flock, Folio, Foolscap, Fourdrinier, FT, Funny, Galley, Garnet, Gazette,
  Gem, Glass(ine), Glumaceous, Government, Grand eagle, Grand Jesus, Graph,
  Greaseproof, Green, Guardian, Hieratica, Imperial, India, Japanese, Jesus, Journal,
  Kent cap, Kraft, Kutch, Lace, Laid, Lavatory, Legal cap, Linen, Litmus, Manifold,
  Manil(l)a, Marble, Mercantile, Mirror, MS, Munimenti, Music(-demy), Needle,
  News(print), Note, Notelet, Oil, Onion-skin, Order, Packing, Pad, Page, Papillote,
  Papyrus, Parchment, Pickwick, Plotting, Position, Post, Pot(t), Pravda, Press, Print,
  Printing, Quair, Quarto, Quire, Rag, Ramee, Rami(e), Ream, Retree, Rhea, Rice,
  Rolled, Rolling, Royal, Safety, Satin, Saxe, Scent, Scotsman, Scrip, Scroll, Scrowl,
  Sheaf, Sheet, Ship's, Silver, Skin, Slipsheet, Spoilt, Stamp, Starch, State, Sugar,
  Sun, Tabloid, Taffeta, Tap(p)a, Tar, TES, Test, Thesis, Thread, Tiger, Tissue, Today,
  Toilet, Torchon, Touch, Tracing, Trade, Transfer, Treatise, Treeware, Turmeric,
  Two-name, Vellum, Velvet, Voucher, Walking, Wall, Waste, Watch, Wax(ed),
  Web, Whatman®, White, Willesden, Wood(chip), Woodfree, Worksheet, Wove,
  Wrapping, Writing, Zine
Paperback Limp(back)
Paper-cutting, Paper-folding Decoupage, Kirigami, Origami, Psaligraphy
Papier-mâché Carton-pierre, Flong
Paprika Spanish
Par Average, Equate, Equivalent, → **NORMAL**, Scratch
Parable Allegory, Fable, Proverb
Parabola Arc, Curve, Hyperbola
Parachute, Parachutist Aeroshell, Aigrette, Brake, Drag, Drogue, Extraction, Float,
  Golden, Jump, Pack, Pappus, Para, Parabrake, Parapente, Red Devil, Ribbon, Silk,
  Sky-diving, Skyman, Thistledown, Umbrella
Parade (ground) Air, Arcade, Cavalcade, Church, Concours d'élégance, Display,
  Dress, Drill, Easter, Emu, Flaunt, Gala, Hit, Identification, Identity, Line-up,
  Maidan, March-past, Monkey-run, Pageantry, Passing-out, Pomp, Procession,
  Prom(enade), Sashay, Show, Sick, Stand-to, Ticker tape, Troop
Paradise Arcadia, Avalon, Bliss, Eden, Elysium, Fool's, Garden,
  Happy-hunting-ground, Heaven, Lost, Malaguetta, Nirvana, Park, Regained,
  Shangri-la, Svarga, Swarga, Swerga, → **UTOPIA**
Paradox(ical) Absurdity, Albers', Cantor's, Contradiction, Dilemma, Electra,
  French, Gilbertian, Hydrostatic, Koan, Liar, Puzzle, Russell's, Sorites, Twin, Zeno's

Paraffin Earthwax, Kerosene, Kerosine, Liquid, Ozocerite, Ozokerite, Photogen(e), Propane
Paragon Model, Non(e)such, Pattern, Pearl, Phoenix, Role model, Rose
Paragraph (mark) Balaam, Causerie, Note, Passage, Piece, Pilcrow
Parakeet Parrot, Popinjay, Rosella
Parallax Annual, Daily, Diurnal, Geocentric, Heliocentric
Parallel Analog, Collimate, Corresponding, Equal, Even, Forty-ninth, Like
Parallelogram Rhomb
Paralysis, Paralyse Apoplexy, Cataplexy, Catatonia, Cramp, Curarise, Cycloplegia, Diplegia, Halt, Hemiplegia, Infantile, Lithyrism, Monoplegia, Numbness, Palsy, Paraplegia, Paresis, Polio, Quadriplegia, Radial, Scram, Shock, Shut, Spastic, Spina bifida, Stun, Torpefy
Paramedic Ambulance-man
Paramilitary Phalangist, SAS, Sena, UDA
Paramount Chief, Dominant, Greatest, Overall, Premier, → SUPREME, Topless, Utmost
Paramour Beau, Franion, Gallant, Leman, Lover, Mistress, Thais
Paranormal Clairvoyant, ESP, Spiritual, Telekinesis
Parapet (space) Barbette, Bartisan, Bartizan, Battlement, Breastwork, Brisure, Bulwark, Crenel, Flèche, Machicolation, Merlon, Rampart, Redan, Surtout, Terreplein, Top, Wall
Paraphernalia Belongings, Equipment, Gear, Trappings
Parasite, Parasitic Ascarid, Autoecious, Aweto, Babesiasis, Bilharzia, Biogenous, Biotroph, Bladder-worm, Bloodsucker, Bonamia, Bot, Candida, Chalcid, Coccus, Conk, Copepod, Crab-louse, Cryptosporidium, Cryptozoite, Dodder, Ectophyte, Endamoeba, Endophyte, Entophyte, Entozoon, Epiphyte, Epizoon, Facultative, Filarium, Flatworm, Flea, Gapeworm, Giardia, Gregarinida, Haematozoon, Hair-eel, Heartworm, Heteroecious, Hook-worm, Ichneumon, Inquiline, Isopod, Kade, Ked, Lackey, Lamprey, Leech, Leishmania, Licktrencher, Liverfluke, Louse, Lungworm, Macdonald, Mallophagous, Measle, Mistletoe, Monogenean, Necrotroph, Nematode, Nit, Obligate, Orobanche, Pinworm, Plasmodium, Puccinia, Pulix, Rafflesia, Redia, Rhipidoptera, Rickettsia, Root, Roundworm, Schistosoma, Scrounger, Shark, Smut-fungus, Sponge(r), Sporozoa(n), Strepsiptera, Strongyle, Strongyloid, Stylops, Sucker, Symphile, Tapeworm, Tick, Toady, Toxoplasma, Trematode, Trencher-friend, Trencher-knight, Trichina, Trichomonad, Tryp(anosoma), Vampire, Viscum, Wheatworm, Whipworm, Worms
Parasol Awning, Brolly, En tout cas, Sunshade, Umbrella
Paratrooper Skyman
Parcel Allocate, Allot, Aret, Bale, Bundle, Holding, Lot, Package, Packet, Sort, Wrap
Parch(ed) Arid, Bake, Dry, Graddan, Hot coppers, Roast, Scorched, Sere, Thirsty, Toast, Torrid
Parchment Diploma, Forel, Mezuzah, Panel, Papyrus, Pell, Pergameneous, Roll, Roule, Scroll, Sheepskin, Vegetable, Vellum, Virgin
Pard Leopard, Pal, Partner
Pardon(able), Pardoner Absolve, Amnesty, Anan, Assoil, Clear, Condone, Eh, Excuse, → FORGIVE, Grace, Mercy, Quaestionary, Qu(a)estor, Release, Remission, Remit, Reprieve, Venial, What
Pare Flaught, Flay, Peel, Shave, Skive, Sliver, Strip, Whittle
Parent(al) Ancestral, Father, Forebear, Genitor, Maternal, Mother, Paternal, Single, Storge

Parenthesis Aside, Brackets, Innuendo
Parhelion Sun-dog
Pariah Ishmael, Leper, Outcast, Pi(e)dog, Pyedog
Paris(ian), Parisienne Abductor, Athene, Elle, Gai, Gay, Grisette, Lutetia (Parisiorum), Lutetian, Maillotin, Midinette, Trojan
Parish Charge, District, Flock, Kirkto(w)n, Parischan(e), Parishen, Parochin(e), Peculiar, Province, Title
Parity Smithsonian
Park(ing) Algonquin, Alton Towers, Amusement, Banff National, Battery, Brecon Beacons, Business, Car, Caravan, Common, Country, Daintree, Dales, Dartmoor, Death Valley, Disneyland, Egmont National, Enclosure, Etosha, Everglades, Exmoor, Fiordland, Forest, Fun, Game, Garage, Gardens, Grand Canyon, Green, Green lung, Grounds, Hwange, Hyde, Industrial, Jasper, Jasper National, Jurassic, Kakadu, Kalahari Gemsbok, Katmai, Kejionkujik, Kobuk Valley, Kruger, Lake District, Lamington, Lassen Volcanic, Lung, Mammoth Cave, Mansfield, Mesa Verde, Motor, Mount Aspiring, Mount Kenya National, Mount McKinley, Mount Rainier, Mungo, Nahanni National, Nairobi, National, Northumberland, Osterley, Oyster, P, Paradise, Peak District, Phoenix, Pitch, Pittie-ward, Prater, Preserve, Rec, Regent's, Riding Mountain, Safari, Sanctuary, Sandown, Science, Sequoia, Sequoia National, Serengeti, Shenandoah National, Siding, Snowdonia, Stand, Stop, Technology, Theme, Trailer, Tsavo, Valet, Wildlife, Wind, Wood Buffalo, Yard, Yellowstone, Yosemite
Parka Atigi
Parker Dorothy, Nos(e)y
Parkleaves Tutsan
Parley Confer, Discourse, Palaver, Speak, Tret
Parliament Addled, Althing, Barebones, Black, Boule, Bundestag, Commons, Congress, Cortes, Council, Cross-bench, Dail, Diet, D(o)uma, Drunken, Eduskunta, European, Folketing, House, Imperial, Knesset, Lack-learning, Lagt(h)ing, Landst(h)ing, Lawless, Legislature, Lok Sabha, Long, Lords, Majlis, Merciless, Mongrel, Odelst(h)ing, Political, Rajya Sabha, Reichsrat, Reichstag, Riksdag, Rump, St Stephens, Sanhedrin, Seanad, Seanad Éireann, Sejm, Short, Stannary, States-general, Stirthing, Stormont, Stort(h)ing, The Beehive, Thing, Tynwald, Tynwald (Court), Unicameral, Unlearned, Useless, Vidhan Sabha, Volkskammer, Volksraad, Westminster
Parliamentarian Cabinet, Fairfax, Ireton, Leveller, Member, MP, Roundhead, Whip
Parlour Beauty, Funeral, Ice-cream, Lounge, Massage, Milking, Salon, Snug, Spence
Parnassus Museum, Verse
Parochial Insular
Parody Burlesque, Cod, Lampoon, Mock, Piss-take, Satire, Send-up, Skit, Spoof, Travesty
Parole Pledge, Promise, Trust, Word
Paronychia Agnail, Felon, Whitlow
Paroxysm Fit, Frenzy, Rapture, Spasm, Subintrant, Throe
Parricide Cenci
Parrot Amazon, Cockatoo, Conure, Copy, Flint, Green leek, Grey, Imitate, Kaka(po), Kea, Lorikeet, Lory, Lovebird, Macaw, Mimic, Nestor, Owl, Parakeet, Paroquet, Poll(y), Popinjay, Psittacine, Quarrion, Repeat, Rosella, Rote, Shell, Stri(n)gops, T(o)uraco
Parrot-bill Glory-pea
Parry Block, Counter, Defend, Dodge, Forestall, Parade, Riposte, Sixte,

Tac-au-tac, Thwart, Ward
Parsee Zoroastrian
Parsimonious, Parsimony Aberdonian, Cheese-paring, Mean, Narrow, Near(ness), Niggardly, Stingy, Tight
Parsley Apiol, Cicely, Dog, Kecks, Kex, Persillade, Pot-herb
Parsnip Buttered, Buttery, Dill, Masterwort, Sium, Skirret
Parson Clergyman, Cleric, Minister, Non juror, Pastor, Priest, Rector, Rev, Sky-pilot, Soul-curer, Yorick
Parsonage Glebe, Manse, Rectory, Vicarage
Part(s), Parting Accession, Aliquot, Antimere, Area, Aught, Bulk, Bye, Cameo, Character, Chunk, Cog, Component, Constituent, Crack, Cue, Dislink, Diverge, Dole, Element, Episode, Escapement, Farewell, Fascicle, Fork, Fraction, Goodbye, Half, Imaginary, Instalment, Into, Lathe, Lead, Leave, Leg, Lill, Lilt, Lines, List, Livraison, Member, Meronym, Parcel, Passus, → **PIECE**, Portion, Primo, Principal, Private, Proportion, Pt, Quota, Rape, Ratio, Region, Rive, Role, Scena, Scene, Secondo, Section, Sector, Segment, Separate, Serial, Sever, Shade, Share, Shed, Sleave, Sle(i)ded, → **SOME**, Spare, Split, Stator, Sunder, Synthon, Tithe, Tranche, Unit, Vaunt, Voice, Walking, Walk on, Wrench
Partake(r) Allottee, Eat, Participate, Share
Parthenogenesis Deuterotoky, Thelytoky
Partial(ity), Partially Biased, Ex-parte, Fan, Favour, Halflins, Imbalance, Incomplete, One-sided, Predilection, Slightly, Unequal, Weakness
Participate, Participant Engage, Join, Partake, Share, Traceur
Participle Dangling, Misrelated, Past, Perfect, Present
Particle(s) Alpha, Anion, Antineutron, Antiproton, Atom, Baryon, Beta, Bit, Boson, Charmonium, Corpuscle, Curn, Dander, Delta, Deuteron, Effluvium, Elementary, Episome, Fermion, Fleck, Fragment, Fundamental, Gauge boson, Gemmule, Globule, Gluon, Grain, Granule, Graviton, Hadron, Heavy, Higgs, Hyperon, Ion, J, Jot, J/psi, Kaon, Lambda, Lemail, Lemel, Lepton, Lipoplast, Liposome, Meson, Micelle, Microsome, Mite, Molecule, Monopole, Mote, Muon, Negatron, Neutralino, Neutrino, Neutron, Nibs, Nobiliary, Omega-minus, Parton, Pentaquark, Photon, Pion, Plasmagene, Platelet, Positon, Positron, Preon, Proton, Psi(on), Quark, Radioactivity, Shives, Shower, Sigma, Singlet, Sinter, Smithereen, Spark, Speck, Strange, Subatom, Submicron, Tachyon, Tardyon, Tau neutrino, Tauon, Thermion, Tittle, Virion, W, Whit, WIMP, X-hyperon, Z
Parti-coloured Fancy, Motley, Piebald, Pied, Variegated
Particular Choosy, Dainty, → **DETAIL**, Endemic, Especial, Essential, Express, Fiky, Fog, Fussy, Item, Itself, London fog, Nice, Niffy-naffy, Own, Pea-souper, Peculiar, Pernickety, Pet, Point, Prim, Proper, → **RESPECT**, Special, Specific, Stickler, Strict, Stripe
Partisan Adherent, Axe, Biased, Carlist, Champion, Devotee, Factional, Fan, Irregular, Partial, Provo, Queenite, Sider, Spear, Supporter, Yorkist
Partition(ed) Abjoint, Bail, Barrier, Brattice, Bretasche, Bulkhead, Cloison, Cubicle, Diaphragm, Dissepiment, Division, Hallan, Mediastinum, Parpane, Parpen(d), Parpent, Parpoint, Perpend, Perpent, Replum, → **SCREEN**, Scriene, Septum, Tabula, Wall, With
Partlet Hen, Overlaid
Partner(ship) Accomplice, Ally, Associate, Bidie-in, Butty, Cahoot(s), Coachfellow, Cohab(itee), Cohabitor, Colleague, Comrade, Confederate, Consort, Copemate, Couple, Dutch, Escort, E-W, Firm, Gigolo, Limited, Mate, N-S, Oppo, Pair, Pal, Pard, Rival, Sidekick, Significant other, Silent, Sleeping, Sparring, Spouse,

Stablemate, Stand, Symbiosis
▷ **Part of** *may indicate* a hidden word
Partridge Bird, Chik(h)or, Chukar, Chukor, Covey, Quail, Red-legged, Tinamou, Ynambu
Party Acid house, Aftershow, Alliance, Apparat, Assembly, At-home, Ba'ath, Ball, Band, Barbecue, Bash, Beano, Bee, Bloc, Blowout, Body, Bottle, Buck's, Bunfight, Bust, Caboodle, Camp, Carousal, Carouse, Caucus, Celebration, Clambake, Cocktail, Commando, Communist, Concert, Congress, Conservative, Contingent, Cookie-shine, Cooperative, Coterie, Cult, Democratic, Detail, Ding, Discotheque, Do, Drum, Faction, Falange, Federalist, Fest, Fête champêtre, Fête Galante, Fianna Fáil, Fine Gael, Firing, Foy, Function, Funfest, Gala, Galravage, Gang, Garden, Ghibel(l)ine, Green, Greenback, Grumbletonian, Guelf, Guelph, Guilty, Hen, High heels, Hoedown, Hooley, Hootenannie, Hootenanny, Hoot(a)nannie, Hoot(a)nanny, House, Housewarming, Hurricane, Irredentist, Jana Sangh, Jol(lities), Junket, Junto, Kettledrum, Kitchen tea, Klat(s)ch, Knees-up, Kuomintang, L, Labour, Launch, Lib, Liberal, Love-in, Low heels, Luau, Mallemaroking, Mollie, Movement, Musicale, National, Necking, Neck-tie, Octobrist, Opposition, Orgy, People's, Person, Petting, Plaid, Posse, Progressive, Prohibition, Pyjama, Rage, Rave, Rave-up, Razzle(-dazzle), Reception, Republican, Reunion, Revel, Ridotto, Rocking, Roister, Rort, Rout, SDP, Search, Sect, Set, Shindig, Shine, Shivoo, Shower, Shower tea, Side, Slumber, Smoker, SNP, Soc(ialist), Social, Social Credit, Social Democratic, Socialise, Soirée, Spree, Squad(rone), Squadrone volante, Stag, Symposium, Tailgate, Tea, Teafight, Third, Thrash, Tory, Treat, Ultramontane, Unionist, United, Wafd, Warehouse, Whig, Whoop-de-do(o), Wine, Wingding, Working
Partygoer Raver, Reveller, Socialite
Party-piece Solo
Parvenu Arriviste, Upstart
Pascal Blaise, Pa, Pressure
Pash Crush, Devotion
Pasha Achmed, Dey, Emir, Ismet
Pass(ed), Passing, Pass on, Past Ago, Agon, Annie Oakley, Aorist, Approve, Arise, Arlberg, Before, Behind, Bernina, Beyond, Boarding, Bolan, Botte, Brenner, Brief, Burgess, By, Bygone, Caudine Forks, Centre, Cerro Gordo, Chal(l)an, Chilkoot, Chine, Chit(ty), Cicilian Gates, Clear, Col, Cote, Cross, Cursory, Death, Defile, Delate, Demise, Diadron, Die, Disappear, Double, Elapse, Emit, Enact, End, Ensue, Ephemeral, Exceed, Exeat, Faena, Flashback, Fleeting, Foist, Forby, Forgone, Former, Forward, Gap, Gate, Gha(u)t, Glencoe, Glide, Go, Go by, Gorge, Great St Bernard, Gulch, Halse, Hand, Happen, Hause, Hospital, Impart, Impermanent, Interval, In transit, Jark, Khyber, Killiecrankie, Kloof, La Cumbre, Lap, Late, Lead, Long syne, Mesmerism, Migrate, Mont Cenis, Moravian Gate, Nek, Nod through, Notch, Nutmeg, Nye, Occur, Oer, OK, Okay, Oke, Omit, One-time, Overhaul, Overshoot, Overslaugh, Overtake, Pa, Palm, Parade, Participle, Perish, Permeate, Permit, Perpetuate, Poll, Poort, Predicament, Preterit(e), Pretty, Proceed, Propagate, Pun(c)to, Qualify, Railcard, Reach, Reeve, Refer, Relay, Retro, Retroactive, Retrospect, Reverse, Roncesvalles, Safe conduct, St Bernard, St Gotthard, San Bernardino, Sanitation, Scissors, Senile, Serve, Shipka, Simplon, Since, Skim, Skip, Skirt, Slap, Sling, Snap, Spend, Stab, State, Thermopylae, Thread, Through, Ticket, Tip, Transient, Transilient, Transitory, Transmit, Transude, Travel, Triptyque, Troop, Uspallata, Veronica, Vet, Visa, Visé, Wall, Wayleave, Weather, While, Wrynose, Yesterday, Yesteryear, Ygoe

Passable Adequate, Fair, Navigable, Tolerable
Passage Adit, Airway, Aisle, Alley(way), Alure, Apostrophe, Arcade, Archway,
Areaway, Arterial, Atresia, Bank, Breezeway, Bridge, Bylane, Cadenza, Caponier(e),
Career, Channel, Chute, Citation, Clarino, Clause, Close, Coda, Conduit, Corridor,
Creep, Crossing, Crush, Cundy, Dead-end, Deambulatory, Defile, Drake, Drift,
Duct, Eel-fare, Episode, Excerpt, Extract, Fare, Fat, Fistula, Flat, Flight, Flue,
Gallery, Gangway, Gap, Gat, Gate, Ghat, Ginnel, Gut, Hall, Head, Inlet, Journey,
Kyle, Labyrinth, Lane, Lapse, Larynx, Lick, Lientery, Loan, Lobby, Locus, Meatus,
Melisma, Meridian, Middle, Mona, Moto perpetuo, Movement, Northeast,
Northwest, Para(graph), Path, Pend, Pericope, Phrase, Pore, Portion, Prelude,
Prose, Purple, Race, Retournelle, Ride, Ripieno, Rite, Ritornell(o), Road, Rough,
Route, Sailing, Screed, Shaft, Shunt, Slap, Slype, Snicket, Sprue, Strait, Street,
Stretta, Stretto, Subway, Sump, Text, Thirl, Thorough(fare), Throat, Tour, Trachea,
Trance, Transe, Transit(ion), Travel, Tunnel, Tutti, Undercast, Unseen, Ureter,
Voyage, Walkway, Way, Windpipe
▷ **Passage of arms** *may indicate* 'sleeve'
Passé Corny, Dated, Ex, Obsolete
Passenger(s) Cad, Commuter, Fare, Payload, Pillion, Rider, Slacker, Steerage,
Straphanger, Transit, Traveller, Voyager, Way, Wayfarer
Passion(ate), Passionately Anger, Appetite, Ardour, Con fuoco, Duende, Fervour,
Fire, Flame, Frampold, Fury, Gust, Gutsy, Hate, Heat, Hot, Hunger, Hwyl, Ileac,
Iliac, Intense, Ire, Irish, Kama, Love, Lust, Mania, Obsession, Oestrus, Rage,
Reverent, Sizzling, Stormy, Sultry, Torrid, Vehement, Violent, Warm, Wax, Wrath,
Yen, Zeal
Passion-fruit Water-lemon
Passion play Oberammergau
Passive (stage) Apathetic, Dormant, Inert, Pathic, Patient, Pupa, Stolid, Supine,
Yielding
Pass out Faint, Graduate, Swarf, Swarve, Swoon
Passover Agadah, Haggada, Omer, Pesach
Passport Access, Clearance, Congé(e), E, ID, Key, Laissez-passer, Nansen, Navicert,
Sea-letter, Visa, Visitor's
Password Code, Countersign, Logon, Nayword, Parole, Sesame, Shibboleth, Sign,
Tessera, Watchword
▶ **Past** *see* PASS
Pasta Agnolotti, Angel hair, Cannelloni, Cappelletti, Cellentani, Conchiglie, Durum,
Eliche, Farfal, Farfel, Fedelini, Fettuc(c)ine, Fusilli, Gnocch(ett)i, Lasagna, Lasagne,
Linguini, Macaroni, Maccheroncini, Manicotti, Noodles, Orecchietti, Orzo, Penne,
Perciatelli, Ravioli, Rigatoni, Ruote, Spaghetti, Spaghettina, Tagliarini, Tagliatelle,
Tortelli(ni), Vermicelli, Ziti
Paste, Pasty Almond, Ashen, Batter, Beat, Berbere, Botargo, Boule, Bridie, Cerate,
Clobber, Cornish, Dentifrice, Dough, Electuary, Fake, Filler, Fondant, Frangipane,
Gentleman's Relish®, Glue, Guarana, Hard, Harissa, Knish, Lute, Magma,
Marchpane, Marzipan, Masala, Mastic, Meat, Miso, Mountant, Pale, Pallid, Pâté,
Patty, Pearl-essence, Pie, Piroshki, Pirozhki, Poonac, Punch, Putty, Rhinestone,
Rout, Samosa, Slip, Slurry, Soft, Spread, Strass, Tahina, Tahini, Tapenade,
Taramasalata, Wan, Wasabi
Pastern Hobble, Knee, Tether
Pastiche Cento, Collage, Medley, Patchwork, Potpourri
Pastille Jujube, Lozenge
Pastime Diversion, Game, Hobby, Recreation, Seesaw, Sport

Past master Champion, Expert, Historian, Pro
Past midnight 1 am
Pastor(al) Arcadia, Bucolic, Curé, Eclogue, Endymion, Idyl(l), Minister, Priest, Rector, Rural, Shepherd, Simple
Pastry Apfelstrudel, Baclava, Bakemeat, Baklava, Beignet, Bouchée, Brik, Calzone, Chausson, Cheese straw, Choux, Clafoutis, Coquile, Creamhorn, Cream puff, Croustade, Cruller, Crust, Danish, Dariole, Dough, Eclair, Empanada, Feuilleté, Filo, Flaky, Flan, Frangipane, French, Gougère, Hamantasch, Millefeuille, Phyllo, Pie, Pie-crust, Pirog, Piroshki, Pirozhki, Profiterole, Puff, Quiche, Rough-puff, Rug(g)elach, Samosa, Shortcrust, Strudel, Tart, Turnover, Vol-au-vent
Pasture Alp, Eadish, Eddish, Feed, Fell, Fodder, Grassland, Graze, Herbage, Kar(r)oo, Lair, Lare, Lay, Lea, Lease, Leasow(e), Leaze, Lee, Ley, Machair, Mead(ow), Moose, Pannage, Potrero, Raik, Rake, Soum, Sowm, Tie, Transhume, Tye
▶ **Pasty** *see* PASTE
Pat Apt, Bog-trotter, Butter, Chuck, Clap, Dab, Glib, Lump, On cue, Postman, Print, Prompt, Rap, Slap, Tap
Patch(y) Bed, Bit, Cabbage, Chloasma, Clout, Coalsack, Cobble, Cooper, Court plaster, Cover, Friar, Fudge, → MEND, Mosaic, Nicotine, Pasty, Piebald, Piece, Plage, Plaque, Plaster, Pot, Purple, Shinplaster, Shoulder, Solder, Tingle, Tinker, Vamp, Variegated
Patchwork Cento, Miscellany, Mosaic, Piecing
Pate, Pâté Crown, Paste, Rillettes, Taramasalata, Terrine
Patent(ed) Breveté, Clear, Copyright, Evident, Letters, Licence, License, Obvious, Overt, Plain, Rolls
Pater(nity) Father, Filiation, Walter
Paterfamilias Coarb, Master
Path(way) Aisle, Allée, Alley, Arc, Berm, Berme, Boreen, Borstal(l), Bridle, Byroad, Causeway, Causey, Clickstream, Corridor, Course, Eclipse, Embden-Meyerhof, Flare, Flight, Garden, Gate, Gennel, Ginnel, Glide, Lane, Ley, Lichwake, Lichway, Locus, Lykewake, Mean-free, Metabolic, Orbit, Pad, Parabola, Peritrack, Primrose, Ride, Ridgeway, Route, Run, Runway, Sidewalk, Spurway, Stie, Sty(e), Swath(e), Taxiway, Tow, Track, Trail, Trajectory, Trod, Walkway, → WAY, Xystus
Pathan Pakhto, Pakhtu, Pashto, Pashtu, Pushto(o), Pushtu
Pathetic(ally) Doloroso, Drip, Forlorn, Piss-poor, Piteous, Poignant, Sad, Saddo, Schnook, Touching
Pathfinder Compass, Explorer, Guide, Pioneer, Scout
Pathological Diseased, Gangrene, Morbid, Septic
Pathos Bathos, Pity, Sadness, Sob-stuff
Patience Calm, Endurance, Forbearance, Fortitude, Indulgence, Longanimity, Monument, Operetta, Solitaire, Stoicism, Virtue
Patient(s) Calm, Case, Clinic, Forbearing, Grisel(da), Grisilda, Invalid, Job, Long-suffering, Passive, Private, Resigned, Stoic, Subject, Ward
Patois Argot, Cant, Dialect, Gumbo, Jargon, Jive, Lingo, Scouse
Patriarch Aaron, Abraham, Abuna, Asher, Catholicos, Ecumenical, Elder, Enoch, Isaac, Job, Levi, Maron, Methuselah, Nestor, Noah, Pope, Simeon, Venerable
Patrician Aristocrat, Noble, Senator
Patrick Mick, Paddy, Pat, Spens
Patrimony Ancestry, Estate, Heritage
Patriot(ic), Patriotism Cavour, Chauvinist, DAR, Emmet, Flag-waving, Flamingant, Garibaldi, Hereward, Irredentist, Jingoism, Loyalist, Maquis, Nationalist, Revere, Tell

Patrol Armilla, Guard, Outguard, Picket, Piquet, Prowl-car, Reconnaissance, Round, Scout, Sentinel, Sentry-go, Shark, Shore, Turm

Patron(age), Patroness, Patronise(d), Patronising Advowson, Aegis, Auspices, Benefactor, Business, Champion, Client, Customer, Donator, Egis, Fautor, Lady Bountiful, Maecenas, Nepotic, Protector, Protégé, Provider, Shopper, → SPONSOR, Stoop, Stoup

Patsy Dupe, Hendren, Scapegoat, Stooge

Patter Backchat, Cant, Jargon, Lingo, Mag, Pitch, Rap, S(c)htick, Schtik, Spiel

Pattern(ed) Agouti, Agouty, Aguti, Argyle, Bird's eye, Blueprint, Branchwork, Broché, Candy stripe, Check, Chequer, Chiné, Chladni figure, Clock, Design, Dévoré, Diaper, Diffraction, Dog's tooth, Draft, Egg and dart, Epitome, Example, Exemplar, Fiddle, Figuration, Format, Fractal, Fret, Gestalt, Grain, Grammadion, Greek key, Greque, Herringbone, Holding, Hound's tooth, Intarsia, Intonation, Koru, Kowhaiwhai, Matel(l)asse, Matrix, Meander, → MODEL, Moire, Moko, Mosaic, Norm, Paisley, Paradigm, Paragon, Pinstripe, Plan, Polka-dot, Pompadour, Precedent, Prototype, Queenstitch, Quincunx, Radiation, Raster, Scansion, Shawl, Stencil, Symmetry, Syndrome, Tala, Talea, Tangram, Tarsia, Tattersall, Template, Tessella, Tessera, Tracery, Traffic, Tread, Type, Willow

Patty Bouchée, Fishcake, Pie

Paul Jones, Oom, Pry, Revere, Robeson, S, St

Pauline Day-boy, Perils

Paunch Belly, Corporation, Gut, Kite, Kyte, Pod, Rumen, Tripe, Tum

Pauper Bankrupt, Beggar, Have-not, Mendicant, Penniless

Pause Break, Breakpoint, Breather, Caesura, Cessation, Cesura, Comma, Desist, Er, Fermata, Hesitate, Interkinesis, Interregnum, Interval, Limma, Lull, Pitstop, Pregnant, → RESPITE, Rest, Selah, Stop, Tacet, Time out

Pave(ment), Paving Causeway, Clint, Cobble, Corsey, Crazy, Diaper, Granolith, Limestone, Moving, Path, Plainstanes, Plainstones, Roadside, Set(t), Sidewalk, Tessellate, Travolator, Trottoir

Pavilion Ear, Gazebo, Jingling Johnny, Kiosk, Marquee, Tent

Paw Kangaroo, Maul, Mitt, Pad, Pat, Pud, Pug

Pawky Dry, Humorous, Shrewd, Sly

Pawn(shop), Pawnbroker, Pawnee Agent, Betel, Chessman, Counter, Derby, Dip, Gage, Gallery, Hanging, Hock, Hockshop, Hostage, Isolated, Leaving-shop, Lumber, Lumberer, Moneylender, Monte-de-piété, Monti di pietà, Nunky, Pan, Passed, Peacock, Piece, Pignerate, Pignorate, Pledge, Pledgee, Pop, Security, Sheeny, Siri, Spout, Stalking horse, Tiddleywink, Tool, Uncle, Usurer, Wadset, Weed

Pax Peace, Truce

Pay(master), Payment, Paid, Pay off, Pay out Aby, Advertise, Agterskot, Amortise, Annat, Annuity, Ante, Arles, Atone, Balloon, Basic, Batta, Blench, Bonus, Bukshee, Bukshi, Cain, Cashier, Cens, Cheque, COD, Commute, Compensate, Consideration, Damage, Defray, Disburse, Discharge, Dividend, Down, Dub, E, Emolument, Endow, Equalisation, Eric, Escot, Farm, Fee, Feu-duty, Finance, Foot, Fork out, Fund, Gale, Gate, Give, Grassum, Grave, Greenmail, Han(d)sel, Hazard, Hire, Hoot(oo), HP, Imburse, Kain, Kickback, Leads and lags, Lobola, Lobolo, Mail, Meet, Merchet, Métayage, Mise, Modus, Overtime, Payola, Pension, Pittance, Pony, Posho, Prebendal, Premium, Primage, Pro, Pro forma, Progress, Purser, Quarterage, Quit(-rent), Ransom, Reap-silver, Redundancy, Refund, Remittance, Remuneration, Rent, Requite, Residual, Respects, Royalty, Salary, Satisfaction, Scot, Screw, Scutage, Settle, Severance, Shell, Shell out, Shot, Sick, Sink, Sold(e),

Soul-scat, Soul-scot, → **SPEND**, Square, Stipend, Strike, Stump, Sub, Subscribe, Sweetener, Table, Take-home, Tar, Tender, Token, Tommy, Transfer, Treasure, Treat, Tribute, Truck, Unpurse, Usance, Veer, Wage, Wardcorn, X-factor
PE Aerobics, Gym
Pea(s) Carling, Chaparral, Chickling, Desert, D(h)al, Dholl, Egyptian, Garbanzo, Goober, Hastings, Legume, Mangetout, Marrow, Marrowfat, Passiform, Petit pois, Pigeon, Pulse, Rounceval, Split, String, Sturt's desert, Sugar
Peace(ful), Peaceable, Peace-keeper, Peace organisation, Peace symbol Ahimsa, Antiwar, Ataraxy, Calm, Ease, Frieda, Frith, Halcyon, Hush, Interceder, Irenic(on), King's, Lee, Lull, Nirvana, Olive, Order, Pacific, Pax, Pbuh, Queen's, Quiet, Repose, Rest, Roskilde, Salem, Serene, Sh, Shalom, Siegfried, Siesta, Silence, Solomon, Still, Tranquil, Truce, UN
Peacemaker ACAS, Arbitrator, Conciliator, Mediator, Trouble-shooter, Wilfred
Peach Blab, Cling, Clingstone, Dish, Dob, Freestone, Inform, Laetrile, Malakatoone, Melba, Melocoto(o)n, Nectarine, Oner, Quandang, Shop, Sneak, Split, Squeak, Stunner, Tattle, Tell, Victorine
Peachum Polly
Peacock Coxcomb, Dandy, Fop, Junonian, Muster, Paiock(e), Pajock(e), Pavo(ne), Pawn, Payock(e), Pown, Sashay
Peak(y) Acme, Aiguille, Alp, Ancohuma, Apex, Ben, Cap, Climax, Comble, Communism, Cone, Crag, Crest, Darien, Drawn, Eiger, Flower, Gable, Gannett, Horn, Matterhorn, Mons, → **MOUNTAIN**, Nevis, Nib, Nunatak, Optimum, Pale, Petermann, Pikes, Pin, Pinnacle, Piton, Pyramidal, Rainier, Sallow, Snowdon, Spire, Stalin, Sukarno, Top, Tor, Visor, Widow's, Zenith
Peal Carillon, Chime, Clap, Toll, Triple
Peanut(s) Arnut, Chickenfeed, Goober, Groundnut, Monkey-nut, Pittance
Pear Aguacate, Alligator, Anchovy, Anjou, Asian, Asparagus, Avocado, Bartlett, Bergamot, Beurré, Blanquet, Carmelite, Catherine, Colmar, Comice, Conference, Cuisse-madame, Dutch admiral, Jargonelle, Muscadel, Muscatel, Musk, Nashi, Neli(e)s, Nelis, Perry, Poperin, Poppering, Poprin, Prickly, Pyrus, Queez-maddam, Seckel, Seckle, Taylor's Gold, Warden, William
Pearl(s), Pearly Barocco, Barock, Baroque, Cultured, False, Gem, Imitated, Jewel, Mabe, Margaret, Margaric, Nacrous, Olivet, Orient, Prize, Rope, Seed, Simulated, String, Sulphur, Unio(n)
Pear-shaped Obconic, Pyriform
Peasant Bogtrotter, Bonhomme, Boor, Bumpkin, Chouan, Churl, Clodhopper, Contadino, Cossack, Cottar, Cott(i)er, Fellah(s), Fellahin, Hick, Jungli, Kern(e), Kisan, Kulak, M(o)ujik, Muzhik, Quashi(e), Raiyat, Roturier, Rustic, Ryot, Swain, Tyrolean, Volost, Whiteboy, Yokel
Pea-shaped Pisiform
Peat(y) Moss-litter, Sod, Turbary, Turbinacious, Turf, Yarfa, Yarpha
Pebble(s), Pebbly Banket, Bibble, Calculus, Cobblestone, Dornick, Dreikanter, Gallet, Gooley, Gravel, Psephism, Pumie, Pumy, Scotch, Scree, Shingle, Ventifact
Peccadillo Mischief, Misdemeanour, Offence
Peccary Mexican hog, Tayassuid
Peck Bill, Bushel, Dab, Forpet, Forpit, Gregory, Kiss, Lip, Lippie, Nibble, Pickle, Tap
Pecksniff Charity
Peculiar(ity) Appropriate, Characteristic, Distinct, Eccentric, Especial, Exclusive, Ferly, Funny, Idiosyncratic, Kink, Kooky, Odd, Own, Proper, Queer, Quirk, Royal, Singular, → **SPECIAL**, Specific, Strange, Unusual
▷ **Peculiar** *may indicate an anagram*

Pedagogue Academic, B.Ed, Teacher
Pedal Bike, Chorus, Clutch, Cycle, Damper, Lever, P, Rat-trap, Soft, Sostenuto, Sustaining, Treadle, Treddle
Pedal-coupler Tirasse
Pedant(ic) Casaubon, Chop logic, Dogmatic, Don, Dryasdust, Elucubrate, Inkhorn, Intellectual, Jobsworth, Lucubrate, Nit-picking, Pedagogue, Pernickety, Pompous, Precisian, Quibbler, Scholastic, Sesquipedalian
Peddle, Pedlar Bodger, Boxwallah, Camelot, Chapman, Cheapjack, Colporteur, Drummer, Duffer, Hawk, Huckster, Jagger, Packman, Pedder, Pether, Sell, Smouch, Smouse(r), Sutler, Tallyman, Tink(er), Yagger
▷ **Peddling** *may indicate* an anagram
Pedestal Acroter(ion), Dado, Footstool, Pillar, Support
Pedestrian Banal, Commonplace, Dull, Earth-bound, Ganger, Hack, Hike, Itinerant, Jaywalker, Laborious, Mundane, Trite, Voetganger, Walker
Pedigree(s) Ancestry, Blood, Breeding, Descent, Genealogy, House, Lineage, Phylogeny, Stemma(ta), Stirp(s), Studbook, Thoroughbred, Whakapapa
Pediment Fronton
Peduncle Scape, Stalk
Peek Eye, Glance, Glimpse, Peep
Peel(er) Bark, Bobby, Candied, Decorticate, Desquamate, Exfoliate, Flype, Orange, Pare, PC, Pill, Rind, Rine, Scale, Shell, Skin, → STRIP, Tirr, Zest
▷ **Peeled** *may indicate* outside letter(s) to be removed from a word
Peep(er), Peephole Cheep, Cook, Crow, Glance, Gledge, Judas, Keek, Kook, Lamp, Nose, Peek, Pink, Pry, Spy, Squeak, Squint, Stime, Styme, Voyeur
Peer(age), Peers Archduke, Aristocrat, Backwoodsman, Baron(et), Burke, Coeval, Daimio, Doucepere, Douzeper(s), Duke, Earl, Egal, Elevation, Equal, Eyeball, Gynt, Life, Lord, Match, Noble, Paladin, Peregal, Pink, Rank, Representative, Scry, Spiritual, Squint, Stare, Stime, Styme, Temporal, Toot, Tweer, Twire
Peerless Matchless, Nonpareil, Supreme
Peevish(ness) Capernoited, Captious, Crabby, Cross, Doddy, Frabbit, Frampal, Frampold, Franzy, Fretful, Lienal, Meldrew, Moody, Nattered, Pet, Petulant, Pindling, Protervity, Querulous, Shirty, Sour, Spleen, Teachie, Testy, Te(t)chy
Peewit Lapwing, Peewee
Peg Cheville, Cleat, Clothespin, Cotter-pin, Crawling, Die, Fix, Freeze, Knag, Leg, Margaret, Nail, Nog, Odontoid, Pin, Piton, Snort, Spigot, Spile, Square, Stengah, Stinger, Support, Tap, Tee, Thole, Tholepin, Thowel, Toggle, Tot, Tuning, Vent, Woffington
Pegboard Solitaire
Pelagic Deep-sea, Marine, Oceanic
Pelf Lucre, Mammon, Money, Notes, Riches
Pelican Alcatras, Bird, Crossing, Golden Hind, LA, Louisiana, Steganopode
Pellagra Maidism
Pellet Birdshot, Bolus, Buckshot, Bullet, Pill, Pithball, Prill, Slug
Pelmet Valance
Pelt Assail, Clod, Fleece, Fur, Hail, Hide, Hie, Lam, Pepper, Random, Sealskin, Shower, Skin, Squail, Stone
Peltast Soldier, Targeteer
Pelvis Ilium, Pubis, Renal
Pen Author, Ballpoint, Bamboo, Bic®, Biro®, Cage, Calamus, Cartridge, Catching, Confine, Coop, Corral, Crawl, Crow-quill, Cru(i)ve, Cub, Cyclostyle, Dabber, Data, Enclosure, Fank, Farm, Felt(-tipped), Fold, Fountain, Gaol, Gladius, Hen,

Highlighter, Hoosegow, J, → **JAIL**, Keddah, Kraal, Lair, Laser, Light, Marker, Mew, Mure, Music, Piggery, Poison, Pound, Quill(-nib), Ree, Reed, Ring, Rollerball, Scribe, Stell, Stie, Stir, Sty(e), Stylet, Stylo, Stylograph, Stylus, Submarine, Swan, Sweatbox, Tank, Write, → **WRITER**
▷ **Pen** *may indicate* a writer
Penal(ize) Cost, Fine, Gate, Handicap, Huff, Mulct, Punitive, Servitude
Penalty Abye, Amende, Card, Cost, Death, Eric, Fine, Fixed, Forfeit, Han(d)sel, Huff, Keltie, Kelty, Pain, Price, Punishment, Rubicon, Sanction, Ticket, Wide
Penance Atonement, Shrift
Penates Lares
Pence D, P, Peter's
Penchant Predilection
Pencil Beam, Ca(l)m, Caum, Charcoal, Chinagraph®, Crayon, Draft, Draw, Eyebrow, Fusain, Grease, Harmonic, Ink, Keelivine, Keelyvine, Lead, Outline, Propelling, Slate, Stump, Styptic, Tortillon
Pendant Albert, Chandelier, Drop, Girandole, Laval(l)ière, Necklace, Poffle, Stalactite
Pending Imminent, In fieri, Unresolved, Until
Pendragon Uther
Pendulous, Pendulum Compensation, Dewlap, Foucault's, Metronome, Noddy, One-way, Swing, Wavering
Penetrate, Penetrating, Penetration Acumen, Acuminate, Bite, Bore, Bridgehead, Cut, Enpierce, Enter, Imbue, Impale, Incisive, Indent, Indepth, Infiltrate, Insight, Into, Intrant, Lance, Permeate, Pierce, Probe, Sagacious, Shear, Thrust, Touch, X-ray
Penguin Adélie, Aeroplane, Anana, Auk, Blue, Emperor, Fairy, Gentoo, King, Korora, Little, Macaroni, Rock-hopper
Penicillin Cloxacillon, Fleming
Peninsula Alaska, Alte, Antarctic, Arabian, Ards, Arm, Avalon, Baja California, Balkan, Banks, Bataan, Black Isle, Boothia, Brittany, Cape, Cape Blanco, Cape Bon, Cape Cod, Cape Verde, Chalcidice, Chersonese, Chukchi, Coromandel, Cowal, Crimea, Deccan, Delmarva, East Cape, Eyre, Florida, Freycinet, Furness, Fylde, Gallipoli, Galloway, Gaspé, Gower, Graham Land, Hispania, Iberia(n), Indo-China, Istria, Jutland, Kamchatka, Kathiawar, Kerch, Kintyre, Kola, Korea, Kowloon, Labrador, Leizhou, Liaodong, Liaotung, Lleyn, Luichow, Malay, Malaysia, Melville, Neck, Northland, Nova Scotia, Olympic, Otago, Palmer, Peloponnese, Portland, Promontory, Quiberon, Rhinns of Galloway, Scandinavian, Seward, Sinai, Spit, Spur, S.W. Malay, Taimyr, Tasman, Taymyr, The Lizard, Upper, Wilson's Promontory, Wirral, Yorke, Yucatan
Penis Archie, Chopper, Cor(e)y, Dick, Dildo(e), Dipstick, Dong, Ferret, Giggle(stick), Horn, Jack, John Thomas, Knob, Langer, Membrum virile, Mojo, Organ, Pecker, Peezle, Percy, Phallus, Pillicock, Pintle, Pisser, Pizzle, Plonker, Prick, Putz, Rod, Roger, Schlong, Shaft, Stiffy, Tallywhacker, Tockley, Todger, Tonk, Tool, W(h)ang, Willie, Willy, Winkle, Yard, Zeppelin
Penitent(iary) Calaboose, Cilice, Clink, Contrite, Gaol, Jail, Jug, Prison, Repenter, Rosary, Stir
Pennant, Pennon Banner, Broad, Bunting, Fane, Flag, Guidon, Streamer
Penniless Bankrupt, Boracic, Broke, Bust, Impecunious, Poor, Skint, Strapped
Penny Bean, Cartwheel, Cent, Copper, D, Dreadful, Gild, Honest, New, P, Pretty, Sen, Sou, Sterling, Stiver, Win(n), Wing
Penny-farthing Bicycle, Ordinary

Pension(er) Allowance, Ann(at), Annuitant, Board, Chelsea, Cod, Cor(r)ody, Gasthaus, Gratuity, Guest-house, Half-board, Hotel, Non-contributory, Occupational, Payment, Personal, Retire(e), Serps, SIPP, Stakeholder, Stipend, Superannuation
Pensive Dreamy, Moody, Musing, Thoughtful, Triste, Wistful
Pentateuch T(h)orah
Pentecost Whit(sun)
Penthouse Cat, Lean-to, Roof, Skyhome
Peon Peasant, Serf, Slave, Ticca
Peony Moutan
People Beings, Bods, Body, Chosen, Commonalty, Commons, Demos, Ecology, Enchorial, Flower, Folk, Fraim, Gens, Grass roots, Guild, Human, Inca, Inhabit, Janata, Kin, Land, Lapith, Lay, Man(kind), Men, Mob, Nair, Nation(s), Nayar, One, Peculiar, Personalities, Phalange, Populace, Proletariat(e), Public, Punters, Quorum, Race, September, Settle, Society, Souls, They, Tribe, Tuath, Volk
Pep Buck, Dash, Enliven, Gism, Go, Jism, Jissom, Stamina, Verve, Vim
Pepper Alligator, All-spice, Ava, Betel, Bird, Black, Caper, Capsicum, Cayenne, Cherry, Chilli, Chipotle, Condiment, Cubeb, Devil, Dittander, Dittany, Ethiopian, Green, Guinea, Habanero, Jalapeno, Jamaica, Kava, Long, Malaguetta, Matico, Negro, Paprika, Pelt, Pim(i)ento, Piper, Piperine, Piquillo, Red, Riddle, Sambal, Spice, Sprinkle, Sweet, Szechwan, Tabasco®, Wall, Water, White, Yaqona, Yellow
Peppercorn Nominal, → PAYMENT, → RENT
Peppermint Bull's Eye, Humbug, Pandrop
Peptide Substance P
Per By, Each, Through
Perambulate, Perambulator Buggy, Expatiate, Pedestrian, Pram, Stroller, Wagon, Walker
Perceive, Perception, Perceptive Acumen, Alert, Anschauung, Apprehend, Astute, Clairvoyance, Clear-eyed, Cryptaesthetic, Descry, Dianoia, Discern, Divine, ESP, Extrasensory, Feel, Insight, Intelligence, Intuit(ion), Kinaesthesia, Notice, Observe, Pan(a)esthesia, Remark, → SEE, Sense, Sensitive, Sentience, Shrewd, Sixth sense, Subliminal, Tact, Taste, Tel(a)esthesia, Telegnosis, Understanding
Percentage Agio, Commission, Contango, Cut, Mark-up, Proportion, Royalty, Scalage, Share, Vigorish
Perch(ing) Aerie, Alight, Anabis, Bass, Comber, Eyrie, Fish, Fogash, Gaper, Insessorial, Lug, Miserere, Ocean, Perca, Pole, Roost, Ruff(e), Seat, Serranid, → SIT, Wall-eye, Zingel
Percolate, Percolation Filter, Infiltrate, Leach, Lixiviate, Ooze, Osmosis, Permeate, Seep, Sipe, Soak, Strain, Sype
Percussion (cap) Amorce, Chinese temple block, Idiophone, Impact, Knee, Knock, Thump, Timbrel
Percy Hotspur, Shelley
Perdition Ades, Hades
Peremptory Absolute, Decisive, Haughty, Imperative, Imperious
Perennial Continual, Enduring, Flower, Livelong, Perpetual, Recurrent
Perfect(ly), Perfection(ist) Absolute, Accomplish, Accurate, Acme, Apple-pie, Bloom, Complete, Consummation, Cross-question, Dead, Develop, Fare-thee-well, Finish, Flawless, Fulfil, Full, Holy, Ideal(ist), Impeccable, Intact, It, Mint, Par, Paragon, Past, Pat, Peace, Pedant, Point-device, Practice, Present, Pure, Quintessential, Refine, Salome, Siddha, Soma, Sound, Spot-on, Stainless, Sublime, The nines, Thorough, Three-pricker, Unblemished, Unqualified, Utopian,

Utter, Whole, Witeless

Perfidy Betrayal, Falsehood, Treachery, Treason

Perforate(d), Perforation, Perforator Cribrate, Cribrose, Drill, Eyelet, Hole, → **PIERCE**, Prick, Punch, Puncture, Riddle, Trephine, Trocar

Perforce Necessarily, Needs

Perform(ed), Performer, Performing Achieve, Act(or), Appear, Artist(e), Basoche, Busk, Carry out, Chansonnier, Comedian, Contortionist, Discharge, Do, Enact, Entertainer, Execute, Exert, Exhibit, Fancy Dan, Fire-eater, Fulfil, Function, Geek, Hand, Headliner, Hersall, Hot dog, Houdini, Implement, Interlocutor, Majorette, Make, Moke, On, Perpetrate, Player, Praxis, Recite, Render, Ripieno, Strongman, Supererogate, Sword-swallower, Throw, Vaudevillian, Virtuoso, Wire-dancer

Performance Accomplishment, Achievement, Act, Auto, Blinder, Bravura, Broadcast, Command, Concert, Dare, Deed, Demonstration, Discharge, Entr'acte, Execution, Gas, Gig, Hierurgy, Holdover, Hootenanny, House, Masterstroke, Matinee, One-night stand, Operation, Perpetration, Practice, Première, Production, Programme, Recital, Rehearsal, Rendering, Rendition, Repeat, Repertoire, Rigmarole, Scene, Show, Showing, Sneak preview, Solo, Specific, Spectacle, Stunt, Theatricals, Track record, Turn

Perfume (box) Abir, Angel water, Aroma, Attar, Bergamot, Cassolette, Chypre, Civet, Cologne, C(o)umarin, Eau de toilette, Enfleurage, Essence, Fragrance, Frangipani, Incense, Ionone, Lavender (water), Linalool, Millefleurs, Muscone, Muskone, Myrrh, Opopanax, Orris, Orrisroot, Otto, Patchouli, Patchouly, Pomander, Potpourri, Redolence, → **SCENT**, Smellies, Terpineol, Toilet water

Perfunctory Apathetic, Careless, Cursory, Indifferent, Token

Perhaps A(i)blins, Belike, Haply, Happen, May(be), Peradventure, Percase, Perchance, Possibly, Relative, Say, Yibbles

▷ **Perhaps** *may indicate* an anagram

Perigee Apsis, Epigeum

Peril(ous) → **DANGER**, Hazard, Jeopardy, Precarious, Risk, Threat, Yellow

Perimeter Boundary, Circuit, Circumference, Limits

Period(ic) Abbevillian, Acheulian, AD, Age, Alcher(ing)a, Andropause, Annual, Archaean, Aurignacian, Azilian, Base, Cal(l)ippic, Cambrian, Carboniferous, Chalcolithic, Chukka, Chukker, Climacteric, Cooling off, Cretaceous, Critical, Curse, Cycle, Day, Decad(e), Devonian, Diapause, Dot, Dreamtime, → **DURATION**, Eocene, Epoch, Excerpt, Floruit, Full-stop, Glacial, Grace, Hercynian, Holocene, Horal, Incubation, Innings, Interregnum, Jurassic, Kalpa, Latency, Latent, Lesson, Liassic, Limit, Meantime, Meanwhile, Menopause, Mesolithic, Mesozoic, Middle Kingdom, Miocene, Monthly, Neocomian, Neolithic, Neozoic, Octave, Olde-worlde, Oligocene, Ordovician, Paleolithic, Permian, Phanerozoic, Phase, Phoenix, Pleistocene, Pliocene, Pre-Cambrian, Proterozoic, Protohistory, Quarter, Quarternary, Reformation, Refractory, Regency, Rent, Riss, Romantic, Safe, Season, Session, Sidereal, Silurian, Span, Spell, Stage, Stop, Stretch, Synodic, Term, Tertiary, Trecento, Triassic, Trimester, Usance, Window

Periodic(al) Catamenia, Comic, Digest, Economist, Etesian, Journal, Liassic, Listener, Mag, New Yorker, Organ, Paper, Phase, Publication, Punch, Rambler, Regency, Review, Solutrean, Solutrian, Spectator, Strand, Stretch, Tatter, Tract

Peripatetic Gadabout, Itinerant, Promenader, Travelling

Periphery Ambit, Bounds, Fringe, Outskirts, Surface

Periscope Eye(-stalk)

Perish(able), Perished, Perishing Brittle, → **DIE**, End, Ephemeral, Expire, Fade, Forfair, Fungibles, Icy, Tine, Tint, Transitory, Tyne, Vanish

Periwinkle Apocynum, Blue, Myrtle
Perjure(d) Forswear, Lie, Mansworn
Perk(s), Perky Brighten, Chipper, Freebie, Freshen, Jaunty, LV, Perquisite
Perm(anent) Abiding, Durable, Enduring, Eternal, Everlasting, Fixed, For keeps, Full-time, Indelible, → LASTING, Marcel, Stable, Standing, Stative, Wave
Permeable, Permeability, Permeate Infiltrate, Leaven, Magnetic, Osmosis, Penetrate, Pervade, Poromeric, Porous, Seep, Transfuse
Permission, Permit(ted) Allow, Authorise, By-your-leave, Carnet, Chop, Clearance, Congé(e), Consent, Copyright, Enable, Give, Grant, Lacet, Laisser-passer, Latitude, Leave, Legal, Let, Liberty, Licence, License, Lief, Luit, Nihil obstat, Ok(e), Pace, Pass, Placet, Planning, Power, Pratique, Privilege, Safe-conduct, Sanction, Stamp-note, Suffer, Ticket, Triptyque, Visa, Vouchsafe, Way-leave, Wear
Pernicious Damnable, Evil, Harmful, Lethal, Noisome, Pestilent, Wicked
Pernickety Fikish, Niggly
Peroration Pirlicue, Purlicue
Peroxide Bleach, Blonde, Colcothar
Perpendicular Aplomb, Apothem, Atrip, Cathetus, Erect, Normal, Orthogonal, Plumb, Sheer, Sine, → UPRIGHT, Vertical
Perpetrate Commit, Effect, Execute
Perpetual Constant, Eternal, Incessant, Sempiternal
Perplex(ed), Perplexity Anan, Baffle, Bamboozle, Beset, Bewilder, Bother, Buffalo, Bumbaze, Cap, Confound, Confuse, Embarrass, Feague, Floor, Flummox, Knotty, Meander, Mystify, Nonplus, Out, Pother, Pudder, Puzzle, Quizzical, Stump, Tangle, Tickle, Tostication
Perquisite Ap(p)anage, Emolument, Extra, Gratuity, → PERK, Tip
Perrier Stoner
Perry Mason
Persecute, Persecution Afflict, Annoy, Badger, Crucify, Dragon(n)ades, Harass, Haze, Intolerant, McCarthyism, Oppress, Pogrom, Ride, Torment, Torture, Witch hunt
Persevere, Perseverance Assiduity, Continue, Fortitude, Insist, Patience, Persist, Plug, Stamina, Steadfastness, Stick, Stickability, Tenacity
Persia(n) Achaemenid, Babee, Babi, Bahai, Cyrus, Dari, Farsi, Iran(ian), Mazdean, Mede, Middle, Pahlavi, Parasang, Parsee, Pehlevi, Pushtu, Samanid, Sassanid, Sohrab, Xerxes, Zoroaster
Persimmon Kaki, Sharon fruit
Persist(ence), Persistent Adhere, Assiduity, Chronic, Continual, Diligent, Doggedness, Endure, Importunate, Labour, Longeval, Lusting, Nag, Persevere, Press, Sedulous, Sneaking, Stick, Tenacity, Urgent
Person(s), Personal(ly) Alter, Artificial, Aymaran, Being, Bird, Bod(y), Chai, Chal, Character, Chav, Chi, Cookie, Displaced, Entity, Everyman, Figure, First, Fish, Flesh, Head, Human, Individual, In propria persona, Natural, One, Own, Party, Passer-by, Pod, Private, Quidam, Second, Selfhood, Skate, Sod, Soul, Specimen, Tales, Third, Walla(h)
Personage, Personality Anima, Celeb(rity), Character, Charisma, Dignitary, Ego, Grandee, Identity, Jekyll and Hyde, Megastar, Multiple, Noble, Notability, Panjandrum, Presence, Psychopath, Sama, Schizoid, Seity, Sel, Self, Sell, Somatotonia, Split, Star, Tycoon, Viscerotonia
Personified, Personification, Personify Embody, Incarnate, Prosopop(o)eia, Represent
Personnel Employees, Hands, Liveware, Manpower, Staff
Perspective Aerial, Attitude, Distance, Linear, Point of view, Proportion, Slant,

View, Vista
Perspicacious Astute, Clear-sighted, Discerning, Keen, Shrewd
Perspiration, Perspire, Perspiring Aglow, Forswatt, Glow, Hidrosis, Sudor, Suint, Sweat, Swelter
Persuade(d), Persuasion, Persuasive Cajole, Coax, Cogent, Conviction, Convince, Disarm, Eloquent, Faith, Feel, Forcible, Geed, Get, Induce, Inveigle, Lead on, Move, Plausible, → **PREVAIL**, Religion, Smooth-talking, Soft sell, Suborn, Truckled, Wheedle, Winning
Pert(ness) Bold, Brisk, Cocky, Dicacity, Flippant, Forward, Fresh, Impertinent, Insolent, Jackanapes, Minx, Quean, Saucy, Tossy
Pertain Apply, Belong, Concern, Effeir, Effere, Relate, Touch
Pertinacious Dogged, Obstinate, Persistent, Stickler, Stubborn
Pertinent Ad rem, Apropos, Apt, Fit, Germane, Relevant, Timely
Perturb(ation) Aerate, Confuse, Dismay, Disturb, Dither, State, Trouble, Upset, Worry
Peru(vian) Inca, PE, Quechua(n), Quichua(n)
Peruse, Perusal Examine, Inspect, Read, Scan, Scrutiny, → **STUDY**
Pervade, Pervasion, Pervasive(ness) Diffuse, Drench, Immanence, Permeate, Saturate
Perverse, Perversion, Pervert(ed), Perversity Aberrant, Abnormal, Algolagnia, Awkward, Awry, Balky, Cam(stairy), Camsteary, Camsteerie, Cantankerous, → **CONTRARY**, Corrupt, Crabbed, Cussed, Deviate, Distort, Donsie, False, Froward, Gee, Kam(me), Kinky, Licentious, Misinterpret, Misuse, Nonce, Paraphilia, Protervity, Refractory, Sadist, Sicko, Stubborn, Thrawn, Traduce, Unnatural, Untoward, Uranism, Warp(ed), Wayward, Wilful, Wrest, Wry
▷ **Perverted** *may indicate* an anagram
Pessimism, Pessimist(ic) Alarmist, Bear, Crapehanger, Crepehanger, Cynic, Defeatist, Dismal Jimmy, Doomwatch, Doomy, Doubter, Downbeat, Fatalist, Glumbum, Jeremiah, Killjoy, Negative
Pest(er) Aggravate, Badger, Bedbug, Blight, Bot, → **BOTHER**, Brat, Breese, Bug, Dim, Disagreeable, Earbash, Fly, Fowl, Greenfly, Harass, Irritate, Mither, Mouse, Nag, Nudnik, Nuisance, Nun, Pize, Plague, Rotter, Scourge, Tease, Terror, Thysanoptera, Vermin, Weevil
Pesticide Botanic(al), DDT, Derris, Heplachlor, Mouser, Permethrin, Synergist, Warfarin
Pestilence, Pestilent Curse, Epidemic, Evil, Lues, Murrain, Murren, Noxious, Outbreak, Pernicious, Plague
Pet Aversion, Cade, Canoodle, Caress, Chou, Coax, Coddle, Cosset, Dandle, Daut(ie), Dawt(ie), Dod, Dort, Ducky, Favourite, Fondle, Glumps, Hamster, Huff, Hump, Ire, Jarta, Jo, Lallygag, Lapdog, Miff, Mouse, Neck, Pique, Rabbit, Smooch, Snog, Spat, Strum, Sulk(s), Tantrum, Teacher's, Tiff, Tout, Towt, Umbrage, Virtual, Yarta
Petal Ala, Keels, Labellum, Leaf, Standard, Vexillum
Petard Firework, Squib
Peter Aumbry, Bell, Dwindle, Grimes, Pan, Principle, Quince, Quint, Rabbit, Safe, Saint, Sellers, Simon, Simple, Wane, Weaken
Petite Dainty, Mignon, Small
Petition(er) Appeal, Beg, Boon, Crave, Entreaty, Litany, Millenary, Orison, Plaintiff, Postulant, Prayer, Representation, Request, Round robin, Solicit, Sue, Suit(or), Suppli(c)ant, Vesper
Pet-name Hypocorisma, Nickname, So(u)briquet
Petrel Bird, Mother Carey's chicken, Nelly, Prion, Procellaria, Stormbird, Stormy, Wilton's

Petrify(ing) Fossilise, Frighten, Lapidescent, Niobe, Numb, Ossify, Scare, Terrify

Petrol(eum) Cetane, Cutting, Diesel, Esso®, Ethyl, Fuel, Gas, High-octane, High-test, Ligroin, Maz(o)ut, Octane, Oilstone, Olein, Refinery, Rock oil, Rock-tar, STP, Unleaded, Vaseline

Petticoat Balmoral, Basquine, Crinoline, Female, Filabeg, Fil(l)ibeg, Jupon, Kilt, Kirtle, Phil(l)abeg, Phil(l)ibeg, Placket, Sarong, Shift, Underskirt, Wylie-coat

Pettifogger Lawmonger

Petty, Pettiness Baubling, Bumbledom, Childish, Little, Mean, Minor, Narrow, Niggling, Nyaff, One-horse, Parvanimity, Picayunish, Pimping, Puisne, Shoestring, Small, Small-minded, Stingy, Tin, Trivial, Two-bit

Petulance, Petulant Fretful, Huff, Moody, Peevish, Perverse, Procacity, Querulous, Sullen, Toutie, Waspish

Pew Box, Carrel, Chair, Seat, Stall

Pewter Trifle, Tutenag

Phaeton Spider

Phalanger Cus-cus, Honey-mouse, Opossum, Petaurist, Phascogale, Possum, Sugar glider, Tait, Tarsipes, Tuan, Wambenger

Phalanx Cohort, Coterie, Legion

Phalarope Lobe-foot

Phallus Linga(m), Penis, Priapus

Phantasist, Phantasm Apparition, Chimera, Spectre, Werewolf

Phantom Apparition, Bogey, Bugbear, Eidolon, Idol, Incubus, Maya, Pepper's ghost, Shade, Spectre, Tut, Wraith

Pharaoh Akhenaton, Amenhotep, Cheops, Egyptian, Rameses, River-dragon, Thutmose, Tut, Tutankhamen, Tutankhamun, Tyrant

Pharisee Formalist, Humbug, Hypocrite, Nicodemus

Pharmacist, Pharmacologist → CHEMIST, Dispenser, MPS, Officinal, Preparator

Phase Coacervate, Colour, Cycle, Form, Period, Post-boost, Primary, Quarter, REM, Stage, State, Synchronise, Transition

Pheasant Argus, Bird, Fireback, Junglefowl, Mona(u)l, Nide, Nye, Peacock, Ring-necked, Tragopan

Phenol Orcine, Orcinol, Resorcinol, Xylenol

Phenomenon Autokinetic, Blip, Effect, Event, Figure ground, Flying saucer, Flysch, Heterography, Marvel, Miracle, Mirage, Paranormal, Phenology, Phi, Psi, Rankshift, Reynaud's, Synergy

Phial Bologna, Bottle, Flask

Phil, Philip Fluter, Macedonia, Pip

Philander(er) Flirt, Lothario, Playboy, Toyer, → TRIFLE, Wolf, Womaniser

Philanthropist, Philanthropy Altruist, Benefactor, Carnegie, Charity, Coram, Donor, Freemason, Humanist, Humanitarian, Nobel, Rockefeller, Samaritan, Shaftesbury, Tate, Wilberforce

Philately Timbromania

Phileas Fogg

▶ **Philip** see PHIL

Philippic Diatribe, Invective, Tirade

Philippine(s) Bisayan, Igorot, Moro, PI, RP, Tagalog, Visayan

Philistine, Philistinism Artless, Ashdod, Barbarian, Foe, Gath, Gaza, Gigman, Goliath, Goth, Lowbrow, Podsnappery, Vandal

Philology Linguistics, Semantics, Speechcraft

Philosopher, Philosophy Academist, Activism, Ahimsa, Analytical, Animism,

Anthrosophy, Antinomianism, Antiochian, Atomist, Attitude, Averr(h)oism,
Cartesian, Casuist, Comtism, Conceptualism, Conservatism, Cracker-barrel,
Critical, Cynic, Deipnosophist, Deontology, Eclectic, Eleatic, Empiricism,
Enlightenment, Epistemology, Ethics, Existentialism, Fatalism, Gymnosophist,
Hedonism, Hobbism, Holist, Humanism, I Ching, Idealism, Ideology,
Instrumentalism, -ism, Kaizen, Linguistic, Logical atomism, Logicism, Logos,
Maieutic, Marxism, Materialism, Megarian, Metaphysician, Metaphysics,
Metempiricism, Monism, Moral(ist), Natural, Neoplatonism, Neoteric, Nihilism,
Nominalism, Occamist, Occam's razor, Opinion, Peripatetic, Phenomenology,
Platonism, Populism, Positivism, Rationalism, Realism, Rosminian, Sage,
Sankhya, Sceptic, Schoolman, Scientology, Sensist, Shankara(-charya), Sophist,
Stoic, Synthetic, Taoism, Theism, Theosophy, Thomist, Transcendentalism,
Ultraism, Utilitarianism, Utopianism, Voluntarism, Weltanschauung, Yoga, Yogi

PHILOSOPHERS

4 letters:
Ayer
Hume
Jedi
Kant
Mach
Mill
Ryle
Weil
Wolf
Zeno

5 letters:
Amiel
Bacon
Comte
Croce
Dewey
Hegel
Locke
Paine
Plato
Quine
Renan
Smith
Sorel
Taine

6 letters:
Agnesi
Cicero
Engels
Godwin
Herder
Hobbes

Olbers
Ortega
Pascal
Popper
Pyrrho
Sartre
Scotus
Seneca
Thales

7 letters:
Abelard
Aquinas
Bentham
Bergson
Diderot
Emerson
Erasmus
Erigena
Herbart
Hypatia
Leibniz
Malthus
Marcion
Marcuse
Mencius
Meng-tse
Ptolemy
Russell
Schlick
Sheffer
Spencer
Spinoza
Steiner
Vedanta

8 letters:
Avicenna
Berkeley
Boethius
Cyreniac
Diogenes
Epicurus
Foucault
Hamilton
Harrison
Menippus
Old Moore
Plotinus
Plutarch
Rousseau
Socrates
Xenophon

9 letters:
Aristotle
Bosanquet
Cleanthes
Confucius
Descartes
Euhemerus
Heidegger
Leucippus
Lucretius
Nietzsche
Santayana
Schelling
Whitehead

10 letters:
Anacharsis

Anaxagoras
Anaximenes
Antiochene
Apemanthus
Apollonius
Aristippus
Campanella
Chrysippus
Democritus
Empedocles
Heraclitus
Hutchinson
Paracelsus
Parmenides
Protagoras
Pythagoras
Saint-Simon
Swedenborg
Von Leibniz
Xenocrates
Xenophanes

11 letters:
Anaximander
Antisthenes
Kierkegaard
Montesquieu

12 letters:
Callisthenes
Schopenhauer
Wittgenstein

Philosophic(al) Rational, Resigned, Thoughtful, Tranquil
Philtre Aphrodisiac, Charm, Drug, Hippomanes, Potion
Phlegm(atic) Calm, Composed, Pituita(ry), Pituite, Stolid, Unperturbed, Unruffled
Phloem Leptome, Liber
Phobia Aversion, Dread, Fear, Thing
Phoebe, Phoebus Apollo, Artemis, Day-star, Deaconess, Moon, Selene, Sol, Sun
Phoenician Tripolitania
Phoenix Bird-of-wonder, Fum, Fung, Paragon, Self-begotten
Phone Bell, Blower, Call, Cellular, Dial, Intercom, Mob(i)e, Mobile, Moby, Pay,
    Picture, Ring, Smart, Talkback, → TELEPHONE, Text
Phonetic(s) Acoustic, Articulatory, Auditory, Mouillé, Oral, Palaeotype, Palatal,
    Plosion, Spoken, Symbol, Synaeresis
▷ **Phonetically** *may indicate* a word sounding like another
Phon(e)y Bogus, Charlatan, Counterfeit, Fake, Hokey, Impostor, Poseur, Quack,
    → SHAM, Specious, Spurious
▷ **Phony** *may indicate* an anagram
Phosphate Monazite, Torbernite, Vivianite, Wavellite, Xenotime
Phosphor(escent), Phosphorescence, Phosphorus Bologna, Briming, Foxfire,
    Friar's lantern, Ignis fatuus, Jack o'lantern, Luminescent, Malathion®, Noctilucent,
    P, Pyrosome, Sarin, Sea-fire, Tabun, Will o' the wisp
Photo(copy), Photograph(y), Photographic, Photo finish Ambrotype,
    Anaglyph, Angiogram, Beefcake, Black and white, Blow-up, Cabinet, Calotype,
    Clog, Close-up, Composite, Contre-jour, Daguerrotype, Diazo, Duplicate, Enprint,
    Exposure, Ferroprint, Ferrotype, Film, Flash, Half-tone, Headshot, Heliochrome®,
    Heliotype, Hologram, Infra-red, Kallitype, Kirlian, Kodak®, Microdot, Microfilm,
    Microgram, Micrograph, Microprint, Monochrome, Montage, Mugshot, Negative,
    Nephogram, Opaline, Panel, Picture, Pinhole, Platinotype, Polaroid®, Positive,
    Print, Resorcin, Rotograph, Rotogravure, Schlieren, Sepia, Shoot, Shot, Shutterbug,
    Slide, Snap, Spirit, Still, Take, Talbotype, Time-lapse, Tintype, Tomography, Topo,
    Trimetrogon, Vignette, Wire, Woodburytype, Xerography, X-ray
Photographer Beaton, Brandt, Cameraman, Cameron, Cartier-Bresson, Daguerre,
    Fox Talbot, Paparazzo, Schlierin, Shutterbug
Phrase Abject, Actant, Asyndeton, Buzzword, Catch(word), Catchcry, Cliché,
    Climacteric, Comma, Expression, Heroic, Hook, Laconism, Leitmotiv, Locution,
    Mantra, Noun, Phr, Refrain, Riff, Slogan, Soundbite, Tag, Term, Trope
Phrygian Midas
Phthisis Decay, TB
Phylactery Amulet, Talisman, Tefillin, Tephillin
Phyllopod Brine-shrimp
Physic(s) Cluster, Cryogenics, Culver's, Cure, Dose, Electrostatics, Geostatics,
    Health, High-energy, Kinematics, Medicine, Nuclear, Nucleonics, Particle,
    Photometry, Purge, Remedy, Rheology, Science, Solid-state, Sonics,
    Thermodynamics, Ultrasonics
Physical Bodily, Carnal, Corpor(e)al, Material, Natural, Tangible
Physician Allopath, Buteyko, Doctor, Galen, Hakim, Hansen, Harvey, Hippocrates,
    Internist, Leech, Linacre, Lister, Medic(o), Menière, Mesmer, Mindererus, Paean,
    Paracelsus, Practitioner, Preceptor, Quack, Roget, Sézary, Stahl, Therapist, Time
Physicist Alfren, Ampère, Angstrom, Appleton, Archimedes, Avogadro, Becquerel,
    Bohr, Bondi, Born, Bose, Bragg, Brewster, Carnot, Cockcroft, Coulomb, Crookes,
    Curie, Dalton, Davisson, Debye, Dicke, Dirac, Einstein, Faraday, Fermi, Friedmann,
    Galileo, Gamow, Gauss, Geiger, Giorgi, Gold, Hahn, Hawking, Heaviside,

Heisenberg, Henry, Hertz, Hooke, Hoyle, Huygens, Joliot-Curie, Josephson, Joule,
Kerv, Kirchhoff, Landau, Lawe, Lodge, Lorentz, Mach, Marconi, Maxwell, Meitner,
Michelson, Morley, Newton, Oersted, Ohm, Oppenheimer, Pauli, Peebles, Penzias,
Pic(c)ard, Planck, Popov, Rankine, Rayleigh, Reaumur, Robertson, Ro(e)ntgen,
Rutherford, Schottky, Schrödinger, Scientist, Sievert, Stark, Torricelli, Tyndall, Van
Allen, Van der Waals, Volta, Watson-Watt, Weber, Wheeler, Wilson, Young
Physiognomist, Physiognomy Face, Features, Lavater
Physiology, Physiologist Malpighi, Pavlov, Wagner, Zoonomia
Physiotherapist Masseur
Physique Body, Build, Figure, Pyknic, Somatotype
Pi, Pious Breast-beater, Craw-thumper, Devotional, Devout, Fraud, Gallio,
God-fearing, Godly, Holy, Holy Willie, Mid-Victorian, Religiose, Sanctimonious,
Savoury, Smug, Wise, Zaddik
Piaffe Spanish-walk
Pianist Anda, Arrau, Hambourg, Hess, Hofmann, Liszt, Mingus, Morton,
Pachmann, Paderewski, Répétiteur, Schnabel, Tatum, Vamper, Virtuoso
Piano Baby grand, Bechstein, Boudoir grand, Celesta, Celeste, Concert grand,
Cottage, Flugel, Forte, Grand, Honkytonk, Keyboard, Mbira, Overstrung, P, Player,
Prepared, Semi-grand, Softly, Steinway, Stride, Thumb, Upright
Piano-maker Erard
Picaresque Roman à tiroirs
Picaroon Brigand, Corsair, Pirate, Rogue
Piccadilly Whist
Piccolo Ottavino
Pick(er), Pickaxe, Picking, Pick up Break, Choice, → CHOOSE, Cream, Cull,
Elite, Flower, Gather, Glean, Gurlet, Hack, Holing, Hopper, Mattock, Nap, Nibble,
Oakum, Plectrum, Pluck, Plum, Select, Single, Sort, Steal, Strum, Tong, Wale
▷ **Picked** *may indicate* an anagram
Picket Demonstrate, Flying, Pale, Palisade, Protester, Stake, Tether, Tie
Pickings Harvest, Profits, Scrounging, Spoils
Pickle(r) Achar, Brine, Cabbage, Caper, Chow-chow, Chutney, Corn, Cucumber,
Cure, Dilemma, Dill, Eisel, Esile, Gherkin, Girkin, Jam, Kimchi, Marinade,
Marinate, Mess, Mull, Olive, Onion, Peculate, Peregrine, Piccalilli, → PLIGHT,
Relish, Samp(h)ire, Scrape, Souse, Trouble, Vinegar, Wolly
Picklock Oustiti, Peterman
Pick-me-up Bracer, Drink, Restorer, Reviver, Tonic
Pickpocket(s) Adept, Bung, Cly-faker, Cutpurse, Dip, Diver, Fagin, File, Nipper,
Swell mob, Wire
Pick-up Arrest, Light o'love, Truck, Ute
Picnic Alfresco, Braaivleis, Burgoo, Clambake, Fun, Outing, Push-over, Spread,
Tailgate, Wase-goose, Wayzgoose
Picture(s) Anaglyph, Arpillera, Art, Bambocciades, Bitmap, Canvas, Collage,
Cutaway, Cyclorama, Decoupage, Depict, Describe, Diptych, Drawing, Drypoint,
Emblem, Envisage, Epitome, Etching, Film, Flick, Fresco, Gouache, Graphic,
Histogram, Icon, Identikit®, Imagery, Inset, Kakemono, Landscape, Likeness,
Lithograph, Montage, Motion, Movie, Moving, Movy, Mugshot, Myriorama,
Oil, Photo, Photofit®, Photogram, Photomontage, Photomosaic, Photomural,
Pin-up, Pix, Plate, Polyptych, Portrait, Predella, Prent, Presentment, Print,
Retraitt, Retrate, Rhyparography, Scene, Shadowgraph, Shot, Slide, Snapshot,
Stereochrome, Stereogram, Stereograph, Stevengraph, Still-life, Table(au), Talkie,
Thermogram, Tone, Topo, Transfer, Transparency, Vanitas, Vectograph, Vision,

Votive, Vraisemblance, Word, Zincograph
Picturesque Idyllic, Scenic
Pidgin Chinook jargon, Creole, Fanagalo, Fanakalo, Japlish, New Guinea, Police Motu, Solomon Islands, Tok Pisin
Pie(s) Anna, Banoffee, Battalia, Bridie, Camp, Chewet, Cobbler, Cottage, Coulibiac, Curry puff, Custard, Deep-dish, Easy, Flan, Floater, Florentine, Hash, Humble, Koulibiaca, Madge, Meat, Mess, Mince, Mud, Mystery bag, Pandowdy, Pastry, Pasty, Patty, Périgord, Pica, Piet, Pirog, Pizza, Printer's, Pyat, Pyet, Pyot, Quiche, Rappe, Resurrection, Shepherd's, Shoofly, Spoil, Squab, Stargaz(e)y, Star(ry)-gazy, Sugar, Tart, Tarte tatin, Torte, Tourtière, Turnover, Tyropitta, Umble, Vol-au-vent, Warden
▷ **Pie** *may indicate* an anagram
Piebald Calico, Dappled, Motley, Pied, Pinto, Skewbald
Piece(s) Add, Bishop, Bit, Blot, Cameo, Cannon, Cent, Charm, → **CHESSMAN**, Chip, Chunk, Coin, Companion, Component, Concerto, Conversation, Crumb, Domino, End, Episode, Extract, Firearm, Flitters, Fragment, Frust, Gat, Goring, → **GUN**, Haet, Hait, Hunk, Item, Join, Mammock, Médaillons, Mite, Money, Morceau, Morsel, Museum, Nip, Novelette, Oddment, Off-cut, Ort, Part, Party, Pastiche, Patch, Pawn, Period, Peso, Pin, Pistareen, Pole, → **PORTION**, Recital, Scliff, Scrap, Section, Set, Shard, Sherd, Skliff, Slice, Sliver, Sou, Speck, String, Stub, Swatch, Tait, Tate, Tile, Toccata, Truncheon, Wedge
Pièce de résistance Star-turn
Piecemeal, Piecework Gradually, Intermittent, Jigsaw, Serial, Tut
Pie-crust Coffin, Lid, Pastry
Pied-à-terre Nest, Pad
Pieman Pastrycook, Shepherd
Pier(s) Anta, Groyne, Jetty, Jutty, Landing, Mole, Plowman, Quay, Slipway, Swiss roll, Wharf
Pierce(d), Piercer, Piercing Accloy, Awl, Broach, Cleave, Cribrose, Dart, Drill, Endart, Fenestrate(d), Fulminant, Gimlet, Gore, Gride, Gryde, Hull, Impale, Jag, Keen, Lance, Lancinate, Lobe, Move, Needle, Penetrate, Perforate, Pike, Pink, Poignant, Punch, Puncture, Riddle, Rive, Shrill, Skewer, Slap, Sleeper, Spear, Spike, Spit, Stab, Steek, Stiletto, Sting, Thirl, Thrill(ant)
Piety Devotion, Purity, Sanctity
Piffle Bilge, Codswallop, Hogwash, Poppycock, Tommy-rot, Twaddle
Pig(s), Piggy, Pigskin Anthony, Babe, Babirusa, Baconer, Barrow, Bartholomew, Bessemer, Bland, Boar, Bonham, British Lop, Bush, Captain Cooker, Doll, Duroc, Elt, Farrow, Fastback, Football, Gadarene, Gilt, Gloucester, Gloucester Old Spot, Glutton, Grice, Grumphie, Gryce, Guffie, Guinea, Gus, Ham, Hog, Ingot, Iron, Javelina, Kentledge, Kintledge, Kunekune, Lacombe, Landrace, Lard, Large Black, Large white, Lingot, Long, Middle White, Napoleon, Old Spot, Peccary, Policeman, Pork(er), Razorback, Rosser, Runt, Saddleback, Shoat, Shot(e), Shott, Slip, Snowball, Sounder, Sow, Squealer, Sucking, Suid(ae), Tamworth, Tayassuid, Tithe, Toe, Tootsie, Truffle, Vietnamese Pot-bellied, Warthog, Welsh, Yelt
Pig-disease Bullnose
Pigeon Archangel, Barb, Bird, Bronze-winged, Cape, Capuchin, Carrier, Clay, Cropper, Culver, Cumulet, Danzig, Dove, Fairy Swallow, Fantail, Goura, Ground, Gull, Homer, Homing, Horseman, Jacobin, Kereru, Kuku, Manumea, New Zealand, Nun, Owl, Passenger, Peristeronic, Piwakawaka, Pouter, Ringdove, Rock(er), Roller, Ront(e), Ruff, Runt, Scandaroon, Solitaire, Spot, Squab, Squealer, Stock-dove, Stool, Stork, Swift, Talkie-talkee, Tippler, Tooth-billed, Tumbler,

Turbit, Wonga(-wonga), Zoozoo
Pigeonhole Classify, Compartment, File, Label, Postpone, Shelve, Slot, Stereotype
Pigeon-house Columbary, Cote, Dovecot(e)
Pig-food Mast, Swill
Pig-headed Self-willed
Pig-iron Kentledge, Kintledge
Pigment(s), Pigmentation Accessory, Anthoclore, Anthocyan(in), Argyria,
Betacyanin, Bilirubin, Biliverdin, Bister, Bistre, Bronzing, Cappagh-brown,
Carmine, Carotene, Carotenoid, Carotin, Carotinoid, Chloasma, Chlorophyll,
Chrome, Chromogen, Cobalt, Colcothar, Colour, Crocus, Curcumin, Dye, Etiolin,
Eumelanin, Flake-white, Flavin(e), Fucoxanthin, Gamboge, Gossypol, Haem,
Hem(e), H(a)ematin, H(a)emocyanin, H(a)emoglobin, Iodopsin, Lake, Lamp-black,
Lithopone, Liverspot, Lutein, Luteolin, Lycopene, Madder, Melanin, Monastral®,
Naevus, Naples yellow, Nigrosine, Ochre, Opsin, Orpiment, Paris-green,
Phthalocyanine, Phycobilin, Phycoerythrin, Phycophaein, Phycoxanthin,
Phytochrome, Porphyrin, Porphyropsin, Pterin, Quercetin, Realgar, Red lead,
Respiratory, Retinene, Rhiboflavin, Rhodophane, Rhodopsin, Saffron, Scheele's
green, Sepia, Sienna, Sinopia, Sinopsis, Smalt, Tapetum, Tempera, Terre-verte,
Tincture, Toner, Ultramarine, Umber, Urobilin, Urochrome, Verditer, Vermilion,
Viridian, Whitewash, Xanthophyll, Xanthopterin(e), Zinc white
Pigtail Braid, Cue, Plait, Queue
Pi jaw Cant
Pike Assegai, Crag, Dory, Fogash, Gar(fish), Ged, Gisarme, Glaive, Hie, Holostei,
Javelin, Lance, Luce, Partisan, Pickerel, Ravensbill, Scafell, Snoek, Spear, Speed,
Spontoon, Vouge, Walleyed
▶ **Pilaster** *see* PILLAR
Pile(d), Piles, Piling Agger, Amass, Atomic, Bing, Bomb, Camp-sheathing,
Camp-shedding, Camp-sheeting, Camp-shot, Clamp, Cock, Column, Crowd, Deal,
Down, Emerods, Farmers, Fender, Fig, Floccus, Fortune, Galvanic, Hair, Haycock,
Heap, Hept, Historic, Hoard, Load, Lot, Marleys, Mass, Moquette, Nap, Pier,
Post, Pyre, Raft, Reactor, Ream(s), Rouleau, Screw, Shag, Sheet, Slush, → STACK,
Starling, Stilt, Trichome, Upheap, Velvet, Voltaic, Wealth, Windrow, Wodge
Pile-driver Tup
Pilfer(ing) Crib, Filch, Finger, Maraud, Miche, Nick, Peculate, Pickery, Pickle, Pinch,
Plagiarise, Plunder, Purloin, Snitch, → STEAL
Pilgrim(age) Aske, Childe Harold, Expedition, Fatima, Gaya, Hadj(i), Haji, Hajj(i),
Karbala, Kerbela, Kum, Loreto, Lourdes, Mathura, Mecca, Nasik, Nikko, Palmer,
Pardoner, Qom, Qum, Reeve, Scallop-shell, Shrine, Voyage, Yatra
Pill(s) Abortion, Ball, Beverley, Bitter, Bolus, Caplet, Capsule, Chill, Dex, Doll, Dose,
Globule, Golfball, Goofball, Lob, Medication, Medicine, Number nine, Peace,
Peel, Pellet, Pep, Pilula, Pilule, Placebo, Poison, Protoplasmal, Radio, Sleeping,
Spansule, Tablet, Troche, Trochisk, Upper
Pillage Booty, Devastate, Plunder, Ransack, Rapine, Ravage, Razzia, Robbery, Sack,
Spoil
Pillar(ed), Pillars Anta, Apostle, Atlantes, Baluster, Balustrade, Boaz, Canton,
Caryatides, Cippus, Columel, Column, Earth, Eustyle, Gendarme, Hercules, Herm,
Impost, Islam, Jachin, Lat, Man, Modiolus, Monolith, Newel, Nilometer, Obelisk,
Pedestal, Peristyle, Pier, Post, Respond, Saddle, Serac, Stalactite, Stalagmite, Stoop,
Telamon, Tetrastyle, Trumeau
Pill-box Hat, Inro
Pillion Cushion, Pad, Rear

Pillory Cang(ue), Cippus, Crucify, Jougs, Little-ease, Pelt, Satirise, Slam
Pillow(case) Bear, Beer, Bere, Bolster, Cod, Cow, Cushion, Headrest, Hop, Lace, Pad, Pulvinar
Pilot Ace, Airman, Auto(matic), Aviator, Captain, → CONDUCT, Experimental, Flier, George, Govern, Guide, Hobbler, Lead, Lodesman, Lodestar, Palinure, Palinurus, Pitt, Prune, Shipman, Steer, Test, Tiphys, Trial, Usher, Wingman
Pimento Allspice
Pimp Apple-squire, Bludger, Fancyman, Fleshmonger, Hoon, Lecher, Mack, Pandarus, Pander, Ponce, Procurer, Solicit, Souteneur
Pimpernel Bastard, Bog, Scarlet, Water, Wincopipe, Wink-a-peep, Yellow
Pimple, Pimply Blackhead, Botch, Bubukle, Button, Gooseflesh, Grog-blossom, Hickey, Horripilation, Milium, Papilla, Papula, Papule, Plook, Plouk, Pock, Pustule, Quat, Rumblossom, Rum-bud, Spot, Tetter, Uredinial, Wen, Whelk, Whitehead, Zit
Pin Bayonet, Belaying, Bolt, Brooch, Candle, Cask, Cotter, Curling, Dowel, Drawing, Drift, End, Fasten, Fid, Firing, Fix, Gam, Gudgeon, Hair, Hairgrip, Hob, Joggle, Kevel, King, Leg, Nail, Needle, Nog, Panel, Peg, Pintle, Pivot, Preen, Rivet, Rolling, Saddle, Safety, Scarf, SCART, Scatter, Shear, Shirt, Skewer, Skittle, Skiver, Spike, Spindle, Split, Staple, Stick, Stump, Swivel, Taper, Thole, Thumbtack, Tie, Tre(e)nail, U-bolt, Woolder, Wrest, Wrist
Pinafore Apron, Brat, HMS, Overall, Pinny, Save-all, Tire
Pinball Pachinko
Pince-nez Nose-nippers
Pincers Chela, Claw, Forceps, Forfex, Nipper, Tweezers
Pinch(ed) Arrest, Bit, Bone, Chack, Constrict, Cramp, Crimp, Crisis, Emergency, Gaunt, Misappropriate, Nab, Nick, Nim, Nip, Peculate, Peel, Pilfer, Pocket, Pook(it), Prig, Pugil, Raft, Rob, Scrimp, Scrounge, Skimp, Smatch, Snabble, Snaffle, Sneak, Sneap, Sneeshing, Snuff, Squeeze, → STEAL, Swipe, Tate, Tweak, Twinge
Pine(s), Pining Arolla, Bristlecone, Celery, Cembra, Chile, Cluster, Cone, Conifer, Cypress, Droop, Dwine, Earn, Erne, Fret, Green, Ground, Hone, Hoop, Huon, Jack, Japanese umbrella, Jeffrey, Kauri, Languish, Languor, Loblolly, Lodgepole, Long, Longleaf, Monkey-puzzle, Moon, Norfolk Island, Norway, Nut, Oregon, Parana, Picea, Pinaster, Pitch, Radiata, Red, Scotch, Scots, Screw, Softwood, Spruce, Starve, Stone, Sugar, Tree, Umbrella, Urman, Waste, White, Yearn
Pineapple Anana, Bomb, Bromelia, Grenade, Piña, Poll, Sorosis, Tillandsia
Ping Knock, Whir(r)
Pinguin Anana(s)
Pinion Fetter, Penne, Pinnoed, Secure, Shackle, Wing
Pink Blush, Carolina, Castory, Cheddar, Clove, Colour, Coral, Dianthus, Dutch, Emperce, FT, Fuchsia, Gillyflower, Indian, Knock, Lake, Lily, Lychnis, Maiden, Moss, Mushroom, Oyster, Peach-blow, Peak, Perce, Pierce, Pompadour, Pounce, Rose(ate), Ruddy, Salmon, Scallop, Sea, Shell, Shocking, Shrimp, Spigelia, Spit, Stab, Tiny
Pinnacle Acme, Apex, Crest, Crown, Gendarme, Height, Needle, Pinnet, Summit
Pinniped Seal
Pin-point Focus, Highlight, Identify, Isolate, Localise
Pint(s) Cab, Jar, Log, Reputed
Pintail Duck, Smeath, Smee(th)
Pin-up Cheesecake, Dish, Star
Pioneer Baird, Bandeirante, Blaze, Boone, Colonist, Emigrant, Explore, Fargo, Fleming, Frontiersman, Harbinger, Innovator, Lead, Marconi, Oecist, Pathfinder,

Planter, Rochdale, Sandgroper, Settler, Spearhead, Trail-blazer, Trekker, Voortrekker, Waymaker, Wells
▸ **Pious** *see* PI
Pip Ace, Acinus, Blackball, Bleep, Hip, Hump, Phil, Pyrene, Seed, Star
Pipe(s), Piper, Pipeline, Piping Antara, Aorta, Aulos, Balance, Barrel, Blub, Boatswain's, Bong, Briar, Briarroot, Broseley, Bubble, Calabash, Call, Calumet, Chanter, Cheep, Cherrywood, Chibouk, Chibouque, Chillum, Churchwarden, Clay, Cob, Conduit, Corncob, Crane, Cutty, Down, Downcomer, Drain, Drill, Drillstring, Dry riser, Duct, Dudeen, Dudheen, Ell, Escape, Exhaust, Faucet, Feed, Fistula, Flue, Flute, Gage, Gas main, Gedact, Gedeckt, Hawse, Hod, Hogger, Hooka(h), Hose, Hubble-bubble, Hydrant, Indian, Irish, Jet, Kalian, Kelly, Mains, Manifold, Marsyas, Meerschaum, Mirliton, Montre, Narghile, Narg(h)il(l)y, Nargile(h), Oat(en), Oboe, Organ, Ottavino, Pan, Peace, Pepper, Pibroch, Piccolo, Pied, Pifferaro, Pitch, Poverty, Pule, Qanat, Quill, Rainwater, Recorder, Ree(d), Rise, Riser, Sack-doudling, Salicional, Sennit, Serpent, Service, Sewer, Shalm, Shawm, Shisha, Shrike, Sing, Siphon, Skirl, Sluice, Soil, Squeak, Stack, Standpipe, Stopcock, Stummel, Sucker, Syrinx, Tail, Tee, Throttle, Tibia, Tootle, Trachea, Tremie, Tube, Tubule, Tweet, U-bend, Uillean(n), Union, Uptake, U-trap, U-tube, Vent, Ventiduct, Volcanic, Waste, Water(-spout), Watermain, Weasand, Whistle, Woodcock's head, Woodnote
Pipefish Sea-adder
Pipe-laying Graft
Pipit Bird, Skylark, Titlark
Pippin Apple, Orange, Ribston
Pipsqueak Nobody
Piquancy, Piquant Pungent, Racy, Relish, Salt, Sharp, Spicy, Tangy
Pique Dod, Huff, Resentment, Titillate
Piranha Caribe, Characinoid, Piraya
Pirate(s), Piratical, Piracy Algerine, Barbarossa, Blackbeard, Boarder, Bootleg, Brigand, Buccaneer, Buccanier, Cateran, Condottier, Conrad, Corsair, Crib, Dampier, Fil(l)ibuster, Flint, Gunn, Hijack, Hook, Kidd, Lift, Loot, Morgan, Penzance, Picaro(on), Pickaroon, Plagiarise, Plunder, Rakish, Rover, Sallee-man, Sallee-rover, Sea-dog, Sea-king, Sea-rat, Sea-robber, Sea-wolf, Silver, Skull and crossbones, Smee, Steal, Teach, Thief, Viking, Water-rat, Water-thief
Pistillate Female
Pistol Air, Ancient, Automatic, Barker, Barking-iron, Colt®, Dag, Derringer, Gat, → GUN, Hackbut, Horse, Iron, Luger®, Pepperbox, Petronel, Pocket, Puffer, Revolver, Rod, Saloon, Shooter, Starter, Starting, Very, Water, Weapon
Piston Four-stroke, Plunger, Ram, Trunk
Pit(ted), Pitting Abyss, Alveolus, Antrum, Bottomless, Catch, Cave, Cesspool, Chasm, Cissing, Cloaca, Colliery, Crater, Den, Depression, Depth, Dungmere, Ensile, Fossa, Fovea, Foxhole, Gehenna, Hangi, Heapstead, Hell, Hole, Hollow, Inferno, Inspection, Khud, Lacunose, Lime, Mark, Match, Measure, → MINE, Mosh, Orchestra, Parterre, Pip, Plague, Play, Pock-mark, Potato, Punctate, Putamen, Pyrene, Ravine, Rifle, Salt, Scrobicule, Silo, Slime, Soakaway, Solar plexus, Stone, Sump, Tar, Tear, Trap, Trous-de-loup, Underarm
Pitch(ed) Absolute, Asphalt, Atilt, Attune, Bitumen, Burgundy, Coal-tar, Concert, Crease, Diamond, Dive, Ela, Elect, Elevator, Encamp, Erect, Establish, Fever, Fling, Fork, Ground, International, Intonation, Key, Knuckleball, Labour, Length, Level, Lurch, Maltha, Mineral, Nets, Neume, Patter, Peck, Perfect, Philosophical, Piceous, Pight, Pin, Plong(e), Plunge, Pop, Purl, Resin, Rock, Ruff(e), Sales, Scend,

Seel, Send, Shape, Sling, Slope, Soprarino, Spiel, Stoit, Tar, Tessitura, Tilt, Tone, Tonemic, Tonus, Tremolo, Tune, Vibrato, Wicket, Wood
Pitchblende Cleveite
Pitcher(-shaped) Aryt(a)enoid, Ascidium, Bowler, Cruse, Ewer, Jug, Steen, Urceolus
Pitchfork Hurl, Toss
Pitfall Ambush, Danger, Hazard, Snare, Trap
Pith(y) Ambatch, Aphorism, Apo(ph)thegm, Core, Down, Essence, Gnomic, Hat-plant, Heart, Marrow, Medulla, Moxa, Nucleus, Rag, Succinct, Terse
Pithead Broo, Brow, Minehead
Pithless Thowless
Pitiless Flint-hearted, Hard, Ruthless
Piton Rurp
Pitt Chatham
Pity, Piteous, Pitiful, Pitiable Ah, Alack, Alas, Commiseration, → COMPASSION, Hapless, Mercy, Pathos, Pilgarlic, Red-leg, Rue, Ruth(ful), Seely, Shame, Sin, Sympathy
Pivot(al) Ax(i)le, Central, Focal, Fulcrum, Gooseneck, Gudgeon, Kingbolt, Revolve, Rotate, Slue, → SWIVEL, Trunnion, Turn, Wheel
Pixie Brownie, Elf, Fairy, Gremlin, Sprite
Pizza Calzone, Pepperoni
Placard Affiche, Bill, Playbill, Poster
Placate Appease, Conciliate, Pacify, Propitiate, Soothe
Place(ment) Ad loc, Aim, Allocate, Area, Berth, Bro, Decimal, Deploy, Deposit, Fix, Habitat, Hither, Howf, Identify, Impose, → IN PLACE OF, Install, Job, Joint, Juxtapose, Lay, Lieu, Locality, Locate, Locus, Parking, Pitch, Plat, Plaza, Point, Posit, → POSITION, Product, Put, Realm, Region, Repose, Resting, Scene, Second, Set, Site, Situate, Situation, Slot, Spot, Stead, Sted(e), Stedd(e), Stratify, Town, Vendôme
Placid Cool, Easy, Easy-osy, Quiet, Tame, Tranquil
Plagiarise, Plagiarist Copy, Crib, Lift, Pirate, Steal
Plague (spot) Annoy, Bane, Bedevil, Black death, Boil, Bubonic, Burden, Cattle, Curse, Dog, Dun, Frogs, Goodyear, Goujeers, Harry, Infestation, Locusts, Lues, Murrain, Murran, Murrin, Murrion, Nag, Pest, Pester, Pox, Press, Scourge, Tease, Token, Torture, Try, Vex
Plaid Maud, Roon, Shepherd's, Tartan, Wales
Plain(s) Abraham, Archimedes, Artless, Ascetic, Au naturel, Bald, Banat, Bare, Blatant, Broad, Campagna, Campo, Candid, Carse, Ceará, Chryse, Clavius, Clear, Cook, Dowdy, Downright, Dry, Esdraelon, Evident, Explicit, Flat, Flood, Girondist, Gran Chaco, Great, Homely, Homespun, Inornate, Jezreel, Kar(r)oo, Lande, Langrenus, Llano, Lombardy, Lowland, Maidan, Manifest, Marathon, Mare, Monochrome, Nullarbor, Obvious, Ocean of Storms, Oceanus Procellarum, Olympia, → ORDINARY, Outspoken, Overt, Packstaff, Pampa(s), Paramo, Patent, Pikestaff, Plateau, Playa, Polje, Prairie, Prose, Ptolemaeus, Purbach, Sabkha(h), Sabkhat, Sailing, Salisbury, Savanna(h), Secco, Serengeti, Sharon, Simple, Sodom, Spoken, Staked, Steppe, Tableland, Thessaly, Tundra, Vega, Veldt, Visible, Walled
Plainchant Canto fermo
Plainsman Llanero
Plainsong Ambrosian, Chant
Plaint(ive) Complaint, Dirge, Lagrimoso, Lament, Melancholy, Sad, Whiny
Plaintiff Doe, Impeacher, Litigant, Suer
Plait Braid, Crimp, Cue, Frounce, Furbelow, Goffer, Intertwine, Pigtail, Plica, Plight, Queue, Ruche, Sennit, Sinnet, Splice

Plan(ned), Planner, Planning Aim, American, Angle, Architect, Arrange,
Axonometric, Blueprint, Brew, Budget, Care, Chart, Commission, Complot,
Contingency, Contrive, Dalton, Dart, Deep-laid, Deliberate, Delors, Design, Desyne,
Device, Devise, Diagram, Draft, Drawing, Elevation, Engineer, European, Family,
Five-Year, Floor, Format, Galveston, Game, Ground, Hang, Ichnography, Idea, Idée,
Instal(l)ment, Intent, Lay(out), Leicester, Leicestershire, Map, Marshall, Master,
Mastermind, Mean, Nominal, Open, Outline, Pattern, Pipe-dream, Plat, Plot, Ploy,
Policy, Premeditate, Prepense, Procedure, Programme, Project, Projet, Proposal,
Prospectus, Protraction, Rapacki, Road map, Scenario, Schedule, Scheme,
Schlieffen, Shape, Spec(ification), Stratagem, Strategy, Subterfuge, System,
Tactician, Town, Wheeze
Plane(s) Aero(dyne), Air, → AIRCRAFT, Airliner, Airship, Bandit, Block, Boeing,
Bomber, Bus, Buttock, Camel, Canard, Cartesian, Chenar, Chinar, Comet,
Concorde, Crate, Dakota, Datum, Delta-wing, Even, Facet, Fault, Fillister, Flat,
Focal, Galactic, Glider, Gliding, Gotha, Homaloid, Hurricane, Icosahedron,
Icosohedra, Inclined, Jack, Jet, Jointer, Jumbo, Level, London, Main, MIG, Mirage,
Mosquito, Moth, Octagon, Perspective, Platan(us), Polygon, Pursuit, Rocket,
Router, Shackleton, Shave, Smooth, Sole, Spitfire, Spokeshave, Spy, Stealth
(bomber), STOL, Surface, Sycamore, Tail, Taube, Thrust, Tow, Trainer, Tree,
Trident, Tropopause, Trying, Viscount
Plane figure Endecagon, Hendecagon
Planet(s), Planetary Alphonsine, Ariel, Asteroid, Body, Cabiri, Ceres, Chiron,
Constellation, Earth, Eros, Extrasolar, Gas giant, Georgian, Giant, House, Hyleg,
Inferior, Inner, Jovian, Jupiter, Lucifer, Major, Mars, Mercury, Minor, Moon,
Neptune, Outer, Pallas, Pluto, Primary, Psyche, Quartile, Red, Satellitium, Saturn,
Sedna, Sphere, Starry, Sun, Superior, Terrestrial, Uranus, Venus, Vista, Vulcan,
World, Zog
Plangent Mournful
Plank Board, Chess, Deal, Duckboard, Garboard, Plonk, Sarking, Slab, Spirketting,
Straik, Strake, Stringer, Weatherboard, Wood, Wrest
Plankton Nekton, Neuston, Pelagic, Red tide, Seston, Spatfall
Plant(s), Plant part Acrogen, Amphidiploid, Anemochore, Annual, Anther,
Aphotoic, Autophyte, Bed, Biennial, Biota, Bloomer, Bryophyte, CAM, Catchfly,
Chamaephyte, Chomophyte, Cotyledon, Cultigen, Cultivar, Dayflower, Dibble,
Ecad, Eccremocarpus, Embed, Endogen, Enrace, Epilithic, Epiphyllous,
Epiphyte, Equisetum, Establish, Factory, Fix, Forb, Geophyte, G(u)ild, Growth,
Gymnosperm, Halophyte, Halosere, Helophyte, Herbage, Herbarium, House,
Humicole, Hydrastus, Hydrophyte, Hygrophyte, Hylophyte, Incross, Insert,
Instil, Inter, Labiate, Land, Lathe, Lithophyte, Livelong, Longday, Machinery,
Mill, Monocotyledon, Ornamental, Phanerogam, Phloem, Pilot, Pitcher, Power,
Protophyte, Ramet, Resurrection, Root, Rosin, Saprophyte, Schizophyte, Sciophyte,
Sclerophyll, Scrambler, Sensitive, Sere, Shortday, Shrub, Simple, Soma, Sow,
Steelworks, Stickseed, Sticktight, Stickweed, Strangler, Streptocarpus, Succulent,
Superweed, Thallophyte, Therophyte, Thickleaf, → TREE, Trifolium, Tropophyte,
Vegetal, Vegetation, Wasabi, Washery, Wilding, Works, Zoophyte

PLANTS

3 letters:			
Dal	Hop	Meu	Set
Hom	Ivy	Pia	Til
	Kex	Rue	Udo

Urd
Yam

4 letters:
Alga
Aloe
Anil
Arum
Beet
Bixa
Chay
Cube
Daal
Dahl
Deme
Dhal
Dill
Fern
Flag
Flax
Geum
Grex
Guar
Herb
Hioi
Homa
Hoya
Ixia
Kali
Loco
More
Musk
Nard
Ombu
Pita
Rape
Reed
Rhus
Rush
Sage
Sego
Sida
Snow
Sola
Sunn
Tare
Taro
Thea
Vine
Weld
Woad

Wort
Yarr

5 letters:
Agave
Ajwan
Anise
Anona
Aroid
Aster
Basil
Benni
Betel
Blite
Bluet
Boree
Broom
Buchu
Bucku
Bugle
Calla
Camas
Canna
Carex
Chara
Chaya
Chufa
Clary
Clote
Cress
Cubeb
Cumin
Daisy
Erica
Ficus
Fouat
Fouet
Gemma
Glaux
Gorse
Guaco
Hosta
Hovea
Inula
Jalap
Kenaf
Kudzu
Laser
Ledum
Liana
Linum

Loofa
Lotus
Luffa
Lupin
Lurgi
Medic
Morel
Murva
Musci
Orach
Orpin
Orris
Oshac
Oxeye
Oxlip
Panax
Pansy
Peony
Phlox
Pilea
Sedge
Sedum
Senna
Shaya
Spink
Stock
Tansy
Tetra
Timbo
Tulip
Urena
Vetch
Vinca
Viola
Vitex
Vitis
Xyris
Yucca
Yulan
Zamia

6 letters:
Acacia
Acorus
Ajowan
Alisma
Allium
Alpine
Althea
Ambari
Ambary

Annona
Arabis
Aralia
Arnica
Azalea
Bablah
Balsam
Bamboo
Bauera
Betony
Borage
Briony
Bryony
Burnet
Cactus
Caltha
Camash
Camass
Cassia
Catnep
Catnip
Celery
Cicuta
Cissus
Cistus
Cleome
Clivia
Clover
Clusia
Cnicus
Cockle
Cohage
Cohash
Coleus
Conium
Coonty
Cornel
Cosmea
Cosmos
Cotton
Cowpea
Crinum
Crocus
Croton
Cummin
Dahlia
Daphne
Darnel
Datura
Derris
Dodder

Echium	Protea	Begonia	Freesia
Endive	Radish	Boneset	Frogbit
Erinus	Ramtil	Brinjal	Fuchsia
Exacum	Rattle	Bugbane	Gazania
Exogen	Reseda	Bugloss	Genista
Fat hen	Retama	Burdock	Gentian
Fennel	Rubber	Burweed	Gerbera
Ferula	Ruscus	Calluna	Ginseng
Funkia	Salvia	Caltrap	Godetia
Garlic	Savory	Caltrop	Gunnera
Gnetum	Scilla	Campion	Haemony
Henbit	Senega	Caraway	Hawkbit
Hoodia	Sesame	Cardoon	Hemlock
Hyssop	Seseli	Carduus	Henbane
Iberis	Silene	Carline	Hogweed
Jojoba	Smilax	Cassava	Ipomoea
Juncus	Sorbus	Catechu	Isoetes
Kentia	Sorrel	Catmint	Jasmine
Kerria	Spider	Cat's ear	Jonquil
Knawel	Spirea	Chayote	Kingcup
Kochia	Spurge	Chelone	Lantana
Korari	Spurry	Chervil	Lettuce
Kumara	Squill	Chicory	Liatris
Kumera	Styrax	Clarkia	Lobelia
Lichen	Sundew	Cocoyam	Logania
Lolium	Teasel	Comfrey	Lucerne
Loofah	Thrift	Compass	Lychnis
Lovage	Tomato	Coontie	Lythrum
Lupine	Tulipa	Cowbane	Madwort
Madder	Turnip	Cowbird	Mahonia
Maguey	Tutsan	Cowhage	Manihot
Mallow	Violet	Cowherb	Maranta
Manioc	Viscum	Cowitch	Mayweed
Medick	Yarrow	Cowslip	Melilot
Mimosa	Yautia	Cudweed	Mercury
Monoao	Zinnia	Curcuma	Milfoil
Moorva		Cushion	Mimulus
Nerine	**7 letters:**	Dasheen	Monarda
Nerium	Absinth	Deutzia	Mugwort
Nettle	Aconite	Diascia	Mullein
Nuphar	Alkanet	Dioecia	Mustard
Orache	All-good	Dittany	Nelumbo
Orchid	Allheal	Dogbane	Nemesia
Orchis	Allseed	Drosera	Nigella
Orpine	Alyssum	Epacris	Nonsuch
Oxalis	Anchusa	Ephedra	Olearia
Oyster	Arachis	Erodium	Opuntia
Pachak	Astilbe	Eugenia	Palmiet
Paeony	Awlwort	Felwort	Pareira
Peanut	Barilla	Filaree	Parsley
Pieris	Bartsia	Fly-trap	Parsnip

Penthia	Vervain	Cilantro	Heuchera
Petunia	Weigela	Cleavers	Hibiscus
Pigface	Zebrina	Clematis	Honewort
Pinguin	Zedoary	Costmary	Hornwort
Potherb		Crowfoot	Horokaka
Primula	**8 letters:**	Crucifer	Hyacinth
Puccoon	Abelmosk	Cucurbit	Hydrilla
Pumpkin	Absinthe	Cumbungi	Hyperium
Ragwort	Abutilon	Cunjevoi	Japonica
Rampion	Acanthus	Cyclamen	Knotweed
Raoulia	Achillea	Daffodil	Kohlrabi
Redroot	Ageratum	Damewort	Krameria
Rhatany	Agrimony	Diandria	Larkspur
Rhodora	Agueweed	Dianthus	Lathyris
Rhubarb	Alocasia	Dicentra	Lavatera
Ricinus	Alumroot	Dielytra	Lavender
Robinia	Angelica	Dogberry	Lungwort
Romneya	Apocynum	Dracaena	Macleaya
Rosebay	Arenaria	Dropwort	Mandrake
Ruellia	Argemone	Duckweed	Marigold
Saffron	Asphodel	Dumbcane	Mariposa
Salfern	Barometz	Eelgrass	Marjoram
Salsify	Bauhinia	Erigeron	Milkweed
Salsola	Bedstraw	Eucharis	Milkwort
Sampire	Bellwort	Euonymus	Miltonia
Sanicle	Bergamot	Feverfew	Monstera
Sawwort	Bergenia	Fireweed	Moonseed
Scandix	Bignonia	Fleabane	Mosspink
Seakale	Bindi-eye	Fleawort	Myosotis
Senecio	Bindweed	Fluellin	Navicula
Setwall	Bluebell	Foxglove	Oleander
Skirret	Bottonia	Fumitory	Opopanax
Solanum	Boxberry	Furcraea	Origanum
Spignel	Brassica	Galangol	Oxtongue
Spinach	Buckbean	Galtonia	Pandanus
Spiraea	Buddleia	Geranium	Paspalum
Spurrey	Buplever	Gesneria	Phacelia
Squilla	Caladium	Gladioli	Phormium
Stachys	Calamint	Gloriosa	Physalis
Stapela	Calathea	Gloxinia	Pinkroot
Statice	Calthrop	Glyceria	Pipewort
Syringa	Camomile	Gnetales	Plantain
Tagetes	Canaigre	Goutweed	Plumbago
Thallus	Cannabis	Gromwell	Pokeroot
Trefoil	Capsicum	Hag-taper	Pokeweed
Triffid	Cardamom	Harakeke	Polygaia
Tritoma	Cardamum	Hardhack	Pondweed
Turbith	Cat's foot	Hawkweed	Primrose
Turpeth	Centaury	Helenium	Prunella
Vanilla	Chenopod	Henequen	Psilotum
Verbena	Chickpea	Hepatica	Psoralea

Psyllium
Purslane
Putchock
Ratsbane
Roly-poly
Sainfoin
Saltwort
Salvinia
Samphire
Sandwort
Scabious
Scammony
Sea-blite
Self-heal
Sept-foil
Shamrock
Sidalcea
Silkweed
Silphium
Snowdrop
Soapwort
Solidago
Sowbread
Sparaxis
Spergula
Stapelia
Staragen
Starwort
Sweet pea
Tamarisk
Tarragon
Tayberry
Tigridia
Trigynia
Trillium
Tritonia
Trollius
Tuberose
Tuckahoe
Turmeric
Turnsole
Valerian
Venidium
Veratrum
Veronica
Viburnum
Viscaria
Wait-a-bit
Wallwort
Wistaria
Wisteria

Withwind
Woodroof
Woodruff
Woodrush
Wormseed

9 letters:
Achimenes
Adderwort
Alfilaria
Alfileria
Amaryllis
Anacharis
Andromeda
Anthurium
Aquilegia
Arracacha
Arrowhead
Arrowroot
Artemisia
Artichoke
Artillery
Asclepias
Asparagus
Astrantia
Aubrietia
Ayabuasca
Bald-money
Baneberry
Birthroot
Birthwort
Breadroot
Bromeliad
Brooklime
Brookweed
Broom-rape
Buckwheat
Burrawang
Butterbur
Buttercup
Calcicole
Calcifuge
Calendula
Campanula
Candytuft
Cardamine
Carnation
Celandine
Centaurea
Chamomile
Cineraria

Claytonia
Clianthus
Clintonia
Colchicum
Colicroot
Colicweed
Collinsia
Colocasia
Colocynth
Coltsfoot
Columbine
Cordaites
Coreopsis
Coriander
Corydalis
Creamcups
Crocosnia
Dandelion
Digitalis
Dittander
Dog fennel
Doronicum
Dulcamara
Echeveria
Echinacea
Edelweiss
Eglantine
Erythrina
Euphorbia
Eyebright
Fenugreek
Feverwort
Forsythia
Fourcroya
Galingale
Germander
Gladiolus
Glasswort
Goldenrod
Goosefoot
Grindelia
Groundnut
Groundsel
Gypsywort
Hardheads
Hellebore
Helophyte
Herb-Paris
Hieracium
Hoarhound
Hollyhock

Horehound
Horsemint
Horse-tail
Houstonia
Hydrangea
Hypericum
Impatiens
Kalanchoe
Kniphofia
Laserwort
Liver-wort
Lousewort
Mare's-tail
Marshwort
Mitrewort
Monandria
Moneywort
Monkshood
Monogynia
Monotropa
Moschatel
Mousetail
Muscadine
Narcissus
Navelwort
Nemophila
Nicotiana
Oenothera
Ouviranda
Patchouli
Pearlwort
Pellitory
Pennywort
Penstemon
Peperomia
Pimpernel
Pineapple
Pokeberry
Polygonum
Portulaca
Quillwort
Rafflesia
Rattlebox
Rocambole
Rosinweed
Rudbeckia
Sabadilla
Safflower
Sagebrush
Santoline
Santonica

Saponaria	Cloudberry	Montbretia	**11 letters:**
Saxifrage	Commiphora	Moonflower	Acidanthera
Screwpine	Coneflower	Motherwort	Antirrhinum
Shoreweed	Corncockle	Nasturtium	Bear's-breech
Sinningia	Cornflower	Nightshade	Bittercress
Snakeroot	Cottonweed	Nipplewort	Bittersweet
Spearmint	Cow parsley	Parkleaves	Bristle-fern
Spearwort	Cow parsnip	Passiflora	Calceolaria
Speedwell	Cranesbill	Pennycress	Callitriche
Spikenard	Deadnettle	Pennyroyal	Convolvulus
Spikerush	Delphinium	Pentagynia	Cotoneaster
Sprekalia	Dragonhead	Pentandria	Dusty-miller
Stinkweed	Dragonroot	Pentstemon	Erythronium
Stone-crop	Dyer's-broom	Peppermint	Forget-me-not
Strapwort	Earth-smoke	Periwinkle	Fothergilla
Sweet-gale	Elecampane	Pimpinella	Gentianella
Taraxacum	Escallonia	Pipsissewa	Gillyflower
Tomatillo	Eupatorium	Poinsettia	Helichrysum
Toothwort	Five-finger	Polemonium	Hippeastrum
Tormentil	Foamflower	Polianthes	Horseradish
Twinberry	Four o'clock	Polyanthus	Hurtleberry
Vaccinium	Fraxinella	Potentilla	Incarvillea
Verbascum	Fritillary	Ranunculus	Lithotripsy
Vetchling	Gaillardia	Rest-harrow	Loosestrife
Wake-robin	Gaultheria	Rhoicissus	Marsh mallow
Wincopipe	Glycophate	Salicornia	Meadowsweet
Witchweed	Gnaphalium	Sarracenia	Monadelphia
Withywind	Goat-sallow	Scindapsus	Nancy-pretty
Wolf's bane	Goatsbeard	Scorzonera	Pachysandra
Woundwort	Goat's-thorn	Silverweed	Paritaniwha
	Goat-willow	Snapdragon	Pelargonium
10 letters:	Goldenseal	Sneezewort	Potamogeton
Agapanthus	Goldilocks	Spiderwort	Saintpaulia
Alexanders	Goldthread	Stavesacre	Sansevieria
Ampelopsis	Gypsophila	Stitchwort	Schizanthus
Anacardium	Hawksbeard	Storksbill	Selaginella
Angiosperm	Heathberry	Strelitzia	Sempervivum
Artocarpus	Helianthus	Thalictrum	Slipperwort
Asarabacca	Heliotrope	Thunbergia	Sparaganium
Aspidistra	Hyoscyamus	Tibouchina	Steeplebush
Astralagus	Icosandria	Tillandsia	Stephanotis
Barrenwort	Illecebrum	Touch-me-not	Strawflower
Beggarweed	Immortelle	Tragacanth	Swiss cheese
Biddy-biddy	Jew's mallow	Tropaeolum	Thimbleweed
Bitterweed	Jimsonweed	Tropaesium	Thoroughwax
Brugmansia	Loganberry	Tumbleweed	Tous-les-mois
Butterwort	Maidenhair	Wallflower	Trumpetweed
Candelilla	Marguerite	Watercress	Vallisneria
Catananche	Masterwort	Yellowroot	Welwitschia
Chionodoxa	Meconopsis	Yellowweed	Wintergreen
Cinquefoil	Mignonette	Yellowwort	Xeranthemum

12 letters:	Pasqueflower	Wandering Jew	14 letters:
Adam's flannel	Philodendron	Water-soldier	Bougainvillaea
Alstroemeria	Phytobenthos	Zantedeschia	Chincherinchee
Aristolochia	Pickerelweed		Lords and ladies
Checkerbloom	Pterydophyte	13 letters:	Partridgeberry
Darlingtonia	Salpiglossis	Bougainvillea	Shepherd's purse
Epacridaceae	Sarsaparilla	Carrion-flower	
Eschscholzia	Scrophularia	Dieffenbachia	16 letters:
Fennelflower	Sempervivium	Eschscholtzia	Mesembrian-
Helianthemum	Southernwood	Passionflower	themum
Lithospermum	Strophanthus	Spathyphyllum	
Midsummermen	Sweet William	Sweet woodruff	17 letters:
Morning glory	Tradescantia	Townhall clock	Mother-of-
None-so-pretty	Venus flytrap	Traveller's joy	thousands
Parsley-piert	Virgin's bower		

Plantagenet Angevin, Broom

Plantain Mato(o)ke, Ribwort, Waybread

Plantation Arboretum, Bosket, Bosquet, Estate, Grove, Hacienda, Pen, Pinetum, Ranch, Tara, Veticetum, Vineyard

Plant disease Anthracnose, Bunt, Club-root, Curlytop, Eyespot, Frogeye, Psillid yellows, Rosette, Smut, Sooty mould

Planted In, Under

Planter Dibber, Farmer, Settler, Trowel

Plaque Calculus, Dental, Plateau, Scale

Plasm Germ

Plasma Dextran, Sigmond

Plaster(ed), Plaster board Bandage, Blister, Blotto, Butterfly clip, Cake, Cataplasm, Clam, Clatch, Compo, Court, Daub, Diachylon, Diachylum, Drunk, Emplastrum, Fresco, Gesso, Grout, Gyprock®, Gypsum, Intonaco, Laying, Leep, Lit, Mud, Mustard, Oiled, Parge(t), Polyfilla®, Porous, Poultice, Render, Roughcast, Scratch-coat, Screed, Secco, Shellac, Sinapism, Smalm, Smarm, Smear, Sowsed, Staff, Sticking, Stookie, Stucco, Teer

Plastic Bakelite®, Cel(luloid), Cling film, Ductile, Fablon®, Fictile, Fluon, Formica®, Ionomer, Laminate, Loid, Lucite®, Melamine, Mylar®, Perspex®, Plexiglass®, Pliant, Polyethylene, Polystyrene, Polythene, Polyvinyl, PVC, Reinforced, Styrene, Styrofoam®, Teflon®, Urea-formaldehyde, Vinyl, Wet-look, Yielding

▷ **Plastic** *may indicate* an anagram

Plastic surgeon McIndoe

Plastic surgery Neoplasty, Nose job, Otoplasty, Rhinoplasty

Plate(s), Plated, Platelet, Plating Acierage, Ailette, Angle, Anode, Armadillo, Armour, Ashet, Baffle, Bakestone, Baleen, Batten, Brass, Butt, Chamfrain, Chape, Charger, Chrome, Coat, Coccolith, Communion, Copper, Cramper, Cribellum, Ctene, Dasypus, Deadman, Denture, Diaphragm, Dinner, Disc, Dish, Echo, Electro, Electrotype, Elytron, Elytrum, Enamel, Entoplastron, Escutcheon, Face, Fashion, Feet, Fine, Fish, Flatware, Foil, Frog, Frons, Futtock, Glacis, Gold, Graal, Ground, Gula, Half, Hasp, Home, Horseshoe, Hot, Illustration, L, Lame, Lamella, Lamina, Lanx, Latten, Licence, Madreporic, Mascle, Mazarine, Nail, Nef, Neural, Nickel, Notum, Number, Ortho, Osteoderm, Paten, Patina, Patine, Pauldron, Peba, Petri, Phototype, Planometer, Plaque, Plastron, Platter, Pleximeter, Poitrel, Prescutum, Print, Quarter, Race, Registration, Riza, Roof, Rove, Salamander, Scale, Screw,

Scrim, Scutcheon, Scute, Scutum, Seg, Selling, Sheffield, Shield, Side, Sieve, Silver, Slab, Soup, Spacer, Spoiler, Squama, Steel, Stencil, Stereo(type), Sternite, Strake, Surface, Swash, T, Tablet, Tace, Tasse(l), Tea, Tectonic, Tergite, Terne, Thali, Theoretical, Tin(ware), Torsel, Touch, Trade, Tramp, Trencher, Trivet, Trophy, Tsuba, Tuill(ett)e, Tymp, Urostegite, Vane, Vanity, Vassail, Vessail, Vessel, Wall, Water, Web, Wet, Whirtle, Whole, Wobble, Workload, Wortle, Wrap(a)round, Zincograph

Plateau Altiplano, Central Karoo, Chota Nagpur, Darling Downs, Dartmoor, Deccan, Durango, Eifel, Field, Fjeld, Had(h)ramaut, Highland, Highveld, Horst, Kalahari, Kar(r)oo, Kurdestan, Kurdistan, La Mancha, Langres, Laurentian, Mat(t)o Grosso, Mesa Verde, Meseta, Nilgiris, Ozark, Paramo, Piedmont, Puna, Shan, Shillong, Tableland, The Kimberleys, Ust Urt, Ustyurt

Platform Accommodation, Almemar, Bandstand, Barbette, Base, Bema, Bier, Catafalque, Catwalk, Crane, Crow's nest, Dais, Deck, Dolly, Drilling, Emplacement, Entablement, Estrade, Exedra, Exhedra, Fighting top, Flake, Footpace, Footplate, Foretop, Gangplank, Gantry, Gauntree, Gauntry, Gravity, Hustings, Kang, Landing stage, Launch-pad, Machan, Oil, Oil-rig, Pad, Paint-bridge, Pallet, Perron, Plank, Podium, Predella, Production, Programme, Pulpit, Raft, Rig, Rostrum, Round-top, Scaffold, Shoe, Skidway, Soapbox, Space, Sponson, → **STAGE**, Stand, Stereobate, Stoep, Stylobate, Tee, Terminal, Thrall, Ticket, Top, Traverser, Tribunal, Tribune, Turntable, Wave-cut, Wharf

Platinum Pt, Ruthenium, Sperrylite

Platitude Bromide, Cliché, Commonplace, Truism

Platocephalus Flat-headed

Platonic, Platonist Academician, Ideal, Spiritual

Platoon Company, Squad, Team

Platter Dish, EP, Graal, Grail, Lanx, LP, Plate, Record, Salver, Trencher

Platypus Duckbill, Duck-mole, Water mole

Plausible, Plausibility Cogent, Credible, Fair, Glib, Logical, Oil, Probable, Proball, Sleek, Smooth, Specious

Play(s), Playing Accompany, Active, Amusement, Antic, Antigone, Brand, Bust, Candida, Caper, Charm, Chronicle, Clearance, Crucible, Curtain-raiser, Daff, Dandle, Docudrama, Doodle, Drama, Echo, Endgame, Epitasis, Equus, Escapade, Everyman, Extended, Fair, Finesse, Foul, Freedom, Frisk, Frolic, Fun, Gamble, Gambol, Game, Ghosts, Grand Guignol, Hamlet, Harp, History, Holiday, Inside, Interlude, Jam, Jape, Jest, Jeu, Kinderspiel, Kitchen-sink, Laik, Lake, Lark, Latitude, Lear, Leeway, Licence, Lilt, Long, Loot, Macbeth, Mask, Masque, Match, Medal, Melodrama, Miracle, Monodrama, Morality, Mousetrap, Mummers, Mysteries, Nativity, Nurse, Oberammergau, On, One-acter, Orestaia, Othello, Parallel, Passion, Pastorale, Perform, Personate, Peter, Portray, Prank, Pretend, Puppet, Recreation, Represent, Riff, Role, Rollick, Romp, Room, Rope, RUR, Satyr, Saw, Screen, Shadow, Shoot, Shuffle, Sketch, Sport, Squeeze, Stage, Straight, Strain, Strike up, Stroke, Strum, Summerstock, Tolerance, Tonguing, Touchback, Toy, Tragedy, Tragicomedy, Trifle, Triple, Tweedle, Twiddle, Two-hander, Vamp, Vent, Whitechapel, Word

▷ **Play** *may indicate* an anagram

Playback Echo, Repeat, Replay

Playboy Casanova, Don Juan, Hedonist, Rake, Roué

Player(s) Actor, Athlete, Back, Backstop, Black, Brass, Bugler, Busker, Cast, CD, Centre, Colt, Contestant, Cornerback, Defenceman, Disc, DVD, E, East, ENSA, Equity, Fetcher, Fiddle, Flanker, Flying wing, Franchise, Fullback, Gary,

Ghetto-blaster, Goalie, Half, Half-back, Half-forward, Harlequin, Hooker,
Infielder, It, Juke-box, Keg(e)ler, Kest, Kicker, Linebacker, Lineman, Lion, Lock,
Long-leg, Longstop, Lutanist, Lutenist, Man, Marquee, Midfield, Mid-on, Mime,
Musician(er), N, Nero, Nickelback, Nightwatchman, North, Ombre, Onside,
Orpheus, Outfielder, Out(side)-half, Pagliacci, Participant, Pianola®, Pitcher,
Pocket, Pone, Pro, Prop, Quarterback, Receiver, Record, Reliever, Rover, S,
Safetyman, Scrape, Scratch, Scrum half, Seagull, Secondo, Seed, Shamateur,
Short-leg, Shortstop, Side, South, Split end, Stand-off, Stand-off half, Stereo,
Striker, Strings, Strolling, Substitute, Super, Sweeper, Target man, Team, Thespian,
Tight end, Troubador, Troupe, Upright, Utility, Virtuosi, W, Walkman®, West,
White, Wing, Winger, Wingman
Playfair Code
Playfellow Actor, Chum, Companion
Playful Arch, Coy, Frisky, Humorous, Jocose, Kittenish, Ludic, Merry, Piacevole,
Scherzo, Skittish, Sportive
Playgirl Actress, Electra
Playgoer Groundling
Playground Adventure, Close, Garden, Park, Rec(reational), Rectangle, Theatre,
Tot lot, Yard
Playhouse Amphitheatre, Cinema, Theatre, Wendy
Playsuit Rompers
Playwright Aeschylus, Albee, Anouilh, Arden, Ayckbourn, Barrie, Barry,
Beaumarchais, Beaumont, Beckett, Behan, Bellow, Bennett, Besier, Bolt, Brecht,
Chekhov, Congreve, Corneille, Coward, Dekker, Delaney, → DRAMATIST,
Dramaturge, Dramaturgist, Drinkwater, Dryden, Euripides, Feydeau, Fletcher,
Frayn, Fry, Gems, Genet, Goldoni, Gorky, Hare, Harwood, Hay, Ibsen, Ionesco,
Jonson, Marlowe, Massinger, Menander, Miller, Molière, Mortimer, O'Casey,
Odets, O'Neill, Orton, Osborne, Pinero, Pinter, Pirandello, Priestley, Racine,
Rattigan, Rostard, Scriptwriter, Shaw, Sheridan, Sherry, Simpson, Sophocles,
Stoppard, Storey, Strindberg, Synge, Tate, Terence, Thespis, Travers, Vanbrugh,
Webster, Wesker, Wilde
Plea(s) Appeal, Claim, Common, Defence, Entreaty, Excuse, Exoration, Nolo
contendere, Orison, Placit(um), Prayer, Rebuttal, Rebutter, Rogation, Suit
Plead(er) Answer, Argue, Beg, Entreat, → IMPLORE, Intercede, Litigate, Moot,
Special, Supplicant, Vakeel, Vakil
Please(d), Pleasant, Pleasing, Pleasure(-seeker) Aggrate, Agreeable, Alcina,
Algolagnia, Amene, Amiable, Amuse, Arride, Benign, Bitte, Braw, Cheerful,
Chuffed, Comely, Comfort, Content, Cordial, Cute, Delectation, Delice, Delight,
Do, Euphonic, Fair, Felicitous, Fit, Flatter, Fun, Genial, Glad, Gladness, Gratify,
Hedonism, Jammy, Joy, Kama, Kindly, Lekker, Lepid, List, Naomi, Oblige, Piacevole,
Primrose path, Prithee, Prythee, Purr, Queme, Satisfy, Suit, Tasty, Tickle, Tickle
pink, Treat, Vanity, Voluptuary, Wally, Will, Winsome, Wrapped, Xanadu List
Pleasure-garden, Pleasure-ground Lung, Oasis, Park, Policy, Ranelagh, Tivoli
Pleat Accordion, Box, Crimp, Fold, French, Frill, Goffer, Gusset, Inverted, Kick,
Knife, Plait, Pranck(e), Prank, Sunburst, Sunray
Pleb(eian) Common, Essex Man, Homely, Laic, Ordinary, Roturier
Pledge Affidavit, Arlene, Arles, Band, Betroth, Bond, Borrow, Bottomry, Dedicate,
Deposit, Earnest(-penny), Engage, Fine, Gage, Gilbert, Giselle, Guarantee, Hock,
Hypothecate, Impignorate, Mortgage, Oath, Pass, Pawn, Pignerate, Pignorate,
Plight, Promise, Propine, Sacrament, Security, Sponsorship, Stake, Surety,
Teetotal, Toast, Troth, Undertake, Vow, Wad, Wage(r), Wed

Pleiades Alcyone, Celaeno, Electra, Maia, Merope, Sterope, Taygete
Plenitude Stouth and routh
Plentiful, Plenty Abounding, Abundance, Abundant, Ample, Bags, Copious, Copy, Easy, Excess, Foison, Fouth, Ful(l)ness, Fushion, Galore, Goshen, Lashings, Lots, Oodles, Pleroma, Profusion, Quantity, Riches, Rife, Routh, Rowth, Scouth, Scowth, Slue, Sonce, Sonse, Umpteen
Plenum Spaceless
Pliable, Pliant Amenable, Flexible, Limber, Limp, Lithe, Malleable, Plastic, Sequacious, Supple, Swack, Swank, Wanle
▸ **Pliers** *see* PLY
Plight Betrothal, Case, Misdight, Peril, Pickle, Pledge, State, Troth
Plimsoll(s) Dap, Gutty, Gym-shoe, Line, Mutton-dummies, Sandshoe, Tacky
Plinth Acroter, Base, Block, Socle, Stand, Zocco
Plod(der) Drudge, Ploughman, Traipse, Tramp, Trog, Trudge
Plonk Rotgut, Wine
Plop Cloop, Drop, Fall, Plap, Plump
Plot(s) Allotment, Babington, Bed, Brew, Carpet, Chart, Cliché, Collude, Connive, Conspiracy, Conspire, Covin, Covyne, Engineer, Erf, Erven, Frame-up, Graden, Graph, Gunpowder, Imbroglio, Intrigue, Locus, Lot, Machination, Map, Meal-tub, Odograph, Pack, Patch, Plan, Plat, Popish, Rye-house, Scenario, → SCHEME, Sect(ion), Seedbed, Shot, Site, Story, Storyline, Taluk, Terf, Turf, Web
Plotter Artist, Brutus, Cabal, Camarilla, Casca, Catesby, Conspirator, Engineer, Incremental, Microfilm, Oates, Schemer
Plough(man), Ploughed, Ploughing Arable, Ard, Arval, Big Dipper, Breaker, Bull tongue, Chamfer, Charles's Wain, Contour, Dipper, Disc, Drail, Drill, Ear, Earth-board, Ere, Fail, Fallow, Farmer, Feer, Flunk, Gadsman, Gang, Great bear, Harrow, Lister, Middlebreaker, Middlebuster, Mouldboard, Piers, Pip, Pleuch, Pleugh, Push, Rafter, Rib, Ridger, Rive, Rotary, Rove, Sand, Scooter, Septentrion(e)s, Sill, Sow, Stump-jump, Swing, Till(er), Trench, Triones, Wheel
Plough-cleaner Pattle, Pettle
Ploughshare Co(u)lter, Sock
Ploughwise Boustrophedon
Plover Bud, Dott(e)rel, Lapwing, Pratincole, Prostitute, Stand, Tewit, Wing
Plowman Piers
Ploy Brinkmanship, Dodge, Gambit, Manoeuvre, M(a)cGuffin, Stratagem, Strike, Tactic, Wile
Pluck(ing), Plucky Avulse, Bare, Carphology, Cock, Courage, Deplume, Epilate, Evulse, Floccillation, Gallus, Game, → GRIT, Guts, Loot, Mettle, Pick, Pinch, Pip, Pizzicato, Plectron, Plectrum, Ploat, Plot, Plunk, Pook(it), Pouk(it), Pull, Race, Scrappy, Snatch, Spin, Spirit, Spunk, Summon, Tug, Twang, Tweak, Tweeze, Vellicate, Yank
Plug Access eye, Ad, Banana, Block, Bung, Caulk, Chew, Commercial, Dam, DIN, Dook, Dossil, Dottle, Douk, Fipple, Fother, Gang, Glow, Go-devil, Heater, Hype, Jack, Lam, Operculum, Pessary, Phono, Prod, Promote, Publicity, Ram, Rawlplug®, Recommendation, Safety, Salt, Scart, Spark(ing), Spile, Spiling, Stop(per), Stopple, Strobili, Suppository, Tampion, Tap, Tent, Tompion, Vent, Volcanic, Wage, Wander, Wedge
Plum Bullace, Cherry, Choice, Damask, Damson, Gage, Greengage, Ground, Jamaica, Japanese, Java, Kaki, Mammee-sapota, Marmalade, Maroon, Mirabelle, Musk, Mussel, Myrobalan, Naseberry, Persimmon, Proin(e), Pruin(e), Prune, Quetsch, Raisin, Sapodilla, Sebesten, Victoria

Plumage, Plume Aigrette, Crest, Eclipse, Egret, Feather, Hackle, Mantle, Panache, Preen, Ptilosis, Quill

Plumb(er) Bullet, Dredge, Fathom, Lead(sman), Perpendicular, Plummet, Sheer, Sound, Test, True, Vertical

Plumbago Graphite, Wad(d), Wadt

Plummet Dive, Drop, Lead, → PLUNGE

Plump(er) Bold, Bonnie, Bonny, Buxom, Choose, Chubbed, Chubby, Cubby, Dumpy, Embonpoint, Endomorph, Fat, Fleshy, Flop, Fubsy, Full, Lie, Matronly, Opt, Plank, Plonk, Plop, Podgy, Portly, Pudgy, Roll-about, Rolypoly, Rotund, Round, Rubenesque, Sonsie, Sonsy, Soss, Souse, Squab, Squat, Stout, Swap, Swop, Tidy, Well-fed

Plunder(er) Berob, Booty, Depredate, Despoil, Devastate, Escheat, Fleece, Forage, Freebooter, Gut, Harry, Haul, Herriment, Herryment, Hership, Loot, Maraud, Peel, Pill(age), Prey, Privateer, → RANSACK, Rape, Rapparee, Raven, Ravin, Ravine, Reave, Reif, Reive, Rieve, Rifle, Rob, Sack, Scoff, Shave, Skoff, Spoil(s), Spoliate, Sprechery, Spuilzie, Spuly(i)e, Spulzie, Swag

Plunge(r) Dasher, Demerge, Dive, Douse, Dowse, Duck, Enew, Immerge, Immerse, La(u)nch, Nose-dive, Plummet, Plump, Raker, Send, Sink, Souse, Swoop, Thrust

Plural Multiply, Pl

Plus Addition, And, Gain, More, Positive

Plush(ed) Die, Luxurious, Rich, Smart, Tint, Velour, Velvet

Pluto(crat), Plutonic Abyssal, Dis, Dog, Hades, Hypogene, Magnate, Nob, Pipeline, Underground

Plutonium Pu

Ply, Plier(s) Bend, Birl, Cab, Exercise, Exert, Gondoliers, Importune, Layer, Practise, Run, Trade, Wield

▷ **Plying** *may indicate* an anagram

Plymouth Brethren Darbyite

PM Addington, Afternoon, Arvo, Asquith, Attlee, Autopsy, Bute, Cabinet-maker, Chatham, De Valera, Disraeli, Gladstone, Major, Melbourne, Peel, Pitt, Portland, Premier, → PRIME MINISTER, Salisbury, Taoiseach

Pneumonia Lobar, Lobular, Visna

Poach Cook, Encroach, Filch, Lag, Steal, Trespass

Pochard Duck, Scaup

Pocket Air, Appropriate, Bag, Bin, Breast, Cavity, Cly, Cup, Enclave, Fob, Glom, Hideaway, Hip, Jenny, Misappropriate, Patch, Placket, Plaid-neuk, Pot, Pouch, Purloin, Purse, Sac, Sky, Slash, Sling, Slit, Steal, Take, Trouser, Watch

Pod(s) Babul, Bean, Belly, Carob, Chilli, Dividivi, Engine, Gumbo, Lablab, Lomentum, Neb-neb, Okra, Pipi, Pregnant, Pudding-pipe, Siliqua, Tamarind, Vanilla

Podgy Roly-poly

Poem(s), Poetry Acmeism, Acrostic, Aeneid, Alcaic, Anthology, Awdl, Ballad(e), Beowulf, Bestiary, Byliny, Caccia, Canzone, Cargoes, Cento, Choliamb, Choriamb, Cicada, Cinquain, Complaint, Concrete, Decastich, Dit(t), Dithyramb, Divan, Dizain, Doggerel, Duan, Dub, Dunciad, Eclogue, Elegy, Elene, Epic(ede), Epigram, Epilogue, Epithalamium, Epode, Epopee, Epopoeia, Epos, Epyllion, Erotic, Fifteener, Finlandia, Gauchesco, Georgic, Ghazal, Graveyard, Haikai, Haiku, Heptastich, Heroic, Hexastich, Hokku, Hull, Hypermeter, Idyll, If, Iliad, Imagism, Inferno, Jazz, Lay, Limerick, Logaoedic, London, Mahabharata(m), Mahabharatum, Meliboean, Melic, Metaphysical, Metre, Mock-heroic, Monostich, Monostrophe, Nostos, Ode, Odyssey, Palinode, Paracrostic, Parnassus, Pastoral, Penill(ion), Pentastich, Performance, Poesy, Prelude, Prose, Prothalamion, Punk, Purana,

Qasida, Quatorzain, Quatrain, Quire, Ramayana, Rat-rhyme, Renga, Rhapsody, Rig-Veda, Rime, Rime riche, Rondeau, Rondel, Rubai(yat), Rune, Scazon (iambus), Senryu, Sestina, Sijo, Sirvente, Song, Sonnet, Sound, Spondee, Stanza, Stornello, Symphonic, Tanka, Telestich, Temora, Tercet, Tetrastich, Thebaid, Title, Tone, Triolet, Tristich, Vers(e), Versicle, Villanelle, Völuspá, Voluspe, Waka

Poet(s), Poetic Amorist, Bard(ling), Beatnik, Cavalier, Cumberland, Cyclic, Elegist, Georgian, Iambist, Imagist, Lake, Laureate, Layman, Lyrist, Maker, Meistersinger, Metaphysical, Metrist, Minnesinger, Minor, Minstrel, Mistral, Monodist, Odist, Parnassian, Performance, PL, Pleiad(e), Poetaster, Rhymer, Rhymester, Rhymist, Rymer, Scald, Scop, Skald, Smart, Sonneteer, Spasmodic, Spasmodic School, Thespis, Tragic, Trench, Troubadour, Trouvère, Trouveur, Vers librist(e), Water

POETS

2 letters:	Cinna	**6 letters:**	Seaman
AE	Clare	Alonso	Shanks
	Dante	Arnold	Sidney
3 letters:	Donne	Austin	Tagore
Gay	Eliot	Barham	Thomas
Poe	Frost	Barnes	Villon
	Gower	Belloc	Virgil
4 letters:	Griot	Borges	Waller
Abse	Heine	Brecht	
Blok	Hesse	Brooke	**7 letters:**
Cory	Homer	Butler	Addison
Dyer	Horne	Clough	Alcaeus
Gray	Hulme	Cowper	Aretino
Gunn	Iqbal	Crabbe	Ariosto
Hogg	Keats	Dowson	Beddoes
Hood	Keyes	Dryden	Belleau
Hugo	Lewis	Dunbar	Bridges
Hunt	Logue	Ennius	Bunting
Lang	Lorca	George	Caedmon
Omar	Lucan	Glycon	Campion
Ovid	Makar	Goethe	Chapman
Owen	Marot	Graves	Chaucer
Pope	Meyer	Hesiod	Collins
Rowe	Moore	Horace	Corinna
Rumi	Nashe	Hughes	Cynwulf
Tate	Noyes	Landor	Emerson
Vega	Plath	Larkin	Flaccus
	Pound	Lawman	Flecker
5 letters:	Prior	Lowell	Heredia
Arion	Rilke	Marini	Herrick
Auden	Rishi	Milton	Hopkins
Blair	Sachs	Morris	Housman
Blake	Tasso	Motion	Juvenal
Burns	Theon	Ossian	Layamon
Byron	Wyatt	Pindar	Martial
Cadou	Yeats	Racine	Marvell
Carew	Young	Sappho	Montale

Newbolt	Catullus	Tyrtaeus	Fitzgerald
Orpheus	Cummings	Verlaine	Longfellow
Pushkin	Cynewulf	Whittier	Propertius
Ronsard	Davenant		Tannhauser
Russell	Day Lewis	**9 letters:**	Theocritus
Sassoon	De la Mare	Aeschylus	Wordsworth
Service	Ginsberg	Bunthorne	
Shelley	Hamilton	Coleridge	**11 letters:**
Sitwell	Kynewulf	Euripides	Apollinaire
Skelton	Laforgue	Goldsmith	Archilochus
Sotades	Langland	Henderson	Asclepiades
Southey	Leopardi	Lamartine	Bildermeier
Spender	Lovelace	Lucretius	Maeterlinck
Spenser	Macaulay	Marinetti	Pherecrates
Statius	Mallarmé	Masefield	
Terence	Menander	Quasimodo	**12 letters:**
Thomson	Petrarch	Shenstone	Archilochian
Vaughan	Rossetti	Simonides	Aristophanes
Whitman	Schiller	Sophocles	
	Shadwell	Stevenson	**14 letters:**
8 letters:	Stephens	Swinburne	Dante Alighieri
Anacreon	Suckling		
Betjeman	Taliesin	**10 letters:**	**15 letters:**
Brentano	Tennyson	Baudelaire	Ettrick Shepherd
Browning	Thompson	Chatterton	
Campbell	Traherne	Drinkwater	

Poetaster Della-Cruscan
Poetess Ingelow, Orinda
Poet laureate Motion, PL
▶ **Poetry** see **POEM**
Po-faced Stolid
Poignant Acute, Biting, Haunting, Keen, Pungent, Stirring, Touching
Point(ed), Pointer, Points Accumulation, Ace, Acerose, Acnode, Acro-, Aculeate,
    Aim, Antinode, Antler, Apex, Aphelion, Apogee, Appui, Apse, Apsis, Ascendant,
    Bar, Barb, Barrow, Basis, Bisque, Boiling, Break(ing), Brownie, Calk, Cape, Cardinal,
    Cash, Catch, Centre, Choke, Clou, Clovis, Clue, Colon, Comma, Compass,
    Compensation, Cone, Conic, Corner, Cover, Crisis, Critical, Crux, Culmination,
    Cultrate, Curie, Cursor, Cusp, Cuss, Cutting, Dead, Decimal, Degree, Descendant,
    Detail, Dew, Diamond, Direct, Dot, Dry, E, Ear, End, Entry, Epanodos, Épée,
    Equant, Equinoctial, Eutectic, Exclamation, Fang, Fastigiate, Feature, Fesse,
    Fielder, Firing, Fitch(e), Five, Fixed, Flash, Focal, Focus, Foreland, Fourteen,
    Freezing, Fulcrum, Gallinas, Game, Germane, Gist, Gnomon, Gold, Hastate,
    Head, High, Hinge, Hint, Home-thrust, Ideal, Index, Indicate, Indicator, Intercept,
    Ippon, Isoelectric, Jag, Jester, Jog, Juncture, Keblah, Kiblah, Kip(p), Knub, Lace,
    Lagrangian, Lance, Lead, Limit, Lizard, Locate, Locus, Low, Mandelbrot set, Mark,
    Match, Melting, Metacentre, Microdot, Moot, Mucro, Muricate, N, Nail, Nasion,
    Near, Neb, Needle, Neel, Ness, Nib, Nocking, Node, Nodus, Nombril, Now, Nub,
    Obconic, Obelion, Obelisk, Objective, Opinion, Ord, Organ, Oscillation, Particle,
    Peak, Pedal, Penalty, Perigee, Perihelion, Perilune, Pin, Pinch, Pinnacle, Place,
    Pour, Power, Pressure, Promontory, Prong, Prow, Punctilio, Punctual, Punctum,

Purpose, Radix, Rallying, Ras, Reef, Respect, Rhumb, Rhumbline, S, Sample, Saturation, Scribe, Seg(h)ol, Set, Shaft, Sheva, Show, Shy, Silly, Socket, Sore, Spearhead, Specie, Spicate, Spick, Spike, Spinode, Spinulose, Stage, Stagnation, Starting, Stationary, Steam, Sticking, Stigme, Stiletto, Sting, Stipule, Strong, Sum, Suspension, Synapse, Tacnode, Talking, Tang, Taper, Tax, Technicality, Tine, → **TIP**, Tongue, Trafficator, Train, Transition, Trig, Trigger, Triple, Turning, Urde(e), Urdy, Use, Vane, Vanishing, Vantage, Verge, Verse, Vertex, Vowel, Voxel, W, Weak, Yad, Yield, Yuko

Pointless Blunt, Curtana, Flat, Futile, Idle, Inane, Inutile, Muticous, Otiose, Stupid, Vain

Point of honour Pundonor

Poise Aplomb, Balance, Composure, P, Serenity

Poison(er), Poisoning, Poisonous Abron, Aconite, Acrolein, Adamsite, Aflatoxin, Aldrin, Amanita, Antiar, Apocynum, Aqua-tofana, Arsenic, Aspic, Atropia, Atropin(e), Bane, Barbasco, Belladonna, Benzidine, Boletus, Borgia, Botulism, Brom(in)ism, Brucine, Bufotalin, Bufotenine, Cacodyl, Cadaverine, Calabar-bean, Cannabin, Cicuta, Colchicine, Coniine, Contact, Cowbane, Coyotillo, Cube, Curare, Curari, Cyanide, Cyanuret, Datura, Daturine, Deadly nightshade, Deleterious, Digitalin, Dioxin, Dumbcane, Durban, Echidnine, Embolism, Emetin(e), Envenom, Ergotise, Exotoxin, Fluorosis, Flybane, Flypaper, Food, Fool's parsley, Formaldehyde, Gelsemin(in)e, Gila, Gila monster, Gossypol, Hebenon, Hebona, Hemlock, Henbane, Hydrargyrism, Hydrastine, Hyoscyamine, Iodism, Jimson weed, Lead, Lewisite, Limberneck, Lindane, Listeriosis, Lobeline, Loco, Locoweed, Malevolent, Manchineal, Mandragora, Mephitic, Methanol, Mezereon, Miasma, Mineral, Monkshood, Muscarine, Mycotoxin, Nerve gas, Neurine, Neurotoxin, Neutron, Nicotine, Noogoora burr, Noxious, Obeism, Ouabain, Ourali, Ourari, Paraquat®, Paris green, Phallin, Phalloidin, Phosphorism, Picrotoxin, Pilocarpine, Plumbism, Ptomaine, Py(a)emia, Raphania, Ratsbane, Rot, Safrole, Salicylism, Salmonella, Samnitis, Santonin, Sapraemia, Sarin, Sassy wood, Saturnism, Saxitoxin, Septic(aemia), Solanine, Solpuga, Soman, Stibine, Stibium, Stonefish, Strophanthus, Strychnine, Sugar of lead, Surinam, Systemic, Tanghin, Tanghinin, Tetro(do)toxin, Thebaine, Thorn-apple, Timbo, Toxaphene, Toxic, Toxicology, Toxicosis, Toxin, Toxoid, Trembles, Tropine, Tutu, Upas, Urali, Urushiol, V-agent, Venefic, Venin, Venom(ous), Veratridine, Veratrin(e), Viperous, Virose, Virous, Virulent, Wabain, Warfarin, Wolfsbane, Woorali, Woorara, Wourali, Yohimbine

Poke, Poky Bonnet, Broddle, Chook, Garget, Itchweed, Jab, Jook, Meddle, Mock, Nousle, Nudge, Nuzzle, Ombu, Peg, Pick, Poach, Pote, Pouch, Powter, → **PRISON**, → **PROD**, Prog, Proke, Punch, Root(le), Rout, Rowt, Sporran, Stab, Thrust

Poker (work) Bugbear, Curate, Draw, Game, High-low, Lowball, Mistigris, Penny ante, Pyrography, Red-hot, Salamander, Strip, Stud(-horse), Texas hold'em, Tickler, Tine

Poland PL, Sarmatia

Polar, Pole(s), Poler Animal, Anode, Antarctic, Arctic, Boathook, Boom, Bowsprit, Bum(p)kin, Caber, Celestial, Clothes, Copernicus, Cowl-staff, Cracovian, Crossbar, Extremity, Fishgig, Fizgy, Flagstaff, Flagstick, Galactic, Gas, Geomagnetic, Icy, Janker, Kent, Liberty, Lug, Magnetic, Mast, May, N, Nadir, Negative, Nib, North, Periscian, Po, Polack, Positive, Punt, Quant, Quarterstaff, Racovian, Range, Ricker, Ripeck, Rood, Ry(e)peck, S, Shaft, Slav, South, Spar, Spindle, Sprit, Staff, Stake, Stanchion, Stang, Starosta, Stilt, Sting, Stobie, Telegraph, Terrestrial, Thyrsos, Thyrsus, Tongue, Topmast, Totem, Utility, Vegetal, Zenith

▷ **Polar** *may indicate* with a pole

Polaris Rhodanic, Rocket, Star
Polecat Ferret, Fitch, Fitchet, Foulmart, Foumart, Weasel
Polemic(al) Argument, Controversy, Debate, Eristic(al)
Police(man), Policewoman Babylon, Bear, Beast, Bizzy, Black and Tans, Blue,
  Bluebottle, Bobby, Bog(e)y, Boss, Boys in blue, Bull, Busy, Carabinero, Carabiniere,
  Catchpole, Centenier, Cheka, Chekist, CID, Constable, Cop(per), Cotwal, Crusher,
  Detective, Dibble, Druzhinnik, Europol, Filth, Flatfoot, Flattie, Flic, Flying Squad,
  Force, Fuzz, Garda, Garda Siochana, Gendarme, Gestapo, Gill, G-man, Guard,
  Gumshoe, Harmanbeck, Heat, Hermandad, Inspector, Interpol, Jamadar, Jemadar,
  John Hop, Keystone, Kitchen, Kotwal, Limb, Mata-mata, Met(ropolitan), Military,
  Morse, Mountie, MP, Mulligan, Nabman, Nark, Ochrana, Officer, OGPU, Ovra,
  Patrolman, PC, Peeler, Peon, Pig, Pointsman, Polis, Polizei, Porn squad, Posse
  (comitatus), Prefect, Provincial, Provost, Puppy-walker, Ranger, Redbreast, Redcap,
  Regulate, RIC, Riot, Robert, Rosser, Roundsman, Rozzer, RUC, Sbirro, SC, Secret,
  Securitate, Securocrat, Sepoy, Shamus, Sleeping, Slop, Smokey, Sowar(ry), Special,
  Special Branch, Stasi, State Trooper, Super, Superintendent, Sureté, Sweeney,
  Texas Rangers, T(h)anadar, The Bill, The Law, Thirdborough, Thought, Trap, Vice
  squad, Vigilante, Walloper, Wolly, Woodentop, Zabtieh, Zaptiah, Zaptieh, Zomo
Police car Black Maria, Panda, Patrol, Prowl
Police station Copshop, Lock-up, Tana, Tanna(h), Thana(h), Thanna(h),
  Watchhouse
Policy Assurance, Ballon d'essai, CAP, Comprehensive, Course, Demesne,
  Endowment, Expedience, First-loss, Floating, Good neighbour, Gradualism,
  Insurance, Knock for knock, Laisser-faire, Lend-lease, Line, Method, Open(-sky),
  Open door, Perestroika, Plank, Platform, Pork-barrel, Practice, Programme,
  Reaganism, Revanchism, Scorched earth, Stop-go, Tack, Tactics, Ticket,
  Traditional, Valued, White Australia
Polish(ed), Polisher Beeswax, Black, Blacklead, Bob, Bruter, Buff, Bull, Burnish,
  Chamois, Complaisant, Edit, Elaborate, Elegant, Emery, Enamel, Finish, French,
  Furbish, Gentlemanly, Glass, Gloss, Heelball, Hone, Inland, Lap, Lustre, Nail,
  Perfect, Planish, Polite, Polverine, Pumice, Refinement, Refurbish, Rottenstone,
  Rub, Sand, Sandblast, Sandpaper, Sejm, Sheen, Shellac, Shine, Slick, Slickenside,
  Sophistication, Supercalender, Svelte, Tutty, Urbane, Veneer, Wax
Polite Civil, Courteous, Genteel, Grandisonian, Mannered, Suave, Urbane,
  Well-bred
Politic(al), Politics Apparat, Body, Chartism, Civic, Diplomacy, Discreet,
  Dog-whistle, Expedient, Falange, Fascism, Gesture, Leftism, Party, Poujadism,
  Power, Practical, Public, Radicalism, Rightism, State, Statecraft, Tactful, Wise,
  Yuppie, Yuppy
Politician(s) Bright, Carpet-bagger, Catiline, Chesterfield, Congressman,
  Coningsby, Demagogue, Demo(crat), Diehard, Disraeli, Eden, Euro-MP, Evita,
  Green, Incumbent, Independent, Ins, Isolationist, Laski, Left, Legislator, Liberal,
  Log-roller, MEP, Minister, Moderate, MP, Octobrist, Parliamentarian, Parnell,
  Politico, Polly, Poujade, Puppet, Rad, Rep, Senator, Socialist, Statesman, Statist,
  Tadpole, Taper, TD, Tory, Trotsky, Unionist, Veep, Warhorse, Whig, Wilberforce
Poll(ing) Advance, Ballot, Bean, Canvass, Count, Cut, Deed, Dod, Election, Exit,
  Gallup, Head, Humlie, Hummel, Lory, MORI, Nestor, Not(t), Opinion, Parrot,
  Pineapple, Pow, Push, Referendum, Scrutiny, Straw, Votes
▷ **Poll** *may indicate* a first letter
Pollack Fish, Lob, Lythe
Pollard Doddered

Pollen, Pollinate(d), Pollination Anemophilous, Beebread, Dust, Errhine, Farina, Fertilised, Geitonogamy, Intine, My(i)ophily, Sternotribe, Witch-meal, Xenia
Pollenbrush Scopa
Pollex Thumb
Pollster Psephologist
Pollute(d), Pollutant, Pollution Adulterate, Contaminate, Defile, Dirty, File, Foul, Impure, Infect, Light, Miasma, Noise, Nox, Oil slick, Rainout, Smog, Soil, Soilure, Stain, Sully, Taint, Violate, Waldsterben
Polly Flinders, Parrot, Peachum
Polo Bicycle, Chukka, Marco, Mint, Navigator, Rink, Water
Polonium Po
Poltergeist Apport, Ghost, Spirit, Trouble-house
Poltroon Coward, Craven, Dastard, Scald, Scaramouch
Polyandry Nair
Polygraph Lie-detector
Polymath Knowall, Toynbee
Polymer Elastomer, Isotactic, Lignin, Oligomer, Resin, Seloxane, Silicone, Tetramer, Trimer
Polymorphic Multiform, Proteus, Variform
Polynesian Moriori, Tahitian, Tongan
Polyp(s) Alcyonaria, Gonophore, Hydra, Hydranth, Nematophore, Obelia, Sea-anemone, Tumour
Polyphony Counterpoint
Polystyrene Expanded
Polyzoan Sea-mat
Pom Choom
Pomander Pounce(t)-box
Pomegranate Punica, Punic apple
Pommel Beat, Knob, Pound, Pummel
Pomp(ous) Big, Bombastic, Budge, Ceremonial, Display, Dogberry, Euphuistic, Fustian, Grandiloquent, Grandiose, Heavy, Highfalutin(g), High-flown, High-muck-a-muck, High-sounding, Hogen-mogen, Inflated, Orotund, Ostentatious, Pageantry, Parade, Pretentious, Sententious, Solemn, Splendour, Starchy, State, Stilted, Stuffed shirt, Stuffy, Turgid
Pom-pom Ball, Tassel
Ponce Pander, Solicit, Souteneur
Poncho Ruana
Pond(s) Curling, Dew, Dub, Flash, Hampstead, Lakelet, Lentic, Mill, Pool, Pound, Puddle, Settling, Shield(ing), Slough, Stank, Stew, Tank, Turlough, Vivarium, Viver
Ponder(ous) Brood, Cogitate, Contemplate, Deliberate, Heavy, Laboured, Mull, Muse, Perpend, Poise, Pore, Reflect, Ruminate, → **THINK**, Vise, Volve, Weight(y), Wonder
Poniard Bodkin, → **DAGGER**, Dirk, Stiletto
Pontiff, Pontifical, Pontificate Aaron, Aaronic, Antipope, Dogmatise, Papal
Pontoon Blackjack, Bridge, Caisson, Chess, Game, Twenty one, Vingt-et-un
Pony Bidet, Canuck, Cayuse, Cow, Dales, Dartmoor, Eriskay, Exmoor, Fell, Garran, Garron, Gen(n)et, GG, Griffin, Griffon, Gryfon, Gryphon, Jennet, Jerusalem, Mustang, New Forest, One-trick, Pit, Polo, Pownie, Sable Island, Shanks', Sheltie, Shetland, Show, Tangun, Tat(too), Timor, Welsh, Welsh Mountain, Western Isles
Poodle Barbet, Swan
Pooh Bah, Bear, Pugh, Winnie, Yah

Pool Backwater, Bank, Bethesda, Billabong, Birthing, Bogey hole, Cenote, Cess, Collect, Combine, Dub, Dump, Flash, Flow, Gene, Hag, Hot, Jackpot, Jacuzzi®, Kitty, Lido, Lin(n), Meer, Mere, Mickery, Mikvah, Mikveh, Millpond, Moon, Natatorium, Piscina, Piscine, Plash, Plesh, Plunge, → POND, Reserve, Share, Siloam, Snooker, Spa, Stank, Stanley, Sump, Tank, Tarn, Water(ing) hole, Wave

Poor(ly) Bad, Bare, Base, Bijwoner, Breadline, Buckeen, Bywoner, Catchpenny, Cheapo, Churchmouse, Conch, Cronk, Destitute, Gritty, Half-pie, Hard-up, Have-nots, Hopeless, Humble, Hungry, Ill(-off), Impecunious, Indigent, Lazarus, Lean, Lo-fi, Lousy, Low, Low-downer, Low-fi, Meagre, Mean, Needy, Obolary, One-horse, Pauper, Peaky, Poxy, Redleg, Roinish, Rop(e)y, Roynish, Sad, Scrub, Shabby, Shitty, Sober, Sorry, Sub, Thin, Third-rate, Trashy, Undeserving, Unwell, Wattle, Wishy-washy

▷ **Poor** *may indicate* an anagram

Poorhouse Union, Workhouse

Pooter Nobody, Nonentity

Pop (off), Popper, Popping Bang, Brit, Burst, Cloop, Crease, Die, → DRUG, Father, Fr, Gingerbeer, Hip-hop, Hock, Insert, Lumber, Mineral, Nip, Party, Pater, Pawn, Pledge, Population, Press-stud, Punk, Sherbet, Soda, Splutter, Weasel

▷ **Pop** *may indicate* an anagram

Pope(s) Adrian, Alexander, Atticus, Benedict, Black, Boniface, Borgia, Clement, Dunciad, Eminence, Fish, Great Schism, Gregory, Hildebrand, Holiness, Innocent, Joan, Leo, Papa, Pius, Pontiff, Ruff(e), Schism, Sixtius, Theocrat, Tiara, Urban, Vatican, Vicar-general of Christ, Vicar of Christ

Pop-gun Bourtree-gun

Popinjay Barbermonger, Coxcomb, Dandy, Fop, Macaroni, Parrot, Prig, Skipjack

Poplar Abele, Aspen, Balsam, Cottonwood, Lombardy, Trembling, Tulip, White, Yellow

Poppet Cutie pie, Valve

Poppy Argemone, Bloodroot, Blue, California, Chicalote, Coquelicot, Corn, Diacodin, Eschscholtzia, Field, Flanders, Horned, Iceland, Matilija, Mawseed, Opium, Papaver, Plume, Ponceau, Prickly, Puccoon, Rhoeadales, Shirley, Tall, Welsh

Poppycock Bosh, Nonsense, Rubbish

Popular(ity) Common, Crowd-pleaser, Cult, Demotic, Enchorial, General, Grass roots, Heyday, Hit, In, Laic, Lay, Mass, Plebeian, Prevalent, Public, Successful, Tipped, Trendy, Vogue

Population, Populace Catchment, Census, Closed, Demography, Inhabitants, Malthusian, Mass, Mob, Optimum, → PEOPLE, Public, Universe

Porcelain Arita, Artificial, Bamboo, Belleek®, Blanc-de-chine, Celadon, Chantilly, Chelsea, China, Coalport, Crackle(ware), Crown Derby, Derby, Dresden, Eggshell, Famille, Famille jaune, Famille noir, Famille rose, Famille verte, Goss, Hard-paste, Hizen, Imari, Ivory, Jasp(er), Jasper(ware), Kakiemon, Limoges, Lithophane, Meissen, Minton, Parian, Sèvres, Softpaste, Spode, Sung, Yuan

Porch Galilee, Lanai, Stoa, Stoep, Veranda(h)

Porcupine Hedgehog, Urson

Pore Browse, Hole, Hydrathode, Lenticel, Muse, Ostium, Outlet, Ponder, Stoma, Study

Porgy Braise, Scup(paug)

Pork(y) Bacon, Boar, Brawn, Chap, Char sui, Crackling, Flitch, Griskin, Ham, Lie, Pancetta, Salt, Scrapple, Scruncheon, Scrunchion, Spare-rib, Spek, Tenderloin

Porn(ography), Pornographic Curiosa, Erotica, Hard, Hard-core, Jazz mag,

Rhyparography, Snuff-film, Soft, Soft-core
Porous Cellular, Permeable, Pumice, Sponge
Porpoise Bucker, Dolphin, Mereswine, Pellach, Pellack, Pellock, Phocaena, Sea pig, Sea swine
Porridge Berry, Bird, Brochan, Brose, Burgoo, Busera, Crowdie, Drammach, Drammock, Gaol, Grits, Grouts, Gruel, Hominy, Kasha, Mabela, Mahewu, Mealie pap, Mielie pap, Oaten, Oatmeal, Parritch, Pease-brose, Polenta, Pottage, Praiseach, Sadza, Samp, Sentence, Skilly, Stirabout, Stretch, Sup(p)awn, Time, Ugali
Porridge stick Thible, Thivel
Port(s) Beeswing, Carry, Cinque, Container (terminal), Entrepot, Free, Gate, Gateway, Geropiga, → **HARBOUR**, Haven, Hinterland, Hithe, Induction, Larboard, Left, Manner, Mien, Outport, Parallel, Serial, Tawny, Treaty, USB, Wine

PORTS

3 letters:	Lima	Arica	Horta
Abo	Linz	Aulis	Hythe
Ayr	Lomé	Bahia	Izmir
Gao	Luda	Bahru	Jaffa
Hué	Naha	Barry	Jedda
Rio	Oban	Basra	Jembi
Rye	Omsk	Batum	Jidda
Tyr	Oran	Beira	Joppa
	Oslo	Belem	Kerch
4 letters:	Oulu	Bharu	Kochi
Acre	Perm	Blyth	Larne
Aden	Pori	Brest	Leith
Akko	Pula	Cadiz	Lulea
Amoy	Puri	Cairo	Mainz
Apia	Ruse	Canea	Malmo
Baku	Safi	Colon	Masan
Bari	Said	Dakar	Merca
Boma	Salé	Davao	Miami
Cobh	Sfax	Derry	Mocha
Cork	Suez	Dilli	Mokpo
Deal	Susa	Dover	Narva
Dill	Suva	Duala	Newry
Doha	Tang	Dubai	Omaha
Eisk	Tema	Eilat	Osaka
Elat	Tvev	Elath	Ostia
Faro	Tyre	Emden	Palos
Gary	Vigo	Gabes	Ponce
Hilo	Wick	Galle	Poole
Hull	Wuhu	Gavie	Pusan
Icel		Genoa	Pylos
I-pin	5 letters:	Ghent	Rabat
Kiel	Akaba	Gijon	Rouen
Kiev	Anzio	Goole	Saida
Kobe	Aqaba	Haifa	Sakai
Kure	Arhus	Hania	Salto

Selby	Cannes	Maputo	Sydney
Sidon	Canton	Matadi	Syzran
Skien	Cavite	Menado	Tacoma
Split	Chania	Mersin	Tajiki
Surat	Chi-lin	Mobile	Timaru
Susah	Cochin	Mumbai	Tobruk
Tajik	Cuiaba	Muscat	Toledo
Tampa	Cuyaba	Namibe	Toulon
Tanga	Da Nang	Nantes	Tromso
Tunis	Danzig	Napier	Tyumen
Turku	Darwin	Naples	Velsen
Vaasa	Dieppe	Narvik	Venice
Varna	Djambi	Nassau	Vyborg
Visby	Douala	Nelson	Weihai
Vlore	Duluth	Newark	Whitby
Volos	Dunbar	Ningbo	Wismar
Yalta	Dundee	Ningpo	Wonsan
Yeisk	Durban	Nizhni	Yangon
Yeysk	Durres	Odense	Yantai
Yibin	Elblag	Odessa	
	Galata	Oporto	**7 letters:**
6 letters:	Galati	Ostend	Aalborg
Aarhus	Gdansk	Padang	Abidjan
Abadan	Gdynia	Patras	Ajaccio
Agadir	Harbin	Peoria	Alesund
Albany	Havana	Pesaro	Almeria
Alborg	Hobart	Quebec	Antalya
Amalfi	Ichang	Quincy	Antibes
Ancona	Iligan	Rabaul	Antwerp
Andong	Iloilo	Ragusa	Aracaju
Annaba	Inchon	Recife	Astoria
Aveiro	Jaffna	Rijeka	Augusta
Balboa	Jarrow	Rimini	Averiro
Bastia	Juneau	Romney	Bangkok
Batumi	Kalmar	Roseau	Bayonne
Bergen	Kisumu	Rostov	Bengasi
Bilbao	Lepaya	Samara	Berbera
Bissao	Lisbon	Samsun	Bizerta
Bissau	Lobito	Santos	Bizerte
Blanca	Lubeck	Sarnia	Bristol
Bombay	Lushun	Sasebo	Buffalo
Bootle	Macelo	Savona	Bushire
Boston	Mackay	Skikda	Calabar
Braila	Madras	Smyrna	Cam Ranh
Bremen	Malabo	Sousse	Canopus
Bukavu	Malaga	Speyer	Cantala
Burgas	Manado	Spires	Cardiff
Cairns	Manama	St John	Catania
Calais	Manaos	St Malo	Changde
Callao	Manaus	St Paul	Changte
Candia	Manila	Suakin	Chicago

Chilung	Masbate	Tampico	Chongjin
Cologne	Massaua	Tangier	Cuxhaven
Colombo	Massawa	Taranto	Drogheda
Conakry	Maulman	Trabzon	Duisburg
Corinth	Memphis	Trapani	Dunleary
Corunna	Messina	Trieste	El Ferrol
Cotonou	Milazzo	Tripoli	Elsinore
Derbent	Mombasa	Ushuaia	Falmouth
Detroit	Moulman	Vitebsk	Flushing
Drammen	Munster	Vitoria	Freetown
Dunedin	Nanjing	Wanxian	Gisborne
Dunkirk	Nanking	Wenchou	Gonaives
El Minya	Nanning	Wenchow	Goteborg
Ephesus	Neusatz	Wenzhou	Greenock
Esbjerg	Newport	Whyalla	Haiphong
Foochow	Niigata	Yakutsk	Hakodate
Fukuoka	Niteroi	Yichang	Halmstad
Funchal	Novi Sad	Yingkou	Hamilton
Geelong	Oakland	Yingkow	Hangchow
Grimsby	Okayama		Hangzhou
Halifax	Onitsha	**8 letters:**	Harfleur
Hamburg	Otranto	Aalesund	Hartford
Harwich	Pahsien	Aberdeen	Hastings
Heysham	Palermo	Acapulco	Helsinki
Hodeida	Pelotas	Alicante	Holyhead
Horsens	Phocaea	Alleppey	Honolulu
Houston	Piraeus	Arbroath	Iraklion
Hungnam	Qingdao	Auckland	Istanbul
Incheon	Randers	Badalona	Jayapura
Iquique	Rangoon	Barletta	Jinjiang
Iquitos	Rapallo	Batangas	Kanazawa
Kaolack	Ravenna	Bathurst	Kawasaki
Karachi	Rosario	Benghazi	Keflavik
Kavalla	Rostock	Benguela	Kingston
Kenitra	Runcorn	Bobruisk	Klaipeda
Kherson	Salerno	Bobryusk	La Coruna
Kinsale	San Remo	Bordeaux	La Guaira
Kolding	Sao Luis	Boulogne	La Guyara
Konakri	Seattle	Brindisi	La Spezia
Kowloon	Sekondi	Brisbane	Lattakia
Kuching	Setubal	Bromberg	Les Cayes
La Plata	Seville	Caesarea	Limassol
Latakia	Shantou	Cagliari	Limerick
Legaspi	Shantow	Calcutta	Luderitz
Le Havre	Sinuiju	Castries	Mariupol
Lepanto	Stettin	Changsha	Matanzas
Liepaja	St John's	Changteh	Maulmain
Livorno	St Louis	Chaochow	Mayaguez
Lorient	Sukhumi	Cheribon	Mazatlan
Makurdi	Swansea	Chimbote	Monrovia
Marsala	Tadzhik	Chingtao	Montreal

Moulmein	Valdivia	Gravesend	Stranraer
Murmansk	Valencia	Guayaquil	Sundsvall
Mytilene	Veracruz	Hangchoio	Takamatsu
Nagasaki	Victoria	Helsinger	Tarragona
Nan-ching	Wanganui	Heraklion	Toamasina
Newhaven	Weymouth	Hiroshima	Trebizond
Nha Trang	Yarmouth	Immingham	Trondheim
Novgorod	Yokohama	Inhambane	Tynemouth
Nykøbing	Yokosuka	Jasselton	Volgograd
Pago Pago	Zaanstad	Kagoshima	Walvis Bay
Paramibo		Kaohsiung	Weihaiwei
Pavlodar	**9 letters:**	King's Lynn	Whangarei
Paysandu	Anchorage	Kingstown	Zamboanga
Peiraeus	Angostura	Kirkcaldy	Zeebrugge
Penzance	Annapolis	Kota Bahru	
Pevensey	Antserana	Kozhikode	**10 letters:**
Plymouth	Archangel	Kronstadt	Alexandria
Pnom Penh	Balaclava	Las Palmas	Belize City
Port Said	Balaklava	Lowestoft	Birkenhead
Pozzuoli	Baltimore	Magdeburg	Bratislava
Qui Nhong	Barcelona	Mahajanga	Bridgeport
Ramsgate	Bass-Terre	Mangalore	Bridgetown
Rio Bravo	Bhavnagar	Maracaibo	Caernarvon
Salvador	Bujumbura	Mariehamn	Cap-Haitien
Samarang	Bydgoszcz	Marseille	Casablanca
Sanarang	Carnarvon	Matamoros	Charleston
Sandakan	Cartagena	Matsuyama	Cheboksary
San Diego	Cherbourg	Melbourne	Chittagong
Sandwich	Chisimaio	Milwaukee	Cienfuegos
Santarem	Chongqing	Morecambe	Copenhagen
Santiago	Chungking	Newcastle	Corrientes
Savannah	Cleveland	Nuku'alofa	Dzerzhinsk
Schiedam	Constanta	Palembang	East London
Selencia	Dartmouth	Phnom Penh	Felixstowe
Semarang	Den Helder	Pontianak	Folkestone
Shanghai	Djajapura	Port Blair	Fray Bentos
Sorrento	Dordrecht	Port Louis	Fredericia
Stockton	Dubrovnik	Port Sudan	Georgetown
Surabaja	Ellesmere	Reykjavik	Gothenburg
Surabaya	Epidaurus	Rotterdam	Hammerfest
Syracuse	Esperance	Santa Cruz	Hartlepool
Szczecin	Essaouira	Santander	Herakleion
Tadzhiki	Europoort	Schleswig	Iskenderun
Taganrog	Famagusta	Sheerness	Joao Pessoa
Takoradi	Fishguard	Singapore	Karlskrona
Tangiers	Fleetwood	Soerabaja	Khabarovsk
Tarshish	Flensburg	Stavanger	Khota Bharu
Tauranga	Fortaleza	St George's	La Rochelle
Teresina	Fremantle	St Nazaire	Launceston
Tjirebon	Gallipoli	Stornoway	Los Angelos
Tsingtao	Gateshead	Stralsund	

Louisville
Matozinhos
Montevideo
Mostaganem
New Bedford
New Orleans
Norrkoping
Paramaribo
Pittsburgh
Pontevedra
Port Gentil
Portobello
Portsmouth
Port Talbot
Providence
Queenstown
Sacramento
Santa Marta
Sebastopol
Sevastopol
Strasbourg
Sunderland
Talcahuano
Thunder Bay
Townsville
Valparaiso
Willemstad
Wilmington
Winchelsea

11 letters:
Antofagusta
Antseranana

Banjarmasin
Banjermasin
Baranquilla
Bremerhaven
Cheng-chiang
Dares Salaam
Fredrikstad
Grangemouth
Helsingborg
Hermoupolis
Kaliningrad
Makhachkala
New Plymouth
Newport News
Nuevo Laredo
Pointe-Noire
Port Moresby
Porto Alegre
Port of Spain
Punta Arenas
Rockhampton
San Fernando
Scarborough
Shimonoseki
Southampton
Telukbetong
Trincomalee
Vizagapatam
Vlaardingen
Vladivostok

12 letters:
Angtofagasta

Bandjarmasin
Bandjermasin
Barranquilla
Buenaventura
Chandemagore
Dun Laoghaire
Ho Chi Min City
Jacksonville
Kota Kinabalu
Kristiansand
Milford Haven
Philadelphia
Pointe-à-Pitre
Ponta Delgada
Port Adelaide
Port-au-Prince
Port Harcourt
Prince Rupert
Rio de Janeiro
San Francisco
San Sebastian
Santo Domingo
South Shields
St Petersburg
Tanjungpriok
Thessaloniki
Ujung Pandang
Usti nad Labem

13 letters:
Chandernagore
Charlottetown
Ciudad Bolivar

Corpus Christi
Florianopolis
Great Yarmouth
Ho Chi Minh City
Port Elizabeth
Tandjungpriok
Teloekbetoeng
Trois Rivières
Visakhapatnam
Wilhelmshaven

14 letters:
Mina Hassen Tani
Nizhni Novgorod
Santiago de Cuba
Vishakhapatnam

15 letters:
Alexandroupolis
Angra-de-Heroismo
Blagoveshchensk
Sault Saint Marie

16 letters:
Reggio di Calabria
Sault Sainte Marie

18 letters:
Castellon de la
Plana

Portable Lapheld, Laptop, Palmtop

Portend, Portent(ous) Augur, Awesome, Bode, Dire, Omen, Ostent, Phenomenon,
Presage, → WARN(ING)

Porter Ale, Bearer, Bellboy, Bellhop, Bummaree, Caddie, Caddy, Cole, Concierge,
Coolie, Door-keeper, Doorman, Dvornik, Entire, Gatekeeper, Hamaul, Ham(m)al,
Humper, Janitor, October, Ostiary, Plain, Red-cap, Stout

Portfolio Holding

Portico Colonnade, Decastyle, Distyle, Dodecastyle, Exedra, Loggia, Narthex,
Parvis(e), Porch, Propylaeum, Prostyle, Stoa, Veranda(h), Xyst(us)

Portion Aliquot, Ann(at), Bit, Deal, Distribute, Dole, Dose, Dotation, Fraction,
Fragment, Helping, Heritage, Hunk, Instalment, Jointure, Lot, Measure, Meed,
Mess, Modicum, Nutlet, Ounce, → PART, Piece, Ratio, Scantle, Scantling, Section,
Segment, Serving, Share, Size, Slice, Something, Spoonful, Tait, Taste, Tate, Tittle,
Tranche, Wodge

Portland Bill, Cement, Stone

Portly Ample, Corpulent, Gaucie, Gaucy, Gawcy, Gawsy, Stout

Portmanteau Bag, Combination, Holdall, Valise

Portrait(ist) Carte de visite, Depiction, Drawing, Eikon, Icon, Identikit®, Ikon, Image, Kit-cat, Lely, Likeness, Painting, Retraitt, Retrate, Sketch, Vignette

Portray(al) Caricature, Depict, Describe, Feature, Image, Limn, Paint, Personate, Render, Represent, → **SHOW**

Portsmouth Pompey

Portugal, Portuguese Lusitania(n), Luso-, Macanese, Senhor

Pose(r), Poseur Aesthete, Affect(ation), Arabesque, Asana, Ask, Contrapposto, Drape, Lotus, Mannequin, Man(n)ikin, Masquerade, Model, Place, Plastique, Posture, Pretend, Problem, Propound, Pseud, Puzzle, Sit, Stance, Sticker, Tickler

Poseidon Earthshaker

Posh Chic, Classy, Grand, Lah-di-dah, Ornate, Ritzy, Swanky, Swish, U

Position Asana, Attitude, Bearing(s), Close, Codille, Delta, Emplacement, Enfilade, False, Fixure, F(o)etal, Foothold, Fowler's, Grade, Instal, Lay, Lie, Location, Locus, Lodg(e)ment, Lotus, Missionary, Mudra, Office, Open, Pass, Peak, Place, Plant, Point, Pole, Possie, Post, Pozzy, Put, Recumbent, Root, Seat, Set(ting), Sextile, Sims, Site, Situ, Situs, Stance, Standing, Standpoint, Station, Status, Strategic, Syzygy, Tagmeme, Thesis, Tierce, Trendelenburg's, Tuck, Viewpoint

Positive, Positivist Absolute, Anode, Assertive, Categorical, → **CERTAIN**, Comte, Definite, Emphatic, False, Plus, Print, Sure, Thetic, Upbeat, Veritable, Yang, Yes

Posse Band, Mob, Vigilantes

Possess(ed), Possession(s), Possessive Adverse, Apostrophe, Asset, Aver, Bedevil, Belonging(s), Demonic, Driven, Energumen, Estate, Have, Haveour, Haviour, Heirloom, His, Hogging, Know, Lares (et) penates, Mad, Obsessed, Occupation, → **OWN**, Sasine, Seisin, Sprechery, Substance, Tenancy, Usucap(t)ion, Vacant, Worth

Possible, Possibility, Possibly Able, Contingency, Feasible, Likely, Maybe, Mayhap, Off-chance, Peradventure, Perchance, Perhaps, Posse, Potential, Prospect, Resort, Viable, Will

▷ **Possibly** *may indicate* an anagram

Possum Burramys, Cataplexy, Opossum, Pygmy, Ringtail, Sugar glider, Sugar squirrel, Tait

Post(s), Postage Affix, After, Assign, Bitt, Bollard, Carrick bitt, Command, Correspondence, Dak, Dawk, Delivery, Dragon's teeth, Emily, Excess, Finger, First, Flagpole, Graded, Gradient, Guardhose, Heel, Hitching, Hovel, Hurter, Jamb, Joggle, King, Last, Listening, Log, Mail, Mast, Newel, Observation, Outstation, Pale, Paling, Parcel, Pendant, Penny, Picket, Pigeon, Pile, Piling, Piquet, Placard, Place, Plant, Plum, Pole, Position, Presidio, Puncheon, Pylon, Queen, Quintain, Quoin, Registered, Remit, Residency, RM, Rubbing, Samson's, Seat, Send, Sheriff's, Snubbing, Sound, Spile, Staff, Staging, Stake, Starting, Station, Stell, Stoop, Stoup, Stud, Studdle, Term(inal), Tom, Tool, Trading, Upright, Vacancy, Waymark, Winning

Postcard(s) Deltiology, Picture

Poster Advertisement, Affiche, Bill, Broadsheet, Placard, Playbill, Sender

Posterior Behind, Bottom, Jacksie, Jacksy, Later, Lumbar, Pygal, Rear, Tail

Post-free Franco

Postman, Postmaster, Postwoman Carrier, Courier, Emily, Hill, Messenger, Nasby, Pat, Portionist, Sorter

Postmark Frank

Post-modern Po-mo

Post mortem Autopsy, Enquiry, Necropsy

Postpone(ment) Adjourn, Backburner, Contango, Defer, Delay, Frist, Hold over,

Lay over, Long-finger, Moratorium, Mothball, Pigeon-hole, Postdate, Prorogue, Put over, Reprieve, Respite, Shelve, Stay, Suspend, Withhold
Postulant Candidate, Noumenon, Novice
Postulate(s) Assert, Assume, Claim, Koch's, Propound
Posture(r), Posturing Affectation, Asana, Attitude, Birkie, Camp, Carriage, Counter-view, Decubitus, Deportment, Mudra, Pose, Pretence, Site, Stance, Vorlage
Posy Bouquet, Buttonhole, Corsage, Nosegay, Tussiemussie, Tuzzi-muzzy
Pot(s), Potting, Potty Abridge, Aludel, Ante, Bankroll, Basil, Belly, Billycan, Cafetière, Ca(u)ldron, Cannabis, Casserole, Ceramic, Chamber, Chanty, Chatti, Chatty, Chimney, Coal, Cocotte, Crewe, Crock(ery), Crucible, Cruse(t), Cupel, Delf(t), Dixie, Ewer, Flesh, Gage, Gallipot, Ganja, Gazunder, Grass, Hash(ish), Helmet, Hemp, In off, Inurn, Jardinière, Jordan, Kettle, Kitty, Livery, Lobster, Lota(h), Maiolica, Majolica, Marijuana, Marmite, Melting, Ming, Monkey, Olla, Olpe, Pan, Papper, Pat, Piñata, Pint, Pipkin, Planter, Po, Pocket, Poot, Posnet, → **POTTERY**, Pottle, Pounce, Pout, Prize, Quart, Samovar, Shoot, Skeet, Skillet, Smudge, Steamer, Stomach, Tajine, Tea, Test, Throw, Togine, Trivet, Tureen, Urn, Vial, Ware, Wash, Wok
Potash Kalinite, Polverine, Sylvine, Sylvite
Potassium K, Kalium, Pearl ash, Saleratus, Saltpetre
Potation Dram, Drink
Potato(es) African, Aloo, Alu, Batata, Chat, Clean, Couch, Datura, Duchesse, Early, Fluke, Hashbrowns, Hog, Hole, Hot, Irish, Jacket, Jersey, Kidney, Kumara, Lyonnaise, Mash, Murphy, Parmentier, Peel-and-eat, Pratie, Praty, Roesti, Rumbledethump(s), Seed, Small, Solanum, Stovies, Sweet, Tatie, Tattie, Teddy, Tuber, Ware, White, Yam
Pot-bearer Trivet
Pot-bellied Kedge, Kedgy, Kidge, Paunchy, Portly, Stout
Potboiler Hob
Pot-boy Basil, Ganymede, Scullion
Potent(ate) Dynamic, Emeer, Emir, Emperor, Huzoor, Influential, Kinglet, Mogul, Nawab, Panjandrum, Powerful, Ras, Ruler, Satrap, Squirearch, Sultan, Virile
Potential(ly) Action, Capacity, Chemical, Electric, Electrode, In posse, Ionization, Making(s), Manqué, Possible, Promise, Resting, Scope, Viable
▷ **Potentially** *may indicate* an anagram
Pothole(r) Chuckhole, Giant's kettle, Spelunker
Pot-house Shebeen, Tavern
Potion Dose, Draught, Drink, Dwale, Love, Mixture, Philtre, Tincture
Pot-pourri Hotchpotch, Medley, Miscellany, Pasticcio, Salmi
Potsherd Ostracon, Ostrakon
Pottage Berry
Potter Cue, Dabbity, Dabble, Dacker, Daidle, Daiker, Daker, Dibble, Dilly-dally, Dodder, Etruscan, Fettle, Fiddle, Footer, Footle, Fouter, Gamesmanship, Harry, Idle, Mess, Minton, Muck, Niggle, One-upmanship, Plouter, Plowter, Poke, Spode, Thrower, Tiddle, Tink(er), Troke, Truck, Wedgewood, Wedgwood
▷ **Potter** *may indicate* a snooker-player
Pottery Agatewear, Bank, Basalt, Bisque, Cameo ware, Celadon, Ceramet, Ceramic, China, Creamware, Crock, Crouch-ware, Dabbity, Delf(t), Earthenware, Encaustic, Etruria(n), Faience, Flatback, Gombroon, Granitewear, Hollowware, Ironstone, Jomon, Lustreware, Maiolica, Majolica, Ming, Minton, Pebbleware, Raku, Red-figured, Satsuma, Scroddled, Sgraffito, Slab, Slipware, Smalto, Spode, Spongeware, Stoneware, Studio, Sung, Terra sigillata, Ware,

Wedgwood®, Wemyss, Whieldon

Pouch(ed) Bag, Brood, Bum-bag, Bursa, Caecum, Cheek, Cisterna, Codpiece, Diverticulum, Fanny pack, Gill, Jockstrap, Marsupial, Marsupium, Poke, Posing, Purse, Sac, Scrip, Scrotum, Spleuchan, Sporran, Tobacco

Poultice Application, Cataplasm, Embrocation, Epithem(a), Lenient, Plaster

Poultry Dorking, Fowl, Gallinaceous, Plymouth Rock, Poot, Pout, Welsummer

Poultry disease Keel, Scaly-leg, Vent gleet

Pounce Claw, Jump, Lunge, Powder, Sere, Souse, Sprinkle, Swoop, Talon

Pound(er) Ache, As, Bar, Bash, Batter, Beat, Bombard, Bradbury, Bray, Broadpiece, Bruise, Catty, Contund, Coop, Drub, Embale, Enclosure, Ezra, Fold, Green, Hammer, Hatter, Imagist, Intern, Iron man, Jail, Jimmy o'goblin, Kiddle, Kidel, Kin, Knevell, L, Lam, Lb, Lock, Mash, Nevel, Nicker, Oncer, One-er, Oner, Pale, Pen, Penfold, Pestle, Pin, Pindar, Pinfold, Powder, Pulverise, Pun, Quid, Quop, Rint, Scots, Smacker, Sov(ereign), Squid, Stamp, Sterling, Strum, Tenderise, Thump, Tower, Troy, Weight

Pour Be mother, Birl(e), Bucket, Cascade, Circumfuse, Decant, Diffuse, Flood, Flow, Jaw, Jirble, Libate, Rain, Seil, Shed, Sile, Skink, Spew, Stream, Teem, Trill, Turn, Vent, Weep, Well

Pout Bib, Blain, Brassy, Eel, Fish, Horn(ed), Mope, Mou(e), Scowl, Sulk, Tout, Towt, Whiting

Poverty Beggary, Dearth, Deprivation, Illth, Indigence, → **LACK**, Locust years, Need, Paucity, Penury, Poortith, Puirtith, Squalor, Want

Powder(ed), Powdery Alumina, Amberite, Araroba, Baking, Ballistite, Bleaching, Boracic, Calamine, Chalk, Chilli, Cosmetic, Crocus, Culm, Curry, Custard, Cuttlefish, Dentifrice, Dover's, Dust, Dusting, Eupad, Explosive, Face, Floury, Fulminating, Giant, Glaucous, Goa, Gregory, Grind, Gun, Hair, Insect, Itching, Kohl, Levigate, Lithia, Litmus, Lupulin, Meal, Mould-facing, Moust, Mu(i)st, Pearl, Pemoline, Percussion, Persian, Plaster of Paris, Plate, Polishing, Pollen, Pounce, Priming, Prismatic, Projecting, Pruinose, Pulver, Pulvil, Putty, Rachel, Rochelle, Rottenstone, Rouge, Saleratus, Seidlitz, Seme(e), Sherbet, Silver iodide, Sitosterol, Smeddum, Smokeless, Snuff, Soap, Spode, Spodium, Talc(um), Talcose, Thimerosal, Toner, Tooth, Triturate, Tutty, Washing, Zein

Power(ful), Powers Ability, Able, Aeon, Aggrandisement, Almighty, Amandla, Arm, Arnold, Atomic, Attorney, Audrey, Autarchy, Authority, Axis, Beef, Big, Chakra, Cham, Charisma, Clairvoyance, Clout, Cogency, Colossus, Command, Corridor, Cube, Danger, Despotic, Diadem, Dioptre, Dominion, Effective, Eminence, Éminence grise, Empathy, Empery, Energy, Eon, Exponent, Facility, Faculty, Fire, Flower, Force, Force majeure, Geothermal, Grey, Gutty, Hands, Hefty, Hegemony, High, Hildebrandic, Horse, Hot, Hp, Hydroelectric, Imperium, Influence, Kami, Kilowatt, Log, Logarithm, Lusty, Mana, Mastery, Megalomania, Might, Mogul, Motive, Motor, Movers and shakers, Muscle, Nature, Nth, Nuclear, Od-force, Omnificent, Omnipotent, Option, P, Panjandrum, People, Pester, Plenipotency, Posse, Potency, Prepollence, Prepotent, Puissant, Punch, Purchasing, Regime, Resolving, Say-so, Siddhi, Sinew, Solar, Soup, Stamina, Staying, Steam, Stiff, Stopping, Strength, → **STRONG**, Supercharge, Supreme, Suzerain, Teeth, Telling, Throne, Tidal, Tycoon, Tyrone, Ulric, Valency, Vertu(e), Vigour, Vis, Volt, Vroom, Water, Watt, Wattage, Wave, Weight, Wind, World, Yeast

Powerless Diriment, Downa-do, Failing, Freewheel, Hamstrung, Helpless, Impotent, Impuissant, Incapable, Inert, Unable, Unarmed, Weak

Powwow Confab, Conference, Council, Meeting

Pox Orf, Pize

Practical, Practicable, Practicalities Active, Applied, Brass tacks, Doable, Easy-care, Hard-boiled, Joker, Logistics, No-nonsense, Nuts and bolts, On, Pragmatic, Realist(ic), Realpolitik, Rule of thumb, Sensible, Shrewd, Useful, Utilitarian, Viable, Virtual

Practice, Practise, Practitioner, Practised Abuse, Adept, Custom, Distributed, Do, Drill, Enure, Exercise, General, Group, Habit, Inure, Ism, Keep, Knock-up, Massed, Meme, Nets, Operate, Order, Ply, Policy, Praxis, Private, Prosecution, Pursuit, Rehearsal, Rehearse, Restrictive, Rite, Rule, Rut, Sadhana, Sharp, Spanish, Target, Teaching, Test-run, Trade, Tradition, Train, Trial, Ure, Usage, Use

Pragmatic, Pragmatist Ad hoc, Busy, Dogmatic, Humanist, Meddling, Officious, Realist

Prairie IL, Illinois, Llano, Plain, Savanna, Steppe, Tundra, Veldt

Prairie dog Whippoorwill, Wishtonwish

Praise(worthy) Acclaim, Adulation, Alleluia, Allow, Anthem, Applause, Belaud, Bless, Blurb, Bouquet, Butter, Carol, Citation, CL, Commend(ation), Compliment, Cry up, Dulia, Ego boost, Encomium, Envy, Eulogise, Eulogium, Eulogy, Exalt, Extol, Gloria, Glory, Hero-worship, Herry, Hery(e), Hosanna, Hymn, Hype, Incense, Kudos, Laud, Lip service, Lo(o)s, Meritorious, Palmary, Panegyric, Puff(ery), Rap, Roose, Tribute

Pram Carriage, Cart, Scow

Prance Brank, Canary, Caper, Cavort, Galumph, Gambol, Jaunce, Jaunse, Prank(le), Swagger, Tittup, Trounce

Prang Accident, Crash, Smash, Whale

Prank(s) Attrap, Bedeck, Bedizen, Caper, Dido, Escapade, Fredaine, Frolic, Gaud, Jape, Lark, Mischief, Pliskie, Rag, Reak, Reik, Rex, Rig, Spoof, Trick, Vagary, Wedgie

Praseodymium Pr

Prat Bottom, → STUPID PERSON

Prate Babble, Boast, Haver, Talk

Prattle Babble, Blat(her), Chatter, Gab(nash), Gas, Gibber, Gossip, Gup, Lalage, Patter, Smatter, Yap

Prawn Banana, Dublin Bay, King, Scampi, School, Shrimp

Pray(ing) Appeal, Bed, Beg, Beseech, Bid, Daven, → ENTREAT, Impetrate, Intone, Invoke, Kneel, Mantis, Solicit, Wrestle

Prayer(s), Prayer book Acoemeti, Act, Amidah, Angelus, Ardas, Ave (Maria), Bead, Beadswoman, Bede, Bene, Bidding, Breviary, Collect, Commination, Common, Confiteor, Cry, Cursus, Daven, Deus det, Devotion, Eleison, Embolism, Entreaty, Epiclesis, Euchologion, Evensong, Geullah, Grace, Habdalah, Hail Mary, Hallan-shaker, Imam, Intercession, Invocation, Kaddish, Khotbah, Khotbeh, Khutbah, Kol Nidre, Kyrie, Kyrie eleison, Lauds, Litany, Lord's, Loulat-ul-qadr, Lychnapsia, Ma(c)hzor, Mantis, Mat(t)ins, Mincha(h), Missal, Morning, Musaf, Novena, Orant, Orarium, Orison, Our Father, Paternoster, Patter, Petition, Phylactery, Placebo, Plea, Preces, Proseucha, Proseuche, Puja, Requiem, Requiescat, Rogation, Rosary, Salat, Secret, Shema, Siddur, State, Stations of the Cross, Suffrage, Te igitur, Tenebrae, Triduum, Venite, Yajur-Veda, Yizkor

▷ **Prayer** *may indicate* one who begs

Preach(er) Ainger, Boanerges, Circuit rider, Dawah, Devil-dodger, Dominican, Donne, Ecclesiastes, Evangelist, Exhort, Gospeller, Graham, Holy Roller, Itinerant, Knox, Lecture, Local, Mar-text, Minister, Moody, → MORALISE, Patercove, Pontificate, Postillate, Predicant, Predicate, Predikant, Priest, Prophet, Pulpiter,

Rant, Revivalist, Spintext, Spurgeon, Teach, Televangelist
Preamble Introduction, Preface, Proem, Prologue
Prearrange(d) Stitch up
Pre-Cambrian Torridonian
Precarious Dangerous, Parlous, Perilous, Risky, Touch and go, Trickle, Uncertain, Unsteady
Precaution Care, Fail-safe, Guard, In case, Prophylaxis, Safeguard
Precede(nce), Precedent Antedate, Example, Forego, Forerun, Head, Herald, Pas, Predate, Preface, Priority, Protocol
Precept(s) Adage, Canon, Commandment, Maxim, Mishna, Motto, Saw
Precession Larmor
Precinct(s) Ambit, Area, Banlieue, Close, Courtyard, District, Environs, Pedestrian, Peribolos, Region, Shopping, Temenos, Verge, Vihara
Precious Adored, Chary, Chichi, Costly, Dear, Dearbought, Ewe-lamb, La-di-da, Murr(h)a, Nice, Owre, Precise, Prissy, Rare, Valuable
Precipice Bluff, Cliff, Crag, Krans, Kran(t)z, Sheer
Precipitate, Precipitation, Precipitous Abrupt, Accelerate, Cause, Deposit, Hailstone, Headlong, Impetuous, Launch, Lees, Pellmell, Pitchfork, Rash, Sca(u)r, Sheer, Shoot, Sleet, Snowflake, Start, → STEEP, White
Précis Abstract, Aperçu, Epitome, Résumé, Summary
Precise(ly), Precisian, Precision Absolute, Accurate, Dry, Exact, Explicit, Fine-drawn, Literal, Minute, Nice(ty), Overnice, Particular, Perfect, Plumb, Point-device, Prig, Prim, Punctilious, Sharpness, Spang, Specific, Starchy, Stringent, Succinct, Surgical, Tight, Very
Preclude Bar, Debar, Estop, Foreclose, Hinder, Impede, Prevent
Precocious(ness) Advanced, Bratpack, Forward, Premature, Protogyny
Preconception Ideating
Precursor Avant-courier, Forerunner, Harbinger
Predator(y) Carnivore, Eagle, Fox, Glede, Harpy-eagle, Jackal, Kestrel, Kite, Lycosa, Marauder, Predacious, Puma, Tanrec, Tarantula, Tenrec
Pre-dawn Antelucan, Ante lucem
Predecessor Ancestor, Forebear, Foregoer
Predestined Doomed, Fated, Tramway
Predicament Box, Dilemma, Embarrassment, Embroglio, Hobble, Hole, Jam, Pass, Peril, Pickle, Plight, Quandary, Scrape, Spot
Predict(ion), Predictable, Predictor Augur, Belomancy, Bet, Damn, Divination, Far-seeing, Forecast, Foreordain, Foresay, Foreshadow, Foreshow, Forespeak, Foretell, Forsay, Horoscope, Nap, Necromancy, Portend, Presage, Previse, Prognosis, Prophecy, Prophesy, Regular, Second-guess, Soothsayer, Spae
Predilection Fancy, Liking, Prejudice, Taste, Tendency
Predisposition Aptitude, Inclination, Parti-pris, Tendency
Predominate Abound, Govern, Overshadow, Prevail, Reign
Pre-eminence, Pre-eminent Arch, Foremost, Palm, Paramount, Primacy, Supreme, Topnotch, Unique
Pre-empt Enter
Preen Perk, Primp, Prink, Prune, Titivate
Prefab(ricated) Quonset, Terrapin®
Preface Foreword, Herald, Intro, Preamble, Precede, Proem, Prolegomenon, Usher
Prefect Prepositor, Pr(a)eposter
Prefer(ence), Preferred Advance, Better, Choose, Discriminate, Elect, Faard, Faurd, Favour, Imperial, Incline, Lean, Liquidity, Predilect(ion), Prefard, Priority,

Proclivity, Promote, Rather, Sooner, Stocks, Taste, Will

Prefix Eka, Introduce, Name

Pregnancy, Pregnant Big, Clucky, Cyesis, Ectopic, Enceinte, Fertile, F(o)etation, Gestation, Gravid(a), Great, Heavy, In foal, In pig, In pup, Knocked-up, Phantom, Pseudocyesis, Pudding-club, Stomack, Up the spout, Up the stick, With child

Prehistoric Ancient, Azilian, Beaker Folk, Boskop, Brontosaurus, Cambrian, Clovis, Cro-Magnon, Eocene, Folsom, Mound Builder, Ogygian, Primeval, Primitive, Pteranodon, Pterodactyl(e), Pterosaur, Saurian, Sinanthropus, Stonehenge, Titanosaurus, Trilith(on)

Prejudice(d) Bias, Bigotry, Derry, Discrimination, Down, Illiberal, Impede, Inequity, Injure, Insular, Intolerance, Partiality, Parti pris, Preoccupy, Prepossession, Racism

Prelate Archiepiscopal, Cardinal, Churchman, Exarch, Monsignor, Odo, Priest

Preliminary Draft, Exploration, Heat, Initial, Introductory, Precursory, Preparatory, Previous, Prodrome, Prolusion, Propaedeutic, Rough, Title-sheet

Prelude Entrée, Forerunner, Intrada, Overture, Proem(ial), Ritornell(e), Ritornello

Premature Early, Precocious, Pre(e)mie, Premy, Previous, Slink, Untimely, Untimeous

Premedication Atropia

Premeditate Anticipate, Foresee, Plan

Premier Chief, Leader, Main, PM, → PRIME MINISTER, Tojo

Premise(s) Assumption, Datum, Epicheirema, Ground, Hypothesis, Inference, Lemma, Major, Postulate, Property, Proposition, Reason

Premium Ap, Bond, Bonus, Discount, Grassum, Pm, Reward, Scarce, Share

Premonition Hunch, Omen, Presentiment, Prodromal, Warning

Preoccupation, Preoccupied, Preoccupy Absorb, Abstracted, Distrait, Engross, Hang-up, Intent, Obsess, Self-centred, Thing

Prepaid Pro-forma, Sae

Prepare(d), Preparation Address, À la, Arrange, Attire, Boun, Bowne, Busk, Calver, Cock, Concoct, Cooper, Countdown, Decoct, Did, Do, Dress, Edit, Forearm, Game, Groom, Ground, Inspan, Key, Lay, Legwork, Lotion, Measure, Mobilise, Parasceve, Pomade, Preliminary, Prime, Procinct, Prothesis, Provide, Psych, → READY, Rehearsal, Ripe, Rustle up, Set, Spadework, Stand-to, Suborn, Train, Truss, Warm-up, Whip up, Yare

▷ **Prepare(d)** *may indicate* an anagram

Preponderance, Preponderant, Preponderate Important, Majority, Outweigh, Paramount, Prevalence, Sway

Preposition Premise

Prepossessing, Prepossession Attractive, Fetching, Predilection, Winsome

Preposterous Absurd, Chimeric, Foolish, Grotesque, Unreasonable

▷ **Preposterous** *may indicate* a word reversed

Pre-Raphaelite Rossetti, Waterhouse

Prerequisite Condition, Essential, Necessity, Sine qua non

Prerogative Faculty, Franchise, Liberty, Privilege, Right, Royal

Presage Abode, Foresight, Omen, Portend, Presentiment, Prophesy

Presbyter(ian) Berean, Blue, Cameronian, Covenanter, Elder, Knox, Macmillanite, Moderator, Sacrarium, Seceder, Secesher, Secession Church, Whig(gamore)

Prescient Clairvoyant, Fly

Prescribe, Prescription Appoint, Assign, Dictate, Enjoin, Impose, Negative, Ordain, Positive, Rule, Scrip, Set

Prescription Cipher, Decree, Direction, Formula, Medicine, R, Rec, Receipt, Ritual, Specific

Presence Aspect, Bearing, Closeness, Company, Debut, Face, Hereness, Real, Shechinah, Shekinah, Spirit

Present(ation), Presented, Presenter, Presently Ad sum, Anchorman, Anon, Assists, Autocutie, Award, Bestow, Bonsela, Boon, Bounty, Box, Breech, By, By and by, Cadeau, Congiary, Coram, Current, Debut, Dee-jay, Deodate, DJ, Donate, Dotal, Douceur, Dower, Emcee, Endew, Endow, Endue, Enow, Étrenne, Existent, Fairing, Feature, Format, Front-man, Gie, → **GIFT**, Give, Going, Grant, Gratuity, Hand, Here, Historical, Hodiernal, Inst, Introduce, Jock(ey), Largess(e), Linkman, MC, Mod, Nonce, Now, Nuzzer, Offering, On hand, Porrect, Potlach, Pr, Prevailing, Produce, Proffer, Pro-tem, Put, Render, Show, Slice, The now, Tip, Today, Vee-jay, Xenium, Yeven

Preserve(d), Preservative, Preserver Bottle, Burnettize, Can, Chill, Chow-chow, Confect, Confiture, Corn, Creosote, Cure, Dehydrate, Dry, Eisel, Embalm, Fixative, Formaldehyde, Formalin, Freeze, Guard, Hain, Hesperides, Jam, Jerk, Keep, Kinin, Kipper, Konfyt, Kyanise, Life, Lifebelt, → **MAINTAIN**, Marmalade, Mummify, On ice, Pectin, Peculiar, Piccalilli, Pickle, Pot, Powellise, Salt, Salve, Saut, Season, Souse, Store, Stratify, Stuff, Tanalith, Tanalized, Tar, Tin, Vinegar, Waterglass

Preshrunk Sanforized®

Preside(nt) Abe, Adams, Banda, Bush, Carter, Chair, Childers, Cleveland, Coolidge, Coty, Dean, De Gaulle, Director, Eisenhower, Ford, Garfield, Grand Pensionary, Grant, Harding, Harrison, Hayes, Hoover, Ike, Johnson, Kennedy, Kruger, Lead, Lincoln, Madison, Mitterand, Moderator, Nixon, Old Hickory, P, Peron, Polk, Pompidou, Pr(a)eses, Prexy, Reagan, Roosevelt, Sa(a)dat, Speaker, Superintendent, Supervisor, Taft, Tito, Truman, Tyler, Veep, Washington, Wilson

Press(ed), Pressing, Pressure Acute, Aldine, Armoire, Atmospheric, Bar, Bench, Blackmail, Blood, Bramah, Button, Cabinet, Chivvy, Clarendon, Closet, Clothes, Coerce, Cram, Crease, Crimp, Critical, Crowd, Crush, Cupboard, Cylinder, Dragoon, Drill, Dun, Durable, Duress, Duresse, Enforcement, Enslave, Exigent, Filter, Flat-bed, Fluid, Fly, Folding, Force, Fourth estate, Full-court, Goad, Greenmail, Gutter, Hasten, Head, Heat, Herd, Hie, High, Hug, Hustle, Hydraulic, Hydrostatic, Impact, Important, Importune, Inarm, Intense, Iron, Isobar, Jam, Jostle, Knead, Leverage, Lie, Lobby, Low, Mangle, Megabar, Microbar, Mill, Minerva, Newspapers, Obligate, Oil, Onus, Osmotic, PA, Partial, Pascal, Peer, Permanent, Persist, Piezo-, Ply, Prease, Printing, Private, Psi, Pump, → **PUSH**, Racket, Ram, Ratpack, Record, Recruit, Reporter, Ridge, Roll, Root, Rotary, Rounce, Rush, Samizdat, Screw, Scrooge, Scrouge, Scrowdge, Scrum, Serr(e), Sit, Speed, Spur, Squash, Squeeze, Stanhope, Static, Stop, Strain(t), Stress, Tension, Thlipsis, Threap, Threep, Throng, Throttle, Thrutch, Torr, Tourniquet, Turgor, → **URGE**, Urgence, Urgency, Vanity, Vapour, Vice, Waid(e), Wardrobe, Weight, Wine, Wring, Yellow

Press agent Flack, Spin doctor

Press-gang Crimp, Force, Impress, Shanghai

Pressman Ed, Journalist, Journo, PRO, Reporter, Twicer

Prestidigitate(r) Conjure, Juggle, Legerdemain, Magician, Palm

Prestige, Prestigious Asma, Cachet, Credit, Distinguished, Fame, Influence, Izzat, Kudos, Notable, Status

Presume, Presumably, Presumption, Presumptuous Allege, Arrogant, Audacity, Believe, Bold, Brass, Cocksure, Cocky, Doubtless, → **EXPECT**, Familiar, Forward, Gall, Impertinent, Insolent, Liberty, Outrecuidance, Pert, Probably, Put upon, Suppose, Uppish, Whipper-snapper

Pretence, Pretend(er), Pretext Act, Affect(ation), Afflict, Assume, Blind, Bluff, Charade, Charlatan, Claim, Claimant, Cover, Cram, Dissemble, Dissimulate,

Dive, Excuse, False, Feign, Feint, Gondolier, Guise, Hokum, Humbug, Hypocrisy, Impostor, Jactitation, Kid(stakes), Lambert Simnel, Let-on, Make-believe, Malinger, Masquerade, Obreption, Old, Parolles, Perkin Warbeck, Pose, Profess, Pseud(o), Quack, Sham, Simulate, Stale, Stalking-horse, Subterfuge, Suppose, Warbeck, Young

Pretentious(ness), Pretension Arty, Bombast, Chi-chi, Fantoosh, Fustian, Gaudy, Grandiose, High-falutin(g), Kitsch, La-di-da, Orotund, Ostentatious, Overblown, Paraf(f)le, Pompous, Ponc(e)y, Pseud(o), Sciolism, Showy, Snob, Snobbish, Squirt, Tat, Tattie-peelin, Tinhorn, Toffee-nosed, Uppity, Wanky, Whippersnapper

Pretty Attractive, Becoming, Chocolate-box, Comely, Cute, Dear, Decorate, Dish, Elegant, Fair(ish), Fairway, Inconie, Incony, Keepsaky, Looker, Moderately, Pass, Peach, Picturesque, Primp, Quite, Sweet, Twee, Winsome

Prevail(ing) Dominate, Endure, Go, Induce, Outweigh, Persist, Persuade, Predominant, Preponderate, Reign, Ring, Triumph, Victor, Win

Prevalent Catholic, Common, Dominant, Endemic, Epidemic, Obtaining, Rife, Set in, Widespread

Prevaricate, Prevarication Equivocate, Hedge, Lie, Runaround, Stall, Whittie-whattie

Prevent(ive) Avert, Bar, Debar, Deter, Disenable, Embar, Estop, Foreclose, Forfend, Help, Impound, Inhibit, Keep, Let, Obstruct, Obviate, Preclude, Prophylactic, Sideline, Stop, Theriac, Trammel

Preview Sneak, Trailer, Vernissage

Previous(ly) Afore, Already, Before, Earlier, Ere(-now), Fore, Foreran, Former, Hitherto, Once, Prior

Prey Booty, Currie, Curry, Feed, Kill, Pelt, Plunder, Predate, Proul, Prowl, Quarry, Raven, Ravin(e), Soyle, Spreagh, Victim

Price(d), Pricing, Price-raising Appraise, Assess, Bride, Charge, Consequence, Contango, → **COST**, Dearth, Due, Evens, Exercise, Expense, Fee, Fiars, Hammer, Hire, Intervention, Issue, Limit, List, Loco, Market, Offer, Packet, Perverse, Predatory, Prestige, Quotation, Quote, Rack, Rate, Regrate, Reserve, Sale, Selling, Shadow, Song, Spot, Starting, Street value, Striking, Subscription, Toll, Trade, Unit, Upset, Value, Vincent, Weregild, Wergeld, Wergild, Worth, Yardage

Prick(ed), Prickle, Prickly Acanaceous, Accloy, Argemone, Arrect, Bearded, Brakier, Bramble, Brog, Bunya, Cactus, Cloy, Cnicus, Echinate, Goad, Gore, Hedgehog, Hedgepig, Impel, Inject, Jab, Jook, Juk, Kali, Penis, Perse, Pierce, Prod, Prog, Puncture, Rowel, Rubus, Ruellia, Seta, Setose, Smart, Spicula, Spinate, Stab, Star-thistle, Stimulus, Sting, Tattoo, Tatu, Teasel, Thistle, Thorn, Tingle, Urge

Prickly heat Miliaria

Prickly-pear Opuntia, Tuna

Pride Bombast, Brag, Conceit, Elation, Esprit de corps, Glory, Hauteur, Hubris, Inordinate, Lions, London, Machismo, Plume, Preen, Purge, Triumphalism, Vainglory, Vanity

Priest(ess), Priests Aaron, Abaris, Abbess, Abbot, Ananias, Annas, Archimandrite, Bacchae, Bacchantes, Baptes, Becket, Bonze, Brahmin, Caiaphas, Cardinal, Clergyman, Cleric, Cohen, Concelebrant, Corybant(es), Curé, Dalai Lama, Druid, Eli, Elisha, Father, Fetial, Flamen, Fr, Habacuc, Habakkuk, Hero, Hieratic, Hierophant, High, H(o)ungan, Io, Jethro, Kohen, Lack-Latin, Lama, Laocoon, Levite, Lucumo, Mage, Magus, Mallet, Mambo, Marabout, Metropolitan, Minister, Missionary, Monsignor, Mufti, Norma, Oratorian, P, Padre, Papa, Parish, Parson, Pastor, Patercove, Patrico, Pawaw, Père, Pontifex, Pontiff, Pope, Pope's knight, Powwow, Pr, Preacher, Prelate, Presbyter, Prior(ess), Pythia, Pythoness,

Rabbi, Rebbe, Rector, Rev, Sacerdotal, Salian, Savonarola, Seminarian, Shaman, Shaveling, Sky pilot, Spoiled, Tohunga, Vicar, Vivaldi, Worker, Zadok
Prig Dandy, Fop, Humbug, Nimmer, Pilfer, Prude, Puritan
Prim Demure, Mun, Neat, Old-maidish, Perjink, Preceese, Precise, Proper, Starchy
Primacy, Primate Angwantibo, Ape, Aye-aye, Bandar, Bigfoot, Biped, Bishop, Bush baby, Cardinal, Ebor, Gibbon, Hanuman, Hominid, Jackanapes, King Kong, Lemur, Loris, Macaque, Magot, Mammal, Marmoset, → MONKEY, Orang, Pongid, Potto, Prosimian, Protohuman, Quadruman, Ramapithecus, Rhesus, Sifaka, Tarsier, Zinjanthropus
Prima donna Diva, Patti, Star
Prime(r), Primary, Priming Arm, Basic, Bloom, Cardinal, Charging, Chief, Choice, Claircolle, Clearcole, Clerecole, Closed, Detonator, Direct, Donat, Donet, Election, Enarm, First, Flower, Heyday, Mature, Open, Original, Paramount, Peak, Radical, Remex, Sell-by-date, Supreme, Thirteen, Tip-top, Totient, Totitive, Valuable, Windac, Windas, Ylem
Prime Minister Asquith, Attlee, Baldwin, Balfour, Begin, Bute, Canning, Chamberlain, Chatham, Dewan, Diefenbaker, Disraeli, Diwan, Eden, Grand Vizier, Grey, Home, Leaderene, Liverpool, North, Number Ten, Peel, Pitt, PM, Premier, Shastri, Tanaiste, Taoiseach, Thatcher, Trudeau, Walpole
Prim(a)eval Ancient, Prehistoric, Primitive
Primitive Aborigine, Amoeba, Antediluvian, Arabic, Archaic, Atavistic, Barbaric, Caveman, Crude, Early, Evolué, Fundamental, Naive, Neanderthal, Neolithic, Old, Persian, Prim(a)eval, Primordial, Pro, Prothyl(e), Protomorphic, Protyl(e), Radical, Rudimentary, Savage, Subman, Turkish, Uncivilised, Ur
Primordial Blastema, Fundamental, Original
Primrose, Primula Auricula, Bear's ear, Cape, Evening, League, Oenothera, Onagra, Ox-lip, Pa(i)gle, Rosebery, Vicar, Yellow
Prince(ly) Ahmed, Albert, Ameer, Amir, Amphitryon, Anchises, Arjuna, Atheling, Barmecide, Black, Cadmus, Caliph, Chagan, Charming, Crown, Czarevich, Elector, Equerry, Eugene, Florizel, Fortinbras, Gaekwar, Gospodar, Guicowar, Hal, Highness, Hospodar, Huzoor, Igor, Inca, Infante, Khan, Ksar, Lavish, Lucumo, Maharaja, Margrave, Meleager, Merchant, Mir, Mirza, Nawab, Nizam, Noble, Otto, P, Pantagruel, Pendragon, Pirithous, Porphyrogenite, Potentate, Rainier, Rajah, Rana, Ras, Rasselas, Ratoo, Ratu, Regal, RH, Rudolph, Rupert, Serene, Sharif, Shereef, Sherif, Siegfried, Student, Tengku, Tereus, Tsar(evich), Tunku, Upper Roger
Princess Andromache, Andromeda, Anne, Ariadne, Begum, Creusa, Czarevna, Czarista, Danae, Di(ana), Electra, Electress, Eudocia, Europa, Helle, Hermione, Hesione, Ida, Imogen, Infanta, Iseult, Isolde, Jezebel, Maharanee, Maharani, Medea, Philomela, Pocahontas, Procne, Rani, Regan, Sara(h), Tou Wan, Tsarevna, Tsarista, Turandot, Yseult
Principal Arch, Capital, Central, → CHIEF, Decuman, Especial, First, Foremost, Head, Leading, Main(stay), Major, Mass, Protagonist, Ringleader, Staple, Star
Principality Andorra, Flanders, Liechtenstein, Moldavia, Moldova, Monaco, Muscovy, Orange, Wales, Wal(l)achia
Principle(s), Principled Accelerator, Animistic, Anthropic, Archimedes, Axiom, Basis, Bernouilli, Brocard, Canon, Carnot, Code, Cosmological, Criterion, Cui bono, Cy pres, D'Alembert's, Doctrine, Dogma, Element, Entelechy, Essential, Exclusion, Fermat's, First, Fourier, Gause's, Generale, Germ, Greatest happiness, Ground rule, Guideline, Heisenberg uncertainty, Honourable, Huygen's, Ideal, Interdeterminacy, Key, Law, Least time, Le Chatelier's, Logos, Methodology, Modus, Object soul,

Occam's razor, Organon, Ormazd, Ormuzd, Pauli-exclusion, Peter, Plank, Platform, Pleasure, Precautionary, Precept, Prescript, Psyche, Purseyism, Rationale, Reality, Reason, Reciprocity, Relativity, Remonstrance, Rudiment, Rule, Sakti, Seed, Shakti, Spirit, Summum bonum, Tenet, Theorem, Ticket, Verification, Vital, Yang, Yin

Prink Beautify, Bedeck, Dress

Print(er), Printing Baskerville, Batik, Benday, Bromide, Calotype, Caveman, Caxton, Chain, Chapel, Chromo, Cibachrome, Cicero, Collotype, Contact, Copperplate, Cyclostyle, Dab, Dot matrix, Electrothermal, Electrotint, Electrotype, Elzevir, Engrave, Etching, Ferrotype, Fine, Flexography, Font, Gravure, Gurmukhi, Gutenberg, Half-tone, Hectograph, Heliotype, Image, Impact, Impress, Incunabula, India, Ink-jet, Intaglio, Italic, Jobbing, Laser, Letterpress, Letterset, Line, Line-engraving, Lino-cut, Lithograph, Logotype, Lower-case, Matrix, Mimeograph®, Monotype®, Moon, Non-impact, Off-line, Offset, Old-face, Oleo, Oleograph, Opaline, Perfector, Phototype, Plate, Platinotype, Positive, Press, Process, Publish, Remarque, Report, Reproduction, Retroussage, Reverse, Rotogravure, Samizdat, Screen, Serigraph, Ship, Silk-screen, Small, Smoot, Splash, Spore, Stamp, Stenochrome, Stereotype, Stonehand, Strike, Thermal, Three-colour, Thumb, Trichromatic, Typesetter, Typography, Typothetae, Whorl, Woodburytype, Woodcut, Xerography, Xylograph, Zincograph

Printing-press Rounce

Prior(ity) Abbot, Afore, Antecedent, Anterior, Aperture, Earlier, Former, Grand, Hitherto, Monk, Overslaugh, Pre-, Precedence, Prefard, Preference, Previous, Privilege, Shutter, Triage, Until

▶ **Prise** see **PRIZE**

Prism(s), Prismatic Catadioptric, Iriscope, Nicol, Periaktos, Rhombohedron, Spectrum, Teinoscope, Wollaston

Prison Albany, Alcatraz, Bagnio, Barracoon, Bastille, Bin, Bird, Boob, Bridewell, Brig, Brixton, Bullpen, Cage, Can, Cell, Chillon, Chok(e)y, Clink, Club, College, Confine, Cooler, Coop, Counter, Dartmoor, Dispersal, Dungeon, Durance, Fleet, Fotheringhay, Gaol, Glass-house, Guardhouse, Guardroom, Gulag, Hokey, Holloway, Hoos(e)gow, Hulk(s), Internment, → JAIL, Jug, Kitty, Labour camp, Limbo, Lob's pound, Lock-up, Logs, Lumber, Marshalsea, Massymore, Mattamore, Maze, Newgate, Nick, Oflag, Open, Panopticon, Pen, Penitentiary, Pentonville, Pit, Pok(e)y, Porridge, Pound, Princetown, Quad, Quod, Rasp-house, Reformatory, Roundhouse, Scrubs, Shop, Sing-Sing, Slammer, Spandau, Stalag, State, Stir, Strangeways, The Leads, Tol(l)booth, Tower, Tronk, Wandsworth, Wormwood Scrubs

Prisoner Canary-bird, Captive, Collegian, Collegiate, Con(vict), Detainee, Detenu, Hostage, Inmate, Internee, Jailbird, Lag, Lifer, Political, POW, Trustee, Trusty, Yardbird, Zek

Pristine Fire-new, Fresh, New, Original, Unmarked, Unspoiled

Private(ly) Ain, Aside, Atkins, Auricular, Buccaneer, Byroom, Clandestine, Close, Closet, Conclave, Confidential, Enisle(d), Esoteric, Homefelt, Hush-hush, In camera, Individual, Inner, Intimate, Non-com, Own, Personal, Piou-piou, Poilu, Postern, Proprietary, Pte, Rank(er), Retired, Sanction, Sapper, Secret, Several, Single soldier, → SOLDIER, Squaddie, Sub rosa, Tommy, Under the rose

Privateer(s) Buccaneer, Corsair, Freebooter, Marque(s), Pirate

Privation Hardship, Penury, Want

Privilege(d) Birthright, Blest, Charter, Curule, Enviable, Exempt, Favour, Franchise, Freedom, Indulgence, Insider, Liberty, Mozarab, Nomenklatura, Octroi,

Parliamentary, Patent, Prerogative, Pryse, Regale, Regalia, Right, Sac
Privy Apprised, Can, Closet, Intimate, Jakes, John, Loo, Necessary, Reredorter,
    Secret, Sedge, Siege
Prize(s), Prizewinner, Prized Acquest, Apple, Archibald, Assess, Award, Best,
    Booby, Booker, Bravie, Capture, Champion, Consolation, Creach, Cup, Dux, Efforce,
    → ESTEEM, Force, Garland, Goncourt, Grice, Honour, Jackpot, Jemmy, Lever,
    Lot, Man Booker, Money, Nobel, Palm, Pearl, Pewter, Pie, Plum, Plunder, Pot,
    Premium, Prix Goncourt, Pulitzer, Purse, Ram, Reprisal, → REWARD, Rollover,
    Scalp, Ship, Spreaghery, Sprechery, Stakes, Taonga, Tern, Treasure, Trophy, Turner,
    Value
Pro Aye, Coach, For, Harlot, Moll, Paid, Tramp, Yea, Yes
▶ **Pro** *see* PROSTITUTE
Probable, Probability Apparent, Belike, Classical, Conditional, Ergodic, Feasible,
    Likely, Marginal, Mathematical, Possible, Posterior, Prior, Verisimilar
Probation(er) Cadet, Novice, Novitiate, Stibbler, Test, Trainee, Trial
Probe Antenna, Bore, Bougie, Canopus, Cassini, Corot, Delve, Dredge, Explore,
    Fathom, Feeler, Fossick, Galileo, Giotto, Inquire, Investigate, Magellan, Mariner,
    Mars Surveyor, Pelican, Pioneer, Poke, Pump, Ranger, → SEARCH, Seeker, Sonde,
    Sound, Space, Stardust, Stylet, Tent, Thrust, Tracer, Venera
Probity Honour, Integrity, Justice
Problem(s) Acrostic, BO, Boyg, Brainteaser, Business, Crisis, Crux, Dilemma,
    Egma, Enigma, Facer, Glitch, Handful, Hang-up, Headache, Hiccup, Hitch, Hurdle,
    Indaba, Knot(ty), Koan, Mind-body, Miniature, Musive, Net, Nuisance, Obstacle,
    Pons asinorum, Poser, Quandary, Question, Re, Rebus, Riddle, Rider, Snag, Sorites,
    Sum, Teaser, Teething, Thing, Tickler, Toughie, Trouble, Tsuris, Yips
Problem-solving Synectics
Proboscis Haustellum, Promuscis, Snout, Trunk
Proceed(s), Proceeding, Procedure Acta, Afoot, Algorithm, Continue, Course,
    Do, Drill, Emanate, Fand, Flow, Fond, Goes, Haul, Issue, Machinery, March,
    Mechanics, Method, Mine, MO, Modal, Move, On, Pass, Practice, Praxis, Process,
    Profit, Protocol, Punctilio, Pursue, Put, Rake, Return, Rigmarole, Rite, Ritual,
    Routine, Sap, Steps, Subroutine, System, Take, Use, Yead(s), Yede, Yeed
Process(ing), Procession, Processor Acromion, Action, Additive, Ala,
    Ambarvalia, Axon, Ben Day, Bessemer, Bosch, Castner, Catalysis, Cavalcade,
    Cibation, Cortège, Cyanide, Demo, Diagonal, Front-end, Haber, Handle, Managing,
    Markov, Method, Moharram, Mond, Motorcade, Muharram, Multiple pounding,
    Odontoid, Open hearth, -osis, Pageant, Parade, Parallel, Paseo, Photosynthesis,
    Pipeline, Planar, Pomp, Primary, Pterygoid, Puddling, Pultrusion, Purex, Recycle,
    Screen, Secondary, Series, Silkscreen, Skimmington, Solvay, Speciation, Sterygoid,
    String, Subtractive, Thermite, Thought, Torchlight, Train, Transverse, Treat, Trial,
    Turn(a)round, Unit, Vermiform, Xiphoid, Zygomatic
Proclaim, Proclamation Announce, Annunciate, Ban, Blaze, Blazon, Boast,
    Broadsheet, Cry, Edict, Enounce, Enunciate, Herald, Indiction, Kerygma, Oyez,
    Preconise, Predicate, Profess, Publish, Ring, Shout, Trumpet, Ukase
Procrastinate, Procrastinating, Procrastinator Cunctator, Defer, Delay, Dilatory,
    Dilly-dally, Linger, Pettifog, Postpone, Shelve, Temporise, Vacillate
Procreate Beget, Engender, Generate, Initiate
Procrustean Conformity
Proctor Agent, King's, Monitor, Prog, Proxy, Queen's
Procurator, Procure(r) Achieve, Aunt, Crimp, Earn, Get, Induce, Naunt, Obtain,
    Pander, Pilate, Pimp, Sort, Suborn

Prod Cattle, Egg, Goad, Impel, Jab, Job, Jog, Nudge, Poke, Pote
Prodigal Costly, Lavish, Profligate, Spendall, Unthrift, Wanton, Wasteful, Waster
Prodigious, Prodigy Abnormal, Amazing, Huge, Immense, Infant, Monster,
  Monument, Mozart, Phenomenal, Portentous, Tremendous, Wonder,
  Wonderwork, Wunderkind
Produce(r), Producing Afford, Bear, Beget, Breed, Cause, Create, Crop, Disney,
  Ean, Edit, Effect, Engender, Evoke, Exhibit, Extend, Fruit, Generate, Get, Grow,
  Home-grown, Impresario, Ingenerate, Issue, Kind, Make, Offspring, Onstream,
  Originate, Output, Propage, Propound, Raise, Son, Spawn, Stage, Supply, Teem,
  Throw, Trot out, Wares, Whelp, Yield
▷ **Produces** *may indicate* an anagram
Product(ion), Productive(ness), Productivity Actualities, Apport, Artefact,
  Ashtareth, Ashtaroth, Astarte, Bore, Cartesian, Coefficient, Commodity, Cross, Dot,
  Drama, End, Factorial, Fecund, Fertile, Fruit, Genesis, Global, Handiwork, Harvest,
  Net domestic, Net national, Output, Outturn, Pair, Partial, Primary, Profilic, Result,
  Rich, Scalar, Secondary, Set, Show, Speiss, Substitution, Uberous, Uberty, Vector,
  Waste, Work, Yield
▷ **Production** *may indicate* an anagram
Proem Foreword, Overture, Pre, Preface
Profane, Profanation, Profanity Coarse, Coprolalia, Desecrate, Impious,
  Irreverent, Sacrilege, Unholy, Violate
Profess(ed), Professor Absent-minded, Academic, Adjoint, Admit, Artist, Aspro,
  Asset, Assistant, Associate, Avow, Challenger, Claim, Declare, Disney, Emeritus,
  Full, Higgins, Hodja, Kho(d)ja, Know-all, Ostensible, Own, Practise, Pundit,
  Regent, Regius, RP, STP, Visiting
Profession(al) Admission, Assurance, Avowal, Buppy, Business, Career, Creed,
  Expert, Métier, Practitioner, Pretence, Pursuit, Regular, Salaried, Skilled, Trade,
  Vocation, Yuppie
Proffer Give, Present, Proposition, Tender
Proficiency, Proficient Able, Adept, Alert, Dan, Expert, Forte, Past master,
  Practised, Skill, Technique
Profile Analysis, Contour, Cross, Half-cheek, Half-face, Long, Loral, Low, Outline,
  Silhouette, Sketch, Statant, T(h)alweg, Vignette
Profit(able), Profiteer, Profits Advantage, Arbitrage, Asset, Avail, Benefit, Boot,
  Bunce, Cere, Clear, Divi(dend), Earn, Economic, Edge, Emblements, Emoluments,
  Exploit, Fat, Gain, Gelt, Graft, Gravy, Grist, Gross, Income, Increment, Issue,
  Jobbery, Juicy, Landshark, Leech, Lucrative, Makings, Margin, Melon, Mesne, Milch
  cow, Mileage, Moneymaker, Negative, Net, Pay(ing), Perk, Pickings, Preacquisition,
  Productive, Rake-off, Return, Reward, Royalty, Scalp, Spoils, Use, Usufruct, Utile,
  Utility, Vail
Profligate Corinthian, Corrupt, Degenerate, Dissolute, Extravagant, Lech(er),
  Libertine, Lorel, Losel(l), Oatmeal, Rakehell, Reprobate, Roué, Spend-all, Wastrel
Profound Altum, Bottomless, Complete, Deep, Intense, Recondite
Profuse, Profusion Abounding, Abundant, Copious, Excess, Free, Galore, Lavish,
  Liberal, Lush, Quantity, Rank, Rich, Two-a-penny
Progenitor, Progenitrix Ancestor, Ma, Predecessor, Sire, Stock
Progeny Burd, Children, Descendants, Fruit, Issue, Offspring, Seed
Prognosis Forecast, Prediction
Prognosticate, Prognostication Augur, Foretell, Omen, Predict, Presage, Prophesy
▶ **Program(ming), Programming language, Programmer**
  see **COMPUTER PROGRAMS**

Programme Agenda, Broadcast, Card, Chat show, Code, Community, Docudrama, Documentary, Docusoap, Dramedy, Est, Event, Faction, Fly-on-the-wall, Infotainment, Linear, Mockumentary, PDL, Phone-in, Pilot, Plan, Playbill, Prank, Radiothon, RECHAR, Regimen, Report, Schedule, Scheme, Sepmag, Shockumentary, Show, Simulcast, Sitcom, Sked, Soap, Software, Sustaining, Syllabus, System, Telecast, Teleplay, Telethon, Timetable

Progress(ive), Progression → ADVANCE, Afoot, Arithmetic, Avant garde, Course, Fabian, Flow, Forge, Forward, Forward-looking, Gain, Geometric, Get along, Go, Growth, Harmonic, Headway, Incede, Knight's, Liberal, Move, Onwards, Paraphonia, Pilgrim's, Prosper, Rack, Radical, Rake's, Reformer, Roll, Run, Sequence, Series, Step, Vaunce, Way, Yead, Yede, Yeed

Prohibit(ed), Prohibition(ist) Ban, Block, Debar, Dry, Embargo, Estop, Forbid, Hinder, Index, Injunct, Interdict, Noli-me-tangere, Off-limits, Prevent, Pussyfoot, Rahui, Suppress, Taboo, Tabu, Verboten, Veto

Project(ile), Projecting, Projection, Projector Aim, Ammo, Antitragus, Assignment, Astral, Astrut, Axonometric, Azimuthal, Ball, Ballistic, Beetle, Bullet, Butt, Buttress, Cam, Cast, Catapult, Channel, Cinerama®, Cog, Conceive, Condyle, Conic, Conical, Console, Corbel, Coving, Crossette, Cutwater, Denticle, Diascope, Discus, Eaves, Echinus, Elance, Enterprise, Episcope, Excrescence, Exsert, Extrapolate, Fet(ter)lock, Flange, Gair, Gore, Guess, Halter(e), Hangover, Helicity, Hoe, Homolosine, Housing, Hurtle, Inion, Jut, Kern, Kinetoscope, Knob, Ledge, Lobe, Lug, Magic lantern, Malleolus, Manhattan, Map, Mercator, Mitraille, Mohole, Mollweide, Mucro, Mutule, Nab, Nose, Nunatak(er), Olecranon, Opaque, Orillion, Orthogonal, Orthographic, Outcrop, Outjet, Outjut, Outshot, Overhang, Overhead, Oversail, Palmation, Peter's, Pitch, Planetarium, Planisphere, Polyconic, Pork barrel, Prickle, Promontory, → PROTRUDE, Proud(er), Pseudopod, Quillon, Raguly, Roach, Rocket, Sail, Salient, Sally, Sanson-Flamsteed, Scaw, Scheme, Screen, Shelf, Shrapnel, Sinusoidal, Skaw, Skeg, Slide, Snag, Snout, Spline, Sponson, Sprocket, Spur, Squarrose, Stand out, Stereopticon, Stick out, Stud, Tang, Tappet, Tenon, Throw, Toe, Tongue, Tracer, Trimetric, Trippet, Trunnion, Turnkey, Turtleback, Tusk, Umbo, Underhung, Undertaking, Villus, Vitascope, Whizzbang, Zenithal

Prolapse Procidence

Proletarian, Proletariat Jamahiriya, People, Plebeian, Popular

Proliferate Expand, Increase, Multiply, Propagate, Snowball

Prolific Abounding, Fecund, Fertile, Fruitful, Profuse, Teeming

Prolix(ity) Lengthy, Prosaic, Rambling, Rigmarole, Verbose, Wire-draw, Wordy

Prologue Introduce, Preface

Prolong(ed) Continue, Extend, Lengthen, Protract, Sostenuto, Spin, Sustain

Prom(enade) Alameda, Boulevard, Cakewalk, Catwalk, Crush-room, Esplanade, Front, Mall, Parade, Paseo, Pier, Sea-front, Stroll, → WALK

Prometheus Fire

Promethium Pm

Prominence, Prominent Antitragus, Blatant, Bold, Colliculus, Condyle, Conspicuous, Egregious, Emphasis, Featured, Gonion, High profile, Important, Insistent, Luminary, Manifest, Marked, Obtrusive, Outstanding, Salient, Signal, Solar, Tall poppy, Teat, Toot, Tragus

Promiscuous, Promiscuity Casual, Chippie, Chippy, Demivierge, Fast, Free, Goer, Hornbag, Horny, Indiscriminate, Licentious, Light, Loslyf, Mixed, Motley, Pell-mell, Skanky(-ho), Slapper, Trollop, Whoredom

Promise, Promising Accept, Assure, Augur, Auspicious, Avoure, Behest, Behight,

Behote, Bode, Coming, Compact, Covenant, Earnest, Engagement, Foretaste, Gratuitous, Guarantee, Hecht, Hest, Hete, Hight, IOU, Likely, Manifest, Parole, Pledge, Plight, Pollicitation, Potential, Pregnant, Recognisance, Recognizance, Rosy, Sign, Sponsor, Swear, Tile, Undertake, Vow, Warranty, Word

Promised land Beulah, Canaan, Israel

Promissory note IOU, PN

Promontory Bill, Cape Sable, Cliff, Flamborough Head, Foreland, Giant's Causeway, Hatteras, → **HEADLAND**, Hoe, Hogh, Mull, Mull of Galloway, Naze, Ness, Nose, Peak, Pillars of Hercules, Ras, Spit, The Lizard, Tintagel Head

Promote(r), Promotion Adman, Advance, → **ADVERTISE**, Advocate, Aggrandise, Aid, Assist, Blurb, Boost, Campaign, Churn, Dog and pony show, Elevate, Encourage, Exponent, Foment, Foster, Further, Help, Hype, Increase, Kick upstairs, Make, Pracharak, Prefer, Prelation, Promulgate, Provoke, Push, Queen, Raise, Rear, Remove, Roadshow, Run, Salutary, Sell, Sponsor, Spruik, Stage, Step, Subserve, Tendencious, Tendentious, Upgrade, Uplead, Uprate

Prompt(er), Promptly, Promptness Actuate, Alacrity, Autocue®, Believe, Celerity, Chop-chop, Cue, Egg, Expeditious, Frack, Idiot-board, Immediate, Incite, Inspire, Instigate, Move, On-the-nail, Opposite, Pernicious, Premove, Punctual, Quick, Ready, Speed(y), Spur, Stage right, Stimulate, Sudden, Tight, Tit(e), Titely, Tyte, Urgent

Promulgate Preach, Proclaim, Publish, Spread

Prone Apt, Groof, Grouf, Grovel, Liable, Lying, Prostrate, Recumbent, Subject, Susceptible

Prong Fang, Fork, Grain, Peg, Tang, Tine

Pronghorn Cabrie, Cabrit

Pronoun Oneself, Personal, Reciprocal, Relative

Pronounce(d), Pronouncement Adjudicate, Affirm, Agrapha, Articulate, Assert, Asseveration, Clear, Conspicuous, Declare, Definite, Dictum, Emphatic, Enunciate, Fiat, Indefinite, Marked, Opinion, Palatalise, Pontificate, Predication, Recite, Utter, Velarise, Vocal, Voice, Vote

Pronto PDQ

Pronunciation Betacism, Cacoepy, Delivery, Diction, Etacism, Itacism, Lallation, Localism, Orthoepy, Phonetics, Plateasm, Proclitic, Received, Rhotacism, Sound, Tense

Proof Apagoge, Argument, Artist's, Assay, Bona fides, Confirmation, Direct, Evidence, Firm, Foundry, Galley, Godel's, Indirect, Justification, Lemma, Positive, Preif(e), Probate, Pull, Quality, Refutation, Remarque, Reproduction, Resistant, Revision, Secure, Slip, Strength, Test, Tight, Token, Trial, Upmake, Validity

Prop Airscrew, Bolster, Buttress, Clothes, Crutch, Dog-shore, Fulcrum, Leg, Loosehead, Misericord(e), Pit, Point d'appui, Punch(eon), Rance, Rest, Scotch, Shore, Sprag, Spur, Staff, Stay, Stempel, Stemple, Stilt, Stoop, Stoup, Studdle, Stull, → **SUPPORT**, Tighthead, Trig, Underpin

Propaganda, Propagandist Agitprop, Ballyhoo, Black, Brainwashing, Chevalier, Doctrine, Exponent, Goebbels, Grey, Promotion, Psyop, Psywar, Publicity, Slogan, Spin doctor, White

Propagate, Propagator, Propagation Breed, Dispread, Generate, Graft, Hatch, Hotbed, Hothouse, Increase, Layering, Produce, Promulgate, Provine, Spread, Tan-bed

Propel(ler) Airscrew, Ca', Drive, Fin, Frogmarch, Launch, Leg, Lox, → **MOVE**, Oar, Paddle, Pedal, Pole, Project, Push, Rotor, Row, Screw, Send, Tail rotor, Throw, Thruster, Vane

Propensity Aptness, Bent, Inclination, Penchant, Tendency
Proper(ly) Ain, Convenance, Correct, Decent, Decorous, Due, Eigen, En règle,
Ethical, → **FIT**, Genteel, Governessy, Kosher, Noun, Ought, Own, Pakka, Pathan,
Prim, Pucka, Pukka, Puritanic, Real, Rightful, Seemly, Suitable, Tao, Trew, True,
Veritable, Well
Property, Properties Assets, Attribute, Aver, Belongings, Capacitance, Chattel,
Chose, Contenement, Dead-hand, Demesne, Des res, Dowry, Effects, Enclave,
Escheat, Escrow, Estate, Fee, Feu, Flavour, Fonds, Freehold, Goods, Haecceity,
Hereditament, Hot, Hotchpot, Immoveable, Inertia, Intellectual, Jointure,
Leasehold, Living, Means, Mortmain, Paraphernalia, Peculium, Personal,
Personalty, Predicate, Premises, Private, Projective, Public, Quale, Quality, Real,
Stock, Stolen, Theft, Thixotropy, Time-share, Timocracy, Trait, Usucapion,
Usucaption
Prophesy, Prophecy, Prophet(s), Prophetess, Prophetic Amos, Augur, Bab,
Balaam, Calchas, Cassandra, Daniel, Deborah, Divine, Druid, Elias, Elijah, Elisha,
Ezekiel, Ezra, Fatal, Fatidical, Forecast, Foretell, Former, Geomancer, Habakkuk,
Haggai, Hosea, Is, Isa, Is(a)iah, Jeremiah, Joel, Jonah, Latter, Mahdi, Mahound,
Major, Malachi, Mani, Mantic, Micah, Minor, Mohammed, Mopsus, Mormon,
Moses, Nahum, Nathan, Nostradamus, Obadiah, Old Mother Shipton, Ominous,
Oracle, Portend, Predictor, Prognosticate, Pythoness, Samuel, Second sight,
Seer, Sibyl, Tipster, Tiresias, Vatic, Vaticinate, Völuspá, Zachariah, Zarathustra,
Zechariah, Zephaniah, Zoroaster, Zwickau
Prophylactic, Prophylaxis Inoculation, Preventive, Serum, Vaccine, Variolation
Propitiate Appease, Atone, Pacify, Reconcile, Sop
Propitious Benign, Favourable, Lucky
Proponent Advocate, Backer, Partisan
Proportion(ate) Commensurable, Dimension, Harmonic, Inverse, Portion, Pro
rata, Quantity, Quota, Ratio, Reason, Regulate, Relation, Sine, Size, Soum, Sowm
Propose(r), Proposal Advance, Bid, Bill, Canvass, Eirenicon, Feeler, Fiancé,
Irenicon, Mean, Motion, Move, Nominate, Offer, Overture, Plan, Pop, Premise,
Proffer, Propound, Recommend, Resolution, Scheme, Slate, Submission,
→ **SUGGEST**, Table, Tender, Volunteer, Woot, Would
Proposition Asses' bridge, Axiom, Convertend, Corollary, Deal, Disjunction, Ergo,
Hypothesis, Identical, Implicature, Lemma, Overture, Pons asinorum, Porism,
Premise, Premiss, Rider, Sorites, Spec, Superaltern, Theorem, Thesis
Propound Advocate, Purpose, State
Proprietor, Propriety Convenance, Correctitude, Decorum, Etiquette, Grundy,
Keeper, Lord, Master, Owner, Patron, Rectitude
Prosaic Common, Drab, Flat, Humdrum, Tedious, Workaday
Proscenium Forestage
Proscribe Exile, Forbid, Outlaw, Prohibit
Prose, Prosy Euphuism, Haikai, Polyphonic, Purple, Purple patch, Saga, Stich,
Verbose, Version, Writing
Prosecute, Prosecutor, Prosecution Allege, Avvogadore, Charge, Crown, Fiscal,
Furtherance, Impeach, Indict, Lord Advocate, Practise, Public, Sue, Wage
Proselytise(r), Proselytism Indoctrination, Propagandism, Souper
Prospect(or) Bellevue, Dowser, Explore, Forty-niner, Fossick, Look-out, Mine,
Opportunity, → **OUTLOOK**, Panorama, Perspective, Pleases, Possibility, Reefer,
Scenery, Search, Sourdough, View, Vista, Visto, Wildcatter
Prospectus Menu, Pathfinder
Prosper(ity), Prospering, Prosperous Aisha, Ay(e)sha, Blessed, Blossom, Boom,

Fair, Fat cat, Flourish, Get ahead, Heyday, Mérimée, Palmy, → SUCCEED, Thee, Thrift, Thrive, Up, Warison, Wealth, Welfare, Well-heeled, Well-to-do

Prostitute, Prostitution Brass, Broad, Bulker, Callet, Catamite, Chippie, Cockatrice, Cocotte, Debase, Dell, Demi-mondaine, Dolly-mop, Doxy, Fancy woman, Fille de joie, Harlot, Hetaera, Hetaira, Hierodule, Ho, Hooker, Jailbait, Lady of the night, Loon, Loose-fish, Loose woman, Lowne, Madam, Magdalen(e), Moll, Mutton, Night-walker, Pict, Plover, Pole-cat, Pro, Punk, Quail, Quiff, Rent-boy, Road, Rough trade, Scrubber, Shippie, Slap, Social evil, Stew, Streetwalker, Strumpet, Tart, Tramp, Trull, Venture, Wench, Whore

Prostrate, Prostration Collapse, Exhausted, Fell, Flat, Flatling, Ko(w)tow, Laid, Obeisance, Overcome, Procumbent, Prone, Repent, Throw

Protactinium Pa

Protean Amoebic, Fusible, Variable

Protect(ed), Protection, Protector Adonise, Aegis, Alexin, Arm, Armour, Asylum, Auspice, Bastion, Bestride, Bield, Buckler, Bullet-proof, Chaffron, Chain mail, Chamfrain, Chamfron, Charm, Cherish, Cloche, Coat, Cocoon, Coleor(r)hiza, Conserve, Copyright, Cosset, Cover, Covert, Cromwell, Cushion, Danegeld, Data, Defend, Defilade, Degauss, Egis, Enamel, Entrenchment, Escort, Estacade, Faun, Fence, Flank, Gobo, Groundsheet, Guard(ian), Gumshield, Hedge, House, Hurter, Immune, Inalienable, Indemnify, Insure, Integument, Keckle, Keep, Kickback, Klendusic, Lee, Mac(k)intosh, Mail, Male, Mollycoddle, Mother, Mouthpiece, Mudguard, Muniment, Noll, Nosey, Oliver, Ombrella, Orillion, Overall, Parados, Patent, Patron, Penthouse, Police, Pomander, Preserve, Rabbit's foot, Raymond, Redome, Revetment, Ride shotgun, Safeguard, Sandbag, Save, Schanse, Schan(t)ze, Screen, Scug, Shadow, Sheathing, Sheeting, Shelter, → SHIELD, Skug, Souteneur, Splashback, Splashboard, Splasher, Starling, Sunscreen, Talisman, Testa, Tribute, Tutelar, Twilled, Umbrella, Underlay, Underseal, Vaccine, Ward(ship), Warhead, Warrant, Weatherboard, Weatherstrip, Windbreaker, Windshield, Wing, Write

Protég(é) Pupil, Tutee, Ward

Protein Abrin, Actin, Actomyosin, Adipsin, Alanine, Albumen, Albumin, Aleuron(e), Allergen, Amandine, Analogon, Angiostatin, Angiotensin, Antibody, Apoenzyme, Aquaporin, Avidin, Bradykinin, Calmodulin, Capsid, Capsomere, Caseinogen, Ceruloplasmin, Collagen, Complement, Conchiolin, Conjugated, Copaxone®, CREB, Cyclin, Cytokine, Dystrophin, Elastin, Enzyme, Factor VIII, Ferritin, Ferrodoxin, Fibrin, Fibrinogen, Fibroin, Flagellin, Gelatin, Gliadin(e), Glob(ul)in, Glutelin, Gluten, Haemoglobin, Haptoglobin, Histone, Hordein, Huntingtin, Immunoglobulin, Incaparina, Integrin, Interferon, Interleukin, Lactalbumin, Lactoglobulin, Lectin, Legumin, Leptin, Leucin(e), Lewy bodies, Luciferin, Lymphokine, Lysin, Meat, Mucin, Myogen, Myoglobin, Myosin, Nuclein, Opsin, Opsonin, Ossein, Ovalbumin, Pepsin(e), Peptide, Phaseolin, Prion, Prolamin(e), Properdin, Protamine, Proteose, Prothrombin, Pyrenoid, Quorn®, Renin, Repressor, Ribosome, Sclerotin, Sericin, Serum albumin, Serum globulin, Single-cell, Soya, Spectrin, Spongin, Tempeh, Thrombogen, Toxalbumin, Transferrin, Tropomyosin, Troponin, TSP, Tubulin, TVP, Ubiquitin, Vitellin, Zein

Protest(er) Abhor, Andolan, Aver, Avouch, Black Bloc(k), Clamour, Come, Démarche, Demo, Demonstrate, Demur, Deprecate, Dharna, Dissent, Expostulate, Gherao, Go-slow, Hartal, Inveigh, Lock-out, Luddite, March, Moonlighter, Nimby, Object, Outcry, Picket, Plea, Refus(e)nik, Remonstrate, Sit-in, Squawk, Squeak, Squeal, Stand, Suffragette, Work-to-rule

Protestant Amish, Anabaptist, Anglo, Arminian, Calvin, Congregationalism, Covenanter, Cranmer, Dissenter, Evangelic, Gospeller, Huguenot, Independent,

Lady, Loyalist, Lutheran, Mennonite, Methodist, Moravian, Neo-Orthodoxy, Nonconformist, Oak-boy, Orangeman, Peep o' day Boys, Pentecostal, Pietism, Prod, Puritan, Religioner, Right-footer, Sacramentarian, Stundist, Swaddler, Wasp, Wesleyan

Protocol Agreement, Code, Convention, Etiquette, Geneva, Kyoto, Point-to-Point

Proton Nucleon, Quark

Protoplasm(ic) Coenocyte, Coenosarc, Cytode, Sarcode

Prototype Blueprint, Exemplar, Model, Original, Pattern

Protozoa(n) Am(o)eba, Foraminifer, Giardia, Globigerina, Gregarine, Heliozoan, Infusoria, Leishmania, Mastigophoran, Moner(a), Moneron, Paramecium, Peritricha, Phagocyte, Radiolaria, Rhizopod, Thrichomonad, Trophozoite, Trypanosome, Volvox, Vorticella

Protract(ed) Delay, → EXTEND, Lengthen, Livelong, Long, Prolong

Protrude, Protrusion Bulge, Eventration, Exsert, Hernia, Jut, Pop, Pout, Project, Pseudopodium, Rectocele, Strout, Tel

Protuberance, Protuberant Apophysis, Bulge, Bump, Burl, Condyle, Crankle, Gibbous, Hump, Knap, Knob, Malleolus, Node, Papillose, Papule, Spadix, Swelling, Tragus, Tuber, Tubersity, Venter

Proud Arrogant, Boaster, Cocky, Conceited, Dic(k)ty, Elated, Flush, Haughty, Haut, Level, Lordly, Orgulous, Protruding, Superb, Vain

Prove(d), Proving Apod(e)ictic, Argue, Ascertain, Assay, Attest, Authenticate, Aver, Confirm, Convince, Deictic, Establish, Evince, Justify, → PROOF, Quote, → SHOW, Substantiate, Test, Trie

Proverb Adage, Axiom, Byword, Gnome, Maxim, Paroemia, Saw

▷ **Proverbial** may refer to the biblical Proverbs

Provide(d), Provident(ial) Afford, Allow, Arrange, Besee, Bring, Cater, Compare, Conditional, Endow, Equip, Far-seeing, Feed, Fend, Find, Furnish, Generate, Give, Grubstake, Heaven sent, If, Lay on, Maintain, Plenish, Proviso, Purvey, Quote, Serve, So, Sobeit, → SUPPLY, Suttle

Province, Provincial(ism) Area, Circar, District, Eparchy, Exclave, Eyalet, Forte, Insular, Land, Mofussil, Narrow, Nomarchy, Nome, Nomos, Oblast, Palatinate, Pale, Petrographic, Realm, Regional, Rural, Sircar, Sirkar, Subah, Suburban, Territory, Vilayet

---

PROVINCES

2 letters:	Hebei	Tirol	Quebec
NI	Henan	Tyrol	Raetia
	Honan		Sanjak
4 letters:	Hopeh	*6 letters:*	Shansi
Gaul	Hopei	Acadia	Shanxi
Ifni	Hubei	Artois	Shensi
Shoa	Hunan	Basque	Sikang
Sind	Jehol	Bengal	Ulster
	Jilin	Fujian	Yunnan
5 letters:	Kansu	Fukien	
Anhui	Kirin	Hainan	*7 letters:*
Anjou	Liege	Kosovo	Alberta
Anwei	Namur	Marche	Almeria
Coorg	Natal	Poitou	Antwerp
Gansu	Otago	Punjab	Brabant

	8 letters:	Aquitaine	Hesse-Nassau
Drenthe	Atlantic	Connaught	Kaliningrad
Eritrea	Chekiang	Flevoland	Paphlagonia
Gascony	Chinghai	Free State	West Prussia
Gauteng	Connacht	Friesland	
Granada	Dauphine	Groningen	12 letters:
Guienne	Hainault	Guangdong	Heilongjiang
Guizhou	Helvetia	Hainan Tao	New Brunswick
Guyenne	Kiaochow	Illyricum	North Brabant
Hainaut	Leinster	Kurdistan	North Holland
Jiangsu	Liaoning	Languedoc	Saskatchewan
Jiangxi	Limousin	Lusitania	South Holland
Jiazhou	Lorraine	Nivernais	
Kiangsi	Lyonnais	North West	13 letters:
Kiangsu	Manitoba	Orleanais	Syrophoenicia
Kwazulu	Maritime	Santa Cruz	
Limpopo	Ninghsia	Sungkiang	14 letters:
Livonia	Normandy	Transvaal	Eastern Rumelia
Munster	Northern		Flemish Brabant
Ningsia	Pashalic	10 letters:	Walloon Brabant
Ontario	Pashalik	Gelderland	
Picardy	Provence	Mpumalanga	15 letters:
Prairie	Shandong	New Castile	British Columbia
Qinghai	Shantung	Overijssel	Orange Free State
Rhaetia	Szechuan	Patavinity	
Satrapy	Szechwan	Roussillon	17 letters:
Shaanxi	Touraine	Wellington	North West Frontier
Sichuan	Tsinghai		
Suiyuan	Zhejiang	11 letters:	23 letters:
Utrecht		Balochistan	Newfoundland and
Western	9 letters:	Baluchistan	Labrador
Zeeland	Apeldoorn	Guelderland	

Provision(s), Provisional Acates, A(p)panage, Board, Fodder, Foresight, Insolvency, Jointure, Larder, Lend-lease, Prog(gins), Scran, Skran, Stock, Supply, Suttle, Viands, Viaticum, Victuals

Proviso, Provisional Caution, Caveat, Clause, Condition, Interim, IRA, Makeshift, Nisi, On trial, Reservation, Salvo, Stipulation, Temporary, Tentative

Provocation, Provocative, Provoke Agacant, Alluring, Egg, Elicit, Erotic, Exacerbate, Excite, Flirty, Gar, Harass, Incense, Induce, Inflame, Instigate, Irk, Irritate, Needle, Nettle, Occasion, Pique, Prompt, Raise, Red rag, Sedition, Spark, Stimulate, Stir, Tar, Tease, Urge, Vex, Wind up

Provost Dean, Keeper, Marshal, Warden

Prow Bow, Cutwater, Fore, Nose, Prore, Stem

Pro-war Hawk

Prowess Ability, Bravery, Forte, Fortitude

Prowl(er) Hunt, Lurch, Lurk, Mooch, Prog, Prole, Rache, Ramble, Ratch, Roam, Rove, Snoke, Snook, Snowk, Tenebrio, Tom

Proxime accessit Next best

Proximity Handiness

Proxy Agent, Attorn, Deputy, PP, Regent, Sub, Surrogate, Vicar, Vice

Prude(nce), Prudent, Prudery Bluenose, Canny, Caution, Circumspect, Comstocker, Conservative, Discreet, Discretion, Far-sighted, Foresight, Frugal, Grundyism, Judicious, Metis, Mrs Grundy, Politic, Prig, Prissy, Provident, Sage, Sensible, Sparing, Strait-laced, Strait-lacer, Thrifty, Tight-laced, Vice-nelly, Victorian, Ware, Wary, Well-advised, Wise

Prune(r) Bill-hook, Clip, Dehorn, Lop, Plum, Proign, Proin(e), Reduce, Reform, Secateur, Shred, Sned, Thin, Trim

Prunella Hedge-sparrow, Self-heal

Prurient Avaricious, Itchy, Lewd, Obscene

Prussia(n) Blue, Junker, Pruce, Spruce, Westphalian

Pry Ferret, Force, Lever, Meddle, Nose, Paul, Peep, Question, Search, Snoop, Stickyback, Toot

Psalm Anthem, Cantate, Chant, Chorale, Hallel, Hymn, Introit, Jubilate, Metrical, Miserere, Neck-verse, Paean, Penitential, Proper, Ps, Song, Tone, Tract, Venite

Pseud(o) Bogus, Mock, Posy, Sham, Spurious

Pseudonym Aka, Alias, Allonym, Anonym, Pen-name, Stage-name

Pshaw Chut, Pooh, Tilley-valley, Tilly-fally, Tilly-vally·

Psyche Ego, Self, Soul, Spirit, Superego

Psychiatrist, Psychologist Adler, Alienist, Clare, Coué, Ellis, Freud, Headshrinker, Jung, Laing, Müller-Lyer, Rat-tamer, Reich, Shrink, Trick-cyclist

Psychic, Psychosis ESP, Korsakoff's, Lodge, Medium, Seer, Telekinesis, Telepathic

Psychological, Psychology, Psychologist Analytical, Behaviourism, Clinical, Comparative, Constitutional, Depth, Dynamic, Educational, Experimental, Eysenck, Gestalt, Hedonics, Humanistic, Industrial, James, Latah, Occupational, Organisational, Piaget, Social, Structural

Psychosis, Psychotic Korsakoff's, Manic-depressive, Organic, Schizophrenia

Psychotherapy Rebirthing

Ptarmigan Rype

Ptomaine Neurine

Pub Bar, Beerhall, Beverage room, Boozer, Chequers, Free-house, Gin-palace, Houf(f), House, Howf(f), Inn, Jerry-shop, Joint, Local, Mughouse, Pothouse, Potshop, Rubbidy, Rubbity, Shanty, Tavern, Tiddlywink

Puberty Adolescence, Hebetic, Teens

Pubescence Tomentum

Public Apert, Bar, Civil, Common, Demos, General, Great unwashed, Inn, Janata, Lay, Limelight, National, Open, Out, Overt, Populace, State, Vulgar, World

Publican Ale-keeper, Bung, Host, Landlord, Licensee, Tapster, Taverner

Publication Announcement, Bluebook, Book, Broadsheet, Edition, Ephemera, Exposé, Festschrift, Issue, → JOURNAL, Lady, Mag, Magazine, Organ, Pictorial, Samizdat, Tabloid, Tatler, Tract, Tribune, Yearbook

Publicist, Publicity Ad(vert), Airing, Ballyhoo, Billing, Build up, Coverage, Exposure, Flack, Glare, Headline, Hype, Leakage, Limelight, Notoriety, Plug, PR(O), Promotion, Propaganda, Réclame, Spin-doctor, Splash

Publish(er), Published, Publishing, Publicise Air, Blaze, Cape, Delator, Desktop, Disclose, Edit, Electronic, Evulgate, Gollancz, Issue, Noise, OUP, Out, Pirate, Plug, Post, Print(er), Proclaim, Propagate, Put about, Release, Run, Stationer, Vanity, Vent, Ventilate

Puck Disc, Elf, Lob, Sprite, Squid

Pucker(ed) Bullate, Cockle, Contract, Gather, Plissé, Purse, Ruck, Shir(r), Wrinkle

Pud Fin, Paw

Pudding Afters, Baked Alaska, Bakewell, Black, Blancmange, Blood, Bread (and butter), Brown Betty, Cabinet, Charlotte, Christmas, Clootie dumpling, College, Crumble, Custard, → **DESSERT**, Drisheen, Duff, Dumpling, Eve's, Flummery, Fritter, Fromenty, Frumenty, Furme(n)ty, Furmity, Haggis, Hasty, Hodge, Hog's, Kugel, Lokshen, Mealie, Milk, Nesselrode, Panada, Pandowdy, Parfait, Pease, Plum, Plum-duff, Popover, Queen's, Rice, Roly-poly, Sago, Savarin, Semolina, Sowens, Sponge, Spotted dick, Stickjaw, Stodge, Suet, Summer, Sundae, Sweet, Tansy, Tapioca, Umbles, White, White hass, White hause, White hawse, Yorkshire, Zabaglione

Puddle Collect, Dub, Flush, Pant, Plash, Plouter, Plowter, Pool, Sop

Puff(ed), Puffer, Puffy Advertise, Blouse, Blow, Blowfish, Blurb, Bouffant, Breath, Chuff, Chug, Cream, Drag, Encomist, Eulogy, Exsufflicate, Fag, Flaff, Flatus, Fluffy, Fuff, Globe-fish, Grampus, Gust, Hype, Lunt, Pech, Pegh, Pluffy, Plug, Powder, Quilt, Recommend, Skiff, Slogan, Smoke, Steam, Swell, Toke, Twilt, Waff, Waft, Waif, Whiff, Whiffle

Puffin Fratercula, Rockbird, Sea-parrot, Tammie Norie, Tam Noddy

Pug(ilist), Pugilism Belcher, Boxer, Bruiser, Carlin, Fancy, Fistic, Monkey, Ring

Pugnacious Aggressive, Belligerent, Combative, Scrappy

Puke Retch, Sick, Vomit

Pukka Authentic, Genuine, Real, True, Valid

Pulchritude Beauty, Cheese-cake, Grace

Pull (up) Adduce, Attraction, Crane, Drag, Draw, Earn, Force, Haul, Heave, Heeze, Hook, → **INFLUENCE**, Lug, Mousle, Pluck, Rein, Ring, Rove, Rug, Saccade, Sally, Sole, Sool(e), Sowl(e), Stop, Tit, Touse, Touze, Tow, Towse, Towze, Trice, Tug, Undertow, Wrest, Yank

Pulley Block, Capstan, Idle(r), Jack-block, Swig, Trice, Trochlea, Truckle

Pullover Jersey, Jumper, Sweater, Sweatshirt, Tank-top, Windcheater

Pullulate Teem

▶ **Pull up** *see* **PULL**

Pulp Cellulose, Chyme, Chymify, Crush, Flong, Gloop, Kenaf, Marrow, Mash, Mush, Pap, Paste, Pomace, Pound, Puree, Rot, Rubbish, Squeeze, Squidge, Wood

Pulpit(e) Ambo(nes), Lectern, Mimbar, Minbar, Pew, Rostrum, Tent, Tub, Wood

Pulsar Geminga

Pulsate Beat, Palpitate, Quiver, Throb, Vibrate

Pulse Adsuki, Adzuki, Alfalfa, → **BEAN**, Beat, Calavance, Caravance, Chickpea, D(h)al, Dholl, Dicrotic, Fava (bean), Flageolet, Garbanzo, Gram, Groundnut, Ictus, Lentil, Lucerne, Pea, Rhythm, Sain(t)foin, Soy beans, Sphygmic, Sync, Systaltic, Systole, Throb

Pulverise Calcine, Comminute, Contriturate, Demolish, Grind, → **POUND**, Powder

Puma Catamount, Cougar, Mountain lion, Panther

Pummel(ling) Beat, Drub, Fib, Knead, Nevel, Pound, Tapotement, Thump

▷ **Pummelled** *may indicate an anagram*

Pump Air, Bellows, Bicycle, Bowser, Breast, Centrifugal, Chain, Compressor, Cross-question, Diaphragm, Donkey, Drive, Electromagnetic, Elicit, Feed, Filter, Force, Geissler, Grease-gun, Grill, Heart, Heat, Hydropult, Inflate, Interrogate, Knee-swell, Lift, Monkey, Mud, Nodding-donkey, Parish, Petrol, Piston, Pulsometer, Question, Rotary, Scavenge, Shoe, Sodium, Stirrup, Stomach, Suction, Turbine, Vacuum, Water, Wind

Pumpernickel Rye (bread)

Pumphandle Sweep

Pumpkin Butternut, Cashaw, Gourd, Pampoen, Quash, Queensland blue

Pun Calembour, Clinch, Equivoque, Paragram, Paronomasia, Quibble, Quip, Ram, Wordplay
Punch(ed) Antic, Bell, Biff, Blow, Boff, Bolo, Box, Bradawl, Bumbo, Card, Centre, Chad, Check, Chop, Clip, Cobbler's, Conk, Dry-beat, Fib, Fid, Fist(ic), Gang, Glogg, Haymaker, Hit, Hook, Horse, Jab, Key, Kidney, Knevell, Knobble, Knubble, KO, Lander, Mat, Milk, Nail set, Nevel, Nubble, One-er, Overhand, Perforate, Pertuse, Planter's, Plug, Poke, Polt, Pommel, Pounce, Prod, Pummel, Rabbit, Roundhouse, Rum, Rumbo, Slosh, Sock, Steed, Sting(o), Stoush, Sucker, Suffolk, Sunday, Swop, Tape, Upper-cut, Wap, Wind, Zest
Punctilious Exact, Formal, Nice, Particular, Picked, Precise, Prim, Stickler
Punctual(ity) Politesse, Prompt, Regular
Punctuate, Punctuation (mark) Apostrophe, Bracket, Close, Colon, Comma, Duckfoot quote, Emphasize, Guillemet, Interabang, Interrobang, Interrupt, Mark, Semicolon
Puncture(d) Bore, Centesis, Criblé, Cribrate, Deflate, Drill, Flat, Hole, Lumbar, Perforate, Pierce, Pounce, Prick, Scarify, Thoracocentesis
Pundit Egghead, Expert, Guru, Maven, Oracle, Sage, Savant, Swami, Teacher
Pungency, Pungent Acid, Acrid, Acrolein, Alum, Ammonia, Bite, Bitter, Caustic, Hot, Mordant, Nidorous, Piquant, Poignant, Point, Racy, Sair, Salt, Spice, Sting, Tangy, Witty
Punish(ment), Punished, Punishing Algates, Amerce, Attainder, Baffle, Bastinado, Beat, Birch, Brasero, Bum rap, Cane, Capital, Cart, Castigate, Chasten, Chastise, Come-uppance, Commination, Corporal, Correct, Cucking-stool, Dam(nation), Defrock, Desert(s), Detention, → DISCIPLINE, Fatigue, Fine, Flog, Gantlope, Gate, Gauntlet, Gruel, Hellfire, Hiding, Horsing, Hot seat, Imposition, Impot, Interdict, Jankers, Jougs, Keelhaul, Knout, Laldie, Laldy, Lambast(e), Lines, Log, Marmalise, Necklace, Nemesis, Pack-drill, Padre Pio, Pandy, Peine forte et dure, Penalise, Penance, Penology, Pensum, Perdition, Picket, Pillory, Pine, Rap, Reprisal, Retribution, Ruler, Scaffold, Scath, Scourge, Sentence, Serve out, Six of the best, Smack, Smite, Spank, Spif(f)licate, Stocks, Strafe, Straff, Strap, Strappado, Swinge(ing), Talion, Tar and feather, Toco, Toko, Tophet, Treadmill, Trim, Tron, Trounce, Tumbrel, Tumbril, Vice anglais, Visit, War(r)ison, What for, Whip, Wild mare, Ywrake, Ywroke
▷ **Punish** *may indicate* an anagram
Punk Goop, Inferior, Ne'er-do-well, Nobody, Touchwood, Worthless
Punnet Basket, Thug
Punt(er), Punting Antepost, Back, Bet, Gamble, Kent, Kick, Pound, Quant, Turfite, Wager
Puny Frail, Inferior, Petty, Reckling, Runtish, Scram, Shilpit, Sickly, Small, Weak
Pup(py) Cub, Whelp
Pupa Chrysalis, Exarate, Neanic, Nymph, Obtect
Pupil Abiturient, Apple, Apprentice, Boarder, Cadet, Catechumen, Dayboy, Daygirl, Disciple, Etonian, Exit, Eyeball, Follower, Gyte, Junior, L, Monitor, Prefect, Preppy, Protégé(e), Scholar, Senior, Student, Tutee, Ward
▷ **Pupil** *may refer to* an eye
Puppet(s), Puppeteer Bunraku, Creature, Doll, Dummy, Fainéant, Fantoccini, Galanty show, Glove, Guignol, Jack-a-lent, Judy, Mammet, Marionette, Mawmet, Mommet, Motion(-man), Pageant, Pawn, Pinocchio, Promotion, Punch(inello), Quisling, Rod, Tool
Purchase(r), Purchasing Acquisition, Bargain, Buy, Coff, Compulsory, Earn, Emption, Gadsden, Get, Grip, Halliard, Halyard, Hold, Layaway, → LEVERAGE,

Louisiana, Money, Offshore, Oligopsony, Parbuckle, Perquisitor, Secure, Shop, Toehold

Pure, Purity Absolute, Cando(u)r, Cathy, Chaste, Chiarezza, Clean(ly), Cleanness, Cosher, Fine, Glenys, Good, Holy, Immaculate, Incorrupt, Innocent, Intemerate, Inviolate, Kathy, Kosher, Lily, Lilywhite, Maidenhood, Me(a)re, Meer, Net(t), Pristine, Quintessence, Sanctity, Sheer, Simon, Simple, Sincere, Snow-white, Stainless, True, Unalloyed, Undrossy, Vertue, Virgin, Virtue, White

Puree Baba ghanoush, Coulis, Dahl, Dal, Dhal, Fool

Purgative, Purge Aloes, Aloetic, Araroba, Aryanise, Cacoon, Calomel, Cascara, Cassia, Castor-oil, Catharsis, Cholagogue, Colquintida, Croton, Delete, Diacatholicon, Diarrh(o)ea, Drastic, Elaterin, Elaterium, Eliminate, Eluant, Emetic, Enos®, Erase, Evacuant, Exonerate, Expiate, Flux, Gleichschaltung, Hiera-picra, Hydragogue, Ipecacuanha, Ipomoea, Jalap, Jalop, Laxative, McCarthyism, Physic, Picra, Pride's, Relaxant, Scour, Scur, Senna, Soil, Turbith, Turpeth, Wahoo

Purification, Purifier, Purify(ing) Absolve, Bowdlerise, Catharsis, Clay, Clean(se), Depurate, Despumate, Dialysis, Distil, Edulcorate, Elution, Exalt, Expurgate, Filter, Fine, Gas-lime, Green vitriol, Lustre, Lustrum, Niyama, Refine, Retort, Samskara, Sanctify, Scorify, Scrub, Smudging, Try

Puritan(ical) Bible belt, Bluenose, Browne, Digger(s), Ireton, Ironsides, Killjoy, Pi, Pilgrim, Plymouth Colony, Precisian, Prig, Prude, Prynne, Roundhead, Seeker, Strait-laced, Traskite, Waldenses, Wowser, Zealot

Purl(er) Cropper, Eddy, Fall, Knit, Ripple, Stream

Purloin Abstract, Annex, Appropriate, Lift, Nab, Pilfer, Snaffle, Sneak, Steal

Purple Amarantin(e), Amethyst, Assai, Aubergine, Burgundy, Cassius, Chlamys, Claret, Corkir, Cudbear, Dubonnet, Eminence, Golp(e), Heather, Heliotrope, Hyacinthine, Imperial, Indigo, Korkir, Lavender, Lilac, Magenta, Mallow, Mauvin(e), Mulberry, Murrey, Orcein, Orcin(e), Orcinol, Pance, Pansy, Plum, Pompadour, Pontiff, Porporate, Proin(e), Prune, Puce, Puke, Punic, Purpure, Rhodopsin, Royal, Solferino, Tyrian, Violet, Visual

Purport Bear, Claim, Drift, Feck, Mean, Tenor

Purpose(ful) Advertent, Aim, Avail, Calculated, Cautel, Design, Errand, Ettle, Goal, Here-to, Idea, → **INTENT**, Marrow, Mean(ing), Meant, Mint, Motive, Object, Plan, Point, Raison d'être, → **REASON**, Resolution, Resolve, Sake, Telic, Telos, Tenor, Use

Purposeless Dysteleology, Futile, Indiscriminate, Otiose

Purr Curr, Rumble

Purse Ad crumenam, Bag, Bung, Caba, Clutch, Crease, Crumenal, Fisc, Fisk, Long Melford, Mermaid's, Pocket, Prim, Privy, Prize, Public, Pucker, Spleuchan, Sporran, Wallet, Whistle

▷ **Pursed** *may indicate* one word within another

Purslane Sea, Water

Pursue(r), Pursuit Alecto, Business, Chase, Chivvy, Course, Dog, Follow, Follow up, Hobby, Hot-trod, Hound, Hunt, Line, Practice, Practise, Proceed, Prosecute, Quest, Scouring, Stalk, Trivial

Pursuivant Blue Mantle

Purulent Mattery

Purvey(or) Cater, Provide, Provisor, Sell, Supply

Pus Empyema, Matter, Purulence, Quitter, Quittor

Push(er), Push in Airscrew, Barge, Birr, Boost, Bunt, Butt, Detrude, Drive, Edge, Effort, Elbow, Fire, Horn, Hustle, Impulse, Invaginate, Jostle, Motivation, Nose, Nudge, Nurdle, Obtrude, Pitchfork, Plod, Ply, Press, Promote, Propel, Railroad,

Ram, Rush, Sell, Shoulder, → **SHOVE**, Snoozle, Subtrude, Thrust, Urge
Pushchair Baby Buggy®, Buggy, Stroller, Trundler
Pushover Doddle, Soda
Pusillanimous Coward, Timid, Weak, Weak-kneed, Yellow
Puss(y) Amentum, → **CAT**, Catkins, Face, Galore, Hare, Malkin, Mouth, Rabbit,
Septic
Pussyfoot Dry, Equivocate, Inch, Paw, Steal, TT
Pustule Blotch, Pimple, Pock
Put (off; on; out; up) Accommodate, Add, Alienate, Bet, Cup, Daff, Defer, Dish, Do,
Don, Douse, Implant, Impose, Incommode, Inn, Lade, Lay, Locate, Lodge, Lump,
Oust, Pit, Place, Plonk, Set, Smore, Snuff, Station, Stow
Put away, Put by Distance, Save, Sheathe, Store, Stow
Put down Abase, Degrade, Demean, Disparage, Floor, Humiliate, Land, Repress,
Reprime, Snuff, Write
▷ **Put off** *may indicate* an anagram
Putrefaction, Putrefy(ing), Putrid Addle, Bitter, Corrupt, Decay, Fester, Mephitic,
Olid, Rot, Sepsis, Septic
Putter Chug, Club
Putt(ing) Gimme, Gobble, Green, Hash, Pigeon, Sink, → **STUPID PERSON**
Put together Assemble, Compile, Synthesize
Putty Glaziers', Jewellers', Painters', Plasterers', Polishers'
Puzzle(r) Acrostic, Baffle, Bemuse, Bewilder, Brainteaser, Chinese, Confuse,
Conundrum, Crossword, Crux, Egma, Elude, Enigma, Fox, Glaik, Gravel, Intrigue,
Jigsaw, Kittle, Logogriph, Magic pyramid, Mind-bender, Monkey, Mystify, Nonplus,
Perplex, Ponder, Pose(r), Rebus, Riddle, Rubik's Cube®, Sorites, Sphinx, Stick(l)er,
Stump, Tangram, Teaser, Tickler, Wordsearch, Wordsquare
Pygmy Atomy, Dwarf, Negrillo, Negrito, Pyknic, Thumbling
Pyjamas Baby-doll, Churidars, Jimjams
Pyramid Cheops, Chephren, Frustum, Magic, Population, Stack, Teocalli
Pyre Bale(-fire), Bonfire, Brasero, Darga, Gha(u)t
Pyrenean Basque
Pyrites Arsenical, Cockscomb, Copper, Fool's gold, Iron, Magnetic, Mispickel,
Mundic, Spear, White
Pyrotechnics Arson, Fireworks
Pyroxene Aegirine, Aegirite, Diopside
Pyrus Service-tree
Pythagoras Samian
Pythian (seat) Delphic, Tripod
Python Anaconda, Diamond, Kaa, Monty, → **SNAKE**, Zombi(e)

Qq

Q Koppa, Quebec, Question
QC Silk
Qua As
Quack Charlatan, Crocus, Dulcamara, Empiric, Fake, Homeopath, → **IMPOSTOR**, Katerfelto, Mountebank, Pretender, Saltimbanco
Quad(rangle) Close, Complete, Compluvium, Court, Em, En, Horse, Pane
Quadrilateral Lambeth, Tetragon, Trapezium, Trapezoid
Quadrille Dance, Lancers, Matador(e), Pantalon
Quaff Carouse, Drink, Imbibe
Quagmire Bog, Fen, Imbroglio, Marsh, Morass, Swamp, Wagmoire
Quahog Clam
Quail Asteria, Bevy, Bird, Blench, Bob-white, Button, Caille, Colin, Flinch, Harlot, Hen, Quake, Shrink, Tremble
Quaint Cute, Naive, Odd, Old-world, Picturesque, Strange, Twee, Wham, Whim(sy)
Quake(r), Quaking Aminadab, Broad-brim, Dither, Dodder, Fox, Friend, Fry, Hicksite, Obadiah, Penn, Quail, Seism, Shake(r), Shiver, → **TREMBLE**, Tremor, Trepid
Qualification, Qualified, Qualify Able, Adapt, Adverb, Capacitate, Caveat, Competent, Condition, Credential, Degree, Diplomatic, Entitle, Fit, Graduate, Habilitate, Higher Still, Meet, Modifier, Nisi, Pass, Past-master, Proviso, Restrict, Temper, Versed
Quality Aroma, Attribute, Body, Calibre, Cast, Charisma, Esse, Essence, Fabric, Fame, First water, Five-star, Flavour, Grade, Inscape, It, Kite-mark, Letter, Long suit, Mystique, Nature, Pitch, Plus, Premium, Primary, Property, Q, Quale, Reception, Savour, Sort, Standard, Stature, Style, Substance, Suchness, Thew, Thisness, Timbre, Tone, Total, Up-market, Vinosity, Virgin, Virtu(e), Water, Worth
Qualm Compunction, Misgiving, Scruple
Quandary Dilemma, Fix, Predicament, Trilemma
Quantity → **AMOUNT**, Analog(ue), Batch, Bundle, Capacity, Deal, Dose, Feck, Fother, Hank, Hundredweight, Idempotent, Intake, Jag, Lock, Lot, Mass, Measure, Melder, Myriad, Nonillion, Number, Ocean(s), Operand, Parameter, Parcel, Peck, Plenty, Posology, Pottle, Qs, Qt, Quire, Quota, Quotient, Ream, Scalar, Slather, Slew, Slue, Sum, Surd, Tret, Unknown, Vector, Warp, Whips
Quantum Graviton, Isospin, Phonon, Photon, Roton
Quarantine Isolate, Lazarette
Quark Flavo(u)r, Strange
Quarrel(some) Affray, Aggress, Altercate, Arrow, Barney, Barratry, Barretry, Bate, Bicker, Brabble, Brattle, Brawl, Breach, Breeze, Broil, Brulyie, Brulzie, Bust-up, Cagmag, Cantankerous, Carraptious, Cat and dog, Caterwaul, Chance-medley, Chide, Clash, Combative, Contretemps, Difference, Disagree, Dispute, Domestic, Dust-up, Eristic, Estrangement, Exchange, Fall out, Feisty, Fracas, Fractious,

Fratch(et)y, Fray, Hassle, Issue, Jar, Loggerheads, Outcast, Outfall, Pugnacious, Ragbolt, Row, Spat, Squabble, Tiff, Tile, Tink, Vendetta, Wap, Whid, Wrangle
Quarry, Quarry face Chalkpit, Chase, Currie, Curry, Game, Heuch, Mine, Pit, Prey, Scabble, Scent, Stone pit, Victim
Quart Winchester
Quarter(ing), Quarters Airt, Barrio, Billet, Canton(ment), Casbah, Casern(e), Chinatown, Clemency, Close, Coshery, District, Dorm, E, Empty, Enclave, Fardel, Farl, First, Fo'c'sle, Forecastle, Forpet, Forpit, Fourth, Ghetto, Ham(s), Harbour, Haunch, Last, Latin, Medina, → MERCY, N, Note, Oda, Pity, Point, Principium, Quadrant, Region, S, Season, Sector, Tail, Trimester, W, Wardroom, Warp, Winter
Quarter-day LD
▷ **Quarterdeck** *may indicate* a suit of cards
Quartet Foursome, Mess, String, Tetrad
Quarto Crown, Demy, Foolscap, Imperial, Medium, Royal, Small
Quartz Agate, Amethyst, Bristol diamond, Buhrstone, Cacholong, Cairngorm, Chalcedony, Chert, Citrine, Flint, Granophyre, Itacolumite, Jasp(er), Morion, Onyx, Plasma, Prase, Rainbow, Rose, Rubasse, Sapphire, Silex, Silica, Smoky, Spanish topaz, Stishovite, Tiger-eye, Tonalite, Whin Sill
Quash Abrogate, Annul, Nullify, Quell, Rebut, Recant, Scotch, Subdue, Suppress, Terminate, Void
Quaver(ing) Shake, Tremulous, Trill, Vibrate, Warble
Quay Bund, Levee, Wharf
Queasy Delicate, Nauseous, Squeamish
Quebec Q
Queen(ly) Adelaide, African, Alcestis, Alexandra, Anna, Anne, Artemesia, Atossa, Balkis, Beauty, Bee, Begum, Bess, Boadicea, Boudicca, Brunhild(e), Camilla, Candace, Card, Caroline, Cleopatra, Closet, Clytemnestra, Coatcard, Dido, Drag, Drama, Eleanor(a), Ellery, Ena, ER, Esther, FD, Gertrude, Guinevere, Hatshepset, Hatshepsut, Hecuba, Helen, Hera, Here, Hermione, Hippolyta, HM, Isabel, Isabella, Ishtar, Isolde, Jocasta, Juno, King, Leda, Maam, Mab, Maeve, Marie Antoinette, Mary, Matilda, May, Medb, Mobled, Monarch, Nance, Nefertiti, Omphale, Pance, Pansy, Parr, Paunce, Pawnce, Pearly, Penelope, Persephone, Phaedra, Prince, Prom, Proserpina, Qu, R, Ranee, Rani, Regal, Regina(l), Sara, Semiramis, Sheba, Sultana, Titania, Vashti, Victoria, Virgin, Warrior
Queen Anne Mrs Morley
Queer(ness) Abnormal, Berdash, Bizarre, Crazy, Cure, Curious, Fey, Fie, Fifish, Gay, Nance, Nancy, → ODD, Outlandish, Peculiar, Pervert, Poorly, Quaint, Rum, Spoil, Uranism, Vert
Quell Alegge, Allay, Calm, Quiet, Repress, Subdue, Suppress
Quench Assuage, Cool, Extinguish, Satisfy, Slake, Slo(c)ken, Sta(u)nch, Yslake
▷ **Query** *see* QUESTION
Quest Goal, Graal, Grail, Hunt, Pursuit, Search, Venture
Question(ing), Questionnaire Appose, Ask, Bi-lateral, Burning, Catechise, Chin, Contest, Conundrum, Cross-examine, Debrief, Dichotomous, Direct, Dispute, Dorothy Dixer, Doubt, Erotema, Eroteme, Erotesis, Examine, Fiscal, Good, Grill, Heckle, Homeric, Impeach, Impugn, Indirect, Information, Innit, Interpellation, Interrogate, Interview, Koan, Leading, Loaded, Maieutic, Matter, Open, Oppugn, Peradventure, Pop, Pose, Previous, Probe, Problem, Pump, Q, Qu, Quaere, Quiz, Rapid-fire, Refute, Rhetorical, Riddle, Speer, Speir, Survey, Suspect, Tag, Teaser, Tickler, Vexed, West Lothian, WH, What, Worksheet
Questionable Ambiguous, Dubious, Fishy, Socratic

Question-master Interrogator, Socrates, Torquemada, Ximenes
Queue Braid, Breadline, Cercus, Crocodile, Cue, Dog, File, Kale, → **LINE**, Pigtail, Plait, Plat, Stack, Tail(back), Track
Quibble(r), Quibbling Balk, Carp, Carriwitchet, Casuist, Cavil, Chicaner, Dodge, Elenchus, Equivocate, Hairsplitting, Nitpick, Pedantry, Pettifoggery, Prevaricate, Pun, Quiddity, Quillet, Quirk, Sophist
Quiche Flan, Tart
Quick(en), Quickening, Quicker, Quickie, Quickly, Quickness Accelerate, Acumen, Adroit, Agile, Alive, Allegr(ett)o, Animate, Apace, Breakneck, Breathing, Brisk, Celerity, Chop-chop, Citigrade, Cito, Con moto, Core, Cracking, Cuticle, Dapper, Deft, Enliven, Existent, Expeditious, Express, Fastness, Festination, Foothot, Gleg, Hasten, Hie, High-speed, Hotfoot, Impulsive, Jiffy, Keen, Lickety-split, Living, Mercurial, Meteoric, Mistress, Mosso, Nailbed, Nimble, Nippy, Nooner, Pdq, Piercing, Piu mosso, Post-haste, Prestissimo, Presto, Prompt, Pronto, Rapid, Rath(e), Ready, Rough and ready, Schnell, Sharp, Skin, Slippy, Smart, Snappy, Snort, Sodain(e), Soon, Spry, Streamline, Stretta, Stretto, Sudden, Swift, Swith, Tout de suite, Trice, Up tempo, Veloce, Vital, Vite, Vivify, Wikiwiki, Yare
Quicksand Flow, Syrtis
Quicksilver Mercury
Quid Chaw, Chew, L, Nicker, Oner, Plug, Pound, Quo, Sov, Tertium, Tobacco
Quid pro quo Mutuum, Tit-for-tat
Quiescence, Quiescent Calm, Di(o)estrus, Inactive, Inert, Latent, Still
Quiet(en), Quietly Accoy, Allay, Appease, Barnacle, Calm, Compose, Conticent, Doggo, Ease, Easeful, Easy, Encalm, Entame, Gag, Grave, Kail, Laconic, Loun(d), Low, Lown(d), Low-profile, Lull, Meek, Mezzo voce, Mp, Muffle, Mute, P, Pacify, Pauciloquent, Pause, Peace, Piano, Pipe down, Plateau, QT, Reserved, Reticent, Sedate, Settle, Sh, Shtoom, Shtum, Silence, Sitzkrieg, Sly, Sober, Soothe, Sotto voce, Still, Stum(m), Subact, Subdued, Tace, Taciturn, Tranquil, Wheesht, Whish, Whisht, Whist
Quill Calamus, Feather, Float, Plectre, Plectron, Plectrum, Plume, Remex
Quillwort Isoetes
Quilt(ed), Quilting Comfort(er), Continental, Counterpane, Cover, Crazy, Doona®, Duvet, Echo, Eiderdown, Futon, Kantha, Matel(l)asse, Patch(work), Puff, Trapunto
Quince Bael, Bel, Bengal, Bhel, Flowering, Japanese, Japonica
Quinine China, Crown-bark, Kina, Quina, Tonic
Quinsy Angina, Cynanche, Garget, Squinancy
Quintessence, Quintessential Classic, Heart, Pith
Quintet Pentad, Trout
Quip Carriwitchet, Crack, Epigram, Gibe, Jest, Jibe, Joke, Taunt, Zinger
Quirk Concert, Foible, Idiosyncrasy, Irony, Kink, Mannerism, Twist
Quisling Collaborator, Traitor
Quit(s) Abandon, Absolve, Ap(p)ay, Cease, Desert, Even(s), Go, Leave, Meet, Resign, → **STOP**
Quite Actually, All, Ap(p)ay, Clean, Dead, Enough, Enow, Fairly, Fully, Mezzo, Precisely, Real, Right, Sheer, Very
Quiver(ing) Aspen, Quake, Shake, Sheath, The yips, Tremble, Tremolo, Tremor, Tremulate, Trepid, Vibrant, Vibrate, Wobble
Qui vive Go-go
Quixote, Quixotic Don, Errant, Impractical
Quiz Bandalore, Bee, Catechism, Examine, Interrogate, I-spy, Mastermind, Oddity,

Probe, Pump, Question, Smoke, Trail, Yo-yo
Quizzical Askance, Curious, Derisive, Odd, Queer, Socratic
Quod Can, Clink, Jail, Prison
Quoit Disc(us), Disk, Ring
Quondam Once, Sometime, Whilom
Quorum Minyan
Quota Numerus clausus, Proportion, Ration, Share
Quotation, Quote(d), Quote Adduce, Citation, Cite, Co(a)te, Duckfoot, Epigraph, Evens, Extract, Forward, Instance, Name, Price, Recite, Reference, Say, Scare, Soundbite, Tag, Verbatim, Wordbite
Quoth Co, Said
Quotient Achievement, Intelligence, Kerma, Quaternion, Ratio, Respiratory

Rr

R Arithmetic, Dog letter, King, Queen, Reading, Recipe, Right, Romeo, Run, Writing
Rabbi Dayan, Mashgiah, Rav, Rebbe
Rabbit Angora, Astrex, Brer, British Lop, Buck, Bun(ny), Chat, Con(e)y, Cottontail,
Daman, Dassie, Doe, Earbash, Harp, Haver, Hyrax, Jabber, Jack, Jaw, Klipdas,
Long White, Lop-eared, Marmot, Muff, Nest, Novice, Oarlap, Palaver, Patzer,
Prate, Rattle, Rex, Rock, Sage, Snowshoe, Tapeti, Terricole, Waffle, Welsh, White,
Witter, Yak, Yap, Yatter
Rabble, Rabble-rousing Canaille, Clamjamphrie, Clanjamfray, Colluvies, Crowd,
Demagoguery, Doggery, Galère, Herd, Hoi-polloi, Horde, Legge, Meinie, Mein(e)y,
Menyie, Mob, Raffle, Rag-tag, Rascaille, Rascal, Riff-raff, Rout, Scaff-raff, Shower,
Tag, Tagrag
Rabelaisian Pantagruel, Panurge
Rabid, Rabies Extreme, Frenzied, Hydrophobia, Lyssa, Mad, Raging, Virulent
Raccoon Coati, Panda, Procyon
Race(course), Racing, Race meeting Aintree, Alpine, Ancestry, Arms, Ascot,
Autocross, Bathtub, Belt, Boat, Boskop, Breed, Broose, Brouze, Bumping,
Cambridgeshire, Career, Catadrome, Catterick, Caucus, Cesarewitch, Chantilly,
Chase, Claiming, Classic, Comrades, Cone, Contest, Corso, Country, Course,
Current, Cursus, Cyclo-cross, Dash, Derby, Doggett's Coat and Badge, Dogs,
Doncaster, Drag, Dromos, Egg and spoon, Enduro, Epsom, Event, F1, Fastnet,
Flapping, Flat, Flow, Formula One, Fun-run, Generation, Ginger, Goodwood, Grand
National, Grand Prix, Guineas, Handicap, Hare and hounds, Harness, Herrenvolk,
Hialeah, High hurdles, Hippodrome, Human(kind), Hurdles, Hurry, Inca, Indy,
Indy car, Kermesse, Kind, Lampadedromy, Lampadephoria, Leat, Leet, Leger, Le
Mans, Lick, Lignage, Line(age), Longchamps, Madison, Man, Marathon, Master,
Meets, Mile, Motocross, Nascar, → NATIONAL, Newmarket, Nursery, Nursery
stakes, Oaks, Obstacle, One-horse, Paceway, Palio, Paper chase, Pattern, Picnic,
Plate, Pluck, Point-to-point, Potato, Pre-Dravidian, Prep, Pursuit, Rallycross,
Rallying, Rapids, Rat, Redcar, Regatta, Relay, Rill, Rod, Ronne, Roost, Run-off,
Sack, St Leger, Scramble, Scratch, Scud, Scurry, Seed, Selling, Shan, Sheep, Slalom,
Slipstream, Sloot, Slot-car, Sluit, Smock, Speedway, Sprint, Stakes, Steeplechase,
Stem, Stirp(s), Stirpes, Stock, Strain, Streak, Strene, Supermoto, Sweepstake, Tail,
Taste, Tear, Thousand Guineas, Three-legged, Tide, Torch, Torpids, Towcester,
Tribe, Trotting, TT, Turf, Two-horse, Two Thousand Guineas, Velodrome,
Volsungs, Walking, Walk-over, Waterway, Welter, Wetherby, Whid, White,
Wincanton
Racehorse, Racer Eclipse, Filly, Go-kart, Hare, Maiden, Novice, Plater, Red Rum,
Steeplechaser, Trotter
Raceme Corymb, Panicle
Racial (area), Racialist Apartheid, Colour, Ethnic, Ghetto, National Front, Quarter
Rack Agonise, Bin, Cloud, Cratch, Drier, Flake, Frame, Hack, Hake, Heck, Pipe,

Plate, Pulley, Roof, Stretcher, Toast, Torment, Torture, Touse, Towse

Racket(eer) Bassoon, → **BAT**, Battledore, Bloop, Brattle, Caterwaul, Chirm, Clamour, Crime, Deen, Din, Discord, Earner, → **FIDDLE**, Gyp, Hubbub, Hustle, → **NOISE**, Noisiness, Protection, Ramp, Rort, Sokaiya, Stridor, Swindle, Tumult, Uproar, Utis

Racy Ethnic, Piquant, Pungent, Ribald, Salty, Spicy, Spirited

Rad Rem

Radar Acronym, Angel, AWACS, Beacon, DEW line, Doppler, Gadget, Gee, Gull, Lidar, Loran, Monopulse, Navar, Rebecca-eureka, Shoran, Surveillance, Teleran®, Tracking

Raddle Hurdle, Ochre, Red

Radial Osteal, Quadrant, Rotula, Spoke, Tire, Tyre

Radiance, Radiant Actinic, Aglow, Aureola, Beamish, Brilliant, Gleam(y), Glory, Glow, Happy, Lustre, Refulgent, Shechina, Sheen, Shekinah

Radiate, Radiating, Radiation, Radiator Actinal, Adaptive, Air-colour, Beam, Bremsstrahlung, Cavity, Characteristic, C(h)erenkov, Disseminate, Dosimetry, Effuse, Emanate, Emit, Exitance, Fluorescence, Gamma, Glow, Hawking, Heater, Infrared, Insolation, Ionizing, Isohel, Laser, Millirem, Non-ionizing, Pentact, Photon, Pulsar, Quasar, Rem(s), Rep, Roentgen, → **SHINE**, Sievert, Soft, Spherics, Spoke, Stellate, Stray, SU, Sun, Synchrotron, Terrestrial, Ultra violet, UVA, UVB, Van Allen, Visible

Radical Acetyl, Allyl, Amide, Ammonium, Amyl, Aryl, Benzil, Benzoyl, Bolshevist, Bolshie, Butyl, Calumba, Carbene, Cetyl, Drastic, Dyad, Ester, Extreme, Free, Fundamental, Gauchist, Genre-busting, Glyceryl, Glycosyl, Hydroxy, Innate, Isopropyl, Jacobin, Leftist, Leveller, Ligand, Maximalist, Methyl, Montagnard, Nitryl, Oxonium, Parsnip, Phenyl, Phosphonium, Pink, Propyl, Red, Revolutionary, Rhizocaul, Root, Rudiment, Sulfone, Sulphone, Trot(sky), Uranyl, Vinyl, Whig, Xylyl

Radio Bluetooth, Boom-box, Cat's whisker, CB, Cellular, Citizen's band, Cognitive, Community, Crystal set, Digital, Ether, Gee, Ghetto-blaster, Local, Loudspeaker, Marconigraph, Receiver, Rediffusion®, Reflex, Rig, Set, Simplex, Sound, Steam, Talk, Talkback, Tranny, Transceiver, Transistor, Transmitter, Transponder, Walkie-talkie, Walkman®, Walky-talky, Wireless

Radioactive, Radioactivity Actinide, Americium, Astatine, Autinite, Bohrium, Cobalt 60, Emanation, Fall-out, Hot, Nucleonics, Plutonium, Radon, Steam, Thorium, Torbernite, Uranite

Radiogram, Radiograph(y) Cable, Telegram, Venography, Ventriculography, Wire

Radiology Interventional

Radish Charlock, Mooli, Runch

Radium Ra

Radius Bone, Long, Schwarzschild, Short

Radon Rn

Raffia Rabanna

Raffle(s) Burglar, Draw, Lottery, Sweepstake

Raft(ing) Balsa, Carley float, Catamaran, Float, Kon-Tiki, Life, Mohiki, Pontoon, Whitewater

Rafter Barge-couple, Beam, Chevron, Jack, Joist, Principal, Ridge, Spar, Timber

Rag(ged), Rags Bait, Bate, Clout, Coral, Daily, Deckle, Dud(s), Duddery, Duddie, Duster, Fent, Figleaf, Glad, Gutter press, Guyed, Haze, Kid, Lap(pie), Lapje, Mop, → **NEWSPAPER**, Nose, Paper, Red, Remnant, Revel, Rivlins, Roast, Rot, Scabrous, S(c)hmatte, Scold, Scrap, → **SHRED**, Slate, Slut, Splore, Tack, Tat(t),

Tatter(demalion), Tatty, Taunt, → **TEASE**, Tiger, Tongue, Uneven
▷ **Rag(ged)** *may indicate* an anagram
Rage, Raging → **ANGER**, Ardour, Bait, Bate, Bayt, Chafe, Conniption, Explode,
Fashion, Fierce, Fit, Fiz(z), Fume, Furibund, Furore, Fury, Gibber, Go, Ire, Mode,
Monkey, Paddy(-whack), Passion, Pelt, Pet, Pique, Rabid, Rail, Ramp, Rant, Road,
See red, Snit, Storm, Tear, Temper, Ton, Trolley, Utis, Wax, Wrath
Raglan Sleeve
Ragout Compot, Goulash, Haricot, Stew
Rag-picker Bunter
Raid(er) Assault, Attack, Baedeker, Bear, Bodrag, Bust, Camisado, Chappow,
Commando, Corporate, Dawn, Do, For(r)ay, Imburst, Incursion, Inroad, Inrush,
Invade, Jameson, Maraud, March-treason, Mosstrooper, Pict, Pillage, Plunder,
Ram, Ransel, Razzia, Reive, Sack, Scrump, Skrimp, Skrump, Smash-and-grab,
Sortie, Spreagh, Storm, Viking
Rail(er), Railing Abuse, Amtrack, Arm, Arris, Balustrade, Ban, Banister, → **BAR**,
Barre, Barrier, Bird, Bullhead, Cloak, Communion, Conductor, Coot, Corncrake,
Crake, Criticise, Dado, Fender, Fiddle, Fife, Flanged, Flat-bottomed, Flow, Gush,
Insult, Inveigh, Light, Live, Metal, Monkey, Neckerchief, Notornis, Parclose,
Picture, Pin, Plate, Post, Pulpit, Pushpit, Rack, Rag, Rate, Rave, Rung, Scold,
Slang-whang, Slate, Slip, Snash, Sneer, Sora, Soree, Spar, T, Taffrail, Takahe,
Taunt, Thersites, Third, Towel, Train, Vituperation, Weka
Raillery Badinage, Banter, Chaff, Persiflage, Sport
Railroad, Railway Aerial, Amtrak, BR, Bulldoze, Cable, Cash, Coerce, Cog,
Crémaillère, Dragoon, El, Elevated, Funicular, Gantlet, GWR, Inclined, L, Light,
Lines, LMS, LNER, Loop-line, Maglev, Marine, Metro, Monorail, Mountain,
Narrow-gauge, Rack, Rack and pinion, Rly, Road, Rollercoaster, Ropeway, ROSCO,
Ry, Scenic, Ship, Siding, SR, Stockton-Darlington, Switchback, Telpher-line, Track,
Train, Tramline, Tramway, Trans-Siberian, Tube, Underground
Railwayman Driver, Fettler, Gandy dancer, Guard, Locoman, NUR, Stephenson,
Stoker, Tracklayer
Raiment Apparel, Clothes, Garb, Ihram
Rain(y), Rainstorm Acid, Brash, Deluge, Drizzle, Flood, Hyad(e)s, Hyetal, Mistle,
Mizzle, Oncome, Onding, Onfall, Pelt, Pelter, Piss, Pluviose, Pluvious, Pour,
Precipitation, Right, Roke, Scat, Seil, Serein, Serene, Shell, Shower, Sile, Silver
thaw, Skiffle, Skit, Smir(r), Smur, Soft, Spat, Spet, Spit, Storm, Thunder-plump,
Virga, Weep, Wet, Yellow
Rainbow(-maker) Arc, Arc-en-ciel, Bifrost, Bruise, Dew-bow, Indescence, Iris,
Moon-bow, Spectroscope, Sunbow, Sundog, Water-gall, Weather-gall, White
Raincoat Burberry®, Gaberdine, Mac, Mino, Oils(kins), Slicker, Waterproof
Raingauge Ombrometer, Udometer
Rain-maker Indra
Rain tree Saman
Raise(d), Raising Advance, Aggrade, Attollent, Boost, Bouse, Bowse, Build, Cat,
Coaming, Cock, Collect, Elate, → **ELEVATE**, Emboss, Enhance, Ennoble, Erect,
Escalate, Exalt, Extol, Fledge, Grow, Heave, Heezie, Heft, High, Hike, Hoick, Hoist,
Increase, Jack, Key, Leaven, Lift, Mention, Overcall, Perk, Rear, Regrate, Repoussé,
Revie, Rouse, Saleratus, Siege, Sky, Snarl, Step-up, Sublimate, Upgrade, Weigh
Rake, Raker, Rakish Casanova, Comb, Corinthian, Croupier, Dapper, Dissolute,
Don Juan, Enfilade, Gay dog, Jaunty, Lecher, Libertine, Lothario, Raff, Reprobate,
Rip, Roué, Scan, Scour, Scowerer, Scratch, Strafe, Stubble, Swash-buckler,
Swinge-buckler, Wagons

Rale Crepitus, Rattle
Rally, Rallying-point Autocross, Autopoint, Badinage, Banter, Demo, Gather,
Jamboree, Meeting, Mobilise, Monte Carlo, Muster, Oriflamme, Persiflage,
Recover, Rely, Rest, Revive, Risorgimento, Roast, Rouse, Scramble, Spirit
Ralph Imp, Nader, Rackstraw
Ram Aries, Battering, Buck, Bunt, Butt, Butter, Corvus, Crash, Drive, Hidder,
Hydraulic, Mendes, Pun, Sheep, Stem, Tamp, Thrust, Tup, Wether
Ramble(r), Rambling Aberrant, Aimless, Digress, Incoherent, Liana, Liane,
Rigmarole, Roam, Rose, Rove, Skimble-skamble, Sprawl, Stray, Stroll, Vagabond,
Wander
Rameses Pharaoh
Ramp Bank, Gradient, Helicline, Incline, Runway, Slipway, Slope, Speed
Rampage Fury, Spree, Storm, Warpath
Rampant Lionel, Predominant, Profuse, Rearing, Rife
▷ **Rampant** *may indicate* an anagram or a reversed word
Rampart Abat(t)is, Brisure, Butt, Defence, Fortification, Parapet, Terreplein, Vallum,
Wall
Ramrod Gunstick
Ramshackle Decrepit, Heath Robinson, Rickety, Rickle
Ranch Bowery, Corral, Dude, Estancia, Farm, Hacienda, Spread, Stump
Rancid Frowy, Reast(y), Reest(y), Reist(y), Sour, Turned
Rancour Gall, Hate, Malice, Resentment, Spite
Rand Border, R, Roon
Random Accidental, Aleatoric, Arbitrary, → **AT RANDOM**, Blind, Casual, Desultory,
Fitful, → **HAPHAZARD**, Harvest, Hit-or-miss, Hobnob, Indiscriminate, Scattershot,
Sporadic, Stochastic, Stray
▷ **Random(ly)** *may indicate* an anagram
Range(r), Rangy Admiralty, Align, Ambit, Andes, Atlas, AZ, Ballpark, Band,
Bowshot, Bushwhack, Capsule, Carry, Cascade, Chain, Cheviot, Compass,
Cotswolds, Course, Darling, Diapason, Dispace, Dolomites, Dynamic, Err,
→ **EXTENT**, Eye-shot, Flinders, Forest, Gamut, Glasgow, Gunshot, Hamersley,
Harmonic, Helicon, Himalayas, Home, Interquartile, Ken(ning), Kolyma, Ladakh,
Leggy, Limit, Line, Long, Massif, Middleback, → **MOUNT**, Orbit, Oven, Owen
Stanley, Palette, Point-blank, Prairie, Purview, Rake, Reach, Register, Repertoire,
Rifle, Roam, Rocket, Scale, Scope, Sc(o)ur, Selection, Serra, Shooting, Short, Sierra,
Sloane, Spectrum, Sphere, Stanovoi, Stanovoy, Stove, Strzelecki, Tape, Tessitura,
Teton, Texas, The Wolds, Tier, Urals, Waldgrave, Wasatch, Waveband, Woomera
Rank(s) Arrant, Assort, Ayatollah, Begum, Brevet, Caste, Category, Cense, Classify,
Cornet, Curule, Degree, Dignity, Downright, Earldom, Estate, État(s), Flight
sergeant, Grade, Graveolent, Gree, Gross, High, Hojatoleslam, Hojatolislam,
Majority, Olid, Parage, Percentile, Place, Range, Rate, Rooty, Row, Seed,
Seigniorage, Sergeant, Serried, Shoulder-strap, Sort, Standing, → **STATION**, Status,
Substantive, Taxi, Tier, → **TITLE**, Titule, Utter, Viscount
Rankle Chafe, Fester, Gall, Irritate, Nag
Ransack Fish, Loot, Pillage, Plunder, Rifle, Ripe, Rob, Rummage
Ransom King's, Redeem, Release, Rescue
Rant(er), Ranting Bombast, Declaim, Fustian, Ham, Harangue, Rail,
Rodomontade, Scold, Slang-whang, Spout, Spruik, Stump, Thunder, Tub-thump
Rap(ped) Blame, Censure, Chat, Clour, Gangsta, Halfpenny, Knock, Ratatat, Shand,
Strike, Swapt, Tack, Tap
Rapacious Accipitrine, Esurient, Exorbitant, Greedy, Harpy, Kite, Predatory,

Ravenous, Ravine

Rape Abuse, Assault, Belinda, Cole-seed, Colza, Creach, Creagh, Date, Deflower, Despoil, Gangbang, Grass(line), Hundred, Lock, Lucretia, Navew, Oilseed, Plunder, Ravish, Statutory, Stuprate, Thack, Tow, Violate

Rapid(ity), Rapidly Chute, Dalle, Double-quick, Express, Fast, Meteoric, Mosso, Presto, Pronto, Quick-fire, Riffle, Sault, Shoot, Skyrocket, Speedy, Stickle, Swift, Tantivy, Veloce, Vibrato, Wildfire

Rapier Sword, Tuck

Rappel Abseil

Rapport Accord, Affinity, Agreement, Harmony

Rapprochement Détente, Reconciliation

Rapt Riveted

Raptor Eagle, Kestrel, Osprey, Standgale, Staniel, Stannel, Stanyel, Stooper

Rapture, Rapturous Bliss, → DELIGHT, Ecstasy, Elation, Joy, Trance

Rare, Rarity Blue moon, Curio, Earth, Geason, Infrequent, Intemerate, One-off, Rear, Recherché, Scarce, Seeld, Seld(om), Singular, Thin, → UNCOMMON, Uncooked, Underdone, Unusual

Rarefied Thin

Rascal(ly) Arrant, Bad hat, Cad, Cullion, Cur, Deer, Devil, Gamin, Hallian, Hallion, Hallyon, → KNAVE, Limner, Loon, Losel, Low, Nointer, Rip, Rogue, Scallywag, Scamp, Scapegrace, Schelm, Skeesicks, Skellum, Skelm, Smaik, Spalpeen, Tinker, Toe-rag, Varlet, Varmint, Villain

Rash(ness), Rasher Acne, Bacon, Barber's, Brash, Collop, Daredevil, Eruption, Erysipelas, Exanthem(a), Fast, Foolhardy, Harum-scarum, → HASTY, Headlong, Heat, Hives, Hotspur, Ill-advised, Impetigo, Impetuous, Imprudent, Impulsive, Lardo(o)n, Lichen, Madbrain, Madcap, Miliaria, Morphew, Nappy, Nettle, Outbreak, Overhasty, Pox, Precipitate, Purpura, Reckless, Road, Roseola, Rubella, Sapego, Scarlatina, Serpigo, Spots, Temerity, Tetter, Thoughtless, Unheeding, Unthinking, Unwise, Urticaria

Rasp(er) File, Grate, Odontophore, Radula, Risp, Rub, Scrape, Scroop, Xyster

Raspberry Berate, Black(cap), Boo, Bronx-cheer, Etaerio, Hindberry, Razz

Rastafarian Dread

Rat(s), Ratty Agouta, Bandicoot, Blackleg, Blackneb, Boodie, Brown, Bug-out, Camass, Cane, Cur, Defect, Desert, Fink, Footra, Foutra, Geomyoid, Gym, Heck, Hood, Hydromys, Informer, Kangaroo, Malabar, Mall, Maori, Mole, Moon, Norway, Pack, Pig, Poppycock, Potoroo, Pouched, Pshaw, Pup(py), Renegade, Renegate, Rice, Rink, Rodent, Roland, Rot(ten), Scab, Sewer, Shirty, Squeal, Stinker, Turncoat, Vole, Water, Wharf, Whiskers, White, Wood

Rat-catcher Cat, Ichneumon, Mongoose, Pied Piper

Rate(s), Rating A, Able, Able-bodied, Apgar, Appreciate, Assess, Base, Basic, Birth, Bit, Carpet, Castigate, Cess, Classify, Conception, Cost, Count, Credit, Deserve, Erk, Estimate, Evaluate, Exchange, Grade, Headline, Hearty, Hurdle, Incidence, Interest, ISO, Lapse, Leading, Mate's, Mortality, Mortgage, MPH, Octane, Ordinary, OS, Pace, Penalty, Percentage, PG, Piece, Poor, Prime (lending), Rag, Rebuke, Red, Refresh, Reproof, Rocket, Row, Sailor, Scold, → SET, Slew, → SPEED, Standing, Starting, Surtax, Take-up, TAM, Tariff, Tax, Tempo, Tog, U, Upbraid, Value, Water, Wig, World-scale, X

Rather Assez, Degree, Fairly, Gey, Instead, Lief, Liever, Loor, More, Prefer, Pretty, Some(what), Sooner, Yes

Ratify Amen, Approve, Confirm, Homologate, Pass, Sanction, Validate

Ratio Advance, Albedo, Aspect, Bypass, Cash, Compound, Compression, Cosine,

Distinctiveness, Duplicate, Focal, Fraction, Gear, Golden, Gyromagnetic, Inverse, Liquidity, Loss, Mass, Neper, PE, Pi, Pogson, Poisson's, Position, Price-dividend, Price-earnings, Proportion, Protection, Quotient, Reserve, Savings, Signal-to-noise, Sin(e), Slip, Space, Tensor, Trigonometric

Ration(s) Allocate, Apportion, Compo, Dole, Étape, Iron, K, Quota, Restrict, Scran, Share, Short commons, Size

Rational(ism), Rationalisation A posteriori, Descartes, Dianoetic, Level-headed, Logical, Lucid, Matter-of-fact, Sane, Sensible, Sine, Sober, Tenable, Wice

Rationale Motive

Rattle (box), Rattling Chatter, Clack, Clank, Clap, Clatter, Clitter, Conductor, Crescelle, Crotalaria, Death, Demoralise, Disconcert, Gas-bag, Hurtle, Jabber, Jangle, Jar, Maraca, Natter, Nonplus, Rale, Rap, Red, Reel, Rhonchus, Ruckle, Sabre, Shake, Sistrum, Sunn, Tirl, Upset, Yellow

Raucous Guttural, Hoarse, Loud, Strident

Ravage Depredation, Desecrate, Despoil, Havoc, Pillage, Prey, Ruin, Sack, Waste

Rave, Raving Boil, Enthuse, Praise, Redwood, Redwud, Storm, Ta(i)ver, Tear

Ravel Disentangle, Explain, Fray, Involve, Snarl, Tangle

Raven(ous) Black, Corbel, Corbie, Corvine, Croaker, Daw, Grip, Hugin, Munin, Unkindness, Wolfish

Ravine Arroyo, Barranca, Barranco, Canada, Canyon, Chasm, Chine, Clough, Coulée, Couloir, Dip, Flume, Ghyll, Gorge, Goyle, Grike, Gulch, Gully, Kedron, Khor, Khud, Kidron, Kloof, Lin(n), Nal(l)a, Nallah, Nulla(h), Pit

Ravish Constuprate, Debauch, Defile, Devour, Rape, Stuprate, Transport, Violate

Raw Brut, Chill, Coarse, Crude, Crudy, Damp, Fresh, Greenhorn, Natural, Recruit, Rude, Uncooked, Wersh

Raw-boned Gaunt, Lanky, Lean, Randle-tree

Ray(s), Rayed Actinic, Alpha, Beam, Beta, Canal, Cathode, Cosmic, Cramp-fish, Death, Delta, Devil, Diactine, Dun-cow, Eagle, Electric, Extraordinary, Fish, Gamma, Grenz, Guitarfish, Homelyn, Manta, Medullary, Monactine, Numbfish, Ordinary, Polyact, Positive, R, Radius, Re, Roentgen, Roker, Röntgen, Sawfish, Sea-devil, Sea-vampire, Sephen, Shaft, Skate, Starburst, Stick, Sting, Stingaree, Tetract, Thornback, Torpedo, Vascular

Rayon Acetate, Faille, Viscose

Raze Annihilate, Bulldoze, Demolish, Destroy, Level

Razor(-maker) Cut-throat, Occam, Safety, Straight

Razorbill Murre

Razor-fish Solen

Razz Raspberry

RE Sappers

Re About, Rhenium, Touching

Reach(ed) Ar(rive), Attain, Boak, Boke, Carry, Come, Get out, Hent, Hit, Key-bugle, Lode, Octave, Peak, Raught, Rax, Retch, Ryke, Seize, Stretch, Touch, Win

Reach-me-downs Slop-clothing

React(or), Reaction(ary) Addition, Allergy, Anaphylaxis, Answer, Backlash, Backwash, Behave, Blimp, Blowback, Bourbon, Breeder, Bristle, Bummer, CANDU, Catalysis, Chain, Chemical, Converter, Convertor, Core, Counterblast, Dark, Dibasic, Diehard, Diels-Adler, Dinosaur, Double-take, Dounreay, Exoergic, Falange, Fast(-breeder), Feedback, Fission, Flareback, Flehmen, Furnace, Fusion, Gas-cooled, Graphite, Gut, Heavy-water, Hydrolysis, Imine, Incomplete, Insulin, Interplay, Junker, Kickback, Knee-jerk, Light, Magnox, Neanderthal, Nuclear, Outcry, Oxidation, Pebble-bed, Photolysis, Pile, Poujade,

Pressure-tube, Pressurized water, Reciprocate, Recoil, Redox, Repercussion, Respond, Reversible, Rigid, Sensitive, Solvolysis, Spallation, Sprocket, Swing-back, Thermal, Thermonuclear, Tokamak, Topochemistry, Ultraconservative, Vaccinia, Wassermann, Water

▷ **Reactionary** *may indicate* reversed or an anagram

Read(ing) Bearing, Browse, Decipher, Decode, Exegesis, First, Grind, Grounden, Haftarah, Haphtarah, Haphtorah, Interpret, Learn, Lection, Lesson, Lu, Maftir, Maw, Paired, Pericope, Peruse, Pore, Rad, Rennet-bag, Scan, Second, See, Skim, Solve, Speed, Stomach, → **STUDY**, Third, Vell, Ycond

Reader(s) ABC, Academic, Alidad(e), Bookworm, Document, Editor, Epistoler, Homeridae, Lay, Lector, Primer, Silas Wegg, Tape, Taster

Readiest, Readily, Readiness, Ready Alacrity, Alamain, Alert, Amber, Apt, Atrip, Available, Boun, Bound, Brass, Cash, Conditional, Dough, Eager, Early, Eftest, Fettle, Fit, Forward, Game, Geared-up, Gelt, Go, Keyed, Latent, Lolly, Masterman, Money, On, Predy, Prepared, Present, Prest, Primed, Prompt, Promptitude, Reckoner, Ripe, Running costs, Set, Soon, Spot, Turnkey, Usable, Wherewithal, Willing, Yare, Yark

Readjust Mend, Regulate, Retrue

Readymade Bought, Precast, Prepared, Prêt-à-porter, Slops, Stock, Store

Reagent Analytical, Grignard, Ninhydrin, Reactor, Schiff's, Titrant

Real, Reality, Realities, Really Actual, Augmented, Bona-fide, Brass tacks, Coin, Deed, De facto, Dinkum, Dinky-di(e), Earnest, Echt, Ens, Entia, Entity, Essence, → **GENUINE**, Honest, Indeed, Mackay, McCoy, McKoy, Naive, Ontic, Positive, Quite, Royal, Simon Pure, Sooth, Sterling, Straight up, Substantial, Tangible, Tennis, Thingliness, True, Verismo, Verity, Very, Virtual

Realgar Rosaker, Zarnec, Zarnich

Realise, Realisation, Realism, Realistic Achieve, Attain, Attuite, Cash, Dirty, Down-to-earth, Embody, Encash, Fetch, Fruition, Fulfil, Learn, Lifelike, Magic, Naive, Practical, Pragmatism, Sell, Sense, Socialist, Suss, Understand, Verité

▷ **Realities, Reality** *see* **REAL**

Realm Domain, Dominion, Field, Kingdom, Land, Notogaea, Region, Special(i)ty, UK

Ream Bore, Foam, Froth, Paper, Printer's, Rime, Screed

Reap(er) Binder, Crop, Death, Earn, Gather, Glean, Harvest, Scythe, Shear, Sickleman, Solitary, Stibbler

Reappear(ance) Emersion, Materialise, Recrudesce

Rear(ing) Aft, Back(side), Background, Baft, Behind, Breeches, Bring-up, Bunt, Cabré, Catastrophe, Derrière, Empennage, Foster, Haunch, Hind, Hindquarters, Loo, Natch, Nousell, Nurture, Prat, → **RAISE**, Serafile, Serrefile, Stern, Tonneau

Rearmament Moral

Rearrange(ment) Adjust, Anagram, Ectopia, Permute, Reorder

Reason(able), Reasoning A fortiori, Analytical, Apagoge, A priori, Argue, Argument, Basis, Call, Casuistry, Cause, Colour, Consideration, Deduce, Economical, Expostulate, Fair, Ground(s), Hypophora, Ijtihad, Inductive, Intelligent, Ipso facto, Justification, Logic, Logical, Logistics, Logos, Metamathematics, Mind, Moderate, Motive, Noesis, Petitio principii, Plausible, Point, Practical, Pretext, Pro, Proof, Pure, Purpose, Ratiocinate, Rational(e), Sanity, Sense, Sensible, Settler, Syllogism, Synthesis, Temperate, Think, Why, Wit

Reave Despoil, Reif, Rob, Spoil

Rebate Diminish, Lessen, Refund, Repayment

Rebecca Sharp

Rebel(s), Rebellion, Rebellious Aginner, Apostate, Arian, Beatnik, Bolshy, Boxer, Cade, Contra, Croppy, Danton, Defiance, Diehard, Disobedient, Emeute, Fifteen, Forty-five, Frondeur, Glendower, Green Mountain Boys, Hampden, Hereward the Wake, Iconoclast, Insurgent, Insurrection, IRA, Jacobite, Jacquerie, Kick, Luddite, Mutine(er), Mutiny, Oates, Pilgrimage of Grace, Putsch, Rebecca, Recalcitrant, Recusant, Reluct, Resist, → REVOLT, Rise, Rum, Scofflaw, Sedition, Sepoy, Spartacus, Steelboy, Straw, Taiping, Ted, Titanism, Tyler, Venner, Warbeck, Wat Tyler, Whiteboy, Zealot

▷ **Rebellious** *may indicate* a word reversed

Rebirth Palingenesis, Reincarnation, Renaissance, Revival, Samsara

Rebound Backfire, Bounce, Cannon, Elastic, Recoil, Repercussion, Ricochet, Snapback

Rebuff Check, Cold-shoulder, Noser, Quelch, Repulse, Retort, Rubber, Setdown, Sneb, Snib, Snub

Rebuke Admonish, Berate, Check, Chide, Earful, Lecture, Neb, Objurgate, Rap, Rate, Razz, Reprimand, Reproof, Reprove, Rollick, Scold, Score, Slap, Slate, Snib, Snub, Strop, Threap, Threep, Tick off, Trim, Tut, Upbraid, Wig

Rebut Disprove, Refute, Repulse, Retreat

Recalcitrant Mulish, Obstinate, Renitent, Unruly, Wilful

Recall(ing) Annul, Echo, Eidetic, Encore, Evocative, Partial, Reclaim, Recollect, Redolent, Remember, Remind, Reminisce, Repeal, Retrace, Revoke, Total, Unsay, Withdraw

Recant(ation) Disclaim, Palinode, Retract, Revoke

Recap(itulate), Recapitulation Epanodos, Summarise

Recapture Rescue

▷ **Recast** *may indicate* an anagram

▶ **Recce** *see* RECONNAISSANCE

Recede Decline, Ebb, Lessen, Regress, Retrograde, Shrink, Withdraw

Receipt(s) Acknowledge, Chit, Docket, Quittance, Recipe, Revenue, Take, Voucher

Receive(d), Receiver Accept, Accoil, Admit, Aerial, Antenna, Assignee, Bailee, Bleeper, Dipole, Dish, Donee, Ear, Fence, Get, Grantee, Greet, Hydrophone, Inherit, Intercom, Official, Pernancy, Phone, Pocket, Radio, Reset, Responser, Responsor, Roger, Set, Sounder, Take, Tap, Transistor, Transponder, Wide

Recent(ly) Alate, Current, Fresh, Hot, Just, Late, Low, Modern, New, Yesterday, Yestereve, Yesterweek

Receptacle Ash-tray, Basket, Bin, Bowl, Box, Chrismatory, Ciborium, Container, Cyst, Hell-box, Locket, Loom, Monstrance, Receiver, Reliquary, Relique, Reservatory, Sacculus, Spermatheca, Tank, Thalamus, Tidy, Tore, Torus, Trash can

Reception, Receptive Accoil, At home, Bel-accoyle, Couchée, Court, Durbar, Entertainment, Greeting, Helpdesk, Infare, Kursaal, Levée, Open, Ovation, Pervious, Ruelle, Saloon, Sensory, Soirée, Superheterodyne, Teleasthetic, Warm, Welcome

Receptor(s) Metabotropic, Steroid

Recess(ion) Alcove, Antrum, Apse, Apsidal, Apsis, Bay, Bole, Bower, Break, Closet, Columbarium, Corner, Corrie, Cove, Croze, Dinette, Ebb, Embrasure, Exedra, Fireplace, Grotto, Hitch, Inglenook, Interval, Loculus, Mortise, → NICHE, Nook, Oriel, Outshot, Rabbet, Rebate, Respite, Rest, Slump, Withdrawal

▷ **Recess** *may indicate* 'reversed'

Rechabite TT

Réchauffé Hachis, Hash, Salmi

Recidivist Relapser

▷ **Recidivist** *may indicate* 'reversed'
Recipe Dish, Formula, Prescription, R, Receipt, Take
Recipient Assignee, Beneficiary, Disponee, Grantee, Heir, Legatee, Receiver, Suscipient
Reciprocal, Reciprocate Corresponding, Elastance, Exchange, Inter(act), Mutual, Repay, Return
Recite(r), Recital, Recitation(ist) Ave, Concert, Declaim, Diseuse, Enumerate, Incantation, Litany, Monologue, Mystic, Parlando, Quote, Reading, Reel, Relate, Rhapsode, Say, Sing, Tell
Reckless(ness) Blindfold, Careless, Catiline, Desperado, Desperate, Devil-may-care, Gadarene, Harum-scarum, Hasty, Headfirst, Headlong, Hell-bent, Irresponsible, Madcap, Perdu(e), Ramstam, Rantipole, → **RASH**, Slapdash, Temerity, Ton-up, Wanton, Wildcat
▷ **Reckless** *may indicate* an anagram
Reckon(ing) Assess, Bet, Calculate, Cast, Census, Computer, Consider, Count, Date, Doomsday, Estimate, Fancy, Figure, Guess, Number, Rate, Settlement, Shot, Tab
Reclaim(ed), Reclamation Assart, Empolder, Impolder, Innings, Novalia, Polder, Recover, Redeem, Restore, Swidden, Tame, Thwaite
Recline, Reclining Accubation, Accumbent, Lean, Lie, Lounge, Rest
Recluse Anchor(et), Anchorite, Ancress, Eremite, Hermit, Solitaire
Recognise(d), Recognition Accept, Acknow(ledge), Admit, Anagnorisis, Appreciate, Ascetic, Character, Cit(ation), Exequatur, Gaydar, Identify, Isolated, Ken, → **KNOW**, Nod, Notice, Oust, Own, Reward, Salute, Scent, Standard, Sung, Voice, Weet, Wot
Recoil Backlash, Bounce, Kick(back), Quail, Rebound, Redound, Repercussion, Resile, Reverberate, Shrink, Shy, Spring, Start, Whiplash
Recollect(ion) Anamnesis, Memory, Pelmanism, Recall, → **REMEMBER**, Reminisce
▷ **Recollection** *may indicate* an anagram
Recommend(ation) Advise, Advocate, Counsel, Direct, Endorse, Exhort, Nap, Praise, Promote, Rider, Suggest, Testimonial, Tip, Tout
Recompense Cognisance, Deodand, Deserts, Expiate, Guerdon, Pay, Remunerate, Repayment, Requite, Restitution, Reward
Reconcile(d) Adapt, Adjust, Affrended, Atone, Harmonise, Henotic, Make up, Mend
Recondite Difficult, Esoteric, Mystic, Obscure, Occult, Profound
Reconnaissance, Reconnoitre Case, Investigate, Recce, Scout, Survey
Reconstitute, Reconstitution Diagenesis
Reconstruction Perestroika
Record(er), Record company, Recording Album, Ampex, Analogue, Annal(ist), Archive, Archivist, Audit trail, Aulos, Bench-mark, Black box, Blue Riband, Book, Campbell-Stokes, Can, Cardiograph, Cartulary, Casebook, CD, Chart, Chronicle, Clickstream, Clock, Clog-almanac, Coat(e), Congressional, Daybook, Diary, Dictaphone®, Dictograph®, Digital, Disc, Document, Dossier, Eloge, Elpee, EMI, Endorsement, English flute, Enter, Entry, EP, Ephemeris, Estreat, Ever, Filater, File, Film, Flight, Flute, Form, Forty-five, Ghetto blaster, Gram, Gramophone, Hansard, Helical scan, Hierogrammat, History, Hologram, Incremental, Indie, Journal, Lap-chart, Ledger, List, Log, Logbook, LP, Marigram, Mark, Maxi-single, Memento, Memo(randum), Memoir, Memorial, Memorise, Meter, Mind, Minute, Mono, Noctuary, Notate, Notch, Note, Odometer, Oscillogram, Pass book, Platter, Playback, Practic(k), Pratique, Pressing, Previous, Protocol, Public, Quadrophonics, Quipo, Quipu, Quote, Rapsheet, Rec, Reel-to-reel, Regest, Register, Release,

Remembrancer, Roll, Score(board), Set down, Seven-inch, Seventy-eight, Shellac,
Single, Spectogram, Sphygmogram, Spirogram, Stenotype®, Studbook, Sunshine,
Tachograph, Tally, Tallyman, Tape, Thirty-three, TiVo®, Toast, Trace, Track,
Transcript, Travelog, Trip, Twelve-inch, VERA, Vid(eo), Videotape, Vote, Wax,
Wire, Wisden, Worksheet, Write
Record-holder Champion, Sleeve
Record-player DJ, Stereo
Recount Describe, Enumerate, → **NARRATE**, Relate, Tell
Recourse Access, Resort
Recover(y) Amend, Clawback, Comeback, Common, Convalescence, Cure, Dead cat
bounce, Get over, Lysis, Over, Perk, Pull through, Rally, Rebound, Reclaim, Recoup,
Redeem, Regain, Rehab, Repaint, Replevin, Replevy, Repo(ssess), Rescript, Rescue,
Resile, → **RETRIEVE**, Revanche, Salvage, Salve, Second-wind, Spontaneous,
Upswing, Upturn
Recreate, Recreation Diversion, Hobby, Palingenesia, Pastime, Play, Revive, Sport
Recriminate, Recrimination Ruction
Recruit(s) Attestor, Bezonian, Choco, Conscript, Crimp, Draft, Employ, Engage,
Enlist, Enrol, Headhunt, Intake, Muster, Nignog, Nozzer, Press, Rookie, Sprog,
Volunteer, Wart, Yardbird, Yobbo
Rectangle, Rectangular Golden, Matrix, Oblong, Quad, Quadrate, Square
Rectifier, Rectify Adjust, Amend, Dephlegmate, Redress, Regulate, → **REMEDY**,
Right, Silicon
Recto Ro
Rector R
Rectum Tewel
Recuperate Convalesce, Rally, Recover
Recur(rent), Recurring Chronic, Quartan, Quintan, Recrudesce, Repeated,
Repetend, Return
▷ **Recurrent** *may indicate* 'reversed'
Recycler, Recycling Freegan
Red(den), Redness Admiral, Alizarin, Angry, Archil, Arun, Ashamed, Auburn, Beet,
Bilirubin, Blush, Bolshevik, Brick, Burgundy, C, Cain-coloured, Carmine, Carroty,
Castory, Cent, Cerise, Cherry, Chica, Chinese, Choy-root, Chrome, Cinnabar, Claret,
Coccineous, Commo, Communist, Congo, Copper, Coquelicot, Coral, Corallin(e),
Corkir, Cramesy, Cremosin, Crimson, Crocoite, Cuprite, Cyanin, Damask, Debit,
Dubonnet, Duster, Embarrassed, Eosin, Eric, Erik, Erythema, Ffion, Flame,
Flaming, Florid, Flush, Foxy, Garnet, Geranium, Ginger, Gory, Grog-blossom,
Gule(s), Guly, Hat, Henna, Herring, Incarnadine, Indian, Indigo, Inflamed,
Infra, Inner, Intertrigo, Iron, Jacqueminot, Keel, Kermes, Korkir, Lac-lake, Lake,
Lateritious, Left(y), Lenin, Letter, Magenta, Maoist, Maroon, Marxist, McIntosh,
Menshevik, Miniate, Minium, Modena, Mulberry, Murrey, Neaten, Orchel,
Orchilla-weed, Orseille, Oxblood, Phenol, Pillar-box, Pinko, Plethoric, Plum,
Pompeian, Ponceau, Poppy, Pyrrhous, Raddle, Radical, Raspberry, Raw, Realgar,
Rhodamine, Rhodopsin, Ridinghood, Roan, Rosaker, Rose, Rot, Rouge, Roy,
Rubefy, Rubella, Rubescent, Rubicund, Rubric, Ruby, Ruddle, Ruddy, Rufescent,
Rufus, Russ(e), Russet, Russian, Rust(y), Rutilant, Sang-de-boeuf, Sanguine,
Santalin, Sard, Scarlet, Sericon, Setter, Solferino, Stammel, Tape, Tidy, Tile, Titian,
Trot, Trotsky, Turacin, Turkey, Tyrian, Venetian, Vermeil, Vermilion, Vermily,
Vinaceous, Wallflower, Wine
▷ **Red** *may indicate* an anagram
Redcoat Rust, Soldier

Redeem(er), Redemption Cross, Liberate, Mathurin, Messiah, Ransom, Retrieve, Salvation, Save
Red-faced Coaita, Florid, Flushed
Red-head Auburn, Blue(y), Carroty, Commissar, Mao, Rufus
Red herring Soldier
▶ **Red Indian** *see* NORTH AMERICAN INDIAN
Redirect Sublimate
▷ **Rediscovered** *may indicate* an anagram
Redolent Aromatic, Fragrant, Reeking, Suggestive
Redoubtable Stalwart
Redress Amends, Offset, Recompense, Rectify, Regrate, Remedy, Right
Redshank Gambet, Totanus
Redskin Indian, Tomato
Red spot Tika
Reduce(r), Reduced, Reduction Abatement, Allay, Alleviate, Amortize, Attenuate, Bate, Beggar, Beneficiate, Clip, Commute, Condense, Contract, Cut, Cutback, Damping, Debase, Decimate, Decrease, Decrement, Demote, Deoxidate, Deplete, Depreciation, Detract, Devalue, Diminish, Diminuendo, Discount, Downgrade, Downsize, Draw-down, Epitomise, Foreshorten, Grind, Hatchet job, Jeff, Kinone, → LESSEN, Lite, Markdown, Mitigate, Moderate, Palliate, Pot, Pulp, Put, Quinol, Razee, Remission, Retrench, Rundown, Scant, Shade, Shorten, Shrinkage, Slash, Strain, Taper, Telescope, Thin, Weaken, Write-off
Redundancy, Redundant Frill, Futile, Needless, Otiose, Pink slip, Pleonasm, Superfluous, Surplus
Redwood Amboyna, Mahogany, Sanders, Wellingtonia
Reed Arundinaceous, Broken, Calamus, Free, Oboe, Papyrus, Pipe, Quill, Raupo, Rush, Sedge, Seg, Sley, Spear, Sudd, Syrinx, Thatch, Twill, Whistle
Reef Atoll, Barrier, Bioherm, Bombora, Bommie, Cay, Coral, Fringing, Great Barrier, Key, Knot, Lido, Motu, Saddle, Sca(u)r, Skerry, Witwatersrand
Reefer Cigarette, Jacket, Joint
Reek Emit, Exude, Stink
Reel Bobbin, Dance, Eightsome, Hoolachan, Hoolican, Lurch, Multiplier, News, Pirn, Spin, Spool, Stagger, Strathspey, Sway, Swift, Swim, Totter, Virgina, Wheel, Whirl, Wintle
Refectory Frater
Refer Advert, Allude, Assign, Cite, Direct, Mention, Pertain, Relate, Remit, Renvoi, Renvoy, See, Submit, Touch, Trade
Referee Arbiter, Commissaire, Mediate, Oddsman, Official, Ref, Umpire, Voucher, Whistler, Zebra
Reference Allusion, Apropos, Biaxal, Character, Coat, Grid, Index, Innuendo, Mention, Passion, Quote, Regard, Renvoi, Respect, Retrospect, Testimonial, Vide
Referendum Mandate, Plebiscite, Vox populi
Refill Replenish
Refine(d), Refinement, Refiner(y) Alembicated, Attic, Catcracker, Couth, Cultivate, Culture, Distinction, Elaborate, Elegance, Exility, Exquisite, Genteel, Grace, Nice, Nicety, Polish(ed), Polite, Précieuse, Pure, Rare(fy), Recherché, Saltern, Sieve, Sift, Smelt, Sophisticated, Spirituel, Sublimate, Subtilise, Tasteful, Try, U, Urbane, Veneer
Reflect(ing), Reflection, Reflective, Reflector Albedo, Blame, Catoptric, Cat's eye®, Chaff, Chew, Cogitate, → CONSIDER, Echo, Glass, Glint, Image, Meditate, Mirror, Muse, Nonspecular, Ponder, Redound, Repercuss, Ricochet, Ruminate,

Spectacular, Speculum, Symmetrical, Tapetum, Thought
Reflex Achilles, Babinski, Bent, Cancrizans, Knee-jerk, Patellar, Pavlovian,
Re-entrant, Single-lens, Tic, Twin-lens
Reform(er) Amend, Apostle, Beveridge, Bloomer, Calvin, Chartism, Chastise,
Correct, Enrage, Fourier, Fry, Gandhi, Gradualism, Howard, Hussite, Improve,
Knox, Land, Lollard, Luther, Meiji, Melanchthon, Mend, Mucker, New Deal,
Owenite, Pietism, PR, Progressionist, Protestant, Proudhon, Puritan, Rad(ical),
Really, Recast, Reclaim, Reconstruction, Rectify, Regenerate, Resipiscence, Ruskin,
Satyagraha, Savonarola, Syncretise, Tariff, Transmute, Tyndale, Wycliffe, Young
Turk, Zwingli
▷ **Reform(ed)** *may indicate* an anagram
Reformatory Borstal, Magdalen(e)
Refract(ion), Refractive, Refractor(y) Anaclastic, Double, Firestone, Obstinate,
Perverse, Prism, Recalcitrant, Refringe, Restive, Stubborn, Sullen, Wayward
Refrain Abstain, Alay, Avoid, Bob, Burden, Chorus, Desist, Epistrophe, Fa-la,
Forbear, Hemistich, Mantra, O(v)erword, Repetend, Ritornello, Rumbelow,
Rum(p)ti-iddity, Rum-ti-tum, Spare, Tag, Tirra-lirra, Tirra-lyra, Turn again,
Undersong, Waive, Wheel
Refresh(ment), Refresher Air, Bait, Be(a)vers, Buffet, Cheer, Elevenses, Enliven,
Food, Four-hours, Nap, New, Nourishment, Purvey, Refection, Reflect, Refocillate,
Reinvigorate, Renew, Repast, Restore, Revive, Seltzer, Shire, Slake, Water
Refrigerator Chill, Chiller, Cooler, Deep freeze, Esky®, Freezer, Freon, Fridge,
Ice-box, Minibar, Reefer
Refuge Abri, Ark, Asylum, Bolthole, Burrow, Dive, Fastness, Funkhole, Girth, Grith,
Harbour, Haven, Hideaway, Hole, Holt, Home, Hospice, Oasis, Port, Reefer, Resort,
Retreat, Sanctuary, Sheet-anchor, → **SHELTER**, Soil, Stronghold, Women's
Refugee(s) Boat people, DP, Economic, Escapist, Fugitive, Grenzganger, Huguenot,
Reffo
Refund Clawback, Repayment
▷ **Refurbished** *may indicate* an anagram
Refusal, Refuse Attle, Bagasse, Ba(u)lk, Bilge, Bin, Black, Blackball, Boycott, Bran,
Brash, Breeze, Brock, Bull, Bunkum, Cane-trash, Chaff, Clap-trap, Crane, Crap,
Cul(t)ch, Debris, Decline, Denay, Deny, Disown, Draff, Drivel, Dross, Dunder, Dung,
Eighty-six, Fag-end, Fenks, Fiddlesticks, Finks, First, Flock, Frass, Garbage, Gob,
Guff, Hards, Hogwash, Hold-out, Hurds, Husk, Interdict, Jews' houses, Jews'
leavings, Jib, Junk, Knickknackery, Knub, Lay-stall, Leavings, Litter, Lumber,
Mahmal, Marc, Megass(e), Midden, Mullock, Mush, Nay(-say), Nill, No, Noser,
Nould, Nub, Offal, Off-scum, Orts, Pellet, Pigwash, Potale, Punk, Radwaste,
Raffle, Rape(cake), Rat(s), Rebuff, Recrement, Recusance, Red(d), Redargue,
Redline, Reest, Regret, Reneg(u)e, Renig, Rot, → **RUBBISH**, Ruderal, Scaff, Scrap,
Scree, Screenings, Scum, Sewage, Shant, Shell heap, Slag, Sordes, Spurn, Sullage,
Sweepings, Swill, Tinpot, Tip, Toom, Tosh, Trade, Trash, Tripe, Trock, Troke,
Trumpery, Turndown, Twaddle, Unsay, Utter, Wash, Waste, Wastrel
▷ **Re-fused** *may indicate* an anagram
Refutation, Refute Deny, Disprove, Elench(us), Rebut, Redargue, Refel
Regain Recoup, Recover, Revanche
▶ **Regal** *see* **ROYAL**
Regalia → **CIGAR**, Mound, Orb, Sceptre
Regard(ing) Anent, As to, Attention, Care, Consider, → **ESTEEM**, Eye, Gaum, Look,
Observe, Odour, Pace, Rate, Re, Repute, Respect, Revere, Sake, Steem, Value,
Vis-à-vis

Regardless Despite, Heedless, Irrespective, Notwithstanding, Rash, Though, Uncaring, Unmindful, Willy-nilly
Regatta Head of the river, Henley
Regenerate Restore
Regent Interrex, Ruler, Viceroy
Regent's Park Zoo
Reggae Ska
Regicide Ireton, Macbeth
Regime(n) Administration, Control, Diet(etics), Method, Reich
Regiment Black Watch, Buffs, Colour(s), Discipline, Greys, Ironsides, Lifeguard, Marching, Monstrous, Nutcrackers, Organise, RA, RE, REME, Rifle, Royals, → SAS, Tercio, Tertia
▷ **Regiment** *may indicate* an anagram
Region Aceh, Alsace, Alsatia, Amhara, Arctogaea, → AREA, Asir, Asturias, Belt, Borders, Brie, Brittany, Bundu, Calabria, Camargue, Cappadocia, Caria, Cariboo, Carniola, Carnnatic, Catalonia, Caucasia, Central, Chald(a)ea, Champagne-Ardenne, Chiasma, Cilicia, Circassia, Climate, Clime, Constantia, Critical, D, Dacia, District, E, Ecosphere, End, F, Guiana, Hinterland, Holarctic, Hundred, Illyria, Ionia, Kashmir, Katanga, Lacustrine, Lothian, Low Countries, Lusitania, Lycia, Lydia, Macao, Macedonia, Maghreb, Manchuria, Mascon, Masuria, Matabeleland, Mauretania, Mecklenburg, Mesopotamia, Midi, Molise, Moravia, Murcia, Mysia, Namaqualand, Negeb, Negev, Nejd, Neogaea, New Castile, New Quebec, Nubia, Nuristan, Offing, Ogaden, Old Castile, Opher, Oriental, Ossetia, Oudh, Pannonia, Pargana, Part, Pergunnah, Persis, Piedmont, Province, Quart(er), Realm, Refugium, Rhizosphere, Ruthenia, Sarmatia, Scythia, Sector, Sogdiana, Stannery, Strathclyde, Subtopia, Sumer, Tagma, Tayside, Territory, Tetrarchate, Thessaly, Thrace, Thule, Tibet, Tigray, Tigré, Tract, Transcaucasia, Transdniestria, Transylvania, Troas, Tundra, Turkestan, Turkistan, Tuscany, Ultima Thule, Umbria, Ungava, Val d'Aosta, Valois, Variable, Vaud, Veneto, Vojvodina, Vuelta Abajo, Weald, Zone, Zululand
Register(ing), Registration, Registry Actuarial, Almanac, Annal, Cadastral, Cadastre, Calendar, Cartulary, Cash, Census, Check-in, Child abuse, Dawn, Diptych, Docket, Enlist, Enrol, Enter, Flag out, Gross, Handicap, Index, Indicate, Inscribe, Inventory, Land, Ledger, List, Lloyd's, Log, Matricula, Menology, NAI, Net, Note, Notitia, Obituary, Parish, Park, Patent, Poll, Quotation, Read, Record, Reg(g)o, Rent-roll, Roll, Roule, Score, Shift(ing), Ship's, Sink in, Soprano, Terrier, Voice
Registrar Actuary, Greffier, Medical, Protocolist, Recorder, Specialist, Surgical
Regress(ion) Backslide, Recidivism, Revert
Regret(ful), Regrettable Alack, Alas, Apologise, Bemoan, Deplore, Deprecate, Ewhow, Forthwink, Ichabod, Lackaday, Lament, Mourn, Otis, Pity, Remorse, Repentance, Repine, Resent, Rew, → RUE, Ruth, Sorrow, Tragic
Regular(ity), Regularly Clockwork, Constant, Custom, Episodic, Even, Giusto, Goer, Habitual, Habitué, Hourly, Insider, Methodic, Nine-to-five, Normal, Often, Orderly, Orthodox, Patron, Peloria, Periodic, Rhythmic, Routine, Set, Smooth, → STANDARD, Stated, Statutory, Steady, Strict, Symmetric, Uniform, Usual, Yearly
Regulate, Regulation, Regulator Adjust, Appestat, Bye-law, Code, Control, Correction, Curfew, Customary, Direct, Gibberellin, Governor, Guide, King's, Logistics, Metrostyle, Order, Ordinance, Police, Queen's, Rule, Snail, Square, Standard, Statute, Stickle, Stopcock, Sumptuary, Thermostat, Valve
Regulus Matte

Regurgitation Trophallaxis
Rehab(ilitate), Rehabilitation AA, Cure, Orthotics, Physio(therapy), Repone
Rehearsal, Rehearse Band-call, Dress, Drill, Dry-block, Dry-run, Dummy-run,
Practice, Practise, Preview, Recite, Repeat, Run through, Trial, Walk through
Reichenbach Falls, Od
Reign Era, Govern, Meiji, Prevail, Raine, Realm, Restoration, → RULE
Reimburse(ment) Indemnity, Recoup, Redress, Repay
Rein(s) Bearing, Check, Control, Curb, Free, Gag, Leading strings, Long, Lumbar,
Restrain, Safety, Tame, Tight
Reindeer Blitzen, Caribou, Comet, Cupid, Dancer, Dasher, Donner, Moss, Prancer,
Rudolf, Tarand, Vixen
Reinforce(ment) Aid, Augment, Beef up, Bolster, Boost, Brace, Buttress, Cleat,
Counterfort, Line, Negative, Partial, Plash, Pleach, Positive, Recruit, Reserve,
→ STRENGTHEN, Support, Tetrapod, Underline
Reinstate Repone
Reinvigorate Recruit
Reiterate(d), Reiteration Battology, Emphasize, Ostinato, Plug, → REPEAT
Reject(ion) Abhor, Abjure, Athetise, Bin, Blackball, Brush off, Cast, Cast off,
Deny, Dice, Disallow, Discard, Disclaim, Discount, Disdain, Disown, Diss, Elbow,
Eliminate, Export, Flout, Frass, Iconoclasm, Jettison, Jilt, Kest, Kill, Knock-back,
Ostracise, Oust, Outcast, Outtake, Pip, Plough, Rebuff, Recuse, Refuse, Reny,
Repel, Reprobate, Repudiate, Repulse, Scout, Scrub, Spet, Spike, Spin, Spit,
→ SPURN, Sputum, Thumbs-down, Turndown, Veto
Rejoice, Rejoicing Celebrate, Exult, Festivity, Gaude, Glory, Joy, Maffick, Sing
Rejoin(der), Rejoined Answer, Counter, Relide, Reply, Response, Retort, Reunite
Rejuvenation Shunamitism
Relapse Backslide, Deteriorate, Hypostrophe, Recidivism, Regress, Revert, Sink
Relate(d), Relation(ship), Relative Account, Affair, Affine, Affinity, Agnate,
Akin, Allied, Antibiosis, Appertain, Associate, Blood, Brer, Brisure, Causality,
Cognate, Commensal, Concern, Connection, Connexion, Consanguinity, Coosen,
Cousin, Coz, Deixis, Dependent, Dispersion, Eme, Enate, Equivalence, External,
False, Formula, German(e), Granny, Guanxi, Heterogeneous, Homologous,
Impart, Industrial, In-law, Internal, Item, Kin, Kinsman, Labour, Liaison, Link,
Love-hate, Mater, Material, Matrix, Mutualism, Narrative, Nooky, One-to-one,
Osculant, Pertain, Phratry, Pi, Plutonic, Poor, Predation, Privity, → PROPORTION,
Proxemics, Public, Race, Rapport, Rapprochement, Ratio, Reciprocity, Recite,
Recount, Rede, Refer(ence), Relevant, Respect(s), Saga, Sib(b), Sibbe, Sibling, Sine,
Sybbe, Symbiosis, Syntax, Tale, Tell, Who
Relating to Of
Relax(ation), Relaxant, Relaxed Abate, Atony, Autogenics, Calm, Chalone, Chill
out, Com(m)odo, Contrapposto, Dégagé, Détente, Diversion, Downbeat, Ease,
Easy-going, Flaccid, Gallamine, Icebreaker, Informal, Laid-back, Leisured, Lesh
states, Lighten, → LOOSEN, Mellow out, Mitigate, Outspan, Peace, Relent, Relief,
Remit, Rest, Settle, Slacken, Sleep, Slump, Toneless, Unbend, Unknit, Unrein,
Untie, Unwind, Veg out
▷ **Relaxed** *may indicate* an anagram
Relay(er) Convey, Medley, Race, Shift, Tell, Telstar, Torch-race, Webcast
▷ **Relay(ing)** *may indicate* an anagram
Release Abreact, Abrogation, Announcement, Bail, Block, Cable, Catharsis, Clear,
Day, Death, Deliver(y), Desorb, Disburden, Discharge, Disclose, Disengage,
Disimprison, Dismiss, Disorb, Emancipate, Enfree, Excuse, Exeem, Exeme,

Extricate, Exude, Free, Handout, Happy, → **LIBERATE**, Manumit, Merciful, Moksa, Nirvana, Parole, Press, Quietus, Quittance, Relinquish, Ripcord, Soft, Spring, Tre corde, Unconfine, Uncouple, Undo, Unhand, Unleash, Unloose, Unpen, Unshackle, Unsnap, Unteam, Untie

Relegate Banish, Consign, Demote, Exile, Marginalise, Sideline, Stellenbosch

Relent Bend, Mollify, Soften, Weaken, Yield

Relentless Cruel, Hard, Hardface, Indefatigable, Inexorable, Pitiless, Rigorous, Stern

Relevance, Relevant Ad rem, Applicable, Apposite, Apropos, Apt, Bearing, Germane, Material, Pertinent, Point, Valid

▶ **Reliable, Reliance** *see* **RELY**

Relic Antique, Ark, Artefact, Fly-in-amber, Fossil, Leftover, Memento, Neolith, Remains, Sangraal, Sangrail, Sangreal, Souvenir, Survival

Relict Survivor, Widow

Relief, Relieve(d) Aid, Air-lift, Allay, Allegeance, Alleviate, Alms, Anaglyph, Anastatic, Anodyne, Assistance, Assuage, Bas, Beet, Beste(a)d, Bete, Cameo, Cavo-relievo, Comfort, Cure, Détente, Ease(ment), Emboss, Emollient, Free, Grisaille, High, Indoor, Let-up, Lighten, Linocut, Low, Lucknow, Mafeking, On the parish, Outdoor, Palliate, Phew, Photo, Pog(e)y, Reassure, Redress, Remedy, Replacement, Repoussé, Reprieve, → **RESCUE**, Respite, Retirement, Rid, Spare, Spell, Stand-in, Stiacciato, Succour, Taper, Tax, Thermoform, Tondo, Toreutics, Wheugh, Whew, Woodcut

Religion, Religious (sect) Animism, Baha'i, Biblist, Bogomil, Brahmanism, Buddhism, Camaldolite, Cargo cult, Carthusian, Celestine, Christadelphian, Christianity, Cistercian, Coenobite, Confucianism, Congregant, Creed, Culdee, Denomination, Devout, Din, Doctrine, Druse, Druz(e), Faith, Falun Gong, Familist, Gilbertine, Gnosticism, God-squad, Gueber, Guebre, Hadith, Hare Krishna, Has(s)id, Hieratic, Hospital(l)er, Ignorantine, Islam, Ismaili, Jain(a), Jansenism, Jehovah's Witness, Jesuit, Jewry, Judaism, Khalsa, Lamaism, Loyola, Lutheran, Macumba, Mahatma, Manichee, Maoism, Mazdaism, Mazdeism, Missionary, Missioner, Mithraism, Moony, Mormonism, New Light, Nun, Oblate, Opium, Orphism, Pagan, Pantheist, Parseeism, Parsism, Pi, Piarist, Pietà, Postulant, Premonstratensian, Progressive, Rastafarian, Reformation, Resurrectionist, Revealed, Revivalism, Ryobu Shinto, Sabbatarian, Sabian, Sacramentarian, Santeria, Scientology®, Serious, Shaker, Shamanism, Shango, Shiism, · Shinto(ism), Sikhism, Sodality, Solifidian, Sons of Freedom, Spike, State, Sunna, Swedenborgian, Taoism, Theatine, Theology, Tractarianism, Tsabian, Utraquist, Voodooism, Whore, Wicca, Zabian, Zarathustric, Zealous, Zend-Avesta, Zoroaster, Zwinglian

Religious book Bible, Koran, Missal, NT, OT, Sefer, Tantra, Targum, T(h)orah

Relinquish Abdicate, Cede, Demit, Discard, Drop, Forlend, Remise, Waive(r), Yield

Reliquary Chef, Encolpion, Encolpium, Simonious, Tope

Relish(ing) Aspic, Botargo, Catsup, Chakalaka, Chow-chow, Condiment, Enjoy, Flavour, Gentleman's, Gout, Gust(o), Ketchup, Lap(-up), Lust, Opsonium, Palate, Pesto, Piccalilli, Pickle, Sapid, Sar, Sauce, Savour, Seasoning, Tang, Tooth, Worcester sauce, Zest

Reluctant Averse, Backward, Chary, Circumspect, Cockshy, Grudging, Half-hearted, Laith, Loath, Loth, Nolition, Renitent, Shy, Under protest, Unwilling

Rely, Reliance, Reliant, Reliable Addiction, Authentic, Bank, Confidence, Constant, Copper-bottomed, → **COUNT**, Dependent, Found, Hope, Jeeves, Leal, Lean, Loyal, Mensch, Presume, Pukka, Rest, Robin, Safe, Secure, Solid, Sound,

Sponge, Stalwart , Stand-by, Staunch, Trustworthy, Trusty, Unfailing
Remain(s), Remainder, Remaining Abide, Ash(es), Balance, Bide, Continue,
Corse, Dreg(s), Dwell, Embers, Estate, Exuviae, Fag-end, Fossils, Kreng, Last, Late,
Lave, Left, Lie, Locorestive, Manet, Nose, Oddment, Orts, Other, Outstand, Persist,
Relic(ts), Reliquae, → **REMNANT**, Residue, Rest, Ruins, Scourings, Scraps, Stay,
Stick, Stub, Surplus, Survive, Tag-end, Talon, Tarry, Wait, Wreck(age)
Remark Aside, Barb, Bromide, Comment(ary), Descry, Dig, Epigram, Generalise,
Mention, Noise, → **NOTE**, Notice, Obiter dictum, Observe, Platitude, Pleasantry,
Reason, Sally, Shot, State
Remarkable, Remarkably Amazing, Arresting, Beauty, Bodacious, Come-on,
Conspicuous, Dilly, Egregious, Extraordinary, Heliozoan, Legendary, Lulu, Mirable,
Notable, Notendum, Noteworthy, Personal, Phenomenal, Rattling, → **SIGNAL**,
Singular, Some, Striking, Tall, Unco, Uncommon, Visible
Remedial, Remedy Adaptogen, Aid, An mo, Antacid, Antibiotic, Antidote,
Antiodontalgic, Antispasmodic, Arcanum, Arnica, Azoth, Bach®, Bach Flower®,
Basilicon, Calomel, Catholicon, Corrective, Cortisone, → **CURE**, Dinic, Drug,
Elixir, Febrifuge, Femiter, Feverfew, Fumitory, Ginseng, Heal, Ipecac, Leechdom,
Medicate, Medicine, Moxa, Nosode, Nostrum, Palliative, Panacea,
Panpharmacon, Paregoric, Poultice, Provisional, Rectify, Redress, Repair,
Rescue®, Salutory, Salve, Simillimum, Simple, Specific, Taraxacum, Therapeutic,
Tonga, Treatment, Tutsan
Remember(ing), Remembrance Bethink, Commemorate, Con, Mem, Memorial,
Memorise, Mention, Mneme, Recall, Recollect, Remind, Reminisce, Retain,
Rosemary, Souvenir
▷ **Remember** *may indicate* RE-member, viz. Sapper
Remind(er) Aftertaste, Aide-memoire, Bookmark, Evocatory, Evoke, Jog, Keepsake,
Mark, Memento, Memo, Mnemonic, Mnemotechnic, Monition, Nudge, Phylactery,
Prod, Prompt, Shades of, Souvenir, Token
Reminiscence(s), Reminiscent Ana, Evocative, Memory, Recall, Recollect,
Remember, Retrospect
Remiss Careless, Derelict, Lax, Lazy, Negligent, Tardy
Remission Abatement, Absolution, Acceptilation, Indulgence, Pardon, Pause,
Spontaneous
Remit Excuse, Forward, Pardon, Postpone
Remnant Butt, End, Fent, Heeltap, Leavings, Left-over, Odd-come-short, Offcut,
Relic, Relict, → **REMAINDER**, Rump, Trace, Vestige, Witness
Remonstrate Argue, Complain, Expostulate, Protest, Reproach
Remorse Angst, Ayenbite, Breast-beating, Compunction, Contrition, Had-i-wist,
Pity, → **REGRET**, Repentance, Rue, Ruing, Ruth, Sorrow, Worm
Remote Aloof, Aphelion, Back blocks, Backveld, Backwater, Backwood, Boondocks,
Bullamakanka, Bundu, → **DISTANT**, Far flung, Forane, Inapproachable, Insular,
Irrelevant, Jericho, Long(inquity), Out(part), Outback, Scrub, Secluded, Shut-out,
Slightest, Surrealistic, Unlikely, Withdrawn, Woop Woop, Wop-wops
Remount(s) Remuda
Removal, Remove(d) Abduct, Ablation, Abstract, Airbrush, Apocope, Asport,
Banish, Blot, Circumcision, Clear, Couch, Declassify, Dele(te), Depilate, Depose,
Deracinate, Detach, Detract, Dishelm, Dislodge, Disloign, Dispel, Doff, Efface,
Eject, Eloi(g)n, Emend, Eradicate, Erase, Esloyne, Estrange, Evacuate, Evict, Exalt,
Excise, Extirpate, Extradite, Extricate, Far, Flit, Huff, Nick, Raise, Raze, Razee,
Recuse, Redline, Remble, Rid, Scratch, Sequester, Shift, Spirit, Sublate, Subtract,
Supplant, Transfer, Transport, Unbelt, Unperson, Unseat, Uproot

Remuneration Pay, Return, Reward, Salary, Solde
Remus Uncle
Renaissance Awakening, Cinquecento, Early, High, Quattrocento, Revival
Rend Cleave, Harrow, Lacerate, Rip, Rive, Rupture, Tear
Render(ing) Construe, Deliver, Do, Gie, Give, Interpretation, Make, Melt,
    Pebble-dash, Plaster, Provide, Recite, Represent, Restore, Setting, Tallow, Try, Yeve
Rendezvous Date, Meeting, Philippi, Tryst, Venue
Rendition Account, Delivery, Interpretation, Translation, Version
René Descartes
Renegade, Renege, Renegue Apostate, Default, Defector, Deserter, Rat(ton),
    Recreant, Traitor, Turncoat, Weasel out
▷ **Renegade** *may indicate* a word reversal
Renew(al) Instauration, Neogenesis, Palingenesis, Refresh, Replace, Resumption,
    Retrace, Revival, Urban
Rennet Steep, Vell
Renounce, Renunciation Abandon, Abdicate, Abjure, Abnegate, Disclaim,
    Disown, For(e)go, For(e)say, Forfeit, Forisfamiliate, Forsake, Forswear, Kenosis,
    Outclaim, Quitclaim, Recede, Relinquish, Renay, Retract, Sacrifice
Renovate(d), Renovation Duff, Face-lift, Instauration, Makeover, Refurbish,
    Renew, Repair, Restore, Revamp, Touch up
Renown(ed) Fame, Glory, Illustrious, Kudos, Lustre, Notoriety, Prestige, Stardom
Rent(er), Renting Broken, Charge, Cornage, Cost, Crack, Cranny, Cuddeehih,
    Cuddy, Division, Economic, Fair, Farm, Fee, Fissure, Gale, Gavel, Ground, → HIRE,
    Lease, Let, List, Mail, Market, Occupy, Penny(-mail), Peppercorn, Quit-rent, Rack,
    Rip, Rived, Riven, Screed, Seat, Slit, Split, Stallage, Subtenant, Tare, Tenant, Tithe,
    Tore, Torn, Tythe, White
Reorganise Rationalise
▷ **Reorganised** *may indicate* an anagram
Reorientate Rabat
Repair(s), Repairer, Reparation Amend(s), Anaplasty, Assythment, Botch,
    Cobble, Damages, Darn, Doctor, Excision, Expiation, Fettle, Fitter, Fix, Go, Haro,
    Harrow, Jury rig, → MEND, Overhaul, Patch, Piece, Recompense, Redress, Refit,
    Reheel, Remedy, Renew, Renovate, Repoint, Resort, Restore, Retouch, Revamp,
    Roadworks, Running, Satisfaction, Stitch, Tenorrhaphy, Ulling, Vamp, Volery
Repartee Backchat, Badinage, Banter, Persiflage, Rejoinder, Retort, Riposte, Wit
Repast Bever, Collection, Food, Meal, Tea, Treat
Repay(ment) Avenge, Compensate, Quit, Refund, Requite, Retaliate, Reward,
    Satisfaction
Repeal Abrogate, Annul, Cancel, Rescind, Revoke
Repeat(ed), Repeatedly, Repetition, Repetitive Again, Alliteration, Anadiplosis,
    Anaphora, Ancora, Battology, Belch, Bis, Burden, Burp, Copy, Ditto(graphy), Do,
    Duplicate, → ECHO, Echolalia, Encore, Epanalepsis, Epistrophe, Epizeuxis, Eruct,
    Facsimile, Habitual, Harp, Image, Imitate, Ingeminate, Iterate, Iterum, Leit-motiv,
    Merism, Ostinato, Palillogy, Parrot, Parrot-fashion, Passion, Perpetuate, Playback,
    Polysyndeton, Recite(r), Redo, Refrain, Regurgitate, Reiterate, Renew, Rep,
    Repetend, Reprise, Rerun, Retail, Rondo, Rosalia, Rote, Same(y), Screed, Segno,
    Symploce, Tautology, Tautophony, Thrum, Trite, Verbigerate
Repel(lent) Estrange, Harsh, Offensive, Rebarbative, Reject, Repulse, Revolt,
    Squalid, Turn-off, Ug(h), Ward
Repent(ant), Repentance Metanoia, Penitent, Regret, Rue, Sackcloth, Yamim
    Nora'im

Repercussion Backlash, Backwash, Echo, Effect, Impact, Recoil
Repertoire, Repertory Company, Depot, Rep, Store
▷ **Repetition** *see* REPEAT
Replace(ment), Replaceable, Replacing Change, Deputise, Diadochy, For, Pre-empt, Prosthesis, Raincheck, Refill, Relief, Replenish, Restore, Stand-in, Substitute, Supersede, Supplant, Surrogate, Taxis, Transform, Transliterate, Understudy, Usurp
Replay Action, Instant, Iso(lated), Segno
Replenish Refill, Refresh, Revictual, Stock, Supply, Top
Replete, Repletion Awash, Full, Gorged, Plenitude, Plethora, Sated, Satiation
Replica Clone, Copy, Duplicate, Facsimile, Image, Repetition, Spit
Reply Accept, Answer, Churlish, Duply, Over, Rejoinder, Replication, Rescript, Response, Retort, Roger, Surrebut, Surrebutter, Surrejoin, Triply
Report(er) Account, Announce, Annual, Auricular, Bang, Beveridge, Blacksmith, Bruit, Bulletin, Cahier, Clap, Columnist, Comment, Commentator, Correspondent, Court, Cover, Crack, Crump, Cub, Debrief, Disclose, Dispatch, Dissertation, Explosion, Fame, Fireman, Grapevine, Hansard, Hearsay, Informant, Item, Jenkins, Journalist, Legman, Libel, News, Newshawk, Newshound, Newsman, Noise, Pop, Powwow, Pressman, Protocol, Rapporteur, Relate, Relay, Representation, Repute, Return, Roorback, Rumour, Sitrep, Sound(bite), Staffer, State(ment), Stringer, Tale, → TELL, Thesis, Transcribe, Tripehound, Troop, Update, Weather, Whang, Wolfenden, Write up
▷ **Reported** *may indicate* the sound of a letter or word
Repose Ease, Kaif, Kef, Kif, Lie, Lig, Peace, Relax, → REST, Serenity
Repository Archive, Ark, Cabinet, Container, Genizah, Reservoir, Sepulchre, Vault
Reprehend Blame, Censure, Criticise, Rebuke, Warn
Represent(ation), Representative, Represented Agent, Ambassador, Anaconic, Caricature, Client, Commercial, Cross-section, Delegate, Depict, Deputation, Describe, Display, Drawing, Drummer, Effigy, Elchee, Eltchi, Emblem, Embody, Emissary, Epitomise, Example, Figurative, Image, Instantiate, John Bull, Legate, Lobby, Map, Mimesis, Mouthpiece, MP, Personate, Personify, Portray, Proportional, Quintessence, Rep, Resemble, Salesman, Senator, Shop steward, Simulacrum, Spokesman, Stand-in, Status, Steward, Symbolic, Syndic, Tableau, Tiki, Transcription, Typical, Vakeel, Vakil, Vernicle
▷ **Represented** *may indicate* an anagram
Repress(ed) Check, Curb, Pent, Quell, Reprime, Sneap, Stifle, Stultify, Subjugate, Withhold
Reprieve Delay, Postpone, Relief, Respite
Reprimand Admonish, Bounce, Carpet, → CENSURE, Chew out, Chide, Dressing-down, Earful, Jobe, Lace, Lambast, Lecture, Rark up, Rating, Rebuke, Reproof, Rocket, Rollicking, Slate, Strafe, Targe, Tick off, Tongue-lashing, Wig
Reprint Copy, Paperback, Replica
Reprisal(s) Marque, Recaption, Retaliation, Revenge
Reproach Blame, Braid, Byword, Chide, Discredit, Dispraise, Exprobate, Gib, Mispraise, Odium, Opprobrium, Rebuke, Ronyon, Runnion, Scold, Shend, Sloan, Stigma, Taunt, Truant, Upbraid, Upcast, Yshend
Reprobate Cur, Lost soul, Outcast, Rascal, Scallywag, Scamp
Reprocess Re-make
Reproduce(r), Reproduction, Reproductive (organ) Amphimixis, Ape, Apomixis, Archegonium, Carpel, Clone, Copy, Counterfeit, Depict, Ectype, Edition, Etch, Eugenics, Gamogenesis, Gemmate, Homogenesis, Isospory, Loins,

Megaspore, Meristematic, Mono, Monogenesis, Monogony, Multiply, Oogamy, Ozalid®, Parthenogenesis, Phon(e)y, Pirate, Playback, Proliferate, Propagate, Pullulation, Refer, Replica, Roneo®, S(h)akti, Schizogony, Seminal, Simulate, Spermatia, Stereo, Strobilation, Syngamy, Syngenesis, Vegetative

▷ **Reproduce** *may indicate* an anagram

Reproof, Reprove Admonish, Berate, Chide, Correction, Correption, Lecture, Rate, Rebuff, Rebuke, Scold, Sloan, Take to task, Tut, Upbraid

Reptile, Reptilian Agamid, Alligarta, Alligator, Base, Basilisk, Caiman, Cayman, Chameleon, Chelonian, Creeper, Crocodile, Cynodont, Diapsid, Dicynodont, Dinosaur, Galliwasp, Goanna, Herpetology, Lacertine, Lizard, Mamba, Pelycosaur, Pteranodon, Pterodactyl, Rhynchocephalian, Sauroid, → SNAKE, Sphenodon, Squamata, Synapsid, Tegu(exin), Thecodont, Therapsid, Theriodontia, Tortoise, Tuatara, Tuatera, Turtle, Worm

Republic(s) Banana, Federal, Fifth, First, Fourth, People's, Second, State, Third, Weimar

---

REPUBLICS

1 letter:	Ghana	Ingush	Ecuador
R	Haiti	Israel	Estonia
	India	Kalmyk	Finland
3 letters:	Italy	Latvia	Georgia
RMM	Kenya	Malawi	Germany
UAR	Khmer	Mari-El	Hungary
USA	Libya	Mexico	Iceland
	Malta	Myanma	Ireland
4 letters:	Nauru	Panama	Jibouti
Chad	Niger	Poland	Kalmuck
Cuba	Palau	Rwanda	Kalmyck
Eire	Sakha	Serbia	Khakass
Fiji	Sudan	Turkey	Lebanon
Iran	Syria	Udmurt	Liberia
Iraq	Tatar	Uganda	Moldova
Komi	Yakut	Venice	Myanmar
Laos	Yemen	Zambia	Namibia
Mali	Zaire		Nigeria
Peru		*7 letters:*	Romania
Togo	*6 letters:*	Adharca	Senegal
Tuva	Adygai	Albania	Somalia
	Adygei	Algeria	Surinam
5 letters:	Angola	Andorra	Tunisia
Adhar	Bharat	Armenia	Ukraine
Altai	Biafra	Austria	Uruguay
Belau	Brazil	Bashkir	Vanuatu
Benin	Bukavu	Belarus	Vietnam
Chile	Buryat	Bolivia	Yakutia
China	France	Burundi	
Congo	Gambia	Chechen	*8 letters:*
Czech	Greece	Chuvash	Botswana
Egypt	Guinea	Comoros	Bulgaria
Gabon	Guyana	Croatia	Buryatia

Cambodia	**9 letters:**	Montenegro	South Vietnam
Cameroon	Argentina	Mordvinian	Turkmenistan
Chechnya	Badakshan	Mozambique	
Colombia	Cape Verde	North Korea	**13 letters:**
Dagestan	Costa Rica	North Yemen	Bashkortostan
Djibouti	Dominican	South Korea	North Ossetian
Dominica	Guatemala	South Yemen	
Esthonia	Indonesia	Tajikistan	**14 letters:**
Honduras	Kazakstan	Ubang-Shari	Czechoslovakia
Karelian	Lithuania	Uzbekistan	
Kiribati	Macedonia	Yugoslavia	**15 letters:**
Malagasy	Mauritius		Gorno-Badakhshan
Maldives	Nicaragua	**11 letters:**	Kabardino-Balkar
Moldavia	San Marino	Afghanistan	Marshall Islands
Mongolia	Singapore	Burkina-Faso	United Provinces
Pakistan	Venezuela	Byelorussia	
Paraguay		Cote d'Ivoire	**16 letters:**
Portugal	**10 letters:**	Nakhichevan	Congo-Brazzaville
Roumania	Azerbaijan	Philippines	Equatorial Guinea
Sinn Fein	Bangladesh	Sierra Leone	Karachai-Cherkess
Slovakia	Belarussia	South Africa	São Tomé e Príncipe
Slovenia	El Salvador	Soviet Union	
Sri Lanka	Gorno-Altai	Switzerland	**17 letters:**
Suriname	Kara-Kalpak	Tadjikistan	Bosnia-Herzegovina
Tanzania	Kazakhstan	West Germany	Mari El-
Zimbabwe	Kyrgyzstan		Nakhichevan
	Madagascar	**12 letters:**	Trinidad and
	Mauritania	Guinea-Bissau	Tobago

Republican Antimonarchist, Democrat, Fenian, Fianna Fáil, Girondist, GOP, International Brigade, IRA, Iraqi, Leveller, Montagnard, Mugwump, Plato, Red, Sansculotte, Sansculottic, Sinn Fein, Whig

Repudiate Abjure, Deny, Discard, Disclaim, Disown, Ignore, Recant, Reject, Renounce, Repel, Retract

Repugnance, Repugnant Abhorrent, Alien, Disgust, Distaste, Fulsome, Horror, Loathing, Nastiness, Revulsion

Repulsive, Repulse Creepy, Grooly, Lo(a)th, Off-putting, Rebuff, Rebut, Refel, Refuse, Repel, Repugnant, Slimy, Squalid, Ugly, Vile

Reputable, Reputation, Repute(d) Bubble, Dit, Estimate, Fame, Good, Izzat, Loos, Los, Name, Note, Notoriety, Odour, Opinion, Prestige, Putative, Regard, Renown, Said, Sar, → STANDING, Status, Stink, Stock, Trustworthy

Request Adjure, Appeal, Apply, Ask, Beg, Desire, D-notice, Entreaty, Invite, Petition, Plea, Prayer, Precatory, Solicit, Supplication

Requiem Agnus Dei, Mass

Require(d), Requirement Charge, Crave, De rigueur, Desire, Enjoin, Entail, Exact, Expect, Incumbent, Lack, Necessity, Need, Prerequisite, Sine qua non, Stipulate

Requisite, Requisition Commandeer, Due, Embargo, Essential, Indent, Necessary, Needful, Order, Press, Simplement

Rescind Abrogate, Annul, Recant, Remove, Repeal

Rescue Aid, Air-sea, Deliver, Free, Liberate, Ransom, Recover, Recower, Redeem, Regain, Relieve, Reprieve, Retrieve, Salvage, Salvation, → SAVE

Research(er) | 618

Research(er) Audience, Boffin, Delve, Dig, Enquiry, Explore, Fieldwork, Investigate, Legwork, Market, MORI, Motivation(al), Near-market, Operational, Pioneer, Psychical, Sus(s), Think-tank

Resell Scalp

Resemblance, Resemble, Resembling Affinity, Apatetic, Approach, Assonant, Dead ringer, Homophyly, Likeness, -oid, -opsis, Replica, Similitude, Simulate

Resent(ful), Resentment Anger, Bridle, Chippy, Choler, Cross, Derry, Dudgeon, Grudge, Indignation, Ire, Jaundiced, Malign, Miff, Mind, Pique, Rankle, Smart, Spite, Umbrage

Reservation, Reserve(d), Reservist(s) Aloof, Arrière-pensée, Backlog, Bashful, Book, By, Capital, Caveat, Central, Cold, Demiss, Detachment, Distant, Earmark, Engage, Ersatz, Except, Fall-back, Federal, Fort Knox, General, Gold, Hold, Husband, Ice, Indian, Introvert, Landwehr, Layby, Locum, Mental, Militiaman, Modesty, Nature, Nest-egg, Nineteenth man, Proviso, Qualification, Reddendum, Res, Rest, Restraint, Retain, Reticence, Retiring, Rez, Salvo, Sanctuary, Save, Scenic, Scruple, Set aside, Special, Spoken for, Stand-by, Stand-offishness, Starch, Stash, Stock(pile), Substitute, TA (men), Twelfth man, Uncommunicate, Understudy, Warren, Waves, Withhold

Reservoir Basin, Cistern, Font, G(h)ilgai, Gilgie, Header tank, Oilcup, Repository, Rybinsk, Service, Stock, Sump, Tank, Water tower

Reset Taxis

Reside(nce), Resident(s), Residential Abode, Address, Amban, Chequers, Commorant, Consulate, Denizen, Domicile, Dwell, Embassy, Establishment, Expatriate, Exurb(anite), Gremial, Guest, Home, In, Indweller, Inholder, Inmate, Intern, Ledger, Lei(d)ger, Lieger, Liveyer(e), Lodger, Metic, Occupant, Pad, Parietal, Permanent, Resiant, Settle, Sojourn, Stay, Tenant, Tenement, Up, Vicinage, Villager, Yamen

Residual, Residue Ash, Astatki, Boneblack, Calx, Caput, Chaff, Cinders, Coke, Crud, Dottle, Draff, Dregs, Expellers, Greaves, Heeltap, Leavings, Maz(o)ut, Mortuum, Prefecture, Remainder, Remanent, Remnant, Scourings, Slag, Slurry, Snuff, Vinasse

Resign(ed), Resignation Abandon, Abdicate, Demit, Fatalism, Heigh-ho, Leave, Meek, → QUIT, Reconcile, Stoic, Submit

Resilience, Resilient Bounce, Buoyant, Elastic, Flexible, Recoil, Springy

Resin Acaroid, Acrylic, Agila, Alkyd, Amber, Amine, Amino, Anime, Arar, Asaf(o)etida, Bakelite®, Bal(sa)m of Gilead, Balsam, Benjamin, Benzoin, Burgundy pitch, Bursera, Cachou, Cannabin, Cannabis, Caranna, Carauna, Catechu, Charas, Cholestyramine, Churrus, Colophony, Conima, Copai(ba), Copaiva, Copal(m), Coumarone, Courbaril, Cutch, Cymene, Dam(m)ar, Dammer, Dragon's blood, Elaterite, Elemi, Epoxy, Frankincense, Galbanum, Galipot, Gambi(e)r, Gamboge, Glyptal, Guaiacum, Gum, Hasheesh, Hashish, Hing, Jalapic, Jalapin, Kino, Labdanum, Lac, Ladanum, Lignaloes, Limonene, Lupulin, Mastic, Melamine, Methacrylate, Myrrh, Natural, Olibanum, Opopanax, Perspex®, Phenolic, Phenoxy, Plastisol, Podophyl(l)in, Polycarbonate, Polyester, Polymer, Polysterene, Polyvinyl, Propolis, Retinite, Roset, Rosin, Rosit, Rozet, Rozit, Sagapenum, Sandarac(h), Saran®, Scammony, Shellac, Silicone, Storax, Styrene, Synthetic, Tacamahac, Tacmahack, Takamaka, Taxin, Thus, Urea, Vinyl, Xylenol

Resist Bristle, Buck, Combat, Contest, Defy, Face, Fend, Gainstrive, Impede, Oppose, Redound, Reluct, Stand (pat), Toughen, → WITHSTAND

Resistance, Resistant, Resistor Barretter, Bleeder, Ceramal, Cermet, Chetnik, Coccidiostat, Combat, Drag, Element, Friction, Hostile, Immunity, Impediment,

Internal, Intifada, Invar, Klendusic, Klepht, Maquis, Maraging, Market, Megohm, Microhm, Negative, Obstacle, Ohm, Passive, Pat, Pull, R, Radiation, Reluctance, Renitent, Resilient, Rheostat, Sales, Satyagraha, Shockproof, Soul-force, Specific, Stability, Stand, Stonde, Stubborn, Tough

Resolute, Resolution Analysis, Bold, Cast-iron, Casuistry, Courage, Decided, Decision, Denouement, Determined, Doughty, → FIRM, Fortitude, Granite, Grim, Grit, Hardiness, Insist, Joint, Pertinacity, Promotion, Rede, Reed(e), Resolve, Stable, Stalwart, Staunch, Stout, Strength, Sturdy, Telic, Tenacity, Unbending, Valiant, Willpower

Resolve(d), Resolver Analyse, Calculate, Decide, Declare, → DETERMINE, Deus ex machina, Factorise, Fix, Hellbent, Intent, Nerve, → PURPOSE, Settle, Steadfast, Tenacity, Vow, Will

▷ **Resolved** *may indicate* an anagram

Resonance, Resonant, Resonator Canorous, Cavity, Electromer, Morphic, Orotund, Parallel, Rhumbatron, Ringing, Sonorous, Timbre, Vibrant

Resort Biarritz, Centre, Dive, Étaples, Expedient, Frame, Frequent, Haunt, Health, Hove, Hydro, Invoke, Lair, Last, Las Vegas, Lowestoft, Malibu, Morecambe, Nassau, Paignton, Pau, Pis aller, Rapallo, Recourse, Repair, Riviera, Southend, Spa(w), Stand by, Use, Watering place, Worthing, Zermatt

▷ **Resort(ing)** *may indicate* an anagram

Resound(ing) Echo, Plangent, Reboant, Reboation, Reverberate, Ring

Resource(s), Resourceful Assets, Beans, Bottom, Chevisance, Clever, Enterprise, Faculty, Funds, Gumption, Human, Ingenious, Input, Inventive, Means, Natural, Renewable, Shared, Sharp, Stock-in-trade, → VERSATILE, Wealth

Respect(ed), Respectable, Respectful Admire, Ahimsa, Aspect, Behalf, Consider, Decent, Deference, Devoir, Duty, Eminent, Esteem, Gigman, Homage, → HONOUR, Intent, Kempt, Kowtowing, Latria, Obeisant, Officious, Pace, Particular, Preppy, Prestige, Proper, Reference, Regard, Relation, Reputable, Revere, Sir, S(t)irrah, U, Venerate, Wellborn, Well-thought-of, Wise, Worthy

Respirator, Respire, Respiration Artificial, Blow, Breathe, Exhale, External, Gasmask, Inhale, Iron lung, Mouth-to-mouth, Pant, Snorkel

Respite Break, Breather, Frist, Interval, Leisure, Let up, Pause, Reprieve, Rest, Stay, Truce

Respond, Response, Responsive Amenable, Answer, Antiphon, Backlash, Bi, Comeback, Conditioned, Counteroffer, Duh, Echo, Feedback, Flechman, Grunt, Immune, Kneejerk, Kyrie, Litany, Nastic, Pavlovian, Photonasty, Prebuttal, Psychogalvanic, React(ion), Reflex, Reply, Repost, Retort, Rheotaxis, Rheotropism, Rise, Stayman, Synapte, Syntonic, Tender, Thigmotropic, Tic, Tropism, Unconditioned, Voice, Warm, Wilco

Responsibility, Responsible Accountable, Anchor, Answerable, Baby, Blame, Buck, Charge, Culpable, Dependable, Diminished, Duty, Frankpledge, Guilty, Hot seat, Incumbent, Instrumental, Liable, Mea culpa, Onus, Pigeon, Sane, Solid, Stayman, Trust

Rest(ing), Rest day Alt, Anchor, Avocation, Balance, Bed, Beulah, Break, Breather, Calm, Catnap, Cetera, Comma, Depend, Dwell, Ease, Easel, Etc, Fermata, Feutre, Fewter, Gite, Half-time, Halt, Inaction, Jigger, Lance, Lave, Lean, Lie, Lie-in, Light, Lodge, Loll, Lound, Lyte, Minim, Nap, Noah, Nooning, Others, Outspan, Overlie, Pause, Quiescence, Quiet, Relâche, Relax, Rely, Remainder, Repose, Requiem, Reserve, Residue, Respite, Sabbath, Siesta, → SLEEP, Slide, Sloom, Slumber, Spell, Spider, Static, Stopover, Support, Surplus, Teabreak, Time out, Y-level

Re-start Da capo, Reboot

Restaurant, Restaurateur Automat, Beanery, Bistro, Brasserie, British, Cabaret, Café, Canteen, Chew'n'spew, Chip-shop, Chophouse, Commissary, Cook shop, Creperie, Diner, Eatery, Eating-house, Estaminet, Greasy spoon, Grill, Grillroom, Grub shop, Luncheonette, Maxim's, Noshery, Padrone, Porter-house, Rathskeller, Ratskeller, Roadhouse, Rotisserie, Slap-bang, Steakhouse, Takeaway, Taqueria, Taverna, Teahouse, Tearoom, Teashop, Trattoria

Rest-home Aggie, Hospice

Resting-place Bed, Couch, Dharmsala, Gite, Grave, Inn, Khan, Serai, She'ol, Stage

Restitute, Restitution Amends, Apocatastasis, Reparation, Restore, Return

Restive, Restless(ness) Chafing, Chorea, Fidgety, Fikish, Free-arm, Itchy, Jactitation, Toey, Unsettled

▷ **Restless** *may indicate* an anagram

Restoration, Restorative, Restore(d) Bring to, Cure, Descramble, Heal, Mend, Pentimento, Pick-me-up, Postliminy, Rally, Recondition, Redeem, Redintegrate, Redux, Refurbish, Regenerate, Rehabilitate, Rejuvenate, Remedial, Renew, Renovate, Replevy, Repone, Restitute, Resuscitate, Retouch, Revamp, Revive, Stet, Tonic, Whole

Restrain(ed), Restraint Abstinence, Ban, Bate, Bit, Bottle, Branks, Bridle, Cage, Chain, Chasten, → CHECK, Checks and balances, Coerce, Cohibit, Compesce, Confinement, Contain, Control, Cramp, Curb, Dam, Decorum, Detent, Dry, Duress, Embargo, Enfetter, Estoppel, Freeze, Halt, Hamshackle, Handcuffs, Harness, Heft, Hinder, Hopple, Impound, Inhibit, Jess, Leg-iron, Lid, Low-key, Manacle, Measure, Mince, Moderation, Muzzle, Patient, Quiet, Rein, Repress, Restrict, Ritenuto, Shackle, Sober, Sobriety, Squeeze, Stay, Stent, Stint, Straitjacket, Temper, Tether, Tie, Trash

Restrict(ed), Restriction Band, Bar, Bind, Bit, Burden, Cage, Catch, Censorship, Chain, Circumscribe, Closet, Condition, Cord, Corset, Cramp, Curb, Curfew, DORA, Fence, Fold, Gate, Ground, Guard, Hamper, Hidebound, Hobble, Inhibit, Intern, Kennel, Let, → LIMIT, Localise, Lock, Mere, Narrow, Net, Nick, No-go, Pale, Parochial, Pen, Pent, Pier, Pin, Pot-bound, Private, Proscribed, Qualify, Regulate, Rein, Rent, Repression, Rope, Safety belt, Scant, Seal, Section, Selected, Shackle, Snare, Squeeze, Stenopaic, Stent, Stint, Stop, Straiten, Stunt, Tether, Tie

Restructure, Restructuring Perestroika

Result(s) After-effect, Aftermath, Ans(wer), Bring, Causal, Consequence, Effect, Emanate, End, Ensue, Entail, Event, Eventuate, Finding, Fruict, Fruits, Issue, Karmic, Knock-on, Lattermath, → OUTCOME, Outturn, Pan, Proceeds, Quotient, Sequel, Side-effect, Sum, Upshot, Wale

Resume, Résumé Continue, Pirlicue, Purlicue, Summary

Resurrect(ion) Anabiosis, Anastasia, Rebirth, Revive, Zomb(ie)

Resuscitate(d), Resuscitation Mouth-to-mouth, Quicken, Redivivus, Restore, Revive

Retail(er) Chandler, Dealer, → NARRATE, Regrate, Sell, Shopkeeper, Symbol, Tell

Retain(er), Retains Brief, Contain, Deposit, Fee, Hold, Hold-all, Keep, Panter, Pantler, Reserve, Retinue, Servant

Retaliate, Retaliation Avenge, Counter, Lex talionis, Quid pro quo, Quit(e), Redress, Repay, Reprisal, Requite, Retort, Talion

Retard(ed) Arrest, Belate, Brake, Cretin, Encumber, Hinder, Slow, Stunt

Retch Boak, Bock, Boke, Cowk, Gap, Heave, Keck, Reach, Vomit

Reticence, Reticent Clam, Coy, Dark, Reserve, Restraint, Secretive, Shy, Taciturn

Reticule, Reticulum Bag, Carryall, Dragnet, Lattice, Net

Retina Detached, Fovea, Macula lutea

Retinue Comitatus, Company, Cortège, Equipage, Following, Meiney, Meinie, Meiny, Menyie, Sowarry, Suite
Retire(d), Retiree, Retirement, Retiring Abed, Aloof, Baccare, Backare, Backpedal, Blate, Bowler-hat, Bow out, Cede, Coy, Depart, Ebb, Emeritus, Essene, Former, Leave, Lonely, Modest, Mothball, Nun, Outgoing, Pension, Perfing, Private, Quit, Recede, Recluse, Reserved, Resign, Retract, Retread, Retreat, Retrocedent, Roost, Rusticate, Scratch, Sequester, Shy, Superannuate, Unassertive, Withdraw
▷ **Retirement** *may indicate* 'bed' around another word, or word reversed
Retort Alembic, Comeback, Courteous, Quip, Repartee, → **REPLY**, Retaliate, Riposte, Still, Tu quoque
Retract(ion) Backpedal, Backtrack, Disavow, Epanorthosis, Palinode, Recall, Recant, Renounce, Revoke
Retreat Abbey, Arbour, Ashram(a), Asylum, Backpedal, Backwater, Bower, Bug, Camp David, Cell, Cloister, Convent, Crawfish, Dacha, Departure, Donjon, Girth, Grith, Hermitage, Hideaway, Hide-out, Hole, Interstadial, Ivory-tower, Katabasis, Lair, Lama(sery), Mew, Monastery, Nest, Neuk, Nook, Recede, Recoil, Recu(i)le, Redoubt, Reduit, Refuge, Retire, Retraite, Right-about, Rout, Shangri-La, Shelter, Skedaddle, Stronghold, Withdraw
Retribution Come-uppance, Deserts, Nemesis, Revenge, Reward, Utu, Vengeance
Retrieve(r), Retrieval Access, Bird-dog, Chesapeake Bay, Field, Gundog, Labrador, Read-out, Recall, Recoup, Recover, Redeem, Rescue, Salvage
Retroflex Cacuminal
Retrograde Backward, Deasi(u)l, Deasoil, Decadent, Decline, Hindward, Rearward, Regrede
Retrospect(ive) Contemplative, Ex post facto, Hindsight, Regardant
Return(s) Agen, Answer, Bricole, Census, Comeback, Day, Diminishing, Dividend, Elect, Er, Extradite, Gain, Nil, Pay, Proceeds, Profit, Rebate, Rebound, Recur, Redound, Regress, Reject, Render, Rent, Repay, Replace, Reply, Requital, Respond, Rest, Restitution, Restore, Retour, Revenue, Reverse, Revert, Riposte, Takings, Tax, Traffic, → **YIELD**
Rev Gun, Minister
Reveal(ing), Revelation Acute, Advertise, Air, Apocalyptic, Bare, Betray, Bewray, Confess, Descry, Disclose, Discover, Discure, → **DIVULGE**, Epiphany, Exhibit, Explain, Expose, Eye-opener, Giveaway, Hierophantic, Impart, Indicate, Ingo, Kythe, Leak, Let on, Manifest, Open, Out, Pentimento, Satori, → **SHOW**, Spill, Tell-tale, Unclose, Uncover, Unfold, Unheal, Unmask, Unveil
Revel(ling), Revelry Ariot, Bacchanalia, Bend, Carnival, Carouse, Comus, Dionysian, Feast, Gloat, Glory, Joy, Merriment, Orgy, Rant, Rejoice, Riot, Roister, Rollicks, Rout, Royst, Saturnalia, Splore, Swig, Upsee, Ups(e)y, Wallow, Wassail, Whoopee
Reveller Bacchant, Birler, Corybant, Guisard, Guiser, Maenad, Merrymaker, Orgiast, Silenus
Revenant Fetch, Ghost, Spectre
Revenge(r), Revengeful Aftergame, Avenge, Commination, Goel, Grenville, Montezuma's, Nightrider, Payback, Reprise, Requite, Retaliation, Revanche, Ultion, Utu, Vindictive
Revenue Capital, Finance, Fisc(al), Fisk, Income, Inland, Internal, Jaghire, Jag(h)ir, Prebend, Primitiae, Rent, Taille, Tax, Turnover, Zamindar, Zemindar
Reverberate Echo, Recoil, Reflect, Repercuss, Resound
Revere(nce) Admire, Awe, Bostonian, Dread, Dulia, Esteem, Fear, Hallow, Hery,

Homage, → **HONOUR**, Hyperdulia, Idolise, Latria, Obeisance, Paul, Respect, Venerate

Reverie Brown study, Daydream, Dream(iness), Fantasy, Memento

Revers Lap(p)el

Reversal, Reverse, Reversing, Reversion, Reversible Antithesis, Antonym, Arsy-versy, Atavism, Back(slide), Change-over, Chiasmus, Commutate, Counter(mand), Escheat, Evaginate, Exergue, Flip, Inversion, Misfortune, → **OPPOSITE**, Overturn, Palindrome, Pile, Regress, Revoke, Rheotropic, Setback, Switchback, Tails, Throwback, Transit, Turn, Turnabout, Two-faced, Un-, Undo, U-turn, Verso, Vice versa, Volte-face, Woman

Revert Annul, Backslide, Regress, Relapse, Resort, Retrogress, Return

Review(er) Appeal, Censor, Credit, Critic, Critique, Editor, Encomium, Feuilleton, Footlights, Inspect, Judicial, Magazine, March-past, Notice, Pan, Peer, Recapitulate, Repeat, Revise, Rundown, Spithead, Summary, Summing-up, Survey, Write-up

▷ **Review** *may indicate* an anagram or a reversed word

Revile, Reviling Abuse, Execrate, Inveigh, Rail, Rayle, Vilify, Vituperate

Revise(r), Revision Alter, Amend, Correct, Diaskeuast, Edit, Peruse, Reappraise, Reassess, Recense, Reform, Rev, Update

▷ **Revise(d)** *may indicate* an anagram

Revive, Revival, Revivify, Reviving Araise, Classical, Enliven, Gothic, Greek, Rake up, Rally, Reanimate, Reawake(n), Rebirth, Redintegrate, Redux, Refresh, Rekindle, Relive, Renaissance, Renascent, Renew, Renovate, Restore, Resurrect, Resuscitate, Risorgimento, Romantic, Rouse, Wake

Revoke Abrogate, Cancel, Countermand, Negate, → **RECALL**, Repeal, Rescind

Revolt(ing), Revolution(ary) Agitator, Agitprop, American, Anarchist, Apostasy, Appal, Bloodless, Bolivar, Bolshevik, Bolshevist, Boxer, Bulldog, Cade, Castro, Chartist, Che, Chinese, Circle, Commune, Coup d'état, Cultural, Cycle, Danton, Defection, Dervish, Desmoulins, Disgust, Emeute, Emmet, Engels, Enrage, February, Fenian, Foul, French, Girondin, Girondist, Glorious, Green, Grody, Guevara, Gyration, Industrial, Inqilab, → **IN REVOLT**, Insurgent, Insurrection, Intifada, IRA, Jacobin, Jacquerie, Komitaji, Lap, Lenin, Marat, Marx, Maximalist, Maypole, Minimalist, Montagnard, Mutiny, Nauseating, Nihilist, October, Orbit, Outbreak, Palace, Paris Commune, Peasants', Poujadist, Putsch, Radical, → **REBEL**, Red, Red Guard, Red Shirt, Reformation, Riot, Rise, Robespierre, Roll, Rotation, Round, Run, Russian, Sandinista, Sansculotte(rie), Sedition, Sicilian Vespers, Spartacus, Syndicalism, The Mountain, Thermidor, Titanomachy, Trot(sky), Twist, Up(rise), → **UPRISING**, Velvet, Villa, Wat Tyler, Weatherman, Whirl, Wolfe Tone, Young Turk, Zapata

▷ **Revolutionary** *may indicate* 'reversed'

Revolve(r), Revolving Carrier, Catherine wheel, Centrifuge, Colt®, Gat, Girandole, Grindstone, → **GUN**, Gyrate, Iron, Klinostat, Lathe, Maelstrom, Peristrephic, Pistol, Pivot, Planet, Roller, Rotate, Rotifer, Rotor, Roundabout, Run, Six-shooter, Spin, Tone, Turn(stile), Turntable, Turret, Wheel, Whirl(igig), Whirlpool

Revue Follies

Reward(ing) Albricias, Bonus, Bounty, Compensate, Consideration, Desert, Emolument, Fee, Guerdon, Head money, Medal, Meed, Payment, Premium, Price, Prize, Profit, Purse, Recompense, Reguerdon, Remuneration, Requital, Requite, S, Shilling, Tanti, Tribute, Wage, War(r)ison

Reword Edit, Paraphrase

Reworking Rifacimento

Rex Priam, R
Reynolds Joshua, PRA
Rhapsodic, Rhapsody Ecstasy, Epic, Music, Unconnected
Rhea Em(e)u, Nandoo, Nandu, Nhandu, Ostrich, Rami
Rhenium Re
Rhesus Bandar, Macaque, Monkey
Rhetoric(al) Alliteration, Anaphora, Antimetabole, Antithesis, Antostrophe,
  Apophasis, Aposiopesis, Assonance, Aureate, Bombast, Brachylogia, Cacophony,
  Catachresis, Chiasmus, Ecbole, Eloquence, Enantiosis, Epanorthosis, Epexegesis,
  Epistrophe, Epizeuxis, Erotema, Eroteme, Erotesis, Euphemism, Hendiadys,
  Hypallage, Hyperbole, Litotes, Metonymy, Oratory, Oxymoron, Paradox,
  Paral(e)ipsis, Periphrasis, Peroration, Platform, Pleonasm, Scesisonomaton,
  Syllepsis, Synoeciosis, Trivium, Zeugma
Rhino Blunt, Bread, Cash, Lolly, Loot, → MONEY, Tin
Rhinoceros Baluchitherium, Keitloa, Square-lipped, Sumatran, White
Rhodes, Rhodesia(n) Cecil, Colossus, Ridgeback, Scholar, Zimbabwe
Rhodium Rh
Rhubarb Pie-plant, Rhapontic, Rheum, Rot, Spat
Rhyme(s), Rhymer, Rhyming Assonance, Clerihew, Closed couplet, Counting out,
  Couplet, Crambo, Cynghanedd, Doggerel, Eye, Feminine, Head, Identical, Internal,
  Jingle, Male, Masculine, Measure, Near, Nursery, Pararhyme, Perfect, Poetry,
  Rich, Riding, Rime riche, Rondel, Royal, Runic, Sight, Slang, Slant, Tail(ed), Tercet,
  Terza-rima, Thomas, Triple, → VERSE, Virelay, Vowel
Rhythm(ic) Agoge, Alpha, Asynartete, Backbeat, Beat, Beta, Bo Diddley beat,
  Breakbeat, Cadence, Circadian, Duple, Hemiol(i)a, In-step, Meter, Movement,
  Oompah, Pulse, Pyrrhic, Rove-over, Rubato, Scotch catch, Scotch snap, Sdrucciola,
  Sesqualtera, Singsong, Sprung, Swing, Syncopation, Tala, Talea, → TEMPO, Time,
  Voltinism
Rib(bed), Ribbing, Rib-joint Bar, Chaff, Chiack, Chip, Chyack, Cod, Costa,
  Cross-springer, Dutch, Eve, False, Fin, Floating, Futtock, Groin, Intercostal, Lierne,
  Nervate, Nervular, Nervure, Ogive, Persiflage, Rack, Rag, Rally, Short, Spare,
  Springer, Subcosta, Taunt, Tease, Tierceron, Tracery, True, Wife
Ribald(ry) Balderdash, Bawdy, Coarse, Scurrilous, Smut, Sotadic, Vulgar
Ribbon Band, Bandeau, Blue, Bow, Braid, Caddis, Caddyss, Cordon, Fattrels, Ferret,
  Fillet, Grosgrain, Hatband, Infula, Multistrike, Pad, Petersham, Radina, Red, Rein,
  Riband, Soutache, Taenia, Tape, Teniate, Tie, Torsade, Yellow
Ribless Ecostate
Rice Arborio, Basmati, Bir(i)yani, Brown, Canada, Carnaroli, Elmer, Entertainer,
  Indian, Kedgeree, Miracle, Paddy, Patna, Pilaf, Pilau, Pilaw, Pillau, Reis, Risotto,
  Spanish, Sushi, Twigs, Water, Wild
Rich(es) Abounding, Abundant, Affluent, Amusing, Bonanza, Buttery, Comic,
  Copious, Croesus, Dives, Edmund, Edwin, Fat, Feast, Fertile, Flamboyant, Flush,
  Fruity, Full, Golconda, Haves, Heeled, High, Larney, Loaded, Luscious, Lush,
  Luxurious, Mammon, Moneybags, Moneyed, Nabob, New, Oberous, → OPULENT,
  Plenteous, Plush, Plutocrat, Resonant, Rolling, Silvertail, Sumptuous, Toff,
  Vulgarian, → WEALTHY, Well-heeled, Well off, Well-to-do
Richard Angevin, Burbage, Dick(y), Lionheart, Rick, Roe
Richthofen Red Baron
Rick (burning) Goaf, Sprain, Swingism, Wrench
Rickets, Rickety Dilapidated, Rachitis, Ramshackle, Rattletrap, Shaky, Unsound
▷ **Rickety** *may indicate* an anagram

Rickshaw Pedicab, Tuktuk

Ricochet Boomerang, Glance, Rebound

Rid Clear, Deliver, Ditch, Eliminate, Eradicate, Expunge, Free, Obviate, Offload, Purge, Scrap, Scrub, Shot

Riddle Boulter, Charade, Colander, Dilemma, Enigma, Koan, Logogriph, Pepper, Perforate, Permeate, Puzzle, Screen, Searce, Search, Seil, Sieve, Sift, Sile, Siler, Sorites, Strain, Tems(e), Trommel

Ride, Riding Annoy, Aquaplane, Bareback, Bestride, Big dipper, Bruise, Canter, Coast, Crog(gy), Cycle, District, Division, Drive, Equitation, Field, Hack, Harass, Haute école, Hitchhike, Merry-go-round, Mount, Pick(-a-)back, Pickpack, Piggyback, Postil(l)ion, Rape, Revere's, Roadstead, Rollercoaster, Sit, Spin, Stang, Switchback, Third, Trot, Weather, Welter, Wheelie, Whip, White-knuckle

Rider(s) Addendum, Adjunct, Appendage, Attachment, Boundary, Bucket, Cavalier, Charioteer, Circuit, Codicil, Condition, Corollary, Dispatch, Equestrian, Eventer, Freedom, Gaucho, Godiva, Guidon, Haggard, Horseman, Jockey, Lochinvar, Messenger, Peloton, Postil(l)ion, Proviso, PS, Revere, Scrub, Spurrer, Transport, Walkyrie

Ridge(pole) Alveolar, Anthelix, Antihelix, Arête, Arris, As(ar), Balk, Bank, Baulk, Berm, Bur(r), Carina, Chine, Clint, Costa, Crease, Crest, Crista, Cuesta, Culmen, Darling Range, Drill, Drum(lin), Dune, Eskar, Esker, Fret, Gonys, Gyrus, Hammock, Hoe, Hogback, Horst, Hummock, Interfluve, Kaim, Kame, Keel, Knur(l), Ledge, Linch, List(er), Lynchet, Mid-Atlantic, Mid-ocean, Missionary, Nek, Nut, Oceanic, Offset, Pressure, Promontory, Ramp, Rand, Raphe, Razor-back, Reef, Rib, Riblet, Rig, Rim, Roof-tree, Sastruga, Screw-thread, Serac, Serpentine, Shoulder, Sowback, Torus, Varix, Verumontanum, Vimy, Wale, Weal, Whelp, Whorl, Windrow, Withers, Witwatersrand, Wrinkle, Yardang, Zastruga

Ridicule, Ridiculous Absurd, Badinage, Bathos, Chaff, Cockamamie, Deride, Derisory, Egregious, Foolish, Gibbet, Gibe, Gird, Guy, Haze, Jibe, Josh, Laughable, Ludicrous, Mimic, Mock, Paradox, Pasquin, Pillory, Pish, Pooh-pooh, Raillery, Rally, Rich, Roast, Satire, Scoff, Scout, Screwy, Send up, Sight, Silly, Skimmington, Taunt, Travesty

Ridinghood Nithsdale, Red

Riding-master RM

Riding-school Manège

Rife Abundant, Manifest, Numerous, Prevalent

Riffle Rapid

Riff-raff Canaille, Hoi polloi, Mob, Populace, Rag-tag, Scaff, Scum, Trash

Rifle Air, Armalite®, Assault, Bone, Browning, Bundook, Burgle, Calic, Carbine, Chassepot, Enfield, Enfield musket, Express, Garand, → GUN, Kalashnikov, Lee Enfield, Loot, Martini®, Martini-Henry, Mauser®, MI, Minié, Pea, Petronel, Pick, Pilfer, Pillage, Ransack, Remington, Repeater, Rob, Ruger, Saloon, Shiloh, Springfield, Winchester®

Rift Altercation, Canyon, Chasm, Chink, Cleft, Crevasse, Fault, Fissure, Gap, Gulf, Split

Rig(ging) Accoutre, Attire, Bermuda, Drilling, Equip, Feer, Gaff, Get-up, Gunter, Hoax, Jack-up, Mainbrace, Manipulate, Marconi, Martingale, Oil, Outfit, Panoply, Ratline, Ropes, Schooner, Semisubmersible, Slant, Sport, Stack, Standing, Strip, Swindle, Tackle, Togs, Top hamper, Trull, Wanton

▷ **Rigged** *may indicate* an anagram

Right(s), Righten, Rightness Accurate, Advowson, Affirmative, Ancient lights, Angary, Animal, Appropriate, Appurtenance, Ay, Befit, Blue-pencil, BNP,

Bote, Cabotage, Champart, Civil, Claim, Competence, Conjugal, Conservative, Copyhold, → **CORRECT**, Cor(r)ody, Coshery, Cuddy, Cure, Curtesy, Customer, Dead on, De jure, Dexter, Direct, Divine, Doctor, Droit, Due, Easement, Eminent domain, Emphyteusis, Equity, Esnecy, Estover, Ethical, Exactly, Faldage, Farren, Fascist, Feu, Fire-bote, Fitting, Forestage, Franchise, Free-bench, Freedom, Gay, Germane, Gunter, Haybote, Hedge-bote, Human, Infangthief, Interest, Isonomy, Iure, Junior, Jural, Jure, Jus (mariti), Leet, Legit, Letters patent, Liberty, Lien, Maritage, Maternity, Meet, Miner's, Moral, Naam, New, Ninepence, Off, Offhand, Offside, OK, Okay, Oke, Okey-dokey, Option, Ortho-, Oughtness, Paine, Passant, Pasturage, Pat, Patent, Paternity, Performing, Pit and gallows, Ploughbote, Pose, Postliminy, Pre-emption, Prerogative, Primogeniture, Priority, Prisage, Privilege, Proper, Property, Pukka, R, Rain, Reason, Recourse, Rectify, Rectitude, Redress, Remainder, Remedy, Repair, Rt, Sac, Sake, Side, So, Soc, Squatter's, Stage, Starboard, Stillicide, Suo jure, Suo loco, Tao, Tenants', Terce, Ticket, Tickety-boo, Title, Trivet, Trover, True, Turbary, User, Usucap(t)ion, Usufruct, Venville, Vert, Warren, Water, Women's

Right-angle(d) Orthogonal
Righteous(ness) Devout, Good, Just, Moral, Pharisee, Prig, Rectitude, Sanctimonious, Tzaddik, Virtuous
Right-hand Dexter, E, Far, Recto, RH, Ro
Right-winger Falangist, Neo-fascist
Rigid(ity) Acierated, Catalepsy, Craton, Extreme, Fixed, Formal, Hard and fast, Hard-set, Hard-shell, Hidebound, Inflexible, Renitent, Rigor, Set, Slavish, Starch(y), Stern, Stiff, Stretchless, Strict, Stringent, Tense, Turgor
Rigmarole Nonsense, Palaver, Paraphernalia, Protocol, Ragman, Ragment, Riddlemeree, Screed
Rigorous, Rigour Accurate, Austere, Cruel, Exact, Firm, Hard, Inclement, Iron-bound, Stern, Strait, Strict, Stringent
Rile Anger, Annoy, Harry, Irritate, → **NETTLE**, Vex
▷ **Rile(y)** *may indicate* an anagram
Rill Purl, Sike
Rim Atlantic, Border, Chimb, Chime, Edge, Felloe, Felly, Flange, Kelyphitic, → **LIP**, Margin, Pacific, Strake, Verge
Rime Crust, Frost, Hoar, Rhyme, Rhythm
Rind Bark, Crackling, Peel, Skin
Ring(ed), Ringer, Ringing, Rings Anchor, Angelus, Annual, Annulus, Anthelion, Arcus, Arena, Band, Bangle, Bayreuth, Bell, Benzine, Boom-iron, Broch, Brogh, Call, Cambridge, Carabiner, Cartel, Cartouche, Change, Chime, Circinate, Circle, Circlet, Circlip, Circus, Claddagh, Clam, Clang, Clink, Coil, Collet, Cordon, Corona, Corral, Corrida, Cramp, Crawl, Cricoid, Cringle, Cromlech, Cycle, Cyclic, Dead, Death's head, Dial, Dicyclic, Ding, Disc, Dohyo, Dong, D(o)uar, Draupnir, Echo, Encircle, Encompass, Engagement, Enhalo, Enlace, Environ, Enzone, Eternity, Extension, Eyelet, Fainne, Fairlead(er), Fairy, Ferrule, Fisherman, Fistic(uffs), Gas, Gimmal, Gird(le), Girr, Gloriole, Groin, Grom(m)et, Growth, Grummet, Guard, Gyges, Gymmal, Gyre, Halo, Hob, → **HOOP**, Hoop-la, Hula-hoop, Ideal, Inner, Inorb, Involucre, Jougs, Jow, Karabiner, Kartell, Keeper, Key, Knell, Knock-out, Kraal, Lifebelt, Link, Loop, Luned, Lute, Magpie, Manacle, Manilla, Marquise, Mourning, Napkin, Newton's, Nibelung, Nimbus, Nose, O, Orb, Outer, Pappus, Parral, Parrel, Peal, Pele, Pen, Phone, Ping, Piston, Potato, Price, Prize, Puteal, Quoit, Resonant, Resound, Retaining, Round, Rove, Rowel, Rundle, Runner, Sale, Scarf, Scraper, Scrunchy, Seal, Signet, Slinger, Slip, Snap-link, Solomon, Sound,

Spell, Split, Stemma, Stemme, Stonehenge, Surround, Swivel, Syndicate, Tang, Tattersall, Teething, Terret, Territ, Thimble, Thumb, Timbre, Ting, Tingle, Tink, Tinnitius, Tintinnabulate, Toe, Token, Toll, Toplady, Tore, Torquate, Torques, Torret, Torus, Travelling, Tree, Trochus, Turret, Tweed, Varvel, Vervel, Vice, Vortex, Wagnerian, Washer, Wedding, Welkin, Withe, Woggle, Zero

Ring-dance Carol

Ring-leader Bell-wether, Fugleman, Instigator

Ringlet Curl(icue), Lock, Tendril, Tress

Ringmaster Wagner

Ringworm Serpigo, Tinea

Rinse Bathe, Blue, Cleanse, Douche, Sind, Sine, Swill, Synd, Syne, Tint, Wash

Riot(er), Riotous(ly), Riots Anarchy, Brawl, Clamour, Demo, Deray, Gordon, Hilarious, Hubbub, Luddite, Medley, Mêlée, Nicker, Orgy, Pandemonium, Peterloo, Petroleur, Porteous, Profusion, Quorum, Race, Rag, Rebecca, Rebel, Roaring, Roister, Rout, Rowdy, Ruction, Ruffianly, Scream, Swing, Tumult

▷ **Rioters, Riotous** *may indicate* an anagram

Rip(per), Ripping Basket, Buller, Cur, Grand, Handful, Horse, Jack, Lacerate, Rent, Rep, Roué, Splendid, Tear, Tide, Topnotch, To-rend, Unseam

Ripe, Ripen(ing) Auspicious, Full, Geocarpy, Mature, Mellow, Rathe, Ready

Riposte Repartee, Retaliate, Retort

Ripple Bradyseism, Fret, Overlap, Popple, Purl, Undulation, Wave, Wavelet, Wrinkle

▷ **Rippling** *may indicate* an anagram

Rise(r), Rising Advance, Appreciate, Ascend, Assurgent, Bull, Butte, Cause, Dutch, Easter, Eger, Elevation, Emerge, Émeute, Eminence, Erect, Escalate, Get up, Hance, Hauriant, Haurient, Heave, Heliacal, Hike, Hill, Hummock, Hunt's up, Improve, Increase, Incremental, Insurgent, Intumesce, Jibe, Knap, Knoll, Lark, Levee, Levitate, Lift, Mount, Mutiny, Orient, Origin, Peripety, Point, Prove, Putsch, Rear, Resurgent, Resurrection, → **REVOLT**, Saleratus, Scarp, Sklim, Soar, Stand, Stie, Sty, Stye, Surface, Surge, The Fifteen, Tor, Tower, Transcend, Up, Upbrast, Upburst, Upgo, Uprest, Upsurge, Upswarm, Upturn, Well

Risk(y) Actuarial, Adventure, Back, Calculated, Chance, Compromise, Counterparty, → **DANGER**, Daring, Dice, Dicy, Emprise, Endanger, Fear, Gamble, Game, Hairy, Hazard, Imperil, Jeopardy, Liability, Peril, Precarious, Security, Shoot the works, Spec, Throw, Touch and go, Touchy, Unsafe, Venture

Risorgimento Renaissance

Risqué Blue, Racy, Salty, Scabrous, Spicy

Rissole(s) Cecils, Croquette, Faggot, Quennelle, Veggieburger

Rite(s) Asperges, Bora, Ceremony, Eastern, Exequies, Initiation, Liturgy, Mystery, Nagmaal, Obsequies, Powwow, Ritual, Sacrament, Sarum use, Superstition, York

Ritual Agadah, Arti, Ceremony, Chanoyu, Customary, Formality, Haggada, Lavabo, Liturgy, Mumbo-jumbo, Puja, Rite, Sacring, Seder, Social, Use

Rival(ry), Rivals Absolute, Acres, Aemule, Binocular, Compete, Contender, Emulate, Emule, Envy, Fo(n)e, → **MATCH**, Needle, Opponent, Retinal, Touch, Vie

River Dalles, Ea, Estuary, Flood, Flower, Fluvial, Potamic, Potamology, R, Riverain, Runner, Stream, Tide, Tributary, Waterway

---

RIVERS

2 letters:		3 letters:	
Ay	Po	Aar	Axe
Ob	Si	Aln	Ayr
	Xi		Bug

Cam	Deva	Saar	Culbá
Dee	Doon	Sava	Dasht
Don	Dove	Soar	Desna
Ems	Drin	Spey	Doubs
Esk	Earn	Styx	Douro
Exe	East	Swan	Drava
Fal	Ebbw	Swat	Drave
Fly	Ebro	Taff	Duero
Fox	Eden	Tana	Dvina
Han	Eder	Tarn	Eblis
Hsi	Elbe	Tees	Firth
Hué	Erne	Teme	Fleet
Inn	Esla	Test	Forth
Lee	Eure	Tone	Gogra
Lot	Gila	Tyne	Green
Luo	Gota	Uele	Havel
Lys	Huon	Ural	Hotan
Mur	Idle	Uvod	Indre
Nar	Isar	Vaal	Indus
Oil	Iser	Waal	Isere
Oka	Isis	Wear	Ishim
Ord	Jiul	Xero	James
Red	Juba	Yalu	Jumna
San	Kama	Yare	Juruá
Tay	Kill	Yate	Kasai
Tet	Kura	Yser	Kaven
Ure	Kwai	Yuan	Kenga
Usk	Lahn	Yuen	Kuban
Wye	Lech		Lethe
Yeo	Lena	**5 letters:**	Liard
	Liao	Abana	Limay
	Luan	Acton	Loire
4 letters:	Lune	Adige	Marne
Abus	Maas	Afton	Mbomu
Abzu	Main	Agate	Meuse
Acis	Meta	Aisne	Minho
Adur	Milk	Aldan	Mosel
Aire	Mino	Apure	Mulla
Alma	Mole	Argun	Mures
Alph	Nene	Avoca	Namoi
Amur	Neva	Benue	Negro
Aran	Nile	Boyne	Neman
Aras	Nith	Broad	Niger
Arno	Oder	Cauca	Ogowe
Aude	Ohio	Chari	Onega
Avon	Oise	Clyde	Oreti
Back	Ouse	Clyst	Peace
Beni	Oxus	Colne	Pearl
Bomu	Prut	Congo	Pecos
Cher	Rock	Conwy	Pelly
Culm	Ruhr	Cross	Piave
Dart			

Pison	Arzina	Medway	Wabash
Plate	Atbara	Mekong	Wairau
Purus	Barcoo	Mersey	Wensum
Rainy	Barrow	Mohawk	Wharfe
Rance	Bio-Bio	Molopo	Wupper
Rhine	Broads	Morava	Yarrow
Rhône	Calder	Moskva	Yellow
Rogue	Canton	Murray	
Saône	Chenab	Neckar	**7 letters:**
Seine	Clutha	Neisse	Acheron
Shari	Colima	Nelson	Aruwimi
Shire	Croton	Nyeman	Bassein
Siang	Crouch	Ogooue	Berbice
Siret	Cydnus	Orange	Berezua
Skien	Danube	Orwell	Bermejo
Slave	Dawson	Ottawa	Buffalo
Snake	Donets	Pahang	Burnett
Snowy	Duddon	Parana	Caqueta
Somme	Durack	Peneus	Cauvery
Spree	Escaut	Platte	Chagres
Staff	Finlay	Pripet	Cocytus
Stour	Fraser	Prosna	Damodar
Swale	Gambia	Rakaia	Darling
Tagus	Ganges	Ribble	Derwent
Tamar	Glomma	Riffle	Detroit
Tapti	Granta	Rother	Dnieper
Tarim	Harlem	Sabine	Dubglas
Teign	Hodder	Salado	Durance
Terek	Hsiang	Sambre	Ettrick
Tiber	Hudson	Santee	Fitzroy
Tisza	Humber	Seneca	Garonne
Tobol	Iguacu	Severn	Genesee
Trent	Ijssel	St John	Gironde
Tweed	Irtish	Struma	Guapore
Volga	Irtysh	Sutlej	Hari Rud
Volta	Irwell	Swanee	Helmand
Warta	Isonzo	Tanana	Hooghly
Weser	Itchen	Tarsus	Huang He
Xiang	Japura	Tevere	Hwangho
Xingu	Javari	Teviot	Iguassu
Yaqui	Javary	Thames	Irawadi
Yarra	Jhelum	Ticino	Kanawha
Yonne	Jordan	Tigris	Krishna
Yssel	Kaduna	Tugela	Lachlan
Yukon	Kagera	Tyburn	Limpopo
	Kennet	Ubangi	Lualaba
6 letters:	Kistna	Ussuri	Madeira
Allier	Kolyma	Vardar	Manning
Amazon	Komati	Vienne	Maranon
Anadyr	Liffey	Vitava	Maritsa
Angara	Mamoré	Vyatka	Mataura

Meander	Araguaia	Suwannee	Cumberland
Moselle	Araguaya	Syr Darya	Great Slave
Narbada	Arkansas	Tonle Sap	Housatonic
Narmada	Berezina	Torridge	Kizil Irmak
Neuquén	Blue Nile	Toulouse	Phlegethon
Niagara	Canadian	Tunguska	Rangitaiki
Nipigon	Charente	Van Hades	Rangitikei
Orinoco	Cherwell	Veronezh	Sacramento
Orontes	Chindwin	Victoria	San Joaquin
Parrett	Chu Kiang	Volturno	Schuylkill
Pechora	Clarence	Wanganui	St Lawrence
Pharpar	Colorado	Windrush	White Volta
Potomac	Columbia	Zhu Jiang	Yesil Irmak
Red Deer	Congaree		
Rubicon	Daintree	**9 letters:**	**11 letters:**
Sabrina	Demerara	Allegheny	Aegospotami
Salinas	Dneister	Ashburton	Assiniboine
Salween	Dordogne	Billabong	Brahmaputra
Salzach	Flinders	Churchill	Connecticut
Sanders	Franklin	Crocodile	Cooper Creek
Scheldt	Gascoyne	Des Moines	Delaguadero
Senegal	Godavari	Essequibo	Guadalentin
Shannon	Granicus	Euphrates	Lesser Slave
Songhua	Guadiana	Irrawaddy	Madre de Dios
St Clair	Hamilton	Kuskokwim	Mississauga
St Croix	Illinois	Mackenzie	Mississippi
St Mary's	Kentucky	Magdalena	Monongahela
Swannee	Klondike	Murchison	Shatt-al-Arab
Tapajos	Kootenay	Parnahiba	Susquehanna
Thomson	Maeander	Perihonca	Yellowstone
Tugaloo	Mahanadi	Pilcomayo	
Ucayali	Manawatu	Porcupine	**12 letters:**
Uruguay	Menderes	Qu'Appelle	Guadalquivir
Vistula	Missouri	Rangitata	Murrumbidgee
Waikato	Mitchell	Richelieu	Saõ Francisco
Washita	Ocmulgee	Rio Branco	Saskatchewan
Wateree	Okanagan	Rio Grande	
Welland	Okavango	Salambria	**13 letters:**
Yangtse	Okovango	Santa Cruz	Little Bighorn
Yenisei	Ouachita	St George's	
Yenisey	Pactolus	White Nile	**17 letters:**
Zambese	Paraguay	Wisconsin	North
Zambezi	Parnaiba		Saskatchewan
	Putumayo	**10 letters:**	South
8 letters:	Rio Negro	Black Volta	Saskatchewan
Amu Darya	Safid Rud	Blackwater	
Anderson	Saguenay	Chao Phraya	
Apurimac	Savannah	Courantyne	

River-bank, Riverside Brim, Carse, Riparian
River-bed T(h)alweg

River-mouth Firth, Frith
Rivet(ing) Bolt, Clinch, Clink, Concentrate, Explosive, Fasten, Fix, Pean, Peen, Stud, Transfix, Unputdownable
Rivulet Beck, Brook, Burn, Gill, Rill, Runnel, Strand
RNA Antisense, → **DNA**, Messenger, Molecule, Retrotransposon, Ribosomal, Ribosome, Ribozyme, Soluble, Transcribe, Transfer, Uracil
Roach Fish, Red-eye
Road(s), Roadside, Road surface A, A1, Access, Anchorage, Arterial, Asphalt, Autobahn, Autopista, Autostrada, Ave(nue), B, Beltway, Blacktop, Boulevard, Burma, Carriageway, Causeway, Clay, Clearway, Close, Cloverleaf, Coach, Concession, Corduroy, Corniche, Course, Cul-de-sac, Dirt, Drift-way, Driveway, Dunstable, Escape, Exit, Expressway, Fairway, Feeder, Fly-over, Fly-under, Foss(e) Way, Freeway, Grid, Hampton, Highway, Horseway, Kerb, Lane, Loan, Loke, Mall, Metal, M1, Motorway, Orbital, Overpass, Parkway, Path, Pike, Post, Private, Rat-run, Rd, Relief, Ride, Ridgeway, Ring, → **ROUTE**, Royal, Service, Shoulder, Shunpike, Side, Skid, Slip, Speedway, Spur(way), St(reet), Superhighway, Switchback, Tarmac, Tar-seal, Thoroughfare, Tobacco, Toby, Track(way), Trunk, Turning, Turnpike, Unadopted, Underpass, Unmade, Verge, Via, Viaduct, Way
Road-block Barrier, Cone, Jam, Toll
Road-keeper Way-warden
Road-maker Drunkard, Macadam, Navigator, Telford, Wade
Roadstead La Hogue
Roam Extravagate, Peregrinate, Rake, Ramble, Rove, Stray, Wander, Wheel
Roan Barbary, Bay, Horse, Leather, Schimmel, Strawberry
Roar(ing) Bawl, Bell(ow), Bluster, Boom, Boys, Cry, Forties, Guffaw, Laugh, Roin, Rote, Rout, Royne, Thunder, Tumult, Vroom, Wuther, Zoom
Roast Bake, Barbecue, Baste, Birsle, Brent, Cabob, Cook, Crab, Crown, Decrepitate, Grill, Kabob, Pan, Pot, Ridicule, Scald, Scathe, Sear, Slate, Tan, Torrefy
Rob(bed), Robber(y) Abduct, Bandalero, Bandit, Barabbas, Bereave, Blag, Brigand, Burgle, Bust, Cabbage, Cacus, Cateran, Clyde, Dacoit, Dakoit, Daylight, Depredation, Despoil, Do, Drawlatch, Fake, Filch, Fleece, Flimp, Footpad, Gilderoy, Heist, Hership, Highjack, High toby, Highwayman, Hijack, Hold-up, Hustle, Job, Kondo, Ladrone, Land-pirate, Larceny, Latrocinium, Latron, Loot, Mill, Moskonfyt, Mosstrooper, Pad, Pandoor, Pandour, Pillage, Pinch, Piracy, Pluck, Plunder, Procrustes, Ramraid, Rapine, Reave, Reft, Reive, Rieve, Rifle, Roberdsman, Robertsman, Roll, Rover, Roy, Rubbet, Rustler, Sack, Sciron, Screw, Short change, Sinis, Skinner, Smash and grab, Snaphaunch, Spoiler, Spoliation, → **STEAL**, Steaming, Stick-up, Sting, Swindle, Thief, Toby, Turn-over, Turpin
Robe(s) Alb, Amice, Amis, Attrap, Buffalo, Camis, Camus, Cassock, Chimer, Chrisom(-cloth), Christom, Dalmatic, Dolman, → **DRESS**, Gown, Ihram, Jilbab, Kanzu, Khalat, Khilat, Kill(a)ut, Kimono, Mantle, Night, Parament, Parliament, Pedro, Peplos, Pontificals, Purple, Regalia, Rochet, Saccos, Sanbenito, Soutane, Sticharion, Stola, Stole, Talar, Tire, Vestment, Yukata
Robert Bob(by), Bridges, Browning, Burns, Cop, Flic, Peel, Rab, Rob
Robin Adair, American, Bird, Cock, Day, Goodfellow, Hob, Hood, Puck(-hairy), Ragged, Redbreast, Reliant, Round, Ruddock, Starveling, Wake
Robot Android, Automaton, Cyborg, Dalek, Golem, Nanobot, Puppet, RUR, Telechir
Robust Hale, Hardy, Healthy, Hearty, Iron, Lusty, Muscular, Sound, Stalwart, Sthenic, Stout, Strapping, Sturdy, Vigorous
Roc Bird, Ruc, Rukh
Rock(s), Rocker, Rocking, Rocky Acid, Ages, Agitate, Astound, Ayers, Cap, Cock,

Country, Cradle, Destabilise, Edinburgh, Erratic, Garage, Gib(raltar), Heavy metal, Hybrid, Mantle, Marciano, Matrix, Native, Nunatak(kr), Permafrost, Petrology, Platform, Plymouth, Punk, Quake, Reel, Reggae, Reservoir, Rip-rap, Rudaceous, Sally, Scare, → SHAKE, Shoogle, Showd, Soft, Stonehenge, Stun, Sway, Swee, Swing, Ted, Teeter, Totter, Tremble, Uluru, Unstable, Unsteady, Weeping, Wind, Windsor

ROCKS

2 letters:
Aa

3 letters:
Gem
Ice
Jow
Tor

4 letters:
Bell
Coal
Crag
Gang
Glam
Jura
Lava
Lias
Noup
Reef
Sill
Sima
Trap
Tufa
Tuff
Wall
Zoic

5 letters:
Arête
Brash
Calpe
Chair
Chalk
Chert
Cliff
Craig
Elvan
Emery
Flint
Geode
Glass
Krans

Loess
Magma
Nappe
Peter
Scalp
Scrae
Scree
Shale
Slate
Solid
Stone
Trass
Wacke

6 letters:
Albite
Aplite
Arkose
Banket
Basalt
Dacite
Desert
Diapir
Dogger
Dunite
Flaser
Flysch
Fossil
Gabbro
Gangue
Garnet
Gibber
Gneiss
Gossan
Gozzan
Inlier
Kingle
Living
Marble
Masada
Norite
Oolite
Oolith

Ophite
Pelite
Pluton
Pumice
Rognon
Sarsen
Schist
Sinter
Skerry
Sklate
S. Peter
Stonen
Synroc
Tephra

7 letters:
Aquifer
Archean
Arenite
Boulder
Breccia
Clastic
Cuprite
Cyanean
Diamond
Diorite
Erathem
Eucrite
Fastnet
Felsite
Geofact
Granite
Greisen
Haplite
Igneous
Lignite
Lorelei
Marlite
Minette
Molasse
Moraine
Needles
Olivine

Ophites
Outcrop
Outlier
Peridot
Picrite
Remanie
Rhaetic
Sinking
Spilite
Stadium
Syenite
Terrane
Thulite
Tripoli
Wenlock

8 letters:
Adularia
Aegirine
Aiguille
Andesite
Aphanite
Archaean
Asbestos
Basanite
Brockram
Burstone
Calcrete
Calc-tufa
Calc-tuff
Ciminite
Diabasic
Dolerite
Dolomite
Eclogite
Eklogite
Elvanite
Eutaxite
Fahlband
Felstone
Footwall
Ganister
Hepatite

Hornfels
Idocrase
Inchcape
Isocline
Laterite
Lenticle
Lopolith
Mesolite
Mudstone
Mylonite
Obsidian
Peperino
Petuntse
Phyllite
Pisolite
Plutonic
Porphyry
Psammite
Psephite
Ragstone
Regolith
Rhyolite
Rocaille
Roe-stone
Saxatile
Saxonite
Scorpion
Sunstone
Taconite
Tarpeian
Tephrite
The Olgas
Tonalite
Trachyte
Trappean
Volcanic
Xenolith

9 letters:
Anticline
Argillite
Batholite
Batholith
Bentonite
Bluestone
Buhrstone
Claystone
Cockhorse

Colluvium
Cornstone
Dalradian
Diatomite
Dolostone
Eddystone
Evaporite
Firestone
Flagstone
Flowstone
Gannister
Goslarite
Granulite
Greensand
Greystone
Greywacke
Gritstone
Hornstone
Impactite
Intrusion
Ironstone
Laccolite
Laccolith
Lardalite
Larvikite
Limestone
Meteorite
Mica-slate
Migmatite
Monadnock
Monocline
Monzonite
Mortstone
Mugearite
Natrolite
Neocomian
Ophiolite
Ottrelite
Pegmatite
Phonolite
Phosphate
Pleonaste
Propylite
Protogine
Quartzite
Sandstone
Saprolite
Scablands

Schistose
Siltstone
Soapstone
Tachylyte
Theralite
Tinguaite
Toadstone
Travertin
Underclay
Variolite
Veinstone
Veinstuff
Ventifact
Vulcanite
Whinstone
White Lias
Whunstane
Zechstein

10 letters:
Ailsa Craig
Amygdaloid
Camptonite
Epidiorite
Foundation
Granophyre
Greenstone
Grey-wether
Hypabyssal
Ignimbrite
Kersantite
Kimberlite
Laurdalite
Laurvikite
Lherzolite
Limburgite
Mica-schist
Novaculite
Orthophyre
Palagonite
Peridotite
Phenocryst
Pitchstone
Pyroxenite
Rupestrian
Schalstein
Serpentine
Sparagmite

Stinkstone
Stonebrash
Syntagmata
Teschenite
Touchstone
Travertine
Troctolite

11 letters:
Agglomerate
Amphibolite
Annabergite
Anorthosite
Carbonatite
Geanticline
Halleflinta
Lamprophyre
Metamorphic
Monchiquite
Napoleonite
Nephelinite
Phillipsite
Pyroclastic
Sedimentary
Symplegades

12 letters:
Babingtonite
Baltic Shield
Coal Measures
Granodiorite
Grossularite
Slickenslide
Straticulate
Stromatolite
Syntagmatite
Thunderstone

13 letters:
Hypersthenite

14 letters:
Roche moutonnée

18 letters:
Scandinavian Shield

Rock-boring Pholas
Rock-cress Arabis

Rocket Arugula, Blue, Booster, Capsule, Carpet, Carrier, Congreve, Dame's, Delta, Drake, Dressing down, Dyer's, Engine, Eruca, Flare, Ion, Jato, Life, London, Missile, Multistage, Onion, Posigrade, Reprimand, Reproof, Retro, Rockoon, Salad, SAM, Sea, Skylark, Soar, Sonde, Sounding, Step, Stephenson, Take-off, Thruster, Tourbillion, Ullage, Upshoot, V1, Vernier, Von Braun, Wall, Warhead, Weld, Yellow, Zero stage

Rock-living Rupicoline, Saxatile, Saxicoline, Saxicolous

Rock-pipit Sea-lark

▷ **Rocky** *may indicate* an anagram

Rococo Baroque, Fancy, Ornate, Quaint

Rod(-shaped), Rodlike, Rods Aaron's, Axle, Baculiform, Bar, Barbe(l)l, Barre, Birch, Caduceus, Caim, Came, Can, Cane, Centre, Connecting, Control, Cue, Cuisenaire®, Dipstick, Divining, Dowser, Drain, Ellwand, Fasces, Filler, Fin-ray, Firearm, Fisher, Fishing, Fly, Fuel, Gold stick, Gun, Handspike, Jacob's staff, Kame, King, Laver, Lightning, Linchpin, Lug, Mapstick, Mopstick, Moses, Napier's bones, Nervure, Newel, Notochord, Perch, Pin, Pistol, Piston, Pitman, Pointer, Poker, Poking-stick, Pole, Pontie, Pontil, Ponty, Probang, Puntee, Punty, Push, Raddle, Regulating, Rhabdoid, Rhabdus, Riding, Rood, Scollop, Shaft, Sounding, Spindle, Spit, Stadia, Stair, Stanchion, Staple, Stave, Stay-bolt, Stick, Strickle, Switch, Tension, Tie, Track, Triblet, Tringle, Trocar, Twig, Urochord, Ventifact, Verge, Virgate, Virgulate, Wand, Welding, Withe

Rod-bearer Lictor

Rode Raid

Rodent Acouchi, Acouchy, Ag(o)uti, Agouty, Bandicoot, Bangsring, Banxring, Beaver, Biscacha, Bizcacha, Bobac, Bobak, Boomer, Capybara, Cavy, Chickaree, Chincha, Chinchilla, Chipmunk, Civet, Coypu, Cricetus, Dassie, Deer-mouse, Delundung, Dormouse, Fieldmouse, Gerbil(le), Glires, Glutton, Gnawer, Gopher, Groundhog, Guinea pig, Ham(p)ster, Hedgehog, Hog-rat, Hutia, Hyrax, Hystricomorph, Jerboa, Jird, Lemming, Marmot, Mole rat, Mouse, Murid, Mus, Musk-rat, Musquash, Ochotona, Ondatra, Paca, Porcupine, Potoroo, Prairie dog, Rat, Ratel, Ratton, Renegade, Runagate, Sciurine, Sewellel, Shrew, Simplicidentate, S(o)uslik, Spermophile, Springhaas, Springhase, Squirrel, Taguan, Taira, Tuco-tuco, Tucu-tuco, Vermin, Viscacha, Vole, Woodchuck, Woodmouse

Roderick Random, Usher

Rodomontade Bluster, Boast, Bombast, Brag, Gas

Roe Avruga, Caviar(e), Coral, Fry, Hard, Melt, Milt(z), Pea, Raun, Rawn, Soft

Roger Ascham, Bacon, Jolly, OK, Rights

Rogue, Roguish(ness) Arch, Bounder, Charlatan, Chiseller, Drole, Dummerer, Elephant, Espiègle(rie), Ganef, Ganev, Ganof, Gonif, Gonof, Greek, Gypsy, Hedge-creeper, Hempy, Herries, Imp, Knave, Latin, Limmer, Monkey, Panurge, Picaresque, Picaroon, Pollard, Rapparee, Ra(p)scal(l)ion, Riderhood, Savage, Scamp, Schellum, Schelm, Scoundrel, Skellum, Sleeveen, Slip-string, Sly, Swindler, Varlet, Villain, Wrong' un

Roil Agitate, Annoy, Churn, Provoke, Vex

Roister(er) Blister, Carouse, Ephesian, Revel, Rollick, Scourer, Scowrer, Swashbuckler, Swinge-buckler

Role Bit, Cameo, Capacity, Function, Gender, Métier, → **PART**, Prima-donna, Stead, Title, Travesty

Roll(ed), Roller, Roll-call, Rolling, Rolls Absence, Bagel, Bap, Barrel, Beigel, Billow, Birmingham, Bolt, Bridge, Brioche, Butterie, Calender, Cambridge, Chamade, Comber, Convolv(ut)e, Cop, Couch, Court, Croissant, Cylinder, Dandy,

Drum, Dutch, Electoral, Enswathe, Eskimo, Even, Fardel, Fardle, Flatten, Forward, Furl, Go, Goggle, Hotdog, Inker, Involute, Labour, List, Loaded, Lurch, Makimono, Mangle, Mano, Matricula, Motmot, Moving, Music, Muster, Notitia, Opulent, Paradiddle, Patent, Paupiette, Pay, Petit-pain, Piano, Pigeon, Pipe, Platen, Rafale, Ragman, Record, Reef, Reel, Register, Ren, Rent, Revolute, Revolve, Rhotacism, Ring, Road, Rob, Rolag, Roster, Rota, Rotate, Rotifer, Roul(e), Roulade, Rouleau, RR, Rub-a-dub, Rumble, Run, Sausage, Schnecke(n), Skin up, Snap, Somersault, Spool, Spring, Sway, Swell, Swiss, Table, Tandem, Taxi, Temple, Tent, Terrier, Thread, Toilet, Tommy, Trill, Trindle, Trundle, Valuation, Victory, Volume, Volutation, Wad, Wallow, Wamble, Waul, Wave, Wawl, Web, Welter, Western, Wince, Wrap, Yaw, Zorbing

Rollick(ing) Frolic, Gambol, Romp, Sport

▷ **Rollicking** *may indicate* an anagram

Roly-poly Chubby

Roman Agricola, Agrippa, Aurelius, Calpurnia, Candle, Catholic, Cato, Consul, CR, Crassus, Decemviri, Decurion, Empire, Flavian, Galba, Holiday, Italian, Jebusite, Latin, Maecenas, Papist, Patrician, PR, Quirites, Raetic, RC, Retarius, Rhaetia, Road, Scipio, Seneca, Sulla, Tarquin, Tiberius, Trebonius, Type, Uriconian, Veneti, Volsci

Romance, Romantic (talk) Affair, Amorous, Byronic, Casanova, Catalan, Dreamy, Fancy, Fantasise, Fib, Fiction, Gest(e), Gothic, Historical, Invention, Ladin(o), Ladinity, Langue d'oc(ian), Langue d'oil, Langue d'oui, Liaison, Lie, Neo-Latin, New, Novelette, Poetic, Quixotic, R(o)uman, Stardust, Tale

▶ **Romanian** *see* RO(U)MANIAN

Romanov Nicholas

▶ **Romany** *see* GYPSY

Rome Holy See, Imperial City

Romeo Casanova, Montagu, R, Swain

Romp(ing) Carouse, Escapade, Fisgig, Fizgig, Frisk, Frolic, Hoyden, Jaunce, Randy, Rig, Rollick, Skylark, Sport, Spree

Ron Glum, Moody

Rondo Rota

Ronnie Biggs

Röntgen R, X-ray

Roo Joey

Roof (edge), Roofing Belfast, Bell, Broach, Ceil, Cl(e)ithral, Cover, Curb, Divot, Dome, Drip, Eaves, French, Gable, Gambrel, Hardtop, Hip(ped), Home, Hypostyle, Imperial, Jerkin-head, Leads, Mansard, Monopitch, Palate, Pavilion, Pent, Pitched, Pop-top, Porte-cochère, Rag top, Rigging, Saddle, Saddleback, Shingle, Skillion, Skirt, Span, Sun(shine), Targa top, Tectiform, Tectum, Tegula, Thatch, Thetch, Tiling, Top, Uraniscus

Roof-climber Stegopholist

Roofless Hypaethral, Upaithric

Rook Bird, Castle, Cheat, Crow, Fleece, Fool, Overcharge, R, Swindle

Rookie Beginner, Colt, Galoot, Greenhorn, Nignog, Novice, Recruit, Tenderfoot, Tyro

Room(s), Roomy Antechamber, Anteroom, Apadana, Apartment, Assembly, Attic, Ben, Berth, Bibby, Boardroom, Boiler, Boudoir, Bower, But, Cabin(et), Camarilla, Camera, Capacity, Casemate, CC, Ceiling, Cell, Cellar, Cenacle, Chamber, Chancellery, Changing, Chat, Chaumer, Closet, Cockloft, Combination, Commodious, Compartment, Composing, Conclave, Consulting, Control, Cubicle,

Cuddy, Cutting, Dark, Day, Delivery, Digs, Dissecting, Divan, Dojo, Drawing, Dressing, Durbar, Elbow, End, Engine, Ex(h)edra, Extension, Foyer, Gap, Garret, Genizah, Green, Grill, Gun, Herbarium, Incident, Kiva, Kursaal, Lab, Latitude, Laura, Lavra, Lebensraum, Leeway, Leg, Library, Living, Locker, Lodge, Loft, Long, Loo, Lounge, Margin, Megaron, Misericord(e), Mould-loft, Music, Oda, Operations, Oratory, Orderly, Oriel, Pad, Palm Court, Panic, Parlour, Parvis, Penetralia, Pentice, Pentise, Powder, Press, Priesthole, Private, Projection, Property, Public, Pump, Reading, Receiving, Reception, Recitation, Recovery, Recreation, Rest, Rm, Robing, Rubber, Rumpus, Sacristy, Sale(s), Salle, Salon, Sanctum, School, Scope, Scriptorium, Scullery, Serdab, Servery, Service, Shebang, Single, Single-end, Sitkamer, Sitting, Smoking, Snug, Solar, Solarium, → **SPACE**, Spacious, Spare, Spence, Spheristerion, Staff, Standing, Steam, Still, Stock, Stowage, Street, Strong, Studio, Study, Suite, Sun, Tap, Tea, Throne, Tiring, Tool, Twin, Two-pair, Ullage, Utility, Vestiary, Vestry, Voorkamer, Waiting, Ward, Wash, Wiggle, Work, Zeta

Roost(er) Cock, Perch, Siskin, Sit

Root(s), Rooted, Rooting Aruhe, Asarum, Beet, Buttress, Calamus, Calumba, Cassava, Cheer, Contrayerva, Costus, Cube, Culver's, Cuscus, Dasheen, Delve, Deracinate, Derivation, Derris, Dig, Eddo, Elecampane, Eradicate, Eringo, Eryngo, Etymic, Etymon, Extirpate, Fern, Fibrous, Foundation, Gelseminine, Ginseng, Grass, Grout, Grub, Heritage, Horseradish, Hurrah, Immobile, Implant, Incorrigible, Insane, Irradicate, Jalap, Jicama, Knee, Lateral, Licorice, Mallee, Mandrake, Mangold, Mishmee, Mishmi, Mooli, More, Myall, Navew, Nousle, Nuzzle, Origins, Orris, Pachak, Pleurisy, Pneumatophore, Poke, Prop, Pry, Putchock, Putchuk, Race, Radical, Radish, Radix, Repent, Rhatany, Rhizic, Rhizoid, Rhizome, Scorzonera, Senega, Sessile, Setwall, Snuzzle, Source, Square, Stilt, Stock, Tap, Taro, Tuber, Tuberous, Tulip, Turbith, Turnip, Turpeth, Vetiver, Yam, Zedoary

Rootless Psilotum

Rope(s) Abaca, Backstay, Ba(u)lk, Becket, Bind, Bobstay, Boltrope, Bracer, Brail, Breeching, Bunt-line, Cable, Cablet, Colt, Cord, Cordage, Cordon, Cringle, Downhaul, Drag, Earing, Fake, Fall, Flemish coil, Fore-brace, Foresheet, Forestay, Funicular, Futtock-shroud, Gantline, Grist, Guest, Guide, Guy, Halliard, Halser, Halter, Halyard, Hawser, Hawser-laid, Headfast, Inhaul, Jack-stay, Jeff, Jib-sheet, Jump, Kernmantel, Knittle, Ladder, Lanyard, Lasher, Lashing, Lasso, Lazo, Leg, Line, Longe, Lunge, Mainbrace, Mainsheet, Manil(l)a, Marlin(e), Match-cord, Messenger, Monkey, Mooring, Nettle, Nip, Noose, Oakum, Outhaul, Painter, Parbuckle, Pastern, Prolonge, Prusik, Pudding, Rawhide, Reef point, Riata, Ridge, Ringstopper, Roband, Robbin, Rode, Runner, St Johnston's ribbon, St Johnston's tippet, Sally, Seal, Selvagee, Sennit, Sheet, Shroud, Sinnet, Span, Spancel, Spun-yarn, Stay, Sternfast, Stirrup, String, Sugan, Swifter, Tackle, Tail, Tether, Tie, Timenoguy, Tippet, Tow(line), Trace, Trail, Triatic, Triatic stay, Vang, Wanty, Warp, Widdy, Wire

Rosalind Ganymede

Rosary Beads, Mala, Paternoster

Rose(-red), Rosie, Rosy Albertine, Amelanchier, Aurorean, Avens, Bear's-foot, Blooming, Bourbon, Breare, Briar, Brier, Burnet, Cabbage, Canker, Ceiling, Cherokee, China, Christmas, Compass, Corn, Damask, Dog, Eglantine, Eglatère, England, Floribunda, Geum, Golden, G(u)elder, Hellebore, Hybrid, Jack, Jacque, Jacqueminot, Lal(age), Lancaster, Lee, Monthly, Moss, Multiflora, Musk, Noisette, Opulus, Peace, Petra, Pink, Potentilla, Promising, Provence, Province, Provincial, Provine, Pyrus, Quillaia, Quillaja, Rambler, Red(dish), Remontant, Rhoda, Rhodo-,

Rock, Rugosa, Scotch, Snowball, Sprinkler, Standard, Sweetbrier, Tea, Tokyo, Tudor, White, Whitethorn, York

Rose-apple Jamboo, Jambu

Rose-bay Oleander

Rosemary Rosmarine

Rosette Buttonhole, Chou, Cockade, Favour, Patera, Rosula

Rosin Colophony, Resin, Roset, Rosit, Rozet, Rozit

Rosinante Jade

Roster List, Register, Scroll, Table

Rostrum Ambo, Bema, Lectern, Podium, Pulpit, Tribune

Rot(ten), Rotting Addle, Baloney, Boo, Bosh, Botrytis, Bull, Caries, Carious, Corrode, Corrupt, Crown, Daddock, Decadent, → DECAY, Decompose, Decrepitude, Degradable, Dotage, Dry, Eat, Erode, Fester, Foot, Foul, Gangrene, Kibosh, Manky, Mildew, Noble, Nonsense, Poppycock, Poxy, Punk, Putid, Putrefy, Putrid, Rail, Rancid, Rank, Rat, Red, Ret, Rhubarb, Ring, Rust, Sapropel, Septic, Soft, Sour, Squish, Twaddle, Vrot, Wet

Rotate, Rotating, Rotation, Rotator Crop, Feather, Gyrate, Laevorotation, Lay-farming, Optical, Pivot, Pronate, Rabat(te), Reamer, Revolve, Roll, Selsyn, Teres, Trundle, Turn, Turntable, Twiddle, Vorticose, Wheel, Windmill

Rote Heart, Memory, Recite, Routine

Rotor Auxiliary, Flywheel, Impeller, Tilt

▶ **Rotten** *see* ROT

▷ **Rotten** *may indicate* an anagram

Rotter Cad, Knave, Stinker, Swine

Rotund Chubby, Corpulent, Plump, Round, Stout, Tubby

Rotunda Pantheon

Roué Debauchee, Decadent, Libertine, Profligate, Rake(-shame), Rip

Rouge Blush, Gild, Jeweller's, Raddle, Redden, Reddle, Ruddy

Rough(en), Roughly, Roughness About, Abrasive, Approximate, Asper(ate), Burr, C, Ca, Choppy, Circa, Coarse, Craggy, Crude, Exasperate, Frampler, Grained, Gross, Gruff, Gurly, Gusty, Hard, Harsh, Hispid, Hoodlum, Hooligan, Impolite, Imprecise, Incondite, Inexact, Irregular, Jagged, Karst, Keelie, Kokobeh, Muricate, Obstreperous, Or so, Push, Ragged, Ramgunshoch, Raspy, Raucle, Rip, Risp, Robust, Row, Rude, Rugged, Rusticate, Rusty, Sandblast, Scabrid, Scabrous, Sea, Shaggy, Sketchy, Some, Spray, Spreathe, Squarrose, Stab, Strong-arm, Stubbly, Swab, Tartar, Tearaway, Ted, Textured, Tousy, Touzy, Towsy, Towzy, Uncut, Violent, Yahoo

Roughage Ballast, Bran, Fodder

Rough breathing Asper, Rale, Wheeze

Roughcast Harl

▷ **Roughly** *may indicate* an anagram

Roulette Russian

Ro(u)manian, Rumanian Ro, R(o)uman, Vlach, Wal(l)achian

Round(ness) About, Ammo, Ball, Beat, Bombe, Bout, Cartridge, Catch, Circle, Complete, Cycle, Dome, Doorstep, Fat, Figure, Full, Global, Globate, Hand, Heat, Jump-off, Lap, Leg, Milk, O, Oblate, Orb, Orbicular, Orbit, Orby, Ought, Patrol, Peri-, Pirouette, Plump, Qualifying, Quarter, Quarter-final, Rev, Ring, Robin, Roly-poly, Ronde, Rondure, Rota, Rotund, Route, Routine, Rundle, Rung, Salvo, Sandwich, Sarnie, Sellinger's, Semi-final, Shot, Skirt, Slice, Sphaer, Sphere, Spherical, Spiral, Step, Table, Tour, Tubby, U-turn

▷ **Round** *may indicate* a word reversed

Roundabout Ambages, Approximately, Bypass, Carousel, Circle, Circuit, Circumambient, Circumbendibus, Circus, Devious, Eddy, → INDIRECT, Merry-go-round, Peripheral, Rotary, Tortuous, Traffic circle, Turntable, Waltzer, Whirligig, Windlass
Round building Tholos, Tholus
Rounders Patball
Round-mouth Hag
Round-up Bang-tail muster, Collate, Corner, Corral, Gather, Herd, Rodeo, Spiral
Roup Auction, Croak, Pip, Roop
Rouse, Rousing Abrade, Abraid, Abray, Amo(o)ve, Animate, Beat, Bestir, Emotive, Enkindle, Firk, Flush, Hearten, Heat, Innate, Kindle, Knock up, Rear, Send, Stimulate, Suscitate, Unbed, Waken, Whip
Rousseau Émile
Rout Clamour, Debacle, Defeat, Drub, Fleme, Flight, Hubbub, Hurricane, Rabble, Retreat, Rhonchal, Snore, Thiasus, Upsee, Upsey, Upsy, Vanquish, Whoobub
Route Arterial, Avenue, Byroad, Causeway, Course, Direction, Itinerary, I-way, Line, Ling, M-way, Path, Red, Road, Stock, Track, Trade, Via, Way
Routine Automatic, Day-to-day, Drill, Everyday, Grind, Groove, Habitual, Heich-how, Heigh-ho, Ho-hum, Jogtrot, Journeywork, Monotony, Pattern, Perfunctory, Pipe-clay, Red tape, Rota, Rote, Round, Rut, S(c)htick, Schtik, Treadmill, Workaday
Rove(r), Roving Car, Discursive, Enrange, Errant, Freebooter, Gad, Globetrotter, Marauder, Nomad, Proler, Prowl, Ralph, Range, → ROAM, Slub(b), Stray, Vagabond, Varangarian, Viking, Wander
Row(er) Align, Altercation, Arew, Argue, Argument, Bank, Barney, Bedlam, Bobbery, Bow, Brattle, Cannery, Colonnade, Death, Debate, Deen, Din, Dispute, Dust-up, Feud, File, Fireworks, Food, Fyle, Hoo-ha, Hullabaloo, Leander, Line(-up), Noise, Note, Oar, Octastich, Paddle, Parade, Peripteral, Pluriserial, Pull, Quarrel, Rammy, Range, Rank, Raunge, Remigate, Reproach, Rew, Rhubarb, Rotten, Ruction, Rumpus, Scene, Scull, Series, Set, Shindig, Shindy, Shine, Skid, Spat, Splore, Stern, Stound, Street, Stridor, Stroke, Stushie, Sweep, Terrace, Tier, Tiff, Tone, Torpid, Wetbob, Wherryman
Rowan Ash, Quicken
Rowdy, Rowdiness Cougan, Hoo, Hooligan, Loud, Noisy, Rorty, Rough, Roughhouse, Ruffian, Scourer, Scozza, Skinhead, Stroppy, Unruly, Uproarious
Roy Rob
Royal(ty), Royalist Academy, Angevin, Basilical, Battle, Bourbon, Emigré, Exchange, Fee, Hanoverian, Imperial, Imposing, Inca, Kingly, King's man, Majestic, Malignant, Palatine, Payment, Pharaoh, Plantagenet, Prince, Princess, Purple, Queenly, Real, Regal, Regis, Regius, Regnal, Sail, Sceptred, Society
Rub(bing), Rubber(y), Rub out Abrade, Attrition, Balata, Buff, Buna®, Bungie, Bungy, Bunje(e), Bunjie, Bunjy, Butyl, Calk, Calque, Camelback, Caoutchouc, Chafe, Cold, Condom, Corrade, Corrode, Cow gum®, Crepe, Cul(t)ch, Destroy, Dunlop®, Ebonite, Efface, Elastic, Elastomer, Embrocate, Emery, Erase, Factice, Factis, Fawn, Foam, Fray, Fret, Friction, Fridge, Frottage, Fudge, Funtumia, Gall, Galoch, Goodyear®, Grate, Graze, Grind, Guayule, Gum elastic, Gutta-percha, Hale, Hard, Hevea, Hule, India, Inunction, Irritate, Isoprene, Jelutong, Lagos, Latex, Leather, Masseur, Negrohead, Neoprene, Nuzzle, Obstacle, Para, Polish, Pontianac, Pontianak, Root, Safe, Sandpaper, Scour, Scrub, Scuff, Seringa, Silastic®, Smoked, Sorbo®, Sponge, Stroke, Synthetic, Towel, Trace, Ule, Vulcanite, Wild, Wipe, Xerotripsis

▷ **Rubbed** *may indicate* an anagram

Rubbish Balls, Brash, Brock, Bull, Bunkum, Cack, Clap-trap, Cobblers, Codswallop, Culch, Debris, Dre(c)k, Drivel, Fiddlesticks, Garbage, Grot, Grunge, Hogwash, Kack, Kak, Landfill, Leavings, Litter, Mullock, Nonsense, Phooey, Piffle, Pish, Raff, Raffle, → REFUSE, Scrap, Sewage, Stuff, Tinpot, Tip, Tom(fool), Tosh, Totting, Trade, Tripe, Trouch, Truck, Trumpery, Twaddle

Rubbish heap Dump, Lay-stall, Sweepings, Toom

Rubble Brash, Debris, Detritus, Moellon, Random, Remains, Riprap, Talus

Rubidium Rb

Ruby Agate, Balas, Brazilian, Colorado, Cuprite, Oriental, Pigeon's blood, Port, Red, Spinel, Star

Ruck Furrow, Scrum, Wrinkle

Rucksack Backpack, Bergen, Pikau

Ruction Ado, Fuss, Quarrel

Rudder Budget, Helm, Steerer

Ruddle Lemnian

Ruddy Bally, Bloody, Flashy, Florid, Red, Roseate, Rubicund, Rufous, Sanguine

Rude Abusive, Barbaric, Bear, Bestial, Bumpkin, Callow, Churlish, Coarse, Discourteous, Elemental, Goustrous, Green, Ill-bred, Impolite, Indecorous, Inficete, Ingram, Ingrum, Insolent, Ocker, Offensive, Peasant, Raw, Risqué, Rough, Simple, Surly, Unbred, Uncomplimentary, Uncourtly, Unlettered, Unmannered, Vulgar

Rudiment(ary), Rudiments ABC, Absey, Anlage, Beginning, Element, Embryo, Foundation, Germ(en), Germinal, Inchoate, Seminal, Vestige

Rudolph Hess, Reindeer

Rue(ful) Boulevard, Dittany, Goat's, Harmala, Harmel, Herb of grace, Meadow, Mourn, Regret, Repent, Rew, Ruta, Sorry, Wall

Ruff Collar, Crest, Fraise, Frill, Mane, Partlet, Pope, Rabato, Rebato, Ree, Trump

Ruffian Apache, Bashi-bazouk, Brute, Bully, Cut-throat, Desperado, Goon(da), Highbinder, Hoodlum, Hooligan, Keelie, Larrikin, Lout, Miscreant, Mohock, Myrmidon, Phansigar, Plug-ugly, Raff, Rowdy, Skinhead, Sweater, Tearaway, Thug, Toe-ragger, Trailbaston, Tumbler

Ruffle(d) Bait, Dishevel, Falbala, Flounce, Fluster, Fret, → FRILL, Gather, Irritate, Jabot, Peplum, Rouse, Ruche, Rumple, Shirty, Tousle

▷ **Ruffle** *may indicate* an anagram

Rug Afghan, Bearskin, Buffalo-robe, Carpet, Drugget, Ensi, Flokati, Gabbeh, Hearth, Herez, Heriz, Kelim, K(h)ilim, Kirman, Lap robe, Mat, Maud, Numdah, Oriental, Prayer, Runner, Rya, Scatter, Tatami, Throw, Travelling

Rugby (player) Back, Fifteen, Forward, Harlequin, Lion, Pack, Quin, RU, Scrum, Sevens, Threequarter, Touch, Wing

Rugged Craggy, Harsh, Knaggy, Rough, Strong

Ruin(ed), Ruins Annihilate, Blast, Blight, Blue, Carcase, Collapse, Corrupt, Crash, Crock, Damn, Decay, Defeat, Demolish, Despoil, Destroy, Devastate, Disfigure, Dish, Disrepair, Dogs, Doom, Downcome, Downfall, End, Fordo, Hamstring, Heap, Hell, Insolvent, Inure, Kaput(t), Kibosh, Loss, Mar, Mocers, Mockers, Mother's, Overthrow, Perdition, Petra, Pigs and whistles, Pot, Puckerood, Ravage, Reck, Relic, Scotch, Scupper, Scuttle, Shatter, Sink, Smash, Spill, → SPOIL, Stramash, Subvert, Undo, Unmade, Ur, Violate, Vitiate, Whelm, Woe, Wrack

▷ **Ruined** *may indicate* an anagram

Rule(r), Rules, Ruling Algorithm, Align, Aristocrat, Arrêt, Article, Bylaw, Caesar, Calliper, Canon, Chain, Club-law, Code, Condominium, Constitution, Control, Criterion, Decree, Domineer, Dominion, Empire, Establishment, Estoppel,

Etiquette, Fatwa, Feint, Fetwa, Fleming's, Formation, Formula, Gag, Global, Golden, Govern, Govern-all, Ground, Home, In, Jackboot, Law, Leibniz's, Lesbian, Lex, Lindley, Liner, Majority, Matriarchy, Maxim, McNa(u)ghten, Mede, Meteyard, Method, Ministrate, Mistress, Mobocracy, Motto, Naismith's, Netiquette, Norm(a), Oppress, Ordinal, Organon, Organum, Parallel, Parallelogram, Phase, Phrase-structure, Pie, Placitum, Plumb, Precedent, Precept, Prescript, Prevail, Principle, Protocol, Pye, Rafferty's, Raine, Realm, Reciprocity, Rector, Regal, Regnant, Regula, Reign, Rewrite, Ring, Rubric, Scammozzi's, Setting, Slide, Squier, Squire, Standard, Statute, Stylebook, Sutra, Sway, Ten-minute, Ten-yard, Three, Thumb, Transformation(al), Trapezoid, T-square, Tycoon, Tyrant, Uti possidetis, Wield

RULERS

1 letter:
K
R

3 letters:
Ban
Bey
Dey
Mir
Oba
Raj
Rex

4 letters:
Amir
Cham
Czar
Doge
Duce
Emir
Imam
Inca
Khan
King
Nero
Pope
Rana
Shah
Tsar
Vali
Wali

5 letters:
Ameer
Ardri
Dewan
Diwan

Henry
Herod
Hoyle
Hyleg
Mogul
Mpret
Mudir
Nawab
Negus
Nizam
Pasha
Queen
Rajah
Shaka
Sheik
Sophi
Sophy
Tenno

6 letters:
Atabeg
Atabek
Bosman
Caliph
Castro
Chagan
Cheops
Dergue
Despot
Dynast
Exarch
Franco
Führer
Gerent
Harold
Hitler
Judges

Kabaka
Kaiser
Mamluk
Manchu
Mikado
Peshwa
Prince
Regent
Ronald
Sachem
Satrap
Sherif
Shogun
Sirdar
Stalin
Sultan
Swaraj
Walter

7 letters:
Abbasid
Ardrigh
Bajayet
Bajazet
Bodicea
Catapan
Chogyal
Elector
Emperor
Gaekwar
Gaikwar
Jamshid
Jamshyd
Khedive
Miranda
Monarch
Omayyad

Pharaoh
Podesta
Richard
Saladin
Serkali
Souldan
Toparch
Umayyad
Viceroy
Zamorin

8 letters:
Archduke
Autocrat
Bismarck
Boudicca
Burgrave
Caligula
Caudillo
Cromwell
Dictator
Ethnarch
Frederic
Heptarch
Hespodar
Hierarch
Maharaja
Mamaluke
Mameluke
Napoleon
Oligarch
Overlord
Padishah
Pericles
Reginald
Roderick
Sagamore

Sassanid	Cleopatra	**10 letters:**	Stadtholder
Suleiman	Cosmocrat	Caractacus	Tutankhamun
Suzerain	Frederick	Plantocrat	
Synarchy	Montezuma	Principate	**12 letters:**
Tetrarch	Ochlocrat	Rajpramukh	Chandragupta
Thearchy	Pendragon	Stratocrat	
	Plutocrat		**13 letters:**
9 letters:	Potentate	**11 letters:**	Haile Selassie
Alexander	President	Charlemagne	
Amenhotep	Sovereign	Genghis Khan	
Bretwalda	Tamerlane	Prester John	
Britannia		Queensberry	

Rule-book Code, Pie, Pye

Rum(mer) Abnormal, Bacardi, Bay, Cachaca, Curious, Daiquiri, Demerara, Eerie, Eery, Glass, Grog, Island, Jamaica, Odd(er), Peculiar, Quaint, Queer, Screech, Strange, Tafia, Weird

▶ **Rumanian** *see* RO(U)MANIAN

Rumble, Rumbling Borborygmus, Brool, Curmurring, Drum-roll, Groan, Growl, Guess, Lumber, Mutter, Rumour, Thunder, Tonneau, Twig

Ruminant, Ruminate Antelope, Cabrie, Camel, Cavicornia, Cervid, Champ, Chew, Contemplate, Cow, Gemsbok, Gnu, Goat, Meditate, Merycism, Nilgai, Nyala, Okapi, Oorial, Palebuck, Pecora

Rummage Delve, Fish, Foray, Jumble, Powter, Ransack, Rifle, Root, Rootle, Scavenge, Search, Tot

Rummy Canasta, Cooncan, Game, Gin, Queer

Rumour Breeze, Bruit, Buzz, Canard, Cry, Fame, Furphy, → GOSSIP, Grapevine, Hearsay, Kite, Kite-flying, Mail, Noise, On-dit, Pig's-whisper, Report, Repute, Say-so, Smear, Tale, Talk, Underbreath, Unfounded, Vine, Voice, Whisper, Word

Rump Arse, Bottom, Buttocks, Croup(e), Croupon, Crupper, Curpel, Derrière, Nates, Parliament, Podex, Pygal, Steak, Uropygium

Rumple Corrugate, Crease, Mess, Muss, Touse, Tousle, Touze, Towse, Towze, Wrinkle

Rumpus Bagarre, Commotion, Noise, Riot, Row, Ruction, Shindig, Shindy, Shine, Stushie, Tirrivee, Uproar

Run(ning), Run away, Run into, Run off, Runny, Runs Admin(ister), Arpeggio, Black, Bleed, Blue, Bolt, Break, Bunk, Bye, Career, Chase, Coop, Corso, Course, Cresta, Cross-country, Current, Cursive, Cut, Dart, Dash, Decamp, Direct, Double, Drive, Dry, Dummy, Enter, Escape, Extra, Fartlek, Flee, Flit, Flow, Fly, Follow, Fun, Fuse, Gad, Gallop, Gauntlet, Go, Green, Ground, Hare, Haste(n), Hennery, Hie, Hightail, Home, Idle, Jog, Jump bail, Ladder, Lauf, Leg, Leg bye, Lienteric, Liquid, Lope, Manage, Marathon, Melt, Milk, Mizzle, Mole, Molt, Monkey, Neume, Now, On, On-line, Operate, Pace, Pacific, Paper chase, Parkour, Pelt, Ply, Pour, Print, Purulent, R, Race, Range, Red, Renne, Rin, Romp, Roulade, Rounder, Ruck, Scamper, Scapa, Scarper, School, Schuss, Scud, Scutter, Scuttle, See, Sequence, Shoot, Single, Skate, Skedaddle, Ski, Skid, Skirr, Skitter, Slalom, Slide, Smuggle, Spew, Split, Spread, Sprint, Sprue, Squitters, Stampede, Straight, Streak, Stream, Taxi, Tear, Tenor, Tie-breaker, Trial, Trickle, Trill, Trot

Runaway Drain, Easy, Escapee, Fugitive, Fugue, Refugee

Run down Asperse, Belie, Belittle, Calumniate, Denigrate, Derelict, Dilapidated, Infame, Knock, Low, Obsolesce(nt), Poorly, Rack, Résumé, Scud, Seedy, Tirade, Traduce

Rune, Runic Ash, Futhark, Futhorc, Futhork, Kri, Ogham, Spell, Thorn, Wen, Wyn(n)
Rung Crossbar, Roundel, Rundle, Stave, Step, Tolled, Tread
Runner(s) Atalanta, Bean, Blade, Bow Street, Carpet, Coe, Courser, Deserter, Emu, Field, Geat, Gentleman, Gillie-wetfoot, Harrier, Hatta, Hencourt, Internuncio, Lampadist, Leg bye, Legman, Messenger, Miler, Milk, Mohr, Mousetrap, Nurmi, Owler, Rug, → RUN(NING), Sarmentum, Scarlet, Series, Slipe, Smuggler, Stolon, Stream, Tailskid, Trial
▷ **Running, Runny** *may indicate* an anagram
Runt Dilling, Oobit, Oubit, Reckling, Scalawag, Scrog, Smallest, Titman, Woobut, Woubit
Run through Impale, Pierce, Rehearsal
Runway Airstrip, Drive, Slipway, Strip, Tarmac®
Run wild Lamp, Rampage
Rupee(s) Lac, Lakh, Re
Rupert Bear
Rupture Breach, Burst, Crack, Hernia, Rend, Rhexis, Rift, Split
Rural Agrarian, Agrestic, Boo(h)ai, Booay, Boondocks, Bucolic, Country, Cracker-barrel, Forane, Georgic, Hick, Mofussil, Platteland, Praedial, Predial, Redneck, Rustic, Sticks, The Shires, Wop-wops
Ruse Artifice, Decoy, Dodge, Engine, Hoax, Pawk, Stratagem, → TRICK
Rush(ed) Accelerate, Barge, Bolt, Bustle, Career, Charge, Dart, Dash, Eriocaulon, Expedite, Faze, Feese, Feeze, Feze, Fly, Frail, Friar, Gad, Gold, Gust, Hare, Hasten, High-tail, → HURRY, Hurtle, Jet, Juncus, Lance, Lash, Leap, Luzula, Moses, Odd-man, Onset, Palmiet, Pellmell, Phase, Pheese, Pheeze, Phese, Plunge, Precipitate, Railroad, Rampa(u)ge, Rash, Rayle, Reed, Rip, Scamp(er), Scirpus, Scour, Scud, Scurry, Sedge, Spate, Speed, Stampede, Star(r), Streak, Streek, Surge, Swoop, Swoosh, Tear, Thrash, Thresh, Tilt, Torrent, Tule, Viretot, Zap, Zoom
Rusk Zwieback
Russell AE, Bertrand, Jack
Russet Rutile
Russia(n), Russian headman, Russian villagers Apparatchik, Ataman, Belorussian, Beria, Bolshevik, Boris, Boyar, Byelorussian, Chechen, Chukchee, Chukchi, Circassian, Cossack, Dressing, D(o)ukhobor, Esth, Igor, Ingush, Ivan, Kabardian, Kalmuk, Kalmyck, Leather, Lett, Mari, Menshevik, Mingrel(ian), Minimalist, Mir, Misha, Muscovy, Octobrist, Osset(e), Red, Romanov, Rus, Russ(niak), Russki, Ruthene, Salad, Serge, Slav, Stakhanovite, SU, Thistle, Udmurt, Uzbeg, Uzbek, Vladimir, Vogul, White, Yakut, Yuri, Zyrian
Rust(y) Aeci(di)um, Blister, Brown, Corrode, Cor(ro)sive, Erode, Etch, Ferrugo, Iron oxide, Iron-stick, Maderise, Oxidise, Puccinia, Rubiginous, Soare, Stem, Teleutospore, Telium, Uredine, Uredo, Verdigris, Yellow
Rust-fungus Aecidiospore
Rustic Arcady, Bacon, Bor(r)el(l), Bucolic, Bumpkin, Chawbacon, Churl, Clodhopper, Clown, Corydon, Cracker-barrel, Culchie, Damon, Doric, Forest, Georgic, Hayseed, Hick, Hillbilly, Hind, Hob, Hobbinoll, Hodge, Homespun, Idyl(l), Pastorale, Peasant, Pr(a)edial, Put(t), Rube, Rural, Strephon, Swain, Sylvan, Uplandish, Villager, Villatic, Yokel
▷ **Rustic** *may indicate* an anagram
Rusticate Banish, Seclude
Rustle(r), Rustling Abactor, Crinkle, Duff, Fissle, Frou-frou, Gully-raker, Poach,

Speagh(ery), Sprechery, Steal, Stir, Susurration, Swish, Thief, Whig
Rust-proof Zinced
Rut Channel, Furrow, Groove, Heat, Routine, Sulcus, Track
Ruth Babe, Compassion, Mercy, Pity, Remorse
Ruthenium Ru
Rutherfordium Rf
Ruthless Brutal, Cruel, Dog eat dog, Fell, Hard, Hardball, Hard-bitten
Rwanda(n) Tutsi
Rye Gentleman, Grain, Grass, Spelt, Whisky

Ss

S Ogee, Saint, Second, Sierra, Society, South, Square
SA It, Lure
Sabbatarian Wee Free
Sabbath Juma, Lord's Day, Rest-day, Shabbat, Sunday, Witches'
Sabbatical Leave
Sabine Horace, Women
Sable American, Black, Jet, Negro, Pean, Zibel(l)ine
Sabotage, Saboteur Cripple, Destroy, Frame-breaker, Hacktivism, Ratten, Spoil, Treachery, Undermine, Vandalise, Worm, Wrecker
Sabre, Sabre rattler Jingo, Sword, Tulwar
Sabrina Severn
Sac Air, Allantois, Amnion, Aneurism, Aneurysm, Bag, Bladder, Bursa, Caecum, Cisterna, Cyst, Diverticulum, Embryo, Follicle, Pericardium, Peritoneum, Pod, Scrotum, Spermatheca, Tylose, Tylosis, Vesica, Vocal, Yolk
Saccharine Dulcite, Dulcose
Sack(cloth), Sacking Bag, Bed, Boot, Bounce, Budget, Burlap, Can, Cashier, Chasse, Chop, Coal, Congé, Congee, Dash, Depredate, Despoil, Discharge, Doss, Fire, Gunny, Havoc, Hessian, Hop-pocket, Jute, Knap, Lay waste, Loot, Mailbag, Maraud, Mitten, Pillage, Plunder, Poke, Push, Rapine, Reave, Replace, Rieve, Road, Rob, Sad, Sanbenito, Sherris, Sherry, Spoliate, Vandalise
▷ **Sacks** *may indicate* an anagram
Sacrament Baptism, Christening, Communion, Confirmation, Eucharist, Extreme unction, Housel, Lord's Supper, Matrimony, Nagmaal, Orders, Penance, Promise, Reconciliation, Ritual, Unction, Viaticum
Sacred (object), Sacred place Adytum, Churinga, Hallowed, Harim, Heart, Hierurgy, → **HOLY**, Ineffable, Manito(u), Nine, Omphalos, Padma, Pietà, Sacrosanct, Sanctum, Taboo, Tapu, Temenos
Sacrifice Alcestic, Cenote, Forego, Gambit, Gehenna, Hecatomb, Holocaust, Immolate, Iphigenia, Isaac, Lay down, Molech, Moloch, Oblation, → **OFFERING**, Peace offering, Relinquish, Sati, Suovetaurilia, Supreme, Surrender, Suttee, Taurobolium, Tophet, Vicarious, Victim
Sacrilege, Sacrilegious Blaspheme, Impiety, Profane, Violation
Sacristan, Sacristy Diaconicon, Sceuophylax, Sexton
Sacrosanct Inviolable
Sad(den), Sadly, Sadness Alas, Attrist, Blue, Con dolore, Dejected, Depressed, Desolate, Disconsolate, Dismal, Doleful, Dolour, Downcast, Drear, Dull, Dumpy, Fadeur, Heartache, Lovelorn, Low, Lugubrious, Mesto, Mournful, Oh, Plangent, Sorrowful, Sorry, Tabanca, Tearful, Tear-jerker, Threnody, Tragic, Triste, Tristesse, Unhappy, Wan, Wo(e)begone
Saddle (bag, cloth, girth, pad) Alforja, Aparejo, Arson, Burden, Cantle, Cinch, Col, Crupper, Demipique, Kajawah, Lumber, Numnah, Oppress, Pack, Pad, Panel,

Pigskin, Pilch, Pillion, Seat, Sell(e), Shabrack, Shabracque, Side, Stock, Tree, Western

Saddle-bow Arson

Saddler Whittaw(er)

Sadie Thompson

Sadism, Sadistic Algolagnia, Cruel

▷ **Sadly** *may indicate* an anagram

Safari Expedition, Hunt

Safe(ty) Active, Allright, Almery, Ambry, Coolgardie, Copper-bottomed, Delouse, Deposit, GRAS, Harmless, Immunity, Impunity, Inviolate, Keister, Meat, Night, Passive, Peter, Reliable, Roadworthy, Sanctuary, Secure, Sound, Strong-box, Strongroom, Sure, Whole-skinned, Worthy

Safeguard Bulwark, Caution, Ensure, Fail-safe, Frithborh, Fuse, Hedge, Palladium, Protection, Register, Ward

Saffron Bastard, Crocus, False, Meadow, Mock, Yellow

Sag(gy) Decline, Dip, Droop, Hang, Hogged, Lop, Slump, Swayback, Wilt

Saga Aga, Chronicle, Edda, Epic, Icelandic, Laxdale, Legend, Odyssey, Volsunga

Sagacity, Sagacious Astute, Commonsense, Depth, Elephant, Judgement, Sapience, Wisdom

Sage(s) Abaris, Aquinian, Bactrian, Bias, Carlyle, Cheronian, Chilo(n), Clary, Cleobulus, Confucius, Counsellor, Egghead, Greybeard, Hakam, Herb, Imhotep, Jerusalem, Maharishi, Mahatma, Malmesbury, Manu, Mirza, Orval, Pandit, Periander, Philosopher, Pittacus, Rishi, Salvia, Savant, Seer, Seven, Solon, Tagore, Thales, Wiseacre, Wood

Sage-brush Nevada

Sago Portland

Sahib Pukka

Said Co, Emir, Port, Quo(th), Related, Reputed, Spoken, Stated

▷ **Said** *may indicate* 'sounding like'

Sail(s), Sailing Balloon, Bunt, Canvas, Circumnavigate, Cloth, Coast, Course, Cross-jack, Cruise, Drag, Drift, Fan, Fore(course), Fore-and-aft, Full, Gaff(-topsail), Genoa, Goose-wing, Head, Jib, Jigger, Jut, Land, Lateen, Leech, Luff, Lug, Moon, Moonraker, Muslin, Navigate, Orthodromy, Parachute spinnaker, Peak, Plain, Plane, Ply, Rag, Reef, Rig, Ring-tail, Royal, Sheet, Shoulder-of-mutton, Solar, Spanker, Spencer, Spinnaker, Spritsail, Square, Staysail, Steer, Studding, Stun, Suit, Top(-gallant), Top-hamper, Van, Vela, Wardrobe, Water, Yard

Sailor(s) AB, Admiral, Anson, Argonaut, Blue-jacket, Boatman, Boatswain, Bos'n, Bos(u)n, Budd, Commodore, Crew, Deckhand, Drake, Evans, Foremastman, Freshwater, Galiongee, Gob, Greenhand, Grommet, Hat, Hearties, Helmsman, Hornblower, Hydronaut, Jack, Janty, Jauntie, Jaunty, Jonty, Khalasi, Killick, Killock, Kroo(boy), Krooman, Kru(boy), Kruman, Lascar, Leadsman, Limey, Loblolly boy, Lt, Lubber, Mariner, Matelot, Matlo(w), Middy, MN, Nelson, Noah, NUS, Oceaner, OS, Polliwog, Pollywog, Popeye, Powder monkey, Privateer, Rating, RN, Salt, Seabee, Seacunny, Sea-dog, Sea-lord, → **SEAMAN**, Serang, Shellback, Sin(d)bad, Stowaway, Submariner, Tar, Tarp(aulin), Tarry-breeks, Tindal, Topman, Triton, Waister, Wandering, Water-dog, Yachtsman

Saint(ly), Saints Agatha, Agnes, Aidan, Alban, Alexis, Aloysius, Alvis, Ambrose, Andrew, Anselm, Anthony, Asaph, Audrey, Augustine, Barbara, Barnabas, Bartholomew, Basil, Bees, Benedict, Bernard, Bernardette, Boniface, Brandan, Brendan, Bridget, Brigid, Canonise, Canonize, Catharine, Cecilia, Chad, Christopher, Clement, Columba(n), Crispian, Crispin(ian), Cuthbert, Cyr, David,

Denis, Denys, Diego, Dominic, Dorothea, Dunstan, Dymphna, Elmo, Eloi, Elvis, Eulalie, Francis, Genevieve, George, Gertrude, Giles, Hagiology, Hallowed, Helena, Hilary, Hilda, Holy, Hugh, Ignatius, Isidor, James, Jerome, John, Joseph, Jude, Just, Kentigern, Kevin, Kilda, Latterday, Lawrence, Leger, Leonard, Linus, Loyola, Lucy, Luke, Malo, Margaret, Mark, Martha, Martin, Matthew, Michael, Monica, Mungo, Nicholas, Ninian, Odyl, Olaf, Oswald, Pancras, Patrick, Patron, Paul(inus), Peter, Pi, Pillar, Plaster, Polycarp, Quentin, Regulus, Ride, Rishi, Roch, Ronan, Roque, Rosalie, Rule, S, Sebastian, Severus, Simeon, Simon, Simon Zelotes, SS, St, Stanislaus, Stephen, Sunday, Swithin, Templar, Teresa, Thecia, Theresa, Thomas, Tobias, Ursula, Valentine, Veronica, Vincent, Vitus, Walstan, Wilfred, William, Winifred

St Anthony's fire Ergotism, Erysipelas
St Elmo's fire Corona discharge, Corposant
St James Scallop-shell
St Jerome Hieronymic
St John's bread Carob
St Lucia WL
St Paul's Wren-ch
St Vincent WV
Sake Account, Behalf, Cause, Drink
Sal Volatile
Salacious, Salacity Fruity, Lewd, Lust, Obscene, Scabrous
Salad Burnet, Caesar, Calaloo, Calalu, Chef's, Chicon, Corn, Cos, Cress, Cucumber, Days, Endive, Escarole, Fennel, Finnochio, Finoc(c)hio, Frisée, Fruit, Greek, Guacamole, Horiatiki, Lactuca, Lamb's lettuce, Lettuce, Lovage, Mesclum, Mesclun, Mixture, Niçoise, Purslane, Radicchio, Radish, Rampion, Rocket, Rojak, Roquette, Russian, Salmagundi, Salmagundy, Slaw, Tabbouleh, Tabbouli, Tomato, Waldorf, Word
▷ **Salad** *may indicate* an anagram
Salamander Axolotl, Congo eel, Ewt, Hellbender, Lizard, Menopome, Mole, Mudpuppy, Olm, Proteus, Siren, Snake, Spring-keeper
Salami, Salami technique Fraud, Peperoni
Salary Emolument, Fee, Hire, Pay, Prebend, Screw, Stipend, → WAGE
Sale(s) Auction, Breeze up, Cant, Car-boot, Clearance, Farm-gate, Fire, Garage, Jumble, Market, Outroop, Outrope, Pitch, Raffle, Retail, Roup, Rummage, Subhastation, Trade, Turnover, Upmarket, Venal, Vend, Vendue, Vent, Voetstoets, Voetstoots, Warrant, Wash, White, Wholesale, Yard
Saleroom Pantechnicon
Salesman Agent, Assistant, Bagman, Broker, Buccaneer, Bummaree, Counterhand, Counter jumper, Drummer, Huckster, Loman, Pedlar, Rep, Retailer, Tallyman, Tout, Traveller
Salient Coign, Jut, Projection, Prominent, Redan, Spur
Salisbury Cecil, Sarum
Saliva Drool, Parotid, Ptyalism, Sial(oid), Slobber, Spawl, Spit(tle), Sputum
Sallow Adust, Pallid, Pasty, Sale, Sauch, Saugh, Wan
Sally Aunt, Boutade, Charge, Dash, Escape, Excursion, Flight, Foray, Issue, Jest, Mot, Pleasantry, Quip, Ride, Sarah, Sortie, Wisecrack, Witticism
Salmagundi Mess
Salmon Alevin, Atlantic, Australian, Baggit, Blueback, Blue-cap, Boaz, Burnett, Chinook, Chum, Cock, Coho(e), Dog, Dorado, Grav(ad)lax, Grilse, Humpback, Kelt, Keta, King, Kipper, Kokanee, Lax, Ligger, Lox, Masu, Mort, Nerka, Oncorhynchus,

Ouananiche, Par(r), Peal, Pink, Quinnat, Red, Redfish, Rock, Samlet, Shedder, Silver, Skegger, Slat, Smelt, Smolt, Smout, Smowt, Sockeye, Sparling, Spirling, Sprod

Salon, Saloon Barrel-house, Car, Hall, Honkytonk, Last chance, Lounge, Nail bar, Pullman, Sedan, Shebang, Tavern

Salt(s), Salty AB, Acid, Alginate, Aluminate, Andalusite, Antimonite, Arsenite, Aspartite, Attic, Aurate, Azide, Base, Bath, Bicarbonate, Bichromate, Borate, Borax, Brackish, Brine, Bromate, Bromide, Capr(o)ate, Caprylate, Carbamate, Carbonate, Carboxylate, Celery, Cerusite, Chlorate, Chlorite, Chromate, Citrate, Complex, Corn, Cure(d), Cyanate, Cyclamate, Datolite, Deer lick, Diazonium, Dichromate, Dioptase, Dithionate, Double, Enos, Epsom, Ferricyanide, Formate, Glauber, Glutamate, Halite, Halo-, Health, Hydrochloride, Hygroscopic, Iodide, Ioduret, Isocyanide, Kosher, Lactate, Lake-basin, Lithate, Liver, Magnesium, Malate, Malonate, Manganate, Mariner, Matelot, Microcosmic, Monohydrate, Mucate, Muriate, NaCl, Nitrate, Nitrite, Oleate, Orthosilicate, Osm(i)ate, Oxalate, Palmitate, Pandermite, Perborate, Perchlorate, Periodate, Phosphate, Phosphite, Phthalate, Picrate, Piquancy, Plumbate, Plumbite, Potassium, Powder, Propionate, Pyruvate, Rating, Reh, Resinate, Rochelle, Rock, Rosinate, Sailor, Sal ammoniac, Salify, Sal volatile, Saut, Sea-dog, Seafarer, Seasoned, Sebate, Selenate, Smelling, Soap, Sodium, Solar, Sorrel, Stannate, Stearate, Suberate, Succinate, Sulfite, Sulphate, Sulphite, Sulphonate, Table, Tannate, Tantalate, Tartrate, Tellurate, Tellurite, Thiocyanate, Thiosulphate, Titanate, Tungstate, Uranin, Urao, Urate, Vanadate, Volatile, Water-dog, White, Wit(ty), Xanthate

Salt meat Mart
Saltpetre Caliche, Chile, Cubic, Nitre, Norway
Salt-water Sea
Salubrious Healthy, Sanitary, Wholesome
Salutary Beneficial, Good, Wholesome
Salutation, Salute Address, Asalam-wa-leikum, Australian, Ave, Banzai, Barcoo, Bid, Cap, Cheer, Command, Coupé(e), Curtsey, Embrace, Feu de joie, Fly-past, Genuflect, Greet, Hail, Hallo, Halse, Homage, Honour, Jambo, Kiss, Middle finger, Namas kar, Namaste, Present, Salaam, Salvo, Sieg Heil, Toast, Tribute, Wassail
Salvador Dali
Salvage Dredge, Lagan, Ligan, Reclaim, Recover, Recycle, Rescue, Retrieve, Tot
Salvation(ist) Booth, Redemption, Rescue, Socinian, Soterial, Yeo
Salve Anele, Anoint, Assuage, Ave, Lanolin(e), Lotion, Ointment, Remedy, Saw, Tolu, Unguent, Weapon
Salver Tray, Waiter
Salvo Fusillade, Salute, Volley
Sal volatile Hartshorn
Sam Browse, Soapy, Uncle, Weller
Samara Ash-key
Samaritan Good
Samarium Sm
Same(ness) Ae, Agnatic, Contemporaneous, Do, Egal, Ejusd(en), Equal, Ib(id), Ibidem, Id, Idem, Identical, Identity, Ilk, Iq, Like, One, Thick(y), Thilk, Uniform, Ylke
Samovar Urn
Samoyed Dog, Uralian, Uralic
Sample, Sampling Amniocentesis, Biopsy, Blad, Browse, Example, Fare, Foretaste, Handout, Matched, Muster, Pattern, Pree, Prospect, Quadrat, Quota, Scantling,

Smear, Specimen, Spread, Stratified, Swatch, Switch, → **TASTE**, Taster, Transect, Try
Samuel Pepys, Smiles
Samurai Ronin
▷ **Sam Weller** *may indicate* the use of 'v' for 'w' or vice versa
Sanctify Consecrate, Purify, Saint
Sanctimonious Banbury, Creeping Jesus, Devout, Goody-goody, Pi, Religiose, Righteous, Saintly
Sanction(s), Sanctioned Allow, Appro, Approbate, Approof, Approve, Authorise, Bar, Countenance, Economic, Endorse, Green light, Imprimatur, Legitimate, Mandate, OK, Pass, Pragmatic, Ratify, Smart, Sustain, Upstay, Warrant
Sanctities, Sanctity Halidom, Holiness, Hollidam, Sonties
Sanctuary, Sanctum Adytum, Asylum, By-room, Cella, Ch, Church, Frithsoken, Frithstool, Girth, Grith, Holy, Kaaba, Lair, Naos, Oracle, Penetralia, Preserve, Refuge, Sacellum, Sacrarium, → **SHELTER**, Shrine, Tabernacle, Temple
Sand(s), Sandbank, Sandbar, Sandy Alec, Alex, Alexander, Areg, Arena(ceous), Arenose, Arkose, As, Atoll, Bar, Barchan(e), Bark(h)an, Beach, Caliche, Dene, Desert, Dogger Bank, Down, Dudevant, Dune, Dupin, Eremic, Erg, Esker, Foundry, Gat, George, Ginger, Goodwin, Grain, Granulose, Hazard, Hurst, Light, Loess, Machair, Nore, Oil, Overslaugh, Podsol, Podzol, Portlandian, Psammite, Ridge, River, Sabulous, Sawney, Seif dune, Shelf, Shoal, Shore, Singing, Tar, Tee, Time, Tombolo
Sandal(s) Alpargata, Buskin, Calceamentum, Chappal, Espadrille, Flip-flop, Ganymede, Geta, Huarache, Jelly, Patten, Pump, Slip-slop, Talaria, Thong, Zori
Sandalwood Algum, Almug, Chypre, Pride, Santal
Sandarac Arar
Sander Pike-perch
Sandhopper Amphipod
Sandhurst RMA
Sand-loving Ammophilous, Psammophil
Sandpiper Bird, Dunlin, Knot, Oxbird, Ree, Ruff, Sandpeep, Stint, Terek
Sandstone Arkose, Calciferous, Cat's brains, Dogger, Fa(i)kes, Flysch, Grit, Hassock, Holystone, Itacolumite, Kingle, Molasse, New Red, Old Red, Psammite, Quartzite, Red, Silica
Sandstorm Haboob, Tebbad
Sandwich(es) Bruschetta, Butty, Club, Clubhouse, Croque-monsieur, Cuban, Doorstep, Earl, Hamburger, Hoagie, Island, Jeely piece, Open, Panini, Piece, Roti, Round, Sanger, Sango, Sarmie, Sarney, Sarnie, Smørbrød, Smörgåsbord, Smørrebrød, Stottie, Sub, Submarine, Tartine, Thumber, Toastie, Toebie, Triple-decker, Twitcher, Victoria, Wad, Zak(o)uski
▷ **Sandwich(es)** *may indicate* a hidden word
Sane, Sanity Compos mentis, Formal, Healthy, Judgement, Rational, Reason, Sensible, Wice
Sangfroid Aplomb, Cool, Poise
Sanguine Confident, Hopeful, Optimistic, Roseate, Ruddy
Sanitary Hygienic, Salubrious, Sterile
Sanskrit Bhagavad-Gita, Panchatantra, Purana, Ramayana, Sutra, Upanishad, Vedic
Santa (Claus) Abonde, Kriss Kringle, Secret
Sap Benzoin, Bleed, Cremor, Drain, Enervate, Entrench, Ichor, Juice, Laser, Latex, Lymph, Mine, Mug, Pulque, Ratten, Resin, Roset, Rosin, Rozet, Rozit, Secretion, Soma, Sura, Swot, Undermine, Weaken

Sapid Flavoursome, Savoury, Tasty
Sapience, Sapient Discernment, Sage, Wisdom
Sapling Ash-plant, Ground-ash, Plant, Tellar, Teller, Tiller, Youth
Sapper(s) Miner, RE
Sapphire Star, Water, White
Sappho Lesbian
Sapwood Alburnum
Sarah Battle, Gamp, Sal
Sarcasm, Sarcastic Acidity, Antiphrasis, Biting, Cutting, Cynical, Derision, Irony, Mordacious, Mordant, Pungent, Quip, Quotha, Sarky, Satire, Sharp, Smartmouth, Snide, Sting, Wisecrack
Sardine Fish, Sard
Sardonic Cutting, Cynical, Ironical, Scornful, Wry
Sargasso Ore, Sea(weed)
Sark Chemise, CI, Shirt
Sarong Sulu
SAS Red Devils
Sash Baldric(k), Band, Belt, Burdash, Cummerbund, Fillister, Obi, Scarf, Window
Sassaby Tsessebe
Sassenach English, Lowlander, Pock-pudding
Satan Adversary, Apollyon, Arch-enemy, Cram, → DEVIL, Eblis, Evil One, Lucifer, Prince of darkness, Shaitan, Tempter
Satchel Bag, Scrip
Sate(d), Satiate Cloy, Glut, Replete, Sad, Surfeit
Satellite Adrastea, Ananke, Ariel, Artificial, Astra, Atlas, Attendant, Aussat, Belinda, Bianca, Bird, Callisto, Calypso, Camenae, Carme, Charon, Communications, Comsat®, Cordelia, Cosmos, Cressida, Deimos, Desdemona, Despina, Dione, Disciple, Early bird, Earth, Echo, Elara, Enceladus, Europa, Explorer, Fixed, Follower, Galatea, Galilean, Ganymede, Geostationary, Helene, Henchman, Himalia, Hipparchus, Hyperion, Iapetus, Intelsat, Io, Janus, Lackey, Larissa, Leda, Lysithea, Meteorological, Metis, Mimas, Miranda, Moon, Mouse, Nereid, Oberon, Ophelia, Orbiter, Pan, Pandora, Pasiphae, Phobos, Phoebe, Portia, Prometheus, Puck, Rhea, Rosalind, Sinope, SPOT, Sputnik, Syncom, Telesto, Telstar, Tethys, Thalassa, Thebe, Tiros, Titan, Titania, Triton, Umbriel, Weather
▶ **Satin** see SILK
Satire, Satirical, Satirist Arbuthnot, Archilochus, Burlesque, Butler, Candide, Chaldee, Dryden, Horace, Iambographer, Juvenal, Lampoon, Lash, Lucian, Mazarinade, Menippean, Mockery, Pantagruel, Parody, Pasquil, Pasquin(ade), Pope, Raillery, Sarky, Sotadic, Spoof, Squib, Swift, Travesty
Satisfaction, Satisfactory, Satisfy(ing), Satisfied, Satisfactorily Agree, Ah, Ap(p)ay, Appease, Assuage, Atone, Change, Compensation, Complacent, → CONTENT, Defrayment, Enough, Feed, Fill, Fulfil, Glut, Gratify, Happy camper, Indulge, Jake, Job, Liking, Meet, OK, Okey-dokey, Pacation, Palatable, Pay, Please, Propitiate, Qualify, Redress, Repay, Replete, Sate, Satiate, Serve, Settlement, Slake, Square, Suffice, Supply, Tickety-boo, Well
Saturate(d) Drench, Glut, Imbue, Impregnate, Infuse, Permeate, → SOAK, Sodden, Steep, Waterlog
Saturday Holy, Sabbatine
Saturn God, Kronos, Lead, Planet, Rocket
Satyr Faun, Leshy, Lesiy, Libertine, Marsyas, Pan, Silen(us), Woodhouse, Woodwose
Sauce, Saucy Agrodolce, Alfredo, Allemanse, Apple, Arch, Baggage, Barbecue,

Béarnaise, Béchamel, Bigarade, Bold(-faced), Bolognese, Bordelaise,
Bourguignonne, Bread, Brown, Caper, Carbonara, Catchup, Catsup, Chasseur,
Chaudfroid, Cheek, Chilli, Chutney, Condiment, Coulis, Cranberry, Cream,
Cumberland, Custard, Dapper, Dip, Dressing, Enchilada, Espagnole, Fenberry,
Fondue, Fu yong, Fu yung, Gall, Garum, Gravy, Hard, Hoisin, Hollandaise,
Horseradish, HP®, Impudence, Jus, Ketchup, Lip, Malapert, Marinade, Marinara,
Matelote, Mayonnaise, Melba, Meunière, Mint, Mirepoix, Mole, Monkeygland,
Mornay, Mousseline, Nam pla, Nerve, Newburg, Nuoc mam, Oxymal, Oyster,
Panada, Parsley, Passata, Peart, Peking, Pert, Pesto, Piert, Piri-piri, Pistou, Ponzu,
Portugaise, Ravigote, Relish, Remoulade, Rouille, Roux, Sabayon, Sal, Salpicon,
Salsa, Salsa verde, Sambal, Sass, Satay, Shoyu, Soja, Soubise, Soy, Soya, Stroganoff,
Sue, Supreme, Sweet and sour, Tabasco®, Tamari, Tartar(e), Tomato, Topping,
Tossy, Velouté, Vinaigrette, White, Wine, Worcester, Worcestershire
Sauceboat-shaped Scaphocephalate
Saucepan Chafer, Goblet, Skillet, Steamer, Stockpot
Saucer Ashtray, Discobolus, Pannikin, UFO
Sauna Bath, Sudatorium, Sudorific
Saunter Amble, Dacker, Da(i)ker, Dander, Lag, Mosey, Promenade, Roam, Shool,
Stroll, Toddle
Sausage(s) Andouille, Andouillette, Banger, Black pudding, Blood, Boerewors,
Bologna, Boudin, Bratwurst, Cervelat, Cheerio, Chipolata, Chorizo, Cumberland,
Devon, Drisheen, Frankfurter, Hot dog, Kishke, Knackwurst, Knockwurst,
Liver(wurst), Mortadella, Mystery bag, Pep(p)eroni, Polony, Pudding, Salami,
Sav(eloy), Snag(s), Snarler, String, Weenie, Weeny, White pudding, Wiener(wurst),
Wienie, Wurst, Zampone
Sausage-shaped Allantoid
Savage Ape, Barbarian, Boor, Brute, Cannibal, Cruel, Feral, Fierce, Frightful, Grim,
Gubbins, Immane, Inhuman, Maul, Noble, Sadistic, Truculent, Vitriolic, Wild
Savanna Plain, Sahel
Savant Expert, Mahatma, Sage, Scholar
Save, Saving(s) Bank, Bar, Besides, But, Capital, Conserve, Cut-rate, Deposit,
Economy, Except, Hain, Hoard, Husband, ISA, Keep, Layby, National, Nest egg,
Nirlie, Nirly, Not, PEPS, Post office, Preserve, Put by, Reclaim, Redeem, Relieve,
Reprieve, → **RESCUE**, Reskew, Sa', Salt, Salvage, Scrape, Scrimp, Shortcut, Slate
club, Soak away, Sock away, Spare, Stokvel, Succour, TESSA, Unless
Saviour Deliverer, Jesu(s), Messiah, Redeemer
Savour(ed), Savoury Aigrette, Bouchée, Canapé, Devils-on-horseback, Essence,
Fag(g)ot, Flavour, Olent, Ramekin, Relish, Resent, Sair, Sapid, Sar, Smack, Starter,
Tang, → **TASTE**, Vol au vent
Savoy Cabbage, Opera
Saw Adage, Aphorism, Apothegm, Azebiki, Back, Band, Beheld, Bucksaw, Buzz,
Chain, Circular, Cliché, Compass, Coping, Cross-cut, Crown, Cut, Dictum, Dovetail,
Dozuki, Flooring, Frame, Fret, Gang, Glimpsed, Gnome, Grooving, Hack, Hand, Jig,
Keyhole, Legend, Log, Maxim, Met, Motto, Pad, Panel, Paroemia, Pitsaw, Proverb,
Pruning, Quarter, Rabbeting, Rack, Ribbon, Rip, Ryoba, Sash, Saying, Scroll, Serra,
Skil®, Skip-tooth, Slogan, Span, Spied, Stadda, Stone, Sweep, Tenon, Trepan,
Trephine, Whip, Witnessed
Sawbones Surgeon
Saw-toothed Runcinate
Saxifrage Astilbe, Bishop's cap, Burnet, Golden, Heuchera, London pride,
Mitre-wort, St Patrick's cabbage

Saxon Cedric, Hengist, Wend
Say, Saying(s) Adage, Agrapha, Allege, Aphorism, Apophthegm, Apostrophise, Articulate, Axiom, Beatitude, Bon mot, Bromide, Byword, Cant, Catchphrase, Cliché, Declare, Dict(um), Eg, Enunciate, Epigram, Express, Fadaise, Gnome, Impute, Logia, Logion, → MAXIM, Mean, Mot, Mouth, Observe, Predicate, Pronounce, Proverb, Put, Quip, Recite, Rede, Relate, Remark, Report, Saine, Saw, Sc, Sententia, → SPEAK, Suppose, Sutra, Utter, Voice, Word
▷ **Say, Saying(s)** *may indicate* a word sounding like another
Scab(by) Blackleg, Crust, Eschar, Leggism, Leprose, Mangy, Rat, Scald, Scall, Sore, Strike-breaker
Scabbard Frog, Pilcher, Sheath, Tsuba
Scabies Itch, Psora, Scotch fiddle
Scabrous Harsh, Rough, Thersites
Scaffold(ing), Scaffolder Gallows, Gantry, Hoarding, Putlock, Putlog, Rig, Spiderman, Stage
Scald Blanch, Burn, Leep, Ploat, Plot
Scale(s), Scaly Analemma, API gravity, Ascend, Balance, Baumé, Beaufort, Binet-Simon, Bismar, Brix, Bud, Burnham, Celsius, Centigrade, Ceterach, Chromatic, → CLIMB, Cottony-cushion, Dandruff, Desquamate, Diagonal, Diatonic, Douglas, Elo, Escalade, Fahrenheit, Flake, Full, Furfur, Gamme, Gamut, Ganoid, Gapped, Gauge, Gravity, Gunter's, Hexachord, Humidex, Indusium, Interval, Kelvin, Ladder, Lamina, Layer, Leaf, Lepid, Lepidote, Leprose, Libra, Ligule, Likert, Lodicule, Loricate, Magnitude, Major, Mercalli, Mesel, Minor, Mohs, Munsell, Natural, Nominal, Octad, Ordinal, Palea, Palet, Patagium, Peel, Pentatonic, Pholidosis, Placoid, Plate, Platform, Ramentum, → RANGE, Rankine, Ratio, Réaumur, Regulo, Richter, San Jose, Scan, Scarious, Scent, Scincoid, Scurf, Scutellate, Shin, Skink, Sliding, Speel, Spring, Squama, Squame(lla), Submediant, Tegmentum, Tegula, Tonal, Tridymite, Tron(e), Unified, Vernier, Wage, Weighbridge, Wentworth, Wind
Scallop(ed) Bivalve, Clam, Coquille, Crenate, Escalop, Frill, Gimp, Mush, Pecten, Queenie, Vandyke
Scallywag Rascal, Scamp, Skeesicks, Whippersnapper
Scalp Cut, Scrape, Skin, Trophy
Scalpel Bistoury, Knife
Scam Ramp
Scamp Fripon, Imp, Limb, Lorel, Lorrell, Losel, Lozell, Neglect, → RASCAL, Reprobate, Rip, Rogue, Scallywag, Skeesicks, Toerag
Scamper Gambol, Lamp, Run, Scurry, Skedaddle, Skelter, Skitter
Scan(ning), Scanner CAT, CT, Examine, Flat-bed, Helical, Interlaced, OCR, Optical, Oversee, Peruse, PET, Rake, Raster, Scrutinise, Sector, SEM, Sequential, SPET, Survey, Tomography, Ultrasound, Vertical, Vet
Scandal(ous), Scandalise Belie, Canard, Commesse, Disgrace, Exposé, Gamy, Hearsay, Muck-raking, Opprobrium, Outrage, Shame, Slander, Stigma, Stink, Watergate
Scandinavian Dane, Finn, Laplander, Lapp, Nordic, Norman, Norseland, Northman, Olaf, Runic, Squarehead, Swede, Varangian, Viking
Scandium Sc
Scant(y) Bare, Brief, Exiguous, Ihram, Jejune, Jimp, Meagre, Poor, Scrimpy, Short, Shy, Skimpy, Slender, Spare, Sparse, Stingy
Scapegoat Butt, Fall-guy, Hazazel, Joe Soap, Patsy, Stooge, Target, Victim, Whipping-boy
Scapula Blade, Omoplate

Scar(face) Al, Blemish, Cheloid, Cicatrix, Cliff, Craig, Epulotic, Hilum, Keloid, Leucoma, Leukoma, Mark, Pockmark, Stigma, Ulosis, Wipe
Scarab Beetle, Gem
Scarce(ly), Scarcity Barely, Dear, Dearth, Famine, Few, Hardly, Ill, Lack, Paucity, Rare, Scanty, Seldom, Short, Strap, Uncommon, Want
Scare(mongering), Scaring Alarmist, Alert, Amaze, Fleg, Fright, Gally, Gliff, Glift, Hairy, Panic, Petrify, Skeer, Spook, Startle
Scarecrow Bogle, Bugaboo, Dudder, Dudsman, Gallibagger, Gallibeggar, Gallicrow, Gallybagger, Gallybeggar, Gallycrow, Malkin, Mawkin, Potato-bogle, Ragman, S(h)ewel, Tattie-bogle
Scarf Babushka, Belcher, Cataract, Comforter, Cravat, Curch, Doek, Dupatta, Fichu, Hai(c)k, Haique, Headsquare, Hyke, Lambrequin, Madras, Mantilla, Muffettee, Muffler, Neckatee, Neckcloth, Neckerchief, Neckgear, Neckpiece, Neckwear, Nightingale, Orarium, Pagri, Palatine, Pashmina, Pugg(a)ree, Rail, Rebozo, Sash, Screen, Stock, Stole, Tallith, Tippet, Trot-cosy, Trot-cozy, Vexillum
Scarifier Scuffler
Scarlet Cinnabar, Cochineal, Crimson, Pimpernel, Pink, Ponceau, Red, Vermilion
Scarper Abscond, Bunk, Run, Shoo, Welsh
Scat Aroint, Dropping
Scathe, Scathing Mordant, Sarcastic, Savage, Severe, Vitriolic
Scatter(ed), Scattering Bestrew, Broadcast, Diaspora, Disject, Dispel, → DISPERSE, Dissipate, Flurr, Inelastic, Interspace, Litter, Rayleigh, Rout, Scail, Skail, Sow, Sparge, Splutter, Sporadic, Spread, Sprinkle, Squander, Straw, Strew
Scatterbrain(ed) Dippy, Ditsy, Tête folie
Scavenge(r) Ant, Dieb, Forage, Hunt, Hy(a)ena, Jackal, Rake, Ratton, Rotten, Scaffie, Sweeper, Totter
Scenario Outline, Plot, Script, Worst case
Scene(ry) Arena, Boscage, Cameo, Coulisse, Decor, Flat(s), Landscape, Locale, Prop, Prospect, Set, Set piece, Sight, Site, Sketch, Stage, Tableau, Tormenter, Tormentor, Transformation, Venue, View
Scent Aroma, Attar, Chypre, Cologne, Eau de cologne, Essence, Fragrance, Frangipani, Fumet(te), Gale, Moschatel, Nose, Odour, Orris, Ottar, Otto, Perfume, Sachet, Smell, Spoor, Vent, Waft, Wind
Scentless Anosmia
Sceptic, Sceptical(ly), Scepticism Agnostic, Askant, Cynic, Doubter, Incredulous, Infidel, Jaundiced, Nihilistic, Nullifidian, Pyrrho(nic), Sadducee, Solipsism
Schedule Agenda, Calendar, Classification, Itinerary, Prioritise, Programme, Register, Slot, Table, Timescale, Timetable
Scheme(r), Scheming CATS, Colour, Concoct, Conspire, Crafty, Cunning, Dare, Darien, Dart, Decoct, Design, Devisal, Diagram, Dodge, Draft, Gin, Honeytrap, Housing, Intrigue, Jezebel, Machiavellian, Machinate, Manoeuvre, Nostrum, Pilot, → PLAN, Plat, Plot, Project, Proposition, Purpose, Put-up job, Racket, Rhyme, Ruse, Set-aside, Stratagem, System, Table, Top-hat, Wangle, Wheeze
Schism(atic) Disunion, Division, Eastern, Great, Greek, Heterodox, Rent, Secession, Split, Western
Schizo(phrenia) Catatonic, Dementia praecox, Hebephrenia
Schmaltz(y) Goo, Slush, Tear-jerker
Schmieder S
Schmuck Gunsel
Schnapps Enzian
Scholar, Scholiast Abelard, Academic, Alcuin, Alumni, Atticus, BA, Bookman,

Boursier, Catachumen, Clergy, Clerisy, Clerk, Commoner, Demy, Disciple, Erasmus, Erudite, Etonian, Exhibitioner, Extern(e), Externat, Goliard, Graduate, Grecian, Hafiz, Inkhorn, Jowett, Literate, Littérateur, MA, Mal(l)am, Masorete, Maulana, Noter, Occam Ulama, Ollamh, Ollav, Pauline, Plutarch, Polymath, Pupil, Rhodes, Sap, Savant, Schoolboy, Sizar, Soph, → **STUDENT**, Tabardar, Taberdar, Taberder, Tom Brown

Scholarship Bursary, Closed, Education, Erudition, Exhibition, Grant, Grant-in-aid, Learning, Lore, Mass, Rhodes

School Academy, Ampleforth, Approved, Ash Can, Barbizon, Bauhaus, Beacon, Benenden, Bluecoat, Board, Boarding, Charm, Charterhouse, Chartreux, Chautauqua, Cheder, Choir, Church, Classical, Coed, Community, Composite, Comprehensive, Conservative, Conservatoire, Conservatory, Cool, Correspondence, Council, Crammer, Cult, Dada, Dame, Day, Direct grant, Dojo, Downside, Drama, Drill, Driving, Dual, Educate, Elementary, Essenes, Eton, Exercise, Externat, Faith, Fettes, Finishing, First, Flemish, Foundation, Frankfurt, Free, Gam, Giggleswick, Gordonstoun, Grade, Graduate, Grammar, Grant-aided, Grant-maintained, Group, Gymnasien, Gymnasium, Harrow, Heder, Hedge, High, Historical, Home, Honour, Hospital, Hostel, Hypermodern, Independent, Industrial, Infant, Institute, Integrated, Intermediate, Ionic, Jim Crow, Junior, Kailyard, Kaleyard, Kant, Kindergarten, Lake, Lancing, Language, Life, List D, Loretto, Lower, LSE, Lycée, Lyceum, Madrassah, Magnet, Mahayana, Maintained, Maintaining, Manchester, Mannheim, Marlborough, Middle, National, Night, Normal, Nursery, Old, Oundle, Palaestra, Parnassian, Parochial, Pensionnat, Perse, Piano, Play, Pod, Poly, Porpoises, Prep, Preparatory, Primary, Private, Progymnasium, Provided, Public, RADA, Ragged, RAM, Ramean, Real, Reformatory, Repton, Residential, Rhodian, Roedean, Rossall, Rydal, Sabbath, Sadducee, St Trinian's, Satanic, Scandalous, Sciences, Scul, Scull(e), Secondary(-modern), Sect, Seminary, Separate, Shoal, Single-sex, Sink, Ski, Slade, Sole charge, Song, Spasmodic, Special, State, Stonyhurst, Stowe, Style, Summer, Sunday, Teach, Tonbridge, Trade, → **TRAIN**, Tutor, Upper, Voluntary(-aided), Voluntary-controlled, Wellington, Whales, Winchester, Writing, Yeshiva

Schoolboy, Schoolgirl Carthusian, Coed, Colleger, East, Etonian, Fag, Gait, Geit, Gyte, Miss, Monitor, Oppidan, Petty, Stalky, Wykehamist

School-leaver Abiturient

Schoolma'am, Schoolman, Schoolmaster, Schoolmistress Aram, Beak, Dominie, Duns, Holofernes, Miss, Occam, Orbilius, Pedagogue, Pedant, Sir, Squeers, Teacher, Tutress, Ursuline

Schooner Glass, Hesperus, Prairie, Ship, Tern

Sciatica Hip-gout

Science Anatomy, Anthropology, Applied, Art, Astrodynamics, Astrophysics, Atmology, Axiology, Biology, Botany, Chemistry, Christian, Cognitive, Computer, Cybernetics, Dismal, Domestic, Earth, Electrodynamics, Entomology, Eth(n)ology, Euphenics, Exact, Geodesy, Geology, Information, Life, Materia medica, Mechanics, Metallurgy, Natural, Noble, Nomology, Occult, Ology, Ontology, Optics, Optometry, Pedagogy, Penology, Physical, Physics, Policy, Political, Pure, Rocket, Rural, Serology, Skill, Social, Soft, Soil, Sonics, Stinks, Stylistics, Tactics, Technics, Technology, Telematics, Thremmatology, Toxicology, Typhlology, Zootechnics

Science fiction Cyberpunk

Scientist Alchemist, Anatomist, Archimedes, Aston, Astronomer, Atomist, Boffin, BSc, Cavendish, Climatologist, Copernicus, Curie, Dalton, Davy, Dopper, Egghead, Einstein, Experimenter, Expert, Faraday, Fourier, FRS, Galileo, Geodesist, Harvey,

Heaviside, Kennelly, Lodge, Lovell, Mendeleev, Newton, Oersted, Pascal, Pasteur, Pauli, Piccard, Potamologist, Réaumur, Researcher, Theremin, Volta

Scimitar Acinaciform, Sword

Scintillate Dazzle, Emicate, Gleam, Glitter, → SPARKLE

Scion Cion, Graft, Imp, Offspring, Sien(t), Sprig, Sprout, Syen

Scissors Clippers, Criss-cross, Cutters, Forfex, Nail, Probe, Shears

Scoff Belittle, Boo, Chaff, Deride, Dor, Eat, Feast, Flout, Food, Gall, Gibe, Gird, Gobble, → JEER, Mock, Rail, Rib, Ridicule, Roast, Scaff, Scorn, Sneer, Taunt

Scold(ing) Admonish, Berate, Callet, Catamaran, Chastise, Chide, Clapperclaw, Cotquean, Do, Earful, Earwig, Flite, Flyte, Fuss, Jaw(bation), Jobation, Lecture, Nag, Objurgate, Philippic, Rant, Rate, → REBUKE, Reprimand, Reprove, Revile, Rouse on, Row, Sas(s)arara, Sis(s)erary, Slang, Slate, Termagant, Threap, Threep, Through-going, Tick-off, Tongue-lash, Trimmer, Upbraid, Virago, Wig, Xant(h)ippe, Yaff, Yankie, Yap

Sconce Candlestick, Crown, Forfeit, Head, Ice, Nole

Scone Drop, Girdle

Scoop Bale, Dipper, Exclusive, Gouge, Grab, Hollow, Ladle, Lap, Pale, Rout, Shovel, Trowel

Scooter Vespa®

Scope Ambit, Bargaining, Diapason, Domain, Elbow-room, Extent, Freedom, Gamut, Ken, Latitude, Leeway, Play, Purview, Range, Remit, Room, Rope, Scouth, Scowth, Size, Sphere

Scorch(er) Adust, Blister, Brasero, → BURN, Char, Destroy, Frizzle, Fry, Parch, Scouther, Scowder, Scowther, Sear, Singe, Soar, Speed, Swale, Swayl, Sweal, Sweel, Torrefy, Torrid, Wither

Score(s), Scoring Apgar, Behind, Bill, Birdie, Bradford, Bye, Capot, Chalk up, Chase, Conversion, Count, Crena, Debt, Eagle, Etch, Full, Groove, Hail, Honours, Ingroove, Ippon, Koka, Law, Lots, Magpie, Make, Music, Net, Nick, Notation, Notch, Nurdle, Open, Partitur(a), Peg, Pique, Point, Record, Repique, Rit(t), Rouge, Run, Rut, Scotch, Scratch, Scribe, Scrive, Set, Single, Spare, Stableford, Stria, String, Sum, Tablature, → TALLY, TE, Twenty, Vocal, Waza-ari, Win

Score-board, Score-sheet Card, Telegraph

▷ **Scorer** *may indicate* a composer

▷ **Scoring** *may indicate* an anagram

Scorn(ful) Arrogant, Bah, Contemn, Contempt, Contumely, Deride, Despise, Dis(s), Disdain, Dislike, Disparagement, Flout, Geck, Haughty, Insult, Meprise, Mock, Opprobrium, Phooey, Putdown, Rebuff, Ridicule, Sarcastic, Sardonic, Sarky, Scoff, Scout, Sdaine, Sdeigne, Sneer, Sniffy, Spurn, Wither

Scorpion Book, Chelifer, False, Father-lasher, Pedipalp(us), Vinegarroon, Water, Whip

Scot(sman), Scots(woman), Scottish Angus, Antenati, Berean, Blue-bonnet, Bluecap, Caledonian, Celt, Clansman, Covenanter, Duni(e)wassal, Dunniewassal, Erse, Fingal, Gael, Highland, Ian, Jock, Kelt, Kiltie, Kitty, Knox, Laird, Lallan(s), Lot, Lowland, Luckie, Lucky, Mac, Mon, Peght, Pict, Ross, Sandy, Sawn(e)y, Shetlander, Stuart, Tartan, Tax, Teuchter, Torridonian

Scotch(man) Censor, Dish, Distiller, Glenlivet®, Notch, Score, Scratch, Thwart, Usquebaugh, Whisky

Scot-free Wreakless

Scotland Alban(y), Albion, Caledonia, Gaeltacht, Gaidhealtachd, Lallans, Lothian, NB, Norland, Scotia

Scoundrel Cad, Cur, Dog, Fink, Heel, Knave, Rat, Reprobate, Scab, Smaik, Varlet, → VILLAIN

Scour Beat, Depurate, Full, Holystone, Purge, Quarter, Scrub
▷ **Scour** *may indicate* an anagram
Scourge Bible-thumper, Cat, Discipline, Flagellate, Knout, Lash, Pest, → **PLAGUE**, Scorpion, Whip, Wire
Scout Akela, Beaver, Bedmaker, Bird dog, Colony, Disdain, Explorer, Flout, Guide, King's, Outrider, Pathfinder, Pickeer, Pioneer, Queen's, Reconnoitre, Rover, Runner, Scoff, Scorn, Scourer, Scurrier, Scurriour, Sea, Sixer, Spial, Spyal, Talent, Tenderfoot, Tonto, Track, Vedette, Venture
Scowl(ing) Frown, Glower, Gnar, Lour, Lower, Sullen
Scrabble Paw
Scrag(gy) Bony, Dewitt, Ewe-necked, Neck, Scrawny
Scram Begone, Hence, Scat, Shoo
Scramble Addle, Clamber, Encode, Grubble, Hurry, Mêlée, Mix, Motocross, Muss(e), Scamble, Sprattle, Sprawl, Swerve, Texas
Scrap(s), Scrappy Abandon, Abrogate, → **BIT**, Cancel, Conflict, Cutting, Discard, Dump, → **FIGHT**, Fisticuffs, Fragment, Fray, Iota, Jot, Junk, Mêlée, Mellay, Morceau, Morsel, Odd, Off-cut, Ort, Ounce, Papier collé, Patch, Piece, Pig's-wash, Rag, Rase, Raze, Remnant, Scarmoge, Scissel, Scissil, Scrub, Set-to, Shard, Sherd, Shred, Skerrick, Skirmish, Snap, Snippet, Spall, Tait, Tate, Tatter, Titbit, Trash, Truculent, Whit
Scrap book Album, Grangerism
Scrap box Tidy
Scrape(r) Abrade, Agar, Bark, Clat, Claw, Comb, Curette, D and C, Erase, Escapade, Grate, Graze, Gride, Harl, Hoe, Hole, Jar, Kowtow, Lesion, Lute, Predicament, Racloir, Rake, Rasorial, Rasp, Rasure, Raze, Razure, Saw, Scalp, Scart, Scrat(ch), Scroop, Scuff, Shave, Skimp, Skive, Squeegee, Strake, Stridulate, Strigil, Xyster
Scraping noise Curr, Scroop
Scrap merchant Didakai, Didakei, Diddicoi, Diddicoy, Didicoi, Didicoy, Gold-end-man, Totter
Scratch(es), Scratched, Scratching Annul, Cancel, Cla(u)t, Claw, Cracked heels, Curry, Devil, Efface, Eradicate, Erase, Grabble, Graze, Mar, Nick, Par, Periwig, Pork, Quit, Race, Rase, Rasp, Rast, Root, Satan, Scarify, Scart, Score, Scrab(ble), Scram(b), Scrape, Scrattle, Scrawm, Scrawp, Scrooch, Scrorp, Scrub, Spag, Streak, Striation, Tease, Teaze, Wig, Withdraw
▷ **Scratch(ed)** *may indicate* an anagram
Scrawl Doodle, Scribble, Squiggle
Scream(er) Bellow, Cariama, Caterwaul, Comedian, Comic, Cry, Eek, Headline, Hern, Kamichi, Laugh, Priceless, Primal, Riot, Scare-line, Screech, Seriema, Shriek, Skirl, Squall, Sutch, Yell
Scree Bahada, Bajada, Eluvium, Talus
Screech(ing) Cry, Screak, Screich, Screigh, Scriech, Scritch, Skreigh, Skriech, Skriegh, Ululant, Whoot
Screed Megillah, Ms, Plastered, Rat-rhyme, Tirade
Screen(s) Abat-jour, Arras, Back projection, Backstop, Blind(age), Block, Blue, Boss, Brise-soleil, Camouflage, Chancel, Check, Chick, Cinerama®, Cloak, Cornea, Coromandel, Cover, Cribble, Curtain, Divider, Dodger, Eyelid, Festoon-blind, Fire, Fluorescent, Glib, Gobo, Grille, Hallan, Help, Hide, Hoard, Hoarding, Iconostas(is), Intensifying, Jube, Lattice, Mantelet, Mask, Net, Nintendo®, Nonny, Obscure, Organ, Over-cover, Parclose, Partition, Part-off, Pella, Plasma, Pulpitum, Purdah, Radar, Reardos, Reredorse, Reredos(se), Retable, Riddle, Rood, Scog, Sconce, Scope, → **SHADE**, Shelter, Shield, Shoji, Show, Sift, Sight, Silver, Skug, Small,

Smoke, Split, Sunblock, Televise, Tems, Test, TFT, Touch, Transenna, Traverse, Umbrella, VDU, Vet, Wide, Windbreak, Window, Windshield, Winnow
Screw Adam, Allen, Archimedes, Butterfly, Cap, Coach, Countersunk, Double-threaded, Dungeoner, Extort, Female, Grub, Ice, Interrupted, Jailer, Jailor, Lag, Lead, Levelling, Lug, Machine, Male, Micrometer, Miser, Monkey-wrench, Niggard, Perpetual, Phillips®, Prop(ellor), Robertson, Salary, Skinflint, Spiral, Swiz(zle), Thumb(i)kins, Twin, Twist, Vice, Whitworth, Worm
Screwdriver Pozidriv®, Ratchet, Stubby, Tweaker
Scribble Doodle, Pen, Scrawl
Scribe Clerk, Ezra, Mallam, Scrivener, Sopherim, Tabellion, Writer, WS
Scrimmage Bully, Maul, Mêlée, Rouge, Scrap, Skirmish, Struggle
Scrimp Economise, Pinch, Save, Scrape, Skrimp
Script Book, Calligraphy, Devanagari, Gurmukhi, Hand, Hiragana, Italic, Jawi, Kana, Libretto, Linear A, Linear B, Lines, Lombardic, Miniscule, Nagari, Nastalik, Nastaliq, Ogam, Prompt book, Ronde, Scenario, Screenplay, Shooting, Writing
Scripture(s), Scriptural version Adi Granth, Agadah, Antilegomena, Avesta, Bible, Gemara, Gematria, Gospel, Granth (Sahib), Guru Granth, Haggada(h), Hermeneutics, Hexapla, Holy book, Holy writ, Koran, K'thibh, Lesson, Lotus Sutra, Mishna(h), OT, Rig-veda, Smriti, Tantra, Targum, Testament, Upanishad, Veda, Vedic, Verse, Vulgate
Scrofula Crewels, Cruel(l)s, King's evil, Struma
Scroll(-work) Cartouche, Dead Sea, Gohonzon, Makimono, Megillah, Mezuza(h), Monkeytail, Parchment, Pell, Roll, Roul(e), Scrow, Sefer Torah, Stemma, Torah, Turbinate, Upcurl, Vitruvian, Volume, Volute
Scrooge Blagueur, Miser
Scrotum Oscheal
Scrounge(r) Blag, Bludge(r), Borrow, Bot, Cadge, Forage, Freeload, Layabout, Ligger, Scunge, Sponge
Scrub(s), Scrubber Cancel, Chaparral, Cleanse, Dele(te), Gar(r)igue, Hog, Holystone, Loofa(h), Luffa, Mallee, Masseur, Negate, Pro, Rub, Scour, Sticks, Tart, Wormwood
▷ **Scrub** *may indicate* 'delete'
Scruff(y) Dog-eared, Grubby, Nape, Raddled, Tatty, Uncombed, Untidy
Scrum(mage) Bajada, Maul, Melée, Mob, Rouge, Ruck
Scrummy, Scrumptious Delectable, Delicious, Toothy, Yum-yum
Scrunt Carl
Scruple(s), Scrupulous Compunction, Conscience, Doubt, Meticulous, Nicety, Precise, Punctilious, Qualm, Queasy, Righteous, Stickle
Scrutinize, Scrutiny Check, Docimasy, Examine, Inspect, Observe, Peruse, Pore, Pry, → SCAN, Size up, Study
Scud East, Scoot, Spark, Spindrift, Spoom, Spoon, Spray
Scuff Brush, Shuffle
Scuffle Bagarre, Brawl, Scarmage, Skirmish, Struggle, Tussle
▷ **Scuffle** *may indicate* an anagram
Scull Oar, Row
Sculpt(ure) Acrolith, Aeginetan, Bas-relief, Boast, Bronze, Calvary, Canephor(a), Canephore, Canephorus, Carve, Chryselephantine, Della-robbia, Figure, Kore, Kouros, Mobile, Nude, Pergamene, Pietà, Relief, Relievo, Sc, Scabble, Scapple, Shape, Stabile, → STATUARY, Topiary
Sculptor Arp, Artist, Bartholdi, Bernini, Brancusi, Canova, Cellini, Daedalus, Della Robbia, Donatello, Giacometti, Gibbons, Gill, Hepworth, Klippel, Landseer,

Michelangelo, Myron, Nollekens, Paclozzi, Phidias, Pisano, Praxiteles, Pygmalion, Rodin, Scopas, Stevens, Wheeler

Scum Confervoid, Dregs, Dross, Epistasis, Glass-gall, Kish, Legge, Mantle, Mother, Pond, Rabble, Sandiver, Scorious, Scruff, Slag, Slime, Spume, Sullage, Vermin

Scupper Drain, Ruin, Scuttle, Sink

Scurf, Scurvy Dander, Dandriff, Dandruff, Furfur, Horson, Lepidote, Lepra, Leprose, Scabrous, Scall, Scorbutic, Whoreson, Yaw(e)y, Yaws

Scurrilous Fescennine, Profane, Ribald, Sotadic, Thersites, Vulgar

Scurry Beetle, Hurry, Scamper, Scutter, Skedaddle, Skelter

Scut Fud, Tail

Scute Plate

Scuttle Abandon, Dan, Hod, Purdonium, Scoop, Scrattle, Scupper, Scurry, Sink, Wreck

Scythe Bushwhacker, Cut, Hook, Sickle, Sieth, Snath(e), Snead, Sneath, Sned

Sea(s) Adriatic, Aegean, Amundsen, Andaman, Arabian, Arafura, Aral, Azov, Baltic, Banda, Barents, Beam, Beaufort, Bellingshausen, Benthos, Bering, Billow, Biscay, Bismarck, Black, Blue, Bosp(h)orus, Brine, Briny, Caribbean, Caspian, Celebes, Celtic, Ceram, Channel, China, Chukchi, Coral, Dead, Ditch, Drink, East China, Euphotic, Euripus, Euxine, Flores, Foam, Four, Galilee, Great, Greenland, Head, Herring-pond, High, Hudson Bay, Icarian, Inland, Ionian, Irish, Japan, Java, Kara, Kattegat, Labrador, Laptev, Ler, Ligurian, Main, Mare, Mare clausum, Mare liberum, Marmara, Marmora, Med, Mediterranean, Narrow, Nordenskjold, North, Norwegian, → **OCEAN**, Offing, Offshore, Oggin, Okhotsk, Pelagic, Philippine, Polynya, Quantity, Red, Ross, Sargasso, Seven, Short, Skagerrak, South, South China, Spanish Main, Strand, Sulu, Tasman, Tethys, Thalassic, Tiberias, Tide, Tide-rip, Timor, Tyrrhenian, Waddenzee, Water, Weddell, White, Yellow, Zee

Sea-anemone Actinia, Zoantharia

Sea-bear Fur-seal, Otary, Seal, Seecatchie

Sea-beast Ellops, Manatee

Sea-bream Carp, Fish, Porgie, Porgy, Tai

Sea-cow Dugong, Lamantin, Manatee, Rhytina, Sirenian

Sea-cucumber Bêche-de-mer, Trepang

Sea-dog Salt, Tar

Sea-ear Abalone, Paua

Sea-fight Naumachy

Seafood Crab, Crevette, → **FISH**, Lobster, Prawn, Shrimp, Zooplankton

Sea-front, Seashore, Seaside Beach, Coast(line), Esplanade, Littoral, Orarian, Prom(enade), Seaboard

Sea-god Neptune, Nereus, Triton

Sea-green Glaucous, Incorruptible, Robespierre

Sea-horse Hippocampus, Hippodame, Lophobranchiate, Morse, Pipefish, Tangie

Seal(s), Sealant, Seal box Airtight, Appose, Atlantic, Bachelor, Bladdernose, Block(ade), Bull(a), Cachet, Cap, Caulk, Chesterfield, Chop, Clinch, Close, Cocket, Common, Consign, Crab-eater, Cylinder, Eared, Earless, Elephant, Emblem, Fob, Fur, Gasket, Great, Greenland, Hair, Harbour, Harp, Hermetic, Hooded, Hudson, Impress, Jark, Lemnian, Lute, Monk, Obsign, O-ring, Otary, Phoca, Pinnipedia, Pintadera, Pod, Privy, Proof, Putty, Quarter, Ribbon, Ringed, Ronan, Rookery, Saddleback, Sea-bear, Sealch, Sea-leopard, Sealgh, Seecatch(ie), Selkie, Sigil, Signet, Silkie, Silky, Size, Skippet, Solomon's, Sphragistics, Stamp, Tar, Wafer, Washer, Water, Weddell, Whitecoat, Womb, Zalophus, Ziplock

Sea-legs Balance, Pleons

Sea-level Geoid
Sea-lily Crinoid, Palmatozoa
Seam Channel, Commissure, Fell, French, Furrow, Join, Layer, Middle-stitching, Monk's, Sew, Suture, Thread, Welt
Seaman, Seamen AB, Crew, Jack, Lascar, Lubber, Mariner, OD, Ordinary, PO, RN, → SAILOR, Salt, Swabby, Tar
Sea-mat Flustra, Hornwrack
Sea-matiness Gam
Sea-monster Kraken, Merman, Wasserman
Sea-mouse Bristle-worm
Séance Communication, Session, Sitting
Sea-parrot Puffin
Sear Brand, Burn, Catch, Cauterise, Frizzle, Parch, Scath(e), Scorch, Singe, Wither
Search(ing) Beat, Body, Comb, Dragnet, Examine, Ferret, Fingertip, → FORAGE, Fossick, Frisk, Global, Google(-whack), Grope, Home, Hunt, Indagate, Inquire, Jerk, Jerque, Kemb, Manhunt, Perquisition, Perscrutation, Probe, Proll, Prospect, Proul, Prowl, Quest, Rake, Rancel, Ransack, Ransel, Ranzel, Ravel, Ripe, Root, Rootle, Rummage, Scan, Scour, Scur, Sker, Skirr, Snoop, Strip, Thumb, Trace, Trawl, Zotetic
Sea-rover Norseman, Viking
Sea-serpent, Sea-snake Ellops, Hydrophidae, Phoca
▶ **Seaside** see SEA-FRONT
Sea-slug Bêche-de-mer, Trepang
Sea-snail Neritidae
Season(able), Seasonal, Seasoned, Seasoning Accustom, Age, Aggrace, Autumn, Betimes, Christmas, Close, Condiment, Devil, Dress, Duxelles, Easter, Enure, Etesian, Fall, Fennel, Festive, Flavour, Garlic, G(h)omasco, Growing, Hiems, High, In, Inure, Lent, Marjoram, Master, Mature, Nutmeg, Open, Paprika, Pepper, Powellise, Practised, Ripen, Salt, Sar, Seal, Seel, Seil, Sele, Silly, Solstice, Spice, Spring, Summer(y), Tahini, Ticket, Tide, Time, Whit, Winter, Xmas
Sea-squirt Ascidian, Cunjevoi
Seat Backside, Banc, Banquette, Beanbag, Bench, Bleachers, Booster, Borne, Bosun's chair, Bottom, Box, Bucket, Bum, Bunker, Buttocks, Canapé, Centre, Chair, Chaise longue, Coit, Couch, Country, Creepie, Croup(e), Croupon, Cushion, Davenport, Deckchair, Derrière, Dick(e)y, Dicky, Divan, Ejector, Epicentre, Faldistory, Faldstool, Foundation, Fud, Fundament, Gradin, Hall, Home, Hot, Houdah, Howdah, Humpty, Hurdies, Judgement, Jump, Knifeboard, Love, Marginal, Marquise, Mercy, Misericord, Natch, Nates, Ottoman, Palanquin, Palfrey, Perch, Pew, Pillion, Pit, Pouffe, Ringside, Rumble, Rumble-tumble, Rump, Saddle, Safe, Sagbag, Sedes, Sedile, Sedilium, See, Sell, Selle, Settee, Settle, Siege, Siege Perilous, Sliding, Sofa, Squab, Stool, Strapontin, Subsellium, Sunk(ie), Sunlounger, Synthronus, Throne, Tonneau, Window, Woolsack
Sea-urchin Asteria, Echinus, Pluteus, Whore's egg
Sea-vampire Manta
Sea-wall Bulwark, Dyke, Groyne
Sea-weed Agar, Alga(e), Arame, Badderlock, Bladderwort, Bladderwrack, Carrag(h)een, Ceylon moss, Chondrus, Conferva, Coralline, Cystocarp, Desmid, Diatom, Driftweed, Dulse, Enteromorpha, Fucus, Gulfweed, Heterocontae, Hornwrack, Karengo, Kelp, Kilp, Kombu, Konbu, Laminaria, Laver, Lemon-weed, Nori, Nullipore, Oarweed, Ore, Peacock's tail, Phyco-, Porphyra, Redware, Rockweed, Sargasso, Seabottle, Sea-furbelow, Sea-girdle, Sea-lace, Sea-lettuce,

Sea-mat, Sea-moss, Sea-tangle, Seaware, Sea-whistle, Sea-wrack, Tang,
Tetraspore, Ulva, Varec(h), Vraic, Wakame, Wakane, Ware, Wrack
Sea-wolf Pirate
Sea-worm Palolo, Spunculid
Sebastian Coe
Secede, Secession(ist) Adullamite, Antiburgher, Defy, Desert, Dissident,
Flamingant, Separatist, Sever, Splinter
Seclude, Seclusion Cloister, Incommunicado, Isolate, Ivory tower, Maroon,
Nook, Privacy, Purdah, Quarantine, Retiracy, Retreat, Secret, Sequester,
Shyness, Solitude
Second(s), Secondary Abet, Alternative, Another (guess), Appurtenance, Assist,
Atomic, Back(er), Beta, Coming, Comprimario, Deuteragonist, Ephemeris,
Flash, Friend, Handler, Imperfect, Indirect, Inferior, Instant, Jiffy, Latter, Leap,
Lesser, Minor, Mo(ment), Nature, Other, Pig's-whisper, Redwood, Runner-up,
Saybolt-Universal, Sec, Shake, Share, Side(r), Sight, Silver, Split, Subsidiary,
Support, Tick, Trice, Twinkling, Universal, Wind
Second-best Worsted
▸ **Second-class** see **SECOND-RATE**
Second coming Parousia
Second earth Antichthon
Second-hand Hand-me-down, Hearsay, Preloved, Reach-me-down, Re-paint,
Tralatitious, Used, Vicarious
Second-rate, Second-class B, Inferior, Mediocre
Second-sight Deuteroscopy, Divination, Tais(c)h
Second tine Bay, Bez
Second-year student Semi(e)(-bajan), Sophomore
Secrecy, Secret(s), Secretive Apocrypha, Arcana, Arcane, Arcanum, Backstairs,
Cabbalistic, Cagey, Clam, Clandestine, Closet, Code, Conventicle, Covert, Cranny,
Cryptadia, Cryptic, Crypto, Dark, Dearn, Deep, Deep-laid, Dern, Devious, Esoteric,
Hidden, Hidling, Hidlin(g)s, Hole and corner, Hugger-mugger, Hush-hush, Hushy,
Inly, Inmost, Latent, Mysterious, Mystical, Mystique, Open, Oyster, Password,
Penetralia, Petto, → **PRIVATE**, Privity, Privy, QT, Rune, Scytale, Shelta, Silent, Slee,
Sly, State, Stealth, Sub rosa, Tight-lipped, Top, Trade, Unbeknown, Undercover,
Underhand, Undescried, Unknown, Unre(a)d, Unrevealed, Untold
Secretary Aide, Amanuensis, Chancellor, Chronicler, CIS, Desk, Desse, Famulus,
Home, Minuteman, Moonshee, Munshi, Notary, Parliamentary, Permanent,
Private, Prot(h)onotary, Scrive, Social, Steno(grapher), Stenotyper, Temp
Secretary-bird Messenger, Serpent-eater
Secrete, Secretion Aequorin, Aldosterone, Allomone, Apocrine, Autacoid,
Cache, Castor, Chalone, Colostrum, Cuckoo-spit, Discharge, Emanation, Exude,
Hide, Honeydew, Hormone, Juice, Lac, Lactate, Lerp, Melatonin, Mucus, Musk,
Osmidrosis, Pruina, Ptyalin, Recrement, Renin, Resin, Rheum, Saliva, Sebum,
Secern, Smegma, Spit(tle), Succus, Trypsin
Sect(arian), Secret society Abelite, Adamite, Ahmadiy(y)ah, Albigenses, Amish,
Anabaptist, Assassin, Babee, Babi, Bahai, Bigendian, Brahmin, Cabal, Cainite,
Calixtine, Camorra, Campbellite, Cathar, Clan, Clapham, Covenantes, Crypto, Cult,
Cynic, Danite, Darbyite, Dissenter, Docate(s), Donatist, Druse, Druze, Dunkard,
Dunker, Ebionite, Encratite, Essene, Familist, Gabar, Gheber, Ghebre, Giaour,
Glassite, Gnostic, Group, Gueber, Guebre, Gymnosophist, Harmonist, Harmonite,
Hassid, Hauhau, Hemerobaptist, Hesychast, Hillmen, Holy Roller, Hutterite,
Illuminati, Ismaili, Jacobite, Jansenist, Jodo, Karaite, Karmathian, Little-endian,

Lollard, Macedonian, Macmillanite, Mandaean, Marcionite, Maronite,
Mendaites, Monothelite, Montanist, Moonie, Mormon, Mucker, Muggletonian,
Nasorean, Nazarine, Noetian, Ophites, Order, Partisan, Patripassian, Paulician,
Perfectionist, Pharisee, Philadelphian, Phrygian, Picard, Pietist, Plymouth
Brethren, Plymouthite, Porch, Pure Land, Rappist, Ribbonism, Sabbatian, Sabian,
Sadducee, Saktas, Sandeman, School, Schwenkfelder, Seekers, Senus(s)i, Seventh
Day Adventist, Sex, Shafiite, S(h)aiva, Shaker, Shembe, Shia(h), Soka Gakkai,
Sons of Freedom, Taliban, Therapeutae, Tunker, Unitarian, Utraquist, Vaishnava,
Valdenses, Vaudois, Wahabee, Wahabi(i)te, Waldenses, Yezdi, Yezidee, Yezidi,
Zealot, Zen, Zezidee
Section, Sector Area, Balkanize, Caesarian, Chapter, Classify, Conic, Cross, Cut,
Division, Ellipse, Empennage, Eyalet, Gan, Golden, Gore, Hyperbola, Lith, Lune,
Meridian, Metamere, Mortice, Movement, Octant, Outlier, Panel, Passus, → PIECE,
Platoon, Private, Public, Pull-out, Quarter, Rhythm, Rib, Segment, Severy, Slice,
Stage, Ungula, Unit, Warm, Zenith, Zone
Secular(ise) Earthly, Laic, Non-CE, Profane, Temporal, Ungod, Worldly
Secure, Security Anchor, Assurance, Bag, Bail, Band, Bar, Batten, Belay, Bellwether,
Belt and braces, Bolt, Bond, Bottomry, Buck Rogers, Calm, Catch, Cement, Chain,
Cheka, Cinch, Clamp, Clasp, Clench, Clinch, Close, Cocoon, Collateral, Collective,
Come by, Consolidate, Consols, Cosy, Cushy, Debenture, Dunnage, Engage,
Enlock, Ensure, Equity, Establishment, Fasten, Fastness, Fortify, Frap, Fungibles,
Gilt, Grith, Guarantee, Guy, Hypothec, Immune, Impregnable, Indemnity, Inlock,
Invest(ment), Knot, Lace, Land, Lash, Latch, Lien, Listed, Lock, Lockaway,
Lockdown, Lockfast, Long-dated, Longs, Medium-dated, Mortgage, Nail, National,
Obtain, Padlock, Patte, Pin, Pledge, Pot, Pre-empt, Preference, Procure, Protect,
Quad, Rope, Rug, → SAFE, Safety, Settle, Snell, Snug, Social, Sound, Stable,
Stanchion, Staple, Staylace, Stock, Strap, Sure(ty), Tack, Take, Tie, Tight, Trap,
Trice, Warrant, Watertight, Wedge, Win
Sedan Battle, Brougham, Chair, Jampan(i), Jampanee, Litter, Palanquin, Palkee,
Palki, Saloon
Sedate Calm, Cool, Decorous, Demure, Dope, Douce, Drug, Sad, Serene,
Sober(sides), Staid, Stand
Sedative Amytal®, Anodyne, Aspirin, Barbitone, Bromal, Bromide, Chloral,
Depressant, Deserpidine, Hypnic, Laurel water, Lenitive, Lupulin, Meprobamate,
Metopryl, Miltown, Morphia, Narcotic, Nembutal®, Opiate, Paraldehyde,
Pethidine, Phenobarbitone, Premed(ication), Roofie, Scopolamine, Seconal®,
Soothing, Temazepam, Thridace, Valerian, Veronal®
Sedentary Inactive, Sessile, Stationary
Sedge Carex, Chufa, Cinnamon, Clubrush, Grey, Seg, Xyris
Sediment Alluvium, Chalk, Deposit, Dregs, F(a)eces, Fecula, Flysch, Foots, Grounds,
Grouts, Lees, Molasse, Placer, Residue, Salt, Sapropel, Silt, Sludge, Terrigenous,
Till, Turbidite, Varve, Warp
Sedition, Seditious Incitement, Insurrection, Revolt, Riot, Treason
Seduce(r), Seductive Allure, Bed, Betray, Bewitch, Bribe, Cuckold-maker, Debauch,
Dishonour, Entice, Honeyed, Honied, Jape, Lothario, Luring, Mislead, Pull, Siren,
Slinky, Tempt, Trepan, Undo, Vamp, Wrong
▷ **Seduce** *may indicate* one word inside another
See(ing) Acknow, Apostolic, Barchester, Behold, Bishopric, C, Consider, Deek,
Descry, Diocesan, Discern, Durham, Ebor, Ecce, Ely, Episcopal, Eye, Get, Glimpse,
Holy, La, Lo, Meet, Norwich, Notice, Observe, Papal, Perceive, Realise, Remark,
Ripon, Rumble, Since, Sodor and Man, Spae, Spot, Spy, Truro, Twig, Understand,

V, Vatican, Vid(e), View, Vision, Visit, Voilà, Witness, York

Seed(s), Seedy Achene, Argan, Arilli, Arillode, Ash-key, Bean, Ben, Best, Blue, Bonduc, Cacoon, Caraway, Carvy, Cebadilla, Cevadilla, Chickpea, Cocoa, Colza, Coriander, Corn, Crabstone, Cum(m)in, Dragon's teeth, Embryo, Endosperm, Ergot, Favourite, Fern, Germ, Grain, Gritty, Issue, Ivory-nut, Kernel, Lima, Lomentum, Mangy, Mawseed, Miliary, Nickar, Nicker, Niger, Nucellous, Nut, Offspring, Ovule, Pea, Pinon, Pip, Poorly, Poppy, Sabadilla, Scuzz, Semen, Seminal, Sesame, Shabby, Shea-nut, Silique, Sorus, Sow, Sperm, Spore, Stone, Terminator, Zoosperm

Seed-case Aril, Bur(r), Endopleura, Husk, Pea(s)cod, Pod, Testa, Theca

Seed-leaf Cotyledon

Seedsman Driller, Nurseryman, Sower

Seek(er) Ask, Beg, Busk, Chase, Court, Endeavour, Ferret out, Gun for, Pursue, Quest, Scur, Search, Skirr, Solicit, Suitor

Seem(ingly) Appear, Look, Ostensible, Purport, Quasi, Think

Seemly Comely, Decent, Decorous, Fit, Suitable

Seep Dribble, Exude, Leak, Ooze, Osmose, Percolate, Permeate

Seer Augur, Auspex, Eye, Melampus, Nahum, Observer, Oculiform, Onlooker, Oracle, Prescience, Prophet, Sage, Sibyl, Soothsayer, T(e)iresias, Witness, Zoroaster

Seesaw Bascule, Teeter(-totter), Teeter-board, Tilt, Vacillate, Wild mare

Seethe(d) Boil, Bubble, Churn, Ferment, Simmer, Smoulder, Sod

Segment Antimere, Arthromere, Cut, Division, Gironny, Gyronny, Intron, Lacinate, Lith, Lobe, Merome, Merosome, Metamere, Part, Piece, Pig, Proglottis, Propodeon, Prothorax, Scliff, Section, Share, Shie, Skliff, Somite, Split, Sternite, Syllable, Tagma, Telson, Trochanter, Urite, Uromere

Segregate, Segregation Apartheid, Exile, Insulate, Intern, → ISOLATE, Jim Crow, Seclude, Separate

Seidlitz Powder, Rochelle

Seismic Terremotive

Seismograph Tromometer

Seize, Seizure Angary, Apprehend, Areach, Arrest, Assume, Attach(ment), Bag, Bone, Capture, Claw, Cleek, Cly, Collar, Commandeer, Confiscate, Distrain, Distress, Extent, For(e)hent, → GRAB, Grip, Hend, Impound, Impress, Maverick, Na(a)m, Nab, Nap, Nim, Point, Possess, Pot, Raid, Replevy, Rifle, Sease, Sequestrate, Smug, Snag, Tackle, Trover, Usurp, Wingding

Seldom Infrequent, Rare, Unoften

Select(ion), Selecting, Selector Artificial, Assortment, Bla(u)d, Cap, Casting, Choice, Choose, Classy, Cull, Darwinism, Discriminate, Draft, Draw, Eclectic, Edit, Elite, Excerpt, Exclusive, Extract, Favour, Garble, Inside, K, Kin, Nap, Natural, Pericope, → PICK, Pot-pourri, Prefer, Recherché, Sample, Seed, Sex, Single, Sort, Stream, Tipster, Triage, UCCA

Selenium Se, Zorgite

Self Atman, Auto, Character, Ego, Person, Psyche, Seity, Sel, Soul

Self-confident, Self-confidence, Self-willed Aplomb, Ego, Headstrong

Self-conscious Guilty

Self-contained Absolute, Reticent, SC, Taciturn

Self-contradictory Absurd, Irish

Self-control, Self-discipline Ascesis, Encraty, Modesty, Patience, Restraint, Temper(ance)

▶ **Self-defence** see MARTIAL (ARTS)

Self-esteem Amour-propre, Conceit, Confidence, Egoism, Pride, Vainglory
Self-evident Axiom, Manifest, Obvious, Patent, Truism, Truth
Self-existence Solipsism
Self-fertilisation, Self-origination Aseity, Autogamy
Self-governing Autonomy, Idior(r)hythmic, Kabele, Kebel, Puritanism, Swaraj
Self-help Smiles
Self-important, Self-indulgent, Self-interested Aristippus, Arrogant, Chesty,
Cocky, Conceited, Immoderate, Jack-in-office, Licentious, Narcissistic, Pompous,
Pragmatic, Profligate, Solipsist, Sybarite
Selfish(ness) Avaricious, Egocentric, Egoist, Grabby, Greedy, Hedonist, Mean,
Solipsism
Selfless(ness) Non-ego, Tuism
Self-limiting Kenotic
▶ **Self-origination** see **SELF-FERTILISATION**
Self-pollinating Cl(e)istogamic
Self-possession Aplomb, Composure, Cool, Nonchalant
Self-satisfied, Self-satisfaction Complacent, Narcissism, Smug, Tranquil
Self-service Automat, Buffet, Cafeteria, Supermarket
Self-sufficient, Self-sufficiency Absolute, Autarky, Complete, Hunter-gatherer
Self-taught Autodidact
Sell(er), Selling Apprize, Auction, Barter, Bear, Betray, Catch, Chant, Chaunt,
Cold-call, Cope, Costermonger, Direct, Dispose, Divest, Do, Fancier, Flog, Go,
Hard, Have, Hawk, Huckster, Hustle, Inertia, Knock down, Market, Marketeer,
Ménage, Merchant, Missionary, Oligopoly, Pardoner, Party, Peddle, Peddler,
Pick-your-own, Purvey, Push, Pyramid, Rabbito(h), Realise, Rep, Retail, Ruse,
Short, Simony, Soft, Stall-man, Sugging, Switch, → **TRADE**, Vend
Selvage Border, Edge, Roon, Rund
Semantics General, Generative, Interpretive, Notional, Onomasiology, Semasiology,
Sematology
Semaphore Signal, Tic-tac, Wigwag
Semblance Aspect, Guise, Likeness, Sign, Verisimilitude
Semen Jis(so)m, Milt, Spunk
Semi-circular D, Hemicycle
Semi-conductor Germanium, LED, Thryristor
Seminar(y) Class, Colloquium, Group, Theologate, Tutorial, Workshop
Semiotics Syntactics
Semi-paralysis Dyaesthesia
Semitic Accadian, Akkadian, Ammonite, Amorite, Arab, Aramaic, Canaanite,
Chaldean, Geez, Jewish, Phoenician
Semitone Pycnon
Senate Council, Curia, Seanad (Eireann)
Senator Antiani, Cicero, Elder, Legislator, Solon
Send, Sent Consign, → **DESPATCH**, Disperse, Emit, Entrance, Issue, Launch, Mail,
Order, Post, Rapt, Ship, Transmit, Transport
Send back Refer, Remand, Remit, Return
Send down Demit, Lower, Refer, Rusticate
Send up Chal(l)an, Lampoon, Promote
Senegal SN
Senescence Age
Senile, Senility Caducity, Dementia, Disoriented, Doddery, Doitit, Dotage, Eild, Eld,
Gaga, Nostology, Twichild

Senior Aîné, Doyen, Elder, Father, Grecian, Mayor, Oubaas, Père, Primus, Superior,
Upper
Senna Bladder
Señor(a) Caballero, Don(a), Hidalga, Hidalgo
Sensation(al) Acolouthite, Anoesis, Aura, Blood, Commotion, Drop-dead, Emotion,
Empfindung, Feeling, Gas, Impression, Lurid, Melodrama, Organic, Par(a)esthesia,
Phosphene, Pyrotechnic, Shocker, Shock-horror, Showstopper, Splash, Stir, Styre,
Synaesthesia, Thrill, Tingle, Vibes, Wow, Yellow
Sense, Sensual, Sensing Acumen, Aura, Carnal, Coherence, Common, Dress,
ESP, Faculty, Feel, Gross, Gumption, Gustation, Hearing, Horse, Idea, Import,
Instinct, Intelligence, Intuition, Lewd, Meaning, Moral, Nous, Olfactory, Palate,
Perceptual, Rational, Receptor, Remote, Rumble-gumption, Rumgumption,
Rum(m)el-gumption, Rum(m)le-gumption, Sight, Sixth, Slinky, Smell, Spirituality,
Sybarite, Synesis, Taste, Touch, Voluptuary, Voluptuous, Wisdom, Wit
Senseless Absurd, Anosmia, Illogical, Inane, Mad, Numb, Stupid, Stupor,
Unconscious, Unwise, Vegetal
Sensible Aware, Clear-headed, Dianoetic, Down to earth, No-nonsense, Prudent,
Raisonné, Rational, Sane, Solid, Well-balanced
Sensitive, Sensitivity Algesia, Alive, Allergic, Atopy, Dainty, Delicate, Erethism,
Erogenous, Hypaesthesia, Keen, Nesh, Nociceptive, Orthochromatic, Passible,
Radiesthesia, Sympathetic, Tactful, Tender, Thermaesthesia, Thin-skinned,
Ticklish, Touchy(-feely), Vulnerable
Sensor(y) Detector, Exteroceptor, Interoceptor, Palpi, Proprioceptor, Remote
Sentence(s) Assize, Bird, Carpet, Clause, Closed, Commit, Complex, Compound,
Condemn, Custodial, Death, Decree(t), Deferred, Doom, Fatwah, Indeterminate,
Judgement, Life, Matrix, Open, Pangram, Paragraph, Period(ic), Porridge,
Predicate, Rap, Rheme, Rune, Simple, Stretch, Suspended, Swy, Tagmene, Time,
Topic, Verdict, Versicle, Weigh off
Sententious Concise, Gnomic, Laconic, Pithy, Pompous, Terse
Sentiment(al), Sentimentality Byronism, Corn, Cornball, Drip, Feeling, Goo,
Govey, Gucky, Gush, Hokey, Icky, Maudlin, Mawkish, Mind, Mush, Namby-pamby,
Nationalism, Nostalgia, Opinion, Romantic, Rose-pink, Rosewater, Saccharin,
Schmaltzy, Sloppy, Smoochy, Soppy, Spoony, Sugary, Tear-jerker, Traveller, Treacly,
Twee, View, Weepy, Yucky
Sentry Custodian, Guard, Jaga, Picket, Sentinel, Vedette, Vidette, Watch
Separate(d), Separation, Separately Abstract, Asunder, Atmolysis, Avulsion,
Comma, Compartmentalise, Cull, Cut, Decollate, Decompose, Decouple, Deduct,
Deglutinate, Demarcate, Demerge, Detach, Dialyse, Diastasis, Diazeuxis,
Diremption, Disally, Discerp, Disconnect, Discrete, Disjunction, Dissociate,
Distance, Distinct, Disunite, Divide, Division, Divorce, Eloi(g)n, Elute, Elutriate,
Esloin, Estrange, Filter, Grade, Gulf, Heckle, Hive, Hyphenate, Insulate, Intervene,
Isolate, Judicial, Laminate, Lease, Legal, Monosy, Part, Particle, Peel off, Piece,
Prescind, Ramify, Red(d), Rift, Scatter, Schism, Screen, Scutch, Secern, Segregate,
Sequester, Sever, Several, Shear, Shed, Shore, Shorn, Sift, Sleave, Sle(i)ded, Solitary,
Sort, → **SPLIT**, Steam-trap, Stream, Sunder, Sundry, Tems(e), Tmesis, Try, Twin(e),
Unclasp, Unravel, Winnow, Wrench, Yandy
Sepia Cuttle, Ink
Seppuku Hara-kiri, Hari-kari
Septic Poisonous, Rotting
Septimus Small
Septum Mediastinum

Sepulchral, Sepulchre Bier, Cenotaph, Charnel, Crypt, Easter, Funeral, Monument, Pyramid, Tomb, Vault, Whited

Sequel After-clap, Consequence, Effect, Outcome, Suite

Sequence Agoge, Algorithm, Byte, Chronological, Consecution, Consensus, Continuity, Continuum, Escape, Fibonacci, Intervening, Intron, Line, Main, Montage, Order, Peptide, Polar, Program(me), Routine, Run, Seriatim, Series, Shot, Signal, Succession, Suit, Suite, Train, Vector

Sequester, Sequestrate Confiscate, Esloin, Esloyne, Impound, Isolate, Retire, Seclude, Separate

Sequin Paillette, Zecchino

Sequoia Redwood

Seraph Abdiel, → ANGEL

Serb(ian) Chetnik

Sere Arid, → DRY, Scorch, Wither

Serenade(r) Aubade, Charivari, Horning, Love song, Minstrel, Nocturne, Shivaree, Sing-song, Wait, Wake

Serene, Serenity Calm, Composed, Impassive, Placid, Repose, Sangfroid, Sedate, Seraphic, Smooth, → TRANQUIL

Serf(dom) Adscript, Bondman, Ceorl, Churl, Helot, Manred, → SLAVE, Thete, Thrall, Vassal, Velle(i)nage, Villein

Serge Russian, Say

Sergeant Buzfuz, Colour, Cuff, Drill, Flight, Havildar, Kite, Lance, Master, → NCO, Platoon, RSM, Sarge, SL, SM, Staff, Technical, Troy

Serial(ism) Episode, Feuilleton, Heft, Livraison, Total

Series Actinide, Actinium, Arithmetical, Balmer, Catena, Chain, Concatenation, Continuum, Course, Cycle, Cyclus, Electromotive, Enfilade, Engrenage, En suite, Episode, Epos, Ethylene, Fibonacci, Fourier, Geometric, Gradation, Harmonic, Homologous, Lanthanide, Line, Links, Loop, Maclaurin's, Methane, Neptunium, Partwork, Pedigree, Power, Process, → PROGRESSION, Radioactive, Rest, Routine, Rubber, Run, Sequence, Ser, Sitcom, String, Succession, Suit, Taylor's, Thorium, Time, Tone, Train, Uranium, World

Serious(ly) Critical, Earnest, Grave, Gravitas, Heavy, Important, Intense, Major, Momentous, Pensive, Sad, Serpentine, Sober, Solemn, Sombre, Staid, Straight(-faced), Very

Sermon Address, Discourse, Gatha, Homily, Khutbah, Lecture, Preachment, Prone, Spital

Serow Goral, Thar

Serpent(ine) Adder, Amphisbaena, Anguine, Apepi, Apophis, Asp, Aspic(k), Basilisk, Boa, Caduceus, Cockatrice, Dipsas, Firedrake, Midgard, Nagas, Ophiolite, Ouroboros, Peridotite, Pharaoh's, Retinalite, Sea-snake, Shesha, → SNAKE, Traitor, Uraeus, Verd-antique, Verde-antico, Viper, Wyvern

Serrate(d) Diprionidian, Saw, Scallop, Serried

Serum Albumin, Antiglobulin, Antilymphocyte, Antitoxin, ATS, Fluid, Globulin, Humoral, Opsonin, Senega

Serval Bush-cat

Servant, Server Aide, Attendant, Ayah, Batman, Bearer, Bedder, Bedmaker, Between-maid, Boot-catcher, Boots, Boy, Butler, Caddie, Chaprassi, Chuprassy, Civil, Columbine, Cook, Daily, Domestic, Dromio, Drudge, Employee, Factotum, Famulus, File, Flunkey, Footboy, Footman, Friday, Gehazi, G(h)illie, Gip, Gully, Gyp, Haiduk, Handmaid, Helot, Henchman, Heyduck, Hind, Hireling, Iras, Jack, Jack-slave, Jeames, Khansama(h), Khidmutgar, Khitmutgar, Kitchen-knave,

Lackey, Lady's maid, Lazy Susan, Maid, Major-domo, Man, Man Friday, Menial, Minion, Mixologist, Muchacha, Muchacho, Myrmidon, Nethinim, Obedient, Page, Pantler, Person, Postman, Public, Retainer, Retinue, Scout, Scrub, Scullion, Servitor, Sewer, Skip, Slavey, Soubrette, Steward, Tablespoon, Tapsman, Tendance, Theow, Thete, Tiger, Tweeny, Underling, Vails, Vales, Valet, Valkyrie, Varlet, Vassal, Waiter, Wash-rag, Weller

Serve, Service(s) Ace, Act, Active, Amenity, Answer, Arriage, Asperges, Assist, ATS, Attendance, Avail, Benediction, Breakfast, Candlemas, Cannonball, Ceefax®, China, Christingle, Civil, Communion, Community, Complin(e), Conscription, Corvée, Credo, Devotional, Dien, Dinnerset, Diplomatic, Dish, Divine, Do, Dow, Drumhead, Duty, Ecosystem, Employ, Evensong, Facility, Fault, Fee, Feudal, Fish, Foreign, Forensic, Forward, → FUNCTION, Further, Go, Help, Helpline, Hour, Ibadat, Ka(e), Kol Nidre, Let, Line, Ling, Lip, Litany, Liturgy, Ma'ariv, Mass, Mat(t)ins, Memorial, Mincha, Minister, Ministry, Missa, National, Nocturn, Nones, Oblige, Office, Oracle, Overarm, Overhaul, Pass, Pay, Personal, Pit stop, Possum, Pottery, Prime, Proper, Public, RAF, Requiem, Rite, RN, Room, Sacrament, Secret, Selective, Senior, Sext, Shacharis, Shaharith, Shuttle, Silver, Social, Sorb, Stead, Sted, Sue, Tableware, Tea, Tenebrae, Tierce, Trental, Uncork, Under-arm, Use, Utility, Vespers, Wait, Waiterage, Watch-night, Wild, Worship, Yeoman('s)

Service-book Hymnal, Hymnary, Missal, Triodion

▷ **Serviceman** *may indicate* a churchman

Servile, Servility Abasement, Base, Crawling, Knee, Kowtowing, Lickspittle, Menial, Obsequious, Slavish, Slimy, Submissive, Suck-hole, Sycophantic, Tintookie, Truckle

Serving Helping, Heuristic, Portion

Servitude Bondage, Domination, Peonism, Slavery, Thirlage, Thrall, Vassalry, Yoke

Sesame Gingelly, Gingili, Grapple-plant, Jinjilli, Semsem, Tahini, Til

Session(s) Bout, Executive, Galah, Jam, Kirk, Meeting, Nightshift, Petty, Poster, Quarter, Rap, Round, Séance, Sederunt, Settle, Sitting, Term

Set(ting) (aside; down; in; off; out; up) Activate, Adjust, Appoint, Arrange, Batch, Bent, Bezel, Boun, Brooch, Cabal, Cake, Case, Cast, Chaton, Class, Claw, Clique, Cliveden, Closed, Coagulate, Cock, Cockshy, Codomain, Collection, Collet, Comp(ositor), Companion, Compose, Congeal, Context, Coterie, Couvert, Crew, Crystal, Cyclorama, Data, Dead, Decline, Decor, Detonate, Diorama, Dispose, Earmark, Earnest, Earth, Enchase, Ensky, Environment, Establish, Explode, Film, Fit, Flagstone, Flash, Flat(s), Found, Garniture, Geal, Gel, Genome, Group, Harden, Ilk, Inchase, Incut, Infinite, Inlay, Jee, Jeel, Jell(y), Jet, Julia, Kit, Laid, Land, Lay, Leg, Locale, Locate, Lot, Mandelbrot, Milieu, Mise en scène, Monture, Mournival, Nail, Nest, Occident, Open, Ordered, Ordinate, Ouch, Pair, Parure, Pavé, Permanent, Physique, Pitch, Place(ment), Plant, Plaste, Ply, Point, Posed, Posit, Power, Put, Radio, Ready, Receiver, Relay, Rigid, Rooted, Rubber, Saw, Scenery, Series, Showcase, Sink, Smart, Solidify, Solution, Squad, Stand, Stationed, Stede, Stell, Stick, Stiffen, Still, Stream, Subscriber, Suit, Suite, Surround, Synchronize, Tar, Tea, Team, Teeth, Televisor, Telly, The four hundred, Tiffany, Till, Toilet, Trannie, Transistor, Trigger, Truth, Tube, Union, Universal, Venn (diagram), Weather, Wide-screen, Yplast

Setback Bodyblow, Checkmate, Hiccup, Jolt, Relapse, Retard, Retreat, Reversal, Scarcement, Sickener, Tes, Vicissitude

Setter Cement, Comp, Dog, English, Gelatin(e), Gordon, Gundog, Irish, Pectin, Red, Smoot, Sphinx, Trend

Settle(d), Settler, Settlement Adjust, Agree, Alight, Appoint, Arrange, Ascertain,

Ausgleich, Avenge, Balance, Bandobast, Bed, Bench, Boer, Borghetto, Botany
Bay, Bundobust, Bustee, Camp, Clear, Clench, Clinch, Colonial, Colonise, Colony,
Compose, Compound, Compromise, Crannog, Decide, Defray, Determine, Diktat,
Discharge, Dispose, Dorp, Dowry, Ekistics, Encamp, Endow, Ensconce, Entail,
Establish, Expat, Faze, Feeze, Finalise, Fix, Foot, Foreclose, Gravitate, Gridironer,
Guilder, Habitant, Hama, Illegitimate, Informal, Jamestown, Jointure, Kibbutz,
Land, Ledge, Light, Lyte, Manyat(t)a, Merino, Mise, Mission, Moreton Bay, Moshav,
Nahal, Nest, Nestle, New Amsterdam, Oecist, Oikist, Opt, Outpost, Over, Pa(h),
Pakka, Pale, Patroon, Pay, Peise, Penal, Perch, Pheazar, Pheese, Pheeze, Phese,
Pilgrim, Pioneer, Placate, Planter, Populate, Port Arthur, Port Nicholson, Presidio,
Pucka, Pueblo, Pukka, Rancheria, Rancherie, Readjust, Reduction, Reimburse,
Remit, Reside, Resolve, Rest, Sate, Satisfaction, Seat, Secure, Sedimentary, Set
fair, Shagroon, Shtetl, Silt, Smoot, Sofa, Soldier, Solve, Soweto, Square, Square up,
State, Still, Straits, Subside, Taurus, Township, Ujamaa, Utu, Vest(ed), Viatical,
Voortrekker
▷ **Settlement** *may indicate* an anagram
▷ **Settler** *may indicate* a coin
Set upon Assail, Attack, Sick
Seven(th), Seven-sided Ages, Days, Dials, Great Bear, Hebdomad, Hepta-, Hills,
Magnificent, Nones, Pleiad(es), S, Sages, Seas, Septenary, Septilateral, Septimal,
Sins, Sisters, Sleepers, Stars, Wonders, Zeta
Seventy S
Seven-week Omer
Sever Amputate, Cut, Detach, Divide, Sunder
Several Divers, Many, Multiple, Some, Sundry
Severe(ly), Severity Acute, Bad, Caustic, Chronic, Cruel, Dour, Draconian, Drastic,
Eager, Extreme, Grave, Grievous, Gruel(ling), Hard, → **HARSH**, Ill, Inclement,
Morose, Penal, Rhadamanthine, Rigo(u)r, Roarming, Roundly, Serious, Sharp,
Snell(y), Sore, Spartan, Stern, Strict, Swingeing
Sew(ing), Sew up Baste, Clinch, Cope, Embroider, Fell, Fine-draw, Machine, Mitre,
Overcast, Overlock, Run, Seam, Seel, Stitch, Tack, Whip
Sewage, Sewer Cesspool, Cloaca, Culvert, Dorcas, → **DRAIN**, Effluence, Jaw-box,
Jaw-hole, Mimi, Needle, Privy, Shore, Soil, Sough, Soughing-tile, Waste
Sex(y), Sexist Bed-hopping, Coupling, Cunnilingus, Erotic, Fair, Favours, Fellatio,
Female, Foreplay, Fornication, French, Gam(ic), Gamahuche, Gamaruche, Gender,
Hanky-panky, Hump, Incest, Intercourse, Kind, Libidinous, Libido, Lingam,
Lumber, Male, Mate, Nookie, Oomph, Opposite, Oral, Outercourse, Paedophilia,
Pederasty, Phallocratic, Phat, Priapean, Race, Randy, Raunchy, Rut(ish), Safe,
Salacious, Screw, Sect, Steamy, Sultry, Teledildonics, Troilism, Unprotected,
Venereal, Venery, VI, Voluptuous, Weaker
Sex appeal It, Oomph, SA
Sexcentenarian Shem
Sexless Agamogenetic, Atoke, N, Neuter
Sextet Over, Six
Sexton Blake, Fossor, Sacristan, Shammes, Warden
Seychelles SY
Sh P, Quiet
Shabby Base, Buckeen, Dog-eared, Down-at-heel, Fusc(ous), Grotty, Mangy, Mean,
Moth-eaten, Old hat, Oobit, Oorie, Oubit, Ourie, Outworn, Owrie, Raunchy, Scaly,
Scruffy, Seedy, Shoddy, Squalid, Tacky, Tatty, Worn, Woubit
Shack Fibro, Heap, Hideout, Hovel, Hut

Shackle(s) Bilboes, Bind, Bracelet, Chain, Darbies, Entrammel, Fetter(lock), Gyve, Hamper, Irons, Manacle, Restrict, Tie, Trammel, Yoke
Shad Allice, Allis, Fish, Twait(e)
Shaddock Grapefruit, Pomelo
Shade(d), Shades, Shading, Shadow, Shady Adumbrate, Arbour, Arcade, Awning, Blend, Blind, Bongrace, Bowery, Brise-soleil, Brocken spectre, Buff, Cast, Chiaroscuro, Chroma, Cloche, Cloud, Cross-hatch, Degree, Dis, Dog, Dubious, Eclipse, Eye, Five o'clock, Galanty, Gamp, Ghost, Gradate, Gray, Hachure, Hell, Herbar, Hint, Hue, Inumbrate, Larva, Lee, Melt, Mezzotint, Nuance, Opaque, Overtone, Parasol, Pastel, Phantom, Presence, Rain, Ray-Bans®, Satellite, Screen, Shroud, Sienna, Silhouette, Silvan, Skia-, Soften, Sound, Spectre, Spirit, Stag, Sunglasses, Swale, Swaly, Tail, Tenebrious, Tinge, Tint, Tone, Ugly, Umbra(tile), Umbrage(ous), Underhand, Velamen, Velar(ium), Velum, Visor
Shadowless Ascian
Shaft(ed), Shafting Arbor, Arrow, Axle tree, Barb, Barrow-train, Beam, Capstan, Cardan, Chimney, Column, Crank, Cue, Diaphysis, Disselboom, Dolly, Drive, Escape, Fil(l), Fust, Gleam, Idler, Incline, Journal, Lamphole, Limber, Loom, Mandrel, Mandril, Manhole, Moon pool, Moulin, Parthian, Passage, Pile, Pit, Pitbrow, Pitch, Pole, Propeller, Quill (drive), Ray, Rib, Scape, Scapus, Shank, Snead, Spindle, Staff, Stairwell, Stale, Steal(e), Steel, Stele, Stem, Stulm, Sunbeam, Telescopic, Thill, Tige, Tomo, Trave, Truncheon, Upcast, Well, Winning, Winze
Shag Cronet, Hair, Intercourse, Nap, Pile, Scart(h), Skart(h), Tire, Tobacco
Shaggy Ainu, Comate, Hairy, Hearie, Hirsute, Horrid, Horror, Nappy, Rough, Rugged, Shock, Shough, Tatty, Tousy, Touzy, Towsy, Towzy, Untidy
Shah Ruler, Sophi, Sophy
Shake(n), Shakes, Shaky Agitate, Ague(-fit), Astonish, Bebung, Brandish, Coggle, Concuss, Dabble, Dick(e)y, Didder, Diddle, Dither, Dodder, → **DT'S**, Feeble, Groggy, Hod, Hotch, Jar, Jiggle, Joggle, Jolt, Jounce, Judder, Jumble, Milk, Mo, Nid-nod, Press flesh, Quake, Quiver, Quooke, Rattle, Rickety, Rickle, → **ROCK**, Rouse, Shimmer, Shiver, Shock, Shog, Shoogle, Shudder, Succuss(ation), Sweat, Tremble, Tremolo, Tremor, Tremulous, Trill(o), Tumbledown, Undulate, Vibrate, Vibrato, Wag, Waggle, Wind, Wobble, Wonky
▷ **Shake** *may indicate* an anagram
Shakedown Blackmail, Chantage, Pallet
Shakespeare Bard, Will, WS
Shale Blaes, Fa(i)kes, Kerogen, Oil, Rock, Till, Torbanite
Shall Sal
Shallot C(h)ibol, Onion, Scallion, Sybo(e), Sybow
Shallow(s) Ebb, Flat, Fleet, Flew, Flue, Justice, Neritic, Sandbar, Shoal, Slight, Superficial
Sham Apocryphal, Bluff, Bogus, Braide, Charade, Counterfeit, Deceit, Fake, → **FALSE**, Hoax, Idol, Impostor, Mimic, Mock, Phony, Pinchbeck, Postiche, Potemkin, Pretence, Pseudo, Repro, Simulated, Snide, Spurious, Straw man
Shamble(s) Abattoir, Bauchle, Butchery, Mess, Shuffle, Totter, Tripple
Shame(ful), Shame-faced Abash, Aidos, Chagrin, Contempt, Crying, Degrade, Discredit, Disgrace, Dishonour, Embarrass, Fi donc, Fie, Gross, Hangdog, Honi, Humiliate, Ignominy, Infamy, Inglorious, Modesty, Mortify, Pity, Pudency, Pudor, Pugh, Shend, Sin, Slander, Stain, Stigma, Yshend
Shameless Audacious, Brash, Brazen, Flagrant, Immodest, Ithyphallic
Shampoo(ing) Massage, Tripsis, Wash
Shandy Drink, Sterne, Tristram

Shanghai Abduct, Kidnap, Trick
Shank Leg, Shaft, Steal(e), Steel, Steil, Stele, Strike
Shanty, Shanty town Boatsong, Bothy, Bustee, Cabin, Dog-hole, Favela, Forebitter, Hutment, Lean-to, Pondok, Sea, Shack, Shypoo, Song
Shape(d), Shapely, Shaping Blancmange, Boast, Bruting, Cast, Contour, Face, Fashion, Figure, Form, Format, Geoid, Gnomon, Headquarters, Hew, Holohedron, Jello, Model, Morph, → **MOULD**, Net, Pendentive, Polyomine, Ream, Rhomb(us), Scabble, Sculpt, Spile, Step-cut, Tromino, Turn, Whittle, Wrought, Zaftig, Zoftig
Shapeless Amorphous, Chaos, Dumpy, Indigest, Vague
Shard Fragment, Sliver, Splinter
Share(d), Shares, Sharing Allocation, Allotment, Apportion, Blue-chip, Bovate, Cahoots, Chop, Co, Cohabit, Coho(e), Common, Communal, Contango, Culter, Cut, Deferred, Divi(dend), Divide, Divvy, Dole, Dutch, Equity, Finger, Founders, Golden, Grubstake, Impart, Interest, Job, Kaffer, Kaf(f)ir, Kangaroo, Lion's, Market, Moiety, Odd lot, Ordinary, Oxgang, Oxgate, Oxland, Parcener, → **PART**, Partake, Participate, Penny, PIBS, Plough, Plough-iron, Portion, Prebend, Pref(erred), Preference, Pro rata, Prorate, Quarter, Quota, Rake off, Ration, Rug, Rundale, Scrip, Security, Shr, Slice, Snack, Snap, Sock, Split, Stock, Taurus, Teene, Time, Tranche, Two-way, Whack
Shareholder Stag
Shark Angel, Basking, Beagle, Blue, Bluepointer, Bonnethead, Bronze-whaler, Bull, Carpet, Cestracion, Cow, Demoiselle, Dog(fish), Flake, Fox, Great white, Gummy, Hammerhead, Houndfish, Huss, Lemonfish, Leopard catshark, Loan, Mackerel, Mako, Miller's dog, Monkfish, Noah, Nurse, Penny-dog, Plagiostomi, Porbeagle, Requiem, Reremai, Rhin(e)odon, Rigg, Sail-fish, Saw, School, Sea-ape, Sea-lawyer, Sevengill, Sharp, Shortfin mako, Shovelhead, Smoothhound, Soupfin, Spotted ragged-tooth, Squaloid, Swindler, Thrasher, Thresher, Tiger, Tope, Usurer, Whale, Whaler, Wobbegong, Zygaena
Sharkskin Shagreen
Sharp(er), Sharpen(er), Sharpness Abrupt, Accidental, Acerose, Acidulous, Acrid, Aculeus, Acumen, Acuminate, Acute, Alert, Angular, Arris, Bateless, Becky, Benchstone, Bitter, Brisk, Cacuminous, Cheat, Clear, Coticular, Cutting, Dital, Edge(r), Fine, Fly, Gleg, Grind, Hone, Hot, Keen, Kurtosis, Massé, Oilstone, Penetrant, Peracute, Piquant, Poignant, Pronto, Pungent, Quick-witted, Razor, Rogue, Rook, Set, Shrewd, Snap, Snell, Sour, Spicate, Strop, Swindler, Tart, Testy, Tomium, Twenty-twenty, Vivid, Volable, Whet
Sharpshooter Bersaglier, Franc-tireur, Sniper, Tirailleur, Voltigeur
Shatter(ing) Astone, Astound, Break, Brisance, Craze, Dash, Explode, Shiver, Smash, Smithereen, Splinter, Unnerve
Shave(r), Shaving(s) Barb(er), Electric, Excelsior, Filings, Flake, Grain, Moslings, Pare, Plane, Pogonotomy, Poll, Raze, Scrape, Skive, Sliver, Splinter, Swarf, Todd, Tonsure, Whittle
Shaw Artie, Green, Spinn(e)y, Wood
Shawl Afghan, Buibui, Cashmere, Chuddah, Chuddar, Dopatta, Dupatta, Fichu, India, Kaffiyeh, Kashmir, Manta, Mantilla, Maud, Paisley, Partlet, Prayer, Serape, Stole, Tallis, Tallit(ot), Tallith, Tonnag, Tozie, Tribon, Whittle, Wrap(per), Zephyr
She A, Hoo
Sheaf Aplustre, Bundle, Folder, Gait, Garb(e), Gerbe, Mow, Shock, Thr(e)ave
Shear(s), Shearer Clip, Cut, Fleece, Greasy, Jaws of life, Pinking, Poll, Pruning, Ring(er), Shave, Snips, Trim, Wind
Sheath Axolemma, Capsule, Case, Cocoon, Coleoptile, Coleorhiza, Condom,

Cover, Extine, Fingerstall, Glume, Medullary, Myelin, Neurilemma, Neurolemma, Oc(h)rea, Perineurium, Periosteum, Quiver, Rhinotheca, Root, Scabbard, Spathe, Thecal, Thumbstall, Urceolus, Vagina, Volva, Wing

Sheave Bee, Clevis

Shed(ding), Shedder Autotomy, Barn, Cast, Cho(u)ltry, Coducity, Cootch, Cwtch, Depot, Discard, Doff, Drop, Ecdysis, Effuse, Emit, Exuviate, Hangar, Hovel, Hut, Infuse, Lair, Lean-to, Linhay, Linn(e)y, Mew, Milking, Moult, Outhouse, Pent, Potting, Salmon, Shearing, Shippen, Shippon, Shuck, Skeo, Skillion, Skio, Slough, Sow, Spend, Spent, Spill, Tilt, Tool

Sheen Glaze, Gloss, Luminance, Lustre, Patina, Schiller, Shine

Sheep(ish) Ammon, Ancon(es), Aoudad, Argali, Barbary, Bell(wether), Bharal, Bident, Bighorn, Black, Blackface, Blate, Border Leicester, Broadtail, Burhel, Burrel(l), Caracul, Charollais, Cheviots, Coopworth, Corriedale, Cotswold, Coy, Crone, Dinmont, Domestic, Dorset Down, Dorset Horn, Down, Drysdale, Embarrassed, Ewe, Exmoor, Fank, Fat-tailed, Flock, Fold, Hair, Hampshire, Hampshire Down, Hangdog, Herdwick, Hidder, Hirsel, Hog(g), Hogget, Jacob, Jemmy, Jumbuck, Karakul, Kent, Kerry Hill, Lamb, Lanigerous, Leicester, Lincoln, Lo(a)ghtan, Loghtyn, Long, Lonk, Marco Polo, Masham, Merino, Mor(t)ling, Mouf(f)lon, Mountain, Muflon, Mug, Mus(i)mon, Mutton, Oorial, Ovine, Oxford Down, Perendale, Portland, Ram, Rambouillet, Romeldale, Romney Marsh, Rosella, Ryeland, Scottish Blackface, Shearling, Shetland, Short, Shorthorn, → **SHY**, Soay, Southdown, Spanish, Stone('s), Suffolk, Sumph, Swaledale, Teeswater, Teg(g), Texel, Theave, Trip, Tup, Two-tooth, Udad, Urial, Vegetable, Welsh Mountain, Wensleydale, Wether, Wiltshire Horn, Woollyback, Yow(e), Yowie

Sheep disease, Sheep problem Black, Blue tongue, Braxy, Dunt, Gid, Hoove, Louping-ill, Orf, Ringwomb, Rubbers, Scabby mouth, Scrapie, Sturdy, Swayback, Variola, Water-brain, Wildfire, Wind

Sheepdog Collie, Huntaway, Maremma, Polish Lowland, Puli

Sheepfold Fank, Pen

Sheepskin Basan, Caracul, Karakul, Mouton, Roan, Wool

Sheeptrack Terracette

Sheer Absolute, Clear, Main, Mere, Peekaboo, Plumb, Precipitous, Pure, Simple, Stark, Steep, Swerve, Thin, Utter

Sheet(s), Sheeting Balance, Cellophane, Cere-cloth, Cerement, Charge, Chart, Clean, Crime, Cutch, Dope, Expanse, Film, Flow, Fly, Folio, Foolscap, Heft, Ice, Inset, Intrusive, Lasagne, Leaf, Membrane, Nappe, Out-hauler, Page, Pane, Pot(t), Pour, Proof, Prospectus, Rap, Ream, Rope, Sail, Scandal, Scratch, Shroud, Stern, Stratus, Taggers, Tarpaulin(g), Tear, Tentorium, Terne, Thunder, Time, Title, Web, White, Winding

Sheet-anchor Letter-weight, Paperweight

Sheet-iron Taggers, Terne(plate)

Sheik(dom) Abu Dhabi, Bahrein, Dubai

Shekel Mina, Sickle

Sheldrake Bergander

Shelf, Shelve(s) Bank, Bar, Bracket, Continental, Counter, Credence, Delay, Dresser, Étagère, Grand Banks, Hob, Ice, Ledge, Leeboard, Mantle, Overmantel, Parcel, Postpone, Rack, Retable, Ross Ice, Shunt, Sidetrack, Sill, Spinsterhood, Whatnot, Windowsill

Shell(ed), Shellfish, Shellwork Abalone, Acorn-shell, Admiral, Ambulacrum, Ammo, Argonaut, Balamnite, Balanus, Balmain bug, Bivalve, Blitz, Boat, Bodywork, Bombard, Buckie, Camera, Capiz, Capsid, Carapace, Cartridge, Casing, Chank,

Chelonia, Chitin, Clam, Clio, Coat-of-mail, Cochlea, Cockle, Cohog, Conch, Cone, Copepoda, Cover, Cowrie, Cowry, Crab, Crustacea, Cuttlebone, Dariole, Deerhorn, Dentalium, Dop, Drill, Electron, Escallop, Eugarie, Foraminifer, Framework, Frustule, Geoduck, Globigerina, Haliotis, Hull, Husk, Hyoplastron, Isopoda, Lamp, Langouste, Limacel, Limpet, Live, Lobster, Lorica, Lyre, Malacostraca, Midas's ear, Mitre, Mollusc, Monocoque, Moreton Bay bug, Mother-of-pearl, Murex, Music, Mussel, Nacre, Nautilus, Olive, Ormer, Ostracod, Ostrea, Otter, Oyster, Paua, Pawa, Pea(s)cod, Peag, Peak, Pecten, Pereia, Periostracum, Periwinkle, Pilgrim's, Pipi, Pipsqueak, Plastron, Pod, Prawn, Projectile, Purple, Putamen, Quahaug, Quahog, Razor, Rocaille, Sal, Scalarium, Scallop, Scollop, Sea-ear, Sea-pen, Shale, Shard, Sheal, Sheel, Shiel, Shill, Shock, Shot, Shrapnel, Shrimp, Shuck, Sial, Smoke-ball, Spend, Spindle, Star, Stomatopod, Stonk, Straddle, Strafe, Stromb(us), Swan-mussel, Tear, Test(a), Thermidor, Toheroa, Tooth, Top, Torpedo, Tracer, Trivalve, Trough, Turbo, Turritella, Tusk, Univalve, Valency, Venus, Wakiki, Wampum, Whelk, Whiz(z)bang, Winkle, Xenophya, Yabbie, Yabby, Zimbi
Shelled Cracked, Kernel
▷ **Shelled** *may indicate* an anagram
Shell money Wakiki, Wampum, Zimbi
Shelter Abri, Anderson, Asylum, Awn, Awning, Belee, Bender, Bield, Billet, Blind, Blockhouse, Booth, Bunker, Burladero, Butt, Cab, Carport, Casemate, Cot(e), Cove, Covert, Coverture, Defence, Dodger, Donga, Dovecote, Dripstone, Dug-out, Fall-out, Garage, Gunyah, Harbour, Haven, Hithe, Hospice, Hostel, House, Hovel, Humpy, Hut, Hutchie, Kipsie, Lee, Lee-gage, Loun, Lound, Lown, Lownd, Mai mai, Mission, Morrison, Nodehouse, Pilothouse, → REFUGE, Retreat, Roof, Sanctuary, Scog, Sconce, Scoog, Scoug, Screen, Scug, Shed, Shiel(ing), Shroud, Skug, Snowshed, Stell, Storm-cellar, Succah, Sukkah, Summerhouse, Tax, Tent, Testudo, Tortoise, Tupik, Twigloo, Umbrage, Weather, Wheelhouse, Wickyup, Wi(c)kiup, Wil(t)ja, Windbreak
Shemozzle Debacle
Shenanigan Antic
Shepherd(ess) Abel, Acis, Amaryllis, Amos, Bergère, Bo-peep, Bucolic, Chloe, Clorin, Conduct, Corin, Corydon, Cuddy, Daphnis, Dorcas, Drover, Endymion, Escort, Ettrick, German, Good, Grubbinol, Gyges, Herdsman, Hobbinol, Lindor, Marshal, Menalcas, Padre, Pastor(al), Pastorella, Phebe, Sheepo, Strephon, Tar-box, Thenot, Thyrsis, Tityrus
Sheriff Bailiff, Deputy, Earp, Grieve, Land-dros(t), Lawman, Process-server, Shireman, Shirra, Shrievalty, Viscount
Sherry Amoroso, Bristol milk, Cobbler, Cream, Cyprus, Doctor, Dry, Fino, Gladstone, Jerez, Manzanilla, Oloroso, Palo cortado, Sack, Solera, Sweet, Whitewash, Xeres
Sherwood Anderson, Forest
Shiah Ismaili
Shibboleth Password
Shield(s), Shield-shaped Ablator, Achievement, Aegis, Ancile, Armour, Arms, Baltic, Biological, Bodyguard, Box, Buckler, Canadian, Cartouche, Clypeus, Defend, Dress, Escutcheon, Fence, Gobo, Guard, Gyron, Hatchment, Heat, Hielaman, Human, Insulate, Laurentian, Lozenge, Mant(e)let, Mask, Pavis(e), Pelta, Plastron, Protect, Randolph, Ranfurly, Riot, Rondache, Scandinavian, Screen, Scute, Scutum, Sheffield, Splashboard, Sternite, Targe(t), Thyroid, Vair, Visor, Water
Shift(er), Shifty Amove, Astatic, Back, Blue, Budge, Change, Chemise, Core, Cymar, Day, Devious, Displace, Dogwatch, Doppler, Einstein, Evasive, Expedient, Fend, Function, Graveyard, Great Vowel, Hedging, Lamb, Landslide, Lateral,

Linen, Louche, Move, Night, Nighty, Paradigm, Red, Relay, Remove, Rota, Ruse,
Scorch, Sell, Shirt, Shovel, Shunt, Simar(re), Slicker, Slip(pery), Sound, Spell, Split,
Stagehand, Stick, Stint, Swing, Tour, Transfer, Tunic, Turn, Vary, Veer, Warp
▷ **Shift(ing)** *may indicate* an anagram
Shilling Bob, Deaner, Falkiner, Hog, King's, Queen's, S, Teston
Shilly-shally Whittie-whattie
Shimmer(ing) Avanturine, Aventurine, Chatoyant, Glint, Glitter, Iridescence, Shine
▷ **Shimmering** *may indicate* an anagram
Shin Clamber, Climb, Cnemial, Leg, Shank, Skink, Swarm
Shindig, Shindy Bobbery, Row, Rumpus, Shivoo, Uproar
Shine(r), Shining, Shiny Aglitter, Aglow, Beam, Bright, Buff, Burnish, Deneb,
Effulge, Excel, Flash, Gleam, Glimmer, Glisten, Glitzy, Gloss, → **GLOW**, Irradiant,
Japan, → **LAMP**, Leam, Leme, Lucent, Luminous, Lustre, Mouse, Nitid, Nugget,
Phoebe, Phosphoresce, Polish, Radiator, Refulgent, Relucent, Resplend, Rutilant,
Skyre, Sleek, Twinkle, Varnish
Shingle(s), Shingly Beach, Chesil, Cut, Dartre, Dartrous, Gravel, Herpes, Herpes
Zoster, Herpetic, Loose metal, Shake, Shale, Stone, Zona, Zoster
Shinpad Greave
Shinty Caman, Camanachd
▷ **Shiny** *may indicate* a star
Ship(s), Shipping Boat, Container, Convoy, Cruiser, → **DISPATCH**, Embark, Export,
Flagship, Flatboat, Her, Hulk, Jolly, Keel, Man, Marine, MV, Post, Privateer, Prize,
Prow, Raft, Ram, Sail, Saique, School, She, Smack, SS, Tall, Transport, Tub, Vessel,
Victualling, Weather

SHIPS

1 letter:		*5 letters:*	
Q	Dory	Aviso	Prahu
	Duck	Barge	Prore
	Fire	Broke	Pucan
2 letters:	Flat	Camel	Razee
PT	Grab	Canoe	Rover
	Isis	Coble	Sabot
3 letters:	Koff	Coper	Saick
Ark	Long	Crare	Scoot
Cat	Nina	Dandy	Screw
Cog	Pink	Dingy	Scull
Dow	Pont	Drake	Shell
Fly	Pram	Ferry	Skiff
Hoy	Prau	Funny	Slave
Kit	Proa	Ketch	Sloop
Red	Ro-ro	Jolly	Tramp
	Saic	Laker	Troop
4 letters:	Scow	Liner	U-boat
Argo	Snow	Moses	Umiak
Bark	Tern	Oiler	Wager
Brig	Trow	Pinky	Whiff
Buss	Yawl	Pinto	Xebec
Cock	Zulu	Plate	Yacht
Cott		Praam	Zabra
Dhow			Zebec

6 letters:
Argosy
Banker
Barque
Bateau
Bawley
Beagle
Bethel
Bireme
Borley
Bottom
Bounty
Caique
Carack
Carvel
Castle
Coaler
Cobble
Codder
Cooper
Crayer
Curagh
Cutter
Decker
Dingey
Dinghy
Dogger
Droger
Dromon
Drover
Dugout
Escort
Flying
Frigot
Galiot
Galley
Gay-you
Goldie
Hooker
Howker
Jigger
Launch
Lorcha
Lugger
Masula
Monkey
Mother
Nuggar
Packet
Pedalo
Pequod

Pinkie
Pirate
Pitpan
Pulwar
Puteli
Randan
Reefer
Sampan
Sandal
Schuit
Schuyt
Settee
Slaver
Tanker
Tartan
Tender
Tonner
Torpid
Trader
Trek-ox
Turret
Whaler
Wherry
Zebeck

7 letters:
Belfast
Bidarka
Bumboat
Capital
Caravel
Carrack
Carract
Carrect
Catboat
Clipper
Coaster
Collier
Consort
Coracle
Counter
Currach
Curragh
Dredger
Drifter
Drogher
Dromond
Factory
Felucca
Flattop
Flyboat

Frigate
Gabbard
Gabbart
Galleon
Galliot
Galloon
Geordie
Gondola
Gunboat
Jetfoil
Kontiki
Liberty
Lymphad
Masoola
Mistico
Monitor
Mudscow
Mystery
Oomiack
Patamar
Pelican
Pinnace
Piragua
Pirogue
Polacca
Polacre
Pontoon
Revenge
Sculler
Shallop
Sharpie
Steamer
Stew-can
Tartane
Titanic
Trawler
Trireme
Tugboat
Vedette
Victory
Vidette

8 letters:
Acapulco
Bilander
Billyboy
Bylander
Cabotage
Corocore
Corocoro
Corvette

Dahabieh
Faldboat
Foldboat
Galleass
Galliass
Gallivat
Hospital
Hoveller
Indiaman
Ironclad
Longboat
Longship
Mackinaw
Mary Rose
Masoolah
Merchant
Monohull
Mosquito
Pinafore
Sallyman
Savannah
Schooner
Shanghai
Showboat
Training

9 letters:
Bucentaur
Catamaran
Cutty Sark
Dahabeeah
Dahabiyah
Dahabiyeh
Discovery
Dromedary
First-rate
Freighter
Frigatoon
Hydrofoil
Klondiker
Klondyker
Lapstrake
Lapstreak
Leviathan
Lightship
Mayflower
Minelayer
Monoxylon
Multihull
Outrigger
Peter-boat

Sallee-man
Shear-hulk
Sheer-hulk
Steamboat
Submarine
Vaporetto
Whale-back
Whaleboat

Knockabout
Mine-hunter
Paddleboat
Quadrireme
Santa Maria
Trekschuit
Triaconter
Windjammer

Dreadnought
Merchantman
Minesweeper
Penteconter
Quinquereme
Side-wheeler
Skidbladnir
Submersible
Supertanker
Three-decker
Three-master
Torpedo boat

12 letters:
East Indiaman
Fore-and-after
Great Eastern
Marie Celeste
Stern-wheeler
Tangle-netter

13 letters:
Paddle steamer

14 letters:
Flying Dutchman
Ocean greyhound

10 letters:
Brigantine
Golden Hind
Hydroplane
Icebreaker

11 letters:
Barquentine
Bellerophon
Berthon-boat
Cockleshell

Shipmate Crew, Hearty, Sailor
Shipping line P and O
Ship's biscuit Dandyfunk, Dunderfunk
Shipshape Apple-pie, Neat, Orderly, Tidy, Trim
Shipwreck Split
Shire County
Shirk(er) Cuthbert, Dodge, Embusqué, Evade, Funk, Malinger, Mike, Pike, Poler, Scrimshank, Skive, Skrimshank, Slack, Soldier
Shirt Black, Boiled, Brown, Bush, Calypso, Camese, Camise, Chemise, Choli, Cilice, Dasheki, Dashiki, Dick(e)y, Dress, Fiesta, Garibaldi, Grandad, Hair, Hawaiian, Hoodie, Jacky Howe, Kaftan, Kaross, K(h)urta, Nessus, Non-iron, Parka, Partlet, Polo, Rash, Red, Rugby, Safari, Sark, Serk, Shift, Smock, Sports, Stuffed, Subucula, Swan(n)dri®, Sweat, T
Shiva Destroyer
Shiver(ing), Shivers, Shivery Aguish, Atingle, Break, Chitter, Crumble, Dash, Dither, Fragile, Frisson, Grew, Grue, Malaria, Nither, Oorie, Ourie, Owrie, Quake, Quiver, → **SHAKE**, Shatter, Shrug, Shudder, Smash, Smither, Smithereens, Splinter, Timbers, Tremble
▷ **Shiver(ed)** *may indicate* an anagram
Shoal Bar, Fish, Quantity, Reef, Run, School, Shallows, Shelf, Tail
Shock(ed), Shocker, Shocking Acoustic, Aghast, Agitate, Anaphylactic, Appal, Astound, Astun, Awhape, Bombshell, Brunt, Bunch, Consternate, Criminal, Culture, Defibrillate, Disgust, Dorlach, Dreadful, Drop, Earthquake, ECT, Egregious, Electric, Electrocute, Épatant, Epiphenomenon, Fleg, Floccus, Forelock, Gait, Galvanism, Gobsmack, Hair, Horrify, Impact, Infamous, Insulin, Jar, Jolt, Live, Mane, Mop, Outrage, Poleaxe, Putrid, Recoil, Return, Revolt, Rick(er), Scandal(ise), Seismic, Shaghaired, Shake, Sheaf, Shell, Shilling, Shog, Shook, Stagger, Start(le), Stitch, Stook, Stound, Stun, Tangle, Thermal, Trauma, Turn
Shock-absorber Buffer, Oleo, Snubber
▷ **Shocked** *may indicate* an anagram
Shod Calced
Shoddy Cagmag, Catchpenny, Cheap, Cheapjack, Cheapo, Cloth, Cowboy, Drecky, Gimcrack, Imitation, Oorie, Ourie, Owrie, Rag-wool, Ropy, Schlock, → **SHABBY**, Slopwork, Tatty, Tawdry, Tinny
Shoe(s) Accessory, Arctic, Athletic, Ballet, Balmoral, Bauchle, Blocked, Boat, → **BOOT**, Bootee, Brake, Brogan, Brogue, Brothel creepers, Buskin, Calceate, Calk(er), Calkin,

Casuals, Caulker, Cawker, Charlier, Chaussures, Chopin(e), Clodhopper, Clog, Co-respondent, Court, Creeper, Dap, Deck, Espadrille, Flattie, Galoche, Galosh, Gatty, Geta, Ghillie, Golosh, Gumboot, Gumshoe, Gym, High-low, High tops, Hot, Hush-puppies®, Jandal®, Jellies, Kletterschue, Kurdaitcha, Launch(ing), Loafer, Mary-Janes®, Mocassin, Moccasin, Muil, Mule, Open-toe, Oxford, Oxonian, Panton, Patten, Peeptoe, Pennyloafer, Pile, Plate, Plimsole, Plimsoll, Poulaine, Pump, Rivlin, Rope-soled, Rubbers, Rullion, Sabaton, Sabot, Saddle, Safety, → **SANDAL**, Sandshoe, Sannie, Scarpetto, Shauchle, Skid, Skimmer, Slingback, Slip-on, → **SLIPPER**, Slip-slop, Sneaker, Snow, Sock, Soft, Solleret, Spike, Stoga, Stogy, Suede, Tackies, Takkies, Tennis, Tie, Topboot, Track, Trainer, Upper, Vamp(er), Veld-schoen, Veldskoen, Velskoen, Vibram®, Vibs, Wagon lock, Wedgie, Welt, Winkle-picker, Zori

Shoeless Barefoot, Discalced

Shoemaker Blacksmith, Clogger, Cobbler, Cordiner, Cordwainer, Cosier, Cozier, Crispi(a)n, Farrier, Gentle craft, Leprechaun, Sachs, Smith, Snob, Soutar, Souter, Sowter, Sutor

Shoe-string Cheap, Lace, Pittance

Shoe-toe Poulaine

Shoo Away, Begone, Hoosh, Off, Scat(ter), Voetsek

Shoot(er), Shooting Ack-ack, Airgun, Arrow, Bine, Bostryx, Braird, Breer, Bud, Bulbil, Catapult, Chit, Cion, Cyme, Dart(le), Delope, Discharge, Drib, Elance, Enate, Eradiate, Film, Fire, Flagellum, Germ, Germain(e), Germen, Germin(ate), Glorious Twelfth, → **GUN**, Gunsel, Head-reach, Hurl, Imp, Layer, Limb, Loose, Offset, Photocall, Photograph, Pluff, Plug, Poot, Pop, Pot, Pout, Ramulus, Rapids, Ratoon, Riddle, Rod, Rove, Runner, Scion, Septembriser, Sien(t), Skeet, Snap, Snipe, Spire, Spirt, Spout, Spray, Sprout, Spurt, Spyre, Start, Stole, Stolon, Strafe, Sucker, Syen, Tellar, Teller, Tendril, Tiller, Trap, Turion, Twelfth, Twig, Udo, Vimen, Wand, Weapon, Whiz(z), Wildfowler, Zap

Shop(s), Shopper Agency, Arcade, Assembly, Atelier, Betray, Body, Boutique, Bucket, Buy, Chain, Charity, Chippy, Closed, Coffee, Commissary, Cook, Co-op, Cop, Corner, Cut-price, Dairy, Delicatessen, Denounce, Dobbin, Dolly, Duddery, Duka, Duty-free, Emporium, Factory, Galleria, Gift, Grass, In bond, Inform, Junk, Luckenbooth, Machine, Mall, Mall-rat, Market, Megastore, Mercat, Muffler, Officinal, Off-licence, Off-sales, Open, Opportunity, Outlet, Parlour, Patisserie, Personal, Precinct, Print, PX, Rat on, Retail, RMA, Salon, Sex, Shambles, Share, Shebang, Spaza, Squat, → **STORE**, Studio, Sundry, Superette, Supermarket, Superstore, Swap, Talking, Tally, Tea, Thrift, Tick, Tommy, Trade, Truck, Tuck, Union, Vintry, Warehouse, Works

Shopkeeper British, Butcher, Chemist, Clothier, Gombeen-man, Greengrocer, Grocer, Haberdasher, Hosier, Ironmonger, Merchant, Newsagent, Provisioner, Retailer, Stationer, Tradesman

Shoplift(er) Boost, Heist

Shore Bank, Beach, Buttress, Coast, Coastline, Coste, Eustatic, Foreside, Landfall, Littoral, Machair, Offing, Prop, Rance, Rivage, Saxon, Seaboard, Strand, Strandline, Support

Short(en), Shortly Abbreviate, Abridge, Abrupt, Anon, Apocope, Brief, Brusque, Close-in, Commons, Compendious, Concise, Contract, Crisp, Cross, Curt, Curtail, Curtal, Diminish, Drink, Eftsoons, Epitomise, Ere-long, Fubsy, Fuse, Inadequate, Lacking, Laconical, Light, Limited, Low, Mini, Near, Nip, Nutshell, Pudsey, Punch, Pyknic, Reduce, Reef, Retrench, Scanty, Scarce, Shrift, Shy, Soon, Sparse, Spirit, Squab, Squat, Squat(ty), Staccato, Stint, Stocky, Strapped, Stubby, Succinct, Syncopate, Systole, Taciturn, Teen(s)y, Temporal, Temporaneous, Terse, Tight, Tot,

Towards, Transient, Wee

Shortage Dearth, Deficit, Drought, Famine, Lack, Need, Paucity, Scarcity, Sparsity, Wantage

Short circuit Varistor

Shortcoming Weakness

Shorthand Gregg, Outline, Phonographic, Pitman, Speedwriting®, Stenography, Stenotypy, Tachygraphy, Tironian, Tironian notes, Triphone, Weblish

Short-headed Brachycephal

Short-lived Ephemeral, Fragile, Meson, Transitory

Shorts Bermuda, Board, Boxer, Briefs, Culottes, Cycling, Hot pants, Kaccha, Lederhosen, Plus-fours, Skort, Stubbies®, Trunks

Short-sight Myopia, Myosis

Short-winded Breathless, Concise, Puffed, Purfled, Pursy, Succinct

Shot(s) Aim, All-in, Ammo, Approach, Attempt, Backhand, Ball, Bank, Barrage, Bisque, Blank, Blast, Bricole, Bull, Bullet, Burl, Canna, Cannonball, Cartridge, Case, Chain, Chatoyant, Chip, Corner, Cover, Crab, Crack, Daisy cutter, Dink, Dolly, Dram, Draw, Drop, Duckhook, Dum dum, Dunk, Elt, Essay, Exhausted, Forehand, Gesse, Get, Glance, Go, Grape, Guess, Gun-stone, Hook, Jump, Langrage, Langrel, Langridge, Lay-up, Longjenny, Magpie, Marksman, Massé, Matte, Money, Moon-ball, Mulligan, Multi-coloured, Musket, Noddy, Pack, Parthian, Parting, Passing, Pelican, Pellet, Penalty, Photo, Plant, Pluff, Pop, Pot, Puff, Push, Rid, Round, Safety, Salvo, Scratch, Shy, Sighter, Silk, Six, Slam-dunk, Slap, Slice, Slug, Slung, Sped, Spell, Spent, Square cut, Stab, Still, Streaked, Tap in, Throw, Tonic, Tracking, Trial, Try, Turn, Volley, Warning, Wrist

Should Ought

Shoulder(-blade) Carry, Cold, Crossette, Epaule, Frozen, Hard, Hump, Joggle, Omohyoid, Omoplate, Pick-a-back, Roadside, Scapula, Shouther, Soft, Spald, Spall, Spaul(d), Speal, Spule, Tote, Withers

Shout(er), Shouting Barrack, Bawl, Bellock, Bellow, Boanerges, Call, Claim, Clamour, Conclamation, Cry, Din, Exclaim, Geronimo, Heckle, Hey, Hoi(cks), Holla, Holla-ho(a), Holler, Hollo, Holloa, Hooch, Hosanna, Howzat, Hue, Oi, Oy, Parnell, Rah, Rant, Root, Round, Sa sa, Treat, Trumpet, Vociferate, Whoop, Yell(och), Yippee, Yoohoo, Yorp

Shove Barge, Birr, Elbow, Jostle, Push, Ram, Spoon, Thrust

Shovel Backhoe, Dustpan, Hat, Loy, Main, Peel, Power, Scoop, Shool, Spade, Steam, Trowel, Van

Show(ing), Shown, Showy Anonyma, Appearance, Aquacade, Bad, Bench, Betray, Branky, Broadcast, Brummagem, Burlesque, Cabaret, Chat, Circus, Come, Con, Cruft's, Demo(nstrate), Depict, Diorama, Display, Do, Dramedy, Dressy, Dumb, Effeir, Effere, Endeictic, Entertainment, Epideictic, Establish, Evince, → **EXHIBIT**, Expo, Extravaganza, Exude, Facade, Fair, Fangled, Farce, Flamboyant, Flash, Flaunt, Floor, Galanty, Game, Garish, Gaudy, Gay, Give, Glitter, Glitz(y), Gloss, Good, Horse, Indicate, Jazzy, Kismet, Light, Loud, Manifest, Matinée, Meritricious, Minstrel, Musical, Naumachy, One-man, Ostensible, Ostentatious, Pageant, Panel game, Pantomime, Parade, Patience, Performance, Phen(o), Point, Pomp, Portray, Presentation, Pretence, Pride, Procession, Prog(ramme), Project, Prominence, Prove, Pseudery, Puff, Puppet, Quiz, Raree, Razzmatazz, Reality, Represent, Reveal, Revue, Road, Roll-out, Ruddigore, Rushes, Screen, Shaw, Sight, Sitcom, Slang, Soap, Son et lumière, Specious, Spectacle, Splash, Splay, Stage, Stunt, Talk, Tamasha, Tattoo, Tawdry, Telecast, Telethon, Theatrical, Three-man, Tinhorn, Tulip, Unbare, Uncover, Usher, Vain,

Variety, Vaudeville, Veneer, Viewy, Wear, Wild west, Zarzuela

Showdown Confrontation, Crunch

Shower Douche, Exhibitor, Flurry, Hail, Indicant, Indicator, Kitchen tea, Meteor, Party, Pelt, Pepper, Precipitation, Rain, Scat, Scouther, Scowther, Skatt, Skit, Snow, Spat, Spet, Spit, Splatter, Spray, Sprinkle, Ticker tape

▷ **Showers** *may indicate* an anagram

Showgirl Evita, Nanette

▷ **Showing, Shown in** *may indicate* a hidden word

Showman Bailey, Barnum, Entertainer, Goon, Impresario, Lord Mayor, MC, Ringmaster

Show-off Coxcomb, Exhibitionist, Extrovert, Jack the lad, Peacock, Poseur, Sport, Swagger, Swank

Showpiece Flagship

Show-place Exhibition, Olympia, Pavilion, Theatre

Shrapnel Fragment, Shell, Splinter

Shred Clout, Filament, Grate, Julienne, Mammock, Mince, Mummock, Rag, Screed, Swarf, Tag, Ta(i)ver, Tatter, Thread, To-tear, Wisp

Shrew Bangsring, Banxring, Callet, Catamaran, Elephant, Fury, Hellcat, Kate, Marabunta, Musk, Nag, Otter, Pygmy, Show, Solenodon, Sondeli, Sorex, Spitfire, Squirrel, Tana, Termagant, Tree, Trull, Tupaia, Virago, Vixen, Water, Xant(h)ippe, Yankie, Yenta

Shrewd Acute, Arch, Argute, Artful, Astucious, Astute, Callid, Canny, Clued-up, Cute, File, Gnostic, Gumptious, Hard-nosed, Judicious, Knowing, Pawky, Politic, Sagacious, Sapient(al), Wily, Wise

Shriek Cry, Scream, Scrike, Shright, Shrike, Shrill, Shritch, Skirl, Yell

Shrift Attention, Penance, Short

Shrike Bird, Butcher-bird

Shrill Argute, High, Keen, Piping, Reedy, Screech, Sharp, Skirl, Treble

Shrimp(s) Brine, Fairy, Freshwater, Krill, Mantis, Midge, Opossum, Potted, Prawn, Runt, Sand, Skeleton, Small, Spectre, Squill(a), Stomatopod

Shrine Adytum, Altar, Dagaba, Dagoba, Dargah, Delphi, Fatima, Feretory, Harem, Holy, Joss house, Kaaba, Marabout, Martyry, Naos, Pagoda, Reliquary, Scrine, Scryne, Stupa, Tabernacle, Temple, Tope, Vimana, Walsingham

Shrink(age), Shrinking, Shrunk Alienist, Analyst, Blanch, Blench, Boggle, Cling, Compress, Constringe, Contract, Cour, Cower, Creep, Crine, Cringe, Dare, Decrew, Depreciate, Dread, Dwindle, Flinch, Funk, Gizzen, Less, Nirl, → **PSYCHIATRIST**, Pycnosis, Quail, Recoil, Reduce, Retract, Sanforised, Shrivel, Shrug, Shy, Sphacelate, Timid, Violet, Wane, Waste, Wince, Wizened

Shrivel(led) Cling, Crine, Desiccate, Dry, Nirl, Parch, Scorch, Scrump, Sear, Shrink, Skrimp, Skrump, Tabid, Welk, Wither, Wizened, Writhled

Shropshire Salop

Shroud(s) Chadri, Chuddah, Chuddar, Cloak, Cloud, Conceal, Cover, Futtock, Grave-cloth, Pall, Rigging, Screen, Sheet, Sindon, Turin, Veil, Winding-sheet, Wrap

Shrub(bery) Arboret, Brush, → **BUSH**, Dead-finish, Horizontal, Plant, Undergrowth, Wintergreen

---

SHRUBS

3 letters:		*4 letters:*	
Kat	Qat	Coca	Dita
	Rue	Cola	Grex
			Hebe

Kava
Nabk
Olea
Rhus
Ruta
Titi
Tutu
Ulex

5 letters:
Aalii
Bosky
Brere
Buaze
Buazi
Buchu
Caper
Gorse
Hakea
Hazel
Henna
Ledum
Maqui
Monte
Mulga
Nebek
Peony
Pyxie
Ramee
Ramie
Salal
Savin
Senna
Thyme
Toyon
Wahoo
Yapon
Yupon
Zamia

6 letters:
Acacia
Alhagi
Ambach
Aucuba
Azalea
Bauera
Cobaea
Correa
Croton
Crowea

Daphne
Fatsia
Feijoa
Frutex
Fynbos
Garrya
Jojoba
Kalmia
Lignum
Manoao
Maquis
Matico
Mimosa
Myrica
Myrtle
Nebbuk
Nebeck
Neinei
Paeony
Pituri
Privet
Protea
Prunus
Savine
Smilax
Storax
Sumach
Tutsan
Yaupon

7 letters:
Acerola
Akiharo
Ambatch
Arbutus
Bauhini
Boronia
Bullace
Cascara
Cytisus
Deutzia
Dogwood
Emubush
Epacris
Ephedra
Filbert
Fuchsia
Guayule
Hop-tree
Jasmine
Juniper

Lantana
Mahonia
Mesquit
Muntrie
Oleacea
Rhatany
Romneya
Rosebay
Savanna
Shallon
Skimmia
Syringa
Tea-tree
Waratah
Weigela

8 letters:
Abutilon
Allspice
Barberry
Bayberry
Berberis
Bignonia
Bilberry
Bluebush
Buddleia
Camellia
Coprosma
Cowberry
Danewort
Euonymus
Gardenia
Hardhack
Heketara
Hibiscus
Horopito
Inkberry
Japonica
Jetbread
Koromiko
Krameria
Lavender
Leadwort
Magnolia
Mairehau
Mezereon
Ninebark
Ocotillo
Oleander
Oleaster
Photinia

Rangiora
Rock rose
Rosemary
Saltbush
Savannah
Shadbush
Sorbaria
Spekboom
Sweetsop
Tamarisk
Viburnum
Waxplant

9 letters:
Andromeda
Bearberry
Buckthorn
Ceanothus
Clianthus
Cordyline
Coreopsis
Coyotillo
Crowberry
Eucryphia
Firethorn
Forsythia
Gelsemium
Grevillia
Hamamelis
Hydrangea
Jaborandi
Jessamine
Kumarahou
Manzanita
Melaleuca
Mistletoe
Patchouli
Pernettya
Perovskia
Rauwolfia
Snowberry
Spicebush
Sterculia

10 letters:
Aphelandra
Cascarilla
Crossandra
Embothrium
Eriostemon
Escallonia

			12 letters:
Fatshedera	Poinsettia	Cotoneaster	Phanerophyte
Frangipani	Potentilla	Honeysuckle	Philadelphus
Gaultheria	Pyracantha	Huckleberry	Rhododendron
Gooseberry	Schefflera	Leatherwood	Serviceberry
Greasewood	Supplejack	Pittosporum	Southernwood
Holodiscus	Twinflower	Staggerbush	Streptosolen
Joshua tree		Steeplebush	Strophanthus
Laurustine	11 letters:	Stephanotis	
Parkleaves	Beautybrush	Wortleberry	
Pilocarpus	Bottlebrush		

Shrug Discard, Toss
Shudder(ing) Abhor, Ashake, Frisson, Grew, Grise, Grue, Horror, Jerk, Quake, Shake, Spasm, Tremble, Tremor
Shuffle(d) Dodge, Drag, Hedge, Make, Mix, Palter, Permute, Redeployment, Riffle, Scuff, Shamble, Shauchle, Soft-shoe, Stack
▷ **Shuffle(d)** *may indicate* an anagram
Shun Attention, Avoid, Eschew, Evade, Forbear, Ignore, Ostracise, Secede, → SPURN
Shunt Move, Shelve, Shuttle, Side-track
Shut (down; in; out; up), Shut(s) Bar, Cage, Close, Confined, Coop, Debar, Embar, Emure, Fasten, Fend, Impale, Impound, Latch, Lay-off, Lock, Occlude, Rid, Scram, Seal, Shet, Slam, Spar, Steek, Telescope, Tine, To
Shutter(s) Blind, B-setting, Dead-lights, Douser, Jalousie, Louvre, Persiennes, Shade
Shuttle Alternate, Commute, Drawer, Flute, Go-between, Navette, Orbiter, Shoot, Shunt, Space, Tat(t), Weave
Shy Bashful, Blate, Blench, Cast, Catapult, Chary, Coy, Deficient, Demure, Farouche, Flinch, Funk, Heave, Jerk, Jib, Laithfu', Leery, Lob, Mim, Mims(e)y, Mousy, Rear, Recoil, Reserved, Reticent, Retiring, Sheepish, Shrinking, Skeigh, Start, Thraw, Throw, Timid, Tongue-tied, Toss, Try, Verecund, Violet, Willyard, Willyart, Withdrawn
Shyster Ambulance chaser
Siamese, Siamese twins Chang, Eng, Parabiosis, Seal-point, T(h)ai
Siberia(n) Chukchi, Evenki, Ostiak, Ostyak, Samo(y)ed, Tungus, Vogul, Yakut, Yupik
Sibilant Hissing, Whistling
Sibling Brother, German, Kin, Sister
Sibyl Oracle, Prophetess, Seer, Soothsayer, Witch
Sicilian Sicanian, Trinacrian
Sick(en), Sickening, Sickliness, Sickly, Sickness Aegrotat, Affection, Ague, Ail, Altitude, Bad, Bends, Cat, Chalky, Chunder, Colic, Crapulence, Crook, Decompression, Delicate, Disorder, Donsie, Gag, Green, Hangover, Icky, Ill, Infection, Leisure, Maid-pale, Mal, Mawkish, Milk, Morbid, Morning, Motion, Mountain, Nauseous, Pale, Peaky, Peelie-wallie, Peely-wally, Pestilent, Pindling, Plague, Puly, Puna, Queachy, Queasy, Queechy, Radiation, Regorge, Repulsive, Retch, Serum, Shilpit, Sleeping, Soroche, Space, Spue, Squeamish, Sweating, Travel, Twee, Uncle Dick, Valetudinarian, Virus, Vomit, Wamble-cropped, Wan
Sick bay San
Sickle(-shaped) Falcate, Falx, Grasshook, Hook, Scythe
Side Abeam, Airs, Ally, B, Beam, Blind, Border, Branch, Camp, Cis-, Distaff, Division, Edge, Effect, Eleven, English, Epistle, Ex intraque parte, Facet, Flank, Flip, Gospel, Gunnel, Hand, Heavy, Hypotenuse, Iliac, Lateral, Lee(ward), Left, Long, Obverse,

Off, On, OP, Pane, Part, Partisan, Party, Port, Pretension, Profile, Prompt, Rave, Reveal, Reverse, Right, Rink, Short, Silver, Slip, Spear, Starboard, Swank, → **TEAM**, Tight, Weak, West, Wind, Windward, Wing, XI
Sideboard(s) Beauf(f)et, Buffet, Cellaret, Commode, Credence, Credenza, Dresser, Whiskers
Side-effect, Side-issue Fall-out, Logograph, Logogriph, Offshoot, Secondary, Spin-off
Sidekick Right-hand man, Satellite
Side-line Hobby, Lye, Siding, Spur
Side-step Crab, Dodge, Evade, Hedge, Maori, Volt
Side-track Distract, Divert, Shunt
Sidewalk Crab, Footpath, Pavement
Sideways Askance, Indirect, Laterally, Laterigrade, Oblique
Siding Alliance, Byway, Lie, Lye, Spur, Turnout
Sidle Edge, Passage
Siege (work) Alamo, Antioch, Antwerp, Beleaguer, Beset, Blockade, Charleston, Gherao, Investment, Khartoum, Ladysmith, Leaguer, Mafeking, Masada, Metz, Obsidional, Perilous, Pleven, Plevna, Poliorcetic, Ravelin, Sarajevo, Surround, Verdun, Vicksburg, Warsaw
Sienese Tuscan
Sienna Burnt, Raw
Siesta Nap, Noonday, Nooning
Sieve, Sift(ing) Analyse, Bolt(er), Boult(er), Bunting, Colander, Coliform, Cribble, Cribrate, Cribrose, Cullender, Eratosthenes, Ethmoid, Filter, Molecular, Riddle, Screen, Searce, Search, Separate, Siler, Strain, Sye, Tamis, Tammy, Tems(e), Trommel, Try, Winnow
Sigh Exhale, Heave, Lackaday, Long, Moan, Sough, Suspire, Welladay
Sight(ed) Aim, Barleycorn, Bead, Conspectuity, Eye(ful), Eyesore, Glimpse, Ken, Long, Oculated, Panoramic, Peep, Prospect, Range, Rear, Riflescope, Scene, Scotopia, Second, See, Short, Spectacle, Taish, Telescopic, Vane, → **VIEW**, Visie, Vision, Vista, Vizy, Vizzie
Sight-screen Eyelid
Sightseer, Sightseeing Lionise, Observer, Rubberneck, Tourist, Tripper, Viewer
Sign(s), Signing, Signpost Accidental, Ache, Addition, Ale-stake, Ampassy, Ampersand, Aquarius, Archer, Aries, Arrow, Auspice, Autograph, Badge, Balance, Beck, Beckon, Board, Brand, Bull, Bush, Call, Cancer, Capricorn, Caract, Caret, Chevron, Clue, Coronis, Crab, Cross, Cue, Dactylology, Dele, Diacritic, Di(a)eresis, Diphone, Division, Dollar, DS, Earmark, Emblem, Endeixis, Endorse, Endoss, Enlist, Evidence, Exit, Fascia, Fish, Gemini, Gesture, Goat, Grammalogue, Hallmark, Hamza(h), Harbinger, Harvey Smith, Hex, Hieroglyphic, Hint, Ideogram, Indian, Indicate, Indication, Indicium, Initial, INRI, Inscribe, Ivy-bush, Leo, Lexigram, Libra, Local, Logogram, Milepost, Milestone, Minus, Mudra, Multiplication, Negative, Neume, Nod, Notice, Obelisk, Obelus, Omen, Peace, Phraseogram, Pisces, Plus, Positive, Pound, Presa, Presage, Prodrome, Prodromus, Radical, Ram, Ratify, Rest, Rune, Sacrament, Sagittarius, Sain, Scorpio, Segno, Semeion, Semiotics, Shingle, Show, Sigil, Sigla, Signal, Star, Subscribe, Subtraction, Superscribe, Symbol, Symptom, Syndrome, Tag, Taurus, Tic(k)tac(k), Tilde, Titulus, Token, Trace, Triphone, Twins, Umlaut, V, Vestige, Virgo, Vital, Warning, Waymark, Word, Zodiac
Signal(ler) Alarm, Aldis lamp, Alert, Amber, Assemble, Baud, Beacon, Bell, Bleep, Bugle, Busy, Buzz, Chamade, Code, Compander, Compandor, Cone, Cue,

Detonator, Diaphone, Distress, Duplex, Earcon, Flag, Flagman, Flare, Flash, Fog, Gantry, Gesticulate, Gong, Griffin, Gun, Harmonic, Heliograph, Heliostat, Herald, Heterodyne, High sign, Hooter, Horse and hattock, Icon, Important, Interrupt, Interval, Luminance, Mark, Mase, Megafog, Message, Modem, Morse, Navar, NICAM, Notation, Noted, Output, Password, Peter, Pinger, Pip, Pollice verso, Prod, Pulsar, Radio, Renowned, Reveille, Robot, Salient, Semaphore, Semiology, Simplex, Singular, Smoke, Sonogram, SOS, Spoiler, Squawk, Taps, Target, Tchick, Telegraph, Teles(e)me, Thumb, Tic(k)-tac(k), Time, Traffic, Troop, Very, Video, V-sign, Waff, Waft, Wave, Wave-off, Wigwag

Signature Alla breve, Allograph, Autograph, By-line, Digital, Hand, John Hancock, John Henry, Key, Mark, Onomastic, Specimen, Subscription, Time

Signet Ring, Seal, Sigil, Sphragistics

Significance, Significant Cardinal, Consequence, Cosmic, Emblem, Great, Impact, Important, Indicative, Key, Magnitude, Major, Material, Matter, Meaningful, Milestone, Moment(ous), Noted, Noteworthy, Other, Paramount, Pith, Pregnant, Salient, Special, Telling

Signify Bemean, Denote, Imply, Indicate, Intimate, Matter, → MEAN, Represent

Sign language Ameslan, Semaphore, Tic(k)tac(k)

Sikh(ism) Granth, Kaccha, Kangha, Kara, Kesh, Khalsa, Kirpan, Mazhbi, Mechanised, Nanak, (Ranjit) Singh

Silas Uncle, Wegg

Silence(r), Silent Amyclaean, Choke-pear, Clam, Clamour, Conticent, Creepmouse, Dumbstruck, Earplug, Gag, Hesychastic, Hist, Hush, Hushkit, Mim(budget), Muffler, Mum(p), Mumchance, Mute, Obmutescent, Omertà, Quench, Quiesce, → QUIET, Reticence, Shtoom, Shush, Speechless, Still, Sulky, Tace(t), Tacit(urn), Throttle, Tight-lipped, Unvoiced, Wheesh(t), Whis(h)t

Silhouette Contour, Outline, Planform, Profile, Shadow figure, Shadowgraph, Shape, Skyline

Silica(te) Albite, Analcite, Andalusite, Chabazite, Chert, Cristobalite, Datolite, Diopside, Dioptase, Fayalite, Float-stone, Gadolinite, Harmotome, Hiddenite, Humite, Iolite, Kieselguhr, Kyanite, Monticellite, Montmorillonite, Olivine, Opal, Pectolite, Penninite, Phillipsite, Pinite, Rhodonite, Riebeckite, Saponite, Scapolite, Silex, Spodumene, Staurolite, Stishovite, Tridymite, Tripoli, Ultrabasic, Vermiculite, Vitreous, Zeolite

Silicon Chip, Si

Silk(y), Silk screen Alamode, Atlas, Barathea, Blonde-lace, Brocade, Bur(r), Charmeuse®, Chenille, Chiffon, Cocoon, Corn, Crape, Crepe, Duchesse, Dupion, Faille, Fibroin, Filature, Filoselle, Florence, Florentine, Flosh, Floss, Flox, Foulard, Gazar, Gazzatum, Georgette, Gimp, Glossy, Grosgrain, KC, Kincob, Lustrine, Lustring, Lutestring, Makimono, Malines, Marabou(t), Matelasse, Mercery, Moiré, Ninon, Oiled, Organza, Ottoman, Paduasoy, Parachute, Peau de soie, Pongee, Prunella, Prunelle, Prunello, Pulu, QC, Raw, Samite, Sars(e)net, Satin, Schappe, Seal(ch), Sendal, Seric, Sericeous, Sericite, Serigraph, Shalli, Shantung, Sien-tsan, Sleave, Sleek, Sle(i)ded, Slipper satin, Smooth, Spun, Surah, Tabaret, Tabby, Taffeta, Tasar, Thistledown, Tiffany, Tram, Tulle, Tussah, Tusseh, Tusser, Tussore, Vegetable, Velvet, Wild

Silkworm (eggs), Silkworm disease Bombyx, Eria, Graine, Multivoltine, Muscardine, Sericulture, Tussore

Sill Ledge, Straining, Threshold

Silly, Silliness Absurd, Anserine, Apish, Brainless, Buffer, Crass, Cuckoo, Daft, Dandy, Ditsy, Divvy, Drippy, Dumb, Dunce, Fatuous, Folly, Fool, Footling, Frivolous,

Goopy, Goosey, Gormless, Hen-witted, Idiotic, Imbecile, Inane, Inept, Infield(er), Liminal, Mid-off, Mid-on, Mopoke, Puerile, Season, Simple, Soft(y), Spoony, → **STUPID**, Tripe, Wacky

▷ **Silly** *may indicate* relating to a sill

Silt Alluvium, Deposit, Dregs, Land, Lees, Loess, Residue, Sullage, Varve

Silver(skin) Ag, Albata, Alpac(c)a, Arg(ent), Argyria, British plate, Cardecue, Cerargyrite, Diana's tree, Electroplate, Free, Fulminating, German, Grey, Horn, Luna, Nickel, One-legged, Pakt(h)ong, Parcel-gilt, Pegleg, Piastre, Plate, Plateresque, Ruby, Stephanite, Sterling, Sycee, Thaler

▷ **Silver** *may indicate* a coin

Silversmith Demetrius, Lamerie, Plater

Simian Apelike, Catar(r)hine

Similar(ity) Analog(ue), Analogical, Corresponding, Equivalent, Etc, Homoeoneric, Homogeneous, Homoiousian, Homologous, Homonym, Isomorphism, Kindred, → **LIKE**, Parallel, Patristic, Resemblance, Samey, Suchlike

Simile Epic

Similitude Parable

Simmer Bubble, Poach, Seethe, Stew

Simon Bolivar, Cellarer, Magus, Peter, Pure, Simple

Simper Bridle, Giggle, Smirk

Simple(r), Simplicity, Simplify, Simply Aefa(u)ld, Afa(w)ld, Arcadian, Artless, Austere, Bald, Bare, Basic, Crude, Daw, Doddle, Doric, → **EASY**, Eath(e), Elegant, ESN, Ethe, Facile, Fee, Folksy, Gomeral, Gotham, Green, Herb(alist), Herborist, Homespun, Idyllic, Incomposite, Inornate, Jaap, Japie, Mere, Moner(on), Naive(té), Naked, Niaiserie, Noddy, One-fold, Open and shut, Ordinary, Paraphrase, Pastoral, Peter, Plain, Pleon, Provincial, Pure, Reduce, Rustic, Saikless, Sapid, Semplice, Sheer, Silly, Simon, Spartan, Stupid, Tout court, Understated, Woollen

Simpleton Abderite, Airhead, Cokes, Cuckoo, Daw, Duffer, Flat, Fool, Gaby, Galah, Gomeral, Gomeril, Greenhorn, Juggins, Spoon, → **STUPID PERSON**, Wiseacre, Zany

Simulate, Simulating Affect, Anti, Feign, Pretend

Simultaneous Coinstantaneous, Contemporaneous, Synchronous, Together

Sin(ful) Aberrant, Accidie, Acedia, Actual, Anger, Avarice, Besetting, Bigamy, Capital, Cardinal, Covetousness, Crime, Deadly, Debt, Depravity, Envy, Err, Evil, Folly, Gluttony, Hamartiology, Harm, Hate, Impious, Lapse, Lust, Misdeed, Misdoing, Mortal, → **OFFENCE**, Original, Peccadillo, Piacular, Pride, Scape, Scarlet, Shirk, Sine, Sloth, Transgress, Trespass, Unrighteous, Venial, Vice, Wicked, Wrath, Wrong

Sinai Horeb, Mount

Since Ago, As, Meantime, Seeing, Sens, Sine, Sinsyne, Sith(en), Syne, Whereas, Ygo(e)

Sincere(ly), Sincerity Bona-fide, Candour, Earnest, Entire, Frank, Genuine, Heartfelt, Honest, Open, Real(ly), True, Verity, Whole-hearted

Sinclair Lewis, Upton

Sine Versed

Sinecure Bludge, Commendam

Sinew(y) Fibre, Ligament, Nerve, String, Tendinous, Tendon

▶ **Sinful** *see* **SIN**

Sing(ing) Antiphony, Barbershop, Bel canto, Belt out, Bhajan, Carol, Chant, Cheep, Chorus, Coloratura, Community, Cough, Croon, Crow, Diaphony, Diddle, Doo-wop, Glee club, Gorgia, Hum, Inform, Intone, Karaoke, Kirtan, La-la, Lilt, Melic,

Parlando, Peach, Pen(n)illion, Pipe, Plainchant, Rand, Rant, Rap, Record, Render, Scat, Second(o), Solmization, Sprechgesang, Sprechstimme, Squeal, Tell, Thrum, Trill, Troll, Vocalise, Warble, Yodel

Singe Burn, Char, Scorch, Swale, Swayl, Sweal, Sweel

Singer(s) Alto, Balladeer, Bard, Baritone, Bass, Beatle, Bing, Bird, Blondel, Buffo, Callas, Canary, Cantabank, Cantatrice, Cantor, Car, Carreras, Caruso, Castrato, Chaliapin, Chanteuse, Chantor, Chazan, Cher, Chorister, Coloratura, Comprimario, Countertenor, Crooner, Dawson, Diva, Dylan, Ella, Falsetto, Folk, Glee club, Gleemaiden, Gleeman, Grass, Haz(z)an, Heldentenor, Isaac, Kettle, Lark, Lauder, Lay clerk, Lead, Lind, Lorelei, Lulu, Mathis, Melba, Minstrel, Opera, Oscine, Patti, Piaf, Pitti, Precentor, Prima donna, Qawwal, Robeson, Semi-chorus, Session, Sinatra, Siren, Snitch, Songstress, Soprano, Soubrette, Stoolie, Succentor, Swan, Tatiana, Tenor, Tenure, Torch, Treble, Troubador, Vocalist, Voice, Wait, Warbler

Single, Singly Ace, Aefa(u)ld, Aefawld, Alone, Azygous, Bachelor, Celibate, Discriminate, EP, Exclusive, Feme sole, Individual, Matchless, Monact, Mono, Odd, One-off, Only, Pick, Run, Sole, Solitary, Spinster, Unary, Unattached, Uncoupled, Uniparous, Unique, Unwed, Versal, Yin

Single-cell Protista

Single-chambered Monothalamous

Singlestick Sword

Singlet Tunic, Vest

Singular(ity) Curious, Especial, Exceptional, Extraordinary, Ferly, Naked, Odd, Once, One, Peculiar, Queer(er), Rare, → UNIQUE, Unusual

Singultus Hiccup

Sinister Bend, Dark, Dirke, Evil, L, Left, Lh, Louche, → OMINOUS

Sink(ing), Sunken Basin, Bog, Cadence, Carbon, Cower, Delapse, Depress, Descend, Devall, Dip, Down, Drain, Draught-house, Drink, Drop, Drown, Ebb, Flag, Founder, Gravitate, Heat, Hole, Immerse, Invest, Jawbox, Kitchen, Lagan, Laigh, Lapse, Ligan, Merger, Pad, Poach, Pot, Prolapse, Put(t), Relapse, Sag, Scupper, Scuttle, Set, Settle, Shipwreck, Slump, Steep-to, Sty, Submerge, Subside, Swag, Swamp

Sinner Evildoer, Malefactor, Offender, Reprobate, Trespasser

Sinuous Curvy, Ogee, Slinky, Snaky, Wavy, Winding

Sinus Cavity, Recess

Sip(ping) Delibate, Hap'orth, Libant, Sample, Sowp, Sup, Taste, Tiff(ing)

Siphon Draw, Rack, Soda, Suck, Transfer

Sir Dan, Dom, K, Knight, Kt, Lord(ing), Sahib, Signor, Sirrah, Stir, Stirra(h), Towkay, Tuan

Sire Beget, Father, Get

Siren Alarm, Alert, Diaphone, Enchanter, Femme fatale, Hooter, Houri, Leucosia, Ligea, Lorelei, Mermaid, Oceanides, Parthenope, Salamander, Shark, Teaser, Temptress, Vamp

Sirenian Dugong, Lamantin, Manatee, Manati, Sea-cow

Sirloin Backsey

Sirree Bo

Sisal Agave

Siskin Aberdevine, Bird, Finch

Sister(s) Anne, Beguine, Lay, Minim, → NUN, Nurse, Out, Religeuse, Sib, Sibling, Sis, Sob, Soul, Swallow, Theatre, Titty, Ugly, Ursuline, Verse, Ward, Weird

Sisyphean Uphill

Sit(ter), Sitting Bestride, Clutch, Dharna, Duck, Gaper, Lime, Lit de justice, Model,

MP, Perch, Pose, Reign, Represent, Roost, Séance, Sederunt, Sejeant, Session, Squat

Site, Siting Area, Arpa, Brownfield, Building, Camp, Caravan, Feng shui, Greenfield, Home-page, Location, Lot, Mirror, Pad, Place, Plot, Ramsar, Rogue, Sacred, Silo, Spot, Stance

Situation Ballpark, Berth, Cart, Case, Catch, Catch-22, Cliff-hanger, Contretemps, Cow, Dilemma, Galère, Hole, Job, Lie, Location, Lurch, Matrix, Nail-biter, Niche, No-win, Office, Plight, Position, Post, Scenario, Schmear, Schmeer, Set-up, Shebang, Showdown, Status quo, Sticky wicket, Strait, Where, Worst case

Six(th) Digamma, French, German, Half(-a)dozen, Hexad, Italian, Neapolitan, Prime, Sax, Senary, Sestette, Sextet, Sice, Size, Vau, VI

Six counties NI

Six days Hexa(e)meron

Six feet Fathom

Sixpence Bender, Kick, Slipper, Tanner, Tester(n), Testril(l), Tizzy, VID, VIP, Zack

Sixteen Sweet

Sixty Degree, Threescore

Size(able) Amplitude, Area, Bulk, Calibre, Clearcole, Countess, Demy, Displacement, → EXTENT, Format, Girth, Glair, Glue, Gum, Imperial, Measure, Particle, Physique, Plus, Pot(t), Princess, Proportion, Tempera, Tidy, Trim

Sizzle Fry, Hiss, Scorch

Skate(r), Skateboard(er), Skating Blade, Bob, Cheap, Choctaw, Cousins, Curry, Dean, Fakie, Figure, Fish, Free, Grommet, In-line, Maid, Mohawk, Rink, Rock(er), Roller, Rollerblade®, Runner, Speed

Skedaddle Scarper, Shoo, Vamoose

Skein Hank, Hasp

Skeleton, Skeletal Anatomy, Atomy, Axial, Bones, Cadaverous, Cadre, Cage, Coenosteum, Corallite, Corallum, Family, Framework, Key, Ossify, Outline, Scenario, Sclere, Tentorium

Sketch(y) Cameo, Character, Charade, Croquis, Delineate, Diagram, Doodle, Draft, → DRAW, Ébauche, Esquisse, Illustration, Limn, Line, Maquette, Modello, Outline, Pencilling, Playlet, Pochade, Précis, Profile, Skit, Summary, Tenuous, Thumbnail, Trick, Vignette, Visual

Skew Agee, Ajee, Oblique, Sheer, Squint, Swerve, Veer

Skewer Brochette, En brochette, Prong, Spit, Transfix

Ski(ing) Aquaplane, Glide, Glissade, Hot-dog, Langlauf, Mogul, Nordic, Schuss, Super G, Telemark, Vorlage, Wedeln

Skid Aquaplane, Drift, Jackknife, Side-slip, Slew, Slide, Slip, Slither, Spinout

▷ **Skidding** *may indicate* an anagram

Skiff Canoe, Dinghy, Outrigger

Skill(ed), Skilful Ability, Able, Ace, Address, Adept, Adroit, Art, Bravura, Canny, Chic, Competence, Craft, Deacon, Deft, Dextrous, Enoch, Expertise, Facility, Feat, Finesse, Flair, Gleg, Habile, Hand, Handicraft, Handy, Hend, Hot, Ingenious, Knack, Know-how, Knowing, Lear(e), Leir, Lere, Masterly, Masterpiece, Mastery, Mean, Métier, Mistery, Mystery, Mystique, Practised, Proficient, Prowess, Quant, Resource, Savvy, Science, Skeely, Sleight, Soft, Speciality, Tactics, Talent, Technic, Technique, Touch, Trade, Trick, Versed, Virtuoso

Skim Cream, Despumate, Flit, Glide, Graze, Plane, Ream, Scan, Scud, Scum, Skiff, Skitter

Skimp Restrict, Scamp, Scrimp, Stint

Skin(s) Agnail, Armour, Bark, Basan, Basil, Box-calf, Bronzed, Calf, Callus, Case,

Cere, Chevrette, Coat, Corium, Cortex, Crackling, Cutaneous, Cuticle, Cutis, Deacon, Deer, Derm(a), Dermatome, Dermis, Dewlap, Disbark, Ectoderm, Enderon, Epicanthus, Epicarp, Epidermis, Eschar, Excoriate, Exterior, Fell, Film, Flaught, Flay, Flench, Flense, Flinch, Forel, Fourchette, Goldbeater's, Hangnail, Hide, Integra®, Jacket, Kip, Kirbeh, Leather, Membrane, Muktuk, Nebris, Pachyderm, Parfleche, Peau, Peel, Pell, Pellicle, Pelt, Perinychium, Plew, Plu(e), Prepuce, Pteryla, Rack, Rape, Rind, Scalp, Scarfskin, Serosa, Shell, Shoder, Spetch, Strip, Swindle, Tegument, Tulchan, Veneer, Water-bouget, Wattle, Woolfell
Skin disease, Skin trouble Boba, Boil, Buba, Causalgia, Chloasma, Chloracne, Cowpox, Cradle cap, Cyanosis, Dartre, Dermatitis, Dermatosis, Dyschroa, EB, Ecthyma, Eczema, Erysipelas, Exanthem(a), Favus, Flay, Framboesia, Gum rash, Herpes, Hives, Ichthyosis, Impetigo, Leishmaniasis, Leucoderma, Lichen, Livedo, Lupus vulgaris, Maidism, Mal del pinto, Mange, Miliaria, Morphew, Morula, Patagium, Pellagra, Pemphigus, Pinta, Pityriasis, Prurigo, Psoriasis, Pyoderma, Rash, Red-gum, Ringworm, Rosacea, Rose-rash, St Anthony's fire, Sapego, Scabies, Sclerodermia, Scurvy, Seborrhoea, Serpigo, Strophulus, Telangiectasis, Tetter, Tinea, Vaccinia, Verruca, Verruga, Vitiligo, Xanthoma, Xerodermia, Yaws, Yawy
Skinflint Cheapo, Dryfist, Miser, Niggard, Pinch-gut, Scrooge, Tightwad
Skinful Drunk, Sausage
Skinhead Not, Punk, Scalp
Skink Seps
Skinless Ecorché
Skinny Barebone, Bony, Dermal, Emaciate, Lean, Scraggy, Thin, Weed
Skint Broke, Ghat, Penniless, Stony
Skip(ped), Skipper Boss, Caper, Captain, Cavort, Drakestone, Dumpster, Elater, Frisk, Hesperian, Jump, Jumping-mouse, Lamb, Luppen, Miss, Omit, Patroon, Ricochet, Saury, Scombresox, Spring, Tittup, Trounce(r)
Skirl Humdudgeon, Pibroch, Pipe, Screigh
Skirmish(er) Brush, Dispute, Escarmouche, Fray, Pickeer, Spar, Tirailleur, Velitation
Skirt(ing) Bases, Bell, Border, Bouffant, Cheongsam, Circle, Coat, Crinoline, Culotte(s), Dado, Dirndl, Edge, Fil(l)ibeg, Fringe, Fustanella, Fustanelle, Girl, Gore, Grass, Harem, Hobble, Hoop, Hug, Hula, Kilt, Lamboys, Lava-lava, Marge, Mini, Mopboard, Pareo, Pareu, Pencil, Peplum, Petticoat, Philibeg, Pinafore, Piu-piu, Plinth, Puffball, Ra-ra, Rim, Sarong, Sidestep, Stringboard, Tace, Tail, Taslet, Tasse(t), Tonlet, Tutu, Washboard, Wrap(a)round, Wrapover
Skit Lampoon, Parody, Sketch
Skittish Coy, Curvetting, Frisky, Restless
Skittle(s) Bayle, Bowl, Kail(s), Kayle, Kingpin, Ninepin, Pin, Spare
Skive(r) Absentee, Scrimshank, Shirk
Skivvy Drudge, Slave
Skrimshank Bludge, Skive
Skulk Lurk, Mooch, Shool
Skull Brainpan, Bregma(ta), Calvaria, Cranium, Fontanel, Harnpan, Head, Malar, Maz(z)ard, Obelion, Occiput, Pannikell, Phrenology, Scalp, Sinciput
Skullcap Ya(r)mulka, Yarmulke, Zucchetto
Skunk Atoc, Atok, Hognosed, Polecat, Pot, Teledu, Zoril(lo)
Sky(-high), Skywards Áir, Azure, Blue, Canopy, Carry, El Al, E-layer, Element, Empyrean, Ether, Firmament, Heaven, Lift, Loft, Mackerel, Occident, Octa, Rangi, Uranus, Welkin

Sky-diver Para
Skylark Aerobatics, Bird
Skylight Abat-jour, Aurora, Comet, Lunette, Star
Skyline Horizon, Rooftops
Sky-pilot Chaplain, Vicar
Slab(s) Briquette, Bunk, Bunk(er), Cake, Cap(e)stone, Chunk, Dalle, Hawk, Ledger,
    Marver, Metope, Mihrab, Mud, Paving-stone, Planch, Plank, Sclate, Sheave, Slate,
    Slice, Stela, Stelene, Tab, Tile, Wood-wool
Slack(en), Slackness Abate, Careless, Crank, Dilatory, Dross, Ease, Easy-going,
    Glen, Idle, Lax(ity), Let-up, Loose, Malinger, Nerveless, Relax, Release, Remiss,
    Shirk, Skive, Slatch, Slow, Surge, Unscrew, Unwind, Veer
Slag Basic, Calx, Cinder, Dross, Scoria, Scum, Sinter, Tap cinder, Tart
Slake Abate, Cool, Quench, Refresh, Satisfy
Slalom Super-G
Slam Crash, Criticise, Dad, Grand, Little, Pan(dy), Small, Sock, Swap, Swop, Vole, Wap
Slander(ous) Asperse, Backbite, Calumny, Defame, Derogatory, Detraction,
    Disparage, Libel, Malediction, Malign, Missay, Mud, Mudslinging, Obloquy,
    Sclaunder, Smear, Traduce, Vilify, Vilipend
Slang Abuse, Argot, Back, Berate, Blinglish, Cant, Colloquial, Ebonics, Flash, Jargon,
    Lingo, Nadsat, Parlyaree, Polari, Rhyming, Slate, Tsotsitaal, Verlan, Zowie
Slant(ed), Slanting Angle, Asklent, Atilt, Bevel, Bias, Brae, Cant, Careen, Chamfer,
    Clinamen, Diagonal, Escarp, Oblique, Prejudice, Slew, → SLOPE, Splay, Squint,
    Talus, Tilt, Virgule
Slap Clatch, Clout, Cuff, Make-up, Pandy, Piston, Sclaff, Scud, Skelp, Smack, Spat,
    Tape, Twank
Slapdash Careless, Hurried, Random
Slash(ed) Chive, Cut, Diagonal, Gash, Hack, Jag, Lacerate, Laciniate, Leak, Oblique,
    Rash, Rast, Reduce, Scorch, Scotch, Separatrix, Slice, Slit, Solidus, Stroke, Virgule,
    Wee
Slat(s) Fish, Jalousie, Louvre
Slate, Slaty, Slating Alum, Berate, Calm, Cam, Caum, Countess, Credit, Criticise,
    Decry, Diatribe, Double, Duchess, Duchy, Enter, Griseous, Imperial, Killas,
    Knotenschiefer, Lady, Marchioness, Ottrelite, Pan, Peggy, Polishing, Princess,
    Queen, Rag(g), Roof, Schalstein, Shingle, Slat, Small, Tomahawk, Viscountess
Slater Hellier, Insect
Slattern Bag, Besom, Drab, Drazel, Frump, Mopsy, Sloven, Slummock, Sozzle,
    Traipse, Trapes, Trollop
Slaughter(house), Slaughterer Abattoir, Behead, Bleed, Bloodshed, Butcher,
    Carnage, Decimate, Hal(l)al, Holocaust, Jhatka, Kill, Mactation, → MASSACRE,
    S(c)hechita(h), Scupper, Shambles, Shochet, Smite
Slav Bohunk, Croat, Czech, Kulak, Lusatia, Polabian, Serb, Sorb, Wend(ic)
Slave(ry), Slaves Addict, Aesop, Aida, Androcles, Barracoon, Blackbird, Bond,
    Bond(s)man, Bondwoman, Bordar, Boy, Caliban, Coffle, Contraband, Dogsbody,
    Drudge, Drug, Dulocracy, Dulosis, Esne, Galley, Gibeonite, Helot, Hierodule,
    Mameluke, Mamluk, Marmaluke, Maroon, Minion, Odalisk, Odali(s)que, Peasant,
    Pr(a)edial, Rhodope, Serf, Servitude, Spartacus, Terence, Theow, Thersites, Thete,
    Thrall, Topsy, Vassal, Villein, Wage, White, Yoke
Slave-driver, Slave-owner Assam, Task-master
Slaver Bespit, Dribble, Drivel, Drool, Slabber, Slobber, Spawl
Slay(er), Slaying Destroy, Execute, Ghazi, → KILL, Mactation, Murder, Quell, Saul,
    Slaughter

Sleazy Flimsy, Red-light, Scuzzy, Seamy, Sordid, Squalid, Thin
Sled(ge), Sleigh(-ride) Bob, Dog train, Dray, Hurdle, Hurly-hacket, Kibitka, Komatik, Lauf, Luge, Mud-boat, Mush, Polack, Pulk(h)(a), Pung, Skeleton bob(sleigh), Skidoo®, Slipe, Stoneboat, Tarboggin, Toboggan, Train, Travois
Sleek Bright, Shine, Silky, Smarm, Smooth, Smug
Sleep, Sleeper(s), Sleepiness, Sleeping, Sleepy Beauty, Bed, Bivouac, Blet, Bundle, Bye-byes, Car, Catnap, Coma, Couchette, Crash, Cross-sill, Cross-tie, Dormant, Dormient, Doss, Doze, Drop off, Drowse, Earring, Endymion, Epimenides, Gowl, Gum, Hibernate, Hypnology, Hypnos, Kip, Lethargic, Lie, Morpheus, Nap, Narcolepsy, Narcosis, Nod, Over, Paradoxical, Petal, Pop off, Psychopannychism, REM, Repast, Repose, Rest, Rip Van Winkle, Rough, Sandman, Seven, Shuteye, Skipper, Sloom, Slumber, Snooz(l)e, Somnolent, Sopor(ose), Sownd, Swone, Tie, Torpid, Twilight, Wink, Zeds, Zizz
Sleeping place Bed, Cot, Dormitory, Kang
Sleeping sickness Trypanosomiasis
Sleepless Wake-rife, Wauk-rife
Sleep-walking Noctambulation
Sleet Graupel, Hail
Sleeve (opening) Arm(hole), Balloon, Batwing, Bishop's, Bush, Cap, Collet, Cover, Dolman, Gatefold, Gigot, Gland, Kimono, Lawn, Leg-o'-mutton, Liner, Magyar, Manche, Pagoda, Pudding, Querpo, Raglan, Record, Sabot, Scye, Slashed, Trunk, Turnbuckle, Wind
▶ **Sleigh** see SLED
Sleight Artifice, Conjury, Cunning, Dodge, Legerdemain, Trick
Slender(ness) Asthenic, Ectomorph, Elongate, Exiguity, Exility, Fine, Flagelliform, Flimsy, Gracile, Jimp, Leptosome, Loris, Narrow, Skinny, Slight, Slim, Small, Spindly, Stalky, Styloid, Svelte, Swank, Sylph, Tenuous, Trim, Waif
Sleuth Bloodhound, Detective, Dick, Eye, Lime-hound, Lyam(-hound), Lyme(-hound)
Slew Number, Skid, Slide, Twist
Slice Cantle, Chip, Collop, Cut, Doorstep, Fade, Frustrum, Lop, Piece, Rasure, Round, Sector, Segment, Share, Sheave, Shive, Slab, Sliver, Spoon, Tranche, Wafer, Whang
▷ **Slice of** may indicate a hidden word
Slick Adroit, Glim, Oil, Sleeveen, Smooth, Suave
Slide Barrette, Chute, Cursor, Diapositive, Drift, Ease, Glissando, Hair, Hirsle, Ice-run, Illapse, Lantern, Mount, Pulka, Schuss, Skid, Skite, Slip, Slippery dip, Slither, Snowboard, Transparency
Slight(ly) Affront, Belittle, Cold shoulder, Cut, Detract, Disparage, Disregard, Facer, Flimsy, Halfway, Insult, Minor, Misprise, Neglect, Nominal, Pet, Petty, Rebuff, Remote, → SLENDER, Slim, Slimsy, Slur, Small, Smattering, Sneaking, Snub, Subtle, Superficial, Sylphine, Tenuous, Thin, Tiny, Wee, Wispy
Slim Bant, Jimp, Macerate, Reduce, Slender, Slight, Sylph, Tenuous, Thin
Slime, Slimy Glair, Glit, Gorydew, Guck, Gunk, Mother, Muc(o)us, Myxomycete, Oily, Ooze, Sapropel, Slake, Sludge, Uliginous
Sling Balista, Catapult, Drink, Fling, Hang, Parbuckle, Prusik, Support, Toss, Trebuchet
Slink Lurk, Skulk, Slope
Slip(ped), Slipping, Slips Boner, Cover, Cutting, Disc, Docket, Drift, EE, Elapse, Elt, Engobe, Error, Faux pas, Fielder, Form, Freudian, Glide, Glissade, Infielder, Label, Landslide, Lapse, Lapsus linguae, Lath, Lauwine, Lingual, Mistake, Muff,

Nod, Oversight, Parapraxis, Petticoat, Pink, Prolapse, Ptosis, Quickset, Rejection, Relapse, Run, Scape, Sc(h)edule, Scoot, Set, Shim, Sin, Ski, Skid, Skin, Skite, Slade, Slidder, Slide, Slither, Slive, Spillican, Stumble, Surge, Ticket, Trip, Tunicle, Underskirt, Unleash, Wage(s)

Slipper(s) Baboosh, Babouche, Babuche, Baffies, Calceolate, Carpet, Eel, Japanese, Mocassin, Moccasin, Moyl, Muil, Mule, Pabouche, Pampootie, Pantable, Pantof(f)le, Panton, Pantoufle, Pump, Rullion, Runner, Ski, Sledge, Sneaker, Sock

Slippery Eely, Foxy, Glid, Icy, Lubric, Shady, Shifty, Skidpan, Slick

Slipshod Careless, Hurried, Jerry, Lax, Slapdash, Slatternly, Sloppy, Slovenly, Toboggan

▷ **Slipshod** *may indicate* an anagram

Slit Buttonhole, Cranny, Cut, Fent, Fissure, Fitchet, Gash, Gill, Loop, Pertus(at)e, Placket, Placket-hole, Race, Rit, Scissure, Spare, Speld(er), Vent

Slithy Tove

Sliver Flake, Fragment, Moslings, Rove, Shaving, Slice, Splinter, Trace

Slob(ber) Drool, Lout, Slaver, Smarm, Wet

Sloe Blackthorn, Slae

Slog(ger) Drag, Strike, Swink, Swot, Traipse, Tramp, Trape, Trauchle, Trudge, Yacker, Yakka, Yakker

Slogan Amandla, Byword, Catchword, Chant, Jai Hind, Masakhane, Mot(to), Murdabad, Phrase, Rallying-cry, Slughorn(e), Tagline, Warcry, Watchword

Sloop Cutter, Hoy, Ship

Slop(s) Cop(per), Gardyloo, Jordeloo, Muck, Policeman, Rossers, Rozzers, Schmaltz, Sop, Spill, Swill

Slope(s), Sloping Acclivity, Angle, Anticline, Bahada, Bajada, Bank, Batter, Bevel, Borrow, Borstal(l), Brae, Breast, Camber, Chamfer, Cuesta, Declivity, Delve, Diagonal, Dip, Dry, Escarp, Fastigate, Fla(u)nch, Foothill, Geanticline, Glacis, Grade, Gradient, Heel, Hill, Incline, Isoclinical, Kant, Lean, Natural, Nursery, Oblique, Pent, Periclinal, Pitch, Rake, Ramp, Rollway, Scarp, Schuss, Scrae, Scree, Shelve, Sideling, Skewback, Slant, Slippery, Slipway, Splay, Steep, Stoss, Talus, Tilt, Verge, Versant, Weather

Sloppily, Sloppy Lagrimoso, Lowse, Madid, Mushy, Remiss, Schmaltzy, Slapdash, Slipshod, Sloven, Slushy, Untidy, Weepie

▷ **Sloppy** *may indicate* an anagram

Slosh(y) Dowse, Fist, Splash, Wet

Slot(ted) Expansion, Graveyard, Groove, Hasp, Hesp, Hole, Key, Keyway, Mortice, Mortise, Seat, Slit, Swanmark, Time

Sloth(ful) Accidie, Acedia, Ai, Bradypus, Edentate, Ground, Idle, Inaction, Indolent, Inertia, Lazy, Lie-abed, Megatherium, Mylodon, Slugabed, Sweer(t), Sweered, Sweir(t), Three-toed, Unau

Slot machine One-armed bandit, Pokey, Pokie

Slouch Lop, Mooch, Mope, Slump

Slough(ing) Cast, Despond, Ecdysis, Eschar, Exuviae, Lerna, Marish, Marsh, Mire, Morass, Paludine, Shed, Shuck, Swamp

Sloven(ly) Careless, Dag(gy), Down-at-heel, D(r)aggle-tail, Frowsy, Grobian, Jack-hasty, Mawkin, Rag-doll, Ratbag, Slaister, Slammakin, Slammerkin, Slattern, Sleazy, Slipshod, Slubberdegullion, Slubberingly, Slummock, Slut, Streel, Untidy

Slow(ing), Slower, Slowly Adagio, Allargando, Andante, Brady, Brake, Broad, Calando, Crawl, Dawdle, Deliberate, Dilatory, Dull, Dumka, ESN, Flag, Gradual, Inchmeal, Lag, Langram, Larghetto, Largo, Lash, Lassu, Late, Lean-witted,

Leisurely, Lentando, Lento, Lifeless, Loiter, Losing, Meno mosso, Obtuse, Pedetentous, Rall(entando), Rein, Reluctant, Retard, Ribattuta, Ritardando, Ritenuto, Slack, Slug, Sluggish, Snaily, Solid, Stem, Tardigrade, Tardive, Tardy, Tardy-gaited

Slowcoach Slowpoke, Slug

Slow-match Portfire

Sludge Activated, Gunge, Mire, Muck, Sapropel, Slob

Slug(s) Ammo, Bêche-de-mer, Blow, Bullet, Cosh, Drink, Limaces, Limax, Linotype®, Mollusc, Nerita, Pellet, Shot, Snail, Trepang

Sluggard Drone, Lazy, Lie-abed, Lusk, Unau

Sluggish Dilatory, Drumble, Idler, Inactive, Inert, Jacent, Lacklustre, Laesie, Languid, Lazy, Lentor, Lethargic, Lug, Phlegmatic, Saturnine, Sleepy, → SLOW, Stagnant, Tardy, Torpid, Unalive

Sluice Aboideau, Aboiteau, Drain, Gutter, Koker, Penstock, Rinse, Sasse

Slum Basti, Bustee, Busti, Cabbagetown, Cardboard city, Ghetto, Pavela, Rookery, Shanty, Slurb, Warren

Slumber Doze, Drowse, Nap, Nod, Sleep, Sloom, Snooze

Slump Decrease, Depression, Deteriorate, Dip, Flop, Recession, Sink, Slouch, Sprawl

Slur(ring) Defame, Drawl, Innuendo, Libel, Opprobrium, Slight, Smear, Synaeresis, Tie

Slush Bathos, Boodle, Bribe, Drip, Money, Mush, Pap, Slop, Sposh, Swash

Slut Candle, Dollymop, Draggle-tail, Dratchell, Drazel, Floosie, Harlot, Slattern, Sow, Tart, Traipse, Trapes, Trollop

Sly Christopher, Clandestine, Coon, Covert, Cunning, Foxy, Furtive, Leery, Peery, Reynard, Secretive, Shifty, Slee, Sleekit, Sleeveen, Slicker, Sneaky, Stallone, Stealthy, Subtle, Surreptitious, Tinker, Tod, Tricky, Weasel, Wily

▷ **Slyly** *may indicate* an anagram

Smack(er) Buss, Cuff, Flavour, Foretaste, Fragrance, Hooker, Kiss, Klap, Lander, Lips, Pra(h)u, Relish, Salt, Saut, Skelp, Slap, Slat, Smatch, Smouch, Soupçon, Spank, Spice, Splat, Tack, → TANG, Taste, Thwack, Tincture, Trace, Twang, X, Yawl

Small (thing) Ateleiosis, Atom, Bantam, Beer, Bijou, Bittie, Bitty, Centesimal, Chotta, Curn, Denier, Diminutive, Dinky, Drib, Elfin, Few, Fry, Grain, Haet, Ha'it, Half-pint, Handful, Hobbit, Holding, Hole-in-the-wall, Hyperosmia, Insect, Ion, Leet, Lilliputian, Limited, Lite, → LITTLE, Lock, Low, Meagre, Mean, Measly, Microscopic, Midget, Mignon, Miniature, Minikin, Minority, Minute, Mite, Modest, Modicum, Peerie, Peewee, Petit(e), Petty, Pigmean, Pigmy, Pink(ie), Pinky, Pint-size, Pittance, Pocket, Poky, Poujadist, Rap, Reduction, Runt, S, Santilla, Scattering, Scrump, Scrunt, Scut, Shrimp, Single, Skerrick, Slight, Slim, Smattering, Smidge(o)n, Smidgin, Smithereen, Smout, Soupçon, Sprinkling, Spud, Stim, Stunted, Tad, Teenty, Thin, Tidd(l)y, Tiny, Titch(y), Tittle, Tot(tie), Totty, Trace, Trivial, Unheroic, Wee, Weedy, Whit

Smallest Least, Minimal, Runt

Smallholder, Smallholding Croft, Nursery, Rundale, Share-cropper, Stead

Small-minded(ness) Parvanimity, Petty

Smallness Exiguity, Exility, Paucity

Smallpox Alastrim, Variola

Smarm(y) Oil, Smoothie, Unctuous

Smart(en), Smartest Ache, Acute, Alec, Astute, Best, Bite, Chic, Classy, Clever, Cute, Dandy, Dapper, Dressy, Elegant, Flash, Flip, Fly, Groom, Gussy up, Kookie, Kooky, Natty, Neat, Nifty, Nip, Nobby, Pac(e)y, Posh, Preen, Primp, Prink, Pusser,

Raffish, Rattling, Ritzy, Saucy, Slick, Sly, Smoke, Smug, Snappy, Soigné(e), Spiff, Sprauncy, Sprightly, Spruce, Sprush, Spry, Sting, Stylish, Swagger, Sweat, Swish, Tiddley, Tippy, Titivate, Toff, U, Well-groomed, Wiseacre

Smash(ed), Smasher, Smashing Atom, Bingle, Brain, Break, Corker, Crush, Demolish, Devastate, Dish, Forearm, High, Jarp, Jaup, Kaput, Kill, Lulu, Shatter, Shiver, Slam, Squabash, Stave, Super, Terrific, Tight, To-brake, → WRECK

▷ **Smash(ed)** *may indicate* an anagram

Smear Assoil, Bedaub, Besmirch, Blur, Borm, Cervical, Clam, Daub, Defile, Denigrate, Discredit, Drabble, Enarm, Gaum, Gild, Gorm, Lick, Oil, Pap(anicolaou), Pay, Plaster, Slairg, Slaister, Slake, Slander, Slather, Slime, Slubber, Slur, Smalm, Smarm, Smudge, Sully, Teer, Traduce, Wax

Smell(ing), Smelly Aroma, Asafoetida, BO, Caproate, Effluvium, Empyreuma, Fetor, F(o)etid, Fug, Gale, Gamy, Graveolent, Guff, Hing, Honk, Hum, Mephitis, Miasm(a), Ming, Musk, Nidor, Niff, Nose, Odour, Olent, Olfact(ory), Osmatic, Perfume, Pong, Ponk, Pooh, Rank, Redolent, Reech, Reek, Sar, Savour, → SCENT, Sniff, Snifty, Snook, Snuff, Steam, Stench, Stifle, Stink, Tang, Whiff

Smelling salts Sal volatile

Smelt(ing) Atherinidae, Melt, Salmon, Scoria, Sparling, Speiss, Spirling

Smile(s), Smiling Agrin, Beam, Cheese, Favour, Gioconda, Grin, Rictus, Samuel, Self-help, Simper, Smirk

Smirk Grimace, Simper

Smite, Smitten Assail, Enamoured, Hit, Strike, Strook

Smith Adam, Farrier, FE, Forger, Hammerman, Mighty, Stan, Vulcan, Wayland

Smithy Forge, Smiddy, Stithy

Smock Blouse, Chemise, Drabbet, Gather, Shift, Slop, Smicket

Smoke(r), Smoking, Smoky Blast, Bloat, Censer, Chain, Chillum, → CIGAR(ETTE), Cure, Drag, Fog, Fuliginous, Fume, Funk, Gasper, Hemp, Incense, Indian hemp, Inhale, Kipper, Latakia, Lum, Lunt, Mainstream, Manil(l)a, Nicotian, Passive, Peat reek, Peaty, Pother, Pudder, Puff, Reech, Reek, Reest, Roke, Smeech, Smeek, Smirting, Smoor, Smoulder, Smudge, Snout, Tear, Toke, Vapour, Viper, Water, Whiff, Wreath

Smoke-hating Misocapnic

Smoking-room Divan

Smollett Tobias

▶ **Smooch** *see* SMOUCH

Smooth(e), Smoother, Smoothly Alabaster, Bald, Bland, Brent, Buff, Chamfer, Clean, Clockwork, Dress, Dub, Easy, Even, Fettle, File, Flat, Fluent, Glabrous, Glare, Glassy, Glib, Goose, Iron, Legato, Level, Levigate, Linish, Mealy-mouthed, Mellifluous, Oil, Plane, Plaster, Rake, Roll, Rub, Sand(er), Satiny, Scrape, Shiny, Sleek, Slick, Slickenslide, Slur, Smug, Snod, Sostenuto, Streamlined, Suave, Swimmingly, Terete, Terse, Trim, Urbane

Smooth-haired Lissotrichous

Smother Burke, Choke, Muffle, Oppress, Overlie, Smoor, Smore, Smoulder, Stifle, Suppress

Smouch Cheat, Kiss, Lallygag, Lollygag, Neck

Smoulder Burn, Seethe

Smudge Blur, Dab, Offset, Slur, Smear, Smooch, Stain

Smug Complacent, Conceited, Goody-goody, Goody-two-shoes, Neat, Oily, Pi, Sanctimonious, Self-satisfied, Trim

Smuggle(d), Smuggler, Smuggling Body-packer, Bootleg, Contraband, Contrabandist, Donkey, Fair trade, Gunrunning, Moonshine, Mule, Owler,

Rum-runner, Run, Secrete, Steal, Traffic

Smut(ty) Bawdy, Blight, Blue, Brand, Burnt-ear, Coom, Filth, Grime, Racy, Soot, Speck, Stinking

Smut-fungus Basidia, Ustilago

Snack Bever, Bhelpuri, Bite, Blintz, Breadstick, Brunch, Butty, Canapé, Chack, Crudités, Elevenses, Entremets, Four-by-two, Gorp, Meze, Nacket, Nibble, Nigiri, Nocket, Nooning, Nuncheon, Padkos, Pie, Popcorn, Rarebit, Refreshment, Samo(o)sa, Sandwich, Sarnie, Savoury, Scroggin, Small chop, Tapa, Taste, Toast(y), Trail mix, Vada, Voidee, Wada, Wrap, Zakuska

Snaffle Bit, Bridoon, Grab, Purloin

Snag Catch, Contretemps, Drawback, Hindrance, Hitch, Impediment, Knob, Nog, Obstacle, Remora, Rub, Snubbe, Stub, Tear

Snail Brian, Cowrie, Cowry, Dew, Dodman, Escargot, Garden, Gasteropod, Giant African, Helix, Hodmandod, Limnaea, Lymnaea, Nautilus, Nerite, Planorbis, Pond, Ramshorn, Roman, Slow, Slug, Strombus, Unicorn-shell, Univalve, Wallfish, Whelk, Wing

Snake Adder, Aesculapian, Amphisbaena, Anaconda, Anguine, Anguis, Apod(e), Asp, Bandy-bandy, Berg-adder, Blacksnake, Blind, Blue-racer, Boa, Boma, Boomslang, Brown, Bull, Bush-master, Camoodi, Carpet, Cerastes, Clotho, Coachwhip, Cobra, Coluber, Congo, Constrictor, Copperhead, Coral, Corn, Cottonmouth, Cribo, Crotalidae, Daboia, Death-adder, Dendrophis, Diamond(-back), Dipsas, Drag, Dugite, Elaeis, Elaps, Ellops, Fer-de-lance, Garter, Glass, Gopher, Grass, Habu, Hamadryad, Hognose, Homorelaps, Hoop, Horned viper, Horsewhip, Hydra, Indigo, Jararaca, Jararaka, Joe Blake, Kaa, K(a)rait, King (cobra), Lachesis, Langaha, Mamba, Massasauga, Massasauger, Meander, Milk, Mocassin, Moccasin, Mulga, Naga, Naia, Naja, Ophidian, Pipe, Pit-viper, Plumber's, Puff-adder, Python, Racer, Rat, Rattler, Reptile, Ribbon, Ringhals, Ringneck, Rinkhals, River jack, Rock, Sand viper, Sea, Seps, → **SERPENT**, Sidewinder, Slowworm, Smooth, Spitting, Squamata, Sucurujú, Surucucu, Taipan, Takshaka, Thirst, Thread, Tiger, Timber rattlesnake, Tree, Uraeus, Vasuki, Viper, Water (moccasin), Whip, Wind, Worm

Snake-charmer Lamia

Snake-in-the-grass Peacher, Rat, Traitor

Snake-root Bistort, Senega, Snakeweed, Virginia, White

Snap(per), Snappy, Snap up Alligator, Autolycus, Bite, Break, Brittle, Camera, Click, Cold, Crack, Crocodile, Cross, Curt, Edgy, Fillip, Girnie, Glom, Gnash, Hanch, Knacker, Knap, Livery, Mugshot, Photo, Photogene, Scotch, Snack, Snatch, Spell, Still, Tetchy, Vigour

Snare Bait, Benet, Engine, Enmesh, Entrap, Gin, Grin, Hook, Illaqueate, Inveigle, Net, Noose, Rat-trap, Springe, Springle, Toil, → **TRAP**, Trapen, Trepan, Web, Weel, Wire

Snarl(ing) Chide, Complicate, Cynic, Enmesh, Girn, Gnar(l), Gnarr, Growl, Grumble, Knar, Knot, Snap, Tangle, Yirr

Snatch Claucht, Claught, Excerpt, Fragment, Glom, Grab, Kidnap, Nip, Pluck, Race, Ramp, Rap, Rase, Raunch, Refrain, Snippet, Song, Spell, Steal, Strain, Take, Tweak, Wrap, Wrest

▷ **Snatch** *may indicate* the first letter of a word

Snazzy Cat

Snead Snath

Sneak(y) Area, Carry-tale, Clipe, Clype, Furtive, Inform, Lurk, Mumblenews, Nim, Peak, Scunge, Skulk, Slink, Slip, Slyboots, Snitch, Snoop, Split, Steal, Stoolie,

Surreptitious, Tell(-tale), Underhand
Sneer(ing) Barb, Critic, Cynical, Fleer, Gibe, Jeer, Scoff, Smirk, Snide, Twitch
Sneeze (at), Sneezing Atishoo, Neese, Neeze, Ptarmic, Scorn, Sternutation
Snick Click, Cut, Edge, Glance
Snicker Snigger, Titter, Whinny
Snide Bitchy, Shand
Sniff Inhale, Nose, Nursle, Nuzzle, Scent, Smell, Snivel, Snort, Snuffle, Vent, Whiff
Snigger Giggle, Laugh, Snicker, Snirtle, Titter, Whicker
Snip(pet) Bargain, Cert, Clip, Cut, Doddle, Piece, Sartor, Snatch, Snick, Tailor
Snipe(r) Bird, Bushwhacker, Criticise, Franc-tireur, Gutter, Heather-bleat(er),
  Heather-bluiter, Heather-blutter, Pick off, Scape, Shoot, Walk, Wisp
Snitch Conk, Konk, Nose
Snivel Blubber, Snotter, Snuffle, Weep, Whine
Snob(bery), Snobbish Cobbler, Crachach, Crispin, High-hat, Inverted, Scab, Side,
  Snooty, Soutar, Souter, Sowter, Toffee-nose, Vain, Vamp
Snooker Pool, Stimie, Stimy, Stym(i)e
Snoop(er) Meddle, Nose, Pry, Tec
Snooty Bashaw, Snob(bish)
Snooze Calk, Caulk, Dove, Doze, Nap, Nod, Siesta, Sleep
Snore, Snoring Rhonchus, Rout, Snort, Snuffle, Stertorous, Zz
Snort(er) Dram, Drink, Grunt, Nare, Nasal, Roncador, Snore, Toot
Snot(ty) Mucoid
Snout Bill, Boko, Cigar, Gasper, Gruntie, Informer, Muzzle, Nose, Nozzle, Proboscis,
  Schnozzle, Tinker, Tobacco, Wall
Snow(y), Snowstorm Brig, Buran, Cocaine, Coke, Corn, Cornice, Crud, Firn, Flake,
  Flurry, Graupel, Half-pipe, Heroin, Marine, Mogul, Neve, Nival, Niveous, Nivose,
  Oncome, Onding, Powder, Red, Sastruga, Sleet, Spotless, Stall, Virga, White-out,
  Wintry, Wreath, Yellow, Zastruga
Snowball Accelerate, Cramp-bark, Cumulative, Guelder-rose, Increase, Magnify,
  Opulus, Pelt, Rose
Snowdrop Avalanche, Eirlys
Snowflake Leucojum, St Agnes' flower
Snow-goose Wav(e)y
Snowman Abominable, Eskimo, Junkie, Sherpa, Yeti
Snowmobile Sno-cat
Snowshoe Bear paw, Racket, Racquet
Snub Cut, Diss, Go-by, Lop, Pug, Put-down, Quelch, Rebuff, Reproof, Retroussé,
  Set-down, Short, Slap, Slight, Sloan, Sneap, Snool, Wither
Snuff(le) Asarabacca, Dout, Errhine, Extinguish, Maccabaw, Maccaboy, Maccoboy,
  Ptarmic, Pulvil, Rappee, Smother, Snaste, Sneesh(an), Sniff, Snift, Snush, Tobacco,
  Vent
Snuffbox Anatomical, Mill, Mull
Snug(gle) Burrow, Cose, → cosy, Couthie, Couthy, Croodle, Cubby, Cuddle,
  Embrace, Lion, Neat, Nestle, Nuzzle, Rug, Snod, Tight, Trim
So Argal, Ergo, Forthy, Hence, Sae, Sic(h), Sol, Therefore, This, Thus, True, Very, Yes
Soak(ed) Bate, Bath(e), Beath, Bewet, Bloat, Blot, Buck, Cree, Deluge, Drench, Drink,
  Drook, Drouk, Drown, Drunk, Duck, Dunk, Embay, Embrue, Fleece, Grog, Imbrue,
  Impregnate, Infuse, Lush, Macerate, Marinate, Mop, Oncome, Permeate, Plastered,
  Rait, Rate, Ret(t), Rinse, Rob, Saturate, Seep, Sipe, Sog, Sop, Souce, Souse,
  Sows(s)e, Steep, Sype, Thwaite, Toper, Wet
Soap(y), Soap opera Cake, Carbolic, Castile, Eluate, Flake, Flannel, Flattery, Green,

Hard, Joe, Lather, Marine, Metallic, Moody, Mountain, Pears®, Pinguid, Saddle, Safrole, Saponaceous, Saponin, Sawder, Shaving, Slime, Soft, Spanish, Suds, Sudser, Sugar, Syndet, Tablet, Tall-oil, Toheroa, Toilet, Washball, Windsor, Yellow

Soapstone French chalk, Spanish chalk, Steatite, Talc

Soar(ing) Ascend, Essorant, Fly, Glide, Hilum, Plane, Rise, Tower, Zoom

Sob (stuff) Blub(ber), Boohoo, Goo, Gulp, Lament, Singult, Singultus, Snotter, Wail, Weep, Yoop

Sober(sides) Abstemious, Calm, Demure, Pensive, Sedate, Staid, Steady, TT

Sobriquet Byname, Cognomen, Nickname, To-name

So-called Alleged, Nominal, Soi-disant

Sociable, Sociability Affable, Cameraderie, Chummy, Clubby, Cosy, Extravert, Extrovert, Folksy, Friendly, Genial, Gregarious, Phatic

Social(ise) Convivial, Hobnob, Hui, Mingle, Mix, Musicale, Phatic, Tea-dance, Yancha

Socialism, Socialist Ba'(a)th, Champagne, Chartist, Dergue, Engels, Fabian, Fourierism, Guild, ILP, International, Karmathian, Lansbury, Left(y), Marxism, Menshevik, Menshevist, National, Nihilism, Owen(ist), Owenite, Parlour pink, Pinko, Red, Revisionist, St Simonist, Sandinista, Spartacist, Utopian, Webb

Socialite Deb, Sloane

Society Affluent, Association, Band of Hope, Beau monde, Benefit, Body, Broederbond, Building, Camorra, Carbonari, Class, Club, College, Company, Conger, Co-op, Cooperative, Culture, Danite, Defenders, Dorcas, Eleutheri, Elite, Elks, Fabian, Fashion, Foresters, Freemans, Freemasons, Friendly, Friends, Glee club, Grand monde, Grotian, Group, Guarantee, Guilds, Haut monde, Hetairia, High, Humane, Illuminati, Institute, Invincibles, John Birch, Ku-Klux-Klan, Kyrle, Law, Linnean, Lodge, Mafia, Malone, Masonic, Mau-Mau, Ménage, Molly Maguire, National, Oddfellows, Oral, Orangemen, Oratory, Order, Permissive, Phi Beta Kappa, Plunket, Plural, Pop, Provident, Repertory, Ribbonism, Rosicrucian, Rotary, Royal, S, School, Secret, Soc, Soroptomist, Sorority, Stakeholder, Surveillance, Tammany, Theosophical, Toc H, Ton, Tong, Triad, U, Whiteboy, World

Sociologist Weber

Sock(s) Argyle, Argyll, Biff, Bobby, Bootee, Digital, Hose(n), Lam, Leg warmer, Punch, Rock, Slipper, Slosh, Strike, Tabi, Trainer, Walk, Wind

Socket Acetabulum, Alveole, Budget, Gudgeon, Hollow, Hosel, Hot shoe, Jack, Nave, Nozzle, Ouch, Outlet, Pod, Point, Port, Power-point, Shoe, Strike, Torulus, Whip

Sock-eye Nerka, Salmon

Socrates, Socratic Ironist, Maieutics, Sage

Sod Clump, Delf, Delph, Divot, Fail, Gazo(o)n, Mool, Mould, Mouls, Scraw, Sward, Turf

Soda, Sodium Acmite, Arfvedsonite, Baking, Barilla, Bicarb, Caustic, Club, Cream, La(u)rvikite, Na, Natrium, Natron, Reh, Saleratus, Splash, Trona, Washing

Sofa Canapé, Chesterfield, Couch, Daybed, Divan, Dos-à-dos, Dosi-do, Ottoman, Settee, Squab, Tête-à-tête

So far (as) As, As yet, Quoad, Until, Yonder

Soft(en), Softener, Softening, Softly Amalgam, Anneal, B, BB, Blet, Boodle, Calm, Casefy, Cedilla, Cree, Dim, Dolcemente, Doughy, Ease, Emolliate, Emollient, Flabby, Gentle, Hooly, Humanise, Intenerate, Lash, Lax, Lenient, Lenition, Limp, Low, Macerate, Malacia, Malax(ate), Malleable, Mardarse, Mardie, Mease, Mellow, Melt, Mild, Milksop, Mitigate, Modulate, Mollify, Mollities, Morendo, Mulch, Mush(y), Mute, Neale, Nesh, Option, P, Palliate, Pastel, Piano, Plushy, Porous, Propitiate, Rait, Rate, Relent, Scumble, Sentimental, Silly, Slack, Squashy, Squidgy,

Squishy, Sumph, Talcose, Temper, → TENDER, Tone, Velvet, Weak
Softness Lenity
▶ **Software** *see* COMPUTER SOFTWARE
Sog(gy) Goop, Sodden
Soil(ed), Soily Acid, Adscript, Agrology, Agronomy, Alkali(ne), Alluvium, Azonal,
  Backfill, Bedraggle, Chemozem, Clay, Cohesive, Defile, Desecrate, Desert, Dinge,
  Dirt(y), Discolour, Earth, Edaphic, Frictional, Gault, Glebe, Grey, Grimy, Ground,
  Gumbo, Hotbed, Humus, Illuvium, Intrazonal, Lair, Land, Latosol, Lithosol, Loam,
  Loess, Lome, Loss, Mire, Mool, Mo(u)ld, Mud, Mulch, Mull, Night, Peat, Ped,
  Pedalfer, Pedocal, Pedology, Phreatic, Planosol, Podsol, Podzol, Prairie, Pure,
  Regar, Regolith, Regosol, Regur, Rendzina, Rhizosphere, Root-ball, Sal, Sedentary,
  Smudge, Smut, Solonchak, Solonetz, Solum, Soot, Stain, Stonebrash, Sub, Sully,
  Tarnish, Tash, Terrain, Terricolous, Tilth, Top, Tschernosem, Udal, Umber, Virgin,
  Yarfa, Yarpha, Zonal
Soirée Drum, Levee, Musicale
Sojourn Abide, Respite, Stay, Tarry
Sol G, Soh, Sun
Solace Cheer, Comfort
Solar(ium) Heliacal, Tannery
Sold Had
Solder Braze, Join, Spelter, Tin, Weld
Soldier(s) Achilles, Alpini, Amazon, Ant, Anzac, Army, Arna(o)ut, Askari, Atkins,
  ATS, Banner, Bashi-Bazouk, Battalion, Bersaglier(e), Blue beret, Bluecoat,
  Bluff, Bod, Bombardier, Borderer, Botha, Brave, Brigade, Buff-coat, Buff-jerkin,
  Butter-nut, Cadet, Caimac(am), Campaigner, Cannoneer, Cannon-fodder,
  Car(a)bineer, Car(a)binier, Cataphract, Centinel(l), Centonel(l), Centurion, Chasseur,
  Chindit, Chocko, Choco, Chocolate, Cohort, Colonel, Colours, Commando,
  Confederate, Contingent, Cornet, Corp(s), Cossack, Crusader, Cuirassier, Ded,
  Desert rat, Detail, Digger, Dog-face, Doughboy, Draftee, Dragoon, Dugout,
  Emmet, Engineer, Enomoty, Evzone, Fag(g)ot, Federal, Fencibles, Fighter,
  Flanker, Foederatus, Foot, Forlorn-hope, Fugleman, Fusilier, Fuzzy-wuzzy,
  Fyrd, Gallo(w)glass, Galoot, General, GI, GI Joe, Gippo, Goorkha, Grenadier,
  Greycoat, Grim dig, Grunt, Guardee, Guardsman, Guerilla, Gurkha, Gyppo,
  Hackbuteer, Hobbler, Hoplite, Hussar, Immortal, Impi, Inf(antry), Iron Duke,
  Ironside, Irregular, Jackman, Janissary, Janizary, Jawan, Joe, Johnny Reb(el),
  Kaimakam, Kern(e), Kitchener, Knight, Lancer, Landsknecht, Lansquenet, Lashkar,
  Leatherneck, Legionary, Legionnaire, Levy, Line, Linesman, Lobster, Maniple,
  Martinet, Men-at-arms, Miles (gloriosus), Militiaman, Miner, Minuteman,
  Missileer, Musketeer, Nahal, Naik, Nasute, Nizam, Non-com, Old Bill, Old
  Contemptibles, Old moustache, OR, Orderly, Palatine, Palikar, Pandoor, Pandour,
  Pandy, Paratroop, Partisan, Peltast, Peon, Perdu(e), Persevere, Phalanx, Pikeman,
  Piou-piou, Pistoleer, Platoon, Poilu, Point man, Pongo, Post, POW, Private, Rajput,
  Ranger, Rank(er), Rank and file, Rapparree, Rat-tail, Reb, Redcoat, Reformado,
  Regiment, Regular, Reiter, Reservist, Retread, Rifleman, Rutter, Sabre, Saddler,
  Sammy, Samurai, SAS, Sebundy, Sentinel, Sepoy, Serviceman, Signaller, Silladar,
  Snarler, So(d)ger, Soldado, Sowar(ee), Sowarry, Spearman, Squaddie, Squaddy,
  Stalhelm(et), Stormtrooper, Strelitz, Subaltern, Swad(dy), Sweat, Targeteer,
  Tarheel, Templar, Terrier, Territorial, Timariot, Tin, Tommy, Toy, Train-band,
  Trencher, Trooper, Troops, Turco(pole), Uhlan, Unknown, Velites, Vet(eran),
  Voltigeur, Volunteer, Wagon, Warhorse, Warmonger, Warrior, Whitecoat, Wild
  Geese, Woodbind, Woodbine, Yardbird, Yeoman, Zouave

▷ **Soldiers** *may indicate* bread for boiled eggs
Sole, Solitaire Alone, Anchoret, Anchorite, Clump, Convex, Dover, Dropped,
Fish, Incommunicado, Lemon, Lonesome, Megrim, Merl, Meunière, Monastical,
Monkish, Only, Pad, Palm, Patience, Pelma, Planta(r), Plantigrade, Platform,
Recluse, Scaldfish, Single(ton), Skate, Slip, Smear-dab, Tap, Thenar, Tread, Unique,
Vibram®, Vola
Solemn Agelast, Austere, Devout, Earnest, Grave, Gravitas, Impressive, Majestic,
Owlish, Po-faced, Sacred, Sedate, Serious, Sober, Sobersides, Sombre
Solent Lee
Solicit Accost, Approach, Ask, Attract, Bash, → **BEG**, Canvass, Commission, Cottage,
Drum up, Importun(at)e, Plead, Ply, Proposition, Speer, Speir, Tout, Woo
Solicitor(s) Advocate, Attorney, Avoué, Beggar, Canvasser, Hallanshaker,
Law-agent, Lawyer, Notary, Official, Side-bar, SL, Tout, Trull, Writer to the Signet,
WS
Solid(arity), Solidify Cake, Chunky, Clot, Clunky, Compact, Comradeship,
Concrete, Cone, Congeal, Consolidate, Cube, Cylinder, Dense, Enneahedron,
Esprit de corps, Ethan, Firm, Foursquare, Freeze, Frustrum, Fuchsin(e), Gel, Hard,
Holosteric, Impervious, Kotahitanga, Masakhane, Merbromin, Octahedron, Pakka,
Petrarchan, Platonic, Polyhedron, Prism, Pucka, Pukka, Purin(e), Robust, Set,
Skatole, Stilbene, Sublimate, Substantial, Tetrahedron, Thick, Unanimous
Solipsism Egotism, Panegoism
Solitary Antisocial, Friendless
▶ **Solitary** *see* **SOLE**
Solitude Privacy, Seclusion
Solo Aria, Cadenza, Cavatine, Concertante, Lone, Monodrama, Monody, Ombre,
One-man, Scena, Variation
Solon Sage
So long Cheerio, Ciao, Goodbye, Tata
Solstice Summer, Tropic, Winter
Soluble Alkaline, Consolute, Surfactant
Solution Acetone, Alkali, Ammonia, Amrit, → **ANSWER**, Austenite, Benedict's,
Collodion, Colloidal, Dakin's, Dobell's, Éclaircissement, Electrolyte, Elixir,
Emulsion, Eusol, Fehling's, Final, Key, Leachate, Limewater, Lixivium, Lye,
Normal, Oleoresin, Rationale, Reducer, Ringer's, Rinse, Rubber, Saline, Solid,
Solvent, Soup, Standard, Suspensoid, Tincture, Titrate, Viscose
▷ **Solution** *may indicate* an anagram
Solve(d), Solver Absolve, Assoil, Calculate, Casuist, Clear, Crack, Decode, Holmes,
Loast, Loose, Read(er), Suss out, Troubleshoot, Unclew, Undo, Unriddle, Work
Solvent Acetaldehyde, Acetone, Afloat, Alcahest, Aldol, Alkahest, Anisole,
Aqua-regia, Banana oil, Chloroform, Cleanser, Cyclohexane, Cyclopentane,
Cymene, Decalin, Diluent, Dioxan(e), Eleunt, Eluant, Ether, Funded, Furan,
Hexane, Ligroin, Megilp, Menstruum, Methanol, Methylal, Naphtha,
Paraldehyde, Picoline, Protomic, Pyridine, Sound, Stripper, Terebene, Terpineol,
Tetrachloromethane, Thinner, Thiophen, Toluene, Toluol, Trike, Trilene,
Turpentine
Sombre Dark, Drab, Drear, Dull, Gloomy, Grave, Morne, Morose, Subfusc, Subfusk,
Sullen, Triste
Some Any, Arrow, Ary, Certain, Divers, Few, One, Part, Portion, Quota, These, They,
Wheen
▷ **Some** *may indicate* a hidden word
Somebody Dignitary, Name, Notable, One, Person, Quidam, Someone, → **VIP**

Somehow Somegate
▷ **Somehow** *may indicate* an anagram
Somersault Back-flip, Barani, Deltcher, Flip(-flap), Flip-flop, Handspring, Pitchpole, Pitchpoll
Something Aliquid, Chattel, Matter, Object, Summat, What, Whatnot
Sometime(s) Erstwhile, Ex, Former, Occasional, Off and on, Quondam
Somewhat Bit, -ish, Mite, Partly, Quasi, Quite, Rather, Relatively
Somewhere Somegate
Son Boy, Descendant, Disciple, Epigon(e), Fils, Fitz, Lad, Lewis, M(a)c, Native, Offspring, Prodigal, Progeny, Scion
Song Air, Amoret, Anthem, Antistrophe, Aria, Art, Aubade, Ayre, Ballad, Ballant, Ballata, Barcarol(l)e, Belter, Berceuse, Bhajan, Blues, Brindisi, Burden, Burthen, Cabaletta, Calypso, Cancionero, Canticle, Cantilena, Cantion, Canzona, Canzone, Canzonet(ta), Carmagnole, Carol, Catch, Cavatina, Chanson, Cha(u)nt, Come-all-ye, Conductus, Corn-kister, Corroboree, Cycle, Descant, Dirge, Dithyramb, Ditty, Epithalamion, Epithalamium, Fado, Fit, Flamenco, Folk, Forebitter, Gita, Glee, Gorgia, Gradual, Hillbilly, Hum, Hymeneal, Hymn, Internationale, Jug(-jug), Lament, Lay, Lied(er), Lilt, Lullaby, Lyric, Madrigal, Magnificat, Marseillaise, Matin, Melic, Melisma, Melody, Mento, Negro spiritual, Noel, Number, Nunc dimittis, Oat, Paean, Pane, Part, Patter, Pennillion, Plain, Plaint, Plantation, Pop, Prick, Prothalamion, Prothalamium, Psalm, Qawwali, Rap, Recitativo, Relish, Rhapsody, Rispetto, Roulade, Roundelay, Rune, Scat, Scolion, Sea-shanty, Secular, Serenade, Shanty, Shosholoza, Siren, Sirvente, Skolion, Sososholoza, Spiritual, Stave, Stomper, Strain, Strophe, Swan, Taps, Tenebrae, Theme, Torch, Trill, Tune, Tyrolienne, Villanella, Volkslied, Waiata, War, Warble, Wassail, Waulking, Yodel, Yodle
Songbook Cancionero, Hymnal, Kommersbuch, Libretto, Psalter
Songsmith, Songwriter Carmichael, Dowland, Espla, Foster, Kern, Minot, Waitz, Zappa
Sonnet Amoret, Elizabethan, English, Italian, Miltonic, Petrarch(i)an, Shakespearean, Shakespearian, Spenserian
Sonometer Monochord
Soon(er) Anon, Directly, Erelong, Lief, OK, Oklahoma, Presently, Shortly, Tight, Timely, Tit(ely), Tite, Tyte
Soot(y) Colly, Coom, Crock, Fuliginous, Gas black, Grime, Lampblack, Smut, Speck
Soothe, Soothing Accoy, Allay, Anetic, Anodyne, Appease, Assuage, Bucku, Calm, Compose, Demulcent, Dulcet, Emollient, Irenic, Lenitive, Lull, Mellifluous, Mollify, Pacific, Paregoric, Poultice, Quell, Rock
Soothsayer Astrologer, Augur, Calchas, Chaldee, Divine, Forecaster, Haruspex, Melampus, Oracle, Picus, Prophet, Pythoness, → **SEER**, Shipton, Tiresias
Sop Appease, Berry, Douceur, Rait, Ret, Sponge
Sophist(ic) Casuist, Elenchic, Quibbler
Sophisticate(d) Blasé, Boulevardier, City slicker, Civilised, Cosmopolitan, Couth, Doctor, High-end, Patrician, Polished, Sative, Slicker, Svelte, Urbane, Worldly
▷ **Sophoclean** *may indicate* Greek (alphabet, etc)
Sophomore Semie
Soporific Barbiturate, Bromide, Drowsy, Halothane, Hypnotic, Lullaby, Narcotic, Opiate, Sedative, Tedious
Soppiness, Soppy Maudlin, Schwärmerei, Sloppy, Slushy
Soprano Caballé, Castrato, Crespin, Descant, Lind, Patti, Treble
Sorb Wend

Sorbet Water ice

Sorcerer, Sorceress, Sorcery Angakok, Ashipu, Circe, Conjury, Diablerie, Hoodoo, Kadaitcha, Kurdaitcha, Lamia, Mage, Magian, Magic(ian), Magus, Medea, Merlin, Morgan le Fay, Mother Shipton, Necromancer, Obi, Pishogue, Shaman, Sortilege, Venefic(ious), Voodoo, Warlock, Witch, Witch knot, Wizard

Sordid Base, Low-life, Miserable, Scungy, Seamy, Sleazy, Squalid, Vile

Sore(ly), Sores Abrasion, Anthrax, Bitter, Blain, Boil, Canker, Chancre, Chap, Chilblain, Cold, Dearnly, Felon, Gall, Impost(h)ume, Ireful, Kibe, Nasty, Pressure, Quitter, Quittor, Raw, Running, Rupia(s), Saddle, Sair, Shiver, Sitfast, Surbate, Ulcer(s), Whitlow, Wound

Sore throat Garget, Prunella, Quinsy, Tonsillitis

Sorghum Kaoliang, Milo

Sorrel Common, French, Hetty, Mountain, Oca, Roman, Sheep, Soar(e), Sore, Sourock

Sorrow(ful) Affliction, Distress, Dole, Dolente, Dolour, Emotion, Fee-grief, → GRIEF, Lament, Misery, Nepenthe, Ochone, Penance, Pietà, Remorse, Rue, Triste, Wae, Waugh, Wirra, Woe, Yoop

Sorry Ashamed, Contrite, Miserable, Oops, Penitent, Pitiful, Poor, Regretful, Relent, Wretched

▷ **Sorry** *may indicate* an anagram

Sort(ing) Arrange, Brand, Breed, Category, Character, Classify, Collate, Drive, Grade, → KIND, Nature, Pranck(e), Prank, Sift, Species, Stamp, Tidy, Triage, Type, Variety

Sortie Attack, Foray, Mission, Outfall, Raid, Sally

▶ **Sorts** *see* OUT OF SORTS

So-so Average, Indifferent, Mediocre, Middling

So to speak Quasi

▷ **So to speak** *may indicate* 'sound of'

Sotto voce Murmur, Whisper

▶ **Soubriquet** *see* SOBRIQUET

Sough Rustle, Sigh

Soul(ful) Alma, Ame, Anima, Animist, Atman, Ba, Bardo, Brevity, Deep, Entelechy, Eschatology, Expressive, Heart, Inscape, Ka, Larvae, Lost, Manes, Object, Person, Pneuma, Psyche, Saul, Shade, Spirit, Universal

Sound(ed), Soundness, Sound system Accurate, Ach-laut, Acoustic, Affricate, Albemarle, Allophone, Alveolar, Amphoric, Audio, Bay, Bleep, Blip, Blow, Boing, Bong, Breathed, Cacophony, Chime, Chirr(e), Chord, Chug, Clam, Clang, Clink, Clop, Clunk, Consistent, Continuant, Dah, Dental, Dit, Dive, Dolby®, Dream, Echo, Euphony, Fast, Fathom, Fere, Fettle, Fit, Foley, Glide, Good, Hale, Harmonics, Healthy, Hearty, Hi-fi, Ich-laut, Inlet, Islay, Jura, Kalmar, Knell, Kyle, Labiodental, Lo-fi, Long Island, Lucid, Mach, Madrilene, McMurdo, Mersey, Milford, Mouillé, Musak, Music, Narrow, → NOISE, Onomatopaeia, Oompah, Optical, Orate, Orthodox, Palatal, Palato-alveolar, Pamlico, Paragog(u)e, Peal, Pectoriloquy, Phone(me), Phonetic, Phonic, Phonology, Pitter(-patter), Plap, Plink, Plonk, Plop, Plosion, Plumb, Plummet, Plunk, Plymouth, Probe, Puget, Put-put, Quadraphonic(s), Quadrophonic(s), Rale, Rational, Real, Reliable, Ring, Roach, Robust, Rong, Rumble, Rustle, Sabin, Safe, Sandhi, Sane, S(c)hwa, Scoresby, Sensurround®, Skirl, Solid, Sonance, Sone, Souffle, Sough, Sowne, Splat, Stereo, Stereophony, Strait, Surround, Swish, Tamber, Tannoy®, Thorough, Timbre, Ting, Tone, Toneme, Trig, Triphthong, Trumpet, Twang, Ultrasonic(s), Unharmed, Uvular, Valid, Viable, Voice, Vowel, Wah-wah, Watertight, Well, Whine, Whistle, Whole(some), Whump, Wolf

Sounder Echo, Lead
Sounding board Abat-voix
Soundproof Deaden
Sound-track Dubbing, Movietone®, Stripe
Soup Alphabet, Avgolemono, Bird's nest, Bisk, Bisque, Borsch, Bouillabaisse,
  Bouillon, Brewis, Broth, Burgoo, Chowder, Cock-a-leekie, Cockieleekie,
  Cockyleeky, Consommé, Duck, Garbure, Gazpacho, Gomb(r)o, Gruel, Gumbo,
  Harira, Hoosh, Julienne, Kail, Kale, Madrilene, Marmite, Mess, Minestrone, Mock
  turtle, Mulligatawny, Oxtail, Palestine, Pea(se), Pot-au-feu, Pot(t)age, Primordial,
  Puree, Ramen, Rice, Rubaboo, Sancoche, Scotch broth, Shchi, Shtchi, Skilligalee,
  Skilligolee, Skilly, Skink, Stock, Tattie-claw, Toheroa, Turtle, Vichyssoise
▷ **Soup** *may indicate* an anagram
Soupçon Thought, Touch
Sour(puss) Acerb, Acescent, Acid, Acidulate, Alegar, Bitter, Citric, Crab, Eager,
  Esile, Ferment, Moody, Stingy, Subacid, → **TART**, Turn, Unamiable, Verjuice,
  Vinegarish
Source Authority, Basis, Bottom, Centre, Closed, Database, Derivation, Egg, Fons,
  Font, Fount, Fountain-head, Germ, Head-stream, Literary, Mine, Mother, Neutron,
  Origin, Parent, Pi, Pion, Point, Provenance, Quarry, Reference, Rise, Riverhead,
  Root, Seat, Seed, Spring, Springhead, Stock, Supply, Urn, Well, Wellhead,
  Wellspring, Widow's cruse, Ylem
Sour milk Curds, Smetana, Whey, Whig, Yogh(o)urt
Souse Beath, Duck, Immerse, Pickle, Plunge, Soak, Spree, Steep
South(ern), Southerner Austral, Confederacy, Dago, Decanal, Decani, Deep,
  Dixieland, Meridian, Meridional, S
South Africa(n) Azania, Bantu, Caper, Ciskei, Grikwa, Griqua, Hottentot, Kaf(f)ir,
  Qwaqwa, SA, Soutie, Soutpiel, Springbok, Swahili, Xhosa, ZA, Zulu
South American Araucanian, Arawak, Argentino, Aymara, Bolivian, Carib, Chibcha,
  Chilean, Galibi, Guarani, Inca, Jivaro, Kechua, Latin, Llanero, Mam, Mapuchi,
  Mayan, Mixe-Zogue, Mixtac, Mochica, Quechua, SA, Shuar, Tapuyan, Tupi
Southwark Boro'
Souvenir Keepsake, Memento, Relic, Remembrance, Scalp, Token, Trophy
Sovereign(ty), Sovereign remedy Anne, Autocrat, Bar, Condominium, Couter,
  Dominant, ER, Goblin, Haemony, Harlequin, Imperial, Imperium, James, King,
  L, Liege, Nizam, Pound, Quid, Rangatiratanga, Royalty, Ruler, Shiner, Supreme,
  Swaraj, Synarchy, Thick' un, Thin' un
Soviet Circassian, Council, Estonian, Russian, Stalin, Supreme, Volost
Sow(ing) Catchcrop, Elt, Foment, Gilt, Inseminate, Plant, Scatter, Seed, Sprue,
  Strew, Yelt
Soya Sitosterol, Tempe(h)
Spa Baden, Baden-Baden, Bath, Buxton, Evian, Godesberg, Harrogate, Hydro,
  Kurhaus, Kursaal, Leamington, Vichy
Space(d), Spacing, Spacious, Spaceman Abyss, Acre, Area, Areola, Bay,
  Bracket, Breathing, Cellule, Cislunar, Clearing, C(o)elom, Coelome, Compluvium,
  Concourse, Contline, Crookes, Cubbyhole, Deep, Diastema, Distal, Distance,
  Elbow-room, Esplanade, Ether, Exergue, Expanse, Extent, Flies, Footprint,
  Forecourt, Freeband, Gagarin, Gap, Glade, Glenn, Goaf, Gob, Gutter, Hair,
  Hash(mark), Headroom, Homaloid, Indention, Inner, Intergalactic, Interim,
  Interlinear, Interplanetary, Interstellar, Interstice, Invader, Kerning, Killogie,
  Kneehole, Lacuna, Lair, Leading, Lebensraum, Legroom, Life, Logie, Lumen,
  Lunar, Lung, Machicolation, Maidan, Metope, Mihrab, Minkowski, Muset,

Musit, Orbit, Outer, Palatial, Parvis(e), Peridrome, Personal, Plenum, Polemics, Pomoerium, Priest hole, Proportional, Quad, Retrochoir, Riemannian, → **ROOM**, Ruelle, Sample, Sheets, Shelf room, Slot, Spandrel, Spandril, Step, Storage, Third, Topological, Tympanum, Ullage, Uncluttered, Vacuole, Vacuum, Vast, Vector, Void

Spacecraft, Space agency, Space object, Spaceship, Space station Apollo, Capsule, Columbia, Deep Space, Explorer, Galileo, Genesis, Giotto, Lander, LEM, Luna, Lunik, Mariner, MIR, Module, NASA, Orbiter, Pioneer, Probe, Quasar, Ranger, Salyut, Shuttle, Skylab, Soyuz, Sputnik, Starship, Tardis, Viking, Vostok, Voyager, Zond

Space walk EVA

Spade Breastplough, Caschrom, Cas crom, Castrato, Detective, Flaughter, Graft, Loy, Negro, Paddle, Pattle, Peat, Pettle, Pick, S, Shovel, Slane, Spit, Suit, Turf, Tus(h)kar, Tus(h)ker, Twiscar

Spain E, Hesperia, Iberia

Spalpeen Sinner

Span Age, Arch, Attention, Bestride, Bridge, Chip, Ctesiphon, Extent, Life, Memory, Range, Timescale

Spangle(d) Avanturine, Aventurine, Glitter, Instar, O, Paillette, Sequin

Spaniard, Spanish Alguacil, Alguazil, Andalusian, Barrio, Basque, Cab, Caballero, Carlist, Castilian, Catalan, Chicano, Dago, Don, Fly, Grandee, Hidalgo, Hispanic, José, Main, Mestizo, Mozarab, Pablo, Papiamento, Señor, Spic(k), Spik

Spaniel Blenheim, Cavalier, Clumber, Cocker, Crawler, Creep, Dog, Fawner, Field, Irish water, King Charles, Maltese, Papillon, Placebo, Skip-kennel, Springer, Sussex, Tibetan, Toad-eater, Toady, Toy, Water, Welsh springer

Spank(ing) Cob, Paddywhack, Rapid, Scud, Slap, Slipper, Sprack

Spanner Arc, Box, Bridge, Clapper, Key, Ring, Shifter, Shifting, Socket, Torque, Wrench

Spar Barite, Barytes, Blue John, Boom, Bowsprit, Box, Cauk, Cawk, Fight, Gaff, Iceland, Jib-boom, Mainyard, Manganese, Martingale, Mast, Nail-head, Outrigger, Rafter, Rail, Ricker, Schiller, Shearleg, Sheerleg, Snotter, Spathic, Sprit, Steeve, Stile, Tabular, Triatic, Whiskerboom, Whiskerpole, Yard

Spare, Sparing Angular, Cast-off, Dup(licate), Economical, Free, Frugal, Gash, Gaunt, Hain, Lean, Lenten, Other, Pardon, Reserve, Rib, Save, Scant, Skimp, Slender, Stint, Subsecive, Thin

Spark Animate, Arc, Beau, Blade, Bluette, Dandy, Flash, Flaught, Funk, Ignescent, Kindle, Life, Muriel, Quenched, Scintilla, Smoulder, Spunk, Trigger, Vital, Zest

Sparkle(r), Sparkling Aerated, Aventurine, Bling, Coruscate, Crémant, Diamanté, Effervesce, Élan, Emicate, Fire, Fizz, Flicker, Frizzante, Glamour, Glint, Glisten, Glitter, Life, Pétillant, Scintillate, Seltzer, Seltzogene, Spangle, Spritzig, Spumante, Twinkle, Verve, Witty, Zap

Sparrow Bird, Cape, Chipping, Hedge, Isaac, Java, Junco, Mah-jong(g), Mossie, Passerine, Piaf, Prunella, Song, Spadger, Speug, Sprug(gy), Titling, Tree

Sparrow-grass Asparagus, Sprue

Sparse Meagre, Rare, Scant, Thin

Spartan(s) Austere, Basic, Enomoty, Hardy, Helot, Heraclid, Lacedaemonian, Laconian, Lysander, Menelaus, Severe, Valiant

Spasm(s), Spasmodic Blepharism, Chorea, Clonus, Convulsive, Cramp, Crick, Fit(ful), Hiccup, Hippus, Hyperkinesis, Intermittent, Irregular, → **JERK**, Kink, Laryngismus, Nystagmus, Paroxysm, Periodical, Start, Strangury, Tetany, Throe, Tonic, Tonus, Trismus, Twinge, Twitch, Vaginismus, Writer's cramp

▷ **Spasmodic** *may indicate* an anagram

Spastic Athetoid, Clonic, Jerky
Spat(s) Bicker, Brattle, Gaiters, Legging, Quarrel, Shower, Tiff
Spate Flood, Sluice, Torrent
Spatter Disject, Ja(u)p, Scatter, Splash, Splosh, Spot, Sprinkle
▷ **Spattered** *may indicate* an anagram
Spawn(ing), Spawning place Anadromous, Blot, Fry, Progeny, Propagate, Redd, Roud, Seed, Spat, Spet, Spit
Speak(er), Speaking Address, Articulate, Broach, Chat, Cicero, Collocuter, Communicate, Converse, Coo, Declaim, Dilate, Discourse, Diseur, Dwell, Effable, Elocution, Eloquent, Expatiate, Express, Extemporise, Filibuster, Intercom, Intone, Inveigh, Jabber, Jaw, Lip, Loq, Mang, Mention, Mike, Mina, Mouth, Mouthpiece, Nark, Native, Open, Orate, Orator, Palaver, Parlance, Parley, Perorate, Pontificate, Prate, Preach, Prelector, Rhetor, → **SAY**, Sayne, Spout, Spruik, Squawk box, Stump, Talk, Tannoy®, Tongue, Trap, Tub-thumper, Tweeter, Utter, Voice, Waffle, Witter, Word
Speakeasy Fluent, Shebeen
Spear Ash, Asparagus, Assagai, Assegai, Barry, Dart, Fishgig, Fizgig, Gad, Gavelock, Gig, Glaive, Gleave, Gum digger's, Gungnir, Hastate, Impale, Javelin, Lance(gay), Launcegaye, Leister, Morris-pike, Partisan, Pierce, Pike, Pilum, Prong, Skewer, Spike, Trident, Trisul(a), Waster
Spear-rest Feutre, Fewter
Special Ad hoc, Constable, Designer, Distinctive, Extra, Important, Notable, Notanda, Particular, Peculiar, S, Specific
Specialise, Specialist(s) Authority, Concentrate, Connoisseur, Consultant, ENT, Expert, Illuminati, Maestro, Major, Quant, Recondite, Technician
Species Class, Genre, Genus, Indicator, Infirma, Kind, Pioneer, Strain, Taxa
Specific(ally), Specified, Specify, Specification Adduce, As, Ascribe, Assign, Concretize, Cure, Define, Detail, Explicit, Full-blown, Itemise, Medicine, Namely, Precise, Quantify, Remedy, Sp, Special, State, Stipulate, Stylesheet, The, Trivial
Specimen(s) Example, Exemplar, Imago, Model, Museum piece, Sample, Slide, Swab, Topotype, Type
Specious False, Glib, Hollow, Pageant, Plausible, Spurious
Speck(led) Atom, Bit, Dot, Fleck, Floater, Freckle, Gay, Muscae volitantes, Particle, Peep(e), Pip, Spot, Spreckle, Stud
Spectacle(s), Spectacled, Spectacular Arresting, Barnacles, Bifocals, Blazers, Blinks, Bossers, Cheaters, Colourful, Epic, Escolar, Giglamps, → **GLASSES**, Goggles, Horn-rims, Lorgnette, Lorgnon, Nose-nippers, Oo, Optical, Outspeckle, Pageant, Pince-nez, Pomp, Preserves, Raree-show, Scene, Show, Sight, Son et lumière, Sunglasses, Tamasha, Tattoo, Trifocal, Varifocals
Spectator(s) Audience, Bystander, Dedans, Etagère, Eyer, Gallery, Gate, Groundling, Kibitzer, Observer, Onlooker, Standerby, Witness
Spectograph, Spectometer Aston, Calutron
Spectral, Spectre Apparition, Boggle, Bogy, Brocken, Eidolon, Empusa, Ghost, Idola, Iridal, Larva, Malmag, Phantasm, Phantom, Phasma, Spirit, Spook, Tarsier, Walking-straw, Wraith
Spectrum Absorption, Band, Continuous, Emission, Iris, Optical, Radio, Rainbow, Sunbow, Sundog, Visible, X-ray
Speculate, Speculative, Speculator, Speculation Agiotage, Arbitrage, Bear, Better, Bull, Conjecture, Flier, Flyer, Gamble, Guess, Ideology, If, Imagine, Meditate, Notional, Operate, Pinhooker, Shark, Stag, Theoretical, Theorise, Theory, Thought, Trade, Wonder

Speech, Speech element Accents, Address, Argot, Articulation, Bunkum, Burr, Curtain, Delivery, Dialect, Diatribe, Diction, Direct, Discourse, Dithyramb, Drawl, Éloge, English, Epilogue, Eulogy, Filibuster, Free, Gab, Glossolalia, Grandiloquence, Harangue, Helium, Idiolect, Idiom, Inaugural, Indirect, Jargon, Keynote, King's, Lallation, → **LANGUAGE**, Lingua franca, Litany, Maiden, Monologue, Morph(eme), Motherese, Musar, Oblique, Occlusive, Oral, Oration, Parabasis, Parle, Peroration, Phasis, Philippic, Phonetics, Prolocution, Prolog(ue), Queen's, Reported, Rhetoric, Sandhi, Scanning, Screed, Sermon, Set, Side, Slang, Soliloquy, Stemwinder, Stump, Tagmeme, Talk, Taxeme, Tirade, Tongue, Uptalk, Vach, Visible, Voice, Wawa, Whaikorero, Whistle-stop, Xenoglossia

Speech defect, Speech disease Alogia, Dysarthria, Dysphasia, Dysphoria, Echolalia, Idioglossia, Lallation, Lisp, Palilalia, Paralalia, Paraphasia, Pararthria, Psellism, Rhinolalia, Stammer, Stutter

Speechless Alogia, Dumb, Dumbstruck, Inarticulate, Mute, Silent, Tongue-tied

Speed(ily), Speedy Accelerate, Alacrity, Amain, Amphetamine, Apace, Average, Bat, Belive, Belt, Breakneck, Burn, Cast, Celerity, Clip, Dart, Despatch, DIN, Dispatch, Expedite, Fang, Fast, Film, Fleet, Further, Gait, Gallop, Goer, Group, Gun, Haste, Hie, Hotfoot, Hypersonic, Induce, Instantaneous, Knot, Landing, Lick, Mach, Merchant, MPH, → **PACE**, Phase, Pike, Post-haste, Pronto, Race, Rapidity, Rate, RPS, Rush, Scorch, Scud, Scurr, Skirr, Soon, Spank, Split, Stringendo, Supersonic, Swift, Tach, Tear, Tempo, Ton up, V, Velocity, Ventre à terre, Vroom, Wave, Whid, Wing

Speedwell Brooklime, Fluellin, Germander, Veronica

Spelaean Troglodyte

Spelk Skelf, Splinter

Spell(ing) Abracadabra, Bewitch, Bout, Cantrip, Charm, Conjuration, Do, Elf-shoot, Enchantment, Entrance, Fit, Go, Gri(s)-gri(s), Hex, Incantation, Innings, Jettatura, Juju, Knock, Knur, → **MAGIC**, Mojo, Need-fire, Nomic, Open sesame, Orthography, Period, Philter, Philtre, Phonetic, Pinyin, Relieve, Ride, Romaji, Run, Rune, Scat, Shot, Signify, Sitting, Snap, Snatch, Sorcery, Sp, Span, Spasm, Splinter, Stint, Stretch, Tack, Tour, Trick, Turn, Weird, Whammy, Witchcraft

Spelling-book ABC, Grimoire

Spencer Topcoat, Tracy, Vest

Spend(er), Spending Anticipate, Birl, Blue, Boondoggling, Consume, Deplete, Disburse, Exhaust, Fritter, Lash out, Lay out, Live, Outlay, Pass, Pay, Shopaholic, Splash, Splash out, Splurge, Ware

Spendthrift Essex Man, High-roller, Prodigal, Profligate, Profuser, Scattergood, Wastrel

Spent Consumed, Dead, Done, Expended, Stale, Tired, Used, Weak, Weary

Sperm Seed, Semen

Spew Eject, Emit, Gush, Spit, Vomit

Sphagnum Moss, Peat

Sphere, Spherical Armillary, Attraction, Celestial, Discipline, Earth, Element, Field, Firmament, Globe, Magic, Mound, Orb(it), Planet, Primum mobile, Prolate, Province, Realm, Schwarzschild, Theatre, Wheel

Sphinx Hawk-moth, Oracle, Riddler

Spice, Spicy Amomum, Anise, Aniseed, Aryl, Caraway, Cardamom, Cardamon, Cardamum, Cassareep, Cassaripe, Cinnamon, Clove, Clow, Coriander, Cubeb, Cum(m)in, Dash, Devil, Garam masala, Ginger, Mace, Malaguetta, Marjoram, Masala, Myrrh, Nutmeg, Oregano, Paprika, Peppercorn, Picante, Pimento, Piperic, Piquant, Salsa verde, Season, Stacte, Staragen, Tamal(e), Tamara, Tansy, Tarragon,

Taste, Turmeric, Vanilla, Variety

Spick Dink, Neat, Spike, Tidy

Spicule Sclere, Tetract

Spider(s) Anancy, Ananse, Arachnid, Aranea, Araneida, Arthrapodal, Attercop, Bird, Black widow, Bobbejaan, Cardinal, Cheesemite, Chelicerate, Citigrade, Diadem, Epeira, Epeirid, Ethercap, Ettercap, Funnel-web, Harvester, Harvestman, House, Hunting, Huntsman, Jumping, Katipo, Lycosa, Mite, Money, Mygale, Orb-weaver, Pan, Phalangid, Podogona, Pycnogonid, Red, Redback, Rest, Ricinulei, Saltigrade, Scorpion, Solifugae, Solpuga, Spinner, Strap, Tarantula, Telary, Trapdoor, Violin, Water, Wolf, Zebra

Spiderwort Tradescantia

Spiel Spruik

Spignel Baldmoney, Meu

Spigot Bung, Plug, Tap

Spike(d) Barb, Brod, Calk, Calt(h)rop, Chape, Cloy, Crampon, Ear, Fid, Foil, Gad, Gadling, Goad, Grama, Herissé, Icicle, Impale, Lace, Locusta, Marlin(e), Nail, Needle, → **PIERCE**, Point, Pricket, Prong, Puseyite, Rod, Sharp, Shod, Skewer, Spadix, Spear, Spicate, Spicule, Spire, Strobiloid, Tang, Thorn, Tine

Spill(age) Divulge, Drop, Fidibus, Jackstraw, Lamplighter, Leakage, Let, Overflow, Overset, Reveal, Scail, Scale, Shed, Skail, Slart, Slop, Stillicide, Taper, Tumble

Spin(ner), Spinning Aeroplane, Arabian, Arachne, Bielmann, Birl, Camel, Centrifuge, Cribellum, Cut, Day trip, Dextrorse, DJ, Flat, Flip, Gimp, Googly, Gymp, Gyrate, Gyre, Gyroscope, Hurl, Isobaric, Isotopic, Lachesis, Mole, Nun, Peg-top, Piecener, Piecer, Pirouette, Pivot, PR, Precess, Prolong, Purl, Reel, Rev(olve), Ride, Rotate, Royal, Screw, Side, Sinistrorse, Slide, Spider, Stator, Strobic, Swirl, Swivel, Throstle, Tirl, Toss, Trill, Trundle, Twirl, Twist, Wheel, Whirl, Whirligig, Work

Spinach Florentine, Orach(e), Popeye, Sa(a)g

Spinal (chord), Spine(d), Spiny Acanthoid, Acerose, Acromion, Aculeus, Areole, Arête, Backbone, Barb, Chine, Coccyx, Column, Doorn, Dorsal, Epidural, Muricate, Myelon, Notochord, Ocotillo, Prickle, Quill, Rachial, R(h)achis, Ray, Thorn, Torso, Tragacanth

Spindle(-shanks), Spindly Arbor, Axle, Bobbin, Capstan, Fusee, Fusiform, Fusil, Mandrel, Mandril, Pin, Scrag, Staff, Triblet

▶ **Spine** *see* **SPINAL**

Spinel Balas, Picotite

Spineless Inerm, Muticous, Timid, Weak

Spinn(e)y Coppice, Shaw, Thicket

Spinning-wheel Chark(h)a

Spinster Discovert, Feme sole, Old maid, Tabby

Spiral Archimedes, Caracol, Chalaza, Cochlea, Coil, Dexiotropic, Dextrorse, Ekman, Gyrate, Helical, Helix, Hyperbolic, Inflationary, Logarithmic, Loxodromical, Parastichy, Screw, Scroll, Sinistrorse, Spin, Tailspin, Turbinate, Vibrio, Volute, Whorl, Wind

Spire(-shaped) Broach, Flèche, Peak, Shaft, Steeple, Thyrsoid

Spirit(s), Spirited Ahriman, Akvavit, Alcohol, Ammonia, Angel, Animal, Animation, Apathodaimon, Applejack, Apsaral, Aquavit, Aqua vitae, Arak, Arch(a)eus, Ardent, Ariel, Arrack, Asmoday, Astral, Bitters, Blithe, Boggart, Bogle, Brandy, Bravura, Brio, Brollachan, Buggan(e), Buggin, Cant, Cherub, Cognac, Courage, Creature, Crouse, Daemon, Dash, Deev, Deva, Distillation, Div, Djinn(i), Domdaniel, → **DRINK**, Dryad, Duende, Duppy, Dybbuk, Eblis, Eidolon, Élan, Element(al), Emit, Empusa, Entrain, Erdgeist, Erl king, Esprit, Essence, Etheric,

Ethos, Eudemon, Fachan, Faints, Familiar, Feints, Feisty, Feni, Fenny, Fetich(e),
Fetish, Fettle, Fight, Firewater, Free, Fuath, Gamy, Geist, Geneva, Genie, Genius,
→ GHOST, Ghoul, Ginger, Ginn, Gism, Glastig, Glendoveer, Go, Grappa, Gremlin,
Grit, Grog, Gumption, Gytrash, Hartshorn, Heart, Hollands, Holy, Huaca, Hugh,
Imp, Incubus, Indwelt, Jann, Jinn(i), Jinnee, Jism, Ka, Kachina, Kehua, Kelpie,
Kindred, Kirsch, Kobold, Larva, Lemur(e), → LIQUOR, Lively, Loki, Manes,
Manito(u), Manitu, Mare, Marid, Metal, Meths, Methyl(ated), Mettle, Mindererus,
Mineral, Mobbie, Mobby, Morale, Mystique, Nain rouge, Neutral, Nis, Nix, Nobody,
Numen, Ondine, Orenda, Panache, Paraclete, Party, Peart, Pecker, Pep, Peri,
Pernod®, Petrol, Phantom, Pluck(y), Pneuma, Poltergeist, Pooka, Potato, Poteen,
Presence, Pride, Proof, Psyche, Puck, Python, Racy, Rakee, Raki, Rakshas(a),
Rectified, Rosicrucian, Ruin, Rum(bullion), Rye, Salt, Samshoo, Samshu, Saul,
Schnapps, Seraph, Shade, Shadow, Shaitan, She'ol, Short, Smeddum, Soul, Spectre,
Spright, Sprite, Spunk, Steam, Strunt, Surgical, Sylph, Tafia, Tangie, Taniwha,
Team, Tequila, Tokoloshe, Ton, Turpentine, Turps, Undine, Verve, Vigour, Vim,
Vodka, Voodoo, Wairua, Water horse, Weltgeist, White, Wili, Wine, Witblits,
Wood, Wraith, Zeitgeist, Zephon, Zing, Zombie
Spiritless Craven, Dowf, Insipid, Languid, Meek, Milksop, Poor, Tame, Vapid
Spirit-level Vial
Spiritual(ism), Spiritualist Aerie, Aery, Coon-song, Ecclesiastic, Ethereous,
Eyrie, Eyry, Incorporeal, Negro, Planchette, Platonic, Psychic, Swedenborg,
Table-rapping, Table-turning
Spirt Gush, Jet, Rush
Spit(ting), Spittle Barbecue, Broach, Brochette, Chersonese, Dead ringer, Dribble,
Drool, Emptysis, Eructate, Expectorate, Fuff, Gob, Golly, Gooby, Goss, Grill, Hawk,
Hockle, Impale, Jack, Lookalike, Peninsula, Ras, Ringer, Rotisserie, Saliva, Skewer,
Slag, Spade(ful), Spawl, Spear, Sputter, Sputum, Tombolo, Yesk, Yex
Spite(ful) Backbite, Bitchy, Catty, Grimalkin, Harridan, Irrespective, Malevolent,
Malgrado, Malgré, Malice, Mau(l)gre, Mean, Nasty, Petty, Pique, Rancour, Spleen,
Venom, Viperish, Waspish
Spitfire Cacafogo, Cacafuego, Wildcat
Spittoon Cuspidor(e)
Spiv Lair, Rorter
Splash Blash, Blue, Dabble, Dash, Dog, Drip, Feature, Flouse, Fl(o)ush, Gardyloo,
Jabble, Ja(u)p, Jirble, Paddle, Plap, Plop, Plowter, Sket, Slosh, Slush, Soda, Soss,
Sozzle, Spairge, Spat(ter), Spectacle, Splat(ch), Splatter, Splodge, Splosh, Splotch,
Spray, Spree, Squatter, Swash, Swatter, Water, Wet
Splay(ed) Curl, Flew, Flue, Patté(e), Spread
Spleen Acrimony, Bite, Lien, Melt, Milt(z), Pip, Stomach, Vitriol, Wrath
Splendid, Splendour Ah, Braw, Brilliant, Bully, Capital, Champion, Clinker,
Dandy, Éclat, Effulgent, Excellent, Fine, Finery, Fulgor, Gallant, Garish, Glitterand,
Glittering, Glorious, Glory, Gorgeous, Grand(eur), Grandiose, Ha, Heroic, Lustrous,
Majestic, Mooi, Noble, Palatial, Panache, Pomp, Proud, Radiant, Rich, Ripping,
Royal, Stunning, Super(b), Wally, Zia
Splice(d) Braid, Eye, Join, Knit, Mainbrace, Wed
▷ **Spliced** *may indicate* an anagram
Splint Airplane, Banjo, Brace, Cal(l)iper, Splenial, T
Splinter(s) Bone-setter, Breakaway, Flinder, Fragment, Matchwood, Shatter, Shiver,
Skelf, Sliver, Spale, Spall, Speel, Spelk, Spell, Spicula, Spill
Split Areolate, Axe, Banana, Bifid, Bifurcate, Bisect, Break, Broach, Burst, Chasm,
Chine, Chop, Clint, Clove(n), Crack, Crevasse, Cut, Decamp, Departmentalise,

Disjoin, Distrix, → **DIVIDE**, Division, Divorce, End, Fissile, Fissure, Flake, Fork(ed), Fragment, Grass, Lacerate, Partition, Red(d), Rift(e), Rip, Rive, Russian, Ryve, Schism, Scissor, Segregate, Separate, Septemfid, Sever, Share, Skive, Slit, Sliver, Spall, Spalt, Speld, Tattle, Tmesis, Told, To-rend, To-tear, Wedge
▷ **Split** *may indicate* a word to become two; one word inside another; or a connection with Yugoslavia

Splodge, Splotch Blot, Drop, Splash

Splurge Binge, Indulge, Lavish, Spend, Splash, Spree

Splutter Chug, Expectorate, Fizz, Gutter, Spray, Stammer

Spoil(s), Spoilt Addle, Agrise, Agrize, Agryze, Blight, Blunk, Booty, Botch, Bribe, Coddle, Corrupt, Crool, → **DAMAGE**, Dampen, Deface, Defect, Deform, Dish, Foul, Gum, Hames, Harm, Impair(ed), Indulge, Loot, Maderise, Maltreat, Mar, Mardy, Mollycoddle, Muck, Mutilate, Mux, Pamper, Pet, Pickings, Pie, Plunder, Prejudicate, Prize, Queer, Rait, Rate, Ravage, Ret, Rot, Ruin, Scupper, Spuly(i)e, Swag, Taint, Tarnish, Vitiate, Wanton, Winnings
▷ **Spoil(ed), Spoilt** *may indicate* an anagram

Spoilsport Damper, Killjoy, Meddler, Party pooper, Wet blanket, Wowser

Spoke(s) Concentric, Radius, Ray, Rung, Said, Sed, Strut
▷ **Spoken** *may indicate* the sound of a word or letter

Spokesman Foreman, Mouthpiece, Orator, Prophet, Representative

Spoliation, Spoliative Devastation, Pillage, Plunder, Predatory, Reif

Sponge(r), Spongy Alcoholic, Ambatch, Argentine, Battenburg, Bum, Cadge, Cake, Cleanse, Diact, Diploe, Fozy, Free-loader, Glass-rope, Hexact, Hyalonema, Leech, Lig, Lithistid(a), Loofa(h), Madeira, Madeleine, Mermaid's glove, Mooch, Mop, Mouch, Mump, Parasite, Parazoa, Pentact, Poachy, Porifera(n), Quandong, Rhabdus, Sarcenchyme, Scambler, Schnorrer, Scrounge, Shark, Shool, Shule, Siphonophora, Smell-feast, Sooner, Sop, Sucker, Swab, Sycophant, Tectratine, Tetract, Tetraxon, Tiramisu, Tylote, Vegetable, Velamen, Venus's flowerbasket, Wangle, Wipe, Zimocca, Zoophyte

Spongewood Sola

Sponsor(ship) Aegis, Angel, Auspice, Backer, Egis, Finance, Godfather, Godparent, Gossip, Guarantor, Lyceum, Patron, Surety

Spontaneous Aleatoric, Autonomic, Gratuitous, Immediate, Impromptu, Improvised, Impulsive, Instant, Intuitive, Natural, Ultroneus, Unasked, Unpremeditated, Unprompted, Unrehearsed

Spoof Chouse, Cozenage, Deception, Delusion, Fallacy, → **HOAX**, Imposture, Ramp, Swindle, Trick

Spook(s), Spooky CIA, Eerie, Fantom, Frightening, Ghost, Phantom, Shade

Spool Bobbin, Capstan, Pirn, Reel, Trundle

Spoon(ful), Spoon-shaped Apostle, Canoodle, Cochlear, Deflagrating, Dollop, Dose, Eucharistic, Gibby, Greasy, Horn, Labis, Ladle, Mote, Neck, Rat-tail, Runcible, Salt, Scoop, Scud, Server, Snuff, Spatula, Sucket, Trolling, Trout, Woo, Wooden

Spoonerism Marrowsky, Metathesis

Spoor Trace, Track, Trail

Sporadic Fitful, Isolated, Occasional, Patchy

Spore(s), Spore case Asexual, Conidium, Ex(t)ine, Fungus, Glomerule, Lenticel, Palynology, Seed, Sexual, Sorus, Spreathed, Telium, Uredinium

Sporran Pock

Sport(s), Sporting, Sportive Amusement, Blood, Breakaway, Brick, By-form, Contact, Daff, Dalliance, Dally, Deviant, Extreme, Field, Freak, Frisky, Frolic, Fun,

→ **GAME**, Gent, In, Joke, Laik, Lake, Lark, Merimake, Merry, Morph, Mutagen, Pal, Recreate, Rogue, Rules, Spectator, Tournament, Tourney, Toy, Wear, Winter

SPORTS

2 letters:	Curling	Canyoning	Table tennis
RU	Fencing	Potholing	Truck racing
	Hurling	Skijoring	Water-skiing
3 letters:	Netball	Skydiving	Windsurfing
Gig	Parkour	Speedball	
	Skating	Twitching	*12 letters:*
4 letters:	Snooker	Water polo	Bar billiards
Polo	Surfing	Wrestling	Boardsailing
Sumo	Tailing		Cross country
		10 letters:	Heli-boarding
5 letters:	*8 letters:*	Cyclo-cross	Orienteering
Basho	Aquatics	Drag-racing	Parascending
Fives	Ballgame	Kickboxing	River bugging
Kendo	Bonspiel	Monoskiing	Sailboarding
	Eventing	Pancratium	Snowboarding
6 letters:	Korfball	Parakiting	Speed-skating
Aikido	Lacrosse	Paraskiing	Steeplechase
Hockey	Langlauf	Rallycross	Trampolining
Karate	Natation	Street luge	Trapshooting
Shinny	Octopush		Wakeboarding
Shinty	Softball	*11 letters:*	
Squash	Speedway	Coasteering	*13 letters:*
Tennis	Swoffing	Fell walking	Bungee-jumping
		Hang-gliding	Prizefighting
7 letters:	*9 letters:*	Paragliding	Weightlifting
Angling	Abseiling	Paralympics	
Archery	Autocross	Parapenting	*17 letters:*
Camogie	Autopoint	Parasailing	Whitewater rafting

▷ **Sport(s)** *may indicate* an anagram

Sportsman, Sportsmen All-rounder, Athlete, Blue, Corinthian, Half-blue, Hunter, Nimrod, Pentathlete, Pitcher, Shamateur, Shikaree, Shikari, Showjumper

Spot(s), Spotted, Spotting, Spotty Ace, Acne, Area, Areola, Areole, Baily's beads, Bausond, Bead, Beauty, Befoul, Blackhead, Blain, Blemish, Blind, Blip, Blister, Blob, Blot, Blotch(ed), Blur, Brind(l)ed, Café-au-lait, Carbuncle, Caruncle, Cash, Check, Cloud, Colon, Comedo, Corner, Curn, Cyst, Dance, Dapple(-bay), Defect, Dick, Dilemma, Discern, Discover, Dot, Drop, Eruption, Espy, Eye, Facula, Flat, Flaw, Fleck, Floater, Fogdog, Foxed, Freak, Freckle, Furuncle, G, Gay, Glimpse, Gout, Gräfenberg, Gricer, Guttate, High, Hot, Identify, Jam, Leaf, Lentago, Light, Little, Liver, Location, Loran, Mackle, Macle, Macul(at)e, Mail, Meal, Measly, Microdot, Milium, Moil, Mole, Morbilli, Mote, Motty, Muscae volitantes, Naevoid, Naevus, Note, Notice, Ocellar, Ocellus, Paca, Papule, Paraselene, Pardal, Parhelion, Patch, Peep(e), Penalty, Perceive, Performance, Petechia, Pied, Pimple, Pin, Pip, Place, Plague, Plight, Plook, Plot, Plouk, Pock, Point, Predicament, Punctuate, Pupil, Pustule, Quat, Radar, Rash, Recognise, Red, Rose-drop, Scene, Scotoma, Situation, Skewbald, Smut, Soft, Speck(le), Speculum, Splodge, Spy, Stigma, Sully, Sun, Sweet,

Taint, Tar, Tight, Touch, Trace, Trouble, Weak, Whelk, Whitehead, Witness, X, Yellow, Zit

Spotless Clean, Immaculate, Pristine, Virginal

Spotlight Ace, Baby, Bon-bon, Brute, Maxi-brute

Spot on To a t

Spouse Companion, Consort, Dutch, Feare, Feer, F(i)ere, Hubby, Husband, Mate, Oppo, Partner, Pheer, Pirrauru, Significant other, Wife, Xant(h)ippe

Spout(er) Adjutage, Erupt, Gargoyle, Geyser, Grampus, Gush, Impawn, Jet, Mouth, Nozzle, Orate, Pawn, Pourer, Raile, Rote, Spurt, Stream, Stroup, Talk, Tap, Vent

Sprain(ed) Crick, Rax, Reckan, Rick, Stave, Strain, Wrench, Wrick

Sprat Brit, Fish, Garvie, Garvock

Sprawl Grabble, Loll, Scamble, Sprangle, Spread, Stretch, Urban

Spray Aerosol, Aigrette, Antiperspirant, Atomiser, Bespatter, Buttonhole, Corsage, Cyme, Egret, Fly, Hair, Mace®, Nasal, Nebuliser, Posy, Rose, Rosula, Shower, Sparge, Spindrift, Splash, Spoondrift, Sprent, Sprig, Sprinkle, Spritz, Strinkle, Syringe, Twig, Wet

▷ **Spray** *may indicate* an anagram

Spread(ing), Spreader Air, Apply, Banquet, Bestrew, Beurre, Blow-out, Branch, Bush, Butter, Carpet, Centre, Circumfuse, Contagious, Couch, Coverlet, Coverlid, Deploy, Diffract, Diffuse, Dilate, Disperse, Dissemination, Distribute, Divulge, Double, Drape, Dripping, Elongate, Emanate, Expand, Extend, Fan, Feast, Flare, Guac(h)amole, Honeycomb, Jam, Lay, Mantle, Marge, Marmite®, Metastasis, Middle-age(d), Multiply, Mushroom, Nutter, Oleo, Open, Overgrow, Paste, Pâté, Patent, Patté, Patulous, Perfuse, Pervade, Picnic, Pour, Propagate, Radiate, Rampant, Ran, Run, Scale, Scatter, Sea-floor, Set, Sheet, Slather, Smear, Smörgåsbord, Sow, Span, Speld, Spelder, Spillover, Splay, Sprawl, Spray, Straddle, Straw, Stretch, Strew, Strow, Suffuse, Systemic, Tath, Teer, Unfold, Unfurl, Unguent, Vegemite®, Widen, Wildfire

▷ **Spread** *may indicate* an anagram

Spree Bat, Batter, Beano, Bender, Binge, Bum, Bust, Buster, Carousal, Frolic, Jag, Jamboree, Juncate, Junket, Lark, Loose, Randan, Rantan, Razzle(-dazzle), Revel, Rouse, Splore, Tear, Ups(e)y

Sprig Brad, Branch, Cion, Cyme, Nail, Scion, Sien, Sient, Spray, Syen, Twig, Youth

Sprightly Agile, Airy, Chipper, Jaunty, Mercurial

Spring(s), Springtime, Springy Aganippe, Air, Alice, Arise, Bolt, Bounce, Bound, Box, Bunt, Cabriole, Caper, Capriole, Castalian, Cavort, Cee, Coil, Dance, Elastic, Eye, Fount(ain), Gambado, Germinate, Geyser, Grass, Hair, Helix, Hippocrene, Hop, Hot, Jump, Leaf, Leap, Lent, Lep, Litt, Low-water, May, Mineral, Originate, Persephone, Pierian, Pounce, Prance, Primavera, Prime, Resilient, Ribbon, Rise, Saddle, Season, Skip, Snap, Source, Spa, Spang, Spaw, Stem, Stot, Submarine, Sulphur, Summer, Thermae, Thermal, Trampoline, Valve, Vault, Vaute, Vawte, Vernal, Voar, Ware, Watch, Waterhole, Weeping, Well(-head), Whip, Winterbourne

▷ **Spring(y)** *may indicate* an anagram

Springbok Amabokoboko

Springless Telega

Springtail Apterygota

Sprinkle(r), Sprinkling Asperge, Aspergill(um), Bedash, Bedrop, Bescatter, Caster, Dredge, Dust, Hyssop, Lard, Pouncet, Powder, Rose, Scatter, Scouthering, Shower, Sow, Spa(i)rge, Spatter, Splash, Spray, Spritz, Strinkle

Sprint(er) Burst, Dash, Race, Rash, Run, Rush, Wells

Sprite Apsaras, Banshee, Croquemitaine, Dobbie, Dobby, Echo, Elf, Fairy, Fiend, Genie, Goblin, Gremlin, Hobgoblin, Icon, Nickel, Ondine, Puck, Spirit, Troll, Trow, Umbriel, Undine

Sprout Braird, Breer, Brussels, Bud, Burgeon, Chit, Crop, Eye, Germ(inate), Grow, Pullulate, Shoot, Spire, Tendron, Vegetate

Spruce Balsam, Dapper, Engelmann, Hemlock, Natty, Neat, Norway, Picea, Pitch-tree, Prink, Shipshape, Sitka, Smart, Spiff, Tidy, Tree, Trim, Tsuga, White

Spry Active, Agile, Constance, Dapper, Nimble, Volable

Spud Murphy, Potato, Spade, Tater, Tatie

Spume Eject, Foam, Froth, Lather, Spet, Spit

Spunk Courage, Grit, Pluck, Tinder

Spur(s) Accourage, Activate, Calcar(ate), Encourage, Fame, Fire, Galvanise, Gee, Gilded, Goad, Groyne, Heel, Incite, Limb, Lye, Needle, Offset, Prick, Rippon, Rowel, Shoot, Spica, Stimulus, Strut, Stud, Tar, Urge

Spurge (tree) Candelilla, Croton, Euphorbia, Kamala, Poinsettia, Ricinus

Spurious Adulterine, Apocryphal, Bogus, Counterfeit, Dog, False, Phoney, Pseudo, Sciolism

▷ **Spurious** *may indicate* an anagram

Spurn Despise, Disdain, Ignore, Jilt, Reject, → **SCORN**, Sdayn, Shun

Spurt Burst, Forge, Geyser, Jet, Outburst, Pump, Spout, Start

Sputter Fizzle, Spit, Splutter, Stutter

Spy(ing), Spies Agent, Beagle, Caleb, CIA, Cicero, Curtain-twitcher, Descry, Dicker, Double agent, Eavesdrop, Emissary, Espionage, Fink, Fuchs, Informer, Keeker, Mata Hari, MI, Mole, Mouchard, Nark, Ninja, Nose, Operative, Pimp, Plant, Pry, Recce, Scout, See, Setter, Shadow, Sinon, Sleeper, Spetsnaz, Spook, Tout, Wait

Spyhole Eyelet, Judas-hole, Oillet, Peephole

Squab Chubby, Cushion, Obese

Squabble Argue, Bicker, Brabble, Quarrel, Rhubarb, Row, Scrap

Squad(ron) Band, Blue, Company, Crew, Death, Drugs, Escadrille, Fifteen, Firing, Flying, Fraud, Hit, Nahal, Platoon, Porn, Red, Snatch, Vice, White, Wing

Squalid, Squalor Abject, Colluvies, Dickensian, Dinge, Dingy, Filth, Frowsy, Grungy, Mean, Poverty, Scuzzy, Seedy, Skid Row, Sleazy, Slum(my), Slurb, Sordid

Squall Blast, Blow, Chubasco, Commotion, Cry, Drow, Flaw, Flurry, Gust, Line, Sumatra, Wail, White, Yell, Yowl

Squander Blow, Blue, Fritter, Frivol, Lash, Mucker, Slather, Splash, Splurge, Ware, → **WASTE**

Square(d), Squares Agree, Anta, Arrière, Ashlar, Ashler, Bang, Barrack, Belgrave, Berkeley, Bevel, Block, Bribe, Chequer, Compone, Compony, Corny, Deal, Dinkum, Even(s), Fair, Fog(e)y, Forty-nine, Fossil, Four, Gobony, Grey, Grosvenor, Latin, Least, Leicester, Level, Magic, Market, Meal, Mitre, Nasik, Neandert(h)aler, Nine, Norma, Old-fashioned, Palm, Passé, Pay, Perfect, Piazza, Place, Platz, Plaza, Quad(rangle), Quadrate, Quarry, Quits, Red, Rood, S, Set(t), Sloane, Solid, Squier, Squire, Straight, T, Tee, Times, Traditionalist, Trafalgar, Try, Unhip

Squash(y) Adpress, Butternut, Conglomerate, Crush, Gourd, Kia-ora®, Knead, Marrow, Mash, Obcompress, Oblate, Pattypan, Press, Pulp, Shoehorn, Silence, Slay, Slew, Slue, Soft, Squeeze, Squidge, Squidgy, Suppress, Torpedo

Squat(ter), Squatting Bywoner, Caganer, Crouch, Croup(e), Cubby, Dumpy, Fubby, Fubsy, Hunker, Occupy, Pudsey, Pyknic, Rook, Ruck, Sit, Spud, Stubby, Stumpy, Swatter, Usucaption

Squaw Kloo(t)chman

Squawk Cackle, Complain, Cry, Scrauch, Scraugh

Squeak(er) Cheep, Creak, Narrow, Near, Peep, Pip, Scroop, Shoat, Squeal
Squeal(er) Blow, Eek, Howl, Inform, Pig, Screech, Sing, Sneak, Tell, Wee, Yelp
Squeamish(ness) Delicate, Disgust, Missish, Nervous, Prudish, Queasy, Reluctant
Squeeze(r) Bleed, Chirt, Coll, Compress, Concertina, Constrict, Cram, Credit,
  Crowd, Crush, Dispunge, Exact, Express, Extort, Extrude, Hug, Jam, Mangle, Milk,
  Preace, Press, Sandwich, Sap, Scrooge, Scrouge, Scrowdge, Scruze, Shoehorn,
  Squash, Squish, Sweat, Thrutch, Thumbscrew, Vice, Wring
Squelch Gurgle, Squash, Squish, Subdue
Squib Banger, Damp, Firework, Lampoon
Squid Calamari, Calamary, Cephalopod, Cuttlefish, Ink-fish, Loligo, Mortar,
  Nautilus, Octopus, Sleeve fish
Squiffy Drunk, Tiddley
▷ **Squiggle** *may indicate* an anagram
Squill Sea, Spring
Squint(ing) Boss-eyed, Cast, Cock-eye, Cross-eye, Glance, Gledge, Glee, Gley,
  Hagioscope, Heterophoria, Louche, Opening, Proptosis, Skellie, Skelly, Sken,
  Squin(n)y, Strabism, Swivel-eye, Vergence, Wall-eye
Squire Armiger(o), Beau, Donzel, Escort, Hardcastle, Headlong, Land-owner,
  Scutiger, Swain, Western, White
Squirm(ing) Fidget, Reptation, Twist, Worm, Wriggle, Writhe
Squirrel, Squirrel's nest Aye-aye, Boomer, Bun, Cage, Chickaree, Chipmuck,
  Chipmunk, Dray, Drey, Flickertail, Flying, Fox, Gopher, Grey, Ground, Hackee,
  Hoard(er), Meerkat, Petaurist, Phalanger, Red, Sciuroid, Sewellel, Skug, S(o)uslik,
  Spermophile, Taguan, Vair, Zizel
Squirt(er) Chirt, Cockalorum, Douche, Jet, Scoosh, Scoot, Skoosh, Spirt, Spout,
  Spritz, Urochorda, Wet, Whiffet, Whippersnapper
Sri Lanka(n) Ceylon, Cingalese, CL, Serendip, Sinhalese, Tamil, Vedda
St Saint, Street
Stab Bayonet, Chib, Crease, Creese, Dag, Effort, Go, Gore, Guess, Jab, Knife, Kreese,
  Kris, Lancinate, Pang, Pierce, Pink, Poniard, Prick, Prong, Stick, Stiletto, Turk,
  Wound
Stabilise(r), Stability Aileron, Balance, Balloonet, Emulsifier, Even, Fin, Maintain,
  Pax Romana, Peg, Permanence, Plateau, Poise, Steady, Tail panel
Stable(s) Augean, Balanced, Barn, Byre, Certain, Constant, Durable, Equerry,
  Equilibrium, Firm, Livery, Loose box, Manger, Mews, Poise, Secure, Solid, Sound,
  Stall, Static(al), Steadfast, Steady, Stud, Sure, Together
Stableman Groom, Lad, Ostler
Stachys Betony
Stack(s) Accumulate, À gogo, Chimney, Clamp, Cock, End, Funnel, Heap, Lum,
  → **PILE**, Rick, Shock, Smoke, Staddle
Stadium Arena, Ballpark, Bowl, Circus, Circus Maximus, Coliseum, Hippodrome,
  Speedway, Velodrome
Staff Aesculapius, Alpenstock, Ash-plant, Bato(o)n, Bourdon, Burden, Caduceus,
  Cane, Crook, Crosier, Cross(e), Crozier, Crutch, Cudgel, Entourage, Equerry,
  État-major, Faculty, Ferula, Ferule, Flagpole, General, Jacob's, Jeddart, Linstock,
  Lituus, Mace, Omlah, Pastoral, Personnel, Pike, Pole, Ragged, Rod, Rung,
  Runic, Sceptre, Seniority, Skeleton, Stave, Stick, Taiaha, Tapsmen, Tau, Thyrsus,
  Truncheon, Verge, Wand, Workers, Workforce, Wring
Stag Actaeon, Brocket, Buck, Deer, For men, Hummel, Imperial, Line, Male, Party,
  Royal, Rutter, Ten-pointer, Wapiti
Stage Act, Anaphase, Apron, Arena, Bardo, Bema, Boards, Catasta, Centre,

Chrysalis, Committee, Diligence, Dog-leg, Estrade, Fare, Fargo, Fit-up, Grade,
Hop, Juncture, Key, Landing, Leg, Level, Metaphase, Milestone, Moment,
Mount, Oidium, Perform, Phase, Phasis, Pier, Pin, Platform, Podium, Point,
Postscenium, Prophase, Proscenium, PS, Puberty, Report, Resting, Rostrum,
Scene, Sensorimeter, Sound, Stadium, Step, Stor(e)y, Subimago, Theatre, Thrust,
Transition, Trek, Yuga, Zoea

Stage-coach Diligence, Thoroughbrace

Stagecraft Pinafore

Stagehand Flyman, Grip

Stagger(ed) Alternate, Amaze, Astichous, Astonish, Awhape, Daidle, Falter,
Floor, Lurch, Recoil, Reel, Rock, Shock, Stoiter, Stot(ter), Stumble, Sway, Teeter,
Thunderstricken, Thunderstruck, Titubate, Tolter, Totter, Wamble, Wintle

▷ **Staggered** *may indicate* an anagram

Stagirite, Stagyrite Aristotle

Stagnant, Stagnation Cholestasis, Foul, Inert, Scummy, Stasis, Static

Staid Decorous, Demure, Formal, Grave, Matronly, Prim, Prudish, Sad, Seemly,
Sober, Stick-in-the-mud

Stain(er) Aniline, Bedye, Besmirch, Blemish, Blob, Blot, Blotch, Discolour,
Dishonour, Dye, Embrue, Ensanguine, Eosin, Fox, Gram's, Grime, Imbrue,
Iodophile, Keel, Maculate, Mail, Meal, Mote, Portwine, Slur, Smirch, Smit, Soil,
Splodge, Splotch, Stigma, Sully, Taint, Tarnish, Tinge, Tint, Vital, Woad

Stair(case), Stairs Apples, Apples and pears, Caracol(e), Cochlea, Companionway,
Escalator, Flight, Moving, Perron, Rung, Scale (and platt), Spiral, Step, Tread,
Turnpike, Vice, Wapping, Winding

Stake(s) Ante, Bet, Claim, Deposit, Gage, Go, Holding, Impale, Impone, Interest,
Lay, Loggat, Mark, Mise, Nursery, Paal, Pale, Paliform, Paling, Palisade, Peel, Peg,
Pele, Picket, Pile, Play, Post, Pot, Punt, Put, Rest, Revie, Risk, Septleva, Spike,
Spile, Stang, Stob, Straddle, Sweep, Tether, Vie, Wager, Welter

Stalactite Dripstone, Dropstone, Helictite, Lansfordite, Soda straw

Stale Aged, Banal, Flat, Fozy, Frowsty, Fusty, Hackneyed, Handle, Hoary, Mouldy,
Musty, Old, Pretext, Rancid, Urine, Worn

▷ **Stale** *may indicate* an obsolete word

Stalemate Deadlock, Dilemma, Hindrance, Impasse, Mexican standoff, Saw-off,
Standoff, Tie, Zugswang

Stalk(s), Stalker Anthophore, Bun, Cane, Caulicle, Follow, Funicle, Garb(e),
Gynophore, Ha(u)lm, Keck(s), Kecksey, Keksye, Kex, Ommatophore, Pedicel,
Pedicle, Peduncle, Petiole, Petiolule, Phyllode, Pursue, Rush, Scape, Seta, Shaw,
Spear, Spire, Stem, Sterigma, Still-hunter, Stipe(s), Stride, Strig, Strut, Stubble,
Stump, Trail, Yolk

Stalking-horse Stale

Stall(s) Arrest, Bay, Booth, Box, Bulk, Crib, → **DELAY**, Floor, Flypitch, Hedge, Kiosk,
Loose-box, Orchestra, Pen, Pew, Prebendal, Seat, Shamble, Sideshow, Stand,
Starting, Stasidion, Temporise, Trap, Traverse, Travis, Trevis(s), Whip, Whipstall

Stallion Cooser, Cuisser, Cusser, Entire, → **HORSE**, Stag, Staig, Stonehorse, Stud

Stalwart Anchor-man, Buirdly, Firm, Manful, Robust, Sturdy, Trusty, Valiant

Stamen(ed) Androecium, Octandria, Polyandria

Stamina Endurance, Fibre, Fortitude, Guts, Last, Stamen, Stay, Steel

Stammer(ing) Balbutient, Er, Hesitate, Hum, Psellism, Sputter, Stumble,
→ **STUTTER**, Waffle

Stamp(s), Stamped Albino, Appel, Cast, Character, Date(r), Die, Dry print, Enface,
Fiscal, Frank, Health, Imperforate, Impress, Imprint, Incuse, Label, Matchmark,

Mint, Pane, Penny black, Perfin, Philately, Pintadera, Postage, Press(ion), Rubber, Seal, Seebeck, Se-tenant, Signet, Spif, Strike, Swage, Tête-bêche, Touch, Touchmark, Trading, Trample, Tread, Tromp, Type

Stamp-collecting Philately, Timbrology, Timbrophily

Stampede Debacle, Flight, Panic, Rampage, → RUSH

Stance Attitude, Ecarté, Pose, Position, Posture, Quinte

Stand(ing), Stand for, Stand up Apron, Arraign, Attitude, Base, Be, Bear, Bide, Binnacle, Bipod, Bristle, Brook, Canterbury, Caste, Confrontation, Cradle, Crease, Dais, Degree, Desk, Dock, Dree, Dumb-waiter, Easel, Epergne, Étagère, Face, Foothold, Freeze, Gantry, Gueridon, Hard, Hob, Importance, Insulator, Klinostat, Last, Lazy Susan, Lectern, Leg, Lime, Music, Nef, Odour, One-night, Ovation, Pedestal, Place, Plant, Podium, Pose, Position, Pou sto, Prestige, Promenade, Protest, Qua, Rack, Rank, Regent, Remain, Represent, Repute, Rise, Stall, Statant, Station, → STATUS, Stay, Stillage, Stock, Stool, Straddle, Straphang, Stroddle, Strut, Table, Tantalus, Taxi, Teapoy, Terrace, Toe, → TREAT, Tree, Tripod, Trivet, Umbrella, Upright, Whatnot, Witness

Standard(s) Banner, Base, Baseline, Basic, Benchmark, Bogey, British, Canon, CAT, Classic(al), Cocker, Colour(s), Criterion, Double, Eagle, English, Ethics, Etiquette, Examplar, Example, Exemplar, Fiducial, Flag, Ga(u)ge, Gold, Gonfalon, Grade, Guidon, Ideal, Labarum, Level, Living, Model, Netiquette, Norm(a), Normal, Numeraire, Old Glory, Oriflamme, Par, Parker Morris, Pennon, Principle, Rate, Regular, Rod, Rose, Routine, Royal, → RULE, Silver, Spec(ification), Staple, Sterling, Stock, Time, Touchstone, Tricolour, Troy, Two-power, Usual, Valuta, Vexillum, Yardstick

Standard-bearer Alferez, Cornet, Ensign, Vexillary

Stand-by Adminicle, Reserve, Substitute, Support, Understudy

Stand-in Double, Locum, Stunt man, Sub(stitute), Surrogate, Temp, Understudy

Standish Miles

Stand-off(ish) Aloof, Remote, Reserved, Stalemate, Upstage

Standpoint Angle, Slant, View

Standstill Deadset, Halt, Jam

Stanley Baldwin, Knife, Rupert

Stannic Tin

Stanza Ballad, Elegiac, Envoi, Envoy, Heroic, Ottava, Ottava rima, Poem, Sixaine, Spenserian, Staff, Stave, Tetrastich, Verse

Staple Basic, Bread, Chief, Maize, Oats, Pin, Rice, Stock, Wool

Star(s) Aster(isk), Binary, Body, Celeb(rity), Companion, Constant, Constellation, Cynosure, Dark, Double, Esther, Exploding, Falling, Feather, Feature, Film, Fixed, Flare, Giant, Headline, Hero, Hester, Hexagram, Idol, Late type, Lead, Lion, Mogen David, Movie, Multiple, Pentacle, Personality, Phad, Pip, Plerion, Pointer, Principal, Pulsating, Seven, Shell, Shine, Shooting, Sidereal, Solomon's seal, Spangle, Starn(ie), Stellar, Stern, Swart, (The) Pointers, Top banana, Top-liner, Ultraviolet, Valentine, Variable, Vedette

---

STARS

3 letters:	*4 letters:*	Lyra	Ursa
Dog	Argo	Mira	Vega
Sol	Beta	Nova	Vela
	Grus	Pavo	Zeta
	Lode	Pole	

5 letters:
Acrux
Agena
Algol
Alpha
Ceres
Comet
Delta
Deneb
Draco
Dubhe
Dwarf
Gamma
Hyads
Indus
Lupus
Mensa
Merak
Mizar
Norma
North
Polar
Radio
Rigel
Rigil
Spica
Theta
Venus
Virgo
Wagon
Whale

6 letters:
Alioth
Alkaid
Altair
Aquila
Auriga
Bootes
Carbon

Carina
Castor
Cygnus
Dorado
Étoile
Fornax
Galaxy
Hyades
Lizard
Megrez
Merope
Meteor
Mullet
Octans
Phecda
Plough
Pollux
Psyche
Pulsar
Puppis
Quasar
Saturn
Sirius
Sothis
Uranus
Vesper
Volans

7 letters:
Antares
Calaeno
Canopus
Capella
Cepheus
Chamber
Columba
Dolphin
Epsilon
Estoile
Evening

Gemingo
Lucifer
Morning
Neutron
Perseus
Phoenix
Polaris
Procyon
Proxima
Regulus
Sabaism
Serpens
Sterope
Triones
Wagoner

8 letters:
Achernar
Arcturus
Barnard's
Circinus
Denebola
Equuleus
Hesperus
Magnetar
Mira Ceti
Pegasean
Phosphor
Pleiades
Praesepe
Red dwarf
Red giant
Scorpius
Synastry
Waggoner

9 letters:
Aldebaran
Andromeda
Bellatrix

Big Dipper
Black hole
Centaurus
Collapsar
Delphinus
Fire-drake
Fomalhaut
Meteorite
Ophiuchus
Pentagram
Rigil-Kent
Supernova
Wolf-Rayet

10 letters:
Betacrucis
Betelgeuse
Betelgeuze
Brown dwarf
Cassiopeia
Orion's Belt
Phosphorus
Supergiant
White dwarf

11 letters:
Circumpolar

12 letters:
Little Dipper

13 letters:
Southern Cross

15 letters:
Proxima Centauri

Starboard Right
Starch(y), Starch producer Amyloid, Animal, Arrowroot, Cassava, Ceremony, Congee, Conjee, Coontie, Coonty, Cycad, Farina, Fecula, Formal, Glycogen, Manioc, Maranta, Pentosan, Sago, Stamina, Statolith, Stiff, Tapioca, Tous-les-mois
Stare Eyeball, Fisheye, Gape, Gapeseed, Gawp, Gaze, Geek, Glare, Goggle, Gorp, Look, Ogle, Outface, Peer, Rubberneck, Scowl
Starfish Asterid, Asteroid(ea), Bipinnaria, Brittlestar, Ophiurid, Radiata
Star-gaze(r), Star-gazing Astrodome, Astronomy, Copernicus
Stark Apparent, Austere, Bald, Bare, Gaunt, Harsh, Naked, Nude, Sheer, Stiff, Utterly

Starling Bird, Gippy, Hill mynah, Murmuration, Pastor, Rosy pastor, Stare
Star of Bethlehem Chincherinchee, Chinkerinchee
Start(ed), Starter Ab ovo, Abrade, Abraid, Abray, Activate, Actuate, Begin, Boggle, Boot-up, Bot, Broach, Bug, Bump, Chance, Commence, Crank, Create, Crudités, Dart, Ean, Embryo, Face-off, False, Fire, Flinch, Float, Flush, Flying, Found, Gambit, Gan, Genesis, Getaway, Gun, Handicap, Head, Hot-wire, Impetus, Imprimis, Incept(ion), Initiate, Instigate, Institute, Intro, Jerk, Judder, Jump, Jump lead, Jump-off, Kick-off, L, Lag, Launch, Lead, Off, Offset, Onset, Ope(n), Ord, Origin, Outset, Preliminary, Prelude, Proband, Push, Put-up, Reboot, Resume, Roll, Roul, Rouse, Scare, Set off, Shy, Slip, Snail, Spring, Spud, String, Tee-off, Wince
▷ **Start** *may indicate* an anagram or first letter(s)
Startle, Startling Alarm, Bewilder, Disturb, Eye-opener, Flush, Frighten, Magical, Rock, Scare
Starvation, Starve(d), Starving Anorexia, Anoxic, Bant, Clem, Cold, Deprive, Diet, Famish, Inanition, Macerate, Perish, Pine, Undernourished
▷ **Starving** *may indicate* an 'o' in the middle of a word
Stash Secrete
State(s), Stateside Affirm, Alle(d)ge, Aread, Arrede, Assert, Assever, Attest, Aver, Avow, Buffer, Case, Circar, Cite, Client, Commonwealth, Condition, Confederate, Country, Critical, Cutch, Declare, Dependency, Emirate, Empire, État, Federal, Fettle, Flap, Free, Habitus, Humour, Kingdom, Land, Lesh, Mess, Name, Nanny, Nation, Native, Palatinate, Papal, Para, Plateau, Plight, Police, Posit, Predicament, Predicate, Premise, Pronounce, Protectorate, Puppet, Quantum, Realm, Republic, Rogue, Samadhi, Satellite, Say, Sircar, Sirkar, Slave, Sorry, Standing, Steady, Succession, Threeness, Uncle Sam, Union, United, Welfare

---

STATES

2 letters:	*4 letters:*	*5 letters:*	
Ga	Abia	Amapa	Nepal
Ia	Acre	Assam	Oshun
Md	Chad	Bahar	Perak
Me	Conn	Benin	Piaui
Mi	Gulf	Benue	Qatar
NC	Iowa	Ceará	Reich
NY	Kano	Dixie	Sabah
Pa	Kogi	Dubai	Samoa
RI	Mass	Gabon	Texas
UK	Ogun	Ghana	
US	Ohio	Hesse	*6 letters:*
Ut	Oman	Idaho	Alaska
Va	Ondo	Kalat	Balkan
	Osun	Kedah	Baltic
3 letters:	Shan	Kutch	Baroda
Ark	Swat	Kwara	Bauchi
Del	Togo	Lippe	Belize
Fla	Utah	Maine	Bremen
Oyo		Malay	Brunei
Wis		Mewar	Cochin
			Colima

Dakota
Hawaii
Jigawa
Johore
Kaduna
Kansas
Kerala
Khelat
Kuwait
Madras
Malawi
Mysore
Nevada
Oaxaca
Oregon
Orissa
Pahang
Parana
Penang
Perlis
Puebla
Punjab
Rivers
Saxony
Sikkim
Sokoto
Sonora
Sparta
Styria
Tonkin

7 letters:
Alabama
Alagoas
Anambra
Andorra
Arizona
Barbary
Bavaria
Buffalo
Chiapos
Durango
Florida
Georgia
Gujarat
Gujerat
Haryana
Hidalgo
Indiana
Ireland
Jalisco

Jamaica
Jodhpur
Kashmir
Malacca
Manipur
Mizoram
Montana
Morelos
Nayarit
New York
Nirvana
Paraiba
Pradesh
Prussia
Roraima
Sarawak
Sergipe
Sinaloa
Tabasco
Tongkin
Tonking
Tripura
Trucial
Udaipur
Vermont
Vietnam
Wyoming
Yucatan

8 letters:
Abu Dhabi
Amazonas
Arkansas
Campeche
Carolina
Coahuila
Colorado
Delaware
Ethiopia
Honduras
Illinois
Jharkand
Kelantan
Kentucky
Maranhao
Maryland
Michigan
Missouri
Nagaland
Nebraska
Oklahoma

Rondonia
Saarland
Sao Paulo
Selangor
Tanzania
Tasmania
Tiaxcala
Tongking
Veracruz
Victoria
Virginia

9 letters:
Chihuahua
Dixieland
Guatemala
Karnataka
Louisiana
Manchukuo
Meghalaya
Michoacán
Minnesota
Nassarawa
New Jersey
New Mexico
Nuevo Léon
Queretaro
Rajasthan
Rajputana
St Vincent
Tamil Nadu
Tennessee
Thuringia
Tocantins
Trengganu
Venezuela
Wisconsin
Zacatecas

10 letters:
California
Guanajuato
Jamahiriya
Jumhouriya
Manchoukuo
Orange Free
Pernambuco
Queensland
Tamaulipas
Tanganyika
Terengganu

Travancore
Washington

11 letters:
Brandenberg
Connecticut
Maharashtra
Mecklenburg
Minas Gerais
Mississippi
North Dakota
Quintana Roo
South Dakota
Uttaranchal
Vatican City

12 letters:
Chhattisgarh
Madhya Bharat
New Hampshire
Pennsylvania
Saxony-Anholt
Uttar Pradesh
West Virginia

13 letters:
Andhra Pradesh
Madhya Pradesh
Massachusetts
Negri Sembilan
New South Wales
San Luis Potosi
Santa Catarina
South Carolina

14 letters:
Rio Grande do Sul
South Australia
Vindhya Pradesh

15 letters:
Himachal Pradesh
Schaumburg-Lippe
St Kitts and Nevis

16 letters:
Rio Grande do
Norte

17 letters:
Schleswig-Holstein

19 letters: *20 letters:*
Rhineland-   North Rhine-
Palatinate   Westphalia

▷ **Stated** *may indicate* a similar sounding word

Stately, Stately home August, Dome, Grand, Imposing, Junoesque, Majestic, Mansion, Noble, Regal

Statement Accompt, Account, Affidavit, Aphorism, Assertion, Asseveration, Attestation, Avowal, Bill, Bulletin, Case, Communiqué, Deposition, Dictum, Diktat, Encyclical, Evidence, Expose, Factoid, Generalisation, Grand Remonstrance, Indictment, Invoice, Jurat, Manifesto, Mission, Outline, Paraphrase, Pleading, Press release, Profession, Pronouncement, Proposition, Protocol, Quotation, Release, Report, Sentence, Shema, Soundbite, Sweeping, Testimony, Theologoumenon, Truism, Utterance, Verb

Stateroom Bibby, Cabin

Statesman American, Attlee, Augustus, Botha, Briand, Bright, Canning, Cato, Clarendon, Diplomat, Disraeli, Draco, Elder, Flaminius, Franklin, Genro, Georgian, Gladstone, Gracchi, Grotius, Guy, Kissinger, Kruger, Lafayette, Lie, Mitterand, Nasser, North, Politician, Politico, Seneca, Smuts, Stein, Talleyrand, Tasmanian, Thiers, Tito, Walpole, Walsingham, Wealsman, Yankee

Static Atmospherics, Becalmed, Electricity, Inert, Maginot-minded, Motionless, Sferics, Stagnant, Stationary

Station(s) Action, Base, Berth, Birth, Camp, Caste, CCS, Coaling, Comfort, Crewe, Deploy, Depot, Docking, Dressing, Euston, Filling, Fire, Garrison, Gas, Generation, Halt, Head, Hill, Hilversum, Ice, Lay, Location, Marylebone, Nick, Outpost, Paddington, Panic, Pay, Petrol, Pitch, Place, Plant, Point, Police, Polling, Post, Power, Powerhouse, Quarter, Radio, Rank, Relay, Rowme, Seat, Service, Sheep, Sit, Space, Stance, Stand, Status, Stond, Subscriber, Tana, Tanna(h), Terminus, Testing, Thana(h), Thanna(h), Tracking, Transfer, Triangulation, Victoria, Waterloo, Waverley, Way, Weather, Work

Stationary Fasten, Fixed, Immobile, Parked, Sessile, Stable, Static

Stationer(y), Stationery-case Continuous, Multi-part, Papeterie

Statistic(ian), Statistics Actuary, Descriptive, Fermi-Dirac, Figure, Gradgrind, Graph, Inferential, Isotype, Lod, Nonparametric, Number, Parametric, Percentage, Quantum, Sampling, Student's t, Vital

Statuary, Statue(tte) Acrolith, Bronze, Bust, Colossus (of Rhodes), Discobolus, Effigy, Figure, Figurine, Galatea, Idol, Image, Kore, Kouros, Liberty, Memnon, Monolith, Monument, Oscar, Palladium, Pietà, Sculpture, Sphinx, Stonework, Stookie, Tanagra, Torso, Xoanon

Stature Growth, Height, Inches, Rank

Status Beacon, Caste, Class, Political, → **POSITION**, Prestige, Quo, Rank, Standing

Statute Act, Capitular, Chapter 11, Chapter 7, Decree, Edict, Law, Novels, Westminster

Staunch Amadou, Leal, Resolute, Steady, Stem, Stout, Styptic, Watertight

Stave Break, Dali, Forestall, Lag, Slat, Stanza, Ward

Stay(s) Alt, Avast, Bide, Board, Bolster, Cohab(it), Corselet, Corset, Embar, Endure, Fulcrum, Gest, Guy, Hawser, Indwell, Jump, Lie, Lig, Linger, Lodge, Manet, Moratorium, Piers, Prop, → **REMAIN**, Reprieve, Restrain, Settle, Sist, Sleepover, Sojourn, Stem, Stop off, Stop-over, Strut, Sustain, Tarry, Triatic, Villeggiatura

Stay-at-home Indoor, Tortoise
STD Aids, Herpes, Telephone, VD
Steadfast Changeless, Constance, Constant, Dilwyn, Firm, Implacable, Resolute, Sad, Stable
Steady Andantino, Ballast, Beau, Boyfriend, Changeless, Composer, Constant, Even, Faithful, Firm, Girlfriend, Measured, Regular, Rock, Stabilise, Stable, Unswerving
Steak Carpet-bag, Chateaubriand, Chuck, Diane, Fillet, Flitch, Garni, Mignon, Minute, Pope's eye, Porterhouse, Rump, Slice, Tartare, T-bone, Tenderloin, Tournedos, Vienna
Steal(ing) Abstract, Bag, Bandicoot, Bone, Boost, Cabbage, Cly, Condiddle, Convey, Creep, Crib, Duff, Edge, Embezzle, Filch, Glom, Grab, Half-inch, Heist, Hotting, Joyride, Kidnap, Knap, Knock down, Knock off, Lag, Liberate, Lift, Loot, Mag(g), Mahu, Mill, Naam, Nam, Nap, Nick, Nim, Nip, Nobble, Nym, Peculate, Phone-jack, Pilfer, Pillage, Pinch, Piracy, Plagiarise, Plunder, Poach, Pocket, Prig, Proll, Purloin, Ram-raid, Remove, Rifle, Rip-off, Rob, Rustle, Scrump, Skrimp, Smug, Snaffle, Snatch, Sneak, Snitch, Souvenir, Swipe, Take, Theft, Thieve, Tiptoe, TWOC, Whip
Stealth(y) Art, Catlike, Covert, Cunning, Furtive, Obreption, Surreptitious, Tiptoe
Steam(ed), Steaming, Steamy Boil, Condensation, Cushion, Dry, Fume, Gaseous, Het, Humid, Live, Livid, Mist, Porn, Radio, Roke, Sauna, Spout, Vapor, Vapour, Wet
Steamer, Steamboat Kettle, Showboat, Side-wheeler, SS, Str, Tramp, Turbine
Steam-hammer Ram
Steed Charger, Horse, Mount
Steel(y) Acierate, Adamant, Bethlehem, Blade, Blister, Bloom, Brace, Carbon, Cast, Chrome, Chromium, Cold, Concrete, Crucible, Damascus, Damask, High-carbon, High-speed, Low-carbon, Magnet, Manganese, Maraging, Martensite, Metal, Mild, Nickel, Pearlite, Ripon, Rolled, Shear, Silver, Sorbite, Spray, Stainless, Structural, Sword, Toledo, Tool, Tungsten, Vanadium, Wootz
Steelyard Bismar
Steep(ening) Abrupt, Arduous, Bold, Brent, Costly, Embay, Expensive, High-pitched, Hilly, Krans, Krantz, Kranz, Macerate, Marinade, Marinate, Mask, Monocline, Precipice, Precipitous, Rait, Rapid, Rate, Ret, Saturate, Scarp, → SHEER, Soak, Sog, Sop, Souse, Stey, Stickle, Tan
Steeple(jack) Spiderman, Spire, Turret
Steer(er), Steering Ackerman, Airt, Buffalo, Bullock, Bum, Cann, Castor, Con(n), Cox, Direct, → GUIDE, Helm, Navaid, Navigate, Ox, Pilot, Ply, Power, Rudder, Stot, Whipstaff, Zebu
Stem Alexanders, Arrow, Axial, Biller, Bine, Bole, Caudex, Caulicle, Caulome, Check, Cladode, Cladophyll, Confront, Corm, Culm, Dam, Epicotyl, Floricane, Ha(u)lm, Kex, Pedicle, Peduncle, Pin, Pseudaxis, Rachis, R(h)achilla, Rhachis, Rhizome, Rise, Rod, Sarment, Scapus, Seta, Shaft, Shank, Sobole(s), Spring, Stalk, Staunch, Stipe, Stolon, Stopple, Straw, Sympodium, Tail
Stench F(o)etor, Funk, Miasma, Odour, Smell, Stink, Whiff
Stencil Copy, Duplicate, Mimeograph®, Pochoir
Stenographer, Stenography Amanuensis, Secretary, Shorthand, Typist
Step(s) Act, Balancé, Chassé, Choctaw, Corbel, Corbie, Curtail, Dance, Degree, Démarche, Echelon, Escalate, False, Flight, Fouetté, Gain, Gait, Glissade, Goose, Grade, Grecian, Greece, Grees(e), Greesing, Grese, Gressing, Grice, Griece, Grise, Grize, Halfpace, Lavolt, Lock, Measure, Move, Notch, Pace, Pas, Pas de souris, Phase, Pigeon('s) wing, Quantal, Raiser, Ratlin(e), Rattlin(e), Rattling, Roundel,

Roundle, Rung, Sashay, Shuffle, Slip, Stage, Stair, Stalk, Stile, Stope, Stride, Toddle, Trap, Tread, Trip, Unison, Waddle, Walk, Whole, Winder

Stephen Martyr, Stainless

Stepmother Novercal

Stepney Spare

Steppe Kyrgyz, Llano, Plain

Stereo IPod®, Personal

Stereotype(d) Hackney, Ritual

Sterile, Sterilise(r), Sterilisation, Sterility Acarpous, Aseptic, Atocia, Autoclave, Barren, Clean, Dead, Fruitless, Impotent, Infertile, Neuter, Pasteurise, Spay, Tubal ligation, Vasectomy

Sterling Excellent, Genuine, Pound, Silver, Sound

Stern Aft, Austere, Back, Counter, Dour, Flinty, Grim, Hard, Implacable, Iron, Isaac, Nates, Poop, Rear, Relentless, Rugged, Stark, Strict, Tailpiece, Transom

Steroid Anabolic, Androsterone, Calciferol, Cortisone, Dexamethasone, Ergosterol, Fusidic, Lipid, Lumisterol, Mifepristone, Nandrolone, Predniso(lo)ne, Spironolactone, Stanozolol, Testosterone, Tetrahydrogestrinone

Sterol Stigmasterol

Stertorous Snore

Stet Restore

Stevedore Docker, Dockhand, Longshoreman, Stower, Wharfinger

Stevenson RLS, Tusitala

Stew(ed), Stews Bagnio, Bath, Blanquette, Boil, Bordel(lo), Bouillabaisse, Bouilli, Braise, Bredie, Brothel, Burgoo, Carbonade, Carbonnade, Casserole, Cassoulet, Cholent, Chowder, Coddle, Colcannon, Compot(e), Daube, Flap, Fuss, Goulash, Haricot, Hash, Hell, Hot(ch)pot(ch), Irish, Jug, Lather, Lobscouse, Maconochie, Matapan, Matelote, Mulligan, Navarin, Olla podrida, Osso bucco, Oyster, Paddy, Paella, Pepperpot, Pot-au-feu, Pot-pourri, Ragout, Ratatouille, Rubaboo, Salmi, Sass, Scouse, Seethe, Simmer, Slumgullion, Squiffy, Stie, Stove, Stovies, Sty, Succotash, Sweat, Swelter, Tajine, Tatahash, Tzimmes, Zamzawed, Zarzuela

Steward Butler, Cellarer, Chamberlain, Chiltern Hundreds, Dewan, Factor, Hind, Malvolio, Manciple, Maormor, Mormaor, Official, Oswald, Panter, Purser, Reeve, Seneschal, Sewer, Shop, Smallboy, Sommelier, Waiter

▷ **Stewed** *may indicate* an anagram

Stibnite Antimony, Kohl

Stick(ing) (out), Sticks, Sticky, Stuck Adhere, Affix, Agglutinant, Aground, Ash, Ashplant, Atlatl, Attach, Bamboo, Bastinado, Bat, Baton, Bauble, Bayonet, Blackthorn, Bludgeon, Bond, Boondocks, Caman, Cambrel, Cammock, Cane, Celery, Cement, Chalk, Chapman, Clag, Clam(my), Clarty, Clave, Cleave, Cleft, Cling, Clog, Club, Cocktail, Cohere, Coinhere, Composing, Control, Crab, Crosier, Cross(e), Crotch, Crozier, Crummack, Crummock, Cue, Distaff, Divining-rod, Dog, Dure, Endure, Fag(g)ot, Firewood, Fix, Flak, Founder, Fuse, Gad(e), Gaid, Gambrel, Gelatine, Glair, Gliadin, Glit, Glue, Goad, Gold, Goo, Gore, Ground-ash, Gum, Gunge, Gunk, Harpoon, Hob, Hurley, Immobile, Impale, Inhere, Isinglass, Jab, Jam, Joss, Jut, Kebbie, Kid, Kierie, Kindling, Kip, Kiri, Knife, Knitch, Knobkerrie, Ko, Lance, Lath(i), Lathee, Lentisk, Limy, Lug, Message, Minder, Molinet, Needle, Orange, Parasitic, Paste, Penang-lawyer, Persist, Phasmid, Piceous, Pierce, Piolet, Plaster, Pogo, Pole, Posser, Pot, Protrude, Protuberant, Pugol, Q-tip, Quarterstaff, Rash, Ratten, Rhubarb, Rhythm, Rod, Ropy, Scouring, Seat, Shillela(g)h, Shooting, Size, Ski, Smudge, Spanish windlass, Spear, Spurtle, Squail(er), Staff, Stand, Stang, Stob, Stodgy, Supplejack, Swagger, Switch, Swizzle, Swordstick, Tacamahac,

Tack(y), Tally, Tar, Thick, Throwing, Toddy, Tokotoko, Truncheon, Trunnion, Twig, Vare, Viscid, Viscous, Waddy, Wait, Walking, Wand, White, Woolder, Woomera(ng), Yardwand
Sticker Araldite®, Barnacle, Bumper, Bur, Glue, Label, Limpet, Partisan, Poster, Slogan
Stickler Pedant, Poser, Problem, Purist, Rigid, Rigorist, Tapist
Stiff, Stiffen(er), Stiffening, Stiffness Anchylosis, Angular, Ankylosis, Baleen, Bandoline, Brace, Buckram, Budge, Corpse, Corpus, Dear, Defunct, Expensive, Formal, Frore(n), Frorn(e), Gammy, Goner, Grommet, Gut, Hard, Lignin, Mort, Myotonia, Petrify, Pokerish, Prim, Ramrod, Rigid, Rigor, Rigor mortis, Sad, Set, Shank-iron, Size, Solid, Starch, Stark, Stay, Steeve, Stieve, Stilted, Stoor, Stour, Stowre, Sture, Trubenize®, Unbending, Unyielding, Whalebone, Wigan, Wooden
Stifle Crush, Dampen, Depress, Funk, Muffle, Scomfish, Smore, Smother, Stive, Strangle
Stigma(tise) Blemish, Brand, Carpel, Discredit, Note, Slur, Smear, Spot, → STAIN, Wound
Stile Gate, Slamming, Steps, Sty
Stiletto Bodkin, Heel, Knife
Still Accoy, Airless, Alembic, Assuage, Becalm, Calm, Check, Current, Doggo, Ene, Even(ness), Freeze-frame, Higher, Howbe, However, Hush, Illicit, Inactive, Inanimate, Inert, Kill, Languid, Limbec(k), Lull, Motionless, Nevertheless, Nonetheless, Patent, Peaceful, Photograph, Placate, Placid, Posé, Pot, Quiescent, Quiet, Resting, Silent, Snapshot, Soothe, Stagnant, Static, Stationary, Though, Yet
Stilt Avocet, Bird, Poaka, Prop, Scatch
Stilted Formal, Pedantic, Stiff, Unruffled, Wooden
Stimulate, Stimulus, Stimulant, Stimulation Activate, Adrenaline, Anilingus, Ankus, Antigen, Aperitif, Arak, Arouse, Auxin, Benny, Caffeine, Cinder, Clomiphene, Coca, Conditioned, Coramine, Cue, Dart, Dex(edrine)®, Digitalin, Digoxin, Egg, Energise, Erotogenic, Evoke, Excitant, Fillip, Foreplay, Fuel, Galvanize, Ginger, Goad, Grains of Paradise, G-spot, Guinea grains, Hormone, Incentive, Incite, Innerve, Inspire, Irritate, Jog, Key, K(h)at, Kick, L-dopa, Mneme, Motivate, Nikethamide, Oestrus, Oxytocin, Paraphilia, Pemoline, Pep, Peyote, Philtre, Pick-me-up, Piquant, Pituitrin, Potentiate, Prod, Promote, Provoke, Psych, Qat, Rim, Roborant, → ROUSE, Rowel, Rub, Sassafras, Sensuous, Spur, Sting, Stir, Tannin, Tar, Theine, Tickle, Tik-tik, Titillate, Tone, Tonic, Tropism, Unconditioned, Upper, Whet(stone), Wintergreen, Winter's bark
Sting(ing) Aculeate, Barb, Bite, Cheat, Cnida, Goad, Nematocyst, Nettle(tree), Overcharge, Perceant, Piercer, Poignant, Prick, Provoke, Pungent, Rile, Scorpion, Sephen, Smart, Spice, Stang, Stimulus, Surcharge, Tang, Tingle, Trichocyst, Urent, Urtica
Sting-ray Sephen, Trygon
Stingy Cheeseparing, Chintzy, Close, Costive, Hard, Illiberal, Mean, Miserly, Narrow, Near, Niggardly, Nippy, Parsimonious, Skimpy, Snippy, Snudge, Tight(wad), Tight-arse
▷ **Stingy** *may indicate* something that stings
Stink(er), Stinking, Stinks Abroma, Atoc, Atok, Brock, Cacodyl, Crepitate, Desman, Fetor, Foumart, Guff, Heel, Hellebore, Malodour, Mephitis, Miasma, Ming, Niff, Noisome, Pong, Ponk, Rasse, Reek, Rich, Science, → SMELL, Sondeli, Stench, Teledu
Stinkbird Hoa(c)tzin
Stint Chore, Economise, Limit, Scamp, Scantle, Scrimp, Share, Skimp

Stipend Ann(at), Annexure, Pay, Prebend, Remuneration, Salary, Wages
Stipulate, Stipulation Clause, Condition, Covenant, Insist, Provision, Proviso, Rider, Specify
Stipule Ocrea
Stir(red), Stirring Accite, Admix, Ado, Afoot, Agitate, Amo(o)ve, Animate, Annoy, Arouse, Awaken, Bird, Bother, Bustle, Buzz, Can, Churn, Cooler, Excite, Foment, Furore, Fuss, Gaol, Hectic, Impassion, Incense, Incite, Inflame, Instigate, Insurrection, Intermix, Jee, Jog, Kitty, Limbo, Live, → **MIX**, Move, Noy, Paddle, Penitentiary, Poach, Poss, Pother, → **PRISON**, Prod, Provoke, Quad, Quatch, Quetch, Quinche, Qui(t)ch, Quod, Rabble, Rear, Roil, Rouse, Roust, Rummage, Rustle, Sod, Steer, Styre, Swizzle, To-do, Upstart, Wake
▷ **Stir(red), Stirring** *may indicate* an anagram
Stirrup (guard) Bone, Footrest, Footstall, Gambado, Iron, Stapes, Tapadera, Tapadero
Stitch(ing), Stitch up Bargello, Basket, Baste, Blanket, Blind, Box, Buttonhole, Cable, Chain, Couching, Crewel, Crochet, Cross, Daisy, Embroider, Fancy, Feather, Fell, Flemish, Florentine, Garter, Gathering, Grospoint, Hem, Herringbone, Honeycomb, Insertion, Kettle, Knit, Lazy daisy, Lock, Middle, Monk's seam, Moss, Needle, Open, Overcast, Overlock, Pearl, Petit point, Pinwork, Plain, Purl, Queen, Rag, Railway, Rib, Rope, Running, Saddle, Satin, Screw, Sew, Slip, Smocking, Spider, Stab, Stay, Steek, Stem, Stockinette, Stocking, Straight, Sutile, Suture, Tack, Tailor's tack, Tent, Topstitch, Vandyke, Wheat-ear, Whip, Whole, Zigzag
Stock(ed), Stocks, Stocky Aerie, Aery, Alpha, Ambulance, Amplosome, Barometer, Blue-chip, Bouillon, Bree, Breech, Brompton, Buffer, But(t), Capital, Cards, Carry, Cattle, Choker, Cippus, Common, Congee, Conjee, Court-bouillon, Cravat, Dashi, Debenture, Delta, Die, Endomorph, Equip, Evening, Fumet, Fund, Gamma, Gear(e), Government, Graft, Gun, Handpiece, He(a)rd, Hilt, Hoosh, Industrial, Intervention, Inventory, Joint, Just-in-time, Kin, Larder, Laughing, Line, Little-ease, Locuplete, Night-scented, Omnium, Pigeonhole, Preferred, Pycnic, Race, Ranch, Recovery, Rep(ertory), Replenish, Reserve, Rolling, Root, Scrip, Seed, Shorts, Soup, Squat, Staple, Steale, Steelbow, Stirp(e)s, → **STORE**, Strain, Stubby, Supply, Surplus, Talon, Tap, Taurus, Team, Tie, Trite, Trust(ee), Utility, Virginian, Water
Stockade Barrier, Eureka, Zare(e)ba, Zereba, Zeriba
Stocking(s) Bas, Body, Boot-hose, Fishnet, Hogger, Hose, Leather, Legwarmer, Moggan, Netherlings, Netherstocking, Nylons, Popsock, Seamless, Sheer, Sock, Spattee, Support, Surgical, Tights
Stockman, Stockbroker Broker, Jobber, Neatherd
Stodge, Stodgy Dull, Filling, Heavy
Stoic(al) Impassive, Job, Logos, Patient, Philosophical, Plato, Porch, Seneca(n), Spartan, Stolid, Zeno
Stoke(r), Stokes Bram, Coal-trimmer, Fire(man), Fuel, S, Shovel
Stole(n) Bent, Epitrachelion, Hot, Maino(u)r, Manner, Manor, Nam, Orarion, Orarium, Reft, Scarf, Soup, Staw, Tippet, Tweedle, Waif, Wrap
Stolid Beefy, Deadpan, Dull, Impassive, Phlegmatic, Po(-faced), Thickset, Wooden
Stomach(ic) Abdomen, Abomasum, Accept, Appetite, Belly, Bible, Bingy, Bonnet, Bread-basket, Brook, C(o)eliac, Corporation, Epigastrium, Epiploon, Fardel-bag, Gaster, Gizzard, Gut, Heart, Jejunum, King's-hood, Kite, Kyte, Little Mary, Manyplies, Mary, Maw, Mesaraic, Midriff, Omasum, Opisthosoma, Paunch, Potbelly, Propodon, Proventriculus, Psalterium, Puku, Pylorus, Read, Rennet, Reticulum, Rumen, Stand, Stick, Swagbelly, → **SWALLOW**, Tripe, Tum, Tun-belly, Urite, Vell, Venter, Wame, Washboard, Wem, Zingiber

Stomach-ache Colic, Colitis, Collywobbles, Gastralgia, Giardiasis, Gripe, Gutrot, Mulligrubs

Stone(s), Stone age, Stoned, Stony Blotto, Cast, Drunk, Henge, Imposing, Ink, Inukshuk, Lucky, Lydian, Mort, Niobe(an), Pelt, Precious, Putting, Rolling, Seeing, Sermon, Standing, Step(ping), Through, Touch, Tusking

STONES

2 letters:
St

3 letters:
Gem
Hog
Pit
Rag
Tin

4 letters:
Bath
Blue
Celt
Door
Flag
Hone
Horn
Iron
Jasp
Kerb
Lias
Lime
Lode
Onyx
Opal
Plum
Ragg
Sard
Skew
Slab
Soap
Tile
Trap

5 letters:
Agate
Amber
Balas
Beryl
Black
Chalk
Chert
Coade

Culch
Drupe
Flint
Gooly
Grape
Jewel
Kenne
Lapis
Logan
Menah
Metal
Mocha
Paste
Prase
Pumie
Quern
Quoin
Quoit
Rubin
Rufus
Rybat
Satin
Scone
Scree
Slate
Slick
Sneck
Stela
Stele
Topaz
Wacke
Wyman

6 letters:
Amazon
Arthur
Ashlar
Ashler
Baetyl
Bezoar
Brinny
Chesil
Chisel
Cobble

Coping
Cultch
Dolmen
Flusch
Fossil
Gibber
Gooley
Goolie
Gravel
Humite
Iolite
Jargon
Jasper
Kidney
Kingle
Ligure
Lithic
Menhir
Metate
Mihrab
Mosaic
Muller
Nutlet
Oamaru
Paving
Pebble
Pot-lid
Pumice
Pyrene
Rip-rap
Samian
Sarsen
Scarab
Summer
Tanist
Yonnie

7 letters:
Asteria
Avebury
Blarney
Bologna
Boulder
Breccia

Callais
Cat's eye
Chuckie
Clinker
Curling
Girasol
Granite
Hyacine
Hyalite
Jargoon
Lia-fail
Lithoid
Moabite
Olivine
Parpane
Parpend
Parpent
Pennant
Peridot
Perpend
Perpent
Petrous
Pudding
Purbeck
Putamen
Rocking
Rosetta
Rubbing
Sardine
Sardius
Sarsden
Scaglia
Schanse
Schanze
Smaragd
Staddle
Tektite
Telamon
Thunder
Trilith
Tripoli
Urolith

8 letters:	Onychite	Chondrite	Chalcedony
Aerolite	Parpoint	Cornelian	Draconites
Aerolith	Peastone	Crossette	Enhydritic
Amethyst	Petrosal	Dichroite	Foundation
Asteroid	Phengite	Firestone	Gastrolith
Baguette	Pisolite	Gannister	Grey-wether
Cabochon	Portland	Greensand	Kimberlite
Calculus	Potstone	Hessonite	Lherzolite
Cinnamon	Rollrich	Hoarstone	Lithophyte
Cromlech	Sapphire	Lithiasis	Pearlstone
Cryolite	Sardonyx	Meteorite	Penny-stone
Ebenezer	Scalpins	Paleolith	Rhinestone
Elf-arrow	Schantze	Pipestone	Sleekstone
Endocarp	Specular	Rubicelle	Slickstone
Essonite	Tonalite	Scagliola	
Ganister	Voussoir	Trilithon	**11 letters:**
Girasole		Turquoise	Pencil-stone
Lapidate	**9 letters:**	Ventifact	Peristalith
Megalith	Alabaster		
Menamber	Asparagus	**10 letters:**	**12 letters:**
Monolith	Cairngorm	Adamantine	Carton-pierre
Nephrite	Carnelian	Alectorian	Philosopher's
Omphalos	Cholelith	Aragonites	

Stone-crop Orpin(e), Sedum, Succulent
Stone-pusher Sisyphus
Stone-thrower Bal(lista), Catapult, David, Mangonel, Onager, Perrier, Sling, Trebuchet
Stone-wall(er) Block, Jackson, Mule, Revet
Stoneware Crouch-ware
Stone-worker Jeweller, Knapper, Sculptor
Stooge Butt, Cat's-paw, Feed, Straight man
Stook(s) Sheaf, Stack, Thr(e)ave
Stool Buffet, Coppy, Cracket, Creepie, Cricket, Cucking, Curule, Cutty, Ducking, Faeces, Hassock, Litany, Milking, Music, Piano, Pouf(fe), Repentance, Ruckseat, Seat, Sir-reverence, Step, Stercoral, Sunkie, Taboret, Tripod, Tripos, Turd
Stoop Bend, Condescend, C(o)urb, Crouch, Daine, Deign, Incline, Porch, Slouch
Stop(page), Stopcock, Stopper, Stopping Abort, Adeem, An(n)icut, Arrest, Avast, Bait, Ba(u)lk, Bide, Blin, Block, Brake, Buffer, Bung, Canting-coin, → CEASE, Cessation, Chapter, Check, Checkpoint, Cheese, Cholestasis, Clarabella, Clarino, Clarion, Clog, Close, Colon, Comfort, Comma, Conclude, Cork, Coupler, Cremo(r)na, Cremorne, Cromorna, Cut, Deactivate, Debar, Demurral, Desist, Deter, Devall, Diapason, Diaphone, Discontinue, Discourage, Dit, Dolce, Dot, Dulciana, Echo, Embargo, End, Fare stage, Field, Fifteenth, Flag, Flue, Flute, Foreclose, Foundation, Fr(a)enum, Freeze, Full, Full point, Gag, Gamba, Gemshorn, Glottal, Gong, Halt, Hamza(h), Hartal, Heave to, Hinder, Hitch, Ho, Hoa, Hoh, Hold, Hoy, Inhibit, Intermit, Ischuria, Jam, Kibosh, Let-up, Lill, Lin, Lute, Media, Mutation, Nasard, Oboe, Obstruent, Obturate, Occlude, Oppilate, Organ, Outage, Outspan, Pause, Period, Piccolo, Pit, Plug, Point, Poop, Preclude, Prevent, Principal, Prorogue, Pull-in, Pull over, Pull-up, Punctuate, Pyramidon, Quash, Quint, Quit, Racket, Red, Reed, Refrain, Register, Rein, Remain, Request, Rest, Salicet,

Salicional, Scotch, Screw-top, Semi-colon, Sese, Sesquialtera, Sext, Sist, Snub,
Solo, Spigot, Stall, Stanch, Standstill, Stash, Stasis, Station, Staunch, Stay, Stent,
Stive, Strike, Subbase, Subbass, Suction, Supersede, Suppress, Suspend, T, Tab,
Tamp(ion), Tap, Tenuis, Terminate, Toby, Toho, Truck, Twelfth, Voix celeste, Vox
angelica, Vox humana, Waldflute, Waldhorn, Waypoint, When, Whistle, Whoa
Stopgap Caretaker, Gasket, Gaskin, Interim, Makeshift, Pis aller, Temporary
Storage, Store(house) Accumulate, Archive, Armoury, Arsenal, Associative,
Backing, Barn, Bin, Bottle, Bottom drawer, Boxroom, Bunker, Buttery, Cache,
Capacitance, Cell, Cellar, Chain, Clamp, Clipboard, Convenience, Co-op(erative),
Co-operative, Cootch, Core, Cupboard, Cutch, Database, Deli, Dene-hole,
Dépanneur, Department(al), Depository, Depot, Dime, Discount, Dolia, Dolly-shop,
Elevator, Emporium, Ensile, Entrepot, Étape, Fund, Galleria, Garner, Genizah,
Girnal, Glory hole, Go-down, Granary, Groceteria, Hive, → HOARD, Hog, Hold,
Hope chest, House, Houseroom, Humidor, Husband, Hypermarket, Imbarn,
Larder, Lastage, Lazaretto, Liquor, Locker, Lumber room, Magazine, Main,
Mart, Mattamore, Memory, Mine, Morgue, Mothball, Mow, Multiple, Nest-egg,
Off-licence, One-stop, Package, Pantechnicon, Pantry, Pithos, Provision, Pumped,
Rack(ing), RAM, Repertory, Reposit, ROM, Root house, Sector, Shed, → SHOP,
Silage, Silo, Spence, Spooling, Springhouse, Squirrel, Stack, Stash, Stock, Stockpile,
Stockroom, Stow, Superbaza(a)r, Superette, Supermarket, Supply, Tack-room,
Tank, Thesaurus, Tithe-barn, Tommy-shop, Virtual, Volutin, Warehouse,
Woodshed, Woodyard, Wool (shed)
▶ **Storey** see STORY
Stork Adjutant, Antigone, Argala, Bird, Jabiru, Marabou(t), Marg, Saddlebill,
Shoebill, Wader, Whale-headed, Wood, Wood ibis
Stork's bill Erodium
Storm(y) Ablow, Adad, Assail, Attack, Baguio, Blizzard, Bluster, Bourasque,
Brouhaha, Buran, Calima, Charge, Cockeye(d) bob, Cyclone, Devil, Dirty, Dust,
Electric, Enlil, Expugn, Furore, Gale, Gusty, Haboob, Hurricane, Ice, Line,
Magnetic, Monsoon, Onset, Oragious, Pelter, Rage(ful), Raid, Rain, Rampage, Rant,
Rave, Red spot, Rugged, Rush, Shaitan, Snorter, Squall, Sumatra, Tea-cup, Tebbad,
Tempest, Tornade, Tornado, Tropical, Unruly, Violent, Weather, Willy-willy,
Wroth, Zu
▷ **Stormy** may indicate an anagram
Story, Storyline, Storey, Stories Account, Allegory, Anecdote, Apocrypha,
Arthuriana, Attic, Bar, Basement, Baur, Bawr, Biog, Blood and thunder, Chestnut,
Clearstory, Clerestory, Cock and bull, Conte, Cover, Decameron, Edda, Epic,
Episode, Étage, Exclusive, Exemplum, Fable, Fabliau, Feature, Fib, Fiction, Flat,
Floor, Folk-tale, Gag, Geste, Ghost, Glurge, Hard-luck, Heptameron, Hitopadesa,
Horror, Idyll, Iliad, Jataka, Lee, Legend, Lie, Mabinogion, Märchen, Mezzanine,
Myth(os), Mythus, Narrative, Nouvelle, Novel(la), Oratorio, Parable, Passus,
Pentameron, Photo, Plot, Rede, Report, Romance, Rumour, Saga, Scoop, Script,
Serial, SF, Shaggy dog, Shocker, Short, Smoke-room, Sob, Spiel, Spine-chiller,
Splash, Stage, Success, Tale, Tall, Thread, Thriller, Tier, Triforium, Upper, Version,
Yarn
Story-teller Aesop, Fibber, Griot, Liar, Munchausen, Narrator, Raconteur,
Shannachie, Tusitala, Uncle Remus
Stoup Benitier, Bucket, Vessel
Stout(ness) Ale, Beer, Black velvet, Burly, Chopping, Chubby, Embonpoint,
Endomorph, Entire, Fat, Fubsy, Hardy, Humpty-dumpty, Lusty, Manful, Milk,
Obese, Overweight, Porter, Portly, Potbelly, Robust, Stalwart, Stalworth, Sta(u)nch,

Strong, Stuggy, Sturdy, Substantial, Tall, Velvet

Stove Baseburner, Break, Calefactor, Chauf(f)er, Cockle, Cooker, Cooktop, Furnace, Gasfire, Oven, Potbelly, Primus®, Range, Salamander

Stow Cram, Flemish (down), Load, Pack, Rummage, Stack, Stash, Steeve

Strabismus Squint

Straddle, Straddling Bestride, Enjamb(e)ment, Strodle

Strafe Bombard, Shell, Shoot

Straggle(r), Straggly Estray, Gad, Meander, Ramble, Rat-tail, Spidery, Sprawl, Stray, Wander

Straight(en), Straightness Align, Bald, Beeline, Correct, Die, Direct, Downright, Dress, Frank, Gain, Het(ero), Home, Honest, Lank, Legit, Level, Neat, Normal, Ortho-, Orthotropous, Rectilineal, Rectitude, Righten, Sheer, Slap, Tidy, True, Unbowed, Uncurl, Unlay, Upright, Veracious, Virgate

Straight edge Lute, Ruler

Straightfaced Agelast

Straightforward Candid, Direct, Downright, Easy, Even, Forthright, Honest, Jannock, Level, Plain sailing, Pointblank, Simple

Straight-haired Leiotrichous

Strain(ed), Strainer, Straining Agonistic, Ancestry, Aria, Breed, Bulk, Carol, Clarify, Colander, Distend, Drawn, Effort, Exert, Filter, Filtrate, Fit, Fitt(e), Force, Fray, Fytt(e), Intense, Kind, Melody, Milsey, Minus, Molimen, Music, Note, Overtask, Passus, Percolate, Plus, Pressure, Pull, Purebred, Rack, Raring, Reck(an), Repetitive, Retch, Rick, Seep, Seil(e), Set, Shear, Sieve, Sift, Sile, Stape, Start, Stirps, Stock, Streak, Stress, Stretch, Sye, Tamis, Tammy, Tax, Tems(e), Tenesmus, Tense, Tension, Threnody, Try, Tune, Unease, Vein, Vice, Work, Wrick

Strait(s) Bab el Mandeb, Basilan, Bass, Bering, Bosp(h)orus, Canso, Channel, Condition, Cook, Crisis, Cut, Dardanelles, Davis, Denmark, Desperate, Dover, Drake Passage, Euripus, Florida, Formosa, Foveaux, Gat, Gibraltar, Golden Gate, Great Belt, Gut, Hainan, Hormuz, Hudson, Johore, Juan de Fuca, Kattegat, Kerch, Korea, Kyle, Little Belt, Lombok, Mackinac, Magellan, Malacca, Menai, Messina, Mona Passage, Narrow, North Channel, Otranto, Palk, Predicament, Soenda, Solent, Sound, St, Sumba, Sunda, Taiwan, Tatar, Tiran, Torres, Tsugaru, Windward Passage

Straiten(ed) Impecunious, Impoverish, Poor, Restrict

Strait-laced Blue-nosed, Narrow, Prig, Primsie, Prudish, Puritan, Stuffy

Strand(ed) Abandon, Aground, Bank, Beach, Desert, Fibre, Haugh, Hexarch, Isolate, Lock, Maroon, Neaped, Ply, Rice, Rope, Shore, Sliver, Thread, Three-ply, Tress, Twist, Wisp

Strange(ness), Stranger Alien, Aloof, Amphitryon, Curious, Dougal, Eerie, Exotic, Ferly, Foreign, Fraim, Frem(d), Fremit, Frenne, Funny, Guest, Jimmy, Malihini, New, Novel, Odd(ball), Outlandish, Outsider, Quare, Queer, Rum, S, Screwy, Selcouth, Singular, Surreal, Tea-leaf, Uncanny, Unco, Uncommon, Unfamiliar, Unked, Unket, Unkid, Unused, Unusual, Wacky, Weird, Wondrous

▷ **Strange** *may indicate* an anagram

Strangle(r) Choke, Garotte, Jugulate, Suppress, Throttle, Thug(gee)

Strap(ping) Able-bodied, Band, Barber, Beat, Bowyangs, Braces, Brail, Braw, Breeching, Browband, Cheekpiece, Crownpiece, Crupper, Cuir-bouilli, Curb, Deckle, Girth, Halter, Harness, Holdback, Jess, Jock(ey), Kicking, Larrup, Lash, Ligule, Lorate, Lore, Manly, Martingale, Nicky-tam, Octopus, Overcheck, Pandy, Rand, Rein, Robust, Shoulder, Sling, Spaghetti, Spider, Strop, Surcingle, Suspender, T, Tab, Taws(e), T-bar, Thong, Throatlash, Throatlatch, Trace,

Tump-line, Wallop, Watch, Watchband

Stratagem, Strategist, Strategy Artifice, Clausewitz, Contrivance, Coup, Deceit, Device, Dodge, Exit, Fetch, Finesse, Fraud, Heresthetic, Kaupapa, Lady Macbeth, Maskirovka, Masterstroke, Maximum, Minimax, Plan, Rope-a-dope, → RUSE, Salami, Scheme, Scorched earth, Sleight, Subterfuge, Tack, Tactic(s), Tactician, Trick, Wile

Stratum, Strata Bed, Coal Measures, Kar(r)oo, Layer, Neogene, Permian, Schlieren, Seam, Syncline

Straw(s), Strawy Balibuntal, Boater, Buntal, Chaff, Cheese, Halm, Hat, Haulm, Hay, Insubstantial, Last, Leghorn, Monkey-pump, Nugae, Oaten, Panama, Parabuntal, Pea(se), Pedal, Rush, Short, Sipper, Stalk, Stramineous, Strammel, Strummel, Stubble, Trifles, Truss, Wisp, Ye(a)lm

Strawberry Alpine, Barren, Birthmark, Fragaria, Fraise, Garden, Hautbois, Hautboy, Potentilla, Wild

Stray Abandoned, Chance, Depart, Deviate, Digress, Err, Forwander, Foundling, Gamin, Maverick, Meander, Misgo, Pye-dog, Ramble, Roam, Sin, Straggle, Streel, Traik, Unowned, Waff, Waif, Wander

Streak(ed), Streaker, Streaky Archimedes, Bended, Blue, Brindle, Comet, Flaser, Flash, Fleck, Freak, Hawked, Highlights, Lace, Layer, Leonid, Lowlight, Marble, Mark, Merle, Mottle, Primitive, Race, Run, Schlieren, Seam, Shot, Striate, Striga, Strip(e), Vein, Venose, Vibex, Waif, Wake, Wale, Yellow

Stream Acheron, Anabranch, Arroyo, Beam, Beck, Bogan, Bourne, Brook, Burn, Consequent, Course, Current, Driblet, Fast, Flow, Flower, Freshet, Gulf, Gush, Headwater, Influent, Jet, Kill, Lade, Lane, Leet, Logan, Meteor, Nala, Nalla(h), Nulla(h), Obsequent, Pokelogan, Pour, Pow, Riffle, Rill, River, Rivulet, Rubicon, Run, Runnel, Sike, Slough, Spill, Spruit, Star, Strand, Streel, Subsequent, Syke, The Fleet, Third, Thrutch, Tide-race, Torrent, Tributary, Trickle, Trout, Watercourse, Water-splash, Winterbourne

Streamer Banderol(e), Bandrol, Banner(all), Bannerol, Pennon, Pinnet, Ribbon, Tape, Tippet, Vane

Streamline(d), Streamliner Clean, Fair, Fairing, Simplify, Sleek, Slim

Street Alley, Ave(nue), Bay, Bowery, Broad, Carey, Carnaby, Cato, Causey, Champs Elysées, Cheapside, Civvy, Close, Corso, Court, Crescent, Downing, Drive, Easy, Fleet, Gate, Grub, Harley, High(way), Kármán vortex, Lane, Lombard, Main, Meuse, Mews, One-way, Parade, Paseo, Queer, Road, Sesame, Side, Sinister, St, Strand, Terrace, Thoroughfare, Threadneedle, Throgmorton, Two-way, Vortex, Wall, Wardour, Watling, Way, Whitehall

Street arab Mudlark

Streetcar Desire, Tram

Strength(en), Strengthened, Strengthening Afforce, Anneal, Asset, Ausforming, Bant, Beef, Brace, Brawn, Build, Confirm, Consolidate, Enable, Energy, Field, Fish, Foison, Force, Forte, Fortify, Freshen, Grit, Heart, Herculean, Horn, Intensity, Iron, Line, Main, Man, Might, Munite, Muscle, Nerve, → POWER, Prepotence, Pre-stress, Proof, Reinforce, Roborant, Shear, Sinew, Spike, Stamina, Steel, Sthenia, Stoutness, → STRONG, Tensile, Thews, Titration, Ultimate, Unity, Vim, Yield

Strenuous Arduous, Effort, Exhausting, Hard, Laborious, Vehement

Strephon Rustic, Wooer

Stress(ed) Accent, Arsis, Birr, Brunt, Careworn, Emphasis, Ictus, Impress, Italicise, Marcato, Orthotonesis, Oxytone, Paroxytone, Post-traumatic, Primary, Proof, PTSD, Rack, Ram, Rhythm, RSI, Secondary, Sentence, Sforzando, Shear, Strain,

Taut, Tense, → TENSION, Try, Underline, Underscore, Urge, Wind shear, Word, Yield (point)
Stretch(able), Stretched, Stretcher, Stretching Belt, Brick, Crane, Distend, Draw, Ectasis, Eke, Elastic, Elongate, Exaggerate, Expanse, Extend, Extensile, Farthingale, Fib, Frame, Give, Gurney, Home, Lengthen, Litter, Narrows, Outreach, Pallet, Pandiculation, Porrect, Procrustes, Prolong, Protend, Pull, Rack, Rax, → REACH, Sentence, Shiner, Span, Spell, Spread, Spreadeagle, Strain, Streak, Taut, Tend, Tense, Tensile, Tenter, Term, Time, Tract, Tractile, Tree, Trolley
Stretcher-bearer Fuzzy-wuzzy angel
Striate Lineolate, Vein
Stricken Beset, Hurt, Overcome, Shattered
Strict Dour, Exacting, Harsh, Literal, Medic, Narrow, Orthodox, Penal, Proper, Puritanical, Rigid, Rigorous, Severe, Spartan, Stern, Strait(-laced), Stringent
Stride Gal(l)umph, Leg, Lope, March, Pace, Piano, Stalk, Sten, Stend, Straddle, Stroam, Strut, Stump
Strident Brassy, Grinding, Harsh, Raucous, Screech
Strife Bargain, Barrat, Bate(-breeding), Colluctation, Conflict, Conteck, Contest, Discord, Disharmony, Dissension, Feud, Food, Friction, Ignoble, Scrap(ping), Sturt
Strike(s), Striker, Striking, Strike out Affrap, Air, Alight, Annul, Appulse, Arresting, Attitude, Backhander, Baff, Band, Bandh, Bang, Bash, Bat, Baton, Batsman, Batter, Beat, Belabour, Better, Biff, Black, Bla(u)d, Bonanza, Bop, British disease, Buff, Buffet, Bund(h), Butt, Cane, Catch, Chime, Chip, Clap, Clash, Clatch, Clip, Clock, Clout, Club, Cob, Collide, Conk, Constitutional, Coup, Cue, Cuff, Dad, Dent, Dev(v)el, Ding, Dint, Dismantle, Distingué, Douse, Dowse, Dramatic, Drive, Dush, Éclat, Événement, Fet(ch), Fillip, Firk, Fist, Flail, Flog, Frap, General, Get, Gnash, Go-slow, Gowf, Hail, Handsome, Hartal, Head-butt, → HIT, Horn, Hour, Hunger, Ictus, Illision, Impact, Impinge, Impress, Jarp, Jaup, Jole, Joll, Joule, Jowl, Knock, Lam, Lambast, Laser, Lay(-off), Lightning, Match, Middle, Mint, Notable, Noticeable, Official, Out, Pash, Pat(ter), Pat, Pean, Peen, Pein, Pene, Percuss, Picket, Pize, Plectrum, Pronounced, Pummel, Punch, Ram, Rap, Remarkable, Rolling, Roquet, Salient, Scrub, Scutch, Shank, Sick out, Sideswipe, Signal, Sitdown, Sit-in, Slam, Slap, Slat, Slog, Slosh, Smack, Smash, Smite, Sock, Souse, Sowce, Sowse, Spank, Stayaway, Stop(page), Stub, Swap, Swat, Swinge, Swipe, Swop, Sympathy, Tan, Tapotement, Tat, Thump, Thwack, Tip, Token, Tonk, Tripper, Twat, Unconstitutional, Unofficial, Walk-out, Wallop, Wap, Whack, Whale, Whang, Whap, Wherret, Who does what, Whomp, Whop, Wick, Wildcat, Wipe, Wondrous, Zap
Strike-breaker Blackleg, Fink, Rat, Scab
String(s), Stringy Band, Bant, Beads, Bootlace, Bow, Bowyang, Cello, Chalaza, Chanterelle, Cord, Cosmic, Creance, Cremaster, Drill, Enfilade, Fiddle, Fillis, First, G, Glass, Gut, Henequin, Heniquin, Hypate, Idiot, Injection, Keyed, Kill, Lace, Lag, Leading, Lichanos, Macramé, Mese, Necklace, Nete, Nicky-tam, Oil, Paramese, Pledget, Production, Proviso, Purse, Quint, Ripcord, Rope, Rough, Second, Series, Shoe(-tie), Sinewy, Snare, Spit, Stable, Straggle, Strand, Sympathetic, Team, Tendon, Thairm, Tie, Tough, Train, Trite, Viola, Violin, Wreathed
String-course Moulding, Table
Stringent Extreme, Rigid, Severe, Strict, Urgent
Strip(ped), Stripper, Striptease Airfield, Armband, Band, Bare, Bark, Batten, Belt, Bereave, Bimetallic, Blowtorch, Casparian, Chippendale, Comic, Cote, Defoliate, Denude, Deprive, Derobe, Despoil, Devest, Disbark, Dismantle, Dismask, Disrobe, Divest, Dosing, Drag, Ecdysiast, Ecdysis, Écorché, Fannel(l), Fiche, Film, Flashing,

Flaught, Flay, Fleece, Flench, Flense, Flight, Flinch, Flounce, Flype, Furring, Gaza, Goujon, Hatband, Infula, Jib, Label, Landing, Lap-dancer, Lardon, Lath, Ledge, Linter, List, Littoral, Loading, Locust, Maniple, Median, Möbius, Panhandle, Parting, Peel, Pillage, Pluck, Pull, Puttee, Puttie, Rand, Raunch, Raw, Ribbon, Ring-bark, Roon, Royne, Rumble, Rund, Runway, Screed, Scrow, Shear, Shed, Shim, Shuck, Skin, Slat, Slit, Sliver, Spellican, Spilikin, Spill(ikin), Splat, Splent, Spline, Splint, Splinter, Spoil, Straik, Strake, Strap, Streak, Strop, Sugar soap, Swath, Sweatband, Tack, Tear, Tee, Thong, Tirl, Tirr, Tongue, Uncase, Unclothe, Undeck, Undress, Unfrock, Unrig, Unrip, Unrobe, Unvaile, Valance, Weather, Widow, Zone

Stripe(d) Band, Bausond, Candy, Chevron, Cingulum, Cove, Endorse, Go-faster, Lance-jack, Laticlave, Line, List, Magnetic, → **NCO**, Ombré, Pale, Paly, Pin, Pirnie, Pirnit, Slash, Snip, Straik, Strake, Streak, Stroke, Tabaret, Tabby, Tiger, Tragelaph(us), Vitta, Weal

Strive, Striving Aim, Aspire, → **ATTEMPT**, Contend, Endeavour, Enter, Kemp, Labour, Nisus, Pingle, Press, Strain, Struggle, Toil, Try, Vie

Stroke Apoplex(y), Backhander, Bat, Bisque, Blow, Boast, Breast, Butterfly, Caress, Carom, Chip, Chop, Counterbuff, Coup, Coy, Crawl, Dash, Dint, Dog(gy)-paddle, Down-bow, Drear(e), Drere, Dropshot, Effleurage, Estrarnazone, Exhaust, Feat, Flick, Fondle, Foozle, Forehand, Glance, Ground, Hairline, Hand(er), Ictus, Inwick, Jenny, Jole, Joll, Joule, Jowl, Knell, Knock, Lash, Lightning, Like, Line, Loft, Long jenny, Loser, Massé, Oarsman, Oblique, Odd, Off-drive, Outlash, Palp, Paw, Pot-hook, Pull, Punto reverso, Put(t), Reverso, Ridding straik, Roquet, Rub, Scart, Scavenge, Sclaff, Scoop, Seizure, Sheffer's, Short jenny, Sider, Sixte, Slash, Smooth, Solidus, Spot, Strike, Stripe, Sweep, Swipe, Tact, Tittle, Touch, Touk, Trait, Trudgen, Trudgeon, Tuck, Upbow, Virgule, Wale, Whang

Stroll(er), Strolling Ambulate, Bummel, Dander, Daun(d)er, Dawner, Flânerie, Flâneur, Idle, Lounge, Ramble, Saunter, Stravaig, Stray, Toddle, Walk, Walkabout, Wander

Strong(est) Able, Boofy, Brawny, Cast-iron, Doughty, Durable, F, Firm, Fit, Forceful, Forcible, Forte, Full-blown, Hale, Heady, Hercules, High-powered, Humming, Husky, Intense, Mighty, Nappy, Pithy, Pollent, Potent, Powerful, Pungent, Racy, Rank, Robust, Samson, Solid, Stalwart, Stark, Steely, Sthenic, Stiff, Stout, Str, Strapping, → **STRENGTH**, Sturdy, Substantial, Suit, Tarzan, Tenable, Thesis, Thickset, Trusty, Vegete, Vehement, Vigorous, Violent, Virile, Well-built, Well-set, Ya(u)ld

Stronghold Acropolis, Aerie, Bastion, Castle, Citadel, Eyrie, Eyry, Fastness, Fortalice, Fortress, Keep, Kremlin, Redoubt, Tower

Strontium Sr

Strop Leather, Sharpen, Strap

Struck Aghast, Raught, Smitten

Structural, Structure Allotrope, Analysis, Anatomy, Armature, Atomic, Building, Catafalque, Cold frame, Compage(s), Conus, Data, Deep, Edifice, Erection, Fabric, Fairing, Format(ion), Formwork, Frame, Galea, Heterarchy, Hyperbolic, Hyperfine, Ice-apron, Kekulé, Lantern, Macrocosm, Mole, Organic, Palmation, Pediment, Pergola, Phloem, Physique, Pod, Power, Protein, Retinaculum, Set-up, Shape, Skeleton, Sponson, Sporocarp, Squinch, Staging, Stand, Starling, Stylobate, Surface, Syntax, System, Tectonic, Telomere, Texas, Texture, Trabecula, Trochlea, Undercarriage

Struggle, Struggling Agon(ise), Agonistes, Amelia, Buckle, Camp, Chore, Class, Conflict, Contend, Contest, Cope, Debatement, Effort, Encounter, Endeavour,

Fight, Flounder, Grabble, Grapple, Jockey, Kampf, Labour, Luctation, Mill, Pingle, Rat-race, Reluct, Scrabble, Scrape, Scrimmage, Scrum, Scrummage, Scuffle, Slugfest, Sprangle, → **STRIVE**, Toil, Tug, Tussle, Uphill, Vie, War(sle), Wrestle

▷ **Struggle** *may indicate* an anagram

Strum Thrum, Twang, Tweedle, Vamp

Strumpet Cocotte, Harlot, Hiren, Lorette, Paramour, Succubus, Wench

Strut(ter), Strutting Bracket, Brank, Bridging, Cock, Dolphin striker, Flounce, Haught(y), Jet, Kingrod, Longeron, Martingale boom, Member, Nervure, Peacock, Pown, Prance, Prop, Scotch, Shore, Spur, Stalk, Stretcher, Strunt, Swagger, Swank, Tail-boom, Tie-beam

Stuart Anne, James, Pretender

Stub(by) Butt, Counterfoil, Dout, Dowt, Dumpy, Squat, Stob, Stocky

Stubble Ar(r)ish, Bristle, Designer, Hair, Ill-shaven, Stump

Stubborn(ness) Adamant, Bigoted, Bull-headed, Contumacious, Cross-grained, Cussed, Diehard, Dogged, Entêté, Hard(-nosed), Hidebound, Intransigent, Inveterate, Moyl(e), Mulish, Mumpsimus, Obdurate, Obstinate, Opinionated, Ornery, Ortus, Pertinacious, Perverse, Recalcitrant, Reesty, Refractory, Rigwiddie, Rigwoodie, Self-willed, Stiff, Stout, Tenacious, Thrawn, Wrong-headed

Stuck Fast, Glued, Jammed, Set, Stopped, Wedged

Stuck-up Chesty, Highty-tighty, Hoity-toity, La(h)-di-da(h), Proud, Sealed, Vain

Stud(ded) Boss, Cooser, Cripple, Cu(i)sser, Doornail, Farm, Frost, He-man, Knob, Nail, Press, Race, Rivet, Seg, Set, Shear, Sire, Stop

Student(s) Abiturient, Alphabetarian, Alumnus, Apprentice, Bajan, Bejant, Bursar, Bursch(en), Cadet, Catechumen, Class, Coed, Commoner, Dan, Dig, Disciple, Dresser, Dux, Exchange, Exhibitioner, Extensionist, External, Form, Fresher, Freshman, Gownsman, Graduand, Green welly, Gyte, Ikey, Internal, Junior, Kommers, Kyu, → **LEARNER**, Magistrand, Matie, Mature, Medical, Nomologist, NUS, Opsimath, Ordinand, Oxonian, Peking duck, Pennal, Plebe, Poll, Postgraduate, Preppy, Pupil, Reader, Rushee, Sap, → **SCHOLAR**, Self-taught, Semi, Seminar, Seminarian, Shark, Sizar, Sizer, Smug, Softa, Soph(omore), Sophister, Spod, Subsizar, Swot, Templar, Tiro, Tosher, Trainee, Tuft, Tukkie, Tutee, Wedge, Witsie, Wonk, Wooden wedge, Wrangler, Year

Studio(s) Atelier, Bottega, Elstree, Gallery, Pinewood, Workshop

Study, Studies, Studied, Studious, Studying Analyse, Bone, Brown, Carol, Case, Classics, Comparability, Con(ne), Conscious, Consider, Course, Cram, Den, Dig, Étude, Eye, Feasibility, Field, Gen up, Isagogics, Learn, Liberal, Lucubrate, Media, Motion, Mug up, Mull, Muse, Nature, Perusal, Peruse, Pilot, Pore, Post-doctoral, Probe, Read, Recce, Reconnoitre, Research, Reverie, Revise, Sanctum, Sap, Scan, Scrutinise, Shiur, Specialize, Stew, Swot, Take, Time and motion, Trade-off, Tutorial, Typto, Voulu, Work

Stuff(iness), Stuffing, Stuffy Airless, Bombast, Canvas, Close, Cloth, Codswallop, Cram, Crap, Dimity, Farce, Feast, Fiddlesticks, Fill, Force, Forcemeat, Frows(t)y, Frowzy, Fug, Gear, Gobble, Gorge, Guff, Havers, Hooey, Horsehair, Hot, Lard, Line, Linen, → **MATERIAL**, Matter, Musty, No-meaning, Nonsense, Overeat, Pad, Pang, Panne, Pompous, Ram, Replete, Rot, Salpicon, Sate, Satiate, Scrap, Sob, Stap, Steeve, Stew, Stifling, Taxidermy, Trig, Upholster, Wad, Youth

Stultify Repress, Ridicule, Smother

Stumble Blunder, Bobble, Daddle, Err, Falter, Flounder, Founder, Lurch, Peck, Snapper, Stoit, Titubate, Trip

Stump(ed), Stumps, Stumpy Black, Butt, Clump, Fag-end, Floor, More, Nog, Nonplus, Orate, Runt, Scrag, Snag, Snooker, Squab, St, Staddle, Stob, Stock, Stool,

Stub(ble), Stud, Tortillon, Tramp, Truncate, Wicket

Stun(ning), Stunned Astonish, Astound, Awhape, Bludgeon, Concuss, Cosh, Daze, Dazzle, Deafen, Donnard, Donnert, Dove, Drop-dead, Glam, KO, Shell-shocked, Shock, Stoun, Stupefy, Taser®

Stunner Belle, Bobby-dazzler, Cheese, Cosh, Doozy, KO, Peach, Taser®

Stunt(ed) Aerobatics, Confine, Droichy, Dwarf, Escapade, Feat, Gimmick, Hot-dog, Hype, Jehad, Jihad, Loop, Nirl, Puny, Ront(e), Runt, Ruse, Scroggy, Scrub(by), Scrunt(y), Stub, Trick, Wanthriven, Wheelie

Stupefaction, Stupefy(ing), Stupefied Amaze(ment), Assot, Benumb, Catatonic, Dozen, Dumbfound, Etherise, Fuddle, Hocus, Moider, Moither, Narcoses, Numb, Stonne, Stun

Stupid, Stupid person Anserine, Asinine, Besotted, Blockish, Braindead, Crass, Daft, Datal, Dense, Desipient, Dim(wit), Donner(e)d, Dozy, Dull(ard), Fatuous, Flat, Foolish, Gormless, Gross, Half-baked, Hammerheaded, Hare-brained, Inane, Insensate, Insipient, Mindless, Natural, Obtuse, Silly, Thick, Thick-witted, Torpid, Vacuous, Wooden(head)

STUPID PERSON

3 letters:	Clot	Meff	Bumbo
Ass	Cony	Mome	Chick
Auf	Coof	Mong	Chump
Bev	Coot	Mook	Clunk
Bob	Dill	Mutt	Cokes
Cod	Ditz	Nana	Cuddy
Daw	Doat	Nerd	Cully
Div	Does	Nerk	Dicky
Fon	Dolt	Nong	Divvy
Git	Dorb	Nurd	Dorba
Jay	Dork	Ouph	Dubbo
Lob	Dote	Poon	Dumbo
Log	Fogy	Poop	Dummy
Nit	Fool	Prat	Dunce
Oaf	Fozy	Putt	Dweeb
Owl	Gaby	Putz	Eejit
Put	Gaga	Rook	Fogey
Sap	Geck	Simp	Galah
Sot	Gelt	Slow	Golem
Twp	Goat	Stot	Goofy
Wof	Goof	Tony	Goose
Yap	Goon	Twit	Hoser
	Goop	Warb	Idiot
4 letters:	Gorm	Yo-yo	Kerky
Berk	Gouk	Zany	Klutz
Bete	Gowk		Looby
Bobb	Gull	**5 letters:**	Loony
Bozo	Gump	Bevan	Lowne
Burk	Hash	Blent	Moron
Cake	Jaap	Bobby	Neddy
Calf	Jerk	Booby	Ninny
Clod	Lown	Brute	Nitty

Noddy
Ocker
Ouphe
Patch
Plank
Prune
Quo-he
Schmo
Simon
Snipe
Spoon
Stock
Stupe
Sumph
Twerp
Waldo
Wally
Yampy

6 letters:
Bampot
Boodle
Buffer
Cretin
Cuckoo
Cuddie
Dawney
Dickey
Dodkin
Donkey
Doofus
Dottle
Drongo
Gander
Gaupus
Gunsel
Ignaro
Ingram
Ingrum
Josser
Lummox
Lurden
Nidget
Nig-nog
Nincum
Nitwit
Noodle
Nudnik
Numpty

Oxhead
Schlep
Schmoe
Scogan
Sucker
Tavert
Thicko
Tosser
Tumphy
Turkey
Turnip
Wommit
Zombie

7 letters:
Airhead
Asinico
Barmpot
Becasse
Buffoon
Charlie
Damfool
Dawbake
Dim bulb
Dizzard
Donnard
Donnart
Donnert
Fuckwit
Gomeral
Gomeril
Gubbins
Half-wit
Haverel
Insulse
Jackass
Juggins
Jughead
Lurdane
Mafflin
Mampara
Muggins
Palooka
Pampven
Pillock
Pinhead
Plonker
Pot-head
Saphead

Schmock
Schmuck
Schnook
Scoggin
Taivert
Thickie
Tosspot
Want-wit
Wazzock

8 letters:
Abderian
Abderite
Baeotian
Boeotian
Bonehead
Boofhead
Clodpole
Clodpoll
Crackpot
Deadhead
Dickhead
Dipstick
Dodipoll
Dotterel
Dottrell
Dumbbell
Flathead
Gobshite
Goofball
Goose-cap
Gormless
Imbecile
Knobhead
Liripipe
Liripoop
Lunkhead
Maffling
Meathead
Moon-calf
Omadhaun
Pea-brain
Shithead
Shot-clog
Softhead
Tom-noddy
Wiseacre
Woodcock

9 letters:
Beccaccia
Blockhead
Capocchia
Chipochia
Clarthead
Doddipoll
Doddypoll
Dottipoll
Dumb-cluck
Gothamite
Ignoramus
Jobernowl
Lamebrain
Malt-horse
Schlemiel
Schlemihl
Simpleton
Thickhead
Woodentop

10 letters:
Analphabet
Changeling
Dummelhead
Dunderhead
Dunderpate
Headbanger
Loggerhead
Muttonhead
Nincompoop
Sheepshead
Thickskull
Thimblewit
Touchstone

11 letters:
Chowderhead
Featherhead
Knucklehead
Leather-head
Ninny-hammer
Simple Simon
Van der Merwe

12 letters:
Featherbrain
Shatterbrain

Stupidity Goosery, Hebetude, Thickness, Torpor

Stupor Catatony, Coma, Daze, Dwa(u)m, Fog, Lethargy, Narcosis, Trance
Sturdy Burly, Dunt, Gid, Hardy, Hefty, Lubbard, Lubber, Lusty, Robust, Stalwart,
Staunch, Steeve, Stieve, Strapping, Strong, Stuffy, Thickset, Turnsick, Vigorous
Sturgeon Beluga, Ellops, Fish, Huso, Osseter, Sevruga, Sterlet
Stutter Hesitate, Stammer
Sty Frank, Hogpen, Hovel, Pen
Stye Eyesore, Hordeolum
Style(s), Stylish, Stylist Adam, À la, A-line, Band, Barocco, Barock, Baroque,
Biedermeier, Blow-dry, Brachylogy, Burin, Call, Cantilena, Carry-on, Chic,
Chinoiserie, Chippendale, Class, Cultism, Cut, Dapper, Dash, Decor, Decorated,
Demotic, Diction, Directoire, Dub, Élan, Elegance, Empire, Entitle, Euphuism,
Execution, Face, Farand, → **FASHION**, Finesse, Flamboyant, Flossy, Form(at),
Free, Genre, Gnomon, Gongorism, Gothic, Grace, Gr(a)ecism, Grand, Groovy,
Hair-do, Hand, Hepplewhite, Heuristic, Hip, Homeric, House, International
(Gothic), Intitule, Katharev(o)usa, Lapidary, Locution, Manner, Marivaudage,
Mod(e), Modernism, Modish, Natty, New, Nib, Nifty, Old, Panache, Pattern, Pen,
Perm, Perpendicular, Personal, Phrase, Pistil, Pointel, Port, Post-modernism,
Preponderant, Probe, Queen Anne, Rakish, Rank, Regency, Rococo, Romanesque,
Sheraton, Silk, Snazzy, Spiffy, Sporty, Street, Swish, Taste, Term, Title, Ton, Tone,
Touch, Traditional, Tuscan, Uncial, Vogue, Way
Stymie Baulk, Frustrate, Thwart
Styptic Alum, Amadou, Matico, Sta(u)nch
Suave Bland, Debonair, Oily, Smooth, Unctuous, Urbane
Sub Advance, Due, Submarine, Subordinate, U-boat, Under
Sub-atomic Mesic
Subconscious Inner, Instinctive, Not-I, Subliminal, Suppressed
Sub-continent India(n)
Subcontract Outsource
Subdivision Arm, Branch, Oblast, Sanjak, Senonian, Sheading, Tepal, Wapentake
Subdominant Fah
Subdue(d) Abate, Adaw, Allay, Chasten, Conquer, Cow, Crush, Dant(on), Daunt(on),
Dominate, Entame, Lick, Low-key, Master, Mate, Mute, Overpower, Quail,
→ **QUELL**, Quieten, Reduce, Refrain, Repress, Slow, Sober, Soft pedal, Subact,
Suppress, Tame, Under
Subfusc, Subfusk Dim, Dressy, Dusky, Evening, Sombre
Subhuman Apeman, Bestial
Subject(s), Subjection, Subject to Amenable, Art, Bethrall, Caitive, Case, Citizen,
Contingent, Core, Cow, Donné(e), Enthrall, Foundation, Gist, Hobby, Hobby-horse,
Inflict, Liable, Liege(man), Matter, National, On, Overpower, PE, People, Poser,
Rayah, RE, RI, Serf, Servient, Servitude, Sitter, Slavery, Snool, Submit, Suit,
Syllabus, → **THEME**, Thirl, Thrall, Topic, Under, Vassal, Villein
Subjugate Enslave, Master, Oppress, Overcome, Reduce, Repress, Suppress
Sublieutenant Cornet
Sublimate(r) Aludel, Cleanse, Suppress, Transfer
Sublime Ali, Alice, August, Empyreal, Grand, Great, Lofty, Majestic, Outstanding,
Perfect, Porte, Splendid
Submarine Diver, Innerspace, Nautilus, Pig-boat, Polaris, Sub, U-boat, Undersea,
X-craft
▷ **Submarine** *may indicate* a fish
Submerge(d) Dip, Dive, Drown, Embathe, Engulf, Imbathe, Lemuria, Overwhelm,
Ria, Sink, Take, Whelm

Submissive, Submit Acquiesce, Bow, Capitulate, Comply, Defer, Docile, File, Knuckle, Meek, Obedient, Obtemperate, Passive, Pathetic, Refer, Render, Resign, Snool, Stepford, Stoop, Succumb, Truckle, → YIELD
Subordinate Adjunct, Dependent, Flunky, Inferior, Junior, Minion, Myrmidon, Offsider, Postpone, Secondary, Second banana, Servient, Stooge, Subject, Subservient, Subsidiary, Surrender, Under(ling), Underman, Under-strapper, Vassal
Subscribe(r), Subscription Abonnement, Approve, Assent, Conform, Due, Pay, Sign(atory), Signature, Undersign, Underwrite
Subsequent(ly) Anon, Consequential, Future, Later, Next, Postliminary, Since, Then, Ulterior
Subservient Kneel, Obedient, Obsequious
Subside, Subsidence, Subsidy Abate, Adaw, Aid, Assuage, Bonus, Diminish, Ebb, Grant, Sink, Sit, Swag
Subsidiary, Subsidise Auxiliar(y), By(e), Feather-bed, Junior, Secondary, Side, Spin-off, Succursal
Subsist(ence) Batta, Bread-line, Dole, Keep, Live, Maintain, Rely, Survive
Substance, Substantial Ambergris, Anethole, Antithrombin, Antitoxin, Blocky, Body, Calyx, Cermet, Chalone, Chemzyne, Chitin, Chromatin, Colloid, Considerable, Content, Cosmin(e), Creatine, Ectocrine, Ectoplasm, Elemi, Enzyme, Essential, Excipient, Extender, Exudate, Fabric, Fixative, Getter, Gist, Gluten, Gossypol, Gravamen, Growth, Guanazolo, Hearty, Hefty, Indol, Inhibitor, Iodoform, Iodophor, Isatin(e), Isomer, Lase, Lecithin, Leucotriene, Linin, Luciferin, Material, Matter, Meaning, Meat(y), Metabolite, Metol, Mineral, Mole, Morphogen, Mucigen, Murr(h)ine, Mutagen, Naloxone, Neurotoxin, Orgone, Papier mâché, Particulate, Phlogiston, Polymer, Protyl(e), Purin(e), Queen (bee), Quid, Reality, Resin, Secretagogue, Sense, Sequestrant, Smectic, Solid, Sorbitol, Stuff, Suint, Sum, Surfactant, Sympathin, Tabasheer, Tabashir, Tangible, Thiouracil, Thiourea, Tusche, Viricide, Volutin, Weighty, Ylem
Substandard Infra dig, Off, Poor, Schlo(c)k, Second, Small
▶ **Substantial** see SUBSTANCE
Substantiate Confirm, Flesh, Prove, Strengthen, Support
Substantive Direct, Noun
Substitute, Substitution Acting, Carborundum®, Change, Changeling, Commute, Creamer, Deputy, Dextran, Double, Dub, Emergency, Ersatz, -ette, Euphemism, Eusystolism, Exchange, Fill-in, Improvise, Instead, Lieu(tenant), Locum, Makeshift, Metonymy, Pinch-hit, Proxy, Regent, Relieve, Replace, Represent, Reserve, Resolution, Ringer, Sentence, Seth, Simulacrum, Stalking-horse, Stand-in, Stead, Stopgap, Subrogate, Succedaneum, Supernumerary, Surrogate, Switch, Swop, Synthetic, Understudy, Vicar(ial), Vicarious
Substructure Base, Foundation, Keelson, Platform, Podium
Subterfuge Artifice, Chicane, Evasion, Hole, Manoeuvre, Off-come, Ruse, Strategy, Trick
Subterranean Concealed, Mattamore, Sunken, Underground, Weem
Subtle(ty) Abstruse, Alchemist, Crafty, Fine(spun), Finesse, Ingenious, Nice, Nice(ty), Refinement, Sly, Suttle, Thin, Wily
Subtle difference Nuance
Subtract(ion) Commission, Deduct, Discount, Sum, Take, Tithe, Withdraw
Suburb(s) Banlieue, Dormitory, Environs, Exurbia, Faubourg, Garden, Metroland, Outskirts, Purlieu, Subtopia
Subversion, Subvert Fifth column, Overthrow, Reverse, Sabotage, Sedition,

Treasonous, Undermine, Upset

Subway Metro, Passage, Tube, Underground

Succeed, Success(ful) Accomplish, Achieve, Arrive, Blockbuster, Boffo, Breakthrough, Chartbuster, Contrive, Coup, Éclat, Effective, Efficacious, Fadge, Felicity, Flourish, Follow, Fortune, Gangbuster, Get, Go, Hit, Hotshot, Inherit, Killing, Landslide, Luck, Made, Manage, Masterstroke, Mega, Midas touch, Offcome, Pass, Prevail, Procure, Prosper, Purple patch, Reach, Replace, Riot, Score, Seal, Seel, Sele, Sell out, Soaraway, Socko, Speed, Stardom, Superstar, Sure thing, Tanistry, Triumph, Up, Up and coming, Upstart, Vault, Weather, W(h)iz(z)kid, Win, Wow, Wunderkind

Succession Apostolic, Chain, Cognate, Dead men's shoes, Line, Order, Reversion, Sequence, Seriatim, Series, Suite

Successor Co(m)arb, Deluge, Descendant, Ensuite, Epigon(e), Heir, Incomer, Inheritor, Khalifa, Next, Syen

Succinct Brief, Cereus, Compact, Concise, Houseleek, Laconic, Pithy, Short

Succour Aid, Assist, Help, Minister, Relieve, Rescue, Sustain

Succulent Agave, Cactus, Echeveria, Juicy, Lush, Rich, Saguaro, Sappy, Spekboom, Tender, Toothy

Succumb Capitulate, Fall, Go under, Surrender, Yield

Such Like, Sae, Sike, Similar, That

Suck(er), Sucking Absorb, Acetabular, Acetabulum, Amphistomous, Antlia, Aphis, Aspirator, Ass, Bull's eye, Culicidae, Dracula, Drink, Dupe, Fawn, Fellatio, Gnat, Graff, Graft, Gull, Haustellum, Haustorium, Hoove, Lamia, Lamprey, Leech, Liquorice, Lollipop, Mammal, Monotremata, Mouth, Mug, Muggins, Osculum, Patsy, Plunger, Remora, Rook, Shoot, Siphon, Slurp, Smarm, Spire, Spyre, Straw, Surculus, Swig, Sycophant, Tellar, Teller, Tick, Tiller, Toad-eater, Turion, Vampire

Suckle Feed, Mother, Nourish, Nurse, Nurture

Suction Adhere, Pump, Siphon

Sud(s) Foam, Lather, Sapples

Sudanese Dinka, Mahdi, Nuba

Sudden(ly) Abrupt, Astart, Astert, Extempore, Ferly, Fleeting, Foudroyant, Fulminant, Hasty, Headlong, Impulsive, Overnight, Precipitate, Rapid, Slap, Sodain, Subitaneous, Subito, Swap, Swop, Unexpected

Sue Ask, Beseech, Dun, Entreat, Implead, Implore, Litigate, Petition, Pray, Process, Prosecute, Woo

Suede Split

Suffer(er), Suffering Abide, Aby(e), Ache, Affliction, Agonise, Auto, Be, → BEAR, Brook, Calvary, Cop, Die, Distress, Dree, Dukkha, Endurance, Endure, Feel, Gethsemane, Golgotha, Grief, Hardship, Have, Incur, Let, Luit, Mafted, Martyr, Pain, Passible, Passion, Passive, Patible, Patience, Pellagrin, Permit, Pine, Plague, Purgatory, Stand, Stomach, Sustain, Thole, Tolerate, Toll, Torment, Trial, Tribulation, Undergo, Use, Victim

Suffering remnant Macmillanite

Suffice, Sufficient Adequate, Ample, Basta, Do, Due, Enough, Enow, Experimental, Run to, Satisfy, Serve

Suffix Enclitic

Suffocate Asphyxiate, Choke, Smoor, Smore, Smother, Stifle, Stive, Strangle, Throttle

Suffrage(tte) Ballot, Feminist, Franchise, Manhood, Vote

Suffuse Colour, Glow, Imbue, Saturate, Spread

Sugar(y), Sugar cane Aldohexose, Aldose, Amygdalin, Arabinose, Barley, Beet,

Blood, Brown, Candy, Cane, Caramel, Carn(e), Cassonade, Caster, Cellobiose, Cellose, Chaptalise, Confectioner's, Daddy, Demerara, Deoxyribose, Dextrose, Disaccharide, Flattery, Fructose, Fucose, Furanose, Galactose, Gallise, Glucose, Glucosoric, Glycosuria, Goo(r), Granulated, Grape, Gur, Heroin, Hexose, Honeydew, Hundreds and thousands, Iced, Icing, Inulin, Invert, Jaggary, Jaggery, Jagghery, Lactose, Laevulose, Loaf, Lump, Maltose, Manna, Mannose, Maple, Milk, Money, Monosaccharide, Muscovado, Nectar, Nucleoside, Palm, Panocha, Pentose, Penuche, Raffinose, Rhamnose, Ribose, Saccharine, Saccharoid, Simple, Sis, Sorbose, Sorg(h)o, Sorghum, Sparrow, Spun, Sweet, Trehalose, Triose, White, Wood, Xylose

Sugar-daddy Lyle, Tate

Suggest(ion), Suggestive Advance, Advice, Advise, Connote, Counter-proposal, Cue, Hint, Idea, Imply, Innuendo, Insinuate, Intimate, Mention, Modicum, Moot, Posit, Posthypnotic, Prompt, Proposal, Propound, Provocative, Racy, Raise, Recommend, Redolent, Reminiscent, Risqué, Savour, Smacks, Soft core, Suspicion, Touch, Trace, Twang, Undertone, Vote, Wind, Wrinkle

Suicide Felo-de-se, Hara-kiri, Hari-kari, Kamikaze, Lemming, Lethal, Sati, Seppuku, Shinju, Suttee

Suit Action, Adapt, Adjust, Agree, Answer, Anti-G, Apply, Appropriate, Become, Befit, Beho(o)ve, Bequest, Beseem, Besit, Birthday, Boiler, Cards, Case, Cat, Clubs, Conform, Courtship, Demob, Diamonds, Dittos, Diving, Do, Drapes, Dress, Effeir, Effere, Etons, Fadge, Fashion, Fit, G, Garb, Gee, Gree, Hearts, Hit, Jump, Lis pendens, Long, Lounge, Major, Mao, Match, Minor, Monkey, NBC, Noddy, Orison, Outcome, Paternity, Petition, Plaint, Play, Plea, Please, Point, Prayer, Pressure, Process, Pyjama, Quarterdeck, Queme, Romper(s), Safari, Sailor, Salopettes, Samfoo, Samfu, Satisfy, Serve, Shell, Siren, Skeleton, Slack, Space, Spades, Strong, Sun, Sunday, Supplicat, Sweat, Swim, Tailleur, Three-piece, Track, Trouser, Trumps, Tsotsi, Twin, Two-piece, Uniform, Union, Wet, Wingsuit, Zoot

Suitable Apposite, Appropriate, Apropos, Apt, Becoming, Capable, Congenial, Consonant, Convenance, Convenient, Due, Expedient, → **FIT**, Giusto, Habile, Keeping, Meet, Opportune, Relevant, Seasonal, Seemly, Sittlichkeit, Very, Worthy

Suite Allemande, Apartment, Chambers, Court, Edit, Ensemble, Entourage, Hospitality, Lounge, Nutcracker, Partita, Retinue, Rooms, Serenade, Set, Skybox, Tail, Three-piece, Train, Two-piece

Suitor Beau, Gallant, John Doe, Lover, Petitioner, Pretender, Suppli(c)ant, Swain, Wooer

Sulk(y), Sulkiness B(r)oody, Disgruntled, Dod, Dort, Gee, Glout(s), Glower, Glum, Grouchy, Grouty, Grumps, Huff, Hump, Jinker, Mardy, Maungy, Mope, Mulligrubs, Mump, Pet, Pique, Pout, Spider, Strunt, Stuffy, Stunkard, Sullen, Tout(ie), Towt, Umbrage

Sullen Dorty, Dour, Farouche, Glum(pish), Grim, Moody, Peevish, Stunkard, Sulky, Surly, Truculent

Sully Assoil, Bedye, Besmirch, Blot, Defile, Glaur(y), Smear, Smirch, Smutch, Soil(ure), Tarnish, Tar-wash

Sulphate, Sulphide Alum, Alunite, Blende, Bluestone, Bornite, Copperas, Coquimbite, Glance, Melanterite, Pyrites, Zarnec, Zarnich

Sulphur Baregine, Brimstone, Cysteine, Hepar, Oleum, S, Stannite, Thionic

Sultan(a), Sultanate Brunei, Caliph, Emir, Grand Seignoir, Grand Turk, Hen, Kalif, Nejd, Oman, Osman, Padishah, Roxane, Saladin, Soldan, Suleiman, Tippoo, Tipu, Wadai

Sultry Humid, Sexy, Smouldering, Steamy, Tropical

Sum(s), Sum up Add(end), Aggregate, All, Amount, Arsmetric, Bomb, Connumerate, Encapsulate, Foot, Logical, Lump, Number, Perorate, Plumule, → QUANTITY, Re-cap, Refund, Remittance, Reversion, Solidum, Total, Vector

Summarize, Summary Abridge, Abstract, Aperçu, Bird's eye, Brief, Compendium, Condense, Conspectus, Digest, Docket, Epanodos, Epitome, Gist, Instant, Memo, Minute, Offhand, Outline, Overview, Précis, Recap, Resume, Résumé, Round-up, Syllabus, Synopsis, Tabloid, Tabulate, Tabulation, Wrap-up

Summer(time) Aestival, August, BST, Computer, Estival, Heyday, Indian, Lintel, Luke, Prime, St Luke's, St Martin's, Season, Solstice, Totter

Summerhouse Belvedere, Chalet, Conservatory, Folly, Gazebo

Summit Acme, Acri-, Apex, Braeheid, Brow, Climax, Conference, → CREST, Crown, Height, Hillcrest, Jole, Peak, Pike, Pinnacle, Spire, Vertex, Vertical, Yalta

Summon(s) Accite, Arrière-ban, Azan, Beck(on), Call, Call in, Cist, Cital, Citation, Command, Conjure, Convene, Convent, Drum, Evoke, Garnishment, Gong, Hail, Invocation, Muster, Order, Page, Post, Preconise, Rechate, Recheat, Reveille, Signal, Sist, Ticket, Warn, Warrant, Whoop, Writ

Sumo Makunouchi, Yokozuna

Sump Bilge, Drain, Pool, Sink

Sumpter Led horse, Pack-horse

Sumptuous Expensive, Lavish, Palatial, Rich(ly), Superb

Sun(-god), Sunlight, Sunny, Sunshine Albedo, Amen-Ra, Amon-Ra, Apollo, Ashine, Aten, Bright, Cheer, Combust, Daily, Day(star), Dry, Earthshine, Eye of the day, Glory, Heater, Helio(s), Helius, Horus, Mean, Midnight, New Mexico, Paranthelion, Parhelion, Pet-day, Phoebean, Photosphere, Ra, Radiant, Rays, Re, Rising, Shamash, Sol(ar), Soleil, Sonne, Surya, Svastika, Swastika, Tabloid, Tan, Titan, UV

Sunbathe Apricate, Bask, Brown, Tan

Sunbeam Car, Ray

Sunblock Parasol

Sunburn Bronze, Combust, Peeling, Tan

Sunday Advent, Best, Cantate, Care, Carle, Carling, Dominical, Easter, Fig, Jubilate, Judica, Laetare, Lord's Day, Lost, Low, Mid-Lent, Mothering, Orthodox, Palm, Passion, Quadragesima, Quasimodo, Quinquagesima, Refection, Refreshment, Remembrance, Rogation, Rose, Rush-bearing, S, Septuagesima, Sexagesima, Stir-up, Tap-up, Trinity, Whit

Sunday school SS

Sunder Divide, Divorce, Part, Separate, Sever, Split

Sundew Drosera, Eyebright

Sundial Analemma, Gnomon, Solarium

Sundry Divers, Several, Various

Sunflower Kansas, KS

Sunglasses Ray-Bans®, Shades

▶ **Sun-god** *see* SUN

▶ **Sunken** *see* SINK

Sunrise, Sun-up Aurora, Cosmical, Dawn, East

Sunset Acronical, Evening

Sunshade Awning, Brise-soleil, Canopy, Chi(c)k, Cloud, Parasol, Umbrella

Sunspot Facula, Freckle, Macula

Sunstroke Heliosis, Siriasis

Sunwise Deasi(u)l, Deasoil, Deis(h)eal, Eutropic

Sun-worshipper Heliolater

Sup Dine, Eat, Feast, Sample, Sip, Swallow
Super A1, Actor, Arch, Extra, Fab(ulous), Great, Grouse, Ideal, Lulu, Paramount, Superb, Terrific, Tip-top, Tops, Walker-on, Wizard
Superadded Advene
Superb A1, Concours, Fine, Grand, Great, Majestic, Peerless, Phat, Splendid, Top-notch
Supercilious Aloof, Arrogant, Bashaw, Cavalier, Haughty, Lordly, Snide, Sniffy, Snooty, Snotty, Snouty, Superior, Toffee-nosed, Upstage
Superficial Cosmetic, Cursenary, Cursory, Dilettante, Exterior, Facile, Glib, Outside, Outward, Overlying, Perfunctory, Shallow, Sketchy, Skindeep, Smattering, Veneer
▷ **Superficial(ly)** *may indicate* a word outside another
Superfluous, Superfluity Cheville, De trop, Extra, Lake, Mountain, Needless, Otiose, Pleonastic, Plethora, Redundant, Spare, Unnecessary
Superhuman Bionic, Herculean, Heroic, Supernatural
Superintend(ent) Boss, Director, Foreman, Guide, Janitor, Oversee(r), Preside, Provost, Sewer, Supercargo, Surveillant, Warden, Zanjero
Superior(ity) Abbess, Abeigh, Above, Advantage, Aloof, Atop, Better, Brahmin, Choice, Condescending, Custos, De luxe, Dinger, Elite, Eminent, Excellent, Exceptional, Finer, Forinsec, Gree, Herrenvolk, High-class, High-grade, Jethro, Lake, Liege, Mastery, Morgue, Mother, Nob, Outstanding, Over, Paramount, Pooh-Bah, Posh, Predominance, Prestige, Pretentious, Prior, Smug, Superordinate, Supremacy, Swell, Top(-loftical), Transcendent(al), U, Udal, Upper(most), Uppish, Upstage
Superlative Best, Exaggerated, Peerless, Smasheroo, Supreme, Utmost
Superman Batman, Bionic, Titan, Übermensch
Supermarket Co-op, Fund, GUM, Self service, Store
Supernatural Divine, Eerie, Fay, Fey, Fie, Fly, Gothic, Kachina, Mana, Metaphysical, Paranormal, Sharp, Siddhi, Uncanny, Unearthly, Wight
Supernova Plerion
Supernumerary Additional, Corollary, Extra, Mute, Orra
Supersede Replace, Stellenbosch, Supplant
Superstition Aberglaube, Abessa, Fable, Folk-lore, Freet, Myth, Pisheog, Pishogue, Uncertainty
Superstructure Mastaba(h)
Supertonic Ray
Supervise(d), Supervision, Supervisor Administer, Chaperone, Check, Direct, Engineer, Floorwalker, Foreman, Grieve, Handle, Honcho, Invigilate, Manager, Monitor, Officiate, Overman, Oversee(r), Probation, Proctor, Shopwalker, Stage-manage, Targe, Under, Walla(h)
Supine Inactive, Inert, Lying, Passive, Protract
Supper Burns, Dinner, → **DRINK(ER)**, Hawkey, Hockey, Horkey, Last, Meal, Nagmaal, Repast, Soirée
Supplant Displace, Exchange, Oust, Overthrow, Pre-empt, Replace, Substitute, Supersede
Supple Compliant, Leish, Limber, Lissom(e), → **LITHE**, Loose, Loose-limbed, Pliable, Souple, Wan(d)le, Wannel, Whippy
Supplement(ary) Addend(um), Addition, And, Annex(e), Appendix, Augment, Auxiliary, Bolt-on, Codicil, Colour, Eche, Eik, Eke, Extra, Incaparina, Paralipomena, Postscript, Relay, Ripienist, Ripieno, Rutin, Weighting
Supplicant, Supplicate Beg, Entreat, Importune, Invoke, Petition, Plead, Request, Schnorr, Sue

Supply, Supplies, Supplier Accommodate, Advance, Afford, Cache, Cater, Commissariat, Contribute, Crop, Endue, Equip, Excess, Exempt, Feed, Fill, Find, Fit, Foison, Fund, Furnish, Give, Grist, Grubstake, Heel, Holp(en), Indue, Issue, Lay on, Lend, Lithely, Mains, Matériel, Pipeline, Plenish, Ply, → **PROVIDE**, Provision, Purvey, RASC, Replenishment, Reservoir, Retailer, Serve, Source, Stake, Stock, → **STORE**, Viands, Vintner, Water, Widow's cruse, Yield

Support(er), Supporting Abacus, Abet, Abutment, Adherent, Adminicle, Advocate, Affirm, Aficionado, Aftercare, Aid, Aidance, Aliment(ative), Ally, Ammunition, Anchor, Ancillary, Andiron, Anta, Appui, Arch, Arm, Assistant, Athletic, Axle, Back(bone), Back-up, Baculum, Baluster, Banister, Bankroll, Barrack, Barre, Base, Batten, Beam, Bear, Befriend, Belt, Bibb, Bier, Bolster, Boom, Bouclée, Bra, Brace, Bracket, Brassiere, Breadwinner, Breast-summer, Bridge, Bridgeboard, Buttress, C(ee)-spring, Chair, Champion, Chaptrel, Circumstantiate, Clientele, Column, Confirm, Console, Corbel, Corbel-table, Cornerstone, Countenance, Cradle, Cross-beam, Crutch, Dado, Diagrid, Dog-shore, Doula, Easel, Encourage, Endorse, Endow, Engager, Enthusiast, Espouse, Family, Fan, Favour, Fid, Finance, Flying buttress, Fly-rail, Footrest, Footstool, For, Friend, Gamb, Gantry, Garter, Girder, Glia, Grass roots, Groundswell, Handrail, Hanger, Harpin(g)s, Headrest, Help, Henchman, Hold with, Horse, Hound, I-beam, Idealogue, Impost, Income, Instantiate, Ite, Jack, Jackstay, Jockstrap, Joist, Keep, Kingpost, Knee, Knighthead, Learning, Lectern, Leg, Lierne, Lifebelt, Lifebuoy, Lobby, Loper, Loyalist, Mahlstick, Mainstay, Maintain, Makefast, Mill-rind, Miserere, Misericord(e), Monial, Moral, Mortsafe, Nervure, Neuroglia, -nik, Nourish, Pack, Paranymph, Parawalker, Partisan, Partizan, Partners, Patronage, Pedestal, Pessary, Phalanx, Pier, Pillar, Pin, Plinth, Poppet, Post, Potent, Price, Prop, Proponent, Prop-root, PTA, Pull-for, Purlin(e), Purlins, Pylon, Raft, Rally round, Reinforce, Relieve, Respond, Rest, Rind, Rod, Roof-plate, Root, Royalist, Rynd, Samaritan, Sanction, Sawhorse, Scaffolding, Second, Shoetree, Shore, Skeg, Skeleton, Skewput, Skid, Sleeper, Sling, Snotter, Socle, Solidarity, Spectator, Splat, Splint, Sponson, Sprag, Spud, Staddle, Staddlestone, Staff, Staging, Stake, Stalwart, Stanchion, Stand(-by), Stay, Steady, Stem(pel), Step, Stick, Stirrup, Stool, Stringer, Strut, Stylobate, Subscribe, Subsidy, Succour, Suffragist, Summer, Suppedaneum, Suspender, Sustain, Tailskid, Technical, Tee, Telamon, Tendril, Third, Tie, Tige, Torsel, Trabecula, Tress(el), Trestle, Tripod, Trivet, Truss, Underlay, Underpin, Understand, Unipod, Uphold, Upkeep, Viva, Walker, Waterwings, Well-wisher, Y-level, Zealot

Suppose(d), Supposition An, Assume, Believe, Daresay, Expect, Guess, Hypothetical, Idea, If, Imagine, Imply, Infer, Opine, Presume, Putative, Said, Sepad, Theory, What if

Suppository Pessary

Suppress(ion) Abolish, Adaw, Burke, Cancel, Censor, Clampdown, Conditioned, Crush, Cushion, Ecthlipsis, Elide, Elision, Gleichschaltung, Hush-up, Mob(b)le, Quash, Quell, Quench, Restrain, Silence, Smother, Squash, Stifle, Submerge, Subreption, Throttle

Suppurate, Suppuration Diapyesis, Discharge, Exude, Fester, Maturate, Ooze, Pus, Pyorrhoea, Rankle

Supreme, Supremacy, Supremo Apical, Baaskap, Caudillo, Consummate, Kronos, Leader, Napoleon, Overlord, Paramount, Peerless, Pre-eminent, Regnant, Sovereign, Sublime, Sudder, Superlative, Top, Utmost, White

Surcharge Addition, Extra, Tax

Surd Voiceless

Sure(ly) Assured, Ay, Bound, Cert(ain), Confident, Definite, Doubtless, Firm, Indeed,

Infallible, Know, Pardi(e), Pardy, Perdie, Positive, Poz, Safe, Secure, Shoo-in, Sicker, Syker, Uh-huh, Yep, Yes

Surety Bail, Frithborth, Guarantee, Mainprise, Security, Sponsional

Surf(er), Surfing Breach, Breaker, Grommet, Internet, Lurk, Rollers, Rote, Sea, Waxhead

Surface Aerofoil, Appear, Area, Arise, Camber, Carpet, Caustic, Control, Day, Dermal, Dermis, Emerge, Epigene, Exterior, External, Face, Facet, Flock, Interface, Macadam, Meniscus, Nanograss, Notaeum, Out, Outcrop, Outward, Paintwork, Patina, Pave, Plane, Reveal, Rise, Salband, Side, Skin, Soffit, Spandrel, Superficial, Superficies, Tarmac®, Tar-seal, Texture, Top, Topping, Toroid, Wearing course, Worktop

Surf-boat, Surfboard(ing) Goofy-footer, Masoola(h), Masula

Surfeit(ed) Blasé, Cloy, Excess, Glut, Overcloy, Plethora, Satiate, Stall, Staw

▷ **Surfer** *may indicate* programming

Surge Billow, Boom, Drive, Gush, Onrush, Seethe, S(c)end, Storm, Sway, Swell, Wind

Surgeon Abernethy, BCh, BS, CHB, CM, Doctor, House, Hunter, Lister, Medic, Operator, Orthopod, Plastic, Sawbones, Staff, Tang, Vet(erinary)

Surgery Anaplasty, Bypass, Cosmetic, Facelift, Keyhole, Knife, Laparotomy, Laser, LASIK, Medicine, Nip and tuck, Nose job, Op, Open-heart, Orthop(a)edics, Osteoplasty, Plastic, Prosthetics, Reconstructive, Repair, Spare-part, Ta(g)liacotian, Thoracoplasty, Zolatrics

Surly Bluff, Cantankerous, Chough, Chuffy, Churl(ish), Crabby, Crusty, Cynic, Glum, Gruff, Grum, Grumpy, Rough, Snarling, Sullen, Truculent

Surmise Extrapolate, Guess, Imagine, Infer, Presume, Suppose

Surmount Beat, Climb, Conquer, Crest, Master, Overcome, Scan, Superate, Tide, Transcend

Surname Cognomen, Patronymic

Surpass Bang, Beat, Best, Cap, Cote, Ding, Eclipse, Efface, Exceed, Excel, Outdo, Outgun, Out-Herod, Outman, Outreach, Outshine, Outstrip, Overshadow, Overtop, Transcend

Surplice Cotta, Ephod, Rochet, Sark, Serk, Vakass

Surplus Excess, Extra, Glut, Lake, Mountain, Out-over, Over, Overabundance, Overage, Overcome, Remainder, Rest, Spare, Surfeit

Surprise(d), Surprising Ag, Alert, Amaze, Ambush, Arrah, Astonish, Aykhona wena, Bewilder, Blimey, Boilover, Bombshell, By Jove, Caramba, Catch, Confound, Coo, Cor, Crick(e)y, Crikey, Criminé, Cripes, Criv(v)ens, Dear, Eye-opener, Gadso, Gee, Geewhiz, Gemini, Geminy, Gemony, Gobsmacked, Golly, Good-lack, Gorblimey, Gordon Bennett, Gosh, Ha, Hah, Hallo, Heavens, Hech, Heck, Heh, Hello, Hey, Ho, Jeepers, Jeepers creepers, Jeez(e), Jinne, Jirre, Law, Lawks, Lor, Lordy, Lumme, Lummy, Man alive, Marry, Musha, My, Nooit, Obreption, Och, Odso, Omigod, Oops, Open-mouthed, Overtake, Phew, Pop-eyed, Really, Sheesh, Shock, Singular, Sjoe, Spot, Stagger, Startle, Strewth, Struth, Stun, Sudden, Treat, Turn-up, Uh, Whew, Whoops, Wonderment, Wow, Wrongfoot, Yikes, Yipes, Yow, Zinger, Zowie

Surrealist Bizarre, Dali, Ernst, Grotesque, Magritte, Man Ray, Miró

Surrender Capitulate, Cave-in, Cession, Enfeoff, Extradite, Fall, Forego, Forfeit, Handover, Hulled, Kamerad, Naam, Recreant, Release, Relinquish, Remise, Rendition, Roll over, Submit, Succumb, Waive, → **YIELD**, Yorktown

Surreptitious Clandestine, Covert, Fly, Furtive, Secret, Slee, Sly, Stealthy, Underhand

Surrey Carriage, Sy

Surrogate Agent, Depute, Deputy, Locum, Proxy

Surround(ed), Surrounding(s) Ambient, Amongst, Architrave, Background, Bathe, Bego, Beset, Bundwall, Circumvallate, Circumvent, Compass, Doughnutting, Ecology, Embail, Encase, → **ENCIRCLE**, Enclave, Enclose, Encompass, Enfold, Entomb, Envelop, Environ, Enwrap, Fence, Gherao, Gird, Hedge, Hem in, Impale, Inorb, Invest, Mid, Orb, Orle, Outflank, Outside, Perimeter, Setting, Wall

Surtees Jorrocks, Sponge

Surveillance, Survey(ing), Surveyor Behold, Cadastre, Case, Census, Chartered, Conspectus, Dialler, Domesday, Doomwatch, Espial, Examination, Eye, Geodesy, Geological, Groma, Look-see, Once-over, Ordnance, Patrol, Poll, Prospect, Quantity, Recce, Reconnaissance, Regard, Review, Scan, Scrutiny, Stakeout, Straw poll, Supervision, Terrier, Theodolite, Triangulate, Trilateration, Vigil, Watch

Survival, Survive, Surviving, Survivor Cope, Die hard, Endure, Extant, Finalist, Hibakusha, Last, Leftover, Live, Outdure, Outlast, Outlive, Outwear, Overlive, Persist, Relic(t), Ride, Street-wise, Viability, Warhorse, Weather

Susan Lazy

Susceptible, Susceptibility Anaphylaxis, Electrical, Impressionable, Liable, Receptive, Vulnerable

Suspect, Suspicion, Suspicious Askance, Assume, Breath, Dodgy, Doubt, Dubious, Fishy, Grain, Grey list, Guess, Hint, Hunch, Jalouse, Jealous, Leery, Misdeem, Misdoubt, Misgiving, Mislippen, Mistrust, Modicum, Notion, Paranoia, Queer, Scent, Smatch, Soupçon, Thought, Tinge, Whiff

▷ **Suspect, Suspicious** may indicate an anagram

Suspend(ed), Suspense, Suspension Abate, Abeyance, Adjourn, Anabiosis, Anti-shock, Cliffhanger, Colloid, Dangle, Defer, Delay, Dormant, Freeze, Ground, → **HANG**, Hydraulic, Independent, Intermit, Lay off, Mist, Moratorium, Nailbiter, Pensile, Poise, Prorogue, Put on ice, Reprieve, Respite, Rub out, Rusticate, Sideline, Sol, Stand off, Swing, Tension, Tenterhooks, Truce, Withhold

▷ **Suspended** may indicate 'ice' (on ice) at the end of a down light

Sussex Rape

Sustain(ed), Sustaining, Sustenance Abide, Afford, Aliment, Bear, Constant, Depend, Endure, Food, Keep, Last, Maintain, Nutrient, Nutriment, Pedal, Prolong, Sostenuto, Succour, Support, Ten(uto), Upbear

Sutler Vivandière

Suture Button, Catgut, Cobbler, Lambda, Pterion, Purse-string, Sagittal, Stitch

Suzanne, Suzie Lenglen, Wong

Svelte Lithe, Slender, Slim

Swab Dossil, Dry, Mop, Pledget, Scour, Sponge, Squeegee, Stupe, Tampon, Tompon, Wipe

Swaddle, Swaddling Bind, Envelop, Incunabula, Swathe, Wrap

Swag Booty, Encarpus, Festoon, Haul, Loot, Maino(u)r, Manner, Matilda, Shiralee, Toran(a)

Swagger(er), Swaggering Birkie, Bluster, Boast, Brag, Bragadisme, Bravado, Bucko, Cock, Crow, Jaunty, Matamore, Nounce, Panache, Pra(u)nce, Roist, Roll, Rollick, Roul, Royster, Ruffle, Side, Strive, Swank, Swash(-buckler), Tigerism

Swain Amoretti, Beau, Churl, Corin, Damon, Hind, Lover, Rustic, Shepherd, Strephon, Wooer

Swallow(able), Swallowing Accept, Aerophagia, Ariel, Barn, Bird, Bolt, Cliff, Consume, Deglutition, Devour, Down, Drink, Eat, Endue, Englut, Engulf, Engulph, Esculent, Glug, Gobble, Gula, Gulp, Hirundine, Incept, Ingest, Ingulf, Ingurgitate,

Itys, Lap, Martin, Martlet, Progne, Quaff, Shift, Sister, Slug, Stomach, Swig, Take, Take off

Swamp(y) Bog, Bunyip, Cowal, Cypress, Deluge, Dismal, Drown, Engulf, Everglade, Flood, Great Dismal, Inundate, Lentic, Lerna, Lerne, Loblolly, Mar(i)sh, Morass, Muskeg, Okavango, Okefenokee, Overrun, Overwhelm, Pakihi, Paludal, Quagmire, Slash, Slough, Sudd, Uliginous, Urman, Vlei, Vly, Wetland

Swan(s) Avon, Bewick's, Bird, Black, Cob, Cygnet, Cygnus, Game, Leda, Lindor, Mute, Pen, Seven, Seward, Song, Stroll, Trumpeter, Whistling, Whooper, Whooping

Swank(y) Boast, Lugs, Pretentious, Side, Style

Swan-song Finale, Last air

Swap, Swop → BARTER, Chop, Commute, Exchange, Scorse, Switch, Trade, Truck

▷ **Swap(ped)** *may indicate* an anagram

Sward Grass, Green, Lawn, Sod, Turf

Swarm(ing) Abound, Alive, Bike, Bink, Byke, Cast, Clamber, Cloud, Crowd, Flood, Geminid, Hoatching, Host, Hotter, Infest, Meteor, Overrun, Pullulate, Rife, Shin, Shoal, Throng

Swarthy Dark, Dusky, Melanotic

Swash Swig, Swill

Swash-buckler Adventurer, Boaster, Braggart, Gascon, Swordsman

Swastika Filfot, Fylfot, Gamma(dion), Hakenkreuz

▶ **Swat** *see* SWOT

Swathe Bind, Enfold, Enroll, Swaddle, Wrap

Sway(ing) Careen, Carry, Command, Diadrom, Domain, Dominion, Flap, Fluctuate, Govern, Hegemony, Influence, Lilt, Oscillate, Prevail, Reel, Reign, Rock, Roll, Rule, Shog, Shoogle, Swag, Swale, Swee, Swing(e), Teeter, Titter, Totter, Vacillate

Swear(ing), Swear word Attest, Avow, Billingsgate, Coprolalia, Curse, Cuss, Depose, Execrate, Expletive, Invective, Jurant, Juratory, Oath, Pledge, Plight, Rail, Sessa, Tarnal, Tarnation, Verify, Vow

Sweat(ing), Sweaty Apocrine, Beads, Clammy, Cold, Dank, Diaphoresis, Excrete, Exude, Flop, Forswatt, Glow, Hidrosis, Lather, Ooze, Osmidrosis, → PERSPIRE, Secretion, Slave, Stew, Sudament, Sudamina, Sudate, Swelter

Sweater Aran, Argyle, Circassian, Circassienne, Cowichan, Fair Isle, Gansey, Guernsey, Indian, Jersey, Polo, Pullover, Roll-neck, Siwash, Skinny-rib, Skivvy, Slip-on, Slop-pouch, Sloppy Joe, Turtleneck, Woolly

Swede Nordic, Rutabaga, Scandinavian, Sven, Turnip

Sweeney Police, Todd

Sweep(er), Sweeping(s) Besom, Broad, Broom, Brush, Chimney, Chummy, Clean, Curve, Debris, Detritus, Expanse, Extensive, Lash, Libero, Lottery, Net, Oars, Pan, Phasing, Police-manure, Range, Scavenger, Scud, Sling, Snowball, Soop, Sooterkin, Street, Stroke, Surge, Swathe, Sway, Vacuum, Waft, Well, Wide

Sweepstake Draw, Gamble, Lottery, Raffle, Tattersall's, Tombola

Sweet(s), Sweeten(er), Sweetmeat, Sweetness Acesulflame-K, Acid drop, Adeline, Afters, Alcorza, Aldose, Amabile, Aspartame, Barley sugar, Bombe, Bonbon, Bonus, Brandyball, Bribe, Bull's eye, Burnt-almonds, Butterscotch, Candy, Candyfloss, Caramel, Chaptalise, Charity, Charming, Cherubic, Choc(olate), Choccy, Cloying, Coconut ice, Comfit, Confect(ion), Confetti, Confiserie, Confit, Conserve, Crème, Cute, Cyclamate, → DESSERT, Dolce, Dolly, Dolly mixture, Douce(t), Dowset, Dragée, Dulcet, Dulcie, Dulcitude, Elecampane, Fairy floss, Flummery, Fondant, Fool, Fragrant, Fresh, Fudge, Glucose, Glycerin, Gob-stopper, Goody, Gum(drop), Gundy, Hal(a)vah, Halva, Honey(ed), Humbug, Hundreds and thousands, Ice, Icky, Indican, Jelly baby, Jelly bean, Jube, Jujube, Kiss, Lavender, Lemon drop, Licorice, Liquorice, Lollipop, Lolly, Lozenge, Luscious, Marchpane, Marshmallow, Marzipan, Melodious, Mint, Mousse, Muscavado, Nanaimo Bar, Nectared, Noisette, Nonpareil, Nougat, Pandrop, Pastille, Pea, Peardrop, Peppermint cream, Peppermint drop, Pet, Pick'n'mix, Pie, Praline, Pud(ding), Redolent, Rock, Romic, Saccharin(e), Scroggin, Seventeen, Sillabub, Sixteen, Solanine, Soot(e), Sop, Sorbet, Spice, Split, Stickjaw, Sucker, Sucrose, Sugar, Sugarplum, Swedger, Syllabub, Syrupy, Tablet, Taffy, Tart, Thaumatin, Toffee, Torte, Trifle, Truffle, Turkish delight, Twee, Uses, William, Wine-gum, Winsome, Xylitol, Zabaglione

Sweetbread Bur(r), Inchpin, Pancreas

Sweetheart Amoret, Amour, Beau, Darling, Dona(h), Dowsabel(l), Doxy, Dulcinea, Flame, Follower, Honey(bunch), Honeybun, Jarta, Jo(e), Lass, Leman, Lover, Masher, Neaera, Peat, Romeo, Steady, Toots(y), True-love, Valentine, Yarta, Yarto

Sweet-seller Butcher, Confectioner

Swell(ing) Adenomata, Ague-cake, Anasarca, Aneurysm, Apophysis, Bag, Balloon, Bellying, Berry, Billow, Blab, Blister, Bloat, Blow, Boil, Boll, Bolster, Botch, Braw, Bubo, Bulb, Bulge, Bump, Bunion, Capellet, Carnosity, Cat, Chancre, Chilblain, Clour, Cratches, Curb, Cyst, Dandy, Desmoid, Diapason, Dilate, → **DISTEND**, Dom, Don, Eche, Ectasia, Eger, Elephantiasis, Encanthis, Enhance, Entasis, Epulis, Excellent, Farcy-bud, Frog, Gall, Gathering, Gent, Goiter, Goitre, Gout, Grandee, Ground, H(a)ematoma, Heave, Heighten, Hove, Hydrocele, Hydroma, Hygroma, Increase, Inflate, Intumesce, Kibe, L, Lampas(se), Lampers, Louden, Lump, Macaroni, Mouse, Nodule, Odontoma, Oedema, OK, Onco-, Ox-warble, Parotitis, Plim, Plump, Protrude, Protuberance, Proud, Pulvinus, Rise, Roil, Scirrhus, Scleriasis, Sea, Shinsplints, Splenomegaly, Strout, Struma, Stye, Stylopodium, Surge, Teratoma, Toff, Torose, Torulose, Tragus, Tuber(cle), Tumefaction, Tumescence, Tumour, Tympany, Upsurge, Varicocele, Venter, Wallow, Warble, Wen, Whelk, Windgall, Xanthoma

▷ **Swelling** *may indicate* a word reversed

Swelter(ing) Perspire, Stew, Sweat, Tropical

Swerve, Swerving Bias, Broach, Careen, Deflect, Deviate, Lean, Sheer, Shy, Stray, Sway, Swee, Swing, Warp, Wheel

Swift(ly) Apace, Bird, Dean, Dromond, Fleet, Flock, Hasty, Martlet, Newt, Nimble, Presto, Prompt, Pronto, Quick, → **RAPID**, Reel, Slick, Spanking, Velocipede, Wight

Swig Drink, Gulp, Nip, Scour, Swill, Tighten

Swill Guzzle, Leavings, Rubbish, Slosh, Swash

▷ **Swilling** *may indicate* an anagram

Swim(ming) Bathe, Bogey, Bogie, Crawl, Dip, Float, Freestyle, Naiant, Natatorial, Paddle, Reel, Run, Skinny-dip, Soom, Synchro(nized), Trudgen, Whim, Whirl

▷ **Swim** *may indicate* an anagram

Swimmer Bather, Cichlid, Copepod(a), Duckbill, Duckmole, Dugong, Frogman, Leander, Pad(d)le, Paidle, Planula, Pleopod, Pobble, Terrapin, Trudgen, Webb

▷ **Swimmer** *may indicate* a fish

Swimming costume Bathers, Bikini, Cossie, Maillot, Monokini, One-piece, Tanga, Tankini, Tog, Trunks

Swindle(r) Beat, Bite, Bucket-shop, Bunco, Bunkosteerer, Cajole, Champerty, → **CHEAT**, Chouse, Con, Crimp, Defraud, Diddle, Do, Escroc, Fake, Fiddle, Finagle, Fineer, Fleece, Fraud, Gazump, Gip, Goose-trap, Graft, Grifter, Gyp, Hocus, Hoser, Hustler, Leg, Leger, Long-firm, Magsman, Mountebank, Mulct, Nobble, Peter Funk, Plant, Racket, Ramp, Rig, Rogue, Scam, Sell, Shakedown, Shark, Sharper,

Shicer, Shyster, Skelder, Skin, Skin game, Slicker, Sting, Stitch-up, Stumer, Suck, Swiz(z), Trick, Twist, Two-time

Swine(herd) Boar, Brute, Cad, Eumaeus, Gadarene, Heel, Hog, Peccary, Pig, Porcine, Pork, Rotter, Sounder, Sow, Sybotic

Swing(er), Swinging Colt, Dangle, Flail, Hang, Hep, Kip(p), Lilt, Metronome, Mod, Music, Oscillate, Pendulate, Pendulum, Reverse, Rock, Rope, Shog, Shoogie, Shuggy, Slew, Swale, Sway, Swee, Swerve, Swey, Swipe, Trapeze, Vibratile, Voop, Wave, Western, Wheel, Whirl, Yaw

Swipe(s) Backhander, Beer, Haymaker, Steal, Strike, Tap-lash

Swirl Eddy, Purl, Swoosh, Tourbill(i)on, Twist, Whirl

▷ **Swirling** *may indicate* an anagram

Swish Cane, Frou-frou, Rustle, Smart, Whir, Whisper

Swiss Genevese, Ladin, Roll, Tell, Vaudois

Switch(ed), Switches, Switching Birch, Change, Convert, Crossbar, Cryotron, Dimmer, Dip, Exchange, Gang, Hairpiece, Knife, Legerdemain, Mercury, Message, Pear, Point, Replace, Retama, Rocker, Rod, Scutch, Thyristor, Time, Toggle, Tress, Trip, Tumbler, Twig, Wave, Zap

▷ **Switched** *may indicate* an anagram

Switzerland CH, Helvetia

Swivel Caster, Pivot, Root, Rotate, Spin, Terret, Territ, Torret, Turret, Wedein

Swiz Chiz(z)

Swollen Blown, Bollen, Bombe, Bulbous, Full, Gourdy, Gouty, Incrassate, Nodose, Puffy, Tumid, Turgescent, Turgid, Varicose, Ventricose, Vesiculate

Swoon Blackout, Collapse, Deliquium, Dover, Dwa(l)m, Dwaum, Faint

Swoop Descend, Dive, Glide, Plummet, Souse

▶ **Swop** *see* **SWAP**

Sword(-like), Swordplay Andrew Ferrara, Anelace, Angurvadel, Anlace, Arondight, Assegai, Balisarda, Balmunc, Balmung, Bilbo, Blade, Brand, Brandiron, Broad(sword), Brondyron, Caliburn, Cemitare, Claymore, Colada, Court, Curtal-ax, Curtana, Curtax, Cutlass, Daisho, Damascene, Damaskin, Damocles, Dance, Dirk, Duranda(l), Durindana, Ensate, Ensiform, Epée, Espada, Estoc, Excalibur, Falchion, Faulchi(o)n, Firangi, Foil, Forte, Fox, Gladius, Glaive, Gleave, Glorious, Hanger, Iai-do, Jacob's staff, Joyeuse, Katana, Kendo, Khanda, Kirpan, Kreese, Kris, Kukri, Kusanagi, Machete, Mandau, Merveilleuse, Mimming, Montanto, Morglay, Nothung, Parang, Philippan, Rapier, Rosse, Sabre, Samurai, Schiavone, Schläger, Scimitar, Semita(u)r, Shabble, Shamshir, Sharp, Sigh, Simi, Skene-dhu, Smallsword, Spadroon, Spirtle, Spit, Spurtle(blade), Steel, Toasting-iron, Toledo, Tuck, Tulwar, Two-edged, Waster, Whinger, Whiniard, Whinyard, White-arm, Xiphoid, Yatag(h)an

Sword-bearer, Swordsman(ship), Swordswoman Aramis, Athos, Blade, Brenda(n), D'Artagnan, Fencer, Frog, Gladiator, Matador, Porthos, Sai-do, Selictar, Spadassin, Spadroon, Spartacus, Swashbuckler, Zorro

Sword-dancer Matachin

Swordfish Espada, Istiophorus, Xiphias

Sword-swallower Samite

Swot Dig, Grind, Kill, Mug, Read up, Smug, Stew, Strike, Swat

Sybarite Aristippus, Epicure, Hedonist, Voluptuary

Sycamore Acer, Maple, Plane, Tree

Sycophant(ic) Apple polisher, Brown-nose, Claqueur, Crawler, Creeper, Damocles, Fawner, Gnathonic, Lickspittle, Parasite, Pickthank, Placebo, Toad-eater, Toady, Yesman

Syllabary Hiragana, Kana, Katakana
Syllable(s) Acatalectic, Anacrusis, Aretinian, Nonsense, Om, Outride, Tonic
Syllabus Program(me), Prospectus, Résumé, Summary, Table, Timetable
Syllogism Argument, Conclusion, Deduction, Enthymeme, Epicheirema, Sorites
Sylph Ariel, Nymph
Symbol(s), Symbolic, Symbolism, Symbolist Acrophony, Agma, Algebra,
Allegory, Ampersand, Aniconic, Ankh, Apostrophus, Aramanth, Asterisk, Badge,
Cachet, Caret, Cedilla, Character, Charactery, Chord, Choropleth, Christogram,
Cipher, Clef, Colon, Crest, Daffodil, Decadent, Del, Descriptor, Diesis, Dingbat,
Double-axe, Eagle, Emblem, Emoticon, Eng, Equal, Fertility, Grammalogue,
Grapheme, Hash, Heitiki, Hieroglyph, Hierogram, Hiragana, Ichthus, Icon,
Iconography, Ideogram, Index, Kalachakra, Kanji, Length mark, Lexigram,
Logo(gram), Logograph, Mandala, Mark, Menorah, Metaphor, Mezuzah, Minus,
Mogen David, Moral, Motif, Mystical, Nabla, Neum(e), Nominal, Notation, Obelus,
Om, One, Operator, Ouroborus, Paragraph, Pentacle, Phonetic, Phonogram,
Phraseogram, Pi, Pictogram, Pictograph, Plus, Presa, Punctuation, Quantifier,
Redon, Rose, Rune, Sacrament, Segno, Semicolon, Semiotic, Sex, Shamrock, Sigla,
Sign, Slur, Smiley, Star of David, Status, Svastika, Swastika, Syllabary, Syllabogram,
Synthetism, Tag, Talisman, Tetragrammaton, Thistle, Tiki, Tilde, Token, Totem,
Trademark, Triskele, Triskelion, Type, Uraeus, Waymark, Wild card, Yoni
Symmetric(al), Symmetry Balance, Bilateral, Digonal, Diphycercal, Even,
Harmony, Isobilateral, Mirror, Pseudocubic, Radial, Regular, Skew
Sympathetic, Sympathise(r), Sympathy Approval, Commiserate, Commiseration,
Compassion, Condole(nce), Condone, Congenial, Crypto, Dear-dear, Empathy,
Fellow-traveller, Humane, Mediagenic, Par, Pathos, Pity, Rapport, Ruth, Side,
Vicarious, Well-disposed
Symphony Concert, Eroica, Farewell, Fifth, Jupiter, Manfred, Music, New World,
Opus, Pastoral, Sinfonia, Sinfonietta, Unfinished
Symposium Assembly, Conference, Synod
Symptom(s) Epiphenomenon, Feature, Indicia, Merycism, Mimesis, Prodrome,
Semiotic, Sign, Syndrome, Token, Trait, Withdrawal
Synagogue Beit Knesset, Beth Knesseth, Shul, Temple
Synchronise(r) Coincide, Genlock, Tune
Syncopated, Syncopation, Syncope Abridged, Breakbeat, Revamp, Vasovagal,
Zoppa, Zoppo
Syndicate Associate, Cartel, Combine, Mafioso, Pool, Ring, Stokvel
Syndrome Adams-Stokes, Asperger's, Carpal tunnel, Cerebellar, Characteristic,
China, Chinese restaurant, Chronic fatigue, Compartment, Couvade, Cri du
chat, Crush, Cushing's, De Clerambault's, Down's, Economy-class, Empty nest,
Fetal alcohol, Fragile X, Goldenhar's, Gorlin, Guillain-Barré, Gulf War, Hughes,
Hutchinson-Gilford, Irritable-bowel, Jerusalem, Klinefelter's, Korsakoff's,
Locked-in, Marfan, ME, Menières, Metabolic, Munch(h)ausen's, Nonne's,
Overuse, Parkinson's, Pattern, POS, Postviral, Prader-Willi, Premenstrual,
Proteus, Reiter's, Rett's, Reye's, SADS, SARS, Savant, Sezary, Sick building, SIDS,
Sjogren's, Stevens-Johnson, Stockholm, Stokes-Adams, Sturge-Weber, Tall-poppy,
Temperomandibular, TMJ, Total allergy, Tourette's, Toxic shock, Turner's, Wag the
dog, Wernicke-Korsakoff, Williams, Wobbler, XYY
Synod Assembly, Conference, Convocation, General, Whitby
Synonym(ous) Comparison, Reciprocal
Synopsis Abstract, Blurb, Conspectus, Digest, Outline, Résumé, Schema,
→ SUMMARY

Syntax Grammar
Synthesis Amalgam, Aperture, Fusion, Merger
Synthesizer Moog®, Vocoder, Wind
Synthetic Empirical, Ersatz, Fake, False, Mock, Plastic, Polyamide, Silicone, Spencerian
Syphilis Chancre, Lues, Pip
Syrian Aramaean, Aramaic, Druse, Druz(e), Hittite, Hurrian, Levantine, Phoenician
Syringe(s) Douche, Flutes, Harpoon, Hypo, Hypodermic, Needle, Reeds, Spray, Squirt, Wash, Works
Syrphid Hoverfly
Syrup Capillaire, Cassareep, Cassis, Cocky's joy, Coquito, Corn, Diacodion, Diacodium, Flattery, Glycerol, Golden, Grenadine, Linctus, Maple, Molasses, Moskonfyt, Orgeat, Quiddany, Rob, Sorghum, Sugar, Treacle
System(s), Systematic ABO, Alpha, An mo, Bertillon, Binary, Bordereau, Braille, Carboniferous, Centauri, Circulatory, Code, Colonial, Compander, → COMPUTER SYSTEMS, Continental, Copernican, Cosmos, Course, Crystal, Decimal, Delsarte, Dewey (Decimal), Distributed, Early warning, Economy, Eocene, Ergodic, Establishment, Expert, Feudal, Fixed, Formal, Fourierism, Froebel, Giorgi, Grading, Harvard, HLA, Honour, Hub and spoke, Iastic, Immune, Imprest, Imputation, Induction loop, Inertial, ISA, Kalamazoo, Kanban, Life-support, Limbic, Lobby, Loop, Lymphatic, Madras, Mercantile, Merit, → METHOD, Metric, Microcosm, Midi, Miocene, Movable, Muschelkalk, Natural, Navigational, Nervous, Network, Nicam, Notation, Number, Octal, Operating, Order, Organon, Panel, Periodic, Permian, Pleiocene, Plenum, Points, Process, Ptolemaic, Public address, Purchase, Quota, Quote-driven, Raisonné, Regime, Regular, Respiratory, Root, Run-time, Scheme, Scientific, Servo, Sexual, SI, Sofar, Solar, Solmisation, Sonar, Sound, Spoils, Sprinkler, Squish lip, Stack(ing), Staff, Stanislavski, Star, Stakhanovism, Structure, Studio, Sweating, Tactic, Talk-down, Tally, Ternary, Theory, Third-rail, Tommy, Touch, Trias(sic), Truck, Turnkey, Tutorial, Two-party, Universe, Unix, Urogenital, Vestibular, VOIP, Warehousing, Water, Water vascular, Weapon

Tt

T Bone, Junction, Potence, Tango, Tau-cross, Tee, Time, Toc(k)
Tab Bill, Check, Decimal, → LABEL, Ring-pull, Stay-on, Tally, Trim, Trimming
Tabby Blabbermouth, Brindled, → CAT, Gossip, Mottled, Spinster, Striped, Trout
Tabitha Gazelle
Table(-like) Alphonsine, Altar, Board, Bradshaw, Breakfast, Calendar, → CHART,
 Coffee, Communion, Console, Contingency, Corbel, Counter, Credence, Credenza,
 Decision, Desk, Diagram, Dinner, Dolmen, Draw-leaf, Draw-top, Dressing,
 Drop-leaf, Drum, Ephemeris, Experience, Food, Gateleg, Gate-legged, Glacier,
 Graph, Green-cloth, Gueridon, High, Imposing, Index, Key, League, Life, Light,
 → LIST, Lord's, Lowboy, Mahogany, Matrix, Mensa(l), Mesa, Monopode, Mortality,
 Multiplication, Occasional, Operating, Orientation, Pembroke, Periodic, Piecrust,
 Pier, Plane, Platen, Pool, Prothesis, Pythagoras, Ready-reckoner, Reckoner,
 Refectory, Roll, Round, Rudolphine, Sand, Schedule, Scheme, Slab, Sofa, Spoon,
 Stall, Statistical, Stone, Taboret, Tabular, Tea, Te(a)poy, Throwing, Tide, Times,
 Toilet, Toning, Top, Traymobile, Trestle, Trolley, Truth, Twelve, Washstand,
 Water, Whirling, Wool, Workbench, Writing
Tableau Semantic
Tablecloth Damask, Linen
Table-land Barkly, Kar(r)oo, Mesa, Plateau, Puna
Table-list Memo, Menu
Tablet Abacus, Album, Aspirin, Caplet, Eugebine, Graphics, Hatch, Medallion,
 Opisthograph, Osculatory, Ostracon, Ostrakon, → PAD, → PILL, Pilule, Plaque,
 Slate, Stele, Stone, Tombstone, Torah, Triglyph, Triptych, Troche, Trochisk, Ugarit,
 Votive
Table-talker Deipnosophist
Table-turner Tartar
Table-ware China, Cutlery, Silver
Taboo, Tabu Ban(ned), Bar, Blackball, Forbidden, Incest, Non dit, No-no, Unclean
Tachograph Spy-in-the-cab
Tacit, Taciturn(ity) Implicit, Laconic, Mumps, Oyster, Reticent, Silent, Understood
Tack(y) Bar, Baste, Beat, Boxhaul, Brass, Cheesy, Cinch, Clubhaul, Cobble, Gybe,
 Leg, Martingale, Nail, Saddlery, Salt-horse, → SEW, Sprig, Stirrup, Tailor's, Veer,
 Wear, White-seam, Yaw, Zigzag
Tackle Accost, Approach, Attempt, Beard, Bobstay, Burton, Cat, Claucht, Claught,
 Clevis, Clew-garnet, Collar, Dead-eye, Fishing, Garnet, Gear, Haliard, Halyard,
 Harness, Jury-rig, Nose, Rig, Rigging, Scrag, Straight-arm, Topping-lift, Undertake
Tact, Tactful Delicacy, Diplomacy, Diplomatic, Discreet, Discretion, Politic,
 Savoir-faire
Tactic(s) Audible, Finesse, Hardball, Manoeuvre, Masterstroke, Plan, Ploy, Ruse,
 Salami, Scare, Shock, Smear, → STRATEGY, Strong-arm, Zwischenzug
Tactless(ness) Blundering, Brash, Crass, Gaffe, Gauche, Indelicate, Maladroit

Tadpole Ascidian, Polliwig, Polliwog, Pollywig, Pollywog, Porwiggle
Taffy Thief, Toffee, Welshman
Tag Aglet, Aiguillette, Cliché, Dog, Electronic, End, Epithet, → FOLLOW, Kabaddi,
Kimball, Label, Meta, Price, Question, Quote, Remnant, Tab, → TICKET, Treasury
Tail, Tailpiece, Tailboard All-flying, Amentum, Apocopate, → APPENDAGE, Bob,
Brush, Caudal, Cercal, Cercus, Coda, Codetta, Colophon, Cue, Dock, Empennage,
Endgate, Fan, Fee, Flag, Floccus, → FOLLOW, Fud, Liripoop, Parson's nose, Pole,
Pope's nose, PS, Queue, Rumple-bane, Scut, Seat, Shirt, Stag, Stern, Telson, → TIP,
Train, Uro(some), Uropygium, Women
Tailless Acaudal, An(o)urous, Fee-simple
Tail-lobes Anisocercal
Tailor(ed) Adapt, Bespoke, Bushel, Cabbager, Couturier, Cutter, Darzi, Draper,
Durzi, Epicene, Feeble, Flint, Merchant, Nine, Outfitter, Pick-the-louse, Pricklouse,
Sartor, Seamster, Snip, Starveling, Style, Whipcat, Whipstitch
▷ **Tailor** *may indicate* an anagram
Taint(ed) Besmirch, Blemish, Fly-blown, High, Infect, Leper, Off, Poison, → SPOIL,
Stain, Stale, Stigma, Tinge, Trace, Unwholesome
Taiwan RC
Take(n), Take in, Taking(s), Take over, Takeover Absorb, → ACCEPT,
Adopt, Assume, Attract, Bag, Beg, Bite, Bone, Borrow, Bottle, → CAPTURE,
Catch, Charming, Claim, Cop, Coup, Detract, Dishy, Distrain, Entr(y)ism, Exact,
Expropriate, Film, Get, Grab, Greenmail, Handle, Haul, Hent, House, Howe, Huff,
Incept, Ingest, Leveraged buy out, Mess, Misappropriate, Nick, Occupy, Pocket,
Quote, R, Rec, Receipt, Receive, Recipe, Reverse, Rob, Seise, Sequester, Ship,
Smitten, Snatch, Sneak, → STEAL, Stomach, Subsume, Swallow, Sweet, Swipe, Toll,
Trump, Turnover, Usher, Usurp, Wan, Winsome, Wrest
Take away, Take-away, Take off Aph(a)eresis, Asport, Carry-out, Deduct,
Dock, Doff, Esloin, Exenterate, Expropriate, Indian, Jato, Minus, Parody, Parrot,
Press-gang, Shanghai, Skit, Subtract, Vertical, VTO(L)
Take care Guard, See, Tend, Watch
▷ **Taken up** *may indicate* reversed
Take part Act, Engage, Side
Talbot House Toc H
Talc Potstone, Rensselaerite, Soapstone, Steatite, Venice
Tale(s) Aga-saga, Allegory, Anecdote, Blood, Boccaccio, Conte, Decameron, Edda,
Fable, Fabliau, Fairy, Fairy story, Fiction, Folk, Gag, Geste, Hadith, Iliad, Jataka,
Jeremiad, Legend, Lie, Mabinogion, Maise, Ma(i)ze, Märchen, Mease, Milesian,
Narrative, Odyssey, Old wives', Pentameron, Rede, Saga, Sandabar, Score, Sinbad,
Sind(a)bad, Sob-story, Spiel, → STORY, Tradition, Traveller's, Weird
Tale-bearer, Tale-teller Gossip, Grass, Informer, Sneak, Tattler, Tusitala
Talent(ed) Ability, Accomplishment, Aptitude, Bent, Dower, Faculty, Flair, Forte,
Genius, Gift, Ingenium, Knack, Long suit, Nous, Prodigy, Schtick, Strong point,
Versatile, Virtuoso, W(h)iz(z), Whiz-kid
Talion Reprisal
Talisman Amulet, Charm, Mascot, Saladin, Sampo, Scarab, Telesm
Talk(ing), Talking point, Talker, Talks Address, Ana, Articulate, Babble,
Bibble-babble, Blab, Blague, Blat, Blather, Blether-skate, Cant, Chalk, Chat,
Chinwag, Chirp, Circumlocution, Colloquy, Commune, Confabulate, Confer,
Converse, Coo, Cross, Descant, Dialog(ue), Diatribe, Dilate, Discourse, Diseur,
Dissert, Double, Earbash, Earful, Express, Fast, Filibuster, Froth, Gab, Gabble,
Gabnash, Gas, Gibber, Gossip, Grandiloquence, Guff, Harp, High-level, Imparl,

Jabber, Jargon, Jaw, Jazz, Korero, Lalage, Lip, Logorrhoea, Macrology, Mang, Maunder, Mince, Monologue, Motormouth, Nashgab, Natter, Noise, Omniana, Palabra, Palaver, Parlance, Parley, Patter, Pawaw, Pep, Perorate, Phraser, Pidgin, Pillow, Pitch, Potter, Powwow, Prate, Prattle, Presentation, Prose, Proximity, Ramble, Rap, Rigmarole, Rote, Sales, SALT, Shop, Slang(-whang), Small, Soliloquy, → **SPEAK**, Spiel, Spout, Straight, Sweet, Table, Tachylogia, Topic, Turkey, Twaddle, Twitter, Unbosom, Up(s), Utter, Vocal, Waffle, Wibble, Witter, Wongi, Wrangle, Yabber, Yack, Yad(d)a-yad(d)a-yad(d)a, Yak, Yalta, Yammer, Yap, Yatter

Talkative Chatty, Fluent, Gabby, Garrulous, Gash, Glib, Loquacious, Vocular, Voluble

Tall Etiolated, Exaggerated, Far-fetched, Hie, High, Hye, Lanky, Lathy, Leggy, Lofty, Long, Order, Procerity, Randle-tree, Rantle-tree, Tangle, Taunt, Tower, Towery

Tallboy Chest, Dresser

Tallow Greaves, Hatchettite, Lead-arming, Mineral, Vegetable, Wax

Tally Accord, → **AGREE**, Census, Correspond, Count, Match, Nickstick, Notch, Record, → **SCORE**, Stick, Stock, Tab, Tag

Talmud Gemara, Mishna

Talon Claw, Ogee, Single

Talus Scree

Tamarind Assam

Tamasha Fuss, To-do

Tame Amenage, Break, Docile, Domesticate, Lapdog, Mail, Mansuete, Meek, Mild, Safe, Snool, Subdue

Tammany Hall, Sachem

Tamp, Tampon Plug

Tamper(ing) Bishop, Cook, Doctor, Fake, Fiddle, Meddle, Medicate, Monkey, Nobble, Phreaking

Tam-tam Gong

Tan(ned), Tanned skin, Tanning Adust, Bablah, Babul, Bark, Basil, Beige, Bisque, Boarding, Bronze, → **BROWN**, Canaigre, Catechu, Furan, Furfuran(e), Insolate, Lambast, Leather, Neb-neb, Paste, Pipi, Puer, Pure, Spank, Sun, Sunbathe, Tenné, Umber, Val(l)onia, Valonea, Ybet

Tandem Duo, Random

Tang Relish, Smack, Taste

Tangent Ratio, Slope, Touching

Tangible Concrete, Palpable, Plain, Solid, Tactual

Tangle Alga, Badderlock, Burble, Dulse, Embroil, Entwine, Fank, Fankle, Heap, Implication, Ket, → **KNOT**, Labyrinth, Laminaria, Lutin, Mat, Mix, Nest, Oarweed, Ore, Perplex, Pleach, → **RAVEL**, Sea-girdle, Seaweed, Skean, Skein, Snarl, Taigle, Taut(it), Tawt, Thicket, Tousle, Varec

▷ **Tangled** *may indicate* an anagram

Tank(ed) Abrams, Alligator, Amphibian, Aquarium, Back boiler, Belly, Bosh, Casspir, Centurion, Cesspool, Challenger, Chieftain, Cistern, Drop, Drunk, Feedhead, Float, Flotation, Gasholder, Header, Keir, Kier, Mouse, Panzer, Pod, Quiescent, → **RESERVOIR**, Ripple, Sedimentation, Septic, Sherman, Shield pond, Sponson, Sump, Surge, Think, Tiger, Valentine, Vat, Ventral, Vivarium, Whippet

Tankard Blackjack, Peg, Pewter, Pot, Stein, Tappit-hen

Tanker Bowser, Lorry, Oiler

Tanner(y) Bender, Currier, Kick, Solarium, Sunbather, Sunshine, Tawery, Tester(n), 'VId', Zack

Tannin Catechu

Tantalise Entice, Tease, Tempt, Torture
Tantalum Ta
Tantivy Alew, Halloo
Tantrum Hissyfit, Paddy, Pet, Rage, Scene, Snit, Tirrivee, Tirrivie
Tanzania EAT
Tap(ping), Taps Accolade, Bibcock, Blip, Bob, Broach, Bug, Cock, Col legno, Drum, Faucet, Fillip, Flick, Hack, Mag, Milk, Mixer, Monitor, Paracentesis, Pat, Patter, Percuss, Petcock, → **RAP**, Screw, Spigot, Spinal, Stopcock, Stroup, Tack, Tat, Tit, Touk, Tuck, Water
Tape Chrome, DAT, → **DRINK**, Duct, Ferret, Finish, Friction, Gaffer, Grip, Idiot, Incle, Inkle, Insulating, Magnetic, Masking, Measure, Metal, Narrowcast, Paper, Passe-partout, Perforated, Punched, Record, Red, Scotch, Sellotape®, Shape, Stay, Sticky, Ticker, Video, Welding
Taper(ed), Tapering Diminish, Fastigiate, Featheredge, Flagelliform, Fusiform, Lanceolate, Morse, Narrow, Nose, Subulate, Tail
Tapestry Alentous, Arras(ene), Aubusson, Bayeux, Bergamot, Crewel-work, Dosser, Gobelin, Hanging, Oudenarde, Petit point, Tapet, Weaving
Tapeworm Echinococcus, Hydatid, Measle, Scolex, Strobila, Taenia, Teniasis
Tapioca Cassava, Pearl, Yuca, Yucca
Tapir Anta, S(e)ladang
Tar, Tar product AB, Bitumen, Carbazole, Coal, Creosote, Egg, Furan, Gladwellise, Gob, Indene, Maltha, Matelot, Matlo, Mineral, Naphtha, Needle, OS, Parcel, Pay, Picamar, Picene, Pine, Pitch, Rating, Retene, Sailor, Salt, Uintahite, Uintaite, Wood, Wood pitch, Xylol
Tardy Behindhand, Dilatory, Late, → **SLOW**
Tare Tine, Vetch
Target → **AIM**, Attainment, Blank, Butt, Clout, Cockshy, Dart, Drogue, End, Hit, Home, Hub, Inner, Magpie, Mark, Motty, → **OBJECT**, Outer, Pelta, Pin, Prey, Prick, Quintain, Sitter, Sitting, Tee, Victim, Wand
Tariff List, Menu, Preferential, Protective, Rate, Revenue, Zabeta
Tarnish Defile, Discolour, Soil, Stain, Sully, Taint
Taro Arum, Coc(c)o, Dasheen, Eddo
Tarot Arcana
Tarpaulin Weathercloth
Tarragon Staragen
Tarry Bide, Dally, Leng, → **LINGER**, Stay, Sticky
Tarsier Malmag
Tarsus Saul
Tart Acetic, Acid, Bakewell, Broad, Charlotte, Cheesecake, Cocotte, Croquante, Cupid, Custard, Dariole, Doxy, Duff, Flam(m), Flan, Flawn, Frock, Harlot, Hussy, Jade, Lemony, Mirliton, Moll, Mort, Nana, Painted woman, → **PIE**, Pinnace, Piquant, Pro, Quean, Quiche, Quine, → **SHARP**, Slapper, Slut, Snappy, Sour, Stew, Strumpet, Tatin, Tramp, Treacle, Trull, Unsweet
Tartan Argyle, Argyll, Maud, Plaid, Set(t), Trews
Tartar Argal, Argol, Beeswing, Calculus, Crust, Hell, Plaque, Rough, Scale, Tam(b)erlane, Zenocrate
Tashkent Uzbek
Task Assignment, Aufgabe, → **CHORE**, Clat, Duty, Errand, Exercise, Fag, Imposition, Mission, Ordeal, Pensum, Stint, Thankless, Vulgus
Tasmania Apple Isle, Van Diemen's Land
Tassel Pompom, Toorie, Tourie, Tsutsith, Tuft

Taste(ful), Taster, Tasty Acquired, Aesthetic, Appetite, Degust, Delibate, Delicious, Discrimination, → **EAT**, Elegant, Fashion, Flavour, Form, Gout, Gust, Gustatory, Hint, Lekker, Lick, Palate, Penchant, Pica, Pree, Refinement, Relish, → **SAMPLE**, Sapor, Sar, Savour, S(c)hme(c)k, Sip, Smack, Smatch, Smattering, Snack, Soupçon, Stomach, Succulent, Tang, Titbit, Toothsome, → **TRY**, Umami, Vertu, Virtu, Waft, Wine

Tasteless Appal, Brassy, Fade, Flat, Insipid, Insulse, Kitsch, Stale, Tacky, Vapid, Vulgar, Watery, Wearish, Wersh

Tat, Tatter, Tatty Rag, Ribbon, Roon, Scrap, Shred, Tag, Ta(i)ver, Tan, Untidy

Tattie-bogle Scarecrow

Tattle(r) Blab, Chatter, Gash, → **GOSSIP**, Prate, Rumour, Sneak, Snitch, Totanus, Willet

Tattoo Devil's, Drum, Edinburgh, Moko, Rataplan, Row-dow, Tat

Tatum Art

Taught Up

Taunt Dig, Fling, Gibe, Gird, → **JEER**, Rag, Ridicule, Twight, Twit

Taut Stiff, Tense

Tavern Bar, Bodega, Bousing-ken, Bush, Fonda, → **INN**, Kiddleywink, Kneipe, Mermaid, Mitre, Mughouse, Pothouse, Shebeen, Taphouse

Taw Alley, Ally, Marble

Tawdry Catchpenny, → **CHEAP**, Flashy, Gaudy, Raffish, Sleazy, Tatty, Tinsey

Tawny Brindle, Dusky, Fawn, Fulvous, Mulatto, Port, Tan

Tawse Cat, Lash, Thong, Whip

Tax(ing), Taxation ACT, Agist, Aid, Alms-fee, Assess, Capitation, Carbon, Carucage, Cense, Cess, → **CHARGE**, Corporation, Council, Custom, Danegeld, Direct, Duty, Energy, EPT, Escot, Escuage, Eurotax, Exact, Excise, Exercise, EZT, Fat, Gabelle, Geld, Gift, Head, Head money, Hearth money, Hidage, Impose, Imposition, Impost, Impute, Indirect, Inheritance, IR, Jaghir(e), Jagir, Land, Levy, Likin, Lot, Murage, Negative, Octroi, Operose, Overwork, Pavage, PAYE, Peter-pence, Poll, Poundage, Precept, Primage, Property, Proportional, PT, Punish, Purchase, Rate, Regressive, Road, Rome-pence, Sales, Scat(t), Scot (and lot), Scutage, Sess, SET, Sin, Single, Skat, Stealth, Stent, Streetage, Stumpage, Super, Taille, Tallage, Talliate, Tariff, Task, Teind, Tithe, Tobin, Toilsome, Toll, Tonnage, Tribute, Try, Turnover, Unitary, Value-added, VAT, Wattle, Wealth, Weary, White rent, Windfall, Window, Withholding, Zakat

Tax area Tahsil, Talooka, Taluk(a)

Tax-collector, Taxman Amildar, Cheater, Exciseman, Farmer, Gabeller, Inspector, IR(S), Publican, Stento(u)r, Tithe-proctor, Tollman, Undertaker, Zemindar

Taxi Cab, Gharri, Gharry, Hackney, Joe baxi, Samlor, Zola Budd

Taxidermist Venus

▶ **Taxman** see **TAX-COLLECTOR**

TB Scrofula

TE Lawrence, Ross, Shaw

Tea Afternoon, Assam, Beef, Black, Bohea, Brew, Brew-up, Brick, Bubble, Bush, Cambric, Camomile, Caper, Ceylon, Cha, Chamomile, Chanoyu, China, Chirping-cup, Congo(u), Cream, Cuppa, Darjeeling, Earl Grey, Grass, Green, Gunfire, Gunpowder, Herb(al), High, Hyson, Indian, Jasmine, K(h)at, Kitchen, Labrador, Lapsang, Lapsang Souchong, Leaves, Ledum, Lemon, Malt, Manuka, Marijuana, Maté, Mexican, Mint, Morning, Mountain, New Jersey, Oolong, Orange pekoe, Oulong, Paraguay, Pekoe, Post and rail, Pot, Qat, Red-root, Rooibos, Rosie Lee, Russian, Sage, Senna, Souchong, Stroupach, Stroupan, Switchel, Tay, Thea,

Theophylline, Tousy, Twankay, Yerba (de Maté)
Teach(er), Teaching (material), Teachings Acharya, Adjoint, Advisory, Agrege,
   AMMA, Anthroposophy, Apostle, Aristotle, Barbe, Beale, BEd, Bhagwan, Buss,
   Catechist, Chalk and talk, Chalkface, → **COACH**, Con(ne), Didactic, Didascalic,
   Docent, Doctrine, Dogma, Dominie, Dressage, Edify, → **EDUCATE**, Educationalist,
   Edutainment, EIS, ELT, Explain, Faculty, Froebel, Gerund-grinder, Gooroo,
   Gospel, Governess, Guru, Head, Heuristic, Hodja, Inculcate, Indoctrinate,
   Inform, Instil, Instruct, Ism, Kho(d)ja, Kumon (Method), Lair, Lancasterian, Larn,
   Lear(e), Lecturer, Leir, Lere, Maam, Maggid, Magister, Maharishi, Mahavira,
   Mallam, Marker, Marm, Master, Maulvi, Mentor, Miss, Mistress, Molla(h),
   Monitor, Montessorian, Moola(h), Moolvi(e), Mufti, Mullah, Munshi, Mwalimu,
   Mystagogue, Nuffield, Paedotribe, Pedagogue, Pedant, Peripetatic, Phonic method,
   Posture-master, Pr(a)efect, Preceptor, Privat-docent, Proctor, Prof, Prog, PT, Pupil,
   Rabbetzin, Rabbi, Rav, Realia, Rebbe, Remedial, Rhetor, Scholastic, Schoolie,
   Schoolman, Scribe, Sensei, Show, Sir, Smriti, Socrates, Sophist, Staff, Starets,
   Staretz, Sunna, Supply, Swami, Tantra, Team, Tonic sol-fa, Train(er), Tutelage,
   Tutor, Tutress, Tutrix, Usher
Teach-in Seminar
Teahouse Sukiya
Teak African, Bastard, White
Team Bafana Bafana, Colts, Crew, Dream, Écurie, Eleven, Équipe, Farm, Fifteen,
   Outfit, Oxen, Panel, Possibles, Probables, Proto, Relay, Scrub, → **SIDE**, Span,
   Special, Spurs, Squad, Squadron, Staff, Tiger, Troupe, Turnout, Unicorn, United, XI
Tea-party Boston, Bunfight, Cookie-shine, Drum, Kettledrum, Shine
Teapot Billycan, Cadogan, Samovar
Tear(s), Tearable, Tearful, Tearing Beano, Claw, Crocodile, Divulsion, Drop,
   Eye-drop, Eye-water, Greeting, Hurry, Lacerate, Laniary, Mammock, Pelt, Ranch,
   Rash, Reave, → **REND**, Rheum, Rip, Rive, Rume, Scag, Screed, Shred, Snag, Split,
   Spree, Tire, Waterworks, Wet, Worry, Wrench, Wrest
Tearaway Get, Hothead, Ned
Tear-jerker Melodrama, Onion
Tear-pit Crumen, Larmier
Tease, Teaser, Teasing Arch, Backcomb, Badinage, Bait, Banter, Card, Chaff, Chap,
   Chiack, Chip, Chyack, Cod, Coquet, Enigma, Grig, Guy, Hank, Imp, Ironic, Itch,
   Josh, Kemb, Kid, Mag, Mamaguy, Nark, Persiflage, → **RAG**, Raillery, Rally, Razz,
   Rib, Rip on, Rot, Strip, → **TANTALISE**, Toaze, Torment(or), Touse, Touze, Towse,
   Towze, Twilly, Twit, Worrit
Teasel Dipsacus, Valerian
Teat Dug, Dummy, Mamilla, Mastoid, Nipple, Pap, Soother, Tit
Tea-time Chat
Teaze Gig, Moze
Technetium Tc
Technical, Technician, Technique Adept, Alexander, Artisan, Brushwork,
   College, Cusum, Delphi, Execution, Foley artist, Footsteps editor, Harmolodics,
   Honey-trap, Junior, Kiwi, Know-how, Layback, Manner, → **METHOD**, Operative,
   Phasing, Pixil(l)ation, Salami, Sandwich, Science, Senior, Serial, Split-screen,
   Stop-motion, Toe and heel
Technology, Technological High, Information, Intermediate, State of the art,
   Stealth
Ted(dy) Bodgie, Dexter, Ducktail, Moult, Widgie, Yob
Tedium, Tedious Boring, Chore, Deadly, Doldrums, Drag, Dreich, Dull, Ennui,

Foozle, Heaviness, Long, Longspun, Longueur, Monotony, Operose, Prosy, Soul-destroying, Tiresome, → **TIRING**, Twaddle, Wearisome, Yawn

Tee Hub, Umbrella, Wind

Teem(ing) Abound, Bustling, Empty, Great, Pullulate, Swarm

Teenager Adolescent, Bobbysoxer, Junior, Juvenile, Minor, Mod, Rocker, Sharpie, Skinhead, Youth

▶ **Teeth** *see* **TOOTH**

Teething ring Coral

Teetotal(ler) Abdar, Blue Ribbon, Nephalist, Rechabite, Temperate, TT, Water-drinker, Wowser

Tegument Seed coat

Telecommunications Cellnet®, Vodafone®

Telegram, Telegraph Bush, Cable, Ems, Facsimile, Fax, Grapevine, Greetings, International, Message, Moccasin, Mulga wire, Overseas, Singing, Telex, Wire

Telepathy, Telepathic Clairvoyance, ESP, Seer

Telephone Ameche, ATLAS, Bell, Blower, BT, Call, Cellphone, Centrex, Cordless, Dial, Dog and bone, Freephone®, GRACE, Handset, Horn, Hotline, Intercom, Line, Lo-call®, Mercury, Mobile, Noki, Pay-station, Pdq, → **PHONE**, POTS, Ring, Snitch line, Squawk box, STD, Textphone, Tie line, Touch-tone, Utility, Vodafone®, Wire

Teleprinter Creed

Telescope Altazimuth, Astronomical, Binocle, Cassegrain(ian), Collimator, Coudé, Electron, Equatorial, Finder, Galilean, Gemini, Glass, Gregorian, Heliometer, Hubble, Intussuscept, Meniscus, Newtonian, Night-glass, Optical, Palomar, Perspective, Radio, Reflecting, Reflector, Refractor, Schmidt, Shorten, Sniperscope, Snooperscope, Spyglass, Stadia, Terrestrial, Tube, X-ray, Zenith

Teletext® Ceefax®, Oracle®

Television, Telly Appointment, Box, Cable, Closed-circuit, Confessional, Digital, Diorama, Docu-soap, Event, Flatscreen, Goggle box, Image orthicon, Interactive, ITV, MAC, Narrowcast, PAL, Pay, Plumbicon®, Projection, RTE, Satellite, SECAM, Set, Small screen, Subscription, Tree and branch, Tube, → **TV**, Video

Tell(ing) Acquaint, Announce, Apprise, Archer, Beads, Blab, Break, Clipe, Clype, Compt, Direct, → **DISCLOSE**, Divulge, Effective, Grass, Impart, Influential, Inform, → **NARRATE**, Noise, Notify, Number, Recite, Recount, Relate, Report, Retail, Rumour, Sneak, Snitch, Spin, Teach, Unbosom, William

Tellurium Te

Temerity Cheek, Gall, Impertinence, Imprudence, Impudence, Incaution, Rashness, Recklessness

Temper, Temperate Abstemious, Abstinent, Allay, Anneal, Assuage, Attune, Balmy, Bile, Blood, Calm, Cantankerous, Choler, Comeddle, Continent, Dander, Delay, Ease, Fireworks, Flaky, Inure, Irish, Leaven, → **MILD**, Mitigate, Moderate, Modify, → **MOOD**, Neal, Paddy, Paddywhack, Pet, Radge, Rage, Season, Short fuse, Snit, Sober, Spitfire, Spleen, Strop, Swage, Tantrum, Techy, Teen, Teetotal, Tetchy, Tiff, Tone, Trim, Tune

Temperament(al) Bent, Blood, Choleric, Crasis, Disposition, Equal, Just, Kidney, Mean-tone, Melancholy, Mettle, Moody, → **NATURE**, Neel, Over-sensitive, Phlegmatic, Prima donna, Sanguine, Unstable, Viscerotonia

Temperance Good Templar, Moderation, Pledge, Rechabite

Temperature Absolute, Celsius, Centigrade, Chambré, Colour, Critical, Curie, Dew point, Eutectic, Fahrenheit, Fever, Flashpoint, Heat, Heterothermal, Hyperthermia, Kelvin, Néel, Permissive, Regulo, Restrictive, Room, Supercritical, T, Thermodynamic, Transition, Weed, Weid

Tempest(uous) Bourasque, Euraquilo, Euroclydon, Gale, High, Marie,
→ STORM(Y), Wrathy
Temple, Temple gate Abu Simbal, Abydos, Adytum, Amphiprostyle, Artemis,
Capitol, Cella, Chapel, Church, Delphi, Delubrum, Ephesus, Erechtheum,
Erechthion, Fane, Gompa, Gurdwara, Haffet, Haffit, Heroon, Inner, Mandir(a),
Masjid, Middle, Monopteron, Monopteros, Mosque, Museum, Naos, Nymphaeum,
Pagod(a), Pantheon, Parthenon, Serapeum, → SHRINE, Shul(n), Teocalli, Teopan,
Torii, Vihara, Wat
Tempo Agoge, Lento, Rate, → RHYTHM, Rubato
Temporal Petrosal, Petrous
Temporary Acting, Caretaker, Cutcha, Ephemeral, Hobjob, Impermanent, Interim,
Kutcha, Locum, Makeshift, Pro tem, Provisional, Quick-fix, Short-term, Stopgap,
Temp, Transient, Transitional
Temporise(r) Politique
Tempt(ation), Tempting, Tempter, Temptress Allure, Apple, Bait, Beguile,
Beset, Circe, Dalilah, Decoy, Delilah, → ENTICE, Eve, Groundbait, Impulse, Lure,
Peccable, Providence, Satan, Seduce, Siren, Snare, Tantalise, Test, Tice, Trial
Ten Commandments, Decad, Dectet, Decury, Denary, Googol, 10, Iota, Long, Tera-,
Tribes, X
Tenacious, Tenacity Clayey, Determined, Dogged, Fast, Guts, Hold, Intransigent,
Persevering, Persistent, Resolute, Retentive, Sticky
Tenancy, Tenant(s) Censuarius, Cosherer, Cottar, Cotter, Cottier, Dreng, Feuar,
Feudatory, Gravelman, Homage, Ingo, Inhabit, Kindly, Leaseholder, Lessee,
→ LODGER, Metayer, Occupier, Periodic, Regulated, Rentaller, Renter, Secure,
Shorthold, Sitting, Socager, Socman, Sokeman, Suckener, Tacksman, Valvassor,
Vassal, Vavasour, Visit
Tend Care, Dress, Herd, Incline, Lean, Liable, Mind, Nurse, Prone, Run, Shepherd,
Verge
Tendency Apt, Bent, Bias, Central, Conatus, Drift, Genius, Idiosyncrasy, Import,
Militant, Penchant, Proclivity, Propensity, Trend
Tender(iser), Tenderly, Tenderness Affettuoso, Amoroso, Bid, Bill, Coin, Con
amore, Crank, Dingey, Ding(h)y, Fond, Frail, Gentle, Green, Humane, Jolly-boat,
Legal, Nesh, Nurse, → OFFER, Painful, Papain, Pinnace, Pra(a)m, Prefer, Present,
Proffer, Proposal, Quotation, Red Cross, Sair, Shepherd, → SOFT, Sore, SRN,
Submit, Sweet, Sympathy, Tendre
Tenderfoot Babe, Chechacho, Chechako, Cub, Greenhorn, Innocent
Tenderloin Psoas, Undercut
Tendon Achilles, Aponeurosis, Hamstring, Kangaroo, Leader, Paxwax, Sinew,
String, Vinculum, Whitleather
Tendril(led) Capreolate, Cirrose, Cirrus, Tentacle
Tenement(s) Dominant, Land, Rookery, Tack
Tenet Adiaphoron, Creed, → DOCTRINE, Dogma
Tenfold Decuple
Tennis Close, Court, Deck, Lawn, LTA, Real, Royal, Set, Short, Sphairistike, Squash,
Table, Wimbledon
Tenon Cog, Dovetail, Lewis, Tusk
Tenor Course, Domingo, → DRIFT, Effect, Ferreras, Gigli, Gist, Heroic, Pavarotti,
Purport, Singer, T, Tide, Timbre, Trial, Vein
Tense Aor, Aorist, Case, Clench, Drawn, Edgy, Electric, Essive, Flex, Imperfect,
Keyed up, Mood(y), Nervy, Overstrung, Past, Perfect, Pluperfect, Preterit, Preterite,
Rigid, Simple, Stiff, Strained, Stressed(-out), Strict, T, → TAUT, Tighten, Uptight

Tensing Sherpa
Tension Creative, High, Isometrics, Isotonic, Meniscus, Nerviness, Premenstrual,
→ STRAIN, Stress, Stretch, Surface, Tone, Tonicity, Tonus, Yips
Tent Bell, Bivvy, Cabana, Douar, Dowar, Duar, Ger, Gur, Kedar, Kibitka, Marquee,
Oxygen, Pavilion, Probe, Pup, Red wine, Ridge, Shamiana(h), Shamiyanah, Shelter,
Tabernacle, Teepee, Tepee, Tilt, Tipi, Top, Topek, Trailer, Tupek, Tupik, Wigwam,
Wine, Y(o)urt
Tentacle Actinal, Cirrate, Feeler, Hectocotylus, Horn, Lophophore
Tentative Empirical, Experimental, Gingerly, Peirastic
Tent-dweller, Tent-maker Camper, Indian, Kedar, Omar, St Paul
Tenth Disme, Teind, Tithe
Ten Thousand Toman
Tenuous Frail, Slender, Slight, Thin, Vague
Tenure Blench, Burgage, Copyhold, Cottier(ism), Drengage, Fee, Fee-farm, Feu,
Frankalmoi(g)n(e), Frank-fee, Gavelkind, Leasehold, Manorial, Occupation,
Raiyatwari, Rundale, Runrig, Ryotwari, Socage, → TERM, Vavasory, Venville,
Zemindar
Tepid Laodicean, Lew, Lukewarm
Terbium Tb
Terete Centric(al)
Term(s), Terminal, Termly Air, Anode, Buffer, Cathode, Coast, Container, Coste,
Designate, Desinant, Distal, Distributed, Dumb, → EPITHET, Euphemism,
Expression, Final, Gnomon, Goal, Half, Hilary, Inkhorn, Intelligent, Law, Lent,
Major, Michaelmas, Middle, Minor, → PERIOD, Point-of-sale, Rail(head), Real,
Removal, Sabbatical, School, Semester, Session, Stint, Stretch, Trimester,
Trimestrial, Trinity, Ultimatum, Waterloo, → WORD, Work station, Zeroth
Termagant Jade, Shrew, Shrow, Spitfire, Vixen
Terminate, Termination, Terminus Abort, Axe, Cease, Conclude, Depot,
Desinent, Earth, → END, Expiry, → FINISH, Goal, Liquidate, Naricorn, Railhead,
Suffix
Termite Duck-ant
Tern Egg-bird, Scray, Three
Terpene Squalene
Terrace Barbette, Beach, Bench, Kop, Linch, Lynchet, Offset, Perron, River, Row
house, Shelf, Stoep, Tarras, Undercliff, Veranda(h)
Terra-cotta Tanagra
Terrain Area, Landscape, Scablands, Tract
Terrapin Diamondback, Emydes, Emys, Slider, Turtle
Terrible, Terribly Appalling, Awful, Deadly, Fell, Frightful, Ghastly, Hellacious,
Horrible, Ivan, Much, Odious, Very
Terrible person Humgruffi(a)n, Ivan, Ogre
Terrier Aberdeen, Airedale, Apsos, Australian, Australian silky, Bedlington, Black
and tan, Border, Boston, Bull, Catalogue, Cesky, Dandie Dinmont, Fox, Glen of
Imaal, Griffon, Irish, Jack Russell, Kerry blue, Lakeland, Maltese, Manchester,
Norfolk, Norwich, Pinscher, Pit bull, Ratter, Register, Schauzer, Scotch, Scottie,
Scottish, Sealyham, Silky, Skye, Soft-coated wheaten, Staffordshire bull, Sydney
silky, TA, Tibetan, Welsh, West Highland, West Highland white, Westie,
Wire-haired, Yorkshire
Terrific, Terrified, Terrify(ing) Affright, Aghast, Agrise, Agrize, Agryze, Appal,
Awe, Blood-curdling, Enorm, Fear, Fine, Fley, Gast, Helluva, Huge, Overawe,
→ PETRIFY, Scare, Superb, Unman, Yippee

Territory Abthane, Ap(p)anage, Colony, Domain, Dominion, Duchy, Emirate,
Enclave, Exclave, Goa, Indian, Latium, Lebensraum, Manor, Margravate,
No-man's-land, Northern, Northwest, Nunavut, Palatinate, Panhandle, Papua,
Petsamo, Principate, Protectorate, Province, Realm, → **REGION**, Rupert's Land,
Scheduled, Sphere, Sultanate, Swazi, Ter(r), Trieste, Trust, Tuath, Union, Yukon
Terror(s) Blue funk, Bugaboo, Bugbear, Eek, → **FEAR**, Fright, Holy, Imp, Night,
Panic, Skrik
Terrorism, Terrorist Alarmist, Al Fatah, Anarchist, Black Hand, Bogeyman,
Bomber, Bully, Cagoulard, Consumer, Desperado, Dynamitard, Eta, Grapo,
Hijacker, Ku Klux Klan, Mau-mau, Maximalist, Mountain, Nightrider, Nihilist,
OAS, Pirate, PLO, Provo, Red Brigade, Robespierre, Ustashi
Terry Ellen, Towel
Terse Abrupt, Brusque, Curt, Laconic, Pithy, Precise, Succinct
Tertiary Cainozoic, Eocene, Miocene, Oligocene, Palaeogene, Pliocene
Tessellation Mosaic
Test(er), Testing Achievement, Acid, Alpha, Ames, Amniocentesis, Apgar,
Appro, Aptitude, Assay, Audition, Barany, Bench, Bender, Benedict, Beta, Blood,
Breath, Breathalyser®, Brinell, Burn-in, Candle, Canopy, Check, Chi-square,
Cis-trans, Cloze, Conn(er), Coomb's, Crash, Criterion, Crucial, Crucible, Crunch,
Dick, Docimastic, Driving, Drop, Dummy-run, Éprouvette, Examine, Exercise,
Experiment, Field, Flame, Frog, Hagberg, Ink-blot, Intelligence, International,
Litmus, Mann-Whitney, Mantoux, Match, Mazzin, Means, Medical, Mom,
MOT, Mug, Neckverse, Needs, Objective, Oral, Ordalian, → **ORDEAL**, Pale, Pap,
Papanicolaou, Paraffin, Patch, Paternity, Performance, Personality, PH, Pilot, Pons
asinorum, Pree, Preeve, Preif, Preve, Probative, Probe, Projective, Proof, Prove,
Proving-ground, Pyx, Q-sort, Qualification, Quiz, Rally, Reagent, Reliability, Road,
Rorschach, SAT, Scalogram, Scan, Schick's, Schilling, Schutz-Charlton, Scratch,
Screen, Shadow, Shibboleth, Showdown, Shroff, Sign, Signed-ranks, Significance,
Sixpence, Skin, Slump, Smear, Smoke, Snellen, Soap, Sound, Sounding, Spinal,
Stanford-Binet, Stress, Tempt, Tensile, Touch, Touchstone, Trial, Trier, Trior, Try,
Turing, Ultrasonic, Viva, Wassermann's, Weigh, Wilcoxon, Zack
Testament Bible, Covenant, Hagographa, Heptateuch, Hexateuch,
Hornolog(o)umena, Midrash, New, Old, Pentateuch, Scripture, Septuagint, Tanach,
Targum, Will
Testicle(s) Ballocks, Balls, Bollix, Bollocks, Bush oyster, Cobblers, Cojones, Cruet,
Family jewels, Gool(e)y, Goolie, Knackers, Monkey-gland, Monorchid, Nads, Nuts,
Orchis, Pills, Ridgel, Ridgil, Rig(gald), Rocks, Stone
Testify, Testimonial, Testimony Character, Chit, Declare, Depone, Deposition,
→ **EVIDENCE**, Rap, Scroll, Tribute, Viva voce, Vouch, Witness
Testy, Tetchy Cross, Narky, Peevish, Ratty
Tetanus Lockjaw
Tête-à-tête A quattr' occhi, Collogue, Confab, Hobnob, Twosome
Tether Cord, Endurance, Hitch, Noose, Picket, Seal, Stringhalt, → **TIE**
Tetrahedrite Fahlerz, Fahlore
Tetrarchy Iturea
Tetrasyllabic Paeon
Tetrode Resnatron
Teuton(ic) Erl-king, German, Goth, Herren, Vandal
Texas Ranger
Text(s), Textbook, Texting ABC, Body, Brahmana, Church, Codex, Donat, Ennage,
Greeked, Harmony, Libretto, Mandaean, Mantra, Mezuzah, Minitel, Octapla,

Op-cit, Philology, Plain, Proof, Pyramid, Quran, Responsa, Rubric, Script, S(h)astra, Shema, SMS, → **SUBJECT**, Sura, Sutra, Tefillin, Tephillin, Tetrapla, Thesis, Topic, Tripitaka, Typography, Upanis(h)ad, Urtext, Variorum, Viewdata, Vulgate, Zohar
Textile Cloth, Fabric, Mercery
Texture Constitution, Feel, Fiber, Fibre, Grain, Open, Set(t), Wale, Weave, Woof
Thai(land) Karen, Lao(s), Mon, Shan, Siam
Thalamus Optic
Thallium Tl
Thames Father, Tamesis
Than And
Thane Banquo, Ross
Thank(s), Thankful, Thanksgiving Appreciate, Collins, Deo gratias, Gloria, Grace, Gramercy, Grateful, Gratitude, Kaddish, Mercy, Roofer
Thankless Ingrate, Vain
That (is), That one As, Cestui, Das heisst, Dh, Exists, How, Id est, Ie, Ille, Namely, Que, Sc, Such, Thence, Thon(der), What, Which, Yon, Yonder, Yt
Thatch(er), Thatching At(t)ap, Daych, Hair, Heard, Hear(i)e, Hele, Hell, Mane, PM, Reed, Straw, Thack, Theek, Wig
Thaw Debacle, Defreeze, Defrost, → **MELT**, Melt-water, Relax
▷ **Thaw** *may indicate* 'ice' *to be removed from a word*
The Der, Die, El, Il, La, Le, Los, T', That, Ye, Ze
Theatre(s), Theatrical(ity) Abbey, Absurd, Adelphi, Arena, Balcony, Broadway, Camp, Cinema, Circle, Coliseum, Criterion, Crucible, Drama, Event, Everyman, Field, Fringe, Gaff, Gaiety, Globe, Grand Guignol, Great White Way, Hall, Haymarket, Hippodrome, Histrionic, House, Kabuki, La Scala, Legitimate, Little, Lyceum, Melodramatic, Mermaid, Music-hall, National, News, Nickelodeon, Noh, Odeon, Odeum, Off-Broadway, Off-off-Broadway, Operating, OUDS, Palladium, Panache, Pennygaff, Pit, Playhouse, Political, Rep(ertory), Sadler's Wells, Shaftesbury, Sheldonian, Shop, Stage, Stalls, Stoll, Straw-hat, Street, Summer stock, Total, Touring, Vic, Windmill, Zarzuela
Theatregoer Circle, Gallery, Gods, Pit, Pittite, Stalls
Theft, Thieving Appropriation, Bluesnarfing, Burglary, Heist, Identity, Kinchinlay, Larceny, Maino(u)r, Manner, Petty larceny, Pilfery, Plagiarism, Plunder, Pugging, Ram-raid, Robbery, Stealth, Stouth(rief), → **THIEF**, Touch, TWOC, Walk-in
Their Her
Theist Believer, Unitarian
Them 'Em, Hem, Tho
Theme Burden, Crab canon, Donnée, Fugue, Idea, Leitmotiv, Lemma, Lemmata, → **MELODY**, Motif, Peg, Question, → **SUBJECT**, Text, Topic, Topos
Then(ce) Already, Away, Next, Since, Sine, So, Syne, Thereupon, Tho
▷ **The northern** *may indicate* t'
Theodolite Diopter, Dioptre, Groma, Tacheometer, Tachymeter, Transit
Theologian, Theologist, Theology Abelard, Aquinas, Barth, Calvin, Christology, Colet, DD, Divine, Eckhart, Erastus, Eschatology, Eusebius, Exegetics, Fideism, Genevan, Hase, Infralapsarian, Irenics, Jansen, Kierkegaard, Knox, Liberation, Luther, Moral, Mullah, Natural, Newman, Niebuhr, Origen, Paley, Pastoral, Pectoral, Pelagius, Pusey, Rabbi, Religious, Sacramentarian, Schoolman, Schwenkfeld, Scotus, Softa, STP, Supralapsarian, Swedenborg, Tertullian, Ulema, Universalist
Theory, Theorem, Theoretical, Theorist Academic, Atomic, Attachment, Attribution, Automata, Band, Bayes(ian), Bernouilli's, Big bang, Binomial, Bohr,

Boo-hurrah, Catastrophe, Chaos, Complexity, Connectionism, Conspiracy, Corpuscular, Darwinian, Decision, Deduction, Dependency, Dictum, Doctrinaire, Domino, Double aspect, Dow, Einstein, Emboîtement, Empiricism, Epigenesist, Exponential, Fermat's (last), Gaia, Galois, Game, Gauge, Germ, Gödel's, Grand Unified, Grotian, Group, Guess, Holism, Hormic, Hypothesis, Ideal, Identity, Ideology, Information, Ism(y), James-Lange, Kinetic, Laingian, Lamarckism, Lemma, Lunar, MAD, Milankovitch, Model, Monism, Mythical, Nernst heat, Notion, Number, Object relations, Perturbation, Petrinism, Pluralism, Poynting, Probability, Proof, Pure, Pythagoras, Quantity, Quantum, Queueing, Random walk, Reception, Relativism, Relativity, Satisfaction, Set, Solipsism, Speculative, Steady state, String, Superdense, Superstring, Supersymmetry, System, Tachyon, TOE, Traducianism, Twistor, Tychism, Utilitarianism, Voluntarism, Vortex, Vulcanist, Wasm, Wave, Wholism, Wolfian

Therapy, Therapeutic Acupressure, Acupuncture, Aura-Soma, Auricular, Aversion, Behaviour, Bowen, Brachytherapy, Cellular, Chavuttithirumal, Chelation, Client-centred, Cognitive, Cognitive-behavioural, Colour, Combination, Craniosacral, Crystal (healing), CST, Curative, Curietherapy, Deep, Dianetics, Drama, ECT, Electric shock, Electroconvulsive, Electroshock, Family, Faradism, Fever, Flotation, Gemstone, Gene, Germ(-line), Gestalt, Group, Heliotherapy, Hellerwork, HRT, Hypnosis, Immunotherapy, Implosive, Insight, Larval, Light, Live cell, Logop(a)edics, Looyenwork, Magnetic, Metamorphic technique, Minimal invasive, MLD, Movement, Music, Narco, Narcotherapy, Natal, Natural, Non directive, Occupational, ORT, Osteopathy, Past life, Pattern, Physical, Phytotherapy, Polarity, Pressure, Primal (scream), Psychodrama, Psychosynthesis, Radiation, Radio, Radium, Rainbow, Reflexology, Regression, Reichian, Reiki, Relaxation, Retail, Rogerian, Rolfing, Röntgenotherapy, Root-canal, Sanatory, Scientology®, Scream, Serum, Sex, SHEN, Shiatsu, Shiatzu, Shock, Sitz-bath, Sound, Speech, Speleotherapy, Supportive, TENS, Thalassotherapy, Theriacal, Thermotherapy, Touch, → TREATMENT, Water cure, X-ray, Zone

There(after), Thereby, Thereupon Attending, Holla, Ipso facto, Present, Thither, Thon, Upon, With that, Y, Yonder

Therefore Argal, Ergo, Forthy, Hence, So, Why

Thermodynamic Enthalpy, Entropy

Thermometer Aethrioscope, Centesimal, Clinical, Gas, Glass, Katathermometer, Maximum and minimum, Psychrometer, Pyrometer, Resistance, Thermograph, Water, Wet and dry bulb, Wet bulb

Thermoplastic Cel(luloid), Resin

Thesaurus Dictionary, Lexicon, Roget, Treasury, Word-finder

These Thir

Theseus Champion

Thesis Argument, Dissertation, Doctorial, Theme

Thespian → ACTOR, Ham, Performer

Thessalonian Lapith

They A

Thick(en), Thickening, Thickener, Thickness, Thickset Abundant, Algin, Burly, Bushy, Callosity, Callus, Clavate, Cloddy, Cruddle, Curdle, Dense, Dextrin(e), Dumose, Engross, Grist, Grouty, Grume, Guar, Gum, Hyperostosis, Incrassate, Inspissate, Kuzu, Liaison, Lush, Nuggety, Pally, Panada, Reduce, Roux, Sclerosis, → SOLID, Soupy, Squat, Stumpy, → STUPID, Thieves, This, Thixotropic, Waulk, Wooden, Xantham

Thick-coated Atheromatous

Thicket Bosk, Brake, Brush, Cane-brake, Chamisal, Chapparal, Coppice, Copse, Dead-finish, Greve, Grove, Macchie, Maquis, Queach, Reedrand, Reedrond, Salicetum, Shola

Thick-lipped Labrose

Thick-skinned Armadillo, Callous, Pachyderm, Tough

Thief, Thieves, Thievish Abactor, Autolycus, Blood, Chummy, Coon, Corsair, Cutpurse, Dismas, Dysmas, Filcher, Flood, Footpad, Freebooter, Furacious, Ganef, Gestas, Gully-raker, Heist, Hotter, Huaquero, Ice-man, Jackdaw, Kiddy, Kondo, Larcener, Light-fingered, Limmer, Looter, Mag, Montith, Nip(per), Nuthook, Pad, Peculator, Pilferer, Pirate, Plagiarist, Poacher, Poddy-dodger, Prig, Raffles, River-rat, → **ROBBER**, Rustler, St Nicholas's clerks, Shark, Shop-lifter, Sneak, Sticky fingers, Taffy, Taker, Tea-leaf, Thick, Twoccer

Thigh Femoral, Gaskin, Ham, Haunch, Hock, Meros

Thin(ner), Thinness Acetone, Atomy, Attenuate, Bald, Beanpole, Bony, Cornstalk, Cull, Diluent, Dilute, Ectomorph, Emaciated, Enseam, Fine, Fine-drawn, Flimsy, Gaunt, Hairline, Hair('s-)breadth, Inseam, Lanky, Lean, Matchstick, Mawger, Puny, Rackabones, Rangy, Rare, Rarefied, Reedy, Scant, Scraggy, Scrannel, Scrawny, Sheer, Sieve, Skeletal, Skimpy, Skinking, Slender, Slim, Slimline, Slink, → **SPARE**, Sparse, Spindly, Stilty, Stringy, Subtle, Taper, Tenuous, Turps, Wafer, Washy, Waste, Watch, Water(y), → **WEAK**, Weedy, Whirtle, Wiry, Wispy, Wortle, Wraith

Thing(s) Alia, Article, Chattel, Chose, Craze, Doodah, Doofer, Entia, Fetish, Fixation, It, Item, Jingbang, Job, Last, Material, Matter, Near, Noumenon, → **OBJECT**, Obsession, Paraphernalia, Phobia, Res, Tool, Vision, Whatnot

Thingummy Dingbat, Dinges, Doodad, Doodah, Doofer, Doohickey, Gubbins, Hoot(a)nanny, Hootenanny, Whatsit, Yoke

Think(er), Thinking Associate, Believe, Brain, Brood, Casuistry, Cogitate, Conjecture, Consider, Contemplant, → **CONTEMPLATE**, Deem, Deliberate, Descartes, Dianoetic, Divergent, Esteem, Fancy, Fear, Feel, Fogramite, Ghesse, Gnostic, Guess, Hegel, Hold, → **IMAGINE**, Judge, Lateral, Meditate, Mentation, Mindset, Mull, Muse, Opine, Pensive, Philosopher, Phrontistery, Ponder, Pore, Presume, Ratiocinate, Rational, Reckon, Reflect, Reminisce, Ruminate, Synectics, Trow, Vertical, Ween, Wishful

Thin-skinned Sensitive

Third, Third rate Bronze, C, Eroica, Gamma, Gooseberry, Interval, Mediant, Minor, Picardy, Quartan, Tertiary, Tertius, Tierce, Trisect

Third man Abel, Lime

Thirst(y) Adry, → **CRAVE**, Dives, Drought, Drouth, Dry, Hydropic, Nadors, Pant, Polydipsia, Thrist

Thirteen Baker's dozen, Devil's dozen, Long dozen, Riddle, Triskaidekaphobia, Unlucky

Thirty Lambda

Thirty nine books All-OT, OT

This Hic, Hoc, The, Thick, Thilk, Thir

Thistle Canada, Carduus, Carline, Cnicus, Creeping, Dayshell, Echinops, Milk, Musk, Rauriki, Russian, Safflower, Scotch, Sow, Spear, Star, Thrissel, Thristle

This year Ha

Thomas Aquinas, Arnold, Christadelphian, De Quincey, Didymus, Doubting, Dylan, Erastus, Hardy, Loco, Parr, Rhymer, Tompion, True, Turbulent

Thomas Aquinas Angelic Doctor

Thong Babiche, Jandal®, Lash, Latchet, Leather, Lore, Riem, Riempie, Shoe-latchet, → **STRAP**, Strop, Taws(e), Whang, Whip

Thor Thunderer
Thorax Chest, Peraeon, Pereion, Scutellum, Throat
Thorium Th
Thorn(y) Acantha, Bael, Bel, Bhel, Bramble, Briar, Coyotillo, Doom, Edh, Eth, Irritation, Jerusalem, Jew's, Mahonia, Mayflower, Nabk, Nebbuk, Nebe(c)k, → **NEEDLE**, Paloverde, Pricker, Prickle, Slae, Spine, Spinescent, Spinulate, Trial, Wagn'bietjie, Y, Ye, Zare(e)ba, Zariba, Zeriba
Thorn-apple Jimpson-weed
Thornless Inerm
Thorough(ly) À fond, Complete, Deep, Even-down, Firm, Fully, Ingrained, Inly, Out, Out and out, Painstaking, Pakka, Pucca, Pukka, Radical, Ripe, Root and branch, Searching, Sound, Strict, Total, Tout à fait, Up
Thoroughbred Arab, Bloodstock, Pedigree
Thoroughfare Avenue, Broadway, Causeway, Freeway, Highway, Parkway, → **ROAD**, Street
Those Thae, Thaim, Them, Tho, Yon
Thou M, Mil
Though Albe, Albeit, All-be, Ever, Tho, Whenas
Thought(s), Thoughtful(ness) Avisandum, Broody, Censed, Cerebration, Cogitation, Concept, Considerate, Contemplation, Dianoetic, Felt, Idea, Indrawn, Innate, Kind, Maieutic, Mind, Musing, Notion, Opinion, Pansy, Pensée, Pensive, Philosophy, Reflection, Rumination, Second
Thoughtless Blindfold, Careless, Heedless, Improvident, Incogitant, Inconsiderate, Pillock, → **RASH**, Reckless, Remiss, Scatter-brained, Vacant, Vain
Thousand(s) Chiliad, Gorilla, K, Lac, Lakh, M, Millenary, Millennium, Myriad, Octillion, Plum, Toman
Thracian Spartacus
Thrall Captive, Esne, Serf, Slave
Thrash(ing) → **BEAT**, Belabour, Belt, Bepelt, Binge, Bless, Cane, Dress, Drub, Flail, Flog, Jole, Joll, Joule, Jowl, Lace, Laidie, Laidy, Lambast, Larrup, Lather, Leather, Lick, Marmelise, Paste, Ploat, Quilt, Slog, Smoke, Strap-oil, Swat, Tank, Targe, Thraiping, Towel, Trim, Trounce, Wallop, Whale, Whap, Writhe
Thread, Threadlike Acme screw, Ariadne, Bar, Bottom, Bride, Buttress, Chalaza, Chromatid, Chromatin, Chromosome, Clew, Clue, Cop(pin), Cord, Coventry blue, Eel-worm, End, Female, Fibre, Filament, File, Filiform, Filose, Filoselle, Float, Flourishing, Gist, Gold, Gossamer, Heddle, Ixtle, Lace, Lap, Lingel, Lingle, Link, Lisle, Lurex®, Male, Meander, Mycellum, Nematode, Nematoid, Organzine, Pack, Pearlin(g), Pick, Plasmodesm, Ravel, Reeve, Sacred, Screw, Sellers screw, Seton, Silver, Single, Spireme, → **STRAND**, Stroma, Suture, Tassel, Tendril, Theme, Thrid, Thrum, Trace, Tram, Trundle, Tussore, Twine, Warp, Watap, Wax(ed), Weft, Whitworth, Whitworth screw, Wick, → **WIND**, Wisp, Worm
Threadbare Hackneyed, Napless, Shabby, Worn
Threadworm Nemathelminth, Strongyl, Vinegar-eel
Threat(en), Threatened, Threatening Baleful, Blackmail, Bluster, Brutum fulmen, Coerce, Comminate, Face, Fatwa, Fraught, Greenmail, Greymail, Hazard, Impend, Imperil, Loom, → **MENACE**, Minacious, Minatory, Mint, Omen, Ominous, Overcast, Overhang, Parlous, Peril, Portent, Ramp, Sabre-rattling, Shore, Strongarm, Ugly, Veiled, Warning
Three, Threefold, Three-wheeler, Thrice Graces, Har, Harpies, Jafenhar, Leash, Muses, Musketeers, Pairial, Pair-royal, Parial, Prial, Ter, Tern, Terzetta, Thrice, Thridi, Tid, T.i.d, Tierce, Tray, Trey, Triad, Tricar, Triennial, Trifid, Trigon, Trilogy,

Sorn, Squat, Stap, Stick, Stoccado, Stoccata, Stock, Stuck, Thrutch, Tilt, Tuck, Venue

Thud Drum, Dump, Flump, Phut, Plod, Thump, Whump

Thug(s) Brute, Gangster, Goon(da), Gorilla, Gurrier, Hoodlum, Loord, Ninja, Ockers, Phansigar, Plug-ugly, Roughneck, SS, Strangler, Ted, Tityre-tu, Tsotsi

Thule Ultima

Thulium Tm

Thumb Bally, Green, Hitch, Midget, Ovolo, Pollex, Scan, Sore, Tom

Thump(ing) Blow, Bonk, Clobber, Cob, Crump, Da(u)d, Dawd, Ding, Dod, Drub, Dub, Hammer, Knevell, Knock, Nevel, Oner, Paik, → **POUND**, Pummel, Slam, Slosh, Souse, Swat, Swingeing, Thud, Trounce, Tund, Whud

Thunder(ing), Thunderstorm Bolt, Boom, Clap, Coup de foudre, Donnerwetter, Foudroyant, Foulder, Fulminate, Intonate, Lei-king, Pil(l)an, Raiden, → **ROAR**, Rumble, Summanus, Tempest, Thor, Tonant

Thursday Chare, Holy, Maundy, Sheer, Shere

Thus Ergo, Sic, So, Therefore

Thwart Baffle, Balk, → **CROSS**, Dash, Dish, Foil, Frustrate, Hamstring, Hogtie, Obstruct, Outwit, Pip, Prevent, Scotch, Snooker, Spike, Spite, Stonker, Stymie, Transverse

Thy Yourn

Thyme Basil, Lemon, Water

Thyroid Goitre, Myxodema

Tiara Cidaris, Crownet, Triple crown

Tiberius Gracchus

Tibetan Lamaist, Naga, Sherpa, Sitsang

Tic Vocal

Tick, Tick off Acarida, Acarus, Beat, Bloodsucker, Check, → **CHIDE**, Click, Cr, → **CREDIT**, Deer, HP, Idle, Instant, Jar, Ked, Mattress, Mile, Mo, Moment, Ricinulei, Second, Sheep, Soft, Strap, Worm

Ticket(s) Billet, Bone, Brief, Carnet, Commutation, Complimentary, Coupon, Day, Docket, Dream, Excursion, Kangaroo, Label, Meal, One-day, One-way, Open-jaw, Parking, Pass, Pass-out, Pawn, Platform, Raffle, Raincheck, Return, Round-trip, Rover, Saver, Scratchcard, Season, Single, Soup, Split, Straight, Stub, Supersaver, → **TAG**, Tempest, Tessera(l), Through, Tix, Transfer, Tyburn, Unity, Voucher, Walking, Zone

Ticket-seller Scalper

Tickle, Ticklish Amuse, Delicate, Divert, Excite, Gratify, Gump, → **ITCH**, Kittle, Queasy, Thrill, Titillate

Tiddler Brit, Tom

Tide, Tidal Current, Drift, Eagre, Easter, Eger, Estuary, Flood, High, High water, Lee, Low, Marigram, Neap, Red, Rising, River, Roost, Sea, Seiche, Slack water, Spring, Surge, Trend, Wave

Tide-gate Aboideau, Aboiteau, Weir

Tidings Gospel, → **NEWS**, Rumour, Word

Tidy Big, Comb, Considerable, Curry, Do, Fair, Fettle, Groom, Kempt, Large, Neat, Neaten, → **ORDER**, Pachyderm, Predy, Preen, Primp, Red(d), Slick, Snug, Sort, Spruce, Trim, Valet

Tie, Tied, Tying Ascot, Attach, Barcelona, Berth, Bind, Black, Bolo, → **BOND**, Bootlace, Bow, Bowyang, Cable, Cope, Cravat, Cup, Dead-heat, Drag, Draw, Four-in-hand, Frap, Halter, Handicap, Harness, Hitch, Holdfast, Kipper, → **KNOT**, Lace, Lash, Level, Ligament, Ligate, Ligature, Link, Marry, Match, Moor, Neck and neck, Oblige, Obstriction, Old School, Oop, Oup, Overlay, Raffia, Restrain, Rod, Scarf, School, Score draw, Scrunchie, Semifinal, Shackle, Shoelace, Shoestring, Sleeper, Slur, Solitaire, Soubise, Splice, Stake, Strap, String, Tawdry-lace, Tether, Together, Trice, Truss, Unite, White, Windsor

Tier Apron, Bank, Gradin(e), Knotter, Layer, Range, Rank, Stage, Storey

Tierce Leash, Tc

Tiff Bicker, Contretemps, Difference, Dispute, Feed, Feud, Huff, Miff, Skirmish, Spat, Squabble

Tiffany Gauze

Tiger Bengal, → CAT, Clemenceau, Demoiselle, Lily, Machairodont, Machairodus, Man-eater, Margay, Paper, Sabre-tooth, Smilodon, Tamil, Tasmanian, Woods

Tight(en), Tightness, Tights Boozy, Bosky, Brace, Cinch, Close(-hauled), Constriction, Cote-hardie, → DRUNK, Fishnet, Fleshings, High, Hose, Jam, Leggings, Leotards, Lit, Loaded, Maillot, Mean, Merry, Niggardly, Oiled, Pang, Pantihose, Phimosis, Pickled, Pinch(penny), Plastered, Prompt, Proof, Rigour, Snug, Squiffy, Stenosis, → STINGY, Stinko, Strict, Stringent, Swift, Swig, Taut, Tense, Tipsy, Trig, Woozy

Tightrope(-walker) Aerialist, Blondin, Equilibrist, Funambulist, Petauriste

Tightwad Cheapskate, → MISER, Scrooge

Tile(s), Tiled Antefix, Arris, Azulejo, Carpet, Chapeau, Dalle, Derby, Dutch, Encaustic, Field, → HAT, Imbrex, Imbricate, Lid, Lino, Mahjong(g), Ostracon, Ostrakon, Peever, Quarrel, Quarry, Rag(g), Ridge, Rooftop, Sclate, Shingle, Slat, → SLATE, Tegular, Tessella, Tessera, Titfer, Topper, Wall, Wally

Till Cashbox, Checkout, Coffer, Ear, Eulenspiegel, Farm, Hasta, Hoe, Husband, Lob, Peter, → PLOUGH, Set, Unto

Tiller Gardener, Helm, Ploughman, Rotavator, Wheel

Tilt Awning, Bank, Camber, Cant, Cock, Dip, Heel, Hut, Joust, Just, → LIST, Quintain, Rock, Tip, Unbalance

Timber Apron, Balk, Batten, Beam, Bolster, Bond, Bridging, Cant-rail, Carapa, Chess, Clapboard, Compass, Coulisse, Cross-tree, Cruck, Dogshores, Dwang, Elmwood, Flitch, Float, Four-by-two, Futchel, Futtock, Greenheart, Groundsell, Hardwood, Harewood, Intertie, Iroko, Ironwood, Joist, Knee, Knighthead, Lauan, Ligger, Lintel, Log, Lumber, Nogging, Nothofagus, Plank-sheer, Purlin(e), Putlock, Putlog, Pyengadu, Radiata, Ramin, Rib, Ridgepole, Roundwood, Rung, Sandalwood, Sapele, Sapodilla, Satinwood, Scantling, Shook, Shorts, Sissoo, Skeg, Sneezewood, Softwood, Souari, Stemson, Stere, Sternpost, Sternson, Straddle, Stud, Stull, Stumpage, Summer, Swing-stock, Tilting fillet, Towing-bitts, Transom, Trestletree, Two-by-four, Wale, Wall plate, Weatherboard, Whitewood, → WOOD, Yang

Timbre Clang, Klang(farbe), Register, → TENOR, Tone

Time(s), Timer Access, African, Agoge, Apparent, Assymetric, Astronomical, Autumn, Awhile, Bird, BST, Central, Chronaxy, Chronic, Chronometer, Chronon, Clock, Closing, Common, Compound, Connect, Core, Counter, Cryptozoic, Date, Day, Dead, Decade, Dimension, Double, Duple, Duration, Early, Eastern, Eastern Standard, Egg-glass, Enemy, Eon, Ephemeris, Epoch, Equinox, Era, European, Eve(ning), Extra, Father, Flexitime, Forelock, Four-four, Free, Full, Gest, Glide, Half, Healer, High, Horologe, Hour, Hourglass, Hr, Idle, Imprisonment, Injury, Innings, Instant, Interlude, Jiff, Juncture, Kalpa, Latent, Lay-day, Lead, Lean, Leisure, Life, Lighting-up, Lilac, Local, Lowsing, Mean, Menopause, Metronome, Mountain standard, Multiple, Needle, Nonce, Nones, Normal, Occasion, Oft, → ON TIME, Opening, Pacific, Paralysis, Part, Period, Phanerozoic, Pinger, Porridge, Post,

Prelapsarian, Prime, Proper, Quadruple, Quality, Question, Quick, Reaction, Real, Reaper, Recovery, Response, Responsum, Reverberation, Rhythm, Run(ning), Sandglass, Seal, → SEASON, Seel, Seil, Semeion, Serial, Session, Shelf-life, Sidereal, Sight, Simple, Sith(e), Slow, Solar, Solstice, Space, Span, Spare, Spell, Spin, Split, Spring, Squeaky-bum, Standard, Stoppage, Stopwatch, Stound, Stownd, Stretch, Summer, Sundial, Sundown, Sythe, T, Tem, Tempo, Tempore, Tense, Thief, Three-four, Thunderer, Tick, Tid, Tide, Trice, Triple, True, Turnaround, Two-four, Universal, Usance, What, While, Winter, X, Yonks, Zero

Timebomb Demographic

Time-keeper, Timepiece Ben, Chronometer, Clock, Hourglass, Ref, Sand-glass, Sundial, Ticker, Tompion, Watch

Timeless Eternal, Nd, Undying

Timely Appropriate, Apropos, Happy, Opportune, Pat, Prompt, Punctual

Timescale Geological

Time-server Prisoner, Trimmer

Timetable Bradshaw, → CHART, Schedule

Timid, Timorous Afraid, Aspen, Bashful, Blate, Chicken, Cowardly, Eerie, Eery, Faint-hearted, Fearful, Hare, Hen-hearted, Milquetoast, Mouse, Mous(e)y, Pavid, Pigeon-hearted, Pusillanimous, Pussy, Quaking, Schnok, Shrinking, → SHY, Skeary, Sook, Yellow

Timothy Cat's-tail, Grass, Phleum

Tin(ned), Tinfoil, Tinny Argentine, Block, Britannia metal, Can, Cash, Debe, Dixie, Maconochie, Mess, → MONEY, Moola(h), Ochre, Plate, Rhino, Sn, Stannary, Stannic, Stream, Tain, Tole

Tincture Arnica, Bufo, Chroma, Elixir, Fur, Infusion, Laudanum, Metal, Or, Sericon, Sol, Spice, Taint, Tenné, Vert

Tinder Amadou, Faggot, Fuel, Funk, Punk, Spark, Spunk, Touchwood

Tine Antler, Bay, Cusp, Grain, Prong, Snag, Surroyal, Trey

Tinge(d) Dye, Eye, Flavour, Gild, → HUE, Infuscate, Taint, Tincture, Tone, Touch

Tingle, Tingling Dinnle, Dirl, Paraesthesia, Pins and needles, Prickle, Thrill, Throb, Tinkle

Tinker Bell, Caird, Coster, Didakai, Didakei, Diddicoy, Didicoy, Didikoi, → FIDDLE, Gypsy, Mender, Pedlar, Potter, Prig, Putter, Repair, Sly, Snout, Tamper, Tramp, Traveller

Tinkle Pink

Tinsel(ly) Clinquant, Gaudy, Glitter, O, Spangle, Turkey

Tint Colour, Henna, Hue, Pigment, → STAIN, Tinct, Tinge, Woad

Tiny Atto-, Baby, Diddy, Dwarf, Ha'it, Infinitesimal, Itsy-bitsy, Lilliputian, Minikin, Minim, Mite, Negligible, Petite, Small, Smidgeon, Stime, Teeny, Tiddl(e)y, Tiddy, Tim, Tine, Tottie, Totty, Toy, Wee

Tip (off), Tipping Apex, Arrowhead, Ash-heap, Asparagus, Backshish, Baksheesh, Batta, Beer-money, Bonsel(l)a, Bonus, B(u)onamono, Cant, Cert, Chape, Counsel, Coup, Cowp, Crown, Cue, Cumshaw, Douceur, Dump, Extremity, Fee, Felt, Ferrule, Filter, Forecast, Glans, Gratillity, Gratuity, Heel, → HINT, Hunch, Inkle, Iridise, Lagniappe, Largess(e), List, Mess, Middenstead, Nap, Nib, Noop, Ord, Perk, Perquisite, Point, Pointer, Pour, Pourboire, Previse, Prong, Straight, Suggestion, Summit, Tag, Tail, Tilt, Toom, Touch, Tronc, Upset, Vail, Vales, Warn, Whisper, Wink, Wrinkle

Tippet Cape, Fur, Scarf

Tipple Bib, Booze, → DRINK, Paint, Pot, Poteen

Tipster Prophet, Tout

Tipsy Bleary, Boozy, Bosky, → **DRUNK**, Elevated, Moony, Nappy, Oiled, On, Rocky, Screwed, Slewed, Slued, Squiffy, Wet

▷ **Tipsy** *may indicate* an anagram

Tiptoe Digitigrade, Spanish, Walk

Tirade Diatribe, Invective, Jobation, Laisse, Philippic, Rand, Rant, Screed, Slang

Tire(d), Tiredness, Tiring All-in, Aweary, Beat, Bore, Bushed, Caparison, Deadbeat, Dress, Drowsy, → **EXHAUST**, Fag, Fagged out, Fatigue, Flag, Fordid, Fordod, Forjeskit, Frazzle, Gruel, Irk, Jack, Jade, Lassitude, Limp, ME, Overspent, Pall, Poop, Puggled, → **ROBE**, Rubber, Sap, Shagged, Sicken, Sleepry, Sleepy, Spent, Swinkt, Tax, Tedious, Tucker, Wabbit, Wappend, Weary, Wrecked

Tiresome Boring, Exhausting, Humdrum, Pill, Tedious, Vexing

Tirl Rattle, Risp, Strip, Turn

▷ **Tiro** *see* **TYRO**

Tissue Adenoid, Adhesion, Adipose, Aerenchyma, Aponeurosis, Archesporium, Callus, Carbon, Cartilage, Cementum, Chalaza, Cheloid, Chlorenchyma, Coenosarc, Collagen, Collenchyma, Commissure, Conducting, Connective, Cortex, Dentine, Diploe, Elastin, Epimysium, Epineurium, Epithelium, Eschar, Evocator, Fabric, Fascia, Flesh, Gamgee, Gauze, Gleba, Glia, Granulation, Gum, Heteroplasia, Histogen, Histoid, Infarct, Keloid, Kleenex®, Lamina, Liber, Lies, Ligament, Luteal, Lymphate, Lymphoid, Macroglia, Marrow, Matrix, Mechanical, Medulla, → **MEMBRANE**, Meristem, Mesenchyme, Mesophyll, Mestom(e), Mole, Muscle, Myelin(e), Myocardium, Neoplasm, Neuroglia, Nucellus, Olivary, Pack, Palisade, Pannus, Paper, Papilla, Parenchyma, Periblem, Perichylous, Pericycle, Peridesmium, Perimysium, Perinephrium, Perineurium, Perisperm, Phellogen, Phloem, Pith, Placenta, Plerome, Polyarch, Pons, Primordium, Procambium, Prosenchyma, Prothallis, Pterygium, Pulp, Radula, Sarcenet, Sars(e)net, Scar, Sclerenchyma, Scleroma, Sequestrum, Sinew, Soft, Somatopleure, Stereome, Stroma, Submucosa, Suet, Tarsus, Tela, Tendon, Tonsil, Tunica, Vascular, Velum, Web, Wound, Xylem, Zoograft

Tit, Tit-bit(s) Analecta, Canapé, Crested, Currie, Curry, Delicacy, Dug, Nag, Nipple, Nun, Pap, Quarry, Sample, Scrap, Snack, Teat, Tug, Twitch, Willow, Wren, Zakuska

Titan(ic), Titaness Atlas, Colossus, Cronos, Cronus, Drone, Enormous, Giant, Huge, Hyperion, Kronos, Large, Leviathan, Liner, Oceanus, Phoebe, Prometheus, Rhea, Themis, Vast

Titanium, Titanite Rutin, Sagenite, Sphene, Ti

Tit for tat Deserts, Revenge, Talion

Tithe Disme, Dyzemas, Frankpledge, Teind, Tenth

Titian Abram, Auburn

Titillate(r) Delight, Excite, Fluffer, Tickle

Titivate Preen, Primp

Title Abbé, → **ADDRESS**, Ag(h)a, Antonomasia, Appellative, Bahadur, Baroness, Baronet, Bart, Bastard, Bhai, Bretwalda, Calif, Caliph, Caption, Charta, Chogyal, Claim, Conveyance, Count(ess), Courtesy, Credit, Dan, Datin, Datuk, Dauphin, Dayan, Deeds, Devi, Dom, Don, Don(n)a, Dowager, Dub, Duchess, Duke, Earl, Effendi, Eminence, Epithet, Esquire, Excellency, Fra, Frau(lein), Gospodin, Grand Master, Gyani, Hafiz, Handle, Header, Heading, Headline, Hojatoleslam, Hon, Honour, Imperator, Interest, Kabaka, Kalif, Kaliph, Kaur, King, Kumari, Lady, Lala, Lemma, → **LIEN**, Lord, Mal(l)am, Marchesa, Marchese, Marquess, Marquis, Master, Masthead, Maulana, Memsahib, Meneer, Mevrou, Miladi, Milady, Milord, Mirza, Mr(s), Name, Native, Negus, Nizam, Nomen, Padishah, Pasha, Peerage, Pir, Polemarch, Prefix, Prince(ss), Queen, → **RANK**, Reb, Reverence, Reverend,

→ **RIGHT**, Rubric, Running, Sahib, Sama, San, Sardar, Say(y)id, Senhor(a), Señor(a), Shri, Singh, Sir, Sirdar, Son, Sowbhagyawati, Sri, Stratum, Tannie, Tenno, Titule, Torrens, Tycoon, U, Worship

Title-holder Cartouche, Champion, Landlord, Noble

Titmouse Bird, Hickymal, Mag, Reedling, Tit

Titter Giggle, Snigger, Tehee

Tittle Jot

Titus Oates

Tizz(y) Pother, Spin, Tanner, Testril, VId

TNT Explosive, Trotyl

To(wards) At, Beside, Inby, Onto, Prone, Shet, Shut, Till

Toad(y) Bootlicker, Bufo, Bumsucker, Cane, Clawback, Cocksucker, Crapaud, Crawler, Fawn, Frog, Horned, Jackal, Jenkins, Knot, Lackey, Lick-platter, Lickspittle, Midwife, Minion, Natterjack, Nototrema, Paddock, Parasite, Pick-thank, Pipa, Placebo, Platanna, Puddock, Queensland cane, Sook, Spade-foot, Surinam, Sycophant, Tree, Tuft-hunter, Walking, Warty, Xenopus, Yesman

Toadstool Amanita, Death-cap, Death-cup, Destroying angel, Fly agaric, → **FUNGUS**, Grisette, Horsehair, Paddock-stool, Parrot, Saffron milk cap, Sickener, Sulphur tuft, Verdigris, Wax cap

Toast(er) Bacchus, Bell, Birsle, Brindisi, → **BROWN**, Bruschetta, Bumper, Cheers, Chin-chin, Crostini, Crouton, Drink-hail, French, Gesundheit, Grace-cup, Grill, Health, Iechyd da, Kia-ora, L'chaim, Lechayim, Loyal, Melba, Pledge, Pop up, Propose, Prosit, Round, Scouther, Scowder, Scowther, Sentiment, Sippet, Skoal, Slainte, Slainte mha(i)th, Soldier, Sunbathe, Wassail, Zwieback

Toastmaster MC, Symposiarch

Tobacco, Tobacco-field Alfalfa, Bacchi, Baccy, Bird's eye, Broadleaf, Burley, Canaster, Capa, Caporal, Cavendish, Chew, Dottle, Filler, Honeydew, Indian, Killikinnick, Kinnikinick, Latakia, Mundungus, Nailrod, Navy-cut, Negro-head, Nicotian, Nicotine, Niggerhead, Perique, Pigtail, Plug, Quid, Rapper, Régie, Returns, Shag, Sneesh, Snout, Snuff, Straight cut, Stripleaf, Turkish, Twist, Vega, Virginia, Weed

Toboggan Sled(ge), Sleigh

Toby Dog, High, Highwayman, Jug, Low

Tocsin Alarm, Siren

Today Hodiernal, Now, Present

Toddle(r) Baim, Gangrel, Mite, Tot, Totter, Trot, Waddle

Toddy Arrack, → **DRINK**, Sura, Whisky

To-do Sensation, Stir

Toe(s) Dactyl, Digit, Fissiped, Hallux, Hammer, Piggy, Pinky, Pointe, Poulaine, Prehallux, Tootsie

Toff Nob, Nut, Swell

Toffee Banket, Butterscotch, Caramel, Cracknel, Gundy, Hard-bake, Hokey-pokey, Humbug, Tom-trot

Toga Palla

Together Among, At-one, Atone, Attone, En bloc, En masse, Gathered, Infere, → **JOINT**, Pari-passu, Sam, Unison, Wed, Y, Yfere, Ysame

Toggle Fastener, Netsuke

Togs Clothes, Gear, Rig, Strip

Toil(s) Drudge, Fag, Industry, → **LABOUR**, Mesh, Net, Seine, Sisyphus, Slog, Sweat, Swink, Tela, Tew, Trap, Trauchle, Travail, Tug, Web, → **WORK**, Wrest, Yacker, Yakka, Yakker

Toilet Can, Chemical, Coiffure, John, Lat(rine), Lavabo, → **LAVATORY**, Loo, Necessary house, Necessary place, Pot, Powder room, Toot, WC

Token Abbey-piece, Buck, Check, Counter, Coupon, Disc, Double-axe, Emblem, Gift, Indication, Mark, → **MEMENTO**, Monument, Nominal, Portend, Seal, Sign, Signal, Slug, Symbol, Symptom, Tessella, Tessera, Valentine

Tolerable Acceptable, Bearable, Mediocre, Passable, So-so

Tolerance, Tolerant, Tolerate(d) Abear, Abide, → **ALLOW**, Bear, Broadminded, Brook, Endure, Enlightened, Good-natured, Hack, Had, Immunological, Latitude, → **LENIENT**, Lump, Mercy, Permit, Stand, Stick, Stomach, Studden, Suffer, Support, Thole, Wear, Zero

Toll Chime, Customs, Due, Duty, Excise, Jole, Joll, Joule, Jowl, Light-dues, Octroi, Pierage, Pike, Pontage, Rates, → **RING**, Scavage, Streetage, Tariff, Tax

Tom(my) Atkins, Bell, Bowling, Bread, Brown, → **CAT**, Collins, Edgar, Gib, Grub, Gun, He-cat, Jerry, Jones, Mog(gy), Nosh, Peeping, Private, Pte, Puss, Ram-cat, Sawyer, Snout, Soldier, Stout, Thos, Thumb, Tiddler, Tucker

Tomato Beef(steak), Cherry, Gooseberry, Husk, Love-apple, Plum, Portuguese, Strawberry, Tamarillo, Tree, Wolf's peach

Tomb(stone) Burial, Catacomb, Catafalque, Cenotaph, Cist, Coffin, Dargah, Durgah, Grave, Hypogeum, Inurn, Kistvaen, Marmoreal, Mastaba, Mausoleum, Megalithic, Monument, Pyramid, Repository, → **SEPULCHRE**, Sepulture, Serdab, Shrine, Speos, Tell el Amarna, Tholos, Tholus, Through-stone, Treasury, Vault

Tombola Draw, Lottery, Raffle

Tomboy Gamine, Gilpey, Gilpy, Hoyden, Ladette, Ramp, Romp

Tome → **BOOK**, Volume

Tomfoolery Caper, Fandangle, Shenanigan

Tomorrow Future, Manana, Morrow

Tompion Watchman

Tom Snout Tinker

Ton(nage) C, Chic, Displacement, Freight, Gross, Hundred, Long, Measurement, Metric, Net register, Register, Shipping, Short, T

Tone, Tonality Aeolian, Brace, Combination, Compound, Dialling, Differential, Engaged, Fifth, Gregorian, Harmonic, Hum, Inflection, Key, Klang, Minor, Ninth, Partial, Passing, Pure, Qualify, Quarter, Resultant, Ringing, Side, → **SOUND**, Strain, Summational, Temper, Tenor, Timbre, Touch, Trite, Whole

Tong(s) Curling, Lazy, Sugar, Wafer

Tongue Brogue, Burr, Chape, Clack, Clapper, Doab, Double, Final, Forked, Glossa, Glossolalia, Glottal, Jinglet, → **LANGUAGE**, Languet(te), Lap, Ligula, Lill, Lingo, Lingual, Lingulate, Mother, Organ, Radula, Ranine, Rasp, Red rag, Single, Spit, Tab, Triple, Voice, Vulgar

Tongue-tied Mush-mouthed

Tongue-twister Jaw-breaker, Shibboleth

Tonic Booster, Bracer, C(h)amomile, Doh, Key, Mease, Medicinal, Mishmee, Mishmi, Myrica, Oporice, Pareira brava, Pick-me-up, Quassia, Refresher, Roborant, Sage tea, Sarsaparilla, Solfa

▷ **Tonic** *may indicate* a musical note

Tonsil, Tonsillitis Amygdala, Antiaditis, Pharyngeal, Quinsy

Tonsure(d) Epilate, Haircut, Peel, Pield

Tony Bête, Chic, Fool, Smart

Too Als(o), As well, Besides, Eke, Excessive, Item, Likewise, Moreover, Oer, Over, Overly, Plus, Troppo

Took Naam, Nam, Set, Stole, Wan, Won

Tool(s) Adze, Aiguille, Airbrush, Auger, Awl, Ax(e), Beetle, Bevel, Billhook, Bit, Broach, Brog, Bur(r), Burin, Calipers, Catspaw, Chaser, Chisel, Chopper, Clippers, Come-along, Croze, Dibber, Dibble, Die, Dolly, Drawknife, Drawshave, Drift(pin), Drill, Eatche, Edge, Elsin, Eolith, Facer, Fid, File, Firmer, Flatter, Float, Float-stone, Former, Fraise, Fretsaw, Froe, Frow, Fuller, Gad, Gimlet, Go-devil, Gouger, Grapnel, Grattoir, Graver, Hammer, Hardware, Hardy, Hob, Hoe, Husker, → IMPLEMENT, Insculp, → INSTRUMENT, Iron, Jackal, Jackhammer, Jemmy, Jim Crow, Jointer, Jumper, Laster, Loggerhead, Loom, Lute, Machine, Mallet, Marlin(e)spike, Microlith, Mitre square, Moon-knife, Muller, Nippers, Oustiti, Outsiders, Palaeolith, Pattle, Pawn, Penis, Percussion, Pestle, Pick, Pickaxe, Picklock, Pitchfork, Piton, Plane, Pliers, Plunger, Power, Pricker, Property, Prunt, Punch, Puncheon, Rabble, Rasp, Reamer, Ripple, Rocking, Roll(er), Rounder, Router, Sander, Saw, Saw set, Scalpel, Scauper, Scissors, Scorper, Scraper, Screwdriver, Scriber, Scutch, Scythe, Seamset, Secateurs, Set, Shoder, Shooting stick, Sickle, Slasher, Slater, Sleeker, Snake, Spade, Spanner, Spirit-level, Spitsticker, Spokeshave, Spudder, Strickle, Strike, Strimmer®, Swage, Swingle, Swipple, Tint, Tjanting, Toothpick, Tranchet, Triblet, Trowel, Try square, Tweezers, Twibill, Upright, Vibrator, Vice, Wimble, Wire-stripper, Wrench

Toot(er) Blow, Horn, Parp, Trumpet

Tooth(ed), Toothy, Teeth Baby, Bicuspid, Bit, Buck, Bunodont, Cadmean, Canine, Carnassial, Chactodon, Cheek tooth, Cog, Comb, Cott's, Crena(te), Ctenoid, Cusp, Denticle, Dentin(e), Dentures, Egg, Eye, False, Fang, Gam, Gat, Gnashers, Grinder, Heterodont, Impacted, Incisor, Ivory, Joggle, Laniary, Milk, Mill, Molar, Nipper, Odontoid, Orthodontics, Overbite, Pawl, Pearly gates, Pectinate, Periodontics, Peristome, Permanent, Phang, Plate, Poison-fang, Pre-molar, Prong, Ratch, Scissor, Secodont, Sectorial, Serration, Set, Snaggle, Sprocket, Store, Sweet, Trophi, Tush, Tusk, Uncinus, Upper, Wallies, Wang, Wiper, Wisdom, Wolf, Zalambdodont

Toothache, Tooth troubles Caries, Odontalgia

Toothless(ness) Anodontia, Edentate, Gummy, Pangolin

Toothpaste Dentifrice

Top (drawer; hole; line; notcher), Topmost, Topper Ace, Acme, Altissimo, A1, Apex, Apical, Behead, Best, Better, Big, Blouse, Blouson, Boob tube, Brow, Bustier, Cacumen, Cap, Capstone, Ceiling, Coma, Cop, Coping, Corking, Cream, → CREST, Crista, Crop, Crown, Culmen, De capo, Decollate, Diabolo, Dog, Dome, Double, Drawer, Dreid(e)l, Dux, Elite, Execute, Fighting, Finial, Flip, Gentry, Gyroscope, Halterneck, Hard, Hat, → HEAD, Height, Hummer, Humming, Imperial, Jumper, Lid, Maillot, Nun, One-er, Optimate, Orb, Parish, → PEAK, Peerie, Peery, Peg, Peplos, Peplus, Pinnacle, Pitch, Replenish, Ridge, Roof, Sawyer, Screw, Secret, Shaw, Shirt, Skim, Slay, Soft, Spinning, Star, Summit, Superate, Superb, Supernal, Supreme, Supremo, Surface, Sweater, Table, Tambour, Targa, Teetotum, Texas, Tile, Trash, T-shirt, Turbinate, Up(most), Uppermost, V, Vertex, Whipping, Whirligig

▷ **Top** *may indicate* first letter

Topaz Citrine, Colorado, Occidental, Oriental, Pycnite, Rose, Scottish, Spanish

Topcoat Finish, Overcoat, Ulster

Tope(r) Boozer, Bouser, Dagaba, Dagoba, → DRUNK, Sot, Tosspot

Topic(al) Head, Hobbyhorse, Item, Local, Motion, Shop, Subject, Text, → THEME

Top-knot Tuft

Topping Grand, Icing, Meringue, Pepperoni, Piecrust, Streusel

Topple Oust, Overbalance, Overturn, Tip, Upend, → UPSET

Topsy Parentless
Topsy-turvy Careen, Cockeyed, Inverted, Summerset, Tapsalteerie, Tapsleteerie
Torah Maftir
Torch Brand, Cresset, Flambeau, Hards, Hurds, Lamp, Lampad, Link, Olympic, Plasma, Roughie, Tead(e), Wisp
Torch-bearer Usherette
Toreador Escamillo, Matador, Picador, Torero
Torment(ed), Tormentor Agony, Anguish, Bait, Ballyrag, Bedevil, Butt, Cruciate, Crucify, Curse, Distress, Excruciate, Frab, Gehenna, Grill, Hag-ridden, Harass, Hell, Martyrdom, Molest, Nag, Nettle, Pang, Pine, Plague, → **RACK**, Sadist, Tantalise, Tease
Tornado Cyclone, Twister, Waterspout
Toronto Hogtown
Torpedo Bangalore, Bomb, Fish, Missile, Ray, Subroc, Tin fish, Weapon
Torpedo-guard Crinoline
Torpid, Torpor Accidie, Acedia, Comatose, Dormant, Inertia, Languid, Lethargic, Sluggish, Slumbering
Torrent Flood, Spate
Torrid Amphiscian, Fiery, Hot, Sultry, Tropical
Torsk Cusk
Torso Body, Midriff, Trunk
Tortilla Pancake, Taco, Tostada
Tortoise Chelonia, Emydes, Emys, Galapagos, Giant, Hic(c)atee, Kurma, Pancake, Snapping-turtle, Terrapin, Testudo, Timothy, Turtle, Water
Tortoiseshell Epiplastra, Hawksbill, Testudo
Tortuous Ambagious, Twisty, Winding
▷ **Tortuous** *may indicate* an anagram
Torture, Torture chamber, Torture instrument Agonise, Auto-da-fé, Bastinade, Bastinado, Boot, Bootikin, Catasta, Chinese burn, Chinese water, Crucify, Engine, Excruciate, Flageolet, Fry, Gadge, Gauntlet, Gyp, Hell, Iron maiden, Knee-cap, Naraka, Persecute, Pilliwinks, Pine, Pinniewinkle, Pinnywinkle, → **RACK**, Sadism, Scaphism, Scarpines, Scavenger's daughter, Scourge, Strappado, Tantalise, Third degree, Thumbscrew, Torment, Tumbrel, Tumbril, Water, Wheel, Wrack
▷ **Tortured** *may indicate* an anagram
Torturer Torquemada
Torus Disc, Stellarator
Tory Abhorrer, Blimp, Blue, C, Opposition, Right, Tantivy, Unionist
Toss(ing), Throw(n) Abject, Bandy, Bounce, Buck, Bung, Buttock, Cant, Canvass, Cast, Catapult, → **CHUCK**, Cottabus, Crabs, Crap, Cross-buttock, Dad, Daud, Dawd, Deal, Disconcert, Dod, Elance, Estrapade, Falcade, → **FLING**, Flip, Flump, Flutter, Flying (head)-mare, Free, Full, Gollum, Haunch, Heave, Hipt, Hoy, → **HURL**, Jack, Jact(it)ation, Jaculation, Jeff, Juggle, Jump, Lance, Lob, Loft, Nick, Pash, Pick, Pitch, Purl, Put(t), Round-arm, Seamer, Shy, Slat, Sling, Squail, Unhorse, Unseat, Upcast
Toss-up Cross and pile, Heads or tails
Tot Add, Babe, Bairn, → **CHILD**, Dop, Dram, Infant, Mite, Nightcap, Nip(per), Nipperkin, Slug, Snifter, Snort, Tad
Total, Toto Absolute, Aggregate, All(-out), All told, Amount, Balance, Be-all, → **COMPLETE**, Entire, Gross, Lot, Mass, Sum, Tale, Tally, Unqualified, Utter, Whole
Totalitarian Autocrat, Despot, Étatiste, Fascist

Tote Bear, → CARRY, Yomp

Totem Fetish, Icon, Image, Pole

Tottenham Hotspur

Totter Abacus, Daddle, Daidle, Didakai, Didakei, Did(d)icoy, Didicoi, Halt, Ragman, Reel, Rock, → STAGGER, Swag, Sway, Topple, Waver

Touch(ed), Touching, Touchy Accolade, Adjoin, Affect, Anent, Badass, Barmy, Cadge, Captious, Carambole, Caress, Carom, Common, Concern, Connivent, Contact, Contiguous, Dash, Emove, → FEEL, Finger, Finishing, Flick, Fondle, Haptic, Heart-warming, Huffy, → IN TOUCH, Iracund, Irascible, J'adoube, Liaison, Libant, Loan, Loco, Midas, Miffy, Near, Nie, Nigh, Nudge, Palp, Pathetic, Paw, Potty, Re, Sense, Shade, Skiff, Soft, Sore, Spice, → SPOT, Tactile, Tactual, Tag, Tangible, Tap, Taste, Tat, Tetchy, Tickle, Tig, Tinderbox, Tinge, Titivate, Trace, Trait, Tuck, Vestige

Touchline Tangent

Touchstone Basanite, Criterion, Norm, Standard

Touchwood Absit omen, Monk, Punk, Spunk, Tinder

Tough(en) Adamantine, Anneal, Apache, Arduous, Ballsy, Burly, → HARD, Hard-boiled, Hard-nosed, Hardy, Heavy duty, He-man, Hood, Hoodlum, Husky, Indurate, Knotty, Leathern, Leathery, Nut, Pesky, Rambo, Rigwiddie, Rigwoodie, Roughneck, Sinewy, Spartan, Steely, Stiff, Strict, String, Sturdy, Teuch, Thewed, Tityre-tu, Virile

Toupee Hairpiece, Rug, Tour, → WIG

Tour(er), Tourism, Tourist Adventure, Barnstorm, Circuit, Cook's, Emmet, Excursion, Gig, Grand, Grockle, GT, Holiday-maker, Itinerate, → JOURNEY, Lionise, Mystery, Outing, Parra, Posting, Roadie, Rubberneck, Safari, Sightsee, Swing, Tiki, → TRAVEL, Trip(per), Viator, Whistle-stop

Tourmaline Indicolite, Indigolite, Schorl, Zeuxite

Tournament American, Basho, Bonspiel, Carousel, Drive, Event, Jereed, Jerid, Joust, Just, Ladder, Plate, Pro-am, Round robin, Royal, Super Twelve, Swiss, Tilt, Tourney, Wimbledon

Tourniquet Garrot, Throttle, Torcular

Tousle Dishevel, Rumple

Tout Barker, Laud, Ply, Praise, Runner, Solicit, Toot, Work-watcher

Tow(ing) Aquaplane, Button, Fibre, → HAUL, Pull, → ROPE, Ski, Skijoring, Stupe, Track

▶ **Towards** see TO

Towel Dry, Jack, Nappy, Roller, Rub, Sanitary, Tea, Tea-cloth, Terry, Turkish

Tower AA, Aspire, Atalaya, Babel, Barbican, Bastille, Bastion, Belfry, Bell, Bloody, Brattice, Brettice, Brogh, Campanile, Clock, Conning, Control, Cooling, Donjon, Dungeon, Edifice, Eiffel, Fly, Fortress, Gantry, Garret, Gate, Giralda, Gopura(m), Guérite, Horologium, Ivory, Keep, Leaning, Loom, Maiden, Martello, Minar(et), Monument, Mooring, Mouse, Nuraghe, Nurhag, Overtop, Peel, Pinnacle, Pisa, Pound, Pylon, Rear, Rise, Rolandseck, Rood, Round, Sail, Sears, Shot, Sikhara, Silo, Ski-lift, Space Needle, Specula, Spire, Stealth, Steeple, Swiss Re, Tête-de-pont, Texas, Tractor, Tugboat, → TURRET, Victoria, Watch, Water, Yagura, Ziggurat, Zikkurat

Town, Township Boom, Borgo, Borough, Bourg, Burg(h), City, Conurbation, County, Deme, Dormitory, Dorp, Favella, Garrison, Ghost, Ham(let), Intraurban, Market, Municipal, Nasik, One-horse, Open, Podunk, Pueblo, Satellite, Shanty, Soweto, Staple, Tinsel, Tp, Twin, Urban, Whistle stop, Wick

Townee, Townsman Cad, Cit(izen), Dude, Freeman, Oppidan, Philister, Resident

Town hall Prytaneum
Toxaemia Eclampsia
Toxic(ity), Toxin Abrin, Aflatoxin, Antigen, Botox®, Botulin, Cadaverine, Cadmium, Chlorin(e), Coumarin, Curare, Deadly, Dioxan, Dioxin, Eclampsia, Fluorin(e), Lethal, Melittin, Muscarine, Phalloidin, Phenol, Phenothiazine, Pre-eclampsia, Psoralen, Ricin, Sepsis, Serology, Venin, Venomous, Virulence, Zootoxin
Toy Bauble, Bull-roarer, Cockhorse, Cyberpet, Dally, Dandle, Dinky®, Doll, Executive, Faddle, Finger, Flirt, Frisbee®, Gewgaw, Golly, Gonk, Jack-in-the-box, Jumping-jack, Kaleidoscope, Kickshaw, Knack, Lego®, Meccano®, Noah's ark, Novelty, Paddle, Pantine, Peashooter, Pinwheel, Plaything, Praxinoscope, Rattle, Russian doll, Scooter, Shoofly, Skipjack, Taste, Teddy, Thaumatrope, Top, → TRIFLE, Trinket, Tu(r)ndun, Whirligig, Windmill, Yoyo, Zoetrope
Trace Atom, Cast, Derive, Describe, Draft, Draw, Dreg, Echo, Footprint, Ghost, → HINT, Leaf, Limn, Mark, Memory, Outline, Relic, Relict, Remnant, Scintilla, Semblance, Sign, Smack, Soupçon, Strap, Tinge, → TOUCH, Track, Vestige, Whiff, Whit
Tracery Filigree
Track(s), Tracker, Tracking, Trackman Aintree, Band, B-road, Caterpillar®, Cinder, Circuit, Course, Crawler, Cycleway, Dog, DOVAP, Drift, Ecliptic, El, Fast, Fettler, Footing, Gandy dancer, Hunt, Ichnite, Ichnolite, Icknield Way, Inside, Lane, Ley, Line, Loipe, Loopline, Mommy, Monitor, Monza, → PATH, Persue, Piste, Pug, Pursue, Race, Raceway, Rail, Railway, Rake, Ridgeway, Riding, Route, Run, Rut, Siding, Sign, Skidway, Sleuth, Slot, Sonar, Speedway, Spoor, Tan, Tan-ride, Taxi, Tenure, Tideway, Title, → TRAIL, Trajectory, Tram, Tramline, Tramroad, Tramway, Tread, Trode, Tug(boat), Twin, Wake, Wallaby, Way, Y
Tract(able), Tracts Area, Belt, Bench, Clime, Colporteur, Common, Dene, Digestive, Enclave, Flysheet, Lande, Leaflet, Monte, Moor, Olfactory, → PAMPHLET, Park, Prairie, Province, Purlieu, Pusey, Region, Screed, Taluk, Tawie, Terrain, Wold
Tractarian(ism) Newman, Oxford movement, Pusey(ism)
Tractor Bombardier®, Bulldozer, Cat, Caterpillar®, Chelsea, Fendalton, Pedrail, Remuera, Skidder, Tower
Trade(r), Tradesman, Trading Arb(itrageur), Art, Banian, Banyan, Bargain, Barter, Bilateral, Bricks and clicks, Bun(n)ia, Burgher, Business, Cabotage, Calling, Carriage, Chaffer, Chandler, Chapman, Cheapjack, Clicks and mortar, Coaster, Comanchero, → COMMERCE, Coster, Costermonger, Crare, Crayer, Deal(er), Dicker, Easterling, Errand, Exchange, Factor, Fair, Floor, Free, Handle, Horse, Hosier, Hot, Importer, Indiaman, Industry, Insider, Ironmonger, Jobber, Logrolling, Line, Merchant, Mercosur, Métier, Middleman, Mister, Monger, Mystery, Occupy, Outfitter, Paralleling, Pitchman, Ply, Program(me), Rag, Retailer, Roaring, Rough, Roundtripping, Scalp, Screen, Sell, Simony, Slave, Stallenger, Stallinger, Stationer, Sutler, Suttle, → SWAP, Traffic, Transit, Trant, Truck, Union, Vaisya, Vend, Wholesaler, Wind
Trademark Brand, Chop, Idiograph, Label, Logo, Tm
Trade union ASLEF, COHSE, Local, Solidarity, Syndicalism, UNISON, USDAW
Trading money, Trading post Cabotage, Fort, Wampum
Tradition(s), Traditional(ist) Ancestral, Classical, Convention, Custom(ary), Eastern, Folksy, Folkway, Hadith, Heritage, Legend, Lore, Mahayana, Misoneist, Old guard, Old-school, Orthodox, Pharisee, Pompier, Practice, Purist, Suburban, Time-honoured, Trad, Tralaticious, Tralatitious, Unwritten
Traduce Abuse, Asperse, Defame, Impugn, Malign, Smear, Vilify

Traffic, Traffic pattern Air, Barter, Broke, Cabotage, Clover-leaf, Commerce, Contraflow, Deal, Negotiate, Passage, Run, Slave trade, Smuggle, Tailback, Through, Trade, Truck, Vehicular

Tragedian, Tragedy, Tragic Aeschylus, Buskin, Calamity, Cenci, Corneille, Dire, → DRAMA, Euripides, Macready, Melpomene, Oedipean, Oresteia, Otway, Pathetic, Seneca, Sophoclean, Thespian, Thespis

Trail(er), Trailing Abature, Advert, Audit, Bedraggle, Caravan, Condensation, Creep, Dissipation, Drag, Draggle, Follow, Ipomaea, Ivy, Lag, Liana, Liane, Nature, Oregon, Paper, Path, Persue, Preview, Promo(tion), Pursue, Repent, Runway, Santa Fe, Scent, Shadow, Sign, Sleuth, Slot, Spoor, Straggle, Stream, Streel, Tag, Trace, → TRACK, Trade, Traipse, Trape, Trauchle, Trayne, Troad, Vapour, Vine, Virga, Wake

Train(er), Training Accommodation, Advanced, APT, Autogenic, BR, Breed, Bullet, Caravan, Cat, Cavalcade, Choo-choo, Circuit, Coach, Commuter, Condition, Cortège, Diesel, Direct, Discipline, Dog, Double-header, Dressage, Drill, Drive, Educate, Entourage, Enure, Epicyclic, Eurostar®, Excursion, Exercise, Express, Fartlek, Field, Flier, Flight simulator, Freightliner®, Fuse, Gear, Ghan, Ghost, Gravy, Grounding, GWR, Handle(r), → INSET, Instruct, Intercity®, Interval, Jerkwater, Journey, Liner, Link, LMS, LNER, Loco, Longe, Lunge, Maglev, Mailcar, Manège, Manrider, Meinie, Mein(e)y, Mentor, Milk, Nopo, Nurture, Nuzzle, Omnibus, Orient Express, Owl, Pack, Paddy, Parliamentary, PE, Pendolino, Personal, Potty, Practise, → PREPARE, Procession, PT, Puffer, Puff-puff, Push-pull, Q, Queue, Rattler, Rehearse, Retinue, Road, Roadwork, Rocket, Ry, Sack, → SCHOOL, Series, Shoe, Shuttle service, Siege, Sinkansen, Skill centre, Sloid, Sloyd, Sowarree, Sowarry, Special, SR, Steer, String, Suite, Tail, Tame, → TEACH, Through, Tire, Tirocinium, Track shoe, Trail, Tube, Twin bill, Wage, Wagon, Wave, Way

▷ **Train(ed)** *may indicate* an anagram

Trainee → APPRENTICE, Cadet, Cub, Intern, Jackaroo, Jackeroo, Learner, Ordinand, Rookie, Rooky

Train-spotter Gricer

Trait Characteristic, Feature, Knack, Ph(a)enotype, Sickle-cell, Strain, Thew, Trick, Vein

Traitor Benedict Arnold, Betrayer, Casement, Dobber-in, Joyce, Judas, Judas Maccabaeus, Nid(d)ering, Nid(d)erling, Nithing, Proditor, Quisling, Renegade, Reptile, Tarpeian, Traditor, Treachetour, Turncoat, Viper, Wallydraigle, Weasel

Trajectory Parabola, Track

▷ **Trammel** *may indicate* an anagram

Tramp, Trample Bog-trotter, Bum, Caird, Clochard, Clump, Crush, Deadbeat, Derelict, Derro, Dingbat, Dosser, Down and out, Estragon, Footslog, Freighter, Gadling, Gangrel, Gook, Hike, Hobo, Knight of the road, Meff, Override, Overrun, Pad, Piker, Plod, Poach, Potch(e), Rover, Scorn, Ship, Splodge, Sundowner, Swagman, → TINKER, Toe-rag(ger), Track, Traipse, Tread, Trek, Trog, Tromp, Truant, Trudge, Tub, Vagabond, Vagrant, Weary Willie

Trampoline Trampet(te)

Trance Catalepsy, Cataplexy, Goa, Narcolepsy

Tranche Gold, Reserve

Tranquil(lity) Ataraxy, Calm, Composure, Easy, Halcyon, Lee, Peaceful, Placid, Quietude, Sedate, → SERENE

Tranquillise(r) Appease, Ataractic, Ataraxic, → CALM, Diazepam, Downer, Hypnone, Hypnotic, Largactil®, Librium®, Nervine, Nitrazepam, Oxazepam,

Placate, Satisfy, Soothe, Still, Valium®
Transaction(s) Affair, Agio, Brokerage, Deal, Escrow, Fasti, Leaseback, Tr
Transcend(ent), Transcendental(ist) Excel, Mystic, Overtop, Surpass, Thoreau
Transcribe, Transcript(ion) Copy, Inclusive, Rescore, Tenor, → TRANSLATE,
Transume
Transfer(ence) Alien, Alienate, → ASSIGN, Attorn, Calk, Calque, Cede, Chargeable,
Communize, Consign, Convey(ance), Credit, Crosstalk, Decal, Demise, Devolve,
Download, Exchange, Explant, Hive off, Make over, Mancipation, Metathesis,
Mortmain, Nuclear, On-lend, Pass, Photomechanical, Print through, Provection,
Reassign, Redeploy, Remit, Remove, Repot, Second, Settlement, Thought,
Transduction, Transfection, Uproot, Vire, Virement
▷ **Transferred** *may indicate* an anagram
Transfix Impale, Rivet, → SKEWER, Spear, Spit
Transform(ation), Transformer Alter, Apotheosis, Balun, Change, Fourier,
Lorentz, Metamorphism, Metamorphose, Metamorphosis, Metaplasia, Metastasis,
Morphallaxis, Morphing, Permute, Rectifier, Sea change, Tinct, Toupee,
Transmogrify, Wig
▷ **Transform(ed)** *may indicate* an anagram
Transfusion Apheresis
Transgress(ion) Encroach, Err, Infringe, Offend, Overstep, Peccancy, → SIN, Violate
Transient, Transit(ion), Transitory Brief, Ephemeral, Fleeting, Fly-by-night,
Forbidden, Fugacious, Hobo, Metabasis, Passage, Passing, Provisional, Seque,
Sfumato, T, Temporary
Transistor Drift, Epitaxial, Field-effect, Junction
Translate, Translation, Translator Calque, Construe, Convert, Coverdale, Crib,
Explain, Free, Horse, Interpret, In vitro, Jerome, Key, Linguist, Loan, Machine,
Metaphrase, Nick, Paraphrase, Pinyin, Polyglot, Pony, Reduce, Render, Rendition,
Rhemist, Simultaneous, Targum, Tr, Transcribe, Transform, Trot, Unseen,
Version(al), Vulgate, Wycliffe
▷ **Translate(d)** *may indicate* an anagram
Transmigrate, Transmigration Exodus, Metempsychosis, Passage, Trek
Transmit(ter), Transmitted, Transmission Air, Allele, Analogue, Automatic,
Band, Baseband, Beacon, Broadband, → BROADCAST, Cable, Carry, CB,
Communicate, Conduct, Consign, Contagion, Convection, Convey, Digital,
Facsimile, Filler, Forward, Gearbox, Gene, Heredity, Impart, Intelsat, Manual,
Mast, Microphone, Modem, Nicol, Permittivity, Pipe, Propagate, Racon, Radiate,
Radio, Receiver, Responser, Simplex, Simulcast, Sonabuoy, Spark, Synchronous,
Tappet, Telautograph®, Telecast, Telegony, Telematics, Telemetry, Teleprinter,
Teletex, Televise, Telex, Tiros, Traduce, Traject, Tralaticious, Tralatitious, UART,
Ultrawideband, Uplink, Upload, Walkie-talkie
Transom Reverse, Traverse
Transparent, Transparency Adularia, Clear, Crystal(line), Diaphanous, Dioptric,
Glassy, Glazed, Hyaloid, Iolite, Leno, Limpid, Lucid, Luminous, Patent, Pellucid,
Sheer, Slide, Tiffany
Transpire Happen, Occur
Transplant Allograft, Anaplasty, Graft, Repot, Reset, Shift
Transport(ed), Transporter, Transportation Active, Aerotrain, Argo, Bear, Bike,
Broomstick, BRS, Bus, Cargo, Carract, → CARRY, Cart, Cat-train, Charm, Convey,
Cycle, Delight, Ecstasy, Electron, Eloin, Enrapt, Enravish, Entrain, Esloin, Estro,
Fishyback, Freight, Haul(age), Helicopter, Jerrican, Joy, Kurvey, Lift, Lug, Maglev,
Mambrane, Matatu, Monorail, Pack animal, Palanquin, Pantechnicon, Public,

Put, Rape, Rapine, Rapture, Roadster, Ship, Shuttle, Sidecar, Sledge, Supersonic, Tandem, Tanker, Tape, Tote, Train, Trap, Tuktuk, Waft, Wheels, Wireway

Transpose, Transposition Anagram, Commute, Convert, Invert, Metathesis, Shift, Spoonerism, Switch, Tr

▷ **Transposed** *may indicate* an anagram

Transsexual Invert

Transubstantiate, Transubstantiation Capernaite

Transverse Across, Crosscut, Diagonal, Obliquid, Thwart

Transvest(it)ism, Transvestite Berdache, Berdash, Cross-dressing, Eonist

Tranter Dolly

Trap(s), Trapdoor, Trapped, Trappings Ambush, → BAGGAGE, Bags, Belongings, Booby, Buckboard, Bunker, Carriage, Catch, Catch-pit, Clapnet, Corner, Cru(i)ve, Deadfall, Death, Decoy, Dogcart, Downfall, Eelset, Emergent, Ensnare, Entrain, Fall, Fit-up, Fly, Flypaper, Frame-up, Fyke, Gig, Gin, Gob, Grin, Hatch, Housings, Ice-bound, Jinri(c)ksha(w), Keddah, Kettle, Kheda, Kiddle, Kidel, Kipe, Kisser, Knur(r), Light, Lime, Live, → LUGGAGE, Lure, Mesh, Mouth, Net, Nur(r), Paraphernalia, Pitfall, Plant, Police, Pot, Poverty, Putcheon, Putcher, Quicksand, Radar, Regalia, Sand, Scruto, → SNARE, Speed, Spell, Spider, Springe, Stake-net, Star, Steam, Stench, Sting, Stink, Sun, Tangle, Tank, Teagle, Toil, Tonga, Trojan horse, Trou-de-loup, Two-wheeler, U, U-bend, Vampire, Web, Weel, Weir, Wire

Trapezist Leotard

Trapper Carson, Voyageur

Trash(y) Bosh, Deface, Dre(c)k, Garbage, Junk, Kitsch, Pulp, → RUBBISH, Schlock, Scum, Tinpot, Trailer, Vandalise, White, Worthless

Trauma Insult, Shock

Travel(ler), Travelling Aeneas, Backpack, Bagman, Bushwhacker, Commercial, Commute, Crustie, Crusty, Drive, Drummer, Fare, Fellow, Fly, Fogg, Geoffrey, Gipsen, Gipsy, Gitano, Globe-trotter, Go, Gulliver, Gypsy, Hike, Interrail, Itinerant, Journey, Long-haul, Marco Polo, Meve, Migrant, Motor, Move, Mush, New Age, Nomad, Passenger, Passepartout, Peregrination, Peripatetic, Pilgrim, Ply, Polo, Pootle, Range, Rep, Ride, Rom(any), Rove, Safari, Sail, Salesman, Samaritan, Space, → TOUR, Trek, Tripper, Tsigane, Viator, Voyage, Wanderjahr, Wayfarer, Wend, Wildfire, Zigan

Traverse Cross, Girdle, Measure, Quest, Trace

Travesty Burlesque, Charade, Distortion, Parody, Show, Skit

Trawl Drag-net, Hose-net, Net

Tray Antler, Bottle-slide, Carrier, Case, Charger, Coaster, Gallery, Joe, Lazy Susan, Plateau, → SALVER, Shower, Tea, Trencher, Typecase, Voider, Waiter

Treacherous, Treachery Bad faith, Deceit, Delilah, Fickle, Ganelon, Guile, Insidious, Judas-kiss, Knife, Mala fide, Medism, Perfidious, Punic (faith), Quicksands, Serpentine, Sleeky, Snaky, Trahison, Traitor, → TREASON, Two-faced, Viper

Treacle Black(jack), Butter, Molasses, Venice

Tread Clamp, Clump, Dance, Pad, Step, Stramp, Track, Trample

Treadle Footboard

Treason Betrayal, Constructive, High, Insurrection, Lèse-majesté, Lese-majesty, Perduellion, Petty, Sedition, → TREACHERY

Treasure(r), Treasury Banker, Bursar, Cache, Camerlengo, Camerlingo, Cherish, Chest, Cimelia, Coffer, Ewe-lamb, Exchequer, Fisc(al), Fisk, Godolphin, Golden, Heritage, Hoard, Montana, Palgrave, Pork barrel, → PRIZE, Procurator, Purser, Relic, Riches, Steward, Taonga, Thesaurus, Trove

Treat, Treatment Action, Acupuncture, Allopathy, Antidote, Archilowe, Arenation, Aromatherapy, Balneotherapy, Beano, Besee, Body wrap, Botox®, Capitulate, Care, Chemotherapy, Chiropractic, Condition, Course, Crymotherapy, Cryotherapy, Cupping, Cure, Deal, Detox(ification), Dialysis, Do, → DOCTOR, Dose, Dress, Dutch, Enantiopathy, Entertain, Est, Facial, Faith-healing, Fango, Figuration, Foment, Frawzey, Handle, Holistic, Homeopathy, HRT, Hydrotherapy, Hypnotherapy, Immunotherapy, Intermediate, Jin shin do, Kenny, Laser, Manage, Massotherapy, Mechanotherapy, Medicate, Moxibustion, Naturopathy, Negotiate, Opotherapy, Organotherapy, Osteopathy, → OUTING, Pasteur, Pedicure, Pelotherapy, Physic, Physiotherapy, Pie, Poultice, Probiotics, Process, Prophylaxis, Psychoanalysis, Psychodrama, Psychotherapy, Radiotherapy, Regale, Rehab(ilitation), Rest cure, Root, Secretage, Serotherapy, Setter, Shout, Shrift, Sironise, Smile, Speleotherapy, → STAND, Tablet, Tebilise®, Thalassotherapy, Themotherapy, Therapy, Titbit, Traction, Twelve-step, Usance, Use, Vet
▷ **Treated** *may indicate* an anagram
Treatise Almagest, Commentary, Didache, Discourse, Dissertation, Essay, Monograph, Pandect, Prodrome, Profound, Summa, Tract(ate), Upanishad, Vedanta
Treaty Agreement, Alliance, Assiento, Concordat, Covenant, Entente, Jay's, Lateran, Locarno, Lunéville, Maastricht, Nijmegen, North Atlantic, → PACT, Paris, Private, Protocol, Rapallo, Rijswijk, Ryswick, San Stefano, Sovetsk, Test-ban, Utrecht, Verdun, Versailles, Yorktown
Treble Castrato, Choirboy, Chorist(er), Pairial, Soprano, → TRIPLE, Triune, Voice
Tree(s) Actor, → ANCESTRY, Axle, Beam, Bluff, Boom, Bosk, Clump, Conifer, Coppice, Corner, Cross, Daddock, Deciduous, Decision, Dendrology, Descent, Family, Fault, Fringe, Gallows, Genealogical, Grove, Hang, Hardwood, Jesse, Nurse, Pedigree, Pole, Rood, Roof, Sawyer, Silva, Softwood, Staddle, Stemma, Summer, Timber, Tyburn, Vista, Wicopy, → WOOD

TREES

2 letters:	Nim	Cade	Ming
Bo	Oak	Coco	Mira
Ti	Oil	Cola	Mott
	Sal	Dali	Mowa
3 letters:	Tea	Dhak	Neem
Ake	Til	Dika	Nipa
Ash	Ule	Dita	Noni
Asp	Wax	Eugh	Olea
Bay	Yew	Gean	Ombu
Bel		Hule	Palm
Ben	4 letters:	Jack	Pine
Box	Acer	Kaki	Pipe
Cow	Akee	Karo	Pith
Elm	Aloe	Kiri	Plum
Fir	Amla	Kola	Poon
Gum	Arar	Lime	Puka
Ita	Atap	Lote	Rain
Jak	Bael	Mako	Rata
Koa	Bhel	Meal	Rhus
Mot	Bito	Milk	Rimu

Sack	Grass	Pipul	Bottle
Shea	Guava	Pitch	Buriti
Silk	Hakea	Plane	Cadaga
Sloe	Hazel	Quina	Cadagi
Soap	Hevea	Ramin	Carapa
Sorb	Holly	Roble	Carica
Tawa	Iroko	Rowan	Cashew
Teak	Ivory	Sabal	Cembra
Teil	Jambu	Saman	Cercis
Titi	Jarul	Sassy	Cerris
Toon	Judas	Scrog	Chaste
Tung	Kapok	Smoke	Chenar
Tutu	Karri	Sumac	Cherry
Upas	Kauri	Tawai	Chinar
Yang	Khaya	Taxus	Citron
	Kiaat	Thorn	Coffee
5 letters:	Kokum	Thuja	Cordon
Abele	Larch	Thuya	Cornel
Abies	Lemon	Tilia	Cornus
Ackee	Lilac	Tsuga	Damson
Afara	Lotus	Tuart	Deodar
Agila	Mahoe	Tulip	Diana's
Alamo	Mahua	Vitex	Dragon
Alder	Mahwa	Wahoo	Durian
Alnus	Maire	Wenge	Durion
Anona	Mamey	Wilga	Emblic
Areca	Mango	Withy	Eumong
Argan	Mapau	Xylem	Eumung
Aspen	Maple	Yacca	Feijoa
Banak	Marri	Yulan	Fustet
Beech	Matai	Zaman	Fustic
Belah	Melia	Zamia	Gallus
Birch	Motte		Garjan
Bodhi	Mowra	**6 letters:**	Gidgee
Boree	Mugga	Abroma	Gidjee
Butea	Mulga	Acacia	Gingko
Cacao	Mvule	Akeake	Ginkgo
Carap	Myall	Alerce	Glinap
Cedar	Ngaio	Angico	Gnetum
Ceiba	Nikau	Annona	Gopher
China	Nyssa	Antiar	Guango
Cocoa	Olive	Arbute	Gurjun
Cocus	Opepe	Arolla	Gympie
Coral	Osier	Babaco	Hupiro
Ebony	Palas	Balsam	Illipe
Elder	Palay	Banyan	Illipi
Fagus	Panax	Baobab	Illupi
Fever	Peach	Bilian	Jarool
Flame	Pecan	Bombax	Jarrah
Fruit	Pinon	Bonsai	Joshua
Genip	Pipal	Bo-tree	Jujube

Kamahi	Sallow	Carbeen	Radiata
Kamala	Samaan	Cascara	Rampick
Kamela	Sapele	Cassava	Rampike
Kapuka	Sapium	Catalpa	Redwood
Karaka	Sapota	Champac	Rock elm
Karamu	Saxaul	Champak	Saksaul
Karite	She-oak	Chayote	Sandbox
Kowhai	Sinder	Coquito	Saouari
Laurel	Sorrel	Corylus	Sapling
Lebbek	Souari	Corypha	Sausage
Linden	Spruce	Cumquat	Sequoia
Locust	Styrax	Dagwood	Seringa
Longan	Sumach	Dogwood	Service
Loquat	Sunder	Dryades	Shittah
Lucuma	Sundra	Durmast	Sourgum
Lungah	Sundri	Geebung	Soursop
Macoya	Tallow	Genipap	Spindle
Mallee	Tamanu	Gluinap	Sundari
Manuka	Tawhai	Gumtree	Taraire
Mastic	Tewart	Hickory	Taupata
Mazard	Thyine	Hog-plum	Tawhiri
Medlar	Titoki	Holm-oak	Trumpet
Mimosa	Tooart	Houhere	Varnish
Missel	Totara	Jipyapa	Wallaba
Mopane	Tupelo	Kumquat	Wirilda
Mopani	Waboom	Lacquer	Witchen
Myrtle	Wandoo	Lagetto	Wych-elm
Nutmeg	Wicken	Lentisk	Xylopia
Obeche	Willow	Logwood	Zelkova
Orange	Witgat	Lumbang	
Orihou	Yarran	Madrono	**8 letters:**
Padauk	Zamang	Mahaleb	Aguacate
Padouk		Manjack	Algaroba
Pagoda	**7 letters:**	Marasca	Aquillia
Papaya	Ailanto	Margosa	Bangalay
Pawpaw	Amboina	Mazzard	Bangalow
Peepul	Apricot	Mesquit	Basswood
Pepper	Arbutus	Moringa	Benjamin
Platan	Avodire	Morrell	Bergamot
Pomelo	Bebeeru	Mustard	Berrigan
Poplar	Bilimbi	Papauma	Blackboy
Popple	Bilsted	Pereira	Blimbing
Protea	Bubinga	Pimento	Bountree
Puriri	Buck-eye	Platane	Bourtree
Quince	Bursera	Pollard	Breadnut
Red-bud	Cajeput	Populus	Brigalow
Red gum	Cajuput	Pukatea	Calabash
Ricker	Calamus	Quassia	Cinchona
Roucou	Camphor	Quicken	Cinnamon
Rubber	Camwood	Quillai	Cocoplum
Sabicu	Canella	Quinain	Coolabah

Coolibah	Quantong	Bully-tree	Pontianac
Corkwood	Quillaia	Bulwaddee	Quebracho
Crabwood	Quillaja	Burrawary	Rauwolfia
Cucumber	Raintree	Butternut	Rose-apple
Cudgerie	Rambutan	Caliatour	Sapodilla
Dendroid	Rangiora	Caliature	Saskatoon
Dracaena	Rewa-rewa	Candlenut	Sassafras
Espalier	Sago-palm	Canoewood	Satinwood
Flittern	Sandarac	Carambola	Shellbark
Fraxinus	Santalum	Casuarina	Simarouba
Garcinia	Sapindus	Chempaduk	Soapberry
Ghost-gum	Sapucaia	Cherimoya	Star-anise
Gnetales	Sasswood	Chincapin	Star-apple
Guaiacum	Sea grape	Chinkapin	Stinkwood
Hagberry	Shagbark	Coachwood	Sweetwood
Hawthorn	Simaruba	Cordyline	Tacamahac
Hinahina	Snowball	Courbaril	Tamarillo
Hornbeam	Snowdrop	Cupressus	Terebinth
Huon-pine	Soapbark	Eaglewood	Toothache
Igdrasil	Sourwood	Evergreen	Torchwood
Inkberry	Standard	Firewheel	Wagenboom
Ironbark	Stinging	Flame-leaf	Wayfaring
Ironwood	Sweet gum	Greenwood	Whitebeam
Jelutong	Sweetsop	Grevillea	Whitewood
Kawakawa	Sycamine	Hackberry	Wineberry
Kingwood	Sycamore	Ivory palm	Wych-hazel
Laburnum	Sycomore	Jacaranda	Yggdrasil
Lacebark	Tamarack	Kahikatea	Zebrawood
Lecythis	Tamarind	Krummholz	
Loblolly	Tamarisk	Kurrajong	**10 letters:**
Magnolia	Taxodium	Lancewood	Arbor Vitae
Mahogany	Umbrella	Lemonwood	Axe-breaker
Makomako	Whitegum	Leylandii	Bitterbark
Mangrove	Wine-palm	Macadamia	Blackbully
Manna-ash	Ygdrasil	Marmalade	Breadfruit
Mesquite		Mirabelle	Bulletwood
Mulberry	**9 letters:**	Mockernut	Buttonball
Ocotillo	Agila-wood	Monkeypot	Buttonwood
Oiticica	Ailantous	Naseberry	Calamondin
Oleaceae	Albespine	Nectarine	Calliature
Oleaster	Angophora	Nux vomica	Candle-wood
Pachouli	Azedarach	Paloverde	Cannonball
Palmetto	Bilimbing	Paperbark	Chamaerops
Pandanus	Bitternut	Patchouli	Chaulmugra
Parapara	Blackbutt	Patchouly	Cheesewood
Pichurim	Blackjack	Paulownia	Chinaberry
Pinaster	Blackwood	Persimmon	Chinquapin
Pithtree	Bloodwood	Pistachio	Cottonwood
Pyinkado	Bolletrie	Pitch-pine	Cowrie-pine
Quandang	Boobialla	Poinciana	Eucalyptus
Quandong	Broadleaf	Ponderosa	Fiddlewood

Flamboyant	Quercitron	Cabbage-palm	Stringybark
Flindersia	Ribbonwood	Chaulmoogra	
Frangipani	Sandalwood	Chokecherry	*12 letters:*
Green-heart	Sappanwood	Copperbeech	African tulip
Hackmatack	Silk-cotton	Cryptomeria	Haemotoxylon
Ilang-ilang	Silverbell	Dipterocarp	Hercules' club
Jaboticaba	Sneezewood	Eriodendron	Liriodendron
Jippi-jappa	Spotted gum	Flamboyante	Mammee-sapota
Kaffirboom	Strawberry	Fothergilla	Masseranduba
Kotokutuku	Tawheowheo	Gingerbread	Monkey-puzzle
Letter-wood	Traveller's	Honey locust	Washingtonia
Lilly-pilly	Turpentine	Jesuit's bark	Wellingtonia
Macrocarpa	Witch-hazel	Leatherwood	
Manchineel	Witgatboom	Lignum vitae	*13 letters:*
Mangabeira	Woollybutt	Liquidambar	Paper-mulberry
Mangosteen	Yellowwood	Maceranduba	
Marblewood	Ylang-ylang	Metasequoia	*14 letters:*
Nithofagus		Pomegranate	Western hemlock
Palisander	*11 letters:*	Purpleheart	
Paper birch	Appleringie	Shittimwood	
Pohutukawa	Bladderwort	Sitka spruce	

Tree-climber, Tree-dweller Monkey, Opossum, Sciurus, Squirrel, Unau
Tree disease Dutch elm, Waldsterben
Tree-man Ent
Tree-moss Usnea
Tree-paeony Moutan
Tree-pecker Picus
Tree-shrew Tana
Trefoil Bird's foot, Clover, Hop, Lotos, Lotus
Trek Hike, Journey, Leg, Odyssey, Safari, Yomp
Trellis Espalier, Lattice, Pergola, Treillage, Treille
Tremble, Trembling, Tremor Aftershock, Ashake, Butterfly, Dither, Dodder, Foreshock, Hotter, Intention, Judder, Marsquake, Moonquake, Palpitate, Quail, Quake, Quaver, Quiver, Seismal, → **SHAKE**, Shiver, Shock, Shudder, Stound, Temblor, Titubation, Trepid, Twitchy, Vibrant, Vibrate, Vibration, Vibratiuncle, Vibrato, Wobble, Wuther, Yips
Tremendous Big, Enormous, Howling, Immense, Marvellous
Tremolo Bebung, Trillo
▶ **Tremor** *see* **TREMBLE**
Tremulous Dithering, Hirrient, Quaking, Shaky, Timorous
Trench(er) Boyau, Cunette, Cuvette, Delf, Delph, Dike(r), → **DITCH**, Dyke(r), Encroach, Fleet, Foss(e), Foxhole, Fur(r), Furrow, Grip, Gullet, Gutter, Leat, Line, Mariana, Moat, Oceanic, Outwork, Rill, Rille, Ring-dyke, Robber, Salient, Sap, Shott, Slit, Sod, Sondage
Trenchant Acid, Cutting
Trend(y), Trendsetter Bent, Bias, Chic, Climate, Drift, Fashion, Hep, In, Mainstream, New Age(r), Newfangled, Pacemaker, Pop, Poserish, Posey, Rage, Right-on, Style, Swim, Tendency, Tendenz, Tenor, Tide, Tonnish
Trespass(ing) Aggravated, Encroach, Errant, Hack, Impinge, Infringe, Offend, Peccancy, Sin, Trench, Wrong

Tress(es) Curl, Lock, Ringlet, Switch, Tallent
Trestle Sawhorse
Triad Chord, Ternion, Trimurti
Trial Adversity, Affliction, Appro, Approbation, Approval, Assize, Attempt, Bane,
    Bernoulli, Bout, Clinical, Compurgation, Corsned, Court-martial, Cow, Cross, Dock,
    Essay, → EXPERIMENT, Field, Fitting, Hearing, Nuremberg, Ordeal, Pilot, Pree,
    Probation, Proof, Rehearsal, Salem, Scramble, Sheepdog, Show, State, Taste, Time
Triangle(d), Triangular Acute, Bermuda, Circular, Cosec, Deltoid, Equilateral,
    Eternal, Gair, Golden, Gore, Gyronny, Isosceles, Obtuse, Pascal's, Pedimental,
    Pendentive, Pyramid, Rack, Right-angled, Scalene, Similar, Spherical, Trigon,
    Triquetral, Tromino, Warning
Trias(sic) Bunter, Keuper, Muschelkalk, Rhaetic
Tribe(s), Tribal, Tribesmen Amalekite, Ammonites, Ashanti, Asher, Benjamin,
    Celt, Cherokee, Clan(nish), Cree, Creek, Dan, D(a)yak, Dinka, Dynasty, Edomites,
    Ephraim, Family, Gad, Gens, Gentes, Gentilic, Gond, Goth, Guarani, Hapu, Helvetii,
    Hittite, Horde, Hottentot, Ibo, Iceni, Israelite, Issachar, Iwi, Jat, Judah, Kaffir,
    Kenite, Kurd, Lashkar, Levi, Levite, Longobardi, Lost, Manasseh, Masai, Moabite,
    Mongol, Moro, Naga, Naphtali, Nation, Nervii, Ngati, Ordovices, Ostrogoths,
    Pathan, Phyle, Picts, → RACE, Reuben, Riff, Rod, Sakai, Salian, Schedule,
    Senones, Senussi, Sept, Shawnee, Silures, Simeon, Strandloper, Tasaday, Teuton,
    Trinobantes, Vandals, Wolof, Wyandot(te), X(h)osa, Zebulun
Tribune, Tribunal Aeropagus, Bema, Bench, → COURT, Divan, Employment,
    Forum, Hague, Industrial, Leader, Platform, Rienzi, Rota, Star-chamber, Waitangi
Tributary Affluent, Bogan, Branch, Creek, Fork
Tribute Cain, Capelline, Citation, Commemoration, Compliment, Dedication,
    Deodate, → DUE, Epitaph, Festschrift, Gavel, Heriot, Homage, Kain, Memento,
    Ode, Panegyric, Peter's pence, → PRAISE, Rome-penny, Rome-scot, Scat(t), Tax,
    Testimonial, Toast, Wreath, Wroth
Trice Flash, Instant
Trichosanthin Q
Trick(ed), Trickery, Tricks(ter), Tricky Antic, Art, Artifice, Attrap, Awkward,
    Bamboozle, Begunk, Book, Bunco, Bunko, Cantrip, Capot, Catch, Cheat,
    Chicane(ry), Chouse, Claptrap, Cod(-act), Cog, Con(fidence), Coyote, Crook,
    Davenport, Deception, Deck, Delicate, Delude, Device, Dirty, → DO, → DODGE,
    Dupe, Elf, Elfin, Elvan, Fard, Feat, Fetch, Fiddle, Finesse, Flam, Flim-flam, Fob,
    Fox, Fraud, Fun, Game, Gaud, Gleek, Glike, Guile, Had, Hanky-panky, Hey
    presto, Hoax, Hocus(-pocus), Hoodwink, Hornswoggle, Hum, Illude, Illusion,
    Illywhacker, Jadery, Jockey, John, Kittle, Knack, Lark, Magsman, Mislead, Monkey,
    Monkey-shine, Murphy's game, Nap, Nasruddin, Palter, Parlour, Pass, Pawk,
    Pleasantry, Pliskie, Prank, Prestige, Put-on, Quick, Ramp, Raven, Reak, Reik,
    Rex, Rig, Rope, Ropery, Roughie, Ruse, Scam, Sell, Set-up, Shanghai, Shavie,
    Shenanigan, Shifty, Shill, Skin-game, Skite, Skul(l)duggery, Skylark, Slam, Sleight,
    Slight, Slinter, Sophism, Spoof, Stall, Stint, Subterfuge, Sug, Swiftie, Thimble-rig,
    Three-card, Ticklish, Tip, Trap, Tregetour, Trump, Turn, Tweedler, Undercraft,
    Underplot, Vole, Wangle, Wheeze, Wile, Wrinkle
▷ **Trick** *may indicate* an anagram
Trickle Drib(ble), Driblet, Dropple, Leak, Rill, Seep
Trickless Misère
Triclinic Anorthic
Trident Fork, Plane, Trisul(a)
Trifle(s), Trifling Bagatelle, Banal, Baubee, Bauble, Bibelot, Birdseed, Bit, Bubkas,

Cent, Chickenfeed, Coquette, Dabble, Dalliance, → **DALLY**, Denier, Desipient,
Dessert, Do, Doit, Faddle, Falderal, Falderol, Fallal, Fattrell, Feather, Fewtril,
Fiddle, Fiddle-faddle, Fig, Fingle-fangle, Flamfew, Fleabite, Flirt, Folderol, Fool,
Footle, Fribble, Frippery, Fritter, Frivol, Gewgaw, Idle, Iota, Kickshaw, Knick-knack,
Luck-penny, Mess, Mite, Nick-nacket, Niff-naff, Nothing, Nugae, Nugatory, Nyaff,
Old song, Palter, Paltry, Peanuts, Peddle, Peppercorn, Petty, Philander, Picayune,
Piddle, Piffle, Pin, Pingle, Pittance, Play, Potty, Quelquechose, Quiddity, Quiddle,
Slight, Small beer, Smatter, Song, Sport, Stiver, Strae, Straw, Sundry, Sweet Fanny
Adams, Tiddle, Tom, Toy, Trinket, Trivia, Whifflery, Whim-wham, Whit
Trig(onometry) Neat, Sech, Spherical, Tosh, Trim
Trigger Activate, Detent, Hair, Instigate, Krytron, Pawl, Precipitate, Schmitt, Start,
Touch off
Trill(ed), Triller, Trilling Burr, Churr, Hirrient, Quaver, Ribattuta, Roll, Staphyle,
Trim, Twitter, Warble
Trilobite Olenellus, Olenus, Paradoxide
Trim(med), Trimmer, Trimming Ballast, Barb, Bleed, Braid, Bray, Chipper, Clip,
Dapper, Dinky, Dress, Ermine, Face, Falbala, Fettle, File, Froufrou, Garni, Garnish,
Garniture, Gimp, Guimpe, Macramé, Macrami, Marabou, Neat, Net(t), Ornament,
Pare, Passament, Passement(erie), Pipe, Plight, Posh, Preen, Proign, Proyn(e),
Pruin(e), Prune, Roach, Robin, Ruche, Sax, Sett, Shipshape, Smirk, Smug, Sned,
Snod, → **SPRUCE**, Straddle, Stroddle, Strodle, Stylist, Svelte, Tiddley, → **TIDY**,
Time-server, Top, Torsade, Trick, Whippersnipper, Wig
Trinidadian Carib
Trinity, Trinitarian Mathurin(e), Prosopon, Triad, Trimurti, Triune, Word
Trinket(s) Bauble, Bibelot, Bijou(terie), Charm, Fallal, Nicknack, Toy, Trankum,
Trumpery
Trio Catch, Graces, Skat, Terzetto, Threesome
Trip(per) Awayday, Cruise, Dance, Day, Ego, Errand, → **FALL**, Field, Flight, Flip,
Guilt, Head, High, Jolly, Journey, Junket, Kilt, Link, Outing, Passage, Pleasure,
Power, Ride, Round, Run, Sail, Sashay, Spin, Spurn, → **STUMBLE**, Tour, Trek, Trial,
Voyage
▷ **Trip** *may indicate* an anagram
Tripe Abracadabra, Bosh, Caen, Entrails, Honeycomb, Offal, Plain, Rot
Triple, Triplet Codon, Hemiol(i)a, Sdrucciola, Ternal, Tiercet, Treble, Trifecta,
Trilling, Trin(e), Tripling
Tripod Cat, Cortina, Highhat, Oracle, Triangle, Trippet, Trivet
Triptych Volet
Trishaw Cycle
Trite Banal, Boilerplate, Cornball, Corny, Hackneyed, Hoary, Laughable, Novelettish,
Platitude, Rinky-dink, Stale, Stock, Time-worn, Worn
Triton Eft, Evet, Ewt, Trumpet-shell
Triumph(ant) Cock-a-hoop, Codille, Cowabunga, Crow, Eureka, Exult, Glory,
Impostor, Killing, Oho, Olé, Ovation, Palm, Prevail, Victorious, → **WIN**
Triumvir Caesar, Crassus, Pompey
Trivet Tripod, Trippet
Trivia(l), Triviality Adiaphoron, Bagatelle, Balaam, Bald, → **BANAL**, Footling,
Frippery, Frothy, Futile, Idle, Inconsequential, Light, Minutiae, Nitpicking,
Nothingism, Paltry, Pap, Peppercorn, Pettifoggery, Petty, Picayune, Piddling,
Piffling, Puerile, Shallow, Small, Small beer, Small fry, Snippety, Squirt, Squit,
Toy(s), Vegie
Trochee Choree

Troglodyte Ape, Caveman, Hermit, Spelean, Wren
Trojan Aeneas, Agamemnon, Dardan, Iliac, Priam, Teucrian, Troic
Troll → FISH, Gnome, Rove, Spoon, Trawl, Warble
Trolley Brute, Cart, Crane, Dolly, Gurney, Hostess, Shopping, Tea, Teacart,
Traymobile, Truck, Trundler
▸ **Trollop** *see* LOOSE WOMAN
Trombone Bass, Posaune, Sackbut, Tenor
Trompe l'oeil Quadratura, Quadrature
Troop(s), Trooper Alpini, Band, BEF, Brigade, Company, Depot, Detachment,
Guard, Horde, Household, Logistics, Midianite, Militia, Pultan, Pulton, Pultoon,
Pultun, SAS, School, Shock, → SOLDIER, Sowar, State, Storm, Subsidiary, Tp,
Turm(e), Velites
Troopship Transport
Trophy Adward, Ashes, → AWARD, Bag, Belt, Cup, Emmy, Memento, Palm, Plate,
→ PRIZE, Scalp, Schneider, Spoils, Tourist, TT
Tropic(al) Cancer, Capricorn, Derris, Jungle, Neogaea, Sultry
Trot(ter), Trot out Air, Clip, Crib, Crubeen, Hag, Job, Jog, Passage, Pettitoes, Piaffe,
Pony, Ranke, Red(-shirt), Rising, Tootsie, Trotskyist
Troth Perfay, Troggs
Trotsky(ist) Entr(y)ism, Leon, Militant Tendency
Troubador Blondel, Griot, Manrico, Minstrel, Singer, Sordello
Trouble(s), Troublemaker, Troublesome Ache, Ado, Affliction, Aggro, Agitate,
Ail, Alarm, Annoy, Bale, Barrat, Beset, → BOTHER, Bovver, Brickle, Burden, Care,
Coil, Concern, Debate, Disaster, Disquiet, Distress, Disturb, Dog, Dolour, Eat,
Esclandre, Exercise, Fash, Fashious, Finger, Firebrand, Fossick, Frondeur, Gram(e),
Grief, Hag-ride, Harass, Harry, Hassle, Hatter, Heat, Heist, Hellion, Hot water,
Howdyedo, Hydra, Inconvenience, Infest, → IN TROUBLE, Jam, Kiaugh, Mess,
Mixer, Moil, Molest, Noy, Perturb, Pester, Pestiferous, Picnic, Plague, Play up,
Poke, Reck, Rub, Scamp, Scrape, Shake, Shtuck, Soup, Spiny, Stir, Storm, Sturt,
Tartar, Teen, Teething, Thorny, Tine, Toil, Trial, Tsouris, Tsuris, Turn-up, Tyne,
Unsettle, Vex, → WORRY
Trouble-free Gallio
Trouble-shooter Ombudsman
▷ **Troublesome** *may indicate* an anagram
Trough Back, Bed, Bucket, Buddle, Channel, Chute, Culvert, Graben, Hod, Hutch,
Langmuir, Launder, Leachtub, Manger, Pneumatic, Puerto Rico, Stock, Straik,
Strake, Syncline, Troffer, Tundish, Tye, Watering
Trounce → BEAT, Hammer, Thump
Trouser(s) Bags, Bell-bottoms, Bloomers, Breeches, Bumsters, Capri pants, Cargo
pants, Churidars, Clam-diggers, Combat, Continuations, Cords, Corduroys,
Cossacks, Culottes, Daks, Denims, Drainpipe, Drawers, Ducks, Dungarees,
Eel-skins, Flannels, Flares, Galligaskins, Gaskins, Gauchos, Hip-huggers, Hipsters,
Inexpressibles, Innominables, Jeans, Jodhpurs, Jog-pants, Kaccha, Ke(c)ks,
Knee cords, Lederhosen, Levis, Longs, Loons, Moleskins, Overalls, Oxford bags,
Palazzo (pants), Palazzos, Pantaloons, Pants, Pedal pushers, Pegtops, Plus-fours,
Plus-twos, Pyjamas, Reach-me-downs, Salopettes, Shalwar, Ski pants, Slacks,
Stirrup pants, Stovepipes, Strides, Strossers, Sweatpants, Thornproofs, Trews,
Trouse, Unmentionables, Unutterables, Utterless
Trout Aurora, Brook, Brown, Bull, Coral, Finnac(k), Finnock, Fish, Gillaroo,
Hag(fish), Herling, Hirling, Kamloops, Peal, Peel, Phinnock, Pogies, Quintet,
Rainbow, Salmon, Sewen, Sewin, Speckled, Splake, Steelhead, Togue, Whitling

Trow Faith, Meseems
Trowel Float, Slicker
Troy Ilium, Laomedon, Sergeant, T, Weight
Truant Absentee, AWOL, Bunk off, Dodge, Hooky, Kip, Mich(e), Mitch, Mooch, Mouch, Wag
Truce Armistice, Barley, Ceasefire, Fainites, Fains, Hudna, Interlude, Keys, Pax, Stillstand, Treague, Treaty
Truck Bakkie, Bogie, Breakdown, Business, Cabover, Cattle, Cocopan, Dealings, Dolly, Dumper, Flatbed, Forklift, Haul, Hopper, Journey, → **LORRY**, Low-loader, Monster, Pallet, Panel, Pick-up, Semi, Sound, Stacking, Tipper, Tommy, Tow(ie), Traffic, Trolley, Trundle, Ute, Utility, Van, Wrecker
Trudge Footslog, Jog, Lumber, Pad, Plod, Stodge, Stramp, Taigle, Traipse, Trash, Trauchle, Trog, Vamp
True Accurate, Actual, Apodictic, Axiomatic, Candid, Constant, Correct, Exact, Factual, Faithful, Genuine, Honest, Indubitable, Leal, Literal, Loyal, Platitude, Plumb, Pure, Real, Realistic, Richt, Right, Sooth, Very
Truffle Tartuffe, Tuber, Tuberaceae
Trug Basket, Wisket
Truly Certainly, Certes, Fegs, Forsooth, Honestly, Indeed, Insooth, Surely, Verily, Yea
Trump(s), Trumpet(er) Agami, Alchemy, Alchymy, Armstrong, Bach, Blare, Blast, Bray, Buccina, Bugle(r), Call, Card, Clang, Clarion, Conch, Cornet, Corona, Crossruff, Crow, Daffodil, Ear, Elephant, Fanfare, Hallali, Honours, → **HORN**, Invent, Jew's, Last, Lituus, Long ten, Lur(e), Lurist, Manille, Marine, Megaphone, → **NO TRUMP**, Overruff, Proclaim, Ram's-horn, Rant, Resurrect, Ruff, Salpingian, Salpinx, Satchmo, Sennet, Shofar, Shophar, Slug-horn, Speaking, Splash, Surpass, Tantara, Tantarara, Tar(at)antara, Theodomas, Tiddy, Triton, Triumph
Trumpery Fattrels, Jimcrack, Paltry, Trashy
Truncate(d) Abrupt, Cut, Dock, Shorten
Truncheon Billie, Billy, Blackjack, Cosh, Night-stick, Warder
Trundle Hump, Roll, Trill, Troll, Wheel
Trunk(s) Aorta(l), A-road, Body, Bole, Box, Bulk, Bus, But(t), Cabin, Carcase, Chest, Coffer, Hose, Imperial, Log, Peduncle, Pollard, Portmanteau, Portmantle, Proboscis, Ricker, Road, Saratoga, Shorts, STD, Stock, Stud, Synangium, Torso, Valise, Wardrobe
Truss → **BIND**, Ligate, Oop, Oup, Sheaf, Tie, Upbind
Trust(y), Trusting, Trustworthy Active, Affy, Apex, Authentic, Belief, Blind, Care, Cartel, Charge, Charitable, Combine, Confide, Credit, Dependable, Discretionary, → **FAITH**, Fiduciary, Gullible, Honest, Hope, Hospital, Investment, Leal, Lippen, Loyal, National, NT, Reliable, Reliance, Rely, Repose, Reputable, Sound, Special, Split, Staunch, Tick, Trojan, Trow, True, Trump, Unit
Trustee Agent, Executor, Fiduciary, Judicial, Pensioneer, Tr
Truth(ful), Truism Accuracy, Alethic, Axiom, Bromide, Cliché, Cold turkey, Dharma, Dialectic, → **FACT**, Facticity, Forsooth, Gospel, Griff, Home, Honesty, Idea(l), Logical, Maxim, Naked, Necessary, Pravda, Principle, Reality, Sooth, Soothfast, Troggs, Veracity, Veridical, Verisimilitude, Verity, Vraisemblance
Try(ing) Aim, Approof, Assay, Attempt, Audition, Bash, Bate, Bid, Birl, Burden, Burl, Conative, Contend, Crack, Effort, Empiric(utic), → **ENDEAVOUR**, Essay, Examine, Experiment, Fand, Fish, Fling, Foretaste, Go, Gun for, Harass, Hard, Hear, Impeach, Importunate, Irk, Noy, Offer, Ordalium, Penalty, Pop, Practise, Pree, Prieve, Prove, Push-over, → **SAMPLE**, Seek, Shot, Sip, Stab, Strain, Strive, Taste, Tax, Tempt, Test, Touchdown, Whirl

Tryst Date, Rendezvous

Tsar(ist) Alexis, Emperor, Godunov, Octobrist, Romanov, Ruler

TT Rechabite

Tub(by), Tubbiness, Tub-thumper Ash-leach, Back, Bath, Boanerges, Bran, Corf, Cowl, Dan, Diogenes, Dolly, Endomorph, Firkin, Keeve, Kid, Kieve, Kit, Luckydip, Mashing, Meat, Pin, Podge, Pot-bellied, Pudge, Pulpit, Seasoning, Stand, Swill, Tun, Twin, Vat, Wash, Whey

Tuba Bombardon, Euphonium, Helicon

Tube, Tubing, Tubular Acorn, Arteriole, Artery, Barrel, Blowpipe, Bronchus, Buckytube, Burette, Calamus, Camera, Canaliculus, Cannula, Capillary, Casing, Catheter, Cathode-ray, Cave, Conduit, Crookes, Digitron, Diode, Discharge, Drain, Draw, Drift, Dropper, Duct, Electron, Endiometer, Epididymis, Eustachian, Extension, Fallopian, Fistula, Flash, Fluorescent, Fulgurite, Geissler, Germ, Glowstick, Grommet, Hose, Iconoscope, Image (orthicon), Inner, Kinescope, Klystron, Macaroni, Malpighian, Matrass, Metro, Morris, Nasogastric, Neural, Nixie, Optic, Orthicon, Oval, Oviduct, Pastille, Pentode, Picture, Pilot-static, → **PIPE**, Pipette, Pitot, Pitot(-static), Pneumatic, Pollen, Postal, Promethean, Salpinx, Saticon®, Saucisse, Saucisson, Schnorkel, Shadow-mask, Shock, Sieve, Siphon, Siphonet, Siphonostele, Siphuncle, Skelp, Skiatron, Sleeve, Slide, Snorkel, Spaghetti, Speaking, Spout, Staple, Static, Stent, Stone canal, Storage, Strae, Straw, Strobotron, Subway, Sucker, Swallet, Telescope, Teletron, Television, Terete, Test, Tetrode, Thermionic, Thyratron, Tile, Torpedo, Torricellian, Trachea, Travelling-wave, Triniscope, Trocar, Trochotron, Trunk, Tunnel, Tuppenny, U, Underground, Ureter, Urethra, Vacuum, Vas, VDU, Vein, Vena, Venturi, Video, Vidicon®, Worm, X-ray

Tuber(s) Arnut, Arracacha, Bulb, Chufa, Coc(c)o, Dahlia, Dasheen, Earth-nut, Eddoes, Jicama, Mashua, Oca, Potato, Salep, Taproot, Taro, Tuckahoe, Yam

Tuberculosis Consumption, Crewels, Cruel(l)s, Decline, King's evil, Lupus, Lupus vulgaris, Phthisis, Scrofula, White plague

Tuck Dart, Friar, Gather, Grub, Hospital corner, Kilt, Pin, Pleat, Scran, Truss, Tummy

Tudor Stockbrokers'

Tuesday Hock, Pancake, Shrove, Super

Tuff Schalstein

Tuft(ed) Aigrette, Amentum, Beard, Candlewick, Catkin, C(a)espitose, Cluster, Coma, Comb, Cowlick, Crest, Dollop, Flaught, Floccus, Flock, Goatee, Hassock, Knop, Lock, Pappus, Penicillate, Quiff, Scopate, Shola, Tait, Tassel, Tate, Toorie, Topknot, Toupee, Tourie, Tussock, Tuzz, Whisk

Tug Drag, Haul, Jerk, Lug, Pug, → **PULL**, Rive, Saccade, Ship, Sole, Soole, Sowl(e), Tit, Tow, Towboat, Yank

Tui Poebird

Tuition Masterclass, Seminal

Tully Cicero

Tumble, Tumbler Acrobat, Cartwheel, Drier, Fall, → **GLASS**, Header, Pitch, Popple, Purl, Realise, Spill, Stumble, Tailer, Topple, Touser, Towser, Trip, Twig, Voltigeur, Welter

▷ **Tumble** *may indicate* an anagram

Tumbledown Decrepit, Dilapidated, Ramshackle, Rickle, Ruinous

Tumbril Caisson

Tummy Belly, Colon, Mary, Paunch, Pod

Tummy-ache Colic, Gripe, Tormina

Tumour Adenoma, Anbury, Angioma, Angiosarcoma, Astroblastoma, Astrocytoma, Burkitt('s) lymphoma, Cancer, Carcinoid, Carcinoma, Carcinosarcoma, Chondroma, Condyloma, Crab(-yaws), Dermoid, Encanthis, Encephaloma, Enchondroma, Endothelioma, Epulis, Exostosis, Fibroid, Fibroma, Ganglion, Germinoma, Gioblastoma, Glioma, Granuloma, Grape, → GROWTH, Gumma, Haemangioma, Haematoma, Hepatoma, Lipoma, Lymphoma, Medullablastoma, Melanoma, Meningioma, Mesothelioma, Metastasis, Mole, Myeloma, Myoma, Myxoma, Neoplasm, Nephroblastoma, Neuroblastoma, Neuroma, Odontoma, -oma, Oncology, Osteoclastoma, Osteoma, Osteosarcoma, Papilloma, Polyp(us), Retinoblastoma, Rhabdomyoma, Sarcoma, Scirrhous, Secondary, Seminoma, Steatoma, Struma, Syphiloma, Talpa, Teratoma, Thymoma, Wart, Warthin's, Wen, Wilm's, Windgall, Wolf, Xanthoma, Yaw

Tumult Brattle, Brawl, Coil, Deray, Ferment, Fracas, Hirdy-girdy, Hubbub, Hurly-burly, Reird, Riot, → ROAR, Romage, Rore, Stoor, Stour, Stowre, Stramash, Tew, Tristan, Tristram, → UPROAR

Tumulus Barrow, How(e), Mote, Motte

Tun Cask, Keg

Tuna Pear, Yellowfin

Tundra Barren Grounds, Barren Lands

Tune(s), Tuneful, Tuner, Tuning Adjust, Air, Aria, Canorous, Carillon, Catch, Choral, Dump, Earworm, Étude, Fine, Fork, Harmony, Hornpipe, Jingle, Key, Maggot, Measure, Melisma, → MELODY, Old Hundred, → OUT OF TUNE, Peg, Planxty, Port, Potpourri, Raga, Rant, Ranz-des-vaches, Signature, Snatch, Song, Spring, Strain, Sweet, Syntonise, Temper, Temperament, Theme, Tone, Toy, Tweak

Tungstate, Tungsten Scheelite, W, Wolfram

Tunic Ao dai, Caftan, Chiton, Choroid, Cote-hardie, Dalmatic, Dashiki, Gymslip, Hauberk, Kabaya, Kaftan, Kameez, K(h)urta, Salwar kameez, → SINGLET, Surcoat, Tabard, Toga

Tunicate Salpa

Tunnel(ler) Blackwall, Bore, Channel, Chunnel, Condie, Countermine, Culvert, Cundy, Earthworm, Euro, Gallery, Head, Mine, Mole, Qanat, Rotherhithe, Simplon, Smoke, Stope, Subway, Syrinx, Tube, Underpass, Water, Wind, Wormhole

Tunny Bonito, Tuna

Turban Bandanna, Hat, Mitral, Pagri, Puggaree, Puggery, Puggree, Sash, Scarf, Tulipant

Turbid Cloudy, Dense, Drumly, Roily

Turbine Francis, Gas, Impulse, Ram air, Reaction, Steam, Water, Wind

Turbulence, Turbulent Atmospheric, Becket, Bellicose, Buller, Factious, Fierce, Overfall, Rapids, Roil, Stormy, Unruly

▷ **Turbulent, Turbulence** *may indicate* an anagram

Turf Caespitose, Clod, Divot, Earth, Fail, Feal, Flaught, Gazo(o)n, → GRASS, Greensward, Peat, Screw, → SOD, Sward

Turk(ish) Anatolian, Bashaw, Bashkir, Bey, Bimbashi, Bostangi, Byzantine, Caimac(am), Crescent, Effendi, Golden Horde, Grand, Gregory, Horse(tail), Irade, Kaimakam, Kazak(h), Kurd, Mameluke, Mutessarif(at), Omar, Osman(li), Ottamite, Ottoman, Ottomite, Rayah, Scanderbeg, Selim, Seljuk(ian), Seraskier, Spahi, Tartar, Tatar, Timariot, Usak, Uzbeg, Uzbek, Yakut, Young

Turkey, Turkey-like Anatolia, Antioch, Brush, Bubbly(-jock), Cold, Curassow, Eyalet, Flop, Gobbler, Norfolk, Plain, Scrub, Sultanate, Talegalla, Talk, TR, Trabzon, Vulturn

Turkish delight Rahat lacoum, Trehala

Turmeric Curcumine
Turmoil Chaos, Din, Ferment, Mess, Pother, Pudder, Stoor, Stour, Tornado, Tracasserie, Tumult, → UPROAR, Welter
▷ **Turn(ing)** *may indicate* an anagram
Turn(ing), Turned away, Turned up, Turns Acescent, Act, Adapt, Addle, Advert, Antrorse, Apostrophe, Apotropaic, Avert, Bad, Bank, Become, Bend, Buggins, Bump, Canceleer, Cancelier, Caracol(e), Careen, Cartwheel, Cast, Chainé, Chandelle, Change, Char(e), Chore, Christiana, Christie, Christy, Churn, Cock, Coil, Crank(le), Cuff, Curd(le), Curve, Defect, Deflect, Demi-volt(e), Detour, Deviate, Dig, Digress, Divert, Ear, Earn, Elbow, Evert, Fadge, Flip, Forfend, Go, Good, Gruppetto, Hairpin, Handbrake, Head-off, Hie, High, Hinge, Hup, Immelmann, Influence, Innings, Intussuscept, Invert, Jar, Jink, Jump, Keel, Kick, Laeotropic, Lodging, Lot, Luff, Mohawk, Number, Obvert, Parallel, Parry, Penchant, Pivot, Plough, Pronate, Prove, PTO, Quarter, Quersprung, Rebut, Refer, Refract, Remuage, Retroflex, Retroussé, Retrovert, Rev, Revolt, Ride, Riffle, Rocker, Roll, Root, → ROTATE, Rote, Roulade, Rout, Routine, Screw, Secund, Sheer, → SHOT, Shout, Sicken, Skit, Slew, Slue, Solstice, Sour, → SPELL, Spin, Spot, Sprain, Star, Start, Stem, Step, Swash, Swing, Swivel, Telemark, Thigmotropism, Three-point, Throw, Tiptilt, Tirl, Torque, Transpose, Trend, Trick, Trie, Trochilic, Turtle, Twiddle, Twist, U, Uey, Up, Veer, Versed, Version, Vertigo, Volta, Volte-face, Volutation, Wap, Warp, Wedeln, Wend, Went, → WHEEL, Whelm, Whirl, Whorl, Wimple, Wind, Wrast, Wrest, Wriggle, Zigzag
Turn-coat Apostate, Cato, Defector, Quisling, Rat, Renegade, Tergiversate, Traitor
Turner Axle, Lana, Lathe, Painter, Pivot, Rose-engine, Spanner, Tina, Worm, Wrench
Turning point Crisis, Crossroads, Landmark, Watershed
Turnip(-shaped) Baggy, Bagie, Hunter, Jicama, Napiform, Navew, Neep, Prairie, Rutabaga, Shaw, → STUPID PERSON, Swede, Tumshie
Turnkey Gaoler, Jailer
Turn-out Eventuate, Gathering, Product, Rig, Splay, Style
Turn over Capsize, Careen, Flip, Inversion, Production, PTO, Somersault, TO, Up-end
Turnpike Highway, Toll
Turnstile Tourniquet
Turntable Racer, Rota, Rotator
Turpentine Galipot, Rosin, Thinner, Turps, Venice
Turquoise Bone, Fossil, Ligure, Occidental, Odontolite, Oriental, Turkey stone
Turret(ed) Barmkin, Bartisan, Garret, Louver, Louvre, Mirador, Pepperbox, Sponson, → TOWER, Turriculate
Turtle, Turtle head Bale, Calipash, Calipee, Chelone, Diamondback, Emys, Floor, Green, Hawk(s)bill, Inverted, Leatherback, Loggerhead, Matamata, Mossback, Mud, Musk, Ridley, Screen, Snapper, Snapping, Soft-shelled, Stinkpot, Terrapin, Thalassian
Tuscany Chiantishire
Tusk Gam, Horn, Ivory, Tooth, Tush
Tusker Dicynodont, Elephant, Mastodon
Tussle Giust, Joust, Mêlée, Scrimmage, Scrum, Scuffle, Skirmish, Touse, Touze, Towse, Towze, Tuilyie, Wrestle
Tussock Hassock, Niggerhead, Tuft
Tut(-tut) Och, Pooh
Tutelary Guardian, Protector

Tutor Abbé, Aristotle, Ascham, Bear, → COACH, Crammer, Don, Instruct, Leader, Mentor, Preceptor, Répétiteur, Supervisor, Teacher
Tuxedo DJ
TV Baird, Box, Cable, Digital, Docusoap, Idiot-box, Lime Grove, Monitor, PAL, Pay, Reality, SECAM, Sky, Tele, → TELEVISION, Telly, Tube, Video
Twaddle Blether, Drivel, Rot, Slipslop, Tripe
Twang Nasal, Pluck, Plunk, Rhinolalia
Tweak Pluck, Primp, Twiddle, Twist, Twitch
Tweed(y) Donegal, Harris®, Homespun, Lovat, Raploch
Tweet Chirrup
Twelfth, Twelve Apostles, Dozen, Epiphany, Glorious, Grouse, Midday, Midnight, N, Night, Noon, Ternion, Twal
Twenty, Twenty-sided Icosahedron, Score, Vicenary, Vicennial, Vicesimal, Vigesimal
Twenty-five, Twentyfifth Pony, Quartern, Semi-jubilee
Twenty-four Thr(e)ave
Twerp Pipsqueak
▸ **Twice** see TWO
Twice-yearly Biennial, Equinox
Twiddle Fidget, Twirl
Twig(s) Besom, Birch, Cotton, Cow, Dig, Grasp, Kow, Osier, Realise, Reis, Rice, Rumble, Sarment, See, Sprig, Sticklac, Switch, Understand, Walking, Wand, Wattle, Whip, Wicker, Withe
Twilight Astronomical, Civil, Cockshut, Crepuscular, Demi-jour, Dimpsy, Dusk, Gloam(ing), Götterdämmerung, Nautical, Summerdim
Twill Cavalry, Chino
Twin(s) Asvins, Castor, Coetaneous, Conjoined, Didymous, Dioscuri, Ditokous, Dizygotic, Double, Fraternal, Gemel, Hemitrope, Identical, Isogeny, Juxtaposition, Kindred, Macle, Monozygotic, Parabiotic, Pigeon-pair, Pollux, Siamese, Thomas, Tweedledee, Tweedledum
Twine Binder, Braid, Coil, Cord, Inosculate, Packthread, Sisal, Snake, String, Twist, Wreathe
Twinge Pang, Scruple, Stab, Twang
Twinkle, Twinkling Glimmer, Glint, Mo(ment), → SPARKLE, Starnie, Trice
Twirl Spin, Swivel, Tirl, Tirlie-wirlie, Trill, Trundle, Twiddle, Twizzle, Whirl
▷ **Twirling** may indicate an anagram
Twist(ed), Twister, Twisting, Twisty Anfractuous, Askant, Askew, Baccy, Becurl, Bought, Braid, Buckle, Card-sharper, Chisel, Coil, Contort, Convolution, Crinkle, Crinkum-crankum, Crisp, Cue, Curl(icue), Cyclone, Deform, Detort, Distort, → DODGE, Entwine, Garrot, Helix, Imposture, Kink, Mangulate, Mat, Möbius strip, Oliver, Pandanaceous, Plait, Quirk, Raddle, Ravel, Rick, Rogue, Rotate, Rove, Serpent, Skew, Slew, Slub(b), Slue, Snake, Snarl, Spin, Spiral, Sprain, Squiggle, Squirm, Swivel, Tendril, Thrawn, Torc, Tornado, Torque, Torsade, Torsion, Torticollis, Tortile, Turn, Tweak, Twiddle, Twine, Twirl, Typhoon, Valgus, Volvulus, Wamble, Warp, Welkt, Wigwag, Wind, Wound-wrap, Wrast, Wreathe, Wrench, Wrest, Wrethe, Wrick, Wriggle, Wring, Writhe, Wry, Zigzag
▷ **Twisted, Twisting** may indicate an anagram
Twit, Twitter Chaff, Cherup, Chirrup, Dotterel, Gear(e), Giber, → JEER, Stupid, Taunt, Tweet, Warble
Twitch(ing), Twitchy Athetosis, Clonic, Fibrillation, Grass, Jerk, Life-blood, Start, Subsultive, Tic, Tig, Tit, Tweak, Twinge, Vellicate, Yips

Two(some), Twofold, Twice Bice, Bis, Bisp, Both, Brace, Couple(t), Deuce, Double, Duad, Dual, Duet, Duo, Duple, Dyad, → **PAIR**, Swy, Tête-à-tête, Twain, Twins, Twister

Two-edged Ancipitous

Two-faced Dihedral, Dorsiventral, Hypocritical, Janus, Redan

Two-gallon Peck

Two-headed Amphisbaenic, Dicephalous, Orthos

Two hundred H

Two hundred and fifty E, K

Two-master Brig

Two-rayed Diactinal

Two-sided Bilateral, Equivocatory

Two thousand Z

Two-up Kip, Swy

Two-wheeler Bicycle, Scooter

Tycoon Baron, Empire-builder, Magnate, Mogul, Nabob, Plutocrat, Shogun

Type(s), Typing A, Agate, Aldine, Antimony, Antique, B, Balaam, Baskerville, Bastard, Beard, Bembo, Black-letter, Block, Blood, Bodoni, Body, Bold face, Bourgeois, Braille, Brand, Brevier, Brilliant, Canon, Caslon, Category, Character, Chase, Cicero, Clarendon, Class, Columbian, Condensed, Cut, Egyptian, Elite, Elzevir, Em, Emblem, Emerald, En(nage), English, Face, Font, Form(e), Founder's, Fount, Fraktur, Fudge, Garamond, Gem, Genre, Gent, Gothic, Great primer, Gutenberg, Hair, Ilk, Image, Kern(e), Key, Kidney, Kind, Late-star, Ligature, Light-faced, Logotype, Longprimer, Ludlow, Mating, Melanochroi, Minion, Modern, Monospaced, Moon, Mould, Non-pareil, Norm, Old English, Old-face, Old Style, Paragon, Pattern, Pearl, Peculiar, Personality, Pi, Pica, Pie, Plantin, Point, Primer, Print, Quad(rat), Roman, Ronde, Ruby, Sanserif, Secretary, Semibold, Serif, Serological, Slug, → **SORT**, Sp, Species, Spectral, Stanhope, Style, Times, Tissue, Touch, Version

▷ **Type of** *may indicate* an anagram

Typewriter Golfball, Portable, Stenograph, Stenotype®, Varityper®

Typhoid, Typhus Camp-fever, Scrub, Tick-borne

Typhoon Cyclone, Hurricane, Monsoon, Tornado, Wind

Typical Average, Characteristic, Classic, Echt, Normal, Representative, Standard, Symbolic, True-bred, Usual

Typist Audio, Copy, Printer, Steno(grapher), Temp

Tyrannise(d) Domineer, Lord, Under

Tyrant, Tyranny, Tyrannical Absolutism, Autocrat, Caligula, Czar, Despot, Dictator, Drawcansir, Gelon, Herod, Lordly, Nero, Oppressor, Pharaoh, Sardanapalus, Satrap, Stalin, Totalitarian, Tsar, Yoke

Tyre(s) Balloon, Cross-ply, Cushion, Earthing, Michelin®, Pericles, Pneumatic, Radial, Radial(-ply), Recap, Remould, Retread, Shoe, Sidewall, Slick, Snow, Spare, Stepney, Tread, Tubeless, Whitewall

Tyro Beginner, Ham, → **NOVICE**, Rabbit, Rookie, Rooky, Starter

Tyrolese R(h)aetian

Uu

U, U-type Gent, Unicorn, Universal, Uranium
Ubiquitous Everywhere, Omnipresent
Udder Bag, Dug
Ugandan Obote
Ugly Butters, Cow, Customer, Eyesore, Foul, Gorgon, Gruesome, Hideous, Homely, Huckery, Loath, Loth, Mean, Ominous, Plain
Ugrian Ostiak, Ostyak, Samo(y)ed, Vogul
UK GB
Ukase Decree
Ukraine Ruthene, UA
Ulcer(ous) Abscess, Aphtha, Bedsore, Canker, Chancre, Chancroid, Decubitus, Duodenal, Enanthema, Gastric, Helcoid, Noli-me-tangere, Noma, Peptic, Phagedaena, Rodent, Rupia, Sore, Varicose, Wolf
Ulster NI, Overcoat, Raincoat, Ulad
Ulterior External, Hidden
Ultimate Absolute, Basic, Deterrent, Eventual, Final, Furthest, Last, Maximum, So, Supreme, Thule
Ultra Drastic, Extreme, Radical
Ultra-modern Space age
Ultra-republican Leveller
Ultrasound Lithotripsy
Ulysses Bloom, Grant, Odysseus
Umbellifer(ous) Angelica, Arnut, Car(r)away, Dill, Honewort, Narthex, Pig-nut, Seseli
Umber Burnt, Mottled, Raw, Waved
Umbrage Offence, Pique, Resentment, Shade
Umbrella(-shaped) Bubble, Bumbershoot, Chatta, Gamp, Gingham, Gloria, Mush(room), Nuclear, Parasol, Sunshade, Tee
Umbria Eugubine, Iguvine
Umpire Arb(iter), Byrlawman, Daysman, Decider, Judge, Oddjobman, Odd(s)man, Overseer, Oversman, Referee, Rule, Stickler, Thirdsman
Unabashed Bare-faced, Brazen, Shameless
Unable Can't, Downa-do, Incapable
Unaccented Atonic, Proclitic
Unacceptable Non-U, Not on, Out, Stigmatic
Unaccompanied A cappella, Alone, High-lone, Secco, Single, Solo, Solus
Unaccustomed Desuetude, New
Unadorned Bald, Plain, Stark
Unadulterated Sincere
Unaffected Artless, Genuine, Homely, Insusceptible, Natural, Plain, Sincere, Unattached
Unaided Single-handed, Solo

Unaltered Constant, Same
Unambiguous Categorical, Univocal
Unanimous Accord, Nem con
Unanswerable Erotema, Irrefragable, Irrefutable
Unappreciated Thankless
Unarguable Erotema
Unarmed Inerm, Naked, Vulnerable
Unashamed Blatant, Brazen, Open
Unassigned Adespota, Anonymous
Unassuming Lowly, Modest
Unattached Freelance, Loose
Unattractive Drac(k), Lemon, Minger, Plain, Plug-ugly, Rebarbative, Seamy, Ugly
Unattributable Anon
Unauthentic Plagal
▷ **Unauthentic** *may indicate* an anagram
Unavail(able), Unavailing Bootless, Futile, Ineluctable, Lost, No use, Off, Useless, Vain
Unavoidable Inevitable, Necessary, Perforce
Unaware Heedless, Ignorant, Incognisant, Innocent, Oblivious
Unbalanced Asymmetric, Deranged, Doolalli, Doolally, Loco, Lopsided, Out to lunch, Uneven
Unbearable Bassington, Intolerable
Unbeaten, Unbeatable All-time, Perfect
Unbecoming, Unbefitting Improper, Infra dig, Shabby, Unfitting, Unseemly, Unsuitable, Unworthy
Unbelievable, Unbeliever Agnostic, Atheist, Cassandra, Doubter, Giaour, Heathen, Incredible, Infidel, Pagan, Painim, Paynim, Sceptic, Tall, Zendik
Unbent Relaxed
Unbiased Fair, Impartial, Just, Neutral, Objective, Unattainted
Unblemished Spotless, Vestal
Unblinking Alert, Astare, Fearless
Unborn Future, Unbred
Unbowed In-kneed, Resolute
Unbreakable Infrangible, Inviolate
Unbridled Fancy free, Footloose, Lawless, Uncurbed, Unrestricted, Unshackled, Untramelled
Unburden Confide, Offload, Relieve, Unload
Uncanny Eerie, Eldritch, Extraordinary, Geason, Rum, Spooky, Weird
Uncastrated Stone
Unceasing Continuous
Uncertain(ty) Acatalepsy, Agnostic, Blate, Broken, Chancy, Chary, Contingent, Delicate, Dicey, Dither, Doubtful, Dubiety, Grey, Heisenberg, Hesitant, Iffy, Indeterminate, Indistinct, Irresolute, Peradventure, Precarious, Queasy, Risky, Slippery, Tentative, Vor, Wide open
▷ **Uncertain** *may indicate* an anagram
Unchallengeable, Unchallenge(d) Irrecusable, Sackless
Unchangeable, Unchanged, Unchanging As is, Enduring, Eternal, Idempotent, Immutable, Monotonous, Pristine, Stable, Standpat
Uncharacteristic Atypical
Uncharged Neutral, Neutron
Unchaste Corrupt, Immodest, Immoral, Impure, Lewd, Wanton

Unchecked Rampant
Uncivil(ised) Barbaric, Benighted, Boondocks, Discourteous, Disrespectful,
  Giant-rude, Goth, Heathen, Impolite, Liberty, Military, Rude, Rudesby
Uncle Abbas, Afrikaner, Arly, Bob, Dutch, Eme, Nunky, Oom, Pawnbroker,
  Pop-shop, Remus, Sam, Tio, Tom, Usurer, Vanya
Unclean Defiled, Dirty, Impure, Obscene, Ordure, Squalid, Tabu, T(e)refa(h)
Unclear Ambitty, Hazy, Nebulous, Obscure
Unclothed Bald, Nude
Uncloven Soliped
Uncommitted Evasive, Laodicean
Uncommon Rara avis, Rare, Sparse, Strange, Unusual
▷ **Uncommon(ly)** *may indicate* an anagram
Uncommunicative Reserved, Tight-lipped
Uncompanionable Threesome
Uncomplimentary Blunt
Uncomprehending Anan, Ignorant
Uncompromising Cutthroat, Hardline, Hardshell, Intransigent, Rigid, Strict, Ultra
Unconcealed Open, Pert
Unconcerned Bland, Careless, Casual, Cold, Indifferent, Insouciant, Nonchalant,
  Strange
Unconditional Absolute, Free, Pure
Unconnected Asyndetic, Detached, Disjointed, Off-line
Unconscious(ness) Asleep, Catalepsy, Cold, Comatose, Instinctive, Non-ego,
  Not-I, Subliminal, Syncope, Trance, Under
Unconsidered Impetuous, Rash
Unconsummated Mariage blanc
Uncontrolled Adrift, Atactic, Free, Incontinent, Loose, Loose cannon, Wild
Unconventional Beatnik, Bohemian, Drop-out, Eccentric, Gonzo, Heretic,
  Heterodox, Hippy, Informal, Irregular, Offbeat, Off-the-wall, Original, Outlandish,
  Outré, Raffish, Spac(e)y, Unorthodox
▷ **Unconventional** *may indicate* an anagram
Unconverted Neat
Unconvincing Farfet(ched), Lame, Thin
Uncoordinated Asynergia, Ataxic, Awkward, Clumsy
Uncorrect Stet
Uncouth(ness) Backwoodsman, Bear, Churlish, Crude, Gothic, Inelegant, Rough,
  Rube, Rude, Rugged, Uncivil
Uncover(ed) Bare, Disclose, Dismask, Expose, Inoperculate, Open, Overt, Peel,
  Reveal, Shave, Shill, Shuck, Uncap, Unveil
Unction, Unctuous(ness) Anele, Balm, Chrism, Extreme, Oil(y), Ointment,
  Oleaginous, Ooze, Smarm, Soapy
Uncultivated, Uncultured Artless, Bundu, Fallow, Ignorant, Incult, Philistine,
  Rude, Tramontane, Wild
Undamaged Intact, Sound, Whole
Undated Sine die
Undecided Doubtful, Moot, Non-committal, Open-ended, Pending, Pendulous,
  Uncertain, Wavering
Undefiled Chaste, Clean, Pure, Virgin
Undeniable Fact, Incontestable, Irrefutable
Under Aneath, Below, Beneath, Hypnotized, Hypo-, Sotto, Sub-, Unconscious,
  Unneath

Underarm Axilla, Lob
Underburnt Samel
Under-butler Bread-chipper
Undercarriage Bogie, Chassis
Undercoat Base, Primer
Undercooked Rare, Raw, Samel
Undercover Espionage, Secret, Veiled
Undercurrent Acheron, Undertone, Undertow
Underdeveloped, Underdevelopment Ateleiosis, Retarded
Underdog Cerberus, Loser, Victim
▶ **Undergarment** see UNDERWEAR
Undergo Bear, Dree, Endure, Solvate, Sustain
Undergraduate Fresher, L, Pup, Sizar, Sophomore, Student, Subsizar, Tuft
Underground (group) Basement, Catacomb, Cellar, Fogou, Hell, Hypogaeous,
   Irgun, Kiva, Macchie, Maquis, Mattamore, Metro, Phreatic, Pict, Plutonia, Pothole,
   Secret, Souterrain, Subsoil, Subterranean, Subway, Tube
Undergrowth Brush, Chaparral, Firth, Frith, Scrub
Underhand Backstair, Dirty, Haunch, Insidious, Lob, Oblique, Secret, Sinister, Sly,
   Sneaky, Surreptitious
Underlease Subtack
Underlie, Underlying Subjacent, Subtend
Underline Emphasise, Insist
Underling Bottle-washer, Cog, Inferior, Jack, Menial, Minion, Munchkin,
   Subordinate
Undermine Erode, Fossick, Sap, Subvert, Tunnel, Weaken
Undernourished Puny, Starveling
Underpass Simplon, Subway
Underside Bed, Soffit
Understand(able), Understanding Accept, Acumen, Agreement, Apprehend,
   Capeesh, Clear, Cognisable, Comprehend, Conceive, Concept, Cotton-on, Deal,
   Dig, Enlighten, Entente, Exoteric, Fathom, Follow, Gather, Gauge, Gaum, Geddit,
   Gorm, Grasp, Have, Head, Heels, Insight, Intuit, Ken, Kind, Knowhow, Learn,
   Light(s), Omniscient, Pact, Plumb, Prajna, Rapport, Rapprochement, Realise,
   Savey, Savvy, See, Sense, Sole, Substance, Tolerance, Treaty, Tumble, Twig,
   Uptak(e), Wisdom, Wit
Understate(d), Understatement Litotes, M(e)iosis, Subtle
Understood Implicit, OK, Perspicuous, Roger, Tacit, Unspoken
Understudy Deputy, Double, Stand-in, Sub
Undertake, Undertaking Attempt, Contract, Covenant, Emprise, Enterprise,
   Essay, Feat, Guarantee, Pledge, Promise, Scheme, Shoulder, Venture, Warranty
Undertaker Entrepreneur, Mortician, Obligor, Sponsor, Upholder
Under-ten Unit, Yarborough
Undertone Murmur, Rhubarb, Sotto voce
Underwater Demersal
Underwear Balbriggan, Balconette, Bloomers, Bodice, Body, Body stocking, Body
   suit, Bra(ssiere), Briefs, Broekies, Butt bra, Camiknickers, Camisole, Chemise,
   Chemisette, Chuddies, Combinations, Combs, Corset, Dainties, Drawers, (French)
   knickers, Frillies, Girdle, Grundies, Innerwear, Jump, Linen, Lingerie, Linings, Long
   johns, Pantalets, Pantaloons, Panties, Pantihose, Panty girdle, Petticoat, Scanties,
   Semmit, Shift, Shorts, Singlet, Skivvy, Slip, Smalls, Stays, Step-ins, Subucula,
   Suspenders, Tanga, Teddy, Thermal, Trunks, Underdaks, Undergarments,

Underpants, Undershirt, Underthings, Undies, Unmentionables, Vest, Wyliecoat, Y-fronts®
Underworld Chthonic, Criminal, Hades, Hell, Lowlife, Mafia, Shades, Tartar(e), Tartarus, Tartary
Underwrite, Underwritten Assure, Endorse, Guarantee, Insure, Lloyds, PS
Undeserving Immeritous
Undesirable Kibitzer
Undeveloped Backward, Depauperate, Green, Inchoate, Latent, Nubbin, Ridgel, Ridgil, Ridgling, Rig, Riggald, Riglin(g), Rudimentary, Seminal
Undifferentiated Thalliform, Thallus
Undigested Crude
Undignified (end) Disaster, Foot, Improper, Infra dig, Unseemly
Undiluted Neat, Pure, Sheer, Straight
Undiminished Entire, Intact, Whole
Undiplomatic Brusque, Tactless
Undisciplined Hothead, Rule-less, Rulesse, Sloppy, Unruly, Wanton
Undisclosed Hidden, In petto
Undisguised Apert, Clear, Plain
Undistinguished Plebeian
Undivided Aseptate, Complete, Entire, Indiscrete, One
Undo(ing) Annul, Defeat, Destroy, Disconnect, Downfall, Dup, Poop, Poupe, Release, Rescind, Ruin, Unravel
Undoctored Neat
Undone Arrears, Left, Postponed, Ran, Ruined
Undoubtedly Certes, Ipso facto, Positively, Sure
Undress(ed) Bare, Disarray, Disrobe, En cuerpo, Expose, Négligé, Nude, Nue, Peel, Querpo, Raw, Rough, Self-faced, Spar, Strip, Unapparelled
Undulate, Undulating Billow, Nebule, Ripple, Roll, Wave
▷ **Unduly** *may indicate* an anagram
Undyed Greige
Undying Amaranthine, Eternal
Unearth(ly) Astral, Dig, Discover, Disentomb, Exhumate, Indagate
Unease, Uneasiness, Uneasy Angst, Anxious, Creeps, Disquiet, Inquietude, Itchy, Malaise, Queasy, Restive, Shy, Tense, The willies, Uptight, Windy, Womble-cropped
Unedifying Idle
Unembarrassed Blasé, Dégagé
Unemotional Bland, Cool, Iceberg, Matter-of-fact, Sober, Stolid
Unemployed, Unemployment Drone, Idle, Laik, Lake, Latent, Lay-off, Redundant, Residual, Stalko, Surfie
Unending Chronic, Eternal, Lasting, Sempiternal
Unenlightened Ignorant, Nighted
Unenthusiastic Cool, Damp, Tepid
Unenveloped Achlamydeous
Unequal(led) Aniso-, Disparate, Non(e)such, Scalene, Unjust
Unerring Dead, Exact, Precise
Unestablished Free
Unethical Amoral, Corrupt, Immoral
Uneven(ness) Accident, Blotchy, Bumpy, Erose, Irregular, Jaggy, Patchy, Ragged, Scratchy
▷ **Unevenly** *may indicate* an anagram

Unexceptional Ordinary, Workaday
Unexpected(ly) Abrupt, Accidental, Adventitious, Fortuitous, Inopinate, Ironic, Snap, Sodain(e), Sudden, Turn-up, Unawares, Unwary
Unexperienced Strange
Unexplained Obscure
Unexploded Live
Unfading Evergreen, Immarcescible
Unfailing Sure
Unfair Bias(s)ed, Crook, Dirty, Inclement, Invidious, Mean, Partial
Unfaithful Disloyal, Godless, Infidel, Traitor, Two-timing
Unfamiliar New, Quaint, Strange
Unfashionable Cube, Dowdy, Out(moded), Out-of-date, Passé, Square
▷ **Unfashionable** *may indicate* 'in' to be removed
Unfasten Undo, Untie, Untruss
Unfathomable Bottomless
Unfavourable Adverse, Ill, Inimical, Poor, Untoward
Unfeeling Adamant, Callous, Cold, Cruel, Dead, Hard, Inhuman(e), Insensate, Iron-witted, Robotic
Unfinished Crude, Inchoate, Raw, Scabble, Scapple, Stickit
Unfit(ting) Cronk, Disabled, Faulty, Ill, Impair, Inept, Outré, Trefa, Tre(i)f, Unable
▷ **Unfit** *may indicate* an anagram
Unfixed Isotropic, Loose
Unfledged Gull
Unflinching Fast, Staunch
Unfold Deploy, Display, Divulge, Evolve, Interpret, Open, Relate, Spread
Unforced Voluntary
Unforeseen Accident, Sudden
Unfortunate(ly) Accursed, Alack, Alas, Hapless, Ill-starred, Luckless, Shameless, Sorry, Star-crossed, Unlucky, Worse luck
Unfounded Groundless
Unfriendly Aloof, Antagonistic, Asocial, Chill(y), Cold, Fraim, Fremd, Fremit, Hostile, Icy, Remote, Surly
Unfruitful Abortive, Barren, Sterile
Unfulfilled Manqué
Ungainly Awkward, Gawkish, Uncouth, Weedy
Ungenerous Small
Ungodliness, Ungodly Impiety, Pagan, Perfidious, Profane
Ungracious Cold, Mesquin(e), Offhand, Rough, Rude
Ungrammatical Anacoluthia
Ungrateful Ingrate, Snaky
Unguent Nard, Pomade, Salve
Ungulate Antelope, Dinoceras, Eland, Equidae, Hoofed, Moose, Rhino, Ruminantia, Takin, Tapir, Tylopoda
Unhappily, Unhappy, Unhappiness Blue, Depressed, Disconsolate, Dismal, Distress, Doleful, Downcast, Down-hearted, Dysphoria, Glumpish, Love-lorn, Lovesick, Miserable, Sad, Sore, Tearful, Unlief, Upset
▷ **Unhappily** *may indicate* an anagram
Unharmed Safe, Scatheless
Unharness Outspan
Unhealthy Bad, Clinic, Diseased, Epinosic, Insalubrious, Morbid, Noxious, Peaky, Prurient, Sickly

Unholy Profane, Wicked
Unhurried Gradual, Patient
Uniat Maronite, Melchite
Unicorn Ch'i-lin, Coin, Monoceros, Moth, Myth, Narwhal
Unidentified Anon, Anonym(ous), Incognito, Ligure
Unification, Unify(ing) Esemplastic, Henotic, Integrate, Risorgimento, Unite
Uniform Abolla, Alike, Battledress, Consistent, Dress, Equable, Equal, Even,
  Flat, Forage-cap, Homogeneous, Homomorphic, Identical, Khaki, Kit, Livery,
  Regimentals, Regular, Rig, Robe, Same, Sole, Standard, Steady, Strip, Unvaried
Unimaginative Banausic, Literalistic, Pedestrian, Pooter
Unimpaired Entire, Intact, Sound
Unimportant Cog, Down-the-line, Expendable, Fiddling, Footling, Frivolous, Idle,
  Immaterial, Inconsequent, Inconsiderable, Insignificant, MacGuffin, Makeweight,
  Minnow, Minutiae, Negligible, Nugatory, Peripheral, Petty, Small-time, Trifling,
  Trivia(l)
Unimpressible Cynical
Uninformed Ingram
Uninhabited Bundu, Deserted, Lonely
Uninhibited Bold, Raunchy
Uninspired Humdrum, Pedestrian, Pompier, Tame
Unintelligent Dumb, Obtuse, Stupid, Witless
Unintelligible Arcane, Code, Greek, Inarticulate
Unintentional Inadvertent, Unwitting
Uninterested, Uninteresting Apathetic, Bland, Dreary, Dry, Dull, Grey, Incurious,
  Nondescript
Uninterrupted Constant, Continuous, Incessant, Running, Steady
Uninvited Gatecrasher, Interloper, Intruder, Sorner, Trespasser, Umbra
Union(ist) Affiance, African, Allegiance, Alliance, Anschluss, Art, Association,
  Bed, Benelux, Bond, Close, Combination, Company, Concert, Confederacy,
  Covalency, Craft, Credit, Customs, Diphthong, Economic, Enosis, Ensemble,
  Equity, EU, European, Fasciation, Federal, Federation, French, Frithgild, Fusion,
  Group, Guild, Heterogamy, Horizontal, Impanation, Industrial, Integration,
  Knight of labour, Latin, Liaison, Liberal, Link-up, Management, Marriage, Match,
  Merger, NUM, Nuptials, NUR, NUS, NUT, Pan-American, Parabiosis, Pearl,
  Postal, Print, RU, Rugby, Samiti, Sex, Sherman, Solidarity, Soviet, Splice,
  Sponsal, Student, Symphysis, Syngamy, Synizesis, Synostosis, Synthesis,
  Syssarcosis, Teamsters, Tenorrhaphy, → TRADE UNION, TU, U, UNISON,
  USDAW, Uxorial, Verein, Vertical, Vienna, Wedding, Wedlock, Wield, ZANU,
  Zollverein, Zygosis
Unique(ness) Alone, A-per-se, Hacceity, Inimitable, Irreplaceable, Lone, Matchless,
  Nonesuch, Nonpareil, Nonsuch, One-off, One(-to)-one, Only, Peerless, Rare,
  Singular, Sole, Sui generis
Unisex(ual) Epicene, Hermaphrodite
Unison Chorus, Harmony, One, Sync
Unit Abampere, Absolute, Ace, Amp, Angstrom, Archine, Archiphoneme,
  Astronomical, Bar, Bargaining, Barn, Base, Baud, Becquerel, Bioblast, Biogen,
  Biophor(e), Bit, Bohr magneton, Brigade, BTU, Byte, Cadre, Calory, Candela,
  Cell, Cent(i)are, Centimorgan, Centipoise, Chaldron, Chronon, Codon, Cohort,
  Commune, Congius, Control, Corps, Coulomb, Crith, Cusec, Dalton, Daraf, Darcy,
  Debye, Degree, Denier, Derived, Dessiatine, Detachment, DIN, Dioptre, Division,
  Dobson, Dol, Dyne, Echelon, Ecosystem, Electromagnetic, Electron, Electrostatic,

Element, Em, EMU, En, Energid, Ensuite, Episome, Erg, Erlang, Farad, Feedlot, Fermi, Field, Flight, Foot-candle, Foot-lambert, Foot-pound, Foot-ton, Fps, Fresnel, Fundamental, Gal, Gauss, Gestalt, GeV, Gigabit, Gigaflop, Gigahertz, Gigawatt, Gilbert, Glosseme, Gram, Grav, Gray, Hank, Hapu, Hartree, Henry, Hertz, Hide, Hogshead, Holon, Home, Hub, Income, Ion, Item, Jansky, Joule, K, Katal, Kelvin, Kilderkin, Kilerg, Kilowatt, Lambert, Langley, Last, League, Lexeme, Lumen, Lux, Maceral, Magneton, Man-hour, Maxwell, Measure, Megabyte, Megahertz, Megaton, Megawatt, Megohm, Message, Metre, Mho, Micella, Micelle, Microcurie, Microinch, Micron, Mil, Module, Mole, Monad, Monetary, Mongo(e), Morgen, Morpheme, Mutchkin, Neper, Nepit, Nest, Newton, Nit, Octa, Oersted, Ohm, Okta, Organelle, Panzer, Parasang, Pascal, Ped, Peninsular, Pennyweight, Period, Peripheral, Phoneme, Phot, Phyton, Pica, Pixel, Ploughgate, Point, Poise, Pond, Poundal, Power, Practical, Probit, Protoplast, Qubit, RA, Radian, Rem, Remen, Rep, Ro(e)ntgen, Rood, Rutherford, Sabin, Sealed, Second, Secure, Semeion, Sememe, Shed, SI, Siemens, Sievert, Singleton, Sink, Slug, Sone, Steradian, Stere, Stilb, Stock, Stoke(s), Strontium, Syllable, Syntagm(a), TA, Tagmeme, Terabyte, Teraflop, Terminal, Tesla, Tetrapody, Tex, Theme, Therblig, Therm, Timocracy, Tog, Token, Torr, Tower, Tripody, Vanitory, Vanity, Var, Vara, Volt, Wall, Watt, Watt-hour, Weber, Wing, X, Yrneh
Unitarian Arian, Paulian, Racovian, Socinian
Unite(d), Unity Accrete, Bind, Coalesce, Combine, Concordant, Connate, Connect, Consolidate, Consubstantiate, Covalent, Ecumenical, Fay, Federal, Federalise, Federate, Fuse, Gene, Graft, Injoint, Inosculate, Join, Kingdom, Knit, Lap, Link, Marry, Meint, Meng, Ment, Merge, Meynt, Ming, Nations, Oop, Oup, Siamese, Solid, States, Tie, Unify, → **WED**, Weld, Yoke
United Ireland Fine Gael
United Kingdom Old Dart, UK
Unity Harmony, One, Solidarity, Sympathy, Togetherness
Univalent Monatomic
Universal, Universe All, Catholic, Cosmos, Creation, Ecumenic(al), Emma, Expanding, General, Global, Infinite, Inflationary, Island, Macrocosm, Mandala, Microcosm, Oscillating, Sphere, U, Via Lactea, World(wide)
University Academe, Academy, Alma mater, Aston, Berkeley, Bonn, Brown, Campus, Civic, College, Columbia, Cornell, Dartmouth, Exeter, Gown, Harvard, Ivy League, Open, OU, Oxbridge, Pennsylvania, Princeton, Reading, Redbrick, St Andrews, Sorbonne, Stamford, Varsity, Whare wanaga, Wittenberg, Yale
Unjust(ified) Groundless, Inequity, Iniquitous, Invalid, Tyrannical
Unkempt Dishevelled, Greebo, Mal soigné, Raddled, Ragged, Raggle-taggle, Scody, Scraggy, Scuzzy, Shaggy, Tousy, Touzy, Towsy, Towzy
Unknown Agnostic, Anon, A.N. Other, Hidden, Ign, Incog(nito), Inconnu, N, Nobody, Noumenon, Occult, Quantity, Secret, Soldier, Strange, Symbolic, Tertium quid, Unchartered, Untold, Warrior, X, Y
Unleavened Azymous
Unless Nisi, Save, Without
Unliable Exempt
Unlicensed Illicit
Unlike(ly) Difform, Disparate, Dubious, Far-fetched, Improbable, Inauspicious, Long shot, Outsider, Remote, Tall, Unlich
Unlimited Almighty, Boundless, Indefinite, Measureless, Nth, Universal, Vast
Unlisted Ex-directory
Unload Disburden, Discharge, Drop, Dump, Jettison, Land, Strip

Unlock(ed) Bald
Unlucky Donsie, Hapless, Ill(-starred), Inauspicious, Infaust, Jonah, Misadventure,
　Misfallen, S(c)hlimazel, Sinister, Stiff, Thirteen, Untoward, Wanchancie,
　Wanchancy
Unman Castrate
Unmannerly Crude, Discourteous, Impolite, Low bred, Rude
Unmarried Bachelor, Common-law, Single, Spinster
Unmask Expose, Rumble
Unmatched Bye, Champion, Orra, Unique
Unmentionable(s) Bra, Foul, No-no, Secret, → **UNDERWEAR**, Undies
Unmindful Heedless, Oblivious
Unmistakable Clear, Manifest, Plain
Unmitigated Absolute, Arrant, Sheer, Ultra
Unmixed Me(a)re, Meer, Neat, Nett, Pure, Raw, Straight
Unmoved, Unmoving Adamant, Doggo, Firm, Serene, Static, Stolid
Unnamed Anon
Unnatural Abnormal, Affected, Cataphysical, Contrived, Eerie, Flat, Geep, Irregular,
　Strange
▷ **Unnaturally** *may indicate* an anagram
Unnecessary De trop, Extra, Gash, Gratuitous, Needless, Otiose, Redundant,
　Superfluous
Unnerve, Unnerving Discouraging, Eerie, Rattle
Unobserved Backstage, Sly, Unseen
Unobtainable Nemesis
Unobtrusive Low profile
Unoccupied Empty, Idle, Otiose, Vacant, Void
Unofficial Disestablish, Fringe, Wildcat
Unoriginal Banal, Copy, Derivative, Imitation, Plagiarised, Slavish
Unorthodox Heretic, Heterodox, Maverick, Off-beat, Off-the-wall, Unconventional
▷ **Unorthodox** *may indicate* an anagram
Unpaid Amateur, Brevet, Hon(orary), Outstanding, Voluntary
Unpaired Azygous, Bye
Unpalatable Acid, Bitter, Unsavoury
Unparalleled Supreme, Unique
Unpartitioned Aseptate
Unperturbed Bland, Calm, Serene
Unplanned Impromptu, Improvised, Spontaneous
Unpleasant, Unpleasant person Cow, Creep, Fink, God-awful, Grim, Grotty,
　Gruesome, Harsh, Hoor, Horrible, Icky, Insalubrious, Invidious, Nasty, Obnoxious,
　Odious, Offensive, Painful, Pejorative, Rank, Rebarbative, Shady, Shitty, Shocker,
　Snarky, Sticky, Thorny, Toerag, Wart
Unploughed Lea-rig
Unpolluted Sterile
Unpopular Detested, Hat(e)able
Unpractical Futile, Orra
Unpredictable Aleatory, Dicy, Erratic, Maverick, Wild card
Unprepared Ad lib, Extempore, Impromptu, Last minute, Unready
Unpretentious Quiet
Unprincipled Amoral, Dishonest, Irregular, Reprobate, Unscrupulous
Unproductive Arid, Atokal, Atokous, Barren, Dead-head, Eild, Fallow, Futile, Lean,
　Poor, Shy, Sterile, Yeld, Yell

Unprofitable Bootless, Fruitless, Lean, Thankless, Wasted
Unprogressive Inert, Square
Unprotected Exposed, Nude, Vulnerable
Unpublished Inedited
Unpunctual Tardy
Unqualified Absolute, Entire, Outright, Perfect, Profound, Pure, Quack, Sheer, Straight, Thorough, Total, Utter
Unquestionably, Unquestioning Absolute, Certain, Doubtless, Implicit
Unravel(ling) Construe, Denouement, Disentangle, Feaze, Fray, Solve
Unreadable Poker-faced
Unready Unripe
Unreal(istic) Eidetic, En l'air, Escapist, Fake, Fancied, Illusory, Insubstantial, Mirage, Oneiric, Phantom, Phon(e)y, Planet Zog, Pseudo, Romantic, Sham, Spurious
Unreasonable, Unreasoning Absurd, Bigot, Extreme, Illogical, Irrational, Misguided, Perverse, Rabid, Steep
Unrecognised Incognito, Inconnu, Invalid, Thankless, Unsung
Unrefined Coarse, Common, Crude, Earthy, Gur, Impure, Rude, Vul(g), Vulgar
Unrehearsed Extempore, Impromptu
Unrelenting Implacable, Remorseless, Severe, Stern
Unreliable Dodgy, Dubious, Erratic, Fair-weather, Fickle, Flighty, Fly-by-night, Shonky, Unstable, Wankle, Weak sister, Wonky
Unremarkable Nondescript
Unremitting Dogged, Intensive
Unresponsive Aloof, Cold, Frigid, Nastic, Rigor
Unrest Discontent, Ferment
Unrestrained Effusive, Extravagant, Free, Hearty, Homeric, Immoderate, Incontinent, Lax, Lowsit, Rampant, Wanton, Wild
Unreturnable Ace
Unrighteousness Adharma
Unrivalled Nonesuch
Unromantic Classic(al), Mundane
Unruffled Calm, Placid, Serene, Smooth, Tranquil
Unruly Anarchic, Bodgie, Buckie, Camstairy, Camsteary, Camsteerie, Coltish, Exception, Fractious, Lawless, Obstreperous, Obstropalous, Ragd(e), Raged, Ragged, Rambunctious, Rampageous, Rattlebag, Riotous, Tartar, Turbulent, Turk, Wanton, Wayward, Zoo
▷ **Unruly** *may indicate* an anagram
Unsafe Deathtrap, Fishy, Insecure, Perilous, Precarious, Vulnerable
Unsatisfactory, Unsatisfying Bad, Lame, Lousy, Meagre, Rocky, Thin, Wanting
Unsavoury Epinosic
Unscramble Decode, Decrypt
Unscripted Ad lib
Unscrupulous Chancer, Rascally, Slippery
Unseasonable, Unseasoned Green, Murken, Raw, Untimely
Unseat Depose, Dethrone, Oust, Overset, Overthrow, Throw
Unseemly Coarse, Improper, Incivil, Indecent, Indecorous, Indign, Seedy, Untoward
Unselfish Altruist, Generous
Unsent Square
Unsettle(d) Faze, Homeless, Hunky, Indecisive, Nervous, Outstanding, Queasy, Restive, Restless, Troublous

▷ **Unsettled** *may indicate* an anagram

Unsexy N, Neuter

Unsheltered Bleak, Exposed, Homeless

Unsight(ed), Unsightly Eyeless, Hideous, Repulsive, Ugly

Unsinning Impeccable, Pure

Unskilled Awkward, Dilutee, Gauche, Green, Inexpert, Raw, Rude

Unsmiling Agelastic

Unsociable Anchoretic, Grouchy, Solitary, Stay-at-home

Unsophisticated Alf, Boondocks, Boonies, Bushie, Cornball, Corny, Cracker-barrel, Direct, Down-home, Faux-naïf, Hillbilly, Homebred, Homespun, Inurbane, Jaap, Jay, Naive, Provincial, Rube, Rustic, Verdant

Unsound Barmy, Infirm, Invalid, Shaky, Wildcat, Wonky

▷ **Unsound** *may indicate* an anagram

Unsparing Severe

Unspeakable Dreadful, Ineffable, Nefandous

Unspecific, Unspecified General, Generic, Somehow, Such, Vague

Unspoiled, Unspoilt Innocent, Natural, Perfect, Pristine, Pure

Unspoken Silent, Tacit

Unstable, Unsteady Anomic, Astatic, Bockedy, Casual, Crank, Crank(y), Dicky, Erratic, Flexuose, Flexuous, Fluidal, Giddy, Groggy, Infirm, Insecure, Labile, Rickety, Shaky, Shifty, Slippy, Tickle, Top-heavy, Tottery, Totty, Variable, Volatile, Walty, Wambling, Wankle, Warby, Wobbly

Unstated Concordat, Tacit, Unknown

▶ **Unsteady** *see* **UNSTABLE**

Unstressed Enclitic

▷ **Unstuck** *may indicate* an anagram

Unsubstantial Aeriform, Airy, Flimsy, Paltry, Shadowy, Slight, Thin, Yeasty

Unsuccessful Abortive, Futile, Joyless, Manqué, Vain

Unsuitable Ill-timed, Impair, Improper, Inapt, Incongruous, Inexpedient, Malapropos, Unbecoming, Unfit

Unsupported, Unsupportable Astylar, Floating, Stroppy, Unfounded

Unsure Hesitant, Tentative

Unsurpassed All-time, Best, Supreme

Unsuspecting Credulous, Innocent, Naive

Unsweetened Brut, Natural

Unsymmetrical Heterauxesis(m), Irregular, Lopsided

Unsympathetic Short shrift

Unthinking Mechanical

Untidy Daggy, Dishevelled, Dowd(y), Frowzy, Litterbug, Ragged, Raunchy, Scruff(y), Slipshod, Slovenly, Tatty

▷ **Untidy** *may indicate* an anagram

Untie Free, Undo, Unlace

Until Hasta

Untilled Fallow

Untiring Assiduous

Untold Secret, Umpteen, Unread, Unred, Vast

Untouchable Burakumin, Dalit, Harijan, Immune, Sacrosanct, Sealed

Untouched Intact, Inviolate, Pristine, Virgin

▷ **Untrained** *may indicate* 'BR' to be removed

Untried New, Virgin

Untroubled Insouciant

Untrue, Untruth Apocryphal, Eccentric, Fabrication, Faithless, False(hood), Lie, Prefabrication, Unleal
Untrustworthy Dishonest, Fickle, Fly-by-night, Mamzer, Momzer, Shifty, Sleeky, Tricky
Untypical Anomalous, Étypic(al), Isolated, Unusual
Unused, Unusable Impracticable, New, Over, Wasted
Unusual(ly) Abnormal, Atypical, Exceptional, Extra(ordinary), Freak, New, Novel, Odd, Offbeat, Out-of-the-way, Outré, Particular, Queer, Rare, Remarkable, Singular, Special, → STRANGE, Unco, Unique, Untypical, Unwonted
▷ **Unusual** *may indicate* an anagram
Unutterable Ineffable
Unvarying Constant, Eternal, Monotonous, Stable, Static, Uniform
Unveil Expose, Honour
Unvoiced Surd
Unwanted De trop, Exile, Gooseberry, Nimby, Outcast, Sorn
Unwashed Grubby
Unwavering Steadfast
Unwed Celibate, Single
Unwelcome, Unwelcoming Frosty, Icy, Lulu, Obtrusive, (Persona) Non grata
Unwell Ailing, Crook, Dicky, Ill, Impure, Poorly, Quazzy, Queasy, Seedy, Shouse, Toxic
Unwholesome Insalutary, Miasmous, Morbid, Noxious
Unwieldy Cumbersome, Elephantine
Unwilling(ness) Averse, Disinclined, Intestate, Loath, Loth, Nolition, Nolo, Obdurate, Perforce, Reluctant
Unwind Relax, Straighten, Unclew, Unreave, Unreeve
▷ **Unwind** *may indicate* an anagram
Unwinnable Catch 22
Unwise Foolish, Ill-advised, Ill-judged, Impolitic, Imprudent, Inexpedient, Injudicious, Rash
Unwitting Accidental, Nescient
Unwonted Inusitate
Unworkable Impossible, Inoperable
Unworried Carefree
Unworthy Below, Beneath, Indign, Inferior, Infra dig
Unwritten Verbal
Unyielding Adamant, Eild, Firm, Hardline, Inexorable, Inextensible, Intransigent, Obdurate, Rigid, Steely, Stubborn, Tough, Unalterable
Unyoke Outspan
Up(on), Upturned, Upper, Uppish A, Acockbill, Afoot, Antidepressant, Arrogant, Astir, Astray, Astride, Cloud-kissing, Erect, Euphoric, Heavenward, Hep, Horsed, Incitant, Off, On, Overhead, Primo, Range, Ride, Riding, Risen, Skyward, Speed, → UPPER CLASS, Vamp, Ventral
Up-anchor Atrip, Weigh
Upbeat Anacrusis, Arsis
Upbraid Abuse, Rebuke, Reproach, Reprove, Scold, Storm, Twit
Upcountry Anabasis, Inland
Update Brief, Renew, Report, Sitrep
Upfront Open
Upheaval Cataclysm, Chaos, Eruption, Rummage, Seismic, Shake out, Stir
▷ **Upheld** *may indicate* 'up' in another word

Uphill Arduous, Borstal, Sisyphean
Uphold Assert, Defend, Maintain
Upholstery Lampas, Moquette, Trim
Upkeep Support
Upland(s) Alps, Downs, Hilly, Wold
Uplift Boost, Edify, Elate, Elevation, Exalt, Hoist, Levitation, Sky
Upper class, Upper crust Aristocrat, County, Crachach, Nobility, Patrician, Posh, Sial, Top-hat, Tweedy, U
Upright(s), Uprightness Aclinic, Anend, Apeak, Apeek, Aplomb, Arrect, Atrip, Erect, Goalpost, Honest, Incorrupt, Jamb, Joanna, Merlon, Moral, Mullion, Orthograde, Perpendicular, Piano, Pilaster(s), Post, Rectitude, Roman, Splat, Stanchion, Stares, Stile, Stud, Vertical, Virtuous
Uprising Incline, Intifada, Meerut, Rebellion, Revolt, Tumulus
Uproar(ious) Ballyhoo, Bedlam, Blatancy, Brouhaha, Charivari, Clamour, Clangour, Collieshangie, Commotion, Cry, Din, Dirdam, Dirdum, Durdum, Emeute, Ferment, Flaw, Fracas, Furore, Garboil, Hell, Hoopla, Hubbub(oo), Hullabaloo, Hurly(-burly), Imbroglio, Katzenjammer, Madhouse, Noise, Noyes, Outcry, Pandemonium, Racket, Raird, Randan, Reird, Riotous, Roister, Romage, Rowdedow, Rowdydow(dy), Ruckus, Ruction, Rumpus, Shemozzle, Stramash, Turmoil, Utis, Whoobub
Uproot Deracinate, Eradicate, Evict, Outweed, Supplant, Weed
Upset(ting) Aggrieve, Alarm, Applecart, Bother, Capsize, Catastrophe, Choked, Coup, Cowp, Crank, Derange, Dip, Discomboberate, Discombobulate, Discomfit, Discomfort, Discommode, Disconcert, Dismay, Disquiet, Distraught, Disturb, Dod, Eat, Fuss, Heart-rending, Inversion, Keel, Miff, Nauseative, Offend, Overthrow, Overturn, Peeve, Perturb, Pip, Pother, Purl, Rattle, Rile, Ruffle, Rumple, Sad, Seel, Shake, Sore, Spill, Tapsalteerie, Tip, Topple, Trauma, Undo, Unsettled
▷ **Upset** *may indicate* an anagram; a word upside down; or 'tes'
Upshot Outcome, Result, Sequel
Upside down Inverted, Resupinate, Tapsie-teerie, Topsy-turvy
Upstart Buckeen, Jumped-up, Mushroom, Parvenu, Vulgarian
▷ **Upstart** *may indicate* 'u'
Upstream Thermal
Upsurge Thrust, Waste
Uptake Shrewdness, Understanding, Wit
Up to Till, Until
Up-to-date Abreast, Contemporary, Current, Mod, New-fashioned, Right-on, State-of-the-art, Swinging, Topical, Trendy
Upwards Acclivious, Aloft, Antrorse, Cabré
Uranium Depleted, Pitchblende, U, Yellowcake
Urban Civic, Megalopolis, Municipal, Town
Urbane Civil, Debonair, Refined, Townly
Urchin Arab, Brat, Crinoid, Crossfish, Cystoid, Echinoderm, Echinoidea, Echinus, Gamin, Guttersnipe, Gutty, Heart, Mudlark, Nipper, Pluteus, Ragamuffin, Sand-dollar, Sea, Sea-egg, Spatangoidea, Spatangus, Street-arab, Townskip
Urge, Urgent Admonish, Ca, Coax, Constrain, Crying, Dire, Drive, Egg, Enjoin, Exhort, Exigent, Goad, Hard, Hie, Hoick, Hunger, Hurry, Id, Immediate, Impel, Impulse, Incense, Incite, Insist(ent), Instance, Instigate, Itch, Kick, Libido, Nag, Peremptory, Persuade, Press(ing), Prod, Push, Scrub, Set on, Spur, Strenuous, Strident, Strong, Threapit, Threepit, Wanderlust, Whig, Yen
▷ **Urgent** *may indicate* 'Ur-gent', viz. Iraqi

Uriah Hittite, Humble, Umble
Urinal Bog, John, Jordan, → LAVATORY, Loo, Pissoir
Urinate, Urine Chamber-lye, Emiction, Enuresis, Lant, Leak, Micturition, Number one, Oliguria, Pee, Piddle, Piss, Planuria, Relieve, Slash, Stale, Strangury, Tiddle, Werris (Creek), Widdle
Urn(s), Urn-shaped Canopic, Cinerarium, Ewer, Grecian, Lachrymal, Olla, Ossuary, Samovar, Storied, Tea, Urceolate, Vase
Us 's, UK, Uns, We
Usage, Use(r), Used, Utilise Application, Apply, Avail, Boot, Consume, Custom, Deploy, Dow, → EMPLOY, End, Ex, Exercise, Exert, Expend, Exploit, Flesh, Habit, Hand-me-down, Inured, Manner, Ply, Practice, Sarum, Spare, Spent, Sport, Take, Tradition, Treat, Try, Ure, Wield, With, Wont
Useful Asset, Availing, Commodity, Dow, Expedient, Invaluable
Useless Base, Bung, Cumber, Cumber-ground, Dead-wood, Dud, Empty, Futile, Gewgaw, Grotty, Ground, Idle, Inane, Ineffective, Lame, Lemon, Nonstarter, Otiose, Plug, Sculpin, Sterile, Swap, US, Vain, Void, Wet
Usher Black Rod, Blue Rod, Chobdar, Commissionaire, Conduct(or), Doorman, Escort, Guide, Herald, Huissier, Macer, Rod, Show, Steward
Usual Common, Customary, Habit(ual), Natural, Normal, Ordinary, Routine, Rule, Solito, Standard, Stock, Typical, Wont
Usurer, Usury Gombeen, Lender, Loanshark, Moneylender, Note-shaver, Shark, Uncle
Usurp(er) Abator, Arrogate, Encroach, Invade
Ut As, Doh, Utah
Utah Ut
Utensil(s) Batterie, Battery, Canteen, Chopsticks, Colander, Cookware, Corer, Double boiler, Fish-kettle, Fork, Funnel, Gadget, Grater, Gridiron, Holloware, Implement, Instrument, Jagger, Knife, Mandolin(e), Ricer, Scoop, Skillet, Spatula, Spoon, Things, Tool, Whisk, Zester
▶ **Utilise** see USE
Utilitarian Benthamite, Mill, Practical, Useful
Utility Elec(tricity), Expected, Gas, Public, Water
Utmost Best, Extreme, Farthest, Maximum, Nth
Utopia(n) Adland, Cloud-cuckoo-land, Ideal, Pantisocracy, Paradise, Perfect, Shangri-la
Utter(ance), Uttered, Utterly Absolute, Accent, Agrapha, Agraphon, Aread, Arrant, Cry, Dead, Deliver, Dictum, Dog, Downright, Ejaculate, Emit, Enunciate, Express, Extreme, Glossolalia, Issue, Judgement, Lenes, Lenis, Locution, Mint, Most, Oracle, Pass, Phonate, Pronounce, Pure, Quo(th), Rank, Rap, Rattle, Remark, Saw, → SAY, Sheer, Speak, Spout, Stark, State, Syllable, Tell, Vend, Vent, Very, Voice
Uvula Staphyle

Vv

V Anti, Bomb, Del, Five, Nabla, See, Sign, Verb, Verse, Versus, Victor(y), Volt, Volume

Vacancy, Vacant Blank, Empty, Glassy, Hole, Hollow, Inane, Place, Space, Vacuum

Vacation Holiday, Leave, Long, Non-term, Outing, Recess, Trip, Voidance

Vaccination, Vaccine Antigen, Antiserum, Bacterin, Cure, HIB, Jenner, MMR, Sabin, Salk, Serum, Subunit

Vacillate, Vacillating Chop, Dither, Feeble, Hesitate, Shilly-shally, Trimmer, Wabble, Wave(r), Whiffle

Vacuous Blank, Empty, Toom, Vacant

Vacuum Blank, Cleaner, Dewar, Emptiness, Magnetron, Nothing, Plenum, Thermos®, Torricellian, Ultra-high, Void

Vade-mecum Ench(e)iridion, Notebook

Vagabond Bergie, Gadling, → **GYPSY**, Hobo, Landlo(u)per, Outcast, Rapparee, Romany, Rover, Runabout, Runagate, Tramp

Vagrant Beachcomber, Bum, Bummer, Caird, Crusty, Derro, Dosser, Drifter, Gangrel, Gang-there-out, Goliard, Gypsy, Hobo, Landlo(u)per, Lazzarone, Nomad, Patercove, Pikey, Rinthereout, Rogue, Romany, Scatterling, Strag, Straggle, Stroller, Swagman, Tinker, → **TRAMP**, Truant, Walker

Vague(ness) Amorphous, Bleary, Blur, Confused, Dim, Equivocal, Hazy, Ill-defined, Ill-headed, Indeterminate, Indistinct, Loose, Mist, Nebulous, Shadowy, Woolly-minded

▷ **Vaguely** *may indicate* an anagram

Vain Bootless, Coxcomb, Coxcomical, Egoistic, Empty, Fruitless, → **FUTILE**, Hollow, Idle, Peacock, Pompous, Profitless, Proud, Strutting, Unuseful, Useless, Vogie

Vainglory Panache

Valance Pand, Pelmet

Vale Addio, Adieu, Cheerio, Coomb, Dean, Dedham, Dene, Ebbw, Enna, Evesham, Glen, Ta-ta, Tempé, Valley

Valediction, Valedictory Apopemptic, Cheerio, Farewell

Valentine Card, Sweetheart

Valerian All-heal, Cetywall, Greek, Red, Setuale, Setwale, Setwall, Spur

Valet Aid, Andrew, Gentleman's gentleman, Jeames, Jeeves, Man, Passepartout, Quint, Servant, Skip-kennel

Valetudinarian Hypochondriac, Invalid

Valiant Brave, Doughty, Heroic, Resolute, Stalwart, Stouthearted, Wight

Valid(ity), Validate Confirm, Establish, Just, Legal, Probate, Rational, Sound

Valise Bag, Case, Dorlach, Satchel

Valkyrie Brynhild

Valley Ajalon, Aosta, Baca, Barossa, Bekaa, Beqaa, Bolson, Cleavage, Clough, Comb(e), Coomb, Cwm, Dale, Dargle, Dean, Death, Defile, Dell, Den, Dene, Dingle, Dip, Drowned, Dry, Gehenna, Ghyll, Glen, Glencoe, Glyn, Graben, Great Glen,

Great Rift, Grindelwald, Hanging, Haugh, Heuch, Hollow, Hope, Humiliation, Hutt, Ladin, Lagan, Lallan, Nemea, Olympia, Ravine, Rhondda, Ria, Rift, San Fernando, Seaton, Silicon, Slack, Slade, Strath(spey), Tempe, Tophet, Trossachs, Umbria, U-shaped, Valdarno, Vale, Vallambrosa, Water, Water gap, Yosemite

Valour Bravery, Courage, Heroism, Merit, Prowess

Valuable, Valuation, Value(s) Absolute, Acid, Appraise, Appreciate, Apprize, Assess(ment), Asset, Bargain, Book, Break up, Calibrate, Carbon, Checksum, Cherish, CIF, Cop, Cost, Crossover, Datum, Denomination, Equity, Esteem, Estimate, Expected, Face, Feck, Hagberg, Intrinsic, Limit, Market, Modulus, Net present, Net realizable, Nominal, Nuisance, Omnium, Par, pH, Place, Precious, Premium, Present, Price, Prize, Prys, Q, Quartile, Rarity, Rate, Rateable, Rating, Regard, Residual, Respect, Rogue, Salt, Sentimental, Set, Snob, Steem, Stent, Store, Street, Surrender, Taonga, Time, Treasure, Tristimulus, Truth, Valuta, → **WORTH**

Valueless Bum, Fig, Mare's nest, Orra, Useless, Worthless

Valve Acorn, Air, Aortic, Ball, Bicuspid, Bleed, Blow, Butterfly, Check, Clack, Cock, Drawgate, Dynatron, Escape, Exhaust, Flip-flop, Foot, Gate, Induction, Magnetron, Mitral, Mixing, Needle, Non-return, Pallet, Pentode, Petcock, Piston, Poppet, Pulmonary, Puppet, Radio, Resnatron, Safety, Seacock, Semilunar, Shut-off, Side, Sleeve, Slide, Sluice, Sluicegate, Snifter, Snifting, Stopcock, Suction, Tap, Tetrode, Thermionic, Throttle, Thyratron, Triode, Turncock, Vacuum, Ventil, Vibroton

Vamoose Abscond, Decamp, Scat, Scram

Vamp Adlib, Charm, Rehash, Seduce, Siren, Strum, Twiddle

Vampire Bat, Dracula, False, Ghoul, Lamia, Lilith, Pontianak, Stringes

Van(guard) Advance, Box-car, Brake, Breakdown, Camper, Cart, Cube, Delivery, Dormobile®, Forefront, Foremost, Front, Furniture, Guard's, Head, Kombi®, Lead, Leader(s), Lorry, Loudspeaker, Luggage, Meat wagon, Panel, Panel-truck, Pantechnicon, Patrol-wagon, Prison, Removal, Spearhead, Truck, Ute, Wagon

Vanadium V

Vandal(ise), Vandalism Desecrate, Hooligan, Hun, Loot, Pillage, Ravage, Rough, Sab(oteur), Sack, Saracen, Skinhead, Slash, Trash

Vandyke Beard, Painter

Vane(s) Dog, Fan, Guide, Rudder, Swirl, Telltale, Vexillum, Weather(cock), Web, Wind (tee), Wing

Vanessa Butterfly

Vanilla Pinole

Vanish(ed), Vanishing Cease, Disappear, Disperse, Dissolve, Evanesce(nt), Evaporate, Extinct, Faint(ed), Mizzle, Slope, Transitory, Unbe

Vanity Amour-propre, Arrogance, Ego, Esteem, Futility, Pomp, Pretension, Pride, Self-conceit, Self-esteem

Vanquish Beat, Conquer, Floor, Master, Overcome, Rout

Vantage (point) Ascendancy, Coign(e), Height

Vaporise, Vapour Boil, Cloud, Contrail, Effluent, Fog, Fume, Halitus, Iodine, Miasma, Mist, Reek, Roke, Skywriting, → **STEAM**, Steme, Water

▶ **Variable, Variance, Variant, Variation** *see* **VARY**

Varicose Haemorrhoids

▶ **Varied, Variety** *see* **VARY**

▷ **Varied** *may indicate* an anagram

Variegate(d) Calico, Dappled, Flecked, Fretted, Motley, Mottle, Pied, Rainbow, Skewbald, Tissue

▷ **Variety of** *may indicate* an anagram

Various Divers(e), Manifold, Multifarious, Separate, Several, Sundry

Various years Vy
Varlet Cad, Knave, Rascal, Rogue
Varnish(ing) Arar, Bee-glue, Copal, Cowdie-gum, Dam(m)ar, Desert, Dope, Dragon's-blood, Glair, Japan, Lacquer, Lentisk, Nail, Nibs, Oil, Resin, Sandarac, Shellac, Spirit, Tung-oil, Tung-tree, Vernis martin, Vernissage
Vary(ing), Variable, Variance, Variant, Variation, Varied, Variety Ablaut, Aelotropy, Alter, Amphoteric, Assortment, Breed, Brew, Cepheid, Change, Chequered, Colour, Contrapuntal, Counterpoint, Daedal(e), Dedal, Dependent, Differ, Discrepancy, Diverse, Diversity, Dummy, Eclectic, Eclipsing, Enigma, Farraginous, Fickle, Fluctuating, Form, Grid, Iid, Inconsistent, Inconstant, Independent, Intervening, Isochor, Isopleth, Isotopy, Line, Local, Medley, Mix, Morph, Morphosis, Multifarious, Multiplicity, Music hall, Mutable, Nimrod, Nuance, Olio, Omniform, Orthogenesis, Parametric, Partita, Protean, Random, Remedy, Response, Smörgåsbord, Sort, Species, Spice, Sport, Stirps, Stochastic, Strain, String, Timeserver, Tolerance, Twistor, Var, Versatile, Versiform, Version, Vicissitude, Vl, Wane, Wax, X, Y, Z
Vase Bronteum, Canopus, Cornucopia, Diota, Hydria, Jardinière, Kalpis, Lachrymal, Lecythus, Lekythos, Moon flask, Murr(h)a, Portland, Pot, Potiche, Stamnos, Urn, Vessel
Vasectomy Desexing
Vassal Client, Daimio, Feoffee, Lackey, Liege, Liegeman, Man, Manred, Servant, Vavaso(u)r
Vast(ness) Big, Cosmic, Cyclopic, Enormous, Epic, Extensive, Huge(ous), Immense, Mighty, Monumental, Ocean, Prodigious
Vat Back, Barrel, Blunger, Chessel, Copper, Cowl, Cuvée, Fat, Girnel, Keir, Kier, Pressfat, Stand, Tank, Tan-pit, Tub, Tun, Winefat
Vatican Rome, V
Vaudeville Zarzuela
Vaughan Silurist
Vault(ed), Vaulting Arch, Barrel, Cavern, Cellar, Chamber, Charnel house, Clear, Cross, Crypt, Cul-de-four, Cupola, Dome, Dungeon, Fan, Firmament, Fornicate, Groin, Hypogeum, Jump, Kiva, Leap(frog), Lierne, Mausoleum, Ossuary, Palm, Pend, Pendentive, Pole, Rib, Safe, Sepulchre, Serdab, Severy, Shade, Souterrain, Tholus, Tomb, Tunnel, Underpitch, Vaut, Wagon, Weem, Wine
▷ **Vault** *may indicate* an anagram
Vaunt Boast, Brag, Crow
Veal Escalope, Fricandeau, Galantine, Scallop, Schnitzel, Wiener schnitzel
Vector, Vector operator Dyad, Nabla, Phasor, Polar, Radius
Veda Yajurveda
Veer Bag, Boxhaul, Broach, Deviate, Draw, Gybe, Splay, Swerve, Tack, Turn, Wear, Yaw
Vegan Parev(e), Parve
Vegetable(s) Alexanders, Allium, Artichoke, Asparagus, Aubergine, Beans, Beet(root), Borecole, Brassica, Broccoli, Cabbage, Calabrese, Calaloo, Calalu, Cardoon, Carrot, Castock, Cataloo, Catalu, Cauliflower, Celeriac, Celery, Chard, Chicory, Chiffonade, Chive, Choko, Chufa, Cocoyam, Colcannon, Cole, Collard, Corn-on-the-cob, Coulis, Courgette, Crout, Cucumber, Custock, Daikon, Endive, Escarole, Eschalot, Fennel, Finocchio, Flora, Garlic, Gherkin, Greens, Guar, Hastings, Inert, Ingan, Jardinière, Jerusalem artichoke, Jicama, Kale, Kohlrabi, Kumara, Kumera, Lablab, Leek, Legume(n), Lettuce, Macedoine, Mangel(-wurzel), Mangetout, Mangold, Marrow(-squash), Mato(o)ke, Mirepoix, Mooli, Navew, Neep,

Oca, Okra, Okro, Olitory, Onion, Orach(e), Parsnip, Pea(se), Pepper, Pimento, Plant, Pomato, Potato, Pottage, Pratie, Primavera, Pulse, Pumpkin, Quinoa, Radicchio, Radish, Rapini, Ratatouille, Rocambole, Root, Rutabaga, Sabji, Salad, Salsify, Samphire, Sauce, Sauerkraut, Savoy, Scorzonera, Shallot, Sibol, Sium, Skirret, Sorrel, Spinach(-beet), Spinage, Sprouts, Spud, Squash, String bean, Succotash, Swede, Sweet corn, Sweet potato, Taro, Tomato, Tonka-bean, Triffid, Truck, Turnip, Udo, Witloof, Wort, Yam, Zucchini

Vegetable extract Solanine

Vegetarian Herbivore, Maigre, Meatless, Parev(e), Parve, Pythagorean, Vegan, Veggie

Vegetate, Vegetator, Vegetation Alga, Brush, Cover, Flora, Fynbos, Gar(r)igue, Greenery, Herb, Lemna, Maquis, Quadrat, Scrub, Stagnate, Sudd, Transect

Vehemence, Vehement(ly) Amain, Ardent, Fervid, Forcible, Frenzy, Heat, Hot, Intense, Violent

Vehicle Ambulance, Amtrack, Artic, Articulated, ATV, Autocycle, Autorickshaw, Brake, Brancard, Buckboard, Buggy, Bus, Cab, Camper, Car, Caravan, Carry-all, Cart, Casspir, Channel, Chariot, Commercial, Conveyance, Crate, Curricle, Cycle, Delta, Dennet, Dog-cart, Dormobile®, Dragster, Dray, Duck, Dune buggy, Estate car, Fiacre, Float, Fly, Four-by-four, Four-seater, Gharri, Gharry, Gladstone, Go-cart, Go-kart, Go-Ped®, Gritter, Growler, Half-track, Hansom, Hatchback, Hearse, Hovercraft, Humvee, Jeep®, Jeepney, Jet-Ski, Jingle, Jinker, Jitney, Juggernaut, Kago, Kart, Koneke, Landau, Land Rover®, Launch, LEM, Limber, Litter, Load-lugger, Lorry, Machine, Mammy wagon, Means, Medium, Micro-scooter, Minibus, Minicab, Minivan, Motor, Motorhome, Multipurpose, Norimon, Offroad, Paddock-basher, Pantechnicon, Pedicab, Penny-farthing, People carrier, People-mover, Perambulator, Personnel carrier, Phaeton, Pick-up, Quad, Recreational, Re-entry, Ricksha(w), Roadroller, Runabout, Rust-bucket, Samlor, Sand-yacht, Scow, Shay, Shuttle, Sidecar, Skibob, Skidoo®, Sled(ge), Sleigh, Sno-Cat®, Snowmobile, Snowplough, Soyuz, Space, Spider, Stanhope, Station wagon, Steam-car, Sulky, Surrey, Tarantas(s), Tardis, Taxi, Tempera, Three-wheeler, Tipcart, Tip-up, Tonga, Tracked, Tractor, Trailer, Tram, Transporter, Trap, Tricar, Tricycle, Trishaw, Troika, Trolley, Trolleybus, Truck, Tuk tuk, Tumble-car(t), Tumbril, Turbo, Two-seater, Two-wheeler, Unicycle, Ute, Utility, Vahana, Velocipede, Vespa®, Volante, Wagon, Wagonette, Weasel, Wheelbarrow, Wheels, Wrecker

Veil Burk(h)a, Calyptra, Chad(d)ar, Chador, Chuddah, Chuddar, Cloud, Cover, Curtain, Envelop, Eucharistic, Hejab, Hijab, Humeral, Kalyptra, Kiss-me, Lambrequin, Mantilla, Mist, Niqab, Obscure, Purdah, Sacramental, Scene, Veale, Volet, Weeper, Wimple, Yashmak

Vein Artery, Azygas, Basilic, Coronary, Costa, Diploic, Epithermal, Fahlband, Gate, H(a)emorrhoid, Hemiazygous, Innominate, Jugular, Ledge, Lode, Mainline, Media, Midrib, Mood, Nervure, Organic, Outcrop, Percurrent, Pipe, Portal, Postcava, Precava, Pulmonary, Rake, Rib, Saphena, Sectorial, Spur, Stockwork, Stringer, Style, Thread, Varicose, Varix, Vena, Venule, Vorticose

Vellum Cutch, Japanese, Kutch, Parchment

Velocity Angular, Escape, Mustard, Muzzle, Orbital, Parabolic, Radial, Rate, Speed, Terminal, V

Velvet Bagheera, Chenille, National, Panné, Pile, Three-pile, Velour, Velure

Venal Corruptible, Mercenary, Sale

Vend(or) Hawk, Peddle, Pedlar, Rep, Sammy, Sell, Sutler

Vendetta Feud

Veneer Facade, Gloss, Varnish
Venerable Aged, August, Augustus, Bede, Guru, Hoary, Sacred, Sage, Vintage
Venerate, Veneration Adore, Awe, Douleia, Dulia, Hallow, Homage, Honour, Hyperdulia, Idolise, Latria, Revere, Worship
Venereal NSU, VD
Venery Chase
Venetian Aldine, Blind, Doge, Gobbo, Polo
Vengeance, Vengeful Commination, Erinyes, Reprisal, Ultion, Vindictive, Wannion, Wrack, Wreak
Venice La Serenissima
Venison Cervena, Deer
Venom(ous) Gall, Gila, Jamestown-weed, Jim(p)son-weed, Poison, Rancour, Solpuga, Spite, Toxic, Virus, Zootoxin
Vent Airway, Aperture, Belch, Chimney, Emit, Express, Fumarole, Hornito, Issue, Ostiole, Outlet, Smoker, Solfatara, Spiracle, Undercast, Wreak
Venter Uterus
Ventilate, Ventilator Air, Air-brick, Air-hole, Discuss, Express, Louvre, Plenum, Shaft, Voice, Windsail, Windway, Winze
Venture(d) Ante, Callet, Chance, Dare, Daur, Durst, Enterprise, Flutter, Foray, Handsel, Hazard, Jump, Opine, Presume, Promotion, Prostitute, Risk, Spec, Throw
Venue Bout, Locale, Place, Showground, Stadium, Stateroom, Tryst, Visne
Venus Cohog, Cytherean, Hesper(us), Love, Lucifer, Morning-star, Phosphorus, Primavera, Quahaug, Quahog, Rokeby, Vesper
Venus fly-trap Dionaea
Veracity, Veracious Accurate, Factual, Sincere, Truth(ful)
Veranda(h) Balcony, Gallery, Lanai, Patio, Piazza, Porch, Sleep-out, Stoep, Stoop, Terrace
Verb(al), Verbs Active, Argy-bargy, Auxiliary, Causative, Conative, Copula, Ergative, Factitive, Infinitive, Intransitive, Irregular, Modal, Passive, Perfective, Performative, Phrasal, Preterite, Stative, Transitive, Vb, Word-of-mouth
Verbascum Mullein
Verbatim Literally
Verbena Vervain
Verbose, Verbosity Padding, Prolix, Talkative, Wordy
Verdant Lush
Verdict Decision, Formal, Judg(e)ment, Majority, Open, Opinion, Pronouncement, Resolution, Ruling, Special
Verdigris Aeruginous, Patina
Verge Border, Brink, → EDGE, Hard shoulder, Incline, Long paddock, Rim
Verger Beadle, Pew-opener
Verify, Verification Affirm, Ascertain, Check, Confirm, Constatation, Control, Crosscheck, Prove, Validate
Verily Yea
Verisimilitude Artistic, Authenticity, Credibility
Verity Fact, Sooth, Truth
Vermifuge Cow(h)age, Cowitch
Vermilion Cinnabar, Minium, Red
Vermin(ous) Carrion, Catawampus, Lice, Mice, Pest, Ratty, → RODENT, Scum
Vermouth Absinthiated, French, It(alian), Martini®
Vernacular Common, Dialect, Idiom, Jargon, Lingo, Native, Patois, Vulgate
Veronica Hebe, Hen-bit, Speedwell

Verruca | 802

Verruca Wart
Versatile Adaptable, All-rounder, Flexible, Handy, Many-sided, Protean, Resourceful
Verse(s), Versed Dactyl, Free, Linked, Logaoedic, Passus, Poetry, Political, Reported, → RHYME

VERSES

1 letter:
V

3 letters:
Fit

4 letters:
Awdl
Blad
Duan
Epic
Epos
Fitt
Hymn
Neck
Poem
Rime
Sijo
Song
Vers

5 letters:
Blank
Blaud
Canto
Comus
Epode
Fitte
Fytte
Gazal
Haiku
Hokku
Ionic
Lyric
Meter
Poesy
Renga
Rubai
Spasm

Stave
Tanka
Tract
Triad

6 letters:
Adonic
Ballad
Burden
Ghazal
Ghazel
Gnomic
Haikai
Heroic
Jingle
Laisse
Miurus
Octave
Pantun
Rondel
Scazon
Stanza
Strain
Tercet

7 letters:
Alcaics
Couplet
Dimeter
Elegiac
Epigram
Fabliau
Huitain
Leonine
Pantoum
Pennill
Prosody
Pythian
Rondeau

Sapphic
Sestina
Sestine
Sixaine
Stiches
Strophe
Tiercet
Triolet
Tripody

8 letters:
Cinquain
Clerihew
Doggerel
Glyconic
Kyrielle
Madrigal
Nonsense
Pindaric
Quatrain
Rhopalic
Rove-over
Rubaiyat
Scansion
Senarius
Sirvente
Syllabic
Terzetta
Trimeter
Tristich
Versicle

9 letters:
Amphigory
Asclepiad
Beatitude
Dithyramb
Ditrochee
Goliardic

Hexameter
Macaronic
Monometer
Octameter
Octastich
Saturnian
Stornello
Terza rima
Vers libre

10 letters:
Asynartete
Catalectic
Cynghanedd
Fescennine
Hypermeter
Mock-heroic
Ottava rima
Pennillion
Pentameter
Rhyme-royal
Serpentine
Tetrameter
Tetrastich
Villanelle

11 letters:
Acatalectic
Alexandrine
Hudibrastic
Riding-rhyme
Septenarius

12 letters:
Archilochian
Asclepiadean
Hudibrastics
Octosyllabic

▷ **Versed** *may indicate* reversed
Versed sine Sagitta
Versifier Lyricist, Poetaster, Rhymer, Rhymester
Version Account, Adaptation, Authorised, Cephalic, Cover, Edition, Form,

Paraphrase, Rede, Rendering, Rendition, Revised, Revision, Rhemish, Standard, Translation

Vertebra(e), Vertebrate Agnathan, Amniote, Amphioxus, Ascidian, Atlas, Axis, Bone, Centrum, Cervical, Chordae, Cyclostome, Dorsal, Gnathostome, Ichthyopsida, Lamprey, Lumbar, Placoderm, Reptile, Sacral, Sauropsida, Spondyl, Tetrapod, Tunicata, Vermis

Vertex Apex, Crest, Crown, Summit, Zenith

Vertical Apeak, Apeek, Atrip, Erect, Lapse, Montant, Ordinate, Perpendicular, Plumb, Prime, Sheer, Standing, Stemmed, Stile, Upright

Vertigo Dinic, Dizziness, Fainting, Giddiness, Megrim, Nausea, Staggers, Whirling

Verve Dash, Energy, Go, Gusto, Panache, Vigour

Very (good, well) A1, Ae, Assai, Awfully, Boffo, Bonzer, Boshta, Boshter, Dashed, Def, Ever, Extreme(ly), Fell, Frightfully, Gey, Grouse, Heap, Hellova, Helluva, Highly, Jolly, Keen, Light, Mighty, Molto, Much, OK, Opt, Precious, Precise, Purler, Real, Right, Self same, So, Sore, Stinking, Très, Unco, Utter, V, VG, Way

Vesicle Ampul, Bladder

Vespers Evensong, Lychnic, Placebo, Sicilian

Vessel → BOAT, Capillary, Container, Craft, Dish, Motor, Pressure, Receptacle, Seed, → SHIP, Utensil, Vascular, Weaker

VESSELS

3 letters:	Snow	Scoop	Dolium
Bin	Vase	Shell	Elutor
Cog	Vein	Sloop	Flagon
Cup	Vena	Stean	Frigot
Dow	Vial	Steen	Galiot
Fat	Zulu	Stoop	Galley
Obo		Stoup	Goblet
Pan	5 letters:	Tazza	Goglet
Pig	Aorta	Varix	Guglet
Pyx	Blood	Xebec	Humpen
Tub	Cogue	Zabra	Jet-ski
Urn	Crare		Kettle
Vas	Crewe	6 letters:	Lorcha
Vat	Crock	Aludel	Mortar
	Cruet	Argyle	Noggin
4 letters:	Cruse	Argyll	Retort
Bowl	Cupel	Artery	Rumkin
Buss	Dandy	Banker	Sailer
Cask	Dixie	Beaker	Sampan
Cowl	Gourd	Bicker	Sconce
Dhow	Ketch	Bouget	Shippo
Etna	Laver	Bucket	Situla
Font	Lotah	Carafe	Steane
Grab	Mazer	Carboy	Tassie
Horn	Oiler	Chatty	Trough
Lota	Phial	Copper	Tureen
Olpe	Pokal	Crayer	Venule
Raft	Quart	Dinghy	Wherry
Skin	Round	Dogger	

7 letters:
Amphora
Ampulla
Canteen
Chalice
Cistern
Costrel
Creamer
Cresset
Cuvette
Cyathus
Dredger
Drifter
Felucca
Frigate
Galleon
Galliot
Gunship
Gurglet
Jugular
Mudscow
Patamar

Pinnace
Pitcher
Polacca
Precava
Steamer
Tankard
Terreen
Vedette
Washpot

8 letters:
Calabash
Cauldron
Ciborium
Colander
Coolamon
Crucible
Cucurbit
Decanter
Figuline
Flatboat
Galleass

Galliass
Gallipot
Gallivat
Hoveller
Hydroski
Jerrican
Longboat
Monteith
Pancheon
Panchion
Pannikin
Sinusoid
Workboat

9 letters:
Alcarraza
Autoclave
Bucentaur
Calandria
Casserole
Cullender
Destroyer

Hydrofoil
Privateer
Tappit-hen

10 letters:
Bathyscaph
Deep-sinker
Jardinière
Triaconter

11 letters:
Aspersorium
Bathyscaphe
Side-wheeler

12 letters:
Fore-and-after
Lachrymatory
Stern-wheeler
Sternwheeler

Vest Beset, Confer, Crop top, Gilet, Modesty, Rash, Semmit, Singlet, Skivvy, Spencer, Sticharion, String, Undercoat, Undershirt, Waistcoat
Vestibule Anteroom, Atrium, Entry, Exedra, Foyer, Hall, Lobby, Narthex, Oeil-de-boeuf, Porch, Portico, Pronaos, Tambour
Vestige Hint, Mark, Mention, Shadow, Sign, Trace
Vestment Alb, Breastplate, Canonicals, Chasuble, Chimar, Chimer(e), Cotta, Dalmatic, Ephod, Fannel, Fanon, Garb, → GARMENT, Maniple, Mantelletta, Omophorion, Pallium, Parament, Ph(a)elonian, Pontificals, Raiment, Rational, Rochet, Rocquet, Sakkos, Sticharion, Stole, Surplice, Tunic(le)
Vestry Common, Sacristy, Select
Vet(ting), Veterinary, Vets Check, Doc(tor), Examine, Ex-serviceman, Inspect, OK, Positive, Screen, Veteran, Zoiatria, Zootherapy
Vetch Bitter, Ers, Fitch, Kidney, Locoweed, Milk, Tare, Tine
Veteran BL, Expert, GAR, Master, Oldster, Old sweat, Old-timer, Old 'un, Retread, Seasoned, Soldier, Stager, Stalwart, Stalworth, Vet, War-horse, Warrior
▷ **Veteran** *may indicate* 'obsolete'
Veto Ban, Bar, Blackball, Debar, Item, Local, Negative, Pocket, Reject, Taboo, Tabu
Vex(ing), Vexed Anger, Annoy, Bother, Chagrin, Debate, Fret, Gall, Grieve, Harass, Irritate, Madden, Mortify, Noy, Pester, Rankle, Rile, Sore, Spite, Tease, Torment, Trouble, Worrisome
Vexation(s) Barrator, Chagrin, Drat, Grief, Nuisance, Pique, Spite, Trouble
Vexatious Trying
Vexillum Web
Via By, Per, Through
Viable Economic, Going, Healthy, Possible
Vial Spirit-level
Viand Cate
Vibrate, Vibration(s), Vibrant Atmosphere, Chatter, Diadrom, Dinnle, Dirl,

Energetic, Flutter, Free, Fremitus, Harmonogram, Hotter, Jar, Judder, Oscillate,
Plangent, Pulse, Quake, Resonance, Resonant, Rumble, Seiche, Shimmy, Shudder,
Thrill, Throb, Tingle, Tremble, Tremor, Trill, Trillo, Twinkle, Uvular, Wag, Whir(r)
Viburnum Opulus
Vicar Apostolic, Bray, Choral, Elton, Forane, General, Incumbent, Lay, Pastoral,
Plenarty, Primrose, Rector, Rev(erend), Trimmer
Vice Clamp, Cramp, Crime, Deputy, Eale, Evil, Foible, Greed, Iniquity, Instead, Jaws,
Regent, Second (in command), → **SIN**, Stair
Vice-president Croupier, Veep
Viceroy Khedive, Nawab, Provost, Satrap, Willingdon
Vichy water Eau
Vicinity Area, Environs, Hereabouts, Locality, Neighbourhood, Region
Vicious Cruel, Flagitious, Hotbed
Victim Abel, Angel, Butt, Casualty, Currie, Curry, Dupe, Fashion, Frame, Host,
Lay-down, Mark, Martyr, Nebbich, Neb(b)ish, Pathic, Patsy, Pigeon, Prey, Quarry,
Sacrifice, Scapegoat, Target
Victor(y) Bangster, Banzai, Beater, Cadmean, Cannae, Captor, Champ(ion),
Conqueror, Conquest, Epinicion, Epinikion, Eunice, Flagship, Fool's mate, Gree,
Gris, Hallelujah, Hugo, Jai, Jai Hind, Kobe, Landslide, Lepanto, Ludorum, Mature,
Moral, Nike, Palm, Philippi, Pyrrhic, Romper, Runaway, Scalp, Signal, Squeaker,
Triumph, VE (day), Vee, Vic, Walk-away, Walkover, Win(ner)
Victoria(n) Aussie, Empress, Plum, Prig, Station
Victualler Caterer, Grocer, Licensed, Purveyor, Supplier, Vivandière
Video(-tape) Betacam®, Digital, Full-motion, Interactive, Laser vision, Minitel,
Pixelation, Promo, Quadruplex, Reverse, Scratch, Still, Vera
Vie Compete, Contend, Emulate, Strive
Vienna Wien
Vietcong Charley, Charlie
Vietnamese Cham
View(er) Aim, Angle, Aspect, Belief, Bird's eye, Cineaste, Consensus, Consider,
Cosmorama, Dekko, Dogma, Doxy, Endoscope, Exploded, Eye, Facet, Gander,
Glimpse, Grandstand, Helicopter, Idea, Introspect, Kaleidoscope, Landscape,
Line, Notion, Opinion, Optic®, Outlook, Pan, Panorama, Point, Private, Profile,
→ **PROSPECT**, Scan, Scape, Scene(ry), See, Sight, Skyscape, Slant, Specular,
Standpoint, Stereoscope, Strain, Synop(sis), Tenet, Terrain, Thanatopsis, Theory,
Vantage-point, Veduta, Vista, Visto, Watch, Witness, Worm's eye
Viewpoint Angle, Attitude, Belvedere, Conspectus, Eyeshot, Grandstand, Instance,
Observatory, Perspective, Sight, Sightline, Voxpop
Vigil, Vigilant(e) Awake, Aware, Baseej, Basij, Deathwatch, Eve, Guardian angel,
Hawk-eyed, Lyke-wake, Pernoctate, Wake, Wake-rife, Wary, Watch, Waukrife,
Whitecap
Vignette Print, Profile, Sketch
Vigorous(ly), Vigour Athletic, Bant, Billy-o, Billy-oh, Birr, Blooming, Brio,
Brisk, Con brio, Cracking, Drastic, Élan, Emphatic, Energetic, Flame, Forceful,
Full-blooded, Furioso, Go, Green, Heart(y), Heterosis, Hybrid, Lush, Lustihood,
Lustique, Lusty, P, Pep, Pith, Potency, Punchy, Pzazz, Racy, Rank, Raucle, Robust,
Round, Rude, Smeddum, Spirit, Sprack, Sprag, Steam, Sthenic, Stingo, Strength,
Strong, Thews, Tireless, Tone, Tooth and nail, Trenchant, Vegete, Vim, Vitality,
Vivid, Vivo, Voema, Zip
▷ **Vigorously** *may indicate* an anagram
Viking Dane, Norseman, Rollo, R(y)urik, Sea king, Sea wolf, Varangian

Vile(ness) Base, Corrupt, Depraved, Dregs, Durance, Earthly, Infamy, Mean, Offensive, Scurvy, Vicious
Vilify Smear
Villa Bastide, Chalet, Dacha, House
Village Aldea, Auburn, Borghetto, Burg, Clachan, Corporate, Dorp, Endship, Global, Gram, Greenwich, Hamlet, Kaik, Kainga, Kampong, Kraal, Manyat(t)a, Mir, Outlet, Pit, Pueblo, Rancheria, Rancherie, Shtetl, Skara Brae, Thorp(e), Ujamaa, Vill, Wick
Villain(y) Baddy, Bluebeard, Bravo, Crim(inal), Crime, Dastard, Dog, Heavy, Iago, Knave, Macaire, Miscreant, Mohock, Nefarious, Ogre, Reprobate, Rogue, Scab, Scelerat, Scoundrel, Skelm, Tearaway, Traitor
Villein Bordar, Churl, Serf
Vim Go, Vigour, Vitality, Zing
Vincent Van Gogh
Vindicate, Vindication Absolve, Acquit, Apologia, Avenge, Clear, Compurgation, Darraign(e), Darrain(e), Darrayn, Defend, Deraign, Justify
Vindictive Hostile, Malevolent, Repay(ing), Spiteful, Vengeful
Vine(yard) Akatea, Ampelopsis, Ayahuasco, Balloon, Balsam apple, Bine, Bush rope, Château, Clinging, Clos, Colocynth, Cross, Cru, Cubeb, Cypress, Dodder, Domaine, Grapery, Hop, Idaean, Kangaroo, Kudzu, Lawyer, Liana, Martha's, Matrimony, Muskmelon, Naboth's, Potato, Puncture, Quinta, Russian, Sarsaparilla, Stephanotis, Supplejack, Swallowwort, Trumpet, Turpeth, Vitis, Winery, Wonga-wonga, Yam, Yquem
Vinegar Acetic, Acetum, Alegar, Balsam, Balsamic, Eisel(l), Esile, Malt, Oxymel, Tarragon, Wine, Wood
Vintage Classic, Crack, Cru, Old, Quality
Viol(a), Violet African, Alto, Amethyst, Archil, Crystal, Dame's, Dog, Dog's tooth, Gamba, Garden, Gentian, Gridelin, Heart's ease, Hesperis, Ianthine, Indole, Ionone, Kiss-me, Lyra, Mauve, Methyl, Neapolitan, Orchil, Pansy, Parma, Prater, Quint(e), Rock, Saintpaulia, Shrinking, Sweet, Tenor, Visual, Water
Violate, Violating, Violation Abuse, Breach, Contravene, Defile, Desecrate, Fract, Infraction, → **INFRINGE**, March-treason, Outrage, Peccant, Rape, Ravish, Solecism, Stuprate, Transgress, Trespass
Violence, Violent(ly) Acquaintance, Amain, Attentat, Bangster, Berserk, Brutal, Brute force, Drastic, Droog, Extreme, Fierce, Flagrant, Force, Frenzied, Furious, Heady, Het, High, Hot, Inbreak, Mighty, Onset, Rage, Rampage, Rampant, Rough, Rough stuff, Rude, Severe, Slap, Stormy, Strongarm, Ta(r)tar, Tearaway, Terrorism, Thuggery, Tinderbox, Tub-thumping, Vehement, Vie, Wrath
▶ **Violet** see **VIOLA**
Violin(ist), Violin-maker, Violin-shaped Alto, Amati, Cremona, Fiddle, Griddle, Gu(e), Guarneri(us), Guarnieri, Kennedy, Kit, Kubelik, Leader, Luthier, Menuhin, Nero, Oistrakh, Paganini, Pandurate, Rebeck, Rote, Stradivarius
VIP Bashaw, Bigshot, Bigwig, Brass, Cheese, Cob, Effendi, Envoy, Grandee, Imago, Kingpin, Magnate, Magnifico, Mugwump, Nabob, Nib, Nob, Pot, Snob, Someone, Swell, Tuft, Tycoon, Worthy
Viper Asp, Cerastes, Gaboon, Horned, Pit, Rattlesnake, River-jack, Russell's, Sand, Saw-scaled, → **SNAKE**, Traitor, Villain
Virago Amazon, Battle-axe, Beldam(e), Harpy, Randy, Shrew
Virgil Maro
Virgin(al), Virginity, Virgin Mary Airline, Blessed, Celibate, Chaste, Cherry, Extra, Intact, Maiden, Maidenhead, Maidenhood, May, New, Pan(h)agia, Parthenos, Pietà, Pucel(l)age, Pucelle, Pure, Queen, Snood, Tarpeia, Theotokos, Untainted, Vestal

Virginia(n) Creeper, Old Dominion, Tuckahoe, Va, Wade
Virile, Virility Energetic, Machismo, Macho, Manly, Red-blooded
Virtu Curio
Virtue(s), Virtuous, Virtual Angelic, Aret(h)a, Assay-piece, Attribute, Cardinal, Caritas, Charity, Chastity, Continent, Dharma, Efficacy, Ethical, Excellent, Faith, Fortitude, Good, Goody-goody, Grace, Hope, Justice, Moral(ity), Natural, Patience, Plaster-saint, Practical, Principal, Prudence, Qua, Say-piece, Squeaky-clean, Temperance, Theological, Upright, Worth
Virtuosity, Virtuoso Artist, Bravura, Excellence, Executant, Maestro, Paganini, Savant
Virulent Acrimonious, Deadly, Hostile, Malign, Noxious, Toxic, Vitriolic, Waspish
Virus AIDS, Antigen, Arbovirus, Bacteriophage, Boot, Capsid, Computer, Contagium, Coxsackie, Defective, EB, Ebola, Echo, Epstein-Barr, Filterable, Fowlpest, Germ, Granulosis, Hantavirus, Hendra, Herpes, HIV negative, HIV positive, Lassa, Latent, Leaf-mosaic, Lentivirus, Michelangelo, Oncogen, Parainfluenza, Parvo(virus), Pathogen, Peach-yellow, Picornavirus, Polyoma, Prophage, Reovirus, Retrovirus, Rhabdovirus, Rhinovirus, Ross River, Rotavirus, SARS, Shingles, Slow, Street, SV40, Tobacco mosaic, Varicella, Virino, Virion, Zoster
Visa Transit
Viscera Bowels, Entrails, Giblets, Guts, Harigal(d)s, Haslet, Innards, Omentum, Splanchnic, Umbles, Vitals
Viscount Vis
Viscous (liquid), Viscosity Absolute, Glaireous, Gluey, Gummy, Kinematic, Slab, Specific, Sticky, Stoke, Tacky, Tar, Thick, Thixotropic
Visible Clear, Conspicuous, Evident, Explicit, Obvious
Visigoth Asaric
Vision(ary) Aery, Aisling, Apparition, Beatific, Bourignian, Double, Dream(er), Emmetropia, Fancy, Fantast, Fey, Idealist, Illusionist, Image, Kef, Moonshine, Mouse-sight, Mystic, Ocular, Phantasm(a), Phantom, Pholism, Photism, Photopia, Rainbow-chaser, Romantic, Seeing, Seer, Sight, Stereo, Sweven, Tunnel, Twenty-twenty, Viewy
Visit(or) Affliction, Alien, Caller, Domiciliary, ET, Event, First-foot, Frequent, Gam, Guest, Habitué, Haunt, Health, Hit, Kursaal, Manuhiri, Prison, See, Sightseer, Stay, Stranger, Take
Visor, Vizor Eyeshade, Mesail, Mezail, Umbrel, Umbr(i)ere, Umbril, Vent(ayle)
Vista Enfilade, Outlook, Scene, View
Visual(ise) Envisage, Ocular, Optical, Visible
Vital(ity) Alive, Central, Critical, Crucial, Energy, Esprit, Essential, Existent, Foison, Gusto, Indispensable, Key, Kick, Life-blood, Linchpin, Lung, Mites, Momentous, Necessary, Oomph, Organ, Pizzazz, Salvation, Sap, Viable, Vigour, Zing, Zoetic
Vitals Numbles, Umbles, Viscera
Vitamin(s) A, Aneurin, Axerophthol, B, Bioflavonoid, Biotin, C, Calciferol, Calcitriol, Citrin, Cobalamin, D, E, Ergocalciferol, Folacin, H, Inositol, K, Linoleic, Menadione, Menaquinone, Niacin, P, Pan(to)thenol, Phylloquinone, Phytonadione, Pyridoxine, Retinene, Retinol, Riboflavin, Ribose, Thiamin(e), Tocopherol, Torulin, Tretinoin
Vitiate(d) Flaw(ed)
Vitreous Glassy, Hyaline
Vitriol(ic) Acid, Acrimonious, Biting, Blue, Caustic, Green, Mordant, White
Vituperate Abuse, Berate, Castigate, Censure, Defame, Inveigh, Lash, Rail, Scold
Viva Oral

Vivacity, Vivacious Animation, Brio, Esprit, Exuberant, Sparkle, Spirit, Verve
Vivid Bright, Brilliant, Dramatic, Eidetic, Fresh, Graphic, Keen, Live, Pictorial,
  Picturesque, Sharp, Violent
Vixen Catamaran, Harridan, Shrew, Virago
Viz Sc, Videlicet
Vizier Pheazar, Wazir
▶ **Vizor** *see* VISOR
Vocabulary Active, Glottochronology, Idiolect, Idioticon, Jargon, (Kata)kana,
  Lexicon, Lexis, Meta-language, Nomenclator, Passive, Wordbook
Vocal(isation), Vocalist Articulate, Doo-wop, Eloquent, Minstrel, Oral, Singer,
  Sprechgesang
Vocation Call, Career, Métier, Mission, Priesthood, Profession, Pursuit, Shop
Vociferous(ly) Clamant, Loud, Ore rotundo, Strident
Vogue Chic, Day, → FASHION, It, Mode, Rage, Style, Ton
Vogul Ugrian, Ugric
Voice(d) Active, Air, Alto, Ancestral, Bass, Chest, Contralto, Countertenor,
  Descant, Edh, Emit, Eth, Express, Falsetto, Glottis, Harp, Head, Intonate, Lyric,
  Mezzo-soprano, Mouth, Opinion, Passive, Phonic, Pipe, Presa, Quill, Say, Sonant,
  Soprano, Speak, Spinto, Sprechstimme, Steven, Syrinx, Tais(c)h, Tenor, Throat,
  Tone, → TONGUE, Treble, Utter, White
Voiceless Aphonia, Aphony, Dumb, Edh, Eth, Mute, Silent, Tacit
Void Abyss, Annul, Belch, Blank, Chasm, Counter, Defeasance, Defecate, Diriment,
  Empty, Evacuate, Gap, Hollow, Inane, Invalid, Irritate, Lapse, Nullify, Quash, Space,
  Vacuum
Volatile Excitable, Explosive, Latin, Live(ly), Mercurial, Temperamental, Terpene
Volcano(es), Volcanic Agglomerate, Black smoker, Burning mountain, Cone,
  Conic, Fumarole, Hornito, Ice, Idocrase, Igneous, Ignimbrite, Monticule, Mud,
  Obsidian, Pele, Pelée, Plinian, Pozz(u)olana, Pumice, Puzzolana, Salse, Sandblow,
  Shield, Soffioni, Solfatara, Stratovolcano, Tephra, Trass, Tuff

---

VOLCANOES

2 letters:	Okmok	El Misti	Mauna Kea
Aa	Thera	Huascan	Mauna Loa
		Iliamna	St Helena
3 letters:	*6 letters:*	Iwo Jima	St Helens
Aso	Ararat	Mofette	Taraniki
Puy	Asosan	Rotorua	Unalaska
	Azores	Ruapehu	Vesuvius
4 letters:	Egmont	Semeroe	
Etna	Erebus	St Kilda	*9 letters:*
Fuji	Ischia	Tambora	Aniakchak
Maui	Katmai		Corcovado
Taal	Kazbek	*8 letters:*	Haleakala
	Lipari	Amygdale	Helgafell
5 letters:	Semeru	Andesite	Huascaran
Askja	Tolima	Antisana	Mount Fuji
Hekla		Cameroon	Nevis Peak
Kauai	*7 letters:*	Cotopaxi	Paricutin
Mayon	Aragats	Jan Mayan	Stromboli
Misti	Comoros	Krakatoa	Tangariro

10 letters:	Mount Erebus	National Park	**17 letters:**
Chimborazo	Mount Katmai	Popocatepetl	Fernando de
Lassen Peak	Mount Kazbek		Noronha
Montserrat	Nyamuragira	**13 letters:**	Warrumbungle
Mount Eigon	Olympus Mons	Mount Demavend	Range
Mount Kenya	Pico de Teide	Mount St Helens	
Mount Pelée	Pico de Teyde		**20 letters:**
Nyiragongo		**14 letters:**	D'Entrecasteau
	12 letters:	Mount Suribachi	Islands
11 letters:	Citlaltépetl	Nevada de Colima	
Erciyas Dagi	Ixtaccahuatl	Nevada de Toluca	
Kilimanjaro	Iztaccahuatl	Soufrière Hills	

Vole Arvicola, Meadow mouse, Muskrat, Musquash, Ondatra

Volition Velleity, Will

Volley Barrage, Boom, Broadside, Platoon, Salvo, Tirade, Tire

Volt(age) BeV, Bias, Grid bias, HT

Voltaire Arouet

Volte face U-turn

Voluble Fluent, Glib

Volume Atomic, Band, Barrel, Book, Bushel, Capacity, CC, Code(x), Content, Critical, Cubage, Gallon, Hin, Loudness, Mass, Ml, Molecular, Omnibus, Peck, Pint, Quart, Quart(o), Roll, Roul(e), Size, Space, Specific, Stere, Swept, Tidal, Tom, Tome, Ullage, Vol

Voluntary, Volunteer Docent, Enlist, Fencible, Free, Free-will, Honorary, Offer, Postlude, Reformado, Spontaneous, Tender, Tennessee, Terrier, TN, Ultroneous, Yeoman

Voluptuary, Voluptuous Carnal, Hedonist, Houri, Luscious, Sensuist, Sensuous, Sybarite

Volute Helix, Roll

Vomit(ing) Anacatharsis, Barf, Black, Boak, Boke, Cascade, Cat, Chuck up, Chunder, Disgorge, Egist, Egurgitate, Emesis, Fetch-up, Haematemesis, Honk, Keck, Kotch, Parbreak, Posset, Puke, Ralph, Regorge, Regurgitate, Retch, Rolf, Spew, Technicolour yawn, Throw up, Upchuck

Voodoo Charm, Jettatura, Kurdaitcha, Macumba, Mambo, Obeah, Sorcery, Zombi(e)

Voracious, Voracity Bulimia, Edacity, Gluttony, Greed, Ravenous, Serrasalmo

Vortex Charybdis, Eddy, Gyre, Trailing, Whirlpool

Votary Adherent, Cenobite, Devotee, Disciple, Fan, Nun, Swinger, Zealot

Vote(r), Votes, Voting Alternative, Assentor, Aye, Ballot, Block, Card, Casting, Choose, Colonist, Coopt, Cross, Crossover, Cumulative, Division, Donkey, Fag(g)ot, Floating, Franchise, Free, Grey, Informal, Mandate, Nay, Negative, No, Opt, People, Placet, Plebiscite, Plump, Plural, Poll, Postal, Pot-wabbler, Pot-waller, Pot-walloner, Pot-walloper, Pot-wobbler, PR, Preferential, Proportional representation, Qualified majority, Referendum, Return, Scrutin de liste, Scrutiny, Show of hands, Side, Single transferable, Straw(-poll), Suffrage, Swinging, Tactical, Ten-pounder, Theta, Ticket, Token, Transferable, Voice, X, Yea, Yes

Vote-catcher Pork

Vouch(er), Vouchsafe Accredit, Assure, Attest, Beteem(e), Book token, Chit, Coupon, Endorse, Gift, Guarantee, Luncheon, Meal-ticket, Receipt, Ticket, Token, Warrant

Voussoir Quoin, Wedge

Vow Baptismal, Behight, Behot(e), Earnest, Ex voto, Hecht, Hest, I do, Nuncupate, → OATH, Pledge, Plight, Promise, Simple, Solemn, Swear, Troth, Vum

Vowel(s) Ablaut, Anaptyxis, Aphesis, Breve, Cardinal, Diphthong, Gradation, Indeterminate, Monophthong, Mutation, Point, Rhyme, S(c)hwa, Seg(h)ol, Svarabhakti, Triphthong

Voyage(r) Anson, Course, Cruise, Launch, Maiden, Passage, Peregrinate, Sinbad, Travel

Voyeur Scopophiliac

VTOL Convertiplane

Vulcan(ite) Blacksmith, Ebonite, Fire, Mulciber, Spock, Wayland

Vulgar(ian) Banausic, Barbaric, Base, Blatant, Blue, Brassy, Buffoon, Canaille, Cheap, Cit, Coarse, Common, Crude, Demotic, Flash, Forward, Gaudy, General, Gent, Gross, Heel, Hussy, Ignorant, Indecent, Laddish, Lavatorial, Lewd, Low(-life), Naff, Obscene, Ostentatious, Pandemian, Plebby, Plebeian, Popular, Proletarian, Raffish, Riff-raff, Rude, Scaff, Scurrilous, Tacky, Tawdry, Threepenny, Tiger, Tink, Upstart, Vulg

Vulnerable Exposed, Open, Susceptible, Unguarded, Wide-open

Vulture Aasvogel, Bearded, Bird, Buzzard, California (condor), Condor, Culture, Falcon, Gallinazo, Gier, Griffon, Gripe, Grype, King, Lammergeier, Lammergeyer, Ossifrage, Predator, Turkey, Urubu, Zopilote

Ww

W Watt, West, Whisky, Women
Wad(ding) Batt(ing), Lump, Pad, Pledget, Roll, Swab, Wodge
Waddle Toddle, Waggle
Waddy Club, Cowboy, Stick
Wade(r), Wading Antigropelo(e)s, Curlew, Dikkop, Egret, Flamingo, Gallae,
Godwit, Grallatorial, Greenshank, Gumboot, Heron, Ibis, Jacksnipe, Limpkin,
Oyster-catcher, Paddle, Phalarope, Plodge, Sarus, Seriema, Shoebill, Splodge,
Stilt(bird), Terek, Virginia
Waesucks Ewhow, O(c)hone
Wafer Biscuit, Cracker, Crisp, Gaufer, Gaufre, Gofer, Gopher, Host, Papad, Seal
Waff Flap, Flutter, Wave
Waffle Adlib, Blather, Equivocate, Gas, Gaufer, Gaufre, Gofer, Gopher, Hedge,
Poppycock, Prate, Rabbit
Waft(ing) Airborne, Aura, Blow, Drift, Float
Wag(gish), Waggle Arch, Card, Comedian, Facetious, Joker, Lick, Niddle-noddle,
Nod, Rogue, Shake, Sway, Wit(snapper), Wobble
Wage(s) Ante, Award, Fee, Hire, Income, Living, Meed, Minimum, Nominal, Pay,
Portage, Practise, Prosecute, Rate, Salary, Screw, Subsistence
Wage-earner Breadwinner, Employee, Proletariat(e)
Wager Ante, Back, → BET, Gamble, Lay, Pascal's, Stake, Wed
Wagon(er) Ar(a)ba, Aroba, Boötes, Boxcar, Brake, Break, Buck, Buckboard, Buggy,
Caisson, Carriage, Cart, Cattle truck, Chuck, Coachman, Cocopan, Conestoga,
Corf, Covered, Democrat, Dray, Flatcar, Fourgon, Gambo, Go-cart, Hopper, Hutch,
Low-loader, Mammy, Paddy, Palabra, Patrol, Plaustral, Police, Prairie schooner,
Rave, Reefer, Rubberneck, Shandry, Station, Tank, Tartana, Telega, Tender, Trap,
Trekker, Truck, Van, Victoria, Wain, Water
Waif Arab, Foundling, Jetsam, Stray, Urchin, Victoria, Wastrel, Water, Weft
Wail(er) Banshee, Bawl, Blubber, Howl, Keen, Lament, Moan, Skirl, Threnody,
Threnos, Ululate, Vagitus, Wah-wah, Yammer
Wain Cart, Dray, Wagon
Waist(band) Belt, Cummerbund, Girdlestead, Girth, Hour-glass, Middle, Midship,
Obi, Sash, Shash, Wasp, Zoster
Waistcoat Gilet, Jerkin, Lorica, MB, Pressure, Sayon, Shawl, Vest, Weskit
Wait(er), Waiting Abid(e), Ambush, Barista, Bide, Busboy, Butler, Buttle, Carhop,
Commis, Cupbearer, Dally, Delay, Estragon, Expect, Flunkey, Frist, Garçon, Hang
on, Hesitate, Hover, Interval, Khidmutgar, Lead time, Lime, Linger, Lurch, Maître
d', Maître d'hôtel, Minority, Omnibus, Pannier, Pause, Pozzo, Remain, Serve(r),
Sommelier, Stacking, Stay, Steward, Suspense, Taihoa, Tarry, Tend(ance), Tray,
Vladimir, Wine, Won
Waitress Hebe, Miss, Mousme(e), Nippy, Server
Waive Abandon, Defer, Forgo, Overlook, Postpone, Relinquish, Renounce

Wake(n) Abrade, Abraid, Abray, Aftermath, Alert, American, Animate, Arouse, Astern, Deathwatch, Excite, Hereward, Keen, Knock-up, Like, Lyke, Prod, Rear, → ROUSE, Train, Wash
Waldo Emerson
Wale(r) Prop, Ridge, Weal
Wales Cambria, Cymru, Dyfed, Principality
Walk(er), Walking, Walkabout, Walkway Alameda, Alley, Alure, Amble, Ambulate, Arcade, Berceau, Birdcage, Charity, Cloister, Clump, Constitutional, Daddle, Dander, Dauner, Emu, Esplanade, EVA, Expatiate, Flânerie, Frescade, Gait, Gallery, Ghost, Go, Gradient, Gressorial, Heel and toe, Hike, Hookey, Hump, Lambeth, Leg, Lumber, Mainstreeting, Mall, March, Mince, Mosey, Pace, Pad, Pasear, Paseo, Passage, Path, Ped, Perambulate, Pergola, Perp, Pipe-opener, Pound, Power, Prance, Prom(enade), Rack, Ramble, Rampart, Random, Ring, Routemarch, Sashay, Shamble, Sidle, Slommock, Space, Spanish, Sponsored, Stalk, Step, Striddle, Stroll, Strut, Stump, Terrace, Toddle, Tramp, Trash, Travolator, Tread, Trog, Truck, Trudge, Turn, Wade, Wend, Widow's, Xyst
Walk-over Doddle, Pie, Scratch
Wall Antonine, Bail, Bailey, Barrier, Berlin, Berm, Cavity, Cell, Chinese, Climbing, Countermure, Crib, Curtain, Dado, Dam, Dike, Dry-stone, Enceinte, Epispore, Exine, Fail-dike, Fourth, Fronton, Frustule, Gable, Great, Hadrian's, Hanging, Hangman, Head, Immure, Intine, Mahjongg, Mani, Merlon, Myocardium, Non-bearing, Parapet, Parietal, Parie(te)s, Parpane, Parpen(d), Parpent, Parpoint, Partition, Party, Peribolos, Pericarp, Perpend, Perpent, Pleuron, Podium, Puteal, Qibla, Retaining, Revet(ment), Ring, River, Roman, Roughcast, Sea, Septum, Severus, Side, Somatopleure, Spandrel, Spandril, Street, Studding, Tambour, Tariff, Trumeau, Vallation, Vallum, Video, Wa', Wailing, Western, Withe, Zooecia
Wallaby Brusher, Dama, Kangaroo, Pad(d)ymelon, Pademelon, Quokka, Tammar, Whiptail
Wallah Competition
Wallaroo Euro
Wall-covering, Wallpaper Anaglypta®, Arras, Burlap, Flock, Lincrusta, Paper, Tapestry, Tapet
Waller Fats, Mason
Wallet Billfold, Case, Flybook, Folder, Notecase, Pochette, Pocket-book, Purse, Scrip
Wallflower Crucifer, Dowd(y), Pariah
Wall-game Eton, Mahjongg
Wallop Bash, Baste, Batter, Beat, Biff, Clout, Cob, → HIT, Lam, Lounder, Polt, Pound, Slog, Strap, Swinge, Tan, Tat, Trounce
Wallow(ing) Bask, Flounder, Luxuriate, Revel, Roll, Splash, Swelter, Tolter, Volutation, Welter
Wall-painting Fresco, Graffiti, Grisaille
▶ **Wallpaper** see WALL-COVERING
Wall-plate Tassel, Torsel
Wall-support Beam, Foundation, Pier, Rear-arch, Rere-arch
Wally Dipstick, Prat
Walnut Black, Butternut, Hickory, Juglans, Satin, White
Walrus Morse, Moustache, Pinniped, Rosmarine, Sea-horse, Tash
Walter Bruno, Mitty, Pater, Scott
Waltz Anniversary, Blue Danube, Boston, Concert, Dance, Hesitation, Rotate, Valse
Wampum Peag(e), Shell-money

Wan Lurid, Pale, Pallid, Pasty, Sanguine, Sorry

Wanchancy Unlucky

Wand Baton, Caduceus, Rod, Runic, Stick, Thyrse, Thyrsus, Vara, Vare

Wander(er), Wandering Aberrance, Amble, Bedouin, Berber, Bum, Caird, Daiker, Delirious, Desultory, Deviate, Digress, Divagate, Drift, Errant, Estray, Evagation, Excursive, Expatiate, Extravagate, Gad(about), Grope, Hobo, Jew, Landloper, Maunder, Meander, Meandrian, Mill, Mither, Moider, Moither, Moon, Nomad(e), Odysseus, Pedder, Peregrine, Peripatetic, Polar, Rache, Ramble, Range, Ratch, Roamer, Romany, Room, Rove, Solivagant, Stooge, Straggle, Stravaig, Stray, Strayve, Streel, Stroam, Stroll, Swan, Ta(i)ver, Tramp, Troll, Truant, Tuareg, Vagabond, Vagile, Vagrant, Vague, Waif, Wend, Wheel, Wilder, Wolves

▷ **Wandering** *may indicate* an anagram

Wane Decline, Decrease, Diminish, Ebb

Wangle Arrange, Finagle, Trick

Want(ing), Wants Absence, Conative, Covet, Crave, Dearth, Defect, Deficient, Derth, Desiderata, → **DESIRE**, Destitution, Envy, Hardship, Indigent, Itch, Lack, Long, Mental, Moldwarp, Mole, Need, Penury, Require, Scarceness, Scarcity, Shortfall, Shy, Void, Wish, Yen

Wanton(ness) Bona-roba, Cadgy, Chamber, Cocotte, Colt's tooth, Deliberate, Demirep, Filly, Flirt-gill, Gammerstang, Giglet, Giglot, Gillflirt, Hussy, Jay, Jezebel, Jillflirt, Lewd, Licentious, Loose, Nice, Protervity, Rig, Roué, Slut, Smicker, Sportive, Sybarite, Toyish, Twigger, Unchaste, Wayward

Wap Blow, Knock, Strike

War(fare), Wars American Civil, American Independence, Ares, Armageddon, Arms, Asymmetrical, Attrition, Bacteriological, Barons', Bate, Battle, Biological, Bishop, Chemical, Civil, Clash, Class, Cod, Cold, Combat, Conflict, Crescentade, Crimean, Crusade, Electronic, Emergency, Feud, → **FIGHT**, Flame, Food, Franco-Prussian, Fray, Germ, Gigantomachy, Great, Guer(r)illa, Gulf, Holy, Hostilities, Hot, Hundred Years', Information, Internecine, Jehad, Jenkins' ear, Jihad, Jugurthine, Korean, Krieg, Limited, Mars, Mexican, Napoleonic, Nuclear, Opium, Peasants', Peloponnesian, Peninsular, Phony, Price, Private, Psychological, Punic, Push-button, Queen Anne's, Rebellion, Revolutionary, Roses, Russo-Japanese, Secession, Seven against Thebes, Seven Years', Shooting, Six Day, Social, Spam, Spanish-American, Spanish Civil, Star, Stoush, Sword, Terrapin, Theomachy, Thirty Years', Total, Trench, Trojan, Turf, Vietnam, Winter, World, Yom Kippur

Warble(r) Carol, Cetti's, Chiff-chaff, Chirl, Fauvette, Peggy, Record, Rel(l)ish, Trill, Vibrate, Yodel, Yodle

War-chant, War-cry Alalagmos, Haka, Slogan

Ward (off) Artemus, Averruncate, Avert, Care, Casual, Casualty, Charge, Defend, District, Fend, Guard, Hand-off, Maternity, Nightingale, Oppose, Parry, Protégé, Pupil, Soc, Soken, Vintry, Wear, Weir

Warden Caretaker, Concierge, Constable, Crossing, Curator, Custodian, Game, Guardian, Keeper, Maori, Meter maid, Pear, Provost, Ranger, Septimus, Spooner, Steward, Traffic, Way

Warder Beefeater, Gaoler, Guardian, Keeper, Provost, Screw, Turnkey, Twirl

Wardrobe Almirah, Capsule, Closet, Clothes, Garderobe, Outfit, Vestuary

Ware(s) Arretine, Basalt, Beware, Biscuit, Cameo, Canton, Chelsea, China, Etruria, Faience, Goods, Jasper, Lustre, Merchandise, Palissy, Queen's, Samian, Sanitary, Satsuma, Shippo, Truck, Wemyss

Warehouse Bonded, Data, Depository, Entrepôt, Freight-shed, Go-down, Hong, Store

▶ **Warfare** *see* **WAR**
War-game Kriegs(s)piel
War-god Ares, Mars, Tiu, Tiw, Tyr
Warhead Atomic, Supremo
Warhorse Charger, Destrier, Fighter
Wariness, Wary Ca'canny, Cagey, Careful, Cautel, Caution, Chary, Discreet,
  Distrust, Guarded, Leery, Mealy-mouthed, Prudent, Sceptical, Suspicious, Tentie,
  Tenty, Vigilant
Warlike Battailous, Bellicose, Gung-ho, Lachlan, Martial, Militant
Warlord Haw-haw, Kitchener, Shogun
Warm(er), Warming, Warmth Abask, Admonish, Air, Ardour, Balmy, British,
  Calefacient, Calid(ity), Cardigan, Chambré, Cordial, Empressement, Enchafe,
  Fervour, Foment, Gemütlich, Genial, Global, Glow, → **HEAT**, Hot, Incalescent,
  Kang, Lew, Logic, Loving, Muff, Muggy, Mull, Radiator, Tepid, Thermal, Toast,
  Toasty
Warm-blooded Homothermal, Homothermic, Homothermous, Idiothermous
Warmonger Hawk
Warn(ing) Admonish, Alarum, Alert, Amber, Aposematic, Apprise, Beacon,
  Beware, Bleep, Buoy, Caution, Caveat, Caveat emptor, Commination, Cone,
  Counsel, Document, Early, En garde, Example, Foghorn, Fore, Foretoken, Gardyloo,
  Garnishment, Griffin, Harbinger, Hazchem, Heads up, Hoot, Horn, Klaxon, Larum,
  Lesson, Light, Maroon, Monition, Nix, Nota bene, Notice, Omen, Pi-jaw, Portent,
  Premonitory, Presage, Prodromal, Profit, Protevangelium, Riot Act, Rumble strip,
  Scaldings, Scarborough, Sematic, Shore, Signal, Storm, Tattler, Threat, Timber,
  Tip-off, Token, Vigia, Vor, Yellow card
Warner Alarm, Fore, Plum, Siren
Warp(ed) Bias, Buckle, Cast, Contort, Distort, Kam, Kedge, Pandation, Time, Twist,
  Weft
Warpath Rampage
▷ **Warped** *may indicate* an anagram
Warrant(y) Able, Authorise, Behight, Behote, Bench, Caption, Certificate, Death,
  Detainer, Distress, Fiat, Fiaunt, Fugle, General, Guarantee, Justify, Mittimus, Peace,
  Permit, Precept, Reprieve, Royal, Search, Sepad, Special, Swear, Transire, Vouch,
  Warn
Warren Burrow, Colony, Hastings, Rabbit
Warrior Achilles, Agamemnon, Ajax, Amazon, Anzac, Berserk(er), Brave, Cold,
  Cossack, Crusader, Eorl, Fianna, Fighter, Finlay, Finley, Geronimo, Ghazi, Heimdall,
  Housecarl, Impi, Lewis, Louis, Myrmidon, Nestor, Rainbow, Rajpoot, Rajput,
  Roger, Samurai, Soldier, Tatar, Unknown, Warhorse, Warwolf, Zulu
Warship Battleship, Castle, Cog, Corvette, Cruiser, Destroyer, Drake, Dromon(d),
  Frigate, Invincible, Man-o-war, Mine-layer, Monitor, Privateer, Ram, Repulse,
  Wooden Walls
Wart(y) Anbury, Angleberry, Blemish, Keratose, Muricate, Plantar, Tuberous,
  Verruca, Wen
Warwick Kingmaker
▶ **Wary** *see* **WARINESS**
Was Erat, Existed, Lived, Past
Wash(ed), Washer, Washing (up), Wash out Ablution, Affusion, Alluvion,
  Bath, Bay(e), Bidet, Bubble-dancing, Bur(r), Calcimine, Circlip, Clean(se), Cradle, D,
  Dashwheel, Dele(te), Dip, Edulcorate, Elute, Elutriate, Enema, Erode, Fen, Flush,
  Freshen, Gargle, Grommet, Grummet, Irrigate, Kalsomine, Lap, → **LAUNDER**,

Lavabo, Lave, Leather, Lip, Lotion, Marsh, Maundy, Mop, Nipter, Pan, Pigswill,
Poss, Purify, Rinse, Sapple, Scrub, Shampoo, Shim, Sind, Sloosh, Sluice, Soogee,
Soojee, Soojey, Squeegie, Stream, Sujee, Swab, Synd, Syne, Tie, Toilette, Top and
tail, Twin tub, Tye, Wake, Wudu, Yellow
Washbasin, Washtub, Washhouse Copper, Lavabo, Steamie
Washerman, Washerwoman Dhobi, Laundress
Washington Wa
Wasn't Nas, Wasna
Wasp(ish) Appledrain, Bembex, Bink, Bite, Chalcid, Cuckoo-fly, Cynipidae,
Cynips, Digger, European, Fig, Fretful, Gall(-fly), Gold, Hornet, Horntail,
Hoverfly, Irritable, Marabunta, Mason, Miffy, Muddauber, Paper, Peevish,
Pompilid, Potter, Ruby-tail, Sand, Seed, Solitary, Spider, Syrphus, Velvet ant,
Vespa, Wood, Yellow jacket
▷ **Wasp** *may indicate* a rugby player
Wasp's nest Bike, Bink, Byke
Wassail Carouse, Pledge, Toast
Wast Wert
Wastage, Waste(d), Wasting, Wasteful, Wasteland Amyotrophy, Atrophy,
Blow, Blue, Boondoggle(r), Cesspit, Cirrhosis, Consume, Contabescent, Coom(b),
Cotton, Crud, Culm, Decay, Dejecta, Desert, Detritus, Devastate, Dilapidate,
Dissipate, Dross, Dung, Dwindle, Dwine, Dystrophy, Effluent, Egesta, Emaciate,
Erode, Estrepe, Excrement, Exhaust, Expend, Exudate, Faeces, Flue, Forpine,
Fribble, Fritter, Garbage, Gash, Gob, Gunge, Haggard, Havoc, Hazardous,
High-level, Husk, Knub, Lavish, Loose, Lose, Loss, Low-level, Marasmus, Merino,
Misspent, Moor, Moulder, Muir, Mullock, Mungo, Natural, Novalia, Nub, Nuclear,
Offal, Oller, Ordure, Pellagra, Phthisis, Pigswill, Pine, Prodigalise, Radioactive,
Rammel, Rank and manger, Ravage, Recrement, Red mud, Red tape, → **REFUSE**,
Reif, Rubble, Ruderal, Schappe, Scissel, Scoria, Scrap, Sewage, Slag, Slurry, Spend,
Spill, Spoil(age), Squander, Sullage, Syntexis, Tabes, Tailing, Thin, Thwaite, Ureal,
Urine, Uropoiesis, Vast, Wanze, Wear, Wilderness, Yearn
▷ **Wasted** *may indicate* an anagram
Wastrel Idler, Profligate, Scattergood, Spend-all, Spendthrift, Stalko, Vagabond
Watch(er) Accutron®, Analog(ue), Analogon, Argus, Await, Bark, Behold, Bird-dog,
Black, Clock, Coastguard, Cock-crow, Digital, Dog, Eryl, Espy, Eyeball, Fob, Glom,
Gregory, Guard, Half-hunter, Huer, Hunter, Kettle, Latewake, Lever, Lo, Look,
Look-out, Middle, Monitor, Morning, Nark, Neighbourhood, Night, Nit, Note,
Nuremberg egg, Observe, Overeye, Patrol, Pernoctation, Posse, Quartz, Regard,
Repeater, Rolex®, Scout, Sentinel, Sentry, Shadow, Spectate, Spotter, Stemwinder,
Suicide, Surveillance, Tend, Ticker, Timekeeper, Timepiece, Timer, Tompion, Tout,
Turnip, Vedette, → **VIGIL**, Voyeur, Wait, Wake, Weather eye, Wrist(let)
Watch-chain Albert, Slang
Watch-control Escapement
Watchful(ness) Alert, Aware, Care, Dragon, Ira, Jealous, Vigilant, Wakerife, Wary,
Waukrife
Watchman Argus, Bellman, Charley, Charlie, Chok(e)y, Cho(w)kidar, Guard,
Sentinel, Sentry, Speculator, Tompion, Viewer
Watch-tower Atalaya, Barbican, Beacon, Mirador, Sentry-go
Watchword Cry, Password, Shibboleth, Slogan
Water(ed), Waters, Watery Adam's ale, Adam's wine, Aerated, Amrit,
Apollinaris, Aq(ua), Aquatic, Aqueous, Barley, Bayou, Bedabble, Bilge, Bound,
Branch, Brine, Broads, Brook, Burn, Canal, Cancer, Chresard, Chuck, Cold,

Compensation, Conductivity, Connate, Dead, Deaw, Deg, Demersal, Dew, Dill,
Dilute, Dribble, Drinking, Eau, Ebb, Echard, Element, Ennerdale, Epilimnion,
Euphotic, Evian®, First, Flood, Ford, Fossil, Functional, Gallise, Gallize, Ganga
jal, Grey, Gripe, Ground, Hard, Heavy, Hectum, Hellespont, High, Holy, Hot,
Hungary, Hydatoid, Irrigate, Javel(le), Kuroshio, Kyle, Lagoon, Lagune, Lake, Lant,
Laurel, Lavender, Leachate, Lentic, Light, Limnology, Lithia, Loch(an), Lode, Lotic,
Lough, Low, Lubricated, Lymph, Melt, Meteoric, Mineral, Miner's inch, Moiré,
Mother, Nappe, North, Oasis®, Oedema, Overfall, Pani, Pawnee, Pee, Perrier®,
Phreatic, Pisces, Polly, Polynia, Polynya, Poppy, Potash, Potass, Pump, Purest,
Quick, Quinine, Rain, Rapids, Rate, Reach, Rice, Rip, Riverine, Rose, Running,
Runny, Rydal, Saltchuck, Scorpio, Sea, Seltzer, Sera, Serous, Serum, Shoal, Shower,
Simpson, Skinkling, Slack, Slick, Sluice, Soda, Sodden, Soft, Solent, Sound, Souse,
Southampton, Stream, Surface, Tabby, Table, Tam, Tap, Tar, Territorial, Thin, Tide,
Toilet, Tonic, Urine, Utility, Vadose, Vichy, Viscous, Vlei, Vly, Wai, Wash(y), Weak,
Wee, Whey, White, White coal, Wild, Wishy-washy
Waterbaby Moses, Tom
Water-boa Anaconda
Water-boatman Notonecta
Water-brash Pyrosis
Water-buckets Noria
Water-carrier Aqueduct, Bheestie, Bheesty, Bhistee, Bhisti, Bucket, Carafe, Chatty,
Furphy, Hose, Hydra, Hydria, Kirbeh, Pail, Pitcher, Rigol
Water-chestnut Saligot
Water-colour Aquarelle, Painting, Pastel, RI
Water-course Arroyo, Billabong, Canal, Ditch, Dyke, Falaj, Furrow, Gutter, Khor,
Lead, Leat, Nala, Nalla(h), Nulla, Nullah, Rean, Rhine, Riverway, Shott, Spruit,
Wadi, Whelm
Watercress Nasturtium
Water-device Shadoof, Shaduf
Water-diviner Dowser, Hydrostat
Waterfall Angel (Falls), Cataract, Churchill, Chute, Cuquenan, Force, Foss, Iguaçú,
Kabiwa, Kaieteur, Kile, Lasher, Lin(n), Mardel, Mtarazi, Niagara, Overfall, Rapid,
Salmon leap, Sault, Sutherland, Takakkaw, Tugela, Victoria, Yellowstone, Yosemite
Water-fern Marsilea, Salvinia
Water-gate Penstock, Sluice, Sluse
Water-god Aleion, Aleyin, Alpheus
Water-hen Gallinule
Water-hole Bore, Gilgai, Oasis
Water-lily Lotus, Nenuphar, Nuphar, Spatterdock, Victoria
Waterloo Rout
Waterman Aquarius, Bargee, Ferryman, Oarsman
Water-monster Nicker
Water-nymph Kelpie, Kelpy, Naiad, Ondine, Rusalka
Water-parsnip Sium, Skirret
Water-plant Alisma, Aquatic, Cress, Crowfoot, Elodea, Gulfweed, Lace-leaf,
Lattice-leaf, Nelumbo, Nenuphar, Nuphar, Ouvirandra, Pontederia, Quillwort,
Reate, Sea-mat, Sedge, Seg, Stratiotes, Urtricularia, Vallisneria
Waterproof, Water-tight Caisson, Camlet, Caulk, Cerecloth, Cofferdam,
Corfam®, Dampcourse, Dubbin(g), Groundsheet, Loden, Mac, Mino, Oilers,
Oilskin, Pay, Seaworthy, Stank, Sta(u)nch, Tarp, Waders
Water-rat Arvicola, Musk-rat, Ratty, Vole

Watershed Divide, Hilltop
Water-spout Gargoyle, Geyser, Hurricano
Water-sprite Kelpie, Kelpy, Nix(ie), Nixy, Tangie, Undine, Water-nymph
Water supply Dewpond, H, Hydrant, Spring, Tank, Tap
Waterway Aqueduct, Billabong, Canal, Channel, Creek, Culvert, Ditch, Igarapé, Illinois, Intracoastal, Lode, River, St Lawrence Seaway, Sny(e), Sound, Straight, Suez
Water-wheel Noria, Pelton, Sakia, Saki(y)eh
Wattle(s) Acacia, Boobialla, Boree, Dewlap, Gills, Golden, Mimosa, Mulga, Sallow, Savanna, Snot
Wave(s), Waved, Wavelength, Wavy Alfven, Alpha, Beachcomber, Beam, Beck, Beta, Billow, Bore, Bow, Brain, Brandish, Breaker, Carrier, Circular polarisation, Clapotis, Cold, Comber, Complex, Continuous, Crenulate, Crest, Crime, Crimp, Crispate, Cymotrichous, De Broglie, Decuman, Delta, Dominant, Dumper, Electromagnetic, Finger, Flap, Flaunt, Float, Flote, Flourish, Gesticulate, Gravitational, Gravity, Graybeard, Ground, Groundswell, Gyrose, Harmonic, Haystack, Head sea, Heat, Hertzian, Internal, Ionospheric, Lee, Long, Longitudinal, Marcel, Matter, Medium, Mexican, Nebule, New, Oundy, Peristalsis, Perm(anent), Plunger, Primary, Pulse, Radar, Radiation, Radio, Rayleigh, Repand, Rip, Ripple, Roller, Rooster, Sastrugi, Scrub, Sea, Secondary, Seiche, Seismic, Shake, Shock, Short, Sine, Sinuate, Sky, Snaky, Soliton, Sound, Spiller, Square, Squiggle, Standing, Stationary, Stream, Supplementary, Surf, Surge, Sway, Tabby, Theta, Third, Thought, Tidal, Tidal bore, Tide, Train, Transverse, Travelling, Tsunami, Ultrasonic, Undate, Unde, Undulate, Vermicular, Waffle, Waft, Wag, Waive, Wash, Waw, Wawe, Whitecap, White-horse, Wigwag
▷ **Wave(s)** *may indicate* an anagram
Wave-band Channel
Wave-detector Coherer
Wavelength Band, Complementary, De Broglie, Ultrashort
Waver(ing), Waverer Dither, Falter, Flag, Gutter, Halt, Hesitate, Oscillate, Stagger, Sway, Swither, Teeter, Trimmer, Vacillate, Waffle, Wet, Wow
Wax(ed), Waxing, Waxy Adipocere, Ambergris, Appal, Bate, Bees, Bone, Brazilian, Candelilla, Carna(h)uba, Cere, Ceresin, Cerumen, Chinese, Cobbler's, Cutin, Earth, Effuse, Enseam, Ethal, Geraldton, Gr(e)aves, Grow, Heelball, Honeycomb, Increase, Increscent, Inseam, Ire, Japan, Kiss, Lecithin, Lipide, Livid, Lost, Lyrical, Mineral, Montan, Mummy, Myrtle, Ozocerite, Ozokerite, Paraffin, Parmacitie, Pela, Petroleum, Propolis, Pruina, Rage, Seal, Sealing, Spermaceti, Suberin, Tallow, Tantrum, Temper, Toxaphene, Vegetable, White, Yielding
Waxwing Cedar-bird, Icarus
Way(s), Wayside Access, Agate, Appian, Autobahn, Avenue, Borstal(l), Budo, Bypass, Companion, Course, Crescent, Defile, Direction, Door, Draw, E, Each, Entrance, Family, Fashion, Flaminian, Foss(e), Gate, Habit, Hatch, Hedge, High, Hither, How, Icknield, Lane, Manner, Means, Method, Milky, MO, Mode, Modus, N, Pass, Path, Pennine, Permanent, Pilgrim's, Procedure, Railroad, Regimen, Ridge, → **ROAD**, Route, S, Sallypost, St(reet), Style, System, Taoism, Technique, Third, Thoroughfare, Thus, Trace, Trail, Troade, Turnpike, Underpass, Untrodden, Via, W, Wise
Wayfarer Commuter, Piepowder, Pilgrim, Traveller, Voyager
Waylay Accost, Ambuscade, Ambush, Beset, Bushwhack, Buttonhole, Molest, Obstruct, Stick up
Way-out Advanced, Bizarre, Egress, Esoteric, Exit, Exotic, Extreme, Offbeat, Trendy

Wayward Capricious, Disobedient, Errant, Erratic, Loup-the-dyke, Obstreperous, Perverse, Stray, Unruly, Wilful

We I and I, Oo, Royal, Us

Weak(er), Weaken(ing), Weakest, Weakness Achilles' heel, Acrasia, Antimnemonic, Aphesis, Appair, Appal, Arsis, Asthenia, Attenuate, Blot, Brickle, Brittle, Cachexia, Cataplexy, Chink, Cripple(d), Debile, Debilitate, Decrease, Delay, Delicate, Dilute, Disable, Effete, Emasculate, Enervate, Enfeeble, Entender, Fade, Faible, Failing, Faint, Fatigue, Feeble, Fissile, Flag, Flaw, Flimsy, Foible, Fragile, Frail(tee), Frailty, Give, Gone, Ham, Hamartia, Helpless, Honeycomb, Impair, Impotence, Infirm, Knock-kneed, Labefaction, Lassitude, Leptosomatic, Low, Low ebb, Meagre, Mild, Milk and water, Myasthenia, Namby-pamby, Pale, Pall, Paraparesis, Paresis, Penchant, Puny, Push-over, Pusillanimous, Reckling, Reduce, Simp, Slack, Soft spot, Tenuous, Thesis, Thin, Thready, Tottery, Unable, Underdog, Undermine, Unnerve, Unstable, Vapid, Velleity, Vessel, Vulnerability, W, Washy, Water(y), Wish(y)-wash(y), Wuss(y)

Weakling Dilling, Drip, Milksop, Nerd, Nisgul, Reed, Softie, Wuss

Weal Ridge, Stripe, Urticant, Wealth, Welfare, Welt, Whelk

Wealth(y) Abundance, Affluence, Bullion, Croesus, Digerati, Ease, Fat-cat, Fortune, Golconda, Jet-set, Klondike, Klondyke, Load(sa), Loaded, Loadsamoney, Lolly, Mammon, Means, Mine, Mint, Moneyed, Nabob, Opulence, Ore, Pelf, Plutocrat, Reich, Rich, Ritzy, Solid, Substance, Treasure, Trustafarian, Untold, Well-heeled, Well-off, Well-to-do

Wean Ablactation, Bairn, Spain, Spane, Spean

Weapon(s) Ammo, Arm, Arsenal, Assault, Binary, Deterrent, Greek fire, Hoplology, Long-range, Missile, Munition, Nuclear, Nuke, Theatre, Tool, Traditional

---

WEAPONS

2 letters:	*5 letters:*	*6 letters:*	Tombco
V1	Arrow	Airgun	Voulge
	Baton	Cestus	
3 letters:	Blade	Cohorn	*7 letters:*
Axe	Estoc	Creese	Arblast
Dag	Flail	Cudgel	Assegai
Gad	Knife	Dagger	Ataghan
	Kukri	Dragon	Bayonet
4 letters:	Lance	Duster	Bazooka
Bill	Lathi	Gingal	Blowgun
Bolo	Maxim	Glaive	Bondook
Bomb	Orgue	Jingal	Caliver
Club	Pilum	Katana	Caltrap
Cosh	Rifle	Lathee	Caltrop
Dart	Sabre	Mauser®	Carbine
Gade	Saker	Mortar	Chopper
Gaid	Spear	Musket	Coehorn
Kris	Staff	Onager	Cutlass
Mere	Stick	Pistol	Dragoon
Pike	Sting	Rapier	Enfield
Spat	Sword	Sparke	Fougade
Sten	Taser®	Sparth	Gingall
	Vouge	Taiaha	Gisarme

Grenade	Bludgeon	**9 letters:**	Smallsword
Halberd	Calthrop	Arquebuse	Swordstick
Halbert	Catapult	Backsword	Throw-stick
Harpoon	Culverin	Battleaxe	
Hatchet	Elf-arrow	Boomerang	**11 letters:**
Javelin	Fougasse	Catchpole	Morgenstern
Longbow	Howitzer	Chainshot	Snickersnee
Machete	Mangonel	Derringer	
Matchet	Nunchaku	Doodlebug	**12 letters:**
Petrary	Partisan	Excalibur	Flamethrower
Poleaxe	Petronel	Flintlock	Quarterstaff
Sandbag	Revolver	Forty-five	
Shotgun	Scimitar	Harquebus	**13 letters:**
Sidearm	Scorpion	Sarbacane	Knuckleduster
Torpedo	Shuriken	Slingshot	Life-preserver
Trident	Skean-dhu	Sword cane	Manrikigusari
	Skene-dhu	Trebuchet	
8 letters:	Spontoon	Truncheon	**14 letters:**
Alderman	Stiletto		Nunchaku sticks
Arbalest	Stinkpot	**10 letters:**	
Armalite®	Tomahawk	Broadsword	
Arquebus	Whirl-bat	Knobkerrie	
Ballista	Whorl-bat	Pea-shooter	
Blowpipe	Yataghan	Shillelagh	

Wear(ing), Wear Out Abate, Ablative, Abrade, Air, Attrition, Chafe, Corrade, Corrode, Deteriorate, Detrition, Efface, Erode, Erosion, Fashion, For(e)spend, Fray, Frazzle, Fret, Garb, Impair, In, Mush, Pack, Scuff, Sport, Stand, Tedy, Tolerate, Utility
▷ **Wear** may indicate the NE (eg Sunderland)
Weariness, Wearisome, Weary(ing) Beat, Bejade, Blethered, Bore, Cloy, Dog-tired, Ennui, Ennuyé, Exhaust, Fag, Fatigate, Fatigue, Harass, Hech, Irk, Jade, Lacklustre, Lassitude, Pall, Puny, Ramfeezle, Sick, Sleepy, Spent, Tire, Tiresome, Trash, Try, Tucker, Wabbit, Worn
Weasel Beech-marten, Cane, Delundung, Ermine, Ferret, Glutton, Grison, Kolinsky, Marten, Mink, Mustela, Pekan, Polecat, Stoat, Taira, Tayra, Vermin, Whitterick, Whit(t)ret, Whittrick, Wolverine, Woodshock
Weather, Weather forecast Atmosphere, Climate, Cyclone, Discolour, Ecoclimate, Elements, El Niño, Endure, Met, Monkey's wedding, Sky, Stand, Survive, Tiros, Undergo, Withstand
Weatherboard Rusticating
Weathercock Barometer, Fane, Vane
Weave(r), Weaves, Weaving Arachne, Basket, Broché, Cane, Complect, Contexture, Entwine, Finch, Fishnet, Folk, Heald, Heddle, Interlace, Jacquard, Lace, Lease, Leno, Lion, Loom, Marner, Osiery, Penelope, Pick, Plain, Plait, Raddle, Ripstop, Rya, Shuttle, Sparrow, Spider, Splice, Stevengraph, Taha, Textorial, Texture, Throstle, Throwster, Tissue, Tweel, Twill, Twine, Wabster, Waggle, Webster, Zigzag
Weaver-bird Amadavat, Avadavat, Quelea, Rice-bird, Taha
Web(bed), Webbing, Web-footed, Web-site Aranea, Fissipalmate, Food, Fourchette, Infomediary, Internet, Mat, Maze, Mesh(work), Offset, Palama,

Palmate, Palmiped(e), Patagium, Pinnatiped, Retiary, Skein, Snare, Spider, Tear, Tela, Tissue, Toil, Totipalmate, World Wide

Webster Spider, Weaver

Wed(ding), Wedlock Alliance, Bet, Diamond, Espousal, Golden, Hymen, Join, Knobstick, Liaison, Link, Marriage, Marry, Mate, Matrimony, Meng(e), Me(i)nt, Meynt, Ming, Monkey's, Nuptials, Pair, Penny, Ruby, Shotgun, Silver, Spousal, → UNION, Unite, White, Y

Wedge(d) Accretionary, Canting-coin, Chock, Chunk, Cleat, Cotter, Cuneal, Doorstop, Feather, Forelock, Gagger, Gib, Impacted, Jack, Jam, Key, Niblick, Pitching, Prop, Quoin, Sand, Scotch, Shim, Sphenic, Stick, Texas, Trig, Vomerine, Voussoir, Whipstock

Wedgwood Benn, China

Wednesday Ash, Midweek, Pulver, Spy

Wee Leak, Little, Pee, Slash, Sma(ll), Tinkle, Tiny, → URINATE, Widdle

▷ **Weed** *may indicate* 'urinated'

Weed(y) Adderwort, Agrestal, Alga, Allseed, Anacharis, Arenaria, Bedstraw, Bell-bind, Blinks, Burdock, Buttercup, Carpetweed, Catch, Charlock, Chickweed, Chlorella, Cigar(ette), Cissy, Clotbur, Clover, Cobbler's pegs, Cockle, Cocklebur, Colonist, Coltsfoot, Corncockle, Couch, Daisy, Dallop, Dandelion, Darnel, Dock, Dollop, Dulse, Elder, Elodea, Ers, Fag, Fat hen, Femitar, Fenitar, Fluellen, Fluellin, Fucoid, Fumitory, Ground elder, Groundsel, Helodea, Hoe, Indian, Joe-pye, Knapweed, Knawel, Knot-grass, Lanky, Lemna, Mare's-tail, Marijuana, Matfelon, Mayweed, Nard, Nettle, Nipplewort, Nostoc, Onion, Oxygen, Paterson's curse, Pearlwort, Pilewort, Pineapple, Piri-piri, Plantain, Potamogeton, Purslane, Ragi, Ragwort, Reate, Rest-harrow, Ribbon, Ribwort, Ruderal, Runch, Sagittaria, Sargasso, Scal(l)awag, Scallywag, Senecio, Softy, Sorrel, Speedwell, Spurge, Spurrey, Sudd, Sun-spurge, Swine's-cress, Tansy, Tare, Thistle, Tine, Tobacco, Tormentil, Twitch, Ulotrichale, Ulva, Vetch, Viper's bugloss, Wartcress, Widow's, Winnow, Yarr

Weedkiller Arsenic, Atrazine, Dalapon, Diquat, Diuron, Herbicide, Paraquat®, Selective, Simazine

Week(s), Weekly Ember, Expectation, Great, Hebdomadary, Holy, Omer, Orientation, Ouk, Oulk, Passion, Periodical, Rag, Rogation, Schoolies, Sennight, Working

Weekday Feria

Weekend K, Sat, Sun

Weep(er), Weepy, Wept Bawl, Blubber, Cry, Grat, Greet, Lachrymose, Lament, Loser, Maudlin, Niobe, Ooze, Pipe, Screet, Seep, Sob, Wail

Weevil Anthonomous, Bean, Boll, Bug, Cornworm, Curculio, Diamond-beetle, Grain, Insect, Pea, Rice, Seed, Snout beetle

Weft Roon, Shot, Texture, Warp, Woof

Weigh(ing), Weigh down, Weight(s), Weighty All-up, Apothecaries', Arroba, Artal, As, Atomic, Avoirdupois, Balance, Bantam, Baric, Bob, Bow, Bulk, Burden, Candie, Candy, Cantar, Carat, Catty, Cental, Centner, Clout, Clove, Consider, Count, Counterpoise, Cruiser, Ct, Dead, Decagram(me), Deliberate, Derham, Dirham, Dirhem, Drachm(a), Drail, Dram, Dumbbell, Emphasis, Equivalent, Feather, Fother, G, Gerah, Grain, Gram, Grammage, Gross, Heft, Importance, Impost, Incumbent, Journey, Kandy, Kantar, Kat(i), Katti, Kerb, Khat, Kin, Kip, Last, Liang, Libra, Lisp(o)und, Live, Load, Mark, Massive, Maund, Metage, Metrology, Mina, Minimum, Mna, Molecular, Moment, Mouse, Nail, Nett, Obol, Oke, Onerous, Oppress, Ounce, Overpoise, Oz, Pease, Peaze, Peck, Peise, Peize, Perpend,

Peyse, Pikul, Plumb-bob, Plummet, Poise, Ponderal, Pood, Pound, Pregnant,
Preponderance, Prey, Pud, Pudge, Quintal, Recul, Rod, Rotl, Rotolo, Sash, Scruple,
Seer, Semuncia, Ser, Sinker, Sit, Slang, Slung-shot, Stone, Stress, Talent, Tare,
Throw, Tical, Tod, Tola, Ton(nage), Tonne, Tophamper, Tron(e), Troy, Truss,
Trutinate, Unce, Unmoor, Welter, Wey, Wt
Weighing machine Bismar, Scales, Steelyard, Tron(e)
Weightless Agravic
Weight-lifter Crane, Lewis, Windlass
Weir Cauld, Dam, Garth, Kiddle, Kidel, Lasher, Pen, Watergate
Weird Bizarre, Curious, Dree, Eerie, Eery, Eldritch, Kookie, Offbeat, Spectral,
Strange, Supernatural, Taisch, Uncanny, Zany
Welch, Welsh Abscond, Cheat, Default, Embezzle, Levant, Rat, Reneg(u)e, Renig,
Skedaddle, Weasel
Welcome, Welcoming Aloha, Ave, Bel-accoyle, Ciao, Embrace, Entertain,
Glad-hand, Greet, Haeremai, Hallo, Halse, Hello, Hi, Hospitable, How, Hullo,
Karanga, Powhiri, Receive, Reception, Salute, Yellow-ribbon
Weld(ing) Arc, Butt, Cold, Explosion, Fillet, Friction, Fuse, Gas, Join, Merge, MIG,
Resistance, Seam, Sinter, Stud, Tack, TIG, Ultrasonic, Unite
Welfare Advantage, Alms, Benison, Ha(y)le, Heal, Health, Sarvodaya, Social, Weal
Welkin Firmament, Sky
Well (done) Artesian, Atweel, Aweel, Bien, Bore(hole), Bravo, Carbon, Casinghead,
Cenote, Chipper, Development, Discovery, Dropping, Dry hole, Euge, Famously,
Fine, Fit, Gas, Gasser, Good, Gosh, Gusher, Hale, → HEALTHY, Hot, Inkpot, Ka
pai, Law, Mickery, My, Namma hole, Odso, Oh, Oil, Phreatic, Potential, Pump, So,
Source, Spa, Spring, Sump, Surge, Teek, Um, Upflow, Wildcat, Zemzem
Wellbeing Atweel, Bien-être, Comfort, Euphoria, Euphory, Good, Health, Oomph,
Welfare
Well-born Eugene
Well-bred Genteel
Well-built Sturdy, Tight
Well-covered Chubby, Padded
Well-curb Puteal
Welles Orson
Wellington, Welly Accelerate, Boot, Green, Gumboot, Iron Duke, Nosey
Well-known Famous, Illustrious, Notorious, Notour, Prominent
Well-off Affluent, Far, Rich, Wealthy
Well part Bucket, Shadoof, Shaduf
Wells Bombardier, Fargo, Sadler's
Well-wisher Friend
▶ **Welsh** see WELCH
Welsh(man) Briton, Brittonic, Brython, Cake, Cambrian, Celtic, Cog, Cym(ric),
Cymry, Dai, Ebbw, Emlyn, Evan, Fluellen, Gareth, Harp, Idris, Ifor, Ivor, Keltic,
P-Celtic, P-Keltic, Rabbit, Rarebit, Rees, Rhys, Sion, Taff(y), Tudor, W
Wen Cyst, Talpa, Tumour, Wart
Wench Blowze, Court, Girl, Gouge, Hussy, Maid, Ramp, Rig, Smock, Strumpet
Wend Meander, Sorb, Steer
Wendy Darling, House
Went Left, Sold, Yode
Werewolf Loup-garou, Lycanthrope, Nazi, Turnskin, Vampire
Wesleyan Epworth, Methodist
West(ern), Westerly Ang mo, Far, Favonian, Hesperian, Mae, Middle, Movie,

Oater, Occidental, Ponent, Spaghetti, Sunset, W, Wild
West African Fantee, Fanti, Kroo, Wolof
▷ **West end** *may indicate* 't' or 'W1'
West Indian Carib, Creole, Jamaican, Taino
Westminster SW1
Wet(ting) Bedabble, Bedraggled, Clammy, Daggle, Damp, Dank, Dew, Dip, Douse,
Dowse, Drench, Drip(ping), Drook, Drouk, Embrue, Enuresis, Feeble, Humect,
Humid, Hyetal, Imbrue, Imbue, Irrigate, Irriguous, Madefy, Madid, Marshy, Moil,
Moist(en), Molly, Namby-pamby, Pee, Piddle, Pouring, Rainy, Ret(t), Roral, Roric,
Runny, Saturate, Shower, Simp(leton), Sipe, Sluice, → **SOAK**, Sodden, Sopping,
Sour, Steep, Tiddle, Tipsy, Urinate, Wat, Wee, Widdle, Wimpy, Wringing
Whack(ed) Belt, Bemaul, Biff, Deadbeat, Joll, Joule, Jowl, Lambast, Lounder, Swat,
Swish, Thump
Whale(meat), Whaling Baleen, Beaked, Beluga, Black, Blower, Blubber, Blue,
Bottlehead, Bottlenose, Bowhead, Bull, Cachalot, Calf, Cetacea(n), Cete, Cow,
Cowfish, Dolphin, Dorado, Fall, Fin(back), Finner, Gam, Glutton, Grampus,
Greenland, Grey, Greyback, Humpback, Killer, Kreng, Leviathan, Manatee, Minke,
Monodon, Mysticeti, Narwhal, Odontoceti, Paste, Physeter, Pilot, Pod, Porpoise,
Right, River dolphin, Rorqual, School, Scrag, Sea-canary, Sea-unicorn, Sei,
Social, Sperm, Spouter, Sulphur-bottom, Thrasher, Toothed, Toothless, White,
Zeuglodon(t)
▷ **Whale** *may indicate* an anagram
Whalebone Busk
Whaler Ahab, Harpooner, Ship, Specksioneer, Specktioneer, Waister
Whales' meat Clio
Wham Bang, Collide
Whang Blow, Flog, Thrash, Whack
Wharf(inger) Dock(er), Jetty, Key, Landing, Pier, Quay, Roustabout, Rouster,
Staith(e)
What Anan, Eh, How, Pardon, Que, Siccan, That, Which
Whatnot, What's-its-name Dinges, Dingus, Doings, Doobrey, Doobrie,
Étagère, Gismo, Jiggamaree, Jiggumbob, Thingamy, Thingumajig, Thingumbob,
Thingummy, Timenoguy
Wheat Amber, Amelcorn, Bald, Beard(ed), Beardless, Blé, Bulg(h)ur, Cone,
Couscous, Cracked, Durum, Einkorn, Emmer, Federation, Fromenty, Frumenty,
Furme(n)ty, Furmity, Grain, Hard, Mummy, Red, Rivet, Sarrasin, Sarrazin, Seiten,
Semolina, Sharps, Soft, Spelt, Spring, Triticum, White, Winter
Wheatsheaf Bale, Gerbe, Stook
Wheedle Banter, Barney, Blandish, Butter up, Cajole, Coax, Cog, Cuiter, Cuittle,
Flatter, Inveigle, Tweedle, Whilly(whaw)
Wheel(er) Balance, Bedel, Bevel, Bicycle, Big, Bogy, Breast, Buff(ing), Caracol(e),
Caster, Castor, Catherine, Chain, Chark(h)a, Circle, Cistern, Count, Crown,
Cycle, Daisy, Disc, Driving, Emery, Epicycloidal, Escape, Fan, Felloe, Felly, Ferris,
Fifth, Fortune, Gear, Grinding, Gyrate, Helm, Hurl, Idle(r), Jagger, Kick, Lantern,
Magnate, Medicine, Mitre, Monkey, Mortimer, Nabob, Nose, Paddle, Pattern,
Pedal, Pelton, Perambulator, Persian, Pin, Pinion, Pitch, Pivot, Planet, Potter's,
Prayer, Pulley, Rag, Ratchet, Rhomb, Roll, Rotate, Roulette, Rowel, Sheave, Snail,
Spider, Spinning, Sprocket, Spur, Star, Steering, Stepney, Stitch, Swing, Tail,
Throwing-table, Tread, Trindle, Trochus, Trolley, Truckle, Trundle, → **TURN**,
Tympan(um), Water, Web, Wharve, Wire, Worm, Zoetrope
Wheelbarrow Monotroch

Wheelhouse Caravan, Paddle-box
Wheel-hub Axle, Nave
Wheelman Cyclist, Ixion
Wheelwright Spokesman
Wheeze Asthma, Jape, Joke, Pant, Ploy, Rale, Reak, Reik, Rhonchus, Ruse, Stridor, Trick, Whaisle, Whaizle
Whelk Buckie, Limpet, Shellfish, Stromb, Triton
Whelm Nalla(h), Nulla(h)
Whelp Bear, Bra(t)chet, Pup
When(ever) Although, As, If, Once, Though, Time
Where(abouts) Location, Neighbourhood, Place, Site, Vicinity, Whaur, Whither
Wherefore Cause, Reason, Why
Whereupon So, When
Wherewithal Finance, Means, Money, Needful, Resources
Wherry Barge, Rowboat
Whet(stone) Coticular, Excite, Hone, Rubstone, Sharpen, Stimulate
Whether Conditional, If
Whey Plasma, Serum, Whig
Which(ever), Which is Anyway, As, QE, Whatna, Whilk, Who
Whiff Breath, Cigarette, Gust, Hum, Puff, Redolence, Smatch, Sniff, Trace, Waft
Whig Adullamite, Jig, Rascal, Tory, Whey
While Although, As, Interim, Since, Space, Span, Spell, Though, Throw, Time, When, Whenas, Whereas, Yet
Whim(s), Whimsical, Whimsy Bizarre, Caprice, Conceit, Crotchet, Fad, Fancy, Fantastic, Fay, Fey, Fie, Flisk, Impulse, Kicksy-wicksy, Kink, Notion, Quaint, Quirk, Tick, Toy, Vagary
Whimper Cry, Grizzle, Mewl, Pule, Snivel, Whine
Whin Furze, Gorse, Ulex
Whine, Whinge Cant, Carp, Complain, Cry, Grumble, Kvetch, Mewl, Moan, Peenge, Pule, Snivel, Whimper, Yammer
Whinny Neigh, Nicker, Whicker
Whip(ped), Whip out, Whipping Beat, Braid, Brede, Bullwhack, Bullwhip, Cat, Cat o' nine tails, Chabouk, Chantilly, Chastise, Chief, Cilium, Colt, Crop, Drive, Feague, Firk, Five-line, Flagellate, Flagellum, Flay, Gad, Hide, Jambok, Knout, K(o)urbash, Larrup, → LASH, Leather, Limber, Lunge, Quirt, Rawhide, Riem, Scourge, Sjambok, Slash, Steal, Stock, Strap-oil, Swinge, Swish, Switch, Taw, Thong, Three-line, Trounce, Welt, West Country, Whap, Whop
Whippersnapper Dandiprat, Dandyprat, Pup, Squirt
Whirl(er), Whirling Bullroarer, Circumgyrate, Dervish, Eddy, Gyrate, → IN A WHIRL, Pivot, Reel, Spin, Swing, Swirl, Vortex, Vortical, Vorticose, Vortiginous, Whirry
Whirlpool Eddy, Gulf, Gurge, Maelstrom, Moulin, Sea purse, Swelchie, Vorago, Vortex, Weel, Wiel
Whirlwind Cyclone, Dust devil, Eddy, Sand-devil, Tornado, Tourbillion, Typho(o)n, Vortex, Willy-willy
Whirr Birr
Whisk Balloon, Chowri, Chowry, Fly, Swish, Switch, Whid, Whip
Whisker(s) Beard, Beater, Burnsides, Cat's, Dundreary, Hackle, Hair, Moustache, Mutton-chop, Samuel, Satyric tuft, Side(-boards), Side-burns, Stibble, Stubble, Vibrissa
Whisk(e)y Alcohol, Barley-bree, Barley-broo, Barley-broth, Bond, Bourbon,

Canadian, Cape smoke, Chain lighting, Corn, Cratur, Crayther, Creature, Fife, Fire-water, Hard stuff, Hard tack, Highball, Hokonui, Hoo(t)ch, Irish, Malt, Monongahela, Moonshine, Morning, Mountain dew, Nip, Peat-reek, Pot(h)een, Ragwater, Red eye, Rye, Scotch, Sourmash, Southern Comfort®, Spunkie, Tanglefoot, Tarantula juice, Usquebaugh, Wheech, Whiss

▷ **Whisky** *may indicate* an anagram

Whisper Breath(e), Bur(r), Hark, Hint, Innuendo, Murmur, Round, Rumour, Rustle, Sigh, Stage, Susurrus, Tittle, Undertone, Whittie-whattie

Whist Dummy, Hush, Long, Progressive, Quiet, Sh, Short, Solo, Whisk and swabbers

Whistle(r) Blow, Boatswain's, Calliope, Catcall, Feedback, Flageolet, Hiss, Marmot, Penny, Ping, Pipe, Ref, Siffle(ur), Sowf(f), Sowth, Steam, Stop, Stridor, Swab(ber), Swanee, Tin, Toot, Tweedle, Tweet, Warbler, Wheeple, Wheugh, Whew, Whiffle, Wolf

Whit Atom, Doit, Figo, Haet, Hait, Hate, Iota, Jot, Particle, Pentecost, Point, Red cent, Straw

White(n), Whitener, Whiteness, White-faced Agene, Agenise, Alabaster, Albedo, Albescent, Albino, Albugineous, Albumen, Argent, Ashen, Au lit, Bakra, Blameless, Blanch, Blanche, Blanco, Bleach, Buckra, Cabbage, Calm, Cam, Camstone, Candid, Candida, Candour, Canescent, Canities, Caucasian, Caum, China, Chinese, Christmas, Cliffs, Collar, Company, Dealbate, Egg, Elephant, Ermine, European, Fang, Fard, Feather, Flag, Flake, French, Glair, Gwen(da), Gwendolen, Gwyn, Hawked, Honorary, Hore, House, Innocent, Ivory, Large, Leucoma, Lie, Lily, Livid, Man, Marbled, Mealy, Niveous, Opal, Oyster, Pakeha, Pale(face), Pallor, Paper, Paris, Pearl, Poor, Pure, Redleg, Russian, Sclerotic, Selborne, Sheep, Silver, Small, Snow(y), Spanish, Taw, Vitiligo, Wan, Wedding, Wyn, Zinc

Whitefish Menominee

Whitefriars Alsatia

Whitehall Ministry

Whitehead Milium

White horse(s) Skipper's daughters, Wave

White man Anglo, Ba(c)kra, Buckra, Caucasian, Corn-cracker, Cracka, Gora, Gub(bah), Haole, Honkie, Honky, Kabloona, Larney, Mzungu, Occidental, Ofay, Pakeha, Paleface, Redleg, Redneck, Umlungu, WASP

Whitewash Calcimine, Excuse, Kalsomine, Lime, Skunk, Trounce

Whitlow Ancome, Felon, Panaritium, Paronychia

Whitsun Pinkster, Pinxter

Whittle Carve, Pare, Sharpen

Whizz Wheech

Who As, Doctor

Whodunit Mystery

Whole, Wholehearted, Wholeness, Wholly All, Cosmos, Eager, Entire(ty), Entity, Fully, Hale, Indiscrete, Intact, Integer, Integrity, Largely, Lot, Sum, Systemic, Thoroughly, Total, Unbroken, Uncut

Wholesale(r) Cutprice, En bloc, Engrosser, Jobber, Root and branch, Stockjobber, Supplier, Sweeping

Wholesome Clean, Good, Healthy, Physical, Sound

Whoop(er), Whooping cough Alew, Celebrate, Chincough, Crane, Cry, Excite, Kink(cough), Kink-host, Pertussis, Swan, War

Whoopee Carouse, Evoe, Hey-go-mad, Roister

Whoosh Birr, Swish

Whopper, Whopping Barn, Crammer, Huge, Immense, Jumbo, Lie, Lig, Oner, Out and outer, Scrouger, Slapper, Slockdolager, Soc(k)dalager, Soc(k)dolager, Soc(k)doliger, Soc(k)dologer, Sogdolager, Sogdoliger, Sogdologer, Stonker, Tale, Taradiddle

Whore Drab, Harlot, Loose woman, Pinnace, Pro, Prostitute, Quail, Road, Strumpet, Tart

Whorl Corolla, Eucyclic, Spiral, Swirl, Verticil, Volute

Why Reason, Yogh

Wick Farm, Rush, Snaste, Snuff, Vill(age)

Wicked(ness) Adharma, Atrocity, → **BAD**, Candle, Criminal, Cru(i)sie, Crusy, Depravity, Devilish, Evil, Facinorous, Flagitious, Goaty, Godless, Heinous, High-viced, Immoral, Impious, Improbity, Iniquity, Lantern, Nefarious, Night-light, Ponerology, Pravity, Rush, Satanic, Scelerate, Sin(ful), Taper, Turpitude, Unholy, Vile

▷ **Wicked** *may indicate* containing a wick

Wicker(work) Basketry, Sale, Seal

Wicket Gate, Hatch, Infield, Pitch, Square, Sticky, Stool, Stump, Yate

Wicket-keeper Stumper

Wide, Widen(ing), Width Abroad, Ample, Bay, Broad, Dilate, Drib, Eclectic, Expand, Extend, Far, Flanch, Flange, Flare, Flaunch, Ga(u)ge, General, Latitude, Miss, Prevalent, Roomy, Set, Spacious, Span, Spread, Sundry, Sweeping, Vast

Wide-awake Alert, Fly, Hat, Wary, Watchful

Widespread Catholic, Diffuse, Epidemic, Extensive, General, Pandemic, Panoramic, Prevalent, Prolate, Rife, Routh(ie), Sweeping

Widow(ed) Bereft, Black, Dame, Dowager, Golf, Grass, Hempen, Jointress, Relict, Sati, Sneerwell, Suttee, Vidual, Viduous, Whydah-bird, Widdy

Wield Brandish, Control, Exercise, Handle, → **MANIPULATE**, Ply, Sound

Wife, Wives Bride, Concubine, Consort, Devi, Dutch, Enid, Evadne, Feme, Feme covert, Fiere, Frau, Goody, Haram, Harem, Harim, Helpmate, Helpmeet, Hen, Her indoors, Kali, Kickie-wickie, Kicksy-wicksy, Kloo(t)chman, Lakshmi, Little woman, Mate, Memsahib, Missis, Missus, Mrs, Mummer's, Partner, Penelope, Pirrauru, Potiphar's, Rib, Seraglio, Spouse, Squaw, Stepford, Trophy, Trouble and strife, Umfazi, Ux(or), Vrou, W

Wig Adonis, Bagwig, Bob(wig), Brigadier, Brutus, Buzz-wig, Cadogan, Campaign, Carpet, Cauliflower, Caxon, Chevelure, Chide, Cockernony, Dalmahoy, Fright, Full-bottomed, Gizz, Gooseberry, Gorgone, Gregorian, Hair(piece), Heare, Jas(e)y, Jazy, Jiz, Macaroni, Major, Periwig, Peruke, Postiche, Ramil(l)ie(s), Rate, Reprimand, Rug, Scold, Scratch, Sheitel, Spencer, Targe, Tie, Toupee, Toupet, Tour

Wiggle, Wiggly Jiggle, Scoleciform, Wobble, Wriggle

Wight Man, Vectis

Wigwam Te(e)pee

Wild Aberrant, Agrestal, Barbarous, Berserk, Bundu, Bush, Chimeric, Crazy, Dionysian, Earl, Errant, Erratic, Extravagant, Farouche, Feral, Frantic, Frenetic, Haggard, Hectic, Lawless, Mad(cap), Manic, Meshugge, Myall, Natural, Rampant, Raver, Riotous, → **SAVAGE**, Unmanageable, Unruly, Violent, Warrigal, West, Woolly

▷ **Wild(ly)** *may indicate* an anagram

Wild beast Eyra, Sapi-utan, Scrubber

Wildcat Lion, Manul, Ocelot, Strike, Tiger

Wilderness Bush, Desert, Ruderal, Sinai, Solitude, Waste

Wild goose Chase, Greylag
Wild oats Haver
Wile, Wily Art, Artful, Artifice, Astute, Braide, → CUNNING, Deceit, Foxy, Peery, Ruse, Shifty, Shrewd, Slee, → SLY, Spider, Stratagem, Streetwise, Subtle, Trick, Versute, Wide
Wilful Deliberate, Headstrong, Heady, Obstinate, Recalcitrant, Wayward
Will, Willing(ly) Alsoon, Amenable, Bard, Bequeath, Bewildered, Biddable, Bill(y), Complaisant, Compliant, Conation, Content, Desire, Devise, Fain, Force, Free, Game, General, Hay, Holographic, Leave, Legator, Leve, Lief, Lieve, Living, Noncupative, Obedient, On, Please, Prone, Purpose, Raring, Rather, Ready, Receptive, Scarlet, Soon, Spirit, Swan, Testament, Testate, Thelma, Volens, Volition, Voluntary, Volunteer, Way, Wimble, Woot
▷ **Will** *may indicate* an anagram
William(s) Bill(y), Conqueror, Occam, Orange, Pear, Rufus, Silent, Sweet, Tell, Tennessee
Will o' the wisp Fen-fire, Friar's lantern, Ignis-fatuus, Jack o'lantern, Min min, Nightfire, Rush, Spunkie
Willow(ing), Willowy Arctic, Crack, Diamond, Lissom(e), Lithe, Osier, Poplar, Port Jackson, Pussy, Salix, Sallow, Sauch, Saugh, Supple, Twilly, Weeping, Withy
Willpower Ab(o)uha, Determination, Strength
Willy-nilly Nolens volens, Perforce
Wilt Decline, Droop, Fade, Flag, Sap, Shalt, Wither
Wiltshireman Moonraker
▶ **Wily** *see* WILE
Wimp(ish) Namby-pamby, Pantywaist, Weed
Wimple Gorget, Meander, Ripple, Turn
▷ **Wimple** *may indicate* an anagram
Win(ner), Winning Achieve, Acquire, Ahead, Appealing, Bangster, Banker, → BEAT, Capot, Champion, Conciliate, Conquer, Cup, Cute, Decider, Disarming, Dormie, Dormy, Earn, Effect, Endearing, First, Gain, Gammon, Hit, Jackpot, Land, Laureate, Lead, Medallist, Motser, Motza, Nice, Pile, Pot, Prevail, Profit, Purler, Repique, Result, Rubicon, Scoop, Shoo-in, Slam, Snip, Success, Sweet, Take, Top dog, → TRIUMPH, Up, Vellet, Velvet, Victor(y), Vole, Walk over, Wrest
Wince Blench, Cringe, Flinch, Recoil
Winch Crab, Crane, Jack, Windlass
Winchester® Rifle
Wind(er), Winding(s), Windy Aeolian, Air, Airstream, Ambages, Anabatic, Anfractuous, Anti-trade, Aquilo(n), Argestes, Auster, Backing, Baguio, Bend, Berg, Bise, Blore, Blow, Bluster, Bora, Boreas, Bottom, Bourasque, Brass, Breeze, Brickfielder, Buran, Burp, Buster, Cape doctor, Capstan, Carminative, Caurus, Chili, Chill, Chinook, Coil, Colic, Cordonazo, Corus, Crank, Creeky, Curl, Curve, Cyclone, Downwash, Draught, Draw, Dust devil, Easterly, Etesian, Euraquilo, Euroclydon, Eurus, Evagation, Favonian, Favonius, Fearful, Firn, Flatulence, Flatus, Flaw, Fo(e)hn, Gale, Gas, G(h)ibli, Greco, Gregale, Gust, Haboob, Harmattan, Heaves, Hurricane, Hurricano, Jet stream, Kamseen, K(h)amsin, Katabatic, Knee-swell, Levant(er), Libecc(h)io, Libs, Link, Maestro, Meander, Meltemi, Mistral, Monsoon, Muzzler, Nervous, Noreast, Norther, Nor(th)wester(ly), Noser, Notus, Ostro, Pampero, Periodic, Ponent, Poop, Prevailing, Puna, Purl, Quarter, Quill, Reeds, Reel, Rip-snorter, Roll, Samiel, Sciroc, Scirocco, Screw, Sea, Second, Series, Serpentine, Shamal, Shimaal, Simoom, Simoon, Sinuous, Sirocco, Slant, Snake, Snifter, Snorter, Solano, Solar, Sough, Souther, Southerly buster, Spiral, Spool,

Squall, Stellar, Sumatra, Surface, Swirl, Tail, Taranaki, Tehuantepecer, Thread, Throw, Tornado, Tortuous, Tourbillon, Trade, Tramontana, Trend, Turn, Twaddle, Twine, Twister, Twisty, Typhon, Typhoon, Vayu, Veer, Veering, Ventose, Volturnus, Waffle, Weave, Wester, Westerly, Whirlblast, White squall, Williwaw, Willy-willy, Winch, Woold, Wrap, Wreathe, Wrest, Wuthering, Zephyr(us), Zonda

Windbag Balloon, Bore, Drogue, Prattler, Whoopee cushion, Zeppelin

Windfall Bonanza, Buckshee, Caduac, Fortune, Godsend, Manna

Windflower Anemone

Windlass Differential, Spanish, Whim, Winch

Windmill Pinwheel, Post, Smock, Whirligig

Window(s) Atmosphere, Bay, Bow, Casement, Catherine-wheel, Companion, Compass, Day, Deadlight, Dormer, Dream-hole, Eye, Eyelids, Fanlight, Fenestella, Fenestra, French, Gable, Garret, Glaze, Guichet, Jalousie, Jesse, Jet, Judas, Lancet, Lattice, Launch, Loop-light, Louver, Louvre, Lozen, Lucarne, Lunette, Luthern, Lychnoscope, Marigold, Mezzanine, Mirador, Monial, Mullion, Oculus, Oeil-de-beouf, Ogive, Orb, Oriel, Ox-eye, Pane, Pede, Picture, Pop-under, Porthole, Quarterlight, Radio, Re-entry, Rosace, Rose, Round, Sash, Sexfoil, Shop, Shot, Spyhole, Storm, Transom, Trellis, Ventana, Weather, Wheel, Wicket, Windock, Winnock

Window-bar, Window-fastening Astragal, Espagnolette

Windpipe Bronchus, Gular, Throat, Trachea, Weasand

Windscale Beaufort

Windsock Drogue, Sleeve

Windswept Scud

Wind-up End, Fright, Liquidate, Span

Windward Ahold, Aloof, Laveer, Luff, Up

Wine Bin, Cabinet, Case, Cup, Cuvée, Doc, Essence, Fortified, Grand cru, Low, Must, Piece, Pigment, Premier cru, Prisage, Rotgut, Rouge, Sparkling, Steen, Terroir, The grape, Tirage, Varietal, Vat, Vintage, Zymurgy

---

WINES

2 letters:	Race	Médoc	6 letters:
It	Rosé	Mirin	Barley
	Rosy	Mosel	Barolo
3 letters:	Sack	Negus	Barsac
Dao	Sekt	Pinot	Beaune
Red	Stum	Plonk	Bishop
Sec	Tent	Rhine	Bubbly
Tun	Tutu	Rioja	Canary
Vin	Vino	Soave	Claret
		Straw	Ginger
4 letters:	5 letters:	Syrah	Graves
Asti	Anjou	Table	Lisbon
Brut	Anker	Tavel	Malaga
Cava	Biddy	Toddy	Merlot
Hock	Blanc	Tokay	Muscat
Mull	Bombo	White	Piment
Palm	Comet	Xeres	Plotty
Pipe	Gallo		Red Ned
Port	Macon		Sherry

Shiraz	Espumoso	Hoccamore	Pouilly-Fumé
Solera	Essencia	Inglenook	Rudesheimer
	Frascati	Lambrusco	Scuppernong
7 letters:	Glühwein	Languedoc	Steinberger
Alicant	Jerepigo	Loll-shrob	
Amoroso	Kabinett	Malvoisie	**12 letters:**
Auslese	Log-juice	Meersault	Johannisberg
Bastard	Malvasia	Minervois	Marcobrunner
Catawba	Malvesie	Muscadine	Supernaculum
Chablis	Montilla	Ordinaire	Valpolicella
Château	Mountain	Pinot noir	Vin ordinaire
Chianti	Muscadel	Sauvignon	
Cowslip	Muscadet	St Emilion	**13 letters:**
Demi-sec	Muscatel	Tafelwein	Beerenauslese
Dessert	Oenology	Tarragona	Entre-Deux-Mers
Eiswein	Pinotage	Zinfandel	Liebfraumilch
Fendant	Pradikat		Montepulciano
Icewine	Red biddy	**10 letters:**	Pouilly-Fuissé
Madeira	Resinata	Beaujolais	
Malmsey	Rheingau	Bull's blood	**14 letters:**
Margaux	Riesling	Chambertin	Gewürztraminer
Marsala	Sancerre	Chardonnay	Johannisberger
Moselle	Sangaree	Constantia	
Oenomel	Sauterne	Elderberry	**15 letters:**
Orvieto	Sémillon	Genevrette	Lachryma Christi
Pomerol	Spätlese	Hochheimer	Liebfrauenmilch
Pommard	Spumante	Loll-shraub	
Retsina	St Julien	Manzanilla	**16 letters:**
Rhenish	Sylvaner	Montrachet	London particular
Sangria	Verdelho	Muscadelle	
Vouvray	Vermouth	Napa Valley	**17 letters:**
		Peter-see-me	Cabernet Sauvignon
8 letters:	**9 letters:**	Piesporter	Châteaux cardboard
Bordeaux	Bacharach	Sangiovese	Nuits Saint Georges
Bucellas	Bardolino	Vinho verde	
Buckfast®	Champagne		**20 letters:**
Burgundy	En primeur	**11 letters:**	Trockenbeeren
Cabernet	Falernian	Amontillado	-auslese
Champers	Gladstone	Dom Perignon	
Charneco	Hermitage	Niersteiner	
Dubonnet®	Hippocras	Petite Sirah	

Wine-cellar, Wine-shop Bistro, Bodega, Vault, Vaut(e)
Wine-glass Flute
Wine-making Gallising, Remuage
Wing(s), Winged, Winger, Wing-like Aerofoil, Ala(r), Alula, Annexe, Appendage, Arm, Bastard, → BIRD, Branch, Buffalo, Canard, Cellar, Corium, Coulisse, Delta, Dipteral, El(l), Elevon, Elytral, Elytriform, Elytron, Elytrum, Fender, Flap, Flew, Flex, Flipper, Flying, Forward, Gull, Halteres, Hurt, Left, Limb, Parascenia, Parascenium, Patagium, Pennate, Pennon, Pinero, Pinion, Pip, Pterygoid, Putto, Right, Rogallo, Sail, Samariform, Scent-scale, Segreant,

Seraphim, Split, Standard, Sweepback, Sweptback, Sweptwing, Swift, Swingwing, Tailplane, Tectrix, Tegmen, Tormentor, Transept, Van, Vol(et), Water, Wound(ed)
Winged sandals Talaria
▷ **Winger** *may indicate* a bird
Wing-footed Aliped, Fleet, Swift
Wingless Apteral
Wink (at) Atone, Bat, Condone, Connive, Eyelid, Flicker, Ignore, Instant, Nap, Nictitate, Pink, Twinkle
Winnie Pooh
Winnow Fan, Riddle, Separate, Sift, Van, Wecht
Winsome Bonny, Engaging, Gay, Pleasant
Winter, Wintry Blackthorn, Bleak, Brumal, Cold, Dec, Fimbul, Frigid, Frore, Hibernate, Hiemal, Hiems, Hodiernal, Jack Frost, Jasmine, Nuclear, Snowy, W
Winter cherry Chinese lantern
Wintergreen Chickweed, Pyrola, Sarcodes
Winter pear Nelis
Winter-sport Ski
Wipe (out), Wiping Abolish, Abrogate, Absterge, Amortise, Cancel, Cleanse, Demolish, Destroy, Deterge, Dicht, Dight, Eradicate, Expunge, Forget, Hanky, Mop, Nose-rag, Null, Purge, Raze, Retroussage, Slorm, Sponge, Tersion, Tissue
Wire(s), Wiry Aerial, Barb(ed), Cable, Cat's whiskers, Chicken, Coil, Earth, Fencing, Filament, Filar, File, Heald, Heddle, High, Kirschner, Lean, Lecher, Live, Marconigram, Mil, Nichrome®, Nipper, Number eight, Piano, Pickpocket, Razor, Sevice, Shroud, Sinewy, Snake, Solenoid, Spit, Staple, Stilet, Strand, String, Stylet, Telegram, Telegraph, Thoth, Thread, Trace
Wireless (operator), Wireless part Baffle, Set, Sparks, Valve
Wise(acre), Wisdom Advisedly, Ancient, Astute, Athena, Athene, Canny, Depth, Ernie, Ganesa, Gothamite, Gudrun, Hep, Hindsight, Judgement, Judicious, Learned, Long-headed, Lore, Manner, Mimir, Minerva, Norman, Oracle, Owl, Penny, Philosopher, Philosophy, Politic, Polymath, Prajna, Profound, Prudence, Sagacity, Sage, Salomonic, Sapience, Savvy, Shrewd, Smartie, Solomon, Solon, Sophia, Tooth, Wice
Wisecrack Dig, One-liner, Quip
Wise man Balthazar, Caspar, Heptad, Melchior, Nestor, Sage, Sapient, Seer, Solomon, Swami, Thales, Tohunga, Worldly
Wish(es) Ache, Ake, Covet, Crave, Death, Desiderate, → **DESIRE**, Hope, List, Long, Pant, Pleasure, Precatory, Regards, Velleity, Want, Yearn
Wishbone Furcula, Marriage-bone, Merrythought, Skipjack
Wishy-washy Bland, Feeble, Insipid, Irresolute, Milksop, Weak, Wheyey
Wisp(y) Cirrate, Frail, Scrap, Shred, Virga, Wase
Wit(s), Witticism, Witty Acumen, Attic, Badinage, Banter, Brevity, Commonsense, Concetto, Cunning, Dry, Epigram, Esprit, Estimation, Eutrapelia, Eutrapely, Facetious, Fantasy, Gnome, Hartford, Humour, Imagination, Intelligence, Irony, Jest, Jeu d'esprit, Joke, Marbles, Marinism, Memory, Mind, Mot, Mother, Native, Nous, Pawky, Pun, Repartee, Rogue, Sally, Salt, Saut, Sconce, → **SENSE**, Shaft, Smart, Videlicet, Viz, Wag, Weet, Wisecrack, Word-play
Witch(craft) Broomstick, Cantrip, Carline, Circe, Coven, Craigfluke, Crone, Cutty Sark, Enchantress, Ensorcell, Galdragon, Glamour, Goety, Gramary(e), Gyre-carlin, Hag, Hecat(e), Hex, Invultuation, Lamia, Magic, Medea, Myal(ism), Necromancy, Night-hag, Obeahism, Obia, Obiism, Pishogue, Pythoness, Salem, Selim, Sibyl, Sieve, Sorceress, Speller, Sycorax, Trout, Valkyrie, Vaudoo, Vilia,

Voodoo, Water, Weird, Wicca

Witch-doctor Boyla, Medicine man, Mganga, Obi, Pawaw, Powwow, Sangoma, Shaman

Witch-hazel Fothergilla, Platan(e), Winter-bloom

Witch-hunter McCarthy

With And, By, Con, Cum, Hereby, In, Mit, Of, Plus, W

Withdraw(al), Withdrawn Abdicate, Alienate, Aloof, Back out, Breakaway, Cold turkey, Cry off, Detach, Disengage, Distrait, Enshell, Evacuate, Hive off, Inshell, Introvert, Leave, Offish, Palinode, Preserve, Recant, Recoil, Repair, Resile, Reticent, Retire, Retract(ion), Retreat, Revoke, Revulsion, Scratch, Secede, Secesh, Sequester, Shrink, Shy, Stand down, Subduce, Subduct, Unreeve, Unsay

Wither(ed), Withering, Withers Arefy, Atrophy, Blight, Burn, Corky, Die, Droop, Dry, Evanish, Fade, Forpine, Googie, Languish, Marcescent, Miff, Nose, Scram, Sere, Shrink, Shrivel, Welk, Welt

Withershins Eastlin(g)s

▷ **With gaucherie** *may indicate* an anagram

Withhold(ing), Withheld Abstain, Conceal, Curt, Deny, Detain, Detinue, Hide, Keep, → RESERVE, Ritenuto, Trover

Within Enclosed, Endo-, Immanent, Indoors, Inside, Interior, Intra

With it Hep, Hip, Syn, Trendy, W

Without Bar, Beyond, Ex, Lack(ing), Less, Minus, Orb, Outdoors, Outside, Sans, Save, Sen, Senza, Sine, X

▷ **Without** *may indicate* one word surrounding another

▷ **Without restraint** *may indicate* an anagram

Without stimulus Nastic

Withstand Blight, Brave, Contest, Defy, Endure, Oppose, Resist, Weather

Witless Crass, → STUPID PERSON

Witness Attend, Attest, Bystander, Catch, Character, Compurgator, Confirm, Crown, Deponent, Depose, Endorse, Evidence, Experience, Expert, Eye, Glimpse, Hostile, Jehovah's, Mark, Martyr, Material, Muggletonian, Note, Notice, Observe, Obtest, Onlooker, Perceive, Proof, → SEE, Show, Sight, Sign, Spy, Stander-by, Survey, Testament, Teste, Testify, Testimony, View, Watch

Witness-box Peter, Stand

▶ **Witticism** *see* WIT

Wizard (priest) Archimage, Carpathian, Conjuror, Expert, Gandalf, Hex, Magician, Merlin, Obiman, Oz, Prospero, Shaman, Sorcerer, Super, Warlock, → WITCH-DOCTOR

Wizen(ed) Dehydrate, Dry, Sere, Shrivel, Sphacelate, Wither

Woad Anil, Dye, Indigo, Isatis, Pastel, Pastil

Wobble, Wobbling, Wobbly Chandler's, Coggle, Precess, Quaver, Reel, Rock, Shimmy, Shoggle, Shoogle, Teeter, Totter, Tremble, Trillo, Unstable, Wag, Waggle, Walty, Waver, Wibble

Wodehouse Plum

Woe(ful) Alack, Alas, Bale, Bane, Distress, Doole, Dule, Ewhow, Execrable, Gram, Grief, Hurt, Jeremiad, Lack-a-day, Misery, Pain, Plague, → SORROW, Torment, Tribulation, Unhappy

Wolds Lincoln(shire), Yorkshire

Wolf(ish), Wolf-like Akela, Assyrian, Bolt, Cancer, Carcajou, Casanova, Coyote, Cram, Dangler, Earth, Engorge, Fenrir, Fenris, Gorge, Grey, Ise(n)grim, Lobo, Lone, Lothario, Lupine, Luster, Lycanthrope, MI, Michigan, Pack, Prairie, Rake, Ravenous, Red, Rip, Roué, Rout, Rudolph, Rye, Scoff, Sea, Strand, Tasmanian,

Thylacine, Tiger, Timber, Wanderer, Were, Whistler
Wolfram Tungsten
Wolf's bane Aconite, Friar's-cap
Wolseley Sir Garnet
Woman(hood), Women Anile, Bellibone, Besom, Biddy, Bimbo, Bint, Bit, Boiler, Broad, Cailleach, Callet, Chai, Chapess, Chook, Citess, Cotquean, Crone, Cummer, Dame, Daughter, Distaff, Doe, Dona(h), Dorcas, Doris, Drab, Duenna, Eve, F, Fair, Fair sex, → **FEMALE**, Feme, Flapper, Floozy, Frail, Frow, Gammer, Gimmer, Gin, Girl, Gyno-, -gyny, Harpy, Harridan, Hen, Her, Ho, Inner, It, Jade, Jane, Kloo(t)chman, Lady, Liberated, Lilith, Lorette, Madam(e), Mademoiselle, Maenad, Mary, Miladi, Milady, Millie, Minge, Mob, Mort, Ms, Muliebrity, Painted, Pandora, Peat, Pict, Piece, Piece of goods, Placket, Popsy, Quean, Queen, Ramp, Rib, Ribibe, Ronyon, Rudas, Runnion, Sabine, Sakti, Scarlet, Shakti, Shawlay, Shawlie, She, Skirt, Sloane Ranger, Sort, Squaw, Tail, Tedesca, Tib, Tiring, Tit, Tottie, Totty, Trot, Umfazi, Vahine, Wahine, Weaker sex, Wifie, Zena
Womaniser Casanova, Lady-killer, Poodle-faker, Wolf
Womb Belly, Matrix, Metritis, Side, Uterus, Ventricle
Women's club, Women's lib S(h)akti, Soroptimist
Won Chon, W
Wonder(s) Admire, Agape, Amazement, AR, Arkansas, Arrah, Awe, Chinless, Colossus, Ferly, Grape-seed, Marle, → **MARVEL**, Meteor, Mirabilia, Miracle, Muse, Nine-day, Phenomenon, Prodigy, Seven, Speculate, Stupor, Suppose, Surprise, Thaumatrope, Wheugh, Whew, Wow
Wonderful(ly) Amazing, Bees' knees, Bitchin(g), Chinless, Épatant, Fantastic, Far-out, Ferly, Geason, Gee-whiz, Glorious, Gramercy, Great, Keen, Lal(l)apalooza, Magic, Mirable, Old, Purely, Ripping, Smashing, Sublime, Superb
Wonder-worker Fakir, Thaumaturgist, Thaumaturgus
Wonky Cockeyed
Wont(ed) Accustomed, Apt, Custom, Habit, Shan't, Used, Winna
Woo(er) Address, Beau, Carve, Court, Seduce, Suitor, Swain
Wood(s), Wooden, Woodland, Woody Arboretum, Batten, Beam, Board, Boord(e), Brake, Cask, Channel, Chipboard, Chuck, Chump, Clapboard, Conductor, Dead, Deadpan, Expressionless, Fardage, Fathom, Fire, Fish, Funk, Furious, Gantry, Gauntree, Hanger, Hard, Hyle, Kindling, Knee, Lath, Lumber, Mad, Magnetic, Miombo, Nemoral, Nemorous, Offcut, Pallet, Plastic, Pulpwood, Punk, Silvan, Slat, Spinney, Splat, Spline, Splint, Stolid, Sylvan, Three-ply, Timber, Tinder, Touch, Treen, Trees, Twiggy, Vert, Xylem, Xyloid

---

WOODS

3 letters:	Bowl	Lima	5 letters:
Ash	Carr	Lime	Agila
Box	Cord	Pine	Algum
Cam	Cork	Rata	Almug
Elm	Deal	Rock	Balsa
Log	Eugh	Shaw	Bavin
Red	Gapó	Soft	Beech
	Holt	Spar	Cedar
4 letters:	Iron	Wild	Copse
Beef	King	Yang	Drive
Bent	Lana		Ebony

Elfin	Citrus	Dunnage	**9 letters:**
Firth	Dingle	Duramen	Briarwood
Frith	Forest	Gambrel	Butternut
Green	Fustet	Gumwood	Caliature
Grove	Fustic	Hadrome	Campeachy
Heben	Fustoc	Hickory	Cocuswood
Hurst	Gaboon	Leopard	Eaglewood
Igapó	Gopher	Meranti	Fruitwood
Iroko	Herman	Palmyra	Heartwood
Jarul	Jarool	Paranym	Ivorywood
Joist	Jarrah	Pimento	Krummholz
Kokra	Letter	Sanders	Matchwood
Lance	Lignum	Sapwood	Partridge
Maple	Loggat	Shawnee	Porcupine
Mazer	Manuka	Shittim	Quebracho
Myall	Obeche	Trumpet	Satinwood
Opepe	Orache	Wallaba	Snakewood
Peach	Orange		Torchwood
Plane	Paddle	**8 letters:**	
Ramin	Poplar	Agalloch	**10 letters:**
Rowan	Raddle	Alburnum	Afrormosia
Sapan	Sabele	Basswood	Blockboard
Spoon	Sabicu	Bushveld	Bulletwood
Stink	Sandal	Caatinga	Calamander
Taiga	Sapele	Coulisse	Candlewood
Thorn	Sappan	Harewood	Cheesewood
Tiger	Sissoo	Hornbeam	Chittagong
Tulip	Sponge	Kingwood	Coromandel
Zante	Tallow	Laburnum	Fiddlewood
Zebra	Waboom	Ligneous	Greenheart
	Walnut	Mahogany	Hackmatack
6 letters:	Wandoo	Masonite®	Nettle-tree
Alerce	Yellow	Mountain	Palisander
Bamboo		Pyengadu	Sneezewood
Beaver	**7 letters:**	Pyinkado	Springwood
Birnam	Amboina	Rosewood	Summerwood
Bocage	Barwood	Sapucaia	
Brazil	Boscage	Shagbark	**11 letters:**
Canary	Brassie	Southern	Lignum-vitae
Carapa	Cambium	Tamarack	Sanderswood
Cheese	Coppice		Slippery elm
Citron	Dudgeon		

▷ **Wood** *may indicate* an anagram (in sense of mad)
Wood-carver Bodger, Gibbons, Whittler
Woodchuck Bobac, Marmot
Woodcock Becasse, Beccaccia, Snipe
Woodlouse Isopod, Oniscus, Slater
Woodman Ali (Baba), Coureur de bois, Feller, Forester, Hewer, Logger, Lumberjack, Sawyer
Woodpecker Bird, Flicker, Hickwall, Picarian, Rainbird, Sapsucker, Saurognathae,

Witwall, Woodspite, Woodwale, Yaffle
Wood-pigeon Bird, Cushat, Que(e)st, Qu(o)ist, Torquate
Wood-sorrel Oca
Wood-tar Furan, Furfuran
Woodwind Bassoon, Clarinet, Cornet, Flute, Oboe, Piccolo, Pipe, Recorder, Reed
Woodwork(er) Ebonist, Intarsia, Marquetrie, Marquetry, Sloid, Sloyd, Tarsia, Termite
Woodworm Gribble, Termes
Wookey Stalactite
Wool(len), Woolly Alpaca, Angora, Aran, Ardil, Bainin, Barège, Beige, Berlin, Botany, Bouclé, Calamanco, Cardi(gan), Cashmere, Cas(s)imere, Clean, Clip, Cotton, Crutchings, Daglock, Delaine, Doeskin, Dog, Doily, Down, Doyley, Drugget, Duffel, Fadge, Fingering, Fleece, Flock, Frib, Frieze, Fuzz, Glass, Greasy, Guernsey, Hank, Hause-lock, Hogget, Indumentum, Jaeger, Jersey, Kashmir, Ket, Lanate, Laniferous, Lanigerous, Lanose, Lock, Loden, Merino, Mineral, Mortling, Moul, Mullein, New, Noil(s), Nun's-veiling, Offsorts, Oo, Pashm, Pelage, Persian, Pine, Qiviut, Rock, Rolag, Sagathy, Saxon, Say, Shahtoosh, Shalloon, Shamina, Shetland, Shoddy, Skein, Skin, Slag, Slipe, Slip-on, Slub, Smart, Spencer, Staple, Steel, Strouding, Swansdown, Tamise, Tammy, Telltale, Thibet, Three-ply, Tod, Tricot, Tweed, Twin set, Vicuña, Virgin, Wire, Wood, Worcester, Yarn, Zephyr, Zibel(l)ine
Wool-gather(er), Woolgathering Argo, Dreamer, Reverie
Wool-holder, Woolsack Bale, Distaff
Woolly-bear Tiger-moth, Woubit
Wool-oil Yolk
Wooster Bertie
Woozy Drunk, Faint, Vague, Woolly
Worcester Wigorn
Word(s), Wording, Wordy Appellative, Bahuvrihi, Buzz, Cheville, Claptrap, Clipped, Clitic, Code, Comment, Content, Dick, Dit(t), Echoic, Embolalia, Enclitic, Epos, Etymon, Faith, Four-letter, Function, Ghost, Grace, Hapax legomenon, Hard, Heteronym, Hint, Homograph, Homonym, Household, Hyponym, → **IN A WORD**, → **IN TWO WORDS**, Janus, Jonah, Key, Last, Lexeme, Lexicon, Lexis, Loan, Logia, Logos, Long-winded, Lyrics, Mantra, Meronym, Message, Morpheme, Mot, Neologism, News, Nonce, Nonsense, Noun, Oracle, Order, Palabra, Paragram, Paranym, Parenthesis, Parole, Paronym, Paroxytone, Particle, Perissology, Peristomenon, Phrase, Piano, Pledge, Pleonasm, Polysemen, Portmanteau, Preposition, Prolix, Promise, Pronoun, Reserved, Rhematic, Rhyme, Rumour, Saying, Selah, Semantics, Signal, Subtitle, Surtitle, Tatpurusha, Term, Tetragram, Text, Trigger, Trope, Typewriter, Verb, Verbiage, Verbose, Vocab(ulary), Vogue, Warcry, Weasel, Wort, Written
Word-blindness Alexia, Dyslexia
Word-play Charade, Paronomasia, Pun
Workable Feasible, Practical
Workaholic, Work(er), Working(-class), Workmen, Workman(ship) Act(ivate), Ant, Appliqué, Apronman, Artefact, Artel, Artifact, Artificer, Artisan, At it, Barmaid, Beaver, Bee, Blue-collar, Blue-singlet, Bohunk, Boondoggle, Boon(er), Bull, Business, Careerist, Casual, Char, Chargehand, Chigga, Chippy, Chore, Claim, Clock, Colon, Community, Coolie, Corvée, Craftsman, Crew, Darg, Do, Dog, Dogsbody, Draft-mule, Droil, Drudge, Drug, Dung, Earn, Effect, Effort, Em, Erg(ataner), Ergatoid, Erg-nine, Ergon, Ergonomics, Erg-ten, Eta, Everything, Evince, Exercise, Exploit, Factotum, Facture, Fast, Fat, Fettler, Field, Flex(i)time,

Floruit, Fret, Fuller, → FUNCTION, Gastarbeiter, Gel, Go, Graft, Grass, Grind,
Grisette, Hand, Harness, Hat, Hobo, Horse, Hot-desking, Hunky, Industry,
Innards, Job, Journeyman, Key, Knead, Kolhoznik, Labour, Laid, Luddite, Lump,
Machinist, Maid, Man, Manipulate, Manpower, McJob, Mechanic, Meng, Menge,
Menial, Midinette, Mine, Ming, MO, Moider, Moil, Moonlight, Movement,
Navvy, Neuter, Number, Oeuvre, On, Op, Opera(tion), Operative, Operator,
Opus, Opusc(u)le, Outside, Ouvrier, Ox, Parergon, Part, Passage, Peasant, Peg,
Pensum, Peon, Pink-collar, Ply, Poker, Portfolio, Potboiler, Practise, Production,
Prole(tariat), Prud'homme, Public, Pursuit, Red-neck, Reduction, Rep, Ride,
Robot, Roughneck, Rouseabout, Roustabout, Run, Salaryman, Samiti, Sandhog,
Satisfactory, Scabble, Scapple, Serve, Service, Servile, Seven, Shift, Shop, Situation,
Skanger, Slogger, Smithy, Social, Spide, Staff, Stakhanovite, Stevedore, Stint, Strap,
Straw, Strive, Support, Surface, Swaggie, Swagman, Sweat, Swink, Take, Tamper,
Task, Team, Telecommuter, Temp, Tenail(le), Tenaillon, Termite, Tew, Tick, Till,
Toccata, Toil, Toreutic, Travail, Treatise, Trojan, TU, TUC, Turk, Tut, Typto, Uphill,
Wage plug, Walla(h), Wark, Welfare, White-collar, Wobblies, Yacker, Yakka,
Yakker, Yarco
Work-basket, Workbox Caba(s), Nécessaire
Workbench Banker, Siege
Workhouse Casual ward, Spike, Union
▷ **Working** *may indicate* an anagram
Working-party Bee, Quilting-bee, Sewing-bee, Squad
Workmate Yokefellow
Work out Deduce
Works, Workshop Atelier, Engine, Factory, Forge, Foundry, Garage, Hacienda,
Hangar, Innards, Lab, Mill, Passage, Plant, Public, Shed, Shop, Skylab, Smithy,
Studio, Sweatshop, Telecottage, Time, Tin, Turnery, Upper
Workshy Indolent, Lazy, Sweer(ed), Sweert, Sweir(t)
World(ly), Worldwide Adland, Carnal, Chthonic, Cosmopolitan, Cosmos,
Cyberspace, Dream, Earth, First, Fleshly, Fourth, Free, Ge, Globe, Kingdom,
Lay, Lower, Mappemond, Meatspace, Microcosm, Mondaine, Mondial, Mould,
Mundane, Nether, New, Old, Orb, Other, Oyster, Planet, Possible, Second, Secular,
Sensual, Society, Sphere, Spirit, Temporal, Terra, Terrene, Terrestrial, Third,
Universe, Vale, Web, Welt
Worm(-like), Worms, Wormy Acorn, Anguillula, Annelid, Annulata, Apod(e),
Apodous, Army, Arrow, Articulata, Ascarid, Bilharzia, Bladder, Blind, Blood,
Bob, Bootlace, Brandling, Bristle, Caddis, Capeworm, Caseworm, Catworm,
Cestode, Cestoid, Chaetopod, Clamworm, Copper, Dew, Diet, Diplozoon, Edge,
Enteropneust, Fan, Filander, Filaria, Flag, Flat, Fluke, Galley, Gape, Gilt-tail,
Gordius, Gourd, Gru-gru, Guinea, Hair, Hair-eel, Hairworm, Heartworm,
Helminth, Hemichordata, Hookworm, Horsehair, Idle, Inchworm, Leech,
Liver-fluke, Lob, Lumbricus, Lytta, Maw, Measuring, Merosome, Miner's, Mopani,
Muck, Nemathelminthes, Nematoda, Nematode, Nematodirus, Nematomorpha,
Nemertea, Nemertina, Nereid, Night-crawler, Oligochaete, Onychophoran, Paddle,
Palmer, Palolo, Paste-eel, Peripatus, Pile, Pin, Piper, Planarian, Platyhelminth,
Polychaete, Ragworm, Ribbon, Roundworm, Sabella, Sand-mason, Schistosome,
Scoleciform, Scolex, Screw, Seamouse, Serpula, Servile, Ship, Sipunculacea,
Sipunculoidea, Stomach, Strawworm, Strongyl(e), Taenia, Tag-tail, Taint,
Tapeworm, Tenioid, Teredo, Termite, Threadworm, Tiger tail, Tongue, Toxocara,
Trematode, Trichin(ell)a, Trichinosed, Triclad, Tube, Tubifex, Turbellaria,
Vermiform, Vinegar, Vinegar eel, Wheat-eel, Wheatworm, Whipworm

Wormkiller Anthelmintic, Santonin
Wormwood Absinth, Appleringie, Artemisia, Moxa, Mugwort, Santonica, Southernwood
Worn (out) Attrite, Bare, Decrepit, Detrition, Effete, Épuisé, Exhausted, Forfairn, Forfoughten, Forjaskit, Forjeskit, Frazzled, Knackered, Old, On, Passé, Raddled, Rag, Seedy, Shabby, Shot, Spent, Stale, Threadbare, Tired, Traikit, Trite, Used, Weathered, Whacked
Worried, Worrier, Worry Agonise, Angst, Annoy, Anxiety, Badger, Bait, Beset, Bother, Brood, Burden, Care(worn), Cark, Chafe, Concern, Deave, Deeve, Distress, Disturb, Dog, Eat, Exercise, Faze, Feeze, Frab, Fret, Fuss, Gnaw, Harass, Harry, Headache, Hyp, Inquietude, Knag, Nag, Perturb, Pester, Pheese, Pheeze, Phese, Pingle, Pium, Preoccupy, Rile, Sool, Stew, Tew, Touse, Towse, Trouble, Unease, Unnerve, Vex, Wherrit, Worn
▷ **Worried** *may indicate* an anagram
Worse(n) Adversely, Degenerate, Deteriorate, Exacerbate, Impair, Inflame, Pejorate, Regress, Relapse, War(re), Waur
Worship(per) Adore, Adulation, Ancestor, Angelolatry, Aniconism, Autolatry, Bless, Churchgoer, Cult, Deify, Devotion, Douleia, Dulia, Epeolatry, Exercise, Fetish, Glorify, Gurdwara, Happy-clappy, Henotheism, Hero, Ibadat, Idolatry, Idolise, Latria, Lauds, Lionise, Liturgics, Lordolatry, Mariolatry, Oncer, Orant, Praise, Puja, Revere, Sabaism, Sakta, Service, Shacharis, Shakta, Sun, Synaxis, Thiasus, Vaishnava, Venerate, Votary, Wodenism
Worst Beat, Best, Defeat, Get, Nadir, Outdo, Overpower, Pessimum, Rock-bottom, Scum, Severest, The pits, Throw, Trounce
Worsted Caddis, Caddyss, Challis, Coburg, Genappe, Lea, Ley, Serge, Shalli, Tamin(e), Whipcord
▷ **Worsted** *may indicate* an anagram
Wort Hopped, Laser, Parkleaves, Plant, Sweet, Tutsan
Worth(while), Worthy, Worthies Admirable, Asset, Be, Cop, Cost, Deserving, Eligible, Estimable, Feck, → MERIT, Nine, Notable, Substance, Tanti, Use, Value, Venerable, Virtuous, Wealth
Worthless (person) Base, Beggarly, Bilge, Blown, Bodger, Bootless, Bum, Catchpenny, Cheapjack, Crumb, Cypher, Damn, Despicable, Docken, Dodkin, Doit, Doitkin, Draffish, Draffy, Dreck, Dross, Duff, Fallal, Footra, Fouter, Foutre, Frippery, Gimcrack, Gingerbread, Glop, Gubbins, Hilding, Javel, Jimcrack, Left, Light, Lorel, Lorrell, Losel, Lozell, Manky, Mare's nest, Mud, Nugatory, Nyaff, Obol, Orra, Otiose, Paltry, Pin, Poxy, Punk, Raca, Rag, Rap, Riffraff, Rubbishy, Scabby, Scrote, Scum, Shinkin, Shotten, Siwash, Sorry, Straw, Tinhorn, Tinpot, Tinsel, Tittle, Toerag, Trangam, Trashy, Trumpery, Tuppenny, Twat, Two-bit, Twopenny, Useless, Vain, Vile, Waff, Wanworthy, Wauff
Wotchermean Anan
Would be Assumed, Pseudo, Soi-disant
Wouldn't Nould(e)
Wound(ed) Battery, Bite, Bless, Blighty, Bruise, Chagrin, Coiled, Crepance, Cut, Dere, Engore, Entry, Exit, Flesh, Ganch, Gash, Gaunch, Gore, Harm, Hurt, Injury, Lacerate, Lesion, Maim, Maul, Molest, Mortify, Offend, Pip, Sabre-cut, Scab, Scar, Scath, Scotch, Scratch, Shoot, Snaked, Snub, Sore, Stab, Sting, Trauma, Twined, Umbrage, Vuln, Vulnerary, Walking, Wing, Wint
Woundwort Clown's, Marsh
Woven Faconne, Inwrought, Knitted, Pirnit, Textile, Wattle
Wow Amaze, Howl, Impress, My, Success

Wrack Destroy, Downfall, Kelp, Ore, Torment, Varec(h), Vengeance
Wraith Apparition, Fetch, Ghost, Phantom, Shadow, Spectre
Wrangle(r), Wrangling Altercate, Argie-bargie, → **ARGUE**, Bandy, Bicker, Brangle,
  Broil, Dispute, Haggle, Horse, Mathematical, Rag, Second, Senior, Vitilitigation
Wrap(per), Wrapping, Wraparound, Wrap up Amice, Amis, Bind, Body, Bubble,
  Bundle, Cellophane®, Cere, Clingfilm, Cloak, Clothe, Cocoon, Conclude, Emboss,
  Enfold, Enrol(l), Ensheath(e), Envelop(e), Enwind, Foil, Folio, Furl, Gladwrap®,
  Hap, Hem, Kimono, Kraft, Lag, Lap, Mail, Mob, Muffle, Negligee, Nori, Outsert,
  Package, Parcel, Plastic, Roll, Rug, Shawl, Sheath(e), Shroud, Stole, Swaddle,
  Swathe, Throw, Tinfoil, Tsutsumu, Velamen, Wap, Wimple
Wrasse Conner, Cunner, Parrot-fish, Scar
Wrath Anger, Cape, Fury, Ire, Passion, Vengeance
Wreak Avenge, Indulge, Inflict
Wreath(e) Adorn, Anadem, Bridal, Chaplet, Coronal, Crown, Entwine, Festoon,
  Garland, Laurel, Lei, Torse, Tortile, Twist
Wreathe(d) Hederated
Wreck(age), Wrecked, Wrecker Blotto, Crab, Debris, Demolish, Devastate,
  Flotsam, Founder, Goner, Hesperus, Hulk, Lagan, Ligan, Loss, Luddite, Mutilate,
  Nervous, Ruin(ate), Sabotage, Shambles, Shatter, Sink, Smash, Subvert, Torpedo,
  Trash, Wrack
▷ **Wrecked** *may indicate* an anagram
Wren Architect, Bird, Fire-crested, Golden-crested, Hannah, Heath, Jenny, Kinglet,
  Rifleman-bird, Sailor, Superb blue, Willow
Wrench Allen, Bobbejaan, Box, Fit, Jerk, Lug, Mole, Monkey, Nut, Pin, Pipe, Pull,
  Screw, Socket, Spanner, Spider, Sprain, Stillson®, Strain, Strap, T-bar, Tear,
  Torque, Twist, Windlass, Wrest
Wrestle(r), Wrestling All-in, Antaeus, Arm, Backbreaker, Basho, Bearhug,
  Bodycheck, Boston crab, Catch-as-catch-can, Catchweight, Clinch, Clothes line,
  Cross press, Featherweight, Flying mare, Folding-press, Freestyle, Full-nelson,
  Gr(a)eco-Roman, Grapple, Grovet, Half-nelson, Hammerlock, Haystacks,
  Headlock, Hip-lock, → **HOLD**, Indian, Judo, Knee-drop, Makunouchi, Milo, Monkey
  climb, Mud, Nelson, Niramiai, Ozeki, Palaestral, Pancratium, Pinfall, Posting,
  Rikishi, Sambo, Stable, Straight arm lift, Struggle, Sumo, Sumotori, Suplex, Tag,
  Tag (team), Tussle, Whip, Wraxle, Wristlock, Writhe, Yokozuna
Wretch(ed) Abject, Bally, Blackguard, Blue, Caitiff, Chap-fallen, Cullion, Donder,
  Forlorn, Git, Hapless, Lorn, Low, Measly, Miser, Miserable, Peelgarlic, Pilgarlick,
  Pipsqueak, Pitiable, Poltroon, Poor, Punk, Rat, Scoundrel, Scroyle, Seely, Snake,
  Unblest, Wo(e), Woeful
▷ **Wretched** *may indicate* an anagram
Wriggle Hirsle, Shimmy, Squirm, Twine, Wiggle, Writhe
Wring(er) Drain, Extort, Mangle, Screw, Squeeze, Twist
Wrinkle(d), Wrinkly Clue, Cockle, Corrugate, Crankle, Crease, Crepy, Crimple,
  Crimpy, Crinkle, Crow's-foot, Crumple, Fold, Frounce, Frown, Frumple, Furrow,
  Gen, Groove, Headline, Hint, Idea, Line, Lirk, Plissé, Plough, Pucker, Purse, Ridge,
  Rimple, Rivel, Rop(e)y, Ruck(le), Rugose, Rumple, Runkle, Seamy, Shrivel, Sulcus,
  Time-worn, Tip, Whelk, Wizened, Wrizled
Wrist Carpus, Radialia, Shackle-bone
Writ(s) Attachment, Audita querela, Capias, Certiorari, Cursitor, Dedimus,
  Distringas, Elegit, Fieri facias, Filacer, Habeas corpus, Holy, Injunction, Jury
  process, Latitat, Law-burrows, Mandamus, Mise, Mittimus, Noverint, Praemunire,
  Process, Quo warranto, Replevin, Scirefacias, Significat, Subpoena, Summons,

Supersedeas, Supplicavit, Tolt, Venire, Venire facias, Warrant
Write(r), Writing Allograph, Amphigory, Annotator, Apocrypha, → **AUTHOR**,
Automatic, Ballpoint, Biographer, Biro®, Bloomsbury Group, Book-hand,
Boustrophedon, Calligraphy, Causerie, Cento, Charactery, Clerk, Clinquant,
Collectanea, Columnist, Continuity, Copperplate, Creative, Cuneiform, Cursive,
Diarist, Dite, Draft, → **DRAMATIST**, Elohist, Endorse, Endoss, Engross,
Epigrammatise, Epistle, → **ESSAYIST**, Expatiate, Farceur, Festschrift, Fist, Form,
Formulary, Freelance, Ghost, Gongorism, Graffiti, Grammatology, Graphite, Hack,
Hairline, Hand, Haplography, Hieratic, Hieroglyphics, Hiragana, Indite, Ink,
Inkhorn-mate, Ink-jerker, Inkslinger, Inscribe, Join-hand, Jot(tings), Journalese,
Journalist, Journo, Kalakana, Kaleyard School, Kana, Kanji, Katakana, Keelivine,
Keelyvine, Leader, Lexigraphy, Lexis, Linear A, Lipogram, Littérateur, Longhand,
Lucubrate, Marivaudage, Memoirist, Minoan, Mirror, Miscellany, Ms(s), Nesk(h),
Nib, Notary, Notate, Novelese, → **NOVELIST**, Paragraphia, Pasigraphy, Pen,
Pencil, Penmanship, Penne, Penny-a-liner, Pentel®, Phrasemonger, Picture,
Pinyin, Planchette, → **POET**, Polemic, Pot-hook, Prosaist, Proser, Pseudepigrapha,
Psychogram, Psychography, Purana, Purple patch, Quill, Roundhand, Samizdat,
Sanskrit, Sci-fi, Scissorer, Scratch, Screed, Screeve, Scribe, Scrip(t), Scripture,
Scrivener, Scrow, Scytale, Secretary, Shaster, Shastra, Sign, Sling-ink, Small-hand,
Space, Spirit, Stichometry, Style, Stylography, Subscript, Superscribe, Sutra,
Syllabary, Syllabic, Syllabism, Syngraph, Tantra, Text, Tractarian, Transcribe,
Treatise, Tushery, Uncial, Wordsmith, Zend-Avesta

WRITERS

3 letters:	Loti	Crane	Lodge
APH	Lyly	Defoe	Lorca
Eco	Mann	Doyle	Mason
Lee	More	Dumas	Milne
Paz	Nash	Eliot	Munro
Poe	Opie	Ellis	Musil
RLS	Ovid	Genet	Nashe
	Pope	Gogol	Orczy
4 letters:	Saki	Gorki	Ouida
Amis	Sand	Gorky	Pater
Asch	Shaw	Gosse	Paton
Aymé	Snow	Greer	Pliny
Bede	Ward	Grimm	Pound
Behn	West	Hardy	Powys
Bolt	Zola	Harte	Reade
Cary		Henty	Renan
Dahl	5 letters:	Hesse	Rilke
Elia	Acton	Heyer	Sagan
Gide	Albee	Homer	Scott
Hope	Auden	Hoyle	Seuss
Hugo	Ayres	Ibsen	Shute
Hunt	Bates	Innes	Spark
King	Blake	James	Stark
Lamb	Caine	Joyce	Stein
Lang	Camus	Kafka	Swift
Loos	Corvo	Lewis	Synge

Twain	Le Fanu	Chekhov	Travers
Verne	London	Cobbett	Wallace
Vidal	Lucian	Cocteau	Walpole
Waugh	Lytton	Colette	Wharton
Wells	Mailer	Collins	Whitman
White	Malory	Cookson	Wyndham
Wilde	Mannin	Coppard	
Woolf	Masoch	Corelli	*8 letters:*
Yates	Miller	Cranmer	Anacreon
Yonge	Milton	Deeping	Andersen
	Morgan	Dickens	Beaumont
6 letters:	Nerval	Dodgson	Bradbury
Ambler	Nesbit	Drabble	Browning
Arnold	Onions	Dreiser	Caldwell
Artaud	Orwell	Durrell	Cartland
Asimov	Proust	Emerson	Chandler
Atwood	Racine	Fenelon	Childers
Austen	Romaji	Forster	Christie
Balzac	Runyon	Gissing	Constant
Baring	Ruskin	Golding	De la Mare
Barrie	Sapper	Haggard	Disraeli
Belloc	Sappho	Herbert	Faulkner
Bellow	Sayers	Hichens	Fielding
Borges	Sendak	Johnson	Flaubert
Borrow	Sewell	Kipling	Forester
Braine	Smiles	Lardner	Goncourt
Bronte	Steele	Marryat	Ishiguro
Buchan	Sterne	Maugham	Kingsley
Bunyan	Stoker	Mauriac	Langland
Butler	Storey	Mérimée	Lawrence
Capote	Thomas	Mitford	Mannheim
Cicero	Updike	Moravia	Meredith
Clarke	Virgil	Murdoch	Perrault
Conrad	Walton	Nabokov	Plutarch
Cowper	Wilder	Naipaul	Proudhon
Cronin		Peacock	Rabelais
Daudet	*7 letters:*	Pushkin	Rattigan
Dryden	Addison	Pynchon	Remarque
Engels	Aldrich	Ransome	Rousseau
Fowles	Aretino	Rostand	Salinger
France	Bagehot	Rushdie	Schiller
Gibbon	Bagnold	Saroyan	Sillitoe
Goethe	Ballard	Sassoon	Smollett
Graves	Beckett	Shelley	Stendhal
Greene	Bennett	Simenon	Taffrail
Heller	Bentley	Sitwell	Traherne
Hobbes	Boileau	Surtees	Trollope
Hughes	Boswell	Terence	Turgenev
Huxley	Burgess	Thoreau	Voltaire
Jerome	Carlyle	Tolkien	Williams
Jonson	Chaucer	Tolstoy	

9 letters:	Lermontov	Wodehouse	Maeterlinck
Aeschylus	Linklater		Shakespeare
Ainsworth	Lovecraft	10 letters:	
Blackmore	Mackenzie	Ballantyne	12 letters:
Boccaccio	Madariaga	Chesterton	Aristophanes
Burroughs	Mansfield	Dostoevsky	Solzhenitsyn
Cervantes	Martineau	Fitzgerald	
Corneille	Oppenheim	Galsworthy	13 letters:
Dos Passos	Pasternak	Mandeville	Chateaubriand
Du Maurier	Priestley	Maupassant	Sackville-West
Edgeworth	Santayana	Richardson	
Goldsmith	Sholokhov	Williamson	15 letters:
Hawthorne	Steinbeck		Somerset Maugham
Hemingway	Stevenson	11 letters:	
Isherwood	Thackeray	Machiavelli	

Write-off Amortise, Annul, Cancel, Scrap
Writhe, Writhing Athetosis, Contort, Curl, Scriggle, Squirm, Thraw, Twist, Wriggle
▷ **Writhing** may indicate an anagram
Writing-case Kalamdan
Writing-room Scriptorium
Wrong(ful) Aggrieve, Agley, Amiss, Astray, Awry, Bad, Bum, Chout, Delict, Disserve, Err, Fallacious, False, Falsism, Harm, Ill, Immoral, Improper, Incorrect, Injury, Mischief, Misintelligence, Misled, Mistake(n), Misuse, Nocent, Offbase, Offend, Pear-shaped, Peccadillo, Perverse, Private, Public, Sin(ful), Tort, Tortious, Transgress, Unethical, Unright, Unsuitable, Withershins, Wryly, X
▷ **Wrong** may indicate an anagram
Wrong opinion Cacodoxy
Wrought (up) Agitated, Beaten, Carved, Created, Excited, Filigree, Freestone, Shaped
Wrung Twisted, Withers
Wry Askew, Contrary, Devious, Distort, Droll, Grimace, Ironic
Wryneck Iynx, Jynx, Torticollis, Yunx
Wycliffian Lollard
Wyoming Wy

X(-shaped) Buss, By, Chi, Christ, Cross, Decussate, Drawn, Kiss, Ten, Times, Unknown, X-ray

Xant(h)ippe Battle-axe, Dragon

Xenon Xe

Xerophyte, Xerophytic Cactus, Cereus, Mesquite, Tamaricaceae, Tamarisk

Xhosan Caffre, Kaf(f)ir

Ximenes Cardinal

▸ **Xmas** *see* CHRISTMAS

X-ray Angiogram, Anticathode, C(A)T-scanner, Cholangiography, Emi-Scanner, Encephalogram, Encephalograph, Fermi, Grenz, Mammogram, Plate, Pyelogram, Radioscopy, Rem, Roentgen, Sciagram, Screening, Skiagram, Tomography, Venogram, Xeroradiography

Xylophone Marimba, Sticcado, Sticcato

Yy

Y Samian, Unknown, Yankee, Yard, Year, Yen, Yttrium
Yacht Britannia, Dragon, Ice, Keelboat, Ketch, Knockabout, Land, Maxi, Sailboat, Sand
Yachtsman, Yachtsmen Chichester, RYS
Yak Gup, Talk
Yale® Key, Lock
Yam Adjigo, Batata, Breadroot, Camote, Dioscorea, Diosgenin, Kumara
Yank(ee) Bet, Carpetbagger, Hitch, Jerk, Jonathan, Lug, Northerner, Pluck, Pull, Rug, Schlep(p), So(o)le, Sowl(e), → TUG, Tweak, Twitch, Wrench, Wrest
▷ **Yank** *may indicate* an anagram
Yap Bark, Yelp
Yard(s) Area, CID, Close, Court, Farm-toun, Garden, Hard, Haw, Hof, Junk, Kail, Knacker's, Main, Marshalling, Mast, Measure, Navy, Patio, Poultry, Prison, Ree(d), Sail, Scotland, Show, Spar, Sprit, Steel, Stick, Stride, Switch, Tilt, Timber, Victualling, Y, Yd
Yarn(s) Abb, Berlin, Bouclé, Caddice, Caddis, Chenille, Clew, Clue, Cop, Cord, Crewel, Fib, Fibroline, Fingering, Genappe, Gimp, Gingham, Guimp(e), Gymp, Homespun, Jaw, Knittle, Knot, Lay, Lea, Ley, Line, Lisle, Lurex®, Marl, Merino, Mohair, Nylon, Organzine, Orlon®, Ply, Rigmarole, Ripping, Rogue's, Rope, Saxony, Schappe, Sennit, Sinnet, Skein, Spun, Story, Strand, Tale, Taradiddle, Thread, Thrid, Thrum(my), Tram, Warp, Weft, Woof, Wool, Worsted, Zephyr
Yarrow Milfoil
Yashmak Veil
Yaw(s) Boba, Buba, Deviate, Framboesia, Lean, Morula, Tack, Veer
Yawn(ing) Boredom, Chasmy, Fissure, Gant, Gape, Gaunt, Greys, Hiant, Oscitation, Pandiculation, Rictus
Yea Certainly, Truly, Verily, Yes
Year(ly), Years A, Age, Anno, Annual, Anomalistic, Astronomical, Calendar, Canicular, Civil, Common, Cosmic, Decennium, Donkey's, Dot, Ecclesiastical, Egyptian, Embolismic, Equinoctial, Financial, Fiscal, Gap, Great, Hebrew, Holy, Indiction, Julian, Leap, Legal, Light, Lunar, Lunisolar, Natural, PA, Perfect, Platonic, Riper, Sabbatical, School, Sidereal, Solar, Sothic, Summer, Sun, Tax, Theban, Time, Towmon(d), Towmont, Tropical, Twelvemonth, Vintage, Wander
Yearbook Annual
Yearling Colt, Hogget, Stirk, Teg
Yearn(ing) Ache, Ake, Aspire, Brame, Burn, Covet, Crave, Curdle, Desire, Erne, Greed, Hanker, Hone, → LONG, Lust, Nostalgia, Pant, Pine, Sigh
▷ **Yearning** *may indicate* an anagram
Year's end Dec
Yeast Barm, Bees, Brewer's, Ferment, Flor, Leaven, Saccharomycete, Torula, Vegemite®

Yell Cry, Hue, Shout, Skelloch, Squall, Thunder, Tiger, Waul, Yoick
Yellow(ish) Abram, Amber, Anthoclore, Auburn, Back, Beige, Bisque, Bistre,
Buff, Butternut, Cadmium, Canary, Chicken, Chrome, Citrine, Cowardly, Craven,
Curcumin(e), Daffadowndilly, Daffodil, Eggshell, Etiolin, Fallow, Fever, Filemot,
Flavescent, Flavin(e), Flavon, Flaxen, Fulvous, Gamboge, Gold, Icteric, Isabel(le),
Isabella, Jack, Jaundiced, King's, Lammer, Lemon(y), Lupulin, Lurid, Lutein,
Luteous, Lutescent, Mustard, Nankeen, Naples, Oaker, Ochery, Ochre(y), Or(eide),
Oroide, Pages, Peril, Pink, Primrose, Queen's, River, Saffron, Sallow, Sand, Sear,
Sherry, Spineless, Straw, Sulphur, Tawny, Topaz, Tow, Vitelline, Weld, Xanthous,
Yolk
Yellowhammer Bunting, Yeldring, Yeldrock, Yite, Yoldring
Yellow-wood Gopher
Yelp Cry, Squeal, Whee, Ya(w)p
Yemeni Adeni, Saba, Sabean, Sheba
Yen Desire, Itch, Longing, Urge, Y, Yearn
Yeoman Beefeater, Exon, Goodman, Goodwife, Salvation
Yep OK, Yes
Yes Ay(e), Da, Indeed, Ja, Jokol, Nod, OK, Oke, Quite, Sure, Truly, Uh-huh, Wilco,
Yea, Yokul, Yup
Yesterday Démodé, Eve, Hesternal, Pridian
Yet But, Even, How-be, Moreover, Nay, Nevertheless, Now, Still, Though
Yeti Abominable snowman, Sasquatch
Yew Podocarp(us), Taxus
Yibbles A(i)blins
Yield(ing), Yielded Abandon, Afford, Bend, Bow, Breed, Capitulate, Catch, Cede,
Come, Comply, Concede, Crack, Crop, Defer, Dividend, Docile, Ductile, Easy,
Elastic, Exert, Facile, Flaccid, Flexible, Give, Harvest, Interest, Knuckle, Knuckle
under, Meek, Meltith, Mess, Output, Pan, Pay, Pliant, Produce, Quantum,
Redemption, Relent, Render, Return, Sag, Soft, → **SUBMIT**, Succumb, Surrender,
Susceptible, Sustained, Temporise, Truckle, Weak-kneed, Yold
Yodel Song, Warble
Yoga, Yogi As(h)tanga, Bear, Bhakti, Fakir, Hatha, Maha, Power, Raja, Sid(d)ha,
Sivananda
Yog(h)urt Dahi, Madzoon, Matzoon, Tzatziki
Yoke Bow, Cang(ue), Collar, Couple, Harness, Inspan, Jugal, Oxbow, Pair, Span,
Square, Tucker
Yokel Boor, Bumpkin, Chaw(-bacon), Clumperton, Culchie, Hayseed, Hick, Jake,
Jock, Peasant, Rustic
Yolk Parablast, Vitellicle, Vitellus, Yelk, Yellow
Yon(der) Distant, Further, O'erby, Thae, There, Thether, Thither
Yore Agone, Olden, Past
Yorick Sterne
York(shire), Yorkshireman Batter, Bowl, Ebor, Pudding, Ridings, Tyke
Yorker Tice
You One, Sie, Thee, Thou, Usted, Wena, Ye
Young (person), Youngster, Youth(ful) Adolescent, Ageless, Amorino, Bev(an),
Bodgie, Boy, Boyhood, Brigham, Bub, Buckie, Buppie, Calf-time, Ch, Charver, Chick,
Chicken, Chiel, Child, Chile, Cion, Cockerel, Cockle, Colt, Comsomol, Cornstalk,
Cub, Day-old, Dell, Dilling, DJ, Early, Ephebe, Ephebus, Esquire, Flapper, Fledgling,
Foetus, Fox, Fry, Gigolo, Gilded, Gillet, Girl, Gunsel, Halfling, Hebe, Hobbledehoy,
Immature, Imp, Infant, Issue, Jeunesse d'orée, Junior, Juvenal, Juvenesce, Juvenile,

Keral, Kid, Kiddo, Kiddy, Kipper, Knave-bairn, Komsomol, Lad, Lamb, Latter-day, Leaping-time, Less, Litter, Little, Loretta, Middle, Minor, Misspent, Mod, Mormon, Mot, Nance, Neanic, Ned(ette), Neophyte, Nestling, New, New Romantic, Nipper, Nurs(e)ling, Nymph, Plant, Popsy, (Pre-)pubescent, Progeny, Protégé(e), Punk, Pup, Sapling, Scent, Scion, Shaveling, Shaver, Sien(t), Skinhead, Slip, Son, Spawn, Sprig, Springal(d), Stripling, Subteen, Swain, Syen, Ted, Teenager, Teens, Teenybopper, Toyboy, Vernal, Well-preserved, Whelp, Whippersnapper, Widge, Wigga, Wigger, Yippy, Yoof, Yopper, Younker, Yumpie, Yuppie

Younger, Youngest Baby, Benjamin, Cadet, Last born, Less, Minimus, Seneca, Wallydrag, Wallydraigle, Yr

Your(s) Thee, Thine, Thy

▸ **Youth** see YOUNG PERSON

Yo-yo Bandalore

Ytterbium Yb

Yttrium Y

Yucatan Maya

Yucca Adam's needle

Yucky Gooey, Grooly, Sickly, Sticky

Yugoslav Croat(ian), Serb, Slovene, Ustashi

Yukon YT

Yuletide Advent, Dec, Noel, Xmas

Zz

Z Izzard, Izzet, Zambia, Zebra
Zamenhof Esperanto
Zander Fogash, Sander
Zany Bor(r)el, Comic, Cuckoo, Idiotic, Mad, Offbeat
Zanzibar Swahili
Zeal(ous) Ardour, Bigotry, Devotion, Eager, Enthusiasm, Evangelic, Fervour, Fire, Hamas, Perfervid, Study
Zealot Bigot, Devotee, Fan(atic), St Simon, Votary
Zebra Convict, Quagga
Zenith Acme, Apogee, Height, Pole, Summit, Vertex
Zeno Colonnade, Elea, Stoic
Zeolite Analcime, Analcite, Gmelinite
Zephyr Breeze, Wind
Zeppelin Airship, Balloon, Dirigible
Zero Absolute, Blob, Cipher, Circle, Donut, Double, Ground, Nil, Nothing, Nought, O, Status, Year, Z
Zest Condiment, Crave, Élan, Enthusiasm, Gusto, Pep, Piquancy, Relish, Spark, Spice, Tang, Zap, Zing
Ziegfeld Flo
Zigzag Crémaillère, Crinkle-crankle, Dancette, Feather-stitch, Indent, Major Mitchell, Ric-rac, Slalom, Stagger, Switchback, Tack, Traverse, Vandyke, Yaw
Zinc Blende, Gahnite, Mossy, Sherardise, Spelter, Sphalerite, Tutenag, Tutty, Willemite, Wurtzite, Zn
Zip(per) Dash, Energy, Fastener, Fly, Go, O, Oomph, Presto, Side fastener, Stingo, Vim, Vivacity, Whirry, Zero
Zircon Hyacinth, Jacinth, Jargo(o)n
Zirconium Baddeleyite, Zr
Zither Autoharp, Cithara, Kantela, Kantele, Koto
Zodiac(al) Aquarius, Archer, Aries, Bull, Cancer, Capricorn, Counter-glow, Crab, Fish, Gegenschein, Gemini, Goat, Horoscope, Leo, Libra, Lion, Ophiuchus, Pisces, Ram, Sagittarius, Scales, Scorpio(n), Taurus, Twins, Virgin, Virgo, Watercarrier
Zola Budd, Emile, Nana, Realism
Zombie Catatonic, Dolt, Robot
Zone(s) Abyssal, Anacoustic, Area, Arid, Auroral, Band, Bathyal, Belt, Benioff, Buffer, Canal, Climate, Collision, Comfort, Convergence, Crumple, Drop, Economic, Ecotone, End, Enterprise, Erogenous, Euro, Exclusion, F layer, Fracture, Free, Fresnel, Frigid, Hadal, Home, Hot, Impact, Ionopause, Krumhole, Low velocity, Neutral, No-fly, Nuclear-free, Precinct, → **REGION**, Rift, Ring, Russian, Sahel, Sector, Shear, Skip, Smokeless, Soviet, Stratopause, Strike, Subduction, T, Temperate, Time, Tolerance, Torrid, Tundra, Twilight
Zoo Bedlam, Circus, Menagerie, Vivarium, Whipsnade

Zoologist, Zoology Biologist, Botanist, Cetology, Naturalist, Primatology
Zoom Close-up, Speed
Zoroastrian Gabar, Gheber, Ghebre, Gueber, Guebre, Magus, Mazdaist, Mazdean, Ormazd, Ormuzd, Parsee, Parsi
Zulu Chaka, Impi, Inkatha, Matabele, Niger, Shaka, Warrior
Zut Crimini

Fantastic English dictionaries from one of Europe 's leading dictionary publishers

The Collins English Dictionary

£35 | 978-0-00-722899 7 | Hardback | 1,888pp

The Collins English Dictionary is a rich source of words for everyone who loves language. Including a much wider range of words than ever before and language notes, giving advice on using the right word in the right place.

The Collins Concise English Dictionary

£20 | 978-0-00-726112 3 | Hardback | 1,984pp

When you buy the Concise English Dictionary you are buying more than just a book. You are buying access to the dictionary whenever and wherever you want it. Learn about current language use and get help with problem words.

The Collins Essential English Dictionary

£12.99 | 978-0-00-718380 7 | Hardback | 1,024pp

Containing up to date and comprehensive coverage of today's English, with detailed language notes to avoid common language pitfalls. A practical supplement created in partnership with Microsoft Office™, makes this hardback dictionary ideal for office use.

Collins Compact English Dictionary

£9.99 | 978-0-00-722392 3 | Paperback flexibind | 1,120pp

A fantastic flexibind edition that opens easily, and stays open at the page. Includes detailed word history and extensive language notes for the language lover.

Collins Pocket English Dictionary

£7.99 | 978-0-00-726136 9 | Paperback vinyl cover | 704pp

This pocket edition is the ideal language companion, helping you to avoid common language mistakes with detailed usage notes. Features coloured headwords and spellings for ease of use.

Collins Paperback English Dictionary

£6.99 | 978-0-00-722384 8 | Paperback | 992pp

Specially tailored to meet your needs at home, school, and the office, the colour Collins Paperback English Dictionary has comprehensive definitions, word tips to provide help with English usage, and weblinked entries to take your knowledge further than a traditional dictionary.

Collins Mini English Dictionary

£5.99 | 978-0-00-722409 8 | Paperback | 704pp

Collins Mini English Dictionary is the perfect dictionary for everyday reference. It contains all the words and definitions you need on a daily basis in a handy portable format that is ideal for carrying to school or work.

Collins Gem English Dictionary

£4.50 | 978-0-00-720877 7 | Paperback vinyl cover | 704pp

Collins Gem English Dictionary, in colour, is the world's best-selling small dictionary. With its clear definitions, spelling and grammar tips, this handy little dictionary is the ideal portable companion for all.